SUMMER OPPORTUNITIES FOR KIDS & TEENAGERS 2005

THOMSON
PETERSON'S™

Australia • Canada • Mexico • Singapore • Spain • United Kingdom • United States

About Thomson Peterson's

Thomson Peterson's (www.petersons.com) is a leading provider of education information and advice, with books and online resources focusing on education search, test preparation, and financial aid. Its Web site offers searchable databases and interactive tools for contacting educational institutions, online practice tests and instruction, and planning tools for securing financial aid. Thomson Peterson's serves 110 million education consumers annually.

For more information, contact Thomson Peterson's, 2000 Lenox Drive, Lawrenceville, NJ 08648; 800-338-3282; or find us on the World Wide Web at: www.petersons.com/about

Editor: Fern A. Oram; Copy Editors: Bret Bollman, Jim Colbert, Michele N. Firestone, Michael Haines, Sally Ross, Jill C. Schwartz, Pam Sullivan, Valerie Bolus Vaughan; Research Project Manager: Jennifer Fishberg; Research Associate: Helen L. Hannan; Programmer: Phyllis Johnson; Manufacturing Manager: Ray Golaszewski; Composition Manager: Linda M. Williams; Client Relations Representatives: Mimi Kaufman, Lois Regina Milton, Mary Ann Murphy, Jim Swinarski, Eric Wallace.

ISSN 0894-9417
ISBN 0-7689-1547-3

Printed in the United States of America

10 9 8 7 6 5 4 3 2 1 06 05 04

Twenty-second Edition

CONTENTS

A LETTER

FROM THE PETERSON'S EDITORS

Welcome to the twenty-second annual edition of *Peterson's Summer Opportunities for Kids & Teenagers.* Our mission: to uncover a mind-boggling array of things to do on your next summer vacation! We'll clue you in on more than 3,200 exciting camps, academic options, travel adventures, community service projects, sports clinics, and arts programs throughout the U.S. and around the world.

First off, you'll want to check out **The Inside Scoop**. There you'll uncover all you need to know about finding the summer program that's right for you, questions to ask before you sign on the dotted line, and how to cope with (gulp) homesickness. Next up, the **Quick-Reference Chart** with the fast facts, at-a-glance rundown on who offers what. This chart gives you important information about the more than 3,200 programs listed in this guide, so you can narrow your search to a manageable size in minutes. Who attends—the number of boys and girls, the age range—the day and boarding options, the types of activities offered, the availability of financial aid, and job opportunities are found here in an easy-to-use format. You'll also quickly be able to zero in on programs around the U.S. and the globe.

Details, details, details—have we got details for you! Find out who attends, what activities are offered, session dates, costs, and financial aid, where to go for more information, program history and accreditations, and job opportunities at more than 3,200 summer programs. Just turn to the **Profiles of Summer Programs** and let your journey begin! Want even more info? The **In-Depth Descriptions** give you an up close and personal look at nearly 250 academic programs, camps, and travel adventures. Finally, check out the **Indexes**. With everything from travel programs to special needs accommodations, you'll be able to narrow your search according to what's important to you!

Peterson's publishes a full line of resources to help you and your family with any information you need to guide you through the process. Peterson's publications can be found at your local bookstore, library, and high school guidance office—or visit us on the Web at www.petersons.com.

Summer camps and programs will be pleased to know that Peterson's helped you in your selection. Staff members are more than happy to answer questions, address specific problems, and help in any way they can. The editors at Peterson's wish you great success in your summer program search. Enjoy the guide and have a dynamite summer!

THE INSIDE Scoop

PERFECT MATCH

There's the kind of summer when you get bored a few weeks after school lets out. When you've listened to all your CDs, aced all your video games, watched one too many soaps, hung out at the same old mall. But summer doesn't have to be this way. You could windsurf on a cool, clear New England lake. Perfect your backhand or golf swing. Horseback ride along breathtaking mountain trails. Trek through spectacular canyonlands or live with a family in Costa Rica, Spain, Switzerland, or Japan. Get a jump on next year's classes. Explore college majors or maybe even careers. Help out on an archeological dig or community service project. And along the way, meet some wonderful people, maybe even make a few lifelong friends.

Interested? Get ready to pack your bags and join the other 5 million kids and teens who'll be having the summer of a lifetime. *Peterson's Summer Opportunities for Kids & Teenagers 2005* lists thousands of terrific camps, academic programs, sports clinics, arts workshops, internships, volunteer opportunities, and travel adventures throughout North America and abroad. Don't have a lump-sum inheritance? Not to worry, there are programs in this guide with costs and fees to meet every budget, from $50 workshops to $4500 world treks, with sessions varying in length from a couple of days to a couple of months.

AND THE CHOICES ARE . . .

Your hardest job will be deciding which one of the summer programs listed in this guide to sign up for. The programs come in many different flavors, but most fit into one of the following categories: traditional, sports, arts, or special-interest camps; academic programs; travel and wilderness adventures; internships; and community service opportunities. Here's a quick rundown on the types of programs described in this guide and what they offer.

CLASSIC CAMPING

Next summer, when 5 million kids enroll in a summer program, most will choose a traditional summer camp. Camps offer a way to learn, grow, have fun, and make friends while enjoying fresh air and sunshine. At a camp, you can learn to skipper a sailboat, ride a horse, master

rock-climbing techniques, develop wilderness survival skills, build a campfire, tell stories, put on a play, learn how to juggle, and even brush up on computer skills.

Camp is also a place to learn cooperation and leadership, take on a little independence, and leave the pressures of school and everyday stuff behind. Friendships made at camp can be special, too.

You'll find camps in some of America's most spectacular natural settings—from the rugged Atlantic coastline of Maine, to the Blue Ridge Mountains of North Carolina, to the canyons of Arizona and the temperate rainforests of the Pacific Northwest.

Many camps also offer specialized programs where fun in the great outdoors is supplemented by weight-loss and fitness programs emphasizing nutrition, support, and supervision for happy, health-enhancing results.

For many campers, summer can also be a time of deepening spiritual commitment. For those who'd like to combine the great outdoors with inner growth, there are camps representing a wide range of religious affiliations.

SUMMER ON CAMPUS

If summer school makes you think of kids sweltering in an all-too-familiar classroom while classmates swim and holler at a nearby pool, you're in for a surprise. Whether you're looking for remedial help or a chance to move ahead, the academic programs in this guide offer learning with a difference. When you're studying under the shady trees of a prep school or college campus, attending small classes, and getting individual attention in the company of kids from different parts of the country or around the world, learning takes on a different meaning. The academic programs in this guide are designed to combine a summer of academic study with the chance to make new friends, discover new places, and still have time for summer fun—from swimming, tennis, and horseback riding to trips to nearby amusement parks and cultural attractions.

EXTRA CREDIT?

You can take another stab at course work that you found difficult during the school year or get a challenging course out of the way at a time when you can focus on it—sometimes for high school or even college credit. Take advantage of the rich curricula many private schools and college programs offer by tackling a course you probably won't find in your local school—there are classes in everything from designing a home page on the Internet to studying the masters of the Italian Renaissance.

You may want to get a preview of what college life will be like and many programs specialize in college preparation. There are programs that can help you improve college entrance scores and study skills and that will work with you to build confidence for the coming school year. Others offer older teens a chance to try college on for size for a few days, a week, or longer. Living in a dorm, sampling college-style courses, and talking with current students and professors can be an exciting and useful experience in getting ready for the major transition to come. There are even college tours that visit representative campuses to help you focus your college search.

FOR THE SPORTS FAN

There's a camp for just about every sport imaginable. There are programs for baseball, basketball, biking, golf, gymnastics, hockey, horseback riding, kayaking, sailing, soccer, tennis, and volleyball—to name just a few! Even skiers will find summer spots for expert instruction—some with snow, some without—in the United States, Canada, Switzerland, and even Australia, where our summer is their winter.

FEELING ADVENTUROUS?

Why just sit there when you can hike, bike, sail, paddle, or climb your way through summer? There are adventure programs that will take you trekking through mountain wilderness, down white-water rapids, and over rugged canyons. Others will have you hiking from

village to village. Still others will have you traveling by canoe, raft, or sailboat, meeting people and soaking in scenery and culture along the way. Whether your destination is a Caribbean island, another country, or a famed American national park, there are summer treks to meet a range of abilities and interests. You don't have to be super-fit or experienced, but you should be open to adventure and new challenges.

EXPLORING YOUR ARTISTIC SIDE

Camps may specialize in advanced, preprofessional studies or may open their doors to kids

just beginning to explore the visual or performing arts. This guide has everything from young playwrights' seminars to dance programs to workshops in sculpture, music, architecture, and graphic design. Arts centers, arts camps, or schools provide the setting, often with professional-quality equipment, facilities, and instruction.

CAREER INTERESTS

Summer can be a great time to check out possible career paths before you have to start thinking about choosing colleges or majors. This guide lists internships and volunteer opportunities that let you see up close and personal what it's like to write for a local newspaper, conduct field studies in a marine science center, work in government or a Wall Street investment firm, or teach children, to name a few options. Whatever your career interest, it can be cultivated in any of the hundreds of special programs offered here.

INTERNATIONAL EXPERIENCES

If languages are your focus, a world of choices awaits. You can sharpen your Spanish skills in Mexico City or Barcelona, learn Japanese in Tokyo, and study French in Geneva or Paris. You'll find dozens of languages—some common, some less so—represented. But you don't have to travel halfway around the world to study them. Many language programs listed here are held at a campus near you.

If cultural immersion is what you're after, check out the international study and travel programs. International study programs are listed by country under **Opportunities Abroad**. Travel programs, where your itinerary includes stays at more than one site, can be found in the special **Travel** section.

WHERE TO GO FROM HERE

Now that we've got your creative juices flowing, make a list of the different activities you'd like to try out. Don't worry if your wish list is all over the place. Eventually, you can focus in on the must-haves. But there's no sense narrowing yourself too soon—you may find a program that has much of what you want. Many summer programs have an incredible variety of activities, spanning a surprising number of interests and ages.

After you've created your list, look it over. Do you see any types of activities again and again? Or is a mix of activities important to you? Depending on your focus, you'll want to stick with generalized or special-interest offerings. The **Indexes** in this guide let you search by activity or subject area.

You'll have to consider your budget as well. If your funds are limited, you may want to concentrate on short-term programs of a week or less. This guide includes a number of low-cost programs offered by nonprofit groups. In addition, many programs offer financial aid. Availability of aid is listed in the **Quick-Reference Chart** as well as in the **Profiles of Summer Programs** and **In-Depth Descriptions** of the programs themselves.

Another concern will be location—how close to home do you want to stay? After you define your limits, you can look for programs by state or country. If you're hoping to roam in the United States or abroad, head for the **Travel** section (which is organized alphabetically by program name).

With your list of must-have activities and essential requirements in hand, dive into the **Profiles of Summer Programs** and **In-Depth Descriptions.** You're sure to find a program that's just what you're looking for. Happy hunting (or skiing, or paragliding, or whatever)!

CHECK IT OUT!

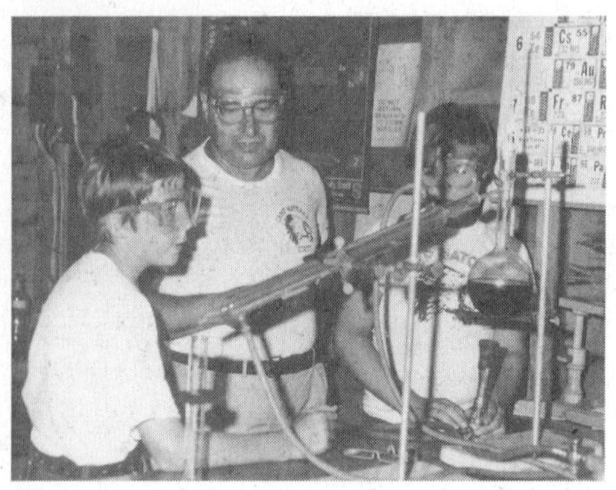

Peterson's Law: How happy you are with a summer program is directly proportionate to the number of questions you asked before you signed up. So here's a list of what to check out where you want to check in:

Who is the director? What are his or her background or credentials? What's the director's philosophy about the program? Directors can be hands-on or take on a more administrative role, depending on the size and type of program. Who will be your primary contact?

What is the program's track record? How long has it been in operation? Is it accredited by an outside organization, such as the American Camping Association (ACA)? Not all programs seek accreditation—some programs may not even fall under an accrediting organization's scope, but it is another piece of information you'll want to weigh when making your decision.

Who are the counselors and instructors? What does the director look for when selecting staff members? What training do they receive? What percentage of staff members return each year? As a guideline, look for a counselor return rate of at least 50 percent.

Are family references provided? There's no better way to get the inside scoop about a program than to ask someone who's been there. Most program directors can supply names and phone numbers of satisfied parents and kids who are willing to talk with prospective families. If a program can't supply references, keep looking.

What are the program's goals? If a program's mission is to help polish future athletes for competition and you like noodling around with a soccer ball on the weekend, you're probably not going to be very happy. Read the program's philosophy and make sure its outlook matches your own.

What if discipline problems arise? Make sure you know the program's rules of conduct and its policy for dealing with violations both small and large. Many program directors recommend that parents and teens discuss the rules—and consequences for breaking them—before the program's start.

How safe is the program? When talking with program directors, ask about the ratio of staff members to participants,

DO YOUR HOMEWORK!

Parents worry—they can't help it. It's in their job description. So how do you make sure the summer program you're dying to go to will get their stamp of approval? By doing a little bit of legwork and some reading between the lines, you can tell a lot about a camp, academic program, or travel group before you sign on the dotted line. Here are some tips on making sure a program is everything you hope it will be:

Start looking early. Give yourself plenty of time to ask around, write away to family references (which most programs are happy to provide), and follow up with the programs directly.

Ask around. Your friends, neighbors, and other family members can give you leads on great summer programs. Don't just ask if they liked a particular camp, course, or tour—ask them what they liked and didn't like about it.

Get brochures from a variety of programs. Comparing materials will help you make a more informed decision—and you might even discover an interest you didn't know you had!

Arrange a tour or visit. Many programs invite families to visit their facilities during the session or off-season. If you can't work in an on-site tour, ask if the program offers a video. Many communities also offer camp fairs where you and your parents can meet with program directors in person.

especially for waterfront and other higher-risk activities. If you'll be living on a campus or traveling, ask about security arrangements and supervision. Less structured, less supervised programs are only appropriate for older teens with a high level of maturity and responsibility.

What provisions are made for medical care and emergencies? Ask about on-site care—is there is a nurse or doctor on staff? If you're bound for a wilderness or travel program, ask if counselors have first aid certification and CPR training. Always ask for the distance to the nearest hospital.

What is the policy on phone calls and family visits? Most camps couldn't function if children were phoning home at all hours. Policies vary, but most programs expect parents and children to stay in touch mainly through letters. If you'll be using pay phones often, look into obtaining calling cards. That way, you won't be scrounging around for quarters every time you want to call home.

How is homesickness handled? Most kids have it, live through it, and are glad that they went away in spite of it. Program directors are more than happy to offer tips for easing the transition to camp and coping with bouts of homesickness.

Who are the other participants? From what areas do they come? What's the age distribution? Nobody wants to find himself or herself in a program that only has a couple of kids in the same grade.

Will I like the food? Most programs offer a variety of food, but if you are a choosy eater, you may want to ask for sample menus. Can substitutions be made? Are special diets accommodated?

Coping with Home-sickness

David G. Richardson, Director
Fay School
Southborough, Massachusetts

Everything was unpacked and put away. I was all moved into my new room. We had explored the entire area. What a great place to be! This was so exciting! I was a lucky person. Then Mom and Dad got into the car to go home. It was time for them to leave.

"Have fun!

"Work hard!

"Love you!

"Make us proud, son!

"We'll see you in a few weeks."

All of a sudden it hit me like a ton of bricks. WAIT A MINUTE, my brain screamed, DON'T LEAVE ME! Instead, I choked back the tears, waved, and said, "I will. See you soon."

My parents drove away and the truth became evident. I missed my home and I felt horrible. What had I done?

Homesickness is a part of life. It's a part of growing up and breaking away. Most people experience the nauseating feeling of being homesick at some time in their lives. Some people may even be homesick later in life when they go away to college or get married. However, most people go through this separation experience when they are much younger. Many people learn to cope with homesickness at a summer camp, and camp is a good place to deal with the feeling of homesickness. Camp is a place for children to learn self-confidence. Camp is a place where children learn about responsibility. Camp is a place to have fun with new friends. Camp is a safe, caring environment where nurturing adults are trained to support children through this sometimes difficult growth process. Homesickness is normal and will go away!

As a parent, you can help your child cope with homesickness without actually mentioning it. While preparing to go to camp, talk about the camp experience with your child and tell him or her what to expect. Talk about the routine and how things may seem strange at first but that this is normal in a new situation. Always be positive and upbeat during any discussions about camp. Talk about friendship—how to make new friends and what constitutes a good friend. Discuss how to be flexible in new situations and how to have fun with change. Point out that you are only a phone call away and explain how the camp can contact you if there is an emergency. Always be honest with your child. Do not leave out important details that will be an unpleasant surprise when your child arrives at camp. If possible, take your child to visit the camp prior to opening day so he or she knows what to expect. In the months leading up to camp, create shorter separation experiences such as an overnight at a friend's house or with another family member to help your child get acclimated to being away from you.

You can expect some letters or telephone calls that sound unhappy. Remember, children can exaggerate quite a bit when they want something. They may not lie, but they may stretch the truth. Sometimes a child will acknowledge his or her homesickness. Although a camper may say, "I miss you" or "I want to come home" or even "I'm homesick," the real message is usually disguised in other statements. For example, you may hear about the bad food or a roommate problem that makes coming home imperative. Or you may hear that no one is nice and the camp is no fun. Of course, "I want to come home" is a plea that cannot be ignored, but you must remember where the message originates and respond in an appropriate manner. Remember, this is not a logical, intellectually motivated call, it is a call from the heart. You must reassure your child of your love and state the importance of completing the camp experience.

During the camp session, there are several things that can help your child adjust to being away from home. Avoid calling! Nothing is tougher for a homesick child than the sound of Mom's or Dad's voice. Many camps ask parents not to call for the first ten days. This is a great idea. Write letters and send postcards that talk about what is happening in the family. Make the correspondence about news. Avoid mentioning how much you miss your child. Instead, write about how you love your child and look forward to hearing about the fun things at camp. In fact, send a letter or package to arrive before opening day so your child receives something right away. Let the adjustment occur! It is a process, and the timetable varies with each individual. Have faith in your child and in the camp staff. Send care packages and include some items to be shared with the counselors and new friends. Always be positive and upbeat.

Remember that camp staff members are trained and prepared to deal with homesick children. If you hear from your child that he or she is homesick, let the staff know. They are probably aware of the situation, but it will not hurt to let them know. It will probably make you feel better about the situation at camp. In fact, counselors have a more difficult time dealing with campsick parents. Homesick campers are with the staff and simply need some assistance to adjust to this new world without Mom and Dad. Campsick parents are somewhere else and are more difficult to assist in adjusting to this new world without the child. Give the staff a chance and let them do the job you originally trusted them to do. Homesickness causes a little pain in the short run for a more self-confident, healthy child in the long run.

Oh—and how did I, the homesick kid in the opening paragraph, do in the horrible place where Mom and Dad left me to suffer by myself? Including time as a staff member, I was only there for twenty years.

How to Use This Guide

Finding the summer program that best suits your wants and needs can be an exciting—and overwhelming—experience. How you find your way through this guide comes down to one question—Are you a *grazer* or a *digger*? If you're a grazer, you'll just dive in, mull over the program options, and write to a bunch of them. That's okay with us. We're sure you'll find some great summer programs using your own finely tuned grazing system. However, if you're a digger, you probably prefer to search more systematically. You'll want to decide what you're looking for, narrow your list of prospects, and contact the remaining choices.

DETAILS, DETAILS

When you're ready to learn about programs that have piqued your interest, turn to the **Profiles of Summer Programs**. This section concisely describes thousands of summer opportunities in the United States and abroad and provides all the info you'll need to narrow down your list of prospects. Here are some highlights of the information you'll find!

General Information Is the program coed or boys or girls only/? Residential or day? When was the program established? Can you earn college credit? What special services are offered? Is there a religious affiliation? Is the program accredited?

Program Focus What's the spotlight on at this program?

Academics/Arts/Special Interest Areas/Sports/Wilderness/Outdoors Whether its government and politics, arts and crafts, community service, soccer, or mountain biking, all the details are given in these categories.

Excursions/Trips Overnight or day? College tours or cultural?

Program Information How long do the sessions last? What are the dates? What are the age ranges? What is the cost? Is financial aid available? Is there a religious affiliation? Is the program accredited?

Housing For travel programs, what kind is offered? Tents? Youth hostels? Cabins?

Application Deadline What date do you need to mark on your calendar or is there a continuous deadline?

Jobs Are they available? For high school students? For college students?

Contact/URL Who to talk to and where to go to get more information.

FOR A CLOSER LOOK

Get the lowdown on nearly 250 summer programs with **In-Depth Descriptions**. Written by program directors exclusively for this guide, the descriptions follow Peterson's own format for easier comparison. These pages give a more complete rundown of program offerings, extra activities, settings, and facilities. You'll learn all the essentials—including enrollment deadlines, staff qualifications, medical care, and transportation arrangements.

FINDING A PERFECT MATCH

If you have a particular interest in mind, check out the **Indexes**. The **Indexes** group programs by seven main search categories: Programs, Program Sponsors, Specialized Programs, Primary Activity, Travel Programs, Special Needs Accommodations, and Religious Affiliation.

ONCE YOU'VE GOT YOUR LIST

Contact the program directly for more information. Keep in mind that it's never too early to start making summer plans. Some programs fill up fast, with many returnees signing up for next year's session at summer's end. So take out your "A" list and mail, phone, fax, or e-mail your favorite programs today!

DATA COLLECTION PROCEDURES

The data contained in *Petersons' Summer Opportunities for Kids & Teenagers* were collected in the spring and summer of 2004. Questionnaires were sent to directors of more than 3,000 summer programs around the globe. Program information included in this edition was submitted by directors of summer programs and supplemented by secondary research when necessary. In addition, most directors were also contacted by Thomson Peterson's research and editorial staffs to verify unusual figures, resolve discrepancies, and obtain additional information. All usable information received in time for publication has been included. Because of the editorial review that takes place in our offices, and because most material comes directly from program directors, we have every reason to believe that the information presented in the guide is accurate. However, readers should check with programs to verify costs, fees, venues, and program offerings, which may have changed since the publication of this edition.

Quick-Reference Chart

SUMMER PROGRAMS AT-A-GLANCE

	GENERAL INFORMATION					PROGRAM INFORMATION						
	Profile Page	Boys D/R†	Girls D/R†	Coed D/R†	Age	Acad	Arts	Sports	Wild/ Outdrs	Special Interest	Jobs	Financial Aid
BY STATE												
Alabama												
Alabama Museum of Natural History Summer Expedition	73			R	14+	•				•	•	•
Alpine Camp for Boys	73	R			7–15			•	•			•
American Allstar Dance Camp	73			R/D	12–17		•	•				
Architecture Summer Camp	74			R	15–18	•	•	•		•		•
Auburn University Design Workshop	74			R	15–18	•	•	•		•		
Birmingham-Southern College Student Leaders in Service Program	74			R	15–17			•		•		
Birmingham-Southern College Summer Scholar Program	74			R/D	16–17	•	•	•	•	•		
Camp Laney for Boys	75	R			8–14		•	•	•	•	•	
Camp Skyline	75		R		6–16		•	•	•	•	•	•
Camp Skyline–Equestrian Program	75		R		9–16			•			•	
Dance Magic	75			R/D	13–18		•					
Half-Time USA	75			R	13–18		•			•	•	
Josten Yearbook Summer Workshop	76			R	13–18	•	•			•		
National Cheerleaders Association Cheerleader Camps	76			R/D	13–19		•	•				
Student Conservation Association–Conservation Crew Program (Alabama)	76			R	15–19	•		•	•	•	•	•
Summer at Altamont	76			D	9–18	•	•	•	•	•	•	
Tuskegee University Vet Step I	76			R	13–15	•				•		•
Tuskegee University Vet Step II	77			R	16–18	•				•		•
Universal Cheerleaders Association and Universal Dance Association Camps	77			R/D	13–18		•	•				
World Affairs Youth Seminar	77			R	14–18	•		•		•		•
Alaska												
AAVE–Alaska	77*				14–18			•	•	•	•	•
Adventures Cross-Country, Alaska Adventure	77*			R	14–18			•	•		•	•
Adventure Treks–Alaska Adventures	78				16–18			•	•			•
Alpengirl–Alaska	78				14–16	•		•	•	•	•	•
Camp Tawonga–Teen Service Learning to Alaska	78					•	•		•	•	•	•
Camp Togowoods	78		R		7–17	•	•	•	•	•	•	•
Cordova 4-H Bluegrass and Old Time Music and Dance Camp	79			R/D	9–18		•		•	•		•
Cordova 4-H Hawaiian Camp	79			D	6–8	•	•	•		•		
EARTHWATCH INSTITUTE–Sea Otters of Alaska	79			R	16+	•				•		•
From the Forest to the Sea	79			R	9–18	•	•	•	•	•	•	•
Longacre Expeditions, Alaska	80*				14–17			•	•		•	
NBC Camps–Basketball Individual Training–Alaska	80			R	9–18			•			•	•
NBC Camps–Basketball Speed–Alaska	80			R	13–19			•			•	•
NBC Camps–Basketball–Team (Boys)–Alaska	80	R						•			•	•
NBC Camps–Basketball–Team (Girls)–Alaska	80		R					•			•	•
NBC Camps–Volleyball–Alaska	80		R		12–18			•			•	•
Outward Bound West–Sea Kayaking and Mountaineering–Alaska	81				16+	•		•	•	•	•	•
Overland: Alaskan Expedition Hiking, Sea-Kayaking, and Rafting	81*				14–19			•	•		•	
Overland: American Community Service, Alaska	81*				15–18			•	•	•	•	
Putney Student Travel–Community Service–Alaska	81*			R	15–18	•		•	•	•		•
Student Conservation Association–Conservation Crew Program (Alaska)	82			R	15–19	•		•	•	•	•	•
Visions–Alaska	82*				14–18	•	•		•	•	•	•
Westcoast Connection–Community Connections Alaska	82*				16+					•		•
Wilderness Ventures–Alaska Leadership	82*				14–18			•	•	•	•	•

**This program is highlighted by a photograph, special note, or in-depth description; see the profile page for more information.*
†D = day camp; R = residential camp

	GENERAL INFORMATION					PROGRAM INFORMATION						
	Profile Page	Boys D/R†	Girls D/R†	Coed D/R†	Age	Acad	Arts	Sports	Wild/ Outdrs	Special Interest	Jobs	Financial Aid
Wilderness Ventures–Alaska Service	83*				14–18			•	•	•	•	•
Wilderness Ventures–Alaska Southcentral	83*				14–18			•	•	•	•	•
Wilderness Ventures–Alaska Southeast	83*				14–18			•	•	•	•	•
Windsor Mountain: Alaska	83*				14–17	•		•	•	•	•	•
Arizona												
Deer Hill Expeditions, Arizona	84			R	13–22	•	•	•	•	•	•	•
EARTHWATCH INSTITUTE–Hopi Ancestors	84			R	16+	•	•			•		•
Landmark Volunteers: Arizona	84*			R	14–18	•			•	•	•	•
Oak Creek Ranch Summer School	84*			R	11–19	•	•	•	•	•		
St. Paul's Preparatory Academy Summer Program	85	R/D			13–17	•	•	•	•	•		
Southwestern Adventures	85*			R/D	11–18	•	•	•	•	•	•	•
Student Conservation Association–Conservation Crew Program (Arizona)	86			R	15–19	•		•	•	•	•	•
Ventures Travel Service–Arizona	86				14–70					•	•	
Arkansas												
Camp Aldersgate–Kota Camp	86			R	6–18		•	•	•	•	•	•
Camp Aldersgate–Med Camps	86			R	6–18		•	•	•	•	•	•
Camp Aldersgate–Respite Care	87			R/D	6–18		•	•	•	•	•	•
Student Conservation Association–Conservation Crew Program (Arkansas)	87			R	15–19	•		•	•	•	•	•
California												
Ability First–Camp Joan Mier	87			R	7+		•	•	•	•	•	•
Ability First–Camp Paivika	88			R	7+		•	•	•	•	•	•
Academic Study Associates–ASA at the University of California, Berkeley	88*			R/D	16–18	•	•	•		•	•	•
Academy by the Sea	88*			R/D	11–17	•	•	•		•	•	
Acting Academy at Pali Overnight Adventures	89			R	9–16	•	•	•	•	•	•	
The Actor's Workshop by Education Unlimited	89*			R/D	10–18		•	•	•		•	•
Adventure Treks–California 19 Adventures	90				13–15			•	•			•
American Academy of Dramatic Arts Summer Program at Hollywood, California	90*			D	14+		•					
American Legal Experience by Education Unlimited–Berkeley, CA	90			R/D	14–18	•				•		•
American Legal Experience by Education Unlimited–Stanford, CA	90			R/D	12+	•				•		•
Arrowsmith Academy Arts and Academics	91			D	13–18	•	•			•		
Art Center College of Design Art Center for Kids	91			D	9–14	•	•			•		•
Bar 717 Ranch/Camp Trinity	91			R	8–16	•	•	•	•	•	•	•
Battlebot Mania at Pali Overnight Adventures	91			R	12–16					•	•	
Bay Area Shakespeare Camp	92			D	7–18		•				•	•
Berklee in L.A. Summer Performance Program	92			R/D	15+	•	•					•
Brighton College Admissions Prep at UCLA	92*			R	15–19	•				•	•	
Britannia Soccer Camp	92			R/D	5–15			•			•	•
California Campus Tours	92				15–24	•			•	•		•
California College of the Arts Pre-College Program	92			R/D	16–18	•	•					•
California Cruzin' Overnight Camp	93				7–13	•	•	•	•	•	•	•
California National Debate Institute	93*			R/D	13–18	•						•
California State Summer School for the Arts/Inner Spark	93*			R	14–18		•	•		•	•	•
Cal Poly State University Young Scholars–Find the College for You!	94			D	14+	•				•		•
Cal Poly State University Young Scholars Prepare for the PSAT & SAT I	94			D	13–18	•						
Camp Exploration Travel Day Camp	94			D	6–13	•	•	•	•	•	•	•
Camp Heartland Summer Camp–California	94			R	7–15		•	•	•	•	•	
Camp James Summer Day Camp	95			D	4–13		•	•	•	•	•	
Camp JCA Shalom	95			R/D	7–17		•	•	•	•	•	•
Camp La Jolla	95*			R	8–29		•	•	•	•	•	
Camp Pacific's Recreational Camp	95*			R	8–16	•	•	•		•	•	
Camp Pacific's Surf and Bodyboard Camp	96*			R	8–16		•	•		•	•	
Camp Tawonga–Call of the Wild	96							•	•		•	•

This program is highlighted by a photograph, special note, or in-depth description; see the profile page for more information.
†D = day camp; R = residential camp

	GENERAL INFORMATION					PROGRAM INFORMATION						
	Profile Page	Boys D/R†	Girls D/R†	Coed D/R†	Age	Acad	Arts	Sports	Wild/ Outdrs	Special Interest	Jobs	Financial Aid
Camp Tawonga–Magical Mystery Tour	96								•	•	•	•
Camp Tawonga–Summer Camp	96			R	7–17		•	•	•	•	•	•
Camp Tawonga–Summertime Family Camp	97			R			•	•	•	•	•	•
Camp Tawonga–Surf 'n Turf Quest	97						•	•	•	•	•	•
Camp Tawonga–Teen Quest: High Sierra	97					•		•	•		•	•
Camp Tawonga–Teen Quest: Yosemite	97							•	•		•	•
Carmel Valley Tennis Camp	97			R	10–17		•	•	•	•	•	
Castilleja Summer Day Camp	98		D		6–12	•	•	•		•	•	•
Catalina Island Camps	98			R	8–15	•	•	•	•	•	•	
Cazadero Family Camp	98			R	2+	•	•	•			•	•
Cazadero Music Camp	98			R	10–18		•	•	•		•	•
The Children's Art Institute	99			D	6–11	•	•	•		•	•	
Children's Creative and Performing Arts Academy Archaeology Adventure Camp	99			D	10–13	•	•				•	•
Children's Creative and Performing Arts Academy Summer Elementary Program	99			D	6–12	•	•	•		•	•	•
Children's Creative and Performing Arts Academy Summer Middle School Program	100			D		•	•	•			•	•
Children's Creative and Performing Arts Academy Summer Program for Preschool/Prekindergarten	100			D	3–5	•	•				•	•
Children's Creative and Performing Arts Academy Summer Programs for High School Students	100			D	14–18	•	•			•	•	•
ClayCamp	100			D	6–16		•				•	
Cloverleaf Ranch Summer Camp	101			R/D	7–15		•	•	•	•	•	
College Admission Prep Camp by Education Unlimited–San Diego	101*			R/D	15–18	•				•		•
College Admission Prep Camp by Education Unlimited–Stanford University	101*			R/D	15–18	•		•		•		•
College Admission Prep Camp by Education Unlimited–UC Berkeley	101*			R/D	15–18	•				•		•
College Admission Prep Camp by Education Unlimited–UCLA	102*			R/D	15–18	•		•		•		•
College Admission Prep Camp Choice by Education Unlimited–Stanford	102*			R/D	16–18	•				•		•
Computer Camp by Education Unlimited–Stanford	102*			R/D	10–18	•		•	•	•	•	•
Computer Camp by Education Unlimited–UC Berkeley	103*			R/D	10–18	•		•	•	•	•	•
Computer Camp by Education Unlimited–UCLA	103*			R/D	10–18	•		•		•	•	•
Crossroads School–Aquatics	103			D				•		•	•	•
Crossroads School– Basketball Camps	103			D	6–12	•		•			•	•
Crossroads School–Jazz Workshop	104			D	8+		•				•	•
Crossroads School–Soccer Camps	104			D	5–12	•		•			•	•
Crossroads School–Summer Educational Journey	104			D		•	•	•	•	•	•	•
Culinary Institute at Pali Overnight Adventures	104			R	12–16					•	•	
Cybercamps–DeAnza College	104			D	7–18	•	•	•		•	•	•
Cybercamps–Stanford University	105			D	7–18	•	•	•		•	•	•
Cybercamps–UCLA	105			R/D	7–18	•	•	•		•	•	
Cybercamps–UC San Diego (UCSD)	105			R/D	7–18	•	•	•		•	•	•
Cybercamps–University of California at Berkeley	105			R/D	7–18	•	•	•		•	•	
Douglas Ranch Camps	106			R	7–14		•	•	•	•	•	
EARTHWATCH INSTITUTE–Mojave Desert Tortoises	106			R	16+	•				•		•
Elite Educational Institute Elementary Enrichment	106*			D		•						
Elite Educational Institute Junior High/PSAT Program	106*			D		•						
Elite Educational Institute SAT I and II Preparation	107*			D		•				•	•	
Elite Educational Institute SAT Summer Bootcamp	107*			D		•				•		
Excel at UC Santa Cruz	107*			R	14+	•	•	•	•	•	•	•
Exploration of Architecture	107*			R	15–18	•					•	•
Film Institute at Pali Overnight Adventures	108			R	9–16	•	•	•	•	•	•	
Gold Arrow Camp	108			R	6–14		•	•	•	•	•	
Great Escapes (Adventure Trips for Teens)–California Beach Escape	108				14–17			•	•	•	•	•
Griffith Park Boys Camp	108	R			6–17	•	•	•	•	•	•	•
Gymnastics Academy at Pali Overnight Adventures	109			R	9–16			•			•	
Harker Summer English Language Institute	109			D	8–15	•						
The Harker Summer Institute	109			D	14–17	•	•					

**This program is highlighted by a photograph, special note, or in-depth description; see the profile page for more information.*
†D = day camp; R = residential camp

	GENERAL INFORMATION					PROGRAM INFORMATION						
	Profile Page	Boys D/R†	Girls D/R†	Coed D/R†	Age	Acad	Arts	Sports	Wild/ Outdrs	Special Interest	Jobs	Financial Aid
Harker Summer Programs	109			D	4–14	•	•	•		•	•	
Hidden Villa Summer Camp	110			R/D	6–18	•	•	•	•	•	•	•
High Sierra Wilderness Camps	110			R	11–17	•	•	•	•	•	•	•
Hollywood Stunt Camp at Pali Overnight Adventures	110			R	9–16		•	•			•	
Horseback Riding Academy at Pali Overnight Adventures	110			R	9–16	•	•	•	•	•	•	
iD Tech Camps–Cal Lutheran University, Thousand Oaks, CA	111*			R/D	7–17	•	•	•		•	•	•
iD Tech Camps–Dominican University, San Rafael, CA	111*			R/D	7–17	•	•	•		•	•	•
iD Tech Camps–Pepperdine University, Malibu, CA	111*			R/D	7–17	•	•	•		•	•	•
iD Tech Camps–Santa Clara University, Santa Clara, CA	112*			R/D	7–17	•	•	•		•	•	•
iD Tech Camps–Stanford University, Palo Alto, CA	112*			R/D	7–17	•	•	•		•	•	•
iD Tech Camps–St. Mary's College, Moraga, CA	112*			R/D	7–17	•	•	•		•	•	•
iD Tech Camps–UC Berkeley, Berkeley, CA	113*			R/D	7–17	•	•	•		•	•	•
iD Tech Camps–UC Irvine, Irvine, CA	113*			R/D	7–17	•	•	•		•	•	•
iD Tech Camps–UCLA, Westwood, CA	114*			R/D	7–17	•	•	•		•	•	•
iD Tech Camps–UC San Diego, La Jolla, CA	114*			R/D	7–17	•	•	•		•	•	•
iD Tech Camps–UC Santa Cruz, Santa Cruz, CA	114*			R/D	7–17	•	•	•		•	•	•
Idyllwild Arts Summer Program–American Experience for International Students	115*			R	13–18	•	•				•	
Idyllwild Arts Summer Program–Children's Center	115*			R/D	5–12		•				•	•
Idyllwild Arts Summer Program–Family Week	115*			R			•	•	•		•	
Idyllwild Arts Summer Program–Junior Artists' Center	115*			R/D	11–13		•				•	•
Idyllwild Arts Summer Program–Youth Arts Center	116*			R/D	13–18		•				•	•
Joe Machnik's No. 1 Academy One and Premier Programs–Claremont, California	116			R/D	9–18			•			•	•
Joe Machnik's No. 1 Academy One and Premier Programs–Rohnert Park, California	116			R/D	9–18			•			•	•
Joe Machnik's No. 1 Mighty Mini, Goalkeeper and Striker Camp–Claremont, California	117			R/D	8–12			•			•	•
Joe Machnik's No. 1 Mighty Mini, Goalkeeper and Striker Camp–Rohnert Park, California	117			R/D	8–12			•			•	•
Julian Krinsky California Teen Tours	117*				13–16			•		•	•	•
Julian Krinsky Yesh Shabbat California Teen Tour	117*				13–16			•		•		•
Junior Statesmen Summer School–Stanford University	117*			R	14–18	•				•		•
Junior Statesmen Symposium on California State Politics and Government	118*			R	14–18	•				•		•
Junior Statesmen Symposium on Los Angeles Politics and Government	118*			R	14–18	•				•		
Landmark Volunteers: California	118*			R	14–18	•		•	•	•	•	•
Leadership Training at Pali Overnight Adventures	119			R	9–16	•	•	•	•	•	•	
Lifeschool Wilderness Adventures–Summer Adventures	119				12–18		•	•	•	•		•
Millennium Entrepreneurs Camp CEO	119			R/D	8–19	•	•	•		•	•	•
Millennium Entrepreneurs "Training Tomorrow's Business Leaders Today"	120			R/D	8–18	•	•	•	•	•	•	
Miracle Makers Summer Camp	120			D	2–12	•	•	•	•	•		•
Monte Vista ESL Intensive Language Institute	120			R	13–17	•	•	•		•		
Mountain Camp	120			R	8–16		•	•	•	•	•	
Mountain Meadow Ranch	121			R	7–17	•	•	•	•	•	•	
Mountain Retreat Overnight Camp	121			R	7–13	•	•	•	•	•	•	•
National Computer Camps at San Francisco State University	121			R/D	8–18	•	•	•		•	•	
National Guitar Workshop–Los Angeles, CA	121			R/D	13–79	•	•				•	•
National Guitar Workshop–San Francisco, CA	122			R/D	13–79	•	•				•	•
The National Music Workshop Day Jams–Los Angeles, CA	122			D	9–15	•	•				•	•
National Student Leadership Conference: Law and Advocacy–California	122*			R	14–18	•		•		•	•	•
NAWA Academy–Girls on the Go	122		R		12–18	•	•	•	•	•	•	•
NAWA Academy–Great Challenge	123			R	12–18	•	•	•	•	•	•	•
NAWA Academy–Lassen Expedition	123			R	12–18	•	•	•	•	•	•	•
NAWA Academy–Trinity Challenge	123			R	10–14	•	•	•	•	•	•	•
NBC Camps–Basketball Individual Training–CA	123			R	9–18			•			•	•
NBC Camps–Basketball Speed Explosion–California	124			R	13–19			•			•	•
NBC Camps–Volleyball–California	124		R		12–18			•			•	•

**This program is highlighted by a photograph, special note, or in-depth description; see the profile page for more information.*
†D = day camp; R = residential camp

	GENERAL INFORMATION					PROGRAM INFORMATION						
	Profile Page	Boys D/R†	Girls D/R†	Coed D/R†	Age	Acad	Arts	Sports	Wild/ Outdrs	Special Interest	Jobs	Financial Aid
NBC Camps–Volleyball Speed Explosion–California	124			R	9–18			•			•	•
The New York Film Academy, Universal Studios, Hollywood, Ca	124*			R	15–18		•					
Ojai Valley School Summer Programs	124*			R/D	8–18	•	•	•	•	•	•	•
Outward Bound West–Climbing and Backpacking–High Sierra, CA	125				14+	•		•	•	•	•	•
Outward Bound West–Sierra Nevada Mountaineering	125				16+	•		•	•	•		•
Oxford School Summer Camp	125			R/D	6–20	•	•	•		•		
Pali Overnight Adventures Camp	126			R	9–16	•	•	•	•	•	•	
Pepperdine University Summer College for High School Students	126*			R/D	15–19	•	•				•	
Power Chord Academy–Los Angeles	126			R	12–18	•	•				•	
Prep Camp Excel by Education Unlimited–Stanford University	126*			R/D	13–16	•		•		•	•	•
Prep Camp Excel by Education Unlimited–UC Berkeley	127*			R/D	13–16	•		•		•	•	•
Prep Camp Excel by Education Unlimited–UCLA	127*			R/D	13–16	•						•
Public Speaking Institute by Education Unlimited–Stanford	127*			R/D	10–18	•		•	•	•	•	•
Public Speaking Institute by Education Unlimited–UC Berkeley	128*			R/D	10–18	•		•	•	•	•	•
Public Speaking Institute by Education Unlimited–UCLA	128*			R/D	10–18	•		•		•	•	•
Quest Scholars Program at Stanford/QuestLeadership	128			R	15–19	•	•	•	•	•	•	•
Rawhide Ranch	129			R	7–15		•	•		•	•	
Redwood National Park Camps	129			R	10–18	•		•	•	•	•	•
River Way Ranch Camp	129			R	7–16	•	•	•	•	•	•	
Rock Star Camp at Pali Overnight Adventures	130			R	9–16		•	•			•	
Salmon Camp Research Team for Native Americans–Redwoods	130			R	15–18	•		•	•	•	•	
Santa Catalina School Summer Camp	130		R/D		8–14	•	•	•		•	•	
Saturday High at Art Center College of Design	130			D	14–18	•	•			•		
Science Program for High School Girls	131		R		15–17	•		•		•		•
Science Program for Middle School Boys on Catalina	131	R			11–15	•		•		•		•
Science Program for Middle School Girls on Catalina	131		R		11–15	•		•		•		•
Scuba Adventures at Pali Overnight Adventures	131			R	12–16	•	•	•	•	•	•	
SEACAMP San Diego	131			R/D	12–18	•		•	•	•		
SeaWorld San Diego Adventure Camp	132*			R/D	3–18	•	•	•		•		
Secret Agent Camp at Pali Overnight Adventures	132			R	9–16	•	•	•	•	•	•	
Sequoia Chamber Music Workshop	132			R	12–20	•	•	•			•	•
Shaffer's High Sierra Camp	133			R	9–16		•	•	•	•	•	•
Skateboarding Academy at Pali Overnight Adventures	133			R	9–16	•	•	•	•	•	•	
Skylake Yosemite Camp	133			R	7–16		•	•	•	•	•	
SoccerPlus Goalkeeper School–Challenge Program–San Diego, CA	133			R/D	10+			•			•	•
SoccerPlus Goalkeeper School–Challenge Program–Stockton, CA	134			R/D	10+			•			•	•
SoccerPlus Goalkeeper School–National Training Center–San Diego, CA	134			R	15+			•			•	
SoccerPlus Goalkeeper School–National Training Center–Stockton, CA	134			R	15+			•			•	•
Southwestern Academy International Summer Semester	134*			R/D	11–19	•	•	•	•	•		
Stanford Discovery Institutes	135*			R/D	15–18	•	•					•
Stanford Jazz Workshop	135			R/D	12+	•	•				•	•
Stanford Jazz Workshop: Jazz Camp	135			R/D	12–17	•	•				•	•
Stanford Jazz Workshop: Jazz Residency	136			R/D	14+	•	•				•	•
Stanford National Forensic Institute	136			R/D	14–18	•						•
Stanford University Summer College for High School Students	136*			R	16–18	•	•	•	•	•		•
Stevenson School Summer Camp	137			R/D	10–15	•	•	•	•	•	•	
Student Conservation Association–Conservation Crew Program (California)	137			R	15–19	•		•	•	•	•	•
Student Conservation Association–Conservation Leadership Corps, Bay Area	137			R/D	15+				•	•		•
Study Tours and Cinema Program in the USA–Oxnard College	137*			R	15+	•	•			•		
Study Tours and Leisure Sports in the USA–Citrus College	138*			R	15+	•		•		•		
Study Tours and Surf Program in the USA–Mira Costa College	138*			R	15+	•		•		•		
Study Tours in the USA–Citrus	138*			R	15+	•		•	•	•		
Study Tours in the USA–Mira Costa College	138*			R	15+	•	•	•	•	•		
Study Tours in the USA–Oxnard	139*			R	15+	•	•	•	•	•		
Summer Discovery at UCLA	139*			R		•	•	•	•	•	•	
Summer Discovery at UC San Diego	140*			R		•	•	•	•	•	•	•

This program is highlighted by a photograph, special note, or in-depth description; see the profile page for more information.
†D = day camp; R = residential camp

	GENERAL INFORMATION					PROGRAM INFORMATION						
	Profile Page	Boys D/R†	Girls D/R†	Coed D/R†	Age	Acad	Arts	Sports	Wild/ Outdrs	Special Interest	Jobs	Financial Aid
Summer Discovery at UC Santa Barbara	140*			R		•	•	•	•	•	•	•
Summer Focus at Berkeley	140*			R/D	14–18	•	•	•		•		•
The Summer Institute for the Gifted at UCLA	141*			R	8–17	•	•	•	•	•	•	•
The Summer Institute for the Gifted at University of California, Berkeley	141*			R	8–17	•					•	•
The Summer Science Program–California Campus	141			R	15–18	•		•	•	•	•	•
SuperCamp–Claremont Colleges	142*			R	9–24	•		•		•	•	•
SuperCamp–Stanford University	142*			R	11–18	•		•	•	•	•	
Technology Encounters–Video Encounter/Computer Encounter–California	142			D	7–13	•	•			•	•	•
Thunderbird Ranch	143			R/D	6–14		•	•	•	•	•	
UC San Diego Academic Connections	143			R	15–18	•	•	•		•	•	
UCSB Alumni Association Santa Barbara Family Vacation Center	143			R	1+		•	•	•	•	•	
University of San Diego Sports Camps–Baseball Camp	143			D	6–15			•			•	
University of San Diego Sports Camps–Boys Basketball High School Team Camp	144	R/D						•			•	
University of San Diego Sports Camps–Boys High School Basketball Camp	144	R/D			13–17			•			•	
University of San Diego Sports Camps–Boys High School Elite Baseball Camp	144	D			6–18			•			•	
University of San Diego Sports Camps–Boys High School Soccer Camp	144	R/D			13–17			•			•	
University of San Diego Sports Camps–Boys Junior Basketball Camp	144	R/D			8–12			•			•	
University of San Diego Sports Camps–Coed Junior Soccer Camp	145			R/D	8–12			•			•	
University of San Diego Sports Camps–Coed Water Polo Camp	145			R/D	11–17			•				•
University of San Diego Sports Camps–Competitive Swim Camp	145			R/D	9–17			•			•	
University of San Diego Sports Camps–Girls Basketball Fundamentals Camp	145		R/D		8–17			•			•	
University of San Diego Sports Camps–Girls Basketball High School Elite Camp	145		R/D					•			•	
University of San Diego Sports Camps–Girls Basketball High School Team Camp	146		R/D					•			•	
University of San Diego Sports Camps–Girls Soccer Camp	146		R/D		8–17			•			•	
University of San Diego Sports Camps–Girls Softball Advanced Camp	146		R/D		9–17			•			•	
University of San Diego Sports Camps–Girls Softball Beginner/Intermediate Camp	146		R/D		9–17			•			•	
University of San Diego Sports Camps–Girls Volleyball Camp	146		R					•			•	
University of San Diego Sports Camps–Sherri Stephens High School Tennis Camp	147			R/D	14–17			•			•	
University of San Diego Sports Camps–Sherri Stephens Junior Tennis Camp	147			R/D	9–17			•			•	
University of San Diego Sports Camps–Sports–N–More All Sports Camp	147			D	6–12		•	•			•	
University of San Diego Sports Camps–Sports–N–More Team Sports Camp	147			D	6–12			•			•	
University of San Diego Sports Camps–Sports–N–More Wet & Wild Sports Camp	148			D	6–12			•		•	•	
University of Southern California Summer Seminars	148			R	15–18	•	•	•		•	•	•
Ventures Travel Service–California	148				14–70					•	•	
Watersports Extravaganza at Pali Overnight Adventures	148			R	9–16	•	•	•	•	•	•	
Westcoast Connection Travel–Adventure California	149*				13–17			•	•	•	•	
Wilderness Ventures–California	149*				14–18			•	•	•	•	•
Wilderness Ventures–High Sierra	149*				14–18				•	•	•	•
Windsor Mountain: California Community Service	149*				13–15	•		•	•	•	•	•
YMCA Camp Oakes Rangers	149			R	8–13	•	•	•	•	•	•	•
YMCA Camp Oakes Teen Leadership	150			R	14–17	•	•	•	•	•	•	•
YMCA Camp Surf	150			R/D	8–17	•	•	•		•	•	•
Yo! Basecamp Rock Climbing Camps	150			R	11–18	•		•	•	•		•
Yosemite Backpacking Adventures	151				13–18	•	•	•	•	•		•
Young Actors Camp	151*			R/D	11–18		•				•	
Colorado												
AAVE–Rocky Mountain Adventure	151*				12–13			•	•	•	•	•

**This program is highlighted by a photograph, special note, or in-depth description; see the profile page for more information.*
†D = day camp; R = residential camp

	GENERAL INFORMATION					PROGRAM INFORMATION						
	Profile Page	Boys D/R†	Girls D/R†	Coed D/R†	Age	Acad	Arts	Sports	Wild/ Outdrs	Special Interest	Jobs	Financial Aid
Adventures Cross-Country, Colorado Adventure	151*			R	13–18			•	•		•	•
Anderson Camps' Colorado River Ranch for Boys/Hilltop Ranch for Girls	152			R	7–17			•	•	•	•	
Anderson Camps' Wilderness Pioneer Camp	152			R	14–17			•	•	•	•	
Bugs to Biospheres	152			R/D	14–18	•						•
Cheley Colorado Camps	153			R	9–17		•	•	•	•	•	
Colorado Academy Summer Programs	153			D	5–16	•	•	•	•	•	•	
The Colorado Mountain Ranch	153			D	7–16	•	•	•	•	•	•	•
Colvig Silver Camps	153			R	7–17	•	•	•	•	•	•	•
Community Sailing of Colorado–Advanced Sailing	154			D	8–17	•		•		•	•	•
Community Sailing of Colorado–Learn to Sail	154			D	8–17			•		•	•	•
Community Sailing of Colorado–Sailboat Racing Camp	154			D	8–17			•		•	•	•
Crow Canyon Archaeological Center High School Excavation Program	154			R	14–18	•	•		•	•		
Crow Canyon Archaeological Center High School Field School	155			R	14–18	•	•		•	•		•
Crow Canyon Archaeological Center Middle School Archaeology Program	155			R	12–14	•	•		•	•		
Deer Hill Expeditions, Colorado	155			R	13–22	•	•	•	•	•	•	
Denver Academy Summer Program	155			D	6–18	•	•				•	
Discovery Camp	156			R	9–16	•	•	•	•	•	•	•
Eagle Lake Bike Camp	156			R	12–20	•		•	•		•	•
Eagle Lake Camp Crew Program	156			R	15–18	•	•	•	•	•	•	•
Eagle Lake Horse Camp	156			R	12–18	•		•	•	•	•	•
Eagle Lake Resident Camp	157			R	8–18	•	•	•	•	•	•	•
Eagle Lake Wilderness Program	157			R	10–21	•		•	•		•	•
EDUCO Summer Adventure Programs	157			R	9–18	•	•	•	•	•	•	•
Flying G Ranch, Tomahawk Ranch	157		R		6–18	•	•	•	•	•	•	•
Geneva Glen Camp	158			R	6–16		•	•	•	•	•	•
Great Escapes (Adventure Trips for Teens)–Rocky Mountain Horsepacking Adventure	158				14–17			•	•	•	•	•
Horizon Adventures Inc.	158			R	13–17	•			•		•	•
iD Tech Camps–Colorado College, Colorado Springs, CO	158*			R/D	7–17	•	•	•		•	•	•
iD Tech Camps–University of Denver, Denver, CO	159*			R/D	7–17	•	•	•		•	•	•
Joe Machnik's No. 1 Academy One and Premier Programs–Colorado Springs, Colorado	159			R/D	9–18			•			•	•
Joe Machnik's No. 1 College Prep Academy–Colorado Springs, Colorado	159			R/D	13–17			•			•	•
Joe Machnik's No. 1 Mighty Mini, Goalkeeper and Striker Camp–Colorado Springs, Colorado	160			R/D	8–12			•			•	•
Keystone Counselor Assistant Program	160			R	15–17	•			•	•	•	•
Keystone Science Adventures	160			R	13–17	•			•	•	•	•
Landmark Volunteers: Colorado	160*			R	14–18	•		•	•	•	•	•
Longacre Expeditions, Leadership Training	160*				17–19			•	•	•	•	
On the Wing	161			R	12–16	•	•		•	•	•	•
Organic Farm Camp	161			R	13–17	•			•	•	•	•
Outpost Wilderness Adventure–Adventure Skills	161			R	11–17			•	•	•		•
Outpost Wilderness Adventure–Alpine Rock and Ice	161				13–17			•	•	•		•
Outpost Wilderness Adventure–Mountain Bike/Rock Camp	162			R	12–17			•	•			•
Outward Bound West–Backpacking, Climbing, and Rafting–Boys	162				12–13	•		•	•	•	•	•
Outward Bound West–Backpacking, Climbing, and Rafting–Colorado	162				14–15	•		•	•	•	•	•
Outward Bound West–Colorado Rockies Lightweight Backpacking	162				16+	•			•	•	•	•
Outward Bound West–Mountaineering–Colorado	163				16+	•			•	•	•	•
Perry-Mansfield Performing Arts School and Camp	163*			R/D	8–25		•	•	•	•	•	•
Poulter Colorado Camps	163			R	9–18	•	•	•	•	•	•	•
Rocky Mountain Village	164			R	7+	•	•	•	•	•	•	•
Sanborn Western Camps: Big Spring Ranch for Boys	164	R			9–17	•	•	•	•	•	•	
Sanborn Western Camps: High Trails Ranch for Girls	164		R		9–17	•	•	•	•	•	•	
Shwayder Camp	165			R	7–16	•	•	•	•	•	•	•
Student Conservation Association–Conservation Crew Program (Colorado)	165			R	15–19	•		•	•	•	•	•
Summer Study at The University of Colorado at Boulder	165*			R	15–18	•	•	•	•	•	•	•

This program is highlighted by a photograph, special note, or in-depth description; see the profile page for more information.
†D = day camp; R = residential camp

	GENERAL INFORMATION					PROGRAM INFORMATION						
	Profile Page	Boys D/R†	Girls D/R†	Coed D/R†	Age	Acad	Arts	Sports	Wild/ Outdrs	Special Interest	Jobs	Financial Aid
Summer Vet	166			R/D	15–18	•				•		•
SuperCamp–Colorado College	166*			R	11–18	•		•		•	•	•
Technology Encounters–Video Encounter/Computer Encounter–Colorado	166			D	7–13	•	•			•	•	•
Trailmark Outdoor Adventures–Colorado–West Elks with Backpack	166				13–14			•	•		•	•
Trailmark Outdoor Adventures–Colorado–West Elks with Horseback	167				13–14			•	•		•	•
WEI Leadership Training	167			R	13–17	•	•		•	•	•	•
Wilderness Adventure	167			R	13–17	•		•	•	•	•	•
Wildlife Camp	167			R	8–13	•	•	•	•	•	•	•
Connecticut												
Boulder Ridge Day Camp	168			D	4–13	•	•	•	•	•	•	
Buck's Rock Performing and Creative Arts Camp	168*			R	11–17	•	•	•	•	•	•	•
Camp Awosting	168	R			6–16	•	•	•	•	•	•	
Camp Chinqueka	169		R		6–16	•	•	•	•	•	•	
Campus Kids–CT	169			R	7–15		•	•	•	•	•	
Camp Wah-Nee	169			R	7–16		•	•	•	•	•	
Center for Creative Youth	170*			R	14–18		•				•	•
Channel 3 Kids Camp	170			R	8–12	•	•	•	•	•	•	•
Cheshire Academy Summer Program	171*			R/D	12–19	•	•	•	•	•		
Choate Rosemary Hall Beginning Writers Workshop	171*			D	10–12	•		•	•			•
Choate Rosemary Hall English Language Institute	171*			R/D	14–19	•	•	•	•			•
Choate Rosemary Hall English Language Institute/Focus Program	172*			R/D	12–14	•	•	•	•			•
Choate Rosemary Hall Focus Program	172*			R/D	12–14	•	•	•	•			•
Choate Rosemary Hall Immersion Program	172*			R/D	14–19	•		•	•			•
Choate Rosemary Hall John F. Kennedy Institute in Government	172*			R/D	15–19	•		•	•			•
Choate Rosemary Hall Math/Science Institute for Girls–CONNECT	173*		R/D		11–14	•		•	•	•		•
Choate Rosemary Hall Summer Arts Conservatory–Playwriting	173*			R/D	12–18		•	•			•	•
Choate Rosemary Hall Summer Arts Conservatory–Theater	174*			R/D	12–18		•	•			•	•
Choate Rosemary Hall Summer Arts Conservatory–Visual Arts Program	174*			R/D	12–18		•	•			•	•
Choate Rosemary Hall Summer Session	174*			R/D	12–19	•	•	•	•	•	•	•
Choate Rosemary Hall Writing Project	175*			R/D	13–18	•	•	•	•			•
Choate Rosemary Hall Young Writers Workshop	175*			R/D	11–14	•	•	•	•			•
Cybercamps–University of Hartford	175			R/D	7–18	•	•	•		•	•	
Exploration Senior Program at Yale University	175*			R/D	15–18	•	•	•	•	•	•	•
Greenhouse: Litchfield Jazz Festival Summer Dance Institute	176			R/D	13+		•	•				•
Hyde School Summer Challenge Program–Woodstock, CT	176*			R	13–18	•	•	•	•	•	•	
iD Tech Camps–Sacred Heart University, Fairfield, CT	176*			R/D	7–17	•	•	•		•	•	•
IMACS–Full Day Summer Camp–Connecticut	177			D	5–18	•				•	•	
IMACS–Individual Summer Programs–Connecticut	177			D	6–18	•				•	•	
Joel Ross Tennis & Sports Camp	177			R	8–18	•	•	•	•		•	
Joe Machnik's No. 1 Academy One and Premier Programs–Windsor, Connecticut	178			R/D	13–17			•			•	•
Joe Machnik's No. 1 College Prep Academy–Windsor, Connecticut	178			R/D	13–17			•			•	•
Joe Machnik's No. 1 Mighty Mini, Goalkeeper and Striker Camp–Windsor, Connecticut	178			R/D	8–12			•			•	•
Junior Statesmen Summer School–Yale University	178*			R	14–18	•				•		•
Kent School Summer Writers Camp	179			R	11–15	•	•	•	•		•	•
Landmark Volunteers: Connecticut	179*			R	14–18	•			•	•	•	•
Litchfield Jazz Festival Summer Music School Program	179			R/D	12+	•	•	•				•
Marvelwood Summer	179*			R/D	11–17	•	•	•	•	•	•	•
Miss Porter's School Athletic Experience	180		R/D		11–15			•				
Miss Porter's School Summer Challenge	180		R		12–15	•	•	•		•	•	•
Miss Porter's School Arts Alive!	180		R		12–15	•	•	•		•	•	•
Mountain Workshop–Bike Touring Days 1	181			D	11–13			•	•	•	•	
Mountain Workshop/Dirt Camp–Mountain Bike Days 1	181			D	12–14			•	•	•	•	
Mountain Workshop/Dirt Camp–Mountain Bike Days 3	181			D	14–17			•	•	•	•	
Mountain Workshop/Dirt Camp–Mountain Bike Days 2	181			D	13–15			•	•	•	•	

**This program is highlighted by a photograph, special note, or in-depth description; see the profile page for more information.*
†D = day camp; R = residential camp

	GENERAL INFORMATION					PROGRAM INFORMATION						
	Profile Page	Boys D/R†	Girls D/R†	Coed D/R†	Age	Acad	Arts	Sports	Wild/ Outdrs	Special Interest	Jobs	Financial Aid
Mountain Workshop–Graduate Awesome Adventures	181			D	11–12			•	•		•	
Mountain Workshop–Junior Awesome Adventures	182			D	9–10			•	•		•	
Mountain Workshop–Original Awesome Adventures	182			D	10–11			•	•		•	
Mountain Workshop–Trailblazer Awesome Adventures	182			D	8–9			•	•		•	
National Computer Camps at Fairfield University	182			R/D	8–18	•	•	•		•	•	
National Guitar Workshop–New Milford, CT	182			R/D	13–79	•	•				•	•
The Oxford Academy Summer Program	183	R			14–20	•	•	•	•		•	
Rainbow Club–Greenwich, Connecticut	183			D	3–16		•	•		•		•
Rectory School Summer Session	183*			R/D	9–15	•	•	•				
Rumsey Hall School Summer Session	184*			R/D	8–15	•		•	•			•
Saint Thomas More School–Summer Academic Camp	184*	R			12–19	•	•	•		•	•	
Salisbury Summer School of Reading and English	185*			R	13–18	•	•	•	•		•	•
The Sarah Porter Leadership Institute	185		R		12–15	•		•		•		
SJ Ranch Riding Camp	185		R		8–16		•	•		•	•	
SoccerPlus FieldPlayer Academy–Kent, CT	186			R/D	11+			•			•	•
SoccerPlus Goalkeeper School–Advanced National Training Center–Connecticut	186			R	12+			•			•	•
SoccerPlus Goalkeeper School–Challenge Program–Kent, CT	186			R/D	10+			•			•	•
SoccerPlus Goalkeeper School–Challenge Program–Suffield, CT	186			R/D	10+			•			•	•
SoccerPlus Goalkeeper School–Competitive Program–Kent, CT	186			R	12+			•			•	•
SoccerPlus Goalkeeper School–Competitive Program–Suffield, CT	186			R	12+			•			•	•
SoccerPlus Goalkeeper School–National Training Center–Kent, CT	187			R	15+			•			•	•
Student Conservation Association–Conservation Crew Program (Connecticut)	187			R	15–19	•		•	•	•	•	•
The Summer Academy at Suffield	187			R/D	12–18	•	•	•	•	•	•	•
The Summer Institute for the Gifted at Fairfield University	187*			D	6–11	•	•	•		•	•	•
Taft Summer School	188*			R/D	12–18	•	•	•			•	•
UCAELI Summer Camp	188			R	13–18	•	•	•		•	•	
United Soccer Academy–Goal Keeping Training Camp, Connecticut	189			R/D	8–14			•			•	
United Soccer Academy–Junior Soccer Squirts, Connecticut	189			D	3–5			•			•	
United Soccer Academy–Recreation Soccer Community Camp, Connecticut	189			R/D	7–14			•			•	
United Soccer Academy–Senior Soccer Squirts, Connecticut	189			D	5–7			•			•	
United Soccer Academy–Team Training Camp, Connecticut	189			R/D	8–14			•			•	
United Soccer Academy–Travel Soccer Community Camp, Connecticut	190			R/D	8–14			•			•	
University of Connecticut Community School of the Arts–Music Camps	190			D	9–18		•					
University of Connecticut Community School of the Arts–World Arts Camps	190			D	6–13		•			•		
University of Connecticut Mentor Connection	190*			R	15–18	•	•			•	•	•
Delaware												
Student Conservation Association–Conservation Crew Program (Delaware)	191			R	15–19	•		•	•	•	•	•
United Soccer Academy–Goal Keeping Training Camp, Delaware	191			R/D	8–14			•			•	
United Soccer Academy–Junior Soccer Squirts, Delaware	191			D	3–5			•			•	
United Soccer Academy–Recreation Soccer Community Camp, Delaware	191			R/D	7–14			•			•	
United Soccer Academy–Senior Soccer Squirts, Delaware	192			D	5–7			•			•	
United Soccer Academy–Team Training Camp, Delaware	192			R/D	8–14			•			•	
United Soccer Academy–Travel Soccer Community Camp, Delaware	192			R/D	8–14			•			•	
University of Delaware Summer College	192*			R	16–18	•		•				•
District of Columbia												
Catholic University Benjamin T. Rome School of Music	193			R/D	11–18	•	•	•			•	•
Catholic University Capitol Classic Debate Institute	193			R/D	14–18	•		•			•	•
Catholic University College Courses for High School Students	193			R/D	15+	•	•	•		•	•	
Catholic University Communication and Media Studies Workshops	194			R/D	14–18	•	•	•			•	
Catholic University Experiences in Architecture	194			R/D	15–18	•		•			•	•
Catholic University Eye on Engineering	194			R	17–18	•		•		•	•	
Catholic University of America–Capitol Mock Trial Institute	194			R/D	14–18	•						•

This program is highlighted by a photograph, special note, or in-depth description; see the profile page for more information.
†D = day camp; R = residential camp

	GENERAL INFORMATION					PROGRAM INFORMATION						
	Profile Page	Boys D/R†	Girls D/R†	Coed D/R†	Age	Acad	Arts	Sports	Wild/ Outdrs	Special Interest	Jobs	Financial Aid
Catholic University of America–the Capitol Hill Lincoln-Douglas Debate Group	195			R/D	14–18	•		•				•
The Congressional Seminar	195			R	15–18	•					•	
Corcoran College of Art and Design–Camp Creativity	195			D	6–15	•	•			•	•	
Corcoran College of Art and Design–Focus on Photojournalism	195			R/D	16+	•	•			•	•	
Corcoran College of Art and Design–Pre-College Summer Portfolio Workshop	195			R/D	16+	•	•			•	•	
Cybercamps–American University	196			R/D	7–18	•	•	•		•	•	•
Diplomacy and Global Affairs Seminar	196			R	15–19	•					•	
Georgetown University College Prep Program	196*			R/D	15–18	•						•
Georgetown University International Relations Program for High School Students	197*			R/D	15–18	•						
Georgetown University Summer College for High School Juniors	197*			R	16–18	•						•
George Washington University Summer Scholars Pre-college Program	197*			R		•	•	•	•		•	•
iD Tech Camps–Georgetown University, Washington, DC	198*			R/D	7–17	•	•	•		•	•	•
Junior Statesmen Summer School–Georgetown University	198*			R	15–18	•				•		•
National Student Leadership Conference: Business and Commerce	199*			R	14–18	•		•		•	•	•
National Student Leadership Conference: International Diplomacy	199*			R	14–18	•		•		•	•	•
National Student Leadership Conference: Law and Advocacy–Washington, DC	199*			R	14–18	•		•		•	•	•
National Student Leadership Conference: Mastering Leadership	200*			R	14–18	•		•		•	•	•
Sidwell Friends Basketball Camp	200			D	7–14			•			•	
Sidwell Friends DaVinci Days Art Studios, Young Artist Academy and Young Scientist Academy	200			D	5–18		•				•	
Sidwell Friends Drama and Dance Workshops with BAPA	200			D	8–18		•					
Sidwell Friends Explorer Day Camp, Explorer Voyagers and ExploreStar	200			D	4	•	•	•		•	•	•
Sidwell Friends Soccer Program with American Soccer Academy	201			D	5–18			•			•	
Sidwell Friends Summer Community Service Programs	201			R/D	5–18	•	•		•	•	•	•
Sidwell Friends Summer Studies	201			D	12–18	•	•			•		
Sidwell Friends Tennis Camp	201			D	6–18			•			•	
Summer Discovery at Georgetown	201*			R		•	•	•		•	•	
Summer JAM (Judaism, Activism, and Mitzvah Work)	202			R	15–18	•	•	•	•	•		•
Washington International School Passport to Summer	202			D	3–15	•	•	•		•	•	•
Washington Internship Experience	202			R	16–20	•					•	
Florida												
Camp Little Palm for the Performing Arts	203			D	7–14		•				•	
Cybercamps–Rollins College	203			R/D	7–18	•	•	•		•	•	•
EARTHWATCH INSTITUTE–Wild Dolphin Societies	203			R	16+	•				•		•
Embry-Riddle Aeronautical University–Aerospace Summer Camp	203			R	12–18	•				•		
Embry-Riddle Aeronautical University–Aviation Career Exploration	204			R	12–18	•				•		
Embry-Riddle Aeronautical University–Flight Exploration	204			R	12–18	•				•		
Embry-Riddle Aeronautical University–Generations	204			R	12+	•				•		
Embry-Riddle Aeronautical University–Sun Flight	204			R	16–18	•				•		
Episcopal High School Academic Camp	204			D	12–18	•	•			•		
Episcopal High School Eagle Arts Camp	205			D	6–16		•	•				
Episcopal High School Sports Camp	205			D	10–18			•				
Florida Air Academy Summer Session	205	R/D			11+	•		•		•		
Fotocamp	205			D	10–17	•	•				•	
FUN-damental Basketball Camp–The Sports Mall	205			D	6–14			•			•	
iD Tech Camps–University of Miami, Coral Gables, FL	206*			R/D	7–17	•	•	•		•	•	•
IMACS–Full Day Summer Camp–Florida	206			D	5–18	•				•	•	
IMACS–Individual Summer Programs–Florida	206			D	6–18	•				•	•	
Joe Machnik's No. 1 Academy One and Premier Programs–Vero Beach, Florida	206			R/D	9–18			•			•	•
Joe Machnik's No. 1 Mighty Mini, Goalkeeper and Striker Camp–Vero Beach, Florida	207			R/D	8–12			•			•	•
Kampus Kampers	207			R	6–13	•	•	•		•	•	

This program is highlighted by a photograph, special note, or in-depth description; see the profile page for more information.
†D = day camp; R = residential camp

	GENERAL INFORMATION					PROGRAM INFORMATION						
	Profile Page	Boys D/R†	Girls D/R†	Coed D/R†	Age	Acad	Arts	Sports	Wild/ Outdrs	Special Interest	Jobs	Financial Aid
Keenan McCardell and Jimmy Smith Football Camp/Sports International	207			R/D	8–18			•			•	
Keenan McCardell Football Camp	207			R/D	8–18			•			•	•
Montverde Academy Summer School	207			R/D	12–18	•	•	•		•		
The New York Film Academy, Disney-MGM Studios, FL	208*			R	14–17		•					
Pine Tree Camps at Lynn University	208			R/D	3–14	•	•	•		•	•	
Ringling School of Art and Design Pre-College Perspective	208			R/D	16–18	•	•					•
Ringling School of Art and Design's Teen Studio	208			D	12–18	•	•					•
St. Johns Summer Camp	209			D	5–13		•	•		•	•	
Seacamp	209*			R	12–17	•	•	•	•	•	•	
SeaWorld/Busch Gardens Tampa Bay Adventure Camp	209*			R	4+	•		•		•	•	
SeaWorld Orlando Adventure Camp	210*			R/D		•				•	•	
Student Conservation Association–Conservation Crew Program (Florida)	210			R	15–19	•		•	•	•	•	•
Tampa Prep–Academic Credit and Enrichment Courses	210			D	12–18	•				•	•	
Tampa Prep–Boys Athletic Camps	211	D			6–18			•			•	
Tampa Prep–Girls Athletic Camps	211		D		10–18			•			•	
Tampa Prep–Terrapin Day Camp	211			D	5–11	•	•	•		•	•	
Technology Encounters–Video Encounter/Computer Encounter–Florida	211			D	7–13	•	•			•	•	•
Teen Tours of America–Golf Camp–Florida Swing	211				12–17			•	•	•	•	
University of Miami Summer Scholar Programs	212*			R	16–17	•	•	•		•		•
Ventures Travel Service–Florida	212				14–70					•	•	
Westcoast Connection–Florida Swing Junior Touring Golf Camp	212*				13–17			•		•	•	•
Georgia												
Atlanta College of Art–Pre-College Program	212			R/D	16–18	•	•			•		•
Camp Barney Medintz	213*			R	8–16	•	•	•	•	•	•	•
Camp WinShape for Boys	213	R			7–16	•	•	•	•	•		
Camp WinShape for Girls	213		R		7–16	•	•	•	•	•		•
Concordia Language Villages–French–Savannah, GA	214			R	7–13	•	•	•	•	•	•	•
Darlington School Summer Camps	214*			R	10–15	•		•	•	•		
Emagination Computer Camps–Georgia	214*			R/D	8–17	•	•	•		•	•	•
iD Tech Camps–Emory University, Atlanta, GA	215*			R/D	7–17	•	•	•		•	•	•
Joe Machnik's No. 1 Academy One and Premier Programs–Rome, Georgia	215			R/D	9–18			•			•	•
Joe Machnik's No. 1 Mighty Mini, Goalkeeper and Striker Camp–Rome, Georgia	215			R/D	8–12			•			•	•
KidzZone Summer Camp	215			D	5–17	•	•	•	•	•	•	•
MidSummer Macon	216			R/D	7–18	•	•				•	•
National Computer Camps at Oglethorpe University	216			R/D	8–18	•	•	•		•	•	
Riverside Military Academy High Adventure Camp	216	R			12–17			•	•			
Riverside Military Academy Summer Opportunity and Academic Review	216	R/D			11–17	•		•		•		
Riverside Military Academy Young Cadet Camp	217	D			10–13			•	•	•		
SoccerPlus FieldPlayer Academy–Rome, GA	217			R/D	11+			•			•	•
SoccerPlus Goalkeeper School–Challenge Program–Rome, GA	217			R/D	10+			•			•	•
SoccerPlus Goalkeeper School–Competitive Program–Rome, GA	217			R	12+			•			•	•
SoccerPlus Goalkeeper School–National Training Center–Rome, GA	217			R	15+			•			•	
Squirrel Hollow Learning Camp	217			R	7–16	•	•	•	•	•	•	•
Student Conservation Association–Conservation Crew Program (Georgia)	218			R	15–19	•		•	•	•	•	•
Valley View Ranch Equestrian Camp	218		R		8–17		•	•	•	•	•	
White Water Learning Center of Georgia Kids Kayaking Summer Day Camp	218			D	9–14			•	•			
Hawaii												
AAC–Aloha Adventure Photo Camp	219			R/D	10–18	•	•	•	•	•	•	
AAC–Aloha Adventure Surf Camp	219			R/D	10–18	•	•	•	•	•	•	•
AAVE–Hawaii	219*				14–18			•	•	•	•	•
Adventures Cross-Country, Hawaii Adventure	219*			R	13–18			•	•	•	•	•
Alpengirl–Hawaii	220				11–17	•		•	•		•	•

**This program is highlighted by a photograph, special note, or in-depth description; see the profile page for more information.*
†D = day camp; R = residential camp

	GENERAL INFORMATION					PROGRAM INFORMATION						
	Profile Page	Boys D/R†	Girls D/R†	Coed D/R†	Age	Acad	Arts	Sports	Wild/ Outdrs	Special Interest	Jobs	Financial Aid
Big Island Volleyball Elite Camp	220*			R/D				•				
Big Island Volleyball Player Camp	220*			R/D				•				
Hawaii Extreme Adventure Scuba Camp	220			R	12–20	•		•	•		•	
Hawaii Preparatory Academy Summer Session	220*			R/D	12–17	•	•	•	•	•	•	
Longacre Expeditions, Hawaii	221*				15–18	•		•	•	•	•	
Maui Surfer Girls	221		R		11–17		•	•	•		•	•
Maui Surfer Girls–Advanced Surf Camp on Kauai	221		R		11–17		•	•	•		•	•
Maui Surfer Girls–Mother/Daughter	222		R/D		11+		•	•	•		•	•
Overland: American Community Service, Hawaii	222*				15–18			•	•	•	•	
Overland: Hawaii Explorer Hiking, Kayaking, Sailing and Snorkeling	222*				14–18			•	•	•	•	
Putney Student Travel–Community Service–Hawaii	222*			R		•		•	•	•		•
RUSTIC PATHWAYS–HAWAIIAN ISLANDS ADVENTURE	222*				13–18			•	•	•	•	
Sidwell Friends Service Expedition to Hawaii	223				13–17					•		
Student Conservation Association–Conservation Crew Program (Hawaii)	223			R	15–19	•		•	•	•	•	•
Surf Quest	223			R	10–17			•	•	•	•	
Wilderness Ventures–Hawaii	223*				13–18			•	•	•	•	•
Windsor Mountain: Hawaii	223*				14–17	•		•	•	•	•	•
World Horizons International–Oahu, Hawaii	224*			R	14–18			•	•	•	•	•
Idaho												
EARTHWATCH INSTITUTE–Restoring the Sagebrush Steppe	224			R	16+	•			•	•		•
Idaho Engineering Science Camp	224			R	13–16	•	•	•		•	•	•
Landmark Volunteers: Idaho	225*			R	14–18	•			•	•	•	•
Student Conservation Association–Conservation Crew Program (Idaho)	225			R	15–19	•		•	•	•	•	•
Illinois												
Alex Brown and Dustin Lyman Football Camp/Sports International	225			R/D	8–18			•			•	
Andy McCollum Football Camp	225			R/D	8–18			•			•	
Camp Cedar Point	225		R		7–17	•	•	•	•	•	•	•
Center for American Archeology/Archeology Field School	226			R	13–17	•	•			•	•	•
Center for American Archeology/Past Lifeways Program	226			R/D	8–18	•	•			•		
Center for Talent Development Summer Academic Program	226*			R/D	4–17	•	•	•		•	•	•
Columbia College Chicago's High School Summer Institute	227			R/D	15–18	•	•			•		•
Cybercamps–Benedictine University	227			R/D	7–18	•	•	•		•	•	
Cybercamps–Concordia University	227			R/D	7–18	•	•	•		•	•	•
EARTHWATCH INSTITUTE–Moundbuilders on the Mississippi	228			R	16+	•				•		•
Emagination Computer Camps–Illinois	228*			R/D	8–17	•	•	•		•	•	
iD Tech Camps–Lake Forest College, Evanston, IL	228*			R/D	7–17	•	•	•		•	•	•
iD Tech Camps–Northwestern University, Chicago, IL	228*			R/D	7–17	•	•	•		•	•	•
Junior Statesmen Summer School–Northwestern University	229*			R	14–18	•				•		•
Kendall College Culinary Camp	229			R/D	14–18					•		
National Guitar Workshop–Chicago, IL	229			R/D	13+		•				•	•
The National Music Workshop Day Jams–Chicago, IL	230			D	9–15	•	•				•	•
Northwestern University's College Preparation Program	230*			R/D	16–18	•	•	•	•			•
Northwestern University's National High School Institute	230*			R	14–18	•	•				•	•
Power Chord Academy–Chicago	231			R	12–18	•	•				•	
SoccerPlus FieldPlayer Academy–Charleston, IL	231			R/D	11+			•			•	•
SoccerPlus Goalkeeper School–Challenge Program–Charleston, IL	231			R/D	10+			•			•	•
SoccerPlus Goalkeeper School–Competitive Program–Charleston, IL	231			R	12+			•			•	•
SoccerPlus Goalkeeper School–National Training Center–Charleston, IL	232			R	15+			•			•	
Student Conservation Association–Conservation Crew Program (Illinois)	232			R	15–19	•		•	•	•	•	•
University of Chicago–Insight	232*			R/D	15–18	•	•			•		•
University of Chicago–Research in the Biological Sciences	232*			R	15–18	•						•
University of Chicago–Summer Quarter for High School Students	233*			R/D	15–18	•	•					•
Indiana												
Ball State University Summer Journalism Workshops	233			R	11–18	•	•				•	•

This program is highlighted by a photograph, special note, or in-depth description; see the profile page for more information.
†D = day camp; R = residential camp

	GENERAL INFORMATION					PROGRAM INFORMATION						
	Profile Page	Boys D/R†	Girls D/R†	Coed D/R†	Age	Acad	Arts	Sports	Wild/ Outdrs	Special Interest	Jobs	Financial Aid
Camp Superkids–Camp Crosley	233			R	7–14		•	•	•	•	•	•
Camp Superkids–Happy Hollow Children's Camp	234			R	7–14		•	•	•	•	•	•
Culver Summer Camps/Culver Specialty Camp– Aviation	234*			R	13–17	•				•	•	•
Culver Summer Camps/Culver Specialty Camp–Equestrian Arts	234*			R	11–16			•		•	•	•
Culver Summer Camps/Culver Specialty Camp–Fencing	235*			R	11–16			•			•	•
Culver Summer Camps/Culver Specialty Camp–Golf	235*			R	11–16			•			•	•
Culver Summer Camps/Culver Specialty Camp–Ice Hockey	235*			R	11–16			•			•	•
Culver Summer Camps/Culver Specialty Camp–Sailing	235*			R	11–16			•		•	•	•
Culver Summer Camps/Culver Specialty Camp–Scuba	236*			R	12–16			•		•	•	•
Culver Summer Camps/Culver Specialty Camp–Soccer	236*			R	11–16			•		•	•	•
Culver Summer Camps/Culver Specialty Camp–Tennis	236*			R	11–16			•			•	•
Culver Summer Camps/Culver Specialty Camp–Water Ski	236*			R	11–16			•		•	•	•
Culver Summer Camps/Upper Camp–Boys	237*	R			13–17	•	•	•	•	•	•	•
Culver Summer Camps/Upper Camp–Girls	237*		R		13–17	•	•	•	•	•	•	•
Culver Summer Woodcraft Camp	238*			R	9–13	•	•	•	•	•	•	•
Explore-A-College	238			R	14–17	•	•				•	•
Indiana University School of Music College Audition Preparation Workshop	238			R	15–18	•	•					
Indiana University School of Music Piano Academy	239			R	10–19	•	•					•
Indiana University School of Music Recorder Academy	239			R	10–19	•	•					•
Indiana University School of Music String Academy	239			R	10–19	•	•					•
OPTIONS for Young Women	239		R		14–18	•		•		•		•
Ramey Summer Riding Camps	240			R/D	10–80			•		•	•	
Student Conservation Association–Conservation Crew Program (Indiana)	240			R	15–19	•		•	•	•	•	•
Iowa												
Camp Courageous of Iowa	240			R	3–80		•	•	•	•	•	•
Camp Hitaga	240			R/D	6–16		•	•	•	•	•	•
Camp Hitaga–Stirrups and Saddles	241			R	10–16		•	•	•	•	•	•
Grinnell Summer Institute	241*			R		•	•	•			•	
Iowa Young Writers' Studio	241			R	14–18	•	•					•
Loras All-Sports Camp	241			R/D	7–13			•	•		•	•
Student Conservation Association–Conservation Crew Program (Iowa)	242			R	15–19	•		•	•	•	•	•
Ventures Travel Service–Iowa	242				14–70					•	•	
Kansas												
Bill Self Kansas Summer Basketball Camp	242	R/D			8–19			•			•	
Future Astronaut Training Program	242			R	12–15	•				•	•	•
Jayhawk Debate Institute	243			R/D	13–18	•					•	
Kansas Journalism Institute	243			R	13–18	•	•			•	•	•
KU Jazz Workshop	243			R/D	13+	•	•				•	
KU Marching Band Camps	243			R/D	13–18		•			•	•	
Mars Academy	243			R	10–12	•				•	•	•
Student Conservation Association–Conservation Crew Program (Kansas)	244			R	15–19	•		•	•	•	•	•
University of Kansas–Boys Soccer Camp	244	R/D			9–13			•			•	
University of Kansas–Duke University Talent Identification Program	244			R	12–18	•	•			•	•	•
University of Kansas–Girls Golf Camp	244		R/D		10–18			•			•	
University of Kansas–Girls Soccer Camp	244		R/D		9–18			•			•	
University of Kansas–Jayhawk Baseball Camps–Little League, Super Skills, and All-Star	245			R/D	7–18			•			•	
University of Kansas–Jayhawk Boys and Girls Tennis Camp	245			R	13–18			•			•	
University of Kansas–Jayhawk Golf Camp–Boys	245	R/D			10–18			•			•	
University of Kansas–Jayhawk Swim Camp	245			R	9–18			•			•	•
University of Kansas–Jayhawk Track and Field/Cross Country Camps	245			R/D	11–18			•			•	
University of Kansas–Jayhawk Volleyball Camp	246			R/D	11–18			•			•	
University of Kansas–Midwestern Music Camp–Junior and Senior Divisions	246			R/D	11–18	•	•				•	•

**This program is highlighted by a photograph, special note, or in-depth description; see the profile page for more information.*
†D = day camp; R = residential camp

	GENERAL INFORMATION					PROGRAM INFORMATION						
	Profile Page	Boys D/R†	Girls D/R†	Coed D/R†	Age	Acad	Arts	Sports	Wild/ Outdrs	Special Interest	Jobs	Financial Aid
University of Kansas–Natural History Museum Summer Workshops	246			D	4–14	•				•	•	•
University of Kansas–Project Discovery	246		R		13–18	•	•	•		•	•	•
University of Kansas–School of Pharmacy Summer Camp	246			R	13–18	•				•	•	•
University of Kansas–Sertoma-Schiefelbush Communication Camp	247			D	4–16	•	•			•	•	•
University of Kansas–Softball–Teen and Advanced Camps	247			R/D	13–18			•			•	
University of Kansas–Sports Skills and Fitness Camp	247			D	7–14			•				•
Kentucky												
Cage Scope/High Potential "Blue-Chip" Basketball Camp	247	R			14–20			•				
EARTHWATCH INSTITUTE–Mammoth Cave	247			R	16+	•	•		•	•		•
Foster Guitar Camp	248			R/D	13+	•	•	•			•	•
Foster High School Band Camp	248			R/D	14–17	•	•	•			•	•
Foster High School Strings Camp	248			R/D	13–18	•	•	•			•	•
Foster Middle School Band Camp	248			R/D	12+	•	•	•			•	•
Foster Middle School Strings Camp	249			R/D	12+	•	•	•			•	•
Foster Piano Camp I	249			R/D	12+	•	•	•			•	•
Foster Piano Camp II	249			R/D	14–17	•	•	•			•	•
Foster Vocal Camp	249			R/D	14–17	•	•	•			•	•
Ramey Summer Tennis Camps	249			R/D	8–80			•			•	
Student Conservation Association–Conservation Crew Program (Kentucky)	250			R	15–19	•		•	•	•	•	•
Ventures Travel Service–Kentucky	250				14–70					•	•	
Louisiana												
Camp Bon Coeur	250			R	8–16	•	•	•	•	•	•	•
Camp Fire Camp Wi-Ta-Wentin	250			R/D	5–12	•	•	•	•	•	•	•
Deuce McCallister Football Camp	251			R/D	8–18			•			•	•
The Governor's Program for Gifted Children	251			R	12–16	•	•	•			•	•
Lady Wildcat Basketball Camp	251		R/D					•				
Louisiana College Center for Academically Talented Students (CATS)	251			D	6–15	•	•	•		•	•	
Louisiana College Summer Superior Program	251			R/D	16–18	•	•	•			•	•
Marydale Resident Camp	252		R		5–17	•	•	•	•	•	•	•
National Guitar Workshop–New Orleans, LA	252			R/D	13–79	•	•				•	•
Student Conservation Association–Conservation Crew Program (Louisiana)	252			R	15–19	•		•	•	•	•	•
Wildcat Basketball Camp	253	R/D						•				
Maine												
Acadia Institute of Oceanography	253*			R	11–19	•		•	•	•		•
Agassiz Village	253			R	8–17	•	•	•	•	•	•	•
Alford Lake Camp	253*		R		8–15		•	•	•	•	•	•
Alford Lake Family Camp	254*			R			•	•	•	•		
Appalachian Mountain Club–Volunteer Trail Crew–Grafton Loop	254			R	16+				•	•	•	
BICYCLE TRAVEL ADVENTURES–Student Hosteling Program–Maine Coast	254*				13–15			•	•	•	•	
Camp All-Star	255			R	9–15	•	•	•	•	•	•	•
Camp Androscoggin	255	R			8–15		•	•	•	•	•	
Camp Arcadia	255*		R		7–17		•	•	•	•	•	•
Camp Chewonki	256	R			8–15	•	•	•	•	•	•	•
Camp Chewonki Adventure Camps	256			R	10–15	•	•	•	•	•	•	•
Camp Chewonki for Girls	256		R		12–17	•	•	•	•	•	•	•
Camp Chewonki Wilderness Expeditions	257			R	12+	•	•	•	•	•	•	•
Camp Encore-Coda for a Great Summer of Music, Sports, and Friends	257*			R	9–17	•	•	•	•	•	•	•
Camp Hawthorne	257			R	7–17	•	•	•	•	•	•	•
Camp Hawthorne Creative Arts Camp	258			R	8–16	•	•	•	•	•	•	•
Camp Kawanhee for Boys	258	R			7–15		•	•	•	•	•	•
Camp Kirkwold	258		R		7–17		•	•	•	•	•	•
Camp Laurel	259			R	8–15		•	•	•	•	•	
Camp Laurel South	259			R	7–15		•	•	•	•	•	

**This program is highlighted by a photograph, special note, or in-depth description; see the profile page for more information.*
†D = day camp; R = residential camp

	GENERAL INFORMATION					PROGRAM INFORMATION						
	Profile Page	Boys D/R†	Girls D/R†	Coed D/R†	Age	Acad	Arts	Sports	Wild/ Outdrs	Special Interest	Jobs	Financial Aid
Camp Matoaka for Girls	259		R		8–15	•	•	•	•	•	•	
Camp Micah	260			R	8–16		•	•	•	•	•	
Camp Modin	260			R	7–16	•	•	•	•	•	•	
Camp Nashoba North	260			R	7–15	•	•	•	•	•	•	
Camp O-AT-KA	261*	R			7–16		•	•	•	•	•	•
Camp Pinehurst	261	R			5–14			•	•	•	•	
Camp Pondicherry	261		R		7–17		•	•	•	•	•	•
Camp Runoia	262		R		8–17	•	•	•	•	•	•	•
Camp Scelkit	262		R		7–13		•			•	•	•
Camp Skylemar	262	R			7–15		•	•	•	•	•	•
Camp Tapawingo	262		R		7–16		•	•	•	•	•	
Camp Timanous	263	R			7–15		•	•	•	•	•	•
Camp Wawenock	263		R		8–17		•	•	•	•	•	
Camp Waziyatah	263*			R	7–15	•	•	•	•	•	•	•
Camp Wekeela for Boys and Girls	264*			R	6–16		•	•	•	•	•	
Camp Winnebago	264	R			8–15	•	•	•	•	•	•	
Chop Point Camp	265			R	12–18	•	•	•	•	•	•	•
Darrow Wilderness Trips–Kayak	265			R	12–17			•	•		•	
Darrow Wilderness Trips–Maine	265				9–17			•	•		•	•
Darrow Wilderness Trips–St. Croix	265				13–15			•	•		•	•
Darrow Wilderness Trips–Voyageurs	266				11–12			•	•		•	•
Darrow Youth Backpacking	266				14+				•		•	•
EARTHWATCH INSTITUTE–Coastal Archaeology of Maine	266			R	16+	•				•		•
EARTHWATCH INSTITUTE–Maine's Island Ecology	266			R	16+	•				•		•
The Festival of Creative Youth	266			D	6–16	•	•	•		•	•	•
Flying Moose Lodge	267	R			10–16	•		•	•	•	•	•
Friends Camp	267			R	7–17		•	•	•	•	•	•
Great Escapes (Adventure Trips for Teens)–Maine Waterways	267				14–17			•	•	•	•	•
Hidden Valley Camp	268*			R	8–14		•	•	•	•	•	
Hurricane Island Outward Bound–Maine Coast and Western Maine Canoeing and Sailing	268				15–17	•		•	•	•	•	•
Hurricane Island Outward Bound–Maine Coast and Western Maine Sailing and Backpacking	268				15+	•		•	•	•	•	•
Hurricane Island Outward Bound–Maine Coast and Western Maine Sea Kayaking and Backpacking	269				15+	•		•	•	•	•	•
Hurricane Island Outward Bound–Maine Coast Sailing/Sailing and Rock Climbing	269				15+	•		•	•	•	•	•
Hurricane Island Outward Bound–Maine Coast Schooner Sailing	269				16+	•		•	•	•	•	•
Hurricane Island Outward Bound–Maine Coast Sea Kayaking	269				16+	•		•	•	•	•	•
Hurricane Island Outward Bound–Maine Woods High School Summer Semester	270				15–17	•		•	•	•	•	•
Hurricane Island Outward Bound–North Woods Maine Allagash and Appalachian Trail Canoeing and Backpacking	270				15–17	•		•	•	•	•	•
Hurricane Island Outward Bound–North Woods Maine Canoeing and Backpacking	270				15+	•		•	•	•	•	•
Hurricane Island Outward Bound–North Woods Maine Expedition Canoeing	270				15–17	•		•	•	•	•	•
Hurricane Island Outward Bound–Western Maine Backpacking and Rock Climbing	271				15+	•		•	•	•	•	•
Hurricane Island Outward Bound–Western Maine Woods Expedition Canoeing	271				14–15	•		•	•	•	•	•
Hyde School Summer Challenge Program–Bath, ME	271*			R	13–18	•	•	•	•	•	•	
Kamp Kohut	271			R	7–16	•	•	•	•	•	•	
Kingsley Pines Camp	272			R	8–15	•	•	•	•	•	•	•
Kippewa for Girls	272*		R		6–16		•	•	•	•	•	
Kroka Expeditions–Coastal Sea Kayaking	273				14–18	•	•	•	•	•	•	•
Landmark Volunteers: Maine	273*			R	14–18	•		•	•	•	•	•
Longacre Expeditions, Downeast	273*				13–17			•	•	•	•	
Longacre Expeditions, Photography	274*				14–17		•	•	•		•	•
Longacre Expeditions, Whales	274*				14–17	•		•	•		•	•

*This program is highlighted by a photograph, special note, or in-depth description; see the profile page for more information.
†D = day camp; R = residential camp

	GENERAL INFORMATION					PROGRAM INFORMATION						
	Profile Page	Boys D/R†	Girls D/R†	Coed D/R†	Age	Acad	Arts	Sports	Wild/ Outdrs	Special Interest	Jobs	Financial Aid
Maine College of Art Early College Program	274			R/D	16–18	•	•				•	•
Maine Conservation School Summer Camps	274			R	8–18	•		•	•	•	•	•
Maine Golf Academy–Family Camp	275			R	8–17		•	•	•	•		•
Maine Golf Academy–Junior Golf Camp	275			R/D	9–17	•	•	•	•	•	•	•
Maine Golf and Tennis Academy–Serve and Turf	275			R	9–17			•	•		•	
Maine Teen Camp	275*			R	13–17	•	•	•	•	•	•	•
Maine Tennis Academy–Junior Tennis Camp	276			R/D	8+	•	•	•	•	•	•	•
Maine Wilderness Adventure Trip	276				13–16			•	•	•	•	
Med-O-Lark Camp	276*			R	11–15	•	•	•	•	•	•	•
Moose River Outpost	277			R	10–16	•	•	•	•	•	•	•
Mountain Workshop–Awesome 5: North Woods of Maine	277				15–16			•	•		•	
Mountain Workshop–Awesome 3: Maine Coast	277				13–14			•	•	•	•	
New England Camping Adventures	278				9–16	•		•	•	•	•	•
OMNI Camp	278*			R	9–17	•	•	•	•	•	•	•
Pine Island Camp	279*	R			9–15		•	•	•	•	•	•
Sailing Program at NE Camping Adventures	279			R	10–17	•	•	•	•	•		•
Snowy Owl Camp for Girls	279		R		7–17		•	•		•	•	
SoccerPlus Goalkeeper School–Challenge Program–Brunswick, ME	279			R/D	10+			•			•	•
SoccerPlus Goalkeeper School–National Training Center–Brunswick, ME	280			R	15+			•			•	
Student Conservation Association–Conservation Crew Program (Maine)	280			R	15–19	•		•	•	•	•	•
Summer Days at the Morris Farm	280			D	6–11	•	•		•	•	•	•
Williwaw Adventures–Maine Mountains and Coast	280				14–18	•		•	•	•	•	•
Winona Camp for Boys	281	R			7–16	•	•	•	•	•	•	•
Wohelo-Luther Gulick Camps	281		R		6–16	•	•	•	•	•	•	•
Maryland												
Art Monk Football Camp/Sports International–Maryland	281			R/D	8–18			•			•	
The Arts! at Maryland	281*			R/D	15–21	•	•			•		•
Camp Airy	281*	R			7–17	•	•	•	•	•	•	•
Camp Louise	282		R		7–17	•	•	•	•	•	•	•
The Community Center Going Places Camp	282			D	11–14		•	•		•	•	•
Cybercamps–Johns Hopkins University	283			D	7–18	•	•	•		•	•	
Cybercamps–University of Maryland	283			R/D	7–18	•	•	•		•	•	•
Georgetown Prep School Summer English Program	283			R/D	13–18	•		•	•	•	•	
Joe Krivak Quarterback Camp, Maryland/Sports International	283			R/D	8–18			•			•	
Johns Hopkins University Zanvyl Krieger School of Arts and Sciences Summer Programs	284*			R/D	15+	•	•	•		•		•
Kids on Campus	284			D	7–17	•	•			•	•	
Lions Camp Merrick Deaf/HOH/KODA Program	284			R	6–16		•	•	•	•	•	•
Lions Camp Merrick Diabetes Program	285			R	5–16		•	•	•	•	•	•
The Marsh	285			D	6–12	•	•	•	•	•	•	•
Montgomery College WDCE–Aspiring Filmmakers	285			D	16+		•					•
Montgomery College WDCE–Biotechnology and Diversity Camp	285			D	12–16	•				•		•
Montgomery College WDCE–Computer Programming Camp–Co-ed	286			D	12–16	•						•
Montgomery College WDCE–Computer Programming Camp for Middle School Girls	286		D		12–16	•						•
Montgomery College WDCE–Culinary Arts–Kids Cook	286			D	11–13					•		•
Montgomery College WDCE–Entrepreneurship Camp 2005	286			D	11–14	•				•		•
Montgomery College WDCE–FIT Summer Camp	287			D	6–13	•		•				•
Montgomery College WDCE–GURL Power	287			D	11–13	•	•			•		•
Montgomery College WDCE–Hands on Art	287			D	8–12		•					•
Montgomery College WDCE–Inventor's Workshop	287			D	8–13	•	•			•		•
Montgomery College WDCE–Joy of Art	288			D	5–10	•	•			•		•
Montgomery College WDCE–Language in Motion	288			D	5–10	•						•
Montgomery College WDCE–Leadership Skills Camp	288			D	11–14					•		•
Montgomery College WDCE–Mathematics Enrichment Program	288			D	9–17	•						•
Montgomery College WDCE–Science Adventures	289			D	5–12	•				•		•

This program is highlighted by a photograph, special note, or in-depth description; see the profile page for more information.
†D = day camp; R = residential camp

	GENERAL INFORMATION					PROGRAM INFORMATION						
	Profile Page	Boys D/R†	Girls D/R†	Coed D/R†	Age	Acad	Arts	Sports	Wild/ Outdrs	Special Interest	Jobs	Financial Aid
Montgomery College WDCE–Summer Dinner Theatre	289			D	16+		•					•
Montgomery College WDCE–Summer Science Camp for Girls	289			D	11–14	•				•		•
Montgomery College WDCE–Summer Student Writing Institute	289			D	8–14	•	•					•
Montgomery College WDCE–Summer Youth Programs	290			D	5–18	•	•	•		•		•
Montgomery College WDCE–Super Sleuths–Meet the Challenge	290			D	8–11	•	•			•		•
Montgomery College WDCE–Web Design Camp for Girls and Boys	290			D	11–13	•				•		•
Montgomery College WDCE–World Events 2005	291			D	11–14	•						•
Montgomery College WDCE–Young Scientist Academy	291			D	6–14	•				•		•
National Debate Institute–DC	291*			R/D	14–18	•						•
The National Music Workshop Day Jams–Baltimore, MD	291			D	9–15	•	•				•	•
The National Music Workshop Day Jams–Rockville, MD	292			D	9–15	•	•				•	•
National Student Leadership Conference: Medicine and Health Care	292*			R	14–18	•		•		•	•	•
St. Andrew's Summer Programs	292			D	9–18	•	•	•		•	•	•
Sidwell Friends Bethesda Day Camp	292			D	3–10	•	•	•		•	•	
Sidwell Friends Camp Corsica	293			R	8–14		•	•		•	•	
Sidwell Friends Overnight Sea Kayaking Trip	293			R	11–17		•	•		•	•	•
Student Conservation Association–Conservation Crew Program (Maryland)	293			R	15–19	•		•	•	•	•	•
Summer Family Conference	293			R/D	1+	•	•	•			•	
Traveling Players Ensemble Camp	293			D	11–18		•	•	•	•	•	•
United Soccer Academy–Goal Keeping Training Camp, Maryland	294			R/D	8–14			•			•	
United Soccer Academy–Junior Soccer Squirts, Maryland	294			D	3–5			•			•	
United Soccer Academy–Recreation Soccer Community Camp, Maryland	294			R/D	7–14			•			•	
United Soccer Academy–Senior Soccer Squirts, Maryland	294			D	5–7			•			•	
United Soccer Academy–Team Training Camp, Maryland	295			R/D	8–14			•			•	
United Soccer Academy–Travel Soccer Community Camp, Maryland	295			R/D	8–14			•			•	
University of Maryland Young Scholars Program	295*			R/D	14–18	•				•		•
West River United Methodist Center	295			R	8–18	•	•	•	•	•	•	•
Massachusetts												
Academic Study Associates–ASA at the University of Massachusetts Amherst	296*			R/D	14–18	•	•	•	•	•	•	
Academic Study Associates–Pathways Program at Amherst College	296			R/D	12–14	•	•	•		•	•	
Adventures in Veterinary Medicine	296			R/D	12+	•				•	•	•
Apogee Outdoor Adventures–Cape Cod and the Islands	297				12–14			•	•	•	•	•
Appalachian Mountain Club–Teen Crews–Alpine Trail, Berkshires	297			R	15+				•	•	•	
Appalachian Mountain Club–Teen Crews–Mount Greylock	297			R	16+				•	•	•	
Appalachian Mountain Club–Trail Crew–Berkshires	297			R	15–18				•	•	•	
Appalachian Mountain Club–Trail Crew–Mount Everett/Alpine Trail	297			R	16+				•	•	•	
Appalachian Mountain Club–Volunteer Trail Crew–Mount Greylock	298			R	16+				•	•	•	
The Art Institute of Boston Pre-College Program	298			R/D	15–18	•	•				•	•
Barton Day Camp–Worcester	298			D	6–12		•	•	•	•	•	•
Belvoir Terrace	298*		R		8–17	•	•	•			•	•
Berklee Business of Music Program	299			R/D	15+	•	•					
Berklee College of Music Summer Performance Program	299			R/D	15+	•	•					•
Berklee Music Production Workshop	299			R/D	15+	•	•					
Berklee Summer Basslines Program	299			R/D	15+	•	•					
Berklee Summer Brass Weekend	300			R/D	15+	•	•					
Berklee Summer Guitar Sessions	300			R/D	15+	•	•					•
Berklee Summer Saxophone Weekend	300			R/D	15+	•	•					
Berklee Summer Songwriting Workshop	300			R/D	15+	•	•					
Berklee Summer String Fling	300			R/D	15+	•	•					
Berklee World Percussion Festival	301			R/D	15+	•	•					
BICYCLE TRAVEL ADVENTURES–Student Hosteling Program–Cape Cod	301*				12–15			•	•	•	•	
Bonnie Castle Riding Camp	301*		R		9–16	•	•	•				
Boston University High School Honors Program	302*			R	16–18	•	•	•				•
Boston University Institute for Television, Film, and Radio Production	302*			R	14–18	•	•	•		•	•	

*This program is highlighted by a photograph, special note, or in-depth description; see the profile page for more information.
†D = day camp; R = residential camp*

	GENERAL INFORMATION					PROGRAM INFORMATION						
	Profile Page	Boys D/R†	Girls D/R†	Coed D/R†	Age	Acad	Arts	Sports	Wild/ Outdrs	Special Interest	Jobs	Financial Aid
Boston University Promys Program	303			R	14–18	•					•	•
Boston University Summer Challenge Program	303			R	14–18	•	•	•				
Boston University Summer Theatre Institute	303			R/D	16–18	•	•					•
Boston University Tanglewood Institute	303*			R	14–18	•	•	•	•		•	•
Brighton College Admissions Prep at Tufts University	304*			R	15–19	•				•	•	
Camp Atwater–Boys Session	304	R			8–16		•	•	•	•	•	•
Camp Atwater–Girls Session	304		R		8–16		•	•	•	•	•	•
Camp Avoda	304	R			7–15	•	•	•	•	•	•	•
Camp Burgess	305	R			7–15		•	•	•	•	•	•
Camp Good News for Young People and Teens	305			R/D	6–15	•	•	•	•	•	•	•
Camp Greylock for Boys	305	R			7–16		•	•	•	•	•	
Camp Hayward	305		R		7–15		•	•	•	•	•	•
Camp Hillside	306			R/D	8–15	•	•	•	•	•		•
Camp Hillside Soccer Program	306			R/D	8–15			•				•
Camp Kingsmont	306			R	7–18		•	•	•	•	•	
Camp Nawaka	306			R	8–16		•	•	•	•	•	•
Camp Watitoh	307			R	7–16	•	•	•	•	•	•	
Camp Wing	307			R	7–13	•	•	•	•	•	•	•
Camp Wingate Kirkland	307			R	8–15		•	•	•	•	•	
Camp Wing Day Camp	308			D	5–16	•	•	•	•	•	•	
Cape Cod Sea Camps–Monomoy/Wono	308			R/D	8–15		•	•	•	•	•	•
Carroll Center for the Blind–Computing for College: Computer and Communication Skills	308			R/D	16–22	•		•		•		•
Carroll Center for the Blind–Real World Work Experience	308			R	16+	•		•		•	•	•
Carroll Center for the Blind–Youth in Transition	309			R/D	15–22	•	•	•	•	•	•	
Center Summer Academy	309			D	15–18	•	•			•		•
Clara Barton Camp	309		R		6–16		•	•	•	•	•	•
Clara Barton Family Camp	309			R			•	•	•	•	•	
College Admission Prep Camp by Education Unlimited–Boston	310*			R/D	15–18	•				•		•
Crane Lake Camp	310			R	7–16	•	•	•		•	•	•
Cushing Academy Summer Session	310*			R/D	12–18	•	•	•	•	•	•	•
Cybercamps–Amherst College	311			R/D	7–18	•	•	•		•	•	•
Cybercamps–Babson College	311			D	7–18	•	•	•		•	•	•
Cybercamps–Bentley College	311			R/D	7–18	•	•	•		•	•	•
Cybercamps–Merrimack College	312			R/D	7–18	•	•	•		•	•	•
Cybercamps–MIT	312			D	7–18	•	•	•		•	•	•
Eaglebrook Summer Semester	312*			R	11–13	•	•	•	•	•	•	•
Eagle Hill School Summer Session	312*			R/D	9–19	•	•	•	•	•	•	
Emagination Computer Camps–Massachusetts	313*			R/D	8–17	•	•	•		•	•	
Excel at Amherst College and Williams College	314*			R	15–18	•	•	•	•	•	•	•
Exploration Intermediate Program at Wellesley College	314*			R/D	13–14	•	•	•	•	•	•	•
Exploration Junior Program at St. Mark's School	315*			R/D	9–12	•	•	•	•	•	•	•
Fay School Day Camp	316			D	4–12		•	•		•	•	
Fay Summer School	316			R/D	6–15	•	•	•	•	•	•	
Fenn School Summer Day Camp	316			D	6–15	•	•	•	•	•	•	•
The Fessenden School Summer ESL Program	316*			R	10–15	•	•	•	•	•	•	
Frontiers Program	317*			R	16–18	•	•	•		•		
Gems: Girls in Engineering, Math and Science	317		R		14–17	•						•
Genesis at Brandeis University	318*			R	15–17	•	•	•		•		•
Great Escapes (Adventure Trips for Teens)–Cape Cod Sail Adventure	318				13–16			•			•	•
Great Escapes (Adventure Trips for Teens)–Cape Cod Underwater Adventure	318				13–16			•	•	•	•	•
Great Escapes (Adventure Trips for Teens)–Cape Escapes	318				13–16			•	•	•	•	•
Harvard University Summer School: Secondary School Program	319*			R/D		•	•	•		•		•
Horizons for Youth	319			R	7–17	•	•	•	•	•	•	•
iD Tech Camps–Emerson College, Boston, MA	320*			R/D	7–17	•	•	•		•	•	•
iD Tech Camps–Merrimack College, North Andover, MA	320*			R/D	7–17	•	•	•		•	•	•
iD Tech Camps–MIT, Cambridge, MA	320*			R/D	7–17	•	•	•		•	•	•

This program is highlighted by a photograph, special note, or in-depth description; see the profile page for more information.
†D = day camp; R = residential camp

	GENERAL INFORMATION					PROGRAM INFORMATION						
	Profile Page	Boys D/R†	Girls D/R†	Coed D/R†	Age	Acad	Arts	Sports	Wild/ Outdrs	Special Interest	Jobs	Financial Aid
iD Tech Camps–Smith College, Northampton, MA	321*			R/D	7–17	•	•	•		•	•	•
Kroka Expeditions–Cape Cod Triple Surfing Bonanza	321			R	13–18	•		•	•	•	•	•
Landmark School Summer Academic Program	321*			R/D	7–20	•	•	•	•			
Landmark Volunteers: Massachusetts	322*			R	14–18	•	•	•	•	•	•	•
Leadership Adventure in Boston	322*		R		11–14	•	•	•	•	•		•
Linden Hill Summer Program	323*			R	7–16	•	•	•	•	•	•	•
Massachusetts College of Art/Creative Vacation	323			D	9–16	•	•			•	•	•
Massachusetts College of Art/Summer Studios	323*			R/D	15–17	•	•			•	•	•
MIT MITE^{2}S (Minority Introduction to Engineering, Entrepreneurship and Science)	324*			R	16–17	•		•		•	•	
Mountain Workshop–Bike 1: Martha's Vineyard and Nantucket	324				11–12			•	•	•	•	
Mountain Workshop–Bike 2	325				12–13			•	•	•	•	
Mount Holyoke College SEARCH (Summer Explorations and Research Collaborations for High School Girls) Program	325		R/D		15–18	•	•	•	•	•	•	•
Mount Holyoke College SummerMath Program	325*		R/D		13–18	•	•	•	•	•	•	•
The National Music Workshop Day Jams–Boston, MA	326			D	9–15	•	•				•	•
Newman School Summer Session	326			D	13–19	•						
The New York Film Academy, Harvard University, Cambridge, MA	326*			R	14–17		•					
Northfield Mount Hermon Summer Session	326*			R/D	12–19	•	•	•		•	•	•
Offense-Defense Golf Camp, Massachusetts	327			R/D	10–18	•		•			•	
Offense-Defense Tennis Camp	327			R/D	9–18	•		•		•	•	
Outward Bound–Connecting with Courage	327		R		12–13			•	•	•	•	•
Outward Bound–Environmental Expeditions	327			R	14–17	•		•	•	•	•	•
Outward Bound–Passages	328	R			12–13			•	•	•	•	•
Overland: Adventure Camp for 5th and 6th Grade Boys	328*	R			10–12			•	•	•	•	
Overland: Adventure Camp for 5th and 6th Grade Girls	328*		R		10–12			•	•	•	•	
Overland: Cape Cod and the Islands Bicycle Touring	328*				13–16			•	•	•	•	
Phillips Academy Summer Session	328*			R/D	13–18	•	•	•		•		•
Ponkapoag Outdoor Center Day Camps	329			D	6–15		•	•	•	•	•	•
Public Speaking Institute by Education Unlimited–Boston	329*			R/D	15–18	•		•		•		•
Research Internship in Science and Engineering	330			R	16–18	•		•				•
Rowe Camp	330			R	9–19		•	•	•	•	•	•
Simon's Rock College of Bard Young Writers Workshop	330*			R	14–18	•	•	•	•			•
Smith College Summer Science and Engineering Program	331*		R		13–18	•	•	•		•	•	•
Snow Farm: The New England Craft Program	331*			R	14–18	•	•					•
SoccerPlus FieldPlayer Academy–Easthampton, MA	331			R/D	11+			•			•	•
SoccerPlus Goalkeeper School–Challenge Program–Franklin, MA	332			R/D	10+			•			•	•
SoccerPlus Goalkeeper School–Competitive Program–Easthampton, MA	332			R	12+			•			•	•
SoccerPlus Goalkeeper School–National Training Center–Franklin, MA	332			R	15+			•			•	
South Shore YMCA Specialty Camp	332			R	7–15		•	•		•	•	•
Springfield College Allied Health Career Exploration Program	332			R	15–18	•				•		
Springfield College Athletic Trainer Workshop	333			R	15–18	•		•		•		
Springfield College Sports Management Career Exploration Program	333			R	15–18	•				•		
Springfield Technical Community College–College for Kids	333			D	7–17	•	•	•		•		•
Stoneleigh–Burnham School: Camp $tart-Up	333*		R		13–18	•				•	•	•
Stoneleigh–Burnham School: Science Camp for Middle School Girls	333*		D		12–14	•				•	•	•
Stoneleigh–Burnham School Softball Camp	334*		R		12–16			•			•	•
Stoneleigh–Burnham School Summer Dance Camp	334*			R	11–17		•	•			•	•
Stoneleigh–Burnham School: Summer Debate and Public Speaking Camp	334*		R		12–17	•					•	
Strive: Exploring Engineering, Math and Science	334			R	14–17	•						•
Student Conservation Association–Conservation Crew Program (Massachusetts)	335			R	15–19	•		•	•	•	•	•
Study Tours and Dance/Theater Camp in the USA–Dean College	335*			R	15+	•	•			•		
Study Tours in the USA–Dean College	335*			R	15+	•	•	•	•	•		
Summer Dance '05	335			R/D	16+	•	•			•	•	
The Summer Institute for the Gifted at Amherst College	336*			R	8–17	•	•	•	•	•	•	•
Summer Summit on Leadership	336*		R		14–18	•	•	•	•	•		•
SuperCamp–Hampshire College	336*			R	11–18	•		•		•	•	•

This program is highlighted by a photograph, special note, or in-depth description; see the profile page for more information.
†D = day camp; R = residential camp

	GENERAL INFORMATION					PROGRAM INFORMATION						
	Profile Page	Boys D/R†	Girls D/R†	Coed D/R†	Age	Acad	Arts	Sports	Wild/ Outdrs	Special Interest	Jobs	Financial Aid
Tabor Academy Summer Program	337*			R/D	9–15	•	•	•		•	•	
Tufts Summer Study	337			D	16–18	•		•			•	•
Wilderness Experiences Unlimited–Explorers Camp	337			R	9–16			•	•	•	•	
Wilderness Experiences Unlimited–Leaders In Training Camp	338			R	14–17			•	•	•	•	
Wilderness Experiences Unlimited–Pathfinders Day Camp	338			D	8–14	•	•	•	•	•		
Wilderness Experiences Unlimited–Trailblazers Camp	338				12–17			•	•		•	
Wilderness Experiences Unlimited/Westfield Water Sports: Scuba Camp	338			R	12+			•			•	
The Winchendon School Summer Session	338*			R	13–20	•	•	•	•	•	•	•

Michigan

	Profile Page	Boys D/R†	Girls D/R†	Coed D/R†	Age	Acad	Arts	Sports	Wild/ Outdrs	Special Interest	Jobs	Financial Aid
American Youth Foundation–Camp Miniwanca	339			R	8–18		•	•	•	•	•	•
American Youth Foundation Leadership Conference	339			R	15–18		•	•	•	•	•	•
Black River Farm and Ranch	340		R		7–15		•	•		•	•	
Blue Lake Fine Arts Camp	340			R	10–18		•	•		•	•	•
Camp Echo	340			R	8–17		•	•	•	•	•	•
Camp Fowler	340			R	6+		•	•	•	•	•	•
Camp Geneva	341			R/D	8–15	•	•	•		•	•	•
Camp Henry	341			R/D	5–17		•	•	•	•	•	•
Camp Henry Offsite: Teen Challenge	341				13–17			•	•		•	•
Camp Lookout	341			R	7–15		•	•	•	•	•	
Camp Maplehurst	342			R	7–17	•	•	•	•	•	•	
Camp Oweki Summer Day Camp	342			D	4–16	•	•	•	•	•	•	•
Camp Roger	342			R	7–16	•	•	•	•	•	•	•
Camp Seagull for Girls	343		R		6–16		•	•	•	•	•	
Cedar Lodge	343			R	8–16		•	•	•	•	•	
Circle Pines Center Summer Camp	343			R	7–17	•	•	•	•	•	•	•
Crystalaire Camp	343			R	8–15		•	•	•	•	•	•
Cybercamps–University of Michigan	344			R/D	7–18	•	•	•		•	•	
CYO Boys Camp	344	R			7–16		•	•	•	•	•	•
CYO Girls Camp	344		R		7–16		•	•	•	•	•	•
EARTHWATCH INSTITUTE–Moose and Wolves	344			R	16+	•			•	•		•
The Glen at Lake of the Woods	345		R		7–13	•	•	•		•	•	•
Greenwoods Camp for Boys	345	R			7–15	•	•	•	•	•	•	•
The Grove at Greenwoods	345	R			7–13	•	•	•	•	•	•	•
Hillsdale College Summer Science Camps	346			R	15–18	•		•				
iD Tech Camps–University of Michigan, Ann Arbor, MI	346*			R/D	7–17	•	•	•		•	•	•
Interlochen Arts Camp	346*			R	8–18	•	•	•			•	•
Joe Machnik's No. 1 Academy One and Premier Programs–Brooklyn, Michigan	347			R/D	9–18			•			•	•
Joe Machnik's No. 1 Mighty Mini, Goalkeeper and Striker Camp–Brooklyn, Michigan	347			R/D	8–12			•			•	•
Lake Ann Baptist Camp	347			R	9+	•	•	•	•	•	•	
Lake of the Woods Camp for Girls	347		R		7–15	•	•	•	•	•	•	
Landmark Volunteers: Michigan	348*			R	14–18	•		•	•	•	•	•
Mah Meh Weh	348		R		10–16		•	•		•		
Michigan State University High School Engineering Institute	348			R	16–18	•				•		•
Michigan Technological University American Indian Workshop	348			R	12–15	•	•			•	•	•
Michigan Technological University Explorations in Engineering Workshop	349			R	14–18	•				•	•	•
Michigan Technological University Honors Orchestra Program	349			R	15–18	•	•				•	•
Michigan Technological University Summer Youth Program	349			R/D	12–18	•	•	•	•	•	•	•
Michigan Technological University Women in Engineering Workshop	349		R		14–18	•				•	•	•
The National Music Workshop Day Jams–Ann Arbor, MI	350			D	9–15	•	•				•	•
Robotics Camp	350	R/D			13–18	•				•		•
Student Conservation Association–Conservation Crew Program (Michigan)	350			R	15–19	•		•	•	•	•	•
Summer Discovery at Michigan	350*			R		•	•	•	•	•	•	
Suzuki Family Camp	351			R/D	2–18		•	•			•	
Women in Technology	351		R/D		13–18	•				•		•

*This program is highlighted by a photograph, special note, or in-depth description; see the profile page for more information.
†D = day camp; R = residential camp

	GENERAL INFORMATION					PROGRAM INFORMATION						
	Profile Page	Boys D/R†	Girls D/R†	Coed D/R†	Age	Acad	Arts	Sports	Wild/ Outdrs	Special Interest	Jobs	Financial Aid
YMCA Camp Pendalouan–Bugs and Bunks	351			R	6–8		•	•		•	•	•
YMCA Camp Pendalouan–Counselor-in-Training	351			R	15–16		•	•	•	•	•	•
YMCA Camp Pendalouan–Resident Camp	352			R	7–13		•	•	•	•	•	•
YMCA Camp Pendalouan–Ropers and Wranglers Horse Camp	352			R	10–15			•			•	•
YMCA Camp Pendalouan–Teen Xtreme	352			R	13–15		•	•	•	•	•	•
Minnesota												
Camp Buckskin	352			R	6–18	•	•	•	•	•	•	
Camp Chippewa for Boys	353	R			7–17			•	•	•	•	
Camp Friendship	353			R/D	5+		•	•	•	•	•	•
Camp Heartland Summer Camp–Minnesota	353			R	7–15		•	•	•	•	•	
Camp Lincoln Fishing Camp	353	R			8–15			•			•	•
Camp Lincoln for Boys/Camp Lake Hubert for Girls	354				8–16		•	•	•	•	•	•
Camp Lincoln for Boys/Camp Lake Hubert for Girls Family Camp	354			R	1+		•	•	•	•	•	•
Camp Lincoln for Boys/Camp Lake Hubert for Girls Golf Camp	354			R	8–16			•			•	•
Camp Lincoln for Boys/Camp Lake Hubert for Girls Tennis Camp	354			R	8–16			•			•	•
Camp Mishawaka for Boys	355	R			9–16		•	•	•	•	•	
Camp Mishawaka for Girls	355		R		9–16		•	•	•	•	•	
Carleton College Summer Writing Program	355			R	16–18	•						•
Catholic Youth Camp	355			R	7–18	•	•	•	•	•	•	•
Concordia Language Villages–Chinese	356			R	7–18	•	•	•	•	•	•	•
Concordia Language Villages–Danish	356			R	7–18	•	•	•	•	•	•	•
Concordia Language Villages–English	356			R	11–20	•	•	•			•	•
Concordia Language Villages–Finnish	356			R	7–18	•	•	•	•	•	•	•
Concordia Language Villages–French–Bemidji	357			R	7–18	•	•	•	•	•	•	•
Concordia Language Villages–French–Camp Holiday	357			R	7–18	•	•	•	•	•	•	•
Concordia Language Villages–French–Fosston	357			R	8–18	•	•	•	•	•	•	•
Concordia Language Villages–French Voyageur	357			R	11–18	•	•	•	•	•	•	•
Concordia Language Villages–German–Bemidji	358			R	7–18	•	•	•	•	•	•	•
Concordia Language Villages–German–Camp Trowbridge	358			R	7–18	•	•	•	•	•	•	•
Concordia Language Villages–Italian	358			R	8–18	•	•	•			•	•
Concordia Language Villages–Japanese	358			R	7–18	•	•	•	•	•	•	•
Concordia Language Villages–Korean	359			R	7–18	•	•	•	•	•	•	•
Concordia Language Villages–Norwegian	359			R	7–18	•	•	•	•	•	•	•
Concordia Language Villages–Russian	359			R	7–18	•	•	•	•	•	•	•
Concordia Language Villages–Spanish–Bemidji	359			R	7–18	•	•	•	•		•	•
Concordia Language Villages–Spanish–Maplelag	360			R	7–18	•	•	•	•	•	•	•
Concordia Language Villages–Spanish–Wilder Forest	360			R	7–18	•	•	•	•	•	•	•
Concordia Language Villages–Swedish	360			R	7–18	•	•	•	•	•	•	•
Cybercamps–University of Minnesota	360			R/D	7–18	•	•	•		•	•	•
Eagle Lake Camp Jaunts–Minnesota Boundary Waters	361				15–18	•		•	•		•	•
Eden Wood Camp	361			R/D	5+		•	•	•	•	•	•
Fort Union Civil War Camp	361			R	11–17	•	•	•	•	•		•
iD Tech Camps–University of Minnesota, Minneapolis, MN	361*			R/D	7–17	•	•	•		•	•	•
Kooch-I-Ching	362	R			7–18			•	•	•	•	•
Landmark Volunteers: Minnesota	362*			R	14–18	•		•		•	•	•
Presbyterian Clearwater Forest	362			R/D	8–17	•	•	•	•	•	•	•
St. Louis County 4-H Camp	363			R/D	8–16		•	•	•	•	•	•
Shattuck–St. Mary's Girls Elite Hockey Camp	363*		R/D		11–17			•			•	
Shattuck–St. Mary's Summer Discovery and English Language Institute	363*			R/D	11–17	•	•	•	•		•	
Shattuck–St. Mary's Boys Elite Hockey Camp	364*	R/D			11–15			•			•	
Student Conservation Association–Conservation Crew Program (Minnesota)	364			R	15–19	•		•	•	•	•	•
Tice Brothers Football Camp	364			R/D	8–18			•			•	
Ventures Travel Service–Minnesota	364				14–70					•	•	
Voyageur Outward Bound–Boundary Waters Wilderness Canoeing	364			R	14+	•		•	•	•	•	•
Voyageur Outward Bound–Boundary Waters Wilderness Canoeing and Climbing XT	365				14+	•		•	•	•	•	•

This program is highlighted by a photograph, special note, or in-depth description; see the profile page for more information.
†D = day camp; R = residential camp

	GENERAL INFORMATION					PROGRAM INFORMATION						
	Profile Page	Boys D/R†	Girls D/R†	Coed D/R†	Age	Acad	Arts	Sports	Wild/ Outdrs	Special Interest	Jobs	Financial Aid
Voyageur Outward Bound–Northwoods Wilderness Canoeing and Backpacking	365				14+	•		•	•	•	•	•
Wilderness Dance Camp	365			R	9+	•	•	•	•		•	•
YMCA Camp Ihduhapi	365			R/D	7–16		•	•	•	•	•	•
YMCA Camp Warren for Boys	366	R			8–16		•	•	•	•	•	•
YMCA Camp Warren for Girls	366		R		8–16		•	•	•	•	•	•
YMCA Camp Widjiwagan	366*			R	12–18			•	•	•	•	•
YMCA Wilderness Camp Menogyn	367				13–18				•		•	•
Mississippi												
Camp Stanislaus	367*	R/D			8–15	•	•	•	•	•	•	
Mississippi Governor's School	367			R	16–18	•	•	•		•	•	
Student Conservation Association–Conservation Crew Program (Mississippi)	368			R	15–19	•		•	•	•	•	•
Missouri												
Camp Sabra	368			R	8–15		•	•	•	•	•	
Cybercamps–Washington University	368			R/D	7–18	•	•	•		•	•	
Girl Scouts of Mid-Continent–Camp Oakledge	369		R		9–16		•	•	•	•	•	•
Girl Scouts of Mid-Continent–Camp Prairie Schooner	369		R		5–12	•	•	•	•	•	•	•
Girl Scouts of Mid-Continent–Juliette Low Camp	369		R		8–18		•	•	•	•	•	•
Girl Scouts of Mid-Continent–Winding River Camp and Ranch	369		R		12–17		•	•	•	•	•	•
IMACS–Full Day Summer Camp–Missouri	370			D	5–18	•				•	•	
IMACS–Individual Summer Programs–Missouri	370			D	6–18	•				•	•	•
Missouri Children's Burn Camp	370			R	6–17		•	•		•		•
Music and Dance Summer Workshops	370		R			•	•				•	
Sciencescape	370		R			•					•	
Student Conservation Association–Conservation Crew Program (Missouri)	371			R	15–19	•		•	•	•	•	•
Ventures Travel Service–Missouri	371				14–70					•	•	
Washington University High School Summer Scholars Program	371*			R	16+	•	•					•
Washington University in St. Louis, School of Art–Portfolio Plus	372*			R/D	16–18	•	•			•		•
Wentworth Military Academy Pathfinder Adventure Camp	372*			R		•		•	•	•		
Wentworth Military Academy Summer School	372*			R		•	•	•	•	•		
Wentworth Military Academy Summer School–Camp LEAD	372*			R		•	•	•	•	•		
Montana												
Adventure Treks–Montana Adventures	373				15–17				•			•
Alpengirl–Montana	373				12–16	•		•	•	•	•	•
Alpengirl–Montana Fitness	373				12–16	•		•	•	•	•	•
Alpengirl–Montana Horse	373				12–16	•		•	•	•	•	•
Apogee Outdoor Adventures–Montana Service Adventure	374				14–17				•	•	•	•
Christikon	374			R	10–19	•	•	•	•	•	•	
Landmark Volunteers: Montana	374*			R	14–18	•		•	•	•	•	•
NBC Camps–Basketball Individual Training–Montana	374			R	9–18			•			•	•
NBC Camps–Basketball–Team–Billings, MT	375			R				•			•	•
Putney Student Travel–Community Service–Montana	375*			R	15–18	•		•	•	•		•
Student Conservation Association–Conservation Crew Program (Montana)	375			R	15–19	•		•	•	•	•	•
Visions–Montana	375*				14–18	•	•	•	•	•		•
Voyageur Outward Bound–Greater Yellowstone Whitewater and Backpacking	376				16+	•			•	•	•	•
Voyageur Outward Bound–Lewis and Clark Alpine Backpacking	376				14+	•			•	•	•	•
Voyageur Outward Bound–Lewis and Clark Alpine Backpacking-Girls	376				14–16	•			•	•	•	•
Voyageur Outward Bound–Montana High Alpine Backpacking	376				14+	•		•	•	•	•	•
Voyageur Outward Bound–Montana Rock Climbing XT	377				16+	•		•	•	•	•	•
Voyageur Outward Bound–Northern Rockies Backpacking Family Adventure	377				14+	•			•	•	•	•

**This program is highlighted by a photograph, special note, or in-depth description; see the profile page for more information.*
†D = day camp; R = residential camp

	GENERAL INFORMATION					PROGRAM INFORMATION						
	Profile Page	Boys D/R†	Girls D/R†	Coed D/R†	Age	Acad	Arts	Sports	Wild/ Outdrs	Special Interest	Jobs	Financial Aid
Nebraska												
Groundwater University	377			R	12–15	•	•	•		•		•
Student Conservation Association–Conservation Crew Program (Nebraska)	377			R	15–19	•		•	•	•	•	•
Nevada												
Student Conservation Association–Conservation Crew Program (Nevada)	378			R	15–19	•		•	•	•	•	•
Study Tours and Hotel and Tourism Management in the USA–Southern Nevada College	378*			R	15+	•				•		
Study Tours in the USA–Southern Nevada	378*			R	15+	•	•	•	•	•		
New Hampshire												
American Youth Foundation–Camp Merrowvista	379			R	8–18		•	•	•	•	•	•
Appalachian Mountain Club–Teen Crews–Pinkham Notch	379			R	15–17				•	•	•	
Appalachian Mountain Club–Teen Crews–Spike	379			R	15–17				•	•	•	
Appalachian Mountain Club–Teen Crews–Two-week Teen Spike	379			R	16–18				•	•	•	
Appalachian Mountain Club–Teen Stewardship Training	380			R	17–19	•			•	•	•	
Appalachian Mountain Club–Trail Crew–White Mountains	380			R	16+				•	•	•	
Appalachian Mountain Club–Volunteer Trail Crew–Alpine/Mount Washington	380			R	16+				•	•	•	
Appalachian Mountain Club–Volunteer Trail Crew–Crawford Notch	380			R	16+				•	•	•	
Appalachian Mountain Club–Volunteer Trail Crew–Hut Crew	381			R	16+				•	•	•	
Appalachian Mountain Club–Wild New Hampshire Trail Crew	381			R	16+				•	•	•	
Appalachian Mountain Club–Women's Trail Crew	381		R		16+				•	•	•	
Brewster Academy Summer Session	381*			R/D	12–17	•	•	•	•	•	•	
Camp Allen	382			R/D	6–90		•	•	•	•	•	•
Camp Brandon for Boys	382	R			8–18		•	•	•	•	•	•
Camp Brookwoods and Deer Run	382			R	8–18	•	•	•	•	•	•	•
Camp Glen Brook	383			R	8–14		•	•	•	•	•	•
Camp Mowglis, School of the Open	383	R			7–14	•	•	•	•	•	•	•
Camp Onaway	383		R		9–15		•	•	•	•	•	•
Camp Pasquaney	383	R			11–16		•	•	•	•	•	•
Camp Quinebarge	384			R	7–15		•	•	•	•	•	•
Camp Robin Hood for Boys and Girls	384			R	7–16	•	•	•	•	•	•	•
Camp Starfish	384			R	7–15	•	•	•	•	•	•	•
Camp Tohkomeupog	385	R			8–16		•	•	•	•	•	•
Camp Walt Whitman	385*			R	7–15	•	•	•	•	•	•	
Camp Wicosuta	385		R		6–16	•	•	•	•	•	•	
The Cardigan Mountain School Summer Session	386*			R/D	9–14	•	•	•	•	•	•	•
Collegiate Summer Program for High School Students	386			R	15–18	•		•	•			•
Cragged Mountain Farm	387			R	5–13		•	•	•	•	•	•
Fleur de Lis Camp	387*		R		8–15		•	•		•	•	
Great Escapes (Adventure Trips for Teens)–White Mountain Adventure	387				13–16			•	•	•	•	•
Landmark Volunteers: New Hampshire	387*			R	14–18	•		•		•		•
North Woods Camp for Boys	388	R			8–18		•	•	•	•	•	•
Paul Hogan's Shooter's Gold Basketball Camp–Alton	388			D				•			•	
Paul Hogan's Shooter's Gold Basketball Camp–Gilford	388			D	6–14			•			•	
Paul Hogan's Shooter's Gold Basketball Camp–Laconia	388			D				•			•	
Paul Hogan's Shooter's Gold Basketball Camp–Lancaster	388			D				•			•	
Paul Hogan's Shooter's Gold Basketball Camp–Littleton	389			D				•			•	
Paul Hogan's Shooter's Gold Basketball Camp–Manchester	389			D				•			•	
Paul Hogan's Shooter's Gold Basketball Camp–Meredith	389			D				•			•	
Paul Hogan's Shooter's Gold Basketball Camp–Tilton	389			D				•			•	
Paul Hogan's Shooter's Gold Basketball Camp–Woodsville	389			D				•			•	
Paul Hogan's Specialty Basketball Camp	389			R/D	10–17			•			•	
Performance PLUS–Positive Learning Using the Stage+Studio+Screen	390*			R	13–18	•	•				•	•
Phillips Exeter Academy Summer School	390*			R/D	13–19	•	•	•	•	•	•	•

**This program is highlighted by a photograph, special note, or in-depth description; see the profile page for more information.*
†D = day camp; R = residential camp

	GENERAL INFORMATION					PROGRAM INFORMATION						
	Profile Page	Boys D/R†	Girls D/R†	Coed D/R†	Age	Acad	Arts	Sports	Wild/ Outdrs	Special Interest	Jobs	Financial Aid
Pleasant Valley Camp for Girls	391		R		8–18		•	•	•	•	•	•
Road's End Farm Horsemanship Camp	391		R		8–16		•	•	•	•	•	
Sandy Island Camp for Families	391			R	3+		•	•		•	•	•
Sargent Center Adventure Camp	391			R	10–17		•	•	•		•	•
Student Conservation Association–Conservation Crew Program (New Hampshire)	392			R	15–19	•		•	•	•	•	•
Wediko Summer Program	392			R	7–17	•	•	•	•	•	•	
Windsor Mountain: Driftwood Stables Ranch Camp	392*			R	12–13			•	•	•		•
Windsor Mountain: Family Camp	392*			R	1+	•	•	•	•	•		•
Windsor Mountain: International Summer Camp	393*			R	8–14	•	•	•	•	•	•	•
Windsor Mountain: Leaders in Action	393*			R	15–17	•	•	•	•	•		•
Wolfeboro: The Summer Boarding School	393*			R/D	11–18	•	•	•	•		•	
YMCA Camp Lincoln–Junior CIT Program	394			D	14+					•	•	•
YMCA Camp Lincoln–On the Road	394			D	12–14					•	•	•
YMCA Camp Lincoln–Outdoor Adventure Camp: Backpacking	394				11–14	•		•	•	•	•	•
YMCA Camp Lincoln–Outdoor Adventure Camp: Everything Outdoors	395				10–13			•	•	•	•	•
YMCA Camp Lincoln–Outdoor Adventure Camp: Mountain Bike	395				10–13			•	•	•	•	•
YMCA Camp Lincoln–Outdoor Adventure Camp: River Runners	395				10–13			•	•	•	•	•
YMCA Camp Lincoln–Senior CIT Program	395			D	15+					•	•	
YMCA Camp Lincoln–Specialty Camps: Archaeology Camp	395			D	9–12	•				•	•	•
YMCA Camp Lincoln–Specialty Camps: Arts & Drama	396			D	9–12		•	•		•	•	•
YMCA Camp Lincoln–Specialty Camps: Horse Camp	396			D	9–12			•		•	•	•
YMCA Camp Lincoln–Specialty Camps: Sports Camp	396			D	9–12			•	•		•	•
YMCA Camp Lincoln–Traditional Day Camp	396			D	5–15	•	•	•	•	•	•	•
YMCA Camp Lincoln–Travel Camp	397			D	5–12			•		•	•	•
New Jersey												
Appel Farm Summer Arts Camp	397*			R	9–17	•	•	•		•	•	•
Bridge to the Future	397			R/D	12–13	•	•		•	•	•	
Camp College–Institute for Arts and Sciences	398			D	7–14	•	•	•	•	•	•	
Camp Discovery–Madison	398			D	6–12	•	•	•		•	•	
Camp Discovery–Teaneck	398			D	6–12	•	•	•		•	•	
Camp Louemma	398			R	7–15	•	•	•	•	•	•	•
Camp Lou Henry Hoover	399		R		7–18	•	•	•	•	•	•	•
Camp Middlesex	399			D	6–18	•	•	•		•	•	
Campus Kids–NJ	399			R	9–15		•	•	•	•	•	
Camp Veritans	399			R/D	5–15	•	•	•	•	•	•	•
Cybercamps–College of St. Elizabeth	400			D	7–18	•	•	•		•	•	•
Cybercamps–FDU Metropolitan Campus	400			D	7–18	•	•	•		•	•	•
Cybercamps–Princeton University	400			R/D	7–18	•	•	•		•	•	•
Drew Summer Music	400			R/D	12–20	•	•	•				•
Dwight-Englewood Summer Academic Session	401			D	11–18	•	•	•		•	•	
Dwight-Englewood Summer Adventures	401			D	6–10	•	•	•		•	•	
Dwight-Englewood Summer Sports Clinics	401			D	11–18			•			•	
Dwight-Englewood Weekly Enrichment	402			D	11–14	•	•			•	•	
ECOES: Exploring Career Options in Engineering and Science	402			R	15–17	•		•		•		•
The Hun School of Princeton American Culture and Language Institute	402*			R/D	13–18	•		•				
The Hun School of Princeton Boys' Basketball Camp	402	D			8–14			•			•	
The Hun School of Princeton Girls' Basketball Camp	403		D		10–14			•			•	
The Hun School of Princeton–Summer Academic Session	403*			R/D	12–18	•		•	•		•	
The Hun School of Princeton Summer Day Camp	403			D	5–12		•	•		•	•	
The Hun School of Princeton Summer Theatre Classics	404*			R/D	13–18		•					
iD Tech Camps–Princeton University, Princeton, NJ	404*			R/D	7–17	•	•	•		•	•	•
Jewish Community Center Day Camp	404			R/D	5–14	•	•	•	•	•	•	•
Junior Statesmen Summer School–Princeton University	404*			R	14–18	•				•		•
Junior Statesmen Symposium on New Jersey State Politics and Government	405*			R	14–18	•				•		•
Lenny Armuth Soccer Academy	405	D			6–17			•			•	•

This program is highlighted by a photograph, special note, or in-depth description; see the profile page for more information.
†D = day camp; R = residential camp

	GENERAL INFORMATION					PROGRAM INFORMATION						
	Profile Page	Boys D/R†	Girls D/R†	Coed D/R†	Age	Acad	Arts	Sports	Wild/ Outdrs	Special Interest	Jobs	Financial Aid
Lindley G. Cook 4-H Camp	405			R	8–16	•	•	•	•	•	•	
Maritime Camp	406				13–17	•	•	•		•	•	
Montclair State University Hi Jump Program	406			D	16–18	•	•	•			•	
Montclair State University Summer Camp for Academically Gifted and Talented Youth	406			D	9–16	•	•	•		•	•	
Newgrange Summer Program	406			D	8–13	•	•					•
Newgrange Summer Tutoring Program	407			D	7–18	•						•
The New York Film Academy, Princeton University, Princeton, NJ	407*			R	14–17		•					
The Peddie School Summer Day School	407			D	12–18	•						
Pingry Academic Camps	407			D	9–18	•						
Pingry Day Camps	407			D	3–14	•	•	•		•	•	
Pingry Lacrosse Camp–Martinsville Campus	408			D	7–14			•			•	
Pingry Lacrosse Camp–Short Hills Campus	408	D			7–14			•			•	
Pingry Soccer Camp	408			D	8–17			•			•	
Pingry Softball Camp	408		D		10–14			•				
Pingry Summer Enrichment Experience	408			D	5–12	•						
PixelNation	408			D	14–18	•	•					•
Princeton Ballet School's Ballet Plus Junior	409			D	9–13	•	•					
Princeton Ballet School's Ballet Plus Senior	409			D	11+		•					
Princeton Ballet School's Summer Intensive	409			R/D	13–21		•				•	
Professional Sports Camps–Big League Baseball Camp	409			R/D	8–18			•			•	
Professional Sports Camps–Hall of Fame Basketball Camp	409			R/D	10–18			•			•	
Professional Sports Camps–Hall of Fame Soccer Camp	410			R/D	7–15			•			•	
Rider University Opportunity for Academically Gifted and Talented High School Students	410			D	15–18	•						
Student Conservation Association–Conservation Crew Program (New Jersey)	410			R	15–19	•		•	•	•	•	•
Summer Academy for the Visual and Performing Arts	410			D	11–14	•	•					•
The Summer Institute for the Gifted at Drew University	411*			R	8–17	•	•	•		•	•	•
The Summer Institute for the Gifted at Moorestown Friends School	411*			D	6–11	•	•	•	•	•	•	•
The Summer Institute for the Gifted at Princeton University	411*			D	6–11	•					•	•
Trail Blazers	411			R	9–18	•	•	•	•	•	•	•
United Soccer Academy–Goal Keeping Training Camp, New Jersey	412			R/D	8–14			•			•	
United Soccer Academy–Junior Soccer Squirts, New Jersey	412			D	3–5			•			•	
United Soccer Academy–Recreation Soccer Community Camp, New Jersey	412			R/D	7–14			•			•	
United Soccer Academy–Regional Academy Camp, New Jersey	412			R/D	8–14			•			•	
United Soccer Academy–Senior Soccer Squirts, New Jersey	413			D	5–7			•			•	
United Soccer Academy–Team Training Camp, New Jersey	413			R/D	8–14			•			•	
United Soccer Academy–Travel Soccer Community Camp, New Jersey	413			R/D	8–14			•			•	
Westminster Choir College Composition Week	413			R	13–18	•	•					•
Westminster Choir College High School Solo Pianist	414			R	14–18	•	•				•	
Westminster Choir College High School Solo Vocal Artist: A Performance Workshop for Singers	414			R	15–18		•				•	
Westminster Choir College Middle School Music Theater	414			R	11–14	•	•					•
Westminster Choir College Middle School Piano Camp	414			R	11–15	•	•				•	
Westminster Choir College Middle School Vocal Camp	414			R	11–14		•				•	
Westminster Choir College Music Theater Workshop	415			R	15–18		•				•	
Westminster Choir College Organ Week	415			R	13–18		•				•	
Westminster Choir College Piano Camp	415			R	13–18		•					
Westminster Choir College Vocal Institute	415			R	15–18	•	•			•		•
Westminster Conservatory of Music–Flute Camp	415			R/D			•					•
Westminster Conservatory of Music–Musical Jamboree	415			D	4–7		•					•
Westminster Conservatory of Music–Summer Ensemble	416			D			•					•
Westminster Conservatory of Music–Try It Out	416			D			•					•
Westminster Conservatory of Music–Youth Opera Workshop	416			D	8–12		•			•		•
YMCA Camp Bernie	416			R	7–16		•	•	•	•	•	•
YMCA Camp Matollionequay	416		R		7–16		•	•	•	•	•	•
YMCA Camp Ockanickon	417	R			7–16		•	•	•	•	•	•

**This program is highlighted by a photograph, special note, or in-depth description; see the profile page for more information.*
†D = day camp; R = residential camp

	GENERAL INFORMATION					PROGRAM INFORMATION						
	Profile Page	Boys D/R†	Girls D/R†	Coed D/R†	Age	Acad	Arts	Sports	Wild/ Outdrs	Special Interest	Jobs	Financial Aid
YMCA Lake Stockwell	417			D	5–15		•	•	•	•	•	•
New Mexico												
Abilene Christian University–Cross Training	417			R	13–18	•	•	•	•	•	•	•
Cottonwood Gulch Family Trek	417			R	5+	•	•	•	•	•	•	
Cottonwood Gulch Mountain Desert Challenge	418				15–19	•	•	•	•	•	•	•
Cottonwood Gulch Outfit Expedition	418			R	10–13	•	•	•	•	•	•	•
Cottonwood Gulch Prairie Trek Expedition	418				13–15	•	•	•	•	•	•	•
Cottonwood Gulch Turquoise Trail Expedition	419				13–15	•	•	•	•	•	•	•
Cottonwood Gulch Wild Country Trek	419				13–15	•	•		•	•	•	•
Deer Hill Expeditions, New Mexico	420			R	15–22	•	•	•	•	•	•	
EARTHWATCH INSTITUTE–Prehistoric Pueblos of the American Southwest	420			R	16+	•				•		•
The Experiment in International Living–Navajo Nation	420*			R	14–19	•	•	•	•	•		•
Landmark Volunteers: New Mexico	420*			R	14–18	•			•	•	•	•
New Mexico Tech Summer Mini-Course	421			R	15–18	•						
Overland: American Community Service, Southwest	421*				15–18				•	•	•	
Student Conservation Association–Conservation Crew Program (New Mexico)	421			R	15–19	•		•	•	•	•	•
The Summer Science Program–New Mexico Campus	421			R	15–18	•		•	•	•	•	•
New York												
Acteen August Academy	422*			R/D	13–20	•	•					
Acteen July Academy	422*			R/D	13–20	•	•					
Acteen June Academy	422*			R	13–20		•					•
Acteen Summer Saturday Academy	422*			D	13–20		•					
Adirondack Alpine Adventures	423			D	14–80				•			
Adirondack Camp	423*			R	7–16		•	•	•	•	•	•
Alfred University Summer Institute in Astronomy	423*			R	15–17	•					•	
Alfred University Summer Institute in Entrepreneurial Leadership	423*			R	15–17	•				•	•	
Alfred University Summer Institute in Writing	424*			R	15–17	•	•				•	
American Academy of Dramatic Arts Summer Program at New York	424*			D	14+		•					
Applejack Teen Camp	425*			R	13–17	•	•	•	•	•	•	•
Barnard's Summer in New York City: A Pre-College Program	425*			R/D	14–18	•	•			•	•	•
Barnard's Summer in New York City: One-Week Mini-Course	425*			R/D	14–18	•				•	•	•
Barnard's Summer in New York City: Young Women's Leadership Institute	426*		R		14–18	•				•		•
Barton Day Camp–Long Island	426			D	6–12		•	•		•	•	•
Barton Day Camp–New York	426			D	6–12		•	•	•	•	•	
Beekman School Summer Session	426			D	13–19	•						
Brant Lake Camp's Dance Centre	427*		R		12–16		•	•	•		•	
Bristol Hills Music Camp	427			R	10–18	•	•	•			•	
Camp Chateaugay	427			R	6–15		•	•	•	•	•	
Camp Dudley	428*	R					•	•	•	•	•	•
Camp Echo in Coleman High Country	428			R	7–17	•	•	•	•	•	•	•
Camp Greenkill–Conservation/Adventure	429			R	10–16	•	•	•	•	•	•	•
Camp Greenkill–Gymnastics	429		R		9–17		•	•			•	•
Camp Greenkill–Judo	429			R	6+		•	•			•	•
Camp Greenkill–Volleyball	429		R		12+			•			•	•
Camp Hilltop	429			R	6–15	•	•	•	•	•	•	•
Camp Kennybrook	430			R	8–15		•	•	•	•	•	
Camp Lakeland	430			R	7–16	•	•	•	•	•	•	•
Camp McAlister	430			R	6–11	•	•	•	•	•	•	•
Camp Monroe	431			R	6–16		•	•	•	•	•	
Camp Pok-O-MacCready	431*			R	6–16	•	•	•	•	•	•	•
Camp Redwood	431			R	5+	•	•	•		•	•	
Camp Regis	432*			R	6–13	•	•	•	•	•	•	•
Camp Scatico	432			R	7–15		•	•	•	•	•	
Camp Talcott	433			R	11–15		•	•	•	•	•	•

This program is highlighted by a photograph, special note, or in-depth description; see the profile page for more information.
†D = day camp; R = residential camp

	GENERAL INFORMATION					PROGRAM INFORMATION						
	Profile Page	Boys D/R†	Girls D/R†	Coed D/R†	Age	Acad	Arts	Sports	Wild/ Outdrs	Special Interest	Jobs	Financial Aid
Camp Treetops	433*			R	8–14	•	•	•	•	•	•	•
Campus Kids–Minisink	433			R	7–15		•	•	•	•	•	
Camp Walden	434			R	6–16	•	•	•	•	•	•	
Career Explorations	434*			R	16–18	•	•	•		•		
Carousel Day School	434			D	3–15	•	•	•		•	•	
Coleman Country Day Camp	435			D	3–15	•	•	•	•	•	•	•
Columbia University Summer Program for High School Students	435			R/D	13–18	•	•	•		•	•	
Cornell University Summer College Programs for High School Students	435*			R	15–19	•	•	•	•	•		•
Cybercamps–Adelphi University	436			R/D	7–18	•	•	•		•	•	•
Cybercamps–Manhattanville College	436			R/D	7–18	•	•	•		•	•	•
Deerfoot Lodge	437	R			8–16	•	•	•	•	•	•	•
Deerkill Day Camp	437			D	3–14		•	•	•	•	•	•
Double "H" Hole in the Woods Ranch Summer Camp	437			R/D	6–16	•	•	•	•	•	•	•
Dunnabeck at Kildonan	438*			R/D	8–16	•	•	•	•		•	•
EARTHWATCH INSTITUTE–Archaeology at West Point Foundry	438			R	16+	•				•		•
Eastern U.S. Music Camp, Inc.	438*			R/D	10–18	•	•	•		•	•	•
Environmental Studies Summer Youth Institute	439*			R	16–18	•	•	•	•	•		•
Forrestel Farm Riding and Sports Camp	440			R	7–15		•	•	•	•	•	
French Woods Festival of the Performing Arts	440			R	7–17	•	•	•	•	•	•	•
FUN-damental Basketball Camp–Morrisville, New York	440			R/D	6–18			•			•	
Girl Scouts of Genesee Valley Day Camp	441		D		6–16		•	•	•	•	•	•
Girl Scouts of Genesee Valley Resident Camp	441		R		9–17	•	•	•	•	•	•	•
GirlSummer at Emma Willard School	441*		R		11–17	•	•	•		•	•	
Gordon Kent's New England Tennis Camp	442*			R/D	9–17			•			•	
The Gow School Summer Program	442*			R/D	8–16	•	•	•	•	•	•	•
Grandparents' and Grandchildren's Camp	443			R	5+	•	•	•		•	•	
Graphic Media Experience	443			R	16–18	•	•				•	•
Houghton Academy Summer ESL	443			R	14–18	•		•	•	•		
iD Tech Camps–Vassar College, Poughkeepsie, NY	443*			R/D	7–17	•	•	•		•	•	•
International Riding Camp	444		R		6–18			•		•	•	
Iroquois Springs	444			R	7–16		•	•	•	•	•	
Ithaca College Summer College for High School Students: Session I	444			R	15–18	•	•	•	•	•	•	•
Ithaca College Summer College for High School Students: Session II	445			R	15–18	•	•	•	•	•	•	•
Ithaca College Summer College for High School Students: Minicourses	445			R	15–18	•		•			•	•
Ithaca College Summer Piano Institute	445			R	12–18		•				•	•
JHS/HS Academic Summer School Program	445			D	10–18	•						
Kutsher's Sports Academy	446			R	7–17	•	•	•	•	•	•	
Landmark Volunteers: New York	446*			R	14–18	•	•	•	•	•	•	•
Maplebrook School's Summer Program	446			R/D	11–18	•	•	•	•	•	•	
Mountain Workshop–Graduate Plus Awesome Adventures	447				11–12			•	•	•	•	
Mountain Workshop–Awesome 1: Adirondacks	447				11–12			•	•	•	•	
Mountain Workshop–Leadership Through Adventure: Adirondacks	447				16–18			•	•	•	•	
The National Music Workshop Day Jams–Long Island, NY	447			D	9–15	•	•				•	•
The National Music Workshop Day Jams–Manhattan, NY	447			D	9–15	•	•				•	•
The National Music Workshop Day Jams–Purchase, NY	448			D	9–15	•	•				•	•
The New York Film Academy, The Dalton School, New York, NY	448*			D	14–17		•					
New York Military Academy–JROTC Summer Program	448			R	14+	•		•	•	•	•	
92nd Street Y Camps–Camp Bari Tov	449			D	5–13		•	•		•	•	•
92nd Street Y Camps–Camp Haverim	449			D	10–12		•	•	•	•	•	•
92nd Street Y Camps–Camp K'Ton Ton	449			D	3–5		•	•		•	•	•
92nd Street Y Camps–Camp Tevah for Science and Nature	449			D	8–11	•	•	•		•	•	•
92nd Street Y Camps–Camp Tova	449			D	6–13		•	•		•	•	•
92nd Street Y Camps–Camp Yaffa for the Arts	450			D	8–11		•	•		•	•	•
92nd Street Y Camps–Camp Yomi	450			D	5–9		•	•		•	•	•
92nd Street Y Camps–Fantastic Gymnastics	450			D	7–13		•	•			•	•
92nd Street Y Camps–Trailblazers	451				12–14		•	•		•	•	•
North Country Camps—Camp Lincoln for Boys	451	R			8–15		•	•	•	•	•	•

**This program is highlighted by a photograph, special note, or in-depth description; see the profile page for more information.*
†D = day camp; R = residential camp

	GENERAL INFORMATION					PROGRAM INFORMATION						
	Profile Page	Boys D/R†	Girls D/R†	Coed D/R†	Age	Acad	Arts	Sports	Wild/ Outdrs	Special Interest	Jobs	Financial Aid
North Country Camps—Camp Whippoorwill for Girls	451		R		8–15		•	•	•	•	•	•
Parsons Pre-College Academy	451			D	9–18	•	•			•	•	•
Parsons Summer Intensive Studies–New York	452			R/D	16+	•	•			•		•
Point O' Pines Camp for Girls	452		R		7–15	•	•	•	•	•	•	
Power Chord Academy–New York City	452			R	12–18	•	•				•	
Pratt Institute Summer Pre-College Program for High School Students	453*			R	16–18	•	•			•		
Purchase Youth Theatre	453			D	9–17		•				•	
The Ranch–Lake Placid Academy	453		R/D		7–17		•	•	•	•	•	
The Ranch–National Golf Camp–Lake Placid	454			R/D	7–17			•	•		•	•
St. John's University Scholars Program	454			D	16+	•	•					
Shakespeare at Purchase	454			D	10–18		•				•	
Shane (Trim-Down) Camp	454*			R	7–25		•	•	•	•	•	
Signature Music Teen Camp	455			R	14–17		•	•			•	
Signature Music Youth Camp	455			R	12–13		•	•		•	•	
Skidmore College–Acceleration Program in Art for High School Students	455*			R/D	15–18	•	•				•	•
Skidmore College–Pre-College Program in the Liberal Arts for High School Students	456*			R/D	16–18	•	•	•	•	•	•	•
SoccerPlus FieldPlayer Academy–Hamilton, NY	456			R/D	11+			•			•	•
SoccerPlus Goalkeeper School–Challenge Program–Hamilton, NY	456			R/D	10+			•			•	•
SoccerPlus Goalkeeper School–Competitive Program–Hamilton, NY	456			R	12+			•			•	•
SoccerPlus Goalkeeper School–National Training Center–Hamilton, NY	457			R	15+			•			•	
Sprucelands Camp	457			R	6–17		•	•		•	•	•
Stagedoor Manor Performing Arts Training Center/Theatre and Dance Camp	457*			R	8–18	•	•	•		•	•	
Stony Brook Summer Music Festival	458			R/D	13–26	•	•	•				•
Stony Brook University–Biotechnology Summer Camp	458			R	14–17	•		•		•		
Stony Brook University–Environmental Education Summer Camp	458			R	11–15	•	•	•	•	•	•	
Stony Brook University–Science Exploration Camp	458			D	11–14	•				•		
Stony Book University–Summer Camp at Stony Brook	459			D	5–12	•	•	•		•	•	
Stony Brook University Summer Sessions College Program	459			D	16+	•					•	
Student Conservation Association–Conservation Crew Program (New York)	459			R	15–19	•		•	•	•	•	•
The Summer Institute for the Gifted at Hofstra University	459*			D	6–11	•					•	•
The Summer Institute for the Gifted at Purchase College	460*			D	6–11	•					•	•
The Summer Institute for the Gifted at Vassar College	460*			R	8–17	•	•	•		•	•	•
"Summer in the City"	460*			R/D	16–24		•					
Summer School at New York Military Academy	461			R	12–18	•		•	•		•	
SummerSkills at Albany Academy for Girls	461			D	10+	•	•	•	•	•		
Summer Theatre Institute–2005	461*			R	14–19	•	•				•	
Surprise Lake Camp	462			R	7–15	•	•	•	•	•	•	•
Syracuse University Summer College	462*			R/D	14–18	•	•	•	•	•		•
Tanager Lodge	463			R	7–14	•	•	•	•	•	•	•
Tannen's Summer Magic Camp	463			R	12–20		•					
Technology Encounters–Video Encounter/Computer Encounter–New York	463			D	7–13	•	•			•	•	•
Tisch School of the Arts–Summer High School Programs	463*			R	15+	•	•					•
United Soccer Academy–Goal Keeping Training Camp, New York	464			R/D	8–14			•			•	
United Soccer Academy–Junior Soccer Squirts, New York	464			D	3–5			•			•	
United Soccer Academy–Recreation Soccer Community Camp, New York	464			R/D	7–14			•			•	
United Soccer Academy–Regional Academy Camp, New York	464			R/D	8–14			•			•	
United Soccer Academy–Senior Soccer Squirts, New York	465			D	5–7			•			•	
United Soccer Academy–Team Training Camp, New York	465			R/D	8–14			•			•	
United Soccer Academy–Travel Soccer Community Camp, New York	465			R/D	8–14			•			•	
Usdan Center for the Creative and Performing Arts	465*			D	6–18	•	•	•		•	•	•
Vassar College Coed Basketball Camp	466			D	7–15			•			•	
Vassar College Coed Soccer Camp	466			D	7–12			•			•	
Vassar College Coed Swim Camp	466			R/D	12–18			•			•	
Vassar College Girl's Field Hockey Camp	466		R/D		10–18			•			•	

**This program is highlighted by a photograph, special note, or in-depth description; see the profile page for more information.*
†D = day camp; R = residential camp

	GENERAL INFORMATION					PROGRAM INFORMATION						
	Profile Page	Boys D/R†	Girls D/R†	Coed D/R†	Age	Acad	Arts	Sports	Wild/ Outdrs	Special Interest	Jobs	Financial Aid
Ventures Travel Service–New York	467				14–70					•	•	
Visual Arts Institute for High School Students	467			D	13+		•				•	
Willow Hill Farm Camp	467			R	7–17			•		•	•	
YMCA Camp Michikamau	467			R	7–14		•	•	•	•	•	•
Young Actors and Playwrights Workshop	467			D	11–17	•	•				•	
Young Artists at Purchase	468			D	7–13	•	•				•	
Young Filmmakers at Purchase	468			D	12–17		•				•	
Young Photographers	468			D	12–17		•				•	
North Carolina												
Adventure Links–North Carolina Expeditions	468				14–17			•	•		•	
All Arts and Sciences Camp–North Carolina State University	468			R/D	7–15	•	•	•		•	•	•
All Arts and Sciences Camp–The University of North Carolina at Greensboro	469			R/D	7–15	•	•	•		•	•	•
Asheville School Summer Academic Adventures	469*			R		•	•	•	•	•	•	•
Blue Star Camps	470			R	6–16	•	•	•	•	•	•	
Brad Hoover and Will Witherspoon Football Camp/Sports International	470			R/D	8–18			•			•	
Brevard Music Center	470			R	14–35	•	•	•	•	•	•	•
Camp Cheerio YMCA	471			R	7–15	•	•	•	•	•	•	•
Camp Chosatonga for Boys	471	R			8–18		•	•	•	•	•	•
Camp Crestridge for Girls	471		R		7–16		•	•	•	•	•	•
Camp Glen Arden for Girls	471		R		6–17		•	•	•	•	•	
Camp Green Cove	472*		R		7–17		•	•	•	•	•	•
Camp High Rocks	472	R			8–16		•	•	•	•	•	
Camp Illahee for Girls	472		R		7–16		•	•	•	•	•	•
Camp Kahdalea for Girls	473		R		8–18		•	•	•	•	•	•
Camp Merrie-Woode	473		R		7–16	•	•	•	•	•	•	•
Camp Mondamin	473*	R			7–17		•	•	•	•	•	•
Camp Pisgah	473		R		7–17		•	•	•	•	•	•
Camp Ridgecrest for Boys	474	R			7–16		•	•	•	•	•	•
Camp Rockmont for Boys	474	R			6–16	•	•	•	•	•	•	•
Camp Sky Ranch, Inc.	474			R	10+		•	•	•	•	•	
Camp Winding Gap	475			R	6–14	•	•	•	•	•	•	•
Constructing Your College Experience	475*			R/D	16–17	•				•	•	•
Cybercamps–Duke University	475			R/D	7–18	•	•	•		•	•	•
Cybercamps–UNC, Chapel Hill	475			R/D	7–18	•	•	•		•	•	
Davidson College July Experience	476			R	16–18	•		•				•
Duke Action: Science Camp for Young Women	476*		R/D		10–13	•			•		•	•
Duke Creative Writers' Workshop	476*			R/D	15–17	•	•			•	•	•
Duke Drama Workshop	476*			R/D	15–17		•			•	•	•
Duke Young Writers Camp	477*			R/D	12–17	•	•	•		•	•	•
Eagle Lake Camp–East	477			R	11–21	•		•	•	•	•	•
Eagle's Nest Camp	477			R	6–17	•	•	•	•	•	•	•
Eastern Music Festival and School	478			R	14–20	•	•	•		•	•	•
EXPRESSIONS! Duke Fine Arts Camp	478*			R/D	10–13		•				•	•
Falling Creek Camp	478	R			7–16		•	•	•	•	•	•
Green River Preserve	478			R	9–14	•	•	•	•	•	•	•
Hante School	479				13–17	•	•	•	•	•	•	•
iD Tech Camps–University of North Carolina at Chapel Hill, Chapel Hill, NC	479*			R/D	7–17	•	•	•		•	•	•
IMACS–Full Day Summer Camp–North Carolina	479			D	5–18	•				•	•	
IMACS–Individual Summer Programs–North Carolina	480			D	6–18	•				•	•	•
Joe Krivak Quarterback Camp, North Carolina/Sports International	480			R/D	8–18			•			•	
Keystone Camp	480		R		7–16		•	•	•	•	•	
Landmark Volunteers: North Carolina	480*			R	14–18	•		•	•	•	•	
Mountain Adventure Guides: Summer Adventure Camp–Blue Ridge Expedition I	481				13–15				•		•	
Mountain Adventure Guides: Summer Adventure Camp–Blue Ridge Expedition II	481				15–17				•		•	

**This program is highlighted by a photograph, special note, or in-depth description; see the profile page for more information.*
†D = day camp; R = residential camp

	GENERAL INFORMATION					PROGRAM INFORMATION						
	Profile Page	Boys D/R†	Girls D/R†	Coed D/R†	Age	Acad	Arts	Sports	Wild/ Outdrs	Special Interest	Jobs	Financial Aid
Mountain Adventure Guides: Summer Adventure Camp–Jr. Adventure Camp	481				11–13				•		•	
Nantahala Outdoor Center–Kids Adventure Sports Camp	481			R	12–15			•	•		•	
Nantahala Outdoor Center–Kids Kayaking Courses	481			R	9–15			•	•		•	
North Carolina Outward Bound–Outer Banks	482				16+			•	•	•	•	•
North Carolina Outward Bound–Southern Appalachian Mountains	482				14+			•	•	•	•	•
North Carolina School of the Arts Summer Session	482			R/D	12+		•					
Oak Ridge Academic Summer Camp	482*			R/D	11–18	•		•		•		
Oak Ridge Summer Leadership Camp	483*			R/D	11–18			•	•	•		
Overland: Blue Ridge Explorer Hiking, Rafting and Kayaking	483*				13–18			•	•	•	•	
Project SUCCEED	483			D	11–17	•					•	•
Rockbrook Camp	484*		R		6–16		•	•	•	•	•	
Skyland Camp for Girls	484		R		6–15		•	•	•	•	•	
SoccerPlus Goalkeeper School–Challenge Program–Fayetteville, NC	484			R/D	10+			•			•	•
SoccerPlus Goalkeeper School–National Training Center–Fayetteville, NC	484			R	15+			•			•	•
Student Conservation Association–Conservation Crew Program (North Carolina)	485			R	15–19	•		•	•	•	•	•
Success Oriented Achievement Realized (SOAR)–North Carolina	485			R	8–18	•		•	•	•	•	•
SuperCamp–Wake Forest University	485*			R	11–18	•		•		•	•	•
Talisman–Academics	485			R	11–17	•				•	•	•
Talisman–INSIGHT	486			R	14–17			•	•	•	•	•
Talisman Mini-Camp	486			R	8–11		•	•	•	•	•	•
Talisman Open Boat Adventures (TOBA)	486			R	14–17			•	•	•	•	
Talisman–SIGHT	486			R	9–14		•	•	•	•	•	
Talisman Summer Camp	487			R	8–13	•	•	•	•	•	•	
Talisman–Trek Hiking Program	487			R	12–17			•	•	•	•	
Talisman–Tri-Adventures	487			R	14–17				•	•	•	•
YMCA Camp Kanata	487			R	6–15		•	•	•	•	•	•
Young Investigators Program in Nuclear Science & Technology	488			R	16+	•				•		•

North Dakota

	Profile Page	Boys D/R†	Girls D/R†	Coed D/R†	Age	Acad	Arts	Sports	Wild/ Outdrs	Special Interest	Jobs	Financial Aid
International Music Camp	488			R	10+	•	•	•			•	
Student Conservation Association–Conservation Crew Program (North Dakota)	488			R	15–19	•		•	•	•	•	•
Ventures Travel Service–North Dakota	488				14–70					•	•	

Ohio

	Profile Page	Boys D/R†	Girls D/R†	Coed D/R†	Age	Acad	Arts	Sports	Wild/ Outdrs	Special Interest	Jobs	Financial Aid
Camp Butterworth	489		R		8–18		•	•	•	•	•	•
Camp Echoing Hills	489			R	7+	•	•	•	•	•	•	•
Camp Joy	489			R/D	7–15	•	•	•	•	•	•	•
Camp Ledgewood	489		R/D		6–17	•	•	•	•	•	•	•
Camp O'Bannon	490			R	9–16		•	•	•	•	•	
Camp Stonybrook	490		R		8–18		•	•	•	•	•	•
Cleveland Institute of Art Portfolio Preparation/Young Artist Programs	490			D	6–18	•	•				•	
Cleveland Institute of Art Pre-College Program	490			R	15–18	•	•					
Cleveland Institute of Art Pre-College Program–Architecture	491			R	15–18	•	•			•		•
Cleveland Institute of Art Pre-College Program–Product and Auto Design	491			R	15–18	•	•					•
Cleveland Institute of Art Pre-College Program–Special Effects and Animation	491			R	15–18	•	•					•
The Country School Farm	491			R	6–12					•		
Explorer Day Camp	491		D		6–9		•	•	•	•	•	•
Falcon Camp	492			R	6–16	•	•	•	•	•	•	
Falcon Horse Lover Camp	492			R	10–15			•		•	•	
Falcon Horse Lover Camp for Girls	492		R		10–15			•		•	•	
Falcon Young Adventure Camp	492	R			6–7	•	•	•	•	•		
Friends Music Camp	493			R	10–18	•	•	•	•		•	•
The Grand River Summer Academy	493*			R/D	13–19	•	•	•	•	•	•	
Harmon's Pine View Camp	493			R	6–12			•	•	•		

**This program is highlighted by a photograph, special note, or in-depth description; see the profile page for more information.*
†D = day camp; R = residential camp

	GENERAL INFORMATION					PROGRAM INFORMATION						
	Profile Page	Boys D/R†	Girls D/R†	Coed D/R†	Age	Acad	Arts	Sports	Wild/ Outdrs	Special Interest	Jobs	Financial Aid
Hidden Hollow Camp	494			R	8–15		•	•		•	•	
Joe Machnik's No. 1 Academy One and Premier Programs–Columbus, Ohio	494			R/D	9–18			•			•	•
Joe Machnik's No. 1 Mighty Mini, Goalkeeper and Striker Camp–Columbus, Ohio	494			R/D	8–12			•			•	•
Junior Statesmen Symposium on Ohio State Politics and Government	494*			R	14–18	•				•		•
Kenyon Review Young Writers	494			R	16–18	•	•					•
Landmark Volunteers: Ohio	495*			R	14–18	•		•		•	•	•
Miami University Junior Scholars Program	495			R	16–18	•	•	•				•
Miami University Summer Sports School	495			R	8–18			•				
National Computer Camps at Notre Dame College	495			R/D	8–18	•	•	•		•	•	
Padua Franciscan High School Sports Camps	496			D	11–17			•				•
Padua Summer Experience	496			D	11–12	•	•	•	•	•		
Purcell Marian High School Cavalier Basketball Camp	496	D						•				
Purcell Marian High School Summer School	496			D		•						
SoccerPlus Goalkeeper School–Challenge Program–Delaware, OH	496			R/D	10+			•			•	•
SoccerPlus Goalkeeper School–National Training Center–Delaware, OH	496			R	15+			•			•	
Student Conservation Association–Conservation Crew Program (Ohio)	497			R	15–19	•		•	•	•	•	•
Summer Biotechnology Institute for High School and Middle School Teachers and Students	497			D		•						
The Summer Institute for the Gifted at Oberlin College	497*			R	8–17	•					•	•
Women in Engineering Summer Camp	497		R		15–18	•						•
Wright State University Residential Camps and Institutes	498			R	10–17	•	•			•	•	
YMCA Camp Tippecanoe–Adventure Camp	498			R/D	7–12	•	•	•	•	•		•
YMCA Camp Tippecanoe–Bike Camp	498			R/D	13–17			•	•	•		•
YMCA Camp Tippecanoe–Equine Camp	498			R/D	14–17		•	•	•	•		•
YMCA Camp Tippecanoe–Girl's & Guy's Corral	498			R/D	10–13		•	•	•	•		•
YMCA Camp Tippecanoe–Horse Pals	499			R/D	7–11			•	•	•		•
YMCA Camp Tippecanoe–Jr. Counselor	499			R/D	15–17		•	•	•	•		•
YMCA Camp Tippecanoe–Teen Camp	499			R/D	13–17		•	•	•	•		•
Oklahoma												
Student Conservation Association–Conservation Crew Program (Oklahoma)	499			R	15–19	•		•	•	•	•	•
Oregon												
Academy	500			R		•	•	•			•	•
Adventures in Learning	500			D	11–14	•	•			•	•	•
Adventure Treks–PAC 16	500				13–14			•	•			•
Camp Namanu	500			R	6–17	•	•	•	•	•	•	•
Cascade Science School	501			R	8–18	•	•	•	•	•	•	•
Cybercamps–Lewis and Clark College	501			R/D	7–18	•	•	•		•	•	
Delphi's Summer Session	501*			R/D	5–18	•	•	•	•	•		•
Expeditions	502			D	8–11	•	•				•	•
Fir Acres Workshop in Writing and Thinking	502			R	13–18	•	•	•	•		•	•
Hancock Field Station	502			R	8–18	•		•	•	•	•	•
High Cascade Snowboard Camp	503			R	9+	•	•	•	•		•	
High Cascade Snowboard Camp Photography Workshop	503			R	15+		•	•		•	•	•
Longacre Expeditions, Peak to Peak	503*				14–17			•	•		•	
Longacre Expeditions, Surf Oregon	503*				14–17			•	•		•	
Longacre Expeditions, Wind and Waves	504*			R	11–12			•	•		•	•
Meadowood Springs Speech and Hearing Camp	504			R	6–16		•	•		•	•	•
NBC Camps–Basketball Individual Training–La Grande, OR	504			R	9–18			•			•	•
NBC Camps–Basketball Individual Training–Newberg, OR	504			R	9–18			•			•	•
NBC Camps–Basketball–Team–La Grande, OR	504							•			•	•
NBC Camps–Volleyball–Oregon	505		R		12–18			•			•	•
OES–Challenge Workshops	505			D	8+	•	•					•
OES–Summer Adventure Camp	505			D	7–11				•	•	•	•
OES–Summer Discovery	505			D	6–11	•	•	•		•	•	•

This program is highlighted by a photograph, special note, or in-depth description; see the profile page for more information.
†D = day camp; R = residential camp

	GENERAL INFORMATION					PROGRAM INFORMATION						
	Profile Page	Boys D/R†	Girls D/R†	Coed D/R†	Age	Acad	Arts	Sports	Wild/ Outdrs	Special Interest	Jobs	Financial Aid
OES–Summer Mini Camps	505			D	6+	•	•	•		•	•	•
OES–Summer Wonder	506			D	3–6	•	•	•		•	•	•
Oregon Summer Music Camps	506			R/D	14–18	•	•	•		•	•	•
Outward Bound West–Backpacking and Whitewater Rafting, Oregon	506				14+	•		•	•	•	•	•
Outward Bound West–Mountaineering and Rafting, Oregon	506				14+	•		•	•	•	•	•
Outward Bound West–Mountaineering, Rafting, and Climbing-XT, Oregon	507				16+	•		•	•	•	•	•
Outward Bound West–Volcanoes Mountaineering–Oregon	507			R	16+	•			•	•	•	•
Pacific Marine Science Camp	507				7–14	•		•	•		•	•
Salmon Camp for Native Americans	507			R	10–14	•		•	•	•	•	
Salmon Camp Research Team for Native Americans–Oregon	508			R	15–18	•		•	•	•	•	•
Shizen Kyampu-Japanese Language Science Camp	508			R	10–14	•		•	•		•	•
Student Conservation Association–Conservation Crew Program (Oregon)	508			R	15–19	•		•	•	•	•	•
Teens-n-Trails	508			R	14–15	•		•	•	•	•	•
Vans Skateboard Camp	509			R	11+	•	•	•	•		•	
Ventures Travel Service–Oregon	509				14–70					•	•	
Wilderness Ventures–Oregon	509*				14–18				•	•	•	•
Young Musicians & Artists	509			R	9–18		•	•				•
Youth Forest Camps	509			R	16–19	•		•	•	•	•	•
Pennsylvania												
Academic Camps at Gettysburg College–Astronomy	510*			R	14–18	•		•				
Academic Camps at Gettysburg College–College Prep & Preview	510*			R	14–18	•		•		•		
Academic Camps at Gettysburg College–Community Service	510*			R	14–18	•		•		•		
Academic Camps at Gettysburg College–Foreign Language Study (Spanish)	510*			R	14–18	•		•		•		
Academic Camps at Gettysburg College–U.S. Civil War	511*			R	14–18	•		•				
Academic Camps at Gettysburg College–Writer's Workshops	511*			R	14–18	•	•	•				
Adventure Camps	511			R/D	12–18	•		•	•		•	•
Antwaan Randle Football Camp/Sports International	511			R/D	8–18			•			•	
Arts Unite	511			D	6–13		•					•
Breezy Point Day Camp	511			D	2–14	•	•	•	•	•	•	
Bryn Mawr College–Writing for College	512*		R		15–18	•	•	•		•	•	•
Camp Ballibay for the Fine and Performing Arts	512*			R	6–16		•	•			•	
Camp Canadensis	513			R	7–16	•	•	•	•	•	•	
Camp Cayuga	513*			R	5–15	•	•	•	•	•	•	
Camp Chen-A-Wanda	514			R	7–16		•	•	•	•	•	
Camp Conrad Weiser	514			R	7–15		•	•	•	•	•	•
Camp Lee Mar	514			R	5–21	•	•	•		•	•	
Camp Lindenmere	515			R	7–17	•	•	•	•	•	•	•
Camp Lohikan in the Pocono Mountains	515*			R	6–15	•	•	•	•	•	•	
Camp Mt. Luther	516			R/D	6–18	•	•	•	•	•	•	•
Camp Nock-A-Mixon	516			R	7–16		•	•	•	•	•	
Camp Pocono Ridge	517			R	8–15	•	•	•	•	•	•	
Camp Saginaw	517			R	6–16	•	•	•	•	•	•	
Camp Shohola	517	R			8–15	•	•	•	•	•	•	
Camp Streamside	518			R	8–16	•	•	•	•	•	•	•
Camp Susquehannock for Boys	518	R			7–16	•	•	•	•	•	•	•
Camp Susquehannock for Girls	518		R		7–17	•	•	•	•	•	•	•
Camp Tioga	519			R	8–15	•	•	•	•	•	•	
Camp Towanda	519			R	6–17	•	•	•	•	•	•	
Camp Watonka	519*	R			7–15	•	•	•	•	•	•	
Camp Wayne for Boys	520	R			6–16		•	•	•	•	•	
Camp Wayne for Girls	520		R		6–16		•	•	•	•	•	
Camp Westmont	520			R	6–16		•	•	•	•	•	
Carnegie Mellon University Advanced Placement Early Admission	521*			R/D	16–18	•						•
Carnegie Mellon University Pre-College Program in the Fine Arts	521*			R/D	16–18	•	•					•

**This program is highlighted by a photograph, special note, or in-depth description; see the profile page for more information.*
†D = day camp; R = residential camp

	GENERAL INFORMATION					PROGRAM INFORMATION						
	Profile Page	Boys D/R†	Girls D/R†	Coed D/R†	Age	Acad	Arts	Sports	Wild/ Outdrs	Special Interest	Jobs	Financial Aid
College for Kids	521			D	6–17	•	•	•	•	•		
College Settlement of Philadelphia	522			R	8–14		•	•	•	•	•	•
Cybercamps–Bryn Mawr College	522			R/D	7–18	•	•	•		•	•	•
Daniel Fox Youth Scholars Institute	522			R	14–17	•	•					•
Dhani Jones Football Camp/Sports International	522			R/D	8–18			•			•	
Dickinson College Research and Writing Workshop	523			R	16–18	•	•	•	•	•		•
Dickinson College Young Writer's Workshop	523			R	16–18	•	•					
Dickinson Summer College Program	523			R	16–18	•	•	•	•	•	•	•
Ensemble Theatre Community School	523*			R	14–18		•	•	•		•	•
Haycock Camping Ministries–Adventure Trails	524	R			13–16	•	•	•	•	•	•	•
Haycock Camping Ministries–Battalion Program	524	R			12–14	•		•	•	•	•	•
Haycock Camping Ministries–Stockade Program	524	R			8–10	•		•	•	•	•	•
Haycock Camping Ministries–Trailbuilders Program	525	R			10–12	•		•	•	•	•	•
High School Scholars (Summer Courses)	525			D	16–18	•						•
Hill Top Summer Programs	525			D	9–18	•	•	•		•		
iD Tech Camps–Carnegie Mellon University, Pittsburgh, PA	525*			R/D	7–17	•	•	•		•	•	•
iD Tech Camps–Villanova University, Villanova, PA	526*			R/D	7–17	•	•	•		•	•	•
IMACS–Full Day Summer Camp–Pennsylvania	526			D	5–18	•				•	•	
IMACS–Individual Summer Programs–Pennsylvania	526			D	6–18	•				•	•	
Indian Head Camp	526			R	7–17	•	•	•	•	•	•	
James Thrash and Hollis Thomas Football Camp/Sports International	527			R/D	8–18			•			•	•
Joe Krivak Quarterback Camp, Pennsylvania/Sports International	527			R/D	8–18			•			•	
Joe Machnik's No. 1 Academy One and Premier Programs–Aston, Pennsylvania	527			R/D	13–17			•			•	•
Joe Machnik's No. 1 Academy One and Premier Programs–Newtown, Pennsylvania	527			R/D	9–18			•			•	•
Joe Machnik's No. 1 College Prep Academy–Newtown/Aston, Pennsylvania	528			R/D	13–17			•			•	•
Joe Machnik's No. 1 Mighty Mini, Goalkeeper and Striker Camp–Aston, Pennsylvania	528			R/D	8–12			•			•	•
Joe Machnik's No. 1 Mighty Mini, Goalkeeper and Striker Camp–Newtown, Pennsylvania	528			R/D	8–12			•			•	•
Julian Krinsky Business School at Haverford College	528*			R/D		•		•		•	•	•
Julian Krinsky Business School at Wharton (Leadership in the Business World)	528*			R		•		•		•		•
Julian Krinsky/Canyon Ranch Young Adult Summer Program " for Smarter Minds and Bodies"	529*			R/D	13–17			•	•	•	•	•
Julian Krinsky Creative and Performing Arts Camp at The Shipley School/Bryn Mawr	529*			D	5–14	•	•	•			•	•
Julian Krinsky Exploring the Majors at the University of Pennsylvania	529*			R	14–17	•		•			•	•
Julian Krinsky Golf Camp at Cabrini College	530*			R/D	8+			•		•	•	•
Julian Krinsky Golf Camp at Haverford College	530*			R/D	8+			•			•	•
Julian Krinsky Junior Enrichment Camp at Cabrini College	530*			R/D	10–14	•	•	•	•	•		•
Julian Krinsky Senior Enrichment Camp at Haverford College	530*			R/D	12–17	•	•	•	•	•	•	•
Julian Krinsky Super Sports Camp at The Shipley School	531*			D	5–14			•			•	•
Julian Krinsky Tennis Camp at Cabrini College	531*			R/D	9–17			•			•	•
Julian Krinsky Tennis Camp at Haverford College	531*			R/D	10–17			•			•	•
Julian Krinsky Yesh Shabbat Summer Camp	531*			R/D	10–17	•	•	•		•	•	•
Jumonville Adventure Camps	532			R	8–17	•		•	•		•	•
Jumonville Baseball/Softball Camp	532			R	13–17	•		•			•	•
Jumonville Basketball Camp	532			R	13–17	•		•			•	•
Jumonville Creative and Performing Arts Camps	532			R	5+	•	•				•	•
Jumonville Discovery Camp	533			R	9+	•	•	•		•	•	•
Jumonville Golf Camp	533			R	13+	•		•			•	•
Jumonville Sampler Camps	533			R	8–17	•	•	•	•	•	•	•
Jumonville Soccer Camp	533			R	10–17	•		•			•	•
Jumonville Spirit and Sport Spectacular–Soccer Camp	534			R	13–17	•		•			•	•
Jumonville Spirit and Sport Spectacular–Swim Camp	534			R	13–17	•		•			•	•
Jumonville Spirit and Sport Spectacular–Tennis Camp	534			R	13–17	•		•			•	•
Jumonville Spirit and Sport Spectacular–Volleyball Camp	534			R	13–17	•		•			•	•

**This program is highlighted by a photograph, special note, or in-depth description; see the profile page for more information.*
†D = day camp; R = residential camp

	GENERAL INFORMATION					PROGRAM INFORMATION						
	Profile Page	Boys D/R†	Girls D/R†	Coed D/R†	Age	Acad	Arts	Sports	Wild/ Outdrs	Special Interest	Jobs	Financial Aid
Jumonville Sports Camp	535			R	9–17	•		•			•	•
Jumonville Youth Mission Work Camp	535			R	14–17	•				•	•	•
Kiski Summer Camp–Junior Division-Boys Grades 5-8	535	R/D			10–13	•	•	•	•	•	•	
Kiski Summer Camp–Senior Division-Boys Grades 9-12	535	R/D			14–18	•	•	•	•	•	•	
Kiski Summer Camp–Senior Division-Girls Grades 9-12	536		D		14–18	•	•	•	•	•	•	
Lebanon Valley College Summer Music Camp	536			R/D	13–18	•	•	•			•	
Ligonier Camp	536			R	8–17	•	•	•	•	•	•	•
Longacre Expeditions, Blue Ridge	537*				12–15			•	•		•	
Longacre Expeditions, Laurel Highlands	537*				12–15			•	•		•	
Longacre Leadership Program	537			R	12–18		•	•	•	•	•	•
Mercersburg Academy Blue Storm Boys Basketball School	538*	R/D			10–18			•			•	•
Mercersburg Academy Blue Storm Football Camp	538*	D						•				
Mercersburg Academy Junior Adventure Camp	538*			R	7–8	•	•	•	•	•	•	
Mercersburg Academy Young Writer's Camp	538*			R	12–16	•	•	•	•	•	•	•
Mercersburg Adventure Camp	538*			R	8–14	•	•	•	•	•	•	•
Mercersburg All-American Wrestling Camp & Junior All-American Wrestling Camp	539*	R/D			6–18			•	•	•	•	•
Mercersburg ESL Plus Program	539*			R	14–18	•	•	•	•	•	•	
Mercersburg Onstage! Young Actors Workshop	539*			R/D	11–14		•				•	
Mercersburg Teen Adventure Camp	540*			R	14–16	•	•	•	•	•	•	
Mercersburg The World's A Stage Theatre Workshop	540*			R/D	14–18		•				•	
Millersville University of Pennsylvania–Summer Language Camps for High School Students	540			R	15–18	•	•	•	•		•	•
Mini-Camp in the Pocono Mountains	540			R	10–15		•	•	•	•	•	
Mountain Workshop–Awesome 4: Pennsylvania	541				14–15			•	•	•	•	
National Computer Camps at La Roche College	541			R/D	8–18	•	•	•		•	•	
The National Music Workshop Day Jams–Philadelphia, PA	541			D	9–15	•	•				•	•
New Jersey YMHA–YWHA Camp Mountaintop	541			R	7–14	•	•	•	•	•	•	•
New Jersey YMHA–YWHA Camp Nah-jee-wah	542			R	6–11	•	•	•	•	•	•	•
New Jersey YMHA–YWHA Camp Nesher	542			R	8–15	•	•	•	•	•	•	•
New Jersey YMHA–YWHA Cedar Lake Camp	542			R	12–14	•	•	•	•	•	•	•
New Jersey YMHA–YWHA Round Lake Camp	543			R	7–18	•	•	•	•	•	•	•
New Jersey YMHA–YWHA Teen Camp	543			R	14–16	•	•	•	•	•	•	•
Next Level Camp	544			R	12–17	•	•	•	•	•	•	•
92nd Street Y Camps–Camp Kesher	544			R	8–11		•	•		•	•	•
92nd Street Y Camps–Camp Kesher Junior	544			R	7–9		•	•		•	•	•
Pathways at Marywood University	544			R/D	13–18	•	•	•	•	•		•
The Performing Arts Institute of Wyoming Seminary	545*			R/D	12–18	•	•			•	•	•
The Phelps School Summer Program	545			R/D	12–19	•	•	•	•	•		•
Pre-College Summer Institute, The University of the Arts	545*			R/D	15–18	•	•					
ProShot Basketball Camp–Boys Camp	546	R/D			10–18			•			•	
ProShot Basketball Camp–Girls Camp	546		R/D		10–18			•			•	•
Saint Vincent College Challenge Program	546			R/D	11–18	•	•	•		•	•	•
Science Quest	547		R/D		11–17	•		•		•	•	•
76ers Basketball Camp	547			R/D	9–17			•			•	
Shippensburg University Academic Camps–Acting & Theatre Arts	547			R			•					
Shippensburg University Academic Camps–Government in Real Life	547		R		14–15	•						•
Shippensburg University Academic Camps–Science Academy for Girls	547		R			•				•		
Shippensburg University Sports Camps–Baseball–Regular Camp	548	R/D			8–18			•				
Shippensburg University Sports Camps–Baseball–Specialist Camp	548	R/D			8–18			•				
Shippensburg University Sports Camps–Boys Basketball	548	R/D			8–18			•				
Shippensburg University Sports Camps–Cross Country	548			R/D	13–18			•				
Shippensburg University Sports Camps–Fast Pitch Softball	548		R/D		9–18			•				
Shippensburg University Sports Camps–Father/Son Basketball Camp	548	R			6–15			•				•
Shippensburg University Sports Camps–Field Hockey	549		R/D					•				
Shippensburg University Sports Camps–Football	549	R/D			8–18			•				
Shippensburg University Sports Camps–Girls Basketball	549		R/D		10–15			•				
Shippensburg University Sports Camps–Jumps	549			R/D				•				•

This program is highlighted by a photograph, special note, or in-depth description; see the profile page for more information.
†D = day camp; R = residential camp

	GENERAL INFORMATION					PROGRAM INFORMATION						
	Profile Page	Boys D/R†	Girls D/R†	Coed D/R†	Age	Acad	Arts	Sports	Wild/ Outdrs	Special Interest	Jobs	Financial Aid
Shippensburg University Sports Camps–Soccer–Boys Camp	549	R/D			11–18			•				
Shippensburg University Sports Camps–Soccer–Day Camp	549			D	6–10			•				
Shippensburg University Sports Camps–Soccer–Girls Camp	550		R/D		11–18			•				
Shippensburg University Sports Camps–Swimming	550			R/D	8–18			•				
Shippensburg University Sports Camps–Tennis	550			R/D				•				
Shippensburg University Sports Camps–Throws Camp	550			R/D				•				•
Shippensburg University Sports Camps–Track & Field	550			R/D				•				
Shippensburg University Sports Camps–Volleyball–Girls Camp	550		R/D					•				
SoccerPlus FieldPlayer Academy–Pottstown, PA	551			R/D	11+			•			•	•
SoccerPlus FieldPlayer Academy–Slippery Rock, PA	551			R/D	11+			•			•	•
SoccerPlus Goalkeeper School–Challenge Program–Pottstown, PA	551			R/D	10+			•			•	•
SoccerPlus Goalkeeper School–Challenge Program–Slippery Rock, PA	551			R/D	10+			•			•	•
SoccerPlus Goalkeeper School–Competitive Program–Pottstown, PA	551			R	12+			•			•	•
SoccerPlus Goalkeeper School–Competitive Program–Slippery Rock, PA	551			R	12+			•			•	•
SoccerPlus Goalkeeper School–National Training Center–Pottstown, PA	552			R	15+			•			•	
SoccerPlus Goalkeeper School–National Training Center–Slippery Rock, PA	552			R	15+			•			•	
Sports and Arts Center at Island Lake	552			R	7–17	•	•	•	•	•	•	
Streamside Camp and Conference Center	553			R	8+	•	•	•	•	•	•	•
Streamside Family Camp	553			R	6+	•	•	•	•	•	•	•
Streamside Pathfinder Adventure Camp	553			R	13–16	•	•	•	•	•	•	•
Student Conservation Association–Conservation Crew Program (Pennsylvania)	554			R	15–19	•		•	•	•	•	•
Study Tours in the USA–Lock Haven	554*			R	15+	•	•	•	•	•		
Summer Academy of Mathematics and Sciences	554*			R/D	16–18	•				•		•
The Summer Institute for the Gifted at Bryn Mawr College	554*			R	8–17	•	•	•	•	•	•	•
Summer Study at Penn State	555*			R	15–18	•	•	•	•	•	•	•
Summit Camp	556			R	8–17	•	•	•	•	•	•	
Susquehanna University Advanced Writers Workshop for High School Students	556			R	15–18	•	•	•				•
Technology Encounters–Video Encounter/Computer Encounter–Pennsylvania	556			D	7–13	•	•			•	•	•
Teen Challenge	557			D	15–18	•	•			•		
Time Travelers Program	557			R/D	11–14	•	•					
United Soccer Academy–Goal Keeping Training Camp, Pennsylvania	557			R/D	8–14			•			•	
United Soccer Academy–Junior Soccer Squirts, Pennsylvania	557			D	3–5			•			•	
United Soccer Academy–Recreation Soccer Community Camp, Pennsylvania	557			R/D	7–14			•			•	
United Soccer Academy–Regional Academy Camp, Pennsylvania	558			R/D	8–14			•			•	
United Soccer Academy–Senior Soccer Squirts, Pennsylvania	558			D	5–7			•			•	
United Soccer Academy–Team Training Camp, Pennsylvania	558			R/D	8–14			•			•	
United Soccer Academy–Travel Soccer Community Camp, Pennsylvania	558			R/D	8–14			•			•	
University of Pennsylvania–Penn Summer Art Studio	558			R/D	16+	•	•					•
University of Pennsylvania–Penn Summer Science Academy	559			R/D	16+	•						•
University of Pennsylvania–Precollege Program	559*			R/D	15+	•	•	•	•	•		•
Valley Forge Military Academy Extreme Tennis Camp	559*			D	8–16			•		•	•	•
Valley Forge Military Academy Summer Band Camp	560*			R/D	12–16	•	•	•		•	•	•
Valley Forge Military Academy Summer Camp for Boys	560*	R/D			8–16	•	•	•	•	•	•	
Valley Forge Military Academy Summer Coed Day Camp	560*			D	6–16	•	•	•	•	•	•	•
Women in Science & Engineering Camp	561		R		16–18	•				•		•
Woodward Freestyle BMX Bicycle, Inline Skate, Skateboarding Camp	561			R	7–17		•	•	•		•	•
Woodward Gymnastics Camp	561			R	7–17		•	•			•	•
Wyoming Seminary–Sem Summer 2005	561*			R/D	12–18	•	•	•			•	•
YMCA Camp Fitch Summer Camp	562			R	8–18	•	•	•	•	•	•	•
YMCA Camp Shand	562			R/D	5–16		•	•	•	•	•	•
Rhode Island												
Alton Jones Day Camp	563			D	5–11	•			•	•	•	•
Alton Jones Earth Camp	563			R	9–13	•		•	•	•	•	•

This program is highlighted by a photograph, special note, or in-depth description; see the profile page for more information.
†D = day camp; R = residential camp

RHODE ISLAND

	GENERAL INFORMATION					PROGRAM INFORMATION						
	Profile Page	Boys D/R†	Girls D/R†	Coed D/R†	Age	Acad	Arts	Sports	Wild/ Outdrs	Special Interest	Jobs	Financial Aid
Brown University Summer Programs–Pre-College Program	563			R/D	12–18	•	•			•	•	•
Camp Canonicus	563			R/D	4–18	•	•	•	•	•	•	•
Damon Huard and Matt Light Football Camp/Sports International	564			R/D	8–18			•			•	
Joe Krivak Quarterback Camp, Rhode Island/Sports International	564			R/D	8–18			•			•	
Landmark Volunteers: Rhode Island	564*			R	14–18	•		•		•	•	•
Portsmouth Abbey Summer School	564*			R/D	13–16	•	•	•			•	•
Rhode Island School of Design Pre-College Program	565*			R/D	16–18	•	•			•		•
St. George's Summer Session	565*			R/D	13–18	•	•	•	•	•		•
Student Conservation Association–Conservation Crew Program (Rhode Island)	566			R	15–19	•		•	•	•	•	•
Teen Expeditions	566			R	12–17	•		•	•	•	•	•
South Carolina												
Camden Military Academy Summer Session/Camp	566*	R				•	•	•	•	•		
Camp Chatuga	567			R	6–16		•	•	•	•	•	
Carolina Master Scholars Adventure Series	567*			R/D	12–18	•	•	•				
Clemson University Economics Summer Camp	567			R	15–18	•						•
Emerging Leaders 2005	568		R		14+	•		•		•		•
Furman University Summer Scholars Program	568			R	16–18	•	•	•	•	•		
IMACS–Full Day Summer Camp–South Carolina	568			D	5–18	•				•	•	
IMACS–Individual Summer Programs–South Carolina	568			D	6–18	•				•	•	•
International Junior Golf Academy	569			R/D	11–19	•	•	•		•	•	
Lead 2005	569		R		14+	•		•		•		•
Student Conservation Association–Conservation Crew Program (South Carolina)	569			R	15–19	•		•	•	•	•	•
Summer Science Program at the South Carolina Governor's School for Science and Math	569			R	13–16	•		•	•	•		•
Ventures Travel Service–South Carolina	570				14–70					•	•	
Visions–South Carolina	570*				14–18	•	•	•	•	•	•	•
South Dakota												
EARTHWATCH INSTITUTE–Mammoth Graveyard	570			R	16+	•				•		•
Student Conservation Association–Conservation Crew Program (South Dakota)	570			R	15–19	•		•	•	•	•	•
Ventures Travel Service–South Dakota	571				14–70					•	•	
Tennessee												
Camp Nakanawa	571		R		8–17		•	•	•	•	•	•
Carson-Newman College–EXCEL Program	571			R/D	16–17	•	•	•	•		•	
Davidson Academy–Academy Arts	571			D	3–16		•	•			•	
Davidson Academy–Bear Country Day Camp	572			D	4–14	•	•			•	•	
Davidson Academy–Sports Camps	572			D	4–14			•			•	
Freed-Hardeman Horizons for Ages 12-18	572			R	12–18	•	•	•		•		
McCallie Sports Camp	572	R			9–15			•			•	•
McCallie Academic Camp	572	R			13–16	•		•	•			
McCallie Lacrosse Camp	573	R			12–15			•			•	•
Montgomery Bell Academy–All-Sports Camps	573	D						•				•
Montgomery Bell Academy–LEAD Program	573			D		•				•		•
Montgomery Bell Academy–Specialty Sports Camps	573			D				•				•
Montgomery Bell Academy–Summer Cooking Camp	573			D						•		•
Montgomery Bell Academy–Summer Music Camp	574			D		•	•	•				•
Montgomery Bell Academy–Summer School	574			D		•	•					•
Montgomery Bell Academy–Summer Science Experience	574			D		•						•
Montgomery Bell Academy–Summer Theater Camp	574			D			•					
National Guitar Workshop–Murfreesboro, TN	574			R/D	13–79	•	•				•	•
Preparatory Academics for Vanderbilt Engineers (PAVE)	574			R/D	16–18	•		•	•	•		
Rhodes Summer Writing Institute	575			R	16–18	•	•	•				•
Student Conservation Association–Conservation Crew Program (Tennessee)	575			R	15–19	•		•	•	•	•	•
Ventures Travel Service–Tennessee	575				14–70					•	•	

**This program is highlighted by a photograph, special note, or in-depth description; see the profile page for more information.*
†D = day camp; R = residential camp

	GENERAL INFORMATION					PROGRAM INFORMATION						
	Profile Page	Boys D/R†	Girls D/R†	Coed D/R†	Age	Acad	Arts	Sports	Wild/ Outdrs	Special Interest	Jobs	Financial Aid
Texas												
Abilene Christian University–Kadesh Life Camp	576			R	14–18	•				•	•	
Abilene Christian University–Learning to Lead	576			R	8–12	•	•	•		•	•	
Abilene Christian University–MPulse	576			R	12–15	•	•	•		•	•	
Abiliene Christian University–KidQuest Day Camp	576			D	6–8	•	•	•		•	•	
Access to Careers in the Sciences (ACES) Camps	576		R		12–18	•						•
Alexander-Smith Academy Summer School	577			D	14+	•						
Arts on the Lake	577			R/D	11–18		•	•	•	•	•	•
Austin Nature and Science Center	577			D	3–16	•	•	•	•	•	•	•
Baylor University High School Summer Science Research Program	577			R	16–18	•						•
Camp La Junta	578	R			6–14		•	•	•	•	•	•
Camp Niwana	578			R/D	6–18		•	•	•	•	•	•
Camp Olympia	578			R	7–16		•	•	•	•	•	
Camp Olympia Junior Golf Academy	578			R	8–16		•	•		•		•
Camp Rio Vista for Boys	579	R			6–16		•	•	•	•	•	
Camp Sierra Vista for Girls	579		R		6–16		•	•	•	•	•	
Clark Scholars Program	579			R	16–18	•	•		•			
Drama Kids International Summer FUN Camp	579			D	5–17	•	•				•	
The Hockaday School Summer Session	580			R/D	4–18	•	•	•	•	•	•	
iD Tech Camps–Southern Methodist University, Dallas, TX	580*			R/D	7–17	•	•	•		•	•	•
iD Tech Camps–UT Austin, Austin, TX	580*			R/D	7–17	•	•	•		•	•	•
Jay Novacek Football Camp/Sports International	581			R/D	8–18			•			•	
JCC Houston: Art Camp	581			D	8–13		•			•	•	•
JCC Houston: Camp Bami	581			D	3–5		•	•		•	•	•
JCC Houston: Camp Kaleidoscope	581			D	6–8		•	•		•	•	•
JCC Houston: Counselor-In-Training	582			D	13–15		•	•		•		•
JCC Houston: Gordon Campsite	582			R/D	5–11		•	•	•	•	•	•
JCC Houston: Gymnastics Camp	582			D	8–13			•			•	•
JCC Houston: Kindercamp	582			D	5–6		•	•		•	•	•
JCC Houston: Sports Camp	582			D	8–13			•			•	•
JCC Houston: Teen Trek	583				11–14			•		•	•	•
JCC Houston: Tennis Camp	583			D	8–14			•			•	•
JCC Houston: Theater Camp	583			D	8–13		•	•			•	•
Joe Machnik's No. 1 Academy One and Premier Programs–Fort Worth, Texas	583			R/D	9–18			•			•	•
Joe Machnik's No. 1 College Prep Academy–Fort Worth, Texas	583			R/D	13–18			•			•	•
Joe Machnik's No. 1 Mighty Mini, Goalkeeper and Striker Camp–Fort Worth, Texas	583			R/D	8–12			•			•	•
The John Cooper School Academic Camps	584			D	4–18	•	•	•		•	•	
The John Cooper School Discovery Camps	584			D	4–12	•	•	•		•	•	
The John Cooper School Recreational Activities and Sports	584			D				•			•	
Junior Statesmen Symposium on Texas Politics and Leadership	584*			R	14–18	•				•		
Kickapoo Kamp	585		R		6–17		•	•	•	•	•	
Longhorn Music Camp: All-State Choir Camp	585			R/D	14–18		•				•	
Longhorn Music Camp: Harp Solo and Ensemble Camp	585			R/D	14–18		•	•			•	
Longhorn Music Camp: High School Band Camp	585			R/D	14–18	•	•				•	
Longhorn Music Camp: Middle School Band Camp	585			R/D	11–14		•	•			•	
Longhorn Music Camp: Middle School String Orchestra Camp	586			R/D	11–14		•				•	
Longhorn Music Camp: Piano Performance Workshop	586			R/D	14–18	•	•	•			•	•
Marbridge Summer Camp	586			R	16–30	•	•	•	•	•	•	
Marine Military Academy English as a Second Language (ESL)	586	R			13–17	•				•		
Marine Military Academy Summer Military Training Camp	586	R			12–17	•		•	•	•		
The Monarch School Summer Camp	587			D	6–19		•	•		•	•	
The Monarch School Summer Course	587			D	13–21	•	•	•		•		
National Guitar Workshop–Austin, TX	587			R/D	13–79	•	•				•	•
Parent/Youth Golf School	587			D	9–18			•				
Sea Camp	587			R	10–18	•		•		•		•

**This program is highlighted by a photograph, special note, or in-depth description; see the profile page for more information.*
†D = day camp; R = residential camp

	GENERAL INFORMATION					PROGRAM INFORMATION						
	Profile Page	Boys D/R†	Girls D/R†	Coed D/R†	Age	Acad	Arts	Sports	Wild/ Outdrs	Special Interest	Jobs	Financial Aid
SeaWorld San Antonio Adventure Camp	588*			R/D	3+	•	•			•	•	•
SoccerPlus Goalkeeper School–Challenge Program–Waco, TX	588			R/D	10+			•			•	•
SoccerPlus Goalkeeper School–National Training Center–Waco, TX	588			R	15+			•			•	
Southern Methodist University–College Experience	589*			R/D	15–18	•	•				•	•
Southern Methodist University TAG (Talented and Gifted)	589*			R	12–15	•	•			•	•	•
Star Ranch Summer Camp	589			R	7–18	•	•	•	•	•	•	•
Student Conservation Association–Conservation Crew Program (Texas)	590			R	15–19	•		•	•	•	•	•
Summer at the Academy	590			D	4–17	•	•	•		•	•	
Ventures Travel Service–Texas	590				14–70					•	•	
WRC Weather Camp	590			D	5–17	•					•	
Utah												
Camp Kostopulos	590			R	7–65	•	•	•	•	•	•	•
Camp Shakespeare	591			R	16+	•	•					
Deer Hill Expeditions, Utah	591			R	13–22	•	•	•	•	•	•	
EARTHWATCH INSTITUTE–Canyonland Creek Ecology	591			R	16+	•			•	•		•
EARTHWATCH INSTITUTE–Wildlife Trails of the American West	592			R	16+	•			•	•		•
Outward Bound West–Southwest Mountaineering, Rafting, and Canyoneering	592				14+	•			•	•	•	•
Outward Bound West–Southwest Mystery Expedition	592				16+	•			•	•	•	•
Outward Bound West–Utah Summer Semester	592				16+	•			•	•	•	•
Student Conservation Association–Conservation Crew Program (Utah)	593			R	15–19	•		•	•	•	•	•
SummerWorks	593			D	4–15		•	•	•	•	•	
World Horizons International–Kanab, Utah	593*			R	14–18			•	•	•	•	•
Vermont												
Aloha Camp	593		R		12–17		•	•	•	•	•	•
Audubon Journeys	594			R	13–16	•		•	•	•	•	•
Audubon Vermont Youth Camp	594			R	10–14	•	•	•	•	•	•	•
Brown Ledge Camp	594		R		10–18		•	•	•	•	•	•
Burklyn Ballet Theatre	594			R/D	12–25		•			•	•	•
Burklyn Ballet Theatre II, The Intermediate Program	595			R	10–12		•	•		•		
Camp Aloha Hive	595		R		7–12		•	•	•	•	•	•
Camp Betsey Cox	595*		R		9–15		•	•	•	•	•	
Camp Billings	596			R	8–15		•	•	•	•	•	•
Camp Catherine Capers	596		R/D		9–15		•	•	•	•	•	•
Camp Kiniya	596		R		6–17		•	•	•	•	•	
Camp Lanakila	596	R			8–14		•	•	•	•	•	•
Camp Sangamon for Boys	597*	R			9–15		•	•	•	•	•	
Craftsbury Running Camps	597			R	13+			•	•			
Craftsbury Sculling Camps	597			R	10+			•	•			
Farm and Wilderness Camps–Barn Day Camp	598			D	3–10	•	•	•	•	•	•	•
Farm and Wilderness Camps–Flying Cloud	598	R			11–14	•	•	•	•	•	•	•
Farm and Wilderness Camps–Indian Brook	598		R		9–14		•	•	•	•	•	•
Farm and Wilderness Camps–Saltash Mountain	599			R	11–14		•	•	•	•	•	•
Farm and Wilderness Camps–Tamarack Farm	599			R	15–17		•	•	•	•	•	•
Farm and Wilderness Camps–Timberlake	599	R			9–14		•	•	•	•	•	•
Future Leader Camp	599*			R	15–18			•	•	•		•
Keewaydin Dunmore	600	R			8–16		•	•	•	•	•	•
Killooleet	600*			R	9–14		•	•	•	•	•	•
Kinhaven Music School	601			R	10–18		•	•	•		•	•
Kroka Expeditions–Adventures for Small People	601			D	7–8	•	•	•	•	•	•	•
Kroka Expeditions–Coming of Age for Young Women	601		R		12–14	•	•	•	•	•	•	•
Kroka Expeditions–Expedition Pre-Columbus	601			R	13–18	•		•	•	•	•	•
Kroka Expeditions–Introduction to Adventure Day Camp	602			D	9–11	•	•	•	•	•	•	•
Kroka Expeditions–Introduction to Adventure Residential Camp	602			R	9–11	•	•	•	•	•	•	•
Kroka Expeditions–Introduction to Rock Climbing	602			R	9–12			•	•	•	•	•
Kroka Expeditions–Introduction to White Water	602			R	9–12	•		•	•	•	•	•

**This program is highlighted by a photograph, special note, or in-depth description; see the profile page for more information.*
†D = day camp; R = residential camp

	GENERAL INFORMATION					PROGRAM INFORMATION						
	Profile Page	Boys D/R†	Girls D/R†	Coed D/R†	Age	Acad	Arts	Sports	Wild/ Outdrs	Special Interest	Jobs	Financial Aid
Kroka Expeditions–Rock 'n Road	602			R	13–18	•		•	•	•	•	•
Kroka Expeditions–Vermont Underground Trail	603			R	13–18			•	•	•	•	•
Kroka Expeditions–Wild Arts and Canoe Adventure	603			R	10–12			•	•	•	•	•
Kroka Expeditions–Wild World of White Water	603			R	12–18	•	•	•	•	•	•	•
Landmark Volunteers: Vermont	603*			R	14+	•	•	•	•	•	•	•
Lochearn Camp for Girls	604		R		8–15	•	•	•	•	•	•	•
Mad River Glen Naturalist Adventure Camp	604			D	7–12	•		•	•	•	•	
Mountain Workshop–Awesome 2: Vermont	604				12–13			•	•	•	•	
Pine Ridge Summer Program	604*			R/D	9–18	•	•	•	•			
Point CounterPoint Chamber Music Camp	605			R	11–17	•	•	•	•		•	•
Program of Audubon Research for Teens (Take P.A.R.T.)	605			R	14–18	•		•	•	•	•	•
The Putney School Summer Arts Program	605*			R/D	14–17	•	•	•	•	•	•	•
The Putney School Summer Program for International Education (ESL)	606*			R	14–17	•	•	•	•	•	•	
The Putney School Summer Writing Program	606*			R/D	14–17	•	•	•	•	•	•	•
Roaring Brook Camp for Boys	607	R			9–16		•	•	•	•	•	
Songadeewin of Keewaydin	607		R		8–15		•	•	•	•	•	•
Student Conservation Association–Conservation Crew Program (Vermont)	607			R	15–19	•		•	•	•	•	•
Summer Discovery at Vermont	607*			R		•	•	•	•	•	•	
Summer Horizons Day Camp	608			D	5–12		•	•	•	•	•	
Summer Sonatina International Piano Camp	608			R	7–16	•	•	•	•	•	•	
University of Vermont Summer Institute for High School Students Discovering Engineering, Computers, and Mathematics	608*			R	15–16	•	•	•		•		•
Vermont Arts Animation Institute	609			R/D	13–18		•	•			•	•
Vermont Arts Dance Institute	609			R/D			•				•	•
Vermont Arts Filmmaking Institute	609			R/D	14–18		•	•			•	•
Vermont Arts Screenwriting Institute	609			R/D	14–18	•	•	•			•	•
Vermont Arts Theatre Camp Institute	610			R/D	12–14		•	•			•	•
Vermont Arts Theatre Institute	610			R/D	14–18		•	•			•	•
Vermont Arts Visual Arts Institute	610			R/D	14–18		•	•			•	•
Windridge Tennis Camp at Craftsbury Common	610			R	9–15		•	•	•		•	
Windridge Tennis Camp at Teela-Wooket, Vermont	611			R	9–15	•	•	•	•	•	•	
YMCA Camp Abnaki	611	R			6–16		•	•	•	•	•	•
YMCA Camp Abnaki–Counselor-in-Training Program	611	R			16–16		•	•	•	•		•
YMCA Camp Abnaki–Family Camp	611			R	1–15		•	•	•	•	•	•
YMCA Camp Abnaki–Mini Camp	612	R			6–8		•	•	•	•	•	•
YMCA Camp Abnaki–Teen Adventure Trips	612				14–16			•	•	•	•	•
Virginia												
Adventure Links–Ultimate Adventure Camps	612			D	8–14			•	•	•	•	
All Arts and Sciences Camp–George Mason University	612			R/D	7–15	•	•	•		•	•	•
All Arts and Sciences Camp–The College of William and Mary	613			R/D	7–15	•	•	•		•	•	•
All Arts and Sciences Camp–Virginia Tech	613			R/D	7–15	•	•	•		•	•	•
Art Monk Football Camp/Sports International–Virginia	613			R/D	8–18			•			•	
Blue Ridge School–Adventure Camps	614	R			11–16	•		•	•	•	•	
Blue Ridge School–Rock Climbing Camp	614	R						•	•	•		
Camp Carysbrook	614		R		6–16		•	•	•	•	•	•
Camp Carysbrook Equestrian	614		R		10–16			•		•	•	
Camp Curtain Call	615			R	10–18		•	•	•	•	•	•
Camp Friendship	615			R	6–16	•	•	•	•	•	•	•
Camp Holiday Trails	615			R	7–17		•	•	•	•	•	•
Camp Horizons Adventure	615			R	13–16		•	•	•		•	
Camp Horizons Discover	616			R	7–9	•	•	•		•	•	
Camp Horizons Explorer	616			R	12–16		•	•	•	•	•	
Camp Horizons Pathfinder	616			R	7–11		•	•	•	•	•	
Camp Horizons Specialty Camp	616			R	10–16		•	•	•		•	
Camp Jordan for Children with Diabetes	617			R	8–15	•	•	•	•	•	•	•
Cheerio Adventures–Appalachian Adventure	617			R	10–15			•	•		•	•

**This program is highlighted by a photograph, special note, or in-depth description; see the profile page for more information.*
†D = day camp; R = residential camp

	GENERAL INFORMATION					PROGRAM INFORMATION						
	Profile Page	Boys D/R†	Girls D/R†	Coed D/R†	Age	Acad	Arts	Sports	Wild/ Outdrs	Special Interest	Jobs	Financial Aid
Cheerio Adventures–Cave/Raft	617			R	13–15				•		•	•
Cheerio Adventures–Mountains to the Sea	617			R	14–17			•	•	•	•	•
Cheerio Adventures–Ocean Odyssey	618			R	14–17			•			•	•
Cheerio Adventures–Rock Climb/Raft	618			R	13–15			•	•		•	•
Cheerio Adventures–Sampler	618			R	10–12			•	•		•	•
Cheerio Adventures–Seekers	618			R	13–15			•	•		•	•
Cheerio Adventures–Standard	618			R	12–14			•	•		•	•
Cybercamps–George Mason University	619			R/D	7–18	•	•	•		•	•	
EARTHWATCH INSTITUTE–Frontier Fort in Virginia	619			R	16+	•				•		•
Fairfax Collegiate School Summer Enrichment Program	619			D	8–17	•	•				•	
Fishburne Summer Session	619*	R/D			12–18	•		•	•	•		
Flint Hill School–"Summer on the Hill"–A Biking Odyssey Day Camp	620			D	11–13			•	•	•	•	
Flint Hill School–"Summer on the Hill"–Academics on the Hill–English and Math Review	620			D	12–18	•					•	
Flint Hill School–"Summer on the Hill"–Academics on the Hill–Geometry for Credit	620			D	14–18	•					•	
Flint Hill School–"Summer on the Hill"–Academics on the Hill–The Reading Clinic	620			D	7–12	•					•	
Flint Hill School–"Summer on the Hill"–Boys Outdoor Adventures! Day Camp	621	D			12–14			•	•	•	•	
Flint Hill School–"Summer on the Hill"–Counselor-in-Training Day Camp	621			D	11–14	•	•	•		•	•	
Flint Hill School–"Summer on the Hill"–Creative Arts on the Hill–Art Camp	621			D	7–14	•	•				•	
Flint Hill School–"Summer on the Hill"–Creative Arts on the Hill–Let the Drums Roll	621			D	11–13	•	•				•	
Flint Hill School–"Summer on the Hill"–Enrichment on the Hill–Gee, Whiz!	622			D	8–11	•	•			•	•	
Flint Hill School–"Summer on the Hill"–Enrichment on the Hill–Investigating Where We Live	622			D	12–16	•	•			•	•	
Flint Hill School–"Summer on the Hill"–Enrichment on the Hill–Junior Great Books	622			D	7–9	•					•	
Flint Hill School–"Summer on the Hill"–Enrichment on the Hill–Scientific Super Sleuths	622			D	11–14	•				•	•	
Flint Hill School–"Summer on the Hill"–Enrichment on the Hill–Spanish Immersion Camp	623			D	7–10	•	•			•	•	
Flint Hill School–"Summer on the Hill"–Enrichment on the Hill–Study Skills for 9th Graders	623			D	13–14	•					•	
Flint Hill School–"Summer on the Hill"–Enrichment on the Hill–Summer Chess Camp	623			D	7–12					•	•	
Flint Hill School–"Summer on the Hill"–Enrichment on the Hill–Summer Service	623			D	14–18					•	•	
Flint Hill School–"Summer on the Hill"–Into the Woods Day Camp	623			D	9–12				•	•	•	
Flint Hill School–"Summer on the Hill"–Junior Day/Day Camps	624			D	5–12	•	•	•		•	•	
Flint Hill School–"Summer on the Hill"–Sports on the Hill–Coed	624			D	5–18			•		•	•	
Flint Hill School–"Summer on the Hill"–Sports on the Hill for Boys	624	D			7–14			•		•	•	
Flint Hill School–"Summer on the Hill"–Sports on the Hill for Girls	624		D		7–14			•		•	•	
Flint Hill School–"Summer on the Hill"–Trips and Travel Day Camp	625			D	11–14			•	•	•	•	
4 Star Academics Junior Camp at the University of Virginia	625			R/D	12–15	•	•	•	•	•	•	
4 Star Academics Scholars at the University of Virginia	625			R/D	16–18	•	•	•	•		•	
4 Star Academics Senior Camp at the University of Virginia	625			R/D	15–18	•	•	•	•	•	•	
4 Star College Prep Tennis at the University of Virginia	626			R/D	15–18			•				
4 Star Golf Camp at the University of Virginia	626			R/D	9–18			•			•	
4 Star Golf Plus All Sports Camp at the University of Virginia	626			R/D	9–18			•	•		•	
4 Star Tennis Camp at the University of Virginia	626			R/D	9–18			•			•	
4 Star Tennis Plus Camp at the University of Virginia	626			R/D	9–18			•	•		•	
4 Star Tennis Plus Golf Camp at the University of Virginia	627			R/D	9–18			•			•	
Hargrave Summer Program	627*	R/D			11–19	•		•	•	•	•	
Hollinsummer	627		R		15–18	•	•	•	•	•		
iD Tech Camps–University of Virginia, Charlottesville, VA	628*			R/D	7–17	•	•	•		•	•	•
Joe Machnik's No. 1 Academy One and Premier Programs–Dyke, Virginia	628			R/D	9–18			•			•	•

**This program is highlighted by a photograph, special note, or in-depth description; see the profile page for more information.*
†D = day camp; R = residential camp

	GENERAL INFORMATION					PROGRAM INFORMATION						
	Profile Page	Boys D/R†	Girls D/R†	Coed D/R†	Age	Acad	Arts	Sports	Wild/ Outdrs	Special Interest	Jobs	Financial Aid
Joe Machnik's No. 1 Mighty Mini, Goalkeeper and Striker Camp–Dyke, Virginia	628			R/D	8–12			•			•	•
Landmark Volunteers: Virginia	628*			R	14–18	•		•	•	•	•	•
Little Keswick School Summer Session	629	R			10–15	•	•	•	•	•	•	•
Makemie Woods Summer Camp	629			R	7–18	•	•	•	•	•	•	•
Massanutten Military Academy Summer Cadet Program	629			R/D	11+	•	•	•	•	•	•	
The National Music Workshop Day Jams–Alexandria, VA	630			D	9–15	•	•				•	•
Oak Hill Academy Summer Program	630			R/D	13–19	•		•	•			
Potomac School Summer Programs	630			D	3–17	•	•	•	•	•	•	•
Randolph-Macon Academy Summer Programs	630*			R/D	11–19	•		•	•	•		
Sidwell Friends Riverview Programs	631			R/D	9–15	•	•	•		•	•	
Sidwell Friends Women's Leadership–St. Margaret's School	631		R		13–18			•		•	•	
Student Conservation Association–Conservation Crew Program (Virginia)	631			R	15–19	•		•	•	•	•	•
Student Conservation Association–Conservation Leadership Corps–Washington, DC Metropolitan Area	631			D	15–18	•			•	•	•	•
Summer Leadership Education and Training	632			R/D	11–19			•	•	•	•	
Summer Programs on the River; Crew/Rowing Camp	632*			R/D	12–17			•			•	
Summer Programs on the River; Marine Science Camp	632*			R	12–17	•		•	•		•	
Summer Programs on the River; Sailing Camp	632*			R/D	10–17			•			•	
Summer Programs on the River; Skills Program	633*			R/D	12–17	•		•			•	
Washington and Lee University Summer Scholars	633			R	16–18	•	•	•	•	•		•
Wilderness Adventure at Eagle Landing	633			R	9–18	•		•	•	•	•	•
Woodberry Forest Basketball Camp	634	R/D			10–14			•		•	•	•
Woodberry Forest Golf Camp	634			D	9–17			•			•	•
Woodberry Forest Junior Adventure	634*			R/D	12–15	•	•	•	•	•	•	•
Woodberry Forest Lacrosse Camp	634	R			10–14			•		•	•	•
Woodberry Forest Senior Adventure	634*			R/D	12–17	•	•	•	•	•	•	•
Woodberry Forest Sports Camp	635	R			10–13			•		•	•	•
Washington												
A.C.E. Intercultural Institute	635			R	16+	•	•	•	•	•		
Adventures in Science and Arts	636			R/D	8–18	•	•	•	•	•	•	
Adventure Treks–Pacific Northwest Adventures	636				13–16			•	•			•
Aerospace Camp Experience	636			D	6–16	•	•	•	•	•	•	•
Alpengirl–Washington	636				12–16	•		•	•	•	•	•
Alpengirl–Washington Alpenguide Training	637				16–17	•		•	•		•	•
Alpengirl–Washington Lil' Alpengirl	637				11–12	•		•	•		•	•
The Art Institute of Seattle–Studio 101	637			R	16–18	•	•			•		
Camp Berachah Ministries–Counselor-In-Training	637			D	13–17	•	•	•	•	•	•	•
Camp Berachah Ministries–Day Camp	638			D	5–12	•	•	•	•	•	•	•
Camp Berachah Ministries–Horse Day Camp	638			D	7–13	•	•	•			•	•
Camp Berachah Ministries–Junior Camp	638			R		•	•	•	•	•	•	•
Camp Berachah Ministries–Leadership Expedition Camp	638			R		•		•	•		•	•
Camp Berachah Ministries–Legend Teen Camp	639			R		•	•	•	•	•	•	•
Camp Berachah Ministries–Overnight Horse Camp	639			R	8–16	•	•	•	•		•	•
Camp Berachah Ministries–Primary Camp	639			R		•	•	•	•	•	•	•
Camp Berachah Ministries–Soccer Camp	639			R	8–16	•	•	•			•	•
Camp Berachah Ministries–Teen Leadership	640			R		•	•	•	•	•	•	•
Camp Berachah Ministries–Wrangler-In-Training	640		R		14–16	•		•		•	•	•
Camp Nor'wester	640			R	9–16		•	•	•	•	•	•
College Quest	640			R	15–18	•	•	•	•	•		
Cybercamps–University of Washington	641			R/D	7–18	•	•	•		•	•	
Cybercamps–University of Washington, Bothell	641			D	7–18	•	•	•		•	•	•
DigiPen Institute of Technology Junior Game Developer Workshop	641*			D		•	•			•	•	•
DigiPen Institute of Technology Robotics Workshop	641*			D		•				•	•	•
DigiPen Institute of Technology 3D Computer Animation Workshop	642*			D	13+	•	•			•	•	
DigiPen Institute of Technology Video Game Programming Workshop	642*			D	14+	•	•			•	•	

This program is highlighted by a photograph, special note, or in-depth description; see the profile page for more information.
†D = day camp; R = residential camp

	GENERAL INFORMATION					PROGRAM INFORMATION						
	Profile Page	Boys D/R†	Girls D/R†	Coed D/R†	Age	Acad	Arts	Sports	Wild/ Outdrs	Special Interest	Jobs	Financial Aid
EARTHWATCH INSTITUTE–Caring for Chimpanzees	642			R	16+	•				•		•
EARTHWATCH INSTITUTE–Conservation Research Initiative–Mountain Meadows of the North Cascades	642			R	16+	•			•	•		•
EARTHWATCH INSTITUTE–Conservation Research Initiative–Restoring Wild Salmon	643			R	16+	•				•		•
EARTHWATCH INSTITUTE–Conservation Research Initiative–Salmon Hotspots of the Skagit River	643			R	16+	•	•	•	•	•		•
EARTHWATCH INSTITUTE–Conservation Research Initiative–Salmon of the Pacific Northwest	643			R	16+	•				•		•
EARTHWATCH INSTITUTE–Conservation Research Initiative–Traditions of Cedar, Salmon, and Gold	643			R	16+	•				•		•
EARTHWATCH INSTITUTE–Orca	643			R	16+	•				•		•
Explore Nor'wester	644			R	7–12		•	•		•		
Forest Ridge Summer Program	644			D	9–19	•	•	•	•	•	•	•
Four Winds * Westward Ho	644			R	9–16	•	•	•	•	•	•	•
GLOBAL WORKS–Adventure Travel-Pacific Northwest-3 weeks	644*				14–18	•	•	•	•	•	•	•
iD Tech Camps–University of Washington, Seattle, WA	645*			R/D	7–17	•	•	•		•	•	•
Joe Machnik's No. 1 Academy One and Premier Programs–Olympia, Washington	645			R/D	9–18			•			•	•
Joe Machnik's No. 1 Mighty Mini, Goalkeeper and Striker Camp–Olympia, Washington	645			R/D	8–12			•			•	•
Junior Institute	645			R	10–17	•	•	•	•	•	•	
Junior Statesmen Symposium on Washington State Politics and Government	646*			R	14–18	•				•		
Landmark Volunteers: Washington	646*			R	14–18	•			•	•	•	•
Marrowstone-in-the-City	646			D	7–14	•	•				•	•
Marrowstone Music Festival	646			R/D	13–23	•	•				•	•
National Guitar Workshop–Seattle, WA	647			R/D	13–79	•	•				•	•
NBC Camps–Basketball–Adult & Child Hoops–Spokane, WA	647			R	6+			•			•	•
NBC Camps–Basketball–Crowell's Intensity–Spokane, WA	647	R			14–19			•			•	•
NBC Camps–Basketball Individual Training (Boys)–Auburn, WA	647	R			9–18			•			•	•
NBC Camps–Basketball Individual Training (Girls)–Auburn, WA	647		R		9–18			•			•	•
NBC Camps–Basketball Individual Training–Spangle, WA	648			R	9–18			•			•	•
NBC Camps–Basketball Individual Training–Spokane, WA	648			R	9–18			•			•	•
NBC Camps–Basketball Point Guard Play–Spangle, WA	648			R				•			•	•
NBC Camps–Basketball Post & Shooting–Spokane, WA	648							•			•	•
NBC Camps–Basketball Speed Explosion–Spokane, WA	648			R	13–19			•			•	•
NBC Camps–Basketball–Team (Girls)–Spangle, WA	649		R					•			•	•
NBC Camps–Soccer–Spangle, WA	649			R	9–19			•			•	•
NBC Camps–Soccer Speed Explosion–Spokane, WA	649			R	9–19			•			•	•
NBC Camps–Volleyball Speed Explosion–Spokane, WA	649			R	9–19			•			•	•
The Northwest School Summer Program	649*			R/D	11–16	•	•	•		•	•	
Outdoor Adventure	650			R/D	11–18	•	•	•	•	•	•	
Outward Bound West–Climbing, Backpacking, and Canoeing–North Cascades, WA	650				12+			•	•	•	•	•
Outward Bound West–Mountaineering–North Cascades, WA	650				14+	•		•	•	•	•	•
Outward Bound West–Sea Kayaking, Backpacking, and Mountaineering–Washington	650				16+	•		•	•	•	•	•
Outward Bound West–Service Course–North Cascades	651				16+	•		•	•	•	•	•
Salmon Camp Research Team for Native Americans–San Juan Island	651			R	15–18	•		•	•	•	•	
San Juan Island Camps	651			R	10–18	•		•	•		•	•
Student Conservation Association–Conservation Crew Program (Washington)	651			R	15–19	•		•	•	•	•	•
Student Conservation Association–Conservation Leadership Corps–Northwest	652			R/D	15–19	•			•	•	•	•
Ventures Travel Service–Washington	652				14–70					•	•	
Westcoast Connection–Community Service	652*				16+			•	•	•	•	•
Whitman National Debate Institute	652			R/D	12–19	•						•
Wilderness Ventures–Cascade-Olympic	653*				14–18			•	•	•	•	
Wilderness Ventures–Puget Sound	653*				13–15			•	•	•	•	•
Wilderness Ventures–Washington Alpine	653*				15–18				•	•	•	•

This program is highlighted by a photograph, special note, or in-depth description; see the profile page for more information.
†D = day camp; R = residential camp

	GENERAL INFORMATION					PROGRAM INFORMATION						
	Profile Page	Boys D/R†	Girls D/R†	Coed D/R†	Age	Acad	Arts	Sports	Wild/ Outdrs	Special Interest	Jobs	Financial Aid
Wilderness Ventures–Washington Mountaineering	653*				16–18				•	•	•	•
YMCA Camp Seymour Summer Camp	654			R	5–18	•	•	•	•	•	•	•
West Virginia												
Buckswood: English Language (ESL) and Activities–West Virginia	654			R	7–16	•	•	•	•	•	•	
Burgundy Center for Wildlife Studies Summer Camp	654			R	8–15	•	•	•	•	•	•	•
Camp Greenbrier for Boys	654	R			7–15	•	•	•	•	•	•	•
Camp Rim Rock–Arts Camp	655		R		9–17		•	•			•	
Camp Rim Rock–General Camp	655		R		6–17		•	•	•	•	•	
Camp Rim Rock–Horseback Riding Camp	655		R		9–17			•			•	
Camp Rim Rock–Mini Camp	655		R				•	•	•	•	•	
Camp Rim Rock–Tennis Camp	655		R		9–17			•			•	
Camp Sandy Cove	656			R	7–15	•	•	•	•	•	•	•
Camp Tall Timbers	656			R	7–16		•	•	•	•	•	
Greenbrier River Outdoor Adventures, Adventure Camp	656			R	10–17		•	•	•	•	•	•
Greenbrier River Outdoor Adventures, Camp Snowshoe	657			D	5–16		•	•		•	•	•
Greenbrier River Outdoor Adventures, Rock and River	657			R	14–17		•	•	•	•	•	•
Greenbrier River Outdoor Adventures, Wilderness Explorer	657			R	11–17		•	•	•	•	•	•
Student Conservation Association–Conservation Crew Program (West Virginia)	657			R	15–19	•		•	•	•	•	•
Wesleyan Summer Gifted Program	658			R	10–17	•		•			•	•
Wisconsin												
American Collegiate Adventures–Wisconsin	658			R	14–18	•	•	•	•	•	•	
Birch Trail Camp for Girls	658		R		8–15	•	•	•	•	•	•	•
Camp Birch Trails	658		R		6–17		•	•	•	•	•	•
Camp Chi	659			R			•	•	•	•	•	•
Camp Highlands for Boys	659	R			8–16		•	•	•	•	•	
Camp Horseshoe	659	R			8–16		•	•	•	•	•	
Camp Menominee	660	R			7–15	•	•	•	•	•	•	•
Camp North Star for Boys	660	R			8–15	•	•	•	•	•	•	•
Camp St. John's Northwestern	660*	R/D			10–16		•	•	•	•		
Timber-lee Science Camp	661			R/D	8–17	•		•	•	•	•	•
Central Wisconsin Environmental Station–Natural Resources Careers Camp	661			R	14–17	•		•	•	•	•	•
Central Wisconsin Environmental Station–Sunset Lake Adventures	661			R	6–17	•	•	•	•	•	•	•
Clearwater Camp for Girls	662*		R		8–16	•	•	•	•	•	•	
Harand Camp of the Theatre Arts	662*			R	8–17	•	•	•		•	•	
Joe Machnik's No. 1 Academy One and Premier Programs–Kenosha, Wisconsin	663			R/D	9–18			•			•	•
Joe Machnik's No. 1 College Prep Academy–Kenosha, Wisconsin	663			R/D	13–17			•			•	•
Joe Machnik's No. 1 Mighty Mini, Goalkeeper and Striker Camp–Kenosha, Wisconsin	663			R/D	8–12			•			•	•
Milwaukee School of Engineering (MSOE)–Discover the Possibilities	663			R	13–18	•				•		
Milwaukee School of Engineering (MSOE)–Focus on Nursing	663			R	13–18	•				•		
Milwaukee School of Engineering (MSOE)–Focus on the Possibilities	664			R	13–18	•				•		
Nelson/Feller Tennis Camp–Lakeland College	664			R/D	10–17			•			•	
Nelson/Feller Tennis Camp–University of Wisconsin–Oshkosh	664			R/D	10–17			•			•	
Point Arts Camp–Music	664			R	12–18	•	•				•	
Red Pine Camp for Girls	664		R		6–16		•	•	•	•	•	
St. John's Northwestern Academic Camp	665	R/D				•	•	•	•	•		
St. John's Northwestern ESL Camp	665	R			10–16	•	•	•	•	•		
Student Conservation Association–Conservation Crew Program (Wisconsin)	665			R	15–19	•		•	•	•	•	•
Summer Music Clinic	666			R	11–18	•	•	•			•	
SuperCamp–University of Wisconsin at Parkside	666*			R	11–18	•		•		•	•	•
Swift Nature Camp–Adventure Camp	666			R	7–15	•	•	•	•	•	•	•
Swift Nature Camp–Discovery Camp	666			R	6–12	•	•	•	•	•	•	•
Swift Nature Camp–Explorer Camp	667			R	7–15	•	•	•	•	•	•	•

This program is highlighted by a photograph, special note, or in-depth description; see the profile page for more information.
†D = day camp; R = residential camp

	GENERAL INFORMATION					PROGRAM INFORMATION						
	Profile Page	Boys D/R†	Girls D/R†	Coed D/R†	Age	Acad	Arts	Sports	Wild/ Outdrs	Special Interest	Jobs	Financial Aid
Timber-lee Creation Camp	667			R		•	•	•	•	•	•	•
Timber-lee Drama Camp	667			R			•	•		•	•	•
Timber-lee Horsemanship Camps	668			R	9–18	•	•	•		•	•	•
Timber-lee Wilderness Trips	668				11–18	•		•	•	•	•	
Timber-lee Youth Camp	668			R/D		•	•	•		•	•	•
Towering Pines Camp	668	R			6–16	•	•	•	•	•	•	•
University of Wisconsin–Green Bay Biz 4 Youth Camp	669			R/D	14–18	•					•	
University of Wisconsin–Green Bay Computer Camp	669			R/D	12–15	•					•	•
University of Wisconsin–Green Bay Ecosystem Investigations	669			R/D	14–18	•					•	
University of Wisconsin–Green Bay Space Trek Camp	669			R/D	12–18	•				•	•	
University of Wisconsin–Green Bay Summer Art Studio	669			R/D	13–18	•	•				•	•
University of Wisconsin–Green Bay Summer Discovery	670			D	4–14	•	•			•	•	•
University of Wisconsin–Green Bay Summer Music Camps	670			R/D	12–18	•	•				•	•
University of Wisconsin–Green Bay Summer Spanish Immersion	670			R/D	13–18	•					•	
University of Wisconsin–Superior Youthsummer 2005	670			R/D	13–17	•		•	•	•	•	•
Ventures Travel Service–Wisconsin	671				14–70					•	•	
William Henderson Football Camp/Sports International	671			R/D	8–18			•			•	•
Woodland	671		R		6–15	•	•	•	•	•	•	•
World Affairs Seminar	671			R	16–18	•	•	•		•	•	•
YMCA Camp Icaghowan	672			R/D	7–16		•	•	•	•	•	•
YMCA Camp Minikani	672			R/D	8–17		•	•	•	•	•	•
YMCA Camp U-Nah-Li-Ya	672			R	7–17	•	•	•	•	•	•	•
YMCA Camp Wabansi	672			D	7–11	•	•	•	•	•	•	•
Wyoming												
EARTHWATCH INSTITUTE–Jackson Hole Bison Dig	673			R	16+	•				•		•
Elk Creek Ranch and Trek Program	673*			R	13–18			•	•	•		
Landmark Volunteers: Wyoming	673*			R	14–18	•	•		•	•	•	•
Outpost Wilderness Adventure–Wind River Expedition	674				13–17	•		•	•	•		•
Outward Bound West–Wyoming Rock Climbing	674				16+	•			•	•	•	•
Overland: Teton Challenge Hiking, Climbing and Kayaking	674*				15–18			•	•	•	•	
Student Conservation Association–Conservation Crew Program (Wyoming)	674			R	15–19	•		•	•	•	•	•
Success Oriented Achievement Realized (SOAR)–Wyoming	675			R	11–18	•		•	•	•	•	•
Teton Valley Ranch Camp–Boys Camp	675	R			10–15		•	•	•	•	•	•
Teton Valley Ranch Camp–Girls Camp	675		R		10–15		•	•	•	•	•	•
University of Chicago–Stones and Bones	676*				15–22	•			•	•		•
Wilderness Ventures–Grand Teton	676*				14–18			•	•	•	•	•
Wilderness Ventures–Jackson Hole	676*				13–15			•	•	•	•	•
Wilderness Ventures–Teton Adventure	677*				14–18			•	•		•	•
Wilderness Ventures–Wyoming Mountaineering	677*				15–18				•	•	•	•
Windsor Mountain: Voices of the Wind River, Wyoming	677*			R	12–14	•			•	•		•

BY COUNTRY

	Profile Page	Boys D/R†	Girls D/R†	Coed D/R†	Age	Acad	Arts	Sports	Wild/ Outdrs	Special Interest	Jobs	Financial Aid
Argentina												
AFS-USA–Community Service–Argentina	678*			R	15–18	•				•		•
AFS-USA–Homestay–Argentina	678*			R	15–18	•				•	•	•
Center for Cultural Interchange–Argentina Independent Homestay	678*			R	16+	•				•		•
EARTHWATCH INSTITUTE–Argentina's Pampas Carnivores	679			R	16+	•				•		•
EARTHWATCH INSTITUTE–Triassic Park	679			R	16+	•				•		•
The Experiment in International Living–Argentina Homestay, Community Service, and Outdoor Ecological Program	679*			R	14–19	•		•		•		•
GIC Arg–Argentinian Cooking	679			R	15+					•		
GIC Arg–Soccer	679			R	15+			•				
GIC Arg–Spanish Language	680			R	15+	•						
GIC Arg–Tango	680			R	15+		•					
Learning Programs International–Argentina	680*			R	14–18	•	•			•		•

This program is highlighted by a photograph, special note, or in-depth description; see the profile page for more information.
†D = day camp; R = residential camp

	GENERAL INFORMATION					PROGRAM INFORMATION						
	Profile Page	Boys D/R†	Girls D/R†	Coed D/R†	Age	Acad	Arts	Sports	Wild/ Outdrs	Special Interest	Jobs	Financial Aid
LSA Buenos Aires, Argentina	680*			R	16+	•				•		•
LSA Cordoba, Argentina	681*			R	16+	•				•		•
Youth for Understanding USA–Argentina	681*			R	15–18	•				•		•
Armenia												
Volunteers for Peace International Work Camp–Armenia	681			R	16+	•				•		
Australia												
AAVE–Australia	681*				14–18			•	•	•	•	
ACTIONQUEST: Australian and Great Barrier Reef Adventures	682*				15–19	•		•	•	•		
AFS-USA–Homestay Plus–Australia	682*			R	15–18	•			•	•		•
BROADREACH Adventures Down Under	682*				15–19	•	•	•	•	•		
Camp Chewonki Eco-Kayak Australia	683				15–17	•	•	•	•	•	•	•
Center for Cultural Interchange–Australia High School Abroad	683*			R	15–18	•			•	•		•
EARTHWATCH INSTITUTE–Conservation Research Initiative–Climate Change in the Rainforest	683			R	16+	•				•		•
EARTHWATCH INSTITUTE–Conservation Research Initiative–Hawksbill Turtles of the Great Barrier Reef	683			R	16+	•				•		•
EARTHWATCH INSTITUTE–Conservation Research Initiative–Queensland Tropical Fish Ecology	684			R	16+	•				•		•
EARTHWATCH INSTITUTE–Echidnas and Goannas of Kangaroo Island	684			R	16+	•				•		•
EARTHWATCH INSTITUTE–Itjaritjari: the Outback's Mysterious Marsupial	684			R	16+	•				•		•
EARTHWATCH INSTITUTE–Koala Ecology	684			R	16+	•				•		•
The Experiment in International Living–Australia Homestay	685*			R	14–19	•		•	•	•		•
LIFEWORKS with the Australian Red Cross	685*				15–19	•	•	•	•	•		•
PAX Abroad to Australia	685				15–18			•	•	•		
RUSTIC PATHWAYS–AWESOME AUSSIE EXPLORER	685*				14–18			•	•	•	•	
RUSTIC PATHWAYS–HIGH ADRENALINE AUSSIE	685*				14–18			•	•	•	•	
RUSTIC PATHWAYS–OUTBACK 4-WHEEL DRIVE SAFARI	686*				14–18				•	•	•	
RUSTIC PATHWAYS–THE SUNSHINE COAST & SYDNEY	686*				14–18			•	•	•	•	
RUSTIC PATHWAYS–TOTALLY DOWNUNDER ADVENTURE	686*				14–18			•	•	•	•	
RUSTIC PATHWAYS–TROPICAL AUSSIE ADVENTURE	686*				14–18			•	•	•	•	
RUSTIC PATHWAYS–ULTIMATE AUSTRALIAN ADVENTURE	686*				14–18			•	•	•	•	
SFS: Tropical Reforestation Studies	687			R	16–25	•		•	•	•		•
Summer Discovery at Australia	687*			R		•	•	•	•	•	•	•
Visions–Australia	687*				14–18	•	•	•	•	•	•	•
Westcoast Connection/On Tour– Australian Outback	688*				15–19			•	•	•		
Wilderness Ventures–Australia	688*				14–18			•	•	•	•	•
Windsor Mountain: Coast of Australia	688*				14–17	•		•	•	•		•
Youth for Understanding USA–Australia	688*				15–18	•			•	•		•
Austria												
Global Teen–Learn German in Vienna, Summer Camp-Ages 12-18	689*			R	12–18	•	•	•		•		•
Global Teen–Learn German in Vienna, Young Adult Summer Camp, Ages 16-18	689*			R	16–18	•	•	•		•		•
LSA Vienna, Austria	689*			R	12+	•	•	•		•	•	
Sprachkurse Ariana, Seefeld-Austria	689			R	10–18	•		•	•		•	
Village Camps–Austria	690*			R	10–17	•	•	•	•	•	•	
Bahamas												
BROADREACH Marine Biology Accredited	690*			R	15–19	•	•	•	•	•		
EARTHWATCH INSTITUTE–Bahamian Reef Survey	690			R	16+	•		•		•		•
EARTHWATCH INSTITUTE–Coastal Ecology of the Bahamas	691			R	16+	•				•		•
EARTHWATCH INSTITUTE–Dolphins and Whales of Abaco Island	691			R	16+	•				•		•
Flint Hill School–"Summer on the Hill"–Trips from the Hill–Ecological Study of Coral Reefs, Bahamas	691				12–18	•		•		•	•	
Barbados												
EARTHWATCH INSTITUTE–Hawksbill Turtles of Barbados	691			R	16+	•				•		•

**This program is highlighted by a photograph, special note, or in-depth description; see the profile page for more information.*
†D = day camp; R = residential camp

	GENERAL INFORMATION					PROGRAM INFORMATION						
	Profile Page	Boys D/R†	Girls D/R†	Coed D/R†	Age	Acad	Arts	Sports	Wild/ Outdrs	Special Interest	Jobs	Financial Aid
Belarus												
EARTHWATCH INSTITUTE–Bogs of Belarus	692			R	16+	•				•		•
Volunteers for Peace International Work Camp–Belarus	692			R	17+	•				•		
Belgium												
Volunteers for Peace International Work Camp–Belgium	692			R	15+	•				•		
Belize												
AAVE–Belize	692*				14–18	•		•	•	•	•	•
BROADREACH Academic Treks–Wilderness Emergency Medicine	693*				15–19	•		•	•	•		
EARTHWATCH INSTITUTE–Manatees in Belize	693			R	16+	•		•		•		•
The Experiment in International Living–Belize Homestay	693*			R	14–19	•		•		•		•
Longacre Expeditions, Belize	693*				15–18			•	•	•	•	
Bolivia												
AFS-USA–Community Service–Bolivia	694*			R	15–18	•			•	•	•	•
LSA Sucre, Bolivia	694*			R	16+	•				•		•
Botswana												
EARTHWATCH INSTITUTE–Crocodiles of the Okavango	694			R	16+	•				•		•
EARTHWATCH INSTITUTE–Health and Nutrition in Botswana	694			R	16+	•				•		•
The Experiment in International Living–Botswana Homestay	694*			R	14–19	•			•	•		•
Brazil												
AFS-USA–Homestay, Outdoor Adventure Amazon–Brazil	695*			R	17–25	•				•		•
AFS-USA–Homestay Plus–Brazil	695*			R	15–18	•		•	•	•		•
Center for Cultural Interchange–Brazil High School Abroad	695*			R	15–17	•				•		•
EARTHWATCH INSTITUTE–Brazil's Marine Wildlife	695			R	16+	•				•		•
EARTHWATCH INSTITUTE–Conservation Research Initiative–Conserving the Pantanal	696			R	16+	•		•	•	•		•
EARTHWATCH INSTITUTE–Dolphins of Brazil	696			R	16+	•				•		•
The Experiment in International Living–Brazil–Ecological Preservation	696*			R	14–19	•			•	•		•
The Experiment in International Living–Brazil Homestay and Community Service	696*			R	14–19	•				•		•
PAX Abroad–Brazil	697				15–18			•				
Putney Student Travel–Community Service–Brazil	697*			R	15–18	•		•	•	•		•
Youth for Understanding USA–Brazil	697*			R	15–18	•				•		•
British Virgin Islands												
ACTIONQUEST: Advanced PADI Scuba Certification and Specialty Voyages	697*				15–19	•		•	•	•		
ACTIONQUEST: British Virgin Islands–Sailing and Scuba Voyages	697*				13–19	•		•	•	•		
ACTIONQUEST: British Virgin Islands-Sailing Voyages	698*				13–19			•	•	•		•
ACTIONQUEST: Junior Advanced Scuba with Marine Biology	698*				13–15	•		•	•	•		
ACTIONQUEST: Rescue Diving Voyages	698*				15–19			•	•	•		
ACTIONQUEST: Tropical Marine Biology Voyages	699*				15–19	•		•	•	•		
!ADVENTURES–AFLOAT: Advanced Scuba Adventure Voyages–British Virgin Islands	699*			R	15–19	•	•	•	•	•	•	
!ADVENTURES–AFLOAT: Scuba and Sailing Discovery Voyages–British Virgin Islands	699*			R	13–19	•	•	•	•	•	•	
LIFEWORKS with the British Virgin Islands Marine Parks and Conservation Department	699*				15–19	•		•	•	•		•
ODYSSEY EXPEDITIONS: Tropical Marine Biology Voyages–British Virgin Islands	700*			R	15–19	•	•	•	•	•	•	
Sail Caribbean–All Levels of Scuba Certification with Sailing	700*				13–18	•	•	•	•	•	•	•
Sail Caribbean–British Virgin Islands	700*				13–18	•		•	•	•	•	•
Sail Caribbean–Community Service	701*				13–18	•		•	•	•	•	•
Sail Caribbean–Marine Biology	701*				13–18	•		•	•	•	•	•
Visions–British Virgin Islands	701*				14–18	•	•	•	•	•	•	•

**This program is highlighted by a photograph, special note, or in-depth description; see the profile page for more information.*
†D = day camp; R = residential camp

	GENERAL INFORMATION					PROGRAM INFORMATION						
	Profile Page	Boys D/R†	Girls D/R†	Coed D/R†	Age	Acad	Arts	Sports	Wild/ Outdrs	Special Interest	Jobs	Financial Aid
Cameroon												
EARTHWATCH INSTITUTE–Community Health in Cameroon	702			R	16+	•				•		•
Canada												
Adventures Cross-Country, Extreme British Columbia Adventure	702*			R	13–18			•	•		•	•
Adventure Treks–Canadian Rockies Adventures	702				14–16			•	•			•
AFS-USA–Homestay Language Study–Canada	702*			R	15–18	•				•	•	•
Appleby College Summer Academy	703			D	11–19	•	•				•	
Appleby College Summer Camps	703			D	4–17		•	•	•	•	•	
Bark Lake Leadership Through Recreation Camp	703			R	11–17	•	•	•	•	•	•	•
BICYCLE TRAVEL ADVENTURES–Student Hosteling Program–Province du Québec	703*				13–17			•	•	•	•	
BICYCLE TRAVEL ADVENTURES–Student Hosteling Program–Province du Québec (short program)	704*				13–17			•	•	•	•	
Bishop's College School Summer School	704*			R/D	11–16	•		•	•		•	
BROADREACH Academic Treks–Marine Mammal Studies	704*				15–19	•		•	•	•		
Camp AK-O-MAK	705		R		7–16	•		•	•	•	•	•
Camp Arowhon–Boys and Girls Camp	705			R	7–16		•	•	•	•	•	
Camp Arowhon–Voyageur Canoe Trip Program	705			R	12–16			•	•	•	•	
Camp Chikopi for Boys	706	R			7–17			•	•	•	•	
Camp Craig Horse Residential Summer Camp	706			R	8–16		•	•	•	•	•	
Camp Craig Sports and Recreation Summer Camp	706			R	8–16		•	•	•	•	•	
Camp Ganadaoweh	706			R/D	5–19	•	•	•	•	•	•	•
Camp Kodiak	707			R	6–18	•	•	•	•	•	•	
Camp Maromac	707			R	6–16	•	•	•	•	•	•	
Camp Mi-A-Kon-Da	707		R		7–17		•	•	•	•	•	
Camp Nominingue	708	R			7–15	•	•	•	•	•	•	
Camp Northway	708		R		7–16		•	•	•	•	•	
Camp Ouareau	708		R		5–15	•	•	•	•	•	•	
Camp Ponacka	709	R			8–15		•	•	•	•	•	
Camps with Meaning–Advanced Horsemanship I & II	709			R	12–15		•	•		•	•	•
Camps with Meaning–Boys Camp	709	R			10–13		•	•		•	•	•
Camps with Meaning–Girls Camp	709		R		10–12		•	•		•	•	•
Camps with Meaning–Junior High/Junior Youth Camp	710			R	11–14		•	•		•	•	•
Camps with Meaning–PreJunior/Junior/Intermediate Camp	710			R	6–12		•	•		•	•	•
Camps with Meaning–Youth Camp	710			R	14–16		•	•		•	•	•
Camp Tawonga–Teen Quest: Canada	710						•	•	•		•	•
Camp Wendigo	711	R			12–16			•	•		•	
Camp Wilvaken	711			R	9–15	•	•	•	•	•	•	
Canadian Rockies Adventurer Camp	711			R	14–18				•		•	
Canadian Rockies Outdoor Leader Camp	711			R	15–18				•	•	•	
Centauri Summer Arts Camp	712			R	9–19	•	•	•		•	•	
Darrow Wilderness Trips–Quebec: Mistassini	712				14–17			•	•		•	•
Deep River Science Academy–Deep River Campus	712			R	14–19	•		•	•		•	•
Deep River Science Academy–Whiteshell Campus	713			R	14–19	•		•	•		•	•
EARTHWATCH INSTITUTE–Climate Change at Arctic's Edge	713			R	16+	•				•		•
EARTHWATCH INSTITUTE–Pine Marten of the Ancient Forest	713			R	16+	•				•		•
EKOCAMP International	713			R	10–16	•		•	•		•	
Excalibur	714	R			10–12			•	•	•	•	•
French Immersion Kayak Expedition	714				14–17	•		•	•	•	•	
French Immersion Summer Camp	714			R	8–17	•	•	•	•	•	•	
Global Teen–Summer Language Adventure in Montreal	714*			R	13–17	•	•	•		•		•
Great Escapes (Adventure Trips for Teens)–Canadian Canoe and Kayak Adventure	715				14–17			•	•		•	•
Guitar Workshop Plus–Bass, Drums, Keyboards	715			R/D	12+	•	•				•	•
Hamilton Learning Centre Summer Fun in the Sun Camp	715			D	6–14	•	•	•	•		•	
Hamilton Learning Centre Summer School	715			D	6	•						•
Hockey Opportunity Camp	716			R/D	7–16			•	•	•	•	

**This program is highlighted by a photograph, special note, or in-depth description; see the profile page for more information.*
†D = day camp; R = residential camp

	GENERAL INFORMATION					PROGRAM INFORMATION						
	Profile Page	Boys D/R†	Girls D/R†	Coed D/R†	Age	Acad	Arts	Sports	Wild/ Outdrs	Special Interest	Jobs	Financial Aid
The Hollows Camp	716			R	7–14			•		•	•	
Kawkawa Summer Camps	716			R/D	7–17	•	•	•	•	•	•	•
Keewaydin Canoe Camp	716*			R	10–18			•	•		•	•
Keewaydin Temagami	717			R	10–18			•	•		•	•
Langskib Wilderness Programs	717	R			10–19			•	•	•	•	•
Learn English and Discover Canada	717			R/D	9–19	•	•	•	•	•	•	
LSA Montreal, Canada–English/French	718*			R	13+	•		•		•		•
Marine and Environmental Science Program	718			R	16–19	•		•	•		•	
Medeba Leader in Training Program	718			R	15–18	•		•	•	•		
Medeba Summer Camp	718			R/D	6–17	•	•	•	•	•	•	
MIMC–Intensive Music Camp	719			R/D	8–25	•	•	•			•	•
MIMC–Language Camp	719			R/D	8–25	•	•	•			•	•
MIMC–Music and Sports Camp	719			R	7–15	•	•	•			•	•
Mountain Workshop–Awesome 6: Quebec	720				15–17			•	•	•	•	
NBC Camps–Basketball Individual Training–Olds, AB Canada	720			R	9–18			•			•	•
NBC Camps–Basketball Individual Training–Three Hills, AB Canada	720			R	15–18			•			•	•
New Strides Day Camp	720			D	10–21		•	•		•	•	•
Northern Lights	720		R		11–14			•	•	•	•	•
Northwaters Wilderness Programs	721			R	13–19	•		•	•	•	•	•
Plato College–English/French Intensive Courses	721			D	14+	•				•		
Pripstein's Camp	721			R	7–16		•	•	•	•	•	
Programs Abroad Travel Alternatives–Canada	721*				15–19	•				•		
St. Margaret's School International Summer ESL Programme	722		R/D		13–25	•						
Sea Kayak Expedition (English)	722				14–17	•		•	•	•	•	
Stanstead College–English as a Second Language	722			R/D	11–16	•	•	•	•	•	•	
Stanstead College–French as a Second Language	722			R/D	11–16	•	•	•	•	•	•	
Summer Music at The Hollows	723			R	7–16	•	•	•			•	
TASC Canadian Wilderness Fishing Camps	723			R	10–17			•	•			
Voyageur Outward Bound–Lake Superior Freshwater Kayaking	723				16+	•		•	•	•	•	•
Westcoast Connection Travel–Quebec Adventure	723*				13–17			•	•	•	•	
Westcoast Connection Travel–Western Canadian Adventure	724*				13–17			•	•	•	•	
The Whale Camp–Youth Programs	724			R	10–17	•	•	•	•	•	•	
Windsor Mountain: Bonjour Quebec	724*				12–13	•		•	•	•		•
YMCA Camp Lincoln–Outdoor Adventure Camp: Canadian Adventure	724				11–14			•	•	•	•	•
YMCA Wanakita Summer Family Camp	725			R	1+	•	•	•	•	•	•	•
YMCA Wanakita Summer Resident and Day Camp	725			R/D	5–17	•	•	•	•	•	•	•
Chile												
AFS-USA–Homestay–Chile	725*			R	15–18	•				•	•	•
BROADREACH Academic Treks–Language Exposure and Service Learning	726*				15–19	•		•	•	•		
Center for Cultural Interchange–Chile Independent Homestay	726*			R	17+	•				•		•
EARTHWATCH INSTITUTE–Chilean Coastal Archaeology	726			R	16+	•				•		•
The Experiment in International Living–Chile North Homestay, Community Service	726*			R	14–19	•			•	•		•
The Experiment in International Living–Chile South Homestay	727*			R	14–19	•		•	•	•		•
Learning Programs International–Chile	727*			R	14–18	•				•		•
LSA Viña del Mar, Chile	727*			R	16+	•				•		•
Youth for Understanding USA–Chile	727*				15–18	•				•		•
China												
AFS-USA–Team Mission–China	728*			R	15–18	•	•	•		•		•
China's Frontiers: Diverse Landscapes and Peoples	728			R	17+	•	•		•	•		•
China Summer Learning Adventures	728			R	16–19	•	•	•		•		
Choate Rosemary Hall Summer in China	728*			R	14–19	•	•			•		•
EARTHWATCH INSTITUTE–China's Ancestral Temples	729			R	16+	•				•		•
EARTHWATCH INSTITUTE–Inner Mongolia's Lost Water	729			R	16+	•				•		•
EF International Language School–Shanghai	729*				16+	•				•		

This program is highlighted by a photograph, special note, or in-depth description; see the profile page for more information.
†D = day camp; R = residential camp

	GENERAL INFORMATION					PROGRAM INFORMATION						
	Profile Page	Boys D/R†	Girls D/R†	Coed D/R†	Age	Acad	Arts	Sports	Wild/ Outdrs	Special Interest	Jobs	Financial Aid
The Experiment in International Living–China North and East Homestay	729*			R	14–19	•			•	•		•
The Experiment in International Living–China South and West Homestay	730*			R	14–19	•			•	•		•
ISB Chinese Language Camp	730*			R	10–18	•	•	•		•	•	
Where There Be Dragons: China	730*				15–20	•	•	•	•	•		•
Where There Be Dragons: Silk Road	730*				15–19	•		•	•	•		•
Where There Be Dragons: Tibet	731*				15–20	•	•		•	•		•
Youth for Understanding USA–China	731*			R	15–18	•		•		•		•
Costa Rica												
AAVE–Costa Rica	732*				14–18	•	•	•	•	•	•	•
Adventure Links–The Costa Rica Experience	732				14–17	•		•	•	•	•	
Adventures Cross-Country, Costa Rica Adventure	732*			R	13–18			•	•		•	•
AFS-USA–Community Service–Costa Rica	732*			R	15–18	•			•	•		•
AFS-USA–Homestay Language Study–Costa Rica	733*			R	15–18	•				•		•
AFS-USA–Homestay Plus–Costa Rica	733*			R	15–18	•				•		•
Blyth Education–Summer Study in Costa Rica	733			R	16–19	•		•	•	•	•	
Brighton in Costa Rica	733*			R	15+	•	•	•	•	•		
BROADREACH Academic Treks–Sea Turtle Studies	734*				15–19	•		•	•	•		•
BROADREACH Costa Rica Experience	734*				15–19	•	•	•	•	•		
Costa Rica ¡Pura Vida!	734				15–17	•			•	•		
Costa Rica Rainforest Outward Bound School–Multi-Element	734				14+	•		•	•	•	•	•
Costa Rica Rainforest Outward Bound School–Summer Semester	735				17+	•		•	•	•	•	•
Costa Rica Rainforest Outward Bound School–Surf Adventure	735				14+	•		•	•	•	•	•
Deer Hill Expeditions, Costa Rica	735			R	15–18	•		•	•	•		•
EARTHWATCH INSTITUTE–Dolphins of Costa Rica	735			R	16+	•	•	•	•	•		•
EARTHWATCH INSTITUTE–Rainforest Caterpillars–Costa Rica	736			R	16+	•				•		•
EARTHWATCH INSTITUTE–Restoring Costa Rica's Rainforest	736			R	16+	•				•		•
The Experiment in International Living–Costa Rica Homestay	736*			R	14–19	•		•	•	•		•
Global Teen–Learn Spanish in Costa Rica	736*			R	12–17	•	•	•	•	•		•
GLOBAL WORKS–Language Exposure-Costa Rica-4 weeks	737*				14–18	•	•	•	•	•	•	•
GLOBAL WORKS–Language Immersion-Costa Rica-4 weeks	737*				15–18	•	•	•	•	•	•	•
Great Escapes (Adventure Trips for Teens)–Costa Rica Rainforest Adventure	737				14–17	•			•	•	•	•
Instituto de Idiomas Geos–Costa Rica	737			R	12–18	•	•	•	•	•		
Learning Programs International–Costa Rica	738*			R	14–18	•	•			•		
LSA Flamingo Beach, Costa Rica	738*			R	16+	•				•		•
LSA San José, Costa Rica	738*			R	13+	•	•			•		•
Overland: Costa Rica Explorer Hiking, Rafting, and Sea-Kayaking	738*				14–18			•	•	•	•	
Overland: Language Study Abroad in Costa Rica	739*			R	14–18	•			•	•	•	
Overland: World Service, Costa Rica	739*			R	14–19					•	•	
Peace Works International–Costa Rica	739*				15–18	•		•	•	•	•	
Poulter Colorado Camps: Adventures Planet Earth–Costa Rica	740				14+	•		•	•	•	•	•
Programs Abroad Travel Alternatives–Costa Rica	740*				15+	•		•	•	•		
Putney Student Travel–Community Service–Costa Rica	740*			R	15–18	•		•	•	•		•
Putney Student Travel–Language Learning–Costa Rica	741*			R	13–18	•		•	•	•		•
RUSTIC PATHWAYS–ACCELERATED SPANISH IMMERSION	741*			R	14–18	•	•		•	•	•	
RUSTIC PATHWAYS–COSTA RICA ADVENTURER	741*				14–18			•	•	•	•	
RUSTIC PATHWAYS–COSTA RICA EXTREME	741*				14–18			•	•	•	•	
RUSTIC PATHWAYS–COSTA RICA NATURAL WONDERS	742*				14–18			•	•	•	•	
RUSTIC PATHWAYS–RAMP UP YOUR SPANISH	742*			R	14–18	•	•	•		•	•	
RUSTIC PATHWAYS–SPANISH LANGUAGE IMMERSION	742*			R	14–18	•	•	•	•	•	•	
RUSTIC PATHWAYS–SURF THE SUMMER–COSTA RICA	742*			R	14–18			•	•	•	•	
RUSTIC PATHWAYS–THE CANO NEGRO SERVICE PROJECT	742*			R	14–18	•		•		•	•	
RUSTIC PATHWAYS–THE TURTLE CONSERVATION PROJECT	743*			R	14–18	•		•		•	•	
RUSTIC PATHWAYS–VOLCANOES AND RAINFORESTS	743*			R	14–18	•		•	•	•	•	
SFS: Sustaining Tropical Ecosystems	743			R	16–25	•		•	•	•		•

**This program is highlighted by a photograph, special note, or in-depth description; see the profile page for more information.*
†D = day camp; R = residential camp

	GENERAL INFORMATION					PROGRAM INFORMATION						
	Profile Page	Boys D/R†	Girls D/R†	Coed D/R†	Age	Acad	Arts	Sports	Wild/ Outdrs	Special Interest	Jobs	Financial Aid
Sidwell Friends Summer Program: Costa Rica	743				13–17	•			•	•		
Wilderness Ventures–Costa Rica	744*				14–18			•	•	•	•	•
World Horizons International–Costa Rica	744*			R	14–18	•		•	•	•	•	•
Cuba												
EARTHWATCH INSTITUTE–Crocodiles of Cuba	744			R	16+	•			•	•		•
Excel Cuba	745*			R	15–18	•	•	•	•	•		•
Putney Student Travel–Cultural Exploration-Creative Writing in Cuba	745*			R	15–18	•	•	•	•	•	•	•
Windsor Mountain: Cuba Friendship Exchange	745*				14–17	•				•		•
Czech Republic												
EARTHWATCH INSTITUTE–Mountain Waters of Bohemia	745			R	16+	•				•		•
Volunteers for Peace International Work Camp–Czech Republic	746			R	16+	•		•	•	•		
Denmark												
Peace in the Modern World	746				15+	•	•	•	•	•		•
Youth for Understanding USA–Denmark	746*			R	15–18	•		•	•	•		•
Dominica												
Putney Student Travel–Community Service–Dominica, West Indies	747*			R	15–18	•		•	•	•		•
Visions–Dominica	747*				14–18	•	•	•	•	•	•	•
World Horizons International–Dominica	747*			R	14–18			•	•	•	•	•
Dominican Republic												
Putney Student Travel–Community Service–Dominican Republic	747*			R	15–18	•		•	•	•		•
SuperCamp–Dominican Republic	748*			R	14–18	•		•			•	•
Visions–Dominican Republic	748*				14–18	•	•	•	•	•	•	•
Ecuador												
AAVE–Ecuador and Galapagos	748*				15–18	•		•	•	•	•	•
ACTIONQUEST: Galapagos Archipelago Expeditions	748*				15–19	•	•	•	•	•		
AFS-USA–Homestay–Ecuador	749*			R	15–18	•				•		•
Blyth Education–Summer Study in the Amazon and the Galapagos Islands	749			R	16–19	•		•	•	•	•	
BROADREACH Academic Treks–Spanish Language Immersion in Ecuador	749*				16–20	•		•	•	•		
BROADREACH Amazon and Galapagos Encounter	749*				15–19	•	•	•	•	•		
EARTHWATCH INSTITUTE–Ecuador Forest Birds	750			R	16+	•				•		•
EF International Language School–Quito	750*				16+	•		•	•	•		
The Experiment in International Living–Ecuador Homestay	750*			R	14–19	•		•	•	•		•
Global Teen–Spanish in Ecuador	750*			R		•	•	•		•		•
GLOBAL WORKS–Language Exposure-Ecuador and the Galapagos-4 weeks	751*				15–18	•	•	•	•	•	•	•
GLOBAL WORKS–Language Immersion-Ecuador and the Galapagos-4 weeks	751*				15–18	•	•	•	•	•	•	•
Ibike Cultural Tours–Ecuador	751				16+	•		•	•	•		•
LIFEWORKS with the Galapagos Islands' National Parks	751*				15–19	•		•	•	•		•
LSA Quito, Ecuador	752*			R	14+	•			•	•		•
PAX Abroad–Ecuador Rainforest Adventure	752				15–18	•		•	•			
PAX Abroad–Ecuador–Spanish Language Immersion	752				15–18	•				•		
Peace Works International–Ecuador	752*				15–18	•		•	•	•	•	
Programs Abroad Travel Alternatives–Ecuador	752*				15–19	•				•		
Putney Student Travel–Community Service–Ecuador	753*			R	15–18	•		•	•	•		•
Visions–Ecuador	753*				16–18	•	•	•	•	•	•	•
Wilderness Ventures–Ecuador and Galapagos	753*				14–18	•			•	•	•	•
Youth for Understanding USA–Ecuador	753*			R	15–18	•			•	•		•
Egypt												
BROADREACH Red Sea Scuba Adventure	754*				15–19	•	•	•	•	•		

**This program is highlighted by a photograph, special note, or in-depth description; see the profile page for more information.*
†D = day camp; R = residential camp

	GENERAL INFORMATION					PROGRAM INFORMATION						
	Profile Page	Boys D/R†	Girls D/R†	Coed D/R†	Age	Acad	Arts	Sports	Wild/ Outdrs	Special Interest	Jobs	Financial Aid
Estonia												
EARTHWATCH INSTITUTE–Baltic Island Wetlands and Wildlife	754			R	16+	•				•		•
Volunteers for Peace International Work Camp–Estonia	754			R	15+	•		•		•		
Fiji												
GLOBAL WORKS–Cultural Exchange-Fiji Islands-4 weeks	755*				14–18	•	•	•	•	•	•	•
RUSTIC PATHWAYS–BIG FIJI EXPLORER	755*				14–18			•	•	•	•	
RUSTIC PATHWAYS–DIVER'S DREAM IN THE FIJI ISLANDS	755*			R	14–18			•		•	•	
RUSTIC PATHWAYS–EXTENDED COMMUNITY SERVICE IN THE FIJI ISLANDS	755*			R	14–18		•	•		•	•	
RUSTIC PATHWAYS–HIGHLANDS COMMUNITY SERVICE IN FIJI	755*				14–18			•		•	•	
RUSTIC PATHWAYS–INTRO TO COMMUNITY SERVICE IN FIJI	756*			R	14–18		•	•	•	•	•	
RUSTIC PATHWAYS–LEARN TO DIVE IN THE FIJI ISLANDS	756*				14–18			•		•	•	
RUSTIC PATHWAYS–SNAPSHOT OF FIJI	756*				15–18			•	•	•	•	
RUSTIC PATHWAYS–SURF THE SUMMER–THE FIJI ISLANDS	756*			R	15–18			•		•	•	
World Horizons International–Fiji	756*			R	15–18			•	•	•	•	•
Finland												
AFS-USA–Homestay–Finland	757*			R	15–18	•				•		•
France												
AAVE–Bike France	757*				14–18	•		•	•	•	•	•
AAVE–Vivons le Français	757*				15–18	•		•	•	•	•	•
Abbey Road Overseas Programs–French Immersion and Homestay	758				13–19	•	•	•	•	•	•	
Abbey Road Overseas Programs–French Study Abroad in Cannes	758				15–19	•	•	•		•	•	
Academic Study Associates–Nice	758			R	14–18	•	•	•	•	•	•	
Academic Study Associates–Royan	758			R	14–18	•		•		•	•	
L' Académie de Paris	759*			R	15–18	•	•	•		•		•
AFS-USA–Homestay–France	759*			R	15–18	•				•		•
Barat Foundation Summer Program in Provence and Paris	759*				13–19	•	•	•	•	•	•	•
Blyth Education–Summer Study in Paris and the South of France	760				14–19	•		•		•	•	
Brighton in Cannes	760*			R	15–19	•		•		•	•	
Brighton in Paris	760*			R	15–19	•		•		•	•	
Center for Cultural Interchange–France High School Abroad	761*			R	15–18	•				•		•
Center for Cultural Interchange–France Independent Homestay	761*			R	16+	•				•		•
Center for Cultural Interchange–France Language School	761*			R	14+	•		•		•		•
Choate Rosemary Hall Summer in Paris	761*			R	14–18	•		•		•		•
Concordia Language Villages–France	762				14–18	•	•	•	•	•	•	
EF International Language School–Nice	762*				16+	•		•	•	•		
EF International Language School–Paris	762*				16+	•				•		
Encore! Ensemble Theatre Workshop	763			R	14–18		•					•
The Experiment in International Living–France, Biking and Homestay	763*			R	14–19	•		•	•	•		•
The Experiment in International Living–France, Five-Week Art and Adventure in Provence	763*			R	14–19	•	•			•		•
The Experiment in International Living–France, Four-Week Brittany Discovery	763*			R	14–19	•				•		•
The Experiment in International Living–France, Four-Week Homestay and Photography	764*			R	14–17	•	•			•		•
The Experiment in International Living–France, Four-Week Homestay and Theatre	764*			R	14–19	•	•			•		•
The Experiment in International Living–France, Four-Week Homestay and Travel–Borders	764*			R	14–19	•			•	•		•
The Experiment in International Living–France, Four-Week Homestay and Travel through Alps	764*			R	14–19	•			•	•		•
The Experiment in International Living–France, Homestay, Language Training, and Cooking	765*			R	14–19	•				•		•
The Experiment in International Living–France, Three-Week Camargue Homestay	765*			R	14–19	•				•		•
The Experiment in International Living–France, Three-Week Homestay and Travel–Borders	765*			R	14–19	•			•	•		•

This program is highlighted by a photograph, special note, or in-depth description; see the profile page for more information.
†D = day camp; R = residential camp

	GENERAL INFORMATION					PROGRAM INFORMATION						
	Profile Page	Boys D/R†	Girls D/R†	Coed D/R†	Age	Acad	Arts	Sports	Wild/ Outdrs	Special Interest	Jobs	Financial Aid
Global Teen–Learn French in Biarritz	765*			R	13–17	•		•	•	•		•
Global Teen–Learn French in Nice	765*			R	15–18	•		•		•		•
Global Teen–Learn French in Paris	766*			R	15–18	•	•	•		•		•
GLOBAL WORKS–Language Immersion-France-4 weeks	766*				15–18	•	•	•	•	•	•	•
International Summer Centre at Biarritz	766			R/D	12–18	•	•	•	•	•		
International Summer Centre at Chatel	766			R/D	11–18	•	•	•	•	•		
International Summer Centre at Paris-Brétigny	767			R/D	13–18	•	•	•		•		
The Loomis Chaffee Summer in France	767			R	14–18	•		•	•	•		•
LSA Amboise, France	767*			R	16+	•				•		•
LSA Antibes, France	767*			R	14+	•		•	•	•	•	•
LSA Argelés-Gazost, France	768*			R	10–18	•	•	•	•			•
LSA Biarritz, France	768*			R	13+	•		•	•	•		
LSA Bordeaux, France	768*			R	17+	•				•	•	
LSA Cannes, France	769*			R	16+	•	•	•	•	•		
LSA Hyères, France	769*			R	11–18	•		•		•		
LSA La Rochelle, France	769*			R	16+	•				•		•
LSA Nice, France	769*			R	13+	•				•	•	•
LSA Paris, France	770*			R	16+	•				•	•	•
LSA Tours, France	770*			R	16+	•				•		•
Mercersburg Academy Summer Study in France	770*				14–18	•				•		
The New York Film Academy in Paris	770*			R	14–17		•					
Overland: Language Study Abroad in France	770*				14–18	•				•	•	
Overland: Paris to the Sea Bicycle Touring	771*				14–18			•	•	•	•	
Parsons Summer Intensive Studies–Paris	771			R/D	16+	•	•			•		
Phillips Exeter Academy French Study Tour	771				15–18	•		•	•	•		
Programs Abroad Travel Alternatives–France	771*				15+	•				•		
Putney Student Travel–Language Learning–France	772*			R	13–18	•		•	•	•		•
Rassias Programs–Arles, France	772*				14–17	•		•		•	•	•
Rassias Programs–Tours, France	772*				14–17	•		•		•	•	•
Service-Learning in Paris	773*			R	16+	•	•			•		•
Summer Study in Paris at The American University of Paris	773*			R	15–18	•	•	•		•	•	•
Taft Summer School Abroad–France	773*				14–18	•				•		
TASIS Arts and Architecture in the South of France	774			R	16–21	•	•	•				
Tisch School of the Arts–International High School Program–Paris	774*			R	15+	•	•					•
Tufts Summit	774			R	16–19	•		•	•	•		•
University of Chicago–ChicaGO! The Traveling Academy	774*				15–18	•						•
Village Camps–France	775*			R	10–16	•	•	•	•	•	•	
Volunteers for Peace International Work Camp–France	775			R	15+	•				•		
Windsor Mountain: Crossroads France	775*				13–15	•		•	•	•	•	•
Woodberry Forest Summer School–France	775*			R	12–17	•		•				•
Youth for Understanding USA–France	776*			R	15–18	•		•		•		•

French Polynesia

	Profile Page	Boys D/R†	Girls D/R†	Coed D/R†	Age	Acad	Arts	Sports	Wild/ Outdrs	Special Interest	Jobs	Financial Aid
ACTIONQUEST: Tahiti and French Polynesian Island Voyages	776*				15–19	•		•	•	•		

Germany

	Profile Page	Boys D/R†	Girls D/R†	Coed D/R†	Age	Acad	Arts	Sports	Wild/ Outdrs	Special Interest	Jobs	Financial Aid
American Association of Teachers of German, German Summer Study Program	776			R	15–18	•						•
Center for Cultural Interchange–Germany High School Abroad	777*			R	15–18	•				•		•
Center for Cultural Interchange–Germany Independent Homestay	777*			R	16+	•				•		•
Center for Cultural Interchange–Germany Language School	777*			R	17+	•				•		•
Concordia Language Villages–Germany	777			R	14–18	•	•	•	•	•	•	
EF International Language School–Munich	778*				16+	•		•	•	•		
The Experiment in International Living–Germany, Four-Week Homestay, Travel, Community Service	778*			R	14–19	•				•		•
Global Teen–German in Bavaria	778*			R	12–17	•	•	•		•		•
Global Teen–German Plus Web Design, Video/Theatre in Berlin	778*			R	12+	•	•	•		•		•
Global Teen–German Summer Camp in Potsdam	779*			R	14–17	•				•		•

This program is highlighted by a photograph, special note, or in-depth description; see the profile page for more information.
†D = day camp; R = residential camp

	GENERAL INFORMATION					PROGRAM INFORMATION						
	Profile Page	Boys D/R†	Girls D/R†	Coed D/R†	Age	Acad	Arts	Sports	Wild/ Outdrs	Special Interest	Jobs	Financial Aid
Global Teen–Learn German in Berlin, Ages 12-15 on Lake Schmockwitz	779*			R	12–15	•	•	•		•		•
Global Teen–Learn German in Berlin-City Centre, Ages 16-19	779*			R	16–19	•	•	•		•		•
Global Teen Summer Sports Camp in Berlin	779*			R	12–17	•		•	•	•		•
GLS Bavarian Summer School	780			R	12–17	•			•	•		
GLS Berlin Summer School	780			R	16–19	•				•		
GLS Potsdam Summer School	780			R	14–17	•			•	•		
GLS Sports and Language Camp Inzell	780			R	10–16	•		•	•			
GLS Summer Camp Blossin	781			R	12–17	•		•	•			
GLS Summer Camp Loewenstein	781			R	12–17	•	•		•			
GLS Summer Camp Schmoeckwitz	781			R	8–15	•		•				
LSA Berlin, Germany	781*			R	8+	•	•	•		•	•	•
LSA Blossin, Germany	781*			R	12–17	•			•			•
LSA Cologne, Germany	782*			R	16+	•				•		•
LSA Hamburg, Germany	782*			R	16+	•				•	•	•
LSA Holzkirchen, Germany	782*			R	12–17	•				•		•
LSA Inzell, Germany	782*			R	10–16	•			•			•
LSA Loewenstein, Germany	783*			R	12–17	•	•					•
LSA Munich, Germany	783*			R	16+	•	•			•	•	•
LSA Potsdam, Germany	783*			R	14–17	•						•
LSA Schmoeckwitz, Germany	783*			R	8–15	•						•
LSA Stuttgart, Germany	783*			R	16+	•				•	•	
Programs Abroad Travel Alternatives–Germany	784*				15+	•				•		
Volunteers for Peace International Work Camp–Germany	784			R	16+	•	•	•	•	•		
Youth for Understanding USA–Germany	784*			R	15–18	•				•		•
Ghana												
AFS-USA–Team Mission–Ghana	784*			R	15–18	•	•			•		•
EARTHWATCH INSTITUTE–Wildlife Conservation in West Africa	785			R	16+	•		•	•	•		•
The Experiment in International Living–Ghana Homestay	785*			R	14–19	•	•			•		•
Youth for Understanding USA–Ghana	785*			R	15–18					•		•
Greece												
Greek Summer	785*				15–18	•	•		•	•		•
Youth for Understanding USA–Greece	786*			R	15–18	•				•		•
Grenada												
EARTHWATCH INSTITUTE–Biodiversity of the Grenadines	786			R	16+	•				•		•
Guadeloupe												
Visions–Guadeloupe	786*				14–18	•	•	•	•	•	•	•
Guatemala												
EARTHWATCH INSTITUTE–Guatemala's Ancient Maya	787			R	16+	•				•		•
LSA Antigua, Guatemala	787*			R	15+	•				•		•
Programs Abroad Travel Alternatives–Guatemala	787*				15–19	•				•		
Where There Be Dragons: Guatemala	787*				16–19	•	•	•	•	•		•
Guyana												
Ibike Cultural Tours–Guyana	788				16+	•		•	•	•		
Honduras												
BROADREACH Honduras Eco-Adventure	788*				15–19	•	•	•	•	•		
Hong Kong												
SuperCamp–Hong Kong	788*			R	9–18	•		•		•	•	•
Hungary												
AFS-USA–Homestay Plus–Hungary	788*			R	15–19	•	•	•	•	•		•
EARTHWATCH INSTITUTE–Europe–Africa Songbird Migrations–Hungary	789			R	16+	•				•		•

**This program is highlighted by a photograph, special note, or in-depth description; see the profile page for more information.*
†D = day camp; R = residential camp

	GENERAL INFORMATION					PROGRAM INFORMATION						
	Profile Page	Boys D/R†	Girls D/R†	Coed D/R†	Age	Acad	Arts	Sports	Wild/ Outdrs	Special Interest	Jobs	Financial Aid
Youth for Understanding USA–Hungary	789*			R	15–18	•		•		•		•
Iceland												
EARTHWATCH INSTITUTE–Icelandic and Alaskan Glaciers	789			R	16+	•				•		•
Longacre Expeditions, Iceland	789*				15–18	•		•	•		•	
World Horizons International–Iceland	790*			R	14–18	•		•		•	•	•
India												
EARTHWATCH INSTITUTE–India's Sacred Groves	790			R	16+	•				•		•
EARTHWATCH INSTITUTE–Maternal and Child Healthcare in India	790			R	16+	•	•			•		•
Ladakh Summer Passage	790				16+	•			•	•	•	•
Putney Student Travel–Community Service-India	791*			R	14–18	•			•	•	•	•
The Sikkim Cultural Immersion Experience	791				15+	•	•	•	•	•		
Tibetan Culture of Northern India	791			R	17–20	•	•		•	•		•
Where There Be Dragons: India Culture and Philosophy	791*				16–20	•	•		•	•		•
Where There Be Dragons: India Zanskar Trek	792*				16–20	•			•	•		•
Indonesia												
Putney Student Travel–Community Service–Nusa Penida and Bali	792*			R	14–18	•		•	•	•	•	•
Ireland												
Adventure Ireland–English Learning Option	792*			R	12–18	•	•	•	•	•		
Adventure Ireland–Irish Studies	793*			R	12–18	•	•	•	•	•		
Adventure Ireland–Surf Camp/Activity Camp	793*			R	12–18			•	•	•		
Celtic Learning and Travel Services–Summer in Ireland	793				14–21	•	•	•		•	•	•
Center for Cultural Interchange–Ireland High School Abroad	794*			R	15–18	•				•		•
Center for Cultural Interchange–Ireland Independent Homestay Program	794*			R	17+	•				•		•
The Experiment in International Living–Ireland/Northern Ireland Homestay and Peace Studies	794*			R	14–19	•				•		•
GLOBAL WORKS–Cultural Exchange-Ireland-4 weeks	794*				14–18	•	•	•	•	•	•	•
Irish Way	795				15+	•	•	•	•	•	•	•
Programs Abroad Travel Alternatives–Ireland	795*				15–19	•				•		
Tisch School of the Arts–International High School Program–Dublin	795*			R	15+	•	•					•
Youth for Understanding USA–Ireland	796*			R	15–18	•				•		•
Israel												
Alexander Muss High School in Israel	796				16–18	•		•	•	•	•	•
Italy												
Abbey Road Overseas Programs–Italy Study Abroad: Language and Culture	796				15–19	•	•	•	•	•	•	
Academic Study Associates–Florence	797			R	15–18	•	•	•		•	•	•
AFS-USA–Homestay Plus–Italy	797*			R	15–18	•	•			•		•
American Collegiate Adventures–Italy	797			R	14–18	•	•	•		•	•	
Blyth Education–Summer Study in Rome and Siena	797			R	14–19	•		•		•	•	
Brighton in Tuscany	798*			R	14–18	•		•		•		
Canadian College Italy/The Renaissance School Summer Academy	798*			R	15–18	•	•	•	•	•		
Center for Cultural Interchange–Italy Language School	798*			R	17+	•				•		•
EARTHWATCH INSTITUTE–Europe–Africa Songbird Migrations–Italy	799			R	16+	•				•		•
EARTHWATCH INSTITUTE–Medicinal Plants of Antiquity	799			R	16+	•				•		•
EF International Language School–Rome	799*				16+	•				•		
The Experiment in International Living–Italy Homestay	799*			R	14–19	•				•		•
Global Teen–Italian and Soccer in Rome	800*			R	16–25	•		•		•		•
Global Teen–Learn Italian in Italy	800*			R	10–16	•	•	•		•		•
Humanities Spring in Assisi	800*				15–22	•	•	•		•	•	•
Humanities Spring on the Road	801				15–21	•	•			•	•	•
Knowledge Exchange Institute–Artist Abroad Program in Italy	801			R	15–19	•	•			•		•
LSA Ascoli, Italy	801*			R	16+	•	•			•		•
LSA Florence, Italy	801*			R	16+	•	•			•		•

**This program is highlighted by a photograph, special note, or in-depth description; see the profile page for more information.*
†D = day camp; R = residential camp

	GENERAL INFORMATION					PROGRAM INFORMATION						
	Profile Page	Boys D/R†	Girls D/R†	Coed D/R†	Age	Acad	Arts	Sports	Wild/ Outdrs	Special Interest	Jobs	Financial Aid
LSA Lignano, Italy–Active Junior Italian Summer Program	802*			R	12–16	•	•	•		•		•
LSA Livorno, Italy	802*			R	16+	•	•	•		•		•
LSA Milan, Italy	802*			R	16+	•				•		•
LSA Orvieto, Italy	802*			R	16+	•				•		•
LSA Rimini, Italy	802*			R	14+	•	•	•		•		
LSA Rome, Italy	803*			R	16+	•				•		•
LSA Siena, Italy	803*			R	16+	•	•			•		•
LSA Taormina, Italy	803*			R	16+	•				•		•
LSA Treviso, Italy	803*			R	6–12	•	•	•	•	•		
The New York Film Academy in Florence, Italy	804*			R	14–17		•					
Operafestival di Roma	804*			R	16+	•	•			•	•	
Programs Abroad Travel Alternatives–Italy	805*				15+	•				•		
Spoleto Study Abroad	805*			R	15–19	•	•	•		•	•	
TASIS Tuscan Academy of Art and Culture	805*			R	15–19	•	•	•	•			
Volunteers for Peace International Work Camp–Italy	805			R	15+	•				•		
Youth for Understanding USA–Italy	806*			R	15–18	•	•			•		•
Jamaica												
EARTHWATCH INSTITUTE–Jamaica's Coral Reefs	806			R	16+	•				•		•
Japan												
AFS-USA–Homestay Language Study–Japan	806*			R	15–18	•				•		•
Center for Cultural Interchange–Japan High School Abroad	806*			R	15–18	•				•		•
Concordia Language Villages–Japan	807			R	14–18	•	•			•	•	•
The Experiment in International Living–Japan Homestay	807*			R	14–19	•				•		•
LSA Kanazawa, Japan	807*			R	16+	•				•		•
Woodberry Forest Summer School–Japan	807*			R	12–17	•		•				•
Youth for Understanding USA–Japan	807*			R	15–18	•				•		•
Kazakhstan												
Youth for Understanding USA–Kazakhstan	808*			R	15–18					•		•
Kenya												
Eagle Lake Camp Jaunts–Kenya Mission Adventure	808				16+	•				•	•	•
EARTHWATCH INSTITUTE–Conservation Research Initiative–Samburu: Communities and Water Resources	808			R	16+	•				•		•
EARTHWATCH INSTITUTE–Conservation Research Initiative–Samburu: Communities and Wildlife Habitat	809			R	16+					•		•
EARTHWATCH INSTITUTE–Conservation Research Initiative–Samburu: Zebras	809			R	16+	•				•		•
EARTHWATCH INSTITUTE–Kenya's Black Rhino	809			R	16+	•				•		•
EARTHWATCH INSTITUTE–Lakes of the Rift Valley	809			R	16+	•				•		•
EARTHWATCH INSTITUTE–Lions of Tsavo	809			R	16+	•				•		•
EARTHWATCH INSTITUTE–Mangroves of the Kenyan Coast	810			R	16+	•			•	•		•
EARTHWATCH INSTITUTE–Rare Plants of Kenya	810			R	16+	•			•	•		•
Knowledge Exchange Institute–African Safari Program	810				15–19	•			•	•		•
SFS: Community Wildlife Management	810			R	16–25	•		•	•	•		•
Youth for Understanding USA–Kenya	811*				15–18	•		•	•	•		•
Latvia												
AFS-USA–Homestay Language Study–Latvia	811*			R	15–18	•				•		•
Lithuania												
Volunteers for Peace International Work Camp–Lithuania	811			R	15+	•	•			•		
Madagascar												
EARTHWATCH INSTITUTE–Carnivores of Madagascar	811			R	16+	•				•		•
Malaysia												
EARTHWATCH INSTITUTE–Malaysian Bat Conservation	812			R	16+	•			•	•		•

**This program is highlighted by a photograph, special note, or in-depth description; see the profile page for more information.*
†D = day camp; R = residential camp

	GENERAL INFORMATION					PROGRAM INFORMATION						
	Profile Page	Boys D/R†	Girls D/R†	Coed D/R†	Age	Acad	Arts	Sports	Wild/ Outdrs	Special Interest	Jobs	Financial Aid
Mexico												
Artes en Mexico	812				15–17	•	•			•		•
Blyth Education–Summer Study in Cozumel	812			R	14–19	•		•		•	•	
BROADREACH Academic Treks–Spanish Immersion in Mexico	812*				15–19	•			•	•		
BROADREACH Baja Extreme–Scuba Adventure	813*				15–19	•	•	•	•	•		•
Center for Cultural Interchange–Mexico High School Abroad	813*			R	14–17	•				•		•
Center for Cultural Interchange–Mexico Language School	813*			R	13+	•				•		•
Cuernavaca Summer Program for Teens	813			R/D	13–18	•	•	•		•	•	
Dickinson College Spanish Language and Cultural Immersion Program	814				16–18	•		•	•	•	•	•
EARTHWATCH INSTITUTE–Cacti and Orchids of the Yucatan	814			R	16+	•				•		•
EARTHWATCH INSTITUTE–Mexican Mangroves and Wildlife	814			R	16+	•		•		•		•
EARTHWATCH INSTITUTE–Mexican Megafauna	814			R	16+	•	•			•		•
EARTHWATCH INSTITUTE–Sea Turtles of Baja	814			R	16+	•				•		•
The Experiment in International Living–Mexico, Community Service, Travel, and Homestay	815*			R	14–19	•				•		•
The Experiment in International Living–Mexico Homestay and Travel	815*			R	14–19	•			•	•		•
Global Teen–Learn Spanish in Mexico	815*			R	13–17	•	•	•				•
GLOBAL WORKS–Language Exposure-Yucatan Peninsula, Mexico-4 weeks	815*				14–18	•	•	•	•	•	•	•
GLOBAL WORKS–Language Immersion-Yucatan Peninsula, Mexico-4 weeks	816*				15–18	•	•	•	•	•	•	•
Knowledge Exchange Institute–Spanish on the Road in Mexico Program	816				15–19	•		•		•		•
Learning Programs International–Mexico	816*			R	14–18	•	•			•		
LSA Cuernavaca, Mexico	816*			R	8–17	•				•		•
LSA Ensenada, Mexico	817*			R	16+	•				•		•
LSA Mérida, Mexico	817*			R	17+	•				•		•
LSA Oaxaca, Mexico	817*			R	6–14	•	•			•		•
LSA Playa Del Carmen, Mexico	817*			R	16+	•		•		•		•
LSA Puebla, Mexico	818*			R	16+	•				•		•
LSA Puerto Vallarta, Mexico	818*			R	16+	•				•		•
MexArt: Art and Spanish	818			R	13–18	•	•	•	•	•	•	
MexArt Dance: Dance and Spanish	818			R	13–18	•	•	•	•	•	•	
Outpost Wilderness Adventure–Copper Canyon Project	819				14–18	•		•	•	•		•
Programs Abroad Travel Alternatives–Mexico	819*				13–19	•				•		
SFS: Conserving Coastal Diversity	819			R	16–25	•		•	•	•		•
SuperCamp–Mexico	819*			R	13–18	•		•		•	•	
Where There Be Dragons: Mexico	820*				15–19	•	•	•	•	•		•
Windsor Mountain: Mexico Community Service	820*				13–18	•			•	•		•
World Horizons International–Mexico	820*			R	14–18	•			•	•	•	•
Monaco												
Global Teen–French Summer Camp in Monte Carlo	820*			R	13–17	•	•	•		•		•
Mongolia												
EARTHWATCH INSTITUTE–Mongolian Argali	821			R	16+	•				•		•
Where There Be Dragons: Mongolia	821*				17–20	•		•	•	•		•
Morocco												
The Experiment in International Living–Morocco Four-Week Arts and Culture Program	821*			R	14–19	•	•			•		•
Namibia												
EARTHWATCH INSTITUTE–Cheetah	821			R	16+	•				•		•
EARTHWATCH INSTITUTE–Desert Elephants of Namibia	822			R	16+	•				•		•
EARTHWATCH INSTITUTE–Namibian Black Rhinos	822			R	16+	•				•		•
EARTHWATCH INSTITUTE–Namibian Wildlife Survey	822			R	16+	•				•		•
Nepal												
Lower Mustang Summer Passage	822				16+	•	•	•	•	•	•	•

**This program is highlighted by a photograph, special note, or in-depth description; see the profile page for more information.*
†D = day camp; R = residential camp

	GENERAL INFORMATION					PROGRAM INFORMATION						
	Profile Page	Boys D/R†	Girls D/R†	Coed D/R†	Age	Acad	Arts	Sports	Wild/ Outdrs	Special Interest	Jobs	Financial Aid
The Nepal Cultural Immersion Experience	822				15+	•	•	•	•	•		
Personal Passage	823				16+	•	•			•	•	•
Netherlands												
AFS-USA–Homestay Plus–Netherlands	823*			R	15–17	•		•	•	•		•
Center for Cultural Interchange–Netherlands High School Abroad	823*			R	15–18	•				•		•
New Zealand												
AFS-USA–Homestay Plus–New Zealand	824*			R	15–18			•	•	•		•
EARTHWATCH INSTITUTE–New Zealand Dolphins	824			R	16+	•				•		•
The Experiment in International Living–New Zealand Homestay	824*			R	14–19	•			•	•		•
Poulter Colorado Camps: Adventures Planet Earth–New Zealand	824				13+	•		•	•	•	•	•
RUSTIC PATHWAYS–SKI AND SNOWBOARD ADVENTURE IN NEW ZEALAND	825*				15–18			•	•		•	
Nicaragua												
Putney Student Travel–Community Service-Nicaragua	825*			R	14–18	•		•	•	•	•	•
Spanish Through Leadership–Nicaragua	825*				14–18	•	•	•	•	•		
Summer Delegation to León, Nicaragua	825				16+					•		•
Norway												
Eagle Lake Camp Jaunts–Norway Mission Adventure	826				16+	•			•	•	•	•
Environmental Studies and Solutions	826				15+	•	•	•	•	•	•	•
Panama												
AFS-USA–Community Service–Panama	826*			R	15–18	•			•	•		•
Paraguay												
AFS-USA–Community Service–Paraguay	827*			R	16+	•				•		•
AFS-USA–Homestay–Paraguay	827*			R	15–18	•				•		•
Peru												
AAVE–Peru and Machu Picchu	827*				14–18	•			•	•	•	•
EARTHWATCH INSTITUTE–Rivers of the Peruvian Amazon	827			R	16+	•				•		•
LSA Cuzco, Peru	828*			R	16+	•			•	•		•
Peace Works International–Peru	828*				15–18	•		•	•	•		
The Peru Cultural Immersion Experience	828				15+	•	•	•	•	•		
Programs Abroad Travel Alternatives–Peru	828*				15–19	•				•		
Visions–Peru	829*				14–18	•	•		•	•	•	•
Where There Be Dragons: Peru	829*				15–19	•	•	•	•	•		•
Poland												
EARTHWATCH INSTITUTE–Poland's Ancient Burials	829			R	16+	•				•		•
The Experiment in International Living–Poland, Homestay, Community Service, and Travel	829*			R	14–19	•			•	•		•
Youth for Understanding USA–Poland	830*			R	15–18	•				•		•
Portugal												
LSA Lisbon, Portugal	830*			R	16+	•	•			•		•
Puerto Rico												
EARTHWATCH INSTITUTE–Puerto Rico's Rainforest	830			R	16+	•			•	•		•
GLOBAL WORKS–Language Exposure-Puerto Rico-3 weeks	830*				14–18	•	•	•	•	•	•	•
GLOBAL WORKS–Language Immersion-Puerto Rico-4 weeks	831*				15–18	•	•	•	•	•	•	•
Windsor Mountain: Puerto Rico	831*				13–16	•		•	•	•		•
World Horizons International–Puerto Rico	831*			R	14–18			•	•	•	•	•
Republic of Korea												
Elite Educational Institute Elementary Enrichment–Korea	831*			D		•						•
Elite Educational Institute Junior High/PSAT Program–Korea	832*			D		•				•		•
Elite Educational Institute SAT Bootcamp–Korea	832*			D		•				•		•

**This program is highlighted by a photograph, special note, or in-depth description; see the profile page for more information.*
†D = day camp; R = residential camp

	GENERAL INFORMATION					PROGRAM INFORMATION						
	Profile Page	Boys D/R†	Girls D/R†	Coed D/R†	Age	Acad	Arts	Sports	Wild/ Outdrs	Special Interest	Jobs	Financial Aid
Elite Educational Institute SAT Preparation–Korea	832*			D		•						•
Youth for Understanding USA–South Korea	832*			R	15–18	•				•		•
Romania												
EARTHWATCH INSTITUTE–Roman Fort on the Danube	833			R	16+	•	•			•		•
Russian Federation												
AFS-USA–Team Mission–Russia	833*			R	14–19	•		•	•	•		•
EARTHWATCH INSTITUTE–Singing Russia	833			R	16+	•	•			•		•
EF International Language School–St. Petersburg	833*				16+	•		•	•	•		
Knowledge Exchange Institute–Research Abroad in Russia	834			R	15–19	•				•		•
LSA Moscow, Russia	834*			R	16+	•				•		•
LSA St. Petersburg, Russia	834*			R	16+	•				•		•
Programs Abroad Travel Alternatives–Russia	834*				15+	•				•		
Volunteers for Peace International Work Camp–Russia	835			R	17+	•				•		
Youth for Understanding USA–Russia	835*			R	15–18	•				•		•
Saint Vincent and The Grenadines												
BROADREACH Adventures in the Grenadines–Advanced Scuba	835*				14–19	•	•	•	•	•		•
Windsor Mountain: Adventures in Filmmaking	835*				15–18	•	•	•				•
Singapore												
SuperCamp–Singapore	836*			R	9–18	•		•			•	•
Slovakia												
Volunteers for Peace International Work Camp–Slovakia	836			R	15+	•		•	•	•		•
South Africa												
Center for Cultural Interchange–South Africa High School Abroad	836*			R	15–18	•				•		•
EARTHWATCH INSTITUTE–Meerkats of the Kalahari	836			R	16+	•				•		•
EARTHWATCH INSTITUTE–South African Penguins	837			R	16+	•				•		•
EARTHWATCH INSTITUTE–South African Wildlife	837			R	16+	•			•	•		•
The Experiment in International Living–South Africa Homestay and Community Service	837*			R	14–19		•			•		•
Youth for Understanding USA–South Africa	837*			R	15–18					•		•
Spain												
AAVE–Inmersión en España	837*				14–18	•		•	•	•	•	•
Abbey Road Overseas Programs–Spanish Immersion and Homestay	838				13–19	•	•	•	•	•	•	
Academic Study Associates–Barcelona	838			R	15–18	•	•	•		•	•	•
Academic Study Associates–Spanish in España	838			R	15–18	•	•	•	•	•	•	
AFS-USA–Homestay–Spain	839*			R	15–18	•				•		•
American Collegiate Adventures–Spain	839				14–18	•	•	•		•	•	•
Bravo Spain–Barcelona	839				16–19	•		•		•		
Center for Cultural Interchange–Spain High School Abroad	839*			R	15–18	•				•		•
Center for Cultural Interchange–Spain Independent Homestay	839*			R	14+	•				•		•
Center for Cultural Interchange–Spain Language School	840*			R	14+	•	•			•		•
Center for Cultural Interchange–Spain Sports and Language Camp	840*			R	10–17	•	•	•	•	•		•
Choate Rosemary Hall Summer in Spain	840*				14–18	•		•		•		•
Columbia University Continuing Education–The Barcelona Experience	841			R	16–18	•					•	
Concordia Language Villages–Spain	841				14–18	•	•		•	•	•	
EARTHWATCH INSTITUTE–Butterflies and Orchids of Spain	841			R	16+	•		•		•		•
EARTHWATCH INSTITUTE–Early Man in Spain	841			R	16+	•				•		•
EARTHWATCH INSTITUTE–Mallorca's Copper Age	841			R	16+	•				•		•
EARTHWATCH INSTITUTE–Spanish Dolphins	842			R	16+	•				•		•
EF International Language School–Barcelona	842*				16+	•		•	•	•		
EF International Language School–Malaga	842*				16+	•		•	•	•		
Enforex–General Spanish–Almuñecar	842*			R	16+	•		•		•		•
Enforex–General Spanish–Barcelona	843*			R	16+	•		•		•		•

**This program is highlighted by a photograph, special note, or in-depth description; see the profile page for more information.*
†D = day camp; R = residential camp

	GENERAL INFORMATION					PROGRAM INFORMATION						
	Profile Page	Boys D/R†	Girls D/R†	Coed D/R†	Age	Acad	Arts	Sports	Wild/ Outdrs	Special Interest	Jobs	Financial Aid
Enforex–General Spanish–Granada	843*			R	16+	•		•		•		•
Enforex–General Spanish–Madrid	843*			R	16+	•		•		•		•
Enforex–General Spanish–Marbella	844*			R	16+	•		•		•		•
Enforex–General Spanish–Salamanca	844*			R	16+	•		•		•		•
Enforex–General Spanish–Valencia	844*			R	16+	•		•		•		•
Enforex Hispanic Culture: Civilization, History, Art, and Literature–Barcelona	844*			R/D	15+	•	•	•		•		
Enforex Hispanic Culture: Civilization, History, Art, and Literature–Granada	845*			R/D	15+	•		•		•		
Enforex Hispanic Culture: Civilization, History, Art, and Literature–Madrid	845*			R/D	15+	•		•		•		
Enforex Homestay Program–Almuñecar	845*			R	13+	•		•		•		
Enforex Homestay Program–Barcelona	846*			R/D	13+	•		•		•		
Enforex Homestay Program–Granada	846*			R	13+	•		•		•		
Enforex Homestay Program–Madrid	846*			R	13+	•		•		•		
Enforex Homestay Program–Marbella	846*			R	13+	•		•		•		•
Enforex Homestay Program–Salamanca	847*			R	13+	•		•		•		
Enforex Residential Youth Summer Camp–Madrid	847*			R	6–18	•	•	•	•	•		
Enforex Residential Youth Summer Camp–Marbella	847*			R	6–18	•	•	•	•	•		
Enforex Residential Youth Summer Camp–Salamanca	848*			R	12–18	•	•	•	•	•		
Enforex Spanish and Golf	848*			R	15+	•		•				
Enforex Spanish and Tennis	848*			R	15+	•		•				
Enforex Study Tour Vacational Program–Madrid	848*			R	15+	•		•		•		•
Excel at Madrid/Barcelona	849*			R	15–18	•	•	•	•	•		•
The Experiment in International Living–Spain, Five-Week Homestay, Travel, Ecology	849*			R	14–19	•				•		•
The Experiment in International Living–Spain, Five-Week Language Training, Travel, and Homestay	849*			R	14–19	•				•		•
The Experiment in International Living–Spain, Four-Week Homestay and Trekking Program	849*			R	14–19	•			•	•		•
The Experiment in International Living–Spain, Four-Week Language Study and Homestay	849*			R	14–19	•				•		•
The Experiment in International Living–Spain–Spanish Culture and Folklore	850*			R	14–19	•	•			•		•
The Experiment in International Living–Spain, Three-Week Homestay	850*			R	14–19	•				•		•
Global Teen–Learn Spanish in Andalusia	850*			R	14–18	•	•	•		•		•
Global Teen–Learn Spanish in Marbella, Ages 6-14	850*			R	6–14	•	•	•		•		•
Global Teen–Learn Spanish in Marbella-Young Adult	851*			R	15–18	•	•	•		•		•
Global Teen–Learn Spanish in Salamanca, Ages 11-18	851*			R	11–18	•	•	•		•		•
Global Teen–Learn Spanish in Salamanca, Ages 13-16	851*			R	13–16	•	•	•		•		•
Global Teen–Learn Spanish in Sevilla	851*			R	14–17	•	•	•		•		•
Global Teen–Spanish in Madrid, Ages 6-14	852*			R	6–14	•	•	•		•		•
Global Teen–Spanish in Malaga-Young Adult, Ages 16-20	852*			R	16–20	•	•	•	•	•		•
Global Teen–Spanish in Palma de Mallorca	852*			R	16–19	•	•			•		•
Global Teen–Spanish Summer Camp in San Sebastian	852*			R	14–16	•		•		•		•
Global Teen–Summer Camp in Barcelona	853*				13–17	•		•		•		•
Global Teen–Summer Camp in Marbella, Ages 14-18	853*			R	14–18	•	•	•		•		•
Global Teen–Vejer Beach Spectacular in Spain	853*			R	13–17	•		•		•		•
Global Teen–Young Adult Summer Camp in Madrid, Ages 14-18	853*			R	14–18	•	•	•		•		•
Global Teen–Young Adult Summer Program in Malaga, Ages 16-20	854*			R	16–20	•	•	•	•	•		•
GLOBAL WORKS–Language Immersion-Spain-4 weeks	854*				15–18	•	•	•	•	•	•	•
iD Tech Camps–Documentary Filmmaking and Cultural Immersion at the University of Cádiz, Spain	854*				14–17	•	•	•		•	•	
Instituto de Idiomas Geos–Granada, Spain	855			R/D	10–18	•	•	•	•	•	•	
Instituto de Idiomas Geos–Marbella, Spain	855			R/D	10–18	•	•	•	•	•	•	
Lacunza Junior Summer Spanish Course	855			R/D	14–17	•	•	•		•		
Learning Programs International–Spain	855*			R	16–18	•	•			•		
The Loomis Chaffee Summer in Spain	856			R	14–18	•				•		•
LSA Alicante, Spain	856*			R	17+	•				•		•
LSA Almuñecar, Spain	856*			R	15+	•	•					•

This program is highlighted by a photograph, special note, or in-depth description; see the profile page for more information.
†D = day camp; R = residential camp

	GENERAL INFORMATION					PROGRAM INFORMATION						
	Profile Page	Boys D/R†	Girls D/R†	Coed D/R†	Age	Acad	Arts	Sports	Wild/ Outdrs	Special Interest	Jobs	Financial Aid
LSA Barcelona, Spain	857*			R	16+	•		•		•		•
LSA El Puerto de Santa Maria, Spain	857*			R	17+	•	•			•		•
LSA Granada, Spain	857*			R	16+	•				•		•
LSA Madrid, Spain	857*			R	6+	•		•		•		
LSA Màlaga, Spain	858*			R	16+	•	•	•		•		•
LSA Marbella, Spain	858*			R	6+	•	•	•		•		•
LSA Nerja, Spain	858*			R	16+	•		•		•		•
LSA Salamanca, Spain	858*			R	14+	•	•	•		•		
LSA San Sebastian, Spain	859*			R	17+	•		•	•	•		•
LSA Sevilla, Spain	859*			R	15+	•	•	•		•		
LSA Tenerife, Spain	859*			R	16+	•				•		•
LSA Valencia, Spain	859*			R	17+	•		•		•		
Mercersburg Academy Summer Study in Spain	860*				14–18	•				•		•
Overland: Language Study Abroad in Spain	860*				14–18	•				•	•	
PAX Abroad–Summer Spain	860				14–18	•						
Poulter Colorado Camps: Adventures Planet Earth–Spain	860				13+	•			•	•	•	•
Programs Abroad Travel Alternatives–Spain	860*				15+	•				•		
Putney Student Travel–Language Learning–Spain	861*			R	13–18	•		•	•	•		•
Rassias Programs–Gijón, Spain	861*				14–17	•		•	•	•	•	•
Rassias Programs–Pontevedra, Spain	861*				14–17	•		•	•	•	•	•
Rassias Programs–Segovia, Spain	861*				14–17	•		•	•	•	•	•
Spanish Language and Flamenco Enforex–Granada	862*			R	15+	•	•	•		•		
Spanish Language and Flamenco Enforex–Madrid	862*			R	15+	•	•	•		•		•
Spanish Language and Flamenco Enforex–Marbella	862*			R		•	•	•		•		•
Study Tour Vacational Program Enforex–Barcelona	862*			R	15+	•		•		•		•
Taft Summer School Abroad–Spain	863*				14–18	•				•		
TASIS Spanish Summer Program	863*			R	13–17	•		•			•	
Wilderness Ventures–Spanish Pyrenees	863*				14–18			•	•	•	•	•
Woodberry Forest Summer School–Spain	863*			R	12–17	•		•				•
Youth for Understanding USA–Spain	864*			R	15–18	•				•		•
Youth Program in Spain	864				15–18	•	•	•				
Sri Lanka												
EARTHWATCH INSTITUTE–Sri Lanka's Temple Monkeys	864			R	16+	•				•		•
Sweden												
Youth for Understanding USA–Sweden	864*			R	15–18	•				•		•
Switzerland												
Atelier des Arts	865			R	16+	•	•		•			
Center for Cultural Interchange–Switzerland Language Camp	865*			R	10–15	•	•	•	•	•		•
Collège du Léman Summer School	865*			R	8–18	•	•	•	•	•	•	
The Experiment in International Living–Switzerland French Language Immersion, Homestay, and Alpine Adventure	866*			R	14–19	•			•	•		•
Institut auf dem Rosenberg	866			R	14–20	•		•	•		•	
International Summer Camp Montana, Switzerland	866*			R	8–17	•	•	•	•	•	•	
Les Elfes–International Summer/Winter Camp	867*			R/D	8–18	•	•	•	•	•	•	
LSA Lausanne, Switzerland	867*			R	16+	•				•		•
Sprachkurse Ariana, Arosa	867			R	7–17	•		•	•		•	
Sprachkurse Ariana, Lenk	868			R	12–18	•		•	•		•	
Summer in Switzerland	868*			R	9–19	•	•	•	•	•	•	•
SuperCamp–Switzerland	868*			R	14–18	•	•	•		•		
Swiss Challenge	869				14–18			•	•	•	•	
TASIS French Language Program in Château–d'Oex, Switzerland	869*			R	13–17	•		•	•			
TASIS Le Château des Enfants	869*			R/D	6–10	•	•	•	•	•	•	
TASIS Middle School Program	869*			R/D	11–13	•	•	•	•	•	•	
TASIS Summer Program for Languages, Arts, and Outdoor Pursuits	870*			R/D	14–18	•	•	•	•	•	•	

**This program is highlighted by a photograph, special note, or in-depth description; see the profile page for more information.*
†D = day camp; R = residential camp

	GENERAL INFORMATION					PROGRAM INFORMATION						
	Profile Page	Boys D/R†	Girls D/R†	Coed D/R†	Age	Acad	Arts	Sports	Wild/ Outdrs	Special Interest	Jobs	Financial Aid
Village Camps–Switzerland	870*			R	7–18	•	•	•	•	•	•	•
Thailand												
AAVE–Thailand	871*				15–18			•	•	•	•	•
Adventures Cross-Country, Thailand Adventure	871*			R	13–18			•	•	•	•	•
AFS-USA–Community Service–Thailand	871*			R	16–19	•	•	•		•		•
AFS-USA–Homestay–Thailand	872*			R	15–17	•	•			•		•
The Experiment in International Living–Thailand Homestay	872*			R	14–19	•			•	•		•
LIFEWORKS with the DPF Foundation in Thailand	872*				15–19	•				•		•
RUSTIC PATHWAYS–ELEPHANTS & AMAZING THAILAND	872*				15–18			•	•	•	•	
RUSTIC PATHWAYS–INTRO TO COMMUNITY SERVICE IN THAILAND	873*			R	14–18		•	•		•	•	
RUSTIC PATHWAYS–PHOTOGRAPHY & ADVENTURE IN THAILAND	873*				16–18		•		•	•	•	
RUSTIC PATHWAYS–RHYTHM IN THE RICEFIELDS	873*			R	14–18	•	•	•	•	•	•	
RUSTIC PATHWAYS–RICEFIELDS, MONKS & SMILING CHILDREN	873*			R	14–18		•	•		•	•	
RUSTIC PATHWAYS–THE AMAZING THAILAND ADVENTURE	874*				15–18		•	•	•	•	•	
RUSTIC PATHWAYS–THE THAI ELEPHANT CONSERVATION PROJECT	874*			R	15–18				•	•	•	
RUSTIC PATHWAYS–THE WONDERS & RICHES OF THAILAND	874*				14–18			•	•	•	•	
SuperCamp–Thailand	874*			R	9–18	•		•			•	
Where There Be Dragons: Thailand	874*				15–20	•	•	•	•	•		•
Youth for Understanding USA–Thailand	875*			R	15–18	•	•	•		•		•
Trinidad and Tobago												
EARTHWATCH INSTITUTE–Trinidad's Leatherback Sea Turtles	875			R	16+	•				•		•
Visions–Trinidad	875*				16–18	•	•	•	•	•	•	•
Turkey												
AFS-USA–Homestay–Turkey	876*			R	15–18	•				•		•
The Experiment in International Living–Turkey Homestay, Community Service, and Travel	876*			R	14–19	•				•		•
Space Camp Turkey 6-Day International Program	876			R	9–16	•					•	
Volunteers for Peace International Work Camp–Turkey	876			R	15+	•		•	•	•		
Turks and Caicos Islands												
SFS: Marine Parks Management Studies	877			R	16–25	•		•	•	•		•
U.S. Virgin Islands												
EARTHWATCH INSTITUTE–Coral Reefs of the Virgin Islands	877			R	16+	•	•	•		•		•
EARTHWATCH INSTITUTE–Saving the Leatherback Turtle	877			R	16+	•				•		•
United Kingdom												
AFS-USA–Community Service–United Kingdom	877*			R	17–21					•	•	•
Blyth Education–Summer Study in London and Oxford University	878			R	14–19	•	•	•		•	•	
Buckswood: English Language (ESL) and Activities–Bradfield, England	878			R	7–16	•	•	•		•	•	
Buckswood: English Language (ESL) and Activities–Plumpton, England	878			R	7–16	•	•	•		•	•	
Cambridge College Programme	878*				14–19	•	•	•		•		
The Cambridge Prep Experience	879*			R	14–15	•	•	•		•		•
The Cambridge Tradition	879*			R	15–18	•	•	•		•		•
Center for Cultural Interchange–United Kingdom Independent Homestay	880*			R	16+	•				•		•
Cross Keys	880			D	4–12		•	•		•	•	
EARTHWATCH INSTITUTE–England's Hidden Kingdom	880			R	16+	•				•		•
EARTHWATCH INSTITUTE–Roman Fort on Tyne	880			R	16+	•				•		•
The Experiment in International Living–The United Kingdom Celtic Odyssey	881*			R	14–19	•				•		•
The Experiment in International Living–United Kingdom Filmmaking Program and Homestay	881*			R	14–19		•			•		•
The Experiment in International Living–United Kingdom Theatre Program	881*			R	14–19	•	•			•		•

**This program is highlighted by a photograph, special note, or in-depth description; see the profile page for more information.*
†D = day camp; R = residential camp

	GENERAL INFORMATION					PROGRAM INFORMATION						
	Profile Page	Boys D/R†	Girls D/R†	Coed D/R†	Age	Acad	Arts	Sports	Wild/ Outdrs	Special Interest	Jobs	Financial Aid
IEI–Digital Media Plus Programme	881*			R	16–18	•	•	•		•	•	
IEI–Fashion and Design Plus Programme	881*			R	16–18	•	•	•		•	•	
IEI–Fine Arts Plus Programme	882*			R	16–18		•	•		•	•	
IEI–Photography Plus Programme	882*			R	16–18	•	•	•		•	•	
IEI–Print and Broadcast Journalism	882*			R	16–18	•	•	•		•	•	
IEI Student Travel–Internship Program in London	882*			R	16–18	•	•	•		•	•	
IEI–Theatre Plus Programme	883*			R	16–18		•	•		•	•	
Longacre Expeditions, British Isles	883*				13–17			•	•	•	•	
Midsummer in London	883*			R	16–18	•	•			•	•	•
Mini Minors	884			D	3–12		•	•		•	•	
NBC Camps–Basketball Individual Training–Isle of Man	884			R	9–18			•			•	•
The New York Film Academy in London	884*			R	14–17		•					
Oxford Advanced Seminars Programme	884			R/D	16+	•	•	•				
Oxford Advanced Studies Program	885*			R/D	15–18	•	•	•		•		
The Oxford Experience	886*			R	15–18	•	•	•		•	•	
Oxford Media School–Film	886*			R	14–18	•	•	•		•		
Oxford Media School–Film Master Class	886*			R	14–18	•	•	•		•		•
Oxford Media School–Newsroom in Europe	887*			R	14–18	•	•	•		•		•
Oxford Media School–Newsroom in Europe, Master Class	887*			R	14–18	•	•	•		•		•
The Oxford Prep Experience	887*			R	13–15	•	•	•		•		•
The Oxford Tradition	888*			R	15–18	•	•	•		•		•
Putney Student Travel–Cultural Exploration–Theatre in Britain	888*			R	15–18		•			•	•	•
Sprachkurse Ariana, Aldenham	888			R	14–19	•		•			•	
Summer Discovery at Cambridge	889*			R		•	•	•		•	•	
TASIS England Summer Program	889*			R/D	12–18	•	•	•			•	
University of St. Andrews Creative Writing Summer Program	889			R	15–18	•	•	•	•			
University of St. Andrews Scottish Studies Summer Program	889			R	15–18	•		•	•			
Village Camps–England	890*			R	7–15	•	•	•	•	•	•	
Woodberry Forest Summer School–England	890*			R	12–17	•		•	•			•
Woodberry Forest Summer School–Scotland	890*			R	12–17	•		•	•			•
XUK	890			R	6–17	•	•	•		•	•	
United Republic of Tanzania												
EARTHWATCH INSTITUTE–Early Man at Olduvai Gorge	891			R	16+	•				•		•
Flint Hill School–"Summer on the Hill"–Trips from the Hill–Tanzania Safari	891				6+	•			•	•	•	
Putney Student Travel–Community Service–Tanzania	891*			R	15–18	•		•	•	•		•
Uruguay												
Youth for Understanding USA–Uruguay	891*			R	15–18	•				•		•
Venezuela												
Youth for Understanding USA–Venezuela	892*			R	15–18	•				•		•
Vietnam												
AAVE–Vietnam	892*				15–18			•	•	•	•	•
EARTHWATCH INSTITUTE–Butterflies of Vietnam	892			R	16+	•				•		•
EARTHWATCH INSTITUTE–Medicinal Plants of Vietnam	893			R	16+	•				•		•
EARTHWATCH INSTITUTE–Restoring Vietnam's Forests	893			R	16+	•	•		•	•		•
Where There Be Dragons: Vietnam	893*				15–20	•	•	•	•	•		•
Youth for Understanding USA–Vietnam	893*			R	15–18					•		•

**This program is highlighted by a photograph, special note, or in-depth description; see the profile page for more information.*
†D = day camp; R = residential camp

	GENERAL INFORMATION		PROGRAM INFORMATION						
	Profile Page	Age	Acad	Arts	Sports	Wild/ Outdrs	Special Interest	Jobs	Financial Aid
TRAVEL PROGRAMS IN THE UNITED STATES									
AAVE–Bold West	894*	14–18			•	•	•	•	•
AAVE–Boot/Saddle/Paddle	894*	14–18	•		•	•	•	•	•
AAVE–Border Cross	894*	13–14			•	•	•	•	•
AAVE–Rock & River	895*	14–18			•	•	•	•	•
AAVE–X–Five	895*	14–18			•	•	•	•	•
Adventure Links	895	8–17			•	•	•	•	
Adventure Links–Appalachian Odyssey	896	14–17			•	•	•	•	
Adventures Cross-Country, Western Adventure	896*	13–18			•	•		•	•
Adventure Treks–California Challenge Adventures	896	15–17			•	•			•
Adventure Treks–Summit Fever	896	17–18			•	•			•
Adventure Treks–Ultimate Northwest Adventures	897	15–17				•			•
Alien Adventure Overnight Camp	897	8–13	•	•	•	•	•	•	•
Alpengirl–Montana Art	897	12–14	•	•	•	•		•	•
Apogee Outdoor Adventures–Burlington to Boston	897	14–17			•	•	•	•	•
Apogee Outdoor Adventures–Coast to Quebec	898	14–17			•	•	•	•	•
Apogee Outdoor Adventures–New England Mountains and Coast	898	11–13			•	•		•	•
ATW: Action America West	898*	13–17			•	•	•	•	
ATW: Adventure Roads	898*	13–15			•	•	•	•	
ATW: American Horizons	898*	13–17			•	•	•	•	
ATW: California Sunset	899*	13–17			•	•	•	•	
ATW: Camp Inn 42	899*	13–18			•	•	•	•	
ATW: Discoverer	899*	13–17			•	•	•	•	
ATW: Fire and Ice	899*	14–17			•	•	•	•	
ATW: Mini Tours	899*	12–15			•	•	•	•	
ATW: Pacific Paradise	900*	13–17			•	•	•	•	
ATW: Skyblazer	900*	14–17			•	•	•	•	
ATW: Sunblazer	900*	13–17			•	•	•	•	
ATW: Wayfarer	900*	13–18			•	•	•	•	
Barton Adventure Camp	901	13–19	•		•	•	•	•	
BICYCLE TRAVEL ADVENTURES–Student Hosteling Program–A Thousand Miles: Massachusetts to Nova Scotia	901*	15–18			•	•	•	•	
BICYCLE TRAVEL ADVENTURES–Student Hosteling Program–Canadian Rockies to California	901*	15–18			•	•	•	•	
BICYCLE TRAVEL ADVENTURES–Student Hosteling Program–Cross-Country America	901*	15–18			•	•	•	•	
BICYCLE TRAVEL ADVENTURES–Student Hosteling Program–Maine-Nova Scotia Coast Loop	902*	13–16			•	•	•	•	
BICYCLE TRAVEL ADVENTURES–Student Hosteling Program–Niagara Falls to Montreal	902*	13–16			•	•	•	•	
BICYCLE TRAVEL ADVENTURES–Student Hosteling Program–Off-Road Vermont	903*	13–16			•	•	•	•	
BICYCLE TRAVEL ADVENTURES–Student Hosteling Program–Pacific Coast Adventure: Washington, Oregon, and California	903*	14–18			•	•	•	•	
BICYCLE TRAVEL ADVENTURES–Student Hosteling Program–Vermont	903*	13–18			•	•	•	•	
BICYCLE TRAVEL ADVENTURES–Student Hosteling Program–Vermont to the Atlantic Ocean	903*	13–18			•	•	•	•	
Camp Chi Teenage Adventure Trips	904	13+			•	•	•	•	•
Camp Friendship Challenge Program	904	11–16			•	•	•	•	•
Camp Tawonga–Teen Quest: Northwest	904			•		•	•	•	•
Camp Tawonga–Teen Quest: Southwest	904		•			•	•	•	•
Cheerio Adventures–5 Rivers in 5 Days	905	14–17				•		•	•
College Impressions	905	15–18	•		•		•		•
Discovery Works New England Community Service Experience	905*	13–15				•	•	•	
East Coast College Tour by Education Unlimited	905	15–19	•				•		•
ExploraMar: Marine Biology Sailing Expeditions–Sea of Cortez, Baja, Mexico	905	13–17	•	•	•	•	•	•	
Flint Hill School–"Summer on the Hill"–Enrichment on the Hill–Women Writers' Adventure	906	14+	•	•		•	•	•	
Four Corners School of Outdoor Education: Southwest Ed-Venture	906	16+	•	•	•	•	•	•	•

This program is highlighted by a photograph, special note, or in-depth description; see the profile page for more information.
†D = day camp; R = residential camp

	GENERAL INFORMATION		PROGRAM INFORMATION						
	Profile Page	Age	Acad	Arts	Sports	Wild/ Outdrs	Special Interest	Jobs	Financial Aid
Geronimo Program	906	15–19	•		•	•	•		
Great Escapes (Adventure Trips for Teens)–Canadian Adventure	906	14–17			•	•	•	•	•
Great Escapes (Adventure Trips for Teens)–Colorado River and Canyons Adventure	907	14–17			•	•	•	•	•
Great Escapes (Adventure Trips for Teens)–Rock and Rapids	907	14–17			•	•		•	•
Great Escapes (Adventure Trips for Teens)–Saddle and Sail	907	13–16			•	•	•	•	•
Hiker's Heaven Overnight Camp	907	7–13	•	•	•	•	•	•	•
Hulbert Voyageurs Youth Wilderness Trips	908	10–17		•	•	•	•	•	•
Hurricane Island Outward Bound–Mid-Atlantic Canoeing, Backpacking, and Rock Climbing	908	14–20	•		•	•	•	•	•
Hurricane Island Outward Bound–Ocean Bound: Tall Ship Sailing and Sea Kayaking Semester	908	16–18	•		•	•	•	•	•
Hurricane Island Outward Bound–Western Maine and New Hampshire Canoeing and Backpacking	909	15–17	•		•	•	•	•	•
Ibike Cultural Tours–Washington/British Columbia	909	16+	•		•	•	•		•
Julian Krinsky Golf Tours	909*	13–17			•			•	•
Kroka Expeditions–Advanced Rock Climbing	909	14–18			•	•	•	•	•
Kroka Expeditions–Paddlers Journey Up North	909	12–18	•		•	•	•	•	•
Longacre Expeditions, Adventure 28	910*	13–17			•	•		•	•
Longacre Expeditions, British Columbia	910*	14–17			•	•		•	
Longacre Expeditions, New England/Canada	910*	13–17			•	•		•	
Longacre Expeditions, Pacific Coast and Inlands	910*	13–17			•	•	•	•	
Longacre Expeditions, Volcanoes	911*	13–15	•		•	•		•	
Longacre Expeditions, Western Challenge	911*	14–17			•	•		•	
Luna Adventures with AAG SummerSkills	911	10–15			•	•	•		
Mountain Workshop/Dirt Camp: Dirt Camp Junior Killington	911	12–17			•	•		•	
Musiker Tours: Action USA	911*	13–17			•	•	•	•	
Musiker Tours: Alaska Aloha	912*	15–18			•		•	•	
Musiker Tours: America Coast to Coast	912*	13–17			•	•	•	•	
Musiker Tours: Cali-Pacific Passport	912*	13–17			•	•	•	•	
Musiker Tours: ComboCamp America	912*	13–17			•	•	•	•	
Musiker Tours: Discover America	913*	13–17			•	•	•	•	
Musiker Tours: Eastcoaster	913*	12–14			•	•	•	•	
Musiker Tours: Westcoaster	913*	13–17			•	•	•	•	
92nd Street Y Camps–The TIYUL	913	15–18	•				•	•	•
Outward Bound West–Cataract Canyon Rafting	913	16+	•		•	•	•	•	•
Overland: Acadia and Prince Edward Island Bicycle Touring and Sea-Kayaking	914*	14–18			•	•	•	•	
Overland: American Challenge Coast-to-Coast Bicycle Touring	914*	15–19			•	•	•	•	
Overland: American Community Service, New England	914*	15–18			•	•	•	•	
Overland: Appalachian Trail Challenge Hiking	914*	15–19				•	•	•	
Overland: Colorado and Utah Mountain Biking and Rafting	915*	13–18			•	•	•	•	
Overland: New England Explorer Hiking, Mountain Biking, and Rafting	915*	13–16			•	•	•	•	
Overland: Pacific Coast Bicycle Touring and Rafting	915*	14–18			•	•	•	•	
Overland: Rocky Mountain Explorer Hiking, Mountain Biking, and Rafting	915*	13–16			•	•	•	•	
Overland: Shasta & the Sierras Backpacking, Climbing and Rafting	915*	14–18			•	•	•	•	
Overland: Vermont & Montreal Bicycle Touring	916*	13–18			•	•	•	•	
Overland: Yellowstone Explorer Backpacking, Rock Climbing, and Rafting	916*	14–18			•	•	•	•	
The Ranch–Lake Placid Teen Travel Camp	916				•	•	•	•	
Rein Teen Tours–American Adventure	917*	13–17			•	•	•	•	
Rein Teen Tours–California Caper	917*	13–17			•	•	•	•	
Rein Teen Tours–Crossroads	917*	13–17			•	•	•	•	
Rein Teen Tours–Eastern Adventure	917*	13–15			•	•	•	•	
Rein Teen Tours–Grand Adventure	918*	13–17			•	•	•	•	
Rein Teen Tours–Hawaiian/Alaskan Adventure	918*	13–17			•	•	•	•	
Rein Teen Tours–Western Adventure	918*	13–17			•	•	•	•	
RUSTIC PATHWAYS–ADVENTURE IN AMERICA'S SOUTHWEST	918*	13–18		•	•	•	•	•	
Summer Conservation Corps	919	16–19	•		•	•	•	•	•
Summit Travel Program	919	16–20				•	•	•	
Swift Nature Camp–Canadian Canoe Trip	919	14–17	•	•	•	•	•	•	•

*This program is highlighted by a photograph, special note, or in-depth description; see the profile page for more information.
†D = day camp; R = residential camp

	GENERAL INFORMATION		PROGRAM INFORMATION						
	Profile Page	Age	Acad	Arts	Sports	Wild/ Outdrs	Special Interest	Jobs	Financial Aid
Teen Tours of America–Alaskan Expedition	919	13–17			•	•	•	•	
Teen Tours of America–Aloha Hawaii	920	13+			•	•	•	•	
Teen Tours of America–New England Journey	920	13–17			•	•	•	•	
Teen Tours of America–Western Adventure	920	12–17			•	•	•	•	•
Teen Tours of America–Western Sprint	920	12–17			•	•	•	•	
Teen Tour USA and Canada	921	13–17	•	•	•	•	•	•	
TENNIS: EUROPE & MORE–North American Teams	921	14–18	•		•	•	•	•	•
Trailmark Outdoor Adventures–New England–Acadia	921	12–16			•	•		•	•
Trailmark Outdoor Adventures–New England–Camden	921	13–16			•	•	•	•	•
Trailmark Outdoor Adventures–New England–Downeast	922	13–16			•	•		•	•
Trailmark Outdoor Adventures–New England–Jr. Acadia	922	11–12			•	•		•	•
Trailmark Outdoor Adventures–New England–Mahoosoc	922	14–16			•	•	•	•	•
Trailmark Outdoor Adventures–New England–Moose River	922	13–14			•	•		•	•
Trailmark Outdoor Adventures–New England–Mt. Desert	922	14–16			•	•		•	•
Trailmark Outdoor Adventures–New England–Rangeley Coed	923	12–14			•	•		•	•
Trailmark Outdoor Adventures–Northern Rockies–Tetons with Backpack	923	13–16			•	•		•	•
Trailmark Outdoor Adventures–Northern Rockies–Tetons with Horseback	923	13–16			•	•		•	•
Trailridge Mountain Camp	923	9–16			•	•	•		
Voyageur Outward Bound–Lake Superior Freshwater Kayaking and Backpacking	923	16+	•		•	•	•	•	•
Voyageur Outward Bound–Manitoba to Montana Summer Semester	924	16+	•		•	•	•	•	•
Weissman Teen Tours–"Aloha–Welcome to Hawaiian Paradise"	924*	14–18			•	•	•	•	
Weissman Teen Tours–U.S. and Western Canada, 4 Weeks	924*	13–17	•		•	•	•	•	•
Weissman Teen Tours–U.S. and Western Canada, 6 Weeks	925*	13–17			•	•	•	•	
Westcoast Connection–American Voyageur	925*	13–17			•	•	•	•	•
Westcoast Connection–Californian Extravaganza	925*	13–17			•	•	•	•	
Westcoast Connection–Hawaiian Spirit	926*	14–17			•	•	•	•	
Westcoast Connection Travel/On Tour–Northwestern Odyssey	926*	17–19			•	•	•		
Westcoast Connection Travel–California and the Canyons	926*	13–17			•	•	•	•	
Westcoast Connection Travel–Canadian Mountain Magic	926*	13–17			•	•	•	•	
Westcoast Connection Travel–Eastcoast Encounter	927*	13–16			•	•	•	•	
Westcoast Connection Travel–Great West Challenge	927*	13–17			•	•	•	•	
Westcoast Connection Travel–Northwestern Odyssey	927*	13–17			•	•	•	•	•
Westcoast Connection Travel/On Tour–Canadian Adventure	927*	17–19			•	•		•	
Westcoast Connection Travel–Ski and Snowboard Sensation	928*	13–17			•	•	•	•	•
Westcoast Connection Travel–Southwesterner	928*	13–17			•	•	•	•	•
Westcoast Connection–U.S. Explorer	928*	13–17			•	•	•	•	•
Wilderness Ventures–Colorado/Utah Mountain Bike	928*	14–18			•	•		•	•
Wilderness Ventures–Great Divide	928*	14–18			•	•	•	•	•
Wilderness Ventures–Great Divide Bike	929*	14–18			•	•		•	•
Wilderness Ventures–Northwest	929*	14–18			•	•	•	•	•
Wilderness Ventures–Pacific Coast Bike	929*	14–18			•	•		•	•
Wilderness Ventures–Pacific Northwest	929*	14–18			•	•	•	•	•
Wilderness Ventures–Rocky Mountain	930*	14–18			•	•	•	•	•
Wilderness Ventures–Yellowstone Fly Fishing	930*	14–18			•	•	•	•	•
Williwaw Adventures–Maine Wilderness	930	14–18	•		•	•	•	•	•
Williwaw Adventures–Pacific Northwest Expedition	930	14–18			•	•	•	•	•
Windsor Mountain: Experiential Summer School	931*	13–17	•			•	•		•
Windsor Mountain: New England Adventure	931*	11–13			•	•	•	•	•
Windsor Mountain: New England Traveling Minstrels	931*	13–15		•	•		•		•
Windsor Mountain: Random Acts of Kindness	931*	13–15	•		•	•	•	•	•

*This program is highlighted by a photograph, special note, or in-depth description; see the profile page for more information.
†D = day camp; R = residential camp

TRAVEL PROGRAMS OUTSIDE THE UNITED STATES

	GENERAL INFORMATION		PROGRAM INFORMATION						
	Profile Page	Age	Acad	Arts	Sports	Wild/ Outdrs	Special Interest	Jobs	Financial Aid
AAVE–Africa	932*	15–18	•		•	•	•	•	•
AAVE–Alps Rider	932*	14–18			•	•	•	•	•
AAVE–Bold Europe	932*	14–18			•	•	•	•	•
AAVE–Wild Isles	933*	14–18			•	•	•	•	•
ACTIONQUEST: Leeward and French Caribbean Island Voyages	933*	14–19	•		•	•	•		
ACTIONQUEST: Mediterranean Sailing Voyage	933*	15–19	•		•	•	•		
!ADVENTURES-AFLOAT: Advanced Scuba Adventure Voyages–Caribbean Islands	934*	13–19	•	•	•	•	•	•	
!ADVENTURES-AFLOAT: Scuba and Sailing Discovery Voyages–Caribbean Islands	934*	13–19	•	•	•	•	•	•	
Adventures Cross-Country, Australia/Fiji Adventure	934*	14–18			•	•		•	
Adventures Cross-Country, Caribbean Adventure	935*	13–18			•	•	•	•	•
Adventures Cross-Country,Southern Europe Adventure	935*	14–18			•	•		•	•
Alpengirl–Scandinavia	935	14–16			•	•	•		•
ATW: European Adventures	936*	15–18			•	•	•	•	
Bicycle Africa Tours	936	16+	•		•	•	•		•
BICYCLE TRAVEL ADVENTURES–Student Hosteling Program–Amsterdam to Paris	936*	14–18			•	•	•	•	
BICYCLE TRAVEL ADVENTURES–Student Hosteling Program–France and Italy	936*	16–18			•	•	•	•	
BICYCLE TRAVEL ADVENTURES–Student Hosteling Program–Ireland and England	937*	13–18			•	•	•	•	
BICYCLE TRAVEL ADVENTURES–Student Hosteling Program–Spain and France	937*	15–18			•	•	•	•	•
Blue Lake International Exchange Program	937	12–18		•			•	•	•
BROADREACH Academic Treks–Marine Park Management	938*	15–19	•		•	•	•		•
BROADREACH Adventures in Scuba and Sailing–Underwater Discoveries	938*	13–19	•	•	•	•	•		
BROADREACH Adventures in the Windward Islands–Advanced Scuba	938*	15–19	•	•	•	•	•		•
BROADREACH Adventures Underwater–Advanced Scuba	938*	13–19	•	•	•	•	•		
BROADREACH Arc of the Caribbean Sailing Adventure	939*	15–19	•	•	•	•	•		
BROADREACH Fiji Solomon Quest	940*	15–19	•	•	•	•	•		
Burklyn Ballet Edinburgh Connection	940	14–25		•			•	•	•
Celtic Learning and Travel Services–Edinburgh and Dublin	940	14–21	•	•	•		•	•	
Celtic Learning and Travel Services–London and Dublin	940	14–21	•	•	•		•	•	
Costa Rica Rainforest Outward Bound School–Tri-Country/Tri-Mester	941	17+	•		•	•	•	•	•
Excel at Oxford/Tuscany	941*	16–18	•	•	•	•	•		•
GLOBAL WORKS–Cultural Exchange-New Zealand and Fiji Islands-4 weeks	941*	14–18	•	•	•	•	•	•	•
Israel Discovery	942	14–18	•		•	•	•	•	•
Kayak Adventures Unlimited	942	12–17			•	•	•	•	
Knowledge Exchange Institute–Discover Spain and Portugal Program	942	15–19	•		•	•	•		•
Knowledge Exchange Institute–European Capitals Program	942	15–19	•				•		•
Longacre Expeditions, Virgin Islands	943*	14–17	•		•	•	•	•	
Musiker Tours: Action Europe	943*	15–18			•		•	•	
ODYSSEY EXPEDITIONS: Tropical Marine Biology Voyages–Caribbean Islands	943*	13–19	•	•	•	•	•	•	
Overland: European Challenge Bicycle Touring from Paris to Rome	944*	15–19			•	•	•	•	
Overland: European Explorer Hiking, Rafting, and Sea Kayaking	944*	14–18			•	•	•	•	
Overland: The Alpine Challenge Leadership Course Backpacking and Hiking	944*	15–18				•	•	•	
Phillips Exeter Academy Taiwan and Beijing Summer Study Tour	944	13+	•	•	•		•		
Poulter Colorado Camps: Adventures Planet Earth–Austria	944	14+	•			•	•	•	•
Putney Student Travel–Cultural Exploration–Australia, New Zealand, and Fiji	945*	16–18	•		•	•	•		•
Putney Student Travel–Cultural Exploration–Eastern European Heritage	945*	14–18	•		•	•	•	•	•
Putney Student Travel–Cultural Exploration–France, Holland, and England	945*	14–15	•		•	•			•
Putney Student Travel–Cultural Exploration–Switzerland, Italy, France, and Holland	945*	16–18	•		•	•	•		•
Putney Student Travel–Cultural Exploration–Thailand and Cambodia	946*	15–18	•			•	•	•	•
Rust College Study Abroad in Africa	946	15+	•	•	•				•
RUSTIC PATHWAYS–BUDDHIST LIFE & ANGKOR WAT	946*	15–18	•				•	•	

**This program is highlighted by a photograph, special note, or in-depth description; see the profile page for more information.*
†D = day camp; R = residential camp

	GENERAL INFORMATION		PROGRAM INFORMATION						
	Profile Page	Age	Acad	Arts	Sports	Wild/ Outdrs	Special Interest	Jobs	Financial Aid
RUSTIC PATHWAYS–EXTREME PLANET	946*	16–18			•	•	•	•	
Sail Caribbean–Leeward Islands	947*	13–18	•		•	•	•	•	•
Spanish Through Leadership–Nicaragua/Costa Rica	947*	14–18	•	•	•	•	•		
TENNIS: EUROPE	947	14–18	•		•	•	•	•	•
Tibetan Summer Passage	948	16+	•	•		•	•	•	•
Weissman Teen Tours–European Experience	948*	14–18	•	•	•	•	•	•	
Westcoast Connection–Australian Outback Plus Hawaii	948*	14–19			•	•	•		•
Westcoast Connection Travel–European Discovery	949*	14–17			•	•	•	•	
Westcoast Connection Travel–European Escape	949*	14–17			•	•	•	•	
Westcoast Connection Travel/On Tour–European Experience	949*	17–19			•	•	•		
Wilderness Ventures–European Alps	949*	14–18	•			•	•	•	•
Windsor Mountain: European Traveling Minstrels	950*	14–18	•	•			•		•
Youth for Understanding USA–Estonia/Latvia-Baltic Summer	950*	15–18	•				•		•

*This program is highlighted by a photograph, special note, or in-depth description; see the profile page for more information.
†D = day camp; R = residential camp

Summer Program Profiles

PPORTUNITIES IN THE UNITED STATES

ALABAMA

ALABAMA MUSEUM OF NATURAL HISTORY SUMMER EXPEDITION

The University of Alabama
Tuscaloosa, Alabama 35487-0340

General Information Coed residential academic program and outdoor program established in 1979. High school or college credit may be earned.
Program Focus Hands-on field science in archaeology and paleontology as well as structured education in areas of natural history.
Academics Archaeology, biology, biology (Advanced Placement), botany, ecology, environmental science, geology/earth science, paleontology.
Special Interest Areas Field research/expeditions, nature study.
Program Information 4 sessions per year. Session length: 6 days in June, July. Ages: 14+. 25 participants per session. Boarding program cost: $350–$400. Financial aid available.
Application Deadline June 1.
Jobs Positions for college students 18 and older.
Contact Randy Mecredy, Education Programs Coordinator / Expedition Leader, Alabama Museum of Natural History, Box 870340, Tuscaloosa, Alabama 35487-0340. Phone: 205-348-2136. Fax: 205-348-9292. E-mail: museum.expedition@ua.edu.
URL www.amnh.ua.edu

ALPINE CAMP FOR BOYS

Alpine Camp for Boys
138 County Road 619
Mentone, Alabama 35984

General Information Boys' residential traditional camp established in 1959. Religious affiliation: Christian. Accredited by American Camping Association.
Sports Archery, basketball, bicycling, canoeing, climbing (wall), cross-country, football, horseback riding, rappelling, riflery, ropes course, soccer, softball, swimming, tennis, volleyball, weight training.
Wilderness/Outdoors Mountain biking, rafting, rock climbing, white-water trips.
Trips Day.
Program Information 3 sessions per year. Session length: 10–25 days in June, July, August. Ages: 7–15. 245 participants per session. Boarding program cost: $1550–$3200. Financial aid available.
Contact Mr. Richard C. O'Ferrall, Jr., Director, PO Box 297, Mentone, Alabama 35984-0297. Phone: 256-634-4404. Fax: 256-634-4405. E-mail: summer@alpinecamp.com.
URL www.alpinecamp.com

AMERICAN ALLSTAR DANCE CAMP

Outreach Program Office at Auburn University
301 O.D. Smith Hall
171 South College Street
Auburn University, Alabama 36849

General Information Coed residential and day sports camp established in 1986.
Program Focus Dance team.
Arts Dance.
Sports Synchronized dancing.

American Allstar Dance Camp (continued)

Program Information 1 session per year. Session length: 4 days in June. Ages: 12–17. 150–300 participants per session. Day program cost: $99. Boarding program cost: $195–$225.
Application Deadline Continuous.
Contact Mr. Robert McKinnell, Program Developer, main address above. Phone: 334-844-5100. Fax: 334-844-3101. E-mail: mckinrr@auburn.edu.
URL www.auburn.edu/summercamps

ARCHITECTURE SUMMER CAMP

Outreach Program Office at Auburn University
301 O.D. Smith Hall
Auburn University, Alabama 36849-5608

General Information Coed residential arts program established in 2002. Specific services available for the physically challenged.
Academics Architecture, art (Advanced Placement).
Arts Arts and crafts (general), drawing, graphic arts, printmaking.
Special Interest Areas Career exploration, leadership training.
Sports Swimming, volleyball.
Program Information 1 session per year. Session length: 6 days in June. Ages: 15–18. 15–20 participants per session. Boarding program cost: $545. Financial aid available.
Application Deadline June 7.
Contact Mr. Scott Greenwood, Program Developer, main address above. E-mail: greens1@auburn.edu.
URL www.auburn.edu/outreach/architecture

AUBURN UNIVERSITY DESIGN WORKSHOP

Outreach Program Office at Auburn University
301 O.D. Smith Hall
Auburn University, Alabama 36849-5608

General Information Coed residential arts program established in 1995. Specific services available for the physically challenged.
Program Focus Introduction to industrial design techniques.
Academics Art (Advanced Placement).
Arts Arts and crafts (general), design, drawing, graphic arts, painting, printmaking, sculpture, woodworking.
Special Interest Areas Career exploration, leadership training.
Sports Swimming, volleyball.
Program Information 1 session per year. Session length: 6 days in June. Ages: 15–18. 15–20 participants per session. Boarding program cost: $545.
Application Deadline June 7.
Contact Scott Greenwood, Program Director, main address above. Phone: 334-844-3107. E-mail: greens1@auburn.edu.
URL www.auburn.edu/outreach/id

BIRMINGHAM-SOUTHERN COLLEGE STUDENT LEADERS IN SERVICE PROGRAM

Birmingham-Southern College
900 Arkadelphia Road
Birmingham, Alabama 35254

General Information Coed residential community service program established in 1994. Formal opportunities for the academically talented.
Program Focus Leadership theories and service learning.
Special Interest Areas Community service, leadership training.
Sports Ropes course.
Trips Cultural.
Program Information 2 sessions per year. Session length: 6 days in June. Ages: 15–17. 30 participants per session. Boarding program cost: $350–$450.
Application Deadline April 10.
Contact Mr. John Hawkins, Assistant Director of Admission, BSC Box 549008, Birmingham, Alabama 35254. Phone: 800-523-5793 Ext.4689. Fax: 205-226-3074. E-mail: jhawkins@bsc.edu.
URL www.bsc.edu

BIRMINGHAM-SOUTHERN COLLEGE SUMMER SCHOLAR PROGRAM

Birmingham-Southern College
900 Arkadelphia Road
Birmingham, Alabama 35254

General Information Coed residential and day academic program established in 1968. High school or college credit may be earned.
Program Focus Combination of academics and extracurricular activities.
Academics English language/literature, SAT/ACT preparation, Spanish language/literature, art (Advanced Placement), art history/appreciation, astronomy, biology, business, chemistry, computer programming, computers, economics, government and politics, health sciences, history, humanities, mathematics, music, precollege program, psychology, religion, social science, social studies, writing.
Arts Drawing, music, music (vocal), painting, photography.
Special Interest Areas Career exploration, community service, field trips (arts and culture), leadership training, team building.
Sports Basketball, bicycling, canoeing, cross-country, golf, racquetball, ropes course, soccer, swimming, tennis, ultimate frisbee, volleyball, weight training.
Wilderness/Outdoors Canoe trips, caving, hiking.
Trips Cultural, day, overnight, shopping.
Program Information 1 session per year. Session length: 50 days in June, July. Ages: 16–17. 50–75 participants per session. Day program cost: $300–$400. Boarding program cost: $1200–$1300.
Application Deadline Continuous.
Contact Mr. David Driskill, Director, BSC Box 549008, Birmingham, Alabama 35254. Phone: 205-226-4684. Fax: 205-226-3074. E-mail: ddriskil@bsc.edu.
URL www.bsc.edu

CAMP LANEY FOR BOYS

Camp Laney for Boys
916 West River Road
Mentone, Alabama 35984

General Information Boys' residential traditional camp established in 1959. Accredited by American Camping Association.
Arts Arts and crafts (general).
Sports Archery, basketball, canoeing, climbing (wall), fishing, football, golf, horseback riding, rappelling, riflery, ropes course, soccer, softball, swimming, tennis, volleyball.
Wilderness/Outdoors Canoe trips, mountain biking, rafting, rock climbing, white-water trips.
Trips Day.
Program Information 4 sessions per year. Session length: 6–13 days in June, July, August. Ages: 8–14. 48–195 participants per session. Boarding program cost: $835–$1665.
Application Deadline Continuous.
Jobs Positions for college students 18 and older.
Contact Rob Hammond, Director, PO Box 289, Mentone, Alabama 35984. Phone: 800-648-2919. Fax: 256-634-4098. E-mail: info@camplaney.com.
URL www.camplaney.com

CAMP SKYLINE

Camp Skyline
4888 Alabama Highway 117
Mentone, Alabama 35984

General Information Girls' residential traditional camp established in 1947. Religious affiliation: Christian non-denominational. Accredited by American Camping Association.
Arts Arts and crafts (general), chorus, circus arts, clowning, dance, dance (jazz), dance (modern), drawing, music (vocal), puppetry, theater/drama.
Special Interest Areas Leadership training, nature study, work camp programs.
Sports Aerobics, archery, basketball, canoeing, cheerleading, climbing (wall), equestrian sports, gymnastics, horseback riding, lacrosse, riflery, ropes course, soccer, softball, swimming, tennis, volleyball.
Wilderness/Outdoors Canoe trips, mountain biking, white-water trips.
Trips Day.
Program Information 7 sessions per year. Session length: 7–13 days in June, July, August. Ages: 6–16. 250–300 participants per session. Boarding program cost: $995–$1795. Financial aid available.
Application Deadline Continuous.
Jobs Positions for high school students 17 and older and college students 19 and older.
Contact Ms. Sally Cash Johnson, Director, PO Box 287, Mentone, Alabama 35984. Phone: 800-448-9279. Fax: 256-634-3018. E-mail: info@campskyline.com.
URL www.campskyline.com

CAMP SKYLINE–EQUESTRIAN PROGRAM

Camp Skyline
4888 Alabama Highway 117
Mentone, Alabama 35984

General Information Girls' residential sports camp established in 1999. Religious affiliation: Christian non-denominational. Accredited by American Camping Association.
Program Focus Equestrian Program with riding and classroom instruction.
Sports Equestrian sports.
Trips Overnight.
Program Information 4 sessions per year. Session length: 13 days in June, July, August. Ages: 9–16. 12–16 participants per session. Boarding program cost: $2395.
Application Deadline Continuous.
Jobs Positions for college students 21 and older.
Contact Ms. Sally Cash Johnson, Director, PO Box 287, Mentone, Alabama 35984. Phone: 800-448-9279. Fax: 256-634-3018. E-mail: info@campskyline.com.
URL www.campskyline.com

DANCE MAGIC

Outreach Program Office at Auburn University
301 O.D. Smith Hall
Auburn University, Alabama 36849-5608

General Information Coed residential and day sports camp.
Arts Dance.
Program Information 1 session per year. Session length: 4 days in July. Ages: 13–18. 100 participants per session. Day program cost: $199. Boarding program cost: $249.
Application Deadline Continuous.
Contact Mr. Robert R. McKinnell, Program Developer, main address above. Phone: 334-844-5100. Fax: 334-844-3101. E-mail: mckinrr@auburn.edu.
URL www.auburn.edu/summercamps

HALF-TIME USA

Outreach Program Office at Auburn University
301 O.D. Smith Hall
Auburn University, Alabama 36849-5608

General Information Coed residential arts program established in 1985.
Arts Band, dance, dance (jazz), dance (modern).
Special Interest Areas Color guard/flag, drum majoring.
Program Information 1 session per year. Session length: 3 days in June, July. Ages: 13–18. 150–250 participants per session. Boarding program cost: $170–$190.
Application Deadline Continuous.
Jobs Positions for college students 20 and older.
Contact Shirley DeVenney, Owner/Camp Director, PO Box 662, Wetumpka, Alabama 36092. Phone: 334-567-7315.
URL www.auburn.edu/summercamps

Josten Yearbook Summer Workshop

Outreach Program Office at Auburn University
301 O.D. Smith Hall
Auburn University, Alabama 36849

General Information Coed residential arts program established in 1986.
Program Focus Yearbook production.
Academics Art (Advanced Placement), journalism.
Arts Creative writing, desktop publishing, graphic arts, photography.
Special Interest Areas Yearbook production.
Program Information 1 session per year. Session length: 3 days in July. Ages: 13–18. 250–350 participants per session. Boarding program cost: $175–$195.
Application Deadline Continuous.
Contact Mr. Sam Burney, Director, Outreach Program, main address above. Phone: 324-844-5100. E-mail: opo@auburn.edu.
URL www.auburn.edu/summercamps

National Cheerleaders Association Cheerleader Camps

Outreach Program Office at Auburn University
301 O.D. Smith Hall
Auburn University, Alabama 36849

General Information Coed residential and day sports camp.
Program Focus Cheerleading.
Arts Dance.
Sports Cheerleading.
Program Information 5 sessions per year. Session length: 4 days in June, July. Ages: 13–19. 150–500 participants per session. Day program cost: $135. Boarding program cost: $223.
Application Deadline Continuous.
Contact Mr. Robert McKinnell, Program Developer, main address above. Phone: 334-844-5100. Fax: 334-844-3101. E-mail: mckinrr@auburn.edu.
URL www.auburn.edu/summercamps

Student Conservation Association–Conservation Crew Program (Alabama)

Student Conservation Association (SCA)
Alabama

General Information Coed residential outdoor program, community service program, and wilderness program established in 1957. High school credit may be earned.
Program Focus Resource management, conservation, environmental education.
Academics Biology, botany, ecology, environmental science, geology/earth science, history.
Special Interest Areas Campcraft, community service, construction, leadership training, nature study, trail maintenance, work camp programs.
Sports Canoeing, fishing, kayaking, swimming.
Wilderness/Outdoors Backpacking, canoe trips, hiking, orienteering, outdoor living skills, rock climbing, wilderness camping.
Trips Cultural, day, overnight.
Program Information 2–3 sessions per year. Session length: 3–5 weeks in June, July, August. Ages: 15–19. 6–8 participants per session. Application fee: $20. Financial aid available. No cost for program; financial aid possible for travel expenses.
Application Deadline Continuous.
Jobs Positions for college students 21 and older.
Contact Recruitment Office, PO Box 550, Charlestown, New Hampshire 03603. Phone: 603-543-1700. Fax: 603-543-1828. E-mail: getreal@thesca.org.
URL www.theSCA.org

Summer at Altamont

The Altamont School
4801 Altamont Road
Birmingham, Alabama 35222

General Information Coed day traditional camp and academic program established in 1975. Formal opportunities for the academically talented. High school credit may be earned.
Academics English language/literature, academics (general), art, computers, ecology, health sciences, history, humanities, mathematics, music, reading, science (general), speech/debate, writing.
Arts Arts, arts and crafts (general), band, creative writing, music (instrumental), music (jazz).
Sports Baseball, basketball, soccer, tennis, volleyball.
Wilderness/Outdoors Hiking.
Trips Cultural, day.
Program Information 1 session per year. Session length: 5–30 days in June, July. Ages: 9–18. 15–300 participants per session. Day program cost: $100–$750.
Application Deadline Continuous.
Jobs Positions for high school students 18 and older and college students 18 and older.
Contact Mr. James M. Wiygul, Director of the Summer Program, main address above. Phone: 205-879-2006. Fax: 205-871-5666. E-mail: jwiygul@altamontschool.org.
URL www.altamontschool.org

Tuskegee University Vet Step I

Tuskegee University College of Veterinary Medicine
Tuskegee, Alabama 36088

General Information Coed residential academic program established in 1991.
Academics Biology (Advanced Placement), chemistry, preveterinary, veterinary science.
Special Interest Areas Animal care, career exploration, college planning, team building.
Trips Day.
Program Information 1 session per year. Session length: 1 week in June. Ages: 13–15. 30 participants per session. Financial aid available. No cost for program.
Application Deadline April 30.
Contact Phillip H. Mitchell, Vet-Step Coordinator, Office of Veterinary Admissions, Tuskegee University,

Tuskegee, Alabama 36088. Phone: 334-727-8309. Fax: 334-727-8177. E-mail: pmitchell@tuskegee.edu.
URL www.tuskegee.edu

Tuskegee University Vet Step II

Tuskegee University College of Veterinary Medicine
Tuskegee, Alabama 36088

General Information Coed residential academic program established in 1991.
Academics Biology (Advanced Placement), chemistry, preveterinary, veterinary science.
Special Interest Areas Animal care, career exploration, college planning, team building.
Trips Day.
Program Information 1 session per year. Session length: 1 week in July. Ages: 16–18. 30 participants per session. Financial aid available. No cost for program.
Application Deadline April 30.
Contact Phillip H. Mitchell, Vet-Step Coordinator, Office of Veterinary Admissions, Tuskegee University, Tuskegee, Alabama 36088. Phone: 334-727-8309. Fax: 334-727-8177. E-mail: pmitchell@tuskegee.edu.
URL www.tuskegee.edu

Universal Cheerleaders Association and Universal Dance Association Camps

Outreach Program Office at Auburn University
301 O.D. Smith Hall
Auburn University, Alabama 36849

General Information Coed residential and day sports camp.
Program Focus Cheerleading and dance.
Arts Dance.
Sports Cheerleading.
Program Information 8–10 sessions per year. Session length: 3–4 days in May, June, July. Ages: 13–18. 150–500 participants per session. Day program cost: $140. Boarding program cost: $210–$225.
Application Deadline Continuous.
Contact Mr. Robert R. McKinnell, Program Developer, main address above. Phone: 334-844-5100. Fax: 334-844-3101. E-mail: mckinrr@auburn.edu.
URL www.auburn.edu/summercamps

World Affairs Youth Seminar

Outreach Program Office at Auburn University
301 O.D. Smith Hall
Auburn University, Alabama 36849-5608

General Information Coed residential academic program established in 1986. Formal opportunities for the academically talented. Specific services available for the physically challenged.
Program Focus Mock international crisis and a model United Nations. Study of the diverse social, political, and religious cultures of the world.
Academics Communications, computers, economics, government and politics, government and politics (Advanced Placement), history, history (Advanced Placement), humanities, international relations, peace education, social science, social studies, speech/debate, writing.
Special Interest Areas Leadership training.
Sports Basketball, soccer, swimming, tennis, volleyball, weight training.
Trips Cultural.
Program Information 1 session per year. Session length: 6 days in July. Ages: 14–18. 75–150 participants per session. Boarding program cost: $399. Financial aid available.
Application Deadline June 18.
Contact Mr. Sam Burney, Director of Outreach Program Office, main address above. Phone: 334-844-5100. E-mail: opo@auburn.edu.
URL www.auburn.edu/summercamps

ALASKA

AAVE–Alaska

AAVE–America's Adventure Ventures Everywhere
Alaska

General Information Coed travel outdoor program, wilderness program, and adventure program established in 1976. Accredited by American Camping Association.
Program Focus Adventure travel.
Special Interest Areas Campcraft, community service, leadership training, team building.
Sports Kayaking, rappelling, sea kayaking, swimming.
Wilderness/Outdoors Backpacking, hiking, ice climbing, mountaineering, orienteering, rafting, survival training, white-water trips, wilderness camping.
Trips Overnight.
Program Information 4–6 sessions per year. Session length: 26 days in June, July, August. Ages: 14–18. 13 participants per session. Cost: $3888. Financial aid available.
Application Deadline Continuous.
Jobs Positions for college students 21 and older.
Contact Mr. Abbott Wallis, Owner, 2245 Stonecrop Way, Golden, Colorado 80401. Phone: 800-222-3595. Fax: 303-526-0885. E-mail: info@aave.com.
URL www.aave.com

For more information, see page 952.

Adventures Cross-Country, Alaska Adventure

Adventures Cross-Country
Alaska

General Information Coed residential outdoor program, wilderness program, and adventure program established in 1983.
Program Focus Multi-activity wilderness program in Alaska.
Sports Sea kayaking.

Adventures Cross-Country, Alaska Adventure (continued)

Wilderness/Outdoors Backpacking, hiking, ice climbing, mountaineering, orienteering, rafting, white-water trips, wilderness camping.
Program Information 2 sessions per year. Session length: 40 days in June, July, August. Ages: 14–18. 8–15 participants per session. Boarding program cost: $4795. Financial aid available.
Application Deadline Continuous.
Jobs Positions for college students 21 and older.
Contact Scott von Eschen, Director, 242 Redwood Highway, Mill Valley, California 94941. Phone: 415-332-5075. Fax: 415-332-2130. E-mail: arcc@adventurescrosscountry.com.
URL www.adventurescrosscountry.com

For more information, see page 972.

Adventure Treks–Alaska Adventures

Adventure Treks, Inc.
Alaska

General Information Coed travel outdoor program, wilderness program, and adventure program established in 1978.
Program Focus Multi-activity adventure programs with a focus on fun, personal growth, leadership, outdoor skills and teamwork.
Sports Sea kayaking.
Wilderness/Outdoors Backpacking, canoe trips, hiking, ice climbing, mountaineering, orienteering, rafting, rock climbing, survival training, white-water trips, wilderness camping.
Program Information 1–2 sessions per year. Session length: 4 weeks in June, July, August. Ages: 16–18. 20–24 participants per session. Cost: $3795. Financial aid available.
Application Deadline Continuous.
Contact John Dockendorf, Director, PO Box 1321, Flat Rock, North Carolina 28731. Phone: 888-954-5555. Fax: 828-696-1663. E-mail: info@advtreks.com.
URL www.adventuretreks.com

Alpengirl–Alaska

Alpengirl, Inc.
Alaska

General Information Girls' travel outdoor program, wilderness program, and adventure program established in 1997. Accredited by American Camping Association.
Program Focus Promoting fitness and health through mountain adventure and outdoor education.
Academics Area studies, ecology, geology/earth science, health sciences, marine studies, science (general).
Special Interest Areas Field research/expeditions, nature study, weight reduction.
Sports Bicycling, canoeing, horseback riding, physical fitness, rappelling, sea kayaking, swimming.
Wilderness/Outdoors Backpacking, bicycle trips, canoe trips, hiking, mountain biking, pack animal trips, rafting, rock climbing, white-water trips, wilderness camping, wilderness/outdoors (general).
Program Information 1 session per year. Session length: 2 weeks in June, July. Ages: 14–16. 10–12 participants per session. Cost: $2030. Financial aid available.
Application Deadline Continuous.
Jobs Positions for college students 21 and older.
Contact Alissa Farley, Camp Director, PO Box 1138, Manhattan, Montana 59741. Phone: 800-585-7476. E-mail: alissa@alpengirl.com.
URL www.alpengirl.com

Camp Tawonga–Teen Service Learning to Alaska

Camp Tawonga (Tawonga Jewish Community Corp.)
Alaska

General Information Coed travel community service program, cultural program, and adventure program established in 2003. Religious affiliation: Jewish. Accredited by American Camping Association. High school credit may be earned.
Program Focus Community service in Juneau, Fairbanks and Arctic villages.
Academics Jewish studies.
Arts Arts and crafts (general), music.
Special Interest Areas Community service, conservation projects, construction, nature study.
Wilderness/Outdoors Hiking.
Program Information 1 session per year. Session length: 20 days in July. 25 participants per session. Cost: $3100. Financial aid available. Open to participants entering grades 10–12.
Application Deadline Continuous.
Jobs Positions for college students 21 and older.
Contact Nina Kaufman, Director of Teen Service Learning, 131 Steuart Street, Suite 460, San Francisco, California 94105. Phone: 415-543-2267. Fax: 415-543-5417. E-mail: nina@taworga.org.
URL www.tawonga.org

Camp Togowoods

Girl Scouts Susitna Council
Wasilla, Alaska 99654

General Information Girls' residential traditional camp, outdoor program, and arts program established in 1958. Accredited by American Camping Association.
Program Focus Three program tracks: outdoor skills, arts, wilderness travel.
Academics Biology, botany, ecology, environmental science, geography, geology/earth science, history, intercultural studies, music, peace education.
Arts Arts, arts and crafts (general), batiking, ceramics, clowning, creative writing, dance, dance (folk), drawing, fabric arts, jewelry making, music, music (vocal), painting, pottery, printmaking, puppetry, sculpture, storytelling, theater/drama, weaving, woodworking.
Special Interest Areas Native American culture, campcraft, culinary arts, gardening, general camp activities, leadership training, nature study.
Sports Bicycling, boating, canoeing, kayaking, sea kayaking, swimming.

Wilderness/Outdoors Backpacking, bicycle trips, canoe trips, hiking, mountain biking, orienteering, rafting, wilderness camping, wilderness/outdoors (general).
Trips Cultural, day, overnight.
Program Information 6–7 sessions per year. Session length: 3–12 days in June, July, August. Ages: 7–17. 80–100 participants per session. Boarding program cost: $115–$455. Financial aid available.
Application Deadline Continuous.
Jobs Positions for college students 18 and older.
Summer Contact Camp Director, HC 35, Box 5400, Wasilla, Alaska 99654. Phone: 907-376-1310. Fax: 907-376-1358. E-mail: camptogo@alaska.net.
Winter Contact Director, Camp Togowoods, 3911 Turnagain East, Anchorage, Alaska 99654. Phone: 907-248-2250. Fax: 907-243-4819.
URL www.girlscouts.ak.org

Cordova 4-H Bluegrass and Old Time Music and Dance Camp

Cordova 4-H
Cordova, Alaska 99574

General Information Coed residential and day arts program established in 1995. Formal opportunities for the academically talented and artistically talented. Specific services available for the physically challenged and visually impaired.
Program Focus Bluegrass and old-time music.
Arts Band, chorus, dance (folk), music, music (folk), music (vocal).
Special Interest Areas Nature study.
Wilderness/Outdoors Hiking.
Trips Day.
Program Information 1 session per year. Session length: 7–9 days in July. Ages: 9–18. 120 participants per session. Day program cost: $200. Financial aid available. $75 for homestay with local 4H family.
Application Deadline Continuous.
Contact Mrs. Linda Brown, 4H Camp Coordinator, Box 1053, Cordova, Alaska 99574. Phone: 907-424-3943. Fax: 907-424-3943. E-mail: cordovabluegrass@hotmail.com.
URL www.bearfootbluegrass.com

Cordova 4-H Hawaiian Camp

Cordova 4-H
Cordova, Alaska 99574

General Information Coed day arts program established in 1995. Formal opportunities for the artistically talented. Specific services available for the physically challenged and visually impaired.
Program Focus Hawaiian music, culture, and crafts.
Academics Intercultural studies.
Arts Arts and crafts (general), dance, fabric arts, music, music (vocal).
Special Interest Areas Nature study.
Sports Swimming.
Trips Day.
Program Information 1 session per year. Session length: 6 days in July. Ages: 6–8. 25 participants per session. Day program cost: $200.
Application Deadline Continuous.
Contact Ms. Linda Brown, 4H Community Coordinator, Box 1053, Cordova, Alaska 99574. Phone: 907-424-3943. Fax: 907-424-3943. E-mail: cordovabluegrass@hotmail.com.
URL www.bearfootbluegrass.com

Earthwatch Institute–Sea Otters of Alaska

Earthwatch Institute
Prince William Sound
Alaska

General Information Coed residential outdoor program and wilderness program.
Program Focus Applying modern technology to the conservation of an ever-popular but declining species.
Academics Biology, environmental science, science (general).
Special Interest Areas Field research/expeditions, nature study.
Program Information 7 sessions per year. Session length: 10 days in June, July, August. Ages: 16+. 6 participants per session. Boarding program cost: $2795–$2895. Financial aid available. Financial aid for high school students and teachers.
Application Deadline Continuous.
Contact General Information Desk, PO Box 75, Maynard, Massachusetts 01754. Phone: 800-776-0188. Fax: 978-461-2332. E-mail: info@earthwatch.org.
URL www.earthwatch.org

From the Forest to the Sea

Prince William Sound Science Center
Cordova, Alaska 99574

General Information Coed residential academic program, outdoor program, and wilderness program established in 1994.
Program Focus Environmental education, science.
Academics Astronomy, biology, botany, communications, ecology, environmental science, geology/earth science, marine studies, oceanography, science (general).
Arts Arts and crafts (general), creative writing, drawing, music, music (vocal).
Special Interest Areas Native American culture, career exploration, conservation projects, leadership training, nature study, team building.
Sports Boating, canoeing, kayaking, sea kayaking, swimming.
Wilderness/Outdoors Canoe trips, hiking, orienteering, outdoor living skills, survival training, wilderness camping.
Trips Day, overnight.
Program Information 4–6 sessions per year. Session length: 3–6 days in June, July, August. Ages: 9–18. 12 participants per session. Boarding program cost: $150–$325. Financial aid available.
Application Deadline Continuous.
Jobs Positions for college students 18 and older.
Contact Ms. Kate Alexander, Education Specialist, Box 705, Cordova, Alaska 99574. Phone: 907-424-5800 Ext. 231. Fax: 907-424-5820. E-mail: kate@pwssc.gen.ak.us.
URL www.pwssc.gen.ak.us/pwssc/educ/camp/camp.htm

Longacre Expeditions, Alaska

Longacre Expeditions
Alaska

General Information Coed travel outdoor program, wilderness program, and adventure program established in 1981. Accredited by American Camping Association.
Program Focus Effective communication skills, responsibility, confidence building.
Sports Sea kayaking.
Wilderness/Outdoors Backpacking, hiking, ice climbing, rafting, white-water trips.
Program Information 1 session per year. Session length: 24 days in July. Ages: 14–17. 10–12 participants per session. Cost: $3895.
Application Deadline Continuous.
Jobs Positions for college students 21 and older.
Contact Meredith Schuler, Director, 4030 Middle Ridge Road, Newport, Pennsylvania 17074. Phone: 717-567-6790. Fax: 717-567-3955. E-mail: longacre@longacreexpeditions.com.
URL www.longacreexpeditions.com

For more information, see page 1200.

NBC Camps–Basketball Individual Training–Alaska

NBC Camps
Alaska

General Information Coed residential sports camp.
Program Focus Well-rounded skill development.
Sports Basketball.
Program Information 2 sessions per year. Session length: 5 days in June. Ages: 9–18. Boarding program cost: $315. Financial aid available.
Application Deadline Continuous.
Jobs Positions for high school students 16 and older and college students.
Contact Ms. Bonnie Tucker, Office Manager, 10003 North Milan Road, #100, Spokane, Washington 99218. Phone: 509-466-4690. Fax: 509-467-6289. E-mail: bonnie@nbccamps.com.
URL www.nbccamps.com

NBC Camps–Basketball Speed–Alaska

NBC Camps
Alaska

General Information Coed residential sports camp.
Program Focus Developing jumping and speed skills.
Sports Basketball.
Program Information 1 session per year. Session length: 2 days in June. Ages: 13–19. Boarding program cost: $150. Financial aid available.
Application Deadline Continuous.
Jobs Positions for high school students 16 and older and college students.
Contact Ms. Bonnie Tucker, Office Manager, 10003 North Milan Road, #100, Spokane, Washington 99218. Phone: 509-466-4690. Fax: 509-467-6289. E-mail: bonnie@nbccamps.com.
URL www.nbccamps.com

NBC Camps–Basketball–Team (Boys)–Alaska

NBC Camps
Alaska

General Information Boys' residential sports camp.
Program Focus Camp for high school basketball teams.
Sports Basketball.
Program Information 1 session per year. Session length: 5 days in June. Boarding program cost: $250. Financial aid available.
Application Deadline Continuous.
Jobs Positions for high school students 16 and older and college students.
Contact Bonnie Tucker, Officer Manager, 10003 North Milan Road, #100, Spokane, Washington 99218. Phone: 509-466-4690. Fax: 509-467-6289. E-mail: bonnie@nbccamps.com.
URL www.nbccamps.com

NBC Camps–Basketball–Team (Girls)–Alaska

NBC Camps
Alaska

General Information Girls' residential sports camp.
Program Focus Camp for high school basketball teams.
Sports Basketball.
Program Information 1 session per year. Session length: 5 days in June. Boarding program cost: $250. Financial aid available.
Application Deadline Continuous.
Jobs Positions for high school students 16 and older and college students.
Contact Danny Beard, 10003 North Milan Road, #100, Spokane, Washington 99218. Phone: 509-466-4690. Fax: 509-467-6289. E-mail: danny@nbccamps.com.
URL www.nbccamps.com

NBC Camps–Volleyball–Alaska

NBC Camps
Alaska

General Information Girls' residential sports camp.
Sports Volleyball.
Program Information 1 session per year. Session length: 5 days in July. Ages: 12–18. Boarding program cost: $315. Financial aid available.
Application Deadline Continuous.
Jobs Positions for high school students 16 and older and college students.
Contact Ms. Bonnie Tucker, Office Manager, 10003 North Milan Road, #100, Spokane, Washington 99218. Phone: 509-466-4690. Fax: 509-467-6289. E-mail: bonnie@nbccamps.com.
URL www.nbccamps.com

Outward Bound West–Sea Kayaking and Mountaineering–Alaska

Outward Bound West/Outward Bound, USA
Prince William Sound and Kenai Mountains
Alaska

General Information Coed travel outdoor program and wilderness program established in 1965. College credit may be earned.
Program Focus Teamwork and leadership wilderness adventure.
Academics Environmental science, oceanography.
Special Interest Areas Campcraft, first aid, leadership training, nature study, personal development, team building.
Sports Sea kayaking.
Wilderness/Outdoors Backpacking, hiking, mountaineering, outdoor adventure, wilderness camping.
Trips Overnight.
Program Information 2 sessions per year. Session length: 22 days in June, July, August. Ages: 16+. Cost: $3495. Application fee: $95. Financial aid available.
Application Deadline Continuous.
Jobs Positions for college students 21 and older.
Contact Admissions Advisor, 910 Jackson Street, Golden, Colorado 80401. Phone: 866-746-9777. Fax: 720-497-2421. E-mail: info@obwest.org.
URL www.outwardboundwest.org

Overland: Alaskan Expedition Hiking, Sea-Kayaking, and Rafting

Overland Travel, Inc.
Alaska

General Information Coed travel outdoor program, wilderness program, and adventure program established in 1985. Accredited by American Camping Association. High school credit may be earned.
Program Focus Explore the wonders of Alaska by foot, raft and kayak.
Sports Sea kayaking.
Wilderness/Outdoors Backpacking, hiking, rafting, white-water trips, wilderness camping.
Trips Cultural, day, overnight.
Program Information 2 sessions per year. Session length: 3 weeks in June, July, August. Ages: 14–19. 8–12 participants per session. Cost: $3695.
Application Deadline Continuous.
Jobs Positions for college students 20 and older.
Contact Ms. Brooks Follansbee, Director, PO Box 31, Williamstown, Massachusetts 01267. Phone: 800-458-0588. Fax: 413-458-5208. E-mail: overland@adelphia.net.
URL www.overlandsummers.com

For more information, see page 1240.

Overland: American Community Service, Alaska

Overland Travel, Inc.
Alaska

General Information Coed travel community service program established in 1985. Accredited by American Camping Association. High school credit may be earned.
Program Focus Community service.
Special Interest Areas Native American culture, community service, conservation projects, field research/expeditions, leadership training, nature study, team building.
Sports Scuba diving, sea kayaking.
Wilderness/Outdoors Backpacking, hiking, rafting, white-water trips, wilderness camping.
Trips Cultural, day, overnight.
Program Information 2–4 sessions per year. Session length: 3 weeks in June, July, August. Ages: 15–18. 12 participants per session. Cost: $3695.
Application Deadline Continuous.
Jobs Positions for college students 20 and older.
Contact Ms. Brooks Follansbee, Director, PO Box 31, Williamstown, Massachusetts 01267. Phone: 800-458-0588. Fax: 413-458-5208. E-mail: overland@adelphia.net.
URL www.overlandsummers.com

For more information, see page 1240.

Putney Student Travel–Community Service–Alaska

Putney Student Travel
Alaska

General Information Coed residential outdoor program, community service program, and wilderness program established in 1951.
Program Focus Community service, cultural exchange, and weekend wilderness excursions from a base in a tiny, exclusively Tlingit native village.
Academics Intercultural studies.
Special Interest Areas Native American culture, community service, construction.
Sports Kayaking.
Wilderness/Outdoors Backpacking, hiking, outdoor adventure, wilderness camping, wilderness/outdoors (general).
Trips Cultural, overnight.
Program Information 2 sessions per year. Session length: 30 days in June, July. Ages: 15–18. 16 participants per session. Boarding program cost: $5100. Financial aid available.
Application Deadline Continuous.
Contact Jeffrey Shumlin, Director, 345 Hickory Ridge Road, Putney, Vermont 05346. Phone: 802-387-5000. Fax: 802-387-4276. E-mail: info@goputney.com.
URL www.goputney.com

For more information, see page 1276.

Student Conservation Association–Conservation Crew Program (Alaska)

Student Conservation Association (SCA)
Alaska

General Information Coed residential outdoor program, community service program, and wilderness program established in 1957. High school credit may be earned.
Program Focus Resource management, conservation and environmental education.
Academics Biology, botany, ecology, environmental science, geology/earth science, history.
Special Interest Areas Campcraft, community service, construction, leadership training, nature study, trail maintenance, work camp programs.
Sports Canoeing, fishing, kayaking, sea kayaking, swimming.
Wilderness/Outdoors Backpacking, canoe trips, hiking, orienteering, outdoor living skills, rock climbing, wilderness camping.
Trips Cultural, day, overnight.
Program Information 2–3 sessions per year. Session length: 3–5 weeks in June, July, August. Ages: 15–19. 6–8 participants per session. Application fee: $20. Financial aid available. No cost for program; financial aid possible for travel expenses.
Application Deadline Continuous.
Jobs Positions for college students 21 and older.
Contact Recruitment Office, PO Box 550, Charlestown, New Hampshire 03603. Phone: 603-543-1700. Fax: 603-543-1828. E-mail: getreal@thesca.org.
URL www.theSCA.org

Visions–Alaska

Visions
Alaska

General Information Coed travel outdoor program, community service program, and cultural program established in 1989. High school credit may be earned.
Program Focus Community service, cross-cultural experience, and outdoor adventure activities.
Academics Intercultural studies.
Arts Carpentry.
Special Interest Areas Native American culture, community service, construction, cross-cultural education, field research/expeditions, field trips (arts and culture), leadership training, nature study.
Wilderness/Outdoors Backpacking, hiking, ice climbing, outdoor adventure, rafting, wilderness camping.
Trips Cultural, day, overnight.
Program Information 2 sessions per year. Session length: 3–4 weeks in June, July, August. Ages: 14–18. 20–25 participants per session. Cost: $2800–$3850. Financial aid available.
Application Deadline Continuous.
Jobs Positions for college students 22 and older.
Contact Joanne Pinaire, Director, PO Box 220, Newport, Pennsylvania 17074. Phone: 717-567-7313. Fax: 717-567-7853. E-mail: info@visionsserviceadventures.com.
URL www.visionsserviceadventures.com

For more information, see page 1382.

Westcoast Connection–Community Connections Alaska

Westcoast Connection
Alaska

General Information Coed travel community service program established in 1982. Accredited by Ontario Camping Association.
Special Interest Areas Community service, touring.
Program Information 1–2 sessions per year. Session length: 3–4 weeks in July, August. Ages: 16+. 13–18 participants per session. Cost: $4699. Financial aid available.
Application Deadline Continuous.
Contact Mr. Mark Segal, Director, 154 East Boston Post Road, Mamaroneck, New York 10543. Phone: 800-767-0227. Fax: 914-835-0798. E-mail: usa@westcoastconnection.com.
URL www.westcoastconnection.com

For more information, see page 1392.

Wilderness Ventures–Alaska Leadership

Wilderness Ventures
Alaska

General Information Coed travel outdoor program, wilderness program, and adventure program established in 1973.
Program Focus Wilderness travel, wilderness skills, leadership skills.
Special Interest Areas Leadership training.
Sports Sea kayaking.
Wilderness/Outdoors Backpacking, hiking, mountaineering, rafting, white-water trips, wilderness camping.
Trips Overnight.
Program Information 1 session per year. Session length: 39 days in June, July, August. Ages: 14–18. 13 participants per session. Cost: $4890. Financial aid available.
Application Deadline Continuous.
Jobs Positions for college students 21 and older.
Contact Mike Cottingham, Director, PO Box 2768, Jackson Hole, Wyoming 83001. Phone: 800-533-2281. Fax: 307-739-1934. E-mail: info@wildernessventures.com.
URL www.wildernessventures.com

For more information, see page 1396.

Wilderness Ventures–Alaska Service

Wilderness Ventures
Alaska

General Information Coed travel outdoor program, community service program, wilderness program, and adventure program established in 1973.
Program Focus Wilderness travel, leadership skills, cultural immersion, community service.
Special Interest Areas Community service, cross-cultural education, leadership training.
Sports Sea kayaking.
Wilderness/Outdoors Backpacking, hiking, white-water trips, wilderness/outdoors (general).
Trips Cultural, overnight.
Program Information 2 sessions per year. Session length: 20 days in June, July, August. Ages: 14–18. 10 participants per session. Cost: $3890. Financial aid available.
Application Deadline Continuous.
Jobs Positions for college students 21 and older.
Contact Mike Cottingham, Director, PO Box 2768, Jackson Hole, Wyoming 83001. Phone: 800-533-2281. Fax: 307-739-1934. E-mail: info@wildernessventures.com.
URL www.wildernessventures.com

For more information, see page 1396.

Wilderness Ventures–Alaska Southcentral

Wilderness Ventures
Alaska

General Information Coed travel outdoor program, wilderness program, and adventure program established in 1973.
Program Focus Wilderness travel, wilderness skills, leadership skills.
Special Interest Areas Leadership training.
Sports Sea kayaking.
Wilderness/Outdoors Backpacking, hiking, rafting, wilderness camping.
Trips Overnight.
Program Information 3 sessions per year. Session length: 15 days in June, July, August. Ages: 14–18. 12 participants per session. Cost: $3390. Financial aid available.
Application Deadline Continuous.
Jobs Positions for college students 21 and older.
Contact Mike Cottingham, Director, PO Box 2768, Jackson Hole, Wyoming 83001. Phone: 800-533-2281. Fax: 307-739-1934. E-mail: info@wildernessventures.com.
URL www.wildernessventures.com

For more information, see page 1396.

Wilderness Ventures–Alaska Southeast

Wilderness Ventures
Alaska

General Information Coed travel outdoor program, wilderness program, and adventure program established in 1973.
Program Focus Wilderness travel, wilderness skills, leadership skills.
Special Interest Areas Leadership training.
Sports Sea kayaking.
Wilderness/Outdoors Backpacking, hiking, mountaineering, rafting.
Trips Overnight.
Program Information 2 sessions per year. Session length: 20 days in June, July, August. Ages: 14–18. 10 participants per session. Cost: $3890. Financial aid available.
Application Deadline Continuous.
Jobs Positions for college students 21 and older.
Contact Mike Cottingham, Director, PO Box 2768, Jackson Hole, Wyoming 83001. Phone: 800-533-2281. Fax: 307-739-1934. E-mail: info@wildernessventures.com.
URL www.wildernessventures.com

For more information, see page 1396.

Windsor Mountain: Alaska

Interlocken at Windsor Mountain
Alaska

General Information Coed travel outdoor program, community service program, cultural program, and adventure program established in 1967.
Program Focus Friendship exchange.
Academics Environmental science, intercultural studies, peace education.
Special Interest Areas Native American culture, community service, leadership training, nature study, team building.
Sports Sea kayaking.
Wilderness/Outdoors Backpacking, hiking, mountaineering, wilderness camping.
Program Information 1 session per year. Session length: 4 weeks in July, August. Ages: 14–17. 13 participants per session. Cost: $3695. Financial aid available.
Application Deadline Continuous.
Jobs Positions for college students 23 and older.
Contact Richard Herman, Director, 19 Interlocken Way, Windsor, New Hampshire 03244. Phone: 800-862-7760. Fax: 603-478-5260. E-mail: mail@windsormountain.org.
URL www.windsormountain.org/xrds

For more information, see page 1162.

ARIZONA

Deer Hill Expeditions, Arizona

Deer Hill Expeditions
Arizona

General Information Coed residential outdoor program, community service program, wilderness program, and cultural program established in 1984. Accredited by Association for Experiential Education. High school credit may be earned.
Program Focus In-depth wilderness adventures, cross-cultural living, and service in the Navajo and Hopi Nations.
Academics Archaeology, area studies, ecology, environmental science, geology/earth science, intercultural studies.
Arts Photography.
Special Interest Areas Native American culture, campcraft, community service, conservation projects, cross-cultural education, first aid, leadership training, nature study, trail maintenance.
Sports Canoeing, kayaking, rappelling.
Wilderness/Outdoors Backpacking, canoe trips, canyoneering, climbing, hiking, mountain biking, mountaineering, orienteering, outdoor camping, outdoor living skills, rafting, rock climbing, white-water trips, wilderness camping, wilderness/outdoors (general).
Trips Cultural, overnight.
Program Information 12–16 sessions per year. Session length: 18–35 days in June, July, August. Ages: 13–22. 12–16 participants per session. Boarding program cost: $2750–$4550. Financial aid available.
Application Deadline Continuous.
Jobs Positions for college students 21 and older.
Contact Ms. Beverly Capelin, Founder and Owner, PO Box 180, Mancos, Colorado 81328. Phone: 800-533-7221. Fax: 970-533-7221. E-mail: info@deerhillexpeditions.com.
URL www.deerhillexpeditions.com

EARTHWATCH INSTITUTE–Hopi Ancestors

Earthwatch Institute
Winslow, Arizona

General Information Coed residential outdoor program and cultural program.
Program Focus Learning about living in cities from one of the original North American civilizations.
Academics Archaeology.
Arts Photography.
Special Interest Areas Native American culture, field research/expeditions.
Program Information 3 sessions per year. Session length: 2 weeks in June, July. Ages: 16+. 12 participants per session. Boarding program cost: $1695–$1795. Financial aid available. Financial aid for high school students and teachers.
Application Deadline Continuous.
Contact General Information Desk, PO Box 75, Maynard, Massachusetts 01754. Phone: 800-776-0188. Fax: 978-461-2332. E-mail: info@earthwatch.org.
URL www.earthwatch.org

Landmark Volunteers: Arizona

Landmark Volunteers, Inc.
Arizona

General Information Coed residential outdoor program and community service program established in 1992. High school credit may be earned.
Program Focus Opportunity for high school students to earn community service credit while working as a team for two weeks serving Canyon de Chelly National Monument. Similar programs offered through Landmark Volunteers at over 60 locations in 21 states.
Academics Archaeology, geology/earth science, social science.
Special Interest Areas Native American culture, career exploration, community service, conservation projects, field research/expeditions, leadership training, team building, work camp programs.
Wilderness/Outdoors Hiking.
Trips Cultural, day.
Program Information 1 session per year. Session length: 2 weeks in June, July, August. Ages: 14–18. 10–13 participants per session. Boarding program cost: $875–$925. Financial aid available.
Application Deadline Continuous.
Jobs Positions for college students.
Contact Ann Barrett, Executive Director, PO Box 455, Sheffield, Massachusetts 01257. Phone: 413-229-0255. Fax: 413-229-2050. E-mail: landmark@volunteers.com.
URL www.volunteers.com

For more information, see page 1182.

Oak Creek Ranch Summer School

Oak Creek Ranch School
West Sedona, Arizona 86340

General Information Coed residential academic program and outdoor program established in 1972. Specific services available for the learning disabled, participant with ADD, and participant with AD/HD. High school credit may be earned.
Program Focus Summer school studies with an outdoor focus for academic underachievers and those seeking to make up credits.
Academics American literature, English as a second language, English language/literature, SAT/ACT preparation, Spanish language/literature, Web page design, academics (general), biology, chemistry, computer programming, computers, economics, geography, geology/earth science, history, mathematics, reading, science (general), social studies, study skills, writing.
Arts Photography.
Sports Archery, baseball, basketball, bicycling, climbing (wall), equestrian sports, fishing, golf, horseback riding, in-line skating, kayaking, paintball, ropes course, softball, swimming, tennis, volleyball, water polo, weight training.

Oak Creek Ranch Summer School

Wilderness/Outdoors Backpacking, bicycle trips, hiking, mountain biking, mountaineering, orienteering, outdoor adventure, pack animal trips, rock climbing, wilderness camping.
Trips College tours, cultural, day, overnight, shopping.
Program Information 3 sessions per year. Session length: 4 weeks in June, July, August. Ages: 11–19. 30–50 participants per session. Boarding program cost: $3950.
Application Deadline Continuous.
Contact Allan Popsack, Director of Admissions, PO Box 4329, West Sedona, Arizona 86340. Phone: 928-634-5571. Fax: 928-634-4915. E-mail: admissions@ocrs.com.
URL www.ocrs.com

For more information, see page 1230.

St. Paul's Preparatory Academy Summer Program

St. Paul's Preparatory Academy
2645 East Osborn Road
Phoenix, Arizona 85016

General Information Boys' residential and day academic program established in 1994. Religious affiliation: Episcopal. Specific services available for the participant with ADD, participant with AD/HD, and youth at risk. High school credit may be earned.
Academics American literature, SAT/ACT preparation, Spanish language/literature, academics (general), art history/appreciation, classical languages/literatures, computers, economics, government and politics, mathematics, writing.
Arts Creative writing, film.
Special Interest Areas Leadership training, nature study.
Sports Baseball, basketball, golf, soccer, swimming.
Wilderness/Outdoors Backpacking, hiking, rock climbing.
Trips Cultural, day, overnight.
Program Information 2 sessions per year. Session length: 25 days in June, July. Ages: 13–17. 3–8 participants per session. Day program cost: $1350–$2700. Boarding program cost: $4100–$8200. Application fee: $50.
Application Deadline Continuous.
Contact Julie Vaughan, Director of Admission, PO Box 32650, Phoenix, Arizona 85064-2650. Phone: 602-956-9090. Fax: 602-956-3018. E-mail: admissions@stpaulsacademy.com.
URL www.stpaulsacademy.com

Southwestern Adventures

Southwestern Academy
Beaver Creek Ranch Campus
Rimrock, Arizona 86335

General Information Coed residential and day traditional camp, academic program, and outdoor program established in 1964. High school credit may be earned.

Southwestern Adventures

Program Focus Academic enrichment and outdoor environmental education, college prep credit classes.
Academics English as a second language, English language/literature, SAT/ACT preparation, Spanish language/literature, academics (general), anthropology, archaeology, area studies, astronomy, biology, botany, chemistry, computers, ecology, environmental science, geology/earth science, government and politics, history, mathematics, physics, physiology, reading, science (general), social science, social studies, study skills, typing, writing.
Arts Arts and crafts (general), ceramics, creative writing, drawing, fabric arts, music, music (instrumental), painting, pottery, printmaking, sculpture.
Special Interest Areas Native American culture, career exploration, community service, conservation projects, nature study.
Sports Baseball, basketball, bicycling, bicycling (BMX), cross-country, fishing, golf, horseback riding, soccer, softball, swimming, volleyball, weight training.
Wilderness/Outdoors Backpacking, hiking, mountain biking, wilderness camping.
Trips College tours, cultural, day, overnight, shopping.
Program Information 3–12 sessions per year. Session length: 14–40 days in June, July, August. Ages: 11–18. 20–30 participants per session. Day program cost: $600–$2400. Boarding program cost: $4000–$6000. Application fee: $100. Financial aid available.
Application Deadline Continuous.

Southwestern Adventures (continued)

Jobs Positions for college students 19 and older.
Contact Mrs. Jane Whitmire, Director of Admissions, Beaver Creek Ranch Campus, HC 64 Box 235, Rimrock, Arizona 86335. Phone: 928-567-4472. Fax: 928-567-5036. E-mail: admissions@southwesternacademy.edu.
URL www.southwesternacademy.edu

For more information, see page 1324.

Student Conservation Association–Conservation Crew Program (Arizona)

Student Conservation Association (SCA)
Arizona

General Information Coed residential outdoor program, community service program, and wilderness program established in 1957. High school credit may be earned.
Program Focus Resource management, conservation and environmental education.
Academics Biology (Advanced Placement), botany, ecology, environmental science, geology/earth science, history.
Special Interest Areas Campcraft, community service, construction, leadership training, nature study, trail maintenance, work camp programs.
Sports Canoeing, fishing, kayaking, swimming.
Wilderness/Outdoors Backpacking, canoe trips, hiking, orienteering, outdoor living skills, rock climbing, wilderness camping.
Trips Cultural, day, overnight.
Program Information 2–3 sessions per year. Session length: 3–5 weeks in June, July, August. Ages: 15–19. 6–8 participants per session. Application fee: $20. Financial aid available. No cost for program; financial aid possible for travel expenses.
Application Deadline Continuous.
Jobs Positions for college students 21 and older.
Contact Recruitment Office, PO Box 550, Charlestown, New Hampshire 03603. Phone: 603-543-1700. Fax: 603-543-1828. E-mail: getreal@thesca.org.
URL www.theSCA.org

Ventures Travel Service–Arizona

Friendship Ventures
Arizona

General Information Coed travel special needs program established in 1985. Specific services available for the developmentally challenged and physically challenged.
Program Focus Provides travel services to older teens and adults with developmental disabilities.
Special Interest Areas Touring.
Program Information 50 sessions per year. Session length: 4–10 days in February, March, April, May, June, July, August, September, October, November, December. Ages: 14–70. 4–8 participants per session. Cost: $395–$2000.
Application Deadline Continuous.
Jobs Positions for college students 18 and older.
Contact Georgann Rumsey, President/CEO, 10509 108th Street, NW, Annandale, Minnesota 55302. Phone: 952-852-0101. Fax: 952-852-0123. E-mail: fv@friendshipventures.org.
URL www.friendshipventures.org

ARKANSAS

Camp Aldersgate–Kota Camp

Camp Aldersgate
2000 Aldersgate Road
Little Rock, Arkansas 72205

General Information Coed residential special needs program established in 2001. Accredited by American Camping Association. Specific services available for the developmentally challenged, hearing impaired, learning disabled, physically challenged, visually impaired, diabetic, participant with cancer, participant with asthma, epileptic, participant with kidney disorders, participant with Cerebral Palsy, and participant with Muscular Dystrophy.
Program Focus For children with medical, physical, and/or developmental challenges and their brothers, sisters and/or friends.
Arts Arts and crafts (general), clowning, music.
Special Interest Areas Native American culture, campcraft, community service, leadership training, nature study, team building.
Sports Archery, basketball, boating, canoeing, fishing, horseback riding, ropes course, scuba diving, soccer, softball, sports (general), swimming.
Wilderness/Outdoors Hiking.
Program Information 8–9 sessions per year. Session length: 6 days in April, June, July, August, October. Ages: 6–18. 35–50 participants per session. Boarding program cost: $25–$350. Financial aid available.
Application Deadline Continuous.
Jobs Positions for high school students 16 and older and college students 18 and older.
Contact Bill Faggard, Director of Programs, main address above. Phone: 501-225-1444. Fax: 501-225-2019. E-mail: info@campaldersgate.net.
URL www.campaldersgate.net

Camp Aldersgate–Med Camps

Camp Aldersgate
2000 Aldersgate Road
Little Rock, Arkansas 72205

General Information Coed residential special needs program established in 1971. Accredited by American Camping Association. Specific services available for the developmentally challenged, hearing impaired, learning disabled, physically challenged, visually impaired, diabetic, participant with heart defects, participant with cancer, participant with asthma, epileptic, participant

with kidney disorders, participant with Cerebral Palsy, participant with Muscular Dystrophy, and participant with hemophilia.
Program Focus For children with medical, physical, and/or developmental challenges.
Arts Arts and crafts (general), clowning, music.
Special Interest Areas Native American culture, campcraft, community service, leadership training, nature study, team building.
Sports Archery, basketball, boating, canoeing, fishing, horseback riding, ropes course, scuba diving, soccer, softball, sports (general), swimming.
Wilderness/Outdoors Hiking.
Program Information 8–9 sessions per year. Session length: 6 days in June, July, August. Ages: 6–18. 35–50 participants per session. Boarding program cost: $450. Financial aid available.
Application Deadline Continuous.
Jobs Positions for high school students 16 and older and college students 18 and older.
Contact Bill Faggard, Director of Programs, main address above. Phone: 501-225-1444. Fax: 501-225-2019. E-mail: info@campaldersgate.net.
URL www.campaldersgate.net

Camp Aldersgate–Respite Care

Camp Aldersgate
2000 Aldersgate Road
Little Rock, Arkansas 72205

General Information Coed residential and day special needs program. Accredited by American Camping Association. Specific services available for the developmentally challenged, hearing impaired, learning disabled, physically challenged, visually impaired, diabetic, participant with cancer, participant with asthma, epileptic, participant with kidney disorders, participant with Cerebral Palsy, and participant with Muscular Dystrophy.
Program Focus Weekend camps for children with disabilities and their families.
Arts Arts and crafts (general), music.
Special Interest Areas Native American culture, campcraft, community service, leadership training, nature study.
Sports Archery, basketball, boating, canoeing, fishing, horseback riding, ropes course, scuba diving, soccer, softball, sports (general), swimming.
Wilderness/Outdoors Hiking.
Program Information 25 sessions per year. Session length: 3 days in January, February, March, April, May, June, July, August, September, October, November, December. Ages: 6–18. 35–50 participants per session. Boarding program cost: $15–$120. Financial aid available.
Application Deadline Continuous.
Jobs Positions for high school students 16 and older and college students 18 and older.
Contact Bill Faggard, Director of Programs, main address above. Phone: 501-225-1444. Fax: 501-225-2019. E-mail: info@campaldersgate.net.
URL www.campaldersgate.net

Student Conservation Association–Conservation Crew Program (Arkansas)

Student Conservation Association (SCA)
Arkansas

General Information Coed residential outdoor program, community service program, and wilderness program established in 1957. High school credit may be earned.
Program Focus Resource management, conservation and environmental education.
Academics Biology (Advanced Placement), botany, ecology, environmental science, geology/earth science, history.
Special Interest Areas Campcraft, community service, construction, leadership training, nature study, trail maintenance, work camp programs.
Sports Canoeing, fishing, kayaking, swimming.
Wilderness/Outdoors Backpacking, canoe trips, hiking, orienteering, outdoor living skills, rock climbing, wilderness camping.
Trips Cultural, day, overnight.
Program Information 2–3 sessions per year. Session length: 3–5 weeks in June, July, August. Ages: 15–19. 6–8 participants per session. Application fee: $20. Financial aid available. No cost for program; financial aid possible for travel expenses.
Application Deadline Continuous.
Jobs Positions for college students 21 and older.
Contact Recruitment Office, PO Box 550, Charlestown, New Hampshire 03603. Phone: 603-543-1700. Fax: 603-543-1828. E-mail: getreal@thesca.org.
URL www.theSCA.org

CALIFORNIA

Ability First–Camp Joan Mier

Ability First
1677 Pacific Coast Highway
Malibu, California 90265

General Information Coed residential special needs program established in 1961. Accredited by American Camping Association. Specific services available for the emotionally challenged, developmentally challenged, hearing impaired, learning disabled, physically challenged, and visually impaired.
Arts Arts and crafts (general), dance.
Sports Horseback riding, swimming.
Wilderness/Outdoors Hiking.
Program Information 6 sessions per year. Session length: 7–8 days in January, February, March, April, June, July, August, November, December. Ages: 7+. 50–55 participants per session. Boarding program cost: $1015–$1160. Financial aid available.
Application Deadline Continuous.
Jobs Positions for college students 18 and older.

Ability First–Camp Joan Mier (continued)

Contact Ms. Brenda Starkins, Social Services Coordinator, 1300 East Green Street, Pasadena, California 91106. Phone: 626-396-1010 Ext.324. Fax: 626-396-1021. E-mail: bstarkins@abilityfirst.org.
URL www.abilityfirst.org/camp_joanmier.htm

Ability First–Camp Paivika

Ability First
600 Playground Drive
Crestline, California 92325

General Information Coed residential special needs program established in 1946. Accredited by American Camping Association. Specific services available for the emotionally challenged, developmentally challenged, hearing impaired, learning disabled, physically challenged, and visually impaired.
Arts Arts and crafts (general), dance.
Sports Horseback riding, swimming.
Wilderness/Outdoors Hiking.
Program Information 6 sessions per year. Session length: 7–8 days in January, February, March, April, June, July, August, November, December. Ages: 7+. 50–55 participants per session. Boarding program cost: $1015–$1160. Financial aid available.
Application Deadline Continuous.
Jobs Positions for college students 18 and older.
Contact Ms. Brenda Starkins, Social Services Coordinator, 1300 East Green Street, Pasadena, California 91106. Phone: 626-396-1010 Ext.324. Fax: 626-396-1021. E-mail: bstarkins@abilityfirst.org.
URL www.abilityfirst.org/camp_paivika.htm

Academic Study Associates–ASA at the University of California, Berkeley

Academic Study Associates, Inc. (ASA)
University of California, Berkeley
Berkeley, California

General Information Coed residential and day academic program established in 2001. Formal opportunities for the academically talented and artistically talented. High school or college credit may be earned.
Program Focus Academic enrichment, college credit, SAT preparation, ESL, TOEFL, and professional sports instruction.
Academics American literature, English as a second language, English language/literature, SAT/ACT preparation, TOEFL/TOEIC preparation, academics (general), anthropology, art (Advanced Placement), art history/appreciation, biology, business, chemistry, computer programming, computers, economics, government and politics, history, humanities, intercultural studies, journalism, mathematics, mathematics (Advanced Placement), music (Advanced Placement), philosophy, physics, precollege program, psychology, social science, social studies, speech/debate, writing.
Arts Arts and crafts (general), creative writing, dance, dance (folk), dance (jazz), dance (modern), drawing, film, graphic arts, painting, photography, theater/drama.

Academic Study Associates–ASA at the University of California, Berkeley

Special Interest Areas Field trips (arts and culture).
Sports Aerobics, basketball, soccer, tennis, volleyball, weight training.
Trips College tours, cultural, day, overnight, shopping.
Program Information 1 session per year. Session length: 6 weeks in July, August. Ages: 16–18. 60–75 participants per session. Boarding program cost: $5995–$6995. Financial aid available.
Application Deadline Continuous.
Jobs Positions for college students 21 and older.
Contact Marcia Evans, President, 10 New King Street, White Plains, New York 10604. Phone: 914-686-7730. Fax: 914-686-7740. E-mail: summer@asaprograms.com.
URL www.asaprograms.com

For more information, see page 956.

Academy by the Sea

The Academy by the Sea/Camp Pacific
2605 Carlsbad Boulevard
Carlsbad, California 92008

General Information Coed residential and day academic program established in 1943. Accredited by American Camping Association. Formal opportunities for the academically talented. High school credit may be earned.
Program Focus Afternoon water sports, camp activities, weekend excursions, academic enrichment, and credit.
Academics American literature, English as a second language, English language/literature, Spanish language/literature, academics (general), art history/appreciation, biology, communications, computers, history, journalism, marine studies, mathematics,

Academy by the Sea

mathematics (Advanced Placement), music, oceanography, precollege program, reading, science (general), social science, social studies, speech/debate, study skills, typing, writing.
Arts Arts and crafts (general), creative writing, dance (folk), drawing, jewelry making, leather working, music, musical productions, painting, photography, pottery, printmaking, radio broadcasting, theater/drama.
Special Interest Areas Campcraft, leadership training.
Sports Baseball, basketball, body boarding, field hockey, football, kayaking, lacrosse, paintball, riflery, scuba diving, sea kayaking, snorkeling, soccer, softball, surfing, swimming, tennis, volleyball, water polo, weight training.
Trips Cultural, day, overnight, shopping.
Program Information 1 session per year. Session length: 5 weeks in July, August. Ages: 11–17. 120–160 participants per session. Day program cost: $600–$2400. Boarding program cost: $3600–$4400. Application fee: $200.
Application Deadline Continuous.
Jobs Positions for college students 21 and older.
Contact Ms. Lori Adlfinger, Associate Director, PO Box 3000, Carlsbad, California 92018-3000. Phone: 760-434-7564. Fax: 760-729-1574. E-mail: info@abts.com.
URL www.abts.com
For more information, see page 958.

Acting Academy at Pali Overnight Adventures

Pali Overnight Adventures
30778 Highway 18
Running Springs, California 92382

General Information Coed residential traditional camp and arts program established in 1990. Accredited by American Camping Association. Formal opportunities for the artistically talented.
Program Focus Performing arts.
Academics Journalism.
Arts Acting, arts and crafts (general), batiking, ceramics, dance, dance (ballet), dance (jazz), dance (modern), film, film production, painting, pottery, theater/drama.
Special Interest Areas Animal care, leadership training, nature study, yearbook production.
Sports Aerobics, archery, basketball, boating, canoeing, climbing (wall), equestrian sports, fencing, field hockey, fishing, football, go-carts, horseback riding, kayaking, lacrosse, martial arts, paintball, rappelling, riflery, ropes course, scuba diving, skateboarding, snorkeling, soccer, softball, swimming, volleyball, waterskiing.
Wilderness/Outdoors Hiking, rafting, rock climbing, survival training, white-water trips.
Trips Day, overnight.
Program Information 5–8 sessions per year. Session length: 1–3 weeks in June, July, August. Ages: 9–16. 8–80 participants per session. Boarding program cost: $1385–$2695.
Application Deadline Continuous.
Jobs Positions for college students 19 and older.
Contact Mr. Andy Wexler, Owner/Founder, PO Box 2237, Running Springs, California 92382. Phone: 909-867-5743. Fax: 909-867-7643. E-mail: info@paliadventures.com.
URL www.paliadventures.com/acting.swf

The Actor's Workshop by Education Unlimited

Education Unlimited
University of California, Berkeley
Berkeley, California 94709

General Information Coed residential and day arts program established in 1997. Formal opportunities for the artistically talented.
Program Focus Acting technique seminar with emphasis on voice, movement, and characters.
Arts Acting, mime, theater/drama.
Sports Basketball, volleyball.
Wilderness/Outdoors Hiking.
Trips Cultural, day.

The Actor's Workshop by Education Unlimited (continued)

The Actor's Workshop by Education Unlimited

Program Information 3 sessions per year. Session length: 13–23 days in July, August. Ages: 10–18. 20–40 participants per session. Boarding program cost: $1796–$2950. Financial aid available.
Application Deadline Continuous.
Jobs Positions for college students 21 and older.
Contact Mr. Andy Spear, Program Director, 1700 Shattuck Avenue, #305, Berkeley, California 94709. Phone: 800-548-6612. Fax: 510-548-0212. E-mail: camps@educationunlimited.com.
URL www.educationunlimited.com
For more information, see page 1096.

ADVENTURE TREKS–CALIFORNIA 19 ADVENTURES

Adventure Treks, Inc.
California

General Information Coed travel outdoor program, wilderness program, and adventure program established in 1978.
Program Focus Multi-activity outdoor adventure with focus on fun, personal growth, teamwork, leadership, building self-confidence, outdoor skills, and community living.
Sports Sea kayaking, swimming.
Wilderness/Outdoors Backpacking, mountain biking, orienteering, rafting, rock climbing, white-water trips, wilderness camping.
Program Information 1–2 sessions per year. Session length: 19 days in June, July, August. Ages: 13–15. 24 participants per session. Cost: $2495. Financial aid available.
Application Deadline Continuous.
Contact John Dockendorf, Director, PO Box 1321, Flat Rock, North Carolina 28731. Phone: 888-954-5555. Fax: 828-696-1663. E-mail: info@advtreks.com.
URL www.adventuretreks.com

AMERICAN ACADEMY OF DRAMATIC ARTS SUMMER PROGRAM AT HOLLYWOOD, CALIFORNIA

American Academy of Dramatic Arts
1336 North LaBrea Avenue
Hollywood, California 90028

General Information Coed day arts program established in 1974. Formal opportunities for the artistically talented.
Program Focus Acting.
Arts Acting, dance, mime, music (vocal), musical productions, stage movement, television/video, theater/drama, vocal production.
Program Information 1 session per year. Session length: 24–30 days in July, August. Ages: 14+. 100–170 participants per session. Day program cost: $1900–$2000. Application fee: $50. Each elective costs $90; admission by audition only.
Application Deadline Continuous.
Contact Dan Justin, Director of Admissions, main address above. Phone: 800-222-2867.
URL www.aada.org
For more information, see page 980.

AMERICAN LEGAL EXPERIENCE BY EDUCATION UNLIMITED–BERKELEY, CA

Education Unlimited
University of California, Berkeley
Berkeley, California

General Information Coed residential and day academic program established in 1997.
Program Focus The American judicial system.
Academics Government and politics, law, speech/debate, writing.
Special Interest Areas Communication skills.
Trips Day.
Program Information 2 sessions per year. Session length: 1 week in June, July. Ages: 14–18. 30–60 participants per session. Boarding program cost: $938. Financial aid available. Open to participants entering grades 9–12.
Application Deadline Continuous.
Contact Director, American Legal Experience, 1700 Shattuck Avenue, #305, Berkeley, California 94709. Phone: 800-548-6612. Fax: 510-548-0212. E-mail: camps@educationunlimited.com.
URL www.educationunlimited.com

AMERICAN LEGAL EXPERIENCE BY EDUCATION UNLIMITED–STANFORD, CA

Education Unlimited
Stanford University
Stanford, California

General Information Coed residential and day academic program established in 1997.
Program Focus The American judicial system.
Academics Government and politics, law, speech/debate.

Special Interest Areas Communication skills.
Trips Day.
Program Information 2 sessions per year. Session length: 1 week in June. Ages: 12+. 30–60 participants per session. Boarding program cost: $1028. Financial aid available. Open to participants entering grades 9–12.
Application Deadline Continuous.
Contact Director, American Legal Experience, 1700 Shattuck Avenue, #305, Berkeley, California 94709. Phone: 800-548-6612. Fax: 510-548-0212. E-mail: camps@educationunlimited.com.
URL www.educationunlimited.com

Arrowsmith Academy Arts and Academics

Arrowsmith Academy
2300 Bancroft Way
Berkeley, California 94704

General Information Coed day academic program and arts program established in 1998. Formal opportunities for the artistically talented. High school credit may be earned.
Academics English as a second language, English language/literature, SAT/ACT preparation, Spanish language/literature, art, biology, mathematics.
Arts Arts, arts and crafts (general), painting, television/video.
Special Interest Areas Driver's education.
Program Information 1 session per year. Session length: 3–6 weeks in June, July. Ages: 13–18. Day program cost: $400–$700.
Application Deadline Continuous.
Contact Mr. William Fletcher, Headmaster, main address above. Phone: 510-540-0440. Fax: 510-540-0541.
URL www.arrowsmith.org

Art Center College of Design Art Center for Kids

Art Center College of Design
Pasadena, California

General Information Coed day arts program established in 2000. Formal opportunities for the artistically talented.
Program Focus Innovation, creativity, visual literacy.
Academics Web page design, architecture.
Arts Arts, arts and crafts (general), design, drawing, film, graphic arts, painting, photography, printmaking, television/video.
Special Interest Areas Problem solving, robotics.
Trips College tours.
Program Information 6 sessions per year. Session length: 5 days in February, March, April, June, July, August, September, October, November, December. Ages: 9–14. 300–400 participants per session. Day program cost: $175. Financial aid available.
Application Deadline Continuous.
Contact Alegria Castro, Program Coordinator, 1700 Lida Street, Pasadena, California 91103. Phone: 626-396-2319. Fax: 626-796-9564. E-mail: kids@artcenter.edu.
URL www.artcenter.edu/kids

Bar 717 Ranch/Camp Trinity

Bar 717 Ranch/Camp Trinity
Hayfork, California 96041

General Information Coed residential traditional camp established in 1930. Accredited by American Camping Association.
Program Focus Mountain ranch living with farming, ranching, and noncompetitive recreational activities chosen by participants.
Academics Area studies, botany, ecology.
Arts Arts and crafts (general), ceramics, dance, jewelry making, leather working, metalworking, photography, pottery, theater/drama, woodworking.
Special Interest Areas Animal care, campcraft, farming, gardening, leadership training, nature study.
Sports Archery, fishing, horseback riding, ropes course, swimming.
Wilderness/Outdoors Backpacking, hiking, pack animal trips, wilderness camping.
Program Information 4 sessions per year. Session length: 2–4 weeks in July, August. Ages: 8–16. 120 participants per session. Day program cost: $117–$122. Boarding program cost: $1700–$3300. Financial aid available.
Application Deadline Continuous.
Jobs Positions for high school students 17 and older and college students 18 and older.
Contact Laura Higley, Assistant Director, Star Route Box 150, Hayfork, California 96041. Phone: 530-628-5992. Fax: 530-628-9392. E-mail: camptrinity@bar717.com.
URL www.bar717.com

Battlebot Mania at Pali Overnight Adventures

Pali Overnight Adventures
30778 Highway 18
Running Springs, California 92382

General Information Coed residential traditional camp and arts program. Accredited by American Camping Association.
Program Focus Battlebot participants design, build, and compete in a series of events.
Special Interest Areas Robotics.
Program Information 5–8 sessions per year. Session length: 1–3 weeks in June, July, August. Ages: 12–16. 8–80 participants per session. Boarding program cost: $1385–$2695.
Application Deadline Continuous.
Jobs Positions for college students 19 and older.
Contact Andy Wexler, Owner/Founder, PO Box 2237, Running Springs, California 92382. Phone: 909-867-5743. Fax: 909-867-7643. E-mail: info@paliadventures.com.
URL www.paliadventures.com/battlebot.html

Bay Area Shakespeare Camp

The San Francisco Shakespeare Festival
San Francisco, California

General Information Coed day arts program established in 1994.
Program Focus Performing Shakespeare's works.
Arts Acting, costume design, set design, theater/drama.
Program Information 28 sessions per year. Session length: 10 days in June, July, August. Ages: 7–18. 40 participants per session. Day program cost: $365–$490. Financial aid available.
Application Deadline Continuous.
Jobs Positions for college students.
Contact Mr. John Western, Marketing Director, PO Box 460937, San Francisco, California 94146. Phone: 415-422-2222. Fax: 415-626-1138. E-mail: sfshakes@sfshakes.org.
URL www.sfshakes.org

Berklee in L.A. Summer Performance Program

Berklee College of Music
Fullerton, California 92832-2095

General Information Coed residential and day arts program. Formal opportunities for the artistically talented.
Program Focus Music performance.
Academics Music, precollege program.
Arts Band, chorus, music, music (ensemble), music (instrumental), music (jazz), music (vocal), musical performance/recitals.
Program Information 1 session per year. Session length: 1 week in August. Ages: 15+. 212 participants per session. Day program cost: $825. Boarding program cost: $1250. Application fee: $25. Financial aid available.
Application Deadline June 15.
Contact Office of Special Programs, 1140 Boylston Street, Boston, Massachusetts 02215. Phone: 617-747-2245. Fax: 617-262-5419. E-mail: summer@berklee.edu.
URL www.berklee.edu/summer/la.html

Brighton College Admissions Prep at UCLA

Brighton
University of California, Los Angeles
Los Angeles, California

General Information Coed residential academic program established in 2003. Formal opportunities for the academically talented.
Program Focus College admissions prep.
Academics SAT/ACT preparation, college tours, writing.
Special Interest Areas College planning.
Trips College tours.
Program Information 2 sessions per year. Session length: 9 days in June, August. Ages: 15–19. 20–30 participants per session. Boarding program cost: $2295.
Application Deadline Continuous.
Jobs Positions for college students 21 and older.
Contact David Allen, Executive Director, 101 East Green Street, Suite 14, Pasadena, California 91105. Phone: 626-795-2985. Fax: 626-795-5564. E-mail: info@brightonedge.org.
URL www.brightonedge.org
For more information, see page 1004.

Britannia Soccer Camp

Ojai Valley School
723 El Paseo Road
Ojai, California 93023

General Information Coed residential and day sports camp established in 1981.
Program Focus Soccer.
Sports Soccer.
Program Information 1 session per year. Session length: 6 days in August. Ages: 5–15. 100–130 participants per session. Day program cost: $390. Boarding program cost: $495–$555. Application fee: $50. Financial aid available.
Application Deadline Continuous.
Jobs Positions for college students.
Contact Mike Hall-Mounsey, Director, main address above. Phone: 805-646-1423. Fax: 805-646-0362. E-mail: mhm@ovs.org.
URL www.ovs.org

California Campus Tours

California Campus Tours
California

General Information Coed travel academic program and adventure program established in 2001.
Program Focus University tours.
Academics SAT/ACT preparation, college tours, precollege program.
Special Interest Areas College planning, touring.
Wilderness/Outdoors Hiking, white-water trips.
Trips College tours, day.
Program Information 1–3 sessions per year. Session length: 10–17 days in June, July, August. Ages: 15–24. 2–80 participants per session. Cost: $1060–$3200. Application fee: $100. Financial aid available.
Application Deadline May 31.
Contact Ms. Nichelle Rodriguez, Director, 305 North 2nd Avenue, #118, Upland, California 91786. Phone: 909-982-8059. Fax: 909-982-5328. E-mail: educationsvc@msn.com.
URL www.californiacampustours.com

California College of the Arts Pre-College Program

California College of the Arts
5212 Broadway
Oakland, California 94618

General Information Coed residential and day arts program established in 1986. Specific services available for the physically challenged. College credit may be earned.

Academics Architecture, art (Advanced Placement), precollege program.
Arts Arts, ceramics, design, drawing, fashion design/ production, graphic arts, painting, photography, pottery, printmaking, sculpture, television/video.
Trips Cultural.
Program Information 1 session per year. Session length: 20 days in July. Ages: 16–18. 200 participants per session. Day program cost: $1800. Boarding program cost: $1800–$2450. Financial aid available.
Application Deadline Continuous.
Contact Kate Wees, Director of Undergraduate Admissions, 1111 Eighth Street, San Francisco, California 94107. Phone: 415-703-9523. Fax: 415-703-9539. E-mail: enroll@cca.edu.
URL www.cca.edu

California Cruzin' Overnight Camp

KidsMakeADifference.org
California

General Information Coed travel traditional camp and outdoor program established in 1994.
Program Focus California laid back beach enjoyment.
Academics Botany, ecology, environmental science, geology/earth science, journalism, music, peace education, writing.
Arts Drawing, music, music (vocal), photography, television/video.
Special Interest Areas Native American culture, campcraft, culinary arts, team building, touring.
Sports Frisbee, miniature golf, swimming.
Wilderness/Outdoors Hiking.
Trips Day, overnight, shopping.
Program Information 1 session per year. Session length: 5 days in July, August. Ages: 7–13. 8 participants per session. Cost: $595. Financial aid available.
Application Deadline Continuous.
Jobs Positions for college students 18 and older.
Contact Dr. Andy Mars, Director, PO Box 24922, West Los Angeles, California 90024-0922. Phone: 818-344-7838.
URL www.kidsmakeadifference.org

California National Debate Institute

Education Unlimited
University of California, Berkeley
Berkeley, California

General Information Coed residential and day academic program established in 1992.
Program Focus Competitive debate.
Academics Communications, economics, government and politics, intercultural studies, linguistics, philosophy, social science, speech/debate, writing.
Program Information 2–3 sessions per year. Session length: 1–3 weeks in June, July. Ages: 13–18. 10–80 participants per session. Day program cost: $500–$825. Boarding program cost: $905–$2425. Financial aid available.
Application Deadline Continuous.
Contact Mr. Robert Thomas, Director, 1700 Shattuck Avenue, #305, Berkeley, California 94709. Phone: 510-548-4800. Fax: 510-548-0212. E-mail: debate@educationunlimited.com.
URL www.educationunlimited.com

For more information, see page 1100.

California State Summer School for the Arts/Inner Spark

California State Summer School for the Arts/Inner Spark
24700 McBean Parkway
Valencia, California 91355

General Information Coed residential arts program established in 1987. Formal opportunities for the artistically talented. College credit may be earned.

California State Summer School for the Arts/Inner Spark

Arts Animation, arts, batiking, ceramics, chorus, clowning, creative writing, dance, dance (ballet), dance (folk), dance (jazz), dance (modern), dance (tap), drawing, fabric arts, film, graphic arts, jewelry making, leather working, metalworking, mime, music, music (chamber), music (classical), music (electronic/synthesized), music (ensemble), music (instrumental), music (jazz), music (vocal), music composition/arrangement, painting, photography, pottery, printmaking, puppetry, radio broadcasting, sculpture, television/video, theater/drama, weaving, woodworking.
Special Interest Areas Career exploration, computer graphics.
Sports Baseball, basketball, soccer, softball, swimming, tennis, volleyball.
Trips Cultural.
Program Information 1 session per year. Session length: 4 weeks in July, August. Ages: 14–18. 470–500 participants per session. Boarding program cost: $2185–$4000. Application fee: $20. Financial aid available.
Application Deadline February 28.
Jobs Positions for college students.
Summer Contact Cynthia Bextine, Office Technician, 1010 Hurley, Suite 185, Sacramento, California 95825. Phone: 916-227-9320. Fax: 916-227-9455. E-mail: cynthia@csssa.org.

California State Summer School for the Arts/Inner Spark (continued)

Winter Contact Cynthia Bextine, Office Technician, PO Box 1077, Sacramento, California 95812-1077. Phone: 916-227-9320. Fax: 916-227-9455. E-mail: cynthia@csssa.org.
URL www.innerspark.us
For more information, see page 1018.

Cal Poly State University Young Scholars—Find the College for You!

California Polytechnic State University, San Luis Obispo
San Luis Obispo, California 93405

General Information Coed day family program established in 1986. Formal opportunities for the academically talented and artistically talented.
Program Focus Help students select colleges based on their interests, abilities, finances, and other needs.
Academics Precollege program.
Special Interest Areas Career exploration, college planning, community service.
Program Information 2–4 sessions per year. Session length: 3–4 days in February, March, April, May, June, August, September, October, November. Ages: 14+. 3–9 participants per session. Day program cost: $70–$90. Financial aid available.
Application Deadline Continuous.
Contact Carroll Busselon, Director, 807 Skyline Drive, San Luis Obispo, California 93405. Phone: 805-544-6777.

Cal Poly State University Young Scholars Prepare for the PSAT & SAT I

California Polytechnic State University, San Luis Obispo
San Luis Obispo, California 93407

General Information Coed day academic program established in 1986. Formal opportunities for the academically talented, artistically talented, and gifted.
Program Focus Prepare students to do their best on the PSAT and SAT I; groom high achievers for competition for National Merit Scholarships.
Academics SAT/ACT preparation, mathematics, precollege program, reading, study skills, tutoring, vocabulary, writing.
Program Information 7–10 sessions per year. Session length: 2–5 days in January, February, March, April, May, June, August, September, October, November. Ages: 13–18. 15–40 participants per session. Day program cost: $80–$165.
Application Deadline Continuous.
Contact Carroll Busselen, Director, 807 Skyline Drive, San Luis Obispo, California 93405. Phone: 805-544-6777.
URL www.calpoly.edu/

Camp Exploration Travel Day Camp

KidsMakeADifference.org
California

General Information Coed day traditional camp and outdoor program established in 1994.
Program Focus Day trips for hiking, amusement park, beaches, museums.
Academics Ecology, environmental science, geology/earth science, journalism, music, peace education, writing.
Arts Arts and crafts (general), drawing, music, music (vocal), painting, photography, television/video, woodworking.
Special Interest Areas Native American culture, animal care, community service, conservation projects, field trips (arts and culture), nature study, team building, touring.
Sports Baseball, bicycling, boating, climbing (wall), croquet, frisbee, in-line skating, miniature golf, soccer, swimming, table tennis/ping-pong, tennis, volleyball.
Wilderness/Outdoors Hiking.
Trips Cultural, day.
Program Information 10 sessions per year. Session length: 5 days in January, March, April, June, July, August, December. Ages: 6–13. 12 participants per session. Day program cost: $300. Financial aid available.
Application Deadline Continuous.
Jobs Positions for college students 18 and older.
Contact Dr. Andy Mars, Director, PO Box 24922, West Los Angeles, California 90024-0922. Phone: 818-344-7838.
URL www.kidsmakeadifference.org

Camp Heartland Summer Camp—California

Camp Heartland
Malibu, California

General Information Coed residential traditional camp and special needs program established in 1993. Specific services available for the participant with HIV/AIDS.
Program Focus Traditional camp for kids living with or affected by HIV/AIDS.
Arts Arts and crafts (general), chorus, creative writing, dance, film.
Sports Archery, baseball, basketball, bicycling, canoeing, climbing (wall), fishing, ropes course.
Wilderness/Outdoors Hiking.
Trips Day, overnight.
Program Information 5 sessions per year. Session length: 6–7 days in July, August. Ages: 7–15. 80 participants per session. No cost for program, airfare provided, $50 registration fee for accepted participants.
Application Deadline Continuous.
Jobs Positions for college students 18 and older.
Contact Ms. Tiffany White, Registrar & Client Services Manager, 3133 Hennepin Avenue, South, Minneapolis, Minnesota 55408. Phone: 612-824-6464. Fax: 612-824-6303. E-mail: tiffany@campheartland.org.
URL www.campheartland.org

Camp James Summer Day Camp

8790 Irvine Center Drive
Irvine, California 92618

General Information Coed day traditional camp established in 1996. Accredited by American Camping Association.
Arts Arts and crafts (general), dance, graphic arts, jewelry making, mime, music, musical productions, puppetry, theater/drama.
Special Interest Areas Community service, leadership training, nature study.
Sports Baseball, boating, cheerleading, climbing (wall), go-carts, martial arts.
Wilderness/Outdoors Rock climbing.
Trips Day.
Program Information Session length: 5–45 days in June, July, August. Ages: 4–13. Day program cost: $230–$2070. Application fee: $20.
Application Deadline Continuous.
Jobs Positions for college students 18 and older.
Contact Scottie Roach, Director, main address above. E-mail: directors@campjames.com.
URL www.campjames.com

Camp JCA Shalom

34342 Mulholland Highway
Malibu, California 90265

General Information Coed residential and day traditional camp established in 1961. Religious affiliation: Jewish. Accredited by American Camping Association.
Program Focus Community camp in a Jewish environment.
Arts Arts and crafts (general), ceramics, chorus, dance (Latin), dance (folk), photography, theater/drama.
Special Interest Areas Gardening.
Sports Archery, basketball, climbing (wall), martial arts, ropes course, sea kayaking, soccer, softball, swimming, volleyball.
Wilderness/Outdoors Backpacking, hiking, outdoor camping, rock climbing.
Trips Day, overnight.
Program Information 15–30 sessions per year. Session length: 5–20 days in June, July, August. Ages: 7–17. Day program cost: $415. Boarding program cost: $395–$2175. Financial aid available.
Application Deadline Continuous.
Jobs Positions for college students 18 and older.
Contact Brandy Ivener, Business Director, main address above. Phone: 818-889-5500. Fax: 818-889-5132. E-mail: shalom_institute@jcc-gla.org.
URL www.campjcashalom.com

Camp La Jolla

Camp La Jolla
University of California, San Diego
10050 North Torrey Pines Road
La Jolla, California 92092

General Information Coed residential outdoor program and special needs program established in 1979. Accredited by American Camping Association. Specific services available for the weight reduction.

Camp La Jolla

Program Focus Fitness and weight loss.
Arts Arts and crafts (general), dance, dance (modern), music, theater/drama.
Special Interest Areas Culinary arts, field trips (arts and culture), nutrition, personal development, weight reduction.
Sports Aerobics, baseball, basketball, bicycling, bicycling (BMX), cheerleading, fishing, football, kayaking, martial arts, physical fitness, racquetball, snorkeling, soccer, softball, sports (general), street/roller hockey, swimming, tennis, track and field, volleyball, weight training.
Wilderness/Outdoors Mountain biking.
Trips Cultural, day, overnight, shopping.
Program Information 6 sessions per year. Session length: 3–9 weeks in June, July, August. Ages: 8–29. 200 participants per session. Boarding program cost: $4595–$7995.
Application Deadline Continuous.
Jobs Positions for college students 19 and older.
Contact Nancy Lenhart, Director, 176 C Avenue, Coronado, California 92118. Phone: 800-825-8746. Fax: 619-435-8188. E-mail: camp@camplajolla.com.
URL www.camplajolla.com
For more information, see page 1028.

Camp Pacific's Recreational Camp

The Academy by the Sea/Camp Pacific
2605 Carlsbad Boulevard
Carlsbad, California 92008

General Information Coed residential traditional camp established in 1943. Accredited by American Camping Association.
Program Focus Water sports, team sports, traditional camp activities, team work, sportsmanship.
Academics English as a second language.
Arts Arts and crafts (general), ceramics, dance, dance (folk), drawing, jewelry making, leather working, music, painting, pottery, printmaking, radio broadcasting, theater/drama.
Special Interest Areas Campcraft.

Camp Pacific's Recreational Camp (continued)

Sports Baseball, basketball, body boarding, football, kayaking, lacrosse, riflery, sea kayaking, snorkeling, soccer, softball, surfing, swimming, tennis, volleyball, water polo, weight training, wrestling.
Trips Cultural, day, shopping.
Program Information 1 session per year. Session length: 3 weeks in June, July, August. Ages: 8–16. 40–60 participants per session. Boarding program cost: $2220–$2300. Application fee: $100.
Application Deadline Continuous.
Jobs Positions for college students 21 and older.
Contact Ms. Lori Adlfinger, Associate Director, PO Box 3000, Carlsbad, California 92018. Phone: 760-434-7564. Fax: 760-729-1574. E-mail: info@abts.com.
URL www.abts.com

For more information, see page 958.

Camp Pacific's Surf and Bodyboard Camp

The Academy by the Sea/Camp Pacific
2605 Carlsbad Boulevard
Carlsbad, California 92008

General Information Coed residential sports camp established in 1943. Accredited by American Camping Association.
Program Focus Surf and bodyboard instruction, sports, recreational activities, field trips, and fun.
Arts Arts and crafts (general), ceramics, dance (folk), drawing, jewelry making, leather working, music, painting, pottery, printmaking, radio broadcasting.
Special Interest Areas Campcraft.
Sports Baseball, basketball, body boarding, football, kayaking, lacrosse, riflery, sea kayaking, snorkeling, soccer, softball, surfing, swimming, tennis, volleyball, water polo, weight training.
Trips Day, shopping.
Program Information 2–3 sessions per year. Session length: 1 week in June, July, August. Ages: 8–16. 40–60 participants per session. Boarding program cost: $775–$850. Application fee: $100.
Application Deadline Continuous.
Jobs Positions for college students 21 and older.
Contact Ms. Lori Adlfinger, Associate Director, PO Box 3000, Carlsbad, California 92018. Phone: 760-434-7564. Fax: 760-729-1574. E-mail: info@abts.com.
URL www.abts.com

For more information, see page 958.

Camp Tawonga–Call of the Wild

Camp Tawonga (Tawonga Jewish Community Corp.)
California

General Information Coed travel wilderness program and adventure program established in 1926. Religious affiliation: Jewish. Accredited by American Camping Association.
Sports Canoeing, climbing (wall), rappelling.
Wilderness/Outdoors Backpacking, hiking, mountaineering, orienteering, outdoor adventure, rafting, rock climbing.
Program Information 1 session per year. Session length: 3 weeks in July. 10–11 participants per session. Cost: $2840. Financial aid available. Open to participants entering grades 9–11.
Application Deadline Continuous.
Jobs Positions for college students 18 and older.
Contact Sara Rubinett, Office Manager, 131 Steuart Street, San Francisco, California 94105. Phone: 415-543-2267. Fax: 415-543-5417. E-mail: info@tawonga.org.
URL www.tawonga.org

Camp Tawonga–Magical Mystery Tour

Camp Tawonga (Tawonga Jewish Community Corp.)
California

General Information Coed travel outdoor program and adventure program established in 1926. Religious affiliation: Jewish. Accredited by American Camping Association.
Special Interest Areas Touring.
Wilderness/Outdoors Backpacking, hiking, mountain biking, rafting, rock climbing, wilderness/outdoors (general).
Program Information 1 session per year. Session length: 2 weeks in June, July. 10–11 participants per session. Cost: $1975. Financial aid available. Open to participants entering grades 9–11.
Application Deadline Continuous.
Jobs Positions for college students 18 and older.
Contact Sara Rubinett, Office Manager, 131 Steuart Street, San Francisco, California 94105. Phone: 415-543-2267. Fax: 415-543-5417. E-mail: info@tawonga.org.
URL www.tawonga.org

Camp Tawonga–Summer Camp

Camp Tawonga (Tawonga Jewish Community Corp.)
Groveland, California 95321

General Information Coed residential traditional camp and outdoor program established in 1926. Religious affiliation: Jewish. Accredited by American Camping Association.
Arts Arts and crafts (general), batiking, ceramics, dance, drawing, fabric arts, jewelry making, leather working, music, painting, pottery, sculpture, theater/drama.
Special Interest Areas Farming, gardening, nature study.
Sports Archery, baseball, basketball, boating, canoeing, climbing (wall), fishing, ropes course, soccer, softball, swimming, volleyball.
Wilderness/Outdoors Backpacking, hiking, mountaineering, orienteering, rafting, rock climbing, white-water trips, wilderness camping.
Trips Cultural, day, overnight.
Program Information 4 sessions per year. Session length: 6–21 days in June, July, August. Ages: 7–17. Boarding program cost: $930–$2840. Financial aid available.
Application Deadline Continuous.
Jobs Positions for college students 18 and older.

Contact Sara Rubinett, Office Manager, 131 Steuart Street, San Francisco, California 94105. Phone: 415-543-2267. Fax: 415-543-5417. E-mail: info@tawonga.org.
URL www.tawonga.org

Camp Tawonga–Summertime Family Camp

Camp Tawonga (Tawonga Jewish Community Corp.)
Groveland, California 95321

General Information Coed residential family program established in 1926. Religious affiliation: Jewish. Accredited by American Camping Association.
Arts Arts and crafts (general), ceramics, dance, dance (folk), jewelry making, music, sing-a-longs.
Special Interest Areas Nature study.
Sports Climbing (wall), ropes course, softball.
Wilderness/Outdoors Hiking.
Program Information 1 session per year. Session length: 4 days in August. Financial aid available. Cost: $270 for adults; $215 for ages 4–18; $125 for ages 3 and under.
Application Deadline Continuous.
Jobs Positions for college students 18 and older.
Contact Sara Rubinett, Office Manager, 131 Steuart Street, San Francisco, California 94105. Phone: 415-543-2267. Fax: 415-543-5417. E-mail: info@tawonga.org.
URL www.tawonga.org

Camp Tawonga–Surf 'n Turf Quest

Camp Tawonga (Tawonga Jewish Community Corp.)
California

General Information Coed travel adventure program established in 1926. Religious affiliation: Jewish. Accredited by American Camping Association.
Arts Arts and crafts (general), dance, music, theater/drama.
Special Interest Areas Touring.
Sports Boating, kayaking, surfing, swimming.
Wilderness/Outdoors Backpacking, hiking, outdoor adventure.
Trips Cultural.
Program Information 1 session per year. Session length: 3 weeks in August. 10–11 participants per session. Cost: $2840. Financial aid available. Open to participants entering grades 8–9.
Application Deadline Continuous.
Jobs Positions for college students 18 and older.
Contact Sara Rubinett, Office Manager, 131 Steuart Street, San Francisco, California 94105. Phone: 415-543-2267. Fax: 415-543-5417. E-mail: info@tawonga.org.
URL www.tawonga.org

Camp Tawonga–Teen Quest: High Sierra

Camp Tawonga (Tawonga Jewish Community Corp.)
California

General Information Coed travel wilderness program and adventure program established in 1926. Religious affiliation: Jewish. Accredited by American Camping Association.
Academics Ecology.
Sports Bicycling, swimming.
Wilderness/Outdoors Bicycle trips, hiking, mountain biking, outdoor adventure, rafting, white-water trips, wilderness camping.
Program Information 1 session per year. Session length: 2 weeks in June, July. 10–11 participants per session. Cost: $1975. Financial aid available. Open to participants entering grades 8–10.
Application Deadline Continuous.
Jobs Positions for college students 18 and older.
Contact Sara Rubinett, Office Manager, 131 Steuart Street, San Francisco, California 94105. Phone: 415-543-2267. Fax: 415-543-5417. E-mail: info@tawonga.org.
URL www.tawonga.org

Camp Tawonga–Teen Quest: Yosemite

Camp Tawonga (Tawonga Jewish Community Corp.)
California

General Information Coed travel wilderness program and adventure program established in 1926. Religious affiliation: Jewish. Accredited by American Camping Association.
Sports Ropes course, swimming.
Wilderness/Outdoors Backpacking, hiking, outdoor adventure, wilderness camping.
Trips Day, overnight.
Program Information 1 session per year. Session length: 6 days in June, August. 10–11 participants per session. Cost: $930. Financial aid available. Open to participants entering grades 7–8.
Application Deadline Continuous.
Jobs Positions for college students 18 and older.
Contact Sara Rubinett, Office Manager, 131 Steuart Street, San Francisco, California 94105. Phone: 415-543-2267. Fax: 415-543-5417. E-mail: info@tawonga.org.
URL www.tawonga.org

Carmel Valley Tennis Camp

20805 Cachagua Road
Carmel Valley, California 93924

General Information Coed residential traditional camp and sports camp established in 1970.
Arts Arts and crafts (general).
Special Interest Areas Nature study.
Sports Archery, basketball, climbing (wall), ropes course, softball, tennis, volleyball.
Wilderness/Outdoors Hiking.
Trips Day.

Carmel Valley Tennis Camp (continued)

Program Information 7–9 sessions per year. Session length: 1–2 weeks in June, July, August. Ages: 10–17. 52–54 participants per session. Boarding program cost: $875–$1750.
Application Deadline Continuous.
Jobs Positions for high school students 18 and older and college students 18 and older.
Contact Ms. Susan Reeder, Owner/Director, main address above. Phone: 831-659-2615. Fax: 831-659-2840. E-mail: cvtcl@aol.com.
URL www.carmelvalleytenniscamp.com

Castilleja Summer Day Camp

Castilleja School
1310 Bryant Street
Palo Alto, California 94301

General Information Girls' day traditional camp established in 1962.
Program Focus Increasing excitement about learning through a wide range of activities.
Academics English language/literature, French language/literature, Spanish language/literature, computers, engineering, environmental science, geology/earth science, mathematics, music, reading, science (general), writing.
Arts Acting, arts and crafts (general), batiking, ceramics, chorus, clowning, creative writing, dance, dance (folk), dance (jazz), dance (modern), dance (tap), drawing, fabric arts, film, graphic arts, jewelry making, music, music (instrumental), music (vocal), painting, puppetry, sculpture, theater/drama, weaving.
Special Interest Areas Culinary arts, gardening, nature study.
Sports Baseball, basketball, football, gymnastics, in-line skating, lacrosse, soccer, softball, swimming, tennis, track and field, volleyball, water polo.
Trips Cultural, day.
Program Information 2 sessions per year. Session length: 20 days in June, July, August. Ages: 6–12. 185–200 participants per session. Day program cost: $1200–$1300. Financial aid available.
Application Deadline February 1.
Jobs Positions for college students 18 and older.
Contact Ms. Katy Roybal, Director of Summer Camp, main address above. Phone: 650-328-3160 Ext.440. Fax: 650-326-8036. E-mail: katy_roybal@castilleja.org.
URL www.castilleja.org

Catalina Island Camps

Catalina Island Camps, Inc.
Howlands Landing
Avalon, California 90704

General Information Coed residential traditional camp established in 1926. Accredited by American Camping Association.
Program Focus Waterfront activities.
Academics Ecology, marine studies.
Arts Arts and crafts (general), leather working, music, theater/drama.
Special Interest Areas Campcraft, gardening, leadership training, nature study, nautical skills.
Sports Archery, boating, canoeing, climbing (wall), kayaking, riflery, ropes course, rowing (crew/sculling), sailing, sea kayaking, snorkeling, soccer, swimming, tennis, volleyball, waterskiing.
Wilderness/Outdoors Canoe trips, hiking, mountain biking.
Trips Overnight.
Program Information 6 sessions per year. Session length: 1–4 weeks in June, July, August. Ages: 8–15. 150–192 participants per session. Boarding program cost: $1200–$3600.
Application Deadline Continuous.
Jobs Positions for college students 19 and older.
Contact Maria Horner, Co-Director, PO Box 94146, Pasadena, California 91109. Phone: 626-296-4040. Fax: 626-794-1401. E-mail: maria@catalinaislandcamps.com.
URL www.catalinaislandcamps.com

Cazadero Family Camp

Cazadero Performing Arts Camp
5000 Austin Creek Road
Cazadero, California 95421

General Information Coed residential family program and arts program. Formal opportunities for the artistically talented.
Program Focus Playing and learning together for families.
Academics Art.
Arts Aboriginal arts, arts and crafts (general), chorus, circus arts, clowning, dance, dance (Latin), guitar, music (chamber), music (jazz), music (piano), music (rock), storytelling, theater/drama.
Sports Badminton, baseball, basketball, softball, swimming, table tennis/ping-pong, volleyball.
Program Information 2 sessions per year. Session length: 1 week in August. Ages: 2+. 100–135 participants per session. Boarding program cost: $635–$2210. Application fee: $35. Financial aid available.
Application Deadline Continuous.
Jobs Positions for high school students 15 and older and college students 18 and older.
Contact Jim Mazzaferro, Camp Director, 9068 Shetland Court, Elk Grove, California 95624. Phone: 916-685-3867. Fax: 916-681-7505. E-mail: jim@cazadero.org.
URL www.cazadero.org

Cazadero Music Camp

Cazadero Performing Arts Camp
5000 Austin Creek Road
Cazadero, California 95421

General Information Coed residential arts program established in 1957. Formal opportunities for the artistically talented.
Program Focus Instrumental music focus—orchestra, jazz band, concert band.
Arts Band, music, music (chamber), music (classical), music (ensemble), music (instrumental), music (jazz), music (orchestral).
Sports Basketball, softball, swimming, volleyball.

Wilderness/Outdoors Hiking.
Program Information 4 sessions per year. Session length: 6–12 days in June, July, August. Ages: 10–18. 135–144 participants per session. Boarding program cost: $660–$1200. Application fee: $35. Financial aid available.
Application Deadline Continuous.
Jobs Positions for high school students 15 and older and college students 18 and older.
Contact Jim Mazzaferro, Camp Director, 9068 Shetland Court, Elk Grove, California 95624. Phone: 916-685-3867. Fax: 916-681-7505. E-mail: jim@cazadero.org.
URL www.cazadero.org

The Children's Art Institute

The Children's Art Institute
14702 Sylvan Street
Van Nuys, California 91411

General Information Coed day arts program established in 2002.
Academics Art.
Arts Arts, arts and crafts (general), batiking, ceramics, clowning, dance, dance (jazz), drawing, fabric arts, music, music (vocal), painting, photography, pottery, printmaking, puppetry, sculpture, theater/drama, woodworking.
Special Interest Areas Culinary arts, nature study.
Sports Fencing.
Program Information 4 sessions per year. Session length: 6–15 days in June, July, August. Ages: 6–11. 60–100 participants per session. Day program cost: $55–$58.
Application Deadline Continuous.
Jobs Positions for high school students 16 and older and college students 18 and older.
Contact David Wohlstadter, Director, main address above. Phone: 818-386-1108. Fax: 818-386-1105. E-mail: artsinstitute2004@yahoo.com.
URL www.childrensartsinstitute.com

Children's Creative and Performing Arts Academy Archaeology Adventure Camp

Children's Creative and Performing Arts Academy of San Diego
4431 Mt. Herbert Avenue
San Diego, California 92117

General Information Coed day traditional camp and academic program. Formal opportunities for the academically talented and artistically talented.
Academics Archaeology, geography, mathematics, science (general), social science, writing.
Arts Arts and crafts (general), illustration.
Program Information 1 session per year. Session length: 20 days in August. Ages: 10–13. 40–60 participants per session. Application fee: $50. Financial aid available. Cost: $150 per week plus $50 materials fee.
Jobs Positions for high school students 16 and older and college students 18 and older.
Contact Janet Cherif, Director, main address above. Phone: 858-279-4744. Fax: 858-279-1243. E-mail: jmcherif@yahoo.com.
URL www.ccpaasd.com

Children's Creative and Performing Arts Academy Summer Elementary Program

Children's Creative and Performing Arts Academy of San Diego
4431 Mt. Herbert Avenue
San Diego, California 92117

General Information Coed day traditional camp, academic program, and arts program established in 1981. Formal opportunities for the academically talented and artistically talented.
Program Focus Exploring creativity through academics, arts and sports.
Academics American literature, English as a second language, English language/literature, Spanish language/literature, academics (general), art (Advanced Placement), biology, chemistry, computers, history, humanities, mathematics, mathematics (Advanced Placement), music, reading, science (general), social science, social studies, study skills, typing, writing.
Arts Acting, arts and crafts (general), band, ceramics, chorus, creative writing, dance, dance (ballet), dance (folk), dance (jazz), dance (modern), dance (tap), drawing, film, graphic arts, jewelry making, music, music (chamber), music (classical), music (ensemble), music (instrumental), music (jazz), music (orchestral), music (vocal), musical productions, painting, photography, pottery, printmaking, sculpture, theater/drama.
Special Interest Areas Community service, homestays.
Sports Aerobics, baseball, basketball, cheerleading, cross-country, field hockey, gymnastics, soccer, softball, track and field, volleyball.
Trips Day.
Program Information 2 sessions per year. Session length: 40–60 days in June, July, August. Ages: 6–12. 100–150 participants per session. Application fee: $45. Financial aid available. Cost: $150 per week.
Application Deadline Continuous.
Jobs Positions for high school students 16 and older and college students 18 and older.
Contact Ms. Janet Cherif, Principal, main address above. Phone: 858-279-4744. Fax: 858-279-1243. E-mail: jmcherif@yahoo.com.
URL www.ccpaasd.com

Children's Creative and Performing Arts Academy Summer Middle School Program

Children's Creative and Performing Arts Academy of San Diego
4431 Mt. Herbert Avenue
San Diego, California 92117

General Information Coed day traditional camp, academic program, and arts program. Formal opportunities for the academically talented and artistically talented.
Academics English language/literature, academics (general), computers, mathematics, social science, typing, writing.
Arts Arts, arts and crafts (general), creative writing, dance (ballet), dance (jazz), dance (tap), drawing, music, music (instrumental), musical productions, painting, theater/drama.
Sports Badminton, basketball, gymnastics, soccer, softball, track and field, volleyball.
Program Information Application fee: $50. Financial aid available. Cost: $150 per week plus $50 materials fee.
Jobs Positions for high school students 16 and older.
Contact Janet Cherif, Director, main address above. Phone: 858-279-4744. Fax: 858-279-1243. E-mail: jmcherif@yahoo.com.
URL www.ccpaasd.com

Children's Creative and Performing Arts Academy Summer Program for Preschool/Prekindergarten

Children's Creative and Performing Arts Academy of San Diego
4431 Mt. Herbert Avenue
San Diego, California 92117

General Information Coed day academic program and arts program. Formal opportunities for the academically talented and artistically talented.
Program Focus Full Montessori curriculum with Spanish language, Beginning Dance Orff, Kodaly Music Training and Art.
Academics Spanish language/literature, academics (general), botany, geography, mathematics, reading, science (general), social studies, writing.
Arts Arts, dance, music.
Program Information Session length: 2–5 days in June, July, August. Ages: 3–5. Day program cost: $60–$150. Application fee: $50. Financial aid available.
Application Deadline Continuous.
Jobs Positions for high school students 16 and older and college students 18 and older.
Contact Janet Cherif, Director, main address above. Phone: 858-279-4744. Fax: 858-279-1243. E-mail: jmcherif@yahoo.com.
URL www.ccpaasd.com

Children's Creative and Performing Arts Academy Summer Programs for High School Students

Children's Creative and Performing Arts Academy of San Diego
4431 Mt. Herbert Avenue
San Diego, California 92117

General Information Coed day traditional camp, academic program, and arts program. Formal opportunities for the academically talented and artistically talented. High school credit may be earned.
Academics American literature, English as a second language, English language/literature, French (Advanced Placement), French language/literature, German language/literature, SAT/ACT preparation, Spanish (Advanced Placement), Spanish language/literature, academics (general), art (Advanced Placement), biology, biology (Advanced Placement), chemistry, computer programming, computer science (Advanced Placement), computers, economics, government and politics, government and politics (Advanced Placement), history, humanities, mathematics, mathematics (Advanced Placement), music, music (Advanced Placement), physics, reading, science (general), social science, social studies, study skills, typing, writing.
Arts Acting, arts and crafts (general), band, ceramics, chorus, creative writing, dance, dance (ballet), dance (folk), dance (jazz), dance (modern), dance (tap), drawing, film, graphic arts, music, music (chamber), music (classical), music (ensemble), music (instrumental), music (jazz), music (orchestral), music (vocal), musical productions, painting, photography, pottery, sculpture, theater/drama.
Special Interest Areas Community service.
Trips Day.
Program Information 2 sessions per year. Session length: 40–60 days in June, July, August. Ages: 14–18. Application fee: $50. Financial aid available. Cost: $450 for 2 semester academic class, $25 book rental; $100 for Drama, Dance, or Musical Theater Workshop.
Application Deadline Continuous.
Jobs Positions for high school students 16 and older and college students 18 and older.
Contact Janet Cherif, Director, main address above. Phone: 858-279-4744. Fax: 858-279-1243. E-mail: jmcherif@yahoo.com.
URL www.ccpaasd.com

ClayCamp

Clayworks Studio
4130 Greenbush Avenue
Sherman Oaks, California 91423

General Information Coed day arts program established in 2002.
Program Focus Ceramics.
Arts Ceramics, pottery.
Program Information 10 sessions per year. Session length: 4–8 days in June, July, August. Ages: 6–16. 8–10 participants per session. Day program cost: $180–$360.
Application Deadline Continuous.

Jobs Positions for high school students 16 and older and college students 18 and older.
Contact Ellen Wohlstadter, Owner, main address above. Phone: 818-905-8300. Fax: 818-386-1105. E-mail: e_wohlstadter@yahoo.com.

Cloverleaf Ranch Summer Camp

3892 Old Redwood Highway
Santa Rosa, California 95403

General Information Coed residential and day traditional camp established in 1947. Accredited by American Camping Association.
Arts Arts and crafts (general), dance.
Special Interest Areas Animal care, leadership training.
Sports Aerobics, archery, baseball, basketball, bicycling, equestrian sports, field hockey, fishing, horseback riding, riflery, ropes course, snorkeling, soccer, softball, swimming, tennis, volleyball.
Wilderness/Outdoors Hiking.
Program Information 5–8 sessions per year. Session length: 7–13 days in June, July, August. Ages: 7–15. 75 participants per session. Day program cost: $300. Boarding program cost: $995–$1990. Application fee: $300. Day program for ages 6-12.
Application Deadline Continuous.
Jobs Positions for college students 18 and older.
Contact Chris Rhodes, Camp Manager, main address above. Phone: 707-545-5906. Fax: 707-545-5908. E-mail: cloverleafranch@netdex.com.
URL www.campchannel.com/cloverleaf

College Admission Prep Camp by Education Unlimited–San Diego

Education Unlimited
University of San Diego
San Diego, California

General Information Coed residential and day academic program established in 1993.
Program Focus The college admission process, SAT preparation.
Academics SAT/ACT preparation, communications, study skills, writing.
Special Interest Areas Career exploration, college planning.
Trips College tours, day.
Program Information 1 session per year. Session length: 9 days in July, August. Ages: 15–18. 40–60 participants per session. Day program cost: $1250. Boarding program cost: $1830. Financial aid available.
Application Deadline Continuous.
Contact Matthew Fraser, Executive Director, 1700 Shattuck Avenue, #305, Berkeley, California 94709. Phone: 800-548-6612. Fax: 510-548-0212. E-mail: camps@educationunlimited.com.
URL www.educationunlimited.com
For more information, see page 1076.

College Admission Prep Camp by Education Unlimited–Stanford University

Education Unlimited
Stanford University
Stanford, California

General Information Coed residential and day academic program established in 1993.

College Admission Prep Camp by Education Unlimited–Stanford University

Program Focus The college admission process, SAT preparation.
Academics SAT/ACT preparation, communications, study skills, writing.
Special Interest Areas Career exploration, college planning.
Sports Basketball, volleyball.
Trips College tours, day.
Program Information 2 sessions per year. Session length: 9 days in July, August. Ages: 15–18. 50–150 participants per session. Day program cost: $1500. Boarding program cost: $2109. Financial aid available.
Application Deadline Continuous.
Contact Matthew Fraser, Executive Director, 1700 Shattuck Avenue, #305, Berkeley, California 94709. Phone: 800-548-6612. Fax: 510-548-0212. E-mail: camps@educationunlimited.com.
URL www.educationunlimited.com
For more information, see page 1076.

College Admission Prep Camp by Education Unlimited–UC Berkeley

Education Unlimited
University of California, Berkeley
Berkeley, California

General Information Coed residential and day academic program established in 1993.
Program Focus The college admission process, SAT preparation.
Academics SAT/ACT preparation, communications, study skills, writing.

College Admission Prep Camp by Education Unlimited–UC Berkeley (continued)

Special Interest Areas Career exploration, college planning.
Trips College tours, day.
Program Information 1–2 sessions per year. Session length: 9 days in June. Ages: 15–18. 40–80 participants per session. Day program cost: $1300. Boarding program cost: $1885. Financial aid available.
Application Deadline Continuous.
Contact Matthew Fraser, Executive Director, 1700 Shattuck Avenue, #305, Berkeley, California 94709. Phone: 800-548-6612. Fax: 510-548-0212. E-mail: camps@educationunlimited.com.
URL www.educationunlimited.com

For more information, see page 1076.

College Admission Prep Camp by Education Unlimited–UCLA

Education Unlimited
University of California, Los Angeles
Los Angeles, California

General Information Coed residential and day academic program established in 1993.
Program Focus The college admission process, SAT preparation.
Academics SAT/ACT preparation, communications, study skills, writing.
Special Interest Areas Career exploration, college planning.
Sports Basketball, volleyball.
Trips College tours, day.
Program Information 1 session per year. Session length: 9 days in July. Ages: 15–18. 40–80 participants per session. Day program cost: $1250. Boarding program cost: $2109. Financial aid available.
Application Deadline Continuous.
Contact Matthew Fraser, Executive Director, 1700 Shattuck Avenue, #305, Berkeley, California 94709. Phone: 800-548-6612. Fax: 510-548-0212. E-mail: camps@educationunlimited.com.
URL www.educationunlimited.com

For more information, see page 1076.

College Admission Prep Camp Choice by Education Unlimited–Stanford

Education Unlimited
Stanford University
Palo Alto, California

General Information Coed residential and day academic program established in 2002.
Program Focus College admission preparation.
Academics SAT/ACT preparation, study skills, writing.
Special Interest Areas College planning.
Trips Day.
Program Information 1 session per year. Session length: 1 week in June, July. Ages: 16–18. 20–60 participants per session. Boarding program cost: $1350. Financial aid available.
Application Deadline Continuous.
Contact Mr. Matthew Fraser, Executive Director, 1700 Shattuck Avenue, #305, Berkeley, California 94709. Phone: 510-548-6612. Fax: 510-548-0212. E-mail: camps@educationunlimited.com.
URL www.educationunlimited.com

For more information, see page 1076.

Computer Camp by Education Unlimited–Stanford

Education Unlimited
Stanford University
Palo Alto, California

General Information Coed residential and day academic program established in 1995.

Computer Camp by Education Unlimited–Stanford

Program Focus Computer use and Java programming.
Academics Web page design, communications, computer programming, computer science (Advanced Placement), computers, journalism, writing.
Special Interest Areas Internet accessibility.
Sports Basketball, volleyball.
Wilderness/Outdoors Hiking.

Trips Day.
Program Information 5 sessions per year. Session length: 1–2 weeks in June, July, August. Ages: 10–18. 48–60 participants per session. Day program cost: $725. Boarding program cost: $1140. Financial aid available.
Application Deadline Continuous.
Jobs Positions for college students 21 and older.
Contact Matthew Fraser, Executive Director, 1700 Shattuck Avenue, #305, Berkeley, California 94709. Phone: 800-548-6612. Fax: 510-548-0212. E-mail: camps@educationunlimited.com.
URL www.educationunlimited.com

For more information, see page 1098.

Computer Camp by Education Unlimited–UC Berkeley

Education Unlimited
University of California, Berkeley
Berkeley, California

General Information Coed residential and day academic program established in 1995.
Program Focus Computer use and programming.
Academics Web page design, communications, computer programming, computer science (Advanced Placement), computers, journalism, writing.
Special Interest Areas Internet accessibility.
Sports Basketball, volleyball.
Wilderness/Outdoors Hiking.
Trips Day.
Program Information 3 sessions per year. Session length: 1 week in July. Ages: 10–18. 48–60 participants per session. Day program cost: $650. Boarding program cost: $1050. Financial aid available.
Application Deadline Continuous.
Jobs Positions for college students 21 and older.
Contact Matthew Fraser, Executive Director, 1700 Shattuck Avenue, #305, Berkeley, California 94709. Phone: 800-548-6612. Fax: 510-548-0212. E-mail: camps@educationunlimited.com.
URL www.educationunlimited.com

For more information, see page 1098.

Computer Camp by Education Unlimited–UCLA

Education Unlimited
University of California, Los Angeles
Los Angeles, California

General Information Coed residential and day academic program established in 1995.
Program Focus Computer use and programming.
Academics Web page design, communications, computer programming, computer science (Advanced Placement), computers, journalism, writing.
Special Interest Areas Internet accessibility.
Sports Basketball, volleyball.
Trips Day.
Program Information 2 sessions per year. Session length: 1 week in June, July. Ages: 10–18. 24–48 participants per session. Day program cost: $650. Boarding program cost: $1050. Financial aid available.
Application Deadline Continuous.
Jobs Positions for college students 21 and older.
Contact Matthew Fraser, Executive Director, 1700 Shattuck Avenue, #305, Berkeley, California 94709. Phone: 800-548-6612. Fax: 510-548-0212. E-mail: camps@educationunlimited.com.
URL www.educationunlimited.com

For more information, see page 1098.

Crossroads School–Aquatics

Crossroads School for Arts and Sciences
1714 21st Street
Santa Monica, California 90404

General Information Coed day family program and sports camp established in 2000.
Program Focus Developing swim and water safety skills, infant to adult.
Special Interest Areas Lifesaving.
Sports Swimming, water aerobics.
Program Information 1–5 sessions per year. Session length: 5–30 days in April, May, June, July, August, September, October. 10–200 participants per session. Day program cost: $64–$350. Application fee: $40. Financial aid available.
Application Deadline Continuous.
Jobs Positions for high school students and college students.
Contact Angela Smith, Director of Summer Programs, main address above. Phone: 310-829-7391 Ext.506. Fax: 310-828-8147. E-mail: summer@xrds.org.
URL www.xrds.org

Crossroads School– Basketball Camps

Crossroads School for Arts and Sciences
1714 21st Street
Santa Monica, California 90404

General Information Coed day sports camp established in 2000.
Academics Computers.
Sports Basketball, swimming.
Program Information 1–2 sessions per year. Session length: 5 days in June, August. Ages: 6–12. 200 participants per session. Day program cost: $350. Application fee: $40. Financial aid available. Open to participants entering grades 1–5.
Application Deadline Continuous.
Jobs Positions for high school students and college students.
Contact Angela Smith, Director of Summer Programs, main address above. Phone: 310-829-7391 Ext.506. Fax: 310-828-8147. E-mail: summer@xrds.org.
URL www.xrds.org

Crossroads School–Jazz Workshop

Crossroads School for Arts and Sciences
1714 21st Street
Santa Monica, California 90404

General Information Coed day arts program established in 2001. High school credit may be earned.
Program Focus Jazz.
Arts Band, music (ensemble), music (instrumental), music (jazz), music theory, musical performance/recitals.
Trips Day.
Program Information 3 sessions per year. Session length: 18–30 days in June, July, August. Ages: 8+. 100 participants per session. Day program cost: $450–$1200. Application fee: $40. Financial aid available.
Application Deadline Continuous.
Jobs Positions for college students.
Contact Angela Smith, Director, Summer Program, main address above. Phone: 310-829-7391 Ext.506. Fax: 310-828-8147. E-mail: summer@xrds.org.
URL www.xrds.org

Crossroads School–Soccer Camps

Crossroads School for Arts and Sciences
1714 21st Street
Santa Monica, California 90404

General Information Coed day sports camp established in 2001.
Academics Computers.
Sports Soccer, swimming.
Program Information 1–2 sessions per year. Session length: 5 days in June, August. Ages: 5–12. 200 participants per session. Day program cost: $350. Application fee: $40. Financial aid available.
Application Deadline Continuous.
Jobs Positions for high school students and college students.
Contact Angela Smith, Director of Summer Programs, main address above. Phone: 310-829-7391 Ext.506. Fax: 310-828-8147. E-mail: summer@xrds.org.
URL www.xrds.org

Crossroads School–Summer Educational Journey

Crossroads School for Arts and Sciences
1714 21st Street
Santa Monica, California 90404

General Information Coed day academic program and arts program established in 1980. High school credit may be earned.
Program Focus Academic credit and enrichment; the arts; sports for infants through adults.
Academics English language/literature, French language/literature, Greek language/literature, Latin language, Spanish language/literature, academics (general), astronomy, biology, chemistry, computer programming, computers, geology/earth science, history, humanities, mathematics, music, oceanography, physics, reading, science (general), social science, social studies, speech/debate, study skills, typing, writing.
Arts Animation, arts, band, cartooning, ceramics, creative writing, dance, dance (jazz), drawing, film, graphic arts, jewelry making, music, music (ensemble), music (instrumental), music (jazz), music (orchestral), music (vocal), musical productions, painting, photography, screenwriting, sculpture, studio arts, television/video, theater/drama.
Special Interest Areas Community service, culinary arts.
Sports Basketball, climbing (wall), flag football, in-line skating, martial arts, physical fitness, sailing, sea kayaking, snorkeling, soccer, street/roller hockey, surfing, swimming, volleyball, water polo, windsurfing, yoga.
Wilderness/Outdoors Rock climbing.
Trips Cultural, day, overnight.
Program Information 1–5 sessions per year. Session length: 5–30 days in April, May, June, July, August, September, October. 300–1,100 participants per session. Day program cost: $64–$1200. Application fee: $40. Financial aid available.
Application Deadline Continuous.
Jobs Positions for high school students 17 and older and college students.
Contact Angela Smith, Director of Summer Programs, Crossroads School, main address above. Phone: 310-829-7391 Ext.506. Fax: 310-828-8147. E-mail: summer@xrds.org.
URL www.xrds.org

Culinary Institute at Pali Overnight Adventures

Pali Overnight Adventures
30778 Highway 18
Running Springs, California 92382

General Information Coed residential traditional camp and arts program. Accredited by American Camping Association.
Program Focus Culinary arts.
Special Interest Areas Culinary arts.
Program Information 5–8 sessions per year. Session length: 1–3 weeks in June, July, August. Ages: 12–16. 10 participants per session. Boarding program cost: $1385–$2695.
Application Deadline Continuous.
Jobs Positions for college students 19 and older.
Contact Mr. Andy Wexler, Owner/Founder, PO Box 2237, Running Springs, California 92382. Phone: 909-867-5743. Fax: 909-867-7643. E-mail: info@paliadventures.com.
URL www.paliadventures.com/culinary.html

Cybercamps–DeAnza College

Cybercamps–Giant Campus, Inc.
Cupertino, California

General Information Coed day academic program established in 1997.
Program Focus High tech computer camps featuring project oriented curriculum in Web design, 3D animation, game design, robotics, digital arts and programming for all ability levels.

Academics Web page design, computer programming, computers, typing.
Arts Animation, creative writing, digital media, graphic arts, photography.
Special Interest Areas Computer game design, computer graphics, robotics, team building.
Sports Frisbee golf, ultimate frisbee.
Program Information 2–9 sessions per year. Session length: 5–30 days in June, July, August. Ages: 7–18. 30–150 participants per session. Day program cost: $599–$849. Financial aid available.
Application Deadline Continuous.
Jobs Positions for high school students 15 and older and college students.
Contact Cybercamps Information Office, 2401 4th Avenue, Suite 1110, Seattle, Washington 98121. Phone: 206-442-4500. Fax: 206-442-4501. E-mail: info@cybercamps.com.
URL www.cybercamps.com

Cybercamps–Stanford University

Cybercamps–Giant Campus, Inc.
Palo Alto, California

General Information Coed day academic program established in 2004.
Academics Web page design, academics (general), computer programming, computers.
Arts Animation, creative writing, digital media, graphic arts, photography.
Special Interest Areas Computer game design, computer graphics, robotics, team building.
Sports Ultimate frisbee.
Program Information 2–9 sessions per year. Session length: 5–30 days in June, July, August. Ages: 7–18. 30–150 participants per session. Day program cost: $599–$849. Financial aid available.
Application Deadline Continuous.
Jobs Positions for high school students 15 and older and college students.
Contact Cybercamps Information Office, 2401 4th Avenue, Suite 1110, Seattle, Washington 98121. Phone: 206-442-4500. Fax: 206-442-4500. E-mail: info@cybercamps.com.
URL www.cybercamps.com

Cybercamps–UCLA

Cybercamps–Giant Campus, Inc.
Los Angeles, California

General Information Coed residential and day academic program established in 1997.
Program Focus High tech computer camps featuring project oriented curriculum in Web design, 3D animation, game design, robotics, digital arts and programming for all ability levels.
Academics Web page design, computer programming, computers.
Arts Animation, creative writing, digital media, graphic arts, photography.
Special Interest Areas Computer game design, computer graphics, robotics, team building.
Sports Frisbee golf, ultimate frisbee.
Program Information 2–9 sessions per year. Session length: 5–30 days in June, July, August. Ages: 7–18. 30–150 participants per session. Day program cost: $599–$849. Boarding program cost: $974–$1224.
Application Deadline Continuous.
Jobs Positions for high school students 15 and older and college students.
Contact Cybercamps Information Office, 2401 4th Avenue, Suite 1110, Seattle, Washington 98121. Phone: 206-442-4500. Fax: 206-442-4501. E-mail: info@cybercamps.com.
URL www.cybercamps.com

Cybercamps–UC San Diego (UCSD)

Cybercamps–Giant Campus, Inc.
La Jolla, California

General Information Coed residential and day academic program established in 1997.
Program Focus High tech computer camps featuring project oriented curriculum in Web design, 3D animation, game design, robotics, digital arts and programming for all ability levels.
Academics Web page design, computer programming, computers.
Arts Animation, creative writing, digital media, graphic arts, photography.
Special Interest Areas Computer game design, computer graphics, robotics, team building.
Sports Frisbee golf, ultimate frisbee.
Program Information 2–9 sessions per year. Session length: 5–30 days in June, July, August. Ages: 7–18. 30–150 participants per session. Day program cost: $599–$849. Boarding program cost: $974–$1224. Financial aid available.
Application Deadline Continuous.
Jobs Positions for high school students 15 and older and college students.
Contact Cybercamps Information Office, 2401 4th Avenue, Suite 1110, Seattle, Washington 98121. Phone: 206-442-4500. Fax: 206-442-4501. E-mail: info@cybercamps.com.
URL www.cybercamps.com

Cybercamps–University of California at Berkeley

Cybercamps–Giant Campus, Inc.
University of California at Berkeley
Berkeley, California

General Information Coed residential and day academic program established in 1997.
Program Focus High tech computer camps featuring project oriented curriculum in Web design, 3D animation, game design, robotics, digital arts and programming for all ability levels.
Academics Web page design, computer programming, computers.
Arts Animation, creative writing, digital media, graphic arts, photography.
Special Interest Areas Career exploration, computer game design, computer graphics, robotics, team building.
Sports Frisbee golf, ultimate frisbee.

Cybercamps–University of California at Berkeley (continued)

Trips College tours, cultural, day, overnight.
Program Information 2–9 sessions per year. Session length: 5–30 days in June, July, August. Ages: 7–18. 30–150 participants per session. Day program cost: $589–$799. Boarding program cost: $909–$1059.
Application Deadline Continuous.
Jobs Positions for high school students 15 and older and college students.
Contact Cybercamps Information Office, 2401 4th Avenue, Suite 1110, Seattle, Washington 98121. Phone: 206-442-4500. Fax: 206-442-4501. E-mail: info@cybercamps.com.
URL www.cybercamps.com

DOUGLAS RANCH CAMPS

Douglas Ranch Camps, Inc.
33200 East Carmel Valley Road
Carmel Valley, California 93924

General Information Coed residential traditional camp established in 1925. Accredited by American Camping Association.
Program Focus Personal development and social skills (confidence, leadership, cooperation, and decision making).
Arts Arts and crafts (general), dance (folk), jewelry making, music (vocal), theater/drama.
Special Interest Areas Campcraft.
Sports Archery, baseball, basketball, equestrian sports, horseback riding, riflery, soccer, swimming, tennis, volleyball, water polo.
Wilderness/Outdoors Hiking, outdoor camping.
Program Information 5 sessions per year. Session length: 2–4 weeks in June, July, August. Ages: 7–14. 70–120 participants per session. Boarding program cost: $2400–$3950.
Application Deadline Continuous.
Jobs Positions for college students 18 and older.
Summer Contact Ms. J. P. O'Connor, Director, main address above. Phone: 831-659-2761. Fax: 831-659-5690. E-mail: director@douglascamp.com.
Winter Contact Ms. J. P. O'Connor, Director, 517 South Griffith Park Drive, Burbank, California 91506. Phone: 818-556-3500. Fax: 818-556-3509. E-mail: director@douglascamp.com.
URL www.douglascamp.com

EARTHWATCH INSTITUTE–MOJAVE DESERT TORTOISES

Earthwatch Institute
Mojave National Preserve
California

General Information Coed residential outdoor program.
Program Focus Understanding how environmental factors affect threatened tortoise populations in order to manage them proactively.
Academics Ecology, environmental science.
Special Interest Areas Animal care, conservation projects, field research/expeditions.
Program Information 8 sessions per year. Session length: 10 days in April, May, June, July. Ages: 16+. 8 participants per session. Boarding program cost: $1595–$1695. Financial aid available. Financial aid for high school students and teachers.
Application Deadline Continuous.
Contact General Information Desk, PO Box 75, Maynard, Massachusetts 01754. Phone: 800-776-0188. Fax: 978-461-2332. E-mail: info@earthwatch.org.
URL www.earthwatch.org

ELITE EDUCATIONAL INSTITUTE ELEMENTARY ENRICHMENT

Elite Educational Institute
California

General Information Coed day academic program established in 1987. Formal opportunities for the academically talented.
Program Focus Elementary enrichment: 2nd-6th grade.
Academics English as a second language, English language/literature, SAT/ACT preparation, mathematics, precollege program, reading, social studies, study skills, writing.
Program Information 3 sessions per year. 10–40 participants per session. Day program cost: $280–$320.
Application Deadline Continuous.
Contact Julian Chou, Program Director, 19735 Colima Road, # 2, Rowland Heights, California 91748. Phone: 909-444-0876. Fax: 909-444-0877.
URL www.eliteprep.com
For more information, see page 1104.

ELITE EDUCATIONAL INSTITUTE JUNIOR HIGH/PSAT PROGRAM

Elite Educational Institute
California

General Information Coed day academic program established in 1987. Formal opportunities for the academically talented.
Academics English as a second language, English language/literature, SAT/ACT preparation, mathematics, reading, study skills, writing.
Program Information 3–4 sessions per year. 40–80 participants per session. Day program cost: $240–$320.
Application Deadline Continuous.
Contact Julian Chou, Program Director, 19735 Colima Road, # 2, Rowland Heights, California 91748. Phone: 909-444-0876. Fax: 909-444-0877.
URL www.eliteprep.com
For more information, see page 1104.

Elite Educational Institute SAT I and II Preparation

Elite Educational Institute
California

General Information Coed day academic program established in 1987. Formal opportunities for the academically talented.
Program Focus SAT I and SAT II preparation.
Academics SAT/ACT preparation, mathematics, precollege program, writing.
Special Interest Areas College planning.
Program Information 3 sessions per year. Session length: 100–350 days in January, February, March, April, May, June, July, August, September, October, November, December. Day program cost: $340–$440.
Application Deadline Continuous.
Jobs Positions for college students.
Contact Julian Chou, Program Director, 19735 Colima Road, # 2, Rowland Heights, California 91748. Phone: 909-444-0876. Fax: 909-444-0877.
URL www.eliteprep.com
For more information, see page 1104.

Elite Educational Institute SAT Summer Bootcamp

Elite Educational Institute
California

General Information Coed day academic program established in 1987. Formal opportunities for the academically talented.
Program Focus Intensive SAT preparation program.
Academics English language/literature, SAT/ACT preparation, mathematics, precollege program, reading, writing.
Special Interest Areas College planning.
Program Information 1 session per year. Session length: 10 weeks in June, July, August. 20–60 participants per session. Day program cost: $2200.
Application Deadline June 15.
Contact Julian Chou, Program Director, 19735 Colima Road, # 2, Rowland Heights, California 91748. Phone: 909-444-0876. Fax: 909-444-0877.
URL www.eliteprep.com
For more information, see page 1104.

Excel at UC Santa Cruz

Putney Student Travel
University of California, Santa Cruz
Santa Cruz, California

General Information Coed residential academic program and arts program established in 1951. Formal opportunities for the academically talented and artistically talented.
Program Focus EXCEL is an innovative precollege program emphasizing small classes and creative interaction among students and faculty. Excursions available to sites of interest in the area.
Academics English as a second language, SAT/ACT preparation, Spanish language/literature, art, biology, business, ecology, environmental science, history, humanities, marine studies, oceanography, precollege program, psychology, social studies, writing.
Arts Arts, arts and crafts (general), creative writing, dance, dance (jazz), dance (modern), drawing, film, music (ensemble), music (instrumental), painting, photography.
Special Interest Areas Community service, field research/expeditions, nature study.
Sports Bicycling, golf, kayaking, soccer, surfing, tennis.
Wilderness/Outdoors Hiking.
Trips College tours, cultural, day.
Program Information 1 session per year. Session length: 30 days in July, August. Ages: 14+. 50–80 participants per session. Boarding program cost: $5500. Financial aid available.
Application Deadline Continuous.
Jobs Positions for college students 20 and older.
Contact Jeffrey Shumlin, Director, 345 Hickory Ridge Road, Putney, Vermont 05346. Phone: 802-387-5000. Fax: 802-387-4276. E-mail: excel@goputney.com.
URL www.goputney.com
For more information, see page 1114.

Exploration of Architecture

University of Southern California, School of Architecture
Watt Hall, Room 204
Los Angeles, California 90089-0291

General Information Coed residential academic program established in 1983. Specific services available for the physically challenged.

Exploration of Architecture

Program Focus Architecture and design.
Academics Architecture.
Trips Cultural.
Program Information 3 sessions per year. Session length: 1–3 weeks in July. Ages: 15–18. 35–100 participants per session. Boarding program cost: $1075–$2450. Application fee: $200. Financial aid available.
Application Deadline Continuous.
Jobs Positions for college students 18 and older.
Contact Ms. Jennifer Park, Director of Undergraduate Admission, USC School of Architecture, Watt Hall 204,

Exploration of Architecture (continued)

Los Angeles, California 90089-0291. Phone: 213-740-2420. Fax: 213-740-8884. E-mail: jenpark@usc.edu.
URL www.usc.edu/dept/architecture/explor/
For more information, see page 1372.

Film Institute at Pali Overnight Adventures

Pali Overnight Adventures
30778 Highway 18
Running Springs, California 92382

General Information Coed residential traditional camp and arts program established in 1990. Accredited by American Camping Association. Formal opportunities for the artistically talented.
Program Focus Film making.
Academics Journalism.
Arts Arts and crafts (general), batiking, ceramics, dance, film, film production, painting, pottery, theater/drama.
Special Interest Areas Animal care, leadership training, nature study, yearbook production.
Sports Aerobics, archery, basketball, boating, canoeing, climbing (wall), equestrian sports, fencing, field hockey, fishing, football, go-carts, horseback riding, kayaking, lacrosse, martial arts, paintball, rappelling, riflery, ropes course, scuba diving, skateboarding, snorkeling, soccer, softball, swimming, volleyball, waterskiing.
Wilderness/Outdoors Hiking, rock climbing, survival training.
Trips Day, overnight.
Program Information 5–8 sessions per year. Session length: 1–3 weeks in June, July, August. Ages: 9–16. 8–80 participants per session. Boarding program cost: $1385–$2695.
Application Deadline Continuous.
Jobs Positions for college students 19 and older.
Contact Mr. Andy Wexler, Owner/Founder, PO Box 2237, Running Springs, California 92382. Phone: 909-867-5743. Fax: 909-867-7643. E-mail: info@paliadventures.com.
URL www.paliadventures.com/film_institute.html

Gold Arrow Camp

Huntington Lake, California 93634

General Information Coed residential traditional camp established in 1933. Accredited by American Camping Association.
Program Focus Noncompetitive outdoor and waterfront activities.
Arts Arts and crafts (general), ceramics, jewelry making, leather working, pottery, radio broadcasting, theater/drama.
Sports Archery, boating, canoeing, climbing (wall), fishing, horseback riding, kayaking, kneeboarding, riflery, ropes course, sailing, wakeboarding, waterskiing, windsurfing.
Wilderness/Outdoors Backpacking, hiking, mountain biking, rock climbing.
Trips Overnight.
Program Information 5–7 sessions per year. Session length: 1–4 weeks in June, July, August. Ages: 6–14. 240–250 participants per session. Boarding program cost: $1045–$4245.
Application Deadline Continuous.
Jobs Positions for college students 19 and older.
Summer Contact Mr. Steven Monke, Director, PO Box 155, Lakeshore, California 93634. Phone: 559-893-6641. Fax: 559-893-6201. E-mail: mail@goldarrowcamp.com.
Winter Contact Mr. Steven Monke, Director, 2900 Bristol Street, Suite A-107, Costa Mesa, California 92626. Phone: 714-424-5484. Fax: 714-424-0844. E-mail: mail@goldarrowcamp.com.
URL www.goldarrowcamp.com

Great Escapes (Adventure Trips for Teens)–California Beach Escape

South Shore YMCA Camps
California

General Information Coed travel outdoor program established in 1989. Religious affiliation: Christian. Accredited by American Camping Association.
Program Focus Surfing lessons, snorkeling, watersports, beach camping.
Special Interest Areas Campcraft.
Sports Body boarding, surfing.
Wilderness/Outdoors Outdoor adventure, outdoor camping.
Program Information 1 session per year. Session length: 13 days in August. Ages: 14–17. 10–12 participants per session. Cost: $1495. Financial aid available.
Application Deadline Continuous.
Jobs Positions for college students 21 and older.
Contact Joe O'Keefe, Great Escapes Director, 75 Stowe Road, Sandwich, Massachusetts 02563. Phone: 508-428-2571 Ext.110. Fax: 508-420-3545. E-mail: joeokeefe@ssymca.org.
URL www.ssymca.org/camps/great_escapes.asp

Griffith Park Boys Camp

City of Los Angeles Department of Recreation and Parks
4730 Crystal Springs Drive
Los Angeles, California 90027

General Information Boys' residential traditional camp established in 1926. Accredited by American Camping Association.
Academics Astronomy, ecology, music.
Arts Arts and crafts (general), ceramics, dance, drawing, film, jewelry making, leather working, music, painting, puppetry, theater/drama, woodworking.
Special Interest Areas Native American culture, campcraft, conservation projects, culinary arts, leadership training, nature study, nautical skills, team building.
Sports Archery, baseball, basketball, climbing (wall), fencing, field hockey, fishing, football, golf, horseback riding, martial arts, ropes course, soccer, softball, street/roller hockey, swimming, tennis, track and field, volleyball, water polo, wrestling.
Wilderness/Outdoors Hiking, orienteering.

Trips Day, overnight.
Program Information 8–10 sessions per year. Session length: 5–6 days in January, February, March, April, May, June, July, August, September, October, November, December. Ages: 6–17. 80–120 participants per session. Boarding program cost: $140–$200. Financial aid available.
Application Deadline Continuous.
Jobs Positions for high school students 18 and older and college students 18 and older.
Contact Karin Fox, Recreation Coordinator, main address above. Phone: 323-664-0571. Fax: 323-913-4170. E-mail: griffithparkboyscamp@rap.lacity.org.
URL www.laparks.org/dos/camps/griffith.htm

Gymnastics Academy at Pali Overnight Adventures

Pali Overnight Adventures
30778 Highway 18
Running Springs, California 92382

General Information Coed residential traditional camp and sports camp. Accredited by American Camping Association.
Program Focus Experienced gymnasts improve their skills and beginners receive a well-rounded introduction.
Sports Gymnastics.
Program Information 5–8 sessions per year. Session length: 1–3 weeks in June, July, August. Ages: 9–16. 8–80 participants per session. Boarding program cost: $1385–$2695.
Application Deadline Continuous.
Jobs Positions for college students 19 and older.
Contact Andy Wexler, Owner/Founder, PO Box 2237, Running Springs, California 92382. Phone: 909-867-5743. Fax: 909-867-7643. E-mail: info@paliadventures.com.
URL www.paliadventures.com/gymnastics.html

Harker Summer English Language Institute

The Harker School
500 Saratoga Avenue
San Jose, California 95129

General Information Coed day academic program established in 1984.
Program Focus English as a second language.
Academics English as a second language.
Trips Cultural, day, overnight.
Program Information 1–5 sessions per year. Session length: 3–8 weeks in June, July, August. Ages: 8–15. 50–80 participants per session. Day program cost: $3500–$8500. Application fee: $50.
Application Deadline Continuous.
Contact Mr. Joe Rosenthal, Executive Director, 500 Saratoga Avenue, San Jose, California 95129. Phone: 408-345-9264. Fax: 408-984-2395. E-mail: joer@harker.org.
URL www.harker.org/summerprograms/international/index.html

The Harker Summer Institute

The Harker School
500 Saratoga Avenue
San Jose, California 95129

General Information Coed day academic program established in 1999. Formal opportunities for the academically talented and artistically talented. High school credit may be earned.
Program Focus Choose from high school classes for academic credit; language studies abroad, academic enrichment and performing arts conservatory.
Academics SAT/ACT preparation, Spanish language/literature, academics (general), computers, mathematics, speech/debate, writing.
Arts Dance, theater/drama.
Program Information 1–3 sessions per year. Session length: 10–35 days in June, July, August. Ages: 14–17. 200–300 participants per session. Day program cost: $240–$1075.
Application Deadline Continuous.
Contact Jada Burrell, Summer Programs Assistant, main address above. Phone: 408-249-2510. Fax: 408-984-2325. E-mail: campinfo@harker.org.
URL www.harker.org

Harker Summer Programs

The Harker School
4300 Bucknall Road
San Jose, California 95130

General Information Coed day traditional camp and academic program established in 1957. Accredited by American Camping Association.
Program Focus Enriched academics and recreation.
Academics English as a second language, English language/literature, academics (general), biology, chemistry, computers, ecology, geology/earth science, health sciences, mathematics, music, reading, science (general), study skills.
Arts Arts and crafts (general), clowning, creative writing, dance, music, theater/drama.
Special Interest Areas Leadership training.
Sports Archery, basketball, climbing (wall), football, in-line skating, soccer, softball, street/roller hockey, swimming, tennis, volleyball.
Trips Day.
Program Information 4 sessions per year. Session length: 10–25 days in June, July, August. Ages: 4–14. 200–400 participants per session. Day program cost: $820–$2860.
Application Deadline Continuous.
Jobs Positions for high school students 16 and older and college students 19 and older.
Contact Kelly Espinosa, Dean Non-Academics, main address above. Phone: 408-871-4622. Fax: 408-871-4320. E-mail: kellye@harker.org.
URL www.harker.org

Hidden Villa Summer Camp

Hidden Villa Trust
26870 Moody Road
Los Altos Hills, California 94022

General Information Coed residential and day traditional camp, outdoor program, and cultural program established in 1945. Accredited by American Camping Association.
Program Focus Multiculturalism and environmentalism.
Academics Environmental science, intercultural studies, natural resource management.
Arts Acting, arts and crafts (general), ceramics, dance, dance (modern), fabric arts, jewelry making, painting, pottery, printmaking.
Special Interest Areas Animal care, campcraft, cross-cultural education, farming, leadership training, nature study.
Sports Archery, ropes course, swimming.
Wilderness/Outdoors Backpacking, hiking, orienteering, rock climbing, wilderness camping.
Trips Overnight.
Program Information 9 sessions per year. Session length: 5–12 days in June, July, August. Ages: 6–18. 12–60 participants per session. Day program cost: $350–$400. Boarding program cost: $350–$1000. Application fee: $50. Financial aid available.
Application Deadline March 1.
Jobs Positions for college students 18 and older.
Contact Ms. Jill Kilty-Newburn, Director, Family and Youth Programs, main address above. Phone: 650-949-8641. Fax: 650-948-1916. E-mail: camp@hiddenvilla.org.
URL www.hiddenvilla.org

High Sierra Wilderness Camps

Southwestern Safaris and Camps and Tours
Idyllwild, California 92549

General Information Coed residential wilderness program established in 1969. Formal opportunities for the academically talented and gifted. Specific services available for the learning disabled.
Academics Astronomy, ecology, environmental science, geography, geology/earth science, science (general).
Arts Music, music (vocal).
Special Interest Areas Campcraft, culinary arts, nature study, work camp programs.
Sports Baseball, fishing, football, swimming.
Wilderness/Outdoors Backpacking, camp fires, hiking, mountaineering, orienteering, rafting, wilderness camping, wilderness/outdoors (general).
Trips Overnight.
Program Information 4 sessions per year. Session length: 12 days in July, August. Ages: 11–17. 5–25 participants per session. Boarding program cost: $750. Financial aid available.
Application Deadline Continuous.
Jobs Positions for high school students 16 and older and college students 21 and older.
Contact Ed Busher, Director, PO Box 651, Idyllwild, California 92549. Phone: 909-659-2998.

Hollywood Stunt Camp at Pali Overnight Adventures

Pali Overnight Adventures
30778 Highway 18
Running Springs, California 92382

General Information Coed residential traditional camp and arts program. Accredited by American Camping Association.
Program Focus Learning high falls, backfalls, and how to choreograph a fight scene.
Arts Acting, stage combat.
Sports Gymnastics.
Program Information 5–8 sessions per year. Session length: 1–3 weeks in June, July, August. Ages: 9–16. 8–80 participants per session. Boarding program cost: $1385–$2695.
Application Deadline Continuous.
Jobs Positions for college students 19 and older.
Contact Andy Wexler, Owner/Founder, PO Box 2237, Running Springs, California 92382. Phone: 909-867-5743. Fax: 909-867-7643. E-mail: info@paliadventures.com.
URL www.paliadventures.com/stunt_camp.html

Horseback Riding Academy at Pali Overnight Adventures

Pali Overnight Adventures
30778 Highway 18
Running Springs, California 92382

General Information Coed residential traditional camp and adventure program established in 1990. Accredited by American Camping Association. Formal opportunities for the artistically talented.
Program Focus Western horseback riding.
Academics Journalism.
Arts Acting, arts and crafts (general), ceramics, dance, dance (jazz), dance (modern), film, film production, painting, pottery, theater/drama.
Special Interest Areas Animal care, leadership training, nature study, robotics, team building, yearbook production.
Sports Aerobics, archery, basketball, boating, canoeing, climbing (wall), equestrian sports, fencing, field hockey, fishing, football, go-carts, gymnastics, horseback riding, kayaking, lacrosse, martial arts, paintball, rappelling, riflery, ropes course, scuba diving, skateboarding, snorkeling, soccer, softball, swimming, tennis, volleyball, waterskiing.
Wilderness/Outdoors Hiking.
Trips Day, overnight.
Program Information 5–8 sessions per year. Session length: 1–2 weeks in June, July, August. Ages: 9–16. 8–80 participants per session. Boarding program cost: $1385–$2695.
Application Deadline Continuous.
Jobs Positions for college students 19 and older.
Contact Mr. Andy Wexler, Owner/Founder, PO Box 2237, Running Springs, California 92382. Phone: 909-867-5743. Fax: 909-867-7643. E-mail: info@paliadventures.com.
URL www.paliadventures.com/horseback_riding.html

iD Tech Camps–Cal Lutheran University, Thousand Oaks, CA

iD Tech Camps
California Lutheran University
Thousand Oaks, California 91360

General Information Coed residential and day academic program established in 1999. Accredited by American Camping Association. Formal opportunities for the academically talented and artistically talented.
Program Focus High-tech computer camps for kids and teens; produce digital movies, create video games, design Web pages, learn programming and robotics, and more; one computer per student, small classes, campers complete a project in a creative and fun learning environment.
Academics Web page design, computer programming, computer science (Advanced Placement), computers, music, precollege program.
Arts Animation, cartooning, cinematography, digital media, drawing, film, film editing, film production, graphic arts, music, television/video.
Special Interest Areas Career exploration, computer graphics, electronics, leadership training, robotics, team building.
Sports Baseball, basketball, soccer, softball, swimming, volleyball.
Trips College tours, cultural, day.
Program Information 5 sessions per year. Session length: 5–7 days in June, July, August. Ages: 7–17. 40–50 participants per session. Day program cost: $639. Boarding program cost: $989. Application fee: $200. Financial aid available.
Application Deadline Continuous.
Jobs Positions for college students 18 and older.
Contact Client Service Representatives, 1885 Winchester Boulevard, Suite 201, Campbell, California 95008. Phone: 888-709-TECH. Fax: 408-871-2228. E-mail: requests@internaldrive.com.
URL www.internaldrive.com

For more information, see page 1156.

iD Tech Camps–Dominican University, San Rafael, CA

iD Tech Camps
Dominican University
San Rafael, California 94901

General Information Coed residential and day academic program established in 1999. Accredited by American Camping Association. Formal opportunities for the academically talented and artistically talented.
Program Focus High-tech computer camps for kids and teens; produce digital movies, create video games, design Web pages, learn programming and robotics, and more; one computer per student, small classes, campers complete a project in a creative and fun learning environment.
Academics Web page design, computer programming, computer science (Advanced Placement), computers, music, precollege program.
Arts Animation, cartooning, cinematography, digital media, drawing, film, film editing, film production, graphic arts, music, television/video.
Special Interest Areas Career exploration, computer graphics, electronics, leadership training, robotics, team building.
Sports Baseball, basketball, soccer, softball, swimming, volleyball.
Trips College tours, cultural, day.
Program Information 5 sessions per year. Session length: 5–7 days in June, July, August. Ages: 7–17. 40–50 participants per session. Day program cost: $639. Boarding program cost: $989. Application fee: $200. Financial aid available.
Application Deadline Continuous.
Jobs Positions for college students 18 and older.
Contact Client Service Representatives, 1885 Winchester Boulevard, Suite 201, Campbell, California 95008. Phone: 888-709-TECH. Fax: 408-871-2228. E-mail: requests@internaldrive.com.
URL www.internaldrive.com

For more information, see page 1156.

iD Tech Camps–Pepperdine University, Malibu, CA

iD Tech Camps
Pepperdine University
Malibu, California 90263

General Information Coed residential and day academic program established in 1999. Accredited by American Camping Association. Formal opportunities for the academically talented and artistically talented.
Program Focus High-tech computer camps for kids and teens; produce digital movies, create video games, design Web pages, learn programming and robotics, and more; one computer per student, small classes, campers complete a project in a creative and fun learning environment.
Academics Web page design, computer programming, computer science (Advanced Placement), computers, music, precollege program.
Arts Animation, cartooning, cinematography, digital media, drawing, film, film editing, film production, graphic arts, music, television/video.
Special Interest Areas Career exploration, computer graphics, electronics, leadership training, robotics, team building.
Sports Baseball, basketball, soccer, softball, swimming, volleyball.
Trips College tours, cultural, day.
Program Information 5 sessions per year. Session length: 5–7 days in June, July, August. Ages: 7–17. 40–50 participants per session. Day program cost: $639. Boarding program cost: $989. Application fee: $200. Financial aid available.
Application Deadline Continuous.
Jobs Positions for college students 18 and older.

iD Tech Camps–Pepperdine University, Malibu, CA (continued)

Contact Client Service Representatives, 1885 Winchester Boulevard, Suite 201, Campbell, California 95008. Phone: 888-709-TECH. Fax: 408-871-2228. E-mail: requests@internaldrive.com.
URL www.internaldrive.com
For more information, see page 1156.

iD Tech Camps–Santa Clara University, Santa Clara, CA

iD Tech Camps
Santa Clara University
Santa Clara, California 95053

General Information Coed residential and day academic program established in 1999. Accredited by American Camping Association. Formal opportunities for the academically talented and artistically talented.
Program Focus High-tech computer camps for kids and teens; produce digital movies, create video games, design Web pages, learn programming and robotics, and more; one computer per student, small classes, campers complete a project in a creative and fun learning environment.
Academics Web page design, computer programming, computer science (Advanced Placement), computers, music, precollege program.
Arts Animation, cinematography, digital media, drawing, film, film editing, film production, graphic arts, music, television/video.
Special Interest Areas Career exploration, computer graphics, electronics, leadership training, robotics, team building.
Sports Baseball, basketball, soccer, softball, swimming, volleyball.
Trips College tours, cultural, day.
Program Information 3 sessions per year. Session length: 5–7 days in June, July, August. Ages: 7–17. 40–50 participants per session. Day program cost: $639. Boarding program cost: $989. Application fee: $200. Financial aid available.
Application Deadline Continuous.
Jobs Positions for college students 18 and older.
Contact Client Service Representatives, 1885 Winchester Boulevard, Suite 201, Campbell, California 95008. Phone: 888-709-TECH. Fax: 408-871-2228. E-mail: requests@internaldrive.com.
URL www.internaldrive.com
For more information, see page 1156.

iD Tech Camps–Stanford University, Palo Alto, CA

iD Tech Camps
Stanford University
Palo Alto, California 94305

General Information Coed residential and day academic program established in 1999. Accredited by American Camping Association. Formal opportunities for the academically talented and artistically talented.
Program Focus High-tech computer camps for kids and teens; produce digital movies, create video games, design Web pages, learn programming and robotics, and more; one computer per student, small classes, campers complete a project in a creative and fun learning environment.
Academics Web page design, computer programming, computer science (Advanced Placement), computers, music, precollege program.
Arts Animation, cartooning, cinematography, digital media, drawing, film, film editing, film production, graphic arts, music, television/video.
Special Interest Areas Career exploration, computer graphics, electronics, leadership training, robotics, team building.
Sports Baseball, basketball, soccer, softball, swimming, volleyball.
Trips College tours, cultural, day.
Program Information 5 sessions per year. Session length: 5–7 days in June, July, August. Ages: 7–17. 90–120 participants per session. Day program cost: $639. Boarding program cost: $989. Application fee: $200. Financial aid available.
Application Deadline Continuous.
Jobs Positions for college students 18 and older.
Contact Client Service Representatives, 1885 Winchester Boulevard, Suite 201, Campbell, California 95008. Phone: 888-709-TECH. Fax: 408-871-2228. E-mail: requests@internaldrive.com.
URL www.internaldrive.com
For more information, see page 1156.

iD Tech Camps–St. Mary's College, Moraga, CA

iD Tech Camps
St. Mary's College
Moraga, California 94575

General Information Coed residential and day academic program established in 1999. Accredited by American Camping Association. Formal opportunities for the academically talented and artistically talented.
Program Focus High-tech computer camps for kids and teens; produce digital movies, create video games, design Web pages, learn programming and robotics, and more; one computer per student, small classes, campers complete a project in a creative and fun learning environment.
Academics Web page design, computer programming, computer science (Advanced Placement), computers, music, precollege program.
Arts Animation, cinematography, digital media, drawing, film, film editing, film production, graphic arts, music, television/video.
Special Interest Areas Computer graphics, electronics, leadership training, robotics, team building.
Sports Baseball, basketball, soccer, softball, swimming, volleyball.
Trips College tours, cultural, day.
Program Information 5 sessions per year. Session length: 5–7 days in June, July, August. Ages: 7–17.

40–50 participants per session. Day program cost: $639. Boarding program cost: $989. Application fee: $200. Financial aid available.
Application Deadline Continuous.
Jobs Positions for college students 18 and older.
Contact Client Service Representatives, 1885 Winchester Boulevard, Suite 201, Campbell, California 95008. Phone: 888-709-TECH. Fax: 408-871-2228. E-mail: requests@internaldrive.com.
URL www.internaldrive.com

For more information, see page 1156.

iD Tech Camps–UC Berkeley, Berkeley, CA

iD Tech Camps
University of California, Berkeley
Berkeley, California 94720

General Information Coed residential and day academic program established in 1999. Accredited by American Camping Association. Formal opportunities for the academically talented and artistically talented.

iD Tech Camps–UC Berkeley, Berkeley, CA

Program Focus High-tech computer camps for kids and teens; produce digital movies, create video games, design Web pages, learn programming and robotics, and more; one computer per student, small classes, campers complete a project in a creative and fun learning environment.
Academics Web page design, computer programming, computer science (Advanced Placement), computers, music, precollege program.
Arts Animation, cartooning, cinematography, digital media, drawing, film, film editing, film production, graphic arts, music, television/video.
Special Interest Areas Career exploration, computer graphics, electronics, leadership training, robotics, team building.
Sports Baseball, basketball, soccer, softball, swimming, volleyball.
Trips College tours, cultural, day.
Program Information 5 sessions per year. Session length: 5–7 days in June, July, August. Ages: 7–17. 40–50 participants per session. Day program cost: $639. Boarding program cost: $989. Application fee: $200. Financial aid available.
Application Deadline Continuous.
Jobs Positions for college students 18 and older.
Contact Client Service Representatives, 1885 Winchester Boulevard, Suite 201, Campbell, California 95008. Phone: 888-709-TECH. Fax: 408-871-2228. E-mail: requests@internaldrive.com.
URL www.internaldrive.com

For more information, see page 1156.

iD Tech Camps–UC Irvine, Irvine, CA

iD Tech Camps
University of California at Irvine
Irvine, California 92697

General Information Coed residential and day academic program established in 1999. Accredited by American Camping Association. Formal opportunities for the academically talented and artistically talented.
Program Focus High-tech computer camps for kids and teens; produce digital movies, create video games, design Web pages, learn programming and robotics, and more; one computer per student, small classes, campers complete a project in a creative and fun learning environment.
Academics Web page design, computer programming, computer science (Advanced Placement), computers, music, precollege program.
Arts Animation, cinematography, digital media, drawing, film, film editing, film production, graphic arts, music, television/video.
Special Interest Areas Career exploration, computer graphics, electronics, leadership training, robotics, team building.
Sports Baseball, basketball, soccer, softball, swimming, volleyball.
Trips College tours, cultural, day.
Program Information 5 sessions per year. Session length: 5–7 days in June, July, August. Ages: 7–17. 40–50 participants per session. Day program cost: $639. Boarding program cost: $989. Application fee: $200. Financial aid available.
Application Deadline Continuous.

iD Tech Camps–UC Irvine, Irvine, CA (continued)

Jobs Positions for college students 18 and older.
Contact Client Service Representatives, 1885 Winchester Boulevard, Suite 201, Campbell, California 95008. Phone: 888-709-TECH. Fax: 408-871-2228. E-mail: requests@internaldrive.com.
URL www.internaldrive.com
For more information, see page 1156.

iD Tech Camps–UCLA, Westwood, CA

iD Tech Camps
University of California, Los Angeles
Westwood, California 90095

General Information Coed residential and day academic program established in 1999. Accredited by American Camping Association. Formal opportunities for the academically talented and artistically talented.
Program Focus High-tech computer camps for kids and teens; produce digital movies, create video games, design Web pages, learn programming and robotics, and more; one computer per student, small classes, campers complete a project in a creative and fun learning environment.
Academics Web page design, computer programming, computer science (Advanced Placement), computers, music, precollege program.
Arts Animation, cartooning, cinematography, digital media, drawing, film, film editing, film production, graphic arts, music, television/video.
Special Interest Areas Career exploration, computer graphics, electronics, leadership training, robotics, team building.
Sports Baseball, basketball, soccer, softball, swimming, volleyball.
Trips College tours, cultural, day.
Program Information 5 sessions per year. Session length: 5–7 days in June, July, August. Ages: 7–17. 40–50 participants per session. Day program cost: $639. Boarding program cost: $989. Application fee: $200. Financial aid available.
Application Deadline Continuous.
Jobs Positions for college students 18 and older.
Contact Client Service Representatives, 1885 Winchester Boulevard, Suite 201, Campbell, California 95008. Phone: 888-709-TECH. Fax: 408-871-2228. E-mail: requests@internaldrive.com.
URL www.internaldrive.com
For more information, see page 1156.

iD Tech Camps–UC San Diego, La Jolla, CA

iD Tech Camps
University of California, San Diego
La Jolla, California 92093

General Information Coed residential and day academic program established in 1999. Accredited by American Camping Association. Formal opportunities for the academically talented and artistically talented.
Program Focus High-tech computer camps for kids and teens; produce digital movies, create video games, design Web pages, learn programming and robotics, and more; one computer per student, small classes, campers complete a project in a creative and fun learning environment.
Academics Web page design, computer programming, computer science (Advanced Placement), computers, music, precollege program.
Arts Animation, cartooning, cinematography, digital media, drawing, film, film editing, film production, graphic arts, music, television/video.
Special Interest Areas Career exploration, computer graphics, electronics, leadership training, robotics, team building.
Sports Baseball, basketball, soccer, softball, swimming, volleyball.
Trips College tours, cultural, day.
Program Information 5 sessions per year. Session length: 5–7 days in June, July, August. Ages: 7–17. 40–50 participants per session. Day program cost: $639. Boarding program cost: $989. Application fee: $200. Financial aid available.
Application Deadline Continuous.
Jobs Positions for college students 18 and older.
Contact Client Service Representatives, 1885 Winchester Boulevard, Suite 201, Campbell, California 95008. Phone: 888-709-TECH. Fax: 408-871-2228. E-mail: requests@internaldrive.com.
URL www.internaldrive.com
For more information, see page 1156.

iD Tech Camps–UC Santa Cruz, Santa Cruz, CA

iD Tech Camps
University of California, Santa Cruz
Santa Cruz, California 95064

General Information Coed residential and day academic program. Accredited by American Camping Association. Formal opportunities for the academically talented and artistically talented.
Program Focus High-tech computer camps for kids and teens; produce digital movies, create video games, design Web pages, learn programming and robotics, and more; one computer per student, small classes, campers complete a project in a creative and fun learning environment.
Academics Web page design, computer programming, computer science (Advanced Placement), computers, music, precollege program.
Arts Animation, cinematography, digital media, drawing, film, film editing, film production, graphic arts, music, television/video.
Special Interest Areas Career exploration, computer graphics, electronics, leadership training, robotics, team building.
Sports Baseball, basketball, soccer, softball, swimming, volleyball.
Trips College tours, cultural, day.
Program Information 5 sessions per year. Session length: 5–7 days in June, July, August. Ages: 7–17.

40–50 participants per session. Day program cost: $639. Boarding program cost: $989. Application fee: $200. Financial aid available.
Application Deadline Continuous.
Jobs Positions for college students 18 and older.
Contact Client Service Representatives, 1885 Winchester Boulevard, Suite 201, Campbell, California 95008. Phone: 888-709-TECH. Fax: 408-871-2228. E-mail: requests@internaldrive.com.
URL www.internaldrive.com

For more information, see page 1156.

IDYLLWILD ARTS SUMMER PROGRAM–AMERICAN EXPERIENCE FOR INTERNATIONAL STUDENTS

Idyllwild Arts Foundation
Idyllwild, California 92549

General Information Coed residential arts program established in 1998.
Program Focus Arts, English, and American culture.
Academics English as a second language.
Arts Arts, band, ceramics, chorus, creative writing, dance, dance (ballet), dance (jazz), dance (modern), dance (tap), drawing, fabric arts, graphic arts, jewelry making, music, music (chamber), music (classical), music (ensemble), music (instrumental), music (jazz), music (orchestral), music (vocal), musical productions, painting, performance art, photography, pottery, sculpture, television/video, theater/drama, visual arts.
Trips Cultural, day, overnight, shopping.
Program Information 1 session per year. Session length: 5 weeks in July, August. Ages: 13–18. 15–40 participants per session. Boarding program cost: $4900.
Application Deadline Continuous.
Jobs Positions for college students 19 and older.
Contact Ms. Diane Dennis, Summer Program Registrar, PO Box 38, Idyllwild, California 92549. Phone: 909-659-2171 Ext.365. Fax: 909-659-5463. E-mail: summer@idyllwildarts.org.
URL www.idyllwildarts.org

For more information, see page 1158.

IDYLLWILD ARTS SUMMER PROGRAM–CHILDREN'S CENTER

Idyllwild Arts Foundation
Idyllwild, California 92549

General Information Coed residential and day arts program established in 1950. Formal opportunities for the artistically talented.
Arts Acting, animation, arts, arts and crafts (general), band, batiking, ceramics, chorus, clowning, creative writing, dance, dance (ballet), dance (jazz), dance (modern), dance (tap), drawing, fabric arts, film, jewelry making, mime, music, music (chamber), music (classical), music (ensemble), music (instrumental), music (jazz), music (orchestral), music (vocal), musical productions, painting, performance art, photography, pottery, printmaking, sculpture, television/video, theater/drama, visual arts.
Program Information 1–2 sessions per year. Session length: 1–2 weeks in July, August. Ages: 5–12. 75–100 participants per session. Day program cost: $230–$1050. Boarding program cost: $1830. Application fee: $25. Financial aid available. Minimum age for boarding is 9.
Application Deadline Continuous.
Jobs Positions for college students 19 and older.
Contact Ms. Diane Dennis, Summer Program Registrar, PO Box 38, Idyllwild, California 92549. Phone: 909-659-2171 Ext.365. Fax: 909-659-5463. E-mail: summer@idyllwildarts.org.
URL www.idyllwildarts.org

For more information, see page 1158.

IDYLLWILD ARTS SUMMER PROGRAM–FAMILY WEEK

Idyllwild Arts Foundation
Idyllwild, California 92549

General Information Coed residential family program and arts program established in 1950. Formal opportunities for the artistically talented.
Arts Arts, arts and crafts (general), batiking, ceramics, chorus, creative writing, dance, drawing, fabric arts, graphic arts, jewelry making, mime, music, musical productions, painting, performance art, photography, pottery, printmaking, puppetry, sculpture, theater/drama, visual arts, weaving, woodworking.
Sports Ropes course, sports (general), swimming.
Wilderness/Outdoors Hiking.
Program Information 1–2 sessions per year. Session length: 1 week in June, July. 75–100 participants per session. Boarding program cost: $1580–$3300.
Application Deadline Continuous.
Jobs Positions for college students 19 and older.
Contact Ms. Diane Dennis, Summer Program Registrar, PO Box 38, Idyllwild, California 92549. Phone: 909-659-2171 Ext.365. Fax: 909-659-5463. E-mail: summer@idyllwildarts.org.
URL www.idyllwildarts.org

For more information, see page 1158.

IDYLLWILD ARTS SUMMER PROGRAM–JUNIOR ARTISTS' CENTER

Idyllwild Arts Foundation
Idyllwild, California 92549

General Information Coed residential and day arts program established in 1950. Formal opportunities for the artistically talented.
Arts Acting, arts, band, ceramics, creative writing, dance, dance (ballet), dance (jazz), dance (modern), dance (tap), drawing, fabric arts, jewelry making, mime, music, music (classical), music (ensemble), music (instrumental), music (jazz), music (orchestral), music (vocal), musical productions, painting, performance art, photography, pottery, printmaking, sculpture, theater/drama, visual arts.
Program Information 1 session per year. Session length: 1–2 weeks in July, August. Ages: 11–13. 75–100

Idyllwild Arts Summer Program–Junior Artists' Center (continued)

participants per session. Day program cost: $915–$1150. Boarding program cost: $1850–$1950. Application fee: $25. Financial aid available.
Application Deadline Continuous.
Jobs Positions for college students.
Contact Ms. Diane Dennis, Summer Program Registrar, PO Box 38, Idyllwild, California 92549. Phone: 909-659-2171 Ext.365. Fax: 909-659-5463. E-mail: summer@idyllwildarts.org.
URL www.idyllwildarts.org
For more information, see page 1158.

Idyllwild Arts Summer Program–Youth Arts Center

Idyllwild Arts Foundation
Idyllwild, California 92549

General Information Coed residential and day arts program established in 1950. Formal opportunities for the artistically talented.

Idyllwild Arts Summer Program–Youth Arts Center

Arts Acting, animation, arts, band, ceramics, chorus, clowning, creative writing, dance, dance (ballet), dance (jazz), dance (modern), dance (tap), drawing, fabric arts, film, graphic arts, jewelry making, mime, music, music (chamber), music (classical), music (ensemble), music (instrumental), music (jazz), music (orchestral), music (vocal), musical productions, musical theater, painting, performance art, photography, pottery, printmaking, sculpture, television/video, theater/drama, visual arts.
Program Information 3 sessions per year. Session length: 2–3 weeks in July, August. Ages: 13–18. 250–400 participants per session. Day program cost: $915–$1150. Boarding program cost: $1750–$1950. Application fee: $25. Financial aid available.
Application Deadline Continuous.
Jobs Positions for college students 19 and older.
Contact Diane Dennis, Registrar, Summer Program, PO Box 38, Idyllwild, California 92549. Phone: 909-659-2171 Ext.365. Fax: 909-659-5463. E-mail: summer@idyllwildarts.org.
URL www.idyllwildarts.org
For more information, see page 1158.

Joe Machnik's No. 1 Academy One and Premier Programs–Claremont, California

Joe Machnik's No. 1 Camps
Claremont McKenna College
Claremont, California

General Information Coed residential and day sports camp established in 1999.
Program Focus Soccer instruction, physical fitness, testing and speed training. Campers gain exposure to top players and are challenged by intense competition.
Sports Soccer, swimming.
Trips Day.
Program Information 1 session per year. Session length: 6 days in July. Ages: 9–18. 50–175 participants per session. Day program cost: $759. Boarding program cost: $819. Financial aid available.
Application Deadline Continuous.
Jobs Positions for college students.
Contact Dr. Joseph Machnik, Director, PO Box 389, 916 Palm Boulevard, Isle of Palms, South Carolina 29451. Phone: 800-622-4645. Fax: 843-886-0885. E-mail: info@no1soccercamps.com.
URL www.no1soccercamps.com

Joe Machnik's No. 1 Academy One and Premier Programs–Rohnert Park, California

Joe Machnik's No. 1 Camps
Sonoma State University
Rohnert Park, California

General Information Coed residential and day sports camp.
Program Focus Soccer instruction, physical fitness, testing and speed training. Campers gain exposure to top players and are challenged by intense competition.

Sports Soccer.
Trips Day.
Program Information 1 session per year. Session length: 6 days in July. Ages: 9–18. Day program cost: $759. Boarding program cost: $819. Financial aid available.
Application Deadline Continuous.
Jobs Positions for college students.
Contact Dr. Joseph Machnik, Director, PO Box 389, 916 Palm Boulevard, Isle of Palms, South Carolina 29451. Phone: 800-622-4645. Fax: 843-886-0885. E-mail: info@no1soccercamps.com.
URL www.no1soccercamps.com

Joe Machnik's No. 1 Mighty Mini, Goalkeeper and Striker Camp–Claremont, California

Joe Machnik's No. 1 Camps
Claremont McKenna College
Claremont, California

General Information Coed residential and day sports camp established in 1977.
Program Focus Soccer instruction. Goalkeepers and strikers compete against each other daily.
Sports Soccer, swimming.
Program Information 1 session per year. Session length: 6 days in July. Ages: 8–12. 100–150 participants per session. Boarding program cost: $459. Financial aid available.
Application Deadline Continuous.
Jobs Positions for college students 17 and older.
Contact Dr. Joseph Machnik, Director, PO Box 389, 916 Palm Boulevard, Isle of Palms, South Carolina 29451. Phone: 800-622-4645. Fax: 843-886-0885. E-mail: info@no1soccercamps.com.
URL www.no1soccercamps.com

Joe Machnik's No. 1 Mighty Mini, Goalkeeper and Striker Camp–Rohnert Park, California

Joe Machnik's No. 1 Camps
Sonoma State University
Rohnert Park, California

General Information Coed residential and day sports camp established in 1977.
Program Focus Soccer instruction. Goalkeepers and strikers compete against each other daily.
Sports Soccer, swimming.
Program Information 1 session per year. Session length: 6 days in July. Ages: 8–12. 100–150 participants per session. Boarding program cost: $459. Financial aid available.
Application Deadline Continuous.
Jobs Positions for college students 17 and older.
Contact Dr. Joseph Machnik, Director, PO Box 389, 916 Palm Boulevard, Isle of Palms, South Carolina 29451. Phone: 800-622-4645. Fax: 843-886-0885. E-mail: info@no1soccerscamps.com.
URL www.no1soccercamps.com

Julian Krinsky California Teen Tours

Julian Krinsky Camps and Programs
California

General Information Coed travel sports camp and cultural program established in 2002.
Program Focus Travel, golf, tennis.
Special Interest Areas Touring.
Sports Golf, tennis.
Trips College tours, cultural, day, overnight, shopping.
Program Information 2 sessions per year. Session length: 3 weeks in June, July, August. Ages: 13–16. 25–100 participants per session. Cost: $4150. Financial aid available.
Application Deadline Continuous.
Jobs Positions for college students 21 and older.
Contact Julian Krinsky, Owner, PO Box 333, Haverford, Pennsylvania 19041. Phone: 610-265-9401. Fax: 610-265-3678. E-mail: info@jkcp.com.
URL www.jkcp.com

For more information, see page 1172.

Julian Krinsky Yesh Shabbat California Teen Tour

Julian Krinsky Camps and Programs
California

General Information Coed travel cultural program. Religious affiliation: Jewish.
Program Focus Travel, golf, tennis.
Special Interest Areas Touring.
Sports Golf, tennis.
Trips College tours, cultural, day, overnight, shopping.
Program Information 1 session per year. Session length: 18 days in July, August. Ages: 13–16. 25–40 participants per session. Cost: $3300. Application fee: $50. Financial aid available.
Application Deadline Continuous.
Contact Julian Krinsky, Owner/Director, 610 South Henderson Road, King of Prussia, Pennsylvania 19406. Phone: 610-265-9401. E-mail: julian@jkcp.com.
URL www.jkcp.com

For more information, see page 1172.

Junior Statesmen Summer School–Stanford University

Junior Statesmen Foundation
Stanford University
Stanford, California 94305

General Information Coed residential academic program established in 1941. Formal opportunities for the academically talented. High school credit may be earned.
Program Focus American government, economics, speech, leadership, political communication, and comparative politics and government.

Junior Statesmen Summer School–Stanford University (continued)

Junior Statesmen Summer School–Stanford University

Academics Communications, economics, government and politics, government and politics (Advanced Placement), journalism, precollege program, social science, social studies, speech/debate.
Special Interest Areas Career exploration, leadership training.
Trips College tours, cultural, day.
Program Information 1 session per year. Session length: 27 days in June, July. Ages: 14–18. 300–350 participants per session. Boarding program cost: $3500. Financial aid available.
Application Deadline Continuous.
Contact Matt Randazzo, National Summer Programs Director, 400 South El Camino Real, Suite 300, San Mateo, California 94402. Phone: 650-347-1600. Fax: 650-347-7200. E-mail: jsa@jsa.org.
URL www.jsa.org
For more information, see page 1174.

Junior Statesmen Symposium on California State Politics and Government

Junior Statesmen Foundation
University of California
Davis, California 95616

General Information Coed residential academic program established in 1990. Formal opportunities for the academically talented.
Program Focus State government, politics, debate, and leadership training.
Academics Communications, government and politics, journalism, precollege program, social science, social studies, speech/debate.
Special Interest Areas Career exploration, leadership training.
Trips College tours, day.
Program Information 1 session per year. Session length: 4 days in August. Ages: 14–18. 40–100 participants per session. Boarding program cost: $395. Financial aid available.
Application Deadline Continuous.
Contact Matt Randazzo, National Summer School Director, 400 South El Camino Real, Suite 300, San Mateo, California 94402. Phone: 650-347-1600. Fax: 650-347-7200. E-mail: jsa@jsa.org.
URL www.jsa.org
For more information, see page 1174.

Junior Statesmen Symposium on Los Angeles Politics and Government

Junior Statesmen Foundation
University of Southern California
Los Angeles, California 90089

General Information Coed residential academic program established in 1977. Formal opportunities for the academically talented.
Program Focus Local government, politics, debate, and leadership training.
Academics Communications, government and politics, journalism, precollege program, social science, social studies, speech/debate.
Special Interest Areas Career exploration, leadership training.
Trips College tours, day.
Program Information 1 session per year. Session length: 5 days in August. Ages: 14–18. 40–80 participants per session. Boarding program cost: $395. Scholarships available to LAUSD inner-city high school students.
Application Deadline Continuous.
Contact Matt Randazzo, National Summer School Director, 400 South El Camino Real, Suite 300, San Mateo, California 94402. Phone: 650-347-1600. Fax: 650-347-7200. E-mail: jsa@jsa.org.
URL www.jsa.org
For more information, see page 1174.

Landmark Volunteers: California

Landmark Volunteers, Inc.
California

General Information Coed residential outdoor program, community service program, and wilderness program established in 1992. High school credit may be earned.
Program Focus Opportunity for high school students to earn community service credit while working as a team for two weeks serving Henry W. Coe State Park. Similar programs offered through Landmark Volunteers at over 60 locations in 21 states.

Academics Biology, ecology, environmental science, science (general), social science.
Special Interest Areas Career exploration, community service, conservation projects, field research/expeditions, leadership training, nature study, team building, trail maintenance, work camp programs.
Sports Swimming.
Wilderness/Outdoors Hiking, wilderness camping.
Trips Cultural, day.
Program Information 1 session per year. Session length: 2 weeks in June, July, August. Ages: 14–18. 10–13 participants per session. Boarding program cost: $875–$925. Financial aid available.
Application Deadline Continuous.
Jobs Positions for college students.
Contact Ann Barrett, Executive Director, PO Box 455, Sheffield, Massachusetts 01257. Phone: 413-229-0255. Fax: 413-229-2050. E-mail: landmark@volunteers.com.
URL www.volunteers.com

For more information, see page 1182.

Leadership Training at Pali Overnight Adventures

Pali Overnight Adventures
30778 Highway 18
Running Springs, California 92382

General Information Coed residential traditional camp and adventure program established in 1990. Accredited by American Camping Association. Formal opportunities for the artistically talented.
Academics Journalism, music, music (Advanced Placement).
Arts Acting, arts and crafts (general), ceramics, dance, dance (jazz), dance (modern), dance (tap), film, film production, painting, pottery, theater/drama.
Special Interest Areas Animal care, counselor-in-training program, culinary arts, leadership training, nature study, robotics, yearbook production.
Sports Aerobics, archery, basketball, boating, canoeing, climbing (wall), equestrian sports, fencing, field hockey, fishing, football, go-carts, gymnastics, horseback riding, kayaking, lacrosse, martial arts, paintball, rappelling, riflery, ropes course, scuba diving, skateboarding, snorkeling, soccer, softball, swimming, tennis, volleyball, waterskiing.
Wilderness/Outdoors Hiking.
Trips Day, overnight.
Program Information 5–8 sessions per year. Session length: 1–2 weeks in June, July, August. Ages: 9–16. 8–80 participants per session. Boarding program cost: $1385–$2695.
Application Deadline Continuous.
Jobs Positions for college students 19 and older.
Contact Mr. Andy Wexler, Owner/Founder, PO Box 2237, Running Springs, California 92382. Phone: 909-867-5743. Fax: 909-867-7643. E-mail: info@paliadventures.com.
URL www.paliadventures.com

Lifeschool Wilderness Adventures–Summer Adventures

Lifeschool Wilderness Adventures and Learning Program
17135 Bodega Highway
Bodega, California 94922

General Information Coed travel outdoor program, wilderness program, and adventure program established in 2000.
Program Focus Life skill building, teamwork, problem solving through wilderness hiking and camping trips in California, Oregon, Washington, Colorado and Hawaii.
Arts Photography.
Special Interest Areas Campcraft, personal development, problem solving, team building.
Sports Sea kayaking.
Wilderness/Outdoors Backpacking, bicycle trips, canoe trips, hiking, mountain biking, orienteering, outdoor adventure, rafting, rock climbing, survival training, white-water trips, wilderness camping.
Program Information 15–30 sessions per year. Session length: 2–20 days in June, July, August. Ages: 12–18. 7–30 participants per session. Cost: $500–$2000. Financial aid available.
Application Deadline Continuous.
Contact Mr. Jim Nevill, Executive Director, PO Box 134, Bodega, California 94922. Phone: 707-876-3071. Fax: 707-876-3072. E-mail: jim@life-school.org.
URL www.life-school.org

Millennium Entrepreneurs Camp CEO

Millennium Entrepreneurs
California

General Information Coed residential and day traditional camp, academic program, and community service program established in 1997. Accredited by American Camping Association. Formal opportunities for the academically talented.
Program Focus Youth entrepreneur training for grades 3-12 located at Pepperdine University and University of San Diego.
Academics English as a second language, business, computers, government and politics, intercultural studies.
Arts Arts and crafts (general), creative writing, jewelry making.
Special Interest Areas Native American culture, community service, leadership training, nature study, touring.
Sports Baseball, basketball, canoeing, fishing, football, soccer, softball, swimming, tennis, volleyball.
Trips College tours, cultural, day, overnight, shopping.
Program Information 2–4 sessions per year. Session length: 3–14 days in March, June, July, August, December. Ages: 8–19. 20–60 participants per session. Day program cost: $500–$800. Boarding program cost: $900–$2400. Financial aid available.
Application Deadline Continuous.
Jobs Positions for high school students 16 and older and college students 19 and older.

Millennium Entrepreneurs Camp CEO (continued)
Summer Contact Ms. Tonja McCoy, Camp Director, PO Box 14, Malibu, California 90265. Phone: 310-589-0235. E-mail: teensceo@yahoo.com.
Winter Contact Ms. Tonja McCoy, Camp Director, PO Box 14, Malibu, California 90265. Phone: 310-589-0235.

Millennium Entrepreneurs "Training Tomorrow's Business Leaders Today"

Millennium Entrepreneurs
California

General Information Coed residential and day traditional camp, academic program, and community service program established in 1997. Accredited by American Camping Association. Formal opportunities for the academically talented.
Program Focus Youth entrepreneur training for grades 3-12 located at Pepperdine University and University of San Diego.
Academics English as a second language, business, computers, government and politics, intercultural studies.
Arts Arts and crafts (general), creative writing, jewelry making, painting, photography.
Special Interest Areas Native American culture, community service, leadership training, nature study, touring.
Sports Baseball, basketball, canoeing, climbing (wall), fishing, football, ropes course, soccer, swimming, tennis, volleyball.
Wilderness/Outdoors Hiking, rock climbing, survival training.
Trips College tours, cultural, day, overnight, shopping.
Program Information 2–7 sessions per year. Session length: 3–14 days in March, June, July, August, December. Ages: 8–18. 20–60 participants per session. Day program cost: $500–$1800. Boarding program cost: $900–$2100. Essay Entrepreneur Scholarship Contest Awards available.
Application Deadline Continuous.
Jobs Positions for college students 19 and older.
Summer Contact Ms. Tonja McCoy, President/Camp Director, PO Box 14, Malibu, California 90265. Phone: 301-582-0235. E-mail: teensceo@yahoo.com.
Winter Contact Ms. Tonja McCoy, President, PO Box 14, Malibu, California 90265. Phone: 301-582-0235. E-mail: teensceo@yahoo.com.

Miracle Makers Summer Camp

Kabbalah Children's Academy-Spirituality for Kids Academy
1046 South Robertson Boulevard
Los Angeles, California 90035

General Information Coed day traditional camp established in 1996. Religious affiliation: Jewish.
Academics Hebrew language, Jewish studies, computers, typing.
Arts Acting, arts and crafts (general), ceramics, dance, dance (jazz), jewelry making, music, music (vocal), musical productions, painting, theater/drama, woodworking.
Special Interest Areas Animal care, culinary arts, leadership training, nature study, team building.
Sports Basketball, field hockey, gymnastics, soccer, swimming, volleyball.
Wilderness/Outdoors Hiking.
Trips Day.
Program Information 3–5 sessions per year. Session length: 5–35 days in June, July, August. Ages: 2–12. 35–80 participants per session. Day program cost: $200–$1400. Financial aid available.
Application Deadline Continuous.
Contact Mrs. Carolyn Strong, Administrator/Principal, main address above. Phone: 310-854-6857. Fax: 310-854-1530. E-mail: kca@kabbalah.com.
URL www.spiritualityforkids.com

Monte Vista ESL Intensive Language Institute

Monte Vista Christian School
Two School Way
Watsonville, California 95076

General Information Coed residential academic program established in 1987. Religious affiliation: Christian. High school credit may be earned.
Program Focus English as a second language.
Academics English as a second language.
Arts Music, television/video, theater/drama.
Special Interest Areas Internet accessibility, culinary arts, touring.
Sports Bicycling, softball, swimming, tennis, volleyball.
Trips Day, overnight, shopping.
Program Information 2 sessions per year. Session length: 24–38 days in June, July. Ages: 13–17. 10–15 participants per session. Boarding program cost: $3300–$4900.
Application Deadline Continuous.
Contact Ms. Susan Bernal, Director of Resident Admissions, main address above. Phone: 831-722-8178 Ext. 128. Fax: 831-722-6003. E-mail: susanbernal@mvcs.org.
URL www.mvcs.org

Mountain Camp

Mountain Camp
Ice House Lake, El Dorado National Forest
Pollock Pines, California 95726

General Information Coed residential traditional camp established in 1966. Accredited by American Camping Association.
Arts Arts and crafts (general), dance, guitar, jewelry making, photography, television/video, theater/drama.
Special Interest Areas Campcraft, leadership training, nature study, team building.
Sports Archery, basketball, bicycling, canoeing, climbing (wall), fencing, fishing, gymnastics, kayaking, martial arts, rappelling, ropes course, sailing, snorkeling, swimming, volleyball, windsurfing.
Wilderness/Outdoors Backpacking, bicycle trips, canoe trips, hiking, mountain biking, orienteering, wilderness camping.
Trips Overnight.

Program Information 6 sessions per year. Session length: 1–2 weeks in June, July, August. Ages: 8–16. 180 participants per session. Boarding program cost: $850–$1745.
Application Deadline Continuous.
Jobs Positions for college students 19 and older.
Contact Don Whipple, Director, 3717 Buchanan Street, Suite 300, San Francisco, California 94123. Phone: 415-351-2267. Fax: 415-351-3939. E-mail: info@mountaincamp.com.
URL www.mountaincamp.com

Mountain Meadow Ranch

Mountain Meadow Ranch
Susanville, California 96130

General Information Coed residential traditional camp and outdoor program established in 1956. Accredited by American Camping Association.
Academics Archaeology, astronomy.
Arts Arts and crafts (general), ceramics, photography, pottery, puppetry, theater/drama.
Special Interest Areas Native American culture, animal care, campcraft, farming, gardening, leadership training, nature study.
Sports Archery, basketball, bicycling, canoeing, climbing (wall), equestrian sports, fencing, fishing, horseback riding, rappelling, riflery, ropes course, sailing, soccer, softball, swimming, tennis, volleyball, waterskiing.
Wilderness/Outdoors Backpacking, caving, hiking, mountain biking, orienteering, rafting, survival training, white-water trips, wilderness camping.
Trips Day, hiking, overnight.
Program Information 3–4 sessions per year. Session length: 7–19 days in June, July, August. Ages: 7–17. 110–120 participants per session. Boarding program cost: $900–$2400.
Application Deadline Continuous.
Jobs Positions for college students 18 and older.
Contact Jack "Chip" Ellena, Owner/Director, P.O. Box 610, Susanville, California 96130. Phone: 530-257-4419. Fax: 530-257-7155. E-mail: info@mountainmeadow.com.
URL www.mountainmeadow.com

Mountain Retreat Overnight Camp

KidsMakeADifference.org
California

General Information Coed residential outdoor program established in 1994.
Program Focus Hiking, vegetarian cooking.
Academics Botany, ecology, environmental science, geology/earth science, journalism, music, peace education, writing.
Arts Drawing, music, music (vocal), photography, television/video.
Special Interest Areas Native American culture, campcraft, culinary arts, nature study, team building.
Sports Baseball, boating, canoeing, frisbee, miniature golf, swimming.
Wilderness/Outdoors Hiking, mountaineering, orienteering.
Trips Day, overnight.
Program Information 1 session per year. Session length: 5 days in July, August. Ages: 7–13. 8 participants per session. Boarding program cost: $695. Financial aid available.
Application Deadline Continuous.
Jobs Positions for college students 18 and older.
Summer Contact Dr. Andy Mars, Director, PO Box 24922, Los Angeles, California 90024-0922. Phone: 818-344-7838.
Winter Contact Dr. Andy Mars, Director, PO Box 24922, Los Angeles, California 90024-0922. Phone: 818-344-7838.
URL www.kidsmakeadifference.org

National Computer Camps at San Francisco State University

National Computer Camps
San Francisco State University
800 Font Boulevard
San Francisco, California 94132

General Information Coed residential and day academic program established in 1977. Formal opportunities for the academically talented.
Program Focus Computer science, programming, Internet, recreation, and sports.
Academics Web page design, computer programming, computer science (Advanced Placement), computers.
Arts Animation, graphic arts.
Special Interest Areas Internet accessibility, electronics, robotics.
Sports Basketball, soccer, swimming, tennis, volleyball.
Program Information 2 sessions per year. Session length: 1 week in July, August. Ages: 8–18. 80–125 participants per session. Day program cost: $595. Boarding program cost: $795.
Application Deadline Continuous.
Jobs Positions for high school students 16 and older and college students 18 and older.
Contact Dr. Michael Zabinski, President, PO Box 585, Orange, Connecticut 06477. Phone: 203-795-9667. E-mail: info@nccamp.com.
URL www.nccamp.com

National Guitar Workshop–Los Angeles, CA

National Guitar Workshop
Loyola Marymount University
7900 LMU Drive
Los Angeles, California 90045

General Information Coed residential and day arts program established in 1984. College credit may be earned.
Program Focus Music education in guitar, bass, drums, and vocals.
Academics Music, music (Advanced Placement).
Arts Guitar, music (classical), music (ensemble), music (instrumental), music (jazz), music (rock), music (vocal).
Program Information 1 session per year. Session length: 1 week in June, July, August. Ages: 13–79.

National Guitar Workshop–Los Angeles, CA (continued)

75–225 participants per session. Day program cost: $670–$720. Boarding program cost: $870–$920. Application fee: $25. Financial aid available.
Application Deadline Continuous.
Jobs Positions for college students 21 and older.
Contact Ms. Emily Flower, Registrar, PO Box 222, Lakeside, Connecticut 06758. Phone: 860-567-3736 Ext. 109. Fax: 860-567-0374. E-mail: emily@guitarworkshop.com.
URL www.guitarworkshop.com

National Guitar Workshop–San Francisco, CA

National Guitar Workshop
Notre Dame de Namer
1500 Ralston Avenue
Belmont, California 94002

General Information Coed residential and day arts program established in 1984. College credit may be earned.
Program Focus Music education in guitar, bass, drums, and vocals.
Academics Music, music (Advanced Placement).
Arts Guitar, music (classical), music (ensemble), music (instrumental), music (jazz), music (rock), music (vocal).
Program Information 1 session per year. Session length: 1 week in June, July, August. Ages: 13–79. 75–225 participants per session. Day program cost: $670–$720. Boarding program cost: $870–$920. Application fee: $25. Financial aid available.
Application Deadline Continuous.
Jobs Positions for college students 21 and older.
Contact Ms. Emily Flower, Registrar, PO Box 222, Lakeside, Connecticut 06758. Phone: 860-567-3736 Ext. 109. Fax: 860-567-0374. E-mail: emily@guitarworkshop.com.
URL www.guitarworkshop.com

The National Music Workshop Day Jams–Los Angeles, CA

National Guitar Workshop
Marymount High School
10643 Sunset Boulevard
Los Angeles, California 90077

General Information Coed day arts program established in 2003. Formal opportunities for the artistically talented.
Program Focus Rock 'n' roll day camp.
Academics Music.
Arts Arts and crafts (general), band, music, music (rock), music (vocal), television/video.
Program Information 2 sessions per year. Session length: 5–10 days in June. Ages: 9–15. 40–60 participants per session. Day program cost: $425–$495. Application fee: $35. Financial aid available.
Application Deadline Continuous.
Jobs Positions for high school students 17 and older and college students 17 and older.
Contact Lynda Wlodarczyk, Associate Director, 407A Bantam Road, Suite 1, Litchfield, Connecticut 06759. Phone: 800-295-5956. Fax: 860-567-0374. E-mail: lynda@dayjams.com.
URL www.dayjams.com

National Student Leadership Conference: Law and Advocacy–California

National Student Leadership Conference
Stanford University
Palo Alto, California

General Information Coed residential academic program established in 1989. Formal opportunities for the academically talented and gifted. College credit may be earned.
Program Focus Leadership, enrichment, law, and the American judicial system.
Academics Communications, prelaw, speech/debate, writing.
Special Interest Areas Career exploration, leadership training, touring.
Sports Ropes course.
Trips Cultural.
Program Information 4–6 sessions per year. Session length: 11 days in June, July, August. Ages: 14–18. 200–250 participants per session. Boarding program cost: $1995. Financial aid available.
Application Deadline Continuous.
Jobs Positions for college students 18 and older.
Contact Mr. Mike Sims, Executive Director, 111 West Jackson Boulevard, 7th Floor, Chicago, Illinois 60604. Phone: 312-322-9999. Fax: 312-765-0081. E-mail: information@nslcleaders.org.
URL www.nslcleaders.org

For more information, see page 1216.

NAWA Academy–Girls on the Go

NAWA Academy
17351 Trinity Mountain Road
French Gulch, California 96033

General Information Girls' residential academic program, outdoor program, and adventure program established in 2001. Specific services available for the learning disabled. High school credit may be earned.
Program Focus Girl empowerment.
Academics English language/literature, biology, economics, geography, geology/earth science, health sciences, history, mathematics, reading, science (general), social science, social studies, writing.
Arts Arts and crafts (general).
Special Interest Areas First aid, leadership training, nature study, team building.
Sports Archery, basketball, bicycling, bicycling (BMX), boating, climbing (wall), fishing, paintball, rappelling, ropes course, swimming, weight training.
Wilderness/Outdoors Backpacking, caving, hiking, mountaineering, rafting, rock climbing, survival training, white-water trips, wilderness camping.
Trips Overnight.

Program Information 2 sessions per year. Session length: 4 weeks in June, July, August. Ages: 12–18. 6–12 participants per session. Boarding program cost: $3654. Financial aid available.
Application Deadline Continuous.
Jobs Positions for college students 18 and older.
Contact Mr. Jason Hull, Director of Admissions and Summer Programs, main address above. Phone: 800-358-6292. Fax: 530-359-2229. E-mail: nawa@concentric.net.
URL www.nawa-academy.com

NAWA Academy–Great Challenge

NAWA Academy
17351 Trinity Mountain Road
French Gulch, California 96033

General Information Coed residential academic program, outdoor program, and adventure program established in 1988. Specific services available for the learning disabled. High school credit may be earned.
Academics English language/literature, biology, economics, geography, geology/earth science, health sciences, history, mathematics, reading, science (general), social science, social studies, writing.
Arts Arts and crafts (general).
Special Interest Areas First aid, leadership training, nature study, team building.
Sports Archery, basketball, bicycling, bicycling (BMX), boating, climbing (wall), fishing, paintball, rappelling, ropes course.
Wilderness/Outdoors Backpacking, caving, hiking, mountaineering, rafting, rock climbing, survival training, white-water trips, wilderness camping.
Trips Overnight.
Program Information 2 sessions per year. Session length: 4 weeks in June, July, August. Ages: 12–18. 6–12 participants per session. Financial aid available.
Application Deadline Continuous.
Jobs Positions for college students 18 and older.
Contact Jason Hull, Director of Admissions and Summer Programs, main address above. Phone: 800-358-6292. Fax: 530-359-2229. E-mail: nawa@concentric.net.
URL www.nawa-academy.com

NAWA Academy–Lassen Expedition

NAWA Academy
17351 Trinity Mountain Road
French Gulch, California 96033

General Information Coed residential academic program, outdoor program, and adventure program established in 1988. Specific services available for the learning disabled. High school credit may be earned.
Academics English language/literature, biology, economics, geography, geology/earth science, health sciences, history, mathematics, reading, science (general), social science, social studies, writing.
Arts Arts and crafts (general).
Special Interest Areas First aid, leadership training, nature study, team building.
Sports Archery, basketball, bicycling, bicycling (BMX), boating, climbing (wall), fishing, paintball, rappelling, ropes course, swimming.
Wilderness/Outdoors Backpacking, caving, hiking, mountaineering, rafting, rock climbing, survival training, white-water trips, wilderness camping.
Trips Overnight.
Program Information 2 sessions per year. Session length: 4 weeks in June, July, August. Ages: 12–18. 6–12 participants per session. Boarding program cost: $3654. Financial aid available.
Application Deadline Continuous.
Jobs Positions for college students 18 and older.
Contact Jason Hull, Director of Admissions and Summer Programs, main address above. Phone: 800-358-6292. Fax: 530-359-2229. E-mail: nawa@concentric.net.
URL www.nawa-academy.com

NAWA Academy–Trinity Challenge

NAWA Academy
17351 Trinity Mountain Road
French Gulch, California 96033

General Information Coed residential outdoor program and adventure program established in 1988. Specific services available for the learning disabled. High school credit may be earned.
Academics Tutoring.
Arts Arts and crafts (general).
Special Interest Areas First aid, leadership training, nature study, team building.
Sports Archery, basketball, bicycling, bicycling (BMX), boating, climbing (wall), fishing, paintball, rappelling, ropes course, swimming, weight training.
Wilderness/Outdoors Backpacking, caving, hiking, mountaineering, rafting, rock climbing, survival training, white-water trips, wilderness camping.
Trips Overnight.
Program Information 2 sessions per year. Session length: 4 weeks in June, July, August. Ages: 10–14. 6–12 participants per session. Boarding program cost: $3488. Financial aid available.
Application Deadline Continuous.
Jobs Positions for college students 18 and older.
Contact Mr. Jason Hull, Director of Admissions and Summer Programs, main address above. Phone: 800-358-6292. Fax: 530-359-2229. E-mail: nawa@concentric.net.
URL www.nawa-academy.com

NBC Camps–Basketball Individual Training–CA

NBC Camps
Simpson College
Redding, California

General Information Coed residential sports camp.
Program Focus Well-rounded skill development.
Sports Basketball.
Program Information 2 sessions per year. Session length: 5 days in July, August. Ages: 9–18. Boarding program cost: $315. Financial aid available.
Application Deadline Continuous.

NBC Camps–Basketball Individual Training–CA (continued)

Jobs Positions for high school students 16 and older and college students.
Contact Ms. Bonnie Tucker, Office Manager, 10003 North Milan Road, #100, Spokane, Washington 99218. Phone: 509-466-4690. Fax: 509-467-6289. E-mail: bonnie@nbccamps.com.
URL www.nbccamps.com

NBC Camps–Basketball Speed Explosion–California

NBC Camps
Simpson College
Redding, California

General Information Coed residential sports camp.
Program Focus Developing jumping and speed skills.
Sports Basketball.
Program Information 1 session per year. Session length: 3 days in August. Ages: 13–19. Boarding program cost: $200. Financial aid available.
Application Deadline Continuous.
Jobs Positions for high school students 16 and older and college students.
Contact Ms. Bonnie Tucker, Office Manager, 10003 North Milan Road, #100, Spokane, Washington 99218. Phone: 509-466-4690. Fax: 509-467-6289. E-mail: bonnie@nbccamps.com.
URL www.nbccamps.com

NBC Camps–Volleyball–California

NBC Camps
Simpson College
Redding, California

General Information Girls' residential sports camp.
Sports Volleyball.
Program Information 1 session per year. Session length: 5 days in August. Ages: 12–18. Boarding program cost: $315. Financial aid available.
Application Deadline Continuous.
Jobs Positions for high school students 16 and older and college students.
Contact Ms. Bonnie Tucker, Office Manager, 10003 North Milan Road, #100, Spokane, Washington 99218. Phone: 509-466-4690. Fax: 509-467-6289. E-mail: bonnie@nbccamps.com.
URL www.nbccamps.com

NBC Camps–Volleyball Speed Explosion–California

NBC Camps
Simpson College
Redding, California

General Information Coed residential sports camp.
Program Focus Developing jumping and speed skills.
Sports Volleyball.
Program Information 1 session per year. Session length: 3 days in August. Ages: 9–18. Boarding program cost: $200. Financial aid available.
Application Deadline Continuous.
Jobs Positions for high school students 16 and older and college students.
Contact Ms. Bonnie Tucker, Office Manager, 10003 North Milan Road, #100, Spokane, Washington 99218. Phone: 509-466-4690. Fax: 509-467-6289. E-mail: bonnie@nbccamps.com.
URL www.nbccamps.com

The New York Film Academy, Universal Studios, Hollywood, CA

New York Film Academy
Los Angeles, California

General Information Coed residential arts program established in 1992. College credit may be earned.
Program Focus "Total immersion" hands-on filmmaking workshop where students write, direct, shoot, and edit their own short 16mm films.
Arts Acting, creative writing, directing, film, film editing, film lighting, film production, screenwriting, sound design, television/video, theater/drama.
Trips Cultural.
Program Information 4 sessions per year. Session length: 6–42 days in June, July, August. Ages: 15–18. Boarding program cost: $1500–$6900.
Application Deadline Continuous.
Contact Admissions, 100 East 17th Street, New York, New York 10003. Phone: 212-674-4300. Fax: 212-477-1414. E-mail: film@nyfa.com.
URL www.nyfa.com
For more information, see page 1218.

Ojai Valley School Summer Programs

Ojai Valley School
723 El Paseo Road
Ojai, California 93023

General Information Coed residential and day traditional camp and academic program established in 1943. Accredited by American Camping Association. High school credit may be earned.
Program Focus General recreation and camping.
Academics English as a second language, English language/literature, academics (general), computers, journalism, mathematics, reading, writing.
Arts Arts and crafts (general), ceramics, creative writing, photography, pottery, theater/drama, woodworking.
Special Interest Areas Campcraft, culinary arts, driver's education.
Sports Archery, basketball, climbing (wall), equestrian sports, martial arts, ropes course, soccer, surfing, swimming, tennis, volleyball, water polo.
Wilderness/Outdoors Backpacking, hiking, rock climbing, wilderness camping.
Trips Day, overnight.
Program Information 3 sessions per year. Session length: 2–6 weeks in June, July, August. Ages: 8–18.

Ojai Valley School Summer Programs

80–150 participants per session. Day program cost: $1175–$3200. Boarding program cost: $2175–$5930. Application fee: $50–$100. Financial aid available.
Application Deadline Continuous.
Jobs Positions for college students 18 and older.
Contact Mr. John Williamson, Director of Admission, main address above. Phone: 805-646-1423. Fax: 805-646-0362. E-mail: admission@ovs.org.
URL www.ovs.org

For more information, see page 1234.

Outward Bound West–Climbing and Backpacking–High Sierra, CA

Outward Bound West/Outward Bound, USA
Sierra Nevada Mountains
California

General Information Coed travel outdoor program and wilderness program established in 1965. College credit may be earned.
Program Focus Teamwork and leadership wilderness adventure.
Academics Environmental science.
Special Interest Areas Campcraft, community service, first aid, leadership training, nature study, outdoor cooking, personal development, team building.
Sports Rappelling.
Wilderness/Outdoors Backpacking, hiking, mountaineering, orienteering, outdoor adventure, rock climbing, wilderness camping.
Trips Overnight.
Program Information 8 sessions per year. Session length: 1–2 weeks in June, July, August, September. Ages: 14+. Cost: $1295–$2395. Application fee: $95. Financial aid available.
Application Deadline Continuous.
Jobs Positions for college students 21 and older.
Contact Admissions Advisor, 910 Jackson Street, Golden, Colorado 80401. Phone: 866-746-9777. Fax: 720-497-2421. E-mail: info@obwest.org.
URL www.outwardboundwest.org

Outward Bound West–Sierra Nevada Mountaineering

Outward Bound West/Outward Bound, USA
Sierra Nevada Mountains
California

General Information Coed travel outdoor program and wilderness program established in 1965. College credit may be earned.
Program Focus Teamwork and leadership wilderness adventure.
Academics Environmental science.
Special Interest Areas Campcraft, community service, conservation projects, first aid, leadership training, personal development, team building.
Sports Rappelling.
Wilderness/Outdoors Backpacking, mountaineering, outdoor adventure, rock climbing, wilderness camping.
Trips Overnight.
Program Information 2 sessions per year. Session length: 22 days in July, August, September. Ages: 16+. Cost: $2895. Application fee: $95. Financial aid available.
Application Deadline Continuous.
Contact Admissions Advisor, 910 Jackson Street, Golden, Colorado 80401. Phone: 866-746-9777. Fax: 720-497-2421. E-mail: info@obwest.org.
URL www.outwardboundwest.org

Oxford School Summer Camp

Oxford School
18760 East Colima Road
Rowland Heights, California 91748

General Information Coed residential and day academic program and cultural program established in 1980.
Program Focus English as a Second Language and multicultural awareness.
Academics American literature, English as a second language, English language/literature, SAT/ACT preparation, art history/appreciation, computers, history, humanities, intercultural studies, music, reading, science (general), social studies, speech/debate, study skills, typing, writing.
Arts Arts and crafts (general), creative writing, drawing, music, music (classical), music (instrumental), painting.
Special Interest Areas Homestays.
Sports Basketball, soccer, softball, volleyball.
Trips Cultural, day, shopping.
Program Information 2 sessions per year. Session length: 20 days in July, August. Ages: 6–20. 100–200 participants per session. Day program cost: $400–$900. Boarding program cost: $1000–$2100. Application fee: $58.
Application Deadline Continuous.
Contact Ms. Michelle Cheng, Coordinator, main address above. Phone: 626-964-9588. Fax: 626-913-3919. E-mail: michelle_c@oxfordschool.org.
URL www.oxfordschool.org

Pali Overnight Adventures Camp

Pali Overnight Adventures
30778 Highway 18
Running Springs, California 92382

General Information Coed residential traditional camp established in 1990. Accredited by American Camping Association.
Academics Journalism.
Arts Arts and crafts (general), ceramics, dance, film, film production, painting, pottery, theater/drama.
Special Interest Areas Animal care, leadership training, nature study, yearbook production.
Sports Aerobics, archery, basketball, boating, canoeing, climbing (wall), equestrian sports, fencing, field hockey, fishing, football, go-carts, horseback riding, kayaking, lacrosse, martial arts, paintball, rappelling, riflery, ropes course, scuba diving, skateboarding, snorkeling, soccer, softball, swimming, tennis, volleyball, waterskiing.
Wilderness/Outdoors Hiking.
Trips Day, overnight.
Program Information 5–8 sessions per year. Session length: 1–2 weeks in June, July, August. Ages: 9–16. 8–80 participants per session. Boarding program cost: $1385–$2695.
Application Deadline Continuous.
Jobs Positions for college students 19 and older.
Contact Mr. Andy Wexler, Owner/Founder, PO Box 2237, Running Springs, California 92382. Phone: 909-867-5743. Fax: 909-867-7643. E-mail: info@paliadventures.com.
URL www.paliadventures.com

Pepperdine University Summer College for High School Students

Pepperdine University
24255 Pacific Coast Highway
Malibu, California 90263

General Information Coed residential and day academic program established in 2000. Religious affiliation: Church of Christ. College credit may be earned.

Pepperdine University Summer College for High School Students

Program Focus Academic program which grants college credit for coursework.
Academics French language/literature, academics (general), astronomy, communications, geology/earth science, history, mathematics.
Arts Arts and crafts (general).
Trips Cultural, day, shopping.
Program Information 1 session per year. Session length: 30 days in June, July. Ages: 15–19. 50–100 participants per session. Day program cost: $5080. Boarding program cost: $6010. Application fee: $35.
Application Deadline April 15.
Jobs Positions for college students 18 and older.
Contact Dana Dudley, Director, Summer School, main address above. Phone: 310-506-6079. Fax: 310-506-4816. E-mail: dana.dudley@pepperdine.edu.
URL seaver.pepperdine.edu/summerschool/

For more information, see page 1252.

Power Chord Academy–Los Angeles

Power Chord Academy
Loyola Marymount University
Los Angeles, California

General Information Coed residential arts program established in 1999. Formal opportunities for the academically talented.
Program Focus Teenage musicians play in a band, record a CD, make a video, play a concert, and gain an unbridled understanding of the music industry.
Academics Art (Advanced Placement), music, music (Advanced Placement).
Arts Band, music, music (chamber), music (classical), music (ensemble), music (instrumental), music (jazz), music (orchestral), music (vocal), music technology/record production, musical performance/recitals, songwriting.
Program Information 1–4 sessions per year. Session length: 1 week in July. Ages: 12–18. 100–120 participants per session. Boarding program cost: $895–$1095.
Application Deadline Continuous.
Jobs Positions for college students 22 and older.
Contact Mr. Bryan J. Wrzesinski, 7336 Santa Monica Boulevard, #107, Los Angeles, California 90046. Phone: 800-897-6677. Fax: 775-306-7923. E-mail: bryan@powerchordacademy.com.
URL www.powerchordacademy.com

Prep Camp Excel by Education Unlimited–Stanford University

Education Unlimited
Stanford University
Stanford, California

General Information Coed residential and day academic program established in 2000.
Program Focus High school and college prep program, PSAT prep.
Academics SAT/ACT preparation, study skills, writing.
Special Interest Areas College planning.
Sports Basketball, volleyball.

Prep Camp Excel by Education Unlimited–Stanford University

Trips College tours, day.
Program Information 2 sessions per year. Session length: 1 week in July, August. Ages: 13–16. 48–120 participants per session. Day program cost: $700. Boarding program cost: $1400. Financial aid available.
Application Deadline Continuous.
Jobs Positions for college students 21 and older.
Contact Mr. Byron Arthur, Director, 1700 Shattuck Avenue, #305, Berkeley, California 94709. Phone: 800-548-6612. Fax: 510-548-0212. E-mail: camps@educationunlimited.com.
URL www.educationunlimited.com
For more information, see page 1272.

Prep Camp Excel by Education Unlimited–UC Berkeley

Education Unlimited
University of California, Berkeley
Berkeley, California

General Information Coed residential and day academic program established in 2000.
Program Focus High school and college prep program, PSAT prep.
Academics SAT/ACT preparation, study skills, writing.
Special Interest Areas College planning.
Sports Basketball, volleyball.
Trips College tours, day.
Program Information 1 session per year. Session length: 1 week in June. Ages: 13–16. 24–60 participants per session. Day program cost: $700. Boarding program cost: $1275. Financial aid available.
Application Deadline Continuous.
Jobs Positions for college students 21 and older.
Contact Mr. Byron Arthur, Director, 1700 Shattuck Avenue, #305, Berkeley, California 94709. Phone: 800-548-6612. Fax: 510-548-0212. E-mail: camps@educationunlimited.com.
URL www.educationunlimited.com
For more information, see page 1272.

Prep Camp Excel by Education Unlimited–UCLA

Education Unlimited
University of California, Los Angeles
Los Angeles, California

General Information Coed residential and day academic program established in 2000.
Program Focus High school and college prep program, PSAT prep.
Academics SAT/ACT preparation, college tours, study skills, writing.
Trips Day.
Program Information 1 session per year. Session length: 1 week in July. Ages: 13–16. 48–64 participants per session. Boarding program cost: $1400. Financial aid available.
Application Deadline Continuous.
Contact Mr. Byron Arthur, Director, 1700 Shattuck Avenue, #305, Berkeley, California 94709. Phone: 510-548-6612. Fax: 510-548-0212. E-mail: camps@educationunlimited.com.
URL www.educationunlimited.com
For more information, see page 1272.

Public Speaking Institute by Education Unlimited–Stanford

Education Unlimited
Stanford University
Palo Alto, California

General Information Coed residential and day academic program established in 1995.
Program Focus Public speaking and leadership training.
Academics Communications, government and politics, speech/debate, writing.
Special Interest Areas Leadership training.
Sports Basketball, volleyball.
Wilderness/Outdoors Hiking.
Trips Day.
Program Information 5 sessions per year. Session length: 1–2 weeks in June, July, August. Ages: 10–18. 48 participants per session. Day program cost: $625. Boarding program cost: $1028. Financial aid available.
Application Deadline Continuous.

Public Speaking Institute by Education Unlimited–Stanford (continued)

Jobs Positions for college students 21 and older.
Contact Matthew Fraser, Executive Director, 1700 Shattuck Avenue, #305, Berkeley, California 94709. Phone: 800-548-6612. Fax: 510-548-0212. E-mail: camps@educationunlimited.com.
URL www.educationunlimited.com

For more information, see page 1100.

PUBLIC SPEAKING INSTITUTE BY EDUCATION UNLIMITED–UC BERKELEY

Education Unlimited
University of California, Berkeley
Berkeley, California

General Information Coed residential and day academic program established in 1995.
Program Focus Public speaking and leadership training.
Academics Communications, government and politics, speech/debate, writing.
Special Interest Areas Leadership training.
Sports Basketball, volleyball.
Wilderness/Outdoors Hiking.
Trips Day.
Program Information 3 sessions per year. Session length: 1–2 weeks in July. Ages: 10–18. 24–48 participants per session. Day program cost: $550. Boarding program cost: $938. Financial aid available.
Application Deadline Continuous.
Jobs Positions for college students 21 and older.
Contact Matthew Fraser, Executive Director, 1700 Shattuck Avenue, #305, Berkeley, California 94709. Phone: 800-548-6612. Fax: 510-548-0212. E-mail: camps@educationunlimited.com.
URL www.educationunlimited.com

For more information, see page 1100.

PUBLIC SPEAKING INSTITUTE BY EDUCATION UNLIMITED–UCLA

Education Unlimited
University of California, Los Angeles
Los Angeles, California

General Information Coed residential and day academic program established in 1995.
Program Focus Public speaking and leadership training.
Academics Communications, government and politics, speech/debate, writing.
Special Interest Areas Leadership training.
Sports Basketball, volleyball.
Trips Day.
Program Information 2 sessions per year. Session length: 1 week in June, July. Ages: 10–18. 20–48 participants per session. Day program cost: $550. Boarding program cost: $938. Financial aid available.
Application Deadline Continuous.
Jobs Positions for college students 21 and older.

Public Speaking Institute by Education Unlimited–UCLA

Contact Matthew Fraser, Executive Director, 1700 Shattuck Avenue, #305, Berkeley, California 94709. Phone: 800-548-6612. Fax: 800-548-0212. E-mail: camps@educationunlimited.com.
URL www.educationunlimited.com

For more information, see page 1100.

QUEST SCHOLARS PROGRAM AT STANFORD/QUESTLEADERSHIP

Quest Scholars Program
Stanford University
Stanford, California 94309

General Information Coed residential academic program, community service program, and cultural program established in 1994. Formal opportunities for the academically talented. High school credit may be earned.
Program Focus College preparatory and leadership training program for talented under-served, low-income high school students..
Academics SAT/ACT preparation, academics (general), biology, business, computers, ecology, economics,

environmental science, geology/earth science, health sciences, intercultural studies, marine studies, precollege program, science (general), speech/debate, study skills, writing.
Arts Dance, music.
Special Interest Areas Career exploration, college planning, community service, conservation projects, field research/expeditions, leadership training, nature study, team building.
Sports Aerobics, martial arts, ropes course.
Wilderness/Outdoors Hiking, orienteering.
Trips College tours, cultural, day.
Program Information 1 session per year. Session length: 35–39 days in June, July, August. Ages: 15–19. 18–22 participants per session. Financial aid available. No cost for program.
Application Deadline March 20.
Jobs Positions for high school students 17 and older and college students.
Contact Ms. Sarah Chandler, Executive Director, PO Box 20054, Stanford, California 94309. Phone: 650-328-8591. Fax: 650-618-1707. E-mail: quest_scholars@yahoo.com.
URL www.questscholars.org

Rawhide Ranch

Rawhide Ranch
6987 West Lilac Road
Bonsall, California 92003

General Information Coed residential traditional camp and outdoor program established in 1964. Accredited by American Camping Association.
Program Focus Horsemanship and animal care.
Arts Arts and crafts (general), creative writing, dance.
Special Interest Areas Animal care, leadership training, outdoor cooking.
Sports Archery, equestrian sports, gymnastics, horseback riding, riflery, swimming.
Program Information 10–12 sessions per year. Session length: 1 week in March, April, June, July, August, December. Ages: 7–15. 200–210 participants per session. Boarding program cost: $695. Application fee: $200.
Application Deadline Continuous.
Jobs Positions for college students 20 and older.
Contact Mr. Paul Tate, Program Director, PO Box 216, Bonsall, California 92003. Phone: 760-758-0083. Fax: 760-758-0440. E-mail: paul@rawhideranch.com.
URL www.rawhideranch.com

Redwood National Park Camps

Oregon Museum of Science and Industry
Wolf Creek Education Center
Orick, California 95555

General Information Coed residential academic program and outdoor program established in 2002. Formal opportunities for the academically talented. High school credit may be earned.
Program Focus Forest ecology, coastal ecology.
Academics Japanese language/literature, archaeology, biology, botany, ecology, environmental science, forestry, marine studies.
Special Interest Areas Field research/expeditions, team building.
Sports Snorkeling.
Wilderness/Outdoors Backpacking, hiking, wilderness camping.
Trips Overnight.
Program Information 5 sessions per year. Session length: 6 days in June, July. Ages: 10–18. 30 participants per session. Boarding program cost: $410–$610. Financial aid available.
Application Deadline Continuous.
Jobs Positions for high school students 16 and older and college students 16 and older.
Contact Travis Neumeyer, Programming Coordinator, 1945 Southeast Water Avenue, Portland, Oregon 97214. Phone: 503-239-7824. Fax: 503-239-7838. E-mail: tneumeyer@omsi.edu.
URL www.omsi.edu

River Way Ranch Camp

6450 Elwood Road
Sanger, California 93657

General Information Coed residential traditional camp and family program established in 1967. Accredited by American Camping Association. High school or college credit may be earned.
Program Focus River Way program offers a waterski camp and horse camp.
Academics Computers.
Arts Acting, arts and crafts (general), ceramics, creative writing, dance, dance (jazz), drawing, fabric arts, film, graphic arts, jewelry making, leather working, music, music (vocal), musical productions, painting, photography, pottery, sculpture, set design, television/video, theater/drama, voice and speech.
Special Interest Areas Animal care, campcraft, homestays, leadership training, model rocketry, nature study.
Sports Aerobics, archery, basketball, boating, canoeing, challenge course, cheerleading, climbing (wall), equestrian sports, fishing, football, go-carts, golf, gymnastics, horseback riding, in-line skating, kayaking, martial arts, minibikes, riflery, ropes course, sailing, snorkeling, soccer, softball, swimming, tennis, trampolining, volleyball, water polo, waterskiing.
Wilderness/Outdoors Canoe trips, hiking, rafting, white-water trips.
Trips Day, overnight.
Program Information 1–3 sessions per year. Session length: 2 weeks in June, July, August. Ages: 7–16. 200–300 participants per session. Call for cost.
Application Deadline Continuous.
Jobs Positions for high school students 16 and older and college students 18 and older.
Contact Nancy Oken Nighbert, Director, main address above. Phone: 800-821-2801. Fax: 559-787-3851. E-mail: rwrcamp@aol.com.
URL www.riverwayranchcamp.com

Rock Star Camp at Pali Overnight Adventures

Pali Overnight Adventures
30778 Highway 18
Running Springs, California 92382

General Information Coed residential traditional camp and arts program. Accredited by American Camping Association. Formal opportunities for the artistically talented.
Program Focus For singers and dancers who want to create musical masterpieces.
Arts Dance, music, music (rock), music (vocal), songwriting, voice and speech.
Sports Gymnastics.
Program Information 5–8 sessions per year. Session length: 1–3 weeks in June, July, August. Ages: 9–16. 8–80 participants per session. Boarding program cost: $1385–$2695.
Application Deadline Continuous.
Jobs Positions for college students 19 and older.
Contact Mr. Andy Wexler, Owner/Founder, PO Box 2237, Running Springs, California 92382. Phone: 909-867-5743. Fax: 909-867-7643. E-mail: info@paliadventures.com.
URL www.paliadventures.com/rockstar_camp.html

Salmon Camp Research Team for Native Americans–Redwoods

Oregon Museum of Science and Industry
Wolf Creek Education Center
Redwoods National Park
Orick, California 95555

General Information Coed residential outdoor program established in 2002. Formal opportunities for the academically talented. High school credit may be earned.
Program Focus Natural resource management field research.
Academics Anthropology, archaeology, biology, botany, ecology, natural resource management.
Special Interest Areas Native American culture, field research/expeditions.
Sports Canoeing.
Wilderness/Outdoors Hiking, wilderness camping.
Trips Cultural, overnight.
Program Information 1 session per year. Session length: 20 days in July. Ages: 15–18. 10 participants per session. No cost for Native Americans.
Application Deadline Continuous.
Jobs Positions for high school students 16 and older and college students 16 and older.
Contact Travis Neumeyer, Programming Coordinator, 1945 Southeast Water Avenue, Portland, Oregon 97214. Phone: 503-239-7824. Fax: 503-239-7838. E-mail: sciencecamps@omsi.edu.
URL www.omsi.edu

Santa Catalina School Summer Camp

Santa Catalina School
1500 Mark Thomas Drive
Monterey, California 93940

General Information Girls' residential and day traditional camp and arts program established in 1953. Religious affiliation: Roman Catholic.
Program Focus Performing arts, fine arts, athletics, and marine biology.
Academics Marine studies.
Arts Ceramics, chorus, creative writing, dance (ballet), dance (jazz), drawing, music (vocal), painting, photography, pottery, theater/drama.
Special Interest Areas Culinary arts, general camp activities.
Sports Diving, equestrian sports, golf, horseback riding, sea kayaking, snorkeling, soccer, swimming, tennis.
Trips Day.
Program Information 2–3 sessions per year. Session length: 18–35 days in June, July. Ages: 8–14. 150–180 participants per session. Day program cost: $1500–$2300. Boarding program cost: $2250–$4000. Application fee: $25.
Application Deadline Continuous.
Jobs Positions for college students 18 and older.
Contact Mrs. Deidre Gonzales, Co-Director of Summer Programs, main address above. Phone: 831-655-9386. Fax: 831-649-3056. E-mail: summercamp@santacatalina.org.
URL www.santacatalina.org

Saturday High at Art Center College of Design

Art Center College of Design
Pasadena, California 91103

General Information Coed day arts program. Formal opportunities for the artistically talented. High school credit may be earned.
Academics Web page design.
Arts Arts, arts and crafts (general), design, drawing, graphic arts, illustration, painting, photography, printing, printmaking, television/video.
Special Interest Areas Robotics.
Trips College tours.
Program Information 3 sessions per year. Session length: 10 days in February, March, April, June, July, August, September, October, November, December. Ages: 14–18. 600–900 participants per session. Day program cost: $175–$350.
Application Deadline Continuous.
Contact Alegria Castro, Program Coordinator, 1700 Lida Street, Pasadena, California 91103. Phone: 626-396-2319. Fax: 626-796-9564. E-mail: saturdayhigh@artcenter.edu.
URL www.artcenter.edu/sat

Science Program for High School Girls

University of Southern California–Summer and Special Programs
Los Angeles, California 90089-1621

General Information Girls' residential academic program established in 2001.
Program Focus Explore the field of oceanography.
Academics Oceanography, science (general).
Special Interest Areas Nature study.
Sports Canoeing, kayaking, scuba diving, snorkeling.
Program Information 1 session per year. Session length: 8 days in August. Ages: 15–17. 20–30 participants per session. Boarding program cost: $1425. Financial aid available.
Application Deadline Continuous.
Contact Mr. Steve Foral, Associate Director, Summer and Special Programs, USC Campus Mail Code 7009, Los Angeles, California 90089-7009. Phone: 213-743-1710. Fax: 213-743-1714. E-mail: sforal@usc.edu.
URL www.usc.edu/summer

Science Program for Middle School Boys on Catalina

University of Southern California–Summer and Special Programs
Wrigley Marine Science Center
Catalina Island, California

General Information Boys' residential academic program established in 2004.
Program Focus Introduction to oceanography.
Academics Oceanography, science (general).
Special Interest Areas Nature study.
Sports Canoeing, kayaking, snorkeling.
Program Information 1 session per year. Session length: 6–8 days in July. Ages: 11–15. 20–30 participants per session. Boarding program cost: $1425. Financial aid available.
Application Deadline Continuous.
Contact Steve Foral, Associate Director, Summer and Special Programs, USC Campus Mail Code 7009, Los Angeles, California 90089-7009. Phone: 213-743-1710. Fax: 213-743-1714. E-mail: sforal@usc.edu.
URL www.usc.edu/summer

Science Program for Middle School Girls on Catalina

University of Southern California–Summer and Special Programs
Wrigley Marine Science Center
Catalina Island, California

General Information Girls' residential academic program established in 1999.
Program Focus Science, discovery, and exploring the aquatic and terrestrial life.
Academics Oceanography, science (general).
Special Interest Areas Nature study.
Sports Canoeing, kayaking, scuba diving, snorkeling.
Program Information 1 session per year. Session length: 8 days in August. Ages: 11–15. 20–30 participants per session. Boarding program cost: $1425. Financial aid available.
Application Deadline Continuous.
Contact Steve Foral, Associate Director, Summer and Special Programs, USC Campus Mail Code 7009, Los Angeles, California 90089-7009. Phone: 213-743-1710. Fax: 213-743-1714. E-mail: sforal@usc.edu.
URL www.usc.edu/summer

Scuba Adventures at Pali Overnight Adventures

Pali Overnight Adventures
30778 Highway 18
Running Springs, California 92382

General Information Coed residential traditional camp and outdoor program established in 1990. Accredited by American Camping Association.
Program Focus Scuba diving certification (PADI).
Academics Journalism.
Arts Arts and crafts (general), batiking, ceramics, dance, film, film production, painting, pottery, theater/drama.
Special Interest Areas Animal care, leadership training, nature study, yearbook production.
Sports Aerobics, archery, basketball, boating, canoeing, climbing (wall), equestrian sports, fencing, field hockey, fishing, football, go-carts, horseback riding, kayaking, lacrosse, martial arts, paintball, rappelling, riflery, ropes course, sailing, scuba diving, skateboarding, snorkeling, soccer, softball, swimming, volleyball, waterskiing.
Wilderness/Outdoors Hiking, rafting, white-water trips.
Trips Day, overnight.
Program Information 5–8 sessions per year. Session length: 1–2 weeks in June, July, August. Ages: 12–16. 8–80 participants per session. Boarding program cost: $1385–$2695.
Application Deadline Continuous.
Jobs Positions for college students 19 and older.
Contact Mr. Andy Wexler, Owner/Founder, PO Box 2237, Running Springs, California 92382. Phone: 909-867-5743. Fax: 909-867-7643. E-mail: info@paliadventures.com.
URL www.paliadventures.com/scuba.html

SEACAMP San Diego

SEACAMP San Diego
1380 Garnet Avenue
PMB E6
San Diego, California 92109

General Information Coed residential and day academic program and outdoor program established in 1987. High school credit may be earned.
Program Focus Marine science and activities.
Academics Biology, biology (Advanced Placement), ecology, environmental science, geology/earth science, marine studies, oceanography, science (general).
Special Interest Areas Career exploration, field research/expeditions, nature study.

SEACAMP San Diego (continued)

Sports Boating, kayaking, scuba diving, snorkeling.
Wilderness/Outdoors Hiking.
Trips Day, overnight.
Program Information 7–9 sessions per year. Session length: 6–13 days in January, February, March, April, May, June, July, August, September, October, November, December. Ages: 12–18. 28–56 participants per session. Day program cost: $575. Boarding program cost: $675–$1525.
Application Deadline Continuous.
Contact Mr. Phil Zerofski, Director, main address above. Phone: 800-SEACAMP. Fax: 619-268-0229. E-mail: seacamp@seacamp.com.
URL www.seacamp.com

SeaWorld San Diego Adventure Camp

SeaWorld Adventure Park
500 SeaWorld Drive
San Diego, California 92109

General Information Coed residential and day academic program and outdoor program established in 1980. Accredited by American Camping Association. Formal opportunities for the academically talented.

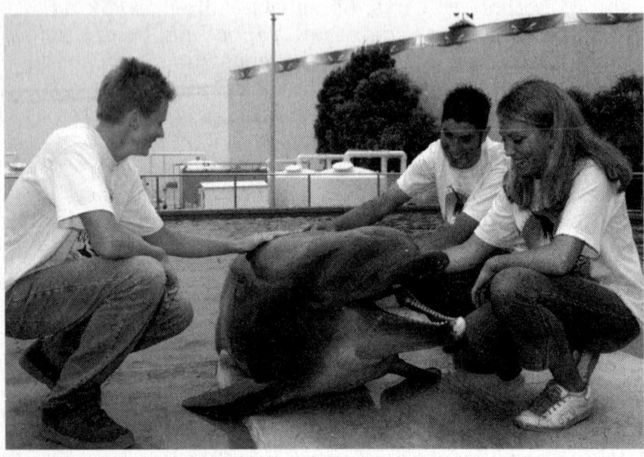

SeaWorld San Diego Adventure Camp

Program Focus Marine science, marine animals.
Academics Biology, ecology, environmental science, geography, geology/earth science, marine studies, science (general).
Arts Arts and crafts (general).
Special Interest Areas Animal care, career exploration, conservation projects, field research/expeditions, nature study.
Sports Kayaking, snorkeling, surfing, swimming.
Trips Day.
Program Information 15–47 sessions per year. Session length: 3–8 days in April, June, July, August. Ages: 3–18. 16–48 participants per session. Day program cost: $75–$180. Boarding program cost: $925–$1050.
Application Deadline Continuous.
Contact Education Reservations, main address above. Phone: 800-237-4268. Fax: 619-226-3634. E-mail: swc.education@seaworld.com.
URL www.seaworld.org
For more information, see page 1304.

Secret Agent Camp at Pali Overnight Adventures

Pali Overnight Adventures
30778 Highway 18
Running Springs, California 92382

General Information Coed residential traditional camp established in 1990. Accredited by American Camping Association.
Academics Journalism.
Arts Arts and crafts (general), batiking, ceramics, dance, film, film production, painting, pottery, theater/drama.
Special Interest Areas Animal care, leadership training, nature study, yearbook production.
Sports Aerobics, all-terrain vehicles, archery, basketball, boating, canoeing, climbing (wall), equestrian sports, fencing, field hockey, fishing, football, go-carts, horseback riding, kayaking, lacrosse, martial arts, motocross, paintball, rappelling, riflery, ropes course, sailing, scuba diving, skateboarding, snorkeling, soccer, softball, swimming, volleyball, waterskiing.
Wilderness/Outdoors Backpacking, hiking, orienteering, rock climbing, survival training.
Trips Day, overnight.
Program Information 5–8 sessions per year. Session length: 1–2 weeks in June, July, August. Ages: 9–16. 8–80 participants per session. Boarding program cost: $1385–$2695.
Application Deadline Continuous.
Jobs Positions for college students 19 and older.
Contact Mr. Andy Wexler, Owner/Founder, PO Box 2237, Running Springs, California 92382-2237. Phone: 909-867-5743. Fax: 909-867-7643. E-mail: info@paliadventures.com.
URL www.paliadventures.com/secretagent.swf

Sequoia Chamber Music Workshop

Humboldt State University
Arcata, California 95521

General Information Coed residential arts program established in 1971. Formal opportunities for the artistically talented.
Program Focus Chamber music; an intensive program of sight reading and performance.
Academics Music.
Arts Music (chamber), music (classical), music (ensemble), music (instrumental), musical performance/recitals.
Sports Table tennis/ping-pong.
Trips Day.
Program Information 2 sessions per year. Session length: 1 week in June, July. Ages: 12–20. 50–60 participants per session. Boarding program cost: $680–$1360. Application fee: $35. Financial aid available.
Application Deadline Continuous.

Jobs Positions for college students 18 and older.
Contact Mr. David Filner, Director, PO Box 131376, Birmingham, Alabama 35213. Phone: 205-591-7325. E-mail: sequoia@humboldt.edu.
URL www.humboldt.edu/sequoiaCMW

Shaffer's High Sierra Camp

Shaffer's High Sierra Camp, Inc.
Tahoe National Forest
38782 State Highway 49
Sattley, California 96124

General Information Coed residential traditional camp and outdoor program established in 2000. Accredited by American Camping Association.
Program Focus A noncompetitive, team-based wilderness adventure program.
Arts Acting, arts and crafts (general), dance, dance (modern), theater/drama.
Special Interest Areas Campcraft, nature study.
Sports Archery, canoeing, horseback riding, kayaking, mountain boarding, rappelling, ropes course, sailing, swimming, volleyball, water polo, windsurfing.
Wilderness/Outdoors Backpacking, bicycle trips, hiking, mountain biking, orienteering, rafting, rock climbing, survival training, white-water trips, wilderness camping.
Trips Day, overnight.
Program Information 4 sessions per year. Session length: 1–2 weeks in June, July, August. Ages: 9–16. 35–55 participants per session. Boarding program cost: $935–$1885. Financial aid available.
Application Deadline Continuous.
Jobs Positions for college students 19 and older.
Summer Contact Scott Shaffer, Co-Director, main address above. Phone: 800-516-3513. Fax: 415-897-0316. E-mail: info@highsierracamp.com.
Winter Contact Lisa Shaffer, Co-Director, 248 San Marin Drive, Novato, California 94945. Phone: 800-516-3513. Fax: 415-897-0316. E-mail: directors@highsierracamp.com.
URL www.highsierracamp.com

Skateboarding Academy at Pali Overnight Adventures

Pali Overnight Adventures
30778 Highway 18
Running Springs, California 92382

General Information Coed residential traditional camp and adventure program established in 1990. Accredited by American Camping Association.
Academics Journalism.
Arts Acting, arts and crafts (general), batiking, ceramics, creative writing, dance, dance (jazz), dance (modern), dance (tap), film, film production, music, music (vocal), musical productions, painting, pottery, theater/drama.
Special Interest Areas Animal care, culinary arts, leadership training, nature study, robotics, team building, yearbook production.
Sports Aerobics, archery, basketball, boating, canoeing, climbing (wall), equestrian sports, fencing, field hockey, fishing, football, go-carts, gymnastics, horseback riding, in-line skating, kayaking, lacrosse, martial arts, paintball, rappelling, riflery, ropes course, sailing, scuba diving, skateboarding, snorkeling, soccer, softball, swimming, volleyball, waterskiing.
Wilderness/Outdoors Hiking, rafting, rock climbing.
Trips Day, overnight.
Program Information 5–8 sessions per year. Session length: 1–2 weeks in June, July, August. Ages: 9–16. 8–80 participants per session. Boarding program cost: $1385–$2695.
Application Deadline Continuous.
Jobs Positions for college students 19 and older.
Contact Mr. Andy Wexler, Owner/Founder, PO Box 2237, Running Springs, California 92382-2237. Phone: 909-867-5743. Fax: 909-867-7643. E-mail: info@paliadventures.com.
URL www.paliadventures.com/skating_mania.html

Skylake Yosemite Camp

37976 Road 222
Wishon, California 93669

General Information Coed residential traditional camp established in 1945. Accredited by American Camping Association.
Arts Arts and crafts (general), ceramics, dance, drawing, jewelry making, leather working, musical productions, painting, pottery.
Special Interest Areas Native American culture, campcraft, culinary arts.
Sports Archery, basketball, bicycling, canoeing, equestrian sports, fishing, horseback riding, kayaking, ropes course, soccer, swimming, tennis, volleyball, wakeboarding, waterskiing, windsurfing.
Wilderness/Outdoors Backpacking, bicycle trips, canoe trips, hiking, mountain biking, orienteering, white-water trips.
Trips Day, overnight.
Program Information 2–4 sessions per year. Session length: 1–4 weeks in June, July, August. Ages: 7–16. 210 participants per session. Boarding program cost: $950–$3400.
Application Deadline Continuous.
Jobs Positions for college students 18 and older.
Contact Jeff Portnoy, Director, main address above. Phone: 559-642-3720. Fax: 559-642-3395. E-mail: jpskylake@aol.com.
URL www.skylakeyosemite.com

SoccerPlus Goalkeeper School–Challenge Program–San Diego, CA

SoccerPlus Camps
University of California, San Diego
San Diego, California

General Information Coed residential and day sports camp.
Program Focus Developing technical and tactical goalkeeping skills.
Sports Soccer.

SoccerPlus Goalkeeper School–Challenge Program–San Diego, CA (continued)

Program Information 2 sessions per year. Session length: 6 days in July. Ages: 10+. Day program cost: $595. Boarding program cost: $695. Financial aid available.
Application Deadline Continuous.
Jobs Positions for college students.
Contact Mr. Shawn Kelly, General Manager, 11 Executive Drive, Suite 202, Farmington, Connecticut 06032. Phone: 800-533-7371. Fax: 860-677-0460. E-mail: info@soccerpluscamps.com.
URL www.soccerpluscamps.com

SoccerPlus Goalkeeper School–Challenge Program–Stockton, CA

SoccerPlus Camps
University of the Pacific
Stockton, California

General Information Coed residential and day sports camp.
Program Focus Developing technical and tactical goalkeeping skills.
Sports Soccer.
Program Information 1 session per year. Session length: 6 days in July, August. Ages: 10+. Day program cost: $595. Boarding program cost: $695. Financial aid available.
Application Deadline Continuous.
Jobs Positions for college students.
Contact Mr. Shawn Kelly, General Manager, 11 Executive Drive, Suite 202, Farmington, Connecticut 06032. Phone: 800-533-7371. Fax: 860-721-8619. E-mail: info@soccerpluscamps.com.
URL www.soccerpluscamps.com

SoccerPlus Goalkeeper School–National Training Center–San Diego, CA

SoccerPlus Camps
University of California, San Diego
San Diego, California

General Information Coed residential sports camp.
Program Focus Developing advanced goalkeeping skills.
Sports Soccer.
Program Information 2 sessions per year. Session length: 6 days in July. Ages: 15+. Boarding program cost: $775.
Application Deadline Continuous.
Jobs Positions for college students.
Contact Mr. Shawn Kelly, General Manager, 11 Executive Drive, Suite 202, Farmington, Connecticut 06032. Phone: 800-533-7371. Fax: 860-677-0460. E-mail: info@soccerpluscamps.com.
URL www.soccerpluscamps.com

SoccerPlus Goalkeeper School–National Training Center–Stockton, CA

SoccerPlus Camps
University of the Pacific
Stockton, California

General Information Coed residential sports camp.
Program Focus Developing advanced goalkeeping skills.
Sports Soccer.
Program Information 1 session per year. Session length: 6 days in July, August. Ages: 15+. Boarding program cost: $775. Financial aid available.
Application Deadline Continuous.
Jobs Positions for college students.
Contact Mr. Shawn Kelly, General Manager, 11 Executive Drive, Suite 202, Farmington, Connecticut 06032. Phone: 800-533-7371. Fax: 860-677-0460. E-mail: info@soccerpluscamps.com.
URL www.soccerpluscamps.com

Southwestern Academy International Summer Semester

Southwestern Academy
2800 Monterey Road
San Marino, California 91108

General Information Coed residential and day academic program established in 1924. Formal opportunities for the artistically talented. High school credit may be earned.
Program Focus English as a second language, college prep credit classes, remedial, academic enhancement.
Academics English as a second language, English language/literature, SAT/ACT preparation, Spanish language/literature, academics (general), area studies, art history/appreciation, astronomy, biology, chemistry, computers, economics, environmental science, geography, geology/earth science, government and politics, history, humanities, intercultural studies, journalism, mathematics, mathematics (Advanced Placement), music, physics, precollege program, psychology, reading, remedial academics, science (general), speech/debate, writing.
Arts Arts and crafts (general), chorus, drawing, jewelry making, music, music (instrumental), painting, photography.
Special Interest Areas Career exploration, college planning, community service.
Sports Baseball, basketball, golf, soccer, softball, swimming, tennis, volleyball, weight training.
Wilderness/Outdoors Hiking.
Trips College tours, cultural, day, overnight, shopping.
Program Information 6 sessions per year. Session length: 30–102 days in June, July, August, September. Ages: 11–19. 45–70 participants per session. Day program cost: $3400–$10,500. Boarding program cost: $3500–$11,500. Application fee: $100. Remedial reading and study classes available.
Application Deadline Continuous.

Contact Mrs. Jane Whitmire, Director of Admissions, main address above. Phone: 626-799-5010 Ext.1204. Fax: 626-799-0407. E-mail: admissions@southwesternacademy.edu.
URL www.southwesternacademy.edu
For more information, see page 1324.

Stanford Discovery Institutes

Stanford University Summer Session
Building 590, Room 103
Stanford, California 94305-3005

General Information Coed residential and day academic program and arts program established in 2000. Formal opportunities for the academically talented and artistically talented. Specific services available for the hearing impaired, learning disabled, physically challenged, and visually impaired. College credit may be earned.

Stanford Discovery Institutes

Program Focus Pre-college program through which students earn university credit from Stanford; topical courses.
Academics Environmental science, philosophy, precollege program.
Arts Creative writing, theater/drama.
Trips Cultural, day.
Program Information 4 sessions per year. Session length: 3 weeks in June, July, August. Ages: 15–18. 30–50 participants per session. Boarding program cost: $3500. Application fee: $50. Financial aid available.
Application Deadline April 9.
Contact Patricia Brandt, Associate Dean and Director, main address above. Phone: 650-723-3109. Fax: 650-725-6080. E-mail: summersession@stanford.edu.
URL summerinstitutes.stanford.edu

Stanford Jazz Workshop

Stanford Jazz Workshop
Braun Music Center
Stanford University
Stanford, California 94309

General Information Coed residential and day arts program established in 1972. Formal opportunities for the artistically talented. College credit may be earned.
Program Focus Jazz music.
Academics Music, music (Advanced Placement).
Arts Music, music (ensemble), music (instrumental), music (jazz), music (vocal).
Trips College tours.
Program Information 2–4 sessions per year. Session length: 3–6 days in July, August. Ages: 12+. 180–200 participants per session. Day program cost: $560–$1698. Boarding program cost: $905–$2804. Application fee: $100. Financial aid available.
Application Deadline Continuous.
Jobs Positions for high school students 17 and older and college students 18 and older.
Contact Mr. Jim Nadel, Executive Director, PO Box 20454, Stanford, California 94309. Phone: 650-736-0324. Fax: 650-856-4155. E-mail: info@stanfordjazz.org.
URL www.stanfordjazz.org

Stanford Jazz Workshop: Jazz Camp

Stanford Jazz Workshop
Braun Music Center
Stanford University
Stanford, California 94309

General Information Coed residential and day arts program established in 1972. Formal opportunities for the artistically talented. College credit may be earned.
Program Focus Jazz music.
Academics Music, music (Advanced Placement).
Arts Music, music (ensemble), music (instrumental), music (jazz), music (vocal), musical performance/recitals.
Trips College tours.
Program Information 2 sessions per year. Session length: 6 days in July, August. Ages: 12–17. 200–250 participants per session. Day program cost: $849–$1698. Boarding program cost: $1372–$2804. Application fee: $100. Financial aid available. Participants will have access to Stanford University's recreational facilities.
Application Deadline Continuous.

Stanford Jazz Workshop: Jazz Camp (continued)

Jobs Positions for high school students 17 and older and college students 18 and older.
Contact Mr. Jim Nadel, Director, PO Box 20454, Stanford, California 94309. Phone: 650-736-0324. Fax: 650-856-4155. E-mail: info@stanfordjazz.org.
URL www.stanfordjazz.org

Stanford Jazz Workshop: Jazz Residency

Stanford Jazz Workshop
Braun Music Center
Stanford University
Stanford, California 94309

General Information Coed residential and day arts program established in 1972. Formal opportunities for the artistically talented. College credit may be earned.
Program Focus Jazz music.
Academics Music, music (Advanced Placement).
Arts Music, music (ensemble), music (instrumental), music (jazz), music (vocal), musical performance/recitals.
Trips College tours.
Program Information 1 session per year. Session length: 6 days in August. Ages: 14+. 200–255 participants per session. Day program cost: $675–$849. Boarding program cost: $905–$1402. Application fee: $100. Financial aid available. Ages 14–17 must audition. Participants will have access to Stanford University's recreational facilities. Jazz Weekend Intensive is available for up to 40 participants. Call for dates and costs.
Application Deadline Continuous.
Jobs Positions for high school students 17 and older and college students 18 and older.
Contact Mr. Jim Nadel, Director, PO Box 20454, Stanford, California 94309. Phone: 650-736-0324. Fax: 650-856-4155. E-mail: info@stanfordjazz.org.
URL www.stanfordjazz.org

Stanford National Forensic Institute

Stanford Debate Society
Stanford University
Palo Alto, California

General Information Coed residential and day academic program established in 1991.
Program Focus Competitive debate.
Academics Communications, ecology, economics, government and politics, intercultural studies, peace education, philosophy, social science, social studies, speech/debate, writing.
Trips Day.
Program Information 5 sessions per year. Session length: 1–4 weeks in July, August. Ages: 14–18. 25–250 participants per session. Day program cost: $925–$2875. Boarding program cost: $1150–$3500. Financial aid available.
Application Deadline Continuous.
Contact Mr. Matthew Fraser, Executive Director, 555 Bryant Street, #599, Palo Alto, California 94301. Phone: 650-723-9086. Fax: 510-548-0212. E-mail: info@snfi.org.
URL www.snfi.org

Stanford University Summer College for High School Students

Stanford University Summer Session
Building 590, Room 103
Stanford, California 94305-3005

General Information Coed residential academic program established in 1960. Formal opportunities for the academically talented. Specific services available for the hearing impaired, learning disabled, physically challenged, and visually impaired. College credit may be earned.
Program Focus Pre-college program through which students earn university credit from Stanford.
Academics American literature, Chinese languages/literature, English language/literature, French language/literature, German language/literature, Greek language/literature, Italian language/literature, Japanese language/literature, Latin language, SAT/ACT preparation, Spanish language/literature, Swahili language, academics (general), aerospace science, anthropology, archaeology, architecture, area studies, art history/appreciation, astronomy, biology, chemistry, classical languages/literatures, communications, computer programming, economics, engineering, geology/earth science, government and politics, history, humanities, marine studies, mathematics, music, philosophy, precollege program, psychology, religion, speech/debate, writing.
Arts Creative writing, dance, music, music (classical), music (instrumental), music (vocal), painting, photography, sculpture, theater/drama.
Special Interest Areas College planning, field trips (arts and culture).
Sports Aerobics, equestrian sports, golf, swimming, tennis, yoga.
Wilderness/Outdoors Backpacking, hiking.
Trips Cultural, day, overnight.
Program Information 1 session per year. Session length: 8 weeks in June, July, August. Ages: 16–18. 250–350 participants per session. Boarding program cost: $8355–$10,753. Application fee: $50. Financial aid available.
Application Deadline April 9.
Contact Patricia Brandt, Associate Dean and Director, main address above. Phone: 650-723-3109. Fax: 650-725-6080. E-mail: summersession@stanford.edu.
URL summersession.stanford.edu/

For more information, see page 1332.

Stevenson School Summer Camp

Stevenson School
3152 Forest Lake Road
Pebble Beach, California 93953

General Information Coed residential and day traditional camp, academic program, and outdoor program established in 1972.
Program Focus Additional emphasis on art classes and sports.
Academics English language/literature, French language/literature, Spanish language/literature, academics (general), geology/earth science, journalism, marine studies, mathematics, music, physics, reading, strategy games, study skills, writing.
Arts Arts and crafts (general), ceramics, creative writing, dance, dance (jazz), dance (modern), drawing, graphic arts, music, music (instrumental), music (jazz), painting, photography, pottery, theater/drama.
Sports Archery, baseball, basketball, bicycling, boating, climbing (wall), fencing, field hockey, golf, kayaking, lacrosse, ropes course, sea kayaking, soccer, softball, swimming, tennis, track and field, volleyball, water polo, weight training.
Wilderness/Outdoors Backpacking, hiking, mountain biking, rock climbing, wilderness camping.
Trips Day, overnight, shopping.
Program Information 1 session per year. Session length: 5 weeks in June, July. Ages: 10–15. 130–160 participants per session. Day program cost: $2100. Boarding program cost: $4400.
Application Deadline May 21.
Jobs Positions for high school students 18 and older and college students 18 and older.
Contact Rosemary Tintle, Administrative Secretary, main address above. Phone: 831-625-8315. Fax: 831-625-5208.
URL www.rlstevenson.org

Student Conservation Association–Conservation Crew Program (California)

Student Conservation Association (SCA)
California

General Information Coed residential outdoor program, community service program, and wilderness program established in 1957. High school credit may be earned.
Program Focus Resource management, conservation and environmental education.
Academics Biology, botany, ecology, environmental science, geology/earth science, history.
Special Interest Areas Campcraft, community service, construction, leadership training, nature study, trail maintenance, work camp programs.
Sports Canoeing, fishing, kayaking, swimming.
Wilderness/Outdoors Backpacking, canoe trips, hiking, orienteering, outdoor living skills, rock climbing, wilderness camping.
Trips Cultural, day, overnight.
Program Information 2–3 sessions per year. Session length: 3–5 weeks in June, July, August. Ages: 15–19. 6–8 participants per session. Application fee: $20. Financial aid available. No cost for program; financial aid possible for travel expenses.
Application Deadline Continuous.
Jobs Positions for college students 21 and older.
Contact Recruitment Office, PO Box 550, Charlestown, New Hampshire 03603. Phone: 603-543-1700. Fax: 603-543-1828. E-mail: getreal@thesca.org.
URL www.theSCA.org

Student Conservation Association–Conservation Leadership Corps, Bay Area

Student Conservation Association (SCA)
655 13th Street, Suite 100
Oakland, California 94612

General Information Coed residential and day outdoor program, community service program, and wilderness program.
Program Focus Conservation education and leadership.
Special Interest Areas Community service, field research/expeditions, leadership training.
Wilderness/Outdoors Wilderness camping.
Trips Day, overnight.
Program Information 1–2 sessions per year. Session length: 104–134 days in January, February, March, April, May, June, July, August, September, October, November, December. Ages: 15+. 8–12 participants per session. Financial aid available. No cost for program; financial aid possible for travel expenses.
Application Deadline Continuous.
Contact Eve Cowen, Regional Program Manager, main address above. Phone: 510-832-1966. Fax: 510-832-4726. E-mail: ecowen@thesca.org.
URL www.theSCA.org

Study Tours and Cinema Program in the USA–Oxnard College

FLS International
Oxnard College
4000 South Rose Avenue
Oxnard, California 93030

General Information Coed residential arts program established in 2003.
Program Focus Cinema and English as a second language.
Academics English as a second language, intercultural studies.
Arts Film, television/video.
Special Interest Areas Homestays.
Trips College tours, cultural, day, shopping.
Program Information 3 sessions per year. Session length: 20 days in June, July, August. Ages: 15+. 5–75 participants per session. Boarding program cost: $1650. Application fee: $100.
Application Deadline Continuous.

Study Tours and Cinema Program in the USA–Oxnard College (continued)

Contact Ms. Veronica Perez, Director of Admissions, 101 East Green Street #14, Pasadena, California 91105. Phone: 626-795-2912. Fax: 626-795-5564. E-mail: veronica@fls.net.
URL www.fls.net
For more information, see page 1128.

Study Tours and Leisure Sports in the USA–Citrus College

FLS International
Citrus College
1000 West Foothill Boulevard
Glendora, California 91741

General Information Coed residential academic program and sports camp.
Program Focus Golf, tennis and English as a second language.
Academics English as a second language, intercultural studies.
Special Interest Areas Homestays.
Sports Golf, tennis.
Trips Day.
Program Information 3 sessions per year. Session length: 19–20 days in June, July, August. Ages: 15+. 15–75 participants per session. Boarding program cost: $1650. Application fee: $100.
Application Deadline Continuous.
Contact Ms. Veronica Perez, Director of Admissions, 101 East Green Street, #14, Pasadena, California 91105. Phone: 626-795-2912. Fax: 626-795-5564. E-mail: veronica@fls.net.
URL www.fls.net
For more information, see page 1128.

Study Tours and Surf Program in the USA–Mira Costa College

FLS International
Mira Costa College
One Barnard Drive
Oceanside, California 92056

General Information Coed residential outdoor program established in 2002. Formal opportunities for the academically talented.
Program Focus English as a second language and surfing.
Academics English as a second language, intercultural studies.
Special Interest Areas Homestays.
Sports Surfing.
Trips College tours, cultural, day, shopping.
Program Information 3 sessions per year. Session length: 20 days in June, July, August. Ages: 15+. 5–75 participants per session. Boarding program cost: $1625. Application fee: $100.
Application Deadline Continuous.
Contact Ms. Veronica Perez, Director of Admissions, 101 East Green Street #14, Pasadena, California 91105. Phone: 626-795-2912. Fax: 626-795-5564. E-mail: veronica@fls.net.
URL www.fls.net
For more information, see page 1128.

Study Tours in the USA–Citrus

FLS International
Citrus College
1000 West Foothill Boulevard
Glendora, California 91741

General Information Coed residential academic program established in 1987. Formal opportunities for the academically talented.
Academics English as a second language, English language/literature, SAT/ACT preparation, college tours, computers, intercultural studies, precollege program, reading, speech/debate, study skills, writing.
Special Interest Areas Career exploration, culinary arts, field trips (arts and culture), homestays.
Sports Basketball, golf, soccer, softball, swimming, tennis.
Wilderness/Outdoors Bicycle trips, hiking.
Trips College tours, cultural, day, overnight, shopping.
Program Information 13 sessions per year. Session length: 19–20 days in January, February, March, April, May, June, July, August, September, October, November, December. Ages: 15+. 15–75 participants per session. Boarding program cost: $1495–$2295. Application fee: $100.
Application Deadline Continuous.
Contact Ms. Veronica Perez, Director of Admissions, 101 East Green Street, #14, Pasadena, California 91105. Phone: 626-795-2912. Fax: 626-795-5564. E-mail: veronica@fls.net.
URL www.fls.net
For more information, see page 1128.

Study Tours in the USA–Mira Costa College

FLS International
Mira Costa College
One Barnard Drive
Oceanside, California 92056

General Information Coed residential academic program established in 1999. Formal opportunities for the academically talented.
Program Focus English as a second language.
Academics English as a second language, English language/literature, SAT/ACT preparation, computers, intercultural studies, precollege program, reading, speech/debate, study skills, writing.
Arts Creative writing.
Special Interest Areas Career exploration, field trips (arts and culture), homestays.
Sports Baseball, basketball, fishing, kayaking, scuba diving, sea kayaking, snorkeling, soccer, softball, tennis.
Wilderness/Outdoors Hiking.
Trips College tours, cultural, day, overnight, shopping.

Program Information 13 sessions per year. Session length: 14–20 days in January, February, March, April, May, June, July, August, September, October, November, December. Ages: 15+. 15–75 participants per session. Boarding program cost: $1495–$2295. Application fee: $100.
Application Deadline Continuous.
Contact Ms. Veronica Perez, Director of Admissions, 101 East Green Street, #14, Pasadena, California 91105. Phone: 626-795-2912. Fax: 626-795-5564. E-mail: veronica@fls.net.
URL www.fls.net
For more information, see page 1128.

Study Tours in the USA–Oxnard

FLS International
Oxnard College
4000 South Rose Avenue
Oxnard, California 93030

General Information Coed residential academic program established in 1987. Formal opportunities for the academically talented.
Program Focus English as a second language.
Academics English as a second language, English language/literature, SAT/ACT preparation, college tours, computers, intercultural studies, precollege program, reading, speech/debate, study skills, writing.
Arts Creative writing, film.
Special Interest Areas Career exploration, culinary arts, field trips (arts and culture), homestays.
Sports Basketball, skiing (downhill), snorkeling, soccer, softball, surfing, swimming, tennis.
Wilderness/Outdoors Bicycle trips, hiking.
Trips College tours, cultural, day, overnight, shopping.
Program Information 13 sessions per year. Session length: 19–20 days in January, February, March, April, May, June, July, August, September, October, November, December. Ages: 15+. 15–75 participants per session. Boarding program cost: $1495–$2295. Application fee: $100.
Application Deadline Continuous.
Contact Ms. Veronica Perez, Director of Admissions, 101 East Green Street, #14, Pasadena, California 91105. Phone: 626-795-2912. Fax: 626-795-5564. E-mail: veronica@fls.net.
URL www.fls.net
For more information, see page 1128.

Summer Discovery at UCLA

Summer Discovery
University of California, Los Angeles
Los Angeles, California 90024

General Information Coed residential academic program established in 1986. High school or college credit may be earned.
Program Focus Pre-college enrichment.
Academics American literature, Chinese languages/literature, English (Advanced Placement), English as a second language, English language/literature, French (Advanced Placement), French language/literature, Italian language/literature, SAT/ACT preparation, Spanish (Advanced Placement), Spanish language/literature, academics (general), anthropology, architecture, art (Advanced Placement), art history/appreciation, astronomy, biology, biology (Advanced Placement), chemistry, chemistry (Advanced Placement), classical languages/literatures, communications, computer science (Advanced Placement), computers, economics, environmental science, geography, government and politics, government and politics (Advanced Placement), history, history (Advanced Placement), humanities, journalism, linguistics, mathematics, mathematics (Advanced Placement), music, philosophy, physics, physics (Advanced Placement), physiology, precollege program, psychology, religion, science (general), social science, social studies, speech/debate, study skills, writing.

Summer Discovery at UCLA

Arts Ceramics, creative writing, dance (ballet), dance (jazz), drawing, film, graphic arts, painting, photography, radio broadcasting, television/video, theater/drama.
Special Interest Areas Career exploration, community service.

Summer Discovery at UCLA (continued)

Sports Aerobics, basketball, bicycling, boating, climbing (wall), football, golf, gymnastics, in-line skating, kayaking, martial arts, racquetball, ropes course, sailing, soccer, softball, swimming, tennis, track and field, volleyball, weight training, windsurfing.
Wilderness/Outdoors Hiking, rafting, rock climbing, white-water trips, wilderness camping.
Trips College tours, cultural, day, overnight.
Program Information 2 sessions per year. Session length: 3–6 weeks in June, July, August. 450 participants per session. Boarding program cost: $4199–$6399. Application fee: $50–$60. Open to participants completing grades 10–12.
Application Deadline Continuous.
Jobs Positions for college students 21 and older.
Contact The Musiker Family, Director, 1326 Old Northern Boulevard, Roslyn Village, New York 11576. Phone: 888-878-6637. Fax: 516-625-3438. E-mail: discovery@summerfun.com.
URL www.summerfun.com

For more information, see page 1338.

Summer Discovery at UC San Diego

Summer Discovery
University of California, San Diego
San Diego, California

General Information Coed residential academic program and outdoor program. High school or college credit may be earned.
Program Focus Pre-college enrichment.
Academics American literature, English as a second language, academics (general), anthropology, archaeology, art (Advanced Placement), art history/appreciation, biology, business, communications, computers, economics, environmental science, geography, government and politics, government and politics (Advanced Placement), history, oceanography, precollege program, psychology, social studies, writing.
Arts Creative writing, drawing, film, music, painting, photography.
Special Interest Areas Career exploration, college planning, leadership training.
Sports Aerobics, basketball, golf, soccer, swimming.
Wilderness/Outdoors Backpacking, bicycle trips, hiking.
Trips College tours, cultural, day, overnight.
Program Information 1 session per year. Session length: 5 weeks in June, July, August. 100–200 participants per session. Boarding program cost: $5699–$6999. Application fee: $60–$70. Financial aid available.
Application Deadline Continuous.
Jobs Positions for college students 21 and older.
Contact The Musiker Family, 1326 Old Northern Boulevard, Roslyn Village, New York 11576. Phone: 888-878-6637. Fax: 516-625-3438. E-mail: discovery@summerfun.com.
URL www.summerfun.com

For more information, see page 1338.

Summer Discovery at UC Santa Barbara

Summer Discovery
University of California, Santa Barbara
Santa Barbara, California

General Information Coed residential academic program. College credit may be earned.
Program Focus Pre-college enrichment.
Academics English language/literature, French language/literature, German language/literature, Italian language/literature, Spanish language/literature, academics (general), anthropology, architecture, art history/appreciation, astronomy, biology, chemistry, communications, computer programming, computers, economics, engineering, geography, geology/earth science, government and politics, history, mathematics, music, philosophy, physics, precollege program, psychology, religion, social science, writing.
Arts Ceramics, dance, dance (jazz), dance (modern), drawing, film, theater/drama.
Special Interest Areas Community service.
Sports Aerobics, basketball, climbing (wall), diving, racquetball, soccer, squash, swimming, tennis, track and field, weight training.
Wilderness/Outdoors Rock climbing.
Trips Cultural, day, shopping.
Program Information 1 session per year. Session length: 6 weeks in June, July, August. 125 participants per session. Boarding program cost: $5699–$5799. Application fee: $60–$70. Financial aid available. Open to participants completing grades 10–12.
Application Deadline Continuous.
Jobs Positions for college students 21 and older.
Contact The Musiker Family, Director, 1326 Old Northern Boulevard, Roslyn Village, New York 11576. Phone: 888-878-6637. Fax: 516-625-3438. E-mail: discovery@summerfun.com.
URL www.summerfun.com

For more information, see page 1338.

Summer Focus at Berkeley

Education Unlimited
University of California, Berkeley
Berkeley, California

General Information Coed residential and day academic program established in 1997. Formal opportunities for the academically talented. High school or college credit may be earned.
Program Focus College credit classes at UC Berkeley.
Academics American literature, English language/literature, SAT/ACT preparation, academics (general), anthropology, area studies, art history/appreciation, astronomy, biology, biology (Advanced Placement), communications, geography, government and politics, government and politics (Advanced Placement), health sciences, history, humanities, intercultural studies, journalism, linguistics, mathematics, music, music (Advanced Placement), peace education, philosophy, physiology, precollege program, psychology, science (general), social science, social services, social studies, speech/debate, study skills, writing.

Summer Focus at Berkeley

Arts Dance, drawing, film, music, theater/drama.
Special Interest Areas Native American culture, cross-cultural education.
Sports Basketball, soccer, tennis, volleyball.
Trips College tours, cultural, day, shopping.
Program Information 1 session per year. Session length: 40–45 days in July, August. Ages: 14–18. 20–60 participants per session. Day program cost: $3100. Boarding program cost: $5075. Financial aid available.
Application Deadline Continuous.
Contact Ms. Lexy Green, Director of Summer Focus, 1700 Shattuck Avenue, #305, Berkeley, California 94709. Phone: 800-548-6612. Fax: 510-548-0212. E-mail: camps@educationunlimited.com.
URL www.educationunlimited.com
For more information, see page 1340.

THE SUMMER INSTITUTE FOR THE GIFTED AT UCLA

Summer Institute for the Gifted
UCLA
Los Angeles, California 90024

General Information Coed residential academic program established in 2004. Formal opportunities for the academically talented and gifted. Specific services available for the hearing impaired, learning disabled, physically challenged, and visually impaired. College credit may be earned.
Academics American literature, English language/literature, French language/literature, Latin language, SAT/ACT preparation, Spanish language/literature, academics (general), aerospace science, archaeology, architecture, art (Advanced Placement), art history/appreciation, biology, business, chemistry, classical languages/literatures, communications, computer programming, computers, engineering, environmental science, history, humanities, marine studies, mathematics, music, philosophy, physics, physiology, precollege program, psychology, science (general), social studies, speech/debate, study skills, writing.
Arts Arts and crafts (general), chorus, creative writing, dance, dance (ballet), dance (folk), dance (jazz), dance (modern), drawing, mime, music, music (chamber), music (classical), music (ensemble), music (instrumental), musical productions, painting, photography, sculpture, theater/drama.
Special Interest Areas Animal care, model rocketry, robotics.
Sports Archery, baseball, basketball, fencing, field hockey, football, lacrosse, martial arts, soccer, squash, swimming, tennis, volleyball.
Wilderness/Outdoors Hiking.
Trips Cultural.
Program Information 1–2 sessions per year. Session length: 3 weeks in June, July, August. Ages: 8–17. 275–300 participants per session. Boarding program cost: $3350. Application fee: $75. Financial aid available.
Application Deadline May 15.
Jobs Positions for college students 19 and older.
Contact Dr. Stephen Gessner, Director, River Plaza, 9 West Broad Street, Stamford, Connecticut 06902-3788. Phone: 866-303-4744. Fax: 203-399-5598. E-mail: sig.info@aifs.com.
URL www.giftedstudy.com
For more information, see page 1342.

THE SUMMER INSTITUTE FOR THE GIFTED AT UNIVERSITY OF CALIFORNIA, BERKELEY

Summer Institute for the Gifted
University of California, Berkeley
Berkeley, California

General Information Coed residential academic program. Formal opportunities for the academically talented and gifted.
Academics Academics (general), precollege program.
Program Information 1–2 sessions per year. Session length: 3 weeks in June, July, August. Ages: 8–17. 200–300 participants per session. Boarding program cost: $3350. Application fee: $75. Financial aid available.
Application Deadline May 15.
Jobs Positions for college students 19 and older.
Contact Dr. Stephen Gessner, Director, River Plaza, 9 West Broad Street, Stamford, Connecticut 06902-3788. Phone: 866-303-4744. Fax: 203-399-5598. E-mail: sig.info@aifs.com.
URL www.giftedstudy.com
For more information, see page 1342.

THE SUMMER SCIENCE PROGRAM–CALIFORNIA CAMPUS

Summer Science Program, Inc.
Happy Valley School
Ojai, California

General Information Coed residential academic program established in 1959. Formal opportunities for the academically talented.
Academics Astronomy, computer programming, mathematics, physics, science (general).
Special Interest Areas Career exploration.
Sports Soccer, swimming, tennis.
Wilderness/Outdoors Hiking.
Trips Day.

The Summer Science Program–California Campus (continued)

Program Information 1 session per year. Session length: 41 days in June, July, August. Ages: 15–18. 30–36 participants per session. Boarding program cost: $3200. Financial aid available.
Application Deadline Continuous.
Jobs Positions for college students 20 and older.
Contact Mr. Richard Bowdon, Executive Director, 108 Whiteberry Drive, Cary, North Carolina 27519. Phone: 866-728-0999. Fax: 419-735-2251. E-mail: info@summerscience.org.
URL www.summerscience.org

SuperCamp–Claremont Colleges

SuperCamp
Claremont Colleges
Claremont, California 91711

General Information Coed residential academic program established in 1981. Accredited by American Camping Association. High school credit may be earned.

SuperCamp–Claremont Colleges

Program Focus Academic enrichment and personal development.
Academics SAT/ACT preparation, academics (general), communications, reading, study skills, writing.
Special Interest Areas Leadership training.
Sports Basketball, ropes course, soccer, swimming, volleyball.
Trips College tours.
Program Information 5–7 sessions per year. Session length: 8–10 days in July, August. Ages: 9–24. 80–125 participants per session. Boarding program cost: $1795–$2295. Application fee: $100. Financial aid available.
Application Deadline Continuous.
Jobs Positions for college students 18 and older.
Contact Enrollments Department, 1725 South Coast Highway, Oceanside, California 92054. Phone: 800-285-3276. Fax: 760-722-3507. E-mail: info@supercamp.com.
URL www.supercamp.com
For more information, see page 1348.

SuperCamp–Stanford University

SuperCamp
Stanford University
Palo Alto, California 94305

General Information Coed residential academic program established in 1981. Accredited by American Camping Association. High school credit may be earned.
Program Focus Academic enrichment and personal development.
Academics SAT/ACT preparation, academics (general), communications, reading, study skills, writing.
Special Interest Areas Leadership training.
Sports Basketball, ropes course, soccer, swimming, volleyball.
Wilderness/Outdoors Outdoor adventure.
Trips College tours.
Program Information 4–6 sessions per year. Session length: 10 days in June, July, August. Ages: 11–18. 112–125 participants per session. Boarding program cost: $2395. Application fee: $100.
Application Deadline Continuous.
Jobs Positions for college students 18 and older.
Contact Enrollments Department, 1725 South Coast Highway, Oceanside, California 92054. Phone: 800-285-3276. Fax: 760-722-3507. E-mail: info@supercamp.com.
URL www.supercamp.com
For more information, see page 1348.

Technology Encounters–Video Encounter/Computer Encounter–California

Ducks in a Row Foundation, Inc./Technology Encounters
California

General Information Coed day arts program established in 2000. Formal opportunities for the academically talented and artistically talented.
Program Focus Local community school district-hosted programs focused on making technology fun, teaching team skills, and using creative energies.
Academics Academics (general), communications, computer programming, computers.
Arts Acting, animation, arts and crafts (general), film, film production, graphic arts, television/video, theater/drama.
Special Interest Areas Computer game design, computer graphics, leadership training.
Program Information 40–50 sessions per year. Session length: 5–10 days in June, July, August. Ages: 7–13. 25–100 participants per session. Day program cost: $195. Financial aid available.
Application Deadline Continuous.
Jobs Positions for high school students 17 and older and college students 17 and older.

Contact Ms. Jane Sandlar, Director, 8 Wemrock Drive, Ocean, New Jersey 07712. Phone: 732-695-0827. Fax: 732-493-4282. E-mail: jane@technologyencounters.com.
URL www.technologyencounters.com

Thunderbird Ranch

9455 Highway 128
Healdsburg, California 95448

General Information Coed residential and day traditional camp established in 1962. Accredited by American Camping Association.
Program Focus Ranch life, western riding, and aquatics.
Arts Arts and crafts (general).
Special Interest Areas Animal care, gardening, nature study.
Sports Aerobics, archery, basketball, bicycling, canoeing, equestrian sports, fishing, gymnastics, horseback riding, soccer, softball, swimming, volleyball, water tubing, waterskiing.
Wilderness/Outdoors Hiking, mountain biking.
Trips Day.
Program Information 8 sessions per year. Session length: 5–14 days in June, July, August. Ages: 6–14. 45–60 participants per session. Day program cost: $335. Boarding program cost: $1090–$2055.
Application Deadline Continuous.
Jobs Positions for college students 18 and older.
Contact Mr. Bruce Johnson, Director, main address above. Phone: 707-433-3729. Fax: 707-433-2960. E-mail: alexvalley@aol.com.

UC San Diego Academic Connections

University of California, San Diego
9500 Gilman Drive
Department 0176-S
La Jolla, California 92093-0176

General Information Coed residential academic program established in 1990. High school or college credit may be earned.
Program Focus Help young people touch the future by exposing them to some of the most exciting fields of research.
Academics Academics (general), biology, communications, economics, engineering, environmental science, government and politics, health sciences, history, humanities, marine studies, music, oceanography, philosophy, physics, precollege program, psychology, science (general), social science, writing.
Arts Arts and crafts (general), dance.
Special Interest Areas Field research/expeditions.
Sports Aerobics, basketball, climbing (wall), gymnastics, kayaking, soccer, softball, swimming, tennis, track and field, volleyball.
Trips Day.
Program Information 1 session per year. Session length: 3 weeks in July. Ages: 15–18. 200–250 participants per session. Boarding program cost: $2700. Application fee: $50.
Application Deadline Continuous.
Jobs Positions for college students 19 and older.
Contact Danielle Nestor, Program Coordinator, 9500 Gilman Drive, La Jolla, California 92093-0179. Phone: 858-534-0804. Fax: 858-822-2619. E-mail: dnestor@ucsd.edu.
URL www.academicconnections.ucsd.edu

UCSB Alumni Association Santa Barbara Family Vacation Center

University of California, Santa Barbara Alumni Association
University of California, Santa Barbara
Santa Barbara, California 93106-1120

General Information Coed residential family program established in 1969.
Program Focus Family vacation and leisure on the beach in Santa Barbara.
Arts Arts and crafts (general), ceramics, dance, dance (jazz), dance (modern), drawing, jewelry making, music, painting, woodworking.
Special Interest Areas College planning, touring.
Sports Basketball, bicycling, fishing, golf, kayaking, noncompetitive sports, sea kayaking, soccer, softball, surfing, swimming, tennis, volleyball.
Wilderness/Outdoors Bicycle trips, hiking, outdoor adventure.
Trips College tours, cultural, day, overnight, shopping.
Program Information 8–10 sessions per year. Session length: 1 week in July, August. Ages: 1+. 260–280 participants per session. Boarding program cost: $550–$750.
Application Deadline Continuous.
Jobs Positions for high school students 13 and older and college students.
Contact Ms. Jean King, Director, UCSB Alumni Association, Santa Barbara, California 93106-1120. Phone: 805-893-3123. Fax: 805-893-2927. E-mail: vacation@ia.ucsb.edu.
URL www.familyvacationcenter.com

University of San Diego Sports Camps–Baseball Camp

University of San Diego Sports Camps
5998 Alcala Park
San Diego, California 92110-2492

General Information Coed day sports camp established in 1978. Religious affiliation: Roman Catholic. Accredited by American Camping Association.
Program Focus Competitive baseball.
Sports Baseball.
Trips College tours.
Program Information 2 sessions per year. Session length: 5 days in June. Ages: 6–15. 60–200 participants per session. Day program cost: $325–$400.
Application Deadline Continuous.
Jobs Positions for college students 19 and older.
Contact Lila Chan, USD Sports Camps, main address above. Phone: 800-991-1873 Ext.2. Fax: 619-260-4185. E-mail: sportscamps@sandiego.edu.
URL camps.sandiego.edu

University of San Diego Sports Camps–Boys Basketball High School Team Camp

University of San Diego Sports Camps
5998 Alcala Park
San Diego, California 92110-2492

General Information Boys' residential and day sports camp established in 1978. Religious affiliation: Roman Catholic. Accredited by American Camping Association.
Program Focus Provides opportunity for teams all over the U.S. to compete with other top teams and receive quality instruction from college coaches.
Sports Basketball.
Trips College tours.
Program Information 1 session per year. Session length: 3 days in June. 60–200 participants per session. Day program cost: $325–$400. Boarding program cost: $450–$525.
Application Deadline Continuous.
Jobs Positions for college students 19 and older.
Contact Lila Chan, USD Sports Camps, main address above. Phone: 800-991-1873 Ext.2. Fax: 619-260-4185. E-mail: sportscamps@sandiego.edu.
URL camps.sandiego.edu

University of San Diego Sports Camps–Boys High School Basketball Camp

University of San Diego Sports Camps
5998 Alcala Park
San Diego, California 92110-2492

General Information Boys' residential and day sports camp established in 1978. Religious affiliation: Roman Catholic. Accredited by American Camping Association.
Program Focus Competitive basketball.
Sports Basketball.
Trips College tours.
Program Information 1 session per year. Session length: 5 days in July. Ages: 13–17. 60–200 participants per session. Day program cost: $325–$400. Boarding program cost: $450–$525.
Application Deadline Continuous.
Jobs Positions for college students 19 and older.
Contact Lila Chan, USD Sports Camps, main address above. Phone: 800-991-1873 Ext.2. Fax: 619-260-4185. E-mail: sportscamps@sandiego.edu.
URL camps.sandiego.edu

University of San Diego Sports Camps–Boys High School Elite Baseball Camp

University of San Diego Sports Camps
5998 Alcala Park
San Diego, California 92110-2492

General Information Boys' day sports camp established in 1978. Religious affiliation: Roman Catholic. Accredited by American Camping Association.
Program Focus Competitive baseball.
Sports Baseball.
Trips College tours.
Program Information 1 session per year. Session length: 5 days in July. Ages: 6–18. 60–200 participants per session. Day program cost: $325–$400.
Application Deadline Continuous.
Jobs Positions for college students 19 and older.
Contact Lila Chan, USD Sports Camps, main address above. Phone: 800-991-1873 Ext.2. Fax: 619-260-4185. E-mail: sportscamps@sandiego.edu.
URL camps.sandiego.edu

University of San Diego Sports Camps–Boys High School Soccer Camp

University of San Diego Sports Camps
5998 Alcala Park
San Diego, California 92110-2492

General Information Boys' residential and day sports camp established in 1978. Religious affiliation: Roman Catholic. Accredited by American Camping Association.
Program Focus Competitive Soccer.
Sports Soccer.
Trips College tours.
Program Information 1 session per year. Session length: 5 days in July. Ages: 13–17. 60–200 participants per session. Day program cost: $325–$400. Boarding program cost: $450–$525.
Application Deadline Continuous.
Jobs Positions for college students 19 and older.
Contact Lila Chan, USD Sports Camps, main address above. Phone: 800-991-1873 Ext.2. Fax: 619-260-4185. E-mail: sportscamps@sandiego.edu.
URL camps.sandiego.edu

University of San Diego Sports Camps–Boys Junior Basketball Camp

University of San Diego Sports Camps
5998 Alcala Park
San Diego, California 92110-2492

General Information Boys' residential and day sports camp established in 1978. Religious affiliation: Roman Catholic. Accredited by American Camping Association.
Program Focus To help participants improve the fundamental skills of basketball.
Sports Basketball.
Trips College tours.
Program Information 1 session per year. Session length: 5 days in July. Ages: 8–12. 60–200 participants per session. Day program cost: $325–$400. Boarding program cost: $450–$525.
Application Deadline Continuous.
Jobs Positions for college students 19 and older.
Contact Lila Chan, USD Sports Camps, main address above. Phone: 800-991-1873 Ext.2. Fax: 619-260-4185. E-mail: sportscamps@sandiego.edu.
URL camps.sandiego.edu

University of San Diego Sports Camps–Coed Junior Soccer Camp

University of San Diego Sports Camps
5998 Alcala Park
San Diego, California 92110-2492

General Information Coed residential and day sports camp established in 1978. Religious affiliation: Roman Catholic. Accredited by American Camping Association.
Program Focus Competitive soccer.
Sports Soccer.
Trips College tours.
Program Information 1 session per year. Session length: 5 days in July. Ages: 8–12. 60–200 participants per session. Day program cost: $325–$400. Boarding program cost: $450–$525.
Application Deadline Continuous.
Jobs Positions for college students 19 and older.
Contact Lila Chan, USD Sports Camps, main address above. Phone: 800-991-1873 Ext.2. Fax: 619-260-4185. E-mail: sportscamps@sandiego.edu.
URL camps.sandiego.edu

University of San Diego Sports Camps–Coed Water Polo Camp

University of San Diego Sports Camps
5998 Alcala Park
San Diego, California 92110-2492

General Information Coed residential and day sports camp established in 1978. Religious affiliation: Roman Catholic. Accredited by American Camping Association.
Program Focus Competitive water polo.
Sports Water polo.
Trips College tours.
Program Information 2 sessions per year. Session length: 5 days in July. Ages: 11–17. 60–200 participants per session. Day program cost: $330–$405. Boarding program cost: $450–$525. Financial aid available.
Application Deadline Continuous.
Contact Lila Chan, USD Sports Camps, main address above. Phone: 800-991-1873 Ext.2. Fax: 619-260-4185. E-mail: sportscamps@sandiego.edu.
URL camps.sandiego.edu

University of San Diego Sports Camps–Competitive Swim Camp

University of San Diego Sports Camps
5998 Alcala Park
San Diego, California 92110-2492

General Information Coed residential and day sports camp established in 1978. Religious affiliation: Roman Catholic. Accredited by American Camping Association.
Program Focus Competitive swimmers with at least one season of high school, summer league or club experience.
Sports Swimming.
Trips College tours.
Program Information 2 sessions per year. Session length: 5 days in June. Ages: 9–17. 60–200 participants per session. Day program cost: $370–$445. Boarding program cost: $500–$575.
Application Deadline Continuous.
Jobs Positions for college students 19 and older.
Contact Lila Chan, USD Sports Camps, main address above. Phone: 800-991-1873 Ext.2. Fax: 619-260-4185. E-mail: sportscamps@sandiego.edu.
URL camps.sandiego.edu

University of San Diego Sports Camps–Girls Basketball Fundamentals Camp

University of San Diego Sports Camps
5998 Alcala Park
San Diego, California 92110-2492

General Information Girls' residential and day sports camp established in 1978. Religious affiliation: Roman Catholic. Accredited by American Camping Association.
Program Focus For players who need to build the basic skills of basketball.
Sports Basketball.
Trips College tours.
Program Information 1 session per year. Session length: 5 days in June. Ages: 8–17. 60–200 participants per session. Day program cost: $325–$400. Boarding program cost: $450–$525.
Application Deadline Continuous.
Jobs Positions for college students 19 and older.
Contact Lila Chan, USD Sports Camps, main address above. Phone: 800-991-1873 Ext.2. Fax: 619-260-4185. E-mail: sportscamps@sandiego.edu.
URL camps.sandiego.edu

University of San Diego Sports Camps–Girls Basketball High School Elite Camp

University of San Diego Sports Camps
5998 Alcala Park
San Diego, California 92110-2492

General Information Girls' residential and day sports camp established in 1978. Religious affiliation: Roman Catholic. Accredited by American Camping Association.
Program Focus Competitive basketball.
Sports Basketball.
Trips College tours.
Program Information 1 session per year. Session length: 3 days in June. 60–200 participants per session. Day program cost: $95–$120. Boarding program cost: $165–$190.
Application Deadline Continuous.
Jobs Positions for college students 19 and older.
Contact Lila Chan, USD Sports Camps, main address above. Phone: 800-991-1873 Ext.2. Fax: 619-260-4185. E-mail: sportscamps@sandiego.edu.
URL camps.sandiego.edu

University of San Diego Sports Camps–Girls Basketball High School Team Camp

University of San Diego Sports Camps
5998 Alcala Park
San Diego, California 92110-2492

General Information Girls' residential and day sports camp established in 1978. Religious affiliation: Roman Catholic. Accredited by American Camping Association.
Program Focus Provides opportunity for teams all over the U.S. to compete with other top teams and receive quality instruction from college coaches.
Sports Basketball.
Trips College tours.
Program Information 1 session per year. Session length: 3 days in June. 60–200 participants per session. Day program cost: $120–$525. Boarding program cost: $420–$625.
Application Deadline Continuous.
Jobs Positions for college students 19 and older.
Contact Lila Chan, USD Sports Camps, main address above. Phone: 800-991-1873 Ext.2. Fax: 619-260-4185. E-mail: sportscamps@sandiego.edu.
URL camps.sandiego.edu

University of San Diego Sports Camps–Girls Soccer Camp

University of San Diego Sports Camps
5998 Alcala Park
San Diego, California 92110-2492

General Information Girls' residential and day sports camp established in 1978. Accredited by American Camping Association.
Program Focus Competitive soccer.
Sports Soccer.
Trips College tours.
Program Information 1 session per year. Session length: 5 days in June, July. Ages: 8–17. 60–200 participants per session. Day program cost: $325–$400. Boarding program cost: $450–$525.
Application Deadline Continuous.
Jobs Positions for college students 19 and older.
Contact Lila Chan, USD Sports Camps, main address above. Phone: 800-991-1873 Ext.2. Fax: 619-260-4185. E-mail: sportscamps@sandiego.edu.
URL camps.sandiego.edu

University of San Diego Sports Camps–Girls Softball Advanced Camp

University of San Diego Sports Camps
5998 Alcala Park
San Diego, California 92110-2492

General Information Girls' residential and day sports camp established in 1978. Religious affiliation: Roman Catholic. Accredited by American Camping Association.
Program Focus Competitive softball for those ready to study the game in depth and learn more advanced techniques.
Sports Softball.
Trips College tours.
Program Information 1 session per year. Session length: 6 days in July. Ages: 9–17. 60–200 participants per session. Day program cost: $325–$400. Boarding program cost: $450–$525.
Application Deadline Continuous.
Jobs Positions for college students 19 and older.
Contact Lila Chan, USD Sports Camps, main address above. Phone: 800-991-1873 Ext.2. Fax: 619-260-4185. E-mail: sportscamps@sandiego.edu.
URL camps.sandiego.edu

University of San Diego Sports Camps–Girls Softball Beginner/ Intermediate Camp

University of San Diego Sports Camps
5998 Alcala Park
San Diego, California 92110-2492

General Information Girls' residential and day sports camp established in 1978. Religious affiliation: Roman Catholic. Accredited by American Camping Association.
Program Focus For players just learning the game or having 1-2 years experience.
Sports Softball.
Trips College tours.
Program Information 1 session per year. Session length: 6 days in July. Ages: 9–17. 60–200 participants per session. Day program cost: $325–$400. Boarding program cost: $450–$525.
Application Deadline Continuous.
Jobs Positions for college students 19 and older.
Contact Lila Chan, USD Sports Camps, main address above. Phone: 800-991-1873 Ext.2. Fax: 619-260-4185. E-mail: sportscamps@sandiego.edu.
URL camps.sandiego.edu

University of San Diego Sports Camps–Girls Volleyball Camp

University of San Diego Sports Camps
5998 Alcala Park
San Diego, California 92110-2492

General Information Girls' residential sports camp established in 1978. Religious affiliation: Roman Catholic. Accredited by American Camping Association.
Program Focus Competitive volleyball.
Sports Volleyball.
Trips College tours.
Program Information 1 session per year. Session length: 4 days in July. 60–200 participants per session. Boarding program cost: $450–$525.
Application Deadline Continuous.
Jobs Positions for college students 19 and older.
Contact Lila Chan, USD Sports Camps, main address above. Phone: 800-991-1873 Ext.2. Fax: 619-260-4185. E-mail: sportscamps@sandiego.edu.
URL camps.sandiego.edu

University of San Diego Sports Camps–Sherri Stephens High School Tennis Camp

University of San Diego Sports Camps
5998 Alcala Park
San Diego, California 92110-2492

General Information Coed residential and day sports camp established in 1978. Religious affiliation: Roman Catholic. Accredited by American Camping Association.
Program Focus For high school players preparing for his/her upcoming tennis season.
Sports Tennis.
Trips College tours.
Program Information 1 session per year. Session length: 6 days in July. Ages: 14–17. 60–200 participants per session. Day program cost: $375–$450. Boarding program cost: $600–$675.
Application Deadline Continuous.
Jobs Positions for college students 19 and older.
Contact Lila Chan, USD Sports Camps, main address above. Phone: 800-991-1873 Ext.2. Fax: 619-260-4185. E-mail: sportscamps@sandiego.edu.
URL camps.sandiego.edu

University of San Diego Sports Camps–Sherri Stephens Junior Tennis Camp

University of San Diego Sports Camps
5998 Alcala Park
San Diego, California 92110-2492

General Information Coed residential and day sports camp established in 1978. Religious affiliation: Roman Catholic. Accredited by American Camping Association.
Program Focus For the intermediate, more aggressive player who is interested in preparing for competitive play.
Sports Tennis.
Trips College tours.
Program Information 1 session per year. Session length: 6 days in July. Ages: 9–17. 60–200 participants per session. Day program cost: $375–$450. Boarding program cost: $600–$675.
Application Deadline Continuous.
Jobs Positions for college students 19 and older.
Contact Lila Chan, USD Sports Camps, main address above. Phone: 800-991-1873 Ext.2. Fax: 619-260-4185. E-mail: sportscamps@sandiego.edu.
URL camps.sandiego.edu

University of San Diego Sports Camps–Sports–N–More All Sports Camp

University of San Diego Sports Camps
5998 Alcala Park
San Diego, California 92110-2492

General Information Coed day sports camp established in 1978. Religious affiliation: Roman Catholic. Accredited by American Camping Association.
Program Focus Competitive sports.
Arts Dance.
Sports Archery, badminton, baseball, basketball, football, golf, soccer, softball, sports (general), street/roller hockey, tennis, ultimate frisbee, volleyball.
Trips College tours.
Program Information 3 sessions per year. Session length: 5 days in June, July. Ages: 6–12. 60–200 participants per session. Day program cost: $120–$225.
Application Deadline Continuous.
Jobs Positions for college students 19 and older.
Contact Lila Chan, USD Sports Camps, main address above. Phone: 800-991-1873 Ext.2. Fax: 619-260-4185. E-mail: sportscamps@sandiego.edu.
URL camps.sandiego.edu

University of San Diego Sports Camps–Sports–N–More Team Sports Camp

University of San Diego Sports Camps
5998 Alcala Park
San Diego, California 92110-2492

General Information Coed day sports camp established in 1978. Religious affiliation: Roman Catholic. Accredited by American Camping Association.
Program Focus General skill instruction in 6-8 competitive sports.
Sports Baseball, basketball, football, soccer, softball, sports (general), tennis, volleyball.
Trips College tours.
Program Information 3 sessions per year. Session length: 5 days in June, July. Ages: 6–12. 60–200 participants per session. Day program cost: $120–$225.
Application Deadline Continuous.
Jobs Positions for college students 19 and older.
Contact Lila Chan, USD Sports Camps, main address above. Phone: 800-991-1873 Ext.2. Fax: 619-260-4185. E-mail: sportscamps@sandiego.edu.
URL camps.sandiego.edu

University of San Diego Sports Camps–Sports-N-More Wet & Wild Sports Camp

University of San Diego Sports Camps
5998 Alcala Park
San Diego, California 92110-2492

General Information Coed day sports camp established in 1978. Religious affiliation: Roman Catholic. Accredited by American Camping Association.
Program Focus Introductory instruction in water sports and activities.
Special Interest Areas Lifesaving.
Sports Diving, snorkeling, sports (general), surfing, swimming, water polo.
Trips College tours.
Program Information 1 session per year. Session length: 5 days in July. Ages: 6–12. 60–200 participants per session. Day program cost: $120–$225.
Application Deadline Continuous.
Jobs Positions for college students 19 and older.
Contact Lila Chan, USD Sports Camps, main address above. Phone: 800-991-1873 Ext.2. Fax: 619-260-4185. E-mail: sportscamps@sandiego.edu.
URL camps.sandiego.edu

University of Southern California Summer Seminars

University of Southern California–Summer and Special Programs
Los Angeles, California 90089-7009

General Information Coed residential academic program established in 1997. Formal opportunities for the academically talented and artistically talented. Specific services available for the hearing impaired, physically challenged, and visually impaired. College credit may be earned.
Academics Academics (general), aerospace science, architecture, art (Advanced Placement), astronomy, biology, communications, computers, engineering, environmental science, journalism, music, physics, physiology, precollege program, psychology, science (general), speech/debate, writing.
Arts Creative writing, film, theater/drama.
Special Interest Areas Career exploration, field research/expeditions.
Sports Baseball, basketball, swimming, tennis, volleyball.
Trips College tours, cultural, day, shopping.
Program Information 1 session per year. Session length: 4 weeks in July. Ages: 15–18. 150–200 participants per session. Boarding program cost: $3975–$4150. Financial aid available.
Application Deadline Continuous.
Jobs Positions for college students 21 and older.
Contact Steve Foral, Director, Summer and Special Programs, USC Campus Mail Code 7009, Los Angeles, California 90089-7009. Phone: 213-743-1710. Fax: 213-743-1714. E-mail: summer@usc.edu.
URL www.usc.edu/summer

Ventures Travel Service–California

Friendship Ventures
California

General Information Coed travel special needs program established in 1985. Specific services available for the developmentally challenged and physically challenged.
Program Focus Provides travel services to older teens and adults with developmental disabilities.
Special Interest Areas Touring.
Program Information 50 sessions per year. Session length: 4–10 days in February, March, April, May, June, July, August, September, October, November, December. Ages: 14–70. 4–8 participants per session. Cost: $395–$2000.
Application Deadline Continuous.
Jobs Positions for college students 18 and older.
Contact Georgann Rumsey, President/CEO, 10509 108th Street, NW, Annandale, Minnesota 55302. Phone: 952-852-0101. Fax: 952-852-0123. E-mail: fv@friendshipventures.org.
URL www.friendshipventures.org

Watersports Extravaganza at Pali Overnight Adventures

Pali Overnight Adventures
30778 Highway 18
Running Springs, California 92382

General Information Coed residential traditional camp and sports camp established in 1990. Accredited by American Camping Association. Formal opportunities for the artistically talented.
Program Focus Watersports.
Academics Journalism.
Arts Acting, arts and crafts (general), batiking, ceramics, dance, dance (jazz), dance (modern), dance (tap), film, film production, music, painting, pottery, theater/drama.
Special Interest Areas Animal care, culinary arts, leadership training, nature study, robotics, team building, yearbook production.
Sports Aerobics, archery, basketball, boating, canoeing, climbing (wall), equestrian sports, fencing, field hockey, fishing, football, go-carts, gymnastics, horseback riding, jet skiing, kayaking, lacrosse, martial arts, paintball, rappelling, riflery, ropes course, sailing, scuba diving, skateboarding, snorkeling, soccer, softball, swimming, volleyball, wakeboarding, waterskiing.
Wilderness/Outdoors Hiking, rafting, white-water trips.
Trips Day, overnight.
Program Information 5–8 sessions per year. Session length: 1–2 weeks in June, July, August. Ages: 9–16. 8–80 participants per session. Boarding program cost: $1385–$2695.
Application Deadline Continuous.
Jobs Positions for college students 19 and older.
Contact Mr. Andy Wexler, Owner/Founder, PO Box 2237, Running Springs, California 92382-2237. Phone: 909-867-5743. Fax: 909-867-7643. E-mail: info@paliadventures.com.
URL www.paliadventures.com/water_sports.html

Westcoast Connection Travel–Adventure California

Westcoast Connection
California

General Information Coed travel outdoor program and adventure program established in 1982. Accredited by Ontario Camping Association.
Program Focus Outdoor adventure in California.
Special Interest Areas Community service.
Sports Bicycling, kayaking, rappelling, ropes course, sea kayaking, snorkeling, surfing, swimming.
Wilderness/Outdoors Caving, hiking, mountain biking, outdoor adventure, rafting, rock climbing, white-water trips.
Program Information 1–2 sessions per year. Session length: 18–27 days in June, July, August. Ages: 13–17. 10–26 participants per session. Cost: $4199.
Application Deadline Continuous.
Jobs Positions for college students 21 and older.
Contact Mr. Mark Segal, Director, 154 East Boston Post Road, Mamaroneck, New York 10543. Phone: 800-767-0227. Fax: 914-835-0798. E-mail: usa@westcoastconnection.com.
URL www.westcoastconnection.com
For more information, see page 1392.

Wilderness Ventures–California

Wilderness Ventures
California

General Information Coed travel outdoor program, wilderness program, and adventure program established in 1973.
Program Focus Wilderness travel, wilderness skills, leadership skills.
Special Interest Areas Leadership training.
Sports Surfing.
Wilderness/Outdoors Backpacking, hiking, rafting, white-water trips, wilderness camping.
Trips Overnight.
Program Information 2 sessions per year. Session length: 3 weeks in June, July, August. Ages: 14–18. 13 participants per session. Cost: $3190. Financial aid available.
Application Deadline Continuous.
Jobs Positions for college students 21 and older.
Contact Mike Cottingham, Director, PO Box 2768, Jackson Hole, Wyoming 83001. Phone: 800-533-2281. E-mail: info@wildernessventures.com.
URL www.wildernessventures.com
For more information, see page 1396.

Wilderness Ventures–High Sierra

Wilderness Ventures
California

General Information Coed travel outdoor program, wilderness program, and adventure program established in 1973.
Program Focus Wilderness travel, wilderness skills, leadership skills.
Special Interest Areas Leadership training.
Wilderness/Outdoors Backpacking, hiking, mountaineering, rafting, rock climbing, white-water trips, wilderness camping.
Trips Overnight.
Program Information 1 session per year. Session length: 26 days in June, July, August. Ages: 14–18. 13 participants per session. Cost: $3590. Financial aid available.
Application Deadline Continuous.
Jobs Positions for college students 21 and older.
Contact Mike Cottingham, Director, PO Box 2768, Jackson Hole, Wyoming 83001. Phone: 800-533-2281. Fax: 307-739-1934. E-mail: info@wildernessventures.com.
URL www.wildernessventures.com
For more information, see page 1396.

Windsor Mountain: California Community Service

Interlocken at Windsor Mountain
California

General Information Coed travel outdoor program, community service program, and adventure program established in 1967.
Program Focus Wilderness adventure, cultural exploration, community service.
Academics Environmental science, intercultural studies.
Special Interest Areas Community service, farming, leadership training, team building.
Sports Rappelling, swimming.
Wilderness/Outdoors Backpacking, hiking, mountaineering, orienteering, rafting, rock climbing, survival training, white-water trips, wilderness camping.
Program Information 1 session per year. Session length: 4 weeks in July, August. Ages: 13–15. 13 participants per session. Cost: $3595. Financial aid available.
Application Deadline Continuous.
Jobs Positions for college students 23 and older.
Contact Richard Herman, Director, 19 Interlocken Way, Windsor, New Hampshire 03244. Phone: 800-862-7760. Fax: 603-478-5260. E-mail: mail@windsormountain.org.
URL www.windsormountain.org/xrds
For more information, see page 1162.

YMCA Camp Oakes Rangers

YMCA of Greater Long Beach
47400 Monte Vista Drive
Big Bear City, California 92314

General Information Coed residential traditional camp and outdoor program established in 1958. Accredited by American Camping Association. Specific services available for the emotionally challenged, developmentally challenged, hearing impaired, learning disabled, physically challenged, visually impaired, and participant with cancer.

YMCA Camp Oakes Rangers (continued)

Program Focus Long-term summer camping up to 3 weeks, attracts broad international cross section, as well as campers from the U.S..
Academics Astronomy.
Arts Arts and crafts (general), leather working, music (vocal).
Special Interest Areas Animal care, campcraft, nature study, nautical skills.
Sports Archery, bicycling, canoeing, climbing (wall), horseback riding, riflery, ropes course, swimming, volleyball.
Wilderness/Outdoors Backpacking, hiking, mountain biking, orienteering, rock climbing.
Trips Day, overnight.
Program Information 1–3 sessions per year. Session length: 6–7 days in June, July. Ages: 8–13. 97 participants per session. Boarding program cost: $479. Financial aid available.
Application Deadline Continuous.
Jobs Positions for high school students 18 and older and college students 18 and older.
Contact Marc Wilson, YMCA Camping Services, PO Box 90995, Long Beach, California 90809-0995. Phone: 562-496-2756. Fax: 562-425-5451. E-mail: camp@lbymca.org.
URL www.campoakes.org

YMCA Camp Oakes Teen Leadership

YMCA of Greater Long Beach
47400 Monte Vista Drive
Big Bear City, California 92314

General Information Coed residential traditional camp and outdoor program established in 1999. Accredited by American Camping Association. Specific services available for the emotionally challenged, developmentally challenged, hearing impaired, learning disabled, physically challenged, and visually impaired.
Program Focus Designed for those who want to develop leadership skills.
Academics Astronomy.
Arts Arts and crafts (general), leather working, music (vocal).
Special Interest Areas Campcraft, leadership training, nature study, nautical skills, team building.
Sports Archery, bicycling, canoeing, climbing (wall), horseback riding, riflery, ropes course, swimming, volleyball.
Wilderness/Outdoors Bicycle trips, mountain biking, mountaineering, rock climbing, wilderness camping.
Trips Day, overnight.
Program Information 1–3 sessions per year. Session length: 6–7 days in June, July. Ages: 14–17. 16–32 participants per session. Boarding program cost: $499. Financial aid available.
Application Deadline Continuous.
Jobs Positions for high school students 18 and older and college students 18 and older.
Contact Marc Wilson, YMCA Camping Services, PO Box 90995, Long Beach, California 90809-0995. Phone: 562-496-2756. Fax: 562-425-5451. E-mail: camp@lbymca.org.
URL www.campoakes.org

YMCA Camp Surf

YMCA Camp Surf
106 Carnation Avenue
Imperial Beach, California 91932

General Information Coed residential and day traditional camp established in 1969. Accredited by American Camping Association.
Program Focus Ocean waterfront activities and leadership training, including open-water lifeguarding.
Academics Ecology, environmental science, geology/earth science, marine studies, oceanography, science (general).
Arts Arts and crafts (general).
Special Interest Areas Leadership training, nature study.
Sports Archery, basketball, bicycling, body boarding, climbing (wall), kayaking, ropes course, sailing, sea kayaking, snorkeling, soccer, softball, surfing, swimming, volleyball.
Trips Day, overnight.
Program Information 10 sessions per year. Session length: 6–13 days in March, April, May, June, July, August, September, October, November. Ages: 8–17. 100–160 participants per session. Day program cost: $125–$170. Boarding program cost: $395–$990. Financial aid available.
Application Deadline Continuous.
Jobs Positions for high school students 18 and older and college students 18 and older.
Contact Zayanne Thompson, Senior Program Director, main address above. Phone: 619-423-5850. Fax: 619-423-4141. E-mail: zgardner@ymca.org.
URL camp.ymca.org

Yo! Basecamp Rock Climbing Camps

Yo! Basecamp Rock Climbing Camps
Sierra Nevada Mountains
California

General Information Coed residential wilderness program and adventure program established in 1998.
Program Focus Rock climbing, three camp levels: Beginning, intermediate, and advanced technical. Minimum impact camping: "Leave no trace" practices.
Academics Ecology, geology/earth science.
Special Interest Areas Campcraft, nature study.
Sports Rappelling.
Wilderness/Outdoors Hiking, mountaineering, rock climbing, wilderness camping.
Trips Day, overnight.
Program Information 6–8 sessions per year. Session length: 4–10 days in June, July, August. Ages: 11–18. 8–14 participants per session. Boarding program cost: $495–$1750. Application fee: $50. Financial aid available.
Application Deadline Continuous.
Contact Ms. Lisa Coleman, Co-Director, 130 McCornick Street, #7, Santa Cruz, California 95062. Phone: 831-673-5918. E-mail: climb@yobasecamp.com.
URL www.yobasecamp.com

Yosemite Backpacking Adventures

Yosemite Institute
Yosemite National Park
Yosemite, California 95389

General Information Coed travel outdoor program, wilderness program, and adventure program established in 1999.
Program Focus 9–11 day wilderness backpacking trips in Yosemite National Park.
Academics Astronomy, botany, ecology, environmental science, geology/earth science.
Arts Creative writing, drawing.
Special Interest Areas Nature study.
Sports Fishing.
Wilderness/Outdoors Backpacking, hiking, mountaineering, orienteering, survival training, wilderness camping.
Trips Day, overnight.
Program Information 4–6 sessions per year. Session length: 9–11 days in June, July, August. Ages: 13–18. 8–12 participants per session. Cost: $799–$1200. Financial aid available.
Application Deadline Continuous.
Summer Contact Ms. Peggy Lovegreen, Administrative Assistant, PO Box 487, Yosemite, California 95389. Phone: 209-379-9511. Fax: 209-379-9510. E-mail: yi@yni.org.
Winter Contact Ms. Leigh Davenport, Executive Director, main address above.
URL www.yni.org/programs/summerprograms.html

Young Actors Camp

Summer Camp for the Young Actor, Inc.
Los Angeles, California

General Information Coed residential and day arts program established in 2000. Formal opportunities for the artistically talented.
Arts Acting, audition technique, film, television/video, theater/drama.
Trips Day.
Program Information 3 sessions per year. Session length: 2 weeks in August. Ages: 11–18. 50–70 participants per session. Boarding program cost: $2040–$4780. Application fee: $50.
Application Deadline May 31.
Jobs Positions for college students 19 and older.
Contact Nichelle Rodriguez, Director, 305 North 2nd Avenue, #118, Upland, California 91786. Phone: 909-982-8059. Fax: 909-982-5328. E-mail: educationsvc@msn.com.
URL www.youngactorscamp.com

For more information, see page 1412.

COLORADO

AAVE–Rocky Mountain Adventure

AAVE–America's Adventure Ventures Everywhere
Colorado

General Information Coed travel outdoor program, wilderness program, and adventure program established in 1976. Accredited by American Camping Association.
Program Focus Adventure travel.
Special Interest Areas Campcraft, community service, leadership training.
Sports Bicycling, horseback riding, rappelling, swimming.
Wilderness/Outdoors Backpacking, bicycle trips, hiking, mountain biking, mountaineering, orienteering, rafting, rock climbing, white-water trips.
Program Information 6–8 sessions per year. Session length: 18 days in June, July, August. Ages: 12–13. 13 participants per session. Cost: $2288. Financial aid available.
Application Deadline Continuous.
Jobs Positions for college students 21 and older.
Contact Mr. Abbott Wallis, Owner, 2245 Stonecrop Way, Golden, Colorado 80401. Phone: 800-222-3595. Fax: 303-526-0885. E-mail: info@aave.com.
URL www.aave.com

For more information, see page 952.

Adventures Cross-Country, Colorado Adventure

Adventures Cross-Country
Colorado

General Information Coed residential outdoor program, wilderness program, and adventure program established in 1983.
Program Focus Multi-activity wilderness adventure in Colorado.
Sports Bicycling.
Wilderness/Outdoors Backpacking, hiking, mountain biking, mountaineering, orienteering, rafting, white-water trips, wilderness camping.
Program Information 3 sessions per year. Session length: 15 days in June, July, August. Ages: 13–18. 8–15 participants per session. Boarding program cost: $2595. Financial aid available.
Application Deadline Continuous.
Jobs Positions for college students 21 and older.

Adventures Cross-Country, Colorado Adventure (continued)

Adventures Cross-Country, Colorado Adventure

Contact Scott von Eschen, Owner, 242 Redwood Highway, Mill Valley, California 94941. Phone: 415-332-5075. Fax: 415-332-2130. E-mail: arcc@adventurescrosscountry.com.
URL www.adventurescrosscountry.com
For more information, see page 972.

Anderson Camps' Colorado River Ranch for Boys/Hilltop Ranch for Girls

Anderson Western Colorado Camps, Ltd.
7177 Colorado River Road
Gypsum, Colorado 81637

General Information Coed residential traditional camp and outdoor program established in 1962. Accredited by American Camping Association.
Program Focus Noncompetitive, individualized outdoor activities.
Special Interest Areas Campcraft, model rocketry.
Sports Archery, baseball, basketball, bicycling, boating, climbing (wall), equestrian sports, fishing, football, horseback riding, rappelling, riflery, ropes course, soccer, softball, swimming, tennis, volleyball.
Wilderness/Outdoors Backpacking, bicycle trips, caving, hiking, mountain biking, mountaineering, orienteering, pack animal trips, rafting, rock climbing, white-water trips, wilderness camping, wilderness/outdoors (general).
Trips Day, overnight.
Program Information 3 sessions per year. Session length: 2–3 weeks in June, July, August. Ages: 7–17. 114–125 participants per session. Boarding program cost: $1795–$2495.
Application Deadline Continuous.
Jobs Positions for high school students 16 and older and college students 18 and older.
Contact Christopher Porter, Director, main address above. Phone: 970-524-7766. Fax: 970-524-7107. E-mail: andecamp@andersoncamps.com.
URL www.andersoncamps.com

Anderson Camps' Wilderness Pioneer Camp

Anderson Western Colorado Camps, Ltd.
7177 Colorado River Road
Gypsum, Colorado 81637

General Information Coed residential outdoor program and wilderness program established in 1969. Accredited by American Camping Association.
Program Focus Wilderness camping, mountaineering, kayaking, rock climbing, and white-water rafting.
Special Interest Areas Campcraft, leadership training.
Sports Boating, climbing (wall), kayaking, rappelling, ropes course, swimming.
Wilderness/Outdoors Backpacking, caving, hiking, mountaineering, orienteering, rafting, rock climbing, white-water trips, wilderness camping.
Trips Overnight.
Program Information 3 sessions per year. Session length: 3 weeks in June, July, August. Ages: 14–17. 20 participants per session. Boarding program cost: $2995.
Application Deadline Continuous.
Jobs Positions for college students 21 and older.
Contact Christopher Porter, Director, main address above. Phone: 970-524-7766. Fax: 970-524-7107. E-mail: andecamp@andersoncamps.com.
URL www.andersoncamps.com

Bugs to Biospheres

Center for Science, Mathematics and Technology Education (CSMATE)
Colorado State University
Fort Collins, Colorado 80523

General Information Coed residential and day academic program.
Program Focus Life sciences.
Academics Biology, chemistry, science (general).
Trips College tours, day.

Program Information 1–2 sessions per year. Session length: 5 days in June. Ages: 14–18. 25–30 participants per session. Day program cost: $190–$350. Boarding program cost: $750. Financial aid available.
Application Deadline May 31.
Contact Ms. Courtney Butler, Assistant to the Director, Colorado State University, Campus Delivery 1802, Fort Collins, Colorado 80523. Phone: 970-491-1700. Fax: 970-491-2005. E-mail: courtney.butler@colostate.edu.
URL www.csmate.colostate.edu

CHELEY COLORADO CAMPS

Estes Park, Colorado 80517

General Information Coed residential traditional camp, outdoor program, family program, wilderness program, and adventure program established in 1921. Accredited by American Camping Association.
Program Focus Horseback riding, wilderness activities, and mountaineering.
Arts Batiking, ceramics, drawing, fabric arts, jewelry making, leather working, painting, pottery, woodworking.
Special Interest Areas Campcraft, leadership training.
Sports Aerobics, archery, basketball, climbing (wall), fishing, horseback riding, rappelling, riflery, ropes course, soccer, weight training.
Wilderness/Outdoors Backpacking, bicycle trips, hiking, mountain biking, mountaineering, orienteering, pack animal trips, rafting, rock climbing, survival training, white-water trips, wilderness camping.
Trips Day, overnight.
Program Information 2 sessions per year. Session length: 27 days in June, July, August. Ages: 9–17. 480 participants per session.
Application Deadline Continuous.
Jobs Positions for college students 19 and older.
Summer Contact Enrollment Manager, PO Box 1170, Estes Park, Colorado 80517. Phone: 970-586-4244. Fax: 970-586-3020. E-mail: office@cheley.com.
Winter Contact Enrollment Manager, PO Box 6525, Denver, Colorado 80206. Phone: 303-377-3616. Fax: 303-377-3605. E-mail: office@cheley.com.
URL www.cheley.com

COLORADO ACADEMY SUMMER PROGRAMS

Colorado Academy
3800 South Pierce Street
Denver, Colorado 80235

General Information Coed day traditional camp and academic program established in 1951.
Academics English language/literature, Spanish language/literature, academics (general), computers, mathematics, reading, science (general), study skills, writing.
Arts Arts and crafts (general), circus arts, photography.
Sports Archery, baseball, basketball, bicycling, climbing (wall), frisbee golf, golf, lacrosse, racquetball, rappelling, soccer, sports (general), tennis, volleyball.
Wilderness/Outdoors Backpacking, rock climbing.
Trips Day.
Program Information 1–4 sessions per year. Session length: 4–10 days in June, July, August. Ages: 5–16. 4–200 participants per session. Day program cost: $200–$250.
Application Deadline Continuous.
Jobs Positions for high school students 16 and older and college students 16 and older.
Contact Ms. Lyn Hills, Registrar, main address above. Phone: 303-914-2531. Fax: 303-914-2532. E-mail: lyhills@mail.coloacad.org.
URL www.coloradoacademy.org

THE COLORADO MOUNTAIN RANCH

10063 Gold Hill Road
Boulder, Colorado 80302

General Information Coed day traditional camp established in 1947. Specific services available for the emotionally challenged, developmentally challenged, hearing impaired, learning disabled, physically challenged, and visually impaired.
Program Focus Confidence-building, noncompetitive specialty programs, and outdoor Western mountain activities.
Academics Mathematics, reading, tutoring, writing.
Arts Arts and crafts (general), creative writing, dance, drawing, fabric arts, jewelry making, leather working, music, music (vocal), painting, pottery, sculpture, theater/drama, weaving, woodworking.
Special Interest Areas Native American culture, animal care, campcraft, leadership training, nature study, team building.
Sports Archery, basketball, climbing (wall), equestrian sports, fishing, gymnastics, horseback riding, riflery, ropes course, soccer, softball, swimming, trampolining, volleyball.
Wilderness/Outdoors Hiking, orienteering, survival training, wilderness camping.
Trips Day, overnight.
Program Information 1–9 sessions per year. Session length: 5–45 days in June, July, August. Ages: 7–16. 100–150 participants per session. Day program cost: $325–$475. Application fee: $35. Financial aid available. 50% tuition scholarships available.
Application Deadline Continuous.
Jobs Positions for college students 18 and older.
Contact Lynn Walker, Director, main address above. Phone: 303-442-4557. Fax: 303-417-9114. E-mail: office@coloradomountainranch.com.
URL www.coloradomountainranch.com

COLVIG SILVER CAMPS

9665 Florida Road
Durango, Colorado 81301

General Information Coed residential traditional camp and outdoor program established in 1969. Accredited by American Camping Association.
Program Focus Traditional camping with wilderness adventure expeditions and outdoor education.

Colvig Silver Camps (continued)

Academics Anthropology, archaeology, area studies, astronomy, ecology, environmental science, geology/earth science.
Arts Arts and crafts (general), batiking, ceramics, drawing, fabric arts, jewelry making, leather working, painting, photography, pottery, puppetry, woodworking.
Special Interest Areas Native American culture, animal care, campcraft, field trips (arts and culture), gardening, leadership training, model rocketry, nature study, team building.
Sports Archery, basketball, bicycling, canoeing, climbing (wall), equestrian sports, fishing, horseback riding, kayaking, riflery, ropes course, swimming, tennis, volleyball, windsurfing.
Wilderness/Outdoors Backpacking, bicycle trips, canoe trips, hiking, mountain biking, mountaineering, orienteering, rafting, rock climbing, survival training, white-water trips, wilderness camping.
Trips Cultural, day, overnight.
Program Information 2–4 sessions per year. Session length: 13–27 days in June, July, August. Ages: 7–17. 100–150 participants per session. Boarding program cost: $1580–$3160. Financial aid available.
Application Deadline Continuous.
Jobs Positions for college students 18 and older.
Contact Clay Colvig, Director, main address above. Phone: 970-247-2564. Fax: 970-247-2547. E-mail: office@colvigsilvercamps.com.
URL www.colvigsilvercamps.com

Community Sailing of Colorado–Advanced Sailing

Community Sailing of Colorado, Ltd.
Cherry Creek State Park
Denver, Colorado

General Information Coed day outdoor program and sports camp established in 1994. Specific services available for the hearing impaired. High school credit may be earned.
Program Focus Sailing as competitive racing and a non-competitive leisure activity.
Academics Meteorology, oceanography.
Special Interest Areas Nautical skills.
Sports Sailing, sea kayaking, windsurfing.
Program Information 9–15 sessions per year. Session length: 5–40 days in May, June, July, August, September, October. Ages: 8–17. 7–24 participants per session. Day program cost: $265–$435. Financial aid available.
Application Deadline Continuous.
Jobs Positions for high school students 17 and older and college students 17 and older.
Contact Steven Frank, Director, Box 102613, Denver, Colorado 80250. Phone: 303-757-7718. Fax: 303-692-9024. E-mail: stevefrank@communitysaiing.org.
URL communitysailing.org

Community Sailing of Colorado–Learn to Sail

Community Sailing of Colorado, Ltd.
Standley Lake Regional Park
Denver, Colorado

General Information Coed day outdoor program and sports camp established in 1994. Specific services available for the hearing impaired. High school credit may be earned.
Program Focus Sailing as a competitive racing and a non-competitive leisure activity.
Special Interest Areas Nautical skills.
Sports Sailing.
Program Information 9 sessions per year. Session length: 5–40 days in June, July, August. Ages: 8–17. 8–24 participants per session. Day program cost: $265–$395. Financial aid available.
Application Deadline Continuous.
Jobs Positions for high school students 17 and older and college students 17 and older.
Contact Steven Frank, Director, Box 102613, Denver, Colorado 80250. Phone: 303-757-7718. Fax: 303-692-9024. E-mail: stevefrank@communitysailing.org.
URL communitysailing.org

Community Sailing of Colorado–Sailboat Racing Camp

Community Sailing of Colorado, Ltd.
Cherry Creek State Park
Greenwood Village
Denver, Colorado

General Information Coed day outdoor program and sports camp established in 1994. Specific services available for the hearing impaired. High school credit may be earned.
Program Focus Competitive sailboat racing for those with solo rating or equivalent sailing experience.
Special Interest Areas Nautical skills.
Sports Sailing, sea kayaking.
Program Information 2–9 sessions per year. Session length: 5–45 days in May, June, July, August, September, October. Ages: 8–17. 7–24 participants per session. Day program cost: $265–$435. Financial aid available.
Application Deadline Continuous.
Jobs Positions for high school students 17 and older and college students 17 and older.
Contact Steven Frank, Director, Box 102613, Denver, Colorado 80250. Phone: 303-757-7718. Fax: 303-692-9024. E-mail: stevefrank@communitysailing.org.
URL communitysailing.org

Crow Canyon Archaeological Center High School Excavation Program

Crow Canyon Archaeological Center
23390 Road K
Cortez, Colorado 81321

General Information Coed residential academic program and cultural program established in 1998.

Program Focus Archaeology.
Academics Anthropology, archaeology, botany, ecology, geography, geology/earth science, history, social science.
Arts Pottery.
Special Interest Areas Native American culture, cross-cultural education.
Wilderness/Outdoors Hiking.
Trips Day.
Program Information 1 session per year. Session length: 5 days in July. Ages: 14–18. 20–24 participants per session. Boarding program cost: $850.
Application Deadline Continuous.
Contact Theresa Titone, School Programs Marketing Manager, main address above. Phone: 800-422-8975 Ext. 130. Fax: 970-565-4859. E-mail: ttitone@crowcanyon.org.
URL www.crowcanyon.org

Crow Canyon Archaeological Center High School Field School

Crow Canyon Archaeological Center
23390 Road K
Cortez, Colorado 81321

General Information Coed residential academic program and cultural program established in 1982. High school or college credit may be earned.
Program Focus Archaeology.
Academics Anthropology, archaeology, botany, ecology, geography, geology/earth science, history, social studies.
Arts Arts and crafts (general), pottery.
Special Interest Areas Native American culture, career exploration, cross-cultural education.
Wilderness/Outdoors Hiking, rafting.
Trips Day, overnight.
Program Information 1 session per year. Session length: 3 weeks in July. Ages: 14–18. 30 participants per session. Boarding program cost: $2900. Financial aid available.
Application Deadline Continuous.
Contact Theresa Titone, School Programs Marketing Manager, main address above. Phone: 800-422-8975 Ext. 130. Fax: 970-565-4859. E-mail: ttitone@crowcanyon.org.
URL www.crowcanyon.org

Crow Canyon Archaeological Center Middle School Archaeology Program

Crow Canyon Archaeological Center
23390 Road K
Cortez, Colorado 81321

General Information Coed residential academic program and cultural program established in 1996.
Program Focus Archaeology.
Academics Anthropology, archaeology, botany, ecology, geography, geology/earth science, history, social science.
Arts Pottery.
Special Interest Areas Native American culture, cross-cultural education.
Wilderness/Outdoors Hiking.
Trips Cultural, day.
Program Information 1 session per year. Session length: 5 days in June. Ages: 12–14. 20–24 participants per session. Boarding program cost: $850.
Application Deadline Continuous.
Contact Theresa Titone, School Programs Marketing Manager, main address above. Phone: 800-422-8975 Ext. 130. Fax: 970-565-4859. E-mail: ttitone@crowcanyon.org.
URL www.crowcanyon.org

Deer Hill Expeditions, Colorado

Deer Hill Expeditions
7850 County Road 41
Mancos, Colorado 81328

General Information Coed residential community service program, wilderness program, and cultural program established in 1984. Accredited by Association for Experiential Education. High school credit may be earned.
Program Focus In-depth wilderness expedition in the canyons, rivers, and mountains of the Southwest, conservation service projects, cross-cultural living and service with Native Americans.
Academics Area studies, environmental science, geology/earth science.
Arts Photography.
Special Interest Areas Native American culture, community service, conservation projects, cross-cultural education, leadership training, nature study, trail maintenance.
Sports Canoeing, fishing, kayaking, rappelling.
Wilderness/Outdoors Backpacking, canoe trips, canyoneering, climbing, hiking, mountain biking, mountaineering, orienteering, outdoor camping, outdoor living skills, rafting, rock climbing, white-water trips, wilderness camping, wilderness/outdoors (general).
Trips Cultural, overnight.
Program Information 12–16 sessions per year. Session length: 21–36 days in June, July, August. Ages: 13–22. 12 participants per session. Boarding program cost: $2800–$4550.
Application Deadline Continuous.
Jobs Positions for college students 21 and older.
Contact Ms. Beverly Capelin, Owner and Director, PO Box 180, Mancos, Colorado 81328. Phone: 800-533-7221. Fax: 970-533-7221. E-mail: info@deerhillexpeditions.com.
URL www.deerhillexpeditions.com

Denver Academy Summer Program

Denver Academy
4400 East Iliff Avenue
Denver, Colorado 80222

General Information Coed day academic program. Specific services available for the learning disabled. High school credit may be earned.
Academics SAT/ACT preparation, academics (general), biology, computer programming, history, mathematics, reading, study skills, writing.
Arts Arts, arts and crafts (general).

Denver Academy Summer Program (continued)
Program Information 15–20 sessions per year. Session length: 24–25 days in June, July, August. Ages: 6–18. 60–90 participants per session. Day program cost: $450–$500.
Application Deadline June.
Jobs Positions for high school students and college students.
Contact Dan Toomey, main address above. Phone: 303-777-5870. Fax: 303-777-5893. E-mail: dtoomey@denveracademy.org.
URL www.denveracademy.org

Discovery Camp

Keystone Science School
1628 Sts. John Road
Keystone, Colorado 80435

General Information Coed residential academic program and outdoor program established in 1988.
Program Focus Outdoor science education.
Academics Academics (general), astronomy, biology, botany, ecology, environmental science, geology/earth science, science (general).
Arts Arts and crafts (general).
Special Interest Areas Campcraft, community service, leadership training, nature study, talent show.
Sports Soccer, ultimate frisbee.
Wilderness/Outdoors Backpacking, hiking, rafting, white-water trips.
Trips Day, overnight.
Program Information 4 sessions per year. Session length: 7–11 days in June, July, August. Ages: 9–16. 45–52 participants per session. Boarding program cost: $600–$1000. Financial aid available.
Application Deadline Continuous.
Jobs Positions for college students 18 and older.
Contact Mr. Steve Remer, Director, main address above. Phone: 970-468-2098. Fax: 970-468-7769. E-mail: amcintyre@keystone.org.
URL www.keystone.org

Eagle Lake Bike Camp

The Navigators
Colorado Springs, Colorado 80934

General Information Coed residential outdoor program, bible camp, and wilderness program established in 1997. Religious affiliation: Christian. Accredited by American Camping Association.
Program Focus Road biking.
Academics Bible study.
Sports Bicycling.
Wilderness/Outdoors Backpacking, bicycle trips, mountain biking, mountaineering, orienteering, rafting, wilderness camping.
Trips Overnight.
Program Information 5–7 sessions per year. Session length: 5–12 days in June, July, August. Ages: 12–20. 12 participants per session. Boarding program cost: $398–$700. Financial aid available.
Application Deadline Continuous.
Jobs Positions for college students 19 and older.
Summer Contact Office Manager, PO Box 6000, Colorado Springs, Colorado 80934. Phone: 719-472-1260. Fax: 719-623-0148. E-mail: registrar_el@navigators.org.
Winter Contact Mr. John Rogers, Director of Excursion Ministries, main address above. Phone: 719-472-1260. Fax: 719-623-0148. E-mail: john_rogers@navigators.org.
URL www.eaglelake.org

Eagle Lake Camp Crew Program

The Navigators
Colorado Springs, Colorado 80934

General Information Coed residential community service program and bible camp established in 1995. Religious affiliation: Christian. Accredited by American Camping Association.
Program Focus Training program for high school students; labor and service is done around camp; involvement in Bible study.
Academics Bible study.
Arts Arts and crafts (general), leather working, music (vocal).
Special Interest Areas Animal care, construction, culinary arts, team building, work camp programs.
Sports Archery, basketball, bicycling, blobbing, canoeing, climbing (wall), fishing, horseback riding, rappelling, riflery, sailing, soccer, swimming, volleyball.
Wilderness/Outdoors Backpacking, bicycle trips, canoe trips, hiking, zip line.
Trips Day, overnight.
Program Information 2 sessions per year. Session length: 34–70 days in June, July, August. Ages: 15–18. 40–45 participants per session. Boarding program cost: $220–$398. Financial aid available.
Application Deadline Continuous.
Jobs Positions for high school students 15 and older and college students 19 and older.
Contact Office Manager, PO Box 6000, Colorado Springs, Colorado 80934. Phone: 719-472-1260. Fax: 719-623-0148. E-mail: registrar_el@navigators.org.
URL www.eaglelake.org

Eagle Lake Horse Camp

The Navigators
3820 North 30th Street
Colorado Springs, Colorado 80934

General Information Coed residential traditional camp and bible camp established in 1994. Religious affiliation: Christian. Accredited by American Camping Association.
Program Focus Horse/equestrian focus; both English and Western.
Academics Bible study.
Special Interest Areas Animal care, work camp programs.
Sports Equestrian sports, horseback riding.
Wilderness/Outdoors Pack animal trips.
Trips Day.

Program Information 6–10 sessions per year. Session length: 5 days in June, July, August. Ages: 12–18. 3–15 participants per session. Boarding program cost: $498–$508. Financial aid available.
Application Deadline Continuous.
Jobs Positions for college students.
Contact Mandy Kerce, Equestrian Program Director, PO Box 6000, Colorado Springs, Colorado 80934. Phone: 719-472-1260. Fax: 719-623-0148. E-mail: tiggerkerce@yahoo.com.
URL www.eaglelake.org

Eagle Lake Resident Camp

The Navigators
Colorado Springs, Colorado 80934

General Information Coed residential traditional camp and bible camp established in 1957. Religious affiliation: Christian. Accredited by American Camping Association.
Academics Bible study.
Arts Arts and crafts (general), leather working.
Special Interest Areas Animal care.
Sports Angle ball, archery, basketball, blobbing, canoeing, fishing, horseback riding, kayaking, mountain boarding, rappelling, riflery, sailing, soccer, swimming, volleyball.
Wilderness/Outdoors Rock climbing, zip line.
Program Information 10 sessions per year. Session length: 5 days in June, July, August. Ages: 8–18. 100–300 participants per session. Boarding program cost: $398–$498. Financial aid available.
Application Deadline Continuous.
Jobs Positions for college students 19 and older.
Contact Office Manager, PO Box 6000, Colorado Springs, Colorado 80934. Phone: 719-472-1260. Fax: 719-623-0148. E-mail: registrar_el@navigators.org.
URL www.eaglelake.org

Eagle Lake Wilderness Program

The Navigators
3820 North 30th Street
Colorado Springs, Colorado 80934

General Information Coed residential outdoor program, bible camp, wilderness program, and adventure program established in 1957. Religious affiliation: Christian. Accredited by American Camping Association.
Program Focus Christian growth and physical challenge.
Academics Bible study.
Sports Bicycling, bicycling (BMX), rappelling, ropes course.
Wilderness/Outdoors Backpacking, bicycle trips, hiking, mountain biking, mountaineering, orienteering, rafting, rock climbing, survival training, white-water trips, wilderness camping.
Trips Overnight.
Program Information 5–10 sessions per year. Session length: 5–12 days in June, July, August. Ages: 10–21. 6–20 participants per session. Boarding program cost: $398–$708. Financial aid available.
Application Deadline Continuous.
Jobs Positions for college students 19 and older.
Contact John Rogers, Director of Excursion Ministries, PO Box 6000, Colorado Springs, Colorado 80934. Phone: 719-472-1260. Fax: 719-623-0148. E-mail: john_rogers@navigators.org.
URL www.eaglelake.org

EDUCO Summer Adventure Programs

EDUCO Colorado
619 South College Avenue, Suite 16
Fort Collins, Colorado 80524

General Information Coed residential outdoor program and wilderness program established in 1969.
Program Focus Leadership, compassion, sense of purpose.
Academics Ecology, environmental science, intercultural studies, science (general).
Arts Arts and crafts (general).
Special Interest Areas Leadership training, nature study.
Sports Kayaking, rappelling, ropes course.
Wilderness/Outdoors Backpacking, hiking, mountaineering, orienteering, rafting, rock climbing, survival training, white-water trips, wilderness camping, wilderness/outdoors (general).
Trips Day, overnight.
Program Information 5–20 sessions per year. Session length: 5–16 days in June, July, August. Ages: 9–18. 12 participants per session. Boarding program cost: $530–$1395. Financial aid available.
Application Deadline Continuous.
Jobs Positions for college students 18 and older.
Contact Kimberly Dazey, Administrator, main address above. Phone: 800-332-7340. Fax: 970-494-0753. E-mail: info@educocolorado.org.
URL www.educointernational.org

Flying G Ranch, Tomahawk Ranch

Flying G Ranch, Tomahawk Ranch–Girl Scouts Mile Hi Council
400 South Broadway
Denver, Colorado 80209-0407

General Information Girls' residential traditional camp established in 1945. Accredited by American Camping Association.
Academics Astronomy, ecology, environmental science, history, music.
Arts Arts and crafts (general), dance, music, theater/drama.
Special Interest Areas Animal care, campcraft, leadership training, nature study, team building.
Sports Archery, horseback riding, ropes course, soccer, softball, volleyball.
Wilderness/Outdoors Backpacking, hiking, orienteering, pack animal trips, rock climbing, wilderness camping.
Trips Overnight.
Program Information 12–14 sessions per year. Session length: 3–13 days in June, July, August. Ages: 6–18.

Flying G Ranch, Tomahawk Ranch (continued)

120–150 participants per session. Boarding program cost: $95–$425. Application fee: $50. Financial aid available.
Application Deadline Continuous.
Jobs Positions for college students 18 and older.
Contact Gretchen Vaughn, Camp Director, 400 South Broadway, PO Box 9407, Denver, Colorado 80209-0407. Phone: 303-778-8774 Ext.281. Fax: 303-733-6345. E-mail: gretchenv@gsmhc.org.
URL www.girlscoutsmilehi.org

GENEVA GLEN CAMP

Geneva Glen Camp, Inc.
5793 Santa Clara Road
Indian Hills, Colorado 80454

General Information Coed residential traditional camp established in 1922. Accredited by American Camping Association.
Program Focus Theme Camp: American Heritage, Knighthood, and World Friendship.
Arts Acting, arts and crafts (general), ceramics, creative writing, dance (folk), drawing, jewelry making, leather working, music, musical productions, photography, pottery, printmaking, radio broadcasting, sculpture, theater/drama.
Special Interest Areas Animal care, campcraft, leadership training, nature study.
Sports Aerobics, archery, basketball, canoeing, climbing (wall), equestrian sports, fencing, horseback riding, lacrosse, rappelling, riflery, ropes course, soccer, softball, sports (general), swimming, volleyball, weight training.
Wilderness/Outdoors Backpacking, canoe trips, caving, hiking, mountaineering, orienteering, rock climbing, wilderness camping.
Trips Day, overnight.
Program Information 5 sessions per year. Session length: 13 days in June, July, August. Ages: 6–16. 225 participants per session. Boarding program cost: $1175. Financial aid available.
Application Deadline February 15.
Jobs Positions for high school students 16 and older and college students 19 and older.
Contact Ken Atkinson, Director, PO Box 248, Indian Hills, Colorado 80454. Phone: 303-697-4621. Fax: 303-697-9429. E-mail: ggcamp@genevaglen.org.
URL www.genevaglen.org

GREAT ESCAPES (ADVENTURE TRIPS FOR TEENS)–ROCKY MOUNTAIN HORSEPACKING ADVENTURE

South Shore YMCA Camps
Colorado

General Information Coed travel outdoor program and adventure program established in 1989. Religious affiliation: Christian. Accredited by American Camping Association.
Program Focus Wilderness horsepacking, horseback riding, hiking.
Special Interest Areas Native American culture, animal care, nature study.
Sports Equestrian sports, horseback riding.
Wilderness/Outdoors Hiking, pack animal trips, white-water trips, wilderness camping.
Program Information 1 session per year. Session length: 13 days in August. Ages: 14–17. 10–12 participants per session. Cost: $1495. Financial aid available.
Application Deadline Continuous.
Jobs Positions for college students 21 and older.
Contact Joseph O'Keefe, Great Escapes Director, 75 Stowe Road, Sandwich, Massachusetts 02563. Phone: 508-428-2571 Ext.110. Fax: 508-420-3545. E-mail: joeokeefe@ssymca.org.
URL www.ssymca.org/camps/great_escapes.asp

HORIZON ADVENTURES INC.

Horizon Adventures, Inc.
Colorado

General Information Coed residential outdoor program and wilderness program established in 1985. Accredited by American Camping Association.
Program Focus Coed program focusing on backcountry safety, wilderness education, and environmental awareness.
Academics Biology, botany, ecology, geology/earth science.
Wilderness/Outdoors Backpacking, mountain biking, mountaineering, orienteering, rafting, rock climbing, survival training, white-water trips, wilderness camping.
Program Information 10 sessions per year. Session length: 6–12 days in June, July, August. Ages: 13–17. 10 participants per session. Boarding program cost: $795–$1295. Financial aid available.
Application Deadline Continuous.
Jobs Positions for college students 21 and older.
Contact Paul Woodward, Director, 1370 Birch Street, Denver, Colorado 80220. Phone: 303-393-7297. Fax: 303-393-7296. E-mail: horizon@earthnet.net.
URL www.horizonadventures.com

ID TECH CAMPS–COLORADO COLLEGE, COLORADO SPRINGS, CO

iD Tech Camps
Colorado College
Colorado Springs, Colorado 80903

General Information Coed residential and day academic program established in 1999. Accredited by American Camping Association. Formal opportunities for the academically talented and artistically talented.
Program Focus High-tech computer camps for kids and teens; produce digital movies, create video games, design Web pages, learn programming and robotics, and more; one computer per student, small classes, campers complete a project in a creative and fun learning environment.
Academics Web page design, computer programming, computer science (Advanced Placement), computers, music, precollege program.

Arts Animation, cinematography, digital media, drawing, film, film editing, film production, graphic arts, music, television/video.
Special Interest Areas Career exploration, computer graphics, electronics, leadership training, robotics, team building.
Sports Baseball, basketball, soccer, softball, swimming, volleyball.
Trips College tours, cultural, day.
Program Information 5 sessions per year. Session length: 5–7 days in June, July, August. Ages: 7–17. 40–50 participants per session. Day program cost: $639. Boarding program cost: $989. Application fee: $200. Financial aid available.
Application Deadline Continuous.
Jobs Positions for college students 18 and older.
Contact Client Service Representatives, 1885 Winchester Boulevard, Suite 201, Campbell, California 95008. Phone: 888-709-TECH. Fax: 408-871-2228. E-mail: requests@internaldrive.com.
URL www.internaldrive.com

For more information, see page 1156.

iD Tech Camps–University of Denver, Denver, CO

iD Tech Camps
University of Denver
Denver, Colorado 80208

General Information Coed residential and day academic program established in 1999. Accredited by American Camping Association. Formal opportunities for the academically talented and artistically talented.
Program Focus High-tech computer camps for kids and teens; produce digital movies, create video games, design Web pages, learn programming and robotics, and more; one computer per student, small classes, campers complete a project in a creative and fun learning environment.
Academics Web page design, computer programming, computer science (Advanced Placement), computers, music, precollege program.
Arts Animation, cinematography, digital media, drawing, film, film editing, film production, graphic arts, music, television/video.
Special Interest Areas Career exploration, computer graphics, electronics, leadership training, robotics, team building.
Sports Baseball, basketball, soccer, softball, swimming, volleyball.
Trips College tours, cultural, day.
Program Information 5 sessions per year. Session length: 5–7 days in June, July, August. Ages: 7–17. 40–50 participants per session. Day program cost: $639. Boarding program cost: $989. Application fee: $200. Financial aid available.
Application Deadline Continuous.
Jobs Positions for college students 18 and older.
Contact Client Service Representatives, 1885 Winchester Boulevard, Suite 201, Campbell, California 95008. Phone: 888-709-TECH. Fax: 408-871-2228. E-mail: requests@internaldrive.com.
URL www.internaldrive.com

For more information, see page 1156.

Joe Machnik's No. 1 Academy One and Premier Programs–Colorado Springs, Colorado

Joe Machnik's No. 1 Camps
Fountain Valley School
Colorado Springs, Colorado

General Information Coed residential and day sports camp.
Program Focus Soccer instruction, physical fitness, testing and speed training. Campers gain exposure to top players and are challenged by intense competition.
Sports Soccer.
Trips Day.
Program Information 3 sessions per year. Session length: 6 days in July. Ages: 9–18. Day program cost: $699. Boarding program cost: $759. Financial aid available.
Application Deadline Continuous.
Jobs Positions for college students.
Contact Dr. Joseph Machnik, Director, PO Box 389, 916 Palm Boulevard, Isle of Palms, South Carolina 29451. Phone: 800-622-4645. Fax: 843-886-0885. E-mail: info@no1soccercamps.com.
URL www.no1soccercamps.com

Joe Machnik's No. 1 College Prep Academy–Colorado Springs, Colorado

Joe Machnik's No. 1 Camps
Fountain Valley School
Colorado Springs, Colorado

General Information Coed residential and day sports camp.
Program Focus Intense soccer instruction for high school students.
Sports Soccer, swimming.
Trips Day.
Program Information 1 session per year. Session length: 12 days in July. Ages: 13–17. 10–20 participants per session. Day program cost: $1449. Boarding program cost: $1549. Financial aid available.
Application Deadline Continuous.
Jobs Positions for college students 17 and older.
Contact Dr. Joseph Machnik, Director, PO Box 389, 916 Palm Boulevard, Isle of Palms, South Carolina 29451. Phone: 800-622-4645. Fax: 843-886-0885. E-mail: info@no1soccercamps.com.
URL www.no1soccercamps.com

Joe Machnik's No. 1 Mighty Mini, Goalkeeper and Striker Camp—Colorado Springs, Colorado

Joe Machnik's No. 1 Camps
Fountain Valley School
Colorado Springs, Colorado

General Information Coed residential and day sports camp established in 1977.
Program Focus Soccer instruction. Goalkeepers and strikers compete against each other daily.
Sports Soccer, swimming.
Program Information 3 sessions per year. Session length: 6 days in July. Ages: 8–12. 100–150 participants per session. Boarding program cost: $429. Financial aid available.
Application Deadline Continuous.
Jobs Positions for college students 17 and older.
Contact Dr. Joseph Machnik, Director, PO Box 389, 916 Palm Boulevard, Isle of Palms, South Carolina 29451. Phone: 800-622-4645. Fax: 843-886-0885. E-mail: info@no1soccercamps.com.
URL www.no1soccercamps.com

Keystone Counselor Assistant Program

Keystone Science School
1628 Sts. John Road
Keystone, Colorado 80435

General Information Coed residential outdoor program established in 1997.
Program Focus Leadership training.
Academics Academics (general), environmental science, geology/earth science, meteorology.
Special Interest Areas Leadership training, nature study, team building.
Wilderness/Outdoors Backpacking, hiking, rafting, white-water trips.
Trips Day, overnight.
Program Information 4 sessions per year. Session length: 7–11 days in June, July, August. Ages: 15–17. 4–8 participants per session. Boarding program cost: $360–$600. Financial aid available.
Application Deadline Continuous.
Jobs Positions for college students 18 and older.
Contact Steve Remer, Summer Programs Director, main address above. Phone: 970-468-2098. Fax: 970-468-7769. E-mail: camp@keystone.org.
URL www.keystone.org

Keystone Science Adventures

Keystone Science School
1628 Sts. John Road
Keystone, Colorado 80435

General Information Coed residential academic program, outdoor program, and adventure program established in 2003.
Academics Academics (general), astronomy, biology, botany, ecology, environmental science, geology/earth science, meteorology, science (general).
Special Interest Areas Nature study.
Wilderness/Outdoors Backpacking, orienteering, wilderness camping.
Trips Overnight.
Program Information 4 sessions per year. Session length: 7–11 days in June, July, August. Ages: 13–17. 10 participants per session. Boarding program cost: $700–$1100. Financial aid available.
Application Deadline Continuous.
Jobs Positions for college students 21 and older.
Contact Steve Remer, Summer Programs Director, main address above. Phone: 970-468-2098. Fax: 970-468-7769. E-mail: camp@keystone.org.
URL www.keystone.org

Landmark Volunteers: Colorado

Landmark Volunteers, Inc.
Colorado

General Information Coed residential outdoor program, community service program, and wilderness program established in 1992. High school credit may be earned.
Program Focus Opportunity for high school students to earn community service credit while working as a team for two weeks serving Chico Basin Ranch, Colorado Trail Foundation, Rock Bottom Ranch, or Rocky Mountain Village. Similar programs offered through Landmark Volunteers at over 60 locations in 21 states.
Academics Biology, ecology, environmental science, natural resource management, science (general), social science, social services.
Special Interest Areas Career exploration, community service, conservation projects, farming, field research/expeditions, leadership training, nature study, team building, trail maintenance, work camp programs.
Sports Swimming.
Wilderness/Outdoors Hiking, wilderness camping.
Trips Cultural, day.
Program Information 4 sessions per year. Session length: 2 weeks in June, July, August. Ages: 14–18. 10–13 participants per session. Boarding program cost: $875–$925. Financial aid available.
Application Deadline Continuous.
Jobs Positions for college students.
Contact Ann Barrett, Executive Director, PO Box 455, Sheffield, Massachusetts 01257. Phone: 413-229-0255. Fax: 413-229-2050. E-mail: landmark@volunteers.com.
URL www.volunteers.com

For more information, see page 1182.

Longacre Expeditions, Leadership Training

Longacre Expeditions
Colorado

General Information Coed travel outdoor program, wilderness program, and adventure program established in 1981. Accredited by American Camping Association.
Program Focus Advanced training in five wilderness skills: backpacking, mountaineering, rock climbing, kayaking, and first aid.

Special Interest Areas Leadership training.
Sports Kayaking.
Wilderness/Outdoors Backpacking, hiking, mountaineering, rock climbing, white-water trips, wilderness camping.
Program Information 1 session per year. Session length: 4 weeks in July. Ages: 17–19. 10–12 participants per session. Cost: $4395.
Application Deadline Continuous.
Jobs Positions for college students 21 and older.
Contact Meredith Schuler, Director, 4030 Middle Ridge Road, Newport, Pennsylvania 17074. Phone: 717-567-6790. Fax: 717-567-3955. E-mail: longacre@longacreexpeditions.com.
URL www.longacreexpeditions.com

For more information, see page 1200.

ON THE WING

Rocky Mountain Bird Observatory
Colorado

General Information Coed residential academic program and outdoor program established in 1993. Accredited by American Camping Association.
Program Focus Field ornithology, research.
Academics Astronomy, biology, biology (Advanced Placement), botany, computers, ecology, environmental science, geology/earth science, ornithology, science (general), speech/debate, study skills, writing.
Arts Arts and crafts (general), drawing.
Special Interest Areas Field research/expeditions.
Wilderness/Outdoors Hiking, wilderness camping.
Trips Day, overnight.
Program Information 1–3 sessions per year. Session length: 10–15 days in June, July. Ages: 12–16. 12 participants per session. Boarding program cost: $625–$1200. Financial aid available.
Application Deadline Continuous.
Jobs Positions for college students.
Contact Ms. Jennie Rectenwald, Camp Director, 1510 South College Avenue, Fort Collins, Colorado 80524. Phone: 970-482-1707. Fax: 303-654-0791. E-mail: jennie.rectenwald@rmbo.org.
URL www.rmbo.org

ORGANIC FARM CAMP

Wilderness Education Institute
Guidestone Organic Farm
Loveland, Colorado 80538

General Information Coed residential outdoor program established in 1999. Formal opportunities for the academically talented.
Program Focus Environmental education, sustainable living, organic farming.
Academics Agricultural sciences, biology, ecology, environmental science, geology/earth science.
Special Interest Areas Animal care, community service, farming, gardening, leadership training, nature study.
Wilderness/Outdoors Backpacking, hiking, mountaineering, rock climbing, wilderness camping.
Trips Day, overnight.
Program Information 1 session per year. Session length: 8 days in June, July, August. Ages: 13–17. 5–10 participants per session. Boarding program cost: $600–$800. Financial aid available.
Application Deadline Continuous.
Jobs Positions for college students 21 and older.
Contact Kevin Snyder, Executive Director, 2260 Baseline Road, Suite 205, Boulder, Colorado 80302. Phone: 877-628-9692. E-mail: information@weiprograms.org.
URL www.weiprograms.org

OUTPOST WILDERNESS ADVENTURE–ADVENTURE SKILLS

Outpost Wilderness Adventure
Lake George, Colorado

General Information Coed residential outdoor program, wilderness program, and adventure program established in 1979. Accredited by Association for Experiential Education.
Program Focus Adventure skills and expeditions. Accredited by American Mountain Guides Association.
Special Interest Areas Campcraft, nature study.
Sports Bicycling, climbing (wall), rappelling.
Wilderness/Outdoors Backpacking, fly fishing, hiking, mountain biking, mountaineering, orienteering, outdoor adventure, rafting, rock climbing, white-water trips, wilderness camping.
Trips Overnight.
Program Information 2 sessions per year. Session length: 19–22 days in June, July. Ages: 11–17. 12–16 participants per session. Boarding program cost: $2200–$2600. Financial aid available.
Application Deadline Continuous.
Summer Contact Quentin Keith, Director, 20859 County Road 77, Lake George, Colorado 80827. Phone: 719-748-3080. Fax: 719-748-3046. E-mail: q@owa.com.
Winter Contact Quentin Keith, Director, 2107 Shovel Mountain Road, Cypress Mill, Texas 78663. Phone: 830-825-3015. Fax: 830-825-3116. E-mail: q@owa.com.
URL www.owa.com

OUTPOST WILDERNESS ADVENTURE–ALPINE ROCK AND ICE

Outpost Wilderness Adventure
Colorado

General Information Coed travel outdoor program, wilderness program, and adventure program established in 1979. Accredited by Association for Experiential Education.
Program Focus Adventure skills and expeditions. Accredited by American Mountain Guides Association.
Special Interest Areas Field research/expeditions.
Sports Rappelling.
Wilderness/Outdoors Backpacking, glacier travel, hiking, ice climbing, mountaineering, orienteering, outdoor adventure, rock climbing, wilderness camping.
Trips Overnight.
Program Information 2 sessions per year. Session length: 3 weeks in June. Ages: 13–17. Cost: $1800. Financial aid available.

Outpost Wilderness Adventure–Alpine Rock and Ice (continued)

Application Deadline Continuous.
Summer Contact Quentin Keith, Director, 20859 County Road 77, Lake George, Colorado 80827. Phone: 719-748-3080. Fax: 719-748-3046. E-mail: q@owa.com.
Winter Contact Quentin Keith, Director, 2107 Shovel Mountain Road, Cypress Mill, Texas 78663. Phone: 830-825-3015. Fax: 830-825-3116. E-mail: q@owa.com.
URL www.owa.com

Outpost Wilderness Adventure–Mountain Bike/Rock Camp

Outpost Wilderness Adventure
20859 County Road 77
Lake George, Colorado 80827

General Information Coed residential outdoor program, wilderness program, and adventure program established in 1979. Accredited by Association for Experiential Education.
Program Focus Adventure skills and expeditions. Accredited by American Mountain Guides Association.
Sports Bicycling, climbing (wall), rappelling.
Wilderness/Outdoors Bicycle trips, hiking, mountain biking, mountaineering, outdoor adventure, rock climbing.
Trips Overnight.
Program Information 2 sessions per year. Session length: 8 days in June, July, August. Ages: 12–17. 10–12 participants per session. Boarding program cost: $960–$1150. Financial aid available.
Application Deadline Continuous.
Summer Contact Quentin Keith, Director, main address above. Phone: 719-748-3080. Fax: 719-748-3046. E-mail: q@owa.com.
Winter Contact Quentin Keith, Director, 2107 Shovel Mountain Road, Cypress Mill, Texas 78663. Phone: 830-825-3015. Fax: 830-825-3116. E-mail: q@owa.com.
URL www.owa.com

Outward Bound West–Backpacking, Climbing, and Rafting–Boys

Outward Bound West/Outward Bound, USA
Rocky Mountains, Leadville Mountain Center
Colorado

General Information Boys' travel outdoor program and wilderness program established in 1965. High school credit may be earned.
Program Focus Teamwork and leadership wilderness adventure.
Academics Environmental science.
Special Interest Areas Campcraft, leadership training, nature study, personal development, team building.
Sports Ropes course.
Wilderness/Outdoors Backpacking, hiking, outdoor adventure, rafting, rock climbing, wilderness camping.
Trips Overnight.
Program Information 2 sessions per year. Session length: 1 week in July, August. Ages: 12–13. Cost: $1395. Application fee: $95. Financial aid available.
Application Deadline Continuous.
Jobs Positions for college students 21 and older.
Contact Admissions Advisor, 910 Jackson Street, Golden, Colorado 80401. Phone: 866-746-9777. Fax: 720-497-2421. E-mail: info@obwest.org.
URL www.outwardboundwest.org

Outward Bound West–Backpacking, Climbing, and Rafting–Colorado

Outward Bound West/Outward Bound, USA
Rocky Mountains, Collegiate Range and Leadville Mountain Center
Colorado

General Information Coed travel outdoor program and wilderness program established in 1965. College credit may be earned.
Program Focus Teamwork and leadership wilderness adventure.
Academics Environmental science.
Special Interest Areas Campcraft, leadership training, nature study, personal development, team building.
Sports Ropes course.
Wilderness/Outdoors Backpacking, outdoor adventure, rafting, rock climbing, wilderness camping.
Trips Overnight.
Program Information 15 sessions per year. Session length: 14–22 days in June, July, August. Ages: 14–15. Cost: $2495–$3095. Application fee: $95. Financial aid available.
Application Deadline Continuous.
Jobs Positions for college students 21 and older.
Contact Admissions Advisor, 910 Jackson Street, Golden, Colorado 80401. Phone: 866-746-9777. Fax: 720-497-2421. E-mail: info@obwest.org.
URL www.outwardboundwest.org

Outward Bound West–Colorado Rockies Lightweight Backpacking

Outward Bound West/Outward Bound, USA
Rocky Mountains, San Juan and Collegiate Ranges
Colorado

General Information Coed travel outdoor program and wilderness program established in 1965. College credit may be earned.
Program Focus Teamwork and leadership wilderness adventure.
Academics Environmental science.
Special Interest Areas Campcraft, community service, leadership training, nature study, personal development, team building.
Wilderness/Outdoors Backpacking, mountaineering, orienteering, survival training, wilderness camping.
Trips Overnight.
Program Information 8 sessions per year. Session length: 14–22 days in June, July, August. Ages: 16+. Cost: $2395–$2895. Application fee: $95. Financial aid available.
Application Deadline Continuous.
Jobs Positions for college students 21 and older.

Contact Admissions Advisor, 910 Jackson Street, Golden, Colorado 80401. Phone: 866-746-9777. Fax: 720-497-2421. E-mail: info@obwest.org.
URL www.outwardboundwest.org

OUTWARD BOUND WEST–MOUNTAINEERING–COLORADO

Outward Bound West/Outward Bound, USA
Rocky Mountains, San Juan Range
Colorado

General Information Coed travel outdoor program and wilderness program established in 1965. College credit may be earned.
Program Focus Teamwork and leadership wilderness adventure.
Academics Environmental science.
Special Interest Areas Campcraft, community service, leadership training, nature study, personal development, team building.
Wilderness/Outdoors Backpacking, hiking, mountaineering, outdoor adventure, rock climbing, wilderness camping.
Trips Overnight.
Program Information 6 sessions per year. Session length: 14–30 days in June, July, August, September. Ages: 16+. Cost: $2395–$3395. Application fee: $95. Financial aid available.
Application Deadline Continuous.
Jobs Positions for college students 21 and older.
Contact Admissions Advisor, 910 Jackson Street, Golden, Colorado 80401. Phone: 866-746-9777. Fax: 720-497-2421. E-mail: info@obwest.org.
URL www.outwardboundwest.org

PERRY-MANSFIELD PERFORMING ARTS SCHOOL AND CAMP

Perry-Mansfield Performing Arts School and Camp
40755 Routt County Road 36
Steamboat Springs, Colorado 80487

General Information Coed residential and day arts program established in 1913. Formal opportunities for the artistically talented and gifted. College credit may be earned.
Program Focus Dance, theater, music, fine arts, horseback riding, and creative writing.
Arts Acting, arts, creative writing, dance, dance (ballet), dance (jazz), dance (modern), dance (tap), drawing, graphic arts, music (vocal), musical productions, theater/drama.
Special Interest Areas Field trips (arts and culture).
Sports Equestrian sports, horseback riding.
Wilderness/Outdoors Hiking, rafting, white-water trips.
Trips Cultural.
Program Information 9 sessions per year. Session length: 1–6 weeks in June, July, August. Ages: 8–25. 25–100 participants per session. Day program cost: $375–$1195. Boarding program cost: $800–$3755. Application fee: $50. Financial aid available. Work study and scholarships available.

Perry-Mansfield Performing Arts School and Camp

Application Deadline Continuous.
Jobs Positions for college students 21 and older.
Contact June Lindenmayer, Executive Director, main address above. Phone: 800-430-2787. Fax: 970-879-5823. E-mail: p-m@perry-mansfield.org.
URL www.perry-mansfield.org
For more information, see page 1258.

POULTER COLORADO CAMPS

Poulter Colorado Camps
Steamboat Springs, Colorado 80477

General Information Coed residential traditional camp, outdoor program, and wilderness program established in 1966. Accredited by American Camping Association.
Program Focus Challenging adventure, teamwork, leadership skills, and wilderness appreciation.
Academics Astronomy, ecology, environmental science, geology/earth science.
Arts Arts and crafts (general), band, batiking, ceramics, clowning, creative writing, dance, dance (modern), drawing, fabric arts, film, graphic arts, jewelry making, leather working, music, music (instrumental), music (vocal), painting, photography, printmaking, puppetry, sculpture, television/video, theater/drama.
Special Interest Areas Animal care, campcraft, community service, leadership training, nature study, team building.
Sports Archery, basketball, boating, canoeing, climbing (wall), fishing, football, horseback riding, kayaking, soccer, softball, sports (general), swimming, tennis, volleyball.

Poulter Colorado Camps (continued)
Wilderness/Outdoors Backpacking, canoe trips, caving, hiking, mountaineering, orienteering, pack animal trips, rafting, rock climbing, white-water trips, wilderness camping.
Trips Day, overnight.
Program Information 4 sessions per year. Session length: 10–28 days in June, July, August, December. Ages: 9–18. 20–80 participants per session. Boarding program cost: $1400–$3000. Financial aid available.
Application Deadline Continuous.
Jobs Positions for college students 19 and older.
Contact Mr. Jay B. Poulter, Director, PO Box 772947, Steamboat Springs, Colorado 80477. Phone: 888-879-4816. Fax: 800-860-3587. E-mail: poulter@poultercamps.com.
URL www.poultercamps.com

Rocky Mountain Village

Easter Seals Colorado
2644 Alvarado Road
Empire, Colorado 80438

General Information Coed residential traditional camp and special needs program established in 1951. Accredited by American Camping Association. Specific services available for the developmentally challenged, hearing impaired, learning disabled, physically challenged, and visually impaired.
Program Focus For children, teens, and adults with disabilities.
Academics Computers, journalism.
Arts Arts and crafts (general), ceramics, clowning, creative writing, dance, jewelry making, leather working, music, painting, photography.
Special Interest Areas Animal care, campcraft, career exploration, gardening, nature study.
Sports Archery, baseball, basketball, bicycling, fishing, golf, horseback riding, rappelling, ropes course, soccer, softball, swimming, tennis, volleyball.
Wilderness/Outdoors Hiking, rafting, rock climbing, white-water trips.
Trips Day, overnight.
Program Information 10–15 sessions per year. Session length: 5 days in June, July, August. Ages: 7+. 40–60 participants per session. Boarding program cost: $700. Application fee: $100. Financial aid available.
Application Deadline Continuous.
Jobs Positions for high school students 16 and older and college students 16 and older.
Contact Roman Krafczyk, Director, PO Box 115, Empire, Colorado 80438. Phone: 303-569-2333 Ext.302. Fax: 303-569-3857. E-mail: campinfo@eastersealscolorado.org.
URL www.eastersealscolorado.org

Sanborn Western Camps: Big Spring Ranch for Boys

Sanborn Western Camps
2000 Old Stage Road
Florissant, Colorado 80816

General Information Boys' residential traditional camp and outdoor program established in 1948. Accredited by American Camping Association.
Program Focus Individual growth and development.
Academics Astronomy, biology, botany, ecology, geology/earth science.
Arts Arts and crafts (general), batiking, ceramics, creative writing, dance (folk), drawing, fabric arts, jewelry making, leather working, metalworking, painting, photography, pottery, printmaking, theater/drama, weaving, woodworking.
Special Interest Areas Campcraft, general camp activities, leadership training, nature study, team building.
Sports Archery, canoeing, fishing, horseback riding, lacrosse, rappelling, ropes course, soccer, softball, sports (general), swimming, tennis, volleyball.
Wilderness/Outdoors Backpacking, bicycle trips, canoe trips, caving, hiking, mountain biking, mountaineering, orienteering, pack animal trips, rafting, rock climbing, wilderness camping.
Trips Day, overnight.
Program Information 2 sessions per year. Session length: 31 days in June, July, August. Ages: 9–17. 150 participants per session. Boarding program cost: $3300.
Application Deadline Continuous.
Jobs Positions for college students 20 and older.
Contact Mike McDonald, Director, PO Box 167, Florissant, Colorado 80816. Phone: 719-748-3341. Fax: 719-748-3259. E-mail: info@sanbornwesterncamps.com.
URL www.sanbornwesterncamps.com

Sanborn Western Camps: High Trails Ranch for Girls

Sanborn Western Camps
2000 Old Stage Road
Florissant, Colorado 80816

General Information Girls' residential traditional camp and outdoor program established in 1948. Accredited by American Camping Association.
Academics Astronomy, biology, botany, ecology, geology/earth science.
Arts Arts and crafts (general), batiking, ceramics, creative writing, dance (folk), drawing, fabric arts, jewelry making, leather working, metalworking, painting, photography, pottery, printmaking, theater/drama, weaving, woodworking.
Special Interest Areas Campcraft, general camp activities, leadership training, nature study, team building.
Sports Archery, canoeing, fishing, horseback riding, lacrosse, rappelling, ropes course, soccer, softball, swimming, tennis, volleyball.

Wilderness/Outdoors Backpacking, bicycle trips, canoe trips, caving, hiking, mountain biking, mountaineering, orienteering, pack animal trips, rafting, rock climbing, wilderness camping.
Trips Day, overnight.
Program Information 2 sessions per year. Session length: 31 days in June, July, August. Ages: 9–17. 150 participants per session. Boarding program cost: $3300.
Application Deadline Continuous.
Jobs Positions for college students 20 and older.
Contact Julie Richardson, Director, PO Box 167, Florissant, Colorado 80816. Phone: 719-748-3341. Fax: 719-748-3259. E-mail: info@sanbornwesterncamps.com.
URL www.sanbornwesterncamps.com

Shwayder Camp

Congregation Emanuel
9118 State Highway 103
Idaho Springs, Colorado 80452

General Information Coed residential traditional camp, outdoor program, and bible camp established in 1948. Religious affiliation: Jewish. Accredited by American Camping Association.
Academics Bible study, Hebrew language, Jewish studies, academics (general), ecology, music, religion.
Arts Acting, arts and crafts (general), chorus, creative writing, dance, drawing, fabric arts, graphic arts, jewelry making, leather working, music, music (instrumental), music (vocal), painting, pottery, sculpture, theater/drama, weaving.
Special Interest Areas Animal care, conservation projects, nature study, team building.
Sports Archery, basketball, fishing, football, horseback riding, ropes course, soccer, softball, volleyball.
Wilderness/Outdoors Backpacking, hiking, outdoor camping, pack animal trips, wilderness camping.
Trips Day, overnight.
Program Information 4 sessions per year. Session length: 6–13 days in June, July, August. Ages: 7–16. 100–120 participants per session. Boarding program cost: $545–$1490. Financial aid available.
Application Deadline Continuous.
Jobs Positions for high school students and college students.
Summer Contact Zim S. A. Zimmerman, Director, main address above. Phone: 303-567-2722. Fax: 303-567-0172. E-mail: info@shwayder.com.
Winter Contact Zim S. A. Zimmerman, Director, 51 Grape Street, Denver, Colorado 80220. Phone: 303-388-4013. Fax: 303-388-6328. E-mail: info@shwayder.com.
URL www.shwayder.com

Student Conservation Association–Conservation Crew Program (Colorado)

Student Conservation Association (SCA)
Colorado

General Information Coed residential outdoor program, community service program, and wilderness program established in 1957. High school credit may be earned.
Program Focus Resource management, conservation and environmental education.
Academics Biology, botany, ecology, environmental science, geology/earth science, history.
Special Interest Areas Campcraft, community service, construction, leadership training, nature study, trail maintenance, work camp programs.
Sports Canoeing, fishing, kayaking, swimming.
Wilderness/Outdoors Backpacking, canoe trips, hiking, orienteering, outdoor living skills, rock climbing, wilderness camping.
Trips Cultural, day, overnight.
Program Information 2–3 sessions per year. Session length: 3–5 weeks in June, July, August. Ages: 15–19. 6–8 participants per session. Application fee: $20. Financial aid available. No cost for program; financial aid possible for travel expenses.
Application Deadline Continuous.
Jobs Positions for college students 21 and older.
Contact Recruitment Office, PO Box 550, Charlestown, New Hampshire 03603. Phone: 603-543-1700. Fax: 603-543-1828. E-mail: getreal@thesca.org.
URL www.theSCA.org

Summer Study at The University of Colorado at Boulder

Summer Study Programs
Boulder, Colorado 80309

General Information Coed residential academic program established in 2001. Formal opportunities for the academically talented. High school or college credit may be earned.
Program Focus Pre-college experience including college credits, enrichment classes, SAT preparation, sports, special outdoor/wilderness activities and weekend trips amidst the Rocky Mountains.
Academics American literature, English as a second language, English language/literature, French (Advanced Placement), SAT/ACT preparation, Spanish (Advanced Placement), academics (general), anthropology, architecture, art (Advanced Placement), art history/appreciation, astronomy, biology, business, chemistry, classical languages/literatures, communications, computer programming, computers, ecology, economics, engineering, environmental science, geology/earth science, government and politics, health sciences, history, humanities, journalism, mathematics, mathematics (Advanced Placement), music, philosophy, physics, physiology, precollege program, psychology, social science, social studies, speech/debate, study skills, writing.

Summer Study at The University of Colorado at Boulder (continued)

Arts Arts and crafts (general), band, ceramics, creative writing, dance, dance (modern), drawing, graphic arts, jewelry making, music, music (instrumental), painting, photography, pottery, theater/drama.
Special Interest Areas Career exploration, community service, nature study, touring.
Sports Aerobics, baseball, basketball, bicycling, canoeing, climbing (wall), cross-country, field hockey, football, golf, horseback riding, lacrosse, racquetball, soccer, softball, squash, swimming, tennis, track and field, volleyball, weight training, wrestling.
Wilderness/Outdoors Backpacking, bicycle trips, canoe trips, caving, hiking, mountain biking, rafting, rock climbing, white-water trips, wilderness/outdoors (general).
Trips Cultural, day, overnight, shopping.
Program Information 2 sessions per year. Session length: 25–34 days in July, August. Ages: 15–18. 150–200 participants per session. Boarding program cost: $3495–$5795. Application fee: $75. Financial aid available.
Application Deadline Continuous.
Jobs Positions for college students 21 and older.
Contact Bill Cooperman, Executive Director, 900 Walt Whitman Road, Melville, New York 11747. Phone: 800-666-2556. Fax: 631-424-0567. E-mail: precollegeprograms@summerstudy.com.
URL www.summerstudy.com
For more information, see page 1344.

Summer Vet

Center for Science, Mathematics and Technology Education (CSMATE)
Colorado State University
Fort Collins, Colorado 80523

General Information Coed residential and day academic program.
Program Focus Veterinary medicine.
Academics Preveterinary, veterinary science.
Special Interest Areas Career exploration.
Trips College tours, day.
Program Information 1–2 sessions per year. Session length: 5 days in June. Ages: 15–18. 25–30 participants per session. Day program cost: $190–$350. Boarding program cost: $750. Financial aid available.
Application Deadline May 31.
Contact Ms. Courtney Butler, Assistant to the Director, Colorado State University, Campus Delivery 1802, Fort Collins, Colorado 80523. Phone: 970-491-1700. Fax: 970-491-2005. E-mail: courtney.butler@colostate.edu.
URL www.csmate.colostate.edu

SuperCamp–Colorado College

SuperCamp
Colorado College
Colorado Springs, Colorado 80903

General Information Coed residential academic program established in 1981. Accredited by American Camping Association. High school credit may be earned.
Program Focus Academic enrichment and personal development.
Academics SAT/ACT preparation, academics (general), communications, reading, study skills, writing.
Special Interest Areas Leadership training.
Sports Basketball, ropes course, soccer, swimming, volleyball.
Trips College tours.
Program Information 3–5 sessions per year. Session length: 8–10 days in July, August. Ages: 11–18. 112–120 participants per session. Boarding program cost: $1795–$2295. Application fee: $100. Financial aid available.
Application Deadline Continuous.
Jobs Positions for college students 18 and older.
Contact Enrollments Department, 1725 South Coast Highway, Oceanside, California 92054. Phone: 800-285-3276. Fax: 760-722-3507. E-mail: info@supercamp.com.
URL www.supercamp.com
For more information, see page 1348.

Technology Encounters–Video Encounter/Computer Encounter–Colorado

Ducks in a Row Foundation, Inc./Technology Encounters
Colorado

General Information Coed day arts program established in 2000. Formal opportunities for the academically talented and artistically talented.
Program Focus Local community school district-hosted programs focused on making technology fun, teaching team skills, and using creative energies.
Academics Academics (general), communications, computer programming, computers.
Arts Acting, animation, arts and crafts (general), film, film production, graphic arts, television/video, theater/drama.
Special Interest Areas Computer game design, computer graphics, leadership training.
Program Information 40–50 sessions per year. Session length: 5–10 days in June, July, August. Ages: 7–13. 25–100 participants per session. Day program cost: $195. Financial aid available.
Application Deadline Continuous.
Jobs Positions for high school students 17 and older and college students 17 and older.
Contact Ms. Jane Sandlar, Director, 8 Wemrock Drive, Ocean, New Jersey 07712. Phone: 732-695-0827. Fax: 732-493-4282. E-mail: jane@technologyencounters.com.
URL www.technologyencounters.com

Trailmark Outdoor Adventures–Colorado–West Elks with Backpack

Trailmark Outdoor Adventures
Colorado

General Information Coed travel outdoor program, wilderness program, and adventure program established in 1985. Accredited by American Camping Association.
Program Focus Coed outdoor adventure.
Sports Rappelling, swimming.

Wilderness/Outdoors Backpacking, hiking, rafting, rock climbing, white-water trips, wilderness camping.
Program Information 1–2 sessions per year. Session length: 15 days in August. Ages: 13–14. 12–18 participants per session. Cost: $2395. Financial aid available.
Application Deadline Continuous.
Jobs Positions for college students 21 and older.
Contact Mr. Rusty Pedersen, Director, 16 Schuyler Road, Nyack, New York 10960. Phone: 845-358-0262. Fax: 845-348-0437. E-mail: info@trailmark.com.
URL www.trailmark.com

Trailmark Outdoor Adventures–Colorado–West Elks with Horseback

Trailmark Outdoor Adventures
Colorado

General Information Coed travel outdoor program, wilderness program, and adventure program established in 1985. Accredited by American Camping Association.
Program Focus Coed outdoor adventure.
Sports Horseback riding, rappelling.
Wilderness/Outdoors Hiking, pack animal trips, rafting, rock climbing, white-water trips, wilderness camping.
Program Information 1 session per year. Session length: 15 days in August. Ages: 13–14. 12–18 participants per session. Cost: $2495. Financial aid available.
Application Deadline Continuous.
Jobs Positions for college students 21 and older.
Contact Mr. Rusty Pedersen, Director, 16 Schuyler Road, Nyack, New York 10960. Phone: 845-358-0262. Fax: 845-348-0437. E-mail: info@trailmark.com.
URL www.trailmark.com

WEI Leadership Training

Wilderness Education Institute
7400 Highway 7
Estes Park, Colorado 80517

General Information Coed residential outdoor program and community service program established in 2000.
Program Focus Leadership development.
Academics Ecology, environmental science.
Arts Arts and crafts (general).
Special Interest Areas Career exploration, community service, leadership training, nature study.
Wilderness/Outdoors Hiking, mountaineering, orienteering, rock climbing, wilderness camping.
Trips Day, overnight.
Program Information 1–2 sessions per year. Session length: 8–14 days in June, July, August. Ages: 13–17. 10 participants per session. Boarding program cost: $750–$1250. Financial aid available.
Application Deadline Continuous.
Jobs Positions for college students 21 and older.
Contact Kevin Snyder, Executive Director, 2260 Baseline Road, Suite 205, Boulder, Colorado 80302. Phone: 877-628-9692. E-mail: information@weiprograms.org.
URL www.weiprograms.org

Wilderness Adventure

Wilderness Education Institute
Colorado

General Information Coed residential outdoor program and wilderness program established in 1998. Formal opportunities for the academically talented.
Program Focus Environmental education.
Academics Area studies, astronomy, biology, botany, ecology, environmental science, geography, geology/earth science, science (general).
Special Interest Areas Community service, field research/expeditions, nature study.
Sports Climbing (wall), ropes course.
Wilderness/Outdoors Backpacking, hiking, mountaineering, orienteering, rock climbing, wilderness camping.
Trips Day, overnight.
Program Information 3–5 sessions per year. Session length: 2 weeks in June, July, August. Ages: 13–17. 15–20 participants per session. Boarding program cost: $1200–$1400. Financial aid available.
Application Deadline Continuous.
Jobs Positions for college students 21 and older.
Contact Kevin Snyder, Executive Director, 2260 Baseline Road, Suite 205, Boulder, Colorado 80302. Phone: 877-628-9692. Fax: 877-628-9692. E-mail: information@weiprograms.org.
URL www.weiprograms.org

Wildlife Camp

Wilderness Education Institute
7400 Highway 7
Estes Park, Colorado 80517

General Information Coed residential traditional camp and outdoor program established in 1998. Formal opportunities for the academically talented.
Program Focus Environmental education.
Academics Astronomy, biology, botany, ecology, environmental science, geography, geology/earth science, science (general).
Arts Arts and crafts (general), batiking, drawing, music.
Special Interest Areas Community service, nature study.
Sports Basketball, canoeing, climbing (wall), ropes course, soccer.
Wilderness/Outdoors Backpacking, hiking, rock climbing, wilderness camping.
Trips Day, overnight.
Program Information 2–3 sessions per year. Session length: 6–14 days in June, July, August. Ages: 8–13. 30–40 participants per session. Boarding program cost: $500–$1200. Financial aid available.
Application Deadline Continuous.
Jobs Positions for college students 18 and older.
Contact Kevin Snyder, Executive Director, 2260 Baseline Road, Suite 205, Boulder, Colorado 80302. Phone: 877-628-9692. Fax: 877-628-9692. E-mail: information@weiprograms.org.
URL www.weiprograms.org

CONNECTICUT

BOULDER RIDGE DAY CAMP

Ebner Camps, Inc.
104 Goose Green Road
Barkhamsted, Connecticut 06063

General Information Coed day traditional camp established in 2004.
Academics Journalism, music.
Arts Arts and crafts (general), ceramics, dance, drawing, jewelry making, music, photography, theater/drama.
Sports Basketball, boating, canoeing, climbing (wall), fencing, golf, gymnastics, kayaking, rappelling, ropes course, soccer, softball, tennis, waterskiing.
Wilderness/Outdoors Hiking, white-water trips.
Trips Day.
Program Information 2–4 sessions per year. Session length: 10–40 days in July, August. Ages: 4–13. 125–150 participants per session. Day program cost: $500–$2000.
Application Deadline Continuous.
Jobs Positions for high school students and college students.
Contact Kevin Ebner, Director, 1 Torrington Office Plaza, Suite 308, Torrington, Connecticut 06790. Phone: 860-379-6500. Fax: 860-626-8301. E-mail: info@boulderday.com.
URL www.boulderday.com

BUCK'S ROCK PERFORMING AND CREATIVE ARTS CAMP

Buck's Rock, LLC
59 Buck's Rock Road
New Milford, Connecticut 06776

General Information Coed residential arts program established in 1943. Accredited by American Camping Association. Formal opportunities for the academically talented and artistically talented.
Program Focus Fine and performing arts, and music, highly motivated participants.
Academics Computer programming, journalism, music, music (Advanced Placement), writing.
Arts Acting, band, batiking, bookbinding, ceramics, chorus, clowning, creative writing, dance, dance (ballet), dance (folk), dance (jazz), dance (modern), dance (tap), drawing, fabric arts, film, glassblowing, graphic arts, jewelry making, leather working, metalworking, mime, music, music (chamber), music (classical), music (ensemble), music (instrumental), music (jazz), music (orchestral), music (vocal), music technology/record production, musical productions, painting, paper making, photography, pottery, printmaking, puppetry, radio broadcasting, sculpture, silk screening, stage managing, television/video, theater/drama, visual arts, weaving, woodworking.
Special Interest Areas Animal care, community service, farming, gardening, organic farming.

Buck's Rock Performing and Creative Arts Camp

Sports Archery, badminton, basketball, equestrian sports, fencing, horseback riding, martial arts, soccer, softball, swimming, table tennis/ping-pong, tennis, ultimate frisbee, volleyball.
Wilderness/Outdoors Caving, hiking, orienteering, wilderness camping.
Trips Cultural, day, overnight.
Program Information 1–2 sessions per year. Session length: 26–54 days in June, July, August. Ages: 11–17. 350–400 participants per session. Boarding program cost: $5240–$7340. Financial aid available.
Application Deadline Continuous.
Jobs Positions for college students 21 and older.
Contact Ms. Laura Morris, Director, main address above. Phone: 860-354-5030. Fax: 860-354-1355. E-mail: bucksrock@bucksrockcamp.com.
URL www.bucksrockcamp.com
For more information, see page 1012.

CAMP AWOSTING

Ebner Camps, Inc.
Litchfield Hills
Bantam, Connecticut 06750

General Information Boys' residential traditional camp established in 1900. Accredited by American Camping Association.

Program Focus Daily elective program of over 30 specialized activities.
Academics English as a second language, computer programming, computers, journalism.
Arts Arts and crafts (general), batiking, ceramics, creative writing, drawing, fabric arts, jewelry making, metalworking, musical productions, painting, photography, pottery, sculpture, television/video, theater/drama, woodworking.
Special Interest Areas Campcraft, leadership training.
Sports Archery, baseball, basketball, bicycling, boating, canoeing, climbing (wall), cross-country, equestrian sports, fencing, fishing, go-carts, golf, gymnastics, horseback riding, kayaking, martial arts, minibikes, rappelling, ropes course, sailing, soccer, softball, sports (general), swimming, tennis, track and field, volleyball, waterskiing, weight training, windsurfing.
Wilderness/Outdoors Canoe trips, hiking, mountain biking, orienteering, white-water trips, wilderness camping.
Trips Cultural, day, overnight.
Program Information 1–4 sessions per year. Session length: 2–8 weeks in July, August. Ages: 6–16. 125–160 participants per session. Boarding program cost: $1750–$5645.
Application Deadline Continuous.
Jobs Positions for college students 19 and older.
Summer Contact Mr. Buzz Ebner, Director, 1 Torrington Office Plaza, Suite 308, Torrington, Connecticut 06790. Phone: 860-567-9678. Fax: 860-485-1681. E-mail: info@awosting.com.
Winter Contact Mr. Buzz Ebner, Director, 2 Breezy Hill, Harwinton, Connecticut 06791. Phone: 860-485-9566. Fax: 860-485-1681. E-mail: buzz@awosting.com.
URL www.awosting.com

Camp Chinqueka

Ebner Camps, Inc.
Litchfield Hills
Bantam, Connecticut 06750

General Information Girls' residential traditional camp established in 1955. Accredited by American Camping Association.
Program Focus Daily elective program of over 30 specialized activities.
Academics English as a second language, computer programming, computers, journalism, music.
Arts Arts and crafts (general), batiking, ceramics, creative writing, dance, dance (jazz), dance (modern), drawing, fabric arts, jewelry making, music, music (vocal), musical productions, painting, photography, pottery, sculpture, television/video, theater/drama, weaving.
Special Interest Areas Campcraft, leadership training.
Sports Aerobics, archery, basketball, bicycling, boating, canoeing, climbing (wall), cross-country, equestrian sports, fencing, field hockey, fishing, go-carts, golf, gymnastics, horseback riding, kayaking, martial arts, minibikes, rappelling, ropes course, sailing, soccer, softball, sports (general), swimming, tennis, track and field, volleyball, waterskiing.
Wilderness/Outdoors Bicycle trips, canoe trips, hiking, mountain biking, orienteering, rafting, white-water trips, wilderness camping.
Trips Cultural, day, overnight.
Program Information 1–4 sessions per year. Session length: 2–8 weeks in July, August. Ages: 6–16. 125–150 participants per session. Boarding program cost: $1750–$5645.
Application Deadline Continuous.
Jobs Positions for college students 19 and older.
Contact Ms. Kristin Martin, Director, 1 Torrington Office Plaza, Suite 308, Torrington, Connecticut 06790. Phone: 860-567-9678. Fax: 860-626-8301. E-mail: info@chinqueka.com.
URL www.chinqueka.com

Campus Kids–CT

CK Summer Camps, Inc.
800 Country Club Road
Waterbury, Connecticut 06723

General Information Coed residential traditional camp established in 1991. Accredited by American Camping Association.
Program Focus Weekday sleep-away camp; transportation provided. Camp during the week and home on the weekends.
Arts Arts and crafts (general), ceramics, creative writing, dance, dance (jazz), dance (modern), drawing, musical productions, photography, theater/drama, woodworking.
Special Interest Areas Campcraft, model rocketry, nature study.
Sports Aerobics, archery, basketball, bicycling, boating, canoeing, fencing, fishing, golf, gymnastics, horseback riding, lacrosse, martial arts, sailing, soccer, softball, street/roller hockey, swimming, tennis, volleyball.
Wilderness/Outdoors Caving, hiking.
Trips Day, overnight.
Program Information 1–4 sessions per year. Session length: 2–8 weeks in June, July, August. Ages: 7–15. 220 participants per session. Boarding program cost: $1575–$5720.
Application Deadline Continuous.
Jobs Positions for college students 18 and older.
Contact Mr. Brad Finkelstein, Director, PO Box 941, Middlebury, Connecticut 06762. Phone: 877-525-2181. E-mail: ckconnecticut@campuskids.com.
URL www.campuskids.com

Camp Wah-Nee

Camp Wah-Nee
Wah-Nee Road
Torrington, Connecticut 06790

General Information Coed residential traditional camp established in 1930. Accredited by American Camping Association.
Arts Arts and crafts (general), ceramics, circus arts, clowning, dance, dance (jazz), dance (modern), dance (tap), drawing, jewelry making, leather working, musical productions, painting, pottery, puppetry, theater/drama, trapeze arts, woodworking.

Camp Wah-Nee (continued)

Special Interest Areas Model rocketry.
Sports Aerobics, baseball, basketball, boating, canoeing, cheerleading, climbing (wall), diving, fishing, gymnastics, in-line skating, kayaking, rappelling, ropes course, rowing (crew/sculling), sailing, snorkeling, soccer, softball, street/roller hockey, swimming, tennis, trampolining, volleyball, water polo, weight training, windsurfing.
Wilderness/Outdoors Hiking, orienteering, rock climbing, white-water trips.
Trips Day, overnight.
Program Information 1 session per year. Session length: 8 weeks in June, July, August. Ages: 7–16. 400 participants per session. Boarding program cost: $6500–$7500. Application fee: $250.
Application Deadline Continuous.
Jobs Positions for college students 18 and older.
Summer Contact Mr. David Stricker, Owner, main address above. Phone: 860-379-2273. Fax: 860-379-2249.
Winter Contact Hal Rosen, Director, 636 Verona Drive, Melville, New York 11747. Phone: 631-424-4443. Fax: 631-732-2626. E-mail: hrunc@aol.com.
URL www.wahnee.com

Center for Creative Youth

Capitol Region Education Council
Wesleyan University
350 High Street
Middletown, Connecticut 06459

General Information Coed residential arts program established in 1977. Formal opportunities for the artistically talented. High school credit may be earned.
Arts Acting, arts, chorus, creative writing, dance, dance (ballet), dance (modern), drawing, film, music, music (chamber), music (classical), music (ensemble), music (instrumental), music (jazz), music (vocal), musical theater, painting, photography, printmaking, sculpture, set design, sound design, stage managing, theater/drama.
Trips Cultural.
Program Information 1 session per year. Session length: 5 weeks in June, July. Ages: 14–18. 200 participants per session. Boarding program cost: $3800. Application fee: $20. Financial aid available.
Application Deadline March 10.
Jobs Positions for college students.
Contact Nancy Wolfe, Director, main address above. Phone: 860-685-3307. Fax: 860-685-3311. E-mail: ccy@wesleyan.edu.
URL www.crec.org/ccy
For more information, see page 1058.

Center for Creative Youth

Channel 3 Kids Camp

Almada Lodge-Times Farm Camp Corporation
73 Times Farm Road
Andover, Connecticut 06232

General Information Coed residential traditional camp established in 1910.
Program Focus Group living, developing interactive skills, for underprivileged children.
Academics Computers, ecology, music, writing.
Arts Arts and crafts (general), creative writing, dance, drawing, film, graphic arts, jewelry making, leather working, painting, photography, radio broadcasting, television/video, theater/drama.
Special Interest Areas Campcraft, gardening.
Sports Archery, baseball, basketball, golf, ropes course, soccer, softball, swimming, volleyball.
Wilderness/Outdoors Hiking, orienteering, rock climbing, wilderness camping.
Trips Overnight.
Program Information 6 sessions per year. Session length: 6–12 days in June, July, August. Ages: 8–12. 120 participants per session. Financial aid available. Cost: $15–$250 per week.
Application Deadline Continuous.
Jobs Positions for high school students 15 and older and college students 18 and older.
Contact David Meizels, Director, main address above. Phone: 860-742-CAMP. Fax: 860-742-3298. E-mail: ch3cc@aol.com.
URL www.channel3kidscamp.org

Cheshire Academy Summer Program

Cheshire Academy
10 Main Street
Cheshire, Connecticut 06410

General Information Coed residential and day traditional camp and academic program established in 1911. Specific services available for the learning disabled. High school credit may be earned.

Cheshire Academy Summer Program

Program Focus Academics, arts and athletics.
Academics English as a second language, Spanish language/literature, academics (general), art history/appreciation, biology, business, chemistry, ecology, history, mathematics, physics, reading, study skills, writing.
Arts Arts, ceramics, dance, drawing, graphic arts, music, music (instrumental), music (vocal), painting, pottery, theater/drama.
Special Interest Areas Communication skills, field research/expeditions, field trips (arts and culture), leadership training.
Sports Basketball, golf, horseback riding, soccer, softball, swimming, tennis, volleyball, weight training.
Wilderness/Outdoors Hiking.
Trips Day, overnight.
Program Information 1 session per year. Session length: 6 weeks in July, August. Ages: 12–19. 125 participants per session. Day program cost: $2600. Boarding program cost: $4700.
Application Deadline Continuous.
Contact Matthew Kallas, Director, main address above. Phone: 203-272-5396. Fax: 203-250-7209. E-mail: summer@cheshireacademy.org.
URL www.cheshireacademy.org

Special Note
Cheshire offers small classes and individual attention. Weekly grade reports are issued so that progress can be monitored. The Writing, Reading, and Study Skills Program tests students for their weaknesses and then works to strengthen or compensate for them. The renowned English as a Second Language Program offers four levels of instruction and caring and experienced faculty members. The Performing Arts Program is designed to satisfy students of all ability levels who share in a love for the performing arts.

For more information, see page 1062.

Choate Rosemary Hall Beginning Writers Workshop

Choate Rosemary Hall
333 Christian Street
Wallingford, Connecticut 06492

General Information Coed day academic program established in 2004.
Program Focus Develop and build skills for effective written communication.
Academics English language/literature, reading, speech/debate, writing.
Sports Aerobics, basketball, climbing (wall), field hockey, in-line skating, lacrosse, softball, squash, swimming, tennis, track and field, volleyball, weight training.
Wilderness/Outdoors Hiking.
Program Information 2 sessions per year. Session length: 10 days in June, July. Ages: 10–12. 10–20 participants per session. Day program cost: $1150. Application fee: $60. Financial aid available.
Application Deadline Continuous.
Contact Mariann Arnold, Director of Admission, main address above. Phone: 203-697-2365. Fax: 203-697-2519. E-mail: marnold@choate.edu.
URL www.choate.edu/summer

For more information, see page 1068.

Choate Rosemary Hall English Language Institute

Choate Rosemary Hall
333 Christian Street
Wallingford, Connecticut 06492

General Information Coed residential and day academic program established in 1994. High school credit may be earned.
Program Focus Strengthening English skills in writing, reading, and speaking.
Academics English as a second language, English language/literature, SAT/ACT preparation, linguistics, mathematics, reading, speech/debate, study skills, typing, writing.
Arts Creative writing, drawing, painting, photography, pottery.
Sports Aerobics, basketball, bicycling, climbing (wall), field hockey, lacrosse, soccer, softball, squash, swimming, tennis, track and field, volleyball, weight training.
Wilderness/Outdoors Hiking.
Trips College tours, cultural, day, overnight, shopping.
Program Information 1 session per year. Session length: 5 weeks in June, July. Ages: 14–19. 75 participants per session. Boarding program cost: $5100. Application fee: $60. Financial aid available. Washington D.C. trip: $385.
Application Deadline Continuous.

Choate Rosemary Hall English Language Institute (continued)

Contact Mariann Arnold, Director of Admission, main address above. Phone: 203-697-2365. Fax: 203-697-2519. E-mail: marnold@choate.edu.
URL www.choate.edu/summer
For more information, see page 1068.

Choate Rosemary Hall English Language Institute/Focus Program

Choate Rosemary Hall
333 Christian Street
Wallingford, Connecticut 06492

General Information Coed residential and day academic program established in 1999.
Program Focus Strengthening English skills in writing, reading, and speaking.
Academics English as a second language, English language/literature, journalism, linguistics, reading, speech/debate, study skills, writing.
Arts Ceramics, creative writing, drawing, painting.
Sports Aerobics, basketball, climbing (wall), field hockey, lacrosse, ropes course, soccer, softball, squash, swimming, tennis, track and field, volleyball, weight training.
Wilderness/Outdoors Hiking.
Trips Cultural, day, overnight, shopping.
Program Information 1 session per year. Session length: 4 weeks in June, July. Ages: 12–14. 35 participants per session. Day program cost: $3100. Boarding program cost: $4150. Application fee: $60. Financial aid available. Washington D.C. trip: $385.
Application Deadline Continuous.
Contact Mariann Arnold, Director of Admission, main address above. Phone: 203-697-2365. Fax: 203-697-2519. E-mail: marnold@choate.edu.
URL www.choate.edu/summer
For more information, see page 1068.

Choate Rosemary Hall Focus Program

Choate Rosemary Hall
333 Christian Street
Wallingford, Connecticut 06492

General Information Coed residential and day academic program established in 1998.
Program Focus Project-based learning.
Academics American literature, Latin language, academics (general), biology, chemistry, computers, economics, environmental science, geology/earth science, government and politics, history, mathematics, physics, reading, social science, social studies, speech/debate, study skills, writing.
Arts Ceramics, drawing.
Sports Aerobics, basketball, climbing (wall), field hockey, lacrosse, soccer, softball, squash, swimming, tennis, track and field, volleyball, weight training.
Wilderness/Outdoors Hiking.
Trips Cultural, day, shopping.
Program Information 1 session per year. Session length: 4 weeks in July. Ages: 12–14. 85 participants per session. Day program cost: $2870. Boarding program cost: $4000. Application fee: $60. Financial aid available.
Application Deadline Continuous.
Contact Mariann Arnold, Director of Admission, main address above. Phone: 203-697-2365. Fax: 203-697-2519. E-mail: marnold@choate.edu.
URL www.choate.edu/summer
For more information, see page 1068.

Choate Rosemary Hall Immersion Program

Choate Rosemary Hall
333 Christian Street
Wallingford, Connecticut 06492

General Information Coed residential and day academic program established in 1999. Formal opportunities for the academically talented. High school credit may be earned.
Program Focus Full-year credit courses during five-week summer session.
Academics French language/literature, Latin language, Spanish language/literature, language study, mathematics, physics.
Sports Aerobics, basketball, bicycling, climbing (wall), field hockey, lacrosse, soccer, softball, squash, swimming, tennis, track and field, volleyball, weight training.
Wilderness/Outdoors Hiking.
Trips College tours, cultural, day, shopping.
Program Information 1 session per year. Session length: 5 weeks in June, July. Ages: 14–19. 10–15 participants per session. Day program cost: $3600. Boarding program cost: $4900. Application fee: $60. Financial aid available.
Application Deadline Continuous.
Contact Mariann Arnold, Director of Admission, main address above. Phone: 203-697-2365. Fax: 203-697-2519. E-mail: marnold@choate.edu.
URL www.choate.edu/summer
For more information, see page 1068.

Choate Rosemary Hall John F. Kennedy Institute in Government

Choate Rosemary Hall
333 Christian Street
Wallingford, Connecticut 06492

General Information Coed residential and day academic program established in 1985. Formal opportunities for the academically talented. High school credit may be earned.
Program Focus Government and political science.
Academics Economics, government and politics, precollege program, speech/debate, writing.
Sports Aerobics, basketball, climbing (wall), field hockey, lacrosse, soccer, softball, squash, swimming, tennis, track and field, volleyball, weight training.
Wilderness/Outdoors Hiking.
Trips College tours, cultural, day, overnight, shopping.

Choate Rosemary Hall John F. Kennedy Institute in Government

Program Information 1 session per year. Session length: 5 weeks in June, July. Ages: 15–19. 20 participants per session. Day program cost: $3550. Boarding program cost: $4800. Application fee: $60. Financial aid available. Washington D.C. trip: $450.
Application Deadline Continuous.
Contact Mariann Arnold, Director of Admission, main address above. Phone: 203-697-2365. Fax: 203-697-2519. E-mail: marnold@choate.edu.
URL www.choate.edu/summer

For more information, see page 1068.

Choate Rosemary Hall Math/ Science Institute for Girls–CONNECT

Choate Rosemary Hall
333 Christian Street
Wallingford, Connecticut 06492

General Information Girls' residential and day academic program established in 1995. Formal opportunities for the academically talented.
Program Focus Mathematics and science project-based group learning.
Academics Biology, chemistry, ecology, environmental science, geology/earth science, health sciences, marine studies, mathematics, physics, science (general), study skills.
Special Interest Areas General camp activities.
Sports Aerobics, basketball, bicycling, climbing (wall), field hockey, lacrosse, soccer, softball, squash, swimming, tennis, track and field, volleyball, weight training.
Wilderness/Outdoors Hiking.
Trips Cultural, day, shopping.
Program Information 1 session per year. Session length: 4 weeks in June, July. Ages: 11–14. 25–30 participants per session. Day program cost: $2870. Boarding program cost: $4000. Application fee: $60. Financial aid available.
Application Deadline Continuous.
Contact Mariann Arnold, Director of Admission, main address above. Phone: 203-697-2365. Fax: 203-697-2519. E-mail: marnold@choate.edu.
URL www.choate.edu/summer

For more information, see page 1068.

Choate Rosemary Hall Summer Arts Conservatory–Playwriting

Choate Rosemary Hall
Paul Mellon Arts Center
333 Christian Street
Wallingford, Connecticut 06492

General Information Coed residential and day arts program established in 1982. Formal opportunities for the artistically talented. High school credit may be earned.
Arts Playwriting, screenwriting.
Sports Racquetball, swimming, tennis.
Trips Cultural, day, overnight, shopping.
Program Information 1 session per year. Session length: 5 weeks in June, July. Ages: 12–18. 12 participants per session. Day program cost: $3400. Boarding program cost: $4400. Application fee: $60. Financial aid available. Optional New York City trip: $425.
Application Deadline Continuous.
Jobs Positions for college students 21 and older.
Contact Mrs. Randi J. Brandt, Admissions Director, Arts Conservatory, main address above. Phone: 203-697-2423. Fax: 203-697-2396. E-mail: rbrandt@choate.edu.
URL www.choate.edu/pmac

For more information, see page 1064.

Choate Rosemary Hall Summer Arts Conservatory–Theater

Choate Rosemary Hall
Paul Mellon Arts Center
333 Christian Street
Wallingford, Connecticut 06492

General Information Coed residential and day arts program established in 1982. Formal opportunities for the artistically talented. High school credit may be earned.

Choate Rosemary Hall Summer Arts Conservatory–Theater

Arts Acting, dance, dance (ballet), dance (jazz), dance (tap), music (vocal), musical productions, musical theater, theater/drama, voice and speech.
Sports Racquetball, swimming, tennis.
Trips Cultural, overnight, shopping.
Program Information 1 session per year. Session length: 5 weeks in June, July. Ages: 12–18. 40 participants per session. Day program cost: $3400. Boarding program cost: $4400. Application fee: $60. Financial aid available. Optional New York City trip: $425.
Application Deadline Continuous.
Jobs Positions for college students 21 and older.
Contact Mrs. Randi J. Brandt, Admissions Director, Arts Conservatory, main address above. Phone: 203-697-2423. Fax: 203-697-2396. E-mail: rbrandt@choate.edu.
URL www.choate.edu/pmac/tickets/other.html
For more information, see page 1064.

Choate Rosemary Hall Summer Arts Conservatory–Visual Arts Program

Choate Rosemary Hall
Paul Mellon Arts Center
333 Christian Street
Wallingford, Connecticut 06492

General Information Coed residential and day arts program established in 1982. Formal opportunities for the artistically talented. High school credit may be earned.
Arts Arts, ceramics, drawing, graphic arts, mixed media, painting, photography, pottery, studio arts, visual arts.
Sports Racquetball, swimming, tennis.
Trips Cultural, day, overnight, shopping.
Program Information 1 session per year. Session length: 5 weeks in June, July. Ages: 12–18. 20 participants per session. Day program cost: $3400. Boarding program cost: $4400. Application fee: $60. Financial aid available. Optional New York City trip: $425.
Application Deadline Continuous.
Jobs Positions for college students 21 and older.
Contact Mrs. Randi J. Brandt, Admissions Director, Arts Conservatory, main address above. Phone: 203-697-2423. Fax: 203-697-2396. E-mail: rbrandt@choate.edu.
URL www.choate.edu/pmac
For more information, see page 1064.

Choate Rosemary Hall Summer Session

Choate Rosemary Hall
333 Christian Street
Wallingford, Connecticut 06492

General Information Coed residential and day academic program established in 1916. High school credit may be earned.
Academics American literature, English as a second language, English language/literature, French language/literature, SAT/ACT preparation, Spanish language/literature, academics (general), anthropology, astronomy, biology, chemistry, computers, economics, environmental science, government and politics, history, humanities, journalism, marine studies, mathematics, physics, pre-college program, psychology, reading, science (general), speech/debate, study skills, typing, writing.
Arts Ceramics, creative writing, drawing, photography, theater/drama.
Special Interest Areas General camp activities.
Sports Aerobics, baseball, basketball, climbing (wall), field hockey, football, lacrosse, soccer, softball, squash, swimming, tennis, track and field, volleyball, weight training.
Wilderness/Outdoors Hiking.
Trips College tours, cultural, day, shopping.
Program Information 1 session per year. Session length: 5 weeks in June, July. Ages: 12–19. 500 participants per session. Day program cost: $760–$3550. Boarding program cost: $4800. Application fee: $60. Financial aid available.
Application Deadline Continuous.
Jobs Positions for college students.
Contact Mariann Arnold, Director of Admission for Summer Programs, main address above. Phone: 203-697-2365. Fax: 203-697-2519. E-mail: marnold@choate.edu.
URL www.choate.edu/summer
For more information, see page 1068.

Choate Rosemary Hall Writing Project

Choate Rosemary Hall
333 Christian Street
Wallingford, Connecticut 06492

General Information Coed residential and day academic program established in 1987. Formal opportunities for the academically talented.
Program Focus Writing skills including creative and expository writing, poetry, and the writing process.
Academics American literature, English language/ literature, journalism, reading, study skills, typing, writing.
Arts Creative writing.
Sports Aerobics, basketball, bicycling, climbing (wall), field hockey, lacrosse, soccer, softball, squash, swimming, tennis, track and field, volleyball, weight training.
Wilderness/Outdoors Hiking.
Trips College tours, cultural, day, shopping.
Program Information 2 sessions per year. Session length: 2 weeks in June, July. Ages: 13–18. 20–25 participants per session. Day program cost: $1500. Boarding program cost: $1970. Application fee: $60. Financial aid available.
Application Deadline Continuous.
Contact Mariann Arnold, Director of Admission, main address above. Phone: 203-697-2365. Fax: 203-697-2519. E-mail: marnold@choate.edu.
URL www.choate.edu/summer

For more information, see page 1068.

Choate Rosemary Hall Young Writers Workshop

Choate Rosemary Hall
333 Christian Street
Wallingford, Connecticut 06492

General Information Coed residential and day academic program established in 1997. Formal opportunities for the academically talented.
Academics American literature, English language/ literature, journalism, reading, study skills, typing, writing.
Arts Creative writing.
Sports Aerobics, basketball, climbing (wall), field hockey, in-line skating, lacrosse, soccer, softball, squash, swimming, tennis, track and field, volleyball, weight training.
Wilderness/Outdoors Hiking.
Trips Cultural, day, shopping.
Program Information 2 sessions per year. Session length: 2 weeks in July. Ages: 11–14. 25–30 participants per session. Day program cost: $1500. Boarding program cost: $1970. Application fee: $60. Financial aid available.
Application Deadline Continuous.
Contact Mariann Arnold, Director of Admission, main address above. Phone: 203-697-2365. Fax: 203-697-2519. E-mail: marnold@choate.edu.
URL www.choate.edu/summer

For more information, see page 1068.

Cybercamps–University of Hartford

Cybercamps–Giant Campus, Inc.
Hartford, Connecticut

General Information Coed residential and day academic program established in 1997.
Program Focus High tech computer camps featuring project oriented curriculum in Web design, 3D animation, game design, robotics, digital arts and programming for all ability levels.
Academics Web page design, computer programming, computers.
Arts Animation, creative writing, digital media, graphic arts, photography.
Special Interest Areas Computer game design, computer graphics, robotics, team building.
Sports Frisbee golf, ultimate frisbee.
Program Information 2–9 sessions per year. Session length: 5–30 days in June, July, August. Ages: 7–18. 30–150 participants per session. Day program cost: $599–$849. Boarding program cost: $974–$1224.
Application Deadline Continuous.
Jobs Positions for high school students 15 and older and college students.
Contact Cybercamps Information Office, 2401 4th Avenue, Suite 1110, Seattle, Washington 98121. Phone: 206-442-4500. Fax: 206-442-4501. E-mail: info@cybercamps.com.
URL www.cybercamps.com

Exploration Senior Program at Yale University

Exploration School, Inc.
Yale University
New Haven, Connecticut 06520

General Information Coed residential and day academic program established in 1977. Formal opportunities for the academically talented and artistically talented. Specific services available for the hearing impaired, learning disabled, physically challenged, and visually impaired.

Exploration Senior Program at Yale University

Program Focus Academic enrichment.

Exploration Senior Program at Yale University (continued)

Academics American literature, English as a second language, English language/literature, SAT/ACT preparation, academics (general), aerospace science, anthropology, architecture, area studies, biology, botany, business, chemistry, communications, computer programming, computers, ecology, economics, engineering, environmental science, geology/earth science, government and politics, health sciences, history, humanities, intercultural studies, journalism, marine studies, mathematics, music, peace education, philosophy, physics, physiology, precollege program, psychology, reading, religion, science (general), social science, social studies, speech/debate, study skills, writing.
Arts Arts and crafts (general), batiking, chorus, clowning, creative writing, dance, dance (jazz), dance (modern), dance (tap), drawing, fabric arts, film, graphic arts, jewelry making, music, music (instrumental), music (jazz), music (vocal), musical productions, painting, photography, pottery, printmaking, sculpture, television/video, theater/drama, woodworking.
Special Interest Areas Career exploration, college planning, community service, construction, culinary arts, electronics, model rocketry.
Sports Aerobics, baseball, basketball, bicycling, boating, canoeing, climbing (wall), field hockey, football, golf, kayaking, lacrosse, martial arts, racquetball, rowing (crew/sculling), sailing, sea kayaking, soccer, softball, sports (general), squash, street/roller hockey, swimming, tennis, volleyball.
Wilderness/Outdoors Canoe trips, hiking, orienteering, rafting, rock climbing, wilderness camping.
Trips College tours, cultural, day, overnight.
Program Information 2 sessions per year. Session length: 3 weeks in June, July, August. Ages: 15–18. 620–650 participants per session. Day program cost: $1725–$3195. Boarding program cost: $3550–$6795. Financial aid available.
Application Deadline Continuous.
Jobs Positions for college students 19 and older.
Summer Contact Mr. Bill Clough, Head of Program, Exploration Senior Program, PO Box 205187, New Haven, Connecticut 06520-5187. Phone: 203-432-1777. Fax: 203-432-2134. E-mail: summer@explo.org.
Winter Contact Barbara Targum, Admissions Coordinator, PO Box 368, 470 Washington Street, Norwood, Massachusetts 02062. Phone: 781-762-7400. Fax: 781-762-7425. E-mail: summer@explo.org.
URL www.explo.org
For more information, see page 1122.

Greenhouse: Litchfield Jazz Festival Summer Dance Institute

Litchfield Performing Arts
Forman School
Litchfield, Connecticut 06759

General Information Coed residential and day arts program established in 2002. Formal opportunities for the artistically talented. High school credit may be earned.
Program Focus Dance education and performance.
Arts Dance, dance (ballet), dance (modern), dance (tap).
Sports Basketball, tennis, volleyball.
Trips Cultural, day.
Program Information 2 sessions per year. Session length: 1–2 weeks in July, August. Ages: 13+. 120–150 participants per session. Day program cost: $745–$1595. Boarding program cost: $795–$2500. Application fee: $50. Financial aid available.
Application Deadline Continuous.
Contact Lindsey Muir, Program Director, PO Box 69, Litchfield, Connecticut 06759. Phone: 860-567-4162. Fax: 860-567-3592. E-mail: lindseymuir@litchfieldjazzfest.com.
URL www.litchfieldjazzfest.com

Hyde School Summer Challenge Program–Woodstock, CT

Hyde School
Woodstock, Connecticut 06281-0237

General Information Coed residential academic program and outdoor program established in 1996.
Program Focus Character education, performing arts, academics, athletics, and wilderness adventure.
Academics Academics (general), mathematics, reading, writing.
Arts Acting, dance, musical productions, theater/drama.
Special Interest Areas Community service, farming, leadership training.
Sports Baseball, basketball, canoeing, football, lacrosse, soccer, track and field, wrestling.
Wilderness/Outdoors Backpacking, canoe trips, hiking, wilderness camping, wilderness/outdoors (general).
Trips Cultural, overnight, shopping.
Program Information 1 session per year. Session length: 35–40 days in July, August. Ages: 13–18. 95–120 participants per session. Boarding program cost: $6000. Application fee: $100. Student bank/bookstore deposit: $500.
Application Deadline Continuous.
Jobs Positions for college students.
Contact Gigi MacMillan, Director of Admissions, PO Box 237, Woodstock, Connecticut 06281-0237. Phone: 860-963-9096. Fax: 860-928-0612. E-mail: gmacmillan@hyde.edu.
URL www.hyde.edu
For more information, see page 1154.

iD Tech Camps–Sacred Heart University, Fairfield, CT

iD Tech Camps
Sacred Heart University
Fairfield, Connecticut 06825

General Information Coed residential and day academic program established in 1999. Accredited by American Camping Association. Formal opportunities for the academically talented and artistically talented.
Program Focus High-tech computer camps for kids and teens; produce digital movies, create video games, design Web pages, learn programming and robotics, and

more; one computer per student, small classes, campers complete a project in a creative and fun learning environment.
Academics Web page design, computer programming, computer science (Advanced Placement), computers, music, precollege program.
Arts Animation, cinematography, digital media, drawing, film, film editing, film production, graphic arts, music, television/video.
Special Interest Areas Career exploration, computer graphics, electronics, leadership training, robotics, team building.
Sports Baseball, basketball, soccer, softball, swimming, volleyball.
Trips College tours, cultural, day.
Program Information 5 sessions per year. Session length: 5–7 days in June, July, August. Ages: 7–17. 40–50 participants per session. Day program cost: $639. Boarding program cost: $989. Application fee: $200. Financial aid available.
Application Deadline Continuous.
Jobs Positions for college students 18 and older.
Contact Client Service Representatives, 1885 Winchester Boulevard, Suite 201, Campbell, California 95008. Phone: 888-709-TECH. Fax: 408-871-2228. E-mail: requests@internaldrive.com.
URL www.internaldrive.com

For more information, see page 1156.

IMACS–Full Day Summer Camp–Connecticut

Institute for Mathematics & Computer Science (IMACS)
Connecticut

General Information Coed day academic program established in 1992. Formal opportunities for the academically talented.
Academics Computer programming, computer science (Advanced Placement), computers, engineering, mathematics.
Special Interest Areas Electronics, robotics.
Program Information 7 sessions per year. Session length: 5 days in January, February, March, April, May, June, July, August, September, October, November, December. Ages: 5–18. 30–50 participants per session. Day program cost: $399–$1224. Supply fee: $50–$200; additional sessions booked at same time $249 plus $50 supply fee.
Application Deadline Continuous.
Jobs Positions for high school students 16 and older and college students 18 and older.
Contact Mr. Terry Kaufman, President, 7435 Northwest 4th Street, Plantation, Florida 33317. Phone: 954-791-2333. Fax: 954-791-0260. E-mail: info@imacs.org.
URL www.imacs.org

IMACS–Individual Summer Programs–Connecticut

Institute for Mathematics & Computer Science (IMACS)
Connecticut

General Information Coed day academic program established in 1992. Formal opportunities for the academically talented.
Academics Computer programming, computer science (Advanced Placement), computers, engineering, mathematics, mathematics (Advanced Placement).
Special Interest Areas Computer graphics, electronics, robotics.
Program Information 5 sessions per year. Session length: 5 days in January, February, March, April, May, June, July, August, September, October, November, December. Ages: 6–18. Day program cost: $79–$199.
Application Deadline Continuous.
Jobs Positions for high school students 16 and older and college students 18 and older.
Contact Mr. Terry Kaufman, President, 7435 Northwest 4th Street, Plantation, Florida 33317. Phone: 954-791-2333. Fax: 954-791-0260. E-mail: info@imacs.org.
URL www.imacs.org

Joel Ross Tennis & Sports Camp

Kent School
Kent, Connecticut 06757

General Information Coed residential sports camp established in 1990. Accredited by American Camping Association.
Program Focus Tennis, golf.
Academics SAT/ACT preparation.
Arts Arts and crafts (general), theater/drama.
Sports Archery, basketball, canoeing, diving, fishing, football, golf, lacrosse, ropes course, soccer, softball, swimming, tennis, track and field, volleyball, water polo.
Wilderness/Outdoors Hiking, rock climbing.
Trips Day.
Program Information 4 sessions per year. Session length: 13 days in June, July, August. Ages: 8–18. 100 participants per session. Boarding program cost: $1995.
Application Deadline Continuous.
Jobs Positions for college students 18 and older.
Summer Contact Joel Ross, Director, main address above. Phone: 860-927-5773. Fax: 860-927-6340. E-mail: rosstennis@aol.com.
Winter Contact Joel Ross, Director, PO Box 62H, Scarsdale, New York 10583. Phone: 914-668-3258. Fax: 914-723-4579. E-mail: rosstennis@aol.com.
URL www.joelrosstennis.com

Joe Machnik's No. 1 Academy One and Premier Programs–Windsor, Connecticut

Joe Machnik's No. 1 Camps
Loomis Chaffee School
Windsor, Connecticut

General Information Coed residential and day sports camp.
Program Focus Soccer instruction, physical fitness, testing and speed training. Campers gain exposure to top players and are challenged by intense competition.
Sports Soccer, swimming.
Trips Day.
Program Information 3 sessions per year. Session length: 6 days in July, August. Ages: 13–17. Day program cost: $699. Boarding program cost: $759. Financial aid available.
Application Deadline Continuous.
Jobs Positions for college students.
Contact Dr. Joseph Machnik, Director, PO Box 389, 916 Palm Boulevard, Isle of Palms, South Carolina 29451. Phone: 800-622-4645. Fax: 843-886-0885. E-mail: info@no1soccercamps.com.
URL www.no1soccercamps.com

Joe Machnik's No. 1 College Prep Academy–Windsor, Connecticut

Joe Machnik's No. 1 Camps
Loomis Chaffee School
Windsor, Connecticut

General Information Coed residential and day sports camp.
Program Focus Intense soccer instruction for high school students.
Sports Soccer, swimming.
Trips Day.
Program Information 2 sessions per year. Session length: 12 days in July, August. Ages: 13–17. 10–20 participants per session. Day program cost: $1449. Boarding program cost: $1549. Financial aid available.
Application Deadline Continuous.
Jobs Positions for college students 17 and older.
Contact Dr. Joseph Machnik, Director, PO Box 389, 916 Palm Boulevard, Isle of Palms, South Carolina 29451. Phone: 800-622-4645. Fax: 843-886-0885. E-mail: info@no1soccercamps.com.
URL www.no1soccercamps.com

Joe Machnik's No. 1 Mighty Mini, Goalkeeper and Striker Camp–Windsor, Connecticut

Joe Machnik's No. 1 Camps
Loomis Chaffee School
Windsor, Connecticut

General Information Coed residential and day sports camp established in 1977.
Program Focus Soccer instruction. Goalkeepers and strikers compete against each other daily.
Sports Soccer, swimming.
Program Information 5 sessions per year. Session length: 6 days in July, August. Ages: 8–12. 100–200 participants per session. Boarding program cost: $429. Financial aid available.
Application Deadline Continuous.
Jobs Positions for college students 17 and older.
Contact Dr. Joseph Machnik, Director, PO Box 389, 916 Palm Boulevard, Isle of Palms, South Carolina 29451. Phone: 800-622-4645. Fax: 843-886-0885. E-mail: info@no1soccercamps.com.
URL www.no1soccercamps.com

Junior Statesmen Summer School–Yale University

Junior Statesmen Foundation
Yale University
New Haven, Connecticut 06520

General Information Coed residential academic program established in 1989. Formal opportunities for the academically talented. High school credit may be earned.

Junior Statesmen Summer School–Yale University

Program Focus Constitutional law, American government, speech, debate, and leadership training.

Academics Communications, government and politics, government and politics (Advanced Placement), journalism, precollege program, prelaw, social science, social studies, speech/debate.
Special Interest Areas Career exploration, leadership training.
Trips College tours, cultural, day.
Program Information 1 session per year. Session length: 4 weeks in June, July. Ages: 14–18. 200–300 participants per session. Boarding program cost: $3500. Financial aid available.
Application Deadline Continuous.
Contact Matt Randazzo, National Summer School Director, 400 South El Camino Real, Suite 300, San Mateo, California 94402. Phone: 650-347-1600. Fax: 650-347-7200. E-mail: jsa@jsa.org.
URL www.jsa.org
For more information, see page 1174.

Kent School Summer Writers Camp

Kent School
Route 341
Kent, Connecticut 06757

General Information Coed residential academic program established in 1995. Accredited by American Camping Association. Formal opportunities for the academically talented.
Program Focus Creative writing and athletic/recreational activities.
Academics English language/literature, journalism, reading, speech/debate, study skills, writing.
Arts Ceramics, creative writing, dance, drawing, painting, theater/drama.
Sports Basketball, fishing, in-line skating, rowing (crew/sculling), soccer, swimming, tennis, weight training.
Wilderness/Outdoors Hiking.
Trips Cultural, day.
Program Information 1 session per year. Session length: 3 weeks in July. Ages: 11–15. 50 participants per session. Boarding program cost: $2300. Application fee: $25. Financial aid available.
Application Deadline Continuous.
Jobs Positions for college students 18 and older.
Contact Ms. Amy Van Sickle, Summer Camp Admissions Director, PO Box 2006, Kent, Connecticut 06757. Phone: 860-927-6114. Fax: 860-927-6109. E-mail: vansicklea@kent-school.edu.
URL www.writerscamp.org

Landmark Volunteers: Connecticut

Landmark Volunteers, Inc.
Connecticut

General Information Coed residential outdoor program and community service program established in 1992. High school credit may be earned.
Program Focus Opportunity for high school students to earn community service credit while working as a team for two weeks serving Hole in the Wall Gang Camp or Sharon Audubon Society. Similar programs offered through Landmark Volunteers at over 60 locations in 21 states.
Academics Biology, botany, ecology, environmental science, social science, social services.
Special Interest Areas Animal care, career exploration, community service, conservation projects, field research/expeditions, leadership training, nature study, team building, trail maintenance, work camp programs.
Wilderness/Outdoors Hiking.
Trips Cultural, day.
Program Information 2 sessions per year. Session length: 14–15 days in March, July, August. Ages: 14–18. 10–13 participants per session. Boarding program cost: $875–$925. Financial aid available.
Application Deadline Continuous.
Jobs Positions for college students.
Contact Ann Barrett, Executive Director, PO Box 455, Sheffield, Massachusetts 01257. Phone: 413-229-0255. Fax: 413-229-2050. E-mail: landmark@volunteers.com.
URL www.volunteers.com
For more information, see page 1182.

Litchfield Jazz Festival Summer Music School Program

Litchfield Performing Arts
Forman School
Litchfield, Connecticut 06759

General Information Coed residential and day arts program established in 1997. Formal opportunities for the artistically talented. High school credit may be earned.
Program Focus Jazz education and performance.
Academics Independent study, music.
Arts Band, chorus, music (instrumental), music (jazz), music (vocal), music composition/arrangement, music theory, musical performance/recitals.
Sports Basketball, tennis, volleyball.
Trips Cultural, day.
Program Information 2 sessions per year. Session length: 1–2 weeks in July, August. Ages: 12+. 120–150 participants per session. Day program cost: $625–$1595. Boarding program cost: $675–$2500. Application fee: $50. Financial aid available.
Application Deadline Continuous.
Contact Lindsey Muir, Program Director, PO Box 69, Litchfield, Connecticut 06759. Phone: 860-567-4162. Fax: 860-567-3592. E-mail: lindseymuir@litchfieldjazzfest.com.
URL www.litchfieldjazzfest.com

Marvelwood Summer

The Marvelwood School
476 Skiff Mountain Road
Kent, Connecticut 06757

General Information Coed residential and day academic program established in 1964. High school credit may be earned.

Marvelwood Summer (continued)

Marvelwood Summer

Program Focus Reading, study skills, math, and English as a second language, outdoor scientific fieldwork.
Academics English as a second language, English language/literature, SAT/ACT preparation, academics (general), biology, computers, ecology, environmental science, journalism, mathematics, reading, science (general), study skills, writing.
Arts Arts and crafts (general), creative writing, drawing, film, film production, music, painting, photography, studio arts, television/video, theater/drama, woodworking.
Special Interest Areas Community service, conservation projects, field research/expeditions.
Sports Aerobics, baseball, basketball, bicycling, boating, canoeing, climbing (wall), equestrian sports, fishing, golf, horseback riding, in-line skating, lacrosse, rappelling, ropes course, sailing, soccer, softball, swimming, tennis, ultimate frisbee, volleyball, weight training.
Wilderness/Outdoors Bicycle trips, canoe trips, hiking, mountain biking, rock climbing, white-water trips.
Trips Cultural, day, shopping.
Program Information 1 session per year. Session length: 36 days in June, July, August. Ages: 11–17. 30–50 participants per session. Day program cost: $4200. Boarding program cost: $5300. Application fee: $35–$60. Financial aid available.
Application Deadline Continuous.
Jobs Positions for college students 21 and older.
Summer Contact Katherine Almquist, Assistant Director of Admissions, 476 Skiff Mountain Road, PO Box 3001, Kent, Connecticut 06757-3001. Phone: 860-927-0047. Fax: 860-927-5325. E-mail: marvelwood.school@snet.net.
Winter Contact Todd Holt, Director of Admissions, 476 Skiff Mountain Road, PO Box 3001, Kent, Connecticut 06757-3001. Phone: 860-927-0047. Fax: 860-927-0021.
URL www.themarvelwoodschool.com

For more information, see page 1204.

Miss Porter's School Athletic Experience

Miss Porter's School
60 Main Street
Farmington, Connecticut 06032

General Information Girls' residential and day sports camp established in 2005.
Program Focus Multi-sport experience offered as an alternative to one-sport, specialized camps.
Sports Athletic training, basketball, field hockey, lacrosse, physical fitness, soccer, softball, sports (general), squash.
Program Information 1 session per year. Session length: 5 days in July. Ages: 11–15. 40 participants per session. Boarding program cost: $600–$800.
Application Deadline June 1.
Contact Elizabeth Conant, Director of Athletics, main address above. Phone: 860-409-3710. Fax: 860-409-3515. E-mail: summer_programs@missporters.org.
URL www.mpsvacationprograms.org

Miss Porter's School Summer Challenge

Miss Porter's School
60 Main Street
Farmington, Connecticut 06032

General Information Girls' residential academic program established in 1995.
Program Focus An interdisciplinary academic program featuring science, mathematics, and technology.
Academics English as a second language, academics (general), astronomy, biology, chemistry, computers, marine studies, mathematics, physics, science (general).
Arts Arts and crafts (general).
Special Interest Areas Field trips (arts and culture).
Sports Basketball, field hockey, lacrosse, martial arts, soccer, softball, squash, swimming, tennis, volleyball.
Trips Day.
Program Information 1–2 sessions per year. Session length: 13–28 days in July. Ages: 12–15. 30–60 participants per session. Boarding program cost: $1800–$3600. Application fee: $30. Financial aid available.
Application Deadline Continuous.
Jobs Positions for college students.
Contact John Barrengos, Director of Summer Programs, main address above. Phone: 860-409-3692. Fax: 860-409-3515. E-mail: summer_programs@missporters.org.
URL www.summerchallenge.org

Miss Porter's School Arts Alive!

Miss Porter's School
60 Main Street
Farmington, Connecticut 06032

General Information Girls' residential academic program and arts program established in 2003.
Program Focus Interdisciplinary academic program featuring studio, performing, and literary arts.

Academics English as a second language, English language/literature, academics (general), music, writing.
Arts Acting, arts, arts and crafts (general), ceramics, creative writing, dance, dance (jazz), dance (modern), drawing, fabric arts, graphic arts, jewelry making, mime, music, painting, photography, pottery, printmaking, studio arts, theater/drama, visual arts.
Special Interest Areas Field trips (arts and culture).
Sports Basketball, field hockey, lacrosse, martial arts, soccer, softball, squash, swimming, tennis, volleyball.
Trips Cultural, day.
Program Information 1–2 sessions per year. Session length: 13–28 days in July. Ages: 12–15. 30–60 participants per session. Boarding program cost: $1800–$3600. Application fee: $30. Financial aid available.
Application Deadline Continuous.
Jobs Positions for college students.
Contact John Barrengos, Director of Summer Programs, main address above. Phone: 860-409-3692. Fax: 860-409-3515. E-mail: summer_programs@missporters.org.
URL www.mpsartsalive.org

Mountain Workshop–Bike Touring Days 1

Mountain Workshop
Connecticut

General Information Coed day outdoor program established in 2000.
Program Focus Road or easy trail riding.
Special Interest Areas Bicycle mechanics.
Sports Bicycling, swimming.
Wilderness/Outdoors Bicycle trips, orienteering.
Trips Day.
Program Information 2 sessions per year. Session length: 5 days in July, August. Ages: 11–13. 13 participants per session. Day program cost: $450.
Application Deadline Continuous.
Jobs Positions for college students 21 and older.
Contact Kent B. Tullo, Director, 9 Brookside Place, West Redding, Connecticut 06896. Phone: 203-544-0555. Fax: 203-544-0333. E-mail: info@mountainworkshop.com.
URL www.mountainworkshop.com

Mountain Workshop/Dirt Camp–Mountain Bike Days 1

Mountain Workshop
Connecticut

General Information Coed day outdoor program established in 1992.
Program Focus For the beginner/intermediate rider.
Special Interest Areas Bicycle mechanics.
Sports Bicycling.
Wilderness/Outdoors Mountain biking.
Trips Day.
Program Information 1–2 sessions per year. Session length: 5 days in July. Ages: 12–14. 13 participants per session. Day program cost: $440.
Application Deadline Continuous.
Jobs Positions for college students 21 and older.
Contact J. J. Jameson, Director, 9 Brookside Place, West Redding, Connecticut 06896. Phone: 203-544-0555. Fax: 203-544-0333. E-mail: jj@dirtcamp.com.
URL www.mountainworkshop.com

Mountain Workshop/Dirt Camp–Mountain Bike Days 3

Mountain Workshop
Connecticut

General Information Coed day outdoor program established in 1995.
Program Focus For the advanced rider.
Special Interest Areas Bicycle mechanics.
Sports Bicycling, swimming.
Wilderness/Outdoors Mountain biking.
Trips Day.
Program Information 1–2 sessions per year. Session length: 5 days in July, August. Ages: 14–17. 13 participants per session. Day program cost: $440.
Jobs Positions for college students 21 and older.
Contact J. J. Jameson, Director, 9 Brookside Place, West Redding, Connecticut 06896. Phone: 203-544-0555. Fax: 203-544-0333. E-mail: jj@dirtcamp.com.
URL www.mountainworkshop.com

Mountain Workshop/Dirt Camp–Mountain Bike Days 2

Mountain Workshop
Connecticut

General Information Coed day outdoor program established in 1995.
Program Focus For the intermediate/advanced rider.
Special Interest Areas Bicycle mechanics.
Sports Bicycling.
Wilderness/Outdoors Mountain biking.
Trips Day.
Program Information 1–2 sessions per year. Session length: 5 days in July. Ages: 13–15. 13 participants per session. Day program cost: $440.
Application Deadline Continuous.
Jobs Positions for college students 21 and older.
Contact J. J. Jameson, Director, 9 Brookside Place, West Redding, Connecticut 06896. Phone: 203-544-0555. Fax: 203-544-0333. E-mail: jj@dirtcamp.com.
URL www.mountainworkshop.com

Mountain Workshop–Graduate Awesome Adventures

Mountain Workshop
Connecticut

General Information Coed day outdoor program established in 1986.
Sports Canoeing, kayaking.
Wilderness/Outdoors Caving, hiking, outdoor adventure, rock climbing.
Trips Day.

Mountain Workshop–Graduate Awesome Adventures (continued)

Program Information 9 sessions per year. Session length: 5 days in June, July, August. Ages: 11–12. Day program cost: $450.
Application Deadline Continuous.
Jobs Positions for college students 21 and older.
Contact Kent B. Tullo, Director, 9 Brookside Place, West Redding, Connecticut 06896. Phone: 203-544-0555. Fax: 203-544-0333. E-mail: info@mountainworkshop.com.
URL www.mountainworkshop.com

Mountain Workshop–Junior Awesome Adventures

Mountain Workshop
Connecticut

General Information Coed day outdoor program established in 1984.
Sports Canoeing, rappelling.
Wilderness/Outdoors Caving, hiking, outdoor adventure.
Trips Day.
Program Information 12 sessions per year. Session length: 5 days in June, July, August. Ages: 9–10. Day program cost: $450.
Application Deadline Continuous.
Jobs Positions for college students 21 and older.
Contact Kent B. Tullo, Director, 9 Brookside Place, West Redding, Connecticut 06896. Phone: 203-544-0555. Fax: 203-544-0333. E-mail: info@mountainworkshop.com.
URL www.mountainworkshop.com

Mountain Workshop–Original Awesome Adventures

Mountain Workshop
Connecticut

General Information Coed day outdoor program established in 1980.
Sports Canoeing, rappelling, sea kayaking.
Wilderness/Outdoors Caving, hiking, outdoor adventure.
Trips Day.
Program Information 11 sessions per year. Session length: 5 days in June, July, August. Ages: 10–11. Day program cost: $450.
Application Deadline Continuous.
Jobs Positions for college students 21 and older.
Contact Kent B. Tullo, Director, 9 Brookside Place, West Redding, Connecticut 06896. Phone: 203-544-0555. Fax: 203-544-0333. E-mail: info@mountainworkshop.com.
URL www.mountainworkshop.com

Mountain Workshop–Trailblazer Awesome Adventures

Mountain Workshop
Connecticut

General Information Coed day outdoor program established in 1980.
Program Focus Outdoor adventure programs.
Sports Canoeing, rappelling, water tubing.
Wilderness/Outdoors Climbing, hiking, outdoor adventure, rock climbing.
Trips Day.
Program Information 10 sessions per year. Session length: 5 days in June, July, August. Ages: 8–9. Day program cost: $450.
Application Deadline Continuous.
Jobs Positions for college students 21 and older.
Contact Kent B. Tullo, Director, 9 Brookside Place, West Redding, Connecticut 06896. Phone: 203-544-0555. Fax: 203-544-0333. E-mail: info@mountainworkshop.com.
URL www.mountainworkshop.com

National Computer Camps at Fairfield University

National Computer Camps
Fairfield University
Fairfield, Connecticut

General Information Coed residential and day academic program established in 1977. Formal opportunities for the academically talented.
Program Focus Computer science, programming, Internet, recreation, and sports.
Academics Web page design, computer programming, computer science (Advanced Placement), computers.
Arts Animation, graphic arts.
Special Interest Areas Electronics, robotics.
Sports Basketball, soccer, swimming, tennis, volleyball.
Program Information 4 sessions per year. Session length: 1 week in June, July. Ages: 8–18. 80–125 participants per session. Day program cost: $595. Boarding program cost: $795.
Application Deadline Continuous.
Jobs Positions for high school students 16 and older and college students 18 and older.
Contact Dr. Michael Zabinski, President, PO Box 585, Orange, Connecticut 06477. Phone: 203-795-9667. E-mail: info@nccamp.com.
URL www.nccamp.com

National Guitar Workshop–New Milford, CT

National Guitar Workshop
Canterbury School
Aspetuck Avenue
New Milford, Connecticut 06776

General Information Coed residential and day arts program established in 1984. College credit may be earned.

Program Focus Music education in guitar, bass, keyboards, drums, and vocals.
Academics Music, music (Advanced Placement).
Arts Guitar, music (classical), music (ensemble), music (instrumental), music (jazz), music (rock), music (vocal).
Program Information 1–6 sessions per year. Session length: 1–6 weeks in June, July, August. Ages: 13–79. 75–225 participants per session. Day program cost: $670–$720. Boarding program cost: $870–$920. Application fee: $25. Financial aid available.
Application Deadline Continuous.
Jobs Positions for college students 21 and older.
Contact Ms. Emily Flower, Registrar, PO Box 222, Lakeside, Connecticut 06758. Phone: 860-567-3736 Ext. 109. Fax: 860-567-0374. E-mail: emily@guitarworkshop.com.
URL www.guitarworkshop.com

The Oxford Academy Summer Program

The Oxford Academy
1393 Boston Post Road
Westbrook, Connecticut 06498

General Information Boys' residential academic program established in 1970. Specific services available for the learning disabled.
Program Focus Remedial academics and postgraduate work on a one-to-one basis. Accelerated course work available.
Academics American literature, English as a second language, English language/literature, French language/literature, German language/literature, Latin language, SAT/ACT preparation, Spanish language/literature, academics (general), astronomy, biology, chemistry, classical languages/literatures, ecology, economics, environmental science, geography, geology/earth science, government and politics (Advanced Placement), history, marine studies, mathematics, mathematics (Advanced Placement), physics, physiology, psychology, reading, remedial academics, science (general), social science, social studies, study skills, writing.
Arts Arts and crafts (general), photography.
Sports Basketball, bicycling, boating, cross-country, fishing, golf, kayaking, martial arts, paintball, sailing, soccer, softball, swimming, tennis, volleyball, weight training, wrestling.
Wilderness/Outdoors Hiking, white-water trips.
Trips Cultural, day, shopping.
Program Information 1 session per year. Session length: 5 weeks in June, July. Ages: 14–20. 25–28 participants per session. Boarding program cost: $6175. Application fee: $65–$125.
Application Deadline Continuous.
Jobs Positions for high school students 16 and older.
Contact Mrs. Michele Deane, Director of Admissions, main address above. Phone: 860-399-6247. Fax: 860-399-6805. E-mail: admissions@oxfordacademy.net.
URL www.oxfordacademy.net

Rainbow Club–Greenwich, Connecticut

The Barton Center for Diabetes Education, Inc.
Round Hill Community Center
397 Round Hill Road
Greenwich, Connecticut

General Information Coed day family program and special needs program established in 2002. Accredited by American Camping Association. Specific services available for the diabetic.
Program Focus Program for children and families living with diabetes.
Arts Acting, arts and crafts (general), clowning, drawing, music, musical productions, painting, television/video, theater/drama.
Special Interest Areas Campcraft, culinary arts, diabetic education.
Sports Aerobics, baseball, basketball, football, soccer, softball, street/roller hockey, swimming, tennis, volleyball.
Trips Day.
Program Information 1 session per year. Session length: 5 days in June. Ages: 3–16. 35–40 participants per session. Financial aid available.
Application Deadline Continuous.
Contact Mary Ellen Flaherty, Regional Director, PO Box 356, 30 Ennis Road, North Oxford, Massachusetts 01537. Phone: 508-987-2056. Fax: 508-987-2002. E-mail: maryellen.flaherty@bartoncenter.org.
URL www.bartoncenter.org

Rectory School Summer Session

The Rectory School
528 Pomfret Street
Pomfret, Connecticut 06258

General Information Coed residential and day academic program established in 1950. Formal opportunities for the academically talented and gifted. Specific services available for the learning disabled.
Program Focus English, mathematics, reading, and study skills.
Academics American literature, English as a second language, English language/literature, academics (general), computers, linguistics, mathematics, reading, study skills, writing.
Arts Arts and crafts (general), batiking, creative writing, drawing, fabric arts, graphic arts, jewelry making, radio broadcasting, woodworking.
Sports Baseball, basketball, bicycling, fishing, football, golf, horseback riding, ropes course, soccer, softball, street/roller hockey, swimming, tennis, volleyball, weight training.
Trips Cultural, day.
Program Information 1 session per year. Session length: 5 weeks in June, July. Ages: 9–15. 35–50 participants per session. Day program cost: $3400. Boarding program cost: $6000. Application fee: $50–$100. Residential program for boys only; coed day program.
Application Deadline Continuous.

Rectory School Summer Session (continued)

Contact Mr. Stephen A. DiPaolo, Director of Admissions, PO Box 68, 528 Pomfret Street, Pomfret, Connecticut 06258. Phone: 860-928-1328. Fax: 860-928-4961. E-mail: admissions@rectoryschool.org.
URL www.rectoryschool.org

Special Note
Located in Connecticut's "quiet corner," Rectory School's beautiful 138-acre campus sits atop Pomfret Hill. The 5-week summer session is for both boarding and day students and develops students' reading, mathematics, and study skills. The program includes daily one-on-one tutoring that is individualized for remediation or enrichment. ESL courses are available. The summer session staff is chosen entirely from the full-time faculty at Rectory, which is a Blue Ribbon School. The small classes average 8 students per class and encourage participation. The student-teacher ratio for the summer session is 3:1. The afternoon schedule is that of a traditional summer camp, with arts and crafts, sports, and swimming. Numerous weekend activities include visits to the beach, a theme park, a science museum, an aquarium, and sporting events.

Rumsey Hall School Summer Session

Rumsey Hall School
201 Romford Road
Washington Depot, Connecticut 06794

General Information Coed residential and day academic program established in 1975. Formal opportunities for the academically talented. Specific services available for the learning disabled. High school credit may be earned.
Academics American literature, English as a second language, English language/literature, art (Advanced Placement), classical languages/literatures, computers, mathematics, mathematics (Advanced Placement), study skills, writing.
Sports Basketball, bicycling, canoeing, equestrian sports, fishing, football, golf, horseback riding, lacrosse, soccer, softball, swimming, tennis.
Wilderness/Outdoors Bicycle trips, hiking, mountain biking.
Trips Cultural, day, shopping.
Program Information 1 session per year. Session length: 5 weeks in July, August. Ages: 8–15. 60–70 participants per session. Day program cost: $1500–$3000. Boarding program cost: $4600–$5800. Application fee: $40–$100. Financial aid available.
Application Deadline Continuous.
Contact Matthew S. Hoeniger, main address above. Phone: 860-868-0535. Fax: 860-868-7907. E-mail: admiss@rumseyhall.org.
URL www.rumseyhall.org

For more information, see page 1288.

Rumsey Hall School Summer Session

Saint Thomas More School–Summer Academic Camp

Saint Thomas More School
45 Cottage Road
Oakdale, Connecticut 06370

General Information Boys' residential traditional camp and academic program established in 1970. Religious affiliation: Roman Catholic. Accredited by American Camping Association. Specific services available for the learning disabled. High school credit may be earned.
Academics American literature, English as a second language, English language/literature, Spanish language/literature, academics (general), art history/appreciation, biology, chemistry, computers, government and politics, history, mathematics, physics, reading, religion, science (general), social science, social studies, study skills.
Arts Arts and crafts (general).
Sports Baseball, basketball, boating, canoeing, fishing, football, sailing, soccer, softball, sports (general), swimming, tennis, volleyball, weight training, windsurfing.
Trips Cultural, day, shopping.

Program Information 1 session per year. Session length: 6 weeks in June, July, August. Ages: 12–19. 80–100 participants per session. Boarding program cost: $5495–$5995. Application fee: $50–$75.
Application Deadline Continuous.
Jobs Positions for college students.
Contact Mr. Timothy Riordan, Director of Admissions, main address above. Phone: 860-823-3861. Fax: 860-823-3863. E-mail: stmadmit@stthomasmoreschool.com.
URL www.stthomasmoreschool.com

For more information, see page 1296.

Salisbury Summer School of Reading and English

Salisbury School
251 Canaan Road
Salisbury, Connecticut 06068

General Information Coed residential academic program established in 1946. Formal opportunities for the academically talented. Specific services available for the learning disabled. High school credit may be earned.

Salisbury Summer School of Reading and English

Program Focus Reading, writing, English, mathematics, and study skills.
Academics English as a second language, English language/literature, SAT/ACT preparation, academics (general), mathematics, reading, study skills, writing.
Arts Creative writing, music, theater/drama.
Sports Aerobics, baseball, basketball, bicycling, canoeing, cross-country, golf, lacrosse, soccer, softball, squash, swimming, tennis, weight training, yoga.
Wilderness/Outdoors Bicycle trips, canoe trips, hiking, mountain biking.
Trips Cultural, day, shopping.
Program Information 1 session per year. Session length: 5–6 weeks in June, July, August. Ages: 13–18. 105–110 participants per session. Boarding program cost: $6500–$6800. Application fee: $30. Financial aid available.
Application Deadline Continuous.
Jobs Positions for college students 20 and older.
Contact Director of Admissions, main address above. Phone: 860-435-5700. Fax: 860-435-5750. E-mail: sss@salisburyschool.org.
URL www.salisburysummerschool.org

For more information, see page 1298.

The Sarah Porter Leadership Institute

Miss Porter's School
60 Main Street
Farmington, Connecticut 06032

General Information Girls' residential academic program established in 2003.
Program Focus The knowledge, skills, and resources girls need to develop their leadership potential.
Academics Communications, speech/debate.
Special Interest Areas Leadership training, personal development, team building.
Sports Climbing (wall), martial arts, ropes course, swimming.
Trips Day.
Program Information 1 session per year. Session length: 4–5 days in July. Ages: 12–15. 30–50 participants per session. Boarding program cost: $500–$800. Application fee: $15.
Application Deadline Continuous.
Contact John Barrengos, Director of Leadership and Summer Programs, main address above. Phone: 860-409-3692. Fax: 860-409-3515. E-mail: summer_programs@missporters.org.
URL www.sarahporterinstitute.org

SJ Ranch Riding Camp

SJ Ranch, Inc.
130 Sandy Beach Road
Ellington, Connecticut 06029

General Information Girls' residential traditional camp and sports camp established in 1956. Accredited by American Camping Association.
Program Focus Horseback riding and horse care.
Arts Arts and crafts (general), drawing, fabric arts, jewelry making, music, painting.
Special Interest Areas Animal care, campcraft, leadership training, nature study.
Sports Archery, basketball, boating, canoeing, equestrian sports, horseback riding, softball, swimming, tennis.
Program Information 4 sessions per year. Session length: 6–20 days in June, July, August. Ages: 8–16. 42–48 participants per session. Day program cost: $160. Boarding program cost: $900–$2450.
Application Deadline Continuous.
Jobs Positions for high school students 18 and older and college students 18 and older.
Contact Ms. Julie Morton, Assistant Director, main address above. Phone: 860-872-4742. Fax: 860-870-4914. E-mail: julie@sjridingcamp.com.
URL www.sjridingcamp.com

SoccerPlus FieldPlayer Academy–Kent, CT

SoccerPlus Camps
Marvelwood School
Kent, Connecticut

General Information Coed residential and day sports camp.
Program Focus Developing overall game skills in a competitive environment with quality goalkeepers.
Sports Soccer.
Program Information 1–2 sessions per year. Session length: 6 days in July, August. Ages: 11+. Day program cost: $595. Boarding program cost: $695. Financial aid available.
Application Deadline Continuous.
Jobs Positions for college students.
Contact Mr. Shawn Kelly, General Manager, 11 Executive Drive, Suite 202, Farmington, Connecticut 06032. Phone: 800-533-7371. Fax: 860-677-0460. E-mail: info@soccerpluscamps.com.
URL www.soccerpluscamps.com

SoccerPlus Goalkeeper School–Advanced National Training Center–Connecticut

SoccerPlus Camps
SoccerPlus Headquarters
Farmington, Connecticut

General Information Coed residential sports camp established in 1982.
Program Focus Bringing the best young goalkeepers in the country together to train with the best goalkeeper coaches.
Sports Soccer.
Program Information 1 session per year. Session length: 6 days in June. Ages: 12+. Boarding program cost: $1195. Financial aid available.
Application Deadline Continuous.
Jobs Positions for college students.
Contact Mr. Shawn Kelly, General Manager, 11 Executive Drive, Suite 202, Farmington, Connecticut 06032. Phone: 800-533-7371. Fax: 860-677-0460. E-mail: info@soccerpluscamps.com.
URL www.soccerpluscamps.com

SoccerPlus Goalkeeper School–Challenge Program–Kent, CT

SoccerPlus Camps
Marvelwood School
Kent, Connecticut

General Information Coed residential and day sports camp.
Program Focus Developing technical and tactical goalkeeping skills.
Sports Soccer.
Program Information 12 sessions per year. Session length: 6 days in August. Ages: 10+. Day program cost: $595. Boarding program cost: $695. Financial aid available.
Application Deadline Continuous.
Jobs Positions for college students.
Contact Mr. Shawn Kelly, General Manager, 11 Executive Drive, Suite 202, Farmington, Connecticut 06032. Phone: 800-533-7371. Fax: 860-677-0460. E-mail: info@soccerpluscamps.com.
URL www.soccerpluscamps.com

SoccerPlus Goalkeeper School–Challenge Program–Suffield, CT

SoccerPlus Camps
Suffield, Connecticut

General Information Coed residential and day sports camp.
Program Focus Developing technical and tactical goalkeeping skills.
Sports Soccer.
Program Information 1 session per year. Session length: 6 days in June. Ages: 10+. Day program cost: $595. Boarding program cost: $695. Financial aid available.
Application Deadline Continuous.
Jobs Positions for college students.
Contact Mr. Shawn Kelly, General Manager, 11 Executive Drive, Suite 202, Farmington, Connecticut 06032. Phone: 800-533-7371. Fax: 860-677-0460. E-mail: info@soccerpluscamps.com.
URL www.soccerpluscamps.com

SoccerPlus Goalkeeper School–Competitive Program–Kent, CT

SoccerPlus Camps
Marvelwood School
Kent, Connecticut

General Information Coed residential sports camp.
Program Focus Developing game skills in a competitive environment with quality field players.
Sports Soccer.
Program Information 1–2 sessions per year. Session length: 6 days in July, August. Ages: 12+. Boarding program cost: $755. Financial aid available.
Application Deadline Continuous.
Jobs Positions for college students.
Contact Mr. Shawn Kelly, General Manager, 11 Executive Drive, Suite 202, Farmington, Connecticut 06032. Phone: 800-533-7371. Fax: 860-677-0460. E-mail: info@soccerpluscamps.com.
URL www.soccerpluscamps.com

SoccerPlus Goalkeeper School–Competitive Program–Suffield, CT

SoccerPlus Camps
Suffield, Connecticut

General Information Coed residential sports camp.

Program Focus Developing game skills in a competitive environment with qualified players.
Sports Soccer.
Program Information 1 session per year. Session length: 6 days in June. Ages: 12+. Boarding program cost: $755. Financial aid available.
Application Deadline Continuous.
Jobs Positions for college students.
Contact Mr. Shawn Kelly, General Manager, 11 Executive Drive, Suite 202, Farmington, Connecticut 06032. Phone: 800-533-7371. Fax: 860-677-0460. E-mail: info@soccerpluscamps.com.
URL www.soccerpluscamps.com

SoccerPlus Goalkeeper School–National Training Center–Kent, CT

SoccerPlus Camps
Marvelwood School
Kent, Connecticut

General Information Coed residential sports camp.
Program Focus Developing advanced goalkeeping skills.
Sports Soccer.
Program Information 2 sessions per year. Session length: 6 days in August. Ages: 15+. Boarding program cost: $775. Financial aid available.
Application Deadline Continuous.
Jobs Positions for college students.
Contact Mr. Shawn Kelly, General Manager, 11 Executive Drive, Suite 202, Farmington, Connecticut 06032. Phone: 800-533-7371. Fax: 860-677-0460. E-mail: info@soccerpluscamps.com.
URL www.soccerpluscamps.com

Student Conservation Association–Conservation Crew Program (Connecticut)

Student Conservation Association (SCA)
Connecticut

General Information Coed residential outdoor program, community service program, and wilderness program established in 1957. High school credit may be earned.
Program Focus Resource management, conservation and environmental education.
Academics Biology, botany, ecology, environmental science, geology/earth science, history.
Special Interest Areas Campcraft, community service, construction, leadership training, nature study, trail maintenance, work camp programs.
Sports Canoeing, fishing, kayaking, swimming.
Wilderness/Outdoors Backpacking, canoe trips, hiking, orienteering, outdoor living skills, wilderness camping.
Trips Cultural, day, overnight.
Program Information 2–3 sessions per year. Session length: 3–5 weeks in June, July, August. Ages: 15–19. 6–8 participants per session. Application fee: $20. Financial aid available. No cost for program; financial aid possible for travel expenses.
Application Deadline Continuous.
Jobs Positions for college students 21 and older.
Contact Recruitment Office, PO Box 550, Charlestown, New Hampshire 03603. Phone: 603-543-1700. Fax: 603-543-1828. E-mail: getreal@thesca.org.
URL www.theSCA.org

The Summer Academy at Suffield

Suffield Academy
185 North Main Street
Suffield, Connecticut 06078

General Information Coed residential and day academic program and arts program established in 1995. Formal opportunities for the academically talented and artistically talented. High school credit may be earned.
Program Focus Innovation and creative project-oriented work in the liberal arts.
Academics American literature, English as a second language, English language/literature, French language/literature, SAT/ACT preparation, Spanish language/literature, TOEFL/TOEIC preparation, academics (general), area studies, biology, business, chemistry, computer programming, computer science (Advanced Placement), computers, history, humanities, journalism, mathematics, music, physics, precollege program, reading, religion, science (general), social science, speech/debate, study skills, typing, writing.
Arts Acting, arts, arts and crafts (general), band, ceramics, chorus, creative writing, drawing, graphic arts, music, music (classical), music (instrumental), music (jazz), music (vocal), musical productions, painting, photography, pottery, radio broadcasting, sculpture, theater/drama, woodworking.
Special Interest Areas Leadership training.
Sports Aerobics, basketball, bicycling, climbing (wall), diving, soccer, squash, swimming, tennis, volleyball, water polo, weight training.
Wilderness/Outdoors Bicycle trips, hiking, mountain biking.
Trips College tours, cultural, day, shopping.
Program Information 1 session per year. Session length: 36 days in July, August. Ages: 12–18. 100–125 participants per session. Day program cost: $2600. Boarding program cost: $4700. Application fee: $45. Financial aid available.
Application Deadline Continuous.
Jobs Positions for college students 19 and older.
Contact Mr. Bryson Tillinghast, Director, Summer Academy Admissions, main address above. Phone: 860-386-4475. Fax: 860-386-4476. E-mail: summer@suffieldacademy.org.
URL www.suffieldsummer.org

The Summer Institute for the Gifted at Fairfield University

Summer Institute for the Gifted
Fairfield University
Fairfield, Connecticut 06824

General Information Coed day academic program established in 2003. Formal opportunities for the

The Summer Institute for the Gifted at Fairfield University (continued)

academically talented and gifted. Specific services available for the hearing impaired, learning disabled, physically challenged, and visually impaired.
Academics American literature, English language/literature, French language/literature, Latin language, SAT/ACT preparation, Spanish language/literature, academics (general), architecture, art history/appreciation, biology, business, chemistry, classical languages/literatures, communications, computers, engineering, environmental science, government and politics, history, marine studies, mathematics, music, philosophy, physics, precollege program, psychology, social studies, speech/debate, study skills, writing.
Arts Chorus, creative writing, dance, dance (jazz), dance (modern), drawing, mime, music, music (chamber), music (classical), music (ensemble), musical productions, painting, photography, sculpture, theater/drama.
Special Interest Areas Electronics, robotics.
Sports Basketball, field hockey, football, lacrosse, martial arts, soccer, squash, swimming, tennis, volleyball.
Program Information 1–2 sessions per year. Session length: 3 weeks in June, July, August. Ages: 6–11. 100–150 participants per session. Day program cost: $1550. Application fee: $75. Financial aid available.
Application Deadline May 15.
Jobs Positions for college students 19 and older.
Contact Dr. Stephen Gessner, Director, River Plaza, 9 West Broad Street, Stamford, Connecticut 06902-3788. Phone: 866-303-4744. Fax: 203-399-5598. E-mail: sig.info@aifs.com.
URL www.giftedstudy.com

For more information, see page 1342.

Taft Summer School

The Taft School
110 Woodbury Road
Watertown, Connecticut 06795

General Information Coed residential and day academic program established in 1982. Accredited by American Camping Association. Formal opportunities for the academically talented.
Program Focus Academic enrichment courses.
Academics American literature, English as a second language, English language/literature, French language/literature, SAT/ACT preparation, Spanish language/literature, academics (general), art history/appreciation, biology, chemistry, computers, environmental science, history, journalism, mathematics, physics, psychology, reading, speech/debate, study skills, writing.
Arts Ceramics, creative writing, drawing, painting, photography, television/video, theater/drama.
Sports Aerobics, basketball, lacrosse, soccer, softball, sports (general), squash, tennis, track and field, volleyball, weight training.
Trips Cultural, day, shopping.
Program Information 1 session per year. Session length: 35–40 days in June, July. Ages: 12–18. 150–160

Taft Summer School

participants per session. Day program cost: $2950–$3350. Boarding program cost: $4950–$5500. Application fee: $50. Financial aid available.
Application Deadline Continuous.
Jobs Positions for college students 21 and older.
Summer Contact Stephen J. McCabe, Jr., Director, main address above. Phone: 860-945-7961. Fax: 860-945-7859. E-mail: summerschool@taftschool.org.
Winter Contact Kristina Kulikauskas, Program Office Manager, main address above. Phone: 860-945-7967. Fax: 860-945-7859. E-mail: summerschool@taftschool.org.
URL www.taftschool.org/summer

For more information, see page 1354.

UCAELI Summer Camp

University of Connecticut American English Language Institute
Storrs, Connecticut 06269

General Information Coed residential academic program and cultural program established in 2000.
Academics English as a second language.
Arts Arts and crafts (general).
Special Interest Areas Touring.
Sports Basketball, soccer, swimming.
Trips College tours, cultural, day, shopping.
Program Information 1 session per year. Session length: 20 days in July, August. Ages: 13–18. 12–30 participants per session. Boarding program cost: $2900–$3200.
Application Deadline June 15.
Jobs Positions for high school students 16 and older and college students 21 and older.

Contact Ms. Kristi Newgarden, Director, main address above. Phone: 860-486-2127. Fax: 860-486-3834. E-mail: kristi.newgarden@uconn.edu.
URL www.ucaeli.uconn.edu

United Soccer Academy–Goal Keeping Training Camp, Connecticut

United Soccer Academy, Inc.
Connecticut

General Information Coed residential and day sports camp established in 1999.
Program Focus All aspects of the keeper position are covered: from techniques to tactical decision-making. Coaches are from international teams and colleges.
Sports Soccer.
Program Information 6 sessions per year. Session length: 5 days in April, June, July, August, September, November. Ages: 8–14. 16–200 participants per session. Day program cost: $145. Boarding program cost: $495. Call for specific locations.
Application Deadline Continuous.
Jobs Positions for college students 18 and older.
Contact Camps Information, 50 Tannery Road, Unit 8, Branchburg, New Jersey 08876. Phone: 908-823-0130. Fax: 908-823-0466. E-mail: info@unitedsocceracademy.com.
URL www.unitedsocceracademy.com

United Soccer Academy–Junior Soccer Squirts, Connecticut

United Soccer Academy, Inc.
Connecticut

General Information Coed day sports camp established in 1999.
Program Focus Introduction to soccer in a camp format with emphasis on fun games and activities in small groups. Coaches are from international soccer teams and college teams.
Sports Soccer.
Program Information 10 sessions per year. Session length: 5 days in April, June, July, August, September, November. Ages: 3–5. 6–48 participants per session. Day program cost: $89. Two sessions daily; parents may stay with camper. Call for specific locations.
Application Deadline Continuous.
Jobs Positions for college students 18 and older.
Contact Camps Information, 50 Tannery Road, Unit 8, Branchburg, New Jersey 08876. Phone: 908-823-0130. Fax: 908-823-0466. E-mail: info@unitedsocceracademy.com.
URL www.unitedsocceracademy.com

United Soccer Academy–Recreation Soccer Community Camp, Connecticut

United Soccer Academy, Inc.
Connecticut

General Information Coed residential and day sports camp established in 1999.
Program Focus Players build on the fundamentals of the game, experiencing a broad range of techniques and skills. Coaches are from international teams and colleges.
Sports Soccer.
Program Information 10 sessions per year. Session length: 5 days in April, June, July, August, September, November. Ages: 7–14. 16–200 participants per session. Day program cost: $145. Boarding program cost: $495. Call for specific locations.
Application Deadline Continuous.
Jobs Positions for college students 18 and older.
Contact Camps Information, 50 Tannery Road, Unit 8, Branchburg, New Jersey 08876. Phone: 908-823-0130. Fax: 908-823-0466. E-mail: info@unitedsocceracademy.com.
URL www.unitedsocceracademy.com

United Soccer Academy–Senior Soccer Squirts, Connecticut

United Soccer Academy, Inc.
Connecticut

General Information Coed day sports camp established in 1999.
Program Focus Introduction to the game in relaxed, fun atmosphere; skills development without competitive environment. Coaches are from international teams and colleges.
Sports Soccer.
Program Information 10 sessions per year. Session length: 5 days in April, June, July, August, September, November. Ages: 5–7. 6–48 participants per session. Day program cost: $89. Two sessions daily; call for specific locations.
Application Deadline Continuous.
Jobs Positions for college students 18 and older.
Contact Camps Information, 50 Tannery Road, Unit 8, Branchburg, New Jersey 08876. Phone: 908-823-0130. Fax: 908-823-0466. E-mail: info@unitedsocceracademy.com.
URL www.unitedsocceracademy.com

United Soccer Academy–Team Training Camp, Connecticut

United Soccer Academy, Inc.
Connecticut

General Information Coed residential and day sports camp established in 1999.
Program Focus Teams of ten or more players receive individualized instruction based on staff discussion with their coach. Structured coaching scrimmages with other teams. Coaches on staff are from international teams and colleges.
Sports Soccer.
Program Information 6 sessions per year. Session length: 5 days in April, June, July, August, September, November. Ages: 8–14. 20–200 participants per session. Day program cost: $125. Boarding program cost: $495. Call for specific locations.
Application Deadline Continuous.

United Soccer Academy–Team Training Camp, Connecticut (continued)

Jobs Positions for college students 18 and older.
Contact Camps Information, 50 Tannery Road, Unit 8, Branchburg, New Jersey 08876. Phone: 908-823-0130. Fax: 908-823-0466. E-mail: info@unitedsocceracademy.com.
URL www.unitedsocceracademy.com

United Soccer Academy–Travel Soccer Community Camp, Connecticut

United Soccer Academy, Inc.
Connecticut

General Information Coed residential and day sports camp established in 1999.
Program Focus Individual player development and team tactics are emphasized. Skills are taught at an accelerated level with practices developing into full game realistic situations. Coaches are from international teams and colleges.
Sports Soccer.
Program Information 10 sessions per year. Session length: 5 days in April, June, July, August, September, November. Ages: 8–14. 16–200 participants per session. Day program cost: $145. Boarding program cost: $495. Call for specific locations.
Application Deadline Continuous.
Jobs Positions for college students 18 and older.
Contact Camps Information, 50 Tannery Road, Unit 8, Branchburg, New Jersey 08876. Phone: 908-823-0130. Fax: 908-823-0466. E-mail: info@unitedsocceracademy.com.
URL www.unitedsocceracademy.com

University of Connecticut Community School of the Arts–Music Camps

University of Connecticut College of Continuing Studies–Community School of the Arts
3 Witryol Place, Unit 5195
Storrs, Connecticut 06269-5195

General Information Coed day arts program established in 2002.
Program Focus Instrumental and musical theater, flute, strings, band, jazz, Broadway.
Arts Acting, band, music, music (chamber), music (classical), music (ensemble), music (instrumental), music (jazz), music (vocal), musical performance/recitals, musical productions, piano, theater/drama.
Program Information 6 sessions per year. Session length: 5 days in July. Ages: 9–18. 10–16 participants per session. Day program cost: $150–$275. Application fee: $10.
Application Deadline Continuous.
Contact Community School of the Arts, main address above. Phone: 860-486-1073. Fax: 860-486-4981. E-mail: csa@uconn.edu.
URL www.continuingstudies.uconn.edu/csa

University of Connecticut Community School of the Arts–World Arts Camps

University of Connecticut College of Continuing Studies–Community School of the Arts
3 Witryol Place, Unit 5195
Storrs, Connecticut 06269-5195

General Information Coed day arts program established in 2002.
Program Focus Arts explorers.
Arts Animation, arts and crafts (general), drawing, fabric arts, mask making, painting, pottery, printmaking, puppetry, sculpture.
Special Interest Areas Culinary arts, gardening.
Program Information 6 sessions per year. Session length: 5 days in June, July. Ages: 6–13. 15 participants per session. Day program cost: $150–$270. Application fee: $10.
Application Deadline Continuous.
Contact Community School of the Arts, main address above. Phone: 860-486-1073. Fax: 860-486-4981. E-mail: csa@uconn.edu.
URL www.continuingstudies.uconn.edu/csa

University of Connecticut Mentor Connection

University of Connecticut
2131 Hillside Road, Unit 3007
Storrs, Connecticut 06269-3007

General Information Coed residential academic program established in 1996. Formal opportunities for the academically talented and artistically talented. College credit may be earned.

University of Connecticut Mentor Connection

Program Focus Students work with a university mentor in field of mutual interest.
Academics American literature, English as a second language, English language/literature, French language/literature, academics (general), anthropology, archaeology, art history/appreciation, astronomy, biology, botany, chemistry, communications, computer programming,

ecology, economics, engineering, environmental science, geology/earth science, history, humanities, independent study, mathematics, music, physics, physiology, psychology, science (general), social science, women's studies, writing.
Arts Arts, creative writing, music, photography, puppetry.
Special Interest Areas Career exploration, field research/expeditions, robotics.
Trips Cultural, day.
Program Information 1 session per year. Session length: 3 weeks in July. Ages: 15–18. 75–80 participants per session. Boarding program cost: $3000. Financial aid available. Open to participants entering grades 11–12.
Application Deadline May 1.
Jobs Positions for college students 21 and older.
Contact Heather Spottiswoode, Program Coordinator, main address above. Phone: 860-486-0283. Fax: 860-486-2900. E-mail: heather.spottiswoode@uconn.edu.
URL www.gifted.uconn.edu/

For more information, see page 1362.

DELAWARE

Student Conservation Association–Conservation Crew Program (Delaware)

Student Conservation Association (SCA)
Delaware

General Information Coed residential outdoor program, community service program, and wilderness program established in 1957. High school credit may be earned.
Program Focus Resource management, conservation and environmental education.
Academics Biology, botany, ecology, environmental science, geology/earth science, history.
Special Interest Areas Campcraft, community service, construction, leadership training, nature study, trail maintenance, work camp programs.
Sports Canoeing, fishing, kayaking, swimming.
Wilderness/Outdoors Backpacking, canoe trips, hiking, orienteering, outdoor living skills, wilderness camping.
Trips Cultural, day, overnight.
Program Information 2–3 sessions per year. Session length: 3–5 weeks in June, July, August. Ages: 15–19. 6–8 participants per session. Application fee: $20. Financial aid available. No cost for program; financial aid possible for travel expenses.
Application Deadline Continuous.
Jobs Positions for college students 21 and older.
Contact Recruitment Office, PO Box 550, Charlestown, New Hampshire 03603. Phone: 603-543-1700. Fax: 603-543-1828. E-mail: getreal@thesca.org.
URL www.theSCA.org

United Soccer Academy–Goal Keeping Training Camp, Delaware

United Soccer Academy, Inc.
Delaware

General Information Coed residential and day sports camp established in 1999.
Program Focus All aspects of the keeper position are covered: from techniques to tactical decision-making. Coaches are from international teams and colleges.
Sports Soccer.
Program Information 6 sessions per year. Session length: 5 days in April, June, July, August, September, November. Ages: 8–14. 16–200 participants per session. Day program cost: $145. Boarding program cost: $495. Call for specific locations.
Application Deadline Continuous.
Jobs Positions for college students 18 and older.
Contact Camps Information, 50 Tannery Road, Unit 8, Branchburg, New Jersey 08876. Phone: 908-823-0130. Fax: 908-823-0466. E-mail: info@unitedsocceracademy.com.
URL www.unitedsocceracademy.com

United Soccer Academy–Junior Soccer Squirts, Delaware

United Soccer Academy, Inc.
Delaware

General Information Coed day sports camp established in 1999.
Program Focus Introduction to soccer in a camp format with emphasis on fun games and activities in small groups. Coaches are from international soccer teams and college teams.
Sports Soccer.
Program Information 10 sessions per year. Session length: 5 days in April, June, July, August, September, November. Ages: 3–5. 6–48 participants per session. Day program cost: $89. Two sessions daily; parents may stay with camper. Call for specific locations.
Application Deadline Continuous.
Jobs Positions for college students 18 and older.
Contact Camps Information, 50 Tannery Road, Unit 8, Branchburg, New Jersey 08876. Phone: 908-823-0130. Fax: 908-823-0466. E-mail: info@unitedsocceracademy.com.
URL www.unitedsocceracademy.com

United Soccer Academy–Recreation Soccer Community Camp, Delaware

United Soccer Academy, Inc.
Delaware

General Information Coed residential and day sports camp established in 1999.
Program Focus Players build on the fundamentals of the game, experiencing a broad range of techniques and skills. Coaches are from international teams and colleges.
Sports Soccer.

United Soccer Academy–Recreation Soccer Community Camp, Delaware (continued)

Program Information 10 sessions per year. Session length: 5 days in April, June, July, August, September, November. Ages: 7–14. 16–200 participants per session. Day program cost: $145. Boarding program cost: $495. Call for specific locations.
Application Deadline Continuous.
Jobs Positions for college students 18 and older.
Contact Camps Information, 50 Tannery Road, Unit 8, Branchburg, New Jersey 08876. Phone: 908-823-0130. Fax: 908-823-0466. E-mail: info@unitedsocceracademy.com.
URL www.unitedsocceracademy.com

United Soccer Academy–Senior Soccer Squirts, Delaware

United Soccer Academy, Inc.
Delaware

General Information Coed day sports camp established in 1999.
Program Focus Introduction to the game in relaxed, fun atmosphere; skills development without competitive environment. Coaches are from international teams and colleges.
Sports Soccer.
Program Information 10 sessions per year. Session length: 5 days in April, June, July, August, September, November. Ages: 5–7. 6–48 participants per session. Day program cost: $89. Two sessions daily; call for specific locations.
Application Deadline Continuous.
Jobs Positions for college students 18 and older.
Contact Camps Information, 50 Tannery Road, Unit 8, Branchburg, New Jersey 08876. Phone: 908-823-0130. Fax: 908-823-0466. E-mail: info@unitedsocceracademy.com.
URL www.unitedsocceracademy.com

United Soccer Academy–Team Training Camp, Delaware

United Soccer Academy, Inc.
Delaware

General Information Coed residential and day sports camp established in 1999.
Program Focus Teams of ten or more players receive individualized instruction based on staff discussion with their coach. Structured coaching scrimmages with other teams. Coaches on staff are from international teams and colleges.
Sports Soccer.
Program Information 6 sessions per year. Session length: 5 days in April, June, July, August, September, November. Ages: 8–14. 20–200 participants per session. Day program cost: $125. Boarding program cost: $495. Call for specific locations.
Application Deadline Continuous.
Jobs Positions for college students 18 and older.
Contact Camps Information, 50 Tannery Road, Unit 8, Branchburg, New Jersey 08876. Phone: 908-823-0130. Fax: 908-823-0466. E-mail: info@unitedsocceracademy.com.
URL www.unitedsocceracademy.com

United Soccer Academy–Travel Soccer Community Camp, Delaware

United Soccer Academy, Inc.
Delaware

General Information Coed residential and day sports camp established in 1999.
Program Focus Individual player development and team tactics are emphasized. Skills are taught at an accelerated level with practices developing into full game realistic situations. Coaches are from international teams and colleges.
Sports Soccer.
Program Information 10 sessions per year. Session length: 5 days in April, June, July, August, September, November. Ages: 8–14. 16–200 participants per session. Day program cost: $145. Boarding program cost: $495. Call for specific locations.
Application Deadline Continuous.
Jobs Positions for college students 18 and older.
Contact Camps Information, 50 Tannery Road, Unit 8, Branchburg, New Jersey 08876. Phone: 908-823-0130. Fax: 908-823-0466. E-mail: info@unitedsocceracademy.com.
URL www.unitedsocceracademy.com

University of Delaware Summer College

University of Delaware
207 Elliott Hall
Newark, Delaware 19716-1256

General Information Coed residential academic program established in 1983. Formal opportunities for the academically talented and gifted. College credit may be earned.
Program Focus College credit for high school students.
Academics English language/literature, academics (general), biology, chemistry, communications, government and politics, history, mathematics, music, philosophy, precollege program, psychology, religion, writing.
Sports Basketball, bicycling, climbing (wall), racquetball, soccer, softball, squash, street/roller hockey, swimming, tennis, volleyball.
Trips Cultural, day.
Program Information 1 session per year. Session length: 5 weeks in June, July. Ages: 16–18. 120–150 participants per session. Boarding program cost: $1795–$3995. Application fee: $35. Financial aid available.
Application Deadline May 15.
Contact Mr. F. Charles Shermeyer, Coordinator, main address above. Phone: 302-831-6560. Fax: 302-831-4339. E-mail: summercollege@udel.edu.
URL www.udel.edu/summercollege/

Special Note
Students earn 6 or 7 University of Delaware (UD) credits in a program that helps academically advanced students ease their transition from high school to college. Freshman-level courses, open only to Summer College participants and taught by UD faculty members, allow students to experience college with their peers. Class enrollment is limited, providing the excitement and challenge of college-level study with an excellent teacher-student ratio. Structured social activities include weekend day trips to nearby metropolitan areas and the Delaware beach. Supervised dorm life helps students develop independence and time-management skills in a supportive environment.

DISTRICT OF COLUMBIA

CATHOLIC UNIVERSITY BENJAMIN T. ROME SCHOOL OF MUSIC

The Catholic University of America
Office of Summer Sessions
620 Michigan Avenue, NE
Washington, District of Columbia 20064

General Information Coed residential and day arts program. Religious affiliation: Roman Catholic. Formal opportunities for the artistically talented. College credit may be earned.
Program Focus Workshops in opera and percussion.
Academics Music, music (Advanced Placement).
Arts Music, music (classical), music (ensemble), music (instrumental), music (orchestral), music (vocal).
Sports Aerobics, racquetball, squash, swimming, tennis, track and field.
Program Information 1 session per year. Session length: 5–15 days in June, July. Ages: 11–18. Day program cost: $250. Financial aid available.
Application Deadline Continuous.
Jobs Positions for college students.
Contact Jessica Madrigal, Director of Summer Sessions, 330 Pangborn Hall, 620 Michigan Avenue, NE, Washington, District of Columbia 20064. Phone: 202-319-5257. Fax: 202-319-6725. E-mail: cua-summers@cua.edu.
URL summer.cua.edu

CATHOLIC UNIVERSITY CAPITOL CLASSIC DEBATE INSTITUTE

The Catholic University of America
Office of Summer Sessions
620 Michigan Avenue, NE
Washington, District of Columbia 20064

General Information Coed residential and day academic program established in 2000. Religious affiliation: Roman Catholic. Formal opportunities for the academically talented.
Program Focus Debate.
Academics Speech/debate.
Sports Aerobics, basketball, racquetball, squash, swimming, tennis, track and field, weight training.
Program Information 1–2 sessions per year. Session length: 3 weeks in June, July. Ages: 14–18. 50–100 participants per session. Boarding program cost: $2795–$3700. Financial aid available.
Application Deadline May 15.
Jobs Positions for college students.
Contact Jessica Madrigal, Director of Summer Sessions, 330 Pangborn Hall, 620 Michigan Avenue, NE, Washington, District of Columbia 20064. Phone: 202-319-5257. Fax: 202-319-6725. E-mail: cua-summers@cua.edu.
URL summer.cua.edu

CATHOLIC UNIVERSITY COLLEGE COURSES FOR HIGH SCHOOL STUDENTS

The Catholic University of America
Office of Summer Sessions
620 Michigan Avenue, NE
Washington, District of Columbia 20064

General Information Coed residential and day academic program. Religious affiliation: Roman Catholic. Formal opportunities for the academically talented. College credit may be earned.
Academics American literature, Bible study, English as a second language, English language/literature, French (Advanced Placement), French language/literature, German language/literature, Greek language/literature, Italian language/literature, Latin language, Spanish (Advanced Placement), Spanish language/literature, academics (general), anthropology, archaeology, architecture, art (Advanced Placement), art history/appreciation, biology, biology (Advanced Placement), business, chemistry, classical languages/literatures, communications, computer programming, computers, ecology, economics, engineering, government and politics, government and politics (Advanced Placement), history, humanities, linguistics, mathematics, music, philosophy, physics, physiology, precollege program, psychology, religion, science (general), social science, social studies, writing.
Arts Ceramics, drawing, music (chamber), music (classical), music (instrumental), music (jazz), music (orchestral), music (vocal), painting, photography, television/video, theater/drama.
Special Interest Areas Robotics.
Sports Aerobics, basketball, racquetball, squash, swimming, tennis, track and field, weight training.

Catholic University College Courses for High School Students (continued)

Program Information 3 sessions per year. Session length: 5–6 weeks in May, June, July. Ages: 15+. 900–1,100 participants per session. Application fee: $20. Cost: $604 per credit.
Application Deadline Continuous.
Jobs Positions for college students.
Contact Jessica Madrigal, Director of Summer Sessions, 330 Pangborn Hall, 620 Michigan Avenue, NE, Washington, District of Columbia 20064. Phone: 202-319-5257. Fax: 202-319-6725. E-mail: cua-summers@cua.edu.
URL summer.cua.edu

Catholic University Communication and Media Studies Workshops

The Catholic University of America
Office of Summer Sessions
620 Michigan Avenue, NE
Washington, District of Columbia 20064

General Information Coed residential and day academic program and arts program established in 2000. Religious affiliation: Roman Catholic. Formal opportunities for the academically talented and artistically talented.
Program Focus Video and new media production.
Academics Communications, computers.
Arts Film, film production, graphic arts, photography, television/video.
Sports Aerobics, basketball, racquetball, squash, swimming, tennis, track and field, weight training.
Trips Day.
Program Information 1 session per year. Session length: 11 days in July. Ages: 14–18. 15–25 participants per session. Day program cost: $500.
Application Deadline Continuous.
Jobs Positions for college students.
Contact Jessica Madrigal, Director of Summer Sessions, 330 Pangborn Hall, 620 Michigan Avenue, NE, Washington, District of Columbia 20064. Phone: 202-319-5257. Fax: 202-319-6725. E-mail: cua-summers@cua.edu.
URL summer.cua.edu

Catholic University Experiences in Architecture

The Catholic University of America
Office of Summer Sessions
620 Michigan Avenue, NE
Washington, District of Columbia 20064

General Information Coed residential and day academic program. Religious affiliation: Roman Catholic. Formal opportunities for the academically talented.
Program Focus Architecture.
Academics Architecture.
Sports Aerobics, basketball, racquetball, squash, swimming, tennis, track and field, weight training.
Trips Day.
Program Information 2 sessions per year. Session length: 3 weeks in June, July. Ages: 15–18. Boarding program cost: $1200–$2200. Financial aid available.
Application Deadline Continuous.
Jobs Positions for college students.
Contact Jessica Madrigal, Director of Summer Sessions, 330 Pangborn Hall, 620 Michigan Avenue, NE, Washington, District of Columbia 20064. Phone: 202-319-5257. E-mail: cua-summers@cua.edu.
URL summer.cua.edu

Catholic University Eye on Engineering

The Catholic University of America
Office of Summer Sessions
620 Michigan Avenue, NE
Washington, District of Columbia 20064

General Information Coed residential academic program. Religious affiliation: Roman Catholic. Formal opportunities for the academically talented.
Program Focus Engineering.
Academics Engineering.
Special Interest Areas Electronics, robotics.
Sports Aerobics, basketball, racquetball, squash, swimming, tennis, track and field, volleyball, weight training.
Trips Day.
Program Information 1 session per year. Session length: 1 week in June. Ages: 17–18. Boarding program cost: $395.
Application Deadline May 31.
Jobs Positions for college students.
Contact Emma Cox, School of Engineering, 102 Pangborn Hall, Washington, District of Columbia 20064. Phone: 202-319-5160. E-mail: coxe@cua.edu.
URL summer.cua.edu

Catholic University of America–Capitol Mock Trial Institute

The Catholic University of America
Office of Summer Sessions
620 Michigan Avenue, NE
Washington, District of Columbia 20064

General Information Coed residential and day academic program established in 2004. Religious affiliation: Roman Catholic. Formal opportunities for the academically talented.
Program Focus Debate.
Academics Academics (general), communications, humanities, speech/debate.
Trips Cultural, day, shopping.
Program Information 1 session per year. Session length: 1 week in June, July. Ages: 14–18. 15–30 participants per session. Day program cost: $3700. Application fee: $100. Financial aid available.
Application Deadline May 7.
Contact Ron Bratt, Director of Debate, 112 Marist Hall, Catholic University of America, 620 Michigan Avenue, NE, Washington, District of Columbia 20064. Phone: 202-319-5447. E-mail: bratt@cua.edu.
URL summer.cua.edu

Catholic University of America–The Capitol Hill Lincoln-Douglas Debate Group

The Catholic University of America
Office of Summer Sessions
620 Michigan Avenue, NE
Washington, District of Columbia 20064

General Information Coed residential and day academic program established in 2003. Religious affiliation: Roman Catholic. Formal opportunities for the academically talented.
Program Focus Debate.
Academics Academics (general), speech/debate.
Sports Aerobics, swimming, tennis, track and field, weight training.
Trips Cultural, day.
Program Information 1 session per year. Session length: 2 weeks in June, July. Ages: 14–18. 60 participants per session. Day program cost: $1970. Financial aid available.
Application Deadline May 15.
Contact Ronald Bratt, Director of Debate, 112 Marist Hall, Catholic University of America, 620 Michigan Avenue, NE, Washington, District of Columbia 20064. Phone: 202-319-5447. E-mail: bratt@cua.edu.
URL summer.cua.edu

The Congressional Seminar

Washington Workshops Foundation
125 Michigan Avenue, NE
Washington, District of Columbia 20017

General Information Coed residential academic program established in 1967. Formal opportunities for the academically talented.
Program Focus American government and politics.
Academics Government and politics, history, social studies.
Trips College tours, cultural.
Program Information 2–3 sessions per year. Session length: 6 days in June, July. Ages: 15–18. 125 participants per session. Boarding program cost: $1095. Application fee: $95.
Application Deadline Continuous.
Jobs Positions for college students 20 and older.
Contact Aaron Corbett, Director, 3222 N Street NW, Suite 340, Washington, District of Columbia 20007. Phone: 800-368-5688. Fax: 202-965-1018. E-mail: info@workshops.org.
URL www.workshops.org

Corcoran College of Art and Design–Camp Creativity

Corcoran College of Art and Design
1801 35th Street, NW
Washington, District of Columbia 20007

General Information Coed day arts program. Formal opportunities for the artistically talented.
Program Focus Hands-on art and fun.
Academics Aerospace science, anthropology, archaeology, architecture, area studies, art history/appreciation, biology, botany, computers, ecology, history, intercultural studies.
Arts Arts, arts and crafts (general), cartooning, digital media, drawing, fabric arts, graphic arts, illustration, jewelry making, leather working, mask making, mixed media, music (instrumental), painting, photography, puppetry, sculpture, storytelling.
Special Interest Areas Native American culture, computer graphics, nature study.
Program Information 1–8 sessions per year. Session length: 4–5 days in June, July, August. Ages: 6–15. 50–60 participants per session. Day program cost: $348–$582.
Application Deadline Continuous.
Jobs Positions for college students 18 and older.
Contact Director of Continuing Education, 500 17th Street, NW, Washington, District of Columbia 20007. Phone: 202-298-2542. Fax: 202-298-2543.
URL www.corcoran.edu/ce/camp_creativity.asp

Corcoran College of Art and Design–Focus on Photojournalism

Corcoran College of Art and Design
1801 35th Street, NW
Washington, District of Columbia 20007

General Information Coed residential and day arts program. Formal opportunities for the artistically talented.
Program Focus Photojournalism with the White House Press Corps.
Academics Area studies, art (Advanced Placement), computers, government and politics, journalism.
Arts Digital media, photography.
Special Interest Areas Career exploration, field trips (arts and culture).
Trips College tours, cultural.
Program Information 7 sessions per year. Session length: 1 week in July, August. Ages: 16+. 50–60 participants per session. Day program cost: $800. Boarding program cost: $1250.
Application Deadline Continuous.
Jobs Positions for college students 18 and older.
Contact Director of Continuing Education, 500 17th Street, NW, Washington, District of Columbia 20007. Phone: 202-298-2542. Fax: 202-298-2543.
URL www.corcoran.edu/ce/focus.asp

Corcoran College of Art and Design–Pre-College Summer Portfolio Workshop

Corcoran College of Art and Design
1801 35th Street, NW
Washington, District of Columbia 20007

General Information Coed residential and day arts program. Formal opportunities for the artistically talented.
Program Focus Fine arts portfolio development.
Academics Art (Advanced Placement).

Corcoran College of Art and Design–Pre-College Summer Portfolio Workshop (continued)

Arts Arts and crafts (general), digital media, drawing, graphic arts, painting, photography, sculpture, studio arts.
Special Interest Areas College planning.
Trips College tours, cultural.
Program Information 1–2 sessions per year. Session length: 10–14 days in July, August. Ages: 16+. 50–60 participants per session. Day program cost: $1200. Boarding program cost: $2200.
Application Deadline Continuous.
Jobs Positions for college students 18 and older.
Contact Director of Continuing Education, 500 17th Street, NW, Washington, District of Columbia 20007. Phone: 202-298-2542. Fax: 202-298-2543.
URL www.corcoran.edu/ce/pre-college.asp

CYBERCAMPS–AMERICAN UNIVERSITY

Cybercamps–Giant Campus, Inc.
Washington, District of Columbia

General Information Coed residential and day academic program.
Academics Web page design, academics (general), computer programming, computers.
Arts Animation, creative writing, digital media, graphic arts, photography.
Special Interest Areas Computer game design, computer graphics, robotics, team building.
Sports Ultimate frisbee.
Program Information 2–9 sessions per year. Session length: 5–30 days in June, July, August. Ages: 7–18. 30–150 participants per session. Day program cost: $599–$849. Boarding program cost: $974–$1224. Financial aid available.
Application Deadline Continuous.
Jobs Positions for high school students 15 and older and college students.
Contact Cybercamps Information Office, 2401 4th Avenue, Suite 1110, Seattle, Washington 98121. Phone: 206-442-4500. Fax: 206-442-4500. E-mail: info@cybercamps.com.
URL www.cybercamps.com

DIPLOMACY AND GLOBAL AFFAIRS SEMINAR

Washington Workshops Foundation
125 Michigan Avenue, NE
Washington, District of Columbia 20017

General Information Coed residential academic program established in 1986. Formal opportunities for the academically talented.
Program Focus International politics and world affairs.
Academics Global issues, government and politics, history, international relations, social studies.
Trips College tours, cultural.
Program Information 2 sessions per year. Session length: 1 week in June, July. Ages: 15–19. 125 participants per session. Boarding program cost: $1095. Application fee: $95.
Application Deadline Continuous.
Jobs Positions for college students 20 and older.
Contact Aaron Corbett, Director, 3222 N Street NW, Suite 340, Washington, District of Columbia 20007. Phone: 800-368-5688. Fax: 202-965-1018. E-mail: info@workshops.org.
URL www.workshops.org

GEORGETOWN UNIVERSITY COLLEGE PREP PROGRAM

Georgetown University
1437 37th Street, NW
Washington, District of Columbia 20057-1010

General Information Coed residential and day academic program.

Georgetown University College Prep Program

Program Focus Math, English, and research/study skills.
Academics English language/literature, mathematics, study skills.
Trips Cultural.
Program Information 1 session per year. Session length: 5 weeks in June, July. Ages: 15–18. 55–70 participants per session. Day program cost: $2600–$2800. Boarding program cost: $4325–$4800. Application fee: $35. Financial aid available.
Application Deadline April 26.
Contact Ms. Emma Harrington, Special Programs Director, School for Summer and Continuing Education,

PO Box 571010, Washington, District of Columbia 20057-1010. Phone: 202-687-5719. Fax: 202-687-8954. E-mail: harringe@georgetown.edu.
URL www.georgetown.edu/ssce/spp/hscp.htm
For more information, see page 1132.

Georgetown University International Relations Program for High School Students

Georgetown University
1437 37th Street, NW
Washington, District of Columbia 20057-1010

General Information Coed residential and day academic program. Formal opportunities for the academically talented.
Program Focus International relations.
Academics Academics (general), government and politics, international relations.
Program Information 1 session per year. Session length: 8 days in July. Ages: 15–18. 125–150 participants per session. Day program cost: $850. Boarding program cost: $1255. Application fee: $15.
Application Deadline April 19.
Contact Ms. Emma Harrington, Special Programs Director, School for Summer and Continuing Education, PO Box 571010, Washington, District of Columbia 20057-1010. Phone: 202-687-5719. Fax: 202-687-8954. E-mail: harringe@georgetown.edu.
URL www.georgetown.edu/ssce/spp/hsir.htm
For more information, see page 1132.

Georgetown University Summer College for High School Juniors

Georgetown University
1437 37th Street, NW
Washington, District of Columbia 20057-1010

General Information Coed residential academic program. Formal opportunities for the academically talented. College credit may be earned.
Academics American literature, English language/literature, French language/literature, German language/literature, Italian language/literature, Spanish language/literature, academics (general), art, art history/appreciation, biology, business, chemistry, computers, economics, government and politics, history, mathematics, music, philosophy, physics, psychology.
Trips Cultural.
Program Information 2 sessions per year. Session length: 5 weeks in June, July, August. Ages: 16–18. 45–95 participants per session. Boarding program cost: $4255–$6700. Application fee: $35. Financial aid available.
Application Deadline April 13.
Contact Ms. Emma Harrington, Special Programs Director, School for Summer and Continuing Education, PO Box 571010, Washington, District of Columbia 20057-1010. Phone: 202-687-5719. Fax: 202-687-8954. E-mail: harringe@georgetown.edu.
URL www.georgetown.edu/ssce/spp/hsj.htm
For more information, see page 1132.

George Washington University Summer Scholars Pre-college Program

George Washington University
2100 Foxhall Road, Mount Vernon Campus
Washington, District of Columbia 20007

General Information Coed residential academic program. College credit may be earned.

George Washington University Summer Scholars Pre-college Program

Program Focus Pre-college/college-prep program.
Academics American literature, English language/literature, French language/literature, Spanish language/literature, academics (general), area studies, art (Advanced Placement), art history/appreciation, biology, economics, government and politics, humanities, mathematics, music, psychology, religion, study skills, writing.
Arts Dance, music, theater/drama.
Sports Basketball, bicycling, ropes course, swimming, tennis, volleyball.

George Washington University Summer Scholars Pre-college Program (continued)
Wilderness/Outdoors Bicycle trips, hiking, rafting, white-water trips.
Trips College tours, cultural, day, shopping.
Program Information 1 session per year. Session length: 43 days in July, August. 35–60 participants per session. Boarding program cost: $5650–$5700. Application fee: $25. Financial aid available. Open to participants entering grade 12.
Application Deadline Continuous.
Jobs Positions for college students.
Contact Ms. Margaret Myers, Program Assistant, main address above. Phone: 202-242-6802. E-mail: memyers@gwu.edu.
URL www.gwu.edu/summer/scholars
For more information, see page 1134.

iD Tech Camps–Georgetown University, Washington, DC

iD Tech Camps
Georgetown University
Washington, District of Columbia 20057

General Information Coed residential and day academic program established in 1999. Accredited by American Camping Association. Formal opportunities for the academically talented and artistically talented.
Program Focus High-tech computer camps for kids and teens; produce digital movies, create video games, design Web pages, learn programming and robotics, and more; one computer per student, small classes, campers complete a project in a creative and fun learning environment.
Academics Web page design, computer programming, computer science (Advanced Placement), computers, music, precollege program.
Arts Animation, cartooning, cinematography, digital media, drawing, film, film editing, film production, graphic arts, music, television/video.
Special Interest Areas Career exploration, computer graphics, electronics, leadership training, robotics, team building.
Sports Baseball, basketball, soccer, softball, swimming, volleyball.
Trips College tours, cultural, day.
Program Information 5 sessions per year. Session length: 5–7 days in June, July, August. Ages: 7–17. 40–50 participants per session. Day program cost: $639. Boarding program cost: $989. Application fee: $200. Financial aid available.
Application Deadline Continuous.
Jobs Positions for college students 18 and older.
Contact Client Service Representatives, 1885 Winchester Boulevard, Suite 201, Campbell, California 95008. Phone: 888-709-TECH. Fax: 408-871-2228. E-mail: requests@internaldrive.com.
URL www.internaldrive.com
For more information, see page 1156.

Junior Statesmen Summer School–Georgetown University

Junior Statesmen Foundation
Georgetown University
Washington, District of Columbia 20057

General Information Coed residential academic program established in 1981. Formal opportunities for the academically talented. High school credit may be earned.

Junior Statesmen Summer School–Georgetown University

Program Focus American government, constitutional law, debate, leadership, and U.S. foreign policy.
Academics Communications, government and politics, government and politics (Advanced Placement), international relations, precollege program, prelaw, social science, social studies, speech/debate, writing.
Special Interest Areas Career exploration, leadership training.
Trips College tours, cultural, day.
Program Information 2 sessions per year. Session length: 3 weeks in June, July, August. Ages: 15–18. 200–300 participants per session. Boarding program cost: $3500. Financial aid available.
Application Deadline Continuous.

Contact Mr. Matthew Randazzo, National Summer School Director, 400 South El Camino Real, Suite 300, San Mateo, California 94402. Phone: 650-347-1600. Fax: 650-347-7200. E-mail: jsa@jsa.org.
URL www.jsa.org
For more information, see page 1174.

National Student Leadership Conference: Business and Commerce

National Student Leadership Conference
American University
Washington, District of Columbia

General Information Coed residential academic program established in 1989. Formal opportunities for the academically talented and gifted. College credit may be earned.
Program Focus Leadership, business and entrepreneurship.
Academics Business, communications, economics, speech/debate, writing.
Special Interest Areas Career exploration, leadership training.
Sports Ropes course.
Trips Cultural.
Program Information 2–6 sessions per year. Session length: 11 days in June, July, August. Ages: 14–18. 100–200 participants per session. Boarding program cost: $1995. Financial aid available.
Application Deadline Continuous.
Jobs Positions for college students 18 and older.
Contact Mr. Mike Sims, Executive Director, 111 West Jackson Boulevard, 7th Floor, Chicago, Illinois 60604. Phone: 312-322-9999. Fax: 312-765-0081. E-mail: information@nslcleaders.org.
URL www.nslcleaders.org
For more information, see page 1216.

National Student Leadership Conference: International Diplomacy

National Student Leadership Conference
American University
Washington, District of Columbia

General Information Coed residential academic program established in 1989. Formal opportunities for the academically talented and gifted. College credit may be earned.
Program Focus Leadership, enrichment, and national and international politics and decision making.
Academics Communications, geography, government and politics, intercultural studies, international relations, speech/debate, writing.
Special Interest Areas Career exploration, leadership training, touring.
Sports Ropes course.
Trips Cultural.
Program Information 4–6 sessions per year. Session length: 11 days in June, July, August. Ages: 14–18. 200–250 participants per session. Boarding program cost: $1995. Financial aid available.
Application Deadline Continuous.

National Student Leadership Conference: International Diplomacy

Jobs Positions for college students 18 and older.
Contact Mr. Mike Sims, Executive Director, 111 West Jackson Boulevard, 7th Floor, Chicago, Illinois 60604. Phone: 312-322-9999. Fax: 312-765-0081. E-mail: information@nslcleaders.org.
URL www.nslcleaders.org
For more information, see page 1216.

National Student Leadership Conference: Law and Advocacy–Washington, DC

National Student Leadership Conference
American University
Washington, District of Columbia

General Information Coed residential academic program established in 1989. Formal opportunities for the academically talented and gifted. College credit may be earned.
Program Focus Leadership, enrichment, law, and the American judicial system.
Academics Communications, prelaw, speech/debate, writing.
Special Interest Areas Career exploration, leadership training, touring.
Sports Ropes course.
Trips Cultural.
Program Information 4–6 sessions per year. Session length: 11 days in June, July, August. Ages: 14–18. 200–250 participants per session. Boarding program cost: $1995. Financial aid available.
Application Deadline Continuous.
Jobs Positions for college students 18 and older.
Contact Mr. Mike Sims, Executive Director, 111 West Jackson Boulevard, 7th Floor, Chicago, Illinois 60604. Phone: 312-322-9999. Fax: 312-765-0081. E-mail: information@nslcleaders.org.
URL www.nslcleaders.org
For more information, see page 1216.

National Student Leadership Conference: Mastering Leadership

National Student Leadership Conference
Washington, District of Columbia

General Information Coed residential academic program established in 1989. Formal opportunities for the academically talented and gifted. College credit may be earned.
Program Focus Leadership training and development.
Academics Communications, speech/debate.
Special Interest Areas Community service, leadership training, touring.
Sports Ropes course, sports (general).
Trips Cultural.
Program Information 4–6 sessions per year. Session length: 6 days in February, March, April, June, July, August, October, November. Ages: 14–18. 150–250 participants per session. Boarding program cost: $1195. Financial aid available.
Application Deadline Continuous.
Jobs Positions for college students 18 and older.
Contact Mr. Mike Sims, Executive Director, 111 West Jackson Boulevard, 7th Floor, Chicago, Illinois 60604. Phone: 312-322-9999. Fax: 312-765-0081. E-mail: information@nslcleaders.org.
URL www.nslcleaders.org

For more information, see page 1216.

Sidwell Friends Basketball Camp

Sidwell Friends School
3825 Wisconsin Avenue, NW
Washington, District of Columbia 20016

General Information Coed day sports camp established in 1939. Religious affiliation: Society of Friends.
Program Focus Basketball.
Sports Basketball.
Program Information 1–4 sessions per year. Session length: 5 days in June, July. Ages: 7–14. 10–100 participants per session. Day program cost: $125–$280. Cost: $125 per week (evenings), or $280 per week (full-day).
Application Deadline Continuous.
Jobs Positions for high school students and college students.
Contact Summer Programs Office, main address above. Phone: 202-537-8133. Fax: 202-537-2483. E-mail: sidwellsummer@yahoo.com.
URL www.sidwell.edu/summer

Sidwell Friends DaVinci Days Art Studios, Young Artist Academy and Young Scientist Academy

Sidwell Friends School
3825 Wisconsin Avenue, NW
Washington, District of Columbia 20016

General Information Coed day arts program established in 1991.
Arts Arts, arts and crafts (general), ceramics, creative writing, dance, dance (ballet), dance (modern), drawing, jewelry making, metalworking, music, painting, photography, pottery, printmaking, puppetry, sculpture, studio arts, theater/drama.
Program Information 1–20 sessions per year. Session length: 5–28 days in June, July, August. Ages: 5–18. 5–20 participants per session. Day program cost: $250–$800.
Application Deadline Continuous.
Jobs Positions for college students.
Contact Summer Programs Office, main address above. Phone: 202-537-8133. Fax: 202-537-2483. E-mail: sidwellsummer@yahoo.com.
URL www.sidwell.edu/summer

Sidwell Friends Drama and Dance Workshops with BAPA

Sidwell Friends School
3825 Wisconsin Avenue, NW
Washington, District of Columbia 20016

General Information Coed day arts program established in 1995.
Program Focus Drama and dance.
Arts Acting, dance, mime, theater/drama.
Program Information 1–8 sessions per year. Session length: 5 days in June, July, August. Ages: 8–18. 10–16 participants per session. Day program cost: $200–$300.
Application Deadline Continuous.
Contact Summer Programs Office, main address above. Phone: 202-537-8133. Fax: 202-537-8138. E-mail: sidwellsummer@yahoo.com.
URL www.sidwell.edu/summer

Sidwell Friends Explorer Day Camp, Explorer Voyagers and ExploreStar

Sidwell Friends School
3825 Wisconsin Avenue, NW
Washington, District of Columbia 20016

General Information Coed day traditional camp and academic program established in 2002. Religious affiliation: Society of Friends.
Program Focus Enrichment-based day camp.
Academics Spanish language/literature, academics (general), computers, mathematics, science (general).
Arts Arts and crafts (general), creative writing, fabric arts, music, television/video.
Special Interest Areas Culinary arts, leadership training, robotics.
Sports Basketball, martial arts, swimming, tennis, yoga.
Trips Day.
Program Information 7 sessions per year. Session length: 5–10 days in June, July, August. Ages: 4. Day program cost: $375–$725. Financial aid available.
Application Deadline Continuous.
Jobs Positions for high school students and college students.

Contact Summer Programs Office, main address above. Phone: 202-537-8133. Fax: 202-537-2483. E-mail: sidwellsummer@yahoo.com.
URL www.sidwell.edu/summer

SIDWELL FRIENDS SOCCER PROGRAM WITH AMERICAN SOCCER ACADEMY

Sidwell Friends School
3825 Wisconsin Avenue, NW
Washington, District of Columbia 20016

General Information Coed day sports camp established in 1974.
Program Focus Soccer.
Sports Soccer.
Program Information 1–5 sessions per year. Session length: 5–35 days in July, August. Ages: 5–18. Day program cost: $170–$300. Cost: $170 per week half-day, $300 per week full-day.
Application Deadline Continuous.
Jobs Positions for high school students and college students.
Contact Summer Programs Office, main address above. Phone: 202-537-8133. Fax: 202-537-2483. E-mail: sidwellsummer@yahoo.com.
URL www.sidwell.edu/summer

SIDWELL FRIENDS SUMMER COMMUNITY SERVICE PROGRAMS

Sidwell Friends School
3825 Wisconsin Avenue, NW
Washington, District of Columbia 20016

General Information Coed residential and day community service program established in 2001. Religious affiliation: Society of Friends.
Program Focus A variety of community service workshops.
Academics Ecology, peace education.
Arts Arts and crafts (general), knitting, music, origami, theater/drama.
Special Interest Areas Babysitting course, community service, work camp programs.
Wilderness/Outdoors Caving, hiking, rafting.
Trips Day.
Program Information 1–12 sessions per year. Session length: 5 days in June, July, August. Ages: 5–18. Day program cost: $100–$475. Boarding program cost: $500–$600. Financial aid available.
Application Deadline Continuous.
Jobs Positions for high school students and college students.
Contact Summer Programs Office, main address above. Phone: 202-537-8133. Fax: 202-537-2483. E-mail: sidwellsummer@yahoo.com.
URL www.sidwell.edu/summer

SIDWELL FRIENDS SUMMER STUDIES

Sidwell Friends School
3825 Wisconsin Avenue, NW
Washington, District of Columbia 20016

General Information Coed day academic program established in 1967. Religious affiliation: Society of Friends. Formal opportunities for the academically talented. High school credit may be earned.
Program Focus Credit courses, review courses, and enrichment courses.
Academics American literature, Chinese languages/literature, English language/literature, French language/literature, German language/literature, SAT/ACT preparation, Spanish language/literature, academics (general), art history/appreciation, biology, chemistry, computer programming, computers, history, mathematics, mathematics (Advanced Placement), physics, reading, social studies, study skills, typing, writing.
Arts Photography, pottery, sculpture.
Special Interest Areas Community service, general camp activities, leadership training.
Program Information 1 session per year. Session length: 3–6 weeks in June, July, August. Ages: 12–18. 9–18 participants per session. Day program cost: $300–$1350.
Application Deadline Continuous.
Contact Summer Programs Office, main address above. Phone: 202-537-8133. Fax: 202-537-2483. E-mail: sidwellsummer@yahoo.com.
URL www.sidwell.edu/summer

SIDWELL FRIENDS TENNIS CAMP

Sidwell Friends School
3825 Wisconsin Avenue, NW
Washington, District of Columbia 20016

General Information Coed day sports camp established in 1963. Religious affiliation: Society of Friends.
Program Focus Tennis.
Sports Tennis.
Program Information 1–10 sessions per year. Session length: 5 days in June, July, August. Ages: 6–18. Day program cost: $150–$350.
Application Deadline Continuous.
Jobs Positions for high school students and college students.
Contact Summer Programs Office, main address above. Phone: 202-537-8133. Fax: 202-537-2483. E-mail: sidwellsummer@yahoo.com.
URL www.sidwell.edu/summer

SUMMER DISCOVERY AT GEORGETOWN

Summer Discovery
Georgetown University
Washington, District of Columbia 20057

General Information Coed residential academic program established in 1994. High school credit may be earned.
Program Focus Pre-college enrichment.

Summer Discovery at Georgetown (continued)

Academics English as a second language, English language/literature, SAT/ACT preparation, academics (general), art history/appreciation, business, communications, economics, environmental science, government and politics, government and politics (Advanced Placement), humanities, journalism, precollege program, psychology, social science, social studies, speech/debate, study skills, writing.
Arts Photography.
Special Interest Areas Community service.
Sports Aerobics, basketball, martial arts, rowing (crew/sculling), tennis, weight training.
Trips College tours, cultural, day, overnight.
Program Information 1 session per year. Session length: 5 weeks in June, July, August. 200 participants per session. Boarding program cost: $5599–$5799. Application fee: $60–$70. Open to participants completing grades 10–12.
Application Deadline Continuous.
Jobs Positions for college students 21 and older.
Contact The Musiker Family, Director, 1326 Old Northern Boulevard, Roslyn Village, New York 11576. Phone: 888-878-6637. Fax: 516-625-3438. E-mail: discovery@summerfun.com.
URL www.summerfun.com

For more information, see page 1338.

SUMMER JAM (JUDAISM, ACTIVISM, AND MITZVAH WORK)

PANIM: The Institute for Jewish Leadership and Values
Washington, District of Columbia

General Information Coed residential academic program and community service program established in 2003. Religious affiliation: Jewish.
Academics Bible study, Jewish studies, government and politics, history, humanities, peace education, religion.
Arts Arts and crafts (general), creative writing, music.
Special Interest Areas Community service, gardening, leadership training, team building, touring.
Sports Bicycling, swimming.
Wilderness/Outdoors Bicycle trips, rafting.
Trips College tours, day, shopping.
Program Information 1–2 sessions per year. Session length: 3 weeks in June, July. Ages: 15–18. 40–60 participants per session. Boarding program cost: $3000. Financial aid available.
Application Deadline Continuous.
Contact Summer JAM, 6101 Montrose Road, Suite 200, Rockville, Maryland 20852. Phone: 301-770-5070. Fax: 301-770-6365. E-mail: summerJAM@panim.org.
URL www.panim.org

WASHINGTON INTERNATIONAL SCHOOL PASSPORT TO SUMMER

Washington International School
3100 Macomb Street, NW
Washington, District of Columbia 20008

General Information Coed day traditional camp and academic program established in 1985.
Program Focus Languages.
Academics English as a second language, French language/literature, Spanish language/literature, language study, mathematics, writing.
Arts Arts, arts and crafts (general), creative writing, drawing, film, music (instrumental), painting, photography, pottery, printmaking, television/video.
Special Interest Areas College planning, counselor-in-training program.
Sports Basketball, soccer, volleyball.
Trips Cultural, day.
Program Information 9 sessions per year. Session length: 1–3 weeks in June, July, August. Ages: 3–15. 200–250 participants per session. Day program cost: $250–$295. Application fee: $150. Financial aid available.
Application Deadline Continuous.
Jobs Positions for high school students 16 and older and college students 18 and older.
Contact Ms. Michelle Broadie, Auxiliary Programs Director, 1690 36th Street, N.W., Washington, District of Columbia 20007. Phone: 202-243-1727. Fax: 202-243-1797. E-mail: broadie@wis.edu.
URL www.wis.edu

WASHINGTON INTERNSHIP EXPERIENCE

Washington Workshops Foundation
125 Michigan Avenue, NE
Washington, District of Columbia 20017

General Information Coed residential academic program established in 1969. Formal opportunities for the academically talented. College credit may be earned.
Program Focus In-depth study of legislative politics.
Academics Government and politics, history, social studies.
Trips College tours, cultural, day, shopping.
Program Information 3 sessions per year. Session length: 3–6 weeks in June, July. Ages: 16–20. 20–30 participants per session. Boarding program cost: $2450–$4700. Application fee: $100.
Application Deadline Continuous.
Jobs Positions for college students 20 and older.
Contact Sharon E. Sievers, Director, 3222 N Street NW, Suite 340, Washington, District of Columbia 20007. Phone: 800-368-5688. Fax: 202-965-1018. E-mail: info@workshops.org.
URL www.workshops.org

FLORIDA

Camp Little Palm for the Performing Arts

Little Palm Family Theatre
Spanish River High School
5100 Jog Road
Boca Raton, Florida 33496

General Information Coed day arts program established in 1997.
Arts Acting, chorus, creative writing, dance, dance (jazz), dance (modern), music, music (vocal), musical performance/recitals, musical productions, musical theater, theater/drama.
Trips Cultural, day.
Program Information 1–3 sessions per year. Session length: 5–40 days in June, July, August. Ages: 7–14. 66–70 participants per session. Day program cost: $195–$995.
Application Deadline Continuous.
Jobs Positions for college students 18 and older.
Contact Ms. Katherine Hoecherl, Operations Manager, 154 NW 16th Street, Boca Raton, Florida 33432. Phone: 561-394-0206. Fax: 561-391-0194. E-mail: info@littlepalm.com.
URL www.littlepalm.org

Cybercamps–Rollins College

Cybercamps–Giant Campus, Inc.
Winter Park, Florida

General Information Coed residential and day academic program established in 2003.
Academics Web page design, academics (general), computer programming, computers.
Arts Animation, creative writing, digital media, graphic arts, photography.
Special Interest Areas Computer game design, computer graphics, robotics, team building.
Sports Ultimate frisbee.
Program Information 2–9 sessions per year. Session length: 5–30 days in June, July, August. Ages: 7–18. 30–150 participants per session. Day program cost: $599–$849. Boarding program cost: $974–$1224. Financial aid available.
Application Deadline Continuous.
Jobs Positions for high school students 15 and older and college students.
Contact Cybercamps Information Office, 2401 4th Avenue, Suite 1110, Seattle, Washington 98121. Phone: 206-442-4500. Fax: 206-442-4500. E-mail: info@cybercamps.com.
URL www.cybercamps.com

Earthwatch Institute–Wild Dolphin Societies

Earthwatch Institute
Sarasota, Florida

General Information Coed residential outdoor program and adventure program.
Program Focus Defining bottlenose dolphin ecology to aid in dolphin conservation.
Academics Ecology, environmental science, marine studies, science (general).
Special Interest Areas Field research/expeditions, nature study.
Program Information 11 sessions per year. Session length: 2 weeks in February, March, April, May, June, July, August, September, October, November, December. Ages: 16+. 5 participants per session. Boarding program cost: $1895–$1995. Financial aid available. Financial aid for high school students and teachers.
Application Deadline Continuous.
Contact General Information Desk, PO Box 75, Maynard, Massachusetts 01754. Phone: 800-776-0188. Fax: 978-461-2332. E-mail: info@earthwatch.org.
URL www.earthwatch.org

Embry-Riddle Aeronautical University–Aerospace Summer Camp

Embry-Riddle Aeronautical University
600 South Clyde Morris Boulevard
Daytona Beach, Florida 32114

General Information Coed residential academic program established in 1994. College credit may be earned.
Program Focus Preparation for college education in an aerospace-related field.
Academics Aerospace science, astronomy, computers, history, physics, precollege program, science (general), writing.
Special Interest Areas Career exploration, field trips (arts and culture), leadership training, model rocketry.
Trips College tours, cultural, day.
Program Information 1 session per year. Session length: 26 days in June, July, August. Ages: 12–18. 12–20 participants per session. Boarding program cost: $1000–$15,000. Application fee: $25. Airfare not included.
Application Deadline June 1.
Contact Pamela Peer, Program Manager, main address above. Phone: 800-359-4550. Fax: 386-226-7630. E-mail: summer@erau.edu.
URL www.erau.edu/summeracademy

Embry-Riddle Aeronautical University–Aviation Career Exploration

Embry-Riddle Aeronautical University
600 South Clyde Morris Boulevard
Daytona Beach, Florida 32114-3900

General Information Coed residential academic program established in 2003.
Program Focus Careers in aviation and aerospace, and college preparation.
Academics Aerospace science, aviation, precollege program.
Special Interest Areas Career exploration.
Trips College tours, day.
Program Information 3–5 sessions per year. Session length: 3–5 days in June, July, August. Ages: 12–18. 10–20 participants per session. Boarding program cost: $1100–$1700. Application fee: $25.
Application Deadline Continuous.
Contact Pamela Peer, Program Manager, main address above. Phone: 800-359-4550. Fax: 386-226-7630. E-mail: summer@erau.edu.
URL www.erau.edu/summeracademy

Embry-Riddle Aeronautical University–Flight Exploration

Embry-Riddle Aeronautical University
600 South Clyde Morris Boulevard
Daytona Beach, Florida 32114

General Information Coed residential academic program established in 1996.
Program Focus Aviation.
Academics Academics (general), aviation, precollege program.
Special Interest Areas Career exploration, flight instruction.
Trips College tours, day.
Program Information 3–5 sessions per year. Session length: 5–6 days in June, July, August. Ages: 12–18. 10–20 participants per session. Boarding program cost: $1700–$1900. Application fee: $25.
Application Deadline Continuous.
Contact Pamela Peer, Program Manager, main address above. Phone: 800-359-4550. Fax: 386-226-7630. E-mail: summer@erau.edu.
URL www.erau.edu/summeracademy

Embry-Riddle Aeronautical University–Generations

Embry-Riddle Aeronautical University
600 South Clyde Morris Boulevard
Daytona Beach, Florida 32114

General Information Coed residential family program established in 2004.
Program Focus Aviation careers and exploration with a family member.
Academics Aerospace science, aviation, meteorology, technology.
Special Interest Areas Career exploration, flight instruction.
Trips College tours, day.
Program Information 1 session per year. Session length: 1 week in July. Ages: 12+. 6–18 participants per session. Boarding program cost: $1600–$1800. Application fee: $25.
Application Deadline June 30.
Contact Ms. Pamela Peer, Summer Academy Manager, main address above. Phone: 800-359-4550. Fax: 386-226-7630. E-mail: pamela.peer@erau.edu.
URL www.erau.edu/db/summer/hs-generations.html

Embry-Riddle Aeronautical University–Sun Flight

Embry-Riddle Aeronautical University
600 South Clyde Morris Boulevard
Daytona Beach, Florida 32114

General Information Coed residential academic program established in 1977. College credit may be earned.
Program Focus Flight instruction leading to a private pilot's license, aviation careers, and college orientation.
Academics Aviation, precollege program.
Special Interest Areas Career exploration, field trips (arts and culture), flight instruction, leadership training.
Trips College tours, cultural, day.
Program Information 4 sessions per year. Session length: 16–60 days in June, July, August. Ages: 16–18. 20 participants per session. Boarding program cost: $3700–$16,000. Application fee: $25. Airfare not included.
Application Deadline June 1.
Contact Pamela Peer, Program Manager, main address above. Phone: 800-359-4550. Fax: 386-226-7630. E-mail: summer@erau.edu.
URL www.erau.edu/summeracademy

Episcopal High School Academic Camp

Episcopal High School of Jacksonville
4455 Atlantic Boulevard
Jacksonville, Florida 32207

General Information Coed day academic program established in 1997. Religious affiliation: Episcopal. High school credit may be earned.
Academics English language/literature, SAT/ACT preparation, academics (general), computers, mathematics, religion, study skills.
Arts Ceramics, dance.
Special Interest Areas Driver's education.
Program Information 8–10 sessions per year. Session length: 5–30 days in June, July, August. Ages: 12–18. 4–70 participants per session. Day program cost: $150–$800.
Application Deadline Continuous.
Contact Mr. G. P. Crandall, Summer Programs Director, main address above. Phone: 904-396-5751. Fax: 904-396-1983. E-mail: gpc3@comcast.com.
URL www.episcopalhigh.org

Episcopal High School Eagle Arts Camp

Episcopal High School of Jacksonville
4455 Atlantic Boulevard
Jacksonville, Florida 32207

General Information Coed day arts program established in 1997. Religious affiliation: Episcopal. High school credit may be earned.
Arts Arts, arts and crafts (general), ceramics, dance, music, set design, storytelling, theater/drama.
Sports Swimming.
Program Information 2 sessions per year. Session length: 5–15 days in June. Ages: 6–16. 4–70 participants per session. Day program cost: $250–$750.
Application Deadline Continuous.
Contact Mr. G. P. Crandall, Summer Programs Director, main address above. Phone: 904-396-5751. Fax: 904-396-1983. E-mail: gpc3@comcast.com.
URL www.episcopalhigh.org

Episcopal High School Sports Camp

Episcopal High School of Jacksonville
4455 Atlantic Boulevard
Jacksonville, Florida 32207

General Information Coed day sports camp established in 1997. Religious affiliation: Episcopal. High school credit may be earned.
Sports Baseball, basketball, football, golf, lacrosse, rowing (crew/sculling), soccer, softball, sports (general), swimming, tennis, track and field, volleyball.
Program Information 8–10 sessions per year. Session length: 5–30 days in June, July, August. Ages: 10–18. 4–70 participants per session. Day program cost: $100–$400.
Application Deadline Continuous.
Contact Mr. G. P. Crandall, Summer Programs Director, main address above. Phone: 904-396-5751. Fax: 904-396-1983. E-mail: gpc3@comcast.com.
URL www.episcopalhigh.org

Florida Air Academy Summer Session

Florida Air Academy
1950 South Academy Drive
Melbourne, Florida 32901

General Information Boys' residential and day academic program established in 1961. Formal opportunities for the academically talented. High school credit may be earned.
Program Focus Flight instruction and computers.
Academics English as a second language, SAT/ACT preparation, computers, history, mathematics, reading, study skills.
Special Interest Areas Driver's education, flight instruction, leadership training, weight reduction.
Sports Basketball, martial arts, scuba diving, soccer, softball, swimming, tennis, volleyball, weight training.
Trips Day, shopping.
Program Information 1 session per year. Session length: 6 weeks in June, July. Ages: 11+. 130–150 participants per session. Day program cost: $2200–$2500. Boarding program cost: $4000–$5000. Application fee: $100.
Application Deadline Continuous.
Contact Maj. Debra Hill, Deputy Director of Admissions, main address above. Phone: 321-723-3211 Ext. 30014. Fax: 321-676-0422. E-mail: dlandis@flair.com.
URL www.flair.com

Fotocamp

Palm Beach Photographic Centre
55 Northeast 2nd Avenue
Delray Beach, Florida 33444

General Information Coed day arts program established in 1996. Formal opportunities for the academically talented and artistically talented. Specific services available for the developmentally challenged, learning disabled, and physically challenged.
Academics Journalism, reading.
Arts Graphic arts, photography.
Trips Day.
Program Information 3 sessions per year. Session length: 10 days in June, July, August. Ages: 10–17. 14–28 participants per session. Day program cost: $545–$575. Application fee: $25.
Application Deadline Continuous.
Jobs Positions for high school students and college students.
Contact Ms. Fatima NeJame, Executive Director, main address above. Phone: 561-276-9797. Fax: 561-276-1932. E-mail: info@fotofusion.org.
URL www.workshop.org

FUN-damental Basketball Camp–The Sports Mall

FUN-damental Basketball Camp, Inc.
The Sports Mall
3650 SW 10th Street
Deerfield Beach, Florida 33442

General Information Coed day sports camp established in 1992.
Program Focus Basketball instruction.
Sports Basketball.
Program Information 1 session per year. Session length: 5–6 days in June. Ages: 6–14. 200–250 participants per session. Day program cost: $180–$195.
Application Deadline Continuous.
Jobs Positions for college students 19 and older.
Contact Mr. Stu Maloff, Owner/Director, PO Box 970446, Boca Raton, Florida 33497-0446. Phone: 561-218-0875. Fax: 561-218-0536. E-mail: basketballcamp@aol.com.
URL www.ebasketballcamps.com

iD Tech Camps–University of Miami, Coral Gables, FL

iD Tech Camps
University of Miami
Coral Gables, Florida 33124

General Information Coed residential and day academic program established in 1999. Accredited by American Camping Association. Formal opportunities for the academically talented and artistically talented.
Program Focus High-tech computer camps for kids and teens; produce digital movies, create video games, design Web pages, learn programming and robotics, and more; one computer per student, small classes, campers complete a project in a creative and fun learning environment.
Academics Web page design, computer programming, computer science (Advanced Placement), computers, music, precollege program.
Arts Animation, cinematography, digital media, drawing, film, film editing, film production, graphic arts, music, television/video.
Special Interest Areas Career exploration, computer graphics, electronics, leadership training, robotics, team building.
Sports Baseball, basketball, soccer, softball, swimming, volleyball.
Trips College tours, cultural, day.
Program Information 5 sessions per year. Session length: 6–7 days in June, July, August. Ages: 7–17. 40–50 participants per session. Day program cost: $639. Boarding program cost: $989. Application fee: $200. Financial aid available.
Application Deadline Continuous.
Jobs Positions for college students 18 and older.
Contact Client Service Representatives, 1885 Winchester Boulevard, Suite 201, Campbell, California 95008. Phone: 888-709-TECH. Fax: 408-871-2228. E-mail: requests@internaldrive.com.
URL www.internaldrive.com

For more information, see page 1156.

IMACS–Full Day Summer Camp–Florida

Institute for Mathematics & Computer Science (IMACS) Florida

General Information Coed day academic program established in 1992. Formal opportunities for the academically talented.
Academics Computer programming, computer science (Advanced Placement), computers, engineering, mathematics.
Special Interest Areas Electronics, robotics.
Program Information 5 sessions per year. Session length: 5 days in January, February, March, April, May, June, July, August, September, October, November, December. Ages: 5–18. 30–50 participants per session. Day program cost: $399–$1224. Supply fee: $50–$200; additional sessions booked at same time $249 plus $50 supply fee.
Application Deadline Continuous.
Jobs Positions for high school students 16 and older and college students 18 and older.
Contact Mr. Terry Kaufman, President, 7435 Northwest 4th Street, Plantation, Florida 33317. Phone: 954-791-2333. Fax: 954-791-0260. E-mail: info@imacs.org.
URL www.imacs.org

IMACS–Individual Summer Programs–Florida

Institute for Mathematics & Computer Science (IMACS) Florida

General Information Coed day academic program established in 1992. Formal opportunities for the academically talented.
Academics Computer programming, computer science (Advanced Placement), computers, engineering, mathematics, mathematics (Advanced Placement).
Special Interest Areas Computer graphics, electronics, robotics.
Program Information 28 sessions per year. Session length: 5 days in January, February, March, April, May, June, July, August, September, October, November, December. Ages: 6–18. Day program cost: $79–$189.
Application Deadline Continuous.
Jobs Positions for high school students 16 and older and college students 18 and older.
Contact Mr. Terry Kaufman, President, 7435 Northwest 4th Street, Plantation, Florida 33317. Phone: 954-791-2333. Fax: 954-791-0260. E-mail: info@imacs.org.
URL www.imacs.org

Joe Machnik's No. 1 Academy One and Premier Programs–Vero Beach, Florida

Joe Machnik's No. 1 Camps
Dodgertown Sports and Conference Center
Vero Beach, Florida

General Information Coed residential and day sports camp.
Program Focus Soccer instruction, physical fitness, testing and speed training. Campers gain exposure to top players and are challenged by intense competition.
Sports Soccer.
Trips Day.
Program Information 1 session per year. Session length: 6 days in June, July. Ages: 9–18. Day program cost: $759. Boarding program cost: $819. Financial aid available.
Application Deadline Continuous.
Jobs Positions for college students.
Contact Dr. Joseph Machnik, Director, PO Box 389, 916 Palm Boulevard, Isle of Palms, South Carolina 29451. Phone: 800-622-4645. Fax: 843-886-0885. E-mail: info@no1soccercamps.com.
URL www.no1soccercamps.com

Joe Machnik's No. 1 Mighty Mini, Goalkeeper and Striker Camp–Vero Beach, Florida

Joe Machnik's No. 1 Camps
Dodgertown Sports and Conference Center
Vero Beach, Florida

General Information Coed residential and day sports camp.
Program Focus Soccer instruction. Goalkeepers and strikers compete against each other daily.
Sports Soccer.
Trips Day.
Program Information 1 session per year. Session length: 6 days in June. Ages: 8–12. 100–150 participants per session. Boarding program cost: $459. Financial aid available.
Application Deadline Continuous.
Jobs Positions for college students.
Contact Dr. Joseph Machnik, Director, PO Box 389, 916 Palm Boulevard, Isle of Palms, South Carolina 29451. Phone: 800-622-4645. Fax: 843-886-0885. E-mail: info@no1soccercamps.com.
URL www.no1soccercamps.com

Kampus Kampers

Lynn University
3601 North Military Trail
Boca Raton, Florida 33431

General Information Coed residential traditional camp established in 1992. Accredited by American Camping Association.
Academics Aerospace science, computers.
Arts Arts and crafts (general), circus arts, dance, dance (ballet), dance (jazz), dance (modern), drawing, magic, music (instrumental), painting, photography, theater/drama.
Special Interest Areas Model rocketry.
Sports Aerobics, archery, baseball, basketball, boating, canoeing, cheerleading, fishing, football, golf, gymnastics, in-line skating, sailing, soccer, softball, street/roller hockey, swimming, tennis, volleyball.
Program Information 3 sessions per year. Session length: 15 days in June, July, August. Ages: 6–13. 170 participants per session. Boarding program cost: $1595–$2350. Application fee: $200.
Application Deadline Continuous.
Jobs Positions for college students 19 and older.
Contact Mrs. Sue Merrill, Camp Director, main address above. Phone: 561-237-7316. Fax: 561-237-7962. E-mail: smerrill@lynn.edu.
URL www.pinetreecamp.com

Keenan McCardell and Jimmy Smith Football Camp/Sports International

Sports International, Inc.
Jacksonville University
Jacksonville, Florida 32211

General Information Coed residential and day sports camp established in 1996.
Sports Football, weight training.
Program Information 1 session per year. Session length: 5 days in June. Ages: 8–18. 300–450 participants per session. Day program cost: $489. Boarding program cost: $599.
Application Deadline Continuous.
Jobs Positions for college students 18 and older.
Contact Customer Service, 8924 McGaw Court, Columbia, Maryland 21045. Phone: 800-555-0801. Fax: 410-309-9962. E-mail: info@footballcamps.com.
URL www.footballcamps.com

Keenan McCardell Football Camp

Sports International, Inc.
Eckherd College
St. Petersburg, Florida 33711

General Information Coed residential and day sports camp.
Program Focus Football.
Sports Football, weight training.
Program Information 1 session per year. Session length: 5 days in June, July. Ages: 8–18. 300–450 participants per session. Day program cost: $489. Boarding program cost: $599. Financial aid available.
Application Deadline Continuous.
Jobs Positions for college students 18 and older.
Contact Customer Service, 8924 McGaw Court, Columbia, Maryland 21045. Phone: 800-555-0801. Fax: 301-625-7723. E-mail: info@footballcamps.com.
URL www.footballcamps.com

Montverde Academy Summer School

Montverde Academy
17235 Seventh Street
Montverde, Florida 34756

General Information Coed residential and day academic program established in 1912. High school credit may be earned.
Academics English as a second language, English language/literature, SAT/ACT preparation, Spanish language/literature, academics (general), biology, business, chemistry, computers, economics, government and politics, health sciences, history, mathematics, physics, reading, science (general), social science, social studies, typing.
Arts Arts and crafts (general).
Special Interest Areas Community service.
Sports Baseball, basketball, soccer, softball, swimming, tennis, track and field, volleyball, waterskiing, weight training.
Trips Day, shopping.
Program Information 1 session per year. Session length: 6 weeks in June, July, August. Ages: 12–18. 30–70 participants per session. Day program cost: $650–$1300. Boarding program cost: $1500–$3000. Application fee: $35.
Application Deadline Continuous.
Contact Mrs. Marie Szymanski, Dean of Admissions, main address above. Phone: 407-469-2561. Fax: 407-469-3711. E-mail: mszymanski@montverde.org.
URL www.montverde.org

The New York Film Academy, Disney-MGM Studios, FL

New York Film Academy
Orlando, Florida

General Information Coed residential arts program established in 1992. College credit may be earned.
Program Focus "Total immersion" hands-on filmmaking workshop where students write, direct, shoot and edit their own 16mm short films.
Arts Acting, creative writing, directing, film, film editing, film lighting, film production, screenwriting, sound design, television/video, theater/drama.
Trips Cultural.
Program Information 2 sessions per year. Session length: 1–6 weeks in June, July, August. Ages: 14–17. Boarding program cost: $1500–$6900.
Application Deadline Continuous.
Contact Admissions, 100 East 17th Street, New York, New York 10003. Phone: 212-674-4300. Fax: 212-477-1414. E-mail: film@nyfa.com.
URL www.nyfa.com

For more information, see page 1218.

Pine Tree Camps at Lynn University

Lynn University
3601 North Military Trail
Boca Raton, Florida 33431

General Information Coed residential and day traditional camp established in 1978. Accredited by American Camping Association.
Program Focus Arts and sports and specialty programs.
Academics Aerospace science, computers, music.
Arts Arts and crafts (general), ceramics, circus arts, clowning, dance, dance (jazz), jewelry making, leather working, music, music (instrumental), painting, photography, sculpture, television/video, theater/drama, weaving.
Special Interest Areas Counselor-in-training program, model rocketry.
Sports Aerobics, archery, baseball, basketball, boating, canoeing, cheerleading, fishing, football, golf, kayaking, lacrosse, martial arts, soccer, softball, street/roller hockey, swimming, tennis, volleyball, water polo.
Trips Day.
Program Information 3 sessions per year. Session length: 15 days in June, July, August. Ages: 3–14. 950–1,000 participants per session. Day program cost: $636–$725. Boarding program cost: $1695. Application fee: $75–$200.
Application Deadline Continuous.
Jobs Positions for college students 18 and older.
Contact Ms. Diane DiCerbo, Director, main address above. Phone: 561-237-7310. Fax: 561-237-7962. E-mail: ddicerbo@lynn.edu.
URL www.pinetreecamp.com

Ringling School of Art and Design Pre-College Perspective

Ringling School of Art and Design
2700 North Tamiami Trail
Sarasota, Florida 34234

General Information Coed residential and day academic program and arts program established in 1989. Formal opportunities for the artistically talented. College credit may be earned.
Program Focus High school juniors and seniors from the U.S. and abroad explore visual art and design while learning contemporary techniques in studio settings. Live on campus and earn three college credits.
Academics Art (Advanced Placement), art history/appreciation, computers, precollege program.
Arts Animation, arts, ceramics, design, digital media, drawing, figure study, graphic arts, illustration, painting, photography, printmaking, sculpture.
Trips Cultural, day.
Program Information 1 session per year. Session length: 4 weeks in June, July. Ages: 16–18. 75–95 participants per session. Day program cost: $2969. Boarding program cost: $3999. Application fee: $30. Financial aid available.
Application Deadline May 13.
Contact Nancee Clark, Director of Continuing Studies and Special Programs, main address above. Phone: 941-955-8866. Fax: 941-955-8801. E-mail: cpe@ringling.edu.
URL www.ringling.edu/precollege

Ringling School of Art and Design's Teen Studio

Ringling School of Art and Design
2700 North Tamiami Trail
Sarasota, Florida 34234

General Information Coed day arts program established in 1999. Formal opportunities for the artistically talented.
Program Focus Allows for opportunity to build college portfolio, computer technology classes offered.
Academics Art (Advanced Placement), art history/appreciation, computers.
Arts Arts, arts and crafts (general), creative writing, drawing, film, graphic arts, illustration, painting, photography, printmaking, sculpture.
Program Information 37 sessions per year. Session length: 5–10 days in June, July. Ages: 12–18. 12–20 participants per session. Day program cost: $140–$495. Financial aid available.
Application Deadline Continuous.
Contact Nancy Godfrey, Program and Marketing Assistant, main address above. Phone: 941-955-8866. Fax: 941-955-8801. E-mail: cpe@ringling.edu.
URL www.ringling.edu/continuingeducation

St. Johns Summer Camp

St. Johns Country Day School
3100 Doctors Lake Drive
Orange Park, Florida 32073

General Information Coed day traditional camp established in 1990.
Arts Arts and crafts (general).
Sports Baseball, basketball, fishing, gymnastics, martial arts, soccer, softball, sports (general), swimming, volleyball.
Trips Day.
Program Information 4 sessions per year. Session length: 10 days in June, July. Ages: 5–13. 90–100 participants per session. Day program cost: $200.
Application Deadline Continuous.
Jobs Positions for high school students 15 and older and college students 18 and older.
Contact Mr. Michael Hilliard, Camp Director, main address above. Phone: 904-264-9572. Fax: 904-264-0375. E-mail: michael_hilliard@stjohnscds.com.

Seacamp

1300 Big Pine Avenue
Big Pine Key, Florida 33043-3336

General Information Coed residential academic program and outdoor program established in 1966. Accredited by American Camping Association. Formal opportunities for the academically talented. High school credit may be earned.

Seacamp

Program Focus Marine science, scuba, sailing.
Academics Biology, botany, ecology, environmental science, geology/earth science, journalism, marine studies, oceanography, science (general), writing.
Arts Arts and crafts (general), batiking, ceramics, creative writing, drawing, fabric arts, jewelry making, music, painting, photography, pottery, printmaking, sculpture, theater/drama.
Special Interest Areas Animal care, career exploration, community service, conservation projects, field research/expeditions, nature study, nautical skills, team building.
Sports Basketball, boating, canoeing, fishing, kayaking, sailing, scuba diving, sea kayaking, snorkeling, swimming, water polo, windsurfing.
Wilderness/Outdoors Ocean expeditions, orienteering.
Trips Cultural, day.
Program Information 3 sessions per year. Session length: 18 days in June, July, August. Ages: 12–17. 145–160 participants per session. Boarding program cost: $2750. Extra fee for scuba: $375 per course.
Application Deadline Continuous.
Jobs Positions for college students 19 and older.
Contact Ms. Grace Upshaw, Director, main address above. Phone: 305-872-2331. Fax: 305-872-2555. E-mail: snorkel&scuba@seacamp.org.
URL www.seacamp.org

For more information, see page 1302.

SeaWorld/Busch Gardens Tampa Bay Adventure Camp

SeaWorld Adventure Park
3605 Bougainvillea Avenue
Tampa, Florida 33674-9157

General Information Coed residential outdoor program and adventure program established in 1997. Accredited by American Camping Association. Formal opportunities for the academically talented. High school credit may be earned.

SeaWorld/Busch Gardens Tampa Bay Adventure Camp

Academics Biology, biology (Advanced Placement), ecology, environmental science, geography, geology/earth science, history, marine studies, science (general).
Special Interest Areas Animal care, career exploration, conservation projects, field research/expeditions, nature study.
Sports Snorkeling, swimming.
Trips Cultural, day.
Program Information 12–20 sessions per year. Session length: 5–7 days in June, July, August. Ages: 4+. 15–25 participants per session. Day program cost: $150–$250. Boarding program cost: $750–$2100.

SeaWorld/Busch Gardens Tampa Bay Adventure Camp (continued)

Application Deadline Continuous.
Jobs Positions for college students.
Contact Education Reservations, PO Box 9157, Tampa, Florida 33674. Phone: 877-248-2267. Fax: 813-987-5878. E-mail: education@buschgardens.org.
URL buschgardens.org
For more information, see page 1014.

SeaWorld Orlando Adventure Camp

SeaWorld Adventure Park
7007 Sea Harbor Drive
Orlando, Florida 32801

General Information Coed residential and day outdoor program. Accredited by American Camping Association. Formal opportunities for the academically talented.

SeaWorld Orlando Adventure Camp

Program Focus Marine science and conservation.
Academics Biology, ecology, environmental science, marine studies, science (general).
Special Interest Areas Career exploration, conservation projects, general camp activities, nature study.
Trips Cultural, day, overnight, shopping.
Program Information 15–30 sessions per year. Session length: 5–10 days in June, July, August. Day program cost: $185–$300. Boarding program cost: $300–$2300.
Application Deadline Continuous.
Jobs Positions for college students.
Contact Education Reservations, main address above. Phone: 866-479-2267. Fax: 407-363-2399. E-mail: education@seaworld.com.
URL seaworld.org
For more information, see page 1306.

Student Conservation Association–Conservation Crew Program (Florida)

Student Conservation Association (SCA)
Florida

General Information Coed residential outdoor program, community service program, and wilderness program established in 1957. High school credit may be earned.
Program Focus Resource management, conservation and environmental education.
Academics Biology, botany, ecology, environmental science, geology/earth science, history.
Special Interest Areas Campcraft, community service, construction, leadership training, nature study, trail maintenance, work camp programs.
Sports Canoeing, fishing, kayaking, sea kayaking, swimming.
Wilderness/Outdoors Backpacking, canoe trips, hiking, orienteering, outdoor living skills, wilderness camping.
Trips Cultural, day, overnight.
Program Information 2–3 sessions per year. Session length: 3–5 weeks in June, July, August. Ages: 15–19. 6–8 participants per session. Application fee: $20. Financial aid available. No cost for program; financial aid possible for travel expenses.
Application Deadline Continuous.
Jobs Positions for college students 21 and older.
Contact Recruitment Office, PO Box 550, Charlestown, New Hampshire 03603. Phone: 603-543-1700. Fax: 603-543-1828. E-mail: getreal@thesca.org.
URL www.theSCA.org

Tampa Prep–Academic Credit and Enrichment Courses

Tampa Preparatory School
727 West Cass Street
Tampa, Florida 33606

General Information Coed day academic program established in 1975. High school credit may be earned.
Academics Japanese language/literature, Spanish language/literature, academics (general), computers, history, mathematics, physical education, physics, reading, speech/debate, study skills, writing.
Special Interest Areas Leadership training.
Program Information 2 sessions per year. Session length: 5–30 days in June, July. Ages: 12–18. 4–24 participants per session. Day program cost: $250–$1550. Open to participants entering grades 6–12.
Application Deadline Continuous.
Jobs Positions for college students 18 and older.
Contact Mrs. Jody Rodriguez, Director of Summer Programs, main address above. Phone: 813-251-8481. Fax: 813-254-2106. E-mail: jrodriguez@tampaprep.org.
URL www.tampaprep.org

Tampa Prep–Boys Athletic Camps

Tampa Preparatory School
727 West Cass Street
Tampa, Florida 33606

General Information Boys' day sports camp established in 1975.
Sports Baseball, basketball, golf, rowing (crew/sculling), soccer, sports (general), swimming, volleyball, wrestling.
Program Information 1–3 sessions per year. Session length: 5 days in June, July. Ages: 6–18. 10–24 participants per session. Day program cost: $100–$150.
Application Deadline Continuous.
Jobs Positions for college students 18 and older.
Contact Mrs. Jody Rodriguez, Director of Summer Programs, main address above. Phone: 813-251-8481. Fax: 813-254-2106. E-mail: jrodriguez@tampaprep.org.
URL www.tampaprep.org

Tampa Prep–Girls Athletic Camps

Tampa Preparatory School
727 West Cass Street
Tampa, Florida 33606

General Information Girls' day sports camp established in 1975.
Sports Basketball, golf, rowing (crew/sculling), soccer, sports (general), swimming, volleyball.
Program Information 1–3 sessions per year. Session length: 5 days in June, July. Ages: 10–18. 10–24 participants per session. Day program cost: $130.
Application Deadline Continuous.
Jobs Positions for college students 18 and older.
Contact Mrs. Jody Rodriguez, Director of Summer Programs, main address above. Phone: 813-251-8481. Fax: 813-254-2106. E-mail: jrodriguez@tampaprep.org.
URL www.tampaprep.org

Tampa Prep–Terrapin Day Camp

Tampa Preparatory School
727 West Cass Street
Tampa, Florida 33606

General Information Coed day traditional camp established in 2003.
Academics Computers, mathematics, science (general).
Arts Arts and crafts (general), dance (ballet), music, painting, puppetry, storytelling, theater/drama.
Special Interest Areas Community service.
Sports Basketball, bowling, diving, gymnastics, kickball, martial arts, soccer, swimming, volleyball.
Program Information 7 sessions per year. Session length: 5 days in June, July. Ages: 5–11. 75–100 participants per session. Day program cost: $100–$1400.
Application Deadline Continuous.
Jobs Positions for college students 18 and older.
Contact Mrs. Jody Rodriguez, Director of Summer Programs, main address above. Phone: 813-251-8481. Fax: 813-254-2106. E-mail: jrodriguez@tampaprep.org.
URL www.tampaprep.org

Technology Encounters–Video Encounter/Computer Encounter–Florida

Ducks in a Row Foundation, Inc./Technology Encounters
Florida

General Information Coed day arts program established in 2000. Formal opportunities for the academically talented and artistically talented.
Program Focus Local community school district-hosted programs focused on making technology fun, teaching team skills, and using creative energies.
Academics Academics (general), communications, computer programming, computers.
Arts Acting, animation, arts and crafts (general), film, film production, graphic arts, television/video, theater/drama.
Special Interest Areas Computer game design, computer graphics, leadership training.
Program Information 40–50 sessions per year. Session length: 5–10 days in June, July, August. Ages: 7–13. 25–100 participants per session. Day program cost: $195. Financial aid available.
Application Deadline Continuous.
Jobs Positions for high school students 17 and older and college students 17 and older.
Contact Ms. Jane Sandlar, Director, 8 Wemrock Drive, Ocean, New Jersey 07712. Phone: 732-695-0827. Fax: 732-493-4282. E-mail: jane@technologyencounters.com.
URL www.technologyencounters.com

Teen Tours of America–Golf Camp–Florida Swing

Teen Tours of America
Florida

General Information Coed travel sports camp established in 1984.
Program Focus Golf instruction and adventure travel experience.
Special Interest Areas Touring.
Sports Basketball, bicycling, boating, fishing, football, golf, snorkeling, swimming, tennis, volleyball, waterskiing, weight training.
Wilderness/Outdoors Bicycle trips, canoe trips, hiking.
Trips College tours, cultural, day, overnight, shopping.
Program Information 1–3 sessions per year. Session length: 21–24 days in June, July, August. Ages: 12–17. 30–40 participants per session. Cost: $3200–$5200.
Application Deadline Continuous.
Jobs Positions for college students 23 and older.
Summer Contact Mr. Ira Solomon, Director, 318 Indian Trace #336, Weston, Florida 33326. Phone: 888-868-7882. Fax: 954-888-9781. E-mail: tourtta@teentoursofamerica.com.
Winter Contact Mr. Ira Solomon, Owner/Director, main address above. E-mail: tourtta@teentoursofamerica.com.
URL www.teengolfcamp.com

University of Miami Summer Scholar Programs

University of Miami
111 Allen Hall
Coral Gables, Florida 33124-1610

General Information Coed residential academic program established in 1991. Formal opportunities for the academically talented. College credit may be earned.
Program Focus Research lab projects and field trips.
Academics Anthropology, art history/appreciation, biology, environmental science, geology/earth science, health sciences, journalism, marine studies, oceanography, precollege program.
Arts Film, television/video.
Special Interest Areas Career exploration.
Sports Aerobics, basketball, racquetball, snorkeling, swimming, tennis, volleyball, weight training.
Trips College tours, cultural, day.
Program Information 1 session per year. Session length: 3 weeks in July. Ages: 16–17. 100–200 participants per session. Application fee: $100. Financial aid available.
Application Deadline Continuous.
Contact Mr. Brian Blythe, Director of High School Programs, 111 Allen Hall, PO Box 248005, Coral Gables, Florida 33124-1610. Phone: 305-284-6107. Fax: 305-284-2620. E-mail: ssp.cstudies@miami.edu.
URL www.miami.edu/summerscholar

For more information, see page 1366.

Ventures Travel Service–Florida

Friendship Ventures
Florida

General Information Coed travel special needs program established in 1985. Specific services available for the developmentally challenged and physically challenged.
Program Focus Provides travel services to older teens and adults with developmental disabilities.
Special Interest Areas Touring.
Program Information 50 sessions per year. Session length: 4–10 days in February, March, April, May, June, July, August, September, October, November, December. Ages: 14–70. 4–8 participants per session. Cost: $395–$2000.
Application Deadline Continuous.
Jobs Positions for college students 18 and older.
Contact Georgann Rumsey, President/CEO, 10509 108th Street, NW, Annandale, Minnesota 55302. Phone: 952-852-0101. Fax: 952-852-0123. E-mail: fv@friendshipventures.org.
URL www.friendshipventures.org

Westcoast Connection–Florida Swing Junior Touring Golf Camp

Westcoast Connection
Florida

General Information Coed travel sports camp established in 1982. Accredited by Ontario Camping Association.
Program Focus Participants receive professional golf instruction, play top rated courses, and enjoy recreation and touring highlights.
Special Interest Areas Touring.
Sports Golf, swimming.
Program Information 1–2 sessions per year. Session length: 3 weeks in July, August. Ages: 13–17. 15–40 participants per session. Cost: $5099. Financial aid available.
Application Deadline Continuous.
Jobs Positions for college students 21 and older.
Contact Mr. Ira Solomon, Director, 154 East Boston Post Road, Mamaroneck, New York 10543. Phone: 800-767-0227. Fax: 914-835-0798. E-mail: usa@westcoastconnection.com.
URL www.westcoastconnection.com

For more information, see page 1392.

GEORGIA

Atlanta College of Art–Pre-College Program

Atlanta College of Art
1280 Peachtree Street, NE
Atlanta, Georgia 30309

General Information Coed residential and day arts program established in 1980. Formal opportunities for the artistically talented. College credit may be earned.
Program Focus Program grants college credit to high school juniors and seniors. Curriculum combines foundation art skills with specialized concentrations.
Academics Art (Advanced Placement), art history/appreciation, precollege program.
Arts Animation, arts, arts and crafts (general), creative writing, drawing, graphic arts, metalworking, painting, photography, printmaking, sculpture, television/video, woodworking.
Special Interest Areas Career exploration, college planning, field trips (arts and culture).
Trips College tours, cultural, day, shopping.
Program Information 1 session per year. Session length: 26 days in June, July. Ages: 16–18. 30–80 participants per session. Day program cost: $1850–$2100. Boarding program cost: $3300–$3600. Application fee: $30. Financial aid available.
Application Deadline June 30.
Contact Director of Pre-College Program, main address above. Phone: 404-733-5202. Fax: 404-733-5007.
URL www.aca.edu

Camp Barney Medintz

Camp Barney Medintz
4165 Highway 129 North
Cleveland, Georgia 30528-2309

General Information Coed residential traditional camp established in 1963. Religious affiliation: Jewish. Accredited by American Camping Association. Formal opportunities for the gifted. Specific services available for the developmentally challenged.
Academics Jewish studies, environmental science, journalism, music.
Arts Arts and crafts (general), batiking, ceramics, chorus, dance (folk), dance (jazz), drawing, fabric arts, graphic arts, jewelry making, music, music (instrumental), music (vocal), painting, photography, pottery, printmaking, puppetry, sculpture, television/video, theater/drama, woodworking.
Special Interest Areas Animal care, campcraft, community service, conservation projects, culinary arts, farming, gardening, leadership training.
Sports Aerobics, archery, baseball, basketball, bicycling, boating, canoeing, climbing (wall), diving, equestrian sports, fishing, football, horseback riding, kayaking, martial arts, rappelling, ropes course, sailing, scuba diving, soccer, softball, street/roller hockey, swimming, tennis, volleyball, water polo, waterskiing, windsurfing.
Wilderness/Outdoors Backpacking, bicycle trips, canoe trips, caving, hiking, mountain biking, mountaineering, rafting, rock climbing, white-water trips, wilderness camping.
Trips Overnight.
Program Information 4 sessions per year. Session length: 2–4 weeks in June, July, August. Ages: 8–16. 475–525 participants per session. Boarding program cost: $1600–$3500. Financial aid available.
Application Deadline Continuous.
Jobs Positions for high school students 17 and older and college students 18 and older.
Summer Contact Mr. Jim Mittenthal, Director, main address above. Phone: 706-865-2715. Fax: 706-865-1495. E-mail: summer@campbarney.org.
Winter Contact Mr. Jim Mittenthal, Director, 5342 Tilly Mill Road, Atlanta, Georgia 30338. Phone: 770-396-3250. Fax: 770-481-0101. E-mail: summer@campbarney.org.
URL www.campbarney.org

Special Note
Camp Barney Medintz, nestled in the foothills of the Blue Ridge and Appalachian Mountains, is located 70 miles northeast of Atlanta. The camp's 500 acres of rolling hills, forests, and twin lakes provide a magnificent setting for this exhilarating, experiential program. Campers make special friendships and gain skills in outdoor adventure programs, including horseback riding, waterskiing, tennis, videography, folk art, theater, mountain biking, white-water rafting, ropes course, camp outs, trips, and much more. The emphasis is on group dynamics, heightened self-esteem, outdoor adventure, and water sports on lakes and in pools—all experienced in a very strong Jewish program (kosher). Boys and girls, ages 8–16, come from the Southeast and throughout the United States. Staff members are sought for their maturity, talent, humor, positive values, and willingness to focus on each child as significant.

Camp WinShape for Boys

Camp WinShape/WinShape Foundation
Berry College
Mount Berry, Georgia 30149

General Information Boys' residential traditional camp established in 1985. Religious affiliation: Christian.
Program Focus Recreational summer camp with a Christian emphasis.
Academics Bible study, science (general).
Arts Arts and crafts (general), pottery.
Special Interest Areas Native American culture, campcraft, leadership training, personal development, team building.
Sports Archery, basketball, flag football, horseback riding, soccer, swimming, tennis, weight training, wrestling.
Wilderness/Outdoors Mountain biking, outdoor camping, outdoor living skills, rock climbing, white-water trips.
Trips Overnight.
Program Information 4–8 sessions per year. Session length: 6–14 days in June, July. Ages: 7–16. 10–100 participants per session. Boarding program cost: $485–$970. Application fee: $50–$100.
Application Deadline Continuous.
Contact David Trejo, Boys Camp Director, 490009 Berry College, Mount Berry, Georgia 30149-0009. Phone: 800-448-6955 Ext.1126. Fax: 706-238-7709. E-mail: speedy@winshape.org.
URL www.winshape.com/camp/boys

Camp WinShape for Girls

Camp WinShape/WinShape Foundation
Berry College
Mount Berry, Georgia 30149

General Information Girls' residential traditional camp established in 1987. Religious affiliation: Christian.
Program Focus Recreational summer camp with a Christian emphasis.
Academics Bible study, science (general).
Arts Arts and crafts (general), dance, pottery, puppetry, theater/drama.
Special Interest Areas Native American culture, leadership training, personal development, team building.
Sports Archery, basketball, cheerleading, flag football, gymnastics, horseback riding, soccer, swimming, tennis, volleyball.
Wilderness/Outdoors Mountain biking, outdoor camping, outdoor living skills, rafting, rock climbing, white-water trips.
Trips Overnight.
Program Information 4–8 sessions per year. Session length: 6–14 days in June, July. Ages: 7–16. 10–100

Camp WinShape for Girls (continued)

participants per session. Boarding program cost: $485–$970. Application fee: $50–$100. Financial aid available.
Application Deadline Continuous.
Contact Trudy White, Girls Camp Director, 490009 Berry College, Mount Berry, Georgia 30149-0009. Phone: 800-448-6955 Ext.1141. Fax: 706-238-7709. E-mail: twhite@winshape.org.
URL www.winshape.com/camp/girls

Concordia Language Villages–French–Savannah, GA

Concordia College
Savannah, Georgia

General Information Coed residential academic program and cultural program established in 1961. Accredited by American Camping Association. Formal opportunities for the academically talented.
Program Focus World languages and culture.
Academics French (Advanced Placement), French language/literature, music, peace education.
Arts Arts and crafts (general), dance, dance (folk), music, music (vocal), weaving.
Special Interest Areas Cross-cultural education.
Sports Canoeing, fencing, soccer, swimming, volleyball.
Wilderness/Outdoors Canoe trips, hiking.
Program Information 3 sessions per year. Session length: 6–13 days in July. Ages: 7–13. 219 participants per session. Boarding program cost: $575–$2585. Financial aid available.
Application Deadline Continuous.
Jobs Positions for high school students 17 and older and college students 18 and older.
Contact Alex Loehrer, Assistant Director, Public Relations, 901 South Eighth Street, Moorhead, Minnesota 56562. Phone: 218-299-4544. Fax: 218-299-3807. E-mail: clv@cord.edu.
URL www.ConcordiaLanguageVillages.org

Darlington School Summer Camps

Darlington School
1014 Cave Spring Road
Rome, Georgia 30161-4700

General Information Coed residential traditional camp and outdoor program established in 2003.
Academics Environmental science.
Special Interest Areas Model rocketry, nature study, robotics.
Sports Basketball, canoeing, climbing (wall), golf, kayaking, ropes course, soccer, softball, sports (general), swimming, tennis, volleyball.
Wilderness/Outdoors Canoe trips, caving, hiking, mountain biking, rafting, rock climbing, white-water trips, wilderness camping.
Trips Day.
Program Information 1–3 sessions per year. Session length: 6–12 days in June, July. Ages: 10–15. 20–150 participants per session. Boarding program cost: $450–$1350.
Application Deadline Continuous.
Contact Ballard Betz, Assistant Director of Summer Programs and Admissions, main address above. Phone: 706-235-6051. Fax: 706-232-3600. E-mail: bbetz@darlingtonschool.org.
URL www.darlingtonschool.org

Special Note
Darlington Summer Camps, located at the Darlington School in Rome, Georgia, offer a variety of 1-week overnight experiences in June and July and Adventure Darlington, a series of 2-week overnight sessions with outdoor activities. Campers entering 6th through 9th grade live in residential houses and enjoy Darlington's many athletic and academic facilities and 500 acres with woodlands and a small lake, as well as the many outdoor activities and cultural offerings in the area. The camps provide unique learning and playing environments; passionate, caring teachers and counselors, with a counselor-camper ratio of 1:5; well-trained and experienced staff members; and jam-packed schedules.

For more information, see page 1086.

Emagination Computer Camps–Georgia

Emagination Computer Camps
Georgia Institute of Technology
Atlanta, Georgia

General Information Coed residential and day academic program. Accredited by American Camping Association. Formal opportunities for the academically talented.
Program Focus Computer science, technology, and art; swimming, tennis, and basketball; Web design; computer music, video, photo, and 3-D animation.
Academics Computer programming, computer science (Advanced Placement), computers, technology.
Arts Graphic arts.
Special Interest Areas ADL skills, Internet accessibility, computer graphics, electronics, field trips (arts and culture), model rocketry, robotics.
Sports Basketball, soccer, swimming, tennis.
Trips Day.
Program Information Ages: 8–17. 150–250 participants per session. Day program cost: $1195–$5830. Boarding program cost: $1995–$7830. Financial aid available.
Application Deadline Continuous.
Jobs Positions for college students 18 and older.
Contact Kathi Rigg, Director, 110 Winn Street, Suite 107, Woburn, Massachusetts 01801. Phone: 888-226-6733. Fax: 781-933-0749. E-mail: camp@computercamps.com.
URL www.computercamps.com

For more information, see page 1106.

iD Tech Camps–Emory University, Atlanta, GA

iD Tech Camps
Emory University
Atlanta, Georgia 30322

General Information Coed residential and day academic program established in 1999. Accredited by American Camping Association. Formal opportunities for the academically talented and artistically talented.
Program Focus High-tech computer camps for kids and teens; produce digital movies, create video games, design Web pages, learn programming and robotics, and more; one computer per student, small classes, campers complete a project in a creative and fun learning environment.
Academics Web page design, computer programming, computer science (Advanced Placement), computers, music, precollege program.
Arts Animation, cartooning, cinematography, digital media, drawing, film, film editing, film production, graphic arts, music, television/video.
Special Interest Areas Career exploration, computer graphics, electronics, leadership training, robotics, team building.
Sports Baseball, basketball, soccer, softball, swimming, volleyball.
Trips College tours, cultural, day.
Program Information 5 sessions per year. Session length: 5–7 days in June, July, August. Ages: 7–17. 40–50 participants per session. Day program cost: $639. Boarding program cost: $989. Application fee: $200. Financial aid available.
Application Deadline Continuous.
Jobs Positions for college students 18 and older.
Contact Client Service Representatives, 1885 Winchester Boulevard, Suite 201, Campbell, California 95008. Phone: 888-709-TECH. Fax: 408-871-2228. E-mail: requests@internaldrive.com.
URL www.internaldrive.com

For more information, see page 1156.

Joe Machnik's No. 1 Academy One and Premier Programs–Rome, Georgia

Joe Machnik's No. 1 Camps
Darlington School
Rome, Georgia

General Information Coed residential and day sports camp.
Program Focus Soccer instruction, physical fitness, testing and speed training. Campers gain exposure to top players and are challenged by intense competition.
Sports Soccer.
Trips Day.
Program Information 1 session per year. Session length: 6 days in June. Ages: 9–18. Day program cost: $699. Boarding program cost: $759. Financial aid available.
Application Deadline Continuous.
Jobs Positions for college students.
Contact Dr. Joseph Machnik, Director, PO Box 389, 916 Palm Boulevard, Isle of Palms, South Carolina 29451. Phone: 800-622-4645. Fax: 843-886-0885. E-mail: info@no1soccercamps.com.
URL www.no1soccercamps.com

Joe Machnik's No. 1 Mighty Mini, Goalkeeper and Striker Camp–Rome, Georgia

Joe Machnik's No. 1 Camps
Darlington School
Rome, Georgia

General Information Coed residential and day sports camp established in 1977.
Program Focus Soccer instruction. Goalkeepers and strikers compete against each other daily.
Sports Soccer, swimming.
Program Information 1 session per year. Session length: 6 days in June. Ages: 8–12. 100–150 participants per session. Boarding program cost: $429. Financial aid available.
Application Deadline Continuous.
Jobs Positions for college students 17 and older.
Contact Dr. Joseph Machnik, Director, PO Box 389, 916 Palm Boulevard, Isle of Palms, South Carolina 29451. Phone: 800-622-4645. Fax: 843-886-0885. E-mail: info@no1soccercamps.com.
URL www.no1soccercamps.com

KidzZone Summer Camp

Church In The Now
1873 Iris Drive
Conyers, Georgia 30013

General Information Coed day traditional camp and bible camp established in 1998. Religious affiliation: Christian.
Program Focus To mentor children in a high activity environment promoting spiritual growth and self-esteem.
Academics Bible study, computers, journalism, music, science (general).
Arts Arts and crafts (general), ceramics, creative writing, dance, drawing, film, graphic arts, painting, pottery, television/video, theater/drama.
Special Interest Areas Campcraft, leadership training.
Sports Archery, basketball, cheerleading, roller skating, soccer, softball, swimming, volleyball.
Wilderness/Outdoors Hiking, outdoor camping.
Trips Day, overnight.
Program Information 10 sessions per year. Session length: 5 days in May, June, July. Ages: 5–17. 100–200 participants per session. Day program cost: $50–$100. Application fee: $50–$75. Financial aid available.
Application Deadline Continuous.
Jobs Positions for high school students 13 and older and college students 18 and older.

KidzZone Summer Camp (continued)

Contact Ms. Melissa Camp-King, Camp Director, main address above. Phone: 678-607-3100. Fax: 678-607-3122. E-mail: mcamp@churchinthenow.org.
URL www.kidzzone.org

MidSummer Macon

Wesleyan College
4760 Forsyth Road
Macon, Georgia 31210-4462

General Information Coed residential and day arts program established in 1989. Formal opportunities for the artistically talented.
Program Focus Music, theatre, visual arts, creative writing, and dance.
Academics Art history/appreciation, music, writing.
Arts Arts, arts and crafts (general), ceramics, chorus, creative writing, dance, dance (ballet), dance (jazz), dance (modern), drawing, illustration, music, music (classical), music (ensemble), music (vocal), painting, pottery, sculpture, theater/drama.
Trips Cultural, day.
Program Information 2 sessions per year. Session length: 1–2 weeks in June. Ages: 7–18. 325–400 participants per session. Day program cost: $175–$350. Boarding program cost: $350–$845. Application fee: $50–$125. Financial aid available.
Application Deadline Continuous.
Jobs Positions for college students 18 and older.
Contact Ms. Jo Ann Green, Executive Director MidSummer Macon, main address above. Phone: 478-757-5174. Fax: 478-757-3990. E-mail: jogreen@wesleyancollege.edu.
URL www.midsummermacon.org

National Computer Camps at Oglethorpe University

National Computer Camps
Oglethorpe University
4484 Peachtree Road, NE
Atlanta, Georgia 30304

General Information Coed residential and day academic program established in 1977. Formal opportunities for the academically talented.
Program Focus Computer science, programming, Internet, recreation, and sports.
Academics Web page design, computer programming, computer science (Advanced Placement), computers.
Arts Animation, graphic arts.
Special Interest Areas Internet accessibility, electronics, robotics.
Sports Basketball, soccer, swimming, tennis, volleyball.
Program Information 2 sessions per year. Session length: 1 week in July, August. Ages: 8–18. 80–125 participants per session. Day program cost: $595. Boarding program cost: $795.
Application Deadline Continuous.
Jobs Positions for high school students 16 and older and college students 18 and older.
Contact Dr. Michael Zabinski, President, PO Box 585, Orange, Connecticut 06477. Phone: 203-795-9667. E-mail: info@nccamp.com.
URL www.nccamp.com

Riverside Military Academy High Adventure Camp

Riverside Military Academy
2001 Riverside Drive
Gainesville, Georgia 30501

General Information Boys' residential outdoor program and adventure program established in 2001.
Sports Canoeing, climbing (wall), kayaking, rappelling, riflery, ropes course, swimming.
Wilderness/Outdoors Backpacking, canoe trips, hiking, outdoor adventure, wilderness camping.
Trips Day, overnight.
Program Information 1 session per year. Session length: 5 days in July. Ages: 12–17. 30 participants per session. Boarding program cost: $775.
Application Deadline Continuous.
Contact Ms. Donna Davis, Admissions Director, main address above. Phone: 800-GO-CADET. Fax: 678-291-3364. E-mail: admissions@cadet.com.
URL www.cadet.com

Riverside Military Academy Summer Opportunity and Academic Review

Riverside Military Academy
2001 Riverside Drive
Gainesville, Georgia 30501

General Information Boys' residential and day academic program established in 2000. High school credit may be earned.
Academics American literature, English as a second language, English language/literature, SAT/ACT preparation, Spanish language/literature, academics (general), biology, chemistry, communications, computers, ecology, economics, government and politics, history, mathematics, science (general), social studies, study skills, writing.
Special Interest Areas Leadership training.
Sports Baseball, basketball, canoeing, climbing (wall), football, rappelling, riflery, ropes course, soccer, softball, swimming, tennis, ultimate frisbee, volleyball, weight training.
Trips Day.
Program Information 1 session per year. Session length: 34 days in June, July. Ages: 11–17. 150–200 participants per session. Day program cost: $2350. Boarding program cost: $3685.
Application Deadline Continuous.
Contact Ms. Donna Davis, Admissions Director, main address above. Phone: 800-GO-CADET. Fax: 678-291-3364. E-mail: admissions@cadet.com.
URL www.cadet.com

Riverside Military Academy Young Cadet Camp

Riverside Military Academy
2001 Riverside Drive
Gainesville, Georgia 30501

General Information Boys' day traditional camp established in 2003.
Special Interest Areas Drill team, leadership training, team building.
Sports Canoeing, climbing (wall), rappelling, riflery, ropes course, swimming.
Wilderness/Outdoors Outdoor adventure.
Program Information 2 sessions per year. Session length: 5 days in July. Ages: 10–13. 30 participants per session. Day program cost: $155.
Application Deadline Continuous.
Contact Ms. Donna Davis, Admissions Director, main address above. Phone: 800-GO-CADET. Fax: 678-291-3364. E-mail: admissions@cadet.com.
URL www.cadet.com

SoccerPlus FieldPlayer Academy–Rome, GA

SoccerPlus Camps
Darlington School
Rome, Georgia

General Information Coed residential and day sports camp.
Program Focus Developing overall game skills in a competitive environment with quality goalkeepers.
Sports Soccer.
Program Information 1 session per year. Session length: 6 days in August. Ages: 11+. Day program cost: $595. Boarding program cost: $695. Financial aid available.
Application Deadline Continuous.
Jobs Positions for college students.
Contact Mr. Shawn Kelly, General Manager, 11 Executive Drive, Suite 202, Farmington, Connecticut 06032. Phone: 800-533-7371. Fax: 860-677-0460. E-mail: info@soccerpluscamps.com.
URL www.soccerpluscamps.com

SoccerPlus Goalkeeper School–Challenge Program–Rome, GA

SoccerPlus Camps
Darlington School
Rome, Georgia

General Information Coed residential and day sports camp.
Program Focus Developing technical and tactical goalkeeping skills.
Sports Soccer.
Program Information 1 session per year. Session length: 6 days in June. Ages: 10+. Day program cost: $595. Boarding program cost: $695. Financial aid available.
Application Deadline Continuous.
Jobs Positions for college students.
Contact Mr. Shawn Kelly, General Manager, 11 Executive Drive, Suite 202, Farmington, Connecticut 06032. Phone: 800-533-7371. Fax: 860-677-0460. E-mail: info@soccerpluscamps.com.
URL www.soccerpluscamps.com

SoccerPlus Goalkeeper School–Competitive Program–Rome, GA

SoccerPlus Camps
Darlington School
Rome, Georgia

General Information Coed residential sports camp.
Program Focus Developing game skills in a competitive environment with quality field players.
Sports Soccer.
Program Information 1 session per year. Session length: 6 days. Ages: 12+. Boarding program cost: $755. Financial aid available.
Application Deadline Continuous.
Jobs Positions for college students.
Contact Mr. Shawn Kelly, General Manager, 11 Executive Drive, Suite 202, Farmington, Connecticut 06032. Phone: 800-533-7371. Fax: 860-677-0460. E-mail: info@soccerpluscamps.com.
URL www.soccerpluscamps.com

SoccerPlus Goalkeeper School–National Training Center–Rome, GA

SoccerPlus Camps
Darlington School
Rome, Georgia

General Information Coed residential sports camp.
Program Focus Developing advanced goalkeeping skills.
Sports Soccer.
Program Information 1 session per year. Session length: 6 days in June. Ages: 15+. Boarding program cost: $775.
Application Deadline Continuous.
Jobs Positions for college students.
Contact Mr. Shawn Kelly, General Manager, 11 Executive Drive, Suite 202, Farmington, Connecticut 06032. Phone: 800-533-7371. Fax: 860-677-0460. E-mail: info@soccerpluscamps.com.
URL www.soccerpluscamps.com

Squirrel Hollow Learning Camp

The Bedford School
2605 Ben Hill Road
East Point, Georgia 30344

General Information Coed residential academic program and special needs program established in 1980. Specific services available for the learning disabled. High school credit may be earned.
Program Focus Program for children with learning disabilities.

Squirrel Hollow Learning Camp (continued)
Academics English language/literature, academics (general), computers, government and politics, mathematics, music, reading, study skills, typing, writing.
Arts Arts and crafts (general), music, theater/drama.
Special Interest Areas Field trips (arts and culture).
Sports Basketball, ropes course, soccer, softball, sports (general), swimming, track and field, volleyball.
Wilderness/Outdoors Backpacking, hiking, rafting, white-water trips.
Trips Cultural, day, overnight.
Program Information 1 session per year. Session length: 34 days in June, July. Ages: 7–16. 60–70 participants per session. Boarding program cost: $3500–$4000. Financial aid available.
Application Deadline June 15.
Jobs Positions for high school students 16 and older and college students 16 and older.
Contact Dr. Betsy E. Box, Director, 5665 Milam Road, Fairburn, Georgia 30213. Phone: 770-774-8001. Fax: 770-774-8005. E-mail: bedfordschool@aol.com.
URL www.thebedfordschool.org

Student Conservation Association–Conservation Crew Program (Georgia)

Student Conservation Association (SCA)
Georgia

General Information Coed residential outdoor program, community service program, and wilderness program established in 1957. High school credit may be earned.
Program Focus Resource management, conservation and environmental education.
Academics Biology, botany, ecology, environmental science, geology/earth science, history.
Special Interest Areas Campcraft, community service, construction, leadership training, nature study, trail maintenance, work camp programs.
Sports Canoeing, fishing, kayaking, swimming.
Wilderness/Outdoors Backpacking, canoe trips, hiking, orienteering, outdoor living skills, wilderness camping.
Trips Cultural, day, overnight.
Program Information 2–3 sessions per year. Session length: 3–5 weeks in June, July, August. Ages: 15–19. 6–8 participants per session. Application fee: $20. Financial aid available. No cost for program; financial aid possible for travel expenses.
Application Deadline Continuous.
Jobs Positions for college students 21 and older.
Contact Recruitment Office, PO Box 550, Charlestown, New Hampshire 03603. Phone: 603-543-1700. Fax: 603-543-1828. E-mail: getreal@thesca.org.
URL www.theSCA.org

Valley View Ranch Equestrian Camp

Valley View Ranch Equestrian Camp
606 Valley View Ranch Road
Cloudland, Georgia 30731

General Information Girls' residential outdoor program and sports camp established in 1954.
Program Focus Equestrian camp.
Arts Arts and crafts (general), drawing, jewelry making, leather working, theater/drama.
Special Interest Areas Native American culture, animal care, nature study.
Sports Archery, canoeing, equestrian sports, horseback riding, swimming.
Wilderness/Outdoors White-water trips.
Trips Day.
Program Information 4 sessions per year. Session length: 2–3 weeks in June, July, August. Ages: 8–17. 60 participants per session. Boarding program cost: $1950–$2800.
Application Deadline Continuous.
Jobs Positions for high school students 17 and older and college students 18 and older.
Contact Ms. Nancy C. Jones, Owner/Director, 606 Valley View Ranch Road, Cloudland, Georgia 30731. Phone: 706-862-2231. Fax: 706-862-6190. E-mail: info@valleyviewranch.com.
URL www.valleyviewranch.com

White Water Learning Center of Georgia Kids Kayaking Summer Day Camp

White Water Learning Center of Georgia
Atlanta, Georgia

General Information Coed day outdoor program established in 1998.
Program Focus Whitewater kayaking.
Sports Kayaking.
Wilderness/Outdoors White-water trips.
Trips Day.
Program Information 5 sessions per year. Session length: 5 days in May, June, July, August. Ages: 9–14. 6–15 participants per session. Day program cost: $350.
Application Deadline Continuous.
Contact Bruce L. Williams, President, 3437 Rockhaven Circle, NE, Atlanta, Georgia 30324-2532. Phone: 404-231-0042. Fax: 404-231-4749. E-mail: mail@whitewatergeorgia.com.
URL www.whitewatergeorgia.com

HAWAII

AAC–Aloha Adventure Photo Camp

AAC–Aloha Adventure Camps
Camp Piiholo
Makawao, Hawaii 96768

General Information Coed residential and day outdoor program, arts program, and cultural program established in 1995. Accredited by American Camping Association.
Program Focus Learning photography while exploring Maui and its culture.
Academics Intercultural studies, marine studies.
Arts Arts and crafts (general), dance, photography.
Special Interest Areas Cross-cultural education, touring.
Sports Bicycling, boating, diving, kayaking, paintball, parasailing, sailing, scuba diving, sea kayaking, snorkeling, swimming, volleyball.
Wilderness/Outdoors Backpacking, bicycle trips, caving, hiking, kayaking trips, mountain biking.
Trips Cultural, day, overnight, shopping.
Program Information 4–5 sessions per year. Session length: 7–30 days in June, July, August. Ages: 10–18. 60–90 participants per session. Day program cost: $650. Boarding program cost: $1150. Application fee: $500.
Application Deadline Continuous.
Jobs Positions for college students 19 and older.
Summer Contact Ms. Kate Stanley, Camp Coordinator, PO Box 12229, Lahaina, Hawaii 96761-7229. Phone: 877-755-2267. Fax: 808-665-0707. E-mail: info@hawaiicamps.com.
Winter Contact Mr. Llew Lazarus, Founder, 3825 McLaughlin Avenue, #201, Los Angeles, California 90066. Phone: 310-391-4601. Fax: 310-391-7738. E-mail: info@hawaiicamps.com.
URL www.hawaiicamps.com

AAC–Aloha Adventure Surf Camp

AAC–Aloha Adventure Camps
Camp Piiholo
Makawao, Hawaii 96768

General Information Coed residential and day sports camp and cultural program.
Program Focus Learn to surf while exploring Maui and its culture.
Academics Intercultural studies, marine studies.
Arts Arts and crafts (general), dance.
Special Interest Areas Cross-cultural education, touring.
Sports Bicycling, boating, diving, kayaking, paintball, parasailing, sailing, scuba diving, sea kayaking, snorkeling, surfing, swimming, volleyball.
Wilderness/Outdoors Backpacking, bicycle trips, caving, hiking, kayaking trips, mountain biking.
Trips Cultural, day, overnight, shopping.
Program Information 4–5 sessions per year. Session length: 7–30 days in June, July, August. Ages: 10–18. 60–90 participants per session. Day program cost: $650. Boarding program cost: $1150. Application fee: $500. Financial aid available.
Application Deadline Continuous.
Jobs Positions for college students 19 and older.
Summer Contact Ms. Kate Stanley, Camp Coordinator, PO Box 12229, Lahaina, Hawaii 96761-7229. Phone: 877-755-2267. Fax: 808-665-0707. E-mail: info@hawaiicamps.com.
Winter Contact Mr. Llew Lazarus, Founder, 5825 McLaughlin Avenue, #201, Los Angeles, California 90066. Phone: 310-391-4601. Fax: 310-391-7738. E-mail: info@hawaiicamps.com.
URL www.hawaiicamps.com

AAVE–Hawaii

AAVE–America's Adventure Ventures Everywhere
Hawaii

General Information Coed travel outdoor program, wilderness program, and adventure program established in 1976. Accredited by American Camping Association.
Program Focus Adventure travel.
Special Interest Areas Campcraft, community service, cross-cultural education, leadership training, nautical skills.
Sports Bicycling, boating, sailing, sea kayaking, snorkeling, surfing, swimming.
Wilderness/Outdoors Backpacking, mountain biking, wilderness camping.
Trips Cultural, day, overnight.
Program Information 4–6 sessions per year. Session length: 3 weeks in June, July, August. Ages: 14–18. 13 participants per session. Cost: $3888. Financial aid available.
Application Deadline Continuous.
Jobs Positions for college students 21 and older.
Contact Mr. Abbott Wallis, Owner, 2245 Stonecrop Way, Golden, Colorado 80401. Phone: 800-222-3595. Fax: 303-526-0885. E-mail: info@aave.com.
URL www.aave.com

For more information, see page 952.

Adventures Cross-Country, Hawaii Adventure

Adventures Cross-Country
Hawaii

General Information Coed residential outdoor program, wilderness program, and adventure program established in 1983.
Program Focus Wilderness adventures in Hawaii.
Special Interest Areas Leadership training.
Sports Sailing, sea kayaking, snorkeling.
Wilderness/Outdoors Backpacking, hiking, orienteering, wilderness camping.
Program Information 2 sessions per year. Session length: 20 days in June, July, August. Ages: 13–18. 8–15 participants per session. Boarding program cost: $3995. Financial aid available.
Application Deadline Continuous.
Jobs Positions for college students 21 and older.

Adventures Cross-Country, Hawaii Adventure (continued)

Contact Scott von Eschen, Director, 242 Redwood Highway, Mill Valley, California 94941. Phone: 415-332-5075. Fax: 415-332-2130. E-mail: arcc@adventurescrosscountry.com.
URL www.adventurescrosscountry.com
For more information, see page 972.

ALPENGIRL–HAWAII

Alpengirl, Inc.
Hawaii

General Information Girls' travel outdoor program, wilderness program, and adventure program. Accredited by American Camping Association.
Program Focus Adventuring on the Big Island and Kauai, Volcanoes National Park.
Academics Area studies, ecology, geology/earth science, science (general).
Sports Sea kayaking, snorkeling, swimming.
Wilderness/Outdoors Backpacking, hiking, wilderness camping.
Trips Cultural, day, overnight, shopping.
Program Information 10 sessions per year. Session length: 7–23 days in June, July, August. Ages: 11–17. 10–12 participants per session. Cost: $700–$3100. Financial aid available.
Application Deadline Continuous.
Jobs Positions for college students 21 and older.
Contact Alissa Farley, Camp Owner, PO Box 1138, Manhattan, Montana 59741. Phone: 800-585-7476. Fax: 406-284-9036. E-mail: alissa@alpengirl.com.
URL www.alpengirl.com

BIG ISLAND VOLLEYBALL ELITE CAMP

Hawaii Preparatory Academy
Waimea, Hawaii

General Information Coed residential and day sports camp established in 2002.
Program Focus Varsity players.
Sports Volleyball.
Program Information 1 session per year. Session length: 4 days in July. Day program cost: $275–$285. Boarding program cost: $495–$505. Open to participants entering grades 10–12.
Application Deadline Continuous.
Contact Special Programs Office, 65-1692 Kohala Mountain Road, Kamuela, Hawaii 96743-8476. Phone: 808-937-2578. E-mail: dcraven@hpa.edu.
URL www.hpa.edu/
For more information, see page 1148.

BIG ISLAND VOLLEYBALL PLAYER CAMP

Hawaii Preparatory Academy
Waimea, Hawaii

General Information Coed residential and day sports camp established in 2002.
Sports Volleyball.
Program Information 1 session per year. Session length: 4 days in July. Day program cost: $185–$195. Boarding program cost: $405–$415. Open to participants entering grades 7–12.
Application Deadline Continuous.
Contact Special Programs Office, 65-1692 Kohala Mountain Road, Kamuela, Hawaii 96743-8476. Phone: 808-937-2578. E-mail: dcraven@hpa.edu.
URL www.hpa.edu/
For more information, see page 1148.

HAWAII EXTREME ADVENTURE SCUBA CAMP

Hawaii Extreme Adventure Scuba Camp
Oahu, Hawaii

General Information Coed residential outdoor program established in 2000. High school or college credit may be earned.
Program Focus Campers earn their PADI open water, or advanced certifications.
Academics Marine studies, oceanography.
Sports Scuba diving, snorkeling, swimming.
Wilderness/Outdoors Hiking.
Trips Cultural, day, shopping.
Program Information 5 sessions per year. Session length: 2 weeks in June, July, August. Ages: 12–20. 6–8 participants per session. Boarding program cost: $2100.
Application Deadline Continuous.
Jobs Positions for college students 22 and older.
Summer Contact Ms. Sophie Miladinovich, Director of Hawaii Extreme Adventure Scuba Camp, main address above. Phone: 925-708-0855. Fax: 925-831-1432. E-mail: scubaforlife@aol.com.
Winter Contact Ms. Sophie Miladinovich, PO Box 696, Danville, California 94526. Phone: 925-708-0855. Fax: 925-831-1432. E-mail: scubaforlife@aol.com.
URL www.hawaiiscubacamp.com

HAWAII PREPARATORY ACADEMY SUMMER SESSION

Hawaii Preparatory Academy
65-1692 Kohala Mountain Road
Kamuela, Hawaii 96743

General Information Coed residential and day academic program established in 1971. Formal opportunities for the academically talented.
Program Focus Academic review and enrichment, Hawaiian studies, marine biology, astronomy, SAT preparation, math and computers.
Academics English as a second language, English language/literature, SAT/ACT preparation, academics (general), area studies, astronomy, computers, environmental science, marine studies, mathematics, reading, science (general), study skills, writing.
Arts Arts and crafts (general), ceramics, creative writing, television/video.
Special Interest Areas Cross-cultural education, driver's education.

Hawaii Preparatory Academy Summer Session

Sports Horseback riding, scuba diving, sea kayaking, snorkeling, soccer, sports (general), swimming, tennis, volleyball, weight training.
Wilderness/Outdoors Hiking, outdoor camping.
Trips Cultural, day, overnight, shopping.
Program Information 1 session per year. Session length: 30 days in June, July. Ages: 12–17. 100–120 participants per session. Day program cost: $475–$2000. Boarding program cost: $3800. Application fee: $25.
Application Deadline April 15.
Jobs Positions for high school students 16 and older and college students 19 and older.
Contact Special Programs Office, main address above. Phone: 808-881-4088. Fax: 808-881-4071. E-mail: summer@hpa.edu.
URL www.hpa.edu/
For more information, see page 1148.

Longacre Expeditions, Hawaii

Longacre Expeditions
Hawaii

General Information Coed travel outdoor program, wilderness program, and adventure program established in 1981. Accredited by American Camping Association.
Program Focus Effective communication skills, responsibility, confidence building.
Academics Intercultural studies, marine studies.
Special Interest Areas Leadership training.
Sports Scuba diving, sea kayaking, snorkeling, swimming.
Wilderness/Outdoors Backpacking, hiking, wilderness camping.
Trips Cultural.
Program Information 1 session per year. Session length: 24 days in July. Ages: 15–18. 10–15 participants per session. Cost: $4550.
Application Deadline Continuous.
Jobs Positions for college students 21 and older.
Summer Contact Meredith Schuler, Director, 4030 Middle Ridge Road, Newport, Pennsylvania 17074. Phone: 717-567-6790. Fax: 717-567-3955. E-mail: longacre@longacreexpeditions.com.
Winter Contact Roger Smith, Director, main address above. Phone: 717-567-6790. Fax: 717-567-3955. E-mail: rog@longacreexpeditions.com.
URL www.longacreexpeditions.com
For more information, see page 1200.

Maui Surfer Girls

Maui Surfer Girls
800 Olowalu Road
Lahaina, Hawaii 96796

General Information Girls' residential outdoor program, sports camp, and cultural program established in 2000.
Program Focus Empowering girls through the sport of surfing.
Arts Creative writing, jewelry making.
Sports Kayaking, sailing, snorkeling, surfing, swimming, windsurfing.
Wilderness/Outdoors Hiking, wilderness camping.
Trips Cultural, day, overnight, shopping.
Program Information 2–4 sessions per year. Session length: 10 days in July, August. Ages: 11–17. 25–30 participants per session. Day program cost: $45–$125. Boarding program cost: $2200–$2500. Financial aid available.
Application Deadline Continuous.
Jobs Positions for college students 20 and older.
Contact Dustin Tester, Director/Founder, PO Box 1158, Puunene, Hawaii 96784. Phone: 808-280-8165. Fax: 808-242-4125. E-mail: dustin@mauisurfergirls.com.
URL www.mauisurfergirls.com

Maui Surfer Girls–Advanced Surf Camp on Kauai

Maui Surfer Girls
800 Olowalu Road
Lahaina, Hawaii 96796

General Information Girls' residential sports camp established in 2002.
Program Focus Empowering girls through the sport of surfing.
Arts Creative writing, jewelry making.
Sports Boating, kayaking, sailing, snorkeling, surfing, swimming, windsurfing.
Wilderness/Outdoors Hiking, wilderness camping.
Trips Cultural, day, overnight, shopping.
Program Information 1 session per year. Session length: 1 week in July, August. Ages: 11–17. 12 participants per session. Boarding program cost: $800. Financial aid available.
Application Deadline Continuous.
Jobs Positions for college students 20 and older.
Contact Dustin Tester, Director/Founder, PO Box 1158, Puunene, Hawaii 96784. Phone: 808-280-8165. Fax: 808-242-4125. E-mail: dustin@mauisurfergirls.com.
URL www.mauisurfergirls.com

Maui Surfer Girls–Mother/ Daughter

Maui Surfer Girls
800 Olowalu Road
Lahaina, Hawaii 96796

General Information Girls' residential and day family program and sports camp established in 2000.
Program Focus Empowering girls and their mothers through surfing.
Arts Creative writing, jewelry making.
Sports Sea kayaking, snorkeling, surfing, windsurfing.
Wilderness/Outdoors Hiking, wilderness camping.
Trips Cultural, day, overnight.
Program Information 2–4 sessions per year. Session length: 1 week in July, August. Ages: 11+. 25–30 participants per session. Day program cost: $45–$125. Boarding program cost: $2100–$2300. Financial aid available.
Application Deadline Continuous.
Jobs Positions for college students 20 and older.
Contact Ms. Dustin Tester, Founder and Director, PO Box 1158, Puunene, Hawaii 96784. Phone: 808-280-8165. Fax: 808-242-4127. E-mail: dustin@mauisurfergirls.com.
URL www.mauisurfergirls.com

Overland: American Community Service, Hawaii

Overland Travel, Inc.
Hawaii

General Information Coed travel community service program established in 1985. Accredited by American Camping Association. High school credit may be earned.
Program Focus Community service.
Special Interest Areas Native American culture, community service, conservation projects, leadership training, nature study, team building.
Sports Sea kayaking.
Wilderness/Outdoors Hiking.
Trips Cultural, day, overnight.
Program Information 2–4 sessions per year. Session length: 3 weeks in June, July, August. Ages: 15–18. 12 participants per session. Cost: $3995.
Application Deadline Continuous.
Jobs Positions for college students 20 and older.
Contact Ms. Brooks Follansbee, Director, PO Box 31, Williamstown, Massachusetts 01267. Phone: 800-458-0588. Fax: 413-458-5208. E-mail: overland@adelphia.net.
URL www.overlandsummers.com

For more information, see page 1240.

Overland: Hawaii Explorer Hiking, Kayaking, Sailing and Snorkeling

Overland Travel, Inc.
Hawaii

General Information Coed travel outdoor program, wilderness program, and adventure program established in 1985. Accredited by American Camping Association. High school credit may be earned.
Program Focus Explore Hawaii by foot and kayak.
Special Interest Areas Leadership training, team building.
Sports Kayaking, sea kayaking, snorkeling.
Wilderness/Outdoors Backpacking, hiking, wilderness camping.
Program Information 2–6 sessions per year. Session length: 3 weeks in June, July, August. Ages: 14–18. 8–12 participants per session. Cost: $3995.
Application Deadline Continuous.
Jobs Positions for college students 20 and older.
Contact Ms. Brooks Follansbee, Director, PO Box 31, Williamstown, Massachusetts 01267. Phone: 800-458-0588. Fax: 413-458-5208. E-mail: overland@adelphia.net.
URL www.overlandsummers.com

For more information, see page 1240.

Putney Student Travel–Community Service–Hawaii

Putney Student Travel
Hawaii

General Information Coed residential community service program.
Program Focus Community service focusing on the Habitat for Humanity, cultural exchange, and local excursions in two sessions per year on Oahu and Kauai.
Academics Intercultural studies.
Special Interest Areas Community service, construction.
Sports Kayaking, swimming.
Wilderness/Outdoors Hiking.
Trips Cultural, day.
Program Information 2 sessions per year. Session length: 30 days in June, July. Boarding program cost: $5100. Financial aid available. Airfare from Los Angeles included.
Application Deadline Continuous.
Contact Jeffrey Shumlin, Director, 345 Hickory Ridge Road, Putney, Vermont 05346. Phone: 802-387-5000. Fax: 802-387-4276. E-mail: excel@goputney.com.
URL www.goputney.com

For more information, see page 1276.

RUSTIC PATHWAYS–HAWAIIAN ISLANDS ADVENTURE

Rustic Pathways
Hawaii

General Information Coed travel cultural program and adventure program established in 2003.
Special Interest Areas Touring.
Sports Kayaking, sailing, snorkeling, swimming.
Wilderness/Outdoors Hiking, outdoor adventure.
Trips Cultural, day, overnight, shopping.
Program Information 4 sessions per year. Session length: 15 days in June, July, August. Ages: 13–18. 10–15 participants per session. Cost: $2895.
Application Deadline Continuous.
Jobs Positions for college students 21 and older.

Contact Mr. Travis Owens, Director, North American Programs, 4121 Erie Street, Willoughby, Ohio 44094. Phone: 440-975-9691. Fax: 440-975-9694. E-mail: travis@rusticpathways.com.
URL www.rusticpathways.com

For more information, see page 1290.

Sidwell Friends Service Expedition to Hawaii

Sidwell Friends School
Hawaii

General Information Coed travel outdoor program and community service program established in 2004. Religious affiliation: Society of Friends.
Program Focus Community service (ecology based) and outdoor adventure.
Special Interest Areas Community service, conservation projects, field research/expeditions, nature study, touring.
Trips Cultural, day, overnight, shopping.
Program Information 1 session per year. Session length: 18 days in July. Ages: 13–17. 15 participants per session. Cost: $2850.
Application Deadline Continuous.
Contact Summer Programs Office, 3825 Wisconsin Avenue, NW, Washington, District of Columbia 20016. Phone: 202-537-8133. Fax: 202-537-2483. E-mail: sidwellsummer@yahoo.com.
URL www.sidwell.edu/summer

Student Conservation Association–Conservation Crew Program (Hawaii)

Student Conservation Association (SCA)
Hawaii

General Information Coed residential outdoor program, community service program, and wilderness program established in 1957. High school credit may be earned.
Program Focus Resource management, conservation and environmental education.
Academics Biology, botany, ecology, environmental science, geology/earth science, history.
Special Interest Areas Campcraft, community service, construction, leadership training, nature study, trail maintenance, work camp programs.
Sports Canoeing, fishing, kayaking, sea kayaking, swimming.
Wilderness/Outdoors Backpacking, canoe trips, hiking, orienteering, outdoor living skills, wilderness camping.
Trips Cultural, day, overnight.
Program Information 2–3 sessions per year. Session length: 3–5 weeks in June, July, August. Ages: 15–19. 6–8 participants per session. Application fee: $20. Financial aid available. No cost for program; financial aid possible for travel expenses.
Application Deadline Continuous.
Jobs Positions for college students 21 and older.
Contact Recruitment Office, PO Box 550, Charlestown, New Hampshire 03603. Phone: 603-543-1700. Fax: 603-543-1828. E-mail: getreal@thesca.org.
URL www.theSCA.org

Surf Quest

Camp Timberline–Kama'aina Kids, Inc.
Camp Timberline
Kapolei, Hawaii 96709

General Information Coed residential outdoor program established in 2002.
Program Focus Surfing.
Special Interest Areas Campcraft, nature study.
Sports Archery, basketball, climbing (wall), ropes course, snorkeling, surfing, swimming.
Wilderness/Outdoors Hiking, wilderness camping.
Trips Day.
Program Information 6 sessions per year. Session length: 7–8 days in July, August. Ages: 10–17. 30 participants per session. Boarding program cost: $1000.
Application Deadline May 30.
Jobs Positions for college students.
Contact Tiffany Sirmans, Program Director, PO Box 700308, Kapolei, Hawaii 96709. Phone: 877-672-4386. E-mail: campprograms@kamaainakids.com.
URL www.surfquesthawaii.com

Wilderness Ventures–Hawaii

Wilderness Ventures
Hawaii

General Information Coed travel outdoor program, wilderness program, and adventure program established in 1973.
Program Focus Wilderness travel, wilderness skills, leadership skills.
Special Interest Areas Leadership training.
Sports Sailing, sea kayaking, snorkeling.
Wilderness/Outdoors Backpacking, hiking, wilderness camping.
Trips Overnight.
Program Information 2 sessions per year. Session length: 3 weeks in June, July, August. Ages: 13–18. 13 participants per session. Cost: $3990. Financial aid available.
Application Deadline Continuous.
Jobs Positions for college students 21 and older.
Contact Mike Cottingham, Director, PO Box 2768, Jackson Hole, Wyoming 83001. Phone: 800-533-2281. Fax: 307-739-1934. E-mail: info@wildernessventures.com.
URL www.wildernessventures.com

For more information, see page 1396.

Windsor Mountain: Hawaii

Interlocken at Windsor Mountain
Hawaii

General Information Coed travel outdoor program, community service program, and adventure program established in 1967.

Windsor Mountain: Hawaii (continued)
Program Focus Culture immersion, friendship exchange.
Academics Environmental science, intercultural studies, peace education.
Special Interest Areas Native American culture, community service, cross-cultural education, nature study, team building.
Sports Snorkeling, swimming.
Wilderness/Outdoors Hiking, outdoor adventure.
Program Information 1 session per year. Session length: 4 weeks in June, July. Ages: 14–17. 13 participants per session. Cost: $4150. Financial aid available.
Application Deadline Continuous.
Jobs Positions for college students 23 and older.
Contact Richard Herman, Director, 19 Interlocken Way, Windsor, New Hampshire 03244. Phone: 800-862-7760. Fax: 603-478-5260. E-mail: mail@windsormountain.org.
URL www.windsormountain.org/xrds
For more information, see page 1162.

WORLD HORIZONS INTERNATIONAL–OAHU, HAWAII

World Horizons International
Honolulu/Oahu, Hawaii

General Information Coed residential community service program and cultural program established in 1993.
Program Focus Community service and cross-cultural education.
Special Interest Areas Community service, conservation projects, cross-cultural education, work camp programs.
Sports Horseback riding, sailing, snorkeling, swimming.
Wilderness/Outdoors Hiking.
Trips Cultural, day, overnight.
Program Information 1–2 sessions per year. Session length: 2–4 weeks in June, July. Ages: 14–18. 10 participants per session. Boarding program cost: $3950–$4950. Application fee: $100. Financial aid available. Airfare from New York to Honolulu included.
Application Deadline Continuous.
Jobs Positions for college students 20 and older.
Contact Mr. Stuart L. Rabinowitz, Executive Director, PO Box 662, Bethlehem, Connecticut 06751. Phone: 800-262-5874. Fax: 230-266-6227. E-mail: worldhorizons@att.net.
URL www.world-horizons.com
For more information, see page 1406.

IDAHO

EARTHWATCH INSTITUTE–RESTORING THE SAGEBRUSH STEPPE

Earthwatch Institute
Dubois, Idaho

General Information Coed residential outdoor program.
Program Focus Testing the efficacy of sheep, fire, and reseeding for restoration of our degraded and invaded rangelands.
Academics Ecology, environmental science.
Special Interest Areas Animal care, field research/expeditions, nature study.
Wilderness/Outdoors Wilderness/outdoors (general).
Program Information 4 sessions per year. Session length: 1 week in June, July, August. Ages: 16+. 8 participants per session. Boarding program cost: $695–$795. Financial aid available. Financial aid for high school students and teachers.
Application Deadline Continuous.
Contact General Information Desk, PO Box 75, Maynard, Massachusetts 01754. Phone: 800-776-0188. Fax: 978-461-2332. E-mail: info@earthwatch.org.
URL www.earthwatch.org

IDAHO ENGINEERING SCIENCE CAMP

Boise State University, College of Engineering
1910 University Drive
Boise, Idaho 83725

General Information Coed residential academic program established in 1997.
Program Focus Science and engineering.
Academics Communications, computers, engineering, science (general).
Arts Design.
Special Interest Areas Career exploration, college planning, computer-aided drafting, electronics.
Sports Volleyball.
Program Information 1 session per year. Session length: 6 days in June. Ages: 13–16. 40–46 participants per session. Boarding program cost: $400. Financial aid available.
Application Deadline May 1.
Jobs Positions for college students 18 and older.
Summer Contact Mr. Joseph C. Sener, Director, 1910 University Drive, MS 2100, Boise, Idaho 83725. Phone: 208-426-4814. Fax: 208-426-4466. E-mail: jsener@boisestate.edu.
Winter Contact Leandra Aburusa-Lete, Student Support Coordinator, College of Engineering, 1910 University Drive, Engineering Technology III, Boise, Idaho 83725-2100. Phone: 208-426-4432. Fax: 208-426-4466. E-mail: laburusa@boisestate.edu.
URL coen.boisestate.edu/aboutus/iesc.htm

Landmark Volunteers: Idaho

Landmark Volunteers, Inc.
Idaho

General Information Coed residential outdoor program and community service program established in 1992. High school credit may be earned.
Program Focus Opportunity for high school students to earn community service credit while working as a team for two weeks serving Craig Mountain Wildlife Management Area/Wolf Research or Sawtooth National Recreation Area. Similar programs offered through Landmark Volunteers at over 60 locations in 21 states.
Academics Biology, botany, ecology, environmental science, science (general).
Special Interest Areas Career exploration, community service, conservation projects, field research/expeditions, leadership training, nature study, team building, trail maintenance, work camp programs.
Wilderness/Outdoors Hiking.
Trips Cultural, day.
Program Information 1 session per year. Session length: 2 weeks in June, July, August. Ages: 14–18. 12–13 participants per session. Boarding program cost: $875–$925. Financial aid available.
Application Deadline Continuous.
Jobs Positions for college students.
Contact Ann Barrett, Executive Director, PO Box 455, Sheffield, Massachusetts 01257. Phone: 413-229-0255. Fax: 413-229-2050. E-mail: landmark@volunteers.com.
URL www.volunteers.com

For more information, see page 1182.

Student Conservation Association–Conservation Crew Program (Idaho)

Student Conservation Association (SCA)
Idaho

General Information Coed residential outdoor program, community service program, and wilderness program. High school credit may be earned.
Program Focus Resource management, conservation and environmental education.
Academics Biology, botany, ecology, environmental science, geology/earth science, history.
Special Interest Areas Campcraft, community service, construction, leadership training, nature study, trail maintenance, work camp programs.
Sports Canoeing, fishing, kayaking, swimming.
Wilderness/Outdoors Backpacking, canoe trips, hiking, orienteering, outdoor living skills, wilderness camping.
Trips Cultural, day, overnight.
Program Information 2–3 sessions per year. Session length: 3–5 weeks in June, July, August. Ages: 15–19. 6–8 participants per session. Application fee: $20. Financial aid available. No cost for program; financial aid possible for travel expenses.
Application Deadline Continuous.
Jobs Positions for college students 21 and older.
Contact Recruitment Office, PO Box 550, Charlestown, New Hampshire 03603. Phone: 603-543-1700. Fax: 603-543-1828. E-mail: getreal@thesca.org.
URL www.theSCA.org

ILLINOIS

Alex Brown and Dustin Lyman Football Camp/Sports International

Sports International, Inc.
Trinity International University
Deerfield, Illinois

General Information Coed residential and day sports camp established in 1983. Accredited by American Camping Association.
Program Focus Football.
Sports Football, weight training.
Program Information 1 session per year. Session length: 5 days in July. Ages: 8–18. 300–450 participants per session. Day program cost: $509. Boarding program cost: $619.
Application Deadline Continuous.
Jobs Positions for college students 18 and older.
Contact Customer Service, 8924 McGaw Court, Columbia, Maryland 21045. Phone: 800-555-0801. Fax: 410-309-9962. E-mail: info@footballcamps.com.
URL www.footballcamps.com

Andy McCollum Football Camp

Sports International, Inc.
Southern Illinois University
Edwardsville, Illinois

General Information Coed residential and day sports camp established in 1983.
Sports Football, weight training.
Program Information 1 session per year. Session length: 5 days in June. Ages: 8–18. 300–450 participants per session. Day program cost: $489. Boarding program cost: $599.
Application Deadline Continuous.
Jobs Positions for college students 18 and older.
Contact Customer Service, 8924 McGaw Court, Columbia, Maryland 21045. Phone: 800-555-0801. Fax: 410-309-9962. E-mail: info@footballcamps.com.
URL www.footballcamps.com

Camp Cedar Point

Girl Scouts of Shagbark Council
1327 Camp Cedar Point Lane
Makanda, Illinois 62958

General Information Girls' residential traditional camp established in 1953. Specific services available for the developmentally challenged.
Program Focus Girl scouting.
Academics Ecology, environmental science.

Camp Cedar Point (continued)

Arts Arts and crafts (general), dance, dance (tap), film, jewelry making, music, pottery.
Special Interest Areas Campcraft, career exploration, leadership training, nature study, team building.
Sports Archery, boating, canoeing, horseback riding, sailing, swimming.
Wilderness/Outdoors Backpacking, canoe trips, caving, hiking, orienteering, wilderness camping.
Trips Day, overnight, shopping.
Program Information 7–20 sessions per year. Session length: 3–6 days in June, July. Ages: 7–17. 150 participants per session. Boarding program cost: $75–$280. Application fee: $10. Financial aid available.
Application Deadline Continuous.
Jobs Positions for high school students 16 and older and college students 18 and older.
Contact Kristi Hettenhausen, Camp Director, 304 North 14th Street, Herrin, Illinois 62948. Phone: 618-457-5924. Fax: 618-942-7153. E-mail: girlscouts@shagbark.org.
URL www.shagbark.org

Center for American Archeology/ Archeology Field School

Center for American Archeology
Kampsville, Illinois 62053

General Information Coed residential academic program established in 1968. Formal opportunities for the academically talented. High school credit may be earned.
Program Focus Archeology and the natural sciences.
Academics Anthropology, archaeology, biology, botany, ecology, environmental science, history, science (general), social science.
Arts Basketry, ceramics, pottery, stone tool production.
Special Interest Areas Native American culture, career exploration, field research/expeditions, gardening, nature study.
Trips Cultural, day.
Program Information 1–4 sessions per year. Session length: 1–4 weeks in June, July. Ages: 13–17. 5–20 participants per session. Boarding program cost: $625–$2500. Financial aid available.
Application Deadline Continuous.
Jobs Positions for college students 21 and older.
Contact Mary Pirkl, Director of Education, PO Box 366, Kampsville, Illinois 62053. Phone: 618-653-4316. Fax: 618-653-4232. E-mail: caa@caa-archeology.org.
URL www.caa-archeology.org

Center for American Archeology/ Past Lifeways Program

Center for American Archeology
Kampsville, Illinois 62053

General Information Coed residential and day academic program established in 1968. Formal opportunities for the academically talented and artistically talented.
Program Focus Prehistoric technologies and archeology.
Academics Anthropology, archaeology, biology, botany, ecology, environmental science, history, humanities, science (general), social science, social studies.
Arts Basketry, ceramics, jewelry making, pottery, stone tool production, weaving, woodworking.
Special Interest Areas Native American culture, career exploration, construction, field research/ expeditions, gardening, nature study.
Trips Day.
Program Information 2 sessions per year. Session length: 1–7 days in April, May, June, July, August, September, October. Ages: 8–18. 10–40 participants per session. Day program cost: $10–$20. Boarding program cost: $85–$425.
Application Deadline Continuous.
Contact Mary Pirkl, Director of Education, PO Box 366, Kampsville, Illinois 62053. Phone: 618-653-4316. Fax: 618-653-4232. E-mail: caa@caa-archeology.org.
URL www.caa-archeology.org

Center for Talent Development Summer Academic Program

Northwestern University's Center for Talent Development
617 Dartmouth Place
Evanston, Illinois 60208

General Information Coed residential and day academic program established in 1983. Formal opportunities for the academically talented. Specific services available for the hearing impaired, physically challenged, and visually impaired. High school credit may be earned.

Center for Talent Development Summer Academic Program

Academics American literature, English language/literature, Latin language, academics (general), architecture, biology, biology (Advanced Placement), chemistry, classical languages/literatures, computer programming, computer science (Advanced Placement), ecology, economics, engineering, environmental science, geology/earth science, government and politics, history, humanities, journalism, mathematics, mathematics (Advanced Placement), philosophy, physics, psychology, religion, science (general), social science, social studies, writing.
Arts Arts and crafts (general), creative writing, drawing.
Special Interest Areas Community service.
Sports Basketball, racquetball, soccer, softball, tennis, weight training.
Trips Cultural, day, shopping.
Program Information 5 sessions per year. Session length: 1–3 weeks in June, July, August. Ages: 4–17. 300–700 participants per session. Day program cost: $200–$1100. Boarding program cost: $2300. Application fee: $50. Financial aid available.
Application Deadline May 7.
Jobs Positions for high school students 17 and older and college students.
Contact Susie Hoffmann, Summer Program Coordinator, main address above. Phone: 847-491-3782. Fax: 847-467-4283. E-mail: ctd@northwestern.edu.
URL www.ctd.northwestern.edu

For more information, see page 1224.

Columbia College Chicago's High School Summer Institute

Columbia College Chicago
600 South Michigan Avenue
Chicago, Illinois 60605

General Information Coed residential and day academic program and arts program established in 1984. Formal opportunities for the artistically talented. College credit may be earned.
Program Focus Visual arts, performing arts, media arts, and communication arts.
Academics Academics (general), art history/appreciation, communications, computers, education, journalism, marketing, music, precollege program, science (general), sign language, writing.
Arts Animation, arts, arts and crafts (general), band, creative writing, dance, dance (modern), digital media, drawing, fashion design/production, film, graphic arts, music, music (ensemble), music (instrumental), music (jazz), music (vocal), music technology/record production, musical productions, painting, photography, radio broadcasting, sculpture, television/video, theater/drama, visual arts.
Special Interest Areas Career exploration, computer graphics.
Trips Cultural.
Program Information 1 session per year. Session length: 25 days in July, August. Ages: 15–18. 500–600 participants per session. Day program cost: $300–$900. Boarding program cost: $1400. Financial aid available. Cost: $150 per credit hour.
Application Deadline June 20.
Contact Ms. Stephanie Strait, Coordinator, Undergraduate Admissions, 600 South Michigan Avenue, Chicago, Illinois 60605. Phone: 312-344-7134. Fax: 312-344-8024. E-mail: sstrait@colum.edu.
URL www.colum.edu

Cybercamps–Benedictine University

Cybercamps–Giant Campus, Inc.
Lisle, Illinois

General Information Coed residential and day academic program established in 1997.
Program Focus High tech computer camps featuring project oriented curriculum in Web design, 3D animation, game design, robotics, digital arts and programming for all ability levels.
Academics Web page design, computer programming, computers.
Arts Animation, creative writing, digital media, graphic arts, photography.
Special Interest Areas Computer game design, computer graphics, robotics, team building.
Sports Frisbee golf, ultimate frisbee.
Program Information 2–9 sessions per year. Session length: 5–30 days in June, July, August. Ages: 7–18. 30–150 participants per session. Day program cost: $589–$799. Boarding program cost: $909–$1059.
Application Deadline Continuous.
Jobs Positions for high school students 15 and older and college students.
Contact Cybercamps Information Office, 2401 4th Avenue, Suite 1110, Seattle, Washington 98121. Phone: 206-442-4500. Fax: 206-442-4501. E-mail: info@cybercamps.com.
URL www.cybercamps.com

Cybercamps–Concordia University

Cybercamps–Giant Campus, Inc.
River Forest, Illinois

General Information Coed residential and day academic program established in 1997.
Program Focus High tech computer camps featuring project oriented curriculum in Web design, 3D animation, game design, robotics, digital arts and programming for all ability levels.
Academics Web page design, computer programming, computers.
Arts Animation, creative writing, digital media, graphic arts, photography.
Special Interest Areas Career exploration, computer game design, computer graphics, electronics, leadership training, robotics, team building.
Sports Frisbee golf, ultimate frisbee.
Program Information 2–9 sessions per year. Session length: 5–30 days in June, July, August. Ages: 7–18. 30–150 participants per session. Day program cost: $599–$849. Boarding program cost: $974–$1224. Financial aid available.
Application Deadline Continuous.
Jobs Positions for high school students 15 and older and college students.

Cybercamps–Concordia University (continued)

Contact Cybercamps Information Office, 2401 4th Avenue, Suite 1110, Seattle, Washington 98121. Phone: 206-442-4500. Fax: 206-442-4501. E-mail: info@cybercamps..com.
URL www.cybercamps.com

EARTHWATCH INSTITUTE–MOUNDBUILDERS ON THE MISSISSIPPI

Earthwatch Institute
Illinois

General Information Coed residential outdoor program.
Program Focus Excavating North America's largest complex of earthen mounds to discover the relationship of their makers with their environment.
Academics Archaeology, geology/earth science.
Special Interest Areas Field research/expeditions.
Program Information 3 sessions per year. Session length: 12 days in May, June, July. Ages: 16+. 15 participants per session. Boarding program cost: $1495–$1595. Financial aid available. Financial aid for high school students and teachers.
Application Deadline Continuous.
Contact General Information Desk, PO Box 75, Maynard, Massachusetts 01754. Phone: 800-776-0188. Fax: 978-461-2332. E-mail: info@earthwatch.org.
URL www.earthwatch.org

EMAGINATION COMPUTER CAMPS–ILLINOIS

Emagination Computer Camps
Lake Forest Academy
1600 West Kennedy Road
Lake Forest, Illinois 60045

General Information Coed residential and day academic program established in 1982. Accredited by American Camping Association. Formal opportunities for the academically talented.
Program Focus Computer science, technology, and art; swimming, tennis, and basketball clinics; Web design, computer music, video, photo, 3-D animation.
Academics Computer programming, computer science (Advanced Placement), computers, technology.
Arts Graphic arts.
Special Interest Areas ADL skills, Internet accessibility, computer graphics, electronics, field trips (arts and culture), model rocketry, robotics.
Sports Basketball, soccer, swimming, tennis.
Trips Day.
Program Information 3 sessions per year. Session length: 10–42 days in June, July, August. Ages: 8–17. 150–250 participants per session. Day program cost: $1195–$5830. Boarding program cost: $1995–$7830.
Application Deadline Continuous.
Jobs Positions for college students 18 and older.
Contact Ms. Kathi Rigg, Director, 110 Winn Street, Suite 207, Woburn, Massachusetts 01801. Phone: 888-226-6733. Fax: 781-933-0749. E-mail: camp@computercamps.com.
URL www.computercamps.com
For more information, see page 1106.

iD TECH CAMPS–LAKE FOREST COLLEGE, EVANSTON, IL

iD Tech Camps
Lake Forest College
Evanston, Illinois 60045

General Information Coed residential and day academic program established in 1999. Accredited by American Camping Association. Formal opportunities for the academically talented and artistically talented.
Program Focus High-tech computer camps for kids and teens; produce digital movies, create video games, design Web pages, learn programming and robotics, and more; one computer per student, small classes, campers complete a project in a creative and fun learning environment.
Academics Web page design, computer programming, computer science (Advanced Placement), computers, music, precollege program.
Arts Animation, cinematography, digital media, drawing, film, film editing, film production, graphic arts, music, television/video.
Special Interest Areas Career exploration, computer graphics, electronics, leadership training, robotics, team building.
Sports Baseball, basketball, soccer, softball, swimming, volleyball.
Trips College tours, cultural, day.
Program Information 5 sessions per year. Session length: 5–7 days in June, July, August. Ages: 7–17. 40–50 participants per session. Day program cost: $639. Boarding program cost: $989. Application fee: $200. Financial aid available.
Application Deadline Continuous.
Jobs Positions for college students 18 and older.
Contact Client Service Representatives, 1885 Winchester Boulevard, Suite 201, Campbell, California 95008. Phone: 888-709-TECH. Fax: 408-871-2228. E-mail: requests@internaldrive.com.
URL www.internaldrive.com
For more information, see page 1156.

iD TECH CAMPS–NORTHWESTERN UNIVERSITY, CHICAGO, IL

iD Tech Camps
Northwestern University
Chicago, Illinois 60208

General Information Coed residential and day academic program established in 1999. Accredited by American Camping Association. Formal opportunities for the academically talented and artistically talented.
Program Focus High-tech computer camps for kids and teens; produce digital movies, create video games, design Web pages, learn programming and robotics, and

more; one computer per student, small classes, campers complete a project in a creative and fun learning environment.
Academics Web page design, computer programming, computer science (Advanced Placement), computers, music, precollege program.
Arts Animation, cartooning, cinematography, digital media, drawing, film, film editing, film production, graphic arts, music, television/video.
Special Interest Areas Career exploration, computer graphics, electronics, leadership training, robotics, team building.
Sports Baseball, basketball, soccer, softball, swimming, volleyball.
Trips College tours, cultural, day.
Program Information 5 sessions per year. Session length: 5–7 days in June, July, August. Ages: 7–17. 40–50 participants per session. Day program cost: $639. Boarding program cost: $989. Application fee: $200. Financial aid available.
Application Deadline Continuous.
Jobs Positions for college students 18 and older.
Contact Client Service Representatives, 1885 Winchester Boulevard, Suite 201, Campbell, California 95008. Phone: 888-709-TECH. Fax: 408-871-2228. E-mail: requests@internaldrive.com.
URL www.internaldrive.com

For more information, see page 1156.

Junior Statesmen Summer School–Northwestern University

Junior Statesmen Foundation
Northwestern University
Evanston, Illinois 60208

General Information Coed residential academic program established in 1995. Formal opportunities for the academically talented. High school credit may be earned.
Program Focus American government, speech, debate, and leadership training.
Academics Communications, government and politics, government and politics (Advanced Placement), journalism, precollege program, social science, social studies, speech/debate.
Special Interest Areas Career exploration, leadership training.
Trips College tours, cultural, day.
Program Information 1 session per year. Session length: 4 weeks in June, July. Ages: 14–18. 80–100 participants per session. Boarding program cost: $3500. Financial aid available.
Application Deadline Continuous.
Contact Matt Randazzo, National Summer School Director, 400 South El Camino Real, Suite 300, San Mateo, California 94402. Phone: 650-347-1600. Fax: 650-347-7200. E-mail: jsa@jsa.org.
URL www.jsa.org

For more information, see page 1174.

Junior Statesmen Summer School–Northwestern University

Kendall College Culinary Camp

Kendall College
900 N. North Branch Street
Chicago, Illinois 60622

General Information Coed residential and day arts program established in 1998.
Program Focus Culinary arts.
Special Interest Areas Culinary arts.
Trips Cultural.
Program Information 10–15 sessions per year. Session length: 5 days in June, July, August. Ages: 14–18. 16 participants per session. Day program cost: $575. Boarding program cost: $885.
Application Deadline Continuous.
Contact Office of Admissions, main address above. Phone: 877-588-8860. Fax: 312-752-2021. E-mail: culinarycamp@kendall.edu.
URL www.kendall.edu

National Guitar Workshop–Chicago, IL

National Guitar Workshop
Judson College
1151 North State Street
Elgin, Illinois 60123-1498

General Information Coed residential and day arts program established in 1984. College credit may be earned.
Program Focus Music education in guitar, bass, drums, and vocals.
Arts Guitar, music (classical), music (ensemble), music (instrumental), music (jazz), music (rock), music (vocal).
Program Information 1 session per year. Session length: 5–6 days in June, July, August. Ages: 13+. 125–

National Guitar Workshop–Chicago, IL (continued)

260 participants per session. Day program cost: $670–$720. Boarding program cost: $870–$920. Application fee: $25. Financial aid available.
Application Deadline Continuous.
Jobs Positions for college students 21 and older.
Contact Emily Flower, Registrar, PO Box 222, Lakeside, Connecticut 06758. Phone: 800-234-6479. Fax: 860-567-0374. E-mail: emily@guitarworkshop.com.
URL www.guitarworkshop.com

THE NATIONAL MUSIC WORKSHOP DAY JAMS–CHICAGO, IL

National Guitar Workshop
Our Lady of Destiny
1880 Ash Street
Des Plaines, Illinois 60018

General Information Coed day arts program established in 2001. Formal opportunities for the artistically talented.
Program Focus Rock 'n' roll day camp.
Academics Music.
Arts Guitar, music, music (rock), music (vocal), television/video.
Program Information 3 sessions per year. Session length: 5–15 days in July. Ages: 9–15. 40–70 participants per session. Day program cost: $425–$495. Application fee: $35. Financial aid available.
Application Deadline Continuous.
Jobs Positions for high school students 17 and older and college students 17 and older.
Contact Lynda Wlodarczyk, Associate Director, 407A Bantam Road, Suite 1, Litchfield, Connecticut 06759. Phone: 800-295-5956. Fax: 860-567-0374. E-mail: lynda@dayjams.com.
URL www.dayjams.com

NORTHWESTERN UNIVERSITY'S COLLEGE PREPARATION PROGRAM

Northwestern University
405 Church Street
Evanston, Illinois 60208

General Information Coed residential and day academic program established in 1987. Formal opportunities for the academically talented. College credit may be earned.
Program Focus Precollege orientation.
Academics American literature, Chinese languages/literature, English language/literature, French language/literature, German language/literature, Italian language/literature, Japanese language/literature, Jewish studies, Russian language/literature, Spanish language/literature, academics (general), anthropology, art history/appreciation, astronomy, biology, business, chemistry, classical languages/literatures, communications, computer programming, computers, economics, government and politics, history, humanities, intercultural studies, journalism, linguistics, mathematics, music, philosophy, physics, physiology, precollege program, psychology, religion, science (general), social science, social studies, speech/debate, writing.

Northwestern University's College Preparation Program

Arts Acting, band, chorus, creative writing, dance, drawing, film, graphic arts, music, music (classical), music (ensemble), music (instrumental), music (jazz), music (orchestral), music (vocal), musical productions, painting, photography, television/video, theater/drama.
Sports Aerobics, basketball, canoeing, golf, kayaking, racquetball, sailing, soccer, sports (general), swimming, tennis, volleyball, weight training, windsurfing.
Wilderness/Outdoors Hiking.
Trips College tours, cultural, day, shopping.
Program Information 1 session per year. Session length: 6–8 weeks in June, July, August. Ages: 16–18. 70–80 participants per session. Day program cost: $3117–$7851. Boarding program cost: $4332–$9471. Application fee: $35–$70. Financial aid available.
Application Deadline Continuous.
Contact Stephanie Teterycz, Associate Director of Summer Sessions, main address above. Phone: 847-491-4358. Fax: 847-491-3660. E-mail: s_teterycz@northwestern.edu.
URL www.northwestern.edu/collegeprep
For more information, see page 1226.

NORTHWESTERN UNIVERSITY'S NATIONAL HIGH SCHOOL INSTITUTE

Northwestern University
617 Noyes Street
Evanston, Illinois 60208

General Information Coed residential academic program and arts program established in 1931. Formal opportunities for the academically talented and artistically talented.
Program Focus Six programs in journalism, music, theatre arts, media arts, forensics, or debate.
Academics Academics (general), journalism, music, speech/debate.
Arts Arts, film, music, radio broadcasting, television/video, theater/drama.
Program Information 1 session per year. Session length: 14–36 days in June, July. Ages: 14–18. 30–200

Northwestern University's National High School Institute

participants per session. Boarding program cost: $2950–$3700. Application fee: $25. Financial aid available.
Application Deadline April 15.
Jobs Positions for college students.
Contact Nick Kanel, Department Assistant, main address above. Phone: 800-662-NHSI. Fax: 847-467-1057. E-mail: nhsi@northwestern.edu.
URL www.northwestern.edu/nhsi

For more information, see page 1228.

Power Chord Academy–Chicago

Power Chord Academy
Saint Xavier University
Chicago, Illinois

General Information Coed residential academic program and arts program. Formal opportunities for the academically talented.
Program Focus Teenage musicians play in a band, record a CD, make a video, play a concert, and gain an unbridled understanding of the music industry.
Academics Art (Advanced Placement), music, music (Advanced Placement).
Arts Band, music, music (chamber), music (classical), music (ensemble), music (instrumental), music (jazz), music (orchestral), music (vocal), music technology/record production, musical performance/recitals, songwriting.
Program Information 1–4 sessions per year. Session length: 1 week in June. Ages: 12–18. 100–120 participants per session. Boarding program cost: $895–$1095.
Application Deadline Continuous.
Jobs Positions for college students 22 and older.
Contact Mr. Bryan J. Wrzesinski, 7336 Santa Monica Boulevard, #107, Los Angeles, California 90046. Phone: 800-897-6677. Fax: 775-306-7923. E-mail: bryan@powerchordacademy.com.
URL www.powerchordacademy.com

SoccerPlus FieldPlayer Academy–Charleston, IL

SoccerPlus Camps
Eastern Illinois University
Charleston, Illinois

General Information Coed residential and day sports camp.
Program Focus Developing overall game skills in a competitive environment with quality goalkeepers.
Sports Soccer.
Program Information 1 session per year. Session length: 6 days in July. Ages: 11+. Day program cost: $595. Boarding program cost: $696. Financial aid available.
Application Deadline Continuous.
Jobs Positions for college students.
Contact Mr. Shawn Kelly, General Manager, 11 Executive Drive, Suite 202, Farmington, Connecticut 06032. Phone: 800-533-7371. Fax: 860-677-0460. E-mail: info@soccerpluscamps.com.
URL www.soccerpluscamps.com

SoccerPlus Goalkeeper School–Challenge Program–Charleston, IL

SoccerPlus Camps
Eastern Illinois University
Charleston, Illinois

General Information Coed residential and day sports camp.
Program Focus Developing technical and tactical goalkeeping skills.
Sports Soccer.
Program Information 2 sessions per year. Session length: 6 days in June, July. Ages: 10+. Day program cost: $595. Boarding program cost: $695. Financial aid available.
Application Deadline Continuous.
Jobs Positions for college students.
Contact Mr. Shawn Kelly, General Manager, 11 Executive Drive, Suite 202, Farmington, Connecticut 06032. Phone: 800-533-7371. Fax: 860-677-0460. E-mail: info@soccerpluscamps.com.
URL www.soccerpluscamps.com

SoccerPlus Goalkeeper School–Competitive Program–Charleston, IL

SoccerPlus Camps
Eastern Illinois University
Charleston, Illinois

General Information Coed residential sports camp.
Program Focus Developing game skills in a competitive environment with quality field players.
Sports Soccer.
Program Information 1 session per year. Session length: 6 days in June, July. Ages: 12+. Boarding program cost: $755. Financial aid available.
Application Deadline Continuous.
Jobs Positions for college students.

SoccerPlus Goalkeeper School–Competitive Program–Charleston, IL (continued)

Contact Mr. Shawn Kelly, General Manager, 11 Executive Drive, Suite 202, Farmington, Connecticut 06032. Phone: 800-533-7371. Fax: 860-677-0460. E-mail: info@soccerpluscamps.com.
URL www.soccerpluscamps.com

SoccerPlus Goalkeeper School–National Training Center–Charleston, IL

SoccerPlus Camps
Eastern Illinois University
Charleston, Illinois

General Information Coed residential sports camp.
Program Focus Developing advanced goalkeeping skills.
Sports Soccer.
Program Information 2 sessions per year. Session length: 6 days in July. Ages: 15+. Boarding program cost: $775.
Application Deadline Continuous.
Jobs Positions for college students.
Contact Mr. Shawn Kelly, General Manager, 11 Executive Drive, Suite 202, Farmington, Connecticut 06032. Phone: 800-533-7371. Fax: 860-677-0460. E-mail: info@soccerpluscamps.com.
URL www.soccerpluscamps.com

Student Conservation Association–Conservation Crew Program (Illinois)

Student Conservation Association (SCA)
Illinois

General Information Coed residential outdoor program, community service program, and wilderness program established in 1957. High school credit may be earned.
Program Focus Resource management, conservation and environmental education.
Academics Biology, botany, ecology, environmental science, geology/earth science, history.
Special Interest Areas Campcraft, community service, construction, leadership training, nature study, trail maintenance, work camp programs.
Sports Canoeing, fishing, kayaking, swimming.
Wilderness/Outdoors Backpacking, canoe trips, hiking, orienteering, outdoor living skills, wilderness camping.
Trips Cultural, day, overnight.
Program Information 2–3 sessions per year. Session length: 3–5 weeks in June, July, August. Ages: 15–19. 6–8 participants per session. Application fee: $20. Financial aid available. No cost for program; financial aid possible for travel expenses.
Application Deadline Continuous.
Jobs Positions for college students 21 and older.
Contact Recruitment Office, PO Box 550, Charlestown, New Hampshire 03603. Phone: 603-543-1700. Fax: 603-543-1828. E-mail: getreal@thesca.org.
URL www.theSCA.org

University of Chicago–Insight

University of Chicago
The Graham School of General Studies, Summer Sessions Office
1427 East 60th Street
Chicago, Illinois 60637

General Information Coed residential and day academic program established in 1998. Formal opportunities for the academically talented and artistically talented. College credit may be earned.
Program Focus "Hands-on" experiential learning.
Academics English language/literature, academics (general), anthropology, archaeology, government and politics, history, humanities, precollege program, psychology, reading, social science, social studies, speech/debate, writing.
Arts Creative writing.
Special Interest Areas Field research/expeditions.
Trips Cultural, day.
Program Information 2 sessions per year. Session length: 3 weeks in June, July. Ages: 15–18. 10–15 participants per session. Day program cost: $2390–$2679. Boarding program cost: $3820–$4120. Application fee: $40–$55. Financial aid available.
Application Deadline May 15.
Contact Ms. Valerie Huston, Secretary, Summer Session Office, main address above. Phone: 773-702-6033. Fax: 773-702-6814. E-mail: uc-summer@uchicago.edu.
URL summer.uchicago.edu/
For more information, see page 1360.

University of Chicago–Research in the Biological Sciences

University of Chicago
Graham School of General Studies, Summer Sessions Office
1427 East 60th Street
Chicago, Illinois 60637

General Information Coed residential academic program established in 1999. Formal opportunities for the academically talented. College credit may be earned.
Program Focus Scientific research.
Academics Biology, genetics, microbiology, precollege program, research skills.
Trips Cultural, day.
Program Information 1 session per year. Session length: 4 weeks in June, July. Ages: 15–18. 24–48 participants per session. Boarding program cost: $6925. Application fee: $40–$55. Financial aid available.
Application Deadline May 15.
Contact Ms. Valerie Huston, Secretary, Summer Session Office, main address above. Phone: 773-702-6033. Fax: 773-702-6814. E-mail: uc-summer@uchicago.edu.
URL summer.uchicago.edu/
For more information, see page 1360.

University of Chicago–Summer Quarter for High School Students

University of Chicago
Graham School of General Studies, Summer Sessions Office
1427 East 60th Street
Chicago, Illinois 60637

General Information Coed residential and day academic program established in 1999. Formal opportunities for the academically talented. College credit may be earned.

University of Chicago–Summer Quarter for High School Students

Program Focus College courses for credit.
Academics American literature, Arabic, Chinese languages/literature, English language/literature, French language/literature, German language/literature, Greek language/literature, Hebrew language, Italian language/literature, Japanese language/literature, Jewish studies, Korean, Latin language, Russian language/literature, Sanskrit, Spanish language/literature, academics (general), anthropology, art history/appreciation, biology, business, classical languages/literatures, computer programming, ecology, economics, environmental science, geology/earth science, government and politics, history, humanities, intercultural studies, law, linguistics, mathematics, music, philosophy, precollege program, psychology, religion, social science, sociology.
Arts Drawing, photography, visual arts.
Trips Cultural, day.
Program Information 1 session per year. Session length: 3–9 weeks in June, July, August. Ages: 15–18. 100–200 participants per session. Day program cost: \$2355–\$6373. Boarding program cost: \$5936–\$9259. Application fee: \$40–\$55. Financial aid available.
Application Deadline May 15.
Contact Ms. Valerie Huston, Secretary, Summer Session Office, main address above. Phone: 773-702-6033. Fax: 773-702-6814. E-mail: uc-summer@uchicago.edu.
URL summer.uchicago.edu/

For more information, see page 1360.

INDIANA

Ball State University Summer Journalism Workshops

Ball State University
Muncie, Indiana 47306-0487

General Information Coed residential academic program established in 1966. Specific services available for the hearing impaired, physically challenged, and visually impaired. College credit may be earned.
Program Focus High school journalism and computer design.
Academics Academics (general), business, communications, computers, journalism, precollege program, typing, writing.
Arts Creative writing, film, graphic arts, photography, radio broadcasting, television/video.
Program Information 2–3 sessions per year. Session length: 3–7 days in June, July, August. Ages: 11–18. 200–400 participants per session. Boarding program cost: \$200–\$550. Financial aid available.
Application Deadline Continuous.
Jobs Positions for college students 18 and older.
Contact Mark Herron, Director, Ball State University, AJ 304, Muncie, Indiana 47306. Phone: 765-285-8900. Fax: 765-285-7997. E-mail: bsuworkshops@bsu.edu.
URL www.bsu.edu/web/bsuworkshops

Camp Superkids–Camp Crosley

American Lung Association of Indiana
165 EMS T2 Lane
North Webster, Indiana 46555

General Information Coed residential special needs program established in 1978. Specific services available for the participant with asthma.
Program Focus For children with moderate to severe asthma.
Arts Arts and crafts (general).

Camp Superkids–Camp Crosley (continued)

Special Interest Areas Nature study.
Sports Archery, basketball, canoeing, climbing (wall), kayaking, ropes course, swimming, volleyball.
Wilderness/Outdoors Hiking.
Program Information 1 session per year. Session length: 6 days in June. Ages: 7–14. 72 participants per session. Boarding program cost: $125. Application fee: $5. Financial aid available.
Application Deadline May 1.
Jobs Positions for college students 18 and older.
Contact Mr. Brett Aschliman, Community Relations Director, 802 West Wayne Street, Fort Wayne, Indiana 46802. Phone: 260-426-1170. Fax: 260-422-4924. E-mail: baschliman@lungin.org.
URL www.lungin.org

Camp Superkids–Happy Hollow Children's Camp

American Lung Association of Indiana
3049 Happy Hollow Road
Nashville, Indiana 47448

General Information Coed residential special needs program established in 1978. Specific services available for the participant with asthma.
Program Focus For children with moderate to severe asthma.
Arts Arts and crafts (general).
Special Interest Areas Nature study.
Sports Archery, basketball, canoeing, horseback riding, kayaking, ropes course, swimming, volleyball.
Wilderness/Outdoors Hiking, mountain biking.
Program Information 1 session per year. Session length: 6 days in July. Ages: 7–14. 125 participants per session. Boarding program cost: $125. Application fee: $5. Financial aid available.
Application Deadline June 1.
Jobs Positions for college students 18 and older.
Contact Mr. Brett Aschliman, Community Relations Director, 802 West Wayne Street, Fort Wayne, Indiana 46802. Phone: 260-426-1170. Fax: 260-422-4924. E-mail: baschliman@lungin.org.
URL www.lungin.org

Culver Summer Camps/Culver Specialty Camp– Aviation

Culver Summer Camps
1300 Academy Road, #138
Culver, Indiana 46511

General Information Coed residential traditional camp. Accredited by American Camping Association.
Program Focus Aviation.
Academics Aviation.
Special Interest Areas Flight instruction, leadership training, team building.
Program Information 1 session per year. Session length: 2 weeks in August. Ages: 13–17. 200 participants per session. Boarding program cost: $1300. Application fee: $75. Financial aid available. Flight time deposit: $900 per 6-week session, $810 per 2-week session.
Application Deadline Continuous.
Jobs Positions for college students 19 and older.
Contact Mr. Anthony T. Mayfield, Director, main address above. Phone: 800-221-2020. Fax: 574-842-8462. E-mail: summer@culver.org.
URL www.culver.org

Special Note
Culver's aviation program began to take off just seventeen years after Orville and Wilbur Wright made their historic flight at Kitty Hawk. Culver provides an opportunity for young people who dream of flying to learn how to fly. The largest precollege school of aviation in the country, Culver features its own ground school and airport. Qualified, experienced instructors help campers develop the skills and habits that can make flying a source of lifelong pleasure. The on-campus airport has two 2,400-foot-long runways: a north/south paved runway and an east/west sod runway. Culver uses six Piper Cherokee training aircraft in which campers receive flight instruction. A flight simulator provides advanced instruction for experienced students. Evenings include movies, dances, all-camp activities, and special events. Campers participate fully in the camp's leadership program and learn more about teamwork, responsibility, self-esteem, and interpersonal skills. There's camp, and then there's Culver!

For more information, see page 1082.

Culver Summer Camps/Culver Specialty Camp–Equestrian Arts

Culver Summer Camps
1300 Academy Road, #138
Culver, Indiana 46511

General Information Coed residential traditional camp and sports camp established in 1902. Accredited by American Camping Association.
Program Focus Horsemanship.
Special Interest Areas Leadership training, team building.
Sports Equestrian sports, horseback riding.
Program Information 1 session per year. Session length: 2 weeks in August. Ages: 11–16. 200 participants per session. Boarding program cost: $1300. Application fee: $75. Financial aid available.
Application Deadline Continuous.
Jobs Positions for college students 19 and older.
Contact Mr. Anthony T. Mayfield, Director, main address above. Phone: 800-221-2020. Fax: 574-842-8462. E-mail: summer@culver.org.
URL www.culver.org

Special Note
Campers use Culver's Vaughn Equestrian Center, the country's largest indoor riding hall, with stabling for 130 horses. The campus also provides a 600-acre bird sanctuary with more than 20 miles of riding trails. Campers learn the balanced seat, proper grooming, equipment use and maintenance, basic stable management skills, and safety techniques. Instruction begins at

the skill level of the rider in combined training, dressage, polo, and trail riding. Upper Campers have the opportunity to join the annual hike, a fun camping and riding experience reminiscent of cavalry days. Evenings include movies, dances, all-camp activities, and special events. Campers participate fully in the camp's leadership program and learn more about teamwork, responsibility, self-esteem, and interpersonal skills. There's camp, and then there's Culver!

For more information, see page 1082.

Culver Summer Camps/Culver Specialty Camp–Fencing

Culver Summer Camps
1300 Academy Road, #138
Culver, Indiana 46511

General Information Coed residential sports camp. Accredited by American Camping Association.
Program Focus Learn to fence, beginner through advanced students in epee, foil, and saber.
Sports Fencing.
Program Information 1 session per year. Session length: 2 weeks in August. Ages: 11–16. Boarding program cost: $1300. Application fee: $75. Financial aid available.
Application Deadline Continuous.
Jobs Positions for college students 19 and older.
Contact Mr. Anthony T. Mayfield, Director, main address above. Phone: 800-221-2020. Fax: 574-842-8462. E-mail: summer@culver.org.
URL www.culver.org

For more information, see page 1082.

Culver Summer Camps/Culver Specialty Camp–Golf

Culver Summer Camps
1300 Academy Road, #138
Culver, Indiana 46511

General Information Coed residential sports camp. Accredited by American Camping Association.
Program Focus Beginner to advanced golf instruction.
Sports Golf.
Program Information 1 session per year. Session length: 2 weeks in August. Ages: 11–16. 300–400 participants per session. Boarding program cost: $1300. Application fee: $75. Financial aid available.
Application Deadline Continuous.
Jobs Positions for college students 19 and older.
Contact Mr. Anthony T. Mayfield, Director, main address above. Phone: 800-221-2020. Fax: 574-842-8462. E-mail: summer@culver.org.
URL www.culver.org

Special Note
For kids ages 11–16 who would like to focus on a favorite activity, Culver Specialty Camps provide 5 hours of daily instruction in one of eleven activities. Two-week programs are offered in sailing, waterskiing, fencing, scuba diving, hockey, soccer, tennis, golf, and equestrian arts. All programs teach beginning through advanced levels, emphasizing safety, proper technique, skills, good sportsmanship, and hands-on experience. In addition, Culver offers an aviation program for ages 13–16, which features dual-flight instruction in aircraft and in a ground instrument trainer. Evening social activities include dances, movies, boat rides, hockey games, bowling, and a farewell dinner dance.

For more information, see page 1082.

Culver Summer Camps/Culver Specialty Camp–Ice Hockey

Culver Summer Camps
1300 Academy Road, #138
Culver, Indiana 46511

General Information Coed residential sports camp. Accredited by American Camping Association.
Program Focus Fundamentals of ice hockey and conditioning techniques.
Sports Ice hockey.
Program Information 1 session per year. Session length: 2 weeks in August. Ages: 11–16. Boarding program cost: $1300. Application fee: $75. Financial aid available.
Application Deadline Continuous.
Jobs Positions for college students 19 and older.
Contact Mr. Anthony T. Mayfield, Director, main address above. Phone: 800-221-2020. Fax: 574-842-8462. E-mail: summer@culver.org.
URL www.culver.org

For more information, see page 1082.

Culver Summer Camps/Culver Specialty Camp–Sailing

Culver Summer Camps
1300 Academy Road, #138
Culver, Indiana 46511

General Information Coed residential sports camp. Accredited by American Camping Association.
Program Focus Practical experience in recreational and competitive sailing.
Special Interest Areas Leadership training, nautical skills, team building.
Sports Sailing.
Program Information 1 session per year. Session length: 2 weeks in August. Ages: 11–16. Boarding program cost: $1300. Application fee: $75. Financial aid available.
Application Deadline Continuous.
Jobs Positions for college students 19 and older.
Contact Mr. Anthony T. Mayfield, Director, main address above. Phone: 800-221-2020. Fax: 574-842-8462. E-mail: summer@culver.org.
URL www.culver.org

For more information, see page 1082.

Culver Summer Camps/Culver Specialty Camp–Scuba

Culver Summer Camps
1300 Academy Road, #138
Culver, Indiana 46511

General Information Coed residential sports camp. Accredited by American Camping Association.
Program Focus Practical experience in fundamentals of skin and scuba diving.
Special Interest Areas Team building.
Sports Scuba diving, skin diving, swimming.
Program Information 1 session per year. Session length: 2 weeks in August. Ages: 12–16. Boarding program cost: $1300. Application fee: $75. Financial aid available.
Application Deadline Continuous.
Jobs Positions for college students 19 and older.
Contact Mr. Anthony T. Mayfield, Director, main address above. Phone: 800-221-2020. Fax: 574-842-8462. E-mail: summer@culver.org.
URL www.culver.org
For more information, see page 1082.

Culver Summer Camps/Culver Specialty Camp–Soccer

Culver Summer Camps
1300 Academy Road, #138
Culver, Indiana 46511

General Information Coed residential sports camp. Accredited by American Camping Association.
Program Focus Rules, tactics, and strategies of soccer while practicing fundamental skills.
Special Interest Areas Team building.
Sports Soccer.
Program Information 1 session per year. Session length: 2 weeks in August. Ages: 11–16. Boarding program cost: $1300. Application fee: $75. Financial aid available.
Application Deadline Continuous.
Jobs Positions for college students 19 and older.
Contact Mr. Anthony T. Mayfield, Director, main address above. Phone: 800-221-2020. Fax: 574-842-8462. E-mail: summer@culver.org.
URL www.culver.org
For more information, see page 1082.

Culver Summer Camps/Culver Specialty Camp–Tennis

Culver Summer Camps
1300 Academy Road, #138
Culver, Indiana 46511

General Information Coed residential sports camp. Accredited by American Camping Association.
Program Focus Mechanics of tennis strokes, rules, strategies, and court demeanor as well as concentration techniques and personal discipline.
Sports Tennis.
Program Information 1 session per year. Session length: 2 weeks in August. Ages: 11–16. Boarding program cost: $1300. Application fee: $75. Financial aid available.
Application Deadline Continuous.
Jobs Positions for college students 19 and older.
Contact Mr. Anthony T. Mayfield, Director, main address above. Phone: 800-221-2020. Fax: 574-842-8462. E-mail: summer@culver.org.
URL www.culver.org
For more information, see page 1082.

Culver Summer Camps/Culver Specialty Camp–Water Ski

Culver Summer Camps
1300 Academy Road, #138
Culver, Indiana 46511

General Information Coed residential sports camp. Accredited by American Camping Association.

Culver Summer Camps / Culver Specialty Camp–Water Ski

Program Focus Beginner to advanced skiers learn basic rescue and life-saving techniques, swimming, diving, and ski form.
Special Interest Areas Leadership training, lifesaving, team building.
Sports Diving, swimming, waterskiing.
Program Information 1 session per year. Session length: 2 weeks in August. Ages: 11–16. Boarding program cost: $1300. Application fee: $75. Financial aid available.
Application Deadline Continuous.
Jobs Positions for college students 19 and older.
Contact Mr. Anthony T. Mayfield, Director, main address above. Phone: 800-221-2020. Fax: 574-842-8462. E-mail: summer@culver.org.
URL www.culver.org
For more information, see page 1082.

Culver Summer Camps/Upper Camp–Boys

Culver Summer Camps
1300 Academy Road, #138
Culver, Indiana 46511

General Information Boys' residential traditional camp and academic program established in 1902. Accredited by American Camping Association.
Program Focus Recreational and academic opportunities.
Academics Bible study, English as a second language, SAT/ACT preparation, aviation, computers, ecology, environmental science, journalism, mathematics, music, physics, reading, speech/debate, writing.
Arts Arts and crafts (general), band, ceramics, chorus, creative writing, dance, dance (ballet), dance (jazz), dance (modern), drawing, film, jewelry making, leather working, music, music (vocal), musical productions, painting, photography, pottery, theater/drama, weaving, woodworking.
Special Interest Areas Native American culture, campcraft, community service, driver's education, flight instruction, leadership training, military program, model rocketry, nature study, nautical skills.
Sports Aerobics, archery, baseball, basketball, boating, canoeing, cheerleading, climbing (wall), cross-country, diving, equestrian sports, fencing, figure skating, fishing, football, golf, horseback riding, ice hockey, in-line skating, kayaking, lacrosse, racquetball, riflery, ropes course, rowing (crew/sculling), sailing, scuba diving, snorkeling, soccer, softball, street/roller hockey, swimming, tennis, track and field, volleyball, waterskiing, weight training, windsurfing, wrestling.
Wilderness/Outdoors Canoe trips, hiking.
Program Information 1 session per year. Session length: 6 weeks in June, July, August. Ages: 13–17. 400 participants per session. Boarding program cost: $4000. Application fee: $200. Financial aid available.
Application Deadline Continuous.
Jobs Positions for college students 19 and older.
Contact Mr. Anthony T. Mayfield, Director, main address above. Phone: 800-221-2020. Fax: 574-842-8462. E-mail: summer@culver.org.
URL www.culver.org

Special Note
Culver is located on the north shore of Indiana's second-largest lake, the 1,864-acre Lake Maxinkuckee. The camp has a fleet of more than 120 sailboats, powerboats, wave runners, and the *R. H. Ledbetter,* one of the largest ships on an inland American lake. Campers with a naval major take sailing for two periods a day. Grouped by skill level, campers receive instruction not only in sailing but also in a variety of boating-related activities. Campers also compete among themselves in sailing, rowing, and other boating-related competitions. Evenings include movies, dances, all-camp activities, and special events. Campers participate fully in the camp's leadership program and learn more about teamwork, responsibility, self-esteem, and interpersonal skills. There's camp, and then there's Culver!

For more information, see page 1082.

Culver Summer Camps/Upper Camp–Girls

Culver Summer Camps
1300 Academy Road, #138
Culver, Indiana 46511

General Information Girls' residential traditional camp and academic program established in 1902. Accredited by American Camping Association.
Program Focus Recreational and academic opportunities.
Academics Bible study, English as a second language, SAT/ACT preparation, aviation, computers, ecology, environmental science, journalism, mathematics, music, physics, reading, speech/debate, writing.
Arts Arts and crafts (general), band, ceramics, chorus, creative writing, dance, dance (ballet), dance (jazz), dance (modern), drawing, film, jewelry making, leather working, music, music (instrumental), music (vocal), musical productions, painting, photography, pottery, theater/drama, weaving, woodworking.
Special Interest Areas Native American culture, campcraft, community service, driver's education, flight instruction, leadership training, model rocketry, nature study, nautical skills.
Sports Aerobics, archery, baseball, basketball, boating, canoeing, cheerleading, climbing (wall), cross-country, diving, equestrian sports, fencing, figure skating, fishing, football, golf, horseback riding, ice hockey, in-line skating, lacrosse, racquetball, riflery, ropes course, rowing (crew/sculling), sailing, scuba diving, snorkeling, soccer, softball, street/roller hockey, swimming, tennis, track and field, volleyball, waterskiing, weight training, windsurfing, wrestling.
Wilderness/Outdoors Canoe trips.
Program Information 1 session per year. Session length: 6 weeks in June, July, August. Ages: 13–17. 300 participants per session. Boarding program cost: $4000. Application fee: $200. Financial aid available.
Application Deadline Continuous.
Jobs Positions for college students 19 and older.
Contact Mr. Anthony T. Mayfield, Director, main address above. Phone: 800-221-2020. Fax: 574-842-8462. E-mail: summer@culver.org.
URL www.culver.org

Special Note
Culver Summer Girls School is a part of Culver Summer Camps' six-week coeducational camp for girls ages 13–17. Girls may choose from more than sixty-five elective activities to fill their six-class-period day. These activities include a wide selection of sports, music, arts, theater, academics, and special courses. Whether sailing, riding horses, flying airplanes, learning modern dance, or preparing for the SAT, girls have the opportunity to learn, grow, and make friends from all over the world. Afternoons are busy with intramural sports competitions. Evenings include movies, dances, all-camp activities, and special events. Girls participate fully in the camp's leadership program and learn more about teamwork, responsibility, self-esteem, and interpersonal skills.

For more information, see page 1082.

Culver Summer Woodcraft Camp

Culver Summer Camps
1300 Academy Road, #138
Culver, Indiana 46511

General Information Coed residential traditional camp established in 1902. Accredited by American Camping Association.
Program Focus Multiple activity/leadership and fun.
Academics Bible study, English as a second language, SAT/ACT preparation, biology, computers, ecology, environmental science, journalism, marine studies, mathematics, music, reading, speech/debate, writing.
Arts Arts and crafts (general), band, ceramics, chorus, creative writing, dance, dance (ballet), dance (jazz), dance (modern), drawing, film, jewelry making, leather working, music, music (instrumental), music (vocal), musical productions, painting, photography, pottery, theater/drama, weaving, woodworking.
Special Interest Areas Native American culture, campcraft, community service, leadership training, model rocketry, nature study, nautical skills, team building.
Sports Archery, baseball, basketball, boating, canoeing, cheerleading, climbing (wall), cross-country, diving, equestrian sports, fencing, figure skating, fishing, football, golf, horseback riding, ice hockey, lacrosse, racquetball, riflery, ropes course, rowing (crew/sculling), sailing, scuba diving, snorkeling, soccer, softball, swimming, tennis, track and field, volleyball, waterskiing, weight training, wrestling.
Wilderness/Outdoors Canoe trips.
Program Information 1 session per year. Session length: 6 weeks in June, July, August. Ages: 9–13. 600 participants per session. Boarding program cost: $4000. Application fee: $200. Financial aid available.
Application Deadline Continuous.
Jobs Positions for college students 19 and older.
Contact Mr. Anthony T. Mayfield, Director, main address above. Phone: 800-221-2020. Fax: 574-842-8462. E-mail: summer@culver.org.
URL www.culver.org

Special Note
Woodcrafters have a rustic, multimillion-dollar campus all their own that is ideal for filling every hour of a six-week camp session with experiences to last a lifetime. On the north shore of 1,864-acre Lake Maxinkuckee, campers live with 9 other youngsters and a counselor in one of sixty-four cabins beside a museum, a library, two authentic pioneer log cabins, classroom cabins, an observatory, and a dining hall. Like the older campers in the Upper Camp, woodcrafters select instruction from more than sixty-five options, including waterskiing, hockey, soccer, Indian lore and dancing, leadership, scuba diving, a variety of academics, fencing, and other options, from traditional camp crafts to programs such as rocketry. Evenings include movies, dances, all-camp activities, and special events. Campers participate fully in the camp's leadership program and learn more about teamwork, responsibility, self-esteem, and interpersonal skills. There's camp, and then there's Culver!

For more information, see page 1082.

Explore-A-College

Earlham College
Richmond, Indiana 47374-4095

General Information Coed residential academic program established in 1982. Religious affiliation: Society of Friends. Formal opportunities for the academically talented. College credit may be earned.
Academics German language/literature, Japanese language/literature, Spanish language/literature, art history/appreciation, humanities, language study, linguistics, peace education, precollege program, psychology, study skills, writing.
Arts Jewelry making, metalworking, photography.
Trips Cultural, day, shopping.
Program Information 1 session per year. Session length: 2 weeks in June, July. Ages: 14–17. 75–100 participants per session. Boarding program cost: $1375. Application fee: $50. Financial aid available.
Application Deadline Continuous.
Jobs Positions for college students.
Contact Dee Johnson, Director of Summer Studies, Drawer 188, Richmond, Indiana 47374-4095. Phone: 800-EARLHAM. Fax: 765-983-1560. E-mail: ballde@earlham.edu.
URL www.earlham.edu/~eac

Indiana University School of Music College Audition Preparation Workshop

Indiana University School of Music Office of Special Programs
Indiana University School of Music
1201 East Third Street
Bloomington, Indiana 47405-7006

General Information Coed residential arts program established in 1998.
Program Focus Preparing aspiring music majors for college auditions.
Academics Music.
Arts Music, music (ensemble), music (instrumental).
Program Information 1 session per year. Session length: 6 days in July. Ages: 15–18. 80 participants per session. Boarding program cost: $600–$825. Application fee: $50.
Application Deadline Continuous.
Contact Helena Walsh, Registration Coordinator, Office of Special Programs, Indiana University School of Music, Bloomington, Indiana 47405-7006. Phone: 812-855-6025. Fax: 812-855-9847. E-mail: musicsp@indiana.edu.
URL www.music.indiana.edu/

Indiana University School of Music Piano Academy

Indiana University School of Music Office of Special Programs
Indiana University School of Music
1201 East Third Street
Bloomington, Indiana 47405-7006

General Information Coed residential arts program established in 1985.
Program Focus Music, piano.
Academics Music, music (Advanced Placement).
Arts Music, music (classical), music (instrumental), piano.
Trips Cultural, day, shopping.
Program Information 1 session per year. Session length: 3 weeks in June, July. Ages: 10–19. 50–60 participants per session. Boarding program cost: $900–$1775. Application fee: $50. Financial aid available.
Application Deadline Continuous.
Contact Helena Walsh, Registration Coordinator, Office of Special Programs, Indiana University School of Music, Bloomington, Indiana 47405-7006. Phone: 812-855-6025. Fax: 812-855-9847. E-mail: musicsp@indiana.edu.
URL www.music.indiana.edu/som/piano_academy/

Indiana University School of Music Recorder Academy

Indiana University School of Music Office of Special Programs
Indiana University School of Music
1201 East Third Street
Bloomington, Indiana 47405-7006

General Information Coed residential arts program established in 1993.
Program Focus Music, recorder.
Academics Music.
Arts Music, music (classical), music (ensemble), music (recorder).
Trips Cultural, shopping.
Program Information 1 session per year. Session length: 15 days in July. Ages: 10–19. 40–60 participants per session. Boarding program cost: $775–$1430. Application fee: $50. Financial aid available.
Application Deadline Continuous.
Contact Helena Walsh, Registration Coordinator, Office of Special Programs, Indiana University School of Music, Bloomington, Indiana 47405-7006. Phone: 812-855-6025. Fax: 812-855-9847. E-mail: musicsp@indiana.edu.
URL www.music.indiana.edu/som/special_programs/

Indiana University School of Music String Academy

Indiana University School of Music Office of Special Programs
Indiana University School of Music
1201 East Third Street
Bloomington, Indiana 47405-7006

General Information Coed residential arts program established in 1984.
Program Focus Music, strings.
Academics Music.
Arts Music, music (chamber), music (classical), music (instrumental), music (orchestral).
Trips Cultural, shopping.
Program Information 1 session per year. Session length: 4 weeks in June, July. Ages: 10–19. 150–200 participants per session. Boarding program cost: $1250–$2450. Application fee: $50. Financial aid available.
Application Deadline Continuous.
Contact Helena Walsh, Registration Coordinator, Office of Special Programs, Indiana University School of Music, Bloomington, Indiana 47405-7006. Phone: 812-855-6025. Fax: 812-855-9847. E-mail: musicsp@indiana.edu.
URL www.indiana.edu/~smsa/

OPTIONS for Young Women

University of Evansville College of Engineering and Computer Science
1800 Lincoln Avenue
Evansville, Indiana 47620

General Information Girls' residential traditional camp and academic program established in 1992. Formal opportunities for the academically talented.
Program Focus Engineering and computer science.
Academics Academics (general), aerospace science, computer programming, computer science (Advanced Placement), computers, engineering, mathematics, physics, precollege program.
Special Interest Areas Career exploration, college planning, leadership training, robotics, team building.
Sports Climbing (wall), ropes course, swimming, volleyball.
Trips College tours, day.
Program Information 1 session per year. Session length: 1 week in July. Ages: 14–18. 20 participants per session. Boarding program cost: $400. Financial aid available.
Application Deadline May 21.
Summer Contact Ms. Tina Newman, Coordinator, OPTIONS, University of Evansville, 1800 Lincoln Avenue, Evansville, Indiana 47722. Phone: 812-479-2651.
Winter Contact Ms. Tina Newman, Coordinator OPTIONS, University of Evansville, 1800 Lincoln Avenue, Evansville, Indiana 47722. Phone: 812-479-2651.
URL csserver.evansville.edu/~options/ad.htm

Ramey Summer Riding Camps

Ramey Tennis and Equestrian Schools
2354 S 200W
Rockport, Indiana 47635

General Information Coed residential and day sports camp established in 1994.
Program Focus Horseback riding instruction; individual program offered year-round.
Special Interest Areas Animal care, touring.
Sports Aerobics, canoeing, equestrian sports, go-carts, horseback riding, miniature golf, swimming, tennis, volleyball.
Trips Day, shopping.
Program Information 10 sessions per year. Session length: 6 days in January, February, March, April, May, June, July, August, September, October, November, December. Ages: 10–80. 2–20 participants per session. Boarding program cost: $690–$730. Application fee: $50.
Application Deadline Continuous.
Jobs Positions for college students 21 and older.
Contact Ms. Joan G. Ramey, Owner/Director, 2354 South 200 West, Rockport, Indiana 47635. Phone: 812-649-2668. E-mail: jramey66@yahoo.com.
URL www.rameycamps.com

Student Conservation Association–Conservation Crew Program (Indiana)

Student Conservation Association (SCA)
Indiana

General Information Coed residential outdoor program, community service program, and wilderness program established in 1957. High school credit may be earned.
Program Focus Resource management, conservation and environmental education.
Academics Biology, botany, ecology, environmental science, geology/earth science, history.
Special Interest Areas Campcraft, community service, construction, leadership training, nature study, trail maintenance, work camp programs.
Sports Canoeing, fishing, kayaking, swimming.
Wilderness/Outdoors Backpacking, canoe trips, hiking, orienteering, outdoor living skills, wilderness camping.
Trips Cultural, day, overnight.
Program Information 2–3 sessions per year. Session length: 3–5 weeks in June, July, August. Ages: 15–19. 6–8 participants per session. Application fee: $20. Financial aid available. No cost for program; financial aid possible for travel expenses.
Application Deadline Continuous.
Jobs Positions for college students 21 and older.
Contact Recruitment Office, PO Box 550, Charlestown, New Hampshire 03603. Phone: 603-543-1700. Fax: 603-543-1828. E-mail: getreal@thesca.org.
URL www.theSCA.org

IOWA

Camp Courageous of Iowa

12007 190th Street
Monticello, Iowa 52310-0418

General Information Coed residential traditional camp and special needs program established in 1972. Accredited by American Camping Association. Specific services available for the developmentally challenged, hearing impaired, learning disabled, physically challenged, visually impaired, participant with ADD, participant with AD/HD, autistic, and brain injured.
Program Focus Adventure activities and respite care.
Arts Arts and crafts (general).
Special Interest Areas Native American culture, animal care, campcraft, leadership training, nature study.
Sports Archery, basketball, canoeing, climbing (wall), fishing, rappelling, ropes course, skiing (cross-country), swimming, volleyball.
Wilderness/Outdoors Backpacking, bicycle trips, canoe trips, caving, hiking, orienteering, outdoor adventure, rock climbing, wilderness camping.
Trips Overnight.
Program Information 40 sessions per year. Session length: 5–6 days in January, February, March, April, May, June, July, August, September, October, November, December. Ages: 3–80. 40–75 participants per session. Boarding program cost: $300–$600. Financial aid available.
Application Deadline Continuous.
Jobs Positions for high school students 18 and older and college students 18 and older.
Contact Ms. Jeanne Muellerleile, Camp Director, 12007 190th Street, PO Box 418, Monticello, Iowa 52310. Phone: 319-465-5916 Ext.206. Fax: 319-465-5919. E-mail: jmuellerleile@campcourageous.org.
URL www.campcourageous.org

Camp Hitaga

Camp Fire USA, Iowana Council
5551 Hitaga Road
Walker, Iowa 52352

General Information Coed residential and day traditional camp and outdoor program established in 1931.
Program Focus Building self-esteem, cooperation, and leadership skills.
Arts Arts and crafts (general), sing-a-longs, storytelling.
Special Interest Areas Campcraft, nature study.
Sports Archery, canoeing, horseback riding, ropes course, swimming.
Wilderness/Outdoors Canoe trips, hiking.
Trips Overnight.
Program Information 4–8 sessions per year. Session length: 4–7 days in June, July, August, December. Ages: 6–16. 50–70 participants per session. Day program cost: $160. Boarding program cost: $140–$260. Application fee: $25. Financial aid available. Open to participants entering grades 1–10.

Application Deadline Continuous.
Jobs Positions for high school students 17 and older and college students 18 and older.
Summer Contact Doug Kelly, Executive Director, PO Box 10075, Cedar Rapids, Iowa 52410. Phone: 319-294-2411. Fax: 319-294-2413. E-mail: okelly777@aol.com.
Winter Contact Doug Kelly, Executive Director, PO Box 10075, Cedar Rapids, Iowa 52410. Phone: 319-294-2411. E-mail: okelly777@aol.com.
URL www.iowanacouncil.org

Camp Hitaga–Stirrups and Saddles

Camp Fire USA, Iowana Council
5551 Hitaga Road
Walker, Iowa 52352

General Information Coed residential traditional camp and outdoor program established in 1984.
Program Focus Horsemanship fundamentals.
Arts Arts and crafts (general), sing-a-longs.
Special Interest Areas Animal care, campcraft.
Sports Canoeing, equestrian sports, horseback riding, ropes course, swimming.
Wilderness/Outdoors Canoe trips, hiking.
Program Information 8 sessions per year. Session length: 4–7 days in June, July, August. Ages: 10–16. 18 participants per session. Boarding program cost: $170–$295. Financial aid available. Level I open to participants entering grades 6–10; Level II participants entering grades 7–10 with previous Level I. Mini-session open to participants entering grades 5–6.
Application Deadline Continuous.
Jobs Positions for high school students 17 and older and college students 18 and older.
Contact Doug Kelly, Executive Director, PO Box 10075, Cedar Rapids, Iowa 52410. Phone: 319-294-2411. Fax: 319-294-2413. E-mail: okelly777@aol.com.
URL www1.cedar-rapids.net/campfire

Grinnell Summer Institute

Grinnell College
Grinnell, Iowa 50112-0810

General Information Coed residential academic program established in 1983. Formal opportunities for the academically talented and gifted.
Program Focus Analytical skills.
Academics Academics (general), government and politics, mathematics, precollege program, social science, study skills, writing.
Arts Acting, theater/drama.
Sports Aerobics, golf, racquetball, soccer, softball, swimming, tennis, volleyball.
Trips Day, shopping.
Program Information 1 session per year. Session length: 4 weeks in June, July. 35–40 participants per session. Boarding program cost: $2250. Open to participants entering grades 11–12.
Application Deadline March 20.
Jobs Positions for college students.
Contact Jim Sumner, Dean of Admissions/Financial Aid, Office of Admissions, 1103 Park Street, Grinnell, Iowa 50112-0810. Phone: 800-247-0113. Fax: 641-269-4800. E-mail: sumnerj@grinnell.edu.
URL www.grinnell.edu/

Special Note
The Grinnell College Summer Institute offers a valuable preview of college life through challenging academic programs, fun, and responsibility. All of the Summer Institute courses are taught by Grinnell College professors, who are committed to helping students refine techniques in writing, researching, analyzing, and discussing. Outside the classroom, much of students' recreational life revolves around friends from the Institute and the numerous activities in which they choose to participate. The Summer Institute promises to make the summer of 2005 a challenging, productive, and exciting experience for students who are curious about college life and want to further develop their academic abilities.

Iowa Young Writers' Studio

The University of Iowa
100 Oakdale Campus W310
Iowa City, Iowa 52242-5000

General Information Coed residential academic program and arts program established in 1999. Formal opportunities for the artistically talented.
Program Focus Creative writing.
Academics American literature, English language/literature, reading, writing.
Arts Creative writing.
Trips College tours, cultural, day.
Program Information 2 sessions per year. Session length: 2 weeks in June, July. Ages: 14–18. 60 participants per session. Boarding program cost: $1395. Financial aid available.
Application Deadline March 1.
Contact Ms. Trish Walsh, Director, main address above. Phone: 319-335-4209. Fax: 319-335-4039. E-mail: iyws@uiowa.edu.
URL www.uiowa.edu/~iyws

Loras All-Sports Camp

Loras College
1450 Alta Vista Street
Dubuque, Iowa 52004

General Information Coed residential and day sports camp established in 1982. Religious affiliation: Roman Catholic. Specific services available for the learning disabled.
Program Focus Developing a broad range of sport skills and good qualities of sportsmanship.
Sports Archery, baseball, basketball, bicycling, bowling, canoeing, cheerleading, climbing (wall), diving, fishing, football, golf, gymnastics, horseback riding, in-line skating, martial arts, racquetball, roller skating, ropes

Loras All-Sports Camp (continued)

course, rugby, soccer, softball, sports (general), swimming, tennis, track and field, volleyball, water polo, wrestling, yoga.
Wilderness/Outdoors Orienteering, rock climbing, trap shooting.
Trips Day.
Program Information 4 sessions per year. Session length: 5 days in June, July. Ages: 7–13. 550–565 participants per session. Day program cost: $300–$325. Boarding program cost: $465–$490. Application fee: $100. Financial aid available.
Application Deadline Continuous.
Jobs Positions for college students 19 and older.
Contact Dr. Robert Tucker, Director, main address above. Phone: 563-588-7196. Fax: 563-588-4975. E-mail: sportscamp@loras.edu.
URL www.loras.edu/~PHE/all_sports

Student Conservation Association–Conservation Crew Program (Iowa)

Student Conservation Association (SCA)
Iowa

General Information Coed residential outdoor program, community service program, and wilderness program established in 1957. High school credit may be earned.
Program Focus Resource management, conservation and environmental education.
Academics Biology, botany, ecology, environmental science, geology/earth science, history.
Special Interest Areas Campcraft, community service, construction, leadership training, nature study, trail maintenance, work camp programs.
Sports Canoeing, fishing, kayaking, swimming.
Wilderness/Outdoors Backpacking, canoe trips, hiking, orienteering, outdoor living skills, wilderness camping.
Trips Cultural, day, overnight.
Program Information 2–3 sessions per year. Session length: 3–5 weeks in June, July, August. Ages: 15–19. 6–8 participants per session. Application fee: $20. Financial aid available. No cost for program; financial aid possible for travel expenses.
Application Deadline Continuous.
Jobs Positions for college students 21 and older.
Contact Recruitment Office, PO Box 550, Charlestown, New Hampshire 03603. Phone: 603-543-1700. Fax: 603-543-1828. E-mail: getreal@thesca.org.
URL www.theSCA.org

Ventures Travel Service–Iowa

Friendship Ventures
Iowa

General Information Coed travel special needs program established in 1985. Specific services available for the developmentally challenged and physically challenged.
Program Focus Provides travel services to older teens and adults with developmental disabilities.
Special Interest Areas Touring.
Program Information 50 sessions per year. Session length: 4–10 days in February, March, April, May, June, July, August, September, October, November, December. Ages: 14–70. 4–8 participants per session. Cost: $395–$2000.
Application Deadline Continuous.
Jobs Positions for college students 18 and older.
Contact Georgann Rumsey, President/CEO, 10509 108th Street, NW, Annandale, Minnesota 55302. Phone: 952-852-0101. Fax: 952-852-0123. E-mail: fv@friendshipventures.org.
URL www.friendshipventures.org

KANSAS

Bill Self Kansas Summer Basketball Camp

University of Kansas
Lawrence, Kansas 66045

General Information Boys' residential and day sports camp.
Program Focus To teach and develop basketball skills.
Sports Basketball.
Program Information 1–2 sessions per year. Session length: 4 days in June. Ages: 8–19. 40–80 participants per session. Day program cost: $300. Boarding program cost: $395.
Application Deadline Continuous.
Jobs Positions for college students 19 and older.
Contact Basketball Camp, Allen Fieldhouse, 1651 Naismith Drive, Lawrence, Kansas 66045. Phone: 785-864-3056. E-mail: mensbasketball@jayhawks.org.
URL www.kuathletics.com/mensbasketball/camp/index.html

Future Astronaut Training Program

Kansas Cosmosphere and Space Center
1100 North Plum
Hutchinson, Kansas 67501

General Information Coed residential academic program established in 1985.
Program Focus Hands-on aerospace education, with emphasis on teamwork and personal achievement.
Academics Aerospace science, astronomy, communications, computers, engineering, environmental science, geology/earth science, health sciences, history, mathematics, physics, physiology, science (general).
Special Interest Areas Career exploration, flight instruction, leadership training, model rocketry, robotics, team building.
Program Information 11 sessions per year. Session length: 5 days in May, June, July, August. Ages: 12–15. 40 participants per session. Boarding program cost: $595. Financial aid available.
Application Deadline Continuous.

Jobs Positions for high school students 15 and older and college students.
Contact Mrs. Laurie Givan, Camp Registrar, main address above. Phone: 800-397-0330 Ext.323. Fax: 620-662-3693. E-mail: laurieg@cosmo.org.
URL www.cosmo.org

JAYHAWK DEBATE INSTITUTE

University of Kansas
Lawrence, Kansas 66045

General Information Coed residential and day academic program established in 1966.
Program Focus Intensive 2 and 3-week camp for high school policy debate.
Academics Speech/debate.
Program Information 2 sessions per year. Session length: 13–20 days in June, July. Ages: 13–18. Day program cost: $500–$750. Boarding program cost: $900–$1200.
Application Deadline Continuous.
Jobs Positions for college students 20 and older.
Contact Jacob Thompson, Associate Debate Institute Director, Department of Communication Studies, 1440 Jayhawk Boulevard—SB 103 Bailey Hall, Lawrence, Kansas 66045. Phone: 785-864-9893. Fax: 785-864-5203. E-mail: coms3@raven.cc.ukans.edu.
URL www.kudebate.org/~coms3/home.html

KANSAS JOURNALISM INSTITUTE

University of Kansas
200 Stauffer-Flint Hall
1435 Jayhawk Boulevard
Lawrence, Kansas 66045

General Information Coed residential academic program established in 1963.
Program Focus Journalism.
Academics Advertising, journalism, photojournalism.
Arts Photography, radio broadcasting, television/video.
Special Interest Areas Yearbook production.
Program Information 1 session per year. Session length: 4 days in June. Ages: 13–18. 165–250 participants per session. Boarding program cost: $310. Financial aid available.
Application Deadline May 5.
Jobs Positions for college students 20 and older.
Contact John Hudnall, Director, main address above. Phone: 785-864-0605. Fax: 785-864-5945. E-mail: kspa@ku.edu.
URL www.ku.edu/~jschool/kji

KU JAZZ WORKSHOP

University of Kansas
452 Murphy Hall
1530 Naismith Drive, #452
Lawrence, Kansas 66045-3120

General Information Coed residential and day arts program established in 1990. Formal opportunities for the artistically talented. College credit may be earned.
Program Focus Jazz instruction and performance.
Academics Music.
Arts Music, music (ensemble), music (jazz), musical performance/recitals.
Program Information 1 session per year. Session length: 6 days in July. Ages: 13+. 100 participants per session. Day program cost: $285. Boarding program cost: $475.
Application Deadline May 5.
Jobs Positions for college students 19 and older.
Contact James Hudson, Director, main address above. Phone: 785-864-4730. Fax: 785-864-5023. E-mail: musicamp@ku.edu.
URL www.ku.edu/~mad/summer/mwmcamp/#content

KU MARCHING BAND CAMPS

University of Kansas
400 Murphy Hall
1530 Naismith Drive
Lawrence, Kansas 66045

General Information Coed residential and day arts program established in 1991. High school credit may be earned.
Program Focus Instruction in flag, rifle, drum major, and student leadership.
Arts Band, dance, music.
Special Interest Areas Color guard/flag, drum majoring.
Program Information 1 session per year. Session length: 4 days in July. Ages: 13–18. 200 participants per session. Day program cost: $175. Boarding program cost: $275.
Application Deadline Continuous.
Jobs Positions for college students 19 and older.
Contact James Hudson, Director, 452 Murphy Hall, 1530 Naismith Drive, #452, Lawrence, Kansas 66045-3120. Phone: 785-864-4730. Fax: 785-864-5023. E-mail: musicamp@ku.edu.
URL www.musiccamp.ku.edu

MARS ACADEMY

Kansas Cosmosphere and Space Center
1100 North Plum
Hutchinson, Kansas 67501

General Information Coed residential academic program established in 2003.
Program Focus Hands-on aerospace education with emphasis on Mars exploration and robotics.
Academics Aerospace science, astronomy, biology, botany, ecology, engineering, geology/earth science, health sciences, mathematics, physics, physiology, science (general).
Special Interest Areas Career exploration, leadership training, robotics, team building.
Program Information 4–6 sessions per year. Session length: 3 days in May, June, July. Ages: 10–12. 40 participants per session. Boarding program cost: $205. Financial aid available.
Application Deadline Continuous.
Jobs Positions for college students.

Mars Academy (continued)

Contact Mrs. Laurie Givan, Education Registrar, main address above. Phone: 800-397-0330 Ext.323. Fax: 620-662-3693. E-mail: laurieg@cosmo.org.
URL www.cosmo.org

Student Conservation Association–Conservation Crew Program (Kansas)

Student Conservation Association (SCA)
Kansas

General Information Coed residential outdoor program, community service program, and wilderness program established in 1957. High school credit may be earned.
Program Focus Resource management, conservation and environmental education.
Academics Biology, botany, ecology, environmental science, geology/earth science, history.
Special Interest Areas Campcraft, community service, construction, leadership training, nature study, trail maintenance, work camp programs.
Sports Canoeing, fishing, kayaking, swimming.
Wilderness/Outdoors Backpacking, canoe trips, hiking, orienteering, outdoor living skills, wilderness camping.
Trips Cultural, day, overnight.
Program Information 2–3 sessions per year. Session length: 3–5 weeks in June, July, August. Ages: 15–19. 6–8 participants per session. Application fee: $20. Financial aid available. No cost for program; financial aid possible for travel expenses.
Application Deadline Continuous.
Jobs Positions for college students 21 and older.
Contact Recruitment Office, PO Box 550, Charlestown, New Hampshire 03603. Phone: 603-543-1700. Fax: 603-543-1828. E-mail: getreal@thesca.org.
URL www.theSCA.org

University of Kansas–Boys Soccer Camp

University of Kansas
Lawrence, Kansas

General Information Boys' residential and day sports camp.
Program Focus Soccer.
Sports Soccer.
Program Information 2–4 sessions per year. Session length: 4–5 days in June, July. Ages: 9–13. 30–60 participants per session. Day program cost: $80–$390. Boarding program cost: $405.
Application Deadline Continuous.
Jobs Positions for college students 19 and older.
Contact Kelly Miller, Kansas Soccer Camps, Inc., Allen Fieldhouse, 1651 Naismith Drive, Lawrence, Kansas 66045. Phone: 785-864-3560. E-mail: kpmiller@ku.edu.
URL www.kuathletics.com/soccer/camp/camp.html

University of Kansas–Duke University Talent Identification Program

University of Kansas
Lawrence, Kansas 66045

General Information Coed residential academic program. Formal opportunities for the academically talented.
Program Focus Challenge program for academically talented students.
Academics Academics (general), aerospace science, architecture, engineering, government and politics, health sciences, humanities, international relations, mathematics (Advanced Placement), philosophy, physics, psychology, science (general), writing.
Arts Cinematography, creative writing, film, television/video.
Special Interest Areas Career exploration, college planning.
Trips College tours.
Program Information 1–2 sessions per year. Session length: 3 weeks in June, July. Ages: 12–18. 160 participants per session. Boarding program cost: $2350. Financial aid available.
Application Deadline Continuous.
Jobs Positions for college students 19 and older.
Contact TIP Program Director, 1121 West Main Street, Durham, North Carolina 27701-2028. Phone: 919-668-9100. Fax: 919-681-7921. E-mail: information@tip.duke.edu.
URL www.tip.duke.edu/ss/kansas.htm

University of Kansas–Girls Golf Camp

University of Kansas
Lawrence, Kansas 66045

General Information Girls' residential and day sports camp.
Program Focus Golf.
Sports Golf.
Program Information 1 session per year. Session length: 5 days in June, July. Ages: 10–18. 15–20 participants per session. Day program cost: $575. Boarding program cost: $675.
Application Deadline June 2.
Jobs Positions for college students 19 and older.
Contact Women's Golf Office, Allen Fieldhouse, 1651 Naismith Drive, Lawrence, Kansas 66045. E-mail: womensgolf@jayhawks.org.
URL www.kuathletics.com/womensgolf/camp/index.html

University of Kansas–Girls Soccer Camp

University of Kansas
Lawrence, Kansas 66045

General Information Girls' residential and day sports camp.
Program Focus Soccer.

Sports Soccer.
Program Information 2–4 sessions per year. Session length: 4–5 days in June, July. Ages: 9–18. 30–60 participants per session. Day program cost: $80–$390. Boarding program cost: $405.
Application Deadline Continuous.
Jobs Positions for college students 19 and older.
Contact Kelly Miller, Kansas Soccer Camps, Inc., Allen Fieldhouse, 1651 Naismith Drive, Lawrence, Kansas 66045. Phone: 785-864-3560. E-mail: kpmiller@ku.edu.
URL www.kuathletics.com/soccer/camp/camp.html

University of Kansas–Jayhawk Baseball Camps–Little League, Super Skills, and All-Star

University of Kansas
Lawrence, Kansas 66045

General Information Coed residential and day sports camp.
Program Focus Baseball instruction at all skill levels.
Sports Baseball.
Program Information 4 sessions per year. Session length: 4–5 days in June, July. Ages: 7–18. 20–40 participants per session. Day program cost: $125–$295. Boarding program cost: $345–$395.
Application Deadline Continuous.
Jobs Positions for college students 19 and older.
Contact Marcia Bagby, Athletics Department, University of Kansas, Allen Fieldhouse, 1651 Naismith Drive, Lawrence, Kansas 66045. Phone: 785-864-7907. E-mail: mlbagby@ku.edu.
URL www.kuathletics.com/baseball/camp/index.html

University of Kansas–Jayhawk Boys and Girls Tennis Camp

University of Kansas
Lawrence, Kansas 66045

General Information Coed residential sports camp.
Program Focus Tennis.
Sports Tennis.
Program Information 1 session per year. Session length: 5 days in June. Ages: 13–18. 5–20 participants per session. Boarding program cost: $400.
Application Deadline Continuous.
Jobs Positions for college students 19 and older.
Contact Jayhawk Tennis Camp, University of Kansas, 1651 Naismith Drive, Lawrence, Kansas 66045. Phone: 785-864-7909.
URL www.kuathletics.com/womenstennis/camp/index.html

University of Kansas–Jayhawk Golf Camp–Boys

University of Kansas
Lawrence, Kansas 66045

General Information Boys' residential and day sports camp.
Program Focus Golf.
Sports Golf.
Program Information 1–2 sessions per year. Session length: 5 days in June. Ages: 10–18. 15–25 participants per session. Day program cost: $600. Boarding program cost: $700.
Jobs Positions for college students 19 and older.
Contact Ross Randall, Ross Randall Golf Camp, Inc., 2104 Inverness Drive, Lawrence, Kansas 66045. Phone: 785-842-1714. E-mail: rossran@ku.edu.
URL www.kuathletics.com/mensgolf/camps/index.html

University of Kansas–Jayhawk Swim Camp

University of Kansas
Emporia State University
Emporia, Kansas

General Information Coed residential sports camp.
Program Focus Swimming techniques camp and skills camp.
Sports Swimming.
Program Information 1–2 sessions per year. Session length: 5–7 days in June. Ages: 9–18. 20–50 participants per session. Boarding program cost: $275–$375. Financial aid available. $599 for both techniques and skills camps.
Application Deadline Continuous.
Jobs Positions for college students 19 and older.
Contact Pam Byrn, Swim Camp Coordinator, main address above. Phone: 785-864-7924. E-mail: pbyrn@ku.edu.
URL www.kuathletics.com/womensswimming/camp/index.html

University of Kansas–Jayhawk Track and Field/Cross Country Camps

University of Kansas
Lawrence, Kansas 66045

General Information Coed residential and day sports camp.
Program Focus Track and field and cross country.
Sports Cross-country, swimming, track and field, volleyball.
Program Information 1 session per year. Session length: 5 days in July. Ages: 11–18. 40–60 participants per session. Day program cost: $295. Boarding program cost: $395.
Application Deadline July 1.
Jobs Positions for college students 19 and older.
Contact Debbie Luman, Jayhawk Track Camps, 1651 Naismith Drive, Lawrence, Kansas 66045. Phone: 785-864-3486. Fax: 785-864-5525. E-mail: dluman@ku.edu.
URL www.kuathletics.com/track/camp/index.html

University of Kansas–Jayhawk Volleyball Camp

University of Kansas
Lawrence, Kansas 66045

General Information Coed residential and day sports camp.
Program Focus Volleyball skills, hitter and setter training.
Sports Volleyball.
Program Information 3–5 sessions per year. Session length: 4–5 days in June, July. Ages: 11–18. 20–40 participants per session. Day program cost: $75. Boarding program cost: $225–$300.
Application Deadline Continuous.
Jobs Positions for college students 19 and older.
Contact Christi Posey, main address above. Phone: 785-864-7959. E-mail: volleyball@jayhawks.org.
URL www.kuathletics.com/volleyball/camp/index.html

University of Kansas–Midwestern Music Camp–Junior and Senior Divisions

University of Kansas
452 Murphy Hall
1530 Naismith Drive #452
Lawrence, Kansas 66045

General Information Coed residential and day arts program established in 1936. Formal opportunities for the artistically talented.
Program Focus Piano, band, orchestra, choir, and jazz ensemble.
Academics Music.
Arts Band, chorus, music, music (chamber), music (classical), music (ensemble), music (instrumental), music (jazz), music (orchestral), music (vocal).
Program Information 2 sessions per year. Session length: 1–2 weeks in June, July. Ages: 11–18. 300–600 participants per session. Day program cost: $250–$450. Boarding program cost: $475–$875. Financial aid available.
Application Deadline May 15.
Jobs Positions for college students 19 and older.
Contact James Hudson, Director, 452 Murphy Hall, 1530 Naismith Drive, #452, Lawrence, Kansas 66045-3120. Phone: 785-864-4730. Fax: 785-864-5023. E-mail: musicamp@ku.edu.
URL www.musiccamp.ku.edu

University of Kansas–Natural History Museum Summer Workshops

University of Kansas
Natural History Museum and Biodiversity Research Center
1345 Jayhawk Boulevard
Lawrence, Kansas 66045

General Information Coed day academic program.
Academics Academics (general), anthropology, archaeology, area studies, biology, botany, ecology, environmental science, geology/earth science, history, humanities, intercultural studies, oceanography, social science.
Special Interest Areas Field research/expeditions.
Program Information 1–2 sessions per year. Session length: 5–7 days in June, July, August. Ages: 4–14. 16–18 participants per session. Day program cost: $65–$75. Financial aid available.
Application Deadline Continuous.
Jobs Positions for college students 19 and older.
Contact Public Education Office, Assistant Director of Public Affairs, main address above. Phone: 785-864-4173. E-mail: kunhm@ku.edu.
URL www.nhm.ku.edu/pubed/summerworkshops.html

University of Kansas–Project Discovery

University of Kansas
School of Engineering, Eaton Hall
1520 West 15th Street
Lawrence, Kansas 66045

General Information Girls' residential academic program.
Program Focus Exploring science and engineering principles in an enlightening, no-pressure setting.
Academics Aerospace science, architecture, chemistry, engineering, mathematics, physics, science (general).
Arts Television/video.
Special Interest Areas Career exploration, college planning, field research/expeditions, team building.
Sports Bowling, swimming.
Trips College tours, day.
Program Information 1–2 sessions per year. Session length: 6–12 days in June. Ages: 13–18. 30–40 participants per session. Boarding program cost: $300–$600. Financial aid available.
Application Deadline May 1.
Jobs Positions for college students 19 and older.
Contact Florence Boldridge, Director of Diversity Programs, main address above. Phone: 785-864-3620. E-mail: fboldridge@ku.edu.
URL www.engr.ku.edu

University of Kansas–School of Pharmacy Summer Camp

University of Kansas
School of Pharmacy, 2056 Malott Hall
1251 Wesoce Hall Drive
Lawrence, Kansas 66045

General Information Coed residential academic program.
Program Focus Learning about career opportunities in the profession of pharmacy.
Academics Anatomy, biology, chemistry, health sciences, medical technology, pharmacology, science (general).
Special Interest Areas Career exploration, college planning, field research/expeditions.
Trips Day.

Program Information 1 session per year. Session length: 5 days in June. Ages: 13–18. 15–20 participants per session. Boarding program cost: $375. Financial aid available.
Application Deadline May 1.
Jobs Positions for college students 19 and older.
Contact Gene Hotchkiss, Pharmacy Summer Camp Coordinator, main address above. Phone: 785-864-3591. E-mail: ghotchkiss@ku.edu.
URL www2.pharm.ku.edu/phpr/camp/camp.html

UNIVERSITY OF KANSAS–SERTOMA-SCHIEFELBUSH COMMUNICATION CAMP

University of Kansas
2101 Haworth Hall
1200 Sunnyside Avenue
Lawrence, Kansas 66045

General Information Coed day traditional camp and special needs program. Specific services available for the hearing impaired and speech impaired.
Program Focus Children and youth with and without communication challenges exploring and improving skills while participating in camp activities.
Academics Intercultural studies.
Arts Arts and crafts (general).
Special Interest Areas Communication skills, field trips (arts and culture), nature study, speech therapy.
Trips Cultural, day.
Program Information 3–5 sessions per year. Session length: 3–6 days in June, July. Ages: 4–16. Day program cost: $75–$100. Financial aid available. For children with communication challenges cost is $15–$20.
Application Deadline Continuous.
Jobs Positions for college students 19 and older.
Contact Jane Wegner, main address above. Phone: 785-864-4690. Fax: 785-864-5094. E-mail: jwegner@ku.edu.
URL www.ku.edu/~splh/CommunicationCamp/

UNIVERSITY OF KANSAS–SOFTBALL–TEEN AND ADVANCED CAMPS

University of Kansas
Lawrence, Kansas 66045

General Information Coed residential and day sports camp.
Program Focus Softball.
Sports Softball.
Program Information 2–5 sessions per year. Session length: 4–10 days in June, July. Ages: 13–18. 30–60 participants per session. Day program cost: $250–$275. Boarding program cost: $300–$315.
Application Deadline Continuous.
Jobs Positions for college students 19 and older.
Contact Christi Musser, Assistant Softball Coach, University of Kansas Softball Camps and Clinics, 1651 Naismith Drive, Lawrence, Kansas 66045. Phone: 785-864-7964. E-mail: cmusser@ku.edu.
URL www.kuathletics.com/softball/camp/index.html

UNIVERSITY OF KANSAS–SPORTS SKILLS AND FITNESS CAMP

University of Kansas
Lawrence, Kansas 66045

General Information Coed day sports camp.
Program Focus Swimming, gymnastics, tennis, soccer, sports skills, and fitness.
Sports Gymnastics, physical fitness, soccer, sports (general), swimming, tennis.
Program Information 1–2 sessions per year. Session length: 3 weeks in June, July. Ages: 7–14. 80–180 participants per session. Day program cost: $180. Financial aid available.
Application Deadline March 1.
Summer Contact Jim La Point, Co-director, HSES Department, Room 104, University of Kansas, 1301 Sunnyside Avenue, Lawrence, Kansas 66045. Phone: 785-864-0785. E-mail: jdl@ku.edu.
Winter Contact Jim La Point, Co-director, University of Kansas, 104 Robinson, Lawrence, Kansas 66045. Phone: 785-864-0785. E-mail: jdl@ku.edu.
URL www.soe.ku.edu/depts/hses/outreach/

KENTUCKY

CAGE SCOPE/HIGH POTENTIAL "BLUE-CHIP" BASKETBALL CAMP

Cage Scope/High Potential "Blue-Chip" Basketball Camp
Georgetown College
Georgetown, Kentucky 40324

General Information Boys' residential sports camp established in 1980.
Sports Basketball.
Program Information 3 sessions per year. Session length: 5 days in June, July. Ages: 14–20. 300 participants per session. Boarding program cost: $360.
Application Deadline Continuous.
Contact Mr. Dave Bones, Co-Director, PO Box 607, Holland, Ohio 43528. Phone: 419-867-8008. Fax: 419-843-4635.
URL www.basketball-camp.net

EARTHWATCH INSTITUTE–MAMMOTH CAVE

Earthwatch Institute
Kentucky

General Information Coed residential outdoor program, cultural program, and adventure program.
Program Focus Hiking to the ends of the world's longest cave system to reconstruct its entire human history.
Academics Archaeology, science (general).
Arts Photography.
Special Interest Areas Field research/expeditions, nature study.
Wilderness/Outdoors Caving, hiking.

EARTHWATCH INSTITUTE–Mammoth Cave (continued)

Program Information 4 sessions per year. Session length: 10 days in July, October. Ages: 16+. 10 participants per session. Boarding program cost: $895–$995. Financial aid available. Financial aid for high school students and teachers.
Application Deadline Continuous.
Contact General Information Desk, PO Box 75, Maynard, Massachusetts 01754. Phone: 800-776-0188. Fax: 978-461-2332. E-mail: info@earthwatch.org.
URL www.earthwatch.org

FOSTER GUITAR CAMP

Eastern Kentucky University Department of Music
521 Lancaster Avenue
Richmond, Kentucky 40475-3102

General Information Coed residential and day arts program. Formal opportunities for the academically talented and artistically talented.
Academics Music, music (Advanced Placement).
Arts Band, chorus, guitar, music, music (chamber), music (classical), music (ensemble), music (instrumental), music (jazz), music (orchestral), music (vocal), music theory, musical performance/recitals, musical productions.
Sports Basketball, diving, football, gymnastics, racquetball, soccer, softball, swimming, tennis, volleyball.
Trips College tours, cultural, day, overnight, shopping.
Program Information 1–8 sessions per year. Session length: 6–13 days in June. Ages: 13+. 30–150 participants per session. Day program cost: $180. Boarding program cost: $265–$625. Financial aid available.
Application Deadline Continuous.
Jobs Positions for college students.
Contact Dr. Joe Allison, Camps Director, main address above. Phone: 859-622-3161. Fax: 859-622-1333.
URL www.fostermusic.eku.edu

FOSTER HIGH SCHOOL BAND CAMP

Eastern Kentucky University Department of Music
521 Lancaster Avenue
Richmond, Kentucky 40475-3102

General Information Coed residential and day arts program. Formal opportunities for the academically talented and artistically talented.
Academics Music, music (Advanced Placement).
Arts Band, chorus, music, music (chamber), music (classical), music (ensemble), music (instrumental), music (jazz), music (orchestral), music (vocal), music theory, musical performance/recitals, musical productions.
Sports Basketball, diving, football, gymnastics, racquetball, soccer, softball, swimming, tennis, volleyball.
Trips College tours, cultural, day, overnight.
Program Information 1 session per year. Session length: 2 weeks in June. Ages: 14–17. 30–150 participants per session. Day program cost: $295. Boarding program cost: $495–$625. Financial aid available.
Application Deadline Continuous.
Jobs Positions for college students.
Contact Dr. Joe Allison, Camps Director, main address above. Phone: 859-622-3161. Fax: 859-622-1333. E-mail: fostercamp@eku.edu.
URL www.fostermusic.eku.edu

FOSTER HIGH SCHOOL STRINGS CAMP

Eastern Kentucky University Department of Music
521 Lancaster Avenue
Richmond, Kentucky 40475-3102

General Information Coed residential and day arts program. Formal opportunities for the academically talented and artistically talented.
Academics Music, music (Advanced Placement).
Arts Band, chorus, music, music (chamber), music (classical), music (ensemble), music (instrumental), music (jazz), music (orchestral), music (vocal), musical performance/recitals, musical productions.
Sports Basketball, diving, football, gymnastics, racquetball, soccer, softball, swimming, volleyball.
Trips College tours, cultural, day, overnight, shopping.
Program Information 1 session per year. Session length: 2 weeks in June. Ages: 13–18. 30–150 participants per session. Day program cost: $295. Boarding program cost: $495–$625. Financial aid available.
Application Deadline Continuous.
Jobs Positions for college students.
Contact Dr. Joe Allison, Camps Director, main address above. Phone: 859-622-3161. Fax: 859-622-1333.
URL www.fostermusic.eku.edu

FOSTER MIDDLE SCHOOL BAND CAMP

Eastern Kentucky University Department of Music
521 Lancaster Avenue
Richmond, Kentucky 40475-3102

General Information Coed residential and day arts program established in 1935. Formal opportunities for the academically talented and artistically talented.
Academics Music, music (Advanced Placement).
Arts Band, chorus, music, music (chamber), music (classical), music (ensemble), music (instrumental), music (jazz), music (orchestral), music (vocal), musical performance/recitals, musical productions.
Sports Basketball, diving, football, gymnastics, racquetball, soccer, softball, swimming, tennis, volleyball.
Trips College tours, cultural, day, overnight, shopping.
Program Information 1 session per year. Session length: 6 days in June. Ages: 12+. 30–150 participants per session. Day program cost: $195. Boarding program cost: $295–$365. Financial aid available.
Application Deadline Continuous.
Jobs Positions for college students.
Contact Dr. Joe Allison, Camps Director, main address above. Phone: 859-622-3161. Fax: 859-622-1333. E-mail: fostercamp@eku.edu.
URL www.fostermusic.eku.edu

Foster Middle School Strings Camp

Eastern Kentucky University Department of Music
521 Lancaster Avenue
Richmond, Kentucky 40475-3102

General Information Coed residential and day arts program. Formal opportunities for the academically talented and artistically talented.
Academics Music, music (Advanced Placement).
Arts Band, chorus, music, music (chamber), music (classical), music (ensemble), music (instrumental), music (jazz), music (orchestral), music (vocal), musical performance/recitals.
Sports Basketball, diving, football, gymnastics, racquetball, soccer, softball, swimming, tennis, volleyball.
Trips College tours, cultural, day, overnight, shopping.
Program Information 1 session per year. Session length: 6 days in June. Ages: 12+. 30–150 participants per session. Day program cost: $275. Boarding program cost: $375. Financial aid available.
Application Deadline Continuous.
Jobs Positions for college students.
Contact Dr. Joe Allison, Camps Director, main address above. Phone: 859-622-3161. Fax: 859-622-1333.
URL www.fostermusic.eku.edu

Foster Piano Camp I

Eastern Kentucky University Department of Music
521 Lancaster Avenue
Richmond, Kentucky 40475-3102

General Information Coed residential and day arts program. Formal opportunities for the academically talented and artistically talented.
Academics Music, music (Advanced Placement).
Arts Band, chorus, music, music (chamber), music (classical), music (ensemble), music (instrumental), music (jazz), music (orchestral), music (vocal), musical performance/recitals, piano.
Sports Basketball, diving, football, gymnastics, racquetball, soccer, softball, swimming, tennis, volleyball.
Trips College tours, cultural, day, overnight, shopping.
Program Information 1 session per year. Session length: 6 days in June. Ages: 12+. 30–150 participants per session. Day program cost: $245. Boarding program cost: $350. Financial aid available.
Application Deadline Continuous.
Jobs Positions for college students.
Contact Dr. Joe Allison, Camps Director, main address above. Phone: 859-622-3161. Fax: 859-622-1333.
URL www.fostermusic.eku.edu

Foster Piano Camp II

Eastern Kentucky University Department of Music
521 Lancaster Avenue
Richmond, Kentucky 40475-3102

General Information Coed residential and day arts program. Formal opportunities for the academically talented and artistically talented.
Academics Music, music (Advanced Placement).
Arts Band, chorus, music, music (chamber), music (classical), music (ensemble), music (instrumental), music (jazz), music (orchestral), music (vocal), musical performance/recitals, piano.
Sports Basketball, diving, football, gymnastics, racquetball, soccer, softball, swimming, tennis, volleyball.
Trips College tours, cultural, day, overnight, shopping.
Program Information 1 session per year. Session length: 6 days in June. Ages: 14–17. 30–150 participants per session. Day program cost: $245. Boarding program cost: $350. Financial aid available.
Application Deadline Continuous.
Jobs Positions for college students.
Contact Dr. Joe Allison, Camps Director, main address above. Phone: 859-622-3161. Fax: 859-622-1333.
URL www.fostermusic.eku.edu

Foster Vocal Camp

Eastern Kentucky University Department of Music
521 Lancaster Avenue
Richmond, Kentucky 40475-3102

General Information Coed residential and day arts program. Formal opportunities for the academically talented and artistically talented.
Academics Music, music (Advanced Placement).
Arts Band, chorus, music, music (chamber), music (classical), music (ensemble), music (instrumental), music (jazz), music (orchestral), music (vocal), musical performance/recitals.
Sports Basketball, diving, football, gymnastics, racquetball, soccer, softball, swimming, tennis, volleyball.
Trips College tours, cultural, day, overnight, shopping.
Program Information 1 session per year. Session length: 6 days in June. Ages: 14–17. 30–150 participants per session. Day program cost: $280. Boarding program cost: $380. Financial aid available.
Application Deadline Continuous.
Jobs Positions for college students.
Contact Dr. Joe Allison, Camps Director, main address above. Phone: 859-622-3161. Fax: 859-622-1333.
URL www.fostermusic.eku.edu

Ramey Summer Tennis Camps

Ramey Tennis and Equestrian Schools
5931 Highway 56
Owensboro, Kentucky 42301-9302

General Information Coed residential and day sports camp established in 1962.
Program Focus Tennis; individual program offered year-round.
Sports Aerobics, basketball, go-carts, horseback riding, miniature golf, tennis, volleyball.
Trips Shopping.
Program Information 10 sessions per year. Session length: 6 days in January, February, March, April, May, June, July, August, September, October, November, December. Ages: 8–80. 2–20 participants per session. Boarding program cost: $690–$730. Application fee: $50.
Application Deadline Continuous.

Ramey Summer Tennis Camps (continued)

Jobs Positions for college students 21 and older.
Contact Ms. Joan G. Ramey, Director/Owner, 2354 S 200W, Rockport, Indiana 47635. Phone: 812-649-2668. E-mail: jramey66@yahoo.com.
URL www.rameycamps.com

Student Conservation Association–Conservation Crew Program (Kentucky)

Student Conservation Association (SCA)
Kentucky

General Information Coed residential outdoor program, community service program, and wilderness program established in 1957. High school credit may be earned.
Program Focus Resource management, conservation and environmental education.
Academics Biology, botany, ecology, environmental science, geology/earth science, history.
Special Interest Areas Campcraft, community service, construction, leadership training, nature study, trail maintenance, work camp programs.
Sports Canoeing, fishing, kayaking, swimming.
Wilderness/Outdoors Backpacking, canoe trips, hiking, orienteering, outdoor living skills, wilderness camping.
Trips Cultural, day, overnight.
Program Information 2–3 sessions per year. Session length: 3–5 weeks in June, July, August. Ages: 15–19. 6–8 participants per session. Application fee: $20. Financial aid available. No cost for program; financial aid possible for travel expenses.
Application Deadline Continuous.
Jobs Positions for college students 21 and older.
Contact Recruitment Office, PO Box 550, Charlestown, New Hampshire 03603. Phone: 603-543-1700. Fax: 603-543-1828. E-mail: getreal@thesca.org.
URL www.theSCA.org

Ventures Travel Service–Kentucky

Friendship Ventures
Kentucky

General Information Coed travel special needs program established in 1985. Specific services available for the developmentally challenged and physically challenged.
Program Focus Provides travel services to older teens and adults with developmental disabilities.
Special Interest Areas Touring.
Program Information 50 sessions per year. Session length: 4–10 days in February, March, April, May, June, July, August, September, October, November, December. Ages: 14–70. 4–8 participants per session. Cost: $395–$2000.
Application Deadline Continuous.
Jobs Positions for college students 18 and older.
Contact Georgann Rumsey, President/CEO, 10509 108th Street, NW, Annandale, Minnesota 55302. Phone: 952-852-0101. Fax: 952-852-0123. E-mail: fv@friendshipventures.org.
URL www.friendshipventures.org

LOUISIANA

Camp Bon Coeur

405 West Main Street
Lafayette, Louisiana 70501

General Information Coed residential special needs program established in 1985. Accredited by American Camping Association. Specific services available for the participant with heart defects.
Program Focus Camp for kids with heart defects.
Academics Area studies.
Arts Arts and crafts (general), fabric arts, film, music, radio broadcasting, theater/drama.
Special Interest Areas Campcraft, cardiac education, nature study.
Sports Archery, basketball, horseback riding, swimming.
Wilderness/Outdoors Hiking.
Trips Cultural, day.
Program Information 2 sessions per year. Session length: 10–13 days in July. Ages: 8–16. 30–50 participants per session. Boarding program cost: $1000–$1350. Application fee: $35. Financial aid available.
Application Deadline April 1.
Jobs Positions for college students 18 and older.
Contact Ms. Susannah Craig, Executive Director, PO Box 53765, Lafayette, Louisiana 70505. Phone: 318-233-8437. Fax: 318-233-4160. E-mail: info@heartcamp.com.
URL www.heartcamp.com

Camp Fire Camp Wi-Ta-Wentin

Camp Fire Council of Sowela
2126 Oak Park Boulevard
Lake Charles, Louisiana 70601

General Information Coed residential and day traditional camp and outdoor program established in 1950. Accredited by American Camping Association.
Academics Computers.
Arts Arts and crafts (general), creative writing, dance, leather working.
Special Interest Areas Native American culture, leadership training, nature study.
Sports Archery, basketball, canoeing, cheerleading, fishing, kayaking, softball, swimming, volleyball.
Wilderness/Outdoors Adventure racing, canoe trips, hiking, wilderness camping.
Program Information 4–6 sessions per year. Session length: 5 days in June, July. Ages: 5–12. 60–100 participants per session. Day program cost: $165. Boarding program cost: $295. Application fee: $25–$50. Financial aid available. Cost: varies.

Application Deadline Continuous.
Jobs Positions for college students 18 and older.
Contact Katheleen M. Mayo, Executive Director, main address above. Phone: 337-478-6550. Fax: 337-478-6551. E-mail: kmkmayo@cox-internet.com.
URL www.freewebs.com/cfusa-sowela

Deuce McCallister Football Camp

Sports International, Inc.
Tulane University
New Orleans, Louisiana 70118

General Information Coed residential and day sports camp established in 2003.
Sports Football, weight training.
Program Information 1 session per year. Session length: 5 days in June, July. Ages: 8–18. 300–450 participants per session. Day program cost: $489. Boarding program cost: $599. Financial aid available.
Application Deadline Continuous.
Jobs Positions for college students.
Contact Customer Service, 8924 McGaw Court, Columbia, Maryland 21045. Phone: 800-555-0801. Fax: 410-309-9962.
URL www.footballcamps.com

The Governor's Program for Gifted Children

The Governor's Program for Gifted Children
McNeese State University
Lake Charles, Louisiana 70609

General Information Coed residential academic program and arts program established in 1959. Formal opportunities for the academically talented and artistically talented. College credit may be earned.
Academics Academics (general), humanities, philosophy, science (general), speech/debate, writing.
Arts Arts, band, chorus, creative writing, drawing, graphic arts, music, music (chamber), music (classical), music (orchestral), music (vocal), musical productions, painting, theater/drama.
Sports Basketball, racquetball, soccer, swimming.
Trips Day, shopping.
Program Information 1 session per year. Session length: 45 days in June, July. Ages: 12–16. 70–80 participants per session. Boarding program cost: $1400–$1900. Application fee: $20. Financial aid available.
Application Deadline Continuous.
Jobs Positions for college students 19 and older.
Contact Dr. George Middleton, Director, Box 91490, Lake Charles, Louisiana 70609. Phone: 800-291-7840. Fax: 337-475-5447. E-mail: office@gpgc.org.
URL www.gpgc.org

Lady Wildcat Basketball Camp

Louisiana College
1140 College Drive
Pineville, Louisiana 71360

General Information Girls' residential and day sports camp. Religious affiliation: Baptist.
Program Focus Basketball camp.
Sports Basketball, swimming.
Program Information 1–3 sessions per year. Session length: 3–4 days in June. Day program cost: $75–$125. Boarding program cost: $150–$250. Application fee: $50. Open to participants entering grades 6–12.
Application Deadline May 15.
Contact Ms. Tonya McIntosh, Head Coach, Women's Basketball, PO Box 543, Pineville, Louisiana 71359. Phone: 318-487-7350.
URL www.lacollege.edu

Louisiana College Center for Academically Talented Students (CATS)

Louisiana College
1140 College Drive
Pineville, Louisiana 71359

General Information Coed day academic program established in 1984. Religious affiliation: Baptist. Formal opportunities for the academically talented.
Program Focus Accelerated enrichment experiences designed to challenge the academic ability of each child. Social activities with peers, independent study projects, and small group field trips.
Academics Academics (general), astronomy, biology, business, communications, intercultural studies, journalism, marine studies, oceanography, science (general).
Arts Arts and crafts (general), creative writing, music, radio broadcasting, television/video.
Special Interest Areas Animal care, career exploration, nature study.
Sports Swimming.
Trips Cultural, day.
Program Information 1 session per year. Session length: 10 days in July. Ages: 6–15. 150 participants per session. Day program cost: $175–$225. Application fee: $30. Open to participants entering grades 1–9.
Application Deadline March 15.
Jobs Positions for high school students 15 and older.
Contact Ms. Pam McLin, Executive Secretary, Academic Affairs, PO Box 567, Pineville, Louisiana 71359. Phone: 318-487-7601. Fax: 318-487-7604. E-mail: mclin@lacollege.edu.
URL www.lacollege.edu/academics/cats/index.html

Louisiana College Summer Superior Program

Louisiana College
1140 College Drive
Pineville, Louisiana 71360

General Information Coed residential and day academic program. Religious affiliation: Baptist. Formal opportunities for the academically talented. College credit may be earned.
Academics American literature, Bible study, French language/literature, Greek language/literature, Hebrew language, Spanish language/literature, academics (general), anthropology, art history/appreciation, biology, botany, business, chemistry, communications, computers,

Louisiana College Summer Superior Program (continued)

economics, engineering, geography, government and politics, health sciences, history, humanities, journalism, mathematics, meteorology, music, philosophy, physics, physiology, precollege program, psychology, religion, social science.
Arts Band, ceramics, chorus, drawing, graphic arts, music (instrumental), music (vocal), musical productions, painting, photography, pottery, radio broadcasting, sculpture, television/video, theater/drama.
Sports Aerobics, basketball, golf, martial arts, racquetball, scuba diving, soccer, swimming, tennis, volleyball, weight training.
Program Information 2 sessions per year. Session length: 20 days in June, July. Ages: 16–18. 1–5 participants per session. Application fee: $25. Financial aid available. Cost: $148 per credit hour; 6 hour limit; additional $500 for 5 weeks room and board.
Application Deadline May 1.
Jobs Positions for high school students 16 and older and college students 18 and older.
Contact Director of Admissions, PO Box 560, Pineville, Louisiana 71359. Phone: 318-487-7439. Fax: 318-487-7550. E-mail: admissions@lacollege.edu.
URL www.lacollege.edu/

Marydale Resident Camp

Girl Scouts–Audubon Council
10317 Marydale Road
St. Francisville, Louisiana 70775

General Information Girls' residential traditional camp established in 1948. Accredited by American Camping Association.
Program Focus Western horseback riding.
Academics Archaeology, ecology, environmental science, geography, science (general).
Arts Acting, arts and crafts (general), ceramics, drawing, fabric arts, jewelry making, leather working, music (vocal), painting, pottery, printmaking, theater/drama.
Special Interest Areas Animal care, community service, conservation projects, leadership training, nature study, touring.
Sports Archery, basketball, canoeing, cheerleading, fishing, horseback riding, ropes course, soccer, softball, swimming, volleyball.
Wilderness/Outdoors Backpacking, canoe trips, hiking, orienteering, rock climbing, survival training, white-water trips, wilderness camping.
Trips Cultural, day, overnight.
Program Information 6 sessions per year. Session length: 6–10 days in June, July. Ages: 5–17. 130–150 participants per session. Boarding program cost: $200–$300. Application fee: $25. Financial aid available.
Application Deadline Continuous.
Jobs Positions for high school students 18 and older and college students 18 and older.
Contact Jill Pollard, Membership/Program Director, 545 Colonial Drive, Baton Rouge, Louisiana 70806-4884. Phone: 800-852-8421. Fax: 225-927-8402. E-mail: info@girlscoutsaudubon.org.

National Guitar Workshop–New Orleans, LA

National Guitar Workshop
Loyola University
6363 St. Charles Avenue
New Orleans, Louisiana 70118

General Information Coed residential and day arts program established in 1984. College credit may be earned.
Program Focus Music education in guitar, bass, drums, and vocals.
Academics Music, music (Advanced Placement).
Arts Guitar, music (classical), music (ensemble), music (instrumental), music (jazz), music (rock), music (vocal).
Program Information 1 session per year. Session length: 1 week in June, July, August. Ages: 13–79. 75–225 participants per session. Day program cost: $670–$720. Boarding program cost: $870–$920. Application fee: $25. Financial aid available.
Application Deadline Continuous.
Jobs Positions for college students 21 and older.
Contact Ms. Emily Flower, Registrar, PO Box 222, Lakeside, Connecticut 06758. Phone: 860-567-3736 Ext. 109. Fax: 860-567-0374. E-mail: emily@guitarworkshop.com.
URL www.guitarworkshop.com

Student Conservation Association–Conservation Crew Program (Louisiana)

Student Conservation Association (SCA)
Louisiana

General Information Coed residential outdoor program, community service program, and wilderness program established in 1957. High school credit may be earned.
Program Focus Resource management, conservation and environmental education.
Academics Biology, botany, ecology, environmental science, geology/earth science, history.
Special Interest Areas Campcraft, community service, construction, leadership training, nature study, trail maintenance, work camp programs.
Sports Canoeing, fishing, kayaking, swimming.
Wilderness/Outdoors Backpacking, hiking, orienteering, outdoor living skills, wilderness camping.
Trips Cultural, day, overnight.
Program Information 2–3 sessions per year. Session length: 3–5 weeks in June, July, August. Ages: 15–19. 6–8 participants per session. Application fee: $20. Financial aid available. No cost for program; financial aid possible for travel expenses.
Application Deadline Continuous.
Jobs Positions for college students 21 and older.
Contact Recruitment Office, PO Box 550, Charlestown, New Hampshire 03603. Phone: 603-543-1700. Fax: 603-543-1828. E-mail: getreal@thesca.org.
URL www.theSCA.org

Wildcat Basketball Camp

Louisiana College
1140 College Drive
Pineville, Louisiana 71360

General Information Boys' residential and day sports camp. Religious affiliation: Baptist.
Program Focus Basketball camp.
Sports Basketball.
Program Information 1 session per year. Session length: 4 days in June. Day program cost: $150–$200. Boarding program cost: $200–$250. Application fee: $30. Open to participants exiting grades 6–12.
Application Deadline May 15.
Contact Gene Rushing, Head Coach, Men's Basketball, PO Box 541, Pineville, Louisiana 71359. Phone: 318-487-7503.
URL www.lacollege.edu

MAINE

Acadia Institute of Oceanography

9 Lower Dunbar Road
Seal Harbor, Maine 04675

General Information Coed residential academic program established in 1975. Formal opportunities for the academically talented and gifted. High school credit may be earned.

Acadia Institute of Oceanography

Program Focus Oceanography.
Academics Biology, botany, chemistry, ecology, environmental science, geology/earth science, marine studies, oceanography, science (general).
Special Interest Areas Career exploration, field research/expeditions, nature study, nautical skills, navigation.
Sports Basketball, snorkeling, soccer, softball, swimming, tennis, volleyball.
Wilderness/Outdoors Hiking, orienteering.
Trips College tours, day, shopping.
Program Information 4–5 sessions per year. Session length: 13 days in June, July, August. Ages: 11–19. 42–45 participants per session. Boarding program cost: $1750. Financial aid available.
Application Deadline Continuous.
Summer Contact Sheryl Christy Gilmore, Director, PO Box 285, Seal Harbor, Maine 04675. Phone: 207-276-9825. Fax: 207-276-9825. E-mail: info@acadiainstitute.com.
Winter Contact Sheryl Christy Gilmore, Executive Director, PO Box 2220, St. Augustine, Florida 32085-2220. Phone: 904-829-1112. Fax: 904-829-1112. E-mail: info@acadiainstitute.com.
URL www.acadiainstitute.com

For more information, see page 960.

Agassiz Village

Agassiz Village, Inc.
71 Agassiz Village Lane
Poland, Maine 04274

General Information Coed residential traditional camp established in 1935. Accredited by American Camping Association. Specific services available for the physically challenged.
Academics Computers, ecology.
Arts Acting, arts and crafts (general), creative writing, dance, drawing, music, musical productions, painting, photography, theater/drama, woodworking.
Special Interest Areas Campcraft, culinary arts, leadership training, nature study.
Sports Archery, baseball, basketball, boating, canoeing, fishing, martial arts, ropes course, sailing, soccer, softball, street/roller hockey, swimming, tennis, volleyball.
Wilderness/Outdoors Backpacking, canoe trips, hiking, wilderness camping.
Trips Day, overnight.
Program Information 4 sessions per year. Session length: 5–11 days in June, July, August. Ages: 8–17. 150–250 participants per session. Day program cost: $200–$400. Boarding program cost: $1000. Financial aid available.
Application Deadline June 1.
Jobs Positions for high school students 14 and older and college students 18 and older.
Contact Lisa M. Gillis, Executive Director, 238 Bedford Street, Suite 8, Lexington, Massachusetts 02420. Phone: 781-860-0200. Fax: 781-860-0352. E-mail: lgillis@agassizvillage.com.
URL www.agassizvillage.com

Alford Lake Camp

Alford Lake Camp
258 Alford Lake Road
Hope, Maine 04847

General Information Girls' residential traditional camp established in 1907. Accredited by American Camping Association.
Arts Arts and crafts (general), ceramics, dance (modern), theater/drama.

Alford Lake Camp (continued)

Alford Lake Camp

Special Interest Areas Campcraft, community service, leadership training.
Sports Archery, canoeing, climbing (wall), gymnastics, horseback riding, kayaking, lacrosse, sailing, soccer, swimming, tennis, windsurfing.
Wilderness/Outdoors Backpacking, canoe trips, hiking.
Trips Overnight.
Program Information 3 sessions per year. Session length: 24–49 days in June, July, August. Ages: 8–15. 180–190 participants per session. Boarding program cost: $3950–$6500. Financial aid available.
Application Deadline Continuous.
Jobs Positions for college students.
Summer Contact Ms. Betsy Brayley, Office Manager/Assistant Director, main address above. Phone: 207-785-2400. Fax: 207-785-5290. E-mail: alc@alfordlake.com.
Winter Contact Ms. Betsy Brayley, Office Manager/Assistant Director, 5 Salt Marsh Way, Cape Elizabeth, Maine 04107. Phone: 207-799-3005. Fax: 207-799-5044. E-mail: alc@alfordlake.com.

Special Note
At Alford Lake, campers experience challenge and fun through a broad, individually elective program. Emphasis is on personal growth and development in a warm, supportive, and values-based community. Living in large, white tents in a simple setting promotes respect for the natural world. In addition, meeting campers and leaders from more than twenty-five states and twenty countries deepens the participants' respect and appreciation for others' differences. The staff-camper ratio of 1:3 allows for individual instruction and encouragement, inspiring tradition, loyalty, and spirit. Established in 1907, Alford Lake is one of the world's oldest girls' camps. Each season brings new friendships and adventures.

For more information, see page 976.

Alford Lake Family Camp

Alford Lake Camp
258 Alford Lake Road
Hope, Maine 04847

General Information Coed residential traditional camp and family program established in 1980. Accredited by American Camping Association.
Program Focus Camp for all ages.
Arts Arts and crafts (general), ceramics.
Sports Archery, canoeing, horseback riding, kayaking, sailing, swimming, tennis, windsurfing.
Wilderness/Outdoors Canoe trips, hiking.
Trips Day.
Program Information 1 session per year. Session length: 5 days in August. 75–150 participants per session. Cost: $90 per day for adults, $50 per day ages 5–15; no charge for children under 5.
Application Deadline Continuous.
Summer Contact Ms. Sue McMullan, Director, main address above. Phone: 207-785-2400. Fax: 207-785-5290. E-mail: alc@alfordlake.com.
Winter Contact Ms. Sue McMullan, Director, 5 Salt Marsh Way, Cape Elizabeth, Maine 04107. Phone: 207-799-3005. Fax: 207-799-5044.

For more information, see page 976.

Appalachian Mountain Club–Volunteer Trail Crew–Grafton Loop

Appalachian Mountain Club
Grafton Notch, Maine

General Information Coed residential outdoor program and wilderness program established in 1980. High school credit may be earned.
Program Focus Stewardship of the land through trail work.
Special Interest Areas Community service, conservation projects, first aid, trail maintenance.
Wilderness/Outdoors Backpacking, hiking, rock climbing.
Trips Day, overnight.
Program Information 1 session per year. Session length: 5 days in July. Ages: 16+. 4–8 participants per session. Boarding program cost: $115–$130. Application fee: $25.
Application Deadline Continuous.
Jobs Positions for college students 18 and older.
Contact North Country Volunteer Coordinator, PO Box 298, Gorham, New Hampshire 03581. Phone: 603-466-2721 Ext.192. Fax: 603-466-2822.
URL www.outdoors.org/trails/

BICYCLE TRAVEL ADVENTURES–Student Hosteling Program–Maine Coast

BICYCLE TRAVEL ADVENTURES–Student Hosteling Program
Maine

General Information Coed travel outdoor program and adventure program established in 1970. Accredited

by American Camping Association. Formal opportunities for the academically talented. Specific services available for the emotionally challenged and learning disabled. High school credit may be earned.
Program Focus A 16-day moderate bicycling/camping tour along the beautiful Maine coast from Pemaquid Point to Bar Harbor.
Special Interest Areas Campcraft, field trips (arts and culture), touring.
Sports Bicycling, boating, canoeing, fishing, sailing, swimming.
Wilderness/Outdoors Bicycle trips, canoe trips, hiking, mountain biking, wilderness camping.
Trips Day, overnight, shopping.
Program Information 1–2 sessions per year. Session length: 16 days in June, July, August. Ages: 13–15. 8–12 participants per session. Cost: $1525.
Application Deadline Continuous.
Jobs Positions for high school students 16 and older and college students 18 and older.
Contact Ted Lefkowitz, Director, 1356 Ashfield Road, PO Box 419, Conway, Massachusetts 01341. Phone: 800-343-6132. Fax: 413-369-4257. E-mail: shpbike@aol.com.
URL www.bicycletrips.com

For more information, see page 994.

CAMP ALL-STAR

Camp All-Star, Inc.
1614 Main Street
Kents Hill, Maine 04349

General Information Coed residential sports camp established in 2001. Accredited by American Camping Association.
Program Focus Campers develop athletic skills in order to build self-esteem.
Academics English as a second language.
Arts Arts and crafts (general), ceramics, drawing, jewelry making, painting, pottery, woodworking.
Special Interest Areas Whale watching.
Sports Aerobics, archery, baseball, basketball, bicycling, boating, canoeing, climbing (wall), equestrian sports, field hockey, figure skating, fishing, football, golf, horseback riding, ice hockey, kayaking, kneeboarding, lacrosse, soccer, softball, swimming, tennis, track and field, volleyball, wakeboarding, waterskiing, weight training.
Wilderness/Outdoors Mountain biking, rafting, white-water trips.
Trips Day.
Program Information 3 sessions per year. Session length: 2–6 weeks in June, July, August. Ages: 9–15. 180 participants per session. Boarding program cost: $1990–$5490. Financial aid available.
Application Deadline Continuous.
Jobs Positions for college students 18 and older.
Summer Contact Mr. Craig H. Rosen, Owner/Director, PO Box 217, Kents Hill, Maine 04349. Phone: 207-685-7242. Fax: 207-685-4169. E-mail: info@campallstar.com.
Winter Contact Mr. Craig H. Rosen, Owner/Director, PO Box 4325, Wayne, New Jersey 07470. Phone: 800-283-3558. Fax: 973-616-9995. E-mail: info@campallstar.com.
URL www.campallstar.com

CAMP ANDROSCOGGIN

Wayne, Maine 04284

General Information Boys' residential traditional camp established in 1907. Accredited by American Camping Association.
Arts Animation, arts and crafts (general), ceramics, drawing, film, music, musical productions, photography, pottery, radio broadcasting, television/video, theater/drama, woodworking.
Special Interest Areas Campcraft, nature study.
Sports Archery, baseball, basketball, bicycling, canoeing, climbing (wall), fishing, football, golf, kayaking, lacrosse, riflery, ropes course, sailing, soccer, street/roller hockey, swimming, tennis, waterskiing, weight training, windsurfing.
Wilderness/Outdoors Backpacking, bicycle trips, canoe trips, hiking, mountain biking, rafting, rock climbing, white-water trips.
Trips Day, overnight.
Program Information 1 session per year. Session length: 53 days in June, July, August. Ages: 8–15. 250 participants per session. Boarding program cost: $7900.
Application Deadline Continuous.
Jobs Positions for college students 19 and older.
Summer Contact Peter Hirsch, Director, main address above. Phone: 207-685-4441. Fax: 207-685-4391. E-mail: info@campandro.com.
Winter Contact Peter Hirsch, Director, 601 West Street, Harrison, New York 10528. Phone: 914-835-5800. Fax: 914-777-2718. E-mail: info@campandro.com.
URL www.campandro.com

CAMP ARCADIA

Route 121
Casco, Maine 04015

General Information Girls' residential traditional camp established in 1916. Accredited by American Camping Association.

Camp Arcadia

Arts Arts and crafts (general), batiking, ceramics, chorus, creative writing, dance, dance (folk), dance

Camp Arcadia (continued)
(jazz), dance (modern), drawing, fabric arts, jewelry making, mime, music, music (vocal), musical productions, painting, photography, pottery, printmaking, theater/drama, weaving.
Special Interest Areas Campcraft, leadership training, nature study.
Sports Archery, boating, canoeing, diving, equestrian sports, gymnastics, horseback riding, kayaking, rowing (crew/sculling), sailing, softball, swimming, tennis, windsurfing.
Wilderness/Outdoors Backpacking, canoe trips, hiking, orienteering, white-water trips, wilderness camping.
Trips Day, overnight.
Program Information 3–4 sessions per year. Session length: 1–7 weeks in June, July, August. Ages: 7–17. 80–160 participants per session. Boarding program cost: $600–$5000. Financial aid available.
Application Deadline Continuous.
Jobs Positions for college students 19 and older.
Summer Contact Anne Henderson Fritts, Director, PO Box 158, Casco, Maine 04015. Phone: 207-627-4605. Fax: 207-627-7162.
Winter Contact Anne Henderson Fritts, Director, Pleasantville Road, PO Box 225, New Vernon, New Jersey 07976. Phone: 973-538-5409. Fax: 973-540-1555. E-mail: cmparcadia@aol.com.
URL www.camparcadia.com

Camp Chewonki

Chewonki Foundation, Inc.
485 Chewonki Neck Road
Wiscasset, Maine 04578

General Information Boys' residential traditional camp and outdoor program established in 1915. Accredited by American Camping Association.
Program Focus Natural history, sailing and wilderness trips.
Academics Astronomy, ecology, environmental science, journalism, marine studies, music, science (general).
Arts Arts and crafts (general), band, creative writing, drawing, music, music (instrumental), music (vocal), painting, photography, pottery, printmaking, weaving, woodworking.
Special Interest Areas Native American culture, animal care, boat building, campcraft, farming, field research/expeditions, gardening, leadership training, nature study, nautical skills, work camp programs.
Sports Archery, baseball, basketball, boating, canoeing, climbing (wall), diving, fishing, football, kayaking, lacrosse, rappelling, ropes course, sailing, sea kayaking, soccer, softball, sports (general), swimming, tennis, track and field, volleyball.
Wilderness/Outdoors Backpacking, canoe trips, hiking, kayaking trips, mountaineering, orienteering, rock climbing, sailing trips, survival training, white-water trips, wilderness camping.
Trips Day, overnight.
Program Information 3 sessions per year. Session length: 25–49 days in June, July, August. Ages: 8–15. 145 participants per session. Boarding program cost: $3650–$5400. Financial aid available.
Application Deadline Continuous.
Jobs Positions for high school students 18 and older and college students 18 and older.
Contact Dick Thomas, Camp Director, main address above. Phone: 207-882-7323. Fax: 207-882-4074. E-mail: camp@chewonki.org.
URL www.chewonki.org

Camp Chewonki Adventure Camps

Chewonki Foundation, Inc.
485 Chewonki Neck Road
Wiscasset, Maine 04578

General Information Coed residential outdoor program and wilderness program established in 2000. Accredited by American Camping Association.
Program Focus Wilderness skills.
Academics Astronomy, ecology, marine studies, science (general).
Arts Creative writing, drawing, photography.
Special Interest Areas Campcraft, farming, general camp activities, nature study.
Sports Canoeing, fishing, ropes course, sea kayaking, swimming.
Wilderness/Outdoors Backpacking, canoe trips, hiking, orienteering, wilderness camping.
Trips Day, overnight.
Program Information 3 sessions per year. Session length: 5–7 days in August. Ages: 10–15. 6–60 participants per session. Boarding program cost: $495–$750. Financial aid available.
Application Deadline Continuous.
Jobs Positions for college students 21 and older.
Contact Dick Thomas, Camp Director, main address above. Phone: 207-882-7323. Fax: 207-882-4074. E-mail: camp@chewonki.org.
URL www.chewonki.org

Camp Chewonki for Girls

Chewonki Foundation, Inc.
485 Chewonki Neck Road
Wiscasset, Maine 04578

General Information Girls' residential outdoor program, wilderness program, and adventure program established in 2000. Accredited by American Camping Association.
Program Focus Natural history, canoeing and wilderness trips.
Academics Ecology, environmental science, journalism, marine studies, music, science (general).
Arts Arts and crafts (general), creative writing, drawing, music, music (vocal), painting, photography.
Special Interest Areas Campcraft, gardening, general camp activities, leadership training, nature study, work camp programs.
Sports Canoeing, climbing (wall), fishing, swimming.
Wilderness/Outdoors Backpacking, canoe trips, hiking, mountaineering, orienteering, rock climbing, survival training, white-water trips, wilderness camping.
Trips Day, overnight.

Program Information 4 sessions per year. Session length: 24 days in June, July, August. Ages: 12–17. 8–10 participants per session. Boarding program cost: $3650. Financial aid available.
Application Deadline Continuous.
Jobs Positions for college students 21 and older.
Contact Dick Thomas, Camp Director, main address above. Phone: 207-882-7323. Fax: 207-882-4074. E-mail: camp@chewonki.org.
URL www.chewonki.org

Camp Chewonki Wilderness Expeditions

Chewonki Foundation, Inc.
485 Chewonki Neck Road
Wiscasset, Maine 04578

General Information Coed residential outdoor program, wilderness program, and adventure program established in 1915. Accredited by American Camping Association.
Program Focus Natural history.
Academics Astronomy, ecology, environmental science, marine studies, science (general).
Arts Creative writing, photography.
Special Interest Areas Boat building, campcraft, community service, leadership training, nature study, nautical skills.
Sports Boating, canoeing, kayaking, ropes course, sailing, sea kayaking, swimming.
Wilderness/Outdoors Backpacking, canoe trips, hiking, kayaking trips, mountaineering, orienteering, rock climbing, sailing trips, survival training, white-water trips, wilderness camping.
Trips Overnight.
Program Information 4–15 sessions per year. Session length: 3–49 days in May, June, July, August, September. Ages: 12+. 8–10 participants per session. Boarding program cost: $200–$5100. Financial aid available.
Application Deadline Continuous.
Jobs Positions for college students 21 and older.
Contact Dick Thomas, Camp Director, main address above. Phone: 207-882-7323. Fax: 207-882-4074. E-mail: camp@chewonki.org.
URL www.chewonki.org

Camp Encore-Coda for a Great Summer of Music, Sports, and Friends

50 Encore/Coda Lane
Sweden, Maine 04040

General Information Coed residential arts program established in 1950. Accredited by American Camping Association. Formal opportunities for the artistically talented and gifted.
Program Focus Music and sports.
Academics Music.
Arts Arts and crafts (general), band, chorus, drawing, jewelry making, music, music (chamber), music (classical), music (ensemble), music (instrumental), music

Camp Encore-Coda for a Great Summer of Music, Sports, and Friends

(jazz), music (orchestral), music (vocal), musical productions, painting, photography, theater/drama.
Special Interest Areas Model rocketry.
Sports Basketball, boating, canoeing, kayaking, sailing, soccer, softball, sports (general), swimming, tennis, track and field, volleyball.
Wilderness/Outdoors Hiking.
Trips Day.
Program Information 2 sessions per year. Session length: 25–50 days in July, August. Ages: 9–17. 140–160 participants per session. Boarding program cost: $3600–$6200. Financial aid available.
Application Deadline Continuous.
Jobs Positions for high school students and college students 18 and older.
Summer Contact James Saltman, Director, main address above. Phone: 207-647-3947. Fax: 207-647-3259. E-mail: jamie@encore-coda.com.
Winter Contact James Saltman, Director, 32 Grassmere Road, Brookline, Massachusetts 02467. Phone: 617-325-1541. Fax: 617-325-7278. E-mail: jamie@encore-coda.com.
URL www.encore-coda.com

Camp Hawthorne

Camp Hawthorne, Inc.
David Plummer Road, Panther Pond
Raymond, Maine 04071

General Information Coed residential traditional camp and outdoor program established in 1919.
Academics Ecology, music, writing.
Arts Acting, arts, arts and crafts (general), band, batiking, ceramics, chorus, clowning, creative writing, dance, dance (ballet), dance (jazz), dance (modern), drawing, fabric arts, film, jewelry making, music, music

Camp Hawthorne (continued)
(ensemble), music (jazz), music (vocal), musical productions, painting, photography, pottery, puppetry, sculpture, television/video, theater/drama, weaving, woodworking.
Special Interest Areas Native American culture, campcraft, construction, culinary arts, field trips (arts and culture), leadership training, nature study, work camp programs.
Sports Archery, basketball, bicycling, boating, canoeing, climbing (wall), cross-country, field hockey, fishing, football, kayaking, martial arts, rappelling, riflery, rowing (crew/sculling), sailing, sea kayaking, snorkeling, soccer, softball, sports (general), street/roller hockey, swimming, track and field, volleyball, waterskiing, windsurfing.
Wilderness/Outdoors Backpacking, bicycle trips, canoe trips, hiking, mountain biking, orienteering, rafting, rock climbing, survival training, white-water trips, wilderness camping, wilderness/outdoors (general).
Trips Overnight.
Program Information 3 sessions per year. Session length: 2–4 weeks in June, July, August. Ages: 7–17. 110–115 participants per session. Boarding program cost: $1295–$2600. Financial aid available.
Application Deadline Continuous.
Jobs Positions for college students 18 and older.
Contact Ronald Furst, Director, 10 Scotland Bridge Road, York, Maine 03909. Phone: 207-363-1773. Fax: 207-363-1773. E-mail: camphaw@maine.rr.com.
URL www.camphawthorne.org

Camp Hawthorne Creative Arts Camp

Camp Hawthorne, Inc.
Panther Pond
Raymond, Maine 04071

General Information Coed residential traditional camp and arts program established in 1987. Formal opportunities for the artistically talented and gifted.
Program Focus Theater and visual arts program taught by professional artists and performers, camp show for parents.
Academics Music, writing.
Arts Arts and crafts (general), band, batiking, ceramics, chorus, creative writing, dance, dance (ballet), dance (jazz), dance (modern), drawing, fabric arts, film, graphic arts, jewelry making, music, music (ensemble), music (jazz), music (vocal), painting, photography, pottery, puppetry, sculpture, television/video, theater/drama, visual arts, weaving, woodworking.
Special Interest Areas Native American culture, campcraft, culinary arts, nature study, work camp programs.
Sports Archery, basketball, boating, canoeing, climbing (wall), field hockey, fishing, kayaking, martial arts, riflery, sailing, sea kayaking, snorkeling, soccer, softball, swimming, volleyball, waterskiing, windsurfing.
Wilderness/Outdoors Hiking.
Trips Day, overnight.
Program Information 2 sessions per year. Session length: 2 weeks in June, July, August. Ages: 8–16. 100–110 participants per session. Boarding program cost: $1395. Financial aid available.
Application Deadline Continuous.
Jobs Positions for college students 18 and older.
Contact Ronald Furst, Director, 10 Scotland Bridge Road, York, Maine 03909. Phone: 207-363-1773. E-mail: camphaw@maine.rr.com.
URL www.camphawthorne.org

Camp Kawanhee for Boys

58 Kawanhee Lane
Weld, Maine 04285

General Information Boys' residential traditional camp established in 1920. Accredited by American Camping Association.
Arts Ceramics, jewelry making, painting, photography, pottery, printmaking, woodworking.
Special Interest Areas Campcraft, leadership training, nature study.
Sports Archery, baseball, basketball, boating, canoeing, climbing (wall), fishing, kayaking, lacrosse, riflery, ropes course, sailing, sea kayaking, soccer, softball, swimming, tennis, volleyball, waterskiing, weight training, wrestling.
Wilderness/Outdoors Canoe trips, hiking, mountain biking, rafting, white-water trips, wilderness camping.
Trips Day, overnight.
Program Information 2 sessions per year. Session length: 4–7 weeks in June, July, August. Ages: 7–15. 130–165 participants per session. Boarding program cost: $3975–$4975. Financial aid available.
Application Deadline Continuous.
Jobs Positions for college students 18 and older.
Summer Contact Mark Nelson, Director, main address above. Phone: 207-585-2210. Fax: 207-585-2620. E-mail: lizmark5@aol.com.
Winter Contact Mark Nelson, Director, PO Box 197, Shelbyville, Indiana 46176. E-mail: lizmark5@aol.com.
URL www.kawanhee.com

Camp Kirkwold

Girl Scouts of Kennebec Council
7 North Wayne Road
Readfield, Maine 04355

General Information Girls' residential traditional camp established in 1970.
Program Focus Girl Scout program.
Arts Arts and crafts (general), music, theater/drama.
Special Interest Areas Campcraft, nature study.
Sports Archery, canoeing, horseback riding, kayaking, swimming, volleyball.
Wilderness/Outdoors Canoe trips, hiking.
Trips Day.
Program Information 6 sessions per year. Session length: 6–13 days in June, July, August. Ages: 7–17. 50–60 participants per session. Boarding program cost: $325–$575. Financial aid available.
Application Deadline Continuous.

Jobs Positions for high school students 16 and older and college students 18 and older.
Contact Anne Johnson, Director of Programs, PO Box 9421, South Portland, Maine 04116-9421. Phone: 207-772-1177. Fax: 207-874-2646. E-mail: annej@gskc.org.
URL www.gskc.org

Camp Laurel

Route 41
Readfield, Maine 04355

General Information Coed residential traditional camp established in 1949. Accredited by American Camping Association.
Arts Ceramics, dance, dance (ballet), dance (modern), dance (tap), drawing, film, jewelry making, music, music (vocal), musical productions, photography, pottery.
Sports Aerobics, archery, baseball, basketball, bicycling, boating, canoeing, climbing (wall), equestrian sports, field hockey, figure skating, fishing, football, golf, gymnastics, horseback riding, ice hockey, kayaking, lacrosse, rappelling, ropes course, rowing (crew/sculling), sailing, snorkeling, soccer, softball, street/roller hockey, swimming, tennis, track and field, volleyball, waterskiing, weight training, windsurfing.
Wilderness/Outdoors Backpacking, rock climbing.
Trips Day, overnight.
Program Information 1 session per year. Session length: 7 weeks in June, July, August. Ages: 8–15. 480 participants per session. Boarding program cost: $8100.
Application Deadline Continuous.
Jobs Positions for college students 19 and older.
Summer Contact Jeremy Sullinger, Director, Box 327, Readfield, Maine 04355. Phone: 207-685-4945. Fax: 207-685-9812. E-mail: summer@camplaurel.com.
Winter Contact Jeremy Sullinger, Director, Box 661, Alpine, New Jersey 07620. Phone: 201-750-0515. Fax: 201-750-0665. E-mail: summer@camplaurel.com.
URL www.camplaurel.com

Camp Laurel South

Camp Laurel South
48 Laurel Road
Casco, Maine 04015

General Information Coed residential traditional camp established in 1921. Accredited by American Camping Association. Formal opportunities for the gifted.
Arts Arts and crafts (general), batiking, ceramics, creative writing, dance, dance (ballet), dance (folk), dance (jazz), dance (modern), drawing, fabric arts, graphic arts, jewelry making, music, music (vocal), musical productions, painting, photography, pottery, printmaking, puppetry, radio broadcasting, sculpture, theater/drama, weaving.
Special Interest Areas Animal care, campcraft, model rocketry, nature study, nautical skills.
Sports Aerobics, archery, baseball, basketball, bicycling, boating, canoeing, climbing (wall), cross-country, equestrian sports, field hockey, fishing, football, golf, gymnastics, horseback riding, in-line skating, kayaking, lacrosse, rappelling, riflery, ropes course, sailing, snorkeling, soccer, softball, sports (general), street/roller hockey, swimming, tennis, volleyball, water polo, waterskiing, weight training, windsurfing.
Wilderness/Outdoors Backpacking, hiking, mountain biking, mountaineering, orienteering, rock climbing, white-water trips, wilderness camping.
Trips Day, hiking, overnight.
Program Information 2 sessions per year. Session length: 25 days in June, July, August. Ages: 7–15. 325 participants per session. Boarding program cost: $4750.
Application Deadline Continuous.
Jobs Positions for college students 19 and older.
Summer Contact Roger Christian, Camp Director, main address above. Phone: 207-627-4334. Fax: 207-627-4255. E-mail: fun@camplaurelsouth.com.
Winter Contact Roger Christian, Camp Director, PO Box 14130, Gainesville, Florida 32604. Phone: 800-327-3506. Fax: 352-331-0014. E-mail: fun@camplaurelsouth.com.
URL www.camplaurelsouth.com

Camp Matoaka for Girls

1 Great Place
Smithfield, Maine 04978-1288

General Information Girls' residential traditional camp established in 1951. Accredited by American Camping Association.
Academics English as a second language, computers, journalism, music, typing, writing.
Arts Arts and crafts (general), batiking, ceramics, chorus, dance, dance (ballet), dance (jazz), dance (modern), dance (tap), drawing, fabric arts, film, jewelry making, leather working, metalworking, mime, music, music (vocal), musical productions, painting, photography, pottery, printmaking, radio broadcasting, sculpture, television/video, theater/drama, weaving, woodworking.
Special Interest Areas Animal care, campcraft, gardening, nature study.
Sports Aerobics, archery, basketball, bicycling, bicycling (BMX), boating, canoeing, cheerleading, climbing (wall), equestrian sports, fishing, golf, gymnastics, horseback riding, kayaking, ropes course, rowing (crew/sculling), sailing, snorkeling, soccer, softball, swimming, tennis, volleyball, water polo, waterskiing, windsurfing.
Wilderness/Outdoors Mountain biking, pack animal trips, rafting, rock climbing, white-water trips.
Trips Day, overnight.
Program Information 2 sessions per year. Session length: 27–53 days in June, July, August. Ages: 8–15. 250–275 participants per session. Boarding program cost: $4250–$6950.
Application Deadline Continuous.
Jobs Positions for college students 19 and older.
Summer Contact Mr. Michael Nathanson, Director, main address above. Phone: 207-362-2500. Fax: 207-362-2525. E-mail: matoaka@matoaka.com.
Winter Contact Mr. Michael Nathanson, Director, 8751 Horseshoe Lane, Boca Raton, Florida 33496. Phone: 800-MATOAKA. Fax: 561-488-6386. E-mail: matoaka@matoaka.com.
URL www.matoaka.com

Camp Micah

Camp Micah
156 Moose Cove Lodge Road
Bridgton, Maine 04009

General Information Coed residential traditional camp established in 2001. Religious affiliation: Jewish. Accredited by American Camping Association.
Arts Acting, arts and crafts (general), band, batiking, ceramics, chorus, dance, dance (folk), dance (modern), drawing, jewelry making, leather working, metalworking, music, music (jazz), musical productions, painting, photography, pottery, radio broadcasting, sculpture, television/video, theater/drama, woodworking.
Special Interest Areas Campcraft, community service, culinary arts, gardening, leadership training, nature study, team building.
Sports Aerobics, archery, baseball, basketball, bicycling, bicycling (BMX), boating, canoeing, cheerleading, climbing (wall), fencing, field hockey, fishing, football, golf, gymnastics, horseback riding, in-line skating, kayaking, lacrosse, martial arts, rappelling, ropes course, sailing, soccer, softball, street/roller hockey, swimming, tennis, volleyball, waterskiing, weight training, windsurfing, wrestling.
Wilderness/Outdoors Backpacking, canoe trips, hiking, mountain biking, mountaineering, orienteering, rafting, rock climbing, white-water trips, wilderness camping.
Trips Day, overnight.
Program Information 1–2 sessions per year. Session length: 26–28 days in June, July, August. Ages: 8–16. 200–250 participants per session. Boarding program cost: $4000–$7200.
Application Deadline Continuous.
Jobs Positions for college students 18 and older.
Summer Contact Mr. Mark H. Lipof, Director, Camp Micah, 156 Moose Cove Lodge Road, Bridgton, Maine 04009. Phone: 207-647-8999. Fax: 207-647-4145. E-mail: markl@campmicah.com.
Winter Contact Mr. Mark H. Lipof, Director, PO Box 67414, Chestnut Hill, Massachusetts 02467. Phone: 617-244-6540. Fax: 617-277-7108. E-mail: markl@campmicah.com.
URL www.campmicah.com

Camp Modin

Modin Way
Belgrade, Maine 04917

General Information Coed residential traditional camp and bible camp established in 1922. Religious affiliation: Jewish. Accredited by American Camping Association.
Program Focus Jewish orientation.
Academics Hebrew language, Jewish studies.
Arts Israeli dance, arts and crafts (general), batiking, ceramics, creative writing, dance, dance (ballet), dance (folk), dance (jazz), dance (modern), dance (tap), drawing, film, jewelry making, leather working, metalworking, music, music (vocal), musical productions, painting, photography, pottery, printmaking, puppetry, radio broadcasting, sculpture, television/video, theater/drama, woodworking.
Special Interest Areas Animal care, campcraft, community service, conservation projects, leadership training, model rocketry, nature study.
Sports Aerobics, archery, baseball, basketball, bicycling, boating, canoeing, climbing (wall), diving, field hockey, fishing, gymnastics, in-line skating, kayaking, lacrosse, martial arts, rappelling, riflery, ropes course, sailing, soccer, softball, sports (general), street/roller hockey, swimming, tennis, volleyball, waterskiing, weight training, windsurfing.
Wilderness/Outdoors Backpacking, bicycle trips, canoe trips, hiking, mountaineering, orienteering, rafting, rock climbing, white-water trips, wilderness camping.
Trips Day, overnight.
Program Information 1–2 sessions per year. Session length: 26–54 days in June, July, August. Ages: 7–16. 350 participants per session. Boarding program cost: $4495–$7050.
Application Deadline Continuous.
Jobs Positions for college students 18 and older.
Summer Contact Howard Salzberg, Director, main address above. Phone: 207-465-4444. Fax: 207-465-4447. E-mail: modin@modin.com.
Winter Contact Howard Salzberg, Director, 401 East 80th Street, Suite 28E/F, New York, New York 10021. Phone: 212-570-1600. Fax: 212-570-1677. E-mail: modin@modin.com.
URL www.modin.com

Camp Nashoba North

198 Raymond Hill Road
Raymond, Maine 04071

General Information Coed residential traditional camp established in 1933. Accredited by American Camping Association.
Program Focus Golf, horseback riding, hiking, and sailing.
Academics English as a second language.
Arts Acting, arts and crafts (general), batiking, candle-making, ceramics, dance, dance (ballet), dance (folk), dance (jazz), dance (modern), dance (tap), drawing, fabric arts, make up, mime, music, music (vocal), musical productions, painting, photography, pottery, puppetry, silk screening, stage movement, theater/drama, tie-dyeing, weaving, woodworking.
Special Interest Areas Animal care, campcraft, farming, nature study.
Sports Aerobics, archery, baseball, basketball, boating, canoeing, climbing (wall), equestrian sports, field hockey, fishing, golf, horseback riding, kayaking, lacrosse, rappelling, ropes course, rowing (crew/sculling), sailing, sea kayaking, snorkeling, soccer, softball, swimming, tennis, volleyball, wakeboarding, water polo, waterskiing, windsurfing.
Wilderness/Outdoors Backpacking, canoe trips, hiking, mountaineering, orienteering, rafting, rock climbing, white-water trips, wilderness camping.
Trips Day, overnight.
Program Information 1–3 sessions per year. Session length: 4–8 weeks in June, July, August. Ages: 7–15. 200 participants per session. Boarding program cost: $4200–$7200.

Application Deadline Continuous.
Jobs Positions for college students 20 and older.
Summer Contact Sarah Seaward, Co-Director, main address above. Phone: 207-655-7170. Fax: 207-655-4063. E-mail: nashobafun@aol.com.
Winter Contact Sarah Seaward, Co-Director, 140 Nashoba Road, Littleton, Massachusetts 01460. Phone: 978-486-8236. Fax: 978-952-2442. E-mail: nashobafun@aol.com.
URL www.campnashoba.com

CAMP O-AT-KA

Camp O-AT-KA, Inc.
593 Sebago Road
Sebago, Maine 04029

General Information Boys' residential traditional camp and outdoor program established in 1906. Accredited by American Camping Association.

Camp O-AT-KA

Program Focus Outdoor living skills, new arts center; sailing; new athletic center.
Arts Arts and crafts (general), ceramics, drawing, fly-tying, leather working, metalworking, music (instrumental), musical productions, photography, pottery, silk screening, stained glass, theater/drama, woodworking.
Special Interest Areas Campcraft, field trips (arts and culture), junior Maine guide program, leadership training, model rocketry, nature study.
Sports Archery, baseball, basketball, boating, canoeing, climbing (wall), cross-country, fishing, kayaking, lacrosse, rappelling, riflery, ropes course, sailing, sea kayaking, soccer, street/roller hockey, swimming, tennis, track and field, volleyball, water polo, waterskiing, windsurfing.
Wilderness/Outdoors Backpacking, bicycle trips, canoe trips, hiking, mountain biking, rafting, rock climbing, white-water trips, wilderness camping.
Trips Day, overnight.
Program Information 6 sessions per year. Session length: 2–7 weeks in June, July, August. Ages: 7–16. 150 participants per session. Boarding program cost: $1950–$4800. Financial aid available.
Application Deadline Continuous.
Jobs Positions for high school students 17 and older and college students.
Contact Keith Reinhardt, Executive Director, main address above. Phone: 800-818-8455. Fax: 207-787-3930. E-mail: director@campoatka.com.
URL www.campoatka.com
For more information, see page 1034.

CAMP PINEHURST

23 Curtis Road
Raymond, Maine 04071

General Information Boys' residential traditional camp established in 1946.
Program Focus A traditional camp that focuses on skill development, outdoor adventure, and teamwork.
Special Interest Areas Campcraft, model rocketry, nature study.
Sports Archery, baseball, basketball, bicycling, boating, canoeing, climbing (wall), fishing, kayaking, riflery, sailing, soccer, softball, swimming, tennis, waterskiing, windsurfing.
Wilderness/Outdoors Backpacking, canoe trips, hiking, mountain biking, rafting, white-water trips, wilderness camping.
Trips Overnight.
Program Information 1–6 sessions per year. Session length: 1–6 weeks in June, July, August. Ages: 5–14. 70–85 participants per session. Boarding program cost: $850–$4650.
Application Deadline Continuous.
Jobs Positions for high school students 15 and older and college students 20 and older.
Summer Contact John Curtis, Director, main address above. Phone: 207-627-4670. Fax: 207-627-4793. E-mail: director@camppinehurst.com.
Winter Contact Jack Curtis, Director, 12 Cider Lane, Nashua, New Hampshire 03063. Phone: 603-880-6287. Fax: 603-880-6287. E-mail: director@camppinehurst.com.
URL www.camppinehurst.com

CAMP PONDICHERRY

Girl Scouts of Kennebec Council
85 Camp Pondicherry Road
Bridgton, Maine 04009

General Information Girls' residential traditional camp established in 1970. Accredited by American Camping Association.
Program Focus Girl Scout program.
Arts Arts and crafts (general), dance, jewelry making, music, puppetry, theater/drama.
Special Interest Areas Campcraft, leadership training, nature study, team building.
Sports Aerobics, canoeing, climbing (wall), ropes course, swimming, volleyball.
Wilderness/Outdoors Backpacking, canoe trips, hiking, orienteering.
Trips Day, overnight.
Program Information 3–6 sessions per year. Session length: 6–13 days in June, July, August. Ages: 7–17.

Camp Pondicherry (continued)

100–150 participants per session. Boarding program cost: $325–$825. Financial aid available. Financial aid available to registered Girl Scouts only.
Application Deadline Continuous.
Jobs Positions for high school students 16 and older and college students 18 and older.
Contact Anne Johnson, Director of Program, PO Box 9421, South Portland, Maine 04116-9421. Phone: 207-772-1177. Fax: 207-874-2646. E-mail: annej@gskc.org.
URL www.gskc.org

Camp Runoia

Camp Runoia
Point Road
Belgrade Lakes, Maine 04918

General Information Girls' residential traditional camp established in 1907. Accredited by American Camping Association.
Program Focus Team building and group process.
Academics Ecology, writing.
Arts Arts and crafts (general), batiking, creative writing, drawing, fabric arts, jewelry making, music (vocal), painting, photography, printmaking, theater/drama, weaving.
Special Interest Areas Campcraft, community service, leadership training, nature study.
Sports Archery, basketball, boating, canoeing, challenge course, climbing (wall), diving, equestrian sports, golf, horseback riding, kayaking, rappelling, riflery, ropes course, sailing, sea kayaking, snorkeling, soccer, softball, sports (general), swimming, tennis, volleyball, windsurfing.
Wilderness/Outdoors Backpacking, canoe trips, hiking, orienteering, rafting, rock climbing, survival training, white-water trips, wilderness camping.
Program Information 2 sessions per year. Session length: 3–7 weeks in June, July, August. Ages: 8–17. 100 participants per session. Boarding program cost: $2700–$5200. Financial aid available. Financial aid deadline is Oct 31.
Application Deadline Continuous.
Jobs Positions for college students 21 and older.
Summer Contact Pamela N. Cobb, Director, PO Box 450, Belgrade Lakes, Maine 04918. Phone: 207-495-2228. Fax: 207-495-2287. E-mail: info@runoia.com.
Winter Contact Pamela N. Cobb, Director, 56 Jackson Street, Cambridge, Massachusetts 02140. Phone: 617-547-4676. Fax: 617-661-1964. E-mail: info@runoia.com.
URL www.runoia.com

Camp Scelkit

Girl Scouts of Kennebec Council
Gerrish Island
Kittery Point, Maine 03905

General Information Girls' residential traditional camp established in 1963.
Arts Arts and crafts (general).
Special Interest Areas Campcraft, nature study.
Trips Day.
Program Information 6 sessions per year. Session length: 3–5 days in June, July, August. Ages: 7–13. 15 participants per session. Boarding program cost: $250–$300. Financial aid available.
Application Deadline Continuous.
Jobs Positions for college students 18 and older.
Contact Anne Johnson, Director of Program, PO Box 9421, South Portland, Maine 04116-9421. Phone: 207-772-1177. Fax: 207-874-2646. E-mail: annej@gskc.org.
URL www.gskc.org

Camp Skylemar

457 Sebago Road
Naples, Maine 04055

General Information Boys' residential traditional camp established in 1948. Accredited by American Camping Association.
Program Focus General sports.
Arts Arts and crafts (general), ceramics, drawing, film, graphic arts, leather working, musical productions, painting, photography, pottery, printmaking, radio broadcasting, television/video, theater/drama, woodworking.
Special Interest Areas Campcraft, gardening, model rocketry, nature study.
Sports Archery, baseball, basketball, bicycling, boating, canoeing, climbing (wall), cross-country, diving, figure skating, fishing, flag football, golf, ice hockey, kayaking, lacrosse, rappelling, riflery, ropes course, sailing, snorkeling, soccer, softball, street/roller hockey, swimming, tennis, track and field, volleyball, water polo, waterskiing, weight training, windsurfing.
Wilderness/Outdoors Backpacking, bicycle trips, canoe trips, hiking, mountain biking, orienteering, survival training, wilderness camping.
Trips Cultural, day, overnight.
Program Information 2 sessions per year. Session length: 4–7 weeks in June, July, August. Ages: 7–15. 160 participants per session. Boarding program cost: $5200–$8100. Financial aid available.
Application Deadline Continuous.
Jobs Positions for college students 18 and older.
Summer Contact Arleen Shepherd, Director, Naples, Maine 04055. Phone: 207-693-6414. Fax: 207-693-3865. E-mail: info@campskylemar.com.
Winter Contact Arleen Shepherd, Director, 16 Bellclare Circle, Sparks, Maryland 21152. Phone: 410-329-3775. Fax: 410-329-5095. E-mail: info@campskylemar.com.
URL www.campskylemar.com

Camp Tapawingo

166 Tapawingo Road
Sweden, Maine 04040

General Information Girls' residential traditional camp established in 1919. Accredited by American Camping Association.
Arts Arts and crafts (general), batiking, ceramics, chorus, dance, drawing, fabric arts, jewelry making, leather working, musical productions, painting, photography, pottery, puppetry, theater/drama.

Sports Aerobics, archery, basketball, boating, canoeing, climbing (wall), diving, equestrian sports, field hockey, gymnastics, horseback riding, kayaking, lacrosse, ropes course, sailing, soccer, softball, swimming, tennis, track and field, volleyball, waterskiing, windsurfing.
Wilderness/Outdoors Backpacking, canoe trips, hiking, rafting, white-water trips, wilderness camping.
Trips Cultural, day, overnight.
Program Information 2 sessions per year. Session length: 26–52 days in June, July, August. Ages: 7–16. 175 participants per session. Boarding program cost: $4500–$7500.
Application Deadline Continuous.
Jobs Positions for college students 19 and older.
Summer Contact Ms. Jane Lichtman, Director, main address above. Phone: 207-647-3351. Fax: 207-647-2232. E-mail: camptap@aol.com.
Winter Contact Ms. Jane Lichtman, Director, PO Box 248, Maplewood, New Jersey 07040. Phone: 973-275-1139. Fax: 973-275-1182. E-mail: camptap@aol.com.
URL www.camptapawingo.com

Camp Timanous

85 Plains Road
Raymond, Maine 04071

General Information Boys' residential traditional camp established in 1917. Accredited by American Camping Association.
Arts Arts and crafts (general), pottery, woodworking.
Special Interest Areas Campcraft.
Sports Archery, baseball, basketball, boating, canoeing, climbing (wall), diving, fishing, kayaking, riflery, sailing, soccer, softball, swimming, tennis, water polo, waterskiing, windsurfing.
Wilderness/Outdoors Backpacking, bicycle trips, canoe trips, hiking, rafting, white-water trips, wilderness camping.
Trips Day, overnight.
Program Information 1–2 sessions per year. Session length: 24–49 days in June, July, August. Ages: 7–15. 110–120 participants per session. Boarding program cost: $3800–$5900. Financial aid available.
Application Deadline Continuous.
Jobs Positions for high school students 17 and older and college students 19 and older.
Summer Contact Ms. Linda Suitor, Director, main address above. Phone: 207-655-4569. Fax: 207-655-5405. E-mail: camptiman@aol.com.
Winter Contact Ms. Linda Suitor, Director, 25 Marlboro Road, Southboro, Massachusetts 01772. Phone: 508-485-8020. Fax: 508-460-6164. E-mail: camptiman@aol.com.
URL www.timanous.com

Camp Wawenock

33 Camp Wawenock Road
Raymond, Maine 04071-6824

General Information Girls' residential traditional camp established in 1910. Accredited by American Camping Association.
Program Focus Human relationships, personal development, and leadership training.
Arts Arts and crafts (general), ceramics, creative writing, dance (jazz), drawing, music, music (orchestral), pottery, theater/drama.
Special Interest Areas Campcraft, leadership training, nature study.
Sports Archery, boating, canoeing, diving, horseback riding, riflery, sailing, swimming, tennis, windsurfing.
Wilderness/Outdoors Canoe trips.
Program Information 1 session per year. Session length: 7 weeks in July, August. Ages: 8–17. 110–115 participants per session. Boarding program cost: $5100–$5300.
Application Deadline Continuous.
Jobs Positions for high school students 17 and older and college students 19 and older.
Contact June W. Gray, Director/Owner, main address above. Phone: 207-655-4657.

Camp Waziyatah

530 Mill Hill Road
Waterford, Maine 04088

General Information Coed residential traditional camp established in 1922. Accredited by American Camping Association.

Camp Waziyatah

Program Focus Waterfront activities, riding, outdoor living skills.
Academics English as a second language, reading.
Arts Acting, arts, arts and crafts (general), batiking, ceramics, chorus, clowning, creative writing, dance, dance (ballet), dance (jazz), dance (modern), drawing, fabric arts, jewelry making, leather working, mime, music, music (vocal), musical productions, painting, photography, pottery, printmaking, sculpture, theater/drama, weaving, woodworking.
Special Interest Areas Animal care, campcraft, leadership training.
Sports Aerobics, archery, baseball, basketball, boating, canoeing, climbing (wall), equestrian sports, fencing, field hockey, fishing, horseback riding, kayaking, martial arts, riflery, sailing, soccer, softball, sports (general),

Camp Waziyatah (continued)

street/roller hockey, swimming, tennis, volleyball, water polo, waterskiing, weight training, windsurfing.
Wilderness/Outdoors Backpacking, canoe trips, hiking, mountaineering, orienteering, rafting, rock climbing, white-water trips.
Trips Overnight.
Program Information 2–3 sessions per year. Session length: 2–4 weeks in June, July, August. Ages: 7–15. 150–200 participants per session. Boarding program cost: $1900–$3500. Financial aid available.
Application Deadline Continuous.
Jobs Positions for college students 19 and older.
Summer Contact Dawn Broussard, Director, main address above. Phone: 207-583-6781. Fax: 207-583-6755. E-mail: info@wazi.com.
Winter Contact Dawn Broussard, Director, 19 Vose Lane, East Walpole, Massachusetts 02032. Phone: 508-668-9758. Fax: 508-668-2665. E-mail: dawn@wazi.com.
URL www.wazi.com

For more information, see page 1046.

Camp Wekeela for Boys and Girls

1750 Bear Pond Road
Hartford, Maine 04220

General Information Coed residential traditional camp established in 1922. Accredited by American Camping Association. Formal opportunities for the artistically talented.

Camp Wekeela for Boys and Girls

Program Focus Competitive swimming, soccer, gymnastics, and tennis.
Arts Acting, arts and crafts (general), batiking, ceramics, creative writing, dance, dance (ballet), dance (folk), dance (jazz), dance (modern), dance (tap), drawing, fabric arts, graphic arts, jewelry making, leather working, music, music (jazz), music (vocal), musical productions, painting, photography, pottery, printmaking, puppetry, radio broadcasting, sculpture, television/video, theater/drama, weaving, woodworking.
Special Interest Areas Campcraft, leadership training, model rocketry, nature study, weight reduction.
Sports Aerobics, archery, baseball, basketball, bicycling, boating, canoeing, cheerleading, climbing (wall), cross-country, equestrian sports, field hockey, fishing, football, golf, gymnastics, horseback riding, kayaking, lacrosse, rappelling, ropes course, sailing, scuba diving, snorkeling, soccer, softball, street/roller hockey, swimming, tennis, track and field, volleyball, water polo, waterskiing, weight training, windsurfing, wrestling.
Wilderness/Outdoors Backpacking, bicycle trips, canoe trips, caving, hiking, mountaineering, orienteering, rafting, rock climbing, white-water trips, wilderness camping.
Trips College tours, cultural, day, overnight.
Program Information 1–5 sessions per year. Session length: 4–8 weeks in June, July, August. Ages: 6–16. 290–300 participants per session. Boarding program cost: $5150–$8475.
Application Deadline Continuous.
Jobs Positions for college students 20 and older.
Summer Contact Eric Scoblionko, Director, main address above. Phone: 207-224-7878. Fax: 207-224-7999. E-mail: wekeela1@aol.com.
Winter Contact Eric Scoblionko, Director, 2807-C Delmar Drive, Columbus, Ohio 43209. Phone: 614-253-3177. Fax: 614-253-3661. E-mail: wekeela1@aol.com.
URL www.campwekeela.com

For more information, see page 1048.

Camp Winnebago

Camp Winnebago
19 Echo Lake Road
Fayette, Maine 04349

General Information Boys' residential traditional camp established in 1919. Accredited by American Camping Association.
Program Focus Individual and group skills; encouragement to participate in all activities.
Academics English as a second language.
Arts Arts and crafts (general), ceramics, drawing, painting, photography, pottery, printmaking, radio broadcasting, sculpture, television/video, theater/drama, weaving, woodworking.
Special Interest Areas Campcraft, community service, nature study.
Sports Archery, baseball, basketball, bicycling, boating, canoeing, climbing (wall), cross-country, diving, fencing, fishing, football, frisbee golf, golf, in-line skating, kayaking, lacrosse, rappelling, riflery, ropes course, sailing, sea kayaking, snorkeling, soccer, softball, street/roller hockey, swimming, tennis, volleyball, water polo, waterskiing, weight training, windsurfing.
Wilderness/Outdoors Backpacking, bicycle trips, canoe trips, hiking, rafting, survival training, white-water trips, wilderness camping.
Trips Day, overnight.
Program Information 1–2 sessions per year. Session length: 26–53 days in June, July, August. Ages: 8–15. 160–170 participants per session. Boarding program cost: $4950–$8000.
Application Deadline Continuous.
Jobs Positions for college students 19 and older.

Summer Contact Andy Lilienthal, Director, 19 Echo Lake Road, Fayette, Maine 04349. Phone: 207-685-4918. Fax: 207-685-9190. E-mail: unkandycw@aol.com.
Winter Contact Andy Lilienthal, Director, 3357 36th Avenue South, Minneapolis, Minnesota 55406. Phone: 612-721-9500. Fax: 612-721-3144. E-mail: unkandycw@aol.com.
URL www.campwinnebago.com

CHOP POINT CAMP

420 Chop Point Road
Woolwich, Maine 04579

General Information Coed residential traditional camp established in 1967. Accredited by American Camping Association.
Program Focus Trips and waterfront activities for teens.
Academics Bible study, English as a second language, mathematics, music.
Arts Arts and crafts (general), batiking, ceramics, chorus, drawing, jewelry making, music, painting, photography, pottery, theater/drama.
Special Interest Areas Campcraft, community service, gardening, homestays.
Sports Aerobics, baseball, basketball, bicycling, boating, canoeing, field hockey, fishing, kayaking, sailing, sea kayaking, soccer, softball, sports (general), swimming, tennis, volleyball, waterskiing, windsurfing.
Wilderness/Outdoors Backpacking, bicycle trips, canoe trips, hiking, mountain biking, rafting, white-water trips, wilderness camping.
Trips Overnight.
Program Information 2 sessions per year. Session length: 3 weeks in June, July, August. Ages: 12–18. 80–85 participants per session. Boarding program cost: $1750–$3200. Financial aid available.
Application Deadline Continuous.
Jobs Positions for high school students and college students 19 and older.
Summer Contact David Wilkinson, Director, main address above. Phone: 207-443-5860. Fax: 207-443-6760. E-mail: wilk@choppoint.org.
Winter Contact Jean Willard, Director, 264 Cedar Grove Road, Dresden, Maine 04342. Phone: 207-737-2725. Fax: 207-737-2684. E-mail: jean@choppoint.org.
URL www.choppoint.org

DARROW WILDERNESS TRIPS–KAYAK

Darrow Foundation
Grand Lake Stream, Maine 04637

General Information Coed residential wilderness program established in 1957. Accredited by American Camping Association.
Program Focus Kayak-lake and coast of Maine.
Sports Kayaking, sea kayaking.
Wilderness/Outdoors Wilderness camping.
Program Information 3 sessions per year. Session length: 1–3 weeks in July, August. Ages: 12–17. 6–8 participants per session. Boarding program cost: $875–$2575.
Jobs Positions for high school students 18 and older and college students 18 and older.
Summer Contact Mr. John Houghton, Director, PO Box 9, Grand Lake Stream, Maine 04637. Phone: 207-592-5827. E-mail: darrow@gwi.net.
Winter Contact Mr. John Houghton, Director, 24 Lunt Road, Brunswick, Maine 04011. Phone: 207-725-4748. Fax: 207-725-4748. E-mail: darrow@gwi.net.
URL www.darrowcamp.org

DARROW WILDERNESS TRIPS–MAINE

Darrow Foundation
Maine

General Information Coed travel wilderness program and adventure program established in 1957. Accredited by American Camping Association.
Program Focus Exploring the rivers of Maine and New Brunswick by canoe, white-water canoeing, and wilderness camping.
Sports Fishing, swimming.
Wilderness/Outdoors Canoe trips, white-water trips, wilderness camping.
Program Information 12 sessions per year. Session length: 1–6 weeks in June, July, August. Ages: 9–17. 6–10 participants per session. Cost: $750–$4800. Application fee: $400. Financial aid available.
Application Deadline Continuous.
Jobs Positions for college students 18 and older.
Summer Contact John Houghton, Director, PO Box 9, Grand Lake Stream, Maine 04637. Phone: 888-854-0810. E-mail: darrow@gwi.net.
Winter Contact John Houghton, Director, 24 Lunt Road, Brunswick, Maine 04011-7288. Phone: 888-854-0810. Fax: 207-725-4748. E-mail: darrow@gwi.net.
URL www.darrowcamp.org

DARROW WILDERNESS TRIPS–ST. CROIX

Darrow Foundation
Maine

General Information Coed travel wilderness program and adventure program established in 1957. Accredited by American Camping Association.
Program Focus Canoeing the lakes and streams of the west Grand Lake systems, white-water canoeing on the St. Croix River, and wilderness camping.
Sports Fishing, swimming.
Wilderness/Outdoors Canoe trips, white-water trips, wilderness camping.
Program Information 3 sessions per year. Session length: 2 weeks in June, July, August. Ages: 13–15. Cost: $1590. Financial aid available.
Application Deadline Continuous.
Jobs Positions for college students 18 and older.
Summer Contact John Houghton, Director, PO Box 9, Grand Lake Stream, Maine 04637. Phone: 888-854-0810. E-mail: darrow@gwi.net.
Winter Contact John Houghton, Director, 24 Lunt Road, Brunswick, Maine 04011-7288. Phone: 888-854-0810. Fax: 207-725-4748. E-mail: darrow@gwi.net.
URL www.darrowcamp.org

DARROW WILDERNESS TRIPS–VOYAGEURS

Darrow Foundation
Maine

General Information Coed travel wilderness program and adventure program established in 1957. Accredited by American Camping Association.
Program Focus Canoeing and camping the way trappers and explorers did 200 years ago.
Sports Fishing, swimming.
Wilderness/Outdoors Canoe trips, wilderness camping.
Program Information 2 sessions per year. Session length: 2 weeks in July, August. Ages: 11–12. Cost: $1440. Financial aid available.
Application Deadline Continuous.
Jobs Positions for college students 18 and older.
Summer Contact John Houghton, Director, PO Box 9, Grand Lake Stream, Maine 04637. Phone: 888-854-0810. E-mail: darrow@gwi.net.
Winter Contact John Houghton, Director, 24 Lunt Road, Brunswick, Maine 04011-7288. Phone: 888-854-0810. Fax: 207-725-4748. E-mail: darrow@gwi.net.
URL www.darrowcamp.org

DARROW YOUTH BACKPACKING

Darrow Foundation
Maine

General Information Coed travel wilderness program and adventure program established in 1957. Accredited by American Camping Association.
Program Focus Hiking and backpacking on the Appalachian Trail.
Wilderness/Outdoors Backpacking, hiking, wilderness camping.
Program Information 2 sessions per year. Session length: 2 weeks in June, July, August. Ages: 14+. Cost: $1650–$3300. Financial aid available.
Application Deadline Continuous.
Jobs Positions for college students 18 and older.
Summer Contact John Houghton, Director, PO Box 9, Grand Lake Stream, Maine 04637. Phone: 888-854-0810. E-mail: darrow@gwi.net.
Winter Contact John Houghton, Director, 24 Lunt Road, Brunswick, Maine 04011-7288. Phone: 888-854-0810. Fax: 207-725-4748. E-mail: darrow@gwi.net.
URL www.darrowcamp.org

EARTHWATCH INSTITUTE–
COASTAL ARCHAEOLOGY OF MAINE

Earthwatch Institute
Muscongus Bay
Maine

General Information Coed residential outdoor program.
Program Focus Excavating shell middens to determine the impact of prehistoric humans on their environment.
Academics Archaeology, biology, ecology, geology/earth science, oceanography.
Special Interest Areas Conservation projects, field research/expeditions.
Program Information 4 sessions per year. Session length: 8 days in July. Ages: 16+. 10 participants per session. Boarding program cost: $1295–$1395. Financial aid available. Financial aid for high school students and teachers.
Application Deadline Continuous.
Contact General Information Desk, PO Box 75, Maynard, Massachusetts 01754. Phone: 800-776-0188. Fax: 978-461-2332. E-mail: info@earthwatch.org.
URL www.earthwatch.org

EARTHWATCH INSTITUTE–
MAINE'S ISLAND ECOLOGY

Earthwatch Institute
Maine

General Information Coed residential outdoor program.
Program Focus Exploring the foraging and breeding ecology of gulls to determine their impact on competing species and intertidal communities.
Academics Ecology, ornithology.
Special Interest Areas Conservation projects, field research/expeditions, nature study.
Program Information 6 sessions per year. Session length: 8 days in May, July. Ages: 16+. 10 participants per session. Boarding program cost: $995–$1095. Financial aid available. Financial aid for high school students and teachers.
Application Deadline Continuous.
Contact General Information Desk, PO Box 75, Maynard, Massachusetts 01754. Phone: 800-776-0188. Fax: 978-461-2332. E-mail: info@earthwatch.org.
URL www.earthwatch.org

THE FESTIVAL OF CREATIVE YOUTH

The University School for the Gifted, Creative and Talented
Portland, Maine 04101

General Information Coed day academic program and arts program established in 1980. Formal opportunities for the academically talented and artistically talented.
Program Focus For gifted and talented students.
Academics French (Advanced Placement), French language/literature, Latin language, academics (general), aerospace science, anthropology, archaeology, architecture, art (Advanced Placement), art history/appreciation, astronomy, biology, chemistry, classical languages/literatures, communications, computer programming, computers, ecology, economics, engineering, environmental science, geology/earth science, government and politics, health sciences, history, humanities, intercultural studies, journalism, marine studies, mathematics, meteorology, music, oceanography, philosophy, physics, psychology, science (general), social science, typing, writing.
Arts Arts, arts and crafts (general), band, ceramics, chorus, clowning, creative writing, dance, dance (ballet), dance (folk), dance (jazz), dance (modern), drawing, film, graphic arts, mime, music, music (instrumental), music

(jazz), music (vocal), musical productions, painting, photography, pottery, printmaking, puppetry, radio broadcasting, sculpture, television/video, theater/drama, weaving.
Special Interest Areas Native American culture, culinary arts, electronics, leadership training, model rocketry, robotics.
Sports Fencing, martial arts.
Trips Day.
Program Information 1 session per year. Session length: 3 weeks in June, July. Ages: 6–16. 250 participants per session. Day program cost: $700–$800. Financial aid available.
Application Deadline Continuous.
Jobs Positions for college students 22 and older.
Contact Mr. John Glynn, Academic Director, PO Box 4353, Portland, Maine 04101. Phone: 207-799-1950.

FLYING MOOSE LODGE

Craig Pond Trail
East Orland, Maine 04431

General Information Boys' residential traditional camp, outdoor program, wilderness program, and adventure program established in 1921.
Program Focus Canoe trips, backpacking, deep woods camping, and fishing.
Academics Area studies, ecology.
Special Interest Areas Campcraft.
Sports Canoeing, fishing, sailing, swimming.
Wilderness/Outdoors Backpacking, canoe trips, hiking, mountaineering, orienteering, white-water trips, wilderness camping.
Trips Day, overnight.
Program Information 2 sessions per year. Session length: 24–49 days in June, July, August. Ages: 10–16. 48–50 participants per session. Boarding program cost: $3400–$4500. Financial aid available.
Application Deadline Continuous.
Jobs Positions for college students 21 and older.
Summer Contact Christopher Price, Director, main address above. Phone: 207-941-9202. E-mail: prices@flyingmooselodge.com.
Winter Contact Shelly Price, Director, PO Box 889, Mt. Desert, Maine 04660. Phone: 207-283-3088. Fax: 207-288-0239. E-mail: prices@flyingmooselodge.com.
URL www.flyingmooselodge.com

FRIENDS CAMP

729 Lakeview Drive
South China, Maine 04358

General Information Coed residential traditional camp established in 1953. Religious affiliation: Society of Friends.
Program Focus Building a noncompetitive Quaker community, emphasis on values and ethics.
Arts Acting, arts and crafts (general), batiking, ceramics, clowning, creative writing, dance, dance (ballet), dance (folk), dance (jazz), dance (modern), drawing, fabric arts, film, jewelry making, leather working, metalworking, mime, music, music (vocal), musical productions, painting, photography, pottery, printmaking, puppetry, sculpture, television/video, theater/drama, weaving, woodworking.
Special Interest Areas Native American culture, campcraft, community service, conservation projects, culinary arts, gardening, model rocketry, nature study, nautical skills, work camp programs.
Sports Aerobics, baseball, basketball, boating, canoeing, fishing, golf, sailing, soccer, softball, swimming, volleyball.
Wilderness/Outdoors Canoe trips, hiking, orienteering.
Trips Day, overnight.
Program Information 4 sessions per year. Session length: 2 weeks in June, July, August. Ages: 7–17. 100 participants per session. Boarding program cost: $585. Financial aid available. Open to all religions.
Application Deadline Continuous.
Jobs Positions for college students 19 and older.
Summer Contact Nat Shed, Director, main address above. Phone: 207-445-2361. Fax: 207-445-5451. E-mail: director@friendscamp.org.
Winter Contact Director, 25 Burleigh Street, Waterville, Maine 04901-1307. Phone: 207-872-5908. Fax: 207-872-5908. E-mail: director@friendscamp.org.
URL www.friendscamp.org

GREAT ESCAPES (ADVENTURE TRIPS FOR TEENS)–MAINE WATERWAYS

South Shore YMCA Camps
Maine

General Information Coed travel outdoor program and adventure program established in 1989. Religious affiliation: Christian. Accredited by American Camping Association.
Program Focus Paddling program, multi-day canoe trip, multi-day sea kayaking trip.
Special Interest Areas Leadership training, nature study.
Sports Boating, canoeing, kayaking, sailing, sea kayaking.
Wilderness/Outdoors Canoe trips, hiking, rafting, white-water trips, wilderness camping, wilderness/outdoors (general).
Program Information 1 session per year. Session length: 13 days in June, July. Ages: 14–17. 10–12 participants per session. Cost: $1095. Financial aid available.
Application Deadline Continuous.
Jobs Positions for college students 21 and older.
Contact Joseph O'Keefe, Great Escapes Director, 75 Stowe Road, Sandwich, Massachusetts 02563. Phone: 508-428-2571 Ext.110. Fax: 508-420-3545. E-mail: joeokeefe@ssymca.org.
URL www.ssymca.org/camps/great_escapes.asp

Hidden Valley Camp

Hidden Valley Camp
161 Hidden Valley Road
Freedom, Maine 04941

General Information Coed residential arts program established in 1946. Accredited by American Camping Association.

Hidden Valley Camp

Program Focus Creative and performing arts and horse care.
Arts Arts, arts and crafts (general), batiking, ceramics, creative writing, dance, dance (ballet), dance (folk), dance (jazz), dance (modern), dance (tap), drawing, fabric arts, jewelry making, music, musical productions, photography, pottery, printmaking, theater/drama, woodworking.
Special Interest Areas Native American culture, animal care, community service, culinary arts, farming, gardening, general camp activities.
Sports Basketball, bicycling, boating, canoeing, equestrian sports, fishing, gymnastics, horseback riding, kayaking, rappelling, ropes course, soccer, softball, swimming, tennis, windsurfing.
Wilderness/Outdoors Backpacking, mountain biking, pack animal trips, white-water trips.
Trips Day, overnight.
Program Information 2 sessions per year. Session length: 4–8 weeks in July, August. Ages: 8–14. 220–270 participants per session. Boarding program cost: $3790–$6190.
Application Deadline Continuous.
Jobs Positions for college students 19 and older.
Contact Meg Kassen, Co-Owner/Director, main address above. Phone: 207-342-5177. Fax: 207-342-5685. E-mail: summer@hiddenvalleycamp.com.
URL www.hiddenvalleycamp.com
For more information, see page 1150.

Hurricane Island Outward Bound–Maine Coast and Western Maine Canoeing and Sailing

Hurricane Island Outward Bound/Outward Bound, USA
Penobscot Bay and Rangely Lakes
Maine

General Information Coed travel wilderness program and adventure program established in 1964. College credit may be earned.
Program Focus Teamwork and leadership wilderness adventure.
Academics Environmental science, marine studies.
Special Interest Areas Campcraft, leadership training, nature study, nautical skills, navigation, personal development, team building.
Sports Canoeing, sailing.
Wilderness/Outdoors Canoe trips, hiking, outdoor adventure, wilderness camping.
Trips Overnight.
Program Information 1 session per year. Session length: 24 days in July, August. Ages: 15–17. Cost: $2995. Application fee: $95. Financial aid available.
Application Deadline Continuous.
Jobs Positions for college students 21 and older.
Contact Admissions Advisor, 75 Mechanic Street, Rockland, Maine 04841. Phone: 866-746-9771. Fax: 207-594-8202. E-mail: admissions@hurricaneisland.org.
URL www.hurricaneisland.org

Hurricane Island Outward Bound–Maine Coast and Western Maine Sailing and Backpacking

Hurricane Island Outward Bound/Outward Bound, USA
Penobscot Bay and Carter-Mahoosuc Range
Maine

General Information Coed travel wilderness program and adventure program established in 1964. College credit may be earned.
Program Focus Teamwork and leadership wilderness adventure.
Academics Environmental science, marine studies.
Special Interest Areas Campcraft, leadership training, nature study, nautical skills, navigation, personal development, team building.
Sports Sailing.
Wilderness/Outdoors Backpacking, canoe trips, hiking, outdoor adventure, wilderness camping.
Trips Overnight.
Program Information 1–3 sessions per year. Session length: 24 days in June, July, August. Ages: 15+. Cost: $2995. Application fee: $95. Financial aid available.
Application Deadline Continuous.
Jobs Positions for college students 21 and older.
Contact Admissions Advisor, 75 Mechanic Street, Rockland, Maine 04841. Phone: 866-746-9771. Fax: 207-594-8202. E-mail: admissions@hurricaneisland.org.
URL www.hurricaneisland.org

Hurricane Island Outward Bound–Maine Coast and Western Maine Sea Kayaking and Backpacking

Hurricane Island Outward Bound/Outward Bound, USA
Penobscot Bay, Carter-Mahoosuc Range, Caribou-Speckled Mountain Wilderness Area
Maine

General Information Coed travel wilderness program and adventure program established in 1964. College credit may be earned.
Program Focus Teamwork and leadership wilderness adventure.
Academics Environmental science, marine studies.
Special Interest Areas Campcraft, conservation projects, leadership training, nature study, nautical skills, navigation, personal development, team building.
Sports Canoeing, sailing, sea kayaking.
Wilderness/Outdoors Backpacking, canoe trips, hiking, outdoor adventure, rock climbing, wilderness camping.
Trips Overnight.
Program Information 1–4 sessions per year. Session length: 22–24 days in June, July, August. Ages: 15+. Cost: $2895–$2995. Application fee: $95. Financial aid available.
Application Deadline Continuous.
Jobs Positions for college students 21 and older.
Contact Admissions Advisor, 75 Mechanic Street, Rockland, Maine 04841. Phone: 866-746-9771. Fax: 207-594-8202. E-mail: admissions@hurricaneisland.org.
URL www.hurricaneisland.org

Hurricane Island Outward Bound–Maine Coast Sailing/Sailing and Rock Climbing

Hurricane Island Outward Bound/Outward Bound, USA
Fox Island, Penobscot Bay, Muscongus Bay
Maine

General Information Coed travel wilderness program and adventure program established in 1964. College credit may be earned.
Program Focus Teamwork and leadership adventure.
Academics Environmental science, history, marine studies.
Special Interest Areas Native American culture, first aid, leadership training, nature study, nautical skills, navigation, personal development, team building.
Sports Sailing.
Wilderness/Outdoors Hiking, outdoor adventure, rock climbing, wilderness camping.
Trips Overnight.
Program Information 11 sessions per year. Session length: 7–27 days in June, July, August. Ages: 15+. Cost: $1295–$2195. Application fee: $95. Financial aid available.
Application Deadline Continuous.
Jobs Positions for college students 21 and older.
Contact Admissions Advisor, 75 Mechanic Street, Rockland, Maine 04841. Phone: 866-746-9771. Fax: 207-594-8202. E-mail: admissions@hurricaneisland.org.
URL www.hurricaneisland.org

Hurricane Island Outward Bound–Maine Coast Schooner Sailing

Hurricane Island Outward Bound/Outward Bound, USA
Penobscot Bay
Maine

General Information Coed travel wilderness program and adventure program established in 1964. College credit may be earned.
Program Focus Teamwork and leadership sailing adventure.
Academics Environmental science, geology/earth science, history, marine studies, oceanography.
Special Interest Areas Native American culture, first aid, leadership training, nature study, nautical skills, navigation, personal development, team building.
Sports Sailing.
Wilderness/Outdoors Outdoor adventure, rock climbing, wilderness camping.
Trips Overnight.
Program Information 2 sessions per year. Session length: 22 days in June, July, August. Ages: 16+. Cost: $3295. Application fee: $95. Financial aid available.
Application Deadline Continuous.
Jobs Positions for college students 21 and older.
Contact Admissions Advisor, 75 Mechanic Street, Rockland, Maine 04841. Phone: 866-746-9771. Fax: 207-594-8202. E-mail: admissions@hurricaneisland.org.
URL www.hurricaneisland.org

Hurricane Island Outward Bound–Maine Coast Sea Kayaking

Hurricane Island Outward Bound/Outward Bound, USA
Fox Island, Penobscot Bay, Muscongus Bay
Maine

General Information Coed travel wilderness program and adventure program established in 1964. College credit may be earned.
Program Focus Teamwork and leadership adventure.
Academics Environmental science, history, marine studies.
Special Interest Areas Native American culture, first aid, leadership training, nature study, nautical skills, navigation, personal development, team building.
Sports Sailing, sea kayaking.
Wilderness/Outdoors Hiking, outdoor adventure, rock climbing, wilderness camping.
Trips Overnight.
Program Information 4 sessions per year. Session length: 7–16 days in June, July, August. Ages: 16+. Cost: $1295–$2495. Application fee: $95. Financial aid available.
Application Deadline Continuous.
Jobs Positions for college students 21 and older.

Hurricane Island Outward Bound–Maine Coast Sea Kayaking (continued)

Contact Admissions Advisor, 75 Mechanic Street, Rockland, Maine 04841. Phone: 866-746-9771. Fax: 207-594-8202. E-mail: admissions@hurricaneisland.org.
URL www.hurricaneisland.org

Hurricane Island Outward Bound–Maine Woods High School Summer Semester

Hurricane Island Outward Bound/Outward Bound, USA
Carter-Mahoosuc Range, Rangely Lakes, Penobscot Bay
Maine

General Information Coed travel wilderness program and adventure program established in 1964. High school or college credit may be earned.
Program Focus Teamwork and leadership wilderness adventure.
Academics Environmental science.
Special Interest Areas Campcraft, community service, field research/expeditions, first aid, leadership training, nature study, nautical skills, navigation, outdoor cooking, personal development, team building.
Sports Canoeing, challenge course, rappelling, sailing.
Wilderness/Outdoors Backpacking, canoe trips, hiking, orienteering, outdoor adventure, rock climbing, wilderness camping.
Trips Overnight.
Program Information 1 session per year. Session length: 7 weeks in June, July, August. Ages: 15–17. Cost: $5895. Application fee: $95. Financial aid available.
Application Deadline Continuous.
Jobs Positions for college students 21 and older.
Contact Admissions Advisor, 75 Mechanic Street, Rockland, Maine 04841. Phone: 866-746-9771. Fax: 207-594-8202. E-mail: admissions@hurricaneisland.org.
URL www.hurricaneisland.org

Hurricane Island Outward Bound–North Woods Maine Allagash and Appalachian Trail Canoeing and Backpacking

Hurricane Island Outward Bound/Outward Bound, USA
Allagash Wilderness, 100-Mile Wilderness, Appalachian Trail
Maine

General Information Coed travel wilderness program and adventure program established in 1964. High school or college credit may be earned.
Program Focus Teamwork and leadership wilderness camp.
Academics Area studies, environmental science.
Special Interest Areas Campcraft, field research/expeditions, leadership training, nature study, outdoor cooking, personal development, team building.
Sports Canoeing.
Wilderness/Outdoors Backpacking, hiking, outdoor adventure, wilderness camping.
Trips Overnight.
Program Information 2 sessions per year. Session length: 22 days in June, July, August. Ages: 15–17. Cost: $2795. Application fee: $95. Financial aid available.
Application Deadline Continuous.
Jobs Positions for college students 21 and older.
Contact Admissions Advisor, 75 Mechanic Street, Rockland, Maine 04841. Phone: 866-746-9771. Fax: 207-594-8202. E-mail: admissions@hurricaneisland.org.
URL www.hurricaneisland.org

Hurricane Island Outward Bound–North Woods Maine Canoeing and Backpacking

Hurricane Island Outward Bound/Outward Bound, USA
Penobscot and Kennebec Watersheds, 100-Mile Wilderness, Appalachian Trail
Maine

General Information Coed travel wilderness program and adventure program established in 1964. College credit may be earned.
Program Focus Teamwork and leadership wilderness adventure.
Academics Area studies, environmental science.
Special Interest Areas Campcraft, community service, conservation projects, field research/expeditions, leadership training, nature study, outdoor cooking, personal development, team building.
Sports Canoeing, rappelling.
Wilderness/Outdoors Backpacking, canoe trips, hiking, outdoor adventure, rock climbing, survival training, white-water trips, wilderness camping.
Trips Overnight.
Program Information 3 sessions per year. Session length: 14–22 days in June, July, August. Ages: 15+. Cost: $2095–$2795. Application fee: $95. Financial aid available.
Application Deadline Continuous.
Jobs Positions for college students 21 and older.
Contact Admissions Advisor, 75 Mechanic Street, Rockland, Maine 04841. Phone: 866-746-9771. Fax: 207-594-8202. E-mail: admissions@hurricaneisland.org.
URL www.hurricaneisland.org

Hurricane Island Outward Bound–North Woods Maine Expedition Canoeing

Hurricane Island Outward Bound/Outward Bound, USA
Penobscot and Kennebec Watersheds
Maine

General Information Coed travel wilderness program and adventure program established in 1964. High school or college credit may be earned.
Program Focus Teamwork and leadership wilderness adventure.
Academics Environmental science, history.

Special Interest Areas Native American culture, campcraft, field research/expeditions, leadership training, nature study, outdoor cooking, personal development, team building.
Sports Canoeing.
Wilderness/Outdoors Canoe trips, outdoor adventure, survival training, wilderness camping.
Trips Overnight.
Program Information 1 session per year. Session length: 2 weeks in August. Ages: 15–17. Cost: $2095. Application fee: $95. Financial aid available.
Application Deadline Continuous.
Jobs Positions for college students 21 and older.
Contact Admissions Advisor, 75 Mechanic Street, Rockland, Maine 04841. Phone: 866-746-9771. Fax: 207-594-8202. E-mail: admissions@hurricaneisland.org.
URL www.hurricaneisland.org

Hurricane Island Outward Bound–Western Maine Backpacking and Rock Climbing

Hurricane Island Outward Bound/Outward Bound, USA
Carter-Mahoosuc and Bigelow Ranges
Maine

General Information Coed travel wilderness program and adventure program established in 1964. High school or college credit may be earned.
Program Focus Teamwork and leadership wilderness adventure.
Academics Environmental science.
Special Interest Areas Campcraft, community service, conservation projects, leadership training, nature study, outdoor cooking, personal development, team building.
Sports Rappelling.
Wilderness/Outdoors Backpacking, hiking, outdoor adventure, rock climbing, wilderness camping.
Trips Overnight.
Program Information 4 sessions per year. Session length: 14–24 days in June, July, August. Ages: 15+. Cost: $2295–$2995. Application fee: $95. Financial aid available.
Application Deadline Continuous.
Jobs Positions for college students 21 and older.
Contact Admissions Advisor, 75 Mechanic Street, Rockland, Maine 04841. Phone: 866-746-9771. Fax: 207-594-8202. E-mail: admissions@hurricaneisland.org.
URL www.hurricaneisland.org

Hurricane Island Outward Bound–Western Maine Woods Expedition Canoeing

Hurricane Island Outward Bound/Outward Bound, USA
Androscoggin Watershed
Maine

General Information Coed travel wilderness program and adventure program established in 1964. College credit may be earned.
Program Focus Teamwork and leadership wilderness adventure.
Academics Environmental science.
Special Interest Areas Native American culture, campcraft, community service, conservation projects, leadership training, nature study, personal development, team building.
Sports Canoeing.
Wilderness/Outdoors Canoe trips, outdoor adventure, wilderness camping.
Trips Overnight.
Program Information 2 sessions per year. Session length: 2 weeks in June, July, August. Ages: 14–15. Cost: $2095. Application fee: $95. Financial aid available.
Application Deadline Continuous.
Jobs Positions for college students 21 and older.
Contact Admissions Advisor, 75 Mechanic Street, Rockland, Maine 04841. Phone: 866-746-9771. Fax: 207-594-8202. E-mail: admissions@hurricaneisland.org.
URL www.hurricaneisland.org

Hyde School Summer Challenge Program–Bath, ME

Hyde School
616 High Street
Bath, Maine 04530-5002

General Information Coed residential academic program and outdoor program established in 1966.
Program Focus Character education, performing arts, academics, athletics, and wilderness adventure.
Academics Academics (general), mathematics, reading, science (general), study skills, writing.
Arts Acting, dance, musical productions, theater/drama.
Special Interest Areas Community service, farming, leadership training.
Sports Basketball, canoeing, kayaking, ropes course, soccer, track and field, wrestling.
Wilderness/Outdoors Backpacking, canoe trips, hiking, wilderness camping, wilderness/outdoors (general).
Trips Cultural, day, overnight.
Program Information 1 session per year. Session length: 35–40 days in July, August. Ages: 13–18. 95–120 participants per session. Boarding program cost: $6000. Application fee: $100. Student bank/bookstore deposit: $300.
Application Deadline Continuous.
Jobs Positions for college students.
Contact Richard K. Truluck, Director of Admission, main address above. Phone: 207-443-7101. Fax: 207-442-9346. E-mail: rtruluck@hyde.edu.
URL www.hyde.edu
For more information, see page 1154.

Kamp Kohut

Kamp Kohut
151 Kohut Road
Oxford, Maine 04270

General Information Coed residential traditional camp established in 1907. Accredited by American

Kamp Kohut (continued)

Camping Association. Specific services available for the developmentally challenged and learning disabled. High school credit may be earned.
Program Focus Nurturing, non-competitive environment; activities focus on instruction and fun.
Academics Web page design, computer programming, reading.
Arts Acting, arts and crafts (general), ceramics, chorus, creative writing, dance, dance (ballet), dance (folk), dance (jazz), dance (modern), dance (tap), drawing, fabric arts, film, graphic arts, jewelry making, leather working, metalworking, music, music (chamber), music (classical), music (ensemble), music (instrumental), music (jazz), music (orchestral), music (vocal), musical productions, painting, photography, pottery, radio broadcasting, sculpture, television/video, theater/drama, woodworking.
Special Interest Areas Campcraft, community service, conservation projects, field research/expeditions, field trips (arts and culture), leadership training, nature study, team building, yearbook production.
Sports Aerobics, archery, baseball, basketball, bicycling, boating, canoeing, cheerleading, climbing (wall), cross-country, diving, field hockey, fishing, football, golf, gymnastics, horseback riding, in-line skating, kayaking, lacrosse, rappelling, ropes course, rowing (crew/sculling), sailing, snorkeling, soccer, softball, street/roller hockey, swimming, tennis, track and field, volleyball, wakeboarding, water polo, waterskiing, windsurfing.
Wilderness/Outdoors Backpacking, bicycle trips, canoe trips, hiking, mountain biking, orienteering, rafting, rock climbing, white-water trips, wilderness camping.
Trips Day, overnight.
Program Information 2 sessions per year. Session length: 26 days in June, July, August. Ages: 7–16. 175 participants per session. Boarding program cost: $4150.
Application Deadline Continuous.
Jobs Positions for college students 19 and older.
Summer Contact Lisa Tripler, Owner / Director, main address above. Phone: 207-539-0966. Fax: 207-539-4701. E-mail: lisa@kampkohut.com.
Winter Contact Lisa Tripler, Owner / Director, 2 Tall Pine Road, Cape Elizabeth, Maine 04107. Phone: 207-767-2406. Fax: 207-767-0604. E-mail: lisa@kampkohut.com.
URL www.kampkohut.com

Kingsley Pines Camp

Kingsley Pines Camp
51 Coughlan Cove Road
Raymond, Maine 04071

General Information Coed residential traditional camp established in 1984. Accredited by American Camping Association.
Program Focus Personal growth, positive reinforcement, decision making, and group living skills.
Academics English as a second language.
Arts Arts and crafts (general), ceramics, dance, dance (modern), drawing, jewelry making, musical productions, painting, photography, pottery, radio broadcasting, sculpture, theater/drama, woodworking.
Special Interest Areas Campcraft, nature study.
Sports Archery, baseball, basketball, boating, canoeing, climbing (wall), fishing, golf, horseback riding, kayaking, lacrosse, ropes course, sailing, soccer, softball, swimming, tennis, waterskiing, windsurfing.
Wilderness/Outdoors Backpacking, canoe trips, hiking, mountain biking, rafting, rock climbing, white-water trips, wilderness camping.
Trips Day, overnight, shopping.
Program Information 3 sessions per year. Session length: 14–55 days in June, July, August. Ages: 8–15. 170–200 participants per session. Boarding program cost: $2098–$7898. Financial aid available.
Application Deadline Continuous.
Jobs Positions for college students 18 and older.
Contact Alan Kissack, Director, main address above. Phone: 207-655-7181. Fax: 207-655-4121. E-mail: staff@kingsleypines.com.
URL www.kingsleypines.com

Kippewa for Girls

1 Kippewa Drive
Monmouth, Maine 04259-6700

General Information Girls' residential traditional camp established in 1957. Accredited by American Camping Association.

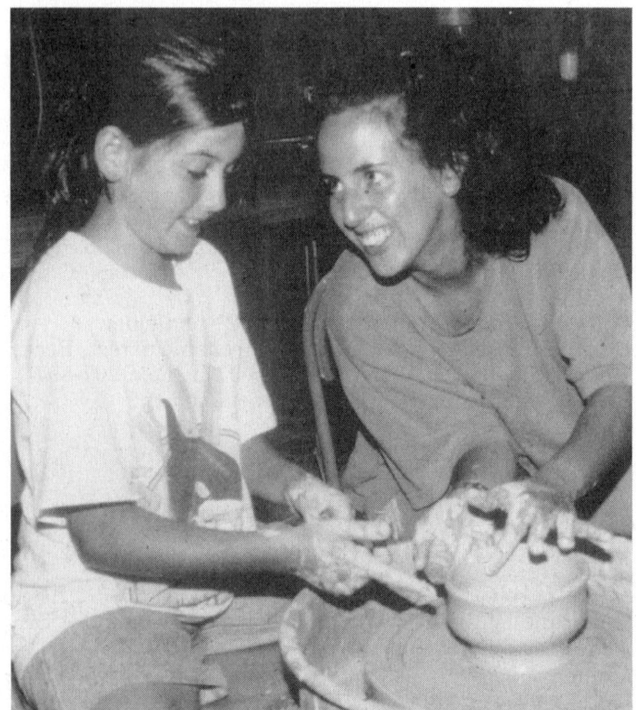

Kippewa for Girls

Program Focus Individual development, group living, and a wide range of traditional activities.

Arts Ceramics, clowning, creative writing, dance, dance (ballet), dance (folk), dance (jazz), dance (modern), dance (tap), drawing, fabric arts, jewelry making, leather working, music, music (vocal), musical productions, painting, photography, pottery, printmaking, puppetry, sculpture, sewing, stained glass, theater/drama, weaving, woodworking.
Special Interest Areas Campcraft.
Sports Aerobics, archery, basketball, canoeing, equestrian sports, field hockey, fishing, football, golf, gymnastics, horseback riding, kayaking, sailing, soccer, softball, swimming, tennis, volleyball, water polo, waterskiing, windsurfing.
Wilderness/Outdoors Backpacking, bicycle trips, canoe trips, hiking, mountain biking, rafting, white-water trips, wilderness camping.
Trips Cultural, overnight.
Program Information 1 session per year. Session length: 4–8 weeks in June, July, August. Ages: 6–16. 140–165 participants per session. Boarding program cost: $4325–$7230.
Application Deadline Continuous.
Jobs Positions for college students 20 and older.
Summer Contact Marty Silverman, Director, main address above. Phone: 207-933-2993. Fax: 207-933-2996. E-mail: info@kippewa.com.
Winter Contact Marty Silverman, Director, 60 Mill Street, PO Box 340, Westwood, Massachusetts 02090-0340. Phone: 800-547-7392. Fax: 781-255-7167. E-mail: info@kippewa.com.
URL www.kippewa.com

For more information, see page 1178.

Kroka Expeditions–Coastal Sea Kayaking

Kroka Expeditions of Vermont
Maine

General Information Coed travel outdoor program, wilderness program, and adventure program established in 1996. Specific services available for the learning disabled and physically challenged.
Program Focus Beginner through advanced level sea kayaking.
Academics Ecology, environmental science, geography, geology/earth science, marine studies.
Arts Arts and crafts (general), basketry.
Special Interest Areas Birdwatching, campcraft, community service, field research/expeditions, leadership training, nature study, nautical skills.
Sports Boating, canoeing, fishing, kayaking, sea kayaking, swimming.
Wilderness/Outdoors Backpacking, canoe trips, hiking, mountaineering, orienteering, rafting, rock climbing, survival training, wilderness camping.
Trips Day, overnight.
Program Information 1 session per year. Session length: 2 weeks in July, August. Ages: 14–18. 8–12 participants per session. Cost: $1750. Financial aid available.
Application Deadline Continuous.
Jobs Positions for college students 18 and older.
Contact Misha Golfman, Executive Director, 659 West Hill Road, Putney, Vermont 05346. Phone: 802-387-5397. Fax: 802-387-4536. E-mail: kroka@sover.net.
URL www.kroka.org

Landmark Volunteers: Maine

Landmark Volunteers, Inc.
Maine

General Information Coed residential outdoor program and community service program established in 1992. High school credit may be earned.
Program Focus Opportunity for high school students to earn community service credit while working as a team for two weeks serving Acadia National Park, Agassiz Village, Aldermere Farm, Atlantic Challenge, Blue Hill Heritage Trust/Kneisel Hall or Camp Sunshine. Similar programs offered through Landmark Volunteers at over 60 locations in 21 states.
Academics Area studies, biology, botany, ecology, environmental science, social science, social services.
Special Interest Areas Animal care, career exploration, community service, conservation projects, field research/expeditions, leadership training, nature study, team building, work camp programs.
Sports Boating.
Wilderness/Outdoors Hiking.
Trips Cultural, day.
Program Information 6 sessions per year. Session length: 14–15 days in June, July, August. Ages: 14–18. 10–13 participants per session. Boarding program cost: $875–$925. Financial aid available.
Application Deadline Continuous.
Jobs Positions for college students.
Contact Ann Barrett, Executive Director, PO Box 455, Sheffield, Massachusetts 01257. Phone: 413-229-0255. Fax: 413-229-2050. E-mail: landmark@volunteers.com.
URL www.volunteers.com

For more information, see page 1182.

Longacre Expeditions, Downeast

Longacre Expeditions
Maine

General Information Coed travel outdoor program, wilderness program, and adventure program established in 1981. Accredited by American Camping Association.
Program Focus Effective communication skills, responsibility, confidence building.
Special Interest Areas Nautical skills, whale watching.
Sports Bicycling, sailing, swimming.
Wilderness/Outdoors Bicycle trips, hiking, rafting, rock climbing, white-water trips.
Program Information 2 sessions per year. Session length: 15 days in June, July, August. Ages: 13–17. 10–16 participants per session. Cost: $2495.
Application Deadline Continuous.
Jobs Positions for college students 21 and older.

Longacre Expeditions, Downeast (continued)

Contact Meredith Schuler, Director, 4030 Middle Ridge Road, Newport, Pennsylvania 17074. Phone: 717-567-6790. Fax: 717-567-3955. E-mail: longacre@longacreexpeditions.com.
URL www.longacreexpeditions.com
For more information, see page 1200.

Longacre Expeditions, Photography

Longacre Expeditions
Maine

General Information Coed travel outdoor program, wilderness program, and adventure program established in 2004. Accredited by American Camping Association.
Program Focus Effective communication skills, photography, confidence building.
Arts Photography.
Sports Sea kayaking, swimming.
Wilderness/Outdoors Bicycle trips, hiking.
Program Information 1 session per year. Session length: 15 days in July. Ages: 14–17. 10–16 participants per session. Cost: $2910. Financial aid available.
Application Deadline Continuous.
Jobs Positions for college students 21 and older.
Contact Meredith Schuler, Director, 4030 Middle Ridge Road, Newport, Pennsylvania 17074. Phone: 717-567-6790. Fax: 717-567-3955. E-mail: longacre@longacreexpeditions.com.
URL www.longacreexpeditions.com
For more information, see page 1200.

Longacre Expeditions, Whales

Longacre Expeditions
Maine

General Information Coed travel outdoor program, wilderness program, and adventure program established in 2004. Accredited by American Camping Association.
Program Focus Effective communication skills, responsibility, confidence building.
Academics Ecology, environmental science, marine studies.
Sports Kayaking, sea kayaking.
Wilderness/Outdoors Bicycle trips, hiking, rafting, white-water trips, wilderness camping.
Program Information 3 sessions per year. Session length: 13 days in July, August. Ages: 14–17. 10–16 participants per session. Cost: $2295. Financial aid available.
Application Deadline Continuous.
Jobs Positions for college students 21 and older.
Contact Meredith Schuler, Director, 4030 Middle Ridge Road, Newport, Pennsylvania 17074. Phone: 717-567-6790. Fax: 717-567-3955. E-mail: longacre@longacrexpeditions.com.
URL www.longacreexpeditions.com
For more information, see page 1200.

Maine College of Art Early College Program

Maine College of Art
97 Spring Street
Portland, Maine 04101

General Information Coed residential and day academic program and arts program established in 1973. Formal opportunities for the artistically talented. College credit may be earned.
Program Focus Visual arts.
Academics Art (Advanced Placement), art history/appreciation, precollege program.
Arts Drawing, film, jewelry making, painting, photography, sculpture, visual arts.
Trips Day.
Program Information 1 session per year. Session length: 4 weeks in July. Ages: 16–18. 30–45 participants per session. Day program cost: $2115. Boarding program cost: $3500. Application fee: $50. Financial aid available.
Application Deadline Continuous.
Jobs Positions for college students 18 and older.
Contact Cheslye Ventimiglia, Director of Continuing Studies, main address above. Phone: 207-775-3052 Ext. 232. Fax: 207-879-5748. E-mail: earlycollege@meca.edu.
URL www.meca.edu/earlycollege

Maine Conservation School Summer Camps

Conservation Education Foundation of Maine
Lakeside Avenue
Bryant Pond, Maine 04219

General Information Coed residential outdoor program and wilderness program established in 1956.
Program Focus Outdoor skills development, conservation theme, connection goals.
Academics Biology, botany, ecology, environmental science, geology/earth science, philosophy, science (general).
Special Interest Areas Campcraft, conservation projects, leadership training, nature study.
Sports Archery, canoeing, fishing, kayaking, riflery, ropes course, swimming.
Wilderness/Outdoors Canoe trips, hiking, hunter safety, mountaineering, orienteering, survival training, wilderness camping.
Program Information 10–12 sessions per year. Session length: 1 week in May, June, July, August, September, October. Ages: 8–18. 100–120 participants per session. Boarding program cost: $400. Financial aid available.
Application Deadline Continuous.
Jobs Positions for high school students and college students.
Contact Scott Olsen, Operations Director, PO Box 188, Bryant Pond, Maine 04219. Phone: 207-665-2068. Fax: 207-665-2768. E-mail: mcsops@megalink.net.
URL www.meconservationschool.org

MAINE GOLF ACADEMY–FAMILY CAMP

Maine Golf and Tennis Academy
Belgrade Lakes
Belgrade, Maine 04917

General Information Coed residential family program and sports camp established in 1907.
Program Focus Golf and camp activities.
Arts Arts and crafts (general), ceramics, creative writing, drawing, photography, television/video.
Special Interest Areas Campcraft, general camp activities, whale watching.
Sports Basketball, boating, canoeing, climbing (wall), fishing, golf, kayaking, rappelling, ropes course, sailing, swimming, tennis, volleyball, waterskiing.
Wilderness/Outdoors Canoe trips, hiking, mountaineering, rafting, rock climbing, white-water trips.
Trips Cultural, day, overnight, shopping.
Program Information 1 session per year. Session length: 1–4 weeks in August. Ages: 8–17. 100–120 participants per session. Boarding program cost: $2395–$4895. Financial aid available.
Application Deadline Continuous.
Contact Joel Lavenson, Director, 35 Golf Academy Drive, Belgrade, Maine 04917. Phone: 800-465-3226. Fax: 207-465-3226. E-mail: fun@golfcamp.com.
URL www.golfcamp.com

MAINE GOLF ACADEMY–JUNIOR GOLF CAMP

Maine Golf and Tennis Academy
Belgrade Lakes
Belgrade, Maine 04917

General Information Coed residential and day traditional camp and sports camp established in 1907.
Program Focus Golf, tennis instruction, and course play plus traditional camp activities.
Academics English as a second language.
Arts Arts and crafts (general), ceramics, creative writing, drawing, photography, television/video.
Special Interest Areas General camp activities, leadership training.
Sports Basketball, boating, canoeing, climbing (wall), fishing, golf, kayaking, rappelling, ropes course, sailing, swimming, tennis, waterskiing.
Wilderness/Outdoors Canoe trips, hiking, rafting, rock climbing, white-water trips, wilderness camping.
Trips Cultural, day, overnight, shopping.
Program Information 5–6 sessions per year. Session length: 2–4 weeks in June, July, August. Ages: 9–17. 100–120 participants per session. Day program cost: $750–$950. Boarding program cost: $2795–$4895. Financial aid available.
Application Deadline Continuous.
Jobs Positions for college students.
Contact Mr. Joel Lavenson, Director, 35 Golf Academy Drive, Belgrade, Maine 04917. Phone: 800-465-3226. Fax: 207-465-3226. E-mail: fun@golfcamp.com.
URL www.golfcamp.com

MAINE GOLF AND TENNIS ACADEMY–SERVE AND TURF

Maine Golf and Tennis Academy
Belgrade Lakes
Belgrade, Maine 04917

General Information Coed residential traditional camp and sports camp established in 1907.
Program Focus Golf and tennis.
Sports Basketball, boating, canoeing, climbing (wall), fishing, golf, kayaking, rappelling, ropes course, sailing, swimming, tennis, waterskiing.
Wilderness/Outdoors Canoe trips, hiking, rafting, rock climbing, white-water trips, wilderness camping.
Trips Cultural, day, overnight, shopping.
Program Information 4 sessions per year. Session length: 2 weeks in June, July, August. Ages: 9–17. 20 participants per session. Boarding program cost: $2795–$2995.
Application Deadline Continuous.
Jobs Positions for college students.
Contact Joel Lavenson, Director, 35 Golf Academy Drive, Belgrade, Maine 04917. Phone: 800-465-3226. Fax: 207-465-3226. E-mail: fun@golfcamp.com.
URL www.golfcamp.com

MAINE TEEN CAMP

Maine Teen Camp
481 Brownfield Road
Porter, Maine 04068

General Information Coed residential traditional camp established in 1985. Accredited by American Camping Association. Formal opportunities for the artistically talented. College credit may be earned.

Maine Teen Camp

Program Focus Teen programs include tennis, waterskiing, arts, music, academics, trips, dance, theater, adventure.
Academics English as a second language, English language/literature, French language/literature, Spanish language/literature, mathematics, music, music (Advanced Placement), reading, science (general), writing.

Maine Teen Camp (continued)

Arts Arts and crafts (general), band, batiking, ceramics, chorus, creative writing, dance, dance (ballet), dance (folk), dance (jazz), dance (modern), dance (tap), drawing, fabric arts, film, graphic arts, jewelry making, metalworking, music, music (ensemble), music (instrumental), music (jazz), music (vocal), musical productions, painting, photography, pottery, printmaking, puppetry, sculpture, television/video, theater/drama.
Special Interest Areas Campcraft, community service, leadership training.
Sports Aerobics, basketball, bicycling, bicycling (BMX), boating, canoeing, cheerleading, climbing (wall), field hockey, fishing, football, golf, kayaking, lacrosse, martial arts, rappelling, ropes course, sailing, snorkeling, soccer, softball, swimming, tennis, track and field, volleyball, waterskiing, weight training, windsurfing.
Wilderness/Outdoors Backpacking, bicycle trips, canoe trips, hiking, mountain biking, rafting, white-water trips, wilderness camping.
Trips Cultural, day, overnight, shopping.
Program Information 2–8 sessions per year. Session length: 2–8 weeks in June, July, August. Ages: 13–17. 260–300 participants per session. Boarding program cost: $1850–$5495. Financial aid available.
Application Deadline Continuous.
Jobs Positions for college students 20 and older.
Summer Contact Ms. Monique Rafuse-Pines, Associate Director, main address above. Phone: 207-625-8581. Fax: 207-625-8738. E-mail: mtc@teencamp.com.
Winter Contact Ms. Monique Rafuse-Pines, Associate Director, 190 Upper Gulph Road, Radnor, Pennsylvania 19087. Phone: 610-527-6759. Fax: 610-520-0182. E-mail: mtc@teencamp.com.
URL www.teencamp.com

For more information, see page 1202.

Maine Tennis Academy–Junior Tennis Camp

Maine Golf and Tennis Academy
Belgrade Lakes
Belgrade, Maine 04917

General Information Coed residential and day traditional camp and sports camp established in 1907.
Program Focus Tennis, golf, course play, plus traditional camp activities.
Academics English as a second language, SAT/ACT preparation.
Arts Arts and crafts (general), ceramics, creative writing, drawing, graphic arts, photography, pottery, television/video, theater/drama.
Special Interest Areas General camp activities, leadership training, work camp programs.
Sports Archery, basketball, boating, canoeing, climbing (wall), fishing, golf, kayaking, rappelling, ropes course, sailing, soccer, softball, swimming, tennis, volleyball, waterskiing.
Wilderness/Outdoors Canoe trips, hiking, rafting, rock climbing, white-water trips, wilderness camping.
Trips Cultural, day, overnight, shopping.
Program Information 5–6 sessions per year. Session length: 2–4 weeks in June, July, August. Ages: 8+. 100–120 participants per session. Day program cost: $750–$950. Boarding program cost: $2795–$4895. Financial aid available.
Application Deadline Continuous.
Jobs Positions for high school students 18 and older and college students 18 and older.
Contact Joel Lavenson, Director, 35 Golf Academy Drive, Belgrade, Maine 04917. Phone: 800-465-3226. Fax: 207-465-3226. E-mail: fun@golfcamp.com.
URL www.tenniscamp.org

Maine Wilderness Adventure Trip

Camp Runoia
Maine

General Information Coed travel outdoor program, wilderness program, and adventure program. Accredited by American Camping Association.
Special Interest Areas Campcraft.
Sports Canoeing, kayaking, sea kayaking.
Wilderness/Outdoors Backpacking, canoe trips, hiking, rafting, rock climbing, white-water trips, wilderness camping.
Trips Overnight.
Program Information 1 session per year. Session length: 23 days in July, August. Ages: 13–16. 10 participants per session. Cost: $3300. Co-sponsored by Birch Rock Camp and Camp Runoia.
Application Deadline Continuous.
Jobs Positions for college students 23 and older.
Summer Contact Pamela N. Cobb, Director, PO Box 450, Belgrade Lakes, Maine 04918. Phone: 207-495-2228. Fax: 207-495-2287. E-mail: info@runoia.com.
Winter Contact Pamela N. Cobb, Director, 56 Jackson Street, Cambridge, Massachusetts 02140. Phone: 617-547-4676. Fax: 617-661-1964. E-mail: info@runoia.com.
URL www.birchrock.org/maine_wilderness_adventure.htm

Med-O-Lark Camp

82 Medolark Road
Washington, Maine 04574

General Information Coed residential traditional camp and arts program established in 1946. Accredited by American Camping Association. Formal opportunities for the artistically talented.
Program Focus Theater, dance, visual arts, and music.
Academics English as a second language, French language/literature, Hebrew language, Russian language/literature, Spanish language/literature, music, writing.
Arts Arts, arts and crafts (general), band, basketry, batiking, candlemaking, ceramics, chorus, clowning, creative writing, dance, dance (ballet), dance (folk), dance (jazz), dance (modern), dance (tap), drawing, fabric arts, film, graphic arts, jewelry making, metalworking, mime, music, music (ensemble), music (instrumental), music (jazz), music (rock), music (vocal),

Med-O-Lark Camp

music technology/record production, musical productions, painting, photography, pottery, printmaking, puppetry, sculpture, stained glass, television/video, theater/drama, visual arts, woodworking.
Special Interest Areas Animal care, community service, culinary arts, field trips (arts and culture), gardening, general camp activities, leadership training, stone carving.
Sports Aerobics, archery, basketball, bicycling, boating, canoeing, cheerleading, equestrian sports, fencing, fishing, gymnastics, horseback riding, kayaking, martial arts, ropes course, rowing (crew/sculling), sailing, sea kayaking, snorkeling, soccer, softball, sports (general), swimming, tennis, volleyball, waterskiing, weight training, windsurfing.
Wilderness/Outdoors Bicycle trips, hiking, mountain biking, pack animal trips, rafting, white-water trips.
Trips Cultural, day, overnight.
Program Information 3 sessions per year. Session length: 4–8 weeks in June, July, August. Ages: 11–15. 275 participants per session. Boarding program cost: $3400–$6000. Financial aid available.
Application Deadline Continuous.
Jobs Positions for college students 20 and older.
Summer Contact Jay R. Stager, Director, main address above. Phone: 800-292-7757. Fax: 207-845-2332. E-mail: medolark@acadia.net.
Winter Contact Jay R. Stager, Director, 214 Atlantic Highway, Northport, Maine 04849. Phone: 207-338-5733. Fax: 207-338-0848. E-mail: medolark@acadia.net.
URL www.medolark.com

For more information, see page 1208.

Moose River Outpost

Christian Camps and Conferences, Inc.
Jackman, Maine 04945

General Information Coed residential traditional camp established in 1999. Religious affiliation: Christian.
Program Focus General camp program.
Academics Bible study.
Arts Arts and crafts (general), music.
Special Interest Areas Campcraft, model rocketry, nature study.
Sports Archery, boating, canoeing, climbing (wall), fishing, swimming, volleyball, water tubing, windsurfing.
Wilderness/Outdoors Hiking, rafting, white-water trips, wilderness camping.
Trips Day, overnight.
Program Information 2 sessions per year. Session length: 2 weeks in June, July, August. Ages: 10–16. 32–75 participants per session. Boarding program cost: $1000–$1500. Financial aid available.
Application Deadline Continuous.
Jobs Positions for college students 18 and older.
Contact Mr. Bob Strodel, Executive Director, 34 Camp Brookwoods Road, Alton, New Hampshire 03809. Phone: 603-875-3600. Fax: 603-875-4606. E-mail: bob@christiancamps.net.
URL www.moose-river-outpost.org

Mountain Workshop–Awesome 5: North Woods of Maine

Mountain Workshop
Maine

General Information Coed travel outdoor program, wilderness program, and adventure program established in 1987.
Program Focus Skill-intensive expedition, canoe experience required.
Sports Canoeing.
Wilderness/Outdoors Canoe trips, hiking, rafting, white-water trips, wilderness camping, wilderness/outdoors (general).
Trips Overnight.
Program Information 1 session per year. Session length: 10 days in July. Ages: 15–16. Cost: $1300.
Application Deadline Continuous.
Jobs Positions for college students 21 and older.
Contact Kent B. Tullo, Director, 9 Brookside Place, West Redding, Connecticut 06896. Phone: 203-544-0555. Fax: 203-544-0333. E-mail: info@mountainworkshop.com.
URL www.mountainworkshop.com

Mountain Workshop–Awesome 3: Maine Coast

Mountain Workshop
Maine

General Information Coed travel outdoor program, wilderness program, and adventure program established in 1986.
Special Interest Areas Nautical skills, team building.
Sports Canoeing, swimming.
Wilderness/Outdoors Canoe trips, hiking, outdoor adventure, rock climbing, wilderness camping.
Trips Overnight.
Program Information 3 sessions per year. Session length: 10 days in June, July, August. Ages: 13–14. Cost: $1500.
Application Deadline Continuous.
Jobs Positions for college students 21 and older.

Mountain Workshop–Awesome 3: Maine Coast (continued)

Contact Kent B. Tullo, Director, 9 Brookside Place, West Redding, Connecticut 06896. Phone: 203-544-0555. Fax: 203-544-0333. E-mail: info@mountainworkshop.com.
URL www.mountainworkshop.com

New England Camping Adventures

Camp Hawthorne, Inc.
Maine

General Information Coed travel outdoor program and wilderness program established in 1986. Formal opportunities for the gifted.
Program Focus Wilderness adventure, backpacking, personal development, sailing, ocean kayaking, white-water canoeing, rafting, and rock climbing.
Academics Ecology, geology/earth science.
Special Interest Areas Campcraft, culinary arts, leadership training, work camp programs.
Sports Baseball, basketball, bicycling, boating, canoeing, climbing (wall), fishing, kayaking, rappelling, riflery, rowing (crew/sculling), sailing, sea kayaking, snorkeling, soccer, softball, swimming, volleyball, waterskiing, windsurfing.
Wilderness/Outdoors Backpacking, bicycle trips, canoe trips, hiking, mountain biking, orienteering, outdoor adventure, rafting, rock climbing, survival training, white-water trips, wilderness camping.
Trips Overnight.
Program Information 4 sessions per year. Session length: 11–28 days in June, July, August. Ages: 9–16. 30–50 participants per session. Cost: $1250–$1450. Financial aid available.
Application Deadline Continuous.
Jobs Positions for college students 18 and older.
Contact Ronald Furst, Director, 10 Scotland Bridge Road, York, Maine 03909. Phone: 207-363-1773. E-mail: camphaw@maine.rr.com.
URL www.camphawthorne.org

OMNI Camp

OMNI Camp
200 Verrill Road
Poland Spring, Maine 04274

General Information Coed residential traditional camp established in 1989. Accredited by American Camping Association.
Program Focus Elective program with choices ranging from arts and theater to outdoor challenge, trips, sports, and waterfront activities.
Academics English as a second language, computers, journalism, peace education.
Arts Acting, animation, arts and crafts (general), band, batiking, ceramics, creative writing, dance, dance (ballet), dance (jazz), dance (modern), dance (tap), drawing, fabric arts, graphic arts, jewelry making, metalworking, music (instrumental), musical productions, painting, photography, pottery, printmaking, sculpture, television/video, theater/drama, weaving, woodworking.

OMNI Camp

Special Interest Areas Animal care, campcraft, community service, conservation projects, culinary arts, field trips (arts and culture), flight instruction, leadership training, nature study, team building.
Sports Aerobics, archery, baseball, basketball, bicycling, boating, canoeing, climbing (wall), field hockey, fishing, golf, gymnastics, horseback riding, kayaking, lacrosse, martial arts, rappelling, ropes course, sailing, soccer, softball, sports (general), swimming, tennis, volleyball, waterskiing, windsurfing.
Wilderness/Outdoors Backpacking, canoe trips, hiking, mountain biking, orienteering, outdoor adventure, rafting, rock climbing, white-water trips, wilderness camping.
Trips Cultural, day, overnight.
Program Information 1–9 sessions per year. Session length: 2–8 weeks in June, July, August. Ages: 9–17. 180–200 participants per session. Boarding program cost: $1850–$6000. Financial aid available.
Application Deadline Continuous.
Jobs Positions for college students 19 and older.
Summer Contact Betsy Roper, Co-Director, main address above. Phone: 207-998-4777. Fax: 207-998-4722. E-mail: info@omnicamp.com.

Winter Contact Mackey Leitch, Program Director / Registrar, P O Box 37, Federalsburg, Maryland 21632. Phone: 888-417-6664. Fax: 410-754-7337. E-mail: enrollment@omnicamp.com.
URL www.omnicamp.com
For more information, see page 1236.

Pine Island Camp

Pine Island Camp
Belgrade Lakes, Maine 04918

General Information Boys' residential traditional camp and outdoor program established in 1902.
Arts Woodworking.
Special Interest Areas Campcraft.
Sports Archery, boating, canoeing, fishing, kayaking, riflery, rowing (crew/sculling), sailing, swimming, tennis.
Wilderness/Outdoors Backpacking, canoe trips, hiking, wilderness camping.
Trips Overnight.
Program Information 1 session per year. Session length: 6 weeks in June, July, August. Ages: 9–15. 85 participants per session. Boarding program cost: $6000. Financial aid available.
Jobs Positions for college students 18 and older.
Contact Benjamin P. Swan, Director, PO Box 242, Brunswick, Maine 04011. Phone: 207-729-7714. Fax: 207-725-1241. E-mail: benswan@pineisland.org.
URL pineisland.org

Special Note
Founded in 1902, Pine Island remains true to the mission described in the 1904 catalog: "To give boys a healthful and beneficial summer outing, to clarify their minds and reinvigorate their bodies, to give them new life and new strength—in a word, to afford them an opportunity for re-creation, not merely recreation." Boys live without electricity in platform tents, each of which houses 4 boys and a counselor. An absence of competitive sports and the island setting make Pine Island unique. Ten in-camp activities are offered daily, including canoeing, sailing, rowing, kayaking, swimming, workshop, archery, riflery, and tennis. More than 40 camping trips leave the island each summer, including hiking, canoeing, and kayaking trips and excursions to the camp's 90-acre saltwater island. In addition, there is a campfire every night by the lake.

Sailing Program at NE Camping Adventures

Camp Hawthorne, Inc.
Panther Pond
Raymond, Maine 04071

General Information Coed residential traditional camp and outdoor program established in 1986. Formal opportunities for the gifted. Specific services available for the learning disabled.
Program Focus Ocean and lake sailing, ocean kayaking, rafting, and rock climbing.
Academics Meteorology, music, writing.
Arts Arts and crafts (general), batiking, ceramics, chorus, creative writing, dance, drawing, film, jewelry making, music (ensemble), music (jazz), painting, photography, pottery, theater/drama.
Special Interest Areas Native American culture.
Sports Archery, baseball, basketball, boating, canoeing, fishing, kayaking, martial arts, rappelling, riflery, sailing, sea kayaking, snorkeling, soccer, softball, swimming, volleyball, waterskiing, windsurfing.
Wilderness/Outdoors Backpacking, canoe trips, hiking, orienteering, rafting, rock climbing, survival training, white-water trips, wilderness camping.
Trips Overnight.
Program Information 2 sessions per year. Session length: 14–20 days in June, July, August. Ages: 10–17. 40 participants per session. Boarding program cost: $1295–$2295. Financial aid available.
Application Deadline Continuous.
Contact Ronald Furst, Director, 10 Scotland Bridge Road, York, Maine 03909. Phone: 207-363-1773. Fax: 207-363-1773. E-mail: camphaw@maine.rr.com.
URL www.camphawthorne.org

Snowy Owl Camp for Girls

Snowy Owl Camp for Girls
Great Moose Lake
Harmony, Maine 04942

General Information Girls' residential traditional camp established in 2003.
Program Focus Water sports.
Arts Acting, arts and crafts (general), dance, musical productions, theater/drama.
Sports Basketball, canoeing, equestrian sports, horseback riding, kayaking, sailing, swimming, tennis, volleyball, waterskiing, windsurfing.
Trips Day, overnight, shopping.
Program Information 2 sessions per year. Session length: 30 days in June, July, August. Ages: 7–17. 50–100 participants per session. Boarding program cost: $3400–$6000. Application fee: $250.
Application Deadline Continuous.
Jobs Positions for college students 18 and older.
Contact Burt Jordan, Director, 74 South Merrill Road, Harmony, Maine 04942. Phone: 866-632-4718. E-mail: info@snowyowlcamp.com.
URL www.snowyowlcamp.com

SoccerPlus Goalkeeper School–Challenge Program–Brunswick, ME

SoccerPlus Camps
Bowdoin College
Brunswick, Maine

General Information Coed residential and day sports camp.
Program Focus Developing technical and tactical goalkeeping skills.
Sports Soccer.
Program Information 1 session per year. Session length: 6 days in July, August. Ages: 10+. Day program cost: $595. Boarding program cost: $695. Financial aid available.

SoccerPlus Goalkeeper School–Challenge Program–Brunswick, ME (continued)
Application Deadline Continuous.
Jobs Positions for college students.
Contact Mr. Shawn Kelly, General Manager, 11 Executive Drive, Suite 202, Farmington, Connecticut 06032. Phone: 800-533-7371. Fax: 860-677-0460. E-mail: info@soccerpluscamps.com.
URL www.soccerpluscamps.com

SoccerPlus Goalkeeper School–National Training Center–Brunswick, ME

SoccerPlus Camps
Bowdoin College
Brunswick, Maine

General Information Coed residential sports camp.
Program Focus Developing advanced goalkeeping skills.
Sports Soccer.
Program Information 1 session per year. Session length: 6 days in July, August. Ages: 15+. Boarding program cost: $775.
Application Deadline Continuous.
Jobs Positions for college students.
Contact Mr. Shawn Kelly, General Manager, 11 Executive Drive, Suite 202, Farmington, Connecticut 06032. Phone: 800-533-7371. Fax: 860-677-0460. E-mail: info@soccerpluscamps.com.
URL www.soccerpluscamps.com

Student Conservation Association–Conservation Crew Program (Maine)

Student Conservation Association (SCA)
Maine

General Information Coed residential outdoor program, community service program, and wilderness program established in 1957. High school credit may be earned.
Program Focus Resource management, conservation and environmental education.
Academics Biology, botany, ecology, environmental science, geology/earth science, history.
Special Interest Areas Campcraft, community service, construction, leadership training, nature study, trail maintenance, work camp programs.
Sports Canoeing, fishing, kayaking, swimming.
Wilderness/Outdoors Backpacking, canoe trips, hiking, orienteering, outdoor living skills, wilderness camping.
Trips Cultural, day, overnight.
Program Information 2–3 sessions per year. Session length: 3–5 weeks in June, July, August. Ages: 15–19. 6–8 participants per session. Application fee: $20. Financial aid available. No cost for program; financial aid possible for travel expenses.
Application Deadline Continuous.
Jobs Positions for college students 21 and older.
Contact Recruitment Office, PO Box 550, Charlestown, New Hampshire 03603. Phone: 603-543-1700. Fax: 603-543-1828. E-mail: getreal@thesca.org.
URL www.theSCA.org

Summer Days at the Morris Farm

The Morris Farm Trust
156 Gardiner Road
Wiscasset, Maine 04578

General Information Coed day outdoor program established in 1996.
Program Focus Farm animals and farm-related activities.
Academics Biology, botany, ecology, environmental science, science (general).
Arts Arts and crafts (general).
Special Interest Areas Animal care, farming, gardening, nature study.
Wilderness/Outdoors Hiking.
Program Information 6 sessions per year. Session length: 5 days in July, August. Ages: 6–11. 25 participants per session. Day program cost: $160–$172. Financial aid available.
Application Deadline Continuous.
Jobs Positions for high school students 15 and older and college students.
Contact Ms. Carey Truebe, Education Coordinator, PO Box 136, Wiscasset, Maine 04578. Phone: 207-882-4080. Fax: 207-882-7390. E-mail: carey_truebe@morrisfarm.org.
URL www.morrisfarm.org

Williwaw Adventures–Maine Mountains and Coast

Williwaw Adventures
Maine

General Information Coed travel outdoor program and wilderness program established in 2002.
Program Focus Wilderness travel.
Academics Astronomy, marine studies, meteorology, oceanography.
Special Interest Areas Leadership training, nautical skills, navigation.
Sports Boating, canoeing, sailing, sea kayaking.
Wilderness/Outdoors Backpacking, canoe trips, hiking, rafting, white-water trips, wilderness camping.
Program Information 2–3 sessions per year. Session length: 14–18 days in June, July, August. Ages: 14–18. 10–12 participants per session. Cost: $2000–$2500. Financial aid available.
Application Deadline Continuous.
Jobs Positions for college students 21 and older.
Contact Mr. Mike Dawson, Director, PO Box 166, Kingston, Massachusetts 02364. Phone: 781-585-3459. Fax: 801-720-4378. E-mail: info@williwawadventures.com.
URL www.williwawadventures.com

Winona Camp for Boys

Winona Road
Moose Pond
Bridgton, Maine 04009

General Information Boys' residential traditional camp established in 1908. Accredited by American Camping Association.
Program Focus Sailing, horseback riding, and outdoor skills, plus athletics.
Academics English as a second language.
Arts Arts and crafts (general), drawing, painting, theater/drama, woodworking.
Special Interest Areas Animal care, campcraft, leadership training, nature study.
Sports Archery, baseball, basketball, boating, canoeing, climbing (wall), equestrian sports, fishing, horseback riding, kayaking, lacrosse, rappelling, riflery, sailing, soccer, softball, swimming, tennis, volleyball, windsurfing.
Wilderness/Outdoors Backpacking, canoe trips, hiking, mountain biking, mountaineering, rock climbing, white-water trips, wilderness camping.
Trips Day, overnight.
Program Information 2–3 sessions per year. Session length: 25–49 days in June, July, August. Ages: 7–16. 275 participants per session. Boarding program cost: $3600–$5750. Financial aid available.
Application Deadline Continuous.
Jobs Positions for college students 19 and older.
Contact Alan Ordway, Director, 35 Winona Road, Bridgton, Maine 04009. Phone: 207-647-3721. Fax: 207-647-2750. E-mail: information@winonacamps.com.
URL www.winonacamps.com

Wohelo-Luther Gulick Camps

South Casco, Maine 04077

General Information Girls' residential traditional camp established in 1907. Accredited by American Camping Association.
Academics Music.
Arts Arts and crafts (general), ceramics, chorus, dance, dance (ballet), dance (folk), dance (jazz), dance (modern), jewelry making, metalworking, music (vocal), painting, pottery, puppetry, theater/drama, weaving.
Special Interest Areas Campcraft, gardening, leadership training, nature study.
Sports Archery, boating, canoeing, diving, kayaking, sailing, swimming, tennis, waterskiing, windsurfing.
Wilderness/Outdoors Canoe trips, hiking.
Trips Day, overnight.
Program Information 1–2 sessions per year. Session length: 25–50 days in June, July, August. Ages: 6–16. 180–200 participants per session. Boarding program cost: $4000–$5500. Financial aid available.
Application Deadline Continuous.
Jobs Positions for high school students 17 and older and college students.
Contact Quincy Van Winkle, Director, PO Box 39, South Casco, Maine 04077. Phone: 207-655-4739. Fax: 207-655-2292. E-mail: quincy@wohelo.com.
URL www.wohelo.com

MARYLAND

Art Monk Football Camp/Sports International–Maryland

Sports International, Inc.
McDaniel College
Westminster, Maryland

General Information Coed residential and day sports camp established in 1983.
Sports Football, weight training.
Program Information 1 session per year. Session length: 5 days in July. Ages: 8–18. 300–450 participants per session. Day program cost: $509. Boarding program cost: $619.
Application Deadline Continuous.
Jobs Positions for college students 18 and older.
Contact Customer Service, 8924 McGaw Court, Columbia, Maryland 21045. Phone: 800-555-0801. Fax: 410-309-9962. E-mail: info@footballcamps.com.
URL www.footballcamps.com

The Arts! at Maryland

University of Maryland, Office of Continuing and Extended Education
2103 Reckord Armory
College Park, Maryland 20742

General Information Coed residential and day arts program established in 2004. Formal opportunities for the academically talented and artistically talented. College credit may be earned.
Academics Art (Advanced Placement), communications, humanities, music.
Arts Acting, arts, creative writing, dance, dance (jazz), dance (modern), music, performance art, theater/drama, visual arts.
Special Interest Areas Career exploration.
Trips College tours, cultural, day, shopping.
Program Information 1 session per year. Session length: 15 days in July. Ages: 15–21. 50–150 participants per session. Day program cost: $1700–$1750. Boarding program cost: $2500–$2600. Application fee: $50. Financial aid available. Open to participants entering grade 11–college sophomores.
Application Deadline Continuous.
Contact Terrie Hruzd, Program Manager, Summer and Special Programs, main address above. Phone: 301-405-8588. Fax: 301-314-9572. E-mail: hruzd@umd.edu.
URL www.summer.umd.edu/arts
For more information, see page 1364.

Camp Airy

Camp Airy and Camp Louise Foundation, Inc.
14938 Old Camp Airy Road
Thurmont, Maryland 21788

General Information Boys' residential traditional camp established in 1924. Religious affiliation: Jewish. Accredited by American Camping Association.

Camp Airy (continued)

Program Focus Athletics, outdoor living, swimming, performing arts, fine arts.
Academics Journalism.
Arts Acting, arts and crafts (general), band, ceramics, creative writing, dance, fabric arts, jewelry making, leather working, mime, music, music (chamber), music (classical), music (ensemble), music (instrumental), music (jazz), music (orchestral), music (vocal), musical productions, painting, photography, pottery, printmaking, radio broadcasting, television/video, theater/drama, woodworking.
Special Interest Areas Campcraft, leadership training, model rocketry, nature study, robotics.
Sports Archery, baseball, basketball, canoeing, climbing (wall), cross-country, fencing, fishing, football, golf, in-line skating, lacrosse, martial arts, mountain boarding, rappelling, riflery, ropes course, soccer, softball, street/roller hockey, swimming, tennis, volleyball, weight training, wrestling.
Wilderness/Outdoors Backpacking, canoe trips, caving, hiking, mountain biking, mountaineering, orienteering, rafting, rock climbing, survival training, white-water trips, wilderness camping.
Trips Cultural, day, overnight.
Program Information 6 sessions per year. Session length: 2–4 weeks in June, July, August. Ages: 7–17. 400 participants per session. Boarding program cost: $1300–$2600. Financial aid available. Financial aid available for Jewish residents of Maryland.
Application Deadline Continuous.
Jobs Positions for college students 18 and older.
Summer Contact Mike Schneider, Executive Director, main address above. Phone: 301-271-4636. Fax: 301-271-1766.
Winter Contact Mike Schneider, Executive Director, 5750 Park Heights Avenue, Baltimore, Maryland 21215. Phone: 410-466-9010. Fax: 410-466-0560. E-mail: airlou@airylouise.org.
URL www.airylouise.org

Special Note

More than 80 summers of full enrollment say Camp Airy and Camp Louise are doing something right. In addition, over two thirds of participants are returning campers. Camp Airy (for boys) and Camp Louise (for girls) are brother/sister camps for Jewish children and are located in the beautiful mountains of western Maryland, only an hour from Baltimore and Washington, D.C. With outstanding and varied programs, top-notch facilities, and a warm, caring, fun-loving staff, parents are assured their camper is in the best of hands at the best of all places. Four 2-week sessions and two 4-week sessions ensure a time frame to fit almost any summer schedule. These camps are traditional summer camps that provide many choices for campers and are liberally sprinkled with an abundance of special guests and activities. Summer's never looked better at Airy and Louise!

Camp Louise

Camp Airy and Camp Louise Foundation, Inc.
24959 Pen Mar Road
Cascade, Maryland 21719

General Information Girls' residential traditional camp established in 1922. Religious affiliation: Jewish. Accredited by American Camping Association.
Program Focus Performing arts, fine arts, athletics, and outdoor living.
Academics Journalism.
Arts Arts, arts and crafts (general), band, batiking, ceramics, chorus, creative writing, dance, dance (ballet), dance (folk), dance (jazz), dance (modern), dance (tap), drawing, fabric arts, film, jewelry making, leather working, mime, music, music (chamber), music (classical), music (ensemble), music (instrumental), music (jazz), music (orchestral), music (vocal), musical productions, painting, photography, pottery, printmaking, puppetry, radio broadcasting, sculpture, television/video, theater/drama.
Special Interest Areas Culinary arts, leadership training, nature study.
Sports Aerobics, archery, basketball, boxing, canoeing, cheerleading, climbing (wall), fencing, field hockey, football, gymnastics, horseback riding, in-line skating, lacrosse, martial arts, rappelling, ropes course, soccer, softball, sports (general), swimming, tennis, volleyball, water polo, weight training.
Wilderness/Outdoors Backpacking, canoe trips, caving, hiking, mountain biking, orienteering, rafting, rock climbing, survival training, white-water trips.
Trips Cultural, day, overnight.
Program Information 6 sessions per year. Session length: 2–4 weeks in June, July, August. Ages: 7–17. 430–440 participants per session. Boarding program cost: $1300–$2600. Financial aid available.
Application Deadline Continuous.
Jobs Positions for college students 18 and older.
Summer Contact Jessie Reter-Choate, Director, main address above. Phone: 301-241-3661. Fax: 301-241-5030. E-mail: airlou@airylouise.org.
Winter Contact Mike Schneider, Executive Director, 5750 Park Heights Avenue, Baltimore, Maryland 21215. Phone: 410-466-9010. Fax: 410-466-0560. E-mail: airlou@airylouise.org.
URL www.airylouise.org

The Community Center Going Places Camp

The Community Center
623 Baltimore-Annapolis Boulevard
Severna Park, Maryland 21146

General Information Coed day traditional camp established in 2000.
Program Focus Visiting local recreational sites.
Arts Arts and crafts (general).
Sports Sports (general), swimming.
Trips Day.
Program Information 5–6 sessions per year. Session length: 5–6 days in June, July, August. Ages: 11–14. 22–25 participants per session. Day program cost: $160. Application fee: $25. Financial aid available.

Application Deadline Continuous.
Jobs Positions for high school students and college students.
Contact Mrs. Patt Haun, Executive Director, main address above. Phone: 410-647-5843. Fax: 410-647-8122. E-mail: phaun@thecommunitycenter.com.
URL www.thecommunitycenter.com

Cybercamps–Johns Hopkins University

Cybercamps–Giant Campus, Inc.
Baltimore, Maryland

General Information Coed day academic program established in 1997.
Program Focus High tech computer camps featuring project oriented curriculum in Web design, 3D animation, game design, robotics, digital arts and programming for all ability levels.
Academics Web page design, computer programming, computers, typing.
Arts Animation, creative writing, digital media, graphic arts, photography.
Special Interest Areas Computer game design, robotics, team building.
Sports Ultimate frisbee.
Program Information 2–9 sessions per year. Session length: 5–30 days in June, July, August. Ages: 7–18. 30–150 participants per session. Day program cost: $599–$849.
Application Deadline Continuous.
Jobs Positions for high school students 15 and older and college students.
Contact Cybercamps Information Office, 2401 4th Avenue, Suite 1110, Seattle, Washington 98121. Phone: 206-442-4500. Fax: 206-442-4501. E-mail: info@cybercamps.com.
URL www.cybercamps.com

Cybercamps–University of Maryland

Cybercamps–Giant Campus, Inc.
College Park, Maryland

General Information Coed residential and day academic program established in 1997.
Program Focus High tech computer camps featuring project oriented curriculum in Web design, 3D animation, game design, robotics, digital arts and programming for all ability levels.
Academics Web page design, computer programming, computers.
Arts Arts and crafts (general), creative writing, digital media, graphic arts, photography.
Special Interest Areas Computer game design, computer graphics, robotics, team building.
Sports Frisbee golf, ultimate frisbee.
Program Information 2–9 sessions per year. Session length: 5–30 days in June, July, August. Ages: 7–18. 30–150 participants per session. Day program cost: $599–$849. Boarding program cost: $974–$1224. Financial aid available.
Application Deadline Continuous.
Jobs Positions for high school students 15 and older and college students.
Contact Cybercamps Information Office, 2401 4th Avenue, Suite 1110, Seattle, Washington 98121. Phone: 206-442-4500. Fax: 206-442-4501. E-mail: info@cybercamps.com.
URL www.cybercamps.com

Georgetown Prep School Summer English Program

Georgetown Preparatory School
10900 Rockville Pike
Rockville, Maryland 20852

General Information Coed residential and day academic program and cultural program established in 1974. Religious affiliation: Roman Catholic. Formal opportunities for the academically talented. Specific services available for the physically challenged. High school credit may be earned.
Program Focus English as a second language.
Academics English as a second language, SAT/ACT preparation, TOEFL/TOEIC preparation, computers, intercultural studies, international relations, linguistics, speech/debate, writing.
Special Interest Areas Political organizing.
Sports Baseball, basketball, fencing, golf, in-line skating, soccer, softball, swimming, tennis, track and field, volleyball, weight training.
Wilderness/Outdoors Canoe trips, rafting, white-water trips.
Trips Cultural, day, shopping.
Program Information 1 session per year. Session length: 42–45 days in June, July, August. Ages: 13–18. 48–110 participants per session. Day program cost: $2875. Boarding program cost: $5200. Application fee: $250.
Application Deadline Continuous.
Jobs Positions for college students 19 and older.
Contact Ms. Rosita Whitman, main address above. Phone: 301-214-1250. Fax: 301-214-8600. E-mail: rwhitman@gprep.org.
URL www.gprep.org/esl/index.cfm

Joe Krivak Quarterback Camp, Maryland/Sports International

Sports International, Inc.
McDaniel College
Westminster, Maryland

General Information Coed residential and day sports camp established in 1983.
Program Focus Quarterback and wide receiver.
Sports Football, weight training.
Program Information 1 session per year. Session length: 5 days in July. Ages: 8–18. 300–450 participants per session. Day program cost: $349. Boarding program cost: $419.
Application Deadline Continuous.
Jobs Positions for college students 18 and older.

Joe Krivak Quarterback Camp, Maryland/Sports International (continued)

Contact Customer Service, 8924 McGaw Court, Columbia, Maryland 21045. Phone: 800-555-0801. Fax: 410-309-9962. E-mail: info@footballcamps.com.
URL www.footballcamps.com

Johns Hopkins University Zanvyl Krieger School of Arts and Sciences Summer Programs

The Johns Hopkins University
3400 North Charles Street
Suite G1/Wyman Park Building
Baltimore, Maryland 21218

General Information Coed residential and day academic program. Formal opportunities for the academically talented. Specific services available for the hearing impaired, learning disabled, physically challenged, and visually impaired. College credit may be earned.

Johns Hopkins University Zanvyl Krieger School of Arts and Sciences Summer Programs

Academics American literature, English as a second language, English language/literature, French (Advanced Placement), French language/literature, German language/literature, Greek language/literature, Italian language/literature, Spanish (Advanced Placement), Spanish language/literature, academics (general), anthropology, art history/appreciation, astronomy, biology, biology (Advanced Placement), business, chemistry, classical languages/literatures, communications, computer programming, computer science (Advanced Placement), computers, economics, engineering, environmental science, geology/earth science, government and politics, government and politics (Advanced Placement), health sciences, history, humanities, mathematics, mathematics (Advanced Placement), music, oceanography, philosophy, physics, physiology, precollege program, psychology, religion, science (general), social science, social studies, writing.
Arts Band, creative writing, drawing, film, music (chamber), music (classical), music (instrumental), painting, photography.
Special Interest Areas Community service.
Sports Baseball, basketball, climbing (wall), racquetball, squash, swimming, tennis, volleyball.
Trips Cultural, day, shopping.
Program Information 2 sessions per year. Session length: 30–35 days in June, July, August. Ages: 15+. 250–300 participants per session. Boarding program cost: $5400. Application fee: $40. Financial aid available. Cost for day program: $515 per credit.
Contact Erin Warhurst, Admissions Assistant, main address above. Phone: 800-548-0548. Fax: 410-516-5585. E-mail: summer@jhu.edu.
URL www.jhu.edu/summer

For more information, see page 1170.

Kids on Campus

Howard Community College
10650 Hickory Ridge Road
Columbia, Maryland 21044

General Information Coed day academic program established in 1986. Formal opportunities for the academically talented.
Academics Chinese languages/literature, French language/literature, Italian language/literature, Japanese language/literature, Latin language, SAT/ACT preparation, Spanish language/literature, academics (general), archaeology, architecture, astronomy, biology, business, classical languages/literatures, communications, computer programming, computers, ecology, engineering, environmental science, geography, geology/earth science, history, journalism, mathematics, mythology, philosophy, psychology, reading, science (general), social science, social studies, speech/debate, study skills, typing, writing.
Arts Arts and crafts (general), creative writing, drawing, film, puppetry.
Special Interest Areas Native American culture, animal care, career exploration, nature study.
Program Information 4 sessions per year. Session length: 5–10 days in June, July, August. Ages: 7–17. 12–20 participants per session. Day program cost: $110–$220.
Application Deadline Continuous.
Jobs Positions for college students 18 and older.
Contact Ms. Sara Baum, Kids on Campus Administrator, 10901 Little Patuxent Parkway, Columbia, Maryland 21044. Phone: 410-772-4976. Fax: 410-772-4986.
URL www.howardcc.edu/

Lions Camp Merrick Deaf/HOH/KODA Program

Lions Club Organization
3650 Rick Hamilton Place
Nanjemoy, Maryland 20662

General Information Coed residential traditional camp and special needs program. Accredited by American Camping Association. Specific services available for the hearing impaired.

Program Focus Traditional camp program for the hearing-impaired.
Arts Arts and crafts (general).
Sports Archery, basketball, canoeing, climbing (wall), fishing, ropes course, soccer, swimming.
Wilderness/Outdoors Hiking.
Program Information 4 sessions per year. Session length: 5 days in June, July. Ages: 6–16. Boarding program cost: $375. Application fee: $25. Financial aid available.
Application Deadline Continuous.
Jobs Positions for high school students 16 and older and college students 16 and older.
Contact Robert J. Rainey, Camp Administrator, PO Box 56, 3650 Rick Hamilton Place, Nanjemoy, Maryland 20662. Phone: 301-870-5858. Fax: 301-246-9108. E-mail: campmerrick@aol.com.
URL www.lionscampmerrick.org

Lions Camp Merrick Diabetes Program

Lions Club Organization
3650 Rick Hamilton Place
Nanjemoy, Maryland 20662

General Information Coed residential traditional camp and special needs program established in 2000. Accredited by American Camping Association. Specific services available for the diabetic.
Program Focus Diabetes education.
Arts Arts and crafts (general).
Special Interest Areas Diabetic education.
Sports Archery, basketball, canoeing, climbing (wall), fishing, ropes course, soccer, softball, swimming, volleyball.
Wilderness/Outdoors Hiking.
Program Information 3–4 sessions per year. Session length: 3–5 days in July, August. Ages: 5–16. Boarding program cost: $150–$600. Financial aid available.
Application Deadline Continuous.
Jobs Positions for high school students 16 and older and college students 16 and older.
Contact Robert J. Rainey, Camp Administrator, PO Box 56, 3650 Rick Hamilton Place, Nanjemoy, Maryland 20662. Phone: 301-870-5858. Fax: 301-246-9108. E-mail: campmerrick@aol.com.
URL www.lionscampmerrick.org

The Marsh

Morning Cheer, Inc.
60 Sandy Cove Road
North East, Maryland 21901

General Information Coed day traditional camp, outdoor program, and bible camp established in 2001. Religious affiliation: Christian. Accredited by American Camping Association.
Academics Bible study.
Arts Arts and crafts (general), jewelry making, tie-dyeing.
Special Interest Areas Campcraft, gardening, nature study, nautical skills, outdoor cooking.
Sports Archery, basketball, boating, canoeing, climbing (wall), fishing, sailing, soccer, swimming, tennis, volleyball.
Wilderness/Outdoors Hiking, outdoor living skills.
Trips Day.
Program Information 9 sessions per year. Session length: 5 days in June, July, August. Ages: 6–12. 35–40 participants per session. Day program cost: $160. Financial aid available.
Application Deadline Continuous.
Jobs Positions for college students 18 and older.
Contact Ms. Jenny Welte, Director, main address above. Phone: 410-287-5433. Fax: 410-287-3196. E-mail: themarsh@sandycove.org.
URL www.sandycove.org/docs/youth.html

Montgomery College WDCE–Aspiring Filmmakers

Montgomery College Workforce Development & Continuing Education Youth Programs
Montgomery College–Rockville Campus
51 Mannakee Street
Rockville, Maryland 20850

General Information Coed day arts program established in 2003. Formal opportunities for the artistically talented.
Program Focus Putting visions and ideas on videotape while learning production techniques.
Arts Cinematography, film, film editing, film production, television/video.
Program Information 1 session per year. Session length: 15 days in July. Ages: 16+. 15–20 participants per session. Day program cost: $1500. Financial aid available. Scholarships available to students in the Montgomery County free and reduced meal program only.
Application Deadline Continuous.
Contact Ms. Sharon Wolfgang, Program Assistant, 51 Mannakee Street, Room 230CC, Rockville, Maryland 20850. Phone: 301-251-7264. Fax: 301-251-7548. E-mail: sharon.wolfgang@montgomerycollege.edu.
URL www.montgomerycollege.edu/wdce/youth.html

Montgomery College WDCE–Biotechnology and Diversity Camp

Montgomery College Workforce Development & Continuing Education Youth Programs
Montgomery College
Maryland

General Information Coed day academic program established in 2003. Formal opportunities for the academically talented.
Program Focus Enrichment and exploration through biotechnology and diversity.
Academics Biology, biotechnology, computers, genetics, intercultural studies, research skills, science (general).
Special Interest Areas Problem solving.
Program Information 4 sessions per year. Session length: 10 days in June, July, August. Ages: 12–16. 15–20 participants per session. Day program cost: $190–

Montgomery College WDCE–Biotechnology and Diversity Camp (continued)

$400. Application fee: $60. Financial aid available. Scholarships available to students in the Montgomery County free and reduced meal program only.
Application Deadline Continuous.
Contact Ms. Sharon Wolfgang, Program Assistant, 51 Mannakee Street, Room 230CC, Rockville, Maryland 20850. Phone: 301-251-7246. Fax: 301-251-7548. E-mail: sharon.wolfgang@montgomerycollege.edu.
URL www.montgomerycollege.edu/wdce/youth.html

Montgomery College WDCE–Computer Programming Camp–Co-ed

Montgomery College Workforce Development & Continuing Education Youth Programs
Montgomery College
Maryland

General Information Coed day traditional camp and academic program established in 2003.
Program Focus Visual Basic computer programming.
Academics Computer programming.
Program Information 1–2 sessions per year. Session length: 10 days in June, July. Ages: 12–16. 15–20 participants per session. Day program cost: $190–$595. Application fee: $35–$50. Financial aid available. Scholarships available to students in the Montgomery County free and reduced meal program only.
Application Deadline Continuous.
Contact Ms. Sharon Wolfgang, Program Assistant, 51 Mannakee Street, Room 230CC, Rockville, Maryland 20850. Phone: 301-251-7264. Fax: 301-251-7548. E-mail: sharon.wolfgang@montgomerycollege.edu.
URL www.montgomerycollege.edu/wdce/youth.html

Montgomery College WDCE–Computer Programming Camp for Middle School Girls

Montgomery College Workforce Development & Continuing Education Youth Programs
Montgomery College–Takoma Park Campus
Takoma Park, Maryland 20912

General Information Girls' day academic program established in 2003.
Program Focus Fundamentals of Visual Basic programming.
Academics Computer programming.
Program Information 1 session per year. Session length: 10 days in August. Ages: 12–16. 15–20 participants per session. Day program cost: $370–$595. Application fee: $50. Financial aid available. Scholarships available to students in the Montgomery County free and reduced meal program only.
Application Deadline Continuous.
Contact Ms. Sharon Wolfgang, Program Assistant, 51 Mannakee Street, Room 230CC, Rockville, Maryland 20850. Phone: 301-251-7264. Fax: 301-251-7548. E-mail: sharon.wolfgang@montgomerycollege.edu.
URL www.montgomerycollege.edu/wdce/youth.html

Montgomery College WDCE–Culinary Arts–Kids Cook

Montgomery College Workforce Development & Continuing Education Youth Programs
Montgomery College–Rockville Campus
51 Mannakee Street
Rockville, Maryland 20850

General Information Coed day arts program established in 2003.
Program Focus Culinary arts camp.
Special Interest Areas Culinary arts.
Trips Day, shopping.
Program Information 1 session per year. Session length: 5 days in July. Ages: 11–13. 15–20 participants per session. Day program cost: $140–$260. Application fee: $50. Financial aid available. Scholarships available to students in the Montgomery County free and reduced meal program only.
Application Deadline Continuous.
Contact Ms. Sharon Wolfgang, Program Assistant, 51 Mannakee Street, Room 230CC, Rockville, Maryland 20850. Phone: 301-251-7264. Fax: 301-215-7548. E-mail: sharon.wolfgang@montgomerycollege.edu.
URL www.montgomerycollege.edu/wdce/youth.html

Montgomery College WDCE–Entrepreneurship Camp 2005

Montgomery College Workforce Development & Continuing Education Youth Programs
Montgomery College–Takoma Park Campus
Takoma Park, Maryland 20912

General Information Coed day academic program established in 2004. Formal opportunities for the academically talented.
Program Focus Business and entrepreneurship, researching patents, writing a business plan.
Academics Business, economics, research skills, social studies.
Special Interest Areas Planning skills.
Program Information 3 sessions per year. Session length: 9–10 days in June, July, August. Ages: 11–14. 15–20 participants per session. Day program cost: $140–$300. Application fee: $40. Financial aid available. Scholarships available to students in the Montgomery County free and reduced meal program only.
Application Deadline Continuous.
Contact Ms. Sharon Wolfgang, Program Assistant, 51 Mannakee Street, Room 230CC, Rockville, Maryland 20850. Phone: 301-251-7264. Fax: 301-251-7548. E-mail: sharon.wolfgang@montgomerycollege.edu.
URL www.montgomerycollege.edu/wdce/youth.html

Montgomery College WDCE–FIT Summer Camp

Montgomery College Workforce Development & Continuing Education Youth Programs
Montgomery College–Takoma Park Campus
7600 Takoma Avenue
Takoma Park, Maryland 20912

General Information Coed day traditional camp and sports camp established in 2002.
Program Focus Fitness and sports.
Academics Academics (general), computers, mathematics, reading, study skills, writing.
Sports Athletic training, basketball, flag football, soccer, sports (general), swimming, tennis.
Program Information 6 sessions per year. Session length: 5 days in July, August. Ages: 6–13. 10–40 participants per session. Day program cost: $140–$280. Application fee: $30. Financial aid available. Scholarships available to students in the Montgomery County free and reduced meal program only.
Application Deadline Continuous.
Contact Ms. Sharon Wolfgang, Program Assistant, 51 Mannakee Street, Room 230CC, Rockville, Maryland 20850. Phone: 301-251-7264. Fax: 301-251-7548. E-mail: sharon.wolfgang@montgomerycollege.edu.
URL www.montgomerycollege.edu/wdce/youth.html

Montgomery College WDCE–GURL Power

Montgomery College Workforce Development & Continuing Education Youth Programs
Montgomery College
Maryland

General Information Coed day arts program established in 2003.
Program Focus Graphics, design, technology, art, and field trips.
Academics Web page design, computer programming.
Arts Arts and crafts (general), graphic arts.
Special Interest Areas Career exploration, computer graphics, field research/expeditions, field trips (arts and culture).
Trips Day.
Program Information 1–2 sessions per year. Session length: 10 days in July. Ages: 11–13. 15–20 participants per session. Day program cost: $360–$595. Application fee: $50. Financial aid available. Scholarships available to students in the Montgomery County free and reduced meal program only.
Application Deadline Continuous.
Contact Ms. Sharon Wolfgang, Program Assistant, 51 Mannakee Street, Room 230CC, Rockville, Maryland 20850. Phone: 301-251-7264. Fax: 301-251-7548. E-mail: sharon.wolfgang@montgomerycollege.edu.
URL www.montgomerycollege.edu/wdce/youth.html

Montgomery College WDCE–Hands on Art

Montgomery College Workforce Development & Continuing Education Youth Programs
Montgomery College–Rockville Campus
51 Mannakee Street
Rockville, Maryland 20850

General Information Coed day arts program established in 2003. Formal opportunities for the artistically talented.
Program Focus Exploring mediums and elements of design.
Arts Arts, design, drawing, painting.
Program Information 2 sessions per year. Session length: 5 days in July, August. Ages: 8–12. 15 participants per session. Day program cost: $115–$235. Application fee: $40. Financial aid available. Scholarships available to students in the Montgomery County free and reduced meal program only.
Application Deadline Continuous.
Contact Ms. Sharon Wolfgang, Program Assistant, 51 Mannakee Street, Room 230CC, Rockville, Maryland 20850. Phone: 301-251-7264. Fax: 301-251-7548. E-mail: sharon.wolfgang@montgomerycollege.edu.
URL www.montgomerycollege.edu/wdce/youth.html

Montgomery College WDCE–Inventor's Workshop

Montgomery College Workforce Development & Continuing Education Youth Programs
Montgomery College–Rockville Campus
51 Mannakee Street
Rockville, Maryland 20850

General Information Coed day academic program and arts program established in 2003. Formal opportunities for the academically talented.
Program Focus Inventions.
Academics Mathematics, physics, research skills, science (general), writing.
Arts Design, drawing.
Special Interest Areas Computer-aided drafting, problem solving, team building.
Program Information 4 sessions per year. Session length: 5–10 days in June, July, August. Ages: 8–13. 15 participants per session. Day program cost: $100–$320. Application fee: $40–$45. Financial aid available. Scholarships available to students in the Montgomery County free and reduced meal program only.
Application Deadline Continuous.
Contact Ms. Sharon Wolfgang, Program Assistant, 51 Mannakee Street, Room 230CC, Rockville, Maryland 20850. Phone: 301-251-7264. Fax: 301-251-7548. E-mail: sharon.wolfgang@montgomerycollege.edu.
URL www.montgomerycollege.edu/wdce/youth.html

Montgomery College WDCE–Joy of Art

Montgomery College Workforce Development & Continuing Education Youth Programs
Montgomery College–Takoma Park Campus
Pavillion of Fine Arts, Room 104
7600 Takoma Avenue
Takoma Park, Maryland 20912

General Information Coed day arts program established in 2003. Formal opportunities for the artistically talented.
Program Focus Exploring India, insects, body art, and American artists.
Academics Art, intercultural studies.
Arts Drawing, painting, sculpture, studio arts.
Special Interest Areas Culinary arts, field trips (arts and culture), nature study.
Trips Day.
Program Information 1–4 sessions per year. Session length: 4–20 days in June, July. Ages: 5–10. 16 participants per session. Day program cost: $90–$870. Application fee: $25–$115. Financial aid available. Scholarships available to students in the Montgomery County free and reduced meal program only.
Application Deadline Continuous.
Contact Ms. Sharon Wolfgang, Program Assistant, 51 Mannakee Street, Room 230CC, Rockville, Maryland 20850. Phone: 301-251-7264. Fax: 301-251-7548. E-mail: sharon.wolfgang@montgomerycollege.edu.
URL www.montgomerycollege.edu/wdce/youth.html

Montgomery College WDCE–Language in Motion

Montgomery College Workforce Development & Continuing Education Youth Programs
Montgomery College–Rockville Campus
51 Mannakee Street
Rockville, Maryland 20850

General Information Coed day academic program established in 2003.
Program Focus Spanish language.
Academics Spanish (Advanced Placement), Spanish language/literature.
Program Information 4 sessions per year. Session length: 5 days in July, August. Ages: 5–10. 15 participants per session. Day program cost: $265–$425. Application fee: $35. Financial aid available. Scholarships available to students in the Montgomery County free and reduced meal program only.
Application Deadline Continuous.
Contact Ms. Sharon Wolfgang, Program Assistant, 51 Mannakee Street, Room 230CC, Rockville, Maryland 20850. Phone: 301-251-7264. Fax: 301-251-1548. E-mail: sharon.wolfgang@montgomerycollege.edu.
URL www.montgomerycollege.edu/wdce/youth.html

Montgomery College WDCE–Leadership Skills Camp

Montgomery College Workforce Development & Continuing Education Youth Programs
Montgomery College–Rockville Campus
51 Mannakee Street
Rockville, Maryland 20850

General Information Coed day academic program established in 2003.
Program Focus Leadership skills activities and techniques.
Special Interest Areas Communication skills, leadership training, planning skills, team building.
Program Information 1 session per year. Session length: 10 days in July. Ages: 11–14. 15–20 participants per session. Day program cost: $250–$390. Application fee: $40. Financial aid available. Scholarships available to students in the Montgomery County free and reduced meal program only.
Application Deadline Continuous.
Contact Ms. Sharon Wolfgang, Program Assistant, 51 Mannakee Street, Room 230CC, Rockville, Maryland 20850. Phone: 301-251-7264. Fax: 301-251-7548. E-mail: sharon.wolfgang@montgomerycollege.edu.
URL www.montgomerycollege.edu/wdce/youth.html

Montgomery College WDCE–Mathematics Enrichment Program

Montgomery College Workforce Development & Continuing Education Youth Programs
Montgomery College–Rockville Campus
51 Mannakee Street
Rockville, Maryland 20850

General Information Coed day academic program established in 2003. Formal opportunities for the academically talented.
Program Focus Pre-algebra through calculus.
Academics SAT/ACT preparation, academics (general), mathematics.
Program Information 2–4 sessions per year. Session length: 5 days in July, August. Ages: 9–17. 15 participants per session. Day program cost: $115–$810. Application fee: $35. Financial aid available. Scholarships available to students in the Montgomery County free and reduced meal program only.
Application Deadline Continuous.
Contact Ms. Sharon Wolfgang, Program Assistant, 51 Mannakee Street, Room 230CC, Rockville, Maryland 20850. Phone: 301-251-7264. Fax: 301-251-7548. E-mail: sharon.wolfgang@montgomerycollege.edu.
URL www.montgomerycollege.edu/wdce/youth.html

Montgomery College WDCE–Science Adventures

Montgomery College Workforce Development & Continuing Education Youth Programs
Montgomery College
Maryland

General Information Coed day academic program established in 2004. Formal opportunities for the academically talented.
Program Focus Flight; robotics; space and rocketry; forensics, and archeology.
Academics Academics (general), aerospace science, archaeology, engineering, mathematics, physics, science (general), technology.
Special Interest Areas Construction, model rocketry, problem solving, robotics, team building.
Program Information 11 sessions per year. Session length: 5 days in June, July, August. Ages: 5–12. 15–40 participants per session. Day program cost: $120–$390. Application fee: $40. Financial aid available. Scholarships available to students in the Montgomery County free and reduced meal program only.
Application Deadline Continuous.
Contact Ms. Sharon Wolfgang, Program Assistant, 51 Mannakee Street, Room 230CC, Rockville, Maryland 20850. Phone: 301-251-7264. Fax: 301-251-7548. E-mail: sharon.wolfgang@montgomerycollege.edu.
URL www.montgomerycollege.edu/wdce/youth.html

Montgomery College WDCE–Summer Dinner Theatre

Montgomery College Workforce Development & Continuing Education Youth Programs
Montgomery College–Rockville Campus
51 Mannakee Street
Rockville, Maryland 20850

General Information Coed day arts program established in 2003.
Program Focus Musical dinner theatre.
Arts Acting, dance, music, musical productions, musical theater, theater/drama.
Program Information 1 session per year. Session length: 72 days in May, June, July. Ages: 16+. 15–30 participants per session. Day program cost: $294–$454. Application fee: $40. Financial aid available. Scholarships available to students in the Montgomery County free and reduced meal program only.
Application Deadline Continuous.
Contact Ms. Sharon Wolfgang, Program Assistant, 51 Mannakee Street, Room 230CC, Rockville, Maryland 20850. Phone: 301-251-7264. Fax: 301-251-7548. E-mail: sharon.wolfgang@montgomerycollege.edu.
URL www.montgomerycollege.edu/wdce/youth.html

Montgomery College WDCE–Summer Science Camp for Girls

Montgomery College Workforce Development & Continuing Education Youth Programs
Montgomery College–Takoma Park Campus
Takoma Park, Maryland 20912

General Information Coed day academic program established in 2004.
Program Focus Hands-on science experiments and discoveries with female science mentors.
Academics Academics (general), biology, health sciences, research skills, science (general).
Special Interest Areas Career exploration, leadership training, problem solving.
Trips College tours.
Program Information 1 session per year. Session length: 9 days in June, July. Ages: 11–14. 15 participants per session. Day program cost: $200–$380. Application fee: $40. Financial aid available. Scholarships available to students in the Montgomery County free and reduced meal program only.
Application Deadline Continuous.
Contact Ms. Sharon Wolfgang, Program Assistant, 51 Mannakee Street, Room 230CC, Rockville, Maryland 20850. Phone: 301-251-7264. Fax: 301-251-7548. E-mail: sharon.wolfgang@montgomerycollege.edu.
URL www.montgomerycollege.edu/wdce/youth.html

Montgomery College WDCE–Summer Student Writing Institute

Montgomery College Workforce Development & Continuing Education Youth Programs
Montgomery College–Rockville Campus
51 Mannakee Street
Rockville, Maryland 20850

General Information Coed day academic program and arts program established in 1982. Formal opportunities for the academically talented.
Program Focus Writing.
Academics Academics (general), writing.
Arts Creative writing.
Program Information 1 session per year. Session length: 15 days in July. Ages: 8–14. 50–75 participants per session. Day program cost: $320–$480. Application fee: $35. Financial aid available. Scholarships available to students in the Montgomery County free and reduced meal program only.
Application Deadline Continuous.
Contact Ms. Sharon Wolfgang, Program Assistant, 51 Mannakee Street, Room 230CC, Rockville, Maryland 20850. Phone: 301-251-7264. Fax: 301-251-7548. E-mail: sharon.wolfgang@montgomerycollege.edu.
URL www.montgomerycollege.edu/wdce/youth.html

Montgomery College WDCE–Summer Youth Programs

Montgomery College Workforce Development & Continuing Education Youth Programs
Montgomery College
Maryland

General Information Coed day traditional camp, academic program, and arts program established in 1982. Formal opportunities for the academically talented and artistically talented.
Program Focus Enrichment activities, exploration, and discovery.
Academics American literature, Arabic, English language/literature, French language/literature, German language/literature, SAT/ACT preparation, Spanish language/literature, Web page design, aerospace science, anthropology, archaeology, architecture, area studies, art history/appreciation, astronomy, aviation, banking/finance, biology, business, cartography, chemistry, communications, computer programming, computers, economics, engineering, environmental science, food science, geography, geology/earth science, health sciences, history, humanities, intercultural studies, journalism, language study, mathematics, physics, physiology, precollege program, reading, research skills, science (general), social studies, strategy games, study skills, typing, word processing, writing.
Arts Acting, animation, arts and crafts (general), bookbinding, cartooning, cinematography, costume design, creative writing, dance, desktop publishing, drawing, film, film production, graphic arts, illustration, music, painting, printing, printmaking, radio broadcasting, sculpture, storytelling, studio arts, television/video, theater/drama.
Special Interest Areas Career exploration, communication skills, computer graphics, computer-aided drafting, conservation projects, culinary arts, field research/expeditions, field trips (arts and culture), first aid, gardening, health education, leadership training, model rocketry, nature study, nutrition, problem solving, robotics, team building, time management, weight reduction.
Sports Noncompetitive sports, physical fitness.
Trips Day.
Program Information 1 session per year. Session length: 40 days in June, July, August. Ages: 5–18. 15–20 participants per session. Day program cost: $80–$420. Financial aid available. Scholarships available to students in the Montgomery County free and reduced meal program only.
Application Deadline Continuous.
Contact Ms. Sharon Wolfgang, Program Assistant, 51 Mannakee Street, Room 230CC, Rockville, Maryland 20850. Phone: 301-251-7264. Fax: 301-251-7548. E-mail: sharon.wolfgang@montgomerycollege.edu.
URL www.montgomerycollege.edu/wdce/youth.html

Montgomery College WDCE–Super Sleuths–Meet the Challenge

Montgomery College Workforce Development & Continuing Education Youth Programs
Montgomery College–Rockville Campus
51 Mannakee Street
Rockville, Maryland 20850

General Information Coed day arts program established in 2003. Formal opportunities for the academically talented.
Program Focus Riddles and mysteries, literature, wits and creative thinking adventure.
Academics English language/literature, reading.
Arts Creative writing.
Special Interest Areas Problem solving.
Program Information 1 session per year. Session length: 5 days in July. Ages: 8–11. 15–20 participants per session. Day program cost: $165–$305. Application fee: $40. Financial aid available. Scholarships available to students in the Montgomery County free and reduced meal program only.
Application Deadline Continuous.
Contact Ms. Sharon Wolfgang, Program Assistant, 51 Mannakee Street, Room 230CC, Rockville, Maryland 20850. Phone: 301-251-7264. Fax: 301-251-7548. E-mail: sharon.wolfgang@montgomerycollege.edu.
URL www.montgomerycollege.edu/wdce/youth.html

Montgomery College WDCE–Web Design Camp for Girls and Boys

Montgomery College Workforce Development & Continuing Education Youth Programs
Montgomery College–Rockville Campus
51 Mannakee Street
Rockville, Maryland 20850

General Information Coed day arts program established in 2003.
Program Focus Graphics and website design.
Academics Web page design, computers.
Special Interest Areas Computer graphics.
Program Information 1 session per year. Session length: 10 days in August. Ages: 11–13. 15–20 participants per session. Day program cost: $190–$330. Application fee: $35. Financial aid available. Scholarships available to students in the Montgomery County free and reduced meal program only.
Application Deadline Continuous.
Contact Ms. Sharon Wolfgang, Program Assistant, 51 Mannakee Street, Room 230CC, Rockville, Maryland 20850. Phone: 301-251-7264. Fax: 301-251-7548. E-mail: sharon.wolfgang@montgomerycollege.edu.
URL www.montgomerycollege.edu/wdce/youth.html

Montgomery College WDCE–World Events 2005

Montgomery College Workforce Development & Continuing Education Youth Programs
Montgomery College–Takoma Park Campus
Takoma Park, Maryland 20912

General Information Coed day academic program established in 2004. Formal opportunities for the academically talented.
Program Focus World events.
Academics Academics (general), area studies, business, communications, current events, economics, government and politics, intercultural studies, philosophy, reading, social studies, sociology.
Program Information 3 sessions per year. Session length: 10 days in June, July, August. Ages: 11–14. 15–20 participants per session. Day program cost: $140–$295. Application fee: $35. Financial aid available. Scholarships available to students in the Montgomery County free and reduced meal program only.
Application Deadline Continuous.
Contact Ms. Sharon Wolfgang, Program Assistant, 51 Mannakee Street, Room 230CC, Rockville, Maryland 20850. Phone: 301-251-7264. Fax: 301-251-7548. E-mail: sharon.wolfgang@montgomerycollege.edu.
URL www.montgomerycollege.edu/wdce/youth.html

Montgomery College WDCE–Young Scientist Academy

Montgomery College Workforce Development & Continuing Education Youth Programs
Montgomery College–Takoma Park Campus
Takoma Park, Maryland 20912

General Information Coed day academic program established in 2003. Formal opportunities for the academically talented.
Program Focus Hands-on scientific investigations, experiments, and research.
Academics Academics (general), biology, computers, health sciences, mathematics, research skills, science (general), study skills.
Special Interest Areas Problem solving, team building.
Trips College tours.
Program Information 3 sessions per year. Session length: 9–10 days in June, July. Ages: 6–14. 15–20 participants per session. Day program cost: $330–$575. Application fee: $50–$100. Financial aid available. Scholarships available to students in the Montgomery County free and reduced meal program only.
Application Deadline Continuous.
Contact Ms. Sharon Wolfgang, Program Assistant, 51 Mannakee Street, Room 230CC, Rockville, Maryland 20850. Phone: 301-251-7264. Fax: 301-251-7548. E-mail: sharon.wolfgang@montgomerycollege.edu.
URL www.montgomerycollege.edu/wdce/youth.html

National Debate Institute–DC

Education Unlimited
University of Maryland, College Park
College Park, Maryland

General Information Coed residential and day academic program established in 1995.
Program Focus Competitive debate and research in the Washington D.C. metro area.
Academics Ecology, economics, government and politics, intercultural studies, peace education, philosophy, social science, social studies, speech/debate, writing.
Trips Cultural.
Program Information 2 sessions per year. Session length: 14–18 days in June, July. Ages: 14–18. 10–60 participants per session. Day program cost: $875–$1250. Boarding program cost: $1685–$2305. Financial aid available.
Application Deadline Continuous.
Contact Mr. Robert Thomas, Associate Director, 1700 Shattuck Avenue, #305, Berkeley, California 94709. Phone: 510-548-4800. Fax: 510-548-0212. E-mail: debate@educationunlimited.com.
URL www.educationunlimited.com

For more information, see page 1100.

The National Music Workshop Day Jams–Baltimore, MD

National Guitar Workshop
Maryvale Preparatory School
11300 Falls Road
Brooklandville, Maryland 21022

General Information Coed day arts program established in 1999. Formal opportunities for the artistically talented.
Program Focus Rock 'n' roll day camp.
Academics Music.
Arts Arts and crafts (general), band, guitar, music, music (rock), music (vocal), television/video.
Program Information 4 sessions per year. Session length: 5–20 days in June, July. Ages: 9–15. 40–70 participants per session. Day program cost: $425–$495. Application fee: $35. Financial aid available.
Application Deadline Continuous.
Jobs Positions for high school students 17 and older and college students 17 and older.
Contact Lynda Wlodarczyk, Associate Director, 407A Bantam Road, Suite 1, Litchfield, Connecticut 06759. Phone: 800-295-5956. Fax: 860-567-0374. E-mail: lynda@dayjams.com.
URL www.dayjams.com

The National Music Workshop Day Jams–Rockville, MD

National Guitar Workshop
St. Elizabeth School
917 Montrose Road
Rockville, Maryland 20852

General Information Coed day arts program established in 1999. Formal opportunities for the artistically talented.
Program Focus Rock 'n' roll day camp.
Academics Music.
Arts Arts and crafts (general), band, guitar, music, music (rock), music (vocal), television/video.
Program Information 4 sessions per year. Session length: 5–20 days in June, July. Ages: 9–15. 40–70 participants per session. Day program cost: $425–$495. Application fee: $35. Financial aid available.
Application Deadline Continuous.
Jobs Positions for high school students 17 and older and college students 17 and older.
Contact Lynda Wlodarczyk, Associate Director, 407A Bantam Road, Suite 1, Litchfield, Connecticut 06759. Phone: 800-295-5956. Fax: 860-567-0374. E-mail: lynda@dayjams.com.
URL www.dayjams.com

National Student Leadership Conference: Medicine and Health Care

National Student Leadership Conference
University of Maryland, College Park
College Park, Maryland

General Information Coed residential academic program established in 1989. Formal opportunities for the academically talented and gifted. College credit may be earned.
Program Focus Leadership training, medicine and health care.
Academics Communications, health sciences, physiology, premed, psychology, social science.
Special Interest Areas Career exploration, leadership training.
Sports Ropes course.
Trips Cultural.
Program Information 4–8 sessions per year. Session length: 11 days in June, July, August. Ages: 14–18. 150–250 participants per session. Boarding program cost: $1995. Financial aid available.
Application Deadline Continuous.
Jobs Positions for college students 18 and older.
Contact Mr. Mike Sims, Executive Director, 111 West Jackson Boulevard, 7th Floor, Chicago, Illinois 60604. Phone: 312-322-9999. Fax: 312-765-0081. E-mail: information@nslcleaders.org.
URL www.nslcleaders.org

For more information, see page 1216.

St. Andrew's Summer Programs

St. Andrew's Episcopal School
8804 Postoak Road
Potomac, Maryland 20854

General Information Coed day traditional camp and academic program established in 1998. High school credit may be earned.
Program Focus Specialty day programs that can be mixed and matched.
Academics English language/literature, SAT/ACT preparation, Spanish language/literature, academics (general), computers, history, mathematics, reading, science (general), study skills, writing.
Arts Acting, animation, arts and crafts (general), band, ceramics, dance, drawing, film, music (instrumental), music (jazz), musical productions, painting, photography, pottery, television/video, theater/drama.
Special Interest Areas Community service, driver's education, leadership training, model rocketry, robotics.
Sports Basketball, lacrosse, soccer, softball, tennis, weight training.
Trips Cultural, day.
Program Information Session length: 5–15 days in June, July. Ages: 9–18. 10–20 participants per session. Day program cost: $100–$400. Financial aid available.
Application Deadline Continuous.
Jobs Positions for high school students 16 and older and college students 18 and older.
Contact Ms. Amanda Macomber, Director of Summer Programs, main address above. Phone: 301-983-5200. Fax: 301-983-4710. E-mail: summerprograms@saes.org.
URL www.saes.org

Sidwell Friends Bethesda Day Camp

Sidwell Friends School
5100 Edgemoor Lane
Bethesda, Maryland 20814

General Information Coed day traditional camp established in 1949. Religious affiliation: Society of Friends.
Academics Spanish language/literature, computers, science (general).
Arts Arts and crafts (general), music.
Sports Basketball, soccer, sports (general), swimming.
Program Information 2 sessions per year. Session length: 3 weeks in June, July, August. Ages: 3–10. 200–250 participants per session. Day program cost: $500–$1500.
Application Deadline Continuous.
Jobs Positions for high school students 18 and older and college students 18 and older.
Contact Summer Programs Office, 3825 Wisconsin Avenue, NW, Washington, District of Columbia 20016. Phone: 202-537-8133. Fax: 202-537-2483. E-mail: sidwellsummer@yahoo.com.
URL www.sidwell.edu/summer

Sidwell Friends Camp Corsica

Sidwell Friends School
Centreville, Maryland 21617

General Information Coed residential traditional camp established in 1993. Religious affiliation: Society of Friends.
Arts Arts and crafts (general).
Sports Boating, canoeing, equestrian sports, fishing, ropes course, sailing, soccer, sports (general), street/roller hockey, swimming, waterskiing, windsurfing.
Program Information 1–4 sessions per year. Session length: 6 days in June, July. Ages: 8–14. 30–50 participants per session. Boarding program cost: $625–$725.
Application Deadline Continuous.
Jobs Positions for college students 18 and older.
Contact Summer Programs Office, 3825 Wisconsin Avenue, NW, Washington, District of Columbia 20016. Phone: 202-537-8133. Fax: 202-537-2483. E-mail: sidwellsummer@yahoo.com.
URL www.sidwell.edu/summer

Sidwell Friends Overnight Sea Kayaking Trip

Sidwell Friends School
Chesapeake Bay
Maryland

General Information Coed residential outdoor program and adventure program. Religious affiliation: Society of Friends.
Program Focus Kayaking on tidal waters, camping, exploring, beachcombing, and swimming.
Arts Creative writing.
Special Interest Areas Campcraft, nature study.
Sports Sea kayaking, sports (general), swimming.
Program Information 2 sessions per year. Session length: 5 days in July. Ages: 11–17. Boarding program cost: $625. Financial aid available.
Application Deadline Continuous.
Jobs Positions for high school students and college students.
Contact Summer Programs Office, main address above. Phone: 202-537-8133. Fax: 202-537-2483. E-mail: sidwellsummer@yahoo.com.
URL www.sidwell.edu/summer

Student Conservation Association–Conservation Crew Program (Maryland)

Student Conservation Association (SCA)
Maryland

General Information Coed residential outdoor program, community service program, and wilderness program established in 1957. High school credit may be earned.
Program Focus Resource management, conservation and environmental education.
Academics Biology, botany, ecology, environmental science, geology/earth science, history.
Special Interest Areas Campcraft, community service, construction, leadership training, nature study, trail maintenance, work camp programs.
Sports Canoeing, fishing, kayaking, swimming.
Wilderness/Outdoors Backpacking, canoe trips, hiking, orienteering, outdoor living skills, wilderness camping.
Trips Cultural, day, overnight.
Program Information 2–3 sessions per year. Session length: 3–5 weeks in June, July, August. Ages: 15–19. 6–8 participants per session. Application fee: $20. Financial aid available. No cost for program; financial aid possible for travel expenses.
Application Deadline Continuous.
Jobs Positions for college students 21 and older.
Contact Recruitment Office, PO Box 550, Charlestown, New Hampshire 03603. Phone: 603-543-1700. Fax: 603-543-1828. E-mail: getreal@thesca.org.
URL www.theSCA.org

Summer Family Conference

Morning Cheer, Inc.
60 Sandy Cove Road
North East, Maryland 21901

General Information Coed residential and day family program and bible camp established in 1946. Religious affiliation: Christian.
Program Focus Christian family conference center.
Academics Bible study.
Arts Arts and crafts (general).
Sports Archery, baseball, basketball, bicycling, boating, canoeing, climbing (wall), diving, horseback riding, ropes course, sailing, soccer, softball, swimming, tennis, volleyball, water polo, weight training.
Trips Cultural, day, shopping.
Program Information 5 sessions per year. Session length: 6 days in June, July, August. Ages: 1+. 100–750 participants per session. Boarding program cost: $400–$1200.
Application Deadline Continuous.
Jobs Positions for college students 18 and older.
Contact Ms. Jean Rae, Human Resources Manager, main address above. Phone: 410-287-5433 Ext.407. Fax: 410-287-3196. E-mail: j.rea@sandycove.org.
URL www.sandycove.org

Traveling Players Ensemble Camp

Traveling Players Ensemble, Inc.
Calleva Campus
Darnestown, Maryland 20874

General Information Coed day outdoor program and arts program established in 2003. Formal opportunities for the artistically talented. High school credit may be earned.
Program Focus Theatre training, backpack off the Appalachian Trail and perform on Skyline Drive.
Arts Acting, costume design, set design, stage combat, stage managing, theater/drama, voice and speech.
Special Interest Areas Campcraft, community service, culinary arts, team building.
Sports Ropes course, swimming.

Traveling Players Ensemble Camp (continued)
Wilderness/Outdoors Backpacking, hiking, wilderness camping.
Trips Cultural, overnight.
Program Information 2 sessions per year. Session length: 4–7 weeks in June, July, August. Ages: 11–18. 12–36 participants per session. Day program cost: $1520–$3200. Financial aid available.
Application Deadline Continuous.
Jobs Positions for college students 18 and older.
Contact Ms. Jeanne Harrison, Artistic Director, 922 Constellation Drive, Great Falls, Virginia 22066. Phone: 301-573-2521. E-mail: info@travelingplayers.org.
URL www.travelingplayers.org

United Soccer Academy–Goal Keeping Training Camp, Maryland

United Soccer Academy, Inc.
Maryland

General Information Coed residential and day sports camp established in 1999.
Program Focus All aspects of the keeper position are covered: from techniques to tactical decision-making. Coaches are from international teams and colleges.
Sports Soccer.
Program Information 6 sessions per year. Session length: 5 days in April, June, July, August, September, November. Ages: 8–14. 16–200 participants per session. Day program cost: $145. Boarding program cost: $495. Call for specific locations.
Application Deadline Continuous.
Jobs Positions for college students 18 and older.
Contact Camps Information, 50 Tannery Road, Unit 8, Branchburg, New Jersey 08876. Phone: 908-823-0130. Fax: 908-823-0466. E-mail: info@unitedsocceracademy.com.
URL www.unitedsocceracademy.com

United Soccer Academy–Junior Soccer Squirts, Maryland

United Soccer Academy, Inc.
Maryland

General Information Coed day sports camp established in 1999.
Program Focus Introduction to soccer in a camp format with emphasis on fun games and activities in small groups. Coaches are from international soccer teams and college teams.
Sports Soccer.
Program Information 20 sessions per year. Session length: 5 days in April, June, July, August, September, November. Ages: 3–5. 6–48 participants per session. Day program cost: $89. Two sessions daily; parents may stay with camper. Call for specific locations.
Application Deadline Continuous.
Jobs Positions for college students 18 and older.
Contact Camps Information, 50 Tannery Road, Unit 8, Branchburg, New Jersey 08876. Phone: 908-823-0130. Fax: 908-823-0466. E-mail: info@unitedsocceracademy.com.
URL www.unitedsocceracademy.com

United Soccer Academy–Recreation Soccer Community Camp, Maryland

United Soccer Academy, Inc.
Maryland

General Information Coed residential and day sports camp established in 1999.
Program Focus Players build on the fundamentals of the game, experiencing a broad range of techniques and skills. Coaches are from international teams and colleges.
Sports Soccer.
Program Information 10 sessions per year. Session length: 5 days in April, June, July, August, September, November. Ages: 7–14. 16–200 participants per session. Day program cost: $145. Boarding program cost: $495. Call for specific locations.
Application Deadline Continuous.
Jobs Positions for college students 18 and older.
Contact Camps Information, 50 Tannery Road, Unit 8, Branchburg, New Jersey 08876. Phone: 908-823-0130. Fax: 908-823-0466. E-mail: info@unitedsocceracademy.com.
URL www.unitedsocceracademy.com

United Soccer Academy–Senior Soccer Squirts, Maryland

United Soccer Academy, Inc.
Maryland

General Information Coed day sports camp established in 1999.
Program Focus Introduction to the game in relaxed, fun atmosphere; skills development without competitive environment. Coaches are from international teams and colleges.
Sports Soccer.
Program Information 10 sessions per year. Session length: 5 days in April, June, July, August, September, November. Ages: 5–7. 6–48 participants per session. Day program cost: $89.
Application Deadline Continuous.
Jobs Positions for college students 18 and older.
Contact Camps Information, 50 Tannery Road, Unit 8, Branchburg, New Jersey 08876. Phone: 908-823-0130. Fax: 908-823-0466. E-mail: info@unitedsocceracademy.com.
URL www.unitedsocceracademy.com

UNITED SOCCER ACADEMY–TEAM TRAINING CAMP, MARYLAND

United Soccer Academy, Inc.
Maryland

General Information Coed residential and day sports camp established in 1999.
Program Focus Teams of ten or more players receive individualized instruction based on staff discussion with their coach. Structured coaching scrimmages with other teams. Coaches on staff are from international teams and colleges.
Sports Soccer.
Program Information 6 sessions per year. Session length: 5 days in April, June, July, August, September, November. Ages: 8–14. 20–200 participants per session. Day program cost: $125. Boarding program cost: $495. Call for specific locations.
Application Deadline Continuous.
Jobs Positions for college students 18 and older.
Contact Camps Information, 50 Tannery Road, Unit 8, Branchburg, New Jersey 08876. Phone: 908-823-0130. Fax: 908-823-0466. E-mail: info@unitedsocceracademy.com.
URL www.unitedsocceracademy.com

UNITED SOCCER ACADEMY–TRAVEL SOCCER COMMUNITY CAMP, MARYLAND

United Soccer Academy, Inc.
Maryland

General Information Coed residential and day sports camp established in 1999.
Program Focus Individual player development and team tactics are emphasized. Skills are taught at an accelerated level with practices developing into full game realistic situations. Coaches are from international teams and colleges.
Sports Soccer.
Program Information 10 sessions per year. Session length: 5 days in April, June, July, August, September, November. Ages: 8–14. 16–200 participants per session. Day program cost: $145. Boarding program cost: $495. Call for specific locations.
Application Deadline Continuous.
Jobs Positions for college students 18 and older.
Contact Camps Information, 50 Tannery Road, Unit 8, Branchburg, New Jersey 08876. Phone: 908-823-0130. Fax: 908-823-0466. E-mail: info@unitedsocceracademy.com.
URL www.unitedsocceracademy.com

UNIVERSITY OF MARYLAND YOUNG SCHOLARS PROGRAM

University of Maryland, Office of Continuing and Extended Education
2103 Reckord Armory
College Park, Maryland 20742

General Information Coed residential and day academic program established in 2002. Formal opportunities for the academically talented. College credit may be earned.
Academics English language/literature, academics (general), architecture, astronomy, biology, biology (Advanced Placement), classical languages/literatures, communications, computer programming, computer science (Advanced Placement), computers, engineering, geography, government and politics, government and politics (Advanced Placement), history, humanities, journalism, mathematics, mathematics (Advanced Placement), precollege program, science (general), social science, social studies.
Special Interest Areas Career exploration.
Trips College tours, cultural, day, shopping.
Program Information 1 session per year. Session length: 15 days in July. Ages: 14–18. 200 participants per session. Day program cost: $1550–$1650. Boarding program cost: $2500–$3000. Application fee: $50. Financial aid available. Open to participants entering grades 11–12.
Application Deadline Continuous.
Contact Ms. Terrie Hruzd, Program Manager, Summer and Special Programs, main address above. Phone: 301-405-8588. Fax: 301-314-9572. E-mail: hruzd@umd.edu.
URL www.summer.umd.edu/youngscholars

For more information, see page 1364.

WEST RIVER UNITED METHODIST CENTER

5100 Chalk Point Road
West River, Maryland 20778

General Information Coed residential traditional camp established in 1951. Religious affiliation: United Methodist. Specific services available for the hearing impaired.
Academics Bible study, sign language.
Arts Arts and crafts (general), music, music (vocal).
Special Interest Areas Nature study.
Sports Basketball, bicycling, canoeing, climbing (wall), fishing, kayaking, ropes course, sailing, soccer, swimming.
Wilderness/Outdoors Bicycle trips.
Trips Overnight.
Program Information 9 sessions per year. Session length: 6 days in June, July, August. Ages: 8–18. 12–30 participants per session. Boarding program cost: $295–$350. Financial aid available.
Application Deadline Continuous.
Jobs Positions for college students 18 and older.
Contact Andrew Thornton, Manager, PO Box 429, Churchton, Maryland 20733. Phone: 410-867-0991. Fax: 410-867-3741. E-mail: westriver.center@verizon.net.
URL www.bwconf.org/camping

MASSACHUSETTS

Academic Study Associates–ASA at the University of Massachusetts Amherst

Academic Study Associates, Inc. (ASA)
University of Massachusetts, Amherst
Amherst, Massachusetts 01002

General Information Coed residential and day academic program established in 1987. Formal opportunities for the academically talented and artistically talented. High school or college credit may be earned.
Program Focus Academic enrichment, college credit, SAT preparation, creative and performing arts, and sports instruction, including professional tennis program.
Academics American literature, English as a second language, English language/literature, French language/literature, SAT/ACT preparation, Spanish language/literature, academics (general), art (Advanced Placement), art history/appreciation, biology (Advanced Placement), business, chemistry, college tours, communications, computer programming, computers, economics, government and politics, history, humanities, journalism, mathematics, music, philosophy, physics, precollege program, psychology, social science, speech/debate, writing.
Arts Arts and crafts (general), creative writing, dance, dance (jazz), dance (modern), drawing, film, graphic arts, music, music (ensemble), music (jazz), music (vocal), musical productions, painting, photography, pottery, radio broadcasting, sculpture, television/video, theater/drama.
Special Interest Areas Community service, field trips (arts and culture).
Sports Aerobics, basketball, golf, horseback riding, soccer, softball, sports (general), swimming, tennis, volleyball, weight training.
Wilderness/Outdoors Hiking, white-water trips.
Trips College tours, cultural, day, overnight, shopping.
Program Information 2 sessions per year. Session length: 19–34 days in June, July. Ages: 14–18. 150–300 participants per session. Day program cost: $750–$2000. Boarding program cost: $3995–$5395.
Application Deadline Continuous.
Jobs Positions for college students 21 and older.
Contact Marcia Evans, President, 10 New King Street, White Plains, New York 10604. Phone: 914-686-7730. Fax: 914-686-7740. E-mail: summer@asaprograms.com.
URL www.asaprograms.com

For more information, see page 956.

Academic Study Associates–Pathways Program at Amherst College

Academic Study Associates, Inc. (ASA)
Amherst College
Amherst, Massachusetts 01002

General Information Coed residential and day academic program established in 1991. Formal opportunities for the academically talented.
Program Focus Academic enrichment and recreation; Judy Dixon tennis instruction.
Academics French language/literature, SAT/ACT preparation, Spanish language/literature, academics (general), business, computers, government and politics, history, journalism, mathematics, physics, reading, science (general), social science, speech/debate, study skills, writing.
Arts Creative writing, drawing, film, painting, television/video, theater/drama.
Special Interest Areas Community service, teen issues.
Sports Aerobics, basketball, soccer, softball, street/roller hockey, swimming, tennis, volleyball.
Trips Cultural, day, overnight.
Program Information 1 session per year. Session length: 4 weeks in June, July. Ages: 12–14. 100 participants per session. Day program cost: $850–$1250. Boarding program cost: $4695. Cost for tennis instruction: $300.
Application Deadline Continuous.
Jobs Positions for college students 21 and older.
Contact Marcia Evans, President, 10 New King Street, White Plains, New York 10604. Phone: 914-686-7730. Fax: 914-686-7740. E-mail: summer@asaprograms.com.
URL www.asaprograms.com

Adventures in Veterinary Medicine

Tufts University School of Veterinary Medicine
200 Westboro Road
North Grafton, Massachusetts 01536

General Information Coed residential and day academic program established in 1991. Formal opportunities for the academically talented.
Program Focus Veterinary medicine.
Academics Academics (general), biology, chemistry, health sciences, preveterinary, science (general), veterinary science.
Special Interest Areas Animal care, career exploration.
Trips College tours, day.
Program Information 9–10 sessions per year. Session length: 5–13 days in April, May, June, July, August. Ages: 12+. 5–40 participants per session. Day program cost: $500–$1465. Boarding program cost: $2095. Application fee: $25. Financial aid available.
Application Deadline Continuous.
Jobs Positions for college students.
Contact Kasey Kobs, Director, Office of Special Programs, Tufts University School of Veterinary Medicine, North Grafton, Massachusetts 01536. Phone: 508-839-7962. Fax: 508-839-7952. E-mail: avm@tufts.edu.
URL www.tufts.edu/vet/avm

Apogee Outdoor Adventures—Cape Cod and the Islands

Apogee Outdoor Adventures
Massachusetts

General Information Coed travel community service program and adventure program established in 2001.
Program Focus Exploring, sightseeing, cycling and whale watching in Martha's Vineyard, Nantucket, Cape Cod and Boston.
Special Interest Areas Community service, touring.
Sports Bicycling.
Wilderness/Outdoors Bicycle trips.
Trips Day.
Program Information 2–4 sessions per year. Session length: 13–15 days in June, July, August. Ages: 12–14. 5–12 participants per session. Cost: $1995–$2095. Financial aid available.
Application Deadline Continuous.
Jobs Positions for college students.
Contact Mr. Kevin Cashman, Director, 40 Bowker Street, Brunswick, Maine 04011. Phone: 207-725-7025. Fax: 509-693-8868. E-mail: info@apogeeadventures.com.
URL www.apogeeadventures.com

Appalachian Mountain Club—Teen Crews—Alpine Trail, Berkshires

Appalachian Mountain Club
Massachusetts

General Information Coed residential outdoor program and wilderness program established in 1980. High school credit may be earned.
Program Focus Stewardship of the land through trail work.
Special Interest Areas Community service, conservation projects, first aid, trail maintenance.
Wilderness/Outdoors Backpacking, hiking, rock climbing, wilderness camping.
Trips Day, overnight.
Program Information 4 sessions per year. Session length: 5 days in July, August. Ages: 15+. 4–8 participants per session. Boarding program cost: $115–$130. Application fee: $25.
Application Deadline Continuous.
Jobs Positions for college students 18 and older.
Contact Regional Trails Coordinator, 964 Main Street, Great Barrington, Massachusetts 01230. Phone: 413-528-6333. Fax: 413-644-8964.
URL www.outdoors.org/trails/

Appalachian Mountain Club—Teen Crews—Mount Greylock

Appalachian Mountain Club
Massachusetts

General Information Coed residential outdoor program established in 1980. High school credit may be earned.
Program Focus Stewardship of the land through trail work.
Special Interest Areas Community service, conservation projects, first aid, trail maintenance.
Wilderness/Outdoors Backpacking, hiking, rock climbing.
Trips Day, overnight.
Program Information 1 session per year. Session length: 5 days in August. Ages: 16+. 4–8 participants per session. Boarding program cost: $115–$130. Application fee: $25.
Application Deadline Continuous.
Jobs Positions for college students 18 and older.
Contact Regional Trails Coordinator, 964 Main Street, Great Barrington, Massachusetts 01230. Phone: 413-528-6333. Fax: 413-644-8964.
URL www.outdoors.org/trails

Appalachian Mountain Club—Trail Crew—Berkshires

Appalachian Mountain Club
Massachusetts

General Information Coed residential outdoor program and wilderness program established in 1980. High school credit may be earned.
Program Focus Stewardship of the land through trail work.
Special Interest Areas Community service, conservation projects, first aid, trail maintenance.
Wilderness/Outdoors Backpacking, hiking, rock climbing.
Trips Day, overnight.
Program Information 1–4 sessions per year. Session length: 5–7 days in July, August. Ages: 15–18. 4–8 participants per session. Boarding program cost: $55–$65. Application fee: $25.
Application Deadline Continuous.
Jobs Positions for college students 18 and older.
Contact Regional Trails Coordinator, 964 Main Street, Great Barrington, Massachusetts 01230. Phone: 413-528-6333. Fax: 413-644-8964.
URL www.outdoors.org/trails/

Appalachian Mountain Club—Trail Crew—Mount Everett/Alpine Trail

Appalachian Mountain Club
Massachusetts

General Information Coed residential outdoor program and wilderness program established in 1980. High school credit may be earned.
Program Focus Stewardship of the land through trail work.
Special Interest Areas Community service, conservation projects, first aid, trail maintenance.
Wilderness/Outdoors Backpacking, hiking, rock climbing.
Trips Day, overnight.
Program Information 1 session per year. Session length: 5–7 days in July. Ages: 16+. 4–8 participants per session. Boarding program cost: $55–$65. Application fee: $25.
Application Deadline Continuous.

Appalachian Mountain Club–Trail Crew–Mount Everett/ Alpine Trail (continued)

Jobs Positions for college students 18 and older.
Contact Regional Trails Coordinator, 964 Main Street, Great Barrington, Massachusetts 01230. Phone: 413-528-6333. Fax: 413-644-8964.
URL www.outdoors.org/trails

Appalachian Mountain Club–Volunteer Trail Crew–Mount Greylock

Appalachian Mountain Club
Massachusetts

General Information Coed residential outdoor program established in 1980. High school credit may be earned.
Program Focus Stewardship of the land through trail work.
Special Interest Areas Community service, conservation projects, first aid, trail maintenance.
Wilderness/Outdoors Backpacking, hiking, rock climbing.
Trips Day, overnight.
Program Information 1–2 sessions per year. Session length: 5 days in June, July, August. Ages: 16+. 4–8 participants per session. Boarding program cost: $55–$65. Application fee: $25.
Application Deadline Continuous.
Jobs Positions for college students 18 and older.
Contact Regional Trails Coordinator, 964 Main Street, Great Barrington, Massachusetts 01230. Phone: 413-528-6333. Fax: 413-644-8964.
URL www.outdoors.org/trails/

The Art Institute of Boston Pre-College Program

The Art Institute of Boston at Lesley University
700 Beacon Street
Boston, Massachusetts 02215-2598

General Information Coed residential and day arts program established in 1912. Formal opportunities for the artistically talented and gifted. College credit may be earned.
Program Focus Artistic development for pre-college students grades 9-12.
Academics Web page design, art (Advanced Placement), art history/appreciation, precollege program.
Arts Animation, arts, arts and crafts (general), ceramics, fashion design/production, film, graphic arts, painting, photography, pottery, printmaking, puppetry, sculpture, woodworking.
Trips College tours, cultural, day, shopping.
Program Information 3 sessions per year. Session length: 1–4 weeks in February, March, April, July, September, October, November. Ages: 15–18. 100–300 participants per session. Day program cost: $115–$140. Boarding program cost: $3250. Application fee: $10–$40. Financial aid available.
Application Deadline Continuous.
Jobs Positions for college students.
Contact Diane Arcadipone, Associate Dean Continuing and Professional Education, 700 Beacon Street, Room 201, Boston, Massachusetts 02215. Phone: 617-585-6729. Fax: 617-585-6721. E-mail: darcadip@aiboston.edu.
URL www.lesley.edu/aib/curriculum/precollege.html

Barton Day Camp–Worcester

The Barton Center for Diabetes Education, Inc.
The Barton Center
North Oxford, Massachusetts 01537

General Information Coed day traditional camp and special needs program established in 2000. Accredited by American Camping Association. Specific services available for the diabetic.
Program Focus Children with diabetes.
Arts Arts and crafts (general), dance, dance (ballet), dance (folk), dance (jazz), dance (modern), dance (tap), drawing, jewelry making, painting, sing-a-longs.
Special Interest Areas Diabetic education.
Sports Aerobics, archery, bicycling, canoeing, field hockey, fishing, gymnastics, lacrosse, soccer, softball, swimming, volleyball.
Wilderness/Outdoors Hiking, rock climbing.
Trips Day.
Program Information 4–5 sessions per year. Session length: 5 days in July. Ages: 6–12. 25–50 participants per session. Day program cost: $500. Application fee: $25. Financial aid available.
Jobs Positions for high school students 18 and older and college students 18 and older.
Contact Kerry Packard, Program Coordinator, PO Box 356, 30 Ennis Road, North Oxford, Massachusetts 01537. Phone: 508-987-3856. Fax: 508-987-2002. E-mail: kerry.packard@bartoncenter.org.
URL www.bartoncenter.org

Belvoir Terrace

80 Cliffwood Street
Lenox, Massachusetts 01240

General Information Girls' residential arts program established in 1954. Accredited by American Camping Association. Formal opportunities for the academically talented, artistically talented, and gifted. High school credit may be earned.
Program Focus Fine and performing arts.
Academics Art (Advanced Placement), music, writing.
Arts Acting, animation, arts, band, ceramics, chorus, creative writing, dance, dance (ballet), dance (jazz), dance (modern), dance (tap), drawing, fabric arts, film, jewelry making, metalworking, music, music (chamber), music (classical), music (ensemble), music (instrumental), music (orchestral), music (vocal), musical productions, painting, photography, pottery, printmaking, sculpture, television/video, theater/drama, weaving.
Sports Aerobics, basketball, bicycling, canoeing, equestrian sports, golf, gymnastics, horseback riding, swimming, tennis.
Trips Cultural.
Program Information 1 session per year. Session length: 7 weeks in June, July, August. Ages: 8–17. 180

Belvoir Terrace

participants per session. Boarding program cost: $8100–$8500. Application fee: $250. Financial aid available. Art studio classes are $50–$100 extra.
Application Deadline Continuous.
Jobs Positions for college students 21 and older.
Summer Contact Ms. Nancy S. Goldberg, Director, 80 Cliffwood Street, Lenox, Massachusetts 01240. Phone: 413-637-0555. Fax: 413-637-4651. E-mail: belvoirt@aol.com.
Winter Contact Ms. Nancy S. Goldberg, Director, 101 West 79th Street, New York, New York 10024. Phone: 212-580-3398. Fax: 212-579-7282. E-mail: info@belvoirterrace.
URL www.belvoirterrace.com

For more information, see page 992.

Berklee Business of Music Program

Berklee College of Music
1140 Boylston Street
Boston, Massachusetts 02215

General Information Coed residential and day arts program. Formal opportunities for the artistically talented.
Academics Business, music, precollege program.
Arts Music.
Trips College tours.
Program Information 1 session per year. Session length: 2 days in June. Ages: 15+. 50–60 participants per session. Day program cost: $345. Boarding program cost: $455. Application fee: $25.
Application Deadline Continuous.
Contact Office of Special Programs, 1140 Boylston Street, MS-155, Boston, Massachusetts 02215. Phone: 617-747-2245. Fax: 617-262-5419. E-mail: summer@berklee.edu.
URL www.berklee.edu/summer/musicbusiness.html

Berklee College of Music Summer Performance Program

Berklee College of Music
1140 Boylston Street
Boston, Massachusetts 02215

General Information Coed residential and day arts program. Formal opportunities for the artistically talented.
Program Focus Music performance.
Academics Music, precollege program.
Arts Band, chorus, music, music (ensemble), music (instrumental), music (jazz), music (vocal), musical performance/recitals.
Trips College tours, cultural, day.
Program Information 1 session per year. Session length: 5 weeks in July, August. Ages: 15+. 600–700 participants per session. Day program cost: $3000. Boarding program cost: $4875. Application fee: $50. Financial aid available.
Application Deadline Continuous.
Contact Office of Special Programs, 1140 Boylston Street, MS-155, Boston, Massachusetts 02215. Phone: 617-747-2245. Fax: 617-262-5419. E-mail: summer@berklee.edu.
URL www.berklee.edu/summer/5week.html

Berklee Music Production Workshop

Berklee College of Music
1140 Boylston Street
Boston, Massachusetts 02215

General Information Coed residential and day arts program. Formal opportunities for the artistically talented.
Academics Engineering, music, precollege program.
Arts Music.
Trips College tours.
Program Information 1 session per year. Session length: 3 days in July. Ages: 15+. 112 participants per session. Day program cost: $525. Boarding program cost: $720. Application fee: $25.
Application Deadline Continuous.
Contact Office of Special Programs, 1140 Boylston Street, MS-155, Boston, Massachusetts 02215. Phone: 617-747-2245. Fax: 617-262-5419. E-mail: summer@berklee.edu.
URL www.berklee.edu/summer/musicproduction.html

Berklee Summer Basslines Program

Berklee College of Music
1140 Boylston Street
Boston, Massachusetts 02215

General Information Coed residential and day arts program. Formal opportunities for the artistically talented.
Program Focus Musical performance.
Academics Music, precollege program.
Arts Music, music (ensemble), music (instrumental), music (jazz), musical performance/recitals.
Trips College tours.

Berklee Summer Basslines Program (continued)
Program Information 1 session per year. Session length: 3 days in June. Ages: 15+. 100–200 participants per session. Day program cost: $385. Boarding program cost: $580. Application fee: $25.
Application Deadline Continuous.
Contact Office of Special Programs, 1140 Boylston Street, MS-155, Boston, Massachusetts 02215. Phone: 617-747-2245. Fax: 617-262-5419. E-mail: summer@berklee.edu.
URL www.berklee.edu/summer/bass.html

Berklee Summer Brass Weekend
Berklee College of Music
1140 Boylston Street
Boston, Massachusetts 02215

General Information Coed residential and day arts program. Formal opportunities for the artistically talented.
Program Focus Music performance.
Academics Music, precollege program.
Arts Band, music, music (ensemble), music (instrumental), music (jazz), musical performance/recitals.
Trips College tours.
Program Information 1 session per year. Session length: 3 days in June. Ages: 15+. 30–40 participants per session. Day program cost: $385. Boarding program cost: $580. Application fee: $25.
Application Deadline Continuous.
Contact Office of Special Programs, 1140 Boylston Street, MS-155, Boston, Massachusetts 02215. Phone: 617-747-2245. Fax: 617-262-5419. E-mail: summer@berklee.edu.
URL www.berklee.edu/summer/brass.html

Berklee Summer Guitar Sessions
Berklee College of Music
1140 Boylston Street
Boston, Massachusetts 02215

General Information Coed residential and day arts program. Formal opportunities for the artistically talented.
Program Focus Musical performance.
Academics Music, precollege program.
Arts Band, music, music (ensemble), music (instrumental), music (jazz), musical performance/recitals.
Trips College tours.
Program Information 1 session per year. Session length: 6 days in August. Ages: 15+. 400–500 participants per session. Day program cost: $675. Boarding program cost: $975. Application fee: $25. Financial aid available.
Application Deadline Continuous.
Contact Office of Special Programs, 1140 Boylston Street, MS-155, Boston, Massachusetts 02215. Phone: 617-747-2245. Fax: 617-262-5419. E-mail: summer@berklee.edu.
URL www.berklee.edu/summer/guitar.html

Berklee Summer Saxophone Weekend
Berklee College of Music
1140 Boylston Street
Boston, Massachusetts 02215

General Information Coed residential and day arts program. Formal opportunities for the artistically talented.
Academics Music, precollege program.
Arts Band, music, music (ensemble), music (instrumental), music (jazz), musical performance/recitals.
Trips College tours.
Program Information 1 session per year. Session length: 3 days in June. Ages: 15+. 50–60 participants per session. Day program cost: $385. Boarding program cost: $580. Application fee: $25.
Application Deadline Continuous.
Contact Office of Special Programs, 1140 Boylston Street, MS-155, Boston, Massachusetts 02215. Phone: 617-747-2245. Fax: 617-262-5419. E-mail: summer@berklee.edu.
URL www.berklee.edu/summer/sax.html

Berklee Summer Songwriting Workshop
Berklee College of Music
1140 Boylston Street
Boston, Massachusetts 02215

General Information Coed residential and day arts program. Formal opportunities for the artistically talented.
Academics Music, precollege program.
Arts Music.
Trips College tours.
Program Information 1 session per year. Session length: 4 days in August. Ages: 15+. 100–200 participants per session. Day program cost: $525. Boarding program cost: $775. Application fee: $25.
Application Deadline Continuous.
Contact Office of Special Programs, 1140 Boylston Street, MS-155, Boston, Massachusetts 02215. Phone: 617-747-2254. Fax: 617-262-5419. E-mail: summer@berklee.edu.
URL www.berklee.edu/summer/songwriting.html

Berklee Summer String Fling
Berklee College of Music
1140 Boylston Street
Boston, Massachusetts 02215

General Information Coed residential and day arts program. Formal opportunities for the artistically talented.
Program Focus Music performance.
Academics Music, precollege program.
Arts Band, music, music (ensemble), music (instrumental), music (jazz), musical performance/recitals.
Trips College tours.

Program Information 1 session per year. Session length: 2 days in July. Ages: 15+. 30–40 participants per session. Day program cost: $385. Boarding program cost: $580. Application fee: $25.
Application Deadline Continuous.
Contact Office of Special Programs, 1140 Boylston Street, MS-155, Boston, Massachusetts 02215. Phone: 617-747-2245. Fax: 617-262-5419. E-mail: summer@berklee.edu.
URL www.berklee.edu/summer/string.html

Berklee World Percussion Festival

Berklee College of Music
1140 Boylston Street
Boston, Massachusetts 02215

General Information Coed residential and day arts program. Formal opportunities for the artistically talented.
Program Focus Music performance.
Academics Music, precollege program.
Arts Band, music, music (ensemble), music (instrumental), music (jazz), musical performance/recitals.
Trips College tours.
Program Information 1 session per year. Session length: 5 days in June. Ages: 15+. 100–200 participants per session. Day program cost: $675. Boarding program cost: $980. Application fee: $25.
Application Deadline Continuous.
Contact Office of Special Programs, 1140 Boylston Street, MS-155, Boston, Massachusetts 02215. Phone: 617-747-2245. Fax: 617-262-5419. E-mail: summer@berklee.edu.
URL www.berklee.edu/summer/wpf.html

BICYCLE TRAVEL ADVENTURES–Student Hosteling Program–Cape Cod

BICYCLE TRAVEL ADVENTURES–Student Hosteling Program
Massachusetts

General Information Coed travel outdoor program and adventure program established in 1970. Accredited by American Camping Association. Formal opportunities for the academically talented. Specific services available for the emotionally challenged and learning disabled. High school credit may be earned.
Program Focus A 15-day easy bicycling/hosteling/camping tour through the islands of Martha's Vineyard and Nantucket and the Cape Cod mainland.
Special Interest Areas Campcraft, field trips (arts and culture), touring.
Sports Bicycling, boating, canoeing, fishing, sailing, sea kayaking, swimming.
Wilderness/Outdoors Bicycle trips, canoe trips, hiking, mountain biking, wilderness camping.
Trips Day, overnight, shopping.
Program Information 1–6 sessions per year. Session length: 16 days in June, July, August. Ages: 12–15. 8–12 participants per session. Cost: $1885–$2030.
Application Deadline Continuous.
Jobs Positions for high school students 16 and older and college students 18 and older.
Contact Ted Lefkowitz, Director, 1356 Ashfield Road, PO Box 419, Conway, Massachusetts 01341. Phone: 800-343-6132. Fax: 413-369-4257. E-mail: shpbike@aol.com.
URL www.bicycletrips.com

For more information, see page 994.

Bonnie Castle Riding Camp

Stoneleigh–Burnham School
574 Bernardston Road
Greenfield, Massachusetts 01301

General Information Girls' residential sports camp established in 1982.

Bonnie Castle Riding Camp

Program Focus Horseback riding.
Academics English language/literature, mathematics.
Arts Arts and crafts (general), ceramics, dance (ballet), dance (jazz), dance (modern), drawing, painting, theater/drama.
Sports Equestrian sports, horseback riding.
Trips Shopping.

Bonnie Castle Riding Camp (continued)

Program Information 3 sessions per year. Session length: 2 weeks in June, July, August. Ages: 9–16. 48 participants per session. Boarding program cost: $1800–$5000. Additional cost for horse boarding, academic tutoring, and per academic subject.
Application Deadline June 15.
Contact Mina Payne Cooper, Director of Riding Program, main address above. Phone: 413-774-2711. Fax: 413-772-2602. E-mail: summerprograms@sbschool.org.
URL www.sbschool.org
For more information, see page 1334.

Boston University High School Honors Program

Boston University Summer Term
755 Commonwealth Avenue, Room 105
Boston, Massachusetts 02215

General Information Coed residential academic program established in 1977. Formal opportunities for the academically talented. College credit may be earned.
Program Focus Liberal arts, sciences, and college credit.
Academics American literature, Chinese languages/literature, English language/literature, French language/literature, German language/literature, Greek language/literature, Italian language/literature, Spanish language/literature, academics (general), anthropology, archaeology, art history/appreciation, astronomy, biology, business, chemistry, classical languages/literatures, communications, computers, economics, engineering, environmental science, geography, geology/earth science, government and politics, history, humanities, intercultural studies, journalism, linguistics, mathematics, music, philosophy, physics, physiology, psychology, religion, social science, social studies, speech/debate, writing.
Arts Drawing, painting, sculpture.
Sports Aerobics, archery, boating, canoeing, fencing, golf, racquetball, rowing (crew/sculling), sailing, scuba diving, swimming, tennis, weight training.
Trips Cultural, day, shopping.
Program Information 1 session per year. Session length: 6 weeks in July, August. Ages: 16–18. 40–60 participants per session. Boarding program cost: $5200–$5400. Financial aid available.
Application Deadline May 15.
Contact Scott Alessandro, Director, High School Honors Program, main address above. Phone: 617-353-1378. Fax: 617-353-5532. E-mail: salessan@bu.edu.
URL www.bu.edu/summer/highschool

Special Note
Rising high school seniors spend an academically challenging and exciting summer in Boston during this 6-week residential program. Highly qualified students choose between the General Honors Program and the Research Internship Program in Science and Engineering. Students in the General Honors Program can earn up to 8 college credits for 2 courses selected from Boston University's scheduled summer courses. The Research Internship Program provides students the opportunity to experience the culture and methodology of a research environment while working on individual projects supervised by a faculty mentor. Outside of class and the lab, students have ample free time to explore Boston.

Boston University Institute for Television, Film, and Radio Production

640 Commonwealth Avenue
Boston, Massachusetts 02215

General Information Coed residential academic program and arts program established in 1989.

Boston University Institute for Television, Film, and Radio Production

Program Focus Television, radio, and film production.
Academics Communications, computers, writing.
Arts Animation, creative writing, film, radio broadcasting, television/video.
Special Interest Areas Career exploration, field trips (arts and culture).
Sports Aerobics, basketball, softball, swimming, volleyball, weight training.
Trips Cultural, day, shopping.
Program Information 1 session per year. Session length: 5 weeks in July, August. Ages: 14–18. 70–85 participants per session. Boarding program cost: $3981. Application fee: $25.
Application Deadline March 30.
Jobs Positions for college students 19 and older.
Contact Christopher Cavalieri, Academic Director, main address above. Phone: 617-353-5015. Fax: 617-353-3405. E-mail: itrp@bu.edu.
URL www.bu.edu/com/itrp
For more information, see page 998.

Boston University PROMYS Program

111 Cummington Street, #142
Boston, Massachusetts 02215

General Information Coed residential academic program established in 1989. Formal opportunities for the academically talented.
Program Focus Mathematics.
Academics Mathematics.
Trips College tours, shopping.
Program Information 1 session per year. Session length: 6 weeks in July, August. Ages: 14–18. 60–75 participants per session. Boarding program cost: $2250. Financial aid available.
Application Deadline June 1.
Jobs Positions for college students 18 and older.
Contact Bridget Walsh, Program Coordinator, main address above. Phone: 617-353-2563. Fax: 617-353-8100. E-mail: promys@math.bu.edu.
URL www.promys.org

Boston University Summer Challenge Program

Boston University Summer Term
755 Commonwealth Avenue, Room 105
Boston, Massachusetts 02215

General Information Coed residential academic program established in 2002.
Program Focus Introduction to college life and academics.
Academics Academics (general), art history/appreciation, biology, business, chemistry, communications, precollege program, science (general), speech/debate, writing.
Arts Creative writing.
Sports Aerobics, boating, soccer, softball, swimming, volleyball.
Trips Cultural, day, shopping.
Program Information 1–2 sessions per year. Session length: 12–14 days in June, July, August. Ages: 14–18. 30–40 participants per session. Boarding program cost: $2400–$2600. Application fee: $25.
Application Deadline Continuous.
Contact Scott Alessandro, Director, Summer Challenge Program, Boston University Summer Term, 755 Commonwealth Avenue, Room 105, Boston, Massachusetts 02215. Phone: 617-353-1378. Fax: 617-353-5532. E-mail: salessan@bu.edu.
URL www.bu.edu/summer/highschool

Boston University Summer Theatre Institute

855 Commonwealth Avenue, #470
Boston, Massachusetts 02215

General Information Coed residential and day arts program established in 1980. Formal opportunities for the artistically talented. College credit may be earned.
Program Focus Theater.
Academics Writing.
Arts Acting, creative writing, dance, directing, music (vocal), theater/drama.
Trips Cultural, day, overnight.
Program Information 1 session per year. Session length: 5 weeks in July, August. Ages: 16–18. 50–65 participants per session. Day program cost: $2500. Boarding program cost: $3850–$4100. Application fee: $60. Financial aid available.
Application Deadline April 15.
Contact Paolo S. DiFabio, Assistant Director, main address above. Phone: 617-353-3390. Fax: 617-353-4363.
URL www.bu.edu/cfa

Boston University Tanglewood Institute

45 West Street
Lenox, Massachusetts 01240

General Information Coed residential arts program established in 1966. Formal opportunities for the artistically talented. College credit may be earned.

Boston University Tanglewood Institute

Academics Music, music (Advanced Placement).
Arts Band, chorus, music, music (chamber), music (classical), music (ensemble), music (instrumental), music (orchestral), music (vocal).
Sports Basketball, soccer, softball, swimming, tennis, volleyball.
Wilderness/Outdoors Hiking.
Trips Cultural.
Program Information 1–3 sessions per year. Session length: 2–8 weeks in June, July, August. Ages: 14–18. 100–275 participants per session. Boarding program cost: $2055–$5615. Application fee: $60. Financial aid available.
Application Deadline March 1.
Jobs Positions for college students.
Contact Ms. Chung-Un Seo, Administrative Director, 855 Commonwealth Avenue, Boston, Massachusetts 02215. Phone: 800-643-4796. Fax: 617-353-7455. E-mail: tanglewd@bu.edu.
URL www.bu.edu/tanglewood

Brighton College Admissions Prep at Tufts University

Brighton
Tufts University
Medford, Massachusetts

General Information Coed residential academic program established in 2003. Formal opportunities for the academically talented.
Program Focus College admissions prep.
Academics SAT/ACT preparation, college tours, writing.
Special Interest Areas College planning.
Trips College tours.
Program Information 1 session per year. Session length: 9 days in August. Ages: 15–19. 20–30 participants per session. Boarding program cost: $2295.
Application Deadline Continuous.
Jobs Positions for college students 21 and older.
Contact David Allen, Executive Director, 101 East Green Street, Suite 14, Pasadena, California 91105. Phone: 626-795-2985. Fax: 626-795-5564. E-mail: info@brightonedge.org.
URL www.brightonedge.org

For more information, see page 1004.

Camp Atwater–Boys Session

Urban League of Springfield, Inc.
20 Shore Road
North Brookfield, Massachusetts 01535

General Information Boys' residential traditional camp established in 1921. Accredited by American Camping Association.
Program Focus Leadership.
Arts Acting, arts and crafts (general), creative writing, dance, drawing, painting.
Special Interest Areas Leadership training, model rocketry, nature study, team building.
Sports Archery, baseball, basketball, boating, canoeing, cheerleading, fishing, football, golf, horseback riding, lacrosse, martial arts, ropes course, sailing, soccer, softball, swimming, tennis, track and field, volleyball.
Wilderness/Outdoors Hiking, orienteering.
Trips College tours, cultural, day.
Program Information 1 session per year. Session length: 2–4 weeks in June, July. Ages: 8–16. 85–135 participants per session. Boarding program cost: $1280–$2560. Application fee: $50. Financial aid available.
Application Deadline Continuous.
Jobs Positions for high school students 17 and older and college students 17 and older.
Contact Camp Office, 765 State Street, Springfield, Massachusetts 01109. Phone: 413-732-7211 Ext.102. Fax: 413-732-9364.
URL www.campatwater.org

Camp Atwater–Girls Session

Urban League of Springfield, Inc.
20 Shore Road
North Brookfield, Massachusetts 01535

General Information Girls' residential traditional camp established in 1921. Accredited by American Camping Association.
Program Focus Leadership development.
Arts Acting, arts and crafts (general), creative writing, dance, drawing, jewelry making, leather working, painting, theater/drama, weaving, woodworking.
Special Interest Areas Leadership training, model rocketry, nature study, team building.
Sports Archery, baseball, basketball, boating, canoeing, cheerleading, fishing, football, golf, horseback riding, lacrosse, martial arts, ropes course, sailing, soccer, softball, swimming, tennis, track and field, volleyball.
Wilderness/Outdoors Hiking, orienteering.
Trips College tours, cultural, day.
Program Information 1 session per year. Session length: 2–4 weeks in July, August. Ages: 8–16. 85–135 participants per session. Boarding program cost: $1280–$2560. Application fee: $50. Financial aid available.
Application Deadline Continuous.
Jobs Positions for high school students 17 and older.
Contact Camp Office, 765 State Street, Springfield, Massachusetts 01109. Phone: 413-739-7211 Ext.102. Fax: 413-732-9364. E-mail: sulcamp@ulspringfield.org.
URL www.campatwater.org

Camp Avoda

Camp Avoda, Inc.
23 Gibbs Road
Middleboro, Massachusetts 02346

General Information Boys' residential traditional camp established in 1927. Religious affiliation: Jewish. Accredited by American Camping Association.
Program Focus Water and land sports.
Academics Jewish studies.
Arts Arts and crafts (general), photography, television/video, woodworking.
Special Interest Areas Campcraft, leadership training.
Sports Archery, basketball, boating, canoeing, fishing, football, golf, in-line skating, kayaking, lacrosse, ropes course, sailing, soccer, softball, sports (general), street/roller hockey, swimming, tennis, volleyball, water polo, waterskiing, weight training, windsurfing, wrestling.
Wilderness/Outdoors Canoe trips, hiking, rafting, white-water trips.
Trips Day, overnight.
Program Information 1–4 sessions per year. Session length: 14–53 days in June, July, August. Ages: 7–15. 140–150 participants per session. Boarding program cost: $2500–$4275. Financial aid available.
Application Deadline Continuous.
Jobs Positions for high school students 18 and older and college students 18 and older.
Summer Contact Mr. Paul G. Davis, Director, main address above. Phone: 508-947-3800. Fax: 508-947-3877. E-mail: campavoda@aol.com.

Winter Contact Mr. Paul G. Davis, Director, 11 Essex Street, Lynnfield, Massachusetts 01940. Phone: 781-334-6275. Fax: 781-334-4779. E-mail: campavoda@aol.com.
URL www.campavoda.org

Camp Burgess

South Shore YMCA Camps
75 Stowe Road
Sandwich, Massachusetts 02563

General Information Boys' residential traditional camp and outdoor program established in 1928. Religious affiliation: Christian. Accredited by American Camping Association.
Arts Arts and crafts (general), ceramics, dance, drawing, music, painting, pottery, theater/drama.
Special Interest Areas Campcraft, leadership training, nature study, nautical skills, team building.
Sports Archery, baseball, basketball, bicycling, boating, canoeing, climbing (wall), field hockey, football, horseback riding, rappelling, ropes course, sailing, snorkeling, soccer, softball, sports (general), street/roller hockey, swimming, tennis, volleyball, water polo, waterskiing, windsurfing.
Wilderness/Outdoors Wilderness camping.
Trips Overnight.
Program Information 6 sessions per year. Session length: 6–12 days in June, July, August. Ages: 7–15. 140–170 participants per session. Boarding program cost: $450–$900. Financial aid available.
Application Deadline Continuous.
Jobs Positions for high school students 17 and older and college students 18 and older.
Contact Lloyd Ewart, Camp Director, main address above. Phone: 508-428-2571. Fax: 508-420-3545. E-mail: camp@ssymca.org.
URL www.ssymca.org

Camp Good News for Young People and Teens

Society for Christian Activities
71 Route 130
Forestdale, Massachusetts 02644

General Information Coed residential and day traditional camp and bible camp established in 1935. Religious affiliation: interdenominational. Accredited by American Camping Association.
Program Focus Positive Christian values.
Academics Bible study.
Arts Arts and crafts (general).
Special Interest Areas Worship.
Sports Archery, baseball, basketball, bicycling, boating, canoeing, fishing, ropes course, sailing, soccer, softball, sports (general), track and field.
Wilderness/Outdoors Bicycle trips, canoe trips, mountaineering.
Trips Cultural, day, overnight, shopping.
Program Information 3 sessions per year. Session length: 2–7 weeks in June, July, August. Ages: 6–15. 180–200 participants per session. Day program cost: $400–$1400. Boarding program cost: $800–$2800. Application fee: $100–$200. Financial aid available. Senior camp trips cost extra.
Application Deadline Continuous.
Jobs Positions for college students 18 and older.
Contact Faith Willard, Director, PO Box 1295, Forestdale, Massachusetts 02644. Phone: 508-477-9731. Fax: 508-477-8016. E-mail: goodnews@intercape.com.
URL www.campgoodnews.org

Camp Greylock for Boys

1525 Main Street
Becket, Massachusetts 01223

General Information Boys' residential traditional camp established in 1916. Accredited by American Camping Association.
Arts Arts and crafts (general), ceramics, leather working, music, musical productions, painting, photography, pottery, radio broadcasting, sculpture, theater/drama, woodworking.
Special Interest Areas Animal care, campcraft, electronics, gardening, leadership training, model rocketry, nature study.
Sports Archery, baseball, basketball, bicycling, bicycling (BMX), boating, canoeing, climbing (wall), cross-country, fencing, fishing, football, golf, in-line skating, kayaking, lacrosse, rappelling, ropes course, sailing, snorkeling, soccer, softball, sports (general), street/roller hockey, swimming, tennis, track and field, volleyball, water polo, waterskiing, weight training, windsurfing.
Wilderness/Outdoors Backpacking, bicycle trips, canoe trips, hiking, mountain biking, mountaineering, orienteering, rafting, rock climbing, white-water trips, wilderness camping.
Trips Cultural, overnight.
Program Information 1 session per year. Session length: 7 weeks in June, July, August. Ages: 7–16. 375 participants per session. Boarding program cost: $7950.
Application Deadline Continuous.
Jobs Positions for college students 19 and older.
Summer Contact Michael Marcus, Director, PO Box 278, Becket, Massachusetts 01223. Phone: 413-623-8921. Fax: 413-623-5049. E-mail: info@campgreylock.com.
Winter Contact Michael Marcus, Director, 200 West 57th Street, Suite 307, New York, New York 10019. Phone: 212-582-1042. Fax: 212-765-8177. E-mail: info@campgreylock.com.
URL www.campgreylock.com

Camp Hayward

South Shore YMCA Camps
75 Stowe Road
Sandwich, Massachusetts 02563

General Information Girls' residential traditional camp established in 1928. Religious affiliation: Christian. Accredited by American Camping Association.
Arts Acting, arts and crafts (general), ceramics, dance, drawing, jewelry making, music, painting, pottery, theater/drama.
Special Interest Areas Campcraft, leadership training, nature study, team building.

Camp Hayward (continued)

Sports Archery, baseball, basketball, boating, canoeing, climbing (wall), horseback riding, ropes course, sailing, soccer, swimming, tennis, windsurfing.
Wilderness/Outdoors Orienteering.
Trips Overnight.
Program Information 6 sessions per year. Session length: 6–12 days in June, July, August. Ages: 7–15. 168 participants per session. Boarding program cost: $485–$985. Financial aid available.
Application Deadline Continuous.
Jobs Positions for high school students 17 and older and college students 18 and older.
Summer Contact Ms. Sacha Johnston, Camp Hayward Director, main address above. Phone: 508-428-2571. Fax: 508-420-3545. E-mail: camp@ssymca.org.
Winter Contact Ms. Sacha Johnston, main address above. Phone: 508-428-2571. Fax: 508-420-3545. E-mail: camp@ssymca.org.
URL www.ssymca.org

CAMP HILLSIDE

Hillside School
404 Robin Hill Road
Marlborough, Massachusetts 01752

General Information Coed residential and day traditional camp and academic program established in 2000. Formal opportunities for the academically talented. Specific services available for the learning disabled.
Academics English as a second language, English language/literature, computer programming, mathematics, reading, study skills, writing.
Arts Creative writing, drawing, painting, woodworking.
Special Interest Areas Animal care, farming, gardening, leadership training, nature study.
Sports Basketball, canoeing, climbing (wall), ropes course, soccer, swimming, volleyball, weight training.
Wilderness/Outdoors Hiking.
Trips Cultural, day.
Program Information 1–5 sessions per year. Session length: 1–5 weeks in July, August. Ages: 8–15. 20–50 participants per session. Day program cost: $500. Boarding program cost: $800–$1000. Financial aid available.
Application Deadline Continuous.
Contact Office of Admissions for Summer Program, main address above. Phone: 508-485-2824. Fax: 508-485-4420. E-mail: admissions@hillsideschool.net.
URL hillsideschool.net

CAMP HILLSIDE SOCCER PROGRAM

Hillside School
404 Robin Hill Road
Marlborough, Massachusetts 01752

General Information Coed residential and day sports camp.
Program Focus Soccer instruction.
Sports Soccer, swimming.
Program Information 4–5 sessions per year. Session length: 1–7 days in July, August. Ages: 8–15. 20–40 participants per session. Day program cost: $250. Boarding program cost: $250–$750. Financial aid available.
Application Deadline Continuous.
Contact Office of Admissions for Summer Programs, main address above. Phone: 508-485-2824. Fax: 508-485-4420. E-mail: admissions@hillsideschool.net.
URL hillsideschool.net

CAMP KINGSMONT

Camp Kingsmont
Hampshire College
893 West Street
Amherst, Massachusetts 01002

General Information Coed residential traditional camp and special needs program established in 1971. Accredited by American Camping Association. Specific services available for the weight reduction.
Program Focus Self-esteem, fitness, weight control, and lifestyle change.
Arts Arts and crafts (general), ceramics, clowning, dance, drawing, fabric arts, jewelry making, musical productions, painting, photography, pottery, radio broadcasting, theater/drama.
Special Interest Areas Campcraft, culinary arts, model rocketry, nature study, weight reduction.
Sports Aerobics, archery, basketball, bicycling, canoeing, fishing, football, horseback riding, kayaking, martial arts, physical fitness, ropes course, soccer, softball, street/roller hockey, swimming, tennis, volleyball, water polo, weight training, yoga.
Wilderness/Outdoors Backpacking, hiking, mountain biking, rafting, white-water trips, wilderness camping.
Trips Cultural, day, overnight, shopping.
Program Information 3 sessions per year. Session length: 3–7 weeks in June, July, August. Ages: 7–18. 150–250 participants per session. Boarding program cost: $2900–$6600. Transportation from Los Angeles or San Francisco to Massachusetts included in program cost.
Application Deadline Continuous.
Jobs Positions for high school students 16 and older and college students 18 and older.
Summer Contact Mr. Marc Manoli, Owner/On-Site Director, main address above. Phone: 800-854-1377. Fax: 413-528-8104. E-mail: info@campkingsmont.com.
Winter Contact Mr. Marc Manoli, Owner/On-Site Director, 195 Main Street, Great Barrington, Massachusetts 01230. Phone: 413-528-8474. Fax: 413-528-8104. E-mail: info@campkingsmont.com.
URL www.campkingsmont.com

CAMP NAWAKA

Camp Fire USA Eastern Massachusetts Council
622 Reservoir Road
East Otis, Massachusetts 01029

General Information Coed residential traditional camp established in 1967. Accredited by American Camping Association.
Program Focus Individualized activities.
Arts Acting, arts and crafts (general), ceramics, creative writing, dance, drawing, fabric arts, jewelry

making, music, music (vocal), musical productions, painting, photography, pottery, sculpture, theater/drama.
Special Interest Areas Campcraft, field trips (arts and culture), leadership training, nature study.
Sports Archery, basketball, boating, canoeing, fishing, horseback riding, lacrosse, sailing, soccer, softball, sports (general), swimming, tennis, volleyball.
Wilderness/Outdoors Backpacking, canoe trips, hiking, orienteering, wilderness camping.
Trips Cultural, day, overnight.
Program Information 13 sessions per year. Session length: 6–21 days in June, July, August. Ages: 8–16. 85–120 participants per session. Boarding program cost: $395–$1200. Financial aid available.
Application Deadline Continuous.
Jobs Positions for high school students 18 and older and college students 18 and older.
Contact Christopher Egan, Camp Director, 56 Roland Street, Suite 305, Boston, Massachusetts 02129. Phone: 617-591-0300 Ext.120. Fax: 617-591-0310. E-mail: egan@nawaka.org.
URL www.nawaka.org

Camp Watitoh

Center Lake
Becket, Massachusetts 01223

General Information Coed residential traditional camp established in 1937. Accredited by American Camping Association.
Academics Astronomy, ecology, journalism, writing.
Arts Arts and crafts (general), batiking, ceramics, chorus, creative writing, dance (folk), dance (modern), drawing, fabric arts, graphic arts, jewelry making, leather working, metalworking, music, music (vocal), musical productions, painting, photography, pottery, printmaking, puppetry, radio broadcasting, sculpture, theater/drama, weaving, woodworking.
Special Interest Areas Native American culture, animal care, campcraft, nature study.
Sports Aerobics, archery, basketball, boating, canoeing, cheerleading, cross-country, field hockey, fishing, football, golf, gymnastics, in-line skating, kayaking, lacrosse, ropes course, rowing (crew/sculling), sailing, snorkeling, soccer, softball, street/roller hockey, swimming, tennis, track and field, volleyball, waterskiing, weight training, windsurfing.
Wilderness/Outdoors Canoe trips, hiking, orienteering, rafting, white-water trips.
Trips Cultural, day, overnight.
Program Information 1 session per year. Session length: 54 days in July, August. Ages: 7–16. 200 participants per session. Boarding program cost: $5600.
Application Deadline Continuous.
Jobs Positions for college students 19 and older.
Summer Contact Mr. William Hoch, Director, main address above. Phone: 413-623-8951. Fax: 413-623-8955. E-mail: info@campwatitoh.com.
Winter Contact Mr. William Hoch, Director, 28 Sammis Lane, White Plains, New York 10605. Phone: 914-428-1894. Fax: 914-428-1648. E-mail: info@campwatitoh.com.
URL www.campwatitoh.com

Camp Wing

Crossroads for Kids
119 Myrtle Street
Duxbury, Massachusetts 02332

General Information Coed residential traditional camp established in 1936. Accredited by American Camping Association. Specific services available for the youth at risk.
Program Focus Youth at risk.
Academics Computer programming, computers, reading, remedial academics.
Arts Arts and crafts (general), ceramics, dance, drawing, fabric arts, jewelry making, music, musical productions, painting, pottery, puppetry, radio broadcasting, theater/drama.
Special Interest Areas Animal care, nature study, team building.
Sports Aerobics, archery, baseball, basketball, bicycling, boating, canoeing, cheerleading, climbing (wall), fishing, football, golf, kayaking, lacrosse, ropes course, sailing, soccer, softball, swimming, tennis, volleyball.
Wilderness/Outdoors Hiking.
Trips Day.
Program Information 3 sessions per year. Session length: 10–21 days in June, July, August. Ages: 7–13. 50–200 participants per session. Boarding program cost: $880–$1760. Application fee: $50. Financial aid available.
Application Deadline Continuous.
Jobs Positions for college students 19 and older.
Contact Pat Cleary, Camp Director, main address above. Phone: 781-834-2700. Fax: 781-834-2701. E-mail: pcleary@crossroads4kids.org.
URL www.crossroads4kids.org

Camp Wingate Kirkland

79 White Rock Road
Yarmouth Port, Massachusetts 02675

General Information Coed residential traditional camp established in 1957. Accredited by American Camping Association.
Program Focus Daily choice in a caring, supportive environment, Cape Cod location.
Arts Arts and crafts (general), batiking, ceramics, creative writing, dance, dance (jazz), dance (modern), drawing, fabric arts, graphic arts, jewelry making, leather working, metalworking, mime, music, music (vocal), musical productions, painting, photography, pottery, printmaking, puppetry, radio broadcasting, sculpture, theater/drama, weaving, woodworking.
Special Interest Areas Campcraft, community service, culinary arts, field trips (arts and culture), gardening, leadership training, model rocketry, nature study.
Sports Aerobics, archery, baseball, basketball, bicycling, boating, canoeing, climbing (wall), cross-country, field hockey, fishing, football, gymnastics, in-line skating, kayaking, lacrosse, martial arts, ropes course, sailing, soccer, softball, sports (general), street/roller hockey, swimming, tennis, track and field, volleyball, weight training.

Camp Wingate Kirkland (continued)
Wilderness/Outdoors Backpacking, bicycle trips, canoe trips, hiking, wilderness camping.
Trips Cultural, day, overnight.
Program Information 3 sessions per year. Session length: 1–7 weeks in June, July, August. Ages: 8–15. 150–175 participants per session. Boarding program cost: $2000–$6550.
Application Deadline Continuous.
Jobs Positions for college students 18 and older.
Summer Contact Will Rubenstein, Director, main address above. Phone: 508-362-3798. Fax: 508-362-1614. E-mail: office@campwk.com.
Winter Contact Mr. Jim Wolfson, Director, 18 Woodridge Road, Wayland, Massachusetts 01778. Phone: 508-358-5816. Fax: 508-358-0249. E-mail: office@campwk.com.
URL www.campwk.com

Camp Wing Day Camp

Crossroads for Kids
119 Myrtle Street
Duxbury, Massachusetts 02332

General Information Coed day traditional camp. Accredited by American Camping Association.
Academics Computer programming, computers, reading.
Arts Arts and crafts (general), ceramics, dance, drawing, fabric arts, jewelry making, music, musical productions, painting, pottery, puppetry, radio broadcasting, theater/drama.
Special Interest Areas Animal care, nature study.
Sports Aerobics, archery, basketball, boating, canoeing, cheerleading, climbing (wall), fishing, football, golf, kayaking, lacrosse, ropes course, sailing, soccer, softball, swimming, tennis, volleyball.
Wilderness/Outdoors Hiking.
Trips Day.
Program Information 5 sessions per year. Session length: 5–10 days in June, July, August. Ages: 5–16. 150 participants per session. Day program cost: $340–$395.
Application Deadline Continuous.
Jobs Positions for college students 19 and older.
Contact Jim Willis, Camp Director, main address above. Phone: 781-834-2700. Fax: 781-834-2701. E-mail: jwillis@crossroads4kids.org.
URL www.crossroads4kids.org

Cape Cod Sea Camps–Monomoy/Wono

Cape Cod Sea Camps, Inc.
3057 Main Street
Brewster, Massachusetts 02631

General Information Coed residential and day traditional camp established in 1922. Accredited by American Camping Association.
Program Focus Sailing and traditional activities.
Arts Arts and crafts (general), batiking, ceramics, creative writing, dance, drawing, graphic arts, painting, photography, pottery, printmaking, theater/drama, woodworking.
Special Interest Areas Leadership training, nature study.
Sports Aerobics, archery, baseball, basketball, bicycling, canoeing, field hockey, fishing, gymnastics, kayaking, lacrosse, riflery, sailing, snorkeling, soccer, softball, swimming, tennis, track and field, volleyball, waterskiing, windsurfing.
Wilderness/Outdoors Bicycle trips, canoe trips.
Trips Day.
Program Information 2 sessions per year. Session length: 10–49 days in July, August. Ages: 8–15. 350–380 participants per session. Day program cost: $480. Boarding program cost: $3800–$6800. Financial aid available. Financial aid deadline is: January 1.
Application Deadline Continuous.
Jobs Positions for college students 19 and older.
Contact David Peterson, Director, Box 1880, Brewster, Massachusetts 02631. Phone: 508-896-3451. Fax: 508-896-8272. E-mail: info@capecodseacamps.com.
URL www.capecodseacamps.com

Carroll Center for the Blind–Computing for College: Computer and Communication Skills

Carroll Center for the Blind
770 Centre Street
Newton, Massachusetts 02458-2597

General Information Coed residential and day special needs program established in 2001. Specific services available for the visually impaired. High school credit may be earned.
Program Focus Visually impaired and blind.
Academics Communications, computers, typing.
Special Interest Areas College planning, communication skills.
Sports Canoeing, fencing, sailing.
Trips Day.
Program Information 1–4 sessions per year. Session length: 2 weeks in June, July, August. Ages: 16–22. 4–5 participants per session. Day program cost: $2800. Boarding program cost: $2800. Financial aid available.
Application Deadline Continuous.
Contact Brian Charlson, main address above. E-mail: charlsonb@carroll.org.
URL www.carroll.org

Carroll Center for the Blind–Real World Work Experience

Carroll Center for the Blind
770 Centre Street
Newton, Massachusetts 02458

General Information Coed residential special needs program established in 2001. Specific services available for the visually impaired. High school credit may be earned.
Program Focus Visually impaired and blind.

Academics Business, communications, computers.
Special Interest Areas Career exploration, work camp programs.
Sports Canoeing, fencing, sailing.
Trips Day.
Program Information 3 sessions per year. Session length: 30 days in June, July, August. Ages: 16+. 4 participants per session. Boarding program cost: $5500. Financial aid available.
Application Deadline Continuous.
Jobs Positions for high school students 16 and older.
Contact Margaret E. Cleary, Director of Admissions, main address above. Phone: 617-969-6200 Ext.216. Fax: 617-969-6204. E-mail: mecleary@carroll.org.
URL www.carroll.org

Carroll Center for the Blind–Youth in Transition

Carroll Center for the Blind
770 Centre Street
Newton, Massachusetts 02458-2597

General Information Coed residential and day special needs program established in 1954. Specific services available for the visually impaired. High school credit may be earned.
Program Focus Visually impaired/blind individuals.
Academics Communications, computers, typing, writing.
Arts Ceramics, dance, music, pottery, woodworking.
Special Interest Areas Career exploration, daily living skills, personal development.
Sports Canoeing, fencing, sailing.
Wilderness/Outdoors Outdoor camping.
Trips Cultural, day, overnight, shopping.
Program Information 2 sessions per year. Session length: 4 weeks in June, July, August. Ages: 15–22. 12 participants per session. Day program cost: $5500. Boarding program cost: $5500. Most fees paid by State Commission for the Blind.
Jobs Positions for college students 18 and older.
Contact Margaret E. Cleary, Director of Admissions, main address above. Phone: 617-969-6200 Ext.216. Fax: 617-969-6204. E-mail: mecleary@carroll.org.
URL www.carroll.org

Center Summer Academy

Boston Architectural Center
320 Newbury Street
Boston, Massachusetts 02115

General Information Coed day academic program established in 1973. Formal opportunities for the academically talented and artistically talented.
Program Focus Architecture and interior design.
Academics Architecture, art (Advanced Placement), art history/appreciation, computers, technology.
Arts Design, drawing, graphic arts, photography, studio arts.
Special Interest Areas Career exploration, field trips (arts and culture).
Trips Day.
Program Information 1 session per year. Session length: 20–30 days in July, August. Ages: 15–18. 60–75 participants per session. Day program cost: $950. Financial aid available.
Application Deadline Continuous.
Contact Ms. Michael Daniels, Coordinator, main address above. Phone: 617-585-0101. Fax: 617-585-0121. E-mail: michael.daniels@the-bac.edu.
URL www.the-bac.edu

Clara Barton Camp

The Barton Center for Diabetes Education, Inc.
30 Ennis Road
North Oxford, Massachusetts 01537

General Information Girls' residential traditional camp and special needs program established in 1932. Accredited by American Camping Association. Specific services available for the diabetic. High school or college credit may be earned.
Program Focus Focus on living well with diabetes.
Arts Arts and crafts (general), batiking, ceramics, dance, dance (ballet), dance (folk), dance (jazz), dance (modern), dance (tap), drawing, jewelry making, music, music (vocal), painting, photography, pottery, theater/drama.
Special Interest Areas Campcraft, diabetic education, health education, leadership training, nature study.
Sports Aerobics, archery, baseball, basketball, bicycling, boating, canoeing, cheerleading, climbing (wall), equestrian sports, field hockey, fishing, gymnastics, horseback riding, lacrosse, ropes course, soccer, softball, sports (general), swimming, tennis, volleyball.
Wilderness/Outdoors Backpacking, hiking, mountain biking, orienteering, wilderness camping.
Trips Day, overnight.
Program Information 5–6 sessions per year. Session length: 5–12 days in June, July, August. Ages: 6–16. 80 participants per session. Boarding program cost: $900–$1800. Application fee: $50. Financial aid available.
Application Deadline Continuous.
Jobs Positions for high school students 18 and older and college students 18 and older.
Contact Gaylen McCann, Resident Camps Director, 30 Ennis Road, PO Box 356, North Oxford, Massachusetts 01537. Phone: 508-987-3856. Fax: 508-987-2002. E-mail: gaylen.mccann@bartoncenter.org.
URL www.bartoncenter.org

Clara Barton Family Camp

The Barton Center for Diabetes Education, Inc.
30 Ennis Road
North Oxford, Massachusetts 01537

General Information Coed residential traditional camp, family program, and special needs program established in 2000. Accredited by American Camping Association. Specific services available for the diabetic.
Program Focus Focus on families living well with diabetes.

Clara Barton Family Camp (continued)

Arts Arts and crafts (general), dance (ballet), dance (folk), dance (jazz), dance (modern), dance (tap), jewelry making, music (vocal), painting, pottery, theater/drama.
Special Interest Areas Campcraft, diabetic education, health education, leadership training, nature study.
Sports Aerobics, archery, baseball, basketball, bicycling, boating, canoeing, cheerleading, climbing (wall), field hockey, fishing, gymnastics, horseback riding, lacrosse, ropes course, soccer, softball, swimming, tennis, volleyball.
Wilderness/Outdoors Backpacking, hiking, mountain biking, orienteering, survival training, wilderness camping.
Trips Day.
Program Information 1 session per year. Session length: 4 days in August. 80 participants per session. Application fee: $50. Cost: $225 per person.
Application Deadline Continuous.
Jobs Positions for high school students 18 and older and college students 18 and older.
Contact Gaylen McCann, Resident Camps Director, 30 Ennis Road, PO Box 356, North Oxford, Massachusetts 01537. Phone: 508-987-3856. Fax: 508-987-2002. E-mail: gaylen.mccann@bartoncenter.org.
URL www.bartoncenter.org

College Admission Prep Camp by Education Unlimited–Boston

Education Unlimited
Tufts University
Boston, Massachusetts

General Information Coed residential and day academic program established in 2004.
Program Focus College admission preparation.
Academics SAT/ACT preparation, college tours, study skills, writing.
Special Interest Areas College planning.
Trips Day.
Program Information 1 session per year. Session length: 10 days in July. Ages: 15–18. 30–40 participants per session. Boarding program cost: $2225. Financial aid available.
Application Deadline Continuous.
Contact Mr. Erby Mitchell, Director, 1700 Shattuck Avenue, # 305, Berkeley, California 94709. Phone: 510-548-6612. Fax: 510-548-0212. E-mail: camps@educationunlimited.com.
URL www.educationunlimited.com

For more information, see page 1076.

Crane Lake Camp

Union for Reform Judaism
Stateline Road
West Stockbridge, Massachusetts 01266

General Information Coed residential traditional camp established in 1998. Religious affiliation: Jewish. Specific services available for the emotionally challenged, learning disabled, and visually impaired.
Program Focus Athletic skill development.
Academics Jewish studies.
Arts Acting, arts and crafts (general), ceramics, dance (folk).
Special Interest Areas Animal care, campcraft, leadership training, nature study, team building.
Sports Aerobics, archery, baseball, basketball, boating, canoeing, climbing (wall), fishing, football, golf, gymnastics, kayaking, lacrosse, ropes course, sailing, soccer, softball, street/roller hockey, swimming, tennis, volleyball, weight training.
Trips Cultural, day, overnight.
Program Information 2 sessions per year. Session length: 4 weeks in July, August. Ages: 7–16. 250–300 participants per session. Boarding program cost: $3080–$6000. Financial aid available.
Application Deadline Continuous.
Jobs Positions for college students 18 and older.
Summer Contact Herbert May, Crane Lake Camp, Stateline Road, West Stockbridge, Massachusetts 01266. Phone: 413-232-4257. E-mail: may@urj.org.
Winter Contact Herbert May, Crane Lake Camp, 301 Route 17 North, Rutherford, New Jersey 07070. E-mail: may@urj.org.
URL urjnecamps.org

Cushing Academy Summer Session

Cushing Academy
39 School Street
Ashburnham, Massachusetts 01430-8000

General Information Coed residential and day academic program, arts program, and community service program established in 1976. Formal opportunities for the academically talented and artistically talented. Specific services available for the learning disabled. High school credit may be earned.

Cushing Academy Summer Session

Program Focus Academic coursework, review, and enrichment.
Academics American literature, English as a second language, English language/literature, SAT/ACT preparation, Spanish language/literature, academics (general), art (Advanced Placement), art history/

appreciation, biology, chemistry, computers, history, mathematics, mathematics (Advanced Placement), physics, reading, research skills, science (general), study skills, writing.
Arts Acting, ceramics, creative writing, dance, drawing, film, graphic arts, jewelry making, metalworking, music, music (instrumental), painting, photography, pottery, radio broadcasting, sculpture, television/video, theater/drama.
Special Interest Areas College planning, community service, field research/expeditions.
Sports Aerobics, basketball, figure skating, golf, ice hockey, martial arts, soccer, swimming, tennis, volleyball.
Wilderness/Outdoors Hiking.
Trips College tours, cultural, day, overnight, shopping.
Program Information 1–2 sessions per year. Session length: 20–40 days in July, August. Ages: 12–18. 300 participants per session. Day program cost: $2600. Boarding program cost: $5450. Application fee: $50. Financial aid available.
Application Deadline Continuous.
Jobs Positions for college students 20 and older.
Contact Mr. Dan Frank, Director of Summer Session, 39 School Street, PO Box 8000, Ashburnham, Massachusetts 01430-8000. Phone: 978-827-7700. Fax: 978-827-6927. E-mail: summersession@cushing.org.
URL www.cushing.org

For more information, see page 1084.

CYBERCAMPS–AMHERST COLLEGE

Cybercamps–Giant Campus, Inc.
Amherst, Massachusetts

General Information Coed residential and day academic program established in 1996.
Program Focus Cybercamps provide a high-tech camp experience for the young inquisitive mind, from beginner to advanced, while also including sports, team building activities, etc.
Academics Web page design, computer programming, computers.
Arts Animation, digital media, graphic arts, photography.
Special Interest Areas Computer game design, computer graphics, robotics, team building.
Sports Frisbee golf, ultimate frisbee.
Program Information 2–9 sessions per year. Session length: 5–30 days in June, July, August. Ages: 7–18. 30–150 participants per session. Day program cost: $599–$849. Boarding program cost: $974–$1224. Financial aid available.
Application Deadline Continuous.
Jobs Positions for high school students 15 and older and college students.
Contact Cybercamps Information Office, 2401 4th Avenue, Suite 1110, Seattle, Washington 98121. Phone: 206-442-4500. Fax: 206-442-4501. E-mail: info@cybercamps.com.
URL www.cybercamps.com

CYBERCAMPS–BABSON COLLEGE

Cybercamps–Giant Campus, Inc.
Wellesley, Massachusetts

General Information Coed day academic program established in 1997.
Program Focus High tech computer camps featuring project oriented curriculum in Web design, 3D animation, game design, robotics, digital arts and programming for all ability levels.
Academics Web page design, computer programming, computers.
Arts Animation, creative writing, digital media, graphic arts, photography.
Special Interest Areas Computer game design, computer graphics, robotics, team building.
Sports Frisbee golf, ultimate frisbee.
Program Information 2–9 sessions per year. Session length: 5–30 days in June, July, August. Ages: 7–18. 30–150 participants per session. Day program cost: $599–$849. Financial aid available.
Application Deadline Continuous.
Jobs Positions for high school students 15 and older and college students.
Contact Cybercamps Information Office, 2401 4th Avenue, Suite 1110, Seattle, Washington 98121. Phone: 206-442-4500. Fax: 206-442-4501. E-mail: info@cybercamps.com.
URL www.cybercamps.com

CYBERCAMPS–BENTLEY COLLEGE

Cybercamps–Giant Campus, Inc.
Waltham, Massachusetts

General Information Coed residential and day academic program established in 1997.
Program Focus High tech computer camps featuring project oriented curriculum in Web design, 3D animation, game design, robotics, digital arts and programming for all ability levels.
Academics Web page design, computer programming, computers.
Arts Animation, creative writing, digital media, drawing, graphic arts, photography.
Special Interest Areas Computer game design, computer graphics, robotics, team building, whale watching.
Sports Frisbee golf, ultimate frisbee.
Program Information 2–9 sessions per year. Session length: 5–30 days in June, July, August. Ages: 7–18. 30–150 participants per session. Day program cost: $589–$799. Boarding program cost: $909–$1059. Financial aid available.
Application Deadline Continuous.
Jobs Positions for high school students 15 and older and college students.
Contact Cybercamps Information Office, 2401 4th Avenue, Suite 1110, Seattle, Washington 98121. Phone: 206-442-4500. Fax: 206-442-4501. E-mail: info@cybercamps.com.
URL www.cybercamps.com

CYBERCAMPS–MERRIMACK COLLEGE

Cybercamps–Giant Campus, Inc.
North Andover, Massachusetts

General Information Coed residential and day academic program.
Academics Web page design, computer programming, computers.
Arts Animation, creative writing, digital media, graphic arts, photography.
Special Interest Areas Computer game design, computer graphics, robotics, team building.
Sports Ultimate frisbee.
Program Information 2–9 sessions per year. Session length: 5–30 days in June, July, August. Ages: 7–18. 30–150 participants per session. Day program cost: \$599–\$849. Boarding program cost: \$974–\$1224. Financial aid available.
Application Deadline Continuous.
Jobs Positions for high school students 15 and older and college students.
Contact Cybercamps Information Office, 2401 4th Avenue, Suite 1110, Seattle, Washington 98121. Phone: 206-442-4500. Fax: 206-442-4501. E-mail: info@cybercamps.com.
URL www.cybercamps.com

CYBERCAMPS–MIT

Cybercamps–Giant Campus, Inc.
Cambridge, Massachusetts

General Information Coed day academic program.
Academics Web page design, computer programming, computers.
Arts Animation, creative writing, digital media, graphic arts, photography.
Special Interest Areas Computer game design, computer graphics, robotics, team building.
Sports Ultimate frisbee.
Program Information 2–9 sessions per year. Session length: 4–5 days in June, July, August. Ages: 7–18. 30–180 participants per session. Day program cost: \$599–\$849. Financial aid available.
Application Deadline Continuous.
Jobs Positions for high school students 15 and older and college students.
Contact Cybercamps Information office, 2401 4th Avenue, Suite 1110, Seattle, Washington 98121. Phone: 206-442-4500. Fax: 206-442-4501. E-mail: info@cybercamps.com.
URL www.cybercamps.com

EAGLEBROOK SUMMER SEMESTER

Eaglebrook School
Deerfield, Massachusetts 01342

General Information Coed residential academic program established in 1996. Formal opportunities for the academically talented.
Academics American literature, English as a second language, English language/literature, French language/literature, Latin language, Spanish language/literature, academics (general), computers, environmental science, history, journalism, mathematics, reading, science (general), study skills, typing, writing.
Arts Arts and crafts (general), ceramics, creative writing, drawing, film, music, painting, photography, pottery, printmaking, sculpture, television/video, theater/drama, woodworking.
Special Interest Areas Field trips (arts and culture), leadership training.
Sports Baseball, basketball, bicycling, canoeing, field hockey, fishing, golf, lacrosse, scuba diving, soccer, softball, sports (general), squash, swimming, tennis, volleyball, water polo.
Wilderness/Outdoors Canoe trips, hiking, orienteering, wilderness camping.
Trips Cultural, day.
Program Information 1 session per year. Session length: 4 weeks in July. Ages: 11–13. 50–60 participants per session. Boarding program cost: \$4500–\$4550. Application fee: \$25–\$50. Financial aid available.
Application Deadline Continuous.
Jobs Positions for college students 19 and older.
Contact Mr. Karl J. Koenigsbauer, Director, main address above. Phone: 413-774-7411. Fax: 413-772-2394.
URL www.eaglebrook.org

Special Note
Eaglebrook's campus is located on 640 wooded acres in western Massachusetts on a hillside that overlooks the village of historic Deerfield. The program offers opportunities for classes in English and math. The Summer Semester relies on the same resources that have already earned Eaglebrook a reputation for excellence: the beauty of its natural setting, family life in dorms and dining room, the excellence of its faculty members, and the variety of classes. The Summer Semester is a four-week boarding adventure for boys and girls ages 11–13. The program is designed to build confidence through achievement and to foster leadership skills in the classroom, on the playing field, and within the school community. Children from every ethnic, racial, economic, and geographic background are welcome. Working and playing together, they discover inner strengths while they expand their knowledge, develop artistic talents, gain physical coordination and strength, and make friends in a multicultural community that encourages shared common interests and respect for differences.

EAGLE HILL SCHOOL SUMMER SESSION

Eagle Hill School
242 Old Petersham Road
Hardwick, Massachusetts 01037

General Information Coed residential and day academic program established in 1967. Specific services available for the learning disabled and participant with ADD.
Program Focus Academic course work, social skills building, camp activities.

Eagle Hill School Summer Session

Academics English language/literature, academics (general), computers, history, mathematics, philosophy, psychology, reading, science (general), social studies, study skills, writing.
Arts Arts and crafts (general), ceramics, creative writing, drawing, graphic arts, painting, photography, pottery, printmaking, sculpture, theater/drama, weaving, woodworking.
Special Interest Areas Culinary arts, field trips (arts and culture), gardening, leadership training, model rocketry.
Sports Aerobics, basketball, bicycling, climbing (wall), equestrian sports, fishing, golf, horseback riding, ropes course, soccer, softball, sports (general), swimming, tennis, volleyball, weight training.
Wilderness/Outdoors Backpacking, bicycle trips, canoe trips, hiking, mountain biking, rafting, whitewater trips, wilderness camping.
Trips Cultural, day, overnight, shopping.
Program Information 1 session per year. Session length: 40 days in July, August. Ages: 9–19. 60–70 participants per session. Day program cost: $5950. Boarding program cost: $5950. Application fee: $35.
Application Deadline Continuous.
Jobs Positions for college students.
Contact Ms. Erin E. Wynne, Director of Admission, PO Box 116, 242 Old Petersham Road, Hardwick, Massachusetts 01037. Phone: 413-477-6000. Fax: 413-477-6837. E-mail: admission@ehs1.org.
URL www.ehs1.org

Special Note
Eagle Hill School runs a six-week summer program for students with learning differences, ages 9 to 19, who have been diagnosed with specific learning disabilities and/or attention deficit disorder. The summer program is primarily designed to remediate academic and social deficits while maintaining progress achieved during the school year. Arts and sports-based electives are combined with academic courses to address the needs of the whole person in a camplike atmosphere. This structured and individualized environment gives bright students the opportunity to flourish. Evening clubs and weekend trips round out the program's offerings and provide for a fun-filled summer.

Emagination Computer Camps–Massachusetts

Emagination Computer Camps
Bentley College
Waltham, Massachusetts

General Information Coed residential and day academic program established in 1982. Accredited by American Camping Association. Formal opportunities for the academically talented.

Emagination Computer Camps–Massachusetts

Program Focus Computer science, technology, and art, swimming, tennis, and basketball clinics; Web design; computer music, video, photo, 3-D animation.
Academics Computer programming, computer science (Advanced Placement), computers, technology.
Arts Graphic arts.
Special Interest Areas ADL skills, Internet accessibility, computer graphics, electronics, field trips (arts and culture), model rocketry, robotics.
Sports Basketball, soccer, swimming, tennis.
Trips Day.
Program Information 4 sessions per year. Session length: 10–56 days in June, July, August. Ages: 8–17. 150–250 participants per session. Day program cost: $1195–$5830. Boarding program cost: $1995–$7830.
Application Deadline Continuous.
Jobs Positions for college students 18 and older.

Emagination Computer Camps–Massachusetts (continued)

Contact Ms. Kathi Rigg, Director, 110 Winn Street, Suite 207, Woburn, Massachusetts 01801. Phone: 888-226-6733. Fax: 781-933-0749. E-mail: camp@computercamps.com.
URL www.computercamps.com
For more information, see page 1106.

Excel at Amherst College and Williams College

Putney Student Travel
Amherst College
Amherst, Massachusetts 01002

General Information Coed residential academic program and arts program established in 1951. Formal opportunities for the academically talented and artistically talented. Specific services available for the learning disabled.

Excel at Amherst College and Williams College

Program Focus EXCEL is an innovative precollege program emphasizing small classes and creative interaction among students and faculty. Excursions available to sites of interest in the Northeast and Canada.
Academics American literature, English as a second language, English language/literature, French language/literature, SAT/ACT preparation, Spanish language/literature, academics (general), anthropology, archaeology, architecture, area studies, art history/appreciation, astronomy, biology, business, college tours, communications, computers, ecology, economics, environmental science, geology/earth science, government and politics, history, humanities, intercultural studies, journalism, mathematics, music, philosophy, physics, physiology, precollege program, psychology, science (general), social science, social studies, speech/debate, study skills, writing.
Arts Arts, arts and crafts (general), batiking, creative writing, dance, dance (jazz), dance (modern), drawing, fabric arts, film, jewelry making, music, music (ensemble), music (instrumental), music (vocal), musical productions, painting, photography, puppetry, sculpture, television/video, theater/drama.
Special Interest Areas Career exploration, community service, field research/expeditions, nature study.
Sports Aerobics, baseball, basketball, bicycling, canoeing, climbing (wall), cross-country, fishing, football, golf, in-line skating, lacrosse, rappelling, sea kayaking, soccer, softball, sports (general), squash, swimming, tennis, volleyball, weight training.
Wilderness/Outdoors Bicycle trips, canoe trips, caving, hiking, mountain biking, rafting, rock climbing, white-water trips.
Trips College tours, cultural, day, overnight.
Program Information 3 sessions per year. Session length: 21–45 days in June, July, August. Ages: 15–18. 90–150 participants per session. Boarding program cost: $4000–$5000. Financial aid available.
Application Deadline Continuous.
Jobs Positions for college students 20 and older.
Contact Tim Weed, Director, 345 Hickory Ridge Road, Putney, Vermont 05346. Phone: 802-387-5000. Fax: 802-387-4276. E-mail: excel@goputney.com.
URL www.goputney.com
For more information, see page 1114.

Exploration Intermediate Program at Wellesley College

Exploration School, Inc.
Wellesley College
Wellesley, Massachusetts 02481-8268

General Information Coed residential and day academic program established in 1983. Formal opportunities for the academically talented and artistically talented. Specific services available for the hearing impaired, learning disabled, physically challenged, and visually impaired.

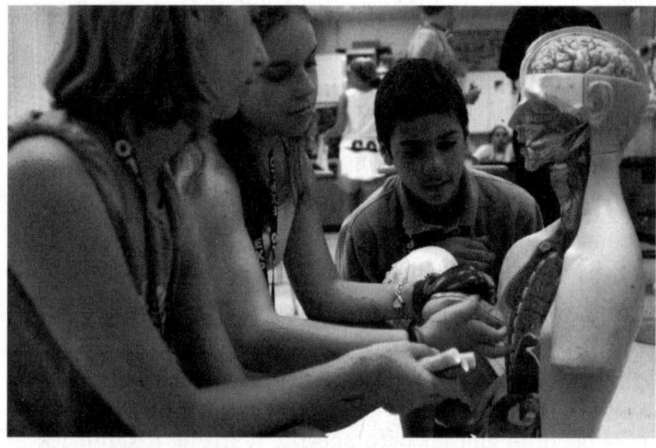

Exploration Intermediate Program at Wellesley College

Program Focus Academic enrichment.
Academics American literature, English as a second language, English language/literature, academics (general), aerospace science, archaeology, architecture, art history/appreciation, astronomy, biology, botany, business, chemistry, communications, ecology, economics, engineering, environmental science, geography, geology/earth science, government and politics, health sciences, history, humanities, journalism, marine studies,

mathematics, meteorology, music, peace education, philosophy, physics, physiology, psychology, reading, religion, science (general), social science, social studies, speech/debate, writing.
Arts Arts and crafts (general), batiking, chorus, clowning, creative writing, dance, dance (ballet), dance (folk), dance (jazz), dance (modern), dance (tap), drawing, fabric arts, film, graphic arts, jewelry making, mime, music, music (classical), music (ensemble), music (instrumental), music (jazz), music (vocal), musical productions, painting, printmaking, puppetry, sculpture, television/video, theater/drama, weaving, woodworking.
Special Interest Areas Career exploration, community service, culinary arts, leadership training, model rocketry, nature study.
Sports Aerobics, baseball, basketball, bicycling, boating, canoeing, cross-country, field hockey, football, golf, lacrosse, martial arts, racquetball, ropes course, sailing, scuba diving, snorkeling, soccer, softball, squash, street/roller hockey, swimming, tennis, track and field, volleyball, water polo.
Wilderness/Outdoors Hiking, orienteering, rock climbing, survival training, wilderness camping.
Trips Cultural, day, overnight.
Program Information 2 sessions per year. Session length: 3 weeks in June, July, August. Ages: 13–14. 550–650 participants per session. Day program cost: $1675–$3095. Boarding program cost: $3450–$6295. Financial aid available.
Application Deadline Continuous.
Jobs Positions for college students 19 and older.
Summer Contact Mary-Ann Sullivan, Head of Program, Wellesley College, 106 Central Street, Wellesley, Massachusetts 02481. Phone: 781-283-3781.
Winter Contact Barbara Targum, Admissions Coordinator, PO Box 368, 470 Washington Street, Norwood, Massachusetts 02062. Phone: 781-762-7400. Fax: 781-762-7425. E-mail: summer@explo.org.
URL www.explo.org
For more information, see page 1118.

EXPLORATION JUNIOR PROGRAM AT ST. MARK'S SCHOOL

Exploration School, Inc.
St. Mark's School
Southborough, Massachusetts 01772

General Information Coed residential and day academic program established in 1994. Formal opportunities for the academically talented and artistically talented. Specific services available for the hearing impaired, learning disabled, physically challenged, and visually impaired.
Program Focus Academic enrichment.
Academics English as a second language, academics (general), aerospace science, anthropology, archaeology, architecture, art history/appreciation, astronomy, biology, botany, business, chemistry, computer programming, computers, ecology, economics, engineering, environmental science, geography, geology/earth science, government and politics, health sciences, history, humanities, journalism, marine studies, mathematics, meteorology,

Exploration Junior Program at St. Mark's School

music, philosophy, physics, physiology, psychology, science (general), social science, social studies, speech/debate, writing.
Arts Arts and crafts (general), band, batiking, ceramics, clowning, creative writing, dance, dance (folk), dance (jazz), dance (modern), dance (tap), drawing, fabric arts, film, graphic arts, jewelry making, music, music (chamber), music (ensemble), music (instrumental), music (jazz), music (vocal), musical productions, painting, photography, pottery, printmaking, puppetry, sculpture, television/video, theater/drama, woodworking.
Special Interest Areas Campcraft, construction, culinary arts, electronics, model rocketry, nature study, robotics.
Sports Aerobics, archery, baseball, basketball, bicycling, canoeing, field hockey, football, golf, in-line skating, lacrosse, martial arts, soccer, softball, street/roller hockey, swimming, tennis, track and field, volleyball, water polo.
Wilderness/Outdoors Canoe trips, hiking, orienteering, survival training.
Trips Cultural, day.
Program Information 2 sessions per year. Session length: 3 weeks in June, July, August. Ages: 9–12. 440 participants per session. Day program cost: $1625–$2995. Boarding program cost: $3350–$6395. Financial aid available.
Application Deadline Continuous.
Jobs Positions for college students 19 and older.
Summer Contact David Torcoletti, Head of Program, Exploration, St. Mark's School, 25 Marlborough Road, Southborough, Massachusetts 01772. Phone: 508-786-1350. Fax: 508-786-1360.
Winter Contact Barbara Targum, Admissions Coordinator, PO Box 368, 470 Washington Street, Norwood, Massachusetts 02062. Phone: 781-762-7400. Fax: 781-762-7425. E-mail: summer@explo.org.
URL www.explo.org
For more information, see page 1120.

Fay School Day Camp

Fay School
48 Main Street
Southborough, Massachusetts 01772

General Information Coed day traditional camp established in 1988.
Program Focus Traditional camp activities and Red Cross swim lessons.
Arts Arts and crafts (general), ceramics, drawing, graphic arts, jewelry making, painting, pottery.
Special Interest Areas Leadership training, nature study.
Sports Archery, basketball, climbing (wall), golf, ropes course, soccer, swimming, tennis.
Program Information 4 sessions per year. Session length: 10 days in June, July, August. Ages: 4–12. 210–250 participants per session. Day program cost: $800. Application fee: $40. 10% discount for campers attending all sessions.
Application Deadline Continuous.
Jobs Positions for high school students 14 and older and college students 18 and older.
Contact Stephen Cariello, Daycamp Director, PO Box 9106, Southborough, Massachusetts 01772. Phone: 508-485-0100 Ext.210. Fax: 508-481-7872. E-mail: scariello@fayschool.org.
URL www.fayschool.org

Fay Summer School

Fay School
48 Main Street
Southborough, Massachusetts 01772

General Information Coed residential and day academic program established in 1988. Specific services available for the learning disabled.
Program Focus Enrichment or remediation classes for students seeking to advance or strengthen their skill base.
Academics English as a second language, English language/literature, Spanish language/literature, academics (general), communications, computers, ecology, history, mathematics, music, reading, science (general), study skills, writing.
Arts Arts and crafts (general), creative writing, painting, printmaking, television/video, theater/drama.
Sports Archery, basketball, climbing (wall), soccer, swimming, tennis.
Wilderness/Outdoors Hiking.
Trips Cultural, day, shopping.
Program Information 3 sessions per year. Session length: 6 weeks in June, July, August. Ages: 6–15. 85–100 participants per session. Day program cost: $350. Boarding program cost: $6050. Application fee: $40. Cost: $250 per class if attended in conjunction with Fay School Day Camp.
Application Deadline Continuous.
Jobs Positions for college students 18 and older.
Contact George Noble, Director of Athletics and Special Programs, PO Box 9106, Southborough, Massachusetts 01772. Phone: 508-485-0100 Ext.220. Fax: 508-481-7872. E-mail: gnoble@fayschool.org.
URL www.fayschool.org

Fenn School Summer Day Camp

The Fenn School
516 Monument Street
Concord, Massachusetts 01742-1894

General Information Coed day traditional camp and outdoor program established in 1999. Accredited by American Camping Association.
Program Focus Summer fun and learning.
Academics American literature, Spanish language/literature, academics (general), computer programming, computers, ecology, environmental science, geology/earth science, history, journalism, mathematics, music, reading, science (general), writing.
Arts Acting, arts, arts and crafts (general), ceramics, creative writing, drawing, film, jewelry making, music, musical productions, painting, photography, pottery, television/video, theater/drama, woodworking.
Special Interest Areas Campcraft, community service, leadership training, nature study.
Sports Baseball, basketball, bicycling, canoeing, climbing (wall), rappelling, ropes course, soccer, softball, swimming, volleyball.
Wilderness/Outdoors Bicycle trips, canoe trips, hiking, mountain biking, orienteering, outdoor adventure, rock climbing, white-water trips.
Trips Cultural, day, overnight.
Program Information 8 sessions per year. Session length: 5–10 days in June, July, August. Ages: 6–15. 200–250 participants per session. Day program cost: $250–$495. Financial aid available.
Application Deadline Continuous.
Jobs Positions for high school students 18 and older and college students 18 and older.
Contact Mr. David A. Platt, Director of Summer Programs, main address above. Phone: 978-318-3614. Fax: 978-318-3683. E-mail: summercamp@fenn.org.
URL www.summerfenn.org

The Fessenden School Summer ESL Program

The Fessenden School
250 Waltham Street
West Newton, Massachusetts 02465

General Information Coed residential academic program, outdoor program, and cultural program established in 1992. Formal opportunities for the academically talented.
Program Focus English as a Second Language instruction.
Academics English as a second language, computers, history, intercultural studies, reading, science (general), study skills, writing.
Arts Arts and crafts (general), creative writing, photography, television/video, theater/drama.
Special Interest Areas Field trips (arts and culture), touring.
Sports Baseball, basketball, canoeing, soccer, softball, swimming, tennis, volleyball.
Wilderness/Outdoors Hiking, wilderness camping.
Trips Cultural, day, overnight, shopping.

The Fessenden School Summer ESL Program

Program Information 1 session per year. Session length: 5 weeks in June, July. Ages: 10–15. 35–42 participants per session. Boarding program cost: $5725. Application fee: $75.
Application Deadline Continuous.
Jobs Positions for college students 17 and older.
Contact Mr. Mark Hansen, Director, main address above. Phone: 617-630-2300. Fax: 617-928-8888. E-mail: esl@fessenden.org.
URL www.fessenden.org
For more information, see page 1124.

FRONTIERS PROGRAM

Worcester Polytechnic Institute
100 Institute Road
Worcester, Massachusetts 01609-2280

General Information Coed residential academic program established in 1982.
Program Focus Science, math, technology and engineering.
Academics Web page design, aerospace science, biology, computer programming, computers, engineering, mathematics, music, physics, precollege program, science (general), speech/debate, writing.
Arts Acting, band, creative writing, music, music (instrumental), music (jazz), music (orchestral), theater/drama.
Special Interest Areas Robotics.
Sports Bowling, volleyball.
Trips Day, shopping.
Program Information 1 session per year. Session length: 13 days in July. Ages: 16–18. 120–130 participants per session. Boarding program cost: $1900. Application fee: $50. Open to participants entering grades 11–12.
Contact Julie Chapman, Frontiers Program/Assistant Director of Admissions, Student Affairs Office, 100 Institute Road, Worcester, Massachusetts 01609-2280. Phone: 508-831-5286. Fax: 508-831-5875. E-mail: frontiers@wpi.edu.
URL www.wpi.edu/+frontiers
For more information, see page 1404.

Frontiers Program

GEMS: GIRLS IN ENGINEERING, MATH AND SCIENCE

Worcester Polytechnic Institute
100 Institute Road
Worcester, Massachusetts 01609

General Information Girls' residential academic program established in 2002. Formal opportunities for the academically talented.
Program Focus Engineering, science and math.
Academics Biology, chemistry, computers, engineering, mathematics, science (general).
Trips College tours, day.
Program Information 1 session per year. Session length: 1 week in July. Ages: 14–17. 50–60 participants per session. Boarding program cost: $250. Financial aid available.
Application Deadline April 30.

Gems: Girls in Engineering, Math and Science (continued)

Contact Dr. Stephanie Blaisdell, Director, Diversity and Women's Programs, main address above. Phone: 508-831-5819. Fax: 508-831-5818. E-mail: diversity@wpi.edu.
URL www.wpi.edu/+ODAWP

Genesis at Brandeis University

415 South Street, MS 085
Waltham, Massachusetts 02454-9110

General Information Coed residential academic program, community service program, and bible camp established in 1997. Religious affiliation: Jewish.
Program Focus Integration of arts, humanities, Jewish studies, community service.
Academics Bible study, Jewish studies, academics (general), area studies, communications, government and politics, history, humanities, journalism, music, religion, social science, writing.
Arts Acting, arts and crafts (general), chorus, creative writing, dance (folk), drawing, graphic arts, mime, music, painting, sculpture, television/video, theater/drama.
Special Interest Areas Community service, culinary arts, field trips (arts and culture), leadership training, team building.
Sports Sports (general).
Trips Day.
Program Information 1 session per year. Session length: 4 weeks in July, August. Ages: 15–17. 70–80 participants per session. Boarding program cost: $4250. Application fee: $40. Financial aid available. Application deadline for need-based aid: March 1; open to participants entering grades 11–12.
Application Deadline Continuous.
Contact Bradley Solmsen, Director, Genesis at Brandeis University, PO Box 549110, MS 085, Waltham, Massachusetts 02454-9110. Phone: 781-736-8416. Fax: 781-736-8122. E-mail: genesis@brandeis.edu.
URL www.brandeis.edu/genesis

Special Note

Students come to Brandeis for a life-changing summer. Genesis at Brandeis University is designed to make connections between intellectual, political, and artistic interests and the richness of the Jewish tradition. Participants take intensive courses fully integrating the arts, humanities, Jewish studies, and social action and enroll in hands-on, multimedia workshops. Field trips within the Boston area, distinguished speakers and artists, community service projects, and seminars make the learning experiences relevant to today's world. Steven Spielberg's Righteous Persons Foundation helped launch this outstanding program and continues to support it.

Great Escapes (Adventure Trips for Teens)–Cape Cod Sail Adventure

South Shore YMCA Camps
75 Stowe Road
Sandwich, Massachusetts 02563

General Information Coed travel outdoor program established in 1989. Religious affiliation: Christian. Accredited by American Camping Association.
Program Focus Small boat sailing, windsurfing, watersports.
Sports Boating, sailing, windsurfing.
Program Information 1 session per year. Session length: 13 days in August. Ages: 13–16. Cost: $1195. Financial aid available.
Application Deadline Continuous.
Jobs Positions for college students 21 and older.
Contact Joseph O'Keefe, Great Escapes Director, main address above. Phone: 508-528-2571 Ext.110. Fax: 508-420-3545. E-mail: joeokeefe@ssymca.org.
URL www.ssymca.org/camps/great_escapes.asp

Great Escapes (Adventure Trips for Teens)–Cape Cod Underwater Adventure

South Shore YMCA Camps
75 Stowe Road
Sandwich, Massachusetts 02563

General Information Coed travel outdoor program established in 1989. Religious affiliation: Christian. Accredited by American Camping Association.
Program Focus SCUBA course, snorkeling, open-water certification.
Special Interest Areas Nature study, whale watching.
Sports Climbing (wall), ropes course, scuba diving, snorkeling, swimming.
Wilderness/Outdoors Outdoor adventure.
Program Information 1 session per year. Session length: 13 days in June, July. Ages: 13–16. 10–12 participants per session. Cost: $995. Financial aid available.
Application Deadline Continuous.
Jobs Positions for college students 21 and older.
Contact Joseph O'Keefe, Great Escapes Director, main address above. Phone: 508-428-2571 Ext.110. Fax: 508-420-3545. E-mail: joeokeefe@ssymca.org.
URL www.ssymca.org/camps/great_escapes.asp

Great Escapes (Adventure Trips for Teens)–Cape Escapes

South Shore YMCA Camps
75 Stowe Road
Sandwich, Massachusetts 02563

General Information Coed travel outdoor program and adventure program established in 1989. Religious affiliation: Christian. Accredited by American Camping Association.
Program Focus Bicycle touring, group travel.
Special Interest Areas Touring.

Sports Bicycling.
Wilderness/Outdoors Bicycle trips, outdoor adventure.
Program Information 3 sessions per year. Session length: 13 days in June, July, August. Ages: 13–16. 10–12 participants per session. Cost: $995. Financial aid available.
Application Deadline Continuous.
Jobs Positions for college students 21 and older.
Contact Joseph O'Keefe, Great Escapes Director, main address above. Phone: 508-428-2571 Ext.110. Fax: 508-420-3545. E-mail: joeokeefe@ssymca.org.
URL www.ssymca.org/camps/great_escapes.asp

Harvard University Summer School: Secondary School Program

Harvard University
51 Brattle Street
Cambridge, Massachusetts 02138

General Information Coed residential and day academic program established in 1975. Formal opportunities for the academically talented. Specific services available for the hearing impaired, learning disabled, physically challenged, and visually impaired. College credit may be earned.

Harvard University Summer School: Secondary School Program

Academics American literature, Chinese languages/literature, English language/literature, French language/literature, German language/literature, Greek language/literature, Hebrew language, Italian language/literature, Japanese language/literature, Latin language, Russian language/literature, Spanish language/literature, academics (general), anthropology, archaeology, art history/appreciation, astronomy, biology, botany, chemistry, classical languages/literatures, college tours, computer programming, computers, economics, government and politics, health sciences, history, journalism, linguistics, marine studies, mathematics, music, philosophy, physics, precollege program, psychology, religion, science (general), social science, study skills, writing.
Arts Band, chorus, creative writing, film, graphic arts, music, music (classical), music (ensemble), music (instrumental), music (orchestral), music (vocal), painting, photography, theater/drama.
Special Interest Areas Community service, touring.
Sports Aerobics, basketball, rowing (crew/sculling), soccer, softball, squash, swimming, tennis, volleyball, weight training.
Trips College tours, cultural, day, shopping.
Program Information 1 session per year. Session length: 8 weeks in June, July, August. 1,000–1,100 participants per session. Day program cost: $1950–$3900. Boarding program cost: $7275–$7385. Application fee: $50. Financial aid available. Participants need to be at least sophomore level.
Application Deadline Continuous.
Contact Mr. William Holinger, Director of Secondary School Programs, main address above. Phone: 617-495-3192. Fax: 617-495-9176. E-mail: ssp@hudce.harvard.edu.
URL www.ssp.harvard.edu
For more information, see page 1146.

Horizons for Youth

Horizons for Youth, Inc.
121 Lakeview Street
Sharon, Massachusetts 02067

General Information Coed residential traditional camp established in 1938. Accredited by American Camping Association. Specific services available for the emotionally challenged, developmentally challenged, learning disabled, and youth at risk.
Program Focus "At risk" youth.
Academics Environmental science.
Arts Acting, arts and crafts (general), batiking, dance, dance (modern), drawing, jewelry making, painting, theater/drama.
Special Interest Areas Community service, gardening, leadership training, nature study.
Sports Baseball, basketball, canoeing, football, ropes course, soccer, softball, swimming, tennis, volleyball.
Wilderness/Outdoors Hiking.
Trips College tours, day.
Program Information 3 sessions per year. Session length: 8–12 days in July, August. Ages: 7–17. 150–160 participants per session. Boarding program cost: $97–$960. Application fee: $20–$45. Financial aid available. Sliding fee scale.

Horizons for Youth (continued)
Application Deadline Continuous.
Jobs Positions for college students 18 and older.
Contact Rebecca O. Lopez, Camp Director, main address above. Phone: 781-828-7550. Fax: 781-784-1287. E-mail: camp@hfy.org.
URL www.hfy.org

iD Tech Camps–Emerson College, Boston, MA

iD Tech Camps
Emerson College
Boston, Massachusetts 02116

General Information Coed residential and day academic program. Accredited by American Camping Association. Formal opportunities for the academically talented and artistically talented.
Program Focus High-tech computer camps for kids and teens; produce digital movies, create video games, design Web pages, learn programming and robotics, and more; one computer per student, small classes, campers complete a project in a creative and fun learning environment.
Academics Web page design, computer programming, computer science (Advanced Placement), computers, music, precollege program.
Arts Animation, cinematography, digital media, drawing, film, film editing, film production, graphic arts, music, television/video.
Special Interest Areas Career exploration, computer graphics, electronics, leadership training, robotics, team building.
Sports Baseball, basketball, soccer, softball, swimming, volleyball.
Trips College tours, cultural, day.
Program Information 5 sessions per year. Session length: 5–7 days in June, July, August. Ages: 7–17. 40–50 participants per session. Day program cost: $639. Boarding program cost: $989. Application fee: $200. Financial aid available.
Application Deadline Continuous.
Jobs Positions for college students 18 and older.
Contact Client Service Representatives, 1885 Winchester Boulevard, Suite 201, Campbell, California 95008. Phone: 888-709-TECH. Fax: 408-871-2228. E-mail: requests@internaldrive.com.
URL www.internaldrive.com

For more information, see page 1156.

iD Tech Camps–Merrimack College, North Andover, MA

iD Tech Camps
Merrimack College
North Andover, Massachusetts 01845

General Information Coed residential and day academic program. Accredited by American Camping Association. Formal opportunities for the academically talented and artistically talented.
Program Focus High-tech computer camps for kids and teens; produce digital movies, create video games, design Web pages, learn programming and robotics, and more; one computer per student, small classes, campers complete a project in a creative and fun learning environment.
Academics Web page design, computer programming, computer science (Advanced Placement), computers, music, precollege program.
Arts Animation, cinematography, digital media, drawing, film, film editing, film production, graphic arts, music, television/video.
Special Interest Areas Career exploration, computer graphics, electronics, leadership training, robotics, team building.
Sports Baseball, basketball, soccer, softball, swimming, volleyball.
Trips College tours, cultural, day.
Program Information 5 sessions per year. Session length: 5–7 days in June, July, August. Ages: 7–17. 40–50 participants per session. Day program cost: $639. Boarding program cost: $989. Application fee: $200. Financial aid available.
Application Deadline Continuous.
Jobs Positions for college students 18 and older.
Contact Client Service Representatives, 1885 Winchester Boulevard, Suite 201, Campbell, California 95008. Phone: 888-709-TECH. Fax: 408-871-2228. E-mail: requests@internaldrive.com.
URL www.internaldrive.com

For more information, see page 1156.

iD Tech Camps–MIT, Cambridge, MA

iD Tech Camps
Massachusetts Institute of Technology
Cambridge, Massachusetts 02139

General Information Coed residential and day academic program established in 1999. Accredited by American Camping Association. Formal opportunities for the academically talented and artistically talented.
Program Focus High-tech computer camps for kids and teens; produce digital movies, create video games, design Web pages, learn programming and robotics, and more; one computer per student, small classes, campers complete a project in a creative and fun learning environment.
Academics Web page design, computer programming, computer science (Advanced Placement), computers, music, precollege program.
Arts Animation, cartooning, cinematography, digital media, drawing, film, film editing, film production, graphic arts, music, television/video.
Special Interest Areas Career exploration, computer graphics, electronics, leadership training, robotics, team building.
Sports Baseball, basketball, soccer, softball, swimming, volleyball.
Trips College tours, cultural, day.
Program Information 5 sessions per year. Session length: 5–7 days in June, July, August. Ages: 7–17. 40–50 participants per session. Day program cost: $639. Boarding program cost: $989. Application fee: $200. Financial aid available.
Application Deadline Continuous.
Jobs Positions for college students 18 and older.

Contact Client Service Representatives, 1885 Winchester Boulevard, Suite 201, Campbell, California 95008. Phone: 888-709-TECH. Fax: 408-871-2228. E-mail: requests@internaldrive.com.
URL www.internaldrive.com

For more information, see page 1156.

iD Tech Camps–Smith College, Northampton, MA

iD Tech Camps
Smith College
Northampton, Massachusetts 01063

General Information Coed residential and day academic program established in 1999. Accredited by American Camping Association. Formal opportunities for the academically talented and artistically talented.
Program Focus High-tech computer camps for kids and teens; produce digital movies, create video games, design Web pages, learn programming and robotics, and more; one computer per student, small classes, campers complete a project in a creative and fun learning environment.
Academics Web page design, computer programming, computer science (Advanced Placement), computers, music, precollege program.
Arts Animation, cartooning, cinematography, digital media, drawing, film, film editing, film production, graphic arts, music, television/video.
Special Interest Areas Career exploration, computer graphics, electronics, leadership training, robotics, team building.
Sports Baseball, basketball, soccer, softball, swimming, volleyball.
Trips College tours, cultural, day.
Program Information 5 sessions per year. Session length: 5–7 days in June, July, August. Ages: 7–17. 40–50 participants per session. Day program cost: $639. Boarding program cost: $989. Application fee: $200. Financial aid available.
Application Deadline Continuous.
Jobs Positions for college students 18 and older.
Contact Client Service Representatives, 1885 Winchester Boulevard, Suite 201, Campbell, California 95008. Phone: 888-709-TECH. Fax: 408-871-2228. E-mail: requests@internaldrive.com.
URL www.internaldrive.com

For more information, see page 1156.

Kroka Expeditions–Cape Cod Triple Surfing Bonanza

Kroka Expeditions of Vermont
Cape Cod, Massachusetts

General Information Coed residential outdoor program and wilderness program established in 1996. Specific services available for the learning disabled and physically challenged.
Program Focus Beginner to advanced level water sports.
Academics Ecology, environmental science, geography, geology/earth science, marine studies.
Special Interest Areas Community service, field research/expeditions, leadership training, nature study, nautical skills.
Sports Bicycling, boating, kayaking, sea kayaking, surfing, swimming, windsurfing.
Wilderness/Outdoors Backpacking, bicycle trips, hiking, mountain biking, orienteering, wilderness camping.
Trips Day, overnight.
Program Information 1 session per year. Session length: 10 days in June. Ages: 13–18. 10 participants per session. Boarding program cost: $1300. Financial aid available.
Application Deadline Continuous.
Jobs Positions for college students 18 and older.
Contact Misha Golfman, Executive Director, 659 West Hill Road, Putney, Vermont 05346. Phone: 802-387-5397. Fax: 802-387-4536. E-mail: kroka@sover.net.
URL www.kroka.org

Landmark School Summer Academic Program

Landmark School
Prides Crossing, Massachusetts 01965-0227

General Information Coed residential and day academic program and special needs program established in 1971. Specific services available for the learning disabled. High school credit may be earned.

Landmark School Summer Academic Program

Program Focus Academic remediation for students with language-based learning disabilities or dyslexia.
Academics English language/literature, marine studies, mathematics, reading, remedial academics, study skills, writing.
Arts Arts and crafts (general).
Sports Baseball, basketball, bicycling, boating, canoeing, fishing, ropes course, sailing, soccer, softball, swimming, tennis, volleyball.
Wilderness/Outdoors Backpacking, hiking.
Trips Day, overnight.
Program Information 1 session per year. Session length: 6 weeks in July, August. Ages: 7–20. 170

Landmark School Summer Academic Program (continued)

participants per session. Day program cost: $3600–$5500. Boarding program cost: $7200–$7600. Application fee: $100.
Application Deadline Continuous.
Contact Director of Admission, PO Box 227, Prides Crossing, Massachusetts 01965-0227. Phone: 978-236-3000. Fax: 978-927-7268. E-mail: jtruslow@landmarkschool.org.
URL www.landmarkschool.org
For more information, see page 1180.

Landmark Volunteers: Massachusetts

Landmark Volunteers, Inc.
Massachusetts

General Information Coed residential outdoor program and community service program established in 1992. High school credit may be earned.

Landmark Volunteers: Massachusetts

Program Focus Opportunity for high school students to earn community service credit while working as a team for two weeks serving Boston Symphony at Tanglewood, Chesterwood, Gould Farm, Norman Rockwell Museum, Plimoth Plantation, Schenob Brook/Bartholomew's Cobble, Shakespeare & Company/Arrowhead, or Ventfort Hall. Similar programs offered through Landmark Volunteers at over 60 locations in 21 states.
Academics Area studies, biology, botany, college tours, ecology, environmental science, history, music, science (general), social science, social services.
Arts Music (orchestral), theater/drama.
Special Interest Areas Animal care, career exploration, community service, conservation projects, farming, field research/expeditions, gardening, leadership training, nature study, team building, work camp programs.
Sports Swimming.
Wilderness/Outdoors Hiking.
Trips Cultural, day.
Program Information 8 sessions per year. Session length: 2 weeks in June, July, August. Ages: 14–18. 10–13 participants per session. Boarding program cost: $875–$925. Financial aid available.
Application Deadline Continuous.
Jobs Positions for college students.
Contact Ann Barrett, Executive Director, PO Box 455, Sheffield, Massachusetts 01257. Phone: 413-229-0255. Fax: 413-229-2050. E-mail: landmark@volunteers.com.
URL www.volunteers.com
For more information, see page 1182.

Leadership Adventure in Boston

Pine Manor College
Center for Inclusive Leadership and Social Responsibility
400 Heath Street
Chestnut Hill, Massachusetts 02467

General Information Girls' residential traditional camp, outdoor program, and community service program established in 1995.

Leadership Adventure in Boston

Program Focus Leadership activities, self-esteem building, community service.
Academics English as a second language.
Arts Arts and crafts (general), creative writing, dance, drawing, fabric arts, jewelry making, music (vocal), painting, photography, television/video.
Special Interest Areas Career exploration, community service, leadership training, team building.
Sports Basketball, canoeing, ropes course, soccer, softball, swimming, tennis, volleyball, weight training.
Wilderness/Outdoors Canoe trips, hiking, wilderness camping.
Trips College tours, cultural, day, overnight, shopping.
Program Information 1 session per year. Session length: 1–2 weeks in July. Ages: 11–14. 25–35 participants per session. Boarding program cost: $550–$1000. Financial aid available.
Application Deadline Continuous.

Contact Ms. Whitney Retallic, Program Director, main address above. Phone: 617-731-7620. Fax: 617-731-7185.
URL www.pmc.edu/ILSR/adventure/camp.html
For more information, see page 1188.

Linden Hill Summer Program

Linden Hill School
154 South Mountain Road
Northfield, Massachusetts 01360-9681

General Information Coed residential traditional camp, academic program, and special needs program established in 1998. Specific services available for the learning disabled. High school credit may be earned.

Linden Hill Summer Program

Program Focus Program offers additional academic support for dyslexia or language-based learning differences.
Academics English as a second language, English language/literature, academics (general), computers, environmental science, journalism, mathematics, music, reading, science (general), study skills, writing.
Arts Acting, arts and crafts (general), creative writing, dance, music, photography, pottery, sculpture, theater/drama, woodworking.
Special Interest Areas Animal care, culinary arts, field trips (arts and culture), leadership training, touring.
Sports Aerobics, archery, basketball, bicycling, climbing (wall), equestrian sports, fishing, golf, horseback riding, in-line skating, ropes course, soccer, softball, swimming, tennis, volleyball.
Wilderness/Outdoors Backpacking, bicycle trips, canoe trips, hiking, mountain biking, orienteering, white-water trips.
Trips Cultural, day, overnight.
Program Information 1 session per year. Session length: 31 days in July, August. Ages: 7–16. 50–60 participants per session. Boarding program cost: $4750. Application fee: $50. Financial aid available.
Application Deadline Continuous.
Jobs Positions for college students 19 and older.
Contact James A. McDaniel, Headmaster and Summer Program Director, main address above. Phone: 413-498-2906. Fax: 413-498-2908. E-mail: admissions@lindenhs.org.
URL www.lindenhs.org
For more information, see page 1198.

Massachusetts College of Art/ Creative Vacation

Massachusetts College of Art
621 Huntington Avenue
Boston, Massachusetts 02115

General Information Coed day arts program established in 1994.
Academics Art (Advanced Placement), art history/appreciation.
Arts Animation, arts, ceramics, drawing, film, graphic arts, painting, photography, pottery, printmaking, sculpture.
Special Interest Areas Career exploration.
Trips Cultural.
Program Information 1 session per year. Session length: 10 days in July. Ages: 9–16. 100–120 participants per session. Day program cost: $525–$1050. Financial aid available. Scholarship deadline is May 7.
Application Deadline May 21.
Jobs Positions for college students.
Contact Nell Agayan, Program Administrative Assistant, main address above. Phone: 617-879-7170. Fax: 617-879-7171. E-mail: nagayan@massart.edu.
URL www.massart.edu/

Massachusetts College of Art/ Summer Studios

Massachusetts College of Art
621 Huntington Avenue
Boston, Massachusetts 02115

General Information Coed residential and day arts program established in 1990. Formal opportunities for the artistically talented.
Academics Art (Advanced Placement), art history/appreciation.
Arts Animation, arts, ceramics, design, drawing, fashion design/production, film, graphic arts, jewelry making, metalworking, painting, photography, pottery, printmaking, sculpture.
Special Interest Areas Career exploration, computer graphics.
Trips College tours, cultural.
Program Information 1 session per year. Session length: 26 days in July, August. Ages: 15–17. 100–110 participants per session. Day program cost: $1890. Boarding program cost: $4015. Financial aid available. Scholarship deadline is June 3.
Application Deadline June 4.
Jobs Positions for college students 19 and older.

Massachusetts College of Art/Summer Studios (continued)

Massachusetts College of Art / Summer Studios

Contact Nell Agayan, Program Administrative Assistant, main address above. Phone: 617-879-7170. Fax: 617-879-7171. E-mail: nagayan@massart.edu.
URL www.massart.edu
For more information, see page 1206.

MIT MITE²S (Minority Introduction to Engineering, Entrepreneurship and Science)

Massachusetts Institute of Technology
77 Massachusetts Avenue, Room 1-123
Cambridge, Massachusetts 02139

General Information Coed residential academic program established in 1975. Formal opportunities for the academically talented and gifted.
Program Focus Science, engineering, and entrepreneurship.
Academics Business, chemistry, computer programming, economics, engineering, humanities, mathematics, physics, precollege program, science (general), study skills, writing.
Special Interest Areas Career exploration, robotics.
Sports Basketball, climbing (wall), racquetball, soccer, swimming, tennis, volleyball, weight training.
Trips College tours, cultural, day.
Program Information 1 session per year. Session length: 6 weeks in June, July, August. Ages: 16–17. 60–80 participants per session. No cost for program.
Application Deadline February 7.
Jobs Positions for college students 19 and older.
Contact Karl W. Reid, Executive Director, Engineering Special Programs, main address above. Phone: 617-253-3298. Fax: 617-253-8549. E-mail: kwreid@mit.edu.
URL mit.edu/mites/www

Special Note
Now in its 29th year, the MIT MITE²S Program offers a rigorous 6-week residential, academic enrichment summer experience to promising rising high school seniors, many of whom are from racial and ethnic groups underrepresented in the fields of engineering and science. The goal of the program is to prepare gifted young men and women for careers in engineering, high-tech entrepreneurship, and science by reinforcing the value and reward of pursuing advanced technical degrees, the academic preparation and skills necessary to achieve success in these disciplines, and the national importance of increasing the representation of minorities pursuing higher education and careers in science and engineering. MITE²S gives selected students the opportunity to experience MIT's demanding academic atmosphere and helps them to build the self-confidence necessary for success. The MITE²S Program is supported by corporations, foundations, individuals, and a grant from the federal government. With additional support from MIT, the program provides each admitted student with full coverage of living and educational expenses.

Mountain Workshop–Bike 1: Martha's Vineyard and Nantucket

Mountain Workshop
Massachusetts

General Information Coed travel outdoor program and adventure program established in 1991.
Program Focus Biking 8-35 miles per day.
Special Interest Areas Touring.
Sports Bicycling, swimming.
Wilderness/Outdoors Bicycle trips.
Trips Cultural, overnight.
Program Information 2–3 sessions per year. Session length: 1 week in July, August. Ages: 11–12. Cost: $1100.
Application Deadline Continuous.
Jobs Positions for college students 21 and older.
Contact Kent B. Tullo, Director, 9 Brookside Place, West Redding, Connecticut 06896. Phone: 203-544-0555. Fax: 203-544-0333. E-mail: info@mountainworkshop.com.
URL www.mountainworkshop.com

Mountain Workshop–Bike 2

Mountain Workshop
Massachusetts

General Information Coed travel outdoor program and adventure program established in 1991.
Program Focus For advanced beginner and intermediate rider.
Special Interest Areas Nature study, touring, whale watching.
Sports Bicycling, kayaking, swimming.
Wilderness/Outdoors Bicycle trips.
Trips Overnight.
Program Information 4 sessions per year. Session length: 7–10 days in June, July, August. Ages: 12–13. Cost: $1100.
Application Deadline Continuous.
Jobs Positions for college students 21 and older.
Contact Kent B. Tullo, Director, 9 Brookside Place, West Redding, Connecticut 06896. Phone: 203-544-0555. Fax: 203-544-0333. E-mail: info@mountainworkshop.com.
URL www.mountainworkshop.com

Mount Holyoke College SEARCH (Summer Explorations and Research Collaborations for High School Girls) Program

Mount Holyoke College
50 College Street
South Hadley, Massachusetts 01075-1441

General Information Girls' residential and day academic program established in 2004. Formal opportunities for the academically talented.
Program Focus Mathematics, collaborative research.
Academics Computers, mathematics.
Arts Arts and crafts (general).
Special Interest Areas Career exploration, college planning.
Sports Basketball, racquetball, swimming, tennis, volleyball, weight training.
Wilderness/Outdoors Hiking.
Trips College tours, cultural, day.
Program Information 1 session per year. Session length: 4 weeks in July. Ages: 15–18. 12–16 participants per session. Day program cost: $2900. Boarding program cost: $3600. Application fee: $25. Financial aid available.
Application Deadline Continuous.
Jobs Positions for college students 19 and older.
Contact Dr. James Morrow, Director, SEARCH, main address above. Phone: 413-538-2608. Fax: 413-538-2002. E-mail: search@mtholyoke.edu.
URL www.mtholyoke.edu/proj/search

Mount Holyoke College SummerMath Program

Mount Holyoke College
50 College Street
South Hadley, Massachusetts 01075-1441

General Information Girls' residential and day academic program established in 1982.

Mount Holyoke College SummerMath Program

Program Focus Mathematics, computer programming, applied workshops.
Academics Architecture, biology, computer programming, computers, economics, engineering, mathematics, social science.
Arts Arts and crafts (general).
Special Interest Areas Career exploration, college planning, robotics.
Sports Basketball, racquetball, swimming, tennis, volleyball, weight training.
Wilderness/Outdoors Hiking.
Trips College tours, cultural, day.
Program Information 1 session per year. Session length: 4 weeks in July. Ages: 13–18. 50–70 participants per session. Day program cost: $3100. Boarding program cost: $3900. Application fee: $25. Financial aid available.
Application Deadline Continuous.
Jobs Positions for college students 19 and older.
Contact Dr. Charlene Morrow, Director, main address above. Phone: 413-538-2608. Fax: 413-538-2002. E-mail: summermath@mtholyoke.edu.
URL www.mtholyoke.edu/proj/summermath
For more information, see page 1212.

The National Music Workshop Day Jams–Boston, MA

National Guitar Workshop
Milton Academy
170 Centre Street
Milton, Massachusetts 02186

General Information Coed day arts program established in 2001. Formal opportunities for the artistically talented.
Program Focus Rock 'n' roll day camp.
Academics Music.
Arts Arts and crafts (general), band, guitar, music, music (rock), music (vocal), television/video.
Program Information 3 sessions per year. Session length: 5–15 days in July. Ages: 9–15. 40–70 participants per session. Day program cost: $425–$495. Application fee: $35. Financial aid available.
Application Deadline Continuous.
Jobs Positions for high school students 17 and older and college students 17 and older.
Contact Lynda Wlodarczyk, Associate Director, 407A Bantam Road, Suite 1, Litchfield, Connecticut 06759. Phone: 800-295-5956. Fax: 860-567-0374. E-mail: lynda@dayjams.com.
URL www.dayjams.com

Newman School Summer Session

The Newman School
247 Marlborough Street
Boston, Massachusetts 02116

General Information Coed day academic program. High school credit may be earned.
Academics English as a second language, English language/literature, French language/literature, Spanish language/literature, biology, chemistry, computers, history, mathematics, study skills, writing.
Program Information 1–3 sessions per year. Session length: 45 days in June, July, August. Ages: 13–19. Day program cost: $850.
Contact Ms. Karen Briggs, Director of Admissions, main address above. Phone: 617-267-4530. Fax: 617-267-7070. E-mail: kbriggs@newmanboston.org.
URL www.newmanboston.org

The New York Film Academy, Harvard University, Cambridge, MA

New York Film Academy
Cambridge, Massachusetts

General Information Coed residential arts program established in 1992. College credit may be earned.
Program Focus "Total immersion" hands-on filmmaking workshop where students write, direct, shoot, and edit their own short 16mm films.
Arts Acting, creative writing, directing, film, film editing, film lighting, film production, screenwriting, sound design, television/video, theater/drama.
Trips Cultural.
Program Information 2–4 sessions per year. Session length: 4–6 weeks in June, July, August. Ages: 14–17. Boarding program cost: $1500–$6900.
Application Deadline Continuous.
Contact Admissions, 100 East 17th Street, New York, New York 10003. Phone: 212-674-4300. Fax: 212-477-1414. E-mail: film@nyfa.com.
URL www.nyfa.com
For more information, see page 1218.

Northfield Mount Hermon Summer Session

Northfield Mount Hermon School
206 Main Street
Northfield, Massachusetts 01360-1089

General Information Coed residential and day academic program established in 1961. Formal opportunities for the academically talented. High school credit may be earned.

Northfield Mount Hermon Summer Session

Academics American literature, English as a second language, English language/literature, SAT/ACT preparation, Spanish language/literature, academics (general), biology, chemistry, history, humanities, journalism, mathematics, music, philosophy, precollege program, reading, science (general), speech/debate, study skills, writing.
Arts Creative writing, dance, dance (jazz), dance (modern), drawing, music (instrumental), painting, photography, printmaking, television/video, theater/drama.
Special Interest Areas Community service.
Sports Basketball, bicycling, soccer, swimming, tennis, volleyball, weight training.
Trips College tours, cultural, day, shopping.
Program Information 1 session per year. Session length: 5 weeks in July, August. Ages: 12–19. 300 participants per session. Day program cost: $2600–$2800. Boarding program cost: $4700–$5000. Application fee: $50–$100. Financial aid available. Apply for financial aid by April 1.
Application Deadline Continuous.

Jobs Positions for college students 21 and older.
Contact Debra J. Frank, Dean of Admission, NMH Summer Session, main address above. Phone: 413-498-3290. Fax: 413-498-3112. E-mail: summer_school@nmhschool.org.
URL www.nmhschool.org/summer
For more information, see page 1222.

Offense-Defense Golf Camp, Massachusetts

The Winchendon School and Golf Facility
Winchendon, Massachusetts 01475

General Information Coed residential and day sports camp established in 1992.
Program Focus Golf.
Academics English as a second language, SAT/ACT preparation.
Sports Basketball, golf, soccer, softball, swimming, tennis, weight training.
Trips Day.
Program Information 3 sessions per year. Session length: 1 week in July. Ages: 10–18. 88 participants per session. Day program cost: $495. Boarding program cost: $940.
Application Deadline Continuous.
Jobs Positions for college students 19 and older.
Contact Mr. Mike Meshken, Director, PO Box 6, Easton, Connecticut 06612. Phone: 203-256-9844. Fax: 203-255-5666. E-mail: golfcamp@localnet.com.
URL www.offensedefensegolf.com

Offense-Defense Tennis Camp

Stonehill College
Easton, Massachusetts 02357

General Information Coed residential and day sports camp established in 1970.
Program Focus Tennis.
Academics English as a second language.
Special Interest Areas Talent show.
Sports Basketball, soccer, tennis, volleyball, weight training.
Trips Cultural, day, shopping.
Program Information 5–6 sessions per year. Session length: 1 week in June, July, August. Ages: 9–18. 40–75 participants per session. Day program cost: $500. Boarding program cost: $840.
Application Deadline Continuous.
Jobs Positions for college students 19 and older.
Contact Mr. Mehdi Belhassan, Director, PO Box 48018, Tampa, Florida 33647. Phone: 813-972-0101. Fax: 813-972-0128. E-mail: mbtennis@aol.com.
URL www.offensedefensetennis.com

Outward Bound–Connecting with Courage

Thompson Island Outward Bound/Outward Bound, USA
Thompson Island
Boston, Massachusetts 02127-0002

General Information Girls' residential outdoor program and wilderness program established in 1988.
Program Focus This program inspires girls to be strong, confident, and courageous.
Special Interest Areas Campcraft, community service, field research/expeditions, leadership training, nature study, nautical skills, team building.
Sports Canoeing, climbing (wall), kayaking, rappelling, ropes course, sailing, sea kayaking, swimming.
Wilderness/Outdoors Backpacking, canoe trips, hiking, mountaineering, orienteering, outdoor adventure, rock climbing, wilderness camping.
Trips Overnight.
Program Information 8 sessions per year. Session length: 10–14 days in June, July, August. Ages: 12–13. 8–12 participants per session. Boarding program cost: $1450–$1860. Application fee: $100. Financial aid available.
Application Deadline Continuous.
Jobs Positions for college students 18 and older.
Contact Mr. Jon Hislop, Director of Admissions, Thompson Island, PO Box 127, Boston, Massachusetts 02127-0002. Phone: 617-328-3900 Ext.142. Fax: 617-328-3710. E-mail: admissions@thompsonisland.org.
URL www.thompsonisland.org

Outward Bound–Environmental Expeditions

Thompson Island Outward Bound/Outward Bound, USA
Thompson Island
Boston, Massachusetts 02127

General Information Coed residential academic program, outdoor program, and wilderness program established in 1988.
Program Focus Marine science and sailing.
Academics Biology, ecology, environmental science, marine studies.
Special Interest Areas Campcraft, community service, field research/expeditions, leadership training, nature study, nautical skills.
Sports Boating, climbing (wall), rappelling, ropes course, sailing, swimming.
Wilderness/Outdoors Orienteering, outdoor adventure, rock climbing, wilderness camping.
Trips Overnight.
Program Information 3 sessions per year. Session length: 2 weeks in June, July, August. Ages: 14–17. 8–12 participants per session. Boarding program cost: $1880. Application fee: $150. Financial aid available.
Application Deadline Continuous.
Jobs Positions for college students 18 and older.
Contact Mr. Jon Hislop, Director of Admissions, Thompson Island, PO Box 127, Boston, Massachusetts 02127. Phone: 617-328-3900 Ext.144. Fax: 617-328-3710. E-mail: admissions@thompsonisland.org.
URL www.thompsonisland.org

Outward Bound–Passages

Thompson Island Outward Bound/Outward Bound, USA
Thompson Island
Boston, Massachusetts 02127-0002

General Information Boys' residential outdoor program and wilderness program established in 1988.
Program Focus This program inspires boys to become leaders by helping them develop both physical and emotional strength, and compassion.
Special Interest Areas Campcraft, field research/ expeditions, leadership training, nautical skills.
Sports Climbing (wall), kayaking, rappelling, ropes course, sailing, sea kayaking.
Wilderness/Outdoors Backpacking, canoe trips, hiking, mountaineering, orienteering, outdoor adventure, rock climbing, wilderness camping.
Trips Overnight.
Program Information 11 sessions per year. Session length: 10–14 days in June, July, August. Ages: 12–13. 8–12 participants per session. Boarding program cost: $1450–$1850. Application fee: $100. Financial aid available.
Application Deadline Continuous.
Jobs Positions for college students 18 and older.
Contact Mr. Jon Hislop, Director of Admissions, PO Box 127, Boston, Massachusetts 02127. Phone: 617-328-3900 Ext.144. Fax: 617-328-3710. E-mail: admissions@ thompsonisland.org.
URL www.thompsonisland.org

Overland: Adventure Camp for 5th and 6th Grade Boys

Overland Travel, Inc.
Williamstown, Massachusetts 01267

General Information Boys' residential outdoor program and adventure program established in 1985. Accredited by American Camping Association.
Program Focus Introductory outdoor adventure program.
Special Interest Areas Campcraft, conservation projects, leadership training, team building.
Sports Bicycling, bicycling (BMX).
Wilderness/Outdoors Backpacking, bicycle trips, hiking, mountain biking, wilderness camping.
Trips Day, overnight.
Program Information 6 sessions per year. Session length: 1 week in June, July, August. Ages: 10–12. 8–12 participants per session. Boarding program cost: $895.
Application Deadline Continuous.
Jobs Positions for college students 20 and older.
Contact Ms. Brooks Follansbee, Director, PO Box 31, Williamstown, Massachusetts 01267. Phone: 800-458-0588. Fax: 413-458-5208. E-mail: overland@adelphia.net.
URL www.overlandsummers.com

For more information, see page 1240.

Overland: Adventure Camp for 5th and 6th Grade Girls

Overland Travel, Inc.
Williamstown, Massachusetts 01267

General Information Girls' residential outdoor program and adventure program established in 1985. Accredited by American Camping Association.
Program Focus Introductory outdoor adventure program.
Special Interest Areas Campcraft, conservation projects, leadership training, team building.
Sports Bicycling.
Wilderness/Outdoors Backpacking, bicycle trips, hiking, mountain biking, wilderness camping.
Trips Day, overnight.
Program Information 6 sessions per year. Session length: 1 week in June, July, August. Ages: 10–12. 8–12 participants per session. Boarding program cost: $895.
Application Deadline Continuous.
Jobs Positions for college students 20 and older.
Contact Ms. Brooks Follansbee, Director, PO Box 31, Williamstown, Massachusetts 01267. Phone: 800-458-0588. Fax: 413-458-5208. E-mail: overland@adelphia.net.
URL www.overlandsummers.com

For more information, see page 1240.

Overland: Cape Cod and the Islands Bicycle Touring

Overland Travel, Inc.
Massachusetts

General Information Coed travel outdoor program and adventure program established in 1985. Accredited by American Camping Association. High school credit may be earned.
Program Focus Bicycle touring on Cape Cod, Nantucket, and Martha's Vineyard, leadership skills.
Special Interest Areas Leadership training, touring, whale watching.
Sports Bicycling.
Wilderness/Outdoors Bicycle trips, outdoor camping.
Program Information 10 sessions per year. Session length: 2 weeks in June, July, August. Ages: 13–16. 8–12 participants per session. Cost: $2495.
Application Deadline Continuous.
Jobs Positions for college students 20 and older.
Contact Ms. Brooks Follansbee, Director, PO Box 31, Williamstown, Massachusetts 01267. Phone: 800-458-0588. Fax: 413-458-5208. E-mail: overland@adelphia.net.
URL www.overlandsummers.com

For more information, see page 1240.

Phillips Academy Summer Session

Phillips Academy (Andover)
180 Main Street
Andover, Massachusetts 01810

General Information Coed residential and day academic program established in 1942. Formal opportunities for the academically talented and artistically talented.

Phillips Academy Summer Session

Program Focus Academic enrichment within a nurturing pre-college environment.
Academics American literature, Chinese languages/literature, English as a second language, English language/literature, French language/literature, Japanese language/literature, Latin language, SAT/ACT preparation, Spanish language/literature, academics (general), art (Advanced Placement), art history/appreciation, biology, chemistry, college tours, computer programming, computers, economics, government and politics, history, journalism, linguistics, marine studies, mathematics, music, philosophy, physics, physiology, precollege program, psychology, social science, speech/debate, writing.
Arts Acting, animation, ceramics, chorus, creative writing, dance, drawing, film, graphic arts, music (chamber), music (classical), music (instrumental), music (jazz), painting, photography, pottery, visual arts.
Special Interest Areas College planning.
Sports Aerobics, basketball, figure skating, physical fitness, power walking, running/jogging, soccer, softball, squash, swimming, tennis, ultimate frisbee, volleyball, weight training, yoga.
Trips College tours, cultural, day, shopping.
Program Information 1 session per year. Session length: 38 days in June, July, August. Ages: 13–18. 500–600 participants per session. Day program cost: $3500–$3900. Boarding program cost: $5000–$5400. Application fee: $50–$80. Financial aid available. Apply for financial aid by March 1.
Application Deadline Continuous.
Contact Ms. Maxine S. Grogan, Dean of Admission, Phillips Academy Summer Session, 180 Main Street, Andover, Massachusetts 01810. Phone: 978-749-4400. Fax: 978-749-4414. E-mail: summersession@andover.edu.
URL www.andover.edu/summersession

Special Note
The nation's oldest incorporated boarding school, situated 25 miles north of Boston, opens a 5-week summer session from the end of June through early August to students from all over the world. Students choose from more than 60 courses, including literature, languages, writing, natural sciences, computer science, mathematics, SAT prep, philosophy, social science, speech and debate, English as a second language, music, and the visual arts. Summer Session students represent an extraordinary diversity of geographic, religious, racial, and economic circumstances. They are students who have strong school records and a serious desire to spend the summer in challenging, disciplined study. With a student-faculty ratio of 7:1 and an average class size of 14, the Phillips Academy Summer Session provides a highly individualized and intensive precollege experience, including an extensive college counseling program, on a beautiful campus with excellent facilities.

For more information, see page 1260.

Ponkapoag Outdoor Center Day Camps

YMCA of Greater Boston–Camping Services Branch
Blue Hills Reservation
Canton, Massachusetts

General Information Coed day traditional camp and outdoor program established in 1985. Accredited by American Camping Association.
Arts Arts and crafts (general), creative writing, dance, dance (modern), drawing, painting.
Special Interest Areas Campcraft, community service, gardening, leadership training, work camp programs.
Sports Archery, baseball, basketball, fishing, ropes course, soccer, softball, street/roller hockey, swimming, volleyball.
Wilderness/Outdoors Hiking.
Program Information 1–6 sessions per year. Session length: 6–13 days in June, July, August. Ages: 6–15. 180–200 participants per session. Day program cost: $130–$320. Application fee: $50. Financial aid available.
Application Deadline Continuous.
Jobs Positions for high school students 16 and older and college students 18 and older.
Contact Jill Gary, Associate Executive Director, 316 Huntington Avenue, Boston, Massachusetts 02115-5019. Phone: 617-927-8220. Fax: 617-927-8156. E-mail: jgary@ymcaboston.org.
URL www.ymcacamp.net

Public Speaking Institute by Education Unlimited–Boston

Education Unlimited
Tufts University
Boston, Massachusetts

General Information Coed residential and day academic program established in 2004.
Program Focus Public speaking and leadership training.
Academics Communications, government and politics, speech/debate, writing.
Special Interest Areas Leadership training.
Sports Basketball, volleyball.

Public Speaking Institute by Education Unlimited–Boston (continued)

Trips Day.
Program Information 1 session per year. Session length: 10 days in July. Ages: 15–18. 20–40 participants per session. Boarding program cost: $1775. Financial aid available.
Application Deadline Continuous.
Contact Mr. Matthew Fraser, Executive Director, 1700 Shattuck Avenue, #305, Berkeley, California 94709. Phone: 510-548-6612. Fax: 510-548-0212. E-mail: camps@educationunlimited.com.
URL www.educationunlimited.com
For more information, see page 1100.

Research Internship in Science and Engineering

Boston University Summer Term
755 Commonwealth Avenue, Room 105
Boston, Massachusetts 02215

General Information Coed residential academic program established in 1979. Formal opportunities for the academically talented.
Program Focus Science and engineering lab work and research.
Academics Aerospace science, astronomy, biology, chemistry, computer science (Advanced Placement), computers, engineering, environmental science, medicine, physics, science (general).
Sports Basketball, boating, racquetball, rowing (crew/sculling), sailing, tennis, volleyball.
Trips Cultural, day, shopping.
Program Information 1 session per year. Session length: 6 weeks in July, August. Ages: 16–18. 25–30 participants per session. Boarding program cost: $4000–$4200. Financial aid available.
Application Deadline May 15.
Contact Mr. Daniel Welty, Physics Department, 590 Commonwealth Avenue, Boston, Massachusetts 02215. Phone: 617-353-1378. Fax: 617-353-5532. E-mail: welty@physics.bu.edu.
URL www.bu.edu/summer/highschool

Rowe Camp

Rowe Camp and Conference Center, Inc.
King's Highway Road
Rowe, Massachusetts 01367

General Information Coed residential traditional camp established in 1924. Religious affiliation: Unitarian Universalist.
Arts Arts and crafts (general), creative writing, dance, fabric arts, jewelry making, music.
Special Interest Areas Native American culture, community service, leadership training.
Sports Basketball, canoeing, climbing (wall), kayaking, rappelling, swimming.
Wilderness/Outdoors Backpacking, hiking, rock climbing, white-water trips, wilderness/outdoors (general).
Trips Day.
Program Information 5 sessions per year. Session length: 1–3 weeks in June, July, August. Ages: 9–19. 64–80 participants per session. Boarding program cost: $500–$1505. Financial aid available.
Application Deadline Continuous.
Jobs Positions for high school students 17 and older and college students 18 and older.
Contact Felicity Pickett, Director, PO Box 273, Rowe, Massachusetts 01367. Phone: 413-339-4954. Fax: 413-339-5728. E-mail: retreat@rowecenter.org.
URL www.rowecenter.org

Simon's Rock College of Bard Young Writers Workshop

Simon's Rock College of Bard
84 Alford Road
Great Barrington, Massachusetts 01230

General Information Coed residential academic program and arts program established in 1983. Formal opportunities for the academically talented and artistically talented.

Simon's Rock College of Bard Young Writers Workshop

Program Focus Creative writing and critical thinking.
Academics American literature, English language/literature, humanities, precollege program, reading, study skills, writing.
Arts Creative writing.
Sports Basketball, bicycling, climbing (wall), handball, racquetball, softball, squash, swimming, tennis, volleyball, weight training.
Wilderness/Outdoors Hiking.
Trips Cultural, day.
Program Information 1 session per year. Session length: 3 weeks in June, July. Ages: 14–18. 70–80 participants per session. Boarding program cost: $1925–$2100. Financial aid available.
Application Deadline Continuous.
Contact Dr. Jamie Hutchinson, Program Director, main address above. Phone: 413-528-7231. Fax: 413-528-7365. E-mail: jamieh@simons-rock.edu.
URL www.simons-rock.edu/young_writers/
For more information, see page 1312.

Smith College Summer Science and Engineering Program

Smith College
Clark Hall
Northampton, Massachusetts 01063

General Information Girls' residential academic program established in 1990. Formal opportunities for the academically talented.

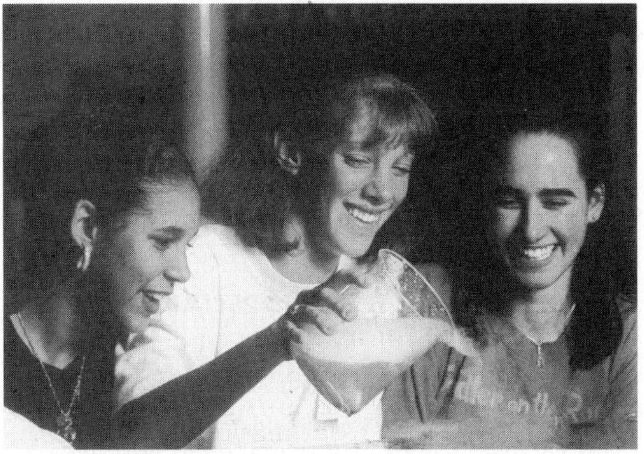

Smith College Summer Science and Engineering Program

Program Focus Hands-on research and science and engineering enrichment program for girls.
Academics Astronomy, biology, botany, chemistry, computer programming, computers, ecology, engineering, environmental science, geology/earth science, health sciences, mathematics, physics, psychology, science (general), writing.
Arts Arts and crafts (general), creative writing, dance, film, jewelry making, music, music (classical), music (jazz), theater/drama.
Special Interest Areas Career exploration, field research/expeditions, leadership training, robotics.
Sports Basketball, bicycling, soccer, softball, sports (general), squash, swimming, tennis, track and field, volleyball, weight training.
Trips College tours, cultural, day.
Program Information 1 session per year. Session length: 4 weeks in July. Ages: 13–18. 100–110 participants per session. Boarding program cost: $3950. Financial aid available.
Application Deadline Continuous.
Jobs Positions for college students 20 and older.
Contact Dr. Gail E. Scordilis, Director of Educational Outreach, main address above. Phone: 413-585-3060. Fax: 413-585-3068. E-mail: gscordil@smith.edu.
URL www.smith.edu/summerprograms/ssep/

For more information, see page 1318.

Snow Farm: The New England Craft Program

5 Clary Road
Williamsburg, Massachusetts 01096

General Information Coed residential arts program established in 1983. Formal opportunities for the artistically talented. High school credit may be earned.

Snow Farm: The New England Craft Program

Program Focus Visual arts.
Academics Art (Advanced Placement), art history/appreciation.
Arts Arts, arts and crafts (general), batiking, ceramics, design, digital media, drawing, fabric arts, figure study, glassblowing, jewelry making, metalworking, painting, photography, pottery, sculpture, silk screening, tie-dyeing, visual arts, wood sculpture.
Trips Cultural.
Program Information 2 sessions per year. Session length: 2–4 weeks in July, August. Ages: 14–18. 55–60 participants per session. Boarding program cost: $2450–$4750. Application fee: $80. Financial aid available.
Application Deadline Continuous.
Contact Mary Colwell, Director, main address above. Phone: 413-268-3101. Fax: 413-268-3163. E-mail: info@snowfarm-art.org.
URL www.snowfarm.org

For more information, see page 1320.

SoccerPlus FieldPlayer Academy–Easthampton, MA

SoccerPlus Camps
Williston Northampton School
Easthampton, Massachusetts

General Information Coed residential and day sports camp.
Program Focus Developing overall game skills in a competitive environment with quality goalkeepers.
Sports Soccer.
Program Information 1 session per year. Session length: 6 days in June. Ages: 11+. Day program cost: $595. Boarding program cost: $695. Financial aid available.

SoccerPlus FieldPlayer Academy–Easthampton, MA (continued)

Application Deadline Continuous.
Jobs Positions for college students.
Contact Mr. Shawn Kelly, General Manager, 11 Executive Drive, Suite 202, Farmington, Connecticut 06032. Phone: 800-533-7371. Fax: 860-677-0460. E-mail: info@soccerpluscamps.com.
URL www.soccerpluscamps.com

SoccerPlus Goalkeeper School–Challenge Program–Franklin, MA

SoccerPlus Camps
Dean College
Franklin, Massachusetts

General Information Coed residential and day sports camp.
Program Focus Developing technical and tactical goalkeeping skills.
Sports Soccer.
Program Information 1 session per year. Session length: 6 days in July. Ages: 10+. Day program cost: $595. Boarding program cost: $695. Financial aid available.
Application Deadline Continuous.
Jobs Positions for college students.
Contact Mr. Shawn Kelly, General Manager, 11 Executive Drive, Suite 202, Farmington, Connecticut 06032. Phone: 800-533-7371. Fax: 860-677-0460. E-mail: info@soccerpluscamps.com.
URL www.soccerpluscamps.com

SoccerPlus Goalkeeper School–Competitive Program–Easthampton, MA

SoccerPlus Camps
Williston Northampton School
Easthampton, Massachusetts

General Information Coed residential sports camp.
Program Focus Developing game skills in a competitive environment with quality field players.
Sports Soccer.
Program Information 1 session per year. Session length: 6 days in June. Ages: 12+. Boarding program cost: $755. Financial aid available.
Application Deadline Continuous.
Jobs Positions for college students.
Contact Mr. Shawn Kelly, General Manager, 11 Executive Drive, Suite 202, Farmington, Connecticut 06032. Phone: 800-533-7371. Fax: 860-677-0460. E-mail: info@soccerpluscamps.com.
URL www.soccerpluscamps.com

SoccerPlus Goalkeeper School–National Training Center–Franklin, MA

SoccerPlus Camps
Dean College
Franklin, Massachusetts

General Information Coed residential sports camp.
Program Focus Developing advanced goalkeeping skills.
Sports Soccer.
Program Information 1 session per year. Session length: 6 days in July. Ages: 15+. Boarding program cost: $775.
Application Deadline Continuous.
Jobs Positions for college students.
Contact Mr. Shawn Kelly, General Manager, 11 Executive Drive, Suite 202, Farmington, Connecticut 06032. Phone: 800-533-7371. Fax: 860-677-0460. E-mail: info@soccerpluscamps.com.
URL www.soccerpluscamps.com

South Shore YMCA Specialty Camp

South Shore YMCA Camps
75 Stowe Road
Sandwich, Massachusetts 02563

General Information Coed residential traditional camp, outdoor program, and special needs program established in 1960. Religious affiliation: Christian. Accredited by American Camping Association. Specific services available for the participant with Phenylketonuria.
Arts Arts and crafts (general), batiking, ceramics, drawing, jewelry making, music, music (instrumental), painting, pottery.
Sports Archery, basketball, boating, canoeing, climbing (wall), equestrian sports, horseback riding, in-line skating, rappelling, ropes course, sailing, soccer, swimming, tennis, volleyball, waterskiing, windsurfing.
Trips Day.
Program Information 1 session per year. Session length: 6 days in August. Ages: 7–15. 168 participants per session. Boarding program cost: $495. Financial aid available.
Application Deadline Continuous.
Jobs Positions for high school students 17 and older and college students 18 and older.
Contact Sacha Johnston, Camp Director, main address above. Phone: 508-428-2571. Fax: 508-420-3545. E-mail: camp@ssymca.org.
URL www.ssymca.org

Springfield College Allied Health Career Exploration Program

Springfield College
263 Alden Street
Springfield, Massachusetts 01108

General Information Coed residential academic program established in 1998.
Program Focus Exploration of careers in allied health.

Academics Health sciences, precollege program.
Special Interest Areas Career exploration.
Trips College tours, day.
Program Information 1 session per year. Session length: 4–5 days in July, August. Ages: 15–18. 50 participants per session. Boarding program cost: $475–$600. Application fee: $100.
Application Deadline Continuous.
Contact Gina Ricciardi, Administrative Secretary, Office of Special Programs, 263 Alden Street, Springfield, Massachusetts 01109. Phone: 413-748-5287. Fax: 413-748-3534. E-mail: gricciardi@spfldcol.edu.
URL www.springfieldcollege.edu

Springfield College Athletic Trainer Workshop

Springfield College
263 Alden Street
Springfield, Massachusetts 01108

General Information Coed residential academic program and sports camp established in 1990.
Program Focus Athletic training and sports medicine.
Academics Health sciences, precollege program.
Special Interest Areas Career exploration.
Sports Athletic training.
Trips Day.
Program Information 1 session per year. Session length: 4–5 days in July. Ages: 15–18. 50 participants per session. Boarding program cost: $525–$550. Application fee: $100.
Application Deadline Continuous.
Contact Gina Ricciardi, Administrative Secretary, Office of Special Programs, 263 Alden Street, Springfield, Massachusetts 01109. Phone: 413-748-5287. Fax: 413-748-3534. E-mail: gricciardi@spfldcol.edu.
URL www.springfieldcollege.edu

Springfield College Sports Management Career Exploration Program

Springfield College
263 Alden Street
Springfield, Massachusetts 01108

General Information Coed residential academic program established in 2000.
Academics Precollege program.
Special Interest Areas Career exploration.
Trips Day.
Program Information 1 session per year. Session length: 4–5 days in July, August. Ages: 15–18. 50 participants per session. Boarding program cost: $600–$675. Application fee: $100.
Application Deadline Continuous.
Contact Gina Ricciardi, Administrative Secretary, Office of Special Programs, 263 Alden Street, Springfield, Massachusetts 01109. Phone: 413-748-5287. Fax: 413-748-3534. E-mail: gricciardi@spfldcol.edu.
URL www.springfieldcollege.edu

Springfield Technical Community College–College for Kids

Springfield Technical Community College
1 Armory Square
Springfield, Massachusetts 01105

General Information Coed day traditional camp and academic program established in 1983. Formal opportunities for the academically talented and artistically talented.
Academics French language/literature, Spanish language/literature, astronomy, biology, business, classical languages/literatures, computer programming, computers, environmental science, mathematics, music, science (general), typing, writing.
Arts Creative writing, drawing, music, painting, photography, printmaking, sculpture, theater/drama.
Special Interest Areas Electronics.
Sports Horseback riding, martial arts, soccer.
Program Information 2 sessions per year. Session length: 2 weeks in July, August. Ages: 7–17. 200 participants per session. Day program cost: $100–$300. Financial aid available.
Application Deadline Continuous.
Contact Mary Breeding, Director, main address above. Phone: 413-755-4501. Fax: 413-755-6319. E-mail: breeding@stcc.edu.
URL cbt.stcc.edu

Stoneleigh–Burnham School: Camp $tart-Up

Stoneleigh–Burnham School
574 Bernardston Road
Greenfield, Massachusetts 01301

General Information Girls' residential academic program. Formal opportunities for the academically talented.
Program Focus Developing skills in business development, enterprise, and leadership.
Academics Business.
Special Interest Areas Career exploration, college planning, leadership training, team building.
Program Information 1 session per year. Session length: 6 days in August. Ages: 13–18. 30 participants per session. Boarding program cost: $550. Financial aid available.
Application Deadline June 1.
Jobs Positions for college students 18 and older.
Contact Joyce Muka, Camp $tartup Director, main address above. Phone: 413-774-2711. Fax: 413-772-2602. E-mail: summerprograms@sbschool.org.
URL www.sbschool.org

For more information, see page 1334.

Stoneleigh–Burnham School: Science Camp for Middle School Girls

Stoneleigh–Burnham School
574 Bernardston Road
Greenfield, Massachusetts 01301

General Information Girls' day academic program.

Stoneleigh–Burnham School: Science Camp for Middle School Girls (continued)

Program Focus "Hands-on, minds-on" experience in a variety of scientific disciplines.
Academics Biology, chemistry, environmental science, geology/earth science, mathematics, physics, science (general).
Special Interest Areas Model rocketry, team building.
Program Information 1 session per year. Session length: 5 days in July. Ages: 12–14. Day program cost: $175. Financial aid available.
Application Deadline Continuous.
Jobs Positions for college students 18 and older.
Contact Dr. Paul C. Bassett, Camp Director, Science Camp. Phone: 413-774-2711. Fax: 413-772-2602. E-mail: summerprograms@sbschool.org.
URL www.sbschool.org
For more information, see page 1334.

Stoneleigh–Burnham School Softball Camp

Stoneleigh–Burnham School
574 Bernardston Road
Greenfield, Massachusetts 01301

General Information Girls' residential sports camp established in 1990.
Program Focus Improving softball skills as hitters, fielders and pitchers; windmill pitching component and catching component are included.
Sports Softball.
Program Information 1 session per year. Session length: 6 days in July. Ages: 12–16. 40–50 participants per session. Boarding program cost: $350. Financial aid available.
Application Deadline July 15.
Jobs Positions for high school students and college students 18 and older.
Contact Dr. Paul C. Bassett, Camp Director, main address above. Phone: 413-774-2711. Fax: 413-772-2602. E-mail: summerprograms@sbschool.org.
URL www.sbschool.org
For more information, see page 1334.

Stoneleigh–Burnham School Summer Dance Camp

Stoneleigh–Burnham School
574 Bernardston Road
Greenfield, Massachusetts 01301

General Information Coed residential arts program established in 1997. Formal opportunities for the artistically talented.
Program Focus Dance: ballet, modern, and jazz and a culminating performance.
Arts Dance, dance (ballet), dance (jazz), dance (modern).
Sports Swimming, tennis, weight training.
Trips Cultural, day.
Program Information 3 sessions per year. Session length: 1 week in June, July. Ages: 11–17. 20–24 participants per session. Boarding program cost: $575. Financial aid available.
Application Deadline Continuous.
Jobs Positions for high school students 17 and older and college students.
Contact Ms. Ann Sorvino, Director, main address above. Phone: 413-774-2711. Fax: 413-772-7602. E-mail: asorvino@sbschool.org.
URL www.sbschool.org
For more information, see page 1334.

Stoneleigh–Burnham School: Summer Debate and Public Speaking Camp

Stoneleigh–Burnham School
574 Bernardston Road
Greenfield, Massachusetts 01301

General Information Girls' residential academic program established in 1998.
Program Focus Debate and public speaking.
Academics Speech/debate.
Program Information 1 session per year. Session length: 5 days in July. Ages: 12–17. 20–40 participants per session. Boarding program cost: $295. Application fee: $100.
Jobs Positions for college students 18 and older.
Contact Dr. Paul C. Bassett, Camp Director, main address above. Phone: 413-774-2711. Fax: 413-772-2602. E-mail: summerprograms@sbschool.org.
URL www.sbschool.org
For more information, see page 1334.

STRIVE: Exploring Engineering, Math and Science

Worcester Polytechnic Institute
100 Institute Road
Worcester, Massachusetts 01609

General Information Coed residential academic program established in 2002. Formal opportunities for the academically talented.
Program Focus Engineering, math and science for minority students.
Academics Biology, chemistry, computers, engineering, mathematics, science (general).
Trips College tours, day.
Program Information 1 session per year. Session length: 1 week in July. Ages: 14–17. 40 participants per session. Boarding program cost: $250. Financial aid available.
Application Deadline April 30.
Contact Calvin R. Hill, Director, Minority Affairs, main address above. Phone: 508-831-5796. Fax: 508-831-5818. E-mail: mao@wpi.edu.
URL www.wpi.edu/+ODAWP

Student Conservation Association–Conservation Crew Program (Massachusetts)

Student Conservation Association (SCA)
Massachusetts

General Information Coed residential outdoor program, community service program, and wilderness program established in 1957. High school credit may be earned.
Program Focus Resource management, conservation and environmental education.
Academics Biology, botany, ecology, environmental science, geology/earth science, history.
Special Interest Areas Campcraft, community service, construction, leadership training, nature study, trail maintenance, work camp programs.
Sports Canoeing, fishing, kayaking, swimming.
Wilderness/Outdoors Backpacking, canoe trips, hiking, orienteering, outdoor living skills, wilderness camping.
Trips Cultural, day, overnight.
Program Information 2–3 sessions per year. Session length: 3–5 weeks in June, July, August. Ages: 15–19. 6–8 participants per session. Application fee: $20. Financial aid available. No cost for program; financial aid possible for travel expenses.
Application Deadline Continuous.
Jobs Positions for college students 21 and older.
Contact Recruitment Office, PO Box 550, Charlestown, New Hampshire 03603. Phone: 603-543-1700. Fax: 603-543-1828. E-mail: getreal@thesca.org.
URL www.theSCA.org

Study Tours and Dance/Theater Camp in the USA–Dean College

FLS International
Dean College
99 Main Street
Franklin, Massachusetts 02038

General Information Coed residential arts program established in 2002. Formal opportunities for the artistically talented.
Program Focus Dance or theater camp and English as a second language.
Academics English as a second language, English language/literature, intercultural studies.
Arts Dance, dance (ballet), dance (folk), dance (jazz), dance (modern), dance (tap), theater/drama.
Special Interest Areas Homestays.
Trips College tours, cultural, day, shopping.
Program Information 1–3 sessions per year. Session length: 20–27 days in June, July, August. Ages: 15+. 3–75 participants per session. Boarding program cost: $1695–$2700. Application fee: $100.
Application Deadline Continuous.
Contact Ms. Veronica Perez, Director of Admissions, 101 East Green Street #14, Pasadena, California 91105. Phone: 626-795-2912. Fax: 626-795-5564. E-mail: veronica@fls.net.
URL www.fls.net

For more information, see page 1128.

Study Tours in the USA–Dean College

FLS International
Dean College
99 Main Street
Franklin, Massachusetts 02038

General Information Coed residential academic program established in 1987. Formal opportunities for the academically talented.
Program Focus English as a second language.
Academics English as a second language, English language/literature, computers, intercultural studies, precollege program, speech/debate, study skills, writing.
Arts Creative writing, dance, dance (ballet), dance (folk), dance (jazz), dance (modern), dance (tap), theater/drama.
Special Interest Areas Career exploration, field trips (arts and culture), homestays.
Sports Basketball, swimming, tennis.
Wilderness/Outdoors Hiking.
Trips College tours, cultural, day, overnight, shopping.
Program Information 13 sessions per year. Session length: 14–20 days in January, February, March, April, May, June, July, August, September, October, November, December. Ages: 15+. 10–75 participants per session. Boarding program cost: $1495–$2295. Application fee: $100.
Application Deadline Continuous.
Contact Ms. Veronica Perez, Director of Admissions, 101 East Green Street #14, Pasadena, California 91105. Phone: 626-795-2912. Fax: 626-795-5564. E-mail: veronica@fls.net.
URL www.fls.net

For more information, see page 1128.

Summer Dance '05

The Boston Conservatory
Dance Division
8 The Fenway
Boston, Massachusetts 02215

General Information Coed residential and day arts program established in 1998. Formal opportunities for the artistically talented. Specific services available for the hearing impaired. College credit may be earned.
Program Focus Stimulate discourse on movement arts.
Academics Intercultural studies.
Arts Dance, dance (ballet), dance (modern), dance (tap), film.
Special Interest Areas Native American culture, field research/expeditions, touring.
Trips College tours, cultural, day.

Summer Dance '05 (continued)

Program Information 2 sessions per year. Session length: 3–6 weeks in June, July. Ages: 16+. 40–60 participants per session. Day program cost: $1440–$2865. Boarding program cost: $2630–$5730. Application fee: $60.
Application Deadline Continuous.
Jobs Positions for college students 18 and older.
Contact Mr. Toby Hanchett, Summer Programs Coordinator, main address above. Phone: 617-912-9166. Fax: 617-247-3159. E-mail: thanchett@bostonconservatory.edu.
URL www.bostonconservatory.edu

THE SUMMER INSTITUTE FOR THE GIFTED AT AMHERST COLLEGE

Summer Institute for the Gifted
Amherst College
Amherst, Massachusetts 01002

General Information Coed residential academic program established in 2000. Formal opportunities for the academically talented and gifted. Specific services available for the hearing impaired, learning disabled, physically challenged, and visually impaired. High school or college credit may be earned.
Academics American literature, English language/literature, French language/literature, Latin language, SAT/ACT preparation, Spanish language/literature, academics (general), aerospace science, archaeology, architecture, art (Advanced Placement), art history/appreciation, biology, business, chemistry, classical languages/literatures, communications, computer programming, computers, engineering, environmental science, government and politics, history, humanities, marine studies, mathematics, music, philosophy, physics, physiology, precollege program, psychology, science (general), social studies, speech/debate, study skills, writing.
Arts Arts and crafts (general), ceramics, chorus, creative writing, dance, dance (ballet), dance (jazz), dance (modern), drawing, graphic arts, mime, music, music (chamber), music (classical), music (ensemble), musical productions, painting, photography, puppetry, sculpture, theater/drama.
Special Interest Areas Electronics, model rocketry, robotics.
Sports Aerobics, archery, baseball, basketball, fencing, field hockey, football, lacrosse, martial arts, soccer, softball, squash, swimming, tennis, volleyball.
Wilderness/Outdoors Hiking.
Trips Cultural.
Program Information 1–2 sessions per year. Session length: 3 weeks in June, July, August. Ages: 8–17. 270–300 participants per session. Boarding program cost: $3350. Application fee: $75. Financial aid available.
Jobs Positions for college students 19 and older.
Contact Dr. Stephen Gessner, Director, River Plaza, 9 West Broad Street, Stamford, Connecticut 06902-3788. Phone: 866-303-4744. Fax: 203-399-5598. E-mail: sig.info@aifs.com.
URL www.giftedstudy.com
For more information, see page 1342.

SUMMER SUMMIT ON LEADERSHIP

Pine Manor College
Center for Inclusive Leadership and Social Responsibility
400 Heath Street
Chestnut Hill, Massachusetts 02467

General Information Girls' residential community service program and cultural program established in 2003.
Program Focus Leadership program.
Academics English as a second language.
Arts Arts and crafts (general), creative writing, fabric arts, jewelry making, painting, television/video.
Special Interest Areas Career exploration, college planning, community service, leadership training, team building.
Sports Basketball, soccer, softball, tennis, volleyball, weight training.
Wilderness/Outdoors Canoe trips.
Trips College tours, cultural, day, shopping.
Program Information 1 session per year. Session length: 6 days in June, July. Ages: 14–18. 20–30 participants per session. Boarding program cost: $500. Financial aid available.
Application Deadline Continuous.
Contact Whitney Retallic, Director of Youth and Student Programs, main address above. Phone: 617-731-7620. Fax: 617-731-7185. E-mail: retalliw@pmc.edu.
URL www.pmc.edu
For more information, see page 1188.

SUPERCAMP–HAMPSHIRE COLLEGE

SuperCamp
Hampshire College
Amherst, Massachusetts

General Information Coed residential academic program established in 1981. Accredited by American Camping Association. High school credit may be earned.
Program Focus Academic enrichment and personal development.
Academics SAT/ACT preparation, academics (general), communications, reading, study skills, writing.
Special Interest Areas Leadership training.
Sports Ropes course, soccer, swimming, volleyball.
Trips College tours.
Program Information 3–5 sessions per year. Session length: 8–10 days in July, August. Ages: 11–18. 80–125 participants per session. Boarding program cost: $1795–$2295. Application fee: $100. Financial aid available.
Application Deadline Continuous.
Jobs Positions for college students 18 and older.
Contact Enrollments Department, 1725 South Coast Highway, Oceanside, California 92054. Phone: 800-285-3276. Fax: 760-722-3507. E-mail: info@supercamp.com.
URL www.supercamp.com
For more information, see page 1348.

Tabor Academy Summer Program

Tabor Academy
66 Spring Street
Marion, Massachusetts 02738

General Information Coed residential and day traditional camp and academic program established in 1917.

Tabor Academy Summer Program

Academics English as a second language, English language/literature, French language/literature, Latin language, SAT/ACT preparation, Spanish language/literature, academics (general), biology, computers, marine studies, mathematics, oceanography, reading, science (general), study skills.
Arts Acting, arts and crafts (general), ceramics, creative writing, drawing, painting, photography, pottery, theater/drama.
Special Interest Areas Nautical skills.
Sports Baseball, basketball, field hockey, golf, lacrosse, sailing, soccer, softball, squash, swimming, tennis, volleyball.
Trips Cultural, day.
Program Information 2 sessions per year. Session length: 4–6 weeks in June, July, August. Ages: 9–15. 160 participants per session. Day program cost: $390–$2050. Boarding program cost: $4300–$5600.
Application Deadline Continuous.
Jobs Positions for high school students 16 and older and college students 18 and older.
Summer Contact William Hrasky, Director, main address above. Phone: 508-748-2000 Ext.2292. Fax: 508-291-8392. E-mail: summer@taboracademy.org.
Winter Contact Richard DaSilva, Jr., Program Director, main address above. Phone: 508-748-2000 Ext.2242. Fax: 508-291-8392. E-mail: summer@taboracademy.org.
URL www.taborsummer.org

For more information, see page 1352.

Tufts Summer Study

Tufts University
108 Packard Avenue
Medford, Massachusetts 02155-7049

General Information Coed day academic program established in 1984. Formal opportunities for the academically talented. College credit may be earned.
Program Focus College exploration, writing, health sciences/medical, ethics, liberal arts.
Academics American literature, English language/literature, French (Advanced Placement), French language/literature, German language/literature, Italian language/literature, Russian language/literature, SAT/ACT preparation, Spanish language/literature, academics (general), architecture, art history/appreciation, astronomy, biology, chemistry, computer programming, computer science (Advanced Placement), computers, economics, geology/earth science, government and politics, health sciences, history, humanities, mathematics, music, oceanography, philosophy, physics, precollege program, psychology, religion, social science, writing.
Sports Aerobics, basketball, racquetball, soccer, softball, squash, swimming, tennis, volleyball, weight training.
Program Information 1 session per year. Session length: 41 days in July, August. Ages: 16–18. 60–80 participants per session. Day program cost: $1360–$3120. Application fee: $25. Financial aid available.
Application Deadline June 1.
Jobs Positions for college students.
Contact Sean Recroft, Manager, Tufts University Summer Study, 108 Packard Avenue, Medford, Massachusetts 02155. Phone: 617-627-3454. Fax: 617-627-3295. E-mail: highschool@tufts.edu.
URL ase.tufts.edu/summer

Wilderness Experiences Unlimited–Explorers Camp

Wilderness Experiences Unlimited, Inc.
Lake Norwich
Huntington, Massachusetts 01050

General Information Coed residential outdoor program, wilderness program, and adventure program.
Special Interest Areas Campcraft, nature study.
Sports Boating, canoeing, climbing (wall), kayaking, scuba diving, snorkeling, swimming, water tubing.
Wilderness/Outdoors Backpacking, hiking, outdoor adventure, outdoor camping.
Trips Day, overnight.
Program Information 8 sessions per year. Session length: 5 days in July, August. Ages: 9–16. 10 participants per session. Boarding program cost: $425–$475.
Application Deadline Continuous.
Jobs Positions for college students 18 and older.
Contact Taylor Scott Cook, Executive Director, 499 Loomis Street, Westfield, Massachusetts 01085. Phone: 888-WEU-CAMP. Fax: 413-562-7431. E-mail: adventures@weu.com.
URL www.weu.com

Wilderness Experiences Unlimited–Leaders In Training Camp

Wilderness Experiences Unlimited, Inc.
Lake Norwich
Huntington, Massachusetts 01050

General Information Coed residential outdoor program, wilderness program, and adventure program established in 1981.
Special Interest Areas Native American culture, campcraft, counselor-in-training program, first aid, leadership training, nature study.
Sports Bicycling, canoeing, climbing (wall), diving, kayaking, rappelling, ropes course, scuba diving, sea kayaking, snorkeling, swimming.
Wilderness/Outdoors Backpacking, bicycle trips, canoe trips, caving, hiking, kayaking trips, mountain biking, orienteering, outdoor adventure, rafting, rock climbing, survival training, white-water trips, wilderness camping.
Trips Day, overnight.
Program Information 8 sessions per year. Session length: 5 days in July, August. Ages: 14–17. 40–50 participants per session. Boarding program cost: $600–$2500. Minimum two-week commitment.
Application Deadline Continuous.
Jobs Positions for college students 18 and older.
Contact Taylor Scott Cook, Executive Director, 499 Loomis Street, Westfield, Massachusetts 01085. Phone: 413-562-7431. Fax: 413-569-6445. E-mail: adventures@weu.com.
URL www.weu.com

Wilderness Experiences Unlimited–Pathfinders Day Camp

Wilderness Experiences Unlimited, Inc.
Southwick, Massachusetts

General Information Coed day traditional camp and outdoor program.
Academics Ecology.
Arts Arts and crafts (general).
Special Interest Areas Nature study.
Sports Canoeing, climbing (wall), kayaking, rappelling, ropes course, scuba diving, sea kayaking, snorkeling, sports (general), swimming.
Wilderness/Outdoors Hiking, outdoor adventure.
Program Information 7 sessions per year. Session length: 5 days in July, August. Ages: 8–14. Day program cost: $199.
Application Deadline Continuous.
Contact Taylor Scott Cook, Executive Director, 499 Loomis Street, Westfield, Massachusetts 01085. Phone: 888-WEU-CAMP. Fax: 413-569-6445. E-mail: adventures@weu.com.
URL www.weu.com

Wilderness Experiences Unlimited–Trailblazers Camp

Wilderness Experiences Unlimited, Inc.
Lake Norwich
Huntington, Massachusetts 01050

General Information Coed travel outdoor program, wilderness program, and adventure program.
Sports Bicycling, canoeing, climbing (wall), kayaking, rappelling, ropes course, scuba diving, sea kayaking, swimming.
Wilderness/Outdoors Backpacking, bicycle trips, canoe trips, caving, mountain biking, outdoor adventure, rafting, rock climbing, white-water trips, wilderness camping.
Trips Day, overnight.
Program Information 8 sessions per year. Session length: 5 days in July, August. Ages: 12–17. Cost: $600–$900.
Application Deadline Continuous.
Jobs Positions for college students 18 and older.
Contact Taylor Scott Cook, Executive Director, 499 Loomis Street, Westfield, Massachusetts 01085. Phone: 888-WEU-CAMP. Fax: 413-569-6445. E-mail: adventures@weu.com.
URL www.weu.com

Wilderness Experiences Unlimited/Westfield Water Sports: Scuba Camp

Wilderness Experiences Unlimited, Inc.
Lake Norwich
Huntington, Massachusetts 01050

General Information Coed residential outdoor program and wilderness program established in 1981.
Program Focus Scuba diving and scuba certification, locations vary for open water training.
Sports Fishing, kayaking, sailing, scuba diving, sea kayaking, snorkeling, swimming.
Trips Overnight.
Program Information 1–4 sessions per year. Session length: 1–2 weeks in July, August. Ages: 12+. 12 participants per session. Boarding program cost: $650–$2200.
Application Deadline Continuous.
Jobs Positions for high school students 16 and older and college students 18 and older.
Contact Taylor Scott Cook, Executive Director, 499 Loomis Street, Westfield, Massachusetts 01085. Phone: 413-562-7431. Fax: 413-569-6445. E-mail: adventures@weu.com.
URL www.weu.com

The Winchendon School Summer Session

The Winchendon School
172 Ash Street
Winchendon, Massachusetts 01475

General Information Coed residential academic program established in 1985. Specific services available for the learning disabled, participant with ADD, and participant with AD/HD. High school credit may be earned.

The Winchendon School Summer Session

Program Focus ESL, learning style differences, and ADD/ADHD, study skills.
Academics American literature, Bible study, English as a second language, English language/literature, French (Advanced Placement), French language/literature, Latin language, SAT/ACT preparation, Spanish (Advanced Placement), Spanish language/literature, TOEFL/TOEIC preparation, academics (general), biology, biology (Advanced Placement), computer programming, computers, health sciences, history, humanities, mathematics, mathematics (Advanced Placement), music, physics, physiology, precollege program, psychology, reading, science (general), social science, social studies, speech/debate, study skills, typing, writing.
Arts Arts and crafts (general), ceramics, creative writing, drawing, graphic arts, music, music (classical), music (instrumental), painting, photography, pottery.
Special Interest Areas College planning, driver's education, homestays.
Sports Basketball, bicycling, bicycling (BMX), cross-country, equestrian sports, fishing, golf, horseback riding, soccer, softball, sports (general), swimming, tennis, volleyball, weight training.
Wilderness/Outdoors Backpacking, bicycle trips, canoe trips, hiking, mountain biking, orienteering, rafting, rock climbing, white-water trips.
Trips Cultural, day, overnight, shopping.
Program Information 1 session per year. Session length: 6 weeks in June, July, August. Ages: 13–20. 50–70 participants per session. Boarding program cost: $5600. Application fee: $50–$100. Financial aid available.
Application Deadline Continuous.
Jobs Positions for high school students 16 and older.
Contact Mr. J. William LaBelle, Headmaster, main address above. Phone: 978-297-1223. Fax: 978-297-0911. E-mail: admissions@winchendon.org.
URL www.winchendon.org

For more information, see page 1398.

MICHIGAN

American Youth Foundation–Camp Miniwanca

American Youth Foundation
8845 West Garfield Road
Shelby, Michigan 49455

General Information Coed residential traditional camp and outdoor program established in 1925. Accredited by American Camping Association.
Program Focus Leadership development in young people, balanced living, and developing personal best.
Arts Arts and crafts (general), ceramics, chorus, creative writing, dance, jewelry making, leather working, music, painting, photography, pottery, theater/drama, woodworking.
Special Interest Areas Campcraft, career exploration, community service, leadership training, nature study, nautical skills, team building.
Sports Aerobics, archery, baseball, basketball, bicycling, boating, canoeing, climbing (wall), fishing, football, golf, kayaking, rappelling, ropes course, sailing, sea kayaking, soccer, softball, swimming, tennis, volleyball, water polo, windsurfing.
Wilderness/Outdoors Backpacking, bicycle trips, canoe trips, hiking, orienteering, rock climbing, wilderness camping.
Trips Day, overnight.
Program Information 3 sessions per year. Session length: 19–40 days in June, July. Ages: 8–18. 300–500 participants per session. Boarding program cost: $1325–$4200. Financial aid available.
Application Deadline Continuous.
Jobs Positions for high school students 16 and older and college students 18 and older.
Contact Lori Greene, Registrar, main address above. Phone: 231-861-4313. Fax: 231-861-5244. E-mail: miniwancacamps@ayf.com.
URL www.ayf.com

American Youth Foundation Leadership Conference

American Youth Foundation
8845 West Garfield Road
Shelby, Michigan 49455

General Information Coed residential academic program and community service program established in 1925. Accredited by American Camping Association. High school or college credit may be earned.
Program Focus Leadership development, openness to diversity, effectiveness in groups.
Arts Arts and crafts (general), creative writing, dance, drawing, jewelry making, leather working.
Special Interest Areas Cross-cultural education, leadership training.
Sports Basketball, boating, canoeing, climbing (wall), fishing, kayaking, rappelling, ropes course, sailing, sea kayaking, soccer, softball, swimming, tennis, volleyball.

American Youth Foundation Leadership Conference (continued)

Wilderness/Outdoors Hiking, orienteering, wilderness camping.
Program Information 1 session per year. Session length: 8 days in July, August. Ages: 15–18. 500 participants per session. Boarding program cost: $550–$650. Application fee: $100. Financial aid available.
Application Deadline Continuous.
Jobs Positions for college students 18 and older.
Contact Ms. Lori Greene, Registrar, Miniwanca Education Center, 8845 West Garfield Road, Shelby, Michigan 49455. Phone: 231-861-4313. Fax: 231-861-5244. E-mail: lori.greene@ayf.com.
URL www.ayf.com

Black River Farm and Ranch

5040 Sheridan Line
Croswell, Michigan 48422

General Information Girls' residential sports camp established in 1962. Accredited by American Camping Association.
Program Focus Western riding.
Arts Arts and crafts (general).
Special Interest Areas Animal care, farming.
Sports Basketball, boating, canoeing, equestrian sports, horseback riding, kayaking, ropes course, soccer, softball, swimming, tennis, trampolining, volleyball.
Program Information 6 sessions per year. Session length: 1–2 weeks in June, July, August. Ages: 7–15. 134 participants per session. Boarding program cost: $950–$1800.
Application Deadline Continuous.
Jobs Positions for college students 18 and older.
Contact Pam Todd, Business Manager, main address above. Phone: 810-679-2505. Fax: 810-679-3188. E-mail: misspam@blackriverfarmandranch.com.
URL www.blackriverfarmandranch.com

Blue Lake Fine Arts Camp

Blue Lake Fine Arts Camp, Inc.
300 East Crystal Lake Road
Twin Lake, Michigan 49457

General Information Coed residential arts program established in 1966. Formal opportunities for the artistically talented.
Arts Arts, arts and crafts (general), band, ceramics, chorus, dance, dance (ballet), dance (jazz), dance (modern), drawing, fabric arts, harp, music, music (chamber), music (classical), music (ensemble), music (instrumental), music (jazz), music (orchestral), music (vocal), musical productions, painting, piano, pottery, theater/drama, visual arts.
Sports Basketball, football, soccer, swimming, track and field, volleyball.
Program Information 4 sessions per year. Session length: 12 days in June, July, August. Ages: 10–18. 1,200 participants per session. Boarding program cost: $880–$1030. Application fee: $150. Financial aid available.
Application Deadline Continuous.
Jobs Positions for college students 18 and older.
Contact Admissions, main address above. Phone: 800-221-3796. Fax: 231-893-5120.
URL www.bluelake.org

Camp Echo

McGaw YMCA
3782 South Triangle Trail
Fremont, Michigan 49412

General Information Coed residential traditional camp and adventure program established in 1902.
Arts Acting, arts and crafts (general), dance, music, photography.
Special Interest Areas Campcraft, nature study.
Sports Archery, baseball, basketball, bicycling, boating, canoeing, fishing, horseback riding, ropes course, sailing, snorkeling, soccer, softball, swimming, tennis, volleyball, waterskiing.
Wilderness/Outdoors Backpacking, bicycle trips, canoe trips, hiking, wilderness camping.
Trips Overnight.
Program Information 5 sessions per year. Session length: 1–2 weeks in June, July, August. Ages: 8–17. 200–275 participants per session. Boarding program cost: $500–$2500. Financial aid available.
Application Deadline Continuous.
Jobs Positions for high school students 16 and older and college students.
Summer Contact Mr. Rob Grierson, Camp Director, main address above. Phone: 231-924-0829. Fax: 231-924-0061. E-mail: rg@mcgawymca.org.
Winter Contact Mr. Rob Grierson, Camp Director, main address above. Phone: 847-475-7400. Fax: 847-475-7959. E-mail: rg@mcgawymca.org.
URL www.ymcacampecho.org

Camp Fowler

The Fowler Center
2315 Harmon Lake Road
Mayville, Michigan 48744

General Information Coed residential traditional camp, outdoor program, and special needs program established in 1957. Accredited by American Camping Association. Specific services available for the emotionally challenged, developmentally challenged, hearing impaired, learning disabled, physically challenged, visually impaired, brain injured, and participant with HIV/AIDS.
Program Focus Program for children and adults with special needs offering traditional camp activities, climbing wall, horseback riding, and camping at a primitive outpost unit.
Arts Arts and crafts (general), batiking, ceramics, clowning, dance, drawing, fabric arts, jewelry making, leather working, music, painting, pottery, puppetry, sculpture, theater/drama, weaving, woodworking.
Special Interest Areas Native American culture, animal care, campcraft, construction, gardening, nature study.
Sports Archery, baseball, basketball, boating, canoeing, climbing (wall), equestrian sports, fishing, football, golf,

horseback riding, ropes course, sailing, skiing (cross-country), soccer, softball, sports (general), swimming, track and field, volleyball.
Wilderness/Outdoors Backpacking, canoe trips, hiking, orienteering, wilderness camping.
Trips Day, overnight.
Program Information 25–30 sessions per year. Session length: 2–14 days in January, February, March, April, May, June, July, August, September, October, November, December. Ages: 6+. 74–95 participants per session. Boarding program cost: $160–$900. Financial aid available.
Application Deadline Continuous.
Jobs Positions for college students 18 and older.
Contact Ms. Pat Jordan, Program Registrar/Office Manager, main address above. Phone: 989-673-2050. Fax: 989-673-6355. E-mail: info@thefowlercenter.org.
URL www.thefowlercenter.org

Camp Geneva

GENEVA Camp & Retreat Center
3995 North Lakeshore Drive
Holland, Michigan 49424

General Information Coed residential and day traditional camp and bible camp established in 1948. Religious affiliation: Reformed Church in America.
Academics Bible study.
Arts Arts and crafts (general), leather working, theater/drama.
Sports Archery, basketball, climbing (wall), in-line skating, soccer, swimming, volleyball.
Program Information 10 sessions per year. Session length: 5–6 days in June, July, August. Ages: 8–15. 75–224 participants per session. Day program cost: $125–$145. Boarding program cost: $170–$350. Financial aid available.
Application Deadline Continuous.
Jobs Positions for high school students 16 and older and college students 18 and older.
Contact Rev. Brian Vander Wege, Program Director, main address above. Phone: 616-399-3150. Fax: 616-399-5180. E-mail: brian@campgeneva.org.
URL www.campgeneva.org

Camp Henry

Westminster Presbyterian Church of Grand Rapids, MI/Camp Henry Board of Directors
5575 Gordon Road
Newaygo, Michigan 49337

General Information Coed residential and day traditional camp established in 1937. Religious affiliation: Presbyterian. Accredited by American Camping Association.
Program Focus Spiritual growth and joyful expression within the experience of the Christian community through traditional and specialty camping.
Arts Arts and crafts (general).
Sports Archery, boating, canoeing, climbing (wall), fishing, horseback riding, ropes course, sailing, swimming, volleyball, waterskiing.
Wilderness/Outdoors Backpacking, canoe trips, hiking, orienteering, rock climbing, white-water trips, wilderness camping.
Trips Day, overnight.
Program Information 8–10 sessions per year. Session length: 3–21 days in April, June, July, August, December. Ages: 5–17. 100–190 participants per session. Day program cost: $175–$205. Boarding program cost: $180–$895. Financial aid available.
Application Deadline Continuous.
Jobs Positions for high school students 16 and older and college students 19 and older.
Summer Contact Jeff Jacobs, Summer Camp Director, 47 Jefferson, SE, Grand Rapids, Michigan 49503. Phone: 231-652-6472 Ext.13. Fax: 231-652-9460. E-mail: jake@camphenry.org.
Winter Contact Tim Horton, Program Director, 5575 Gordon Rd, Newayso, Michigan 49337. Phone: 231-652-6472. Fax: 231-652-9460. E-mail: tim@camphenry.org.
URL www.camphenry.org

Camp Henry Offsite: Teen Challenge

Westminster Presbyterian Church of Grand Rapids, MI/Camp Henry Board of Directors
Michigan

General Information Coed travel adventure program established in 1937. Religious affiliation: Presbyterian. Accredited by American Camping Association.
Sports Canoeing, climbing (wall), horseback riding, ropes course, sea kayaking, skiing (downhill).
Wilderness/Outdoors Backpacking, canoe trips, hiking, rafting, rock climbing, white-water trips, wilderness camping.
Trips Overnight.
Program Information 2–6 sessions per year. Session length: 1–2 weeks in April, June, July, August. Ages: 13–17. 8–24 participants per session. Cost: $395–$895. Financial aid available.
Application Deadline Continuous.
Jobs Positions for high school students 17 and older and college students 19 and older.
Contact Chris McClain, Business Office Manager, 47 Jefferson, SE, Grand Rapids, Michigan 49503. Phone: 616-459-2267. Fax: 616-732-6374. E-mail: chris@camphenry.org.
URL www.camphenry.org

Camp Lookout

Crystalaire Camp, Inc.
4410 Lookout Road
Frankfort, Michigan 49635

General Information Coed residential traditional camp and family program established in 1930.
Program Focus Individualized program in a noncompetitive, rustic, simple setting.
Arts Arts and crafts (general), batiking, ceramics, creative writing, drawing, jewelry making, music, painting, pottery, puppetry, sculpture.
Special Interest Areas Campcraft, community service.

Camp Lookout (continued)
Sports Aerobics, bicycling, boating, canoeing, fishing, horseback riding, kayaking, sea kayaking, soccer, swimming, volleyball, waterskiing, windsurfing.
Wilderness/Outdoors Backpacking, bicycle trips, canoe trips, hiking, mountain biking.
Trips Day.
Program Information 4–8 sessions per year. Session length: 3–14 days in June, July, August. Ages: 7–15. 25–45 participants per session. Boarding program cost: $400–$1500.
Application Deadline Continuous.
Jobs Positions for college students 19 and older.
Contact Ms. Katherine M. Houston, Director, 2768 South Shore Road East, Frankfort, Michigan 49635. Phone: 231-352-7589. Fax: 231-352-6609. E-mail: camp_info@crystalairecamp.com.
URL www.crystalairecamp.com

Camp Maplehurst

12055 Waring Road
Kewadin, Michigan 49648

General Information Coed residential traditional camp established in 1955. Accredited by American Camping Association. Formal opportunities for the academically talented and artistically talented. College credit may be earned.
Academics Psychology.
Arts Arts and crafts (general), ceramics, creative writing, dance, drawing, jewelry making, leather working, painting, photography, printmaking, theater/drama, weaving.
Special Interest Areas Leadership training, model rocketry.
Sports Archery, basketball, boating, canoeing, equestrian sports, fencing, fishing, golf, gymnastics, horseback riding, kayaking, martial arts, sailing, scuba diving, sea kayaking, snorkeling, soccer, softball, street/roller hockey, swimming, tennis, track and field, volleyball, water polo, waterskiing, weight training, windsurfing.
Wilderness/Outdoors Backpacking, canoe trips, hiking, mountain biking, survival training, wilderness camping.
Trips Cultural, day, overnight.
Program Information 4 sessions per year. Session length: 2–8 weeks in June, July, August. Ages: 7–17. 100–150 participants per session. Boarding program cost: $1800–$5600.
Application Deadline Continuous.
Jobs Positions for high school students 17 and older and college students 18 and older.
Contact Dr. Laurence Cohn, Director, 1455 Quarton Road, Birmingham, Michigan 48009. Phone: 231-264-9675. Fax: 231-264-5041. E-mail: info@campmaplehurst.com.
URL www.campmaplehurst.com

Camp Oweki Summer Day Camp

Camp Fire USA North Oakland
Independence Oaks County Park
9501 Sashabaw Road
Clarkston, Michigan 48348

General Information Coed day traditional camp and outdoor program established in 1952. Specific services available for the emotionally challenged, developmentally challenged, learning disabled, and physically challenged.
Academics Peace education.
Arts Arts and crafts (general).
Special Interest Areas Leadership training, nature study, weight reduction.
Sports Archery, boating, fishing, swimming.
Wilderness/Outdoors Hiking, orienteering, survival training.
Program Information 3–4 sessions per year. Session length: 5 days in May, July. Ages: 4–16. 100 participants per session. Day program cost: $100–$120. Financial aid available.
Application Deadline Continuous.
Jobs Positions for high school students 14 and older and college students 18 and older.
Contact Barb Zelinski, Program Director, 4450 Walton Boulevard, Suite C, Waterford, Michigan 48329. Phone: 248-618-9050. Fax: 248-618-9052. E-mail: barbizelinski@aol.com.
URL www.comnet.org/campfirenoc

Camp Roger

Camp Roger
8356 Belding Road
Rockford, Michigan 49341

General Information Coed residential outdoor program and bible camp established in 1941. Religious affiliation: Christian. Accredited by American Camping Association.
Program Focus Explore God's World, Discover God's Love.
Academics Bible study.
Arts Acting, arts and crafts (general), dance, leather working, theater/drama.
Special Interest Areas Campcraft, nature study.
Sports Archery, blobbing, boating, canoeing, climbing (wall), fishing, riflery, ropes course, snorkeling, swimming, volleyball.
Wilderness/Outdoors Backpacking, canoe trips, hiking, orienteering, outdoor adventure.
Trips Overnight.
Program Information 9–10 sessions per year. Session length: 4–7 days in June, July, August. Ages: 7–16. 130–150 participants per session. Boarding program cost: $220–$280. Financial aid available.
Application Deadline Continuous.
Jobs Positions for high school students 16 and older and college students 18 and older.
Contact Mr. Jim Van Wingerden, Executive Director, main address above. Phone: 616-874-7286. Fax: 616-874-5734. E-mail: jimvwg@juno.com.
URL www.camproger.org

Camp Seagull for Girls

Camp Seagull
08580 Boyne City Road
Charlevoix, Michigan 49720

General Information Girls' residential traditional camp established in 1955. Accredited by American Camping Association.
Arts Arts, arts and crafts (general), batiking, ceramics, dance (modern), drawing, fabric arts, jewelry making, leather working, musical productions, painting, pottery, theater/drama, weaving, woodworking.
Special Interest Areas Campcraft, leadership training, nature study, nautical skills.
Sports Aerobics, archery, baseball, basketball, bicycling, boating, canoeing, climbing (wall), equestrian sports, field hockey, fishing, football, golf, horseback riding, kayaking, lacrosse, rappelling, ropes course, sailing, sea kayaking, snorkeling, soccer, softball, sports (general), swimming, tennis, volleyball, water polo, waterskiing, windsurfing.
Wilderness/Outdoors Backpacking, bicycle trips, canoe trips, hiking, mountain biking, orienteering, pack animal trips, wilderness camping.
Trips Day, overnight.
Program Information 1–6 sessions per year. Session length: 1–6 weeks in June, July, August. Ages: 6–16. 80–100 participants per session. Boarding program cost: $1975–$3975.
Application Deadline Continuous.
Jobs Positions for high school students 18 and older and college students 18 and older.
Contact Mr. Bill Schulman, Director, 301 Mercer Boulevard, Charleviox, Michigan 49720. Phone: 231-547-6556. E-mail: seagull@freeway.net.
URL www.campseagull.com

Cedar Lodge

47000 52nd Street
Lawrence, Michigan 49064

General Information Coed residential traditional camp and sports camp established in 1964. Accredited by American Camping Association.
Program Focus Horsemanship, primarily English, including competitive jumping.
Arts Arts and crafts (general), dance, dance (folk), dance (modern), drawing, fabric arts, jewelry making, leather working, mime, music, music (instrumental), music (vocal), painting, puppetry, theater/drama, weaving, woodworking.
Special Interest Areas Animal care, campcraft, construction, nature study, nautical skills, work camp programs.
Sports Archery, baseball, basketball, bicycling, boating, canoeing, diving, equestrian sports, fishing, football, gymnastics, horseback riding, sailing, soccer, softball, swimming, tennis, volleyball.
Wilderness/Outdoors Bicycle trips, canoe trips, hiking, mountain biking.
Trips Day, overnight.
Program Information 8 sessions per year. Session length: 1 week in June, July, August. Ages: 8–16. 60 participants per session. Boarding program cost: $485–$3300. Riding program fee: $105.
Application Deadline Continuous.
Jobs Positions for high school students 17 and older and college students 19 and older.
Contact Amy Edwards, Program Director, PO Box 218, Lawrence, Michigan 49064. Phone: 269-674-8071. Fax: 269-674-3143. E-mail: info@cedarlodge.com.
URL www.cedarlodge.com

Circle Pines Center Summer Camp

8650 Mullen Road
Delton, Michigan 49046

General Information Coed residential traditional camp established in 1938. Accredited by American Camping Association.
Program Focus To teach peace, justice, ecology and cooperation.
Academics Current events, environmental science, intercultural studies, music, peace education.
Arts Arts and crafts (general), dance (folk), music (vocal), musical productions, photography, pottery, theater/drama.
Special Interest Areas Native American culture, animal care, campcraft, community service, construction, culinary arts, gardening, leadership training, nature study, work camp programs.
Sports Canoeing, soccer, swimming, ultimate frisbee.
Wilderness/Outdoors Hiking.
Trips Day.
Program Information 3–4 sessions per year. Session length: 1–2 weeks in June, July, August. Ages: 7–17. 50–60 participants per session. Boarding program cost: $350–$700. Financial aid available.
Application Deadline Continuous.
Jobs Positions for college students.
Contact Mr. Kyle Hodnett, Summer Camp Director, main address above. Phone: 269-623-5555. Fax: 269-623-9054. E-mail: circle@net-link.net.
URL www.circlepinescenter.org

Crystalaire Camp

Crystalaire Camp, Inc.
2768 South Shore Road East
Frankfort, Michigan 49635

General Information Coed residential traditional camp established in 1924.
Program Focus Individualized programs in a noncompetitive atmosphere, including art, sailing, and trips.
Arts Arts and crafts (general), batiking, ceramics, creative writing, drawing, fabric arts, jewelry making, leather working, painting, pottery, printmaking, puppetry, sculpture.
Special Interest Areas Animal care, campcraft, community service, gardening, work camp programs.
Sports Aerobics, basketball, bicycling, boating, canoeing, fishing, horseback riding, kayaking, sailing, scuba

Crystalaire Camp (continued)
diving, sea kayaking, snorkeling, soccer, swimming, tennis, volleyball, water polo, waterskiing, windsurfing.
Wilderness/Outdoors Backpacking, bicycle trips, canoe trips, hiking, mountain biking, wilderness/outdoors (general).
Trips Day, overnight.
Program Information 3 sessions per year. Session length: 12–19 days in June, July, August. Ages: 8–15. 90 participants per session. Boarding program cost: $900–$1500. Financial aid available.
Application Deadline Continuous.
Jobs Positions for college students 19 and older.
Contact David P. Reid, Director, main address above. Phone: 231-352-7589. Fax: 231-352-6609. E-mail: camp_info@crystalairecamp.com.
URL www.crystalairecamp.com

Cybercamps–University of Michigan

Cybercamps–Giant Campus, Inc.
Ann Arbor, Michigan

General Information Coed residential and day academic program established in 1997.
Program Focus High tech computer camps featuring project oriented curriculum in Web design, 3D animation, game design, robotics, digital arts and programming for all ability levels.
Academics Web page design, computer programming, computers.
Arts Animation, creative writing, digital media, graphic arts, photography.
Special Interest Areas Computer graphics, robotics, team building.
Sports Frisbee golf, ultimate frisbee.
Program Information 2–9 sessions per year. Session length: 5–30 days in June, July, August. Ages: 7–18. 30–150 participants per session. Day program cost: $599–$849. Boarding program cost: $974–$1224.
Application Deadline Continuous.
Jobs Positions for high school students 15 and older and college students.
Contact Cybercamps Information Office, 2401 4th Avenue, Suite 1110, Seattle, Washington 98121. Phone: 206-442-4500. Fax: 206-442-4501. E-mail: info@cybercamps.com.
URL www.cybercamps.com

CYO Boys Camp

Catholic Youth Organization
1295 South Lakeshore Road
Carsonville, Michigan 48419

General Information Boys' residential traditional camp established in 1946. Religious affiliation: Roman Catholic. Accredited by American Camping Association.
Arts Arts and crafts (general).
Special Interest Areas Animal care, community service, leadership training, nautical skills, team building.
Sports Archery, baseball, basketball, boating, climbing (wall), kayaking, ropes course, sailing, swimming.
Wilderness/Outdoors Canoe trips, hiking.
Trips Day.
Program Information 5–10 sessions per year. Session length: 4–10 days in June, July, August. Ages: 7–16. 10–100 participants per session. Boarding program cost: $215–$540. Application fee: $35. Financial aid available.
Application Deadline Continuous.
Jobs Positions for high school students 17 and older and college students 18 and older.
Contact Caroline Krucker, Director of Parish Services and Camps, 305 Michigan Avenue, Detroit, Michigan 48226. Phone: 313-963-7172 Ext.168. Fax: 313-963-7179. E-mail: ckrucker@cyodetroit.org.
URL www.cyocamps.org

CYO Girls Camp

Catholic Youth Organization
1564 North Lakeshore Road
Port Sanilac, Michigan 48469

General Information Girls' residential traditional camp established in 1952. Religious affiliation: Roman Catholic. Accredited by American Camping Association.
Arts Arts and crafts (general).
Special Interest Areas Animal care, campcraft, community service, leadership training, nautical skills, team building.
Sports Archery, basketball, boating, climbing (wall), kayaking, ropes course, sailing, softball, swimming, volleyball.
Wilderness/Outdoors Canoe trips, hiking.
Trips Day.
Program Information 5–10 sessions per year. Session length: 4–10 days in June, July, August. Ages: 7–16. 10–100 participants per session. Boarding program cost: $215–$540. Application fee: $35. Financial aid available.
Application Deadline Continuous.
Jobs Positions for high school students 17 and older and college students 18 and older.
Contact Caroline Krucker, Director of Parish Services and Camps, 305 Michigan Avenue, Detroit, Michigan 48226. Phone: 313-963-7172 Ext.168. Fax: 313-963-7179. E-mail: ckrucker@cyodetroit.org.
URL www.cyocamps.org

Earthwatch Institute–Moose and Wolves

Earthwatch Institute
Isle Royale
Michigan

General Information Coed residential outdoor program, wilderness program, and adventure program.
Program Focus Clarifying the role of predators in controlling prey populations.
Academics Ecology, environmental science, science (general).
Special Interest Areas Field research/expeditions, nature study.
Wilderness/Outdoors Hiking.
Program Information 4 sessions per year. Session length: 9 days in May, June, August. Ages: 16+. 10

participants per session. Boarding program cost: $795–$895. Financial aid available. Financial aid for high school students and teachers.
Application Deadline Continuous.
Contact General Information Desk, PO Box 75, Maynard, Massachusetts 01754. Phone: 800-776-0188. Fax: 978-461-2332. E-mail: info@earthwatch.org.
URL www.earthwatch.org

The Glen at Lake of the Woods

Lake of the Woods Camp for Girls and Greenwoods Camp for Boys
84600 47½ Street
Decatur, Michigan 49045

General Information Girls' residential traditional camp established in 2004. Accredited by American Camping Association.
Academics Hebrew language, computer programming.
Arts Acting, ceramics, dance (jazz), dance (modern), drawing, jewelry making, photography, theater/drama.
Special Interest Areas Campcraft, model rocketry.
Sports Aerobics, archery, basketball, canoeing, cheerleading, climbing (wall), equestrian sports, gymnastics, horseback riding, in-line skating, riflery, ropes course, sailing, soccer, swimming, tennis, waterskiing, windsurfing.
Trips Day.
Program Information 2 sessions per year. Session length: 2 weeks in June, July. Ages: 7–13. 95 participants per session. Boarding program cost: $1900. Financial aid available.
Application Deadline Continuous.
Jobs Positions for college students 19 and older.
Summer Contact Dayna Hardin, Director, main address above. Phone: 269-423-3091. Fax: 269-423-8889. E-mail: lwcgwc@aol.com.
Winter Contact Dayna Hardin, Owner / Director, 227 Mary Street, Winnetka, Illinois 60093. Phone: 888-459-2492. Fax: 847-242-0008. E-mail: lwcgwc@aol.com.
URL lakeofthewoodsglen.com

Greenwoods Camp for Boys

Lake of the Woods Camp for Girls and Greenwoods Camp for Boys
84600 47½ Street
Decatur, Michigan 49045

General Information Boys' residential traditional camp established in 1935. Accredited by American Camping Association.
Program Focus Waterski and horseback riding specialty with 40 other activities.
Academics English as a second language, Hebrew language, computers, music, reading.
Arts Arts and crafts (general), ceramics, leather working, music, pottery, television/video, theater/drama, woodworking.
Special Interest Areas Animal care, campcraft, farming, model rocketry.
Sports Archery, baseball, basketball, boating, canoeing, climbing (wall), cross-country, diving, equestrian sports, fishing, football, go-carts, golf, gymnastics, horseback riding, in-line skating, riflery, ropes course, sailing, snorkeling, soccer, sports (general), street/roller hockey, swimming, tennis, track and field, volleyball, waterskiing, windsurfing, wrestling.
Wilderness/Outdoors Canoe trips, orienteering, rock climbing.
Trips Day, overnight.
Program Information 3 sessions per year. Session length: 21–55 days in June, July, August. Ages: 7–15. 130 participants per session. Boarding program cost: $2950–$6000. Financial aid available.
Application Deadline Continuous.
Jobs Positions for college students 19 and older.
Summer Contact Dayna Hardin, Director, main address above. Phone: 269-423-3091. Fax: 269-423-8889. E-mail: lwcgwc@aol.com.
Winter Contact Dayna Hardin, Owner/Director, 227 Mary Street, Winnetka, Illinois 60093. Phone: 888-459-2492. Fax: 847-242-0008. E-mail: lwcgwc@aol.com.
URL www.greenwoodscamp.com

The Grove at Greenwoods

Lake of the Woods Camp for Girls and Greenwoods Camp for Boys
84600 47½ Street
Decatur, Michigan 49045

General Information Boys' residential traditional camp established in 1935. Accredited by American Camping Association.
Academics English as a second language, Hebrew language, computers, music, reading.
Arts Arts and crafts (general), ceramics, leather working, music, pottery, television/video, theater/drama, woodworking.
Special Interest Areas Animal care, campcraft, farming, model rocketry.
Sports Archery, baseball, basketball, boating, canoeing, climbing (wall), cross-country, diving, fishing, football, golf, gymnastics, in-line skating, riflery, ropes course, sailing, snorkeling, soccer, sports (general), street/roller hockey, swimming, tennis, track and field, volleyball, wrestling.
Wilderness/Outdoors Canoe trips, orienteering, rock climbing.
Trips Day, overnight.
Program Information 2 sessions per year. Session length: 2 weeks in July, August. Ages: 7–13. Boarding program cost: $1900. Financial aid available.
Application Deadline Continuous.
Jobs Positions for college students 19 and older.
Summer Contact Dayna Hardin, Director, main address above. Phone: 269-423-3091. Fax: 269-423-8889. E-mail: lwcgwc@aol.com.
Winter Contact Dayna Hardin, Owner / Director, 227 Mary Street, Winnetka, Illinois 60093. Phone: 888-459-2492. Fax: 847-242-0008. E-mail: lwcgwc@aol.com.
URL www.greenwoodscamp.com

Hillsdale College Summer Science Camps

Hillsdale College
33 East College Street
Hillsdale, Michigan 49242

General Information Coed residential academic program established in 1989. College credit may be earned.
Program Focus Hands-on science camps in molecular biology, physics and chemistry, mathematics and computer science.
Academics Biology, chemistry, computers, mathematics, physics, science (general).
Sports Basketball, racquetball, swimming, tennis.
Trips College tours.
Program Information 3 sessions per year. Session length: 6 days in June. Ages: 15–18. 20 participants per session. Application fee: $50. No cost for program.
Application Deadline March 1.
Contact Dr. Francis X. Steiner, Professor of Biology/Dean of Natural Sciences, Biology Department, Hillsdale, Michigan 49242. Phone: 517-607-2399. Fax: 517-607-2252. E-mail: fxs@hillsdale.edu.
URL www.hillsdale.edu

iD Tech Camps–University of Michigan, Ann Arbor, MI

iD Tech Camps
University of Michigan
Ann Arbor, Michigan 48109

General Information Coed residential and day academic program established in 1999. Accredited by American Camping Association. Formal opportunities for the academically talented and artistically talented.
Program Focus High-tech computer camps for kids and teens; produce digital movies, create video games, design Web pages, learn programming and robotics, and more; one computer per student, small classes, campers complete a project in a creative and fun learning environment.
Academics Web page design, computer programming, computer science (Advanced Placement), computers, music, precollege program.
Arts Animation, cinematography, digital media, drawing, film, film editing, film production, graphic arts, music, television/video.
Special Interest Areas Career exploration, computer graphics, electronics, leadership training, robotics, team building.
Sports Baseball, basketball, soccer, softball, swimming, volleyball.
Trips College tours, cultural, day.
Program Information 5 sessions per year. Session length: 5–7 days in June, July, August. Ages: 7–17. 40–50 participants per session. Day program cost: $639. Boarding program cost: $989. Application fee: $200. Financial aid available.
Application Deadline Continuous.
Jobs Positions for college students 18 and older.
Contact Client Service Representatives, 1885 Winchester Boulevard, Suite 201, Campbell, California 95008. Phone: 888-709-TECH. Fax: 408-871-2228. E-mail: requests@internaldrive.com.
URL www.internaldrive.com

For more information, see page 1156.

Interlochen Arts Camp

Interlochen Center for the Arts
4000 Highway M-137
Interlochen, Michigan 49643

General Information Coed residential arts program established in 1928. Accredited by American Camping Association. Formal opportunities for the artistically talented.

Interlochen Arts Camp

Program Focus Fine arts, visual arts, theatre arts, dance, music, and creative writing.
Academics Art (Advanced Placement), environmental science, music, music (Advanced Placement), writing.
Arts Arts, arts and crafts (general), band, ceramics, chorus, creative writing, dance, dance (ballet), dance (jazz), dance (modern), drawing, fabric arts, jewelry making, metalworking, music, music (chamber), music (classical), music (ensemble), music (instrumental), music (jazz), music (orchestral), music (vocal), musical productions, painting, photography, pottery, printmaking, puppetry, radio broadcasting, sculpture, theater/drama, weaving.
Sports Aerobics, archery, basketball, boating, canoeing, football, ropes course, sailing, soccer, softball, swimming, tennis, volleyball.
Trips Cultural, day, overnight, shopping.
Program Information 1–2 sessions per year. Session length: 4–8 weeks in June, July, August. Ages: 8–18. 1,500–1,700 participants per session. Boarding program cost: $3495–$5250. Application fee: $35. Financial aid available.
Application Deadline February 15.
Jobs Positions for college students 18 and older.

Contact Tom Bewley, Director of Admissions, PO Box 199, Interlochen, Michigan 49643. Phone: 231-276-7472. Fax: 231-276-7464. E-mail: admissions@interlochen.org.
URL www.interlochen.org/

For more information, see page 1160.

Joe Machnik's No. 1 Academy One and Premier Programs–Brooklyn, Michigan

Joe Machnik's No. 1 Camps
Sauk Valley Sports Center
Brooklyn, Michigan

General Information Coed residential and day sports camp.
Program Focus Soccer instruction, physical fitness, testing and speed training. Campers gain exposure to top players and are challenged by intense competition.
Sports Soccer.
Trips Day.
Program Information 1 session per year. Session length: 6 days in June. Ages: 9–18. Day program cost: $699. Boarding program cost: $759. Financial aid available.
Application Deadline Continuous.
Jobs Positions for college students.
Contact Dr. Joseph Machnik, Director, PO Box 389, 916 Palm Boulevard, Isle of Palms, South Carolina 29451. Phone: 800-622-4645. Fax: 843-886-0885. E-mail: info@no1soccercamps.com.
URL www.no1soccercamps.com

Joe Machnik's No. 1 Mighty Mini, Goalkeeper and Striker Camp–Brooklyn, Michigan

Joe Machnik's No. 1 Camps
Sauk Valley Sports Center
Brooklyn, Michigan

General Information Coed residential and day sports camp established in 1977.
Program Focus Soccer instruction. Goalkeepers and strikers compete against each other daily.
Sports Soccer, swimming.
Program Information 1 session per year. Session length: 6 days in June. Ages: 8–12. 100–150 participants per session. Boarding program cost: $429. Financial aid available.
Application Deadline Continuous.
Jobs Positions for college students 17 and older.
Contact Dr. Joseph Machnik, Director, PO Box 389, 916 Palm Boulevard, Isle of Palms, South Carolina 29451. Phone: 800-622-4645. Fax: 843-886-0885. E-mail: info@no1soccercamps.com.
URL www.no1soccercamps.com

Lake Ann Baptist Camp

18215 Baptist Camp Trail
Lake Ann, Michigan 49650-0109

General Information Coed residential traditional camp and bible camp established in 1948. Religious affiliation: Baptist. Accredited by American Camping Association.
Academics Bible study.
Arts Arts and crafts (general), ceramics, leather working.
Special Interest Areas Campcraft, nature study.
Sports Archery, basketball, canoeing, climbing (wall), fishing, paintball, rappelling, ropes course, soccer, sports (general), swimming, volleyball.
Wilderness/Outdoors Bicycle trips, canoe trips, hiking, mountain biking, rafting.
Trips Overnight.
Program Information 40 sessions per year. Session length: 6 days in June, July, August. Ages: 9+. 24–508 participants per session. Boarding program cost: $259–$399.
Application Deadline Continuous.
Jobs Positions for college students 20 and older.
Contact Dan Good, Director of Guest Relations, PO Box 109, 18215 Baptist Camp Trail, Lake Ann, Michigan 49650. Phone: 800-223-5722. Fax: 231-275-5174. E-mail: info@lakeanncamp.com.
URL www.lakeanncamp.com

Lake of the Woods Camp for Girls

Lake of the Woods Camp for Girls and Greenwoods Camp for Boys
84600 47½ Street
Decatur, Michigan 49045

General Information Girls' residential traditional camp established in 1935. Accredited by American Camping Association.
Program Focus Waterskiing and horseback riding specialties with 40 other activities.
Academics English as a second language, Hebrew language, computers, music, reading.
Arts Batiking, ceramics, dance, dance (jazz), dance (modern), drawing, jewelry making, music, music (vocal), painting, photography, pottery, printmaking, television/video, theater/drama, weaving.
Special Interest Areas Animal care, campcraft, farming, gardening, model rocketry.
Sports Aerobics, archery, basketball, bicycling, bicycling (BMX), boating, canoeing, cheerleading, climbing (wall), cross-country, diving, equestrian sports, figure skating, fishing, golf, gymnastics, horseback riding, in-line skating, riflery, sailing, snorkeling, soccer, softball, sports (general), swimming, tennis, track and field, volleyball, waterskiing, windsurfing.
Wilderness/Outdoors Canoe trips, orienteering, rock climbing.
Trips Day, overnight.
Program Information 3 sessions per year. Session length: 21–55 days in June, July, August. Ages: 7–15. 160 participants per session. Boarding program cost: $2950–$6000.
Application Deadline Continuous.

Lake of the Woods Camp for Girls (continued)
Jobs Positions for college students 19 and older.
Summer Contact Dayna Hardin, Director, main address above. Phone: 269-423-3091. Fax: 269-423-8889. E-mail: lwcgwc@aol.com.
Winter Contact Dayna Hardin, Director, 227 Mary Street, Winnetka, Illinois 60093. Phone: 888-459-2492. Fax: 847-242-0008. E-mail: lwcgwc@aol.com.
URL www.lakeofthewoodscamp.com

Landmark Volunteers: Michigan

Landmark Volunteers, Inc.
Michigan

General Information Coed residential outdoor program and community service program established in 1992. High school credit may be earned.
Program Focus Opportunity for high school students to earn community service credit while working as a team for two weeks serving Lakes of the Upper Peninsula. Similar programs offered through Landmark Volunteers at over 60 locations in 21 states.
Academics Biology, ecology, environmental science, science (general).
Special Interest Areas Career exploration, community service, conservation projects, field research/expeditions, leadership training, nature study, team building, trail maintenance, work camp programs.
Sports Swimming.
Wilderness/Outdoors Hiking.
Trips Cultural, day.
Program Information 1 session per year. Session length: 2 weeks in June. Ages: 14–18. 10–13 participants per session. Boarding program cost: $875–$926. Financial aid available.
Application Deadline Continuous.
Jobs Positions for college students.
Contact Ann Barrett, Executive Director, PO Box 455, Sheffield, Massachusetts 01257. Phone: 413-229-0255. Fax: 413-229-2050. E-mail: landmark@volunteers.com.
URL www.volunteers.com

For more information, see page 1182.

Mah Meh Weh

The Fowler Center
2315 Harmon Lake Road
Mayville, Michigan 48744

General Information Girls' residential traditional camp. Accredited by American Camping Association.
Program Focus Horseback riding at all skill levels with an emphasis on English riding; stable management.
Arts Arts and crafts (general), dance.
Special Interest Areas Animal care, nature study.
Sports Horseback riding, sports (general), swimming.
Program Information 2–3 sessions per year. Session length: 6 days in July, August. Ages: 10–16. 16 participants per session. Boarding program cost: $275.
Application Deadline Continuous.
Contact Ms. Pat Jordan, Program Registrar/Office Manager, main address above. Phone: 989-673-2050. Fax: 989-673-6355. E-mail: info@thefowlercenter.org.
URL www.thefowlercenter.org

Michigan State University High School Engineering Institute

Michigan State University
1410 Engineering Building
East Lansing, Michigan 48824

General Information Coed residential academic program established in 1962.
Program Focus Six-day summer residential program designed to encourage students to consider engineering as a career option.
Academics Computers, engineering, mathematics, physics.
Special Interest Areas Career exploration.
Program Information 1 session per year. Session length: 5 days in July. Ages: 16–18. 100–120 participants per session. Boarding program cost: $400–$500. Financial aid available. Open to participants entering grade 10.
Application Deadline May 28.
Contact Jonathan Lembright, Director, High School Engineering Institute, main address above. Phone: 517-355-6616 Ext.6. Fax: 517-432-1350. E-mail: lembrigh@egr.msu.edu.
URL www.egr.msu.edu/egr/programs/bachelors/hsei.php

Michigan Technological University American Indian Workshop

Michigan Technological University
1400 Townsend Drive
Houghton, Michigan 49931-1295

General Information Coed residential academic program established in 1988.
Program Focus Native American study, computers, math, biology, physiology, and ecology.
Academics Biology, computers, ecology, environmental science, health sciences, mathematics, physiology, science (general), technology.
Arts Arts and crafts (general), dance.
Special Interest Areas Native American culture, career exploration, field research/expeditions.
Trips College tours, cultural, day.
Program Information 1 session per year. Session length: 1 week in June, July. Ages: 12–15. 50–70 participants per session. Financial aid available. No cost for Michigan residents; $465 for out-of-state residents.
Application Deadline April 30.
Jobs Positions for college students 18 and older.
Contact John Lehman, Youth Programs Coordinator, main address above. Phone: 906-487-2219. Fax: 906-487-3101. E-mail: yp@mtu.edu.
URL youthprograms.mtu.edu

Michigan Technological University Explorations in Engineering Workshop

Michigan Technological University
1400 Townsend Drive
Houghton, Michigan 49931-1295

General Information Coed residential academic program established in 1988. Formal opportunities for the academically talented.
Program Focus Engineering, science, and mathematics.
Academics Computers, engineering, geology/earth science, mathematics, physics, science (general).
Special Interest Areas Career exploration, electronics, robotics, team building.
Trips College tours, cultural, day.
Program Information 1 session per year. Session length: 1 week in July. Ages: 14–18. 100–120 participants per session. Financial aid available. Cost (excluding travel and registration fee) covered by scholarship.
Application Deadline April 9.
Jobs Positions for college students 18 and older.
Contact John Lehman, Youth Programs Coordinator, main address above. Phone: 906-487-2219. Fax: 906-487-3101. E-mail: yp@mtu.edu.
URL youthprograms.mtu.edu

Michigan Technological University Honors Orchestra Program

Michigan Technological University
1400 Townsend Drive
Houghton, Michigan 49931-1295

General Information Coed residential arts program established in 1994. Formal opportunities for the artistically talented.
Program Focus Honors orchestra environment, masters classes, career investigation while performing alongside professionals in an opera setting.
Academics Music (Advanced Placement).
Arts Band, music, music (chamber), music (classical), music (ensemble), music (instrumental), music (jazz), music (orchestral), musical performance/recitals, musical productions.
Trips College tours, cultural, day, overnight.
Program Information 1 session per year. Session length: 14–22 days in June, July. Ages: 15–18. 20–30 participants per session. Application fee: $10. Financial aid available. Cost (excluding travel and registration fee) covered by scholarship.
Application Deadline March 1.
Jobs Positions for college students 18 and older.
Contact John Lehman, Youth Programs Coordinator, main address above. Phone: 906-487-2219. Fax: 906-487-3101. E-mail: yp@mtu.edu.
URL youthprograms.mtu.edu

Michigan Technological University Summer Youth Program

Michigan Technological University
1400 Townsend Drive
Houghton, Michigan 49931

General Information Coed residential and day academic program, outdoor program, and arts program established in 1973.
Program Focus Explorations in careers and knowledge; university residential living.
Academics English as a second language, Spanish language/literature, academics (general), aerospace science, biology, business, chemistry, computer programming, computer science (Advanced Placement), computers, ecology, engineering, environmental science, geology/earth science, health sciences, physiology, precollege program, science (general), writing.
Arts Acting, arts, arts and crafts (general), ceramics, creative writing, dance (folk), drawing, fabric arts, painting, photography, pottery, theater/drama.
Special Interest Areas College planning, electronics, field research/expeditions, model rocketry, nature study, robotics.
Sports Rappelling.
Wilderness/Outdoors Backpacking, hiking, mountaineering, orienteering, outdoor adventure, outdoor camping, rock climbing, wilderness/outdoors (general).
Trips College tours, cultural, day, overnight.
Program Information 70–80 sessions per year. Session length: 1 week in July, August. Ages: 12–18. 10–20 participants per session. Day program cost: $290. Boarding program cost: $495–$720. Financial aid available.
Application Deadline Continuous.
Jobs Positions for college students 18 and older.
Contact John Lehman, Youth Programs Coordinator, main address above. Phone: 906-487-2219. Fax: 906-487-3101. E-mail: yp@mtu.edu.
URL youthprograms.mtu.edu

Michigan Technological University Women in Engineering Workshop

Michigan Technological University
1400 Townsend Drive
Houghton, Michigan 49931-1295

General Information Girls' residential academic program established in 1973. Formal opportunities for the academically talented.
Program Focus Engineering, science, and mathematics.
Academics Computers, engineering, geology/earth science, mathematics, physics, science (general).
Special Interest Areas Career exploration, electronics, robotics, team building.
Trips College tours, cultural, day.
Program Information 1 session per year. Session length: 1 week in June, July. Ages: 14–18. 100–120 participants per session. Financial aid available. Cost (excluding travel and registration fee) covered by scholarship.
Application Deadline April 9.
Jobs Positions for college students 18 and older.

Michigan Technological University Women in Engineering Workshop (continued)

Contact Mr. John Lehman, Youth Programs Coordinator, main address above. Phone: 906-487-2219. Fax: 906-487-3101. E-mail: yp@mtu.edu.
URL youthprograms.mtu.edu

THE NATIONAL MUSIC WORKSHOP DAY JAMS–ANN ARBOR, MI

National Guitar Workshop
Rudolph Steiner School
2230 Pontiac Trail
Ann Arbor, Michigan 48105

General Information Coed day arts program established in 1999. Formal opportunities for the artistically talented.
Program Focus Rock 'n' roll day camp.
Academics Music.
Arts Arts and crafts (general), band, guitar, music, music (rock), music (vocal).
Program Information 2 sessions per year. Session length: 5–10 days in July. Ages: 9–15. 40–70 participants per session. Day program cost: $425–$495. Application fee: $35. Financial aid available.
Application Deadline Continuous.
Jobs Positions for high school students 17 and older and college students 17 and older.
Contact Lynda Wlodarczyk, Associate Director, 407A Bantam Road, Suite 1, Litchfield, Connecticut 06759. Phone: 800-295-5956. Fax: 860-567-0374. E-mail: lynda@dayjams.com.
URL www.dayjams.com

ROBOTICS CAMP

School of Engineering and Technology/Lake Superior State University
650 West Easterday Avenue
Sault Ste. Marie, Michigan 49783

General Information Boys' residential and day academic program established in 1990. Formal opportunities for the academically talented.
Program Focus Hands-on experiences with computer programming, industrial robots, automation, data acquisition, computer animation and electronics.
Academics Computer programming, computer science (Advanced Placement), engineering, technology.
Special Interest Areas Robotics.
Trips College tours, day, shopping.
Program Information 1–2 sessions per year. Session length: 5 days in July. Ages: 13–18. 16 participants per session. Day program cost: $595. Boarding program cost: $695. Financial aid available.
Application Deadline Continuous.
Contact Ms. Jeanne Shibley, Special Assistant to the Provost, main address above. Phone: 906-635-2597. Fax: 906-635-6663. E-mail: jmshibly@lssu.edu.
URL engineering.lssu.edu

STUDENT CONSERVATION ASSOCIATION–CONSERVATION CREW PROGRAM (MICHIGAN)

Student Conservation Association (SCA)
Michigan

General Information Coed residential outdoor program, community service program, and wilderness program established in 1957. High school credit may be earned.
Program Focus Resource management, conservation and environmental education.
Academics Biology, botany, ecology, environmental science, geology/earth science, history.
Special Interest Areas Campcraft, community service, construction, leadership training, nature study, trail maintenance, work camp programs.
Sports Canoeing, fishing, kayaking, swimming.
Wilderness/Outdoors Backpacking, hiking, orienteering, outdoor living skills, wilderness camping.
Trips Cultural, day, overnight.
Program Information 2–3 sessions per year. Session length: 3–5 weeks in June, July, August. Ages: 15–19. 6–8 participants per session. Application fee: $20. Financial aid available. No cost for program; financial aid possible for travel expenses.
Application Deadline Continuous.
Jobs Positions for college students 21 and older.
Contact Recruitment Office, PO Box 550, Charlestown, New Hampshire 03603. Phone: 603-543-1700. Fax: 603-543-1828. E-mail: getreal@thesca.org.
URL www.theSCA.org

SUMMER DISCOVERY AT MICHIGAN

Summer Discovery
University of Michigan
Ann Arbor, Michigan 48109

General Information Coed residential academic program established in 1991. High school credit may be earned.
Program Focus Pre-college enrichment.
Academics American literature, English as a second language, English language/literature, Russian language/literature, SAT/ACT preparation, academics (general), archaeology, architecture, art (Advanced Placement), art history/appreciation, business, communications, computers, economics, environmental science, government and politics, history, humanities, journalism, mathematics, mathematics (Advanced Placement), music, philosophy, precollege program, psychology, reading, social science, social studies, speech/debate, study skills, writing.
Arts Arts and crafts (general), band, ceramics, creative writing, drawing, jewelry making, metalworking, music, music (instrumental), music (vocal), painting, photography, printmaking, sculpture, television/video, theater/drama.
Special Interest Areas Career exploration, community service, driver's education.
Sports Aerobics, basketball, boating, football, golf, rowing (crew/sculling), soccer, softball, sports (general), swimming, tennis, volleyball, weight training.

Wilderness/Outdoors Canoe trips, hiking, wilderness camping.
Trips College tours, cultural, day, overnight.
Program Information 3 sessions per year. Session length: 3–6 weeks in June, July, August. 400 participants per session. Boarding program cost: $3699–$5699. Application fee: $60–$70. Open to participants completing grades 9–11.
Application Deadline Continuous.
Jobs Positions for college students 21 and older.
Contact The Musiker Family, Director, 1326 Old Northern Boulevard, Roslyn Village, New York 11576. Phone: 888-878-6637. Fax: 516-625-3438. E-mail: discovery@summerfun.com.
URL www.summerfun.com

For more information, see page 1338.

Suzuki Family Camp

Blue Lake Fine Arts Camp, Inc.
300 East Crystal Lake Road
Twin Lake, Michigan 49457

General Information Coed residential and day arts program established in 1972. Formal opportunities for the artistically talented.
Program Focus Suzuki method of music instruction.
Arts Arts and crafts (general), music, music (chamber), music (classical), music (instrumental), music (orchestral).
Sports Basketball, football, soccer, swimming, track and field.
Program Information 3 sessions per year. Session length: 3 days in June. Ages: 2–18. 350 participants per session. Boarding program cost: $250–$425. Application fee: $30.
Application Deadline Continuous.
Jobs Positions for college students 18 and older.
Contact Admissions, Blue Lake Fine Arts Camp, main address above. Phone: 800-221-3796. Fax: 231-893-5120.
URL www.bluelake.org

Women in Technology

School of Engineering and Technology/Lake Superior State University
650 West Easterday Avenue
Sault Ste. Marie, Michigan 49783

General Information Girls' residential and day academic program established in 1991. Formal opportunities for the academically talented.
Program Focus Hands-on experiences with computer programming, industrial robots, automation, data acquisition, computer animation and electronics.
Academics Computer programming, computer science (Advanced Placement), engineering, technology.
Special Interest Areas Robotics.
Trips College tours, day, shopping.
Program Information 1–2 sessions per year. Session length: 5 days in June. Ages: 13–18. 16 participants per session. Day program cost: $595. Boarding program cost: $695. Financial aid available.
Application Deadline Continuous.
Contact Ms. Jeanne Shibley, Special Assistant to the Provost, main address above. Phone: 906-635-2597. Fax: 906-635-6663. E-mail: jmshibly@lssu.edu.
URL engineering.lssu.edu

YMCA Camp Pendalouan–Bugs and Bunks

YMCA Camp Pendalouan
1243 East Fruitvale Road
Montague, Michigan 49437

General Information Coed residential traditional camp. Accredited by American Camping Association.
Arts Arts and crafts (general), music.
Special Interest Areas Nature study.
Sports Archery, basketball, canoeing, climbing (wall), fishing, swimming.
Program Information 4–7 sessions per year. Session length: 3 days in June, July, August. Ages: 6–8. Boarding program cost: $150. Financial aid available.
Application Deadline Continuous.
Jobs Positions for high school students 17 and older and college students 18 and older.
Contact Darryl Thompson Powell, Summer Camp Director, main address above. Phone: 231-894-4538. Fax: 231-894-4448. E-mail: summer@pendalouan.org.
URL www.pendalouan.org

YMCA Camp Pendalouan–Counselor-in-Training

YMCA Camp Pendalouan
1243 East Fruitvale Road
Montague, Michigan 49437

General Information Coed residential traditional camp. Accredited by American Camping Association.
Program Focus Teen leadership training.
Arts Arts and crafts (general), music, theater/drama.
Special Interest Areas Counselor-in-training program, leadership training, nature study.
Sports Archery, basketball, canoeing, climbing (wall), fishing, horseback riding, riflery, ropes course, sailing, windsurfing.
Wilderness/Outdoors Backpacking, bicycle trips, canoe trips, hiking.
Program Information 1 session per year. Session length: 12 days in June. Ages: 15–16. Boarding program cost: $285. Financial aid available.
Application Deadline Continuous.
Jobs Positions for high school students 18 and older and college students 18 and older.
Contact Darryl Thompson Powell, Summer Camp Director, main address above. Phone: 231-894-4538. Fax: 231-894-4448. E-mail: summer@pendalouan.org.
URL www.pendalouan.org

YMCA Camp Pendalouan–Resident Camp

YMCA Camp Pendalouan
1243 East Fruitvale Road
Montague, Michigan 49437

General Information Coed residential traditional camp established in 1925. Accredited by American Camping Association.
Arts Arts and crafts (general), music, photography, theater/drama.
Special Interest Areas Nature study.
Sports Archery, basketball, canoeing, climbing (wall), fishing, horseback riding, riflery, ropes course, sailing, windsurfing.
Wilderness/Outdoors Backpacking, bicycle trips, canoe trips, hiking.
Program Information 7 sessions per year. Session length: 6 days in June, July, August. Ages: 7–13. 135 participants per session. Boarding program cost: $355. Financial aid available.
Application Deadline Continuous.
Jobs Positions for high school students 18 and older and college students 18 and older.
Contact Darryl Thompson Powell, Summer Camp Director, main address above. Phone: 231-894-4538. Fax: 231-894-4448. E-mail: summer@pendalouan.org.
URL www.pendalouan.org

YMCA Camp Pendalouan–Ropers and Wranglers Horse Camp

YMCA Camp Pendalouan
1243 East Fruitvale Road
Montague, Michigan 49437

General Information Coed residential traditional camp established in 1925. Accredited by American Camping Association.
Program Focus Horseback riding.
Sports Horseback riding, ropes course, swimming.
Program Information 7 sessions per year. Session length: 6 days in June, July, August. Ages: 10–15. 10–20 participants per session. Boarding program cost: $445. Financial aid available.
Application Deadline Continuous.
Jobs Positions for high school students 18 and older and college students 18 and older.
Contact Darryl Thompson Powell, Summer Camp Director, main address above. Phone: 231-894-4538. Fax: 231-894-4448. E-mail: summer@pendalouan.org.
URL www.pendalouan.org

YMCA Camp Pendalouan–Teen Xtreme

YMCA Camp Pendalouan
1243 East Fruitvale Road
Montague, Michigan 49437

General Information Coed residential traditional camp. Accredited by American Camping Association.
Arts Arts and crafts (general), music, theater/drama.
Special Interest Areas Nature study.
Sports Archery, basketball, canoeing, climbing (wall), fishing, horseback riding, riflery, ropes course, sailing, windsurfing.
Wilderness/Outdoors Backpacking, bicycle trips, canoe trips.
Trips Day, overnight.
Program Information 7 sessions per year. Session length: 6 days in June, July, August. Ages: 13–15. Boarding program cost: $375. Financial aid available.
Application Deadline Continuous.
Jobs Positions for college students 21 and older.
Contact Darryl Thompson Powell, Summer Camp Director, main address above. Phone: 231-894-4538. Fax: 231-894-4448. E-mail: summer@pendalouan.org.
URL www.pendalouan.org

MINNESOTA

Camp Buckskin

9830 Fredrickson Lane
Ely, Minnesota 55731

General Information Coed residential traditional camp, academic program, and special needs program established in 1959. Accredited by American Camping Association. Specific services available for the learning disabled, participant with AD/HD, and participant with Aspergers Syndrome. High school credit may be earned.
Program Focus To improve social skills along with some academic skills so campers can experience and enjoy greater success.
Academics Environmental science, reading, remedial academics, science (general), study skills, writing.
Arts Beading, creative writing, drawing, jewelry making, music, painting, sculpture, tie-dyeing, weaving.
Special Interest Areas Campcraft, career exploration, leadership training, nature study, social skills development, weight reduction.
Sports Aerobics, archery, baseball, basketball, canoeing, field hockey, fishing, football, frisbee, hacky sack, riflery, soccer, softball, swimming, volleyball, water polo, weight training.
Wilderness/Outdoors Backpacking, canoe trips, hiking, orienteering, wilderness camping.
Trips Cultural, overnight.
Program Information 2 sessions per year. Session length: 30 days in June, July, August. Ages: 6–18. 140 participants per session. Boarding program cost: $2825–$2925.
Application Deadline Continuous.
Jobs Positions for high school students 17 and older and college students 18 and older.
Summer Contact Tom Bauer, Director, PO Box 389, Ely, Minnesota 55731. Phone: 218-365-2121. Fax: 218-365-2880. E-mail: buckskin@spacestar.net.
Winter Contact Tom Bauer, Director, 8700 West 36th Street, Suite 6W, St. Louis Park, Minnesota 55426. Phone: 952-930-3544. Fax: 952-938-6996. E-mail: buckskin@spacestar.net.
URL www.campbuckskin.com

Camp Chippewa for Boys

Camp Chippewa Foundation
22767 Cap Endres Road
Chippewa National Forest
Cass Lake, Minnesota 56633

General Information Boys' residential traditional camp established in 1935. Accredited by American Camping Association.
Program Focus A broad program balanced between land and water.
Special Interest Areas Campcraft, leadership training, nature study.
Sports Archery, boating, canoeing, diving, fencing, fishing, kayaking, riflery, sailing, soccer, softball, swimming, tennis, volleyball, waterskiing, windsurfing.
Wilderness/Outdoors Canoe trips, wilderness camping.
Trips Day, overnight.
Program Information 6 sessions per year. Session length: 2–8 weeks in June, July, August. Ages: 7–17. 70 participants per session. Boarding program cost: $1600–$5700.
Application Deadline Continuous.
Jobs Positions for college students 19 and older.
Summer Contact Michael K. Thompson, Director, main address above. Phone: 218-335-8807. Fax: 218-335-7742. E-mail: mike@campchippewa.com.
Winter Contact Michael K. Thompson, Director, 15 East 5th Street, Suite 4022, Tulsa, Oklahoma 74103. Phone: 800-262-1544. Fax: 918-582-7896. E-mail: mike@campchippewa.com.
URL www.campchippewa.com

Camp Friendship

Friendship Ventures
10509 108th Street, NW
Annandale, Minnesota 55302

General Information Coed residential and day traditional camp and special needs program established in 1965. Accredited by American Camping Association. Specific services available for the developmentally challenged and physically challenged.
Program Focus Provide resident camp services to children and adults with developmental disabilities.
Arts Arts and crafts (general), dance, jewelry making, leather working, music, puppetry.
Special Interest Areas Nature study.
Sports Archery, bicycling, boating, canoeing, climbing (wall), fishing, golf, horseback riding, ropes course, sailing, swimming.
Wilderness/Outdoors Bicycle trips, hiking.
Trips Day, overnight.
Program Information 12 sessions per year. Session length: 6–14 days in January, June, July, August, December. Ages: 5+. 60–125 participants per session. Day program cost: $77–$118. Boarding program cost: $595–$1800. Financial aid available.
Application Deadline Continuous.
Jobs Positions for high school students 16 and older and college students 18 and older.
Contact Georgann Rumsey, President/CEO, main address above. Phone: 952-852-0101. Fax: 952-852-0123. E-mail: fv@friendshipventures.org.
URL www.friendshipventures.org

Camp Heartland Summer Camp–Minnesota

Camp Heartland
Willow River
Minnesota

General Information Coed residential traditional camp and special needs program established in 1993. Specific services available for the participant with HIV/AIDS.
Program Focus Traditional camp for kids living with or affected by HIV/AIDS.
Arts Arts and crafts (general), chorus, creative writing, dance, film.
Sports Archery, baseball, basketball, bicycling, canoeing, climbing (wall), fishing, ropes course.
Wilderness/Outdoors Hiking.
Trips Day, overnight.
Program Information 5 sessions per year. Session length: 6–7 days in July, August. Ages: 7–15. 80 participants per session. No cost for program, airfare provided, $50 registration fee for accepted participants.
Application Deadline Continuous.
Jobs Positions for college students 18 and older.
Contact Ms. Tiffany White, Registrar & Client Services Manager, 3133 Hennepin Avenue, South, Minneapolis, Minnesota 55408. Phone: 612-824-6464. Fax: 612-824-6303. E-mail: tiffany@campheartland.org.
URL www.campheartland.org

Camp Lincoln Fishing Camp

Camp Lincoln/Camp Lake Hubert
Lake Hubert, Minnesota 56459

General Information Boys' residential sports camp established in 1995. Accredited by American Camping Association.
Program Focus Fishing.
Sports Archery, basketball, bicycling, fishing, horseback riding, riflery, sailing, swimming.
Program Information 2 sessions per year. Session length: 6–7 days in June. Ages: 8–15. 16 participants per session. Boarding program cost: $780. Financial aid available.
Application Deadline Continuous.
Jobs Positions for college students 19 and older.
Summer Contact Sam Cote, Director, Box 1308, Lake Hubert, Minnesota 56459. Phone: 218-963-2339. Fax: 218-963-2447. E-mail: home@lincoln-lakehubert.com.
Winter Contact Sam Cote, Director, 10179 Crosstown Circle, Eden Prairie, Minnesota 55344. Phone: 800-242-1909. Fax: 952-922-7149. E-mail: home@lincoln-lakehubert.com.
URL www.lincoln-lakehubert.com

Camp Lincoln for Boys/Camp Lake Hubert for Girls

Camp Lincoln/Camp Lake Hubert
Lake Hubert, Minnesota 56459

General Information Residential traditional camp established in 1909. Accredited by American Camping Association.
Arts Arts and crafts (general), ceramics, dance, dance (jazz), dance (modern), leather working, painting, photography, pottery, theater/drama, weaving, woodworking.
Special Interest Areas Campcraft, leadership training, nature study.
Sports Aerobics, archery, baseball, basketball, bicycling, canoeing, cheerleading, climbing (wall), fishing, golf, gymnastics, horseback riding, kayaking, lacrosse, riflery, ropes course, rowing (crew/sculling), sailing, snorkeling, soccer, softball, sports (general), swimming, tennis, volleyball, water polo, windsurfing, wrestling.
Wilderness/Outdoors Backpacking, bicycle trips, canoe trips, hiking, mountain biking, orienteering, rock climbing, white-water trips.
Trips Overnight.
Program Information 13 sessions per year. Session length: 12–27 days in June, July, August. Ages: 8–16. 200 participants per session. Boarding program cost: $1695–$3100. Financial aid available.
Application Deadline Continuous.
Jobs Positions for college students 19 and older.
Summer Contact Sam Cote, Director, Box 1308, Lake Hubert, Minnesota 56459. Phone: 218-963-2339. Fax: 218-963-2447. E-mail: home@lincoln-lakehubert.com.
Winter Contact Bill Jones, Director, 10179 Crosstown Circle, Eden Prairie, Minnesota 55344. Phone: 800-242-1909. Fax: 952-922-7149. E-mail: home@lincoln-lakehubert.com.
URL www.lincoln-lakehubert.com

Camp Lincoln for Boys/Camp Lake Hubert for Girls Family Camp

Camp Lincoln/Camp Lake Hubert
Lake Hubert, Minnesota 56459

General Information Coed residential family program established in 1909. Accredited by American Camping Association.
Arts Arts and crafts (general), ceramics, fabric arts, leather working, photography, pottery.
Sports Archery, basketball, bicycling, boating, canoeing, fishing, golf, horseback riding, kayaking, riflery, ropes course, sailing, soccer, softball, swimming, tennis, volleyball, water polo, windsurfing.
Wilderness/Outdoors Hiking.
Program Information 1 session per year. Session length: 5 days in August. Ages: 1+. 120 participants per session. Boarding program cost: $475–$595. Financial aid available.
Application Deadline Continuous.
Jobs Positions for college students 19 and older.
Summer Contact Sam Cote, Director, Box 1308, Lake Hubert, Minnesota 56459. Phone: 218-963-2339. Fax: 218-963-2447. E-mail: home@lincoln-lakehubert.com.
Winter Contact Bill Jones, Director, 10179 Crosstown Circle, Eden Prairie, Minnesota 55344. Phone: 800-242-1909. Fax: 952-922-7149. E-mail: home@lincoln-lakehubert.com.
URL www.lincoln-lakehubert.com

Camp Lincoln for Boys/Camp Lake Hubert for Girls Golf Camp

Camp Lincoln/Camp Lake Hubert
Lake Hubert, Minnesota 56459

General Information Coed residential sports camp established in 1990. Accredited by American Camping Association.
Program Focus Golf.
Sports Archery, bicycling, canoeing, fishing, golf, horseback riding, riflery, sailing, soccer, swimming, windsurfing.
Program Information 3 sessions per year. Session length: 4–6 days in June, July, August. Ages: 8–16. 16–28 participants per session. Boarding program cost: $780–$835. Financial aid available.
Application Deadline Continuous.
Jobs Positions for college students 19 and older.
Summer Contact Sam Cote, Director, Box 1308, Lake Hubert, Minnesota 56459. Phone: 218-963-2339. Fax: 218-963-2447. E-mail: home@lincoln-lakehubert.com.
Winter Contact Sam Cote, Director, 10179 Crosstown Circle, Eden Prairie, Minnesota 55344. Phone: 800-242-1909. Fax: 952-922-7149. E-mail: home@lincoln-lakehubert.com.
URL www.lincoln-lakehubert.com

Camp Lincoln for Boys/Camp Lake Hubert for Girls Tennis Camp

Camp Lincoln/Camp Lake Hubert
Lake Hubert, Minnesota 56459

General Information Coed residential sports camp established in 1972. Accredited by American Camping Association.
Program Focus Tennis.
Sports Archery, basketball, bicycling, canoeing, horseback riding, kayaking, riflery, ropes course, sailing, soccer, swimming, tennis, volleyball, water polo, windsurfing.
Program Information 2–3 sessions per year. Session length: 6–7 days in August. Ages: 8–16. 40 participants per session. Boarding program cost: $780. Financial aid available.
Application Deadline Continuous.
Jobs Positions for college students 19 and older.
Summer Contact Sam Cote, Director, Box 1308, Lake Hubert, Minnesota 56459. Phone: 218-963-2339. Fax: 218-963-2447. E-mail: home@lincoln-lakehubert.com.

Winter Contact Sam Cote, Director, 10179 Crosstown Circle, Eden Prairie, Minnesota 55344. Phone: 800-242-1909. Fax: 952-922-7149. E-mail: home@lincoln-lakehubert.com.
URL www.lincoln-lakehubert.com

Camp Mishawaka for Boys

New Camps, Inc.
Grand Rapids, Minnesota 55744

General Information Boys' residential traditional camp established in 1910. Accredited by American Camping Association.
Arts Arts and crafts (general), ceramics, drawing, music, pottery, theater/drama, woodworking.
Special Interest Areas Campcraft, leadership training, model rocketry, nature study.
Sports Archery, badminton, baseball, basketball, bicycling, boating, canoeing, climbing (wall), fishing, floor hockey, horseback riding, kayaking, riflery, ropes course, sailing, snorkeling, soccer, softball, sports (general), street/roller hockey, swimming, table tennis/ping-pong, tennis, volleyball, waterskiing, weight training, windsurfing.
Wilderness/Outdoors Backpacking, canoe trips, hiking, mountain biking, rafting, white-water trips, wilderness camping.
Trips Cultural, day, overnight.
Program Information 5 sessions per year. Session length: 2–8 weeks in June, July, August. Ages: 9–16. 140 participants per session. Boarding program cost: $1600–$5000.
Application Deadline Continuous.
Jobs Positions for college students 18 and older.
Contact Steve Purdum, Executive Director, PO Box 368, Grand Rapids, Minnesota 55744. Phone: 218-326-5011. Fax: 218-326-9228. E-mail: info@campmishawaka.com.
URL www.campmishawaka.com/boys.php

Camp Mishawaka for Girls

New Camps, Inc.
Grand Rapids, Minnesota 55744

General Information Girls' residential traditional camp established in 1910. Accredited by American Camping Association.
Arts Arts and crafts (general), ceramics, drawing, music, pottery, theater/drama, woodworking.
Special Interest Areas Campcraft, leadership training, model rocketry, nature study.
Sports Archery, baseball, basketball, bicycling, boating, canoeing, climbing (wall), fishing, horseback riding, kayaking, riflery, ropes course, sailing, snorkeling, soccer, softball, street/roller hockey, swimming, tennis, volleyball, waterskiing, weight training, windsurfing.
Wilderness/Outdoors Backpacking, canoe trips, hiking, mountain biking, rafting, white-water trips, wilderness camping.
Trips Day, overnight.
Program Information 5 sessions per year. Session length: 2–8 weeks in June, July, August. Ages: 9–16. 140 participants per session. Boarding program cost: $1600–$5000.
Application Deadline Continuous.
Jobs Positions for college students 18 and older.
Contact Steve Purdum, Executive Director, PO Box 368, Grand Rapids, Minnesota 55744. Phone: 218-326-5011. Fax: 218-326-9228. E-mail: info@campmichawaka.com.
URL www.campmishawaka.com/girls.php

Carleton College Summer Writing Program

Carleton College
1 North College Street
Northfield, Minnesota 55057-4016

General Information Coed residential academic program established in 1976. Formal opportunities for the academically talented. College credit may be earned.
Program Focus Writing, literature, writing college-level papers.
Academics American literature, English language/literature, writing.
Trips Cultural.
Program Information 1 session per year. Session length: 20 days in July. Ages: 16–18. 80–90 participants per session. Boarding program cost: $1900–$2100. Financial aid available.
Application Deadline April 1.
Contact Becky Fineran-Gardner, Director of Summer Academic Programs, main address above. Phone: 507-646-4038. Fax: 507-646-4540. E-mail: swp@carleton.edu.
URL www.webapps.acs.Carleton.edu/campus/SAP/writing/

Catholic Youth Camp

Catholic Youth Camp
19590 520th Lane
McGregor, Minnesota 55760

General Information Coed residential traditional camp and bible camp established in 1947. Religious affiliation: Roman Catholic. Accredited by American Camping Association.
Academics Religion.
Arts Arts and crafts (general), clowning, creative writing, dance, dance (folk), fabric arts, leather working, music, theater/drama.
Special Interest Areas Leadership training, nature study, team building.
Sports Archery, baseball, basketball, boating, canoeing, fishing, football, ropes course, soccer, softball, swimming, volleyball.
Wilderness/Outdoors Canoe trips, hiking, wilderness camping.
Trips Day, overnight.
Program Information 9 sessions per year. Session length: 4–10 days in June, July, August. Ages: 7–18. 120–150 participants per session. Boarding program cost: $210–$380. Application fee: $50. Financial aid available.

Catholic Youth Camp (continued)

Application Deadline Continuous.
Jobs Positions for high school students 16 and older and college students 18 and older.
Summer Contact Ms. Maggie Braun, Co-Director, main address above. Phone: 218-426-3383. Fax: 218-426-4675. E-mail: camp@cycamp.org.
Winter Contact Ms. Maggie Braun, Co-Director, 2131 Fairview Avenue North, Suite 200, Roseville, Minnesota 55113. Phone: 651-636-1645. Fax: 651-628-9323. E-mail: office@cycamp.org.
URL www.cycamp.org

Concordia Language Villages–Chinese

Concordia College
Bemidji, Minnesota

General Information Coed residential academic program and cultural program established in 1961. Accredited by American Camping Association. Formal opportunities for the academically talented. High school credit may be earned.
Program Focus World languages and culture.
Academics Chinese languages/literature, music, peace education.
Arts Arts and crafts (general), batiking, ceramics, chorus, dance, dance (folk), drawing, jewelry making, leather working, music, music (vocal), painting, pottery, radio broadcasting, theater/drama, weaving.
Special Interest Areas Cross-cultural education.
Sports Canoeing, martial arts, swimming.
Wilderness/Outdoors Hiking.
Trips Cultural.
Program Information 5 sessions per year. Session length: 6–28 days in July, August. Ages: 7–18. 142 participants per session. Boarding program cost: $575–$2585. Financial aid available.
Application Deadline Continuous.
Jobs Positions for high school students 17 and older and college students 18 and older.
Contact Alex Loehrer, Assistant Director, Public Relations, 901 South Eighth Street, Moorhead, Minnesota 56562. Phone: 218-299-4544. Fax: 218-299-3807. E-mail: clv@cord.edu.
URL www.ConcordiaLanguageVillages.org

Concordia Language Villages–Danish

Concordia College
Bemidji, Minnesota

General Information Coed residential academic program and cultural program established in 1961. Accredited by American Camping Association. Formal opportunities for the academically talented. High school credit may be earned.
Program Focus World languages and culture.
Academics Danish language/literature, music, peace education.
Arts Arts and crafts (general), batiking, ceramics, dance, dance (folk), jewelry making, music, music (vocal), weaving.
Special Interest Areas Cross-cultural education.
Sports Archery, baseball, canoeing, soccer, swimming, volleyball.
Wilderness/Outdoors Canoe trips, hiking.
Program Information 3 sessions per year. Session length: 6–28 days in August. Ages: 7–18. 85 participants per session. Boarding program cost: $575–$2585. Financial aid available.
Application Deadline Continuous.
Jobs Positions for high school students 17 and older and college students 18 and older.
Contact Alex Loehrer, Assistant Director, Public Relations, 901 South Eighth Street, Moorhead, Minnesota 56562. Phone: 218-299-4544. Fax: 218-299-3807. E-mail: clv@cord.edu.
URL www.ConcordiaLanguageVillages.org

Concordia Language Villages–English

Concordia College
901 South Eighth Street
Moorhead, Minnesota 56562

General Information Coed residential academic program and cultural program established in 1961. Accredited by American Camping Association.
Program Focus Language.
Academics English as a second language, language study, music, peace education.
Arts Arts and crafts (general), dance, music, musical productions.
Sports Baseball, soccer, swimming.
Trips Cultural, day, overnight, shopping.
Program Information 5 sessions per year. Session length: 13–34 days in July, August. Ages: 11–20. 25–50 participants per session. Boarding program cost: $1520–$3400. Application fee: $80. Financial aid available.
Application Deadline Continuous.
Jobs Positions for high school students 18 and older and college students 18 and older.
Contact Alex Loehrer, Assistant Director, Public Relations, main address above. Phone: 800-222-4750. Fax: 218-299-3807. E-mail: clv@cord.edu.
URL www.ConcordiaLanguageVillages.org

Concordia Language Villages–Finnish

Concordia College
Bemidji, Minnesota

General Information Coed residential academic program and cultural program established in 1961. Accredited by American Camping Association. Formal opportunities for the academically talented. High school credit may be earned.
Program Focus World languages and culture.
Academics Finnish language/literature, music, peace education.
Arts Arts and crafts (general), batiking, dance, dance (folk), jewelry making, music, music (vocal), weaving.
Special Interest Areas Cross-cultural education.

Sports Archery, baseball, canoeing, soccer, swimming, volleyball.
Wilderness/Outdoors Canoe trips, hiking.
Program Information 5 sessions per year. Session length: 6–28 days in June, July. Ages: 7–18. 185 participants per session. Boarding program cost: \$575–\$2585. Financial aid available.
Application Deadline Continuous.
Jobs Positions for high school students 17 and older and college students 18 and older.
Contact Alex Loehrer, Assistant Director, Public Relations, 901 South Eighth Street, Moorhead, Minnesota 56562. Phone: 218-299-4544. Fax: 218-299-3807. E-mail: clv@cord.edu.
URL www.ConcordiaLanguageVillages.org

Concordia Language Villages–French–Bemidji

Concordia College
Bemidji, Minnesota

General Information Coed residential academic program and cultural program established in 1961. Accredited by American Camping Association. Formal opportunities for the academically talented. High school or college credit may be earned.
Program Focus World languages and culture.
Academics French (Advanced Placement), French language/literature, music (Advanced Placement), peace education.
Arts Arts and crafts (general), batiking, dance, dance (folk), jewelry making, leather working, music (vocal).
Special Interest Areas Cross-cultural education.
Sports Archery, canoeing, fencing, swimming, volleyball.
Wilderness/Outdoors Canoe trips, hiking.
Program Information 9 sessions per year. Session length: 6–28 days in June, July, August. Ages: 7–18. 128 participants per session. Boarding program cost: \$575–\$2870. Financial aid available.
Application Deadline Continuous.
Jobs Positions for high school students 17 and older and college students 18 and older.
Contact Alex Loehrer, Assistant Director, Public Relations, 901 South Eighth Street, Moorhead, Minnesota 56562. Phone: 218-299-4544. Fax: 218-299-3807. E-mail: clv@cord.edu.
URL www.ConcordiaLanguageVillages.org

Concordia Language Villages–French–Camp Holiday

Concordia College
Hackensack, Minnesota

General Information Coed residential academic program and cultural program established in 1961. Accredited by American Camping Association. Formal opportunities for the academically talented. High school credit may be earned.
Program Focus World language and culture.
Academics French (Advanced Placement), French language/literature, music, peace education.
Arts Arts and crafts (general), dance, dance (folk), music, music (vocal).
Special Interest Areas Cross-cultural education.
Sports Canoeing, fencing, soccer, swimming, volleyball.
Wilderness/Outdoors Canoe trips, hiking.
Program Information 6 sessions per year. Session length: 6–26 days in June, July, August. Ages: 7–18. 526 participants per session. Boarding program cost: \$575–\$2585. Financial aid available.
Application Deadline Continuous.
Jobs Positions for high school students 17 and older and college students 18 and older.
Contact Alex Loehrer, Assistant Director, Public Relations, 901 South Eighth Street, Moorhead, Minnesota 56562. Phone: 218-299-4544. Fax: 218-299-3807. E-mail: clv@cord.edu.
URL www.ConcordiaLanguageVillages.org

Concordia Language Villages–French–Fosston

Concordia College
Fosston, Minnesota

General Information Coed residential academic program and cultural program established in 1961. Accredited by American Camping Association. Formal opportunities for the academically talented. High school credit may be earned.
Program Focus World languages and culture.
Academics French (Advanced Placement), French language/literature, music, peace education.
Arts Arts and crafts (general), dance, dance (folk), music, music (vocal).
Special Interest Areas Cross-cultural education.
Sports Canoeing, fencing, soccer, swimming, volleyball.
Wilderness/Outdoors Canoe trips, hiking.
Program Information 4 sessions per year. Session length: 6–28 days in July, August. Ages: 8–18. 157 participants per session. Boarding program cost: \$575–\$2585. Financial aid available.
Application Deadline Continuous.
Jobs Positions for high school students 17 and older and college students 18 and older.
Contact Alex Loehrer, Assistant Director, Public Relations, 901 South Eighth Street, Moorhead, Minnesota 56562. Phone: 218-299-4544. Fax: 218-299-3807. E-mail: clv@cord.edu.
URL www.ConcordiaLanguageVillages.org

Concordia Language Villages–French Voyageur

Concordia College
Bemidji, Minnesota

General Information Coed residential academic program, wilderness program, and cultural program established in 1961. Accredited by American Camping Association. High school credit may be earned.
Program Focus World languages and culture.
Academics French language/literature, music, peace education.

Concordia Language Villages–French Voyageur (continued)

Arts Arts and crafts (general), jewelry making, leather working, music (vocal).
Special Interest Areas Cross-cultural education.
Sports Canoeing, ropes course, swimming.
Wilderness/Outdoors Backpacking, canoe trips, hiking, survival training, wilderness camping.
Program Information 8 sessions per year. Session length: 6–28 days in June, July, August. Ages: 11–18. 102 participants per session. Boarding program cost: $575–$2585. Financial aid available.
Application Deadline Continuous.
Jobs Positions for high school students 17 and older and college students 18 and older.
Contact Alex Loehrer, Assistant Director, Public Relations, 901 South Eighth Street, Moorhead, Minnesota 56562. Phone: 218-299-4544. Fax: 218-299-3807. E-mail: clv@cord.edu.
URL www.ConcordiaLanguageVillages.org

Concordia Language Villages–German–Bemidji

Concordia College
Bemidji, Minnesota

General Information Coed residential academic program and cultural program established in 1961. Accredited by American Camping Association. Formal opportunities for the academically talented. High school or college credit may be earned.
Program Focus World languages and culture.
Academics German language/literature, music, peace education.
Arts Arts and crafts (general), dance, dance (folk), music, music (vocal), weaving.
Special Interest Areas Cross-cultural education.
Sports Canoeing, fencing, ropes course, soccer, swimming, volleyball.
Wilderness/Outdoors Canoe trips, hiking.
Program Information 10 sessions per year. Session length: 6–26 days in June, July, August. Ages: 7–18. 176 participants per session. Boarding program cost: $575–$2585. Financial aid available.
Application Deadline Continuous.
Jobs Positions for high school students 17 and older and college students 18 and older.
Contact Alex Loehrer, Assistant Director, Public Relations, 901 South Eighth Street, Moorhead, Minnesota 56562. Phone: 218-299-4544. Fax: 218-299-3807. E-mail: clv@cord.edu.
URL www.ConcordiaLanguageVillages.org

Concordia Language Villages–German–Camp Trowbridge

Concordia College
Vergas, Minnesota

General Information Coed residential academic program and cultural program established in 1961. Accredited by American Camping Association. High school credit may be earned.
Program Focus World languages and culture.
Academics German language/literature, music, peace education.
Arts Arts and crafts (general), dance, dance (folk), music, music (vocal), weaving.
Special Interest Areas Cross-cultural education.
Sports Canoeing, fencing, ropes course, soccer, swimming, volleyball.
Wilderness/Outdoors Canoe trips, hiking.
Program Information 4 sessions per year. Session length: 6–26 days in June, July. Ages: 7–18. 100 participants per session. Boarding program cost: $575–$2585. Financial aid available.
Application Deadline Continuous.
Jobs Positions for high school students 17 and older and college students 18 and older.
Contact Alex Loehrer, Assistant Director, Public Relations, 901 South Eighth Street, Moorhead, Minnesota 56562. Phone: 218-299-4544. Fax: 218-299-3807. E-mail: clv@cord.edu.
URL www.ConcordiaLanguageVillages.org

Concordia Language Villages–Italian

Concordia College
Hackensack, Minnesota

General Information Coed residential academic program and cultural program established in 2003. Accredited by American Camping Association. Formal opportunities for the academically talented. High school credit may be earned.
Program Focus Italian language and culture.
Academics Italian language/literature.
Arts Arts and crafts (general), dance (folk).
Sports Soccer.
Program Information 3 sessions per year. Session length: 13–28 days in July, August. Ages: 8–18. 48–72 participants per session. Boarding program cost: $1165–$2585. Financial aid available.
Application Deadline Continuous.
Jobs Positions for high school students 17 and older and college students 18 and older.
Contact Alex Loehrer, Assistant Director, Public Relations, main address above. Phone: 800-222-4750. Fax: 218-299-3807. E-mail: clv@cord.edu.
URL www.ConcordiaLanguageVillages.org

Concordia Language Villages–Japanese

Concordia College
Dent, Minnesota

General Information Coed residential academic program and cultural program established in 1961. Accredited by American Camping Association. Formal opportunities for the academically talented. High school credit may be earned.
Program Focus World languages and culture.
Academics Japanese language/literature, music, peace education.
Arts Arts and crafts (general), ceramics, dance, dance (folk), drawing, music, music (vocal), pottery, weaving.
Special Interest Areas Cross-cultural education.

Sports Canoeing, swimming, volleyball.
Wilderness/Outdoors Canoe trips, hiking.
Program Information 9 sessions per year. Session length: 6–26 days in June, July, August. Ages: 7–18. 90 participants per session. Boarding program cost: $575–$2585. Financial aid available.
Application Deadline Continuous.
Jobs Positions for high school students 17 and older and college students 18 and older.
Contact Alex Loehrer, Assistant Director, Public Relations, 901 South Eighth Street, Moorhead, Minnesota 56562. Phone: 218-299-4544. Fax: 218-299-3807. E-mail: clv@cord.edu.
URL www.ConcordiaLanguageVillages.org

Concordia Language Villages–Korean

Concordia College
Hackensack, Minnesota

General Information Coed residential academic program and cultural program established in 1961. Accredited by American Camping Association. Formal opportunities for the academically talented. High school credit may be earned.
Program Focus World languages and culture.
Academics Korean, music, peace education.
Arts Arts and crafts (general), dance, dance (folk), music, music (vocal), weaving.
Special Interest Areas Cross-cultural education.
Sports Canoeing, martial arts, swimming, volleyball.
Wilderness/Outdoors Canoe trips, hiking.
Program Information 4 sessions per year. Session length: 6–26 days in August. Ages: 7–18. 100 participants per session. Boarding program cost: $575–$2585. Financial aid available.
Application Deadline Continuous.
Jobs Positions for high school students 17 and older and college students 18 and older.
Contact Alex Loehrer, Assistant Director, Public Relations, 901 South Eighth Street, Moorhead, Minnesota 56562. Phone: 218-299-4544. Fax: 218-299-3807. E-mail: clv@cord.edu.
URL www.ConcordiaLanguageVillages.org

Concordia Language Villages–Norwegian

Concordia College
Bemidji, Minnesota

General Information Coed residential academic program and cultural program established in 1961. Accredited by American Camping Association. Formal opportunities for the academically talented. High school credit may be earned.
Program Focus World languages and culture.
Academics Norwegian language/literature, music, peace education.
Arts Arts and crafts (general), dance, dance (folk), music, music (vocal), weaving.
Special Interest Areas Cross-cultural education.
Sports Canoeing, soccer, swimming, volleyball.
Wilderness/Outdoors Canoe trips, hiking.
Program Information 7 sessions per year. Session length: 6–13 days in June, July, August. Ages: 7–18. 450 participants per session. Boarding program cost: $575–$2585. Financial aid available.
Application Deadline Continuous.
Jobs Positions for high school students 17 and older and college students 18 and older.
Contact Alex Loehrer, Assistant Director, Public Relations, 901 South Eighth Street, Moorhead, Minnesota 56562. Phone: 218-299-4544. Fax: 218-299-3807. E-mail: clv@cord.edu.
URL www.ConcordiaLanguageVillages.org

Concordia Language Villages–Russian

Concordia College
Vergas, Minnesota

General Information Coed residential academic program and cultural program established in 1961. Accredited by American Camping Association. Formal opportunities for the academically talented. High school credit may be earned.
Program Focus World languages and culture.
Academics Russian language/literature, music, peace education.
Arts Arts and crafts (general), dance, dance (folk), music, music (vocal), weaving.
Special Interest Areas Cross-cultural education.
Sports Canoeing, swimming, volleyball.
Wilderness/Outdoors Canoe trips, hiking.
Program Information 4 sessions per year. Session length: 6–26 days in July, August. Ages: 7–18. 100 participants per session. Boarding program cost: $575–$2585. Financial aid available.
Application Deadline Continuous.
Jobs Positions for high school students 17 and older and college students 18 and older.
Contact Alex Loehrer, Assistant Director, Public Relations, 901 South Eighth Street, Moorhead, Minnesota 56562. Phone: 218-299-4544. Fax: 218-299-3807. E-mail: clv@cord.edu.
URL www.ConcordiaLanguageVillages.org

Concordia Language Villages–Spanish–Bemidji

Concordia College
Bemidji, Minnesota

General Information Coed residential academic program and cultural program established in 1961. Accredited by American Camping Association. Formal opportunities for the academically talented. High school or college credit may be earned.
Program Focus World languages and culture.
Academics Spanish language/literature.
Arts Arts and crafts (general), dance, dance (folk), music, theater/drama, weaving.
Sports Canoeing, soccer, swimming, volleyball.
Wilderness/Outdoors Hiking.

Concordia Language Villages–Spanish–Bemidji (continued)

Program Information 9 sessions per year. Session length: 6–28 days in June, July, August. Ages: 7–18. 60 participants per session. Boarding program cost: $575–$2585. Financial aid available.
Application Deadline Continuous.
Jobs Positions for high school students 18 and older and college students 18 and older.
Contact Alex Loehrer, Assistant Director, Public Relations, 901 South Eighth Street, Moorhead, Minnesota 56562. Phone: 800-222-4750. Fax: 218-299-3807. E-mail: clv@cord.edu.
URL www.ConcordiaLanguageVillages.org

Concordia Language Villages–Spanish–Maplelag

Concordia College
Maplelag, Minnesota

General Information Coed residential academic program and cultural program established in 1961. Accredited by American Camping Association. Formal opportunities for the academically talented. High school credit may be earned.
Program Focus World languages and culture.
Academics Spanish (Advanced Placement), Spanish language/literature, music, peace education.
Arts Arts and crafts (general), dance, dance (folk), music, music (vocal), weaving.
Special Interest Areas Cross-cultural education.
Sports Canoeing, soccer, swimming, volleyball.
Wilderness/Outdoors Canoe trips, hiking.
Program Information 10 sessions per year. Session length: 6–26 days in June, July, August. Ages: 7–18. 154 participants per session. Boarding program cost: $575–$2585. Financial aid available.
Application Deadline Continuous.
Jobs Positions for high school students 17 and older and college students 18 and older.
Contact Alex Loehrer, Assistant Director, Public Relations, 901 South Eighth Street, Moorhead, Minnesota 56562. Phone: 218-299-4544. Fax: 218-299-3807. E-mail: clv@cord.edu.
URL www.ConcordiaLanguageVillages.org

Concordia Language Villages–Spanish–Wilder Forest

Concordia College
Marine on the St. Croix, Minnesota

General Information Coed residential academic program and cultural program established in 1961. Accredited by American Camping Association. Formal opportunities for the academically talented. High school credit may be earned.
Program Focus World languages and culture.
Academics Spanish (Advanced Placement), Spanish language/literature, music, peace education.
Arts Arts and crafts (general), dance, dance (folk), music, music (vocal), weaving.
Special Interest Areas Cross-cultural education.
Sports Canoeing, soccer, swimming, volleyball.
Wilderness/Outdoors Canoe trips, hiking.
Program Information 8 sessions per year. Session length: 6–26 days in June, July, August. Ages: 7–18. Boarding program cost: $575–$2585. Financial aid available.
Application Deadline Continuous.
Jobs Positions for high school students 17 and older and college students 18 and older.
Contact Alex Loehrer, Assistant Director, Public Relations, 901 South Eighth Street, Moorhead, Minnesota 56562. Phone: 218-299-4544. Fax: 218-299-3807. E-mail: clv@cord.edu.
URL www.ConcordiaLanguageVillages.org

Concordia Language Villages–Swedish

Concordia College
Bemidji, Minnesota

General Information Coed residential academic program and cultural program established in 1961. Accredited by American Camping Association. Formal opportunities for the academically talented. High school credit may be earned.
Program Focus World languages and culture.
Academics Swedish language/literature, music, peace education.
Arts Arts and crafts (general), dance, dance (folk), music, music (vocal), weaving.
Special Interest Areas Cross-cultural education.
Sports Canoeing, soccer, swimming, volleyball.
Wilderness/Outdoors Canoe trips, hiking.
Program Information 4 sessions per year. Session length: 6–26 days in July, August. Ages: 7–18. 85 participants per session. Boarding program cost: $575–$2585. Financial aid available.
Application Deadline Continuous.
Jobs Positions for high school students 17 and older and college students 18 and older.
Contact Alex Loehrer, Assistant Director, Public Relations, 901 South Eighth Street, Moorhead, Minnesota 56562. Phone: 218-299-4544. Fax: 218-299-3807. E-mail: clv@cord.edu.
URL www.ConcordiaLanguageVillages.org

Cybercamps–University of Minnesota

Cybercamps–Giant Campus, Inc.
Minneapolis, Minnesota

General Information Coed residential and day academic program established in 1997.
Program Focus High tech computer camps featuring project oriented curriculum in Web design, 3D animation, game design, robotics, digital arts and programming for all ability levels.
Academics Web page design, computer programming, computers.
Arts Animation, creative writing, digital media, graphic arts, photography.
Special Interest Areas Computer game design, computer graphics, robotics, team building.
Sports Frisbee golf, ultimate frisbee.

Program Information 2–9 sessions per year. Session length: 5–30 days in June, July, August. Ages: 7–18. 30–150 participants per session. Day program cost: $599–$849. Boarding program cost: $974–$1224. Financial aid available.
Application Deadline Continuous.
Jobs Positions for high school students 15 and older and college students.
Contact Cybercamps Information Office, 2401 4th Avenue, Suite 1110, Seattle, Washington 98121. Phone: 206-442-4500. Fax: 206-442-4501. E-mail: info@cybercamps.com.
URL www.cybercamps.com

Eagle Lake Camp Jaunts–Minnesota Boundary Waters

The Navigators
Minnesota

General Information Coed travel outdoor program, bible camp, and wilderness program established in 1997. Religious affiliation: Christian. Accredited by American Camping Association.
Academics Bible study.
Sports Canoeing.
Wilderness/Outdoors Backpacking, canoe trips, hiking, wilderness camping.
Trips Overnight.
Program Information 1–2 sessions per year. Session length: 5–6 days in June, July, August. Ages: 15–18. 12 participants per session. Cost: $438. Financial aid available.
Application Deadline Continuous.
Jobs Positions for college students 19 and older.
Summer Contact Office Manager, PO Box 6000, Colorado Springs, Colorado 80934. Phone: 719-472-1260. Fax: 719-623-0148. E-mail: registrar_el@navigators.org.
Winter Contact Mr. John Rogers, Wilderness Director, main address above. Phone: 719-472-1260. Fax: 719-623-0148. E-mail: john_rogers@navigators.org.
URL www.eaglelake.org

Eden Wood Camp

Friendship Ventures
6350 Indian Chief Road
Eden Prairie, Minnesota 55346

General Information Coed residential and day traditional camp and special needs program established in 1958. Accredited by American Camping Association. Specific services available for the developmentally challenged and physically challenged.
Program Focus Provides services to children and adults with developmental disabilities.
Arts Arts and crafts (general), dance, music.
Special Interest Areas Nature study.
Sports Archery, bicycling, canoeing, climbing (wall), fishing, ropes course, swimming.
Wilderness/Outdoors Hiking.
Trips Day, overnight.
Program Information 6–8 sessions per year. Session length: 6–14 days in June, July, August. Ages: 5+. 25–35 participants per session. Day program cost: $107–$148. Boarding program cost: $595–$1800. Financial aid available.
Application Deadline Continuous.
Jobs Positions for high school students 16 and older and college students 18 and older.
Contact Georgann Rumsey, President/CEO, 10509 108th Street, NW, Annandale, Minnesota 55302. Phone: 952-852-0101. Fax: 952-852-0123. E-mail: fv@friendshipventures.org.
URL www.friendshipventures.org

Fort Union Civil War Camp

Historical Experiences
Flandrau Group Camp, Flandrau State Park
1300 Summit Avenue
New Ulm, Minnesota 56073-3364

General Information Coed residential outdoor program established in 1995. Formal opportunities for the academically talented and artistically talented.
Program Focus Students learn all about the American Civil War by emulating soldiers and experiencing life as they did.
Academics History, social studies, strategy games.
Arts Dance, dance (folk).
Special Interest Areas Leadership training, military program, touring.
Sports Riflery, swimming.
Wilderness/Outdoors Hiking.
Trips Day, overnight.
Program Information 1 session per year. Session length: 5 days in June. Ages: 11–17. 55–60 participants per session. Boarding program cost: $650. Application fee: $50. Financial aid available.
Application Deadline Continuous.
Contact Arn Kind, Camp Director, 20150 589th Avenue, Mankato, Minnesota 56001. Phone: 507-625-8011. E-mail: akind1@mail.isd77.k12.mn.us.
URL www.civilwarcamp.com

iD Tech Camps–University of Minnesota, Minneapolis, MN

iD Tech Camps
University of Minnesota
Minneapolis, Minnesota

General Information Coed residential and day academic program established in 1999. Formal opportunities for the academically talented and artistically talented.
Program Focus High-tech computer camps for kids and teens; produce digital movies, create video games, design Web pages, learn programming and robotics, and more; one computer per student, small classes, campers complete a project in a creative and fun learning environment.
Academics Web page design, computer programming, computer science (Advanced Placement), computers, music, precollege program.
Arts Animation, cinematography, digital media, drawing, film, film editing, film production, graphic arts, music, television/video.

iD Tech Camps–University of Minnesota, Minneapolis, MN (continued)

Special Interest Areas Career exploration, computer graphics, electronics, leadership training, robotics, team building.
Sports Baseball, basketball, soccer, softball, swimming, volleyball.
Program Information 5 sessions per year. Session length: 5–7 days in June, July, August. Ages: 7–17. 40–50 participants per session. Day program cost: $639. Boarding program cost: $989. Application fee: $200. Financial aid available.
Application Deadline Continuous.
Jobs Positions for college students 18 and older.
Contact Client Service Representatives, 1885 Winchester Boulevard, Suite 201, Campbell, California 95008. Phone: 888-709-TECH. Fax: 408-871-2228. E-mail: requests@internaldrive.com.
URL www.internaldrive.com

For more information, see page 1156.

Kooch-I-Ching

Camping and Education Foundation
International Falls, Minnesota 56649

General Information Boys' residential traditional camp, outdoor program, and wilderness program established in 1924. Accredited by American Camping Association.
Program Focus Canoe, backpacking, and climbing trips.
Special Interest Areas Native American culture, campcraft, community service, construction, leadership training, nature study, nautical skills, team building.
Sports Archery, baseball, basketball, boating, canoeing, climbing (wall), fishing, riflery, ropes course, sailing, swimming, tennis, waterskiing, weight training.
Wilderness/Outdoors Backpacking, canoe trips, hiking, rock climbing, white-water trips, wilderness camping.
Trips Overnight.
Program Information 4 sessions per year. Session length: 10–56 days in June, July, August. Ages: 7–18. 15–150 participants per session. Boarding program cost: $1250–$6045. Financial aid available.
Application Deadline Continuous.
Jobs Positions for college students 18 and older.
Summer Contact David M. Plain, Executive Director, Box 271, International Falls, Minnesota 56649. Phone: 218-286-3141. Fax: 218-286-3255. E-mail: office@koochiching.org.
Winter Contact David M. Plain, Executive Director, 230 Northland Boulevard, Suite 206, Cincinnati, Ohio 45246. Phone: 513-772-7479. Fax: 513-772-5673. E-mail: office@koochiching.org.
URL www.kooch-i-ching.org

Landmark Volunteers: Minnesota

Landmark Volunteers, Inc.
Minnesota

General Information Coed residential outdoor program and community service program established in 1992. High school credit may be earned.
Program Focus Opportunity for high school students to earn community service credit while working as a team for two weeks serving Confidence Learning Center or Friendship Ventures. Similar programs offered through Landmark Volunteers at over 60 locations in 21 states.
Academics Social science, social services.
Special Interest Areas Career exploration, community service, construction, leadership training, team building, work camp programs.
Sports Swimming.
Trips Cultural, day.
Program Information 2 sessions per year. Session length: 14–15 days in July, August. Ages: 14–18. 10–12 participants per session. Boarding program cost: $875–$925. Financial aid available.
Application Deadline Continuous.
Jobs Positions for college students.
Contact Ann Barrett, Executive Director, PO Box 455, Sheffield, Massachusetts 01257. Phone: 413-229-0255. Fax: 413-229-2050. E-mail: landmark@volunteers.com.
URL www.volunteers.com

For more information, see page 1182.

Presbyterian Clearwater Forest

16595 Crooked Lake Road
Deerwood, Minnesota 56444-8173

General Information Coed residential and day traditional camp, outdoor program, and bible camp established in 1954. Religious affiliation: Presbyterian. Accredited by American Camping Association.
Program Focus Christian education and outdoor activities.
Academics Astronomy.
Arts Arts and crafts (general), creative writing, drawing, music, music (vocal), painting, photography, pottery, printmaking, theater/drama, woodworking.
Special Interest Areas Campcraft, leadership training, nature study, work camp programs.
Sports Archery, bicycling, canoeing, equestrian sports, fishing, golf, horseback riding, kayaking, ropes course, sailing, sea kayaking, skiing (cross-country), soccer, swimming, volleyball.
Wilderness/Outdoors Backpacking, bicycle trips, canoe trips, hiking, orienteering, rafting, survival training, white-water trips, wilderness camping.
Trips Day, overnight.
Program Information 20–30 sessions per year. Session length: 3–14 days in January, February, March, April, May, June, July, August, September, October, November, December. Ages: 8–17. 30–200 participants per session. Day program cost: $36–$50. Boarding program cost: $275–$595. Financial aid available.
Application Deadline Continuous.
Jobs Positions for high school students 17 and older and college students 18 and older.

Contact David Jeremiason, Director, main address above. Phone: 218-678-2325. Fax: 218-678-3196. E-mail: dj@clearwaterforest.org.
URL www.clearwaterforest.org

St. Louis County 4-H Camp

St. Louis County Promotional Bureau
Lake Eshquagama
Gilbert, Minnesota 55741

General Information Coed residential and day traditional camp established in 1935.
Arts Arts and crafts (general).
Special Interest Areas Gardening, nature study.
Sports Archery, baseball, basketball, boating, canoeing, field hockey, fishing, football, kayaking, riflery, soccer, softball, swimming, volleyball, water tubing, waterskiing.
Wilderness/Outdoors Canoe trips, wilderness camping.
Trips Day, overnight.
Program Information 7 sessions per year. Session length: 5–6 days in June, July, August. Ages: 8–16. 80–90 participants per session. Day program cost: $125. Boarding program cost: $185–$245. Financial aid available.
Application Deadline Continuous.
Jobs Positions for high school students 16 and older and college students.
Contact Mr. Walter Hautala, Business Manager, 5088 Maple Drive, Gilbert, Minnesota 55741. Phone: 218-865-4247. Fax: 218-865-4247. E-mail: fourhcamp@rangenet.com.
URL www.4hcampmn.com

Shattuck–St. Mary's Girls Elite Hockey Camp

Shattuck-St. Mary's School
1000 Shumway Avenue
Faribault, Minnesota

General Information Girls' residential and day sports camp established in 2000.
Program Focus Girls ice hockey.
Sports Ice hockey.
Program Information 1 session per year. Session length: 1 week in July. Ages: 11–17. 80–100 participants per session. Boarding program cost: $700–$800.
Application Deadline Continuous.
Jobs Positions for college students 18 and older.
Contact Gordon Stafford, Director of SSM Girls Elite Hockey Camp, main address above. Phone: 800-617-8469. Fax: 507-333-1591. E-mail: gstafford@s-sm.org.
URL www.s-sm.org
For more information, see page 1310.

Shattuck-St. Mary's Summer Discovery and English Language Institute

Shattuck-St. Mary's School
1000 Shumway Avenue
Faribault, Minnesota 55021

General Information Coed residential and day academic program established in 1988. Formal opportunities for the academically talented and artistically talented. High school credit may be earned.

Shattuck-St. Mary's Summer Discovery and English Language Institute

Program Focus Academic course work, enrichment, and review.
Academics American literature, English as a second language, English language/literature, academics (general), computers, mathematics, writing.
Arts Ceramics, creative writing, dance, drawing, painting, photography, pottery, sculpture.
Sports Basketball, bicycling, canoeing, figure skating, football, golf, in-line skating, snorkeling, soccer, softball, swimming, tennis, track and field, volleyball, water polo, weight training.
Wilderness/Outdoors Bicycle trips, canoe trips, hiking, orienteering, wilderness camping.
Trips Cultural, day, shopping.
Program Information 1 session per year. Session length: 4 weeks in July. Ages: 11–17. 60–80 participants per session. Boarding program cost: $2400–$2850. Application fee: $50.
Application Deadline Continuous.
Jobs Positions for college students 18 and older.
Contact Mike Frankenfield, Director of Summer Programs, Box 218, Faribault, Minnesota 55021. Phone: 507-333-1674. Fax: 507-333-1591. E-mail: mfrankenfield@s-sm.org.
URL www.s-sm.org
For more information, see page 1310.

Shattuck-St. Mary's Boys Elite Hockey Camp

Shattuck-St. Mary's School
1000 Shumway Avenue
Faribault, Minnesota 55021

General Information Boys' residential and day sports camp established in 1998.
Program Focus Boys ice hockey.
Sports Ice hockey.
Program Information 2 sessions per year. Session length: 1 week in July, August. Ages: 11–15. 80–100 participants per session. Boarding program cost: $750–$850.
Application Deadline Continuous.
Jobs Positions for college students 18 and older.
Contact Gordon Stafford, Director of SSM Boys Elite Hockey Camp, main address above. Phone: 800-617-8469. Fax: 507-333-1591. E-mail: gstafford@s-sm.org.
URL www.s-sm.org

For more information, see page 1310.

Student Conservation Association–Conservation Crew Program (Minnesota)

Student Conservation Association (SCA)
Minnesota

General Information Coed residential outdoor program, community service program, and wilderness program established in 1957. High school credit may be earned.
Program Focus Resource management, conservation and environmental education.
Academics Biology, botany, ecology, environmental science, geology/earth science, history.
Special Interest Areas Campcraft, community service, construction, leadership training, nature study, trail maintenance, work camp programs.
Sports Canoeing, fishing, kayaking, swimming.
Wilderness/Outdoors Backpacking, hiking, orienteering, outdoor living skills, wilderness camping.
Trips Cultural, day, overnight.
Program Information 2–3 sessions per year. Session length: 3–5 weeks in June, July, August. Ages: 15–19. 6–8 participants per session. Application fee: $20. Financial aid available. No cost for program; financial aid possible for travel expenses.
Application Deadline Continuous.
Jobs Positions for college students 21 and older.
Contact Recruitment Office, PO Box 550, Charlestown, New Hampshire 03603. Phone: 603-543-1700. Fax: 603-543-1828. E-mail: getreal@thesca.org.
URL www.theSCA.org

Tice Brothers Football Camp

Sports International, Inc.
University of St. Thomas
St. Paul, Minnesota

General Information Coed residential and day sports camp established in 1997.
Program Focus Football.
Sports Football, weight training.
Program Information 1 session per year. Session length: 5 days in June. Ages: 8–18. 300–450 participants per session. Day program cost: $509. Boarding program cost: $619.
Application Deadline Continuous.
Jobs Positions for college students 18 and older.
Contact Customer Service, 8924 McGaw Court, Columbia, Maryland 21045. Phone: 800-555-0801. Fax: 410-309-9962. E-mail: info@footballcamps.com.
URL www.footballcamps.com

Ventures Travel Service–Minnesota

Friendship Ventures
Minnesota

General Information Coed travel special needs program established in 1985. Specific services available for the developmentally challenged and physically challenged.
Program Focus Provides travel services to older teens and adults with developmental disabilities.
Special Interest Areas Touring.
Program Information 50 sessions per year. Session length: 4–10 days in February, March, April, May, June, July, August, September, October, November, December. Ages: 14–70. 4–8 participants per session. Cost: $395–$2000.
Application Deadline Continuous.
Jobs Positions for college students 18 and older.
Contact Georgann Rumsey, President/CEO, 10509 108th Street, NW, Annandale, Minnesota 55302. Phone: 952-852-0101. Fax: 952-852-0123. E-mail: fv@friendshipventures.org.
URL www.friendshipventures.org

Voyageur Outward Bound–Boundary Waters Wilderness Canoeing

Voyageur Outward Bound/Outward Bound, USA
Boundary Waters Canoe Area Wilderness
Minnesota

General Information Coed residential outdoor program and wilderness program established in 1964. High school or college credit may be earned.
Program Focus Teamwork and leadership wilderness adventure.
Academics Environmental science.
Special Interest Areas Campcraft, community service, leadership training, nature study, personal development, team building.
Sports Canoeing, rappelling.
Wilderness/Outdoors Backpacking, canoe trips, orienteering, outdoor adventure, rock climbing, wilderness camping.
Trips Overnight.
Program Information 7 sessions per year. Session length: 10–22 days in July, August. Ages: 14+. Boarding

program cost: $1495–$2895. Application fee: $95. Financial aid available. Deadline 30 days prior to course start date.
Jobs Positions for college students 21 and older.
Contact Anne DesLauriers, Admissions Advisor, 101 East Chapman Street, Ely, Minnesota 55731. Phone: 800-328-2943. Fax: 218-365-7079. E-mail: info@vobs.com.
URL www.vobs.org

Voyageur Outward Bound–Boundary Waters Wilderness Canoeing and Climbing XT

Voyageur Outward Bound/Outward Bound, USA
Boundary Waters
Minnesota

General Information Coed travel outdoor program and wilderness program established in 1964. High school or college credit may be earned.
Program Focus Teamwork and leadership wilderness adventure.
Academics Ecology, environmental science.
Special Interest Areas Campcraft, community service, leadership training, nature study, outdoor cooking, personal development, team building.
Sports Canoeing, challenge course, climbing (wall), rappelling, ropes course.
Wilderness/Outdoors Canoe trips, orienteering, outdoor adventure, rock climbing, survival training, wilderness camping.
Trips Overnight.
Program Information 5 sessions per year. Session length: 15–22 days in June, July, August. Ages: 14+. Cost: $2295–$2995. Application fee: $95. Financial aid available. Deadline 30 days prior to course start date.
Jobs Positions for college students 21 and older.
Contact Anne DesLauriers, Admissions Advisor, 101 East Chapman Street, Ely, Minnesota 55731. Phone: 800-328-2943. Fax: 218-365-7079. E-mail: info@vobs.org.
URL www.vobs.org

Voyageur Outward Bound–Northwoods Wilderness Canoeing and Backpacking

Voyageur Outward Bound/Outward Bound, USA
Boundary Waters, Superior Hiking Trail
Minnesota

General Information Coed travel outdoor program and wilderness program established in 1964. High school or college credit may be earned.
Program Focus Teamwork and leadership wilderness adventure.
Academics Environmental science.
Special Interest Areas Campcraft, community service, leadership training, nature study, personal development, team building.
Sports Canoeing, challenge course, ropes course.
Wilderness/Outdoors Backpacking, canoe trips, hiking, orienteering, outdoor adventure, rock climbing, survival training, wilderness camping.
Trips Overnight.
Program Information 5–6 sessions per year. Session length: 22–29 days in June, July, August. Ages: 14+. Cost: $2895–$3295. Application fee: $95. Financial aid available. Deadline 30 days prior to course start date.
Jobs Positions for college students 21 and older.
Contact Anne DesLauriers, Admissions Advisor, 101 East Chapman Street, Ely, Minnesota 55731. Phone: 800-328-2943. Fax: 218-365-7079. E-mail: info@vobs.org.
URL www.vobs.org

Wilderness Dance Camp

Wilderness Dance Camp, Inc.
10251 Lyndale Avenue South
Bloomington, Minnesota 55420

General Information Coed residential arts program established in 1997. Formal opportunities for the artistically talented.
Program Focus Training dancers in ballet, tap, jazz, modern, and musical theatre.
Academics Anatomy.
Arts Dance, dance (ballet), dance (jazz), dance (modern), dance (tap).
Sports Bicycling, canoeing, swimming.
Wilderness/Outdoors Hiking.
Program Information 1–6 sessions per year. Session length: 6 days in June, July, August. Ages: 9+. 30–60 participants per session. Boarding program cost: $585–$3190. Application fee: $50–$200. Financial aid available.
Application Deadline Continuous.
Jobs Positions for high school students 16 and older and college students 18 and older.
Contact Ms. Chandra Saign, Director, main address above. Phone: 952-884-6009. E-mail: info@dancecamp.org.
URL www.dancecamp.org/

YMCA Camp Ihduhapi

YMCA of Metropolitan Minneapolis
Loretto, Minnesota 55357

General Information Coed residential and day traditional camp established in 1930. Accredited by American Camping Association.
Program Focus Traditional resident camp with a variety of activities.
Arts Arts and crafts (general).
Special Interest Areas Campcraft, nature study.
Sports Archery, basketball, canoeing, climbing (wall), fishing, horseback riding, kayaking, ropes course, sailing, soccer, softball, sports (general), swimming, volleyball, windsurfing.
Wilderness/Outdoors Canoe trips.
Trips Overnight.
Program Information 7 sessions per year. Session length: 3–11 days in June, July, August. Ages: 7–16. 160

YMCA Camp Ihduhapi (continued)

participants per session. Day program cost: $90–$160. Boarding program cost: $195–$825. Financial aid available.
Application Deadline Continuous.
Jobs Positions for high school students 17 and older and college students 18 and older.
Contact Brian Burns, Summer Camp Director, Box 37, Loretto, Minnesota 55357. Phone: 763-479-1146. Fax: 763-479-1333. E-mail: info@campihduhapi.org.
URL www.ymcacamps.org

YMCA Camp Warren for Boys

YMCA of Metropolitan Minneapolis
3726 Miller Trunk Road
Eveleth, Minnesota 55734

General Information Boys' residential traditional camp established in 1922. Accredited by American Camping Association.
Program Focus Single gender camping for boys.
Arts Arts and crafts (general), ceramics, jewelry making, photography, pottery, theater/drama.
Special Interest Areas Campcraft, leadership training, nature study.
Sports Archery, basketball, boating, canoeing, climbing (wall), equestrian sports, fishing, horseback riding, kayaking, rowing (crew/sculling), sailing, soccer, swimming, tennis, windsurfing.
Wilderness/Outdoors Canoe trips, wilderness camping.
Trips Overnight.
Program Information 3 sessions per year. Session length: 6–13 days in June, July, August. Ages: 8–16. 80–100 participants per session. Boarding program cost: $390–$1250. Financial aid available.
Application Deadline Continuous.
Jobs Positions for high school students 16 and older and college students 19 and older.
Contact Cheri Keepers, Camp Director, 4 West Rustic Lodge, Minneapolis, Minnesota 55409. Phone: 612-821-2903. Fax: 612-823-2482. E-mail: info@campwarren.org.
URL www.ymcacamps.org

YMCA Camp Warren for Girls

YMCA of Metropolitan Minneapolis
3726 Miller Trunk Road
Eveleth, Minnesota 55734

General Information Girls' residential traditional camp established in 1922. Accredited by American Camping Association.
Program Focus Single gender camping for girls.
Arts Arts and crafts (general), photography, pottery.
Special Interest Areas Campcraft, leadership training, nature study.
Sports Archery, boating, canoeing, fishing, horseback riding, sailing, swimming, tennis.
Wilderness/Outdoors Canoe trips.
Trips Overnight.
Program Information 3 sessions per year. Session length: 6–13 days in June, July, August. Ages: 8–16. 100 participants per session. Boarding program cost: $390–$1250. Financial aid available.
Application Deadline Continuous.
Jobs Positions for high school students 16 and older and college students 19 and older.
Contact Cheri Keepers, Camp Director, 4 West Rustic Lodge, Minneapolis, Minnesota 55409. Phone: 612-821-2903. Fax: 612-823-2482. E-mail: info@campwarren.org.
URL www.ymcacamps.org

YMCA Camp Widjiwagan

YMCA Camp Widjiwagan
2125 East Hennepin Avenue
Minneapolis, Minnesota 55413

General Information Coed residential outdoor program and wilderness program established in 1929. Accredited by American Camping Association.
Program Focus Canoe and backpack trips.
Special Interest Areas Native American culture, campcraft, leadership training, nature study, work camp programs.
Sports Canoeing.
Wilderness/Outdoors Backpacking, canoe trips, hiking, mountaineering, orienteering, white-water trips, wilderness camping.
Trips Overnight.
Program Information Session length: 10–55 days in June, July, August. Ages: 12–18. 5–50 participants per session. Boarding program cost: $820–$6500. Financial aid available.
Application Deadline Continuous.
Jobs Positions for college students 19 and older.
Contact Alissa Johnson, Program Director, 2125 East Hennepin Avenue, Minneapolis, Minnesota 55413. Phone: 612-465-0489. Fax: 651-646-5521. E-mail: info@widji.org.
URL www.widji.org

Special Note
Widjiwagan is not a typical summer camp for youth; it offers extended backcountry wilderness expeditions. Located just north of Ely, Minnesota, on the edge of the Boundary Waters Canoe Area (BWCA) wilderness, Widjiwagan has provided canoe and backpack adventures for teens since 1929. Travel is in small groups (5 campers and 1 or 2 experienced leaders), either canoeing the spectacular waterways of the BWCA or hiking among the inspiring peaks of the Rocky Mountains of Wyoming. Widji's wilderness programs, which range from 10 to 21 days for first-time campers, promote leadership, teamwork, and self-confidence. Through their wilderness adventures, Widji campers develop a deep care and respect for themselves, the environment, and each other.

YMCA Wilderness Camp Menogyn

YMCA of Metropolitan Minneapolis
55 Menogyn Trail
Grand Marais, Minnesota 55604

General Information Coed travel wilderness program established in 1922. Accredited by American Camping Association.
Program Focus Backpacking, canoeing, and rock climbing.
Wilderness/Outdoors Backpacking, canoe trips, hiking, rock climbing, wilderness camping.
Trips Overnight.
Program Information 35 sessions per year. Session length: 8–21 days in June, July, August. Ages: 13–18. 8–100 participants per session. Cost: $580–$1695. Financial aid available.
Application Deadline Continuous.
Jobs Positions for college students 19 and older.
Contact Mr. Paul Danicic, Camp Director, 4 West Rustic Lodge, Minneapolis, Minnesota 55409. Phone: 612-821-2905. Fax: 612-823-2482. E-mail: info@campmenogyn.org.
URL www.ymcacamps.org

MISSISSIPPI

Camp Stanislaus

Camp Stanislaus
304 South Beach Boulevard
Bay St. Louis, Mississippi 39520

General Information Boys' residential and day traditional camp established in 1928. Religious affiliation: Roman Catholic.
Program Focus The development of young men through a recreational and learning experience.
Academics English language/literature, computers, marine studies, mathematics, reading, writing.
Arts Arts and crafts (general), ceramics, creative writing, drawing, painting, photography.
Special Interest Areas Leadership training.
Sports Archery, baseball, basketball, boating, canoeing, climbing (wall), fishing, football, horseback riding, riflery, sailing, sea kayaking, soccer, softball, swimming, tennis, volleyball, water polo, waterskiing, weight training.
Wilderness/Outdoors Canoe trips.
Trips Day.
Program Information 3 sessions per year. Session length: 1–6 weeks in June, July. Ages: 8–15. 150–170 participants per session. Day program cost: $325–$1350. Boarding program cost: $600–$2750. Application fee: $100–$200.
Application Deadline Continuous.
Jobs Positions for high school students 16 and older and college students 18 and older.

Camp Stanislaus

Contact Mr. Michael Reso, Camp Director, main address above. Phone: 228-467-9057 Ext.222. Fax: 228-466-2972. E-mail: mreso@ststan.com.
URL www.campstanislaus.com

Mississippi Governor's School

Mississippi University for Women
1100 College Street
MUW 129
Columbus, Mississippi 39701-5800

General Information Coed residential academic program established in 1981. Formal opportunities for the academically talented. Specific services available for the hearing impaired, physically challenged, and visually impaired. College credit may be earned.
Program Focus Leadership, community service, and creativity.
Academics American literature, English language/literature, academics (general), architecture, area studies, biology, computers, history, humanities, journalism, marine studies, mathematics, music, philosophy, precollege program, science (general), speech/debate, writing.

Mississippi Governor's School (continued)
Arts Acting, creative writing, dance (modern), film, graphic arts, music (classical), music (instrumental), photography, television/video, theater/drama.
Special Interest Areas Community service, culinary arts, field research/expeditions, leadership training.
Sports Aerobics, basketball, racquetball, scuba diving, soccer, softball, swimming, tennis, volleyball, weight training.
Trips Cultural, day, shopping.
Program Information 1 session per year. Session length: 20 days in June. Ages: 16–18. 120–150 participants per session. No cost for program. Open to Mississippi residents only.
Application Deadline February 15.
Jobs Positions for college students 21 and older.
Contact Dr. Robert W. Seney, Program Director, Columbus, Mississippi 39701-5800. Phone: 601-329-7110. Fax: 601-329-8515. E-mail: bseney@muw.edu.
URL www.muw.edu/govschool/

Student Conservation Association–Conservation Crew Program (Mississippi)

Student Conservation Association (SCA)
Mississippi

General Information Coed residential outdoor program, community service program, and wilderness program established in 1957. High school credit may be earned.
Program Focus Resource management, conservation and environmental education.
Academics Biology, botany, ecology, environmental science, geology/earth science, history.
Special Interest Areas Campcraft, community service, construction, leadership training, nature study, trail maintenance, work camp programs.
Sports Canoeing, fishing, kayaking, swimming.
Wilderness/Outdoors Backpacking, canoe trips, hiking, orienteering, outdoor living skills, wilderness camping.
Trips Cultural, day, overnight.
Program Information 2–3 sessions per year. Session length: 3–5 weeks in June, July, August. Ages: 15–19. 6–8 participants per session. Application fee: $20. Financial aid available. No cost for program; financial aid possible for travel expenses.
Application Deadline Continuous.
Jobs Positions for college students 21 and older.
Contact Recruitment Office, PO Box 550, Charlestown, New Hampshire 03603. Phone: 603-543-1700. Fax: 603-543-1828. E-mail: getreal@thesca.org.
URL www.theSCA.org

MISSOURI

Camp Sabra

St. Louis Jewish Community Center
30750 Camp Sabra Road
Rocky Mount, Missouri 65072

General Information Coed residential traditional camp established in 1938. Religious affiliation: Jewish. Accredited by American Camping Association.
Arts Arts and crafts (general), ceramics, dance, music, photography, pottery, television/video, theater/drama.
Special Interest Areas Campcraft, leadership training, nature study.
Sports Archery, basketball, bicycling, canoeing, cheerleading, climbing (wall), fishing, football, golf, horseback riding, lacrosse, ropes course, sailing, soccer, softball, street/roller hockey, swimming, tennis, volleyball, waterskiing.
Wilderness/Outdoors Backpacking, canoe trips, hiking, mountain biking, orienteering.
Trips Day, overnight.
Program Information 2–4 sessions per year. Session length: 2–4 weeks in June, July, August. Ages: 8–15. 325 participants per session. Boarding program cost: $1400–$2900.
Application Deadline Continuous.
Jobs Positions for high school students 17 and older and college students 17 and older.
Contact Mr. Randy Comensky, Director, 16801 Baxter Road, Chesterfield, Missouri 63005. Phone: 314-442-3426 Ext.3426. Fax: 314-442-3404. E-mail: rcomensky@jcc.stl.org.
URL www.campsabra.com

Cybercamps–Washington University

Cybercamps–Giant Campus, Inc.
St. Louis, Missouri

General Information Coed residential and day academic program established in 1997.
Program Focus High tech computer camps featuring project oriented curriculum in Web design, 3D animation, game design, robotics, digital arts and programming for all ability levels.
Academics Web page design, computer programming, computers.
Arts Animation, creative writing, digital media, graphic arts, photography.
Special Interest Areas Computer game design, computer graphics, robotics, team building.
Sports Frisbee golf, ultimate frisbee.
Program Information 2–9 sessions per year. Session length: 5–30 days in June, July, August. Ages: 7–18. 30–150 participants per session. Day program cost: $599–$849. Boarding program cost: $974–$1224.
Application Deadline Continuous.
Jobs Positions for high school students 15 and older and college students.

Contact Cybercamps Information Office, 2401 4th Avenue, Suite 1110, Seattle, Washington 98121. Phone: 206-442-4500. Fax: 206-442-4501. E-mail: info@cybercamps.com.
URL www.cybercamps.com

Girl Scouts of Mid-Continent–Camp Oakledge

Girl Scouts of Mid-Continent Council
Warsaw, Missouri 65355

General Information Girls' residential outdoor program established in 1946. Accredited by American Camping Association.
Program Focus Traditional camp for girls.
Arts Arts and crafts (general), jewelry making, music.
Special Interest Areas Campcraft, team building.
Sports Archery, boating, canoeing, fishing, kayaking, rappelling, sailing, softball, swimming.
Wilderness/Outdoors Backpacking, canoe trips, caving, hiking, orienteering, wilderness camping.
Trips Day, overnight.
Program Information 5 sessions per year. Session length: 10 days in June, July, August. Ages: 9–16. 160–180 participants per session. Boarding program cost: $100–$250. Financial aid available.
Application Deadline Continuous.
Jobs Positions for high school students 18 and older and college students 18 and older.
Contact Ms. Robyn E. Ratcliff, Outdoor Program Specialist, 8383 Blue Parkway Drive, Kansas City, Missouri 64133. Phone: 816-358-8750. Fax: 816-358-5714. E-mail: campjobs@girlscoutsmcc.org.
URL www.girlscoutsmcc.org

Girl Scouts of Mid-Continent–Camp Prairie Schooner

Girl Scouts of Mid-Continent Council
Kansas City, Missouri 64136

General Information Girls' residential traditional camp established in 1953. Accredited by American Camping Association.
Program Focus Traditional camp for young girls.
Academics Computers, ecology, environmental science.
Arts Arts and crafts (general), dance, music.
Special Interest Areas Campcraft.
Sports Archery, rappelling, soccer, softball, swimming, volleyball.
Wilderness/Outdoors Hiking.
Trips Day.
Program Information 7 sessions per year. Session length: 1 week in June, July, August. Ages: 5–12. 100–150 participants per session. Boarding program cost: $100–$250. Financial aid available.
Application Deadline Continuous.
Jobs Positions for high school students 18 and older and college students 18 and older.
Contact Ms. Robyn E. Ratcliff, Outdoor Program Specialist, 8383 Blue Parkway Drive, Kansas City, Missouri 64133. Phone: 816-358-8750. Fax: 816-358-5714. E-mail: campjobs@girlscoutsmcc.org.
URL www.girlscoutsmcc.org

Girl Scouts of Mid-Continent–Juliette Low Camp

Girl Scouts of Mid-Continent Council
Kansas City, Missouri 64136

General Information Girls' residential special needs program established in 1980. Specific services available for the developmentally challenged, hearing impaired, physically challenged, and visually impaired.
Arts Arts and crafts (general), music.
Special Interest Areas Campcraft.
Sports Swimming.
Wilderness/Outdoors Hiking.
Program Information 2 sessions per year. Session length: 8 days in June, July, August. Ages: 8–18. 25–50 participants per session. Boarding program cost: $100–$250. Financial aid available.
Application Deadline Continuous.
Jobs Positions for high school students 18 and older and college students 18 and older.
Contact Ms. Robyn E. Ratcliff, Outdoor Program Specialist, 8383 Blue Parkway Drive, Kansas City, Missouri 64133. Phone: 816-358-8750. Fax: 816-358-5714. E-mail: campjobs@girlscoutsmcc.org.
URL www.girlscoutsmcc.org

Girl Scouts of Mid-Continent–Winding River Camp and Ranch

Girl Scouts of Mid-Continent Council
Dearborn, Missouri 64439

General Information Girls' residential traditional camp established in 1995.
Program Focus Horseback riding.
Arts Arts and crafts (general).
Special Interest Areas Animal care, campcraft.
Sports Archery, equestrian sports, horseback riding.
Wilderness/Outdoors Hiking.
Program Information 5 sessions per year. Session length: 10 days in June, July, August. Ages: 12–17. 45–60 participants per session. Boarding program cost: $100–$250. Financial aid available.
Application Deadline Continuous.
Jobs Positions for high school students 18 and older and college students 18 and older.
Contact Ms. Robyn E. Ratcliff, Outdoor Program Specialist, 8383 Blue Parkway Drive, Kansas City, Missouri 64133. Phone: 816-358-8750. Fax: 816-358-5714. E-mail: campjobs@girlscoutsmcc.org.
URL www.girlscoutsmcc.org

IMACS–Full Day Summer Camp–Missouri

Institute for Mathematics & Computer Science (IMACS)
Missouri

General Information Coed day academic program established in 1992. Formal opportunities for the academically talented.
Academics Computer programming, computer science (Advanced Placement), computers, engineering, mathematics.
Special Interest Areas Electronics, robotics.
Program Information 7 sessions per year. Session length: 5 days in January, February, March, April, May, June, July, August, September, October, November, December. Ages: 5–18. 30–50 participants per session. Day program cost: $399–$1224. Supply fee: $50–$200; additional sessions booked at same time $249 plus $50 supply fee.
Application Deadline Continuous.
Jobs Positions for high school students 16 and older and college students 18 and older.
Contact Mr. Terry Kaufman, President, 7435 Northwest 4th Street, Plantation, Florida 33317. Phone: 954-791-2333. Fax: 954-791-0260. E-mail: info@imacs.org.
URL www.imacs.org

IMACS–Individual Summer Programs–Missouri

Institute for Mathematics & Computer Science (IMACS)
Missouri

General Information Coed day academic program established in 1992. Formal opportunities for the academically talented.
Academics Computer programming, computer science (Advanced Placement), computers, engineering, mathematics, mathematics (Advanced Placement).
Special Interest Areas Computer graphics, electronics, robotics.
Program Information 5 sessions per year. Session length: 5 days in January, February, March, April, May, June, July, August, September, October, November, December. Ages: 6–18. Day program cost: $79–$199. Financial aid available.
Application Deadline Continuous.
Jobs Positions for high school students 16 and older and college students 18 and older.
Contact Mr. Terry Kaufman, President, 7435 Northwest 4th Street, Plantation, Florida 33317. Phone: 954-791-2333. Fax: 954-791-0260. E-mail: info@imacs.org.
URL www.imacs.org

Missouri Children's Burn Camp

Burns Recovered Support Group
Lake of the Ozarks
Rocky Mount, Missouri

General Information Coed residential special needs program established in 1997. Specific services available for the burn survivor.
Arts Arts and crafts (general).
Sports Archery, canoeing, climbing (wall), fishing, horseback riding, ropes course, sailing, swimming, waterskiing.
Program Information 1 session per year. Session length: 1 week in August. Ages: 6–17. 70–90 participants per session. Financial aid available. No cost for program.
Application Deadline Continuous.
Contact Ms. Linda Hansen, Camp Director, 11710 Administration Drive, Suite 2B, Saint Louis, Missouri 63146. Phone: 314-997-2757. Fax: 314-997-0903. E-mail: brsg@sbcglobal.net.
URL www.brsg.org

Music and Dance Summer Workshops

Cottey College
1000 West Austin
Nevada, Missouri 64772

General Information Girls' residential arts program established in 1999. Formal opportunities for the artistically talented.
Academics Music.
Arts Chorus, dance, dance (ballet), dance (jazz), dance (modern), music, music (ensemble), music (instrumental), music (orchestral), music (vocal).
Program Information 1 session per year. Session length: 6 days in June. 36 participants per session. Boarding program cost: $300. Application fee: $10. Open to participants entering grades 9–11.
Application Deadline April 1.
Jobs Positions for college students 18 and older.
Contact Denise Carrick, Coordinator of P.E.O. Relations, main address above. Phone: 417-667-8181. Fax: 417-667-8103. E-mail: peorelations@cottey.edu.
URL www.cottey.edu

Sciencescape

Cottey College
1000 West Austin
Nevada, Missouri 64772

General Information Girls' residential academic program established in 1993. Formal opportunities for the academically talented.
Program Focus Science and math.
Academics Astronomy, biology, chemistry, computers, mathematics, philosophy, psychology, science (general).
Trips Day.
Program Information 1 session per year. Session length: 6 days in June. 36 participants per session. Boarding program cost: $300. Application fee: $10. Open to participants entering grades 6–7.

Application Deadline April 1.
Jobs Positions for college students 18 and older.
Contact Denise Carrick, Coordinator of P.E.O. Relations, main address above. Phone: 417-667-8181. Fax: 417-667-8103. E-mail: dcarrick@cottey.edu.
URL www.cottey.edu

Student Conservation Association–Conservation Crew Program (Missouri)

Student Conservation Association (SCA)
Missouri

General Information Coed residential outdoor program, community service program, and wilderness program established in 1957. High school credit may be earned.
Program Focus Resource management, conservation and environmental education.
Academics Biology, botany, ecology, environmental science, geology/earth science, history.
Special Interest Areas Campcraft, community service, construction, leadership training, nature study, trail maintenance, work camp programs.
Sports Canoeing, fishing, kayaking, swimming.
Wilderness/Outdoors Backpacking, canoe trips, hiking, orienteering, outdoor living skills, wilderness camping.
Trips Cultural, day, overnight.
Program Information 2–3 sessions per year. Session length: 3–5 weeks in June, July, August. Ages: 15–19. 6–8 participants per session. Application fee: $20. Financial aid available. No cost for program; financial aid possible for travel expenses.
Application Deadline Continuous.
Jobs Positions for college students 21 and older.
Contact Recruitment Office, PO Box 550, Charlestown, New Hampshire 03603. Phone: 603-543-1700. Fax: 603-543-1828. E-mail: getreal@thesca.org.
URL www.theSCA.org

Ventures Travel Service–Missouri

Friendship Ventures
Missouri

General Information Coed travel special needs program established in 1985. Specific services available for the developmentally challenged and physically challenged.
Program Focus Provides travel services to older teens and adults with developmental disabilities.
Special Interest Areas Touring.
Program Information 50 sessions per year. Session length: 4–10 days in February, March, April, May, June, July, August, September, October, November, December. Ages: 14–70. 4–8 participants per session. Cost: $395–$2000.
Application Deadline Continuous.
Jobs Positions for college students 18 and older.
Contact Georgann Rumsey, President/CEO, 10509 108th Street, NW, Annandale, Minnesota 55302. Phone: 952-852-0101. Fax: 952-852-0123. E-mail: fv@friendshipventures.org.
URL www.friendshipventures.org

Washington University High School Summer Scholars Program

Washington University in St. Louis
1 Brookings Drive
St. Louis, Missouri 63130-4899

General Information Coed residential academic program established in 1988. Formal opportunities for the academically talented. College credit may be earned.

Washington University High School Summer Scholars Program

Program Focus Pre-college academic enrichment.
Academics English language/literature, French language/literature, German language/literature, Italian language/literature, Russian language/literature, Spanish (Advanced Placement), archaeology, art history/appreciation, biology, chemistry, communications, economics, environmental science, geology/earth science, government and politics, history, humanities, mathematics, music, philosophy, physics, precollege program, psychology, science (general), social science, social studies, writing.
Arts Dance, music, television/video, theater/drama.
Trips Day.
Program Information 2 sessions per year. Session length: 5 weeks in June, July, August. Ages: 16+. 70–80 participants per session. Boarding program cost: $4565. Application fee: $35. Financial aid available. Up to 7 units of college credit may be earned.
Application Deadline May 7.
Contact Ms. Marsha Hussung, Director, High School Summer Scholars Program, Campus Box 1145, 1 Brookings Drive, St. Louis, Missouri 63130. Phone: 314-935-6834. Fax: 314-935-4847. E-mail: mhussung@wustl.edu.
URL ucollege.wustl.edu/hssp
For more information, see page 1384.

Washington University in St. Louis, School of Art–Portfolio Plus

Washington University in St. Louis, School of Art
1 Brookings Drive
St. Louis, Missouri 63130

General Information Coed residential and day arts program established in 2004. Formal opportunities for the academically talented and artistically talented. College credit may be earned.
Program Focus Portfolio preparation, visual arts studies.
Academics Art (Advanced Placement).
Arts Arts, ceramics, design, drawing, fashion design/production, painting, photography, printmaking, sculpture, visual arts.
Special Interest Areas Career exploration, college planning.
Trips College tours, cultural.
Program Information 1 session per year. Session length: 1 day in June, July. Ages: 16–18. 50 participants per session. Day program cost: $2282. Boarding program cost: $4565. Application fee: $25. Financial aid available.
Application Deadline May 1.
Contact Belinda Lee, Director, Study Abroad, Washington University in St. Louis, School of Art, Box 1031, One Brookings Drive, St. Louis, Missouri 63130. Phone: 314-935-8456. Fax: 314-935-4862. E-mail: bslee@art.wustl.edu.
URL www.artsci.wustl.edu/~artweb/washUSoa/
For more information, see page 1386.

Wentworth Military Academy Pathfinder Adventure Camp

Wentworth Military Academy and Junior College
1880 Washington Avenue
Lexington, Missouri 64067

General Information Coed residential adventure program.
Academics History.
Special Interest Areas Military program.
Sports Canoeing, climbing (wall), paintball, rappelling, swimming.
Wilderness/Outdoors Canoe trips, hiking, orienteering, survival training.
Trips Day, overnight.
Program Information 1 session per year. Session length: 1 week in June, July. 50–100 participants per session. Boarding program cost: $695. Application fee: $50.
Application Deadline May 31.
Contact Maj. Todd Kitchen, Director of Admissions, main address above. Phone: 800-962-7682. Fax: 660-259-2677. E-mail: admissions@wma1880.org.
URL www.wma1880.org
For more information, see page 1390.

Wentworth Military Academy Summer School

Wentworth Military Academy and Junior College
1880 Washington Avenue
Lexington, Missouri 64067-1799

General Information Coed residential academic program established in 1940. High school credit may be earned.

Wentworth Military Academy Summer School

Academics English as a second language, English language/literature, academics (general), biology, computers, geography, history, mathematics.
Arts Arts and crafts (general), ceramics, pottery.
Special Interest Areas Leadership training, model rocketry.
Sports Archery, basketball, canoeing, golf, rappelling, sports (general).
Wilderness/Outdoors Canoe trips.
Trips Cultural, day.
Program Information 1 session per year. Session length: 40 days in June, July. 100 participants per session. Boarding program cost: $4800. Application fee: $100. Open to boys entering grades 7–12 and girls entering grades 10–12.
Application Deadline Continuous.
Contact Maj. Todd Kitchen, Director of Admissions, main address above. Phone: 800-962-7682. Fax: 660-259-2677. E-mail: admissions@wma1880.org.
URL www.wma1880.org
For more information, see page 1390.

Wentworth Military Academy Summer School–Camp LEAD

Wentworth Military Academy and Junior College
1880 Washington Avenue
Lexington, Missouri 64067

General Information Coed residential academic program. High school credit may be earned.
Program Focus Developing stronger leadership skills.
Academics English as a second language, English language/literature, biology, computers, geography, history, mathematics.

Arts Arts and crafts (general), chorus, pottery.
Special Interest Areas Leadership training.
Sports Archery, basketball, canoeing, golf, rappelling, sports (general).
Wilderness/Outdoors Canoe trips.
Trips Day.
Program Information Session length: 40 days in June, July. 100 participants per session. Boarding program cost: $4560. Open to boys entering grades 7–12 and girls entering grades 10–12.
Application Deadline Continuous.
Contact Maj. Todd Kitchen, Director of Admissions, main address above. Phone: 800-962-7682. Fax: 660-259-2677. E-mail: admissions@wma1880.org.
URL www.wma1880.org

For more information, see page 1390.

MONTANA

Adventure Treks–Montana Adventures

Adventure Treks, Inc.
Montana

General Information Coed travel outdoor program, wilderness program, and adventure program established in 1978.
Program Focus Multi-activity outdoor adventures with a focus on fun, personal growth, teamwork, leadership, building self-confidence, outdoor skills, and community living.
Wilderness/Outdoors Backpacking, hiking, mountain biking, mountaineering, orienteering, rafting, rock climbing, white-water trips, wilderness camping.
Program Information 1 session per year. Session length: 24 days in July, August. Ages: 15–17. 24 participants per session. Cost: $3095. Financial aid available.
Application Deadline Continuous.
Contact John Dockendorf, Director, PO Box 1321, Flat Rock, North Carolina 28731. Phone: 888-954-5555. Fax: 828-696-1663. E-mail: info@advtreks.com.
URL www.adventuretreks.com

Alpengirl–Montana

Alpengirl, Inc.
Manhattan, Montana 59741

General Information Girls' travel outdoor program, wilderness program, and adventure program established in 1997. Accredited by American Camping Association.
Program Focus Promoting fitness and health through mountain adventure and outdoor education.
Academics Area studies, ecology, geology/earth science, science (general).
Special Interest Areas Field research/expeditions, nature study, weight reduction.
Sports Bicycling, canoeing, horseback riding, physical fitness, rappelling, sea kayaking, swimming.
Wilderness/Outdoors Backpacking, bicycle trips, canoe trips, fly fishing, hiking, mountain biking, pack animal trips, rafting, rock climbing, white-water trips, wilderness camping, wilderness/outdoors (general).
Trips Cultural, day, overnight, shopping.
Program Information 2 sessions per year. Session length: 2 weeks in July, August. Ages: 12–16. 10–12 participants per session. Cost: $1890. Financial aid available.
Application Deadline Continuous.
Jobs Positions for college students 21 and older.
Contact Alissa Farley, Camp Director, PO Box 1138, Manhattan, Montana 59741. Phone: 800-585-7476. E-mail: alissa@alpengirl.com.
URL www.alpengirl.com

Alpengirl–Montana Fitness

Alpengirl, Inc.
Manhattan, Montana 59741

General Information Girls' travel outdoor program, wilderness program, and adventure program.
Program Focus Promoting fitness and health through mountain adventure and outdoor education.
Academics Area studies, ecology, geology/earth science, science (general).
Special Interest Areas Field research/expeditions, nature study, weight reduction.
Sports Bicycling, canoeing, horseback riding, physical fitness, rappelling, sea kayaking, swimming, yoga.
Wilderness/Outdoors Backpacking, bicycle trips, canoe trips, fly fishing, hiking, mountain biking, pack animal trips, rafting, rock climbing, white-water trips, wilderness camping, wilderness/outdoors (general).
Trips Cultural, day, overnight, shopping.
Program Information 2 sessions per year. Session length: 3 weeks in June, July. Ages: 12–16. 10–12 participants per session. Cost: $3150. Financial aid available.
Application Deadline Continuous.
Jobs Positions for college students 21 and older.
Contact Alissa Farley, Camp Director, PO Box 1138, Manhattan, Montana 59741. Phone: 800-585-7476. E-mail: alissa@alpengirl.com.
URL www.alpengirl.com

Alpengirl–Montana Horse

Alpengirl, Inc.
Manhattan, Montana 59741

General Information Girls' travel outdoor program, wilderness program, and adventure program.
Program Focus Promoting fitness and health through mountain adventure and outdoor education.
Academics Area studies, ecology, geology/earth science, science (general).
Special Interest Areas Field research/expeditions, nature study, weight reduction.
Sports Bicycling, canoeing, horseback riding, physical fitness, rappelling, sea kayaking, swimming.
Wilderness/Outdoors Backpacking, bicycle trips, canoe trips, fly fishing, hiking, mountain biking, pack

Alpengirl–Montana Horse (continued)

animal trips, rafting, rock climbing, white-water trips, wilderness camping, wilderness/outdoors (general).
Trips Cultural, day, overnight, shopping.
Program Information 1 session per year. Session length: 2 weeks in July. Ages: 12–16. 10–12 participants per session. Cost: $2100. Financial aid available.
Application Deadline Continuous.
Jobs Positions for college students 21 and older.
Contact Alissa Farley, Camp Director, PO Box 1138, Manhattan, Montana 59741. Phone: 800-585-7476. E-mail: alissa@alpengirl.com.
URL www.alpengirl.com

Apogee Outdoor Adventures–Montana Service Adventure

Apogee Outdoor Adventures
Montana

General Information Coed travel outdoor program, community service program, and adventure program established in 2004.
Special Interest Areas Community service, conservation projects.
Wilderness/Outdoors Bicycle trips, hiking, rafting.
Program Information 1 session per year. Session length: 3 weeks in July, August. Ages: 14–17. 6–12 participants per session. Cost: $2995–$3295. Financial aid available.
Application Deadline Continuous.
Jobs Positions for college students.
Contact Mr. Kevin Cashman, Director, 40 Bowker Street, Brunswick, Maine 04011. Phone: 207-725-7025. Fax: 509-693-8868. E-mail: info@apogeeadventures.com.
URL www.apogeeadventures.com

Christikon

4661 Boulder Road
McLeod, Montana 59052

General Information Coed residential traditional camp, outdoor program, family program, bible camp, and wilderness program established in 1951. Religious affiliation: Evangelical Lutheran Church in America. Accredited by American Camping Association. Specific services available for the developmentally challenged.
Program Focus Christian faith development and personal/social growth.
Academics Bible study.
Arts Arts and crafts (general), dance, music.
Special Interest Areas Work camp programs.
Sports Volleyball.
Wilderness/Outdoors Backpacking, hiking, wilderness camping.
Trips Overnight.
Program Information 10–13 sessions per year. Session length: 3–8 days in June, July, August. Ages: 10–19. 50–120 participants per session. Boarding program cost: $139–$312.
Application Deadline Continuous.
Jobs Positions for college students 19 and older.
Summer Contact Bob Quam, Pastor/Director, main address above. Phone: 406-932-6300. Fax: 406-932-6300. E-mail: christikon@aol.com.
Winter Contact Bob Quam, Pastor/Director, 1108 24th Street West, Billings, Montana 59102. Phone: 406-656-1969. Fax: 406-656-1969. E-mail: christikon@aol.com.
URL www.christikon.org

Landmark Volunteers: Montana

Landmark Volunteers, Inc.
Montana

General Information Coed residential outdoor program and community service program established in 1992. High school credit may be earned.
Program Focus Opportunity for high school students to earn community service credit while working as a team for two weeks serving Center Pole Foundation, Glacier Institute/Glacier National Park, or Spotted Bear Ranger District. Similar programs offered through Landmark Volunteers at over 60 locations in 21 states.
Academics Biology, ecology, environmental science, geology/earth science, natural resource management, science (general).
Special Interest Areas Career exploration, community service, conservation projects, field research/expeditions, leadership training, nature study, team building, trail maintenance, work camp programs.
Sports Swimming.
Wilderness/Outdoors Hiking.
Trips Cultural, day.
Program Information 3 sessions per year. Session length: 2 weeks in July, August. Ages: 14–18. 10–13 participants per session. Boarding program cost: $875–$925. Financial aid available.
Application Deadline Continuous.
Jobs Positions for college students.
Contact Ann Barrett, Executive Director, PO Box 455, Sheffield, Massachusetts 01257. Phone: 413-229-0255. Fax: 413-229-2050. E-mail: landmark@volunteers.com.
URL www.volunteers.com
For more information, see page 1182.

NBC Camps–Basketball Individual Training–Montana

NBC Camps
Rocky Mountain College
Billings, Montana

General Information Coed residential sports camp.
Program Focus Well-rounded skill development.
Sports Basketball.
Program Information 2 sessions per year. Session length: 5 days in July. Ages: 9–18. Boarding program cost: $315. Financial aid available.
Application Deadline Continuous.
Jobs Positions for high school students 16 and older and college students.
Contact Ms. Bonnie Tucker, Office Manager, 10003 North Milan Road, #100, Spokane, Washington 99218. Phone: 509-466-4690. Fax: 509-467-6289. E-mail: bonnie@nbccamps.com.
URL www.nbccamps.com

NBC Camps–Basketball–Team–Billings, MT

NBC Camps
Rocky Mountain College
Billings, Montana

General Information Coed residential sports camp.
Program Focus Camp for high school basketball teams.
Sports Basketball.
Program Information 1 session per year. Session length: 5 days in July. Boarding program cost: $280. Financial aid available.
Application Deadline Continuous.
Jobs Positions for high school students 16 and older and college students.
Contact Danny Beard, 10003 North Milan Road, #100, Spokane, Washington 99218. Phone: 509-466-4690. Fax: 509-467-6289. E-mail: danny@nbccamps.com.
URL www.nbccamps.com

Putney Student Travel–Community Service–Montana

Putney Student Travel
Montana

General Information Coed residential outdoor program, community service program, and cultural program established in 1951.
Program Focus Community service, cultural exchange, and weekend wilderness excursions from a base in Browning, Montana on the Blackfeet Reservation.
Academics Intercultural studies.
Special Interest Areas Native American culture, community service.
Sports Horseback riding.
Wilderness/Outdoors Hiking, rafting.
Trips Cultural.
Program Information 1 session per year. Session length: 30 days in June, July. Ages: 15–18. 16 participants per session. Boarding program cost: $4400. Financial aid available.
Application Deadline Continuous.
Contact Jeffrey Shumlin, Director, 345 Hickory Ridge Road, Putney, Vermont 05346. Phone: 802-387-5000. Fax: 802-387-4276. E-mail: info@goputney.com.
URL www.goputney.com
For more information, see page 1276.

Student Conservation Association–Conservation Crew Program (Montana)

Student Conservation Association (SCA)
Montana

General Information Coed residential outdoor program, community service program, and wilderness program established in 1957. High school credit may be earned.
Program Focus Resource management, conservation and environmental education.
Academics Biology, botany, ecology, environmental science, geology/earth science, history.
Special Interest Areas Campcraft, community service, construction, leadership training, nature study, trail maintenance, work camp programs.
Sports Canoeing, fishing, kayaking, swimming.
Wilderness/Outdoors Backpacking, canoe trips, hiking, orienteering, outdoor living skills, rock climbing, wilderness camping.
Trips Cultural, day, overnight.
Program Information 2–3 sessions per year. Session length: 3–5 weeks in June, July, August. Ages: 15–19. 6–8 participants per session. Application fee: $20. Financial aid available. No cost for program; financial aid possible for travel expenses.
Application Deadline Continuous.
Jobs Positions for college students 21 and older.
Contact Recruitment Office, PO Box 550, Charlestown, New Hampshire 03603. Phone: 603-543-1700. Fax: 603-543-1828. E-mail: getreal@thesca.org.
URL www.theSCA.org

Visions–Montana

Visions
Montana

General Information Coed travel outdoor program, community service program, and cultural program established in 1989. High school credit may be earned.
Program Focus Community service, cross-cultural experience, outdoor adventure activities.
Academics Intercultural studies.
Arts Carpentry.
Special Interest Areas Native American culture, community service, construction, cross-cultural education, field research/expeditions, field trips (arts and culture), leadership training, nature study.
Sports Horseback riding, swimming.
Wilderness/Outdoors Backpacking, hiking, outdoor adventure, rafting, rock climbing, wilderness camping.
Trips Cultural, day, overnight.
Program Information 2 sessions per year. Session length: 3–4 weeks in June, July, August. Ages: 14–18. 20–25 participants per session. Cost: $2700–$3550. Financial aid available.
Application Deadline Continuous.
Contact Joanne Pinaire, Director, PO Box 220, Newport, Pennsylvania 17074. Phone: 717-567-7313. Fax: 717-567-7853. E-mail: info@visionsserviceadventures.com.
URL www.visionsserviceadventures.com
For more information, see page 1382.

Voyageur Outward Bound–Greater Yellowstone Whitewater and Backpacking

Voyageur Outward Bound/Outward Bound, USA
Yellowstone River, Beartooth Mountains
Montana

General Information Coed travel outdoor program and wilderness program established in 1964. High school or college credit may be earned.
Program Focus Teamwork and leadership wilderness adventure.
Academics Environmental science.
Special Interest Areas Campcraft, community service, leadership training, nature study, personal development, team building.
Wilderness/Outdoors Backpacking, hiking, mountaineering, outdoor adventure, rafting, survival training, white-water trips, wilderness camping.
Trips Overnight.
Program Information 1 session per year. Session length: 22 days in July. Ages: 16+. Cost: $2995. Application fee: $95. Financial aid available. Deadline 30 days prior to course start date.
Jobs Positions for college students 21 and older.
Contact Anne DesLauriers, Admissions Advisor, 101 East Chapman Street, Ely, Minnesota 55731. Phone: 800-328-2943. Fax: 218-365-7079. E-mail: info@vobs.org.
URL www.vobs.org

Voyageur Outward Bound–Lewis and Clark Alpine Backpacking

Voyageur Outward Bound/Outward Bound, USA
Beaverhead Mountains/Continental Divide
Montana

General Information Coed travel outdoor program and wilderness program established in 1964. High school or college credit may be earned.
Program Focus Teamwork and leadership wilderness adventure.
Academics Environmental science.
Special Interest Areas Campcraft, community service, leadership training, nature study, personal development, team building.
Wilderness/Outdoors Backpacking, hiking, mountaineering, outdoor adventure, rock climbing, survival training, wilderness camping.
Trips Overnight.
Program Information 2 sessions per year. Session length: 15–22 days in June, July. Ages: 14+. Cost: $2295–$2895. Application fee: $95. Financial aid available. Deadline 30 days prior to course start date.
Jobs Positions for college students 21 and older.
Contact Anne DesLauriers, Admissions Advisor, 101 East Chapman Street, Ely, Minnesota 55731. Phone: 800-328-2943. Fax: 218-365-7079. E-mail: info@vobs.org.
URL www.vobs.org

Voyageur Outward Bound–Lewis and Clark Alpine Backpacking-Girls

Voyageur Outward Bound/Outward Bound, USA
Beaverhead Mountains/Continental Divide
Montana

General Information Girls' travel outdoor program and wilderness program established in 1964. High school or college credit may be earned.
Program Focus Teamwork and leadership wilderness adventure.
Academics Environmental science.
Special Interest Areas Campcraft, community service, leadership training, nature study, personal development, team building.
Wilderness/Outdoors Backpacking, hiking, mountaineering, outdoor adventure, rock climbing, survival training, wilderness camping.
Trips Overnight.
Program Information 1 session per year. Session length: 15 days in June. Ages: 14–16. Cost: $2295. Application fee: $95. Financial aid available. Deadline 30 days prior to course start date.
Jobs Positions for college students 21 and older.
Contact Anne DesLauriers, Admissions Advisor, 101 East Chapman Street, Ely, Minnesota 55731. Phone: 800-328-2943. Fax: 218-365-7079. E-mail: info@vobs.org.
URL www.vobs.org

Voyageur Outward Bound–Montana High Alpine Backpacking

Voyageur Outward Bound/Outward Bound, USA
Absaroka-Beartooth Wilderness Area
Montana

General Information Coed travel outdoor program and wilderness program established in 1964. High school or college credit may be earned.
Program Focus Teamwork and leadership wilderness adventure.
Academics Environmental science.
Special Interest Areas Campcraft, community service, leadership training, nature study, personal development, team building.
Sports Rappelling.
Wilderness/Outdoors Backpacking, hiking, mountaineering, outdoor adventure, rock climbing, survival training, wilderness camping.
Trips Overnight.
Program Information 6 sessions per year. Session length: 15–22 days in June, July, August. Ages: 14+. Cost: $2195–$2895. Application fee: $95. Financial aid available. Deadline 30 days prior to course start date.
Jobs Positions for college students 21 and older.
Contact Anne DesLauriers, Admissions Advisor, 101 East Chapman Street, Ely, Minnesota 55731. Phone: 800-328-2943. Fax: 218-365-7079. E-mail: info@vobs.org.
URL www.vobs.org

Voyageur Outward Bound–Montana Rock Climbing XT

Voyageur Outward Bound/Outward Bound, USA
Humbug Spires and Highland Mountains
Montana

General Information Coed travel outdoor program and wilderness program established in 1964. High school or college credit may be earned.
Program Focus Teamwork and leadership wilderness adventure.
Academics Environmental science.
Special Interest Areas Campcraft, community service, leadership training, nature study, personal development, team building.
Sports Rappelling.
Wilderness/Outdoors Backpacking, outdoor adventure, rock climbing, survival training, wilderness camping.
Trips Overnight.
Program Information 2 sessions per year. Session length: 10 days in July, August. Ages: 16+. Cost: $1695. Application fee: $95. Financial aid available. Deadline 30 days prior to course start date.
Jobs Positions for college students 21 and older.
Contact Anne DesLauriers, Admissions Advisor, 101 East Chapman Street, Ely, Minnesota 55731. Phone: 800-328-2943. Fax: 218-365-7079. E-mail: info@vobs.org.
URL www.vobs.org

Voyageur Outward Bound–Northern Rockies Backpacking Family Adventure

Voyageur Outward Bound/Outward Bound, USA
Pioneer Mountains
Montana

General Information Coed travel outdoor program and wilderness program established in 1964. High school or college credit may be earned.
Program Focus Teamwork and leadership wilderness adventure.
Academics Environmental science.
Special Interest Areas Campcraft, community service, leadership training, nature study, personal development, team building.
Wilderness/Outdoors Backpacking, mountaineering, outdoor adventure, rock climbing, survival training, wilderness camping.
Trips Overnight.
Program Information 1 session per year. Session length: 8 days in August. Ages: 14+. Cost: $1295. Application fee: $95. Financial aid available. Deadline 30 days prior to course start date.
Jobs Positions for college students 21 and older.
Contact Anne DesLauriers, Admissions Advisor, 101 East Chapman Street, Ely, Minnesota 55731. Phone: 800-328-2943. Fax: 218-365-7079. E-mail: info@vobs.org.
URL www.vobs.org

NEBRASKA

Groundwater University

The Groundwater Foundation
Nebraska

General Information Coed residential academic program, outdoor program, and community service program established in 1994.
Program Focus Participants learn about groundwater and the related environment through fun hands-on activities, experiments, and tours.
Academics Ecology, environmental science, geography, geology/earth science, natural resource management, science (general).
Arts Arts and crafts (general).
Special Interest Areas Career exploration, community service, conservation projects, field research/expeditions, nature study.
Sports Fishing, horseback riding, swimming, tennis.
Trips Day.
Program Information 1 session per year. Session length: 3 days in June. Ages: 12–15. 10–20 participants per session. Boarding program cost: $175. Financial aid available.
Application Deadline April 30.
Contact Ms. Carla Mansfield, Camp Director, 5561 South 48th Street, #215, Lincoln, Nebraska 68516. Phone: 800-858-4844. Fax: 402-434-2742. E-mail: gu@groundwater.org.
URL www.groundwater.org

Student Conservation Association–Conservation Crew Program (Nebraska)

Student Conservation Association (SCA)
Nebraska

General Information Coed residential outdoor program, community service program, and wilderness program established in 1957. High school credit may be earned.
Program Focus Resource management, conservation, and environmental education.
Academics Biology, botany, ecology, environmental science, geology/earth science, history.
Special Interest Areas Campcraft, community service, construction, leadership training, nature study, trail maintenance, work camp programs.
Sports Canoeing, fishing, kayaking, swimming.
Wilderness/Outdoors Backpacking, canoe trips, hiking, orienteering, outdoor living skills, wilderness camping.
Trips Cultural, day, overnight.
Program Information 2–3 sessions per year. Session length: 3–5 weeks in June, July, August. Ages: 15–19. 6–8 participants per session. Application fee: $20. Financial aid available. No cost for program; financial aid possible for travel expenses.
Application Deadline Continuous.
Jobs Positions for college students 21 and older.

Student Conservation Association–Conservation Crew Program (Nebraska) (continued)

Contact Recruitment Office, PO Box 550, Charlestown, New Hampshire 03603. Phone: 603-543-1700. Fax: 603-543-1828. E-mail: getreal@thesca.org.
URL www.theSCA.org

NEVADA

Student Conservation Association–Conservation Crew Program (Nevada)

Student Conservation Association (SCA)
Nevada

General Information Coed residential outdoor program, community service program, and wilderness program established in 1957. High school credit may be earned.
Program Focus Resource management, conservation and environmental education.
Academics Biology, botany, ecology, environmental science, geology/earth science, history.
Special Interest Areas Campcraft, community service, construction, leadership training, nature study, trail maintenance, work camp programs.
Sports Canoeing, fishing, kayaking, swimming.
Wilderness/Outdoors Backpacking, hiking, orienteering, outdoor living skills, wilderness camping.
Trips Cultural, day, overnight.
Program Information 2–3 sessions per year. Session length: 3–5 weeks in June, July, August. Ages: 15–19. 6–8 participants per session. Application fee: $20. Financial aid available. No cost for program; financial aid possible for travel expenses.
Application Deadline Continuous.
Jobs Positions for college students 21 and older.
Contact Recruitment Office, PO Box 550, Charlestown, New Hampshire 03603. Phone: 603-543-1700. Fax: 603-543-1828. E-mail: getreal@thesca.org.
URL www.theSCA.org

Study Tours and Hotel and Tourism Management in the USA–Southern Nevada College

FLS International
Southern Nevada College
6375 West Charleston Boulevard
Las Vegas, Nevada 89102

General Information Coed residential academic program established in 2002. Formal opportunities for the academically talented.
Program Focus Hotel, tourism management and English as a second language.
Academics English as a second language, English language/literature, business, study skills.
Special Interest Areas Career exploration, homestays, hotel management.
Trips College tours, cultural, day, shopping.
Program Information 3 sessions per year. Session length: 20 days in June, July, August. Ages: 15+. 5–75 participants per session. Boarding program cost: $1525. Application fee: $100.
Application Deadline Continuous.
Contact Ms. Veronica Perez, Director of Admissions, 101 East Green Street #14, Pasadena, California 91105. Phone: 626-795-2912. Fax: 626-795-5564. E-mail: veronica@fls.net.
URL www.fls.net

For more information, see page 1128.

Study Tours in the USA–Southern Nevada

FLS International
Southern Nevada College
6375 West Charleston Boulevard
Las Vegas, Nevada 89102-1124

General Information Coed residential academic program established in 1987. Formal opportunities for the academically talented.
Program Focus English as a second language.
Academics English as a second language, English language/literature, SAT/ACT preparation, college tours, computers, intercultural studies, precollege program, reading, speech/debate, study skills, writing.
Arts Arts and crafts (general), creative writing.
Special Interest Areas Career exploration, culinary arts, field trips (arts and culture), homestays.
Sports Basketball, bicycling, ice hockey, skiing (downhill), soccer, softball, swimming, tennis.
Wilderness/Outdoors Bicycle trips, hiking, rafting, white-water trips.
Trips College tours, cultural, day, overnight, shopping.
Program Information 13 sessions per year. Session length: 19–20 days in January, February, March, April, May, June, July, August, September, October, November, December. Ages: 15+. 15–75 participants per session. Boarding program cost: $1495–$2295. Application fee: $100.
Application Deadline Continuous.
Contact Ms. Veronica Perez, Director of Admissions, 101 East Green Street, #14, Pasadena, California 91105. Phone: 626-795-2912. Fax: 626-795-5564. E-mail: veronica@fls.net.
URL www.fls.net

For more information, see page 1128.

NEW HAMPSHIRE

American Youth Foundation–Camp Merrowvista

American Youth Foundation
147 Canaan Road
Center Tuftonboro, New Hampshire 03816

General Information Coed residential traditional camp and outdoor program established in 1925. Accredited by American Camping Association and Association for Experiential Education.
Program Focus Leadership development and balanced living in a noncompetitive atmosphere.
Arts Arts and crafts (general), batiking, creative writing, drawing, jewelry making, pottery, theater/drama, weaving, woodworking.
Special Interest Areas Campcraft, leadership training, nature study.
Sports Aerobics, archery, basketball, bicycling, boating, canoeing, climbing (wall), field hockey, fishing, lacrosse, ropes course, sailing, soccer, softball, swimming, volleyball, windsurfing.
Wilderness/Outdoors Backpacking, bicycle trips, canoe trips, hiking, orienteering, rock climbing, wilderness camping.
Trips Overnight.
Program Information 6 sessions per year. Session length: 1–4 weeks in February, July, August. Ages: 8–18. 180–200 participants per session. Boarding program cost: $710–$2900. Financial aid available.
Application Deadline Continuous.
Jobs Positions for college students 18 and older.
Contact Lisa Boucher, Merrowvista Registrar, main address above. Phone: 603-539-6607. Fax: 603-539-7504. E-mail: merrowvista@ayf.com.
URL www.ayf.com

Appalachian Mountain Club–Teen Crews–Pinkham Notch

Appalachian Mountain Club
New Hampshire

General Information Coed residential outdoor program and wilderness program established in 1980. High school credit may be earned.
Program Focus Stewardship of the land through trail work.
Special Interest Areas Community service, conservation projects, first aid, trail maintenance.
Wilderness/Outdoors Backpacking, hiking, rock climbing.
Trips Day, overnight.
Program Information 1 session per year. Session length: 5 days in June, July. Ages: 15–17. 4–8 participants per session. Boarding program cost: $115–$130. Application fee: $25.
Application Deadline Continuous.
Jobs Positions for college students 18 and older.
Contact North Country Volunteer Coordinator, PO Box 298, Gorham, New Hampshire 03581. Phone: 603-466-2721 Ext.192. Fax: 603-466-2822.
URL www.outdoors.org/trails

Appalachian Mountain Club–Teen Crews–Spike

Appalachian Mountain Club
New Hampshire

General Information Coed residential outdoor program and wilderness program established in 1980. High school credit may be earned.
Program Focus Stewardship of the land through trail work.
Special Interest Areas Community service, conservation projects, first aid, trail maintenance.
Wilderness/Outdoors Backpacking, hiking, rock climbing, wilderness camping.
Trips Day, overnight.
Program Information 3 sessions per year. Session length: 5 days in July, August. Ages: 15–17. 4–8 participants per session. Boarding program cost: $115–$130. Application fee: $25.
Application Deadline Continuous.
Jobs Positions for college students 18 and older.
Contact North Country Volunteer Coordinator, PO Box 298, Gorham, New Hampshire 03581. Phone: 603-466-2721 Ext.192. Fax: 603-466-2822.
URL www.outdoors.org/trails/

Appalachian Mountain Club–Teen Crews–Two-week Teen Spike

Appalachian Mountain Club
New Hampshire

General Information Coed residential outdoor program and wilderness program established in 1980. High school credit may be earned.
Program Focus Stewardship of the land through trail work.
Special Interest Areas Community service, conservation projects, first aid, trail maintenance.
Wilderness/Outdoors Backpacking, hiking, rock climbing, wilderness camping.
Trips Day, overnight.
Program Information 2 sessions per year. Session length: 10–14 days in June, July, August. Ages: 16–18. 4–8 participants per session. Boarding program cost: $325–$350. Application fee: $25.
Application Deadline Continuous.
Jobs Positions for college students 18 and older.
Contact North Country Volunteer Coordinator, PO Box 298, Gorham, New Hampshire 03581. Phone: 603-466-2721 Ext.192. Fax: 603-466-2822.
URL www.outdoors.org/trails/

Appalachian Mountain Club–Teen Stewardship Training

Appalachian Mountain Club
New Hampshire

General Information Coed residential outdoor program and wilderness program. High school credit may be earned.
Program Focus Stewardship education.
Academics Ecology, environmental science, geology/earth science.
Special Interest Areas Career exploration, community service, conservation projects, field research/expeditions, first aid, nature study, trail maintenance.
Wilderness/Outdoors Backpacking, hiking, rock climbing, wilderness camping.
Trips Day, overnight.
Program Information 1 session per year. Session length: 15–21 days in July, August. Ages: 17–19. 8–12 participants per session. Boarding program cost: $600–$675. Application fee: $25.
Application Deadline Continuous.
Jobs Positions for college students 18 and older.
Contact North Country Volunteer Coordinator, PO Box 298, Gorham, New Hampshire 03581. Phone: 603-466-2721 Ext.192. Fax: 603-466-2822.
URL www.outdoors.org/trails

Appalachian Mountain Club–Trail Crew–White Mountains

Appalachian Mountain Club
Camp Dodge
Gorham, New Hampshire 03581

General Information Coed residential outdoor program and wilderness program established in 1980. High school credit may be earned.
Program Focus Stewardship of the land through trail work.
Special Interest Areas Community service, conservation projects, first aid, trail maintenance.
Wilderness/Outdoors Backpacking, hiking.
Trips Day, overnight.
Program Information 1 session per year. Session length: 5–7 days in July. Ages: 16+. 4–8 participants per session. Boarding program cost: $55–$65. Application fee: $25.
Application Deadline Continuous.
Jobs Positions for college students 18 and older.
Contact North Country Volunteer Coordinator, PO Box 298, Gorham, New Hampshire 03581. Phone: 603-466-2721 Ext.192. Fax: 603-466-2822.
URL www.outdoors.org/trails

Appalachian Mountain Club–Volunteer Trail Crew–Alpine/Mount Washington

Appalachian Mountain Club
Gorham, New Hampshire

General Information Coed residential outdoor program and wilderness program established in 1980. High school credit may be earned.
Program Focus Stewardship of the land through trail work.
Special Interest Areas Community service, conservation projects, first aid, trail maintenance.
Wilderness/Outdoors Backpacking, hiking, rock climbing.
Trips Day, overnight.
Program Information 3 sessions per year. Session length: 5–7 days in July, August. Ages: 16+. 4–8 participants per session. Boarding program cost: $115–$130. Application fee: $25.
Application Deadline Continuous.
Jobs Positions for college students 18 and older.
Contact North Country Volunteer Coordinator, PO Box 298, Gorham, New Hampshire 03581. Phone: 603-466-2721 Ext.192. Fax: 603-466-2822.
URL www.outdoors.org/trails/

Appalachian Mountain Club–Volunteer Trail Crew–Crawford Notch

Appalachian Mountain Club
Gorham, New Hampshire

General Information Coed residential outdoor program and wilderness program established in 1980. High school credit may be earned.
Program Focus Stewardship of the land through trail work.
Special Interest Areas Community service, conservation projects, first aid, trail maintenance.
Wilderness/Outdoors Backpacking, hiking, rock climbing.
Trips Day, overnight.
Program Information 1 session per year. Session length: 5–7 days in July. Ages: 16+. 4–8 participants per session. Boarding program cost: $115–$130. Application fee: $25.
Application Deadline Continuous.
Jobs Positions for college students 18 and older.
Contact North Country Volunteer Coordinator, PO Box 298, Gorham, New Hampshire 03581. Phone: 603-466-2721 Ext.192. Fax: 603-466-2822.
URL www.outdoors.org/trails/

Appalachian Mountain Club–Volunteer Trail Crew–Hut Crew

Appalachian Mountain Club
Camp Dodge
Gorham, New Hampshire

General Information Coed residential outdoor program and wilderness program established in 1980. High school credit may be earned.
Program Focus Stewardship of the land through trail work.
Special Interest Areas Community service, conservation projects, first aid, trail maintenance.
Wilderness/Outdoors Backpacking, hiking, rock climbing.
Trips Day, overnight.
Program Information 1 session per year. Session length: 5 days in June. Ages: 16+. 4–8 participants per session. Boarding program cost: $200–$225. Application fee: $25.
Application Deadline Continuous.
Jobs Positions for college students 18 and older.
Contact North Country Volunteer Coordinator, PO Box 298, Gorham, New Hampshire 03581. Phone: 603-466-2721 Ext.192. Fax: 603-466-2822.
URL www.outdoors.org/trails/

Appalachian Mountain Club–Wild New Hampshire Trail Crew

Appalachian Mountain Club
New Hampshire

General Information Coed residential outdoor program and wilderness program established in 1980. High school credit may be earned.
Program Focus Stewardship of the land through trail work.
Special Interest Areas Community service, conservation projects, first aid, trail maintenance.
Wilderness/Outdoors Backpacking, hiking, rock climbing, wilderness camping.
Trips Day, overnight.
Program Information 1 session per year. Session length: 5 days in June. Ages: 16+. 4–8 participants per session. Boarding program cost: $115–$130. Application fee: $25.
Application Deadline Continuous.
Jobs Positions for college students 18 and older.
Contact North Country Volunteer Coordinator, PO Box 298, Gorham, New Hampshire 03581. Phone: 603-466-2721 Ext.192. Fax: 603-466-2822.
URL www.outdoors.org/trails

Appalachian Mountain Club–Women's Trail Crew

Appalachian Mountain Club
New Hampshire

General Information Girls' residential outdoor program and wilderness program established in 1980. High school credit may be earned.
Program Focus Stewardship of the land through trail work.
Special Interest Areas Community service, conservation projects, first aid, trail maintenance.
Wilderness/Outdoors Backpacking, hiking, rock climbing, wilderness camping.
Trips Day, overnight.
Program Information 1 session per year. Session length: 5 days in July. Ages: 16+. 4–8 participants per session. Boarding program cost: $115–$130. Application fee: $25.
Application Deadline Continuous.
Jobs Positions for college students 18 and older.
Contact North Country Volunteer Coordinator, PO Box 298, Gorham, New Hampshire 03581. Phone: 603-466-2721 Ext.192. Fax: 603-466-2822.
URL www.outdoors.org/trails/

Brewster Academy Summer Session

Brewster Academy
80 Academy Drive
Wolfeboro, New Hampshire 03894

General Information Coed residential and day academic program and outdoor program established in 1994. Formal opportunities for the academically talented. Specific services available for the learning disabled. High school credit may be earned.

Brewster Academy Summer Session

Program Focus Academics (including for-credit courses in English and math), ESL, science, computer graphics and design, video editing, technology, instructional skills (organization, study, time management, reading/writing, etc.), and mentored study halls.
Academics English as a second language, English language/literature, computers, environmental science, humanities, language study, mathematics, reading, research skills, science (general), study skills, writing.
Arts Digital media, film, film editing, graphic arts, photography, studio arts, television/video.
Special Interest Areas Internet accessibility, campcraft, community service, computer graphics, time management.

Brewster Academy Summer Session (continued)

Sports Aerobics, baseball, basketball, bicycling, boating, canoeing, climbing (wall), fishing, kayaking, rappelling, ropes course, sailing, scuba diving, sea kayaking, snorkeling, soccer, softball, swimming, tennis, volleyball, weight training.
Wilderness/Outdoors Backpacking, bicycle trips, canoe trips, hiking, mountaineering, orienteering, rock climbing, survival training, wilderness camping.
Trips Cultural, day, shopping.
Program Information 1 session per year. Session length: 6 weeks in July, August. Ages: 12–17. 40–60 participants per session. Day program cost: $3400–$3500. Boarding program cost: $5795–$6000. Application fee: $35–$75.
Application Deadline Continuous.
Jobs Positions for college students 21 and older.
Contact Ms. Christine Brown, Summer Programs Manager, main address above. Phone: 603-569-7155. Fax: 603-569-7050. E-mail: summer@brewsteracademy.org.
URL www.brewsteracademy.org

For more information, see page 1002.

CAMP ALLEN

Manchester, NH Lions and Boston, MA Kiwanis Clubs
56 Camp Allen Road
Bedford, New Hampshire 03110

General Information Coed residential and day special needs program established in 1931. Specific services available for the developmentally challenged, hearing impaired, physically challenged, and visually impaired.
Arts Arts and crafts (general).
Special Interest Areas Campcraft, gardening, nature study.
Sports Baseball, basketball, sports (general), swimming.
Wilderness/Outdoors Hiking, outdoor camping, wilderness camping.
Trips Day.
Program Information 8–10 sessions per year. Session length: 6–12 days in June, July, August. Ages: 6–90. 40–65 participants per session. Day program cost: $275–$425. Boarding program cost: $575–$1485. Financial aid available.
Application Deadline Continuous.
Jobs Positions for high school students 18 and older and college students 18 and older.
Contact Mary C. Constance, Executive Director, main address above. Phone: 603-622-8471. Fax: 603-626-4295. E-mail: campallennh@aol.com or campallenmary@aol.com.
URL www.campallennh.org

CAMP BRANDON FOR BOYS

Northern Sports and Recreation
Wolfeboro, New Hampshire

General Information Boys' residential traditional camp and special needs program established in 1998. Specific services available for the participant with enuresis and participant with encopresis.
Program Focus For boys who suffer from enuresis/encopresis.
Arts Woodworking.
Special Interest Areas Campcraft, model rocketry.
Sports Basketball, kayaking, sailing, skateboarding, soccer, sports (general), swimming, tennis, track and field, volleyball, water polo, windsurfing.
Wilderness/Outdoors Backpacking, canoe trips, hiking.
Trips Day.
Program Information 4 sessions per year. Session length: 1 week in February, July, August, September, October. Ages: 8–18. 10–50 participants per session. Boarding program cost: $875–$6500. Financial aid available.
Application Deadline May 1.
Jobs Positions for high school students 14 and older and college students 18 and older.
Contact Mr. Richard Cooper, Director, 29 Morrison Avenue, Plattsburgh, New York 12901. Phone: 800-255-1980. Fax: 518-561-3672. E-mail: cbrandon@westelcom.com.
URL www.four-starheritagegroup.com

CAMP BROOKWOODS AND DEER RUN

Christian Camps and Conferences, Inc.
34 Camp Brookwoods Road
Alton, New Hampshire 03809

General Information Coed residential traditional camp established in 1944. Religious affiliation: Christian. Accredited by American Camping Association.
Academics Bible study.
Arts Arts and crafts (general), ceramics, music, photography, woodworking.
Special Interest Areas Campcraft, leadership training, model rocketry, nature study.
Sports Aerobics, archery, baseball, basketball, bicycling, boating, canoeing, climbing (wall), equestrian sports, field hockey, fishing, gymnastics, horseback riding, kayaking, lacrosse, rappelling, riflery, ropes course, sailing, scuba diving, sea kayaking, snorkeling, soccer, softball, swimming, tennis, volleyball, waterskiing, windsurfing.
Wilderness/Outdoors Backpacking, bicycle trips, canoe trips, hiking, mountain biking, rafting, rock climbing, white-water trips, wilderness camping.
Trips Day, overnight.
Program Information 4 sessions per year. Session length: 2–4 weeks in June, July, August. Ages: 8–18. 300 participants per session. Boarding program cost: $1285–$2275. Financial aid available.
Application Deadline Continuous.
Jobs Positions for college students 18 and older.
Contact Mr. Bob Strodel, Executive Director, main address above. Phone: 603-875-3600. Fax: 603-875-4606. E-mail: bob@brookwoods.org.
URL www.christiancamps.net

Camp Glen Brook

35 Glenbrook Road
Marlborough, New Hampshire 03455-2207

General Information Coed residential traditional camp and outdoor program established in 1946. Accredited by American Camping Association.
Arts Acting, arts and crafts (general), ceramics, chorus, dance (folk), drawing, music (vocal), musical productions, painting, photography, pottery, sculpture, weaving, woodworking.
Special Interest Areas Animal care, campcraft, gardening, model rocketry, nature study, team building.
Sports Archery, baseball, basketball, bicycling, canoeing, climbing (wall), fishing, ice hockey, ice skating, kayaking, ropes course, skiing (cross-country), snowshoeing, soccer, softball, swimming, tennis, volleyball.
Wilderness/Outdoors Canoe trips, caving, hiking, mountain biking, rafting, rock climbing, wilderness camping.
Trips Day, overnight.
Program Information 2 sessions per year. Session length: 3–6 weeks in February, June, July, August. Ages: 8–14. 60–75 participants per session. Boarding program cost: $2375–$4200. Financial aid available.
Application Deadline Continuous.
Jobs Positions for high school students 14 and older and college students 18 and older.
Contact James Madsen, Director, main address above. Phone: 603-876-3342. Fax: 603-876-3763. E-mail: glenbrook@glenbrook.org.
URL www.glenbrook.org

Camp Mowglis, School of the Open

Route 3A
Hebron, New Hampshire 03241

General Information Boys' residential traditional camp and outdoor program established in 1903.
Program Focus Individual growth in a traditional camping environment.
Academics Forestry, meteorology, music, tutoring.
Arts Acting, arts and crafts (general), chorus, creative writing, drawing, jewelry making, leather working, music, music (instrumental), painting, photography, pottery, theater/drama, woodworking.
Special Interest Areas Campcraft, model rocketry, nature study, team building.
Sports Archery, baseball, basketball, boating, canoeing, climbing (wall), diving, fishing, football, kayaking, rappelling, riflery, ropes course, rowing (crew/sculling), sailing, soccer, softball, swimming, tennis, track and field, volleyball, waterskiing, windsurfing.
Wilderness/Outdoors Backpacking, canoe trips, hiking, mountain biking, mountaineering, orienteering, rock climbing, white-water trips, wilderness camping.
Trips Day, overnight.
Program Information 1 session per year. Session length: 7 weeks in June, July, August. Ages: 7–14. 85–95 participants per session. Boarding program cost: $4600. Financial aid available.
Application Deadline Continuous.
Jobs Positions for high school students 15 and older and college students 18 and older.
Contact K. Robert Bengtson, Director, PO Box 9, Hebron, New Hampshire 03241. Phone: 603-744-8095. Fax: 603-744-9350. E-mail: campoffice@mowglis.org.
URL www.mowglis.org

Camp Onaway

Onaway Camp Trust
27 Camp Onaway Road
Hebron, New Hampshire 03241

General Information Girls' residential traditional camp established in 1911.
Arts Arts and crafts (general), ceramics, chorus, creative writing, dance, dance (ballet), dance (jazz), dance (tap), drawing, fabric arts, music (instrumental), music (vocal), painting, photography, pottery, printmaking, theater/drama, woodworking.
Special Interest Areas Campcraft, community service, leadership training, nature study.
Sports Aerobics, boating, canoeing, rowing (crew/sculling), sailing, swimming, tennis, volleyball.
Wilderness/Outdoors Backpacking, canoe trips, hiking, white-water trips, wilderness camping.
Trips Day, overnight.
Program Information 1 session per year. Session length: 7 weeks in June, July, August. Ages: 9–15. 84–92 participants per session. Boarding program cost: $4900. Financial aid available.
Application Deadline Continuous.
Jobs Positions for high school students 17 and older and college students 19 and older.
Summer Contact Anne Conolly, Director, main address above. Phone: 603-744-2180. Fax: 603-744-2180.
Winter Contact Anne Conolly, Director, PO Box 444, Kinderhook, New York 12106. Phone: 518-758-2337. Fax: 518-758-2337. E-mail: aconolly@camponaway.org.
URL www.camponaway.org

Camp Pasquaney

19 Pasquaney Lane
Hebron, New Hampshire 03241

General Information Boys' residential traditional camp established in 1895.
Arts Theater/drama, woodworking.
Special Interest Areas Campcraft, nature study.
Sports Baseball, boating, canoeing, diving, fishing, rowing (crew/sculling), sailing, swimming, tennis.
Wilderness/Outdoors Backpacking, canoe trips, hiking, wilderness camping.
Trips Day, overnight.
Program Information 1 session per year. Session length: 50 days in June, July, August. Ages: 11–16. 95 participants per session. Boarding program cost: $4400. Financial aid available.
Application Deadline Continuous.
Jobs Positions for college students 18 and older.
Summer Contact Vincent J. Broderick, Director, main address above. Phone: 603-744-8043. E-mail: office@pasquaney.org.

Camp Pasquaney (continued)

Winter Contact Vincent J. Broderick, Director, 5 South State Street, Concord, New Hampshire 03301. Phone: 603-225-4065. Fax: 603-225-4015. E-mail: office@pasquaney.org.

URL www.pasquaney.org

CAMP QUINEBARGE

PO Box 608
Center Harbor, New Hampshire 03226

General Information Coed residential traditional camp established in 1936. Accredited by American Camping Association.

Arts Arts and crafts (general), ceramics, drawing, jewelry making, leather working, painting, photography, pottery, theater/drama, woodworking.

Special Interest Areas Animal care, campcraft, nature study.

Sports Aerobics, archery, basketball, bicycling, boating, canoeing, climbing (wall), fishing, horseback riding, kayaking, rappelling, ropes course, sailing, soccer, softball, swimming, tennis, volleyball, windsurfing.

Wilderness/Outdoors Backpacking, bicycle trips, canoe trips, hiking, mountain biking, rafting, rock climbing, white-water trips, wilderness camping.

Trips Cultural, day, overnight.

Program Information 4 sessions per year. Session length: 2–7 weeks in June, July, August. Ages: 7–15. 100 participants per session. Boarding program cost: $1500–$4200. Financial aid available.

Application Deadline Continuous.

Jobs Positions for high school students 18 and older and college students 19 and older.

Contact David Hurley, Director, PO Box 608, Center Harbor, New Hampshire 03226. Phone: 603-253-6029. Fax: 603-253-6027.

URL www.campquinebarge.com

CAMP ROBIN HOOD FOR BOYS AND GIRLS

65 Robin Hood Lane
Freedom, New Hampshire 03836

General Information Coed residential traditional camp established in 1927. Accredited by American Camping Association.

Program Focus Skill development, interpersonal relationships, independence, self-esteem, and fun.

Academics English as a second language, mathematics, reading.

Arts Arts and crafts (general), ceramics, dance, dance (modern), drawing, jewelry making, leather working, metalworking, music (rock), musical productions, painting, photography, pottery, sculpture, theater/drama, woodworking.

Special Interest Areas Campcraft, model rocketry, nature study, work camp programs.

Sports Archery, baseball, basketball, boating, canoeing, cheerleading, diving, field hockey, figure skating, fishing, football, golf, gymnastics, horseback riding, ice hockey, kayaking, lacrosse, riflery, sailing, soccer, softball, sports (general), street/roller hockey, swimming, tennis, track and field, volleyball, water polo, waterskiing, windsurfing.

Wilderness/Outdoors Backpacking, canoe trips, hiking, rafting, white-water trips, wilderness camping.

Trips Day, overnight.

Program Information 4 sessions per year. Session length: 4–8 weeks in June, July, August. Ages: 7–16. 175–250 participants per session. Boarding program cost: $4250–$6700. Financial aid available.

Application Deadline Continuous.

Jobs Positions for high school students 18 and older and college students 19 and older.

Summer Contact Jamie Cole, Owner/Director, main address above. Phone: 603-539-4500. Fax: 603-539-4599. E-mail: dc@camprobinhood.com.

Winter Contact Jamie Cole, Owner/Director, 3330 Somerset Drive, Shaker Heights, Ohio 44122. Phone: 216-491-2267. Fax: 216-491-2268. E-mail: dc@camprobinhood.com.

URL www.camprobinhood.com

CAMP STARFISH

Camp Starfish
East Monomonac Road
Rindge, New Hampshire 03451

General Information Coed residential traditional camp and special needs program established in 1998. Specific services available for the emotionally challenged, developmentally challenged, and learning disabled.

Program Focus Camp Starfish is a special camp with a one to one camper to staff ratio, for children with emotional, behavioral, and learning problems.

Academics Computers, reading, science (general), technology.

Arts Acting, arts and crafts (general), ceramics, creative writing, dance, drawing, jewelry making, music, painting, pottery, theater/drama.

Special Interest Areas Community service, gardening, leadership training, nature study, team building.

Sports Basketball, boating, canoeing, football, kayaking, martial arts, ropes course, sailing, soccer, street/roller hockey, swimming, tennis, volleyball.

Wilderness/Outdoors Hiking.

Program Information 1–3 sessions per year. Session length: 19 days in July, August. Ages: 7–15. 47–55 participants per session. Boarding program cost: $500–$2850. Financial aid available.

Application Deadline Continuous.

Jobs Positions for high school students 16 and older and college students 16 and older.

Contact Todd A. Zeff, Associate Director, 31 Heath Street, Boston, Massachusetts 02130. Phone: 617-522-9800. Fax: 617-522-9181. E-mail: todd@campstarfish.org.

URL www.campstarfish.org

Camp Tohkomeupog

2151 East Madison Road
East Madison, New Hampshire 03849

General Information Boys' residential traditional camp established in 1932. Accredited by American Camping Association.
Arts Arts and crafts (general).
Special Interest Areas Campcraft, leadership training, nature study, work camp programs.
Sports Archery, baseball, basketball, bicycling, boating, canoeing, climbing (wall), diving, fishing, golf, in-line skating, lacrosse, rappelling, riflery, ropes course, sailing, scuba diving, snorkeling, soccer, softball, street/roller hockey, swimming, tennis, track and field, volleyball, water polo, waterskiing, weight training.
Wilderness/Outdoors Backpacking, bicycle trips, canoe trips, hiking, mountain biking, rock climbing, white-water trips, wilderness camping.
Trips Day, overnight.
Program Information 1–4 sessions per year. Session length: 13–52 days in June, July, August. Ages: 8–16. 120 participants per session. Boarding program cost: $1395–$4790. Financial aid available.
Application Deadline Continuous.
Jobs Positions for college students 19 and older.
Contact Andrew Mahoney, Director, 1251 Eaton Road, Madison, New Hampshire 03849. Phone: 603-367-8362. Fax: 603-367-8664. E-mail: tohko@tohko.com.
URL www.tohko.com

Camp Walt Whitman

Camp Walt Whitman
1000 Cape Moonshine Road
Piermont, New Hampshire 03779

General Information Coed residential traditional camp established in 1948. Accredited by American Camping Association.
Program Focus Skill development in community-oriented values.
Academics Mathematics, reading, study skills, tutoring, writing.
Arts Arts and crafts (general), batiking, ceramics, chorus, creative writing, dance, dance (folk), dance (jazz), dance (modern), dance (tap), drawing, fabric arts, jewelry making, leather working, metalworking, musical productions, painting, photography, pottery, printmaking, puppetry, radio broadcasting, television/video, theater/drama, weaving, woodworking.
Special Interest Areas Campcraft, community service, culinary arts, leadership training, model rocketry, nature study.
Sports Aerobics, archery, baseball, basketball, bicycling, boating, canoeing, climbing (wall), field hockey, fishing, golf, gymnastics, horseback riding, in-line skating, kayaking, lacrosse, martial arts, rappelling, ropes course, sailing, snorkeling, soccer, softball, street/roller hockey, swimming, tennis, track and field, volleyball, water polo, waterskiing, weight training, windsurfing, wrestling.
Wilderness/Outdoors Backpacking, bicycle trips, canoe trips, hiking, mountaineering, orienteering, rafting, rock climbing, white-water trips, wilderness camping.
Trips Cultural, day, overnight.
Program Information 3 sessions per year. Session length: 21–51 days in June, July, August. Ages: 7–15. 400 participants per session. Boarding program cost: $7500–$8000. 3 and 4-week programs available for participants entering grades 3–4.
Application Deadline Continuous.
Jobs Positions for college students 18 and older.
Summer Contact Jed Dorfman, Associate Director, main address above. Phone: 603-764-5521. Fax: 603-764-9146. E-mail: campwalt@aol.com.
Winter Contact Jed Dorfman, Associate Director, PO Box 938, Bedford, New York 10506. Phone: 914-234-5484. Fax: 914-234-5487. E-mail: campwalt@aol.com.
URL www.campwalt.com

Special Note
Camp Walt Whitman is located on a 300-acre campsite on its own crystal-clear lake in the White Mountains of New Hampshire. The camp has extensive sports and waterfront activities and facilities, including 11 clay tennis courts and a heated swimming pool. The camp offers team and individual sports, creative and performing arts, hiking, camping, and special trips. Activities are taught by highly qualified coaches and specialists who emphasize skill development and fun. Campers who want more competition have the opportunity to participate in intercamp games. Owned and operated by the same family since 1948, Camp Walt Whitman has provided a caring environment for 3 generations of campers. Directors Bill, Jancy, and Jed Dorfman run the camp and participate in programs with their campers and staff members. They know every camper, so they ensure that each has a successful and happy summer experience.

Camp Wicosuta

21 Wicosuta Drive
Hebron, New Hampshire 03241

General Information Girls' residential traditional camp established in 1920. Accredited by American Camping Association.
Program Focus Sports, arts, and wilderness adventure.
Academics Art (Advanced Placement), ecology.
Arts Arts and crafts (general), batiking, ceramics, chorus, dance, dance (jazz), dance (modern), drawing, film, jewelry making, leather working, musical productions, painting, photography, pottery, printmaking, sculpture, theater/drama.
Special Interest Areas Campcraft, culinary arts, gardening, leadership training, nature study.
Sports Aerobics, archery, basketball, canoeing, climbing (wall), equestrian sports, figure skating, fishing, golf,

Camp Wicosuta (continued)

gymnastics, handball, horseback riding, lacrosse, rappelling, ropes course, sailing, soccer, softball, swimming, tennis, track and field, volleyball, waterskiing, windsurfing.
Wilderness/Outdoors Backpacking, bicycle trips, canoe trips, caving, hiking, mountain biking, mountaineering, orienteering, rafting, rock climbing, white-water trips, wilderness camping.
Trips Day, overnight.
Program Information 2 sessions per year. Session length: 26 days in June, July, August. Ages: 6–16. 270 participants per session. Boarding program cost: $4500–$4900.
Application Deadline Continuous.
Jobs Positions for college students 18 and older.
Summer Contact Cole Kelly, Co-Director, main address above. Phone: 603-744-3301. Fax: 603-744-5570. E-mail: campwicosuta@campwicosuta.com.
Winter Contact Cole Kelly, Co-Director, 48 MacArthur Road, Natick, Massachusetts 01760. Phone: 800-846-9426. Fax: 781-455-1486. E-mail: campwicosuta@campwicosuta.com.
URL www.campwicosuta.com

The Cardigan Mountain School Summer Session

Cardigan Mountain School
62 Alumni Drive
Canaan, New Hampshire 03741

General Information Coed residential and day traditional camp and academic program established in 1951. Formal opportunities for the academically talented, artistically talented, and gifted. Specific services available for the learning disabled.

The Cardigan Mountain School Summer Session

Program Focus Study skills, academic enrichment, and recreational activities.
Academics American literature, English as a second language, English language/literature, French language/literature, Latin language, Spanish language/literature, academics (general), art history/appreciation, biology, botany, classical languages/literatures, computer programming, computers, ecology, environmental science, geology/earth science, journalism, marine studies, mathematics, music, reading, science (general), study skills, typing, writing.
Arts Arts and crafts (general), ceramics, chorus, creative writing, drawing, fabric arts, graphic arts, music, music (vocal), musical productions, painting, photography, pottery, printmaking, theater/drama, weaving, woodworking.
Special Interest Areas Native American culture, construction, field research/expeditions, model rocketry, nature study, nautical skills, robotics.
Sports Aerobics, baseball, basketball, bicycling, boating, canoeing, climbing (wall), cross-country, equestrian sports, fishing, golf, horseback riding, in-line skating, kayaking, lacrosse, rappelling, riflery, ropes course, sailing, scuba diving, snorkeling, soccer, softball, sports (general), street/roller hockey, swimming, tennis, volleyball, weight training, windsurfing, wrestling.
Wilderness/Outdoors Backpacking, bicycle trips, canoe trips, hiking, mountain biking, mountaineering, rafting, rock climbing, wilderness camping.
Trips Cultural, day, overnight.
Program Information 1 session per year. Session length: 6 weeks in June, July, August. Ages: 9–14. 150–180 participants per session. Day program cost: $3500. Boarding program cost: $6700. Application fee: $35–$75. Financial aid available.
Application Deadline Continuous.
Jobs Positions for college students 21 and older.
Contact Mr. Thomas S. Pastore, Director of the Summer Session, 62 Alumni Drive, Cardigan Mountain School, Canaan, New Hampshire 03741-9307. Phone: 603-523-3528. Fax: 603-523-3565. E-mail: tpastore@cardigan.org.
URL www.cardigan.org

For more information, see page 1050.

Collegiate Summer Program for High School Students

Thomas More College of Liberal Arts
6 Manchester Street
Merrimack, New Hampshire 03054

General Information Coed residential academic program established in 1975. Religious affiliation: Roman Catholic.
Program Focus Liberal arts.
Academics American literature, English language/literature, academics (general), government and politics, philosophy, reading, religion, writing.
Sports Basketball, soccer, swimming.
Wilderness/Outdoors Hiking.
Trips Day.
Program Information 2 sessions per year. Session length: 2 weeks in July, August. Ages: 15–18. 25–35 participants per session. Boarding program cost: $975. Application fee: $10. Financial aid available.
Application Deadline Continuous.

Contact Ms. Joanne K. Geiger, Director of Admissions, 6 Manchester Street, Merrimack, New Hampshire 03054. Phone: 800-880-8308. Fax: 603-880-9280. E-mail: admissions@thomasmorecollege.edu.
URL www.thomasmorecollege.edu

Cragged Mountain Farm

239 Cold Brook Road
Freedom, New Hampshire 03836

General Information Coed residential traditional camp established in 1927.
Program Focus Camping, hiking, and canoeing.
Arts Arts and crafts (general), music, photography, pottery.
Special Interest Areas Nature study.
Sports Canoeing, climbing (wall), ropes course, soccer, softball, swimming.
Wilderness/Outdoors Backpacking, canoe trips, hiking, orienteering, white-water trips, wilderness camping.
Trips Day, overnight.
Program Information 1–2 sessions per year. Session length: 2–4 weeks in July, August. Ages: 5–13. 55–75 participants per session. Boarding program cost: $900–$1800. Financial aid available.
Application Deadline Continuous.
Jobs Positions for high school students 16 and older and college students 17 and older.
Contact Ben Utter, Owner/Director, 239 Cold Brook Road, Freedom, New Hampshire 03836. Phone: 603-539-4070.

Fleur de Lis Camp

Fleur de Lis Camp, Inc.
120 Howeville Road
Fitzwilliam, New Hampshire 03447-3465

General Information Girls' residential traditional camp established in 1929. Accredited by American Camping Association.
Arts Arts and crafts (general), theater/drama.
Sports Archery, basketball, boating, canoeing, diving, field hockey, horseback riding, kayaking, riflery, ropes course, sailing, soccer, softball, swimming, tennis, volleyball, waterskiing, windsurfing.
Trips Overnight.
Program Information 2 sessions per year. Session length: 4 weeks in June, July, August. Ages: 8–15. 100–110 participants per session. Boarding program cost: $1525–$4100. Application fee: $25.
Application Deadline Continuous.
Jobs Positions for college students 18 and older.
Summer Contact Liz Young, Director, main address above. Phone: 603-585-7751. Fax: 603-585-7751. E-mail: fdlcamp@aol.com.
Winter Contact Liz Young, Director, Box 659, Lincoln, Massachusetts 01773-0659. Phone: 508-757-1402. Fax: 508-757-1402. E-mail: fdlcamp@aol.com.
URL www.fleurdeliscamp.org

Special Note
While swimming, boating, or waterskiing, Fleur-de-Lis campers have a perfect view of Mt. Monadnock. This beautiful spot on Laurel Lake in Fitzwilliam, New Hampshire, offers girls a wide range of activities, from arts and crafts to tennis and windsurfing. Many of the staff members have grown up through the program, ensuring that the camp's unique traditions and values are passed on. Every year, a small number of new staff members come from abroad, bringing with them their own diverse views of the world and a willingness to share their cultures with campers. Fleur-de-Lis girls grow and mature in an environment of caring and nurturing. Campers are encouraged to share their own special talents and uniqueness with one another.

Great Escapes (Adventure Trips for Teens)–White Mountain Adventure

South Shore YMCA Camps
New Hampshire

General Information Coed travel outdoor program and adventure program established in 1989. Religious affiliation: Christian. Accredited by American Camping Association.
Program Focus Climbing school canoe expedition.
Special Interest Areas Leadership training.
Sports Canoeing, rappelling.
Wilderness/Outdoors Canoe trips, hiking, mountaineering, orienteering, rock climbing, white-water trips, wilderness camping, wilderness/outdoors (general).
Program Information 1 session per year. Session length: 13 days in July, August. Ages: 13–16. 10–12 participants per session. Cost: $995. Financial aid available.
Application Deadline Continuous.
Jobs Positions for college students 21 and older.
Contact Joseph O'Keefe, Great Escapes Director, 75 Stowe Road, Sandwich, Massachusetts 02563. Phone: 508-428-2571 Ext.110. Fax: 508-420-3545. E-mail: joeokeefe@ssymca.org.
URL www.ssymca.org/camps/great_escapes.asp

Landmark Volunteers: New Hampshire

Landmark Volunteers, Inc.
New Hampshire

General Information Coed residential outdoor program and community service program established in 1992. High school credit may be earned.
Program Focus Opportunity for high school students to earn community service credit while working as a team for two weeks serving Hidden Valley or Strawberry Banke. Similar programs offered through Landmark Volunteers at over 60 locations in 21 states.
Academics History, social science, social services.
Special Interest Areas Career exploration, community service, conservation projects, leadership training, team building, work camp programs.
Sports Swimming.
Trips Cultural, day.

Landmark Volunteers: New Hampshire (continued)

Program Information 1 session per year. Session length: 2 weeks in June, July, August. Ages: 14–18. 10–13 participants per session. Boarding program cost: $875–$925. Financial aid available.
Application Deadline Continuous.
Contact Ann Barrett, Executive Director, PO Box 455, Sheffield, Massachusetts 01257. Phone: 413-229-0255. Fax: 413-229-2050. E-mail: landmark@volunteers.com.
URL www.volunteers.com

For more information, see page 1182.

North Woods Camp for Boys

YMCA of Greater Boston–Camping Services Branch
Lake Winnipesaukee
Route 109N, Northwoods Road
Mirror Lake, New Hampshire 03853

General Information Boys' residential traditional camp and outdoor program established in 1929. Accredited by American Camping Association.
Arts Acting, arts and crafts (general), ceramics, creative writing, film, leather working, music, painting, photography, radio broadcasting, theater/drama, woodworking.
Special Interest Areas Campcraft, conservation projects, leadership training, team building.
Sports Archery, baseball, basketball, bicycling, boating, canoeing, challenge course, climbing (wall), equestrian sports, field hockey, fishing, football, horseback riding, kayaking, lacrosse, riflery, ropes course, sailing, snorkeling, soccer, softball, swimming, tennis, volleyball, waterskiing, windsurfing.
Wilderness/Outdoors Backpacking, bicycle trips, canoe trips, hiking, mountain biking, wilderness camping.
Trips Day, overnight.
Program Information 2–4 sessions per year. Session length: 13–18 days in July, August. Ages: 8–18. 140–150 participants per session. Boarding program cost: $800–$885. Financial aid available.
Application Deadline Continuous.
Jobs Positions for high school students 16 and older and college students 18 and older.
Contact Ms. Amy Goodman, Registrar, PO Box 230, Mirror Lake, New Hampshire 03853. Phone: 603-569-2725. Fax: 603-569-5869. E-mail: agoodman@ymcaboston.org.
URL www.ymcacamp.net

Paul Hogan's Shooter's Gold Basketball Camp–Alton

Paul Hogan Sports Camps
Alton, New Hampshire

General Information Coed day sports camp established in 1990.
Program Focus Basketball.
Sports Basketball.
Program Information 2 sessions per year. Session length: 5 days in June, July. Day program cost: $50–$115. Open to participants entering grades 1–8.
Application Deadline Continuous.
Jobs Positions for high school students and college students.
Contact Mr. Paul Hogan, Director, PO Box 1136, Concord, New Hampshire 03302. Phone: 603-340-1719. Fax: 603-271-6431. E-mail: paul@hogancamps.com.
URL www.hogancamps.com

Paul Hogan's Shooter's Gold Basketball Camp–Gilford

Paul Hogan Sports Camps
Gilford, New Hampshire

General Information Coed day sports camp established in 1990.
Program Focus Basketball.
Sports Basketball.
Program Information 2 sessions per year. Session length: 5 days in June, July. Ages: 6–14. Day program cost: $50–$115. Open to participants entering grades 1–8.
Application Deadline Continuous.
Jobs Positions for college students.
Contact Mr. Paul Hogan, Director, PO Box 1136, Concord, New Hampshire 03302. Phone: 603-340-1719. Fax: 603-271-6431. E-mail: paul@hogancamps.com.
URL www.hogancamps.com

Paul Hogan's Shooter's Gold Basketball Camp–Laconia

Paul Hogan Sports Camps
Laconia, New Hampshire

General Information Coed day sports camp established in 1990.
Program Focus Basketball.
Sports Basketball.
Program Information 2 sessions per year. Session length: 5 days in June, July. Day program cost: $50–$115. Open to participants entering grades 1–8.
Application Deadline Continuous.
Jobs Positions for high school students 16 and older and college students.
Contact Mr. Paul Hogan, Director, PO Box 1136, Concord, New Hampshire 03302. Phone: 603-340-1719. Fax: 603-271-6431. E-mail: paul@hogancamps.com.
URL www.hogancamps.com

Paul Hogan's Shooter's Gold Basketball Camp–Lancaster

Paul Hogan Sports Camps
Lancaster, New Hampshire

General Information Coed day sports camp established in 1990.
Program Focus Basketball.
Sports Basketball.
Program Information 2 sessions per year. Session length: 5 days in June, July. Day program cost: $50–$115. Open to participants entering grades 1–8.
Application Deadline Continuous.

Jobs Positions for college students.
Contact Mr. Paul Hogan, Director, PO Box 1136, Concord, New Hampshire 03302. Phone: 603-340-1719. Fax: 603-271-6431. E-mail: paul@hogancamps.com.
URL www.hogancamps.com

Paul Hogan's Shooter's Gold Basketball Camp–Littleton

Paul Hogan Sports Camps
Littleton, New Hampshire

General Information Coed day sports camp established in 1990.
Program Focus Basketball.
Sports Basketball.
Program Information 2 sessions per year. Session length: 5 days in June, July. Day program cost: $50–$115. Open to participants entering grades 1–8.
Application Deadline Continuous.
Jobs Positions for high school students 16 and older and college students.
Contact Mr. Paul Hogan, Director, PO Box 1136, Concord, New Hampshire 03302. Phone: 603-340-1719. Fax: 603-271-6431. E-mail: paul@hogancamps.com.
URL www.hogancamps.com

Paul Hogan's Shooter's Gold Basketball Camp–Manchester

Paul Hogan Sports Camps
Manchester, New Hampshire

General Information Coed day sports camp established in 1990.
Program Focus Basketball.
Sports Basketball.
Program Information 2 sessions per year. Session length: 5 days in June, July. Day program cost: $50–$115. Open to participants entering grades 1–8.
Application Deadline Continuous.
Jobs Positions for college students.
Contact Mr. Paul Hogan, Director, PO Box 1136, Concord, New Hampshire 03302. Phone: 603-340-1719. Fax: 603-271-6431. E-mail: paul@hogancamps.com.
URL www.hogancamps.com

Paul Hogan's Shooter's Gold Basketball Camp–Meredith

Paul Hogan Sports Camps
Meredith, New Hampshire

General Information Coed day sports camp established in 1990.
Program Focus Basketball.
Sports Basketball.
Program Information 2 sessions per year. Session length: 5 days in July. Day program cost: $50–$115. Open to participants entering grades 1–8.
Application Deadline Continuous.
Jobs Positions for college students.
Contact Mr. Paul Hogan, Director, PO Box 1136, Concord, New Hampshire 03302. Phone: 603-340-1719. Fax: 603-271-6431. E-mail: paul@hogancamps.com.
URL www.hogancamps.com

Paul Hogan's Shooter's Gold Basketball Camp–Tilton

Paul Hogan Sports Camps
Tilton, New Hampshire

General Information Coed day sports camp established in 1990.
Program Focus Basketball.
Sports Basketball.
Program Information 2 sessions per year. Session length: 5 days in July. Day program cost: $50–$115. Open to participants entering grades 1–8.
Application Deadline Continuous.
Jobs Positions for college students.
Contact Mr. Paul Hogan, Director, PO Box 1136, Concord, New Hampshire 03302. Phone: 603-340-1719. Fax: 603-271-6431. E-mail: paul@hogancamps.com.
URL www.hogancamps.com

Paul Hogan's Shooter's Gold Basketball Camp–Woodsville

Paul Hogan Sports Camps
Woodsville, New Hampshire

General Information Coed day sports camp established in 1990.
Program Focus Basketball.
Sports Basketball.
Program Information 2 sessions per year. Session length: 5 days in June. Day program cost: $50–$115. Open to participants entering grades 1–8.
Application Deadline Continuous.
Jobs Positions for college students.
Contact Mr. Paul Hogan, Director, PO Box 1136, Concord, New Hampshire 03302. Phone: 603-340-1719. Fax: 603-271-7139. E-mail: paul@hogancamps.com.
URL www.hogancamps.com

Paul Hogan's Specialty Basketball Camp

Paul Hogan Sports Camps
New Hampshire Technical Institute
31 College Drive
Concord, New Hampshire 03301

General Information Coed residential and day sports camp established in 1990.
Program Focus Basketball.
Sports Basketball.
Program Information 1 session per year. Session length: 5 days in July, August. Ages: 10–17. 120 participants per session. Day program cost: $200–$275. Boarding program cost: $410–$450. Open to participants entering grades 5–10.
Application Deadline Continuous.

Paul Hogan's Specialty Basketball Camp (continued)

Jobs Positions for high school students 17 and older and college students.
Contact Mr. Paul Hogan, Director, PO Box 1136, Concord, New Hampshire 03302. Phone: 603-340-1719. Fax: 603-271-6431. E-mail: paul@hogancamps.com.
URL www.hogancamps.com

Performance PLUS–Positive Learning Using the Stage + Studio + Screen

Performance PLUS
New Hampton School
Main Street
New Hampton, New Hampshire 03256

General Information Coed residential arts program established in 2000. Formal opportunities for the artistically talented. High school credit may be earned.

Performance PLUS–Positive Learning Using the Stage+Studio+Screen

Program Focus Performing arts: film, music, dance, theatre arts, and/or technical production.
Academics Music.
Arts Acting, arts, audition technique, band, chorus, cinematography, costume design, creative writing, dance, dance (ballet), dance (jazz), dance (modern), dance (tap), design, digital media, directing, film, film editing, film lighting, film production, guitar, music, music (classical), music (ensemble), music (instrumental), music (jazz), music (rock), music (vocal), music composition/arrangement, music technology/record production, musical productions, musical theater, performance art, screenwriting, set design, sound design, stage combat, stage managing, stage movement, television/video, theater/drama, vocal production, voice and speech.
Trips Cultural, day, shopping.
Program Information 1 session per year. Session length: 22 days in July. Ages: 13–18. 70–80 participants per session. Boarding program cost: $3600. Application fee: $300. Financial aid available.
Application Deadline Continuous.
Jobs Positions for college students 21 and older.
Contact Lori Murphy, Producing Director, Performance PLUS at New Hampton School, PO Box 579, New Hampton, New Hampshire 03256. Phone: 603-677-3403. Fax: 603-677-3481. E-mail: lmurphy@performanceplus.org.
URL www.performanceplus.org
For more information, see page 1254.

Phillips Exeter Academy Summer School

Phillips Exeter Academy
20 Main Street
Exeter, New Hampshire 03833-2460

General Information Coed residential and day academic program established in 1919. Formal opportunities for the academically talented and artistically talented.
Academics American literature, Chinese languages/literature, English as a second language, English language/literature, French language/literature, German language/literature, Italian language/literature, Japanese language/literature, Latin language, Russian language/literature, SAT/ACT preparation, Spanish language/literature, academics (general), archaeology, architecture, art history/appreciation, astronomy, biology, chemistry, classical languages/literatures, computer programming, computers, ecology, economics, environmental science, government and politics, government and politics (Advanced Placement), history, humanities, journalism, marine studies, mathematics, music, physics, physiology, psychology, science (general), social science, social studies, speech/debate, study skills, writing.
Arts Band, ceramics, chorus, creative writing, dance, dance (ballet), dance (jazz), dance (modern), dance (tap), drawing, film, graphic arts, jewelry making, music, music (chamber), music (classical), music (ensemble), music (instrumental), music (jazz), music (orchestral), music (vocal), painting, photography, sculpture, theater/drama.
Special Interest Areas Career exploration, community service, electronics, field trips (arts and culture).
Sports Aerobics, basketball, cross-country, field hockey, golf, in-line skating, lacrosse, soccer, softball, squash, swimming, tennis, track and field, volleyball, water polo, weight training.
Wilderness/Outdoors Hiking.
Trips College tours, cultural, day, shopping.
Program Information 1 session per year. Session length: 5 weeks in July, August. Ages: 13–19. 580–590 participants per session. Day program cost: $975–$3395. Boarding program cost: $5295–$5595. Application fee: $60–$95. Financial aid available.
Application Deadline Continuous.
Jobs Positions for college students.
Contact Richard A. Hardej, Dean of Admissions, main address above. Phone: 603-777-3488. Fax: 603-777-4385. E-mail: summer@exeter.edu.
URL www.exeter.edu/summer
For more information, see page 1262.

Pleasant Valley Camp for Girls

YMCA of Greater Boston–Camping Services Branch
Lake Winnipesaukee
Route 109N, Northwoods Road
Mirror Lake, New Hampshire 03853

General Information Girls' residential traditional camp established in 1969. Accredited by American Camping Association.
Arts Acting, arts and crafts (general), ceramics, dance, drawing, fabric arts, film, jewelry making, leather working, music, painting, photography, radio broadcasting, sculpture, theater/drama, woodworking.
Special Interest Areas Campcraft, conservation projects, gardening, leadership training, team building.
Sports Archery, baseball, basketball, bicycling, boating, canoeing, climbing (wall), equestrian sports, field hockey, fishing, horseback riding, kayaking, lacrosse, riflery, ropes course, sailing, snorkeling, soccer, softball, swimming, tennis, volleyball, waterskiing, windsurfing.
Wilderness/Outdoors Backpacking, bicycle trips, canoe trips, hiking, mountain biking, wilderness camping.
Trips Day, overnight.
Program Information 2–4 sessions per year. Session length: 18 days in July, August. Ages: 8–18. 140–150 participants per session. Boarding program cost: $800–$885. Financial aid available.
Application Deadline Continuous.
Jobs Positions for high school students 16 and older and college students 18 and older.
Contact Ms. Amy Goodman, Registrar, PO Box 230, Mirror Lake, New Hampshire 03853. Phone: 617-569-2725. Fax: 603-569-5869. E-mail: agoodman@ymcaboston.org.
URL www.ymcacamp.net

Road's End Farm Horsemanship Camp

Road's End Farm
Jackson Hill Road
Chesterfield, New Hampshire 03443-0197

General Information Girls' residential traditional camp established in 1958.
Program Focus English pleasure riding and care of horses.
Arts Arts and crafts (general).
Special Interest Areas Animal care, gardening.
Sports Canoeing, horseback riding, swimming.
Wilderness/Outdoors Canoe trips, hiking.
Trips Day.
Program Information 7 sessions per year. Session length: 13–55 days in June, July, August, October. Ages: 8–16. 60–65 participants per session. Boarding program cost: $1680–$6320.
Application Deadline Continuous.
Jobs Positions for college students 19 and older.
Contact Mr. Thomas E. Woodman, Owner/Director, main address above. Phone: 603-363-4900. Fax: 603-363-4949.
URL www.roadsendfarm.com

Sandy Island Camp for Families

YMCA of Greater Boston–Camping Services Branch
Lake Winnipesaukee
New Hampshire

General Information Coed residential traditional camp, outdoor program, and family program established in 1898.
Program Focus Camping experience for children of all ages and their parents.
Arts Arts and crafts (general), batiking, creative writing, dance, dance (modern), drawing, music (instrumental), painting.
Special Interest Areas Campcraft.
Sports Aerobics, basketball, boating, canoeing, climbing (wall), equestrian sports, fishing, horseback riding, kayaking, ropes course, sailing, snorkeling, softball, swimming, tennis, volleyball, waterskiing, windsurfing.
Program Information 1–10 sessions per year. Session length: 3–7 days in June, July, August, September. Ages: 3+. 140–150 participants per session. Boarding program cost: $255–$550. Financial aid available.
Application Deadline Continuous.
Jobs Positions for high school students 16 and older and college students 18 and older.
Contact Jill Gary, Associate Executive Director, 316 Huntington Avenue, Boston, Massachusetts 02115-5019. Phone: 617-927-8220. Fax: 617-927-8156. E-mail: jgary@ymcaboston.org.
URL www.ymcacamp.net

Sargent Center Adventure Camp

Sargent Center Adventure Camp
36 Sargent Camp Road
Hancock, New Hampshire 03449

General Information Coed residential outdoor program and adventure program established in 1993. Accredited by American Camping Association.
Arts Arts and crafts (general).
Sports Archery, canoeing, climbing (wall), kayaking, rappelling, ropes course, sea kayaking, swimming.
Wilderness/Outdoors Backpacking, canoe trips, hiking, mountain biking, outdoor adventure, rock climbing, wilderness camping.
Program Information 36 sessions per year. Session length: 3–20 days in July, August. Ages: 10–17. 150–170 participants per session. Boarding program cost: $480–$1575. Financial aid available.
Application Deadline Continuous.
Jobs Positions for high school students 18 and older and college students 21 and older.
Contact Ms. Marijean Parry, Director, Adventure Camp, main address above. Phone: 603-525-3311. Fax: 603-525-4151. E-mail: mj@busc.mv.com.
URL www.bu.edu/outdoor/adventure

Student Conservation Association–Conservation Crew Program (New Hampshire)

Student Conservation Association (SCA)
New Hampshire

General Information Coed residential outdoor program, community service program, and wilderness program established in 1957. High school credit may be earned.
Program Focus Resource management, conservation and environmental education.
Academics Biology, botany, ecology, environmental science, geology/earth science, history.
Special Interest Areas Campcraft, community service, construction, leadership training, nature study, trail maintenance, work camp programs.
Sports Canoeing, fishing, kayaking, swimming.
Wilderness/Outdoors Backpacking, canoe trips, hiking, orienteering, outdoor living skills, rock climbing, wilderness camping.
Trips Cultural, day, overnight.
Program Information 2–3 sessions per year. Session length: 3–5 weeks in June, July, August. Ages: 15–19. 6–8 participants per session. Application fee: $20. Financial aid available. No cost for program; financial aid possible for travel expenses.
Application Deadline Continuous.
Jobs Positions for college students 21 and older.
Contact Recruitment Office, PO Box 550, Charlestown, New Hampshire 03603. Phone: 603-543-1700. Fax: 603-543-1828. E-mail: getreal@thesca.org.
URL www.theSCA.org

Wediko Summer Program

Wediko Children's Services
11 Bobcat Boulevard
Windsor, New Hampshire 03244

General Information Coed residential special needs program established in 1934. Specific services available for the emotionally challenged, developmentally challenged, and learning disabled.
Program Focus A multi-modality, comprehensively structured therapeutic summer program for children at high psychological risk.
Academics English language/literature, mathematics, science (general).
Arts Arts and crafts (general), dance, music, theater/drama.
Special Interest Areas Animal care.
Sports Archery, baseball, basketball, boating, canoeing, fishing, gymnastics, kayaking, soccer, softball, swimming.
Wilderness/Outdoors Hiking, mountain biking.
Program Information 1 session per year. Session length: 45 days in July, August. Ages: 7–17. 120 participants per session. Boarding program cost: $8050–$8250.
Application Deadline Continuous.
Jobs Positions for college students 20 and older.
Summer Contact Bonnie Thompson-Yezukevich, Administrative Coordinator, Wediko Children's Services, 72-74 East Dedham Street, Boston, Massachusetts 02118. Phone: 617-292-9200. Fax: 617-292-9275. E-mail: bthompson@wediko.org.
Winter Contact Dolores Kane, Co-Director, Admissions, Windsor, New Hampshire 03244. Phone: 603-478-5236. Fax: 603-478-2040. E-mail: dkane@wediko-nh.org.
URL www.wediko.org

Windsor Mountain: Driftwood Stables Ranch Camp

Interlocken at Windsor Mountain
Driftwood Stables
Windsor Road
Hillsboro, New Hampshire

General Information Coed residential outdoor program established in 2001.
Program Focus Horsemanship—Western and English.
Special Interest Areas Animal care, community service.
Sports Horseback riding.
Wilderness/Outdoors Pack animal trips.
Program Information 1 session per year. Session length: 3 weeks in July, August. Ages: 12–13. 13 participants per session. Boarding program cost: $3450. Financial aid available.
Application Deadline Continuous.
Contact Richard Herman, Director, RR #2, Box 165, Hillsboro, New Hampshire 03244. Phone: 603-478-3166. Fax: 603-478-5260. E-mail: mail@windsormountain.org.
URL www.driftwoodstables.com/ranchcam.htm
For more information, see page 1162.

Windsor Mountain: Family Camp

Interlocken at Windsor Mountain
19 Interlocken Way
Windsor, New Hampshire 03244

General Information Coed residential family program established in 1961. Accredited by American Camping Association.
Academics English as a second language, ecology, environmental science, journalism, music.
Arts Acting, arts and crafts (general), batiking, ceramics, clowning, creative writing, dance, dance (ballet), dance (folk), dance (jazz), dance (modern), drawing, fabric arts, jewelry making, metalworking, mime, music, music (jazz), painting, photography, pottery, printmaking, puppetry, sculpture, theater/drama, weaving, woodworking.
Special Interest Areas Native American culture, animal care, campcraft, community service, conservation projects, construction, culinary arts, farming, gardening, leadership training, nature study, team building, work camp programs.
Sports Aerobics, archery, basketball, bicycling, boating, canoeing, climbing (wall), cross-country, diving, fishing, gymnastics, kayaking, lacrosse, martial arts, rappelling, ropes course, sailing, soccer, softball, swimming, tennis, volleyball, water polo, windsurfing.
Wilderness/Outdoors Bicycle trips, canoe trips, hiking, mountain biking, orienteering, rock climbing.

Program Information 1 session per year. Session length: 5 days in August, September. Ages: 1+. 100 participants per session. Financial aid available. Cost: $280 per person; $995 for family of 4, $200 per additional person.
Application Deadline Continuous.
Contact Tom Herman, Marketing Director, 19 Interlocken Way, Windsor, New Hampshire 03244. Phone: 603-478-3166 Ext.20. Fax: 603-478-5260. E-mail: mail@windsormountain.org.
URL www.windsormountain.org
For more information, see page 1162.

Windsor Mountain: International Summer Camp

Interlocken at Windsor Mountain
19 Interlocken Way
Hillsboro, New Hampshire 03244

General Information Coed residential traditional camp established in 1961. Accredited by American Camping Association.

Windsor Mountain: International Summer Camp

Program Focus Individualized programming, cross-cultural understanding, creative and performing arts, wilderness adventure and leadership development.
Academics English as a second language, ecology, environmental science, journalism, music.
Arts Acting, arts and crafts (general), batiking, ceramics, clowning, creative writing, dance, dance (ballet), dance (folk), dance (jazz), dance (modern), drawing, fabric arts, jewelry making, metalworking, mime, music, music (jazz), painting, photography, pottery, printmaking, puppetry, sculpture, theater/drama, weaving, woodworking.
Special Interest Areas Native American culture, animal care, campcraft, community service, conservation projects, construction, cross-cultural education, culinary arts, driver's education, farming, gardening, leadership training, nature study, team building, work camp programs.
Sports Aerobics, archery, basketball, bicycling, boating, canoeing, climbing (wall), cross-country, diving, fishing, gymnastics, kayaking, lacrosse, martial arts, rappelling, ropes course, sailing, soccer, softball, swimming, tennis, volleyball, windsurfing.
Wilderness/Outdoors Backpacking, bicycle trips, canoe trips, caving, hiking, mountain biking, mountaineering, orienteering, rock climbing, survival training, white-water trips, wilderness camping.
Trips Overnight.
Program Information 2 sessions per year. Session length: 4–8 weeks in July, August. Ages: 8–14. 180 participants per session. Boarding program cost: $3525–$7050. Financial aid available.
Application Deadline Continuous.
Jobs Positions for college students 20 and older.
Contact Jon Poto, Assistant Director, 19 Interlocken Way, Windsor, New Hampshire 03244. Phone: 800-862-7760. Fax: 603-478-5260. E-mail: mail@windsormountain.org.
URL www.windsormountain.org/isc
For more information, see page 1162.

Windsor Mountain: Leaders in Action

Interlocken at Windsor Mountain
Hillsboro, New Hampshire 03244

General Information Coed residential community service program established in 1967. Accredited by American Camping Association.
Program Focus Leadership training and community service.
Academics Education.
Arts Arts and crafts (general).
Special Interest Areas Community service, leadership training, work camp programs.
Sports Bicycling, ropes course, sports (general), swimming.
Wilderness/Outdoors Hiking.
Program Information 1 session per year. Session length: 24 days in July. Ages: 15–17. 13 participants per session. Boarding program cost: $3395. Financial aid available.
Application Deadline Continuous.
Contact Tom Herman, Marketing Director, 19 Interlocken Way, Windsor, New Hampshire 03244. Phone: 603-478-3166 Ext.20. Fax: 603-478-5260. E-mail: tom@windsormountain.org.
URL www.windsormountain.org/xrds/lia.html
For more information, see page 1162.

Wolfeboro: The Summer Boarding School

93 Camp School Road
Wolfeboro, New Hampshire 03894

General Information Coed residential and day academic program and outdoor program established in 1910. High school credit may be earned.
Program Focus Wolfeboro emphasizes the development of student confidence, study skills, accountability, and success.

Wolfeboro: The Summer Boarding School (continued)

Wolfeboro: The Summer Boarding School

Academics American literature, English as a second language, English language/literature, French language/literature, Greek language/literature, Latin language, SAT/ACT preparation, Spanish language/literature, academics (general), biology, chemistry, ecology, history, mathematics, physics, reading, science (general), social studies, study skills, vocabulary, writing.
Arts Ceramics, drawing, painting, pottery, sculpture.
Sports Aerobics, baseball, basketball, boating, canoeing, cross-country, fishing, horseback riding, lacrosse, sailing, soccer, softball, swimming, tennis, volleyball, weight training.
Wilderness/Outdoors Backpacking, hiking, wilderness camping.
Trips Day, overnight.
Program Information 1 session per year. Session length: 45 days in June, July, August. Ages: 11–18. 200 participants per session. Day program cost: $1000–$2300. Boarding program cost: $8850.
Application Deadline Continuous.
Jobs Positions for college students 20 and older.
Contact Edward A. Cooper, Assistant Head of School, main address above. Phone: 603-569-3451. Fax: 603-569-4080. E-mail: wolfe@wolfeboro.org.
URL www.wolfeboro.org

For more information, see page 1400.

YMCA Camp Lincoln–Junior CIT Program

YMCA Camp Lincoln
67 Ball Road
Kingston, New Hampshire 03848

General Information Coed day traditional camp. Accredited by American Camping Association.
Special Interest Areas Cardiac education, counselor-in-training program, first aid, leadership training, substance abuse education.
Trips Overnight.
Program Information 2 sessions per year. Session length: 30 days in June, July, August. Ages: 14+. Day program cost: $400. Financial aid available.
Application Deadline Continuous.
Jobs Positions for high school students and college students.
Contact Chris Burke, Director, PO Box 729, 67 Ball Road, Kingston, New Hampshire 03848. Phone: 603-642-3361. Fax: 603-642-4340. E-mail: chris@ymcacamplincoln.org.
URL www.ymcacamplincoln.org

YMCA Camp Lincoln–On the Road

YMCA Camp Lincoln
New Hampshire

General Information Coed day adventure program. Accredited by American Camping Association.
Special Interest Areas Field trips (arts and culture), planning skills.
Trips Cultural, day.
Program Information 8 sessions per year. Session length: 5 days in June, July, August. Ages: 12–14. Day program cost: $190. Financial aid available.
Application Deadline Continuous.
Jobs Positions for high school students and college students.
Contact Chris Burke, Director, PO Box 729, 67 Ball Road, Kingston, New Hampshire 03848. Phone: 603-642-3361. Fax: 603-642-4340. E-mail: chris@ymcacamplincoln.org.
URL www.ymcacamplincoln.org

YMCA Camp Lincoln–Outdoor Adventure Camp: Backpacking

YMCA Camp Lincoln
New Hampshire

General Information Coed travel outdoor program, wilderness program, and adventure program. Accredited by American Camping Association.
Academics Ecology.
Special Interest Areas Communication skills, leadership training, nature study, team building.
Sports Ropes course.
Wilderness/Outdoors Backpacking, hiking, orienteering, outdoor adventure, outdoor living skills, wilderness camping.
Program Information 1 session per year. Session length: 6 days in June, July, August. Ages: 11–14. 8–12 participants per session. Cost: $390. Application fee: $25. Financial aid available.
Application Deadline Continuous.
Jobs Positions for high school students and college students.
Contact Chris Braun, Outdoor/Adventure Program Director, PO Box 729, 67 Ball Road, Kingston, New Hampshire 03848. Phone: 603-642-3361. Fax: 603-642-4340. E-mail: cbraun@ymcacamplincoln.org.
URL www.ymcacamplincoln.org

YMCA Camp Lincoln–Outdoor Adventure Camp: Everything Outdoors

YMCA Camp Lincoln
New Hampshire

General Information Coed travel outdoor program, wilderness program, and adventure program. Accredited by American Camping Association.
Special Interest Areas Communication skills, team building.
Sports Bicycling, canoeing, kayaking, ropes course.
Wilderness/Outdoors Backpacking, hiking, mountain biking, outdoor adventure, outdoor living skills, rock climbing, wilderness camping.
Program Information 1 session per year. Session length: 6 days in June, July, August. Ages: 10–13. 8–12 participants per session. Cost: $390. Application fee: $25. Financial aid available.
Application Deadline Continuous.
Jobs Positions for high school students and college students.
Contact Chris Braun, Outdoor/Adventure Program Director, PO Box 729, 67 Ball Road, Kingston, New Hampshire 03848. Phone: 603-642-3361. Fax: 603-642-4340. E-mail: cbraun@ymcacamplincoln.org.
URL www.ymcacamplincoln.org

YMCA Camp Lincoln–Outdoor Adventure Camp: Mountain Bike

YMCA Camp Lincoln
New Hampshire

General Information Coed travel outdoor program, wilderness program, and adventure program. Accredited by American Camping Association.
Special Interest Areas Bicycle mechanics, communication skills, team building.
Sports Bicycling, ropes course.
Wilderness/Outdoors Mountain biking, orienteering, outdoor adventure, outdoor living skills, wilderness camping.
Program Information 1 session per year. Session length: 6 days in July, August. Ages: 10–13. 8–12 participants per session. Cost: $390. Application fee: $25. Financial aid available.
Application Deadline Continuous.
Jobs Positions for high school students and college students.
Contact Chris Braun, Outdoor/Adventure Program Director, PO Box 729, 67 Ball Road, Kingston, New Hampshire 03848. Phone: 603-642-3361. Fax: 603-642-4340. E-mail: cbraun@ymcacamplincoln.org.
URL www.ymcacamplincoln.org

YMCA Camp Lincoln–Outdoor Adventure Camp: River Runners

YMCA Camp Lincoln
New Hampshire

General Information Coed travel outdoor program, wilderness program, and adventure program. Accredited by American Camping Association.
Special Interest Areas Communication skills, team building.
Sports Canoeing, kayaking, ropes course.
Wilderness/Outdoors Canoe trips, hiking, outdoor adventure, outdoor living skills, wilderness camping.
Program Information 1 session per year. Session length: 6 days in June, July, August. Ages: 10–13. 8–12 participants per session. Cost: $390. Application fee: $25. Financial aid available.
Application Deadline Continuous.
Jobs Positions for high school students and college students.
Contact Chris Braun, Outdoor/Adventure Program Director, PO Box 729, 67 Ball Road, Kingston, New Hampshire 03848. Phone: 603-642-3361. Fax: 603-642-4340. E-mail: cbraun@ymcacamplincoln.org.
URL www.ymcacamplincoln.org

YMCA Camp Lincoln–Senior CIT Program

YMCA Camp Lincoln
New Hampshire

General Information Coed day traditional camp. Accredited by American Camping Association.
Special Interest Areas Cardiac education, counselor-in-training program, first aid, leadership training, substance abuse education.
Program Information 1 session per year. Session length: 45 days in June, July, August. Ages: 15+. No cost for junior CIT program graduates; call for interview.
Application Deadline Continuous.
Jobs Positions for high school students and college students.
Contact Chris Burke, Director, PO Box 729, 67 Ball Road, Kingston, New Hampshire 03848. Phone: 603-642-3361. Fax: 603-642-4340. E-mail: chris@ymcacamplincoln.org.
URL www.ymcacamplincoln.org

YMCA Camp Lincoln–Specialty Camps: Archaeology Camp

YMCA Camp Lincoln
New Hampshire

General Information Coed day adventure program established in 1998. Accredited by American Camping Association.
Academics Archaeology.
Special Interest Areas Field research/expeditions.
Trips Day.

YMCA Camp Lincoln–Specialty Camps: Archaeology Camp (continued)

Program Information 1 session per year. Session length: 10 days in July, August. Ages: 9–12. 13–20 participants per session. Day program cost: $390. Financial aid available.
Application Deadline Continuous.
Jobs Positions for high school students and college students.
Contact Chris Burke, Director, PO Box 729, 67 Ball Road, Kingston, New Hampshire 03848. Phone: 603-642-3361. Fax: 603-642-4340. E-mail: chris@ymcacamplincoln.org.
URL www.ymcacamplincoln.org

YMCA Camp Lincoln–Specialty Camps: Arts & Drama

YMCA Camp Lincoln
New Hampshire

General Information Coed day arts program established in 1998. Accredited by American Camping Association.
Arts Arts, arts and crafts (general), batiking, leather working, painting, paper making, pottery, theater/drama.
Special Interest Areas Campcraft.
Sports Boating, swimming.
Program Information 2 sessions per year. Session length: 10 days in June, July, August. Ages: 9–12. 13–20 participants per session. Day program cost: $350. Financial aid available.
Application Deadline Continuous.
Jobs Positions for high school students and college students.
Contact Chris Burke, Director, PO Box 729, 67 Ball Road, Kingston, New Hampshire 03848. Phone: 603-642-3361. Fax: 603-642-4340. E-mail: chris@ymcacamplincoln.org.
URL www.ymcacamplincoln.org

YMCA Camp Lincoln–Specialty Camps: Horse Camp

YMCA Camp Lincoln
New Hampshire

General Information Coed day outdoor program established in 1998. Accredited by American Camping Association.
Special Interest Areas Animal care.
Sports Equestrian sports, horseback riding.
Program Information 1 session per year. Session length: 10 days in June. Ages: 9–12. 13–20 participants per session. Day program cost: $490. Financial aid available.
Application Deadline Continuous.
Jobs Positions for high school students and college students.
Contact Chris Burke, Director, PO Box 729, 67 Ball Road, Kingston, New Hampshire 03848. Phone: 603-642-3361. Fax: 603-642-4340. E-mail: chris@ymcacamplincoln.org.
URL www.ymcacamplincoln.org

YMCA Camp Lincoln–Specialty Camps: Sports Camp

YMCA Camp Lincoln
New Hampshire

General Information Coed day sports camp established in 1998. Accredited by American Camping Association.
Sports Baseball, boating, soccer, sports (general), swimming, volleyball.
Wilderness/Outdoors Mountain biking.
Program Information 2 sessions per year. Session length: 10 days in June, July, August. Ages: 9–12. 13–20 participants per session. Day program cost: $350. Financial aid available.
Application Deadline Continuous.
Jobs Positions for high school students and college students.
Contact Chris Burke, Director, PO Box 729, 67 Ball Road, Kingston, New Hampshire 03848. Phone: 603-642-3361. Fax: 603-642-4340. E-mail: chris@ymcacamplincoln.org.
URL www.ymcacamplincoln.org

YMCA Camp Lincoln–Traditional Day Camp

YMCA Camp Lincoln
67 Ball Road
Kingston, New Hampshire 03848

General Information Coed day traditional camp established in 1924. Accredited by American Camping Association.
Academics Archaeology, environmental science, history, intercultural studies, music, peace education, science (general).
Arts Arts and crafts (general), ceramics, creative writing, dance, drawing, music, musical productions, painting, pottery, theater/drama, woodworking.
Special Interest Areas Campcraft, community service.
Sports Archery, baseball, basketball, bicycling, boating, canoeing, climbing (wall), equestrian sports, field hockey, fishing, football, horseback riding, kayaking, rappelling, ropes course, soccer, softball, street/roller hockey, swimming, volleyball, windsurfing.
Wilderness/Outdoors Canoe trips, hiking, mountain biking.
Trips Cultural, day, overnight.
Program Information 5 sessions per year. Session length: 5–10 days in June, July, August. Ages: 5–15. 350 participants per session. Day program cost: $150–$350. Application fee: $25. Financial aid available. Open to participants entering grades K–8.
Application Deadline Continuous.
Jobs Positions for high school students and college students.

Contact Chris Burke, Director, PO Box 729, 67 Ball Road, Kingston, New Hampshire 03848. Phone: 603-642-3361. Fax: 603-642-4340. E-mail: chris@ymcacamplincoln.org.
URL www.ymcacamplincoln.org

YMCA Camp Lincoln–Travel Camp

YMCA Camp Lincoln
67 Ball Road
Kingston, New Hampshire 03848

General Information Coed day adventure program. Accredited by American Camping Association.
Special Interest Areas Field trips (arts and culture), touring.
Sports Bowling, ice skating, miniature golf, roller skating, swimming.
Trips Day.
Program Information 8 sessions per year. Session length: 5 days in June, July, August. Ages: 5–12. Day program cost: $190. Application fee: $25. Financial aid available.
Application Deadline Continuous.
Jobs Positions for high school students and college students.
Contact Chris Burke, Director, PO Box 729, 67 Ball Road, Kingston, New Hampshire 03848. Phone: 603-642-3361. Fax: 603-642-4340. E-mail: chris@ymcacamplincoln.org.
URL www.ymcacamplincoln.org

NEW JERSEY

Appel Farm Summer Arts Camp

Appel Farm Arts and Music Center
457 Shirley Road
Elmer, New Jersey 08318-0888

General Information Coed residential arts program established in 1959. Accredited by American Camping Association. Formal opportunities for the artistically talented.
Academics Journalism, writing.
Arts Acting, arts, arts and crafts (general), band, batiking, ceramics, chorus, creative writing, dance, dance (ballet), dance (folk), dance (jazz), dance (modern), dance (tap), drawing, fabric arts, film, graphic arts, jewelry making, metalworking, mime, music, music (chamber), music (classical), music (ensemble), music (instrumental), music (jazz), music (orchestral), music (rock), music (vocal), musical productions, painting, photography, pottery, printmaking, puppetry, sculpture, television/video, theater/drama.
Special Interest Areas Campcraft, community service, gardening, model rocketry.
Sports Aerobics, basketball, soccer, softball, swimming, tennis, volleyball.
Trips Day.

Appel Farm Summer Arts Camp

Program Information 2 sessions per year. Session length: 4–8 weeks in July, August. Ages: 9–17. 190–215 participants per session. Boarding program cost: $3500–$5800. Financial aid available.
Application Deadline Continuous.
Jobs Positions for college students 20 and older.
Contact Mr. Matt Sisson, Director, PO Box 888, Elmer, New Jersey 08318-0888. Phone: 856-358-2472. Fax: 856-358-6513. E-mail: appelcamp@aol.com.
URL www.appelfarm.org
For more information, see page 984.

Bridge to the Future

The Hun School of Princeton
176 Edgerstoune Road
Princeton, New Jersey 08540

General Information Coed residential and day academic program established in 1991. Specific services available for the learning disabled.
Academics Academics (general), computers, history, mathematics, writing.
Arts Creative writing.
Special Interest Areas Field trips (arts and culture).
Wilderness/Outdoors Canoe trips.
Trips Cultural, day, overnight.
Program Information 1 session per year. Session length: 25 days in June, July. Ages: 12–13. 12 participants per session. No cost for program.
Application Deadline May 1.
Jobs Positions for college students 18 and older.
Summer Contact Mr. Doug Harmon, Bridge Program Coordinator, main address above. Phone: 609-921-7600. Fax: 609-924-2170.
Winter Contact Ms. Donna O'Sullivan, Coordinator of Summer Programs, main address above. Phone: 609-921-7600 Ext.2265. Fax: 609-924-2170. E-mail: summer@hunschool.org.
URL www.hunschool.org

Camp College–Institute for Arts and Sciences

Mercer County Community College
1200 Old Trenton Road
West Windsor Campus
Trenton, New Jersey 08690

General Information Coed day academic program and arts program established in 1980.
Program Focus Program can be customized to focus on arts, sciences or sports.
Academics Academics (general), archaeology, computers, marine studies, science (general).
Arts Arts, arts and crafts (general), chorus, graphic arts, painting.
Special Interest Areas Chess, culinary arts, field research/expeditions, general camp activities, model rocketry, nature study, robotics.
Sports Aerobics, baseball, canoeing, cheerleading, fishing, golf, kayaking, rappelling, soccer, swimming, tennis.
Wilderness/Outdoors Rock climbing.
Program Information 1–3 sessions per year. Session length: 4–5 days in June, July, August. Ages: 7–14. 20–25 participants per session. Day program cost: $125–$350.
Application Deadline Continuous.
Jobs Positions for high school students 17 and older and college students 17 and older.
Contact Sharon Vlasac, Director, Youth Programs, PO Box B, Trenton, New Jersey 08690. Phone: 609-586-4800 Ext.3267. Fax: 609-890-6338. E-mail: campcollege@mccc.edu.
URL www.mccc.edu

Camp Discovery–Madison

Fairleigh Dickinson University
Madison, New Jersey

General Information Coed day traditional camp and academic program established in 1996.
Program Focus Science, art, theater, sports and field trips.
Academics Aerospace science, archaeology, biology, botany, chemistry, physics, science (general).
Arts Arts and crafts (general), jewelry making, painting, puppetry, sculpture, theater/drama.
Special Interest Areas Nature study.
Sports Basketball, soccer, softball, street/roller hockey, swimming, tennis, volleyball.
Trips Day.
Program Information 1–3 sessions per year. Session length: 10 days in June, July, August. Ages: 6–12. 300 participants per session. Day program cost: $545–$1635. Application fee: $20.
Application Deadline Continuous.
Jobs Positions for high school students 16 and older and college students 16 and older.
Contact Ms. Karen Nelson, Senior Program Director, 1000 River Road, HDHI-02, Teaneck, New Jersey 07666. Phone: 201-692-6500. Fax: 201-692-6505.
URL www.fdu.edu/academic/ce/campmain.htm

Camp Discovery–Teaneck

Fairleigh Dickinson University
Teaneck, New Jersey

General Information Coed day traditional camp and academic program established in 1996.
Academics Aerospace science, archaeology, biology, botany, chemistry, physics, science (general).
Arts Arts and crafts (general), jewelry making, painting, puppetry, sculpture, theater/drama.
Special Interest Areas Nature study.
Sports Basketball, soccer, softball, street/roller hockey, swimming, tennis, volleyball.
Trips Day.
Program Information 1–3 sessions per year. Session length: 10 days in June, July, August. Ages: 6–12. 300 participants per session. Day program cost: $545–$1635. Application fee: $20.
Application Deadline Continuous.
Jobs Positions for high school students 16 and older and college students 16 and older.
Contact Karen Nelson, Senior Program Director, 1000 River Road, HDHI-02, Teaneck, New Jersey 07666. Phone: 201-692-6500. Fax: 201-692-6505.
URL www.fdu.edu/academic/ce/campmain.htm

Camp Louemma

Camp Louemma, Inc.
43 Louemma Lane
Sussex, New Jersey 07461

General Information Coed residential traditional camp established in 1941. Religious affiliation: Jewish. Accredited by American Camping Association.
Academics Jewish studies.
Arts Arts and crafts (general), ceramics, dance, dance (modern), jewelry making, music, painting, photography, pottery, radio broadcasting, television/video, theater/drama, woodworking.
Special Interest Areas Campcraft, culinary arts, work camp programs.
Sports Aerobics, archery, boating, canoeing, cheerleading, climbing (wall), field hockey, fishing, football, golf, gymnastics, in-line skating, kayaking, martial arts, snorkeling, soccer, softball, street/roller hockey, swimming, tennis, volleyball.
Wilderness/Outdoors Hiking, orienteering.
Trips Day.
Program Information 3 sessions per year. Session length: 16–18 days in June, July, August. Ages: 7–15. 200 participants per session. Boarding program cost: $1250–$1400. Application fee: $125. Financial aid available.
Application Deadline Continuous.
Jobs Positions for high school students 16 and older and college students 18 and older.
Contact Hal Pugach, Director, 214-45 42nd Avenue, Bayside, New York 11361. Phone: 973-316-0362. Fax: 973-316-0980. E-mail: camplouemma@aol.com.
URL www.camplouemma.com

Camp Lou Henry Hoover

Girl Scouts of Washington Rock Council
961 West Shore Drive
Middleville, New Jersey 07855

General Information Girls' residential traditional camp established in 1953. Accredited by American Camping Association.
Program Focus Girl Scout values, human relations, and personal development.
Academics Ecology.
Arts Arts and crafts (general), ceramics, dance, dance (ballet), dance (folk), dance (jazz), dance (modern), dance (tap), drawing, fabric arts, jewelry making, leather working, painting, photography, pottery, printmaking, theater/drama, weaving, woodworking.
Special Interest Areas Campcraft, career exploration, community service, leadership training, nature study.
Sports Boating, canoeing, equestrian sports, fishing, gymnastics, horseback riding, ropes course, rowing (crew/sculling), sailing, soccer, softball, swimming, volleyball, windsurfing.
Wilderness/Outdoors Backpacking, canoe trips, hiking, orienteering, survival training.
Trips Day, overnight.
Program Information 6 sessions per year. Session length: 1–2 weeks in July, August, September. Ages: 7–18. 200–225 participants per session. Boarding program cost: $190–$710. Financial aid available.
Application Deadline Continuous.
Jobs Positions for high school students 16 and older and college students 18 and older.
Contact Deborah Hooker, Camp Director, 201 Grove Street East, Westfield, New Jersey 07090. Phone: 908-232-3236 Ext.1226. Fax: 908-232-2140. E-mail: hookie@ix.netcom.com.
URL www.camphoover.org

Camp Middlesex

Middlesex County College
2600 Woodbridge Avenue
Edison, New Jersey 08818

General Information Coed day traditional camp, academic program, and arts program established in 1969.
Program Focus Campers may attend 1-8 weeks by selecting their choice of half-day, usually one week, specialty camps. There are over 40 choices.
Academics Spanish language/literature, academics (general), business, communications, computers, economics, journalism, mathematics, reading, science (general), writing.
Arts Acting, arts and crafts (general), chorus, clowning, creative writing, dance, dance (ballet), dance (jazz), dance (modern), drawing, fabric arts, film, jewelry making, musical productions, painting, photography, puppetry, sculpture, theater/drama.
Special Interest Areas Construction, culinary arts, electronics, general camp activities, robotics.
Sports Aerobics, baseball, basketball, cheerleading, golf, martial arts, soccer, sports (general), tennis.
Program Information 1–16 sessions per year. Session length: 5–15 days in June, July, August. Ages: 6–18. 100–150 participants per session. Day program cost: $160–$320. Cost: $160 for one week half-day programs, $1350 for 8-week full-day Theater Camp.
Application Deadline Continuous.
Jobs Positions for college students 18 and older.
Contact Elaine Berlin, Assistant Director, Professional and Community Programs, 2600 Woodbridge Avenue, Attn : Mill Gate, Edison, New Jersey 08818. Phone: 732-906-7740. Fax: 732-906-7741. E-mail: eberlin@middlesexcc.us.
URL www.middlesexcc.edu

Campus Kids–NJ

CK Summer Camps, Inc.
400 Jefferson Street
Hackettstown, New Jersey 07840

General Information Coed residential traditional camp established in 1991. Accredited by American Camping Association.
Program Focus Weekday sleep-away camp; transportation provided. Camp during the week and home on the weekends.
Arts Arts and crafts (general), ceramics, creative writing, dance, dance (jazz), dance (modern), drawing, jewelry making, leather working, musical productions, painting, photography, theater/drama, woodworking.
Special Interest Areas Model rocketry, nature study.
Sports Aerobics, archery, basketball, boating, canoeing, fencing, fishing, gymnastics, horseback riding, lacrosse, soccer, softball, street/roller hockey, swimming, tennis, volleyball.
Wilderness/Outdoors Hiking.
Trips Day, overnight.
Program Information 1–4 sessions per year. Session length: 2–8 weeks in June, July, August. Ages: 9–15. 220 participants per session. Boarding program cost: $1575–$5720.
Application Deadline Continuous.
Jobs Positions for college students 18 and older.
Contact Mr. Tom Riddleberger, Director, PO Box 1058, Chatham, New Jersey 07928. Phone: 973-635-2300. Fax: 973-635-1217. E-mail: campuskids@aol.com.
URL www.campuskids.com

Camp Veritans

YM-YWHA of North Jersey
1 Pike Drive
Wayne, New Jersey 07470

General Information Coed residential and day traditional camp established in 1927. Religious affiliation: Jewish. Specific services available for the emotionally challenged, developmentally challenged, and learning disabled.
Academics Hebrew language, Jewish studies, journalism, music, science (general).
Arts Acting, arts and crafts (general), ceramics, creative writing, dance, dance (folk), dance (jazz), dance (modern), drawing, fabric arts, leather working, music, music (vocal), musical productions, painting, pottery, printmaking, puppetry, theater/drama, woodworking.

Camp Veritans (continued)

Special Interest Areas Animal care, campcraft, community service, culinary arts, leadership training, model rocketry, nature study.
Sports Archery, baseball, basketball, cheerleading, climbing (wall), field hockey, football, gymnastics, in-line skating, lacrosse, martial arts, ropes course, snorkeling, soccer, softball, street/roller hockey, swimming, tennis, volleyball.
Wilderness/Outdoors Hiking, mountaineering, orienteering, survival training, white-water trips.
Trips Cultural, day, overnight, shopping.
Program Information 1–2 sessions per year. Session length: 4 weeks in June, July, August. Ages: 5–15. 450–500 participants per session. Day program cost: $1590–$3020. Boarding program cost: $2430–$3785. Financial aid available.
Application Deadline Continuous.
Jobs Positions for high school students 16 and older and college students.
Summer Contact Ms. Robin Rosenfeld, Director, 225 Pompton Road, Haledon, New Jersey 07508. Phone: 973-956-1220. Fax: 973-956-5751. E-mail: campveritans@ymha-nj.org.
Winter Contact Ms. Robin Rosenfeld, Director, 1 Pike Drive, Wayne, New Jersey 07470. Phone: 973-595-0100. Fax: 973-595-7480. E-mail: rosenfeldr@ymha-nj.org.
URL ymha-nj.org

Cybercamps–College of St. Elizabeth

Cybercamps–Giant Campus, Inc.
Morristown, New Jersey

General Information Coed day academic program established in 2004.
Academics Web page design, academics (general), computer programming, computers.
Arts Animation, creative writing, digital media, graphic arts, photography.
Special Interest Areas Computer game design, computer graphics, robotics, team building.
Sports Ultimate frisbee.
Program Information 2–9 sessions per year. Session length: 5–30 days in June, July, August. Ages: 7–18. 30–150 participants per session. Day program cost: $599–$849. Financial aid available.
Application Deadline Continuous.
Jobs Positions for high school students 15 and older and college students.
Contact Cybercamps Information Office, 2401 4th Avenue, Suite 1110, Seattle, Washington 98121. Phone: 206-442-4500. Fax: 206-442-4500. E-mail: info@cybercamps.com.
URL www.cybercamps.com

Cybercamps–FDU Metropolitan Campus

Cybercamps–Giant Campus, Inc.
Hackensack, New Jersey

General Information Coed day academic program established in 2002.
Program Focus High tech computer camps featuring project oriented curriculum in Web design, 3D animation, game design, digital arts and programming for all ability levels.
Academics Web page design, computer programming, computers.
Arts Animation, creative writing, digital media, graphic arts, photography.
Special Interest Areas Computer game design, computer graphics, robotics, team building.
Sports Frisbee golf, ultimate frisbee.
Program Information 2–9 sessions per year. Session length: 5–30 days in June, July, August. Ages: 7–18. 30–150 participants per session. Day program cost: $599–$849. Financial aid available.
Application Deadline Continuous.
Jobs Positions for high school students 15 and older and college students.
Contact Cybercamps Information Office, 2401 4th Avenue, Suite 1110, Seattle, Washington 98121. Phone: 206-442-4500. Fax: 206-442-4501. E-mail: info@cybercamps.com.
URL www.cybercamps.com

Cybercamps–Princeton University

Cybercamps–Giant Campus, Inc.
Princeton, New Jersey

General Information Coed residential and day academic program established in 2003.
Academics Web page design, academics (general), computer programming, computers.
Arts Animation, creative writing, digital media, graphic arts, photography.
Special Interest Areas Computer game design, computer graphics, robotics, team building.
Sports Frisbee.
Program Information 2–9 sessions per year. Session length: 5–30 days in June, July, August. Ages: 7–18. 30–150 participants per session. Day program cost: $599–$849. Boarding program cost: $974–$1224. Financial aid available.
Application Deadline Continuous.
Jobs Positions for high school students 15 and older and college students.
Contact Cybercamps Information Office, 2401 4th Avenue, Suite 1110, Seattle, Washington 98121. Phone: 206-442-4500. Fax: 206-442-4500. E-mail: info@cybercamps.com.
URL www.cybercamps.com

Drew Summer Music

Drew University Music Department
Drew University
36 Madison Avenue
Madison, New Jersey 07940

General Information Coed residential and day arts program established in 1995. Formal opportunities for the artistically talented.
Program Focus Chamber music.
Academics Music.

Arts Music, music (chamber), music (classical), music (ensemble), music (instrumental), music (vocal), music composition/arrangement.
Sports Racquetball, swimming, tennis, volleyball.
Program Information 1 session per year. Session length: 8 days in June. Ages: 12–20. 70 participants per session. Day program cost: $700. Boarding program cost: $800. Application fee: $50. Financial aid available. Master classes available.
Application Deadline February 1.
Contact Dr. Virginia Schulze-Johnson, Director, main address above. Phone: 973-408-3428. Fax: 973-408-3885. E-mail: vschulze@drew.edu.
URL www.depts.drew.edu/music/beyond/dsm/dsmindex.htm

Dwight-Englewood Summer Academic Session

Dwight-Englewood School
315 East Palisade Avenue
Englewood, New Jersey 07631

General Information Coed day academic program established in 1972. Formal opportunities for the academically talented, artistically talented, and gifted. High school credit may be earned.
Academics English as a second language, English language/literature, SAT/ACT preparation, academics (general), astronomy, biology, biology (Advanced Placement), chemistry, computers, geology/earth science, health sciences, mathematics, mathematics (Advanced Placement), physics, reading, science (general), study skills, writing.
Arts Arts and crafts (general), ceramics, creative writing, drawing, music, music (ensemble), music (instrumental), music (jazz), music (vocal), musical productions, painting, photography, pottery, sculpture, television/video, theater/drama.
Special Interest Areas Driver's education, leadership training, robotics.
Sports Aerobics, baseball, basketball, field hockey, lacrosse, soccer, softball, tennis.
Trips Day.
Program Information 1–6 sessions per year. Session length: 12–28 days in June, July. Ages: 11–18. 16 participants per session. Day program cost: $300–$450. Application fee: $35.
Application Deadline Continuous.
Jobs Positions for high school students 16 and older and college students 17 and older.
Contact Mr. Mark A. Shultz, Summer School Principal, main address above. Phone: 201-569-9500 Ext.3501. Fax: 201-568-5018. E-mail: shultm@d-e.org.
URL www.d-e.org

Dwight-Englewood Summer Adventures

Dwight-Englewood School
315 East Palisade Avenue
Englewood, New Jersey 07631

General Information Coed day traditional camp established in 1987. Formal opportunities for the academically talented, artistically talented, and gifted.
Academics English as a second language, academics (general), computers, environmental science, geology/earth science, health sciences, intercultural studies, mathematics, music, reading, science (general), social studies, writing.
Arts Arts and crafts (general), dance, juggling, music, painting, theater/drama.
Special Interest Areas Culinary arts.
Sports Baseball, basketball, soccer, softball.
Trips Day.
Program Information 6 sessions per year. Session length: 5 days in June, July. Ages: 6–10. 125–160 participants per session. Day program cost: $325. Application fee: $35.
Application Deadline Continuous.
Jobs Positions for high school students 16 and older and college students 17 and older.
Contact Mark A. Shultz, Summer School Principal, main address above. Phone: 201-569-9500 Ext.3501. Fax: 201-568-5018. E-mail: shultm@d-e.org.
URL www.d-e.org

Dwight-Englewood Summer Sports Clinics

Dwight-Englewood School
315 East Palisade Avenue
Englewood, New Jersey 07631

General Information Coed day sports camp established in 1987.
Sports Baseball, basketball, field hockey, lacrosse, soccer, softball, tennis, track and field.
Program Information 24 sessions per year. Session length: 5 days in June, July. Ages: 11–18. 30 participants per session. Day program cost: $95. Application fee: $35.
Application Deadline Continuous.
Jobs Positions for high school students 16 and older and college students 18 and older.
Contact Mr. Mark Shultz, Summer School Principal, main address above. Phone: 201-569-9500 Ext.3501. Fax: 201-568-5018. E-mail: shultm@d-e.org.
URL www.d-e.org

Dwight-Englewood Weekly Enrichment

Dwight-Englewood School
315 East Palisade Avenue
Englewood, New Jersey 07631

General Information Coed day traditional camp and academic program established in 1987. Formal opportunities for the academically talented, artistically talented, and gifted.
Program Focus Enrichment.
Academics Academics (general), astronomy, business, communications, computer programming, computer science (Advanced Placement), computers, economics, geology/earth science, history, journalism, mathematics, music, speech/debate, study skills, typing, writing.
Arts Arts and crafts (general), ceramics, chorus, creative writing, dance, drawing, film, graphic arts, music, music (chamber), music (ensemble), music (instrumental), music (vocal), musical productions, painting, photography, pottery, puppetry, radio broadcasting, sculpture, television/video, theater/drama.
Special Interest Areas Robotics.
Program Information 24 sessions per year. Session length: 5 days in June, July. Ages: 11–14. 14–18 participants per session. Application fee: $35. Cost: $100–$195 per class. Open to participants entering grades 5–8.
Application Deadline Continuous.
Jobs Positions for high school students 16 and older and college students 17 and older.
Contact Mr. Mark A. Shultz, Summer School Principal, main address above. Phone: 201-569-9500 Ext.3501. Fax: 201-568-5018. E-mail: shultm@d-e.org.
URL www.d-e.org

ECOES: Exploring Career Options in Engineering and Science

Stevens Institute of Technology
Castle Point on Hudson
Hoboken, New Jersey 07030

General Information Coed residential academic program established in 1978. Formal opportunities for the academically talented. Specific services available for the physically challenged.
Program Focus To teach interested high school students about careers in science and engineering.
Academics Aerospace science, biology, chemistry, engineering, environmental science, health sciences, oceanography, physics, physiology, precollege program, science (general).
Special Interest Areas Career exploration, field research/expeditions, leadership training, robotics.
Sports Basketball, climbing (wall), racquetball, soccer, swimming, tennis, volleyball.
Trips College tours, cultural, day, shopping.
Program Information 1 session per year. Session length: 13 days in July. Ages: 15–17. 65–70 participants per session. Boarding program cost: $895–$950. Financial aid available.
Application Deadline May 9.
Contact Ms. Rae Talerico, Director, Pre-College Programs, Lore-El Center, Castle Point on Hudson, Hoboken, New Jersey 07030. Phone: 201-216-5245. Fax: 201-216-5175. E-mail: ataleric@stevens.edu.
URL www.stevens.edu/lore-el/pre-college/ecoes/

The Hun School of Princeton American Culture and Language Institute

The Hun School of Princeton
176 Edgerstoune Road
Princeton, New Jersey 08540

General Information Coed residential and day academic program and cultural program established in 1994. Formal opportunities for the academically talented.
Program Focus English as a second language and TOEFL preparation.
Academics English as a second language, computers, reading, writing.
Sports Basketball, bicycling, canoeing, soccer, softball, swimming, tennis, volleyball.
Trips Cultural, day, overnight.
Program Information 1 session per year. Session length: 25 days in July. Ages: 13–18. 20–25 participants per session. Day program cost: $2650. Boarding program cost: $5870. Application fee: $100–$250. Residential student minimum age: 13.
Application Deadline Continuous.
Summer Contact Ms. Dianne Somers, Director, main address above. Phone: 609-921-7600. Fax: 609-683-4410. E-mail: summer@hunschool.org.
Winter Contact Ms. Donna O'Sullivan, Coordinator of Summer Programs, main address above. Phone: 609-921-7600. Fax: 609-924-2170. E-mail: summer@hunschool.org.
URL www.hunschool.org

For more information, see page 1152.

The Hun School of Princeton Boys' Basketball Camp

The Hun School of Princeton
176 Edgerstoune Road
Princeton, New Jersey 08540

General Information Boys' day sports camp established in 2001.
Program Focus Basketball.
Sports Basketball.
Program Information 1 session per year. Session length: 5 days in August. Ages: 8–14. 55–60 participants per session. Day program cost: $185.
Application Deadline Continuous.
Jobs Positions for high school students and college students 18 and older.
Summer Contact Mr. Jonathan Stone, Varsity Basketball Coach, main address above. Phone: 609-921-7600 Ext.3137. Fax: 609-683-4410. E-mail: jstone@hunschool.org.

Winter Contact Ms. Donna O'Sullivan, Coordinator Summer Programs, main address above. Phone: 609-921-7600. Fax: 609-924-2170. E-mail: summer@hunschool.org.
URL www.hunschool.org

The Hun School of Princeton Girls' Basketball Camp

The Hun School of Princeton
176 Edgerstoune Road
Princeton, New Jersey 08540

General Information Girls' day sports camp established in 2001.
Program Focus Basketball.
Sports Basketball.
Program Information 1 session per year. Session length: 5 days in June. Ages: 10–14. 30–40 participants per session. Day program cost: $185.
Application Deadline Continuous.
Jobs Positions for high school students and college students 18 and older.
Summer Contact Bill Holup, Summer Programs Office, main address above. Phone: 609-921-7600 Ext. 2265. Fax: 609-924-2170.
Winter Contact Ms. Donna O'Sullivan, Coordinator of Summer Programs, main address above. Phone: 609-921-7600 Ext.2265. Fax: 609-924-2170. E-mail: summer@hunschool.org.
URL www.hunschool.org

The Hun School of Princeton–Summer Academic Session

The Hun School of Princeton
176 Edgerstoune Road
Princeton, New Jersey 08540

General Information Coed residential and day academic program established in 1990. Formal opportunities for the academically talented. High school credit may be earned.

The Hun School of Princeton–Summer Academic Session

Academics American literature, English as a second language, English language/literature, SAT/ACT preparation, academics (general), biology, chemistry, computers, mathematics, physics, reading, writing.
Sports Basketball, bicycling, canoeing, in-line skating, soccer, softball, sports (general), swimming, tennis, volleyball.
Wilderness/Outdoors Canoe trips.
Trips Cultural.
Program Information 1 session per year. Session length: 5 weeks in July, August. Ages: 12–18. 115–125 participants per session. Day program cost: $1120–$1975. Boarding program cost: $4785. Application fee: $100–$250. Open to participants entering grades 9–12.
Application Deadline Continuous.
Jobs Positions for college students 21 and older.
Summer Contact Ms. LeRhonda Greats, Summer Academic Director, main address above. Phone: 609-921-7600 Ext.2258. Fax: 609-683-4410. E-mail: summer@hunschool.org.
Winter Contact Ms. Donna O'Sullivan, Coordinator of Summer Program, main address above. Phone: 609-921-7600 Ext.2265. Fax: 609-924-2170. E-mail: summer@hunschool.org.
URL www.hunschool.org
For more information, see page 1152.

The Hun School of Princeton Summer Day Camp

The Hun School of Princeton
176 Edgerstoune Road
Princeton, New Jersey 08540

General Information Coed day traditional camp established in 1988. Specific services available for the developmentally challenged and learning disabled.
Arts Arts and crafts (general), dance, mime, music, puppetry, theater/drama.
Special Interest Areas Culinary arts, nature study.
Sports Archery, basketball, fishing, soccer, softball, swimming, tennis.
Program Information 1 session per year. Session length: 5 days in July, August. Ages: 5–12. 135–145 participants per session. Day program cost: $650–$1300. Application fee: $50. Minimum 2 week commitment (weeks need not be consecutive).
Application Deadline Continuous.
Jobs Positions for college students 21 and older.
Summer Contact William Long, Director Summer Day Camp, main address above. Phone: 609-921-7600 Ext. 2251. Fax: 609-683-4410.
Winter Contact Ms. Donna O'Sullivan, Coordinator of Summer Programs, main address above. Phone: 609-921-7600 Ext.2265. Fax: 609-924-2170. E-mail: summer@hunschool.org.
URL www.hunschool.org

The Hun School of Princeton Summer Theatre Classics

The Hun School of Princeton
176 Edgerstoune Road
Princeton, New Jersey 08540

General Information Coed residential and day arts program established in 1995. Formal opportunities for the artistically talented.
Program Focus Intensive drama workshop.
Arts Theater/drama.
Program Information 1 session per year. Session length: 20 days in July. Ages: 13–18. 8–14 participants per session. Day program cost: $805. Boarding program cost: $3825. Application fee: $100–$250. Residential student minimum age: 14.
Application Deadline Continuous.
Summer Contact Ms. Julia Ohm, Summer Programs Office, main address above. Phone: 609-921-7600 Ext. 2339. E-mail: summer@hunschool.org.
Winter Contact Ms. Donna O'Sullivan, Coordinator of Summer Programs, main address above. Phone: 609-921-7600 Ext.2265. Fax: 609-924-2170. E-mail: summer@hunschool.org.
URL www.hunschool.org
For more information, see page 1152.

iD Tech Camps–Princeton University, Princeton, NJ

iD Tech Camps
Princeton University
Princeton, New Jersey 08544

General Information Coed residential and day academic program established in 1999. Accredited by American Camping Association. Formal opportunities for the academically talented and artistically talented.
Program Focus High-tech computer camps for kids and teens; produce digital movies, create video games, design Web pages, learn programming and robotics, and more; one computer per student, small classes, campers complete a project in a creative and fun learning environment.
Academics Web page design, computer programming, computer science (Advanced Placement), computers, music, precollege program.
Arts Animation, cinematography, digital media, drawing, film, film editing, film production, graphic arts, music, television/video.
Special Interest Areas Career exploration, computer graphics, electronics, leadership training, robotics, team building.
Sports Baseball, basketball, soccer, softball, swimming, volleyball.
Trips College tours, cultural, day.
Program Information 5 sessions per year. Session length: 5–7 days in June, July, August. Ages: 7–17. 40–50 participants per session. Day program cost: $639. Boarding program cost: $989. Application fee: $200. Financial aid available.
Application Deadline Continuous.
Jobs Positions for college students 18 and older.
Contact Client Service Representatives, 1885 Winchester Boulevard, Suite 201, Campbell, California 95008. Phone: 888-709-TECH. Fax: 408-871-2228. E-mail: requests@internaldrive.com.
URL www.internaldrive.com
For more information, see page 1156.

Jewish Community Center Day Camp

Jewish Community Center of Greater Monmouth
100 Grant Avenue
Deal Park, New Jersey 07723

General Information Coed residential and day traditional camp and special needs program. Religious affiliation: Jewish. Specific services available for the developmentally challenged and learning disabled.
Academics Jewish studies.
Arts Arts and crafts (general), ceramics, dance, dance (ballet), dance (folk), dance (jazz), dance (modern), dance (tap), drawing, film, jewelry making, leather working, music (vocal), photography, puppetry, woodworking.
Special Interest Areas Touring.
Sports Aerobics, baseball, basketball, boating, canoeing, climbing (wall), fishing, football, golf, gymnastics, horseback riding, martial arts, racquetball, ropes course, soccer, softball, street/roller hockey, swimming, tennis, track and field, volleyball.
Wilderness/Outdoors Canoe trips.
Trips Day, overnight.
Program Information 2 sessions per year. Session length: 19–38 days in June, July, August. Ages: 5–14. 800–1,000 participants per session. Day program cost: $1000–$2700. Boarding program cost: $1775–$2525. Financial aid available.
Application Deadline Continuous.
Jobs Positions for high school students and college students.
Contact Jeff Weisenberg, Camp Director, main address above. Phone: 732-531-9100 Ext.171. Fax: 732-531-4718. E-mail: jweisenberg@msn.com.
URL www.jcc.yehud.com/camp

Junior Statesmen Summer School–Princeton University

Junior Statesmen Foundation
Princeton University
Princeton, New Jersey 08544

General Information Coed residential academic program established in 1997. Formal opportunities for the academically talented. High school credit may be earned.
Program Focus American government and politics, debate, leadership, speech, economics.
Academics Communications, economics, government and politics, government and politics (Advanced Placement), journalism, precollege program, social science, social studies, speech/debate.
Special Interest Areas Career exploration, leadership training.
Trips College tours, cultural, day.

Junior Statesmen Summer School–Princeton University

Program Information 1 session per year. Session length: 27 days in June, July. Ages: 14–18. 200–300 participants per session. Boarding program cost: $3500. Financial aid available.
Application Deadline Continuous.
Contact Matt Randazzo, National Summer School Director, 400 South El Camino Real, Suite 300, San Mateo, California 94402. Phone: 650-347-1600. Fax: 650-347-7200. E-mail: jsa@jsa.org.
URL www.jsa.org
For more information, see page 1174.

Junior Statesmen Symposium on New Jersey State Politics and Government

Junior Statesmen Foundation
Princeton University
Princeton, New Jersey 08544

General Information Coed residential academic program established in 1996. Formal opportunities for the academically talented.
Program Focus State government, politics, debate, and leadership training.
Academics Communications, government and politics, journalism, precollege program, social science, social studies, speech/debate.
Special Interest Areas Career exploration, leadership training.
Trips College tours, day.
Program Information 1 session per year. Session length: 4 days in August. Ages: 14–18. 100–150 participants per session. Boarding program cost: $395. Financial aid available.
Application Deadline Continuous.
Contact Matt Randazzo, National Summer School Director, 400 South El Camino Real, Suite 300, San Mateo, California 94402. Phone: 650-347-1600. Fax: 650-347-7200. E-mail: jsa@jsa.org.
URL www.jsa.org
For more information, see page 1174.

Lenny Armuth Soccer Academy

Drew University
36 Madison Avenue
Madison, New Jersey 07940

General Information Boys' day sports camp established in 1995.
Program Focus Soccer; mastering the fundamentals and playing at a higher level.
Sports Soccer.
Program Information 1 session per year. Session length: 5 days in July. Ages: 6–17. 100–175 participants per session. Day program cost: $265. Financial aid available.
Application Deadline Continuous.
Jobs Positions for college students 18 and older.
Contact Lenny Armuth, Director, main address above. Phone: 973-408-3135. Fax: 973-408-3014. E-mail: larmuth@drew.edu.
URL www.depts.drew.edu/ath/soccerm/camps.php

Lindley G. Cook 4-H Camp

Rutgers Cooperative Extension System/Rutgers University
100 Struble Road
Branchville, New Jersey 07826

General Information Coed residential traditional camp established in 1951.
Academics Ecology, environmental science, geology/earth science, marine studies, meteorology.
Arts Arts and crafts (general), ceramics, creative writing, leather working, theater/drama.
Special Interest Areas Campcraft, counselor-in-training program, leadership training, nature study, team building.
Sports Archery, boating, canoeing, fishing, kayaking, riflery, swimming.
Wilderness/Outdoors Backpacking, hiking, orienteering, survival training, wilderness camping.
Program Information 6–8 sessions per year. Session length: 5 days in July, August. Ages: 8–16. 80–150 participants per session. Boarding program cost: $285–$305. 4-H members receive discount.
Application Deadline Continuous.
Jobs Positions for high school students 16 and older and college students 18 and older.

Lindley G. Cook 4-H Camp (continued)

Contact James Tavares, Director, main address above. Phone: 973-948-3550. Fax: 973-948-0735. E-mail: tavares@aesop.rutgers.edu.
URL http://nj4hcamp.rutgers.edu

Maritime Camp

Bayshore Discovery Project
New Jersey

General Information Coed travel outdoor program established in 1996. High school credit may be earned.
Program Focus Participants sail in a historic sailing vessel from Liberty State Park, NJ to Cape May, NJ learning sailing skills and the ecology of the area.
Academics Area studies, ecology, environmental science, history, marine studies, oceanography.
Arts Arts and crafts (general).
Special Interest Areas Campcraft, nature study, nautical skills, team building.
Sports Sailing.
Trips Overnight.
Program Information 1–2 sessions per year. Session length: 5–8 days in July, August. Ages: 13–17. 6 participants per session. Cost: $700–$1100.
Application Deadline Continuous.
Jobs Positions for college students 18 and older.
Contact Ms. Lindsay Smith, Program Coordinator, 2800 High Street (Bivalve), Port Norris, New Jersey 08349. Phone: 856-785-2060 Ext.152. Fax: 856-785-2893. E-mail: ajmeerwald@snip.net.
URL www.ajmeerwald.org

Montclair State University Hi Jump Program

Montclair State University
876 Valley Road
Upper Montclair, New Jersey 07043

General Information Coed day academic program established in 1976. Formal opportunities for the academically talented and artistically talented. College credit may be earned.
Program Focus Academic enrichment through college courses in a wide variety of subjects.
Academics American literature, English as a second language, English language/literature, French language/literature, German language/literature, Italian language/literature, Latin language, Spanish language/literature, academics (general), anthropology, art history/appreciation, astronomy, biology, business, chemistry, communications, computers, economics, environmental science, geography, geology/earth science, government and politics, history, humanities, linguistics, marine studies, mathematics, meteorology, music, oceanography, philosophy, physics, psychology, reading, religion, science (general), social science, speech/debate, writing.
Arts Arts and crafts (general), ceramics, creative writing, dance, music, music (instrumental), painting, theater/drama.
Sports Swimming, tennis.
Program Information 3–9 sessions per year. Session length: 30–80 days in January, February, March, April, May, June, July, August, September, October, November, December. Ages: 16–18. 10–15 participants per session. Call for college course tuition.
Application Deadline Continuous.
Jobs Positions for college students 18 and older.
Contact Stevens A. Nash, Gifted Program Director, main address above. Phone: 973-655-4104. Fax: 973-655-7895. E-mail: nashs@mail.montclair.edu.
URL www.montclair.edu/gifted

Montclair State University Summer Camp for Academically Gifted and Talented Youth

Montclair State University
876 Valley Road
Upper Montclair, New Jersey 07043

General Information Coed day academic program and arts program established in 1983. Formal opportunities for the academically talented and gifted.
Program Focus Recreational courses are also offered.
Academics SAT/ACT preparation, academics (general), architecture, astronomy, biology, chemistry, communications, computers, engineering, government and politics, history, humanities, mathematics, physics, science (general), study skills, writing.
Arts Animation, arts, arts and crafts (general), cartooning, creative writing, drawing, music (ensemble), music (jazz), photography, printmaking, theater/drama.
Special Interest Areas Electronics, model rocketry, robotics.
Sports Diving, fencing, figure skating, golf, ice hockey, physical fitness, sports (general), swimming, tennis, volleyball, weight training.
Program Information 2 sessions per year. Session length: 15 days in June, July, August. Ages: 9–16. 225–250 participants per session. Day program cost: $1100–$1400. Application fee: $75. Application deadline: Session 1, May 25; Session 2, June 15.
Jobs Positions for college students 18 and older.
Contact Dr. Richard Taubald, Director, Academically Gifted/Talented Youth Programs, main address above. Phone: 973-655-4104. Fax: 973-655-7895. E-mail: taubaldr@mail.montclair.edu.
URL www.montclair.edu/gifted

Newgrange Summer Program

The Newgrange School
526 South Olden Avenue
Hamilton, New Jersey 08629

General Information Coed day academic program and special needs program. Specific services available for the learning disabled.
Program Focus For students with language-based learning disabilities.
Academics Academics (general), aerospace science, art (Advanced Placement), mathematics, reading, science (general), technology.
Arts Arts and crafts (general).

Program Information 1 session per year. Session length: 17 days in June, July. Ages: 8–13. 50 participants per session. Day program cost: $450. Financial aid available.
Application Deadline Continuous.
Contact Miss Heather Rose, Office Manager, main address above. Phone: 609-584-1800. Fax: 609-584-6166. E-mail: hrose@thenewgrange.org.
URL www.thenewgrange.org

Newgrange Summer Tutoring Program

The Newgrange School
526 South Olden Avenue
Hamilton, New Jersey 08629

General Information Coed day academic program and special needs program.
Program Focus Tutoring for students.
Academics Academics (general), aerospace science, mathematics, reading, science (general), technology, tutoring.
Program Information Ages: 7–18. Financial aid available. Cost: $85 per session.
Application Deadline Continuous.
Contact Miss Heather Rose, Office Manager, main address above. Phone: 609-584-1800. Fax: 609-584-6166. E-mail: hrose@thenewgrange.org.
URL www.thenewgrange.org

The New York Film Academy, Princeton University, Princeton, NJ

New York Film Academy
Princeton, New Jersey 08544

General Information Coed residential arts program established in 1992. College credit may be earned.
Program Focus "Total immersion" hands-on filmmaking workshop where students write, direct, shoot, and edit their own short 16mm films.
Arts Acting, creative writing, directing, film, film editing, film lighting, film production, screenwriting, sound design, television/video, theater/drama.
Trips Cultural.
Program Information 4 sessions per year. Session length: 1–6 weeks in June, July, August. Ages: 14–17. Boarding program cost: $1500–$6900.
Application Deadline Continuous.
Contact Admissions, 100 East 17th Street, New York, New York 10003. Phone: 212-674-4300. Fax: 212-477-1414. E-mail: film@nyfa.com.
URL www.nyfa.com
For more information, see page 1218.

The Peddie School Summer Day School

The Peddie School
Ward at South Main
Hightstown, New Jersey 08520

General Information Coed day academic program established in 1921. Formal opportunities for the academically talented and gifted. High school credit may be earned.
Academics American literature, English language/literature, Latin language, Spanish language/literature, academics (general), biology, chemistry, classical languages/literatures, mathematics, physics, writing.
Program Information 1 session per year. Session length: 30 days in June, July, August. Ages: 12–18. 300 participants per session. Day program cost: $700–$1300. Application fee: $25.
Application Deadline Continuous.
Contact Dr. David G. Martin, Director, PO Box A, Hightstown, New Jersey 08520. Phone: 609-490-7520. E-mail: dmartin@peddie.org.
URL www.peddie.org/community/summer/schoolasp

Pingry Academic Camps

The Pingry School
Martinsville Road
Martinsville, New Jersey 08836

General Information Coed day academic program.
Program Focus Academic enrichment.
Academics German language/literature, academics (general), mathematics, mathematics (Advanced Placement), reading, study skills, writing.
Program Information 1 session per year. Session length: 30 days in June, July, August. Ages: 9–18. Day program cost: $1040–$2000.
Application Deadline Continuous.
Contact Mr. Norman LaValette, Program Director/Chair, Foreign Language Department, The Pingry School, Box 366, Martinsville, New Jersey 08836. Phone: 908-647-5555. Fax: 908-647-3037. E-mail: info@pingry.org.
URL www.pingry.org

Pingry Day Camps

The Pingry School
Martinsville Road
Martinsville, New Jersey 08836

General Information Coed day traditional camp. Accredited by American Camping Association.
Academics German language/literature, computers, mathematics, reading, study skills, writing.
Arts Arts and crafts (general), ceramics, music, pottery, theater/drama.
Sports Basketball, soccer, swimming, tennis.
Program Information 1–3 sessions per year. Session length: 3–5 days in June, July, August. Ages: 3–14. Day program cost: $1320–$3935.
Application Deadline Continuous.
Jobs Positions for high school students 15 and older and college students 16 and older.

Pingry Day Camps (continued)
Contact Mr. Emanuel Tramontana, Camp Director/ Chair, Mathematics Department, The Pingry School, Box 366, Martinsville, New Jersey 08836. Phone: 908-647-5555. Fax: 908-647-3703. E-mail: info@pingry.org.
URL www.pingry.org

Pingry Lacrosse Camp–Martinsville Campus

The Pingry School
Martinsville Road
Martinsville, New Jersey 08836

General Information Coed day sports camp.
Program Focus Beginner and intermediate lacrosse.
Sports Lacrosse.
Program Information 1 session per year. Session length: 4–5 days in June. Ages: 7–14. 75 participants per session. Call for costs.
Application Deadline Continuous.
Jobs Positions for high school students 16 and older and college students 16 and older.
Contact Mr. Mike Webster, Program Director—Lacrosse, The Pingry School, Box 366, Martinsville, New Jersey 08836. Phone: 908-647-5555. Fax: 908-647-3703. E-mail: mwebster@pingry.org.
URL www.pingry.org

Pingry Lacrosse Camp–Short Hills Campus

The Pingry School
Country Day Drive
Short Hills, New Jersey 07078

General Information Boys' day sports camp.
Program Focus Beginner and intermediate lacrosse.
Sports Lacrosse.
Program Information 1 session per year. Session length: 4–5 days in June. Ages: 7–14. 75 participants per session. Call for costs.
Application Deadline Continuous.
Jobs Positions for high school students 16 and older and college students 16 and older.
Contact Mr. Mike Webster, Program Director—Lacrosse, The Pingry School, Box 366, Martinsville, New Jersey 08836. Phone: 908-647-5555. Fax: 908-647-3703. E-mail: mwebster@pingry.org.
URL www.pingry.org

Pingry Soccer Camp

The Pingry School
Martinsville Road
Martinsville, New Jersey 08836

General Information Coed day sports camp. Accredited by American Camping Association.
Program Focus Soccer.
Sports Soccer.
Program Information 1 session per year. Session length: 5 days in August. Ages: 8–17. Day program cost: $280.
Application Deadline Continuous.
Jobs Positions for high school students 16 and older and college students 16 and older.
Contact Mr. Miller Bugliari, Special Assistant to the Headmaster, The Pingry School, Box 366, Martinsville, New Jersey 08836. Phone: 908-647-5555. Fax: 908-647-3037. E-mail: info@pingry.org.
URL www.pingry.org

Pingry Softball Camp

The Pingry School
Martinsville Road
Martinsville, New Jersey 08836

General Information Girls' day sports camp.
Program Focus Softball.
Sports Softball.
Program Information 1 session per year. Session length: 5 days in June. Ages: 10–14. Day program cost: $125.
Application Deadline Continuous.
Contact Mr. Emanuel Tramontana, Director of Summer Camps/Chair, Mathematics Department, The Pingry School, Box 366, Martinsville, New Jersey 08836. Phone: 908-647-5555. Fax: 908-647-3037. E-mail: info@pingry.org.
URL www.pingry.org

Pingry Summer Enrichment Experience

The Pingry School
Short Hills Campus
Country Day Drive
Short Hills, New Jersey 07078

General Information Coed day academic program. Formal opportunities for the academically talented.
Program Focus Academic enrichment.
Academics Spanish language/literature, academics (general), art history/appreciation, mathematics, reading, writing.
Program Information 1–3 sessions per year. Session length: 5–10 days in June. Ages: 5–12. 10–12 participants per session. Day program cost: $150–$280.
Application Deadline Continuous.
Contact Ms. Carolyn Gibson, Assistant Director—Lower School, The Pingry School—Summer Enrichment Experience, Country Day Drive, Short Hills, New Jersey 07078. Phone: 973-379-4550. Fax: 973-379-1861. E-mail: info@pingry.org.
URL www.pingry.org

PixelNation

Institute for Arts and Humanities Education
Highland Park and Lawrenceville
New Jersey

General Information Coed day arts program established in 2002.
Program Focus Experimental film.
Academics Art (Advanced Placement).
Arts Animation, film, television/video.

Trips College tours, cultural, day.
Program Information 1 session per year. Session length: 25 days in June, July. Ages: 14–18. 20–25 participants per session. Day program cost: $485–$850. Financial aid available.
Application Deadline June 4.
Contact Ms. Maureen Heffernan, Executive Director, 100 Jersey Avenue, Suite B104, Box B17, New Brunswick, New Jersey 08901. Phone: 732-220-1600. Fax: 732-220-1515. E-mail: iahe@iahenj.org.
URL www.iahenj.org

Princeton Ballet School's Ballet Plus Junior

Princeton Ballet School
301 North Harrison Street
Princeton, New Jersey 08540

General Information Coed day arts program established in 1999. Formal opportunities for the artistically talented.
Program Focus Ballet, body conditioning, choreography, variations.
Academics Music.
Arts Dance, dance (ballet), dance (folk), dance (modern), music.
Program Information 5 sessions per year. Session length: 5 days in June, July. Ages: 9–13. 8–18 participants per session. Day program cost: $525–$1065.
Application Deadline Continuous.
Contact Ms. Mary Pat Robertson, Director, main address above. Phone: 609-921-7758. Fax: 609-921-3249.
URL www.arballet.org

Princeton Ballet School's Ballet Plus Senior

Princeton Ballet School
29 North Main Street
Cranbury, New Jersey 08512

General Information Coed day arts program established in 1980. Formal opportunities for the artistically talented.
Program Focus Dance/Ballet.
Arts Dance, dance (ballet), dance (jazz), dance (modern).
Program Information 6 sessions per year. Session length: 10–30 days in June, July, August. Ages: 11+. 20–40 participants per session. Day program cost: $545–$1300.
Application Deadline Continuous.
Contact Ms. Mary Pat Robertson, Director, 301 North Harrison Street, Princeton, New Jersey 08540. Phone: 609-921-7758. Fax: 609-921-3249.
URL www.arballet.org

Princeton Ballet School's Summer Intensive

Princeton Ballet School
301 North Harrison Street
Princeton, New Jersey 08540

General Information Coed residential and day arts program established in 1976. Formal opportunities for the artistically talented.
Program Focus Ballet.
Arts Dance, dance (ballet), dance (folk), dance (jazz), dance (modern).
Trips Cultural.
Program Information 1 session per year. Session length: 30 days in June, July. Ages: 13–21. 80 participants per session. Day program cost: $1450. Boarding program cost: $3400. Application fee: $25.
Application Deadline Continuous.
Jobs Positions for college students 21 and older.
Contact Ms. Mary Pat Robertson, Director, main address above. Phone: 609-921-7758. Fax: 609-921-3249.
URL www.arballet.org

Professional Sports Camps–Big League Baseball Camp

Professional Sports Camps
Montclair State University
Upper Montclair, New Jersey 07043

General Information Coed residential and day sports camp established in 1947.
Sports Baseball, swimming.
Trips Day.
Program Information 7 sessions per year. Session length: 6 days in June, July, August. Ages: 8–18. 40–150 participants per session. Day program cost: $325. Boarding program cost: $625.
Application Deadline Continuous.
Jobs Positions for college students 19 and older.
Contact Mr. Vincent Carlesi, Camp Director, PO Box 15, Sparta, New Jersey 07871. Phone: 973-691-0070. Fax: 973-347-5832. E-mail: sportscamp@aol.com.
URL www.psccamps.com

Professional Sports Camps–Hall of Fame Basketball Camp

Professional Sports Camps
Montclair State University
Upper Montclair, New Jersey 07043

General Information Coed residential and day sports camp established in 1947.
Sports Basketball, swimming.
Trips Day.
Program Information 7 sessions per year. Session length: 6 days in June, July, August. Ages: 10–18. 40–150 participants per session. Day program cost: $325. Boarding program cost: $625.
Application Deadline Continuous.
Jobs Positions for college students 19 and older.

Professional Sports Camps–Hall of Fame Basketball Camp (continued)

Contact Mr. Vincent Carlesi, Camp Director, PO Box 15, Sparta, New Jersey 07871. Phone: 973-691-0070. Fax: 973-347-5832. E-mail: sportscamp@aol.com.
URL www.psccamps.com

Professional Sports Camps–Hall of Fame Soccer Camp

Professional Sports Camps
Montclair State University
Upper Montclair, New Jersey 07043

General Information Coed residential and day sports camp established in 1947.
Sports Soccer, swimming.
Trips Day.
Program Information 6 sessions per year. Session length: 6 days in June, July, August. Ages: 7–15. 40–120 participants per session. Day program cost: $300. Boarding program cost: $585.
Application Deadline Continuous.
Jobs Positions for college students 19 and older.
Contact Mr. Vincent Carlesi, Camp Director, PO Box 15, Sparta, New Jersey 07871. Phone: 973-691-0070. Fax: 973-347-5832. E-mail: sportscamp@aol.com.
URL www.psccamps.com

Rider University Opportunity for Academically Gifted and Talented High School Students

Rider University
2083 Lawrenceville Road
Lawrenceville, New Jersey 08648

General Information Coed day academic program established in 1980. Formal opportunities for the academically talented. College credit may be earned.
Academics English language/literature, Spanish language/literature, academics (general), art history/appreciation, biology, business, chemistry, communications, geology/earth science, government and politics, history, humanities, journalism, marine studies, mathematics, music, oceanography, philosophy, physics, psychology, science (general), social science.
Program Information 2 sessions per year. Session length: 5 weeks in May, June, July, August. Ages: 15–18. 3–4 participants per session. Day program cost: $2190. Application fee: $40. Cost: $990 per 3-credit course.
Application Deadline Continuous.
Contact Susan Christian, Dean of Enrollment, main address above. Phone: 609-896-5042. Fax: 609-895-6645. E-mail: christian@rider.edu.
URL www.rider.edu

Student Conservation Association–Conservation Crew Program (New Jersey)

Student Conservation Association (SCA)
New Jersey

General Information Coed residential outdoor program, community service program, and wilderness program established in 1957. High school credit may be earned.
Program Focus Resource management, conservation and environmental education.
Academics Biology, botany, ecology, environmental science, geology/earth science, history.
Special Interest Areas Campcraft, community service, construction, leadership training, nature study, trail maintenance, work camp programs.
Sports Canoeing, fishing, kayaking, swimming.
Wilderness/Outdoors Backpacking, hiking, orienteering, outdoor living skills, wilderness camping.
Trips Cultural, day, overnight.
Program Information 2–3 sessions per year. Session length: 3–5 weeks in June, July, August. Ages: 15–19. 6–8 participants per session. Application fee: $20. Financial aid available. No cost for program; financial aid possible for travel expenses.
Application Deadline Continuous.
Jobs Positions for college students 21 and older.
Contact Recruitment Office, PO Box 550, Charlestown, New Hampshire 03603. Phone: 603-543-1700. Fax: 603-543-1828. E-mail: getreal@thesca.org.
URL www.theSCA.org

Summer Academy for the Visual and Performing Arts

Red Bank Regional High School
101 Ridge Road
Little Silver, New Jersey 07739

General Information Coed day academic program and arts program established in 2000. Formal opportunities for the artistically talented.
Academics English language/literature, art history/appreciation, humanities, music.
Arts Arts and crafts (general), chorus, creative writing, dance, drawing, graphic arts, music, music (ensemble), music (vocal), musical productions, musical theater, painting, photography, pottery, sculpture, theater/drama, visual arts.
Trips Cultural, day.
Program Information 1–2 sessions per year. Session length: 10–25 days in July, August. Ages: 11–14. 10–81 participants per session. Day program cost: $250–$600. Application fee: $50. Financial aid available.
Application Deadline June 15.
Contact Mr. Kristopher L. Zook, Director, main address above. Phone: 732-842-8000 Ext.227. Fax: 732-842-4868. E-mail: zookak@hotmail.com.

The Summer Institute for the Gifted at Drew University

Summer Institute for the Gifted
Drew University
Madison, New Jersey 07940

General Information Coed residential academic program established in 1994. Formal opportunities for the academically talented and gifted. Specific services available for the hearing impaired, learning disabled, physically challenged, and visually impaired. College credit may be earned.
Academics American literature, English language/literature, French language/literature, Latin language, SAT/ACT preparation, Spanish language/literature, academics (general), architecture, art history/appreciation, biology, business, chemistry, classical languages/literatures, communications, computers, engineering, environmental science, history, marine studies, mathematics, music, philosophy, physics, physiology, precollege program, psychology, social studies, speech/debate, study skills, writing.
Arts Chorus, creative writing, dance, dance (modern), drawing, mime, music, music (chamber), music (classical), music (ensemble), music (instrumental), musical productions, painting, photography, sculpture, theater/drama.
Special Interest Areas Animal care, electronics, robotics.
Sports Archery, baseball, basketball, fencing, field hockey, football, lacrosse, martial arts, soccer, squash, swimming, tennis.
Trips Cultural.
Program Information 1–2 sessions per year. Session length: 3 weeks in June, July, August. Ages: 8–17. 275–325 participants per session. Boarding program cost: $3350. Application fee: $75. Financial aid available.
Application Deadline May 15.
Jobs Positions for college students 19 and older.
Contact Dr. Stephen Gessner, Director, River Plaza, 9 West Broad Street, Stamford, Connecticut 06902-3788. Phone: 866-303-4744. Fax: 203-399-5598. E-mail: sig.info@aifs.com.
URL www.giftedstudy.com

For more information, see page 1342.

The Summer Institute for the Gifted at Moorestown Friends School

Summer Institute for the Gifted
Moorestown Friends School
Moorestown, New Jersey 08057

General Information Coed day academic program established in 2003. Formal opportunities for the academically talented and gifted. Specific services available for the hearing impaired, learning disabled, physically challenged, and visually impaired.
Academics American literature, English language/literature, French language/literature, Latin language, SAT/ACT preparation, Spanish language/literature, academics (general), aerospace science, archaeology, architecture, art (Advanced Placement), art history/appreciation, biology (Advanced Placement), business, chemistry, classical languages/literatures, communications, computer programming, computers, engineering, environmental science, government and politics, history, humanities, marine studies, mathematics, music, philosophy, physics, physiology, precollege program, psychology, science (general), social studies, speech/debate, study skills, writing.
Arts Arts and crafts (general), ceramics, chorus, creative writing, dance, dance (ballet), dance (jazz), dance (modern), drawing, graphic arts, mime, music, music (chamber), music (classical), music (ensemble), musical productions, painting, photography, puppetry, sculpture, theater/drama.
Special Interest Areas Electronics, model rocketry, robotics.
Sports Aerobics, baseball, basketball, field hockey, football, lacrosse, martial arts, soccer, softball, squash, swimming, tennis, volleyball.
Wilderness/Outdoors Hiking.
Program Information 1–2 sessions per year. Session length: 3 weeks in June, July, August. Ages: 6–11. 100–150 participants per session. Day program cost: $1550. Application fee: $75. Financial aid available.
Application Deadline May 15.
Jobs Positions for college students 19 and older.
Contact Dr. Stephen Gessner, Director, River Plaza, 9 West Broad Street, Stamford, Connecticut 06902-3788. Phone: 866-303-4744. Fax: 203-399-5598. E-mail: sig.info@aifs.com.
URL www.giftedstudy.com

For more information, see page 1342.

The Summer Institute for the Gifted at Princeton University

Summer Institute for the Gifted
Princeton University
Princeton, New Jersey

General Information Coed day academic program. Formal opportunities for the academically talented and gifted.
Academics Academics (general), precollege program.
Program Information 1–2 sessions per year. Session length: 3 weeks in June, July, August. Ages: 6–11. 200–300 participants per session. Day program cost: $1550. Application fee: $75. Financial aid available.
Application Deadline May 15.
Jobs Positions for college students 19 and older.
Contact Dr. Stephen Gessner, Director, River Plaza, 9 West Broad Street, Stamford, Connecticut 06902-3788. Phone: 866-303-4744. Fax: 203-399-5598. E-mail: sig.info@aifs.com.
URL www.giftedstudy.com

For more information, see page 1342.

Trail Blazers

210 Deckertown Turnpike
Montague, New Jersey 07827

General Information Coed residential outdoor program and wilderness program established in 1887. Accredited by American Camping Association.

Trail Blazers (continued)
Program Focus Outdoor living skills for economically disadvantaged children.
Academics Astronomy, ecology, environmental science, history, music, reading, science (general), social studies, writing.
Arts Arts and crafts (general), ceramics, creative writing, drawing, jewelry making, leather working, music, pottery, theater/drama, weaving, woodworking.
Special Interest Areas Native American culture, animal care, campcraft, career exploration, community service, gardening, leadership training, nature study.
Sports Boating, canoeing, fishing, ropes course, swimming.
Wilderness/Outdoors Backpacking, canoe trips, hiking, orienteering, outdoor living skills, wilderness camping.
Trips Overnight.
Program Information 2 sessions per year. Session length: 24 days in June, July, August. Ages: 9–18. 75–99 participants per session. Financial aid available. Sliding fee scale.
Application Deadline June 1.
Jobs Positions for college students 19 and older.
Summer Contact Jean Lynch, Program Director, main address above. Phone: 973-875-4116. Fax: 973-875-8562. E-mail: jlynch@trailblazers.org.
Winter Contact Jean Lynch, Program Director, 45 East 20th Street, 9th Floor, New York, New York 10003. Phone: 212-529-5113 Ext.204. Fax: 212-529-2704. E-mail: jlynch@trailblazers.org.
URL trailblazers.org

UNITED SOCCER ACADEMY–GOAL KEEPING TRAINING CAMP, NEW JERSEY

United Soccer Academy, Inc.
New Jersey

General Information Coed residential and day sports camp established in 1999.
Program Focus All aspects of the keeper position are covered: from techniques to tactical decision-making. Coaches are from international teams and colleges.
Sports Soccer.
Program Information 25 sessions per year. Session length: 5 days in April, June, July, August, September, November. Ages: 8–14. 16–200 participants per session. Day program cost: $145. Boarding program cost: $495. Call for specific locations.
Application Deadline Continuous.
Jobs Positions for college students 18 and older.
Contact Camps Information, 50 Tannery Road, Unit 8, Branchburg, New Jersey 08876. Phone: 908-823-0130. Fax: 908-823-0466. E-mail: info@unitedsocceracademy.com.
URL www.unitedsocceracademy.com

UNITED SOCCER ACADEMY–JUNIOR SOCCER SQUIRTS, NEW JERSEY

United Soccer Academy, Inc.
New Jersey

General Information Coed day sports camp established in 1999.
Program Focus Introduction to soccer in a camp format with emphasis on fun games and activities in small groups. Coaches are from international soccer teams and college teams.
Sports Soccer.
Program Information 100 sessions per year. Session length: 5 days in April, June, July, August, September, November. Ages: 3–5. 6–48 participants per session. Day program cost: $89. Two sessions daily; parents may stay with camper. Call for specific locations.
Application Deadline Continuous.
Jobs Positions for college students 18 and older.
Contact Camps Information, 50 Tannery Road, Unit 8, Branchburg, New Jersey 08876. Phone: 908-823-0130. Fax: 908-823-0466. E-mail: info@unitedsocceracademy.com.
URL www.unitedsocceracademy.com

UNITED SOCCER ACADEMY–RECREATION SOCCER COMMUNITY CAMP, NEW JERSEY

United Soccer Academy, Inc.
New Jersey

General Information Coed residential and day sports camp established in 1999.
Program Focus Players build on the fundamentals of the game, experiencing a broad range of techniques and skills. Coaches are from international teams and colleges.
Sports Soccer.
Program Information 170 sessions per year. Session length: 5 days in April, June, July, August, September, November. Ages: 7–14. 16–200 participants per session. Day program cost: $145. Boarding program cost: $495. Call for specific locations.
Application Deadline Continuous.
Jobs Positions for college students 18 and older.
Contact Camps Information, 50 Tannery Road, Unit 8, Branchburg, New Jersey 08876. Phone: 908-823-0130. Fax: 908-823-0466. E-mail: info@unitedsocceracademy.com.
URL www.unitedsocceracademy.com

UNITED SOCCER ACADEMY–REGIONAL ACADEMY CAMP, NEW JERSEY

United Soccer Academy, Inc.
New Jersey

General Information Coed residential and day sports camp established in 1999.
Program Focus Intense program aimed at the dedicated travel and select soccer player. Sites are regionalized to ensure high quality competition.

Advanced techniques and skills taught, tactical game analysis, position assessment. Coaches are from international teams and colleges.
Sports Soccer.
Program Information 10 sessions per year. Session length: 5 days in June, July, August. Ages: 8–14. 16–200 participants per session. Day program cost: $165. Boarding program cost: $495. Call for specific locations.
Application Deadline Continuous.
Jobs Positions for high school students and college students 18 and older.
Contact Camps Information, 50 Tannery Road, Unit 8, Branchburg, New Jersey 08876. Phone: 908-823-0130. Fax: 908-823-0466. E-mail: info@unitedsocceracademy.com.
URL www.unitedsocceracademy.com

UNITED SOCCER ACADEMY–SENIOR SOCCER SQUIRTS, NEW JERSEY

United Soccer Academy, Inc.
New Jersey

General Information Coed day sports camp established in 1999.
Program Focus Introduction to the game in relaxed, fun atmosphere; skills development without competitive environment. Coaches are from international teams and colleges.
Sports Soccer.
Program Information 150 sessions per year. Session length: 5 days in April, June, July, August, September, November. Ages: 5–7. 6–48 participants per session. Day program cost: $89. Two sessions daily; call for specific locations.
Application Deadline Continuous.
Jobs Positions for college students 18 and older.
Contact Camps Information, 50 Tannery Road, Unit 8, Branchburg, New Jersey 08876. Phone: 908-823-0130. Fax: 908-823-0466. E-mail: info@unitedsocceracademy.com.
URL www.unitedsocceracademy.com

UNITED SOCCER ACADEMY–TEAM TRAINING CAMP, NEW JERSEY

United Soccer Academy, Inc.
New Jersey

General Information Coed residential and day sports camp established in 1999.
Program Focus Teams of ten or more players receive individualized instruction based on staff discussion with their coach. Structured coaching scrimmages with other teams. Coaches on staff are from international teams and colleges.
Sports Soccer.
Program Information 50 sessions per year. Session length: 5 days in April, June, July, August, September, November. Ages: 8–14. 20–200 participants per session. Day program cost: $125. Boarding program cost: $495. Call for specific locations.
Application Deadline Continuous.
Jobs Positions for college students 18 and older.
Contact Camps Information, 50 Tannery Road, Unit 8, Branchburg, New Jersey 08876. Phone: 908-823-0130. Fax: 908-823-0466. E-mail: info@unitedsocceracademy.com.
URL www.unitedsocceracademy.com

UNITED SOCCER ACADEMY–TRAVEL SOCCER COMMUNITY CAMP, NEW JERSEY

United Soccer Academy, Inc.
New Jersey

General Information Coed residential and day sports camp established in 1999.
Program Focus Individual player development and team tactics are emphasized. Skills are taught at an accelerated level with practices developing into full game realistic situations. Coaches are from international teams and colleges.
Sports Soccer.
Program Information 170 sessions per year. Session length: 5 days in April, June, July, August, September, November. Ages: 8–14. 16–200 participants per session. Day program cost: $145. Boarding program cost: $495. Call for specific locations.
Application Deadline Continuous.
Jobs Positions for college students 18 and older.
Contact Camps Information, 50 Tannery Road, Unit 8, Branchburg, New Jersey 08876. Phone: 908-823-0130. Fax: 908-823-0466. E-mail: info@unitedsocceracademy.com.
URL www.unitedsocceracademy.com

WESTMINSTER CHOIR COLLEGE COMPOSITION WEEK

Westminster Choir College of Rider University
101 Walnut Lane
Princeton, New Jersey 08540-3899

General Information Coed residential arts program. Formal opportunities for the artistically talented.
Program Focus Provides young composers with concentrated study in the fundamentals of composition.
Academics Music.
Arts Chorus, music, music (ensemble), music (instrumental), music composition/arrangement.
Program Information 1 session per year. Session length: 6 days in July. Ages: 13–18. 20 participants per session. Boarding program cost: $715. Financial aid available. Letter of recommendation from music teacher required.
Application Deadline Continuous.
Contact Scott R. Hoerl, Director of Continuing Education, main address above. Phone: 609-924-7416. Fax: 609-921-6187. E-mail: woce@rider.edu.
URL westminster.rider.edu

Westminster Choir College High School Solo Pianist

Westminster Choir College of Rider University
101 Walnut Lane
Princeton, New Jersey 08540-3899

General Information Coed residential arts program established in 2000. Formal opportunities for the artistically talented.
Program Focus Piano.
Academics Music.
Arts Music (classical), piano.
Trips Day.
Program Information 1 session per year. Session length: 6 days in July. Ages: 14–18. 10–15 participants per session. Boarding program cost: $790. Letter of recommendation from piano teacher and audition tape required.
Application Deadline March 15.
Jobs Positions for college students.
Contact Scott R. Hoerl, Director of Continuing Education, main address above. Phone: 609-924-7416. Fax: 609-921-6187. E-mail: woce@rider.edu.
URL westminster.rider.edu

Westminster Choir College High School Solo Vocal Artist: A Performance Workshop for Singers

Westminster Choir College of Rider University
101 Walnut Lane
Princeton, New Jersey 08540-3899

General Information Coed residential arts program established in 1999. Formal opportunities for the artistically talented.
Program Focus Music; art of solo performances.
Arts Music, music (chamber), music (classical), music (ensemble), music (vocal).
Program Information 1 session per year. Session length: 6 days in July. Ages: 15–18. 35 participants per session. Boarding program cost: $790. Letter of recommendation from music teacher and audition tape required.
Application Deadline March 15.
Jobs Positions for college students.
Contact Scott R. Hoerl, Director of Continuing Education, main address above. Phone: 609-924-7416. Fax: 609-921-6187. E-mail: woce@rider.edu.
URL westminster.rider.edu/

Westminster Choir College Middle School Music Theater

Westminster Choir College of Rider University
101 Walnut Lane
Princeton, New Jersey 08540-3899

General Information Coed residential arts program established in 2004.
Program Focus Music and theater arts.
Academics Music.
Arts Chorus, dance, music (ensemble), music (vocal), musical productions, musical theater, theater/drama.
Trips Cultural.
Program Information 1 session per year. Session length: 1 week in August. Ages: 11–14. 45 participants per session. Boarding program cost: $775. Financial aid available. Letter of recommendation from music director required.
Application Deadline Continuous.
Contact Scott R. Hoerl, Director of Continuing Education, main address above. Phone: 609-924-7416. Fax: 609-921-6187. E-mail: woce@rider.edu.
URL westminster.rider.edu

Westminster Choir College Middle School Piano Camp

Westminster Choir College of Rider University
101 Walnut Lane
Princeton, New Jersey 08540-3899

General Information Coed residential arts program established in 2000. Formal opportunities for the artistically talented.
Program Focus Piano.
Academics Music.
Arts Music (classical), piano.
Trips Day.
Program Information 1 session per year. Session length: 5 days in June. Ages: 11–15. 24 participants per session. Boarding program cost: $715. Letter of recommendation from piano teacher required.
Application Deadline Continuous.
Jobs Positions for college students.
Contact Scott R. Hoerl, Director of Continuing Education, main address above. Phone: 609-924-7416. Fax: 609-921-6187. E-mail: woce@rider.edu.
URL westminster.rider.edu

Westminster Choir College Middle School Vocal Camp

Westminster Choir College of Rider University
101 Walnut Lane
Princeton, New Jersey 08540-3899

General Information Coed residential arts program established in 1995. Formal opportunities for the artistically talented.
Program Focus Music.
Arts Chorus, music, music (classical), music (vocal), painting, theater/drama.
Trips Cultural, day.
Program Information 1 session per year. Session length: 6 days in June. Ages: 11–14. 60 participants per session. Boarding program cost: $715. Letter of recommendation from music director required.
Application Deadline Continuous.
Jobs Positions for college students.
Contact Scott R. Hoerl, Director of Continuing Education, main address above. Phone: 609-924-7416. Fax: 609-921-6187. E-mail: woce@rider.edu.
URL westminster.rider.edu

Westminster Choir College Music Theater Workshop

Westminster Choir College of Rider University
101 Walnut Lane
Princeton, New Jersey 08540-3899

General Information Coed residential arts program established in 1995.
Program Focus Music and theater arts.
Arts Chorus, dance, music (ensemble), music (vocal), musical theater, theater/drama.
Trips Cultural.
Program Information 1 session per year. Session length: 1 week in August. Ages: 15–18. 45 participants per session. Boarding program cost: $800. Letter of recommendation from music director required.
Application Deadline Continuous.
Jobs Positions for college students.
Contact Scott R. Hoerl, Director of Continuing Education, main address above. Phone: 609-924-7416. Fax: 609-921-6187. E-mail: woce@rider.edu.
URL westminster.rider.edu

Westminster Choir College Organ Week

Westminster Choir College of Rider University
101 Walnut Lane
Princeton, New Jersey 08540-3899

General Information Coed residential arts program. Formal opportunities for the artistically talented.
Program Focus Organ lessons.
Arts Music, organ.
Trips Cultural, day.
Program Information 1 session per year. Session length: 6 days in July. Ages: 13–18. 20 participants per session. Boarding program cost: $715. Letter of recommendation from music director required.
Application Deadline Continuous.
Jobs Positions for college students.
Contact Scott R. Hoerl, Director of Continuing Education, main address above. Phone: 609-924-7416. Fax: 609-921-6187. E-mail: woce@rider.edu.
URL westminster.rider.edu/

Westminster Choir College Piano Camp

Westminster Choir College of Rider University
101 Walnut Lane
Princeton, New Jersey 08540-3899

General Information Coed residential arts program. Formal opportunities for the artistically talented.
Program Focus Piano.
Arts Music, piano.
Program Information 2 sessions per year. Session length: 5 days in July, August. Ages: 13–18. 24 participants per session. Boarding program cost: $715. Letter of recommendation from music director required.
Application Deadline Continuous.
Contact Scott R. Hoerl, Director of Continuing Education, main address above. Phone: 609-924-7416. Fax: 609-921-6187. E-mail: woce@rider.edu.
URL westminster.rider.edu/

Westminster Choir College Vocal Institute

Westminster Choir College of Rider University
101 Walnut Lane
Princeton, New Jersey 08540-3899

General Information Coed residential arts program established in 1948. Formal opportunities for the artistically talented.
Program Focus Vocal music.
Academics Music.
Arts Chorus, dance, music, music (vocal).
Special Interest Areas Career exploration.
Trips Cultural, day.
Program Information 1 session per year. Session length: 2 weeks in July. Ages: 15–18. 160 participants per session. Boarding program cost: $1000. Financial aid available. Letter of recommendation from music director required.
Application Deadline Continuous.
Contact Scott R. Hoerl, Director of Continuing Education, main address above. Phone: 609-924-7416. Fax: 609-921-6187. E-mail: woce@rider.edu.
URL westminster.rider.edu

Westminster Conservatory of Music–Flute Camp

Westminster Conservatory of Music
Westminster Choir College of Rider University
101 Walnut Lane
Princeton, New Jersey 08540-3899

General Information Coed residential and day arts program.
Arts Music, music (instrumental).
Program Information 1 session per year. Session length: 1 week in July, August. Financial aid available. Open to participants entering grades 6–12; call for costs.
Contact Conservatory Office, main address above. Phone: 609-921-7104. Fax: 609-921-7296. E-mail: wccconserv@rider.edu.
URL www.rider.edu/westminster/conserv/

Westminster Conservatory of Music–Musical Jamboree

Westminster Conservatory of Music
Unitarian Universalist Church
Route 206 and Cherry Hill Road
Princeton, New Jersey 08540-3899

General Information Coed day arts program.
Arts Arts and crafts (general), music, sing-a-longs.
Program Information 2 sessions per year. Session length: 5 days in July, August. Ages: 4–7. Financial aid available. Call for costs.

Westminster Conservatory of Music–Musical Jamboree (continued)

Contact Conservatory Office, 101 Walnut Lane, Princeton, New Jersey 08540-3899. Phone: 609-921-7104. Fax: 609-921-7296. E-mail: wccconserv@rider.edu.
URL www.rider.edu/westminster/conserv/

Westminster Conservatory of Music–Summer Ensemble

Westminster Conservatory of Music
Unitarian Universalist Church
Route 206 and Cherry Hill Road
Princeton, New Jersey 08540-3899

General Information Coed day arts program.
Program Focus Experienced string, wind, brass, or piano students.
Arts Music, music (chamber), music (ensemble), music (instrumental), music (jazz), music (orchestral), music (vocal).
Program Information Financial aid available. Open to participants entering grades 6–8; call for costs.
Contact Conservatory Office, 101 Walnut Lane, Princeton, New Jersey 08540-3899. Phone: 609-921-7104. Fax: 609-921-7296. E-mail: wccconserv@rider.edu.
URL www.rider.edu/westminster/conserv

Westminster Conservatory of Music–Try It Out

Westminster Conservatory of Music
Unitarian Universalist Church
Route 206 and Cherry Hill Road
Princeton, New Jersey 08540-3899

General Information Coed day arts program.
Arts Guitar, music, music (instrumental), piano.
Program Information 1 session per year. Session length: 10 days in July, August. Financial aid available. Open to participants entering grades 1–5; call for costs.
Contact Conservatory Office, 101 Walnut Lane, Princeton, New Jersey 08540-3899. Phone: 609-921-7104. Fax: 609-921-7296. E-mail: wccconserv@rider.edu.
URL www.rider.edu/westminster/conserv/

Westminster Conservatory of Music–Youth Opera Workshop

Westminster Conservatory of Music
Unitarian Universalist Church
Route 206 and Cherry Hill Road
Princeton, New Jersey 08540-3899

General Information Coed day arts program.
Program Focus Introduction to the integral elements of opera performance.
Arts Acting, audition technique, make up, stage movement.
Special Interest Areas Opera.
Program Information 1 session per year. Session length: 10 days in July, August. Ages: 8–12. Financial aid available. Call for costs.
Contact Conservatory Office, 101 Walnut Lane, Princeton, New Jersey 08540-3899. Phone: 609-921-7104. Fax: 609-921-7296. E-mail: wccconserv@rider.edu.
URL www.rider.edu/westminster/conserv

YMCA Camp Bernie

Ridgewood YMCA
327 Turkey Top Road
Port Murray, New Jersey 07865

General Information Coed residential traditional camp established in 1957. Accredited by American Camping Association.
Program Focus Trips to Maine, Ontario, Massachusetts, and Virginia.
Arts Arts and crafts (general), creative writing, jewelry making, painting.
Special Interest Areas Animal care, campcraft, model rocketry, nature study.
Sports Archery, basketball, bicycling, boating, canoeing, climbing (wall), equestrian sports, fishing, football, horseback riding, minibikes, rappelling, ropes course, soccer, swimming, volleyball.
Wilderness/Outdoors Backpacking, canoe trips, hiking, mountain biking, rock climbing, wilderness camping.
Trips Overnight.
Program Information 4 sessions per year. Session length: 12–26 days in June, July, August. Ages: 7–16. 180–200 participants per session. Boarding program cost: $860–$1735. Financial aid available.
Application Deadline Continuous.
Jobs Positions for high school students 16 and older and college students 18 and older.
Contact David Shelanskey, Summer Camp Director, main address above. Phone: 908-832-5315. Fax: 908-832-9078. E-mail: dshelanskey@campbernieymca.org.
URL www.campbernieymca.org

YMCA Camp Matollionequay

YMCA Camp Ockanickon, Inc.
1303 Stokes Road
Medford, New Jersey 08055

General Information Girls' residential traditional camp established in 1937. Accredited by American Camping Association. Specific services available for the participant with HIV/AIDS.
Arts Acting, arts and crafts (general), ceramics, chorus, creative writing, dance, dance (modern), drawing, fabric arts, film, music, musical productions, painting, photography, pottery, theater/drama.
Special Interest Areas Campcraft, leadership training, nature study, team building.
Sports Archery, basketball, boating, canoeing, climbing (wall), equestrian sports, field hockey, fishing, horseback riding, kayaking, ropes course, soccer, softball, swimming, tennis, volleyball.
Wilderness/Outdoors Backpacking, canoe trips, hiking, orienteering, wilderness camping.
Trips Overnight.
Program Information 5–10 sessions per year. Session length: 5–28 days in June, July, August. Ages: 7–16.

200–230 participants per session. Boarding program cost: $500–$1400. Application fee: $125. Financial aid available.
Application Deadline Continuous.
Jobs Positions for high school students 17 and older and college students 17 and older.
Contact Mr. Tom Rapine, Associate Executive Director, main address above. Phone: 609-654-8225. Fax: 609-654-8895. E-mail: info@ycamp.org.
URL www.ycamp.org

YMCA Camp Ockanickon

YMCA Camp Ockanickon, Inc.
1303 Stokes Road
Medford, New Jersey 08055

General Information Boys' residential traditional camp established in 1906. Accredited by American Camping Association.
Arts Acting, arts and crafts (general), ceramics, dance, drawing, music, painting, photography, theater/drama.
Special Interest Areas Leadership training, nature study, team building.
Sports Archery, basketball, boating, canoeing, climbing (wall), equestrian sports, fishing, horseback riding, kayaking, ropes course, soccer, swimming, tennis, volleyball.
Wilderness/Outdoors Backpacking, canoe trips, hiking, orienteering, wilderness camping.
Trips Overnight.
Program Information 5–10 sessions per year. Session length: 5–28 days in June, July, August. Ages: 7–16. 150–200 participants per session. Boarding program cost: $500–$1400. Application fee: $125. Financial aid available.
Application Deadline Continuous.
Jobs Positions for high school students 17 and older and college students 17 and older.
Contact Mr. Tom Rapine, Associate Executive Director, main address above. Phone: 609-654-8225. Fax: 609-654-8895. E-mail: info@ycamp.org.
URL www.ycamp.org

YMCA Lake Stockwell

YMCA Camp Ockanickon, Inc.
1303 Stokes Road
Medford, New Jersey 08055

General Information Coed day traditional camp established in 1990. Accredited by American Camping Association.
Arts Arts and crafts (general), ceramics, drawing, painting, theater/drama.
Special Interest Areas Leadership training, nature study.
Sports Archery, basketball, boating, canoeing, climbing (wall), horseback riding, kayaking, ropes course, soccer, swimming, volleyball.
Wilderness/Outdoors Hiking, orienteering, wilderness camping.
Trips Overnight.
Program Information 5–11 sessions per year. Session length: 5–28 days in June, July, August. Ages: 5–15. 200–250 participants per session. Day program cost: $180–$1200. Application fee: $50–$200. Financial aid available.
Application Deadline Continuous.
Jobs Positions for high school students 16 and older and college students 17 and older.
Contact Mr. Tom Rapine, Associate Executive Director, main address above. Phone: 609-654-8225. Fax: 609-654-8895. E-mail: info@ycamp.org.
URL www.ycamp.org

NEW MEXICO

Abilene Christian University–Cross Training

Abilene Christian University
Sipapu Ski and Summer Resort
Sipapu, New Mexico

General Information Coed residential outdoor program, bible camp, and adventure program established in 2002. Religious affiliation: Church of Christ.
Program Focus Youth leadership training.
Academics Bible study.
Arts Arts and crafts (general), music (vocal).
Special Interest Areas Community service, leadership training, team building, worship.
Sports Climbing (wall), frisbee golf, ropes course.
Wilderness/Outdoors Hiking, orienteering, rafting.
Program Information 1 session per year. Session length: 1 week in August. Ages: 13–18. 50 participants per session. Boarding program cost: $395. Financial aid available.
Application Deadline Continuous.
Jobs Positions for college students 19 and older.
Contact Dr. Jan Meyer, Director of Leadership Camps, ACU Box 29004, 129 McKinzie Hall, Abilene, Texas 79699-9004. Phone: 325-674-2033. Fax: 325-674-6475. E-mail: leadership.camps@campuslife.acu.edu.
URL www.acucamps.com

Cottonwood Gulch Family Trek

Cottonwood Gulch Foundation
Thoreau, New Mexico 87323

General Information Coed residential outdoor program, family program, and cultural program established in 1978.
Program Focus Adventure and fun in the Southwest for the whole family.
Academics Anthropology, archaeology, ecology, environmental science, geography, geology/earth science, government and politics, history, intercultural studies, social science, social studies.
Arts Arts, arts and crafts (general), drawing, jewelry making, leather working, painting, photography, pottery, weaving, woodworking.

Cottonwood Gulch Family Trek (continued)

Special Interest Areas Native American culture, campcraft, nature study.
Sports Swimming.
Wilderness/Outdoors Caving, hiking, orienteering, outdoor adventure, wilderness camping.
Trips Cultural, day, overnight, shopping.
Program Information 1 session per year. Session length: 8 days in August. Ages: 5+. 10–25 participants per session. Boarding program cost: $450–$950.
Application Deadline Continuous.
Jobs Positions for college students 21 and older.
Summer Contact Mr. Jeff Zemsky, Executive Director, PO Box 969, Thoreau, New Mexico 87323. Phone: 505-862-7503. Fax: 505-862-7503. E-mail: jeff@cottonwoodgulch.org.
Winter Contact Mr. Seth Battis, Assistant Director, PO Box 3915, Albuquerque, New Mexico 87190-3915. Phone: 800-246-8735. Fax: 505-248-0563. E-mail: seth@cottonwoodgulch.org.
URL www.cottonwoodgulch.org/groups/familytrek/

Cottonwood Gulch Mountain Desert Challenge

Cottonwood Gulch Foundation
Thoreau, New Mexico 87323

General Information Coed travel outdoor program, wilderness program, cultural program, and adventure program established in 1951. Formal opportunities for the academically talented and artistically talented.
Program Focus Wilderness, Native American culture, arts, anthropology and adventure.
Academics Anthropology, archaeology, area studies, art history/appreciation, astronomy, biology, botany, ecology, environmental science, geography, geology/earth science, government and politics, history, intercultural studies, journalism, music, philosophy, science (general), social science, social studies, speech/debate, writing.
Arts Arts, arts and crafts (general), creative writing, drawing, fabric arts, jewelry making, leather working, painting, photography, pottery, weaving, woodworking.
Special Interest Areas Native American culture, campcraft, community service, conservation projects, construction, field research/expeditions, gardening, leadership training, nature study, team building.
Sports Canoeing, rappelling, ropes course, swimming.
Wilderness/Outdoors Backpacking, canoe trips, caving, hiking, mountaineering, orienteering, outdoor adventure, rock climbing, white-water trips, wilderness camping.
Trips Cultural, day, overnight.
Program Information 1–2 sessions per year. Session length: 44 days in June, July, August. Ages: 15–19. 10–14 participants per session. Cost: $3795. Financial aid available.
Application Deadline Continuous.
Jobs Positions for college students 21 and older.
Summer Contact Mr. Jeff Zemsky, Executive Director, PO Box 969, Thoreau, New Mexico 87323. Phone: 505-862-7503. Fax: 505-862-7503. E-mail: jeff@cottonwoodgulch.org.
Winter Contact Mr. Seth Battis, Assistant Director, PO Box 3915, Albuquerque, New Mexico 87190-3815. Phone: 800-246-8735. Fax: 505-248-0563. E-mail: seth@cottonwoodgulch.org.
URL www.cottonwoodgulch.org/groups/mdc/

Cottonwood Gulch Outfit Expedition

Cottonwood Gulch Foundation
Thoreau, New Mexico 87323

General Information Coed residential outdoor program and cultural program established in 1960. Formal opportunities for the academically talented and artistically talented.
Program Focus Camping, adventure, hiking, and fun tailored to 10-13 year old boys and girls.
Academics Anthropology, archaeology, art history/appreciation, astronomy, biology, botany, ecology, environmental science, geography, geology/earth science, government and politics, history, intercultural studies, music, science (general), social science, social studies, writing.
Arts Arts, arts and crafts (general), creative writing, fabric arts, jewelry making, leather working, music, painting, photography, pottery, weaving, woodworking.
Special Interest Areas Native American culture, campcraft, community service, field research/expeditions, gardening, nature study, team building.
Sports Ropes course, swimming.
Wilderness/Outdoors Caving, hiking, orienteering, outdoor adventure, wilderness camping.
Trips Cultural, day, overnight.
Program Information 2 sessions per year. Session length: 13–28 days in June, July. Ages: 10–13. 10–20 participants per session. Boarding program cost: $1225–$2300. Financial aid available.
Application Deadline Continuous.
Jobs Positions for college students 21 and older.
Summer Contact Mr. Jeff Zemsky, Executive Director, PO Box 969, Thoreau, New Mexico 87323. Phone: 505-862-7503. Fax: 505-862-7503. E-mail: jeff@cottonwoodgulch.org.
Winter Contact Mr. Seth Battis, Assistant Director, PO Box 3915, Albuquerque, New Mexico 87190-3915. Phone: 800-246-8735. Fax: 505-248-0563. E-mail: seth@cottonwoodgulch.org.
URL www.cottonwoodgulch.org/groups/outfit/

Cottonwood Gulch Prairie Trek Expedition

Cottonwood Gulch Foundation
Thoreau, New Mexico 87323

General Information Boys' travel outdoor program, community service program, wilderness program, cultural program, and adventure program established in 1926. Formal opportunities for the academically talented and artistically talented.
Program Focus Wilderness, Southwestern history and art, and adventure tailored to 13-15 year old boys.

Academics American literature, anthropology, archaeology, art history/appreciation, astronomy, biology, botany, ecology, environmental science, geography, geology/earth science, government and politics, history, intercultural studies, journalism, music, philosophy, science (general), social science, social studies, writing.
Arts Arts, arts and crafts (general), creative writing, fabric arts, jewelry making, leather working, music, photography, pottery, weaving, woodworking.
Special Interest Areas Native American culture, campcraft, community service, conservation projects, construction, field research/expeditions, gardening, leadership training, nature study, team building.
Sports Canoeing, rappelling, ropes course, swimming.
Wilderness/Outdoors Backpacking, canoe trips, caving, hiking, mountaineering, orienteering, outdoor adventure, rock climbing, white-water trips, wilderness camping.
Trips Cultural, day, overnight.
Program Information 1 session per year. Session length: 36 days in June, July, August. Ages: 13–15. 10–20 participants per session. Cost: $2965. Financial aid available.
Application Deadline Continuous.
Jobs Positions for college students 21 and older.
Summer Contact Mr. Jeff Zemsky, Executive Director, PO Box 969, Thoreau, New Mexico 87323. Phone: 505-862-7503. Fax: 505-862-7503. E-mail: jeff@cottonwoodgulch.org.
Winter Contact Mr. Seth Battis, Assistant Director, PO Box 3915, Albuquerque, New Mexico 87190-3915. Phone: 800-246-8735. Fax: 505-248-0563. E-mail: seth@cottonwoodgulch.org.
URL www.cottonwoodgulch.org/groups/trek/

Cottonwood Gulch Turquoise Trail Expedition

Cottonwood Gulch Foundation
Thoreau, New Mexico 87323

General Information Girls' travel outdoor program, community service program, wilderness program, cultural program, and adventure program established in 1934. Formal opportunities for the academically talented and artistically talented.
Program Focus Wilderness, Native American culture, arts, anthropology, and adventure tailored to 13-15 year old girls.
Academics American literature, anthropology, archaeology, art history/appreciation, astronomy, biology, botany, ecology, environmental science, geography, geology/earth science, government and politics, history, intercultural studies, music, philosophy, science (general), social science, social studies, writing.
Arts Arts, arts and crafts (general), creative writing, drawing, fabric arts, jewelry making, leather working, painting, photography, pottery, weaving, woodworking.
Special Interest Areas Native American culture, campcraft, community service, conservation projects, construction, field research/expeditions, gardening, leadership training, nature study, team building.
Sports Canoeing, rappelling, ropes course, swimming.
Wilderness/Outdoors Backpacking, canoe trips, caving, hiking, mountaineering, orienteering, outdoor adventure, rock climbing, white-water trips, wilderness camping.
Trips Cultural, day, overnight.
Program Information 1 session per year. Session length: 36 days in June, July, August. Ages: 13–15. 10–20 participants per session. Cost: $2965. Financial aid available.
Application Deadline Continuous.
Jobs Positions for college students 21 and older.
Summer Contact Mr. Jeff Zemsky, Executive Director, PO Box 969, Thoreau, New Mexico 87323. Phone: 505-862-7503. Fax: 505-862-7503. E-mail: jeff@cottonwoodgulch.org.
Winter Contact Mr. Seth Battis, Assistant Director, PO Box 3915, Albuquerque, New Mexico 87190-3915. Phone: 800-246-8735. Fax: 505-248-0563. E-mail: seth@cottonwoodgulch.org.
URL www.cottonwoodgulch.org/groups/tt

Cottonwood Gulch Wild Country Trek

Cottonwood Gulch Foundation
Thoreau, New Mexico 87323

General Information Coed travel outdoor program, wilderness program, and adventure program established in 2004.
Program Focus Outdoor adventure and wilderness skills in the Southwest for boys and girls 13-15.
Academics Anthropology, archaeology, area studies, art history/appreciation, astronomy, biology, botany, ecology, environmental science, geography, geology/earth science, history, music, philosophy, science (general), social science, social studies, writing.
Arts Arts and crafts (general), creative writing, fabric arts, jewelry making, leather working, music, painting, photography, pottery, weaving, woodworking.
Special Interest Areas Campcraft, community service, conservation projects, construction, field research/expeditions, gardening, leadership training, nature study, team building.
Wilderness/Outdoors Backpacking, caving, hiking, orienteering, outdoor adventure, rock climbing, wilderness camping.
Trips Cultural, day, overnight.
Program Information 1 session per year. Session length: 13 days in July. Ages: 13–15. 10–14 participants per session. Cost: $1560. Financial aid available.
Application Deadline Continuous.
Jobs Positions for college students 21 and older.
Summer Contact Mr. Jeff Zemsky, Executive Director, PO Box 969, Thoreau, New Mexico 87323. Phone: 505-862-7503. Fax: 505-862-7503. E-mail: jeff@cottonwoodgulch.org.
Winter Contact Mr. Seth Battis, Assistant Director, PO Box 3915, Albuquerque, New Mexico 87190-3915. Phone: 800-246-8735. Fax: 505-248-0563. E-mail: seth@cottonwoodgulch.org.
URL www.cottonwoodgulch.org/groups/wct/

Deer Hill Expeditions, New Mexico

Deer Hill Expeditions
Navajo Nation
New Mexico

General Information Coed residential community service program, wilderness program, and cultural program established in 1984. Accredited by Association for Experiential Education. High school credit may be earned.
Program Focus Wilderness expeditions, community service and cross-cultural living with Native Americans.
Academics Area studies, ecology, environmental science, geology/earth science, intercultural studies.
Arts Photography.
Special Interest Areas Native American culture, community service, conservation projects, cross-cultural education, first aid, leadership training, nature study, trail maintenance.
Sports Canoeing, kayaking, rappelling.
Wilderness/Outdoors Backpacking, canoe trips, canyoneering, climbing, hiking, mountain biking, mountaineering, orienteering, outdoor camping, outdoor living skills, rafting, white-water trips, wilderness camping, wilderness/outdoors (general).
Trips Cultural, overnight.
Program Information 12–16 sessions per year. Session length: 21–36 days in June, July, August. Ages: 15–22. 12–16 participants per session. Boarding program cost: $2750–$4550.
Application Deadline Continuous.
Jobs Positions for college students 21 and older.
Contact Ms. Beverly Capelin, Owner and Director, PO Box 180, Mancos, Colorado 81328. Phone: 800-533-7221. Fax: 970-533-7221. E-mail: info@deerhillexpeditions.com.
URL www.deerhillexpeditions.com

EARTHWATCH INSTITUTE–
Prehistoric Pueblos of the American Southwest

Earthwatch Institute
Rio Alamosa, New Mexico

General Information Coed residential outdoor program and cultural program.
Program Focus Excavating settlements in a cultural borderland to discover the relationships between ancient Pueblo peoples.
Academics Anthropology, archaeology, history, science (general).
Special Interest Areas Field research/expeditions.
Program Information 2 sessions per year. Session length: 1–2 weeks in June, October. Ages: 16+. 12 participants per session. Boarding program cost: $1295–$1795. Financial aid available. Financial aid for high school students and teachers.
Application Deadline Continuous.
Contact General Information Desk, PO Box 75, Maynard, Massachusetts 01754. Phone: 800-776-0188. Fax: 978-461-2332. E-mail: info@earthwatch.org.
URL www.earthwatch.org

The Experiment in International Living–Navajo Nation

The Experiment in International Living
Farmington, New Mexico

General Information Coed residential outdoor program, community service program, cultural program, and adventure program established in 1932.
Program Focus Youth travel, homestay, Navajo culture.
Academics Navajo language, ecology.
Arts Arts and crafts (general), jewelry making.
Special Interest Areas Native American culture, community service, homestays, nature study, touring.
Sports Horseback riding.
Wilderness/Outdoors Backpacking, hiking, white-water trips.
Trips Cultural, day, overnight.
Program Information 1 session per year. Session length: 4 weeks in July, August. Ages: 14–19. 10–15 participants per session. Boarding program cost: $3000. Financial aid available.
Application Deadline May 1.
Contact Annie Thompson, Enrollment Director, Summer Abroad, Kipling Road, PO Box 676, Brattleboro, Vermont 05302-0676. Phone: 800-345-2929. Fax: 802-258-3428. E-mail: eil@worldlearning.org.
URL www.usexperiment.org
For more information, see page 1116.

Landmark Volunteers: New Mexico

Landmark Volunteers, Inc.
New Mexico

General Information Coed residential outdoor program and community service program established in 1992. High school credit may be earned.
Program Focus Opportunity for high school students to earn community service credit while working as a team for two weeks serving Chaco Culture/Salmon Ruins Heritage Park. Similar programs offered through Landmark Volunteers at over 60 locations in 21 states.
Academics Archaeology, environmental science, social science.
Special Interest Areas Native American culture, career exploration, community service, conservation projects, field research/expeditions, nature study.
Wilderness/Outdoors Hiking.
Trips Cultural, day.
Program Information 1 session per year. Session length: 2 weeks in July, August. Ages: 14–18. 10–13 participants per session. Boarding program cost: $875–$925. Financial aid available.
Application Deadline Continuous.
Jobs Positions for college students.
Contact Ann Barrett, Executive Director, PO Box 455, Sheffield, Massachusetts 01257. Phone: 413-229-0255. Fax: 413-229-2050. E-mail: landmark@volunteers.com.
URL www.volunteers.com
For more information, see page 1182.

NEW MEXICO TECH SUMMER MINI-COURSE

New Mexico Institute of Mining and Technology
801 Leroy Place
Socorro, New Mexico 87801

General Information Coed residential academic program. Formal opportunities for the academically talented. College credit may be earned.
Academics Academics (general), biology, chemistry, computer programming, computer science (Advanced Placement), computers, engineering, environmental science, geology/earth science, mathematics, physics, precollege program, psychology, science (general).
Trips Day.
Program Information 2 sessions per year. Session length: 5–6 days in July. Ages: 15–18. 20–50 participants per session. Boarding program cost: $399–$450.
Application Deadline June 1.
Contact Ms. Marcelle England, Assistant Director of Admissions, 801 Leroy Place, Socorro, New Mexico 87801. Phone: 505-835-5424. Fax: 505-835-5989. E-mail: admissions@admin.nmt.edu.
URL www.nmt.edu

OVERLAND: AMERICAN COMMUNITY SERVICE, SOUTHWEST

Overland Travel, Inc.
Santa Fe, New Mexico

General Information Coed travel community service program established in 1985. Accredited by American Camping Association. High school credit may be earned.
Program Focus Community service.
Special Interest Areas Native American culture, community service, conservation projects, construction, leadership training, team building.
Wilderness/Outdoors Hiking.
Trips Cultural, day, overnight.
Program Information 2–4 sessions per year. Session length: 2 weeks in June, July, August. Ages: 15–18. 10–12 participants per session. Cost: $2895.
Application Deadline Continuous.
Jobs Positions for college students 20 and older.
Contact Ms. Brooks Follansbee, Director, PO Box 31, Williamstown, Massachusetts 01267. Phone: 800-458-0588. Fax: 413-458-5208. E-mail: overland@adelphia.net.
URL www.overlandsummers.com

For more information, see page 1240.

STUDENT CONSERVATION ASSOCIATION–CONSERVATION CREW PROGRAM (NEW MEXICO)

Student Conservation Association (SCA)
New Mexico

General Information Coed residential outdoor program, community service program, and wilderness program established in 1957. High school credit may be earned.
Program Focus Resource management, conservation and environmental education.
Academics Biology, botany, ecology, environmental science, geology/earth science, history.
Special Interest Areas Campcraft, community service, construction, leadership training, nature study, trail maintenance, work camp programs.
Sports Canoeing, fishing, kayaking, swimming.
Wilderness/Outdoors Backpacking, canoe trips, hiking, orienteering, outdoor living skills, wilderness camping.
Trips Cultural, day, overnight.
Program Information 2–3 sessions per year. Session length: 3–5 weeks in June, July, August. Ages: 15–19. 6–8 participants per session. Application fee: $20. Financial aid available. No cost for program; financial aid possible for travel expenses.
Application Deadline Continuous.
Jobs Positions for college students 21 and older.
Contact Recruitment Office, PO Box 550, Charlestown, New Hampshire 03603. Phone: 603-543-1700. Fax: 603-543-1828. E-mail: getreal@thesca.org.
URL www.theSCA.org

THE SUMMER SCIENCE PROGRAM–NEW MEXICO CAMPUS

Summer Science Program, Inc.
New Mexico Institute of Technology
Socorro, New Mexico

General Information Coed residential academic program established in 2003. Formal opportunities for the academically talented.
Academics Astronomy, computer programming, mathematics, physics, science (general).
Special Interest Areas Career exploration.
Sports Golf, racquetball, soccer, swimming, tennis.
Wilderness/Outdoors Hiking.
Trips Day.
Program Information 1 session per year. Session length: 41 days in June, July. Ages: 15–18. 30–36 participants per session. Boarding program cost: $3200. Financial aid available.
Application Deadline Continuous.
Jobs Positions for college students 20 and older.
Contact Mr. Richard D. Bowdon, Executive Director, 108 Whiteberry Drive, Cary, North Carolina 27519. Phone: 866-728-0999. Fax: 419-735-2251. E-mail: info@summerscience.org.
URL www.summerscience.org

NEW YORK

Acteen August Academy

Acteen
35 West 45th Street
New York, New York 10036

General Information Coed residential and day arts program established in 1978. Formal opportunities for the artistically talented.

Acteen August Academy

Program Focus Film and television acting, videotape camera work.
Academics Writing.
Arts Acting, audition technique, creative writing, film, music (vocal), musical theater, stage movement, television/video, theater/drama, voice and speech.
Trips Cultural.
Program Information 1 session per year. Session length: 17–18 days in August. Ages: 13–20. 20–30 participants per session. Day program cost: $250–$1950. Boarding program cost: $800–$2400. Application fee: $25.
Application Deadline Continuous.
Contact Rita Litton, Acteen Director, main address above. Phone: 212-391-5915. Fax: 212-768-8918. E-mail: rita@acteen.com.
URL www.acteen.com

For more information, see page 962.

Acteen July Academy

Acteen
35 West 45th Street
New York, New York 10036

General Information Coed residential and day arts program established in 1978. Formal opportunities for the artistically talented.
Program Focus Film and television acting.
Academics Writing.
Arts Acting, directing, film, music (vocal), musical theater, playwriting, screenwriting, stage movement, television/video, theater/drama, voice and speech.
Trips Cultural.
Program Information 1 session per year. Session length: 4 weeks in July. Ages: 13–20. 40–60 participants per session. Day program cost: $300–$2350. Boarding program cost: $800–$3000. Application fee: $25.
Application Deadline Continuous.
Contact Rita Litton, Acteen Director, main address above. Phone: 212-391-5915. Fax: 212-768-8918. E-mail: rita@acteen.com.
URL www.acteen.com

For more information, see page 962.

Acteen June Academy

Acteen
35 West 45th Street
New York, New York 10036

General Information Coed residential arts program established in 2004. Formal opportunities for the artistically talented.
Program Focus Film and television acting, videotape camera work.
Arts Acting, audition technique, film, mime, stage movement, television/video, theater/drama, voice and speech.
Program Information 1 session per year. Session length: 9 days in June. Ages: 13–20. 12–24 participants per session. Day program cost: $1200–$1300. Boarding program cost: $1500–$2100. Application fee: $25. Financial aid available.
Application Deadline Continuous.
Contact Rita Litton, Director, main address above. Phone: 212-391-5915. Fax: 212-768-8918. E-mail: rita@acteen.com.
URL www.acteen.com

For more information, see page 962.

Acteen Summer Saturday Academy

Acteen
35 West 45th Street
New York, New York 10036

General Information Coed day arts program established in 1978. Formal opportunities for the artistically talented.
Program Focus Film and television acting.
Arts Acting, audition technique, film, television/video, theater/drama, voice and speech.
Program Information 1 session per year. Session length: 6 days in July, August. Ages: 13–20. 30–50 participants per session. Day program cost: $275–$1075. Application fee: $25.
Application Deadline Continuous.
Contact Rita Litton, Acteen Director, main address above. Phone: 212-391-5915. Fax: 212-768-8918. E-mail: rita@acteen.com.
URL www.acteen.com

For more information, see page 962.

Adirondack Alpine Adventures

Alpine Adventures, Inc.
10873 Route 9 North
Keene, New York 12942

General Information Coed day outdoor program and wilderness program established in 1985.
Program Focus Development of technical skills as well as experience in adventure rock climbing, ice climbing, and mountaineering.
Wilderness/Outdoors Hiking, ice climbing, mountaineering, rock climbing.
Trips Day, overnight.
Program Information 70–120 sessions per year. Session length: 2–5 days in January, February, March, April, May, June, July, August, September, October, December. Ages: 14–80. 2–6 participants per session. Day program cost: $379–$999.
Application Deadline Continuous.
Contact Mr. R. L. Stolz, President, PO Box 179, 10873 Route 9 North, Keene, New York 12942. Phone: 518-576-9881. E-mail: mail@alpineadven.com.
URL www.alpineadven.com

Adirondack Camp

Warrick Road
Putnam Station, New York 12861-0097

General Information Coed residential traditional camp established in 1904.

Adirondack Camp

Arts Arts and crafts (general), ceramics, drawing, fabric arts, jewelry making, music (vocal), painting, pottery, puppetry, sculpture, theater/drama, woodworking.
Special Interest Areas Native American culture, animal care, campcraft, culinary arts, leadership training, nature study.
Sports Aerobics, archery, baseball, basketball, boating, canoeing, climbing (wall), fencing, fishing, frisbee, golf, in-line skating, kayaking, lacrosse, rappelling, ropes course, rowing (crew/sculling), sailing, scuba diving, sea kayaking, snorkeling, soccer, softball, street/roller hockey, swimming, tennis, volleyball, waterskiing, windsurfing.
Wilderness/Outdoors Backpacking, bicycle trips, canoe trips, hiking, mountain biking, mountaineering, orienteering, rafting, rock climbing, white-water trips, wilderness camping.
Trips Day, overnight.
Program Information 4 sessions per year. Session length: 2–8 weeks in June, July, August. Ages: 7–16. 160–175 participants per session. Boarding program cost: $2350–$6000. Financial aid available.
Application Deadline Continuous.
Jobs Positions for high school students 17 and older and college students 18 and older.
Contact Matt Basinet, Director, PO Box 97, Putnam Station, New York 12861. Phone: 518-547-8261. Fax: 518-547-8973. E-mail: matt@adirondackcamp.com.
URL www.adirondackcamp.com

For more information, see page 966.

Alfred University Summer Institute in Astronomy

Alfred University
Saxon Drive
Alfred, New York 14802-1215

General Information Coed residential academic program established in 1998. Formal opportunities for the academically talented.
Program Focus Astronomy.
Academics Astronomy.
Program Information 1–2 sessions per year. Session length: 5–6 days in June, July. Ages: 15–17. 25–30 participants per session. Boarding program cost: $500–$600.
Application Deadline May 23.
Jobs Positions for college students 19 and older.
Contact Ms. Melody McLay, Director of Summer Programs, Alumni Hall, Saxon Drive, Alfred, New York 14802-1205. Phone: 607-871-2612. Fax: 607-871-2045. E-mail: summerpro@alfred.edu.
URL www.alfred.edu/summer/html/astronomy.html

For more information, see page 978.

Alfred University Summer Institute in Entrepreneurial Leadership

Alfred University
Saxon Drive
Alfred, New York 14802-1215

General Information Coed residential academic program established in 1998. Formal opportunities for the academically talented.
Program Focus Business/leadership training.
Academics Business, marketing.
Special Interest Areas Leadership training.
Program Information 1 session per year. Session length: 5 days in June, July. Ages: 15–17. 20–30 participants per session. Boarding program cost: $500–$600.
Application Deadline May 23.
Jobs Positions for college students 19 and older.

Alfred University Summer Institute in Entrepreneurial Leadership (continued)

Contact Ms. Melody McLay, Director of Summer Programs, Alumni Hall, Saxon Drive, Alfred, New York 14802-1205. Phone: 607-871-2612. Fax: 607-871-2045. E-mail: summerpro@alfred.edu.
URL www.alfred.edu/summer/html/entrepreneurial.html
For more information, see page 978.

Alfred University Summer Institute in Writing

Alfred University
Saxon Drive
Alfred, New York 14802

General Information Coed residential academic program established in 2000. Formal opportunities for the academically talented.

Alfred University Summer Institute in Writing

Program Focus Creative writing.
Academics Writing.
Arts Creative writing.
Program Information 1–3 sessions per year. Session length: 5–6 days in July. Ages: 15–17. 25–30 participants per session. Boarding program cost: $500–$600.
Application Deadline May 23.
Jobs Positions for college students 19 and older.
Contact Ms. Melody McLay, Director of Summer Programs, Alumni Hall, Saxon Drive, Alfred, New York 14802-1205. Phone: 607-871-2612. E-mail: summerpro@alfred.edu.
URL www.alfred.edu/summer
For more information, see page 978.

American Academy of Dramatic Arts Summer Program at New York

American Academy of Dramatic Arts
120 Madison Avenue
New York, New York 10016

General Information Coed day arts program established in 1884. Formal opportunities for the artistically talented.

American Academy of Dramatic Arts Summer Program at New York

Program Focus Acting.
Arts Acting, dance, music (vocal), musical productions, stage movement, television/video, theater/drama, vocal production, voice and speech.
Program Information 1 session per year. Session length: 24–30 days in July, August. Ages: 14+. 100–170 participants per session. Day program cost: $1900–$2000. Application fee: $50. Each elective costs $90; admission by audition only.
Application Deadline Continuous.
Contact Ms. Karen Higginbotham, Director of Admissions, main address above. Phone: 800-463-8990. Fax: 212-685-8093. E-mail: admissions-ny@aada.org.
URL www.aada.org
For more information, see page 980.

Applejack Teen Camp

Camp Regis, Inc.
Paul Smiths, New York 12970

General Information Coed residential traditional camp established in 1946. Religious affiliation: Friends United Meeting. Accredited by American Camping Association.
Program Focus Waterfront activities, sports, and wilderness experiences.
Academics English as a second language.
Arts Arts and crafts (general), band, batiking, ceramics, chorus, creative writing, dance, dance (folk), dance (jazz), dance (modern), drawing, jewelry making, leather working, music, music (classical), music (instrumental), music (vocal), musical productions, painting, photography, pottery, sculpture, theater/drama, weaving, woodworking.
Special Interest Areas Native American culture, animal care, campcraft, community service, field trips (arts and culture), leadership training, nature study, touring.
Sports Aerobics, archery, basketball, boating, canoeing, cross-country, diving, equestrian sports, field hockey, fishing, football, golf, gymnastics, horseback riding, kayaking, lacrosse, sailing, snorkeling, soccer, softball, street/roller hockey, swimming, tennis, track and field, volleyball, water polo, waterskiing, windsurfing.
Wilderness/Outdoors Backpacking, bicycle trips, canoe trips, hiking, mountain biking, mountaineering, orienteering, rafting, wilderness camping.
Trips Cultural, day, overnight.
Program Information 3 sessions per year. Session length: 4–8 weeks in June, July, August. Ages: 13–17. 280 participants per session. Boarding program cost: $2800–$5100. Financial aid available. Deposit of $600 required. Applications accepted during winter and spring.
Application Deadline Continuous.
Jobs Positions for college students 19 and older.
Summer Contact Michael P. Humes, Director, PO Box 245, Paul Smiths, New York 12970. Phone: 518-327-3117. Fax: 518-327-3193. E-mail: campregis@aol.com.
Winter Contact Michael P. Humes, Director, 60 Lafayette Road West, Princeton, New Jersey 08540-2428. Phone: 609-688-0368. Fax: 609-688-0369. E-mail: campregis@aol.com.
URL www.campregis-applejack.com
For more information, see page 1036.

Barnard's Summer in New York City: A Pre-College Program

Barnard College/Columbia University
3009 Broadway
112 Hewitt Hall
New York, New York 10027-6598

General Information Coed residential and day academic program established in 1985. Formal opportunities for the academically talented. Specific services available for the learning disabled. High school credit may be earned.
Program Focus Exploring New York City.

Barnard's Summer in New York City: A Pre-College Program

Academics American literature, English language/literature, architecture, art history/appreciation, environmental science, history, humanities, intercultural studies, philosophy, precollege program, psychology, religion, social science, writing.
Arts Acting, creative writing, dance, dance (ballet), dance (modern), film, theater/drama.
Special Interest Areas Career exploration, community service, field trips (arts and culture), leadership training.
Trips Cultural, day.
Program Information 1–3 sessions per year. Session length: 6–35 days in June, July. Ages: 14–18. 40–170 participants per session. Day program cost: $900–$2400. Boarding program cost: $1200–$3600. Application fee: $35–$65. Financial aid available.
Application Deadline May 1.
Jobs Positions for college students.
Contact Dr. Bari Meltzer, Director of Pre-College Programs, Barnard College, 3009 Broadway, New York, New York 10023. Phone: 212-854-8866. Fax: 212-854-8867. E-mail: pcp@barnard.edu.
URL www.barnard.edu/pcp
For more information, see page 990.

Barnard's Summer in New York City: One-Week Mini-Course

Barnard College/Columbia University
New York, New York 10027

General Information Coed residential and day academic program established in 1985. Formal opportunities for the academically talented. Specific services available for the learning disabled. High school credit may be earned.
Program Focus Exploring New York City.
Academics American literature, English language/literature, academics (general), architecture, art history/appreciation, history, humanities, intercultural studies, precollege program, psychology, social science, writing.
Special Interest Areas Career exploration, field trips (arts and culture), leadership training.
Trips Cultural, day.

Barnard's Summer in New York City: One-Week Mini-Course (continued)

Program Information 1 session per year. Session length: 1 week in June. Ages: 14–18. 42–52 participants per session. Day program cost: $900. Boarding program cost: $1500. Application fee: $35–$65. Financial aid available.
Application Deadline May 1.
Jobs Positions for college students.
Contact Dr. Bari Meltzer, Director of Pre-College Programs, main address above. Phone: 212-854-8866. Fax: 212-854-8867. E-mail: pcp@barnard.edu.
URL www.barnard.edu/pcp

For more information, see page 990.

Barnard's Summer in New York City: Young Women's Leadership Institute

Barnard College/Columbia University
3009 Broadway
New York, New York 10027

General Information Girls' residential academic program established in 2003. Formal opportunities for the academically talented. Specific services available for the learning disabled. High school credit may be earned.
Program Focus Leadership training.
Academics Academics (general), area studies, humanities, intercultural studies, precollege program, social science, social studies, speech/debate, writing.
Special Interest Areas Career exploration, community service, field research/expeditions, field trips (arts and culture), leadership training.
Trips Cultural, day.
Program Information 1 session per year. Session length: 1 week in July. Ages: 14–18. 35–40 participants per session. Boarding program cost: $1200. Application fee: $35–$65. Financial aid available.
Application Deadline May 1.
Contact Dr. Bari Meltzer, Director of Pre-College Programs, main address above. Phone: 212-854-8866. Fax: 212-854-8867. E-mail: pcp@barnard.edu.
URL www.barnard.edu/pcp

For more information, see page 990.

Barton Day Camp–Long Island

The Barton Center for Diabetes Education, Inc.
Henry Kaufman Campground
Wheatley Heights, New York

General Information Coed day traditional camp and special needs program established in 2002. Accredited by American Camping Association. Specific services available for the diabetic.
Program Focus Children with diabetes.
Arts Arts and crafts (general), drawing, sing-a-longs, theater/drama.
Special Interest Areas Culinary arts, diabetic education.
Sports Aerobics, baseball, basketball, cheerleading, soccer, softball, street/roller hockey, swimming, tennis, volleyball.
Trips Day.
Program Information 1 session per year. Session length: 10 days in July, August. Ages: 6–12. 25 participants per session. Day program cost: $1000. Application fee: $25. Financial aid available. Transportation additional.
Application Deadline Continuous.
Jobs Positions for high school students 16 and older and college students.
Contact Ms. Kerry Packard, Program Coordinator, PO Box 356, 30 Ennis Road, North Oxford, Massachusetts 01537. Phone: 508-987-3856. Fax: 508-987-2002. E-mail: kerry.packard@bartoncenter.org.
URL www.bartoncenter.org

Barton Day Camp–New York

The Barton Center for Diabetes Education, Inc.
Central Park
New York, New York

General Information Coed day traditional camp and special needs program established in 2000. Accredited by American Camping Association. Specific services available for the diabetic.
Program Focus Children with diabetes.
Arts Arts and crafts (general), dance, dance (ballet), dance (folk), dance (jazz), dance (modern), dance (tap), drawing, jewelry making, painting, sing-a-longs.
Special Interest Areas Diabetic education.
Sports Aerobics, archery, boating, canoeing, field hockey, fishing, soccer, softball, swimming, volleyball.
Wilderness/Outdoors Hiking, rock climbing.
Trips Day.
Program Information 1 session per year. Session length: 5 days in August. Ages: 6–12. 25–30 participants per session. Day program cost: $500. Application fee: $25.
Application Deadline Continuous.
Jobs Positions for high school students 18 and older and college students 18 and older.
Contact Kerry Packard, Program Coordinator, PO Box 356, 30 Ennis Road, North Oxford, Massachusetts 01537. Phone: 508-987-2056. Fax: 508-987-2002. E-mail: kerry.packard@bartoncenter.org.
URL www.bartoncenter.org

Beekman School Summer Session

The Beekman School
220 East 50th Street
New York, New York 10022

General Information Coed day academic program established in 1980. Formal opportunities for the academically talented. Specific services available for the learning disabled. High school credit may be earned.
Program Focus Accelerated or repeated course work and academic enrichment.
Academics American literature, English as a second language, English language/literature, French (Advanced Placement), French language/literature, SAT/ACT preparation, Spanish (Advanced Placement), Spanish language/literature, academics (general), astronomy, biology, chemistry, computers, ecology, economics,

environmental science, government and politics, government and politics (Advanced Placement), health sciences, history, mathematics, mathematics (Advanced Placement), physics, reading, science (general), social studies, study skills, writing.
Program Information 1–2 sessions per year. Session length: 16–32 days in June, July, August. Ages: 13–19. 40–80 participants per session. Day program cost: $1400–$5200. Cost: $1400 per course.
Application Deadline June 30.
Contact George Higgins, Headmaster, main address above. Phone: 212-755-6666. Fax: 212-888-6085. E-mail: georgeh@beekmanschool.org.
URL www.beekmanschool.org

Brant Lake Camp's Dance Centre

Brant Lake Camp
7586 State Route 8
Brant Lake, New York 12815

General Information Girls' residential arts program established in 1980. Accredited by American Camping Association.

Brant Lake Camp's Dance Centre

Program Focus Professional dance classes in a camp environment.
Arts Arts and crafts (general), ceramics, dance, dance (ballet), dance (jazz), dance (modern), dance (tap), drawing, jewelry making, leather working, music (vocal), painting, photography, pottery, printmaking, television/video, theater/drama, weaving, woodworking.
Sports Aerobics, bicycling, boating, canoeing, climbing (wall), golf, ropes course, sailing, swimming, tennis, volleyball, waterskiing, weight training.
Wilderness/Outdoors Bicycle trips, canoe trips, hiking.
Trips Cultural, day, overnight.
Program Information 2 sessions per year. Session length: 21–43 days in June, July, August. Ages: 12–16. 45–60 participants per session. Boarding program cost: $3500–$6000.
Application Deadline Continuous.
Jobs Positions for college students 19 and older.
Contact Ms. Kirstin Been Spielman, Director, main address above. Phone: 518-494-2406. Fax: 518-494-7372. E-mail: brantlakec@aol.com.
URL www.blcdance.com

For more information, see page 1000.

Bristol Hills Music Camp

Bristol Hills Music Camp, Inc.
Ontario County 4H Camp
Kear Road
Canandaigua, New York 14424

General Information Coed residential arts program established in 1962. Formal opportunities for the artistically talented.
Program Focus Music study and performance; private music lessons.
Academics Music.
Arts Band, chorus, music, music (chamber), music (classical), music (ensemble), music (instrumental), music (jazz), music (orchestral), music (vocal).
Sports Basketball, soccer, swimming, volleyball.
Program Information 1 session per year. Session length: 1 week in August. Ages: 10–18. 135–165 participants per session. Boarding program cost: $420.
Application Deadline Continuous.
Jobs Positions for college students 18 and older.
Contact Irene Hebert, Registrar, 4304 Hepatica Hill Road, Manlius, New York 13104. Phone: 315-682-6786. E-mail: rhebert694@earthlink.net.
URL www.bristolhillsmusiccamp.com

Camp Chateaugay

233 Gadway Road
Merrill, New York 12955

General Information Coed residential traditional camp established in 1946. Accredited by American Camping Association.
Program Focus Water and land sports, arts and crafts, wilderness activities, and theater.
Arts Arts and crafts (general), batiking, ceramics, dance, dance (jazz), dance (modern), drawing, fabric arts, jewelry making, leather working, musical productions, painting, photography, pottery, printmaking, sculpture, theater/drama, woodworking.
Special Interest Areas Animal care, campcraft, model rocketry, nature study.
Sports Aerobics, archery, baseball, basketball, bicycling, boating, canoeing, climbing (wall), diving, equestrian sports, figure skating, fishing, football, golf, gymnastics, horseback riding, in-line skating, kayaking, lacrosse, martial arts, ropes course, rowing (crew/sculling), sailing, skiing (downhill), soccer, softball, sports (general), swimming, tennis, volleyball, water polo, waterskiing, weight training, windsurfing.
Wilderness/Outdoors Backpacking, bicycle trips, canoe trips, hiking, mountain biking, rafting, rock climbing, white-water trips, wilderness camping.
Trips Overnight.

Camp Chateaugay (continued)

Program Information 2 sessions per year. Session length: 25–49 days in July, August. Ages: 6–15. 230–250 participants per session. Boarding program cost: $3950–$6300.
Application Deadline Continuous.
Jobs Positions for college students 19 and older.
Summer Contact Hal Lyons, Owner/Director, main address above. Phone: 518-425-6888. Fax: 518-425-3487.
Winter Contact Hal Lyons, Director, 34 Old Roxbury Road, Roxbury, Connecticut 06783. Phone: 800-431-1184. Fax: 860-350-8809. E-mail: chateaugay@aol.com.
URL www.chateaugay.com

Camp Dudley

Camp Dudley
126 Dudley Road
Westport, New York 12993-9711

General Information Boys' residential traditional camp established in 1885. Religious affiliation: Christian. Accredited by American Camping Association.

Camp Dudley

Program Focus Provides boys with activities meant to engender leadership, social skills, and spiritual development.
Arts Arts and crafts (general), band, ceramics, chorus, creative writing, drawing, fabric arts, music, music (ensemble), music (instrumental), music (jazz), music (vocal), musical productions, painting, photography, pottery, printmaking, sculpture, television/video, theater/drama, woodworking.
Special Interest Areas Campcraft, community service, gardening, leadership training, nature study.
Sports Archery, baseball, basketball, boating, canoeing, climbing (wall), cross-country, fishing, football, golf, kayaking, lacrosse, rappelling, riflery, ropes course, rowing (crew/sculling), sailing, snorkeling, soccer, softball, sports (general), swimming, tennis, track and field, volleyball, water polo.
Wilderness/Outdoors Backpacking, canoe trips, hiking, outdoor camping, rock climbing.
Trips Day, overnight.
Program Information 2 sessions per year. Session length: 4 weeks in June, July, August. 350 participants per session. Boarding program cost: $3500–$6000. Financial aid available. Ages 10½–16.
Application Deadline February 1.
Jobs Positions for high school students 17 and older and college students 18 and older.
Contact Andy Bisselle, Director, main address above. Phone: 518-962-4720. Fax: 518-962-4320. E-mail: andy@campdudley.org.
URL www.campdudley.org

For more information, see page 1026.

Camp Echo in Coleman High Country

Coleman Family Camps
Burlingham, New York 12722

General Information Coed residential traditional camp established in 1924. Accredited by American Camping Association.
Academics Hebrew language, ecology, environmental science, geology/earth science.
Arts Acting, arts and crafts (general), batiking, ceramics, chorus, creative writing, dance, dance (ballet), dance (jazz), dance (modern), drawing, fabric arts, film, jewelry making, leather working, music, music (instrumental), music (vocal), musical productions, painting, photography, pottery, sculpture, television/video, theater/drama, woodworking.
Special Interest Areas Animal care, campcraft, community service, culinary arts, electronics, leadership training, model rocketry, nature study, robotics, team building, touring.
Sports Archery, baseball, basketball, bicycling, boating, canoeing, climbing (wall), diving, equestrian sports, fishing, golf, gymnastics, horseback riding, in-line skating, kayaking, lacrosse, martial arts, rappelling, ropes course, soccer, softball, sports (general), street/roller hockey, swimming, tennis, track and field, volleyball, water polo, weight training.
Wilderness/Outdoors Canoe trips, hiking, mountain biking, orienteering, outdoor adventure, rafting, rock climbing, white-water trips.
Trips College tours, day, overnight.
Program Information 1–2 sessions per year. Session length: 26–53 days in June, July, August. Ages: 7–17. 320–350 participants per session. Boarding program cost: $4100–$7200. Financial aid available.
Application Deadline Continuous.
Jobs Positions for college students 18 and older.
Summer Contact Ms. Jessica Pearson, Assistant Director, 210 Echo Road, PO Box 105, Burlingham, New York 12722. Phone: 516-620-4301. Fax: 516-620-4330. E-mail: jessica@campecho.com.
Winter Contact Ms. Jessica Pearson, Assistant Director, PO Box 34, Merrick, New York 11566. Phone: 516-620-4300. Fax: 516-620-4329. E-mail: jessica@campecho.com.
URL colemanfamilycamps.com/highcountry

Camp Greenkill–Conservation/ Adventure

YMCA Camping Services of Greater New York
300 Big Pond Road
Huguenot, New York 12746

General Information Coed residential outdoor program established in 1972. Accredited by American Camping Association.
Program Focus Specialty program focusing on conservation/adventure.
Academics Archaeology, astronomy, biology, botany, ecology, environmental science, geography, geology/earth science, science (general).
Arts Arts and crafts (general), jewelry making, photography.
Special Interest Areas Native American culture, campcraft, conservation projects, gardening, leadership training, nature study, team building.
Sports Archery, basketball, boating, canoeing, climbing (wall), fishing, horseback riding, kayaking, ropes course, soccer, softball, swimming, tennis, volleyball.
Wilderness/Outdoors Backpacking, canoe trips, hiking, mountaineering, orienteering, outdoor adventure, rafting, rock climbing, survival training, white-water trips, wilderness camping.
Trips Day, overnight.
Program Information 6 sessions per year. Session length: 6 days in June, July, August. Ages: 10–16. 40 participants per session. Boarding program cost: $495. Financial aid available.
Application Deadline Continuous.
Jobs Positions for high school students 17 and older and college students 18 and older.
Contact Chris Scheuer, Director of Camping, PO Box B, 300 Big Pond Road, Huguenot, New York 12746. Phone: 845-858-2200. Fax: 845-858-7823. E-mail: camps@ymcanyc.org.
URL www.ymcanyc.org/camps

Camp Greenkill–Gymnastics

YMCA Camping Services of Greater New York
300 Big Pond Road
Huguenot, New York 12746

General Information Girls' residential sports camp established in 1972. Accredited by American Camping Association.
Program Focus Specialty program focusing on gymnastics.
Arts Arts and crafts (general).
Sports Boating, canoeing, gymnastics, swimming.
Program Information 2 sessions per year. Session length: 6 days in June, July. Ages: 9–17. 80–100 participants per session. Boarding program cost: $510. Financial aid available.
Application Deadline Continuous.
Jobs Positions for high school students 17 and older and college students 18 and older.
Contact Chris Scheuer, Director of Camping, PO Box B, 300 Big Pond Road, Huguenot, New York 12746. Phone: 845-858-2200. Fax: 845-858-7823. E-mail: camps@ymcanyc.org.
URL www.ymcanyc.org/camps

Camp Greenkill–Judo

YMCA Camping Services of Greater New York
300 Big Pond Road
Huguenot, New York 12746

General Information Coed residential sports camp established in 1972. Accredited by American Camping Association.
Program Focus Specialty program focusing on judo.
Arts Arts and crafts (general).
Sports Boating, canoeing, martial arts, swimming.
Program Information 1 session per year. Session length: 6 days in August. Ages: 6+. 50–150 participants per session. Boarding program cost: $495. Financial aid available.
Application Deadline Continuous.
Jobs Positions for college students 18 and older.
Contact Chris Scheuer, Director of Camping, PO Box B, 300 Big Pond Road, Huguenot, New York 12746. Phone: 845-858-2200. Fax: 845-858-7823. E-mail: camps@ymcanyc.org.
URL www.ymcanyc.org/camps

Camp Greenkill–Volleyball

YMCA Camping Services of Greater New York
300 Big Pond Road
Huguenot, New York 12746

General Information Girls' residential sports camp established in 1972. Accredited by American Camping Association.
Program Focus Specialty program focusing on volleyball.
Sports Boating, canoeing, swimming, volleyball.
Trips Day, shopping.
Program Information 5 sessions per year. Session length: 6 days in July, August. Ages: 12+. 80–145 participants per session. Boarding program cost: $505. Financial aid available.
Application Deadline Continuous.
Jobs Positions for college students 18 and older.
Contact Chris Scheuer, Director of Camping, PO Box B, 300 Big Pond Road, Huguenot, New York 12746. Phone: 845-858-2200. Fax: 845-858-7823. E-mail: camps@ymcanyc.org.
URL www.ymcanyc.org/camps

Camp Hilltop

7825 County Highway 67
Hancock, New York 13783

General Information Coed residential traditional camp established in 1924. Accredited by American Camping Association.
Program Focus Family values-oriented traditional camping.
Academics Computers.
Arts Arts and crafts (general), batiking, ceramics, clowning, dance, dance (jazz), drawing, fabric arts, jewelry making, leather working, metalworking, mime, music, music (instrumental), painting, photography, pottery, printmaking, puppetry, theater/drama, weaving, woodworking.

Camp Hilltop (continued)

Special Interest Areas Animal care, campcraft, farming, model rocketry, nature study.
Sports Aerobics, archery, baseball, basketball, bicycling, boating, canoeing, climbing (wall), equestrian sports, field hockey, fishing, golf, gymnastics, horseback riding, lacrosse, riflery, ropes course, sailing, snorkeling, soccer, softball, swimming, tennis, volleyball, waterskiing, windsurfing.
Wilderness/Outdoors Bicycle trips, canoe trips, hiking, mountain biking, orienteering, rafting.
Trips Day, overnight.
Program Information 10 sessions per year. Session length: 2–8 weeks in June, July, August. Ages: 6–15. 230 participants per session. Boarding program cost: $1625–$5600. Financial aid available.
Application Deadline Continuous.
Jobs Positions for college students 19 and older.
Contact Bill Young, Owner/Director, main address above. Phone: 607-637-5201. Fax: 607-637-2389. E-mail: hilltop@hancock.net.
URL www.camphilltop.com

Camp Kennybrook

Camp Kennybrook, Inc.
Camp Road
Monticello, New York 12701

General Information Coed residential traditional camp established in 1947. Accredited by American Camping Association.
Arts Acting, arts and crafts (general), ceramics, dance, drawing, fabric arts, jewelry making, music, musical productions, painting, photography, pottery, printmaking, sculpture, theater/drama, woodworking.
Special Interest Areas Culinary arts, model rocketry.
Sports Aerobics, archery, baseball, basketball, bicycling (BMX), boating, canoeing, cheerleading, climbing (wall), equestrian sports, field hockey, fishing, football, golf, gymnastics, horseback riding, in-line skating, kayaking, lacrosse, martial arts, ropes course, scuba diving, soccer, softball, street/roller hockey, swimming, tennis, track and field, volleyball, waterskiing, weight training.
Wilderness/Outdoors Backpacking, canoe trips, hiking, mountain biking, rafting.
Trips College tours, day, overnight.
Program Information 1 session per year. Session length: 28–54 days in June, July, August. Ages: 8–15. 300 participants per session. Boarding program cost: $6200–$7300.
Application Deadline Continuous.
Jobs Positions for college students 18 and older.
Summer Contact Howard Landman, Owner/Director, main address above. Phone: 845-794-5320. Fax: 845-791-4738. E-mail: kennybrook@aol.com.
Winter Contact Howard Landman, Owner/Director, 633 Saw Mill River Road, Ardsley, New York 10502. Phone: 914-693-3037. Fax: 914-693-7678. E-mail: kennybrook@aol.com.
URL www.kennybrook.com

Camp Lakeland

Jewish Community Center of Greater Buffalo
3510 Bear Creek Road
Franklinville, New York 14737

General Information Coed residential traditional camp established in 1910. Religious affiliation: Jewish. Accredited by American Camping Association.
Academics Hebrew language, Jewish studies, art (Advanced Placement), computers, ecology, music.
Arts Arts and crafts (general), batiking, ceramics, dance, drawing, fabric arts, film, jewelry making, leather working, music, music (instrumental), musical productions, painting, photography, pottery, puppetry, radio broadcasting, television/video, theater/drama, woodworking.
Special Interest Areas Animal care, campcraft, gardening, leadership training.
Sports Baseball, basketball, bicycling, boating, canoeing, climbing (wall), equestrian sports, fishing, football, golf, horseback riding, in-line skating, kayaking, ropes course, sailing, soccer, softball, street/roller hockey, swimming, tennis, track and field, volleyball, water polo, waterskiing, windsurfing.
Wilderness/Outdoors Backpacking, bicycle trips, canoe trips, hiking, mountain biking, orienteering, rafting, white-water trips.
Trips Day, overnight.
Program Information 2–6 sessions per year. Session length: 7–50 days in June, July, August. Ages: 7–16. 200–250 participants per session. Boarding program cost: $729–$4269. Financial aid available.
Application Deadline Continuous.
Jobs Positions for high school students 17 and older and college students 17 and older.
Contact David Miller, Director, 787 Delaware Avenue, Buffalo, New York 14209. Phone: 716-886-3145. Fax: 716-961-0863. E-mail: summer@camplakeland.com.
URL www.camplakeland.com

Camp McAlister

YMCA Camping Services of Greater New York
300 Big Pond Road
Huguenot, New York 12746

General Information Coed residential traditional camp established in 1946. Accredited by American Camping Association.
Academics Botany, ecology.
Arts Arts and crafts (general), ceramics, drawing, jewelry making, leather working, painting, photography, pottery, woodworking.
Special Interest Areas Animal care, campcraft, farming, gardening, nature study, team building.
Sports Archery, basketball, boating, canoeing, climbing (wall), fishing, football, horseback riding, lacrosse, ropes course, soccer, softball, swimming, volleyball.
Wilderness/Outdoors Hiking, orienteering.
Trips Day, overnight.
Program Information 4 sessions per year. Session length: 13 days in June, July, August. Ages: 6–11. 140–160 participants per session. Boarding program cost: $415–$830. Financial aid available. Mainstreaming program for special needs is offered.

Application Deadline Continuous.
Jobs Positions for high school students 17 and older and college students 18 and older.
Contact Chris Scheuer, Director of Camping, PO Box B, 300 Big Pond Road, Huguenot, New York 12746. Phone: 845-858-2200. Fax: 845-858-7823. E-mail: camps@ymcanyc.org.
URL www.ymcanyc.org/camps

Camp Monroe

Monroe, New York 10950

General Information Coed residential traditional camp established in 1941. Religious affiliation: Jewish. Accredited by American Camping Association.
Program Focus Help to build positive character traits and self-esteem.
Arts Arts and crafts (general), ceramics, dance, drawing, fabric arts, jewelry making, leather working, metalworking, music, musical productions, painting, photography, pottery, radio broadcasting, theater/drama.
Special Interest Areas Animal care, model rocketry, nature study.
Sports Aerobics, archery, basketball, boating, canoeing, equestrian sports, fishing, golf, gymnastics, horseback riding, kayaking, martial arts, miniature golf, ropes course, soccer, softball, street/roller hockey, swimming, tennis, volleyball, waterskiing.
Wilderness/Outdoors Canoe trips, orienteering.
Trips Cultural, day, overnight.
Program Information 2 sessions per year. Session length: 4 weeks in July, August. Ages: 6–16. 350 participants per session. Boarding program cost: $3500–$5900.
Application Deadline Continuous.
Jobs Positions for college students.
Contact Stanley Felsinger, Director, PO Box 475, Monroe, New York 10950. Phone: 845-782-8695. Fax: 845-782-2247.

Camp Pok-O-MacCready

112 Reber Road, North
Willsboro, New York 12996

General Information Coed residential traditional camp established in 1905. Accredited by American Camping Association.
Academics English as a second language, tutoring.
Arts Acting, arts and crafts (general), blacksmithing, ceramics, creative writing, drawing, metalworking, music, musical productions, painting, photography, pottery, puppetry, sculpture, theater/drama, weaving, woodworking.
Special Interest Areas Native American culture, animal care, campcraft, construction, farming, gardening, general camp activities, leadership training, nature study, team building.
Sports Archery, baseball, basketball, bicycling, bicycling (BMX), boating, canoeing, climbing (wall), cross-country, diving, equestrian sports, fishing, football, gymnastics, horseback riding, in-line skating, kayaking, lacrosse, martial arts, rappelling, riflery, ropes course,

Camp Pok-O-MacCready

sailing, snorkeling, soccer, softball, street/roller hockey, swimming, tennis, track and field, volleyball, water polo, weight training, windsurfing, wrestling.
Wilderness/Outdoors Backpacking, bicycle trips, canoe trips, hiking, kayaking trips, mountain biking, mountaineering, orienteering, pioneer skills, rock climbing, survival training, wilderness camping, wilderness/outdoors (general).
Trips Cultural, day, overnight.
Program Information 3 sessions per year. Session length: 3–7 weeks in June, July, August. Ages: 6–16. 200–250 participants per session. Boarding program cost: $2170–$4850. Financial aid available.
Application Deadline Continuous.
Jobs Positions for high school students 17 and older and college students 18 and older.
Summer Contact Chris Durlacher, Director of Admissions, PO Box 397, Willsboro, New York 12996. Phone: 518-963-8366. Fax: 518-963-1128. E-mail: pokomac@aol.com.
Winter Contact Chris Durlacher, Director of Admissions, PO Box 397, Willsboro, New York 12996. Phone: 518-963-7656. Fax: 518-963-4165. E-mail: pokomac@aol.com.
URL www.pokomac.com

For more information, see page 1266.

Camp Redwood

576 Rock Cut Road
Walden, New York 12586

General Information Coed residential traditional camp established in 1961. Accredited by American Camping Association. High school credit may be earned.
Program Focus Noncompetitive sports instruction for every level.
Academics English as a second language, mathematics, reading.
Arts Arts and crafts (general), dance, dance (ballet), dance (folk), dance (jazz), dance (modern), dance (tap), music, theater/drama, woodworking.
Special Interest Areas Campcraft, flight instruction, model rocketry, nature study, weight reduction.
Sports Aerobics, archery, basketball, boating, canoeing, cheerleading, diving, field hockey, fishing, flag football,

Camp Redwood (continued)

gymnastics, horseback riding, in-line skating, kayaking, lacrosse, riflery, sailing, soccer, softball, sports (general), street/roller hockey, swimming, tennis, volleyball, waterskiing, weight training.
Trips Cultural, day, shopping.
Program Information 1–5 sessions per year. Session length: 2–8 weeks in June, July, August. Ages: 5+. 150 participants per session. Boarding program cost: $1695–$5195.
Application Deadline Continuous.
Jobs Positions for college students 19 and older.
Summer Contact Irma Estis, Co-Director, main address above. Phone: 888-600-6655. Fax: 845-564-1128. E-mail: info@camp-redwood.com.
Winter Contact John Estis, Co-Director, 576 Rock Cut Road, Walden, New York 12586. Phone: 888-600-6655. Fax: 845-564-1128. E-mail: info@camp-redwood.com.
URL www.campredwood.net

CAMP REGIS

Camp Regis, Inc.
Paul Smiths, New York 12970

General Information Coed residential traditional camp established in 1946. Religious affiliation: Friends United Meeting. Accredited by American Camping Association.

Camp Regis

Program Focus Sports, wilderness experiences, and waterfront activities.
Academics English as a second language.
Arts Arts and crafts (general), band, batiking, ceramics, chorus, creative writing, dance, dance (ballet), dance (folk), dance (jazz), dance (modern), drawing, jewelry making, leather working, music, music (classical), music (vocal), musical productions, painting, photography, pottery, sculpture, theater/drama, weaving, woodworking.
Special Interest Areas Native American culture, animal care, campcraft, field trips (arts and culture), leadership training, nature study.
Sports Archery, basketball, boating, canoeing, cross-country, diving, equestrian sports, field hockey, fishing, football, golf, gymnastics, horseback riding, kayaking, lacrosse, sailing, snorkeling, soccer, softball, street/roller hockey, swimming, tennis, track and field, volleyball, water polo, waterskiing, windsurfing.
Wilderness/Outdoors Backpacking, bicycle trips, canoe trips, hiking, mountain biking, mountaineering, orienteering, rafting, wilderness camping.
Trips Cultural, day, overnight.
Program Information 3 sessions per year. Session length: 4–8 weeks in June, July, August. Ages: 6–13. 280 participants per session. Boarding program cost: $2800–$5100. Financial aid available. Deposit of $600 required. Applications accepted during winter and spring.
Application Deadline Continuous.
Jobs Positions for college students 19 and older.
Summer Contact Michael P. Humes, Director, PO Box 245, Paul Smiths, New York 12970. Phone: 518-327-3117. Fax: 518-327-3193. E-mail: campregis@aol.com.
Winter Contact Michael P. Humes, Director, 60 Lafayette Road West, Princeton, New Jersey 08540-2428. Phone: 609-688-0368. Fax: 609-688-0369. E-mail: campregis@aol.com.
URL www.campregis-applejack.com
For more information, see page 1036.

CAMP SCATICO

Camp Scatico, Inc
1558 Route 19
Elizaville, New York 12523

General Information Coed residential traditional camp established in 1921. Accredited by American Camping Association.
Program Focus Team building, leadership skills, personal growth.
Arts Acting, arts and crafts (general), batiking, ceramics, creative writing, dance (jazz), dance (modern), drawing, jewelry making, leather working, music (vocal), musical productions, painting, photography, pottery, radio broadcasting, sculpture, television/video, theater/drama, woodworking.
Special Interest Areas Animal care, campcraft, culinary arts, gardening, leadership training, model rocketry, nature study.
Sports Aerobics, archery, baseball, basketball, boating, canoeing, climbing (wall), cross-country, equestrian sports, field hockey, fishing, football, golf, gymnastics, horseback riding, in-line skating, kayaking, lacrosse, martial arts, mountain boarding, rappelling, riflery, sailing, soccer, softball, street/roller hockey, swimming, tennis, track and field, volleyball, weight training, windsurfing, wrestling.
Wilderness/Outdoors Backpacking, canoe trips, caving, hiking, orienteering, rafting, rock climbing.
Trips Cultural, day, overnight.
Program Information 1–3 sessions per year. Session length: 7–50 days in July, August. Ages: 7–15. 250 participants per session. Boarding program cost: $1000–$6600.
Application Deadline Continuous.
Jobs Positions for college students 19 and older.

Summer Contact Mr. David Fleischner, Director, 1558 Route 19, PO Box 6, Elizaville, New York 12523. Phone: 845-756-4040. Fax: 845-756-2298. E-mail: info@scatico.com.
Winter Contact David Fleischner, Director, main address above. Phone: 914-632-7791. E-mail: info@scatico.com.
URL www.scatico.com

CAMP TALCOTT

YMCA Camping Services of Greater New York
300 Big Pond Road
Huguenot, New York 12746

General Information Coed residential traditional camp established in 1920. Accredited by American Camping Association.
Arts Arts and crafts (general), ceramics, chorus, creative writing, dance, drawing, fabric arts, film, jewelry making, leather working, painting, photography, pottery, woodworking.
Special Interest Areas Campcraft, leadership training, nature study, team building.
Sports Aerobics, archery, basketball, boating, canoeing, climbing (wall), fishing, football, horseback riding, lacrosse, rappelling, ropes course, sailing, snorkeling, soccer, softball, swimming, tennis, volleyball, waterskiing.
Wilderness/Outdoors Backpacking, hiking, rafting.
Trips Day, overnight.
Program Information 5 sessions per year. Session length: 6–13 days in June, July, August. Ages: 11–15. 170–200 participants per session. Boarding program cost: $415–$830. Financial aid available. Mainstreaming program for special needs is offered.
Application Deadline Continuous.
Jobs Positions for college students 18 and older.
Contact Chris Scheuer, Director of Camping, PO Box B, 300 Big Pond Road, Huguenot, New York 12746. Phone: 845-858-2200. Fax: 845-858-7823. E-mail: camps@ymcanyc.org.
URL www.ymcanyc.org/camps

CAMP TREETOPS

North Country School
Lake Placid, New York 12946

General Information Coed residential traditional camp and outdoor program established in 1921. Accredited by American Camping Association. Formal opportunities for the artistically talented.
Program Focus Organic farming, wilderness program, and the arts.
Academics Astronomy, ecology, environmental science, music.
Arts Arts, arts and crafts (general), batiking, ceramics, creative writing, dance, dance (ballet), dance (folk), drawing, fabric arts, jewelry making, leather working, music, musical productions, painting, photography, pottery, printmaking, puppetry, sculpture, theater/drama, weaving, woodworking.

Camp Treetops

Special Interest Areas Native American culture, animal care, campcraft, culinary arts, farming, field trips (arts and culture), gardening, nature study, nautical skills.
Sports Baseball, basketball, boating, canoeing, climbing (wall), diving, equestrian sports, fishing, gymnastics, horseback riding, kayaking, rappelling, rowing (crew/sculling), sailing, snorkeling, soccer, softball, swimming, tennis, water polo.
Wilderness/Outdoors Backpacking, canoe trips, hiking, mountaineering, orienteering, pack animal trips, rock climbing, wilderness camping.
Trips Cultural, day, overnight.
Program Information 1 session per year. Session length: 7 weeks in June, July, August. Ages: 8–14. 150–160 participants per session. Boarding program cost: $5700. Financial aid available.
Application Deadline Continuous.
Jobs Positions for high school students 18 and older and college students 18 and older.
Contact Karen Culpepper, Director, PO Box 187, Lake Placid, New York 12946. Phone: 518-523-9329 Ext.112. Fax: 518-523-4858. E-mail: ctt@nct.org.
URL www.camptreetops.com

For more information, see page 1044.

CAMPUS KIDS–MINISINK

CK Summer Camps, Inc.
Team USA Way
Port Jervis, New York 12771

General Information Coed residential traditional camp established in 2001. Accredited by American Camping Association.
Program Focus Weekday sleep-away camp; transportation provided. Camp during the week and home on the weekends.
Arts Arts and crafts (general), ceramics, creative writing, dance, dance (jazz), dance (modern), drawing, musical productions, photography, puppetry, theater/drama, woodworking.
Special Interest Areas Campcraft, model rocketry, nature study.
Sports Archery, basketball, bicycling, boating, canoeing, climbing (wall), fencing, fishing, golf, gymnastics,

Campus Kids–Minisink (continued)
horseback riding, kayaking, lacrosse, martial arts, ropes course, sailing, soccer, softball, street/roller hockey, swimming, tennis, volleyball.
Wilderness/Outdoors Hiking, mountain biking, orienteering.
Trips Day, overnight.
Program Information 1–4 sessions per year. Session length: 2–8 weeks in June, July, August. Ages: 7–15. 250 participants per session. Boarding program cost: $1575–$5720.
Application Deadline Continuous.
Jobs Positions for college students 18 and older.
Contact Ms. Jani Brokaw Williams, Director, PO Box 422, Mahopac, New York 10541. Phone: 845-621-2193. Fax: 845-621-2383. E-mail: ckminisink@aol.com.
URL www.campuskids.com

Camp Walden

Camp Walden, LLC
429 Trout Lake Road
Diamond Point, New York 12824

General Information Coed residential traditional camp established in 1931. Religious affiliation: Jewish. Accredited by American Camping Association.
Academics Hebrew language, Jewish studies.
Arts Arts and crafts (general), ceramics, dance, drawing, graphic arts, guitar, jewelry making, leather working, music, musical productions, painting, photography, piano, pottery, puppetry, radio broadcasting, sculpture, television/video, theater/drama.
Special Interest Areas Gardening, leadership training, lifesaving, model rocketry, nature study, team building, touring.
Sports Aerobics, archery, baseball, basketball, boating, canoeing, cheerleading, climbing (wall), equestrian sports, fencing, fishing, football, golf, gymnastics, horseback riding, in-line skating, kayaking, lacrosse, martial arts, rappelling, ropes course, rowing (crew/sculling), sailing, snorkeling, soccer, softball, street/roller hockey, swimming, tennis, track and field, volleyball, water polo, waterskiing, weight training, windsurfing.
Wilderness/Outdoors Backpacking, hiking, mountaineering, orienteering, rafting, rock climbing, white-water trips, wilderness camping.
Trips Day, overnight.
Program Information 1–4 sessions per year. Session length: 26–52 days in June, July, August. Ages: 6–16. 220–225 participants per session. Boarding program cost: $3700–$6300. Application fee: $50.
Application Deadline Continuous.
Jobs Positions for high school students 17 and older and college students 18 and older.
Summer Contact Mrs. Renee Pitt, Owner/Director, main address above. Phone: 518-644-9441. Fax: 518-644-2929. E-mail: waldenmail@yahoo.com.
Winter Contact Mrs. Renee Pitt, Owner/Director, PO Box 2640, Windermere, Florida 34786. Phone: 407-523-1917. Fax: 775-535-6627. E-mail: waldenmail@yahoo.com.
URL www.campwalden.org

Career Explorations

Career Explorations, LLC
The Juilliard School, Samuel B. and David Rose Building
60 Lincoln Center Plaza
New York, New York 10023-6588

General Information Coed residential academic program and arts program established in 2003.

Career Explorations

Program Focus Residential summer professional program with possible internships with NY Times (journalism), Putnam Lowell (finance) and various companies in a variety of fields.
Academics Anthropology, architecture, art history/appreciation, business, communications, computer science (Advanced Placement), economics, government and politics, intercultural studies, journalism, music, social science, writing.
Arts Creative writing, drawing, fabric arts, music, radio broadcasting.
Special Interest Areas Career exploration, community service, electronics, internships, leadership training.
Sports Baseball, basketball, football, softball, swimming.
Trips College tours, cultural, day, overnight, shopping.
Program Information 1 session per year. Session length: 28–30 days in June, July. Ages: 16–18. 20–25 participants per session. Boarding program cost: $5495. Application fee: $50.
Application Deadline April 15.
Contact Josh Flowerman, Director, 119 Headquarters Plaza, Morristown, New Jersey 07960. Phone: 973-984-8808. Fax: 973-984-5666. E-mail: jflowerman@ceinternships.com.
URL www.ceinternships.com
For more information, see page 1052.

Carousel Day School

9 West Avenue
Hicksville, New York 11801

General Information Coed day traditional camp established in 1956. Accredited by American Camping Association.

Program Focus Day tripping and swimming (Red Cross instruction).
Academics Computers.
Arts Arts and crafts (general), ceramics, chorus, drawing, jewelry making, leather working, music (vocal), painting, radio broadcasting, woodworking.
Sports Aerobics, archery, baseball, basketball, field hockey, football, lacrosse, ropes course, soccer, softball, street/roller hockey, swimming, volleyball.
Trips Day.
Program Information 3 sessions per year. Ages: 3–15. 200 participants per session. Cost: $1825–$2800 for 8 weeks.
Application Deadline Continuous.
Jobs Positions for high school students 16 and older and college students 18 and older.
Summer Contact Mr. Gene Formica, Director/Owner, main address above. Phone: 516-938-1137. Fax: 516-822-9269.
Winter Contact Kathy Cordaro, Director, Programs and Personnel, main address above. Phone: 516-938-1137. Fax: 516-822-9269. E-mail: kathy@carouseldayschool.com.
URL www.carouseldayschool.com

Coleman Country Day Camp

Coleman Family Camps
Merrick, New York 11566

General Information Coed day traditional camp established in 1982. Accredited by American Camping Association. Specific services available for the learning disabled.
Academics Computers, ecology, environmental science, geology/earth science, music, science (general).
Arts Acting, arts and crafts (general), ceramics, clowning, dance, dance (modern), drawing, fabric arts, jewelry making, leather working, music, music (vocal), musical productions, painting, pottery, sculpture, theater/drama, woodworking.
Special Interest Areas Animal care, campcraft, leadership training, model rocketry, nature study, team building.
Sports Archery, baseball, basketball, boating, climbing (wall), equestrian sports, gymnastics, horseback riding, rappelling, ropes course, soccer, softball, street/roller hockey, swimming, tennis, volleyball.
Wilderness/Outdoors Rock climbing.
Trips Day.
Program Information 1–2 sessions per year. Session length: 20–40 days in June, July, August. Ages: 3–15. 500–800 participants per session. Day program cost: $2650–$4675. Financial aid available.
Application Deadline Continuous.
Jobs Positions for high school students 16 and older and college students 18 and older.
Contact Mr. Ross Coleman, Director, PO Box 34, Merrick, New York 11566. Phone: 516-620-4300. Fax: 516-620-4329. E-mail: ross@colemancountry.com.
URL www.colemancountry.com

Columbia University Summer Program for High School Students

Columbia University Continuing Education
2970 Broadway
New York, New York 10027

General Information Coed residential and day academic program established in 1987. Formal opportunities for the academically talented. Specific services available for the physically challenged.
Academics American literature, English language/literature, SAT/ACT preparation, academics (general), art history/appreciation, bioengineering, biology, business, chemistry, computer programming, computers, ecology, economics, engineering, environmental science, government and politics, law, mathematics, physics, precollege program, reading, religion, social science, study skills, urban studies, writing.
Arts Creative writing, theater/drama.
Special Interest Areas Career exploration, community service.
Sports Aerobics, basketball, racquetball, squash, swimming, tennis, volleyball, weight training.
Trips Cultural, day.
Program Information 2 sessions per year. Session length: 20–25 days in July, August. Ages: 13–18. 500–700 participants per session. Day program cost: $2675–$2800. Boarding program cost: $5240–$5365. Application fee: $35–$50.
Application Deadline April 5.
Jobs Positions for college students 18 and older.
Contact Ms. Darlene Giraitis, Director of Secondary School Programs, Columbia University, 2970 Broadway, Mail Code 4110, New York, New York 10027. Phone: 212-854-3771. Fax: 212-854-5861. E-mail: hsp@columbia.edu.
URL www.ce.columbia.edu/hs/

Cornell University Summer College Programs for High School Students

Cornell University
B20 Day Hall
Ithaca, New York 14853-2801

General Information Coed residential academic program established in 1962. Formal opportunities for the academically talented. Specific services available for the emotionally challenged, hearing impaired, learning disabled, physically challenged, and visually impaired. College credit may be earned.
Academics American literature, English as a second language, English language/literature, French language/literature, German language/literature, Italian language/literature, Jewish studies, Latin language, Russian language/literature, Spanish (Advanced Placement), Spanish language/literature, academics (general), anthropology, archaeology, architecture, art history/appreciation, astronomy, biology, botany, business, chemistry, classical languages/literatures, communications, computer programming, computers, economics, engineering, environmental science, geology/earth science, government and politics, government and politics (Advanced Placement), history, humanities, linguistics,

Cornell University Summer College Programs for High School Students (continued)

Cornell University Summer College Programs for High School Students

mathematics, music, oceanography, philosophy, physics, precollege program, psychology, religion, speech/debate, study skills.
Arts Chorus, dance, drawing, fabric arts, film, painting, photography, television/video.
Special Interest Areas Animal care, career exploration.
Sports Basketball, bicycling, climbing (wall), equestrian sports, golf, sailing, swimming, tennis, volleyball, weight training, windsurfing.
Wilderness/Outdoors Hiking.
Program Information 2 sessions per year. Session length: 3–6 weeks in June, July, August. Ages: 15–19. 150–600 participants per session. Boarding program cost: $4150–$6960. Application fee: $50–$100. Financial aid available.
Application Deadline Continuous.
Contact Abby H. Eller, Director, main address above. Phone: 607-255-6203. Fax: 607-255-6665. E-mail: summer_college@cornell.edu.
URL www.summercollege.cornell.edu
For more information, see page 1080.

Cybercamps–Adelphi University

Cybercamps–Giant Campus, Inc.
Garden City, New York

General Information Coed residential and day academic program established in 1996.
Program Focus Cybercamps provide a high-tech camp experience for the young inquisitive mind, from beginner to advanced, while also including sports, team building activities, etc.
Academics Web page design, computer programming, computers.
Arts Animation, creative writing, digital media, graphic arts, photography.
Special Interest Areas Computer game design, computer graphics, robotics, team building.
Sports Frisbee golf, ultimate frisbee.
Program Information 2–9 sessions per year. Session length: 5–30 days in June, July, August. Ages: 7–18. 30–150 participants per session. Day program cost: $599–$849. Boarding program cost: $974–$1224. Financial aid available.
Application Deadline Continuous.
Jobs Positions for high school students 15 and older and college students.
Contact Cybercamps Information Office, 2401 4th Avenue, Suite 1110, Seattle, Washington 98121. Phone: 206-442-4500. Fax: 206-442-4501. E-mail: info@cybercamps.com.
URL www.cybercamps.com

Cybercamps–Manhattanville College

Cybercamps–Giant Campus, Inc.
Purchase, New York

General Information Coed residential and day academic program established in 2003.
Academics Web page design, academics (general), computer programming, computers.
Arts Animation, creative writing, digital media, graphic arts, photography.
Special Interest Areas Computer game design, computer graphics, robotics, team building.
Sports Ultimate frisbee.
Program Information 2–9 sessions per year. Session length: 5–30 days in June, July, August. Ages: 7–18. 30–150 participants per session. Day program cost: $599–$849. Boarding program cost: $974–$1224. Financial aid available.
Application Deadline Continuous.
Jobs Positions for high school students 15 and older and college students.
Contact Cybercamps Information Office, 2401 4th Avenue, Suite 1110, Seattle, Washington 98121. Phone: 206-442-4500. Fax: 206-442-4500. E-mail: info@cybercamps.com.
URL www.cybercamps.com

Deerfoot Lodge

Christian Camps, Inc.
Whitaker Lake
Route 30
Speculator, New York 12164

General Information Boys' residential traditional camp and outdoor program established in 1930. Religious affiliation: interdenominational. Accredited by American Camping Association.
Program Focus Building godly young men in a Christ-centered environment of wilderness camping.
Academics Bible study.
Arts Leather working, pottery.
Special Interest Areas Campcraft, leadership training, nature study.
Sports Archery, baseball, basketball, boating, canoeing, climbing (wall), fishing, kayaking, riflery, ropes course, sailing, soccer, softball, swimming, volleyball.
Wilderness/Outdoors Backpacking, canoe trips, hiking, mountaineering, orienteering, survival training, wilderness camping.
Trips Overnight.
Program Information 4 sessions per year. Session length: 2 weeks in June, July, August. Ages: 8–16. 140–170 participants per session. Boarding program cost: $795. Financial aid available.
Application Deadline Continuous.
Jobs Positions for high school students 17 and older and college students.
Contact Ron Mackey, Director, Deerfoot Lodge, PO Box 228, Speculator, New York 12164. Phone: 518-548-5277. Fax: 518-924-7203. E-mail: dl12164@attglobal.net.
URL www.deerfoot.org

Deerkill Day Camp

54 Wilder Road
Suffern, New York 10901

General Information Coed day traditional camp established in 1958. Accredited by American Camping Association.
Arts Acting, arts and crafts (general), batiking, ceramics, creative writing, dance, dance (folk), dance (jazz), dance (modern), drawing, fabric arts, film, graphic arts, jewelry making, painting, photography, pottery, printmaking, sculpture, theater/drama, woodworking.
Special Interest Areas Animal care, electronics, farming, gardening, model rocketry, nature study, team building.
Sports Archery, basketball, boating, climbing (wall), diving, equestrian sports, field hockey, fishing, football, gymnastics, horseback riding, in-line skating, lacrosse, martial arts, racquetball, ropes course, soccer, softball, squash, swimming, tennis, track and field, volleyball, water polo.
Wilderness/Outdoors Hiking.
Trips Cultural, day.
Program Information 4–8 sessions per year. Session length: 20–39 days in July, August. Ages: 3–14. 450 participants per session. Day program cost: $2165–$5175. Application fee: $50. Financial aid available.
Application Deadline Continuous.
Jobs Positions for high school students 16 and older and college students 17 and older.
Contact Dr. Robert I. Rhodes, Director, main address above. Phone: 845-354-1466. Fax: 845-362-4597. E-mail: deerkill@att.net.
URL www.deerkilldaycamp.com

Double "H" Hole in the Woods Ranch Summer Camp

Double "H" Hole in the Woods Ranch
97 Hidden Valley Road
Lake Luzerne, New York 12846

General Information Coed residential and day family program and special needs program established in 1993. Accredited by American Camping Association. Specific services available for the emotionally challenged, developmentally challenged, hearing impaired, learning disabled, physically challenged, visually impaired, participant with cancer, participant with HIV/AIDS, participant with hemophilia, and participant with Sickle Cell Anemia.
Program Focus Serves children with chronic illness and their families. Camp focuses on adventure, health and safety.
Academics Environmental science, music, typing, writing.
Arts Arts and crafts (general), batiking, ceramics, creative writing, dance, drawing, fabric arts, film, jewelry making, leather working, music, musical productions, painting, photography, pottery, sculpture, television/video, theater/drama, weaving, woodworking.
Special Interest Areas ADL skills, animal care, campcraft, culinary arts, gardening, leadership training, model rocketry, nature study, nautical skills.
Sports Baseball, basketball, boating, fishing, football, horseback riding, ropes course, skiing (cross-country), skiing (downhill), soccer, softball, swimming, tennis, volleyball.
Wilderness/Outdoors Backpacking, hiking, mountaineering, orienteering, rafting, white-water trips, wilderness camping.
Trips Day, overnight.
Program Information 8 sessions per year. Session length: 6–7 days in January, February, March, April, May, June, July, August, September, October, November, December. Ages: 6–16. 128 participants per session. Financial aid available. No cost for program.
Application Deadline Continuous.
Jobs Positions for high school students 17 and older and college students 18 and older.
Contact Peter Carner, Camp Director, main address above. Phone: 518-696-5676. Fax: 518-696-4528. E-mail: petecarner@doublehranch.org.
URL www.doublehranch.org

Dunnabeck at Kildonan

Kildonan School
425 Morse Hill Road
Amenia, New York 12501

General Information Coed residential and day academic program and special needs program established in 1955. Specific services available for the learning disabled.

Dunnabeck at Kildonan

Program Focus Language training for dyslexic students.
Academics Academics (general), computers, reading, study skills, writing.
Arts Arts and crafts (general), ceramics, drawing, painting, woodworking.
Sports Archery, baseball, basketball, bicycling, boating, canoeing, equestrian sports, fishing, horseback riding, sailing, soccer, swimming, tennis, waterskiing, windsurfing.
Wilderness/Outdoors Rock climbing.
Trips Cultural, day, overnight.
Program Information 1 session per year. Session length: 42–50 days in June, July, August. Ages: 8–16. 75–100 participants per session. Day program cost: $3725–$5725. Boarding program cost: $7300. Application fee: $50. Financial aid available.
Application Deadline Continuous.
Jobs Positions for college students 21 and older.
Contact Ronald A. Wilson, Headmaster, main address above. Phone: 845-373-8111. Fax: 845-373-9793. E-mail: bsattler@kildonan.org.
URL www.kildonan.org

For more information, see page 1092.

Earthwatch Institute–Archaeology at West Point Foundry

Earthwatch Institute
Cold Spring, New York

General Information Coed residential outdoor program.
Program Focus Teasing out technological, economic, and social history from the ruins of a 19th-century foundry.
Academics Archaeology, history.
Special Interest Areas Field research/expeditions.
Program Information 4 sessions per year. Session length: 1–2 weeks in June. Ages: 16+. 15 participants per session. Boarding program cost: $995–$1695. Financial aid available. Financial aid for high school students and teachers.
Application Deadline Continuous.
Contact General Information Desk, PO Box 75, Maynard, Massachusetts 01754. Phone: 800-776-0188. Fax: 978-461-2332. E-mail: info@earthwatch.org.
URL www.earthwatch.org

Eastern U.S. Music Camp, Inc.

Colgate University
Dana Arts Center
Hamilton, New York 13346-1398

General Information Coed residential and day arts program established in 1976. Accredited by American Camping Association. Formal opportunities for the artistically talented and gifted. High school credit may be earned.
Program Focus Bands, jazz ensembles, jazz combos, orchestras, chamber ensemble, string quartets, wind ensemble, choirs, private lessons, small ensembles (all areas), piano, voice, guitar, organ, harp, music theory, harmony, improvisation, composition-arranging, conducting, recitals, concerts, recreation, trip, and guest artists.
Academics Computers, music, music (Advanced Placement).
Arts Arts and crafts (general), band, chorus, creative writing, guitar, harp, music, music (chamber), music (classical), music (ensemble), music (instrumental), music (jazz), music (orchestral), music (vocal), music composition/arrangement, music conducting, music theory, musical performance/recitals, organ, performance art, piano.
Special Interest Areas Career exploration, leadership training, weight reduction.

Eastern U.S. Music Camp, Inc.

Sports Basketball, diving, golf, racquetball, softball, sports (general), swimming, tennis, track and field, volleyball.
Trips Day.
Program Information 1–3 sessions per year. Session length: 2–4 weeks in June, July. Ages: 10–18. 150–175 participants per session. Day program cost: $579–$1158. Boarding program cost: $1459–$2859. Financial aid available.
Application Deadline Continuous.
Jobs Positions for high school students 16 and older and college students 18 and older.
Summer Contact Dr. Thomas A. Brown, Director, main address above. Phone: 315-228-7041. Fax: 315-228-7557. E-mail: eusmc@hotmail.com.
Winter Contact Dr. Thomas A. Brown, Director, 7 Brook Hollow Road, Ballston Lake, New York 12019. Phone: 866-777-7841. Fax: 518-877-4943. E-mail: eusmc@hotmail.com.
URL www.easternusmusiccamp.com

Special Note
Eastern U.S. Music Camp is located in picturesque central New York State on the beautiful Colgate University campus in Hamilton. Colgate has a tradition of excellence in education. The program offers an exciting array of musical, social, and recreational opportunities, including jazz ensembles, jazz combos, concert band, wind ensemble, orchestras, chamber ensemble, concert choir, swing, and women's, men's, and madrigal choirs. Ensembles at all levels of proficiency include percussion, brass, harp, string, woodwinds, guitar, piano, flute, saxophone, vocal, jazz, and combos. All styles of music are performed. There are classes in theory, harmony, composition/arranging, and conducting. Private instruction is offered in all instruments, plus piano, voice, guitar, harp, and pipe organ. Public concerts and recitals are presented weekly. Master classes and coaching with professional artists/educators is included. All rehearsals and concerts are held in a multimillion-dollar, air-conditioned Fine Arts Center. Students are housed in modern college dormitories, with separate dorms for girls and boys. A nationally renowned staff includes college faculty members and experienced, world-renowned clinicians/artists in this friendly environment. Outstanding recreational facilities and activities are provided, as is a trip. Students can obtain credit when enrolled for the full four-week session, which is recommended for its greater musical and social benefits.

For more information, see page 1094.

Environmental Studies Summer Youth Institute

Hobart and William Smith Colleges
Geneva, New York 14456-3397

General Information Coed residential academic program and outdoor program established in 1993. Formal opportunities for the academically talented and artistically talented. College credit may be earned.

Environmental Studies Summer Youth Institute

Program Focus Two-week interdisciplinary approach to environmental studies, field work centered.

Environmental Studies Summer Youth Institute (continued)

Academics Area studies, art history/appreciation, biology, botany, chemistry, ecology, economics, environmental science, geography, geology/earth science, government and politics, history, humanities, philosophy, science (general), social science, social studies, writing.
Arts Photography.
Special Interest Areas Field research/expeditions, nature study.
Sports Canoeing.
Wilderness/Outdoors Canoe trips, hiking.
Trips Cultural, day, overnight.
Program Information 1 session per year. Session length: 2 weeks in July. Ages: 16–18. 32–38 participants per session. Boarding program cost: $1700. Application fee: $25. Financial aid available.
Application Deadline Continuous.
Contact Prof. Brooks McKinney, Director, ESSYI, main address above. Phone: 315-781-4401. Fax: 315-781-4400. E-mail: essyi@hws.edu.
URL academic.hws.edu/enviro

For more information, see page 1112.

Forrestel Farm Riding and Sports Camp

4536 South Gravel Road
Medina, New York 14103

General Information Coed residential traditional camp established in 1981.
Program Focus Horseback riding, sports, and outdoor adventure.
Arts Arts and crafts (general), painting, woodworking.
Special Interest Areas Animal care, campcraft, farming, gardening, nature study.
Sports Aerobics, archery, baseball, basketball, bicycling, canoeing, climbing (wall), equestrian sports, fishing, football, golf, horseback riding, lacrosse, riflery, ropes course, soccer, softball, sports (general), street/roller hockey, swimming, tennis, volleyball, water polo.
Wilderness/Outdoors Bicycle trips, canoe trips, mountain biking, orienteering, outdoor adventure, pack animal trips, survival training, wilderness camping.
Trips Overnight.
Program Information 4 sessions per year. Session length: 12 days in June, July, August. Ages: 7–15. 60–75 participants per session. Day program cost: $350. Boarding program cost: $1200–$1500.
Application Deadline May 1.
Jobs Positions for college students 19 and older.
Contact Mary Herbert, Owner/Director, main address above. Phone: 585-798-2222. Fax: 585-798-0941. E-mail: summer@ffridingsportscamp.com.
URL www.ffridingsportscamp.com

French Woods Festival of the Performing Arts

350 Bouchoux Brook Road
Hancock, New York 13783

General Information Coed residential arts program established in 1970. Accredited by American Camping Association. Formal opportunities for the artistically talented. Specific services available for the learning disabled. High school credit may be earned.
Program Focus Performing and visual arts, sports, and circus arts.
Academics SAT/ACT preparation, computers, music.
Arts Acting, arts, arts and crafts (general), band, batiking, ceramics, chorus, circus arts, clowning, creative writing, dance, dance (ballet), dance (folk), dance (jazz), dance (modern), dance (tap), drawing, fabric arts, film, graphic arts, jewelry making, leather working, metalworking, mime, music, music (chamber), music (classical), music (ensemble), music (instrumental), music (jazz), music (orchestral), music (rock), music (vocal), music technology/record production, musical productions, painting, photography, pottery, printmaking, puppetry, radio broadcasting, sculpture, television/video, theater/drama, visual arts, weaving, woodworking.
Special Interest Areas Campcraft, culinary arts, model rocketry.
Sports Aerobics, baseball, basketball, bicycling, bicycling (BMX), boating, canoeing, climbing (wall), cross-country, equestrian sports, fencing, field hockey, fishing, football, golf, gymnastics, horseback riding, in-line skating, kayaking, martial arts, rappelling, ropes course, sailing, soccer, softball, street/roller hockey, swimming, tennis, track and field, volleyball, water polo, waterskiing, weight training, windsurfing, wrestling.
Wilderness/Outdoors Bicycle trips, canoe trips, hiking, mountain biking, rock climbing.
Trips Cultural.
Program Information 3 sessions per year. Session length: 3–9 weeks in June, July, August. Ages: 7–17. 400–500 participants per session. Boarding program cost: $2850–$7500. Financial aid available.
Application Deadline Continuous.
Jobs Positions for college students 18 and older.
Summer Contact Mr. Ronald Schaefer, Director, PO Box 609, Hancock, New York 13783. Phone: 845-887-5600. E-mail: admin@frenchwoods.com.
Winter Contact Mr. Ronald Schaefer, Director, PO Box 770100, Coral Springs, Florida 33077-0100. Phone: 954-346-7455. E-mail: admin@frenchwoods.com.
URL www.frenchwoods.com

FUN-damental Basketball Camp–Morrisville, New York

FUN-damental Basketball Camp, Inc.
State University of New York at Morrisville
Morrisville, New York 13408

General Information Coed residential and day sports camp established in 1992.
Program Focus Basketball instruction.
Sports Basketball, swimming.

Program Information 1 session per year. Session length: 5–6 days in June, July. Ages: 6–18. 200–250 participants per session. Day program cost: $180–$195. Boarding program cost: $395–$415.
Application Deadline Continuous.
Jobs Positions for college students 19 and older.
Contact Mr. Stu Maloff, Owner/Director, PO Box 970446, Boca Raton, Florida 33497-0446. Phone: 877-545-8423. Fax: 561-218-0536. E-mail: basketballcamp@aol.com.
URL www.ebasketballcamps.com

Girl Scouts of Genesee Valley Day Camp

Girl Scouts of Genesee Valley
New York

General Information Girls' day traditional camp established in 1967. Accredited by American Camping Association.
Arts Arts and crafts (general), jewelry making, leather working.
Special Interest Areas Campcraft, nature study.
Sports Archery, canoeing, fishing, horseback riding, ropes course, sports (general), swimming.
Wilderness/Outdoors Orienteering.
Program Information 4 sessions per year. Session length: 5 days in July, August. Ages: 6–16. 75–125 participants per session. Day program cost: $120–$270. Financial aid available. Open to participants entering grades 1–12.
Application Deadline Continuous.
Jobs Positions for high school students 16 and older and college students 18 and older.
Contact Ms. Mary McDowell, Director of Outdoor Program, 1020 John Street, West Henrietta, New York 14586. Phone: 585-239-7915. Fax: 585-292-1086. E-mail: marym@gsgv.org.
URL www.gsgv.org

Girl Scouts of Genesee Valley Resident Camp

Girl Scouts of Genesee Valley
Arkport, New York 14807

General Information Girls' residential traditional camp. Accredited by American Camping Association.
Academics Environmental science.
Arts Arts and crafts (general), jewelry making, leather working, theater/drama, weaving, woodworking.
Special Interest Areas Campcraft, general camp activities, leadership training, nature study.
Sports Archery, boating, canoeing, fishing, horseback riding, ropes course, swimming.
Wilderness/Outdoors Backpacking, canoe trips, caving, hiking, orienteering, rafting, white-water trips, wilderness camping.
Trips Day, overnight.
Program Information 5–6 sessions per year. Session length: 6–12 days in July, August. Ages: 9–17. 75–100 participants per session. Boarding program cost: $260–$625. Financial aid available. Open to participants entering grades 1–12.
Application Deadline Continuous.
Jobs Positions for high school students 16 and older and college students 18 and older.
Contact Ms. Mary McDowell, Director of Outdoor Program, 1020 John Street, West Henrietta, New York 14586. Phone: 585-239-7915. Fax: 585-292-1086. E-mail: marym@gsgv.org.
URL www.gsgv.org

GirlSummer at Emma Willard School

Emma Willard School
285 Pawling Avenue
Troy, New York 12180

General Information Girls' residential academic program and arts program established in 2003.

GirlSummer at Emma Willard School

Program Focus Students choose from one of ten academic tracks: college prep; Spanish; French; computers, science & technology; writer's workshop; performing arts; fine arts; AP US history; AP English language & composition; AP English literature & composition. All students visit Manhattan at least once on a program-specific field trip.
Academics American literature, English language/literature, French language/literature, SAT/ACT preparation, Spanish language/literature, academics (general), computer programming, computers, precollege program, science (general), writing.
Arts Acting, arts, arts and crafts (general), creative writing, painting, photography, theater/drama.
Special Interest Areas College planning, culinary arts, robotics.
Sports Aerobics, basketball, field hockey, soccer, softball, swimming, tennis, weight training.
Trips College tours, cultural, day, shopping.
Program Information 3 sessions per year. Session length: 13 days in June, July, August. Ages: 11–17. 40–100 participants per session. Boarding program cost: $2295. Open to participants entering grades 7–12.
Application Deadline Continuous.

GirlSummer at Emma Willard School (continued)

Jobs Positions for college students.
Summer Contact Doug Murphy, Director, main address above. Phone: 866-EWS-CAMP. Fax: 212-815-9256. E-mail: girlsummer@emmawillard.org.
Winter Contact Doug Murphy, Director, 101 Murray Street, Suite 427, New York, New York 10007. Phone: 866-EWS-CAMP. Fax: 212-815-9256. E-mail: girlsummer@emmawillard.org.
URL www.emmawillard.org/summer/camps.shtml
For more information, see page 1108.

Gordon Kent's New England Tennis Camp

Gordon Kent's New England Tennis Camp
Trinity-Pauling School
700 Route 22
Pawling, New York 12564

General Information Coed residential and day sports camp established in 1965.

Gordon Kent's New England Tennis Camp

Program Focus Tennis.
Sports Baseball, basketball, bowling, soccer, softball, tennis, volleyball.
Trips Day.
Program Information 4 sessions per year. Session length: 13 days in June, July, August. Ages: 9–17. 75 participants per session. Day program cost: $1150. Boarding program cost: $1700.
Application Deadline Continuous.
Jobs Positions for college students.
Summer Contact Gordon Kent, Director/Owner, PO Box 840, Pawling, New York 12564. Phone: 800-528-2752. Fax: 845-855-9661. E-mail: netennis@aol.com.
Winter Contact Gordon Kent, Director/Owner, PO Box 212, New York, New York 10044. Phone: 212-750-3810. Fax: 212-750-3704. E-mail: netennis@aol.com.
URL www.netennis.com
For more information, see page 1138.

The Gow School Summer Program

The Gow School
2491 Emery Road
South Wales, New York 14139

General Information Coed residential and day traditional camp and academic program established in 1990. Accredited by American Camping Association. Specific services available for the learning disabled.

The Gow School Summer Program

Program Focus Camping, academics, sports, arts, and weekend overnight trips.
Academics English language/literature, academics (general), communications, computers, humanities, journalism, mathematics, reading, science (general), speech/debate, study skills, writing.
Arts Arts and crafts (general), ceramics, chorus, creative writing, dance, drawing, fabric arts, film, graphic arts, jewelry making, leather working, music, musical productions, painting, photography, pottery, printmaking, television/video, theater/drama.
Special Interest Areas Leadership training.
Sports Aerobics, archery, baseball, basketball, bicycling, canoeing, climbing (wall), cross-country, equestrian sports, fishing, football, golf, gymnastics, horseback riding, in-line skating, lacrosse, rappelling, ropes course, soccer, softball, squash, street/roller hockey, swimming, tennis, track and field, volleyball, weight training, wrestling.

Wilderness/Outdoors Backpacking, bicycle trips, canoe trips, hiking, mountain biking, orienteering, rock climbing, white-water trips, wilderness camping.
Trips Day, overnight.
Program Information 1 session per year. Session length: 5 weeks in July, August. Ages: 8–16. 115 participants per session. Day program cost: $2800–$3800. Boarding program cost: $5800. Application fee: $50. Financial aid available.
Application Deadline Continuous.
Jobs Positions for college students 18 and older.
Contact Mr. Robert Garcia, Director of Admissions, 2491 Emery Road, PO Box 85, South Wales, New York 14139. Phone: 716-652-3450. Fax: 716-687-2003. E-mail: summer@gow.org.
URL www.gow.org

Special Note
The Gow School Summer Program was created for girls and boys who have experienced academic difficulties or have learning differences but possess the potential for success. The program is composed of a carefully considered balance between academics, traditional camp activities, and weekend overnight trips. In short, the program balances learning and fun. The Summer Program provides the camper-students with the academic growth they need and the fun that all kids deserve in the summer. The goal is for camper-students to go home at the end of the summer feeling confident, relaxed, and prepared for the coming school year. The Gow School Summer Program is accredited by the New York State Association of Independent Schools and is a member of the American Camping Association.

For more information, see page 1140.

Grandparents' and Grandchildren's Camp

Sagamore Institute of the Adirondacks
Great Camp Sagamore, Sagamore Road
Raquette Lake, New York 13436

General Information Coed residential traditional camp and family program established in 1986.
Program Focus Camp activities with intergenerational emphasis.
Academics Ecology.
Arts Arts and crafts (general), music.
Sports Canoeing, swimming.
Trips Cultural, day.
Program Information 4–6 sessions per year. Session length: 5 days in July, August. Ages: 5+. 60 participants per session. Boarding program cost: $430–$800.
Application Deadline Continuous.
Jobs Positions for college students 18 and older.
Summer Contact Dr. M. Wilson, Associate Director, PO Box 40, Raquette Lake, New York 13436-0040. Phone: 315-354-5311 Ext.21. Fax: 315-354-5851. E-mail: sagamore@telenet.net.
Winter Contact Dr. M. Wilson, main address above. Phone: 518-891-1718. Fax: 518-891-2561. E-mail: mwilson@northnet.org.
URL www.sagamore.org

Graphic Media Experience

Rochester Institute of Technology
School of Printing Management and Sciences
69 Lomb Memorial Drive
Rochester, New York 14623-5603

General Information Coed residential academic program and arts program. Formal opportunities for the academically talented.
Program Focus Includes industry tours and other activities.
Academics Communications, computers, digital press run.
Arts Graphic arts, printing.
Trips College tours, day.
Program Information 1 session per year. Session length: 3 days in June. Ages: 16–18. 18–20 participants per session. Boarding program cost: $245. Financial aid available.
Application Deadline May 17.
Jobs Positions for college students.
Contact Marcia Carrol, main address above. Phone: 716-475-5992.
URL www.rit.edu/

Houghton Academy Summer ESL

Houghton Academy
9790 Thayer Street
Houghton, New York 14744

General Information Coed residential academic program and cultural program established in 1995. Religious affiliation: Wesleyan Church. High school credit may be earned.
Program Focus Orientation to American culture.
Academics English as a second language, computers, history, reading, writing.
Special Interest Areas Homestays.
Sports Basketball, canoeing, soccer, swimming, tennis, volleyball.
Wilderness/Outdoors Canoe trips, hiking.
Trips Cultural, day, overnight, shopping.
Program Information 1 session per year. Session length: 6 weeks in July, August. Ages: 14–18. 10–30 participants per session. Boarding program cost: $2500.
Application Deadline Continuous.
Contact Mr. Ron Bradbury, Director of Admissions, main address above. Phone: 716-567-8115. Fax: 716-567-8048. E-mail: admissions@houghtonacademy.org.
URL www.houghtonacademy.org

iD Tech Camps–Vassar College, Poughkeepsie, NY

iD Tech Camps
Vassar College
Poughkeepsie, New York 12604

General Information Coed residential and day academic program established in 1999. Accredited by American Camping Association. Formal opportunities for the academically talented and artistically talented.
Program Focus High-tech computer camps for kids and teens; produce digital movies, create video games,

iD Tech Camps–Vassar College, Poughkeepsie, NY (continued)

design Web pages, learn programming and robotics, and more; one computer per student, small classes, campers complete a project in a creative and fun learning environment.
Academics Web page design, computer programming, computer science (Advanced Placement), computers, music, precollege program.
Arts Animation, cartooning, cinematography, digital media, drawing, film, film editing, film production, graphic arts, music, television/video.
Special Interest Areas Career exploration, computer graphics, electronics, leadership training, robotics, team building.
Sports Baseball, basketball, soccer, softball, swimming, volleyball.
Trips College tours, cultural, day.
Program Information 5 sessions per year. Session length: 5–7 days in June, July, August. Ages: 7–17. 40–50 participants per session. Day program cost: $639. Boarding program cost: $989. Application fee: $200. Financial aid available.
Application Deadline Continuous.
Jobs Positions for college students 18 and older.
Contact Client Service Representatives, 1885 Winchester Boulevard, Suite 201, Campbell, California 95008. Phone: 888-709-TECH. Fax: 408-871-2228. E-mail: requests@internaldrive.com.
URL www.internaldrive.com

For more information, see page 1156.

International Riding Camp

Birchall Road
Greenfield Park, New York 12435

General Information Girls' residential sports camp established in 1978. Accredited by American Camping Association.
Program Focus Horseback riding and polo.
Special Interest Areas Animal care.
Sports Aerobics, basketball, boating, equestrian sports, fishing, horseback riding, polo, tennis, waterskiing.
Program Information 10 sessions per year. Session length: 1–10 weeks in June, July, August. Ages: 6–18. 40–60 participants per session. Boarding program cost: $1150–$8525.
Application Deadline Continuous.
Jobs Positions for high school students and college students 18 and older.
Contact Arno Mares, Director, main address above. Phone: 845-647-3240. Fax: 845-647-3286. E-mail: ope135@hvi.net.
URL www.horseridingcamp.com

Iroquois Springs

Iroquois Springs
Bowers Road
Rock Hill, New York 12775

General Information Coed residential traditional camp established in 1932. Accredited by American Camping Association.
Arts Arts and crafts (general), batiking, ceramics, dance (jazz), dance (modern), drawing, fabric arts, jewelry making, leather working, metalworking, music, musical productions, painting, photography, pottery, sculpture, theater/drama, woodworking.
Special Interest Areas Campcraft, community service, leadership training, model rocketry.
Sports Aerobics, archery, baseball, basketball, bicycling, boating, canoeing, climbing (wall), equestrian sports, fencing, fishing, football, golf, gymnastics, horseback riding, in-line skating, kayaking, lacrosse, martial arts, rappelling, ropes course, sailing, scuba diving, soccer, softball, street/roller hockey, swimming, tennis, volleyball, water polo, waterskiing, weight training.
Wilderness/Outdoors Bicycle trips, canoe trips, hiking, mountain biking, rock climbing, white-water trips.
Trips College tours, day, overnight.
Program Information 2 sessions per year. Session length: 3–6 weeks in June, July, August. Ages: 7–16. 300 participants per session. Boarding program cost: $3375–$6000.
Application Deadline Continuous.
Jobs Positions for college students.
Summer Contact Mr. Mark Newfield, Owner/Director, PO Box 487, Bowers Road, Rock Hill, New York 12775. Phone: 845-434-6500. Fax: 845-434-6508. E-mail: summers@iroquoissprings.com.
Winter Contact Ms. Laura Newfield, Owner/Director, PO Box 20126, Dix Hills, New York 11746. Phone: 631-462-2550. Fax: 631-462-0779. E-mail: summers@iroquoissprings.com.
URL www.iroquoissprings.com

Ithaca College Summer College for High School Students: Session I

Ithaca College Division of Continuing Education and Summer Sessions
Ithaca, New York 14850-7141

General Information Coed residential academic program established in 1997. Formal opportunities for the academically talented. College credit may be earned.
Program Focus Participants earn three college credits.
Academics English language/literature, biology, communications, health sciences, humanities, precollege program, psychology, science (general), social science, social studies, writing.
Arts Acting, theater/drama.
Special Interest Areas Community service.
Sports Basketball, horseback riding, soccer, swimming, tennis.
Wilderness/Outdoors Hiking.
Trips Day, shopping.
Program Information 1 session per year. Session length: 20 days in July. Ages: 15–18. 40–60 participants per session. Boarding program cost: $2900–$3200. Application fee: $40. Financial aid available.
Application Deadline May 1.
Jobs Positions for college students 18 and older.
Contact Mr. E. Kimball Milling, Director of Continuing Education and Summer Sessions, 120 Towers Concourse,

Ithaca, New York 14850-7141. Phone: 607-274-3143. Fax: 607-274-1263. E-mail: cess@ithaca.edu.
URL www.ithaca.edu/summercollege

Ithaca College Summer College for High School Students: Session II

Ithaca College Division of Continuing Education and Summer Sessions
Ithaca, New York 14850-7141

General Information Coed residential academic program established in 1998. Formal opportunities for the academically talented. College credit may be earned.
Program Focus Participants earn six freshman level college credits.
Academics English language/literature, communications, health sciences, humanities, journalism, philosophy, precollege program, psychology, science (general), social science, writing.
Arts Acting, film, musical productions, television/video, theater/drama.
Special Interest Areas Community service.
Sports Basketball, horseback riding, soccer, swimming, tennis.
Wilderness/Outdoors Hiking.
Trips Day, shopping.
Program Information 1 session per year. Session length: 34 days in June, July. Ages: 15–18. 50–60 participants per session. Boarding program cost: $5300–$5700. Application fee: $40. Financial aid available.
Application Deadline May 1.
Jobs Positions for college students 18 and older.
Contact Mr. E. Kimball Milling, Director of Continuing Education and Summer Sessions, 120 Towers Concourse, Ithaca, New York 14850-7141. Phone: 607-274-3143. Fax: 607-274-1263. E-mail: cess@ithaca.edu.
URL www.ithaca.edu/summercollege

Ithaca College Summer College for High School Students: Minicourses

Ithaca College Division of Continuing Education and Summer Sessions
Ithaca, New York 14850-7141

General Information Coed residential academic program established in 2002. Formal opportunities for the academically talented.
Program Focus Students participate in noncredit college preparatory workshops.
Academics English language/literature, biology, communications, health sciences, humanities, precollege program, psychology, science (general), social science, writing.
Sports Soccer, swimming, tennis.
Trips Day, shopping.
Program Information 2 sessions per year. Session length: 6 days in July. Ages: 15–18. 25–40 participants per session. Boarding program cost: $975–$1050. Application fee: $40. Financial aid available.
Application Deadline May 1.
Jobs Positions for college students 18 and older.
Contact Mr. E. Kimball Milling, Director of Continuing Education and Summer Sessions, 120 Towers Concourse, Ithaca, New York 14850-7141. Phone: 607-274-3143. Fax: 607-274-1263. E-mail: cess@ithaca.edu.
URL www.ithaca.edu/summercollege

Ithaca College Summer Piano Institute

Ithaca College Division of Continuing Education and Summer Sessions
Ithaca, New York 14850-7141

General Information Coed residential arts program established in 2000. Formal opportunities for the artistically talented.
Program Focus A comprehensive and intensive week of varied musical experiences for young pianists.
Arts Music (ensemble), music (instrumental), music (piano), piano.
Trips Day.
Program Information 1 session per year. Session length: 6 days in July. Ages: 12–18. 15–35 participants per session. Boarding program cost: $730–$800. Application fee: $25. Financial aid available.
Application Deadline April 30.
Jobs Positions for college students 18 and older.
Contact Mr. E. Kimball Milling, Director of Continuing Education and Summer Sessions, 120 Towers Concourse, Ithaca, New York 14850-7141. Phone: 607-274-3143. Fax: 607-274-1263. E-mail: cess@ithaca.edu.
URL www.ithaca.edu/cess

JHS/HS Academic Summer School Program

The Windsor School
136-23 Sanford Avenue
Flushing, New York 11355

General Information Coed day academic program established in 1973. Formal opportunities for the academically talented. High school credit may be earned.
Program Focus Courses may be taken for preview, enrichment, advanced credit or repeating.
Academics English as a second language, English language/literature, French language/literature, SAT/ACT preparation, Spanish language/literature, academics (general), biology, chemistry, economics, environmental science, geography, geology/earth science, government and politics, history, mathematics, mathematics (Advanced Placement), physics, reading, science (general), social science, social studies.
Program Information 1 session per year. Session length: 30 days in July, August. Ages: 10–18. 5–20 participants per session. Day program cost: $430.
Application Deadline Continuous.
Contact Dr. Philip A. Stewart, Director, main address above. Phone: 718-359-8300. Fax: 718-359-1876. E-mail: admin@thewindsorschool.com.
URL www.windsorschool.com

Kutsher's Sports Academy

Anawana Lake Road
Monticello, New York 12701

General Information Coed residential traditional camp established in 1968. Accredited by American Camping Association.
Academics SAT/ACT preparation, study skills.
Arts Acting, arts and crafts (general), ceramics, dance, dance (ballet), dance (folk), dance (jazz), dance (modern), dance (tap), drawing, leather working, painting, photography, pottery, sculpture, theater/drama, woodworking.
Special Interest Areas College planning, weight reduction.
Sports Aerobics, baseball, basketball, bicycling, bicycling (BMX), boating, canoeing, cheerleading, climbing (wall), cross-country, field hockey, figure skating, fishing, golf, gymnastics, horseback riding, in-line skating, lacrosse, martial arts, sailing, soccer, softball, sports (general), street/roller hockey, swimming, tennis, track and field, volleyball, water polo, waterskiing, weight training, wrestling.
Wilderness/Outdoors Bicycle trips, hiking, mountain biking, white-water trips.
Trips Cultural, day, overnight, shopping.
Program Information 3 sessions per year. Session length: 3–7 weeks in June, July, August. Ages: 7–17. 400–500 participants per session. Boarding program cost: $3200–$6200.
Application Deadline Continuous.
Jobs Positions for college students 19 and older.
Summer Contact Marc White, Executive Director, main address above. Phone: 845-794-5400.
Winter Contact Marc White, Executive Director, 7 Mine Hill Road, Bridgewater, Connecticut 06752. Phone: 860-350-3819. Fax: 860-350-3819. E-mail: kutsport@warwick.net.
URL www.ksacad.com

Landmark Volunteers: New York

Landmark Volunteers, Inc.
New York

General Information Coed residential outdoor program, community service program, and wilderness program established in 1992. High school credit may be earned.
Program Focus High school students may earn community service credit while working as a team for two weeks serving Adirondack Mountain Club, Boys and Girls Harbor, Clearpool, Glimmerglass Opera and Farmers' Museum, Institute of Ecosystem Studies, Paleontological Research Institution, Pathfinder Village, Scenic Hudson, Shaker Museum North Family Site, Snug Harbor Cultural Center, Wagon Road Camp, or Wilderstein Preservation.
Academics Archaeology, area studies, biology, ecology, environmental science, history, science (general), social science, social services.
Arts Carpentry, music, music (vocal), musical productions.
Special Interest Areas Campcraft, career exploration, community service, conservation projects, construction, field research/expeditions, leadership training, nature study, team building, work camp programs.
Sports Swimming.
Wilderness/Outdoors Backpacking, hiking, wilderness camping.
Trips Cultural, day.
Program Information 12 sessions per year. Session length: 14–18 days in June, July, August. Ages: 14–18. 10–13 participants per session. Boarding program cost: $875–$925. Financial aid available.
Application Deadline Continuous.
Jobs Positions for college students.
Contact Ann Barrett, Executive Director, PO Box 455, Sheffield, Massachusetts 01257. Phone: 413-229-0255. Fax: 413-229-2050. E-mail: landmark@volunteers.com.
URL www.volunteers.com

For more information, see page 1182.

Maplebrook School's Summer Program

Maplebrook School
5142 Route 22
Amenia, New York 12501

General Information Coed residential and day academic program and special needs program established in 1945. Specific services available for the learning disabled.
Program Focus Students with learning differences, Attention Deficit Disorder, and low average intellectual abilities; stress academics, social skills, and self-esteem.
Academics English language/literature, SAT/ACT preparation, academics (general), communications, computers, mathematics, reading, study skills, technology, typing, writing.
Arts Arts and crafts (general), ceramics, chorus, creative writing, dance, drawing, fabric arts, music, painting, photography, pottery, radio broadcasting, sculpture, theater/drama, woodworking.
Special Interest Areas Campcraft, community service, driver's education, leadership training, personal development, social skills development.
Sports Aerobics, basketball, bicycling (BMX), equestrian sports, fishing, golf, horseback riding, in-line skating, martial arts, soccer, softball, swimming, tennis, volleyball, weight training.
Wilderness/Outdoors Backpacking, bicycle trips, hiking, mountain biking, orienteering, wilderness camping.
Trips Cultural, day, overnight, shopping.
Program Information 1–3 sessions per year. Session length: 2–6 weeks in July, August. Ages: 11–18. 50–55 participants per session. Boarding program cost: $2332–$7000. Cost for day program varies.
Application Deadline Continuous.
Jobs Positions for college students 20 and older.
Contact Jennifer L. Scully, Director of Admissions, main address above. Phone: 845-373-8191. Fax: 845-373-7029. E-mail: mbsecho@aol.com.

Mountain Workshop–Graduate Plus Awesome Adventures

Mountain Workshop
New York

General Information Coed travel outdoor program, wilderness program, and adventure program established in 2002.
Program Focus Outdoor leadership development focusing on planning, logistics, instruction.
Special Interest Areas Communication skills, leadership training, planning skills, team building.
Sports Canoeing.
Wilderness/Outdoors Caving, hiking, rock climbing, wilderness camping.
Trips Overnight.
Program Information 3–4 sessions per year. Session length: 5 days in June, July, August. Ages: 11–12. Cost: $540.
Application Deadline Continuous.
Jobs Positions for college students 21 and older.
Contact Kent B. Tullo, Director, 9 Brookside Place, West Redding, Connecticut 06896. Phone: 203-544-0555. Fax: 203-544-0333. E-mail: info@mountainworkshop.com.
URL www.mountainworkshop.com

Mountain Workshop–Awesome 1: Adirondacks

Mountain Workshop
New York

General Information Coed travel outdoor program, wilderness program, and adventure program established in 1985.
Special Interest Areas Campcraft, team building.
Sports Canoeing, ropes course, swimming.
Wilderness/Outdoors Canoe trips, caving, hiking, outdoor adventure, outdoor living skills, wilderness camping.
Trips Overnight.
Program Information 3 sessions per year. Session length: 1 week in June, July, August. Ages: 11–12. 13 participants per session. Cost: $950.
Application Deadline Continuous.
Jobs Positions for college students 21 and older.
Contact Kent B. Tullo, Director, 9 Brookside Place, West Redding, Connecticut 06896. Phone: 203-544-0555. Fax: 203-544-0333. E-mail: info@mountainworkshop.com.
URL www.mountainworkshop.com

Mountain Workshop–Leadership Through Adventure: Adirondacks

Mountain Workshop
New York

General Information Coed travel outdoor program, wilderness program, and adventure program established in 1996.
Program Focus Outdoor leadership development focusing on planning, logistics, instruction techniques, hard skills.
Special Interest Areas Communication skills, leadership training, planning skills, team building.
Sports Canoeing.
Wilderness/Outdoors Backpacking, caving, hiking, wilderness camping.
Trips Overnight.
Program Information 1 session per year. Session length: 1 week in June. Ages: 16–18. 8 participants per session. Cost: $1100.
Jobs Positions for college students 21 and older.
Contact Kent B. Tullo, Director, 9 Brookside Place, West Redding, Connecticut 06896. Phone: 203-544-0555. Fax: 203-544-0333. E-mail: info@mountainworkshop.com.
URL www.mountainworkshop.com

The National Music Workshop Day Jams–Long Island, NY

National Guitar Workshop
St. Aidan Lower School
525 Willis Avenue
Williston Park, New York 11596

General Information Coed day arts program established in 2003. Formal opportunities for the artistically talented.
Academics Music.
Arts Arts and crafts (general), band, music, music (rock), music (vocal).
Program Information 2 sessions per year. Session length: 5–10 days in July. Ages: 9–15. 50–65 participants per session. Day program cost: $425–$495. Application fee: $35. Financial aid available.
Application Deadline Continuous.
Jobs Positions for high school students 17 and older and college students 17 and older.
Contact Ms. Lynda Wlodarczyk, Associate Director, 407A Bantam Road, Suite 1, Litchfield, Connecticut 06759. Phone: 800-295-5956. Fax: 860-567-0374. E-mail: lynda@dayjams.com.
URL www.dayjams.com

The National Music Workshop Day Jams–Manhattan, NY

National Guitar Workshop
Manhattan Country School
7 East 96th Street
New York, New York 10128

General Information Coed day arts program established in 1999. Formal opportunities for the artistically talented.
Program Focus Rock 'n' roll day camp.
Academics Music.
Arts Arts and crafts (general), band, guitar, music, music (rock), music (vocal), television/video.
Program Information 4 sessions per year. Session length: 5–20 days in June, July. Ages: 9–15. 40–70

The National Music Workshop Day Jams–Manhattan, NY (continued)

participants per session. Day program cost: $425–$495. Application fee: $35. Financial aid available.
Application Deadline Continuous.
Jobs Positions for high school students 17 and older and college students 17 and older.
Contact Ms. Lynda Wlodarczyk, Associate Director, 407A Bantam Road, Suite 1, Litchfield, Connecticut 06759. Phone: 800-295-5956. Fax: 860-567-0374. E-mail: lynda@dayjams.com.
URL www.dayjams.com

THE NATIONAL MUSIC WORKSHOP DAY JAMS–PURCHASE, NY

National Guitar Workshop
Keio Academy
3 College Road
Purchase, New York 10577

General Information Coed day arts program established in 1999. Formal opportunities for the artistically talented.
Program Focus Rock 'n' roll day camp.
Academics Music.
Arts Arts and crafts (general), band, guitar, music, music (rock), music (vocal), television/video.
Program Information 4 sessions per year. Session length: 5–20 days in June, July. Ages: 9–15. 70–80 participants per session. Day program cost: $425–$495. Application fee: $35. Financial aid available.
Application Deadline Continuous.
Jobs Positions for high school students 17 and older and college students 17 and older.
Contact Lynda Wlodarczyk, Associate Director, 407A Bantam Road, Suite 1, Litchfield, Connecticut 06759. Phone: 800-295-5956. Fax: 860-567-0374. E-mail: lynda@dayjams.com.
URL www.dayjams.com

THE NEW YORK FILM ACADEMY, THE DALTON SCHOOL, NEW YORK, NY

New York Film Academy
New York, New York

General Information Coed day arts program established in 1992. College credit may be earned.
Program Focus "Total immersion" hands-on filmmaking workshop where students write, direct, shoot, and edit their own short 16mm films.
Arts Acting, creative writing, directing, film, film editing, film lighting, film production, screenwriting, sound design, television/video, theater/drama.
Trips Cultural.
Program Information 4–30 sessions per year. Session length: 6–42 days in June, July, August. Ages: 14–17. 6–16 participants per session. Day program cost: $1500–$6900.
Application Deadline Continuous.

The New York Film Academy, The Dalton School, New York, NY

Contact Admissions, 100 East 17th Street, New York, New York 10003. Phone: 212-674-4300. Fax: 212-477-1414. E-mail: film@nyfa.com.
URL www.nyfa.com

For more information, see page 1218.

NEW YORK MILITARY ACADEMY–JROTC SUMMER PROGRAM

New York Military Academy
78 Academy Avenue
Cornwall-on-Hudson, New York 12520

General Information Coed residential academic program. High school credit may be earned.
Program Focus Character and leadership development.
Academics English as a second language, English language/literature, SAT/ACT preparation, Spanish language/literature, academics (general), biology, chemistry, computers, history, mathematics, reading, science (general), social studies, study skills.
Special Interest Areas Leadership training.
Sports Basketball, horseback riding, paintball, riflery, soccer, softball, swimming, tennis, volleyball, weight training.
Wilderness/Outdoors Rafting, white-water trips.
Trips Cultural, day, shopping.
Program Information 2 sessions per year. Session length: 3–5 weeks in June, July. Ages: 14+. 15–125 participants per session. Boarding program cost: $3400–$5500. Application fee: $300.
Application Deadline June 27.
Jobs Positions for college students.
Contact Maureen T. Kelly, Director of Admissions, main address above. Phone: 845-534-3710 Ext.4233. Fax: 845-534-7699. E-mail: admissions@nyma.ouboces.org.
URL www.nyma.org

92nd Street Y Camps–Camp Bari Tov

92nd Street YM–YWHA
1395 Lexington Avenue
New York, New York 10128

General Information Coed day traditional camp and special needs program established in 1955. Religious affiliation: Jewish. Accredited by American Camping Association. Specific services available for the developmentally challenged.
Program Focus For children with developmental disabilities who require one-to-one supervision.
Arts Arts and crafts (general), music.
Special Interest Areas Campcraft, nature study.
Sports Swimming.
Trips Day.
Program Information 1 session per year. Session length: 39 days in June, July, August. Ages: 5–13. 15–20 participants per session. Financial aid available.
Application Deadline Continuous.
Jobs Positions for high school students 18 and older and college students.
Contact Alan Saltz, Director of Camp Programs, main address above. Phone: 212-415-5600. Fax: 212-415-5637. E-mail: camps@92y.org.
URL www.92y.org/camps

92nd Street Y Camps–Camp Haverim

92nd Street YM–YWHA
1395 Lexington Avenue
New York, New York 10128

General Information Coed day traditional camp established in 1955. Religious affiliation: Jewish. Accredited by American Camping Association.
Program Focus One night sleepovers, 5-day, 4-night trip to camp in the Poconos.
Arts Arts and crafts (general), ceramics, chorus, dance, drawing, jewelry making, music, painting, pottery, theater/drama.
Special Interest Areas Campcraft, model rocketry, nature study.
Sports Archery, baseball, basketball, boating, climbing (wall), football, golf, horseback riding, in-line skating, martial arts, ropes course, soccer, softball, swimming, tennis, volleyball.
Wilderness/Outdoors Rafting.
Trips Day, overnight.
Program Information 3 sessions per year. Session length: 20–40 days in June, July, August. Ages: 10–12. 150–200 participants per session. Day program cost: $2650–$4150. Financial aid available. Open to participants entering grades 5–6.
Application Deadline Continuous.
Jobs Positions for high school students 18 and older and college students.
Contact Alan Saltz, Director of Camp Programs, main address above. Phone: 212-415-5600. Fax: 212-415-5637. E-mail: camps@92y.org.
URL www.92y.org/camps

92nd Street Y Camps–Camp K'Ton Ton

92nd Street YM–YWHA
1395 Lexington Avenue
New York, New York 10128

General Information Coed day traditional camp established in 1955. Religious affiliation: Jewish. Accredited by American Camping Association.
Arts Arts and crafts (general), drawing, jewelry making, music, painting, theater/drama.
Special Interest Areas Campcraft.
Sports Swimming.
Program Information 1 session per year. Session length: 30 days in June, July, August. Ages: 3–5. 150 participants per session. Day program cost: $3300–$4300. Financial aid available.
Application Deadline Continuous.
Jobs Positions for high school students 18 and older and college students.
Contact Alan Saltz, Director of Camp Programs, main address above. Phone: 212-415-5600. Fax: 212-415-5637. E-mail: camps@92y.org.
URL www.92y.org/camps

92nd Street Y Camps–Camp Tevah for Science and Nature

92nd Street YM–YWHA
New York

General Information Coed day traditional camp and outdoor program established in 1955. Religious affiliation: Jewish. Accredited by American Camping Association.
Program Focus Exploring science and nature.
Academics Science (general).
Arts Arts and crafts (general).
Special Interest Areas Campcraft, nature study.
Sports Archery, baseball, basketball, boating, climbing (wall), football, golf, horseback riding, in-line skating, martial arts, ropes course, soccer, softball, swimming, tennis, volleyball.
Trips Day.
Program Information 1 session per year. Session length: 30 days in June, July, August. Ages: 8–11. 35–45 participants per session. Day program cost: $3350. Financial aid available.
Application Deadline Continuous.
Jobs Positions for high school students 18 and older and college students.
Contact Alan Saltz, Director of Camp Programs, 1395 Lexington Avenue, New York, New York 10128. Phone: 212-415-5600. Fax: 212-415-5637. E-mail: camps@92y.org.
URL www.92y.org/camps

92nd Street Y Camps–Camp Tova

92nd Street YM–YWHA
New York

General Information Coed day traditional camp and special needs program established in 1955. Religious

92nd Street Y Camps–Camp Tova (continued)
affiliation: Jewish. Accredited by American Camping Association. Specific services available for the emotionally challenged, learning disabled, and physically challenged.
Program Focus Designed to foster each child's emotional, social, and physical growth.
Arts Arts and crafts (general), music, painting, sculpture.
Special Interest Areas Campcraft, nature study.
Sports Archery, basketball, ropes course, soccer, softball, sports (general), swimming.
Program Information 1 session per year. Session length: 40 days in June, July, August. Ages: 6–13. 60–75 participants per session. Day program cost: $3950. Financial aid available.
Application Deadline Continuous.
Jobs Positions for high school students 18 and older and college students.
Contact Alan Saltz, Director of Camp Programs, 1395 Lexington Avenue, New York, New York 10128. Phone: 212-415-5600. Fax: 212-415-5637. E-mail: camps@92y.org.
URL www.92y.org/camps

92nd Street Y Camps–Camp Yaffa for the Arts

92nd Street YM–YWHA
1395 Lexington Avenue
New York, New York 10128

General Information Coed day traditional camp and arts program established in 1955. Religious affiliation: Jewish. Accredited by American Camping Association. Formal opportunities for the artistically talented.
Program Focus Workshops in dance, visual arts, and drama; multidisciplinary performance and exhibition.
Arts Arts, arts and crafts (general), ceramics, chorus, dance, drawing, jewelry making, music, painting, pottery, theater/drama.
Special Interest Areas Campcraft, model rocketry.
Sports Archery, baseball, basketball, boating, climbing (wall), football, golf, horseback riding, in-line skating, martial arts, ropes course, soccer, softball, swimming, tennis, volleyball.
Trips Day.
Program Information 1 session per year. Session length: 30 days in June, July, August. Ages: 8–11. 35–45 participants per session. Day program cost: $3350. Financial aid available.
Application Deadline Continuous.
Jobs Positions for high school students 18 and older and college students.
Contact Alan Saltz, Director of Camp Programs, main address above. Phone: 212-415-5600. Fax: 212-415-5637. E-mail: camps@92y.org.
URL www.92y.org/camps

92nd Street Y Camps–Camp Yomi

92nd Street YM–YWHA
1395 Lexington Avenue
New York, New York 10128

General Information Coed day traditional camp established in 1955. Religious affiliation: Jewish. Accredited by American Camping Association.
Arts Animation, arts and crafts (general), ceramics, chorus, dance, drawing, jewelry making, music, painting, pottery, sculpture, television/video, theater/drama.
Special Interest Areas Campcraft, model rocketry, nature study.
Sports Archery, baseball, basketball, boating, football, golf, gymnastics, horseback riding, in-line skating, martial arts, ropes course, soccer, softball, swimming, tennis, volleyball.
Trips Overnight.
Program Information 2 sessions per year. Session length: 20–40 days in June, July, August. Ages: 5–9. 600 participants per session. Day program cost: $2550–$4050. Application fee: $50. Financial aid available. Open to participants entering grades K–4.
Application Deadline Continuous.
Jobs Positions for high school students 16 and older and college students.
Contact Alan Saltz, Director of Camp Programs, main address above. Phone: 212-415-5600. Fax: 212-415-5637. E-mail: camps@92y.org.
URL www.92y.org/camps

92nd Street Y Camps–Fantastic Gymnastics

92nd Street YM–YWHA
1395 Lexington Avenue
New York, New York 10128

General Information Coed day sports camp established in 1955. Religious affiliation: Jewish. Accredited by American Camping Association.
Program Focus Gymnastics instruction and exhibition.
Arts Arts and crafts (general), dance.
Sports Gymnastics, swimming.
Program Information 3 sessions per year. Session length: 10–30 days in June, July, August. Ages: 7–13. 50 participants per session. Day program cost: $2000–$3800. Financial aid available. Open to participants entering grades 2–8.
Application Deadline Continuous.
Jobs Positions for high school students 18 and older and college students.
Contact Alan Saltz, Director of Camp Programs, main address above. Phone: 212-415-5600. Fax: 212-415-5637. E-mail: camps@92y.org.
URL www.92y.org/camps

92nd Street Y Camps–Trailblazers

92nd Street YM–YWHA
New York

General Information Coed travel traditional camp established in 1955. Religious affiliation: Jewish. Accredited by American Camping Association.
Program Focus Day-travel program where campers go on a diverse range of one-day trips to various destinations.
Arts Arts and crafts (general).
Special Interest Areas Campcraft.
Sports Archery, baseball, basketball, boating, football, in-line skating, ropes course, soccer, softball, swimming, tennis, volleyball.
Trips Day, overnight.
Program Information 2 sessions per year. Session length: 20–40 days in June, July, August. Ages: 12–14. 60–90 participants per session. Cost: $2800–$4300. Financial aid available. Open to participants entering grades 7–8.
Application Deadline Continuous.
Jobs Positions for college students 19 and older.
Contact Alan Saltz, Director of Camp Programs, 1395 Lexington Avenue, New York, New York 10128. Phone: 212-415-5600. Fax: 212-415-5637. E-mail: camps@92y.org.
URL www.92y.org/camps

North Country Camps—Camp Lincoln for Boys

North Country Camps
395 Frontage Road
Keeseville, New York 12944

General Information Boys' residential traditional camp established in 1920. Accredited by American Camping Association.
Program Focus Activities, skills, and attitudes to last a lifetime.
Arts Arts and crafts (general), batiking, ceramics, creative writing, dance, dance (folk), drawing, fabric arts, music, music (vocal), painting, photography, pottery, printmaking, theater/drama, woodworking.
Special Interest Areas Animal care, campcraft, community service, construction, gardening, leadership training, nature study, work camp programs.
Sports Archery, baseball, basketball, bicycling, boating, canoeing, climbing (wall), diving, equestrian sports, fishing, football, horseback riding, kayaking, lacrosse, rappelling, ropes course, sailing, sea kayaking, snorkeling, soccer, softball, swimming, tennis, volleyball, water polo, windsurfing.
Wilderness/Outdoors Backpacking, bicycle trips, canoe trips, hiking, mountain biking, mountaineering, pack animal trips, rock climbing, wilderness camping.
Trips Day, overnight.
Program Information 1 session per year. Session length: 52 days in July, August. Ages: 8–15. 90 participants per session. Boarding program cost: $5000. Financial aid available.
Application Deadline Continuous.
Jobs Positions for college students 19 and older.
Summer Contact Nancy Gucker Birdsall, Director, main address above. Phone: 518-834-5152. Fax: 518-834-5527. E-mail: nancy@nccamps.com.
Winter Contact Nancy Gucker Birdsall, Director, 166 Morgan Road, Town of Tinmouth, West Rutland, Vermont 05777. Phone: 802-235-2908. Fax: 802-235-2908. E-mail: nancy@nccamps.com.
URL www.nccamps.com

North Country Camps—Camp Whippoorwill for Girls

North Country Camps
395 Frontage Road
Keeseville, New York 12944

General Information Girls' residential traditional camp established in 1931. Accredited by American Camping Association.
Program Focus Activities, skills, and attitudes to last a lifetime.
Arts Arts and crafts (general), batiking, ceramics, creative writing, dance, dance (folk), dance (jazz), dance (modern), drawing, fabric arts, jewelry making, music, music (vocal), painting, photography, pottery, printmaking, theater/drama, weaving, woodworking.
Special Interest Areas Animal care, campcraft, community service, construction, gardening, leadership training, nature study, work camp programs.
Sports Aerobics, archery, basketball, bicycling, boating, canoeing, climbing (wall), equestrian sports, fishing, horseback riding, kayaking, rappelling, ropes course, sailing, sea kayaking, snorkeling, soccer, softball, swimming, tennis, volleyball, windsurfing.
Wilderness/Outdoors Backpacking, bicycle trips, canoe trips, hiking, mountain biking, mountaineering, pack animal trips, rock climbing, wilderness camping.
Trips Day, overnight.
Program Information 1 session per year. Session length: 52 days in July, August. Ages: 8–15. 85 participants per session. Boarding program cost: $5000. Financial aid available.
Application Deadline Continuous.
Jobs Positions for college students 19 and older.
Summer Contact Nancy Gucker Birdsall, Director, main address above. Phone: 518-834-5152. Fax: 518-834-5527. E-mail: nancy@nccamps.com.
Winter Contact Nancy Gucker Birdsall, Director, 166 Morgan Road, Town of Tinmouth, West Rutland, Vermont 05777. Phone: 802-235-2908. Fax: 802-235-2908. E-mail: nancy@nccamps.com.
URL www.nccamps.com

Parsons Pre-College Academy

Parsons School of Design
66 Fifth Avenue
New York, New York 10011

General Information Coed day arts program established in 2000. Formal opportunities for the artistically talented.
Program Focus Studio art and design courses.
Academics Architecture, communications, computers, precollege program.

Parsons Pre-College Academy (continued)

Arts Animation, design, drawing, fashion design/ production, graphic arts, painting, photography, studio arts, television/video.
Special Interest Areas Career exploration, college planning, robotics.
Trips Cultural, day.
Program Information 3 sessions per year. Session length: 10–11 days in February, March, April, May, August, October, November, December. Ages: 9–18. 250–350 participants per session. Day program cost: $290–$720. Application fee: $7. Financial aid available.
Application Deadline Continuous.
Jobs Positions for college students 19 and older.
Contact Charlotte Rice, Director, Pre-Enrollment Programs, main address above. Phone: 212-229-8925. Fax: 212-229-8975. E-mail: summer@newschool.edu.
URL www.parsons.edu/academy

Parsons Summer Intensive Studies–New York

Parsons School of Design
66 Fifth Avenue
New York, New York 10011

General Information Coed residential and day arts program established in 1977. Formal opportunities for the artistically talented. College credit may be earned.
Program Focus Studio art and design courses.
Academics Architecture, art (Advanced Placement), computers, precollege program.
Arts Animation, design, drawing, fashion design/ production, graphic arts, painting, photography, studio arts.
Special Interest Areas Career exploration, college planning, robotics.
Trips College tours, cultural, day.
Program Information 1 session per year. Session length: 4 weeks in June, July. Ages: 16+. 250–350 participants per session. Day program cost: $2200. Boarding program cost: $3600. Financial aid available.
Application Deadline Continuous.
Contact Ms. Charlotte Rice, Director, Pre-Enrollment Programs, main address above. Phone: 212-229-8925. Fax: 212-229-8975. E-mail: summer@newschool.edu.
URL www.parsons.edu/summer

Point O' Pines Camp for Girls

Point O' Pines Camp
7201 State Route 8
Brant Lake, New York 12815-2236

General Information Girls' residential traditional camp established in 1957. Accredited by American Camping Association.
Program Focus Traditional program featuring field sports, tennis, performing arts (drama and dance).
Academics Music.
Arts Arts and crafts (general), ceramics, dance, dance (jazz), dance (modern), dance (tap), drawing, fabric arts, film, jewelry making, magic, music (vocal), painting, photography, pottery, puppetry, television/video, theater/ drama.
Special Interest Areas Culinary arts, nature study.
Sports Aerobics, baseball, basketball, boating, canoeing, equestrian sports, field games, field hockey, fishing, golf, gymnastics, horseback riding, lacrosse, physical fitness, ropes course, sailing, soccer, softball, swimming, tennis, track and field, volleyball, waterskiing, windsurfing.
Wilderness/Outdoors Backpacking, canoe trips, hiking, mountaineering, orienteering, rafting, wilderness camping.
Trips Overnight.
Program Information 1 session per year. Session length: 54 days in June, July, August. Ages: 7–15. 320 participants per session. Boarding program cost: $8300.
Application Deadline Continuous.
Jobs Positions for college students 18 and older.
Contact Ms. Sue Himoff, Director, main address above. Phone: 518-494-3213 Ext.11. Fax: 518-494-3489. E-mail: sue@pointopines.com.
URL www.pointopines.com

Power Chord Academy–New York City

Power Chord Academy
New York, New York

General Information Coed residential arts program. Formal opportunities for the academically talented.
Program Focus Teenage musicians play in a band, record a CD, make a video, play a concert, and gain an unbridled understanding of the music industry.
Academics Art (Advanced Placement), music, music (Advanced Placement).
Arts Band, music, music (chamber), music (classical), music (ensemble), music (instrumental), music (jazz), music (orchestral), music (vocal), music technology/ record production, musical performance/recitals, songwriting.
Program Information 1–4 sessions per year. Session length: 1 week in July. Ages: 12–18. 100–120 participants per session. Boarding program cost: $895–$1095.
Application Deadline Continuous.
Jobs Positions for college students 22 and older.
Contact Mr. Bryan J. Wrzesinski, 7336 Santa Monica Boulevard, #107, Los Angeles, California 90046. Phone: 800-897-6677. Fax: 775-306-7923. E-mail: bryan@ powerchordacademy.com.
URL www.powerchordacademy.com

Pratt Institute Summer Pre-College Program for High School Students

Pratt Institute
200 Willoughby Avenue
113 Engineering Building
Brooklyn, New York 11205

General Information Coed residential academic program and arts program. Formal opportunities for the academically talented and artistically talented. College credit may be earned.

Pratt Institute Summer Pre-College Program for High School Students

Program Focus The development of a portfolio and academic skills in art, design, and architecture.
Academics Architecture, art (Advanced Placement), art history/appreciation, intercultural studies, precollege program, writing.
Arts Arts, arts and crafts (general), creative writing, design, fabric arts, fashion design/production, film, graphic arts, illustration, photography, sculpture.
Special Interest Areas Career exploration, industrial arts.
Trips Cultural, day.
Program Information 1 session per year. Session length: 30 days in July. Ages: 16–18. 300–400 participants per session. Boarding program cost: $1850–$3541. Application fee: $25. Tuition scholarship available by competitive application. Call for program costs.
Application Deadline April 1.
Contact Ms. Johndell Wilson, Program Assistant, main address above. Phone: 718-636-3453. Fax: 718-399-4410. E-mail: precollege@pratt.edu.
URL www.pratt.edu/precollege/

For more information, see page 1270.

Purchase Youth Theatre

Purchase College, State University of New York
735 Anderson Hill Road
Purchase, New York 10577-1400

General Information Coed day arts program established in 1984.
Program Focus Musical theater.
Arts Chorus, dance, dance (jazz), dance (modern), dance (tap), music (vocal), musical productions, musical theater, theater/drama.
Program Information 1 session per year. Session length: 24 days in June, July, August. Ages: 9–17. 80 participants per session. Day program cost: $825–$995.
Application Deadline June 3.
Jobs Positions for college students 18 and older.
Contact Stephanie Nieves, Youth Programs Coordinator, main address above. Phone: 914-251-6500. Fax: 914-251-6515. E-mail: stephanie.nieves@purchase.edu.
URL www.purchase.edu/ce/youth_programs

The Ranch–Lake Placid Academy

The Ranch–Lake Placid Academy
RR #1
Forest Home Road
Lake Clear, New York 12945

General Information Girls' residential and day traditional camp and outdoor program established in 1989. Accredited by American Camping Association.
Program Focus English/Western riding program.
Arts Arts and crafts (general), ceramics, dance, dance (ballet), dance (folk), dance (jazz), dance (modern), drawing, jewelry making, leather working, metalworking, music, musical productions, painting, photography, pottery, printmaking, sculpture, television/video, theater/drama, weaving.
Special Interest Areas Native American culture, animal care, nature study.
Sports Archery, baseball, basketball, climbing (wall), equestrian sports, fishing, golf, gymnastics, horseback riding, ropes course, soccer, softball, swimming, tennis, volleyball.
Wilderness/Outdoors Backpacking, canoe trips, hiking, pack animal trips, rafting, white-water trips, wilderness camping.
Trips Day, overnight, shopping.
Program Information 4 sessions per year. Session length: 2–8 weeks in June, July, August. Ages: 7–17. 50 participants per session. Day program cost: $1400–$5600. Boarding program cost: $1450–$5800.
Application Deadline Continuous.
Jobs Positions for high school students 18 and older and college students 18 and older.
Contact Marleen Goodman, Admissions, 4 Yankee Glen, Madison, Connecticut 06443. Phone: 518-891-5684. Fax: 518-891-6350. E-mail: marleengoodman@hotmail.com.
URL www.childrenscamps.com

The Ranch–National Golf Camp–Lake Placid

The Ranch–Lake Placid Academy
Lake Clear, New York 12945

General Information Coed residential and day sports camp established in 1994.
Program Focus Golf.
Sports Aerobics, archery, basketball, canoeing, equestrian sports, golf, horseback riding, soccer, softball, swimming, tennis, volleyball.
Wilderness/Outdoors Backpacking, hiking, orienteering, pack animal trips, rafting.
Trips Day.
Program Information 8 sessions per year. Session length: 6 days in June, July, August. Ages: 7–17. 1–50 participants per session. Day program cost: $75. Boarding program cost: $999. Financial aid available.
Application Deadline Continuous.
Jobs Positions for college students.
Contact Marleen Goodman, Admissions, 4 Yankee Glen, Madison, Connecticut 06443. Phone: 518-891-5684. Fax: 518-891-6350. E-mail: marleengoodman@hotmail.com.
URL www.childrenscamps.com

St. John's University Scholars Program

St. John's University
8000 Utopia Parkway
Jamaica, New York 11439

General Information Coed day academic program established in 1976. Formal opportunities for the academically talented and gifted. Specific services available for the physically challenged. College credit may be earned.
Program Focus Academic course work.
Academics American literature, English language/literature, academics (general), business, chemistry, communications, computers, government and politics, government and politics (Advanced Placement), history, humanities, mathematics, music, physics, social science, writing.
Arts Drawing, graphic arts.
Program Information 3 sessions per year. Session length: 20–65 days in January, February, March, April, May, June, July, August, September, October, November, December. Ages: 16+. 20–30 participants per session. Day program cost: $900–$1100.
Application Deadline May 10.
Contact Cecelia M. Russo, Director, Pre-Admission Programs, main address above. Phone: 718-990-6565. Fax: 718-990-2158. E-mail: russoc@stjohns.edu.
URL www.stjohns.edu

Shakespeare at Purchase

Purchase College, State University of New York
735 Anderson Hill Road
Purchase, New York 10577

General Information Coed day arts program established in 2004. Formal opportunities for the artistically talented.
Program Focus Shakespearean plays.
Arts Acting, theater/drama.
Program Information 3 sessions per year. Session length: 2 weeks in June, July, August. Ages: 10–18. 20–25 participants per session. Day program cost: $630–$680.
Application Deadline June 25.
Jobs Positions for college students 19 and older.
Contact Ms. Stephanie Nieves, Director of Youth Programs, main address above. Phone: 914-251-6508. Fax: 914-251-6515. E-mail: stephanie.nieves@purchase.edu.
URL www.purchase.edu/ce/youth_programs

Shane (Trim-Down) Camp

302 Harris Road
Ferndale, New York 12734

General Information Coed residential special needs program established in 1968. Accredited by American Camping Association. Specific services available for the weight reduction.

Shane (Trim-Down) Camp

Program Focus Weight loss.
Arts Arts and crafts (general), batiking, ceramics, dance, dance (jazz), dance (modern), drawing, fabric arts, jewelry making, leather working, music, musical productions, painting, photography, pottery, printmaking, radio broadcasting, sculpture, television/video, theater/drama, woodworking.
Special Interest Areas Culinary arts, leadership training, model rocketry, nutrition, weight reduction.
Sports Aerobics, archery, basketball, bicycling, boating, canoeing, cheerleading, climbing (wall), fishing, football, go-carts, horseback riding, lacrosse, physical fitness,

riflery, ropes course, scuba diving, soccer, softball, swimming, tennis, volleyball, water polo, waterskiing, weight training.
Wilderness/Outdoors Backpacking, bicycle trips, canoe trips, hiking, mountain biking.
Trips Day, overnight.
Program Information 3–5 sessions per year. Session length: 20–60 days in June, July, August. Ages: 7–25. 400–500 participants per session. Boarding program cost: $2900–$6400.
Application Deadline Continuous.
Jobs Positions for college students 18 and older.
Summer Contact David Ettenberg, Certified Camp Director, main address above. Phone: 845-292-4644. Fax: 845-292-8636. E-mail: office@campshane.com.
Winter Contact David Ettenberg, Director, 134 Teatown Road, Croton-on-Hudson, New York 10520. Phone: 914-271-4141. Fax: 914-271-2103. E-mail: office@campshane.com.
URL www.campshane.com

For more information, see page 1042.

Signature Music Teen Camp

Signature Music Camp
Ithaca College
Ithaca, New York 14850

General Information Coed residential arts program established in 1993. Formal opportunities for the artistically talented.
Program Focus Instrumental and vocal music, including jazz ensembles, show choirs, concert band, and concert choir.
Arts Band, chorus, music (chamber), music (classical), music (ensemble), music (instrumental), music (jazz), music (vocal).
Sports Soccer, swimming.
Program Information 1 session per year. Session length: 2 weeks in June, July. Ages: 14–17. 80–100 participants per session. Boarding program cost: $1600.
Application Deadline Continuous.
Jobs Positions for college students 20 and older.
Contact Dr. Richard W. Ford, Executive Director, 138 Fellows Avenue, Syracuse, New York 13210. Phone: 315-478-7480. Fax: 315-478-0962. E-mail: director@signaturemusiccamp.org.
URL www.signaturemusiccamp.org

Signature Music Youth Camp

Signature Music Camp
Ithaca College
Ithaca, New York 14850

General Information Coed residential arts program established in 1998. Formal opportunities for the artistically talented.
Program Focus Music.
Arts Band, chorus, music (chamber), music (classical), music (ensemble), music (instrumental), music (jazz), music (vocal).
Special Interest Areas Career exploration.
Sports Soccer, swimming, volleyball.
Program Information 1 session per year. Session length: 1 week in July. Ages: 12–13. 80–100 participants per session. Boarding program cost: $800. Camperships available; assistance given families in receiving local sponsorships.
Application Deadline Continuous.
Jobs Positions for college students 20 and older.
Contact Dr. Richard W. Ford, Executive Director, 138 Fellows Avenue, Syracuse, New York 13210. Phone: 315-478-7840. Fax: 315-478-0962.
URL www.signaturemusiccamp.org

Skidmore College–Acceleration Program in Art for High School Students

Skidmore College
815 North Broadway
Saratoga Springs, New York 12866

General Information Coed residential and day arts program established in 1985. Formal opportunities for the artistically talented. College credit may be earned.

Skidmore College–Acceleration Program in Art for High School Students

Program Focus Visual arts and art history.
Academics Art (Advanced Placement), art history/appreciation, precollege program.
Arts Arts and crafts (general), ceramics, drawing, fabric arts, film, graphic arts, painting, photography, pottery, printmaking, sculpture, weaving, woodworking.
Trips Cultural, day.
Program Information 1 session per year. Session length: 24–30 days in July, August. Ages: 15–18. 50–75 participants per session. Day program cost: $780–$2600. Boarding program cost: $3200–$4500. Application fee: $30. Financial aid available.
Application Deadline Continuous.
Jobs Positions for college students.
Contact Ms. Marianne Needham, Coordinator, main address above. Phone: 518-580-5052. Fax: 518-580-5029. E-mail: mneedham@skidmore.edu.
URL www.skidmore.edu/academics/art/summersix/

For more information, see page 1314.

Skidmore College–Pre-College Program in the Liberal Arts for High School Students

Skidmore College
815 North Broadway
Saratoga Springs, New York 12866

General Information Coed residential and day academic program and arts program established in 1978. Formal opportunities for the academically talented. High school or college credit may be earned.

Skidmore College–Pre-College Program in the Liberal Arts for High School Students

Program Focus College credit-bearing courses offered in the liberal arts.
Academics American literature, English language/literature, French language/literature, Spanish language/literature, academics (general), anthropology, archaeology, area studies, art (Advanced Placement), biology, business, chemistry, ecology, economics, environmental science, geology/earth science, government and politics, history, humanities, intercultural studies, mathematics, music, oceanography, philosophy, physics, precollege program, psychology, religion, science (general), social science, writing.
Arts Arts and crafts (general), ceramics, creative writing, drawing, graphic arts, music, painting, photography, sculpture.
Special Interest Areas Career exploration, field trips (arts and culture).
Sports Basketball, cross-country, diving, equestrian sports, horseback riding, racquetball, soccer, softball, sports (general), squash, swimming, tennis, volleyball, weight training.
Wilderness/Outdoors Hiking.
Trips Cultural, day.
Program Information 1 session per year. Session length: 37 days in July, August. Ages: 16–18. 45–60 participants per session. Day program cost: $3000–$3100. Boarding program cost: $4250–$4400. Application fee: $30. Financial aid available.
Application Deadline Continuous.
Jobs Positions for college students 19 and older.
Contact Dr. James Chansky, Director of Summer Special Programs, main address above. Phone: 518-580-5590. Fax: 518-580-5548. E-mail: jchansky@skidmore.edu.
URL www.skidmore.edu/summer
For more information, see page 1316.

SoccerPlus FieldPlayer Academy–Hamilton, NY

SoccerPlus Camps
Colgate University
Hamilton, New York

General Information Coed residential and day sports camp.
Program Focus Developing overall game skills in a competitive environment with quality goalkeepers.
Sports Soccer.
Program Information 1 session per year. Session length: 6 days in July. Ages: 11+. Day program cost: $595. Boarding program cost: $695. Financial aid available.
Application Deadline Continuous.
Jobs Positions for college students.
Contact Mr. Shawn Kelly, General Manager, 11 Executive Drive, Suite 202, Farmington, Connecticut 06032. Phone: 800-533-7371. Fax: 860-677-0460. E-mail: info@soccerpluscamps.com.
URL www.soccerpluscamps.com

SoccerPlus Goalkeeper School–Challenge Program–Hamilton, NY

SoccerPlus Camps
Colgate University
Hamilton, New York

General Information Coed residential and day sports camp.
Program Focus Developing technical and tactical goalkeeping skills.
Sports Soccer.
Program Information 1 session per year. Session length: 6 days in July. Ages: 10+. Day program cost: $595. Boarding program cost: $695. Financial aid available.
Application Deadline Continuous.
Jobs Positions for college students.
Contact Mr. Shawn Kelly, General Manager, 11 Executive Drive, Suite 202, Farmington, Connecticut 06032. Phone: 800-533-7371. Fax: 860-677-0460. E-mail: info@soccerpluscamps.com.
URL www.soccerpluscamps.com

SoccerPlus Goalkeeper School–Competitive Program–Hamilton, NY

SoccerPlus Camps
Colgate University
Hamilton, New York

General Information Coed residential sports camp.

Program Focus Developing game skills in a competitive environment with quality field players.
Sports Soccer.
Program Information 1 session per year. Session length: 6 days in July. Ages: 12+. Boarding program cost: $755. Financial aid available.
Application Deadline Continuous.
Jobs Positions for college students.
Contact Mr. Shawn Kelly, General Manager, 11 Executive Drive, Suite 202, Farmington, Connecticut 06032. Phone: 800-533-7371. Fax: 860-677-0460. E-mail: info@soccerpluscamps.com.
URL www.soccerpluscamps.com

SoccerPlus Goalkeeper School–National Training Center–Hamilton, NY

SoccerPlus Camps
Colgate University
Hamilton, New York

General Information Coed residential sports camp.
Program Focus Developing advanced goalkeeping skills.
Sports Soccer.
Program Information 1 session per year. Session length: 6 days in July. Ages: 15+. Boarding program cost: $775.
Application Deadline Continuous.
Jobs Positions for college students.
Contact Mr. Shawn Kelly, General Manager, 11 Executive Drive, Suite 202, Farmington, Connecticut 06032. Phone: 800-533-7371. Fax: 860-677-0460. E-mail: info@soccerpluscamps.com.
URL www.soccerpluscamps.com

Sprucelands Camp

Sprucelands Equestrian Center and Summer Camp
1316 Pit Road
Java Center, New York 14082

General Information Coed residential traditional camp and sports camp established in 1935. Specific services available for the learning disabled.
Program Focus Skills-oriented horsemanship, horse care/riding, leadership training with overall emphasis on responsibility, self-confidence, independence and teamwork.
Arts Arts and crafts (general), creative writing.
Special Interest Areas Animal care, leadership training.
Sports Basketball, canoeing, equestrian sports, horseback riding, kayaking, softball, swimming, tennis, volleyball.
Program Information 1–4 sessions per year. Session length: 13–56 days in July, August. Ages: 6–17. 55–60 participants per session. Boarding program cost: $1300–$4960. Application fee: $200. Financial aid available. Accredited by the Certified Horsemanship Association (CHA). Early registration discounts offered September-May.
Application Deadline Continuous.
Jobs Positions for high school students 17 and older and college students 17 and older.
Contact Ms. Eileen Thompson, Owner/Director, 1316 Pit Road, PO Box 54, Java Center, New York 14082. Phone: 585-457-4150. Fax: 585-457-4150. E-mail: spruceland@aol.com.
URL www.sprucelands.com

Stagedoor Manor Performing Arts Training Center/Theatre and Dance Camp

116 Karmel Road
Loch Sheldrake, New York 12759-5308

General Information Coed residential arts program established in 1975. Formal opportunities for the artistically talented and gifted. High school credit may be earned.

Stagedoor Manor Performing Arts Training Center/Theatre and Dance Camp

Program Focus Theater, dance, voice, television, film, and modeling.
Academics Music, precollege program, speech/debate, writing.
Arts Acting, arts and crafts (general), batiking, chorus, creative writing, dance, dance (ballet), dance (folk), dance (jazz), dance (modern), dance (tap), film, film production, mime, modeling, music, music (vocal), musical productions, television/video, theater/drama, voice and speech.
Special Interest Areas Career exploration.
Sports Aerobics, basketball, horseback riding, soccer, softball, swimming, tennis, volleyball.
Trips Day.
Program Information 3 sessions per year. Session length: 3 weeks in June, July, August. Ages: 8–18. 245 participants per session. Boarding program cost: $3700–$3985.
Application Deadline Continuous.
Jobs Positions for college students 21 and older.

Stagedoor Manor Performing Arts Training Center/ Theatre and Dance Camp (continued)

Summer Contact Barbara Martin, Director, main address above. Phone: 888-STAGE 88. Fax: 888-STAGE 88.
Winter Contact Barbara Martin, Director, 3658 Churchville Avenue, Churchville, Virginia 24421. Phone: 888-STAGE 88. Fax: 888-STAGE 88. E-mail: stagedoormanor@aol.com.
URL www.stagedoormanor.com
For more information, see page 1330.

Stony Brook Summer Music Festival

Stony Brook University, State University of New York
Stony Brook, New York 11794-5475

General Information Coed residential and day arts program established in 1998. Formal opportunities for the artistically talented.
Program Focus Talented and enthusiastic string, woodwind, brass, piano and percussion musicians.
Academics Music (Advanced Placement), precollege program.
Arts Chorus, music, music (chamber), music (classical), music (ensemble), music (instrumental), music (jazz), music (orchestral), music composition/arrangement, music technology/record production, music theory, musical performance/recitals.
Sports Sports (general).
Trips Cultural, day.
Program Information 1 session per year. Session length: 15 days in July, August. Ages: 13–26. 50 participants per session. Day program cost: $1200. Boarding program cost: $1850. Application fee: $25–$45. Financial aid available.
Application Deadline April 16.
Contact Dr. Linda M. Sinanian, Director, Stony Brook Summer Music Festival, Department of Music, Stony Brook, New York 11794-5475. Phone: 631-220-0911. Fax: 631-632-7404. E-mail: lsinanian@notes1.cc.sunysb.edu.
URL www.stonybrook.edu/music

Stony Brook University–Biotechnology Summer Camp

Stony Brook University, State University of New York
Stony Brook, New York 11794-5215

General Information Coed residential academic program established in 1995. Formal opportunities for the academically talented.
Program Focus Research in biotechnology.
Academics Academics (general), biology, biotechnology, botany, chemistry, genetics, mathematics, microbiology, precollege program, research skills, science (general).
Special Interest Areas Problem solving.
Sports Aerobics, basketball, swimming, volleyball, weight training.
Trips College tours.
Program Information 1 session per year. Session length: 26 days in July, August. Ages: 14–17. 24 participants per session. Boarding program cost: $1895.
Application Deadline April 1.
Contact Judy Nimmo, Administrator, Department of Biochemistry and Cell Biology, State University of New York at Stony Brook, Stony Brook, New York 11794-5215. Phone: 631-632-9750. Fax: 631-632-9791. E-mail: jnimmo@notes.cc.sunysb.edu.
URL www.stonybrook.edu/ligase/

Stony Brook University–Environmental Education Summer Camp

Stony Brook University, State University of New York
Peconic Dunes
Southold, New York

General Information Coed residential academic program and outdoor program established in 1965.
Program Focus Students participate in environmentally-oriented activities.
Academics Ecology, environmental science, geology/earth science, precollege program, science (general).
Arts Arts and crafts (general).
Special Interest Areas Field research/expeditions, nature study.
Sports Archery, baseball, basketball, canoeing, equestrian sports, fishing, kayaking, sailing, softball, swimming, volleyball.
Wilderness/Outdoors Orienteering.
Program Information 3 sessions per year. Session length: 1 week in July, August. Ages: 11–15. Boarding program cost: $485.
Jobs Positions for college students 18 and older.
Contact Mr. Richard Hilary, Camp Director, Stony Brook, New York. Phone: 631-852-8629.
URL www.stonybrook.edu/summer/precollege/index.html

Stony Brook University–Science Exploration Camp

Stony Brook University, State University of New York
Stony Brook, New York 11794-5215

General Information Coed day academic program established in 1996. Formal opportunities for the academically talented.
Program Focus For middle school students interested in exploring different areas of science.
Academics Academics (general), biology, botany, chemistry, computers, ecology, environmental science, genetics, microbiology, physics, precollege program, reading, research skills, science (general), writing.
Special Interest Areas Problem solving.
Trips College tours.
Program Information 3 sessions per year. Session length: 12 days in July, August. Ages: 11–14. 24 participants per session. Day program cost: $350.
Application Deadline Continuous.
Contact Judy Nimmo, Administrator, Department of Biochemistry and Cell Biology, Stony Brook University, Stony Brook, New York 11794-5215. Phone: 631-632-5215. Fax: 631-632-9791. E-mail: jnimmo@notes.cc.sunysb.edu.
URL www.stonybrook.edu/ligase/

Stony Book University–Summer Camp at Stony Brook

Stony Brook University, State University of New York
Long Island
Stony Brook, New York 11794-3500

General Information Coed day traditional camp and academic program established in 2000.
Program Focus A camp program that offers a unique combination of educational and athletic activities.
Academics English language/literature, academics (general), biology, computers, ecology, environmental science, geography, geology/earth science, history, humanities, intercultural studies, mathematics, music, science (general), social science.
Arts Arts and crafts (general), dance, dance (jazz), painting.
Special Interest Areas Gardening, leadership training, nature study, robotics.
Sports Baseball, basketball, football, lacrosse, martial arts, soccer, softball, swimming, tennis, volleyball.
Program Information 2–8 sessions per year. Session length: 14–40 days in June, July, August. Ages: 5–12. 200–350 participants per session. Day program cost: $696–$2784. Application fee: $50.
Application Deadline March 27.
Jobs Positions for high school students 17 and older and college students 18 and older.
Contact Ms. Janice Maggio, The Summer Camp at Stony Brook, Director, Stony Brook Sports Complex, Stony Brook University, Stony Brook, New York 11794-3500. Phone: 631-632-4550. Fax: 631-632-7122. E-mail: summercamp@stonybrook.edu.
URL www.stonybrook.edu/daycamp

Stony Brook University Summer Sessions College Program

Stony Brook University, State University of New York
Stony Brook, New York 11794-1970

General Information Coed day academic program established in 1965. Formal opportunities for the academically talented. College credit may be earned.
Academics American literature, Chinese languages/literature, English language/literature, French language/literature, German language/literature, Italian language/literature, Japanese language/literature, Spanish language/literature, academics (general), art history/appreciation, astronomy, business, classical languages/literatures, economics, government and politics, history, humanities, marine studies, mathematics, music, philosophy, psychology, religion.
Program Information 2 sessions per year. Session length: 30 days in June, July, August. Ages: 16+. Cost for NY state residents: $181 per credit; for out-of-state residents: $429 per credit plus fees.
Application Deadline Continuous.
Jobs Positions for college students.
Contact Director, Summer Sessions, Summer Sessions Office, Stony Brook, New York 11794-1970. Phone: 631-632-7790. Fax: 631-632-7302. E-mail: summerschool@notes.cc.sunysb.edu.
URL www.stonybrook.edu/summer

Student Conservation Association–Conservation Crew Program (New York)

Student Conservation Association (SCA)
New York

General Information Coed residential outdoor program, community service program, and wilderness program established in 1957. High school credit may be earned.
Program Focus Resource management, conservation and environmental education.
Academics Biology, botany, ecology, environmental science, geology/earth science, history.
Special Interest Areas Campcraft, community service, construction, leadership training, nature study, trail maintenance, work camp programs.
Sports Canoeing, fishing, kayaking, swimming.
Wilderness/Outdoors Backpacking, hiking, orienteering, outdoor living skills, wilderness camping.
Trips Cultural, day, overnight.
Program Information 2–3 sessions per year. Session length: 3–5 weeks in June, July, August. Ages: 15–19. 6–8 participants per session. Application fee: $20. Financial aid available. No cost for program; financial aid possible for travel expenses.
Application Deadline Continuous.
Jobs Positions for college students 21 and older.
Contact Recruitment Office, PO Box 550, Charlestown, New Hampshire 03603. Phone: 603-543-1700. Fax: 603-543-1828. E-mail: getreal@thesca.org.
URL www.theSCA.org

The Summer Institute for the Gifted at Hofstra University

Summer Institute for the Gifted
Hofstra University
Hempstead, New York

General Information Coed day academic program. Formal opportunities for the academically talented and gifted.
Academics Academics (general), precollege program.
Program Information 1–2 sessions per year. Session length: 3 weeks in June, July, August. Ages: 6–11. 200–300 participants per session. Day program cost: $1550. Application fee: $75. Financial aid available.
Application Deadline May 15.
Jobs Positions for college students 19 and older.
Contact Dr. Stephen Gessner, Director, River Plaza, 9 West Broad Street, Stamford, Connecticut 06902-3788. Phone: 866-303-4744. Fax: 203-399-5598. E-mail: sig.info@aifs.com.
URL www.giftedstudy.com

For more information, see page 1342.

The Summer Institute for the Gifted at Purchase College

Summer Institute for the Gifted
Purchase College, SUNY
Purchase, New York

General Information Coed day academic program. Formal opportunities for the academically talented and gifted.
Academics Academics (general), precollege program.
Program Information 1–2 sessions per year. Session length: 3 weeks in June, July, August. Ages: 6–11. 200–300 participants per session. Day program cost: $1550. Application fee: $75. Financial aid available.
Application Deadline May 15.
Jobs Positions for college students 19 and older.
Contact Dr. Stephen Gessner, Director, River Plaza, 9 West Broad Street, Stamford, Connecticut 06902-3788. Phone: 866-303-4744. Fax: 203-399-5598. E-mail: sig.info@aifs.com.
URL www.giftedstudy.com
For more information, see page 1342.

The Summer Institute for the Gifted at Vassar College

Summer Institute for the Gifted
Vassar College
Poughkeepsie, New York 12603

General Information Coed residential academic program established in 1992. Formal opportunities for the academically talented and gifted. Specific services available for the learning disabled, physically challenged, and visually impaired. College credit may be earned.
Academics American literature, English language/literature, French language/literature, Latin language, SAT/ACT preparation, Spanish language/literature, academics (general), architecture, art history/appreciation, astronomy, biology, business, chemistry, classical languages/literatures, communications, computers, engineering, environmental science, history, marine studies, mathematics, music, philosophy, physics, physiology, precollege program, psychology, social studies, speech/debate, study skills, writing.
Arts Ceramics, chorus, creative writing, dance, dance (modern), drawing, mime, music, music (chamber), music (classical), music (ensemble), music (instrumental), musical productions, painting, photography, sculpture, theater/drama.
Special Interest Areas Electronics, robotics.
Sports Archery, baseball, basketball, fencing, field hockey, lacrosse, martial arts, soccer, squash, swimming, tennis, volleyball.
Trips Cultural.
Program Information 1–2 sessions per year. Session length: 3 weeks in June, July, August. Ages: 8–17. 300–350 participants per session. Boarding program cost: $3350. Application fee: $75. Financial aid available.
Application Deadline May 15.
Jobs Positions for college students 19 and older.
Contact Dr. Stephen Gessner, Director, River Plaza, 9 West Broad Street, Stamford, Connecticut 06902-3788. Phone: 866-303-4744. Fax: 203-399-5598. E-mail: sig.info@aifs.com.
URL www.giftedstudy.com
For more information, see page 1342.

"Summer in the City"

The School for Film and Television
39 West 19th Street, 12th Floor
New York, New York 10011

General Information Coed residential and day academic program and arts program. College credit may be earned.

"Summer in the City"

Program Focus A six-week acting intensive geared towards on-camera acting.
Arts Acting, film, television/video, theater/drama.
Trips Cultural, day.
Program Information 1–2 sessions per year. Session length: 30 days in June, July, August. Ages: 16–24. 98 participants per session. Day program cost: $3550. Boarding program cost: $5500. Application fee: $30.
Application Deadline Continuous.

Contact Mr. Steven Chinni, Director of Admission, main address above. Phone: 888-645-0030 Ext.772. Fax: 212-624-0117. E-mail: schinni@sft.edu.
URL www.sft.edu
For more information, see page 1300.

Summer School at New York Military Academy

New York Military Academy
78 Academy Avenue
Cornwall-on-Hudson, New York 12520

General Information Coed residential academic program established in 1954. High school credit may be earned.
Academics English as a second language, English language/literature, SAT/ACT preparation, Spanish language/literature, academics (general), biology, chemistry, computers, geography, history, mathematics, reading, science (general), social studies, study skills.
Sports Basketball, horseback riding, paintball, riflery, soccer, softball, swimming, tennis, volleyball, weight training.
Wilderness/Outdoors Rafting, white-water trips.
Trips Cultural, day, shopping.
Program Information 2 sessions per year. Session length: 3–5 weeks in June, July, August. Ages: 12–18. 100–150 participants per session. Boarding program cost: $3400–$5500. Application fee: $300.
Application Deadline June 27.
Jobs Positions for college students.
Contact Maureen T. Kelly, Director of Admissions, main address above. Phone: 845-534-3710 Ext.4233. Fax: 845-534-7699. E-mail: admissions@nyma.ouboces.org.
URL www.nyma.org

SummerSkills at Albany Academy for Girls

Albany Academy for Girls
140 Academy Road
Albany, New York 12208

General Information Coed day academic program established in 1999. Formal opportunities for the academically talented.
Program Focus Enrichment courses geared towards developing and enhancing various skills.
Academics English language/literature, Web page design, academics (general), computers, humanities, mathematics, writing.
Arts Creative writing.
Special Interest Areas College planning, culinary arts, driver's education, robotics.
Sports Aerobics, basketball, bicycling, climbing (wall), sea kayaking.
Wilderness/Outdoors Backpacking, bicycle trips, hiking, mountain biking, rafting, rock climbing, white-water trips.
Trips Overnight.
Program Information 3–6 sessions per year. Session length: 5–10 days in June, July, August. Ages: 10+. 50–100 participants per session. Day program cost: $50–$425.
Application Deadline Continuous.
Contact Mrs. Donna Keegan, Program Director, main address above. Phone: 518-463-2201. Fax: 518-463-5096. E-mail: keegand@albanyacademyforgirls.org.
URL www.albanyacadmyforgirls.org/

Summer Theatre Institute–2005

Youth Theatre of New Jersey's Teen Program in Residence at Columbia University, NYC
Columbia University
New York, New York

General Information Coed residential arts program established in 1989. Formal opportunities for the artistically talented.

Summer Theatre Institute–2005

Program Focus Professional theater training program for teens.

Summer Theatre Institute–2005 (continued)

Arts Acting, clowning, creative writing, dance, dance (ballet), dance (jazz), dance (modern), dance (tap), directing, mime, musical productions, musical theater, playwriting, puppetry, stage movement, theater/drama, voice and speech.
Trips Cultural, day.
Program Information 1 session per year. Session length: 27 days in June, July. Ages: 14–19. 25–50 participants per session. Boarding program cost: $4850–$4975. Application fee: $60. Discounts available if enrolled before May 20.
Application Deadline June 25.
Jobs Positions for college students 22 and older.
Contact Ms. Allyn Sitjar, Artistic Director, 23 Tomahawk Trail, Sparta, New Jersey 07871. Phone: 201-415-5329. Fax: 973-729-3654. E-mail: youththeatreallyn@yahoo.com.

For more information, see page 1346.

Surprise Lake Camp

Cold Spring, New York 10516

General Information Coed residential traditional camp established in 1902. Religious affiliation: Jewish. Accredited by American Camping Association.
Academics Hebrew language, Jewish studies, ecology, environmental science, music.
Arts Arts and crafts (general), batiking, ceramics, dance, dance (folk), jewelry making, music, music (instrumental), musical productions, photography, pottery, theater/drama.
Special Interest Areas Animal care, nature study, work camp programs.
Sports Aerobics, archery, basketball, boating, canoeing, climbing (tower), climbing (wall), diving, field hockey, fishing, football, golf, kayaking, ropes course, sailing, soccer, softball, street/roller hockey, swimming, tennis, volleyball, water polo, weight training, windsurfing.
Wilderness/Outdoors Backpacking, canoe trips, hiking, white-water trips, wilderness camping.
Trips Cultural, day, overnight.
Program Information 2–5 sessions per year. Session length: 1–4 weeks in July, August. Ages: 7–15. 480 participants per session. Boarding program cost: $1150–$4450. Financial aid available.
Application Deadline Continuous.
Jobs Positions for high school students 16 and older and college students 18 and older.
Summer Contact Ms. Sylvie Erlich, Executive Assistant/Registrar, Lake Surprise Road, Cold Spring, New York 10516. Phone: 845-265-3616. Fax: 845-265-3646. E-mail: info@surpriselake.org.
Winter Contact Ms. Sylvie Erlich, Executive Assistant/Registrar, 307 Seventh Avenue, Suite 900, New York, New York 10001. Phone: 212-924-3131. Fax: 212-924-5112. E-mail: info@surpriselake.org.
URL www.surpriselake.org

Syracuse University Summer College

Syracuse University
111 Waverly Avenue
Suite 240
Syracuse, New York 13244-1270

General Information Coed residential and day academic program and arts program established in 1961. Formal opportunities for the academically talented and artistically talented. College credit may be earned.

Syracuse University Summer College

Program Focus General academic, earn college credits.
Academics American literature, English language/literature, academics (general), aerospace science, anthropology, archaeology, architecture, art history/appreciation, astronomy, biology, business, chemistry, communications, computer programming, computers, ecology, economics, engineering, environmental science, geography, geology/earth science, government and politics, history, humanities, journalism, mathematics, meteorology, philosophy, physics, physiology, precollege program, psychology, reading, religion, science (general), social science, social studies, speech/debate, writing.

Arts Ceramics, chorus, creative writing, dance, dance (ballet), dance (folk), dance (jazz), dance (modern), dance (tap), drawing, fabric arts, graphic arts, music, music (vocal), musical productions, painting, photography, pottery, printmaking, radio broadcasting, sculpture, television/video, theater/drama, weaving.
Special Interest Areas Career exploration, community service, field research/expeditions, leadership training, model rocketry, robotics.
Sports Aerobics, basketball, racquetball, ropes course, softball, sports (general), squash, swimming, tennis, volleyball, weight training.
Wilderness/Outdoors Hiking.
Trips College tours, cultural, day, shopping.
Program Information 1 session per year. Session length: 6 weeks in July, August. Ages: 14–18. 175–225 participants per session. Day program cost: $3428–$3800. Boarding program cost: $5050–$5750. Application fee: $50. Financial aid available.
Application Deadline May 3.
Contact Jack Carr, Interm Director, main address above. Phone: 315-443-5297. Fax: 315-443-3976. E-mail: sumcoll@syr.edu.
URL www.summercollege.syr.edu/

For more information, see page 1350.

TANAGER LODGE

85 Youngs Road
Merrill, New York 12955

General Information Coed residential traditional camp and outdoor program established in 1925.
Program Focus Fostering understanding and appreciation for the natural world.
Arts Arts and crafts (general), basketry, drawing, woodworking.
Special Interest Areas Native American culture, campcraft, nature study, paddle-making.
Sports Archery, boating, canoeing, diving, fishing, kayaking, sailing, snorkeling, swimming, windsurfing.
Wilderness/Outdoors Backpacking, canoe trips, hiking, mountaineering, orienteering, outdoor camping, rock climbing.
Trips Day, overnight.
Program Information 1 session per year. Session length: 7 weeks in July, August. Ages: 7–14. 48 participants per session. Boarding program cost: $3600. Financial aid available.
Application Deadline Continuous.
Jobs Positions for high school students 16 and older and college students 18 and older.
Summer Contact Mr. Tad Welch, Director, main address above. Phone: 518-425-3386.
Winter Contact Mr. Tad Welch, Director, 602 Park Avenue, Greensboro, North Carolina 27405. Phone: 336-389-9716. E-mail: tadandali@tanagerlodge.com.
URL www.tanagerlodge.com

TANNEN'S SUMMER MAGIC CAMP

Tannen's Magic, Inc.
New York Institute of Technology-Central Islip
Central Islip, New York 11722

General Information Coed residential arts program established in 1974.
Program Focus Magic.
Arts Magic.
Program Information 1 session per year. Session length: 8 days in July, August. Ages: 12–20. 120–150 participants per session. Boarding program cost: $1095.
Application Deadline July 31.
Contact Director, 24 West 25th Street, 2nd Floor, New York, New York 10010. Phone: 212-929-4500. Fax: 212-929-4565. E-mail: camp@tannens.com.
URL www.tannens.com

TECHNOLOGY ENCOUNTERS–VIDEO ENCOUNTER/COMPUTER ENCOUNTER–NEW YORK

Ducks in a Row Foundation, Inc./Technology Encounters
New York

General Information Coed day arts program established in 2000. Formal opportunities for the academically talented and artistically talented.
Program Focus Local community school district-hosted programs focused on making technology fun, teaching team skills, and using creative energies.
Academics Academics (general), communications, computer programming, computers.
Arts Acting, animation, arts and crafts (general), film, film production, graphic arts, television/video, theater/drama.
Special Interest Areas Computer game design, computer graphics, leadership training.
Program Information 40–50 sessions per year. Session length: 5–10 days in June, July, August. Ages: 7–13. 25–100 participants per session. Day program cost: $195. Financial aid available.
Application Deadline Continuous.
Jobs Positions for high school students 17 and older and college students 17 and older.
Contact Ms. Jane Sandlar, Director, 8 Wemrock Drive, Ocean, New Jersey 07712. Phone: 732-695-0827. Fax: 732-493-4282. E-mail: jane@technologyencounters.com.
URL www.technologyencounters.com

TISCH SCHOOL OF THE ARTS–SUMMER HIGH SCHOOL PROGRAMS

New York University
721 Broadway
New York, New York 10003

General Information Coed residential academic program and arts program established in 2001. Formal opportunities for the academically talented and artistically talented. College credit may be earned.
Program Focus College-level training in the performing and media arts.

Tisch School of the Arts–Summer High School Programs (continued)

Tisch School of the Arts–Summer High School Programs

Academics Classical languages/literatures, communications, precollege program, writing.
Arts Acting, animation, creative writing, dance, dance (jazz), dance (modern), dance (tap), drawing, film, music (vocal), musical productions, musical theater, television/video, theater/drama.
Trips Cultural, day.
Program Information 1 session per year. Session length: 28–30 days in July, August. Ages: 15+. 8–20 participants per session. Boarding program cost: $7645–$8645. Application fee: $50. Financial aid available. Open to participants entering grade 12.
Application Deadline March 10.
Contact Josh Murray, Assistant Director of Recruitment, main address above. Phone: 212-998-1500. Fax: 212-995-4578. E-mail: tisch.special.info@nyu.edu.
URL http://specialprograms.tisch.nyu.edu

For more information, see page 1220.

United Soccer Academy–Goal Keeping Training Camp, New York

United Soccer Academy, Inc.
New York

General Information Coed residential and day sports camp established in 1999.
Program Focus All aspects of the keeper position are covered: from techniques to tactical decision-making. Coaches are from international teams and colleges.
Sports Soccer.
Program Information 5 sessions per year. Session length: 5 days in April, June, July, August, September, November. Ages: 8–14. 16–200 participants per session. Day program cost: $145. Boarding program cost: $495. Call for specific locations.
Application Deadline Continuous.
Jobs Positions for college students 18 and older.
Contact Camps Information, 50 Tannery Road, Unit 8, Branchburg, New Jersey 08876. Phone: 908-823-0130. Fax: 908-823-0466. E-mail: info@unitedsocceracademy.com.
URL www.unitedsocceracademy.com

United Soccer Academy–Junior Soccer Squirts, New York

United Soccer Academy, Inc.
New York

General Information Coed day sports camp established in 1999.
Program Focus Introduction to soccer in a camp format with emphasis on fun games and activities in small groups. Coaches are from international soccer teams and college teams.
Sports Soccer.
Program Information 20 sessions per year. Session length: 5 days in April, June, July, August, September, November. Ages: 3–5. 6–48 participants per session. Day program cost: $89. Two sessions daily; parents may stay with camper. Call for specific locations.
Application Deadline Continuous.
Jobs Positions for college students 18 and older.
Contact Camps Information, 50 Tannery Road, Unit 8, Branchburg, New Jersey 08876. Phone: 908-823-0130. Fax: 908-823-0466. E-mail: info@unitedsocceracademy.com.
URL www.unitedsocceracademy.com

United Soccer Academy–Recreation Soccer Community Camp, New York

United Soccer Academy, Inc.
New York

General Information Coed residential and day sports camp established in 1999.
Program Focus Players build on the fundamentals of the game, experiencing a broad range of techniques and skills. Coaches are from international teams and colleges.
Sports Soccer.
Program Information 20 sessions per year. Session length: 5 days in April, June, July, August, September, November. Ages: 7–14. 16–200 participants per session. Day program cost: $145. Boarding program cost: $495. Call for specific locations.
Application Deadline Continuous.
Jobs Positions for college students 18 and older.
Contact Camps Information, 50 Tannery Road, Unit 8, Branchburg, New Jersey 08876. Phone: 908-823-0130. Fax: 908-823-0466. E-mail: info@unitedsocceracademy.com.
URL www.unitedsocceracademy.com

United Soccer Academy–Regional Academy Camp, New York

United Soccer Academy, Inc.
New York

General Information Coed residential and day sports camp established in 1999.
Program Focus Intense program aimed at the dedicated travel and select soccer player. Sites are regionalized to ensure high quality competition.

Advanced techniques and skills taught, tactical game analysis, position assessment. Coaches are from international teams and colleges.
Sports Soccer.
Program Information 5 sessions per year. Session length: 5 days in June, July, August. Ages: 8–14. 16–200 participants per session. Day program cost: $165. Boarding program cost: $495. Call for specific locations.
Application Deadline Continuous.
Jobs Positions for college students 18 and older.
Contact Camps Information, 50 Tannery Road, Unit 8, Branchburg, New Jersey 08876. Phone: 908-823-0130. Fax: 908-823-0466. E-mail: info@unitedsocceracademy.com.
URL www.unitedsocceracademy.com

United Soccer Academy–Senior Soccer Squirts, New York

United Soccer Academy, Inc.
New York

General Information Coed day sports camp established in 1999.
Program Focus Introduction to the game in relaxed, fun atmosphere; skills development without competitive environment. Coaches are from international teams and colleges.
Sports Soccer.
Program Information 20 sessions per year. Session length: 5 days in April, June, July, August, September, November. Ages: 5–7. 6–48 participants per session. Day program cost: $89. Two sessions daily; call for specific locations.
Application Deadline Continuous.
Jobs Positions for college students 18 and older.
Contact Camps Information, 50 Tannery Road, Unit 8, Branchburg, New Jersey 08876. Phone: 908-823-0130. Fax: 908-823-0466. E-mail: info@unitedsocceracademy.com.
URL www.unitedsocceracademy.com

United Soccer Academy–Team Training Camp, New York

United Soccer Academy, Inc.
New York

General Information Coed residential and day sports camp established in 1999.
Program Focus Teams of ten or more players receive individualized instruction based on staff discussion with their coach. Structured coaching scrimmages with other teams. Coaches on staff are from international teams and colleges.
Sports Soccer.
Program Information 10 sessions per year. Session length: 5 days in April, June, July, August, September, November. Ages: 8–14. 20–200 participants per session. Day program cost: $125. Boarding program cost: $495. Call for specific locations.
Application Deadline Continuous.
Jobs Positions for college students 18 and older.
Contact Camps Information, 50 Tannery Road, Unit 8, Branchburg, New Jersey 08876. Phone: 908-823-0130. Fax: 908-823-0466. E-mail: info@unitedsocceracademy.com.
URL www.unitedsocceracademy.com

United Soccer Academy–Travel Soccer Community Camp, New York

United Soccer Academy, Inc.
New York

General Information Coed residential and day sports camp established in 1999.
Program Focus Individual player development and team tactics are emphasized. Skills are taught at an accelerated level with practices developing into full game realistic situations. Coaches are from international teams and colleges.
Sports Soccer.
Program Information 20 sessions per year. Session length: 5 days in April, June, July, August, September, November. Ages: 8–14. 16–200 participants per session. Day program cost: $145. Boarding program cost: $495. Call for specific locations.
Application Deadline Continuous.
Jobs Positions for college students 18 and older.
Contact Camps Information, 50 Tannery Road, Unit 8, Branchburg, New Jersey 08876. Phone: 908-823-0130. Fax: 908-823-0466. E-mail: info@unitedsocceracademy.com.
URL www.unitedsocceracademy.com

Usdan Center for the Creative and Performing Arts

185 Colonial Springs Road
Wheatley Heights, New York 11798

General Information Coed day arts program established in 1968. Formal opportunities for the academically talented, artistically talented, and gifted. College credit may be earned.

Usdan Center for the Creative and Performing Arts

Usdan Center for the Creative and Performing Arts (continued)

Program Focus Visual and performing arts.
Academics Botany, ecology, music, writing.
Arts Band, cartooning, ceramics, chorus, creative writing, dance, dance (ballet), dance (jazz), dance (modern), dance (tap), drawing, film, graphic arts, jewelry making, metalworking, music, music (chamber), music (classical), music (ensemble), music (instrumental), music (jazz), music (orchestral), music (vocal), musical productions, musical theater, painting, photography, pottery, sculpture, television/video, theater/drama.
Special Interest Areas Chess, computer graphics, gardening, nature study.
Sports Archery, basketball, swimming, tennis, volleyball.
Program Information 2 sessions per year. Session length: 4–5 weeks in June, July, August. Ages: 6–18. 1,600–1,800 participants per session. Day program cost: $2100–$3000. Financial aid available. Transportation fee assessed according to home address.
Application Deadline Continuous.
Jobs Positions for college students 18 and older.
Summer Contact Ms. Ruth Starr, Director of L.I. Admissions, main address above. Phone: 631-643-7900. E-mail: info@usdan.com.
Winter Contact Ms. Allison Bitz, Assistant Director, 420 East 79th Street, New York, New York 10021. Phone: 212-772-6060. E-mail: info@usdan.com.
URL www.usdan.com

For more information, see page 1376.

Vassar College Coed Basketball Camp

Vassar College
124 Raymond Avenue
Poughkeepsie, New York 12604-0720

General Information Coed day sports camp established in 1997.
Program Focus Basketball.
Sports Basketball.
Program Information 1 session per year. Session length: 5 days in June, July. Ages: 7–15. 50–80 participants per session. Day program cost: $195. Application fee: $30.
Application Deadline Continuous.
Jobs Positions for high school students and college students.
Contact Antonia Sweet, Assistant Director, Conferences and Summer Programs, Box 720, 124 Raymond Avenue, Poughkeepsie, New York 12604-0720. Phone: 845-437-5904. Fax: 845-437-7209. E-mail: answeet@vassar.edu.
URL www.vassar.edu/summer/

Vassar College Coed Soccer Camp

Vassar College
124 Raymond Avenue
Poughkeepsie, New York 12604-0720

General Information Coed day sports camp established in 1999.
Program Focus Soccer.
Sports Soccer.
Program Information 1 session per year. Session length: 5 days in July. Ages: 7–12. 40–70 participants per session. Day program cost: $190–$210. Application fee: $50.
Application Deadline June 14.
Jobs Positions for high school students and college students.
Contact Antonia Sweet, Assistant Director, Conferences and Summer Programs, Box 720, 124 Raymond Avenue, Poughkeepsie, New York 12604-0720. Phone: 845-437-5904. Fax: 845-437-7209. E-mail: answeet@vassar.edu.
URL www.vassar.edu/summer/

Vassar College Coed Swim Camp

Vassar College
124 Raymond Avenue
Poughkeepsie, New York 12604-0720

General Information Coed residential and day sports camp established in 2004.
Program Focus Swimming.
Sports Swimming.
Program Information 1 session per year. Session length: 6 days in June, July. Ages: 12–18. 50–80 participants per session. Day program cost: $325. Boarding program cost: $400–$450. Application fee: $100.
Application Deadline May 15.
Jobs Positions for high school students and college students.
Contact Antonia Sweet, Assistant Director, Conferences and Summer Programs, Box 720, Vassar College, Poughkeepsie, New York 12604-0720. Phone: 845-437-5904. Fax: 845-437-7209. E-mail: answeet@vassar.edu.
URL www.vassar.edu/summer/

Vassar College Girl's Field Hockey Camp

Vassar College
124 Raymond Avenue
Poughkeepsie, New York 12604-0720

General Information Girls' residential and day sports camp established in 2000.
Program Focus Field hockey.
Sports Field hockey.
Program Information 1 session per year. Session length: 5 days in July. Ages: 10–18. 50–150 participants per session. Day program cost: $300. Boarding program cost: $425. Application fee: $75.
Application Deadline June 30.
Jobs Positions for high school students and college students.
Contact Antonia Sweet, Assistant Director, Conferences and Summer Programs, Box 720, 124 Raymond Avenue, Poughkeepsie, New York 12604-0720. Phone: 845-437-5904. Fax: 845-437-7209. E-mail: answeet@vassar.edu.
URL www.vassar.edu/summer/

Ventures Travel Service–New York

Friendship Ventures
New York

General Information Coed travel special needs program established in 1985. Specific services available for the developmentally challenged and physically challenged.
Program Focus Provides travel services to older teens and adults with developmental disabilities.
Special Interest Areas Touring.
Program Information 50 sessions per year. Session length: 4–10 days in February, March, April, May, June, July, August, September, October, November, December. Ages: 14–70. 4–8 participants per session. Cost: $395–$2000.
Application Deadline Continuous.
Jobs Positions for college students 18 and older.
Contact Georgann Rumsey, President/CEO, 10509 108th Street, NW, Annandale, Minnesota 55302. Phone: 952-858-0101. Fax: 952-852-0123. E-mail: fv@friendshipventures.org.
URL www.friendshipventures.org

Visual Arts Institute for High School Students

Purchase College, State University of New York
735 Anderson Hill Road
Purchase, New York 10577

General Information Coed day arts program established in 1991. Formal opportunities for the artistically talented. High school credit may be earned.
Arts Ceramics, film, metalworking, painting, photography, printmaking, sculpture, visual arts.
Program Information 1 session per year. Session length: 16 days in July, August. Ages: 13+. 60 participants per session. Day program cost: $1295.
Application Deadline June 3.
Jobs Positions for college students.
Contact Stephanie Nieves, Director of Youth Programs, main address above. Phone: 914-251-6508. Fax: 914-251-6515. E-mail: stephanie.nieves@purchase.edu.
URL www.purchase.edu/ce/youth_programs

Willow Hill Farm Camp

75 Cassidy Road
Keeseville, New York 12944

General Information Coed residential sports camp established in 1980. Accredited by American Camping Association.
Program Focus Program teaches all disciplines of English riding plus total horse care.
Special Interest Areas Animal care.
Sports Equestrian sports, horseback riding, polocrosse, squash, swimming, volleyball.
Trips Day.
Program Information 5 sessions per year. Session length: 2–9 weeks in June, July, August. Ages: 7–17. 36 participants per session. Boarding program cost: $1900–$6000.
Application Deadline Continuous.
Jobs Positions for college students 18 and older.
Contact Col. Gerald Edwards, Owner/Director, main address above. Phone: 518-834-9746. Fax: 518-834-9476. E-mail: edwardsj@westelcom.com.
URL www.willowhillfarm.com

YMCA Camp Michikamau

YMCA of Greater Bergen County
Harriman State Park
Bear Mountain, New York 10911

General Information Coed residential traditional camp established in 1929.
Program Focus Arts, crafts, sports, low ropes course, and traditional camping.
Arts Arts and crafts (general), ceramics.
Special Interest Areas Native American culture, leadership training.
Sports Archery, canoeing, fishing, kayaking, ropes course, sailing, snorkeling, softball, swimming, volleyball.
Wilderness/Outdoors Backpacking, canoe trips, hiking, orienteering, rock climbing.
Program Information 4 sessions per year. Session length: 12–13 days in July, August. Ages: 7–14. 90–105 participants per session. Boarding program cost: $450–$460. Financial aid available.
Application Deadline Continuous.
Jobs Positions for high school students 16 and older and college students 18 and older.
Contact Ken Riscinti, Director, 360 Main Street, Hackensack, New Jersey 07601. Phone: 201-487-6600. Fax: 201-487-4539. E-mail: kriscinti@ymcagbc.org.
URL www.ymcagbc.org

Young Actors and Playwrights Workshop

Purchase College, State University of New York
735 Anderson Hill Road
Purchase, New York 10577

General Information Coed day arts program established in 1984.
Program Focus Playwriting.
Academics Writing.
Arts Acting, creative writing, playwriting, theater/drama.
Program Information 1 session per year. Session length: 20 days in June, July, August. Ages: 11–17. 20–30 participants per session. Day program cost: $875.
Application Deadline June 3.
Jobs Positions for college students 18 and older.
Contact Stephanie Nieves, Director of Youth Programs, main address above. Phone: 914-251-6500. Fax: 914-251-6515. E-mail: stephanie.nieves@purchase.edu.
URL www.purchase.edu/ce/youth_programs

YOUNG ARTISTS AT PURCHASE

Purchase College, State University of New York
735 Anderson Hill Road
Purchase, New York 10577

General Information Coed day arts program established in 1988. Formal opportunities for the artistically talented.
Academics Music, writing.
Arts Arts and crafts (general), creative writing, dance (jazz), painting, sculpture.
Trips Cultural.
Program Information 2–3 sessions per year. Session length: 8–24 days in January, February, March, April, June, July, August, September, October, November. Ages: 7–13. 15–68 participants per session. Day program cost: $350–$995.
Application Deadline June 3.
Jobs Positions for college students 18 and older.
Contact Stephanie Nieves, Director of Youth Programs, main address above. Phone: 914-251-6508. Fax: 914-251-6515. E-mail: stephanie.nieves@purchase.edu.
URL www.purchase.edu/ce/youth_programs

YOUNG FILMMAKERS AT PURCHASE

Purchase College, State University of New York
735 Anderson Hill Road
Purchase, New York 10577

General Information Coed day arts program established in 2001. Formal opportunities for the artistically talented.
Program Focus Filmmaking.
Arts Film, film production.
Program Information 1 session per year. Session length: 20 days in July, August. Ages: 12–17. 40 participants per session. Day program cost: $825.
Application Deadline June 4.
Jobs Positions for college students.
Contact Ms. Stephanie Nieves, M.S. Ed., Director of Youth Programs, main address above. Phone: 914-251-6508. Fax: 914-251-6515. E-mail: stephanie.nieves@purchase.edu.
URL www.purchase.edu/ce/youth_programs

YOUNG PHOTOGRAPHERS

Purchase College, State University of New York
735 Anderson Hill Road
Purchase, New York 10577

General Information Coed day arts program established in 2001. Formal opportunities for the artistically talented.
Program Focus Photography.
Arts Photography.
Program Information 1 session per year. Session length: 16 days in June, July. Ages: 12–17. 20–25 participants per session. Day program cost: $895.
Application Deadline June 4.
Jobs Positions for college students 19 and older.
Contact Ms. Stephanie Nieves, M.S. Ed., Director of Youth Programs, main address above. Phone: 914-251-6508. Fax: 914-251-6515. E-mail: stephanie.nieves@purchase.edu.
URL www.purchase.edu/ce/youth_programs

NORTH CAROLINA

ADVENTURE LINKS–NORTH CAROLINA EXPEDITIONS

Adventure Links
North Carolina

General Information Coed travel wilderness program and adventure program established in 2003. Accredited by American Camping Association.
Program Focus Rock climbing, white water kayaking.
Sports Climbing (wall), kayaking.
Wilderness/Outdoors Backpacking, rock climbing, survival training, white-water trips, wilderness camping.
Trips Overnight.
Program Information 1 session per year. Session length: 2 weeks in July. Ages: 14–17. 13 participants per session. Cost: $1495.
Application Deadline Continuous.
Jobs Positions for high school students 18 and older and college students 18 and older.
Contact Elena Gonzalez, Director, 21498 Blue Ridge Mountain Road, Paris, Virginia 20130. Phone: 540-592-3682. Fax: 540-592-3316. E-mail: elena@adventurelinks.net.
URL www.adventurelinks.net

ALL ARTS AND SCIENCES CAMP–NORTH CAROLINA STATE UNIVERSITY

All Arts and Sciences Camp
North Carolina State University
Raleigh, North Carolina 27695

General Information Coed residential and day academic program and arts program established in 1991. Formal opportunities for the academically talented and artistically talented.
Program Focus Citizenship and civic virtues through discussion of famous individuals exemplifying certain values, such as Mother Teresa or Martin Luther King.
Academics Academics (general), anthropology, architecture, biology, botany, chemistry, computers, ecology, environmental science, geology/earth science, history, journalism, marine studies, mathematics, meteorology, music, physics, psychology, science (general), social science, veterinary science, writing.
Arts Arts, arts and crafts (general), ceramics, clowning, creative writing, dance, dance (modern), drawing, film, jewelry making, mime, painting, photography, pottery, printmaking, sculpture, theater/drama.

Special Interest Areas Leadership training, nature study.
Sports Lacrosse, soccer, softball, volleyball.
Trips College tours.
Program Information 1 session per year. Session length: 6 days in June. Ages: 7–15. 300–500 participants per session. Day program cost: $500. Boarding program cost: $600. Financial aid available.
Application Deadline Continuous.
Jobs Positions for high school students 16 and older and college students 18 and older.
Contact Kisha Carmichael, Camp Director, PO Box 26170, Greensboro, North Carolina 27402-6170. Phone: 336-334-5414. Fax: 336-334-4733. E-mail: allarts@uncg.edu.
URL allarts.uncg.edu/dcl/web/youth.asp

All Arts and Sciences Camp–The University of North Carolina at Greensboro

All Arts and Sciences Camp
1100 West Market Street
The University of North Carolina at Greensboro
Greensboro, North Carolina 27402

General Information Coed residential and day academic program and arts program established in 1991. Formal opportunities for the academically talented and artistically talented.
Program Focus Citizenship and civic virtues through discussion of famous individuals exemplifying certain values, such as Mother Teresa or Martin Luther King.
Academics Academics (general), anthropology, architecture, biology, botany, chemistry, computers, ecology, environmental science, geology/earth science, history, journalism, marine studies, mathematics, meteorology, music, physics, psychology, science (general), social science, veterinary science, writing.
Arts Arts, arts and crafts (general), ceramics, clowning, creative writing, dance, dance (modern), drawing, film, jewelry making, mime, painting, photography, pottery, printmaking, sculpture, theater/drama.
Special Interest Areas Leadership training, nature study.
Sports Lacrosse, soccer, softball, volleyball.
Trips College tours.
Program Information 2 sessions per year. Session length: 6 days in June, July, August. Ages: 7–15. 300–500 participants per session. Day program cost: $500. Boarding program cost: $600. Financial aid available.
Application Deadline Continuous.
Jobs Positions for high school students 16 and older and college students 18 and older.
Contact Kisha Carmichael, Camp Director, PO Box 26170, Greensboro, North Carolina 27402-6170. Phone: 336-334-5414. Fax: 336-334-4733. E-mail: allarts@uncg.edu.
URL allarts.uncg.edu/dcl/web/youth.asp

Asheville School Summer Academic Adventures

Asheville School
360 Asheville School Road
Asheville, North Carolina 28806

General Information Coed residential academic program established in 1982. Formal opportunities for the academically talented and artistically talented.

Asheville School Summer Academic Adventures

Program Focus Academic enrichment and English as a second language.
Academics American literature, English as a second language, English language/literature, academics (general), art history/appreciation, biology, botany, chemistry, computer programming, computers, ecology, economics, environmental science, geology/earth science, government and politics, history, humanities, intercultural studies, mathematics, philosophy, physics, psychology, reading, science (general), speech/debate, study skills, writing.
Arts Acting, arts and crafts (general), creative writing, drawing, graphic arts, painting, pottery, theater/drama.

Asheville School Summer Academic Adventures (continued)

Special Interest Areas Campcraft, field research/ expeditions, field trips (arts and culture), leadership training, nature study.
Sports Basketball, climbing (wall), kayaking, rappelling, ropes course, soccer, swimming, tennis, volleyball, water polo, weight training.
Wilderness/Outdoors Backpacking, canoe trips, caving, hiking, mountain biking, mountaineering, orienteering, rafting, rock climbing, survival training, white-water trips, wilderness camping.
Trips Cultural, day, overnight.
Program Information 2 sessions per year. Session length: 3 weeks in June, July. 80–90 participants per session. Boarding program cost: $2550–$4895. Application fee: $30. Financial aid available. Open to participants entering grades 7–11.
Application Deadline Continuous.
Jobs Positions for college students 18 and older.
Contact Ms. Elysia Versen, Director, main address above. Phone: 828-254-6345. Fax: 828-252-8666. E-mail: saa@ashevilleschool.org.
URL www.ashevilleschool.org

For more information, see page 986.

Blue Star Camps

Blue Star Way
Crab Creek Road
Hendersonville, North Carolina 28793-1029

General Information Coed residential traditional camp established in 1948. Religious affiliation: Jewish. Accredited by American Camping Association.
Program Focus A sanctuary from stress of the "real world" and a thread woven into a camper's tapestry of Jewish-American experiences.
Academics Hebrew language, Jewish studies.
Arts Arts and crafts (general), ceramics, creative writing, dance, dance (folk), dance (jazz), dance (modern), drawing, fabric arts, film, jewelry making, leather working, music, musical productions, painting, photography, pottery, puppetry, television/video, theater/drama, weaving.
Special Interest Areas Animal care, campcraft, community service, farming, gardening, leadership training, nature study.
Sports Aerobics, archery, basketball, bicycling, bicycling (BMX), boating, canoeing, climbing (wall), equestrian sports, fishing, football, golf, horseback riding, kayaking, martial arts, rappelling, riflery, ropes course, soccer, softball, swimming, tennis, track and field, volleyball, water polo, waterskiing, weight training.
Wilderness/Outdoors Backpacking, bicycle trips, canoe trips, hiking, mountain biking, mountaineering, orienteering, rafting, rock climbing, white-water trips, wilderness camping.
Trips Cultural, day, overnight.
Program Information 2 sessions per year. Session length: 27 days in June, July, August. Ages: 6–16. 750 participants per session. Boarding program cost: $3800–$6900.
Application Deadline Continuous.
Jobs Positions for college students 18 and older.
Summer Contact Rodger Popkin, Co-Director/Owner, PO Box 1029, Crab Creek Road, Hendersonville, North Carolina 28793. Phone: 828-692-3591. Fax: 828-692-7030. E-mail: info@bluestarcamps.com.
Winter Contact Jason Popkin, Co-Director/Owner, 3595 Sheridan Street, Suite 107, Hollywood, Florida 33021. Phone: 954-963-4494. Fax: 954-963-2145. E-mail: info@bluestarcamps.com.
URL www.bluestarcamps.com

Brad Hoover and Will Witherspoon Football Camp/Sports International

Sports International, Inc.
Queens University of Charlotte
Charlotte, North Carolina 28274

General Information Coed residential and day sports camp established in 1996.
Sports Football, weight training.
Program Information 1 session per year. Session length: 5 days in June. Ages: 8–18. 300–450 participants per session. Day program cost: $489. Boarding program cost: $599.
Application Deadline Continuous.
Jobs Positions for college students 18 and older.
Contact Customer Service, 8924 McGaw Court, Columbia, Maryland 21045. Phone: 800-555-0801. Fax: 401-309-9962. E-mail: info@footballcamps.com.
URL www.footballcamps.com

Brevard Music Center

Brevard Music Center
1000 Probart Street
Brevard, North Carolina 28712

General Information Coed residential arts program established in 1936. Formal opportunities for the artistically talented. College credit may be earned.
Program Focus Music.
Academics Music, music (Advanced Placement).
Arts Band, music, music (chamber), music (classical), music (ensemble), music (instrumental), music (jazz), music (orchestral), music (vocal), musical productions.
Special Interest Areas Career exploration.
Sports Basketball, canoeing, soccer, softball, swimming, volleyball.
Wilderness/Outdoors Canoe trips, white-water trips.
Program Information 1 session per year. Session length: 46 days in June, July, August. Ages: 14–35. 390 participants per session. Boarding program cost: $3900. Application fee: $50. Financial aid available.
Application Deadline Continuous.
Jobs Positions for college students 20 and older.
Contact Dorothy Knowles, Admissions Coordinator and Registrar, PO Box 312, Brevard, North Carolina 28712. Phone: 828-862-2140. Fax: 828-884-2036. E-mail: bmcadmission@brevardmusic.org.
URL www.brevardmusic.org

CAMP CHEERIO YMCA

YMCA of Greater High Point, North Carolina, Inc.
1430 Camp Cheerio Road
Glade Valley, North Carolina 28627-9731

General Information Coed residential traditional camp established in 1960. Religious affiliation: Christian. Accredited by American Camping Association.
Academics Journalism.
Arts Arts and crafts (general), creative writing, dance (modern), photography.
Special Interest Areas Campcraft, leadership training, model rocketry, nature study, team building.
Sports Aerobics, archery, basketball, canoeing, cheerleading, climbing (wall), fishing, football, golf, gymnastics, horseback riding, kayaking, lacrosse, rappelling, riflery, ropes course, soccer, softball, swimming, tennis, volleyball, water polo.
Wilderness/Outdoors Backpacking, canoe trips, caving, hiking, orienteering, rock climbing.
Trips Day, overnight.
Program Information 7 sessions per year. Session length: 1–2 weeks in June, July, August. Ages: 7–15. 220–225 participants per session. Boarding program cost: $675–$1350. Financial aid available.
Application Deadline Continuous.
Jobs Positions for high school students 17 and older and college students 18 and older.
Summer Contact Mr. Michaux Crocker, Director, main address above. Phone: 336-363-2604. Fax: 336-363-3671. E-mail: director@campcheerio.org.
Winter Contact Mr. Michaux Crocker, Director, PO Box 6258, High Point, North Carolina 27262. Phone: 336-869-0195. Fax: 336-869-2736. E-mail: director@campcheerio.org.
URL www.campcheerio.org

CAMP CHOSATONGA FOR BOYS

Camps Kahdalea for Girls and Chosatonga for Boys
2500 Morgan Mill Road
Brevard, North Carolina 28712

General Information Boys' residential traditional camp and outdoor program established in 1977.
Arts Arts and crafts (general), leather working, music (instrumental), musical productions, pottery.
Special Interest Areas Campcraft, community service, model rocketry, nature study, work camp programs.
Sports Archery, bicycling, canoeing, climbing (wall), equestrian sports, fishing, horseback riding, kayaking, rappelling, riflery, ropes course, soccer, swimming, tennis, volleyball, weight training, wrestling.
Wilderness/Outdoors Backpacking, bicycle trips, canoe trips, caving, hiking, mountain biking, mountaineering, orienteering, rafting, rock climbing, white-water trips, wilderness camping.
Trips Cultural, day, overnight.
Program Information 2 sessions per year. Session length: 24–35 days in June, July, August. Ages: 8–18. 80 participants per session. Boarding program cost: $2400–$3100. Financial aid available.
Application Deadline Continuous.
Jobs Positions for college students 18 and older.
Contact Mr. David Trufant, President, main address above. Phone: 828-884-6834. Fax: 828-884-6834. E-mail: office@kahdalea.com.
URL www.chosatonga.com

CAMP CRESTRIDGE FOR GIRLS

Lifeway Christian Resources
Ridgecrest, North Carolina 28770

General Information Girls' residential traditional camp established in 1955. Religious affiliation: Christian. Accredited by American Camping Association.
Program Focus Christian camping.
Arts Arts and crafts (general), chorus, music (vocal), woodworking.
Special Interest Areas Campcraft, nature study.
Sports Aerobics, archery, basketball, canoeing, cheerleading, golf, gymnastics, horseback riding, martial arts, riflery, soccer, softball, swimming, tennis, volleyball.
Wilderness/Outdoors Backpacking, hiking, rafting, rock climbing, wilderness camping.
Trips Day.
Program Information 6 sessions per year. Session length: 2–4 weeks in June, July, August. Ages: 7–16. 200 participants per session. Boarding program cost: $1100–$2000. Financial aid available.
Application Deadline Continuous.
Jobs Positions for high school students 17 and older and college students 18 and older.
Contact Ron Springs, Director, PO Box 279, Ridgecrest, North Carolina 28770. Phone: 800-968-1630. Fax: 828-669-5512. E-mail: uncron@aol.com.
URL www.ridgecrestcamps.com

CAMP GLEN ARDEN FOR GIRLS

Camp Glen Arden
1261 Cabin Creek Road
Tuxedo, North Carolina 28784

General Information Girls' residential traditional camp established in 1951. Formal opportunities for the artistically talented.
Arts Arts and crafts (general), ceramics, chorus, dance, dance (ballet), dance (jazz), dance (modern), drawing, music, music (classical), music (ensemble), music (instrumental), music (vocal), musical productions, photography, pottery, theater/drama, weaving, woodworking.
Special Interest Areas Counselor-in-training program, gardening, leadership training, nature study, wood carving.
Sports Archery, baseball, basketball, canoeing, climbing (wall), diving, equestrian sports, gymnastics, horseback riding, kayaking, riflery, ropes course, sailing, soccer, softball, sports (general), swimming, tennis, track and field, volleyball.
Wilderness/Outdoors Backpacking, canoe trips, hiking, mountaineering, orienteering, rock climbing, survival training, white-water trips, wilderness camping.
Trips Cultural, day, overnight.

Camp Glen Arden for Girls (continued)

Program Information 2–3 sessions per year. Session length: 10–49 days in June, July, August. Ages: 6–17. 60–180 participants per session. Boarding program cost: $1400–$5300.
Application Deadline Continuous.
Jobs Positions for college students 19 and older.
Contact Ms. Casey Thurman, Director/Owner, PO Box 7, Tuxedo, North Carolina 28784. Phone: 828-692-8362. Fax: 828-692-6259. E-mail: tajarden@aol.com.
URL www.campglenarden.com

CAMP GREEN COVE

Camps Mondamin and Green Cove
South Lake Summit Road
Tuxedo, North Carolina 28784

General Information Girls' residential traditional camp and outdoor program established in 1945. Accredited by Association for Experiential Education.

Camp Green Cove

Program Focus Waterfront activities, wilderness trips, and horseback riding.
Arts Arts and crafts (general), batiking, ceramics, drawing, fabric arts, jewelry making, painting, photography, pottery, printmaking, sculpture, theater/drama, weaving.
Special Interest Areas Animal care, campcraft, nature study.
Sports Archery, bicycling, boating, canoeing, climbing (wall), equestrian sports, horseback riding, kayaking, rappelling, riflery, ropes course, sailing, swimming, tennis.
Wilderness/Outdoors Backpacking, bicycle trips, canoe trips, hiking, mountain biking, mountaineering, outdoor adventure, rafting, rock climbing, white-water trips, wilderness camping.
Trips Overnight.
Program Information 3 sessions per year. Session length: 7–38 days in June, July, August. Ages: 7–17. 190 participants per session. Boarding program cost: $790–$4175. Financial aid available.
Application Deadline Continuous.
Jobs Positions for college students 18 and older.
Contact Ms. Nancy Bell, Director, PO Box 38, Tuxedo, North Carolina 28784. Phone: 828-692-6355. Fax: 828-696-8895. E-mail: greencove@greencove.com.
URL www.greencove.com
For more information, see page 1032.

CAMP HIGH ROCKS

Greenville Highway
Cedar Mountain, North Carolina 28718

General Information Boys' residential traditional camp established in 1958. Accredited by Association for Experiential Education.
Arts Arts and crafts (general), ceramics, leather working, pottery.
Sports Archery, canoeing, climbing (wall), horseback riding, kayaking, rappelling, riflery, ropes course, sailing, soccer, swimming, tennis.
Wilderness/Outdoors Backpacking, canoe trips, hiking, mountain biking, orienteering, rock climbing, white-water trips, wilderness camping.
Trips Day, overnight.
Program Information 3 sessions per year. Session length: 13–27 days in June, July, August. Ages: 8–16. 129 participants per session. Boarding program cost: $2025–$3575.
Application Deadline Continuous.
Jobs Positions for college students 19 and older.
Contact Mr. Henry Birdsong, Director, PO Box 210, Cedar Mountain, North Carolina 28718-0210. Phone: 828-885-2153. Fax: 828-884-4612. E-mail: mail@highrocks.com.
URL www.highrocks.com

CAMP ILLAHEE FOR GIRLS

500 Illahee Road
Brevard, North Carolina 28712-0272

General Information Girls' residential traditional camp established in 1921. Religious affiliation: Christian Churches and Churches of Christ. Accredited by American Camping Association.
Arts Arts and crafts (general), ceramics, dance (jazz), fabric arts, painting, pottery, puppetry, theater/drama, weaving, woodworking.
Special Interest Areas Campcraft, leadership training, nature study.
Sports Aerobics, archery, basketball, canoeing, climbing (wall), diving, equestrian sports, field hockey, gymnastics, horseback riding, kayaking, lacrosse, martial arts, rappelling, riflery, ropes course, soccer, softball, swimming, tennis, volleyball.
Wilderness/Outdoors Canoe trips, hiking, rock climbing, white-water trips.
Trips Day, overnight.
Program Information 4 sessions per year. Session length: 5–27 days in June, July, August. Ages: 7–16. 225 participants per session. Boarding program cost: $975–$3400. Financial aid available.
Jobs Positions for college students 18 and older.

Contact Ms. Laurie Strayhorn, Director, main address above. Phone: 828-883-2181. Fax: 828-883-8738. E-mail: info@campillahee.com.
URL www.campillahee.com

Camp Kahdalea for Girls

Camps Kahdalea for Girls and Chosatonga for Boys
2500 Morgan Mill Road
Brevard, North Carolina 28712

General Information Girls' residential traditional camp established in 1962.
Arts Acting, arts and crafts (general), ceramics, dance, drawing, fabric arts, jewelry making, leather working, music (instrumental), music (vocal), musical productions, painting, pottery, sculpture, theater/drama.
Special Interest Areas Campcraft, community service, leadership training, nature study.
Sports Archery, basketball, bicycling, canoeing, climbing (wall), diving, equestrian sports, fishing, gymnastics, horseback riding, kayaking, rappelling, riflery, ropes course, soccer, softball, swimming, tennis, volleyball.
Wilderness/Outdoors Backpacking, bicycle trips, canoe trips, caving, hiking, mountain biking, mountaineering, orienteering, rafting, rock climbing, white-water trips, wilderness camping.
Trips Cultural, day, overnight.
Program Information 2 sessions per year. Session length: 24–35 days in June, July, August. Ages: 8–18. 150 participants per session. Boarding program cost: $2400–$3100. Financial aid available.
Application Deadline Continuous.
Jobs Positions for college students 18 and older.
Contact Mr. David Trufant, President, main address above. Phone: 828-884-6834. Fax: 828-884-6834. E-mail: office@kahdalea.com.
URL www.kahdalea.com

Camp Merrie-Woode

100 Merrie-Woode Road
Sapphire, North Carolina 28774

General Information Girls' residential traditional camp established in 1919. Religious affiliation: Christian non-denominational. Accredited by American Camping Association.
Academics Music.
Arts Arts and crafts (general), ceramics, dance, dance (ballet), dance (folk), dance (jazz), dance (modern), music, photography, pottery, theater/drama, weaving, woodworking.
Sports Aerobics, archery, boating, canoeing, climbing (wall), equestrian sports, gymnastics, horseback riding, kayaking, sailing, soccer, swimming, tennis.
Wilderness/Outdoors Backpacking, canoe trips, hiking, mountaineering, rock climbing, white-water trips.
Trips Day, overnight.
Program Information 3 sessions per year. Session length: 2–5 weeks in June, July, August. Ages: 7–16. 200 participants per session. Boarding program cost: $1700–$3800. Financial aid available.
Application Deadline Continuous.
Jobs Positions for college students 19 and older.
Contact Ms. Denice Dunn, Director, main address above. Phone: 828-743-3300. Fax: 828-743-5846. E-mail: denice@merriewoode.com.
URL www.merriewoode.com

Camp Mondamin

Camps Mondamin and Green Cove
Mondamin Road
Tuxedo, North Carolina 28784

General Information Boys' residential traditional camp and outdoor program established in 1922. Accredited by Association for Experiential Education.
Program Focus Waterfront activities, wilderness trips, and horseback riding.
Arts Arts and crafts (general), ceramics, leather working, metalworking, photography, pottery, woodworking.
Special Interest Areas Native American culture, animal care, campcraft, field research/expeditions, leadership training, nature study.
Sports Archery, bicycling, boating, canoeing, climbing (wall), diving, equestrian sports, fishing, horseback riding, kayaking, rappelling, riflery, ropes course, sailing, swimming, tennis.
Wilderness/Outdoors Backpacking, bicycle trips, canoe trips, hiking, mountain biking, mountaineering, outdoor adventure, pack animal trips, rafting, rock climbing, white-water trips, wilderness camping.
Trips Overnight.
Program Information 3 sessions per year. Session length: 7–38 days in June, July, August. Ages: 7–17. 180 participants per session. Boarding program cost: $790–$4175. Financial aid available.
Application Deadline Continuous.
Jobs Positions for college students 18 and older.
Contact Frank D. Bell, Director, PO Box 8, Tuxedo, North Carolina 28784. Phone: 828-693-7446. Fax: 828-696-8895. E-mail: mondamin@mondamin.com.
URL www.mondamin.com

For more information, see page 1032.

Camp Pisgah

Girl Scouts of Western North Carolina Pisgah Council
570 Girl Scout Camp Road
Brevard, North Carolina 28712

General Information Girls' residential traditional camp established in 1953. Accredited by American Camping Association.
Arts Acting, arts and crafts (general), ceramics, clowning, dance (folk), fabric arts, jewelry making, leather working, music, painting, photography, pottery, puppetry, theater/drama.
Special Interest Areas Native American culture, animal care, campcraft, community service, leadership training, nature study, team building.
Sports Archery, basketball, bicycling, boating, canoeing, climbing (wall), equestrian sports, fishing, horseback riding, kayaking, rappelling, ropes course, soccer, softball, swimming, volleyball.

Camp Pisgah (continued)
Wilderness/Outdoors Backpacking, bicycle trips, canoe trips, caving, hiking, mountain biking, orienteering, pack animal trips, rafting, rock climbing, white-water trips, wilderness camping.
Trips Cultural, day, overnight.
Program Information 7 sessions per year. Session length: 1–2 weeks in June, July. Ages: 7–17. 100–140 participants per session. Boarding program cost: $110–$550. Financial aid available.
Application Deadline Continuous.
Jobs Positions for college students 18 and older.
Summer Contact Ms. Michele Hathcock, Camp Director, PO Box 8249, Asheville, North Carolina 28814. Phone: 828-252-4442. Fax: 828-255-8306. E-mail: camppisgah@girlscoutswnc.org.
Winter Contact Ms. Molly de Mattos, Program Specialist, PO Box 8249, Asheville, North Carolina 28814. Phone: 828-252-4442. Fax: 828-255-8306. E-mail: camppisgah@girlscoutswnc.org.
URL www.girlscoutswnc.org

Camp Ridgecrest for Boys

Lifeway Christian Resources
Ridgecrest, North Carolina 28770

General Information Boys' residential traditional camp established in 1929. Religious affiliation: Christian. Accredited by American Camping Association.
Program Focus Christian camping.
Arts Arts and crafts (general), woodworking.
Special Interest Areas Native American culture, campcraft, model rocketry, nature study.
Sports Archery, baseball, basketball, bicycling, canoeing, climbing (wall), football, gymnastics, horseback riding, martial arts, riflery, soccer, softball, swimming, tennis, volleyball, weight training.
Wilderness/Outdoors Backpacking, canoe trips, hiking, mountain biking, rafting, rock climbing, white-water trips, wilderness camping.
Trips Day.
Program Information 6 sessions per year. Session length: 2–4 weeks in June, July, August. Ages: 7–16. 150–200 participants per session. Boarding program cost: $1100–$2000. Financial aid available.
Application Deadline Continuous.
Jobs Positions for high school students 17 and older and college students 18 and older.
Contact Ron Springs, Director, PO Box 279, Ridgecrest, North Carolina 28770. Phone: 800-968-1630. Fax: 828-669-5512. E-mail: uncron@aol.com.
URL www.ridgecrestcamps.com

Camp Rockmont for Boys

375 Lake Eden Road
Black Mountain, North Carolina 28711

General Information Boys' residential traditional camp and bible camp established in 1956. Religious affiliation: interdenominational. Accredited by American Camping Association.
Academics Bible study.
Arts Arts and crafts (general), ceramics, drawing, pottery.
Special Interest Areas Farming, gardening, homestays, model rocketry, nature study.
Sports Archery, baseball, basketball, canoeing, climbing (wall), field hockey, fishing, flag football, horseback riding, kayaking, lacrosse, paintball, riflery, ropes course, sailing, soccer, softball, swimming, tennis, track and field, ultimate frisbee, volleyball, waterskiing, weight training.
Wilderness/Outdoors Backpacking, canoe trips, caving, hiking, mountain biking, rafting, rock climbing, white-water trips, wilderness camping.
Trips Day, overnight.
Program Information 4 sessions per year. Session length: 6–27 days in June, July, August. Ages: 6–16. 400 participants per session. Boarding program cost: $1725–$2950. Financial aid available. Counselors-in-training pay a reduced rate; there is an additional charge for horseback riding and trap shooting.
Application Deadline Continuous.
Jobs Positions for high school students 17 and older and college students 18 and older.
Contact R. David Bruce, Director, main address above. Phone: 828-686-3885. Fax: 828-686-7332. E-mail: info@rockmont.com.
URL www.rockmont.com

Camp Sky Ranch, Inc.

634 Sky Ranch Road
Blowing Rock, North Carolina 28605-9738

General Information Coed residential traditional camp and special needs program established in 1948. Specific services available for the developmentally challenged, hearing impaired, learning disabled, physically challenged, and visually impaired.
Program Focus Mentally challenged.
Arts Dance, music.
Special Interest Areas Nature study.
Sports Archery, basketball, boating, fishing, horseback riding, softball, swimming, volleyball.
Wilderness/Outdoors Hiking.
Program Information 3 sessions per year. Session length: 13–14 days in June, July, August. Ages: 10+. 100–110 participants per session. Boarding program cost: $850.
Application Deadline Continuous.
Jobs Positions for college students 19 and older.
Summer Contact Ms. Jack L. Sharp (Betty), Owner, main address above. Phone: 828-264-8600. Fax: 828-265-2339.
Winter Contact Ms. Jack L. Sharp (Betty), Owner, 515 Hobbs Road, Greensboro, North Carolina 27403. Phone: 336-854-1141. Fax: 336-852-1987. E-mail: jsharpl@triad.rr.com.
URL www.campskyranch.com

Camp Winding Gap

Camp Winding Gap
500 Winding Gap Road
Lake Toxaway, North Carolina 28747

General Information Coed residential traditional camp, wilderness program, and adventure program established in 1979. Accredited by American Camping Association.
Program Focus Western horseback riding, farm animals, mountain adventures.
Academics Tutoring.
Arts Arts and crafts (general), dance, drawing, fabric arts, film, guitar, jewelry making, painting, photography, puppetry, television/video, theater/drama, woodworking.
Special Interest Areas Animal care, campcraft, culinary arts, farming, gardening, leadership training, model rocketry, nature study.
Sports Aerobics, archery, bicycling, canoeing, climbing (wall), equestrian sports, fishing, horseback riding, kayaking, martial arts, riflery, soccer, swimming, volleyball.
Wilderness/Outdoors Backpacking, bicycle trips, canoe trips, hiking, mountain biking, mountaineering, orienteering, pack animal trips, rafting, rock climbing, white-water trips, wilderness camping.
Trips Day, overnight.
Program Information 5 sessions per year. Session length: 6–20 days in June, July, August. Ages: 6–14. 85 participants per session. Boarding program cost: $750–$5700. Financial aid available.
Application Deadline Continuous.
Jobs Positions for high school students 18 and older and college students 18 and older.
Contact Mrs. Ann S. Hertzberg, Director, Route 1, Box 56, Lake Toxaway, North Carolina 28747. Phone: 888-CWG-CAMP. Fax: 828-883-8720. E-mail: campwgap@citcom.net.
URL www.campwindinggap.com

Constructing Your College Experience

Duke Youth Programs–Duke University Continuing Studies
Duke University
Durham, North Carolina 27708

General Information Coed residential and day academic program established in 1998.
Program Focus Exploration of the college selection process and navigation of the college admissions process.
Academics SAT/ACT preparation, writing.
Special Interest Areas Career exploration, college planning, leadership training.
Trips College tours, day.
Program Information 1 session per year. Session length: 1 week in July, August. Ages: 16–17. 50–65 participants per session. Day program cost: $900–$1000. Boarding program cost: $1150–$1200. Financial aid available.
Application Deadline Continuous.
Jobs Positions for college students 18 and older.
Contact Youth Program Director, 203 Bishop's House, Box 90702, Durham, North Carolina 27708. Phone: 919-684-6259. Fax: 919-681-8235. E-mail: youth@duke.edu.
URL www.learnmore.duke.edu/youth

For more information, see page 1090.

Cybercamps–Duke University

Cybercamps–Giant Campus, Inc.
Durham, North Carolina

General Information Coed residential and day academic program established in 2004.
Academics Web page design, academics (general), computer programming, computers.
Arts Animation, creative writing, digital media, graphic arts, photography.
Special Interest Areas Computer game design, computer graphics, robotics, team building.
Sports Ultimate frisbee.
Program Information 2–9 sessions per year. Session length: 5–30 days in June, July, August. Ages: 7–18. 30–150 participants per session. Day program cost: $599–$849. Boarding program cost: $974–$1224. Financial aid available.
Application Deadline Continuous.
Jobs Positions for high school students 15 and older and college students.
Contact Cybercamps Information Office, 2401 4th Avenue, Suite 1110, Seattle, Washington 98121. Phone: 206-442-4500. Fax: 206-442-4500. E-mail: info@cybercamps.com.
URL www.cybercamps.com

Cybercamps–UNC, Chapel Hill

Cybercamps–Giant Campus, Inc.
Chapel Hill, North Carolina

General Information Coed residential and day academic program established in 1997.
Program Focus High tech computer camps featuring project oriented curriculum in Web design, 3D animation, game design, robotics, digital arts and programming for all ability levels.
Academics Web page design, computer programming, computers.
Arts Animation, creative writing, digital media, graphic arts, photography.
Special Interest Areas Computer game design, computer graphics, robotics, team building.
Sports Frisbee golf, ultimate frisbee.
Program Information 2–9 sessions per year. Session length: 5–30 days in June, July, August. Ages: 7–18. 30–150 participants per session. Day program cost: $599–$849. Boarding program cost: $974–$1224.
Application Deadline Continuous.
Jobs Positions for high school students 15 and older and college students.
Contact Cybercamps Information Office, 2401 4th Avenue, Suite 1110, Seattle, Washington 98121. Phone: 206-442-4500. Fax: 206-442-4501. E-mail: info@cybercamps.com.
URL www.cybercamps.com

DAVIDSON COLLEGE JULY EXPERIENCE

Davidson College
Davidson, North Carolina 28035

General Information Coed residential academic program established in 1975. Formal opportunities for the academically talented.
Academics American literature, English language/literature, academics (general), anthropology, biology, economics, government and politics, history, mathematics, music, physics, physiology, psychology, social science.
Sports Basketball, boating, canoeing, climbing (wall), golf, racquetball, sailing, swimming, tennis, volleyball, waterskiing.
Trips College tours, day, shopping.
Program Information 1 session per year. Session length: 3 weeks in July. Ages: 16–18. 60–75 participants per session. Boarding program cost: $2100. Financial aid available.
Application Deadline April 1.
Contact Evelyn Gerdes, Director, July Experience, Box 7151, Davidson, North Carolina 28035-7151. Phone: 704-894-2508. Fax: 704-894-2645. E-mail: julyexp@davidson.edu.
URL www.davidson.edu/academic/education/julyexp.html

DUKE ACTION: SCIENCE CAMP FOR YOUNG WOMEN

Duke Youth Programs–Duke University Continuing Studies
Duke University
Durham, North Carolina 27708

General Information Girls' residential and day academic program established in 1991.

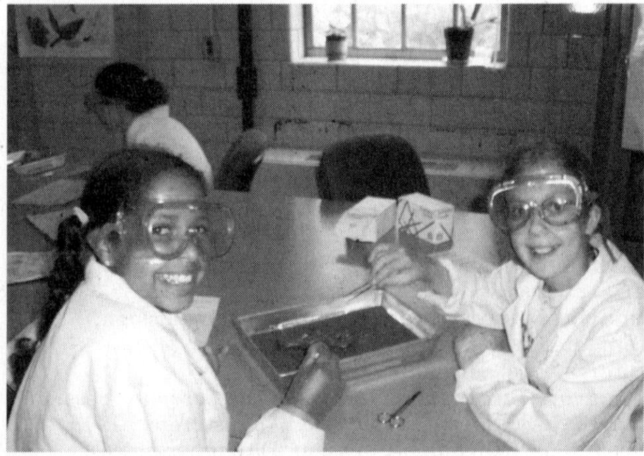

Duke Action: Science Camp for Young Women

Program Focus Scientific discovery through field and laboratory experiences.
Academics Biology, botany, chemistry, ecology, environmental science, geology/earth science, health sciences, science (general).
Wilderness/Outdoors Canoe trips, hiking.
Trips Cultural, day.
Program Information 1 session per year. Session length: 12 days in June, July. Ages: 10–13. 40–60 participants per session. Day program cost: $865–$875. Boarding program cost: $1655–$1700. Financial aid available.
Application Deadline Continuous.
Jobs Positions for college students 18 and older.
Contact Youth Program Director, 203 Bishop's House, Box 90702, Durham, North Carolina 27708. Phone: 919-684-6259. Fax: 919-681-8235. E-mail: youth@duke.edu.
URL www.learnmore.duke.edu/youth

For more information, see page 1090.

DUKE CREATIVE WRITERS' WORKSHOP

Duke Youth Programs–Duke University Continuing Studies
Duke University
Durham, North Carolina 27708

General Information Coed residential and day academic program established in 1993. Formal opportunities for the academically talented and artistically talented.
Program Focus Creative writing in all genres for advanced writers.
Academics Writing.
Arts Creative writing.
Special Interest Areas Field trips (arts and culture).
Trips Cultural, day.
Program Information 1 session per year. Session length: 12 days in July. Ages: 15–17. 35–45 participants per session. Day program cost: $1025. Boarding program cost: $1565–$1600. Financial aid available.
Application Deadline Continuous.
Jobs Positions for college students 18 and older.
Contact Youth Program Director, 203 Bishop's House, Box 90702, Durham, North Carolina 27708. Phone: 919-684-6259. Fax: 919-681-8235. E-mail: youth@duke.edu.
URL www.learnmore.duke.edu/youth

For more information, see page 1090.

DUKE DRAMA WORKSHOP

Duke Youth Programs–Duke University Continuing Studies
Duke University
Durham, North Carolina 27708

General Information Coed residential and day arts program established in 1996. Formal opportunities for the academically talented and artistically talented.
Program Focus Intense experience in acting and other aspects of theater.
Arts Acting, dance, music (vocal), musical productions, theater/drama.
Special Interest Areas Field trips (arts and culture).
Trips Cultural, day.
Program Information 1 session per year. Session length: 12 days in July. Ages: 15–17. 36–50 participants per session. Day program cost: $1025. Boarding program cost: $1565–$1600. Financial aid available.
Application Deadline Continuous.
Jobs Positions for college students 18 and older.

Contact Program Director, 203 Bishop's House, Box 90702, Durham, North Carolina 27708. Phone: 919-684-6259. Fax: 919-681-8235. E-mail: youth@duke.edu.
URL www.learnmore.duke.edu/youth

For more information, see page 1090.

Duke Young Writers Camp

Duke Youth Programs–Duke University Continuing Studies
Duke University
Durham, North Carolina 27708

General Information Coed residential and day academic program established in 1983. Formal opportunities for the academically talented and artistically talented.
Program Focus The development of creative and analytical processes of writing.
Academics Communications, journalism, strategy games, writing.
Arts Arts and crafts (general), creative writing, dance, theater/drama.
Special Interest Areas Community service.
Sports Basketball, soccer, sports (general), tennis, volleyball.
Trips Cultural.
Program Information 3 sessions per year. Session length: 11–12 days in June, July. Ages: 12–17. 140–160 participants per session. Day program cost: $775–$800. Boarding program cost: $1565–$1600. Financial aid available.
Application Deadline Continuous.
Jobs Positions for college students 18 and older.
Contact Youth Program Director, 203 Bishop's House, Box 90702, Durham, North Carolina 27708. Phone: 919-684-6259. Fax: 919-681-8235. E-mail: youth@duke.edu.
URL www.learnmore.duke.edu/youth

For more information, see page 1090.

Eagle Lake Camp–East

The Navigators
Asheville, North Carolina

General Information Coed residential outdoor program, bible camp, wilderness program, and adventure program established in 1993. Religious affiliation: Christian. Accredited by American Camping Association.
Academics Bible study.
Special Interest Areas Nature study.
Sports Bicycling, canoeing, kayaking, rappelling, sea kayaking, swimming.
Wilderness/Outdoors Backpacking, bicycle trips, canoe trips, hiking, mountain biking, mountaineering, orienteering, rafting, rock climbing, white-water trips, wilderness camping.
Trips Day, overnight.
Program Information 3–10 sessions per year. Session length: 5–12 days in June, July, August. Ages: 11–21. 12–20 participants per session. Boarding program cost: $388–$1008. Financial aid available.
Application Deadline Continuous.
Jobs Positions for college students 19 and older.
Summer Contact Office Manager, PO Box 6000, Colorado Springs, Colorado 80934. Phone: 719-472-1260. Fax: 719-623-0148. E-mail: registrar_el@navigators.org.
Winter Contact John Rogers, Director of Excursion Ministries, PO Box 6000, Colorado Springs, Colorado 80934. Phone: 719-472-1260. Fax: 719-623-0148. E-mail: john_rogers@navigators.org.
URL www.eaglelake.org

Eagle's Nest Camp

Eagle's Nest Foundation
43 Hart Road
Pisgah Forest, North Carolina 28768

General Information Coed residential traditional camp and outdoor program established in 1927. Accredited by American Camping Association. Formal opportunities for the artistically talented. High school credit may be earned.
Program Focus Wilderness expeditions, art, music, and drama.
Academics Area studies, art (Advanced Placement), art history/appreciation, biology, botany, ecology, environmental science, geography, geology/earth science, intercultural studies, music, music (Advanced Placement), science (general), writing.
Arts Acting, arts, arts and crafts (general), batiking, ceramics, creative writing, dance, dance (ballet), dance (folk), dance (jazz), dance (modern), drawing, fabric arts, jewelry making, leather working, metalworking, mime, music, music (chamber), music (classical), music (ensemble), music (folk), music (instrumental), music (jazz), music (vocal), musical productions, painting, photography, pottery, printmaking, puppetry, sculpture, theater/drama, weaving, woodworking.
Special Interest Areas Native American culture, campcraft, community service, culinary arts, field research/expeditions, gardening, leadership training, nature study, team building.
Sports Aerobics, archery, baseball, basketball, bicycling, canoeing, climbing (wall), equestrian sports, fishing, gymnastics, horseback riding, kayaking, ropes course, soccer, softball, sports (general), swimming, tennis, track and field, volleyball.
Wilderness/Outdoors Backpacking, bicycle trips, canoe trips, caving, hiking, mountain biking, mountaineering, orienteering, rock climbing, survival training, white-water trips, wilderness camping, wilderness/outdoors (general).
Trips Cultural, day, overnight.
Program Information 3 sessions per year. Session length: 3 weeks in June, July, August. Ages: 6–17. 150–190 participants per session. Boarding program cost: $2215–$2320. Application fee: $50. Financial aid available.
Application Deadline Continuous.
Jobs Positions for college students 18 and older.
Summer Contact R. Emmylou Ferris, Assistant Camp Director, main address above. Phone: 828-877-4349. Fax: 828-884-2788. E-mail: promotions@enf.org.

Eagle's Nest Camp (continued)

Winter Contact R. Emmylou Ferris, Assistant Camp Director, PO Box 5127, Winston-Salem, North Carolina 27113-5127. Phone: 336-761-1040. Fax: 336-727-0030. E-mail: promotions@enf.org.
URL www.enf.org

Eastern Music Festival and School

Greensboro, North Carolina 27420

General Information Coed residential arts program established in 1962. Formal opportunities for the artistically talented.
Program Focus Classical music performance and instruction.
Academics Music.
Arts Music, music (chamber), music (classical), music (ensemble), music (instrumental), music (orchestral), piano.
Special Interest Areas Career exploration.
Sports Baseball, basketball, racquetball, soccer, softball, swimming, tennis, weight training.
Trips Day, shopping.
Program Information 1 session per year. Session length: 35–40 days in June, July, August. Ages: 14–20. 185–195 participants per session. Boarding program cost: $3900. Application fee: $50. Financial aid available.
Application Deadline March 1.
Jobs Positions for college students 21 and older.
Contact Dr. Melissa M. Edwards, Director of Admissions, PO Box 22026, Greensboro, North Carolina 27420. Phone: 336-333-7450 Ext.27. Fax: 336-333-7454. E-mail: admissions@easternmusicfestival.org.
URL www.easternmusicfestival.org

EXPRESSIONS! Duke Fine Arts Camp

Duke Youth Programs–Duke University Continuing Studies
Duke University
Durham, North Carolina 27708

General Information Coed residential and day arts program established in 1995.
Program Focus A fine arts experience that explores: dance, drama, visual art, and musical theatre.
Arts Acting, arts, arts and crafts (general), dance, drawing, fabric arts, music (vocal), musical productions, painting, sculpture, theater/drama.
Program Information 1 session per year. Session length: 10 days in June. Ages: 10–13. 40 participants per session. Day program cost: $825–$850. Boarding program cost: $1565–$1600. Financial aid available.
Application Deadline Continuous.
Jobs Positions for college students 18 and older.
Contact Youth Program Director, 203 Bishop's House, Box 90702, Durham, North Carolina 27708. Phone: 919-684-6259. Fax: 919-681-8235. E-mail: youth@duke.edu.
URL www.learnmore.duke.edu/youth

For more information, see page 1090.

Falling Creek Camp

Falling Creek Camp Road
Tuxedo, North Carolina 28784

General Information Boys' residential traditional camp established in 1969. Accredited by American Camping Association.
Arts Arts and crafts (general), drawing, pottery, woodworking.
Special Interest Areas Native American culture, nature study.
Sports Archery, basketball, canoeing, climbing (wall), fishing, horseback riding, kayaking, lacrosse, riflery, ropes course, sailing, soccer, softball, swimming, tennis, track and field, volleyball.
Wilderness/Outdoors Backpacking, canoe trips, mountain biking, mountaineering, orienteering, rock climbing, white-water trips, wilderness camping.
Trips Overnight.
Program Information 3 sessions per year. Session length: 10–29 days in June, July, August. Ages: 7–16. 217 participants per session. Boarding program cost: $1500–$3500. Financial aid available.
Application Deadline Continuous.
Jobs Positions for college students 19 and older.
Contact Donnie Bain, Director, Box 98, Tuxedo, North Carolina 28784. Phone: 828-692-0262. Fax: 828-696-1616. E-mail: mail@fallingcreek.com.
URL www.fallingcreek.com

Green River Preserve

Green River Preserve
301 Green River Road
Cedar Mountain, North Carolina 28718

General Information Coed residential outdoor program established in 1988. Accredited by American Camping Association. Formal opportunities for the academically talented and artistically talented.
Program Focus Co-ed summer camp for young naturalists who are advanced learners in grades 4-8.
Academics Ecology.
Arts Arts and crafts (general), creative writing, painting, pottery.
Special Interest Areas Campcraft, field research/expeditions, gardening, nature study.
Sports Archery, canoeing, climbing (wall), fencing, fishing, riflery, swimming.
Wilderness/Outdoors Backpacking, hiking, mountaineering, orienteering, rock climbing, wilderness camping.
Trips Day, overnight.
Program Information 4 sessions per year. Session length: 1–3 weeks in June, July, August. Ages: 9–14. 98 participants per session. Boarding program cost: $900–$2600. Financial aid available.
Application Deadline Continuous.
Jobs Positions for college students 18 and older.
Contact Mrs. Missi Schenck, Founder/Director, main address above. Phone: 828-698-8828. Fax: 828-698-9201. E-mail: grpreserve@citcom.net.
URL www.greenriverpreserve.com

HANTE SCHOOL

Eagle's Nest Foundation
43 Hart Road
Pisgah Forest, North Carolina 28768

General Information Coed travel outdoor program, wilderness program, cultural program, and adventure program established in 1973. Accredited by American Camping Association. Formal opportunities for the academically talented and artistically talented. High school credit may be earned.
Program Focus Leadership and personal development through wilderness trekking in various states and international travel in the Hante tradition of "I went away and learned.".
Academics Spanish (Advanced Placement), Spanish language/literature, archaeology, architecture, area studies, art history/appreciation, biology, botany, ecology, environmental science, geography, geology/earth science, music, music (Advanced Placement), philosophy, science (general), writing.
Arts Arts and crafts (general), batiking, creative writing, dance, drawing, fabric arts, jewelry making, leather working, metalworking, music, photography, weaving.
Special Interest Areas Native American culture, campcraft, community service, conservation projects, construction, culinary arts, field research/expeditions, gardening, leadership training, nature study, team building, touring, work camp programs.
Sports Bicycling, canoeing, climbing (wall), fishing, ropes course, swimming.
Wilderness/Outdoors Backpacking, bicycle trips, canoe trips, caving, hiking, mountain biking, mountaineering, orienteering, outdoor adventure, rock climbing, survival training, white-water trips, wilderness camping, wilderness/outdoors (general).
Trips Cultural, day, overnight.
Program Information 9 sessions per year. Session length: 3 weeks in June, July, August. Ages: 13–17. 10–12 participants per session. Cost: $2575–$3500. Application fee: $50. Financial aid available.
Application Deadline Continuous.
Jobs Positions for college students 18 and older.
Contact Mr. John Carrico, Hante Director, main address above. Phone: 828-877-4349. Fax: 828-884-2788. E-mail: hante@enf.org.
URL www.enf.org

iD TECH CAMPS–UNIVERSITY OF NORTH CAROLINA AT CHAPEL HILL, CHAPEL HILL, NC

iD Tech Camps
University of North Carolina at Chapel Hill
Chapel Hill, North Carolina 27599

General Information Coed residential and day academic program established in 1999. Accredited by American Camping Association. Formal opportunities for the academically talented and artistically talented.
Program Focus High-tech computer camps for kids and teens; produce digital movies, create video games, design Web pages, learn programming and robotics, and more; one computer per student, small classes, campers complete a project in a creative and fun learning environment.
Academics Web page design, computer programming, computer science (Advanced Placement), computers, music, precollege program.
Arts Animation, cinematography, digital media, drawing, film, film editing, film production, graphic arts, music, television/video.
Special Interest Areas Career exploration, computer graphics, electronics, leadership training, robotics, team building.
Sports Baseball, basketball, soccer, softball, swimming, volleyball.
Trips College tours, cultural, day.
Program Information 5 sessions per year. Session length: 6–7 days in June, July, August. Ages: 7–17. 40–50 participants per session. Day program cost: $639. Boarding program cost: $989. Application fee: $200. Financial aid available.
Application Deadline Continuous.
Jobs Positions for college students 18 and older.
Contact Client Service Representatives, 1885 Winchester Boulevard, Suite 201, Campbell, California 95008. Phone: 888-709-TECH. Fax: 408-871-2228. E-mail: requests@internaldrive.com.
URL www.internaldrive.com

For more information, see page 1156.

IMACS–FULL DAY SUMMER CAMP–NORTH CAROLINA

Institute for Mathematics & Computer Science (IMACS)
North Carolina

General Information Coed day academic program established in 1992. Formal opportunities for the academically talented.
Academics Computer programming, computer science (Advanced Placement), computers, engineering, mathematics.
Special Interest Areas Electronics, robotics.
Program Information 5 sessions per year. Session length: 5 days in January, February, March, April, May, June, July, August, September, October, November, December. Ages: 5–18. 30–50 participants per session. Day program cost: $399–$1224. Supply fee: $50–$200; additional sessions booked at same time $249 plus $50 supply fee.
Application Deadline Continuous.
Jobs Positions for high school students 16 and older and college students 18 and older.
Contact Mr. Terry Kaufman, President, 7435 Northwest 4th Street, Plantation, Florida 33317. Phone: 954-791-2333. Fax: 954-791-0260. E-mail: info@imacs.org.
URL www.imacs.org

IMACS–Individual Summer Programs–North Carolina

Institute for Mathematics & Computer Science (IMACS)
North Carolina

General Information Coed day academic program established in 1992. Formal opportunities for the academically talented.
Academics Computer programming, computer science (Advanced Placement), computers, engineering, mathematics, mathematics (Advanced Placement).
Special Interest Areas Computer graphics, electronics, robotics.
Program Information 5 sessions per year. Session length: 5 days in January, February, March, April, May, June, July, August, September, October, November, December. Ages: 6–18. Day program cost: $79–$199. Financial aid available.
Application Deadline Continuous.
Jobs Positions for high school students 16 and older and college students 18 and older.
Contact Mr. Terry Kaufman, President, 7435 Northwest 4th Street, Plantation, Florida 33317. Phone: 954-791-2333. Fax: 954-791-0260. E-mail: info@imacs.org.
URL www.imacs.org

Joe Krivak Quarterback Camp, North Carolina/Sports International

Sports International, Inc.
Catawba College
Salisbury, North Carolina

General Information Coed residential and day sports camp established in 1983.
Program Focus Quarterback and wide receiver.
Sports Football, weight training.
Program Information 1 session per year. Session length: 5 days in July. Ages: 8–18. 300–450 participants per session. Day program cost: $349. Boarding program cost: $419.
Application Deadline Continuous.
Jobs Positions for college students 18 and older.
Contact Customer Service, 8924 McGaw Court, Columbia, Maryland 21045. Phone: 800-555-0801. Fax: 410-309-9962. E-mail: info@footballcamps.com.
URL www.footballcamps.com

Keystone Camp

Cashiers Valley Road
Brevard, North Carolina 28712

General Information Girls' residential traditional camp established in 1916.
Program Focus Daily horseback riding and horsemanship.
Arts Arts and crafts (general), ceramics, dance, dance (ballet), dance (jazz), dance (modern), dance (tap), drawing, fabric arts, jewelry making, painting, pottery, puppetry, theater/drama, weaving, woodworking.
Special Interest Areas Native American culture, animal care, campcraft, leadership training, nature study, team building.
Sports Aerobics, archery, baseball, basketball, canoeing, climbing (wall), equestrian sports, golf, gymnastics, horseback riding, rappelling, riflery, ropes course, soccer, softball, swimming, synchronized swimming, tennis, volleyball.
Wilderness/Outdoors Backpacking, canoe trips, hiking, orienteering, rock climbing, white-water trips, wilderness camping.
Trips Day, overnight.
Program Information 3–5 sessions per year. Session length: 13–27 days in June, July, August. Ages: 7–16. 125 participants per session. Boarding program cost: $2000–$3550.
Application Deadline Continuous.
Jobs Positions for college students 18 and older.
Contact Ms. Mary Boyd, Associate Director, PO Box 829, Brevard, North Carolina 28712. Phone: 828-884-9125. Fax: 828-884-9125. E-mail: mary@keystonecamp.com.
URL www.keystonecamp.com

Landmark Volunteers: North Carolina

Landmark Volunteers, Inc.
North Carolina

General Information Coed residential outdoor program and community service program established in 1992. High school credit may be earned.
Program Focus Opportunity for high school students to earn community service credit while working as a team for two weeks serving CooperRiis. Similar programs offered through Landmark Volunteers at over 60 locations in 21 states.
Academics Environmental science.
Special Interest Areas Career exploration, community service, conservation projects, leadership training, nature study, team building, work camp programs.
Sports Swimming.
Wilderness/Outdoors Hiking.
Trips Cultural, day.
Program Information 1 session per year. Session length: 2 weeks in June, July. Ages: 14–18. 10–13 participants per session. Boarding program cost: $875–$925.
Application Deadline Continuous.
Jobs Positions for college students 18 and older.
Contact Ann Barrett, Executive Director, PO Box 455, Sheffield, Massachusetts 01257. Phone: 413-229-0255. Fax: 413-229-2050. E-mail: landmark@volunteers.com.
For more information, see page 1182.

Mountain Adventure Guides: Summer Adventure Camp–Blue Ridge Expedition I

Mountain Adventure Guides
13490 US Highway 25/70
Marshall, North Carolina 28753

General Information Coed travel wilderness program and adventure program established in 1999.
Wilderness/Outdoors Backpacking, mountain biking, rafting, rock climbing, white-water trips, wilderness camping.
Trips Day, overnight.
Program Information 3 sessions per year. Session length: 12 days in June, July, August. Ages: 13–15. 8–12 participants per session. Cost: $1300–$1500.
Application Deadline Continuous.
Jobs Positions for college students 19 and older.
Contact Mr. Richard Dulworth, Director, 13490 US Highway 25/70, Marshall, North Carolina 28753. Phone: 866-813-5210. Fax: 828-649-0561. E-mail: guide@mtwadventure.guides.com.
URL www.mtnadventureguides.com

Mountain Adventure Guides: Summer Adventure Camp–Blue Ridge Expedition II

Mountain Adventure Guides
13490 US Highway 25/70
Marshall, North Carolina 28753

General Information Coed travel wilderness program and adventure program established in 1999.
Wilderness/Outdoors Backpacking, mountain biking, rafting, rock climbing, white-water trips, wilderness camping.
Trips Day, overnight.
Program Information 3 sessions per year. Session length: 18 days in June, July, August. Ages: 15–17. 8–12 participants per session. Cost: $1800.
Application Deadline Continuous.
Jobs Positions for college students 19 and older.
Contact Mr. Richard Dulworth, Director, 13490 US Highway 25/70, Marshall, North Carolina 28753. Phone: 866-813-5210. Fax: 828-649-0561. E-mail: guide@mtnadventureguides.com.
URL www.mtnadventureguides.com

Mountain Adventure Guides: Summer Adventure Camp–Jr. Adventure Camp

Mountain Adventure Guides
13490 US Highway 25/70
Marshall, North Carolina 28753

General Information Coed travel wilderness program and adventure program established in 1999.
Wilderness/Outdoors Backpacking, mountain biking, rafting, rock climbing, white-water trips, wilderness camping.
Trips Day, overnight.
Program Information 1 session per year. Session length: 1 week in July. Ages: 11–13. 8–12 participants per session. Cost: $800.
Application Deadline Continuous.
Jobs Positions for college students 19 and older.
Contact Mr. Richard Dulworth, Director, 13490 US Highway 25/70, Marshall, North Carolina 28753. Phone: 866-813-5210. Fax: 828-649-0561. E-mail: guide@mtnadventureguides.com.
URL www.mtnadventureguides.com

Nantahala Outdoor Center–Kids Adventure Sports Camp

Nantahala Outdoor Center
13077 Highway 19 West
Bryson City, North Carolina 28713

General Information Coed residential outdoor program established in 1984.
Program Focus Kayaking and mountain biking instruction in a fun atmosphere.
Sports Bicycling, kayaking, ropes course.
Wilderness/Outdoors Mountain biking, white-water trips.
Trips Day, overnight.
Program Information 1 session per year. Session length: 5 days in June. Ages: 12–15. 3–10 participants per session. Boarding program cost: $1000.
Application Deadline Continuous.
Jobs Positions for high school students 16 and older and college students 18 and older.
Contact NOC Guest Relations Office, main address above. Phone: 800-232-7238. Fax: 828-488-0301. E-mail: programs@noc.com.
URL www.noc.com

Nantahala Outdoor Center–Kids Kayaking Courses

Nantahala Outdoor Center
13077 Highway 19 West
Bryson City, North Carolina 28713

General Information Coed residential outdoor program established in 1984.
Program Focus Kayaking skills development, for novice to advanced paddlers.
Sports Kayaking.
Wilderness/Outdoors White-water trips.
Trips Day, overnight.
Program Information 6 sessions per year. Session length: 5–7 days in June, July. Ages: 9–15. 3–10 participants per session. Boarding program cost: $1000.
Application Deadline Continuous.
Jobs Positions for high school students 16 and older and college students 18 and older.
Contact NOC Guest Relations Office, main address above. Phone: 800-232-7238. Fax: 828-488-0301. E-mail: programs@noc.com.
URL www.noc.com

North Carolina Outward Bound–Outer Banks

North Carolina Outward Bound/Outward Bound, USA
Outer Banks
North Carolina

General Information Coed travel outdoor program, wilderness program, and adventure program established in 1966. High school or college credit may be earned.
Program Focus Programs are designed to promote personal growth and focus on these core values: self-reliance, fitness, craftsmanship, leadership, environmental stewardship and compassion.
Special Interest Areas Campcraft, community service, leadership training, nature study, team building.
Sports Sea kayaking.
Wilderness/Outdoors Hiking, orienteering, wilderness camping, wilderness/outdoors (general).
Trips Overnight.
Program Information 5–7 sessions per year. Session length: 8–14 days in May, June, July, August, September. Ages: 16+. 10–12 participants per session. Cost: $1195–$2095. Application fee: $95. Financial aid available.
Application Deadline Continuous.
Jobs Positions for college students 18 and older.
Contact Student Services Representative, 2582 Riceville Road, Asheville, North Carolina 28805. Phone: 877-776-2627. Fax: 828-299-3928. E-mail: challenge@ncobs.org.
URL www.ncoutwardbound.org

North Carolina Outward Bound–Southern Appalachian Mountains

North Carolina Outward Bound/Outward Bound, USA
North Carolina

General Information Coed travel outdoor program, wilderness program, and adventure program established in 1966. High school or college credit may be earned.
Program Focus Programs promote personal growth and focus on these core values: self-reliance, leadership, craftsmanship, fitness, environmental stewardship and compassion.
Special Interest Areas Campcraft, community service, leadership training, nature study, team building.
Sports Canoeing, rappelling, ropes course.
Wilderness/Outdoors Backpacking, canoe trips, hiking, orienteering, rock climbing, white-water trips, wilderness camping, wilderness/outdoors (general).
Trips Overnight.
Program Information 40–60 sessions per year. Session length: 4–28 days in March, April, May, June, July, August, September, October. Ages: 14+. 10–12 participants per session. Cost: $695–$3095. Application fee: $95. Financial aid available.
Application Deadline Continuous.
Jobs Positions for college students 18 and older.
Contact Student Services Representative, 2582 Riceville Road, Asheville, North Carolina 28805. Phone: 877-776-2627. Fax: 828-299-3928. E-mail: challenge@ncobs.org.
URL www.ncoutwardbound.org

North Carolina School of the Arts Summer Session

North Carolina School of the Arts
1533 South Main Street
Winston-Salem, North Carolina 27127

General Information Coed residential and day arts program established in 1967. Formal opportunities for the artistically talented. High school or college credit may be earned.
Arts Acting, arts, ceramics, chorus, clowning, creative writing, dance, dance (ballet), dance (modern), drawing, film, graphic arts, metalworking, mime, music, music (chamber), music (classical), music (ensemble), music (instrumental), music (orchestral), music (vocal), painting, pottery, sculpture, television/video, theater/drama.
Trips Cultural, day, shopping.
Program Information 1 session per year. Session length: 5 weeks in June, July. Ages: 12+. 530 participants per session. Day program cost: $1790. Boarding program cost: $2169–$3145. Application fee: $50. Minimum age for participants varies by department.
Application Deadline May 14.
Contact Sheeler Lawson, Assistant Director of Admissions for Summer Session, main address above. Phone: 336-770-3290. Fax: 336-770-3370. E-mail: admissions@ncarts.edu.
URL www.ncarts.edu

Oak Ridge Academic Summer Camp

Oak Ridge Military Academy
Oak Ridge, North Carolina 27310

General Information Coed residential and day traditional camp and academic program established in 1980. Formal opportunities for the academically talented. High school credit may be earned.
Program Focus Academic enrichment, enhancement, acceleration.
Academics American literature, English as a second language, English language/literature, academics (general), chemistry, government and politics, history, mathematics, science (general).
Special Interest Areas Leadership training.
Sports Football, paintball, rappelling, riflery, scuba diving, soccer, swimming, volleyball.
Trips Day, overnight.
Program Information 2 sessions per year. Session length: 3 weeks in June, July. Ages: 11–18. 50–85 participants per session. Day program cost: $900. Boarding program cost: $1800–$2300. Application fee: $100.
Application Deadline Continuous.
Contact Sgt. Maj. Dan Carpinetti, Vice President of Admissions, PO Box 498, Oak Ridge, North Carolina 27310. Phone: 336-643-4131 Ext.132. Fax: 336-643-1797. E-mail: dcarpinetti@ormila.com.
URL www.oakridgemilitary.com
For more information, see page 1232.

Oak Ridge Academic Summer Camp

Oak Ridge Summer Leadership Camp

Oak Ridge Military Academy
Oak Ridge, North Carolina 27310

General Information Coed residential and day outdoor program and adventure program established in 1980.
Program Focus Leadership training, athletic/recreational activities, and challenge/adventure training.
Special Interest Areas Campcraft, communication skills, leadership training, planning skills, team building.
Sports Boating, canoeing, challenge course, climbing (tower), football, martial arts, obstacle course, paintball, rappelling, riflery, ropes course, scuba diving, soccer, softball, swimming.
Wilderness/Outdoors Orienteering, survival training, wilderness camping.
Trips Day, overnight.
Program Information 2 sessions per year. Session length: 3 weeks in June, July. Ages: 11–18. 60–90 participants per session. Day program cost: $900. Boarding program cost: $1800–$2300. Application fee: $100.
Application Deadline Continuous.
Contact Sgt. Maj. Dan Carpinetti, Vice President of Admissions, PO Box 498, Oak Ridge, North Carolina 27310. Phone: 336-643-4131 Ext.132. Fax: 336-643-1797. E-mail: dcarpinetti@ormila.com.
URL www.oakridgemilitary.com
For more information, see page 1232.

Overland: Blue Ridge Explorer Hiking, Rafting and Kayaking

Overland Travel, Inc.
Blue Ridge Mountains
North Carolina

General Information Coed travel outdoor program, wilderness program, and adventure program established in 1985. Accredited by American Camping Association. High school credit may be earned.
Program Focus Backpacking, rafting, kayaking and climbing in the Blue Ridge Mountains.
Special Interest Areas Leadership training, team building.
Sports Kayaking.
Wilderness/Outdoors Backpacking, hiking, mountaineering, rafting, white-water trips, wilderness camping.
Program Information 3–6 sessions per year. Session length: 2 weeks in June, July, August. Ages: 13–18. 8–12 participants per session. Cost: $2495.
Application Deadline Continuous.
Jobs Positions for college students 20 and older.
Contact Tom Costley, Director, PO Box 31, Williamstown, Massachusetts 01267. Phone: 800-458-0588. Fax: 413-458-5208. E-mail: overland@adelphia.net.
URL www.overlandsummers.com
For more information, see page 1240.

Project SUCCEED

Shodor Education Foundation, Inc.
923 Broad Street
Suite 100
Durham, North Carolina 27705

General Information Coed day academic program established in 1996. Formal opportunities for the academically talented. Specific services available for the hearing impaired. High school credit may be earned.
Program Focus Computational science and math workshops in a hands-on, collaborative, and exploratory environment.
Academics Aerospace science, anthropology, archaeology, astronomy, biology, chemistry, communications, computer programming, computers, ecology, engineering, environmental science, geology/earth science, health sciences, mathematics, meteorology, physics, physiology, science (general).
Program Information 7–12 sessions per year. Session length: 5–15 days in February, March, April, June, July, August, October, November. Ages: 11–17. 3–14 participants per session. Day program cost: $175–$300. Financial aid available.
Application Deadline Continuous.
Jobs Positions for high school students 14 and older and college students 18 and older.

Project SUCCEED (continued)

Contact Mr. Matthew Lathrop, Project SUCCEED Director, main address above. Phone: 919-286-1911. Fax: 919-286-7876. E-mail: mlathrop@shodor.org.
URL www.shodor.org/succeed

Rockbrook Camp

4000 Greenville Highway
Brevard, North Carolina 28712

General Information Girls' residential traditional camp established in 1921. Accredited by American Camping Association.

Rockbrook Camp

Program Focus Horseback riding, pottery, drama, gymnastics, tennis, and outdoor activities in a noncompetitive environment.
Arts Arts and crafts (general), batiking, ceramics, dance, drawing, fabric arts, jewelry making, leather working, music, music (vocal), musical productions, pottery, sculpture, theater/drama, weaving.
Special Interest Areas Campcraft, nature study.
Sports Aerobics, archery, basketball, bicycling, boating, canoeing, climbing (wall), equestrian sports, golf, gymnastics, horseback riding, kayaking, rappelling, riflery, ropes course, soccer, softball, swimming, tennis.
Wilderness/Outdoors Backpacking, bicycle trips, canoe trips, hiking, mountain biking, orienteering, rafting, rock climbing, white-water trips, wilderness camping.
Trips Day, overnight.
Program Information 8 sessions per year. Session length: 7–27 days in June, July, August. Ages: 6–16. 190 participants per session. Boarding program cost: $1825–$3025.
Application Deadline Continuous.
Jobs Positions for college students 19 and older.
Contact Brenda Ivers, Office Manager, PO Box 792, Brevard, North Carolina 28712. Phone: 828-884-6151. Fax: 828-884-6459. E-mail: office@rockbrookcamp.com.
URL www.rockbrookcamp.com

For more information, see page 1286.

Skyland Camp for Girls

317 Spencer Street
Clyde, North Carolina 28721

General Information Girls' residential traditional camp established in 1917.
Program Focus Horseback riding, overnight horse trips, tennis, and Appalachian trips.
Arts Arts and crafts (general), chorus, dance, dance (folk), dance (jazz), drawing, jewelry making, leather working, music, music (vocal), musical productions, painting, pottery, theater/drama.
Special Interest Areas Campcraft, nature study.
Sports Archery, canoeing, cheerleading, equestrian sports, horseback riding, ropes course, softball, swimming, tennis, volleyball, water tubing.
Wilderness/Outdoors Backpacking, hiking, rafting, white-water trips.
Trips Cultural, day, overnight.
Program Information 3–6 sessions per year. Session length: 2–7 weeks in June, July, August. Ages: 6–15. 85 participants per session. Boarding program cost: $1500–$4500.
Application Deadline Continuous.
Jobs Positions for high school students 17 and older and college students 18 and older.
Contact Ms. Sherry Brown, Director, PO Box 128, Clyde, North Carolina 28721. Phone: 828-627-2470. Fax: 828-627-2071. E-mail: info@skylandcamp.com.
URL www.skylandcamp.com

SoccerPlus Goalkeeper School–Challenge Program–Fayetteville, NC

SoccerPlus Camps
Methodist College
Fayetteville, North Carolina

General Information Coed residential and day sports camp.
Program Focus Developing technical and tactical goalkeeping skills.
Sports Soccer.
Program Information 1 session per year. Session length: 6 days in June. Ages: 10+. Day program cost: $595. Boarding program cost: $695. Financial aid available.
Application Deadline Continuous.
Jobs Positions for college students.
Contact Mr. Shawn Kelly, General Manager, 11 Executive Drive, Suite 202, Farmington, Connecticut 06032. Phone: 800-533-7371. Fax: 860-677-0460. E-mail: info@soccerpluscamps.com.
URL www.soccerpluscamps.com

SoccerPlus Goalkeeper School–National Training Center–Fayetteville, NC

SoccerPlus Camps
Methodist College
Fayetteville, North Carolina

General Information Coed residential sports camp.

Program Focus Developing advanced goalkeeping skills.
Sports Soccer.
Program Information 1 session per year. Session length: 6 days in June. Ages: 15+. Boarding program cost: $775. Financial aid available.
Application Deadline Continuous.
Jobs Positions for college students.
Contact Mr. Shawn Kelly, General Manager, 11 Executive Drive, Suite 202, Farmington, Connecticut 06032. Phone: 800-533-7371. Fax: 860-677-0460. E-mail: info@soccerpluscamps.com.
URL www.soccerpluscamps.com

Student Conservation Association–Conservation Crew Program (North Carolina)

Student Conservation Association (SCA)
North Carolina

General Information Coed residential outdoor program, community service program, and wilderness program established in 1957. High school credit may be earned.
Program Focus Resource management, conservation and environmental education.
Academics Biology, botany, ecology, environmental science, geology/earth science, history.
Special Interest Areas Campcraft, community service, construction, leadership training, nature study, trail maintenance, work camp programs.
Sports Canoeing, fishing, kayaking, swimming.
Wilderness/Outdoors Backpacking, canoe trips, hiking, orienteering, outdoor living skills, wilderness camping.
Trips Cultural, day, overnight.
Program Information 2–3 sessions per year. Session length: 3–5 weeks in June, July, August. Ages: 15–19. 6–8 participants per session. Application fee: $20. Financial aid available. No cost for program; financial aid possible for travel expenses.
Application Deadline Continuous.
Jobs Positions for college students 21 and older.
Contact Recruitment Office, PO Box 550, Charlestown, New Hampshire 03603. Phone: 603-543-1700. Fax: 603-543-1828. E-mail: getreal@thesca.org.
URL www.theSCA.org

Success Oriented Achievement Realized (SOAR)–North Carolina

Success Oriented Achievement Realized (SOAR)
226 SOAR Lane
Balsam, North Carolina 28707

General Information Coed residential outdoor program, wilderness program, special needs program, and adventure program established in 1975. Accredited by Association for Experiential Education. Formal opportunities for the academically talented. Specific services available for the learning disabled, participant with ADD, and participant with AD/HD.
Program Focus Youth diagnosed with learning disabilities and Attention Deficit Disorder in an adventure-based setting.
Academics English language/literature, academics (general), mathematics, study skills.
Special Interest Areas Career exploration.
Sports Canoeing, climbing (wall), fishing, horseback riding, kayaking, rappelling, ropes course, scuba diving, sea kayaking, snorkeling.
Wilderness/Outdoors Backpacking, caving, hiking, mountain biking, mountaineering, orienteering, pack animal trips, rafting, rock climbing, white-water trips, wilderness camping.
Trips Overnight.
Program Information 15 sessions per year. Session length: 12–26 days in January, February, March, April, May, June, July, August, September, October, November, December. Ages: 8–18. 7–21 participants per session. Boarding program cost: $1750–$3600. Financial aid available.
Application Deadline Continuous.
Jobs Positions for college students 20 and older.
Contact Ed Parker, Admissions Director, PO Box 388, Balsam, North Carolina 28707. Phone: 828-456-3435. Fax: 828-456-3449. E-mail: ed@soarnc.org.
URL www.soarnc.org

SuperCamp–Wake Forest University

SuperCamp
Wake Forest University
Winston-Salem, North Carolina 27106

General Information Coed residential academic program established in 1981. Accredited by American Camping Association.
Program Focus Academic enrichment and personal development.
Academics SAT/ACT preparation, academics (general), communications, reading, study skills, writing.
Special Interest Areas Leadership training.
Sports Basketball, ropes course, soccer, swimming, volleyball.
Trips College tours.
Program Information 2–3 sessions per year. Session length: 10 days in June, July. Ages: 11–18. 80–125 participants per session. Boarding program cost: $2095. Application fee: $100. Financial aid available.
Application Deadline Continuous.
Jobs Positions for college students 18 and older.
Contact Enrollments Department, 1725 South Coast Highway, Oceanside, California 92054. Phone: 800-285-3276. Fax: 760-722-3507. E-mail: info@supercamp.com.
URL www.supercamp.com
For more information, see page 1348.

Talisman–Academics

Talisman Summer Programs
64 Gap Creek Road
Zirconia, North Carolina 28790

General Information Coed residential academic program, outdoor program, and special needs program. Accredited by American Camping Association. Specific

Talisman–Academics (continued)
services available for the learning disabled, participant with AD/HD, autistic, and participant with Aspergers Syndrome.
Program Focus Teaching methods of learning and proper study skills, and to boost self esteem.
Academics Academics (general).
Program Information 2 sessions per year. Session length: 13–19 days in June, July, August. Ages: 11–17. Boarding program cost: $2000–$3000. Financial aid available.
Application Deadline Continuous.
Jobs Positions for college students 18 and older.
Contact Linda Tatsapaugh, Director, main address above. Phone: 828-692-3568. Fax: 828-669-2521. E-mail: summer@stonemountainschool.com.
URL www.talismansummercamp.com/academics.html

TALISMAN–INSIGHT

Talisman Summer Programs
64 Gap Creek Road
Zirconia, North Carolina 28790

General Information Coed residential outdoor program and special needs program. Accredited by American Camping Association. Specific services available for the autistic and participant with Aspergers Syndrome.
Program Focus Outdoor activities designed to boost confidence and build communication skills for participants with Asperger's syndrome and high-functioning autism.
Special Interest Areas Leadership training.
Sports Canoeing.
Wilderness/Outdoors Backpacking, climbing, hiking.
Program Information 1 session per year. Session length: 1 week in July. Ages: 14–17. 14 participants per session. Boarding program cost: $1200. Financial aid available.
Application Deadline Continuous.
Jobs Positions for college students 18 and older.
Contact Linda Tatsapaugh, Director, main address above. Phone: 828-692-3568. Fax: 828-669-2521. E-mail: summer@stonemountainschool.com.
URL www.talismansummercamp.com/sight.html

TALISMAN MINI-CAMP

Talisman Summer Programs
64 Gap Creek Road
Zirconia, North Carolina 28790

General Information Coed residential outdoor program and special needs program. Accredited by American Camping Association. Specific services available for the participant with AD/HD.
Program Focus Wilderness experiences, working together to improve individual and group communication skills.
Arts Arts and crafts (general).
Sports Sports (general), swimming.
Wilderness/Outdoors Backpacking, white-water trips.
Program Information 1 session per year. Session length: 2 weeks in June. Ages: 8–11. Boarding program cost: $1800. Financial aid available.
Application Deadline Continuous.
Jobs Positions for college students 18 and older.
Contact Linda Tatsapaugh, Director, main address above. Phone: 828-692-3568. Fax: 828-669-2521. E-mail: summer@stonemountainschool.com.
URL www.talismansummercamp.com

TALISMAN OPEN BOAT ADVENTURES (TOBA)

Talisman Summer Programs
64 Gap Creek Road
Zirconia, North Carolina 28790

General Information Coed residential outdoor program, wilderness program, and special needs program established in 1999. Accredited by American Camping Association. Specific services available for the emotionally challenged, learning disabled, and participant with AD/HD.
Program Focus Whitewater and flatwater tandem canoeing.
Special Interest Areas Campcraft, leadership training.
Sports Canoeing, climbing (wall), ropes course, swimming.
Wilderness/Outdoors Canoe trips, rafting, rock climbing, white-water trips, wilderness camping.
Trips Day, overnight.
Program Information 2 sessions per year. Session length: 20 days in June, July. Ages: 14–17. 6 participants per session. Boarding program cost: $2800.
Application Deadline Continuous.
Jobs Positions for college students 21 and older.
Contact Linda Tatsapaugh, Director, 126 Camp Elliott Road, Black Mountain, North Carolina 28711. Phone: 828-692-3568. Fax: 828-669-2521. E-mail: summer@stonemountainschool.com.
URL www.talismansummercamp.com

TALISMAN–SIGHT

Talisman Summer Programs
64 Gap Creek Road
Zirconia, North Carolina 28790

General Information Coed residential outdoor program and special needs program established in 2001. Accredited by American Camping Association. Specific services available for the autistic and participant with Aspergers Syndrome.
Program Focus Developing social skills for Autistic and Aspergers campers.
Arts Arts and crafts (general).
Special Interest Areas Native American culture, campcraft, nature study.
Sports Canoeing, fishing, horseback riding, ropes course.
Wilderness/Outdoors Backpacking, hiking, rock climbing.
Trips Cultural, day, overnight.

Program Information 3 sessions per year. Session length: 2–3 weeks in June, July. Ages: 9–14. 16 participants per session. Boarding program cost: $1800–$3700.
Application Deadline Continuous.
Jobs Positions for college students 18 and older.
Contact Linda Tatsapaugh, Director, 126 Camp Elliott Road, Black Mountain, North Carolina 28711. Phone: 828-692-3568. Fax: 828-669-2521. E-mail: summer@stonemountainschool.com.
URL www.talismansummercamp.com

Talisman Summer Camp

Talisman Summer Programs
64 Gap Creek Road
Zirconia, North Carolina 28790

General Information Coed residential traditional camp, academic program, outdoor program, and special needs program established in 1980. Accredited by American Camping Association. Specific services available for the emotionally challenged, learning disabled, and participant with AD/HD.
Program Focus Self-esteem and decision-making skills.
Academics Academics (general).
Arts Arts and crafts (general), music, theater/drama.
Special Interest Areas Native American culture, campcraft, leadership training, nature study.
Sports Canoeing, climbing (wall), fishing, rappelling, ropes course, swimming.
Wilderness/Outdoors Backpacking, canoe trips, hiking, orienteering, rafting, rock climbing, wilderness camping.
Trips Day, overnight.
Program Information 3 sessions per year. Session length: 2–3 weeks in June, July. Ages: 8–13. 48 participants per session. Boarding program cost: $1800–$3000.
Application Deadline Continuous.
Jobs Positions for college students 18 and older.
Contact Ms. Linda Tatsapaugh, Director, 126 Camp Elliott Road, Black Mountain, North Carolina 28711. Phone: 828-692-3568. Fax: 828-669-2521. E-mail: summer@stonemountainschool.com.
URL www.talismansummercamp.com

Talisman–Trek Hiking Program

Talisman Summer Programs
64 Gap Creek Road
Zirconia, North Carolina 28790

General Information Coed residential outdoor program, wilderness program, special needs program, and adventure program established in 1997. Accredited by American Camping Association. Specific services available for the emotionally challenged, learning disabled, and participant with AD/HD.
Program Focus Backpacking and leadership skill-building.
Special Interest Areas Native American culture, campcraft, nature study.
Sports Ropes course, swimming.
Wilderness/Outdoors Backpacking, hiking, mountaineering, rafting, rock climbing, wilderness camping.
Trips Day, overnight.
Program Information 3 sessions per year. Session length: 14–20 days in June, July. Ages: 12–17. 8 participants per session. Boarding program cost: $1800–$2700.
Application Deadline Continuous.
Jobs Positions for college students 18 and older.
Contact Linda Tatsapaugh, Director, 126 Camp Elliott Road, Black Mountain, North Carolina 28711. Phone: 828-692-3568. Fax: 828-669-2521. E-mail: summer@stonemountainschool.com.
URL www.talismansummercamp.com

Talisman–Tri-Adventures

Talisman Summer Programs
64 Gap Creek Road
Zirconia, North Carolina 28790

General Information Coed residential outdoor program and special needs program. Accredited by American Camping Association.
Program Focus Multi-skills course of outdoor sports and social interaction lessons.
Special Interest Areas Social skills development.
Wilderness/Outdoors Backpacking, canoe trips, climbing.
Program Information 2 sessions per year. Session length: 3 weeks in June, July, August. Ages: 14–17. Boarding program cost: $2700. Financial aid available.
Application Deadline Continuous.
Jobs Positions for college students 18 and older.
Contact Linda Tatsapaugh, Director, main address above. Phone: 828-692-3568. Fax: 828-669-2521. E-mail: summer@stonemountainschool.com.
URL www.talismansummercamp.com/triadventures.html

YMCA Camp Kanata

YMCA of the Triangle
13524 Camp Kanata Road
Wake Forest, North Carolina 27587

General Information Coed residential traditional camp established in 1954. Accredited by American Camping Association.
Program Focus Building friendships.
Arts Arts and crafts (general), dance, theater/drama.
Special Interest Areas Campcraft, leadership training.
Sports Aerobics, archery, basketball, canoeing, cheerleading, climbing (wall), cross-country, equestrian sports, fishing, football, horseback riding, riflery, ropes course, sailing, snorkeling, soccer, swimming, tennis.
Wilderness/Outdoors Hiking, orienteering.
Trips Day.
Program Information 10 sessions per year. Session length: 6 days in June, July, August. Ages: 6–15. 190–200 participants per session. Boarding program cost: $508. Financial aid available.
Application Deadline Continuous.
Jobs Positions for college students 18 and older.

YMCA Camp Kanata (continued)

Contact Mr. Richard R. Hamilton, Director of Camping Services, main address above. Phone: 919-556-2661. Fax: 919-556-9459. E-mail: campkanata@ymcatriangle.org.
URL ymcatriangle.org/Camp_Kanata.aspx

Young Investigators Program in Nuclear Science & Technology

North Carolina State University
Raleigh, North Carolina 27695-7909

General Information Coed residential academic program established in 1980. Formal opportunities for the academically talented.
Program Focus Focus on nuclear science fundamentals and it's applications.
Academics Chemistry, computers, engineering, environmental science, government and politics, mathematics, physics, science (general), technology.
Special Interest Areas Electronics.
Trips College tours, cultural, day, shopping.
Program Information 1 session per year. Session length: 19–21 days in July. Ages: 16+. 25–30 participants per session. Boarding program cost: $900. Financial aid available.
Application Deadline April 15.
Contact Lisa Marshall, Director of Outreach Programs, Department of Nuclear Engineering, Box 7909, Raleigh, North Carolina 27695-7909. Phone: 919-515-5876. Fax: 919-515-5115. E-mail: lisa.marshall@ncsu.edu.
URL www.ne.ncsu.edu

NORTH DAKOTA

International Music Camp

International Peace Garden
Dunseith, North Dakota 58329

General Information Coed residential arts program established in 1956. Accredited by American Camping Association. Formal opportunities for the academically talented and artistically talented.
Program Focus Fine arts.
Academics Music.
Arts Acting, arts, arts and crafts (general), band, chorus, creative writing, dance, dance (ballet), dance (jazz), dance (modern), drawing, music, music (chamber), music (ensemble), music (instrumental), music (jazz), music (orchestral), music (vocal), painting, theater/drama.
Sports Cheerleading.
Program Information 7 sessions per year. Session length: 1 week in June, July. Ages: 10+. 10–440 participants per session. Boarding program cost: $230–$250. Application fee: $75.
Application Deadline May 15.
Jobs Positions for college students 18 and older.
Summer Contact Joseph T. Alme, Director, RR #1, Box 116 A, Dunseith, North Dakota 58329. Phone: 701-263-4211. Fax: 701-263-4212.
Winter Contact Joseph T. Alme, Director, 1930 23rd Avenue, SE, Minot, North Dakota 58701-6081. Phone: 701-838-8472. Fax: 701-838-8472. E-mail: info@internationalmusiccamp.com.
URL www.internationalmusiccamp.com

Student Conservation Association–Conservation Crew Program (North Dakota)

Student Conservation Association (SCA)
North Dakota

General Information Coed residential outdoor program, community service program, and wilderness program established in 1957. High school credit may be earned.
Program Focus Resource management, conservation and environmental education.
Academics Biology, botany, ecology, environmental science, geology/earth science, history.
Special Interest Areas Campcraft, community service, construction, leadership training, nature study, trail maintenance, work camp programs.
Sports Canoeing, fishing, kayaking, swimming.
Wilderness/Outdoors Backpacking, canoe trips, hiking, orienteering, outdoor living skills, wilderness camping.
Trips Cultural, day, overnight.
Program Information 2–3 sessions per year. Session length: 3–5 weeks in June, July, August. Ages: 15–19. 6–8 participants per session. Application fee: $20. Financial aid available. No cost for program; financial aid possible for travel expenses.
Application Deadline Continuous.
Jobs Positions for college students 21 and older.
Contact Recruitment Office, PO Box 550, Charlestown, New Hampshire 03603. Phone: 603-543-1700. Fax: 603-543-1828. E-mail: getreal@thesca.org.
URL www.theSCA.org

Ventures Travel Service–North Dakota

Friendship Ventures
North Dakota

General Information Coed travel special needs program established in 1985. Specific services available for the developmentally challenged and physically challenged.
Program Focus Provides travel services to older teens and adults with developmental disabilities.
Special Interest Areas Touring.
Program Information 50 sessions per year. Session length: 4–10 days in February, March, April, May, June, July, August, September, October, November, December. Ages: 14–70. 4–8 participants per session. Cost: $395–$2000.
Application Deadline Continuous.
Jobs Positions for college students 18 and older.

Contact Georgann Rumsey, President/CEO, 10509 108th Street, NW, Annandale, Minnesota 55302. Phone: 952-852-0101. Fax: 952-852-0123. E-mail: fv@friendshipventures.org.
URL www.friendshipventures.org

OHIO

Camp Butterworth

Girl Scouts–Great Rivers Council, Inc.
8551 Butterworth Road
Maineville, Ohio 45039

General Information Girls' residential traditional camp established in 1935. Accredited by American Camping Association.
Arts Arts and crafts (general), batiking, ceramics, creative writing, dance, dance (modern), fabric arts, jewelry making, photography, theater/drama, woodworking.
Special Interest Areas Campcraft, culinary arts, leadership training, nature study.
Sports Archery, bicycling, canoeing, climbing (wall), horseback riding, in-line skating, ropes course, swimming.
Wilderness/Outdoors Backpacking, bicycle trips, canoe trips, caving, hiking, mountain biking, rafting, rock climbing, white-water trips, wilderness camping.
Trips Day, overnight.
Program Information 7 sessions per year. Session length: 2–6 days in June, July, August. Ages: 8–18. 60–100 participants per session. Boarding program cost: $198–$440. Financial aid available.
Application Deadline Continuous.
Jobs Positions for high school students 18 and older and college students 18 and older.
Contact Kellee Echeverria, Program Services Manager, 4930 Cornell Road, Cincinnati, Ohio 45242. Phone: 513-489-1025. Fax: 513-489-1417. E-mail: kecheverria@grgsc.org.
URL www.grgsc.org

Camp Echoing Hills

36272 County Road 79
Warsaw, Ohio 43844

General Information Coed residential bible camp and special needs program established in 1966. Religious affiliation: Christian non-denominational. Accredited by American Camping Association. Specific services available for the emotionally challenged, developmentally challenged, hearing impaired, learning disabled, physically challenged, and visually impaired.
Academics Bible study.
Arts Arts and crafts (general), leather working, music.
Special Interest Areas Animal care, leadership training, nature study, touring.
Sports Archery, fishing, go-carts, horseback riding, swimming.
Wilderness/Outdoors Hiking.
Trips Cultural, day, overnight.
Program Information 9 sessions per year. Session length: 6 days in April, June, July, August, October. Ages: 7+. 50–85 participants per session. Boarding program cost: $450–$500. Application fee: $30. Financial aid available.
Application Deadline Continuous.
Jobs Positions for high school students 16 and older and college students 18 and older.
Contact Shaker Samuel, Camp Administrator, main address above. Phone: 740-327-2311. Fax: 740-327-6371.
URL www.campechoinghills.org

Camp Joy

Joy Outdoor Education Center
10117 Old 3-C Highway
Clarksville, Ohio 45113

General Information Coed residential and day traditional camp established in 1938. Accredited by American Camping Association. Specific services available for the emotionally challenged and developmentally challenged.
Academics Environmental science.
Arts Arts and crafts (general), dance, dance (modern), drawing, music, theater/drama.
Special Interest Areas Campcraft, gardening, nature study, team building.
Sports Archery, baseball, basketball, bicycling, canoeing, climbing (wall), ropes course, soccer, sports (general), swimming.
Wilderness/Outdoors Camp fires, canoe trips, hiking, mountain biking.
Trips Day.
Program Information 5 sessions per year. Session length: 5 days in June, July, August. Ages: 7–15. 100–120 participants per session. Day program cost: $25–$105. Boarding program cost: $25–$250. Application fee: $25. Financial aid available.
Application Deadline Continuous.
Jobs Positions for high school students 16 and older and college students 18 and older.
Contact Dan McKay, Associate Program Director, PO Box 157, Clarksville, Ohio 45113. Phone: 800-300-7094. Fax: 937-289-3179. E-mail: summercampregistrar@joec.org.
URL www.joec.org

Camp Ledgewood

Girl Scouts of the Western Reserve, Inc.
Peninsula, Ohio 44264

General Information Girls' residential and day traditional camp and outdoor program established in 1931. Accredited by American Camping Association.
Academics Astronomy, botany, ecology, environmental science, geology/earth science, intercultural studies.
Arts Arts and crafts (general), dance, drawing, jewelry making, leather working, music (vocal), painting, puppetry.
Special Interest Areas Campcraft, leadership training, nature study, team building.

Camp Ledgewood (continued)

Sports Archery, canoeing, horseback riding, soccer, softball, swimming, volleyball.
Wilderness/Outdoors Backpacking, canoe trips, hiking, wilderness camping.
Trips Day, overnight.
Program Information 7 sessions per year. Session length: 3–12 days in June, July, August. Ages: 6–17. 50–120 participants per session. Day program cost: $125–$225. Boarding program cost: $150–$325. Application fee: $25. Financial aid available.
Application Deadline Continuous.
Jobs Positions for high school students 16 and older and college students 18 and older.
Summer Contact Ms. Susana Barba, Resident Camp Specialist, main address above. Phone: 330-650-4743. Fax: 330-655-9593. E-mail: sbarba@girlscoutswr.org.
Winter Contact Ms. Susana Barba, Resident Camp Specialist, 345 White Pond Drive, Akron, Ohio 44320-1155. Phone: 330-864-9933. Fax: 330-864-5720. E-mail: sbarba@girlscoutswr.org.
URL www.girlscoutswr.org

Camp O'Bannon

Camp O'Bannon
9688 Butler Road, NE
Newark, Ohio 43055

General Information Coed residential traditional camp, outdoor program, and special needs program established in 1922. Accredited by American Camping Association. Specific services available for the emotionally challenged, developmentally challenged, and learning disabled.
Program Focus Learning self-esteem through noncompetitive activities.
Arts Arts and crafts (general).
Special Interest Areas Campcraft, community service, gardening, leadership training, team building.
Sports Archery, basketball, canoeing, climbing (wall), fishing, rappelling, ropes course, softball, swimming.
Wilderness/Outdoors Hiking, rock climbing.
Trips Day.
Program Information 6 sessions per year. Session length: 6–12 days in June, July, August. Ages: 9–16. 65–70 participants per session. No cost for program; participants must reside in Licking County and be referred by a social services agency or school.
Application Deadline Continuous.
Jobs Positions for college students 18 and older.
Contact Ted Cobb, Camp Director, main address above. Phone: 740-345-8295. Fax: 740-349-5093. E-mail: campobannon@alltel.net.
URL www.campobannon.org

Camp Stonybrook

Girl Scouts–Great Rivers Council, Inc.
4491 East State Route 73
Waynesville, Ohio 45068

General Information Girls' residential traditional camp established in 1966. Accredited by American Camping Association.
Arts Arts and crafts (general), jewelry making, painting, photography, weaving.
Special Interest Areas Campcraft, leadership training, nature study.
Sports Archery, basketball, bicycling, canoeing, ropes course, soccer, swimming, volleyball.
Wilderness/Outdoors Hiking.
Program Information 8 sessions per year. Session length: 2–6 days in June, July, August. Ages: 8–18. 120 participants per session. Boarding program cost: $62–$125. Financial aid available.
Application Deadline Continuous.
Jobs Positions for high school students 15 and older and college students 18 and older.
Contact Kellee Echeverria, Program Services Manager, 4930 Cornell Road, Cincinnati, Ohio 45242. Phone: 513-489-1025. Fax: 513-489-1417. E-mail: kecheverria@grgsc.org.
URL www.grgsc.org

Cleveland Institute of Art Portfolio Preparation/Young Artist Programs

The Cleveland Institute of Art
11141 East Boulevard
Cleveland, Ohio 44106

General Information Coed day arts program established in 1950. Formal opportunities for the artistically talented. High school credit may be earned.
Program Focus Learning how to prepare a portfolio for entrance into an art school or college.
Academics Architecture, precollege program.
Arts Arts, ceramics, jewelry making, painting, photography, pottery, theater/drama, visual arts.
Trips Cultural.
Program Information 3 sessions per year. Session length: 12–35 days in January, February, March, April, May, June, September, October, November, December. Ages: 6–18. 10–25 participants per session. Day program cost: $220–$1000. Cost includes materials.
Application Deadline Continuous.
Jobs Positions for college students.
Contact William Martin Jean, Director of Continuing Education, main address above. Phone: 216-421-7460. Fax: 216-421-7438. E-mail: wjean@gate.cia.edu.
URL www.cia.edu

Cleveland Institute of Art Pre-College Program

The Cleveland Institute of Art
11141 East Boulevard
Cleveland, Ohio 44106

General Information Coed residential arts program established in 1999. Formal opportunities for the artistically talented.
Program Focus Arts enrichment, portfolio development.
Academics Precollege program.
Arts Arts and crafts (general), drawing, visual arts.
Trips Cultural, day.

Program Information 1 session per year. Session length: 1 week in June. Ages: 15–18. 20–30 participants per session. Boarding program cost: $771.
Application Deadline May 1.
Contact Admissions Office, main address above. Phone: 216-421-7418. Fax: 216-421-7438. E-mail: summer@gate.cia.edu.
URL www.cia.edu

Cleveland Institute of Art Pre-College Program–Architecture

The Cleveland Institute of Art
11141 East Boulevard
Cleveland, Ohio 44106

General Information Coed residential arts program established in 1999. Formal opportunities for the artistically talented.
Program Focus Architectural design.
Academics Architecture, precollege program.
Arts Design, drawing, modeling.
Special Interest Areas Field trips (arts and culture).
Trips Cultural, day.
Program Information 1 session per year. Session length: 9 days in June, July. Ages: 15–18. 12 participants per session. Boarding program cost: $620. Financial aid available.
Application Deadline May 1.
Contact Admissions Office, main address above. Phone: 216-421-7418. Fax: 216-421-7438. E-mail: summer@gate.cia.edu.
URL www.cia.edu

Cleveland Institute of Art Pre-College Program–Product and Auto Design

The Cleveland Institute of Art
11141 East Boulevard
Cleveland, Ohio 44106

General Information Coed residential arts program established in 1999. Formal opportunities for the artistically talented.
Program Focus Product and auto design.
Academics Precollege program.
Arts Design, drawing.
Trips Cultural, day.
Program Information 1 session per year. Session length: 10 days in June. Ages: 15–18. 15 participants per session. Boarding program cost: $670. Financial aid available.
Application Deadline May 1.
Contact Admissions Office, main address above. Phone: 216-421-7418. Fax: 216-421-7438. E-mail: summer@gate.cia.edu.
URL www.cia.edu

Cleveland Institute of Art Pre-College Program–Special Effects and Animation

The Cleveland Institute of Art
11141 East Boulevard
Cleveland, Ohio 44106

General Information Coed residential arts program established in 1999. Formal opportunities for the artistically talented.
Program Focus Special effects and animation.
Academics Computers, precollege program.
Arts Animation, drawing, graphic arts, television/video.
Trips Cultural, day.
Program Information 1 session per year. Session length: 10 days in June. Ages: 15–18. 20 participants per session. Boarding program cost: $860. Financial aid available.
Application Deadline May 1.
Contact Admissions Office, main address above. Phone: 216-421-7418. Fax: 216-421-7438. E-mail: summer@gate.cia.edu.
URL www.cia.edu

The Country School Farm

The Country School Farm
3516 Township Road 124
Becks Mills, Ohio 44654

General Information Coed residential outdoor program established in 1976.
Program Focus Life on a turn-of-the-century Amish farmstead; activities include animal care and farm life skills, nondenominational, Montessori.
Special Interest Areas Animal care, farming, gardening.
Trips Cultural.
Program Information 10 sessions per year. Session length: 5 days in June, July, August. Ages: 6–12. 25 participants per session. Boarding program cost: $700.
Application Deadline Continuous.
Contact Mr. Richard Barker, Director / Owner, main address above. Phone: 330-231-2963. E-mail: barkers@thecountryschool.com.
URL www.thecountryschool.com

Explorer Day Camp

Girl Scouts–Great Rivers Council, Inc.
8551 Butterworth Road
Maineville, Ohio 45039

General Information Girls' day traditional camp established in 1998.
Arts Arts and crafts (general).
Special Interest Areas Campcraft, career exploration, leadership training, nature study.
Sports Horseback riding, soccer, swimming.
Wilderness/Outdoors Hiking.
Program Information 6–9 sessions per year. Session length: 5 days in June, July, August. Ages: 6–9. 24–48 participants per session. Day program cost: $110. Financial aid available.

Explorer Day Camp (continued)
Application Deadline Continuous.
Jobs Positions for college students 18 and older.
Contact Kellee Echeverria, Program Services Manager, 4930 Cornell Road, Cincinnati, Ohio 45242. Phone: 513-489-1025. Fax: 513-489-1417. E-mail: kecheverria@grgsc.org.
URL www.grgsc.org

FALCON CAMP

Falcon Camp
4251 Delta Road, SW
Carrollton, Ohio 44615-9251

General Information Coed residential traditional camp established in 1959. Accredited by American Camping Association.
Academics English as a second language, ecology.
Arts Acting, arts and crafts (general), dance, drawing, fabric arts, jewelry making, leather working, musical productions, theater/drama, woodworking.
Special Interest Areas Animal care, campcraft, construction, leadership training, model rocketry, nature study.
Sports Aerobics, archery, basketball, boating, canoeing, diving, equestrian sports, fishing, horseback riding, in-line skating, lacrosse, riflery, ropes course, sailing, soccer, softball, sports (general), swimming, tennis, volleyball, weight training.
Wilderness/Outdoors Backpacking, canoe trips, hiking, orienteering, rock climbing, survival training, wilderness camping.
Trips Overnight.
Program Information 1–4 sessions per year. Session length: 2–8 weeks in June, July, August. Ages: 6–16. 110 participants per session. Boarding program cost: $1450–$4800.
Application Deadline Continuous.
Jobs Positions for college students 19 and older.
Summer Contact Mr. David Devey, Director, main address above. Phone: 330-627-4269. Fax: 330-627-2220. E-mail: falconcampoffice@aol.com.
Winter Contact Mr. David Devey, Director, 22232 Rye Road, Shaker Heights, Ohio 44122. Phone: 800-837-CAMP. Fax: 216-991-4908. E-mail: falconcampoffice@aol.com.
URL www.falconcamp.com

FALCON HORSE LOVER CAMP

Falcon Camp
4251 Delta Road, SW
Carrollton, Ohio 44615

General Information Coed residential sports camp established in 1959. Accredited by American Camping Association.
Program Focus Horseback riding and equestrian sports.
Special Interest Areas Animal care.
Sports Canoeing, equestrian sports, fishing, horseback riding, sailing, swimming.
Program Information 1 session per year. Session length: 1 week in August. Ages: 10–15. 20 participants per session. Boarding program cost: $700.
Application Deadline Continuous.
Jobs Positions for college students 19 and older.
Summer Contact Emily Devey, Director, main address above. Phone: 800-837-CAMP. Fax: 330-627-2220. E-mail: falconhorsecamp@aol.com.
Winter Contact Emily Devey, Director, 22232 Rye Road, Shaker Heights, Ohio 44122. Phone: 800-837-CAMP. Fax: 216-991-4908. E-mail: falconhorsecamp@aol.com.
URL www.falconcamp.com

FALCON HORSE LOVER CAMP FOR GIRLS

Falcon Camp
4251 Delta Road, SW
Carrollton, Ohio 44615

General Information Girls' residential sports camp established in 1959. Accredited by American Camping Association.
Program Focus Horseback riding and equestrian sports.
Special Interest Areas Animal care.
Sports Canoeing, equestrian sports, fishing, horseback riding, sailing, swimming.
Program Information 8 sessions per year. Session length: 1 week in June, July, August. Ages: 10–15. 10 participants per session. Boarding program cost: $700.
Application Deadline Continuous.
Jobs Positions for college students 19 and older.
Summer Contact Ms. Emily Devey, Director, main address above. Phone: 800-837-CAMP. Fax: 330-627-2220. E-mail: falconhorsecamp@aol.com.
Winter Contact Ms. Emily Devey, Director, 22232 Rye Road, Shaker Heights, Ohio 44122. Phone: 800-837-CAMP. Fax: 216-991-4908. E-mail: falconhorsecamp@aol.com.
URL www.falconcamp.com

FALCON YOUNG ADVENTURE CAMP

Falcon Camp
4251 Delta Road SW
Carrollton, Ohio 44615

General Information Boys' residential traditional camp established in 1959. Accredited by American Camping Association.
Program Focus Introduction to camping.
Academics Ecology.
Arts Arts and crafts (general), theater/drama, woodworking.
Special Interest Areas Animal care, campcraft, model rocketry.
Sports Archery, basketball, boating, canoeing, equestrian sports, fishing, horseback riding, riflery, sailing, soccer, softball, swimming, tennis, volleyball.
Wilderness/Outdoors Hiking.
Program Information 4 sessions per year. Session length: 1 week in June, August. Ages: 6–7. 6 participants per session. Boarding program cost: $650.
Application Deadline Continuous.

Summer Contact Mr. Dave Devey, Director, main address above. Phone: 800-837-CAMP. Fax: 330-627-2220. E-mail: falconcampoffice@aol.com.
Winter Contact Mr. Dave Devey, Director, 22232 Rye Road, Shaker Heights, Ohio 44122. Phone: 216-991-2489. Fax: 216-991-4908. E-mail: falconcampoffice@aol.com.
URL www.falconcamp.com

Friends Music Camp

Friends Music Institute, Inc.
61830 Sandy Ridge Road
Barnesville, Ohio 43713

General Information Coed residential arts program established in 1980. Religious affiliation: Society of Friends.
Program Focus Music, Quaker values, and community.
Academics Music, peace education.
Arts Band, chorus, dance (folk), music, music (chamber), music (classical), music (ensemble), music (instrumental), music (jazz), music (orchestral), music (vocal), musical productions, theater/drama.
Sports Canoeing, soccer, swimming, tennis, volleyball.
Wilderness/Outdoors Canoe trips.
Trips Day.
Program Information 1 session per year. Session length: 2–4 weeks in July, August. Ages: 10–18. 75–80 participants per session. Boarding program cost: $950–$1500. Application fee: $100. Financial aid available.
Application Deadline Continuous.
Jobs Positions for college students 19 and older.
Summer Contact Peg Champney, Director, main address above. Phone: 740-425-3655. E-mail: musicfmc@yahoo.com.
Winter Contact Peg Champney, Director, PO Box 427, Yellow Springs, Ohio 45387. Phone: 937-767-1311. Fax: 937-767-2254. E-mail: musicfmc@yahoo.com.
URL www.quaker.org/friends-music-camp/

The Grand River Summer Academy

The Grand River Academy
3042 College Street
Austinburg, Ohio 44010

General Information Coed residential and day academic program established in 1990. High school credit may be earned.
Program Focus Remedial and advanced academics with full afternoon activity program.
Academics English as a second language, English language/literature, French language/literature, SAT/ACT preparation, Spanish language/literature, academics (general), art history/appreciation, biology, chemistry, computers, economics, environmental science, geography, geology/earth science, government and politics, health sciences, history, journalism, mathematics, physics, reading, science (general), social science, social studies, study skills, typing, writing.
Arts Arts and crafts (general), ceramics, creative writing, drawing, film, painting, photography, pottery, printmaking, sculpture.

The Grand River Summer Academy

Special Interest Areas Community service, driver's education, field trips (arts and culture).
Sports Baseball, basketball, bicycling, canoeing, cross-country, equestrian sports, fishing, football, golf, horseback riding, in-line skating, kayaking, paintball, soccer, softball, sports (general), swimming, tennis, volleyball, weight training.
Wilderness/Outdoors Bicycle trips, canoe trips, hiking, wilderness camping.
Program Information 1 session per year. Session length: 6 weeks in June, July, August. Ages: 13–19. 80–100 participants per session. Day program cost: $1200. Boarding program cost: $3300–$3500. Application fee: $25. Open to participants entering grades 9–12.
Application Deadline Continuous.
Jobs Positions for college students 18 and older.
Contact Sam Corabi, Director of Admission, main address above. Phone: 440-275-2811 Ext.25. Fax: 440-275-1825. E-mail: academy@grandriver.org.
URL www.grandriver.org

For more information, see page 1142.

Harmon's Pine View Camp

Candlewood Lake
Galion, Ohio 44833

General Information Coed residential traditional camp established in 1975.
Special Interest Areas Karaoke.
Sports Archery, baseball, basketball, billiards, boating, canoeing, diving, fishing, horseback riding, kayaking, sailing, soccer, swimming, table tennis/ping-pong, trampolining, volleyball, waterskiing.
Wilderness/Outdoors White-water trips.
Program Information 1–4 sessions per year. Session length: 1–4 weeks in July. Ages: 6–12. 36 participants per session. Boarding program cost: $470–$1880.
Application Deadline Continuous.
Contact Ms. Lee Harmon, Director, PO Box 644, Candlewood Lake, Galion, Ohio 44833. Phone: 419-947-3197.
URL www.harmonspineview.com

Hidden Hollow Camp

Friendly House
5127 Opossum Run Road
Bellville, Ohio 44813-9134

General Information Coed residential traditional camp established in 1940. Accredited by American Camping Association.
Arts Arts and crafts (general), theater/drama, woodworking.
Sports Archery, baseball, basketball, canoeing, fishing, horseback riding, swimming, tennis.
Program Information 5 sessions per year. Session length: 6 days in July, August. Ages: 8–15. 188 participants per session. Boarding program cost: $215.
Application Deadline Continuous.
Jobs Positions for high school students 16 and older and college students 18 and older.
Contact Thelda J. Dillon, Director, 380 North Mulberry Street, Mansfield, Ohio 44902. Phone: 419-522-0521. Fax: 419-522-2166.

Joe Machnik's No. 1 Academy One and Premier Programs–Columbus, Ohio

Joe Machnik's No. 1 Camps
Capital University
Columbus, Ohio

General Information Coed residential and day sports camp.
Program Focus Soccer instruction, physical fitness, testing and speed training. Campers gain exposure to top players and are challenged by intense competition.
Sports Soccer.
Trips Day.
Program Information 1 session per year. Session length: 6 days in June. Ages: 9–18. Day program cost: $699. Boarding program cost: $759. Financial aid available.
Application Deadline Continuous.
Jobs Positions for college students.
Contact Dr. Joseph Machnik, Director, PO Box 389, 916 Palm Boulevard, Isle of Palms, South Carolina 29451. Phone: 800-622-4645. Fax: 843-886-0885. E-mail: info@no1soccercamps.com.
URL www.no1soccercamps.com

Joe Machnik's No. 1 Mighty Mini, Goalkeeper and Striker Camp–Columbus, Ohio

Joe Machnik's No. 1 Camps
Capital University
Columbus, Ohio

General Information Coed residential and day sports camp.
Program Focus Soccer instruction. Goalkeepers and strikers compete against each other daily.
Sports Soccer.
Trips Day.
Program Information 1 session per year. Session length: 6 days in June. Ages: 8–12. 100–150 participants per session. Boarding program cost: $429. Financial aid available.
Application Deadline Continuous.
Jobs Positions for college students.
Contact Dr. Joseph Machnik, Director, PO Box 389, 916 Palm Boulevard, Isle of Palms, South Carolina 29451. Phone: 800-622-4645. Fax: 843-886-0885. E-mail: info@no1soccercamps.com.
URL www.no1soccercamps.com

Junior Statesmen Symposium on Ohio State Politics and Government

Junior Statesmen Foundation
Ohio State University
Columbus, Ohio

General Information Coed residential academic program established in 1998. Formal opportunities for the academically talented.
Program Focus State government, politics, debate, and leadership training.
Academics Communications, government and politics, journalism, precollege program, social science, social studies, speech/debate.
Special Interest Areas Career exploration, leadership training.
Trips College tours, day.
Program Information 1 session per year. Session length: 4 days in August. Ages: 14–18. 50–70 participants per session. Boarding program cost: $285. Financial aid available.
Application Deadline Continuous.
Contact Matt Randazzo, National Summer School Director, 400 South El Camino Real, Suite 300, San Mateo, California 94402. Phone: 650-347-1600. Fax: 650-347-7200. E-mail: jsa@jsa.org.
URL www.jsa.org
For more information, see page 1174.

Kenyon Review Young Writers

Kenyon College/The Kenyon Review
Gambier, Ohio 43022-9623

General Information Coed residential academic program and arts program established in 1989. Formal opportunities for the academically talented and artistically talented.
Program Focus Creative writing.
Academics English language/literature, reading, writing.
Arts Creative writing.
Trips College tours.
Program Information 1 session per year. Session length: 2 weeks in June, July. Ages: 16–18. 50–60 participants per session. Boarding program cost: $1800–$1900. Financial aid available.
Application Deadline March 1.
Contact David Lynn, Walton House, Gambier, Ohio 43022. Phone: 740-427-5208. Fax: 740-427-5417. E-mail: kenyonreview@kenyon.edu.
URL www.kenyonreview.org/writing/young/

Landmark Volunteers: Ohio

Landmark Volunteers, Inc.
Joy Outdoor Education Center
Clarksville, Ohio

General Information Coed residential outdoor program and community service program established in 1992. High school credit may be earned.
Program Focus Opportunity for high school students to earn community service credit while working as a team for two weeks serving Joy Outdoor Education Center. Similar programs offered through Landmark Volunteers at over 60 locations in 21 states.
Academics Social science, social services.
Special Interest Areas Career exploration, community service, leadership training, team building, work camp programs.
Sports Swimming.
Trips Cultural, day.
Program Information 1 session per year. Session length: 2 weeks in July. Ages: 14–18. 10–13 participants per session. Boarding program cost: $875–$925. Financial aid available.
Application Deadline Continuous.
Jobs Positions for college students.
Contact Ann Barrett, Executive Director, PO Box 455, Sheffield, Massachusetts 01257. Phone: 413-229-0255. Fax: 413-229-2050. E-mail: landmark@volunteers.com.
URL www.volunteers.com

For more information, see page 1182.

Miami University Junior Scholars Program

Miami University
301 South Patterson Avenue
Room 202
Oxford, Ohio 45056-3414

General Information Coed residential academic program established in 1982. Formal opportunities for the academically talented. College credit may be earned.
Program Focus College credit for academically talented rising high school seniors.
Academics American literature, English language/literature, French language/literature, German language/literature, Russian language/literature, Spanish language/literature, academics (general), anthropology, architecture, art (Advanced Placement), astronomy, biology, botany, business, classical languages/literatures, communications, computer programming, computers, ecology, economics, geography, geology/earth science, government and politics, history, humanities, mathematics, music, philosophy, physics, physiology, precollege program, psychology, religion, science (general), social science, speech/debate, writing.
Arts Drawing, painting.
Sports Aerobics, basketball, climbing (wall), diving, figure skating, soccer, softball, sports (general), squash, street/roller hockey, swimming, tennis, volleyball.
Trips Cultural, day, shopping.
Program Information 1 session per year. Session length: 6 weeks in June, July, August. Ages: 16–18. 60–85 participants per session. Boarding program cost: $1800–$2900. Financial aid available. Each qualified applicant receives a scholarship.
Application Deadline May 15.
Contact Dr. Robert S. Smith, Director, main address above. Phone: 513-529-5825. Fax: 513-529-1498. E-mail: juniorscholars@muohio.edu.
URL www.muohio.edu/JuniorScholars/

Miami University Summer Sports School

Miami University
220 Millet Hall
Oxford, Ohio 45056

General Information Coed residential sports camp established in 1973.
Sports Basketball, figure skating, ice hockey, soccer, sports (general), volleyball.
Program Information 20–25 sessions per year. Session length: 2–5 days in June, July. Ages: 8–18. 48–200 participants per session. Boarding program cost: $150–$540. Application fee: $50–$75.
Application Deadline Continuous.
Contact Sharon Tabler, main address above. Phone: 513-529-2472. Fax: 513-529-6404.
URL www.muohio.edu/

National Computer Camps at Notre Dame College

National Computer Camps
Notre Dame College
South Euclid, Ohio

General Information Coed residential and day academic program. Formal opportunities for the academically talented.
Program Focus Computer science, computer programming, Internet, recreation, and sports.
Academics Web page design, computer programming, computer science (Advanced Placement), computers.
Arts Animation, graphic arts.
Special Interest Areas Internet accessibility, electronics, robotics.
Sports Basketball, soccer, swimming, tennis, volleyball.
Program Information 3 sessions per year. Session length: 1–3 weeks in July. Ages: 8–18. 80–125 participants per session. Day program cost: $695–$2085. Boarding program cost: $895–$2475.
Application Deadline Continuous.
Jobs Positions for high school students 16 and older and college students 18 and older.
Contact Dr. Michael Zabinski, President, PO Box 585, Orange, Connecticut 06477. Phone: 203-795-9667. E-mail: info@nccamp.com.
URL www.nccamp.com

Padua Franciscan High School Sports Camps

Padua Franciscan High School
6740 State Road
Parma, Ohio 44134

General Information Coed day sports camp.
Program Focus Build skills in soccer, basketball, baseball, volleyball, and football.
Sports Baseball, basketball, football, soccer, volleyball, wrestling.
Program Information Session length: 5–10 days in June, July, August. Ages: 11–17. 40–100 participants per session. Day program cost: $80. Financial aid available.
Contact Mr. Ken Dworznik, Athletic Director, main address above. Phone: 440-845-0442. Fax: 440-845-5710. E-mail: kdworznic@paduafranciscan.com.
URL www.paduafranciscan.com

Padua Summer Experience

Padua Franciscan High School
6740 State Road
Parma, Ohio

General Information Coed day traditional camp established in 2004.
Academics Computers, history, science (general).
Arts Acting, arts and crafts (general), dance (folk), music (vocal), painting, photography, theater/drama.
Special Interest Areas Culinary arts, robotics.
Sports Football, volleyball.
Wilderness/Outdoors Orienteering.
Program Information 1 session per year. Session length: 5 days in June. Ages: 11–12. 5–30 participants per session. Day program cost: $100.
Application Deadline June 7.
Contact Mrs. Lillian Gathers, Director of Admissions and Marketing, main address above. Phone: 440-845-2444 Ext.111. Fax: 440-845-5710. E-mail: lgathers@paduafranciscan.com.
URL www.paduafranciscan.com

Purcell Marian High School Cavalier Basketball Camp

Purcell Marian High School
2935 Hackberry Street
Cincinnati, Ohio 45206

General Information Boys' day sports camp. Religious affiliation: Roman Catholic.
Sports Basketball.
Program Information 1 session per year. Session length: 4 days in June. Day program cost: $50–$60. Open to participants entering grades 4–9.
Application Deadline May 28.
Contact Mr. Randy Reeder, Head Varsity Basketball Coach, main address above. Phone: 513-751-1230 Ext. 306. Fax: 513-751-1395. E-mail: randyreeder@purcellmarian.org.
URL www.purcellmarian.org

Purcell Marian High School Summer School

Purcell Marian High School
2935 Hackberry Street
Cincinnati, Ohio 45206

General Information Coed day academic program established in 1972. Religious affiliation: Roman Catholic. Specific services available for the developmentally challenged, learning disabled, and physically challenged. High school credit may be earned.
Academics English language/literature, Spanish language/literature, academics (general), biology (Advanced Placement), chemistry, geography, government and politics, health sciences, history, mathematics, physical education, religion, science (general).
Program Information 2 sessions per year. Session length: 25 days in June, July. 400 participants per session. Day program cost: $200. Open to participants entering grades 9–12.
Application Deadline June 14.
Contact Mr. Thomas Strotman, Summer School Principal, main address above. Phone: 513-751-1230. Fax: 513-751-1395. E-mail: tomstrotman@purcellmarian.org.
URL www.purcellmarian.org

SoccerPlus Goalkeeper School–Challenge Program–Delaware, OH

SoccerPlus Camps
Ohio Wesleyan University
Delaware, Ohio

General Information Coed residential and day sports camp.
Program Focus Developing technical and tactical goalkeeping skills.
Sports Soccer.
Program Information 2 sessions per year. Session length: 6 days in June. Ages: 10+. Day program cost: $595. Boarding program cost: $695. Financial aid available.
Application Deadline Continuous.
Jobs Positions for college students.
Contact Mr. Shawn Kelly, General Manager, 11 Executive Drive, Suite 202, Farmington, Connecticut 06032. Phone: 800-533-7371. Fax: 860-677-0460. E-mail: info@soccerpluscamps.com.
URL www.soccerpluscamps.com

SoccerPlus Goalkeeper School–National Training Center–Delaware, OH

SoccerPlus Camps
Ohio Wesleyan University
Delaware, Ohio

General Information Coed residential sports camp.
Program Focus Developing advanced goal keeping skills.
Sports Soccer.

Program Information 2 sessions per year. Session length: 6 days in June. Ages: 15+. Boarding program cost: $775.
Application Deadline Continuous.
Jobs Positions for college students.
Contact Mr. Shawn Kelly, General Manager, 11 Executive Drive, Suite 202, Farmington, Connecticut 06032. Phone: 800-533-7371. Fax: 860-677-0460. E-mail: info@soccerpluscamps.com.
URL www.soccerpluscamps.com

STUDENT CONSERVATION ASSOCIATION–CONSERVATION CREW PROGRAM (OHIO)

Student Conservation Association (SCA)
Ohio

General Information Coed residential outdoor program, community service program, and wilderness program established in 1957. High school credit may be earned.
Program Focus Resource management, conservation and environmental education.
Academics Biology, botany, ecology, environmental science, geology/earth science, history.
Special Interest Areas Campcraft, community service, construction, leadership training, nature study, trail maintenance, work camp programs.
Sports Canoeing, fishing, kayaking, swimming.
Wilderness/Outdoors Backpacking, canoe trips, hiking, orienteering, outdoor living skills, wilderness camping.
Trips Cultural, day, overnight.
Program Information 2–3 sessions per year. Session length: 3–5 weeks in June, July, August. Ages: 15–19. 6–8 participants per session. Application fee: $20. Financial aid available. No cost for program; financial aid possible for travel expenses.
Application Deadline Continuous.
Jobs Positions for college students 21 and older.
Contact Recruitment Office, PO Box 550, Charlestown, New Hampshire 03603. Phone: 603-543-1700. Fax: 603-543-1828. E-mail: getreal@thesca.org.
URL www.theSCA.org

SUMMER BIOTECHNOLOGY INSTITUTE FOR HIGH SCHOOL AND MIDDLE SCHOOL TEACHERS AND STUDENTS

Case Western Reserve University and Howard Hughes Medical Institute
2080 Adelbert Road
Cleveland, Ohio 44106

General Information Coed day academic program established in 1992. Formal opportunities for the academically talented.
Program Focus Molecular biology techniques; biotechnology.
Academics Biology, science (general).
Trips Day.
Program Information 1 session per year. Session length: 10 days in June. 12 participants per session. Open to Cleveland area participants entering grades 9–10. No cost for program.
Application Deadline Continuous.
Contact Dr. Jens Cavallius, CWRU—Biology Department, DeGrace 206, 10900 Euclid Avenue, Cleveland, Ohio 44106-7080. Phone: 216-368-3557. Fax: 216-368-4672. E-mail: jens.cavallius@case.edu.
URL www.case.edu/artsci/biol/hhmi/biotechhome.htm

THE SUMMER INSTITUTE FOR THE GIFTED AT OBERLIN COLLEGE

Summer Institute for the Gifted
Oberlin College
Oberlin, Ohio 44074

General Information Coed residential academic program. Formal opportunities for the academically talented and gifted.
Academics Academics (general), precollege program.
Program Information 1–2 sessions per year. Session length: 3 weeks in June, July, August. Ages: 8–17. 200–300 participants per session. Boarding program cost: $3350. Application fee: $75. Financial aid available.
Application Deadline May 15.
Jobs Positions for college students 19 and older.
Contact Dr. Stephen Gessner, Director, River Plaza, 9 West Broad Street, Stamford, Connecticut 06902-3788. Phone: 866-303-4744. Fax: 203-399-5598. E-mail: sig.info@aifs.com.
URL www.giftedstudy.com

For more information, see page 1342.

WOMEN IN ENGINEERING SUMMER CAMP

University of Dayton
300 College Park, Kettering Labs
Dayton, Ohio 45469-0228

General Information Girls' residential academic program established in 1974.
Program Focus Engineering.
Academics Engineering.
Program Information 1 session per year. Session length: 6 days in July. Ages: 15–18. 100 participants per session. Boarding program cost: $325. Financial aid available.
Application Deadline June 15.
Contact Ms. Annette Packard, Program Coordinator, main address above. Phone: 937-229-3296. Fax: 937-229-2756. E-mail: wie@udayton.edu.
URL engineering.udayton.edu/wie

Wright State University Residential Camps and Institutes

Wright State University Pre-College Programs
120 Millett Hall
3640 Colonel Glenn Highway
Dayton, Ohio 45435-0001

General Information Coed residential academic program and arts program established in 1990. Accredited by American Camping Association. Formal opportunities for the academically talented and artistically talented.
Academics Academics (general), aviation, biology, chemistry, computers, ecology, mathematics, precollege program, science (general), writing.
Arts Acting, arts and crafts (general), creative writing, television/video, theater/drama.
Special Interest Areas Leadership training.
Trips Cultural, day.
Program Information 6–7 sessions per year. Session length: 6–13 days in June, July, August. Ages: 10–17. 16–32 participants per session. Boarding program cost: $550–$750. Application fee: $75.
Application Deadline Continuous.
Jobs Positions for college students 19 and older.
Contact Chris S. Hoffman, Assistant Director, Pre-College Programs, 120 Millet Hall, Wright State University, Dayton, Ohio 45435-0001. Phone: 937-775-3135. Fax: 937-775-4883. E-mail: precollege@wright.edu.
URL www.wright.edu/academics/precollege/

YMCA Camp Tippecanoe–Adventure Camp

YMCA of Central Stark County
81300 YMCA Road
Tippecanoe, Ohio 44699

General Information Coed residential and day traditional camp. Accredited by American Camping Association. Specific services available for the emotionally challenged, hearing impaired, and learning disabled.
Program Focus Traditional overnight camp.
Academics Astronomy, intercultural studies, journalism, writing.
Arts Arts and crafts (general), creative writing, dance, theater/drama.
Special Interest Areas Campcraft, nature study.
Sports Boating, canoeing, horseback riding, softball, swimming, volleyball.
Wilderness/Outdoors Canoe trips, hiking, outdoor camping.
Program Information 6 sessions per year. Session length: 5 days in June, July, August. Ages: 7–12. Boarding program cost: $315–$330. Application fee: $50. Financial aid available.
Application Deadline Continuous.
Contact Patrick Dunlop, Program Director, main address above. Phone: 800-922-0679. Fax: 740-922-1152. E-mail: ycamptippe@aol.com.
URL www.ymcastark.org

YMCA Camp Tippecanoe–Bike Camp

YMCA of Central Stark County
81300 YMCA Road
Tippecanoe, Ohio 44699

General Information Coed residential and day traditional camp. Accredited by American Camping Association. Specific services available for the emotionally challenged, hearing impaired, and learning disabled.
Sports Bicycling, canoeing.
Wilderness/Outdoors Bicycle trips, mountain biking, outdoor camping.
Program Information 1 session per year. Session length: 5 days in June. Ages: 13–17. Boarding program cost: $380–$395. Application fee: $50. Financial aid available.
Application Deadline Continuous.
Contact Patrick Dunlop, Program Director, main address above. Phone: 800-922-0679. Fax: 740-922-1152. E-mail: ycamptippe@aol.com.
URL www.ymcastark.org

YMCA Camp Tippecanoe–Equine Camp

YMCA of Central Stark County
81300 YMCA Road
Tippecanoe, Ohio 44699

General Information Coed residential and day traditional camp. Accredited by American Camping Association. Specific services available for the emotionally challenged, hearing impaired, and learning disabled.
Program Focus Riding instruction, horseback events, trail rides.
Arts Arts and crafts (general).
Special Interest Areas Animal care, nature study.
Sports Boating, canoeing, equestrian sports, horseback riding, swimming.
Wilderness/Outdoors Hiking, outdoor camping.
Program Information 1 session per year. Session length: 5 days in July. Ages: 14–17. Boarding program cost: $480–$495. Application fee: $50. Financial aid available.
Application Deadline Continuous.
Contact Patrick Dunlop, Program Director, main address above. Phone: 800-922-0679. Fax: 740-922-1152. E-mail: ycamptippe@aol.com.
URL www.ymcastark.org

YMCA Camp Tippecanoe–Girl's & Guy's Corral

YMCA of Central Stark County
81300 YMCA Road
Tippecanoe, Ohio 44699

General Information Coed residential and day traditional camp. Accredited by American Camping Association. Specific services available for the emotionally challenged, hearing impaired, and learning disabled.

Program Focus Riding instruction, horse care.
Arts Arts and crafts (general).
Special Interest Areas Animal care, campcraft, nature study.
Sports Boating, canoeing, equestrian sports, horseback riding.
Wilderness/Outdoors Hiking, outdoor camping.
Program Information 4–9 sessions per year. Session length: 5 days in June, July, August. Ages: 10–13. Boarding program cost: $425–$440. Application fee: $50. Financial aid available.
Application Deadline Continuous.
Contact Patrick Dunlop, Program Director, main address above. Phone: 800-922-0679. Fax: 740-922-1152. E-mail: ycamptippe@aol.com.
URL www.ymcastark.org

YMCA Camp Tippecanoe–Horse Pals

YMCA of Central Stark County
81300 YMCA Road
Tippecanoe, Ohio 44699

General Information Coed residential and day traditional camp. Accredited by American Camping Association. Specific services available for the emotionally challenged, hearing impaired, and learning disabled.
Program Focus Riding instruction and basic horse care.
Special Interest Areas Animal care, campcraft.
Sports Canoeing, equestrian sports, horseback riding.
Wilderness/Outdoors Hiking, outdoor camping.
Program Information 7 sessions per year. Session length: 5 days in June, July, August. Ages: 7–11. Boarding program cost: $380–$395. Application fee: $50. Financial aid available.
Application Deadline Continuous.
Contact Patrick Dunlop, Program Director, main address above. Phone: 800-922-0679. Fax: 740-922-1152. E-mail: ycamptippe@aol.com.
URL www.ymcastark.org

YMCA Camp Tippecanoe–Jr. Counselor

YMCA of Central Stark County
81300 YMCA Road
Tippecanoe, Ohio 44699

General Information Coed residential and day traditional camp. Accredited by American Camping Association. Specific services available for the emotionally challenged, hearing impaired, and learning disabled.
Program Focus Junior Counselor and Summer Camp staff member program.
Arts Arts and crafts (general).
Special Interest Areas Campcraft, counselor-in-training program, leadership training, nature study, team building.
Sports Boating, canoeing.
Wilderness/Outdoors Hiking.
Program Information 7 sessions per year. Session length: 5 days in June, July, August. Ages: 15–17. Boarding program cost: $130. Application fee: $50. Financial aid available.
Application Deadline Continuous.
Contact Patrick Dunlop, Program Director, main address above. Phone: 800-922-0679. Fax: 740-922-1152. E-mail: ycamptippe@aol.com.
URL www.ymcastark.org

YMCA Camp Tippecanoe–Teen Camp

YMCA of Central Stark County
81300 YMCA Road
Tippecanoe, Ohio 44699

General Information Coed residential and day traditional camp. Accredited by American Camping Association. Specific services available for the emotionally challenged, hearing impaired, and learning disabled.
Arts Arts and crafts (general), dance.
Special Interest Areas Campcraft, leadership training, nature study.
Sports Boating, canoeing, horseback riding, sailing, swimming.
Wilderness/Outdoors Canoe trips, hiking, outdoor camping.
Program Information 2 sessions per year. Session length: 5 days in July. Ages: 13–17. Boarding program cost: $325–$355. Application fee: $50. Financial aid available.
Application Deadline Continuous.
Contact Patrick Dunlop, Program Director, main address above. Phone: 800-922-0679. Fax: 740-922-1152. E-mail: ycamptippe@aol.com.
URL www.ymcastark.org

OKLAHOMA

Student Conservation Association–Conservation Crew Program (Oklahoma)

Student Conservation Association (SCA)
Oklahoma

General Information Coed residential outdoor program, community service program, and wilderness program established in 1957. High school credit may be earned.
Program Focus Resource management, conservation and environmental education.
Academics Biology, botany, ecology, environmental science, geology/earth science, history.
Special Interest Areas Campcraft, community service, construction, leadership training, nature study, trail maintenance, work camp programs.
Sports Canoeing, fishing, kayaking, swimming.

Student Conservation Association–Conservation Crew Program (Oklahoma) (continued)

Wilderness/Outdoors Backpacking, canoe trips, hiking, orienteering, outdoor living skills, wilderness camping.
Trips Cultural, day, overnight.
Program Information 2–3 sessions per year. Session length: 3–5 weeks in June, July, August. Ages: 15–19. 6–8 participants per session. Application fee: $20. Financial aid available. No cost for program; financial aid possible for travel expenses.
Application Deadline Continuous.
Jobs Positions for college students 21 and older.
Contact Recruitment Office, PO Box 550, Charlestown, New Hampshire 03603. Phone: 603-543-1700. Fax: 603-543-1828. E-mail: getreal@thesca.org.
URL www.theSCA.org

OREGON

ACADEMY

Southern Oregon University Youth Programs
1250 Siskiyou Boulevard
Ashland, Oregon 97520

General Information Coed residential academic program established in 1980. Formal opportunities for the academically talented and artistically talented.
Program Focus Academic program for talented and gifted students.
Academics English language/literature, academics (general), biology, communications, computers, engineering, history, humanities, mathematics, music, precollege program, science (general), social studies, writing.
Arts Acting, animation, ceramics, creative writing, dance, drawing, mime, music, painting, radio broadcasting, sculpture, television/video, theater/drama.
Sports Basketball, climbing (wall), swimming.
Trips College tours, cultural, day.
Program Information 3 sessions per year. Session length: 1 week in June, July. 100–200 participants per session. Boarding program cost: $565–$595. Application fee: $50. Financial aid available. Open to participants entering grades 6–9.
Application Deadline Continuous.
Jobs Positions for college students 18 and older.
Contact Carol Jensen, Director, Youth Programs, main address above. Phone: 541-552-6326. Fax: 541-552-6047. E-mail: jensen@sou.edu.
URL www.sou.edu/ecp/youth

ADVENTURES IN LEARNING

Oregon State University
100 Education Hall
Corvallis, Oregon 97331-3502

General Information Coed day academic program established in 1984. Formal opportunities for the academically talented.
Program Focus Education for gifted, talented, and creative learners.
Academics Academics (general), archaeology, astronomy, biology, chemistry, computer programming, computers, mathematics, oceanography, physics, precollege program, science (general), writing.
Arts Creative writing, drawing, painting, photography, radio broadcasting, television/video, theater/drama.
Special Interest Areas Animal care, model rocketry.
Program Information 1 session per year. Session length: 10 days in June, July. Ages: 11–14. 200 participants per session. Day program cost: $385. Financial aid available.
Application Deadline Continuous.
Jobs Positions for college students.
Contact Ms. Judy Michael, Program Director, main address above. Phone: 541-737-1289. Fax: 541-737-2040. E-mail: TAG@oregonstate.edu.
URL oregonstate.edu/precollege/ail

ADVENTURE TREKS–PAC 16

Adventure Treks, Inc.
Oregon

General Information Coed travel outdoor program, wilderness program, and adventure program established in 1978.
Program Focus Multi-activity outdoor adventures with a focus on fun, personal growth, teamwork, leadership, building self-confidence, outdoor skills, and community living.
Sports Sea kayaking.
Wilderness/Outdoors Backpacking, hiking, mountaineering, orienteering, rafting, rock climbing, white-water trips, wilderness camping.
Program Information 1–2 sessions per year. Session length: 16 days in June, July, August. Ages: 13–14. 24 participants per session. Cost: $2095. Financial aid available.
Application Deadline Continuous.
Contact John Dockendorf, Director, PO Box 1321, Flat Rock, North Carolina 28731. Phone: 888-954-5555. Fax: 828-696-1663. E-mail: info@advtreks.com.
URL www.adventuretreks.com

CAMP NAMANU

Camp Fire USA Portland Metro Council
10300 Camp Namanu Road
Sandy, Oregon 97055

General Information Coed residential traditional camp established in 1923. Accredited by American Camping Association. Specific services available for the participant with asthma.
Academics Ecology, environmental science.
Arts Arts and crafts (general), fabric arts, theater/drama, weaving.
Special Interest Areas Campcraft, general camp activities, leadership training, nature study, team building.
Sports Archery, baseball, basketball, boating, canoeing, climbing (wall), equestrian sports, fishing, horseback riding, kayaking, ropes course, swimming.

Wilderness/Outdoors Backpacking, hiking, orienteering, rafting, white-water trips.
Trips Overnight.
Program Information 7 sessions per year. Session length: 6 days in July, August. Ages: 6–17. 170–220 participants per session. Boarding program cost: $300–$425. Financial aid available.
Application Deadline Continuous.
Jobs Positions for college students 18 and older.
Contact Brian Hayes, Camp Director, 619 Southwest 11th Avenue, Suite 200, Portland, Oregon 97205. Phone: 503-224-7800. Fax: 503-223-3916. E-mail: info@portlandcampfire.org.
URL www.portlandcampfire.org

Cascade Science School

Oregon Museum of Science and Industry
16125 Skyliner's Road
Bend, Oregon 97701

General Information Coed residential outdoor program established in 1993. Formal opportunities for the academically talented. High school credit may be earned.
Program Focus Ecology, geology, wilderness skills, backpacking, marine science, astronomy, paleontology.
Academics Japanese language/literature, anthropology, archaeology, astronomy, biology, botany, ecology, environmental science, geology/earth science, marine studies, oceanography, science (general).
Special Interest Areas Native American culture, campcraft, field research/expeditions, nature study.
Sports Canoeing, climbing (wall).
Wilderness/Outdoors Backpacking, canoe trips, caving, hiking, orienteering, rafting, survival training, wilderness camping, wilderness/outdoors (general).
Trips Cultural, overnight.
Program Information 30 sessions per year. Session length: 6–30 days in March, June, July, August. Ages: 8–18. 10–30 participants per session. Boarding program cost: $410–$615. Financial aid available.
Application Deadline Continuous.
Jobs Positions for high school students 16 and older and college students 16 and older.
Contact Travis Neumeyer, Programming Coordinator, 1945 Southeast Water Avenue, Portland, Oregon 97214. Phone: 503-239-7824. Fax: 503-239-7838. E-mail: tneumeyer@omsi.edu.
URL www.omsi.edu

Cybercamps–Lewis and Clark College

Cybercamps–Giant Campus, Inc.
Lewis and Clark College
Portland, Oregon

General Information Coed residential and day academic program established in 1997.
Program Focus High tech computer camps featuring project oriented curriculum in Web design, 3D animation, game design, robotics, digital arts and programming for all ability levels.
Academics Web page design, computer programming, computers, typing.
Arts Animation, creative writing, digital media, graphic arts, photography.
Special Interest Areas Computer game design, computer graphics, robotics, team building.
Sports Ultimate frisbee.
Program Information 2–9 sessions per year. Session length: 5–30 days in June, July, August. Ages: 7–18. 30–150 participants per session. Day program cost: $599–$849. Boarding program cost: $974–$1224.
Application Deadline Continuous.
Jobs Positions for high school students 15 and older and college students.
Contact Cybercamps Information Office, 2401 4th Avenue, Suite 1110, Seattle, Washington 98121. Phone: 206-442-4500. Fax: 206-442-4501. E-mail: info@cybercamps.com.
URL www.cybercamps.com

Delphi's Summer Session

The Delphian School
20950 Southwest Rock Creek Road
Sheridan, Oregon 97378

General Information Coed residential and day traditional camp and academic program established in 1973. Formal opportunities for the academically talented and gifted. High school credit may be earned.

Delphi's Summer Session

Program Focus Leadership, personal development, and study skills.
Academics American literature, English (Advanced Placement), English as a second language, English language/literature, academics (general), art history/appreciation, astronomy, biology, biology (Advanced Placement), botany, business, chemistry, chemistry (Advanced Placement), communications, computer programming, computer science (Advanced Placement), computers, ecology, economics, environmental science, geography, geology/earth science, government and politics, health sciences, history, history (Advanced

Delphi's Summer Session (continued)

Placement), humanities, journalism, linguistics, mathematics, mathematics (Advanced Placement), meteorology, music, music (Advanced Placement), philosophy, physics, physics (Advanced Placement), physiology, reading, religion, science (general), social science, social studies, study skills, typing, writing.
Arts Arts and crafts (general), ceramics, creative writing, dance (modern), drawing, music, music (classical), music (instrumental), music (jazz), music (orchestral), music (vocal), painting, photography, pottery, theater/drama.
Special Interest Areas Community service, leadership training, model rocketry.
Sports Aerobics, archery, baseball, basketball, equestrian sports, golf, horseback riding, racquetball, soccer, softball, swimming, tennis, volleyball, weight training.
Wilderness/Outdoors Canoe trips, hiking, rafting, white-water trips, wilderness camping.
Trips Cultural, day, overnight, shopping.
Program Information 1–2 sessions per year. Session length: 4–6 weeks in June, July, August. Ages: 5–18. 300 participants per session. Day program cost: $2294–$2842. Boarding program cost: $4522–$5806. Application fee: $50. Financial aid available.
Application Deadline Continuous.
Contact Donetta Phelps, Director of Admissions, Department 18, 20950 Southwest Rock Creek Road, Sheridan, Oregon 97378. Phone: 800-626-6610. Fax: 503-843-4158. E-mail: info@delphian.org.
URL www.summeratdelphi.org

Special Note
The Delphian School Summer Program in Oregon emphasizes academic and personal enrichment by offering a wide variety of more than 250 challenging classes and summer activities that help prepare students for life. Students come from all over the world to study at the Delphian School and to learn the effective study method developed by American philosopher and educator L. Ron Hubbard. This study method represents a great breakthrough in education. The skills that students acquire are essential tools for life and learning. The 4- to 6-week summer program balances academics with application in real-life situations. Many recreational activities are offered, as are weekend trips into the magnificent Northwest environment.

For more information, see page 1336.

Expeditions

Oregon State University
100 Education Hall
Corvallis, Oregon 97331-3502

General Information Coed day academic program established in 1996. Formal opportunities for the academically talented.
Program Focus Education for gifted, talented, and creative learners.
Academics Spanish language/literature, academics (general), chemistry, computers, mathematics, music, precollege program, writing.
Arts Arts and crafts (general), ceramics, creative writing, drawing, painting, puppetry, theater/drama.
Program Information 1 session per year. Session length: 10 days in June, July. Ages: 8–11. 150 participants per session. Day program cost: $195. Financial aid available.
Application Deadline March 31.
Jobs Positions for high school students 16 and older and college students.
Contact Ms. Carol Brown, Program Coordinator, main address above. Phone: 541-737-2670. Fax: 541-737-2040. E-mail: carol.brown@oregonstate.edu.
URL oregonstate.edu/precollege/expeditions

Fir Acres Workshop in Writing and Thinking

Fir Acres Writing Workshop
Lewis and Clark College
0615 SW Palatine Hill Road
Portland, Oregon 97219-7899

General Information Coed residential academic program and arts program established in 1989.
Program Focus How narrative, poetry, reflection, argument, and experimental writing are complementary habits of a mind both engaged by and committed to inquiry.
Academics College tours, computers, writing.
Arts Creative writing.
Sports Swimming, tennis.
Wilderness/Outdoors Hiking.
Trips College tours, cultural, day, shopping.
Program Information 1 session per year. Session length: 12 days in July. Ages: 13–18. 42–50 participants per session. Boarding program cost: $1400. Financial aid available.
Application Deadline Continuous.
Jobs Positions for college students 18 and older.
Contact Molly Miles, Department Specialist, main address above. Phone: 503-768-7200. Fax: 503-768-7205. E-mail: miles@lclark.edu.
URL www.lclark.edu/org/firacres

Hancock Field Station

Oregon Museum of Science and Industry
39472 Highway 218
Fossil, Oregon 97830

General Information Coed residential academic program and outdoor program established in 1951. Formal opportunities for the academically talented. High school credit may be earned.
Program Focus Fossils, ecology, geology, and astronomy.
Academics Japanese language/literature, anthropology, archaeology, astronomy, biology, botany, ecology, environmental science, geology/earth science.
Special Interest Areas Native American culture, field research/expeditions, nature study.
Sports Canoeing, climbing (wall).

Wilderness/Outdoors Backpacking, canoe trips, hiking, orienteering, rafting, survival training, wilderness camping.
Trips Cultural, overnight.
Program Information 20 sessions per year. Session length: 6–30 days in June, July, August. Ages: 8–18. 10–50 participants per session. Boarding program cost: $410–$610. Financial aid available.
Application Deadline Continuous.
Jobs Positions for high school students 16 and older and college students 16 and older.
Contact Mr. Travis Neumeyer, Programming Coordinator, 1945 Southeast Water Avenue, Portland, Oregon 97214. Phone: 503-239-7824. Fax: 503-239-7838. E-mail: tneumeyer@omsi.edu.
URL www.omsi.edu

High Cascade Snowboard Camp

High Cascade Snowboard Camp
Mt. Hood, Oregon 97028

General Information Coed residential sports camp established in 1989. Accredited by American Camping Association.
Program Focus Snowboard skill development.
Academics Japanese language/literature.
Arts Arts and crafts (general), knitting, photography.
Sports Baseball, basketball, bicycling, bicycling (BMX), boating, field games, fishing, golf, skateboarding, snowboarding, soccer, softball, swimming, volleyball, wakeboarding, waterskiing, yoga.
Wilderness/Outdoors Hiking, mountain biking, rafting, white-water trips.
Trips Day.
Program Information 7 sessions per year. Session length: 8–10 days in June, July, August. Ages: 9+. 160–180 participants per session. Day program cost: $700. Boarding program cost: $1095.
Application Deadline Continuous.
Jobs Positions for high school students 18 and older and college students 21 and older.
Summer Contact Meagan Stein, Camp Administrator, PO Box 368, Government Camp, Oregon 97028. Phone: 800-334-4272. Fax: 503-272-3637. E-mail: highcascade@highcascade.com.
Winter Contact Meagan Stein, Camp Administrator, 50 SE Scott Street, Bend, Oregon 97702. Phone: 800-334-4272. Fax: 541-389-6371. E-mail: highcascade@highcascade.com.
URL www.highcascade.com

High Cascade Snowboard Camp Photography Workshop

High Cascade Snowboard Camp
Mt. Hood
Government Camp, Oregon 97028

General Information Coed residential outdoor program and arts program established in 2001.
Program Focus Action sports photography training.
Arts Photography.
Special Interest Areas Lecture series.
Sports Snowboarding.
Trips Day.
Program Information 1 session per year. Session length: 5 days in July. Ages: 15+. 30 participants per session. Boarding program cost: $1325. Financial aid available.
Application Deadline Continuous.
Jobs Positions for college students 21 and older.
Summer Contact Ms. Christy Chaloux, Sales and Promotions Coordinator, PO Box 368, Government Camp, Oregon 97028. Fax: 503-272-3037. E-mail: highcascade@highcascade.com.
Winter Contact Ms. Christy Chaloux, Sales and Promotions Coordinator, 50 SE Scott Street, Bend, Oregon 97702. Fax: 541-389-6371. E-mail: highcascade@highcascade.com.
URL www.hcscphotoworkshop.com

Longacre Expeditions, Peak to Peak

Longacre Expeditions
Oregon

General Information Coed travel outdoor program, wilderness program, and adventure program established in 1981. Accredited by American Camping Association.
Program Focus Effective communication skills, responsibility, confidence building.
Sports Snowboarding, swimming, windsurfing.
Wilderness/Outdoors Backpacking, mountain biking, rafting, rock climbing, wilderness camping.
Program Information 1 session per year. Session length: 24 days in July. Ages: 14–17. 10 participants per session. Cost: $3795.
Application Deadline Continuous.
Jobs Positions for college students 21 and older.
Contact Meredith Schuler, Director, 4030 Middle Ridge Road, Newport, Pennsylvania 17074. Phone: 717-567-6790. Fax: 717-567-3955. E-mail: longacre@longacreexpeditions.com.
URL www.longacreexpeditions.com
For more information, see page 1200.

Longacre Expeditions, Surf Oregon

Longacre Expeditions
Oregon

General Information Coed travel outdoor program, wilderness program, and adventure program established in 2002. Accredited by American Camping Association.
Program Focus Effective communication skills, responsibility, confidence building.
Sports Bicycling, sandboarding, skiing (glacial), snowboarding, surfing, swimming.
Wilderness/Outdoors Bicycle trips, hiking, rafting, white-water trips, wilderness camping.
Program Information 1 session per year. Session length: 18 days in July. Ages: 14–17. 10–16 participants per session. Cost: $2995.
Application Deadline Continuous.
Jobs Positions for college students 21 and older.

Longacre Expeditions, Surf Oregon (continued)

Contact Meredith Schuler, Director, 4030 Middle Ridge Road, Newport, Pennsylvania 17074. Phone: 717-567-6790. Fax: 717-567-3955. E-mail: longacre@longacreexpeditions.com.
URL www.longacreexpeditions.com

For more information, see page 1200.

Longacre Expeditions, Wind and Waves

Longacre Expeditions
Oregon

General Information Coed residential outdoor program, wilderness program, and adventure program established in 1981. Accredited by American Camping Association.
Program Focus Effective communication skills, responsibility, confidence building.
Sports Bicycling, sandboarding, sea kayaking, surfing, swimming, windsurfing.
Wilderness/Outdoors Hiking, outdoor adventure, outdoor camping.
Program Information 2 sessions per year. Session length: 2 weeks in June, July, August. Ages: 11–12. 10–16 participants per session. Boarding program cost: $2195. Financial aid available.
Application Deadline Continuous.
Jobs Positions for college students 21 and older.
Contact Meredith Schuler, Director, 4030 Middle Ridge Road, Newport, Pennsylvania 17074. Phone: 717-567-6790. Fax: 717-567-3955. E-mail: longacre@longacreexpeditions.com.
URL www.longacreexpeditions.com

For more information, see page 1200.

Meadowood Springs Speech and Hearing Camp

The Institute for Rehabilitation, Research, and Recreation, Inc.
77650 Meadowood Road
Weston, Oregon 97886

General Information Coed residential special needs program established in 1964. Specific services available for the developmentally challenged, hearing impaired, learning disabled, and speech impaired.
Program Focus Speech, language, and hearing therapy for the learning impaired.
Arts Arts and crafts (general).
Special Interest Areas Hearing therapy, nature study, speech therapy.
Sports Canoeing, field games, swimming.
Program Information 2 sessions per year. Session length: 10–14 days in July. Ages: 6–16. 50–60 participants per session. Boarding program cost: $1100. Application fee: $25. Financial aid available.
Application Deadline May 15.
Jobs Positions for high school students 18 and older and college students 18 and older.
Contact Rhonda Hack, Executive Administrator, PO Box 1025, Pendleton, Oregon 97801-0030. Phone: 541-276-2752. Fax: 541-276-7227. E-mail: meadowood@oregontrail.net.
URL www.meadowoodsprings.com

NBC Camps–Basketball Individual Training–La Grande, OR

NBC Camps
Eastern Oregon State College
La Grande, Oregon

General Information Coed residential sports camp.
Program Focus Well-rounded skill development.
Sports Basketball.
Program Information 2 sessions per year. Session length: 5 days in June, July. Ages: 9–18. Boarding program cost: $315. Financial aid available.
Application Deadline Continuous.
Jobs Positions for high school students 16 and older and college students.
Contact Ms. Bonnie Tucker, Office Manager, 10003 North Milan Road, #100, Spokane, Washington 99218. Phone: 509-466-4690. Fax: 509-467-6289. E-mail: bonnie@nbccamps.com.
URL www.nbccamps.com

NBC Camps–Basketball Individual Training–Newberg, OR

NBC Camps
George Fox University
Newberg, Oregon

General Information Coed residential sports camp.
Program Focus Well-rounded skill development.
Sports Basketball.
Program Information 1 session per year. Session length: 5 days in July. Ages: 9–18. Boarding program cost: $315. Financial aid available.
Application Deadline Continuous.
Jobs Positions for high school students 16 and older and college students.
Contact Ms. Bonnie Tucker, Office Manager, 10003 North Milan Road, #100, Spokane, Washington 99218. Phone: 509-466-4690. Fax: 509-467-6289. E-mail: bonnie@nbccamps.com.
URL www.nbccamps.com

NBC Camps–Basketball–Team–La Grande, OR

NBC Camps
Eastern Oregon State College
La Grande, Oregon

General Information Residential sports camp.
Program Focus Camp for high school basketball teams.
Sports Basketball.
Program Information 1 session per year. Session length: 5 days in July. Boarding program cost: $280. Financial aid available.

Application Deadline Continuous.
Jobs Positions for high school students and college students.
Contact Danny Beard, 10003 North Milan Road, #100, Spokane, Washington 99218. Phone: 509-466-4690. Fax: 509-467-6289. E-mail: danny@nbccamps.com.
URL www.nbccamps.com

NBC Camps–Volleyball–Oregon

NBC Camps
Eastern Oregon State University
La Grande, Oregon

General Information Girls' residential sports camp.
Sports Volleyball.
Program Information 1 session per year. Session length: 5 days in July. Ages: 12–18. Boarding program cost: $315. Financial aid available.
Application Deadline Continuous.
Jobs Positions for high school students 16 and older and college students.
Contact Ms. Bonnie Tucker, Office Manager, 10003 North Milan Road, #100, Spokane, Washington 99218. Phone: 509-466-4690. Fax: 509-467-6287. E-mail: bonnie@nbccamps.com.
URL www.nbccamps.com

OES–Challenge Workshops

Oregon Episcopal School
Oregon

General Information Coed day academic program established in 2003. Religious affiliation: Episcopal.
Program Focus Technology and academics.
Academics English language/literature, SAT/ACT preparation, Web page design, academics (general), computer programming, computers, mathematics, music, study skills, writing.
Arts Animation.
Program Information 18–22 sessions per year. Session length: 5–10 days in June, July, August. Ages: 8+. 8–16 participants per session. Day program cost: $125–$395. Application fee: $50. Financial aid available.
Application Deadline Continuous.
Contact Ms. Joan Lowe, Program Director, 6300 SW Nicol Road, Portland, Oregon 97223. Phone: 503-768-3145. Fax: 503-416-9801. E-mail: lowej@oes.edu.
URL www.oes.edu/summer

OES–Summer Adventure Camp

Oregon Episcopal School
Oregon

General Information Coed day outdoor program established in 1974. Religious affiliation: Episcopal.
Special Interest Areas Touring.
Wilderness/Outdoors Hiking, outdoor adventure.
Trips Day, shopping.
Program Information 1 session per year. Session length: 5 days in July, August. Ages: 7–11. Day program cost: $325. Financial aid available.
Application Deadline Continuous.
Jobs Positions for high school students 15 and older and college students 18 and older.
Contact Joan Lowe, Program Director, 6300 Southwest Nicol Road, Portland, Oregon 97223. Phone: 503-768-3145. Fax: 503-416-9801. E-mail: lowej@oes.edu.
URL www.oes.edu/Summer/Adventure.html

OES–Summer Discovery

Oregon Episcopal School
6300 Southwest Nicol Road
Portland, Oregon 97223

General Information Coed day traditional camp established in 1974. Religious affiliation: Episcopal.
Academics Science (general).
Arts Acting, arts and crafts (general), dance, music, painting.
Special Interest Areas Nature study.
Sports Sports (general).
Trips Day, overnight.
Program Information 4 sessions per year. Session length: 10 days in June, July, August. Ages: 6–11. 40 participants per session. Day program cost: $435–$475. Financial aid available. Extended care available for $110 per week.
Application Deadline Continuous.
Jobs Positions for high school students 15 and older and college students 18 and older.
Contact Joan Lowe, Program Director, main address above. Phone: 503-768-3145. Fax: 503-452-3517. E-mail: lowej@oes.edu.
URL www.oes.edu/Summer/Discovery.html

OES–Summer Mini Camps

Oregon Episcopal School
6300 Southwest Nicol Road
Portland, Oregon 97223

General Information Coed day traditional camp established in 1974. Religious affiliation: Episcopal.
Academics Academics (general), mathematics, music.
Arts Arts and crafts (general), ceramics, creative writing, music (electronic/synthesized), music (ensemble), music (instrumental), music (jazz), paper making, pottery, puppetry, tie-dyeing.
Special Interest Areas Chess, culinary arts.
Sports Basketball, fencing, flag football, soccer, tennis.
Program Information 25 sessions per year. Session length: 5–10 days in June, July, August. Ages: 6+. 6–15 participants per session. Day program cost: $125–$295. Financial aid available. Extended care available for $110 per week, $25 per day.
Application Deadline Continuous.
Jobs Positions for high school students 15 and older and college students 18 and older.
Contact Joan Lowe, Program Director, main address above. Phone: 503-768-3145. Fax: 503-452-3517. E-mail: lowej@oes.edu.
URL www.oes.edu/summer

OES–Summer Wonder

Oregon Episcopal School
6300 Southwest Nicol Road
Portland, Oregon 97223

General Information Coed day traditional camp established in 1974. Religious affiliation: Episcopal.
Academics Science (general).
Arts Arts and crafts (general), dance, music, painting.
Special Interest Areas Nature study.
Sports Sports (general).
Program Information 4 sessions per year. Session length: 10 days in June, July, August. Ages: 3–6. Day program cost: $220–$375. Financial aid available. Extended care available for $110 per week, $25 per day.
Application Deadline Continuous.
Jobs Positions for high school students 15 and older and college students 18 and older.
Contact Joan Lowe, Program Director, main address above. Phone: 503-768-3145. Fax: 503-416-9801. E-mail: lowej@oes.edu.
URL www.oes.edu/Summer/Wonder.html

Oregon Summer Music Camps

University of Oregon
1225 University of Oregon
School of Music
Eugene, Oregon 97403-1225

General Information Coed residential and day arts program established in 1946. Formal opportunities for the artistically talented.
Program Focus Band, drum major, and jazz improvisation, color guard/flag, marching percussion.
Academics Music.
Arts Band, music, music (chamber), music (classical), music (ensemble), music (instrumental), music (jazz).
Special Interest Areas Color guard/flag, drum majoring, leadership training.
Sports Basketball, swimming, ultimate frisbee, volleyball.
Program Information 4 sessions per year. Session length: 1 week in June, July. Ages: 14–18. 30–200 participants per session. Day program cost: $225–$385. Boarding program cost: $385. Application fee: $50. Financial aid available.
Application Deadline Continuous.
Jobs Positions for college students.
Summer Contact Todd Zimbelman, Director, main address above. Phone: 541-346-5668. Fax: 541-346-6188. E-mail: tzimbelm@oregon.uoregon.edu.
Winter Contact Todd Zimbelman, Director of the University of Oregon Summer Music Camps, main address above. Phone: 541-346-5668. Fax: 541-346-6188. E-mail: tzimbelm@oregon.uoregon.edu.
URL music.uoregon.edu/EventsNews/Camps/campsgen.html

Outward Bound West–Backpacking and Whitewater Rafting, Oregon

Outward Bound West/Outward Bound, USA
Deschutes River and Central Cascades
Oregon

General Information Coed travel outdoor program and wilderness program established in 1965. College credit may be earned.
Program Focus Teamwork and leadership wilderness adventure.
Academics Environmental science.
Special Interest Areas Native American culture, campcraft, first aid, leadership training, outdoor cooking, personal development, team building.
Sports Rappelling, swimming.
Wilderness/Outdoors Backpacking, hiking, mountaineering, orienteering, outdoor adventure, rafting, rock climbing, white-water trips, wilderness camping.
Trips Overnight.
Program Information 2–3 sessions per year. Session length: 14–15 days in June, July, August. Ages: 14+. Cost: $1995–$2795. Application fee: $95. Financial aid available.
Application Deadline Continuous.
Jobs Positions for college students 21 and older.
Contact Admissions Advisor, 910 Jackson Street, Golden, Colorado 80401. Phone: 866-746-9777. Fax: 720-497-2421. E-mail: info@obwest.org.
URL www.outwardboundwest.org

Outward Bound West–Mountaineering and Rafting, Oregon

Outward Bound West/Outward Bound, USA
Deschutes River and Central Cascades
Oregon

General Information Coed travel outdoor program and wilderness program established in 1965. College credit may be earned.
Program Focus Teamwork and leadership wilderness adventure.
Academics Environmental science.
Special Interest Areas Native American culture, campcraft, first aid, leadership training, outdoor cooking, personal development, team building.
Sports Rappelling, swimming.
Wilderness/Outdoors Hiking, mountaineering, orienteering, outdoor adventure, rafting, rock climbing, white-water trips, wilderness camping.
Trips Overnight.
Program Information 9 sessions per year. Session length: 15–22 days in June, July, August, September. Ages: 14+. Cost: $2695–$3295. Application fee: $95. Financial aid available.
Application Deadline Continuous.
Jobs Positions for college students 21 and older.
Contact Admissions Advisor, 910 Jackson Street, Golden, Colorado 80401. Phone: 866-746-9777. Fax: 720-497-2421. E-mail: info@obwest.org.
URL www.outwardboundwest.org

Outward Bound West–Mountaineering, Rafting, and Climbing-XT, Oregon

Outward Bound West/Outward Bound, USA
Deschutes River and Central Cascades
Oregon

General Information Coed travel outdoor program and wilderness program established in 1965. College credit may be earned.
Program Focus Teamwork and leadership wilderness adventure.
Academics Environmental science.
Special Interest Areas Native American culture, campcraft, first aid, leadership training, outdoor cooking, personal development, team building.
Sports Rappelling, swimming.
Wilderness/Outdoors Hiking, mountaineering, orienteering, outdoor adventure, rafting, rock climbing, white-water trips, wilderness camping.
Trips Overnight.
Program Information 1–2 sessions per year. Session length: 15–30 days in July, September. Ages: 16+. Cost: \$3000–\$3695. Application fee: \$95. Financial aid available.
Application Deadline Continuous.
Jobs Positions for college students 21 and older.
Contact Admissions Advisor, 910 Jackson Street, Golden, Colorado 80401. Phone: 866-746-9777. Fax: 720-497-2421. E-mail: info@obwest.org.
URL www.outwardboundwest.org

Outward Bound West–Volcanoes Mountaineering–Oregon

Outward Bound West/Outward Bound, USA
Cascade Mountains
Redmond, Oregon

General Information Coed residential outdoor program and wilderness program established in 1965. College credit may be earned.
Program Focus Teamwork and leadership wilderness adventure.
Academics Environmental science.
Special Interest Areas Campcraft, first aid, leadership training, outdoor cooking, personal development, team building.
Wilderness/Outdoors Backpacking, hiking, mountaineering, orienteering, outdoor adventure, rock climbing, wilderness camping.
Trips Overnight.
Program Information 1 session per year. Session length: 30 days in June, July. Ages: 16+. Boarding program cost: \$3395. Application fee: \$95. Financial aid available.
Application Deadline Continuous.
Jobs Positions for college students 21 and older.
Contact Admissions Advisor, 910 Jackson Street, Golden, Colorado 80401. Phone: 866-746-9777. Fax: 720-497-2421. E-mail: info@obwest.org.
URL www.outwardboundwest.org

Pacific Marine Science Camp

Oregon Museum of Science and Industry
Oregon

General Information Coed travel academic program and outdoor program established in 1962. Formal opportunities for the academically talented. High school credit may be earned.
Program Focus Coastal ecology, marine biology.
Academics Japanese language/literature, anthropology, biology, ecology, forestry, geology/earth science, marine studies, science (general).
Sports Canoeing, snorkeling.
Wilderness/Outdoors Canoe trips, hiking, orienteering, wilderness camping.
Trips Day, overnight.
Program Information 30 sessions per year. Session length: 6 days in June, July, August. Ages: 7–14. 30–50 participants per session. Cost: \$410. Financial aid available.
Application Deadline Continuous.
Jobs Positions for high school students and college students.
Contact Travis Neumeyer, Programming Coordinator, 1945 Southeast Water Avenue, Portland, Oregon 97214. Phone: 503-239-7824. Fax: 503-239-7838. E-mail: tneumeyer@omsi.edu.
URL www.omsi.edu

Salmon Camp for Native Americans

Oregon Museum of Science and Industry
Hancock Field Station
39472 Highway 218
Fossil, Oregon 97830

General Information Coed residential outdoor program established in 1993. Formal opportunities for the academically talented. High school credit may be earned.
Program Focus Natural science and natural resource management.
Academics Archaeology, astronomy, biology (Advanced Placement), botany, ecology, environmental science, geology/earth science, marine studies, natural resource management.
Special Interest Areas Native American culture, nature study.
Sports Canoeing, snorkeling.
Wilderness/Outdoors Canoe trips, hiking, orienteering, rafting.
Trips Cultural, overnight.
Program Information 2 sessions per year. Session length: 6 days in March, August. Ages: 10–14. 25 participants per session. No cost for Native Americans.
Application Deadline Continuous.
Jobs Positions for high school students 16 and older and college students 18 and older.
Contact Travis Neumeyer, Programming Coordinator, 1945 Southeast Water Avenue, Portland, Oregon 97214. Phone: 503-239-7824. Fax: 503-239-7838. E-mail: tneumeyer@omsi.edu.
URL www.omsi.edu

Salmon Camp Research Team for Native Americans–Oregon

Oregon Museum of Science and Industry
Hancock Field Station
39472 Highway 218
Fossil, Oregon 97830

General Information Coed residential outdoor program. Formal opportunities for the academically talented. High school credit may be earned.
Program Focus Natural resource management.
Academics Astronomy, biology, botany, ecology, geology/earth science, natural resource management.
Special Interest Areas Native American culture, field research/expeditions.
Sports Canoeing, snorkeling.
Wilderness/Outdoors Hiking, rafting, white-water trips, wilderness camping.
Trips Cultural.
Program Information 2 sessions per year. Session length: 20 days in March, June, July. Ages: 15–18. 10 participants per session. Financial aid available. No cost for Native Americans.
Application Deadline Continuous.
Jobs Positions for high school students 16 and older and college students 16 and older.
Contact Travis Neumeyer, Programming Coordinator, 1945 Southeast Water Avenue, Portland, Oregon 97214. Phone: 503-239-7824. Fax: 503-239-7838. E-mail: sciencecamps@omsi.edu.
URL www.omsi.edu

Shizen Kyampu-Japanese Language Science Camp

Oregon Museum of Science and Industry
Camp Kiwanilong
Warrenton, Oregon 97146

General Information Coed residential academic program, outdoor program, and cultural program established in 1993. Formal opportunities for the academically talented. High school credit may be earned.
Program Focus Coastal ecology.
Academics Japanese language/literature, biology, botany, ecology, marine studies.
Sports Boating.
Wilderness/Outdoors Hiking.
Trips Cultural, day.
Program Information 1 session per year. Session length: 6 days in August. Ages: 10–14. 70 participants per session. Boarding program cost: $415. Financial aid available.
Application Deadline Continuous.
Jobs Positions for high school students 16 and older and college students 16 and older.
Contact Travis Neumeyer, Programming Coordinator, 1945 Southeast Water Avenue, Portland, Oregon 97214. Phone: 503-239-7824. Fax: 503-239-7838. E-mail: tneumeyer@omsi.edu.
URL www.omsi.edu

Student Conservation Association–Conservation Crew Program (Oregon)

Student Conservation Association (SCA)
Oregon

General Information Coed residential outdoor program, community service program, and wilderness program established in 1957. High school credit may be earned.
Program Focus Resource management, conservation and environmental education.
Academics Biology, botany, ecology, environmental science, geology/earth science, history.
Special Interest Areas Campcraft, community service, construction, leadership training, nature study, trail maintenance, work camp programs.
Sports Canoeing, fishing, kayaking, swimming.
Wilderness/Outdoors Backpacking, hiking, orienteering, outdoor living skills, wilderness camping.
Trips Cultural, day, overnight.
Program Information 2–3 sessions per year. Session length: 3–5 weeks in June, July, August. Ages: 15–19. 6–8 participants per session. Application fee: $20. Financial aid available. No cost for program; financial aid possible for travel expenses.
Application Deadline Continuous.
Jobs Positions for college students 21 and older.
Contact Recruitment Office, PO Box 550, Charlestown, New Hampshire 03603. Phone: 603-543-1700. Fax: 603-543-1828. E-mail: getreal@thesca.org.
URL www.theSCA.org

Teens-n-Trails

Northwest Youth Corps
2621 Augusta Street
Eugene, Oregon 97403

General Information Coed residential outdoor program. High school credit may be earned.
Academics Environmental science, science (general).
Special Interest Areas Nature study, trail maintenance, work camp programs.
Sports Fishing, swimming.
Wilderness/Outdoors Backpacking, hiking, rafting, wilderness camping.
Trips Overnight.
Program Information 2 sessions per year. Session length: 4 weeks in June, July, August. Ages: 14–15. 10 participants per session. Boarding program cost: $595. Financial aid available.
Application Deadline Continuous.
Jobs Positions for high school students 14 and older.
Contact Elizabeth Wartluft, Youth Services Coordinator, main address above. Phone: 541-349-5055 Ext.236. Fax: 541-349-5060. E-mail: nyc@nwyouthcorps.org.
URL www.nwyouthcorps.org

VANS SKATEBOARD CAMP

High Cascade Snowboard Camp
Mt. Hood, Oregon 97028

General Information Coed residential sports camp established in 2001.
Program Focus Skateboard skill development.
Academics Japanese language/literature.
Arts Arts and crafts (general).
Sports Basketball, bicycling (BMX), skateboarding, snowboarding, soccer, swimming, volleyball, wakeboarding, yoga.
Wilderness/Outdoors Hiking, mountain biking.
Trips Day.
Program Information 6 sessions per year. Session length: 8–10 days in June, July, August. Ages: 11+. 30–60 participants per session. Boarding program cost: $995–$1095.
Application Deadline Continuous.
Jobs Positions for high school students 18 and older and college students 21 and older.
Summer Contact Ms. Meagan Stein, Camp Administrator, PO Box 368, Government Camp, Oregon 97028. Phone: 800-334-4272. Fax: 503-272-3637. E-mail: highcascade@highcascade.com.
Winter Contact Ms. Meagan Stein, Camp Administrator, 50 Southeast Scott Street, Bend, Oregon 97702. Phone: 800-334-4272. Fax: 541-389-6371. E-mail: highcascade@highcascade.com.
URL www.vansskatecamp.com

VENTURES TRAVEL SERVICE–OREGON

Friendship Ventures
Oregon

General Information Coed travel special needs program established in 1985. Specific services available for the developmentally challenged and physically challenged.
Program Focus Provides travel services to older teens and adults with developmental disabilities.
Special Interest Areas Touring.
Program Information 50 sessions per year. Session length: 4–10 days in February, March, April, May, June, July, August, September, October, November, December. Ages: 14–70. 4–8 participants per session. Cost: $395–$2000.
Application Deadline Continuous.
Jobs Positions for college students 18 and older.
Contact Georgann Rumsey, President/CEO, 10509 108th Street, NW, Annandale, Minnesota 55302. Phone: 952-852-0101. Fax: 952-852-0123. E-mail: fv@friendshipventures.org.
URL www.friendshipventures.org

WILDERNESS VENTURES–OREGON

Wilderness Ventures
Oregon

General Information Coed travel outdoor program, wilderness program, and adventure program established in 1973.
Program Focus Wilderness travel, wilderness skills, leadership skills.
Special Interest Areas Leadership training.
Wilderness/Outdoors Backpacking, hiking, rafting, rock climbing, white-water trips, wilderness camping.
Trips Overnight.
Program Information 3 sessions per year. Session length: 16 days in June, July, August. Ages: 14–18. 10 participants per session. Cost: $2590. Financial aid available.
Application Deadline Continuous.
Jobs Positions for college students 21 and older.
Contact Mike Cottingham, Director, PO Box 2768, Jackson Hole, Wyoming 83001. Phone: 800-533-2281. Fax: 307-739-1934. E-mail: info@wildernessventures.com.
URL www.wildernessventures.com

For more information, see page 1396.

YOUNG MUSICIANS & ARTISTS

Young Musicians & Artists
Willamette University
Salem, Oregon 97301

General Information Coed residential arts program established in 1965.
Arts Band, ceramics, chorus, clowning, creative writing, dance, dance (ballet), dance (jazz), dance (tap), drawing, music, music (chamber), music (classical), music (ensemble), music (instrumental), music (jazz), music (orchestral), music (vocal), musical productions, painting, photography, pottery, printmaking, sculpture, theater/drama, visual arts.
Sports Soccer, softball, swimming, tennis, volleyball, weight training.
Program Information 2 sessions per year. Session length: 13 days in June, July. Ages: 9–18. 145 participants per session. Boarding program cost: $1010. Application fee: $200. Financial aid available.
Application Deadline Continuous.
Contact Brian M. Biggs, Executive Director, PO Box 13277, Portland, Oregon 97213. Phone: 503-281-9528. E-mail: brian@ymainc.org.
URL www.ymainc.org

YOUTH FOREST CAMPS

Northwest Youth Corps
2621 Augusta Street
Eugene, Oregon 97403

General Information Coed residential outdoor program established in 1984. High school credit may be earned.
Academics Environmental science, science (general).
Special Interest Areas Career exploration, field research/expeditions, nature study, trail maintenance, work camp programs.
Sports Fishing, swimming.
Wilderness/Outdoors Backpacking, hiking, rafting, wilderness camping.
Trips Day, overnight.

Youth Forest Camps (continued)
Program Information 4 sessions per year. Session length: 5 weeks in June, July, August. Ages: 16–19. 10 participants per session. Financial aid available. Cost: program fee/tuition $200.
Application Deadline Continuous.
Jobs Positions for high school students 16 and older and college students 16 and older.
Contact Elizabeth Wartluft, Youth Services Coordinator, main address above. Phone: 541-349-5055 Ext.236. Fax: 541-349-5060. E-mail: nyc@nwyouthcorps.org.
URL www.nwyouthcorps.org

PENNSYLVANIA

Academic Camps at Gettysburg College–Astronomy

Gettysburg College
300 North Washington Street
Gettysburg, Pennsylvania 17325

General Information Coed residential academic program established in 2004.
Academics Academics (general), astronomy.
Sports Baseball, basketball, ropes course, softball, track and field.
Trips College tours, cultural, day, shopping.
Program Information 2 sessions per year. Session length: 15 days in June, July. Ages: 14–18. 50 participants per session. Boarding program cost: $2395.
Application Deadline Continuous.
Contact Doug Murphy, Director, 101 Murray Street, Suite 427, New York, New York 10007. Phone: 800-289-7029. Fax: 212-815-9256. E-mail: academiccamps@gettysburg.edu.
URL www.gettysburg.edu/homepage/academiccamps/
For more information, see page 954.

Academic Camps at Gettysburg College–College Prep & Preview

Gettysburg College
300 North Washington Street
Gettysburg, Pennsylvania 17325

General Information Coed residential academic program established in 2004.
Academics SAT/ACT preparation, academics (general), college tours, precollege program.
Special Interest Areas College planning.
Sports Baseball, basketball, ropes course, softball, track and field.
Trips College tours, cultural, day, shopping.
Program Information 2 sessions per year. Session length: 15 days in June, July. Ages: 14–18. 50 participants per session. Boarding program cost: $2395.
Application Deadline Continuous.
Contact Doug Murphy, Director, 101 Murray Street, Suite 427, New York, New York 10007. Phone: 800-289-7029. Fax: 212-815-9256. E-mail: academiccamps@gettysburg.edu.
URL www.gettysburg.edu/homepage/academiccamps/
For more information, see page 954.

Academic Camps at Gettysburg College–Community Service

Gettysburg College
300 North Washington Street
Gettysburg, Pennsylvania 17325

General Information Coed residential academic program and community service program established in 2004.
Academics Academics (general).
Special Interest Areas Community service, leadership training, team building.
Sports Baseball, basketball, ropes course, softball, track and field.
Trips College tours, cultural, day, shopping.
Program Information 2 sessions per year. Session length: 15 days in June, July. Ages: 14–18. 50 participants per session. Boarding program cost: $2395.
Application Deadline Continuous.
Contact Doug Murphy, Director, 101 Murray Street, Suite 427, New York, New York 10007. Phone: 800-289-7029. Fax: 212-815-9256. E-mail: academiccamps@gettysburg.edu.
URL www.gettysburg.edu/homepage/academiccamps/
For more information, see page 954.

Academic Camps at Gettysburg College–Foreign Language Study (Spanish)

Gettysburg College
300 North Washington Street
Gettysburg, Pennsylvania 17325

General Information Coed residential academic program established in 2004.
Academics Spanish language/literature, academics (general).
Special Interest Areas Cross-cultural education.
Sports Baseball, basketball, ropes course, softball, track and field.
Trips College tours, cultural, day, shopping.
Program Information 2 sessions per year. Session length: 15 days in June, July. Ages: 14–18. 50 participants per session. Boarding program cost: $2395.
Application Deadline Continuous.
Contact Doug Murphy, Director, 101 Murray Street, Suite 427, New York, New York 10007. Phone: 800-289-7029. Fax: 212-815-9256. E-mail: academiccamps@gettysburg.edu.
URL www.gettysburg.edu/homepage/academiccamps/
For more information, see page 954.

Academic Camps at Gettysburg College–U.S. Civil War

Gettysburg College
300 North Washington Street
Gettysburg, Pennsylvania 17325

General Information Coed residential academic program established in 2004.
Academics Academics (general), history.
Sports Baseball, basketball, ropes course, softball, track and field.
Trips College tours, cultural, day, shopping.
Program Information 2 sessions per year. Session length: 15 days in June, July. Ages: 14–18. 50 participants per session. Boarding program cost: $2395.
Application Deadline Continuous.
Contact Doug Murphy, Director, 101 Murray Street, Suite 427, New York, New York 10007. Phone: 800-289-7029. Fax: 212-815-9256. E-mail: academiccamps@gettysburg.edu.
URL www.gettysburg.edu/homepage/academiccamps/
For more information, see page 954.

Academic Camps at Gettysburg College–Writer's Workshops

Gettysburg College
300 North Washington Street
Gettysburg, Pennsylvania 17325

General Information Coed residential academic program established in 2004.
Academics Academics (general), writing.
Arts Creative writing.
Sports Baseball, basketball, ropes course, softball, track and field.
Trips College tours, cultural, day, shopping.
Program Information 2 sessions per year. Session length: 15 days in June, July. Ages: 14–18. 50 participants per session. Boarding program cost: $2395.
Application Deadline Continuous.
Contact Doug Murphy, Director, 101 Murray Street, Suite 427, New York, New York 10007. Phone: 800-289-7029. Fax: 212-815-9256. E-mail: academiccamps@gettysburg.edu.
URL www.gettysburg.edu/homepage/academiccamps/
For more information, see page 954.

Adventure Camps

Ligonier Camp and Conference Center
188 Macartney Lane
Ligonier, Pennsylvania 15658

General Information Coed residential and day traditional camp, outdoor program, and wilderness program established in 1993. Religious affiliation: Presbyterian. Accredited by American Camping Association.
Program Focus Traditional camps with adventure focus and wilderness program.
Academics Bible study.
Sports Climbing (wall), ropes course.
Wilderness/Outdoors Backpacking, caving, hiking, orienteering, rafting, rock climbing, white-water trips, wilderness camping.
Program Information 7–10 sessions per year. Session length: 3–14 days in June, July, August. Ages: 12–18. 10–216 participants per session. Day program cost: $15–$50. Boarding program cost: $250–$300. Financial aid available.
Application Deadline Continuous.
Jobs Positions for high school students 16 and older and college students 19 and older.
Contact Registrar, LCCC. Phone: 724-238-6428. Fax: 724-238-6971. E-mail: ligcamp@ligoniercamp.org.
URL www.ligoniercamp.org

Antwaan Randle Football Camp/ Sports International

Sports International, Inc.
Slippery Rock University
Slippery Rock, Pennsylvania

General Information Coed residential and day sports camp established in 1993.
Program Focus Football.
Sports Football, weight training.
Program Information 1 session per year. Session length: 5 days in June. Ages: 8–18. 300–450 participants per session. Day program cost: $489. Boarding program cost: $599.
Application Deadline Continuous.
Jobs Positions for college students 18 and older.
Contact Customer Service, 8924 McGaw Court, Columbia, Maryland 21045. Phone: 800-555-0801. Fax: 410-309-9962. E-mail: info@footballcamps.com.
URL www.footballcamps.com

Arts Unite

The University of Scranton
University of Scranton
Scranton, Pennsylvania 18510-4625

General Information Coed day arts program.
Arts Arts, creative writing, dance, music, puppetry, storytelling, theater/drama.
Program Information 1 session per year. Session length: 15 days in July. Ages: 6–13. 20–30 participants per session. Day program cost: $650. Financial aid available.
Application Deadline Continuous.
Contact Gary P. Celli, Director of Special Projects, main address above. Phone: 570-941-7580. Fax: 570-941-5819. E-mail: cellig2@scranton.edu.
URL www.scranton.edu

Breezy Point Day Camp

Breezy Point
1126 Bridgetown Pike
Langhorne, Pennsylvania 19053

General Information Coed day traditional camp established in 1955. Accredited by American Camping Association.

Breezy Point Day Camp (continued)

Academics Computers, environmental science.
Arts Arts and crafts (general), dance, musical productions, photography, theater/drama, woodworking.
Special Interest Areas Nature study.
Sports Archery, baseball, basketball, bicycling, bicycling (BMX), boating, canoeing, cheerleading, climbing (wall), fishing, football, golf, ropes course, soccer, softball, street/roller hockey, swimming, tennis, track and field, volleyball, water polo.
Wilderness/Outdoors Hiking.
Trips Day.
Program Information 30–60 sessions per year. Session length: 4–8 weeks in June, July, August. Ages: 2–14. 500–600 participants per session.
Application Deadline Continuous.
Jobs Positions for high school students 15 and older and college students 18 and older.
Contact Mr. Bill Wright, Sr., Program Director, main address above. Phone: 215-752-1987.
URL www.breezypoints.com

Bryn Mawr College–Writing for College

Bryn Mawr College
101 North Merion Avenue
Bryn Mawr, Pennsylvania 19010-2899

General Information Girls' residential academic program established in 1993. Formal opportunities for the academically talented.
Program Focus College preparation, critical and creative writing.
Academics English language/literature, college tours, humanities, journalism, precollege program, study skills, writing.
Arts Creative writing.
Special Interest Areas Field trips (arts and culture).
Sports Swimming, tennis, weight training.
Trips College tours, cultural, day, shopping.
Program Information 1 session per year. Session length: 3–4 weeks in June, July. Ages: 15–18. 50 participants per session. Boarding program cost: $2700–$3500. Application fee: $40. Financial aid available.
Application Deadline May 1.
Jobs Positions for college students 20 and older.
Contact Ms. Ann Brown, Coordinator, main address above. Phone: 610-526-5376. Fax: 610-526-7471. E-mail: writingforcollege@brynmawr.edu.
URL www.brynmawr.edu/writingforcollege
For more information, see page 1408.

Camp Ballibay for the Fine and Performing Arts

1 Ballibay Road
Camptown, Pennsylvania 18815

General Information Coed residential arts program established in 1964. Accredited by American Camping Association.
Program Focus Fine and performing arts.

Bryn Mawr College–Writing for College

Arts Arts, arts and crafts (general), batiking, ceramics, chorus, clowning, creative writing, dance, dance (ballet), dance (folk), dance (jazz), dance (modern), dance (tap), drawing, fabric arts, film, graphic arts, jewelry making, mime, music, music (chamber), music (classical), music (ensemble), music (instrumental), music (jazz), music (orchestral), music (rock), music (vocal), musical productions, painting, performance art, photography, pottery, printmaking, puppetry, radio broadcasting, sculpture, television/video, theater/drama, weaving, woodworking.
Sports Archery, basketball, boating, canoeing, equestrian sports, fencing, fishing, golf, horseback riding, kayaking, martial arts, soccer, softball, swimming, tennis, volleyball.
Program Information 4 sessions per year. Session length: 2–9 weeks in June, July, August. Ages: 6–16. 150 participants per session.
Application Deadline Continuous.
Jobs Positions for college students 19 and older.
Contact Gerard J. Jannone, Director, Box 1, Camptown, Pennsylvania 18815. Phone: 570-746-3223. Fax: 570-746-3691. E-mail: jannone@ballibay.com.
URL www.ballibay.com
For more information, see page 1022.

Camp Ballibay for the Fine and Performing Arts

Camp Canadensis

Lake Road
Canadensis, Pennsylvania 18325

General Information Coed residential traditional camp established in 1941. Religious affiliation: Jewish. Accredited by American Camping Association.
Program Focus Tennis, athletics, waterfront sports, drama, crafts, and outdoor adventure.
Academics Astronomy.
Arts Acting, arts and crafts (general), ceramics, creative writing, dance, dance (modern), drawing, fabric arts, jewelry making, leather working, music, musical productions, painting, photography, pottery, radio broadcasting, sculpture, television/video, theater/drama, woodworking.
Special Interest Areas Culinary arts, model rocketry, nature study, robotics.
Sports Aerobics, archery, baseball, basketball, bicycling, bicycling (BMX), boating, canoeing, cheerleading, climbing (wall), fishing, golf, gymnastics, horseback riding, in-line skating, kayaking, lacrosse, martial arts, rappelling, ropes course, sailing, scuba diving, snorkeling, soccer, softball, street/roller hockey, swimming, tennis, track and field, volleyball, water polo, waterskiing, weight training, windsurfing, wrestling.
Wilderness/Outdoors Backpacking, bicycle trips, canoe trips, hiking, mountain biking, rock climbing.
Trips Day, overnight.
Program Information 1 session per year. Session length: 50 days in June, July, August. Ages: 7–16. 450 participants per session. Boarding program cost: $6885.
Application Deadline Continuous.
Jobs Positions for college students 18 and older.
Summer Contact Steven Smilk, Director, RR2, Box 2350, Lake Road, Canadensis, Pennsylvania 18325. Phone: 570-595-7461. Fax: 570-595-9290. E-mail: camp4you@aol.com.
Winter Contact Steven Smilk, Director, Box 182, Wyncote, Pennsylvania 19095. Phone: 215-572-8222. Fax: 215-572-8298. E-mail: camp4you@aol.com.
URL www.canadensis.com

Camp Cayuga

Pocono Mountains
Niles Pond Road, Suite Petg
Honesdale, Pennsylvania 18431

General Information Coed residential traditional camp established in 1957. Accredited by American Camping Association.

Camp Cayuga

Program Focus Over 60 activities including paintball, extreme sport jumping, scuba, horseback riding, flying trapeze, tennis, Honda ATVs, and fun trips.
Academics English as a second language, SAT/ACT preparation, journalism, mathematics, reading, writing.
Arts Arts and crafts (general), batiking, ceramics, chorus, circus arts, clowning, creative writing, dance, dance (ballet), dance (folk), dance (jazz), dance (modern), dance (tap), drawing, fabric arts, film, graphic arts, jewelry making, juggling, leather working, music, music (instrumental), music (vocal), painting, photography, pottery, printmaking, puppetry, radio broadcasting, sculpture, television/video, theater/drama, trapeze arts, weaving, woodworking.
Special Interest Areas Animal care, campcraft, model rocketry, nature study.
Sports Aerobics, all-terrain vehicles, archery, baseball, basketball, bicycling, boating, bungee jumping, canoeing,

Camp Cayuga (continued)

cheerleading, climbing (wall), cross-country, dodge ball, equestrian sports, field hockey, fishing, flag football, football, golf, gymnastics, horseback riding, in-line skating, kayaking, kickball, lacrosse, martial arts, paintball, rappelling, riflery, roller skating, ropes course, rugby, sailing, skateboarding, soccer, softball, street/roller hockey, swimming, table tennis/ping-pong, tennis, tetherball, track and field, trampolining, ultimate frisbee, unicycling, volleyball, water polo, water tubing, weight training, windsurfing, wrestling.
Wilderness/Outdoors Backpacking, canoe trips, hiking, mountain biking, mountaineering, orienteering, outdoor camping, pack animal trips, rafting, rock climbing, white-water trips, wilderness camping.
Trips Cultural, day, overnight, shopping.
Program Information 4 sessions per year. Session length: 13–54 days in June, July, August. Ages: 5–15. 390 participants per session. Boarding program cost: $1400–$6400. Sibling credit available: $400 for 8 weeks, $200 for 4 weeks; tuition discounts available for early registration.
Application Deadline Continuous.
Jobs Positions for college students 19 and older.
Summer Contact Mr. Brian B. Buynak, Camp Director, Pocono Mountains, Niles Pond Road, Suite Petg, Honesdale, Pennsylvania 18431. Phone: 570-253-3133. Fax: 570-253-3194. E-mail: info@campcayuga.com.
Winter Contact Mr. Brian B. Buynak, Camp Director, PO Box 151, Suite PETG, Peapack, New Jersey 07977. Phone: 800-422-9842. Fax: 908-470-1228. E-mail: info@campcayuga.com.
URL www.campcayuga.com

For more information, see page 1024.

Camp Chen-A-Wanda

Thompson, Pennsylvania 18465

General Information Coed residential traditional camp established in 1939. Accredited by American Camping Association.
Arts Arts and crafts (general), ceramics, dance, dance (folk), dance (jazz), dance (modern), dance (tap), jewelry making, leather working, musical productions, painting, pottery, radio broadcasting, woodworking.
Special Interest Areas Model rocketry.
Sports Aerobics, all-terrain vehicles, archery, baseball, basketball, bicycling, bicycling (BMX), boating, canoeing, cheerleading, climbing (wall), diving, fishing, football, frisbee golf, go-carts, golf, gymnastics, horseback riding, in-line skating, kayaking, lacrosse, martial arts, mountain boarding, rappelling, ropes course, sailing, soccer, softball, street/roller hockey, swimming, tennis, track and field, volleyball, waterskiing, weight training, windsurfing, wrestling.
Wilderness/Outdoors Mountain biking, rock climbing, white-water trips.
Trips Day, overnight.
Program Information 1 session per year. Session length: 50 days in June, July, August. Ages: 7–16. 400 participants per session. Boarding program cost: $6400.
Application Deadline Continuous.
Jobs Positions for college students 18 and older.
Summer Contact Morey Baldwin, Director, RR #1, Box 32, Thompson, Pennsylvania 18465. Phone: 570-756-2016. Fax: 570-756-2086. E-mail: carlyma@aol.com.
Winter Contact Morey Baldwin, Director, 8 Claverton Court, Dix Hills, New York 11747. Phone: 631-643-5878. Fax: 631-643-0920. E-mail: cneier@aol.com.
URL www.campchen-a-wanda.com

Camp Conrad Weiser

South Mountain YMCA
201 Cushion Peak Road
Wernersville, Pennsylvania 19565

General Information Coed residential traditional camp and outdoor program established in 1948. Accredited by American Camping Association. Specific services available for the learning disabled. College credit may be earned.
Program Focus Outdoor living skills, horsemanship, mountain biking, sailing, and adventure.
Arts Acting, arts and crafts (general), creative writing, dance, drawing, film, photography, theater/drama.
Special Interest Areas Native American culture, campcraft, leadership training, nature study.
Sports Archery, baseball, basketball, bicycling, canoeing, climbing (wall), diving, equestrian sports, football, golf, horseback riding, kayaking, mountain boarding, rappelling, riflery, ropes course, sailing, scuba diving, soccer, softball, sports (general), street/roller hockey, swimming, tennis, volleyball.
Wilderness/Outdoors Backpacking, canoe trips, caving, hiking, mountain biking, orienteering, rafting, survival training, white-water trips, wilderness camping.
Trips Overnight.
Program Information 4–5 sessions per year. Session length: 2 weeks in June, July, August. Ages: 7–15. 184–230 participants per session. Boarding program cost: $875–$2000. Financial aid available.
Application Deadline Continuous.
Jobs Positions for high school students 18 and older and college students 18 and older.
Contact Gideon A. Fetterolf, Director of Resident Camping, PO Box 147, Wernersville, Pennsylvania 19565. Phone: 610-670-2267. Fax: 610-670-5010. E-mail: jmarquis@smymca.org.
URL www.smymca.org

Camp Lee Mar

450 Route 590
Lackawaxen, Pennsylvania 18435

General Information Coed residential traditional camp, academic program, and special needs program established in 1953. Accredited by American Camping Association. Specific services available for the developmentally challenged, learning disabled, and participant with Aspergers Syndrome. College credit may be earned.
Program Focus Camp for children with developmental challenges.
Academics Academics (general), computers, mathematics, reading.

Arts Arts and crafts (general), dance, drawing, painting, theater/drama.
Special Interest Areas Daily living skills, speech therapy.
Sports Aerobics, basketball, soccer, softball, swimming, tennis, volleyball.
Trips Day, overnight.
Program Information 1 session per year. Session length: 7 weeks in July, August. Ages: 5–21. 155 participants per session. Boarding program cost: $6600.
Application Deadline Continuous.
Jobs Positions for college students 19 and older.
Summer Contact Mr. Ariel Segal, Executive Director, main address above. Phone: 570-685-7188. E-mail: gtour400@aol.com.
Winter Contact Mr. Ariel Segal, Executive Director, 805 Redgate Road, Dresher, Pennsylvania 19025. Phone: 215-658-1708. Fax: 215-658-1710. E-mail: gtour400@aol.com.
URL www.leemar.com

Camp Lindenmere

Henryville, Pennsylvania 18332

General Information Coed residential traditional camp established in 1998. Accredited by American Camping Association. Formal opportunities for the artistically talented.
Program Focus Each child chooses his or her activities for the day.
Academics Computers, music.
Arts Acting, arts and crafts (general), batiking, ceramics, circus arts, clowning, creative writing, dance, dance (ballet), dance (jazz), dance (modern), dance (tap), drawing, fabric arts, film, graphic arts, jewelry making, leather working, music, music (vocal), musical productions, painting, photography, pottery, printmaking, radio broadcasting, sculpture, television/video, theater/drama, trapeze arts, woodworking.
Special Interest Areas Electronics, nature study.
Sports Aerobics, archery, baseball, basketball, bicycling, boating, canoeing, climbing (wall), fencing, figure skating, fishing, gymnastics, horseback riding, ice hockey, in-line skating, kayaking, lacrosse, martial arts, mountain boarding, ropes course, skateboarding, snorkeling, soccer, softball, street/roller hockey, swimming, tennis, volleyball, weight training.
Wilderness/Outdoors Canoe trips, hiking, mountain biking, survival training.
Trips Cultural, day, overnight.
Program Information 3 sessions per year. Session length: 18–63 days in June, July, August. Ages: 7–17. 300 participants per session. Boarding program cost: $2150–$5600. Financial aid available.
Application Deadline Continuous.
Jobs Positions for college students 18 and older.
Summer Contact Ms. Enid R. Marcus, Co-Director, RR #1, Box 1765, Henryville, Pennsylvania 18332. Phone: 570-629-0240. Fax: 208-723-3288. E-mail: admin@camplindenmere.com.
Winter Contact Jerry Marcus, Co-Director, 12773 West Forest Hill Boulevard, Suite 1216, Wellington, Florida 33414. Phone: 888-220-4773. Fax: 208-723-3288. E-mail: admin@camplindenmere.com.
URL www.camplindenmere.com

Camp Lohikan in the Pocono Mountains

Camp Lohikan in the Pocono Mountains
24 Wallerville Road
Lake Como, Pennsylvania 18437

General Information Coed residential traditional camp established in 1957. Accredited by American Camping Association.

Camp Lohikan in the Pocono Mountains

Program Focus Horseback riding, tennis, jet skiing, and sixty other activities.
Academics English as a second language, SAT/ACT preparation, astronomy, computers, environmental science, history, mathematics, music, reading, science (general), social science, social studies, typing, writing.
Arts Acting, arts and crafts (general), batiking, ceramics, circus arts, clowning, creative writing, dance, dance (ballet), dance (folk), dance (jazz), dance (modern), dance (tap), drawing, fabric arts, graphic arts, jewelry making, leather working, metalworking, mime, music, music (instrumental), music (rock), music (vocal), musical

Camp Lohikan in the Pocono Mountains (continued)

productions, painting, photography, pottery, printmaking, puppetry, radio broadcasting, sculpture, television/video, theater/drama, trapeze arts, weaving, woodworking.
Special Interest Areas Native American culture, animal care, campcraft, chess, culinary arts, gardening, leadership training, model rocketry, nature study, team building.
Sports Aerobics, all-terrain vehicles, archery, badminton, baseball, basketball, bicycling, billiards, boating, canoeing, challenge course, cheerleading, climbing (tower), climbing (wall), cross-country, diving, dodge ball, equestrian sports, field games, fishing, flag football, football, frisbee golf, go-carts, golf, gymnastics, horseback riding, in-line skating, jet skiing, kayaking, lacrosse, martial arts, minibikes, mountain boarding, noncompetitive sports, obstacle course, paintball, physical fitness, rappelling, riflery, roller skating, ropes course, running/jogging, sailing, scuba diving, skateboarding, snorkeling, soccer, softball, sports (general), street/roller hockey, swimming, table tennis/ping-pong, tennis, tetherball, track and field, ultimate frisbee, unicycling, volleyball, wakeboarding, water polo, water tubing, waterskiing, weight training, windsurfing, wrestling.
Wilderness/Outdoors Backpacking, bicycle trips, canoe trips, hiking, mountain biking, mountaineering, orienteering, pack animal trips, rafting, rock climbing, survival training, white-water trips, wilderness camping, zip line.
Trips Cultural, day, overnight, shopping.
Program Information 3 sessions per year. Session length: 4–54 days in June, July, August. Ages: 6–15. 390 participants per session. Boarding program cost: $1500–$5900.
Application Deadline Continuous.
Jobs Positions for college students 19 and older.
Summer Contact Mr. Mark Buynak, CCD, Director, 24 Wallerville Road, PO Box 217, Lake Como, Pennsylvania 18473. Phone: 908-798-2707. Fax: 908-470-9319. E-mail: info@lohikan.com.
Winter Contact Mr. Mark Buynak, CCD, Director, PO Box 189, Department PETG, Gladstone, New Jersey 07934. Phone: 908-470-9317. Fax: 908-470-9319. E-mail: info@lohikan.com.
URL www.lohikan.com

For more information, see page 1030.

Camp Mt. Luther

355 Mt. Luther Lane
Mifflinburg, Pennsylvania 17844

General Information Coed residential and day traditional camp, outdoor program, and bible camp established in 1963. Religious affiliation: Lutheran. Accredited by American Camping Association.
Academics Bible study, environmental science, peace education.
Arts Arts and crafts (general), batiking, jewelry making, leather working, music, musical productions, photography, theater/drama.
Special Interest Areas Campcraft, leadership training, nature study.
Sports Archery, bicycling, canoeing, fishing, rappelling, ropes course, skiing (cross-country), soccer, softball, sports (general), swimming, track and field, volleyball, water polo.
Wilderness/Outdoors Backpacking, bicycle trips, canoe trips, caving, hiking, mountain biking, orienteering, rafting, rock climbing, survival training, white-water trips, wilderness camping.
Trips Overnight.
Program Information 8 sessions per year. Session length: 5–10 days in June, July, August. Ages: 6–18. 60–80 participants per session. Day program cost: $75–$105. Boarding program cost: $275–$305. Financial aid available.
Application Deadline Continuous.
Jobs Positions for high school students 16 and older and college students 18 and older.
Contact Chad Hershberger, Director, main address above. Phone: 570-922-1587. Fax: 570-922-1118. E-mail: cml@campmountluther.org.
URL www.campmountluther.org

Camp Nock-A-Mixon

249 Traugers Crossing Road
Kintnersville, Pennsylvania 18930

General Information Coed residential traditional camp established in 1938. Accredited by American Camping Association.
Arts Arts and crafts (general), batiking, ceramics, dance, dance (ballet), dance (jazz), dance (modern), drawing, guitar, jewelry making, leather working, photography, piano, pottery, radio broadcasting, theater/drama, woodworking.
Special Interest Areas Chess, culinary arts, model rocketry, self-defense.
Sports Aerobics, archery, baseball, basketball, canoeing, cheerleading, climbing (wall), fencing, field hockey, fishing, frisbee golf, golf, gymnastics, horseback riding, ice hockey, in-line skating, lacrosse, martial arts, riflery, ropes course, sailing, soccer, softball, street/roller hockey, swimming, tennis, volleyball, weight training, wrestling.
Wilderness/Outdoors Canoe trips, hiking, zip line.
Trips Cultural, day, overnight.
Program Information 1 session per year. Session length: 50 days in June, July, August. Ages: 7–16. 375 participants per session. Boarding program cost: $5575.
Application Deadline Continuous.
Jobs Positions for high school students 18 and older and college students 18 and older.
Summer Contact Mark Glaser, Director, main address above. Phone: 610-847-5963. Fax: 610-847-2199. E-mail: info@campnockamixon.com.
Winter Contact Mark Glaser, Director, 16 Gum Tree Lane, Lafayette Hill, Pennsylvania 19444. Phone: 610-941-0128. Fax: 610-941-1307. E-mail: mglaser851@aol.com.
URL www.campnockamixon.com

Camp Pocono Ridge

1 Pine Grove Road
South Sterling, Pennsylvania 18460

General Information Coed residential traditional camp and outdoor program established in 1957. Accredited by American Camping Association.
Program Focus An all-around program including optional camping adventures to Ohio and New England.
Academics English as a second language, academics (general), archaeology, computer programming, computers, ecology, environmental science, geology/earth science, journalism, music, reading, typing, writing.
Arts Acting, arts, arts and crafts (general), basketry, batiking, ceramics, chorus, clowning, creative writing, dance, dance (ballet), dance (jazz), dance (modern), drawing, fabric arts, film, graphic arts, jewelry making, leather working, metalworking, music, music (ensemble), music (instrumental), music (vocal), musical productions, painting, photography, pottery, printmaking, radio broadcasting, sculpture, television/video, theater/drama, woodworking.
Special Interest Areas Native American culture, animal care, community service, construction, culinary arts, electronics, gardening, leadership training, model rocketry, nature study, team building.
Sports Aerobics, archery, baseball, basketball, bicycling, boating, canoeing, cheerleading, climbing (wall), diving, equestrian sports, fencing, field hockey, fishing, flag football, golf, gymnastics, horseback riding, in-line skating, kayaking, lacrosse, martial arts, mountain boarding, rappelling, riflery, ropes course, scuba diving, skateboarding, snorkeling, soccer, softball, sports (general), street/roller hockey, swimming, tennis, volleyball, water polo, waterskiing, weight training, wrestling.
Wilderness/Outdoors Backpacking, canoe trips, hiking, mountain biking, mountaineering, rafting, rock climbing, white-water trips.
Trips Day, overnight.
Program Information 4 sessions per year. Session length: 1–8 weeks in June, July, August. Ages: 8–15. 250 participants per session. Day program cost: $126–$142. Boarding program cost: $1000–$6200. Application fee: $50.
Application Deadline Continuous.
Jobs Positions for college students 19 and older.
Summer Contact Ms. Shellie Santay Visinski, Director, main address above. Phone: 570-676-3478. Fax: 570-676-9823. E-mail: poconoridge@aol.com.
Winter Contact M. Santay Visinski, Director, 49 North State Home Road, Monroe Township, New Jersey 08831. Phone: 732-521-3211. Fax: 732-521-8250. E-mail: poconoridge@aol.com.
URL www.poconoridge.com

Camp Saginaw

740 Saginaw Road
Oxford, Pennsylvania 19363-2167

General Information Coed residential traditional camp established in 1930. Accredited by American Camping Association.
Academics Environmental science.
Arts Acting, arts and crafts (general), ceramics, dance, dance (jazz), drawing, film, jewelry making, leather working, musical productions, painting, photography, pottery, radio broadcasting, sculpture, television/video, theater/drama, woodworking.
Special Interest Areas Campcraft, community service, culinary arts, gardening, leadership training, model rocketry, nature study.
Sports Aerobics, archery, baseball, basketball, canoeing, climbing (wall), diving, field hockey, fishing, football, go-carts, golf, gymnastics, horseback riding, in-line skating, kayaking, lacrosse, martial arts, minibikes, rappelling, riflery, ropes course, scuba diving, soccer, softball, sports (general), street/roller hockey, swimming, tennis, volleyball, waterskiing, weight training.
Wilderness/Outdoors Backpacking, canoe trips, hiking, orienteering.
Trips Day, overnight.
Program Information 3 sessions per year. Session length: 14–53 days in June, July, August. Ages: 6–16. 400 participants per session. Boarding program cost: $3600–$6300.
Application Deadline Continuous.
Jobs Positions for college students 18 and older.
Summer Contact Jay Petkov, Director, main address above. Phone: 610-932-8467. Fax: 610-932-3313. E-mail: campsaginaw@comcast.net.
Winter Contact Jay Petkov, Director, 1010 Old Egg Harbor Road, Suite 200, Voorhees, New Jersey 08043-4770. Phone: 856-782-9080. Fax: 856-782-2750. E-mail: campsaginaw@comcast.net.
URL www.campsaginaw.com

Camp Shohola

Camp Shohola
105 Weber Road
Greeley, Pennsylvania 18425

General Information Boys' residential traditional camp established in 1943. Accredited by American Camping Association.
Program Focus Waterfront program, optional trips program.
Academics Computer programming, computers.
Arts Jewelry making, photography, pottery, radio broadcasting, stained glass, television/video, woodworking.
Special Interest Areas Electronics, model rocketry, nature study, wood carving.
Sports Archery, baseball, basketball, bicycling, boating, canoeing, climbing (wall), equestrian sports, fishing, golf, horseback riding, kayaking, lacrosse, martial arts, rappelling, riflery, ropes course, sailing, soccer, softball, sports (general), street/roller hockey, swimming, table tennis/ping-pong, tennis, track and field, volleyball, waterskiing, windsurfing, wrestling.
Wilderness/Outdoors Backpacking, bicycle trips, canoe trips, hiking, mountain biking, rafting, rock climbing, white-water trips, wilderness camping.
Trips Day, overnight.

Camp Shohola (continued)

Program Information 2 sessions per year. Session length: 4–8 weeks in June, July, August. Ages: 8–15. 155 participants per session. Boarding program cost: $3000–$4800.
Application Deadline Continuous.
Jobs Positions for college students 21 and older.
Contact Mr. Duncan Barger, Director, 105 Weber Road, Greeley, Pennsylvania 18425. Phone: 570-685-7186. Fax: 570-685-4563. E-mail: duncan@shohola.com.
URL www.shohola.com

Camp Streamside

Streamside Foundation, Inc./BCM International
Possinger Drive
Stroudsburg, Pennsylvania 18360

General Information Coed residential traditional camp and bible camp established in 1942. Religious affiliation: Christian.
Program Focus Christian camping for inner-city children, youth and families.
Academics Bible study, botany, ecology, environmental science, geology/earth science, history, music, religion, sign language.
Arts Arts and crafts (general), chorus, clowning, creative writing, dance, dance (folk), drawing, jewelry making, leather working, mime, music, music (vocal), origami, puppetry, television/video, theater/drama.
Special Interest Areas Animal care, campcraft, leadership training, nature study, work camp programs.
Sports Aerobics, archery, baseball, basketball, boating, canoeing, cheerleading, cricket, diving, equestrian sports, fishing, football, horseback riding, ropes course, soccer, softball, swimming, volleyball.
Wilderness/Outdoors Backpacking, canoe trips, hiking, mountaineering, orienteering, outdoor camping, survival training, wilderness camping.
Trips Overnight.
Program Information 6–8 sessions per year. Session length: 5–6 days in June, July, August. Ages: 8–16. 100–150 participants per session. Boarding program cost: $50–$300. Financial aid available.
Application Deadline Continuous.
Jobs Positions for high school students 15 and older and college students 17 and older.
Contact Dale L. Schoenwald, Director, RR #3, Box 3307, Possinger Drive, Stroudsburg, Pennsylvania 18360. Phone: 570-629-1902. Fax: 570-629-9650. E-mail: summercamp@streamside.org.
URL www.streamside.org

Camp Susquehannock for Boys

Camp Susquehannock, Inc.
Brackney, Pennsylvania 18812

General Information Boys' residential traditional camp established in 1905. Accredited by American Camping Association. College credit may be earned.
Academics English as a second language, English language/literature, Latin language, biology, mathematics, reading.
Arts Arts and crafts (general), ceramics, leather working, painting, pottery, woodworking.
Special Interest Areas Campcraft, leadership training, nature study, work camp programs.
Sports Archery, baseball, basketball, bicycling, canoeing, climbing (wall), diving, equestrian sports, fishing, football, golf, horseback riding, lacrosse, martial arts, ropes course, sailing, snorkeling, soccer, softball, street/roller hockey, swimming, tennis, volleyball, weight training, windsurfing, wrestling.
Wilderness/Outdoors Canoe trips, mountain biking, orienteering.
Trips Day, overnight, shopping.
Program Information 2–5 sessions per year. Session length: 14–53 days in June, July, August. Ages: 7–16. 125–150 participants per session. Boarding program cost: $1800–$4500. Financial aid available.
Application Deadline Continuous.
Jobs Positions for college students.
Summer Contact Dave Williams, Executive Director, Box 1375, RR #1, Brackney, Pennsylvania 18812. Phone: 570-967-2323. Fax: 570-967-2631. E-mail: info@susquehannock.com.
Winter Contact Dave Williams, Executive Director, PO Box 3, Huntingdon Valley, Pennsylvania 19006. Phone: 215-947-5384. Fax: 215-947-5385. E-mail: davewilliams@susquehannock.com.
URL www.susquehannock.com

Camp Susquehannock for Girls

Camp Susquehannock, Inc.
Lake Choconut
Carmalt Road
Friendsville, Pennsylvania 18818

General Information Girls' residential traditional camp established in 1986. Accredited by American Camping Association.
Program Focus Team and individual sports.
Academics English as a second language, mathematics, reading, study skills.
Arts Arts and crafts (general), ceramics, dance, dance (folk), jewelry making, music (vocal), painting, pottery, woodworking.
Special Interest Areas Animal care, campcraft, leadership training, nature study.
Sports Aerobics, archery, basketball, boating, canoeing, climbing (wall), equestrian sports, field hockey, fishing, gymnastics, horseback riding, lacrosse, ropes course, sailing, soccer, softball, sports (general), swimming, tennis, track and field, volleyball.
Wilderness/Outdoors Canoe trips, orienteering.
Trips Overnight.
Program Information 2 sessions per year. Session length: 20–55 days in June, July, August. Ages: 7–17. 75–85 participants per session. Boarding program cost: $1800–$4500. Financial aid available.
Application Deadline Continuous.
Jobs Positions for high school students 14 and older and college students 18 and older.
Summer Contact Tarryn Larson Rozen, Site Director, PO Box 48, Lake Choconut, Friendsville, Pennsylvania 18818. Phone: 570-553-2343. E-mail: tarryn@susquehannock.com.

Winter Contact Mr. Dave Williams, Executive Director, PO Box 3, Huntingdon Valley, Pennsylvania 19006. Phone: 215-947-5384. Fax: 215-947-5385. E-mail: davewilliams@susquehannock.com.
URL www.susquehannock.com

Camp Tioga

Camp Tioga
Thompson, Pennsylvania 18465

General Information Coed residential traditional camp established in 1998. Accredited by American Camping Association.
Program Focus More than 80 activities to choose from.
Academics Aerospace science, astronomy, computers, ecology, environmental science.
Arts Arts and crafts (general), ceramics, dance, drawing, film, film production, jewelry making, leather working, metalworking, music, musical productions, painting, photography, pottery, puppetry, radio broadcasting, sculpture, television/video, theater/drama, woodworking.
Special Interest Areas Native American culture, animal care, construction, culinary arts, model rocketry, nature study, weight reduction.
Sports Aerobics, archery, baseball, basketball, bicycling, bicycling (BMX), boating, canoeing, cheerleading, climbing (wall), equestrian sports, field hockey, fishing, football, golf, horseback riding, in-line skating, kayaking, lacrosse, martial arts, physical fitness, ropes course, sailing, scuba diving, snorkeling, soccer, softball, street/roller hockey, swimming, tennis, trampolining, volleyball, water polo, weight training, windsurfing.
Wilderness/Outdoors Bicycle trips, hiking, mountain biking, rock climbing, white-water trips.
Trips Day, overnight, shopping.
Program Information 3 sessions per year. Session length: 26–51 days in July, August. Ages: 8–15. 225–250 participants per session. Boarding program cost: $3895–$6495.
Application Deadline Continuous.
Jobs Positions for college students 19 and older.
Summer Contact Mr. Ron Kuznetz, Director/Owner, RD 1, Box 54, Thompson, Pennsylvania 18465. Phone: 570-756-2660. Fax: 516-938-3184. E-mail: info@camptioga.com.
Winter Contact Mr. Ron Kuznetz, Director/Owner, 1191 Old Country Road, Plainview, New York 11803. Phone: 516-938-0894. Fax: 516-938-3184. E-mail: info@camptioga.com.
URL www.camptioga.com

Camp Towanda

Camp Towanda
Camp Towanda Road
Honesdale, Pennsylvania 18431-9798

General Information Coed residential traditional camp established in 1923. Religious affiliation: Jewish. Accredited by American Camping Association. Formal opportunities for the artistically talented. College credit may be earned.
Program Focus Friendship, skill development.
Academics English as a second language, SAT/ACT preparation, art (Advanced Placement), astronomy.
Arts Acting, arts and crafts (general), ceramics, dance, dance (jazz), dance (modern), jewelry making, painting, pottery, radio broadcasting, sculpture, television/video, theater/drama, woodworking.
Special Interest Areas Animal care, campcraft, community service, conservation projects, farming, gardening, leadership training, model rocketry.
Sports Aerobics, archery, baseball, basketball, bicycling, bicycling (BMX), boating, canoeing, cheerleading, climbing (wall), cross-country, field hockey, fishing, football, golf, gymnastics, horseback riding, in-line skating, kayaking, lacrosse, martial arts, rappelling, ropes course, sailing, scuba diving, soccer, softball, street/roller hockey, swimming, tennis, track and field, volleyball, water polo, waterskiing, weight training, windsurfing, wrestling.
Wilderness/Outdoors Backpacking, bicycle trips, canoe trips, hiking, mountain biking, rafting, rock climbing, white-water trips, wilderness camping.
Trips College tours, cultural, day, overnight.
Program Information 1 session per year. Session length: 7 weeks in June, July, August. Ages: 6–17. 400 participants per session. Boarding program cost: $7700.
Application Deadline Continuous.
Jobs Positions for college students 19 and older.
Summer Contact Mr. Mitch Reiter, Director, Camp Towanda Road, RR #1, Box 1585, Honesdale, Pennsylvania 18431-9798. Phone: 570-253-3266. Fax: 570-253-6334. E-mail: staff@camptowanda.com.
Winter Contact Mr. Mitch Reiter, Director, 4 York Court, New City, New York 10956. Phone: 845-639-4582. E-mail: mitch@camptowanda.com.
URL www.camptowanda.com

Camp Watonka

Hawley, Pennsylvania 18428

General Information Boys' residential traditional camp and academic program established in 1963. Accredited by American Camping Association. Formal opportunities for the academically talented.

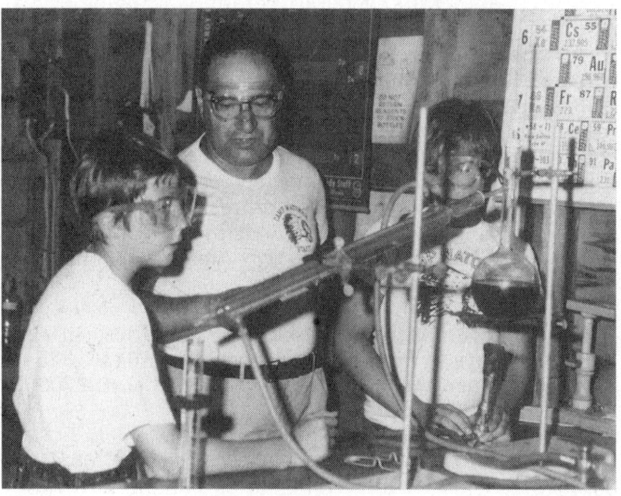

Camp Watonka

Camp Watonka (continued)

Program Focus Science.
Academics Academics (general), astronomy, biology, botany, chemistry, communications, computer programming, computers, ecology, environmental science, geology/earth science, marine studies, meteorology, physics, science (general).
Arts Arts and crafts (general), batiking, drawing, film, leather working, painting, photography, sculpture, television/video, weaving, woodworking.
Special Interest Areas Campcraft, electronics, model rocketry, nature study, robotics.
Sports Archery, baseball, basketball, bicycling, boating, canoeing, climbing (wall), fishing, kayaking, minibikes, rappelling, riflery, ropes course, rowing (crew/sculling), sailing, soccer, softball, street/roller hockey, swimming, tennis, volleyball, windsurfing.
Wilderness/Outdoors Backpacking, canoe trips, hiking, mountain biking, orienteering, rafting, wilderness camping.
Trips Cultural, day, overnight.
Program Information 3 sessions per year. Session length: 4–8 weeks in June, July, August. Ages: 7–15. 130 participants per session. Boarding program cost: $2895–$5195.
Application Deadline Continuous.
Jobs Positions for college students 19 and older.
Contact Mr. Donald P. Wacker, Director, PO Box 127, Hawley, Pennsylvania 18428. Phone: 570-857-1401. E-mail: donwackr@voicenet.com.
URL www.watonka.com

Camp Wayne for Boys

Camp Wayne
Preston Park, Pennsylvania 18455

General Information Boys' residential traditional camp established in 1921. Accredited by American Camping Association.
Arts Arts and crafts (general), ceramics, drawing, painting, photography, pottery, radio broadcasting, woodworking.
Special Interest Areas Model rocketry, nature study.
Sports Archery, baseball, basketball, bicycling, boating, canoeing, climbing (wall), fishing, football, golf, ice hockey, in-line skating, kayaking, lacrosse, martial arts, rappelling, ropes course, sailing, soccer, sports (general), street/roller hockey, swimming, tennis, track and field, volleyball, weight training, windsurfing, wrestling.
Wilderness/Outdoors Canoe trips, hiking, mountain biking, orienteering, rock climbing.
Trips Day, overnight.
Program Information 1 session per year. Session length: 51 days in June, July, August. Ages: 6–16. 325 participants per session. Boarding program cost: $7000.
Application Deadline Continuous.
Jobs Positions for college students 18 and older.
Summer Contact Peter Corpuel, Director, HC 60, Box 30, Preston Park, Pennsylvania 18455. Phone: 570-798-2511. Fax: 570-798-2193. E-mail: info@campwayne.com.
Winter Contact Peter Corpuel, Director, 55 Channel Drive, Port Washington, New York 11050. Phone: 513-883-3067. Fax: 516-883-2985. E-mail: info@campwayne.com.
URL www.campwayne.com

Camp Wayne for Girls

Camp Wayne
Route 247
Preston Park, Pennsylvania 18455

General Information Girls' residential traditional camp established in 1921. Accredited by American Camping Association.
Arts Arts and crafts (general), ceramics, dance, drawing, jewelry making, musical productions, painting, photography, pottery, printmaking, radio broadcasting, sculpture, theater/drama, woodworking.
Special Interest Areas Model rocketry, nature study.
Sports Aerobics, archery, baseball, basketball, bicycling, boating, canoeing, cheerleading, climbing (wall), field hockey, fishing, football, golf, gymnastics, horseback riding, ice hockey, in-line skating, kayaking, lacrosse, martial arts, rappelling, ropes course, sailing, soccer, sports (general), street/roller hockey, swimming, tennis, track and field, volleyball, waterskiing, weight training, windsurfing, wrestling.
Wilderness/Outdoors Bicycle trips, canoe trips, hiking, mountain biking, orienteering, rock climbing.
Trips Day, overnight.
Program Information 1 session per year. Session length: 51 days in June, July, August. Ages: 6–16. 325 participants per session. Boarding program cost: $7400.
Application Deadline Continuous.
Jobs Positions for college students 18 and older.
Summer Contact Mr. Matt Brown, Director, HC 60, Box 27, Preston Park, Pennsylvania 18455. Phone: 570-798-2591. Fax: 570-798-2674. E-mail: info@campwaynegirls.com.
Winter Contact Mr. Matt Brown, Director, 12 Allevard Street, Lido Beach, New York 11561. Phone: 516-889-3217. Fax: 516-897-7339. E-mail: info@campwaynegirls.com.
URL www.campwaynegirls.com

Camp Westmont

Route 370
Poyntelle, Pennsylvania 18454

General Information Coed residential traditional camp established in 1980. Accredited by American Camping Association.
Program Focus Sports instruction and play including all watersports, strong arts and crafts program, nature, and trapeze.
Arts Arts and crafts (general), batiking, ceramics, circus arts, clowning, creative writing, dance, dance (jazz), dance (tap), drawing, fabric arts, jewelry making, juggling, leather working, musical productions, painting, photography, pottery, radio broadcasting, television/video, theater/drama, trapeze arts, weaving, woodworking.

Special Interest Areas Animal care, campcraft, leadership training, model rocketry, nature study.
Sports Aerobics, archery, baseball, basketball, bicycling, boating, canoeing, cheerleading, climbing (tower), climbing (wall), cross-country, diving, fishing, football, golf, gymnastics, horseback riding, in-line skating, kayaking, lacrosse, martial arts, ropes course, sailing, soccer, softball, sports (general), street/roller hockey, swimming, tennis, track and field, trampolining, unicycling, volleyball, water polo, waterskiing, weight training, windsurfing, wrestling.
Wilderness/Outdoors Bicycle trips, canoe trips, hiking, mountain biking, rafting.
Trips Cultural, day, overnight.
Program Information 1 session per year. Session length: 52 days in July, August. Ages: 6–16. 450 participants per session. Boarding program cost: $6500–$6750.
Application Deadline Continuous.
Jobs Positions for college students 18 and older.
Summer Contact Jack Pinsky, Camp Director, PO Box 15, Poyntelle, Pennsylvania 18454. Phone: 570-448-2500. Fax: 570-448-2063. E-mail: westmont4u@aol.com.
Winter Contact Jack Pinsky, Camp Director, 2116 Merrick Avenue, Merrick, New York 11566. Phone: 516-771-3660. Fax: 516-771-2654. E-mail: westmont4u@aol.com.
URL www.campwestmont.com

Carnegie Mellon University Advanced Placement Early Admission

Carnegie Mellon University
5000 Forbes Avenue
Pittsburgh, Pennsylvania 15213-3890

General Information Coed residential and day academic program established in 1974. Formal opportunities for the academically talented. College credit may be earned.
Program Focus Advanced Placement study.
Academics English (Advanced Placement), Spanish language/literature, academics (general), biology (Advanced Placement), chemistry, chemistry (Advanced Placement), computer science (Advanced Placement), economics, engineering, history, history (Advanced Placement), humanities, mathematics (Advanced Placement), philosophy, physics, physics (Advanced Placement), precollege program, social science, writing.
Trips Cultural, day.
Program Information 1 session per year. Session length: 6 weeks in June, July, August. Ages: 16–18. 120–150 participants per session. Day program cost: $2285–$4537. Boarding program cost: $6347. Application fee: $30. Financial aid available.
Application Deadline May 1.
Contact Mr. Joel Ripka, Office of Admission, Pre-College Programs, main address above. Phone: 412-268-2082. Fax: 412-268-7838. E-mail: precollege@andrew.cmu.edu.
URL www.cmu.edu/enrollment/pre-college/
For more information, see page 1054.

Carnegie Mellon University Pre-College Program in the Fine Arts

Carnegie Mellon University
5000 Forbes Avenue
Pittsburgh, Pennsylvania 15213-3890

General Information Coed residential and day arts program established in 1955. Formal opportunities for the artistically talented. College credit may be earned.

Carnegie Mellon University Pre-College Program in the Fine Arts

Program Focus Architecture, arts, design, drama, and music.
Academics Architecture, art (Advanced Placement), music, precollege program.
Arts Arts, dance, dance (jazz), dance (modern), dance (tap), design, drawing, graphic arts, metalworking, music, music (instrumental), music (jazz), music (orchestral), music (vocal), painting, photography, printmaking, sculpture, theater/drama.
Trips Cultural.
Program Information 1 session per year. Session length: 6 weeks in June, July, August. Ages: 16–18. 250–300 participants per session. Day program cost: $3345. Boarding program cost: $5155. Application fee: $30. Financial aid available.
Application Deadline May 1.
Contact Mr. Joel Ripka, Office of Admission, Pre-College Programs, main address above. Phone: 412-268-2082. Fax: 412-268-7838. E-mail: precollege@andrew.cmu.edu.
URL www.cmu.edu/enrollment/pre-college
For more information, see page 1054.

College for Kids

The Pennsylvania State University at Erie, The Behrend College
5091 Station Road
Erie, Pennsylvania 16563

General Information Coed day traditional camp established in 1993.
Program Focus Enrichment opportunities in a diverse group of disciplines.

College for Kids (continued)

Academics Biology, computer programming, computers, ecology, mathematics, science (general).
Arts Acting, arts and crafts (general), drawing, painting, theater/drama.
Special Interest Areas Career exploration, model rocketry, nature study.
Sports Golf, martial arts.
Wilderness/Outdoors Survival training.
Trips College tours.
Program Information 16 sessions per year. Session length: 5 days in June, July, August. Ages: 6–17. 10–16 participants per session. Day program cost: $65–$95.
Application Deadline Continuous.
Contact Ms. Mary Trott, Program Coordinator, Student Affairs, Penn State Erie, 5091 Station Road, Erie, Pennsylvania 16563. Phone: 814-898-6212. Fax: 814-898-6024. E-mail: met7@psu.edu.
URL www.pserie.psu.edu/kids

College Settlement of Philadelphia

600 Witmer Road
Horsham, Pennsylvania 19044

General Information Coed residential traditional camp and outdoor program established in 1922. Accredited by American Camping Association.
Program Focus Nature appreciation and environmental awareness.
Arts Arts and crafts (general), ceramics, creative writing, dance, drawing, music, painting, pottery, weaving.
Special Interest Areas Native American culture, animal care, campcraft, community service, farming, gardening, nature study.
Sports Archery, baseball, basketball, bicycling, boating, canoeing, climbing (wall), fishing, ropes course, soccer, softball, swimming, tennis.
Wilderness/Outdoors Backpacking, bicycle trips, caving, hiking, orienteering, rafting, rock climbing, white-water trips, wilderness camping.
Trips Day, overnight.
Program Information 4 sessions per year. Session length: 2 weeks in June, July, August. Ages: 8–14. 140 participants per session. Boarding program cost: $200–$1000. Application fee: $30. Financial aid available.
Application Deadline Continuous.
Jobs Positions for college students 19 and older.
Contact Marjorie Byers, Executive Assistant, main address above. Phone: 215-542-7974. Fax: 215-542-7457. E-mail: camps@collegesettlement.org.
URL www.collegesettlement.org

Cybercamps–Bryn Mawr College

Cybercamps–Giant Campus, Inc.
Bryn Mawr, Pennsylvania

General Information Coed residential and day academic program established in 1997.
Program Focus High tech computer camps featuring project oriented curriculum in Web design, 3D animation, game design, robotics, digital arts and programming for all ability levels.
Academics Web page design, computer programming, computers.
Arts Animation, creative writing, digital media, graphic arts, photography.
Special Interest Areas Computer game design, computer graphics, robotics, team building.
Sports Frisbee golf, ultimate frisbee.
Program Information 2–9 sessions per year. Session length: 5–30 days in June, July, August. Ages: 7–18. 30–150 participants per session. Day program cost: $589–$799. Boarding program cost: $909–$1059. Financial aid available.
Application Deadline Continuous.
Jobs Positions for high school students 15 and older and college students.
Contact Cybercamps Information Office, 2401 4th Avenue, Suite 1110, Seattle, Washington 98121. Phone: 206-442-4500. Fax: 206-442-4501. E-mail: info@cybercamps.com.
URL www.cybercamps.com

Daniel Fox Youth Scholars Institute

Lebanon Valley College
College Avenue
Annville, Pennsylvania 17003

General Information Coed residential academic program established in 1974. Formal opportunities for the academically talented. Specific services available for the learning disabled and physically challenged.
Academics French (Advanced Placement), Spanish language/literature, biology, chemistry, classical languages/literatures, computer programming, education, environmental science, health sciences, history, mathematics, psychology.
Arts Acting.
Program Information 1 session per year. Session length: 5 days in June. Ages: 14–17. 150–200 participants per session. Boarding program cost: $410. Financial aid available.
Application Deadline March 22.
Summer Contact Ms. Susie Greenawalt, Assistant, Continuing Education Graduate Studies, Lebanon Valley College, College Avenue, Annville, Pennsylvania 17003. Phone: 717-867-6213. E-mail: greenawa@lvc.edu.
Winter Contact Dr. Dale Erskine, Professor of Biology, Biology Department, Lebanon Valley College, Annville, Pennsylvania 17003. Phone: 717-867-6176. E-mail: erskine@lvc.edu.

Dhani Jones Football Camp/Sports International

Sports International, Inc.
East Stroudsburg University
East Stroudsburg, Pennsylvania

General Information Coed residential and day sports camp established in 1994.
Program Focus Football.
Sports Football, weight training.

Program Information 1 session per year. Session length: 5 days in June. Ages: 8–18. 300–450 participants per session. Day program cost: $529. Boarding program cost: $639.
Application Deadline Continuous.
Jobs Positions for college students 18 and older.
Contact Customer Service, 8924 McGaw Court, Columbia, Maryland 21045. Phone: 800-555-0801. Fax: 410-309-9962. E-mail: info@footballcamps.com.
URL www.footballcamps.com

Dickinson College Research and Writing Workshop

Dickinson College Summer Programs
Carlisle, Pennsylvania 17013

General Information Coed residential academic program established in 2002.
Program Focus Research and writing workshop for students undertaking a teacher-guided research project, independent study, senior project, or extended essays.
Academics Academics (general), research skills, writing.
Arts Acting, theater/drama.
Special Interest Areas College planning.
Sports Basketball, canoeing, climbing (wall), fishing, kayaking, racquetball, ropes course, swimming, tennis, weight training.
Wilderness/Outdoors Canoe trips, hiking.
Trips College tours, day, shopping.
Program Information 1 session per year. Session length: 3 weeks in June, July, August. Ages: 16–18. 10–20 participants per session. Boarding program cost: $2925–$3200. Application fee: $35. Financial aid available.
Application Deadline Continuous.
Contact Jennifer Howland, Office of Summer Programs, PO Box 1773, Carlisle, Pennsylvania 17013. Phone: 717-254-8782. Fax: 717-245-1972. E-mail: summer@dickinson.edu.
URL www.dickinson.edu/summer

Dickinson College Young Writer's Workshop

Dickinson College Summer Programs
Carlisle, Pennsylvania 17013

General Information Coed residential academic program established in 2004.
Program Focus Creative writing: fiction and poetry.
Academics English language/literature, writing.
Arts Creative writing.
Program Information 1 session per year. Session length: 1 week in July. Ages: 16–18. 30–50 participants per session. Boarding program cost: $975–$1100. Application fee: $35.
Application Deadline Continuous.
Contact Ms. Jennifer Howland, Office of Summer Programs, PO Box 1773, Carlisle, Pennsylvania 17013. Phone: 717-254-8782. Fax: 717-245-1972. E-mail: summer@dickinson.edu.
URL www.dickinson.edu/summer

Dickinson Summer College Program

Dickinson College Summer Programs
Carlisle, Pennsylvania

General Information Coed residential academic program established in 2001. College credit may be earned.
Academics English as a second language, English language/literature, German language/literature, Jewish studies, SAT/ACT preparation, Spanish language/literature, academics (general), anthropology, astronomy, business, communications, computer science (Advanced Placement), computers, economics, environmental science, government and politics, history, humanities, intercultural studies, journalism, law, mathematics, music, philosophy, precollege program, psychology, religion, science (general), speech/debate, writing.
Arts Acting, photography.
Special Interest Areas College planning, community service, team building.
Sports Canoeing, climbing (wall), fishing, kayaking, ropes course, swimming, tennis, weight training.
Wilderness/Outdoors Canoe trips, hiking.
Trips College tours, cultural, day, overnight, shopping.
Program Information 1 session per year. Session length: 5 weeks in July, August. Ages: 16–18. 30–50 participants per session. Boarding program cost: $4650–$5000. Application fee: $35. Financial aid available.
Application Deadline Continuous.
Jobs Positions for college students.
Contact Ms. Jennifer Howland, Office of Summer Programs, PO Box 1773, Carlisle, Pennsylvania 17013. Phone: 717-254-8782. Fax: 717-245-1972. E-mail: summer@dickinson.edu.
URL www.dickinson.edu/summer

Ensemble Theatre Community School

Player's Lodge, Pennsylvania Avenue
Eagles Mere, Pennsylvania 17731

General Information Coed residential arts program established in 1984. Formal opportunities for the artistically talented. High school or college credit may be earned.
Program Focus Theater, acting, movement, and music.
Arts Acting, clowning, costume design, creative writing, dance, dance (jazz), dance (modern), mime, music, music (instrumental), music (vocal), musical productions, painting, puppetry, set design, theater/drama.
Sports Basketball, bicycling, fencing, swimming, tennis.
Wilderness/Outdoors Hiking.
Trips Cultural, hiking.
Program Information 1 session per year. Session length: 40–42 days in June, July, August. Ages: 14–18. 18–22 participants per session. Boarding program cost: $4000–$4500. Financial aid available.
Application Deadline Continuous.
Jobs Positions for college students 19 and older.
Summer Contact Seth Orbach, Associate Director, PO Box 188, Eagles Mere, Pennsylvania 17731. Phone: 570-525-3043. Fax: 570-525-3548. E-mail: info@etcschool.org.

Ensemble Theatre Community School (continued)
Winter Contact Seth Orbach, Associate Director, 43 Lyman Circle, Shaker Heights, Ohio 44122. Phone: 216-464-1688. E-mail: info@etcschool.org.
URL www.etcschool.org

Special Note
At ETC, students learn the craft and process of acting by balancing intensive class work with practical experience in performance. Located in a beautiful mountain setting, ETC emphasizes cooperation and collaboration in a supportive, noncompetitive environment. The atmosphere encourages self-discovery and trust; the small program size and experienced professional faculty ensure that a student's training is extremely personal. Living as a community presents special challenges to each member of the group, both onstage and off. Students beginning in the theater, as well as those who have more experience, are encouraged to apply. ETC does extraordinary theater with exceptional people.

Haycock Camping Ministries—Adventure Trails

Haycock Camping Ministries
3100 School Road
Kintnersville, Pennsylvania 18930

General Information Boys' residential traditional camp, outdoor program, and bible camp established in 1964. Religious affiliation: Christian non-denominational. Accredited by American Camping Association.
Academics Bible study.
Arts Music.
Special Interest Areas Model rocketry, team building.
Sports Archery, bicycling (BMX), canoeing, climbing (wall), horseback riding, kayaking, riflery, ropes course, sailing, soccer, swimming, volleyball, windsurfing.
Wilderness/Outdoors Backpacking, canoe trips, hiking, outdoor adventure, rafting, rock climbing, white-water trips.
Trips Day, overnight.
Program Information 7 sessions per year. Session length: 6 days in June, July, August. Ages: 13–16. 10–20 participants per session. Boarding program cost: $240–$270. Financial aid available.
Application Deadline Continuous.
Jobs Positions for college students 18 and older.
Contact Chris Hendrickson, Traditional Camp and Family Ministries Director, main address above. Phone: 610-346-7155. Fax: 610-346-8927. E-mail: info@haycock.org.
URL www.haycock.org

Haycock Camping Ministries—Battalion Program

Haycock Camping Ministries
3100 School Road
Kintnersville, Pennsylvania 18930

General Information Boys' residential traditional camp, outdoor program, and bible camp established in 2001. Religious affiliation: Christian non-denominational. Accredited by American Camping Association.
Academics Bible study.
Special Interest Areas Campcraft, model rocketry.
Sports Archery, basketball, canoeing, horseback riding, riflery, ropes course, soccer, swimming, volleyball.
Wilderness/Outdoors Canoe trips, hiking, rock climbing, wilderness camping.
Trips Day.
Program Information 7 sessions per year. Session length: 6 days in June, July, August. Ages: 12–14. 20–30 participants per session. Boarding program cost: $250. Financial aid available.
Application Deadline Continuous.
Jobs Positions for college students 18 and older.
Contact Chris Hendrickson, Traditional Camp and Family Ministries Director, main address above. Phone: 610-346-7155. Fax: 610-346-8927. E-mail: info@haycock.org.
URL www.haycock.org

Haycock Camping Ministries—Stockade Program

Haycock Camping Ministries
3100 School Road
Kintnersville, Pennsylvania 18930

General Information Boys' residential traditional camp, outdoor program, and bible camp established in 1964. Religious affiliation: Christian non-denominational. Accredited by American Camping Association.
Academics Bible study.
Special Interest Areas Campcraft, general camp activities, nature study, wood carving.
Sports Archery, basketball, horseback riding, riflery, ropes course, soccer, swimming, volleyball.
Wilderness/Outdoors Hiking.
Trips Day.
Program Information 7 sessions per year. Session length: 6 days in June, July, August. Ages: 8–10. 20–30 participants per session. Boarding program cost: $240. Financial aid available.
Application Deadline Continuous.
Jobs Positions for college students 18 and older.
Contact Chris Hendrickson, Traditional Camp and Family Ministries Director, main address above. Phone: 610-346-7155. Fax: 610-346-8927. E-mail: info@haycock.org.
URL www.haycock.org

Haycock Camping Ministries–Trailbuilders Program

Haycock Camping Ministries
3100 School Road
Kintnersville, Pennsylvania 18930

General Information Boys' residential traditional camp, outdoor program, and bible camp established in 1995. Religious affiliation: Christian non-denominational. Accredited by American Camping Association.
Academics Bible study.
Special Interest Areas Campcraft, general camp activities, model rocketry, nature study.
Sports Archery, basketball, canoeing, horseback riding, riflery, ropes course, soccer, swimming, volleyball.
Wilderness/Outdoors Hiking, outdoor living skills, wilderness camping.
Trips Day.
Program Information 7 sessions per year. Session length: 6 days in June, July, August. Ages: 10–12. 20–30 participants per session. Boarding program cost: $245. Financial aid available.
Application Deadline Continuous.
Jobs Positions for college students 18 and older.
Contact Chris Hendrickson, Traditional Camp and Family Ministries Director, main address above. Phone: 610-346-7155. Fax: 610-346-8927. E-mail: info@haycock.org.
URL www.haycock.org

High School Scholars (Summer Courses)

The University of Scranton
University of Scranton
Scranton, Pennsylvania 18510

General Information Coed day academic program. College credit may be earned.
Academics English language/literature, academics (general), computers, history, mathematics, philosophy, physics, psychology, science (general), social science, social studies, writing.
Program Information 2 sessions per year. Session length: 16 days in June, July, August. Ages: 16–18. 20–30 participants per session. Day program cost: $300. Application fee: $30–$50. Financial aid available. Open to participants entering grades 11–12 with a minimum B+ grade average.
Application Deadline Continuous.
Contact Holly Waner, Coordinator, High School Scholars, main address above. Phone: 570-941-5919. E-mail: warnerh2@scranton.edu.
URL www.scranton.edu

Hill Top Summer Programs

The Hill Top Preparatory School
737 South Ithan Avenue
Rosemont, Pennsylvania 19010

General Information Coed day traditional camp and academic program established in 1999. Specific services available for the learning disabled. High school credit may be earned.
Program Focus Social and academic development for bright, learning-disabled and AD/HD students.
Academics English language/literature, computers, mathematics, remedial academics.
Arts Arts and crafts (general), ceramics, photography, woodworking.
Special Interest Areas Campcraft.
Sports Basketball, swimming.
Trips Day.
Program Information 1–2 sessions per year. Session length: 2–3 weeks in June, July. Ages: 9–18. 10–30 participants per session. Day program cost: $1850–$2600. Application fee: $35.
Application Deadline Continuous.
Contact Dr. Natan Gottesman, Director, Hill Top Summer Programs, main address above. Phone: 610-527-3230. Fax: 610-527-7683. E-mail: natangottesman@hilltopprep.org.
URL www.hilltopprep.org

iD Tech Camps–Carnegie Mellon University, Pittsburgh, PA

iD Tech Camps
Carnegie Mellon University
Pittsburgh, Pennsylvania 15213

General Information Coed residential and day academic program established in 1999. Accredited by American Camping Association. Formal opportunities for the academically talented and artistically talented.
Program Focus High-tech computer camps for kids and teens; produce digital movies, create video games, design Web pages, learn programming and robotics, and more; one computer per student, small classes, campers complete a project in a creative and fun learning environment.
Academics Web page design, computer programming, computer science (Advanced Placement), computers, music, precollege program.
Arts Animation, cinematography, digital media, drawing, film, film editing, film production, graphic arts, music, television/video.
Special Interest Areas Career exploration, computer graphics, electronics, leadership training, robotics, team building.
Sports Baseball, basketball, soccer, softball, swimming, volleyball.
Trips College tours, cultural, day.
Program Information 5 sessions per year. Session length: 5–7 days in June, July, August. Ages: 7–17. 40–50 participants per session. Day program cost: $639. Boarding program cost: $989. Application fee: $200. Financial aid available.
Application Deadline Continuous.
Jobs Positions for college students 18 and older.

iD Tech Camps–Carnegie Mellon University, Pittsburgh, PA (continued)

Contact Client Service Representatives, 1885 Winchester Boulevard, Suite 201, Campbell, California 95008. Phone: 888-709-TECH. Fax: 408-871-2228. E-mail: requests@internaldrive.com.
URL www.internaldrive.com

For more information, see page 1156.

iD TECH CAMPS–VILLANOVA UNIVERSITY, VILLANOVA, PA

iD Tech Camps
Villanova University
Villanova, Pennsylvania 19085

General Information Coed residential and day academic program established in 1999. Accredited by American Camping Association. Formal opportunities for the academically talented and artistically talented.
Program Focus High-tech computer camps for kids and teens; produce digital movies, create video games, design Web pages, learn programming and robotics, and more; one computer per student, small classes, campers complete a project in a creative and fun learning environment.
Academics Web page design, computer programming, computer science (Advanced Placement), computers, music, precollege program.
Arts Animation, cinematography, digital media, drawing, film, film editing, film production, graphic arts, music, television/video.
Special Interest Areas Career exploration, computer graphics, electronics, leadership training, robotics, team building.
Sports Baseball, basketball, soccer, softball, swimming, volleyball.
Trips College tours, cultural, day.
Program Information 5 sessions per year. Session length: 5–7 days in June, July, August. Ages: 7–17. 40–50 participants per session. Day program cost: $639. Boarding program cost: $989. Application fee: $200. Financial aid available.
Application Deadline Continuous.
Jobs Positions for college students 18 and older.
Contact Client Service Representatives, 1885 Winchester Boulevard, Suite 201, Campbell, California 95008. Phone: 888-709-TECH. Fax: 408-871-2228. E-mail: requests@internaldrive.com.
URL www.internaldrive.com

For more information, see page 1156.

IMACS–FULL DAY SUMMER CAMP–PENNSYLVANIA

Institute for Mathematics & Computer Science (IMACS)
Pennsylvania

General Information Coed day academic program established in 1992. Formal opportunities for the academically talented.
Academics Computer programming, computer science (Advanced Placement), computers, engineering, mathematics.
Special Interest Areas Electronics, robotics.
Program Information 5 sessions per year. Session length: 5 days in January, February, March, April, May, June, July, August, September, October, November, December. Ages: 5–18. 30–50 participants per session. Day program cost: $399–$1224. Supply fee: $50–$200; additional sessions booked at same time $249 plus $50 supply fee.
Application Deadline Continuous.
Jobs Positions for high school students 16 and older and college students 18 and older.
Contact Mr. Terry Kaufman, President, 7435 Northwest 4th Street, Plantation, Florida 33317. Phone: 954-791-2333. Fax: 954-791-0260. E-mail: info@imacs.org.
URL www.imacs.org

IMACS–INDIVIDUAL SUMMER PROGRAMS–PENNSYLVANIA

Institute for Mathematics & Computer Science (IMACS)
Pennsylvania

General Information Coed day academic program established in 1992. Formal opportunities for the academically talented.
Academics Computer programming, computer science (Advanced Placement), computers, engineering, mathematics, mathematics (Advanced Placement).
Special Interest Areas Computer graphics, electronics, robotics.
Program Information 5 sessions per year. Session length: 5 days in January, February, March, April, May, June, July, August, September, October, November, December. Ages: 6–18. Day program cost: $79–$199.
Application Deadline Continuous.
Jobs Positions for high school students 16 and older and college students 18 and older.
Contact Mr. Terry Kaufman, President, 7435 Northwest 4th Street, Plantation, Florida 33317. Phone: 954-791-2333. Fax: 954-791-0260. E-mail: info@imacs.org.
URL www.imacs.org

INDIAN HEAD CAMP

Honesdale, Pennsylvania 18431

General Information Coed residential traditional camp established in 1940. Accredited by American Camping Association.
Academics English language/literature, mathematics.
Arts Acting, arts and crafts (general), ceramics, dance, dance (ballet), dance (jazz), dance (modern), drawing, jewelry making, leather working, painting, photography, pottery, stained glass, television/video, theater/drama, woodworking.
Special Interest Areas Campcraft, community service, leadership training, model rocketry.
Sports Aerobics, archery, baseball, basketball, bicycling, bicycling (BMX), boating, canoeing, climbing (wall), field hockey, fishing, football, golf, gymnastics, in-line skating, kayaking, lacrosse, martial arts, rappelling, ropes course, sailing, snorkeling, soccer, softball,

street/roller hockey, swimming, tennis, track and field, volleyball, water polo, waterskiing, weight training, windsurfing.
Wilderness/Outdoors Backpacking, bicycle trips, canoe trips, caving, hiking, mountain biking, orienteering, rafting, rock climbing, wilderness camping.
Trips Cultural, day, overnight.
Program Information 1 session per year. Session length: 51 days in July, August. Ages: 7–17. 450 participants per session. Boarding program cost: $7950–$8250. Application fee: $250.
Application Deadline Continuous.
Jobs Positions for college students 19 and older.
Summer Contact Joel Rutkowski, Assistant Director, PO Box 2005, Honesdale, Pennsylvania 18431. Phone: 570-224-4111. Fax: 570-224-4067. E-mail: joel@indianhead.com.
Winter Contact Joel Rutkowski, Assistant Director, PO Box 1199, Scarsdale, New York 10583. Phone: 914-345-2155. Fax: 914-345-2479. E-mail: joel@indianhead.com.
URL www.indianhead.com

James Thrash and Hollis Thomas Football Camp/Sports International

Sports International, Inc.
Albright University
Reading, Pennsylvania

General Information Coed residential and day sports camp established in 1995.
Program Focus Football.
Sports Football, weight training.
Program Information 1 session per year. Session length: 5 days in July. Ages: 8–18. 300–450 participants per session. Day program cost: $529. Boarding program cost: $639. Financial aid available.
Application Deadline Continuous.
Jobs Positions for college students 18 and older.
Contact Customer Service, 8924 McGaw Court, Columbia, Maryland 21045. Phone: 800-555-0811. Fax: 410-309-9962. E-mail: info@footballcamps.com.
URL www.footballcamps.com

Joe Krivak Quarterback Camp, Pennsylvania/Sports International

Sports International, Inc.
Slippery Rock University
Slippery Rock, Pennsylvania

General Information Coed residential and day sports camp established in 1983.
Program Focus Quarterback and wide receiver.
Sports Football, weight training.
Program Information 1 session per year. Session length: 5 days in June. Ages: 8–18. 300–450 participants per session. Day program cost: $349. Boarding program cost: $419.
Application Deadline Continuous.
Jobs Positions for college students 18 and older.
Contact Customer Service, 8924 McGaw Court, Columbia, Maryland 21045. Phone: 800-555-0801. Fax: 410-309-9962. E-mail: info@footballcamps.com.
URL www.footballcamps.com

Joe Machnik's No. 1 Academy One and Premier Programs–Aston, Pennsylvania

Joe Machnik's No. 1 Camps
Neumann College
Aston, Pennsylvania

General Information Coed residential and day sports camp.
Program Focus Soccer instruction, physical fitness, testing and speed training. Campers gain exposure to top players and are challenged by intense competition.
Sports Soccer.
Trips Day.
Program Information 1 session per year. Session length: 6 days in July. Ages: 13–17. Day program cost: $699. Boarding program cost: $759. Financial aid available.
Application Deadline Continuous.
Jobs Positions for college students.
Contact Dr. Joseph Machnik, Director, PO Box 389, 916 Palm Boulevard, Isle of Palms, South Carolina 29451. Phone: 800-622-4645. Fax: 843-886-0885. E-mail: info@no1soccercamps.com.
URL www.no1soccercamps.com

Joe Machnik's No. 1 Academy One and Premier Programs–Newtown, Pennsylvania

Joe Machnik's No. 1 Camps
George School
Newtown, Pennsylvania

General Information Coed residential and day sports camp.
Program Focus Soccer instruction, physical fitness, testing and speed training. Campers gain exposure to top players and are challenged by intense competition.
Sports Soccer.
Trips Day.
Program Information 1 session per year. Session length: 6 days in July. Ages: 9–18. Day program cost: $699. Boarding program cost: $759. Financial aid available.
Application Deadline Continuous.
Jobs Positions for college students.
Contact Dr. Joseph Machnik, Director, PO Box 389, 916 Palm Boulevard, Isle of Palms, South Carolina 29451. Phone: 800-622-4645. Fax: 843-886-0885. E-mail: info@no1soccercamps.com.
URL www.no1soccercamps.com

Joe Machnik's No. 1 College Prep Academy–Newtown/Aston, Pennsylvania

Joe Machnik's No. 1 Camps
Pennsylvania

General Information Coed residential and day sports camp.
Program Focus Intense soccer instruction for high school students.
Sports Soccer, swimming.
Trips Day.
Program Information 1 session per year. Session length: 12 days in July. Ages: 13–17. 10–20 participants per session. Day program cost: $1449. Boarding program cost: $1549. Financial aid available.
Application Deadline Continuous.
Jobs Positions for college students 17 and older.
Contact Dr. Joseph Machnik, Director, PO Box 389, 916 Palm Boulevard, Isle of Palms, South Carolina 29451. Phone: 800-622-4645. Fax: 843-886-0885. E-mail: info@no1soccercamps.com.
URL www.no1soccercamps.com

Joe Machnik's No. 1 Mighty Mini, Goalkeeper and Striker Camp–Aston, Pennsylvania

Joe Machnik's No. 1 Camps
Neumann College
Aston, Pennsylvania

General Information Coed residential and day sports camp.
Program Focus Soccer instruction. Goalkeepers and strikers compete against each other daily.
Sports Soccer.
Trips Day.
Program Information 1 session per year. Session length: 6 days in July. Ages: 8–12. 100–150 participants per session. Boarding program cost: $429. Financial aid available.
Application Deadline Continuous.
Jobs Positions for college students.
Contact Dr. Joseph Machnik, Director, PO Box 389, 916 Palm Boulevard, Isle of Palms, South Carolina 29451. Phone: 800-622-4645. Fax: 843-886-0885. E-mail: info@no1soccercamps.com.
URL www.no1soccercamps.com

Joe Machnik's No. 1 Mighty Mini, Goalkeeper and Striker Camp–Newtown, Pennsylvania

Joe Machnik's No. 1 Camps
The George School
Newtown, Pennsylvania

General Information Coed residential and day sports camp established in 1977.
Program Focus Soccer instruction. Goalkeepers and strikers compete against each other daily.
Sports Soccer, swimming.
Program Information 1 session per year. Session length: 6 days in July. Ages: 8–12. 100–175 participants per session. Boarding program cost: $429. Financial aid available.
Application Deadline Continuous.
Jobs Positions for college students 17 and older.
Contact Dr. Joseph Machnik, Director, PO Box 389, 916 Palm Boulevard, Isle of Palms, South Carolina 29451. Phone: 800-622-4645. Fax: 843-886-0885. E-mail: info@no1soccercamps.com.
URL www.no1soccercamps.com

Julian Krinsky Business School at Haverford College

Julian Krinsky Camps and Programs
Haverford College
Haverford, Pennsylvania 19041

General Information Coed residential and day academic program established in 1995. Formal opportunities for the academically talented.
Program Focus American and international world of business.
Academics Advertising, banking/finance, business, communications, computers, economics, government and politics, marketing, mathematics, precollege program, writing.
Special Interest Areas Career exploration, leadership training.
Sports Baseball, basketball, golf, soccer, softball, squash, swimming, tennis, volleyball.
Trips College tours, cultural, day, overnight, shopping.
Program Information 3 sessions per year. Session length: 14–22 days in June, July, August. 75–100 participants per session. Boarding program cost: $2190–$3200. Financial aid available. Open to participants entering grades 9–12.
Application Deadline Continuous.
Jobs Positions for college students 21 and older.
Contact Julian Krinsky, Owner, PO Box 333, Haverford, Pennsylvania 19041-0333. Phone: 800-TRY-JKST. E-mail: info@jkcp.com.
URL www.jkcp.com

For more information, see page 1172.

Julian Krinsky Business School at Wharton (Leadership in the Business World)

Julian Krinsky Camps and Programs
Wharton School of the University of Pennsylvania
Pennsylvania

General Information Coed residential academic program. Formal opportunities for the academically talented.
Academics Advertising, banking/finance, business, communications, computers, economics, government and politics, marketing, mathematics, precollege program, reading, speech/debate, writing.
Special Interest Areas Leadership training.
Sports Golf, swimming, tennis, volleyball.

Trips Cultural, day.
Program Information 1 session per year. Session length: 4 weeks in July, August. Boarding program cost: $4000. Financial aid available. Open to participants entering grade 12.
Application Deadline Continuous.
Contact Julian Krinsky, PO Box 333, Haverford, Pennsylvania 19041-0333. Phone: 800-TRY-JKST. E-mail: info@jkcp.com.
URL www.jkcp.com
For more information, see page 1172.

Julian Krinsky/Canyon Ranch Young Adult Summer Program " for Smarter Minds and Bodies"

Julian Krinsky Camps and Programs
Bryn Mawr College
Bryn Mawr, Pennsylvania

General Information Coed residential and day outdoor program and sports camp established in 2002.

Julian Krinsky/Canyon Ranch Young Adult Summer Program "for Smarter Minds and Bodies."

Program Focus Health and wellness.
Special Interest Areas Health education.
Sports Aerobics, bicycling, climbing (wall), cross-country, golf, gymnastics, in-line skating, martial arts, squash, tennis, weight training.
Wilderness/Outdoors Bicycle trips, hiking, mountain biking.
Trips Cultural, day, shopping.
Program Information 3 sessions per year. Session length: 2 weeks in June, July, August. Ages: 13–17. 50–150 participants per session. Boarding program cost: $2750. Financial aid available.
Application Deadline Continuous.
Jobs Positions for college students 23 and older.
Contact Julian Krinsky, Owner, PO Box 333, Haverford, Pennsylvania 19041. Phone: 610-265-9401. Fax: 610-265-3678. E-mail: info@jkcp.com.
URL www.jkcp.com
For more information, see page 1172.

Julian Krinsky Creative and Performing Arts Camp at The Shipley School/Bryn Mawr

Julian Krinsky Camps and Programs
Bryn Mawr College
Bryn Mawr, Pennsylvania 19010

General Information Coed day arts program established in 1990. Formal opportunities for the artistically talented.
Program Focus Music, dance, theater, fine and folk art, photography, videography, and computers.
Academics Computers.
Arts Arts, arts and crafts (general), ceramics, dance, dance (folk), dance (jazz), dance (modern), dance (tap), drawing, fabric arts, film, jewelry making, music, music (vocal), musical productions, painting, photography, pottery, printmaking, sculpture, theater/drama.
Sports Swimming.
Trips Cultural, day.
Program Information 4 sessions per year. Session length: 10 days in June, July, August. Ages: 5–14. 100–200 participants per session. Day program cost: $720. Financial aid available.
Application Deadline Continuous.
Jobs Positions for college students 20 and older.
Contact Julian Krinsky, Owner, PO Box 333, Haverford, Pennsylvania 19041-0333. Phone: 800-TRY-JKST. Fax: 610-265-3678. E-mail: info@jkcp.com.
URL www.jkcp.com
For more information, see page 1172.

Julian Krinsky Exploring the Majors at the University of Pennsylvania

Julian Krinsky Camps and Programs
University of Pennsylvania
Philadelphia, Pennsylvania

General Information Coed residential academic program. Formal opportunities for the academically talented.
Program Focus College preparation.
Academics American literature, English language/literature, SAT/ACT preparation, academics (general), biology, business, communications, computer programming, computers, economics, engineering, government and politics, health sciences, history, philosophy, psychology, writing.
Sports Golf, tennis.
Trips College tours, cultural, day, shopping.
Program Information 2 sessions per year. Session length: 3 weeks in June, July, August. Ages: 14–17. 100 participants per session. Boarding program cost: $3450. Application fee: $50. Financial aid available.
Application Deadline Continuous.
Jobs Positions for college students 21 and older.
Contact Julian Krinsky, Owner, 610 South Henderson Road, King of Prussia, Pennsylvania 19416. Phone: 610-265-9401. E-mail: julian@jkcp.com.
URL www.jkcp.com
For more information, see page 1172.

Julian Krinsky Golf Camp at Cabrini College

Julian Krinsky Camps and Programs
Cabrini College
Radnor, Pennsylvania

General Information Coed residential and day sports camp.
Program Focus Golf camp.
Special Interest Areas ADL skills.
Sports Golf.
Trips Day, shopping.
Program Information 13 sessions per year. Session length: 5–7 days in June, July, August. Ages: 8+. 150 participants per session. Day program cost: $485. Boarding program cost: $1145. Application fee: $50. Financial aid available.
Application Deadline Continuous.
Jobs Positions for college students 21 and older.
Contact Julian Krinsky, 610 South Hendeson Road, King of Prussia, Pennsylvania 19406. Phone: 610-265-9401. E-mail: info@jkcp.com.
URL www.jkcp.com
For more information, see page 1172.

Julian Krinsky Golf Camp at Haverford College

Julian Krinsky Camps and Programs
Haverford College
Haverford, Pennsylvania

General Information Coed residential and day sports camp.
Program Focus Golf camp.
Sports Golf, tennis.
Trips Day, shopping.
Program Information 13 sessions per year. Session length: 5–7 days in June, July, August. Ages: 8+. 150 participants per session. Day program cost: $485. Boarding program cost: $1145. Application fee: $50. Financial aid available.
Application Deadline Continuous.
Jobs Positions for college students 21 and older.
Contact Julian Krinsky, PO Box 333, Haverford, Pennsylvania 19041-0333. Phone: 800-TRY-JKST. E-mail: info@jkcp.com.
URL www.jkcp.com
For more information, see page 1172.

Julian Krinsky Junior Enrichment Camp at Cabrini College

Julian Krinsky Camps and Programs
Cabrini College
Radnor, Pennsylvania

General Information Coed residential and day academic program and arts program established in 2003. Formal opportunities for the academically talented, artistically talented, and gifted.
Program Focus Enrichment courses and activities in a college setting.
Academics American literature, English as a second language, English language/literature, academics (general), art (Advanced Placement), art history/appreciation, business, communications, computer programming, computers, economics, government and politics, history, humanities, intercultural studies, journalism, music, reading, speech/debate, study skills, writing.
Arts Arts and crafts (general), graphic arts, jewelry making, music, music (ensemble), music (instrumental), music (jazz), music (orchestral), music (vocal), musical productions, painting, photography, pottery, radio broadcasting, sculpture, television/video, theater/drama.
Special Interest Areas Culinary arts, leadership training.
Sports Basketball, fencing, golf, in-line skating, martial arts, scuba diving, soccer, softball, squash, swimming, tennis, volleyball.
Wilderness/Outdoors Hiking.
Trips College tours, cultural, day, shopping.
Program Information 3 sessions per year. Session length: 2–3 weeks in June, July, August. Ages: 10–14. 100–200 participants per session. Boarding program cost: $2300–$3450. Financial aid available.
Application Deadline Continuous.
Contact Julian Krinsky, PO Box 333, Haverford, Pennsylvania 19041-0333. Phone: 800-TRY-JKCP. E-mail: info@jkcp.com.
URL www.jkcp.com
For more information, see page 1172.

Julian Krinsky Senior Enrichment Camp at Haverford College

Julian Krinsky Camps and Programs
Haverford College
Haverford, Pennsylvania 19041

General Information Coed residential and day academic program and arts program established in 1991. Formal opportunities for the academically talented, artistically talented, and gifted.
Program Focus Precollege experience and enrichment courses and activities.
Academics American literature, English as a second language, English language/literature, SAT/ACT preparation, academics (general), anthropology, art (Advanced Placement), art history/appreciation, business, college tours, communications, computer programming, computers, economics, government and politics, history, humanities, intercultural studies, journalism, music, psychology, reading, speech/debate, study skills, writing.
Arts Arts and crafts (general), band, batiking, ceramics, clowning, creative writing, dance, dance (ballet), dance (folk), dance (jazz), dance (modern), dance (tap), drawing, fabric arts, film, graphic arts, jewelry making, music, music (ensemble), music (instrumental), music (jazz), music (orchestral), music (vocal), musical productions, painting, photography, pottery, radio broadcasting, sculpture, television/video, theater/drama.
Special Interest Areas Culinary arts, leadership training.

Sports Basketball, climbing (wall), fencing, field hockey, golf, in-line skating, martial arts, scuba diving, soccer, softball, squash, swimming, tennis, volleyball.
Wilderness/Outdoors Hiking.
Trips College tours, cultural, day, shopping.
Program Information 3 sessions per year. Session length: 2–3 weeks in June, July, August. Ages: 12–17. 125–200 participants per session. Boarding program cost: $2300–$3450. Financial aid available.
Application Deadline Continuous.
Jobs Positions for college students 21 and older.
Contact Julian Krinsky, Owner/Director, PO Box 333, Haverford, Pennsylvania 19041-0333. Phone: 800-TRY-JKST. Fax: 610-265-3678. E-mail: info@jkcp.com.
URL www.jkcp.com
For more information, see page 1172.

Julian Krinsky Super Sports Camp at The Shipley School

Julian Krinsky Camps and Programs
Shipley School
Yarrow Street
Bryn Mawr, Pennsylvania 19010

General Information Coed day sports camp established in 1990.
Program Focus Serious sports taught by educators and professional coaches.
Sports Baseball, basketball, climbing (wall), field hockey, golf, in-line skating, lacrosse, ropes course, skateboarding, soccer, softball, sports (general), squash, street/roller hockey, swimming, tennis, volleyball.
Trips Day.
Program Information 9 sessions per year. Session length: 5 days in June, July, August. Ages: 5–14. 200 participants per session. Day program cost: $360. Financial aid available.
Application Deadline Continuous.
Jobs Positions for high school students 18 and older and college students 20 and older.
Contact Adrian Castelli, Owner, PO Box 333, Haverford, Pennsylvania 19041-0333. Phone: 800-TRY-JKST. Fax: 610-265-3678. E-mail: info@jkcp.com.
URL www.jkcp.com
For more information, see page 1172.

Julian Krinsky Tennis Camp at Cabrini College

Julian Krinsky Camps and Programs
Cabrini College
Radnor, Pennsylvania

General Information Coed residential and day sports camp established in 1977.
Program Focus Tennis, golf, squash and tournament training.
Sports Golf, squash, tennis.
Trips Day, shopping.
Program Information 13 sessions per year. Session length: 5–7 days in June, July, August. Ages: 9–17. 175–200 participants per session. Day program cost: $425. Boarding program cost: $945–$995. Financial aid available.
Application Deadline Continuous.
Jobs Positions for college students 21 and older.
Contact Julian Krinsky, Owner/Director, 610 South Henderson Road, King of Prussia, Pennsylvania 19406. Phone: 610-265-9401. E-mail: info@jkcp.com.
URL www.jkcp.com
For more information, see page 1172.

Julian Krinsky Tennis Camp at Haverford College

Julian Krinsky Camps and Programs
Haverford College
Haverford, Pennsylvania 19041

General Information Coed residential and day sports camp established in 1977.
Program Focus Tennis, golf, squash, and tournament training.
Sports Basketball, golf, squash, swimming, tennis.
Trips Day, shopping.
Program Information 13 sessions per year. Session length: 5–7 days in June, July, August. Ages: 10–17. 175–200 participants per session. Day program cost: $425. Boarding program cost: $945–$995. Financial aid available.
Application Deadline Continuous.
Jobs Positions for college students 20 and older.
Contact Julian Krinsky, Owner/Director, PO Box 333, Haverford, Pennsylvania 19041-0333. Phone: 800-TRY-JKST. Fax: 610-265-3678. E-mail: info@jkcp.com.
URL www.jkcp.com
For more information, see page 1172.

Julian Krinsky Yesh Shabbat Summer Camp

Julian Krinsky Camps and Programs
Arcadia University
Glenside, Pennsylvania

General Information Coed residential and day academic program, arts program, and sports camp established in 2002. Religious affiliation: Jewish. Formal opportunities for the academically talented and artistically talented.
Program Focus Basketball, tennis, golf, arts and academics.
Academics Jewish studies.
Arts Arts and crafts (general), ceramics, creative writing, dance, dance (modern), drawing, music, musical productions, painting.
Special Interest Areas Leadership training.
Sports Basketball, golf, swimming, tennis.
Trips Cultural, day, shopping.
Program Information 3 sessions per year. Session length: 2–3 weeks in June, July, August. Ages: 10–17. 50–200 participants per session. Boarding program cost: $1755–$2970. Financial aid available.
Application Deadline Continuous.
Jobs Positions for college students 21 and older.

Julian Krinsky Yesh Shabbat Summer Camp (continued)

Contact Steven Bernstein, Director, PO Box 333, Haverford, Pennsylvania 19041. Phone: 610-265-9401. Fax: 610-265-3678. E-mail: info@jkcp.com.
URL www.jkcp.com
For more information, see page 1172.

Jumonville Adventure Camps

Camping and Retreat Ministries of Western Pennsylvania Conference of the United Methodist Church
887 Jumonville Road
Hopwood, Pennsylvania 15445

General Information Coed residential outdoor program, bible camp, and adventure program established in 1941. Religious affiliation: United Methodist.
Academics Bible study.
Sports Climbing (wall), mountain boarding, rappelling, ropes course.
Wilderness/Outdoors Bicycle trips, canoe trips, caving, hiking, mountain biking, outdoor adventure, rock climbing, white-water trips.
Trips Day.
Program Information 17 sessions per year. Session length: 3–7 days in June, July, August. Ages: 8–17. 18–20 participants per session. Boarding program cost: $154–$497. Financial aid available.
Application Deadline Continuous.
Jobs Positions for high school students 16 and older and college students 16 and older.
Contact Jane Fiedler, Camp Registrar, PO Box 5002, Cranberry Township, Pennsylvania 16066. Phone: 800-886-3382. Fax: 724-776-1355. E-mail: umcamp@umchurch.org.
URL www.jumonville.org

Jumonville Baseball/Softball Camp

Camping and Retreat Ministries of Western Pennsylvania Conference of the United Methodist Church
887 Jumonville Road
Hopwood, Pennsylvania 15445

General Information Coed residential sports camp and bible camp established in 1941. Religious affiliation: United Methodist.
Program Focus Baseball/softball skills improvement and daily games.
Academics Bible study.
Sports Baseball, softball.
Trips Day.
Program Information 1 session per year. Session length: 1 week in July. Ages: 13–17. 18–38 participants per session. Boarding program cost: $337. Financial aid available.
Application Deadline Continuous.
Jobs Positions for high school students 16 and older and college students 16 and older.
Contact Jane Fiedler, Camp Registrar, PO Box 5002, Cranberry Township, Pennsylvania 16066. Phone: 800-886-3382. Fax: 724-776-1355. E-mail: umcamp@umchurch.org.
URL www.jumonville.org

Jumonville Basketball Camp

Camping and Retreat Ministries of Western Pennsylvania Conference of the United Methodist Church
887 Jumonville Road
Hopwood, Pennsylvania 15445

General Information Coed residential sports camp and bible camp established in 1941. Religious affiliation: United Methodist.
Program Focus Improve basketball skills and game play.
Academics Bible study.
Sports Basketball.
Trips Day.
Program Information 1 session per year. Session length: 1 week in July. Ages: 13–17. 18–20 participants per session. Boarding program cost: $337. Financial aid available.
Application Deadline Continuous.
Jobs Positions for high school students 16 and older and college students 16 and older.
Contact Jane Fiedler, Camp Registrar, PO Box 5002, Cranberry Township, Pennsylvania 16066. Phone: 800-886-3382. Fax: 724-776-1355. E-mail: umcamp@umchurch.org.
URL www.jumonville.org

Jumonville Creative and Performing Arts Camps

Camping and Retreat Ministries of Western Pennsylvania Conference of the United Methodist Church
887 Jumonville Road
Hopwood, Pennsylvania 15445

General Information Coed residential family program, arts program, and bible camp established in 1941. Religious affiliation: United Methodist.
Program Focus Choose from arts and crafts, choir, drama, dance, or clowning.
Academics Bible study.
Arts Arts, arts and crafts (general), clowning, dance, leather working, metalworking, music, music (vocal), musical productions, stained glass, theater/drama, weaving.
Trips Day.
Program Information 3–4 sessions per year. Session length: 1 week in June, July. Ages: 5+. 18–120 participants per session. Boarding program cost: $60–$316. Financial aid available.
Application Deadline Continuous.
Jobs Positions for high school students 16 and older and college students 16 and older.

Contact Jane Fiedler, Camp Registrar, PO Box 5002, Cranberry Township, Pennsylvania 16066. Phone: 800-886-3382. Fax: 724-776-1355. E-mail: umcamp@umchurch.org.
URL www.jumonville.org

JUMONVILLE DISCOVERY CAMP

Camping and Retreat Ministries of Western Pennsylvania Conference of the United Methodist Church
887 Jumonville Road
Hopwood, Pennsylvania 15445

General Information Coed residential bible camp and special needs program established in 1941. Religious affiliation: United Methodist. Specific services available for the mentally challenged.
Program Focus Mentally handicapped persons.
Academics Bible study.
Arts Arts and crafts (general).
Sports Swimming.
Trips Day.
Program Information 1–2 sessions per year. Session length: 1 week in June, July. Ages: 9+. 18–40 participants per session. Boarding program cost: $325–$379. Financial aid available.
Application Deadline Continuous.
Jobs Positions for high school students 16 and older and college students 16 and older.
Contact Jane Fiedler, Camp Registrar, PO Box 5002, Cranberry Township, Pennsylvania 16066. Phone: 800-886-3382. E-mail: umcamp@umchurch.org.
URL www.jumonville.org

JUMONVILLE GOLF CAMP

Camping and Retreat Ministries of Western Pennsylvania Conference of the United Methodist Church
887 Jumonville Road
Hopwood, Pennsylvania 15445

General Information Coed residential sports camp and bible camp established in 1941. Religious affiliation: United Methodist.
Program Focus Learn or improve skills in golf.
Academics Bible study.
Sports Golf.
Trips Day.
Program Information 1–2 sessions per year. Session length: 5–7 days in June. Ages: 13+. 14–20 participants per session. Boarding program cost: $366–$441. Financial aid available.
Application Deadline Continuous.
Jobs Positions for high school students 16 and older and college students 16 and older.
Contact Jane Fiedler, Camp Registrar, PO Box 5002, Cranberry Township, Pennsylvania 16066. Phone: 800-866-3382. Fax: 724-766-1355. E-mail: umcamp@umchurch.org.
URL www.jumonville.org

JUMONVILLE SAMPLER CAMPS

Camping and Retreat Ministries of Western Pennsylvania Conference of the United Methodist Church
887 Jumonville Road
Hopwood, Pennsylvania 15445

General Information Coed residential traditional camp and bible camp established in 1941. Religious affiliation: United Methodist.
Academics Bible study.
Arts Arts and crafts (general), sing-a-longs.
Sports Archery, climbing (wall), mountain boarding, rappelling, ropes course, sports (general), swimming, tennis, volleyball.
Wilderness/Outdoors Camp fires, hiking.
Trips Day.
Program Information 6–8 sessions per year. Session length: 3–7 days in June, July, August. Ages: 8–17. 18–40 participants per session. Boarding program cost: $163–$317. Financial aid available.
Application Deadline Continuous.
Jobs Positions for high school students 16 and older and college students 16 and older.
Contact Jane Fiedler, Camp Registrar, PO Box 5002, Cranberry Township, Pennsylvania 16066. Phone: 800-886-3382. Fax: 724-766-1355. E-mail: umcamp@umchurch.org.
URL www.jumonville.org

JUMONVILLE SOCCER CAMP

Camping and Retreat Ministries of Western Pennsylvania Conference of the United Methodist Church
887 Jumonville Road
Hopwood, Pennsylvania 15445

General Information Coed residential sports camp and bible camp established in 1941. Religious affiliation: United Methodist.
Program Focus Soccer for beginners.
Academics Bible study.
Sports Soccer.
Trips Day.
Program Information 2 sessions per year. Session length: 6 days in June, July. Ages: 10–17. 14–18 participants per session. Boarding program cost: $296–$337. Financial aid available.
Application Deadline Continuous.
Jobs Positions for high school students 16 and older and college students 16 and older.
Contact Jane Fiedler, Camp Registrar, PO Box 5002, Cranberry Township, Pennsylvania 16066. Phone: 800-886-3382. Fax: 724-776-1355. E-mail: umcamp@umchurch.org.
URL www.jumonville.org

Jumonville Spirit and Sport Spectacular–Soccer Camp

Camping and Retreat Ministries of Western Pennsylvania Conference of the United Methodist Church
887 Jumonville Road
Hopwood, Pennsylvania 15445

General Information Coed residential sports camp and bible camp established in 1941. Religious affiliation: United Methodist.
Program Focus Soccer fundamentals with emphasis on position playing and strategy.
Academics Bible study.
Sports Soccer.
Trips Day.
Program Information 1 session per year. Session length: 1 week in July. Ages: 13–17. 10–18 participants per session. Boarding program cost: $320. Financial aid available.
Application Deadline Continuous.
Jobs Positions for high school students 16 and older and college students 16 and older.
Contact Jane Fiedler, Camp Registrar, PO Box 5002, Cranberry Township, Pennsylvania 16066. Phone: 800-886-3382. Fax: 724-775-1355. E-mail: umcamp@umchurch.org.
URL www.jumonville.org

Jumonville Spirit and Sport Spectacular–Swim Camp

Camping and Retreat Ministries of Western Pennsylvania Conference of the United Methodist Church
887 Jumonville Road
Hopwood, Pennsylvania 15445

General Information Coed residential sports camp and bible camp established in 1941. Religious affiliation: United Methodist.
Program Focus Competitive and regular swimming, instruction available.
Academics Bible study.
Sports Swimming.
Trips Day.
Program Information 1 session per year. Session length: 1 week in July. Ages: 13–17. 10–18 participants per session. Boarding program cost: $320. Financial aid available.
Application Deadline Continuous.
Jobs Positions for high school students 16 and older and college students 16 and older.
Contact Jane Fiedler, Camp Registrar, PO Box 5002, Cranberry Township, Pennsylvania 16066. Phone: 800-886-3382. Fax: 724-776-1355. E-mail: umcamp@umchurch.org.
URL www.jumonville.org

Jumonville Spirit and Sport Spectacular–Tennis Camp

Camping and Retreat Ministries of Western Pennsylvania Conference of the United Methodist Church
887 Jumonville Road
Hopwood, Pennsylvania 15445

General Information Coed residential sports camp and bible camp established in 1941. Religious affiliation: United Methodist.
Program Focus Tennis for all skill levels.
Academics Bible study.
Sports Tennis.
Trips Day.
Program Information 1 session per year. Session length: 1 week in July. Ages: 13–17. 10–18 participants per session. Boarding program cost: $320. Financial aid available.
Application Deadline Continuous.
Jobs Positions for high school students 16 and older and college students 16 and older.
Contact Jane Fiedler, Camp Registrar, PO Box 5002, Cranberry Township, Pennsylvania 16066. Phone: 800-886-3382. Fax: 724-775-1355. E-mail: umcamp@umchurch.org.
URL www.jumonville.org

Jumonville Spirit and Sport Spectacular–Volleyball Camp

Camping and Retreat Ministries of Western Pennsylvania Conference of the United Methodist Church
887 Jumonville Road
Hopwood, Pennsylvania 15445

General Information Coed residential sports camp and bible camp established in 1941. Religious affiliation: United Methodist.
Program Focus Volleyball.
Academics Bible study.
Sports Volleyball.
Trips Day.
Program Information 1 session per year. Session length: 1 week in July. Ages: 13–17. 10–18 participants per session. Boarding program cost: $320. Financial aid available.
Application Deadline Continuous.
Jobs Positions for high school students 16 and older and college students 16 and older.
Contact Jane Fiedler, Camp Registrar, PO Box 5002, Cranberry Township, Pennsylvania 16066. Phone: 800-886-3382. Fax: 724-776-1355. E-mail: umcamp@umchurch.org.
URL www.jumonville.org

Jumonville Sports Camp

Camping and Retreat Ministries of Western Pennsylvania Conference of the United Methodist Church
887 Jumonville Road
Hopwood, Pennsylvania 15445

General Information Coed residential sports camp and bible camp established in 1941. Religious affiliation: United Methodist.
Program Focus Develop fundamental skills and improve in your favorite sport.
Academics Bible study.
Sports Archery, baseball, basketball, field hockey, flag football, ropes course, soccer, softball, sports (general), swimming, tennis, volleyball.
Trips Day.
Program Information 3 sessions per year. Session length: 1 week in June, July. Ages: 9–17. Boarding program cost: $291. Financial aid available.
Application Deadline Continuous.
Jobs Positions for high school students 16 and older and college students 16 and older.
Contact Jane Fiedler, Camp Registrar, PO Box 5002, Cranberry Township, Pennsylvania 16066. Phone: 800-886-3382. Fax: 724-776-1355. E-mail: umcamp@umchurch.org.
URL www.jumonville.org

Jumonville Youth Mission Work Camp

Camping and Retreat Ministries of Western Pennsylvania Conference of the United Methodist Church
887 Jumonville Road
Hopwood, Pennsylvania 15445

General Information Coed residential community service program and bible camp established in 1941. Religious affiliation: United Methodist.
Academics Bible study.
Special Interest Areas Community service, work camp programs.
Program Information 1 session per year. Session length: 1 week in August. Ages: 14–17. 14–24 participants per session. Boarding program cost: $217. Financial aid available.
Application Deadline Continuous.
Jobs Positions for high school students 16 and older and college students 16 and older.
Contact Jane Fiedler, Camp Registrar, PO Box 5002, Cranberry Township, Pennsylvania 16066. Phone: 800-886-3382. Fax: 724-776-1355. E-mail: umcamp@umchurch.org.
URL www.jumonville.org

Kiski Summer Camp–Junior Division-Boys Grades 5-8

The Kiski School
1888 Brett Lane
Saltsburg, Pennsylvania 15681

General Information Boys' residential and day traditional camp and academic program. Formal opportunities for the academically talented.
Program Focus Integrated subjects driven thematically by famous people from all walks of life.
Academics American literature, English language/literature, architecture, biology, botany, communications, computer programming, computers, ecology, environmental science, geography, geology/earth science, government and politics, history, intercultural studies, mathematics, reading, science (general), social studies, study skills, writing.
Arts Arts and crafts (general), creative writing, dance, drawing, theater/drama.
Special Interest Areas Community service, gardening, model rocketry.
Sports Baseball, basketball, bicycling (BMX), canoeing, climbing (wall), cross-country, diving, fishing, football, golf, kayaking, lacrosse, soccer, softball, swimming, tennis, track and field, volleyball, weight training, wrestling.
Wilderness/Outdoors Backpacking, canoe trips, hiking, mountain biking, orienteering, rafting, white-water trips, wilderness camping.
Trips Cultural, day, overnight, shopping.
Program Information 2 sessions per year. Session length: 2 weeks in June, July. Ages: 10–13. 18–40 participants per session. Day program cost: $600. Boarding program cost: $1000.
Application Deadline Continuous.
Jobs Positions for high school students 16 and older and college students 18 and older.
Contact Mr. David Melgard, Director, main address above. Phone: 724-639-3586. Fax: 724-639-8596. E-mail: david.melgard@kiski.org.
URL www.kiski.org

Kiski Summer Camp–Senior Division-Boys Grades 9-12

The Kiski School
1888 Brett Lane
Saltsburg, Pennsylvania 15681

General Information Boys' residential and day traditional camp and academic program. Formal opportunities for the academically talented.
Program Focus Integrated subjects driven thematically by famous people from all walks of life.
Academics American literature, English language/literature, SAT/ACT preparation, architecture, astronomy, biology, botany, communications, computer programming, computers, ecology, environmental science, geography, geology/earth science, government and politics, history, intercultural studies, mathematics, reading, science (general), social studies, study skills, technology, writing.

Kiski Summer Camp–Senior Division-Boys Grades 9-12 (continued)

Arts Arts and crafts (general), creative writing, dance, drawing, theater/drama, woodworking.
Special Interest Areas Community service, gardening, model rocketry.
Sports Baseball, basketball, bicycling (BMX), canoeing, climbing (wall), cross-country, diving, fishing, football, golf, kayaking, lacrosse, soccer, softball, swimming, tennis, track and field, volleyball, weight training, wrestling.
Wilderness/Outdoors Backpacking, canoe trips, hiking, mountain biking, orienteering, rafting, white-water trips, wilderness camping.
Trips Cultural, day, overnight, shopping.
Program Information 2 sessions per year. Session length: 2 weeks in June, July. Ages: 14–18. 18–40 participants per session. Day program cost: $600. Boarding program cost: $1000.
Application Deadline Continuous.
Jobs Positions for high school students 16 and older and college students 18 and older.
Contact Mr. John Lombardo, Director, main address above. Phone: 724-639-3586. Fax: 724-639-8596. E-mail: john.lombardo@kiski.org.
URL www.kiski.org

Kiski Summer Camp–Senior Division-Girls Grades 9-12

The Kiski School
1888 Brett Lane
Saltsburg, Pennsylvania 15681

General Information Girls' day traditional camp and academic program. Formal opportunities for the academically talented.
Program Focus Integrated subjects driven thematically by famous people from all walks of life, girls day camp division with co-ed activities and classes.
Academics American literature, English language/literature, SAT/ACT preparation, architecture, astronomy, biology, botany, communications, computer programming, computers, ecology, environmental science, geography, geology/earth science, government and politics, history, intercultural studies, mathematics, reading, science (general), social studies, study skills, technology, writing.
Arts Arts and crafts (general), creative writing, dance, drawing, theater/drama, woodworking.
Special Interest Areas Community service, gardening, model rocketry.
Sports Baseball, basketball, bicycling (BMX), canoeing, climbing (wall), cross-country, diving, fishing, football, golf, kayaking, lacrosse, soccer, softball, swimming, tennis, track and field, volleyball, weight training, wrestling.
Wilderness/Outdoors Backpacking, canoe trips, hiking, mountain biking, orienteering, rafting, white-water trips, wilderness camping.
Trips Cultural, day, overnight, shopping.
Program Information 2 sessions per year. Session length: 2 weeks in June, July. Ages: 14–18. 18–40 participants per session. Day program cost: $600.
Application Deadline Continuous.
Jobs Positions for high school students 16 and older and college students 18 and older.
Contact Mr. John Lombardo, Director, main address above. Phone: 724-639-3586. Fax: 724-639-8596. E-mail: john.lombardo@kiski.org.
URL www.kiski.org

Lebanon Valley College Summer Music Camp

Lebanon Valley College
101 North College Avenue
Annville, Pennsylvania 17003

General Information Coed residential and day arts program established in 1987. Formal opportunities for the academically talented and artistically talented.
Program Focus Music.
Academics Music.
Arts Band, music, music (chamber), music (classical), music (ensemble), music (instrumental), music (jazz), music (orchestral), music technology/record production.
Sports Basketball, racquetball, softball, swimming, tennis, volleyball.
Trips College tours, day.
Program Information 1 session per year. Session length: 1 week in July. Ages: 13–18. 90–110 participants per session. Day program cost: $345. Boarding program cost: $495.
Application Deadline June 15.
Jobs Positions for college students 19 and older.
Contact Dr. Robert H. Hearson, Director, Summer Music Camp, main address above. Phone: 717-867-6289. Fax: 717-867-6390. E-mail: hearson@acad.lvc.edu.
URL www.lvc.edu/music-camp

Ligonier Camp

Ligonier Camp and Conference Center
188 Macartney Lane
Ligonier, Pennsylvania 15658

General Information Coed residential traditional camp, outdoor program, and bible camp established in 1914. Religious affiliation: Presbyterian. Accredited by American Camping Association.
Program Focus Traditional Christian camp program with emphasis on adventure education.
Academics Bible study, environmental science.
Arts Arts and crafts (general), jewelry making, painting, theater/drama.
Special Interest Areas Nature study, team building.
Sports Archery, basketball, bicycling, canoeing, climbing (tower), climbing (wall), fishing, lacrosse, riflery, ropes course, soccer, sports (general), swimming, tennis, ultimate frisbee, volleyball.
Wilderness/Outdoors Backpacking, bicycle trips, caving, hiking, mountain biking, rafting, rock climbing, white-water trips, wilderness camping, wilderness/outdoors (general), zip line.
Trips Day, overnight.

Program Information 6–7 sessions per year. Session length: 6–13 days in June, July, August. Ages: 8–17. 200–216 participants per session. Boarding program cost: $280–$600. Financial aid available.
Application Deadline Continuous.
Jobs Positions for high school students 16 and older and college students 19 and older.
Contact Sal Hanna, Summer Camp Director, main address above. Phone: 724-238-6428. Fax: 724-238-6971. E-mail: shanna@ligoniercamp.org.
URL www.ligoniercamp.org

Longacre Expeditions, Blue Ridge

Longacre Expeditions
Pennsylvania

General Information Coed travel outdoor program, wilderness program, and adventure program established in 1981. Accredited by American Camping Association.
Program Focus Effective communication skills, responsibility, confidence building.
Sports Bicycling, climbing (wall), kayaking.
Wilderness/Outdoors Bicycle trips, hiking, rafting, rock climbing, wilderness camping.
Program Information 2 sessions per year. Session length: 20–24 days in June, July, August. Ages: 12–15. 10–16 participants per session. Cost: $3150.
Application Deadline Continuous.
Jobs Positions for college students 21 and older.
Contact Meredith Schuler, Director, 4030 Middle Ridge Road, Newport, Pennsylvania 17074. Phone: 717-567-6790. Fax: 717-567-3955. E-mail: longacre@longacreexpeditions.com.
URL www.longacreexpeditions.com

For more information, see page 1200.

Longacre Expeditions, Laurel Highlands

Longacre Expeditions
Pennsylvania

General Information Coed travel outdoor program, wilderness program, and adventure program established in 1981. Accredited by American Camping Association.
Program Focus Effective communication skills, responsibility, confidence building.
Sports Kayaking.
Wilderness/Outdoors Backpacking, hiking, rafting, rock climbing, white-water trips, wilderness camping.
Program Information 3 sessions per year. Session length: 15 days in July, August. Ages: 12–15. 10–16 participants per session. Cost: $2295.
Application Deadline Continuous.
Jobs Positions for college students 21 and older.
Contact Meredith Schuler, Director, 4030 Middle Ridge Road, Newport, Pennsylvania 17074. Phone: 717-567-6790. Fax: 717-567-3955. E-mail: longacre@longacreexpeditions.com.
URL www.longacreexpeditions.com

For more information, see page 1200.

Longacre Expeditions, Laurel Highlands

Longacre Leadership Program

Longacre Farm
Newport, Pennsylvania 17074

General Information Coed residential outdoor program and community service program established in 1975.
Program Focus Experiential education including construction, outdoor adventure, community service, horseback riding, and farming.
Arts Arts and crafts (general), batiking, carpentry, ceramics, creative writing, dance, drawing, fabric arts, jewelry making, music, painting, pottery, theater/drama, woodworking.
Special Interest Areas Animal care, community service, conservation projects, construction, culinary arts, farming, field trips (arts and culture), gardening, leadership training, nature study, team building, work camp programs.
Sports Basketball, bicycling, canoeing, climbing (wall), fishing, horseback riding, lacrosse, ropes course, soccer, softball, swimming, tennis, volleyball.
Wilderness/Outdoors Backpacking, bicycle trips, caving, hiking, mountain biking, rafting, rock climbing, white-water trips, wilderness camping.
Trips Cultural, day, overnight.
Program Information 2 sessions per year. Session length: 4–6 weeks in June, July, August. Ages: 12–18. 72 participants per session. Boarding program cost: $3670–$5090. Financial aid available.
Application Deadline Continuous.
Jobs Positions for college students 21 and older.
Contact Susan Smith, Director, 4028 Middle Ridge Road, Newport, Pennsylvania 17074. Phone: 717-567-3349. Fax: 717-567-3955. E-mail: connect@longacre.com.
URL www.longacre.com

Mercersburg Academy Blue Storm Boys Basketball School

Mercersburg Academy Summer and Extended Programs
300 East Seminary Street
Mercersburg, Pennsylvania 17236

General Information Boys' residential and day sports camp established in 1996.
Program Focus Basketball.
Sports Aerobics, basketball, swimming, weight training.
Trips Day.
Program Information 1–2 sessions per year. Session length: 4–5 days in June. Ages: 10–18. 40–75 participants per session. Day program cost: $240. Boarding program cost: $315. Financial aid available.
Application Deadline Continuous.
Jobs Positions for high school students 17 and older and college students 18 and older.
Contact Mr. Rick Hendrickson, Director of Summer and Extended Programs, main address above. Phone: 717-328-6225. Fax: 717-328-9072. E-mail: summerprograms@mercersburg.edu.
URL www.mercersburg.edu

For more information, see page 1210.

Mercersburg Academy Blue Storm Football Camp

Mercersburg Academy Summer and Extended Programs
300 East Seminary Street
Mercersburg, Pennsylvania 17236

General Information Boys' day sports camp established in 2004.
Program Focus Football fundamentals.
Sports Football.
Program Information 1 session per year. Session length: 5 days in July. Day program cost: $100.
Application Deadline Continuous.
Contact Mr. Rick Hendrickson, Director of Summer and Extended Programs, main address above. Phone: 717-328-6225. Fax: 717-328-9072. E-mail: summerprograms@mercersburg.edu.
URL www.mercersburg.edu

For more information, see page 1210.

Mercersburg Academy Junior Adventure Camp

Mercersburg Academy Summer and Extended Programs
300 East Seminary Street
Mercersburg, Pennsylvania 17236

General Information Coed residential traditional camp established in 2003.
Program Focus Enrichment, outdoors.
Academics Computers, ecology, environmental science, science (general), writing.
Arts Arts and crafts (general), creative writing, fabric arts, puppetry.
Special Interest Areas Culinary arts.
Sports Aerobics, canoeing, frisbee golf, kickball, swimming.
Wilderness/Outdoors Canoe trips, hiking.
Trips Cultural, day.
Program Information 1–2 sessions per year. Session length: 6 days in July, August. Ages: 7–8. 30–40 participants per session. Boarding program cost: $650.
Application Deadline Continuous.
Jobs Positions for college students 18 and older.
Contact Mr. Rick Hendrickson, Director of Summer and Extended Programs, main address above. Phone: 717-328-6225. Fax: 717-328-9072. E-mail: summerprograms@mercersburg.edu.
URL www.mercersburg.edu

For more information, see page 1210.

Mercersburg Academy Young Writer's Camp

Mercersburg Academy Summer and Extended Programs
300 East Seminary Street
Mercersburg, Pennsylvania 17236

General Information Coed residential academic program and outdoor program established in 2003. Formal opportunities for the academically talented.
Academics American literature, English language/literature, area studies, writing.
Arts Creative writing.
Special Interest Areas Nature study.
Sports Bicycling.
Wilderness/Outdoors Canoe trips, hiking, mountain biking, orienteering, wilderness camping.
Trips Cultural, day, overnight.
Program Information 1 session per year. Session length: 2 weeks in July. Ages: 12–16. 20–40 participants per session. Day program cost: $1000. Boarding program cost: $1400. Financial aid available.
Application Deadline Continuous.
Jobs Positions for college students 18 and older.
Contact Mr. Rick Hendrickson, Director of Summer and Extended Programs, main address above. Phone: 717-328-6225. Fax: 717-328-9072. E-mail: summerprograms@mercersburg.edu.
URL www.mercersburg.edu

For more information, see page 1210.

Mercersburg Adventure Camp

Mercersburg Academy Summer and Extended Programs
300 East Seminary Street
Mercersburg, Pennsylvania 17236

General Information Coed residential traditional camp established in 1999.
Program Focus Enrichment, sports, outdoor and wilderness activities.
Academics Spanish language/literature, chemistry, computers, ecology, journalism, music, physics.
Arts Arts and crafts (general), dance, graphic arts, painting, pottery, radio broadcasting, sculpture, theater/drama.
Special Interest Areas Culinary arts, nature study.

Mercersburg Adventure Camp

Sports Aerobics, basketball, bicycling, canoeing, climbing (wall), diving, equestrian sports, fishing, flag football, floor hockey, golf, horseback riding, in-line skating, kayaking, kickball, lacrosse, martial arts, rappelling, ropes course, soccer, softball, squash, swimming, tennis, track and field, volleyball, water polo.
Wilderness/Outdoors Hiking, mountain biking, orienteering, rafting, rock climbing, white-water trips, wilderness camping.
Trips Cultural, day, overnight.
Program Information 3–4 sessions per year. Session length: 2–6 weeks in June, July, August. Ages: 8–14. 40–75 participants per session. Boarding program cost: $1490–$4350. Financial aid available.
Application Deadline Continuous.
Jobs Positions for high school students 16 and older and college students 18 and older.
Contact Mr. Rick Hendrickson, Director of Summer and Extended Programs, main address above. Phone: 717-328-6225. Fax: 717-328-9072. E-mail: summerprograms@mercersburg.edu.
URL www.mercersburg.edu
For more information, see page 1210.

Mercersburg All-American Wrestling Camp & Junior All-American Wrestling Camp

Mercersburg Academy Summer and Extended Programs
300 East Seminary Street
Mercersburg, Pennsylvania 17236

General Information Boys' residential and day sports camp established in 1994.
Program Focus Wrestling.
Special Interest Areas Weight reduction.
Sports Aerobics, dodge ball, swimming, weight training, wrestling.
Wilderness/Outdoors Hiking.
Trips Day.
Program Information 2–3 sessions per year. Session length: 3–5 days in June, July. Ages: 6–18. 26–100 participants per session. Day program cost: $145–$235. Boarding program cost: $175–$285. Financial aid available.
Application Deadline Continuous.
Jobs Positions for high school students 17 and older and college students.
Contact Mr. Rick Hendrickson, Director of Summer and Extended Programs, main address above. Phone: 717-328-6225. Fax: 717-328-9072. E-mail: summerprograms@mercersburg.edu.
URL www.mercersburg.edu
For more information, see page 1210.

Mercersburg ESL Plus Program

Mercersburg Academy Summer and Extended Programs
300 East Seminary Street
Mercersburg, Pennsylvania 17236

General Information Coed residential academic program established in 1999. High school credit may be earned.
Program Focus Orientation of international students to American school life and culture.
Academics American literature, English as a second language, English language/literature, SAT/ACT preparation, art (Advanced Placement), communications, computers, humanities, linguistics, reading, study skills.
Arts Dance, graphic arts, music, photography.
Special Interest Areas Cross-cultural education.
Sports Sports (general), swimming, tennis.
Wilderness/Outdoors Hiking, rafting.
Trips College tours, cultural, day, overnight, shopping.
Program Information 1 session per year. Session length: 32 days in July, August. Ages: 14–18. 10–25 participants per session. Boarding program cost: $2800–$4650. Application fee: $50.
Application Deadline Continuous.
Jobs Positions for high school students 17 and older and college students 18 and older.
Contact Mr. Rick Hendrickson, Director of Summer and Extended Programs, main address above. Phone: 717-328-6225. Fax: 717-328-9072. E-mail: summerprograms@mercersburg.edu.
URL www.mercersburg.edu
For more information, see page 1210.

Mercersburg Onstage! Young Actors Workshop

Mercersburg Academy Summer and Extended Programs
300 East Seminary Street
Mercersburg, Pennsylvania 17236

General Information Coed residential and day arts program established in 2001.
Program Focus Theatre, acting, producing, directing.
Arts Acting, directing, theater/drama.
Trips Cultural, day.
Program Information 1 session per year. Session length: 5 days in July, August. Ages: 11–14. 15–25 participants per session. Day program cost: $265. Boarding program cost: $350.
Application Deadline Continuous.

Mercersburg Onstage! Young Actors Workshop (continued)

Jobs Positions for college students 18 and older.
Contact Mr. Rick Hendrickson, Director of Summer and Extended Programs, main address above. Phone: 717-328-6225. Fax: 717-328-9072. E-mail: summerprograms@mercersburg.edu.
URL www.mercersburg.edu
For more information, see page 1210.

Mercersburg Teen Adventure Camp

Mercersburg Academy Summer and Extended Programs
300 East Seminary Street
Mercersburg, Pennsylvania 17236

General Information Coed residential traditional camp established in 2001.
Program Focus Enrichment, outdoors.
Academics Web page design, architecture, business, chemistry, computers, ecology, physics, writing.
Arts Ceramics, creative writing, drawing, fashion design/production, graphic arts, music (instrumental), painting, photography, pottery, sculpture, theater/drama.
Special Interest Areas Native American culture, culinary arts, nature study.
Sports Bicycling (BMX), canoeing, climbing (wall), equestrian sports, fishing, horseback riding, kayaking, ropes course, soccer, swimming, tennis, track and field.
Wilderness/Outdoors Hiking, mountain biking, orienteering, rafting, rock climbing, white-water trips, wilderness camping.
Trips Cultural, day, overnight.
Program Information 1–2 sessions per year. Session length: 12 days in June, July. Ages: 14–16. 40–65 participants per session. Boarding program cost: $1490–$2825.
Application Deadline Continuous.
Jobs Positions for high school students 17 and older and college students 19 and older.
Contact Mr. Rick Hendrickson, Director of Teen Adventure Camp, main address above. Phone: 717-328-6225. Fax: 717-328-9072. E-mail: summerprograms@mercersburg.edu.
URL www.mercersburg.edu
For more information, see page 1210.

Mercersburg The World's A Stage Theatre Workshop

Mercersburg Academy Summer and Extended Programs
300 East Seminary Street
Mercersburg, Pennsylvania 17236

General Information Coed residential and day arts program.
Arts Acting, audition technique, stage combat, theater/drama.
Trips Day.
Program Information 1 session per year. Session length: 6 days in July, August. Ages: 14–18. Day program cost: $350. Boarding program cost: $430.
Application Deadline Continuous.
Jobs Positions for college students 18 and older.
Contact Mr. Rick Hendrickson, Director of Summer and Extended Programs, main address above. Phone: 717-328-6225. Fax: 717-328-9072. E-mail: summerprograms@mercersburg.edu.
URL www.mercersburg.edu
For more information, see page 1210.

Millersville University of Pennsylvania–Summer Language Camps for High School Students

Millersville University of Pennsylvania
Millersville, Pennsylvania 17551-0302

General Information Coed residential academic program and cultural program established in 1981.
Program Focus Language camp in Spanish, French, German or Russian with learning activities, sports, songs, and games.
Academics French language/literature, German language/literature, Russian language/literature, Spanish language/literature, academics (general), computers, humanities, intercultural studies, language study, music.
Arts Arts and crafts (general), creative writing, dance (folk), film, music, television/video, theater/drama.
Sports Basketball, soccer, softball, swimming, tennis, volleyball.
Wilderness/Outdoors Hiking.
Trips Day.
Program Information 1 session per year. Session length: 6 days in July, August. Ages: 15–18. 25–35 participants per session. Boarding program cost: $350. Financial aid available.
Application Deadline Continuous.
Jobs Positions for college students 21 and older.
Contact Dr. Christine Gaudry-Hudson, Chair, Department of Foreign Languages, Millersville University, PO Box 1002, Millersville, Pennsylvania 17551-0302. Phone: 717-872-3526. Fax: 717-871-2482. E-mail: camps@millersville.edu.
URL www.millersville.edu/~forlang

Mini-Camp in the Pocono Mountains

Camp Lohikan in the Pocono Mountains
24 Wallerville Road
Lake Como, Pennsylvania 18437

General Information Coed residential traditional camp established in 1984.
Arts Arts and crafts (general), circus arts, drawing, fabric arts, graphic arts, jewelry making, leather working, metalworking, trapeze arts.
Special Interest Areas Animal care, campcraft, team building.
Sports All-terrain vehicles, archery, baseball, basketball, boating, canoeing, cheerleading, climbing (wall), equestrian sports, football, horseback riding, in-line skating, jet skiing, kayaking, paintball, rappelling, riflery, ropes course, rowing (crew/sculling), soccer, softball, tennis.
Wilderness/Outdoors Hiking, zip line.

Program Information 3 sessions per year. Session length: 4–7 days in August. Ages: 10–15. 120–140 participants per session. Boarding program cost: $400–$750.
Application Deadline Continuous.
Jobs Positions for college students 19 and older.
Summer Contact Mr. Mark Buynak, CCD, Director, 24 Wallerville Road, PO Box 217, Dept PETG, Lake Como, Pennsylvania 18437. Phone: 908-798-2707. Fax: 908-470-9319. E-mail: info@lohikan.com.
Winter Contact Mr. Mark Buynak, CCD, Director, PO Box 189, Dept PETG, Gladstone, New Jersey 07934. Phone: 908-470-9317. Fax: 908-470-9319. E-mail: info@lohikan.com.
URL www.lohikan.com/1week.htm

Mountain Workshop–Awesome 4: Pennsylvania

Mountain Workshop
Pennsylvania

General Information Coed travel outdoor program, wilderness program, and adventure program established in 1986.
Special Interest Areas Team building.
Sports Kayaking.
Wilderness/Outdoors Caving, outdoor adventure, rafting, rock climbing, white-water trips.
Trips Overnight.
Program Information 3 sessions per year. Session length: 1 week in June, July, August. Ages: 14–15. Cost: $1100.
Application Deadline Continuous.
Jobs Positions for college students 21 and older.
Contact Kent B. Tullo, Director, 9 Brookside Place, West Redding, Connecticut 06896. Phone: 203-544-0555. Fax: 203-544-0333. E-mail: info@mountainworkshop.com.
URL www.mountainworkshop.com

National Computer Camps at La Roche College

National Computer Camps
La Roche College
9000 Babcock Boulevard
Pittsburgh, Pennsylvania 15237

General Information Coed residential and day academic program established in 1998. Formal opportunities for the academically talented.
Program Focus Computer science, programming, Internet recreation and sports.
Academics Web page design, computer programming, computer science (Advanced Placement), computers.
Arts Animation, graphic arts.
Special Interest Areas Internet accessibility, electronics, robotics.
Sports Basketball, soccer, swimming, tennis, volleyball.
Program Information 2 sessions per year. Session length: 1 week in July. Ages: 8–18. 80–125 participants per session. Day program cost: $595. Boarding program cost: $795.
Application Deadline Continuous.
Jobs Positions for high school students 16 and older and college students 18 and older.
Contact Dr. Michael Zabinski, President, PO Box 585, Orange, Connecticut 06477. Phone: 203-795-9667. E-mail: info@nccamp.com.
URL www.nccamp.com

The National Music Workshop Day Jams–Philadelphia, PA

National Guitar Workshop
Gwynedd Valley Mercy Academy
1345 Sumneytown Pike
Gwynedd Valley, Pennsylvania 19437

General Information Coed day arts program established in 2001. Formal opportunities for the artistically talented.
Program Focus Rock 'n' roll day camp.
Academics Music.
Arts Arts and crafts (general), band, guitar, music, music (rock), music (vocal).
Program Information 2 sessions per year. Session length: 5–10 days in July. Ages: 9–15. 40–70 participants per session. Day program cost: $425–$495. Application fee: $35. Financial aid available.
Application Deadline Continuous.
Jobs Positions for high school students 17 and older and college students 17 and older.
Contact Lynda Wlodarczyk, Associate Director, 407A Bantam Road, Suite 1, Litchfield, Connecticut 06759. Phone: 800-295-5956. Fax: 860-567-0374. E-mail: lynda@dayjams.com.
URL www.dayjams.com

New Jersey YMHA–YWHA Camp Mountaintop

New Jersey YMHA–YWHA Camps
570 Sawkill Road
Milford, Pennsylvania 18337

General Information Coed residential traditional camp established in 1996. Religious affiliation: Jewish. Accredited by American Camping Association.
Program Focus Short-term sleepaway and introductory experience.
Academics Jewish studies, computers.
Arts Arts and crafts (general), ceramics, dance, dance (folk), dance (modern), drawing, fabric arts, jewelry making, metalworking, music, music (vocal), painting, photography, pottery, printmaking, radio broadcasting, television/video, theater/drama, woodworking.
Special Interest Areas Animal care, campcraft, culinary arts, model rocketry, nature study.
Sports Aerobics, archery, basketball, bicycling, bicycling (BMX), boating, canoeing, climbing (wall), cross-country, fishing, football, gymnastics, in-line skating, kayaking, rappelling, ropes course, sailing, soccer, softball, street/roller hockey, swimming, tennis, track and field, volleyball, weight training.
Wilderness/Outdoors Hiking, mountain biking, orienteering.

New Jersey YMHA–YWHA Camp Mountaintop (continued)

Program Information 4–6 sessions per year. Session length: 5–14 days in July, August. Ages: 7–14. 30–100 participants per session. Boarding program cost: $400–$650. Financial aid available.
Application Deadline Continuous.
Jobs Positions for college students 18 and older.
Summer Contact Leonard Robinson, Executive Director, main address above. Phone: 570-296-8596 Ext.120. Fax: 570-296-6381.
Winter Contact Leonard Robinson, Executive Director, 21 Plymouth Street, Fairfield, New Jersey 07004. Phone: 973-575-3333. Fax: 973-575-4188.
URL www.njycamps.org

New Jersey YMHA–YWHA Camp Nah-jee-wah

New Jersey YMHA–YWHA Camps
570 Sawkill Road
Milford, Pennsylvania 18337

General Information Coed residential traditional camp established in 1920. Religious affiliation: Jewish. Accredited by American Camping Association.
Academics English as a second language, Hebrew language, computer programming, computers.
Arts Arts and crafts (general), ceramics, dance, drawing, fabric arts, leather working, music (instrumental), musical productions, painting, photography, pottery, puppetry, radio broadcasting, theater/drama, woodworking.
Special Interest Areas Animal care, campcraft, culinary arts, gardening, model rocketry, nature study.
Sports Archery, baseball, basketball, bicycling, boating, canoeing, cheerleading, climbing (wall), diving, fishing, football, gymnastics, horseback riding, in-line skating, ropes course, sailing, soccer, softball, street/roller hockey, swimming, tennis, track and field, volleyball.
Wilderness/Outdoors Canoe trips, hiking.
Trips Day.
Program Information 2 sessions per year. Session length: 27–54 days in June, July, August. Ages: 6–11. 350–380 participants per session. Boarding program cost: $2700–$5400. Financial aid available.
Application Deadline Continuous.
Jobs Positions for high school students 17 and older and college students 18 and older.
Summer Contact Anne Tursky, Resident Director, main address above. Phone: 570-296-8596 Ext.125. Fax: 570-296-6381.
Winter Contact Anne Tursky, Resident Director, 21 Plymouth Street, Fairfield, New Jersey 07004. Phone: 973-575-3333 Ext.125. Fax: 973-575-4188. E-mail: njw@njycamps.org.
URL www.njycamps.org

New Jersey YMHA–YWHA Camp Nesher

New Jersey YMHA–YWHA Camps
Lake Como, Pennsylvania 18437

General Information Coed residential traditional camp established in 1996. Religious affiliation: Jewish (Orthodox). Accredited by American Camping Association.
Program Focus Modern Jewish Orthodox tradition.
Academics Jewish studies.
Arts Arts and crafts (general), ceramics, chorus, dance, musical productions, painting, theater/drama, woodworking.
Special Interest Areas Culinary arts, model rocketry.
Sports Archery, baseball, basketball, bicycling, boating, canoeing, football, golf, horseback riding, in-line skating, martial arts, ropes course, sailing, soccer, softball, street/roller hockey, swimming, tennis, volleyball.
Wilderness/Outdoors Canoe trips, hiking, mountain biking, orienteering, rafting.
Trips Day, overnight.
Program Information 3 sessions per year. Session length: 25–50 days in June, July, August. Ages: 8–15. 250–370 participants per session. Boarding program cost: $3450–$5870. Financial aid available.
Application Deadline Continuous.
Jobs Positions for high school students 16 and older and college students.
Summer Contact Mr. Jeff Braverman, Director, HCR 60, Box 5000, Lake Como, Pennsylvania 18437. Phone: 570-798-2373. Fax: 570-798-2663. E-mail: nesher@njycamps.org.
Winter Contact Mr. Jeff Braverman, Director, 21 Plymouth Street, Fairfield, New Jersey 07004. Phone: 973-575-3333 Ext.111. Fax: 973-575-4188. E-mail: nesher@njycamps.org.
URL www.campnesher.org

New Jersey YMHA–YWHA Cedar Lake Camp

New Jersey YMHA–YWHA Camps
570 Sawkill Road
Milford, Pennsylvania 18337

General Information Coed residential traditional camp established in 1920. Religious affiliation: Jewish. Accredited by American Camping Association.
Academics Computers.
Arts Animation, arts and crafts (general), ceramics, dance, dance (jazz), dance (modern), drawing, fabric arts, graphic arts, jewelry making, leather working, magic, metalworking, music, music (instrumental), painting, photography, television/video, theater/drama, woodworking.
Special Interest Areas Campcraft, culinary arts, model rocketry, nature study.
Sports Aerobics, archery, basketball, bicycling, bicycling (BMX), boating, canoeing, cheerleading, climbing (wall), cross-country, diving, field hockey, fishing, football, golf, gymnastics, horseback riding, in-line skating, jet skiing, kayaking, lacrosse, martial arts, rappelling, ropes course, rowing (crew/sculling), sailing, scuba

diving, soccer, softball, sports (general), street/roller hockey, swimming, tennis, track and field, volleyball, water polo, weight training, windsurfing.
Wilderness/Outdoors Backpacking, bicycle trips, canoe trips, hiking, mountain biking.
Trips Day.
Program Information 2 sessions per year. Session length: 26–53 days in June, July, August. Ages: 12–14. 550 participants per session. Boarding program cost: $2740–$5350. Financial aid available.
Application Deadline Continuous.
Jobs Positions for high school students 17 and older and college students 19 and older.
Summer Contact Walter Synalovski, Assistant Executive Director, main address above. Phone: 570-296-8596 Ext.124. Fax: 570-296-6381. E-mail: clc@njycamps.org.
Winter Contact Walter Synalovski, Resident Director, 21 Plymouth Street, Fairfield, New Jersey 07004. Phone: 973-575-3333 Ext.124. Fax: 973-575-4188. E-mail: clc@njycamps.org.
URL www.njycamps.org

New Jersey YMHA–YWHA Round Lake Camp

New Jersey YMHA–YWHA Camps
Lake Como, Pennsylvania

General Information Coed residential special needs program established in 1983. Religious affiliation: Jewish. Accredited by American Camping Association. Specific services available for the emotionally challenged, developmentally challenged, learning disabled, participant with ADD, and participant with AD/HD.
Program Focus Learning disabilities, ADD, and ADHD.
Academics English language/literature, Hebrew language, Jewish studies, SAT/ACT preparation, academics (general), aerospace science, astronomy, biology, communications, computer programming, computers, environmental science, geography, geology/earth science, history, humanities, mathematics, meteorology, music, reading, religion, remedial academics, science (general), social science, social studies, study skills, typing, writing.
Arts Acting, arts and crafts (general), batiking, ceramics, chorus, creative writing, dance, dance (folk), dance (jazz), dance (modern), drawing, fabric arts, graphic arts, leather working, metalworking, music, music (instrumental), music (vocal), musical productions, painting, photography, pottery, television/video, theater/drama, woodworking.
Special Interest Areas Animal care, campcraft, career exploration, community service, culinary arts, electronics, farming, gardening, leadership training, model rocketry, nature study, nautical skills, team building, work camp programs.
Sports Aerobics, baseball, basketball, bicycling, bicycling (BMX), boating, canoeing, climbing (wall), diving, fishing, football, gymnastics, horseback riding, in-line skating, jet skiing, kayaking, martial arts, ropes course, sailing, soccer, softball, street/roller hockey, swimming, tennis, track and field, trampolining, volleyball.
Wilderness/Outdoors Backpacking, bicycle trips, canoe trips, hiking, mountain biking, mountaineering, orienteering, rock climbing.
Trips Day, overnight.
Program Information 3 sessions per year. Session length: 21–50 days in June, July, August. Ages: 7–18. 200 participants per session. Boarding program cost: $3200–$7000. Financial aid available.
Application Deadline Continuous.
Jobs Positions for high school students and college students.
Contact Sheira L. Director-Nowack, Assistant Director, 21 Plymouth Street, Fairfield, New Jersey 07004. Phone: 570-798-2551. Fax: 570-798-2784. E-mail: rlc@njycamps.org.
URL www.roundlakecamp.org

New Jersey YMHA–YWHA Teen Camp

New Jersey YMHA–YWHA Camps
570 Sawkill Road
Milford, Pennsylvania 18337

General Information Coed residential traditional camp and community service program established in 1959. Religious affiliation: Jewish.
Academics Hebrew language, Jewish studies, computers, ecology.
Arts Ceramics, chorus, dance, dance (jazz), dance (modern), dance (tap), drawing, fabric arts, jewelry making, metalworking, painting, photography, pottery, printmaking, television/video, theater/drama, woodworking.
Special Interest Areas Culinary arts, leadership training, model rocketry, nature study.
Sports Aerobics, archery, baseball, basketball, bicycling, bicycling (BMX), boating, canoeing, climbing (wall), field hockey, fishing, football, golf, gymnastics, horseback riding, in-line skating, jet skiing, kayaking, martial arts, rappelling, ropes course, rowing (crew/sculling), sailing, scuba diving, soccer, softball, street/roller hockey, swimming, tennis, track and field, volleyball, water polo, weight training, windsurfing, wrestling.
Wilderness/Outdoors Backpacking, bicycle trips, canoe trips, hiking, mountain biking, rafting.
Trips Cultural, day, hiking, overnight.
Program Information 2 sessions per year. Session length: 27–54 days in June, July, August. Ages: 14–16. 150 participants per session. Boarding program cost: $3300–$5900. Financial aid available.
Application Deadline Continuous.
Jobs Positions for college students 21 and older.
Summer Contact Gali Scharf, Teen Camp Director, main address above. Phone: 570-296-8596 Ext.169.
Winter Contact Gali Scharf, 21 Plymouth Street, Fairfield, New Jersey 07004. Phone: 973-575-3333 Ext.169. Fax: 973-575-4188.
URL www.njycamps.org

NEXT LEVEL CAMP

Ligonier Camp and Conference Center
188 Macartney Lane
Ligonier, Pennsylvania 15658

General Information Coed residential traditional camp, outdoor program, and bible camp. Religious affiliation: Presbyterian. Accredited by American Camping Association.
Program Focus Traditional Christian camp program with greater emphasis on adventure education.
Academics Bible study, environmental science.
Arts Arts and crafts (general), jewelry making, painting, theater/drama.
Special Interest Areas Nature study, team building.
Sports Archery, basketball, bicycling, canoeing, climbing (tower), climbing (wall), fishing, lacrosse, mountain boarding, riflery, ropes course, soccer, sports (general), swimming, tennis, ultimate frisbee, volleyball.
Wilderness/Outdoors Backpacking, bicycle trips, caving, hiking, mountain biking, rafting, rock climbing, white-water trips, wilderness camping, wilderness/outdoors (general), zip line.
Trips Day, overnight.
Program Information 1–3 sessions per year. Session length: 6 days in June, July. Ages: 12–17. 100–200 participants per session. Boarding program cost: $295. Financial aid available.
Application Deadline Continuous.
Jobs Positions for high school students 16 and older and college students 19 and older.
Contact Sal Hanna, Summer Camp Director, main address above. Phone: 724-238-6428. Fax: 724-238-6971. E-mail: shanna@ligoniercamp.org.
URL www.ligoniercamp.org

92ND STREET Y CAMPS–CAMP KESHER

92nd Street YM–YWHA
Milford, Pennsylvania

General Information Coed residential traditional camp established in 1955. Religious affiliation: Jewish. Accredited by American Camping Association.
Program Focus Tailored for campers who may struggle while being away from home.
Arts Arts and crafts (general), music, painting, photography, pottery, woodworking.
Special Interest Areas Campcraft, model rocketry, nature study.
Sports Archery, baseball, basketball, bicycling, boating, climbing (wall), gymnastics, in-line skating, ropes course, soccer, softball, sports (general), street/roller hockey, swimming.
Program Information 1 session per year. Session length: 13 days in July, August. Ages: 8–11. 90–100 participants per session. Boarding program cost: $1750. Financial aid available. Open to participants entering grades 3–6.
Application Deadline Continuous.
Jobs Positions for college students 18 and older.
Contact Alan Saltz, Director of Camp Programs, 1395 Lexington Avenue, New York, New York 10128. Phone: 212-415-5600. Fax: 212-415-5637. E-mail: camps@92y.org.
URL www.92y.org/camps

92ND STREET Y CAMPS–CAMP KESHER JUNIOR

92nd Street YM–YWHA
Milford, Pennsylvania

General Information Coed residential traditional camp established in 1955. Religious affiliation: Jewish. Accredited by American Camping Association.
Program Focus Tailored for campers who may struggle while being away from home.
Arts Arts and crafts (general), ceramics, drawing, music, painting, woodworking.
Special Interest Areas Campcraft, model rocketry, nature study.
Sports Archery, basketball, bicycling, in-line skating, ropes course, sports (general), swimming.
Program Information 1 session per year. Session length: 1 week in July. Ages: 7–9. 40–50 participants per session. Boarding program cost: $900. Financial aid available. Open to participants entering grades 2–4.
Application Deadline Continuous.
Jobs Positions for college students 18 and older.
Contact Alan Saltz, Director of Camp Programs, 1395 Lexington Avenue, New York, New York 10128. Phone: 212-415-5600. Fax: 212-415-5637. E-mail: camps@92y.org.
URL www.92y.org/camps

PATHWAYS AT MARYWOOD UNIVERSITY

Marywood University
2300 Adams Avenue
Scranton, Pennsylvania 18509

General Information Coed residential and day academic program established in 1984. Formal opportunities for the academically talented and artistically talented. College credit may be earned.
Program Focus College preparation.
Academics American literature, English language/literature, French language/literature, Latin language, SAT/ACT preparation, Spanish language/literature, academics (general), architecture, art (Advanced Placement), art history/appreciation, biology, business, chemistry, classical languages/literatures, communications, computers, ecology, economics, education, geography, government and politics, health sciences, history, humanities, journalism, mathematics, music, philosophy, physiology, precollege program, psychology, reading, science (general), social science, social studies, study skills, typing, writing.
Arts Acting, ceramics, creative writing, dance (modern), drawing, film, graphic arts, jewelry making, music, music (instrumental), music (jazz), music (vocal), painting, photography, pottery, printmaking, radio broadcasting, sculpture, television/video, theater/drama.
Special Interest Areas Career exploration, college planning, leadership training, nutrition.

Sports Aerobics, baseball, basketball, boating, canoeing, fishing, golf, martial arts, racquetball, soccer, softball, swimming, tennis, volleyball, weight training.
Wilderness/Outdoors Hiking.
Trips College tours, cultural, day, shopping.
Program Information 1 session per year. Session length: 10–14 days in July. Ages: 13–18. 50–80 participants per session. Day program cost: $225–$1195. Boarding program cost: $750–$1500. Financial aid available.
Application Deadline June 30.
Contact Meg Cullen-Brown, Program Director, Pathways, main address above. Phone: 800-724-0399. Fax: 570-961-4776. E-mail: brownm@ac.marywood.edu.
URL www.marywood.edu

The Performing Arts Institute of Wyoming Seminary

Wyoming Seminary College Preparatory School
201 North Sprague Avenue
Kingston, Pennsylvania 18704

General Information Coed residential and day arts program established in 1998. Religious affiliation: United Methodist. Formal opportunities for the artistically talented.

The Performing Arts Institute of Wyoming Seminary

Program Focus Performing arts: dance, music, and musical theater.
Academics Music, music (Advanced Placement), precollege program.
Arts Band, chorus, dance, dance (ballet), dance (jazz), dance (modern), music, music (chamber), music (classical), music (ensemble), music (instrumental), music (jazz), music (orchestral), music (vocal), musical productions, theater/drama.
Special Interest Areas Career exploration.
Trips Cultural.
Program Information 1–2 sessions per year. Session length: 3–6 weeks in June, July, August. Ages: 12–18. 125–150 participants per session. Day program cost: $800–$1600. Boarding program cost: $2250–$4250. Application fee: $25. Financial aid available.
Application Deadline Continuous.
Jobs Positions for high school students 17 and older and college students 18 and older.
Contact Nancy Sanderson, Director, The Performing Arts Institute of Wyoming Seminary, main address above. Phone: 570-270-2186. Fax: 570-270-2198. E-mail: onstage@wyomingseminary.org.
URL www.wyomingseminary.org/pai

For more information, see page 1256.

The Phelps School Summer Program

The Phelps School
583 Sugartown Road
Malvern, Pennsylvania 19355-0476

General Information Coed residential and day academic program established in 1970. Specific services available for the learning disabled. High school credit may be earned.
Program Focus Remedial.
Academics English as a second language, English language/literature, computers, mathematics, reading, remedial academics, study skills.
Arts Creative writing, photography.
Special Interest Areas Driver's education.
Sports Baseball, basketball, canoeing, equestrian sports, horseback riding, rappelling, soccer, softball, swimming, tennis, volleyball, weight training.
Wilderness/Outdoors White-water trips.
Trips Cultural, day, shopping.
Program Information 1 session per year. Session length: 30–35 days in July. Ages: 12–19. 30–40 participants per session. Day program cost: $3000. Boarding program cost: $4000–$5000. Financial aid available.
Application Deadline Continuous.
Contact Mr. F. Christopher Chirieleison, Director of Admissions, 583 Sugartown Road, PO Box 476, Malvern, Pennsylvania 19355-0476. Phone: 610-644-1754. Fax: 610-644-6679. E-mail: admis@phelpsschool.org.
URL www.thephelpsschool.org

Pre-College Summer Institute, The University of the Arts

The University of the Arts
320 South Broad Street
Philadelphia, Pennsylvania 19102

General Information Coed residential and day arts program established in 1981. Formal opportunities for the artistically talented and gifted.
Program Focus Four week visual and performing arts (musical theater and drama) and media and communication program, as well as a two-week jazz performance: instrumental and voice program.
Academics Art (Advanced Placement), art history/appreciation, communications, computers, music, precollege program, writing.
Arts Acting, animation, arts and crafts (general), band, ceramics, creative writing, dance, drawing, fabric arts, film, graphic arts, jewelry making, metalworking, music, music (ensemble), music (instrumental), music (jazz),

Pre-College Summer Institute, The University of the Arts (continued)

Pre-College Summer Institute, The University of the Arts

music (vocal), musical productions, painting, photography, pottery, printmaking, sculpture, television/video, theater/drama, weaving.
Trips Cultural.
Program Information 1 session per year. Session length: 2–4 weeks in July, August. Ages: 15–18. 250–300 participants per session. Application fee: $100. Contact the Pre-College Department for tuition information.
Application Deadline April 29.
Contact Erin Elman, Director, Pre-College Programs, main address above. Phone: 215-717-6430. Fax: 215-717-6433. E-mail: precollege@uarts.edu.
URL www.uarts.edu/precollege

For more information, see page 1374.

ProShot Basketball Camp–Boys Camp

ProShot Basketball Camp
142 Buck River Road
Thornhurst, Pennsylvania 18424

General Information Boys' residential and day sports camp established in 1989.
Program Focus Basketball shooting and offensive skills.
Sports Basketball.
Program Information 8–18 sessions per year. Session length: 3 days in June, July, August, September. Ages: 10–18. 18–25 participants per session. Day program cost: $120. Boarding program cost: $170.
Application Deadline Continuous.
Jobs Positions for college students 18 and older.
Contact John Szela, Director, main address above. Phone: 570-842-7044. Fax: 570-842-7044. E-mail: info@proshot.us.
URL www.proshot.us/

ProShot Basketball Camp–Girls Camp

ProShot Basketball Camp
142 Buck River Road
Thornhurst, Pennsylvania 18424

General Information Girls' residential and day sports camp established in 1989.
Program Focus Basketball shooting and offensive skills.
Sports Basketball.
Program Information 8–18 sessions per year. Session length: 3 days in June, July, August, September. Ages: 10–18. 18–25 participants per session. Day program cost: $120. Boarding program cost: $170. Financial aid available.
Jobs Positions for college students 18 and older.
Contact John Szela, Director, main address above. Phone: 570-842-7044. Fax: 570-842-7044. E-mail: info@proshot.us.
URL www.proshot.us/

Saint Vincent College Challenge Program

Saint Vincent College
300 Fraser Purchase Road
Latrobe, Pennsylvania 15650

General Information Coed residential and day traditional camp and academic program established in 1985. Formal opportunities for the academically talented and artistically talented.
Academics Academics (general), aerospace science, archaeology, architecture, area studies, art (Advanced Placement), biology, botany, chemistry, communications, computer programming, computer science (Advanced Placement), computers, ecology, engineering, environmental science, government and politics, government and politics (Advanced Placement), health sciences, history, humanities, physics, precollege program, prelaw, psychology, science (general), social science, speech/debate.
Arts Acting, batiking, film, photography, pottery, sculpture, television/video, theater/drama.
Special Interest Areas College planning, conservation projects, field research/expeditions, model rocketry, nature study, team building.
Sports Basketball, climbing (wall), golf, lacrosse, ropes course, swimming, tennis, volleyball.
Trips College tours, cultural, day.

Program Information 2 sessions per year. Session length: 6 days in July. Ages: 11–18. 75–100 participants per session. Day program cost: $500. Boarding program cost: $600. Financial aid available.
Application Deadline June 30.
Jobs Positions for college students 19 and older.
Contact Ms. Joanne Krynicky, Challenge Director-Saint Vincent College, main address above. Phone: 724-532-5093.
URL www.stvincent.edu/

SCIENCE QUEST

Seton Hill University
Seton Hill Drive
Greensburg, Pennsylvania 15601

General Information Girls' residential and day academic program established in 1992. Religious affiliation: Roman Catholic. Formal opportunities for the academically talented. College credit may be earned.
Program Focus Hands-on science and computer lab activities.
Academics Biology, chemistry, computers, ecology, environmental science, mathematics, science (general).
Special Interest Areas Field research/expeditions, nature study, nutrition.
Sports Basketball, softball, swimming, tennis, volleyball.
Trips College tours, day.
Program Information 1–2 sessions per year. Session length: 6 days in July. Ages: 11–17. 30–48 participants per session. Day program cost: $200. Boarding program cost: $400. Financial aid available.
Application Deadline Continuous.
Jobs Positions for college students 21 and older.
Contact Dr. Susan Yochum, SC, Science Quest Director, main address above. Phone: 724-830-1044. Fax: 724-830-1571. E-mail: yochum@setonhill.edu.
URL www.setonhill.edu

76ERS BASKETBALL CAMP

Stroudsburg, Pennsylvania 18360

General Information Coed residential and day sports camp established in 1971.
Program Focus Basketball.
Sports Basketball, boating, canoeing, fishing.
Trips Day.
Program Information 7 sessions per year. Session length: 6 days in July, August. Ages: 9–17. 275 participants per session. Day program cost: $375. Boarding program cost: $525.
Application Deadline Continuous.
Jobs Positions for college students 18 and older.
Summer Contact Sonny Elia, Director, RD #1, Box 1454, Stroudsburg, Pennsylvania 18360. Phone: 610-668-7676. Fax: 610-668-7799. E-mail: sonny@sixerscamps.com.
Winter Contact Sonny Elia, Director, PO Box 1073, Bala Cynwyd, Pennsylvania 19004. Phone: 610-668-7676. Fax: 610-668-7799. E-mail: sonny@sixerscamps.com.
URL www.sixerscamps.com

SHIPPENSBURG UNIVERSITY ACADEMIC CAMPS–ACTING & THEATRE ARTS

Shippensburg University of Pennsylvania
1871 Old Main Drive
Shippensburg, Pennsylvania 17257-2299

General Information Coed residential arts program.
Arts Acting, costume design, make up, stage combat, theater/drama.
Program Information 1 session per year. Session length: 1 week in June. 25–40 participants per session. Boarding program cost: $420. Open to participants entering grades 8–12.
Application Deadline Continuous.
Contact Mr. Randal Hammond, Director of Conferences, main address above. Phone: 717-477-1256. Fax: 717-477-4014.
URL www.ship.edu/camps

SHIPPENSBURG UNIVERSITY ACADEMIC CAMPS–GOVERNMENT IN REAL LIFE

Shippensburg University of Pennsylvania
1871 Old Main Drive
Shippensburg, Pennsylvania 17257-2299

General Information Girls' residential academic program.
Academics Government and politics.
Program Information 1 session per year. Session length: 5 days in July. Ages: 14–15. 25–40 participants per session. Boarding program cost: $395. Financial aid available.
Application Deadline Continuous.
Contact Mr. Randal Hammond, Director of Conferences, main address above. Phone: 717-477-1256. Fax: 717-477-4014.
URL www.ship.edu/camps

SHIPPENSBURG UNIVERSITY ACADEMIC CAMPS–SCIENCE ACADEMY FOR GIRLS

Shippensburg University of Pennsylvania
1871 Old Main Drive
Shippensburg, Pennsylvania 17257-2299

General Information Girls' residential academic program.
Academics Science (general).
Special Interest Areas Career exploration.
Program Information 1 session per year. Session length: 4 days. 25–40 participants per session. Boarding program cost: $375. Open to participants entering grades 6–8.
Application Deadline Continuous.
Contact Mr. Randal Hammond, Director of Conferences, main address above. Phone: 717-477-1256. Fax: 717-477-4014.
URL www.ship.edu/camps

SHIPPENSBURG UNIVERSITY SPORTS CAMPS–BASEBALL–REGULAR CAMP

Shippensburg University of Pennsylvania
1871 Old Main Drive
Shippensburg, Pennsylvania 17257-2299

General Information Boys' residential and day sports camp.
Sports Baseball.
Program Information 3 sessions per year. Session length: 4 days in July. Ages: 8–18. 24–150 participants per session. Day program cost: $195. Boarding program cost: $305.
Application Deadline Continuous.
Contact Mr. Randal Hammond, Director of Conferences, main address above. Phone: 717-477-1256. Fax: 717-477-4014.
URL www.ship.edu/camps

SHIPPENSBURG UNIVERSITY SPORTS CAMPS–BASEBALL–SPECIALIST CAMP

Shippensburg University of Pennsylvania
1871 Old Main Drive
Shippensburg, Pennsylvania 17257-2299

General Information Boys' residential and day sports camp.
Sports Baseball.
Program Information 1 session per year. Session length: 3 days in July. Ages: 8–18. 24–150 participants per session. Day program cost: $175. Boarding program cost: $235. Participants will select one or two of the following concentration areas: pitching, catching, and hitting.
Application Deadline Continuous.
Contact Mr. Randal Hammond, Director of Conferences, main address above. Phone: 717-477-1256. Fax: 717-477-4014.
URL www.ship.edu/camps

SHIPPENSBURG UNIVERSITY SPORTS CAMPS–BOYS BASKETBALL

Shippensburg University of Pennsylvania
1871 Old Main Drive
Shippensburg, Pennsylvania 17257-2299

General Information Boys' residential and day sports camp.
Sports Basketball.
Program Information 2 sessions per year. Session length: 4 days in June, July. Ages: 8–18. 24–150 participants per session. Day program cost: $200. Boarding program cost: $305.
Application Deadline Continuous.
Contact Mr. Randal Hammond, Director of Conferences, main address above. Phone: 717-477-1256. Fax: 717-477-4014.
URL www.ship.edu/camps

SHIPPENSBURG UNIVERSITY SPORTS CAMPS–CROSS COUNTRY

Shippensburg University of Pennsylvania
1871 Old Main Drive
Shippensburg, Pennsylvania 17257-2299

General Information Coed residential and day sports camp.
Sports Cross-country.
Program Information 1 session per year. Session length: 4 days in July, August. Ages: 13–18. 24–150 participants per session. Day program cost: $195. Boarding program cost: $305. Open to participants entering grades 9–12.
Application Deadline Continuous.
Contact Mr. Randal Hammond, Director of Conferences, main address above. Phone: 717-477-1256. Fax: 717-477-4014.
URL www.ship.edu/camps

SHIPPENSBURG UNIVERSITY SPORTS CAMPS–FAST PITCH SOFTBALL

Shippensburg University of Pennsylvania
1871 Old Main Drive
Shippensburg, Pennsylvania 17257-2299

General Information Girls' residential and day sports camp.
Sports Softball.
Program Information 2 sessions per year. Session length: 4 days in June, July. Ages: 9–18. 24–150 participants per session. Day program cost: $195. Boarding program cost: $300.
Application Deadline Continuous.
Contact Mr. Randal Hammond, Director of Conferences, main address above. Phone: 717-477-1256. Fax: 717-477-4014.
URL www.ship.edu/camps

SHIPPENSBURG UNIVERSITY SPORTS CAMPS–FATHER/SON BASKETBALL CAMP

Shippensburg University of Pennsylvania
1871 Old Main Drive
Shippensburg, Pennsylvania 17257-2299

General Information Boys' residential family program and sports camp.
Sports Basketball.
Program Information 1 session per year. Session length: 2 days in June. Ages: 6–15. 25–100 participants per session. Boarding program cost: $210. Financial aid available. $50 per additional son.
Application Deadline Continuous.
Contact Mr. Randal Hammond, Director of Conferences, main address above. Phone: 717-477-1256. Fax: 717-477-4014.
URL www.ship.edu/camps

Shippensburg University Sports Camps–Field Hockey

Shippensburg University of Pennsylvania
1871 Old Main Drive
Shippensburg, Pennsylvania 17257-2299

General Information Girls' residential and day sports camp.
Sports Field hockey.
Program Information 1 session per year. Session length: 4 days in July. 24–150 participants per session. Day program cost: $220. Boarding program cost: $325. Open to participants entering grade 9–college freshmen.
Application Deadline Continuous.
Contact Mr. Randal Hammond, Director of Conferences, main address above. Phone: 717-477-1256. Fax: 717-477-4014.
URL www.ship.edu/camps

Shippensburg University Sports Camps–Football

Shippensburg University of Pennsylvania
1871 Old Main Drive
Shippensburg, Pennsylvania 17257-2299

General Information Boys' residential and day sports camp.
Sports Football.
Program Information 1 session per year. Session length: 4 days in June. Ages: 8–18. 24–150 participants per session. Day program cost: $190. Boarding program cost: $295.
Application Deadline Continuous.
Contact Mr. Randal Hammond, Director of Conferences, main address above. Phone: 717-477-1256. Fax: 717-477-4014.
URL www.ship.edu/camps

Shippensburg University Sports Camps–Girls Basketball

Shippensburg University of Pennsylvania
1871 Old Main Drive
Shippensburg, Pennsylvania 17257-2299

General Information Girls' residential and day sports camp.
Sports Basketball.
Program Information 1 session per year. Session length: 4 days in June. Ages: 10–15. 24–150 participants per session. Day program cost: $200. Boarding program cost: $305.
Application Deadline Continuous.
Contact Mr. Randal Hammond, Director of Conferences, main address above. Phone: 717-477-1256. Fax: 717-477-4014.
URL www.ship.edu/camps

Shippensburg University Sports Camps–Jumps

Shippensburg University of Pennsylvania
1871 Old Main Drive
Shippensburg, Pennsylvania 17257-2299

General Information Coed residential and day sports camp.
Program Focus Track and field jumps.
Sports Track and field.
Program Information 1 session per year. Session length: 4 days in July, August. 24–50 participants per session. Day program cost: $195. Boarding program cost: $305. Financial aid available. Open to participants entering grades 7–12.
Application Deadline Continuous.
Contact Mr. Randal Hammond, Director of Conferences, main address above. Phone: 717-477-1256. Fax: 717-477-4014.
URL www.ship.edu/camps

Shippensburg University Sports Camps–Soccer–Boys Camp

Shippensburg University of Pennsylvania
1871 Old Main Drive
Shippensburg, Pennsylvania 17257-2299

General Information Boys' residential and day sports camp.
Sports Soccer.
Program Information 1 session per year. Session length: 4 days in June. Ages: 11–18. 24–150 participants per session. Day program cost: $205. Boarding program cost: $305.
Application Deadline Continuous.
Contact Mr. Randal Hammond, Director of Conferences, main address above. Phone: 717-477-1256. Fax: 717-477-4014.
URL www.ship.edu/camps

Shippensburg University Sports Camps–Soccer–Day Camp

Shippensburg University of Pennsylvania
1871 Old Main Drive
Shippensburg, Pennsylvania 17257-2299

General Information Coed day sports camp.
Sports Soccer.
Program Information 1 session per year. Session length: 5 days in July. Ages: 6–10. 24–150 participants per session. Day program cost: $160.
Application Deadline Continuous.
Contact Mr. Randal Hammond, Director of Conferences, main address above. Phone: 717-477-1256. Fax: 717-477-4014.
URL www.ship.edu/camps

Shippensburg University Sports Camps–Soccer–Girls Camp

Shippensburg University of Pennsylvania
1871 Old Main Drive
Shippensburg, Pennsylvania 17257-2299

General Information Girls' residential and day sports camp.
Sports Soccer.
Program Information 1 session per year. Session length: 4 days in June. Ages: 11–18. 24–150 participants per session. Day program cost: $205. Boarding program cost: $305.
Application Deadline Continuous.
Contact Mr. Randal Hammond, Director of Conferences, main address above. Phone: 717-477-1256. Fax: 717-477-4014.
URL www.ship.edu/camps

Shippensburg University Sports Camps–Swimming

Shippensburg University of Pennsylvania
1871 Old Main Drive
Shippensburg, Pennsylvania 17257-2299

General Information Coed residential and day sports camp.
Sports Swimming.
Program Information 1 session per year. Session length: 4 days in June. Ages: 8–18. 24–50 participants per session. Day program cost: $195. Boarding program cost: $300.
Application Deadline Continuous.
Contact Mr. Randal Hammond, Director of Conferences, main address above. Phone: 717-477-1256. Fax: 717-477-4014.
URL www.ship.edu/camps

Shippensburg University Sports Camps–Tennis

Shippensburg University of Pennsylvania
1871 Old Main Drive
Shippensburg, Pennsylvania 17257-2299

General Information Coed residential and day sports camp.
Sports Tennis.
Program Information 3 sessions per year. Session length: 4 days in June, July. 24 participants per session. Day program cost: $195. Boarding program cost: $305. Open to participants entering grades 9–12.
Application Deadline Continuous.
Contact Mr. Randal Hammond, Director of Conferences, main address above. Phone: 717-477-1256. Fax: 717-477-4014.
URL www.ship.edu/camps

Shippensburg University Sports Camps–Throws Camp

Shippensburg University of Pennsylvania
1871 Old Main Drive
Shippensburg, Pennsylvania 17257-2299

General Information Coed residential and day sports camp.
Program Focus Throws-specific camp.
Sports Track and field.
Program Information 1 session per year. Session length: 4 days in June. Day program cost: $165. Boarding program cost: $270. Financial aid available. Open to participants entering grades 7–12.
Application Deadline Continuous.
Contact Mr. Randal Hammond, Director of Conferences, main address above. Phone: 717-477-1256. Fax: 717-477-4014.
URL www.ship.edu/camps

Shippensburg University Sports Camps–Track & Field

Shippensburg University of Pennsylvania
1871 Old Main Drive
Shippensburg, Pennsylvania 17257-2299

General Information Coed residential and day sports camp.
Sports Track and field.
Program Information 1 session per year. Session length: 4 days in June. 24–150 participants per session. Day program cost: $195. Boarding program cost: $305. Open to participants entering grades 7–12.
Application Deadline Continuous.
Contact Mr. Randal Hammond, Director of Conferences, main address above. Phone: 717-477-1256. Fax: 717-477-4014.
URL www.ship.edu/camps

Shippensburg University Sports Camps–Volleyball–Girls Camp

Shippensburg University of Pennsylvania
1871 Old Main Drive
Shippensburg, Pennsylvania 17257-2299

General Information Girls' residential and day sports camp.
Sports Volleyball.
Program Information 2 sessions per year. Session length: 4 days in July. 24–150 participants per session. Day program cost: $195. Boarding program cost: $300. Open to participants entering grades 6–12.
Application Deadline Continuous.
Contact Mr. Randal Hammond, Director of Conferences, main address above. Phone: 717-477-1256. Fax: 717-477-4014.
URL www.ship.edu/camps

SoccerPlus FieldPlayer Academy–Pottstown, PA

SoccerPlus Camps
The Hill School
Pottstown, Pennsylvania

General Information Coed residential and day sports camp.
Program Focus Developing overall game skills in a competitive environment with quality goalkeepers.
Sports Soccer.
Program Information 1 session per year. Session length: 6 days in July. Ages: 11+. Day program cost: $595. Boarding program cost: $695. Financial aid available.
Application Deadline Continuous.
Jobs Positions for college students.
Contact Mr. Shawn Kelly, General Manager, 11 Executive Drive, Suite 202, Farmington, Connecticut 06032. Phone: 800-533-7371. Fax: 860-677-0460. E-mail: info@soccerpluscamps.com.
URL www.soccerpluscamps.com

SoccerPlus FieldPlayer Academy–Slippery Rock, PA

SoccerPlus Camps
Slippery Rock University
Slippery Rock, Pennsylvania

General Information Coed residential and day sports camp.
Program Focus Developing overall game skills in a competitive environment with quality goalkeepers.
Sports Soccer.
Program Information 1 session per year. Session length: 6 days in July. Ages: 11+. Day program cost: $595. Boarding program cost: $695. Financial aid available.
Application Deadline Continuous.
Jobs Positions for college students.
Contact Mr. Shawn Kelly, General Manager, 11 Executive Drive, Suite 202, Farmington, Connecticut 06032. Phone: 800-533-7371. Fax: 860-677-0460. E-mail: info@soccerpluscamps.com.
URL www.soccerpluscamps.com

SoccerPlus Goalkeeper School–Challenge Program–Pottstown, PA

SoccerPlus Camps
The Hill School
Pottstown, Pennsylvania

General Information Coed residential and day sports camp.
Program Focus Developing technical and tactical goalkeeping skills.
Sports Soccer.
Program Information 1 session per year. Session length: 6 days in June. Ages: 10+. Day program cost: $595. Boarding program cost: $695. Financial aid available.
Application Deadline Continuous.
Jobs Positions for college students.
Contact Mr. Shawn Kelly, General Manager, 11 Executive Drive, Suite 202, Farmington, Connecticut 06032. Phone: 800-533-7371. Fax: 860-677-0460. E-mail: info@soccerpluscamps.com.
URL www.soccerpluscamps.com

SoccerPlus Goalkeeper School–Challenge Program–Slippery Rock, PA

SoccerPlus Camps
Slippery Rock University
Slippery Rock, Pennsylvania

General Information Coed residential and day sports camp.
Program Focus Developing technical and tactical goalkeeping skills.
Sports Soccer.
Program Information 2 sessions per year. Session length: 6 days in June, July. Ages: 10+. Day program cost: $595. Boarding program cost: $695. Financial aid available.
Application Deadline Continuous.
Jobs Positions for college students.
Contact Mr. Shawn Kelly, General Manager, 11 Executive Drive, Suite 202, Farmington, Connecticut 06032. Phone: 800-533-7371. Fax: 860-677-0460. E-mail: info@soccerpluscamps.com.
URL www.soccerpluscamps.com

SoccerPlus Goalkeeper School–Competitive Program–Pottstown, PA

SoccerPlus Camps
The Hill School
Pottstown, Pennsylvania

General Information Coed residential sports camp.
Program Focus Developing game skills in a competitive environment with quality field players.
Sports Soccer.
Program Information 1 session per year. Session length: 6 days in July. Ages: 12+. Boarding program cost: $755. Financial aid available.
Application Deadline Continuous.
Jobs Positions for college students.
Contact Mr. Shawn Kelly, General Manager, 11 Executive Drive, Suite 202, Farmington, Connecticut 06032. Phone: 800-533-7371. Fax: 860-677-0460. E-mail: info@soccerpluscamps.com.
URL www.soccerpluscamps.com

SoccerPlus Goalkeeper School–Competitive Program–Slippery Rock, PA

SoccerPlus Camps
Slippery Rock University
Slippery Rock, Pennsylvania

General Information Coed residential sports camp.

SoccerPlus Goalkeeper School–Competitive Program–Slippery Rock, PA (continued)

Program Focus Developing game skills in a competitive environment with quality field players.
Sports Soccer.
Program Information 1 session per year. Session length: 6 days in July. Ages: 12+. Boarding program cost: $755. Financial aid available.
Application Deadline Continuous.
Jobs Positions for college students.
Contact Mr. Shawn Kelly, General Manager, 11 Executive Drive, Suite 202, Farmington, Connecticut 06032. Phone: 800-533-7371. Fax: 860-677-0460. E-mail: info@soccerpluscamps.com.
URL www.soccerpluscamps.com

SoccerPlus Goalkeeper School–National Training Center–Pottstown, PA

SoccerPlus Camps
The Hill School
Pottstown, Pennsylvania

General Information Coed residential sports camp.
Program Focus Developing advanced goalkeeping skills.
Sports Soccer.
Program Information 1 session per year. Session length: 6 days in July. Ages: 15+. Boarding program cost: $775.
Application Deadline Continuous.
Jobs Positions for college students.
Contact Mr. Shawn Kelly, General Manager, 11 Executive Drive, Suite 202, Farmington, Connecticut 06032. Phone: 800-533-7371. Fax: 860-677-0460. E-mail: info@soccerpluscamps.com.
URL www.soccerpluscamps.com

SoccerPlus Goalkeeper School–National Training Center–Slippery Rock, PA

SoccerPlus Camps
Slippery Rock University
Slippery Rock, Pennsylvania

General Information Coed residential sports camp.
Program Focus Developing advanced goalkeeping skills.
Sports Soccer.
Program Information 2 sessions per year. Session length: 6 days in July. Ages: 15+. Boarding program cost: $775.
Application Deadline Continuous.
Jobs Positions for college students.
Contact Mr. Shawn Kelly, General Manager, 11 Executive Drive, Suite 202, Farmington, Connecticut 06032. Phone: 800-533-7671. Fax: 860-677-0460. E-mail: info@soccerpluscamps.com.
URL www.soccerpluscamps.com

Sports and Arts Center at Island Lake

Island Lake Road
Starrucca, Pennsylvania 18462

General Information Coed residential academic program, arts program, and sports camp established in 1986. Accredited by American Camping Association.
Program Focus Individually programmed sports and arts.
Academics Astronomy, biology, botany, chemistry, computers, environmental science, geology/earth science, music, physics, reading, science (general).
Arts Arts, arts and crafts (general), band, batiking, ceramics, chorus, circus arts, clowning, creative writing, dance, dance (ballet), dance (folk), dance (jazz), dance (modern), dance (tap), drawing, fabric arts, film, graphic arts, jewelry making, leather working, magic, metalworking, mime, music, music (instrumental), music (vocal), musical productions, painting, photography, pottery, printmaking, puppetry, radio broadcasting, sculpture, television/video, theater/drama, weaving, woodworking.
Special Interest Areas Electronics, field trips (arts and culture), model rocketry, nature study.
Sports Aerobics, archery, baseball, basketball, bicycling, boating, canoeing, cheerleading, climbing (wall), diving, equestrian sports, fencing, field hockey, fishing, football, golf, gymnastics, horseback riding, in-line skating, kayaking, lacrosse, martial arts, rappelling, ropes course, sailing, soccer, softball, sports (general), street/roller hockey, swimming, tennis, volleyball, waterskiing, weight training, windsurfing, wrestling.
Wilderness/Outdoors Backpacking, bicycle trips, canoe trips, hiking, mountain biking, mountaineering, orienteering, rock climbing, survival training, whitewater trips, wilderness camping.
Trips Day, overnight.
Program Information 3 sessions per year. Session length: 14–53 days in June, July, August. Ages: 7–17. 400–500 participants per session. Boarding program cost: $2550–$7350. Financial aid available for session 3 only.
Application Deadline Continuous.
Jobs Positions for college students 18 and older.
Summer Contact Beverly Stoltz, Co-Director, main address above. Phone: 570-798-2550. Fax: 570-798-2346. E-mail: info@islandlake.com.
Winter Contact Beverly Stoltz, Co-Director, 136 East 57th Street, Suite 1001, New York, New York 10022. Phone: 212-753-7777. Fax: 212-753-7761. E-mail: info@islandlake.com.
URL www.islandlake.com

Streamside Camp and Conference Center

Streamside Foundation, Inc./BCM International
Possinger Drive
Stroudsburg, Pennsylvania 18360

General Information Coed residential traditional camp and bible camp established in 1965. Religious affiliation: Christian.
Program Focus Quality conference retreat center for Christ-centered resident camping programs.
Academics Bible study, environmental science, history, music, religion, sign language.
Arts Arts and crafts (general), chorus, clowning, creative writing, dance, dance (folk), drawing, leather working, mime, music, music (vocal), origami, puppetry, television/video, theater/drama.
Special Interest Areas Animal care, campcraft, leadership training, nature study, outdoor cooking, work camp programs.
Sports Aerobics, archery, baseball, basketball, boating, canoeing, cheerleading, cricket, diving, equestrian sports, fishing, football, horseback riding, ropes course, soccer, softball, swimming, volleyball.
Wilderness/Outdoors Backpacking, canoe trips, hiking, mountaineering, orienteering, outdoor camping, survival training, wilderness camping.
Trips Day, overnight, shopping.
Program Information 4–6 sessions per year. Session length: 4–6 days in August. Ages: 8+. 150–250 participants per session. Boarding program cost: $120–$250. Financial aid available. Food service program rebate, multi-child discount, and campership funds available.
Application Deadline Continuous.
Jobs Positions for high school students 15 and older and college students 17 and older.
Contact Dale L. Schoenwald, Director, RR #3, Box 3307, Stroudsburg, Pennsylvania 18360. Phone: 570-629-1902. Fax: 570-629-9650. E-mail: retreats@streamside.org.
URL www.streamside.org

Streamside Family Camp

Streamside Foundation, Inc./BCM International
Possinger Drive
Stroudsburg, Pennsylvania 18360

General Information Coed residential traditional camp, family program, and bible camp established in 1995. Religious affiliation: Christian.
Program Focus Learning and fun together-a family adventure with God.
Academics Bible study, botany, ecology, environmental science, geology/earth science, history, music, religion, sign language.
Arts Arts and crafts (general), chorus, clowning, creative writing, dance, dance (folk), drawing, jewelry making, mime, music, music (vocal), origami, puppetry, television/video, theater/drama.
Special Interest Areas Animal care, campcraft, leadership training, nature study, work camp programs.
Sports Archery, baseball, basketball, boating, canoeing, cheerleading, cricket, equestrian sports, fishing, football, horseback riding, ropes course, slingshot, soccer, softball, swimming, volleyball.
Wilderness/Outdoors Backpacking, hiking, mountaineering, orienteering, outdoor camping, survival training, wilderness camping.
Program Information 1 session per year. Session length: 3 days in June. Ages: 6+. 100–150 participants per session. Boarding program cost: $60. Financial aid available.
Application Deadline Continuous.
Jobs Positions for high school students 15 and older and college students 17 and older.
Contact Dale L. Schoenwald, Director, RR #3, Box 3307, Stroudsburg, Pennsylvania 18360. Phone: 570-629-1902. Fax: 570-629-9650. E-mail: summercamp@streamside.org.
URL www.streamside.org

Streamside Pathfinder Adventure Camp

Streamside Foundation, Inc./BCM International
Possinger Drive
Stroudsburg, Pennsylvania 18360

General Information Coed residential outdoor program, bible camp, wilderness program, and adventure program established in 1977. Religious affiliation: Christian.
Program Focus Making the beauty and challenge of God's creation available and accessible to inner-city youth.
Academics Bible study, astronomy, botany, environmental science, geography, geology/earth science, meteorology.
Arts Music (vocal).
Special Interest Areas Campcraft, nature study, outdoor cooking.
Sports Canoeing, climbing (wall), rappelling, ropes course, snorkeling, swimming.
Wilderness/Outdoors Backpacking, bicycle trips, canoe trips, hiking, mountaineering, orienteering, rafting, rock climbing, survival training, white-water trips, wilderness camping.
Trips Day, overnight.
Program Information 2 sessions per year. Session length: 8–12 days in June, July. Ages: 13–16. 8–12 participants per session. Boarding program cost: $250–$300. Financial aid available.
Application Deadline Continuous.
Jobs Positions for college students 17 and older.
Contact Mr. Dale Schoenwald, Director, RR #3, Box 3307, Stroudsburg, Pennsylvania 18360. Phone: 570-629-1902. Fax: 570-629-9650. E-mail: summercamp@streamside.org.
URL www.streamside.org

Student Conservation Association–Conservation Crew Program (Pennsylvania)

Student Conservation Association (SCA)
Pennsylvania

General Information Coed residential outdoor program, community service program, and wilderness program established in 1957. High school credit may be earned.
Program Focus Resource management, conservation and environmental education.
Academics Biology, botany, ecology, environmental science, geology/earth science, history.
Special Interest Areas Campcraft, community service, construction, leadership training, nature study, trail maintenance, work camp programs.
Sports Canoeing, fishing, kayaking, swimming.
Wilderness/Outdoors Backpacking, canoe trips, hiking, orienteering, outdoor living skills, wilderness camping.
Trips Cultural, day, overnight.
Program Information 2–3 sessions per year. Session length: 3–5 weeks in June, July, August. Ages: 15–19. 6–8 participants per session. Application fee: $20. Financial aid available. No cost for program; financial aid possible for travel expenses.
Application Deadline Continuous.
Jobs Positions for college students 21 and older.
Contact Recruitment Office, PO Box 550, Charlestown, New Hampshire 03603. Phone: 603-543-1700. Fax: 603-543-1828. E-mail: getreal@thesca.org.
URL www.theSCA.org

Study Tours in the USA–Lock Haven

FLS International
Lock Haven University
Courthouse Annex
151 Susquehanna Avenue
Lock Haven, Pennsylvania 17745

General Information Coed residential academic program established in 1987. Formal opportunities for the academically talented.
Program Focus English as a second language.
Academics English as a second language, English language/literature, art (Advanced Placement), art history/appreciation, intercultural studies, precollege program, reading, study skills, writing.
Arts Arts and crafts (general), creative writing, drawing, painting, theater/drama.
Special Interest Areas Community service, homestays.
Sports Baseball, basketball, bicycling, canoeing, horseback riding, kayaking, skiing (cross-country), skiing (downhill), soccer, swimming, track and field, wrestling.
Wilderness/Outdoors Bicycle trips, canoe trips, caving, hiking.
Trips College tours, cultural, day, overnight, shopping.
Program Information 13 sessions per year. Session length: 19–20 days in January, February, March, April, May, June, July, August, September, October, November, December. Ages: 15+. 15–75 participants per session. Boarding program cost: $1495–$2295. Application fee: $100.
Application Deadline Continuous.
Contact Veronica Perez, Director of Admissions, 101 East Green Street, #14, Pasadena, California 91105. Phone: 626-795-2912. Fax: 626-795-5564. E-mail: veronica@fls.net.
URL www.fls.net

For more information, see page 1128.

Summer Academy of Mathematics and Sciences

Carnegie Mellon University
5000 Forbes Avenue
Pittsburgh, Pennsylvania 15213-3890

General Information Coed residential and day academic program established in 2001. Formal opportunities for the academically talented.
Program Focus African American, Hispanic American, and Native American students entering their junior or senior year who are considering careers in engineering, science, and other math based disciplines are eligible to participate in this program.
Academics English language/literature, SAT/ACT preparation, academics (general), computers, engineering, mathematics, precollege program, social studies, study skills.
Special Interest Areas Career exploration, field trips (arts and culture).
Trips Cultural, day.
Program Information 1 session per year. Session length: 6 weeks in June, July, August. Ages: 16–18. 100 participants per session. Financial aid available. No cost for tuition, housing, or dining fees. Participant responsible for books, supplies, transportation and recreational activities.
Application Deadline April 1.
Contact Office of Admission, main address above. Phone: 412-268-2082. Fax: 412-268-7838. E-mail: precollege@andrew.cmu.edu.
URL www.cmu.edu/enrollment/summerprogramsfordiversity/pgsc.html

For more information, see page 1054.

The Summer Institute for the Gifted at Bryn Mawr College

Summer Institute for the Gifted
Bryn Mawr College
Bryn Mawr, Pennsylvania 19010

General Information Coed residential academic program established in 1991. Formal opportunities for the academically talented and gifted. Specific services available for the hearing impaired, learning disabled, physically challenged, and visually impaired. College credit may be earned.
Academics American literature, English language/literature, French language/literature, Latin language, SAT/ACT preparation, Spanish language/literature, academics (general), aerospace science, archaeology,

architecture, art (Advanced Placement), art history/appreciation, biology, business, chemistry, classical languages/literatures, communications, computer programming, computers, engineering, environmental science, history, humanities, marine studies, mathematics, music, philosophy, physics, physiology, precollege program, psychology, science (general), social studies, speech/debate, study skills, writing.
Arts Arts and crafts (general), chorus, creative writing, dance, dance (modern), drawing, graphic arts, mime, music, music (chamber), music (classical), music (ensemble), musical productions, painting, photography, sculpture, theater/drama.
Special Interest Areas Electronics, model rocketry, robotics.
Sports Archery, baseball, basketball, fencing, field hockey, football, lacrosse, martial arts, soccer, squash, swimming, tennis, volleyball.
Wilderness/Outdoors Hiking.
Trips Cultural.
Program Information 1–2 sessions per year. Session length: 3 weeks in June, July, August. Ages: 8–17. 275–300 participants per session. Boarding program cost: $3350. Application fee: $75. Financial aid available.
Application Deadline May 15.
Jobs Positions for college students 19 and older.
Contact Dr. Stephen Gessner, Director, River Plaza, 9 West Broad Street, Stamford, Connecticut 06902-3788. Phone: 866-303-4744. Fax: 203-399-5598. E-mail: sig.info@aifs.com.
URL www.giftedstudy.com
For more information, see page 1342.

SUMMER STUDY AT PENN STATE

Summer Study Programs
University Park, Pennsylvania 16802

General Information Coed residential academic program established in 1991. Formal opportunities for the academically talented and artistically talented. High school or college credit may be earned.
Program Focus Pre-college experience including college credit courses, enrichment classes, SAT preparation, sports, and touring of different college campuses.
Academics American literature, English as a second language, English language/literature, French (Advanced Placement), French language/literature, German language/literature, Russian language/literature, SAT/ACT preparation, Spanish (Advanced Placement), Spanish language/literature, academics (general), anthropology, architecture, art (Advanced Placement), art history/appreciation, astronomy, biology, business, chemistry, classical languages/literatures, college tours, communications, computer programming, computers, ecology, economics, engineering, environmental science, geography, geology/earth science, government and politics, government and politics (Advanced Placement), health sciences, history, humanities, journalism, mathematics, mathematics (Advanced Placement), music, philosophy, physics, physiology, precollege program, psychology, religion, social science, social studies, study skills, writing.
Arts Arts and crafts (general), band, ceramics, creative writing, dance, dance (modern), drawing, graphic arts,

Summer Study at Penn State

jewelry making, music, music (instrumental), music (vocal), painting, photography, pottery, theater/drama.
Special Interest Areas Career exploration, community service, driver's education, touring.
Sports Aerobics, baseball, basketball, bicycling, boating, canoeing, climbing (wall), diving, field hockey, football, golf, gymnastics, ice hockey, in-line skating, lacrosse, martial arts, racquetball, soccer, softball, sports (general), squash, street/roller hockey, swimming, tennis, track and field, volleyball, water polo, weight training, wrestling.
Wilderness/Outdoors Hiking.
Trips College tours, cultural, day, overnight.
Program Information 2 sessions per year. Session length: 25–42 days in June, July, August. Ages: 15–18. 450–500 participants per session. Boarding program cost: $3795–$5995. Application fee: $75. Financial aid available.
Application Deadline Continuous.
Jobs Positions for college students 21 and older.

Summer Study at Penn State (continued)
Contact Mr. Bill Cooperman, Executive Director, 900 Walt Whitman Road, Melville, New York 11747. Phone: 800-666-2556. Fax: 631-424-0567. E-mail: precollegeprograms@summerstudy.com.
URL www.summerstudy.com
For more information, see page 1344.

Summit Camp

Summit Camp
Honesdale, Pennsylvania 18431

General Information Coed residential special needs program established in 1969. Accredited by American Camping Association. Specific services available for the emotionally challenged, learning disabled, participant with ADD, participant with Aspergers Syndrome, and participant with Tourette's Syndrome.
Program Focus Recreation and socialization skills for children with Attention-Deficit Disorders and/or non-verbal learning disabilities, Asperger's Syndrome, Tourette's Syndrome.
Academics Computers.
Arts Arts and crafts (general), ceramics, creative writing, dance (folk), jewelry making, leather working, metalworking, music, pottery, puppetry, radio broadcasting, television/video, theater/drama, woodworking.
Special Interest Areas Animal care, campcraft, culinary arts, model rocketry, nature study, social skills development, work camp programs.
Sports Aerobics, baseball, basketball, bicycling, boating, canoeing, climbing (wall), diving, field hockey, fishing, gymnastics, in-line skating, kayaking, martial arts, ropes course, sailing, soccer, softball, swimming, tennis, track and field, volleyball, windsurfing.
Wilderness/Outdoors Bicycle trips, canoe trips, hiking, mountain biking.
Trips Cultural, day.
Program Information 3 sessions per year. Session length: 10–53 days in June, July, August. Ages: 8–17. 300 participants per session. Boarding program cost: $1845–$9500.
Application Deadline Continuous.
Jobs Positions for college students 20 and older.
Summer Contact Ms. Regina Skyer, Director, RR 5, Box 5230, Honesdale, Pennsylvania 18431. Phone: 570-253-4381. Fax: 570-253-2937. E-mail: summitcamp@aol.com.
Winter Contact Ms. Regina Skyer, Director, 18 East 41st Street, # 402, NY, New York 10017. Phone: 212-689-3880. Fax: 212-689-4347. E-mail: summitcamp@aol.com.
URL www.summitcamp.com

Susquehanna University Advanced Writers Workshop for High School Students

Susquehanna University
Selinsgrove, Pennsylvania 17870

General Information Coed residential academic program established in 1988. Formal opportunities for the academically talented, artistically talented, and gifted.
Program Focus Creative writing.
Academics Writing.
Arts Creative writing.
Sports Swimming.
Trips College tours.
Program Information 1 session per year. Session length: 1 week in July. Ages: 15–18. 45 participants per session. Boarding program cost: $525. Financial aid available.
Application Deadline May 10.
Contact Gary Fincke, Workshop Director, main address above. Phone: 570-372-4164. Fax: 570-372-2774. E-mail: gfincke@susqu.edu.
URL www.susqu.edu/writers

Technology Encounters–Video Encounter/Computer Encounter–Pennsylvania

Ducks in a Row Foundation, Inc./Technology Encounters
Pennsylvania

General Information Coed day arts program established in 2000. Formal opportunities for the academically talented and artistically talented.
Program Focus Local community school district-hosted programs focused on making technology fun, teaching team skills and using creative energies.
Academics Academics (general), communications, computer programming, computers.
Arts Acting, animation, arts and crafts (general), film, film production, graphic arts, television/video, theater/drama.
Special Interest Areas Computer game design, computer graphics, leadership training.
Program Information 40–50 sessions per year. Session length: 5–10 days in June, July, August. Ages: 7–13. 25–100 participants per session. Day program cost: $195. Financial aid available.
Application Deadline Continuous.
Jobs Positions for high school students 17 and older and college students 17 and older.
Contact Ms. Jane Sandlar, Director, 8 Wemrock Drive, Ocean, New Jersey 07712. Phone: 732-695-0827. Fax: 732-496-4282. E-mail: jane@technologyencounters.com.
URL www.technologyencounters.com

Teen Challenge

The Pennsylvania State University at Erie, The Behrend College
5091 Station Road
Erie, Pennsylvania 16563

General Information Coed day academic program established in 2003. Formal opportunities for the academically talented and artistically talented.
Academics Academics (general), art (Advanced Placement), biology, chemistry, engineering, physics.
Arts Drawing, painting, pottery.
Special Interest Areas Electronics, robotics.
Program Information 5 sessions per year. Session length: 5 days in June, July, August. Ages: 15–18. 8–12 participants per session. Day program cost: $175–$235. Application fee: $25.
Application Deadline Continuous.
Contact Ms. Mary Trott, Program Coordinator, Office of Student Affairs, Penn State Erie, 5091 Station Road, Erie, Pennsylvania 16563. Phone: 814-898-6212. Fax: 814-898-6024. E-mail: met7@psu.edu.
URL www.pserie.psu.edu/affairs/cfk/teenchallenge.htm

Time Travelers Program

The University of Scranton
University of Scranton
Scranton, Pennsylvania 18510-4625

General Information Coed residential and day academic program. Formal opportunities for the academically talented.
Academics English language/literature, academics (general), mathematics, music, science (general).
Arts Performance art, visual arts.
Program Information 1 session per year. Session length: 18 days in July. Ages: 11–14. 40 participants per session. Day program cost: $985. Boarding program cost: $1800. Open to participants entering grades 6–8.
Application Deadline Continuous.
Contact Gary P. Celli, Director of Special Projects, main address above. Phone: 570-941-7580. Fax: 570-941-5819. E-mail: cellig2@scranton.edu.
URL www.scranton.edu

United Soccer Academy–Goal Keeping Training Camp, Pennsylvania

United Soccer Academy, Inc.
Pennsylvania

General Information Coed residential and day sports camp established in 1999.
Program Focus All aspects of the keeper position are covered: from techniques to tactical decision-making. Coaching staff is selected from international teams and colleges.
Sports Soccer.
Program Information 10 sessions per year. Session length: 5 days in April, June, July, August, September, November. Ages: 8–14. 16–200 participants per session. Day program cost: $145. Boarding program cost: $495. Call for specific locations.
Application Deadline Continuous.
Jobs Positions for college students 18 and older.
Contact Camps Information, 50 Tannery Road, Unit 8, Branchburg, New Jersey 08876. Phone: 908-823-0130. Fax: 908-823-0466. E-mail: info@unitedsocceracademy.com.
URL www.unitedsocceracademy.com

United Soccer Academy–Junior Soccer Squirts, Pennsylvania

United Soccer Academy, Inc.
Pennsylvania

General Information Coed day sports camp established in 1999.
Program Focus Introduction to soccer in a camp format with emphasis on fun games and activities in small groups. Coaches are from international soccer teams and college teams.
Sports Soccer.
Program Information 50 sessions per year. Session length: 5 days in April, June, July, August, September, November. Ages: 3–5. 6–48 participants per session. Day program cost: $89. Two sessions daily; parents may stay with camper. Call for specific locations.
Application Deadline Continuous.
Jobs Positions for college students 18 and older.
Contact Camps Information, 50 Tannery Road, Unit 8, Branchburg, New Jersey 08876. Phone: 908-823-0130. Fax: 908-823-0466. E-mail: info@unitedsocceracademy.com.
URL www.unitedsocceracademy.com

United Soccer Academy–Recreation Soccer Community Camp, Pennsylvania

United Soccer Academy, Inc.
Pennsylvania

General Information Coed residential and day sports camp established in 1999.
Program Focus Players build on the fundamentals of the game, experiencing a broad range of techniques and skills. Coaches are from international teams and colleges.
Sports Soccer.
Program Information 75 sessions per year. Session length: 5 days in April, June, July, August, September, November. Ages: 7–14. 16–200 participants per session. Day program cost: $145. Boarding program cost: $495. Call for specific locations.
Application Deadline Continuous.
Jobs Positions for college students 18 and older.
Contact Camps Information, 50 Tannery Road, Unit 8, Branchburg, New Jersey 08876. Phone: 908-823-0130. Fax: 908-823-0466. E-mail: info@unitedsocceracademy.com.
URL www.unitedsocceracademy.com

UNITED SOCCER ACADEMY–REGIONAL ACADEMY CAMP, PENNSYLVANIA

United Soccer Academy, Inc.
Pennsylvania

General Information Coed residential and day sports camp established in 1999.
Program Focus Intense program aimed at the dedicated travel and select soccer player. Sites are regionalized to ensure high quality competition. Advanced techniques and skills taught, tactical game analysis, position assessment. Coaches are from international teams and colleges.
Sports Soccer.
Program Information 5 sessions per year. Session length: 5 days in June, July, August. Ages: 8–14. 16–200 participants per session. Day program cost: $165. Boarding program cost: $495. Call for specific locations.
Application Deadline Continuous.
Jobs Positions for college students 18 and older.
Contact Camps Information, 50 Tannery Road, Unit 8, Branchburg, New Jersey 08876. Phone: 908-823-0130. Fax: 908-823-0466. E-mail: info@unitedsocceracademy.com.
URL www.unitedsocceracademy.com

UNITED SOCCER ACADEMY–SENIOR SOCCER SQUIRTS, PENNSYLVANIA

United Soccer Academy, Inc.
Pennsylvania

General Information Coed day sports camp established in 1999.
Program Focus Introduction to the game in relaxed, fun atmosphere; skills development without competitive environment. Coaches are from international teams and colleges.
Sports Soccer.
Program Information 50 sessions per year. Session length: 5 days in April, June, July, August, September, November. Ages: 5–7. 6–48 participants per session. Day program cost: $89. Two sessions daily; call for specific locations.
Application Deadline Continuous.
Jobs Positions for college students 18 and older.
Contact Camps Information, 50 Tannery Road, Unit 8, Branchburg, New Jersey 08876. Phone: 908-823-0130. Fax: 908-823-0466. E-mail: info@unitedsocceracademy.com.
URL www.unitedsocceracademy.com

UNITED SOCCER ACADEMY–TEAM TRAINING CAMP, PENNSYLVANIA

United Soccer Academy, Inc.
Pennsylvania

General Information Coed residential and day sports camp established in 1999.
Program Focus Teams of ten or more players receive individualized instruction based on staff discussion with their coach. Structured coaching scrimmages with other teams. Coaches on staff are from international teams and colleges.
Sports Soccer.
Program Information 25 sessions per year. Session length: 5 days in April, June, July, August, September, November. Ages: 8–14. 20–200 participants per session. Day program cost: $125. Boarding program cost: $495. Call for specific locations.
Application Deadline Continuous.
Jobs Positions for college students 18 and older.
Contact Camps Information, 50 Tannery Road, Unit 8, Branchburg, New Jersey 08876. Phone: 908-823-0130. Fax: 908-823-0466. E-mail: info@unitedsocceracademy.com.
URL www.unitedsocceracademy.com

UNITED SOCCER ACADEMY–TRAVEL SOCCER COMMUNITY CAMP, PENNSYLVANIA

United Soccer Academy, Inc.
Pennsylvania

General Information Coed residential and day sports camp established in 1999.
Program Focus Individual player development and team tactics are emphasized. Skills are taught at an accelerated level with practices developing into full game realistic situations. Coaches are from international teams and colleges.
Sports Soccer.
Program Information 75 sessions per year. Session length: 5 days in April, June, July, August, September, November. Ages: 8–14. 16–200 participants per session. Day program cost: $145. Boarding program cost: $495. Call for specific locations.
Application Deadline Continuous.
Jobs Positions for college students 18 and older.
Contact Camps Information, 50 Tannery Road, Unit 8, Branchburg, New Jersey 08876. Phone: 908-823-0130. Fax: 908-823-0466. E-mail: info@unitedsocceracademy.com.
URL www.unitedsocceracademy.com

UNIVERSITY OF PENNSYLVANIA–PENN SUMMER ART STUDIO

University of Pennsylvania
3440 Market Street, Suite 100
Philadelphia, Pennsylvania 19104-3335

General Information Coed residential and day arts program established in 2002. Formal opportunities for the academically talented and artistically talented. College credit may be earned.
Academics Architecture.
Arts Animation, digital media, drawing, film, graphic arts, painting, photography, television/video.
Trips Cultural, day, shopping.
Program Information 1 session per year. Session length: 4 weeks in June, July. Ages: 16+. 300

participants per session. Day program cost: $2700. Boarding program cost: $4700. Application fee: $50–$100. Financial aid available.
Application Deadline April 15.
Contact Mr. Matthew Palmer, Coordinator of Summer Sessions, main address above. Phone: 215-746-6901. Fax: 215-573-2053. E-mail: hsprogs@sas.upenn.edu.
URL www.upenn.edu/summer

University of Pennsylvania–Penn Summer Science Academy

University of Pennsylvania
3440 Market Street, Suite 100
Philadelphia, Pennsylvania 19104-3335

General Information Coed residential and day academic program. Formal opportunities for the academically talented.
Academics Astronomy, biology, biology (Advanced Placement), chemistry, ecology, physics.
Trips Cultural, day, shopping.
Program Information 1 session per year. Session length: 4 weeks in June, July. Ages: 16+. 300 participants per session. Day program cost: $2600. Boarding program cost: $4500. Application fee: $50–$100. Financial aid available.
Application Deadline April 15.
Contact Mr. Matthew Palmer, Coordinator of Summer Sessions, main address above. Phone: 215-746-6901. Fax: 215-573-2053. E-mail: hsprogs@sas.upenn.edu.
URL www.upenn.edu/summer

University of Pennsylvania–Precollege Program

University of Pennsylvania
3440 Market Street, Suite 100
Philadelphia, Pennsylvania 19104-3335

General Information Coed residential and day academic program established in 1981. Formal opportunities for the academically talented and gifted. College credit may be earned.
Academics American literature, Chinese languages/literature, English as a second language, English language/literature, Jewish studies, SAT/ACT preparation, Spanish language/literature, anthropology, archaeology, art history/appreciation, astronomy, biology, business, chemistry, classical languages/literatures, communications, computer programming, economics, geology/earth science, government and politics, government and politics (Advanced Placement), history, humanities, linguistics, mathematics, music, philosophy, physics, precollege program, prelaw, premed, psychology, religion, social science, study skills, writing.
Arts Creative writing, film.
Special Interest Areas Career exploration, community service, leadership training.
Sports Basketball, bicycling, fishing, golf, horseback riding, soccer, softball, swimming, tennis, volleyball.
Wilderness/Outdoors Bicycle trips, canoe trips, hiking, mountain biking, white-water trips.
Trips Cultural, day, shopping.

University of Pennsylvania–Precollege Program

Program Information 1 session per year. Session length: 6 weeks in June, July, August. Ages: 15+. 300 participants per session. Boarding program cost: $4950–$7150. Application fee: $50–$100. Financial aid available.
Application Deadline April 15.
Contact Mr. Matthew Palmer, Coordinator of Summer Sessions, main address above. Phone: 215-746-6901. Fax: 215-573-2053. E-mail: precoll@sas.upenn.edu.
URL www.upenn.edu/summer

For more information, see page 1368.

Valley Forge Military Academy Extreme Tennis Camp

Valley Forge Military Academy and College
1001 Eagle Road
Wayne, Pennsylvania 19087-3695

General Information Coed day sports camp.
Program Focus Tennis, good sportsmanship, and character-building program.
Special Interest Areas Leadership training.
Sports Swimming, tennis.
Program Information 6 sessions per year. Session length: 5–30 days in June, July. Ages: 8–16. 5–10 participants per session. Day program cost: $400–$2300. Application fee: $125. Financial aid available.
Application Deadline Continuous.
Jobs Positions for high school students 18 and older and college students 18 and older.
Summer Contact Maj. Jeffrey Bond, Director of Summer Camps, main address above. Phone: 610-989-1253. Fax: 610-688-1260. E-mail: summercamp@vfmac.edu.
Winter Contact Lt. Col. Kelly M. DeShane, USAR, Dean of Admissions, main address above. Phone: 610-989-1300. Fax: 610-688-1545. E-mail: admissions@vfmac.edu.
URL www.vfmac.edu

For more information, see page 1378.

VALLEY FORGE MILITARY ACADEMY SUMMER BAND CAMP

Valley Forge Military Academy and College
1001 Eagle Road
Wayne, Pennsylvania 19087-3695

General Information Coed residential and day traditional camp and arts program established in 1945.
Program Focus Day and overnight coed band camp.
Academics Music.
Arts Arts and crafts (general), band, music (instrumental).
Special Interest Areas Leadership training.
Sports Archery, baseball, basketball, canoeing, climbing (wall), equestrian sports, go-carts, golf, horseback riding, in-line skating, martial arts, paintball, rappelling, riflery, ropes course, scuba diving, soccer, softball, sports (general), street/roller hockey, swimming, tennis, track and field, volleyball, water polo, weight training.
Trips Cultural, day, overnight.
Program Information 1 session per year. Session length: 4 weeks in June, July. Ages: 12–16. 25–75 participants per session. Day program cost: $1900. Boarding program cost: $2900. Application fee: $125. Financial aid available.
Application Deadline Continuous.
Jobs Positions for high school students 18 and older and college students 18 and older.
Summer Contact Maj. Jeffrey Bond, Director of Summer Camps, main address above. Phone: 610-989-1253. Fax: 610-688-1260. E-mail: summercamp@vfmac.edu.
Winter Contact Lt. Col. Kelly M. DeShane, Dean of Admissions, main address above. Phone: 610-989-1300. Fax: 610-688-1545. E-mail: admissions@vfmac.edu.
URL www.vfmac.edu

For more information, see page 1378.

VALLEY FORGE MILITARY ACADEMY SUMMER CAMP FOR BOYS

Valley Forge Military Academy and College
1001 Eagle Road
Wayne, Pennsylvania 19087-3695

General Information Boys' residential and day traditional camp and outdoor program established in 1945.
Academics Bible study, English language/literature, mathematics, music, reading.
Arts Arts and crafts (general), band, music (instrumental).
Special Interest Areas Campcraft, leadership training, team building.
Sports Archery, baseball, basketball, boating, canoeing, climbing (wall), equestrian sports, go-carts, golf, horseback riding, in-line skating, martial arts, paintball, rappelling, riflery, ropes course, scuba diving, soccer, softball, sports (general), street/roller hockey, swimming, tennis, volleyball, water polo, weight training.
Wilderness/Outdoors Canoe trips, hiking, orienteering, survival training, wilderness camping.
Trips Cultural, day, overnight.
Program Information 1 session per year. Session length: 4 weeks in June, July. Ages: 8–16. 320–400

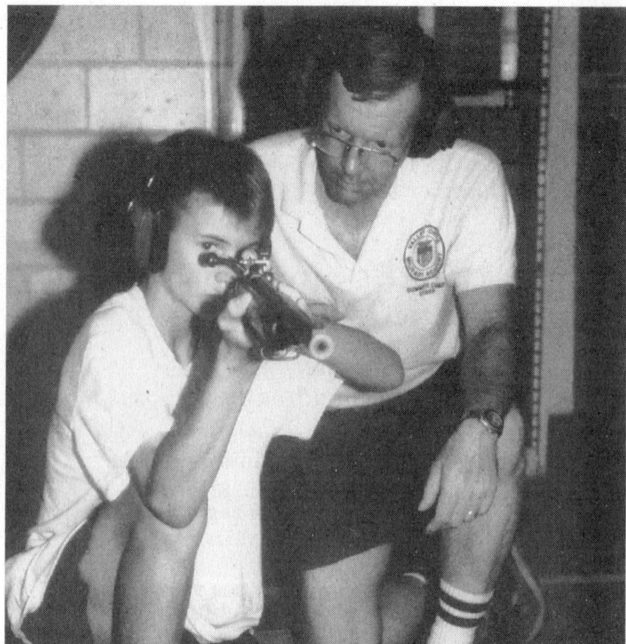

Valley Forge Military Academy Summer Camp for Boys

participants per session. Boarding program cost: $3100–$3200. Application fee: $125. $175 spending allowance required; additional classes and activities: $250–$900.
Application Deadline Continuous.
Jobs Positions for high school students 18 and older and college students 18 and older.
Summer Contact Maj. Jeffrey Bond, Director of Summer Camps, main address above. Phone: 610-989-1253. Fax: 610-688-1260. E-mail: summercamp@vfmac.edu.
Winter Contact Ltc. Kelly M. DeShane, USAR, Dean of Admissions, main address above. Phone: 610-989-1300. Fax: 610-688-1545. E-mail: admissions@vfmac.edu.
URL www.vfmac.edu

For more information, see page 1378.

VALLEY FORGE MILITARY ACADEMY SUMMER COED DAY CAMP

Valley Forge Military Academy and College
1001 Eagle Road
Wayne, Pennsylvania 19087-3695

General Information Coed day traditional camp and outdoor program established in 2004.
Academics English language/literature, mathematics, music, reading.
Arts Arts and crafts (general), band, music (instrumental).
Special Interest Areas Field trips (arts and culture), leadership training.
Sports Archery, baseball, basketball, canoeing, climbing (wall), equestrian sports, go-carts, golf, horseback riding, in-line skating, martial arts, paintball, rappelling, riflery, ropes course, scuba diving, soccer, softball, sports (general), street/roller hockey, swimming, tennis, volleyball, water polo, weight training.

Wilderness/Outdoors Canoe trips, hiking, orienteering, survival training, wilderness camping.
Trips Cultural, day, overnight.
Program Information 1–6 sessions per year. Session length: 5–30 days in June, July. Ages: 6–16. 150–200 participants per session. Day program cost: $300–$1700. Application fee: $125. Financial aid available. $175 spending allowance required; additional classes and activities for 6-week participants only: $250–$900.
Application Deadline Continuous.
Jobs Positions for high school students 18 and older and college students 18 and older.
Summer Contact Maj. Jeffrey Bond, Director of Summer Camps, main address above. Phone: 610-989-1253. Fax: 610-688-1260. E-mail: summercamp@vfmac.edu.
Winter Contact Lt. Col. Kelly M. DeShane, USAR, Dean of Admissions, main address above. Phone: 610-989-1300. Fax: 610-688-1545. E-mail: admissions@vfmac.edu.
URL www.vfmac.edu

For more information, see page 1378.

Women in Science & Engineering Camp

The Pennsylvania State University–WISE
University Park, Pennsylvania 16802

General Information Girls' residential academic program established in 1992.
Academics Aerospace science, archaeology, biology, botany, chemistry, computers, ecology, engineering, environmental science, geography, geology/earth science, health sciences, mathematics, meteorology, physics, physiology, science (general).
Special Interest Areas Career exploration.
Program Information 1 session per year. Session length: 1 week in June, July. Ages: 16–18. 32–36 participants per session. Boarding program cost: $350. Financial aid available.
Application Deadline April 1.
Contact Katie Rung, Assistant Director, 111G Kern Building, University Park, Pennsylvania 16802. Phone: 814-865-3342. Fax: 814-863-0085. E-mail: cxg1@psu.edu.
URL www.equity.psu.edu/wise

Woodward Freestyle BMX Bicycle, Inline Skate, Skateboarding Camp

Woodward Camp, Inc.
134 Sports Camp Drive
Woodward, Pennsylvania 16882

General Information Coed residential sports camp established in 1984.
Program Focus Taught by professional instructors.
Arts Arts and crafts (general), ceramics, fabric arts, jewelry making, leather working, photography, pottery, weaving.
Sports Basketball, bicycling (BMX), cheerleading, climbing (wall), go-carts, gymnastics, horseback riding, in-line skating, paintball, ropes course, skateboarding, swimming, volleyball, weight training.
Wilderness/Outdoors Rock climbing.
Program Information 14 sessions per year. Session length: 6 days in June, July, August. Ages: 7–17. 350–500 participants per session. Financial aid available. Cost: $895 for one week, $845 each additional week.
Application Deadline Continuous.
Jobs Positions for college students 18 and older.
Contact Russ Haerer, Manager, PO Box 93, 134 Sports Camp Drive, Woodward, Pennsylvania 16882. Phone: 814-349-5633. Fax: 814-349-5643. E-mail: office@woodwardcamp.com.
URL www.woodwardcamp.com

Woodward Gymnastics Camp

Woodward Camp, Inc.
134 Sports Camp Drive
Woodward, Pennsylvania 16882

General Information Coed residential sports camp established in 1970.
Program Focus Taught by professional coaches.
Arts Arts and crafts (general), ceramics, fabric arts, jewelry making, leather working, photography, pottery, weaving.
Sports Basketball, bicycling (BMX), cheerleading, climbing (wall), go-carts, gymnastics, horseback riding, in-line skating, paintball, ropes course, swimming, volleyball, weight training.
Program Information 11 sessions per year. Session length: 6 days in June, July, August. Ages: 7–17. 150–330 participants per session. Financial aid available. Cost: $725 for one week, $675 each additional week.
Application Deadline Continuous.
Jobs Positions for college students 18 and older.
Contact Russ Haerer, Manager, PO Box 93, 134 Sports Camp Drive, Woodward, Pennsylvania 16882. Phone: 814-349-5633. Fax: 814-349-5643. E-mail: office@woodwardcamp.com.
URL www.woodwardcamp.com

Wyoming Seminary–Sem Summer 2005

Wyoming Seminary College Preparatory School
Wyoming Seminary
201 North Sprague Avenue
Kingston, Pennsylvania 18704

General Information Coed residential and day academic program established in 1991. Religious affiliation: United Methodist. Formal opportunities for the academically talented and artistically talented. High school credit may be earned.
Program Focus Academic enrichment and science discovery.
Academics Bible study, English as a second language, French language/literature, Latin language, SAT/ACT preparation, Spanish language/literature, academics (general), art history/appreciation, biology, chemistry, communications, computers, ecology, environmental science, health sciences, history, humanities, journalism, marine studies, mathematics, music, music (Advanced Placement), physics, precollege program, reading, religion, science (general), speech/debate, study skills, writing.

Wyoming Seminary–Sem Summer 2005 (continued)

Wyoming Seminary–Sem Summer 2005

Arts Arts and crafts (general), band, ceramics, chorus, dance, dance (ballet), dance (jazz), dance (modern), drawing, music, music (chamber), music (classical), music (ensemble), music (instrumental), music (jazz), music (orchestral), music (vocal), musical productions, photography, pottery, theater/drama.
Sports Basketball, field hockey, soccer, softball, swimming, tennis, volleyball.
Trips Cultural, day, overnight, shopping.
Program Information 1–2 sessions per year. Session length: 14–60 days in June, July, August. Ages: 12–18. 325–425 participants per session. Day program cost: $60–$1000. Boarding program cost: $2800–$8600. Application fee: $25–$50. Financial aid available.
Application Deadline Continuous.
Jobs Positions for high school students 17 and older and college students 19 and older.
Contact John R. Eidam, Dean of Admissions/Director of International and Summer Programs, main address above. Phone: 570-270-2187. Fax: 570-270-2198. E-mail: semsum@wyomingseminary.org.
URL www.wyomingseminary.org/summer
For more information, see page 1410.

YMCA Camp Fitch Summer Camp

YMCA Camp Fitch
12600 Ables Road
North Springfield, Pennsylvania 16430

General Information Coed residential traditional camp and academic program established in 1914. Accredited by American Camping Association.
Program Focus Broad-based program with an emphasis on waterfront activities and including specialty camps for soccer, computers, swimming, running, music, CIT, and diabetic and orthopedic camps.
Academics Computer programming, computers, music.
Arts Arts and crafts (general), leather working, music (instrumental).
Special Interest Areas Animal care, campcraft, leadership training, model rocketry, nautical skills.
Sports Archery, baseball, bicycling, boating, canoeing, climbing (wall), cross-country, equestrian sports, fishing, football, horseback riding, kayaking, rappelling, riflery, sailing, sea kayaking, snorkeling, soccer, softball, swimming, volleyball, waterskiing.
Wilderness/Outdoors Bicycle trips, canoe trips, climbing, rock climbing.
Program Information 8 sessions per year. Session length: 1 week in June, July, August. Ages: 8–18. 200–300 participants per session. Boarding program cost: $350–$380. Financial aid available.
Application Deadline Continuous.
Jobs Positions for high school students 16 and older and college students.
Contact Mr. William Lyder, Executive Camp Director, 17 N. Champion Street, Youngstown, Ohio 44501-1287. Phone: 330-744-8411. Fax: 330-744-8416. E-mail: campfitch@hotmail.com.
URL www.campfitch.com

YMCA Camp Shand

Lancaster Family YMCA
Lancaster, Pennsylvania

General Information Coed residential and day traditional camp established in 1894. Accredited by American Camping Association.
Arts Arts and crafts (general), ceramics, dance, drawing, jewelry making, leather working, painting, theater/drama, woodworking.
Special Interest Areas Native American culture, animal care, campcraft, community service, leadership training, model rocketry, nature study, nautical skills.
Sports Archery, baseball, basketball, bicycling, boating, canoeing, climbing (wall), equestrian sports, field hockey, fishing, football, golf, horseback riding, lacrosse, ropes course, soccer, softball, street/roller hockey, swimming, volleyball, water polo.
Wilderness/Outdoors Backpacking, canoe trips, hiking, mountain biking, orienteering, rafting, survival training, white-water trips, wilderness camping.
Trips Day, overnight.
Program Information 10 sessions per year. Session length: 5–6 days in June, July, August. Ages: 5–16. 60–90 participants per session. Day program cost: $130–$150. Boarding program cost: $305–$335. Financial aid available.

Application Deadline Continuous.
Jobs Positions for high school students 16 and older and college students 18 and older.
Contact Ms. Brenda Barrett, Camp Director, 572 North Queen Street, Lancaster, Pennsylvania 17603. Phone: 717-397-7474 Ext.104. Fax: 717-397-7815. E-mail: ymcacampshand@dejazzd.com.
URL www.LancasterYMCA.org

RHODE ISLAND

ALTON JONES DAY CAMP

University of Rhode Island
West Alton Jones Campus
401 Victory Highway
West Greenwich, Rhode Island 02817

General Information Coed day outdoor program established in 1990. Accredited by American Camping Association.
Program Focus Farming and ecology.
Academics Ecology, environmental science.
Special Interest Areas Animal care, campcraft, farming, gardening, nature study.
Wilderness/Outdoors Hiking.
Program Information 8 sessions per year. Session length: 5 days in July, August. Ages: 5–11. 80 participants per session. Day program cost: $185–$195. Financial aid available.
Application Deadline Continuous.
Jobs Positions for high school students 14 and older and college students 18 and older.
Contact Mr. John Jacques, Manager, main address above. Phone: 401-397-3304 Ext.6043. Fax: 401-397-3293. E-mail: urieec@etal.uri.edu.
URL www.uri.edu/ajc/eec/

ALTON JONES EARTH CAMP

University of Rhode Island
West Alton Jones Campus
401 Victory Highway
West Greenwich, Rhode Island 02817

General Information Coed residential outdoor program established in 1963. Accredited by American Camping Association.
Program Focus Ecology and the environment.
Academics Astronomy, ecology, environmental science, marine studies.
Special Interest Areas Native American culture, animal care, campcraft, farming, gardening, nature study.
Sports Canoeing, swimming.
Wilderness/Outdoors Backpacking, hiking, wilderness camping.
Trips Day, overnight.
Program Information 7 sessions per year. Session length: 6 days in July, August. Ages: 9–13. 100 participants per session. Boarding program cost: $410–$595. Financial aid available.
Application Deadline Continuous.
Jobs Positions for high school students 15 and older and college students 18 and older.
Contact Mr. John Jacques, Manager, main address above. Phone: 401-397-3304 Ext.6043. Fax: 401-397-3293. E-mail: urieec@etal.uri.edu.
URL www.uri.edu/ajc/eec/

BROWN UNIVERSITY SUMMER PROGRAMS–PRE-COLLEGE PROGRAM

Brown University
133 Waterman Street
Providence, Rhode Island 02912-9120

General Information Coed residential and day academic program established in 1982. Formal opportunities for the academically talented. College credit may be earned.
Program Focus Environmental leadership lab, students camp at the site for 2 weeks.
Academics American literature, English as a second language, English language/literature, Latin language, academics (general), anthropology, art history/appreciation, astronomy, biology, chemistry, communications, computer programming, computer science (Advanced Placement), computers, ecology, economics, engineering, environmental science, geology/earth science, government and politics, history, humanities, intercultural studies, journalism, marine studies, mathematics, music, oceanography, philosophy, physiology, precollege program, psychology, religion, speech/debate, writing.
Arts Creative writing, dance, music.
Special Interest Areas Career exploration, electronics, leadership training.
Trips Cultural, day.
Program Information 1–6 sessions per year. Session length: 1–7 weeks in June, July, August. Ages: 12–18. 75–700 participants per session. Day program cost: $1050–$4400. Boarding program cost: $1320–$7500. Application fee: $50–$100. Financial aid available.
Application Deadline Continuous.
Jobs Positions for college students.
Contact Ms. Karen H. Sibley, Dean of Summer Studies, 133 Waterman Street, Box T, Providence, Rhode Island 02912-9120. Phone: 401-863-7900. Fax: 401-863-7908. E-mail: summer@brown.edu.
URL www.brown.edu/summer

CAMP CANONICUS

Canonicus Camp and Conference Center
54 Exeter Road
Exeter, Rhode Island 02822

General Information Coed residential and day traditional camp established in 1948. Religious affiliation: American Baptist Churches in the USA. Accredited by American Camping Association.

Camp Canonicus (continued)

Program Focus Christian focus; regular Bible studies and worship.
Academics Bible study.
Arts Arts and crafts (general), music (vocal), musical productions, theater/drama.
Special Interest Areas Campcraft, leadership training, model rocketry, nature study, work camp programs.
Sports Archery, basketball, boating, canoeing, cheerleading, equestrian sports, fishing, horseback riding, in-line skating, kayaking, ropes course, soccer, swimming, volleyball, windsurfing.
Wilderness/Outdoors Backpacking, canoe trips, hiking, rock climbing, white-water trips, wilderness camping.
Trips Day, overnight.
Program Information 8 sessions per year. Session length: 5–8 days in June, July, August. Ages: 4–18. 40–80 participants per session. Day program cost: $125–$195. Boarding program cost: $130–$575. Financial aid available.
Application Deadline Continuous.
Jobs Positions for college students 18 and older.
Contact Mr. Mark Bates, Director of Camping and Conferencing, PO Box 330, Exeter, Rhode Island 02822-0330. Phone: 800-294-6318 Ext.100. Fax: 401-294-7780. E-mail: mark@canonicus.org.
URL www.canonicus.org

Damon Huard and Matt Light Football Camp/Sports International

Sports International, Inc.
Bryant College
Smithfield, Rhode Island 02917

General Information Coed residential and day sports camp established in 1983.
Sports Football, weight training.
Program Information 1 session per year. Session length: 5 days in July. Ages: 8–18. 300–450 participants per session. Day program cost: $529. Boarding program cost: $639.
Application Deadline Continuous.
Jobs Positions for college students 18 and older.
Contact Customer Service, 8924 McGaw Court, Columbia, Maryland 21045. Phone: 800-555-0801. Fax: 401-309-9962. E-mail: info@footballcamps.com.
URL www.footballcamps.com

Joe Krivak Quarterback Camp, Rhode Island/Sports International

Sports International, Inc.
Bryant College
Smithfield, Rhode Island

General Information Coed residential and day sports camp established in 1983.
Program Focus Quarterback and wide receiver.
Sports Football, weight training.
Program Information 1 session per year. Session length: 5 days in July. Ages: 8–18. 300–450 participants per session. Day program cost: $349. Boarding program cost: $419.
Application Deadline Continuous.
Jobs Positions for college students 18 and older.
Contact Customer Service, 8924 McGaw Court, Columbia, Maryland 21045. Phone: 800-555-0801. Fax: 410-309-9962. E-mail: info@footballcamps.com.
URL www.footballcamps.com

Landmark Volunteers: Rhode Island

Landmark Volunteers, Inc.
Rhode Island

General Information Coed residential community service program established in 1992. High school credit may be earned.
Program Focus Opportunity for high school students to earn community service credit while working as a team for two weeks serving Tennis Hall of Fame. Similar programs offered through Landmark Volunteers at over 60 locations in 21 states.
Academics Area studies, history.
Special Interest Areas Career exploration, community service, leadership training, team building.
Sports Tennis.
Trips Cultural, day.
Program Information 1 session per year. Session length: 14–17 days in June, July. Ages: 14–18. 10–13 participants per session. Boarding program cost: $875–$925. Financial aid available.
Application Deadline Continuous.
Jobs Positions for college students.
Contact Ann Barrett, Executive Director, PO Box 455, Sheffield, Massachusetts 01257. Phone: 413-229-0255. Fax: 413-229-2050. E-mail: landmark@volunteers.com.
URL www.volunteers.com

For more information, see page 1182.

Portsmouth Abbey Summer School

Portsmouth Abbey School
285 Corys Lane
Portsmouth, Rhode Island 02871-1352

General Information Coed residential and day academic program established in 1943. Religious affiliation: Roman Catholic.
Program Focus Academic enrichment.
Academics English as a second language, English language/literature, French language/literature, Latin language, SAT/ACT preparation, Spanish language/literature, academics (general), classical languages/literatures, computers, economics, geology/earth science, government and politics, health sciences, history, journalism, marine studies, mathematics, physiology, reading, speech/debate, study skills, writing.
Arts Acting, arts and crafts (general), ceramics, creative writing, drawing, painting, photography, pottery.
Sports Basketball, equestrian sports, horseback riding, sailing, soccer, softball, squash, tennis, track and field, volleyball, weight training.

Portsmouth Abbey Summer School

Trips Cultural, day, shopping.
Program Information 1 session per year. Session length: 5 weeks in June, July. Ages: 13–16. 60–70 participants per session. Day program cost: $2300. Boarding program cost: $4400. Application fee: $55. Financial aid available.
Application Deadline Continuous.
Jobs Positions for college students 21 and older.
Contact Mr. Robert Sahms, Director of Summer School, Portsmouth Abbey School, Portsmouth, Rhode Island 02871. Phone: 401-683-2000 Ext.225. Fax: 401-683-5888. E-mail: summer@portsmouthabbey.org.
URL www.portsmouthabbey.org
For more information, see page 1268.

Rhode Island School of Design Pre-College Program

Rhode Island School of Design
2 College Street
Providence, Rhode Island 02903-2787

General Information Coed residential and day arts program established in 1970. Formal opportunities for the artistically talented.
Program Focus Art and design.
Academics Art (Advanced Placement), art history/appreciation, precollege program.

Rhode Island School of Design Pre-College Program

Arts Arts, ceramics, design, drawing, fabric arts, film, graphic arts, jewelry making, painting, photography, pottery, printmaking, sculpture, weaving.
Special Interest Areas Field trips (arts and culture).
Trips Cultural, day, shopping.
Program Information 1 session per year. Session length: 6 weeks in June, July. Ages: 16–18. 400–500 participants per session. Day program cost: $3075. Boarding program cost: $4515. Financial aid available. Rhode Island Resident Scholarships, Balfour Minority Scholarship.
Application Deadline Continuous.
Contact Mr. Marc Torick, Continuing Education Office/Summer Programs, main address above. Phone: 401-454-6200. Fax: 401-454-6218. E-mail: cemail@risd.edu.
URL www.risd.edu/precollege.cfm
For more information, see page 1284.

St. George's Summer Session

St. George's School
Newport, Rhode Island 02840

General Information Coed residential and day academic program established in 1944.

St. George's Summer Session

St. George's Summer Session (continued)

Academics American literature, Chinese languages/literature, English as a second language, English language/literature, Latin language, SAT/ACT preparation, Spanish (Advanced Placement), Spanish language/literature, TOEFL/TOEIC preparation, academics (general), art (Advanced Placement), astronomy, biology, biology (Advanced Placement), chemistry, chemistry (Advanced Placement), computer science (Advanced Placement), computers, history, history (Advanced Placement), journalism, marine studies, mathematics, mathematics (Advanced Placement), music, philosophy, precollege program, reading, science (general), speech/debate, study skills, writing.
Arts Acting, ceramics, creative writing, drawing, music (instrumental), painting, photography, pottery, sculpture, theater/drama.
Special Interest Areas College planning.
Sports Basketball, bicycling, sailing, soccer, softball, tennis, volleyball, weight training, windsurfing.
Wilderness/Outdoors Hiking.
Trips Cultural, day, shopping.
Program Information 1 session per year. Session length: 5 weeks in June, July, August. Ages: 13–18. 150 participants per session. Day program cost: $2400. Boarding program cost: $4800. Application fee: $50. Financial aid available.
Application Deadline Continuous.
Contact Anthony T.T. Jaccaci, Director of Summer Session, PO Box 1910, Newport, Rhode Island 02840-0190. Phone: 401-842-6712. Fax: 401-842-6763. E-mail: tony_jaccaci@stgeorges.edu.
URL www.stgeorges.edu/summerschool

For more information, see page 1294.

Student Conservation Association–Conservation Crew Program (Rhode Island)

Student Conservation Association (SCA)
Rhode Island

General Information Coed residential outdoor program, community service program, and wilderness program established in 1957. High school credit may be earned.
Program Focus Resource management, conservation and environmental education.
Academics Biology, botany, ecology, environmental science, geology/earth science, history.
Special Interest Areas Campcraft, community service, construction, leadership training, nature study, trail maintenance, work camp programs.
Sports Canoeing, fishing, kayaking, swimming.
Wilderness/Outdoors Backpacking, canoe trips, hiking, orienteering, outdoor living skills, wilderness camping.
Trips Cultural, day, overnight.
Program Information 2–3 sessions per year. Session length: 3–5 weeks in June, July, August. Ages: 15–19. 6–8 participants per session. Application fee: $20. Financial aid available. No cost for program; financial aid possible for travel expenses.
Application Deadline Continuous.
Jobs Positions for college students 21 and older.
Contact Recruitment Office, PO Box 550, Charlestown, New Hampshire 03603. Phone: 603-543-1700. Fax: 603-543-1828. E-mail: getreal@thesca.org.
URL www.theSCA.org

Teen Expeditions

University of Rhode Island
West Alton Jones Campus
401 Victory Highway
West Greenwich, Rhode Island 02817

General Information Coed residential outdoor program and wilderness program established in 1975. Accredited by American Camping Association.
Program Focus Ecology and the environment.
Academics Ecology, environmental science, marine studies.
Special Interest Areas Campcraft, nature study.
Sports Canoeing, kayaking, rappelling, ropes course, sea kayaking, swimming.
Wilderness/Outdoors Backpacking, canoe trips, caving, hiking, orienteering, rafting, rock climbing, survival training, wilderness camping.
Trips Overnight.
Program Information 7 sessions per year. Session length: 5–7 days in July, August. Ages: 12–17. 8–12 participants per session. Boarding program cost: $510–$645. Financial aid available.
Application Deadline Continuous.
Jobs Positions for college students 20 and older.
Contact Mr. John Jacques, Manager, main address above. Phone: 401-397-3304 Ext.6043. Fax: 401-397-3293. E-mail: urieec@etal.uri.edu.
URL www.uri.edu/ajc/eec/

SOUTH CAROLINA

Camden Military Academy Summer Session/Camp

Camden Military Academy
Camden, South Carolina 29020

General Information Boys' residential traditional camp and academic program established in 1994. High school credit may be earned.
Program Focus Summer school program for grades 6-12 plus summer camp for grades 6-8 in a 2 week or 5 week session.
Academics English language/literature, French language/literature, Spanish language/literature, academics (general), biology, chemistry, computers, history, mathematics, reading, science (general), social studies.
Arts Television/video.
Special Interest Areas Campcraft, field trips (arts and culture), flight instruction, leadership training, outdoor cooking.

Sports Billiards, boating, golf, gymnastics, paintball, riflery, scuba diving, swimming, tennis, track and field, weight training.
Wilderness/Outdoors White-water trips.
Trips Overnight.
Program Information 1–2 sessions per year. Session length: 20–36 days in June, July. 80–100 participants per session. Boarding program cost: $1895–$3995. Application fee: $100. Open to participants entering grades 6–11.
Application Deadline Continuous.
Contact Mr. Casey Robinson, Director of Admissions, 520 Highway 1, North, Camden, South Carolina 29020. Phone: 803-432-6001. Fax: 803-425-1020. E-mail: admissions@camdenmilitary.com.
URL www.camdenmilitary.com

Special Note
Camden Military Academy is a college-preparatory military boarding school for young men in grades 7–12 and postgraduate. The Academy is in historic Camden, South Carolina. The modern campus features air-conditioned classrooms and dorms as well as a new track and pool. Small classes and a teacher-supervised study hall combine to help each student reach their potential. The summer program is nonmilitary, and each student takes 2 academic subjects.

Camp Chatuga

291 Camp Chatuga Road
Mountain Rest, South Carolina 29664

General Information Coed residential traditional camp established in 1956. Accredited by American Camping Association.
Arts Arts and crafts (general), chorus, creative writing, dance, drawing, fabric arts, jewelry making, music, music (instrumental), music (vocal), painting, photography, theater/drama.
Special Interest Areas Animal care, campcraft, culinary arts, farming, gardening, nature study, work camp programs.
Sports Aerobics, archery, basketball, bicycling, boating, canoeing, cheerleading, climbing (wall), diving, fishing, flag football, horseback riding, martial arts, riflery, soccer, softball, swimming, tennis, track and field, ultimate frisbee, volleyball, waterskiing, weight training.
Wilderness/Outdoors Backpacking, canoe trips, hiking, mountain biking, orienteering, wilderness camping.
Trips Day, overnight.
Program Information 5 sessions per year. Session length: 6–35 days in June, July, August. Ages: 6–16. 175 participants per session. Boarding program cost: $455–$2000. Transportation included.
Application Deadline Continuous.
Jobs Positions for college students 19 and older.
Contact Ms. Kelly G. Moxley, Director/Personnel, main address above. Phone: 864-638-3728. Fax: 864-638-0898. E-mail: mail@campchatuga.com.
URL www.campchatuga.com

Carolina Master Scholars Adventure Series

University of South Carolina Continuing Education
University of South Carolina
Columbia, South Carolina 29208

General Information Coed residential and day academic program and arts program established in 2002. Formal opportunities for the academically talented and artistically talented.

Carolina Master Scholars Adventure Series

Academics SAT/ACT preparation, academics (general), aerospace science, architecture, art (Advanced Placement), art history/appreciation, astronomy, biology (Advanced Placement), business, chemistry, computer programming, criminal justice, health sciences, humanities, law, mathematics, physics, science (general), study skills, writing.
Arts Arts, ceramics, creative writing, drawing, fabric arts, film, graphic arts, painting, photography, pottery.
Sports Swimming.
Trips College tours, cultural, day, overnight.
Program Information 14 sessions per year. Session length: 6 days in June, July. Ages: 12–18. 10–20 participants per session. Day program cost: $500. Boarding program cost: $450–$800.
Application Deadline Continuous.
Contact Continuing Education, Summer Academic Programs, 1600 Hampton Street Annex, Suite 203, Columbia, South Carolina 29208. Phone: 803-777-9444. Fax: 803-777-2663. E-mail: confs@gwm.sc.edu.
URL www.rcce.sc.edu/adventures

For more information, see page 1370.

Clemson University Economics Summer Camp

Clemson University Department of Economics
Clemson, South Carolina 29634

General Information Coed residential academic program established in 2003.
Program Focus Economics.
Academics Economics.
Trips College tours, cultural, day.

Clemson University Economics Summer Camp (continued)

Program Information 1 session per year. Session length: 6 days in July. Ages: 15–18. 30–40 participants per session. Financial aid available.
Application Deadline May 9.
Contact Dr. Robert C. McCormick, Professor of Economics, 201-C Sirrine Hall, Box 341309, Clemson, South Carolina 29634-1309. Phone: 864-656-4877. Fax: 864-656-4532.
URL business.clemson.edu/bbtcenter

Emerging Leaders 2005

Columbia College Leadership Institute
The Leadership Institute
1301 Columbia College Drive
Columbia, South Carolina 29203

General Information Girls' residential academic program established in 2001. Formal opportunities for the academically talented.
Program Focus Leadership experience designed to provide 9th grade girls with the skills necessary for academic and personal success in the high school environment.
Academics Business, communications, computers, environmental science, intercultural studies, precollege program, speech/debate, study skills, writing.
Special Interest Areas Community service, leadership training, self-defense, team building.
Sports Ropes course, swimming, tennis.
Trips College tours, cultural, day.
Program Information 1 session per year. Session length: 6 days in July. Ages: 14+. 70 participants per session. Boarding program cost: $600. Financial aid available. Open to participants entering grade 9.
Application Deadline May 21.
Contact Ms. Candy Waites, Coordinator, main address above. Phone: 803-786-3108. Fax: 803-786-3806. E-mail: cwaites@colacoll.edu.

Furman University Summer Scholars Program

Furman University
3300 Poinsett Highway
Greenville, South Carolina 29613

General Information Coed residential academic program established in 2000. Formal opportunities for the academically talented.
Academics French language/literature, academics (general), computer programming, computers, health sciences, law, psychology, writing.
Arts Acting, creative writing, graphic arts, theater/drama.
Special Interest Areas Computer graphics, leadership training.
Sports Ropes course, swimming, volleyball.
Wilderness/Outdoors Hiking.
Trips Day.
Program Information 7–10 sessions per year. Session length: 6–13 days in June, July. Ages: 16–18. 11–21 participants per session. Boarding program cost: $775–$1300. Open to participants entering grades 11–12.
Application Deadline Continuous.
Contact Ms. Anne Chubb, Summer Scholars Manager, Furman University, Continuing Education, 3300 Poinsett Highway, Greenville, South Carolina 29613. Phone: 864-294-2155. Fax: 864-294-3378. E-mail: anne.chubb@furman.edu.
URL www.furman.edu/summerscholars

IMACS–Full Day Summer Camp–South Carolina

Institute for Mathematics & Computer Science (IMACS)
South Carolina

General Information Coed day academic program established in 1992. Formal opportunities for the academically talented.
Academics Computer programming, computer science (Advanced Placement), computers, engineering, mathematics.
Special Interest Areas Electronics, robotics.
Program Information 5 sessions per year. Session length: 5 days in January, February, March, April, May, June, July, August, September, October, November, December. Ages: 5–18. 30–50 participants per session. Day program cost: $399–$1224. Supply fee: $50–$200; additional sessions booked at same time $249 plus $50 supply fee.
Application Deadline Continuous.
Jobs Positions for high school students 16 and older and college students 18 and older.
Contact Mr. Terry Kaufman, President, 7435 Northwest 4th Street, Plantation, Florida 33317. Phone: 954-791-2333. Fax: 954-791-0260. E-mail: info@imacs.org.
URL www.imacs.org

IMACS–Individual Summer Programs–South Carolina

Institute for Mathematics & Computer Science (IMACS)
South Carolina

General Information Coed day academic program established in 1992. Formal opportunities for the academically talented.
Academics Computer programming, computer science (Advanced Placement), computers, engineering, mathematics, mathematics (Advanced Placement).
Special Interest Areas Computer graphics, electronics, robotics.
Program Information 28 sessions per year. Session length: 5 days in January, February, March, April, May, June, July, August, September, October, November, December. Ages: 6–18. Day program cost: $79–$189. Financial aid available.
Application Deadline Continuous.
Jobs Positions for high school students 16 and older and college students 18 and older.

Contact Mr. Terry Kaufman, President, 7435 Northwest 4th Street, Plantation, Florida 33317. Phone: 954-791-2333. Fax: 954-791-0260. E-mail: info@imacs.org.
URL www.imacs.org

International Junior Golf Academy

Golf Academy of Hilton Head Island
7 Office Park Road
Suite 105
Hilton Head Island, South Carolina 29938

General Information Coed residential and day academic program and sports camp established in 1995. High school or college credit may be earned.
Program Focus Golf instruction, physical fitness, psychology of golf, and tournament preparedness.
Academics American literature, English as a second language, English language/literature, SAT/ACT preparation, Spanish (Advanced Placement), Spanish language/literature, academics (general), area studies, art (Advanced Placement), biology, biology (Advanced Placement), chemistry, computer programming, computer science (Advanced Placement), computers, economics, environmental science, government and politics, history, mathematics, mathematics (Advanced Placement), physics, precollege program, reading, science (general), social studies, study skills.
Arts Arts and crafts (general), drawing, painting.
Special Interest Areas Career exploration, driver's education.
Sports Golf.
Trips College tours, cultural, day.
Program Information 1–10 sessions per year. Session length: 7–270 days in January, February, March, April, May, June, July, August, September, October, November, December. Ages: 11–19. 12–30 participants per session. Cost: $1550 per week for residential program; $1095 per week for day program; $35,000 for full-year golf and academic program.
Application Deadline Continuous.
Jobs Positions for college students 19 and older.
Contact Thomas R. Layer, Program Director, PO Box 5580, Hilton Head, South Carolina 29938. Phone: 843-785-4540. Fax: 843-785-5116. E-mail: tom@ijga.com.
URL www.ijga.com

Lead 2005

Columbia College Leadership Institute
The Leadership Institute
1301 Columbia College Drive
Columbia, South Carolina 29203

General Information Girls' residential academic program established in 2001. Formal opportunities for the academically talented.
Program Focus Leadership training.
Academics Business, communications, computers, environmental science, intercultural studies, precollege program, speech/debate, study skills, writing.
Special Interest Areas College planning, community service, leadership training, self-defense, team building.
Sports Ropes course, swimming, tennis.
Trips Cultural, day.
Program Information 1 session per year. Session length: 6 days in June. Ages: 14+. 70 participants per session. Boarding program cost: $600. Financial aid available. Open to participants entering grade 10.
Application Deadline May 21.
Contact Ms. Candy Waites, Coordinator, main address above. Phone: 803-786-3108. Fax: 803-786-3806. E-mail: cwaites@colacoll.edu.
URL www.columbiacollegesc.edu/

Student Conservation Association–Conservation Crew Program (South Carolina)

Student Conservation Association (SCA)
South Carolina

General Information Coed residential outdoor program, community service program, and wilderness program established in 1957. High school credit may be earned.
Program Focus Resource management, conservation and environmental education.
Academics Biology, botany, ecology, environmental science, geology/earth science, history.
Special Interest Areas Campcraft, community service, construction, leadership training, nature study, trail maintenance, work camp programs.
Sports Canoeing, fishing, kayaking, swimming.
Wilderness/Outdoors Backpacking, canoe trips, hiking, orienteering, outdoor living skills, wilderness camping.
Trips Cultural, day, overnight.
Program Information 2–3 sessions per year. Session length: 3–5 weeks in June, July, August. Ages: 15–19. 6–8 participants per session. Application fee: $20. Financial aid available. No cost for program; financial aid possible for travel expenses.
Application Deadline Continuous.
Jobs Positions for college students 21 and older.
Contact Recruitment Office, PO Box 550, Charlestown, New Hampshire 03603. Phone: 603-543-1700. Fax: 603-543-1828. E-mail: getreal@thesca.org.
URL www.theSCA.org

Summer Science Program at the South Carolina Governor's School for Science and Math

South Carolina Governor's School for Science and Math
401 Railroad Avenue
Hartsville, South Carolina 29550

General Information Coed residential academic program established in 1990. Formal opportunities for the academically talented.
Academics Academics (general), biology, botany, chemistry, computer programming, engineering, marine studies, mathematics, meteorology, physics.
Special Interest Areas Electronics, robotics.
Sports Basketball, soccer, swimming, volleyball.
Wilderness/Outdoors Backpacking, hiking.

Summer Science Program at the South Carolina Governor's School for Science and Math (continued)
Trips Day, overnight.
Program Information 4 sessions per year. Session length: 1 week in June, July. Ages: 13–16. 100 participants per session. Boarding program cost: $465–$695. Financial aid available.
Application Deadline Continuous.
Contact Dr. Clyde J. Smith, SSP Director, GSSM, main address above. Phone: 843-383-3937. Fax: 843-383-3903. E-mail: smith@gssm.k12.sc.us.
URL www.gssm.k12.sc.us/summerscience/index.htm

Ventures Travel Service–South Carolina

Friendship Ventures
South Carolina

General Information Coed travel special needs program established in 1985. Specific services available for the developmentally challenged and physically challenged.
Program Focus Provides travel services to older teens and adults with developmental disabilities.
Special Interest Areas Touring.
Program Information 50 sessions per year. Session length: 4–10 days in February, March, April, May, June, July, August, September, October, November, December. Ages: 14–70. 4–8 participants per session. Cost: $395–$2000.
Application Deadline Continuous.
Jobs Positions for college students 18 and older.
Contact Georgann Rumsey, President/CEO, 10509 108th Street, NW, Annandale, Minnesota 55302. Phone: 952-852-0101. Fax: 952-852-0123. E-mail: fv@friendshipventures.org.
URL www.friendshipventures.org

Visions–South Carolina

Visions
South Carolina

General Information Coed travel outdoor program, community service program, and cultural program established in 1989. High school credit may be earned.
Program Focus Community service, cross-cultural experience, and outdoor adventure activities.
Academics Intercultural studies.
Arts Carpentry, painting.
Special Interest Areas Community service, construction, cross-cultural education, field research/expeditions, field trips (arts and culture), leadership training, nature study.
Sports Climbing (wall), sea kayaking, swimming.
Wilderness/Outdoors Backpacking, hiking, outdoor adventure, rock climbing, wilderness/outdoors (general).
Trips Cultural, day, overnight.
Program Information 1 session per year. Session length: 3–4 weeks in June, July, August. Ages: 14–18. 20–25 participants per session. Cost: $3500. Financial aid available.
Application Deadline Continuous.
Jobs Positions for college students 22 and older.
Contact Joanne Pinaire, Director, PO Box 220, Newport, Pennsylvania 17074. Phone: 717-567-7313. Fax: 717-567-7853. E-mail: info@visionsserviceadventures.com.
URL www.visionsserviceadventures.com
For more information, see page 1382.

SOUTH DAKOTA

Earthwatch Institute–Mammoth Graveyard

Earthwatch Institute
Hot Springs, South Dakota

General Information Coed residential outdoor program, cultural program, and adventure program.
Program Focus Piecing together the life and world of the Columbian mammoth at a world-class site.
Academics Anthropology, geology/earth science, science (general).
Special Interest Areas Field research/expeditions, nature study.
Program Information 2 sessions per year. Session length: 15 days in June, July. Ages: 16+. 12 participants per session. Boarding program cost: $1995–$2095. Financial aid available. Financial aid for high school students and teachers.
Application Deadline Continuous.
Contact General Information Desk, PO Box 75, Maynard, Massachusetts 01754. Phone: 800-776-0188. Fax: 978-461-2332. E-mail: info@earthwatch.org.
URL www.earthwatch.org

Student Conservation Association–Conservation Crew Program (South Dakota)

Student Conservation Association (SCA)
South Dakota

General Information Coed residential outdoor program, community service program, and wilderness program established in 1957. High school credit may be earned.
Program Focus Resource management, conservation and environmental education.
Academics Biology, botany, ecology, environmental science, geology/earth science, history.
Special Interest Areas Campcraft, community service, construction, leadership training, nature study, trail maintenance, work camp programs.
Sports Canoeing, fishing, kayaking, swimming.
Wilderness/Outdoors Backpacking, canoe trips, hiking, orienteering, outdoor living skills, wilderness camping.
Trips Cultural, day, overnight.
Program Information 2–3 sessions per year. Session length: 3–5 weeks in June, July, August. Ages: 15–19.

6–8 participants per session. Application fee: $20. Financial aid available. No cost for program; financial aid possible for travel expenses.
Application Deadline Continuous.
Jobs Positions for college students 21 and older.
Contact Recruitment Office, PO Box 550, Charlestown, New Hampshire 03603. Phone: 603-543-1700. Fax: 603-543-1828. E-mail: getreal@thesca.org.
URL www.theSCA.org

Ventures Travel Service–South Dakota

Friendship Ventures
South Dakota

General Information Coed travel special needs program established in 1985. Specific services available for the developmentally challenged and physically challenged.
Program Focus Provides travel services to older teens and adults with developmental disabilities.
Special Interest Areas Touring.
Program Information Session length: 4–10 days in February, March, April, May, June, July, August, September, October, November, December. Ages: 14–70. 4–8 participants per session. Cost: $395–$2000.
Application Deadline Continuous.
Jobs Positions for college students 18 and older.
Contact Georgann Rumsey, President/CEO, 10509 108th Street, NW, Annandale, Minnesota 55302. Phone: 952-852-0101. Fax: 952-852-0123. E-mail: fv@friendshipventures.org.
URL www.friendshipventures.org

TENNESSEE

Camp Nakanawa

Camp Nakanawa, Inc.
1084 Camp Nakanawa Road
Crossville, Tennessee 38571-2146

General Information Girls' residential traditional camp established in 1920.
Program Focus Program designed to help young ladies gain confidence and reach their potential in a positive and fun-filled environment.
Arts Acting, arts and crafts (general), ceramics, chorus, dance (jazz), dance (modern), drawing, fabric arts, music (vocal), musical productions, painting, pottery, printmaking, theater/drama.
Special Interest Areas Nature study.
Sports Aerobics, archery, basketball, boating, canoeing, climbing (wall), cross-country, diving, equestrian sports, fencing, fishing, golf, gymnastics, horseback riding, rappelling, riflery, sailing, soccer, softball, swimming, tennis, volleyball.
Wilderness/Outdoors Canoe trips, caving, hiking, rafting, white-water trips.
Trips Day, overnight.
Program Information 2 sessions per year. Session length: 2–4 weeks in June, July. Ages: 8–17. 240 participants per session. Boarding program cost: $1400–$2400. Application fee: $300. Financial aid available.
Application Deadline Continuous.
Jobs Positions for college students 18 and older.
Contact Pepe Perron, Owner/Director, main address above. Phone: 931-277-3711. Fax: 931-277-5552. E-mail: campnak@tnaccess.com.
URL www.campnakanawa.com

Carson-Newman College–EXCEL Program

Carson-Newman College
1646 Russell Avenue
Jefferson City, Tennessee 37760

General Information Coed residential and day academic program established in 1978. Religious affiliation: Baptist. Formal opportunities for the academically talented. College credit may be earned.
Program Focus Students earn 3-6 semester hours of college coursework.
Academics Bible study, academics (general), art history/appreciation, biology, business, communications, computers, geography, geology/earth science, government and politics, history, humanities, mathematics, music, psychology, religion, social science, social studies, speech/debate.
Arts Music, photography.
Sports Basketball, racquetball, swimming, tennis, volleyball.
Wilderness/Outdoors Backpacking, hiking, rafting, white-water trips.
Trips Day, shopping.
Program Information 3 sessions per year. Session length: 3–6 weeks in June, July. Ages: 16–17. 20–30 participants per session. Day program cost: $300–$600. Boarding program cost: $780–$1580. Application fee: $25.
Application Deadline May 15.
Jobs Positions for college students.
Contact Sheryl M. Gray, Director of Admissions, C-N Box 72025, Jefferson City, Tennessee 37760. Phone: 865-471-3223. Fax: 865-471-3502. E-mail: sgray@cn.edu.
URL www.cn.edu

Davidson Academy–Academy Arts

Davidson Academy
1414 Old Hickory Boulevard
Nashville, Tennessee 37207

General Information Coed day arts program. Religious affiliation: Christian.
Arts Dance, dance (ballet), dance (jazz), dance (tap), guitar, music, piano.
Sports Gymnastics.
Trips Day.
Program Information 1–9 sessions per year. Session length: 5 days in June, July. Ages: 3–16. Day program cost: $48–$135.
Application Deadline Continuous.

Davidson Academy–Academy Arts (continued)
Jobs Positions for high school students and college students.
Contact Ms. Beverly Willis, Director of Extended Programs, main address above. Phone: 615-860-5310. E-mail: bwillis@davidsonacademy.com.
URL www.davidsonacademy.com

DAVIDSON ACADEMY–BEAR COUNTRY DAY CAMP

Davidson Academy
1414 Old Hickory Boulevard
Nashville, Tennessee 37207

General Information Coed day traditional camp. Religious affiliation: Christian.
Academics Computers, mathematics, reading, science (general), sign language, study skills, tutoring.
Arts Arts and crafts (general), dance, drawing, music, music (instrumental), pottery, sculpture.
Special Interest Areas Culinary arts, etiquette, robotics.
Trips Day.
Program Information 1–23 sessions per year. Session length: 1–5 days in June, July, August. Ages: 4–14. Day program cost: $15–$150.
Application Deadline Continuous.
Jobs Positions for college students 18 and older.
Contact Ms. Beverly Willis, Director of Extended Programs, main address above. Phone: 615-860-5310. E-mail: bwillis@davidsonacademy.com.
URL www.davidsonacademy.com

DAVIDSON ACADEMY–SPORTS CAMPS

Davidson Academy
1414 Old Hickory Boulevard
Nashville, Tennessee 37207

General Information Coed day sports camp. Religious affiliation: Christian.
Sports Baseball, basketball, cheerleading, football, golf, soccer, softball, swimming, volleyball.
Trips Day.
Program Information 1–14 sessions per year. Session length: 3–5 days in June, July. Ages: 4–14. Day program cost: $35–$75.
Application Deadline Continuous.
Jobs Positions for high school students and college students.
Contact Beverly Willis, Director of Extended Programs, main address above. Phone: 615-860-5310. E-mail: bwillis@davidsonacademy.com.
URL www.davidsonacademy.com

FREED-HARDEMAN HORIZONS FOR AGES 12-18

Freed-Hardeman University
158 East Main Street
Henderson, Tennessee 38340

General Information Coed residential bible camp established in 1982. Religious affiliation: Christian.
Program Focus Christian leadership development.
Academics Bible study.
Arts Chorus.
Special Interest Areas Leadership training.
Sports Baseball, basketball, soccer, softball, swimming, tennis.
Program Information 2 sessions per year. Session length: 6 days in July. Ages: 12–18. 500–700 participants per session. Boarding program cost: $180.
Application Deadline Continuous.
Contact Hope Shull, Director, Horizons, main address above. Phone: 901-989-6067. Fax: 901-989-6065. E-mail: hshull@fhu.edu.
URL www.fhu.edu/

MCCALLIE SPORTS CAMP

The McCallie School
Missionary Ridge
500 Dodds Avenue
Chattanooga, Tennessee 37404

General Information Boys' residential sports camp established in 1979. Religious affiliation: Christian.
Program Focus To provide boys of various athletic abilities an action-oriented camp with an emphasis on fun and participation.
Sports Baseball, basketball, football, golf, lacrosse, soccer, softball, sports (general), swimming, tennis, track and field, volleyball, water polo.
Trips Day.
Program Information 3 sessions per year. Session length: 13 days in June, July. Ages: 9–15. 120 participants per session. Boarding program cost: $1650. Financial aid available.
Application Deadline Continuous.
Jobs Positions for high school students and college students.
Contact Mike Wood, Director, main address above. Phone: 800-MSC-CAMP. E-mail: mwood@mccallie.org.
URL www.mccallie.org/summerprograms/sports_camp.htm

MCCALLIE ACADEMIC CAMP

The McCallie School
Missionary Ridge
500 Dodds Avenue
Chattanooga, Tennessee 37404

General Information Boys' residential academic program.
Academics English language/literature, academics (general), journalism, mathematics, science (general), study skills, writing.
Sports Basketball, climbing (wall), football, golf, lacrosse, racquetball, soccer, softball, swimming, tennis.

Wilderness/Outdoors Hiking, rafting, rock climbing, white-water trips.
Trips Cultural, day, shopping.
Program Information 1 session per year. Session length: 20–21 days in June. Ages: 13–16. 25–35 participants per session. Boarding program cost: $2500.
Application Deadline Continuous.
Contact Mr. Bill Eiselstein, Director of Summer Programs, main address above. Phone: 423-493-5852. Fax: 423-629-2852. E-mail: wce@mccallie.org.
URL www.mccallie.org/summerprograms/academic_camp.htm

McCallie Lacrosse Camp

The McCallie School
Missionary Ridge
500 Dodds Avenue
Chattanooga, Tennessee 37404

General Information Boys' residential sports camp.
Program Focus All aspects of team play, with emphasis on fundamental development and the mechanics of individual offense and defense.
Sports Lacrosse.
Program Information 1 session per year. Session length: 6 days in July. Ages: 12–15. 50–60 participants per session. Boarding program cost: $475. Financial aid available.
Application Deadline Continuous.
Jobs Positions for high school students and college students.
Contact Mr. Troy Kemp, Lacrosse Head Coach, main address above. Phone: 800-MSC-CAMP. E-mail: tkemp@mccallie.org.
URL www.mccallie.org/summerprograms/lacrosse_camp.htm

Montgomery Bell Academy–All-Sports Camps

Montgomery Bell Academy
4001 Harding Road
Nashville, Tennessee 37205

General Information Boys' day sports camp.
Sports Baseball, basketball, football, kickball, sports (general), tennis, wrestling.
Trips Day.
Program Information 3 sessions per year. Session length: 5 days in June. Day program cost: $180–$530. Financial aid available. Open to participants entering grades 1–7.
Contact Floyd Elliot, Sports Camp Director, main address above. Phone: 615-298-5514 Ext.340. Fax: 615-297-0271. E-mail: elliotf@montgomerybell.com.
URL www.montgomerybell.com

Montgomery Bell Academy–LEAD Program

Montgomery Bell Academy
4001 Harding Road
Nashville, Tennessee 37205

General Information Coed day academic program.
Academics English language/literature, computers, mathematics, science (general), social science, technology.
Special Interest Areas Communication skills, leadership training, problem solving.
Program Information 2 sessions per year. Session length: 5 days in July. Day program cost: $325. Financial aid available. Open to participants entering grades 5–6.
Contact Thomas Wims, MBA LEAD Coordinator, main address above. Phone: 615-298-5514 Ext.266. Fax: 615-297-0271. E-mail: wimst@montgomerybell.com.
URL www.montgomerybell.com

Montgomery Bell Academy–Specialty Sports Camps

Montgomery Bell Academy
4001 Harding Road
Nashville, Tennessee 37205

General Information Coed day sports camp.
Sports Baseball, basketball, football, lacrosse, riflery, soccer, sports (general), tennis, track and field, weight training, wrestling.
Program Information Session length: 5 days in June, July. Day program cost: $50–$200. Financial aid available. Open to participants entering grades 1–12.
Contact Floyd Elliot, Sports Camp Director, main address above. Phone: 615-298-5514 Ext.340. Fax: 615-297-0271. E-mail: elliotf@montgomerybell.com.
URL www.montgomerybell.com

Montgomery Bell Academy–Summer Cooking Camp

Montgomery Bell Academy
4001 Harding Road
Nashville, Tennessee 37205

General Information Coed day academic program.
Special Interest Areas Culinary arts.
Program Information 1 session per year. Session length: 10 days in June. 12 participants per session. Day program cost: $395. Financial aid available. Open to participants entering grade 10–college freshmen.
Contact Malcolm Morrison, Cooking Camp Coordinator, main address above. Phone: 615-298-5514 Ext.347. Fax: 615-297-0271. E-mail: morrism@montgomerybell.com.
URL www.montgomerybell.com

Montgomery Bell Academy–Summer Music Camp

Montgomery Bell Academy
4001 Harding Road
Nashville, Tennessee 37205

General Information Coed day arts program.
Academics Music.
Arts Music, music (instrumental), music (vocal), musical theater.
Sports Weight training.
Program Information 1 session per year. Session length: 5 days in June. Day program cost: $165. Financial aid available.
Contact David Cassel, Summer Music Camp Coordinator, main address above. Phone: 615-298-5514 Ext.247. Fax: 615-297-0271. E-mail: casseld@montgomerybell.com.
URL www.montgomerybell.com

Montgomery Bell Academy–Summer School

Montgomery Bell Academy
4001 Harding Road
Nashville, Tennessee 37205

General Information Coed day academic program. High school credit may be earned.
Academics English language/literature, French language/literature, German language/literature, Latin language, SAT/ACT preparation, Spanish language/literature, academics (general), art, chemistry, computers, geography, history, mathematics, physics, study skills, writing.
Arts Creative writing, digital media, drawing, mixed media, painting, printmaking.
Program Information 1–2 sessions per year. Session length: 5–30 days in June, July, August. Day program cost: $175–$750. Financial aid available. Open to participants entering grades 5–12.
Contact Nita Snow, Summer School Coordinator, main address above. Phone: 615-369-5380. Fax: 615-297-0271. E-mail: snown@montgomerybell.com.
URL www.montgomerybell.com

Montgomery Bell Academy–Summer Science Experience

Montgomery Bell Academy
4001 Harding Road
Nashville, Tennessee 37205

General Information Coed day academic program.
Academics Biology, chemistry, physics, science (general).
Program Information 2 sessions per year. Session length: 10 days in June, July. 20 participants per session. Day program cost: $525. Financial aid available. Open to participants entering grades 5–8.
Contact Mr. Chris Spiegl, MBA Summer Science Coordinator, main address above. Phone: 615-298-5514 Ext.329. Fax: 615-297-0271. E-mail: spiegl@montgomerybell.com.
URL www.montgomerybell.com

Montgomery Bell Academy–Summer Theater Camp

Montgomery Bell Academy
4001 Harding Road
Nashville, Tennessee 37205

General Information Coed day arts program.
Arts Dance, music, playwriting, songwriting, stage movement, theater/drama.
Program Information 1 session per year. Session length: 15 days in June. 30 participants per session. Day program cost: $500.
Contact Malcolm Morrison, Summer Theater Coordinator, main address above. Phone: 615-298-5514 Ext.347. Fax: 615-297-0271. E-mail: morrism@montgomerybell.com.
URL www.montgomerybell.com

National Guitar Workshop–Murfreesboro, TN

National Guitar Workshop
Middle Tennessee State University–Falkenberry
Murfreesboro, Tennessee 37132

General Information Coed residential and day arts program established in 1984. College credit may be earned.
Program Focus Music education in guitar, bass, drums, and vocals.
Academics Music, music (Advanced Placement).
Arts Guitar, music (classical), music (ensemble), music (instrumental), music (jazz), music (rock), music (vocal).
Program Information 1 session per year. Session length: 1 week in June, July, August. Ages: 13–79. 75–225 participants per session. Day program cost: $670–$720. Boarding program cost: $870–$920. Application fee: $25. Financial aid available.
Application Deadline Continuous.
Jobs Positions for college students 21 and older.
Contact Ms. Emily Flower, Registrar, PO Box 222, Lakeside, Connecticut 06758. Phone: 860-567-3736 Ext. 109. Fax: 860-567-0374. E-mail: emily@guitarworkshop.com.
URL www.guitarworkshop.com

Preparatory Academics for Vanderbilt Engineers (PAVE)

Vanderbilt University
Vanderbilt University
Nashville, Tennessee 37235

General Information Coed residential and day academic program established in 1991. Formal opportunities for the academically talented. Specific services

available for the hearing impaired and physically challenged. High school credit may be earned.
Program Focus Science, engineering, problem solving, technical writing, and computer skills.
Academics Aerospace science, architecture, biology, chemistry, chemistry (Advanced Placement), computer programming, computers, engineering, environmental science, mathematics, mathematics (Advanced Placement), physics, physics (Advanced Placement), precollege program, science (general), study skills, writing.
Special Interest Areas Career exploration, construction, electronics, robotics.
Sports Baseball, basketball, bicycling, canoeing, football, golf, horseback riding, soccer, swimming, tennis, volleyball, weight training.
Wilderness/Outdoors Backpacking, bicycle trips, canoe trips, caving, rafting, white-water trips.
Trips Cultural, day.
Program Information 1 session per year. Session length: 6 weeks in June, July, August. Ages: 16–18. 80 participants per session. Day program cost: $3670. Boarding program cost: $4880.
Application Deadline April 20.
Contact Prof. John Veillette, Director/Associate Dean, Pre-College Division, Box 351736, Station B, Nashville, Tennessee 37235-1736. Phone: 615-322-7827. Fax: 615-322-3297. E-mail: pave-req@vuse.vanderbilt.edu.
URL www.vuse.vanderbilt.edu/~pave-req

Rhodes Summer Writing Institute

Rhodes College
2000 North Parkway
Memphis, Tennessee 38112

General Information Coed residential academic program established in 1987. Formal opportunities for the academically talented. College credit may be earned.
Program Focus Creative and expository writing, liberal arts, pre-college.
Academics American literature, English language/literature, academics (general), government and politics, history, humanities, precollege program, psychology, social science, social studies, writing.
Arts Creative writing, film, theater/drama.
Sports Swimming, tennis, track and field, volleyball.
Trips Cultural.
Program Information 1 session per year. Session length: 2 weeks in June. Ages: 16–18. 50–70 participants per session. Boarding program cost: $1400. Financial aid available.
Application Deadline May 1.
Contact Dr. Rebecca Finlayson, Director, Rhodes College Summer Writing Institute, Department of English, 2000 North Parkway, Memphis, Tennessee 38112. Phone: 901-843-3293. Fax: 901-843-3728. E-mail: finlayson@rhodes.edu.
URL www.rhodes.edu/writinginstitute

Student Conservation Association–Conservation Crew Program (Tennessee)

Student Conservation Association (SCA)
Tennessee

General Information Coed residential outdoor program, community service program, and wilderness program established in 1957. High school credit may be earned.
Program Focus Resource management, conservation and environmental education.
Academics Biology, botany, ecology, environmental science, geology/earth science, history.
Special Interest Areas Campcraft, community service, construction, leadership training, nature study, trail maintenance, work camp programs.
Sports Canoeing, fishing, kayaking, swimming.
Wilderness/Outdoors Backpacking, canoe trips, hiking, orienteering, outdoor living skills, wilderness camping.
Trips Cultural, day, overnight.
Program Information 2–3 sessions per year. Session length: 3–5 weeks in June, July, August. Ages: 15–19. 6–8 participants per session. Application fee: $20. Financial aid available. No cost for program; financial aid possible for travel expenses.
Application Deadline Continuous.
Jobs Positions for college students 21 and older.
Contact Recruitment Office, PO Box 550, Charlestown, New Hampshire 03603. Phone: 603-543-1700. Fax: 603-543-1828. E-mail: getreal@thesca.org.
URL www.theSCA.org

Ventures Travel Service–Tennessee

Friendship Ventures
Tennessee

General Information Coed travel special needs program established in 1985. Specific services available for the developmentally challenged and physically challenged.
Program Focus Provides travel services to older teens and adults with developmental disabilities.
Special Interest Areas Touring.
Program Information 50 sessions per year. Session length: 4–10 days in February, March, April, May, June, July, August, September, October, November, December. Ages: 14–70. 4–8 participants per session. Cost: $395–$2000.
Application Deadline Continuous.
Jobs Positions for college students 18 and older.
Contact Georgann Rumsey, President/CEO, 10509 108th Street, NW, Annandale, Minnesota 55302. Phone: 952-852-0101. Fax: 952-852-0123. E-mail: fv@friendshipventures.org.
URL www.friendshipventures.org

TEXAS

Abilene Christian University–Kadesh Life Camp

Abilene Christian University
129 McKinzie Hall
Abilene, Texas 79699-9004

General Information Coed residential bible camp established in 1982. Religious affiliation: Church of Christ.
Program Focus Youth leadership training.
Academics Bible study.
Special Interest Areas Community service, leadership training, worship.
Program Information 4 sessions per year. Session length: 6 days in June, July. Ages: 14–18. 200 participants per session. Boarding program cost: $275.
Application Deadline Continuous.
Jobs Positions for college students 19 and older.
Contact Jan Meyer, Director of Leadership Camps, ACU Box 29004, 127 McKinzie Hall, Abilene, Texas 79699-9004. Phone: 325-674-2033. Fax: 325-674-6475. E-mail: leadership.camps@campuslife.acu.edu.
URL www.acucamps.com

Abilene Christian University–Learning to Lead

Abilene Christian University
129 McKinzie Hall
Abilene, Texas 79699-9004

General Information Coed residential bible camp established in 1986. Religious affiliation: Church of Christ.
Program Focus Youth leadership training.
Academics Bible study.
Arts Creative writing, drawing, music (vocal), theater/drama.
Special Interest Areas Community service, leadership training, worship.
Sports Swimming.
Program Information 3 sessions per year. Session length: 6 days in June, July. Ages: 8–12. 150 participants per session. Boarding program cost: $250.
Application Deadline Continuous.
Jobs Positions for college students 19 and older.
Contact Jan Meyer, Director of Leadership Camps, ACU Box 29004, Abilene, Texas 79699-9004. Phone: 325-674-2033. Fax: 325-674-6475. E-mail: leadership.camps@campuslife.acu.edu.
URL www.acucamps.com

Abilene Christian University–MPulse

Abilene Christian University
129 McKinzie Hall
Abilene, Texas 79699-9004

General Information Coed residential bible camp established in 1997. Religious affiliation: Church of Christ.
Program Focus Youth leadership training.
Academics Bible study.
Arts Chorus, creative writing, drawing, music (vocal), theater/drama.
Special Interest Areas Community service, leadership training, worship.
Sports Swimming.
Program Information 3 sessions per year. Session length: 6 days in June, July. Ages: 12–15. 200 participants per session. Boarding program cost: $250.
Application Deadline Continuous.
Jobs Positions for college students 19 and older.
Contact Jan Meyer, Director of Leadership Camps, ACU Box 29004, Abilene, Texas 79699-9004. Phone: 325-674-2033. Fax: 325-674-6475. E-mail: leadership.camps@campuslife.acu.edu.
URL www.acucamps.com

Abiliene Christian University–KidQuest Day Camp

Abilene Christian University
129 McKinzie Hall
Abilene, Texas 79699-9004

General Information Coed day bible camp established in 1999. Religious affiliation: Church of Christ.
Academics Bible study, computers.
Arts Arts and crafts (general), chorus, creative writing, drawing, music, theater/drama.
Special Interest Areas Leadership training, worship.
Sports Swimming.
Program Information 3 sessions per year. Session length: 5 days in June, July. Ages: 6–8. 50 participants per session. Day program cost: $150.
Application Deadline Continuous.
Jobs Positions for college students 19 and older.
Contact Jan Meyer, Director of Leadership Camps, ACU Box 29004, 127 McKinzie Hall, Abilene, Texas 79699-9004. Phone: 325-674-2033. Fax: 325-674-6475. E-mail: leadership.camps@campuslife.acu.edu.
URL www.acucamps.com

Access to Careers in the Sciences (ACES) Camps

Texas Woman's University
Science and Math Center for Women
Denton, Texas 76204-5846

General Information Girls' residential academic program established in 1988. Formal opportunities for the academically talented.
Program Focus Career opportunities for women in the mathematics and science fields.

Academics Anthropology, archaeology, astronomy, biology, chemistry, computer programming, computers, ecology, engineering, geology/earth science, health sciences, marine studies, mathematics, meteorology, physics, science (general), technology.
Trips Day.
Program Information 2 sessions per year. Session length: 13 days in June, July. Ages: 12–18. 20–60 participants per session. Boarding program cost: $900. Application fee: $30. Financial aid available. Open to participants entering grades 7–10.
Application Deadline April 29.
Contact DeAnna Taylor, Project Coordinator, Science and Math Center, PO Box 425846, Denton, Texas 76204-5846. Phone: 800-860-2237. Fax: 940-898-2767. E-mail: dtaylor@twu.edu.
URL www.twu.edu/smcw/aces.html

Alexander-Smith Academy Summer School

Alexander Smith Academy
10255 Richmond Avenue
Houston, Texas 77042-4117

General Information Coed day academic program established in 1968. Formal opportunities for the academically talented. High school credit may be earned.
Academics American literature, English language/literature, Spanish language/literature, biology, business, chemistry, computers, economics, geography, government and politics, history, mathematics, psychology, science (general), social studies.
Program Information 2 sessions per year. Session length: 17 days in June, July. Ages: 14+. 25 participants per session. Day program cost: $1500–$6000. Application fee: $150.
Application Deadline June 5.
Contact David Arnold, President, main address above. Phone: 713-266-0920 Ext.16. Fax: 713-266-8857. E-mail: darnold@alexandersmith.com.
URL www.alexandersmith.com

Arts on the Lake

St. Stephen's Episcopal School
2900 Bunny Run
Austin, Texas 78746

General Information Coed residential and day arts program established in 1996. Formal opportunities for the artistically talented.
Arts Arts, ceramics, dance, dance (ballet), dance (folk), dance (jazz), dance (modern), dance (tap), drawing, music, music (vocal), musical productions, painting, photography, pottery, printmaking, sculpture, theater/drama, visual arts.
Special Interest Areas Field trips (arts and culture).
Sports Swimming, tennis.
Wilderness/Outdoors Hiking.
Trips Cultural, day.
Program Information 1–6 sessions per year. Session length: 5–14 days in June, July. Ages: 11–18. 10–25 participants per session. Day program cost: $130–$750. Boarding program cost: $1250–$1600. Financial aid available.
Application Deadline Continuous.
Jobs Positions for college students 19 and older.
Contact Elizabeth Hansing Moon, Director, main address above. Phone: 512-327-1213. Fax: 512-327-1311. E-mail: emoon@sstx.org.
URL www.sstx.org

Austin Nature and Science Center

301 Nature Center Drive
Austin, Texas 78746

General Information Coed day academic program and outdoor program established in 1962. Formal opportunities for the academically talented and gifted.
Program Focus Environmental education and adventure activities.
Academics Archaeology, astronomy, biology, botany, chemistry, ecology, environmental science, geography, geology/earth science, marine studies, meteorology, physics, science (general).
Arts Arts and crafts (general), drawing, leather working, painting, theater/drama.
Special Interest Areas Campcraft, career exploration, gardening, leadership training, nature study.
Sports Archery, bicycling, canoeing, climbing (wall), fishing, kayaking, rappelling, ropes course, swimming.
Wilderness/Outdoors Backpacking, bicycle trips, canoe trips, caving, hiking, mountain biking, orienteering, outdoor living skills, rock climbing, wilderness camping.
Trips Day, overnight.
Program Information 9–11 sessions per year. Session length: 4–10 days in May, June, July, August. Ages: 3–16. 60–150 participants per session. Day program cost: $80–$365. Financial aid available.
Application Deadline Continuous.
Jobs Positions for college students 18 and older.
Contact Janice Sturrock, Education Director, main address above. Phone: 512-327-8181 Ext.13. Fax: 512-327-8745. E-mail: janice.sturrock@ci.austin.tx.us.
URL www.cityofaustin.org/ansc

Baylor University High School Summer Science Research Program

Baylor University
Waco, Texas

General Information Coed residential academic program established in 1991. College credit may be earned.
Program Focus Science research.
Academics Academics (general), aerospace science, biology, biology (Advanced Placement), botany, chemistry, computer science (Advanced Placement), engineering, environmental science, geology/earth science, health sciences, mathematics, mathematics (Advanced Placement), physics, psychology, research skills, science (general).
Trips Day.

Baylor University High School Summer Science Research Program (continued)

Program Information 1 session per year. Session length: 5 weeks in June. Ages: 16–18. 10 participants per session. Boarding program cost: $500–$600. Application fee: $45. Financial aid available.
Application Deadline April 5.
Contact Ms. Bernice Helpert, Administrative Associate to Associate Deans, College of Arts and Sciences, Baylor University, One Bear Place #97344, Waco, Texas 76798-7344. Phone: 254-710-4288. Fax: 254-710-3639. E-mail: hsssrp@baylor.edu.
URL www.baylor.edu/summerscience

CAMP LA JUNTA

Camp La Junta
1585 Highway 39
Hunt, Texas 78024

General Information Boys' residential traditional camp established in 1928.
Program Focus Individualized programs and recreation.
Arts Arts and crafts (general).
Special Interest Areas Campcraft, driver's education, flight instruction, leadership training, model rocketry, nature study.
Sports Archery, baseball, basketball, bicycling, boating, canoeing, climbing (wall), equestrian sports, fishing, football, golf, horseback riding, kayaking, rappelling, riflery, ropes course, sailing, scuba diving, snorkeling, soccer, softball, swimming, tennis, volleyball, waterskiing.
Wilderness/Outdoors Canoe trips, hiking, mountain biking, orienteering, pack animal trips, rock climbing, survival training, wilderness camping.
Trips Day, overnight.
Program Information 6 sessions per year. Session length: 13–26 days in June, July. Ages: 6–14. 100–200 participants per session. Boarding program cost: $1500–$2750. Financial aid available.
Application Deadline Continuous.
Jobs Positions for college students 18 and older.
Contact Blake W. Smith, Camp Director, PO Box 136, Hunt, Texas 78024. Phone: 830-238-4621. Fax: 830-238-4888. E-mail: lajunta@ktc.com.
URL www.lajunta.com

CAMP NIWANA

Camp Fire USA Southeast Texas Council, Inc.
525 FM 256
Woodville, Texas 75979

General Information Coed residential and day traditional camp and outdoor program established in 1951.
Arts Arts and crafts (general).
Special Interest Areas Native American culture, campcraft, nature study.
Sports Archery, canoeing, fishing, gymnastics, riflery, ropes course, softball, swimming, volleyball.
Wilderness/Outdoors Backpacking, bicycle trips, canoe trips, hiking, outdoor adventure.
Trips Day.
Program Information 4 sessions per year. Session length: 1–2 weeks in June, July. Ages: 6–18. 80–120 participants per session. Day program cost: $100. Boarding program cost: $240. Financial aid available.
Application Deadline Continuous.
Jobs Positions for high school students 16 and older and college students 18 and older.
Contact Ms. Barbara Waters, Outdoor Program Director, 3037 25th Street, Port Arthur, Texas 77642. Phone: 409-985-3386. Fax: 409-985-7887. E-mail: setxcf1927@sbcglobal.net.

CAMP OLYMPIA

Camp Olympia
723 Olympia Drive
Trinity, Texas 75862

General Information Coed residential traditional camp established in 1968. Religious affiliation: Christian. Accredited by American Camping Association.
Arts Arts and crafts (general), dance, dance (modern), photography, theater/drama.
Special Interest Areas Campcraft, nature study.
Sports Aerobics, archery, baseball, basketball, bicycling, boating, canoeing, cheerleading, climbing (wall), diving, equestrian sports, fishing, football, golf, gymnastics, horseback riding, martial arts, rappelling, riflery, ropes course, sailing, scuba diving, snorkeling, soccer, softball, swimming, tennis, track and field, volleyball, water polo, waterskiing, weight training, windsurfing.
Wilderness/Outdoors Backpacking, mountaineering, orienteering, rafting, rock climbing.
Trips Overnight.
Program Information 4 sessions per year. Session length: 2–3 weeks in May, June, July, August. Ages: 7–16. 322 participants per session. Boarding program cost: $2170–$2920.
Application Deadline Continuous.
Jobs Positions for college students 18 and older.
Contact Tommy Ferguson, Director, main address above. Phone: 936-594-2541 Ext.409. Fax: 936-594-8143. E-mail: tferguson@campolympia.com.
URL www.campolympia.com

CAMP OLYMPIA JUNIOR GOLF ACADEMY

Camp Olympia
723 Olympia Drive
Trinity, Texas 75862

General Information Coed residential sports camp established in 1996. Religious affiliation: Christian. Accredited by American Camping Association.
Program Focus Golf.
Arts Arts and crafts (general), chorus, dance, photography, theater/drama.
Special Interest Areas Nature study.
Sports Aerobics, archery, baseball, basketball, bicycling, boating, canoeing, cheerleading, climbing (wall), diving, equestrian sports, fishing, football, golf, gymnastics, horseback riding, martial arts, rappelling, riflery, ropes course, sailing, scuba diving, snorkeling,

soccer, softball, swimming, tennis, track and field, volleyball, water polo, waterskiing, weight training, windsurfing.
Program Information 4 sessions per year. Session length: 2–3 weeks in May, June, July, August. Ages: 8–16. 25–30 participants per session. Boarding program cost: $2495–$3370. Financial aid available.
Application Deadline Continuous.
Contact Tommy Ferguson, Director, main address above. Phone: 936-594-2541. Fax: 936-594-8143. E-mail: tferguson@campolympia.com.
URL www.jrgolfacademy.com

Camp Rio Vista for Boys

Vista Camps
Highway 39 West
Ingram, Texas 78025

General Information Boys' residential traditional camp established in 1921.
Program Focus Providing a safe, wholesome, and fun-filled learning experience.
Arts Arts and crafts (general), jewelry making, leather working, music (instrumental), photography, television/video, theater/drama.
Special Interest Areas Animal care, campcraft, leadership training, nature study.
Sports Archery, basketball, canoeing, climbing (wall), equestrian sports, fencing, fishing, football, golf, horseback riding, kayaking, lacrosse, martial arts, rappelling, riflery, ropes course, sailing, soccer, softball, sports (general), swimming, tennis, track and field, volleyball, waterskiing, weight training, wrestling.
Wilderness/Outdoors Canoe trips, hiking, orienteering.
Program Information 6 sessions per year. Session length: 13–26 days in June, July, August. Ages: 6–16. 100–150 participants per session. Boarding program cost: $1550–$2575. Application fee: $25. Payment plans available.
Application Deadline Continuous.
Jobs Positions for high school students 18 and older and college students 19 and older.
Contact Mr. Freddie Hawkins, Owner/Director of Vista Camps, 175 Rio Vista Road, Ingram, Texas 78025. Phone: 830-367-5353. Fax: 830-367-4044. E-mail: riovista@ktc.com.
URL www.vistacamps.com

Camp Sierra Vista for Girls

Vista Camps
Highway 39 West
Ingram, Texas 78025

General Information Girls' residential traditional camp established in 1982.
Program Focus Providing a safe, wholesome, and fun-filled learning experience.
Arts Arts and crafts (general), dance, fabric arts, jewelry making, leather working, music (instrumental), photography, television/video, theater/drama.
Special Interest Areas Animal care, campcraft, leadership training, nature study.
Sports Aerobics, archery, basketball, canoeing, cheerleading, climbing (wall), equestrian sports, fencing, fishing, golf, horseback riding, kayaking, martial arts, rappelling, riflery, ropes course, sailing, soccer, softball, sports (general), swimming, tennis, track and field, volleyball, waterskiing, weight training.
Wilderness/Outdoors Canoe trips, hiking, orienteering.
Program Information 6 sessions per year. Session length: 13–26 days in June, July, August. Ages: 6–16. 95–105 participants per session. Boarding program cost: $1550–$2575. Application fee: $25. Payment plans available.
Application Deadline Continuous.
Jobs Positions for high school students 18 and older and college students 19 and older.
Contact Mrs. Debbie Griffin, Camp Director, 175 Rio Vista Road, Ingram, Texas 78025. Phone: 830-367-5353. Fax: 830-367-4044. E-mail: dgriffin@vistacamps.com.
URL www.vistacamps.com

Clark Scholars Program

Texas Tech University
Department of Biological Sciences
Lubbock, Texas 79409-3131

General Information Coed residential academic program established in 1991. Formal opportunities for the academically talented.
Program Focus Individual research with faculty mentor.
Academics English language/literature, academics (general), biology, chemistry, classical languages/literatures, communications, computer programming, computer science (Advanced Placement), ecology, economics, engineering, environmental science, food science, geology/earth science, health sciences, history, horticulture, journalism, mathematics, music, paleontology, philosophy, physics, psychology, science (general).
Arts Theater/drama.
Wilderness/Outdoors Hiking.
Trips Day, overnight.
Program Information 1 session per year. Session length: 1 week in June, July, August. Ages: 16–18. 12 participants per session. No cost for program; $750 stipend upon completion of oral and written report.
Application Deadline March 2.
Contact Ms. Lynda Durham, Clark Scholar Program Coordinator, Texas Tech University, Department of Biological Sciences, Box 43131, Lubbock, Texas 79409-3131. Phone: 806-742-2883 Ext.5. Fax: 806-742-2963. E-mail: lynda.durham@ttu.edu.
URL www.clarkscholars.ttu.edu

Drama Kids International Summer FUN Camp

Drama Kids International–Houston Central
Houston, Texas

General Information Coed day arts program established in 2004.
Academics Communications, music, speech/debate.

Drama Kids International Summer FUN Camp (continued)

Arts Acting, arts and crafts (general), clowning, dance, mime, musical productions, painting, puppetry, radio broadcasting, theater/drama.
Trips Cultural, day.
Program Information 4 sessions per year. Session length: 10–14 days in January, February, March, April, May, June, July, August, September, October, November, December. Ages: 5–17. Day program cost: $175–$310.
Application Deadline Continuous.
Jobs Positions for college students 18 and older.
Contact Liz Starn, Director, 4730 Warm Springs Road, Houston, Texas 77035. Phone: 713-721-5200. Fax: 713-721-5202. E-mail: dramakidshouston@aol.com.
URL dramakids.com

The Hockaday School Summer Session

The Hockaday School
11600 Welch Road
Dallas, Texas 75229

General Information Coed residential and day traditional camp and academic program established in 1983. High school credit may be earned.
Program Focus ESL program, creative arts day camp.
Academics American literature, English as a second language, English language/literature, French language/literature, SAT/ACT preparation, Spanish language/literature, academics (general), art history/appreciation, chemistry, communications, computer programming, computers, geography, government and politics, journalism, mathematics, music, physics, reading, science (general), social science, social studies, speech/debate, study skills, typing, writing.
Arts Animation, arts, arts and crafts (general), ceramics, creative writing, dance, dance (jazz), music, music (vocal), painting, photography, printmaking, theater/drama.
Special Interest Areas Career exploration, general camp activities, leadership training.
Sports Basketball, fencing, field hockey, football, martial arts, soccer, swimming, tennis, track and field.
Wilderness/Outdoors Canoe trips, outdoor adventure.
Trips Cultural, day, overnight.
Program Information 2–3 sessions per year. Session length: 1–3 weeks in June, July. Ages: 4–18. 750–850 participants per session. Day program cost: $150–$1250. Boarding program cost: $1900–$3500. Application fee: $25.
Application Deadline Continuous.
Jobs Positions for high school students 16 and older and college students 16 and older.
Contact Nancy Gale, Director of Summer Session, main address above. Phone: 214-360-6586. Fax: 214-739-8867. E-mail: ngale@mail.hockaday.org.
URL www.hockaday.org

iD Tech Camps–Southern Methodist University, Dallas, TX

iD Tech Camps
Southern Methodist University
Dallas, Texas 75205

General Information Coed residential and day academic program established in 1999. Accredited by American Camping Association. Formal opportunities for the academically talented and artistically talented.
Program Focus High-tech computer camps for kids and teens; produce digital movies, create video games, design Web pages, learn programming and robotics, and more; one computer per student, small classes, campers complete a project in a creative and fun learning environment.
Academics Web page design, computer programming, computer science (Advanced Placement), computers, music, precollege program.
Arts Animation, cinematography, digital media, drawing, film, film editing, film production, graphic arts, music, television/video.
Special Interest Areas Career exploration, computer graphics, electronics, leadership training, robotics, team building.
Sports Baseball, basketball, soccer, softball, swimming, volleyball.
Trips College tours, cultural, day.
Program Information 5 sessions per year. Session length: 5–7 days in June, July, August. Ages: 7–17. 40–50 participants per session. Day program cost: $639. Boarding program cost: $989. Application fee: $200. Financial aid available.
Application Deadline Continuous.
Jobs Positions for college students 18 and older.
Contact Client Service Representatives, 1885 Winchester Boulevard, Suite 201, Campbell, California 95008. Phone: 888-709-TECH. Fax: 408-871-2228. E-mail: requests@internaldrive.com.
URL www.internaldrive.com

For more information, see page 1156.

iD Tech Camps–UT Austin, Austin, TX

iD Tech Camps
The University of Texas at Austin
Austin, Texas 78712

General Information Coed residential and day academic program established in 1999. Accredited by American Camping Association. Formal opportunities for the academically talented and artistically talented.
Program Focus High-tech computer camps for kids and teens; produce digital movies, create video games, design Web pages, learn programming and robotics, and more; one computer per student, small classes, campers complete a project in a creative and fun learning environment.
Academics Web page design, computer programming, computer science (Advanced Placement), computers, music, precollege program.

Arts Animation, cinematography, digital media, drawing, film, film editing, film production, graphic arts, music, television/video.
Special Interest Areas Career exploration, computer graphics, electronics, leadership training, robotics, team building.
Sports Baseball, basketball, soccer, softball, swimming, volleyball.
Trips College tours, day.
Program Information 5 sessions per year. Session length: 5–7 days in June, July, August. Ages: 7–17. 40–50 participants per session. Day program cost: $639. Boarding program cost: $989. Application fee: $200. Financial aid available.
Application Deadline Continuous.
Jobs Positions for college students 18 and older.
Contact Client Service Representatives, 1885 Winchester Boulevard, Suite 201, Campbell, California 95008. Phone: 888-709-TECH. Fax: 408-871-2228. E-mail: requests@internaldrive.com.
URL www.internaldrive.com

For more information, see page 1156.

Jay Novacek Football Camp/Sports International

Sports International, Inc.
University of North Texas
Denton, Texas

General Information Coed residential and day sports camp established in 1983.
Program Focus Football camp.
Sports Football, weight training.
Program Information 1 session per year. Session length: 5 days in July. Ages: 8–18. 300–450 participants per session. Day program cost: $509. Boarding program cost: $619.
Application Deadline Continuous.
Jobs Positions for college students 18 and older.
Contact Customer Service, 8924 McGaw Court, Columbia, Maryland 21045. Phone: 800-555-0801. Fax: 410-309-9962. E-mail: info@footballcamps.com.
URL www.footballcamps.com

JCC Houston: Art Camp

Jewish Community Center of Houston
5601 South Braeswood Boulevard
Houston, Texas 77096

General Information Coed day arts program established in 1969. Religious affiliation: Jewish. Formal opportunities for the artistically talented. Specific services available for the emotionally challenged, developmentally challenged, hearing impaired, learning disabled, and physically challenged.
Arts Arts, arts and crafts (general), ceramics, drawing, jewelry making, painting, photography.
Special Interest Areas Campcraft.
Trips Day.
Program Information 4 sessions per year. Session length: 5–19 days in June, July, August. Ages: 8–13. 25–35 participants per session. Day program cost: $225–$750. Financial aid available.
Application Deadline Continuous.
Jobs Positions for high school students 15 and older and college students 18 and older.
Contact Mr. Jordan Shenker, Assistant Executive Director, main address above. Phone: 713-551-7208. Fax: 713-551-7223. E-mail: jshenker@jcchouston.org.
URL www.jcchouston.org

JCC Houston: Camp Bami

Jewish Community Center of Houston
5601 South Braeswood Boulevard
Houston, Texas 77096

General Information Coed day traditional camp established in 1942. Religious affiliation: Jewish. Specific services available for the emotionally challenged, developmentally challenged, hearing impaired, learning disabled, physically challenged, and visually impaired.
Arts Arts and crafts (general), music.
Sports Gymnastics, swimming.
Program Information 3 sessions per year. Session length: 15–19 days in June, July, August. Ages: 3–5. 160 participants per session. Day program cost: $430–$750. Financial aid available.
Application Deadline Continuous.
Jobs Positions for high school students 15 and older and college students 18 and older.
Contact Mr. Jordan Shenker, Assistant Executive Director, main address above. Phone: 715-551-7208. Fax: 715-551-7223. E-mail: jshenker@jcchouston.org.
URL www.jcchouston.org

JCC Houston: Camp Kaleidoscope

Jewish Community Center of Houston
9000 South Rice
Houston, Texas 77096

General Information Coed day traditional camp established in 1942. Religious affiliation: Jewish. Specific services available for the emotionally challenged, developmentally challenged, hearing impaired, learning disabled, physically challenged, and visually impaired.
Arts Arts and crafts (general), dance (folk).
Sports Basketball, climbing (wall), soccer, swimming, tennis.
Trips Day.
Program Information 2 sessions per year. Session length: 15–19 days in June, July, August. Ages: 6–8. 90–120 participants per session. Day program cost: $425–$710. Financial aid available.
Application Deadline Continuous.
Jobs Positions for high school students 15 and older and college students 18 and older.
Summer Contact Mr. Eric Bishop, Camp Director, 5601 South Braeswood Boulevard, Houston, Texas 77096. Phone: 713-838-7200. Fax: 713-551-7223. E-mail: ebishop@jcchouston.org.

JCC Houston: Camp Kaleidoscope (continued)
Winter Contact Mr. Eric Bishop, main address above. Phone: 713-729-3200.
URL www.jcchouston.org

JCC Houston: Counselor-In-Training

Jewish Community Center of Houston
5601 South Braeswood Boulevard
Houston, Texas 77096

General Information Coed day traditional camp established in 1985. Religious affiliation: Jewish.
Arts Arts and crafts (general), dance (folk).
Special Interest Areas Leadership training.
Sports Basketball, climbing (wall), soccer, swimming, tennis.
Trips Day.
Program Information 1 session per year. Session length: 33 days in June, July, August. Ages: 13–15. 10–20 participants per session. Day program cost: $250. Financial aid available.
Application Deadline June 1.
Summer Contact Mr. Eric Bishop, Camp Director, 9000 South Rice, Houston, Texas 77096. Phone: 713-838-7200. Fax: 713-551-7223. E-mail: ebishop@jcchouston.org.
Winter Contact Mr. Eric Bishop, main address above. Phone: 713-729-3200.
URL www.jcchouston.org

JCC Houston: Gordon Campsite

Jewish Community Center of Houston
Richmond, Texas 77469

General Information Coed residential and day traditional camp and outdoor program established in 1978. Religious affiliation: Jewish.
Arts Arts and crafts (general).
Sports Archery, basketball, canoeing, equestrian sports, soccer, swimming, volleyball.
Wilderness/Outdoors Canoe trips.
Trips Day, overnight.
Program Information 1 session per year. Session length: 19 days in June, July. Ages: 5–11. 100–200 participants per session. Day program cost: $450–$900. Boarding program cost: $525–$1375. Financial aid available.
Application Deadline Continuous.
Jobs Positions for high school students 15 and older and college students 17 and older.
Contact Mr. Jordan Shenker, Assistant Executive Director, 5601 South Braeswood Boulevard, Houston, Texas 77096. Phone: 713-1551-7208. Fax: 713-551-7223. E-mail: jshenker@jcchouston.org.
URL www.jcchouston.org

JCC Houston: Gymnastics Camp

Jewish Community Center of Houston
5601 South Braeswood Boulevard
Houston, Texas 77096

General Information Coed day sports camp established in 1985. Religious affiliation: Jewish.
Sports Climbing (wall), gymnastics, swimming.
Program Information 3 sessions per year. Session length: 15 days in June, July, August. Ages: 8–13. 30–60 participants per session. Day program cost: $225–$750. Financial aid available.
Application Deadline Continuous.
Jobs Positions for high school students 16 and older and college students 18 and older.
Contact Mr. Jordan Shenker, Assistant Executive Director, main address above. Phone: 713-551-7208. Fax: 713-551-7223. E-mail: jshenker@jcchouston.org.
URL www.jcchouston.org

JCC Houston: Kindercamp

Jewish Community Center of Houston
5601 South Braeswood Boulevard
Houston, Texas 77096

General Information Coed day traditional camp established in 1942. Religious affiliation: Jewish.
Arts Arts and crafts (general).
Sports Swimming.
Program Information 3 sessions per year. Session length: 15–19 days in June, July, August. Ages: 5–6. 60–75 participants per session. Day program cost: $585–$975. Financial aid available.
Application Deadline Continuous.
Jobs Positions for high school students 15 and older and college students 18 and older.
Contact Mr. Jordan Shenker, Assistant Executive Director, main address above. Phone: 713-551-7208. Fax: 713-551-7223. E-mail: jshenker@jcchouston.org.
URL www.jcchouston.org

JCC Houston: Sports Camp

Jewish Community Center of Houston
5601 South Braeswood Boulevard
Houston, Texas 77096

General Information Coed day sports camp established in 1969. Religious affiliation: Jewish.
Sports Baseball, basketball, bowling, climbing (wall), field hockey, football, gymnastics, racquetball, soccer, swimming, tennis, volleyball.
Program Information 1–9 sessions per year. Session length: 5–19 days in June, July, August. Ages: 8–13. 14–30 participants per session. Day program cost: $225–$750. Financial aid available.
Application Deadline Continuous.
Jobs Positions for high school students 16 and older and college students 18 and older.
Contact Mr. Jordan Shenker, Assistant Executive Director, main address above. Phone: 713-551-7208. Fax: 713-551-7223. E-mail: jshenker@jcchouston.org.
URL www.jcchouston.org

JCC Houston: Teen Trek

Jewish Community Center of Houston
Houston, Texas

General Information Coed travel traditional camp established in 1969. Religious affiliation: Jewish.
Special Interest Areas Community service, touring.
Sports Climbing (wall), swimming.
Trips Cultural, day, overnight, shopping.
Program Information 3 sessions per year. Session length: 15–19 days in June, July, August. Ages: 11–14. 30–50 participants per session. Cost: $485–$875. Financial aid available.
Application Deadline Continuous.
Jobs Positions for college students 18 and older.
Contact Mr. Jordan Shenker, Assistant Executive Director, 5601 South Braeswood Boulevard, Houston, Texas 77096. Phone: 713-551-7208. Fax: 713-551-7223. E-mail: jshenker@jcchouston.org.
URL www.jcchouston.org

JCC Houston: Tennis Camp

Jewish Community Center of Houston
5601 South Braeswood Boulevard
Houston, Texas 77096

General Information Coed day sports camp established in 1969. Religious affiliation: Jewish.
Sports Swimming, tennis.
Program Information 1–10 sessions per year. Session length: 5–19 days in June, July, August. Ages: 8–14. 10–15 participants per session. Day program cost: $225–$750. Financial aid available.
Application Deadline Continuous.
Jobs Positions for high school students 15 and older and college students 18 and older.
Contact Mr. Jordan Shenker, Assistant Executive Director, main address above. Phone: 713-551-7208. Fax: 713-551-7223. E-mail: jshenker@jcchouston.org.
URL www.jcchouston.org

JCC Houston: Theater Camp

Jewish Community Center of Houston
5601 South Braeswood Boulevard
Houston, Texas 77096

General Information Coed day arts program established in 1969. Religious affiliation: Jewish. Formal opportunities for the artistically talented.
Arts Dance, music (vocal), musical productions, puppetry, theater/drama.
Sports Swimming.
Program Information 1 session per year. Session length: 15 days in June, July. Ages: 8–13. 20–40 participants per session. Day program cost: $610. Financial aid available.
Application Deadline Continuous.
Jobs Positions for high school students 16 and older and college students 18 and older.
Contact Mr. Jordan Shenker, Assistant Executive Director, main address above. Phone: 713-551-7208. Fax: 713-551-7223. E-mail: jshenker@jcchouston.org.
URL www.jcchouston.org

Joe Machnik's No. 1 Academy One and Premier Programs–Fort Worth, Texas

Joe Machnik's No. 1 Camps
Texas Christian University
Fort Worth, Texas

General Information Coed residential and day sports camp.
Program Focus Soccer instruction, physical fitness, testing and speed training. Campers gain exposure to top players and are challenged by intense competition.
Sports Soccer.
Trips Day.
Program Information 2 sessions per year. Session length: 6 days in June. Ages: 9–18. 50–175 participants per session. Day program cost: $699. Boarding program cost: $759. Financial aid available.
Application Deadline Continuous.
Jobs Positions for college students.
Contact Dr. Joseph Machnik, Director, PO Box 389, 916 Palm Boulevard, Isle of Palms, South Carolina 29451. Phone: 800-622-4645. Fax: 843-886-0885. E-mail: info@no1soccercamps.com.
URL www.no1soccercamps.com

Joe Machnik's No. 1 College Prep Academy–Fort Worth, Texas

Joe Machnik's No. 1 Camps
Texas Christian University
Fort Worth, Texas

General Information Coed residential and day sports camp.
Program Focus Intense soccer instruction for high school students.
Sports Soccer, swimming.
Trips Day.
Program Information 1 session per year. Session length: 12 days in June. Ages: 13–18. 10–20 participants per session. Day program cost: $1449. Boarding program cost: $1549. Financial aid available.
Application Deadline Continuous.
Jobs Positions for college students 17 and older.
Contact Dr. Joseph Machnik, Director, PO Box 389, 916 Palm Boulevard, Isle of Palms, South Carolina 29451. Phone: 800-622-4645. Fax: 843-886-0885. E-mail: info@no1soccercamps.com.
URL www.no1soccercamps.com

Joe Machnik's No. 1 Mighty Mini, Goalkeeper and Striker Camp–Fort Worth, Texas

Joe Machnik's No. 1 Camps
Texas Christian University
Fort Worth, Texas

General Information Coed residential and day sports camp established in 1977.
Program Focus Soccer instruction. Goalkeepers and strikers compete against each other daily.

Joe Machnik's No. 1 Mighty Mini, Goalkeeper and Striker Camp–Fort Worth, Texas (continued)

Sports Soccer, swimming.
Program Information 2 sessions per year. Session length: 6 days in June. Ages: 8–12. 100–175 participants per session. Boarding program cost: $429. Financial aid available.
Application Deadline Continuous.
Jobs Positions for college students 17 and older.
Contact Dr. Joseph Machnik, Director, PO Box 389, 916 Palm Boulevard, Isle of Palms, South Carolina 29451. Phone: 800-622-4645. Fax: 843-886-0885. E-mail: info@no1soccercamps.com.
URL www.no1soccercamps.com

THE JOHN COOPER SCHOOL ACADEMIC CAMPS

The John Cooper School
One John Cooper Drive
The Woodlands, Texas 77381

General Information Coed day academic program established in 1991. High school credit may be earned.
Academics English as a second language, SAT/ACT preparation, Spanish language/literature, academics (general), aerospace science, architecture, computers, law, mathematics, reading, study skills, writing.
Arts Acting, arts and crafts (general), creative writing, photography, pottery, printmaking, weaving, woodworking.
Special Interest Areas Robotics.
Sports Baseball, basketball, fencing, soccer, volleyball.
Trips Day.
Program Information 3 sessions per year. Session length: 10 days in June, July. Ages: 4–18. 300–500 participants per session. Day program cost: $115–$465.
Application Deadline Continuous.
Jobs Positions for high school students 15 and older and college students 18 and older.
Contact Ms. Cheryl Dickinson, Summer Program Director, main address above. Phone: 281-367-0900 Ext. 319. Fax: 281-292-9201. E-mail: cheryl_dickinson@johncooper.org.
URL www.johncooper.org/summerprogram

THE JOHN COOPER SCHOOL DISCOVERY CAMPS

The John Cooper School
One John Cooper Drive
The Woodlands, Texas 77381

General Information Coed day traditional camp established in 1991.
Academics Computers, science (general).
Arts Arts and crafts (general), photography, pottery, printmaking, theater/drama.
Special Interest Areas Culinary arts.
Sports Baseball, fencing, soccer, softball, sports (general), tennis, volleyball.
Trips Day.
Program Information 2 sessions per year. Session length: 10 days in June, July. Ages: 4–12. 300–500 participants per session. Day program cost: $255–$290.
Application Deadline Continuous.
Jobs Positions for high school students 15 and older and college students 18 and older.
Contact Ms. Cheryl Dickinson, Summer Program Director, main address above. Phone: 281-367-0900 Ext. 319. E-mail: cheryl_dickinson@johncooper.org.
URL www.johncooper.org/summerprogram

THE JOHN COOPER SCHOOL RECREATIONAL ACTIVITIES AND SPORTS

The John Cooper School
One John Cooper Drive
The Woodlands, Texas 77381

General Information Coed day sports camp established in 1991.
Sports Baseball, fencing, soccer, softball, sports (general), tennis, volleyball.
Program Information 2 sessions per year. Session length: 10 days in June, July. 300–500 participants per session. Day program cost: $115–$130. Open to participants entering grades 2–12.
Application Deadline Continuous.
Jobs Positions for high school students 15 and older and college students 18 and older.
Contact Cheryl Dickinson, Summer Program Director, main address above. Phone: 281-367-0900 Ext.319. E-mail: cheryl_dickinson@johncooper.org.
URL www.johncooper.org/summerprogram

JUNIOR STATESMEN SYMPOSIUM ON TEXAS POLITICS AND LEADERSHIP

Junior Statesmen Foundation
The University of Texas at Austin
Austin, Texas 78712-1157

General Information Coed residential academic program established in 1999. Formal opportunities for the academically talented.
Program Focus Leadership at the national, state, and high school level.
Academics Communications, government and politics, journalism, social science, social studies, speech/debate.
Special Interest Areas Career exploration, leadership training.
Trips College tours, cultural, day.
Program Information 1 session per year. Session length: 4 days in June. Ages: 14–18. 100–150 participants per session. Boarding program cost: $325.
Application Deadline Continuous.
Contact Matt Randazzo, National Summer School Director, 400 South El Camino Real, Suite 300, San Mateo, California 94402. Phone: 800-334-5353. Fax: 650-347-7200. E-mail: jsa@jsa.org.
URL www.jsa.org

For more information, see page 1174.

Kickapoo Kamp

216 Hummingbird Lane
Kerrville, Texas 78028

General Information Girls' residential traditional camp established in 1925.
Arts Arts and crafts (general), dance (modern), leather working, music (vocal).
Special Interest Areas Campcraft.
Sports Aerobics, archery, basketball, canoeing, cheerleading, fishing, gymnastics, horseback riding, riflery, softball, swimming, tennis, volleyball, waterskiing.
Wilderness/Outdoors Hiking.
Program Information 3 sessions per year. Session length: 1–3 weeks in June, July. Ages: 6–17. 110 participants per session. Boarding program cost: $1550–$2000.
Application Deadline Continuous.
Jobs Positions for college students 18 and older.
Contact Bimmie Findlay, Owner, main address above. Phone: 830-257-5731. Fax: 830-895-5729.
URL www.kickapookamp.com

Longhorn Music Camp: All-State Choir Camp

The University of Texas at Austin, School of Music
Austin, Texas 78712-0435

General Information Coed residential and day arts program established in 1979. Formal opportunities for the artistically talented. Specific services available for the physically challenged.
Program Focus Choral performance, intensive study of the All-State Repertoire.
Arts Chorus, music (ensemble), music (vocal).
Trips Shopping.
Program Information 1 session per year. Session length: 4 days in June. Ages: 14–18. 160 participants per session. Day program cost: $200. Boarding program cost: $350.
Application Deadline May 31.
Jobs Positions for college students 18 and older.
Contact Ms. Lynne V. Lange, Program Coordinator, 1 University Station E3100, Austin, Texas 78712-0435. Phone: 512-232-2080. Fax: 512-232-3907. E-mail: lmc@www.utexas.edu.
URL www.longhornmusiccamp.org

Longhorn Music Camp: Harp Solo and Ensemble Camp

The University of Texas at Austin, School of Music
Austin, Texas 78712-0435

General Information Coed residential and day arts program established in 1979. Formal opportunities for the artistically talented. Specific services available for the physically challenged.
Program Focus Develop the skills harpists will need to succeed in the music industry.
Arts Music (chamber), music (ensemble).
Sports Volleyball.
Trips Shopping.
Program Information 1 session per year. Session length: 1 week in June. Ages: 14–18. 16 participants per session. Day program cost: $375–$405. Boarding program cost: $545–$575.
Application Deadline May 31.
Jobs Positions for college students 18 and older.
Contact Ms. Lynne V. Lange, Program Coordinator, 1 University Station E3100, Austin, Texas 78712-0435. Phone: 512-232-2080. Fax: 512-232-3907. E-mail: lmc@www.utexas.edu.
URL www.longhornmusiccamp.org

Longhorn Music Camp: High School Band Camp

The University of Texas at Austin, School of Music
Austin, Texas 78712-0435

General Information Coed residential and day arts program established in 1979. Formal opportunities for the artistically talented. Specific services available for the physically challenged.
Program Focus High school band.
Academics Music.
Arts Band, music (ensemble), music (instrumental).
Trips Shopping.
Program Information 1 session per year. Session length: 1 week in June, July. Ages: 14–18. 376 participants per session. Day program cost: $350–$380. Boarding program cost: $520–$550.
Application Deadline May 31.
Jobs Positions for college students 18 and older.
Contact Ms. Lynne V. Lange, Program Coordinator, 1 University Station E3100, Austin, Texas 78712-0435. Phone: 512-232-2080. Fax: 512-232-3907. E-mail: lmc@www.utexas.edu.
URL www.longhornmusiccamp.org

Longhorn Music Camp: Middle School Band Camp

The University of Texas at Austin, School of Music
Austin, Texas 78712-0435

General Information Coed residential and day arts program established in 1979. Formal opportunities for the artistically talented. Specific services available for the physically challenged.
Program Focus Band camp.
Arts Band, music (ensemble), music (instrumental).
Sports Volleyball.
Trips Shopping.
Program Information 1 session per year. Session length: 1 week in June. Ages: 11–14. 470 participants per session. Day program cost: $350–$380. Boarding program cost: $520–$550.
Application Deadline May 31.
Jobs Positions for college students.
Contact Ms. Lynne V. Lange, Program Coordinator, 1 University Station E3100, Austin, Texas 78712-0435. Phone: 512-232-2080. Fax: 512-232-3907. E-mail: lmc@www.utexas.edu.
URL www.longhornmusiccamp.org

Longhorn Music Camp: Middle School String Orchestra Camp

The University of Texas at Austin, School of Music
Austin, Texas 78712-0435

General Information Coed residential and day arts program established in 1979. Formal opportunities for the artistically talented. Specific services available for the physically challenged.
Program Focus String orchestra.
Arts Music (ensemble), music (orchestral).
Trips Shopping.
Program Information 1 session per year. Session length: 1 week in June. Ages: 11–14. 168 participants per session. Day program cost: $350–$380. Boarding program cost: $520–$550.
Application Deadline May 31.
Jobs Positions for college students 18 and older.
Contact Ms. Lynne V. Lange, Program Coordinator, 1 University Station E3100, Austin, Texas 78712-0435. Phone: 512-232-2080. Fax: 512-232-3907. E-mail: lmc@www.utexas.edu.
URL www.longhornmusiccamp.org

Longhorn Music Camp: Piano Performance Workshop

The University of Texas at Austin, School of Music
Austin, Texas 78712-0435

General Information Coed residential and day arts program established in 1979. Formal opportunities for the artistically talented. Specific services available for the physically challenged.
Program Focus Piano performance.
Academics Music, music (Advanced Placement).
Arts Music (classical), music (instrumental), piano.
Sports Swimming.
Trips Day, shopping.
Program Information 1 session per year. Session length: 10–11 days in July. Ages: 14–18. 20 participants per session. Day program cost: $275–$305. Boarding program cost: $575–$605. Financial aid available.
Application Deadline May 31.
Jobs Positions for college students 18 and older.
Contact Ms. Lynne V. Lange, Program Coordinator, 1 University Station E3100, Austin, Texas 78712-0435. Phone: 512-232-2080. Fax: 512-232-3907. E-mail: lmc@www.utexas.edu.
URL www.longhornmusiccamp.org

Marbridge Summer Camp

Marbridge Foundation, Inc.
2310 Bliss Spillar Road
Manchaca, Texas 78652

General Information Coed residential special needs program established in 1999. Specific services available for the developmentally challenged.
Program Focus To offer a transition opportunity from high school or home to a more independent lifestyle.
Academics Bible study, computers, music, writing.
Arts Arts and crafts (general), dance (modern), music (vocal), painting.
Special Interest Areas Animal care, daily living skills, gardening, nature study, personal development, planning skills, problem solving, social skills development.
Sports Basketball, boules, horseback riding, softball, swimming, volleyball.
Wilderness/Outdoors Hiking.
Trips Day.
Program Information 8 sessions per year. Session length: 1 week in June, July. Ages: 16–30. 8 participants per session. Boarding program cost: $350. Application fee: $150.
Application Deadline Continuous.
Jobs Positions for college students 18 and older.
Contact Ms. Connie Brashear, Camp Director, PO Box 2250, Manchaca, Texas 78652. Phone: 512-282-1144. Fax: 512-282-3723. E-mail: info@marbridge.org.
URL www.marbridge.org

Marine Military Academy English as a Second Language (ESL)

Marine Military Academy
320 Iwo Jima Boulevard
Harlingen, Texas 78550

General Information Boys' residential academic program established in 1999.
Program Focus English as a second language.
Academics English as a second language, aerospace science.
Special Interest Areas Military program.
Program Information 1 session per year. Session length: 4 weeks in July. Ages: 13–17. 50 participants per session. Boarding program cost: $2850. Application fee: $150.
Application Deadline Continuous.
Contact Ms. Jay Perez, Admissions, main address above. Phone: 956-423-6006 Ext.252. Fax: 956-412-3848. E-mail: admissions@mma-tx.org.
URL www.mma-tx.org

Marine Military Academy Summer Military Training Camp

Marine Military Academy
320 Iwo Jima Boulevard
Harlingen, Texas 78550

General Information Boys' residential outdoor program established in 1977.
Program Focus Military training.
Academics Aerospace science.
Special Interest Areas Flight instruction, leadership training, military program.
Sports Aerobics, basketball, climbing (wall), football, rappelling, riflery, ropes course, soccer, softball, sports (general), swimming, volleyball.
Wilderness/Outdoors Backpacking, hiking, wilderness camping.
Program Information 1 session per year. Session length: 4 weeks in July. Ages: 12–17. 300 participants

per session. Boarding program cost: $3000. Application fee: $150. Optional aerospace training: $750.
Application Deadline Continuous.
Contact Ms. Jay Perez, Admissions Officer, main address above. Phone: 956-423-6006 Ext.251. Fax: 956-412-3848. E-mail: admissions@mma-tx.org.
URL www.mma-tx.org

The Monarch School Summer Camp

The Monarch School
1231 Wirt Road
Houston, Texas 77055

General Information Coed day special needs program established in 1999. Specific services available for the developmentally challenged and learning disabled. High school credit may be earned.
Program Focus Relationship practice, executive functioning.
Arts Woodworking.
Special Interest Areas Construction, gardening, robotics, social skills development.
Sports Aerobics, martial arts.
Trips Day.
Program Information 1 session per year. Session length: 20 days in June, July. Ages: 6–19. 35–40 participants per session. Day program cost: $1500–$2250. Application fee: $150.
Application Deadline May 15.
Jobs Positions for high school students and college students.
Contact Debrah Hall, Summer Program Director, main address above. Phone: 713-479-0811. Fax: 713-464-7499. E-mail: dhall@monarchschool.org.
URL www.monarchschool.org

The Monarch School Summer Course

The Monarch School
1231 Wirt Road
Houston, Texas 77055

General Information Coed day academic program and special needs program established in 2004. Specific services available for the developmentally challenged and learning disabled. High school credit may be earned.
Academics Academics (general), biology, chemistry, environmental science, mathematics (Advanced Placement), music, social studies, study skills.
Arts Animation, music (vocal), theater/drama, woodworking.
Special Interest Areas Leadership training, nature study, robotics.
Sports Swimming.
Program Information Ages: 13–21. 30–40 participants per session. Cost: $525 per course.
Application Deadline May 20.
Contact Debra Hall, Program Director, Summer Camp, main address above. Phone: 713-479-0800. Fax: 713-464-7900. E-mail: dhall@monarchschool.org.
URL www.monarchschool.org

National Guitar Workshop–Austin, TX

National Guitar Workshop
St. Stephens Episcopal School
2900 Bunny Run Road
Austin, Texas 78746

General Information Coed residential and day arts program established in 1984. College credit may be earned.
Program Focus Music education in guitar, bass, drums, and vocals.
Academics Music, music (Advanced Placement).
Arts Guitar, music (classical), music (ensemble), music (instrumental), music (jazz), music (rock), music (vocal).
Program Information 1 session per year. Session length: 1 week in June, July, August. Ages: 13–79. 75–225 participants per session. Day program cost: $670–$720. Boarding program cost: $870–$920. Application fee: $25. Financial aid available.
Application Deadline Continuous.
Jobs Positions for college students 21 and older.
Contact Ms. Emily Flower, Registrar, PO Box 222, Lakeside, Connecticut 06758. Phone: 860-567-3736 Ext. 109. Fax: 860-567-0374. E-mail: emily@guitarworkshop.com.
URL www.guitarworkshop.com

Parent/Youth Golf School

The Academy of Golf Dynamics
45 Club Estates Parkway
Austin, Texas 78738

General Information Coed day family program and sports camp.
Program Focus Three-day golf academy for parents or grandparents and their kids, grandkids, or youth.
Sports Golf.
Program Information 35–40 sessions per year. Session length: 3 days in June, July, August, September, October, November, December. Ages: 9–18. 2–22 participants per session. Day program cost: $750–$850.
Application Deadline Continuous.
Contact Mr. Kevin Hunt, Office Manager, main address above. Phone: 800-879-2008. Fax: 512-261-8168. E-mail: info@golfdynamics.com.
URL www.golfdynamics.com

Sea Camp

Texas A&M University at Galveston
Galveston, Texas 77553

General Information Coed residential academic program and outdoor program established in 1986. Formal opportunities for the academically talented.
Program Focus Marine biology/ecology.
Academics Biology, botany, ecology, environmental science, marine studies, oceanography.
Special Interest Areas Conservation projects, field research/expeditions, nature study.
Sports Fishing, swimming.
Trips College tours, day, shopping.

Sea Camp (continued)
Program Information 16 sessions per year. Session length: 1 week in June, July. Ages: 10–18. 52 participants per session. Boarding program cost: $725–$775. Financial aid available.
Application Deadline Continuous.
Contact Daisy Duerson, Administrative Assistant, PO Box 1675, Galveston, Texas 77553. Phone: 409-740-4525. Fax: 409-740-4894. E-mail: seacamp@tamug.tamu.edu.
URL www.tamug.edu/seacamp

SeaWorld San Antonio Adventure Camp

SeaWorld Adventure Park
10500 SeaWorld Drive
San Antonio, Texas 78251-3002

General Information Coed residential and day academic program, outdoor program, and family program established in 1990. Accredited by American Camping Association. Formal opportunities for the academically talented. High school or college credit may be earned.

SeaWorld San Antonio Adventure Camp

Program Focus Marine science, marine animals.
Academics Area studies, biology, ecology, environmental science, geography, geology/earth science, marine studies, science (general).
Arts Arts and crafts (general).
Special Interest Areas Animal care, career exploration, conservation projects, field research/expeditions, nature study, team building.
Trips Day, overnight.
Program Information 90–150 sessions per year. Session length: 3–10 days in January, February, March, April, May, June, July, August, September, October, November. Ages: 3+. 10–88 participants per session. Day program cost: $50–$200. Boarding program cost: $300–$1400. Financial aid available.
Application Deadline Continuous.
Jobs Positions for college students 19 and older.
Contact Ann Quinn, Director of Education, 10500 SeaWorld Drive, San Antonio, Texas 78251-3002. Phone: 210-523-3608. Fax: 210-523-3898. E-mail: ann.quinn@seaworld.com.
URL seaworld.org
For more information, see page 1016.

SoccerPlus Goalkeeper School–Challenge Program–Waco, TX

SoccerPlus Camps
Baylor University
Waco, Texas

General Information Coed residential and day sports camp.
Program Focus Developing technical and tactical goalkeeping skills.
Sports Soccer.
Program Information 1 session per year. Session length: 6 days in June, July. Ages: 10+. Day program cost: $595. Boarding program cost: $695. Financial aid available.
Application Deadline Continuous.
Jobs Positions for college students.
Contact Mr. Shawn Kelly, General Manager, 11 Executive Drive, Suite 202, Farmington, Connecticut 06032. Phone: 800-533-7371. Fax: 860-677-0460. E-mail: info@soccerpluscamps.com.
URL www.soccerpluscamps.com

SoccerPlus Goalkeeper School–National Training Center–Waco, TX

SoccerPlus Camps
Baylor University
Waco, Texas

General Information Coed residential sports camp.
Program Focus Developing advanced goalkeeping skills.
Sports Soccer.
Program Information 1 session per year. Session length: 6 days in June, July. Ages: 15+. Boarding program cost: $775.
Application Deadline Continuous.
Jobs Positions for college students.
Contact Mr. Shawn Kelly, General Manager, 11 Executive Drive, Suite 202, Farmington, Connecticut 06032. Phone: 800-533-7371. Fax: 860-677-0460. E-mail: info@soccerpluscamps.com.
URL www.soccerpluscamps.com

Southern Methodist University–College Experience

Southern Methodist University
Dallas, Texas 75275

General Information Coed residential and day academic program established in 1978. Formal opportunities for the academically talented and gifted. College credit may be earned.
Academics American literature, English language/literature, academics (general), anthropology, art history/appreciation, chemistry, computer programming, computers, economics, engineering, geology/earth science, government and politics, history, journalism, mathematics, philosophy, precollege program, psychology, writing.
Arts Creative writing, film.
Trips Cultural.
Program Information 1 session per year. Session length: 25–30 days in July, August. Ages: 15–18. 70 participants per session. Day program cost: $900–$1800. Boarding program cost: $3100–$3500. Application fee: $25. Financial aid available.
Application Deadline Continuous.
Jobs Positions for college students 21 and older.
Contact Marilyn Swanson, Assistant Director of Pre-College Programs, PO Box 750383, Dallas, Texas 75275. Phone: 214-768-0123. Fax: 214-768-3147. E-mail: gifted@smu.edu.
URL www.smu.edu/ce

For more information, see page 1322.

Southern Methodist University TAG (Talented and Gifted)

Southern Methodist University
Dallas, Texas 75275

General Information Coed residential academic program established in 1978. Formal opportunities for the academically talented and gifted. College credit may be earned.

Southern Methodist University TAG (Talented and Gifted)

Academics American literature, English language/literature, academics (general), engineering, geography, government and politics, humanities, mathematics, philosophy, precollege program, psychology, science (general), social science, writing.
Arts Creative writing, drawing, music, painting, photography, television/video, theater/drama.
Special Interest Areas Leadership training, model rocketry.
Trips Cultural.
Program Information 1 session per year. Session length: 3 weeks in July. Ages: 12–15. 125–175 participants per session. Boarding program cost: $2450–$2600. Application fee: $25. Financial aid available.
Application Deadline Continuous.
Jobs Positions for college students 19 and older.
Contact Ms. Marilyn Swanson, Assistant Director of Pre-College Programs, PO Box 750383, Dallas, Texas 75275. Phone: 214-768-0123. Fax: 214-768-3147. E-mail: gifted@smu.edu.
URL www.smu.edu/tag

For more information, see page 1322.

Star Ranch Summer Camp

Star Programs, Inc.
149 Camp Scenic Loop
Ingram, Texas 78025-5086

General Information Coed residential academic program, bible camp, and special needs program established in 1990. Religious affiliation: Christian. Specific services available for the emotionally challenged, developmentally challenged, hearing impaired, learning disabled, participant with ADD, and participant with AD/HD.
Program Focus Christian educational summer camp for children with learning differences, including ADD/ADHD, that focuses on building self-confidence, experience, and independence.
Academics Bible study, academics (general), journalism, mathematics, reading, study skills, writing.
Arts Acting, arts and crafts (general), dance, drawing, music, painting, photography.
Special Interest Areas Animal care, campcraft, gardening, nature study, team building.
Sports Archery, basketball, bicycling, canoeing, fishing, kayaking, rappelling, riflery, snorkeling, soccer, softball, swimming, volleyball, weight training.
Wilderness/Outdoors Hiking, rock climbing.
Trips Day.
Program Information 7 sessions per year. Session length: 1 week in June, July, August. Ages: 7–18. 45–50 participants per session. Boarding program cost: $635–$1270. Financial aid available.
Application Deadline Continuous.
Jobs Positions for college students 18 and older.
Contact Mrs. Valerie Chambers, Camp Administrative Assistant, main address above. Phone: 830-367-4868. Fax: 830-367-2814. E-mail: vchambers@starranch.org.
URL www.starranch.org/summer_camp.htm

Student Conservation Association–Conservation Crew Program (Texas)

Student Conservation Association (SCA)
Texas

General Information Coed residential outdoor program, community service program, and wilderness program established in 1957. High school credit may be earned.
Program Focus Resource management, conservation and environmental education.
Academics Biology, botany, ecology, environmental science, geology/earth science, history.
Special Interest Areas Campcraft, community service, construction, leadership training, nature study, trail maintenance, work camp programs.
Sports Canoeing, fishing, kayaking, swimming.
Wilderness/Outdoors Backpacking, hiking, orienteering, outdoor living skills, wilderness camping.
Trips Cultural, day, overnight.
Program Information 2–3 sessions per year. Session length: 3–5 weeks in June, July, August. Ages: 15–19. 6–8 participants per session. Application fee: $20. Financial aid available. No cost for program; financial aid possible for travel expenses.
Application Deadline Continuous.
Jobs Positions for college students 21 and older.
Contact Recruitment Office, PO Box 550, Charlestown, New Hampshire 03603. Phone: 603-543-1700. Fax: 603-543-1828. E-mail: getreal@thesca.org.
URL www.theSCA.org

Summer at the Academy

San Antonio Academy
117 East French Place
San Antonio, Texas 78212

General Information Coed day traditional camp established in 1986.
Academics Spanish language/literature, biology, botany, chemistry, computers, mathematics, music, science (general), study skills, writing.
Arts Arts and crafts (general), ceramics, creative writing, dance, dance (folk), drawing, jewelry making, metalworking, music (instrumental), musical productions, painting, photography, pottery, puppetry, television/video, woodworking.
Special Interest Areas Community service, culinary arts, model rocketry.
Sports Basketball, cheerleading, cross-country, football, golf, lacrosse, martial arts, soccer, softball, tennis.
Program Information 8 sessions per year. Session length: 1–2 weeks in June, July. Ages: 4–17. 10–30 participants per session. Day program cost: $64–$176. Application fee: $15.
Application Deadline Continuous.
Jobs Positions for college students 18 and older.
Contact Ms. Yulanee McKnight, Summer Registrar, main address above. Phone: 210-733-7331 Ext.237. Fax: 210-734-0711. E-mail: yulanee@yahoo.com.
URL www.sa-academy.org

Ventures Travel Service–Texas

Friendship Ventures
Texas

General Information Coed travel special needs program established in 1985. Specific services available for the developmentally challenged and physically challenged.
Program Focus Provides travel services to older teens and adults with developmental disabilities.
Special Interest Areas Touring.
Program Information 50 sessions per year. Session length: 4–10 days in February, March, April, May, June, July, August, September, October, November, December. Ages: 14–70. 4–8 participants per session. Cost: $395–$2000.
Application Deadline Continuous.
Jobs Positions for college students 18 and older.
Contact Georgann Rumsey, President/CEO, 10509 108th Street, NW, Annandale, Minnesota 55302. Phone: 952-852-0101. Fax: 952-852-0123. E-mail: fv@friendshipventures.org.
URL www.friendshipventures.org

WRC Weather Camp

Weather Research Center
3227 Audley Street
Houston, Texas 77098

General Information Coed day academic program established in 1993.
Program Focus Weather, weather safety, meteorology.
Academics Computers, geography, mathematics, meteorology, oceanography, physics, science (general).
Program Information 25–30 sessions per year. Session length: 1 day in June, July. Ages: 5–17. 5–10 participants per session. Day program cost: $55–$75.
Application Deadline Continuous.
Jobs Positions for high school students 16 and older and college students 18 and older.
Contact Ms. Jill F. Hasling, Program Coordinator, main address above. Phone: 713-529-3076. Fax: 713-528-3538. E-mail: wrc@wxresearch.org.
URL www.weathercamp.org

UTAH

Camp Kostopulos

Kostopulos Dream Foundation
2500 Emigration Canyon
Salt Lake City, Utah 84108

General Information Coed residential traditional camp, outdoor program, and special needs program established in 1967. Accredited by American Camping Association. Specific services available for the emotionally challenged, developmentally challenged, hearing

impaired, learning disabled, physically challenged, visually impaired, participant with Neurofibromatosis, and organ transplant recipient.
Program Focus Traditional summer camp activities adapted for people with disabilities.
Academics Environmental science, music.
Arts Arts and crafts (general), ceramics, dance, drawing, fabric arts, jewelry making, leather working, music, music (instrumental), painting, photography, pottery, puppetry, theater/drama.
Special Interest Areas Animal care, campcraft, leadership training, nature study.
Sports Baseball, basketball, boating, canoeing, climbing (wall), fishing, football, horseback riding, ropes course, soccer, swimming, volleyball, waterskiing.
Wilderness/Outdoors Hiking, outdoor adventure, rafting, white-water trips, wilderness camping, wilderness/outdoors (general).
Trips Cultural, day, overnight.
Program Information 10–12 sessions per year. Session length: 5 days in June, July, August. Ages: 7–65. 40–50 participants per session. Boarding program cost: $320. Financial aid available.
Application Deadline Continuous.
Jobs Positions for high school students 16 and older and college students 18 and older.
Contact Amy Stoeger, Program Director, main address above. Phone: 801-582-0700. Fax: 801-583-5176. E-mail: astoeger@campk.org.
URL www.campk.org

Camp Shakespeare

Southern Utah University
351 Center Street
Cedar City, Utah 84720

General Information Coed residential academic program and arts program established in 1980. College credit may be earned.
Program Focus The plays of William Shakespeare.
Academics Humanities.
Arts Theater/drama.
Program Information 1 session per year. Session length: 5 days in July. Ages: 16+. 80–100 participants per session. Boarding program cost: $1040. Application fee: $50.
Application Deadline Continuous.
Contact Dr. Michael Flachmann, Program Director, Camp Shakespeare, c/o Department of English, CSUB, 9001 Stockdale Highway, Bakersfield, California 93311-1099. Phone: 661-664-2121. E-mail: mflachmann@csub.edu.
URL www.csub.edu/campshakespeare

Deer Hill Expeditions, Utah

Deer Hill Expeditions
Utah

General Information Coed residential outdoor program, community service program, wilderness program, and cultural program established in 1984. Accredited by Association for Experiential Education. High school or college credit may be earned.
Program Focus In-depth wilderness adventure and conservation service in the canyons, rivers, and mountains of the Southwest.
Academics Archaeology, area studies, ecology, environmental science, geology/earth science, intercultural studies.
Arts Photography.
Special Interest Areas Native American culture, community service, conservation projects, cross-cultural education, first aid, leadership training, nature study, trail maintenance.
Sports Canoeing, kayaking, rappelling.
Wilderness/Outdoors Backpacking, canoe trips, canyoneering, climbing, hiking, mountain biking, mountaineering, orienteering, outdoor camping, outdoor living skills, rafting, rock climbing, white-water trips, wilderness camping, wilderness/outdoors (general).
Trips Cultural, overnight.
Program Information 12–16 sessions per year. Session length: 3–5 weeks in June, July, August. Ages: 13–22. 12 participants per session. Boarding program cost: $2750–$4550.
Application Deadline Continuous.
Jobs Positions for college students 21 and older.
Contact Ms. Beverly Capelin, Owner and Director, PO Box 180, Mancos, Colorado 81328. Phone: 800-533-7221. Fax: 970-533-7221. E-mail: info@deerhillexpeditions.com.
URL www.deerhillexpeditions.com

Earthwatch Institute–Canyonland Creek Ecology

Earthwatch Institute
Canyonlands National Park
Utah

General Information Coed residential outdoor program, cultural program, and adventure program.
Program Focus Discovering the impact of wilderness roads on desert stream ecology.
Academics Ecology, environmental science, science (general).
Special Interest Areas Field research/expeditions, nature study.
Wilderness/Outdoors Hiking.
Program Information 5 sessions per year. Session length: 16 days in May, June, July, August, September. Ages: 16+. 10 participants per session. Boarding program cost: $1595–$1695. Financial aid available. Financial aid for high school students and teachers.
Application Deadline Continuous.
Contact General Information Desk, PO Box 75, Maynard, Massachusetts 01754. Phone: 800-776-0188. Fax: 978-461-2332. E-mail: info@earthwatch.org.
URL www.earthwatch.org

EARTHWATCH INSTITUTE–WILDLIFE TRAILS OF THE AMERICAN WEST

Earthwatch Institute
Red Butte Canyon, Utah

General Information Coed residential outdoor program.
Program Focus Studying wildlife trail ecology and traffic to design efficient wildlife corridors.
Academics Ecology, environmental science.
Special Interest Areas Internet accessibility, field research/expeditions, nature study.
Wilderness/Outdoors Hiking, wilderness/outdoors (general).
Program Information 3 sessions per year. Session length: 8 days in January, February, May, June, October. Ages: 16+. 15 participants per session. Boarding program cost: $1495–$1595. Financial aid available. Financial aid for high school students and teachers.
Application Deadline Continuous.
Contact General Information Desk, PO Box 75, Maynard, Massachusetts 01754. Phone: 800-776-0188. Fax: 978-461-2332. E-mail: info@earthwatch.org.
URL www.earthwatch.org

OUTWARD BOUND WEST–SOUTHWEST MOUNTAINEERING, RAFTING, AND CANYONEERING

Outward Bound West/Outward Bound, USA
Utah or La Sal Mountains; Green or Colorado Rivers
Utah

General Information Coed travel outdoor program and wilderness program established in 1965. College credit may be earned.
Program Focus Teamwork and leadership wilderness adventure.
Academics Environmental science.
Special Interest Areas Campcraft, community service, leadership training, nature study, personal development, team building.
Wilderness/Outdoors Backpacking, canyoneering, hiking, mountaineering, rafting, rock climbing, wilderness camping.
Trips Overnight.
Program Information 15 sessions per year. Session length: 15–22 days in June, July, August. Ages: 14+. Cost: $2695–$3295. Application fee: $95. Financial aid available.
Application Deadline Continuous.
Jobs Positions for college students 21 and older.
Contact Admissions Advisor, 910 Jackson Street, Golden, Colorado 80401. Phone: 866-746-9777. Fax: 720-497-2421. E-mail: info@obwest.org.
URL www.outwardboundwest.org

OUTWARD BOUND WEST–SOUTHWEST MYSTERY EXPEDITION

Outward Bound West/Outward Bound, USA
Canyon Country
Utah

General Information Coed travel outdoor program and wilderness program established in 1965. College credit may be earned.
Program Focus Teamwork and leadership wilderness adventure.
Academics Environmental science.
Special Interest Areas Campcraft, leadership training, nature study, personal development, team building.
Wilderness/Outdoors Backpacking, canyoneering, hiking, mountaineering, outdoor adventure, wilderness camping.
Trips Overnight.
Program Information 1 session per year. Session length: 10 days in August. Ages: 16+. Cost: $1795. Application fee: $95. Financial aid available.
Application Deadline Continuous.
Jobs Positions for college students 21 and older.
Contact Admissions Advisor, 910 Jackson Street, Golden, Colorado 80401. Phone: 866-746-9777. Fax: 720-497-2421. E-mail: info@obwest.org.
URL www.outwardboundwest.org

OUTWARD BOUND WEST–UTAH SUMMER SEMESTER

Outward Bound West/Outward Bound, USA
La Sal and Henry Mountains, Colorado River, Lake Powell
Utah

General Information Coed travel outdoor program and wilderness program established in 1965. College credit may be earned.
Program Focus Teamwork and leadership wilderness adventure.
Academics Environmental science.
Special Interest Areas Campcraft, community service, leadership training, nature study, personal development, team building.
Wilderness/Outdoors Backpacking, canyoneering, hiking, mountaineering, outdoor adventure, rafting, rock climbing, white-water trips, wilderness camping.
Trips Overnight.
Program Information 1 session per year. Session length: 50 days in June, July, August. Ages: 16+. Cost: $5395. Application fee: $95. Financial aid available.
Application Deadline Continuous.
Jobs Positions for college students 21 and older.
Contact Admissions Advisor, 910 Jackson Street, Golden, Colorado 80401. Phone: 866-746-9777. Fax: 720-497-2421. E-mail: info@obwest.org.
URL www.outwardboundwest.org

Student Conservation Association–Conservation Crew Program (Utah)

Student Conservation Association (SCA)
Utah

General Information Coed residential outdoor program, community service program, and wilderness program established in 1957. High school credit may be earned.
Program Focus Resource management, conservation and environmental education.
Academics Biology, botany, ecology, environmental science, geology/earth science, history.
Special Interest Areas Campcraft, community service, construction, leadership training, nature study, trail maintenance, work camp programs.
Sports Canoeing, fishing, kayaking, swimming.
Wilderness/Outdoors Backpacking, canoe trips, hiking, orienteering, outdoor living skills, wilderness camping.
Trips Cultural, day, overnight.
Program Information 2–3 sessions per year. Session length: 3–5 weeks in June, July, August. Ages: 15–19. 6–8 participants per session. Application fee: $20. Financial aid available. No cost for program; financial aid possible for travel expenses.
Application Deadline Continuous.
Jobs Positions for college students 21 and older.
Contact Recruitment Office, PO Box 550, Charlestown, New Hampshire 03603. Phone: 603-543-1700. Fax: 603-543-1828. E-mail: getreal@thesca.org.
URL www.theSCA.org

SummerWorks

Rowland Hall-St. Mark's School
720 South Guardsman Way
Salt Lake City, Utah 84108

General Information Coed day traditional camp.
Arts Arts and crafts (general), ceramics, dance, photography, theater/drama.
Special Interest Areas Counselor-in-training program, culinary arts, field trips (arts and culture), leadership training, team building.
Sports Archery, martial arts, soccer, swimming, tennis.
Wilderness/Outdoors Hiking, orienteering, wilderness camping.
Trips Day, overnight.
Program Information 9 sessions per year. Session length: 5 days in June, July, August. Ages: 4–15. 60–90 participants per session. Day program cost: $200–$240.
Application Deadline Continuous.
Jobs Positions for high school students 16 and older and college students 18 and older.
Contact Rich Weeks, Director, main address above. Phone: 801-355-7485. Fax: 801-355-0388. E-mail: richweeks@rowland-hall.org.
URL www.rhsm.org

World Horizons International–Kanab, Utah

World Horizons International
Utah

General Information Coed residential outdoor program, community service program, and cultural program established in 1996.
Program Focus Working with abused and abandoned animals in conjunction with "Best Friends Animal Sanctuary" and doing trail maintenance at Zion National Park.
Special Interest Areas Animal care, career exploration, community service, conservation projects, trail maintenance.
Sports Horseback riding, swimming.
Wilderness/Outdoors Backpacking, canoe trips, hiking, white-water trips.
Trips Cultural, day, overnight.
Program Information 1–2 sessions per year. Session length: 17–28 days in July. Ages: 14–18. 10 participants per session. Boarding program cost: $2950–$4100. Application fee: $100. Financial aid available. Airfare from New York to Utah included.
Application Deadline Continuous.
Jobs Positions for college students 20 and older.
Contact Stuart L. Rabinowitz, Executive Director, PO Box 662, Bethlehem, Connecticut 06751. Phone: 800-262-5874. Fax: 203-266-6227. E-mail: worldhorizons@att.net.
URL www.world-horizons.com

For more information, see page 1406.

VERMONT

Aloha Camp

Aloha Foundation, Inc.
2039 Lake Morey Road
Fairlee, Vermont 05045

General Information Girls' residential traditional camp established in 1905. Accredited by American Camping Association.
Arts Arts and crafts (general), batiking, ceramics, dance, drawing, fabric arts, jewelry making, leather working, metalworking, music, music (vocal), musical productions, painting, photography, pottery, printmaking, puppetry, theater/drama, weaving, woodworking.
Special Interest Areas Campcraft, leadership training, nature study.
Sports Archery, basketball, bicycling, boating, canoeing, diving, equestrian sports, fencing, field hockey, horseback riding, kayaking, riflery, ropes course, rowing (crew/sculling), sailing, snorkeling, soccer, softball, sports (general), swimming, tennis, volleyball, windsurfing.

Aloha Camp (continued)

Wilderness/Outdoors Backpacking, bicycle trips, canoe trips, hiking, mountain biking, survival training, white-water trips, wilderness camping.
Trips Day, overnight.
Program Information 3 sessions per year. Session length: 26–50 days in July, August. Ages: 12–17. 130–150 participants per session. Boarding program cost: $4300–$6400. Financial aid available.
Application Deadline Continuous.
Jobs Positions for high school students 18 and older and college students 18 and older.
Summer Contact Nancy L. Pennell, Director, main address above. Phone: 802-333-3410. Fax: 802-333-3404. E-mail: nancy_pennell@alohafoundation.org.
Winter Contact Nancy L. Pennell, Director, 465 Pennell Road, Chester, Vermont 05143. Phone: 802-875-3410. Fax: 802-875-3410. E-mail: nancy_pennell@alohafoundation.org.
URL www.alohafoundation.org

Audubon Journeys

Audubon Vermont
2658 High Pond Road
Brandon, Vermont 05733

General Information Coed residential outdoor program, wilderness program, and adventure program established in 1999.
Program Focus Environmental stewardship and habitat restoration, minimum impact camping.
Academics Astronomy, biology, botany, ecology, environmental science, herpetology, ornithology.
Special Interest Areas Campcraft, career exploration, community service, conservation projects, nature study, team building.
Sports Canoeing, swimming.
Wilderness/Outdoors Canoe trips, hiking, orienteering, survival training, wilderness camping.
Trips Day, overnight.
Program Information 1 session per year. Session length: 10 days in July, August. Ages: 13–16. 8–16 participants per session. Boarding program cost: $875–$900. Financial aid available.
Application Deadline Continuous.
Jobs Positions for college students 20 and older.
Contact Mr. Ryan Young, Director, 255 Sherman Hollow Road, Huntington, Vermont 05462. Phone: 802-434-3068. Fax: 802-434-4686. E-mail: ryoung@audubon.org.
URL www.vt.audubon.org/highpond.html

Audubon Vermont Youth Camp

Audubon Vermont
2658 High Pond Road
Brandon, Vermont 05733

General Information Coed residential academic program and outdoor program established in 1995.
Program Focus Environmental and science education.
Academics Astronomy, biology, botany, ecology, environmental science, geology/earth science, herpetology, ornithology.
Arts Arts and crafts (general).
Special Interest Areas Nature study, team building.
Sports Swimming, ultimate frisbee, volleyball.
Wilderness/Outdoors Backpacking, hiking, orienteering, wilderness camping.
Trips Cultural, day, overnight.
Program Information 2–3 sessions per year. Session length: 10 days in June, July, August. Ages: 10–14. 30 participants per session. Boarding program cost: $775–$850. Financial aid available.
Application Deadline Continuous.
Jobs Positions for high school students 16 and older and college students 21 and older.
Contact Mr. Ryan Young, Director, 255 Sherman Hollow Road, Huntington, Vermont 05462. Phone: 802-434-3068. Fax: 802-434-4686. E-mail: ryoung@audubon.org.
URL www.vt.audubon.org/highpond.html

Brown Ledge Camp

71 Brown Ledge Road
Colchester, Vermont 05446

General Information Girls' residential traditional camp established in 1926. Accredited by American Camping Association.
Program Focus Horsemanship, theatre, and waterfront.
Arts Arts and crafts (general), drawing, theater/drama.
Sports Archery, canoeing, diving, equestrian sports, horseback riding, riflery, sailing, swimming, tennis, waterskiing, windsurfing.
Wilderness/Outdoors Canoe trips.
Trips Overnight.
Program Information 3 sessions per year. Session length: 4–8 weeks in June, July, August. Ages: 10–18. 180 participants per session. Boarding program cost: $3400–$4900. Financial aid available.
Application Deadline Continuous.
Jobs Positions for college students 19 and older.
Contact Co-Director, 25 Wilson Street, Burlington, Vermont 05401. Phone: 802-862-2442. Fax: 802-658-1614. E-mail: blc@brownledge.org.
URL www.brownledge.org

Burklyn Ballet Theatre

Burklyn Ballet Theatre, Inc.
337 College Hill
Johnson State College
Johnson, Vermont 05656

General Information Coed residential and day arts program established in 1976. Formal opportunities for the artistically talented. Specific services available for the hearing impaired. College credit may be earned.
Program Focus Classical ballet training and performance opportunities.
Arts Dance, dance (ballet), dance (folk), dance (jazz), dance (modern), mime, music (classical), musical productions, theater/drama.
Special Interest Areas Field trips (arts and culture).
Trips Cultural, shopping.
Program Information 3 sessions per year. Session length: 2–8 weeks in June, July, August. Ages: 12–25.

65–80 participants per session. Day program cost: $900–$1800. Boarding program cost: $2000–$4400. Application fee: $25. Financial aid available.
Application Deadline Continuous.
Jobs Positions for college students 20 and older.
Summer Contact Joanne Whitehill, Artistic Director, PO Box 302, Johnson, Vermont 05656-0302. Phone: 802-635-1390. E-mail: burklyn@aol.com.
Winter Contact Joanne Whitehill, Artistic Director, PO Box 907, Island Heights, New Jersey 08732. Phone: 732-288-2660. Fax: 732-288-2663. E-mail: burklyn@aol.com.
URL www.burklynballet.com

Burklyn Ballet Theatre II, The Intermediate Program

Burklyn Ballet Theatre, Inc.
337 College Hill
Johnson State College
Johnson, Vermont 05656

General Information Coed residential arts program established in 1995. Formal opportunities for the artistically talented. Specific services available for the hearing impaired.
Program Focus Classical ballet training and performance opportunities.
Arts Arts and crafts (general), costume design, dance, dance (ballet), dance (folk), dance (jazz), dance (modern), fabric arts, jewelry making, mime, music (classical), painting, television/video, theater/drama.
Special Interest Areas Field trips (arts and culture).
Sports Swimming.
Trips Cultural, day, shopping.
Program Information 1 session per year. Session length: 2 weeks in July. Ages: 10–12. 18–24 participants per session. Boarding program cost: $2100–$3200. Application fee: $25.
Application Deadline Continuous.
Summer Contact Joanne Whitehill, Artistic Director, PO Box 302, Johnson, Vermont 05656-0302. Phone: 802-635-1390. E-mail: burklyn@aol.com.
Winter Contact Joanne Whitehill, Director, PO Box 907, Island Heights, New Jersey 08732-0907. Phone: 732-288-2660. Fax: 732-288-2663. E-mail: burklyn@aol.com.
URL www.burklynballet.com

Camp Aloha Hive

Aloha Foundation, Inc.
846 Vermont Route 244
Fairlee, Vermont 05045

General Information Girls' residential traditional camp established in 1915. Accredited by American Camping Association.
Arts Arts and crafts (general), ceramics, chorus, dance, drawing, jewelry making, music, music (instrumental), musical productions, painting, photography, pottery, printmaking, puppetry, theater/drama.
Special Interest Areas Campcraft, nature study.
Sports Archery, basketball, canoeing, equestrian sports, field hockey, gymnastics, horseback riding, kayaking, lacrosse, ropes course, sailing, soccer, softball, sports (general), swimming, tennis, volleyball, windsurfing.
Wilderness/Outdoors Backpacking, canoe trips, hiking, wilderness camping.
Trips Day, overnight.
Program Information 3 sessions per year. Session length: 26–50 days in July, August. Ages: 7–12. 130–150 participants per session. Boarding program cost: $4300–$6400. Financial aid available.
Application Deadline Continuous.
Jobs Positions for high school students 17 and older and college students 17 and older.
Summer Contact Helen Rankin Butler, Director, main address above. Phone: 802-333-3420. Fax: 802-333-3404. E-mail: helen_rankinbutler@alohafoundation.org.
Winter Contact Helen Rankin Butler, Director, PO Box 477, Gates Mills, Ohio 44040. Phone: 440-423-0521. Fax: 440-423-0521. E-mail: helen_rankinbutler@alohafoundation.org.
URL www.alohafoundation.org

Camp Betsey Cox

Camp Betsey Cox/Camp Sangamon for Boys, Inc.
140 Betsey Cox Lane
Pittsford, Vermont 05763

General Information Girls' residential traditional camp established in 1953. Accredited by American Camping Association. Formal opportunities for the artistically talented.
Program Focus Individual development and decision making; strong emphasis on arts and crafts and individual sports.
Arts Arts and crafts (general), batiking, dance, dance (jazz), dance (modern), drawing, painting, photography, pottery, theater/drama, weaving, woodworking.
Special Interest Areas Animal care, campcraft, community service, construction, farming, gardening, model rocketry.
Sports Archery, bicycling, canoeing, equestrian sports, fishing, horseback riding, kayaking, ropes course, sailing, sea kayaking, soccer, softball, swimming, tennis.
Wilderness/Outdoors Backpacking, bicycle trips, canoe trips, caving, hiking, rock climbing.
Trips Day, overnight.
Program Information 3–4 sessions per year. Session length: 2–3 weeks in June, July, August. Ages: 9–15. 85 participants per session. Boarding program cost: $1425–$2130.
Application Deadline Continuous.
Jobs Positions for college students 20 and older.
Summer Contact Lorrie Byrom, Director, main address above. Phone: 802-483-6611. E-mail: betcoxvt@aol.com.
Winter Contact Mike Byrom, Executive Director, PO Box 886, Key Largo, Florida 33037. Phone: 888-345-9193. E-mail: betcoxvt@aol.com.
URL www.campbetseycox.com
For more information, see page 1040.

Camp Billings

1452 Route 244
Fairlee, Vermont 05045-9620

General Information Coed residential traditional camp established in 1907. Accredited by American Camping Association.
Arts Acting, arts and crafts (general), chorus, dance, dance (folk), dance (jazz), dance (modern), drawing, jewelry making, music, music (vocal), musical productions, painting, photography, puppetry, theater/drama.
Special Interest Areas Campcraft, gardening, leadership training, nature study.
Sports Aerobics, archery, baseball, basketball, boating, canoeing, cross-country, diving, fishing, football, gymnastics, kayaking, lacrosse, martial arts, rowing (crew/sculling), sailing, snorkeling, soccer, softball, sports (general), street/roller hockey, swimming, tennis, track and field, volleyball, water polo, waterskiing, windsurfing.
Wilderness/Outdoors Backpacking, canoe trips, hiking, orienteering, white-water trips.
Trips Day, overnight.
Program Information 4 sessions per year. Session length: 2 weeks in June, July, August. Ages: 8–15. 160–170 participants per session. Boarding program cost: $700. Application fee: $50. Financial aid available.
Application Deadline Continuous.
Jobs Positions for high school students 18 and older and college students 18 and older.
Summer Contact Mr. Bob Green, Director, main address above. Phone: 802-333-4317. E-mail: campbillings@juno.com.
Winter Contact Mr. Bob Green, Director, 11955 Classic Drive, Coral Springs, Florida 33071. Phone: 954-345-7290. E-mail: campbillings@juno.com.
URL www.campbillings.org

Camp Catherine Capers

Lake St. Catherine
127 West Lake Road
Wells, Vermont 05774

General Information Girls' residential and day traditional camp established in 1952. Accredited by American Camping Association.
Program Focus Horseback riding, water sports, camping trips, and horse and animal care.
Arts Arts and crafts (general), chorus, drawing, jewelry making, leather working, photography.
Special Interest Areas Animal care, campcraft, field trips (arts and culture), leadership training.
Sports Archery, canoeing, diving, equestrian sports, horseback riding, riflery, sailing, swimming, tennis, waterskiing, windsurfing.
Wilderness/Outdoors Backpacking, canoe trips, hiking, wilderness camping.
Trips Day, overnight.
Program Information 5 sessions per year. Session length: 1–8 weeks in June, July, August. Ages: 9–15. 60 participants per session. Day program cost: $200–$600. Boarding program cost: $1055–$9440. Financial aid available.
Application Deadline Continuous.
Jobs Positions for college students 18 and older.
Contact Liz Ambuhl, Co-Director, PO Box 68, West Pawlet, Vermont 05775. Phone: 802-645-0216. Fax: 802-645-9818. E-mail: info@campcatherinecapers.com.
URL www.campcatherinecapers.com

Camp Kiniya

1281 Camp Kiniya Road
Colchester, Vermont 05446

General Information Girls' residential traditional camp established in 1919. Accredited by American Camping Association.
Arts Arts and crafts (general), chorus, dance (ballet), dance (folk), dance (jazz), dance (modern), dance (tap), drawing, jewelry making, music (vocal), musical productions, painting, theater/drama, weaving.
Special Interest Areas Animal care, campcraft, leadership training.
Sports Archery, baseball, basketball, canoeing, equestrian sports, gymnastics, horseback riding, kayaking, rowing (crew/sculling), sailing, soccer, softball, swimming, tennis, waterskiing.
Wilderness/Outdoors Backpacking, canoe trips, hiking, mountaineering.
Trips Day, overnight.
Program Information 4 sessions per year. Session length: 1–7 weeks in June, July, August. Ages: 6–17. 100–130 participants per session. Day program cost: $108–$121. Boarding program cost: $850–$5300.
Application Deadline Continuous.
Jobs Positions for college students 20 and older.
Contact Marnie Williams, Associate Director, main address above. Phone: 802-893-7849. Fax: 802-893-7849. E-mail: marnieatkiniya@aol.com.
URL www.kiniya.com

Camp Lanakila

Aloha Foundation, Inc.
2899 Lake Morey Road
Fairlee, Vermont 05045

General Information Boys' residential traditional camp established in 1922. Accredited by American Camping Association.
Arts Arts and crafts (general), drawing, jewelry making, metalworking, music, music (instrumental), music (vocal), musical productions, painting, photography, theater/drama, woodworking.
Special Interest Areas Campcraft, leadership training, model rocketry, nature study.
Sports Archery, baseball, basketball, bicycling, boating, canoeing, diving, riflery, ropes course, sailing, soccer, softball, sports (general), swimming, tennis, volleyball.
Wilderness/Outdoors Backpacking, bicycle trips, canoe trips, hiking, rock climbing, white-water trips, wilderness camping.
Trips Day, overnight.
Program Information 3 sessions per year. Session length: 26–50 days in July, August. Ages: 8–14. 140–160 participants per session. Boarding program cost: $4300–$6400. Financial aid available.
Application Deadline Continuous.

Jobs Positions for high school students 18 and older and college students 18 and older.
Summer Contact D. Barnes Boffey, Director, main address above. Phone: 802-333-3430. Fax: 802-333-3404. E-mail: barnes_boffey@alohafoundation.org.
Winter Contact D. Barnes Boffey, Director, 113 True's Brook Road, West Lebanon, New Hampshire 03784. Phone: 603-298-1010. Fax: 603-298-1010. E-mail: barnes_boffey@alohafoundation.org.
URL www.alohafoundation.org

Camp Sangamon for Boys

Camp Betsey Cox/Camp Sangamon for Boys, Inc.
382 Camp Lane
Pittsford, Vermont 05763

General Information Boys' residential traditional camp established in 1922. Accredited by American Camping Association. Formal opportunities for the artistically talented.

Camp Sangamon for Boys

Program Focus Individual development, decision making, and traditional camping; strong emphasis on arts and crafts and individual sports.
Arts Arts and crafts (general), drawing, graphic arts, photography, pottery, theater/drama, weaving, woodworking.
Special Interest Areas Animal care, campcraft, construction, farming, gardening, model rocketry.
Sports Archery, basketball, bicycling, canoeing, fishing, horseback riding, kayaking, sailing, sea kayaking, snorkeling, soccer, softball, swimming, tennis.
Wilderness/Outdoors Backpacking, bicycle trips, canoe trips, caving, hiking, rock climbing.
Trips Day, overnight.
Program Information 4 sessions per year. Session length: 2–3 weeks in June, July, August. Ages: 9–15. 85–90 participants per session. Boarding program cost: $1425–$2130.
Application Deadline Continuous.
Jobs Positions for college students 20 and older.
Summer Contact Mike Byrom, Executive Director, main address above. Phone: 802-483-2862. E-mail: sangamonvt@aol.com.
Winter Contact Mike Byrom, Executive Director, PO Box 886, Key Largo, Florida 33037. Phone: 888-345-9193.
URL www.campsangamon.com
For more information, see page 1040.

Craftsbury Running Camps

Craftsbury Outdoor Center
535 Lost Nation Road
Craftsbury Common, Vermont 05827

General Information Coed residential sports camp established in 1977.
Program Focus Distance running and triathlon.
Sports Bicycling, canoeing, cross-country, fishing, kayaking, rowing (crew/sculling), running/jogging, sailing, skiing (cross-country), swimming, tennis, volleyball, weight training.
Wilderness/Outdoors Hiking, mountain biking, orienteering.
Trips Day.
Program Information 6 sessions per year. Session length: 6–8 days in June, July, August. Ages: 13+. 20–40 participants per session. Boarding program cost: $598–$788.
Application Deadline Continuous.
Contact Craftsbury Running Camp, main address above. Phone: 802-586-7767. Fax: 802-586-7768. E-mail: stay@craftsbury.com.
URL www.craftsbury.com

Craftsbury Sculling Camps

Craftsbury Outdoor Center
535 Lost Nation Road
Craftsbury Common, Vermont 05827

General Information Coed residential sports camp established in 1976.
Program Focus Sculling.
Sports Bicycling, canoeing, cross-country, fishing, kayaking, rowing (crew/sculling), sailing, skiing (cross-country), swimming, tennis, volleyball, weight training.
Wilderness/Outdoors Hiking, mountain biking, orienteering.
Trips Day.

Craftsbury Sculling Camps (continued)
Program Information 35 sessions per year. Session length: 3–6 days in May, June, July, August, September, October. Ages: 10+. 20–40 participants per session. Boarding program cost: $465–$895.
Application Deadline Continuous.
Contact Craftsbury Sculling Camp, main address above. Phone: 802-586-7767. Fax: 802-586-7768. E-mail: stay@craftsbury.com.
URL www.craftsbury.com

Farm and Wilderness Camps–Barn Day Camp

Farm and Wilderness Camps
263 Farm and Wilderness Road
Plymouth, Vermont 05056

General Information Coed day traditional camp and outdoor program established in 1984. Religious affiliation: Society of Friends. Accredited by American Camping Association.
Program Focus Creative activities, wilderness activities, organic gardening, farm animals.
Academics Environmental science, natural resource management.
Arts Arts and crafts (general), leather working, music (instrumental), music (vocal), pottery, weaving, woodworking.
Special Interest Areas Animal care, campcraft, gardening, nature study, team building.
Sports Canoeing, climbing (wall), noncompetitive sports, swimming.
Wilderness/Outdoors Backpacking, canoe trips, caving, hiking, orienteering, rock climbing, wilderness camping.
Trips Day, overnight.
Program Information 3 sessions per year. Session length: 10 days in July, August. Ages: 3–10. 84 participants per session. Day program cost: $650–$900. Financial aid available.
Application Deadline Continuous.
Jobs Positions for high school students 18 and older and college students 18 and older.
Contact Linda Berryhill, Registrar, main address above. Phone: 802-422-3761. Fax: 802-422-8660. E-mail: fandw@fandw.org.
URL www.fandw.org

Farm and Wilderness Camps–Flying Cloud

Farm and Wilderness Camps
263 Farm and Wilderness Road
Plymouth, Vermont 05056

General Information Boys' residential outdoor program and wilderness program established in 1965. Religious affiliation: Society of Friends. Accredited by American Camping Association.
Program Focus Remote simple living camp honoring rustic living skills, community, respect for each other and the land on which we live.
Academics Natural resource management.
Arts Arts and crafts (general), beading, dance (folk), leather working, music (vocal), pottery, woodworking.
Special Interest Areas Campcraft, community service, leadership training, nature study.
Sports Archery, canoeing.
Wilderness/Outdoors Canoe trips, hiking, orienteering, outdoor living skills, tracking, wilderness camping, wilderness/outdoors (general).
Trips Day, overnight.
Program Information 1–2 sessions per year. Session length: 28–54 days in June, July, August. Ages: 11–14. 35 participants per session. Boarding program cost: $3550–$5550. Financial aid available.
Application Deadline Continuous.
Jobs Positions for high school students 18 and older and college students 18 and older.
Contact Linda Berryhill, Registrar, main address above. Phone: 802-422-3761. Fax: 802-422-8660. E-mail: fandw@fandw.org.
URL www.fandw.org

Farm and Wilderness Camps–Indian Brook

Farm and Wilderness Camps
263 Farm and Wilderness Road
Plymouth, Vermont 05056

General Information Girls' residential traditional camp, outdoor program, and wilderness program established in 1940. Religious affiliation: Society of Friends. Accredited by American Camping Association.
Program Focus Farming, wilderness experiences, and gender empowerment.
Arts Arts and crafts (general), batiking, ceramics, dance (folk), drawing, fabric arts, jewelry making, leather working, music (instrumental), music (vocal), painting, pottery, sculpture, theater/drama, weaving, woodworking.
Special Interest Areas Animal care, campcraft, community service, construction, farming, gardening, leadership training, nature study, team building.
Sports Canoeing, climbing (wall), rappelling, swimming.
Wilderness/Outdoors Backpacking, canoe trips, hiking, orienteering, rock climbing, wilderness camping, wilderness/outdoors (general).
Trips Day, overnight.
Program Information 1–2 sessions per year. Session length: 28–54 days in June, July, August. Ages: 9–14. 125 participants per session. Boarding program cost: $3550–$5550. Financial aid available.
Application Deadline Continuous.
Jobs Positions for high school students 18 and older and college students 18 and older.
Contact Linda Berryhill, Registrar, main address above. Phone: 802-422-3761. Fax: 802-422-8660. E-mail: fandw@fandw.org.
URL www.fandw.org

Farm and Wilderness Camps–Saltash Mountain

Farm and Wilderness Camps
263 Farm and Wilderness Road
Plymouth, Vermont 05056

General Information Coed residential outdoor program and wilderness program established in 1962. Religious affiliation: Society of Friends. Accredited by American Camping Association.
Program Focus Wilderness experiences, backpacking, canoeing, music.
Arts Arts and crafts (general), dance (folk), drawing, fabric arts, leather working, music (instrumental), music (vocal), theater/drama.
Special Interest Areas Campcraft, community service, leadership training, nature study.
Sports Canoeing, rappelling, swimming.
Wilderness/Outdoors Backpacking, canoe trips, hiking, orienteering, rock climbing, survival training, wilderness camping, wilderness/outdoors (general).
Trips Overnight.
Program Information 1–2 sessions per year. Session length: 28–54 days in June, July, August. Ages: 11–14. 40 participants per session. Boarding program cost: $3550–$5550. Financial aid available.
Application Deadline Continuous.
Jobs Positions for college students 21 and older.
Contact Linda Berryhill, Registrar, main address above. Phone: 802-422-3761. Fax: 802-422-8660. E-mail: fandw@fandw.org.
URL www.fandw.org

Farm and Wilderness Camps–Tamarack Farm

Farm and Wilderness Camps
263 Farm and Wilderness Road
Plymouth, Vermont 05056

General Information Coed residential traditional camp, outdoor program, and community service program established in 1951. Religious affiliation: Society of Friends. Accredited by American Camping Association.
Program Focus Organic farming, construction, and community work projects.
Arts Arts and crafts (general), batiking, ceramics, dance, dance (folk), drawing, fabric arts, jewelry making, leather working, metalworking, music (instrumental), music (vocal), painting, photography, pottery, puppetry, sculpture, theater/drama, weaving, woodworking.
Special Interest Areas Animal care, community service, construction, farming, gardening, leadership training, work camp programs.
Sports Climbing (wall), frisbee, soccer, swimming.
Wilderness/Outdoors Backpacking, canoe trips, hiking, rock climbing, wilderness camping.
Trips Day, overnight.
Program Information 1 session per year. Session length: 54 days in June, July, August. Ages: 15–17. 65–72 participants per session. Boarding program cost: $5550. Financial aid available.
Application Deadline Continuous.
Jobs Positions for college students 22 and older.
Contact Linda Berryhill, Registrar, main address above. Phone: 802-422-3761. Fax: 802-422-8660. E-mail: fandw@fandw.org.
URL www.fandw.org

Farm and Wilderness Camps–Timberlake

Farm and Wilderness Camps
263 Farm and Wilderness Road
Plymouth, Vermont 05056

General Information Boys' residential traditional camp, outdoor program, and wilderness program established in 1939. Religious affiliation: Society of Friends. Accredited by American Camping Association.
Program Focus Wilderness activities, construction projects, leadership development, organic farming.
Arts Arts and crafts (general), batiking, ceramics, dance (folk), drawing, jewelry making, leather working, metalworking, music (instrumental), music (vocal), painting, pottery, theater/drama, weaving, woodworking.
Special Interest Areas Animal care, campcraft, construction, farming, field research/expeditions, gardening, leadership training, nature study.
Sports Archery, basketball, canoeing, climbing (wall), rappelling, soccer, swimming.
Wilderness/Outdoors Backpacking, canoe trips, hiking, orienteering, rock climbing, survival training, wilderness camping, wilderness/outdoors (general).
Trips Day, overnight.
Program Information 1–2 sessions per year. Session length: 28–54 days in June, July, August. Ages: 9–14. 50–70 participants per session. Boarding program cost: $3550–$5550. Financial aid available.
Application Deadline Continuous.
Jobs Positions for high school students 18 and older and college students 18 and older.
Contact Linda Berryhill, Registrar, main address above. Phone: 802-422-3761. Fax: 802-422-8660. E-mail: fandw@fandw.org.
URL www.fandw.org

Future Leader Camp

Norwich University
27 I. D. White Avenue
Northfield, Vermont 05663

General Information Coed residential outdoor program established in 1998.
Program Focus Leadership and team skills development for active participants in community service, sports, scouting and youth groups.
Special Interest Areas Career exploration, college planning, first aid, leadership training, team building.
Sports Archery, climbing (wall), physical fitness, rappelling, riflery, ropes course.
Wilderness/Outdoors Backpacking, hiking, orienteering, outdoor adventure, rock climbing, survival training, wilderness camping.
Trips College tours, day, overnight.
Program Information 2 sessions per year. Session length: 2 weeks in July. Ages: 15–18. 80 participants per

Future Leader Camp (continued)

Future Leader Camp

session. Boarding program cost: $1325. Application fee: $25. Financial aid available. Open to participants entering grades 10–12.
Application Deadline Continuous.
Contact Lt. Col. Skip Davison, Director FLC, main address above. Phone: 802-485-2531. Fax: 802-485-2739. E-mail: flc@norwich.edu.
URL www.norwich.edu/flc
For more information, see page 1130.

Keewaydin Dunmore

Keewaydin Foundation
10 Keewaydin Road
Salisbury, Vermont 05769

General Information Boys' residential traditional camp and outdoor program established in 1910. Accredited by American Camping Association.
Program Focus Canoeing and backpacking trips plus full in-camp program.
Arts Arts and crafts (general), photography, theater/drama.
Special Interest Areas Campcraft, nature study.
Sports Archery, baseball, basketball, boxing, canoeing, diving, fencing, fishing, golf, kayaking, martial arts, rappelling, riflery, sailing, snorkeling, soccer, softball, swimming, tennis, windsurfing, wrestling.
Wilderness/Outdoors Backpacking, canoe trips, caving, hiking, mountaineering, rock climbing, white-water trips, wilderness camping.
Trips Cultural, day, overnight.
Program Information 1–2 sessions per year. Session length: 4–8 weeks in June, July, August. Ages: 8–16. 215 participants per session. Boarding program cost: $4300–$5650. Financial aid available.
Application Deadline Continuous.
Jobs Positions for college students 18 and older.
Contact Mr. Peter Hare, Director, main address above. Phone: 802-352-4770. Fax: 802-352-4772. E-mail: pete@keewaydin.org.
URL www.keewaydin.org

Killooleet

Route 100
Hancock, Vermont 05748-0070

General Information Coed residential traditional camp established in 1927. Accredited by American Camping Association. Formal opportunities for the artistically talented.

Killooleet

Program Focus Personal development and leadership skills.
Arts Acting, arts, arts and crafts (general), band, batiking, ceramics, creative writing, dance, drawing, fabric arts, graphic arts, guitar, jewelry making, metalworking, music, music (folk), music (jazz), music (rock), music (vocal), musical productions, painting, photography, pottery, stained glass, television/video, theater/drama, weaving, woodworking.
Special Interest Areas Campcraft, electronics, gardening, leadership training, model rocketry, nature study, team building.
Sports Archery, basketball, bicycling, boating, canoeing, diving, fencing, fishing, horseback riding, kayaking, martial arts, rappelling, riflery, sailing, soccer, softball, sports (general), swimming, tennis, volleyball, windsurfing.
Wilderness/Outdoors Backpacking, bicycle trips, canoe trips, caving, hiking, mountain biking, mountaineering, rock climbing, wilderness/outdoors (general).
Trips Day, overnight.
Program Information 1 session per year. Session length: 50–55 days in June, July, August. Ages: 9–14. 100–105 participants per session. Boarding program cost: $5900. Financial aid available.
Application Deadline Continuous.
Jobs Positions for college students 19 and older.
Summer Contact Ms. Kate Seeger, Director, PO Box 70, Hancock, Vermont 05748. Phone: 802-767-3152.
Winter Contact Ms. Kate Seeger, Director, 70 Trull Street, Somerville, Massachusetts 02145. Phone: 617-666-1484. Fax: 617-666-0378. E-mail: camp05748@aol.com.
URL www.killooleet.com
For more information, see page 1176.

Kinhaven Music School

Kinhaven Music School
354 Lawrence Hill Road
Weston, Vermont 05161

General Information Coed residential arts program established in 1952.
Program Focus Chamber music.
Arts Chorus, dance (folk), music, music (chamber), music (classical), music (ensemble), music (instrumental), music (orchestral), pottery.
Sports Soccer, swimming, volleyball.
Wilderness/Outdoors Hiking.
Program Information 2 sessions per year. Session length: 15–45 days in June, July, August. Ages: 10–18. 60–95 participants per session. Boarding program cost: $2025–$5100. Financial aid available.
Application Deadline Continuous.
Jobs Positions for college students 21 and older.
Summer Contact Ms. Nancy Bidlack, Admissions Director, PO Box 68, Weston, Vermont 05161. Phone: 802-824-4332. Fax: 802-824-4332.
Winter Contact Ms. Nancy Bidlack, Admissions Director, 1704 Sycamore Street, Bethlehem, Pennsylvania 18017. Phone: 610-868-9200. Fax: 610-868-9200.
URL www.kinhaven.org

Kroka Expeditions–Adventures for Small People

Kroka Expeditions of Vermont
Newfane, Vermont 05345

General Information Coed day outdoor program and adventure program established in 1996.
Program Focus Day school offering age-appropriate adventures.
Academics Ecology, geography, geology/earth science.
Arts Arts and crafts (general), sing-a-longs.
Special Interest Areas Campcraft, field research/expeditions, leadership training, nature study, social skills development.
Sports Canoeing, kayaking, rappelling, swimming.
Wilderness/Outdoors Canoe trips, hiking, orienteering, outdoor adventure, rafting, rock climbing, white-water trips.
Trips Day.
Program Information 1 session per year. Session length: 5 days in July. Ages: 7–8. 8–12 participants per session. Day program cost: $250–$350. Financial aid available.
Application Deadline Continuous.
Jobs Positions for college students 18 and older.
Contact Misha Golfman, Executive Director, 659 West Hill Road, Putney, Vermont 05346. Phone: 802-387-5397. Fax: 802-387-4536. E-mail: kroka@sover.net.
URL www.kroka.org

Kroka Expeditions–Coming of Age for Young Women

Kroka Expeditions of Vermont
Vermont

General Information Girls' residential outdoor program and wilderness program established in 1996. Specific services available for the learning disabled and physically challenged.
Program Focus Rites of passage.
Academics Ecology, environmental science, geography, geology/earth science, marine studies.
Arts Arts and crafts (general), basketry.
Special Interest Areas Campcraft, field research/expeditions, leadership training, nature study, nautical skills, personal development.
Sports Canoeing, fishing, kayaking, swimming.
Wilderness/Outdoors Backpacking, canoe trips, hiking, mountaineering, orienteering, outdoor living skills, rafting, survival training, white-water trips, wilderness camping.
Trips Day, overnight.
Program Information 1 session per year. Session length: 10 days in July. Ages: 12–14. 8–12 participants per session. Boarding program cost: $1250. Financial aid available.
Application Deadline Continuous.
Jobs Positions for college students 18 and older.
Contact Misha Golfman, Executive Director, 659 West Hill Road, Putney, Vermont 05346. Phone: 802-387-5397. Fax: 802-389-4536. E-mail: kroka@sover.net.
URL www.kroka.org

Kroka Expeditions–Expedition Pre-Columbus

Kroka Expeditions of Vermont
Vermont

General Information Coed residential outdoor program and wilderness program established in 1996.
Program Focus Intermediate to advanced level wilderness living.
Academics Geology/earth science, history.
Special Interest Areas Campcraft, nature study, team building.
Sports Canoeing, swimming.
Wilderness/Outdoors Hiking, orienteering, wilderness camping.
Program Information 1 session per year. Session length: 11 days in August. Ages: 13–18. 8–12 participants per session. Boarding program cost: $1375. Financial aid available.
Application Deadline Continuous.
Jobs Positions for college students 18 and older.
Contact Misha Golfman, Executive Director, 659 West Hill Road, Putney, Vermont 05346. Phone: 802-387-5397. Fax: 802-387-4536. E-mail: kroka@sover.net.
URL www.kroka.org

KROKA EXPEDITIONS–INTRODUCTION TO ADVENTURE DAY CAMP

Kroka Expeditions of Vermont
Newfane, Vermont

General Information Coed day outdoor program established in 1996. Specific services available for the learning disabled and physically challenged.
Program Focus Day school offering age-appropriate adventures.
Academics Ecology, environmental science, geology/earth science.
Arts Arts and crafts (general).
Special Interest Areas Campcraft, field research/expeditions, leadership training, nature study, team building.
Sports Canoeing, kayaking, rappelling, swimming.
Wilderness/Outdoors Hiking, orienteering, outdoor adventure, rafting, rock climbing, white-water trips, wilderness/outdoors (general).
Trips Day.
Program Information 1 session per year. Session length: 5 days in July. Ages: 9–11. 8–12 participants per session. Day program cost: $350. Financial aid available.
Application Deadline Continuous.
Jobs Positions for college students 18 and older.
Contact Misha Golfman, Executive Director, 659 West Hill Road, Putney, Vermont 05346. Phone: 802-387-5397. Fax: 802-387-4536. E-mail: kroka@sover.net.
URL www.kroka.org

KROKA EXPEDITIONS–INTRODUCTION TO ADVENTURE RESIDENTIAL CAMP

Kroka Expeditions of Vermont
Newfane, Vermont 05345

General Information Coed residential outdoor program, wilderness program, and adventure program established in 1996. Specific services available for the learning disabled and physically challenged.
Academics Ecology, environmental science, geology/earth science.
Arts Arts and crafts (general).
Special Interest Areas Campcraft, field research/expeditions, leadership training, nature study, team building.
Sports Canoeing, kayaking, rappelling, ropes course, swimming.
Wilderness/Outdoors Hiking, orienteering, outdoor adventure, outdoor camping, rafting, rock climbing, white-water trips, wilderness camping.
Trips Day.
Program Information 1 session per year. Session length: 1 week in August. Ages: 9–11. 8–12 participants per session. Boarding program cost: $875. Financial aid available.
Application Deadline Continuous.
Jobs Positions for college students 18 and older.
Contact Misha Golfman, Executive Director, 659 West Hill Road, Putney, Vermont 05346. Phone: 802-387-5397. Fax: 802-387-4536. E-mail: kroka@sover.net.
URL www.kroka.org

KROKA EXPEDITIONS–INTRODUCTION TO ROCK CLIMBING

Kroka Expeditions of Vermont
Vermont

General Information Coed residential outdoor program and wilderness program established in 1996.
Program Focus Beginner level rock climbing.
Special Interest Areas Campcraft.
Sports Rappelling.
Wilderness/Outdoors Backpacking, caving, hiking, mountaineering, rock climbing.
Trips Day, overnight.
Program Information 1 session per year. Session length: 1 week in June, July. Ages: 9–12. 8–12 participants per session. Boarding program cost: $875. Financial aid available.
Application Deadline Continuous.
Jobs Positions for college students 18 and older.
Contact Misha Golfman, Executive Director, 659 West Hill Road, Putney, Vermont 05346. Phone: 802-387-5397. Fax: 802-387-4536. E-mail: kroka@sover.net.
URL www.kroka.org

KROKA EXPEDITIONS–INTRODUCTION TO WHITE WATER

Kroka Expeditions of Vermont
Newfane, Vermont

General Information Coed residential outdoor program, wilderness program, and adventure program established in 1996. Specific services available for the learning disabled and physically challenged.
Program Focus Beginner level white-water paddling instruction.
Academics Ecology, environmental science, geography, geology/earth science, marine studies.
Special Interest Areas Campcraft, community service, field research/expeditions, leadership training, nature study, nautical skills.
Sports Boating, canoeing, kayaking, sea kayaking.
Wilderness/Outdoors Backpacking, canoe trips, hiking, kayaking trips, orienteering, rafting, survival training, white-water trips, wilderness camping.
Trips Day, overnight.
Program Information 1 session per year. Session length: 1 week in June. Ages: 9–12. 8–12 participants per session. Boarding program cost: $875. Financial aid available.
Application Deadline Continuous.
Jobs Positions for college students 18 and older.
Contact Misha Golfman, Executive Director, 659 West Hill Road, Putney, Vermont 05346. Phone: 802-387-5397. Fax: 802-387-4536. E-mail: kroka@sover.net.
URL www.kroka.org

KROKA EXPEDITIONS–ROCK 'N ROAD

Kroka Expeditions of Vermont
Vermont

General Information Coed residential outdoor program, wilderness program, and adventure program

established in 1996. Specific services available for the learning disabled and physically challenged.
Program Focus Beginner to intermediate level rock climbing.
Academics Ecology, environmental science, geography, geology/earth science, marine studies.
Special Interest Areas Campcraft, field research/ expeditions, leadership training, nature study, nautical skills.
Sports Climbing (wall), rappelling, swimming.
Wilderness/Outdoors Backpacking, caving, hiking, mountaineering, orienteering, rafting, rock climbing, survival training, white-water trips, wilderness camping.
Trips Day, overnight.
Program Information 1 session per year. Session length: 2 weeks in July. Ages: 13–18. 8–12 participants per session. Boarding program cost: $1750. Financial aid available.
Application Deadline Continuous.
Jobs Positions for college students 18 and older.
Contact Misha Golfman, Executive Director, 659 West Hill Road, Putney, Vermont 05346. Phone: 802-387-5397. Fax: 802-387-4536. E-mail: kroka@sover.net.
URL www.kroka.org

Kroka Expeditions–Vermont Underground Trail

Kroka Expeditions of Vermont
Vermont

General Information Coed residential outdoor program and wilderness program established in 1996.
Program Focus Intermediate to advanced level rock climbing and caving, wilderness living.
Special Interest Areas Campcraft.
Sports Rappelling.
Wilderness/Outdoors Backpacking, caving, hiking, mountaineering, rock climbing.
Program Information 1 session per year. Session length: 3 weeks in June, July. Ages: 13–18. 10 participants per session. Boarding program cost: $2100. Financial aid available.
Application Deadline Continuous.
Jobs Positions for college students 18 and older.
Contact Misha Golfman, Executive Director, 659 West Hill Road, Putney, Vermont 05346. Phone: 802-387-5397. Fax: 802-387-4536. E-mail: kroka@sover.net.
URL www.kroka.org

Kroka Expeditions–Wild Arts and Canoe Adventure

Kroka Expeditions of Vermont
Vermont

General Information Coed residential outdoor program and wilderness program established in 1996.
Program Focus Beginner to intermediate level canoeing, wilderness living.
Special Interest Areas Campcraft, nature study, team building.
Sports Canoeing, kayaking, rappelling, swimming.
Wilderness/Outdoors Hiking, orienteering, wilderness camping.
Program Information 1 session per year. Session length: 1 week in June, July. Ages: 10–12. 8–12 participants per session. Boarding program cost: $875. Financial aid available.
Application Deadline Continuous.
Jobs Positions for college students 18 and older.
Contact Misha Golfman, Executive Director, 659 West Hill Road, Putney, Vermont 05346. Phone: 802-387-5397. Fax: 802-387-4536. E-mail: kroka@sover.net.
URL www.kroka.org

Kroka Expeditions–Wild World of White Water

Kroka Expeditions of Vermont
Vermont

General Information Coed residential outdoor program, wilderness program, and adventure program established in 1996. Specific services available for the learning disabled and physically challenged.
Program Focus Beginner to intermediate level white-water paddling instruction.
Academics Ecology, environmental science, geography, geology/earth science, marine studies.
Arts Arts and crafts (general).
Special Interest Areas Campcraft, community service, field research/expeditions, leadership training, nature study, nautical skills.
Sports Boating, canoeing, fishing, kayaking, sea kayaking.
Wilderness/Outdoors Canoe trips, hiking, rafting, survival training, white-water trips, wilderness camping.
Trips Day, overnight.
Program Information 1 session per year. Session length: 2 weeks in June, July. Ages: 12–18. 8–12 participants per session. Boarding program cost: $1750. Financial aid available.
Application Deadline Continuous.
Jobs Positions for college students 18 and older.
Contact Misha Golfman, Executive Director, 659 West Hill Road, Putney, Vermont 05346. Phone: 802-387-5397. Fax: 802-387-4536. E-mail: kroka@sover.net.
URL www.kroka.org

Landmark Volunteers: Vermont

Landmark Volunteers, Inc.
Vermont

General Information Coed residential outdoor program and community service program established in 1992. High school credit may be earned.
Program Focus Opportunity for high school students to earn community service credit while working as a team for two weeks serving Calvin Coolidge, Marsh-Billings-Rockefeller National Historical Park, Morgan Horse Farm/Eddy Farm School, Shelburne Museum/ Shelburne Farms, or Vermont State Parks. Similar programs offered through Landmark Volunteers at over 60 locations in 21 states.

Landmark Volunteers: Vermont (continued)

Academics Architecture, art history/appreciation, ecology, environmental science, history.
Arts Arts and crafts (general).
Special Interest Areas Animal care, career exploration, community service, farming, leadership training, team building, trail maintenance, work camp programs.
Sports Swimming.
Wilderness/Outdoors Hiking, wilderness camping.
Trips Cultural, day.
Program Information 5 sessions per year. Session length: 2 weeks in June, July, August. Ages: 14+. 10–13 participants per session. Boarding program cost: $875–$923. Financial aid available.
Application Deadline Continuous.
Jobs Positions for college students.
Contact Ann Barrett, Executive Director, PO Box 455, Sheffield, Massachusetts 01257. Phone: 413-229-0255. Fax: 413-229-2050. E-mail: landmark@volunteers.com.
URL www.volunteers.com

For more information, see page 1182.

Lochearn Camp for Girls

Lake Fairlee
1061 Robinson Hill Road
Post Mills, Vermont 05058

General Information Girls' residential traditional camp established in 1916. Accredited by American Camping Association.
Academics Reading.
Arts Arts and crafts (general), basketry, ceramics, chorus, creative writing, dance, dance (jazz), drawing, jewelry making, music, musical productions, pottery, theater/drama.
Special Interest Areas Leadership training.
Sports Aerobics, archery, basketball, canoeing, cross-country, diving, equestrian sports, field hockey, gymnastics, horseback riding, lacrosse, sailing, snorkeling, soccer, softball, swimming, tennis, volleyball, waterskiing.
Wilderness/Outdoors Hiking.
Trips Day, overnight.
Program Information 2 sessions per year. Session length: 27 days in June, July, August. Ages: 8–15. 170 participants per session. Boarding program cost: $4050. Financial aid available.
Application Deadline Continuous.
Jobs Positions for college students 18 and older.
Contact Ginny Maxson, Director, Lake Fairlee, PO Box 400, Post Mills, Vermont 05058. Phone: 802-333-4211. Fax: 802-333-4856. E-mail: ginny@lochearncamp.com.
URL www.lochearncamp.com

Mad River Glen Naturalist Adventure Camp

Mad River Glen Cooperative
Route 17 West, 62 Mad River Road
Waitsfield, Vermont 05673

General Information Coed day outdoor program established in 1998.
Program Focus Adventure activities and naturalist skills, plus environmental education in a day camp setting.
Academics Biology, botany, ecology, environmental science, geology/earth science, science (general).
Special Interest Areas Field research/expeditions, nature study.
Sports Bicycling, canoeing, climbing (wall), fishing, kayaking, rappelling, ropes course.
Wilderness/Outdoors Backpacking, canoe trips, hiking, mountain biking, rock climbing, wilderness camping.
Trips Day, overnight.
Program Information 1 session per year. Session length: 1–31 days in June, July, August. Ages: 7–12. 6–13 participants per session. Day program cost: $40–$50. Application fee: $15.
Application Deadline Continuous.
Jobs Positions for college students 18 and older.
Contact Mr. Sean T. Lawson, Naturalist Program Director, PO Box 1089, Waitsfield, Vermont 05673. Phone: 802-496-3551 Ext.17. Fax: 802-496-3562. E-mail: sean@madriverglen.com.
URL www.madriverglen.com/naturalist

Mountain Workshop–Awesome 2: Vermont

Mountain Workshop
Vermont

General Information Coed travel outdoor program, wilderness program, and adventure program established in 1985.
Special Interest Areas Team building.
Sports Rappelling, swimming.
Wilderness/Outdoors Backpacking, caving, hiking, outdoor adventure, wilderness camping.
Trips Overnight.
Program Information 3 sessions per year. Session length: 1 week in July, August. Ages: 12–13. Cost: $950.
Application Deadline Continuous.
Jobs Positions for college students 21 and older.
Contact Kent B. Tullo, Director, 9 Brookside Place, West Redding, Connecticut 06896. Phone: 203-544-0555. Fax: 203-544-0333. E-mail: info@mountainworkshop.com.
URL www.mountainworkshop.com

Pine Ridge Summer Program

Pine Ridge School
9505 Williston Road
Williston, Vermont 05495

General Information Coed residential and day special needs program established in 1968. Specific services available for the learning disabled.
Program Focus Learning disabilities.
Academics English language/literature, mathematics, writing.
Arts Arts and crafts (general).
Sports Basketball, canoeing, fishing, ropes course, softball, swimming, volleyball.
Wilderness/Outdoors Hiking, mountain biking.

Pine Ridge Summer Program

Trips Cultural, day, overnight.
Program Information 1 session per year. Session length: 6 weeks in July, August. Ages: 9–18. 45 participants per session. Day program cost: $5300. Boarding program cost: $7000. Application fee: $25.
Application Deadline Continuous.
Contact Mr. Joshua Doyle, Director of Admissions, main address above. Phone: 802-434-6915. Fax: 802-434-5512. E-mail: jdoyle@pineridgeschool.com.
URL www.pineridgeschool.com

For more information, see page 1264.

Point CounterPoint Chamber Music Camp

Lake Dunemore, Vermont 05733

General Information Coed residential arts program established in 1963. Formal opportunities for the artistically talented.
Program Focus Chamber music for strings and piano.
Academics Music.
Arts Arts and crafts (general), creative writing, music, music (chamber), music (classical), music (instrumental).
Sports Basketball, canoeing, rowing (crew/sculling), soccer, swimming, tennis, waterskiing.
Wilderness/Outdoors Hiking.
Program Information 3 sessions per year. Session length: 3–7 weeks in June, July, August. Ages: 11–17. 45–50 participants per session. Boarding program cost: $2600–$5600. Application fee: $30. Financial aid available.
Application Deadline Continuous.
Jobs Positions for college students 19 and older.
Summer Contact Dr. Paul Roby, Director, 1361 Hooker Road, Brandon, Vermont 05733. Phone: 802-247-8467. Fax: 802-247-8467. E-mail: pointcp@aol.com.
Winter Contact Dr. Paul Roby, Director, PO Box 3181, Terre Haute, Indiana 47803. Phone: 812-877-3745. Fax: 812-877-2174. E-mail: pointcp@aol.com.
URL www.pointcp.com

Program of Audubon Research for Teens (Take P.A.R.T.)

Audubon Vermont
2658 High Pond Road
Brandon, Vermont 05733

General Information Coed residential academic program, outdoor program, and wilderness program established in 1997.
Program Focus Field science and conservation research.
Academics Archaeology, astronomy, biology, botany, ecology, environmental science, geology/earth science, herpetology, ornithology, science (general).
Special Interest Areas Field research/expeditions, nature study, team building.
Sports Swimming, ultimate frisbee, volleyball.
Wilderness/Outdoors Hiking, orienteering, outdoor camping, wilderness camping.
Trips Cultural, day, overnight.
Program Information 1–3 sessions per year. Session length: 10 days in July, August. Ages: 14–18. 30 participants per session. Boarding program cost: $900–$1000. Financial aid available.
Application Deadline Continuous.
Jobs Positions for college students 20 and older.
Contact Mr. Ryan Young, Director, 255 Sherman Hollow Road, Huntington, Vermont 05462. Phone: 802-434-3068. Fax: 802-434-4686. E-mail: ryoung@audubon.org.
URL www.vt.audubon.org/highpond.html

The Putney School Summer Arts Program

The Putney School
Elm Lea Farm
418 Houghton Brook Road
Putney, Vermont 05346

General Information Coed residential and day arts program established in 1987. Formal opportunities for the artistically talented.
Program Focus Visual and performing arts, music, and theater.
Academics Art (Advanced Placement), music, music (Advanced Placement), writing.
Arts Arts, ceramics, creative writing, dance, dance (modern), fabric arts, film, jewelry making, metalworking, music, music (chamber), music (classical), music (ensemble), music (instrumental), music (orchestral), music (vocal), music composition/arrangement, painting, performance art, photography, playwriting, printmaking, sculpture, songwriting, stained glass, studio arts, theater/drama, visual arts, weaving, woodworking.
Special Interest Areas Animal care, community service, farming, gardening.
Sports Basketball, bicycling, canoeing, fencing, horseback riding, running/jogging, soccer, softball, swimming, volleyball.
Wilderness/Outdoors Backpacking, canoe trips, hiking, mountain biking.
Trips Cultural, day.
Program Information 2 sessions per year. Session length: 3 weeks in June, July, August. Ages: 14–17.

The Putney School Summer Arts Program (continued)

The Putney School Summer Arts Program

90–100 participants per session. Day program cost: $950–$1650. Boarding program cost: $2750–$5300. Application fee: $30. Financial aid available.
Application Deadline Continuous.
Jobs Positions for college students 21 and older.
Contact Maria Ogden, Administrative Coordinator, main address above. Phone: 802-387-6297. Fax: 802-387-6216. E-mail: summer@putneyschool.org.
URL www.putneyschool.org/summer

For more information, see page 1274.

THE PUTNEY SCHOOL SUMMER PROGRAM FOR INTERNATIONAL EDUCATION (ESL)

The Putney School
Elm Lea Farm
418 Houghton Brook Road
Putney, Vermont 05346

General Information Coed residential academic program established in 1990. High school credit may be earned.
Program Focus English as a second language, cultural exchange.
Academics English as a second language, English language/literature, computers, intercultural studies, reading, social studies, speech/debate, study skills, writing.
Arts Ceramics, creative writing, dance, dance (modern), drawing, fabric arts, graphic arts, jewelry making, metalworking, music, painting, photography, printmaking, sculpture, theater/drama, weaving, woodworking.
Special Interest Areas Animal care, community service, cross-cultural education, farming, field trips (arts and culture), gardening.
Sports Basketball, bicycling, canoeing, fencing, horseback riding, running/jogging, soccer, softball, swimming, volleyball.
Wilderness/Outdoors Backpacking, canoe trips, hiking, mountain biking.
Trips Cultural, day.
Program Information 2 sessions per year. Session length: 3 weeks in June, July, August. Ages: 14–17. 20–30 participants per session. Boarding program cost: $3000–$5600. Application fee: $30.
Application Deadline Continuous.
Jobs Positions for college students 21 and older.
Contact Maria Ogden, Administrative Coordinator, main address above. Phone: 802-387-6297. Fax: 802-387-6216. E-mail: summer@putneyschool.org.
URL www.putneyschool.org/summer

For more information, see page 1274.

THE PUTNEY SCHOOL SUMMER WRITING PROGRAM

The Putney School
Elm Lea Farm
418 Houghton Brook Road
Putney, Vermont 05346

General Information Coed residential and day academic program and arts program established in 1997. Formal opportunities for the academically talented, artistically talented, and gifted.
Program Focus Creative writing, fiction and poetry.
Academics Writing.
Arts Arts, ceramics, creative writing, dance, drawing, fabric arts, graphic arts, jewelry making, metalworking, music, music (chamber), music (orchestral), painting, photography, playwriting, printmaking, sculpture, theater/drama, weaving, woodworking.
Special Interest Areas Animal care, community service, field trips (arts and culture), gardening.
Sports Basketball, bicycling, canoeing, fencing, horseback riding, soccer, softball, swimming, volleyball.
Wilderness/Outdoors Backpacking, canoe trips, hiking.
Trips Cultural, day.
Program Information 2 sessions per year. Session length: 3 weeks in July, August. Ages: 14–17. 12–15 participants per session. Day program cost: $950–$1650. Boarding program cost: $2750–$5300. Application fee: $30. Financial aid available.
Application Deadline Continuous.
Jobs Positions for college students 21 and older.
Contact Maria Ogden, Administrative Coordinator, main address above. Phone: 802-387-6297. Fax: 802-387-6216. E-mail: summer@putneyschool.org.
URL www.putneyschool.org/summer

For more information, see page 1274.

Roaring Brook Camp for Boys

480 Roaring Brook Road
Bradford, Vermont 05033

General Information Boys' residential wilderness program established in 1965. Accredited by American Camping Association.
Program Focus Outdoor adventure and wilderness backpack/canoe trips.
Arts Blacksmithing, fly-tying, leather working, metalworking, woodworking.
Special Interest Areas Native American culture, campcraft, leadership training, nature study.
Sports Archery, canoeing, fishing, kayaking, rappelling, riflery, ropes course, swimming.
Wilderness/Outdoors Backpacking, canoe trips, hiking, mountain biking, mountaineering, orienteering, outdoor living skills, rafting, rock climbing, survival training, white-water trips, wilderness camping, wilderness/outdoors (general).
Trips Overnight.
Program Information 3 sessions per year. Session length: 2–6 weeks in June, July, August. Ages: 9–16. 45 participants per session. Boarding program cost: $1700–$5000.
Application Deadline Continuous.
Jobs Positions for college students 21 and older.
Summer Contact Dr. J. Thayer Raines, Director/Owner, main address above. Phone: 802-222-5702.
Winter Contact Dr. Candice L. Raines, Director/Owner, 300 Grove Street, #4, Rutland, Vermont 05701. Phone: 800-832-4295. Fax: 802-786-0653. E-mail: rainest@sover.net.
URL www.roaringbrookcamp.com

Songadeewin of Keewaydin

Keewaydin Foundation
500 Rustic Lane
Salisbury, Vermont 05769

General Information Girls' residential traditional camp and outdoor program established in 1999. Accredited by American Camping Association.
Program Focus Canoeing and backpacking trip plus full in-camp program.
Arts Arts and crafts (general), dance, music (vocal), photography.
Special Interest Areas Campcraft, nature study.
Sports Archery, basketball, canoeing, field hockey, golf, kayaking, lacrosse, riflery, sailing, soccer, softball, swimming, tennis, volleyball.
Wilderness/Outdoors Backpacking, canoe trips, hiking, rock climbing, white-water trips, wilderness camping.
Trips Cultural, day, overnight.
Program Information 1–2 sessions per year. Session length: 4–8 weeks in June, July, August. Ages: 8–15. 100–108 participants per session. Boarding program cost: $4300–$5650. Financial aid available.
Application Deadline Continuous.
Jobs Positions for college students.
Contact Ellen Flight, Director, main address above. Phone: 802-352-9860. Fax: 802-352-4772. E-mail: ellen@keewaydin.org.
URL www.keewaydin.org

Student Conservation Association–Conservation Crew Program (Vermont)

Student Conservation Association (SCA)
Vermont

General Information Coed residential outdoor program, community service program, and wilderness program established in 1957. High school credit may be earned.
Program Focus Resource management, conservation and environmental education.
Academics German language/literature, biology, botany, ecology, environmental science, history.
Special Interest Areas Campcraft, community service, construction, leadership training, nature study, trail maintenance, work camp programs.
Sports Canoeing, fishing, kayaking, swimming.
Wilderness/Outdoors Backpacking, canoe trips, hiking, orienteering, outdoor living skills, wilderness camping.
Trips Cultural, day, overnight.
Program Information 2–3 sessions per year. Session length: 3–5 weeks in June, July, August. Ages: 15–19. 6–8 participants per session. Application fee: $20. Financial aid available. No cost for program; financial aid possible for travel expenses.
Application Deadline Continuous.
Jobs Positions for college students 21 and older.
Contact Recruitment Office, PO Box 550, Charlestown, New Hampshire 03603. Phone: 603-543-1700. Fax: 603-543-1828. E-mail: getreal@thesca.org.
URL www.theSCA.org

Summer Discovery at Vermont

Summer Discovery
University of Vermont
Burlington, Vermont 05401

General Information Coed residential academic program and outdoor program established in 1990. High school or college credit may be earned.
Program Focus Pre-college enrichment.
Academics American literature, English as a second language, English language/literature, SAT/ACT preparation, Spanish language/literature, academics (general), anthropology, archaeology, biology, computers, environmental science, government and politics, history, journalism, mathematics, mathematics (Advanced Placement), precollege program, psychology, reading, social science, social studies, speech/debate, study skills, writing.
Arts Ceramics, creative writing, film, jewelry making, music, painting, photography, television/video, theater/drama.
Special Interest Areas Career exploration, community service, culinary arts, driver's education.

Summer Discovery at Vermont (continued)

Sports Aerobics, basketball, bicycling, climbing (wall), equestrian sports, golf, horseback riding, in-line skating, kayaking, racquetball, ropes course, sailing, scuba diving, sea kayaking, soccer, softball, swimming, tennis, volleyball, waterskiing, weight training.
Wilderness/Outdoors Backpacking, bicycle trips, caving, hiking, mountain biking, mountaineering, rafting, rock climbing, white-water trips, wilderness camping.
Trips College tours, cultural, day, overnight.
Program Information 1 session per year. Session length: 5 weeks in July, August. 200 participants per session. Boarding program cost: $5299–$5599. Application fee: $60–$70. Open to participants completing grades 10–12.
Application Deadline Continuous.
Jobs Positions for college students 21 and older.
Contact The Musiker Family, Director, 1326 Old Northern Boulevard, Roslyn Village, New York 11576. Phone: 888-878-6637. Fax: 516-625-3438. E-mail: discovery@summerfun.com.
URL www.summerfun.com

For more information, see page 1338.

Summer Horizons Day Camp

Aloha Foundation, Inc.
43 Middlebrook Road
Fairlee, Vermont 05045

General Information Coed day traditional camp established in 1997. Accredited by American Camping Association.
Arts Arts and crafts (general), music, music (vocal), theater/drama.
Special Interest Areas Nature study.
Sports Archery, basketball, boating, canoeing, gymnastics, ropes course, sailing, swimming, tennis.
Wilderness/Outdoors Hiking.
Trips Day.
Program Information 3 sessions per year. Session length: 10 days in July, August. Ages: 5–12. 100–125 participants per session. Day program cost: $650. Discount available for residents of Fairlee, West Fairlee, Vershire, VT; and Orford, NH.
Application Deadline Continuous.
Jobs Positions for high school students 16 and older and college students 18 and older.
Summer Contact Danny Kerr, Director, 2968 Lake Morey Road, Fairlee, Vermont 05045. Phone: 802-333-3450. Fax: 802-333-3404. E-mail: danny_kerr@alohafoundation.org.
Winter Contact Danny Kerr, Director, George School, Box 4410, Newtown, Pennsylvania 18940. Phone: 215-579-0759. Fax: 215-579-0759. E-mail: danny_kerr@alohafoundation.org.
URL www.alohafoundation.org

Summer Sonatina International Piano Camp

Sonatina Enterprises
5 Catamount Lane
Bennington, Vermont 05201

General Information Coed residential arts program established in 1969. Formal opportunities for the artistically talented.
Program Focus Piano performance.
Academics Music, music (Advanced Placement).
Arts Arts and crafts (general), chorus, music, music (chamber), music (classical), music (ensemble), music (jazz), music (vocal), musical productions, piano.
Special Interest Areas Field trips (arts and culture).
Sports Bicycling, football, soccer, sports (general), swimming, table tennis/ping-pong, tennis, ultimate frisbee, volleyball.
Wilderness/Outdoors Bicycle trips, hiking.
Trips Cultural, day.
Program Information 1–5 sessions per year. Session length: 1–5 weeks in June, July. Ages: 7–16. 32–40 participants per session. Boarding program cost: $875–$4375.
Application Deadline Continuous.
Jobs Positions for high school students 15 and older and college students 19 and older.
Contact Ms. Polly van der Linde, Director, 5 Catamount Lane, Department PSO, Bennington, Vermont 05201. Phone: 802-442-9197. Fax: 802-447-0140. E-mail: piano@sonatina.com.
URL www.sonatina.com

University of Vermont Summer Institute for High School Students Discovering Engineering, Computers, and Mathematics

University of Vermont, College of Engineering and Mathematics
Votey 109
Burlington, Vermont 05405

General Information Coed residential academic program established in 1990. Formal opportunities for the academically talented. Specific services available for the physically challenged.
Program Focus Firsthand insight into civil, electrical, mechanical, environmental, aerospace, and biomedical engineering, computer science, and mathematics. Laboratory experiences in mechanical, civil, and electrical engineering are offered. Robots are built by students for a robot war.
Academics English language/literature, aerospace science, computer science (Advanced Placement), computers, engineering, mathematics, music.
Arts Music.
Special Interest Areas Robotics, team building.
Sports Volleyball.
Trips Day.

Program Information 1 session per year. Session length: 9 days in June. Ages: 15–16. 60–80 participants per session. Boarding program cost: $950. Financial aid available.
Application Deadline Continuous.
Contact Dawn Densmore, Director, College of Engineering and Mathematics, 109 Votey Building, Burlington, Vermont 05405. Phone: 802-656-8748. Fax: 802-656-8802.
URL www.emba.uvm.edu/summer/2002

Special Note
The 2004 UVM/GIV Engineering, Mathematics, and Computer Sciences Summer Institute, scheduled for June 20–27, 2004, provides information on how engineering, mathematics, and computer science impact the world. During this institute, students will build robots using the power supplies from computer hard drives and remote-control cars. Each robot must climb a ramp and raise a flag during the Robot War at the University Mall. Students also tour the Materials Reclamation Center, the Burlington Waste Treatment Facility, Burlington Composting, Husky, and Ocean Arks International. Tours show the impact waste has on the world. For pictures and more information on this program, students should visit http://www.emba.uvm.edu/summer/2003.

Vermont Arts Animation Institute

Vermont Arts Institute at Lyndon Institute
Lyndon Center, Vermont 05850

General Information Coed residential and day arts program established in 2003. Formal opportunities for the artistically talented.
Program Focus Clay, computer generated and hand-drawn animation.
Arts Animation, film, graphic arts.
Sports Basketball, soccer, swimming, volleyball.
Trips Day.
Program Information 1 session per year. Session length: 5 days in July. Ages: 13–18. 12 participants per session. Day program cost: $500–$550. Boarding program cost: $650. Application fee: $15. Financial aid available.
Application Deadline Continuous.
Jobs Positions for college students 21 and older.
Contact Ms. Mary B. Thomas, Director of Admissions, Lyndon Institute, PO Box 127, College Road, Lyndon Center, Vermont 05850. Phone: 802-626-5232. Fax: 802-626-6138. E-mail: mthomas@lyndon.k12.vt.us.
URL www.vermontarts.org

Vermont Arts Dance Institute

Vermont Arts Institute at Lyndon Institute
Lyndon Center, Vermont 05850

General Information Coed residential and day arts program. Formal opportunities for the artistically talented.
Program Focus Dance training designed to expose students to graduated levels of conditioning, toning, and technique in a variety of movement styles.
Arts Dance, dance (ballet), dance (jazz), dance (modern).
Program Information 1 session per year. Session length: 5 days in July. Day program cost: $350. Boarding program cost: $500. Application fee: $15. Financial aid available. Open to participants entering grades 7–12.
Application Deadline Continuous.
Jobs Positions for college students 21 and older.
Contact Ms. Mary B. Thomas, Director of Admissions, Lyndon Institute, PO Box 127, College Road, Lyndon Center, Vermont 05850. Phone: 802-626-5232. Fax: 802-626-6138. E-mail: mthomas@lyndon.k12.vt.us.
URL www.vermontarts.org

Vermont Arts Filmmaking Institute

Vermont Arts Institute at Lyndon Institute
Lyndon Center, Vermont 05850

General Information Coed residential and day arts program established in 2002. Formal opportunities for the artistically talented.
Program Focus Hands-on experience in film acting, directing and production.
Arts Acting, directing, film, film production.
Sports Basketball, soccer, swimming, volleyball.
Trips Day.
Program Information 1 session per year. Session length: 2 weeks in July. Ages: 14–18. 25–30 participants per session. Day program cost: $1650–$1750. Boarding program cost: $1950–$2350. Application fee: $15. Financial aid available.
Application Deadline Continuous.
Jobs Positions for college students 21 and older.
Contact Ms. Mary B. Thomas, Director of Admissions, Lyndon Institute, PO Box 127, College Road, Lyndon Center, Vermont 05850. Phone: 802-626-5232. Fax: 802-626-6138. E-mail: mthomas@lyndon.k12.vt.us.
URL www.vermontarts.org

Vermont Arts Screenwriting Institute

Vermont Arts Institute at Lyndon Institute
Lyndon Center, Vermont 05850

General Information Coed residential and day arts program established in 2002. Formal opportunities for the artistically talented.
Program Focus Students develop their own screenplay.
Academics Writing.
Arts Creative writing, screenwriting.
Sports Basketball, soccer, swimming, volleyball.
Trips Day.
Program Information 1 session per year. Session length: 5 days in July. Ages: 14–18. 8–12 participants per session. Day program cost: $500–$560. Boarding program cost: $650–$750. Application fee: $15. Financial aid available.
Application Deadline Continuous.

Vermont Arts Screenwriting Institute (continued)
Jobs Positions for college students 21 and older.
Contact Ms. Mary B. Thomas, Director of Admissions, Lyndon Institute, PO Box 127, College Road, Lyndon Center, Vermont 05850. Phone: 802-626-5232. Fax: 802-626-6138. E-mail: mthomas@lyndon.k12.vt.us.
URL www.vermontarts.org

Vermont Arts Theatre Camp Institute

Vermont Arts Institute at Lyndon Institute
Lyndon Center, Vermont 05850

General Information Coed residential and day arts program established in 2002. Formal opportunities for the artistically talented.
Program Focus Theatre arts.
Arts Acting, theater/drama.
Sports Basketball, soccer, swimming, volleyball.
Trips Day.
Program Information 1 session per year. Session length: 5 days in July. Ages: 12–14. Day program cost: $300–$360. Boarding program cost: $450–$500. Application fee: $15. Financial aid available.
Application Deadline Continuous.
Jobs Positions for college students 21 and older.
Contact Ms. Mary B. Thomas, Director of Admissions, Lyndon Institute, PO Box 127, College Road, Lyndon Center, Vermont 05850. Phone: 802-626-5232. Fax: 802-626-6138. E-mail: mthomas@lyndon.k12.vt.us.
URL www.vermontarts.org

Vermont Arts Theatre Institute

Vermont Arts Institute at Lyndon Institute
Lyndon Center, Vermont 05850

General Information Coed residential and day arts program established in 2002. Formal opportunities for the artistically talented.
Program Focus Theatre arts.
Arts Acting, stage combat, stage movement, theater/drama.
Sports Basketball, soccer, swimming, volleyball.
Trips Day.
Program Information 1 session per year. Session length: 2 weeks in July. Ages: 14–18. 45–55 participants per session. Day program cost: $1000–$1120. Boarding program cost: $1400–$1600. Application fee: $15. Financial aid available.
Application Deadline Continuous.
Jobs Positions for college students 21 and older.
Contact Ms. Mary B. Thomas, Director of Admissions, Lyndon Institute, PO Box 127, College Road, Lyndon Center, Vermont 05850. Phone: 802-626-5232. Fax: 802-626-6138. E-mail: mthomas@lyndon.k12.vt.us.
URL www.vermontarts.org

Vermont Arts Visual Arts Institute

Vermont Arts Institute at Lyndon Institute
Lyndon Center, Vermont 05850

General Information Coed residential and day arts program established in 2002. Formal opportunities for the artistically talented.
Program Focus Drawing, painting and printmaking.
Arts Drawing, painting, printmaking, visual arts.
Sports Basketball, soccer, swimming, volleyball.
Trips Day.
Program Information 1 session per year. Session length: 5 days in July. Ages: 14–18. 8–12 participants per session. Day program cost: $350–$400. Boarding program cost: $500. Application fee: $15. Financial aid available.
Application Deadline Continuous.
Jobs Positions for college students 21 and older.
Contact Ms. Mary B. Thomas, Director of Admissions, Lyndon Institute, PO Box 127, College Road, Lyndon Center, Vermont 05850. Phone: 802-626-5232. Fax: 802-626-6138. E-mail: mthomas@lyndon.k12.vt.us.
URL www.vermontarts.org

Windridge Tennis Camp at Craftsbury Common

Windridge Tennis Camps
76 Windridge Lane
Craftsbury Common, Vermont 05827

General Information Coed residential sports camp established in 1973. Accredited by American Camping Association.
Program Focus Tennis and waterfront activities.
Arts Arts and crafts (general), batiking, photography, pottery, printmaking, theater/drama.
Sports Archery, basketball, canoeing, fishing, golf, kayaking, rowing (crew/sculling), sailing, snorkeling, soccer, swimming, tennis, volleyball, windsurfing.
Wilderness/Outdoors Mountain biking, wilderness camping.
Trips Day.
Program Information 3 sessions per year. Session length: 3–4 weeks in June, July, August. Ages: 9–15. 110 participants per session. Boarding program cost: $1975–$3975.
Application Deadline Continuous.
Jobs Positions for college students 18 and older.
Summer Contact Charles Witherell, Director, PO Box 27, Craftsbury Common, Vermont 05827. Phone: 802-586-9646. Fax: 802-586-8033. E-mail: wcampsmichelle@pshift.com.
Winter Contact Charles Witherell, Director, PO Box 1298, Jeffersonville, Vermont 05464. Phone: 888-386-7859. Fax: 802-644-6300. E-mail: wcampsmichelle@pshift.com.
URL www.windridgetenniscamps.com

Windridge Tennis Camp at Teela-Wooket, Vermont

Windridge Tennis Camps
1215 Roxbury Road
Roxbury, Vermont 05669

General Information Coed residential sports camp established in 1986. Accredited by American Camping Association.
Program Focus Tennis, soccer, and horseback riding.
Academics English as a second language.
Arts Arts and crafts (general), drawing, fabric arts, jewelry making, painting, photography, theater/drama.
Special Interest Areas Leadership training.
Sports Aerobics, archery, basketball, bicycling, equestrian sports, horseback riding, in-line skating, soccer, softball, street/roller hockey, swimming, tennis.
Wilderness/Outdoors Bicycle trips, hiking, mountain biking.
Trips Day.
Program Information 4 sessions per year. Session length: 2–4 weeks in June, July, August. Ages: 9–15. 168 participants per session. Boarding program cost: $2600–$3800. Additional cost for horseback riding.
Application Deadline Continuous.
Jobs Positions for college students 18 and older.
Summer Contact Deb Fennell, Director, main address above. Phone: 802-485-5400. Fax: 802-485-8092. E-mail: wcampsdeb@pshift.com.
Winter Contact Deb Fennell, Director, PO Box 1298, Jeffersonville, Vermont 05464. Phone: 888-386-7859. E-mail: wcampsdeb@pshift.com.
URL www.windridgetenniscamps.com

YMCA Camp Abnaki

Greater Burlington YMCA
1252 Abnaki Road
North Hero, Vermont 05474

General Information Boys' residential traditional camp and outdoor program established in 1901. Accredited by American Camping Association. Specific services available for the participant with asthma.
Program Focus Character development.
Arts Arts and crafts (general), creative writing, jewelry making, pottery, theater/drama, woodworking.
Special Interest Areas Native American culture, campcraft, community service, leadership training, nature study, nautical skills, team building.
Sports Archery, baseball, basketball, bicycling, boating, canoeing, climbing (wall), fishing, football, kayaking, martial arts, rappelling, sailing, snorkeling, soccer, softball, swimming, tennis, track and field, volleyball, water polo, weight training, windsurfing.
Wilderness/Outdoors Backpacking, bicycle trips, canoe trips, hiking, mountain biking, rock climbing, wilderness camping.
Trips Day, overnight.
Program Information 5–7 sessions per year. Session length: 1–2 weeks in June, July, August. Ages: 6–16. 150–160 participants per session. Boarding program cost: $475–$850. Financial aid available.
Application Deadline Continuous.
Jobs Positions for high school students 17 and older and college students 17 and older.
Summer Contact Jon Kuypers, Camp Director, main address above. Phone: 802-372-8275. E-mail: jkuypers@gbymca.org.
Winter Contact Jon Kuypers, Camp Director, 266 College Street, Burlington, Vermont 05401. Phone: 802-862-9622. Fax: 802-862-9984.
URL www.campabnaki.org

YMCA Camp Abnaki–Counselor-in-Training Program

Greater Burlington YMCA
1252 Abnaki Road
North Hero, Vermont 05474

General Information Boys' residential traditional camp and outdoor program established in 1960. Accredited by American Camping Association.
Program Focus Counselor-in-training.
Arts Arts and crafts (general), jewelry making, pottery, woodworking.
Special Interest Areas Campcraft, community service, leadership training, team building.
Sports Archery, baseball, basketball, bicycling, boating, canoeing, climbing (wall), fishing, football, kayaking, lacrosse, martial arts, sailing, snorkeling, swimming, tennis, volleyball, windsurfing.
Wilderness/Outdoors Bicycle trips, canoe trips, hiking, rock climbing.
Program Information 2 sessions per year. Session length: 4–8 weeks in June, July, August. Ages: 16. 8–10 participants per session. Boarding program cost: $1650–$3300. Financial aid available.
Application Deadline Continuous.
Summer Contact Jon Kuypers, Camp Director, main address above. Phone: 802-372-8275. E-mail: jkuypers@gbymca.org.
Winter Contact Jon Kuypers, Camp Director, 266 College Street, Burlington, Vermont 05401. Phone: 802-862-9622. Fax: 802-862-9984.
URL www.campabnaki.org

YMCA Camp Abnaki–Family Camp

Greater Burlington YMCA
1252 Abnaki Road
North Hero, Vermont 05474

General Information Coed residential traditional camp and family program. Accredited by American Camping Association.
Arts Arts and crafts (general), creative writing, theater/drama, woodworking.
Special Interest Areas Native American culture, campcraft, nature study.
Sports Archery, baseball, basketball, bicycling, boating, canoeing, climbing (wall), fishing, football, kayaking, martial arts, rappelling, sailing, snorkeling, soccer, softball, swimming, tennis, track and field, volleyball, water polo, weight training, windsurfing.
Wilderness/Outdoors Hiking, rock climbing, wilderness camping.

YMCA Camp Abnaki–Family Camp (continued)

Program Information 1 session per year. Session length: 4 days in August, September. Ages: 1–15. Boarding program cost: $75–$125. Financial aid available. No cost for program for participants age 6 and under.
Application Deadline Continuous.
Jobs Positions for high school students 17 and older.
Summer Contact Jon Kuypers, Camp Director, main address above. Phone: 802-372-8275. E-mail: jkuypers@gbymca.org.
Winter Contact Jon Kuypers, Camp Director, 266 College Street, Burlington, Vermont 05401. Phone: 802-862-9622. Fax: 802-862-9984.
URL www.campabnaki.org

YMCA Camp Abnaki–Mini Camp

Greater Burlington YMCA
1252 Abnaki Road
North Hero, Vermont 05474

General Information Boys' residential traditional camp. Accredited by American Camping Association.
Arts Arts and crafts (general), creative writing, theater/drama, woodworking.
Special Interest Areas Native American culture, campcraft, nature study.
Sports Archery, baseball, basketball, bicycling, boating, canoeing, climbing (wall), fishing, football, kayaking, martial arts, rappelling, sailing, snorkeling, soccer, softball, swimming, tennis, track and field, volleyball, water polo, windsurfing.
Wilderness/Outdoors Hiking, wilderness camping.
Program Information 2 sessions per year. Session length: 4 days in June, July. Ages: 6–8. Boarding program cost: $275. Financial aid available.
Application Deadline Continuous.
Jobs Positions for high school students 17 and older and college students 17 and older.
Summer Contact Jon Kuypers, Camp Director, main address above. Phone: 802-375-8275. E-mail: jkuypers@gbymca.org.
Winter Contact Jon Kuypers, Camp Director, 266 College Street, Burlington, Vermont 05401. Phone: 802-862-9622. Fax: 802-862-9984.
URL www.campabnaki.org

YMCA Camp Abnaki–Teen Adventure Trips

Greater Burlington YMCA
Vermont

General Information Boys' travel outdoor program and adventure program. Accredited by American Camping Association.
Special Interest Areas Nautical skills.
Sports Bicycling, kayaking, sailing.
Wilderness/Outdoors Backpacking, bicycle trips, canoe trips, hiking, outdoor adventure, rock climbing, sailing trips, white-water trips.
Program Information 5 sessions per year. Session length: 2 weeks in June, July, August. Ages: 14–16. Cost: $900. Financial aid available.
Application Deadline Continuous.
Jobs Positions for college students 21 and older.
Summer Contact Jon Kuypers, Camp Director, 1252 Abnaki Road, North Hero, Vermont 05474. Phone: 802-372-8275. E-mail: jkuypers@gbymca.org.
Winter Contact Jon Kuypers, Camp Director, 266 College Street, Burlington, Vermont 05401. Phone: 802-862-9622. Fax: 802-862-9984.
URL www.campabnaki.org

VIRGINIA

Adventure Links–Ultimate Adventure Camps

Adventure Links
21498 Blue Ridge Mountain Road
Paris, Virginia 20130

General Information Coed day outdoor program, wilderness program, and adventure program established in 1994. Accredited by American Camping Association.
Special Interest Areas Campcraft.
Sports Canoeing, climbing (wall), kayaking, ropes course.
Wilderness/Outdoors Backpacking, canoe trips, caving, hiking, mountain biking, orienteering, rafting, rock climbing.
Trips Day, overnight.
Program Information 9 sessions per year. Session length: 5 days in June, July, August. Ages: 8–14. 15–20 participants per session. Day program cost: $325–$365.
Application Deadline Continuous.
Jobs Positions for high school students 17 and older and college students 17 and older.
Summer Contact David Kocher, Summer Camp Director, 31498 Blue Ridge Mountain Road, Paris, Virginia 20130. Phone: 540-592-3682. Fax: 540-592-3316. E-mail: dave@adventurelinks.net.
Winter Contact Austin Birch, Owner, 31498 Blue Ridge Mountain Road, Paris, Virginia 20130. Phone: 800-877-0954. Fax: 540-592-3316. E-mail: programs@adventurelinks.net.
URL www.adventurelinks.net

All Arts and Sciences Camp–George Mason University

All Arts and Sciences Camp
George Mason University
Fairfax, Virginia 22030

General Information Coed residential and day academic program and arts program established in 1991. Formal opportunities for the academically talented and artistically talented.
Program Focus Citizenship and civic virtues through discussion of famous individuals exemplifying certain values, such as Mother Teresa or Martin Luther King.

Academics Academics (general), anthropology, architecture, biology, botany, chemistry, computers, ecology, environmental science, geology/earth science, history, journalism, marine studies, mathematics, meteorology, music, physics, psychology, science (general), social science, veterinary science, writing.
Arts Arts, arts and crafts (general), ceramics, clowning, creative writing, dance, dance (modern), drawing, film, jewelry making, mime, painting, photography, pottery, printmaking, sculpture, theater/drama.
Special Interest Areas Leadership training, nature study.
Sports Lacrosse, soccer, softball, volleyball.
Trips College tours.
Program Information 1 session per year. Session length: 6 days in July. Ages: 7–15. 300–500 participants per session. Day program cost: $550. Boarding program cost: $650. Financial aid available.
Application Deadline Continuous.
Jobs Positions for high school students 16 and older and college students 18 and older.
Contact Kisha Carmichael, Camp Director, PO Box 26170, Greensboro, North Carolina 27402-6170. Phone: 336-334-5414. Fax: 336-334-4733. E-mail: allarts@uncg.edu.
URL allarts.uncg.edu/dcl/web/youth.asp

All Arts and Sciences Camp–The College of William and Mary

All Arts and Sciences Camp
The College of William and Mary
Williamsburg, Virginia 23187

General Information Coed residential and day academic program and arts program established in 1991. Formal opportunities for the academically talented and artistically talented.
Program Focus Citizenship and civic virtues through discussion of famous individuals exemplifying certain values, such as Mother Teresa or Martin Luther King.
Academics Academics (general), anthropology, architecture, biology, botany, chemistry, computers, ecology, environmental science, geology/earth science, history, journalism, marine studies, mathematics, meteorology, music, physics, psychology, science (general), social science, veterinary science, writing.
Arts Arts, arts and crafts (general), ceramics, clowning, creative writing, dance, dance (modern), drawing, film, jewelry making, mime, painting, photography, pottery, printmaking, sculpture, theater/drama.
Special Interest Areas Leadership training, nature study.
Sports Lacrosse, soccer, softball, volleyball.
Trips College tours.
Program Information 1 session per year. Session length: 6 days in July. Ages: 7–15. 300–500 participants per session. Day program cost: $550. Boarding program cost: $650. Financial aid available.
Application Deadline Continuous.
Jobs Positions for high school students 16 and older and college students 18 and older.
Contact Kisha Carmichael, Camp Director, PO Box 26170, Greensboro, North Carolina 27402-6170. Phone: 336-334-5414. Fax: 336-334-4733. E-mail: allarts@uncg.edu.
URL allarts.uncg.edu/dcl/web/youth.asp

All Arts and Sciences Camp–Virginia Tech

All Arts and Sciences Camp
Virginia Polytechnic Institute and State University
Blacksburg, Virginia 24061

General Information Coed residential and day academic program and arts program established in 1991. Formal opportunities for the academically talented and artistically talented.
Program Focus Citizenship and civic virtues through discussion of famous individuals exemplifying certain values, such as Mother Teresa or Martin Luther King.
Academics Academics (general), anthropology, architecture, biology, botany, chemistry, computers, ecology, environmental science, geology/earth science, history, journalism, marine studies, mathematics, meteorology, music, physics, psychology, science (general), social science, veterinary science, writing.
Arts Arts, arts and crafts (general), ceramics, clowning, creative writing, dance, dance (modern), drawing, film, jewelry making, mime, painting, photography, pottery, printmaking, sculpture, theater/drama.
Special Interest Areas Leadership training, nature study.
Sports Lacrosse, soccer, softball, volleyball.
Trips College tours.
Program Information 1 session per year. Session length: 6 days in July. Ages: 7–15. 300–500 participants per session. Day program cost: $550. Boarding program cost: $650. Financial aid available.
Application Deadline Continuous.
Jobs Positions for high school students 16 and older and college students 18 and older.
Contact Kisha Carmichael, Camp Director, PO Box 26170, Greensboro, North Carolina 27402-6170. Phone: 336-334-5414. Fax: 336-334-4733. E-mail: allarts@uncg.edu.
URL allarts.uncg.edu/dcl/web/youth.asp

Art Monk Football Camp/Sports International–Virginia

Sports International, Inc.
George Mason University
Fairfax, Virginia

General Information Coed residential and day sports camp established in 1983.
Program Focus Football camp.
Sports Football, weight training.
Program Information 1 session per year. Session length: 5 days in June, July. Ages: 8–18. 300–450 participants per session. Day program cost: $509. Boarding program cost: $619.
Application Deadline Continuous.
Jobs Positions for college students 18 and older.

Art Monk Football Camp/Sports International–Virginia (continued)

Contact Customer Service, 8924 McGaw Court, Columbia, Maryland 21045. Phone: 800-555-0801. Fax: 401-309-9962. E-mail: info@footballcamps.com.
URL www.footballcamps.com

BLUE RIDGE SCHOOL–ADVENTURE CAMPS

The Blue Ridge School
Highway 627
St. George, Virginia 22935

General Information Boys' residential outdoor program, wilderness program, and adventure program established in 2001.
Academics Astronomy, botany, communications, ecology.
Special Interest Areas Campcraft, culinary arts, gardening, leadership training, team building.
Sports Bicycling (BMX), canoeing, climbing (wall), football, kayaking, rappelling, ropes course, swimming.
Wilderness/Outdoors Backpacking, bicycle trips, canoe trips, caving, climbing, hiking, mountain biking, orienteering, rock climbing, survival training, white-water trips, wilderness camping.
Trips Day, overnight.
Program Information 2–3 sessions per year. Session length: 4–10 days in June, July. Ages: 11–16. 4–10 participants per session. Boarding program cost: $400–$900. Open to participants in grades 6–9.
Application Deadline Continuous.
Jobs Positions for college students.
Contact Tony Brown, Director of Outdoor Programs, main address above. Phone: 434-985-2811. Fax: 434-985-7215. E-mail: tbrown@blueridgeschool.com.
URL www.blueridgeschool.com

BLUE RIDGE SCHOOL–ROCK CLIMBING CAMP

The Blue Ridge School
Highway 627
St. George, Virginia 22935

General Information Boys' residential outdoor program, wilderness program, and adventure program established in 2002.
Special Interest Areas Leadership training, team building.
Sports Climbing (wall), rappelling, ropes course.
Wilderness/Outdoors Backpacking, rock climbing, wilderness camping.
Trips Day, overnight.
Program Information Session length: 4–9 days in July, August. Boarding program cost: $400–$900. Open to participants in grades 6–9.
Application Deadline Continuous.
Contact Tony Brown, Director of Outdoor Programs, main address above. Phone: 434-985-2811. Fax: 434-985-7215. E-mail: tbrown@blueridgeschool.com.
URL www.blueridgeschool.com

CAMP CARYSBROOK

Camp Carysbrook
3500 Camp Carysbrook Road
Riner, Virginia 24149

General Information Girls' residential traditional camp established in 1923. Accredited by American Camping Association.
Arts Arts and crafts (general), batiking, ceramics, chorus, clowning, creative writing, dance, dance (ballet), dance (folk), dance (jazz), dance (modern), dance (tap), drawing, jewelry making, leather working, painting, pottery, theater/drama, weaving, woodworking.
Special Interest Areas Campcraft, leadership training, nature study.
Sports Aerobics, archery, basketball, canoeing, climbing (wall), equestrian sports, fencing, field hockey, fishing, gymnastics, horseback riding, lacrosse, rappelling, riflery, soccer, softball, swimming, tennis, volleyball.
Wilderness/Outdoors Backpacking, canoe trips, caving, hiking, rock climbing, wilderness camping.
Trips Day, overnight.
Program Information 12 sessions per year. Session length: 1–8 weeks in June, July, August. Ages: 6–16. 85–100 participants per session. Boarding program cost: $675–$3700. Financial aid available.
Application Deadline Continuous.
Jobs Positions for high school students 18 and older and college students 18 and older.
Contact Sarah Baughman, Owner/Director, main address above. Phone: 540-382-1670. E-mail: sarah@campcarysbrook.com.
URL www.campcarysbrook.com

CAMP CARYSBROOK EQUESTRIAN

Camp Carysbrook
3500 Camp Carysbrook Road
Riner, Virginia 24149

General Information Girls' residential sports camp established in 1987. Accredited by American Camping Association.
Program Focus Equestrian.
Special Interest Areas General camp activities.
Sports Equestrian sports, horseback riding.
Trips Overnight.
Program Information 3 sessions per year. Session length: 1–2 weeks in August. Ages: 10–16. 20 participants per session. Boarding program cost: $750–$1400.
Application Deadline Continuous.
Jobs Positions for high school students 18 and older and college students 18 and older.
Contact Rachel Baughman, Owner/Director, main address above. Phone: 540-382-1670. E-mail: sarah@campcarysbrook.com.
URL www.campcarysbrook.com

Camp Curtain Call

849 River Road
Dugspur, Virginia 24325

General Information Coed residential traditional camp and arts program established in 2001. Formal opportunities for the artistically talented.
Arts Acting, arts and crafts (general), chorus, circus arts, clowning, dance, dance (ballet), dance (jazz), dance (modern), dance (tap), drawing, fabric arts, graphic arts, jewelry making, leather working, magic, mime, music, music (ensemble), music (instrumental), music (jazz), music (vocal), musical productions, painting, photography, puppetry, theater/drama, woodworking.
Special Interest Areas Chess, model rocketry.
Sports Aerobics, basketball, bicycling, canoeing, croquet, fencing, fishing, football, golf, horseshoes, kayaking, martial arts, ropes course, soccer, softball, swimming, tennis, volleyball, weight training.
Wilderness/Outdoors Hiking.
Trips Cultural, day, shopping.
Program Information 3 sessions per year. Session length: 3 weeks in June, July, August. Ages: 10–18. 50–60 participants per session. Boarding program cost: $2650–$6950. Financial aid available.
Application Deadline Continuous.
Jobs Positions for high school students 17 and older and college students 19 and older.
Summer Contact Eddie Armbrister, Director, main address above. Phone: 276-730-0233. Fax: 276-730-0233. E-mail: info@campcurtaincall.com.
Winter Contact Eddie Armbrister, Director, 7804 Sagefield Drive, Knoxville, Tennessee 37920. Phone: 865-573-7002. Fax: 865-573-7002. E-mail: info@campcurtaincall.com.
URL www.CampCurtainCall.com

Camp Friendship

Camp Friendship
Highway 15
Palmyra, Virginia 22963

General Information Coed residential traditional camp established in 1966. Accredited by American Camping Association.
Academics English as a second language.
Arts Acting, arts and crafts (general), band, dance, dance (jazz), dance (modern), drawing, leather working, music, music (instrumental), musical productions, painting, photography, pottery, television/video, theater/drama.
Special Interest Areas Campcraft, leadership training, nature study.
Sports Archery, basketball, bicycling, canoeing, cheerleading, cross-country, diving, equestrian sports, fencing, field hockey, fishing, golf, gymnastics, hang gliding, horseback riding, kayaking, lacrosse, mountain boarding, rappelling, riflery, ropes course, soccer, swimming, tennis, volleyball, waterskiing.
Wilderness/Outdoors Backpacking, bicycle trips, canoe trips, caving, hiking, rafting, rock climbing, white-water trips, wilderness camping.
Program Information 5–11 sessions per year. Session length: 6–13 days in June, July, August. Ages: 6–16. 400–425 participants per session. Boarding program cost: $650–$1300. Financial aid available.
Application Deadline Continuous.
Jobs Positions for high school students 16 and older and college students 19 and older.
Contact Ray Ackenbom, Co-Director, PO Box 145, Palmyra, Virginia 22963. Phone: 800-873-3223. Fax: 434-589-5880. E-mail: info@campfriendship.com.
URL www.campfriendship.com

Camp Holiday Trails

Holiday Trails, Inc.
400 Holiday Trails Lane
Charlottesville, Virginia 22903

General Information Coed residential special needs program established in 1973. Accredited by American Camping Association. Specific services available for the diabetic, participant with heart defects, participant with cancer, participant with HIV/AIDS, organ transplant recipient, participant with asthma, epileptic, participant with kidney disorders, participant with hemophilia, participant with Sickle Cell Anemia, participant with Cystic Fibrosis, and participant with arthritis.
Program Focus Children with chronic illness and special health needs.
Arts Acting, arts and crafts (general), creative writing, dance, music, photography, pottery, theater/drama.
Special Interest Areas Campcraft, community service, conservation projects, gardening, leadership training, nature study, team building, weight reduction.
Sports Archery, basketball, canoeing, challenge course, climbing (wall), equestrian sports, fishing, horseback riding, rappelling, ropes course, swimming, tennis, volleyball.
Wilderness/Outdoors Hiking, orienteering.
Trips Day.
Program Information 3 sessions per year. Session length: 13 days in June, July, August. Ages: 7–17. 50–70 participants per session. Boarding program cost: $1120. Application fee: $60. Financial aid available.
Application Deadline Continuous.
Jobs Positions for high school students 18 and older and college students 19 and older.
Contact Tina La Roche, Executive Director, main address above. Phone: 434-977-3781. Fax: 434-977-8814. E-mail: tina.laroche.cht@nexet.net.
URL www.avenue.org/cht

Camp Horizons Adventure

Camp Horizons
3586 Horizons Way
Harrisonburg, Virginia 22802

General Information Coed residential outdoor program established in 1983. Accredited by American Camping Association.
Program Focus Hang gliding, scuba diving, ropes course, white-water rafting, rock climbing, and caving.
Arts Jewelry making.

Camp Horizons Adventure (continued)

Sports Canoeing, climbing (wall), hang gliding, kayaking, ropes course, scuba diving, swimming.
Wilderness/Outdoors Backpacking, canoe trips, caving, hiking, mountain biking, outdoor adventure, rafting, rock climbing, white-water trips, wilderness camping.
Trips Day, overnight.
Program Information 4 sessions per year. Session length: 2 weeks in June, July, August. Ages: 13–16. 50–60 participants per session. Boarding program cost: $1500.
Application Deadline Continuous.
Jobs Positions for college students 18 and older.
Contact John Hall, Director/Owner, 3586 Horizons Way, Harrisonburg, Virginia 22802. Phone: 800-729-9230. Fax: 540-896-5455. E-mail: camp@horizonsva.com.
URL www.camphorizonsva.com

Camp Horizons Discover

Camp Horizons
3586 Horizons Way
Harrisonburg, Virginia 22802

General Information Coed residential traditional camp established in 2003. Accredited by American Camping Association.
Program Focus Geared towards first-time campers, ages 7-9.
Academics Sign language.
Arts Acting, arts and crafts (general), creative writing, dance, dance (modern), drawing, film, music, photography, theater/drama, woodworking.
Special Interest Areas Campcraft, model rocketry, nature study.
Sports Archery, canoeing, climbing (wall), diving, golf, horseback riding, soccer, softball, swimming, tennis, volleyball.
Program Information 2 sessions per year. Session length: 1 week in June. Ages: 7–9. 16–24 participants per session. Boarding program cost: $700.
Application Deadline Continuous.
Jobs Positions for college students 18 and older.
Contact Kim Betts, Associate Director, main address above. Phone: 800-729-9230. Fax: 540-896-5455. E-mail: camp@horizonava.com.
URL www.camphorizonsva.com

Camp Horizons Explorer

Camp Horizons
3586 Horizons Way
Harrisonburg, Virginia 22802

General Information Coed residential traditional camp and outdoor program established in 1983. Accredited by American Camping Association.
Program Focus A traditional camp with choice of adventure or performing arts activities.
Arts Acting, arts, arts and crafts (general), creative writing, dance, dance (jazz), dance (modern), drawing, fabric arts, film, magic, music (instrumental), painting, photography, radio broadcasting, television/video, theater/drama.
Special Interest Areas Campcraft, general camp activities, model rocketry, nature study.
Sports Archery, basketball, bicycling, canoeing, climbing (wall), golf, horseback riding, kayaking, ropes course, soccer, softball, swimming, tennis, volleyball, water tubing.
Wilderness/Outdoors Caving, hiking, mountain biking, orienteering, outdoor adventure, rock climbing.
Trips Day.
Program Information 4 sessions per year. Session length: 2 weeks in June, July, August. Ages: 12–16. 80–110 participants per session. Boarding program cost: $1400.
Application Deadline Continuous.
Jobs Positions for college students 18 and older.
Contact John Hall, Director/Owner, main address above. Phone: 800-729-9230. Fax: 540-896-5455. E-mail: camp@horizonsva.com.
URL www.camphorizonsva.com

Camp Horizons Pathfinder

Camp Horizons
3586 Horizons Way
Harrisonburg, Virginia 22802

General Information Coed residential traditional camp and outdoor program established in 1983. Accredited by American Camping Association.
Program Focus Outdoor activities; newspaper; videography; photography.
Arts Acting, arts and crafts (general), creative writing, dance, dance (jazz), dance (modern), drawing, fabric arts, magic, music (instrumental), painting, photography, radio broadcasting, television/video, theater/drama.
Special Interest Areas Campcraft, model rocketry, nature study.
Sports Archery, basketball, boating, canoeing, climbing (wall), golf, horseback riding, kayaking, kickball, ropes course, soccer, softball, swimming, tennis, volleyball.
Wilderness/Outdoors Hiking, orienteering.
Program Information 4 sessions per year. Session length: 2 weeks in June, July, August. Ages: 7–11. 100–120 participants per session. Boarding program cost: $1300.
Application Deadline Continuous.
Jobs Positions for college students 18 and older.
Contact John Hall, Director/Owner, main address above. Phone: 800-729-9230. Fax: 540-896-5455. E-mail: camp@horizonsva.com.
URL www.camphorizonsva.com

Camp Horizons Specialty Camp

Camp Horizons
3586 Horizons Way
Harrisonburg, Virginia 22802

General Information Coed residential outdoor program and arts program established in 2003. Accredited by American Camping Association.
Program Focus Campers select one focus area: photography, movie making, paddling, rock climbing, mountain biking, or guitar music.

Arts Acting, arts, music, music (instrumental), photography, television/video.
Sports Canoeing, kayaking, swimming.
Wilderness/Outdoors Bicycle trips, canoe trips, mountain biking, outdoor adventure, rock climbing.
Trips Day.
Program Information 1 session per year. Session length: 1 week in August. Ages: 10–16. 40–60 participants per session. Boarding program cost: $700.
Application Deadline Continuous.
Jobs Positions for college students 18 and older.
Contact John Hall, Director/Owner, main address above. Phone: 540-896-7600. Fax: 540-896-5455. E-mail: camp@horizonsva.com.
URL www.camphorizonsva.com

Camp Jordan for Children with Diabetes

Presbytery of Eastern Virginia
Makemie Woods
3700 Ropers Church Road
Lanexa, Virginia 23089

General Information Coed residential traditional camp and special needs program established in 1966. Religious affiliation: Presbyterian. Accredited by American Camping Association. Specific services available for the diabetic.
Program Focus Self reliance and self-esteem.
Academics Bible study.
Arts Acting, arts and crafts (general), music (folk), music (vocal), theater/drama.
Special Interest Areas Campcraft, health education, nature study, nutrition, outdoor cooking, worship.
Sports Archery, boating, canoeing, horseback riding, ropes course, sailing, soccer, swimming.
Wilderness/Outdoors Canoe trips, rafting, rock climbing, white-water trips.
Trips Overnight.
Program Information 1 session per year. Session length: 10 days in July, August. Ages: 8–15. 8–25 participants per session. Boarding program cost: $675. Financial aid available.
Application Deadline Continuous.
Jobs Positions for high school students 16 and older and college students 18 and older.
Contact Ms. Karen Broughman, Office Manager, 23011, Barhamsville, Virginia 23011. Phone: 800-566-1496. Fax: 757-566-8803. E-mail: makwoods@makwoods.org.
URL www.makwoods.org/cjordan/index.html

Cheerio Adventures–Appalachian Adventure

YMCA of Greater High Point, North Carolina, Inc.
754 Fox Knob Road
Mouth of Wilson, Virginia 24363

General Information Coed residential wilderness program and adventure program established in 1982. Religious affiliation: Christian. Accredited by American Camping Association.
Sports Canoeing, kayaking, rappelling.
Wilderness/Outdoors Canoe trips, caving, hiking, mountain biking, rafting, rock climbing, white-water trips, wilderness/outdoors (general).
Trips Day, overnight.
Program Information 2 sessions per year. Session length: 1 week in June, July. Ages: 10–15. 30 participants per session. Boarding program cost: $765. Financial aid available.
Application Deadline Continuous.
Jobs Positions for college students 19 and older.
Contact Keith Russell, Director, 1430 Camp Cheerio Road, Glade Valley, North Carolina 28627. Phone: 336-363-2604. Fax: 336-363-3671. E-mail: krussell@campcheerio.org.
URL www.cheerioadventures.com

Cheerio Adventures–Cave/Raft

YMCA of Greater High Point, North Carolina, Inc.
754 Fox Knob Road
Mouth of Wilson, Virginia 24363

General Information Coed residential wilderness program and adventure program established in 1982. Religious affiliation: Christian. Accredited by American Camping Association.
Wilderness/Outdoors Caving, hiking, rafting, white-water trips, wilderness camping.
Trips Day, overnight.
Program Information 1 session per year. Session length: 1 week in July. Ages: 13–15. 10 participants per session. Boarding program cost: $795. Financial aid available.
Application Deadline Continuous.
Jobs Positions for college students 19 and older.
Contact Keith Russell, Director, 1430 Camp Cheerio Road, Glade Valley, North Carolina 28627. Phone: 336-363-2604. Fax: 336-363-3671. E-mail: krussell@campcheerio.org.
URL www.cheerioadventures.com

Cheerio Adventures–Mountains to the Sea

YMCA of Greater High Point, North Carolina, Inc.
754 Fox Knob Road
Mouth of Wilson, Virginia 24363

General Information Coed residential wilderness program and adventure program established in 1982. Religious affiliation: Christian. Accredited by American Camping Association.
Special Interest Areas Campcraft, leadership training.
Sports Canoeing, kayaking, rappelling, sailing, sea kayaking, windsurfing.
Wilderness/Outdoors Backpacking, caving, hiking, rafting, rock climbing, white-water trips, wilderness camping, wilderness/outdoors (general).
Trips Day, overnight.
Program Information 2 sessions per year. Session length: 2 weeks in June, July, August. Ages: 14–17. 10 participants per session. Boarding program cost: $1495. Financial aid available.

Cheerio Adventures–Mountains to the Sea (continued)
Application Deadline Continuous.
Jobs Positions for college students 19 and older.
Contact Keith Russell, Director, 1430 Camp Cheerio Road, Glade Valley, North Carolina 28627. Phone: 336-363-2604. Fax: 336-363-3671. E-mail: krussell@campcheerio.org.
URL www.cheerioadventures.com

Cheerio Adventures–Ocean Odyssey

YMCA of Greater High Point, North Carolina, Inc.
754 Fox Knob Road
Mouth of Wilson, Virginia 24363

General Information Coed residential wilderness program and adventure program established in 1982. Religious affiliation: Christian. Accredited by American Camping Association.
Sports Sailing, sea kayaking, surfing, windsurfing.
Trips Overnight.
Program Information 1–2 sessions per year. Session length: 11 days in June, July. Ages: 14–17. 10–12 participants per session. Boarding program cost: $1495. Financial aid available.
Application Deadline Continuous.
Jobs Positions for college students 19 and older.
Contact Keith Russell, Director, 1430 Camp Cheerio Road, Glade Valley, North Carolina 28627. Phone: 336-363-2604. Fax: 336-363-3671. E-mail: krussell@campcheerio.org.
URL www.cheerioadventures.com

Cheerio Adventures–Rock Climb/Raft

YMCA of Greater High Point, North Carolina, Inc.
754 Fox Knob Road
Mouth of Wilson, Virginia 24363

General Information Coed residential wilderness program and adventure program established in 1982. Accredited by American Camping Association.
Sports Rappelling.
Wilderness/Outdoors Rafting, rock climbing, wilderness camping.
Trips Day, overnight.
Program Information 1 session per year. Session length: 1 week in July. Ages: 13–15. 10 participants per session. Boarding program cost: $795. Financial aid available.
Application Deadline Continuous.
Jobs Positions for college students 19 and older.
Contact Keith Russell, Director, 1430 Camp Cheerio Road, Glade Valley, North Carolina 28627. Phone: 336-363-2604. Fax: 336-363-3671. E-mail: krussell@campcheerio.org.
URL www.cheerioadventure.com

Cheerio Adventures–Sampler

YMCA of Greater High Point, North Carolina, Inc.
754 Fox Knob Road
Mouth of Wilson, Virginia 24363

General Information Coed residential wilderness program and adventure program established in 1982. Religious affiliation: Christian. Accredited by American Camping Association.
Program Focus Wilderness adventure and trips.
Sports Canoeing, kayaking, rappelling.
Wilderness/Outdoors Backpacking, canoe trips, caving, hiking, outdoor adventure, rafting, rock climbing, white-water trips, wilderness camping.
Trips Day, overnight.
Program Information 8 sessions per year. Session length: 1 week in June, July, August. Ages: 10–12. 12 participants per session. Boarding program cost: $765. Financial aid available.
Application Deadline Continuous.
Jobs Positions for college students 19 and older.
Contact Keith Russell, Director, 1430 Camp Cheerio Road, Glade Valley, North Carolina 28627. Phone: 336-363-2604. Fax: 336-363-3671. E-mail: krussell@campcheerio.org.
URL www.cheerioadventures.com

Cheerio Adventures–Seekers

YMCA of Greater High Point, North Carolina, Inc.
754 Fox Knob Road
Mouth of Wilson, Virginia 24363

General Information Coed residential wilderness program and adventure program established in 1982. Religious affiliation: Christian. Accredited by American Camping Association.
Sports Bicycling, canoeing, kayaking, rappelling.
Wilderness/Outdoors Backpacking, canoe trips, caving, hiking, mountain biking, rafting, rock climbing, white-water trips, wilderness camping, wilderness/outdoors (general).
Trips Day, overnight.
Program Information 2 sessions per year. Session length: 2 weeks in June, July, August. Ages: 13–15. 8 participants per session. Boarding program cost: $1435. Financial aid available.
Application Deadline Continuous.
Jobs Positions for college students 19 and older.
Contact Keith Russell, Director, 1430 Camp Cheerio Road, Glade Valley, North Carolina 28627. Phone: 336-363-2604. Fax: 336-363-3671. E-mail: krussell@campcheerio.org.
URL www.cheerioadventure.com

Cheerio Adventures–Standard

YMCA of Greater High Point, North Carolina, Inc.
754 Fox Knob Road
Mouth of Wilson, Virginia 24363

General Information Coed residential wilderness program and adventure program established in 1982. Religious affiliation: Christian. Accredited by American Camping Association.

Sports Canoeing, kayaking, rappelling.
Wilderness/Outdoors Backpacking, canoe trips, caving, hiking, mountain biking, rafting, rock climbing, white-water trips, wilderness camping, wilderness/outdoors (general).
Trips Day, overnight.
Program Information 2 sessions per year. Session length: 2 weeks in June, July, August. Ages: 12–14. 8 participants per session. Boarding program cost: $1435. Financial aid available.
Application Deadline Continuous.
Jobs Positions for college students 19 and older.
Contact Keith Russell, Director, 1430 Camp Cheerio Road, Glade Valley, North Carolina 28627. Phone: 336-363-2604. Fax: 336-363-3671. E-mail: krussell@campcheerio.org.
URL www.cheerioadventure.com

Cybercamps–George Mason University

Cybercamps–Giant Campus, Inc.
Fairfax, Virginia

General Information Coed residential and day academic program established in 1997.
Program Focus High tech computer camps featuring project oriented curriculum in Web design, 3D animation, game design, robotics, digital arts and programming for all ability levels.
Academics Web page design, computer programming, computers, typing.
Arts Animation, creative writing, digital media, drawing, graphic arts, photography.
Special Interest Areas Computer game design, computer graphics, robotics, team building.
Sports Ultimate frisbee.
Program Information 2–9 sessions per year. Session length: 5–30 days in June, July, August. Ages: 7–18. 30–150 participants per session. Day program cost: $599–$849. Boarding program cost: $974–$1224.
Application Deadline Continuous.
Jobs Positions for high school students 15 and older and college students.
Contact Cybercamps Information Office, 2401 4th Avenue, Suite 1110, Seattle, Washington 98121. Phone: 206-442-4500. Fax: 206-442-4501. E-mail: info@cybercamps.com.
URL www.cybercamps.com

EARTHWATCH INSTITUTE–Frontier Fort in Virginia

Earthwatch Institute
Fort Christanna
Lawrenceville, Virginia

General Information Coed residential outdoor program, cultural program, and adventure program.
Program Focus Investigating how culturally different populations develop alliances over time.
Academics Archaeology, history, science (general).
Special Interest Areas Field research/expeditions.
Program Information 3 sessions per year. Session length: 13 days in June, July. Ages: 16+. 10 participants per session. Boarding program cost: $1795–$1895. Financial aid available. Financial aid for high school students and teachers.
Application Deadline Continuous.
Contact General Information Desk, PO Box 75, Maynard, Massachusetts 01754. Phone: 800-776-0188. Fax: 978-461-2332. E-mail: info@earthwatch.org.
URL www.earthwatch.org

Fairfax Collegiate School Summer Enrichment Program

Fairfax Collegiate School
St. Katherine's Greek Orthodox Church
3149 Glen Carlyn Road
Falls Church, Virginia 22041

General Information Coed day academic program established in 1993. Formal opportunities for the academically talented.
Academics SAT/ACT preparation, Spanish language/literature, academics (general), computer programming, computers, journalism, mathematics, typing, writing.
Arts Acting, creative writing, film, television/video, theater/drama.
Program Information 5 sessions per year. Session length: 10 days in June, July, August. Ages: 8–17. 100 participants per session. Cost: $360 per course, $585 for 2 courses.
Application Deadline Continuous.
Jobs Positions for high school students and college students.
Contact Jennifer Nossal, Summer Program Director, 2101 Crystal Plaza, ARC 232, Arlington, Virginia 22202. Phone: 703-486-1787. Fax: 703-486-1788. E-mail: jennifer_nossal@fairfaxcollegiate.com.
URL www.fairfaxcollegiate.com

Fishburne Summer Session

Fishburne Military School
Waynesboro, Virginia 22980

General Information Boys' residential and day academic program established in 1955. High school credit may be earned.
Program Focus Academic review and enrichment—intensive individual instruction.
Academics English as a second language, English language/literature, French language/literature, SAT/ACT preparation, Spanish language/literature, academics (general), biology, chemistry, computers, environmental science, geology/earth science, government and politics, history, mathematics, science (general), social studies.
Special Interest Areas Driver's education.
Sports Basketball, fishing, golf, horseback riding, martial arts, riflery, soccer, softball, swimming, tennis, volleyball, weight training.
Wilderness/Outdoors Hiking.
Trips Day.
Program Information 1 session per year. Session length: 5 weeks in June, July, August. Ages: 12–18. 90

Fishburne Summer Session (continued)

Fishburne Summer Session

participants per session. Day program cost: $950. Boarding program cost: $2950. Application fee: $50.
Application Deadline Continuous.
Contact Capt. Carl Lambert, Director of Admissions, PO Box 988E, Waynesboro, Virginia 22980. Phone: 800-946-7773. Fax: 540-946-7738. E-mail: lambert@fishburne.org.
URL www.fishburne.org

For more information, see page 1126.

Flint Hill School–"Summer on the Hill"–A Biking Odyssey Day Camp

Flint Hill School
East Campus
10409 Academic Drive
Oakton, Virginia 22124

General Information Coed day outdoor program.
Program Focus Bike lovers adventure.
Special Interest Areas Bicycle mechanics.
Sports Bicycling, bicycling (BMX).
Wilderness/Outdoors Bicycle trips, outdoor adventure.
Trips Day.
Program Information 1 session per year. Session length: 5 days in July. Ages: 11–13. 2–20 participants per session. Day program cost: $450.
Application Deadline Continuous.
Jobs Positions for high school students 16 and older and college students 18 and older.
Contact Ms. Peggy Laurent, Director of Special and Summer Programs, 3320 Jermantown Road, Oakton, Virginia 22124. Phone: 703-584-2315. Fax: 703-242-0718. E-mail: plaurent@flinthill.org.
URL www.flinthill.org

Flint Hill School–"Summer on the Hill"–Academics on the Hill–English and Math Review

Flint Hill School
East Campus
10409 Academic Drive
Oakton, Virginia 22124

General Information Coed day academic program.
Program Focus English, Math or Algebra review.
Academics English language/literature, mathematics, reading, remedial academics, study skills, writing.
Program Information 1–5 sessions per year. Session length: 10–30 days in June, July. Ages: 12–18. 2–80 participants per session. Day program cost: $475–$795.
Application Deadline Continuous.
Jobs Positions for high school students 16 and older and college students 18 and older.
Contact Ms. Peggy Laurent, Director of Special and Summer Programs, 3320 Jermantown Road, Oakton, Virginia 22124. Phone: 703-584-2315. Fax: 703-242-0718. E-mail: plaurent@flinthill.org.
URL www.flinthill.org

Flint Hill School–"Summer on the Hill"–Academics on the Hill–Geometry for Credit

Flint Hill School
West Campus
3320 Jermantown Road
Oakton, Virginia 22124

General Information Coed day academic program. College credit may be earned.
Program Focus 120 hours of classroom instruction in college preparatory geometry.
Academics Mathematics.
Program Information 1–2 sessions per year. Session length: 30 days in June, July. Ages: 14–18. 2–6 participants per session. Day program cost: $1435.
Application Deadline Continuous.
Jobs Positions for high school students 16 and older and college students 18 and older.
Contact Ms. Peggy Laurent, Director of Special and Summer Programs, 3320 Jermantown Road, Oakton, Virginia 22124. Phone: 703-584-2315. Fax: 703-242-0718. E-mail: plaurent@flinthill.org.
URL www.flinthill.org

Flint Hill School–"Summer on the Hill"–Academics on the Hill–The Reading Clinic

Flint Hill School
East Campus
10409 Academic Drive
Oakton, Virginia 22124

General Information Coed day academic program. Specific services available for the speech impaired.
Program Focus Intensive summer reading clinic.

Academics Reading, remedial academics, study skills.
Program Information 1–6 sessions per year. Session length: 5–30 days in June, July. Ages: 7–12. 2–6 participants per session. Day program cost: $475–$2200.
Application Deadline Continuous.
Jobs Positions for high school students 16 and older and college students 18 and older.
Contact Ms. Peggy Laurent, Director of Special and Summer Programs, 3320 Jermantown Road, Oakton, Virginia 22124. Phone: 703-584-2315. Fax: 703-242-0718. E-mail: plaurent@flinthill.org.
URL www.flinthill.org

FLINT HILL SCHOOL–"SUMMER ON THE HILL"–BOYS OUTDOOR ADVENTURES! DAY CAMP

Flint Hill School
East Campus
10409 Academic Drive
Oakton, Virginia 22124

General Information Boys' day outdoor program.
Program Focus Basics of camping.
Special Interest Areas Campcraft, nature study, outdoor cooking.
Sports Fishing.
Wilderness/Outdoors Backpacking, fly fishing, hiking, orienteering, outdoor adventure, outdoor camping.
Trips Day, overnight.
Program Information 1 session per year. Session length: 5 days in July. Ages: 12–14. 2–20 participants per session. Day program cost: $500.
Application Deadline Continuous.
Jobs Positions for high school students 16 and older and college students 18 and older.
Contact Ms. Peggy Laurent, Director of Special and Summer Programs, 3320 Jermantown Road, Oakton, Virginia 22124. Phone: 703-584-2315. Fax: 703-242-0718. E-mail: plaurent@flinthill.org.
URL www.flinthill.org

FLINT HILL SCHOOL–"SUMMER ON THE HILL"–COUNSELOR-IN-TRAINING DAY CAMP

Flint Hill School
East Campus
10409 Academic Drive
Oakton, Virginia 22124

General Information Coed day traditional camp and academic program.
Program Focus Counselor-in-Training program.
Academics Academics (general), writing.
Arts Arts and crafts (general).
Special Interest Areas Campcraft, counselor-in-training program, first aid, health education, leadership training, team building.
Sports Sports (general).
Trips Day.
Program Information 1–2 sessions per year. Session length: 15 days in June, July. Ages: 11–14. 2–40 participants per session. Day program cost: $785.
Application Deadline Continuous.
Jobs Positions for high school students 16 and older and college students 18 and older.
Contact Ms. Peggy Laurent, Director of Special and Summer Programs, 3320 Jermantown Road, Oakton, Virginia 22124. Phone: 703-584-2315. Fax: 703-242-0718. E-mail: plaurent@flinthill.org.
URL www.flinthill.org

FLINT HILL SCHOOL–"SUMMER ON THE HILL"–CREATIVE ARTS ON THE HILL–ART CAMP

Flint Hill School
East Campus
10409 Academic Drive
Oakton, Virginia 22124

General Information Coed day arts program.
Program Focus Art, clay animation, drawing, knitting, ceramics.
Academics Art.
Arts Animation, arts, arts and crafts (general), ceramics, drawing, knitting, mixed media.
Program Information 1–5 sessions per year. Session length: 5–30 days in June, July. Ages: 7–14. 2–80 participants per session. Day program cost: $120–$388.
Application Deadline Continuous.
Jobs Positions for high school students 16 and older and college students 18 and older.
Contact Ms. Peggy Laurent, Director of Special and Summer Programs, 3320 Jermantown Road, Oakton, Virginia 22124. Phone: 703-584-2315. Fax: 703-242-0718. E-mail: plaurent@flinthill.org.
URL www.flinthill.org

FLINT HILL SCHOOL–"SUMMER ON THE HILL"–CREATIVE ARTS ON THE HILL–LET THE DRUMS ROLL

Flint Hill School
East Campus
10409 Academic Drive
Oakton, Virginia 22124

General Information Coed day arts program.
Program Focus Drumming.
Academics Music.
Arts Music, music (folk), music (instrumental), music (rock).
Program Information 1 session per year. Session length: 5 days in June, July. Ages: 11–13. 2–30 participants per session. Day program cost: $370.
Application Deadline Continuous.
Jobs Positions for high school students 16 and older and college students 18 and older.

Flint Hill School–"Summer on the Hill"–Creative Arts on the Hill–Let the Drums Roll (continued)

Contact Ms. Peggy Laurent, Director of Special and Summer Programs, 3320 Jermantown Road, Oakton, Virginia 22124. Phone: 703-584-2315. Fax: 703-242-0718. E-mail: plaurent@flinthill.org.
URL www.flinthill.org

Flint Hill School–"Summer on the Hill"–Enrichment on the Hill–Gee, Whiz!

Flint Hill School
East Campus
10409 Academic Drive
Oakton, Virginia 22124

General Information Coed day academic program.
Program Focus Investigating chemistry, physics, biology, math, and art.
Academics Art history/appreciation, biology, chemistry, computers, mathematics, physics, science (general).
Arts Animation.
Special Interest Areas Field research/expeditions.
Trips Day.
Program Information 1 session per year. Session length: 5 days in July. Ages: 8–11. 2–40 participants per session. Day program cost: $460.
Application Deadline Continuous.
Jobs Positions for high school students 16 and older and college students 18 and older.
Contact Ms. Peggy Laurent, Director of Special and Summer Programs, 3320 Jermantown Road, Oakton, Virginia 22124. Phone: 703-584-2315. Fax: 703-242-0718. E-mail: plaurent@flinthill.org.
URL www.flinthill.org

Flint Hill School–"Summer on the Hill"–Enrichment on the Hill–Investigating Where We Live

Flint Hill School
West Campus
3320 Jermantown Road
Oakton, Virginia 22124

General Information Coed day arts program. High school credit may be earned.
Program Focus A program developed by the National Building Museum for young people to explore the suburban landscape through photography, art and design.
Academics Architecture, urban design.
Arts Drawing, photography.
Special Interest Areas Field research/expeditions, field trips (arts and culture).
Trips Cultural, day.
Program Information 1 session per year. Session length: 10 days in July. Ages: 12–16. 2–30 participants per session. Day program cost: $800.
Application Deadline Continuous.
Jobs Positions for high school students 16 and older and college students 18 and older.
Contact Ms. Peggy Laurent, Director of Special and Summer Programs, main address above. Phone: 703-584-2315. Fax: 703-242-0718. E-mail: plaurent@flinthill.org.
URL www.flinthill.org

Flint Hill School–"Summer on the Hill"–Enrichment on the Hill–Junior Great Books

Flint Hill School
East Campus
10409 Academic Drive
Oakton, Virginia 22124

General Information Coed day academic program.
Program Focus Reading, writing and learning to interpret what you've read.
Academics English language/literature, reading, study skills, writing.
Program Information 1 session per year. Session length: 10 days in July. Ages: 7–9. 2–40 participants per session. Day program cost: $200.
Application Deadline Continuous.
Jobs Positions for high school students 16 and older and college students 18 and older.
Contact Ms. Peggy Laurent, Director of Special and Summer Programs, 3320 Jermantown Road, Oakton, Virginia 22124. Phone: 703-584-2315. Fax: 703-242-0718. E-mail: plaurent@flinthill.org.
URL www.flinthill.org

Flint Hill School–"Summer on the Hill"–Enrichment on the Hill–Scientific Super Sleuths

Flint Hill School
East Campus
10409 Academic Drive
Oakton, Virginia 22124

General Information Coed day academic program.
Program Focus Fun with science.
Academics Biology, chemistry, ecology, environmental science, science (general).
Special Interest Areas Field research/expeditions.
Trips Day.
Program Information 1 session per year. Session length: 5 days in June. Ages: 11–14. 2–40 participants per session. Day program cost: $460.
Application Deadline Continuous.
Jobs Positions for high school students 16 and older and college students 18 and older.
Contact Ms. Peggy Laurent, Director of Special and Summer Programs, 3320 Jermantown Road, Oakton, Virginia 22124. Phone: 703-584-2315. Fax: 703-242-0718. E-mail: plaurent@flinthill.org.
URL www.flinthill.org

Flint Hill School–"Summer on the Hill"–Enrichment on the Hill–Spanish Immersion Camp

Flint Hill School
East Campus
10409 Academic Drive
Oakton, Virginia 22124

General Information Coed day academic program and cultural program.
Program Focus Spanish immersion.
Academics Spanish language/literature, intercultural studies, reading, study skills, writing.
Arts Arts and crafts (general), dance, dance (Latin), music.
Special Interest Areas Culinary arts, field trips (arts and culture).
Trips Cultural, day.
Program Information 1 session per year. Session length: 15 days in July. Ages: 7–10. 2–30 participants per session. Day program cost: $1350.
Application Deadline Continuous.
Jobs Positions for high school students 16 and older and college students 18 and older.
Contact Ms. Peggy Laurent, Director of Special and Summer Programs, 3320 Jermantown Road, Oakton, Virginia 22124. Phone: 703-584-2315. Fax: 703-242-0718. E-mail: plaurent@flinthill.org.
URL www.flinthill.org

Flint Hill School–"Summer on the Hill"–Enrichment on the Hill–Study Skills for 9th Graders

Flint Hill School
West Campus
3320 Jermantown Road, Room B132
Oakton, Virginia 22124

General Information Coed day academic program. High school credit may be earned.
Program Focus Study skills and class management.
Academics Academics (general), reading, study skills, writing.
Program Information 1 session per year. Session length: 10 days in July. Ages: 13–14. 2–40 participants per session. Day program cost: $325.
Application Deadline Continuous.
Jobs Positions for high school students 16 and older and college students 18 and older.
Contact Ms. Peggy Laurent, Director of Special and Summer Programs, 3320 Jermantown Road, Oakton, Virginia 22124. Phone: 703-584-2315. Fax: 703-242-0718. E-mail: plaurent@flinthill.org.
URL www.flinthill.org

Flint Hill School–"Summer on the Hill"–Enrichment on the Hill–Summer Chess Camp

Flint Hill School
East Campus
10409 Academic Drive
Oakton, Virginia 22124

General Information Coed day sports camp.
Program Focus Chess.
Special Interest Areas Chess.
Program Information 1 session per year. Session length: 10 days in June, July. Ages: 7–12. 2–40 participants per session. Day program cost: $260.
Application Deadline Continuous.
Jobs Positions for high school students 16 and older and college students 18 and older.
Contact Ms. Peggy Laurent, Director of Special and Summer Programs, 3320 Jermantown Road, Oakton, Virginia 22124. Phone: 703-584-2315. Fax: 703-242-0718. E-mail: plaurent@flinthill.org.
URL www.flinthill.org

Flint Hill School–"Summer on the Hill"–Enrichment on the Hill–Summer Service

Flint Hill School
West Campus
3320 Jermantown Road
Oakton, Virginia 22124

General Information Coed day community service program. High school credit may be earned.
Special Interest Areas Community service.
Trips Day.
Program Information 1 session per year. Session length: 5 days in June, July. Ages: 14–18. 2–80 participants per session. Day program cost: $220.
Application Deadline Continuous.
Jobs Positions for high school students 16 and older and college students 18 and older.
Contact Ms. Peggy Laurent, Director of Special and Summer Programs, main address above. Phone: 703-584-2315. Fax: 703-242-0718. E-mail: plaurent@flinthill.org.
URL www.flinthill.org

Flint Hill School–"Summer on the Hill"–Into the Woods Day Camp

Flint Hill School
East Campus
10409 Academic Drive
Oakton, Virginia 22124

General Information Coed day outdoor program and adventure program.
Special Interest Areas Campcraft, nature study, outdoor cooking.
Wilderness/Outdoors Backpacking, hiking, orienteering, outdoor adventure, outdoor camping, outdoor living skills.

Flint Hill School–"Summer on the Hill"–Into the Woods Day Camp (continued)

Trips Day, overnight.
Program Information 1 session per year. Session length: 5 days in July. Ages: 9–12. 2–20 participants per session. Day program cost: $450.
Application Deadline Continuous.
Jobs Positions for high school students 16 and older and college students 18 and older.
Contact Ms. Peggy Laurent, Director of Special and Summer Programs, 3320 Jermantown Road, Oakton, Virginia 22124. Phone: 703-584-2315. Fax: 703-242-0718. E-mail: plaurent@flinthill.org.
URL www.flinthill.org

FLINT HILL SCHOOL–"SUMMER ON THE HILL"–JUNIOR DAY/DAY CAMPS

Flint Hill School
East Campus
10409 Academic Drive
Oakton, Virginia 22124

General Information Coed day traditional camp.
Program Focus Junior day camp for rising kindergarten and 1st grade, and day camp for rising 2nd-6th grade.
Academics English language/literature, academics (general), aerospace science, computers, language study, reading, science (general), writing.
Arts Acting, animation, arts and crafts (general), cartooning, ceramics, dance, drawing, fabric arts, jewelry making, music (instrumental), music (vocal), painting, photography, puppetry.
Special Interest Areas Culinary arts, nature study.
Sports Baseball, basketball, bicycling, football, lacrosse, soccer, tennis.
Trips Day.
Program Information 1–2 sessions per year. Session length: 15 days in June, July. Ages: 5–12. 2–80 participants per session. Day program cost: $785.
Application Deadline Continuous.
Jobs Positions for high school students 16 and older and college students 18 and older.
Contact Ms. Peggy Laurent, Director of Special and Summer Programs, 3320 Jermantown Road, Oakton, Virginia 22124. Phone: 703-584-2315. Fax: 703-242-0718. E-mail: plaurent@flinthill.org.
URL www.flinthill.org

FLINT HILL SCHOOL–"SUMMER ON THE HILL"–SPORTS ON THE HILL–COED

Flint Hill School
West Campus
3320 Jermantown Road
Oakton, Virginia 22124

General Information Coed day sports camp.
Program Focus Baseball, football, soccer, tennis, strength and conditioning.
Special Interest Areas Team building.
Sports Baseball, football, soccer, tennis, weight training.
Program Information 1–13 sessions per year. Session length: 5–30 days in June, July. Ages: 5–18. 2–80 participants per session. Day program cost: $110–$315.
Application Deadline Continuous.
Jobs Positions for high school students 16 and older and college students 18 and older.
Contact Ms. Peggy Laurent, Director of Special and Summer Programs, main address above. Phone: 703-584-2315. Fax: 703-242-0718. E-mail: plaurent@flinthill.org.
URL www.flinthill.org

FLINT HILL SCHOOL–"SUMMER ON THE HILL"–SPORTS ON THE HILL FOR BOYS

Flint Hill School
West Campus
3320 Jermantown Road
Oakton, Virginia 22124

General Information Boys' day sports camp.
Program Focus Boys basketball and lacrosse.
Special Interest Areas Team building.
Sports Basketball, lacrosse.
Program Information 1–3 sessions per year. Session length: 5–15 days in June, July. Ages: 7–14. 2–80 participants per session. Day program cost: $135–$160.
Application Deadline Continuous.
Jobs Positions for high school students 16 and older and college students 18 and older.
Contact Ms. Peggy Laurent, Director of Special and Summer Programs, main address above. Phone: 703-584-2315. Fax: 703-242-0718. E-mail: plaurent@flinthill.org.
URL www.flinthill.org

FLINT HILL SCHOOL–"SUMMER ON THE HILL"–SPORTS ON THE HILL FOR GIRLS

Flint Hill School
West Campus
3320 Jermantown Road
Oakton, Virginia 22124

General Information Girls' day sports camp.
Program Focus Girls' soccer, basketball, volleyball, and lacrosse camps.
Special Interest Areas Team building.
Sports Basketball, lacrosse, soccer, volleyball.
Program Information 1–5 sessions per year. Session length: 5–30 days in June, July. Ages: 7–14. 2–80 participants per session. Day program cost: $110–$160.
Application Deadline Continuous.
Jobs Positions for high school students 16 and older and college students 18 and older.
Contact Ms. Peggy Laurent, Director of Special and Summer Programs, main address above. Phone: 703-584-2315. Fax: 703-242-0718. E-mail: plaurent@flinthill.org.
URL www.flinthill.org

Flint Hill School–"Summer on the Hill"–Trips and Travel Day Camp

Flint Hill School
East Campus
10409 Academic Drive
Oakton, Virginia 22124

General Information Coed day traditional camp.
Program Focus Amusement parks, water parks, movies, trips and outdoor fun.
Special Interest Areas Field trips (arts and culture).
Sports Bicycling, canoeing, football.
Wilderness/Outdoors Backpacking, bicycle trips, canoe trips, hiking, outdoor adventure.
Trips Cultural, day.
Program Information 1–2 sessions per year. Session length: 5 days in June, July. Ages: 11–14. 2–30 participants per session. Day program cost: $465.
Application Deadline Continuous.
Jobs Positions for high school students 16 and older and college students 18 and older.
Contact Ms. Peggy Laurent, Director of Special and Summer Programs, 3320 Jermantown Road, Oakton, Virginia 22124. Phone: 703-584-2315. Fax: 703-242-0718. E-mail: plaurent@flinthill.org.
URL www.flinthill.org

4 Star Academics Junior Camp at the University of Virginia

4 Star Summer Camps at the University of Virginia
Charlottesville, Virginia 22905

General Information Coed residential and day traditional camp and academic program established in 1995.
Program Focus Wide variety of enrichment courses; academic courses can be combined with a half day of tennis, golf, recreational sports, informal excursions, or seminars.
Academics English as a second language, English language/literature, academics (general), art (Advanced Placement), business, mathematics, reading, speech/debate, study skills, writing.
Arts Creative writing, drawing, film, photography, television/video, theater/drama.
Special Interest Areas Electronics, field trips (arts and culture).
Sports Basketball, canoeing, figure skating, golf, horseback riding, soccer, swimming, tennis, volleyball.
Wilderness/Outdoors Canoe trips, hiking, white-water trips.
Trips College tours, cultural, day, shopping.
Program Information 3 sessions per year. Session length: 12 days in June, July, August. Ages: 12–15. 60–80 participants per session. Day program cost: $1850. Boarding program cost: $2350.
Application Deadline Continuous.
Jobs Positions for college students 19 and older.
Contact Ms. Marietta Naramore, Admissions Director, PO Box 3387, Falls Church, Virginia 22043-0387. Phone: 800-334-7827. Fax: 703-866-7775. E-mail: info@4starcamps.com.
URL www.4starcamps.com

4 Star Academics Scholars at the University of Virginia

4 Star Summer Camps at the University of Virginia
Charlottesville, Virginia 22905

General Information Coed residential and day academic program established in 2002. Formal opportunities for the academically talented. College credit may be earned.
Program Focus Pre-college experience, academic courses for college credit and enrichment courses, recreational sports, golf or tennis instruction, informal excursions.
Academics English language/literature, Italian language/literature, SAT/ACT preparation, Spanish language/literature, academics (general), anthropology, art history/appreciation, astronomy, biology, environmental science, geography, history, mathematics, music, philosophy, psychology, religion, social science, study skills.
Arts Creative writing, drawing, film, photography, television/video, theater/drama.
Sports Basketball, canoeing, golf, horseback riding, soccer, swimming, tennis, volleyball.
Wilderness/Outdoors Hiking, white-water trips.
Trips College tours, cultural, day, shopping.
Program Information 1 session per year. Session length: 31 days in July, August. Ages: 16–18. 60–80 participants per session. Day program cost: $4325–$4575. Boarding program cost: $5450–$5695. Application fee: $50.
Application Deadline Continuous.
Jobs Positions for college students 19 and older.
Contact Ms. Marietta Naramore, Admissions Director, PO Box 3387, Falls Church, Virginia 22043-0387. Phone: 800-334-7827. Fax: 703-866-7775. E-mail: info@4starcamps.com.
URL www.4starcamps.com

4 Star Academics Senior Camp at the University of Virginia

4 Star Summer Camps at the University of Virginia
Charlottesville, Virginia 22905

General Information Coed residential and day traditional camp and academic program established in 1995.
Program Focus Wide variety of enrichment courses; academic courses can be combined with a half day of tennis, golf, recreational sports, informal excursions, or seminars.
Academics English as a second language, English language/literature, SAT/ACT preparation, academics (general), art (Advanced Placement), business, mathematics, philosophy, psychology, reading, speech/debate, study skills, writing.
Arts Creative writing, drawing, film, photography, television/video, theater/drama.
Special Interest Areas Field trips (arts and culture).
Sports Basketball, canoeing, figure skating, golf, horseback riding, soccer, swimming, tennis, volleyball.
Wilderness/Outdoors Canoe trips, hiking, white-water trips.

4 Star Academics Senior Camp at the University of Virginia (continued)

Trips College tours, cultural, day, shopping.
Program Information 3 sessions per year. Session length: 12 days in June, July, August. Ages: 15–18. 60–80 participants per session. Day program cost: $1850. Boarding program cost: $2350.
Application Deadline Continuous.
Jobs Positions for college students 19 and older.
Contact Ms. Marietta Naramore, Admissions Director, PO Box 3387, Falls Church, Virginia 22043-0387. Phone: 800-334-7827. Fax: 703-866-7775. E-mail: info@4starcamps.com.
URL www.4starcamps.com

4 Star College Prep Tennis at the University of Virginia

4 Star Summer Camps at the University of Virginia
Charlottesville, Virginia 22905

General Information Coed residential and day sports camp established in 1998.
Program Focus Tennis instruction including coaching from college coaches and college style team matches.
Sports Tennis.
Trips College tours.
Program Information 1 session per year. Session length: 5 days in July. Ages: 15–18. 40–50 participants per session. Day program cost: $795. Boarding program cost: $995.
Application Deadline Continuous.
Contact Marietta Naramore, Admissions Director, PO Box 3387, Falls Church, Virginia 22043-0387. Phone: 800-334-7827. Fax: 703-866-7775. E-mail: info@4starcamps.com.
URL www.4starcamps.com

4 Star Golf Camp at the University of Virginia

4 Star Summer Camps at the University of Virginia
Charlottesville, Virginia 22905

General Information Coed residential and day sports camp established in 2002.
Program Focus Golf instruction and play.
Sports Golf.
Program Information 3 sessions per year. Session length: 5 days in June, July, August. Ages: 9–18. 40–50 participants per session. Day program cost: $795. Boarding program cost: $995.
Application Deadline Continuous.
Jobs Positions for college students 19 and older.
Contact Marietta Naramore, Admissions Director, PO Box 3387, Falls Church, Virginia 22043-0387. Phone: 800-334-7827. Fax: 703-866-7775. E-mail: info@4starcamps.com.
URL www.4starcamps.com

4 Star Golf Plus All Sports Camp at the University of Virginia

4 Star Summer Camps at the University of Virginia
Charlottesville, Virginia 22905

General Information Coed residential and day sports camp established in 1998.
Program Focus Combines a half-day of golf with recreational sports such as swimming, basketball, hiking, canoeing, and horseback riding.
Sports Basketball, canoeing, figure skating, golf, horseback riding, soccer, sports (general), swimming, volleyball.
Wilderness/Outdoors Canoe trips, hiking, white-water trips.
Trips Day.
Program Information 1–6 sessions per year. Session length: 5 days in June, July, August. Ages: 9–18. 60–80 participants per session. Day program cost: $695. Boarding program cost: $895.
Application Deadline Continuous.
Jobs Positions for college students 19 and older.
Contact Marietta Naramore, Admissions Director, PO Box 3387, Falls Church, Virginia 22043. Phone: 800-334-7827. Fax: 703-866-7775. E-mail: info@4starcamps.com.
URL www.4starcamps.com

4 Star Tennis Camp at the University of Virginia

4 Star Summer Camps at the University of Virginia
Charlottesville, Virginia 22905

General Information Coed residential and day sports camp established in 1975.
Program Focus Tennis instruction, match play, private lessons.
Sports Tennis.
Program Information 1–6 sessions per year. Session length: 5 days in June, July, August. Ages: 9–18. 60–80 participants per session. Day program cost: $595. Boarding program cost: $795.
Application Deadline Continuous.
Jobs Positions for college students 19 and older.
Contact Marietta Naramore, Admissions Director, PO Box 3387, Falls Church, Virginia 22043-0387. Phone: 800-334-7827. Fax: 703-866-7775. E-mail: info@4starcamps.com.
URL www.4starcamps.com

4 Star Tennis Plus Camp at the University of Virginia

4 Star Summer Camps at the University of Virginia
Charlottesville, Virginia 22905

General Information Coed residential and day sports camp established in 1998.
Program Focus Combine a half day of tennis with other recreational sports such as hiking, canoeing, horseback riding, swimming, basketball.
Sports Basketball, canoeing, figure skating, golf, horseback riding, soccer, sports (general), swimming, tennis, volleyball.

Wilderness/Outdoors Canoe trips, hiking, white-water trips.
Trips Day.
Program Information 1–6 sessions per year. Session length: 5 days in June, July, August. Ages: 9–18. 60–80 participants per session. Day program cost: $595–$695. Boarding program cost: $795–$895.
Application Deadline Continuous.
Jobs Positions for college students 19 and older.
Contact Marietta Naramore, Admissions Director, PO Box 3387, Falls Church, Virginia 22043-0387. Phone: 800-334-7827. Fax: 703-866-7775. E-mail: info@4starcamps.com.
URL www.4starcamps.com

4 Star Tennis Plus Golf Camp at the University of Virginia

4 Star Summer Camps at the University of Virginia
Charlottesville, Virginia 22905

General Information Coed residential and day sports camp established in 1998.
Program Focus Tennis and golf instruction and play.
Sports Golf, tennis.
Trips Day.
Program Information 1–6 sessions per year. Session length: 5 days in June, July, August. Ages: 9–18. 60–80 participants per session. Day program cost: $695. Boarding program cost: $895.
Application Deadline Continuous.
Jobs Positions for college students 19 and older.
Contact Marietta Naramore, Admissions Director, PO Box 3387, Falls Church, Virginia 22043-0387. Phone: 800-334-7827. Fax: 703-866-7775. E-mail: info@4starcamps.com.
URL www.4starcamps.com

Hargrave Summer Program

Hargrave Military Academy
Chatham, Virginia 24531

General Information Boys' residential and day academic program, outdoor program, and sports camp established in 1923. Religious affiliation: Baptist. High school credit may be earned.
Program Focus All students are required to choose at least one sports camp to attend in the afternoon session.
Academics English as a second language, English language/literature, SAT/ACT preparation, Spanish language/literature, academics (general), biology, computers, geography, government and politics, history, mathematics, mathematics (Advanced Placement), reading, science (general), social studies, study skills, writing.
Special Interest Areas Leadership training.
Sports Archery, baseball, basketball, canoeing, climbing (wall), fishing, football, rappelling, riflery, soccer, sports (general), swimming, tennis, weight training.
Wilderness/Outdoors Backpacking, canoe trips, hiking, orienteering, rock climbing.
Trips Day, overnight, shopping.
Program Information 1 session per year. Session length: 32–35 days in June, July. Ages: 11–19. 180–200 participants per session. Day program cost: $800. Boarding program cost: $3500. Application fee: $75.
Application Deadline June 15.
Jobs Positions for college students 19 and older.
Contact Frank Martin, Director of Admissions, main address above. Phone: 800-432-2480. Fax: 434-432-3129.
URL www.hargrave.edu

Special Note
Hargrave Military Academy is located in a beautiful setting of hills and valleys in southern Virginia. The campus is in proximity to historic battlefields and museums. The 214-acre campus is located within the town limits of Chatham. Chatham is 65 miles north of Greensboro, North Carolina, and 40 miles south of Lynchburg, Virginia, on U.S. Highway 29. The Academy opened its doors in 1909. The summer school was established in 1923. The summer school provides the opportunity for students to accelerate an academic program, strengthen weak areas, improve reading skills, learn study skills, and enjoy recreational and athletic experiences through the Academy's sports camp. It also gives the fall school applicant an opportunity to familiarize himself with school routine and the life of a boarding student and to spend a profitable and enjoyable summer. Hargrave also has a mandatory study period in the evening in order to enhance students' organizational and study habits.

Hollinsummer

Hollins University
Roanoke, Virginia 24020

General Information Girls' residential academic program and arts program established in 1983.
Program Focus Interdisciplinary courses focusing on the theme of creativity.
Academics Precollege program, premed, psychology, writing.
Arts Creative writing, dance (modern), film, film production, mask making, painting, photography, television/video.
Special Interest Areas Leadership training.
Sports Climbing (wall), ropes course, swimming, tennis, volleyball.
Wilderness/Outdoors Hiking.
Trips Cultural, day, shopping.
Program Information 1 session per year. Session length: 12 days in July. Ages: 15–18. 80–100 participants per session. Boarding program cost: $1045–$1100. Open to participants entering grades 9–12.
Application Deadline Continuous.
Contact Ms. Julie Aavatsmark, Sr. Assistant Director of Admissions, PO Box 9707, Roanoke, Virginia 24020. Phone: 800-456-4595. Fax: 540-362-6218. E-mail: jaavatsmark@hollins.edu.
URL www.hollins.edu/

iD Tech Camps–University of Virginia, Charlottesville, VA

iD Tech Camps
University of Virginia
Charlottesville, Virginia 22904

General Information Coed residential and day academic program established in 1999. Accredited by American Camping Association. Formal opportunities for the academically talented and artistically talented.
Program Focus High-tech computer camps for kids and teens; produce digital movies, create video games, design Web pages, learn programming and robotics, and more; one computer per student, small classes, campers complete a project in a creative and fun learning environment.
Academics Web page design, computer programming, computer science (Advanced Placement), computers, music, precollege program.
Arts Animation, cartooning, cinematography, digital media, drawing, film, film editing, film production, graphic arts, music, television/video.
Special Interest Areas Career exploration, computer graphics, electronics, leadership training, robotics, team building.
Sports Baseball, basketball, soccer, softball, swimming, volleyball.
Trips College tours, cultural, day.
Program Information 5 sessions per year. Session length: 5–7 days in June, July, August. Ages: 7–17. 40–50 participants per session. Day program cost: $639. Boarding program cost: $989. Application fee: $200. Financial aid available.
Application Deadline Continuous.
Jobs Positions for college students 18 and older.
Contact Client Service Representatives, 1885 Winchester Boulevard, Suite 201, Campbell, California 95008. Phone: 888-709-TECH. Fax: 408-871-2228. E-mail: requests@internaldrive.com.
URL www.internaldrive.com

For more information, see page 1156.

Joe Machnik's No. 1 Academy One and Premier Programs–Dyke, Virginia

Joe Machnik's No. 1 Camps
Blue Ridge School
Dyke, Virginia

General Information Coed residential and day sports camp.
Program Focus Soccer instruction, physical fitness, testing and speed training. Campers gain exposure to top players and are challenged by intense competition.
Sports Soccer.
Trips Day.
Program Information 1 session per year. Session length: 6 days in August. Ages: 9–18. Day program cost: $699. Boarding program cost: $759. Financial aid available.
Application Deadline Continuous.
Jobs Positions for college students.
Contact Dr. Joseph Machnik, Director, PO Box 389, 916 Palm Boulevard, Isle of Palms, South Carolina 29451. Phone: 800-622-4645. Fax: 843-886-0885. E-mail: info@no1soccercamps.com.
URL www.no1soccercamps.com

Joe Machnik's No. 1 Mighty Mini, Goalkeeper and Striker Camp–Dyke, Virginia

Joe Machnik's No. 1 Camps
Blue Ridge School
Dyke, Virginia

General Information Coed residential and day sports camp.
Program Focus Soccer instruction. Goalkeepers and strikers compete against each other daily.
Sports Soccer.
Trips Day.
Program Information 1 session per year. Session length: 6 days in August. Ages: 8–12. 100–150 participants per session. Boarding program cost: $429. Financial aid available.
Application Deadline Continuous.
Jobs Positions for college students.
Contact Dr. Joseph Machnik, Director, PO Box 389, 916 Palm Boulevard, Isle of Palms, South Carolina 29451. Phone: 800-622-4645. Fax: 843-886-0885. E-mail: info@no1soccercamps.com.
URL www.no1soccercamps.com

Landmark Volunteers: Virginia

Landmark Volunteers, Inc.
Virginia

General Information Coed residential outdoor program and community service program established in 1992. High school credit may be earned.
Program Focus Opportunity for high school students to earn community service credit while working as a team for two weeks serving Colonial National Historic Park/Jamestown-Yorktown Foundation, Kerr Reservoir & Wildlife Management Area or Virginia Center for the Creative Arts. Similar programs offered through Landmark Volunteers at over 60 locations in 21 states.
Academics Art (Advanced Placement), biology, ecology, environmental science, history, science (general).
Special Interest Areas Community service, conservation projects, construction, field research/expeditions, gardening, leadership training, nature study, team building, trail maintenance, work camp programs.
Sports Swimming.
Wilderness/Outdoors Hiking.
Trips Cultural, day.
Program Information 3 sessions per year. Session length: 2 weeks in June, July, August. Ages: 14–18. 10–13 participants per session. Boarding program cost: $875–$925. Financial aid available. $50 late application fee after April 1.
Application Deadline Continuous.
Jobs Positions for college students.

Contact Ann Barrett, Executive Director, PO Box 455, Sheffield, Massachusetts 01257. Phone: 413-229-0255. Fax: 413-229-2050. E-mail: landmark@volunteers.com.
URL www.volunteers.com
For more information, see page 1182.

Little Keswick School Summer Session

Little Keswick School
500 Little Keswick Lane
Keswick, Virginia 22947

General Information Boys' residential traditional camp and special needs program established in 1963. Formal opportunities for the academically talented. Specific services available for the emotionally challenged, developmentally challenged, and learning disabled. High school credit may be earned.
Academics English language/literature, mathematics, music, reading, writing.
Arts Arts and crafts (general), music, painting, woodworking.
Special Interest Areas Animal care.
Sports Basketball, canoeing, equestrian sports, fishing, horseback riding, lacrosse, soccer, swimming.
Wilderness/Outdoors Hiking.
Trips Cultural, day, overnight, shopping.
Program Information 1 session per year. Session length: 41 days in July, August. Ages: 10–15. 31–40 participants per session. Boarding program cost: $5585. Financial aid available.
Application Deadline Continuous.
Jobs Positions for college students 21 and older.
Contact Ms. Terry Columbus, Director, PO Box 24, Keswick, Virginia 22947. Phone: 434-295-0457. Fax: 434-977-1892. E-mail: columbuslks@aol.com.
URL www.avenue.org/lks

Makemie Woods Summer Camp

Presbytery of Eastern Virginia
3700 Ropers Church Road
Lanexa, Virginia 23089

General Information Coed residential bible camp established in 1964. Religious affiliation: Presbyterian. Accredited by American Camping Association.
Program Focus Developing self-esteem and fostering spiritual growth.
Academics Bible study.
Arts Acting, arts and crafts (general), music (folk), music (vocal), musical instrument construction/repair, photography, theater/drama.
Special Interest Areas Campcraft, community service, leadership training, nature study, outdoor cooking, worship.
Sports Archery, boating, canoeing, horseback riding, ropes course, sailing, soccer, swimming.
Wilderness/Outdoors Canoe trips, rafting, rock climbing, white-water trips.
Trips Overnight.
Program Information 37 sessions per year. Session length: 2–14 days in June, July, August. Ages: 7–18. 8–25 participants per session. Boarding program cost: $100–$500. Financial aid available.
Application Deadline Continuous.
Jobs Positions for high school students 16 and older and college students 18 and older.
Contact Ms. Karen Broughman, Office Manager, PO Box 39, Barhamsville, Virginia 23011. Phone: 800-566-1496. Fax: 757-566-8803. E-mail: makwoods@makwoods.org.
URL www.makwoods.org/sumcamp/sumcamp.htm

Massanutten Military Academy Summer Cadet Program

Massanutten Military Academy
614 South Main Street
Woodstock, Virginia 22664

General Information Coed residential and day academic program established in 1899. Religious affiliation: United Church of Christ. Formal opportunities for the academically talented. High school credit may be earned.
Program Focus Army JROTC.
Academics American literature, English as a second language, English language/literature, French language/literature, German language/literature, Greek language/literature, Russian language/literature, SAT/ACT preparation, Spanish language/literature, academics (general), biology, chemistry, computers, government and politics, history, mathematics, precollege program, reading, science (general), social science, social studies, study skills.
Arts Arts and crafts (general), drawing, painting.
Special Interest Areas Career exploration, leadership training.
Sports Baseball, basketball, football, riflery, soccer, softball, swimming, weight training.
Wilderness/Outdoors Mountaineering, orienteering.
Trips Cultural, day, shopping.
Program Information 1 session per year. Session length: 25 days in June, July. Ages: 11+. 150–200 participants per session. Day program cost: $1450–$2610. Boarding program cost: $2150–$3310. Application fee: $100.
Application Deadline June 26.
Jobs Positions for high school students 16 and older and college students 18 and older.
Contact Frank Thomas, Director of Admissions, main address above. Phone: 877-466-6222 Ext.263. Fax: 540-459-5421. E-mail: admissions@militaryschool.com.
URL www.militaryschool.com

The National Music Workshop Day Jams–Alexandria, VA

National Guitar Workshop
St. Stephens and St. Agnes School
4401 West Braddock Road
Alexandria, Virginia 22304

General Information Coed day arts program established in 1999. Formal opportunities for the artistically talented.
Program Focus Rock 'n' roll day camp.
Academics Music.
Arts Arts and crafts (general), band, guitar, music, music (rock), music (vocal), television/video.
Program Information 3 sessions per year. Session length: 5–15 days in July. Ages: 9–15. 40–70 participants per session. Day program cost: $425–$495. Application fee: $35. Financial aid available.
Application Deadline Continuous.
Jobs Positions for high school students 17 and older and college students 17 and older.
Contact Lynda Wlodarczyk, Associate Director, 407A Bantam Road, Suite 1, Litchfield, Connecticut 06759. Phone: 800-295-5956. Fax: 860-567-0374. E-mail: lynda@dayjams.com.
URL www.dayjams.com

Oak Hill Academy Summer Program

Oak Hill Academy
2635 Oak Hill Road
Mouth of Wilson, Virginia 24363

General Information Coed residential and day academic program established in 1878. Religious affiliation: Southern Baptist. High school credit may be earned.
Academics English language/literature, Spanish language/literature, academics (general), biology, chemistry, geography, government and politics, history, mathematics, science (general), social studies.
Sports Basketball, canoeing, horseback riding, soccer, softball, swimming, tennis, volleyball, weight training.
Wilderness/Outdoors Hiking.
Program Information 1 session per year. Session length: 36 days in June, July. Ages: 13–19. 65–70 participants per session. Boarding program cost: $3575. Application fee: $50. Day program costs negotiated individually.
Application Deadline Continuous.
Contact Dr. Michael D. Groves, Director of Admissions, main address above. Phone: 276-579-2619. Fax: 276-579-4722. E-mail: info@oak-hill.net.
URL www.oak-hill.net

Potomac School Summer Programs

The Potomac School
1301 Potomac School Road
McLean, Virginia 22101

General Information Coed day traditional camp established in 1965. High school credit may be earned.
Academics Chemistry, humanities, study skills.
Arts Acting, arts and crafts (general), band, batiking, chorus, creative writing, dance, drawing, fabric arts, film, music, music (chamber), music (instrumental), music (vocal), musical productions, photography, theater/drama, weaving.
Special Interest Areas Nature study, robotics.
Sports Basketball, canoeing, lacrosse, soccer, street/roller hockey, swimming, tennis.
Wilderness/Outdoors Canoe trips, hiking, rock climbing.
Trips Day, overnight.
Program Information 3 sessions per year. Session length: 5–15 days in June, July, August. Ages: 3–17. 660 participants per session. Day program cost: $200–$1200. Financial aid available.
Application Deadline Continuous.
Jobs Positions for high school students 16 and older and college students 16 and older.
Contact Ms. Jennifer Van Horn, Assistant to the Director, PO Box 430, McLean, Virginia 22101. Phone: 703-749-6317. Fax: 703-883-9031. E-mail: jennifer_vanhorn@potomacschool.org.
URL www.potomacschool.org

Randolph-Macon Academy Summer Programs

Randolph-Macon Academy
200 Academy Drive
Front Royal, Virginia 22630

General Information Coed residential and day academic program established in 1966. Religious affiliation: United Methodist. High school credit may be earned.

Randolph-Macon Academy Summer Programs

Academics English as a second language, English language/literature, French language/literature, Latin language, Spanish language/literature, academics (general), biology, chemistry, computers, government and politics, history, mathematics, physics, science (general), social studies, study skills, writing.
Special Interest Areas Flight instruction.
Sports Baseball, basketball, soccer, softball, swimming, tennis, volleyball, weight training.
Wilderness/Outdoors Hiking.

Trips Day.
Program Information 1 session per year. Session length: 27 days in July. Ages: 11–19. 220–240 participants per session. Day program cost: $285–$800. Boarding program cost: $3000–$3560. Application fee: $75–$200.
Application Deadline Continuous.
Contact Mr. Frank Gardner, Recruiter, main address above. Phone: 800-272-1172. Fax: 540-636-5419. E-mail: admissions@rma.edu.
URL www.rma.edu

For more information, see page 1278.

Sidwell Friends Riverview Programs

Sidwell Friends School
444 Water Lane
Tappahannock, Virginia 22560

General Information Coed residential and day traditional camp and academic program established in 2000. Religious affiliation: Society of Friends.
Program Focus Hands-on enrichment workshops in a college-prep environment.
Academics Archaeology, computers, environmental science, journalism, marine studies, mathematics, psychology, science (general), speech/debate, study skills, writing.
Arts Arts and crafts (general), dance, theater/drama.
Special Interest Areas Community service, culinary arts, leadership training, nautical skills.
Sports Canoeing, golf, lacrosse, sailing, soccer, swimming, tennis, waterskiing.
Trips Day, overnight.
Program Information 2 sessions per year. Session length: 6–12 days in July, August. Ages: 9–15. 30–80 participants per session. Day program cost: $300–$375. Boarding program cost: $625–$1400.
Application Deadline Continuous.
Jobs Positions for college students.
Contact Sidwell Friends Summer Programs, 3825 Wisconsin Avenue, NW, Washington, District of Columbia 20016. Phone: 202-537-8133. Fax: 202-537-2483. E-mail: sidwellsummer@yahoo.com.
URL www.sidwell.edu/summer

Sidwell Friends Women's Leadership–St. Margaret's School

Sidwell Friends School
Tappahannock, Virginia 22560

General Information Girls' residential academic program and outdoor program established in 1995. Religious affiliation: Society of Friends.
Program Focus Leadership, team building, self-esteem, personal growth, skill building.
Special Interest Areas Leadership training, self-defense.
Sports Canoeing, ropes course, sailing, swimming.
Trips College tours.
Program Information 1 session per year. Session length: 1 week in July, August. Ages: 13–18. 30 participants per session. Boarding program cost: $775–$825.
Application Deadline Continuous.
Jobs Positions for college students.
Contact Sidwell Friends Summer Programs, 3825 Wisconsin Avenue, NW, Washington, District of Columbia 20016. Phone: 202-537-8133. Fax: 202-537-2483. E-mail: sidwellsummer@yahoo.com.
URL www.sidwell.edu/summer

Student Conservation Association–Conservation Crew Program (Virginia)

Student Conservation Association (SCA)
Virginia

General Information Coed residential outdoor program, community service program, and wilderness program established in 1957. High school credit may be earned.
Program Focus Resource management, conservation and environmental education.
Academics Biology, botany, ecology, environmental science, geology/earth science, history.
Special Interest Areas Campcraft, community service, construction, leadership training, nature study, trail maintenance, work camp programs.
Sports Canoeing, fishing, kayaking, swimming.
Wilderness/Outdoors Backpacking, canoe trips, hiking, orienteering, outdoor living skills, wilderness camping.
Trips Cultural, day, overnight.
Program Information 2–3 sessions per year. Session length: 3–5 weeks in June, July, August. Ages: 15–19. 6–8 participants per session. Application fee: $20. Financial aid available. No cost for program; financial aid possible for travel expenses.
Application Deadline Continuous.
Jobs Positions for college students 21 and older.
Contact Recruitment Office, PO Box 550, Charlestown, New Hampshire 03603. Phone: 603-543-1700. Fax: 603-543-1828. E-mail: getreal@thesca.org.
URL www.theSCA.org

Student Conservation Association–Conservation Leadership Corps–Washington, DC Metropolitan Area

Student Conservation Association (SCA)
1800 North Kent Street, Suite 102
Arlington, Virginia 22209

General Information Coed day outdoor program and community service program established in 1996.
Program Focus Conservation service for students in the District of Columbia, Maryland and Virginia.
Academics Biology, botany, ecology, environmental science, geology/earth science.
Special Interest Areas Community service, leadership training, nature study, work camp programs.
Wilderness/Outdoors Canoe trips, hiking.
Trips Cultural, day, overnight.
Program Information Session length: 6 weeks in January, February, March, April, May, June, July,

Student Conservation Association–Conservation Leadership Corps–Washington, DC Metropolitan Area (continued)

August, September, October, November, December. Ages: 15–18. 54 participants per session. Financial aid available. No cost for program; financial aid possible for travel expenses.
Application Deadline May 15.
Jobs Positions for high school students 15 and older and college students.
Contact Mr. James Corcoran, Conservation Service Coordinator, main address above. Phone: 703-524-2441. Fax: 703-524-2451. E-mail: jcorcoran@thesca.org.
URL www.theSCA.org

Summer Leadership Education and Training

Massanutten Military Academy
614 South Main Street
Woodstock, Virginia 22664

General Information Coed residential and day academic program established in 2003. Religious affiliation: United Church of Christ. High school credit may be earned.
Program Focus Army JROTC.
Special Interest Areas Leadership training, military program.
Sports Baseball, basketball, cheerleading, football, riflery, soccer, softball, swimming, weight training.
Wilderness/Outdoors Mountaineering, orienteering.
Trips Cultural, day, shopping.
Program Information 1 session per year. Session length: 25 days in July. Ages: 11–19. 10–30 participants per session. Day program cost: $1450–$2610. Boarding program cost: $2150–$3310. Application fee: $100.
Application Deadline June 26.
Jobs Positions for high school students 16 and older and college students 18 and older.
Contact Mr. Frank Thomas, Director of Admissions, main address above. Phone: 540-459-2167 Ext.263. Fax: 540-459-5421. E-mail: admissions@militaryschool.com.
URL www.militaryschool.com

Summer Programs on the River; Crew/Rowing Camp

Christchurch School
49 Seahorse Lane
Christchurch, Virginia 23031

General Information Coed residential and day sports camp established in 1995. Religious affiliation: Episcopal.
Program Focus Crew/rowing camp.
Sports Baseball, basketball, canoeing, fishing, lacrosse, rowing (crew/sculling), sailing, soccer, softball, swimming, tennis, volleyball.
Trips Day.
Program Information 1–4 sessions per year. Session length: 6–28 days in June, July. Ages: 12–17. 30–35 participants per session. Day program cost: $380–$1900. Boarding program cost: $630–$3660.
Application Deadline Continuous.
Jobs Positions for high school students 16 and older and college students 17 and older.
Contact Admissions at Christchurch School, main address above. Phone: 800-296-2306. Fax: 804-758-0721. E-mail: admission@christchurchschool.org.
URL www.christchurchschool.org

For more information, see page 1072.

Summer Programs on the River; Marine Science Camp

Christchurch School
49 Seahorse Lane
Christchurch, Virginia 23031

General Information Coed residential outdoor program established in 1984. Religious affiliation: Episcopal.
Program Focus Marine science camps.
Academics Marine studies.
Sports Baseball, basketball, canoeing, fishing, lacrosse, rowing (crew/sculling), sailing, soccer, softball, swimming, tennis, volleyball.
Wilderness/Outdoors Canoe trips.
Trips Day.
Program Information 1–2 sessions per year. Session length: 2 weeks in June, July. Ages: 12–17. 17–20 participants per session. Day program cost: $380–$1900. Boarding program cost: $630–$3660.
Application Deadline Continuous.
Jobs Positions for high school students 17 and older and college students 18 and older.
Contact Admissions at Christchurch School, main address above. Phone: 800-296-2306. Fax: 804-758-0721. E-mail: admission@christchurchschool.org.
URL www.christchurchschool.org

For more information, see page 1072.

Summer Programs on the River; Sailing Camp

Christchurch School
49 Seahorse Lane
Christchurch, Virginia 23031

General Information Coed residential and day sports camp established in 1921. Religious affiliation: Episcopal.
Program Focus Sailing camp.
Sports Baseball, basketball, canoeing, fishing, lacrosse, rowing (crew/sculling), sailing, soccer, softball, swimming, tennis, volleyball.
Trips Day.
Program Information 1–4 sessions per year. Session length: 6–28 days in June, July. Ages: 10–17. 30–40 participants per session. Day program cost: $380–$1900. Boarding program cost: $630–$3660.
Application Deadline Continuous.
Jobs Positions for high school students 16 and older and college students 17 and older.

Summer Programs on the River; Sailing Camp

Contact Admissions at Christchurch School, main address above. Phone: 800-296-2306. Fax: 804-758-0721. E-mail: admission@christchurchschool.org.
URL www.christchurchschool.org
For more information, see page 1072.

Summer Programs on the River; Skills Program

Christchurch School
49 Seahorse Lane
Christchurch, Virginia 23031

General Information Coed residential and day academic program established in 1921. Religious affiliation: Episcopal.
Program Focus Skills program: math, writing, and study; sailing or crew/rowing.
Academics Mathematics, study skills, writing.
Sports Baseball, basketball, canoeing, fishing, lacrosse, rowing (crew/sculling), sailing, soccer, softball, tennis, volleyball.
Trips Day.
Program Information 1 session per year. Session length: 4 weeks in June, July. Ages: 12–17. 9–27 participants per session. Day program cost: $500–$2200. Boarding program cost: $3500–$3800.
Application Deadline Continuous.
Jobs Positions for college students 21 and older.
Contact Admissions at Christchurch School, main address above. Phone: 800-296-2306. Fax: 804-758-0721. E-mail: admission@christchurchschool.org.
URL www.christchurchschool.org
For more information, see page 1072.

Washington and Lee University Summer Scholars

Washington and Lee University
Hill House
Lexington, Virginia 24450

General Information Coed residential academic program established in 1981. Formal opportunities for the academically talented and gifted.
Program Focus Pre-college orientation.
Academics English language/literature, academics (general), biology, business, chemistry, communications, computers, economics, environmental science, government and politics, history, humanities, journalism, music, philosophy, psychology, writing.
Arts Chorus, drawing, music (vocal).
Special Interest Areas Community service.
Sports Basketball, golf, lacrosse, racquetball, soccer, softball, swimming, tennis, volleyball.
Wilderness/Outdoors Hiking.
Trips Cultural, day.
Program Information 1 session per year. Session length: 4 weeks in July. Ages: 16–18. 150–160 participants per session. Boarding program cost: $2500. Financial aid available.
Application Deadline Continuous.
Contact Dr. Mimi Milner Elrod, Director, main address above. Phone: 540-458-8727. Fax: 540-458-8113. E-mail: summerscholars@wlu.edu.
URL summerscholars.wlu.edu

Wilderness Adventure at Eagle Landing

Route #2
New Castle, Virginia 24127

General Information Coed residential outdoor program and wilderness program established in 1990. Accredited by American Camping Association.
Program Focus Wilderness experience, development of leadership skills, teamwork, and self-confidence.
Academics Ecology, environmental science, geology/earth science.
Special Interest Areas Native American culture, community service, leadership training, nature study, team building.
Sports Bicycling, canoeing, climbing (wall), kayaking, rappelling, ropes course, scuba diving, sea kayaking, snorkeling.
Wilderness/Outdoors Backpacking, bicycle trips, canoe trips, caving, hiking, mountain biking, mountaineering, orienteering, outdoor living skills, rafting, rock climbing, survival training, white-water trips, wilderness camping, zip line.
Trips Cultural, overnight.
Program Information 65–75 sessions per year. Session length: 1–4 weeks in January, February, March, April, May, June, July, August, September, October, November, December. Ages: 9–18. 12 participants per session. Boarding program cost: $545–$2830. Financial aid available.
Application Deadline Continuous.

Wilderness Adventure at Eagle Landing (continued)
Jobs Positions for high school students 17 and older and college students 18 and older.
Contact Dave Cohan, Director of Administration, PO Box 760, New Castle, Virginia 24127. Phone: 800-782-0779. Fax: 540-864-6800. E-mail: info@wilderness-adventure.com.
URL www.wilderness-adventure.com

Woodberry Forest Basketball Camp

Woodberry Forest School
Woodberry Station
Woodberry Forest, Virginia 22989

General Information Boys' residential and day sports camp.
Program Focus Basketball.
Special Interest Areas Team building.
Sports Basketball.
Program Information 1–2 sessions per year. Session length: 5 days in July. Ages: 10–14. 40–50 participants per session. Day program cost: $130. Boarding program cost: $437–$450. Application fee: $50. Financial aid available.
Application Deadline Continuous.
Jobs Positions for college students 21 and older.
Contact Summer Admissions, 272 Woodberry Station, Woodberry Forest, Virginia 22989. Phone: 540-672-6047. E-mail: wfs_summer@woodberry.org.
URL www.woodberry.org

Woodberry Forest Golf Camp

Woodberry Forest School
Woodberry Station
Woodberry Forest, Virginia 22989

General Information Coed day sports camp.
Program Focus Golf.
Sports Golf.
Program Information 1–5 sessions per year. Session length: 5 days in July. Ages: 9–17. 12 participants per session. Day program cost: $325. Application fee: $50. Financial aid available.
Application Deadline Continuous.
Jobs Positions for college students 21 and older.
Contact Summer Admissions, 272 Woodberry Station, Woodberry Forest, Virginia 22989. Phone: 540-672-6047. E-mail: wfs_summer@woodberry.org.
URL www.woodberry.org

Woodberry Forest Junior Adventure

Woodberry Forest School
354 Woodberry Station
Woodberry Forest, Virginia 22989

General Information Coed residential and day academic program established in 1998. Formal opportunities for the academically talented and artistically talented.
Program Focus Gifted and talented.
Academics Academics (general), art history/appreciation, astronomy, computer programming, computers, history, humanities, mathematics, music, physics, reading, science (general), writing.
Arts Arts and crafts (general), ceramics, creative writing, dance, film, music, painting, photography, pottery, television/video, theater/drama.
Special Interest Areas Career exploration, community service, field research/expeditions, nature study, touring.
Sports Baseball, basketball, bicycling, canoeing, climbing (wall), cross-country, fishing, football, golf, kayaking, racquetball, ropes course, soccer, softball, swimming, tennis, track and field, volleyball.
Wilderness/Outdoors Backpacking, bicycle trips, canoe trips, hiking, mountain biking, rafting, rock climbing, white-water trips.
Trips Cultural, day, overnight.
Program Information 1 session per year. Session length: 3 weeks in June, July. Ages: 12–15. 25–40 participants per session. Day program cost: $1900. Boarding program cost: $2839. Application fee: $50. Financial aid available.
Application Deadline Continuous.
Jobs Positions for college students 21 and older.
Summer Contact Dr. W. David McRae, Director, Woodberry Forest Summer Experience, Woodberry Forest, Virginia 22989. Phone: 540-672-6047. Fax: 540-672-9076. E-mail: wfs_summer@woodberry.org.
Winter Contact Holly Baker, Woodberry Forest Summer Experience, Woodberry Forest, Virginia 22989. Phone: 540-672-6047. Fax: 540-672-9076. E-mail: wfs_summer@woodberry.org.
URL www.woodberry.org
For more information, see page 1402.

Woodberry Forest Lacrosse Camp

Woodberry Forest School
Woodberry Station
Woodberry Forest, Virginia 22989

General Information Boys' residential sports camp.
Program Focus Lacrosse.
Special Interest Areas Team building.
Sports Lacrosse.
Program Information 1 session per year. Session length: 5 days in July. Ages: 10–14. 70–80 participants per session. Boarding program cost: $468. Application fee: $50. Financial aid available.
Application Deadline Continuous.
Jobs Positions for college students 21 and older.
Contact Summer Admissions, 272 Woodberry Station, Woodberry Forest, Virginia 22989. Phone: 540-672-6047. E-mail: wfs_summer@woodberry.org.
URL www.woodberry.org

Woodberry Forest Senior Adventure

Woodberry Forest School
Woodberry Station
Woodberry Forest, Virginia 22989

General Information Coed residential and day academic program established in 1922. Formal opportunities for the academically talented and artistically talented.

Woodberry Forest Senior Adventure

Academics English as a second language, English language/literature, French language/literature, SAT/ACT preparation, Spanish language/literature, academics (general), art history/appreciation, biology, computers, history, journalism, mathematics, music, reading, speech/debate, study skills, writing.
Arts Arts and crafts (general), creative writing, dance, drawing, music, painting, photography, pottery, theater/drama.
Special Interest Areas Community service, driver's education, field research/expeditions.
Sports Baseball, basketball, bicycling, canoeing, climbing (wall), cross-country, fishing, football, golf, horseback riding, in-line skating, kayaking, racquetball, rappelling, ropes course, soccer, softball, squash, swimming, tennis, track and field, volleyball, weight training.
Wilderness/Outdoors Backpacking, bicycle trips, canoe trips, hiking, mountain biking, rafting, rock climbing, white-water trips, wilderness camping.
Trips Cultural, day, overnight, shopping.
Program Information 1 session per year. Session length: 27 days in June, July. Ages: 12–17. 100–160 participants per session. Day program cost: $2600. Boarding program cost: $3822. Application fee: $50. Financial aid available.
Application Deadline Continuous.
Jobs Positions for college students 21 and older.
Summer Contact Dr. W. David McRae, Director of Summer Programs, 354 Woodberry Station, Woodberry Forest, Virginia 22989. Phone: 540-672-6047. Fax: 540-672-9076. E-mail: wfs_summer@woodberry.org.
Winter Contact Lori Brown, Summer Programs Assistant, 354 Woodberry Station, Woodberry Forest, Virginia 22989. Phone: 540-672-6047. Fax: 540-672-9076. E-mail: wfs_summer@woodberry.org.
URL www.woodberry.org

For more information, see page 1402.

Woodberry Forest Sports Camp

Woodberry Forest School
Woodberry Station
Woodberry Forest, Virginia 22989

General Information Boys' residential sports camp established in 1967.
Program Focus Team and individual sports.
Special Interest Areas Field research/expeditions, leadership training, team building.
Sports Baseball, basketball, bicycling, canoeing, climbing (wall), cross-country, fishing, football, golf, horseback riding, in-line skating, kayaking, racquetball, rappelling, ropes course, soccer, softball, sports (general), squash, swimming, tennis, track and field, volleyball, weight training.
Trips Day.
Program Information 1 session per year. Session length: 20–28 days in June, July. Ages: 10–13. 70–80 participants per session. Boarding program cost: $3276. Application fee: $50. Financial aid available.
Application Deadline Continuous.
Jobs Positions for college students 21 and older.
Contact Assistant Athletic Director, 272 Woodberry Station, Woodberry Forest, Virginia 22989. Phone: 540-672-6044. E-mail: wfs_summer@woodberry.org.
URL www.woodberry.org

WASHINGTON

A.C.E. Intercultural Institute

American Cultural Exchange
Seattle Pacific University
Seattle, Washington

General Information Coed residential traditional camp, academic program, and cultural program established in 1996.
Program Focus Campers include American and international youths.
Academics English as a second language, English language/literature, Japanese language/literature, Spanish language/literature, computers, intercultural studies.
Arts Arts and crafts (general), music, painting, puppetry.
Special Interest Areas Cross-cultural education, homestays, touring.
Sports Boating, soccer, softball, swimming, volleyball.
Wilderness/Outdoors Hiking.
Trips Day.
Program Information 4 sessions per year. Session length: 8–21 days in July, August. Ages: 16+. 12 participants per session. Boarding program cost: $845–$1935. Application fee: $100–$300.
Application Deadline Continuous.
Contact Mr. Chris Gilman, Program Coordinator, 200 West Mercer Street, Suite 504, Seattle, Washington 98119. Phone: 206-217-9644. Fax: 206-217-9641. E-mail: cgilman@cultural.org.
URL www.cultural.org

Adventures in Science and Arts

Western Washington University
516 High Street
Bellingham, Washington 98225

General Information Coed residential and day academic program and arts program established in 1982. Formal opportunities for the academically talented. Specific services available for the hearing impaired and physically challenged.
Program Focus Science, arts, academic enrichment, and personal development.
Academics Academics (general), architecture, art history/appreciation, astronomy, biology, chemistry, economics, engineering, environmental science, geology/earth science, humanities, journalism, marine studies, mathematics, physics, precollege program, science (general), social studies, technology, writing.
Arts Arts, arts and crafts (general), batiking, creative writing, drawing, painting, photography, television/video, theater/drama.
Special Interest Areas Internet accessibility, career exploration, nature study.
Sports Noncompetitive sports, swimming.
Wilderness/Outdoors Hiking.
Trips College tours, day.
Program Information 5 sessions per year. Session length: 5 days in June, July. Ages: 8–18. 85–100 participants per session. Day program cost: $250. Boarding program cost: $525.
Application Deadline May 31.
Jobs Positions for college students 18 and older.
Contact Debbie Young Gibbons, Program Manager, Extended Education and Summer Programs, Mail Stop 5293, 516 High Street, Bellingham, Washington 98225. Phone: 360-650-6820. Fax: 360-650-6858. E-mail: adventures@wwu.edu.
URL www.wwu.edu/~adventur

Adventure Treks–Pacific Northwest Adventures

Adventure Treks, Inc.
Washington

General Information Coed travel outdoor program, wilderness program, and adventure program established in 1978.
Program Focus Multi-activity outdoor adventure program with an emphasis on fun, personal growth, leadership, teamwork, and outdoor skills.
Sports Sea kayaking.
Wilderness/Outdoors Backpacking, hiking, mountaineering, orienteering, rafting, rock climbing, white-water trips, wilderness camping.
Program Information 3–4 sessions per year. Session length: 16–20 days in June, July, August. Ages: 13–16. 24 participants per session. Cost: $2095–$2595. Financial aid available.
Application Deadline Continuous.
Contact John Dockendorf, Director, PO Box 1321, Flat Rock, North Carolina 28731. Phone: 888-954-5555. Fax: 828-696-1663. E-mail: info@advtreks.com.
URL www.adventuretreks.com

Aerospace Camp Experience

The Museum of Flight
9404 East Marginal Way South
Seattle, Washington 98108

General Information Coed day academic program established in 1965. Accredited by American Camping Association. Formal opportunities for the academically talented and artistically talented.
Program Focus Aviation and aerospace.
Academics Aerospace science, astronomy, biology, chemistry, communications, computers, engineering, geography, geology/earth science, history, humanities, mathematics, meteorology, physics, physiology, reading, science (general), writing.
Arts Arts and crafts (general), drawing, graphic arts.
Special Interest Areas Career exploration, flight instruction, leadership training, model rocketry, robotics.
Sports Swimming.
Wilderness/Outdoors Hiking, orienteering, survival training.
Trips Day, overnight.
Program Information 11 sessions per year. Session length: 5 days in June, July, August. Ages: 6–16. 15–40 participants per session. Day program cost: $250–$410. Application fee: $25. Financial aid available.
Application Deadline Continuous.
Jobs Positions for college students 19 and older.
Contact Mr. Erik Oost, Ace Coordinator, The Museum of Flight. Phone: 206-768-7141. Fax: 206-764-5707. E-mail: ace@museumofflight.org.
URL www.museumofflight.org/ace

Alpengirl–Washington

Alpengirl, Inc.
Olympic National Park
Washington

General Information Girls' travel outdoor program, wilderness program, and adventure program established in 1997. Accredited by American Camping Association.
Program Focus Promoting fitness and health through mountain adventure and outdoor education.
Academics Area studies, ecology, geology/earth science, marine studies, science (general).
Special Interest Areas Field research/expeditions, nature study, weight reduction.
Sports Bicycling, canoeing, horseback riding, physical fitness, rappelling, sailing, sea kayaking, swimming.
Wilderness/Outdoors Backpacking, bicycle trips, canoe trips, hiking, pack animal trips, rafting, rock climbing, white-water trips, wilderness camping, wilderness/outdoors (general).
Trips Cultural, day, overnight.
Program Information 2 sessions per year. Session length: 2 weeks in August. Ages: 12–16. 10 participants per session. Cost: $1775. Financial aid available.
Application Deadline Continuous.
Jobs Positions for college students 21 and older.
Contact Alissa Farley, Camp Director, PO Box 1138, Manhattan, Montana 59741. Phone: 800-585-7476. E-mail: alissa@alpengirl.com.
URL www.alpengirl.com

Alpengirl–Washington Alpenguide Training

Alpengirl, Inc.
Washington

General Information Girls' travel outdoor program, wilderness program, and adventure program. Accredited by American Camping Association.
Program Focus Wilderness first aid and CPR certification, trip planning, budgeting, leadership, teaching, back packing, adventures.
Academics Area studies, ecology, geology/earth science, science (general).
Sports Sailing, sea kayaking, swimming.
Wilderness/Outdoors Backpacking, hiking, wilderness camping.
Trips Cultural, day, overnight, shopping.
Program Information 1 session per year. Session length: 23 days in July, August. Ages: 16–17. 10–12 participants per session. Cost: $2300. Financial aid available.
Application Deadline Continuous.
Jobs Positions for college students 21 and older.
Contact Alissa Farley, Camp Owner, PO Box 1138, Manhattan, Montana 59741. Phone: 800-585-7476. Fax: 406-284-9036. E-mail: alissa@alpengirl.com.
URL www.alpengirl.com

Alpengirl–Washington Lil' Alpengirl

Alpengirl, Inc.
Washington

General Information Girls' travel outdoor program, wilderness program, and adventure program. Accredited by American Camping Association.
Program Focus Beach back packing, rain forest hiking, outdoor education, tent camping.
Academics Area studies, ecology, geology/earth science, science (general).
Sports Swimming.
Wilderness/Outdoors Backpacking, hiking, wilderness camping.
Trips Cultural, day, overnight, shopping.
Program Information 1 session per year. Session length: 1 week in August. Ages: 11–12. 10–12 participants per session. Cost: $700. Financial aid available.
Application Deadline Continuous.
Jobs Positions for college students 21 and older.
Contact Alissa Farley, Camp Owner, PO Box 1138, Manhattan, Montana 59741. Phone: 800-585-7476. Fax: 406-284-9036. E-mail: alissa@alpengirl.com.
URL www.alpengirl.com

The Art Institute of Seattle–Studio 101

The Art Institute of Seattle
2323 Elliott Avenue
Seattle, Washington 98121

General Information Coed residential arts program established in 1985. Specific services available for the physically challenged.
Program Focus Insight into career possibilities in art.
Academics Art (Advanced Placement).
Arts Animation, design, fashion design/production, graphic arts, interior design, photography, television/video.
Special Interest Areas Computer graphics, culinary arts, industrial arts.
Trips College tours, day, overnight.
Program Information 1 session per year. Session length: 3–4 days in June. Ages: 16–18. 100–120 participants per session. Boarding program cost: $350.
Application Deadline June 4.
Contact Mr. Chris Galbraith, High School Admissions Information Specialist, main address above. Phone: 800-275-2471. Fax: 206-269-0275. E-mail: cgalbraith@aii.edu.
URL www.ais.edu

Camp Berachah Ministries–Counselor-In-Training

Camp Berachah Ministries Christian Camps and Conferences
19830 South East 328th Place
Auburn, Washington 98092-2212

General Information Coed day traditional camp and bible camp established in 1990. Religious affiliation: Christian.
Program Focus Counselor-in-training program.
Academics Bible study, religion.
Arts Arts and crafts (general).
Special Interest Areas Counselor-in-training program, leadership training, team building.
Sports Archery, basketball, bicycling, bicycling (BMX), canoeing, climbing (wall), equestrian sports, golf, riflery, ropes course, swimming, volleyball.
Wilderness/Outdoors Mountain biking.
Trips Day.
Program Information 11 sessions per year. Ages: 13–17. 5–25 participants per session. Day program cost: $30. Application fee: $30. Financial aid available.
Application Deadline May 1.
Jobs Positions for high school students 16 and older and college students.
Contact Mr. Steve Altick, Executive Director, main address above. Phone: 800-859-CAMP. Fax: 253-833-7027. E-mail: staff@campberachah.org.
URL www.berachahcamp.org

Camp Berachah Ministries–Day Camp

Camp Berachah Ministries Christian Camps and Conferences
19830 South East 328th Place
Auburn, Washington 98092-2212

General Information Coed day traditional camp and bible camp. Religious affiliation: Christian. Specific services available for the developmentally challenged and hearing impaired.
Academics Bible study, religion.
Arts Arts and crafts (general).
Sports Archery, basketball, bicycling, bicycling (BMX), climbing (wall), equestrian sports, horseback riding, riflery, ropes course, soccer, softball, swimming, volleyball.
Wilderness/Outdoors Hiking, mountain biking.
Trips Day, overnight.
Program Information 11 sessions per year. Session length: 5 days in June, July, August. Ages: 5–12. Day program cost: $115. Application fee: $30. Financial aid available.
Application Deadline Continuous.
Jobs Positions for high school students 16 and older and college students 18 and older.
Contact Mr. Steve Altick, Executive Director, main address above. Phone: 800-859-CAMP. Fax: 253-833-7027. E-mail: staff@campberachah.org.
URL www.berachahcamp.org

Camp Berachah Ministries–Horse Day Camp

Camp Berachah Ministries Christian Camps and Conferences
Red Barn Ranch
17601 South East Lake Money Smith Road
Auburn, Washington 98092

General Information Coed day traditional camp and bible camp. Religious affiliation: Christian. Specific services available for the developmentally challenged and hearing impaired.
Program Focus Horseback riding.
Academics Bible study.
Arts Arts and crafts (general).
Sports Equestrian sports, horseback riding, swimming.
Program Information 10 sessions per year. Session length: 5 days in June, July, August. Ages: 7–13. 24 participants per session. Day program cost: $175. Application fee: $30. Financial aid available.
Application Deadline Continuous.
Jobs Positions for high school students 16 and older and college students 18 and older.
Contact Mr. Steve Altick, Executive Director, main address above. Phone: 800-859-CAMP. Fax: 253-833-7027. E-mail: staff@campberachah.org.
URL www.berachahcamp.org

Camp Berachah Ministries–Junior Camp

Camp Berachah Ministries Christian Camps and Conferences
19830 South East 328th Place
Auburn, Washington 98092-2212

General Information Coed residential traditional camp and bible camp. Religious affiliation: Christian. Specific services available for the developmentally challenged and hearing impaired.
Academics Bible study, religion.
Arts Arts and crafts (general).
Sports Archery, basketball, bicycling, bicycling (BMX), boating, canoeing, climbing (wall), equestrian sports, horseback riding, riflery, ropes course, soccer, softball, swimming, volleyball.
Wilderness/Outdoors Hiking, mountain biking.
Trips Day.
Program Information 3 sessions per year. Session length: 6 days in July, August. 150–300 participants per session. Boarding program cost: $220. Application fee: $30. Financial aid available. Open to participants entering grades 5–7.
Application Deadline Continuous.
Jobs Positions for high school students 16 and older and college students 18 and older.
Contact Mr. Steve Altick, Executive Director, main address above. Phone: 800-859-CAMP. Fax: 253-833-7027. E-mail: staff@campberachah.org.
URL www.berachahcamp.org

Camp Berachah Ministries–Leadership Expedition Camp

Camp Berachah Ministries Christian Camps and Conferences
Washington

General Information Coed residential outdoor program, bible camp, and adventure program. Religious affiliation: Christian. Specific services available for the developmentally challenged and hearing impaired.
Academics Bible study, religion.
Sports Bicycling, challenge course, climbing (wall), ropes course, swimming.
Wilderness/Outdoors Backpacking, hiking, mountain biking, orienteering, outdoor adventure, rafting, rock climbing, wilderness camping.
Trips Day, overnight.
Program Information 5 sessions per year. Session length: 5–6 days in July, August. 13 participants per session. Boarding program cost: $295–$315. Application fee: $30. Financial aid available. Open to participants entering grade 8–college freshmen.
Application Deadline Continuous.
Jobs Positions for high school students 16 and older and college students 18 and older.
Contact Mr. Steve Altick, Executive Director, main address above. Phone: 800-859-CAMP. Fax: 253-833-7027. E-mail: staff@campberachah.org.
URL www.berachahcamp.org

Camp Berachah Ministries–Legend Teen Camp

Camp Berachah Ministries Christian Camps and Conferences
19830 South East 328th Place
Auburn, Washington 98092-2212

General Information Coed residential traditional camp and bible camp. Religious affiliation: Christian. Specific services available for the developmentally challenged and hearing impaired.
Academics Bible study, religion.
Arts Arts and crafts (general).
Special Interest Areas Leadership training.
Sports Archery, baseball, basketball, bicycling, bicycling (BMX), canoeing, climbing (wall), equestrian sports, horseback riding, riflery, ropes course, soccer, softball, swimming, volleyball, waterskiing.
Wilderness/Outdoors Hiking, mountain biking.
Trips Day.
Program Information 1 session per year. Session length: 6 days in July. Boarding program cost: $225. Application fee: $30. Financial aid available. Open to participants entering grade 7–college freshmen.
Application Deadline Continuous.
Jobs Positions for high school students 16 and older and college students 18 and older.
Contact Mr. Steve Altick, Executive Director, main address above. Phone: 800-859-CAMP. Fax: 253-833-7027. E-mail: staff@campberachah.org.
URL www.berachahcamp.org

Camp Berachah Ministries–Overnight Horse Camp

Camp Berachah Ministries Christian Camps and Conferences
19830 South East 328th Place
Auburn, Washington 98092-2212

General Information Coed residential traditional camp and bible camp. Religious affiliation: Christian. Specific services available for the developmentally challenged and hearing impaired.
Program Focus Horseback riding.
Academics Bible study.
Arts Arts and crafts (general).
Sports Archery, basketball, bicycling, bicycling (BMX), canoeing, cross-country, equestrian sports, horseback riding, riflery, ropes course, soccer, softball, swimming, volleyball.
Wilderness/Outdoors Mountain biking.
Program Information 11 sessions per year. Session length: 5 days in June, July, August. Ages: 8–16. Boarding program cost: $275. Application fee: $30. Financial aid available. One coed session for all skill levels, other sessions available for girls only or boys only at specific skill levels, contact camp for details.
Application Deadline Continuous.
Jobs Positions for high school students 16 and older and college students 18 and older.
Contact Mr. Steve Altick, Executive Director, main address above. Phone: 800-859-CAMP. Fax: 253-833-7027. E-mail: staff@campberachah.org.
URL www.berachahcamp.org

Camp Berachah Ministries–Primary Camp

Camp Berachah Ministries Christian Camps and Conferences
19830 South East 328th Place
Auburn, Washington 98092-2212

General Information Coed residential traditional camp and bible camp. Religious affiliation: Christian. Specific services available for the developmentally challenged and hearing impaired.
Academics Bible study, religion.
Arts Arts and crafts (general).
Sports Archery, basketball, bicycling, canoeing, climbing (wall), equestrian sports, horseback riding, riflery, ropes course, soccer, softball, swimming, volleyball.
Wilderness/Outdoors Canoe trips, hiking, mountain biking.
Program Information 2 sessions per year. Session length: 3 days in June, July. Boarding program cost: $99–$115. Application fee: $30. Financial aid available. Open to participants entering grades 2–4.
Application Deadline Continuous.
Jobs Positions for high school students 16 and older and college students 18 and older.
Contact Mr. Steve Altick, Executive Director, main address above. Phone: 800-859-CAMP. Fax: 253-833-7027. E-mail: staff@campberachah.org.
URL www.berachahcamp.org

Camp Berachah Ministries–Soccer Camp

Camp Berachah Ministries Christian Camps and Conferences
19830 South East 328th Place
Auburn, Washington 98092-2212

General Information Coed residential sports camp and bible camp. Religious affiliation: Christian. Specific services available for the developmentally challenged and hearing impaired.
Program Focus Soccer.
Academics Bible study, religion.
Arts Arts and crafts (general).
Sports Archery, bicycling, bicycling (BMX), canoeing, climbing (wall), equestrian sports, horseback riding, ropes course, soccer, swimming, volleyball.
Program Information 1 session per year. Session length: 4 days in July, August. Ages: 8–16. Boarding program cost: $325–$330. Application fee: $30. Financial aid available.
Application Deadline Continuous.
Jobs Positions for high school students 16 and older and college students 18 and older.

Camp Berachah Ministries–Soccer Camp (continued)
Contact Mr. Steve Altick, Executive Director, main address above. Phone: 800-859-CAMP. Fax: 253-833-7027. E-mail: staff@campberachah.org.
URL www.berachahcamp.org

Camp Berachah Ministries–Teen Leadership

Camp Berachah Ministries Christian Camps and Conferences
19830 South East 328th Place
Auburn, Washington 98092-2212

General Information Coed residential traditional camp and bible camp. Religious affiliation: Christian. Specific services available for the developmentally challenged and hearing impaired.
Academics Bible study, religion.
Arts Arts and crafts (general).
Special Interest Areas Leadership training.
Sports Archery, basketball, bicycling, bicycling (BMX), canoeing, climbing (wall), equestrian sports, horseback riding, riflery, ropes course, soccer, softball, swimming, volleyball.
Wilderness/Outdoors Hiking, mountain biking.
Program Information 1 session per year. Session length: 6 days in July. Boarding program cost: $225–$230. Application fee: $30. Financial aid available. Open to participants entering grade 10–college freshmen.
Application Deadline Continuous.
Jobs Positions for high school students 16 and older and college students 18 and older.
Contact Mr. Steve Altick, Executive Director, main address above. Phone: 800-859-CAMP. Fax: 253-833-7027. E-mail: staff@campberachah.org.
URL www.berachahcamp.org

Camp Berachah Ministries–Wrangler-In-Training

Camp Berachah Ministries Christian Camps and Conferences
19830 South East 328th Place
Auburn, Washington 98092-2212

General Information Girls' residential traditional camp and bible camp. Religious affiliation: Christian. Specific services available for the developmentally challenged and hearing impaired.
Program Focus Horseback riding.
Academics Bible study.
Special Interest Areas Leadership training.
Sports Climbing (wall), equestrian sports, horseback riding, ropes course, swimming.
Program Information 9 sessions per year. Session length: 5 days in June, July, August. Ages: 14–16. Boarding program cost: $130. Application fee: $30. Financial aid available. One coed session available.
Application Deadline Continuous.
Jobs Positions for high school students 16 and older and college students 18 and older.
Contact Mr. Steve Altick, Executive Director, main address above. Phone: 800-859-CAMP. Fax: 253-833-7027. E-mail: staff@campberachah.org.
URL www.berachahcamp.org

Camp Nor'wester

Camp Nor'wester
262 Weeks Road
Lopez Island, Washington 98261

General Information Coed residential traditional camp and outdoor program established in 1935.
Program Focus Development of group living skills, self-confidence and environmental awareness.
Arts Arts and crafts (general), batiking, ceramics, dance (folk), drawing, fabric arts, graphic arts, jewelry making, leather working, metalworking, music, painting, pottery, printmaking, theater/drama, weaving, woodworking.
Special Interest Areas Native American culture, campcraft, gardening, nature study, nautical skills, team building.
Sports Archery, bicycling, boating, canoeing, kayaking, ropes course, sailing, sea kayaking, soccer, swimming, volleyball.
Wilderness/Outdoors Backpacking, bicycle trips, canoe trips, hiking, mountaineering, outdoor camping.
Trips Day, overnight.
Program Information 2 sessions per year. Session length: 12–28 days in June, July, August. Ages: 9–16. 140–180 participants per session. Boarding program cost: $1500–$3000. Application fee: $100. Financial aid available.
Application Deadline Continuous.
Jobs Positions for high school students 18 and older and college students 19 and older.
Summer Contact Mr. Paul S. Henriksen, Director, PO Box 4395, Roche Harbor, Washington 98250. Phone: 360-468-2225. Fax: 360-468-2472. E-mail: norwester@rockisland.com.
Winter Contact Mr. Paul S. Henriksen, Director, PO Box 668, Lopez Island, Washington 98261. Phone: 360-468-2225. Fax: 360-468-2472. E-mail: norwester@rockisland.com.
URL www.norwester.org

College Quest

Western Washington University
516 High Street
Bellingham, Washington 98225

General Information Coed residential academic program established in 2000. Formal opportunities for the academically talented. Specific services available for the hearing impaired, physically challenged, and visually impaired. College credit may be earned.
Program Focus Pre-college earning credit.
Academics Environmental science, humanities, journalism, precollege program, study skills.
Arts Arts and crafts (general), creative writing.
Special Interest Areas Leadership training.
Sports Noncompetitive sports, swimming.
Wilderness/Outdoors Hiking.

Trips College tours, day.
Program Information 1 session per year. Session length: 6 days in August. Ages: 15–18. 20–50 participants per session. Boarding program cost: $750.
Application Deadline June 15.
Contact Debbie Young Gibbons, Program Manager, Extended Education and Summer Programs, Mail Stop 5293, 516 High Street, Bellingham, Washington 98225. Phone: 360-650-6820. Fax: 360-650-6858. E-mail: adventures@wwu.edu.
URL www.wwu.edu/~adventur

Cybercamps–University of Washington

Cybercamps–Giant Campus, Inc.
University of Washington
Seattle, Washington

General Information Coed residential and day academic program established in 1997.
Program Focus High tech computer camps featuring project oriented curriculum in Web design, 3D animation, game design, robotics, digital arts and programming for all ability levels.
Academics Web page design, computer programming, computers.
Arts Animation, creative writing, digital media, graphic arts, photography.
Special Interest Areas Computer game design, computer graphics, robotics, team building.
Sports Frisbee golf, ultimate frisbee.
Program Information 2–9 sessions per year. Session length: 5–30 days in June, July, August. Ages: 7–18. 30–150 participants per session. Day program cost: $599–$849. Boarding program cost: $974–$1224.
Application Deadline Continuous.
Jobs Positions for high school students 15 and older and college students.
Contact Cybercamps Information Office, 2401 4th Avenue, Suite 1110, Seattle, Washington 98121. Phone: 206-442-4500. Fax: 206-442-4501. E-mail: info@cybercamps.com.
URL www.cybercamps.com

Cybercamps–University of Washington, Bothell

Cybercamps–Giant Campus, Inc.
Bothell, Washington

General Information Coed day academic program established in 1997.
Program Focus High tech computer camps featuring project oriented curriculum in Web design, 3D animation, game design, robotics, digital arts and programming for all ability levels.
Academics Web page design, computer programming, computers.
Arts Animation, creative writing, digital media, graphic arts, photography.
Special Interest Areas Computer game design, computer graphics, robotics, team building.
Sports Frisbee golf, ultimate frisbee.
Program Information 2–9 sessions per year. Session length: 5–30 days in June, July, August. Ages: 7–18. 30–150 participants per session. Day program cost: $589–$799. Financial aid available.
Application Deadline Continuous.
Jobs Positions for high school students 15 and older and college students.
Contact Cybercamps Information Office, 2401 4th Avenue, Suite 1110, Seattle, Washington 98121. Phone: 206-442-4500. Fax: 206-442-4501. E-mail: info@cybercamps.com.
URL www.cybercamps.com

DigiPen Institute of Technology Junior Game Developer Workshop

DigiPen Institute of Technology
5001 150th Avenue, NE
Redmond, Washington 98052

General Information Coed day academic program and arts program. High school credit may be earned.
Program Focus Video game development process.
Academics Computers.
Arts Digital media, graphic arts.
Special Interest Areas Career exploration, computer game design, computer graphics.
Program Information 5 sessions per year. Session length: 2 weeks in June, July, August. 15–40 participants per session. Day program cost: $600. Application fee: $50. Financial aid available. Open to participants entering grades 5–7.
Application Deadline Continuous.
Jobs Positions for college students 18 and older.
Contact Ms. Gina Corpening, Admissions and Outreach Coordinator, main address above. Phone: 425-558-0299. Fax: 425-558-0378. E-mail: gcorpeni@digipen.edu.
URL workshops.digipen.edu
For more information, see page 1088.

DigiPen Institute of Technology Robotics Workshop

DigiPen Institute of Technology
5001 150th Avenue, NE
Redmond, Washington 98052

General Information Coed day academic program and arts program. High school credit may be earned.
Program Focus Robotics mechanics, electronics, and software.
Academics Computers.
Special Interest Areas Electronics, robotics.
Program Information 5 sessions per year. Session length: 2 weeks in June, July, August. 15–40 participants per session. Day program cost: $845. Application fee: $50. Financial aid available. Open to participants entering grade 8 or above.
Application Deadline Continuous.
Jobs Positions for college students 18 and older.

DigiPen Institute of Technology Robotics Workshop (continued)

Contact Ms. Gina Corpening, Admissions and Outreach Coordinator, main address above. Phone: 425-558-0299. Fax: 425-558-0378. E-mail: gcorpeni@digipen.edu.
URL workshops.digipen.edu
For more information, see page 1088.

DigiPen Institute of Technology 3D Computer Animation Workshop

DigiPen Institute of Technology
5001 150th Avenue, NE
Redmond, Washington 98052

General Information Coed day academic program and arts program established in 1998. High school credit may be earned.
Program Focus 3-D animation production.
Academics Computers.
Arts Animation, digital media, graphic arts, television/video.
Special Interest Areas Career exploration, computer game design, computer graphics.
Program Information 5 sessions per year. Session length: 2 weeks in June, July, August. Ages: 13+. 15–40 participants per session. Day program cost: $795. Application fee: $50. Level one or level two available to participants depending on background.
Application Deadline Continuous.
Jobs Positions for college students 18 and older.
Contact Ms. Gina Corpening, Admissions and Outreach Coordinator, main address above. Phone: 425-558-0299. Fax: 425-558-0378. E-mail: gcorpeni@digipen.edu.
URL workshops.digipen.edu
For more information, see page 1088.

DigiPen Institute of Technology Video Game Programming Workshop

DigiPen Institute of Technology
5001 150th Avenue, NE
Redmond, Washington 98052

General Information Coed day academic program established in 1998. High school credit may be earned.
Program Focus Video game programming.
Academics Computer programming, computers.
Arts Graphic arts.
Special Interest Areas Career exploration, computer game design.
Program Information 5 sessions per year. Session length: 2 weeks in June, July, August. Ages: 14+. 15–40 participants per session. Day program cost: $795. Application fee: $50. Level one or level two available to participants depending on background.
Application Deadline Continuous.
Jobs Positions for college students 18 and older.
Contact Ms. Gina Corpening, Admissions and Outreach Coordinator, main address above. Phone: 425-558-0299. Fax: 425-558-0378. E-mail: gcorpeni@digipen.edu.
URL workshops.digipen.edu
For more information, see page 1088.

Earthwatch Institute–Caring for Chimpanzees

Earthwatch Institute
Ellensburg, Washington

General Information Coed residential outdoor program and adventure program.
Program Focus Evaluating captive chimpanzee environments to improve primate care.
Academics Biology, ecology, environmental science, science (general).
Special Interest Areas Animal care, field research/expeditions, nature study.
Program Information 8 sessions per year. Session length: 2 weeks in March, April, June, July, August, October, November. Ages: 16+. 12 participants per session. Boarding program cost: $1995–$2095. Financial aid available. Financial aid for high school students and teachers.
Application Deadline Continuous.
Contact General Information Desk, PO Box 75, Maynard, Massachusetts 01754. Phone: 800-776-0188. Fax: 978-461-2332. E-mail: info@earthwatch.org.
URL www.earthwatch.org

Earthwatch Institute–Conservation Research Initiative–Mountain Meadows of the North Cascades

Earthwatch Institute
Washington

General Information Coed residential outdoor program and wilderness program.
Program Focus Collecting baseline data on the status of the mountain meadows to aid in their conservation and the restoration of the Skagit watershed.
Academics Botany, ecology, environmental science.
Special Interest Areas Field research/expeditions, nature study.
Wilderness/Outdoors Backpacking, hiking, wilderness camping.
Program Information 2 sessions per year. Session length: 12 days in July, August. Ages: 16+. 8 participants per session. Boarding program cost: $1795–$1895. Financial aid available. Financial aid for high school students and teachers.
Application Deadline Continuous.
Contact General Information Desk, PO Box 75, Maynard, Massachusetts 01754. Phone: 800-776-0188. Fax: 978-461-2332. E-mail: info@earthwatch.org.
URL www.earthwatch.org

EARTHWATCH INSTITUTE–CONSERVATION RESEARCH INITIATIVE–RESTORING WILD SALMON

Earthwatch Institute
Washington

General Information Coed residential outdoor program, cultural program, and adventure program.
Program Focus Evaluating experiments in rehabilitating salmon habitat.
Academics Ecology, environmental science, science (general).
Special Interest Areas Field research/expeditions, nature study.
Program Information 2 sessions per year. Session length: 10 days in June, July. Ages: 16+. 6 participants per session. Boarding program cost: $1795–$1895. Financial aid available. Financial aid for high school students and teachers.
Application Deadline Continuous.
Contact General Information Desk, PO Box 75, Maynard, Massachusetts 01754. Phone: 800-776-0188. Fax: 978-461-2332. E-mail: info@earthwatch.org.
URL www.earthwatch.org

EARTHWATCH INSTITUTE–CONSERVATION RESEARCH INITIATIVE–SALMON HOTSPOTS OF THE SKAGIT RIVER

Earthwatch Institute
Skagit River
Washington

General Information Coed residential outdoor program.
Program Focus Determining the role of tributaries in maintaining biodiversity and habitat quality for endangered Pacific salmon.
Academics Ecology, environmental science, marine studies.
Arts Television/video.
Special Interest Areas Animal care, field research/expeditions, nature study.
Sports Fishing, snorkeling, swimming.
Wilderness/Outdoors Climbing, hiking, wilderness/outdoors (general).
Program Information 2 sessions per year. Session length: 12 days in June, July. Ages: 16+. 8 participants per session. Boarding program cost: $1795–$1895. Financial aid available. Financial aid for high school students and teachers.
Application Deadline Continuous.
Contact General Information Desk, PO Box 75, Maynard, Massachusetts 01754. Phone: 800-776-0188. Fax: 978-461-2332. E-mail: info@earthwatch.org.
URL www.earthwatch.org

EARTHWATCH INSTITUTE–CONSERVATION RESEARCH INITIATIVE–SALMON OF THE PACIFIC NORTHWEST

Earthwatch Institute
Washington

General Information Coed residential outdoor program.
Program Focus Assessing stream and riparian restoration projects to benefit threatened salmon populations.
Academics Ecology.
Special Interest Areas Conservation projects, field research/expeditions, nature study.
Program Information 5 sessions per year. Session length: 1 week in June, July, August, September, November. Ages: 16+. 8 participants per session. Boarding program cost: $1195–$1295. Financial aid available. Financial aid for high school students and teachers.
Application Deadline Continuous.
Contact General Information Desk, PO Box 75, Maynard, Massachusetts 01754. Phone: 800-776-0188. Fax: 978-461-2332. E-mail: info@earthwatch.org.
URL www.earthwatch.org

EARTHWATCH INSTITUTE–CONSERVATION RESEARCH INITIATIVE–TRADITIONS OF CEDAR, SALMON, AND GOLD

Earthwatch Institute
Washington

General Information Coed residential outdoor program.
Program Focus Documenting cultural transitions in historic resource use in the Pacific Northwest to guide future management.
Academics Archaeology, forestry, history.
Special Interest Areas Field research/expeditions.
Program Information 3 sessions per year. Session length: 12 days in May, August, September. Ages: 16+. 12 participants per session. Boarding program cost: $1795–$1895. Financial aid available. Financial aid for high school students and teachers.
Application Deadline Continuous.
Contact General Information Desk, PO Box 75, Maynard, Massachusetts 01754. Phone: 800-776-0188. Fax: 978-461-2332. E-mail: info@earthwatch.org.
URL www.earthwatch.org

EARTHWATCH INSTITUTE–ORCA

Earthwatch Institute
Puget Sound
Washington

General Information Coed residential outdoor program and adventure program.
Program Focus Investigating human impact on a top marine predator.
Academics Biology, ecology, environmental science, marine studies, science (general).

EARTHWATCH INSTITUTE–Orca (continued)

Special Interest Areas Field research/expeditions, nature study.
Program Information 9 sessions per year. Session length: 11 days in June, July, August, September, October. Ages: 16+. 8 participants per session. Boarding program cost: $2195–$2295. Financial aid available. Financial aid for high school students and teachers.
Application Deadline Continuous.
Contact General Information Desk, PO Box 75, Maynard, Massachusetts 01754. Phone: 800-776-0188. Fax: 978-461-2332. E-mail: info@earthwatch.org.
URL www.earthwatch.org

Explore Nor'wester

Camp Nor'wester
John's Island
Washington

General Information Coed residential family program established in 2002.
Program Focus Introduce families to Camp Nor'wester program.
Arts Arts and crafts (general), ceramics, dance (folk), drawing, fabric arts, painting, pottery, printmaking.
Special Interest Areas Native American culture, nature study.
Sports Archery, canoeing, kayaking.
Program Information 1 session per year. Session length: 4 days in August. Ages: 7–12. 60 participants per session. Boarding program cost: $150.
Application Deadline Continuous.
Summer Contact Mr. Paul Henriksen, Director, PO Box 4395, Roche Harbor, Washington 98250. Phone: 360-468-2225. Fax: 360-468-2472. E-mail: norwester@rockisland.com.
Winter Contact Mr. Paul Henriksen, Director, PO Box 668, Lopez Island, Washington 98261. Phone: 360-468-2225. Fax: 360-468-2472. E-mail: norwester@rockisland.com.
URL www.norwester.org

Forest Ridge Summer Program

Forest Ridge School of the Sacred Heart
4800 139th Avenue, SE
Bellevue, Washington 98006

General Information Coed day traditional camp established in 2002.
Program Focus Sports, technology, and arts as well as traditional camp offerings.
Academics English language/literature, SAT/ACT preparation, Spanish language/literature, academics (general), computers, environmental science, intercultural studies, journalism, mathematics, writing.
Arts Acting, arts and crafts (general), creative writing, drawing, film, jewelry making, painting, television/video, theater/drama.
Special Interest Areas Gardening.
Sports Basketball, climbing (wall), lacrosse, soccer, sports (general), tennis, volleyball.
Wilderness/Outdoors Rock climbing.
Trips Cultural, day.
Program Information 2–4 sessions per year. Session length: 5–10 days in June, July, August. Ages: 9–19. 30–100 participants per session. Day program cost: $125–$600. Financial aid available.
Application Deadline Continuous.
Jobs Positions for high school students 16 and older and college students 18 and older.
Contact Ms. Melissa Miller, Summer Program Director, main address above. Phone: 425-641-0700 Ext.1113. Fax: 425-643-3881. E-mail: mmiller@forestridge.org.
URL www.forestridge.org

Four Winds * Westward Ho

Four Winds, Inc.
286 Four Winds Lane
Deer Harbor, Washington 98243

General Information Coed residential traditional camp established in 1927. Accredited by American Camping Association.
Academics Ecology.
Arts Arts and crafts (general), batiking, ceramics, dance (folk), drawing, fabric arts, music (vocal), painting, photography, pottery, printmaking, theater/drama, weaving, woodworking.
Special Interest Areas Animal care, campcraft, gardening, leadership training, work camp programs.
Sports Archery, basketball, canoeing, equestrian sports, fishing, horseback riding, kayaking, lacrosse, sailing, sea kayaking, soccer, softball, tennis, volleyball.
Wilderness/Outdoors Backpacking, canoe trips.
Trips Overnight.
Program Information 2 sessions per year. Session length: 4 weeks in June, July, August. Ages: 9–16. 160–170 participants per session. Boarding program cost: $3450. Application fee: $50. Financial aid available.
Application Deadline Continuous.
Jobs Positions for college students 18 and older.
Contact Michael Douglas, Interim Director, PO Box 140, Deer Harbor, Washington 98243. Phone: 360-376-2277. E-mail: info@fourwindscamp.org.
URL www.fourwindscamp.org

GLOBAL WORKS–Adventure Travel-Pacific Northwest-3 weeks

GLOBAL WORKS
Washington

General Information Coed travel community service program and adventure program established in 1988. High school credit may be earned.
Program Focus Community service, adventure travel.
Academics Biology, ecology, environmental science.
Arts Arts and crafts (general).
Special Interest Areas Community service, conservation projects, construction, field research/expeditions.
Sports Basketball, kayaking, sea kayaking, soccer, volleyball.
Wilderness/Outdoors Hiking, outdoor adventure, rock climbing, wilderness camping.
Trips Cultural, day, overnight.

Program Information 2 sessions per year. Session length: 3 weeks in June, July, August. Ages: 14–18. 16 participants per session. Cost: $2950–$3050. Application fee: $100. Financial aid available.
Application Deadline Continuous.
Jobs Positions for college students 23 and older.
Contact Mr. Erik Werner, Director, 1113 South Allen Street, State College, Pennsylvania 16801. Phone: 814-867-7000. Fax: 814-867-2717. E-mail: info@globalworksinc.com.
URL www.globalworksinc.com

For more information, see page 1136.

iD Tech Camps–University of Washington, Seattle, WA

iD Tech Camps
University of Washington
Seattle, Washington 98195

General Information Coed residential and day academic program established in 1999. Accredited by American Camping Association. Formal opportunities for the academically talented and artistically talented.
Program Focus High-tech computer camps for kids and teens; produce digital movies, create video games, design Web pages, learn programming and robotics, and more; one computer per student, small classes, campers complete a project in a creative and fun learning environment.
Academics Web page design, computer programming, computer science (Advanced Placement), computers, music, precollege program.
Arts Animation, cinematography, digital media, drawing, film, film editing, film production, graphic arts, music, television/video.
Special Interest Areas Career exploration, computer graphics, electronics, leadership training, robotics, team building.
Sports Baseball, basketball, soccer, softball, swimming, volleyball.
Trips College tours, cultural, day.
Program Information 5 sessions per year. Session length: 5–7 days in June, July, August. Ages: 7–17. 40–50 participants per session. Day program cost: $639. Boarding program cost: $989. Application fee: $200. Financial aid available.
Application Deadline Continuous.
Jobs Positions for college students 18 and older.
Contact Client Service Representatives, 1885 Winchester Boulevard, Suite 201, Campbell, California 95008. Phone: 888-709-TECH. Fax: 408-871-2228. E-mail: requests@internaldrive.com.
URL www.internaldrive.com

For more information, see page 1156.

Joe Machnik's No. 1 Academy One and Premier Programs–Olympia, Washington

Joe Machnik's No. 1 Camps
Evergreen State University
Olympia, Washington

General Information Coed residential and day sports camp.
Program Focus Soccer instruction, physical fitness, testing and speed training. Campers gain exposure to top players and are challenged by intense competition.
Sports Soccer.
Trips Day.
Program Information 1 session per year. Session length: 6 days in July, August. Ages: 9–18. Day program cost: $699. Boarding program cost: $759. Financial aid available.
Application Deadline Continuous.
Jobs Positions for college students.
Contact Dr. Joseph Machnik, Director, PO Box 389, 916 Palm Boulevard, Isle of Palms, South Carolina 29451. Phone: 800-622-4645. Fax: 843-886-0885. E-mail: info@no1soccercamps.com.
URL www.no1soccercamps.com

Joe Machnik's No. 1 Mighty Mini, Goalkeeper and Striker Camp–Olympia, Washington

Joe Machnik's No. 1 Camps
The Evergreen State College
Olympia, Washington

General Information Coed residential and day sports camp established in 1977.
Program Focus Soccer instruction. Goalkeepers and strikers compete against each other daily.
Sports Soccer, swimming.
Program Information 1 session per year. Session length: 6 days in July. Ages: 8–12. 100–150 participants per session. Boarding program cost: $429. Financial aid available.
Application Deadline Continuous.
Jobs Positions for college students 17 and older.
Contact Dr. Joseph Machnik, Director, PO Box 389, 916 Palm Boulevard, Isle of Palms, South Carolina 29451. Phone: 800-622-4645. Fax: 843-886-0885. E-mail: info@no1soccercamps.com.
URL www.no1soccercamps.com

Junior Institute

American Cultural Exchange
Seattle Pacific University
Seattle, Washington 98119

General Information Coed residential traditional camp, academic program, and cultural program established in 1994. High school credit may be earned.
Program Focus English as a second language, sight seeing, host families, San Juan Islands trip.

Junior Institute (continued)
Academics English as a second language, academics (general).
Arts Arts and crafts (general), music (vocal).
Special Interest Areas Campcraft, cross-cultural education, homestays, nature study.
Sports Archery, baseball, basketball, bicycling, canoeing, climbing (wall), horseback riding, in-line skating, kayaking, sea kayaking, soccer, softball, swimming, volleyball.
Wilderness/Outdoors Hiking.
Trips College tours, cultural, day, overnight, shopping.
Program Information 4 sessions per year. Session length: 8–21 days in July, August. Ages: 10–17. 12 participants per session. Boarding program cost: $895–$2085. Application fee: $100–$300.
Application Deadline Continuous.
Jobs Positions for college students 19 and older.
Contact Mr. Chris Gilman, Junior Institute Coordinator, 200 West Mercer Street #504, Seattle, Washington 98119. Phone: 206-217-9644. Fax: 206-812-2257. E-mail: cgilman@cultural.org.
URL www.cultural.org

Junior Statesmen Symposium on Washington State Politics and Government

Junior Statesmen Foundation
University of Washington
Seattle, Washington 98195

General Information Coed residential academic program established in 1979. Formal opportunities for the academically talented.
Program Focus State government, politics, debate, and leadership training.
Academics Communications, government and politics, journalism, precollege program, social science, social studies, speech/debate.
Special Interest Areas Career exploration, leadership training.
Trips College tours, day.
Program Information 1 session per year. Session length: 4 days in August. Ages: 14–18. 40–60 participants per session. Boarding program cost: $320.
Application Deadline Continuous.
Contact Matt Randazzo, National Summer School Director, 400 South El Camino Real, Suite 300, San Mateo, California 94402. Phone: 650-347-1600. Fax: 650-347-7200. E-mail: jsa@jsa.org.
URL www.jsa.org

For more information, see page 1174.

Landmark Volunteers: Washington

Landmark Volunteers, Inc.
Washington

General Information Coed residential outdoor program, community service program, and wilderness program established in 1992. High school credit may be earned.
Program Focus Opportunity for high school students to earn community service credit while working as a team for two weeks in Washington State serving Olympic National Park, Cape Disappointment, or Washington Trails Association. Similar programs offered through Landmark Volunteers at over 60 locations in 21 states.
Academics Botany, ecology, environmental science, history, science (general).
Special Interest Areas Career exploration, community service, conservation projects, construction, field research/expeditions, gardening, leadership training, nature study, team building, trail maintenance, work camp programs.
Wilderness/Outdoors Hiking.
Trips Cultural, day.
Program Information 2 sessions per year. Session length: 2 weeks in June, July. Ages: 14–18. 12–14 participants per session. Boarding program cost: $875–$925. Financial aid available.
Application Deadline Continuous.
Jobs Positions for college students.
Contact Ann Barrett, Executive Director, PO Box 455, Sheffield, Massachusetts 01257. Phone: 413-229-0255. Fax: 413-229-2050. E-mail: landmark@volunteers.com.
URL www.volunteers.com

For more information, see page 1182.

Marrowstone-in-the-City

Seattle Youth Symphony Orchestras
Shorecrest High School; The Overlake School
Seattle, Washington

General Information Coed day arts program established in 1992. Formal opportunities for the artistically talented.
Program Focus Orchestral and chamber music.
Academics Music.
Arts Music, music (chamber), music (classical), music (ensemble), music (instrumental), music (orchestral).
Trips Day.
Program Information 2 sessions per year. Session length: 2 weeks in July, August. Ages: 7–14. 150–200 participants per session. Day program cost: $325–$350. Application fee: $25. Financial aid available.
Application Deadline Continuous.
Jobs Positions for high school students.
Contact John Empey, MITC Coordinator, 11065 5th Avenue, NE, Suite A, Seattle, Washington 98125. Phone: 206-362-2300. Fax: 206-361-9254. E-mail: mitc@syso.org.
URL www.marrowstone.org

Marrowstone Music Festival

Seattle Youth Symphony Orchestras
Western Washington University
Bellingham, Washington 98225

General Information Coed residential and day arts program established in 1943. Formal opportunities for the artistically talented. College credit may be earned.
Program Focus Orchestral and chamber music.
Academics Music, music (Advanced Placement).

Arts Music, music (chamber), music (classical), music (ensemble), music (instrumental), music (orchestral), music composition/arrangement.
Trips College tours, cultural, day, shopping.
Program Information 1–3 sessions per year. Session length: 2–3 weeks in July, August. Ages: 13–23. 170–250 participants per session. Day program cost: $1275–$1400. Boarding program cost: $1500–$1800. Application fee: $35–$50. Financial aid available.
Application Deadline Continuous.
Jobs Positions for high school students 13 and older and college students 18 and older.
Contact Mary Jensen, Marrowstone Music Festival Coordinator, 11065 5th Avenue, NE, Suite A, Seattle, Washington 98125. Phone: 206-362-2300. Fax: 206-361-9254. E-mail: marrowstone@syso.org.
URL www.syso.org/

National Guitar Workshop–Seattle, WA

National Guitar Workshop
Seattle Pacific University
3307 Third Avenue West
Seattle, Washington 98119

General Information Coed residential and day arts program established in 1984. College credit may be earned.
Program Focus Music education in guitar, bass, drums, and vocals.
Academics Music, music (Advanced Placement).
Arts Guitar, music (classical), music (ensemble), music (instrumental), music (jazz), music (rock), music (vocal).
Program Information 1 session per year. Session length: 1 week in June, July, August. Ages: 13–79. 75–225 participants per session. Day program cost: $670–$720. Boarding program cost: $870–$920. Application fee: $25. Financial aid available.
Application Deadline Continuous.
Jobs Positions for college students 21 and older.
Contact Ms. Emily Flower, Registrar, PO Box 222, Lakeside, Connecticut 06758. Phone: 860-567-3736 Ext. 109. Fax: 860-567-0374. E-mail: emily@guitarworkshop.com.
URL www.guitarworkshop.com

NBC Camps–Basketball–Adult & Child Hoops–Spokane, WA

NBC Camps
Whitworth College
Spokane, Washington

General Information Coed residential family program and sports camp.
Program Focus Adult and child weekend mini-camp.
Sports Basketball.
Program Information 1 session per year. Session length: 3 days in August. Ages: 6+. Boarding program cost: $225. Financial aid available.
Application Deadline Continuous.
Jobs Positions for high school students 16 and older and college students.
Contact Ms. Bonnie Tucker, Office Manager, 10003 North Milan Road, #100, Spokane, Washington 99218. Phone: 509-466-4690. Fax: 509-467-6289. E-mail: bonnie@nbccamps.com.
URL www.nbccamps.com

NBC Camps–Basketball–Crowell's Intensity–Spokane, WA

NBC Camps
Spokane, Washington

General Information Boys' residential sports camp.
Program Focus Intense 10-day basketball camp.
Sports Basketball.
Program Information 1 session per year. Session length: 10 days in August. Ages: 14–19. Boarding program cost: $980. Financial aid available.
Application Deadline Continuous.
Jobs Positions for high school students 16 and older and college students.
Contact Ms. Bonnie Tucker, Office Manager, 10003 North Milan Road, #100, Spokane, Washington 99218. Phone: 509-466-4690. Fax: 509-467-6289. E-mail: bonnie@nbccamps.com.
URL www.nbccamps.com

NBC Camps–Basketball Individual Training (Boys)–Auburn, WA

NBC Camps
Auburn Adventist Academy
Auburn, Washington

General Information Boys' residential sports camp.
Program Focus Well-rounded skill development.
Sports Basketball.
Program Information 2 sessions per year. Session length: 5 days in July. Ages: 9–18. Boarding program cost: $325. Financial aid available.
Application Deadline Continuous.
Jobs Positions for high school students 16 and older and college students.
Contact Ms. Bonnie Tucker, Office Manager, 10003 North Milan Road, #100, Spokane, Washington 99218. Phone: 509-466-4690. Fax: 509-467-6289. E-mail: bonnie@nbccamps.com.
URL www.nbccamps.com

NBC Camps–Basketball Individual Training (Girls)–Auburn, WA

NBC Camps
Auburn Adventist Academy
Auburn, Washington

General Information Girls' residential sports camp.
Program Focus Well-rounded skill development.
Sports Basketball.
Program Information 2 sessions per year. Session length: 5 days in July, August. Ages: 9–18. Boarding program cost: $325. Financial aid available.
Application Deadline Continuous.

NBC Camps–Basketball Individual Training (Girls)–Auburn, WA (continued)

Jobs Positions for high school students 16 and older and college students.
Contact Ms. Bonnie Tucker, Office Manager, 10003 North Milan Road, #100, Spokane, Washington 99218. Phone: 509-466-4690. Fax: 509-467-6289. E-mail: bonnie@nbccamps.com.
URL www.nbccamps.com

NBC Camps–Basketball Individual Training–Spangle, WA

NBC Camps
Spangle, Washington

General Information Coed residential sports camp.
Program Focus Well-rounded skill development.
Sports Basketball.
Program Information 3 sessions per year. Session length: 5 days in July, August. Ages: 9–18. Boarding program cost: $315. Financial aid available.
Application Deadline Continuous.
Jobs Positions for high school students 16 and older and college students.
Contact Ms. Bonnie Tucker, Office Manager, 10003 North Milan Road, #100, Spokane, Washington 99218. Phone: 509-466-4690. Fax: 509-467-6289. E-mail: bonnie@nbccamps.com.
URL www.nbccamps.com

NBC Camps–Basketball Individual Training–Spokane, WA

NBC Camps
Whitworth College
Spokane, Washington

General Information Coed residential sports camp.
Program Focus Well-rounded skill development.
Sports Basketball.
Program Information 1 session per year. Session length: 5 days in July. Ages: 9–18. Boarding program cost: $325. Financial aid available.
Application Deadline Continuous.
Jobs Positions for high school students 16 and older and college students.
Contact Ms. Bonnie Tucker, Office Manager, 10003 North Milan Road, #100, Spokane, Washington 99218. Phone: 509-466-4690. Fax: 509-467-6289. E-mail: bonnie@nbccamps.com.
URL www.nbccamps.com

NBC Camps–Basketball Point Guard Play–Spangle, WA

NBC Camps
Spangle, Washington

General Information Coed residential sports camp.
Program Focus Point guard specific instruction.
Sports Basketball.
Program Information 1 session per year. Session length: 5 days in June. Boarding program cost: $315. Financial aid available. Point guards must be age 14+; for non-point guards, this camp is identical to Individual Training Camp.
Application Deadline Continuous.
Jobs Positions for high school students 16 and older and college students.
Contact Ms. Bonnie Tucker, Office Manager, 10003 North Milan Road, #100, Spokane, Washington 99218. Phone: 509-466-4690. Fax: 509-467-6289. E-mail: bonnie@nbccamps.com.
URL www.nbccamps.com

NBC Camps–Basketball Post & Shooting–Spokane, WA

NBC Camps
Whitworth College
Spokane, Washington

General Information Residential sports camp.
Program Focus Emphasis on shooting and post position improvement.
Sports Basketball.
Program Information 1 session per year. Session length: 5 days in July, August. Boarding program cost: $325. Financial aid available. Ages: Shooting, 9—18; Post, 14+.
Application Deadline Continuous.
Jobs Positions for high school students 16 and older and college students.
Contact Ms. Bonnie Tucker, Office Manager, 10003 North Milan Road, #100, Spokane, Washington 99218. Phone: 509-466-4690. Fax: 509-467-6289. E-mail: bonnie@nbccamps.com.
URL www.nbccamps.com

NBC Camps–Basketball Speed Explosion–Spokane, WA

NBC Camps
Whitworth College
Spokane, Washington

General Information Coed residential sports camp.
Program Focus Developing jumping and speed skills.
Sports Basketball.
Program Information 1 session per year. Session length: 3 days in July. Ages: 13–19. Boarding program cost: $200. Financial aid available.
Application Deadline Continuous.
Jobs Positions for high school students 16 and older and college students.
Contact Ms. Bonnie Tucker, Office Manager, 10003 North Milan Road, #100, Spokane, Washington 99218. Phone: 509-466-4690. Fax: 509-467-6289. E-mail: bonnie@nbccamps.com.
URL www.nbccamps.com

NBC Camps–Basketball–Team (Girls)–Spangle, WA

NBC Camps
Spangle, Washington

General Information Girls' residential sports camp.
Program Focus Camp for high school basketball teams.
Sports Basketball.
Program Information 1 session per year. Session length: 5 days in June. Boarding program cost: $280. Financial aid available.
Application Deadline Continuous.
Jobs Positions for high school students and college students.
Contact Danny Beard, 10003 North Milan Road, #100, Spokane, Washington 99218. Phone: 509-466-4690. Fax: 509-467-6289. E-mail: danny@nbccamps.com.
URL www.nbccamps.com

NBC Camps–Soccer–Spangle, WA

NBC Camps
Spangle, Washington

General Information Coed residential sports camp established in 1971.
Sports Soccer.
Program Information 1 session per year. Session length: 5 days in July. Ages: 9–19. Boarding program cost: $315. Financial aid available.
Application Deadline Continuous.
Jobs Positions for high school students 16 and older and college students.
Contact Ms. Bonnie Tucker, Office Manager, 10003 North Milan Road, #100, Spokane, Washington 99218. Phone: 509-466-4690. Fax: 509-467-6289. E-mail: bonnie@nbccamps.com.
URL www.nbccamps.com

NBC Camps–Soccer Speed Explosion–Spokane, WA

NBC Camps
Whitworth College
Spokane, Washington

General Information Coed residential sports camp.
Program Focus Developing jumping and speed skills.
Sports Soccer.
Program Information 1 session per year. Session length: 3 days in July. Ages: 9–19. Boarding program cost: $200. Financial aid available.
Application Deadline Continuous.
Jobs Positions for high school students 16 and older and college students.
Contact Ms. Bonnie Tucker, Office Manager, 10003 North Milan Road, #100, Spokane, Washington 99218. Phone: 509-466-4690. Fax: 509-467-6289. E-mail: bonnie@nbccamps.com.
URL www.nbccamps.com

NBC Camps–Volleyball Speed Explosion–Spokane, WA

NBC Camps
Whitworth College
Spokane, Washington

General Information Coed residential sports camp.
Program Focus Developing jumping and speed skills.
Sports Volleyball.
Program Information 1 session per year. Session length: 3 days in July. Ages: 9–19. Boarding program cost: $200. Financial aid available.
Application Deadline Continuous.
Jobs Positions for high school students 16 and older and college students.
Contact Ms. Bonnie Tucker, Office Manager, 10003 North Milan Road, #100, Spokane, Washington 99218. Phone: 509-466-4690. Fax: 509-467-6289. E-mail: bonnie@nbccamps.com.
URL www.nbccamps.com

The Northwest School Summer Program

The Northwest School
1415 Summit Avenue
Seattle, Washington 98122

General Information Coed residential and day academic program and arts program established in 1990.

The Northwest School Summer Program

Program Focus Special interest, enrichment, ESL, computers.
Academics English as a second language, English language/literature, academics (general), business, communications, computers, intercultural studies, journalism, mathematics, music, philosophy, reading, writing.
Arts Animation, arts, arts and crafts (general), batiking, cartooning, ceramics, chorus, creative writing, dance, drawing, fabric arts, film, music, painting, photography, pottery, printmaking, sculpture, television/video, theater/drama.

The Northwest School Summer Program (continued)
Special Interest Areas Community service, culinary arts, field trips (arts and culture), homestays, leadership training, problem solving, robotics.
Sports Basketball, climbing (wall), field hockey, martial arts, soccer, volleyball.
Trips Cultural, day, shopping.
Program Information 3 sessions per year. Session length: 2 weeks in July, August. Ages: 11–16. 150–200 participants per session. Day program cost: $75–$750. Boarding program cost: $1255–$1545.
Application Deadline June 11.
Jobs Positions for college students 21 and older.
Contact Ms. Susan Mueller, Summer Program Director, main address above. Phone: 206-682-7309. Fax: 206-467-7353.
URL northwestschool.org

Outdoor Adventure

Western Washington University
Bellingham, Washington 98225

General Information Coed residential and day traditional camp and outdoor program established in 2000. Formal opportunities for the academically talented. Specific services available for the hearing impaired.
Program Focus Leadership development, activity skill development.
Academics Writing.
Arts Arts and crafts (general).
Special Interest Areas Leadership training, team building.
Sports Bicycling, canoeing, climbing (wall), kayaking, ropes course, swimming.
Wilderness/Outdoors Backpacking, bicycle trips, hiking, kayaking trips, mountain biking, mountaineering, orienteering, rock climbing, wilderness camping.
Trips Day, overnight.
Program Information 2 sessions per year. Session length: 5 days in July, August. Ages: 11–18. 20–40 participants per session. Day program cost: $425. Boarding program cost: $600–$895.
Application Deadline June 15.
Jobs Positions for college students 18 and older.
Contact Debbie Young Gibbons, Program Manager, Extended Education and Summer Programs, Mail Stop 5293, 516 High Street, Bellingham, Washington 98225. Phone: 360-650-6820. Fax: 360-650-6858. E-mail: adventures@wwu.edu.
URL www.wwu.edu/~adventur

Outward Bound West–Climbing, Backpacking, and Canoeing–North Cascades, WA

Outward Bound West/Outward Bound, USA
North Cascades
Washington

General Information Coed travel outdoor program and wilderness program established in 1965. College credit may be earned.
Program Focus Teamwork and leadership wilderness adventure.
Special Interest Areas Campcraft, conservation projects, first aid, leadership training, outdoor cooking, personal development, team building.
Sports Canoeing, rappelling.
Wilderness/Outdoors Backpacking, canoe trips, hiking, outdoor adventure, rock climbing, wilderness camping.
Trips Overnight.
Program Information 4 sessions per year. Session length: 1–2 weeks in July, August, September. Ages: 12+. Cost: $1995–$2195. Application fee: $95. Financial aid available.
Application Deadline Continuous.
Jobs Positions for college students 21 and older.
Contact Admissions Advisor, 910 Jackson Street, Golden, Colorado 80401. Phone: 866-746-9777. Fax: 720-497-2421. E-mail: info@obwest.org.
URL www.outwardboundwest.org

Outward Bound West–Mountaineering–North Cascades, WA

Outward Bound West/Outward Bound, USA
Washington

General Information Coed travel outdoor program and wilderness program established in 1965.
Program Focus Teamwork and leadership wilderness adventure.
Academics Environmental science.
Special Interest Areas Leadership training, personal development, team building.
Sports Rappelling.
Wilderness/Outdoors Mountaineering, outdoor adventure, rock climbing, wilderness camping.
Trips Overnight.
Program Information 4 sessions per year. Session length: 14–22 days in June, July, August. Ages: 14+. Cost: $2195–$2895. Application fee: $95. Financial aid available.
Application Deadline Continuous.
Jobs Positions for college students 21 and older.
Contact Admissions Advisor, 910 Jackson Street, Golden, Colorado 80401. Phone: 866-746-9777. Fax: 720-497-2421. E-mail: info@obwest.org.
URL www.outwardboundwest.org

Outward Bound West–Sea Kayaking, Backpacking, and Mountaineering–Washington

Outward Bound West/Outward Bound, USA
Puget Sound and North Cascades
Washington

General Information Coed travel outdoor program and wilderness program established in 1965. College credit may be earned.
Program Focus Teamwork and leadership wilderness adventure.

Academics Environmental science, oceanography.
Special Interest Areas Campcraft, first aid, leadership training, nautical skills, personal development, team building.
Sports Sea kayaking.
Wilderness/Outdoors Backpacking, hiking, mountaineering, outdoor adventure, wilderness camping.
Trips Overnight.
Program Information 4 sessions per year. Session length: 14–22 days in June, July, August, September. Ages: 16+. Cost: $2595–$3095. Application fee: $95. Financial aid available.
Application Deadline Continuous.
Jobs Positions for college students 21 and older.
Contact Admissions Advisor, 910 Jackson Street, Golden, Colorado 80401. Phone: 866-746-9777. Fax: 720-497-2421. E-mail: info@obwest.org.
URL www.outwardboundwest.org

Outward Bound West–Service Course–North Cascades

Outward Bound West/Outward Bound, USA
Washington

General Information Coed travel outdoor program and wilderness program established in 1965. College credit may be earned.
Program Focus Teamwork and leadership wilderness adventure.
Academics Environmental science.
Special Interest Areas Campcraft, community service, conservation projects, first aid, leadership training, personal development, team building.
Sports Rappelling.
Wilderness/Outdoors Backpacking, hiking, mountaineering, outdoor adventure, rock climbing, wilderness camping.
Trips Overnight.
Program Information 1 session per year. Session length: 2 weeks in June. Ages: 16+. Cost: $1395. Application fee: $95. Financial aid available.
Application Deadline Continuous.
Jobs Positions for college students 21 and older.
Contact Admissions Advisor, 910 Jackson Street, Golden, Colorado 80401. Phone: 866-746-9777. Fax: 720-497-2421. E-mail: info@obwest.org.
URL www.outwardboundwest.org

Salmon Camp Research Team for Native Americans–San Juan Island

Oregon Museum of Science and Industry
San Juan Island National Historic Park
San Juan Island, Washington

General Information Coed residential outdoor program established in 2002. Formal opportunities for the academically talented. High school credit may be earned.
Program Focus Natural resource management field research.
Academics Archaeology, astronomy, biology, botany, ecology, environmental science, geology/earth science, marine studies, natural resource management.
Special Interest Areas Native American culture, field research/expeditions, nature study.
Sports Canoeing, snorkeling.
Wilderness/Outdoors Canoe trips, hiking.
Trips Cultural, overnight.
Program Information 2 sessions per year. Session length: 20 days in July, August. Ages: 15–18. 10 participants per session. No cost for Native Americans.
Application Deadline Continuous.
Jobs Positions for high school students 16 and older and college students 16 and older.
Contact Travis Neumeyer, Programming Coordinator, 1945 Southeast Water Avenue, Portland, Oregon 97214. Phone: 503-239-7824. Fax: 503-239-7838. E-mail: sciencecamps@omsi.edu.
URL www.omsi.edu

San Juan Island Camps

Oregon Museum of Science and Industry
San Juan National Historic Park
San Juan Island, Washington

General Information Coed residential outdoor program established in 1999. Formal opportunities for the academically talented. High school credit may be earned.
Program Focus Marine biology, coastal ecology.
Academics Archaeology, biology, botany, ecology, geology/earth science, marine studies.
Sports Canoeing, snorkeling.
Wilderness/Outdoors Hiking.
Trips Cultural.
Program Information 7 sessions per year. Session length: 6–13 days in June, July, August. Ages: 10–18. 10–30 participants per session. Boarding program cost: $440–$610. Financial aid available.
Application Deadline Continuous.
Jobs Positions for high school students 16 and older and college students 18 and older.
Contact Travis Neumeyer, Programming Coordinator, 1945 Southeast Water Avenue, Portland, Oregon 97214. Phone: 503-239-7824. Fax: 503-239-7838. E-mail: teumeyer@omsi.edu.
URL www.omsi.edu

Student Conservation Association–Conservation Crew Program (Washington)

Student Conservation Association (SCA)
Washington

General Information Coed residential outdoor program, community service program, and wilderness program established in 1957. High school credit may be earned.
Program Focus Resource management, conservation and environmental education.
Academics Biology, botany, ecology, environmental science, geology/earth science, history.

Student Conservation Association–Conservation Crew Program (Washington) (continued)

Special Interest Areas Campcraft, community service, construction, leadership training, nature study, trail maintenance, work camp programs.
Sports Canoeing, fishing, kayaking, swimming.
Wilderness/Outdoors Backpacking, canoe trips, hiking, orienteering, outdoor living skills, wilderness camping.
Trips Cultural, day, overnight.
Program Information 2–3 sessions per year. Session length: 3–5 weeks in June, July, August. Ages: 15–19. 6–8 participants per session. Application fee: $20. Financial aid available. No cost for program; financial aid possible for travel expenses.
Application Deadline Continuous.
Jobs Positions for college students 21 and older.
Contact Recruitment Office, PO Box 550, Charlestown, New Hampshire 03603. Phone: 603-543-1700. Fax: 603-543-1828. E-mail: getreal@thesca.org.
URL www.theSCA.org

Student Conservation Association–Conservation Leadership Corps–Northwest

Student Conservation Association (SCA)
Washington

General Information Coed residential and day outdoor program and community service program. High school credit may be earned.
Program Focus Environmental stewardship, education, leadership development and conservation service.
Academics Biology, ecology, environmental science, geography, geology/earth science, intercultural studies, social studies.
Special Interest Areas Career exploration, community service, construction, leadership training, nature study, trail maintenance.
Wilderness/Outdoors Backpacking, hiking, survival training, wilderness camping.
Trips Day, overnight.
Program Information Session length: 15–28 days in January, February, March, April, May, July, August, September, October, November, December. Ages: 15–19. 6–8 participants per session. Financial aid available. No cost for program; financial aid possible for travel expenses.
Application Deadline Continuous.
Jobs Positions for high school students 15 and older and college students.
Contact Mandy Putney, Regional Program Manager, 1265 South Main Street, Suite 210, Seattle, Washington 98144. Phone: 206-324-4649 Ext.22. Fax: 206-324-4998. E-mail: mputney@thesca.org.
URL www.theSCA.org

Ventures Travel Service–Washington

Friendship Ventures
Washington

General Information Coed travel special needs program established in 1985. Specific services available for the developmentally challenged and physically challenged.
Program Focus Provides travel services to older teens and adults with developmental disabilities.
Special Interest Areas Touring.
Program Information 50 sessions per year. Session length: 4–10 days in February, March, April, May, June, July, August, September, October, November, December. Ages: 14–70. 4–8 participants per session. Cost: $395–$2000.
Application Deadline Continuous.
Jobs Positions for college students 18 and older.
Contact Georgann Rumsey, President/CEO, 10509 108th Street, NW, Annandale, Minnesota 55302. Phone: 952-852-0101. Fax: 952-852-0123. E-mail: fv@friendshipventures.org.
URL www.friendshipventures.org

Westcoast Connection–Community Service

Westcoast Connection
Washington

General Information Coed travel community service program established in 1982. Accredited by Ontario Camping Association.
Program Focus Community service of 120 hours over 4 weeks combined with touring and adventure highlights.
Special Interest Areas Community service.
Sports Sea kayaking.
Wilderness/Outdoors Hiking, rafting.
Program Information 1–2 sessions per year. Session length: 27 days in July, August. Ages: 16+. 13–18 participants per session. Cost: $4199. Financial aid available.
Application Deadline Continuous.
Jobs Positions for college students 21 and older.
Contact Mr. Mark Segal, Director, 154 East Boston Post Road, Mamaroneck, New York 10543. Phone: 800-767-0227. Fax: 914-835-0798. E-mail: usa@westcoastconnection.com.
URL www.westcoastconnection.com

For more information, see page 1392.

Whitman National Debate Institute

Whitman College
345 Boyer Avenue
Walla Walla, Washington 99362

General Information Coed residential and day academic program established in 2000. Formal opportunities for the gifted.
Program Focus Debate for high school students.
Academics Speech/debate.
Trips Day.

Program Information 1 session per year. Ages: 12–19. 50–100 participants per session. Day program cost: $900–$1300. Boarding program cost: $1200–$1600. Application fee: $100. Financial aid available.
Application Deadline Continuous.
Contact Jim Hanson, Director of Forensics, main address above. Phone: 509-527-5499. Fax: 509-527-4959. E-mail: hansonjb@whitman.edu.
URL www.whitman.edu/rhetoric/camp/

Wilderness Ventures–Cascade-Olympic

Wilderness Ventures
Washington

General Information Coed travel outdoor program, wilderness program, and adventure program established in 1973.
Program Focus Wilderness travel, wilderness skills, leadership skills.
Special Interest Areas Leadership training.
Sports Sea kayaking.
Wilderness/Outdoors Backpacking, hiking, mountaineering, rafting, wilderness camping.
Trips Overnight.
Program Information 2 sessions per year. Session length: 25 days in July, August. Ages: 14–18. 10 participants per session. Cost: $3690.
Application Deadline Continuous.
Jobs Positions for college students 21 and older.
Contact Mike Cottingham, Director, PO Box 2768, Jackson Hole, Wyoming 83001. Phone: 800-533-2281. Fax: 307-739-1934. E-mail: info@wildernessventures.com.
URL www.wildernessventures.com

For more information, see page 1396.

Wilderness Ventures–Puget Sound

Wilderness Ventures
Washington

General Information Coed travel outdoor program, wilderness program, and adventure program established in 1973.
Program Focus Wilderness travel, wilderness skills, leadership skills.
Special Interest Areas Leadership training.
Sports Sea kayaking.
Wilderness/Outdoors Backpacking, hiking, rafting, white-water trips, wilderness camping.
Trips Overnight.
Program Information 2 sessions per year. Session length: 3 weeks in June, July, August. Ages: 13–15. 10 participants per session. Cost: $3590. Financial aid available.
Application Deadline Continuous.
Jobs Positions for college students 21 and older.
Contact Mike Cottingham, Director, PO Box 2768, Jackson Hole, Wyoming 83001. Phone: 800-533-2281. Fax: 307-739-1934. E-mail: info@wildernessventures.com.
URL www.wildernessventures.com

For more information, see page 1396.

Wilderness Ventures–Washington Alpine

Wilderness Ventures
Washington

General Information Coed travel outdoor program, wilderness program, and adventure program established in 1973.
Program Focus Wilderness travel, wilderness skills, leadership skills.
Special Interest Areas Leadership training.
Wilderness/Outdoors Backpacking, rafting, white-water trips, wilderness camping.
Trips Overnight.
Program Information 2 sessions per year. Session length: 16 days in June, July. Ages: 15–18. 10 participants per session. Cost: $3390. Financial aid available.
Application Deadline Continuous.
Jobs Positions for college students 21 and older.
Contact Mike Cottingham, Director, PO Box 2768, Jackson Hole, Wyoming 83001. Phone: 800-533-2281. Fax: 307-739-1934. E-mail: info@wildernessventures.com.
URL www.wildernessventures.com

For more information, see page 1396.

Wilderness Ventures–Washington Mountaineering

Wilderness Ventures
Washington

General Information Coed travel outdoor program, wilderness program, and adventure program established in 1973.
Program Focus Wilderness travel, wilderness skills, leadership skills.
Special Interest Areas Leadership training.
Wilderness/Outdoors Backpacking, hiking, mountaineering, wilderness camping.
Trips Overnight.
Program Information 2 sessions per year. Session length: 25 days in June, July, August. Ages: 16–18. 10 participants per session. Cost: $3690. Financial aid available.
Application Deadline Continuous.
Jobs Positions for college students 21 and older.
Contact Mike Cottingham, Director, PO Box 2768, Jackson Hole, Wyoming 83001. Phone: 800-533-2281. Fax: 307-739-1934. E-mail: info@wildernessventures.com.
URL www.wildernessventures.com

For more information, see page 1396.

YMCA Camp Seymour Summer Camp

YMCA Camp Seymour
9725 Cramer Road KPN
Gig Harbor, Washington 98329

General Information Coed residential traditional camp established in 1905. Accredited by American Camping Association.
Academics Marine studies.
Arts Arts and crafts (general), dance, painting, photography, printmaking, theater/drama, woodworking.
Special Interest Areas Campcraft, leadership training, nature study, team building.
Sports Archery, basketball, boating, canoeing, climbing (wall), kayaking, ropes course, sailing, sea kayaking, soccer, street/roller hockey, swimming, volleyball.
Wilderness/Outdoors Backpacking, canoe trips, hiking, kayaking trips, orienteering, rafting, rock climbing, wilderness camping.
Trips Day, overnight.
Program Information 8 sessions per year. Session length: 4–14 days in June, July, August. Ages: 5–18. 150–200 participants per session. Boarding program cost: $180–$810. Application fee: $50–$75. Financial aid available.
Application Deadline Continuous.
Jobs Positions for high school students 17 and older and college students 18 and older.
Contact Ms. Magill Lange, Camping Director, main address above. Phone: 253-884-3392. Fax: 253-460-8897. E-mail: campseymour@ymcatocoma.org.
URL www.campseymour.org

WEST VIRGINIA

Buckswood: English Language (ESL) and Activities–West Virginia

Buckswood Summer Programs
Marlinton, West Virginia

General Information Coed residential traditional camp, academic program, and cultural program established in 1978.
Program Focus Buckswood classic EFL offers English language tuition with activity program.
Academics English as a second language.
Arts Arts and crafts (general), dance, musical productions.
Sports Aerobics, archery, baseball, basketball, boating, canoeing, equestrian sports, fishing, football, golf, horseback riding, soccer, softball, swimming, tennis, volleyball, waterskiing.
Wilderness/Outdoors Backpacking, hiking, orienteering.
Program Information 2–4 sessions per year. Session length: 2 weeks in July, August. Ages: 7–16. 40–60 participants per session. Boarding program cost: $1695–$1895.
Application Deadline Continuous.
Jobs Positions for college students 20 and older.
Contact Ms. Katie Black, Buckswood Summer Programmes, Belle Vue House, 259 Greenwich High Road, London SE10 8NB, United Kingdom. Phone: 44-(0) 208-269-0044. Fax: 44-(0) 208-293-1199. E-mail: info@buckswood.com.
URL www.buckswood.com

Burgundy Center for Wildlife Studies Summer Camp

Burgundy Farm School
Capon Bridge, West Virginia 26711

General Information Coed residential outdoor program established in 1963. Accredited by American Camping Association. Formal opportunities for the academically talented.
Program Focus Nature study.
Academics Biology, botany, ecology, environmental science, geology/earth science, zoology.
Arts Arts and crafts (general), photography.
Special Interest Areas Campcraft, conservation projects, gardening, nature study.
Sports Swimming.
Wilderness/Outdoors Backpacking, hiking, orienteering.
Trips Overnight.
Program Information 5 sessions per year. Session length: 1–2 weeks in June, July, August. Ages: 8–15. 32 participants per session. Boarding program cost: $700–$1200. Financial aid available.
Application Deadline Continuous.
Jobs Positions for high school students 16 and older and college students.
Summer Contact Lavinia Schoene, Director, HC 83, Box 38DD, Capon Bridge, West Virginia 26711. Phone: 304-856-3758. Fax: 304-856-3758. E-mail: bcws2@earthlink.net.
Winter Contact Lavinia Schoene, Director, 3700 Burgundy Road, Alexandria, Virginia 22303. Phone: 703-960-3431. Fax: 703-960-5056. E-mail: bcws2@earthlink.net.
URL camppage.com/bcws

Camp Greenbrier for Boys

Camp Greenbrier for Boys
Route 12
Alderson, West Virginia 24910

General Information Boys' residential traditional camp established in 1898. Accredited by American Camping Association.
Program Focus A tradition of fun.
Academics English as a second language, English language/literature, mathematics, reading.
Arts Arts and crafts (general), creative writing, drawing, leather working, painting, pottery, weaving, woodworking.
Special Interest Areas Campcraft, nature study.
Sports Archery, baseball, basketball, canoeing, climbing (wall), cross-country, fishing, golf, kayaking, lacrosse, rappelling, riflery, snorkeling, soccer, softball, sports (general), swimming, tennis, track and field, volleyball, wrestling.

Wilderness/Outdoors Backpacking, canoe trips, caving, hiking, orienteering, rock climbing, white-water trips.
Trips Day, overnight.
Program Information 3 sessions per year. Session length: 24–48 days in June, July, August. Ages: 7–15. 150 participants per session. Boarding program cost: $1850–$3390. Financial aid available.
Application Deadline Continuous.
Jobs Positions for high school students 16 and older and college students 18 and older.
Summer Contact Mr. Will Harvie, Director, Route 2, Box 5A, Alderson, West Virginia 24910. Phone: 304-445-7168. Fax: 304-445-7168. E-mail: woofus@juno.com.
Winter Contact Mr. Will Harvie, Director, Box 585, Exmore, Virginia 23350. Phone: 888-226-7427. Fax: 757-789-3477. E-mail: woofus@juno.com.
URL www.campgreenbrier.com

Camp Rim Rock–Arts Camp

Camp Rim Rock
Yellow Spring, West Virginia 26865

General Information Girls' residential arts program established in 2002. Accredited by American Camping Association.
Program Focus Oriented toward final performance in dance and drama.
Arts Acting, arts, arts and crafts (general), chorus, dance, drawing, jewelry making, music, painting, sculpture, theater/drama.
Sports Swimming.
Program Information 4 sessions per year. Session length: 1 week in June, August. Ages: 9–17. 20–40 participants per session. Boarding program cost: $875.
Application Deadline Continuous.
Jobs Positions for college students 19 and older.
Contact Deborah Matheson, Director, PO Box 69, Yellow Spring, West Virginia 26865. Phone: 800-662-4650. Fax: 304-856-3201. E-mail: office@camprimrock.com.
URL www.camprimrock.com

Camp Rim Rock–General Camp

Camp Rim Rock
Yellow Spring, West Virginia 26865

General Information Girls' residential traditional camp established in 1952. Accredited by American Camping Association.
Program Focus Equestrian program, the arts, aquatics, land sports.
Arts Acting, art (folk), arts and crafts (general), chorus, dance, dance (folk), dance (jazz), dance (modern), drawing, fabric arts, jewelry making, mime, painting, pottery, puppetry, sculpture, theater/drama.
Sports Archery, basketball, canoeing, equestrian sports, field games, horseback riding, lacrosse, soccer, softball, swimming, tennis, volleyball.
Wilderness/Outdoors Hiking.
Program Information 6 sessions per year. Session length: 2–4 weeks in June, July, August. Ages: 6–17. 260–280 participants per session. Boarding program cost: $1600–$3400.
Application Deadline Continuous.
Jobs Positions for college students 19 and older.
Contact Deborah Matheson, Director, PO Box 69, Yellow Spring, West Virginia 26865. Phone: 800-662-4650. Fax: 304-856-3201. E-mail: office@camprimrock.com.
URL www.camprimrock.com

Camp Rim Rock–Horseback Riding Camp

Camp Rim Rock
Yellow Spring, West Virginia 26865

General Information Girls' residential sports camp. Accredited by American Camping Association.
Program Focus Horseback riding.
Sports Equestrian sports, horseback riding, swimming.
Program Information 4 sessions per year. Session length: 1 week in June, August. Ages: 9–17. Boarding program cost: $1000.
Application Deadline Continuous.
Jobs Positions for college students 19 and older.
Contact Deborah Matheson, Director, PO Box 69, Yellow Spring, West Virginia 26865. Phone: 800-662-4650. Fax: 304-856-3201. E-mail: office@camprimrock.com.
URL www.camprimrock.com

Camp Rim Rock–Mini Camp

Camp Rim Rock
Yellow Spring, West Virginia 26865

General Information Girls' residential traditional camp. Accredited by American Camping Association.
Arts Arts and crafts (general), chorus, dance, dance (folk), dance (jazz), dance (modern), drawing, fabric arts, jewelry making, mime, music (vocal), painting, puppetry, sculpture, theater/drama.
Sports Archery, basketball, canoeing, equestrian sports, field games, horseback riding, soccer, softball, swimming, tennis, volleyball.
Wilderness/Outdoors Hiking.
Program Information 9 sessions per year. Session length: 1 week in June, July, August. Boarding program cost: $850. Open to participants entering grades 1–3.
Application Deadline Continuous.
Jobs Positions for college students 19 and older.
Contact Deborah Matheson, Director, PO Box 69, Yellow Spring, West Virginia 26865. Phone: 800-662-4650. Fax: 304-856-3201. E-mail: office@camprimrock.com.
URL www.camprimrock.com

Camp Rim Rock–Tennis Camp

Camp Rim Rock
Yellow Spring, West Virginia 26865

General Information Girls' residential sports camp established in 2004.
Program Focus Tennis.
Sports Swimming, tennis.
Program Information 4 sessions per year. Session length: 1 week in June, August. Ages: 9–17. Boarding program cost: $875.
Application Deadline Continuous.

Camp Rim Rock–Tennis Camp (continued)
Jobs Positions for college students.
Contact Deborah Matheson, Director, PO Box 69, Yellow Spring, West Virginia 26865. Phone: 304-856-2869. Fax: 304-856-3201. E-mail: office@camprimrock.com.
URL www.camprimrock.com

Camp Sandy Cove

Morning Cheer, Inc.
High View, West Virginia 26801

General Information Coed residential traditional camp, outdoor program, and bible camp established in 1950. Religious affiliation: Christian. Accredited by American Camping Association.
Program Focus Helping young people develop a relationship with their Creator.
Academics Bible study.
Arts Arts and crafts (general), ceramics, photography, television/video.
Special Interest Areas Native American culture, campcraft, leadership training, nature study.
Sports Archery, baseball, basketball, bicycling, canoeing, climbing (wall), equestrian sports, field hockey, fishing, gymnastics, horseback riding, in-line skating, martial arts, rappelling, ropes course, soccer, sports (general), street/roller hockey, swimming, tennis, volleyball.
Wilderness/Outdoors Bicycle trips, canoe trips, hiking, mountain biking, orienteering, rafting, rock climbing, white-water trips, wilderness camping.
Trips Day, overnight.
Program Information 8 sessions per year. Session length: 1 week in June, July, August. Ages: 7–15. 200 participants per session. Boarding program cost: $350–$400. Financial aid available.
Application Deadline Continuous.
Jobs Positions for high school students 17 and older and college students 18 and older.
Summer Contact Tim Nielsen, Director, Rt. 1, Box 471, High View, West Virginia 26801. Phone: 304-856-2959. Fax: 304-856-1683. E-mail: chieftimn@aol.com.
Winter Contact Tim Nielsen, Director, 60 Sandy Cove Road, North East, Maryland 21901. Phone: 800-234-COVE Ext.454. Fax: 410-287-3196. E-mail: chieftimn@aol.com.
URL www.campsandycove.org

Camp Tall Timbers

Route 1
High View, West Virginia 26808

General Information Coed residential traditional camp established in 1970. Accredited by American Camping Association.
Arts Arts and crafts (general), ceramics, chorus, creative writing, dance, dance (ballet), dance (modern), dance (tap), drawing, jewelry making, leather working, music, music (vocal), musical productions, painting, photography, pottery, radio broadcasting, television/video, theater/drama.
Special Interest Areas Animal care, model rocketry, nature study.
Sports Aerobics, archery, baseball, basketball, bicycling, bicycling (BMX), canoeing, cheerleading, climbing (wall), cross-country, equestrian sports, field hockey, fishing, football, golf, gymnastics, horseback riding, in-line skating, kayaking, lacrosse, martial arts, mountain boarding, racquetball, rappelling, riflery, ropes course, soccer, softball, street/roller hockey, swimming, tennis, track and field, volleyball, water polo, waterskiing, weight training, wrestling.
Wilderness/Outdoors Backpacking, bicycle trips, canoe trips, hiking, mountain biking, orienteering, rafting, rock climbing, white-water trips.
Trips Day, overnight.
Program Information 2–4 sessions per year. Session length: 12–24 days in June, July, August. Ages: 7–16. 150–175 participants per session. Boarding program cost: $1600–$3000.
Application Deadline Continuous.
Jobs Positions for high school students 17 and older and college students 18 and older.
Summer Contact Glenn Smith, Director, Route 1, Box 472, High View, West Virginia 26808. Phone: 304-856-3722. Fax: 304-856-3765. E-mail: funcamp@aol.com.
Winter Contact Glenn Smith, Director, 3735 Spicebush Drive, Urbana, Maryland 21704. Phone: 301-874-0111. Fax: 301-874-0113. E-mail: funcamp@aol.com.
URL www.camptalltimbers.com

Greenbrier River Outdoor Adventures, Adventure Camp

Greenbrier River Outdoor Adventures
Bartow, West Virginia 24920

General Information Coed residential traditional camp, outdoor program, and wilderness program established in 1992.
Program Focus Wilderness adventure.
Arts Arts and crafts (general).
Special Interest Areas Campcraft, community service, leadership training.
Sports Basketball, canoeing, climbing (wall), fishing, kayaking, rappelling, ropes course, swimming.
Wilderness/Outdoors Adventure racing, backpacking, bicycle trips, canoe trips, caving, climbing, hiking, mountain biking, rock climbing, white-water trips, wilderness camping.
Trips Day, overnight.
Program Information 6 sessions per year. Session length: 1–2 weeks in June, July, August. Ages: 10–17. 8–12 participants per session. Boarding program cost: $750–$1700. Financial aid available.
Application Deadline Continuous.
Jobs Positions for high school students and college students 21 and older.
Contact Tom Bryant, Camp Director, HC77, Box 117, Bartow, West Virginia 24920. Phone: 304-456-5191. Fax: 304-456-5572. E-mail: groa@groa.com.
URL www.groa.com

Greenbrier River Outdoor Adventures, Camp Snowshoe

Greenbrier River Outdoor Adventures
West Virginia

General Information Coed day traditional camp and outdoor program established in 2004.
Arts Acting, animation, arts and crafts (general), beading, cartooning, dance, drawing, film, jewelry making, music, painting, television/video.
Special Interest Areas Campcraft, community service, conservation projects, team building.
Sports Baseball, bicycling, boating, canoeing, climbing (wall), fishing, soccer, softball, swimming, track and field, volleyball.
Trips Day, overnight.
Program Information 8 sessions per year. Session length: 1–14 days in June, July, August, September, October. Ages: 5–16. Day program cost: $35–$55. Financial aid available.
Application Deadline Continuous.
Jobs Positions for college students 18 and older.
Contact Danica Kilander, Director, HC77, Box 117, Bartow, West Virginia 24920. Phone: 304-456-5191. Fax: 304-456-5572. E-mail: groa@groa.com.
URL www.groa.com

Greenbrier River Outdoor Adventures, Rock and River

Greenbrier River Outdoor Adventures
West Virginia

General Information Coed residential outdoor program and wilderness program.
Program Focus Whitewater kayaking, whitewater rafting, and challenge courses.
Arts Arts and crafts (general).
Special Interest Areas Campcraft, community service.
Sports Basketball, canoeing, climbing (wall), fishing, kayaking, rappelling, ropes course, swimming.
Wilderness/Outdoors Canoe trips, climbing, hiking, mountain biking, rafting, rock climbing, white-water trips, wilderness camping.
Trips Day, overnight.
Program Information 1–3 sessions per year. Session length: 2 weeks in July. Ages: 14–17. 8–12 participants per session. Boarding program cost: $750–$1700. Financial aid available.
Application Deadline Continuous.
Jobs Positions for high school students and college students 21 and older.
Contact Tom Bryant, Camp Director, HC77, Box 117, Bartow, West Virginia 24920. Phone: 304-456-5191. Fax: 304-456-5572. E-mail: groa@groa.com.
URL www.groa.com

Greenbrier River Outdoor Adventures, Wilderness Explorer

Greenbrier River Outdoor Adventures
West Virginia

General Information Coed residential outdoor program and wilderness program.
Program Focus Wilderness adventure.
Arts Arts and crafts (general).
Special Interest Areas Campcraft, community service.
Sports Basketball, canoeing, climbing (wall), fishing, kayaking, rappelling, ropes course, swimming.
Wilderness/Outdoors Adventure racing, backpacking, bicycle trips, canoe trips, caving, climbing, hiking, mountain biking, orienteering, rock climbing, white-water trips, wilderness camping.
Trips Day, overnight.
Program Information 2 sessions per year. Session length: 2 weeks in June, July, August. Ages: 11–17. 8–12 participants per session. Boarding program cost: $1450. Financial aid available.
Application Deadline Continuous.
Jobs Positions for college students 21 and older.
Contact Tom Bryant, Camp Director, HC77, Box 117, Bartow, West Virginia 24920. Phone: 304-456-5191. Fax: 304-456-5572. E-mail: groa@groa.com.
URL www.groa.com

Student Conservation Association–Conservation Crew Program (West Virginia)

Student Conservation Association (SCA)
West Virginia

General Information Coed residential outdoor program, community service program, and wilderness program established in 1957. High school credit may be earned.
Program Focus Resource management, conservation and environmental education.
Academics Biology, botany, ecology, environmental science, geology/earth science, history.
Special Interest Areas Campcraft, community service, construction, leadership training, nature study, trail maintenance, work camp programs.
Sports Canoeing, fishing, kayaking, swimming.
Wilderness/Outdoors Backpacking, canoe trips, hiking, orienteering, outdoor living skills, wilderness camping.
Trips Cultural, day, overnight.
Program Information 2–3 sessions per year. Session length: 3–5 weeks in June, July, August. Ages: 15–19. 6–8 participants per session. Application fee: $20. Financial aid available. No cost for program; financial aid possible for travel expenses.
Application Deadline Continuous.
Jobs Positions for college students 21 and older.
Contact Recruitment Office, PO Box 550, Charlestown, New Hampshire 03603. Phone: 603-543-1700. Fax: 603-543-1828. E-mail: getreal@thesca.org.
URL www.theSCA.org

Wesleyan Summer Gifted Program

West Virginia Wesleyan College
59 College Avenue
Buckhannon, West Virginia 26201

General Information Coed residential academic program established in 1983. Formal opportunities for the academically talented and gifted. College credit may be earned.
Program Focus Residential academic program for gifted students in grades 6-12.
Academics English language/literature, astronomy, biology, computers, geology/earth science, history, mathematics, physics, precollege program, writing.
Sports Soccer, swimming, tennis.
Trips Day.
Program Information 2 sessions per year. Session length: 2 weeks in June, July. Ages: 10–17. 100 participants per session. Boarding program cost: $900–$1000. Financial aid available.
Application Deadline May 1.
Jobs Positions for college students 20 and older.
Contact Dr. Joseph E. Wiest, Founder, Box 89, Buckhannon, West Virginia 26201. Phone: 304-473-8072. E-mail: sgp@wvwc.edu.
URL www.wvwc.edu/wvwc/gifted/giftcamp.html

WISCONSIN

American Collegiate Adventures–Wisconsin

American Collegiate Adventures
University of Wisconsin–Madison
Madison, Wisconsin

General Information Coed residential academic program. Accredited by American Camping Association. High school credit may be earned.
Academics American literature, English as a second language, French language/literature, SAT/ACT preparation, academics (general), advertising, biology, business, chemistry, college tours, computers, environmental science, humanities, journalism, language study, mathematics, music, oceanography, physics, precollege program, prelaw, psychology, reading, science (general), social science, sociology, speech/debate, women's studies, writing.
Arts Acting, arts and crafts (general), creative writing, desktop publishing, drawing, fashion design/production, graphic arts, music, music composition/arrangement, painting, photography, radio broadcasting, screenwriting, television/video.
Special Interest Areas Internet accessibility, career exploration, community service, culinary arts, driver's education.
Sports Aerobics, baseball, basketball, bicycling, canoeing, football, golf, kayaking, martial arts, racquetball, soccer, softball, swimming, tennis, volleyball, weight training.
Wilderness/Outdoors Outdoor adventure.
Trips College tours, cultural, day, overnight, shopping.
Program Information 3 sessions per year. Session length: 2–6 weeks in June, July, August. Ages: 14–18. 100–200 participants per session. Boarding program cost: $2895–$6295. Application fee: $75.
Application Deadline Continuous.
Jobs Positions for college students.
Contact Jason Lubar, Director of Summer Programs, 1811 W. North Avenue, Suite 201, Chicago, Illinois 60622. Phone: 800-509-SUMR. Fax: 773-342-0246. E-mail: info@acasummer.com.
URL www.acasummer.com

Birch Trail Camp for Girls

Minong, Wisconsin 54859

General Information Girls' residential traditional camp established in 1959. Accredited by American Camping Association.
Academics Journalism.
Arts Acting, arts and crafts (general), batiking, ceramics, chorus, creative writing, dance, dance (ballet), dance (folk), dance (jazz), dance (modern), drawing, fabric arts, film, jewelry making, music, music (jazz), musical productions, painting, photography, pottery, printmaking, radio broadcasting, sculpture, television/video, theater/drama, weaving.
Special Interest Areas Campcraft, lecture series, nature study.
Sports Aerobics, archery, baseball, basketball, boating, canoeing, cheerleading, climbing (wall), diving, equestrian sports, field hockey, fishing, football, golf, gymnastics, horseback riding, kayaking, martial arts, rappelling, ropes course, sailing, soccer, softball, swimming, tennis, volleyball, waterskiing, windsurfing.
Wilderness/Outdoors Backpacking, bicycle trips, canoe trips, hiking, mountain biking, mountaineering, orienteering, rock climbing, survival training, whitewater trips, wilderness camping.
Trips Day, overnight.
Program Information 3 sessions per year. Session length: 4–8 weeks in June, July, August. Ages: 8–15. 195–215 participants per session. Boarding program cost: $3500–$5900. Financial aid available.
Application Deadline Continuous.
Jobs Positions for college students 18 and older.
Contact Mr. Gabriel Chernov, Director, PO Box 527, Minong, Wisconsin 54859. Phone: 715-466-2216. Fax: 715-466-2217. E-mail: gabe@birchtrail.com.
URL www.birchtrail.com

Camp Birch Trails

Girl Scouts of the Fox River Area, Inc.
W5860 Olivotti Lake Road
Irma, Wisconsin 54442

General Information Girls' residential traditional camp established in 1965. Accredited by American Camping Association.
Program Focus Wilderness trips.
Arts Arts and crafts (general), dance.
Special Interest Areas Campcraft, leadership training, nature study, team building.

Sports Archery, bicycling, boating, canoeing, fishing, golf, horseback riding, kayaking, ropes course, sea kayaking, snorkeling, soccer, swimming, volleyball.
Wilderness/Outdoors Backpacking, bicycle trips, canoe trips, hiking, orienteering, white-water trips, wilderness camping.
Trips Overnight.
Program Information 8–10 sessions per year. Session length: 4–21 days in June, July, August. Ages: 6–17. 50–120 participants per session. Boarding program cost: $160–$625. Financial aid available.
Application Deadline Continuous.
Jobs Positions for high school students 16 and older and college students 18 and older.
Contact Ms. Carrie Schroyer, Program/Resident Camp Director, 4693 North Lynndale Drive, Appleton, Wisconsin 54913-9614. Phone: 920-734-4559. Fax: 920-734-1304. E-mail: cschroyer@girlscoutsfoxriverarea.org.
URL www.girlscoutsfoxriverarea.org

Camp Chi

Camp Chi/Jewish Community Center of Chicago
Lake Delton, Wisconsin 53940

General Information Coed residential traditional camp established in 1921. Religious affiliation: Jewish. Accredited by American Camping Association.
Arts Animation, arts and crafts (general), batiking, ceramics, chorus, creative writing, dance, dance (jazz), dance (modern), drawing, fabric arts, film, jewelry making, metalworking, music, music (instrumental), musical productions, painting, photography, pottery, radio broadcasting, stained glass, television/video, theater/drama, woodworking.
Special Interest Areas Campcraft.
Sports Aerobics, archery, baseball, basketball, bicycling (BMX), boating, canoeing, cheerleading, climbing (wall), equestrian sports, field hockey, fishing, football, golf, horseback riding, in-line skating, kayaking, lacrosse, ropes course, sailing, scuba diving, soccer, softball, street/roller hockey, swimming, tennis, volleyball, waterskiing.
Wilderness/Outdoors Canoe trips, hiking, mountain biking, orienteering, rock climbing, survival training.
Trips Overnight.
Program Information 2 sessions per year. Session length: 4–8 weeks in June, July, August. 400–600 participants per session. Boarding program cost: $2800–$5425. Financial aid available. Open to participants entering grades 4–10.
Application Deadline Continuous.
Jobs Positions for high school students and college students.
Summer Contact Mr. Ron Levin, Director, PO Box 104, Lake Delton, Wisconsin 53940. Phone: 608-253-1681. Fax: 608-253-4302. E-mail: info@campchi.com.
Winter Contact Mr. Ron Levin, Director, 3050 Woodridge Road, Northbrook, Illinois 60062. Phone: 847-272-2301. Fax: 847-272-5357. E-mail: info@campchi.com.
URL www.campchi.com

Camp Highlands for Boys

8450 Camp Highlands Road
Sayner, Wisconsin 54560

General Information Boys' residential traditional camp established in 1904.
Arts Arts and crafts (general), leather working, music, photography, television/video.
Special Interest Areas Campcraft, model rocketry, nature study, nautical skills.
Sports Archery, baseball, basketball, boating, canoeing, climbing (wall), cross-country, diving, fishing, football, golf, kayaking, lacrosse, rappelling, riflery, ropes course, sailing, sea kayaking, snorkeling, soccer, softball, sports (general), swimming, tennis, track and field, volleyball, water polo, waterskiing, weight training, windsurfing.
Wilderness/Outdoors Backpacking, canoe trips, hiking, white-water trips, wilderness camping.
Trips Overnight.
Program Information 3 sessions per year. Session length: 3–7 weeks in June, July, August. Ages: 8–16. 150 participants per session. Boarding program cost: $2100–$4350.
Application Deadline Continuous.
Jobs Positions for college students 20 and older.
Summer Contact Michael P. Bachmann, Director, main address above. Phone: 715-542-3443. Fax: 715-542-3868. E-mail: chmike@aol.com.
Winter Contact Michael P. Bachmann, Director, 4146 Lawn Avenue, Western Springs, Illinois 60558. Phone: 708-246-1238. Fax: 708-246-3216. E-mail: chmike@aol.com.
URL www.camphighlands.com

Camp Horseshoe

Camp Horseshoe
4151 Camp Brinoffen Road
Rhinelander, Wisconsin 54501

General Information Boys' residential traditional camp established in 1932.
Arts Arts and crafts (general), radio broadcasting, theater/drama.
Special Interest Areas Campcraft, nature study, team building.
Sports Archery, baseball, basketball, bicycling, boating, canoeing, climbing (wall), cross-country, diving, fencing, field hockey, fishing, football, golf, ice hockey, in-line skating, kayaking, lacrosse, riflery, ropes course, sailing, soccer, softball, street/roller hockey, swimming, tennis, track and field, volleyball, waterskiing, windsurfing.
Wilderness/Outdoors Backpacking, bicycle trips, canoe trips, hiking, mountain biking, orienteering, wilderness camping.
Trips Overnight.
Program Information 4–8 sessions per year. Session length: 28–54 days in June, July, August. Ages: 8–16. 100–200 participants per session. Boarding program cost: $3450–$5700.
Application Deadline Continuous.
Jobs Positions for college students 19 and older.

Camp Horseshoe (continued)

Summer Contact Jordan Shiner, Director, PO Box 458, Rhinelander, Wisconsin 54501. Phone: 715-362-2000. Fax: 715-362-2001. E-mail: fun@camphorseshoe.com.
Winter Contact Director, 821 Kimball Road, Highland Park, Illinois 60035. Phone: 847-433-9140. E-mail: fun@camphorseshoe.com.
URL www.camphorseshoe.com

Camp Menominee

4985 County Road D
Eagle River, Wisconsin 54521

General Information Boys' residential traditional camp established in 1928. Accredited by American Camping Association.
Program Focus Building boys' self-esteem and character through traditional activities as well as sports.
Academics Hebrew language, computers, journalism, mathematics, reading.
Arts Arts and crafts (general), ceramics, creative writing, film, graphic arts, jewelry making, leather working, metalworking, music, painting, photography, pottery, radio broadcasting, television/video, theater/drama, woodworking.
Special Interest Areas Campcraft, model rocketry, nature study.
Sports Archery, baseball, basketball, boating, canoeing, climbing (wall), cross-country, field hockey, fishing, football, golf, in-line skating, kayaking, lacrosse, racquetball, rappelling, riflery, rowing (crew/sculling), sailing, soccer, softball, street/roller hockey, swimming, tennis, track and field, volleyball, waterskiing, weight training, windsurfing, wrestling.
Wilderness/Outdoors Canoe trips, hiking, rafting, rock climbing, white-water trips.
Trips Day, overnight, shopping.
Program Information 2 sessions per year. Session length: 26–27 days in June, July, August. Ages: 7–15. 140–180 participants per session. Boarding program cost: $600–$700. Financial aid available.
Application Deadline May 1.
Jobs Positions for high school students 17 and older and college students.
Summer Contact Mr. Steve Kanefsky, Owner/Director, main address above. Phone: 715-479-2267. Fax: 715-479-5512. E-mail: fun@campmenominee.com.
Winter Contact Mr. Steve Kanefsky, Owner/Director, 15253 North 104th Way, Scottsdale, Arizona 85255. Phone: 480-515-5474. Fax: 480-515-5475. E-mail: fun@campmenominee.com.
URL www.campmenominee.com

Camp North Star for Boys

10970 West Boys Camp Road
Hayward, Wisconsin 54843

General Information Boys' residential traditional camp established in 1945. Accredited by American Camping Association.
Academics Ecology.
Arts Arts and crafts (general), ceramics, film, leather working, music (vocal), painting, photography, pottery, sculpture, theater/drama, woodworking.
Special Interest Areas Campcraft, leadership training, model rocketry.
Sports Archery, basketball, bicycling, boating, canoeing, climbing (wall), fishing, football, golf, horseback riding, kayaking, lacrosse, rappelling, riflery, ropes course, sailing, snorkeling, soccer, softball, swimming, tennis, track and field, volleyball, waterskiing, weight training, windsurfing, wrestling.
Wilderness/Outdoors Backpacking, bicycle trips, canoe trips, hiking, mountain biking, rock climbing, white-water trips, wilderness camping.
Trips Cultural, overnight.
Program Information 2 sessions per year. Session length: 27 days in June, July, August. Ages: 8–15. 150 participants per session. Boarding program cost: $3350–$5700. Financial aid available.
Application Deadline Continuous.
Jobs Positions for college students 20 and older.
Summer Contact Robert Lebby, Director, main address above. Phone: 715-462-3254. Fax: 715-462-9278. E-mail: leb@northstarcamp.com.
Winter Contact Robert Lebby, Director, 6101 East Paseo Cimarron, Tucson, Arizona 85750. Phone: 520-577-7925. Fax: 520-529-2140. E-mail: leb@northstarcamp.com.
URL www.northstarcamp.com

Camp St. John's Northwestern

St. John's Northwestern Military Academy
1101 North Genesee Street
Delafield, Wisconsin 53018

General Information Boys' residential and day traditional camp established in 1995. Religious affiliation: nondenominational. Accredited by American Camping Association.

Camp St. John's Northwestern

Program Focus Leadership training, military adventure, athletics, recreation, teamwork, skills, and self-confidence building activities.
Arts Photography.

Special Interest Areas First aid, leadership training, lifesaving, team building.
Sports Archery, basketball, canoeing, climbing (wall), fishing, golf, martial arts, obstacle course, paintball, rappelling, riflery, ropes course, sailing, scuba diving, snorkeling, swimming, volleyball.
Wilderness/Outdoors Canoe trips, hiking, orienteering, survival training.
Trips Day.
Program Information 4 sessions per year. Session length: 6–13 days in July. Ages: 10–16. 40–125 participants per session. Day program cost: $475–$850. Boarding program cost: $800–$1400. Application fee: $75.
Application Deadline Continuous.
Contact Director of Camp Enrollment, main address above. Phone: 800-SJ-CADET. Fax: 262-646-7128. E-mail: admissions@sjnma.org.
URL www.sjnma.org

For more information, see page 1038.

Timber-lee Science Camp

Camp Timber-lee
N8705 Scout Road
East Troy, Wisconsin 53120

General Information Coed residential and day traditional camp, academic program, outdoor program, and bible camp established in 1972. Religious affiliation: Evangelical Free Church of America. Accredited by American Camping Association.
Academics Bible study, astronomy, biology, botany, chemistry, ecology, marine studies, meteorology, science (general).
Special Interest Areas Nature study, team building.
Sports Canoeing, climbing (wall), ropes course.
Wilderness/Outdoors Outdoor adventure.
Trips Day, overnight.
Program Information 4–6 sessions per year. Session length: 1 week in June, July, August. Ages: 8–17. 25–40 participants per session. Boarding program cost: $345–$445. Financial aid available.
Application Deadline Continuous.
Jobs Positions for high school students 17 and older and college students 17 and older.
Contact Mr. Tom Parsons, Director, Human Resources, main address above. Phone: 262-642-7345. Fax: 262-642-7517. E-mail: tomp@timber-lee.com.
URL www.timber-lee.com

Central Wisconsin Environmental Station–Natural Resources Careers Camp

Central Wisconsin Environmental Station/University of Wisconsin–Stevens Point
10186 County Road MM
Amherst Junction, Wisconsin 54407

General Information Coed residential academic program, outdoor program, and wilderness program established in 1975. College credit may be earned.
Program Focus Career education, natural resources, environmental awareness, outdoor skills, leadership skills.
Academics Astronomy, biology, botany, ecology, environmental science, geology/earth science, precollege program.
Special Interest Areas Campcraft, career exploration, field research/expeditions, leadership training, nature study, team building.
Sports Archery, boating, canoeing, fishing, ropes course, swimming, volleyball.
Wilderness/Outdoors Backpacking, canoe trips, hiking, orienteering, survival training, wilderness camping.
Trips College tours, day, overnight.
Program Information 1 session per year. Session length: 3–6 days in June, July, August. Ages: 14–17. 50–60 participants per session. Boarding program cost: $290–$915. Financial aid available.
Application Deadline Continuous.
Jobs Positions for college students 18 and older.
Contact Ms. Rebecca Franzen, Program Manager, main address above. Phone: 715-824-2428. Fax: 715-824-3201. E-mail: bfranzen@uwsp.edu.
URL www.uwsp.edu/cnr/cwes

Central Wisconsin Environmental Station–Sunset Lake Adventures

Central Wisconsin Environmental Station/University of Wisconsin–Stevens Point
10186 County Road MM
Amherst Junction, Wisconsin 54407

General Information Coed residential traditional camp, outdoor program, and wilderness program established in 1975.
Program Focus Environmental awareness and natural history.
Academics Astronomy, biology, botany, ecology, environmental science, geology/earth science, music, science (general).
Arts Arts and crafts (general), creative writing, dance, drawing, jewelry making, music, musical productions, painting, puppetry.
Special Interest Areas Native American culture, campcraft, career exploration, nature study.
Sports Archery, boating, canoeing, challenge course, climbing (wall), fishing, ropes course, swimming.
Wilderness/Outdoors Backpacking, canoe trips, hiking, orienteering, outdoor living skills, survival training, wilderness camping.
Trips Day, overnight.
Program Information 4–8 sessions per year. Session length: 3–11 days in June, July, August. Ages: 6–17. 50–60 participants per session. Boarding program cost: $130–$520. Financial aid available.
Application Deadline Continuous.
Jobs Positions for college students 18 and older.
Summer Contact Rebecca Franzen, Program Manager, main address above. Phone: 715-824-2428. Fax: 715-824-3201. E-mail: bfranzen@uwsp.edu.
Winter Contact Rebecca Franzen, Program Manager, main address above. Phone: 715-824-2428. Fax: 715-824-3201. E-mail: bfranzen@uwsp.edu.
URL www.uwsp.edu/cnr/cwes

Clearwater Camp for Girls

Clearwater Camp, Inc.
7490 Clearwater Road
Minocqua, Wisconsin 54548

General Information Girls' residential traditional camp established in 1933. Accredited by American Camping Association.

Clearwater Camp for Girls

Academics Ecology.
Arts Arts and crafts (general), ceramics, creative writing, photography, pottery.
Special Interest Areas Campcraft, leadership training, nature study.
Sports Archery, basketball, boating, canoeing, equestrian sports, fishing, horseback riding, kayaking, sailing, swimming, tennis, volleyball, waterskiing, windsurfing.
Wilderness/Outdoors Backpacking, canoe trips, hiking, wilderness camping.
Trips Day, overnight.
Program Information 1–2 sessions per year. Session length: 25–49 days in June, July, August. Ages: 8–16. 120–130 participants per session. Boarding program cost: $2800–$5000.
Application Deadline Continuous.
Jobs Positions for high school students 16 and older and college students 19 and older.
Summer Contact Sunny Moore, Executive Director, main address above. Phone: 715-356-5030. Fax: 715-356-3124. E-mail: clearwatercamp@newnorth.net.
Winter Contact Sunny Moore, Director, main address above. Phone: 800-399-5030.
URL www.clearwatercamp.com

For more information, see page 1074.

Harand Camp of the Theatre Arts

Carthage on the Lake
2001 Alford Park Drive
Kenosha, Wisconsin 53140-1994

General Information Coed residential arts program established in 1955. Accredited by American Camping Association.
Program Focus Participation and preparation for musical spectaculars, reviews, and productions; sports.
Academics Music, speech/debate, writing.
Arts Arts and crafts (general), chorus, creative writing, dance, dance (ballet), dance (jazz), dance (modern), dance (tap), drawing, film, jewelry making, mime, music, music (ensemble), music (instrumental), music (vocal), musical productions, painting, photography, puppetry, television/video, theater/drama.
Special Interest Areas Community service.
Sports Aerobics, basketball, cheerleading, golf, gymnastics, racquetball, soccer, softball, swimming, tennis, track and field, volleyball, water polo, weight training.
Trips Day.
Program Information 2 sessions per year. Session length: 3 weeks in June, July, August. Ages: 8–17. 190–200 participants per session. Boarding program cost: $2125–$4250.
Application Deadline Continuous.
Jobs Positions for college students 18 and older.
Summer Contact Sulie Harand, Director, main address above. Phone: 920-885-4517. Fax: 920-885-4521. E-mail: harandcamp@aol.com.
Winter Contact Sulie Harand, Director, 708 Church Street, #231, Evanston, Illinois 60201. Phone: 847-864-1500. Fax: 847-864-1588. E-mail: harandcamp@aol.com.
URL www.harandcamp.com

Special Note
Harand Camp of Theatre Arts & Sports was established in 1955 and was formerly located in Elkhart Lake, Wisconsin. Harand is now located in Beaver Dam, Wisconsin, on the campus of Wayland Academy. Harand Camp provides boys and girls ages 8–18 with all the fun, sports, recreational activities, and camaraderie of camp life under the guidance and leadership of well-trained, caring professionals, teaching staff members, and counselors. In addition, regardless of ability or talent, each camper participates in the camp's specialized musical theater program. This excellent program includes drama, singing, dance, and arts, and participants appear in outstanding musical productions directed by dedicated, talented professionals. All of this is accomplished in a noncompetitive and caring family environment where "each one is a star" and "no one is an island." Through the years, Harand Camp has trained and developed youngsters who have then gone on to professional careers in a variety of areas. Harand Camp develops poise, confidence, self-esteem, leadership abilities, theater knowledge, and arts appreciation and provides excellent experience onstage and backstage. Each art and skill enhances the other, and the combination of the arts and skills, plus sports, ultimately helps each camper to become a well-rounded, whole person.

Harand Camp means family to thousands of Haranders all over the world. Harand proudly raises the curtain on its 50th happy season.

Joe Machnik's No. 1 Academy One and Premier Programs–Kenosha, Wisconsin

Joe Machnik's No. 1 Camps
Carthage College
Kenosha, Wisconsin

General Information Coed residential and day sports camp.
Program Focus Soccer instruction, physical fitness, testing and speed training. Campers gain exposure to top players and are challenged by intense competition.
Sports Soccer.
Trips Day.
Program Information 2 sessions per year. Session length: 6 days in June, July. Ages: 9–18. Day program cost: $699. Boarding program cost: $759. Financial aid available.
Application Deadline Continuous.
Jobs Positions for college students.
Contact Dr. Joseph Machnik, Director, PO Box 389, 916 Palm Boulevard, Isle of Palms, South Carolina 29451. Phone: 800-622-4645. Fax: 843-886-0885. E-mail: info@no1soccercamps.com.
URL www.no1soccercamps.com

Joe Machnik's No. 1 College Prep Academy–Kenosha, Wisconsin

Joe Machnik's No. 1 Camps
Carthage College
Kenosha, Wisconsin

General Information Coed residential and day sports camp.
Program Focus Intense soccer instruction for high school students.
Sports Soccer.
Trips Day.
Program Information 1 session per year. Session length: 12 days in July. Ages: 13–17. 10–20 participants per session. Day program cost: $1449. Boarding program cost: $1549. Financial aid available.
Application Deadline Continuous.
Jobs Positions for college students.
Contact Dr. Joseph Machnik, Director, PO Box 389, 916 Palm Boulevard, Isle of Palms, South Carolina 29451. Phone: 800-622-4645. Fax: 843-886-0885. E-mail: info@no1soccercamps.com.
URL www.no1soccercamps.com

Joe Machnik's No. 1 Mighty Mini, Goalkeeper and Striker Camp–Kenosha, Wisconsin

Joe Machnik's No. 1 Camps
Carthage College
Kenosha, Wisconsin

General Information Coed residential and day sports camp.
Program Focus Soccer instruction. Goalkeepers and strikers compete against each other daily.
Sports Soccer.
Trips Day.
Program Information 2 sessions per year. Session length: 6 days in July. Ages: 8–12. 100–150 participants per session. Boarding program cost: $429. Financial aid available.
Application Deadline Continuous.
Jobs Positions for college students.
Contact Dr. Joseph Machnik, Director, PO Box 389, 916 Palm Boulevard, Isle of Palms, South Carolina 29451. Phone: 800-622-4645. Fax: 843-886-0885. E-mail: info@no1soccercamps.com.
URL www.no1soccercamps.com

Milwaukee School of Engineering (MSOE)–Discover the Possibilities

Milwaukee School of Engineering
1025 North Broadway
Milwaukee, Wisconsin 53202

General Information Coed residential academic program established in 1999.
Program Focus Explores the exciting field of engineering through study, expos, and industry visits.
Academics Computers, engineering.
Special Interest Areas Career exploration, construction.
Trips Cultural, day, shopping.
Program Information 2 sessions per year. Session length: 5 days in July. Ages: 13–18. 50–90 participants per session. Boarding program cost: $650.
Application Deadline Continuous.
Contact Ms. Linda Levandowski, Special Events Coordinator MSOE, main address above. Phone: 800-332-6763. Fax: 414-277-7475. E-mail: levandow@msoe.edu.
URL www.msoe.edu/admiss/summer

Milwaukee School of Engineering (MSOE)–Focus on Nursing

Milwaukee School of Engineering
1025 North Broadway
Milwaukee, Wisconsin 53202

General Information Coed residential academic program established in 2004.
Program Focus Explore the field of nursing.
Academics Health sciences, medicine.
Special Interest Areas Career exploration.
Trips Cultural, day, shopping.

Milwaukee School of Engineering (MSOE)–Focus on Nursing (continued)

Program Information 1 session per year. Session length: 5 days in July. Ages: 13–18. 15–24 participants per session. Boarding program cost: $650.
Application Deadline Continuous.
Contact Ms. Linda Levandowski, Special Events Coordinator, MSOE, main address above. Phone: 800-332-6763. Fax: 414-277-7475. E-mail: levandow@msoe.edu.
URL www.msoe.edu/admiss/summer

MILWAUKEE SCHOOL OF ENGINEERING (MSOE)–FOCUS ON THE POSSIBILITIES

Milwaukee School of Engineering
1025 North Broadway
Milwaukee, Wisconsin 53202

General Information Coed residential academic program established in 1999.
Program Focus Participant pursues a track of activities in one area of engineering/construction: biomedical, architectural, building, computers, electrical, or mechanical.
Academics Computers, engineering.
Special Interest Areas Career exploration, construction.
Trips Cultural, day, shopping.
Program Information 6 sessions per year. Session length: 5 days in July, August. Ages: 13–18. 10–25 participants per session. Boarding program cost: $650.
Application Deadline Continuous.
Contact Ms. Linda Levandowski, Special Events Coordinator, MSOE, main address above. Phone: 800-332-6763. Fax: 414-277-7475. E-mail: levandow@msoe.edu.
URL www.msoe.edu/admiss/summer

NELSON/FELLER TENNIS CAMP–LAKELAND COLLEGE

Nelson/Feller Tennis Camp
Lakeland College
Sheboygan, Wisconsin 53082-0359

General Information Coed residential and day sports camp established in 1991.
Program Focus Tennis instruction and strategy.
Sports Aerobics, basketball, tennis, volleyball.
Program Information 1–3 sessions per year. Session length: 5 days in July, August. Ages: 10–17. 48–60 participants per session. Day program cost: $300–$325. Boarding program cost: $375–$400.
Application Deadline Continuous.
Jobs Positions for high school students 18 and older and college students 18 and older.
Contact Mr. Bob Feller, Co-Director, 3925 Seneca Lane, Manitowoc, Wisconsin 54220. Phone: 920-684-0830. Fax: 920-684-3641. E-mail: nftc@lsol.net.
URL www.nelson-feller.com

NELSON/FELLER TENNIS CAMP–UNIVERSITY OF WISCONSIN–OSHKOSH

Nelson/Feller Tennis Camp
University of Wisconsin–Oshkosh
Oshkosh, Wisconsin 54901

General Information Coed residential and day sports camp established in 1991.
Program Focus Tennis instruction and strategy.
Sports Aerobics, basketball, tennis, volleyball.
Program Information 1–2 sessions per year. Session length: 5 days in July. Ages: 10–17. 48–60 participants per session. Day program cost: $300–$325. Boarding program cost: $375–$400.
Application Deadline Continuous.
Jobs Positions for high school students 18 and older and college students 18 and older.
Contact Mr. Bob Feller, Co-Director, 3925 Seneca Lane, Manitowoc, Wisconsin 54220. Phone: 920-684-0830. Fax: 920-684-3641. E-mail: nftc@lsol.net.
URL www.nelson-feller.com

POINT ARTS CAMP–MUSIC

University of Wisconsin–Stevens Point
Stevens Point, Wisconsin 54481

General Information Coed residential arts program established in 1950. Formal opportunities for the artistically talented.
Program Focus Music.
Academics Music, music (Advanced Placement).
Arts Band, chorus, music, music (chamber), music (classical), music (ensemble), music (instrumental), music (jazz), music (vocal).
Program Information 2 sessions per year. Session length: 1 week in June. Ages: 12–18. 100–200 participants per session. Boarding program cost: $465–$495. Application fee: $50.
Application Deadline Continuous.
Jobs Positions for college students.
Contact Ruth Daniels, Program Assistant, 1101 Reserve Street, CAC 324, Stevens Point, Wisconsin 54481. Phone: 715-346-3956. Fax: 715-346-2718. E-mail: rdaniels@uwsp.edu.
URL www.uwsp.edu/cofac/pointartscamps/

RED PINE CAMP FOR GIRLS

Minocqua, Wisconsin 54548

General Information Girls' residential traditional camp established in 1937. Accredited by American Camping Association.
Program Focus Individual attention, noncompetitive programs, and professional instruction with strong equestrian and waterfront programs. Canadian canoe trip and trip to Apostle Islands in Michigan.
Arts Arts and crafts (general), dance, dance (ballet), dance (jazz), dance (modern), drawing, music (vocal), musical productions, painting, printmaking, theater/drama.
Special Interest Areas Campcraft, gardening, leadership training, nature study.

Sports Aerobics, archery, basketball, bicycling, boating, canoeing, cheerleading, equestrian sports, field hockey, fishing, gymnastics, horseback riding, kayaking, lacrosse, martial arts, sailing, sea kayaking, soccer, softball, swimming, tennis, volleyball, waterskiing, windsurfing.
Wilderness/Outdoors Backpacking, bicycle trips, canoe trips, hiking, mountain biking, white-water trips, wilderness camping.
Trips Day, overnight.
Program Information 1–4 sessions per year. Session length: 2–8 weeks in June, July, August. Ages: 6–16. 125 participants per session. Boarding program cost: $1690–$5600. Additional cost for daily riding: $500–$950.
Application Deadline Continuous.
Jobs Positions for college students 18 and older.
Contact Sarah Rolley, Director, PO Box 69, Minocqua, Wisconsin 54548. Phone: 715-356-6231. Fax: 715-356-1077. E-mail: redpinec@newnorth.net.
URL www.redpinecamp.com

St. John's Northwestern Academic Camp

St. John's Northwestern Military Academy
1101 North Genesee Street
Delafield, Wisconsin 53018

General Information Boys' residential and day traditional camp and academic program established in 2004. Religious affiliation: nondenominational. Accredited by American Camping Association. High school credit may be earned.
Program Focus Leadership training, military adventure, athletics, recreation, teamwork skills, and self-confidence building activities, and earn ½ credit (high school).
Academics Academics (general), government and politics, history, mathematics, science (general).
Arts Photography.
Special Interest Areas Leadership training, team building.
Sports Archery, basketball, canoeing, climbing (wall), fishing, golf, martial arts, obstacle course, paintball, rappelling, riflery, ropes course, sailing, scuba diving, snorkeling, swimming, volleyball.
Wilderness/Outdoors Canoe trips, hiking, orienteering, survival training.
Trips Day.
Program Information 1 session per year. Session length: 3 weeks in July. 5–20 participants per session. Boarding program cost: $3500. Application fee: $75. Open to participants entering grades 9–11.
Application Deadline Continuous.
Contact Director of Camp Enrollment, main address above. Phone: 800-SJ-CADET. Fax: 262-646-7128. E-mail: admissions@sjnma.org.
URL www.sjnma.org

St. John's Northwestern ESL Camp

St. John's Northwestern Military Academy
1101 North Genesee Street
Delafield, Wisconsin 53018

General Information Boys' residential traditional camp and academic program established in 1996. Religious affiliation: nondenominational. Accredited by American Camping Association.
Program Focus Leadership training, military adventure, athletics, recreation, teamwork skills, and self-confidence building activities and English instruction.
Academics English as a second language, computers.
Arts Photography.
Special Interest Areas Leadership training, team building.
Sports Archery, basketball, canoeing, climbing (wall), fishing, golf, martial arts, obstacle course, paintball, rappelling, riflery, ropes course, sailing, scuba diving, snorkeling, swimming, volleyball.
Wilderness/Outdoors Canoe trips, hiking, orienteering, survival training.
Trips Day.
Program Information 1 session per year. Session length: 3 weeks in July. Ages: 10–16. 5–40 participants per session. Boarding program cost: $3000. Application fee: $75.
Application Deadline Continuous.
Contact Director of Enrollment, main address above. Phone: 800-SJ-CADET. Fax: 262-646-7128.
URL www.sjnma.org

Student Conservation Association–Conservation Crew Program (Wisconsin)

Student Conservation Association (SCA)
Wisconsin

General Information Coed residential outdoor program, community service program, and wilderness program established in 1957. High school credit may be earned.
Program Focus Resource management, conservation and environmental education.
Academics Biology, botany, ecology, environmental science, geology/earth science, history.
Special Interest Areas Campcraft, community service, construction, leadership training, nature study, trail maintenance, work camp programs.
Sports Canoeing, fishing, kayaking, swimming.
Wilderness/Outdoors Backpacking, canoe trips, hiking, orienteering, outdoor living skills, wilderness camping.
Trips Cultural, day, overnight.
Program Information 2–3 sessions per year. Session length: 3–5 weeks in June, July, August. Ages: 15–19. 6–8 participants per session. Application fee: $20. Financial aid available. No cost for program; financial aid possible for travel expenses.
Application Deadline Continuous.
Jobs Positions for college students 21 and older.

Student Conservation Association–Conservation Crew Program (Wisconsin) (continued)
Contact Recruitment Office, PO Box 550, Charlestown, New Hampshire 03603. Phone: 603-543-1700. Fax: 603-543-1828. E-mail: getreal@thesca.org.
URL www.theSCA.org

SUMMER MUSIC CLINIC

University of Wisconsin–Madison
5554 Humanities
455 North Park Street
Madison, Wisconsin 53706

General Information Coed residential arts program established in 1929. Formal opportunities for the artistically talented.
Academics Art history/appreciation, computers, music.
Arts Arts and crafts (general), band, chorus, dance, music, music (chamber), music (classical), music (ensemble), music (instrumental), music (orchestral), music (vocal), musical productions, theater/drama.
Sports Basketball, volleyball.
Trips Cultural.
Program Information 3 sessions per year. Session length: 5–7 days in June, July. Ages: 11–18. 600 participants per session. Boarding program cost: $520–$570. Application fee: $50.
Application Deadline May 1.
Jobs Positions for college students 20 and older.
Contact Anne Aley, Program Manager, main address above. Phone: 608-263-2242. Fax: 608-265-0452. E-mail: maaley@facstaff.wisc.edu.
URL www.wisc.edu/smc

SUPERCAMP–UNIVERSITY OF WISCONSIN AT PARKSIDE

SuperCamp
University of Wisconsin at Parkside
Kenosha, Wisconsin 53141

General Information Coed residential academic program established in 1981. Accredited by American Camping Association. High school credit may be earned.
Program Focus Academic enrichment and personal development.
Academics SAT/ACT preparation, academics (general), communications, reading, study skills, writing.
Special Interest Areas Leadership training.
Sports Basketball, ropes course, soccer, swimming, volleyball.
Program Information 3–5 sessions per year. Session length: 8–10 days in July, August. Ages: 11–18. 80–125 participants per session. Boarding program cost: $1795–$2295. Application fee: $100. Financial aid available.
Application Deadline Continuous.
Jobs Positions for college students 18 and older.
Contact Enrollments Department, 1725 South Coast Highway, Oceanside, California 92054. Phone: 800-285-3276. Fax: 760-722-3507. E-mail: info@supercamp.com.
URL www.supercamp.com
For more information, see page 1348.

SWIFT NATURE CAMP–ADVENTURE CAMP

Swift Nature Camp
W7471 Ernie Swift Road
Minong, Wisconsin 54859

General Information Coed residential traditional camp established in 1964. Specific services available for the emotionally challenged and learning disabled.
Program Focus Environmental education, nature study.
Academics Astronomy, biology, ecology, science (general).
Arts Arts and crafts (general), clowning, leather working, music (vocal), musical productions, sculpture.
Special Interest Areas Animal care, campcraft, field research/expeditions, nature study, nautical skills, team building.
Sports Archery, baseball, basketball, bicycling, bicycling (BMX), boating, canoeing, fishing, football, horseback riding, kayaking, riflery, ropes course, rowing (crew/sculling), sailing, scuba diving, skin diving, soccer, softball, swimming, volleyball, waterskiing.
Wilderness/Outdoors Backpacking, bicycle trips, canoe trips, hiking, mountain biking, rafting, white-water trips, wilderness camping.
Trips Day, overnight.
Program Information 1–3 sessions per year. Session length: 12–40 days in June, July, August. Ages: 7–15. 100 participants per session. Boarding program cost: $1000–$3000. Financial aid available.
Application Deadline Continuous.
Jobs Positions for college students 18 and older.
Summer Contact Mr. Jeff Lorenz, Director, main address above. Phone: 715-466-5666. Fax: 715-466-5666. E-mail: swiftcamp@aol.com.
Winter Contact Mr. Jeff Lorenz, Director, 25 Baybrook Lane, Oak Brook, Illinois 60523. Phone: 630-654-8036. Fax: 630-654-8036. E-mail: swiftcamp@aol.com.
URL www.swiftnaturecamp.com

SWIFT NATURE CAMP–DISCOVERY CAMP

Swift Nature Camp
W7471 Ernie Swift Road
Minong, Wisconsin 54859

General Information Coed residential traditional camp established in 2000. Specific services available for the emotionally challenged and learning disabled.
Program Focus Environmental education, nature study.
Academics Astronomy, biology, ecology, science (general).
Arts Arts and crafts (general), clowning, leather working, music (vocal), musical productions, sculpture.
Special Interest Areas Native American culture, animal care, campcraft, field research/expeditions, nature study, nautical skills.
Sports Archery, baseball, basketball, bicycling, bicycling (BMX), boating, canoeing, fishing, football, horseback riding, kayaking, riflery, ropes course, rowing (crew/sculling), sailing, scuba diving, snorkeling, soccer, softball, swimming, volleyball, waterskiing.

Wilderness/Outdoors Backpacking, bicycle trips, canoe trips, hiking, mountain biking, orienteering, rafting, white-water trips, wilderness camping.
Trips Day.
Program Information 1 session per year. Session length: 12 days in June. Ages: 6–12. 100 participants per session. Boarding program cost: $1000. Financial aid available.
Application Deadline Continuous.
Jobs Positions for college students 18 and older.
Summer Contact Jeff Lorenz, Director, main address above. Phone: 715-466-5666. Fax: 715-466-5666. E-mail: swiftscamp@aol.com.
Winter Contact Jeff Lorenz, Director, 25 Baybrook Lane, Oak Brook, Illinois 60823. Phone: 630-654-8036. Fax: 630-654-8036. E-mail: swiftcamp@aol.com.
URL www.swiftnaturecamp.com

SWIFT NATURE CAMP–EXPLORER CAMP

Swift Nature Camp
W7471 Ernie Swift Road
Minong, Wisconsin 54859

General Information Coed residential traditional camp established in 1964. Specific services available for the emotionally challenged and learning disabled.
Program Focus Environmental education, nature study.
Academics Astronomy, biology, ecology, science (general).
Arts Arts and crafts (general), clowning, leather working, music (vocal), musical productions, painting, sculpture.
Special Interest Areas Native American culture, animal care, campcraft, field research/expeditions, nature study, nautical skills, team building.
Sports Archery, baseball, basketball, bicycling, bicycling (BMX), boating, canoeing, fishing, football, horseback riding, kayaking, riflery, ropes course, rowing (crew/sculling), sailing, scuba diving, snorkeling, soccer, softball, swimming, volleyball, waterskiing.
Wilderness/Outdoors Backpacking, bicycle trips, canoe trips, hiking, mountain biking, orienteering, rafting, white-water trips, wilderness camping.
Trips Day, overnight.
Program Information 2 sessions per year. Session length: 3 weeks in June, July, August. Ages: 7–15. 100 participants per session. Boarding program cost: $1400–$1600. Financial aid available.
Application Deadline Continuous.
Jobs Positions for college students 18 and older.
Summer Contact Jeff Lorenz, Director, main address above. Phone: 715-466-5666. Fax: 715-466-5666. E-mail: swiftcamp@aol.com.
Winter Contact Jeff Lorenz, Director, 25 Bay Brook, Oak Brook, Illinois 60523. Phone: 630-654-8036. Fax: 630-654-8036. E-mail: swiftcamp@aol.com.
URL www.swiftnaturecamp.com

TIMBER-LEE CREATION CAMP

Camp Timber-lee
N8705 Scout Road
East Troy, Wisconsin 53120

General Information Coed residential traditional camp, outdoor program, bible camp, and adventure program established in 1972. Religious affiliation: Evangelical Free Church of America. Accredited by American Camping Association.
Academics Botany, chemistry, ecology, environmental science, marine studies, ornithology.
Arts Leather working.
Special Interest Areas Campcraft, field research/expeditions, nature study, team building.
Sports Archery, canoeing, climbing (wall), fishing, horseback riding, ropes course, soccer.
Wilderness/Outdoors Adventure racing, backpacking, canoe trips, caving, hiking, outdoor adventure, rafting, rock climbing, white-water trips, wilderness camping.
Program Information 6–8 sessions per year. Session length: 1 week in June, July, August. 40–400 participants per session. Boarding program cost: $405–$445. Financial aid available. Open to participants entering grades 3–8.
Application Deadline Continuous.
Jobs Positions for high school students 17 and older and college students 17 and older.
Contact Mr. Tom Parsons, Director, Human Resources, main address above. Phone: 262-642-7348. Fax: 262-642-7517. E-mail: timber-lee@timber-lee.com.
URL www.timber-lee.com

TIMBER-LEE DRAMA CAMP

Camp Timber-lee
N8705 Scout Road
East Troy, Wisconsin 53120

General Information Coed residential traditional camp, arts program, and bible camp established in 1972. Religious affiliation: Evangelical Free Church of America. Accredited by American Camping Association.
Arts Acting, mime, theater/drama.
Special Interest Areas Nature study.
Sports Climbing (wall), ropes course, swimming.
Program Information 1 session per year. Session length: 1 week in July. 40 participants per session. Boarding program cost: $405–$445. Financial aid available. Open to participants entering grades 7–12.
Application Deadline Continuous.
Jobs Positions for high school students 17 and older and college students 17 and older.
Contact Mr. Tom Parsons, Director, Human Resources, main address above. Phone: 262-642-7348. Fax: 262-642-7517. E-mail: timber-lee@timber-lee.com.
URL www.timber-lee.com

Timber-lee Horsemanship Camps

Camp Timber-lee
N8705 Scout Road
East Troy, Wisconsin 53120

General Information Coed residential sports camp and bible camp established in 1972. Religious affiliation: Evangelical Free Church of America. Accredited by American Camping Association.
Academics Bible study.
Arts Leather working.
Special Interest Areas Nature study.
Sports Archery, canoeing, climbing (wall), horseback riding, ropes course, swimming.
Program Information 7–8 sessions per year. Session length: 1 week in June, July, August. Ages: 9–18. 24–48 participants per session. Boarding program cost: $395–$445. Financial aid available.
Jobs Positions for high school students 17 and older and college students 17 and older.
Contact Mr. Tom Parsons, Director, Human Resources, main address above. Phone: 262-642-7345. Fax: 262-642-7517. E-mail: timber-lee@timber-lee.com.
URL www.timber-lee.com

Timber-lee Wilderness Trips

Camp Timber-lee
N8705 Scout Road
East Troy, Wisconsin 53120

General Information Coed travel bible camp, wilderness program, and adventure program established in 1972. Religious affiliation: Evangelical Free Church of America. Accredited by American Camping Association.
Academics Bible study.
Special Interest Areas Campcraft, nature study.
Sports Bicycling, canoeing, climbing (wall), ropes course.
Wilderness/Outdoors Backpacking, bicycle trips, canoe trips, caving, hiking, mountain biking, orienteering, rock climbing, white-water trips, wilderness camping, wilderness/outdoors (general).
Trips Overnight.
Program Information 10–20 sessions per year. Session length: 3–7 days in January, February, March, April, May, June, July, August, September, October, November, December. Ages: 11–18. 10–20 participants per session. Cost: $250–$450.
Jobs Positions for college students 18 and older.
Contact Mr. Tom Parsons, Director, Human Resources, main address above. Phone: 262-642-7345. Fax: 262-642-7517. E-mail: timber-lee@timber-lee.com.
URL www.timber-lee.com

Timber-lee Youth Camp

Camp Timber-lee
N8705 Scout Road
East Troy, Wisconsin 53120

General Information Coed residential and day traditional camp and bible camp established in 1972. Religious affiliation: Evangelical Free Church of America. Accredited by American Camping Association.
Academics Bible study.
Arts Arts and crafts (general), ceramics, leather working.
Special Interest Areas Campcraft, nature study.
Sports Archery, canoeing, fishing, horseback riding, ropes course, skateboarding, skiing (cross-country), soccer, softball, swimming.
Trips Day, overnight.
Program Information 8 sessions per year. Session length: 1 week in June, July, August. 400 participants per session. Day program cost: $115–$161. Boarding program cost: $345–$445. Financial aid available. Open to participants entering grades 3–12.
Application Deadline Continuous.
Jobs Positions for high school students 17 and older and college students 17 and older.
Contact Mr. Tom Parsons, Director, Human Resources, main address above. Phone: 262-642-7348. Fax: 262-642-7517. E-mail: timber-lee@timber-lee.com.
URL www.timber-lee.com

Towering Pines Camp

Towering Pines Camp
5586 County D
Eagle River, Wisconsin 54521

General Information Boys' residential traditional camp established in 1946. Accredited by American Camping Association. Formal opportunities for the academically talented.
Program Focus Sailing and tutoring.
Academics English as a second language, computers, ecology, mathematics, study skills, typing.
Arts Batiking, ceramics, dance (jazz), dance (modern), fabric arts, jewelry making, leather working, metalworking, musical productions, painting, photography, pottery, television/video, theater/drama, weaving, woodworking.
Special Interest Areas Nature study.
Sports Archery, boating, canoeing, diving, equestrian sports, fencing, fishing, golf, gymnastics, horseback riding, kayaking, riflery, rowing (crew/sculling), sailing, soccer, softball, swimming, tennis, track and field, volleyball, waterskiing, windsurfing.
Wilderness/Outdoors Canoe trips, hiking, wilderness camping.
Trips Overnight.
Program Information 2 sessions per year. Session length: 4–6 weeks in June, July, August. Ages: 6–16. 100 participants per session. Boarding program cost: $2950–$3900. Financial aid available.
Application Deadline Continuous.
Jobs Positions for college students 19 and older.
Summer Contact John M. Jordan, Director, main address above. Phone: 715-479-4540. Fax: 715-466-7710.
Winter Contact John M. Jordan, Director, 242 Bristol Street, Northfield, Illinois 60093. Phone: 715-446-7311. Fax: 715-446-7710. E-mail: towpines@aol.com.
URL www.toweringpinescamp.com

University of Wisconsin–Green Bay Biz 4 Youth Camp

University of Wisconsin–Green Bay
2420 Nicolet Drive
Green Bay, Wisconsin 54311

General Information Coed residential and day academic program established in 2004.
Academics Business.
Trips Day, shopping.
Program Information 1 session per year. Session length: 6 days in June, July. Ages: 14–18. 30–50 participants per session. Day program cost: $239. Boarding program cost: $465.
Application Deadline Continuous.
Jobs Positions for college students 19 and older.
Contact Ms. Mona Christensen, Director of Youth Opportunities, main address above. Phone: 920-465-CAMP (2267). Fax: 920-465-2552. E-mail: summercamps@uwgb.edu.
URL www.uwgbsummercamps.com

University of Wisconsin–Green Bay Computer Camp

University of Wisconsin–Green Bay
2420 Nicolet Drive
Green Bay, Wisconsin 54311-7001

General Information Coed residential and day academic program established in 1999.
Program Focus Computers: web and multimedia design.
Academics Web page design, computer programming, computers.
Trips Cultural, shopping.
Program Information 1–2 sessions per year. Session length: 5–6 days in June. Ages: 12–15. 30–40 participants per session. Day program cost: $205. Boarding program cost: $400–$445. Financial aid available. Financial aid available for minority students in Wisconsin who meet specific requirements.
Application Deadline Continuous.
Jobs Positions for college students 20 and older.
Contact Mona Christensen, Director of Youth Opportunities, main address above. Phone: 920-465-CAMP (2267). Fax: 920-465-2552. E-mail: summercamps@uwgb.edu.
URL www.uwgbsummercamps.com

University of Wisconsin–Green Bay Ecosystem Investigations

University of Wisconsin–Green Bay
2420 Nicolet Drive
Green Bay, Wisconsin 54311

General Information Coed residential and day academic program established in 2004.
Academics Environmental science, geology/earth science.
Trips Day, shopping.
Program Information 1 session per year. Session length: 6 days in June. Ages: 14–18. 30–50 participants per session. Day program cost: $239. Boarding program cost: $465.
Application Deadline Continuous.
Jobs Positions for college students 19 and older.
Contact Ms. Mona Christensen, Director of Youth Opportunities, main address above. Phone: 920-465-CAMP (2267). Fax: 920-465-2552. E-mail: summercamps@uwgb.edu.
URL www.uwgbsummercamps.com

University of Wisconsin–Green Bay Space Trek Camp

University of Wisconsin–Green Bay
2420 Nicolet Drive
Green Bay, Wisconsin 54311

General Information Coed residential and day academic program established in 2004.
Academics Aerospace science.
Special Interest Areas Model rocketry, robotics.
Trips Day, shopping.
Program Information 1 session per year. Session length: 6 days in July, August. Ages: 12–18. 100–150 participants per session. Day program cost: $239. Boarding program cost: $465.
Application Deadline Continuous.
Jobs Positions for college students 19 and older.
Contact Ms. Mona Christensen, Director of Youth Opportunities, main address above. Phone: 920-465-CAMP (2267). Fax: 920-465-2552. E-mail: summercamps@uwgb.edu.
URL www.uwgbsummercamps.com

University of Wisconsin–Green Bay Summer Art Studio

University of Wisconsin–Green Bay
2420 Nicolet Drive
Green Bay, Wisconsin 54311-7001

General Information Coed residential and day arts program established in 1957. Formal opportunities for the artistically talented.
Academics Art (Advanced Placement).
Arts Arts, ceramics, drawing, fabric arts, film, graphic arts, jewelry making, metalworking, painting, photography, pottery, printmaking, sculpture, studio arts, visual arts, weaving.
Trips Cultural, day, shopping.
Program Information 2 sessions per year. Session length: 5–6 days in July. Ages: 13–18. 100–200 participants per session. Day program cost: $175. Boarding program cost: $395. Financial aid available. Financial aid available for minority students in Wisconsin who meet specific requirements.
Application Deadline Continuous.
Jobs Positions for college students 19 and older.

University of Wisconsin–Green Bay Summer Art Studio (continued)

Contact Mona Christensen, Director of Youth Opportunities, main address above. Phone: 920-465-CAMP (2267) Ext... Fax: 920-465-2552. E-mail: summercamps@uwgb.edu.
URL www.uwgbsummercamps.com

University of Wisconsin–Green Bay Summer Discovery

University of Wisconsin–Green Bay
2420 Nicolet Drive
Green Bay, Wisconsin 54311-7001

General Information Coed day traditional camp and academic program established in 1992.
Program Focus Enrichment.
Academics English language/literature, Spanish language/literature, academics (general), astronomy, communications, computers, ecology, geography, mathematics, music, psychology, reading, science (general), social studies, writing.
Arts Acting, arts and crafts (general), ceramics, drawing, jewelry making, music, painting, photography, theater/drama.
Special Interest Areas Animal care, culinary arts, model rocketry, nature study.
Program Information 3 sessions per year. Session length: 5 days in July, August. Ages: 4–14. 150–200 participants per session. Day program cost: $60–$146. Application fee: $10. Financial aid available.
Application Deadline Continuous.
Jobs Positions for high school students 15 and older and college students 18 and older.
Contact Mona Christensen, Director of Youth Opportunities, main address above. Phone: 920-465-CAMP (2267). Fax: 920-465-2552. E-mail: summercamps@uwgb.edu.
URL www.uwgbsummercamps.com

University of Wisconsin–Green Bay Summer Music Camps

University of Wisconsin–Green Bay
2420 Nicolet Drive
Green Bay, Wisconsin 54311-7001

General Information Coed residential and day arts program established in 1965. Formal opportunities for the artistically talented.
Program Focus Music.
Academics Music.
Arts Band, chorus, music, music (chamber), music (classical), music (ensemble), music (instrumental), music (jazz), music (orchestral), music (vocal).
Trips Cultural, shopping.
Program Information 7 sessions per year. Session length: 6–7 days in June, July, August. Ages: 12–18. 40–675 participants per session. Day program cost: $160–$200. Boarding program cost: $360–$425. Financial aid available. Financial aid available for minority students in Wisconsin who meet specific requirements.
Application Deadline Continuous.
Jobs Positions for college students 20 and older.
Contact Mona Christensen, Director of Youth Opportunities, main address above. Phone: 920-465-CAMP (2267). Fax: 920-465-2552. E-mail: summercamps@uwgb.edu.
URL www.uwgbsummercamps.com

University of Wisconsin–Green Bay Summer Spanish Immersion

University of Wisconsin–Green Bay
2420 Nicolet Drive
Green Bay, Wisconsin 54311-7001

General Information Coed residential and day academic program and cultural program established in 2003. Formal opportunities for the academically talented.
Academics Spanish language/literature.
Trips Cultural, day, shopping.
Program Information 1 session per year. Session length: 6 days in July. Ages: 13–18. 20–75 participants per session. Day program cost: $240. Boarding program cost: $455.
Application Deadline Continuous.
Jobs Positions for college students 20 and older.
Contact Ms. Mona Christensen, Director of Youth Opportunities, main address above. Phone: 920-465-CAMP. Fax: 920-465-2552. E-mail: summercamps@uwgb.edu.
URL www.uwgbsummercamps.com

University of Wisconsin–Superior Youthsummer 2005

University of Wisconsin–Superior
1800 Grand Avenue
Superior, Wisconsin 54880

General Information Coed residential and day traditional camp and academic program established in 1972. Specific services available for the physically challenged.
Program Focus Career orientation.
Academics SAT/ACT preparation, aerospace science, astronomy, biology, business, ecology, environmental science, geography, health sciences, humanities, intercultural studies, marine studies, physics, precollege program, psychology, reading, science (general), social science, social studies, writing.
Special Interest Areas Native American culture, animal care, career exploration, college planning, community service, field research/expeditions, field trips (arts and culture), flight instruction, leadership training, nautical skills.
Sports Basketball, bicycling, boating, canoeing, climbing (wall), golf, kayaking, rowing (crew/sculling), sailing, sea kayaking, swimming, tennis.
Wilderness/Outdoors Backpacking, canoe trips, hiking, mountain biking, wilderness camping.
Trips College tours, cultural, day, overnight.
Program Information 5 sessions per year. Session length: 5 days in June, July. Ages: 13–17. 90–120

participants per session. Day program cost: $220–$470. Boarding program cost: $365–$615. Application fee: $50. Financial aid available.
Application Deadline Continuous.
Jobs Positions for college students.
Contact Gregory Burke, Director, Rothwell Student Center, Room 50, PO Box 2000, Superior, Wisconsin 54880. Phone: 715-394-8173. Fax: 715-394-8445. E-mail: gburke@uwsuper.edu.
URL www2.uwsuper.edu/youth

Ventures Travel Service–Wisconsin

Friendship Ventures
Wisconsin

General Information Coed travel special needs program established in 1985. Specific services available for the developmentally challenged and physically challenged.
Program Focus Provides travel services to older teens and adults with developmental disabilities.
Special Interest Areas Touring.
Program Information 50 sessions per year. Session length: 4–10 days in February, March, April, May, June, July, August, September, October, November, December. Ages: 14–70. 4–8 participants per session. Cost: $395–$2000.
Application Deadline Continuous.
Jobs Positions for college students 18 and older.
Contact Georgann Rumsey, President/CEO, 10509 108th Street, NW, Annandale, Minnesota 55302. Phone: 952-852-0101. Fax: 952-852-0123. E-mail: fv@friendshipventures.org.
URL www.friendshipventures.org

William Henderson Football Camp/Sports International

Sports International, Inc.
St. Norbert College
De Pere, Wisconsin

General Information Coed residential and day sports camp established in 1998.
Program Focus Football.
Sports Football, weight training.
Program Information 1 session per year. Session length: 5 days in July. Ages: 8–18. 300–450 participants per session. Day program cost: $489. Boarding program cost: $599. Financial aid available.
Application Deadline Continuous.
Jobs Positions for college students 18 and older.
Contact Customer Service, 8924 McGaw Court, Columbia, Maryland 21045. Phone: 800-555-0801. Fax: 410-309-9962. E-mail: info@footballcamps.com.
URL www.footballcamps.com

Woodland

Towering Pines Camp
5513 Highway D
Eagle River, Wisconsin 54521

General Information Girls' residential traditional camp established in 1941. Accredited by American Camping Association. Formal opportunities for the academically talented and artistically talented.
Academics English as a second language, computers, ecology.
Arts Arts and crafts (general), ceramics, dance (jazz), dance (modern), fabric arts, jewelry making, music, painting, photography, pottery, theater/drama, weaving.
Special Interest Areas Animal care, campcraft, leadership training, nature study.
Sports Aerobics, archery, basketball, boating, canoeing, diving, equestrian sports, fencing, fishing, horseback riding, riflery, ropes course, sailing, swimming, tennis, volleyball, waterskiing, windsurfing.
Wilderness/Outdoors Canoe trips.
Trips Cultural, day, overnight.
Program Information 1–2 sessions per year. Session length: 4–6 weeks in June, July, August. Ages: 6–15. 65–70 participants per session. Boarding program cost: $2950–$3900. Financial aid available.
Application Deadline Continuous.
Jobs Positions for college students 19 and older.
Summer Contact Anne G. Jordan, Director, main address above. Phone: 715-479-4540. Fax: 715-466-7710.
Winter Contact Anne G. Jordan, Director, 242 Bristol Street, Northfield, Illinois 60093. Phone: 800-882-7034. Fax: 715-446-7710. E-mail: towpines@aol.com.
URL www.campwoodland.com

World Affairs Seminar

Wisconsin World Affairs Council, Inc.
University of Wisconsin–Whitewater
800 West Main Street
Whitewater, Wisconsin 53190

General Information Coed residential academic program and cultural program established in 1977. Specific services available for the physically challenged.
Program Focus In association with University of Wisconsin-Whitewater and District 6270 of Rotary International, seminar deals with issues and events shaping world affairs. Program approved by National Association of Secondary School Principals.
Academics Area studies, government and politics, peace education.
Arts Acting, dance (folk), music, music (ensemble).
Special Interest Areas Career exploration, community service, team building.
Sports Basketball, cross-country, diving, football, gymnastics, in-line skating, lacrosse, racquetball, soccer, softball, squash, swimming, tennis, track and field, volleyball, water polo, weight training.
Trips College tours.
Program Information 1 session per year. Session length: 1 week in June. Ages: 16–18. 900–1,200 participants per session. Boarding program cost: $400–$440. Financial aid available.
Application Deadline Continuous.

World Affairs Seminar (continued)
Jobs Positions for college students 19 and older.
Contact Mr. Frederick R. Luedke, General Manager, 800 West Main Street, University of Wisconsin-Whitewater, Whitewater, Wisconsin 53190. Phone: 888-404-4049. Fax: 262-472-5210. E-mail: was@uww.edu.
URL www.worldaffairsseminar.org

YMCA Camp Icaghowan

YMCA of Metropolitan Minneapolis
899-A 115th Street
Amery, Wisconsin 54001

General Information Coed residential and day traditional camp established in 1909. Accredited by American Camping Association.
Program Focus YMCA values and environmental awareness.
Arts Arts and crafts (general).
Special Interest Areas Leadership training, nature study.
Sports Archery, canoeing, fishing, horseback riding, ropes course, sailing, skateboarding, swimming.
Wilderness/Outdoors Backpacking, canoe trips, climbing, rock climbing.
Trips Overnight.
Program Information 10 sessions per year. Session length: 3–6 days in June, July, August. Ages: 7–16. 120–160 participants per session. Day program cost: $95–$110. Boarding program cost: $195–$990. Financial aid available.
Application Deadline Continuous.
Jobs Positions for high school students 17 and older and college students 18 and older.
Contact Peter Wieczorek, Camp Director, 4 West Rustic Lodge, Minneapolis, Minnesota 55409. Phone: 612-821-2904. Fax: 612-823-2482. E-mail: info@campicaghowan.org.
URL www.ymcacamps.org

YMCA Camp Minikani

YMCA of Metropolitan Milwaukee
860 Amy Belle Lake Road
Hubertus, Wisconsin 53033

General Information Coed residential and day traditional camp and outdoor program established in 1919. Religious affiliation: Christian. Accredited by American Camping Association.
Arts Arts and crafts (general).
Special Interest Areas Campcraft, leadership training, nature study.
Sports Archery, boating, canoeing, climbing (wall), diving, horseback riding, riflery, ropes course, sailing, snorkeling, swimming.
Wilderness/Outdoors Backpacking, canoe trips, caving, hiking, mountain biking, orienteering, outdoor adventure, rock climbing, white-water trips, wilderness camping.
Trips Day, overnight.
Program Information 12–15 sessions per year. Session length: 5–14 days in June, July, August. Ages: 8–17. 10–200 participants per session. Day program cost: $154–$179. Boarding program cost: $300–$1150. Financial aid available.
Application Deadline Continuous.
Jobs Positions for college students 18 and older.
Contact Donna Buckmaster, Administrative Director, 860 Amy Belle Lake Road, Hubertus, Wisconsin 53033. Phone: 262-251-9080. Fax: 262-628-4051. E-mail: dbuckmaster.mi@ymcamke.org.
URL www.minikani.org

YMCA Camp U-Nah-Li-Ya

Greater Green Bay YMCA
Nicolet National Forest
Wisconsin

General Information Coed residential traditional camp established in 1937. Accredited by American Camping Association.
Academics Astronomy.
Arts Arts and crafts (general), dance.
Special Interest Areas Gardening, leadership training, nature study.
Sports Archery, baseball, basketball, boating, canoeing, climbing (wall), fishing, horseback riding, rappelling, ropes course, sailing, soccer, swimming, volleyball.
Wilderness/Outdoors Backpacking, canoe trips, hiking, mountain biking, rock climbing, survival training, white-water trips, wilderness camping.
Trips Overnight.
Program Information 8–10 sessions per year. Session length: 4–15 days in January, February, March, April, May, June, July, August, September, October, December. Ages: 7–17. 80–140 participants per session. Boarding program cost: $250–$500. Financial aid available.
Application Deadline Continuous.
Jobs Positions for college students 18 and older.
Contact Kathleen McKee, Program Director, 13654 South Shore Drive, Suring, Wisconsin 54174. Phone: 715-276-7116. Fax: 715-276-1701. E-mail: mckeeka@greenbayymca.org.
URL www.greenbayymca.org

YMCA Camp Wabansi

Greater Green Bay YMCA
Dykesville, Wisconsin

General Information Coed day traditional camp. Accredited by American Camping Association.
Academics Astronomy.
Arts Arts and crafts (general), dance.
Special Interest Areas Nature study.
Sports Archery, boating, fishing, horseback riding, swimming, volleyball.
Wilderness/Outdoors Backpacking, hiking, mountain biking.
Trips Overnight.
Program Information 8–10 sessions per year. Session length: 5 days in June, July, August. Ages: 7–11. 80–140 participants per session. Financial aid available.
Application Deadline Continuous.
Jobs Positions for college students 18 and older.

Contact Ms. Kathleen McKee, Program Director, 13654 South Shore Drive, Suring, Wisconsin 54174. Phone: 715-276-7116. Fax: 715-276-1701. E-mail: mckeeka@greenbayymca.org.
URL www.greenbayymca.org

WYOMING

EARTHWATCH INSTITUTE–JACKSON HOLE BISON DIG

Earthwatch Institute
Jackson Hole, Wyoming

General Information Coed residential outdoor program, cultural program, and adventure program.
Program Focus Excavating a prehistoric site to determine the role of bison in Native American life.
Academics Archaeology, ecology, science (general).
Special Interest Areas Field research/expeditions.
Program Information 3 sessions per year. Session length: 2 weeks in June, July. Ages: 16+. 12 participants per session. Boarding program cost: $1595–$1695. Financial aid available. Financial aid for high school students and teachers.
Application Deadline Continuous.
Contact General Information Desk, PO Box 75, Maynard, Massachusetts 01754. Phone: 800-776-0188. Fax: 978-461-2332. E-mail: info@earthwatch.org.
URL www.earthwatch.org

ELK CREEK RANCH AND TREK PROGRAM

Cody, Wyoming 82414

General Information Coed residential outdoor program and wilderness program established in 1957.

Elk Creek Ranch and Trek Program

Special Interest Areas Animal care, construction, first aid, general camp activities.
Sports Fishing, horseback riding, riflery, ropes course, swimming.
Wilderness/Outdoors Backpacking, hiking, mountaineering, orienteering, pack animal trips, rafting, rock climbing, white-water trips, wilderness camping, wilderness/outdoors (general).
Trips Overnight.
Program Information 2–6 sessions per year. Session length: 4 weeks in June, July, August. Ages: 13–18. 10–45 participants per session. Boarding program cost: $3200–$5100.
Application Deadline Continuous.
Summer Contact Susan Ridgway, Co-Director, PO Box 1476, Cody, Wyoming 82414. Phone: 307-587-3902.
Winter Contact Susan Ridgway, Co-Director, 31A Academy Street, South Berwick, Maine 03908. Phone: 207-384-5361. E-mail: rockinrrranch@aol.com.
URL www.elkcreekranch.com

Special Note
Elk Creek Ranch, located in the Shoshone National Forest, has operated for forty-three years. The Ranch Program is for teenagers seeking a wilderness experience. The program includes horseback riding, work projects, backpacking, fishing, glacier skiing, horse pack trips, and other activities. The Trek Program spends twenty-five days in the rugged wilderness. Each trek introduces basic wilderness skills, including diet, first aid, map and compass work, survival techniques, and low-impact camping. In addition, each program stresses small-group dynamics, nurturing individual growth in a close community.

LANDMARK VOLUNTEERS: WYOMING

Landmark Volunteers, Inc.
Wyoming

General Information Coed residential outdoor program and community service program established in 1992. High school credit may be earned.
Program Focus Opportunity for high school students to earn community service credit while working as a team for two weeks serving Grand Teton Music Festival/Jackson Hole or National Elk Refuge. Similar programs offered through Landmark Volunteers at over 60 locations in 21 states.
Academics Biology, ecology, environmental science, music.
Arts Music, music (chamber), music (classical), music (orchestral).
Special Interest Areas Career exploration, community service, conservation projects, construction, field research/expeditions, leadership training, nature study, team building, trail maintenance, work camp programs.
Wilderness/Outdoors Hiking.
Trips Cultural, day.
Program Information 2 sessions per year. Session length: 2 weeks in June, July. Ages: 14–18. 10–12 participants per session. Boarding program cost: $875–$925. Financial aid available.
Application Deadline Continuous.
Jobs Positions for college students.

Landmark Volunteers: Wyoming (continued)

Contact Ann Barrett, Executive Director, PO Box 455, Sheffield, Massachusetts 01257. Phone: 413-229-0255. Fax: 413-229-2050. E-mail: landmark@volunteers.com.
URL www.volunteers.com
For more information, see page 1182.

Outpost Wilderness Adventure–Wind River Expedition

Outpost Wilderness Adventure
Wind River Range
Lander, Wyoming

General Information Coed travel outdoor program, wilderness program, and adventure program established in 1979.
Program Focus Adventure skills and expeditions.
Academics Ecology.
Special Interest Areas Campcraft, field research/expeditions, nature study.
Sports Fishing, rappelling.
Wilderness/Outdoors Backpacking, fly fishing, hiking, mountaineering, orienteering, outdoor adventure, rock climbing, wilderness camping.
Trips Overnight.
Program Information 1 session per year. Session length: 15 days in July, August. Ages: 13–17. Cost: $1800. Financial aid available.
Application Deadline Continuous.
Summer Contact Quentin Keith, Director, 20859 County Road 77, Lake George, Colorado 80827. Phone: 719-748-3080. Fax: 719-748-3046. E-mail: q@owa.com.
Winter Contact Quentin Keith, Director, 2107 Shovel Mountain Road, Cypress Mill, Texas 78663. Phone: 830-825-3015. Fax: 830-825-3116. E-mail: q@owa.com.
URL www.owa.com

Outward Bound West–Wyoming Rock Climbing

Outward Bound West/Outward Bound, USA
Medicine Bow National Forest, Vedauwoo
Wyoming

General Information Coed travel outdoor program and wilderness program established in 1965. College credit may be earned.
Program Focus Teamwork and leadership wilderness adventure.
Academics Environmental science.
Special Interest Areas Campcraft, community service, leadership training, nature study, personal development, team building.
Wilderness/Outdoors Hiking, outdoor adventure, rock climbing, wilderness camping.
Trips Overnight.
Program Information 2 sessions per year. Session length: 1 week in June, August. Ages: 16+. Cost: $1295. Application fee: $95. Financial aid available.
Application Deadline Continuous.
Jobs Positions for college students 21 and older.
Contact Admissions Advisor, 910 Jackson Street, Golden, Colorado 80401. Phone: 866-746-9777. Fax: 720-497-2421. E-mail: info@obwest.org.
URL www.outwardboundwest.org

Overland: Teton Challenge Hiking, Climbing and Kayaking

Overland Travel, Inc.
Wyoming

General Information Coed travel outdoor program, wilderness program, and adventure program established in 1985. Accredited by American Camping Association. High school credit may be earned.
Program Focus Participants will climb the Grand Teton.
Special Interest Areas Leadership training, team building.
Sports Kayaking, rappelling.
Wilderness/Outdoors Backpacking, hiking, mountaineering, rafting, rock climbing, white-water trips, wilderness camping.
Program Information 2 sessions per year. Session length: 3 weeks in June, July, August. Ages: 15–18. 8–12 participants per session. Cost: $3695.
Application Deadline Continuous.
Jobs Positions for college students 20 and older.
Contact Ms. Brooks Follansbee, Director, PO Box 31, Williamstown, Massachusetts 01267. Phone: 800-458-0588. Fax: 413-458-5208. E-mail: overland@adelphia.net.
URL www.overlandsummers.com
For more information, see page 1240.

Student Conservation Association–Conservation Crew Program (Wyoming)

Student Conservation Association (SCA)
Wyoming

General Information Coed residential outdoor program, community service program, and wilderness program established in 1957. High school credit may be earned.
Program Focus Resource management, conservation and environmental education.
Academics Biology, botany, ecology, environmental science, geology/earth science, history.
Special Interest Areas Campcraft, community service, construction, leadership training, nature study, trail maintenance, work camp programs.
Sports Canoeing, fishing, kayaking, swimming.
Wilderness/Outdoors Backpacking, canoe trips, hiking, orienteering, outdoor living skills, wilderness camping.
Trips Cultural, day, overnight.
Program Information 2–3 sessions per year. Session length: 3–5 weeks in June, July, August. Ages: 15–19. 6–8 participants per session. Application fee: $20. Financial aid available. No cost for program; financial aid possible for travel expenses.
Application Deadline Continuous.
Jobs Positions for college students 21 and older.

Contact Recruitment Office, PO Box 550, Charlestown, New Hampshire 03603. Phone: 603-543-1700. Fax: 603-543-1828. E-mail: getreal@thesca.org.
URL www.theSCA.org

Success Oriented Achievement Realized (SOAR)–Wyoming

Success Oriented Achievement Realized (SOAR)
184 Uphill Road
Dubois, Wyoming 82513

General Information Coed residential outdoor program, wilderness program, special needs program, and adventure program established in 1997. Accredited by Association for Experiential Education. Formal opportunities for the academically talented. Specific services available for the learning disabled, participant with ADD, and participant with AD/HD.
Program Focus Youth diagnosed with learning disabilities and Attention Deficit Disorder in an adventure-based setting.
Academics English as a second language, academics (general), mathematics, study skills.
Special Interest Areas Career exploration.
Sports Canoeing, climbing (wall), fishing, horseback riding, kayaking, rappelling, ropes course, scuba diving, sea kayaking, snorkeling.
Wilderness/Outdoors Backpacking, caving, hiking, mountaineering, orienteering, pack animal trips, rafting, rock climbing, white-water trips, wilderness camping.
Trips Overnight.
Program Information 12 sessions per year. Session length: 12–26 days in January, February, March, April, May, June, July, August, September, October, November, December. Ages: 11–18. 10–14 participants per session. Boarding program cost: $1950–$3600. Financial aid available.
Application Deadline Continuous.
Jobs Positions for college students 20 and older.
Contact Ed Parker, Admissions Director, PO Box 388, Balsam, North Carolina 28707. Phone: 828-456-3435. Fax: 828-456-3449. E-mail: ed@soarnc.org.
URL www.soarwy.org

Teton Valley Ranch Camp–Boys Camp

Teton Valley Ranch Camp Education Foundation
Dubois, Wyoming 82513

General Information Boys' residential traditional camp, outdoor program, and wilderness program established in 1939. Accredited by American Camping Association.
Program Focus Western mountain adventures in a great ranch community with wilderness trips on foot and horseback.
Arts Arts and crafts (general), drawing, jewelry making, leather working, musical productions, painting, photography, theater/drama.
Special Interest Areas Native American culture, animal care, campcraft, community service, field trips (arts and culture), gold panning, leadership training, nature study, rodeo arts, stone carving.
Sports Archery, equestrian sports, fishing, horseback riding, riflery, swimming.
Wilderness/Outdoors Backpacking, hiking, orienteering, outdoor adventure, pack animal trips, wilderness camping, wilderness/outdoors (general).
Trips Day, overnight, shopping.
Program Information 1 session per year. Session length: 30 days in June, July. Ages: 10–15. 100–125 participants per session. Boarding program cost: $3800–$4000. Financial aid available.
Application Deadline Continuous.
Jobs Positions for high school students 18 and older and college students 18 and older.
Contact Mr. Jim Walter, Director, PO Box 3968, Jackson, Wyoming 83001. Phone: 307-733-2958. Fax: 307-733-0258. E-mail: mailbag@tvrcamp.org.
URL www.tvrcamp.org

Teton Valley Ranch Camp–Girls Camp

Teton Valley Ranch Camp Education Foundation
Dubois, Wyoming 82513

General Information Girls' residential traditional camp, outdoor program, and wilderness program established in 1939. Accredited by American Camping Association.
Program Focus Western mountain adventures in a great ranch community with wilderness trips on foot and horseback.
Arts Arts and crafts (general), drawing, jewelry making, leather working, musical productions, painting, photography, theater/drama.
Special Interest Areas Native American culture, animal care, campcraft, community service, field trips (arts and culture), gold panning, leadership training, nature study, rodeo arts, stone carving.
Sports Archery, equestrian sports, fishing, horseback riding, riflery, swimming.
Wilderness/Outdoors Backpacking, hiking, orienteering, outdoor adventure, pack animal trips, wilderness camping, wilderness/outdoors (general).
Trips Day, overnight, shopping.
Program Information 1 session per year. Session length: 30 days in July, August. Ages: 10–15. 100–125 participants per session. Boarding program cost: $3800–$4000. Financial aid available.
Application Deadline Continuous.
Jobs Positions for high school students 18 and older and college students 18 and older.
Contact Mr. Jim Walter, Director, PO Box 3968, Jackson, Wyoming 83001. Phone: 307-733-2958. Fax: 307-733-0258. E-mail: mailbag@tvrcamp.org.
URL www.tvrcamp.org

University of Chicago–Stones and Bones

University of Chicago
Wyoming

General Information Coed travel academic program and outdoor program established in 2001. Formal opportunities for the academically talented. College credit may be earned.
Program Focus Paleontology, field work.
Academics Biology, geology/earth science, precollege program.
Special Interest Areas Field research/expeditions.
Wilderness/Outdoors Outdoor camping.
Trips Cultural, day.
Program Information 1 session per year. Session length: 4 weeks in June, July. Ages: 15–22. 15–20 participants per session. Cost: $6993–$7429. Application fee: $40–$55. Financial aid available.
Application Deadline May 15.
Contact Ms. Valerie Huston, Secretary, Summer Session Office, Graham School of General Studies, The University of Chicago, 1427 East 60th Street, Chicago, Illinois 60637. Phone: 773-702-6033. Fax: 773-702-6814. E-mail: uc-summer@uchicago.edu.
URL summer.uchicago.edu/
For more information, see page 1360.

Wilderness Ventures–Grand Teton

Wilderness Ventures
Wyoming

General Information Coed travel outdoor program, wilderness program, and adventure program established in 1973.
Program Focus Wilderness travel, wilderness skills, leadership skills.
Special Interest Areas Leadership training.
Sports Sea kayaking.
Wilderness/Outdoors Backpacking, hiking, rafting, rock climbing, wilderness camping.
Trips Overnight.
Program Information 4 sessions per year. Session length: 22 days in June, July, August. Ages: 14–18. 13 participants per session. Cost: $3490. Financial aid available.
Jobs Positions for college students 21 and older.
Contact Mike Cottingham, Director, PO Box 2768, Jackson Hole, Wyoming 83001. Phone: 800-533-2281. Fax: 307-739-1934. E-mail: info@wildernessventures.com.
URL www.wildernessventures.com
For more information, see page 1396.

Wilderness Ventures–Jackson Hole

Wilderness Ventures
Wyoming

General Information Coed travel outdoor program, wilderness program, and adventure program established in 1973.

Wilderness Ventures–Grand Teton

Program Focus Wilderness travel, wilderness skills, leadership skills.
Special Interest Areas Leadership training.
Sports Sea kayaking.
Wilderness/Outdoors Backpacking, canoe trips, hiking, rafting, rock climbing, wilderness camping.
Trips Overnight.
Program Information 2 sessions per year. Session length: 22 days in June, July, August. Ages: 13–15. 13 participants per session. Cost: $3490. Financial aid available.
Application Deadline Continuous.
Jobs Positions for college students 21 and older.
Contact Mike Cottingham, Director, PO Box 2768, Jackson Hole, Wyoming 83001. Phone: 800-533-2281. Fax: 307-739-1934. E-mail: info@wildernessventures.com.
URL www.wildernessventures.com
For more information, see page 1396.

Wilderness Ventures–Teton Adventure

Wilderness Ventures
Wyoming

General Information Coed travel outdoor program, wilderness program, and adventure program established in 1973.
Program Focus Wilderness travel, wilderness skills, leadership skills.
Sports Kayaking, sea kayaking.
Wilderness/Outdoors Backpacking, mountain biking, white-water trips.
Trips Overnight.
Program Information 4 sessions per year. Session length: 16 days in June, July, August. Ages: 14–18. 12 participants per session. Cost: $2490. Financial aid available.
Application Deadline Continuous.
Jobs Positions for college students 21 and older.
Contact Mike Cottingham, Director, PO Box 2768, Jackson Hole, Wyoming 83001. Phone: 800-533-2281. Fax: 307-739-1934. E-mail: info@wildernessventures.com.
URL www.wildernessventures.com

For more information, see page 1396.

Wilderness Ventures–Wyoming Mountaineering

Wilderness Ventures
Wyoming

General Information Coed travel outdoor program, wilderness program, and adventure program established in 1973.
Program Focus Wilderness travel, wilderness skills, leadership skills.
Special Interest Areas Leadership training.
Wilderness/Outdoors Backpacking, hiking, mountaineering, rock climbing, wilderness camping.
Trips Overnight.
Program Information 2 sessions per year. Session length: 3 weeks in July, August. Ages: 15–18. 10 participants per session. Cost: $3490. Financial aid available.
Application Deadline Continuous.
Jobs Positions for college students 21 and older.
Contact Mike Cottingham, Director, PO Box 2768, Jackson Hole, Wyoming 83001. Phone: 800-533-2281. Fax: 307-739-1934. E-mail: info@wildernessventures.com.
URL www.wildernessventures.com

Special Note
Since 1973, Wilderness Ventures has been conducting exciting expeditions for beginners and experienced young adults, ages 13–20. Expeditions visit a variety of wilderness environments in Alaska, Australia, Canada, Central America, Europe, Hawaii, South America, and the western United States for extended periods. Students learn outdoor and group leadership skills and gain an appreciation for varied wilderness environments. The professional staff consists of outdoor educators, whose ages range from 21 to 32. Participants come from nearly every state and several countries. Enrollment is limited, and applicants must submit school references prior to admission. Previous wilderness experience is not necessary.

For more information, see page 1396.

Windsor Mountain: Voices of the Wind River, Wyoming

Interlocken at Windsor Mountain
Riverton, Wyoming

General Information Coed residential outdoor program, community service program, and cultural program established in 1967.
Academics Geology/earth science, history, intercultural studies, science (general), writing.
Special Interest Areas Community service, conservation projects.
Wilderness/Outdoors Backpacking, fly fishing, hiking, outdoor adventure, rafting, rock climbing, white-water trips.
Trips Cultural, day, overnight.
Program Information 1 session per year. Session length: 3 weeks in June, July. Ages: 12–14. 15 participants per session. Boarding program cost: $2995. Financial aid available.
Application Deadline April 1.
Contact David Love, Director, 19 Interlocken Way, Windsor, New Hampshire 03244. Phone: 603-478-3166. Fax: 603-478-5260. E-mail: david@windsormountain.org.
URL www.windsormountain.org/xrds

For more information, see page 1162.

ARGENTINA

AFS-USA–Community Service–Argentina

AFS-USA
Argentina

General Information Coed residential community service program and cultural program. High school credit may be earned.
Program Focus Living with a host family in Argentina. Volunteering in community organization on projects with social or environmental focus.
Academics Spanish language/literature.
Special Interest Areas Community service, cross-cultural education, homestays.
Trips Cultural, day, overnight.
Program Information 1 session per year. Session length: 30 days in July. Ages: 15–18. 80–90 participants per session. Boarding program cost: $4165–$4465. Application fee: $75. Financial aid available. International airfare and volunteer homestay support included.
Application Deadline Continuous.
Contact Manager, AFS Info Center, 506 Southwest 6th Avenue, 2nd Floor, Portland, Oregon 97204. Phone: 800-AFS-INFO. Fax: 503-248-4076. E-mail: afsinfo@afs.org.
URL www.afs.org/usa
For more information, see page 974.

AFS-USA–Homestay–Argentina

AFS-USA
Argentina

General Information Coed residential academic program and cultural program.
Program Focus Living with a host family while attending school.
Academics Spanish language/literature.
Special Interest Areas Homestays.
Trips Cultural, day, overnight.
Program Information 1 session per year. Session length: 6 weeks in June, July, August. Ages: 15–18. Boarding program cost: $4165–$4665. Application fee: $75. Financial aid available. International airfare and volunteer homestay support included.
Application Deadline Continuous.
Jobs Positions for college students.
Contact Manager, AFS Info Center, 506 Southwest 6th Avenue, 2nd Floor, Portland, Oregon 97204. Phone: 800-AFS-INFO. Fax: 503-248-4076. E-mail: afsinfo@afs.org.
URL www.afs.org/usa
For more information, see page 974.

Center for Cultural Interchange–Argentina Independent Homestay

Center for Cultural Interchange
Argentina

General Information Coed residential cultural program established in 1985.
Program Focus Homestay program.
Academics Independent study, language study.
Special Interest Areas Homestays.
Trips Cultural, day, shopping.

Program Information Session length: 1–6 weeks in January, February, March, April, May, June, July, August, September, October, November, December. Ages: 16+. Boarding program cost: $985–$1120. Financial aid available.
Application Deadline Continuous.
Contact Ms. Juliet Jones, Outbound Programs Director, 325 West Huron, Suite 706, Chicago, Illinois 60610. Phone: 866-684-9675. Fax: 312-944-2644. E-mail: info@cci-exchange.com.
URL www.cci-exchange.com
For more information, see page 1060.

EARTHWATCH INSTITUTE–ARGENTINA'S PAMPAS CARNIVORES

Earthwatch Institute
Parque Provincial Ernesto Tornquist
Argentina

General Information Coed residential outdoor program, cultural program, and adventure program.
Program Focus Using the status of carnivores to measure and mitigate human impact on Argentina's prairies.
Academics Biology, ecology, environmental science, science (general).
Special Interest Areas Field research/expeditions, nature study.
Program Information 5 sessions per year. Session length: 10 days in March, April, May, June, July, September, October. Ages: 16+. 5 participants per session. Boarding program cost: $1695–$1795. Financial aid available. Financial aid for high school students and teachers.
Application Deadline Continuous.
Contact General Information Desk, PO Box 75, Maynard, Massachusetts 01754. Phone: 800-776-0188. Fax: 978-461-2332. E-mail: info@earthwatch.org.
URL www.earthwatch.org

EARTHWATCH INSTITUTE–TRIASSIC PARK

Earthwatch Institute
Ischigualasto Provincial Park
Argentina

General Information Coed residential outdoor program.
Program Focus Reconstructing the dawn of the age of dinosaurs.
Academics Paleontology.
Special Interest Areas Field research/expeditions.
Program Information 4 sessions per year. Session length: 13 days in April, August, September, October. Ages: 16+. 15 participants per session. Boarding program cost: $1895–$1995. Financial aid available. Financial aid for high school students and teachers.
Application Deadline Continuous.
Contact General Information Desk, PO Box 75, Maynard, Massachusetts 01754. Phone: 800-776-0188. Fax: 978-461-2332. E-mail: info@earthwatch.org.
URL www.earthwatch.org

THE EXPERIMENT IN INTERNATIONAL LIVING–ARGENTINA HOMESTAY, COMMUNITY SERVICE, AND OUTDOOR ECOLOGICAL PROGRAM

The Experiment in International Living
Argentina

General Information Coed residential outdoor program, community service program, cultural program, and adventure program established in 1932.
Program Focus International youth travel, homestays, ecological trek.
Academics Spanish language/literature.
Special Interest Areas Community service, homestays, nature study, touring.
Sports Horseback riding.
Trips Cultural, day, overnight.
Program Information 1 session per year. Session length: 4 weeks in July, August. Ages: 14–19. 10–15 participants per session. Boarding program cost: $4750. Financial aid available.
Application Deadline May 1.
Contact Annie Thompson, Enrollment Director, Summer Abroad, Kipling Road, PO Box 676, Brattleboro, Vermont 05302-0676. Phone: 800-345-2929. Fax: 802-258-3428. E-mail: eil@worldlearning.org.
URL www.usexperiment.org
For more information, see page 1116.

GIC ARG–ARGENTINIAN COOKING

GIC Arg–Cultural Exchange Group of Argentina
Buenos Aires
Argentina

General Information Coed residential arts program established in 2002.
Program Focus Argentinian cooking at Escuela Superior de Cocina de Alicia Berger.
Special Interest Areas Culinary arts.
Trips Cultural, day.
Program Information Session length: 4 days in January, February, March, April, May, June, July, August, September, October, November, December. Ages: 15+. 2–20 participants per session. Boarding program cost: $480.
Application Deadline Continuous.
Contact Mr. Marcos M. Salusso, Director, Lavalle 397-1-1, Buenos Aires C1047AAG, Argentina. Phone: 54-11-43151000. Fax: 54-11-43151000. E-mail: info@gicarg.org.
URL www.gicarg.org

GIC ARG–SOCCER

GIC Arg–Cultural Exchange Group of Argentina
Buenos Aires
Argentina

General Information Coed residential sports camp established in 2002.
Program Focus Soccer.
Sports Soccer.
Trips Cultural, day.

GIC Arg–Soccer (continued)

Program Information 3–10 sessions per year. Session length: 30–90 days in January, February, March, April, May, June, July, August, September, October, November, December. Ages: 15+. 2–30 participants per session. Boarding program cost: $600–$1200.
Application Deadline Continuous.
Contact Mr. Marcos M. Salusso, Director, Lavalle 397-1-1, Buenos Aires C1047AAG, Argentina. Phone: 54-11-43151000. Fax: 54-11-43151000. E-mail: info@gicarg.org.
URL www.gicarg.org

GIC Arg–Spanish Language

GIC Arg–Cultural Exchange Group of Argentina
Buenos Aires
Argentina

General Information Coed residential academic program established in 2002. High school or college credit may be earned.
Program Focus Spanish as a second language.
Academics Spanish (Advanced Placement), Spanish language/literature.
Trips Day, shopping.
Program Information 12–14 sessions per year. Session length: 30–90 days in January, February, March, May, June, July, August, September, October, December. Ages: 15+. 5–20 participants per session. Boarding program cost: $1070–$3170.
Application Deadline Continuous.
Contact Mr. Marcos M. Salusso, Director, Lavalle 397-1-1, Buenos Aires C1047AAG, Argentina. Phone: 54-11-43151000. Fax: 54-11-43151000. E-mail: info@gicarg.org.
URL www.gicarg.org

GIC Arg–Tango

GIC Arg–Cultural Exchange Group of Argentina
Buenos Aires
Argentina

General Information Coed residential arts program established in 2002.
Program Focus Tango dance.
Arts Dance.
Trips Cultural, day.
Program Information 25–30 sessions per year. Session length: 5–120 days in January, February, March, April, May, June, July, August, September, October, November, December. Ages: 15+. 2–10 participants per session. Boarding program cost: $265–$3440.
Application Deadline Continuous.
Contact Mr. Marcos Salusso, Director, Lavalle 397-1-1, Buenos Aires C1047AAG, Argentina. Phone: 54-11-43151000. Fax: 54-11-43151000. E-mail: info@gicarg.org.
URL www.gicarg.org

Learning Programs International–Argentina

Learning Programs International
Buenos Aires
Argentina

General Information Coed residential academic program and cultural program established in 2004. Formal opportunities for the academically talented. High school or college credit may be earned.
Program Focus Language acquisition.
Academics Spanish (Advanced Placement), Spanish language/literature.
Arts Dance.
Special Interest Areas Community service, homestays.
Trips Cultural, day, overnight.
Program Information 5 sessions per year. Session length: 8–28 days in January, February, March, June, July, December. Ages: 14–18. 10–30 participants per session. Boarding program cost: $1180. Financial aid available. Airfare not included.
Application Deadline Continuous.
Contact Michelle McRaney, Program Director, 901 West 24th Street, Austin, Texas 78705. Phone: 800-259-4439. Fax: 512-480-8866. E-mail: lpi@studiesabroad.com.
URL www.lpiabroad.com

For more information, see page 1190.

LSA Buenos Aires, Argentina

Language Studies Abroad, Inc.
Buenos Aires
Argentina

General Information Coed residential academic program and cultural program established in 2002. Formal opportunities for the academically talented. High school or college credit may be earned.
Program Focus Language and culture.
Academics Spanish (Advanced Placement), Spanish language/literature, academics (general), intercultural studies.
Special Interest Areas Homestays.
Trips Cultural, day.
Program Information 1–26 sessions per year. Session length: 13–360 days in January, February, March, April, May, June, July, August, September, October, November, December. Ages: 16+. 30–60 participants per session. Application fee: $100. Financial aid available.
Application Deadline Continuous.
Contact Director, 1801 Highway 50 East, Suite I, Carson City, Nevada 89701. Phone: 800-424-5522. Fax: 775-883-2266. E-mail: info@languagestudiesabroad.com.
URL www.languagestudiesabroad.com

For more information, see page 1186.

LSA Cordoba, Argentina

Language Studies Abroad, Inc.
Cordoba
Argentina

General Information Coed residential academic program and cultural program established in 2002. Formal opportunities for the academically talented. High school or college credit may be earned.
Program Focus Language and culture.
Academics Spanish (Advanced Placement), Spanish language/literature, academics (general), intercultural studies.
Special Interest Areas Homestays.
Trips Cultural, day.
Program Information 1–26 sessions per year. Session length: 13–360 days in January, February, March, April, May, June, July, August, September, October, November, December. Ages: 16+. Boarding program cost: $475–$1700. Application fee: $100. Financial aid available.
Application Deadline Continuous.
Contact Director, 1801 Highway 50 East, Suite I, Carson City, Nevada 89701. Phone: 800-424-5522. Fax: 775-883-2266. E-mail: info@languagestudiesabroad.com.
URL www.languagestudiesabroad.com

For more information, see page 1186.

Youth for Understanding USA–Argentina

Youth for Understanding USA
Argentina

General Information Coed residential academic program and cultural program established in 1951. High school or college credit may be earned.
Program Focus Living with a host family and learning Spanish language in Argentina.
Academics Spanish language/literature, area studies, intercultural studies, social studies.
Special Interest Areas Cross-cultural education, homestays.
Trips Cultural, day, overnight, shopping.
Program Information 1 session per year. Session length: 35–45 days in June, July, August. Ages: 15–18. 10–50 participants per session. Boarding program cost: $5595. Application fee: $75. Financial aid available. Round-trip domestic and international airfare is included in the tuition.
Application Deadline March 15.
Contact Admissions Counselor, 6400 Goldsboro Road, Suite 100, Bethesda, Maryland 20817. Phone: 800-TEENAGE (833-6243). Fax: 240-235-2174. E-mail: admissions@us.yfu.org.
URL www.yfu-usa.org

For more information, see page 1414.

ARMENIA

Volunteers for Peace International Work Camp–Armenia

Volunteers for Peace International Work Camps
Yerevan
Armenia

General Information Coed residential community service program established in 1981. Specific services available for the hearing impaired and physically challenged. College credit may be earned.
Program Focus International work camps.
Academics Intercultural studies, peace education.
Special Interest Areas Community service, construction, work camp programs.
Trips Cultural, day, overnight.
Program Information Session length: 2–3 weeks in July, August. Ages: 16+. 12–20 participants per session. Boarding program cost: $250–$600.
Application Deadline Continuous.
Contact Peter Coldwell, Director, 1034 Tiffany Road, Belmont, Vermont 05730. Phone: 802-259-2759. Fax: 802-259-2922. E-mail: vfp@vfp.org.
URL www.vfp.org

AUSTRALIA

AAVE–Australia

AAVE–America's Adventure Ventures Everywhere
Australia

General Information Coed travel outdoor program, wilderness program, and adventure program established in 1976. Accredited by American Camping Association.
Program Focus Watersports.
Special Interest Areas Campcraft, leadership training, nautical skills.
Sports Sailing, scuba diving, snorkeling, surfing, swimming.
Wilderness/Outdoors Backpacking, hiking, orienteering, wilderness camping.
Trips Cultural, day, overnight.
Program Information 2–4 sessions per year. Session length: 3 weeks in June, July, August. Ages: 14–18. 14 participants per session. Cost: $3888.
Application Deadline Continuous.
Jobs Positions for college students 21 and older.
Contact Mr. Abbott Wallis, Owner, 2245 Stonecrop Way, Golden, Colorado 80401. Phone: 800-222-3595. Fax: 303-526-0885. E-mail: info@aave.com.
URL www.aave.com

For more information, see page 952.

ACTIONQUEST: Australian and Great Barrier Reef Adventures

ActionQuest
Australia

General Information Coed travel outdoor program, cultural program, and adventure program established in 1986.

ACTIONQUEST: Australian and Great Barrier Reef Adventures

Program Focus Sailing and land exploration of Sydney, Great Barrier Reef, Whitsunday Islands, and Queensland. Voyage includes PADI scuba certifications, sail training, and shore adventures.
Academics Intercultural studies, marine studies.
Special Interest Areas Leadership training, nautical skills, team building, touring.
Sports Sailing, scuba diving, snorkeling, surfing.
Wilderness/Outdoors Hiking, white-water trips.
Trips Cultural, day, overnight.
Program Information 3 sessions per year. Session length: 3 weeks in June, July, August. Ages: 15–19. 10–18 participants per session. Cost: $4570.
Application Deadline Continuous.
Contact James Stoll, Director, PO Box 5517, Sarasota, Florida 34277. Phone: 800-317-6789. Fax: 941-924-6075. E-mail: info@actionquest.com.
URL www.actionquest.com
For more information, see page 964.

AFS-USA–Homestay Plus–Australia

AFS-USA
Australia

General Information Coed residential outdoor program and cultural program.
Program Focus Living with a host family, participating in activities such as rock climbing, mountain biking, and canoeing and completing an internship in a field of interest.
Academics Area studies, social science, social studies.
Special Interest Areas Campcraft, career exploration, homestays.
Wilderness/Outdoors Backpacking, canoe trips, hiking, mountaineering, outdoor adventure, rock climbing, wilderness camping.
Trips Cultural, day, overnight.
Program Information 1 session per year. Session length: 7 weeks in June, July, August. Ages: 15–18. 35–60 participants per session. Boarding program cost: $4865–$5365. Application fee: $75. Financial aid available. International airfare and volunteer homestay support included.
Application Deadline Continuous.
Contact Manager, AFS Info Center, 506 Southwest 6th Avenue, 2nd Floor, Portland, Oregon 97204. Phone: 800-AFS-INFO. Fax: 503-248-4076. E-mail: afsinfo@afs.org.
URL www.afs.org/usa
For more information, see page 974.

BROADREACH Adventures Down Under

Broadreach
Australia

General Information Coed travel outdoor program, wilderness program, and adventure program established in 1992.

BROADREACH Adventures Down Under

Program Focus Coed program exploring the "Land Down Under" including the Great Barrier Reef, rain

forests, rivers, and the Outback. A week of live-aboard scuba diving includes scuba certification and hands-on marine research.
Academics Environmental science, intercultural studies, marine studies.
Arts Photography.
Special Interest Areas Aboriginal studies, field research/expeditions, leadership training, nature study.
Sports Canoeing, rappelling, sailing, scuba diving, sea kayaking, snorkeling.
Wilderness/Outdoors Backpacking, canoe trips, hiking, rafting, rock climbing, white-water trips, wilderness camping.
Trips Cultural.
Program Information 2 sessions per year. Session length: 25 days in June, July, August. Ages: 15–19. 10–14 participants per session. Cost: $4900.
Application Deadline Continuous.
Contact Carlton Goldthwaite, Director, PO Box 27076, Raleigh, North Carolina 27611-7076. Phone: 888-833-1907. Fax: 919-833-2129. E-mail: info@gobroadreach.com.
URL www.gobroadreach.com
For more information, see page 1010.

Camp Chewonki Eco-Kayak Australia

Chewonki Foundation, Inc.
Australia

General Information Coed travel wilderness program, cultural program, and adventure program established in 2003. Accredited by American Camping Association. Formal opportunities for the academically talented.
Program Focus Ecology, sea kayaking.
Academics Area studies, biology, ecology, geography, marine studies, oceanography, science (general), writing.
Arts Photography.
Special Interest Areas Campcraft, field research/expeditions.
Sports Sea kayaking, swimming.
Wilderness/Outdoors Backpacking, hiking, wilderness camping.
Trips Overnight.
Program Information 1 session per year. Session length: 5 weeks in June, July, August. Ages: 15–17. 8 participants per session. Cost: $4600. Financial aid available.
Application Deadline Continuous.
Jobs Positions for college students 21 and older.
Contact Dick Thomas, Camp Director, 485 Chewonki Neck Road, Wiscasset, Maine 04578. Phone: 207-882-7323. Fax: 207-882-4074. E-mail: camp@chewonki.org.
URL www.chewonki.org

Center for Cultural Interchange–Australia High School Abroad

Center for Cultural Interchange
Australia

General Information Coed residential academic program and cultural program established in 1985. High school credit may be earned.
Program Focus High school abroad, homestay and adventure program.
Academics Academics (general), independent study, precollege program.
Special Interest Areas Cross-cultural education, homestays.
Wilderness/Outdoors Hiking.
Trips Cultural, day, overnight.
Program Information 2 sessions per year. Session length: 150–300 days in January, February, March, April, May, June, July, August, September, October, November, December. Ages: 15–18. Boarding program cost: $8400–$14,400. Financial aid available. Early Bird discount.
Application Deadline Continuous.
Contact Ms. Juliet Jones, Outbound Programs Director, 325 West Huron, Suite 706, Chicago, Illinois 60610. Phone: 866-684-9675. Fax: 312-944-2644. E-mail: info@cci-exchange. com.
URL www.cci-exchange.com
For more information, see page 1060.

Earthwatch Institute–Conservation Research Initiative–Climate Change in the Rainforest

Earthwatch Institute
Queensland
Australia

General Information Coed residential outdoor program.
Program Focus Understanding species patterns to predict the impact of climate change on biodiversity.
Academics Ecology.
Special Interest Areas Conservation projects, field research/expeditions, nature study.
Program Information 4 sessions per year. Session length: 15 days in January, February, April, July, October. Ages: 16+. 12 participants per session. Boarding program cost: $2195–$2295. Financial aid available. Financial aid for high school students and teachers.
Application Deadline Continuous.
Contact General Information Desk, PO Box 75, Maynard, Massachusetts 01754. Phone: 800-776-0188. Fax: 978-461-2332. E-mail: info@earthwatch.org.
URL www.earthwatch.org

Earthwatch Institute–Conservation Research Initiative–Hawksbill Turtles of the Great Barrier Reef

Earthwatch Institute
Australia

General Information Coed residential outdoor program.
Program Focus Monitoring key nesting and foraging populations of a critically endangered species to develop sustainable management plans.
Academics Ecology, marine studies.

EARTHWATCH INSTITUTE–Conservation Research Initiative–Hawksbill Turtles of the Great Barrier Reef (continued)

Special Interest Areas Conservation projects, field research/expeditions, nature study.
Program Information 2 sessions per year. Session length: 16 days in July. Ages: 16+. 10 participants per session. Boarding program cost: $2095–$2195. Financial aid available. Financial aid for high school students and teachers.
Application Deadline Continuous.
Contact General Information Desk, PO Box 75, Maynard, Massachusetts 01754. Phone: 800-776-0188. Fax: 978-461-2332. E-mail: info@earthwatch.org.
URL www.earthwatch.org

EARTHWATCH INSTITUTE–CONSERVATION RESEARCH INITIATIVE–QUEENSLAND TROPICAL FISH ECOLOGY

Earthwatch Institute
Douglas Shire, Queensland
Australia

General Information Coed residential outdoor program.
Program Focus Assessing the impact of floodplain riparian restoration on stream ecology.
Academics Ecology.
Special Interest Areas Conservation projects, field research/expeditions, nature study.
Program Information 4 sessions per year. Session length: 13 days in March, June, September, December. Ages: 16+. 8 participants per session. Boarding program cost: $1995–$2095. Financial aid available. Financial aid for high school students and teachers.
Application Deadline Continuous.
Contact General Information Desk, PO Box 75, Maynard, Massachusetts 01754. Phone: 800-776-0188. Fax: 978-461-2332. E-mail: info@earthwatch.org.
URL www.earthwatch.org

EARTHWATCH INSTITUTE–ECHIDNAS AND GOANNAS OF KANGAROO ISLAND

Earthwatch Institute
Kangaroo Island
Australia

General Information Coed residential outdoor program, cultural program, and adventure program.
Program Focus Learning about sustainable living by studying the world's oldest mammal and its only predator.
Academics Ecology, science (general).
Special Interest Areas Field research/expeditions, nature study.
Program Information 5 sessions per year. Session length: 2 weeks in February, May, June, July, September, October. Ages: 16+. 7 participants per session. Boarding program cost: $2095–$2195. Financial aid available. Financial aid for high school students and teachers.
Application Deadline Continuous.
Contact General Information Desk, PO Box 75, Maynard, Massachusetts 01754. Phone: 800-776-0188. Fax: 978-461-2332. E-mail: info@earthwatch.org.
URL www.earthwatch.org

EARTHWATCH INSTITUTE–ITJARITJARI: THE OUTBACK'S MYSTERIOUS MARSUPIAL

Earthwatch Institute
Anangu-Pitjantjatjara Lands
Australia

General Information Coed residential outdoor program, cultural program, and adventure program.
Program Focus Discovering the habits and habitats of a little-known marsupial mole to establish its conservation needs.
Academics Ecology, science (general), zoology.
Special Interest Areas Field research/expeditions, nature study.
Program Information 3 sessions per year. Session length: 15 days in May, July, September. Ages: 16+. 8 participants per session. Boarding program cost: $1995–$2095. Financial aid available. Financial aid for high school students and teachers.
Application Deadline Continuous.
Contact General Information Desk, PO Box 75, Maynard, Massachusetts 01754. Phone: 800-776-0188. Fax: 978-461-2332. E-mail: info@earthwatch.org.
URL www.earthwatch.org

EARTHWATCH INSTITUTE–KOALA ECOLOGY

Earthwatch Institute
St. Bees Island, Queensland
Australia

General Information Coed residential outdoor program, cultural program, and adventure program.
Program Focus Investigating the ecology of a healthy koala population to improve conservation elsewhere.
Academics Biology, ecology, science (general).
Special Interest Areas Animal care, field research/expeditions, nature study.
Program Information 4 sessions per year. Session length: 13 days in January, February, May, July, October. Ages: 16+. 13 participants per session. Boarding program cost: $2095–$2195. Financial aid available. Financial aid for high school students and teachers.
Application Deadline Continuous.
Contact General Information Desk, PO Box 75, Maynard, Massachusetts 01754. Phone: 800-776-0188. Fax: 978-461-2332. E-mail: info@earthwatch.org.
URL www.earthwatch.org

The Experiment in International Living–Australia Homestay

The Experiment in International Living
Australia

General Information Coed residential outdoor program, cultural program, and adventure program established in 1932. Specific services available for the hearing impaired and visually impaired.
Program Focus International youth travel, homestay, ecology.
Academics Ecology.
Special Interest Areas Homestays.
Sports Snorkeling, swimming.
Wilderness/Outdoors Backpacking, hiking.
Trips Cultural, day, overnight.
Program Information 1 session per year. Session length: 5 weeks in July, August. Ages: 14–19. 10–15 participants per session. Boarding program cost: $4700. Financial aid available. Airfare included.
Application Deadline May 1.
Contact Annie Thompson, Enrollment Director, Summer Abroad, Kipling Road, PO Box 676, Brattleboro, Vermont 05302-0676. Phone: 800-345-2929. Fax: 802-258-3428. E-mail: eil@worldlearning.org.
URL www.usexperiment.org

For more information, see page 1116.

LIFEWORKS with the Australian Red Cross

LIFEWORKS International
Australia

General Information Coed travel outdoor program, community service program, and cultural program established in 1986. High school credit may be earned.
Program Focus Working with the Australian Red Cross, students participate primarily in aboriginal community projects. During the program, students travel to Sydney, Queensland, and the Northern Territories.
Academics Marine studies.
Arts Aboriginal arts.
Special Interest Areas Aboriginal studies, community service, touring.
Sports Snorkeling.
Wilderness/Outdoors Hiking.
Trips Cultural, day, overnight.
Program Information 1 session per year. Session length: 22 days in June, July. Ages: 15–19. 8–15 participants per session. Cost: $3760. Financial aid available.
Application Deadline Continuous.
Contact James Stoll, Director, PO Box 5517, Sarasota, Florida 34277. Phone: 800-808-2115. Fax: 941-924-6075. E-mail: info@lifeworks-international.com.
URL www.lifeworks-international.com

For more information, see page 1196.

PAX Abroad to Australia

PAX Abroad
Australia

General Information Coed travel cultural program established in 1999.
Special Interest Areas Homestays, touring.
Sports Scuba diving, snorkeling.
Wilderness/Outdoors Hiking.
Trips Cultural, day, overnight, shopping.
Program Information 2 sessions per year. Session length: 4 weeks in July. Ages: 15–18. 15–20 participants per session. Cost: $3350–$3850. Application fee: $100. Airfare from Los Angeles included.
Application Deadline April 15.
Contact Ms. Libby Cryer, Director, PAX Abroad, 71 Arch Street, Greenwich, Connecticut 06830. Phone: 800-555-6211. Fax: 203-629-0486. E-mail: academicexchange@pax.org.
URL www.pax.org

Rustic Pathways–Awesome Aussie Explorer

Rustic Pathways
Australia

General Information Coed travel cultural program and adventure program established in 1982.
Special Interest Areas Cross-cultural education, touring.
Sports Surfing, swimming.
Wilderness/Outdoors Outdoor adventure.
Trips Cultural, day, overnight, shopping.
Program Information 2 sessions per year. Session length: 17 days in June, July. Ages: 14–18. 10–15 participants per session. Cost: $2895.
Application Deadline Continuous.
Jobs Positions for college students 21 and older.
Contact Ms. Jessie Woodard, Director, Business Development, 4121 Erie Street, Willoughby, Ohio 44094. Phone: 440-975-9691. Fax: 440-975-9694. E-mail: jessie@rusticpathways.com.
URL www.rusticpathways.com

For more information, see page 1290.

Rustic Pathways–High Adrenaline Aussie

Rustic Pathways
Australia

General Information Coed travel cultural program and adventure program established in 1982.
Special Interest Areas Cross-cultural education, touring.
Sports Horseback riding, sailing, scuba diving, snorkeling, swimming.
Wilderness/Outdoors Hiking, outdoor adventure, rafting, white-water trips.
Trips Cultural, day, overnight, shopping.
Program Information 3 sessions per year. Session length: 10 days in June, July, August. Ages: 14–18. 10–15 participants per session. Cost: $1495.

RUSTIC PATHWAYS–HIGH ADRENALINE AUSSIE (continued)

Application Deadline Continuous.
Jobs Positions for college students 21 and older.
Contact Ms. Jessie Woodard, Director, Australia Programs, 4121 Erie Street, Willoughby, Ohio 44094. Phone: 440-975-9691. Fax: 440-975-9694. E-mail: jessie@rusticpathways.com.
URL www.rusticpathways.com

For more information, see page 1290.

RUSTIC PATHWAYS–OUTBACK 4-WHEEL DRIVE SAFARI

Rustic Pathways
Australia

General Information Coed travel cultural program and adventure program established in 1982.
Special Interest Areas Aboriginal studies, cross-cultural education, touring.
Wilderness/Outdoors Hiking, outdoor adventure, safari, wilderness camping.
Trips Cultural, day, overnight, shopping.
Program Information 3 sessions per year. Session length: 10 days in June, July, August. Ages: 14–18. 10–15 participants per session. Cost: $1495.
Application Deadline Continuous.
Jobs Positions for college students 21 and older.
Contact Ms. Jessie Woodard, Director, Australian Programs, 4121 Erie Street, Willoughby, Ohio 44094. Phone: 440-975-9691. Fax: 440-975-9694. E-mail: jessie@rusticpathways.com.
URL www.rusticpathways.com

For more information, see page 1290.

RUSTIC PATHWAYS–THE SUNSHINE COAST & SYDNEY

Rustic Pathways
Australia

General Information Coed travel cultural program and adventure program established in 1982.
Special Interest Areas Cross-cultural education, touring.
Sports Surfing.
Wilderness/Outdoors Hiking, outdoor adventure.
Trips Cultural, day, overnight, shopping.
Program Information 2 sessions per year. Session length: 10 days in June, July. Ages: 14–18. 10–15 participants per session. Cost: $1495.
Application Deadline Continuous.
Jobs Positions for college students 21 and older.
Contact Ms. Jessie Woodard, Director, Australian Programs, 4121 Erie Street, Willoughby, Ohio 44094. Phone: 440-975-9691. Fax: 440-975-9694. E-mail: jessie@rusticpathways.com.
URL www.rusticpathways.com

For more information, see page 1290.

RUSTIC PATHWAYS–TOTALLY DOWNUNDER ADVENTURE

Rustic Pathways
Australia

General Information Coed travel cultural program and adventure program established in 1982.
Special Interest Areas Aboriginal studies, cross-cultural education, touring.
Sports Horseback riding, sailing, scuba diving, snorkeling, surfing, swimming.
Wilderness/Outdoors Hiking, outdoor adventure, rafting, white-water trips.
Trips Cultural, day, overnight, shopping.
Program Information 2 sessions per year. Session length: 17 days in June, July, August. Ages: 14–18. 10–15 participants per session. Cost: $2895.
Application Deadline Continuous.
Jobs Positions for college students 21 and older.
Contact Ms. Jessie Woodard, Director, Australia Programs, 4121 Erie Street, Willoughby, Ohio 44094. Phone: 440-975-9691. Fax: 440-975-9694. E-mail: jessie@rusticpathways.com.
URL www.rusticpathways.com

For more information, see page 1290.

RUSTIC PATHWAYS–TROPICAL AUSSIE ADVENTURE

Rustic Pathways
Australia

General Information Coed travel cultural program and adventure program established in 1982.
Special Interest Areas Aboriginal studies, cross-cultural education, touring.
Sports Boating, horseback riding, sailing, scuba diving, snorkeling, swimming.
Wilderness/Outdoors Outdoor adventure, rafting, white-water trips, wilderness camping.
Trips Cultural, day, overnight, shopping.
Program Information 3 sessions per year. Session length: 17 days in June, July, August. Ages: 14–18. 10–15 participants per session. Cost: $2895.
Application Deadline Continuous.
Jobs Positions for college students 21 and older.
Contact Ms. Jessie Woodard, Director, Australia Programs, 4121 Erie Street, Willoughby, Ohio 44094. Phone: 440-975-9691. Fax: 440-975-9694. E-mail: jessie@rusticpathways.com.
URL www.rusticpathways.com

For more information, see page 1290.

RUSTIC PATHWAYS–ULTIMATE AUSTRALIAN ADVENTURE

Rustic Pathways
Australia

General Information Coed travel cultural program and adventure program established in 1982.
Special Interest Areas Aboriginal studies, cross-cultural education, touring.

Sports Boating, horseback riding, sailing, scuba diving, snorkeling, surfing, swimming.
Wilderness/Outdoors Hiking, outdoor adventure, rafting, white-water trips, wilderness camping.
Trips Cultural, day, overnight, shopping.
Program Information 5 sessions per year. Session length: 24 days in June, July, August. Ages: 14–18. 10–15 participants per session. Cost: $4295.
Application Deadline Continuous.
Jobs Positions for college students 21 and older.
Contact Ms. Jessie Woodard, Director, Australia Programs, 4121 Erie Street, Willoughby, Ohio 44094. Phone: 440-975-9691. Fax: 440-975-9694. E-mail: jessie@rusticpathways.com.
URL www.rusticpathways.com
For more information, see page 1290.

SFS: Tropical Reforestation Studies

The School for Field Studies
Center for Rainforest Studies
Yungaburra
Australia

General Information Coed residential academic program, outdoor program, and cultural program established in 1980. Formal opportunities for the academically talented. College credit may be earned.
Program Focus Environmental field research and environmental problem solving.
Academics Anthropology, area studies, biology, botany, ecology, economics, environmental science, forestry, geography, geology/earth science, intercultural studies, science (general), social science, social studies, writing.
Special Interest Areas Community service, field research/expeditions, nature study.
Sports Baseball, basketball, scuba diving, snorkeling, soccer, volleyball.
Wilderness/Outdoors Backpacking, hiking, wilderness camping.
Trips Cultural, day, overnight.
Program Information 2 sessions per year. Session length: 30 days in May, June, July. Ages: 16–25. 32 participants per session. Boarding program cost: $3810. Application fee: $45. Financial aid available. Airfare not included.
Application Deadline Continuous.
Contact Lili Folsom, Director of Admissions and Alumni Services, 10 Federal Street, Salem, Massachusetts 01970-3853. Phone: 800-989-4418. Fax: 978-741-3551. E-mail: admissions@fieldstudies.org.
URL www.fieldstudies.org

Summer Discovery at Australia

Summer Discovery
Sydney University
Sydney
Australia

General Information Coed residential academic program and outdoor program. High school or college credit may be earned.
Program Focus Pre-college enrichment.
Academics American literature, English as a second language, academics (general), anthropology, archaeology, art (Advanced Placement), art history/appreciation, biology, business, communications, computers, economics, environmental science, geography, government and politics, government and politics (Advanced Placement), history, oceanography, precollege program, psychology, social studies, writing.
Arts Creative writing, drawing, film, music, painting, photography.
Special Interest Areas Career exploration, college planning, leadership training.
Sports Aerobics, basketball, golf, soccer, swimming.
Wilderness/Outdoors Backpacking, bicycle trips, hiking.
Trips College tours, cultural, day, overnight.
Program Information 1 session per year. Session length: 5 weeks in June, July, August. 100–200 participants per session. Boarding program cost: $5699–$6999. Application fee: $60–$70. Financial aid available.
Application Deadline Continuous.
Jobs Positions for college students 21 and older.
Contact The Musiker Family, 1326 Old Northern Boulevard, Roslyn Village, New York 11576. Phone: 888-878-6637. E-mail: discovery@summerfun.com.
URL www.summerfun.com
For more information, see page 1338.

Visions–Australia

Visions
Queensland
Australia

General Information Coed travel outdoor program, community service program, and cultural program established in 1989. High school credit may be earned.
Program Focus Community service, cross-cultural experience, and outdoor adventure activities.
Academics Intercultural studies.
Arts Carpentry.
Special Interest Areas Community service, construction, cross-cultural education, field research/expeditions, field trips (arts and culture), gardening, leadership training, nature study.
Sports Kayaking, ropes course, scuba diving, sea kayaking, snorkeling, swimming.
Wilderness/Outdoors Backpacking, bicycle trips, outdoor adventure.
Trips Cultural, day, overnight.
Program Information 1–2 sessions per year. Session length: 3–4 weeks in June, July, August. Ages: 14–18. 20–25 participants per session. Cost: $2900–$3980. Financial aid available.
Application Deadline Continuous.
Jobs Positions for college students 22 and older.
Contact Ms. Joanne Pinaire, Director, PO Box 220, Newport, Pennsylvania 17074. Phone: 717-567-7313. E-mail: info@visionsserviceadventures.com.
URL www.visionsserviceadventures.com
For more information, see page 1382.

Westcoast Connection/On Tour–Australian Outback

Westcoast Connection
Australia

General Information Coed travel outdoor program and adventure program established in 1982. Accredited by Ontario Camping Association.
Program Focus A balance of touring, recreation, and adventure.
Special Interest Areas Touring.
Sports Kayaking, scuba diving, sea kayaking, snorkeling, surfing, swimming.
Wilderness/Outdoors Hiking, mountain biking, outdoor adventure, rafting, white-water trips.
Program Information 1–2 sessions per year. Session length: 30 days in July. Ages: 15–19. 15–30 participants per session. Cost: $6499.
Application Deadline Continuous.
Contact Mr. Mark Segal, Director, 154 East Boston Post Road, Mamaroneck, New York 10543. Phone: 800-767-0227. Fax: 914-835-0798. E-mail: usa@westcoastconnection.com.
URL www.westcoastconnection.com

For more information, see page 1392.

Wilderness Ventures–Australia

Wilderness Ventures
Australia

General Information Coed travel outdoor program, wilderness program, cultural program, and adventure program established in 1973.
Program Focus Wilderness travel, cultural immersion, leadership skills.
Special Interest Areas Aboriginal studies, leadership training.
Sports Scuba diving, snorkeling.
Wilderness/Outdoors Backpacking, canoe trips, hiking, rafting, white-water trips.
Trips Cultural, overnight.
Program Information 1 session per year. Session length: 32 days in June, July, August. Ages: 14–18. 15 participants per session. Cost: $6290. Financial aid available.
Application Deadline Continuous.
Jobs Positions for college students 21 and older.
Contact Mike Cottingham, Director, PO Box 2768, Jackson Hole, Wyoming 83001. Phone: 800-533-2281. Fax: 307-739-1934. E-mail: info@wildernessventures.com.
URL www.wildernessventures.com

For more information, see page 1396.

Windsor Mountain: Coast of Australia

Interlocken at Windsor Mountain
Australia

General Information Coed travel outdoor program and cultural program established in 1967.
Program Focus Surfing, scuba, sailing.
Academics Intercultural studies.
Special Interest Areas Cross-cultural education, homestays, team building.
Sports In-line skating, sailing, scuba diving, snorkeling, surfing, swimming.
Wilderness/Outdoors Hiking, rock climbing.
Trips Cultural, day.
Program Information 1 session per year. Session length: 4 weeks in July, August. Ages: 14–17. 12–16 participants per session. Cost: $3995. Financial aid available.
Application Deadline Continuous.
Contact Tom Herman, Marketing Director, 19 Interlocken Way, Windsor, New Hampshire 03244. Phone: 603-478-3166 Ext.20. Fax: 603-478-5260. E-mail: mail@windsormountain.org.
URL www.windsormountain.org/xrds

For more information, see page 1162.

Youth for Understanding USA–Australia

Youth for Understanding USA
Australia

General Information Coed travel academic program, cultural program, and adventure program established in 1951. High school or college credit may be earned.
Program Focus Living with a host family, participating in activities such as hiking and mountain biking, and traveling throughout Australia.
Academics Area studies, intercultural studies, social studies.
Special Interest Areas Homestays, touring.
Wilderness/Outdoors Hiking, mountain biking.
Trips Cultural, day, overnight, shopping.
Program Information 1 session per year. Session length: 35–45 days in June, July, August. Ages: 15–18. 50–100 participants per session. Cost: $6295. Application fee: $75. Financial aid available. Round-trip domestic and international airfare is included in the tuition.
Application Deadline Continuous.
Contact Admissions Counselor, 6400 Goldsboro Road, Suite 100, Bethesda, Maryland 20817. Phone: 800-TEENAGE (833-6243). Fax: 202-895-1104. E-mail: admissions@us.yfu.org.
URL www.yfu-usa.org

For more information, see page 1414.

AUSTRIA

Global Teen–Learn German in Vienna, Summer Camp-Ages 12-18

Language Liaison
Vienna
Austria

General Information Coed residential academic program established in 1956. High school or college credit may be earned.
Program Focus German language study and cultural immersion.
Academics German language/literature, area studies, intercultural studies, reading, writing.
Arts Dance, theater/drama.
Special Interest Areas Field trips (arts and culture).
Sports Aerobics, badminton, basketball, football, horseback riding, swimming, tennis, volleyball.
Trips Cultural, day.
Program Information 2–6 sessions per year. Session length: 2–5 weeks in July, August. Ages: 12–18. 2–15 participants per session. Boarding program cost: $1604–$3643. Application fee: $85. Financial aid available. Cultural specials and tennis lessons extra.
Application Deadline Continuous.
Contact Nancy Forman, President, PO Box 1772, Pacific Palisades, California 90272. Phone: 800-284-4448. Fax: 310-454-1706. E-mail: learn@languageliaison.com.
URL www.languageliaison.com

For more information, see page 1184.

Global Teen–Learn German in Vienna, Young Adult Summer Camp, Ages 16-18

Language Liaison
Vienna
Austria

General Information Coed residential academic program. High school or college credit may be earned.
Program Focus German language study and cultural immersion.
Academics German language/literature, area studies, intercultural studies, reading, writing.
Arts Dance, theater/drama.
Special Interest Areas Field trips (arts and culture).
Sports Aerobics, badminton, basketball, football, horseback riding, swimming, tennis, volleyball.
Trips Cultural, day.
Program Information 2–6 sessions per year. Session length: 2–5 weeks in July, August. Ages: 16–18. 2–15 participants per session. Boarding program cost: $1699–$3888. Application fee: $85. Financial aid available. Cultural specials and tennis lessons extra.
Application Deadline Continuous.
Contact Ms. Nancy Forman, President, PO Box 1772, Pacific Palisades, California 90272. Phone: 800-284-4448. Fax: 310-454-1706. E-mail: learn@languageliaison.com.
URL www.languageliaison.com

For more information, see page 1184.

LSA Vienna, Austria

Language Studies Abroad, Inc.
Vienna
Austria

General Information Coed residential academic program and cultural program established in 1988. High school or college credit may be earned.
Program Focus Learning language, culture, and music.
Academics German language/literature, intercultural studies, language study, music, music (Advanced Placement).
Arts Dance, music, music (chamber), music (classical), music (instrumental), music (orchestral), music (vocal), music theory, musical performance/recitals, theater/drama.
Special Interest Areas Homestays.
Sports Badminton, equestrian sports, football, skiing (downhill), snowboarding, swimming, table tennis/ping-pong, tennis, volleyball.
Trips College tours, cultural, day, overnight, shopping.
Program Information 1–26 sessions per year. Session length: 14–360 days in January, February, March, April, May, June, July, August, September, October, November, December. Ages: 12+. 90–400 participants per session. Boarding program cost: $688–$2237. Application fee: $100.
Application Deadline Continuous.
Jobs Positions for high school students and college students 18 and older.
Contact Director, 1801 Highway 50 East, Suite I, Carson City, Nevada 89701. Phone: 800-424-5522. Fax: 775-883-2266. E-mail: info@languagestudiesabroad.com.
URL www.languagestudiesabroad.com

For more information, see page 1186.

Sprachkurse Ariana, Seefeld-Austria

Sprachkurse Ariana AG
Seefeld 6100
Austria

General Information Coed residential academic program established in 1985.
Academics English as a second language, French language/literature, German language/literature.
Sports Basketball, golf, gymnastics, horseback riding, soccer, sports (general), swimming, tennis, volleyball.
Wilderness/Outdoors Hiking.
Trips Cultural, day, shopping.
Program Information 1 session per year. Session length: 2–5 weeks in July, August. Ages: 10–18. 80 participants per session. Boarding program cost: 2520–6300 Swiss francs.
Application Deadline Continuous.
Jobs Positions for college students 20 and older.

Sprachkurse Ariana, Seefeld-Austria (continued)

Contact Ms. M. Schmid, Director, Hoehenweg 60, St. Gallen 9000, Switzerland. Phone: 41-71-277-9291. Fax: 41-71-277-7253. E-mail: info@ariana.ch.
URL www.ariana.ch

Village Camps–Austria

Village Camps
Notburgahof
Piesendorf/Furth 150 5721
Austria

General Information Coed residential traditional camp and academic program established in 1972.
Program Focus German language, video making.
Academics German language/literature, environmental science, language study, linguistics.
Arts Arts and crafts (general), dance, dance (modern), drawing, fabric arts, film, jewelry making, painting, photography, television/video, theater/drama.
Special Interest Areas Campcraft, leadership training, nature study.
Sports Aerobics, archery, baseball, basketball, bicycling, bicycling (BMX), climbing (wall), figure skating, in-line skating, rappelling, ropes course, sailing, skiing (downhill), soccer, softball, sports (general), squash, swimming, tennis, volleyball, waterskiing, windsurfing.
Wilderness/Outdoors Hiking, mountain biking, orienteering, rafting, rock climbing, wilderness/outdoors (general).
Trips Cultural, day, overnight, shopping.
Program Information 2 sessions per year. Session length: 2 weeks in July, August. Ages: 10–17. 80 participants per session. Boarding program cost: $1900–$2880.
Application Deadline Continuous.
Jobs Positions for college students 21 and older.
Contact Roger Ratner, Director, 14 Rue de la Morâche, Nyon CH-1260, Switzerland. Phone: 41-22-990-9400. Fax: 41-22-990-9494. E-mail: camps@villagecamps.ch.
URL www.villagecamps.com

For more information, see page 1380.

BAHAMAS

BROADREACH Marine Biology Accredited

Broadreach
The Island School on Cape Eleuthera
Bahamas

General Information Coed residential academic program and outdoor program established in 1992. High school or college credit may be earned.
Program Focus Coed program focusing on marine biology, marine studies, scuba, advanced and specialty dive certifications as well as high school and college credit.

BROADREACH Marine Biology Accredited

Academics Biology, ecology, environmental science, marine studies, oceanography.
Arts Photography.
Special Interest Areas Community service, conservation projects, field research/expeditions, nature study.
Sports Bicycling, boating, fishing, sailing, scuba diving, sea kayaking, snorkeling, volleyball, waterskiing.
Wilderness/Outdoors Hiking.
Trips Cultural, day.
Program Information 2 sessions per year. Session length: 25 days in June, July, August. Ages: 15–19. 14–18 participants per session. Boarding program cost: $4480.
Application Deadline Continuous.
Contact Carlton Goldthwaite, Director, PO Box 27076, Raleigh, North Carolina 27611-7076. Phone: 888-833-1907. Fax: 919-833-2129. E-mail: info@gobroadreach.com.
URL www.gobroadreach.com

For more information, see page 1008.

EARTHWATCH INSTITUTE–Bahamian Reef Survey

Earthwatch Institute
San Salvador Island
Bahamas

General Information Coed residential outdoor program, cultural program, and adventure program.
Program Focus Measuring changes to understand the coral reef environment and the causes of bleaching and other coral diseases.
Academics Ecology, environmental science, marine studies, science (general).
Special Interest Areas Field research/expeditions, nature study.
Sports Swimming.
Program Information 3 sessions per year. Session length: 8–11 days in February, June, July, November. Ages: 16+. 20 participants per session. Boarding program cost: $1795–$1995. Financial aid available. Financial aid for high school students and teachers.
Application Deadline Continuous.

Contact General Information Desk, PO Box 75, Maynard, Massachusetts 01754. Phone: 800-776-0188. Fax: 978-461-2332. E-mail: info@earthwatch.org.
URL www.earthwatch.org

EARTHWATCH INSTITUTE–COASTAL ECOLOGY OF THE BAHAMAS

Earthwatch Institute
Bahamas

General Information Coed residential outdoor program, cultural program, and adventure program.
Program Focus Testing a model for assessing and mitigating damage to nearshore habitats.
Academics Biology, ecology, environmental science, marine studies, science (general).
Special Interest Areas Field research/expeditions, nature study.
Program Information 4 sessions per year. Session length: 11 days in June, July. Ages: 16+. 10 participants per session. Boarding program cost: $1795–$1895. Financial aid available. Financial aid for high school students and teachers.
Application Deadline Continuous.
Contact General Information Desk, PO Box 75, Maynard, Massachusetts 01754. Phone: 800-776-0188. Fax: 978-461-2332. E-mail: info@earthwatch.org.
URL www.earthwatch.org

EARTHWATCH INSTITUTE–DOLPHINS AND WHALES OF ABACO ISLAND

Earthwatch Institute
Great Abaco Island
Bahamas

General Information Coed residential outdoor program, cultural program, and adventure program.
Program Focus Gathering fundamental data on a diversity of cetaceans to guide regional conservation and tourism.
Academics Biology, ecology, environmental science, marine studies, oceanography, science (general).
Special Interest Areas Field research/expeditions, nature study.
Program Information 9 sessions per year. Session length: 11 days in January, February, March, June, July, August. Ages: 16+. 8 participants per session. Boarding program cost: $1995–$2095. Financial aid available. Financial aid for high school students and teachers.
Application Deadline Continuous.
Contact General Information Desk, PO Box 75, Maynard, Massachusetts 01754. Phone: 800-776-0188. Fax: 978-461-2332. E-mail: info@earthwatch.org.
URL www.earthwatch.org

FLINT HILL SCHOOL–"SUMMER ON THE HILL"–TRIPS FROM THE HILL–ECOLOGICAL STUDY OF CORAL REEFS, BAHAMAS

Flint Hill School
Andros Island Research Station
College of the Bahamas
Andros Island
Bahamas

General Information Coed travel academic program and outdoor program.
Program Focus Coral reef ecology, mangrove wetlands on Andros Island, Bahamas.
Academics Biology, ecology, environmental science, intercultural studies, marine studies, oceanography, science (general).
Special Interest Areas Field research/expeditions.
Sports Boating, snorkeling, swimming.
Program Information 1 session per year. Session length: 10–12 days in July. Ages: 12–18. 2–30 participants per session. Cost: $2500. 12-13 year old must be accompanied by an adult.
Application Deadline Continuous.
Jobs Positions for high school students 16 and older and college students 18 and older.
Contact Ms. Peggy Laurent, Director of Special and Summer Programs, 3320 Jermantown Road, Oakton, Virginia 22124. Phone: 703-584-2315. Fax: 703-242-0718. E-mail: plaurent@flinthill.org.
URL www.flinthill.org

BARBADOS

EARTHWATCH INSTITUTE–HAWKSBILL TURTLES OF BARBADOS

Earthwatch Institute
Barbados

General Information Coed residential outdoor program, wilderness program, and cultural program.
Program Focus Monitoring the nesting success and ecology of endangered sea turtles to aid in their recovery.
Academics Biology, ecology, marine studies, oceanography, science (general).
Special Interest Areas Field research/expeditions, nature study.
Program Information 9 sessions per year. Session length: 12 days in June, July, August, September. Ages: 16+. 8 participants per session. Boarding program cost: $2095–$2195. Financial aid available. Financial aid for high school students and teachers.
Application Deadline Continuous.
Contact General Information Desk, PO Box 75, Maynard, Massachusetts 01754. Phone: 800-776-0188. Fax: 978-461-2332. E-mail: info@earthwatch.org.
URL www.earthwatch.org

BELARUS

EARTHWATCH INSTITUTE–BOGS OF BELARUS

Earthwatch Institute
Belarus

General Information Coed residential outdoor program.
Program Focus Surveying the botanical diversity of unique wetlands to make conservation recommendations.
Academics Botany, ecology.
Special Interest Areas Conservation projects, field research/expeditions, nature study.
Program Information 4 sessions per year. Session length: 2 weeks in June, July, August. Ages: 16+. 10 participants per session. Boarding program cost: $1695–$1795. Financial aid available. Financial aid for high school students and teachers.
Application Deadline Continuous.
Contact General Information Desk, PO Box 75, Maynard, Massachusetts 01754. Phone: 800-776-0188. Fax: 978-461-2332. E-mail: info@earthwatch.org.
URL www.earthwatch.org

VOLUNTEERS FOR PEACE INTERNATIONAL WORK CAMP–BELARUS

Volunteers for Peace International Work Camps
Minsk
Belarus

General Information Coed residential community service program established in 1981. Specific services available for the hearing impaired and physically challenged. College credit may be earned.
Program Focus International work camps.
Academics Intercultural studies, peace education.
Special Interest Areas Community service, work camp programs.
Trips Cultural, day, overnight.
Program Information Session length: 2–3 weeks in July, August. Ages: 17+. 12–20 participants per session. Boarding program cost: $250–$600.
Application Deadline Continuous.
Contact Peter Coldwell, Director, 1034 Tiffany Road, Belmont, Vermont 05730. Phone: 802-259-2759. Fax: 802-259-2922. E-mail: vfp@vfp.org.
URL www.vfp.org

BELGIUM

VOLUNTEERS FOR PEACE INTERNATIONAL WORK CAMP–BELGIUM

Volunteers for Peace International Work Camps
Brussels
Belgium

General Information Coed residential community service program established in 1981. Specific services available for the hearing impaired and physically challenged. College credit may be earned.
Program Focus International work camps.
Academics Intercultural studies, peace education.
Special Interest Areas Community service, work camp programs.
Trips Cultural, day, overnight.
Program Information Session length: 2–3 weeks in May, July, August, September. Ages: 15+. 12–20 participants per session. Boarding program cost: $250–$600.
Application Deadline Continuous.
Contact Peter Coldwell, Director, 1034 Tiffany Road, Belmont, Vermont 05730. Phone: 802-259-2759. Fax: 802-259-2922. E-mail: vfp@vfp.org.
URL www.vfp.org

BELIZE

AAVE–BELIZE

AAVE–America's Adventure Ventures Everywhere
Belize

General Information Coed travel outdoor program, community service program, wilderness program, cultural program, and adventure program established in 1976. Accredited by American Camping Association.
Program Focus Adventure travel.
Academics Area studies, intercultural studies.
Special Interest Areas Community service, homestays, leadership training.
Sports Canoeing, sea kayaking, snorkeling, swimming.
Wilderness/Outdoors Backpacking, canoe trips, caving, hiking, outdoor adventure, white-water trips.
Trips Cultural, day, overnight.
Program Information 3–5 sessions per year. Session length: 3 weeks in June, July, August. Ages: 14–18. 13–15 participants per session. Cost: $3688. Financial aid available.
Application Deadline Continuous.
Jobs Positions for college students 21 and older.
Contact Mr. Abbott Wallis, Owner, 2245 Stonecrop Way, Golden, Colorado 80401. Phone: 800-222-3595. Fax: 303-526-0885. E-mail: info@aave.com.
URL www.aave.com
For more information, see page 952.

BROADREACH ACADEMIC TREKS–WILDERNESS EMERGENCY MEDICINE

Broadreach
Belize

General Information Coed travel academic program, outdoor program, community service program, and cultural program established in 1992. High school or college credit may be earned.
Program Focus Program focuses on Wilderness First Responder (WFR) certification, clinic and hospital service work, cultural immersion; hiking.
Academics Academics (general), area studies, health sciences, medicine.
Special Interest Areas Career exploration, community service, cross-cultural education, first aid, leadership training.
Sports Sea kayaking.
Wilderness/Outdoors Hiking, wilderness camping.
Trips Cultural.
Program Information 2 sessions per year. Session length: 25 days in June, July, August. Ages: 15–19. 10–14 participants per session. Cost: $3800–$4700.
Application Deadline Continuous.
Contact Carlton Goldthwaite, Director, PO Box 27076, Raleigh, North Carolina 27611-7076. Phone: 888-833-1907. Fax: 919-833-2129. E-mail: info@gobroadreach.com or info@academictreks.com.
URL www.academictreks.com

For more information, see page 1010.

EARTHWATCH INSTITUTE–MANATEES IN BELIZE

Earthwatch Institute
The Drowned Cayes
Belize

General Information Coed residential outdoor program, wilderness program, and cultural program.
Program Focus Conducting a baseline survey of endangered manatees and their habitat.
Academics Biology, environmental science, marine studies, oceanography, science (general).
Special Interest Areas Field research/expeditions, nature study.
Sports Swimming.
Program Information 8 sessions per year. Session length: 2 weeks in February, March, April, June, July, August. Ages: 16+. 8 participants per session. Boarding program cost: $1895–$1995. Financial aid available. Financial aid for high school students and teachers.
Application Deadline Continuous.
Contact General Information Desk, PO Box 75, Maynard, Massachusetts 01754. Phone: 800-776-0188. Fax: 978-461-2332. E-mail: info@earthwatch.org.
URL www.earthwatch.org

THE EXPERIMENT IN INTERNATIONAL LIVING–BELIZE HOMESTAY

The Experiment in International Living
Belize

General Information Coed residential outdoor program, community service program, and cultural program established in 1932.
Program Focus International youth travel, homestay, community service, ecology.
Academics Ecology.
Special Interest Areas Community service, homestays.
Sports Snorkeling, swimming.
Trips Cultural, day, overnight.
Program Information 1 session per year. Session length: 4 weeks in July, August. Ages: 14–19. 10–15 participants per session. Boarding program cost: $3400. Financial aid available.
Application Deadline May 1.
Contact Annie Thompson, Enrollment Director, Summer Abroad, Kipling Road, PO Box 676, Brattleboro, Vermont 05302-0676. Phone: 800-345-2929. Fax: 802-258-3428. E-mail: eil@worldlearning.org.
URL www.usexperiment.org

For more information, see page 1116.

LONGACRE EXPEDITIONS, BELIZE

Longacre Expeditions
Belize

General Information Coed travel outdoor program, wilderness program, and adventure program established in 1981. Accredited by American Camping Association.
Program Focus Effective communication skills, responsibility, confidence building in a developing country. Trip to Mayan ruins is included.
Special Interest Areas Community service.
Sports Scuba diving.
Wilderness/Outdoors Backpacking, hiking, wilderness camping.
Trips Cultural.
Program Information 1 session per year. Session length: 22 days in July. Ages: 15–18. 10–16 participants per session. Cost: $3995.
Application Deadline Continuous.
Jobs Positions for college students 21 and older.
Contact Meredith Schuler, Director, 4030 Middle Ridge Road, Newport, Pennsylvania 17074. Phone: 717-567-6790. Fax: 717-567-3955. E-mail: longacre@longacreexpeditions.com.
URL www.longacreexpeditions.com

For more information, see page 1200.

BOLIVIA

AFS-USA–Community Service–Bolivia

AFS-USA
Bolivia

General Information Coed residential community service program and cultural program. High school credit may be earned.
Program Focus Chance to help with reforestation, and help in a shelter for children. Participants will tour the ruins of Tiahnanaco and explore the wonders of La Paz, Chabamba, and Lake Titicaca.
Academics Spanish language/literature.
Special Interest Areas Animal care, community service, farming, homestays, nature study, touring.
Wilderness/Outdoors Hiking.
Trips Cultural, day, overnight.
Program Information 1 session per year. Session length: 4 weeks in July. Ages: 15–18. 15–20 participants per session. Boarding program cost: $3865–$4165. Application fee: $75. Financial aid available. International airfare and volunteer homestay support included.
Application Deadline Continuous.
Jobs Positions for high school students.
Contact Manager, AFS Info Center, 506 Southwest 6th Avenue, 2nd Floor, Portland, Oregon 97204. Phone: 800-AFS-INFO. Fax: 503-248-4076. E-mail: afsinfo@afs.org.
URL www.afs.org/usa

For more information, see page 974.

LSA Sucre, Bolivia

Language Studies Abroad, Inc.
Sucre
Bolivia

General Information Coed residential academic program and cultural program established in 2002. Formal opportunities for the academically talented. High school or college credit may be earned.
Program Focus Language and culture.
Academics Spanish (Advanced Placement), Spanish language/literature, academics (general), intercultural studies.
Special Interest Areas Homestays.
Trips Cultural, day.
Program Information 1–26 sessions per year. Session length: 13–360 days in January, February, March, April, May, June, July, August, September, October, November, December. Ages: 16+. 30–60 participants per session. Boarding program cost: $575–$2100. Application fee: $100. Financial aid available.
Application Deadline Continuous.
Contact Director, 1801 Highway 50 East, Suite I, Carson City, Nevada 89701. Phone: 800-424-5522. Fax: 775-883-2266. E-mail: info@languagestudiesabroad.com.
URL www.languagestudiesabroad.com

For more information, see page 1186.

BOTSWANA

Earthwatch Institute–Crocodiles of the Okavango

Earthwatch Institute
Botswana

General Information Coed residential outdoor program, cultural program, and adventure program.
Program Focus Investigating the ecology of a keystone species to balance its wetland ecosystem.
Academics Biology, ecology, science (general).
Special Interest Areas Field research/expeditions, nature study.
Program Information 9 sessions per year. Session length: 2 weeks in February, March, April, July, August, September, October, November, December. Ages: 16+. 8 participants per session. Boarding program cost: $2595–$2695. Financial aid available. Financial aid for high school students and teachers.
Application Deadline Continuous.
Contact General Information Desk, PO Box 75, Maynard, Massachusetts 01754. Phone: 800-776-0188. Fax: 978-461-2332. E-mail: info@earthwatch.org.
URL www.earthwatch.org

Earthwatch Institute–Health and Nutrition in Botswana

Earthwatch Institute
Botswana

General Information Coed residential community service program and cultural program.
Program Focus Gathering baseline information on emerging health issues to guide national health policy.
Academics Health sciences, intercultural studies.
Special Interest Areas Community service, field research/expeditions, nutrition.
Program Information 4 sessions per year. Session length: 12 days in July, August. Ages: 16+. 10 participants per session. Boarding program cost: $2195–$2295. Financial aid available. Financial aid for high school students and teachers.
Application Deadline Continuous.
Contact General Information Desk, PO Box 75, Maynard, Massachusetts 01754. Phone: 800-776-0188. Fax: 978-461-2332. E-mail: info@earthwatch.org.
URL www.earthwatch.org

The Experiment in International Living–Botswana Homestay

The Experiment in International Living
Botswana

General Information Coed residential outdoor program, community service program, cultural program, and adventure program established in 1932.
Program Focus International youth travel, homestay, community service.
Academics Setswana language, academics (general).

Special Interest Areas Community service, homestays.
Wilderness/Outdoors Backpacking, wilderness/ outdoors (general).
Trips Cultural, day, overnight.
Program Information 1 session per year. Session length: 5 weeks in July, August. Ages: 14–19. 10–15 participants per session. Boarding program cost: $4700. Financial aid available.
Application Deadline May 1.
Contact Annie Thompson, Enrollment Director, Summer Abroad, Kipling Road, PO Box 676, Brattleboro, Vermont 05302-0676. Phone: 800-345-2929. Fax: 802-258-3428. E-mail: eil@worldlearning.org.
URL www.usexperiment.org
For more information, see page 1116.

BRAZIL

AFS-USA–Homestay, Outdoor Adventure Amazon–Brazil

AFS-USA
Brazil

General Information Coed residential outdoor program and cultural program established in 2002.
Program Focus Ecology and biology of the Amazon.
Academics Portuguese language/literature, biology, ecology, geology/earth science.
Special Interest Areas Homestays.
Trips Cultural, day, overnight.
Program Information 1 session per year. Session length: 45 days in July, August. Ages: 17–25. 40–60 participants per session. Boarding program cost: $5265–$5765. Application fee: $75. Financial aid available. International airfare and volunteer homestay support included.
Application Deadline Continuous.
Contact Manager, AFS Info Center, 506 Southwest 6th Avenue, 2nd Floor, Portland, Oregon 97204. Phone: 800-AFS-INFO. Fax: 503-248-4076. E-mail: afsinfo@afs.org.
URL www.afs.org/usa
For more information, see page 974.

AFS-USA–Homestay Plus–Brazil

AFS-USA
Brazil

General Information Coed residential outdoor program, cultural program, and adventure program.
Program Focus Living with a host family for 5 weeks, exploring Brazil's ecosystem, participating in outdoor activities such as hiking, canoeing, and camping for the remainder of program.
Academics Portuguese language/literature.
Special Interest Areas Homestays.
Sports Swimming.
Wilderness/Outdoors Backpacking, canoe trips, caving, hiking, mountaineering, outdoor adventure.
Trips Cultural, day, overnight.
Program Information 1 session per year. Session length: 7 weeks in June, July, August. Ages: 15–18. 20–30 participants per session. Boarding program cost: $4465–$4765. Application fee: $75. Financial aid available. International airfare and volunteer homestay support included.
Application Deadline Continuous.
Contact Manager, AFS Info Center, 506 Southwest 6th Avenue, 2nd Floor, Portland, Oregon 97204. Phone: 800-AFS-INFO. Fax: 503-248-4076. E-mail: afsinfo@afs.org.
URL www.afs.org/usa
For more information, see page 974.

Center for Cultural Interchange–Brazil High School Abroad

Center for Cultural Interchange
Brazil

General Information Coed residential academic program and cultural program established in 1985. High school credit may be earned.
Program Focus High school abroad, homestay program, cultural immersion.
Academics Academics (general), precollege program.
Special Interest Areas Cross-cultural education, homestays.
Trips Cultural, day.
Program Information 2 sessions per year. Session length: 150–300 days in January, February, March, April, May, June, July, August, September, October, November, December. Ages: 15–17. Boarding program cost: $4450–$4950. Financial aid available.
Application Deadline Continuous.
Contact Ms. Juliet Jones, Outbound Programs Director, 325 West Huron, Suite 706, Chicago, Illinois 60610. Phone: 866-684-9675. Fax: 312-944-2644. E-mail: info@cci-exchange.com.
URL www.cci-exchange.com
For more information, see page 1060.

EARTHWATCH INSTITUTE–Brazil's Marine Wildlife

Earthwatch Institute
Ilha de Cardoso State Park
São Paulo
Brazil

General Information Coed residential outdoor program.
Program Focus Monitoring dolphins in a rich estuary ecosystem to support responsible tourism development.
Academics Ecology, marine studies.
Special Interest Areas Conservation projects, field research/expeditions, nature study.
Program Information 5 sessions per year. Session length: 11 days in January, February, July, August, September. Ages: 16+. 8 participants per session. Boarding program cost: $1895–$1995. Financial aid available. Financial aid for high school students and teachers.

EARTHWATCH INSTITUTE–Brazil's Marine Wildlife (continued)

Application Deadline Continuous.
Contact General Information Desk, PO Box 75, Maynard, Massachusetts 01754. Phone: 800-776-0188. Fax: 978-461-2332. E-mail: info@earthwatch.org.
URL www.earthwatch.org

EARTHWATCH INSTITUTE–CONSERVATION RESEARCH INITIATIVE–CONSERVING THE PANTANAL

Earthwatch Institute
Mato Grosso do Sul
Brazil

General Information Coed residential outdoor program.
Program Focus Conducting a comprehensive research program to conserve an outstanding ecosystem.
Academics Ecology, environmental science.
Special Interest Areas Field research/expeditions, nature study.
Sports Boating, horseback riding.
Wilderness/Outdoors Wilderness/outdoors (general).
Program Information 33 sessions per year. Session length: 7–12 days in February, March, April, May, June, July, August, September, October, November, December. Ages: 16+. 10–14 participants per session. Boarding program cost: $1795–$2495. Financial aid available. Financial aid for high school students and teachers.
Application Deadline Continuous.
Contact General Information Desk, PO Box 75, Maynard, Massachusetts 01754. Phone: 800-776-0188. Fax: 978-461-2332. E-mail: info@earthwatch.org.
URL www.earthwatch.org

EARTHWATCH INSTITUTE–DOLPHINS OF BRAZIL

Earthwatch Institute
Baía Norte
Brazil

General Information Coed residential outdoor program, cultural program, and adventure program.
Program Focus Identifying the unique habits of marine tucuxi dolphin to improve conservation policy.
Academics Environmental science, marine studies, science (general).
Special Interest Areas Field research/expeditions, nature study.
Program Information 8 sessions per year. Session length: 12 days in February, March, May, June, July, August, October, November. Ages: 16+. 3 participants per session. Boarding program cost: $1895–$1995. Financial aid available. Financial aid for high school students and teachers.
Application Deadline Continuous.
Contact General Information Desk, PO Box 75, Maynard, Massachusetts 01754. Phone: 800-776-0188. Fax: 978-461-2332. E-mail: info@earthwatch.org.
URL www.earthwatch.org

THE EXPERIMENT IN INTERNATIONAL LIVING–BRAZIL–ECOLOGICAL PRESERVATION

The Experiment in International Living
Brazil

General Information Coed residential outdoor program, cultural program, and adventure program established in 1932.
Program Focus International youth travel, homestay, ecology.
Academics Ecology.
Special Interest Areas Homestays, nature study, touring.
Wilderness/Outdoors Backpacking, hiking, whitewater trips.
Trips Cultural, day, overnight.
Program Information 1 session per year. Session length: 5 weeks in July, August. Ages: 14–19. 10–15 participants per session. Boarding program cost: $4800. Application fee: $75. Financial aid available.
Application Deadline May 1.
Contact Ms. Annie Thompson, Enrollment Director, Summer Abroad, Kipling Road, PO Box 676, Brattleboro, Vermont 05302-0676. Phone: 800-345-2929. Fax: 802-258-3428. E-mail: eil@worldlearning.org.
URL www.usexperiment.org

For more information, see page 1116.

THE EXPERIMENT IN INTERNATIONAL LIVING–BRAZIL HOMESTAY AND COMMUNITY SERVICE

The Experiment in International Living
Brazil

General Information Coed residential community service program and cultural program established in 1932.
Program Focus International youth travel, homestay, community service.
Academics Portuguese language/literature.
Special Interest Areas Community service, homestays, touring.
Trips Cultural, day, overnight.
Program Information 1 session per year. Session length: 5 weeks in July, August. Ages: 14–19. 10–15 participants per session. Boarding program cost: $4800. Financial aid available.
Application Deadline May 1.
Contact Ms. Annie Thompson, Enrollment Director, Summer Abroad, Kipling Road, PO Box 676, Brattleboro, Vermont 05302-0676. Phone: 800-345-2929. Fax: 802-258-3428. E-mail: eil@worldlearning.org.
URL www.usexperiment.org

For more information, see page 1116.

PAX Abroad–Brazil

PAX Abroad
Brazil

General Information Coed travel sports camp established in 2000.
Sports Soccer.
Trips Cultural, day, overnight, shopping.
Program Information 1 session per year. Session length: 3 weeks in July. Ages: 15–18. 10–20 participants per session. Cost: $3650–$4150. Application fee: $100. Airfare from New York included.
Application Deadline April 15.
Contact Ms. Libby Cryer, Director, PAX Abroad, 71 Arch Street, Greenwich, Connecticut 06830. Phone: 800-555-6211. Fax: 203-629-0486. E-mail: academicexchange@pax.org.
URL www.pax.org

Putney Student Travel–Community Service–Brazil

Putney Student Travel
Brazil

General Information Coed residential community service program and cultural program established in 1951.
Program Focus Community service, cultural exchange, and weekend excursions from a base in a small, rural community.
Academics Intercultural studies.
Special Interest Areas Community service, construction, farming.
Sports Soccer.
Wilderness/Outdoors Hiking, white-water trips.
Trips Cultural, day.
Program Information 1 session per year. Session length: 30 days in June, July. Ages: 15–18. 16 participants per session. Boarding program cost: $5800. Financial aid available. Airfare from Miami included.
Application Deadline Continuous.
Contact Jeffrey Shumlin, Director, 345 Hickory Ridge Road, Putney, Vermont 05346. Phone: 802-387-5000. Fax: 802-387-4276. E-mail: info@goputney.com.
URL www.goputney.com
For more information, see page 1276.

Youth for Understanding USA–Brazil

Youth for Understanding USA
Brazil

General Information Coed residential academic program and cultural program established in 1951. High school or college credit may be earned.
Program Focus Learning about environment, studying the rainforest, and experiencing diverse Brazilian culture.
Academics Portuguese language/literature, area studies, biology, botany, ecology, environmental science, intercultural studies, social studies.
Special Interest Areas Homestays, nature study.
Trips Cultural, day, overnight.
Program Information 2 sessions per year. Session length: 35–45 days in June, July, August. Ages: 15–18. 10–50 participants per session. Boarding program cost: $4595–$5795. Application fee: $75. Financial aid available. Round trip domestic and international airfare is included in the tuition.
Application Deadline Continuous.
Contact Admissions Counselor, 6400 Goldsboro Road, Suite 100, Bethesda, Maryland 20817. Phone: 800-TEENAGE (833-6243). Fax: 202-895-1104. E-mail: admissions@us.yfu.org.
URL www.yfu-usa.org
For more information, see page 1414.

BRITISH VIRGIN ISLANDS

ActionQuest: Advanced PADI Scuba Certification and Specialty Voyages

ActionQuest
British Virgin Islands

General Information Coed travel outdoor program and adventure program established in 1986.
Program Focus Live-aboard program offering PADI advanced and specialty scuba certifications.
Academics Marine studies, oceanography.
Special Interest Areas Field research/expeditions, leadership training, nature study, nautical skills, team building.
Sports Sailing, scuba diving, snorkeling, wakeboarding, waterskiing.
Wilderness/Outdoors Hiking.
Trips Cultural, day.
Program Information 3 sessions per year. Session length: 3 weeks in June, July, August. Ages: 15–19. 12–24 participants per session. Cost: $3670–$4470.
Application Deadline Continuous.
Contact James Stoll, Director, PO Box 5517, Sarasota, Florida 34277. Phone: 800-317-6789. Fax: 941-924-6075. E-mail: info@actionquest.com.
URL www.actionquest.com
For more information, see page 964.

ActionQuest: British Virgin Islands–Sailing and Scuba Voyages

ActionQuest
British Virgin Islands

General Information Coed travel outdoor program and adventure program established in 1986.
Program Focus Live-aboard adventures for teenagers offering sailing and scuba diving certifications with associated watersports.

ACTIONQUEST: British Virgin Islands–Sailing and Scuba Voyages (continued)

ACTIONQUEST: British Virgin Islands–Sailing and Scuba Voyages

Academics Marine studies.
Special Interest Areas Leadership training, nature study, nautical skills, team building.
Sports Sailing, scuba diving, snorkeling, wakeboarding, waterskiing, windsurfing.
Wilderness/Outdoors Hiking.
Trips Day.
Program Information 3 sessions per year. Session length: 18–21 days in June, July, August. Ages: 13–19. 66–84 participants per session. Cost: $3670–$4470. No experience necessary.
Application Deadline Continuous.
Contact James Stoll, Director, PO Box 5517, Sarasota, Florida 34277. Phone: 800-317-6789. Fax: 941-924-6075. E-mail: info@actionquest.com.
URL www.actionquest.com
For more information, see page 964.

ACTIONQUEST: British Virgin Islands–Sailing Voyages

ActionQuest
British Virgin Islands

General Information Coed travel outdoor program and adventure program established in 1986.
Program Focus Live-aboard adventures for teenagers offering sailing and American Red Cross certifications with associated watersports.
Special Interest Areas Leadership training, lifesaving, nature study, nautical skills, team building.
Sports Sailing, snorkeling, wakeboarding, waterskiing, windsurfing.
Wilderness/Outdoors Hiking.
Trips Day.
Program Information 3 sessions per year. Session length: 18–21 days in June, July, August. Ages: 13–19. 12–48 participants per session. Cost: $3470–$4270. Financial aid available.
Application Deadline Continuous.
Contact James Stoll, Director, PO Box 5517, Sarasota, Florida 34277. Phone: 800-317-6789. Fax: 941-924-6075. E-mail: info@actionquest.com.
URL www.actionquest.com
For more information, see page 964.

ACTIONQUEST: Junior Advanced Scuba with Marine Biology

ActionQuest
British Virgin Islands

General Information Coed travel outdoor program and adventure program established in 1986.
Program Focus Live-aboard program focusing on PADI junior advanced scuba and specialty certifications with introduction to marine biology.
Academics Ecology, marine studies, oceanography.
Special Interest Areas Field research/expeditions, leadership training, nature study, nautical skills, team building.
Sports Sailing, scuba diving, snorkeling, waterskiing.
Wilderness/Outdoors Hiking.
Trips Cultural, day.
Program Information 3 sessions per year. Session length: 3 weeks in June, July, August. Ages: 13–15. 12 participants per session. Cost: $3670–$4470.
Application Deadline Continuous.
Contact James Stoll, Director, PO Box 5517, Sarasota, Florida 34277. Phone: 800-317-6789. Fax: 941-924-6075. E-mail: info@actionquest.com.
URL www.actionquest.com
For more information, see page 964.

ACTIONQUEST: Rescue Diving Voyages

ActionQuest
British Virgin Islands

General Information Coed travel outdoor program and adventure program established in 1986.
Program Focus Live-aboard program focusing on PADI Rescue certification and diver safety, search and recovery, underwater navigation.
Special Interest Areas Cardiac education, first aid, leadership training, nature study, nautical skills, team building.
Sports Sailing, scuba diving, snorkeling, waterskiing.
Wilderness/Outdoors Hiking.
Trips Day.
Program Information 3 sessions per year. Session length: 3 weeks in June, July, August. Ages: 15–19. 12 participants per session. Cost: $3670–$4470.
Application Deadline Continuous.
Contact James Stoll, Director, PO Box 5517, Sarasota, Florida 34277. Phone: 800-317-6789. Fax: 941-924-6075. E-mail: info@actionquest.com.
URL www.actionquest.com
For more information, see page 964.

ACTIONQUEST: Tropical Marine Biology Voyages

ActionQuest
British Virgin Islands

General Information Coed travel academic program, outdoor program, and adventure program established in 1986. High school credit may be earned.
Program Focus Live-aboard program focusing on PADI specialty certifications and marine biology with research scuba diving.
Academics Biology, ecology, environmental science, marine studies, oceanography.
Special Interest Areas Field research/expeditions, leadership training, nature study, nautical skills, team building.
Sports Sailing, scuba diving, snorkeling, waterskiing.
Wilderness/Outdoors Hiking.
Trips Cultural, day.
Program Information 3 sessions per year. Session length: 3 weeks in June, July, August. Ages: 15–19. 10 participants per session. Cost: $3670–$4470.
Application Deadline Continuous.
Contact James Stoll, Director, PO Box 5517, Sarasota, Florida 34277. Phone: 800-317-6789. Fax: 941-924-6075. E-mail: info@actionquest.com.
URL www.actionquest.com

For more information, see page 964.

!ADVENTURES–AFLOAT: Advanced Scuba Adventure Voyages–British Virgin Islands

!Adventures–Afloat/Odyssey Expeditions
British Virgin Islands

General Information Coed residential outdoor program and adventure program established in 1995. College credit may be earned.
Program Focus Advanced PADI scuba certifications, sail training, island exploration, and watersports.
Academics Biology, ecology, marine studies, oceanography.
Arts Photography, television/video.
Special Interest Areas Community service, field research/expeditions, leadership training, nature study, nautical skills.
Sports Boating, diving, fishing, kayaking, sailing, scuba diving, sea kayaking, snorkeling, waterskiing, windsurfing.
Wilderness/Outdoors Hiking.
Trips Cultural.
Program Information 3 sessions per year. Session length: 3 weeks in June, July, August. Ages: 15–19. 10 participants per session. Boarding program cost: $4290.
Application Deadline Continuous.
Jobs Positions for college students 21 and older.
Contact Jason Buchheim, Director, 650 Southeast Paradise Point Road, #100, Crystal River, Florida 34429. Phone: 800-929-7749. Fax: 801-340-5000. E-mail: odyssey@usa.net.
URL www.odysseyexpeditions.org

For more information, see page 970.

!ADVENTURES–AFLOAT: Scuba and Sailing Discovery Voyages–British Virgin Islands

!Adventures–Afloat/Odyssey Expeditions
British Virgin Islands

General Information Coed residential outdoor program and adventure program established in 1995. High school or college credit may be earned.
Program Focus PADI scuba certification, sail training, island exploration, and watersports.
Academics Biology, ecology, marine studies, oceanography.
Arts Photography, television/video.
Special Interest Areas Community service, field research/expeditions, leadership training, nature study, nautical skills.
Sports Boating, diving, sailing, scuba diving, sea kayaking, waterskiing, windsurfing.
Wilderness/Outdoors Hiking.
Trips Cultural.
Program Information 3 sessions per year. Session length: 3 weeks in June, July, August. Ages: 13–19. 10 participants per session. Boarding program cost: $4290.
Application Deadline Continuous.
Jobs Positions for college students 21 and older.
Contact Jason Buchheim, Director, 650 Southeast Paradise Point Road, #100, Crystal River, Florida 34429. Phone: 800-929-7749. Fax: 801-340-5000. E-mail: odyssey@usa.net.
URL www.odysseyexpeditions.org

For more information, see page 970.

LIFEWORKS with the British Virgin Islands Marine Parks and Conservation Department

LIFEWORKS International
British Virgin Islands

General Information Coed travel outdoor program, community service program, cultural program, and adventure program established in 1986. High school credit may be earned.
Program Focus Live-aboard program sailing throughout British Virgin Islands, working on both marine and land-based service projects.
Academics Marine studies.
Special Interest Areas Community service, field research/expeditions, leadership training, nautical skills, team building.
Sports Sailing, snorkeling.
Wilderness/Outdoors Hiking.
Trips Cultural, day.
Program Information 3 sessions per year. Session length: 17–21 days in June, July, August. Ages: 15–19. 8–26 participants per session. Cost: $3060–$3560. Financial aid available.
Application Deadline Continuous.

LIFEWORKS with the British Virgin Islands Marine Parks and Conservation Department (continued)

LIFEWORKS with the British Virgin Islands Marine Parks and Conservation Department

Contact James Stoll, Director, PO Box 5517, Sarasota, Florida 34277. Phone: 800-808-2115. Fax: 941-924-6075. E-mail: info@lifeworks-international.com.
URL www.lifeworks-international.com
For more information, see page 1196.

ODYSSEY EXPEDITIONS: Tropical Marine Biology Voyages–British Virgin Islands

!Adventures–Afloat/Odyssey Expeditions
British Virgin Islands

General Information Coed residential academic program, outdoor program, and adventure program established in 1995. College credit may be earned.
Program Focus Coed marine biology field studies program featuring underwater research, scuba certifications, sailing, and island exploration.
Academics Biology, ecology, geology/earth science, marine studies, oceanography.
Arts Photography, television/video.
Special Interest Areas Field research/expeditions, nature study, nautical skills.
Sports Boating, diving, fishing, sailing, scuba diving, sea kayaking, waterskiing, windsurfing.
Wilderness/Outdoors Hiking.
Trips Day, overnight.
Program Information 3 sessions per year. Session length: 3 weeks in June, July, August. Ages: 15–19. 10 participants per session. Boarding program cost: $4290.
Application Deadline Continuous.
Jobs Positions for college students 21 and older.
Contact Jason Buchheim, Director, 650 Southeast Paradise Point Road, #100, Crystal River, Florida 34429. Phone: 800-929-7749. Fax: 801-340-5000. E-mail: odyssey@usa.net.
URL www.odysseyexpeditions.org
For more information, see page 970.

Sail Caribbean–All Levels of Scuba Certification with Sailing

Sail Caribbean
British Virgin Islands

General Information Coed travel outdoor program and adventure program established in 1979. High school or college credit may be earned.
Program Focus Scuba certifications and teaching sailing, racing, and seamanship.
Academics Marine studies, oceanography.
Arts Photography.
Special Interest Areas Community service, leadership training, lifesaving, team building.
Sports Boating, diving, kayaking, sailing, scuba diving, snorkeling, swimming, volleyball, waterskiing, windsurfing.
Wilderness/Outdoors Hiking.
Trips Cultural, shopping.
Program Information 3 sessions per year. Session length: 2–3 weeks in June, July, August. Ages: 13–18. 50–80 participants per session. Cost: $3375–$4575. Financial aid available.
Application Deadline Continuous.
Jobs Positions for college students 20 and older.
Contact Michael Liese, Director, 79 Church Street, Northport, New York 11768. Phone: 800-321-0994. Fax: 631-754-3362. E-mail: info@sailcaribbean.com.
URL www.sailcaribbean.com
For more information, see page 1292.

Sail Caribbean–British Virgin Islands

Sail Caribbean
British Virgin Islands

General Information Coed travel outdoor program and adventure program established in 1979. High school or college credit may be earned.

Sail Caribbean–British Virgin Islands

Program Focus Teaching sailing, racing, and seamanship.
Academics Marine studies, oceanography.

Special Interest Areas Leadership training, lifesaving, team building.
Sports Boating, kayaking, sailing, scuba diving, snorkeling, swimming, volleyball, waterskiing, windsurfing.
Wilderness/Outdoors Hiking.
Trips Cultural, shopping.
Program Information 7 sessions per year. Session length: 2–3 weeks in June, July, August. Ages: 13–18. 50–80 participants per session. Cost: $3375–$4575. Financial aid available.
Application Deadline Continuous.
Jobs Positions for college students 20 and older.
Contact Michael Liese, Director, 79 Church Street, Northport, New York 11768. Phone: 800-321-0994. Fax: 631-754-3362. E-mail: info@sailcaribbean.com.
URL www.sailcaribbean.com
For more information, see page 1292.

Sail Caribbean–Community Service

Sail Caribbean
British Virgin Islands

General Information Coed travel outdoor program, community service program, and adventure program established in 1979. High school credit may be earned.
Academics Biology, marine studies, oceanography.
Special Interest Areas Community service, leadership training, team building.
Sports Boating, kayaking, sailing, scuba diving, snorkeling, volleyball, waterskiing, windsurfing.
Wilderness/Outdoors Hiking.
Trips Cultural, shopping.
Program Information 3 sessions per year. Session length: 2–3 weeks in June, July, August. Ages: 13–18. 10–20 participants per session. Cost: $3375–$4395. Financial aid available.
Application Deadline Continuous.
Jobs Positions for college students 20 and older.
Contact Mr. Michael Liese, Director, 79 Church Street, Northport, New York 11768. Phone: 800-321-0994. Fax: 631-754-3362. E-mail: info@sailcaribbean.com.
URL www.sailcaribbean.com
For more information, see page 1292.

Sail Caribbean–Marine Biology

Sail Caribbean
British Virgin Islands

General Information Coed travel outdoor program, community service program, and adventure program established in 1979. High school credit may be earned.
Academics Biology, marine studies, oceanography.
Special Interest Areas Community service, leadership training, nature study, team building.
Sports Boating, kayaking, sailing, scuba diving, sea kayaking, snorkeling, volleyball, waterskiing, windsurfing.
Wilderness/Outdoors Hiking.
Trips Cultural, day, shopping.
Program Information 3 sessions per year. Session length: 2–3 weeks in June, July, August. Ages: 13–18. 50–80 participants per session. Cost: $3375–$4395. Financial aid available.
Application Deadline Continuous.
Jobs Positions for college students 20 and older.
Contact Mr. Michael Liese, Director, 79 Church Street, Northport, New York 11768. Phone: 800-321-0994. Fax: 631-754-3362. E-mail: info@sailcaribbean.com.
URL www.sailcaribbean.com
For more information, see page 1292.

Visions–British Virgin Islands

Visions
British Virgin Islands

General Information Coed travel outdoor program, community service program, and cultural program established in 1989. High school credit may be earned.

Visions–British Virgin Islands

Program Focus Community service, cross-cultural experience, and outdoor adventure activities.
Academics Intercultural studies.
Arts Carpentry.
Special Interest Areas Community service, construction, cross-cultural education, field research/expeditions, field trips (arts and culture), leadership training, nature study.
Sports Scuba diving, sea kayaking, snorkeling, swimming.
Wilderness/Outdoors Hiking, outdoor adventure.
Trips Cultural, day, overnight.
Program Information 2–3 sessions per year. Session length: 3–4 weeks in June, July, August. Ages: 14–18. 20–25 participants per session. Cost: $2800–$3825. Financial aid available.
Application Deadline Continuous.
Jobs Positions for college students 22 and older.

Visions–British Virgin Islands (continued)

Contact Joanne Pinaire, Director, PO Box 220, Newport, Pennsylvania 17074. Phone: 717-567-7313. Fax: 717-567-7853. E-mail: info@visionsserviceadventures.com.
URL www.visionsserviceadventures.com
For more information, see page 1382.

CAMEROON

EARTHWATCH INSTITUTE–COMMUNITY HEALTH IN CAMEROON

Earthwatch Institute
Djohong
Cameroon

General Information Coed residential outdoor program, cultural program, and adventure program.
Program Focus Measuring the impact of public health efforts on intestinal parasites in remote villages.
Academics Biology, health sciences, science (general).
Special Interest Areas Community service, field research/expeditions, nature study.
Program Information 5 sessions per year. Session length: 13 days in January, March, May, July, November, December. Ages: 16+. 7 participants per session. Boarding program cost: $1895–$1995. Financial aid available. Financial aid for high school students and teachers.
Application Deadline Continuous.
Contact General Information Desk, PO Box 75, Maynard, Massachusetts 01754. Phone: 800-776-0188. Fax: 978-461-2332. E-mail: info@earthwatch.org.
URL www.earthwatch.org

CANADA

ADVENTURES CROSS-COUNTRY, EXTREME BRITISH COLUMBIA ADVENTURE

Adventures Cross-Country
British Columbia
Canada

General Information Coed residential outdoor program, wilderness program, and adventure program established in 1983.
Program Focus Wilderness adventure in British Columbia.
Sports Sea kayaking, skiing (cross-country).
Wilderness/Outdoors Backpacking, hiking, mountain biking, orienteering, rafting, rock climbing, white-water trips, wilderness camping.
Program Information 3 sessions per year. Session length: 20–23 days in July, August. Ages: 13–18. 8–15 participants per session. Boarding program cost: $3595–$3895. Financial aid available.
Application Deadline Continuous.
Jobs Positions for college students 21 and older.
Contact Scott von Eschen, Director, 242 Redwood Highway, Mill Valley, California 94941. Phone: 415-332-5075. Fax: 415-332-2130. E-mail: arcc@adventurescrosscountry.com.
URL www.adventurescrosscountry.com
For more information, see page 972.

ADVENTURE TREKS–CANADIAN ROCKIES ADVENTURES

Adventure Treks, Inc.
British Columbia
Canada

General Information Coed travel outdoor program, wilderness program, and adventure program established in 1978.
Program Focus Multi-activity outdoor adventure programs with a focus on fun, personal growth, leadership, outdoor skills, and teamwork.
Sports Canoeing, swimming.
Wilderness/Outdoors Backpacking, canoe trips, hiking, mountaineering, orienteering, rafting, rock climbing, white-water trips, wilderness camping.
Program Information 3–4 sessions per year. Session length: 21–22 days in June, July, August. Ages: 14–16. 24 participants per session. Cost: $2795. Financial aid available.
Application Deadline Continuous.
Contact John Dockendorf, Director, PO Box 1321, Flat Rock, North Carolina 28731. Phone: 888-954-5555. Fax: 828-696-1663. E-mail: info@advtreks.com.
URL www.adventuretreks.com

AFS-USA–HOMESTAY LANGUAGE STUDY–CANADA

AFS-USA
Quebec
Canada

General Information Coed residential academic program and cultural program.
Program Focus Beginners' French language study in Canada, homestay with French-speaking family.
Academics French language/literature.
Special Interest Areas Homestays.
Trips Cultural, day.
Program Information 1 session per year. Session length: 6 weeks in June, July, August. Ages: 15–18. Boarding program cost: $3665–$3965. Application fee: $75. Financial aid available. International airfare and volunteer homestay support included.
Application Deadline Continuous.
Jobs Positions for college students.

Contact Manager, AFS Info Center, 506 Southwest 6th Avenue, 2nd Floor, Portland, Oregon 97204. Phone: 800-AFS-INFO. Fax: 503-248-4076. E-mail: afsinfo@afs.org.
URL www.afs.org/usa
For more information, see page 974.

Appleby College Summer Academy

Appleby College
540 Lakeshore Road West
Oakville, Ontario L6K 3P1
Canada

General Information Coed day academic program established in 2001. High school credit may be earned.
Program Focus Academic credit and enrichment courses.
Academics French language/literature, SAT/ACT preparation, Spanish language/literature, academics (general), biology, chemistry, computers, geography, history, mathematics, mathematics (Advanced Placement), reading, writing.
Arts Arts and crafts (general), creative writing.
Trips Day.
Program Information 1–4 sessions per year. Session length: 5–25 days in July, August. Ages: 11–19. 10–12 participants per session. Day program cost: 275–1350 Canadian dollars.
Application Deadline Continuous.
Jobs Positions for high school students 16 and older and college students.
Contact Mr. Yigin Wu, Director, Summer Academy, main address above. Phone: 905-845-4681 Ext.269. Fax: 905-845-9828. E-mail: ywu@appleby.on.ca.
URL www.appleby.on.ca

Appleby College Summer Camps

Appleby College
540 Lakeshore Road West
Oakville, Ontario L6K 3P1
Canada

General Information Coed day traditional camp established in 1990.
Arts Arts and crafts (general), dance, drawing, mask making, music, painting, puppetry, sculpture, theater/drama, visual arts.
Special Interest Areas Internet accessibility.
Sports Badminton, baseball, basketball, bowling, canoeing, climbing (wall), field hockey, golf, lacrosse, physical fitness, soccer, softball, sports (general), swimming, tennis, track and field, volleyball.
Wilderness/Outdoors Canoe trips.
Program Information 1–8 sessions per year. Session length: 5–10 days in June, July, August. Ages: 4–17. 10–60 participants per session. Day program cost: 120–500 Canadian dollars.
Application Deadline Continuous.
Jobs Positions for high school students 16 and older and college students.
Contact Summer Programmes, main address above. Phone: 905-845-4681 Ext.366. Fax: 905-845-9828. E-mail: campprogrammes@appleby.on.ca.
URL www.appleby.on.ca

Bark Lake Leadership Through Recreation Camp

Bark Lake Leadership Centre
Highway 503
Irondale, Ontario K0M 1X0
Canada

General Information Coed residential traditional camp, academic program, outdoor program, and adventure program established in 1998. Accredited by Ontario Camping Association. Formal opportunities for the academically talented and artistically talented. Specific services available for the emotionally challenged, developmentally challenged, hearing impaired, learning disabled, physically challenged, and visually impaired. High school credit may be earned.
Program Focus ESL (English As a Second Language) camp, leadership, team building.
Academics English as a second language, astronomy, ecology, environmental science, music, science (general).
Arts Arts and crafts (general), band, music, music (ensemble), music (instrumental).
Special Interest Areas Leadership training, nature study, touring.
Sports Archery, baseball, basketball, canoeing, climbing (wall), fishing, kayaking, ropes course, soccer, swimming, volleyball, windsurfing.
Wilderness/Outdoors Canoe trips, hiking, orienteering, rock climbing, survival training, wilderness camping.
Trips College tours, day, overnight, shopping.
Program Information 4–5 sessions per year. Session length: 2–4 weeks in March, July, August. Ages: 11–17. Boarding program cost: 1120–2800 Canadian dollars. Financial aid available.
Application Deadline Continuous.
Jobs Positions for college students 20 and older.
Contact Mr. Brent Gordon, Camp Director, 1033 Main Street West, Hamilton, Ontario L8S 1B7, Canada. Phone: 905-577-0705. Fax: 905-577-0704. E-mail: info@barklake.com.
URL www.barklake.com

BICYCLE TRAVEL ADVENTURES–Student Hosteling Program–Province du Québec

BICYCLE TRAVEL ADVENTURES–Student Hosteling Program
Quebec
Canada

General Information Coed travel outdoor program, cultural program, and adventure program established in 2003. Accredited by American Camping Association. Formal opportunities for the academically talented. Specific services available for the emotionally challenged and learning disabled. High school credit may be earned.
Program Focus A moderate 24-day camping/hosteling trip cycling through the countryside of Quebec and touring the cities of Montreal and Quebec.
Special Interest Areas Campcraft, field trips (arts and culture), touring.

BICYCLE TRAVEL ADVENTURES–Student Hosteling Program–Province du Québec (continued)
Sports Bicycling, boating, swimming.
Wilderness/Outdoors Bicycle trips, hiking, wilderness camping.
Trips Cultural, day, overnight, shopping.
Program Information 2–3 sessions per year. Session length: 24 days in July, August. Ages: 13–17. 8–12 participants per session. Cost: $2625.
Application Deadline Continuous.
Jobs Positions for high school students 16 and older and college students 18 and older.
Contact Ted Lefkowitz, Director, 1356 Ashfield Road, PO Box 419, Conway, Massachusetts 01341. Phone: 800-343-6132. Fax: 413-369-4257. E-mail: shpbike@aol.com.
URL www.bicycletrips.com
For more information, see page 994.

BICYCLE TRAVEL ADVENTURES–STUDENT HOSTELING PROGRAM–PROVINCE DU QUÉBEC (SHORT PROGRAM)

BICYCLE TRAVEL ADVENTURES–Student Hosteling Program
Quebec
Canada

General Information Coed travel outdoor program, cultural program, and adventure program established in 2004. Accredited by American Camping Association. Formal opportunities for the academically talented. Specific services available for the emotionally challenged and learning disabled. High school credit may be earned.
Special Interest Areas Campcraft, field trips (arts and culture), touring.
Sports Bicycling, boating, swimming.
Wilderness/Outdoors Bicycle trips, hiking, wilderness camping.
Trips Cultural, day, overnight, shopping.
Program Information 2 sessions per year. Session length: 17 days in August. Ages: 13–17. 8–12 participants per session. Cost: $1875.
Application Deadline Continuous.
Jobs Positions for high school students 16 and older and college students 18 and older.
Contact Ted Lefkowitz, Director, 1356 Ashfield Road, PO Box 419, Conway, Massachusetts 01341. Phone: 800-343-6132. Fax: 413-369-4257. E-mail: shpbike@aol.com.
URL www.bicycletrips.com
For more information, see page 994.

BISHOP'S COLLEGE SCHOOL SUMMER SCHOOL

Bishop's College School
80 Moulton Hill
Lennoxville, Quebec J1M 1Z8
Canada

General Information Coed residential and day academic program established in 1960.

Bishop's College School Summer School

Program Focus French or English as a second language.
Academics English as a second language, French language/literature.
Sports Basketball, canoeing, climbing (wall), football, golf, horseback riding, kayaking, skateboarding, soccer, softball, squash, swimming, tennis, track and field, volleyball, waterskiing.
Wilderness/Outdoors Rock climbing.
Trips Cultural, day, shopping.
Program Information 1 session per year. Session length: 4 weeks in July. Ages: 11–16. 150–180 participants per session. Day program cost: 1550–1600 Canadian dollars. Boarding program cost: 2550–2600 Canadian dollars.
Application Deadline Continuous.
Jobs Positions for high school students 17 and older and college students 18 and older.
Contact Ms. Denise Addona, Coordinator Summer School, main address above. Phone: 819-566-0227. Fax: 819-822-8917. E-mail: daddona@bishopscollegeschool.com.
URL www.bishopscollegeschool.com
For more information, see page 996.

BROADREACH ACADEMIC TREKS–MARINE MAMMAL STUDIES

Broadreach
British Columbia
Canada

General Information Coed travel academic program, outdoor program, and adventure program established in 1992. High school or college credit may be earned.
Program Focus Academic adventure program focusing on whale and dolphin studies, community service, sea kayaking, hiking, exploration and high school/college credit.
Academics Academics (general), area studies, biology, ecology, environmental science, marine studies.
Special Interest Areas Native American culture, career exploration, community service, conservation projects, field research/expeditions, leadership training.
Sports Sea kayaking, swimming.

Wilderness/Outdoors Backpacking, hiking, wilderness camping.
Trips Cultural.
Program Information 2 sessions per year. Ages: 15–19. 10–14 participants per session. Cost: $3800–$4700.
Application Deadline Continuous.
Contact Carlton Goldthwaite, Director, PO Box 27076, Raleigh, North Carolina 27611. Phone: 888-833-1907. Fax: 919-833-2129. E-mail: info@gobroadreach.com or info@academictreks.com.
URL www.academictreks.com
For more information, see page 1010.

Camp AK-O-MAK

Camp AK-O-MAK
1 AK-O-MAK Road
Ahmic Harbour, Ontario P0A 1A0
Canada

General Information Girls' residential traditional camp, outdoor program, and sports camp established in 1928. Accredited by Ontario Camping Association.
Program Focus Competitive swimming and paddling (canoe/kayak).
Academics English as a second language.
Special Interest Areas Leadership training, nature study, nautical skills.
Sports Aerobics, archery, basketball, bicycling, boating, canoeing, climbing (wall), croquet, cross-country, diving, fencing, field hockey, fishing, football, golf, handball, kayaking, lacrosse, rappelling, ropes course, rugby, sailing, sea kayaking, soccer, softball, sports (general), street/roller hockey, swimming, tennis, track and field, ultimate frisbee, volleyball, water polo, weight training, windsurfing, wrestling.
Wilderness/Outdoors Backpacking, bicycle trips, canoe trips, hiking, mountain biking, mountaineering, orienteering, pack animal trips, survival training, wilderness camping, wilderness/outdoors (general).
Trips Day, overnight.
Program Information 4 sessions per year. Session length: 2–7 weeks in June, July, August. Ages: 7–16. 80–100 participants per session. Boarding program cost: $450–$500. Financial aid available.
Application Deadline Continuous.
Jobs Positions for college students 17 and older.
Summer Contact Mr. Pat Kennedy, Director, General Delivery, 240 AK-O-MAK Road, Ahmic Harbour, Ontario P0A 1A0, Canada. Phone: 705-387-3810. Fax: 705-387-4838. E-mail: akomak@aol.com.
Winter Contact Mr. Pat Kennedy, Director, PO Box 787, Kankakee, Illinois 60901. Phone: 815-928-9840. Fax: 815-928-8971. E-mail: akomak@aol.com.
URL www.campakomak.com

Camp Arowhon–Boys and Girls Camp

Camp Arowhon, Ltd.
Algonquin Park
Ontario P1H 2G6
Canada

General Information Coed residential traditional camp established in 1934. Accredited by Ontario Camping Association.
Arts Arts and crafts (general), ceramics, jewelry making, leather working, pottery, theater/drama, woodworking.
Special Interest Areas Leadership training, nature study, team building.
Sports Archery, baseball, basketball, canoeing, climbing (wall), equestrian sports, horseback riding, kayaking, rappelling, ropes course, sailing, soccer, softball, swimming, tennis, volleyball, windsurfing.
Wilderness/Outdoors Canoe trips, hiking, rock climbing, wilderness camping.
Trips Day, overnight.
Program Information 2–6 sessions per year. Session length: 14–54 days in July, August. Ages: 7–16. 300 participants per session. Boarding program cost: 1700–5800 Canadian dollars.
Application Deadline Continuous.
Jobs Positions for high school students 17 and older and college students 18 and older.
Contact Joanne Kates, Director, 72 Lyndhurst Avenue, Toronto, Ontario M5R 2Z7, Canada. Phone: 416-975-9060. Fax: 416-975-0130. E-mail: info@camparowhon.com.
URL www.camparowhon.com

Camp Arowhon–Voyageur Canoe Trip Program

Camp Arowhon, Ltd.
Algonquin Park
Ontario P1H 2G6
Canada

General Information Coed residential adventure program established in 1934. Accredited by Ontario Camping Association.
Special Interest Areas Nature study.
Sports Canoeing.
Wilderness/Outdoors Canoe trips, hiking, wilderness camping.
Trips Overnight.
Program Information 4 sessions per year. Session length: 16–27 days in July, August. Ages: 12–16. Boarding program cost: 2060–6400 Canadian dollars.
Application Deadline Continuous.
Jobs Positions for high school students 17 and older and college students 18 and older.
Contact Joanne Kates, Director, 72 Lyndhurst Avenue, Toronto, Ontario M5R 2Z7, Canada. Phone: 416-975-9060. Fax: 416-975-0130. E-mail: info@camparowhon.com.
URL www.camparowhon.com

Camp Chikopi for Boys

Camp Chikopi
1 Chikopi Road
Ahmic Harbour, Ontario P0A 1A0
Canada

General Information Boys' residential traditional camp established in 1920. Accredited by Ontario Camping Association.
Program Focus Provides the setting for campers to improve self-confidence and think more positively in every challenge that arises.
Special Interest Areas Leadership training.
Sports Aerobics, archery, baseball, basketball, bicycling, canoeing, climbing (wall), cricket, croquet, cross-country, diving, field hockey, fishing, football, golf, gymnastics, kayaking, lacrosse, martial arts, ropes course, rugby, sailing, soccer, softball, sports (general), swimming, tennis, track and field, volleyball, water polo, weight training, windsurfing, wrestling.
Wilderness/Outdoors Backpacking, canoe trips, hiking, mountain biking, mountaineering, orienteering, survival training, wilderness camping.
Trips Day, overnight.
Program Information 4 sessions per year. Session length: 2–7 weeks in June, July, August. Ages: 7–17. 100 participants per session. Boarding program cost: 425–695 Canadian dollars.
Application Deadline Continuous.
Jobs Positions for college students 20 and older.
Summer Contact Mr. Bob Duenkel, Director, main address above. Phone: 705-387-3811. Fax: 705-387-4747. E-mail: campchikopi@aol.com.
Winter Contact Mr. Bob Duenkel, Director, 2132 Northeast 17 Terrace, Ft. Lauderdale, Florida 33305. Phone: 954-566-8235. Fax: 954-525-4031. E-mail: campchikopi@aol.com.
URL www.campchikopi.com

Camp Craig Horse Residential Summer Camp

Camp Craig
98 Main Street
Ailsa Craig, Ontario N0M 1A0
Canada

General Information Coed residential traditional camp and outdoor program established in 1990.
Program Focus Horseback riding.
Arts Arts and crafts (general), dance, dance (folk).
Special Interest Areas Native American culture, animal care, leadership training.
Sports Archery, bicycling (BMX), canoeing, horseback riding, obstacle course, soccer, softball, sports (general), swimming, volleyball.
Wilderness/Outdoors Hiking.
Program Information 9 sessions per year. Session length: 1 week in July, August. Ages: 8–16. 45 participants per session. Boarding program cost: 420 Canadian dollars.
Application Deadline Continuous.
Jobs Positions for high school students 17 and older and college students.
Contact Angela Robinson, Owner, Box 265, Ailsa Craig, Ontario N0M 1A0, Canada. Phone: 519-293-3484. E-mail: angelaandbob@msn.com.
URL www.campcraig.com

Camp Craig Sports and Recreation Summer Camp

Camp Craig
98 Main Street
Ailsa Craig, Ontario N0M 1A0
Canada

General Information Coed residential traditional camp established in 1990.
Program Focus Horseback riding, sports.
Arts Arts and crafts (general), dance, dance (folk).
Special Interest Areas Animal care.
Sports Archery, bicycling (BMX), canoeing, horseback riding, soccer, softball, swimming, volleyball.
Wilderness/Outdoors Hiking.
Program Information 9–10 sessions per year. Session length: 1 week in July, August. Ages: 8–16. 45 participants per session. Boarding program cost: 420 Canadian dollars.
Application Deadline Continuous.
Jobs Positions for high school students 17 and older and college students.
Contact Angela Robinson, Owner, Box 265, Ailsa Craig, Ontario N0M 1A0, Canada. Phone: 519-293-3484. E-mail: angelaandbob@msn.com.
URL www.campcraig.com

Camp Ganadaoweh

Camp Ganadaoweh
Ayr, Ontario N0B 1E0
Canada

General Information Coed residential and day traditional camp, outdoor program, and bible camp established in 1959. Religious affiliation: United Church of Canada. Accredited by Ontario Camping Association.
Program Focus Community-building, wilderness and residential programs.
Academics Bible study, religion.
Arts Arts and crafts (general), music (vocal).
Special Interest Areas Campcraft, leadership training, nature study.
Sports Archery, basketball, canoeing, ropes course, soccer, swimming, volleyball.
Wilderness/Outdoors Canoe trips, orienteering.
Program Information 7–20 sessions per year. Session length: 3–11 days in July, August. Ages: 5–19. 12–60 participants per session. Day program cost: 110–115 Canadian dollars. Boarding program cost: 175–420 Canadian dollars. Financial aid available.
Application Deadline Continuous.
Jobs Positions for high school students 17 and older and college students 17 and older.
Contact Ms. M. Hipkin, Director, main address above. Phone: 519-632-7559. Fax: 519-632-9607. E-mail: camp@ganadaoweh.ca.
URL www.ganadaoweh.ca

Camp Kodiak

4069 Pheasant Run
Mississauga, Ontario L5L 2C2
Canada

General Information Coed residential traditional camp, academic program, and special needs program established in 1991. Accredited by Ontario Camping Association. Specific services available for the learning disabled, participant with ADD, and participant with AD/HD. High school credit may be earned.
Academics American literature, English as a second language, English language/literature, French (Advanced Placement), French language/literature, Hebrew language, academics (general), area studies, biology, business, chemistry, communications, computer programming, computers, ecology, environmental science, geography, geology/earth science, government and politics, government and politics (Advanced Placement), history, humanities, mathematics, mathematics (Advanced Placement), music, physics, reading, remedial academics, science (general), social science, social studies, study skills, typing, writing.
Arts Arts and crafts (general), batiking, ceramics, chorus, creative writing, dance, dance (jazz), dance (modern), drawing, fabric arts, film, graphic arts, jewelry making, leather working, music, music (instrumental), music (vocal), musical productions, painting, photography, pottery, printmaking, puppetry, radio broadcasting, sculpture, stained glass, television/video, theater/drama, weaving, woodworking.
Special Interest Areas Campcraft, career exploration, culinary arts, leadership training, model rocketry, nature study, social skills development.
Sports Aerobics, archery, baseball, basketball, boating, canoeing, climbing (wall), diving, equestrian sports, fishing, football, golf, gymnastics, horseback riding, kayaking, martial arts, rappelling, ropes course, sailing, snorkeling, soccer, softball, swimming, tennis, volleyball, wakeboarding, water polo, waterskiing, weight training, windsurfing, wrestling.
Wilderness/Outdoors Backpacking, canoe trips, hiking, survival training, wilderness camping.
Trips Day, overnight.
Program Information 2 sessions per year. Session length: 3–4 weeks in July, August. Ages: 6–18. 200 participants per session. Boarding program cost: $2275–$4875.
Application Deadline Continuous.
Jobs Positions for college students 20 and older.
Summer Contact Mr. David Stoch, Director, General Delivery, McKellar, Ontario P0G 1C0, Canada. Phone: 705-389-1910. Fax: 705-389-1911. E-mail: dave@campkodiak.com.
Winter Contact Mr. David Stoch, Director, 4069 Pheasant Run, Mississauga, Ontario L5L 2C2, Canada. Phone: 905-569-7595. Fax: 905-569-6045. E-mail: dave@campkodiak.com.
URL www.campkodiak.com

Camp Maromac

Camp Maromac
231 Chemin Lac Quenouille
Val des Lacs, Quebec J0T 2P0
Canada

General Information Coed residential traditional camp and outdoor program established in 1968. Accredited by Quebec Camping Association.
Program Focus Fun, friends, adventure. All activities have certified experienced instructors.
Academics English language/literature, art (Advanced Placement).
Arts Acting, arts, arts and crafts (general), ceramics, dance, dance (jazz), dance (modern), drawing, jewelry making, music, music (vocal), musical productions, painting, printmaking, puppetry, sculpture, theater/drama, woodworking.
Special Interest Areas Counselor-in-training program, work camp programs.
Sports Aerobics, baseball, basketball, bicycling, bicycling (BMX), boating, canoeing, climbing (wall), field hockey, fishing, football, golf, gymnastics, in-line skating, kayaking, rappelling, sailing, soccer, softball, street/roller hockey, swimming, tennis, track and field, volleyball, water polo, waterskiing, windsurfing.
Wilderness/Outdoors Backpacking, bicycle trips, canoe trips, hiking, mountain biking, rafting, rock climbing, white-water trips.
Trips Cultural, day, overnight, shopping.
Program Information 3–4 sessions per year. Session length: 14–47 days in June, July, August. Ages: 6–16. 200 participants per session. Boarding program cost: $2760–$4590.
Application Deadline Continuous.
Jobs Positions for college students 18 and older.
Summer Contact Joseph Marovitch, Director/Owner, 4999 Rue Ste. Catherine Ouest, Suite 232, Montreal, Quebec H3Z 1T3, Canada. Phone: 800-884-2267. Fax: 514-485-1124. E-mail: info@maromac.com.
Winter Contact Joseph Marovitch, Director/Owner, 4999 Rue Ste. Catherine Ouest, Suite 232, Montreal, Quebec H3Z 1T3, Canada. Phone: 800-884-2267. Fax: 514-485-1124. E-mail: info@maromac.com.
URL www.maromac.com

Camp Mi-A-Kon-Da

132 Seymour Drive
Ancaster, Ontario L9G 4N6
Canada

General Information Girls' residential traditional camp established in 1955. Accredited by Ontario Camping Association.
Program Focus Waterfront activities and canoe trips.
Arts Arts and crafts (general), theater/drama, woodworking.
Special Interest Areas Campcraft, leadership training, nature study.
Sports Archery, bicycling, canoeing, climbing (wall), kayaking, ropes course, sailing, swimming, windsurfing.
Wilderness/Outdoors Canoe trips, hiking, rock climbing, wilderness camping.

Camp Mi-A-Kon-Da (continued)

Program Information 6 sessions per year. Session length: 2–8 weeks in July, August. Ages: 7–17. 98 participants per session. Boarding program cost: 1200–2200 Canadian dollars.
Application Deadline Continuous.
Jobs Positions for high school students 17 and older and college students 17 and older.
Summer Contact Pam Lamont, Director, RR #2, Dunchurch, Ontario P0A 1G0, Canada. Phone: 705-389-1462.
Winter Contact Pam Lamont, Director, 132 Seymour Drive, Ancaster, Ontario L9G 4N6, Canada. Phone: 905-648-9382. Fax: 905-648-1305. E-mail: plamont@sympatico.ca.
URL www.miakonda.com

Camp Nominingue

1889 Chemin des Mesanges
Nominingue, Quebec J0W 1R0
Canada

General Information Boys' residential traditional camp and outdoor program established in 1925. Accredited by Ontario Camping Association and Quebec Camping Association.
Program Focus Wilderness canoe trips.
Academics English as a second language, French language/literature.
Arts Arts and crafts (general), leather working, theater/drama, woodworking.
Special Interest Areas Campcraft, leadership training, nature study.
Sports Archery, basketball, boating, canoeing, diving, fishing, football, golf, kayaking, lacrosse, riflery, sailing, soccer, softball, sports (general), swimming, tennis, volleyball, windsurfing.
Wilderness/Outdoors Canoe trips, hiking, mountain biking, orienteering, wilderness camping.
Trips Day, overnight.
Program Information 6 sessions per year. Session length: 14–47 days in June, July, August. Ages: 7–15. 200 participants per session. Day program cost: 100–800 Canadian dollars. Boarding program cost: 1400–3900 Canadian dollars.
Application Deadline Continuous.
Jobs Positions for high school students 17 and older and college students.
Summer Contact Grant McKenna, Executive Director, 1889 Chemin des Mésanges, Nominingue, Quebec J0W 1R0, Canada. Phone: 819-278-3383. Fax: 819-278-1307. E-mail: camp@axess.com.
Winter Contact Grant McKenna, Executive Director, 2700 rue Halpern, St. Laurent, Quebec H4S 1R6, Canada. Phone: 514-856-1333. Fax: 514-856-8001. E-mail: camp@axess.com.
URL www.nominingue.com

Camp Northway

Camp Northway
Cache Lake
Algonquin Provincial Park
Huntsville, Ontario P1H 2G7
Canada

General Information Girls' residential traditional camp and outdoor program established in 1906. Accredited by Ontario Camping Association.
Arts Arts and crafts (general), painting, theater/drama.
Sports Canoeing, fishing, kayaking, sailing, swimming.
Wilderness/Outdoors Bicycle trips, canoe trips, hiking, mountain biking, wilderness camping.
Trips Overnight.
Program Information 4 sessions per year. Session length: 13–50 days in July, August. Ages: 7–16. 50 participants per session. Boarding program cost: 1287–3950 Canadian dollars.
Application Deadline Continuous.
Jobs Positions for high school students 17 and older and college students 17 and older.
Summer Contact Mr. Brookes Prewitt, Director, Box 10003 Cache Lake, Algonquin Park, Huntsville, Ontario P1H 2G7, Canada. Phone: 705-633-5595.
Winter Contact Mr. Brookes Prewitt, Director, 294 Regent Street, Box 1184, Niagara-on-the-Lake, Ontario L0S 1J0, Canada. Phone: 905-468-4455. E-mail: northway@sprint.ca.
URL www.campnorthway.com

Camp Ouareau

Camp Ouareau
2494 Route 125 South
St. Donat, Quebec J0T 2C0
Canada

General Information Girls' residential traditional camp established in 1922. Accredited by Quebec Camping Association and Ontario Camping Association.
Program Focus French and English languages and water sports.
Academics English as a second language, French language/literature, language study.
Arts Arts and crafts (general), musical productions, theater/drama.
Special Interest Areas Campcraft.
Sports Archery, boating, canoeing, climbing (wall), kayaking, ropes course, sailing, swimming, tennis, windsurfing.
Wilderness/Outdoors Backpacking, canoe trips, hiking, mountaineering, rock climbing.
Trips Overnight.
Program Information 4 sessions per year. Session length: 2–8 weeks in June, July, August. Ages: 5–15. 106–124 participants per session. Boarding program cost: 1350–4700 Canadian dollars.
Application Deadline Continuous.
Jobs Positions for high school students 18 and older and college students 18 and older.
Contact Ms. Jacqui Raill, Director, main address above. Phone: 819-424-2662. Fax: 819-424-4145. E-mail: info@ouareau.com.
URL www.ouareau.com

Camp Ponacka

376 Ponacka Road
Highland Grove, Ontario K0L 2A0
Canada

General Information Boys' residential traditional camp established in 1947. Accredited by Ontario Camping Association.
Arts Arts and crafts (general), batiking, ceramics, fabric arts, jewelry making, leather working, music (vocal), pottery, theater/drama, woodworking.
Special Interest Areas Campcraft, leadership training, nature study.
Sports Archery, basketball, bicycling, boating, canoeing, climbing (wall), equestrian sports, fishing, horseback riding, kayaking, ropes course, rowing (crew/sculling), sailing, scuba diving, snorkeling, swimming, waterskiing, windsurfing.
Wilderness/Outdoors Backpacking, bicycle trips, canoe trips, caving, hiking, mountain biking, rock climbing, white-water trips, wilderness camping.
Trips Day, overnight.
Program Information 2–4 sessions per year. Session length: 2–4 weeks in July, August. Ages: 8–15. 155 participants per session. Boarding program cost: 1400–2700 Canadian dollars. Application fee: 75 Canadian dollars.
Application Deadline Continuous.
Jobs Positions for high school students 17 and older and college students 17 and older.
Contact Don Bocking, Co-Director, 1674 Killoran Road, RR #4, Peterborough, Ontario K9J 6X5, Canada. Phone: 705-748-9470. Fax: 705-748-3880. E-mail: info@ponacka.com.
URL www.ponacka.com

Camps with Meaning–Advanced Horsemanship I & II

Camps with Meaning
Camp Assiniboia
Winnipeg, Manitoba
Canada

General Information Coed residential traditional camp, outdoor program, and bible camp established in 1950. Religious affiliation: Mennonite. Accredited by Manitoba Camping Association.
Program Focus Advanced horsemanship at Camp Assiniboia.
Arts Acting, arts and crafts (general).
Special Interest Areas Nature study.
Sports Archery, canoeing, climbing (wall), horseback riding, kayaking, ropes course, swimming, windsurfing.
Program Information 2 sessions per year. Session length: 5–7 days in August. Ages: 12–15. Boarding program cost: 281 Canadian dollars. Financial aid available.
Application Deadline Continuous.
Jobs Positions for high school students and college students.
Summer Contact Ms. Sandy W. Plett, Director, Summer Camp & Youth Ministries, 200-600 Shaftesbury Boulevard, Winnipeg, Manitoba R3P 2J1, Canada. Phone: 204-896-1616. Fax: 204-832-7804. E-mail: splett@mennochurch.mb.ca.
Winter Contact Mrs. Eva Loewen, Administrative Assistant, 200-600 Shaftesbury Boulevard, Winnipeg, Manitoba R3P 2J1, Canada. Phone: 204-895-2267. Fax: 204-832-7804. E-mail: camps@mennochurch.mb.ca.
URL www.campswithmeaning.org

Camps with Meaning–Boys Camp

Camps with Meaning
Camp Koinonia
Winnipeg, Manitoba
Canada

General Information Boys' residential traditional camp, outdoor program, and bible camp established in 1950. Religious affiliation: Mennonite. Accredited by Manitoba Camping Association.
Arts Acting, arts and crafts (general).
Special Interest Areas Nature study.
Sports Archery, canoeing, climbing (wall), kayaking, ropes course, swimming, windsurfing.
Program Information 1 session per year. Session length: 5–7 days in August. Ages: 10–13. 42–90 participants per session. Boarding program cost: 176 Canadian dollars. Financial aid available.
Application Deadline Continuous.
Jobs Positions for high school students and college students.
Summer Contact Ms. Sandy W. Plett, Director, Summer Camp & Youth Ministries, 200-600 Shaftesbury Boulevard, Winnipeg, Manitoba R3P 2J1, Canada. Phone: 204-896-1616. Fax: 204-832-7804. E-mail: splett@mennochurch.mb.ca.
Winter Contact Mrs. Eva Loewen, Administrative Assistant, 200-600 Shaftesbury Boulevard, Winnipeg, Manitoba R3P 2J1, Canada. Phone: 204-895-2267. Fax: 204-832-7804. E-mail: camps@mennochurch.mb.ca.
URL www.campswithmeaning.org

Camps with Meaning–Girls Camp

Camps with Meaning
Camp Assiniboia
Winnipeg, Manitoba
Canada

General Information Girls' residential traditional camp, outdoor program, and bible camp established in 1950. Religious affiliation: Mennonite. Accredited by Manitoba Camping Association.
Arts Acting, arts and crafts (general).
Special Interest Areas Nature study.
Sports Archery, canoeing, climbing (wall), horseback riding, kayaking, ropes course, swimming, windsurfing.
Program Information 1 session per year. Session length: 5–7 days in July. Ages: 10–12. 42–90 participants per session. Boarding program cost: 197 Canadian dollars. Financial aid available.
Application Deadline Continuous.
Jobs Positions for high school students and college students.

Camps with Meaning–Girls Camp (continued)

Summer Contact Ms. Sandy W. Plett, Director, Summer Camp & Youth Ministries, 200-600 Shaftesbury Boulevard, Winnipeg, Manitoba R3P 2J1, Canada. Phone: 204-896-1616. Fax: 204-832-7804. E-mail: splett@mennochurch.mb.ca.
Winter Contact Mrs. Eva Loewen, Administrative Assistant, 200-600 Shaftesbury Boulevard, Winnipeg, Manitoba R3P 2J1, Canada. Phone: 204-895-2267. Fax: 204-832-7804. E-mail: camps@mennochurch.mb.ca.
URL www.campswithmeaning.org

Camps with Meaning–Junior High/Junior Youth Camp

Camps with Meaning
Winnipeg, Manitoba
Canada

General Information Coed residential traditional camp, outdoor program, and bible camp established in 1950. Religious affiliation: Mennonite. Accredited by Manitoba Camping Association.
Program Focus Junior high and junior youth programs at Camps Assiniboia, Koinonia and Moose Lake.
Arts Acting, arts and crafts (general).
Special Interest Areas Nature study.
Sports Archery, canoeing, climbing (wall), horseback riding, kayaking, ropes course, swimming, windsurfing.
Program Information 1–5 sessions per year. Session length: 5–7 days in July, August. Ages: 11–14. 42–90 participants per session. Boarding program cost: 159–197 Canadian dollars. Financial aid available.
Application Deadline Continuous.
Jobs Positions for high school students and college students.
Summer Contact Ms. Sandy W. Plett, Director, Summer Camps & Youth Ministries, 200-600 Shaftesbury Boulevard, Winnipeg, Manitoba R3P 2J1, Canada. Phone: 204-896-1616. Fax: 204-832-7804. E-mail: splett@mennochurch.mb.ca.
Winter Contact Mrs. Eva Loewen, Administrative Assistant, 200-600 Shaftesbury Boulevard, Winnipeg, Manitoba R3P 2J1, Canada. Phone: 204-895-2267. Fax: 204-832-7804. E-mail: camps@mennochurch.mb.ca.
URL www.campswithmeaning.org

Camps with Meaning–PreJunior/Junior/Intermediate Camp

Camps with Meaning
Camp Assiniboia
Winnipeg, Manitoba
Canada

General Information Coed residential traditional camp, outdoor program, and bible camp established in 1950. Religious affiliation: Mennonite. Accredited by Manitoba Camping Association.
Program Focus Pre Junior for first time campers plus Junior and Intermediate programs at Camp Assiniboia.
Arts Acting, arts and crafts (general).
Special Interest Areas Nature study.
Sports Archery, canoeing, climbing (wall), horseback riding, kayaking, ropes course, swimming, windsurfing.
Program Information 1–5 sessions per year. Session length: 5–7 days in July, August. Ages: 6–12. 42–90 participants per session. Boarding program cost: 106–197 Canadian dollars. Financial aid available.
Application Deadline Continuous.
Jobs Positions for high school students and college students.
Summer Contact Ms. Sandy W. Plett, Director, Summer Camp and Youth Ministries, 200-600 Shaftesbury Boulevard, Winnipeg, Manitoba R3P 2J1, Canada. Phone: 204-896-1616. Fax: 204-832-7804. E-mail: splett@mennochurch.mb.ca.
Winter Contact Mrs. Eva Loewen, Administrative Assistant, 200-600 Shaftesbury Boulevard, Winnipeg, Manitoba R3P 2J1, Canada. Phone: 204-895-2267. Fax: 204-832-7804. E-mail: camps@mennochurch.mb.ca.
URL www.campswithmeaning.org

Camps with Meaning–Youth Camp

Camps with Meaning
Winnipeg, Manitoba
Canada

General Information Coed residential traditional camp, outdoor program, and bible camp established in 1950. Religious affiliation: Mennonite. Accredited by Manitoba Camping Association.
Program Focus Youth camp at Camps Koinonia and Moose Lake.
Arts Acting, arts and crafts (general).
Special Interest Areas Nature study.
Sports Archery, canoeing, climbing (wall), kayaking, ropes course, swimming, windsurfing.
Program Information 1–2 sessions per year. Session length: 5–7 days in July, August. Ages: 14–16. 42–90 participants per session. Boarding program cost: 210 Canadian dollars. Financial aid available.
Application Deadline Continuous.
Jobs Positions for high school students and college students.
Summer Contact Ms. Sandy W. Plett, Director, Summer Camp & Youth Ministries, 200-600 Shaftesbury Boulevard, Winnipeg, Manitoba R3P 2J1, Canada. Phone: 204-896-1616. Fax: 204-832-7804. E-mail: splett@mennochurch.mb.ca.
Winter Contact Mrs. Eva Loewen, Administrative Assistant, 200-600 Shaftesbury Boulevard, Winnipeg, Manitoba R3P 2J1, Canada. Phone: 204-895-2267. Fax: 204-832-7804. E-mail: camps@mennochurch.mb.ca.
URL www.campswithmeaning.org

Camp Tawonga–Teen Quest: Canada

Camp Tawonga (Tawonga Jewish Community Corp.)
British Columbia
Canada

General Information Coed travel wilderness program and adventure program established in 1926. Religious affiliation: Jewish. Accredited by American Camping Association.
Arts Arts and crafts (general), music.

Sports Boating, sea kayaking.
Wilderness/Outdoors Backpacking, hiking, outdoor adventure, rock climbing.
Program Information 1 session per year. Session length: 3 weeks in August. 10–11 participants per session. Cost: $2840. Financial aid available. Open to participants entering grades 10–12. Airfare included in cost.
Application Deadline Continuous.
Jobs Positions for college students 18 and older.
Contact Sara Rubinett, Office Manager, 131 Steuart Street, San Francisco, California 94105. Phone: 415-543-2267. Fax: 415-534-5417. E-mail: info@tawonga.org.
URL www.tawonga.org

Camp Wendigo

Camp Northway
Cache Lake
Algonquin Provincial Park
Huntsville, Ontario P1H 2G7
Canada

General Information Boys' residential outdoor program and wilderness program established in 1965. Accredited by Ontario Camping Association.
Program Focus Canoe-tripping camp.
Sports Canoeing.
Wilderness/Outdoors Canoe trips, wilderness camping.
Trips Overnight.
Program Information 4 sessions per year. Session length: 13–50 days in July, August. Ages: 12–16. 7 participants per session. Boarding program cost: 1287–3950 Canadian dollars.
Application Deadline Continuous.
Jobs Positions for high school students 17 and older and college students 17 and older.
Summer Contact Mr. Brookes Prewitt, Director, Box 10003 Cache Lake, Algonquin Park, Huntsville, Ontario P1H 2G7, Canada. Phone: 705-633-5595.
Winter Contact Mr. Brookes Prewitt, Director, 294 Regent Street, Box 1184, Niagara-on-the-Lake, Ontario L0S 1J0, Canada. Phone: 905-468-4455. E-mail: northway@sprint.ca.
URL www.campnorthway.com

Camp Wilvaken

241 Chemin Willis
Magog, Quebec J1X 3W2
Canada

General Information Coed residential traditional camp established in 1958. Accredited by Ontario Camping Association and Quebec Camping Association.
Program Focus Informal use of French and English in a camp setting.
Academics English language/literature, French language/literature, language study.
Arts Arts and crafts (general), batiking, drawing, music (vocal), painting, pottery, printmaking, theater/drama.
Special Interest Areas Campcraft, leadership training, nature study, nautical skills.
Sports Archery, basketball, boating, canoeing, diving, equestrian sports, fishing, horseback riding, kayaking, riflery, sailing, soccer, softball, sports (general), swimming, tennis, volleyball, waterskiing, windsurfing.
Wilderness/Outdoors Backpacking, canoe trips, hiking, orienteering, wilderness camping.
Trips Day, overnight.
Program Information 6 sessions per year. Session length: 2–8 weeks in July, August. Ages: 9–15. 100 participants per session. Boarding program cost: 1300–4800 Canadian dollars.
Application Deadline Continuous.
Jobs Positions for high school students 17 and older and college students 18 and older.
Summer Contact Maya Willis, Co-Director, main address above. Phone: 819-843-5353. Fax: 819-843-3024. E-mail: wilvaken@wilvaken.com.
Winter Contact Maya Willis, Co-Director, PO Box 141, Hudson Heights, Quebec J0P 1J0, Canada. Phone: 450-458-5051. Fax: 450-458-2581. E-mail: wilvaken@wilvaken.com.
URL www.wilvaken.com

Canadian Rockies Adventurer Camp

Howling Wolf Adventures
Canadian Rocky Mountains
British Columbia
Canada

General Information Coed residential outdoor program, wilderness program, and adventure program established in 2004.
Wilderness/Outdoors Backpacking, bicycle trips, canoe trips, hiking, mountain biking, rafting, white-water trips, wilderness camping.
Trips Overnight.
Program Information 2 sessions per year. Session length: 18 days in July, August. Ages: 14–18. 12 participants per session. Boarding program cost: $2199.
Application Deadline Continuous.
Jobs Positions for college students 21 and older.
Contact Mr. Todd Hebert, Camp Director, 411 13th Avenue South, Cranbrook, British Columbia V1C 2W3, Canada. Phone: 250-426-7989. Fax: 250-426-3933. E-mail: info@howlingwolfadventures.com.
URL www.howlingwolfadventures.com

Canadian Rockies Outdoor Leader Camp

Howling Wolf Adventures
British Columbia
Canada

General Information Coed residential outdoor program, wilderness program, and adventure program established in 2004.
Program Focus Leadership.
Special Interest Areas First aid, leadership training.
Wilderness/Outdoors Backpacking, bicycle trips, hiking, mountain biking, rafting, white-water trips, wilderness camping.
Trips Overnight.

Canadian Rockies Outdoor Leader Camp (continued)
Program Information 2 sessions per year. Session length: 20 days in July, August. Ages: 15–18. 12 participants per session. Boarding program cost: $2300.
Application Deadline Continuous.
Jobs Positions for college students 21 and older.
Contact Mr. Todd Herbert, Camp Director, 411 13th Avenue South, Cranbrook, British Columbia V1C 2W3, Canada. Phone: 250-426-7989. Fax: 250-426-3933. E-mail: info@howlingwolfadventures.com.
URL www.howlingwolfadventures.com

Centauri Summer Arts Camp

Centauri Summer Arts Camp
Wellandport, Ontario L0R 2J0
Canada

General Information Coed residential arts program established in 1993. Accredited by Ontario Camping Association. Formal opportunities for the artistically talented.
Program Focus Specialist arts training, leadership programs.
Academics English as a second language, English language/literature, art (Advanced Placement), art history/appreciation, journalism, speech/debate, writing.
Arts Acting, animation, arts, arts and crafts (general), band, cartooning, chorus, clowning, creative writing, dance, dance (ballet), dance (folk), dance (jazz), dance (modern), dance (tap), drawing, film, jewelry making, mime, music (jazz), music (vocal), musical productions, painting, photography, pottery, printmaking, puppetry, sculpture, television/video, theater/drama.
Special Interest Areas Career exploration, leadership training, touring.
Sports Baseball, basketball, climbing (wall), football, soccer, softball, swimming, volleyball.
Trips Cultural, day.
Program Information 4 sessions per year. Session length: 10–14 days in July, August. Ages: 9–19. 125–140 participants per session. Boarding program cost: 780–1020 Canadian dollars.
Application Deadline Continuous.
Jobs Positions for high school students 19 and older and college students 19 and older.
Summer Contact Julie Hartley, Director, c/o Robert Land Academy, RR #3, Wellandport, Ontario L0R 2J0, Canada. Phone: 416-766-7124. Fax: 416-766-7655. E-mail: directors@centauri.on.ca.
Winter Contact Julie Hartley, Director, 19 Harshaw Avenue, Toronto, Ontario M6S 1X9, Canada. Phone: 416-766-7124. Fax: 416-766-7655. E-mail: directors@centauri.on.ca.
URL www.centauri.on.ca

Darrow Wilderness Trips–Quebec: Mistassini

Darrow Foundation
Quebec
Canada

General Information Coed travel wilderness program and adventure program established in 1957. Accredited by American Camping Association.
Program Focus 300-mile canoeing and camping expedition in the area of the Mistassini River in northern Quebec.
Sports Fishing.
Wilderness/Outdoors Canoe trips, wilderness camping.
Program Information 1 session per year. Session length: 6 weeks in July, August. Ages: 14–17. Cost: $4800. Financial aid available.
Jobs Positions for college students 18 and older.
Summer Contact John Houghton, Director, PO Box 9, Grand Lake Stream, Maine 04637. Phone: 888-854-0810. E-mail: darrow@gwi.net.
Winter Contact John Houghton, Director, 24 Lunt Road, Brunswick, Maine 04011-7288. Phone: 888-854-0810. Fax: 207-725-4748. E-mail: darrow@gwi.net.
URL www.darrowcamp.org

Deep River Science Academy–Deep River Campus

The Deep River Science Academy
20 Forest Avenue
Deep River, Ontario K0J 1P0
Canada

General Information Coed residential academic program established in 1986. Formal opportunities for the academically talented. High school credit may be earned.
Program Focus Scientific research experience.
Academics Archaeology, biology, chemistry, engineering, environmental science, geology/earth science, health sciences, mathematics, physics, research skills, science (general).
Sports Basketball, canoeing, rowing (crew/sculling), swimming, volleyball.
Wilderness/Outdoors Hiking.
Trips Day, overnight.
Program Information 1 session per year. Session length: 6 weeks in July, August. Ages: 14–19. 40 participants per session. Boarding program cost: 1300–4150 Canadian dollars. Application fee: 50 Canadian dollars. Financial aid available.
Application Deadline March 15.
Jobs Positions for college students 19 and older.
Contact Ms. Mary MacCafferty, National Registrar, Box 600, 20 Forest Avenue, Deep River, Ontario K0J 1P0, Canada. Phone: 613-584-4541. Fax: 613-584-9597. E-mail: info@drsa.ca.
URL www.drsa.ca

Deep River Science Academy–Whiteshell Campus

The Deep River Science Academy
Pinawa, Manitoba R0E 1L0
Canada

General Information Coed residential academic program established in 1993. Formal opportunities for the academically talented. High school credit may be earned.
Program Focus Scientific research experience.
Academics Archaeology, biology, chemistry, environmental science, health sciences, mathematics, physics, research skills, science (general).
Sports Boating, canoeing, rowing (crew/sculling), sailing, swimming, volleyball.
Wilderness/Outdoors Canoe trips, hiking.
Trips Day, overnight.
Program Information 1 session per year. Session length: 6 weeks in July, August. Ages: 14–19. 20 participants per session. Boarding program cost: 1300–4000 Canadian dollars. Application fee: 50 Canadian dollars. Financial aid available.
Application Deadline March 15.
Jobs Positions for college students 19 and older.
Contact Ms. Mary MacCafferty, National Registrar, Box 600, 20 Forest Avenue, Deep River, Ontario K0J 1P0, Canada. Phone: 613-584-4541. Fax: 613-584-9597. E-mail: info@drsa.ca.
URL www.drsa.ca

EARTHWATCH INSTITUTE–Climate Change at Arctic's Edge

Earthwatch Institute
Churchill, Manitoba
Canada

General Information Coed residential outdoor program, cultural program, and adventure program.
Program Focus How the diversity of the northern forest and tundra respond to global warming.
Academics Ecology, science (general).
Special Interest Areas Field research/expeditions, nature study.
Program Information 5 sessions per year. Session length: 10 days in February, June, July, August, October. Ages: 16+. 11 participants per session. Boarding program cost: $1995–$2095. Financial aid available. Financial aid for high school students and teachers.
Application Deadline Continuous.
Contact General Information Desk, PO Box 75, Maynard, Massachusetts 01754. Phone: 800-776-0188. Fax: 978-461-2332. E-mail: info@earthwatch.org.
URL www.earthwatch.org

EARTHWATCH INSTITUTE–Pine Marten of the Ancient Forest

Earthwatch Institute
Temagami Region
Ontario
Canada

General Information Coed residential outdoor program, cultural program, and adventure program.
Program Focus Documenting the habitat needs of key species in Canada's last old-growth pine stands.
Academics Ecology, environmental science, science (general).
Special Interest Areas Field research/expeditions, nature study.
Program Information 3 sessions per year. Session length: 13 days in July, August. Ages: 16+. 14 participants per session. Boarding program cost: $1495–$1595. Financial aid available. Financial aid for high school students and teachers.
Application Deadline Continuous.
Contact General Information Desk, PO Box 75, Maynard, Massachusetts 01754. Phone: 800-776-0188. Fax: 978-461-2332. E-mail: info@earthwatch.org.
URL www.earthwatch.org

EKOCAMP International

EKOCAMP
4433 Rive
Val-Morin, Quebec J0T 2R0
Canada

General Information Coed residential traditional camp, academic program, outdoor program, and cultural program established in 1970.
Program Focus The benefits of living in an international environment, language training (French and English), and a Canadian wilderness experience.
Academics English as a second language, French language/literature.
Sports Archery, basketball, canoeing, fishing, horseback riding, ice hockey, kayaking, skiing (cross-country), skiing (downhill), soccer, softball, swimming, volleyball, waterskiing.
Wilderness/Outdoors Backpacking, canoe trips, hiking, mountaineering, orienteering, rafting, rock climbing, wilderness camping, wilderness/outdoors (general).
Trips Cultural, day, overnight.
Program Information 9 sessions per year. Session length: 1 week in July, August. Ages: 10–16. 150 participants per session. Boarding program cost: $560.
Application Deadline Continuous.
Jobs Positions for college students 18 and older.
Contact Louis Gibeau, President, main address above. Phone: 819-322-7051. Fax: 819-322-2872. E-mail: info@ekocamp.com.
URL www.ekocamp.com

Excalibur

Langskib Wilderness Programs
Temagami, Ontario P0H 2H0
Canada

General Information Boys' residential outdoor program, wilderness program, and adventure program established in 1990. Accredited by Ontario Camping Association.
Program Focus Introduction to wilderness travel.
Special Interest Areas Native American culture, campcraft, leadership training, nature study, team building.
Sports Canoeing, climbing (wall), fishing, ropes course, swimming.
Wilderness/Outdoors Canoe trips, hiking, white-water trips, wilderness camping.
Trips Day, overnight.
Program Information 1 session per year. Session length: 2 weeks in July. Ages: 10–12. 24–32 participants per session. Boarding program cost: $1450. Financial aid available.
Application Deadline Continuous.
Jobs Positions for high school students 18 and older and college students 19 and older.
Summer Contact Mr. Clay Stephens, Program Director, PO Box 358, Temagami, Ontario P0H 2H0, Canada. Phone: 518-962-4869. Fax: 518-962-8768. E-mail: canoe@langskib.com.
Winter Contact Mr. C. G. Stephens, Program Director, PO Box 205, Westport, New York 12993. Phone: 518-962-4869. Fax: 518-962-8768. E-mail: canoe@langskib.com.
URL www.langskib.com/excalibur.html

French Immersion Kayak Expedition

Centre Nautique de L'Istorlet
100 Istorlet Road
Havre-Aubert
Iles-de-la-Madeleine, Quebec G4T 9E5
Canada

General Information Coed travel outdoor program, wilderness program, and adventure program established in 1995. Accredited by Quebec Camping Association. Specific services available for the developmentally challenged.
Program Focus French immersion; participation in kayak expedition while speaking in French for the duration of the program.
Academics French language/literature.
Special Interest Areas Nautical skills.
Sports Archery, bicycling, boating, fishing, kayaking, sailing, sea kayaking, snorkeling, swimming, windsurfing.
Wilderness/Outdoors Kayaking trips, orienteering, wilderness camping.
Trips Day, overnight.
Program Information 1 session per year. Session length: 5 days in June, July, August. Ages: 14–17. 6–12 participants per session. Cost: 450 Canadian dollars. Application fee: 50 Canadian dollars.
Application Deadline Continuous.
Jobs Positions for high school students 18 and older and college students 20 and older.
Contact Ms. Rita Castonguay, Camp Director, 100 Istorlet Road, Havre-Aubert, Iles-de-la-Madeleine, Quebec G0B 1J0, Canada. Phone: 888-937-8166. Fax: 418-937-9028. E-mail: istorlet@sympatico.ca.
URL www.istorlet.qc.ca

French Immersion Summer Camp

Centre Nautique de L'Istorlet
100 Istorlet Road
Havre-Aubert
Iles-de-la-Madeleine, Quebec G4T 9E5
Canada

General Information Coed residential traditional camp and outdoor program established in 1988. Accredited by Quebec Camping Association.
Program Focus French immersion; participation in nautical activities while speaking in French for the duration of the camp.
Academics French language/literature.
Arts Arts and crafts (general), mime, music, sculpture, theater/drama.
Special Interest Areas Birdwatching, nautical skills.
Sports Archery, bicycling (BMX), canoeing, fishing, kayaking, sailing, sea kayaking, snorkeling, swimming, windsurfing.
Wilderness/Outdoors Bicycle trips, canoe trips, mountain biking, orienteering.
Trips Cultural, day.
Program Information 8 sessions per year. Session length: 6–12 days in June, July, August. Ages: 8–17. 25–35 participants per session. Boarding program cost: 350 Canadian dollars. Application fee: 50 Canadian dollars.
Application Deadline Continuous.
Jobs Positions for high school students 18 and older and college students 18 and older.
Contact Ms. Rita Castonguay, Director, 100 Istorlet Road, Havre-Aubert, Iles-de-la-Madeleine, Quebec G4T 9E5, Canada. Phone: 888-937-8166. Fax: 418-937-9028. E-mail: istorlet@sympatico.ca.
URL www.istorlet.qc.ca

Global Teen–Summer Language Adventure in Montreal

Language Liaison
Montreal, Quebec
Canada

General Information Coed residential academic program established in 1965. High school or college credit may be earned.
Program Focus French language study and cultural immersion.
Academics French language/literature, area studies, intercultural studies, reading, writing.
Arts Painting, pottery.
Special Interest Areas Field trips (arts and culture), homestays, touring.
Sports Bicycling, boating, in-line skating, jet skiing, miniature golf, soccer.

Trips Cultural.
Program Information 7 sessions per year. Session length: 2–4 weeks in June, July, August. Ages: 13–17. 2–10 participants per session. Boarding program cost: $1409–$2019. Application fee: $100. Financial aid available. Additional week: $705.
Application Deadline Continuous.
Contact Nancy Forman, President, PO Box 1772, Pacific Palisades, California 90272. Phone: 800-284-4448. Fax: 310-454-1706. E-mail: learn@languageliaison.com.
URL www.languageliaison.com
For more information, see page 1184.

Great Escapes (Adventure Trips for Teens)–Canadian Canoe and Kayak Adventure

South Shore YMCA Camps
Quebec
Canada

General Information Coed travel outdoor program and adventure program established in 1989. Religious affiliation: Christian. Accredited by American Camping Association.
Program Focus Canoe and river kayak skills.
Sports Boating, canoeing, kayaking.
Wilderness/Outdoors Canoe trips, white-water trips.
Program Information 1 session per year. Session length: 13 days in July. Ages: 14–17. 10–12 participants per session. Cost: $1208; including airfare. Financial aid available.
Application Deadline Continuous.
Jobs Positions for college students 21 and older.
Contact Joseph O'Keefe, Great Escapes Director, 75 Stowe Road, Sandwich, Massachusetts 02563. Phone: 508-428-2571 Ext.110. Fax: 508-420-3545. E-mail: joeokeefe@ssymca.org.
URL www.ssymca.org/camps/great_escapes.asp

Guitar Workshop Plus–Bass, Drums, Keyboards

Guitar Workshop Plus
Toronto, Ontario
Canada

General Information Coed residential and day academic program and arts program established in 2003. Formal opportunities for the artistically talented.
Program Focus Music education in guitar, bass, drums, and keyboards.
Academics Music.
Arts Guitar, music, music (classical), music (ensemble), music (instrumental), music (jazz), music (rock), piano.
Program Information 1–3 sessions per year. Session length: 5–7 days in June, July, August. Ages: 12+. 100–150 participants per session. Day program cost: 550 Canadian dollars. Boarding program cost: 810 Canadian dollars. Financial aid available.
Application Deadline Continuous.
Jobs Positions for high school students 16 and older and college students 18 and older.
Contact Mr. Brian Murray, Director, PO Box 21207, Meadowvale Postal Outlet, Mississauga, Ontario L5N 6A2, Canada. Phone: 905-785-7087. Fax: 905-785-2831. E-mail: info@guitarworkshopplus.com.
URL www.guitarworkshopplus.com

Hamilton Learning Centre Summer Fun in the Sun Camp

Hamilton Learning Centre
1603 Main Street West
Hamilton, Ontario L8S 1E6
Canada

General Information Coed day traditional camp, academic program, and special needs program established in 2003. Formal opportunities for the academically talented. Specific services available for the learning disabled.
Program Focus Especially for children with learning exceptionalities.
Academics English as a second language, English language/literature, mathematics, reading, remedial academics, study skills, typing, writing.
Arts Arts and crafts (general).
Sports Basketball, floor hockey, soccer, softball, volleyball.
Wilderness/Outdoors Hiking.
Trips Day.
Program Information 4–8 sessions per year. Session length: 5 days in July, August. Ages: 6–14. 10 participants per session. Day program cost: 275 Canadian dollars.
Application Deadline Continuous.
Jobs Positions for high school students 16 and older and college students.
Contact Ms. Maureen Pangan, Director, main address above. Phone: 905-521-1333. Fax: 905-521-1106. E-mail: info@hamiltonlearningcentre.com.
URL www.hamiltonlearningcentre.com

Hamilton Learning Centre Summer School

Hamilton Learning Centre
1603 Main Street West
Hamilton, Ontario L8S 1E6
Canada

General Information Coed day academic program and special needs program established in 1989. Formal opportunities for the academically talented. Specific services available for the learning disabled. High school credit may be earned.
Program Focus Remediation/enrichment.
Academics English as a second language, English language/literature, French (Advanced Placement), French language/literature, Hebrew language, Jewish studies, SAT/ACT preparation, academics (general), art history/appreciation, biology, biology (Advanced Placement), business, chemistry, computer science (Advanced Placement), computers, economics, geography, history,

Hamilton Learning Centre Summer School (continued)
mathematics, mathematics (Advanced Placement), philosophy, physics, reading, science (general), social studies, study skills, typing, writing.
Trips Day.
Program Information 4–8 sessions per year. Session length: 6–10 days in July, August. Ages: 6. 20–50 participants per session. Day program cost: 45–206 Canadian dollars. Financial aid available. $45 per hour.
Application Deadline Continuous.
Contact Maureen Pangan, Director, 1603 Main St. W., Hamilton, Ontario L8S IE6, Canada. Phone: 905-521-1333. Fax: 905-521-1106. E-mail: info@hamiltonlearningcentre.com.
URL www.hamiltonlearningcentre.com

HOCKEY OPPORTUNITY CAMP

Sundridge, Ontario P0A 1Z0
Canada

General Information Coed residential and day sports camp established in 1966. Accredited by Ontario Camping Association.
Program Focus Hockey, waterskiing, and mountain biking.
Special Interest Areas Campcraft, leadership training, nature study.
Sports Archery, basketball, bicycling, canoeing, climbing (wall), fishing, ice hockey, in-line skating, kayaking, snorkeling, swimming, volleyball, waterskiing, weight training, windsurfing.
Wilderness/Outdoors Backpacking, mountain biking, wilderness camping.
Trips Overnight.
Program Information 8 sessions per year. Session length: 6–13 days in July, August. Ages: 7–16. 220–240 participants per session. Day program cost: 280 Canadian dollars. Boarding program cost: 600–650 Canadian dollars.
Application Deadline Continuous.
Jobs Positions for high school students 16 and older and college students 19 and older.
Contact Lance Barrs, Director, Box 448, Sundridge, Ontario P0A 1Z0, Canada. Phone: 888-576-2752. Fax: 705-386-0179. E-mail: lance@learnhockey.com.
URL www.learnhockey.com

THE HOLLOWS CAMP

The Hollows Camp, Ltd.
RR #3, 3309 13th Line
Cookstown, Ontario L0L 1L0
Canada

General Information Coed residential traditional camp established in 1982. Accredited by Ontario Camping Association.
Program Focus English riding program.
Sports Archery, bicycling, canoeing, equestrian sports, fishing, horseback riding, in-line skating, kayaking, rappelling, ropes course, swimming, tennis.
Program Information 4 sessions per year. Session length: 12 days in June, July, August, September. Ages: 7–14. 40–50 participants per session. Boarding program cost: 675–1475 Canadian dollars.
Application Deadline Continuous.
Jobs Positions for high school students 18 and older and college students 18 and older.
Contact Mrs. Janet Fine, Director, main address above. Phone: 905-775-2694. Fax: 905-775-2694. E-mail: fine@hollowscamp.com.
URL www.hollowscamp.com

KAWKAWA SUMMER CAMPS

Kawkawa Camp and Retreat
66706 Kawkawa Lake Road
Hope, British Columbia V0X 1L1
Canada

General Information Coed residential and day traditional camp, family program, and bible camp established in 1974. Religious affiliation: The Christian and Missionary Alliance. Accredited by British Columbia Camping Association.
Academics Bible study.
Arts Arts and crafts (general), ceramics, leather working, pottery.
Special Interest Areas Campcraft, leadership training, work camp programs.
Sports Archery, boating, canoeing, fishing, kayaking, riflery, soccer, swimming, volleyball, wakeboarding, waterskiing.
Wilderness/Outdoors Hiking, orienteering.
Program Information 8–10 sessions per year. Session length: 4–7 days in July, August. Ages: 7–17. 70–80 participants per session. Boarding program cost: 208–335 Canadian dollars. Financial aid available.
Application Deadline Continuous.
Jobs Positions for college students.
Contact Office Administrator, main address above. Phone: 604-869-2200. Fax: 604-869-2878. E-mail: office@kawkawa.com.
URL www.kawkawa.com

KEEWAYDIN CANOE CAMP

Keewaydin Camps Corporation
Temagami, Ontario P0H 2H0
Canada

General Information Coed residential outdoor program, wilderness program, and adventure program established in 1893. Accredited by Ontario Camping Association.
Program Focus Canoe trips, white water trips, team and personal growth.
Sports Canoeing, swimming.
Wilderness/Outdoors Canoe trips, white-water trips, wilderness camping.
Trips Overnight.
Program Information 2–3 sessions per year. Session length: 3–7 weeks in June, July, August. Ages: 10–18. 24–100 participants per session. Boarding program cost: $3000–$4800. Financial aid available.
Application Deadline Continuous.

Keewaydin Canoe Camp

Jobs Positions for high school students 17 and older and college students 18 and older.
Contact Mr. Doug Mosle, Director, 10 Keewaydin Road, Salisbury, Vermont 05769. Phone: 802-352-4709. Fax: 802-352-4772. E-mail: doug@keewaydin.org.
URL www.keewaydin.org

KEEWAYDIN TEMAGAMI

Keewaydin Foundation
Lake Temagami
Temagami, Ontario P0H 2H0
Canada

General Information Coed residential outdoor program, wilderness program, and adventure program established in 1893. Accredited by Ontario Camping Association.
Program Focus To develop independence, self confidence and leadership skills.
Sports Canoeing, fishing, swimming.
Wilderness/Outdoors Canoe trips, hiking, orienteering, white-water trips, wilderness camping.
Trips Overnight.
Program Information 3 sessions per year. Session length: 3–6 weeks in June, July, August. Ages: 10–18. 40–60 participants per session. Boarding program cost: $3000–$4800. Financial aid available.
Application Deadline Continuous.
Jobs Positions for high school students 18 and older and college students 18 and older.
Contact Mr. Doug Mosle, Director, 10 Keewaydin Road, Salisbury, Vermont 05769. Phone: 802-352-4709. Fax: 802-352-4772. E-mail: doug@keewaydin.org.
URL www.keewaydin.org

LANGSKIB WILDERNESS PROGRAMS

Langskib Wilderness Programs
Temagami, Ontario P0H 2H0
Canada

General Information Boys' residential outdoor program, wilderness program, and adventure program established in 1979. Accredited by Ontario Camping Association.
Program Focus Leadership and community building skills.
Special Interest Areas Native American culture, campcraft, leadership training, nature study, team building.
Sports Canoeing, climbing (wall), fishing, ropes course, swimming.
Wilderness/Outdoors Canoe trips, hiking, white-water trips, wilderness camping.
Trips Day, overnight.
Program Information 2 sessions per year. Session length: 24 days in July, August. Ages: 10–19. 30–50 participants per session. Boarding program cost: $2650. Financial aid available.
Application Deadline Continuous.
Jobs Positions for high school students 18 and older and college students 19 and older.
Summer Contact Mr. Clay Stephens, Program Director, PO Box 358, Temagami, Ontario P0H 2H0, Canada. Phone: 518-962-4869. Fax: 518-962-8768. E-mail: canoe@langskib.com.
Winter Contact Mr. Clay Stephens, Program Director, PO Box 205, Westport, New York 12993. Phone: 518-962-4869. Fax: 518-962-8768. E-mail: canoe@langskib.com.
URL www.langskib.com

LEARN ENGLISH AND DISCOVER CANADA

Columbia International College of Canada
1003 Main Street West
Hamilton, Ontario L8S 4P3
Canada

General Information Coed residential and day academic program, outdoor program, and cultural program established in 1991. Formal opportunities for the academically talented and artistically talented.
Program Focus ESL (English As a Second Language) camp.
Academics English as a second language, English language/literature, chemistry, communications, computer programming, computers, engineering, science (general), speech/debate.
Arts Arts and crafts (general), jewelry making, music (vocal), painting, pottery, printmaking, sculpture, theater/drama.
Special Interest Areas Leadership training, model rocketry, robotics.
Sports Archery, baseball, basketball, canoeing, climbing (wall), field hockey, fishing, football, golf, kayaking, racquetball, ropes course, soccer, softball, swimming, tennis, track and field, volleyball, water polo, windsurfing.
Wilderness/Outdoors Canoe trips, hiking, orienteering, rock climbing, survival training.

Learn English and Discover Canada (continued)

Trips College tours, cultural, day, overnight, shopping.
Program Information 2–5 sessions per year. Session length: 3–4 weeks in June, July, August. Ages: 9–19. 100–150 participants per session. Day program cost: 2055–2625 Canadian dollars. Boarding program cost: 2500–3185 Canadian dollars.
Application Deadline Continuous.
Jobs Positions for college students 20 and older.
Contact Mrs. Ping Tse, Liaison Director, main address above. Phone: 905-572-7883 Ext.2816. Fax: 905-572-9332. E-mail: liaison01@cic-totalcare.com.
URL www.cic-TotalCare.com

LSA Montreal, Canada–English/French

Language Studies Abroad, Inc.
Montreal, Quebec
Canada

General Information Coed residential academic program and cultural program established in 1962. Formal opportunities for the academically talented and artistically talented. High school or college credit may be earned.
Program Focus Learning language and culture.
Academics English as a second language, English language/literature, French (Advanced Placement), French language/literature, intercultural studies, language study.
Special Interest Areas Homestays, touring.
Sports Boating, canoeing, in-line skating, soccer, swimming, volleyball.
Trips College tours, cultural, day, overnight, shopping.
Program Information 1–26 sessions per year. Session length: 14–360 days in January, February, March, April, May, June, July, August, September, October, November, December. Ages: 13+. 150–450 participants per session. Boarding program cost: $960–$3360. Application fee: $100. Financial aid available.
Application Deadline Continuous.
Contact Director, 1801 Highway 50 East, Suite I, Carson City, Nevada 89701. Phone: 800-424-5522. Fax: 775-883-2266. E-mail: info@languagestudiesabroad.com.
URL www.languagestudiesabroad.com

For more information, see page 1186.

Marine and Environmental Science Program

Ocean Educations, Ltd.
Lester B. Pearson College of the Pacific
650 Pearson College Drive
Victoria, British Columbia V9C 4H7
Canada

General Information Coed residential academic program and outdoor program established in 1997. Formal opportunities for the academically talented. High school credit may be earned.
Program Focus Marine, oceanographic and environmental studies with scuba diving.
Academics Environmental science, marine studies, oceanography.
Sports Canoeing, scuba diving, sea kayaking, snorkeling.
Wilderness/Outdoors Hiking.
Trips Day, overnight.
Program Information 2 sessions per year. Session length: 3 weeks in July, August. Ages: 16–19. 16 participants per session. Boarding program cost: $3000. Participants receive scuba certification.
Application Deadline Continuous.
Jobs Positions for college students 21 and older.
Contact Ian Mitchell, Director, 341 Price Road, Salt Spring Island, British Columbia V8K 2E9, Canada. Phone: 250-537-8464. Fax: 250-537-8465. E-mail: ian@oceaned.com.
URL www.oceaned.com

Medeba Leader in Training Program

Medeba
West Guilford, Ontario K0M 2S0
Canada

General Information Coed residential traditional camp, outdoor program, and bible camp established in 1959. Religious affiliation: Christian. Accredited by Ontario Camping Association.
Program Focus Leadership training.
Academics Bible study.
Special Interest Areas Campcraft, leadership training, nature study.
Sports Archery, bicycling, canoeing, climbing (wall), kayaking, rappelling, riflery, ropes course, swimming.
Wilderness/Outdoors Canoe trips, caving, hiking, mountain biking, orienteering, rock climbing, whitewater trips, wilderness camping.
Trips Day, overnight.
Program Information 2 sessions per year. Session length: 4 weeks in July, August. Ages: 15–18. 15–20 participants per session. Boarding program cost: 1400 Canadian dollars.
Application Deadline Continuous.
Contact Mr. Bruce Dunning, General Director/LIT Director, Box 138, West Guilford, Ontario K0M 250, Canada. Phone: 800-461-6523. Fax: 705-754-1530. E-mail: bruce@medeba.com.
URL www.medeba.com

Medeba Summer Camp

Medeba
West Guilford, Ontario K0M 2S0
Canada

General Information Coed residential and day traditional camp, outdoor program, and bible camp established in 1952. Religious affiliation: Christian. Accredited by Ontario Camping Association. Specific services available for the developmentally challenged and learning disabled.
Program Focus Traditional summer camp that specializes in adventure experiences.
Academics Bible study.

Arts Arts and crafts (general), puppetry, theater/drama, woodworking.
Special Interest Areas Campcraft, model rocketry.
Sports Archery, baseball, basketball, boating, canoeing, climbing (wall), diving, fishing, football, kayaking, rappelling, riflery, ropes course, soccer, softball, swimming, volleyball.
Wilderness/Outdoors Canoe trips, caving, hiking, mountain biking, orienteering, rock climbing, whitewater trips.
Trips Day, overnight.
Program Information 8 sessions per year. Session length: 6 days in July, August. Ages: 6–17. 80–90 participants per session. Boarding program cost: 469–509 Canadian dollars.
Application Deadline Continuous.
Jobs Positions for high school students 17 and older and college students.
Contact Glenda Dunning, Registrar, General Delivery, West Guilford, Ontario K0M 2S0, Canada. Phone: 705-754-2444. Fax: 705-754-1530. E-mail: glenda@medeba.com.
URL www.medeba.com

MIMC–Intensive Music Camp

MIMC
5000 rue Clément Lockquell
St. Augustin-de-Desmaures
Québec City, Quebec G3A 1B3
Canada

General Information Coed residential and day academic program and arts program established in 1998. Formal opportunities for the artistically talented.
Program Focus Music performance.
Academics Music, music (Advanced Placement).
Arts Arts and crafts (general), chorus, dance, music, music (chamber), music (classical), music (ensemble), music (instrumental), music (jazz), music (orchestral), music (vocal), musical productions.
Sports Swimming.
Trips Day, overnight.
Program Information 1 session per year. Session length: 2 weeks in July, August. Ages: 8–25. 200–300 participants per session. Day program cost: 350–575 Canadian dollars. Boarding program cost: 1500–2500 Canadian dollars. Application fee: 25–200 Canadian dollars. Financial aid available.
Application Deadline May 31.
Jobs Positions for college students 18 and older.
Contact Carl Urquhart, Senior Director, 500 Place d'Armes, Suite 1600, Montreal, Quebec H2Y 2W2, Canada. Phone: 514-875-1116. Fax: 514-875-0660. E-mail: curquhart@unitam.com.
URL www.mimc.ca

MIMC–Language Camp

MIMC
Campus Notre-Dame-de-Foy
Québec City, Quebec
Canada

General Information Coed residential and day academic program established in 1998.
Academics English as a second language, English language/literature, French language/literature, language study, linguistics, music.
Arts Chorus, music (chamber), music (classical), music (ensemble), music (instrumental), music (orchestral), music (vocal), musical productions.
Sports Soccer, swimming, volleyball.
Trips Day, overnight.
Program Information 1 session per year. Session length: 2 weeks in July, August. Ages: 8–25. 100–120 participants per session. Day program cost: 350–575 Canadian dollars. Boarding program cost: 1500–2500 Canadian dollars. Application fee: 25–200 Canadian dollars. Financial aid available.
Application Deadline May 31.
Jobs Positions for college students 18 and older.
Contact Carl Urquhart, Senior Director, 500 Place d'Armes, Suite 1600, Montreal, Quebec H2Y 2W2, Canada. Phone: 514-875-1116. Fax: 514-875-0660. E-mail: curquhart@unitam.com.
URL www.mimc.ca

MIMC–Music and Sports Camp

MIMC
Campus Notre-Dame-de-Foy
Québec City, Quebec
Canada

General Information Coed residential arts program and sports camp. Formal opportunities for the artistically talented.
Program Focus Provides an introduction to music and a variety of sports.
Academics Music.
Arts Music, music (instrumental), music (jazz), music (orchestral), music (vocal), musical productions.
Sports Basketball, soccer, sports (general), swimming, volleyball.
Trips Day, overnight.
Program Information 2 sessions per year. Session length: 2 weeks in July, August. Ages: 7–15. Boarding program cost: 365–1515 Canadian dollars. Financial aid available.
Application Deadline May 31.
Jobs Positions for college students 18 and older.
Contact Carl Urquhart, Senior Director, 1 Place Ville Marie, Suite 2715, Montreal, Quebec H3B 4G4, Canada. Phone: 514-875-1116. Fax: 514-875-0660. E-mail: curquhart@unitam.com.
URL www.mimc.ca

Mountain Workshop–Awesome 6: Quebec

Mountain Workshop
Quebec
Canada

General Information Coed travel outdoor program, wilderness program, cultural program, and adventure program established in 2000.
Special Interest Areas Nature study, touring.
Sports Kayaking, sea kayaking.
Wilderness/Outdoors Backpacking, hiking, outdoor adventure, wilderness camping.
Trips Overnight.
Program Information 1 session per year. Session length: 11 days in August. Ages: 15–17. Cost: $1800.
Application Deadline Continuous.
Jobs Positions for college students 21 and older.
Contact Kent B. Tullo, Director, 9 Brookside Place, West Redding, Connecticut 06896. Phone: 203-544-0555. Fax: 203-544-0333. E-mail: info@mountainworkshop.com.
URL www.mountainworkshop.com

NBC Camps–Basketball Individual Training–Olds, AB Canada

NBC Camps
Olds College
Olds, Alberta
Canada

General Information Coed residential sports camp.
Program Focus Well-rounded skill development.
Sports Basketball.
Program Information 2 sessions per year. Session length: 5 days in August. Ages: 9–18. Boarding program cost: $395. Financial aid available.
Application Deadline Continuous.
Jobs Positions for high school students 16 and older and college students.
Contact Ms. Bonnie Tucker, Office Manager, 10003 North Milan Road, #100, Spokane, Washington 99218. Phone: 509-466-4690. Fax: 509-467-6289. E-mail: bonnie@nbccamps.com.
URL www.nbccamps.com

NBC Camps–Basketball Individual Training–Three Hills, AB Canada

NBC Camps
Prairie Bible Institute
Three Hills, Alberta
Canada

General Information Coed residential sports camp.
Program Focus Well-rounded skill development.
Sports Basketball.
Program Information 1 session per year. Session length: 5 days in July, August. Ages: 15–18. Boarding program cost: $395. Financial aid available.
Application Deadline Continuous.
Jobs Positions for high school students 16 and older and college students.
Contact Ms. Bonnie Tucker, Office Manager, 10003 North Milan Road, #100, Spokane, Washington 99218. Phone: 509-466-4690. Fax: 509-467-6289. E-mail: bonnie@nbccamps.com.
URL www.nbccamps.com

New Strides Day Camp

City of Toronto Parks and Recreation West District
Etobicoke Civic Centre
399 The West Mall
Etobicoke, Ontario M9C 2Y2
Canada

General Information Coed day traditional camp, community service program, and special needs program established in 1977. Accredited by Ontario Camping Association. Specific services available for the emotionally challenged, developmentally challenged, hearing impaired, learning disabled, physically challenged, and visually impaired.
Program Focus A specialized day camp serving children and teens with at wide variety of disabilities.
Arts Arts and crafts (general), creative writing, dance, drawing, music, painting, photography, theater/drama.
Special Interest Areas Community service, leadership training.
Sports Horseback riding, miniature golf, noncompetitive sports, sailing, soccer, softball, swimming, tennis.
Trips Cultural, day, overnight, shopping.
Program Information 7 sessions per year. Session length: 5 days in July, August. Ages: 10–21. 15–20 participants per session. Day program cost: 125–250 Canadian dollars. Financial aid available. Financial aid available through Ministry of Community Social Service and the City of Etobicoke. TTY/TTD: 416-394-8534.
Application Deadline Continuous.
Jobs Positions for high school students 18 and older and college students 18 and older.
Contact Miss Sarah Bumstead, Adapted/Integrated Programs Recreationist, main address above. Phone: 416-394-8533. Fax: 416-394-8935. E-mail: sbumste@toronto.ca.
URL www.toronto.ca

Northern Lights

Northwaters Wilderness Programs
Temagami, Ontario P0H 2H0
Canada

General Information Girls' residential outdoor program, wilderness program, and adventure program established in 1990. Accredited by Ontario Camping Association.
Program Focus Introduction to wilderness camping.
Special Interest Areas Campcraft, leadership training, nature study, team building.
Sports Canoeing, climbing (wall), fishing, ropes course, swimming.
Wilderness/Outdoors Canoe trips, hiking, white-water trips, wilderness camping.
Trips Day, overnight.

Program Information 2 sessions per year. Session length: 2 weeks in July, August. Ages: 11–14. 24–32 participants per session. Boarding program cost: $1450. Financial aid available.
Application Deadline Continuous.
Jobs Positions for high school students 18 and older and college students 19 and older.
Summer Contact Mr. C. G. Stephens, Program Director, PO Box 358, Temagami, Ontario P0H 2H0, Canada. Phone: 518-962-4869. Fax: 518-962-8768. E-mail: canoe@northwaters.com.
Winter Contact Mr. C. G. Stephens, Program Director, PO Box 205, Westport, New York 12993. Phone: 518-962-4869. Fax: 518-962-8768. E-mail: canoe@northwaters.com.
URL www.northwaters.com/northern.html

Northwaters Wilderness Programs

Northwaters Wilderness Programs
Temagami, Ontario P0H 2H0
Canada

General Information Coed residential outdoor program, wilderness program, and adventure program established in 1986. Accredited by Ontario Camping Association.
Program Focus Leadership skills and community building.
Academics Ecology, environmental science.
Special Interest Areas Native American culture, campcraft, leadership training, nature study, team building.
Sports Canoeing, climbing (wall), fishing, ropes course, swimming.
Wilderness/Outdoors Canoe trips, hiking, white-water trips, wilderness camping.
Trips Day, overnight.
Program Information 2 sessions per year. Session length: 23–40 days in July, August. Ages: 13–19. 30–60 participants per session. Boarding program cost: $2650–$4600. Financial aid available.
Application Deadline Continuous.
Jobs Positions for high school students 18 and older and college students 19 and older.
Summer Contact Clay Stephens, Program Director, PO Box 358, Temagami, Ontario P0H 2H0, Canada. Phone: 518-962-4869. Fax: 518-962-8768. E-mail: canoe@northwaters.com.
Winter Contact Clay Stephens, Program Director, PO Box 205, Westport, New York 12993. Phone: 518-962-4869. Fax: 518-962-8768. E-mail: canoe@northwaters.com.
URL www.northwaters.com

Plato College–English/French Intensive Courses

Plato College
4521 Park Avenue
Montreal, Quebec H2V 4E4
Canada

General Information Coed day academic program established in 1957.
Academics English as a second language, English language/literature, French (Advanced Placement), French language/literature, German language/literature, Greek language/literature, Hebrew language, Italian language/literature, Japanese language/literature, Latin language, Russian language/literature, Spanish (Advanced Placement), Spanish language/literature, academics (general), linguistics.
Special Interest Areas Homestays.
Trips Cultural, day, overnight, shopping.
Program Information Session length: 4–48 weeks in January, February, March, April, May, June, July, August, September, October, November, December. Ages: 14+. 8–15 participants per session. Day program cost: 675–3200 Canadian dollars. Application fee: 45 Canadian dollars.
Application Deadline Continuous.
Contact Mr. Chris Kavathas, Vice President, main address above. Phone: 514-281-1016. Fax: 514-281-6275. E-mail: info@collegeplaton.com.
URL www.collegeplaton.com

Pripstein's Camp

St. Adolphe D'Howard, Quebec J0T 2B0
Canada

General Information Coed residential traditional camp established in 1938. Accredited by Ontario Camping Association.
Arts Arts and crafts (general), ceramics, dance (jazz), fabric arts, jewelry making, leather working, photography, pottery, printmaking, theater/drama.
Sports Aerobics, archery, baseball, basketball, bicycling, boating, canoeing, climbing (wall), football, golf, gymnastics, in-line skating, kayaking, ropes course, sailing, soccer, softball, street/roller hockey, swimming, tennis, volleyball, waterskiing, windsurfing.
Wilderness/Outdoors Bicycle trips, canoe trips, hiking, rafting, rock climbing.
Trips Day, overnight.
Program Information 2 sessions per year. Session length: 3–7 weeks in June, July, August. Ages: 7–16. 250 participants per session. Boarding program cost: $2600–$4950.
Application Deadline Continuous.
Jobs Positions for high school students 19 and older and college students 19 and older.
Contact Ronnie Braverman, Director, 5702 Cote Saint Luc Road, Suite 202, Montreal, Quebec H3X 2E7, Canada. Phone: 866-481-1875. Fax: 514-481-7863. E-mail: ronnie@pripsteinscamp.com.
URL www.pripsteinscamp.com

Programs Abroad Travel Alternatives–Canada

Programs Abroad Travel Alternatives
Quebec
Canada

General Information Coed travel academic program established in 1996. Formal opportunities for the academically talented. College credit may be earned.

Programs Abroad Travel Alternatives–Canada (continued)

Program Focus Immersion for foreign language students.
Academics French language/literature, Spanish language/literature, art history/appreciation, history, intercultural studies.
Special Interest Areas Cross-cultural education, homestays, touring.
Trips Cultural, overnight.
Program Information 2–3 sessions per year. Session length: 9–34 days in March, June, July. Ages: 15–19. 1–30 participants per session. Cost: $1500–$4500. Application fee: $90.
Application Deadline Continuous.
Contact Heather Kenley, Director of Operations, 6200 Adel Cove, Austin, Texas 78749. Phone: 888-777-PATA. Fax: 512-282-7076. E-mail: immerse@gopata.com.
URL www.gopata.com

For more information, see page 1248.

St. Margaret's School International Summer ESL Programme

St. Margaret's School
1080 Lucas Avenue
Victoria, British Columbia V8X 3P7
Canada

General Information Girls' residential and day academic program.
Academics English as a second language.
Program Information 1 session per year. Session length: 4 weeks in July. Ages: 13–25. Boarding program cost: 3700 Canadian dollars. Application fee: 100 Canadian dollars.
Application Deadline May 1.
Contact ESL Summer Programme Director, St. Margaret's School, 1080 Lucas Avenue, Victoria, British Columbia V8X 3P7, Canada. Phone: 250-479-7171. Fax: 250-479-8976. E-mail: stmarg@stmarg.ca.
URL www.stmarg.ca

Sea Kayak Expedition (English)

Centre Nautique de L'Istorlet
100 Istorlet Road
Havre-Aubert
Iles-de-la-Madeleine, Quebec G4T 9E5
Canada

General Information Coed travel outdoor program, wilderness program, and adventure program established in 1999. Accredited by Quebec Camping Association.
Program Focus Participation in sea kayak expedition in a wilderness setting.
Academics Ecology.
Special Interest Areas Nautical skills.
Sports Fishing, sea kayaking, snorkeling, swimming.
Wilderness/Outdoors Wilderness camping.
Trips Overnight.
Program Information 2 sessions per year. Session length: 5 days in July, August. Ages: 14–17. 6–12 participants per session. Cost: 450 Canadian dollars. Application fee: 50 Canadian dollars.
Application Deadline Continuous.
Jobs Positions for college students 21 and older.
Contact Ms. Rita Castonguay, Director, 100 Istorlet Road, Havre-Aubert, Iles-de-la-Madeleine, Quebec G4T 9E5, Canada. Phone: 888-937-8166. Fax: 418-937-9028. E-mail: istorlet@sympatico.ca.
URL www.istorlet.qc.ca

Stanstead College–English as a Second Language

Stanstead College
450 Dufferin Street
Stanstead, Quebec J0B 3E0
Canada

General Information Coed residential and day academic program established in 1987.
Program Focus Interactive language learning.
Academics English as a second language, French language/literature.
Arts Arts and crafts (general), dance, film, theater/drama.
Special Interest Areas Campcraft, touring.
Sports Basketball, canoeing, soccer, softball, swimming, volleyball, water polo.
Wilderness/Outdoors Hiking.
Trips Cultural, day, overnight.
Program Information 1 session per year. Session length: 3 weeks in July. Ages: 11–16. 110 participants per session. Day program cost: 995 Canadian dollars. Boarding program cost: 1920 Canadian dollars. Application fee: 300 Canadian dollars.
Application Deadline June 10.
Jobs Positions for high school students 18 and older and college students 20 and older.
Contact Mrs. Louise Retchless, Summer School Director, main address above. Phone: 819-876-7891 Ext.246. Fax: 819-876-5891. E-mail: lretchless@stansteadcollege.com.
URL www.stansteadcollege.com/scla

Stanstead College–French as a Second Language

Stanstead College
450 Dufferin Street
Stanstead, Quebec J0B 3E0
Canada

General Information Coed residential and day academic program established in 1987.
Program Focus Interactive language learning.
Academics French language/literature.
Arts Arts and crafts (general), dance, film, theater/drama.
Special Interest Areas Campcraft, touring.
Sports Basketball, canoeing, soccer, softball, swimming, volleyball, water polo.
Wilderness/Outdoors Hiking.

Trips Cultural, day, overnight.
Program Information 1 session per year. Session length: 3 weeks in July. Ages: 11–16. 50 participants per session. Day program cost: 995 Canadian dollars. Boarding program cost: 1920 Canadian dollars. Application fee: 330 Canadian dollars.
Application Deadline June 10.
Jobs Positions for high school students 18 and older and college students 20 and older.
Contact Mrs. Louise Retchless, Summer School Director, main address above. Phone: 819-876-7891 Ext.246. Fax: 819-876-5891. E-mail: lretchless@stansteadcollege.com.
URL www.stansteadcollege.com/scla

Summer Music at The Hollows

The Hollows Camp, Ltd.
RR #3, 3309 13th Line
Cookstown, Ontario L0L 1L0
Canada

General Information Coed residential traditional camp and arts program established in 1998. Accredited by Ontario Camping Association.
Academics Music, music (Advanced Placement).
Arts Music, music (chamber), music (ensemble), music (orchestral).
Sports Archery, bicycling, canoeing, equestrian sports, in-line skating, kayaking, rappelling, swimming, tennis.
Program Information 1 session per year. Session length: 1 week in July, August. Ages: 7–16. 40 participants per session. Boarding program cost: 675 Canadian dollars.
Application Deadline Continuous.
Jobs Positions for high school students 17 and older and college students 17 and older.
Contact Mrs. Janet Fine, Director, main address above. Phone: 905-775-2694. Fax: 905-775-2694. E-mail: fine@hollowscamp.com.
URL www.hollowscamp.com

TASC Canadian Wilderness Fishing Camps

TASC for Teens
Tatachikapika Lake
Gogama, Ontario
Canada

General Information Coed residential outdoor program established in 1976.
Program Focus Fishing camp.
Sports Boating, canoeing, fishing, snorkeling, swimming.
Wilderness/Outdoors Canoe trips, wilderness camping.
Trips Day, overnight.
Program Information 2 sessions per year. Session length: 2 weeks in June, July, August. Ages: 10–17. 10–16 participants per session. Boarding program cost: $1795–$1895.
Application Deadline Continuous.
Contact Mr. Paul Oesterreicher, Director, 5439 Countryside Circle, Jeffersonton, Virginia 22724. Phone: 800-296-8272. Fax: 540-937-8272. E-mail: tasc@peoplepc.com.
URL www.tascforteens.com

Voyageur Outward Bound–Lake Superior Freshwater Kayaking

Voyageur Outward Bound/Outward Bound, USA
Rossport Islands, Lake Superior
Ontario
Canada

General Information Coed travel outdoor program and wilderness program established in 1964. High school or college credit may be earned.
Program Focus Teamwork and leadership wilderness adventure.
Academics Environmental science.
Special Interest Areas Campcraft, community service, leadership training, nature study, personal development, team building.
Sports Kayaking, rappelling.
Wilderness/Outdoors Orienteering, outdoor adventure, rock climbing.
Trips Overnight.
Program Information 1 session per year. Session length: 15 days in August. Ages: 16+. Cost: $2295. Application fee: $95. Financial aid available. Deadline 30 days prior to course start date.
Jobs Positions for college students 21 and older.
Contact Anne DesLauriers, Admissions Advisor, 101 East Chapman Street, Ely, Minnesota 55731. Phone: 800-328-2943. Fax: 218-365-7079. E-mail: info@vobs.com.
URL www.vobs.org

Westcoast Connection Travel–Quebec Adventure

Westcoast Connection
Quebec
Canada

General Information Coed travel outdoor program and adventure program established in 1982. Accredited by Ontario Camping Association.
Program Focus A challenging outdoor adventure with whitewater rafting, canoeing, rock climbing, and mountain biking with visits to Quebec City and Montreal.
Special Interest Areas Community service.
Sports Bicycling, canoeing, horseback riding, in-line skating, kayaking, rappelling, ropes course, swimming, windsurfing.
Wilderness/Outdoors Bicycle trips, canoe trips, hiking, mountain biking, outdoor adventure, rafting, rock climbing, white-water trips, wilderness camping, wilderness/outdoors (general).
Program Information 2–3 sessions per year. Session length: 3 weeks in July, August. Ages: 13–17. 12–25 participants per session. Cost: $2899.
Application Deadline Continuous.

Westcoast Connection Travel–Quebec Adventure (continued)

Jobs Positions for college students 21 and older.
Contact Mr. Mark Segal, Director, 154 East Boston Post Road, Mamaroneck, New York 10543. Phone: 800-767-0227. Fax: 914-835-0798. E-mail: usa@westcoastconnection.com.
URL www.westcoastconnection.com
For more information, see page 1392.

Westcoast Connection Travel–Western Canadian Adventure

Westcoast Connection
Alberta
Canada

General Information Coed travel outdoor program and adventure program established in 1982. Accredited by Ontario Camping Association.
Program Focus A challenging outdoor adventure in Whistler and the Canadian Rockies, with a visit to Vancouver.
Special Interest Areas Community service.
Sports Bicycling, canoeing, horseback riding, in-line skating, rappelling, ropes course, sea kayaking, skiing (downhill), snowboarding, swimming.
Wilderness/Outdoors Caving, hiking, mountain biking, outdoor adventure, rafting, rock climbing, white-water trips, wilderness/outdoors (general).
Program Information 8–12 sessions per year. Session length: 18–40 days in July, August. Ages: 13–17. 12–25 participants per session. Cost: $2799–$5299.
Application Deadline Continuous.
Jobs Positions for college students 21 and older.
Contact Mr. Mark Segal, Director, 154 East Boston Post Road, Mamaroneck, New York 10543. Phone: 800-767-0227. Fax: 914-835-0798. E-mail: usa@westcoastconnection.com.
URL www.westcoastconnection.com
For more information, see page 1392.

The Whale Camp–Youth Programs

The Whale Camp
Grand Manan Island, New Brunswick
Canada

General Information Coed residential academic program, outdoor program, and adventure program established in 1984. Formal opportunities for the academically talented and artistically talented.
Program Focus Research whales, marine mammals, and environmental issues.
Academics Astronomy, biology, botany, ecology, economics, environmental science, geography, geology/earth science, history, marine studies, meteorology, oceanography, research skills, writing.
Arts Drawing, film, photography.
Special Interest Areas Nature study, nautical skills, navigation, whale watching.
Sports Boating, fishing, kayaking, sailing, sea kayaking, softball, swimming, volleyball.
Wilderness/Outdoors Backpacking, hiking, orienteering.
Trips Overnight.
Program Information 8–11 sessions per year. Session length: 1–4 weeks in June, July, August. Ages: 10–17. 36–38 participants per session. Boarding program cost: $1050–$3495.
Application Deadline Continuous.
Jobs Positions for college students 21 and older.
Contact Dennis Bowen, President, 183 Locksley Road, PO Box 63, Cheyney, Pennsylvania 19319. Phone: 888-54-WHALE. E-mail: info@whalecamp.com.
URL www.whalecamp.com

Windsor Mountain: Bonjour Quebec

Interlocken at Windsor Mountain
Quebec
Canada

General Information Coed travel outdoor program, cultural program, and adventure program established in 1967.
Program Focus Wilderness adventure, French language and cross-cultural learning.
Academics French language/literature.
Special Interest Areas Native American culture, animal care, bicycle mechanics, campcraft, community service, cross-cultural education, farming, homestays, leadership training.
Sports Boating, canoeing, climbing (wall), kayaking, rappelling, sea kayaking.
Wilderness/Outdoors Backpacking, hiking, rafting, rock climbing, white-water trips, wilderness camping.
Program Information 1 session per year. Session length: 4 weeks in July, August. Ages: 12–13. 13 participants per session. Cost: $3295. Financial aid available.
Application Deadline Continuous.
Contact Tom Herman, Director, Marketing, 19 Interlocken Way, Windsor, New Hampshire 03244. Phone: 800-862-7760. Fax: 603-478-5260. E-mail: mail@windsormountain.org.
URL www.windsormountain.org/xrds/Quebec.html
For more information, see page 1162.

YMCA Camp Lincoln–Outdoor Adventure Camp: Canadian Adventure

YMCA Camp Lincoln
Nova Scotia
Canada

General Information Coed travel outdoor program and adventure program. Accredited by American Camping Association.
Special Interest Areas Communication skills, team building, touring.
Sports Bicycling, ropes course.
Wilderness/Outdoors Hiking, outdoor adventure, outdoor living skills, rafting, wilderness camping.

Program Information 1 session per year. Session length: 13 days in July, August. Ages: 11–14. 8–10 participants per session. Cost: $775. Application fee: $25. Financial aid available.
Application Deadline Continuous.
Jobs Positions for high school students and college students.
Contact Chris Braun, Outdoor/Adventure Program Director, PO Box 729, 67 Ball Road, Kingston, New Hampshire 03848. Phone: 603-642-3361. Fax: 603-642-4340. E-mail: cbraun@ymcacamplincoln.org.
URL www.ymcacamplincoln.org

YMCA Wanakita Summer Family Camp

YMCA of Hamilton/Burlington
YMCA Wanakita
RR #2
Koshlong Lake
Haliburton, Ontario K0M 1S0
Canada

General Information Coed residential traditional camp and family program established in 1969. Accredited by Ontario Camping Association. Specific services available for the emotionally challenged, developmentally challenged, hearing impaired, learning disabled, and physically challenged.
Academics Ecology, environmental science.
Arts Arts and crafts (general), chorus, dance, drawing, leather working, musical productions, painting, theater/drama, woodworking.
Special Interest Areas Campcraft, career exploration, community service, leadership training, model rocketry, nature study, team building, work camp programs.
Sports Archery, baseball, basketball, boating, canoeing, climbing (wall), fishing, football, ice hockey, kayaking, rappelling, ropes course, sailing, skiing (cross-country), snorkeling, soccer, softball, swimming, volleyball, water polo, windsurfing.
Wilderness/Outdoors Backpacking, canoe trips, hiking, orienteering, survival training, wilderness camping.
Program Information 9 sessions per year. Session length: 1 week in July, August. Ages: 1+. 180–250 participants per session. Boarding program cost: 210–345 Canadian dollars. Financial aid available. Cost: $345 for adults, $240 for children 10–16, $210 for children 3–9, children under 3 free.
Application Deadline Continuous.
Jobs Positions for high school students 17 and older and college students 17 and older.
Contact Mr. Steve Heming, General Manager, main address above. Phone: 705-457-2132. Fax: 705-457-1597. E-mail: info@ymca-wanakita.on.ca.
URL www.ymca-wanakita.on.ca

YMCA Wanakita Summer Resident and Day Camp

YMCA of Hamilton/Burlington
YMCA Wanakita
RR #2
Koshlong Lake Road
Haliburton, Ontario K0M 1S0
Canada

General Information Coed residential and day traditional camp and special needs program established in 1953. Accredited by Ontario Camping Association. Specific services available for the emotionally challenged, developmentally challenged, hearing impaired, learning disabled, and physically challenged.
Program Focus Year-round camp for all ages and abilities.
Academics Ecology, environmental science.
Arts Arts and crafts (general), drawing, leather working, painting, theater/drama, woodworking.
Special Interest Areas Campcraft, career exploration, leadership training, nature study, work camp programs.
Sports Aerobics, archery, baseball, basketball, canoeing, challenge course, climbing (wall), fishing, football, ice hockey, kayaking, rappelling, ropes course, sailing, skiing (cross-country), soccer, softball, swimming, volleyball, water polo, windsurfing.
Wilderness/Outdoors Backpacking, canoe trips, hiking, orienteering, survival training, wilderness camping.
Trips Day, overnight.
Program Information 6–10 sessions per year. Session length: 5–28 days in January, February, March, April, May, June, July, August, September, October, November, December. Ages: 5–17. 40–320 participants per session. Day program cost: 130 Canadian dollars. Boarding program cost: 485–1710 Canadian dollars. Financial aid available. Day camper age: 5—14; residential camper age: 7—16.
Application Deadline Continuous.
Jobs Positions for high school students 17 and older and college students 17 and older.
Contact Mr. Steve Heming, General Manager, main address above. Phone: 705-457-2132. Fax: 705-457-1597. E-mail: info@ymca-wanakita.on.ca.
URL www.ymca-wanakita.on.ca

CHILE

AFS-USA–Homestay–Chile

AFS-USA
Chile

General Information Coed residential academic program and cultural program.
Program Focus Living with a host family while attending school.
Academics Spanish language/literature.
Special Interest Areas Homestays.
Trips Cultural, day, overnight.

AFS-USA–Homestay–Chile (continued)

Program Information 1 session per year. Session length: 6 weeks in June, July, August. Ages: 15–18. Boarding program cost: $3665–$3965. Application fee: $75. Financial aid available. International airfare and volunteer homestay support included.
Application Deadline Continuous.
Jobs Positions for college students.
Contact Manager, AFS Info Center, 506 Southwest 6th Avenue, 2nd Floor, Portland, Oregon 97204. Phone: 800-AFS-INFO. Fax: 503-248-4076. E-mail: afsinfo@afs.org.
URL www.afs.org/usa

For more information, see page 974.

BROADREACH ACADEMIC TREKS–LANGUAGE EXPOSURE AND SERVICE LEARNING

Broadreach
Chile

General Information Coed travel academic program, outdoor program, and community service program established in 1992. High school or college credit may be earned.
Program Focus Adventure program focusing on language exposure, service learning, cultural immersion, and hiking in Chile.
Academics Spanish language/literature, area studies, intercultural studies.
Special Interest Areas Community service, cross-cultural education, leadership training.
Sports Horseback riding.
Wilderness/Outdoors Hiking.
Trips Cultural.
Program Information 2 sessions per year. Session length: 3 weeks in June, July, August. Ages: 15–19. 12–14 participants per session. Cost: $3800–$4700.
Application Deadline Continuous.
Contact Carlton Goldthwaite, Director, PO Box 27076, Raleigh, North Carolina 27611. Phone: 888-833-1907. Fax: 919-833-2129. E-mail: info@gobroadreach.com or info@academictreks.com.
URL www.academictreks.com

For more information, see page 1010.

CENTER FOR CULTURAL INTERCHANGE–CHILE INDEPENDENT HOMESTAY

Center for Cultural Interchange
Chile

General Information Coed residential cultural program established in 1985.
Program Focus Cultural immersion, independent homestay program.
Academics Spanish language/literature, area studies, independent study.
Special Interest Areas Homestays.
Trips Cultural, day.
Program Information Session length: 1–4 weeks in January, February, March, April, May, June, July, August, September, October, November, December. Ages: 17+. Boarding program cost: $790–$1090. Financial aid available.
Application Deadline Continuous.
Contact Ms. Juliet Jones, Outbound Programs Director, 325 West Huron, Suite 706, Chicago, Illinois 60610. Phone: 866-684-9675. Fax: 312-944-2644. E-mail: info@cci-exchange.com.
URL www.cci-exchange.com

For more information, see page 1060.

EARTHWATCH INSTITUTE–CHILEAN COASTAL ARCHAEOLOGY

Earthwatch Institute
Pisagua
Chile

General Information Coed residential outdoor program.
Program Focus Unearthing evidence of two radically different but contemporaneous societies from 3,000 years ago.
Academics Archaeology, history.
Special Interest Areas Field research/expeditions.
Program Information 4 sessions per year. Session length: 12 days in May, June, July. Ages: 16+. 15 participants per session. Boarding program cost: $1995–$2095. Financial aid available. Financial aid for high school students and teachers.
Application Deadline Continuous.
Contact General Information Desk, PO Box 75, Maynard, Massachusetts 01754. Phone: 800-776-0188. Fax: 978-461-2332. E-mail: info@earthwatch.org.
URL www.earthwatch.org

THE EXPERIMENT IN INTERNATIONAL LIVING–CHILE NORTH HOMESTAY, COMMUNITY SERVICE

The Experiment in International Living
Chile

General Information Coed residential outdoor program, community service program, cultural program, and adventure program established in 1932.
Program Focus International youth travel, homestay, community service.
Academics Spanish language/literature.
Special Interest Areas Community service, homestays, touring.
Wilderness/Outdoors Hiking.
Trips Cultural, day, overnight.
Program Information 1 session per year. Session length: 4 weeks in July, August. Ages: 14–19. 10–15 participants per session. Boarding program cost: $4100. Financial aid available.
Application Deadline May 1.

Contact Ms. Annie Thompson, Enrollment Director, Summer Abroad, Kipling Road, PO Box 676, Brattleboro, Vermont 05302-0676. Phone: 800-345-2929. Fax: 802-258-3428. E-mail: eil@worldlearning.org.
URL www.usexperiment.org
For more information, see page 1116.

The Experiment in International Living–Chile South Homestay

The Experiment in International Living
Chile

General Information Coed residential outdoor program, community service program, and cultural program established in 1932.
Program Focus International youth travel, homestay, community service.
Academics Spanish language/literature.
Special Interest Areas Community service, homestays, touring.
Sports Horseback riding.
Wilderness/Outdoors Hiking.
Trips Cultural, day, overnight.
Program Information 1 session per year. Session length: 4 weeks in July, August. Ages: 14–19. 10–15 participants per session. Boarding program cost: $4100. Financial aid available.
Application Deadline May 1.
Contact Annie Thompson, Enrollment Director, Summer Abroad, Kipling Road, PO Box 676, Brattleboro, Vermont 05302-0676. Phone: 800-345-2929. Fax: 802-258-3428. E-mail: eil@worldlearning.org.
URL www.usexperiment.org
For more information, see page 1116.

Learning Programs International–Chile

Learning Programs International
Valparaiso
Chile

General Information Coed residential academic program and cultural program established in 2004. Formal opportunities for the academically talented. High school or college credit may be earned.
Program Focus Language acquisition.
Academics Spanish (Advanced Placement), Spanish language/literature.
Special Interest Areas Community service, homestays.
Trips Cultural, day, overnight.
Program Information 4 sessions per year. Session length: 16–28 days in May, June, July. Ages: 14–18. 10–30 participants per session. Boarding program cost: $1200. Financial aid available. Airfare not included.
Application Deadline Continuous.
Contact Michelle McRaney, Program Director, 901 West 24th Street, Austin, Texas 78705. Phone: 800-259-4439. Fax: 512-480-8866. E-mail: lpi@studiesabroad.com.
URL www.lpiabroad.com
For more information, see page 1190.

LSA Viña del Mar, Chile

Language Studies Abroad, Inc.
Viña del Mar
Chile

General Information Coed residential academic program and cultural program. Formal opportunities for the academically talented. High school or college credit may be earned.
Program Focus Language and culture.
Academics Spanish (Advanced Placement), Spanish language/literature, academics (general), intercultural studies.
Special Interest Areas Homestays.
Trips Cultural, day.
Program Information 1–26 sessions per year. Session length: 13–300 days in January, February, March, April, May, June, July, August, September, October, November, December. Ages: 16+. Application fee: $100. Financial aid available.
Application Deadline Continuous.
Contact Director, 1801 Highway 50 West, Suite I, Carson City, Nevada 89701. Phone: 800-424-5522. Fax: 775-883-2266. E-mail: info@languagestudiesabroad.com.
URL www.languagestudiesabroad.com
For more information, see page 1186.

Youth for Understanding USA–Chile

Youth for Understanding USA
Chile

General Information Coed travel academic program and cultural program established in 1951. High school or college credit may be earned.
Program Focus Living with a host family, exploring Easter Island (most remote island on earth), and learning about Chilean culture.
Academics Spanish language/literature, archaeology, area studies, ecology, history, intercultural studies, social studies.
Special Interest Areas Field research/expeditions, homestays.
Trips Cultural, day, overnight.
Program Information 1 session per year. Session length: 25–35 days in July, August. Ages: 15–18. 10–50 participants per session. Cost: $6495. Application fee: $75. Financial aid available. Round-trip domestic and international airfare is included in the tuition.
Application Deadline Continuous.
Contact Admissions Counselor, 6400 Goldsboro Road, Suite 100, Bethesda, Maryland 20817. Phone: 800-TEENAGE (833-6243). Fax: 202-895-1104. E-mail: admissions@us.yfu.org.
URL www.yfu-usa.org
For more information, see page 1414.

CHINA

AFS-USA–Team Mission–China

AFS-USA
China

General Information Coed residential academic program, community service program, and cultural program established in 1995. High school credit may be earned.
Program Focus Participants take morning classes in Chinese language and culture; opportunity to tutor Chinese students in English, sightsee, and be involved with a community service program with an adult team leader.
Academics Chinese languages/literature, intercultural studies.
Arts Calligraphy, painting.
Special Interest Areas Community service, cross-cultural education, culinary arts, homestays.
Sports Martial arts.
Trips Cultural, day, overnight.
Program Information 1 session per year. Session length: 4 weeks in July. Ages: 15–18. 15 participants per session. Boarding program cost: $4565–$5065. Application fee: $75. Financial aid available. International airfare and volunteer homestay support included.
Application Deadline Continuous.
Contact Manager, AFS Info Center, 506 Southwest 6th Avenue, 2nd Floor, Portland, Oregon 97204. Phone: 800-AFS-INFO. Fax: 503-248-4076. E-mail: afsinfo@afs.org.
URL www.afs.org/usa
For more information, see page 974.

China's Frontiers: Diverse Landscapes and Peoples

Pacific Village Institute
Dali, Lijiang
China

General Information Coed residential community service program and cultural program established in 2002. High school or college credit may be earned.
Academics Chinese languages/literature, academics (general), anthropology, art history/appreciation, ecology, environmental science, humanities, intercultural studies, peace education, religion, writing.
Arts Arts and crafts (general).
Special Interest Areas Community service, homestays.
Wilderness/Outdoors Hiking.
Trips Cultural, overnight.
Program Information 1–2 sessions per year. Session length: 30–40 days in June, July, August. Ages: 17+. 10–14 participants per session. Boarding program cost: $3000–$5000. Financial aid available.
Application Deadline Continuous.
Contact Ms. Carey Moore, Executive Director, 1122 East Pike Street #545, Seattle, Washington 98112. Phone: 206-860-4050. E-mail: carey@pacificvillage.org.
URL www.pacificvillage.com

China Summer Learning Adventures

Xi'an Jiao Tong University Campus/Xi'an Winning Training Center
Gaoxin Qu Kejilu 39 Hao
Yamei Dasha Juxiang Ge 901
Xi'an 710075
China

General Information Coed residential cultural program established in 2003.
Program Focus Sight-seeing: terracotta soldiers, emperors' tombs, pagodas, old city, merchants' barter market, 6000-year-old archeological dig, Buddhist temples.
Academics Chinese languages/literature, computers, geography, history, intercultural studies.
Arts Calligraphy, painting, photography.
Special Interest Areas Internet accessibility, touring.
Sports Martial arts.
Trips College tours, cultural, day, overnight, shopping.
Program Information 4 sessions per year. Session length: 2 weeks in June, July, August. Ages: 16–19. 4–16 participants per session. Boarding program cost: $1950.
Application Deadline May 31.
Contact David Schoon, USA Representative / China Link Company, LLC, 2150 44th Street, SE, Suite 309, Grand Rapids, Michigan 49508. Phone: 616-281-0000. Fax: 616-281-2118. E-mail: dbschoon@chinalinkcompanyllc.com.
URL www.usapmp.com

Choate Rosemary Hall Summer in China

Choate Rosemary Hall
China

General Information Coed residential academic program and cultural program established in 2000. High school credit may be earned.
Program Focus Chinese culture and language.
Academics Chinese languages/literature, art history/appreciation.
Arts Calligraphy, painting.
Special Interest Areas Cross-cultural education, homestays, touring.
Trips Cultural, day, overnight.
Program Information 1 session per year. Session length: 5 weeks in June, July. Ages: 14–19. 20–25 participants per session. Boarding program cost: $6055. Application fee: $60. Financial aid available. Airfare from USA to China included. Participants housed in college dormitories and hotels.
Application Deadline Continuous.
Contact Dr. Carol S. Chen-Lin, Director Summer in China, 333 Christian Street, Wallingford, Connecticut 06492. Phone: 203-697-2080. Fax: 203-697-2519. E-mail: cchen@choate.edu.
URL www.crhsummerabroad.org
For more information, see page 1070.

Choate Rosemary Hall Summer in China

EARTHWATCH INSTITUTE–CHINA'S ANCESTRAL TEMPLES

Earthwatch Institute
Jinhua
China

General Information Coed residential outdoor program, cultural program, and adventure program.
Program Focus Documenting the history and architecture of family lineage compounds to encourage their preservation.
Academics Architecture, history, intercultural studies.
Special Interest Areas Cross-cultural education, field research/expeditions.
Program Information 2 sessions per year. Session length: 15 days in June, July. Ages: 16+. 10 participants per session. Boarding program cost: $2295–$2395. Financial aid available. Financial aid for high school students and teachers.
Application Deadline Continuous.
Contact General Information Desk, PO Box 75, Maynard, Massachusetts 01754. Phone: 800-776-0188. Fax: 978-461-2332. E-mail: info@earthwatch.org.
URL www.earthwatch.org

EARTHWATCH INSTITUTE–INNER MONGOLIA'S LOST WATER

Earthwatch Institute
Gobi Desert
China

General Information Coed residential outdoor program, cultural program, and adventure program.
Program Focus Assessing the hydrological history of the Gobi to learn how deserts grow.
Academics Ecology, environmental science, geology/earth science, intercultural studies, meteorology, science (general).
Special Interest Areas Field research/expeditions, nature study.
Program Information 5 sessions per year. Session length: 19 days in July, August, September, October. Ages: 16+. 8 participants per session. Boarding program cost: $2395–$2495. Financial aid available. Financial aid for high school students and teachers.
Application Deadline Continuous.
Contact General Information Desk, PO Box 75, Maynard, Massachusetts 01754. Phone: 800-776-0188. Fax: 978-461-2332. E-mail: info@earthwatch.org.
URL www.earthwatch.org

EF INTERNATIONAL LANGUAGE SCHOOL–SHANGHAI

EF International Language Schools
218 South Xi Zang Road
19th Floor, Silver Tower
Shanghai
China

General Information Coed travel academic program and cultural program established in 2004.
Program Focus Language and cultural immersion.
Academics Chinese languages/literature.
Special Interest Areas Field trips (arts and culture).
Trips Cultural, day, overnight.
Program Information Session length: 14–365 days in January, February, March, April, May, June, July, August, September, October, November, December. Ages: 16+. 50–100 participants per session. Call for costs.
Application Deadline Continuous.
Contact Ms. Katie Mahon, Director of Admissions, One Education Street, Cambridge, Massachusetts 02141. Phone: 800-992-1892. Fax: 800-590-1125. E-mail: ils@ef.com.
URL www.ef.com
For more information, see page 1102.

THE EXPERIMENT IN INTERNATIONAL LIVING–CHINA NORTH AND EAST HOMESTAY

The Experiment in International Living
China

General Information Coed residential cultural program and adventure program established in 1932.

The Experiment in International Living–China North and East Homestay (continued)

Program Focus International youth travel, homestay, travel with Chinese high school students.
Academics Chinese languages/literature.
Special Interest Areas Homestays, touring.
Wilderness/Outdoors Hiking.
Trips Cultural, day, overnight.
Program Information 1 session per year. Session length: 4 weeks in July, August. Ages: 14–19. 10–20 participants per session. Boarding program cost: $4900. Financial aid available.
Application Deadline May 1.
Contact Annie Thompson, Enrollment Director, Summer Abroad, Kipling Road, PO Box 676, Brattleboro, Vermont 05302-0676. Phone: 800-345-2929. Fax: 802-258-3428. E-mail: eil@worldlearning.org.
URL www.usexperiment.org

For more information, see page 1116.

The Experiment in International Living–China South and West Homestay

The Experiment in International Living
China

General Information Coed residential cultural program and adventure program established in 1932.
Program Focus International youth travel, homestays, travel with Chinese high school students.
Academics Chinese languages/literature.
Special Interest Areas Homestays, touring.
Wilderness/Outdoors Hiking.
Trips Cultural, day, overnight.
Program Information 1 session per year. Session length: 4 weeks in July, August. Ages: 14–19. 10–20 participants per session. Boarding program cost: $4900. Financial aid available.
Application Deadline May 1.
Contact Annie Thompson, Enrollment Director, Summer Abroad, Kipling Road, PO Box 676, Brattleboro, Vermont 05302-0676. Phone: 800-345-2929. Fax: 802-258-3428. E-mail: eil@worldlearning.org.
URL www.usexperiment.org

For more information, see page 1116.

ISB Chinese Language Camp

International School of Beijing–Shunyi
10 An Hua Road
Shunyi
Beijing, 101300
China

General Information Coed residential academic program and cultural program established in 2003. Formal opportunities for the academically talented and artistically talented. Specific services available for the developmentally challenged.
Program Focus Immersion program for students to learn Chinese language, culture, and people while exploring the city of Beijing.
Academics Chinese languages/literature, intercultural studies.
Arts Arts and crafts (general), dance (folk), painting.
Special Interest Areas Cross-cultural education, leadership training.
Sports Baseball, basketball, climbing (wall), martial arts, soccer, swimming, tennis, volleyball.
Trips Cultural, day, overnight, shopping.
Program Information 1 session per year. Session length: 25 days in June, July. Ages: 10–18. 20–40 participants per session. Boarding program cost: $2500.
Application Deadline May 31.
Jobs Positions for college students 19 and older.
Contact Ms. Theresa Chao, Chinese Program Principal, main address above. Phone: 86-10-8046-2345 Ext.1050. Fax: 86-10-8046-2001. E-mail: tchao@isb.bj.edu.cn.
URL chinese.isb.bj.edu.cn

For more information, see page 1164.

Where There Be Dragons: China

Where There Be Dragons
China

General Information Coed travel academic program, outdoor program, cultural program, and adventure program established in 1993. Formal opportunities for the academically talented.
Program Focus Rugged and off the beaten path travel introduces a wide range of development issues.
Academics Chinese languages/literature, anthropology, area studies, art history/appreciation, business, ecology, geography, government and politics, history, intercultural studies, journalism, philosophy, religion, social studies.
Arts Painting.
Special Interest Areas Field research/expeditions, leadership training.
Sports Bicycling.
Wilderness/Outdoors Backpacking, hiking, pack animal trips, wilderness camping.
Trips Cultural, overnight.
Program Information 2 sessions per year. Session length: 6 weeks in June, July, August. Ages: 15–20. 12 participants per session. Cost: $5900. Financial aid available. Airfare included.
Application Deadline Continuous.
Contact Chris Yager, Director, PO Box 4651, Boulder, Colorado 80306. Phone: 800-982-9203. Fax: 303-413-0857. E-mail: info@wheretherebedragons.com.
URL www.wheretherebedragons.com

For more information, see page 1394.

Where There Be Dragons: Silk Road

Where There Be Dragons
China

General Information Coed travel academic program, outdoor program, cultural program, and adventure program established in 1993. Formal opportunities for the academically talented.

Program Focus Survey Central-Asian cultures. Rugged and off the beaten path travel that introduces a wide range of development issues.
Academics Chinese languages/literature, anthropology, area studies, art history/appreciation, ecology, economics, geography, government and politics, government and politics (Advanced Placement), history, intercultural studies, peace education, philosophy, religion, social studies.
Special Interest Areas Animal care, field research/expeditions, leadership training, nature study.
Sports Horseback riding.
Wilderness/Outdoors Backpacking, bicycle trips, hiking, wilderness camping.
Trips Cultural, overnight.
Program Information 2 sessions per year. Session length: 6 weeks in June, July, August. Ages: 15–19. 12 participants per session. Cost: $5900. Financial aid available. Airfare included.
Application Deadline Continuous.
Contact Chris Yager, Director, PO Box 4651, Boulder, Colorado 80306. Phone: 800-982-9203. Fax: 303-413-0857. E-mail: info@wheretherebedragons.com.
URL www.wheretherebedragons.com

For more information, see page 1394.

Where There Be Dragons: Tibet

Where There Be Dragons
China

General Information Coed travel academic program, outdoor program, community service program, wilderness program, cultural program, and adventure program established in 1993. Formal opportunities for the academically talented.
Program Focus Tibetan studies program that takes place in Tibet. Rugged off the beaten path travel introduces a wide range of development issues.
Academics Academics (general), anthropology, area studies, art history/appreciation, ecology, geography, government and politics (Advanced Placement), intercultural studies, peace education, philosophy, religion, social studies.
Arts Batiking, ceramics, fabric arts, music (instrumental), photography, weaving.
Special Interest Areas Community service, field research/expeditions, homestays, leadership training, nature study.
Wilderness/Outdoors Backpacking, hiking, mountaineering, orienteering, pack animal trips, wilderness camping.
Trips Cultural, overnight.
Program Information 3 sessions per year. Session length: 6 weeks in June, July, August. Ages: 15–20. 12 participants per session. Cost: $5500–$6000. Financial aid available. Airfare included.
Application Deadline Continuous.
Contact Chris Yager, Director, PO Box 4651, Boulder, Colorado 80306. Phone: 800-982-9203. Fax: 303-413-0857. E-mail: info@wheretherebedragons.com.
URL www.wheretherebedragons.com

For more information, see page 1394.

Where There Be Dragons: Tibet

Youth for Understanding USA–China

Youth for Understanding USA
China

General Information Coed residential academic program and cultural program established in 1951. High school or college credit may be earned.
Program Focus Living with a host family, participating in activities such as martial arts, and traveling throughout China.
Academics Chinese languages/literature, area studies, intercultural studies, social studies.
Special Interest Areas Homestays, touring.
Sports Martial arts.
Trips Cultural, day, overnight, shopping.
Program Information 1 session per year. Session length: 20–25 days in July, August. Ages: 15–18. 10–50 participants per session. Boarding program cost: $4995. Application fee: $75. Financial aid available. Round-trip domestic and international airfare is included in the tuition.
Application Deadline Continuous.

Youth for Understanding USA–China (continued)

Contact Admissions Counselor, 6400 Goldsboro Road, Suite 100, Bethesda, Maryland 20817. Phone: 800-TEENAGE (833-6243). Fax: 202-895-1104. E-mail: admissions@us.yfu.org.
URL www.yfu-usa.org

For more information, see page 1414.

COSTA RICA

AAVE–Costa Rica

AAVE–America's Adventure Ventures Everywhere
Costa Rica

General Information Coed travel academic program, outdoor program, community service program, cultural program, and adventure program established in 1976. Accredited by American Camping Association.
Program Focus One week of academic Spanish language study/3 weeks Spanish immersion.
Academics Latin language, Spanish language/literature.
Arts Dance, drawing.
Special Interest Areas Campcraft, community service, homestays, leadership training, nature study.
Sports Bicycling, horseback riding, sailing, snorkeling, surfing, swimming.
Wilderness/Outdoors Hiking, mountain biking, rafting, white-water trips.
Trips Cultural, day, overnight.
Program Information 4 sessions per year. Session length: 3 weeks in June, July, August. Ages: 14–18. 13–15 participants per session. Cost: $3688. Financial aid available.
Application Deadline Continuous.
Jobs Positions for college students 21 and older.
Contact Abbott Wallis, Owner/Director, 2245 Stonecrop Way, Golden, Colorado 80401. Phone: 800-222-3595. Fax: 303-526-0806. E-mail: info@aave.com.
URL www.aave.com

For more information, see page 952.

Adventure Links–The Costa Rica Experience

Adventure Links
Costa Rica

General Information Coed travel community service program, wilderness program, cultural program, and adventure program established in 2003. Accredited by American Camping Association.
Program Focus Experiential/cultural learning.
Academics Spanish language/literature, environmental science, intercultural studies.
Special Interest Areas Cross-cultural education, homestays, nature study, team building, touring.
Sports Kayaking, sea kayaking, snorkeling, swimming.
Wilderness/Outdoors Backpacking, hiking, mountaineering, orienteering, survival training, white-water trips, wilderness camping.
Trips Cultural, overnight.
Program Information 1 session per year. Session length: 18 days in July, August. Ages: 14–17. 13 participants per session. Cost: $2750.
Application Deadline Continuous.
Jobs Positions for high school students 18 and older and college students 18 and older.
Contact Elena Gonzalez, Director, 21498 Blue Ridge Mountain Road, Paris, Virginia 20130. Phone: 540-592-3682. Fax: 540-592-3316. E-mail: elena@adventurelinks.net.
URL www.adventurelinks.net

Adventures Cross-Country, Costa Rica Adventure

Adventures Cross-Country
Costa Rica

General Information Coed residential outdoor program, wilderness program, and adventure program established in 1983.
Program Focus Exploring Costa Rica's rainforest, beaches, jungles, and rivers.
Sports Sea kayaking.
Wilderness/Outdoors Backpacking, hiking, orienteering, rafting, white-water trips, wilderness camping.
Program Information 2 sessions per year. Session length: 22 days in June, July, August. Ages: 13–18. 8–15 participants per session. Boarding program cost: $3995. Financial aid available.
Application Deadline Continuous.
Jobs Positions for college students 21 and older.
Contact Scott von Eschen, Director, 242 Redwood Highway, Mill Valley, California 94941. Phone: 415-332-5075. Fax: 415-332-2130. E-mail: arcc@adventurescrosscountry.com.
URL www.adventurescrosscountry.com

For more information, see page 972.

AFS-USA–Community Service–Costa Rica

AFS-USA
Costa Rica

General Information Coed residential community service program and cultural program. High school credit may be earned.
Program Focus Community service program with an ecological focus and a short homestay experience.
Academics Spanish language/literature.
Special Interest Areas Community service, homestays, nature study, touring.
Wilderness/Outdoors Hiking.
Trips Cultural, day, overnight.
Program Information 1 session per year. Session length: 4–6 weeks in June, July, August. Ages: 15–18. 30–45 participants per session. Boarding program cost:

$3965–$4265. Application fee: $75. Financial aid available. International airfare and volunteer homestay support included.
Application Deadline Continuous.
Contact Manager, AFS Info Center, 506 Southwest 6th Avenue, 2nd Floor, Portland, Oregon 97204. Phone: 800-AFS-INFO. Fax: 503-248-4076. E-mail: afsinfo@afs.org.
URL www.afs.org/usa
For more information, see page 974.

AFS-USA–Homestay Language Study–Costa Rica

AFS-USA
Costa Rica

General Information Coed residential cultural program.
Program Focus Language study program.
Academics Spanish language/literature.
Special Interest Areas Homestays, touring.
Trips Cultural, day, overnight.
Program Information 1 session per year. Session length: 36–42 days in June, July, August. Ages: 15–18. 40 participants per session. Boarding program cost: $4765–$5265. Application fee: $75. Financial aid available. International airfare and volunteer homestay support included.
Application Deadline Continuous.
Contact Manager, AFS Info Center, 506 Southwest 6th Avenue, 2nd Floor, Portland, Oregon 97204. Phone: 800-AFS-INFO. Fax: 503-248-4076. E-mail: afsinfo@afs.org.
URL www.afs.org/usa
For more information, see page 974.

AFS-USA–Homestay Plus–Costa Rica

AFS-USA
Costa Rica

General Information Coed residential cultural program.
Program Focus Live with a host family, perform community service and go on nature bus trips with expert guides.
Academics Spanish language/literature.
Special Interest Areas Community service, homestays, nature study.
Trips Cultural, day, overnight.
Program Information 1 session per year. Session length: 6 weeks in June, July, August. Ages: 15–18. Boarding program cost: $3865–$4165. Application fee: $75. Financial aid available. International airfare and volunteer homestay support included.
Application Deadline Continuous.
Contact Manager, AFS Info Center, 506 Southwest 6th Avenue, 2nd Floor, Portland, Oregon 97204. Phone: 800-AFS-INFO. Fax: 503-248-4076. E-mail: afsinfo@afs.org.
URL www.afs.org/usa
For more information, see page 974.

Blyth Education–Summer Study in Costa Rica

Blyth Education
Costa Rica

General Information Coed residential academic program and cultural program established in 1998. High school credit may be earned.
Program Focus Experience the ecology and culture of Costa Rica.
Academics Academics (general), biology, science (general), social science.
Special Interest Areas Community service, touring.
Sports Horseback riding, scuba diving, snorkeling, soccer, volleyball.
Wilderness/Outdoors Backpacking, hiking.
Trips Cultural, day, overnight.
Program Information 1 session per year. Session length: 25–30 days in July. Ages: 16–19. 40–50 participants per session. Boarding program cost: 3995 Canadian dollars. Airfare from Toronto or New York included.
Application Deadline Continuous.
Jobs Positions for college students 25 and older.
Contact Blyth Education, 9 Sultan Street, Suite 300, Toronto, Ontario M5S 1L6, Canada. Phone: 416-960-3552. Fax: 416-960-9506. E-mail: info@blytheducation.com.
URL www.blytheducation.com

Brighton in Costa Rica

Brighton
Costa Rica

General Information Coed residential academic program established in 2003. Formal opportunities for the academically talented. College credit may be earned.
Program Focus Language and cultural immersion.
Academics Spanish language/literature.
Arts Dance, pottery.
Special Interest Areas Cross-cultural education, culinary arts, homestays, touring.
Sports Horseback riding, rappelling.
Wilderness/Outdoors Hiking.
Trips Cultural, day, shopping.
Program Information 5 sessions per year. Session length: 1–6 weeks in June, July, August. Ages: 15+. 30–35 participants per session. Boarding program cost: $850–$2350.
Application Deadline Continuous.
Contact David Allen, Executive Director, 101 East Green Street, Suite 14, Pasadena, California 91105. Phone: 626-795-2985. Fax: 626-795-5564. E-mail: info@brightonedge.org.
URL www.brightonedge.org
For more information, see page 1004.

BROADREACH Academic Treks–Sea Turtle Studies

Broadreach
Costa Rica

General Information Coed travel academic program, outdoor program, community service program, and adventure program established in 1992. High school or college credit may be earned.
Program Focus Academic adventure program focusing on sea turtle field studies and research, community service, scuba diving, marine science, hiking, high school and college credit.
Academics Academics (general), biology, ecology, environmental science, marine studies.
Special Interest Areas Community service, conservation projects, field research/expeditions, leadership training.
Sports Scuba diving, sea kayaking, snorkeling, swimming.
Wilderness/Outdoors Hiking, white-water trips.
Trips Cultural, day.
Program Information 2 sessions per year. Session length: 3 weeks in June, July, August. Ages: 15–19. 10–14 participants per session. Cost: $3800–$4700. Financial aid available.
Application Deadline Continuous.
Contact Carlton Goldthwaite, Director, PO Box 27076, Raleigh, North Carolina 27611-7076. Phone: 888-833-1907. Fax: 919-833-2129. E-mail: info@gobroadreach.com.
URL www.academictreks.com
For more information, see page 1010.

BROADREACH Costa Rica Experience

Broadreach
Costa Rica

General Information Coed travel outdoor program, wilderness program, and adventure program established in 1992.
Program Focus Coed program focusing on adventure travel, whitewater rafting, sea kayaking, ecosystem exploration, rain forest ecology, and community service.
Academics Ecology, environmental science, geology/earth science, intercultural studies.
Arts Photography.
Special Interest Areas Community service, conservation projects, field research/expeditions, leadership training, nature study.
Sports Horseback riding, rappelling, sea kayaking, snorkeling, surfing.
Wilderness/Outdoors Backpacking, hiking, kayaking trips, rafting, white-water trips, wilderness camping.
Trips Cultural.
Program Information 2 sessions per year. Session length: 22 days in June, July, August. Ages: 15–19. 12 participants per session. Cost: $3800.
Application Deadline Continuous.
Contact Carlton Goldthwaite, Director, PO Box 27076, Raleigh, North Carolina 27611-7076. Phone: 888-833-1907. Fax: 919-833-2129. E-mail: info@gobroadreach.com.
URL www.gobroadreach.com
For more information, see page 1010.

Costa Rica ¡Pura Vida!

Interamerican University Studies Institute
San Pedro
Costa Rica

General Information Coed travel academic program, outdoor program, and cultural program.
Academics Spanish language/literature, biology.
Special Interest Areas Homestays, nature study, touring.
Wilderness/Outdoors Hiking, white-water trips.
Trips Cultural, day, overnight.
Program Information 2 sessions per year. Session length: 30 days in June, July, August. Ages: 15–17. 8 participants per session. Cost: $3600–$4000.
Application Deadline Continuous.
Contact Ms. Amber Thacher, Program Assistant, PO Box 10958, Eugene, Oregon 97440. Phone: 800-345-4874. Fax: 541-686-5947. E-mail: office@iusi.org.
URL www.iusi.org

Costa Rica Rainforest Outward Bound School–Multi-Element

Costa Rica Rainforest Outward Bound School
Costa Rica

General Information Coed travel outdoor program, wilderness program, cultural program, and adventure program established in 1994. High school or college credit may be earned.
Program Focus Leadership skills, teamwork and personal development.
Academics Spanish language/literature, anthropology, biology, botany, ecology, environmental science, geography, intercultural studies, oceanography, science (general).
Special Interest Areas Campcraft, community service, homestays, leadership training, nature study.
Sports Climbing (wall), kayaking, rappelling, scuba diving, sea kayaking, snorkeling, surfing, swimming.
Wilderness/Outdoors Backpacking, hiking, mountaineering, rafting, white-water trips, wilderness camping.
Trips Cultural, day, overnight.
Program Information 25–35 sessions per year. Session length: 15–24 days in May, June, July, August. Ages: 14+. 8–12 participants per session. Cost: $1995–$2595. Application fee: $60. Financial aid available.
Application Deadline Continuous.
Jobs Positions for college students 21 and older.
Contact Student Administrator, Box 1817-2050, San Pedro-San Jose, Costa Rica. Phone: 011-506-278-6058. Fax: 011-506-278-6059. E-mail: info@crrobs.org.
URL www.crrobs.org

Costa Rica Rainforest Outward Bound School–Summer Semester

Costa Rica Rainforest Outward Bound School
Costa Rica

General Information Coed travel outdoor program, wilderness program, cultural program, and adventure program established in 1994. High school or college credit may be earned.
Program Focus Leadership skills, teamwork, and personal development.
Academics Spanish language/literature, anthropology, biology, botany, ecology, environmental science, geography, intercultural studies, oceanography, science (general).
Special Interest Areas Campcraft, community service, homestays, leadership training, nature study.
Sports Climbing (wall), kayaking, rappelling, scuba diving, sea kayaking, snorkeling, surfing, swimming.
Wilderness/Outdoors Backpacking, hiking, mountaineering, rafting, white-water trips, wilderness camping.
Trips Cultural, day, overnight.
Program Information 25–35 sessions per year. Session length: 60 days in June, July, August. Ages: 17+. 8–12 participants per session. Cost: $5595. Application fee: $60. Financial aid available.
Application Deadline Continuous.
Jobs Positions for college students 21 and older.
Contact Student Administrator, Box 1817-2050, San Pedro-San Jose, Costa Rica. Phone: 011-506-278-6058. Fax: 011-506-278-6059. E-mail: info@crrobs.org.
URL www.crrobs.org

Costa Rica Rainforest Outward Bound School–Surf Adventure

Costa Rica Rainforest Outward Bound School
Costa Rica

General Information Coed travel outdoor program, wilderness program, cultural program, and adventure program established in 1994. High school or college credit may be earned.
Program Focus Leadership skills, teamwork, and personal development.
Academics Spanish language/literature, anthropology, biology, botany, ecology, environmental science, geography, intercultural studies, oceanography, science (general).
Special Interest Areas Campcraft, community service, homestays, leadership training, nature study.
Sports Surfing, swimming, yoga.
Wilderness/Outdoors Backpacking, hiking, mountaineering, outdoor camping, wilderness camping.
Trips Cultural, day, overnight.
Program Information 25–35 sessions per year. Session length: 15–30 days in May, June, July, August. Ages: 14+. 8–12 participants per session. Cost: $1995–$2995. Application fee: $60. Financial aid available.
Application Deadline Continuous.
Jobs Positions for college students 21 and older.
Contact Student Administrator, Box 1817-2050, San Pedro-San Jose, Costa Rica. Phone: 011-506-278-6058. Fax: 011-506-278-6059. E-mail: info@crrobs.org.
URL www.crrobs.org

Deer Hill Expeditions, Costa Rica

Deer Hill Expeditions
Costa Rica

General Information Coed residential community service program, wilderness program, and cultural program established in 1984. Accredited by Association for Experiential Education. High school credit may be earned.
Program Focus Wilderness expeditions, service, and native cultures.
Academics Spanish language/literature, area studies, ecology, environmental science, geology/earth science, intercultural studies.
Special Interest Areas Campcraft, community service, conservation projects, cross-cultural education, gardening, homestays, leadership training, nature study.
Sports Kayaking.
Wilderness/Outdoors Backpacking, hiking, mountain biking, rafting, white-water trips, wilderness camping.
Trips Cultural, overnight.
Program Information 2 sessions per year. Session length: 3 weeks in June, July, August. Ages: 15–18. 12 participants per session. Boarding program cost: $3600. Financial aid available.
Application Deadline Continuous.
Contact Ms. Beverly Capelin, Founder and Owner, PO Box 180, Mancos, Colorado 81328. Phone: 800-533-7221. Fax: 970-533-7221. E-mail: info@deerhillexpeditions.com.
URL www.deerhillexpeditions.com

EARTHWATCH INSTITUTE–Dolphins of Costa Rica

Earthwatch Institute
Talamanca
Costa Rica

General Information Coed residential outdoor program.
Program Focus Monitoring the interactions between two dolphin species and tourists to create a more sustainable tourism industry.
Academics Ecology, environmental science, marine studies.
Arts Photography, television/video.
Special Interest Areas Field research/expeditions.
Sports Boating, kayaking, snorkeling, swimming.
Wilderness/Outdoors Hiking.
Trips Cultural.
Program Information 6 sessions per year. Session length: 9 days in August, September, October, November. Ages: 16+. 6 participants per session. Boarding program cost: $1995–$2095. Financial aid available. Financial aid for high school students and teachers.
Application Deadline Continuous.

EARTHWATCH INSTITUTE–Dolphins of Costa Rica (continued)

Contact General Information Desk, PO Box 75, Maynard, Massachusetts 01754. Phone: 800-776-0188. Fax: 978-461-2332. E-mail: info@earthwatch.org.
URL www.earthwatch.org

EARTHWATCH INSTITUTE–RAINFOREST CATERPILLARS–COSTA RICA

Earthwatch Institute
La Selva Biological Station
Costa Rica

General Information Coed residential outdoor program, wilderness program, and cultural program.
Program Focus Exploring caterpillar defenses to better understand and protect their habitat.
Academics Ecology, environmental science, science (general).
Special Interest Areas Field research/expeditions, nature study.
Program Information 4 sessions per year. Session length: 11–13 days in January, May, June, December. Ages: 16+. 14 participants per session. Boarding program cost: $1895–$1995. Financial aid available. Financial aid for high school students and teachers.
Application Deadline Continuous.
Contact General Information Desk, PO Box 75, Maynard, Massachusetts 01754. Phone: 800-776-0188. Fax: 978-461-2332. E-mail: info@earthwatch.org.
URL www.earthwatch.org

EARTHWATCH INSTITUTE–RESTORING COSTA RICA'S RAINFOREST

Earthwatch Institute
Agua Buena
Costa Rica

General Information Coed residential outdoor program.
Program Focus Conducting a large-scale reforestation experiment to develop strategies for restoring tropical forests.
Academics Ecology.
Special Interest Areas Conservation projects, field research/expeditions, nature study.
Program Information 3 sessions per year. Session length: 12 days in June, July. Ages: 16+. 12 participants per session. Boarding program cost: $1795–$1895. Financial aid available. Financial aid for high school students and teachers.
Application Deadline Continuous.
Contact General Information Desk, PO Box 75, Maynard, Massachusetts 01754. Phone: 800-776-0188. Fax: 978-461-2332. E-mail: info@earthwatch.org.
URL www.earthwatch.org

THE EXPERIMENT IN INTERNATIONAL LIVING–COSTA RICA HOMESTAY

The Experiment in International Living
Costa Rica

General Information Coed residential outdoor program, community service program, cultural program, and adventure program established in 1932.
Program Focus International youth travel, homestay, ecology.
Academics Spanish language/literature, ecology.
Special Interest Areas Community service, homestays.
Sports Snorkeling, swimming.
Wilderness/Outdoors Hiking, white-water trips.
Trips Cultural, day, overnight.
Program Information 1 session per year. Session length: 4 weeks in July, August. Ages: 14–19. 10–15 participants per session. Boarding program cost: $3950. Financial aid available.
Application Deadline May 1.
Contact Annie Thompson, Enrollment Director, Summer Abroad, Kipling Road, PO Box 676, Brattleboro, Vermont 05302-0676. Phone: 800-345-2929. Fax: 802-258-3428. E-mail: eil@worldlearning.org.
URL www.usexperiment.org
For more information, see page 1116.

GLOBAL TEEN–LEARN SPANISH IN COSTA RICA

Language Liaison
San Jose
Costa Rica

General Information Coed residential academic program established in 1974. High school or college credit may be earned.
Program Focus Spanish language study and cultural immersion.
Academics Spanish language/literature, area studies, art, intercultural studies, reading, writing.
Arts Dance (Latin).
Special Interest Areas Community service, culinary arts, field research/expeditions, field trips (arts and culture), nature study, whale watching.
Sports Basketball, boating, diving, fishing, horseback riding, jet skiing, kayaking, snorkeling, surfing, swimming, volleyball.
Wilderness/Outdoors Hiking, white-water trips.
Trips Cultural, day.
Program Information 3 sessions per year. Session length: 2–3 weeks in June, July, August. Ages: 12–17. 2–5 participants per session. Boarding program cost: $1956–$2933. Application fee: $85. Financial aid available. Additional week: $977.
Application Deadline Continuous.
Contact Nancy Forman, President, PO Box 1772, Pacific Palisades, California 90272. Phone: 800-284-4448. Fax: 310-454-1706. E-mail: learn@languageliaison.com.
URL www.languageliaison.com
For more information, see page 1184.

GLOBAL WORKS–Language Exposure-Costa Rica-4 weeks

GLOBAL WORKS
Costa Rica

General Information Coed travel community service program, cultural program, and adventure program established in 1988. High school credit may be earned.
Program Focus Environmental and community service, language exposure and cultural exchange.
Academics Spanish language/literature, environmental science, intercultural studies.
Arts Arts and crafts (general), dance (Latin), painting.
Special Interest Areas Community service, construction, cross-cultural education, field trips (arts and culture), homestays.
Sports Basketball, horseback riding, rappelling, soccer, swimming, volleyball.
Wilderness/Outdoors Backpacking, hiking, outdoor adventure, rafting, white-water trips.
Trips Cultural, day, overnight.
Program Information 1 session per year. Session length: 4 weeks in June, July. Ages: 14–18. 15–16 participants per session. Cost: $3650–$3790. Application fee: $100. Financial aid available. Airfare not included.
Application Deadline Continuous.
Jobs Positions for college students 23 and older.
Contact Erik Werner, Director, 1113 South Allen Street, State College, Pennsylvania 16801. Phone: 814-867-7000. Fax: 814-867-2717. E-mail: info@globalworksinc.com.
URL www.globalworksinc.com

For more information, see page 1136.

GLOBAL WORKS–Language Immersion-Costa Rica-4 weeks

GLOBAL WORKS
Costa Rica

General Information Coed travel community service program, cultural program, and adventure program established in 1988. High school credit may be earned.
Program Focus Environmental and community service, language immersion, and cultural exchange.
Academics Spanish language/literature, ecology, intercultural studies.
Arts Arts and crafts (general), dance (Latin), painting.
Special Interest Areas Community service, construction, field trips (arts and culture), homestays.
Sports Horseback riding, ropes course, soccer, sports (general), swimming, volleyball.
Wilderness/Outdoors Backpacking, hiking, outdoor adventure, rafting, white-water trips.
Trips Cultural, day, overnight.
Program Information 5–6 sessions per year. Session length: 28–29 days in June, July, August. Ages: 15–18. 15–16 participants per session. Cost: $3650–$3750. Application fee: $100. Financial aid available. Airfare not included.
Application Deadline Continuous.
Jobs Positions for college students 23 and older.
Contact Mr. Erik Werner, Director, 1113 South Allen Street, State College, Pennsylvania 16801. Phone: 814-867-7000. Fax: 814-867-2717. E-mail: info@globalworksinc.com.
URL www.globalworksinc.com

For more information, see page 1136.

Great Escapes (Adventure Trips for Teens)–Costa Rica Rainforest Adventure

South Shore YMCA Camps
Costa Rica

General Information Coed travel outdoor program and adventure program established in 1989. Religious affiliation: Christian. Accredited by American Camping Association.
Program Focus Cross-cultural experience, Spanish lessons, rainforest exploration.
Academics Spanish language/literature, ecology, environmental science, geography, geology/earth science.
Special Interest Areas Community service, cross-cultural education, leadership training, nature study, touring.
Wilderness/Outdoors Wilderness camping, wilderness/outdoors (general).
Program Information 1 session per year. Session length: 13 days in July, August. Ages: 14–17. 10 participants per session. Cost: $1995. Financial aid available.
Application Deadline Continuous.
Jobs Positions for college students 21 and older.
Contact Joseph O'Keefe, Great Escapes Director, 75 Stowe Road, Sandwich, Massachusetts 02563. Phone: 508-428-2571 Ext.110. Fax: 508-420-3545. E-mail: joeokeefe@ssymca.org.
URL www.ssymca.org/camps/great_escapes.asp

Instituto de Idiomas Geos–Costa Rica

Instituto de Idiomas Geos
Centro Commercial Boulevard, Local 2
Escazu
San José
Costa Rica

General Information Coed residential academic program, cultural program, and adventure program established in 2002.
Academics English as a second language, Spanish (Advanced Placement), Spanish language/literature.
Arts Dance, film, music, television/video.
Special Interest Areas Culinary arts, homestays.
Sports Aerobics, bicycling, boating, canoeing, climbing (wall), cross-country, diving, equestrian sports, fishing, golf, horseback riding, kayaking, sailing, scuba diving, sea kayaking, soccer, squash, swimming, tennis, volleyball, waterskiing, windsurfing.
Wilderness/Outdoors Bicycle trips, canoe trips, hiking, mountain biking, mountaineering, pack animal trips, rafting, rock climbing.
Trips College tours, cultural, day, overnight, shopping.

Instituto de Idiomas Geos–Costa Rica (continued)
Program Information 4–8 sessions per year. Session length: 1–4 weeks in January, February, March, April, May, June, July, August, September, October, November, December. Ages: 12–18. 5–30 participants per session. Boarding program cost: $480–$2425. Application fee: $50.
Application Deadline Continuous.
Contact Mr. Tetsuko Motte, Admissions, main address above. Phone: 506-288-8576. E-mail: geoscr@racsa.co.cr.
URL www.geosspanish.com

LEARNING PROGRAMS INTERNATIONAL–COSTA RICA

Learning Programs International
San José
Costa Rica

General Information Coed residential academic program and cultural program established in 1998. Formal opportunities for the academically talented. High school or college credit may be earned.
Program Focus Language acquisition.
Academics Spanish (Advanced Placement), Spanish language/literature.
Arts Dance.
Special Interest Areas Community service, homestays.
Trips Cultural, day, overnight.
Program Information 4 sessions per year. Session length: 14–30 days in June, July. Ages: 14–18. 10–30 participants per session. Boarding program cost: $1170–$3300. Airfare not included.
Application Deadline Continuous.
Contact Michelle McRaney, Program Director, 901 West 24th Street, Austin, Texas 78705. Phone: 800-259-4439. Fax: 512-480-8866. E-mail: lpi@studiesabroad.com.
URL www.lpiabroad.com

For more information, see page 1190.

LSA FLAMINGO BEACH, COSTA RICA

Language Studies Abroad, Inc.
Flamingo Beach
Costa Rica

General Information Coed residential academic program and cultural program established in 2002. Formal opportunities for the academically talented. High school or college credit may be earned.
Program Focus Language and culture.
Academics Spanish (Advanced Placement), Spanish language/literature, academics (general), intercultural studies.
Special Interest Areas Homestays.
Trips Cultural, day.
Program Information 1–26 sessions per year. Session length: 13–300 days in January, February, March, April, May, June, July, August, September, October, November, December. Ages: 16+. 30–60 participants per session. Boarding program cost: $775–$2900. Application fee: $100. Financial aid available.
Application Deadline Continuous.
Contact Director, 1801 Highway 50 East, Suite I, Carson City, Nevada 89701. Phone: 800-424-5522. Fax: 775-883-2266. E-mail: info@languagestudiesabroad.com.
URL www.languagestudiesabroad.com/

For more information, see page 1186.

LSA SAN JOSÉ, COSTA RICA

Language Studies Abroad, Inc.
San José
Costa Rica

General Information Coed residential academic program and cultural program established in 1979. Formal opportunities for the academically talented and artistically talented. College credit may be earned.
Program Focus Learning language and culture.
Academics Spanish (Advanced Placement), Spanish language/literature, business, intercultural studies, language study.
Arts Dance.
Special Interest Areas Homestays.
Trips College tours, cultural, day, overnight, shopping.
Program Information 1–26 sessions per year. Session length: 14–360 days in January, February, March, April, May, June, July, August, September, October, November, December. Ages: 13+. 40–80 participants per session. Boarding program cost: $1370–$1890. Application fee: $100. Financial aid available.
Application Deadline Continuous.
Contact Director, 1801 Highway 50 East, Suite I, Carson City, Nevada 89701. Phone: 800-424-5522. Fax: 775-883-2266. E-mail: info@languagestudiesabroad.com.
URL www.languagestudiesabroad.com

For more information, see page 1186.

OVERLAND: COSTA RICA EXPLORER HIKING, RAFTING, AND SEA-KAYAKING

Overland Travel, Inc.
Costa Rica

General Information Coed travel outdoor program, wilderness program, cultural program, and adventure program established in 1985. Accredited by American Camping Association. High school credit may be earned.
Program Focus Backpacking, sea-kayaking and cultural exploration of Costa Rica's mountains and rain forests.
Special Interest Areas Leadership training, team building, touring.
Sports Kayaking, sea kayaking.
Wilderness/Outdoors Backpacking, hiking, outdoor camping, rafting, white-water trips, wilderness camping.
Trips Cultural.
Program Information 2 sessions per year. Session length: 3 weeks in June, July, August. Ages: 14–18. 8–21 participants per session. Cost: $3995.
Application Deadline Continuous.
Jobs Positions for college students 20 and older.

Contact Ms. Brooks Follansbee, Director, PO Box 31, Williamstown, Massachusetts 01267. Phone: 800-458-0588. Fax: 413-458-5208. E-mail: overland@adelphia.net.
URL www.overlandsummers.com
For more information, see page 1240.

Overland: Language Study Abroad in Costa Rica

Overland Travel, Inc.
Costa Rica

General Information Coed residential academic program and cultural program established in 1985. Accredited by American Camping Association. High school credit may be earned.
Program Focus Spanish language study and cultural exploration of Costa Rica.
Academics Spanish language/literature.
Special Interest Areas Cross-cultural education, homestays.
Wilderness/Outdoors Outdoor adventure.
Trips Cultural, day, overnight.
Program Information 2 sessions per year. Session length: 32 days in June, July, August. Ages: 14–18. 8–12 participants per session. Boarding program cost: $5995.
Application Deadline Continuous.
Jobs Positions for college students 20 and older.
Contact Ms. Brooks Follansbee, Director, PO Box 31, Williamstown, Massachusetts 01267. Phone: 800-458-0588. Fax: 413-458-5208. E-mail: overland@adelphia.net.
URL www.overlandsummers.com
For more information, see page 1240.

Overland: World Service, Costa Rica

Overland Travel, Inc.
Costa Rica

General Information Coed residential community service program and cultural program established in 1985. Accredited by American Camping Association. High school credit may be earned.
Program Focus Community service and cultural exploration.
Special Interest Areas Community service, conservation projects, construction, cross-cultural education, leadership training, team building.
Trips Cultural, day, overnight.
Program Information 2 sessions per year. Session length: 3 weeks in June, July, August. Ages: 14–19. 8–12 participants per session. Boarding program cost: $3995.
Application Deadline Continuous.
Jobs Positions for college students 20 and older.
Contact Ms. Brooks Follansbee, Director, PO Box 31, Williamstown, Massachusetts 01267. Phone: 800-458-0588. Fax: 413-458-5208. E-mail: overland@adelphia.net.
URL www.overlandsummers.com
For more information, see page 1240.

Peace Works International–Costa Rica

Peace Works International
Costa Rica

General Information Coed travel community service program, cultural program, and adventure program established in 1994.

Peace Works International–Costa Rica

Academics Spanish language/literature, intercultural studies, peace education.
Special Interest Areas Community service, construction, cross-cultural education, homestays, leadership training.
Sports Bicycling, horseback riding, rappelling, soccer, surfing, volleyball.
Wilderness/Outdoors Backpacking, hiking.
Trips Cultural, overnight.
Program Information 4 sessions per year. Session length: 26 days in June, July, August. Ages: 15–18. 16–18 participants per session. Cost: $3695–$3895. Airfare included.
Application Deadline Continuous.
Jobs Positions for college students 22 and older.
Contact Mr. Christopher Kealey, Executive Director, PO Box 70905, Pasadena, California 91117. Phone: 626-798-5221. Fax: 626-798-2959. E-mail: info@peaceworksintl.org.
URL www.peaceworksintl.org
For more information, see page 1250.

Poulter Colorado Camps: Adventures Planet Earth–Costa Rica

Poulter Colorado Camps
Costa Rica

General Information Coed travel outdoor program and cultural program established in 1966. Accredited by American Camping Association.
Program Focus Exciting international experiences combining adventure travel with cultural immersion.
Academics Intercultural studies.
Special Interest Areas Community service, homestays, leadership training, nature study, touring.
Sports Ropes course, snorkeling.
Wilderness/Outdoors Backpacking, hiking, rafting, white-water trips.
Trips Cultural, day, overnight, shopping.
Program Information 2 sessions per year. Session length: 10–20 days in June, July, August. Ages: 14+. 6–10 participants per session. Cost: $2450–$3500. Financial aid available.
Application Deadline April 15.
Jobs Positions for college students 21 and older.
Contact Jay B. Poulter, Director, PO Box 772947, Steamboat Springs, Colorado 80477. Phone: 888-879-4816. Fax: 888-860-3587. E-mail: poulter@poultercamps.com.
URL www.poultercamps.com

Programs Abroad Travel Alternatives–Costa Rica

Programs Abroad Travel Alternatives
San Jose
Costa Rica

General Information Coed travel academic program and cultural program established in 1996. Formal opportunities for the academically talented. College credit may be earned.
Program Focus Immersion for foreign language students.
Academics Spanish language/literature, art history/appreciation, ecology, history, intercultural studies.
Special Interest Areas Cross-cultural education, homestays, touring.
Sports Ropes course.
Wilderness/Outdoors Backpacking, hiking.
Trips Cultural, day, overnight.
Program Information 2–3 sessions per year. Session length: 9–34 days in March, June, July. Ages: 15+. 3–30 participants per session. Cost: $1500–$4500. Application fee: $90. Participant must be in high school.
Application Deadline Continuous.
Summer Contact Rose Potter, Founder/CEO, 6200 Adel Cove, Austin, Texas 78749. Phone: 888-777-PATA. Fax: 512-282-7076. E-mail: immerse@gopata.com.
Winter Contact Ms. Heather Kenley, Director, main address above. E-mail: studyabroad@gopata.com.
URL www.gopata.com
For more information, see page 1248.

Programs Abroad Travel Alternatives–Costa Rica

Putney Student Travel–Community Service–Costa Rica

Putney Student Travel
Costa Rica

General Information Coed residential community service program and cultural program established in 1951.
Program Focus Community service, cultural exchange, and weekend excursions from a base in a small, rural community.
Academics Intercultural studies.
Special Interest Areas Community service, construction.
Sports Horseback riding, soccer, swimming.
Wilderness/Outdoors Hiking, white-water trips.
Trips Cultural, day.
Program Information 4–5 sessions per year. Session length: 28–30 days in June, July, August. Ages: 15–18. 16 participants per session. Boarding program cost: $5100. Financial aid available. Airfare from Miami included.
Application Deadline Continuous.

Contact Jeffrey Shumlin, Admissions Director, 345 Hickory Ridge Road, Putney, Vermont 05346. Phone: 802-387-5000. Fax: 802-387-4276. E-mail: info@goputney.com.
URL www.goputney.com
For more information, see page 1276.

Putney Student Travel–Language Learning–Costa Rica

Putney Student Travel
Costa Rica

General Information Coed residential academic program and cultural program. Formal opportunities for the academically talented.
Program Focus Spanish language immersion in the context of community service. Participants housed in host-family homes and hotels. Enrollment limited to those who are studying Spanish.
Academics Spanish (Advanced Placement), Spanish language/literature, art history/appreciation, intercultural studies.
Special Interest Areas Homestays.
Sports Horseback riding, rappelling, sailing, soccer, swimming, windsurfing.
Wilderness/Outdoors Bicycle trips, hiking, mountaineering, rock climbing.
Trips Cultural, day, overnight.
Program Information 2 sessions per year. Session length: 28–30 days in June, July, August. Ages: 13–18. 16–18 participants per session. Boarding program cost: $5800. Financial aid available. Airfare from Miami included.
Application Deadline Continuous.
Contact Jeffrey Shumlin, Admissions Director, 345 Hickory Ridge Road, Putney, Vermont 05346. Phone: 802-387-5000. Fax: 802-387-4276. E-mail: info@goputney.com.
URL www.goputney.com
For more information, see page 1276.

RUSTIC PATHWAYS–ACCELERATED SPANISH IMMERSION

Rustic Pathways
Escazu, Alajuela
Costa Rica

General Information Coed residential academic program and cultural program established in 2002.
Academics Spanish (Advanced Placement), Spanish language/literature.
Arts Dance.
Special Interest Areas Cross-cultural education, homestays, touring.
Wilderness/Outdoors Hiking.
Trips Cultural, day, overnight, shopping.
Program Information 8 sessions per year. Session length: 15 days in June, July, August. Ages: 14–18. 5–10 participants per session. Boarding program cost: $2995.
Application Deadline Continuous.
Jobs Positions for college students 21 and older.
Contact Mr. Chris Stakich, Business Development Director, 4121 Erie Street, Willoughby, Ohio 44094. Phone: 440-975-9691. Fax: 440-975-9694. E-mail: chris@rusticpathways.com.
URL www.rusticpathways.com
For more information, see page 1290.

RUSTIC PATHWAYS–COSTA RICA ADVENTURER

Rustic Pathways
Costa Rica

General Information Coed travel cultural program and adventure program established in 2002.
Special Interest Areas Cross-cultural education, touring.
Sports Bicycling, horseback riding, kayaking, rappelling, sailing, snorkeling, soccer, swimming.
Wilderness/Outdoors Hiking, outdoor adventure, rafting, white-water trips.
Trips Cultural, day, overnight, shopping.
Program Information 4 sessions per year. Session length: 15 days in June, July, August. Ages: 14–18. 10–15 participants per session. Cost: $2295.
Application Deadline Continuous.
Jobs Positions for college students 21 and older.
Contact Mr. Chris Stakich, Business Development Director, 4121 Erie Street, Willoughby, Ohio 44094. Phone: 440-975-9691. Fax: 440-975-9694. E-mail: chris@rusticpathways.com.
URL www.rusticpathways.com
For more information, see page 1290.

RUSTIC PATHWAYS–COSTA RICA EXTREME

Rustic Pathways
Costa Rica

General Information Coed travel cultural program and adventure program established in 2002.
Special Interest Areas Touring.
Sports Bicycling, horseback riding, kayaking, rappelling, sailing, snorkeling, soccer, swimming.
Wilderness/Outdoors Hiking, outdoor adventure, rafting, white-water trips.
Trips Cultural, day, overnight, shopping.
Program Information 4 sessions per year. Session length: 22 days in June, July. Ages: 14–18. 10–15 participants per session. Cost: $3495.
Application Deadline Continuous.
Jobs Positions for college students 21 and older.
Contact Mr. Chris Stakich, Business Development Director, 4121 Erie Street, Willoughby, Ohio 44094. Phone: 440-975-9691. Fax: 440-975-9694. E-mail: chris@rusticpathways.com.
URL www.rusticpathways.com
For more information, see page 1290.

RUSTIC PATHWAYS–COSTA RICA NATURAL WONDERS

Rustic Pathways
Costa Rica

General Information Coed travel outdoor program and adventure program established in 2002.
Special Interest Areas Nature study, touring.
Sports Kayaking, rappelling, sea kayaking, snorkeling, soccer, swimming.
Wilderness/Outdoors Hiking, wilderness camping.
Trips Cultural, day, overnight, shopping.
Program Information 2 sessions per year. Session length: 8 days in June, July, August. Ages: 14–18. 10–15 participants per session. Cost: $1295.
Application Deadline Continuous.
Jobs Positions for college students 21 and older.
Contact Mr. Chris Stakich, Business Development Director, 4121 Erie Street, Willoughby, Ohio 44094. Phone: 440-975-9691. Fax: 440-975-9694. E-mail: chris@rusticpathways.com.
URL www.rusticpathways.com

For more information, see page 1290.

RUSTIC PATHWAYS–RAMP UP YOUR SPANISH

Rustic Pathways
Escazu, Alajuela
Costa Rica

General Information Coed residential academic program and cultural program established in 2002.
Academics Spanish (Advanced Placement), Spanish language/literature.
Arts Dance.
Special Interest Areas Homestays.
Sports Bicycling, soccer.
Trips Cultural, day, overnight, shopping.
Program Information 9 sessions per year. Session length: 8 days in June, July, August. Ages: 14–18. 15–20 participants per session. Boarding program cost: $995.
Jobs Positions for college students 21 and older.
Contact Mr. Chris Stakich, Business Development Director, 4121 Erie Street, Willoughby, Ohio 44094. Phone: 440-975-9691. Fax: 440-975-9694. E-mail: chris@rusticpathways.com.
URL www.rusticpathways.com

For more information, see page 1290.

RUSTIC PATHWAYS–SPANISH LANGUAGE IMMERSION

Rustic Pathways
Escazu, Alajuela
Costa Rica

General Information Coed residential academic program and cultural program.
Academics Spanish (Advanced Placement), Spanish language/literature.
Arts Dance.
Special Interest Areas Cross-cultural education, homestays, touring.
Sports Soccer.
Wilderness/Outdoors Hiking.
Trips Cultural, day, overnight, shopping.
Program Information 8 sessions per year. Session length: 15 days in June, July, August. Ages: 14–18. 15–20 participants per session. Boarding program cost: $1895.
Application Deadline Continuous.
Jobs Positions for college students 21 and older.
Contact Mr. Chris Stakich, Business Development Director, 4121 Erie Street, Willoughby, Ohio 44094. Phone: 440-975-9691. Fax: 440-975-9694. E-mail: chris@rusticpathways.com.
URL www.rusticpathways.com

For more information, see page 1290.

RUSTIC PATHWAYS–SURF THE SUMMER–COSTA RICA

Rustic Pathways
Costa Rica

General Information Coed residential sports camp and adventure program established in 2002.
Special Interest Areas Touring.
Sports Bicycling, horseback riding, kayaking, sailing, sea kayaking, snorkeling, soccer, surfing, swimming, volleyball.
Wilderness/Outdoors Hiking.
Trips Cultural, day, overnight, shopping.
Program Information 9 sessions per year. Session length: 8–15 days in June, July, August. Ages: 14–18. 10–15 participants per session. Boarding program cost: $985–$1885.
Application Deadline Continuous.
Jobs Positions for college students 21 and older.
Contact Mr. Chris Stakich, Business Development Director, 4121 Erie Street, Willoughby, Ohio 44094. Phone: 440-975-9691. Fax: 440-975-9694. E-mail: chris@rusticpathways.com.
URL www.rusticpathways.com

For more information, see page 1290.

RUSTIC PATHWAYS–THE CANO NEGRO SERVICE PROJECT

Rustic Pathways
Caño Negro
Costa Rica

General Information Coed residential community service program and cultural program established in 2003.
Academics Biology.
Special Interest Areas Animal care, community service, construction, cross-cultural education.
Sports Bicycling, horseback riding, sea kayaking.
Trips Cultural, day, overnight.
Program Information 9 sessions per year. Session length: 8–15 days in June, July, August. Ages: 14–18. 10–15 participants per session. Boarding program cost: $765–$1465.

Application Deadline Continuous.
Jobs Positions for college students 21 and older.
Contact Mr. Jessemin Sheyda-Losick, Manager, Global Community Service Initiatives, 4121 Erie Street, Willoughby, Ohio 44094. Phone: 440-975-9691. Fax: 440-975-9694. E-mail: jessemin@rusticpathways.com.
URL www.rusticpathways.com

For more information, see page 1290.

RUSTIC PATHWAYS–THE TURTLE CONSERVATION PROJECT

Rustic Pathways
Punta Judas
Costa Rica

General Information Coed residential outdoor program and community service program established in 2002.
Academics Biology, ecology, marine studies.
Special Interest Areas Animal care, community service, conservation projects, construction, cross-cultural education.
Sports Horseback riding, soccer, swimming, volleyball.
Trips Cultural, day, overnight, shopping.
Program Information 6 sessions per year. Session length: 8 days in July, August. Ages: 14–18. 10–15 participants per session. Boarding program cost: $885.
Application Deadline Continuous.
Jobs Positions for college students 21 and older.
Contact Mr. Jessemin Sheyda-Losick, Manager, Community Service Global Initiative, 4121 Erie Street, Willoughby, Ohio 44094. Phone: 440-975-9691. Fax: 440-975-9694. E-mail: jessemin@rusticpathways.com.
URL www.rusticpathways.com

For more information, see page 1290.

RUSTIC PATHWAYS–VOLCANOES AND RAINFORESTS

Rustic Pathways
Arenal Volcano Park Station
Fortuna
Costa Rica

General Information Coed residential outdoor program and community service program established in 2002.
Academics Environmental science, geology/earth science.
Special Interest Areas Community service, conservation projects, construction, gardening, nature study, trail maintenance.
Sports Soccer, swimming.
Wilderness/Outdoors Hiking.
Trips Cultural, day, overnight, shopping.
Program Information 9 sessions per year. Session length: 8–15 days in June, July, August. Ages: 14–18. 10–15 participants per session. Boarding program cost: $695–$1325.
Application Deadline Continuous.
Jobs Positions for college students 21 and older.
Contact Mr. Jessemin Sheyda-Losick, Manager, Global Community Service Initiative, 4121 Erie Street, Willoughby, Ohio 44094. Phone: 440-975-9691. Fax: 440-975-9694. E-mail: jessemin@rusticpathways.com.
URL www.rusticpathways.com

For more information, see page 1290.

SFS: SUSTAINING TROPICAL ECOSYSTEMS

The School for Field Studies
Center for Sustainable Development Studies
Atenas
Costa Rica

General Information Coed residential academic program, outdoor program, and community service program established in 1980. Formal opportunities for the academically talented. College credit may be earned.
Program Focus Environmental field research and environmental problem solving.
Academics Spanish language/literature, anthropology, area studies, biology, botany, ecology, economics, environmental science, geography, geology/earth science, government and politics, intercultural studies, science (general), social science, social studies, writing.
Special Interest Areas Community service, field research/expeditions, homestays, nature study.
Sports Baseball, basketball, soccer, volleyball.
Wilderness/Outdoors Backpacking, hiking, wilderness camping.
Trips Cultural, day, overnight.
Program Information 2 sessions per year. Session length: 30 days in June, July, August. Ages: 16–25. 32 participants per session. Boarding program cost: $3410. Application fee: $45. Financial aid available. Airfare not included.
Application Deadline Continuous.
Contact Lili Folsom, Director of Admissions and Alumni Services, 10 Federal Street, Salem, Massachusetts 01970-3853. Phone: 800-989-4418. Fax: 978-741-3551. E-mail: admissions@fieldstudies.org.
URL www.fieldstudies.org

SIDWELL FRIENDS SUMMER PROGRAM: COSTA RICA

Sidwell Friends School
San Jose
Costa Rica

General Information Coed travel academic program, outdoor program, and community service program established in 1998.
Program Focus Spanish immersion and community service.
Academics Spanish language/literature, marine studies, peace education.
Special Interest Areas Community service, touring.
Wilderness/Outdoors Hiking, mountain biking, rafting, white-water trips, wilderness/outdoors (general).
Trips Cultural, day, overnight, shopping.
Program Information 1 session per year. Session length: 13 days in July, August. Ages: 13–17. 12–15

Sidwell Friends Summer Program: Costa Rica (continued)

participants per session. Cost: $2975. Airfare from Washington, DC to San Jose, Costa Rica included.
Application Deadline Continuous.
Contact Summer Programs Office, 3825 Wisconsin Avenue, NW, Washington, District of Columbia 20016. Phone: 202-537-8133. Fax: 202-537-2483. E-mail: sidwellsummer@yahoo.com.
URL www.sidwell.edu/summer

Wilderness Ventures–Costa Rica

Wilderness Ventures
Costa Rica

General Information Coed travel outdoor program, wilderness program, cultural program, and adventure program established in 1973.
Program Focus Wilderness travel, cultural immersion, leadership skills.
Special Interest Areas Leadership training.
Sports Sea kayaking.
Wilderness/Outdoors Backpacking, hiking, rafting, white-water trips, wilderness camping.
Trips Cultural, overnight.
Program Information 2 sessions per year. Session length: 3 weeks in June, July, August. Ages: 14–18. 13 participants per session. Cost: $3890. Financial aid available.
Application Deadline Continuous.
Jobs Positions for college students 21 and older.
Contact Mike Cottingham, Director, PO Box 2768, Jackson Hole, Wyoming 83001. Phone: 800-533-2281. Fax: 307-739-1934. E-mail: info@wildernessventures.com.
URL www.wildernessventures.com

For more information, see page 1396.

World Horizons International–Costa Rica

World Horizons International
Costa Rica

General Information Coed residential community service program and cultural program established in 1988. Formal opportunities for the academically talented and artistically talented.
Program Focus Community service, intercultural travel abroad, and foreign language immersion.
Academics Spanish language/literature.
Special Interest Areas Community service, cross-cultural education, work camp programs.
Sports Horseback riding, snorkeling.
Wilderness/Outdoors Hiking, rafting.
Trips Cultural, day, overnight.
Program Information 1–2 sessions per year. Session length: 2–4 weeks in June, July, August. Ages: 14–18. 10–12 participants per session. Boarding program cost: $3000–$4500. Application fee: $100. Financial aid available. Airfare from Miami to San Jose included.
Application Deadline Continuous.
Jobs Positions for college students 20 and older.

World Horizons International–Costa Rica

Contact Stuart L. Rabinowitz, Executive Director, PO Box 662, Bethlehem, Connecticut 06751. Phone: 800-262-5874. Fax: 203-266-6227. E-mail: worldhorizons@att.net.
URL www.world-horizons.com

For more information, see page 1406.

CUBA

Earthwatch Institute–Crocodiles of Cuba

Earthwatch Institute
Province Las Tunas
Cuba

General Information Coed residential outdoor program.
Program Focus Exploring the natural history of a rare reptile to improve its management.
Academics Ecology, environmental science.

Special Interest Areas Animal care, conservation projects, field research/expeditions.
Wilderness/Outdoors Wilderness/outdoors (general).
Program Information 3 sessions per year. Session length: 2 weeks in May, June, August. Ages: 16+. 6 participants per session. Boarding program cost: $2695–$2795. Financial aid available. Financial aid for high school students and teachers.
Application Deadline Continuous.
Contact General Information Desk, PO Box 75, Maynard, Massachusetts 01754. Phone: 800-776-0188. Fax: 978-461-2332. E-mail: info@earthwatch.org.
URL www.earthwatch.org

Excel Cuba

Putney Student Travel
Cuba

General Information Coed residential academic program, arts program, and cultural program established in 1951. Formal opportunities for the academically talented and artistically talented.
Program Focus Excel is an innovative precollege program that emphasizes small classes, creative interactions among students and faculty, and cultural exchange.
Academics Spanish language/literature, academics (general), art history/appreciation, government and politics, history, humanities, intercultural studies, linguistics, music, social science, writing.
Arts Arts, creative writing, dance, dance (folk), drawing, film, music, music (jazz), painting, photography, television/video.
Special Interest Areas Field research/expeditions.
Sports Baseball, basketball, horseback riding, soccer, swimming, tennis.
Wilderness/Outdoors Hiking.
Trips Cultural, day.
Program Information 1 session per year. Session length: 4 weeks in June, July, August. Ages: 15–18. 60–65 participants per session. Boarding program cost: $6000. Financial aid available.
Application Deadline Continuous.
Contact Tim Weed, Director, 345 Hickory Ridge Road, Putney, Vermont 05346. Phone: 802-387-5000. Fax: 802-387-4276. E-mail: info@goputney.com.
URL www.goputney.com

For more information, see page 1114.

Putney Student Travel–Cultural Exploration-Creative Writing in Cuba

Putney Student Travel
Santiago/Havana
Cuba

General Information Coed residential arts program established in 1951.
Program Focus A group of aspiring writers hone their skills while experiencing the unique life and culture of Cuba.
Academics Writing.
Arts Creative writing.
Special Interest Areas Cross-cultural education.
Sports Bicycling, snorkeling, swimming.
Wilderness/Outdoors Hiking.
Trips Cultural, day, overnight.
Program Information 1 session per year. Session length: 28–34 days in June, July, August. Ages: 15–18. 25 participants per session. Boarding program cost: $6400. Financial aid available.
Application Deadline Continuous.
Jobs Positions for college students 21 and older.
Contact Jeffrey Shumlin, Director, 345 Hickory Ridge Road, Putney, Vermont 05346. Phone: 802-387-5000. Fax: 802-387-4276. E-mail: info@goputney.com.
URL www.goputney.com

For more information, see page 1276.

Windsor Mountain: Cuba Friendship Exchange

Interlocken at Windsor Mountain
Cuba

General Information Coed travel community service program and cultural program established in 1967.
Program Focus Community service, family stays, cross-cultural exploration, language training.
Academics Spanish (Advanced Placement), Spanish language/literature, intercultural studies, social studies.
Special Interest Areas Community service, cross-cultural education, homestays.
Program Information 1 session per year. Session length: 4 weeks in July, August. Ages: 14–17. 13 participants per session. Cost: $4995. Financial aid available.
Application Deadline Continuous.
Contact Tom Herman, Director, Marketing, 19 Interlocken Way, Windsor, New Hampshire 03244. Phone: 603-478-3166 Ext.20. Fax: 603-478-5260. E-mail: tom@windsormountain.org.
URL www.windsormountain.org/xrds/cuba.html

For more information, see page 1162.

CZECH REPUBLIC

EARTHWATCH INSTITUTE–MOUNTAIN WATERS OF BOHEMIA

Earthwatch Institute
Jizera Mountains
Czech Republic

General Information Coed residential outdoor program, cultural program, and adventure program.
Program Focus Restoring the vital links of ecosystems damaged by acid rain.
Academics Biology, environmental science, forestry, science (general).
Special Interest Areas Field research/expeditions, nature study.

EARTHWATCH INSTITUTE–Mountain Waters of Bohemia (continued)

Program Information 3 sessions per year. Session length: 15 days in May, June, July. Ages: 16+. 8 participants per session. Boarding program cost: $2095–$2195. Financial aid available. Financial aid for high school students and teachers.
Application Deadline Continuous.
Contact General Information Desk, PO Box 75, Maynard, Massachusetts 01754. Phone: 800-776-0188. Fax: 978-461-2332. E-mail: info@earthwatch.org.
URL www.earthwatch.org

Volunteers for Peace International Work Camp–Czech Republic

Volunteers for Peace International Work Camps
Prague
Czech Republic

General Information Coed residential community service program established in 1981. Specific services available for the hearing impaired and physically challenged. College credit may be earned.
Program Focus International work camps.
Academics Intercultural studies, peace education.
Special Interest Areas Community service, construction, work camp programs.
Sports Canoeing, swimming, volleyball.
Wilderness/Outdoors Hiking.
Trips Cultural, day, overnight.
Program Information Session length: 2–3 weeks in April, May, August, October. Ages: 16+. 12–20 participants per session. Boarding program cost: $250–$600.
Application Deadline Continuous.
Contact Peter Coldwell, Director, 1034 Tiffany Road, Belmont, Vermont 05730. Phone: 802-259-2759. Fax: 802-259-2922. E-mail: vfp@vfp.org.
URL www.vfp.org

DENMARK

Peace in the Modern World

Scandinavian Seminar
Denmark

General Information Coed travel academic program and cultural program established in 2005. Formal opportunities for the academically talented. High school credit may be earned.
Academics Academics (general), anthropology, area studies, economics, government and politics, history, humanities, intercultural studies, music, oceanography, peace education, philosophy, precollege program, social science, social studies.
Arts Arts and crafts (general), dance (folk), weaving, woodworking.
Special Interest Areas Career exploration, conservation projects, farming, field research/expeditions, nature study.
Sports Boating, fishing, sailing, swimming.
Wilderness/Outdoors Hiking.
Trips Cultural, day, overnight.
Program Information 1 session per year. Session length: 2 weeks in July. Ages: 15+. 15–30 participants per session. Cost: $2250. Financial aid available.
Application Deadline March 15.
Contact Leslie Evans, Student Program Director, 24 Dickinson Street, Amherst, Massachusetts 01002. Phone: 413-253-9736. Fax: 413-253-5282. E-mail: evans@scandinavianseminar.org.
URL www.scandinavianseminar.com/files/globalpeace2.pdf

Youth for Understanding USA–Denmark

Youth for Understanding USA
Denmark

General Information Coed residential academic program and cultural program established in 1951. High school or college credit may be earned.
Program Focus Living with a host family, learning about other cultures, attending an International Relations and Perspectives Retreat, and improving language and communication skills.
Academics Danish language/literature, area studies, environmental science, intercultural studies, social science.
Special Interest Areas Cross-cultural education, homestays.
Sports Bicycling, kayaking, sea kayaking, swimming.
Wilderness/Outdoors Bicycle trips.
Trips Cultural, day, overnight.
Program Information 1 session per year. Session length: 35–45 days in June, July. Ages: 15–18. 10–50 participants per session. Boarding program cost: $5195. Application fee: $75. Financial aid available. Round-trip domestic and international airfare is included in the tuition.
Application Deadline Continuous.
Contact Admissions Counselor, 6400 Goldsboro Road, Suite 100, Bethesda, Maryland 20817. Phone: 800-TEENAGE (833-6243). Fax: 202-895-1104. E-mail: admissions@us.yfu.org.
URL www.yfu-usa.org

For more information, see page 1414.

DOMINICA

Putney Student Travel–Community Service–Dominica, West Indies

Putney Student Travel
Dominica

General Information Coed residential community service program and cultural program established in 1951.
Program Focus Community service, cultural exchange, and weekend excursions from a small rural community.
Academics Intercultural studies.
Special Interest Areas Community service, construction, farming.
Sports Sailing, snorkeling, soccer, swimming.
Wilderness/Outdoors Canoe trips, hiking.
Trips Cultural, day.
Program Information 1 session per year. Session length: 4 weeks in June, July. Ages: 15–18. 16 participants per session. Boarding program cost: $5100. Financial aid available. Airfare included.
Application Deadline Continuous.
Contact Jeffrey Shumlin, Admissions Director, 345 Hickory Ridge Road, Putney, Vermont 05346. Phone: 802-387-5000. Fax: 802-387-4276. E-mail: info@goputney.com.
URL www.goputney.com
For more information, see page 1276.

Visions–Dominica

Visions
Dominica

General Information Coed travel outdoor program, community service program, and cultural program established in 1989. High school credit may be earned.
Program Focus Community service, cross-cultural experience, and outdoor adventure activities.
Academics Intercultural studies.
Arts Carpentry, painting.
Special Interest Areas Community service, construction, cross-cultural education, field research/expeditions, field trips (arts and culture), leadership training, nature study, whale watching.
Sports Canoeing, snorkeling, swimming.
Wilderness/Outdoors Backpacking, hiking, outdoor adventure.
Trips Cultural, day, overnight.
Program Information 1 session per year. Session length: 4 weeks in June, July. Ages: 14–18. 20–25 participants per session. Cost: $3750. Financial aid available.
Application Deadline Continuous.
Jobs Positions for college students 22 and older.
Contact Joanne Pinaire, Director, PO Box 220, Newport, Pennsylvania 17074. Phone: 717-567-7313. Fax: 717-567-7853. E-mail: info@visionsserviceadventures.com.
URL www.visionsserviceadventures.com
For more information, see page 1382.

World Horizons International–Dominica

World Horizons International
Dominica

General Information Coed residential community service program and cultural program established in 1988.
Program Focus Community service and intercultural travel abroad.
Special Interest Areas Community service, conservation projects, cross-cultural education, work camp programs.
Sports Snorkeling, swimming.
Wilderness/Outdoors Backpacking, hiking.
Trips Cultural, day, overnight.
Program Information 1–2 sessions per year. Session length: 10–28 days in June, July, December. Ages: 14–18. 10–12 participants per session. Boarding program cost: $2750–$4500. Application fee: $100. Financial aid available. Airfare from Miami to Dominica included.
Application Deadline Continuous.
Jobs Positions for college students 20 and older.
Contact Stuart L. Rabinowitz, Executive Director, PO Box 662, Bethlehem, Connecticut 06751. Phone: 800-262-5874. Fax: 203-266-6227. E-mail: worldhorizons@att.net.
URL www.world-horizons.com
For more information, see page 1406.

DOMINICAN REPUBLIC

Putney Student Travel–Community Service–Dominican Republic

Putney Student Travel
Dominican Republic

General Information Coed residential community service program and cultural program established in 1951.
Program Focus Community service, cultural exchange, and weekend excursions from a base in a small, rural community.
Academics Intercultural studies.
Special Interest Areas Community service, construction, farming.
Sports Baseball, soccer, swimming.
Wilderness/Outdoors Caving, hiking.
Trips Cultural, day.

Putney Student Travel–Community Service–Dominican Republic (continued)

Program Information 2 sessions per year. Session length: 28–29 days in June, July. Ages: 15–18. 16 participants per session. Boarding program cost: $5100. Financial aid available. Airfare from Miami included.
Application Deadline Continuous.
Contact Jeffrey Shumlin, Admissions Director, 345 Hickory Ridge Road, Putney, Vermont 05346. Phone: 802-387-5000. Fax: 802-387-4276. E-mail: info@goputney.com.
URL www.goputney.com

For more information, see page 1276.

SuperCamp–Dominican Republic

SuperCamp
La Vega
Dominican Republic

General Information Coed residential academic program established in 2002.
Program Focus Academic enrichment and personal development.
Academics SAT/ACT preparation, academics (general), communications, reading, study skills, writing.
Sports Ropes course, soccer, swimming, volleyball.
Program Information 1–4 sessions per year. Session length: 10 days in July. Ages: 14–18. 50–100 participants per session. Boarding program cost: $1200–$1300. Application fee: $100. Financial aid available.
Application Deadline Continuous.
Jobs Positions for college students 18 and older.
Contact Enrollments Department, 1725 South Coast Highway, Oceanside, California 92054. Phone: 800-285-3276. Fax: 760-722-3507. E-mail: info@supercamp.com.
URL www.supercamp.com

For more information, see page 1348.

Visions–Dominican Republic

Visions
Santo Domingo
Dominican Republic

General Information Coed travel outdoor program, community service program, and cultural program established in 1989. High school credit may be earned.
Program Focus Community service, cross-cultural experience, language immersion, and outdoor adventure activities.
Academics Spanish language/literature, intercultural studies, language study.
Arts Carpentry.
Special Interest Areas Community service, construction, cross-cultural education, field trips (arts and culture), homestays, leadership training, nature study.
Sports Snorkeling, swimming.
Wilderness/Outdoors Backpacking, hiking.
Trips Cultural, day, overnight, shopping.
Program Information 2 sessions per year. Session length: 3–4 weeks in June, July, August. Ages: 14–18. 20–25 participants per session. Cost: $2800–$3750. Financial aid available.
Application Deadline Continuous.
Jobs Positions for college students 22 and older.
Contact Joanne Pinaire, Director, PO Box 220, Newport, Pennsylvania 17074. Phone: 717-567-7313. Fax: 717-567-7853. E-mail: info@visionsserviceadventures.com.
URL www.visionsserviceadventures.com

For more information, see page 1382.

ECUADOR

AAVE–Ecuador and Galapagos

AAVE–America's Adventure Ventures Everywhere
Ecuador

General Information Coed travel outdoor program, cultural program, and adventure program established in 1976. Accredited by American Camping Association.
Program Focus Cultural and outdoor experience; travel to Galapagos Islands and the Amazon.
Academics Area studies, ecology, intercultural studies.
Special Interest Areas Community service, leadership training, nature study, touring.
Sports Bicycling, boating, horseback riding, sailing, snorkeling, swimming.
Wilderness/Outdoors Hiking.
Trips Cultural, day, overnight.
Program Information 2–4 sessions per year. Session length: 3 weeks in June, July, August. Ages: 15–18. 12 participants per session. Cost: $4288. Financial aid available.
Application Deadline Continuous.
Jobs Positions for college students 21 and older.
Contact Mr. Abbott Wallis, Owner, America's Adventure, 2245 Stonecrop Way, Golden, Colorado 80401. Phone: 800-222-3595. Fax: 303-526-0885. E-mail: info@aave.com.
URL www.aave.com

For more information, see page 952.

ActionQuest: Galapagos Archipelago Expeditions

ActionQuest
Ecuador

General Information Coed travel outdoor program, cultural program, and adventure program established in 1986.
Program Focus Live-aboard; land exploration of the Galapagos Islands, with emphasis on ecology and nature study. Voyage includes a three-day Amazon rainforest trek.
Academics Ecology, environmental science, geology/earth science, intercultural studies, marine studies, oceanography.
Arts Photography.

Special Interest Areas Community service, field research/expeditions, leadership training, nature study, team building, touring.
Sports Scuba diving, snorkeling.
Wilderness/Outdoors Hiking, white-water trips.
Trips Cultural, day, overnight.
Program Information 2 sessions per year. Session length: 3 weeks in June, July, August. Ages: 15–19. 14 participants per session. Cost: $4470.
Application Deadline Continuous.
Contact James Stoll, Director, PO Box 5517, Sarasota, Florida 34277. Phone: 800-317-6789. Fax: 941-924-6075. E-mail: info@actionquest.com.
URL www.actionquest.com
For more information, see page 964.

AFS-USA–Homestay–Ecuador

AFS-USA
Ecuador

General Information Coed residential cultural program.
Program Focus Living with a host family and taking part in activities with other teenagers.
Academics Spanish language/literature.
Special Interest Areas Homestays, touring.
Trips Cultural, day, overnight.
Program Information 1 session per year. Session length: 6 weeks in June, July, August. Ages: 15–18. 10 participants per session. Boarding program cost: $3665–$3965. Application fee: $75. Financial aid available. International airfare and volunteer homestay support included.
Application Deadline Continuous.
Contact Manager, AFS Info Center, 506 Southwest 6th Avenue, 2nd Floor, Portland, Oregon 97204. Phone: 800-AFS-INFO. Fax: 503-248-4076. E-mail: afsinfo@afs.org.
URL www.afs.org/usa
For more information, see page 974.

Blyth Education–Summer Study in the Amazon and the Galapagos Islands

Blyth Education
Ecuador

General Information Coed residential academic program, cultural program, and adventure program established in 2000. High school credit may be earned.
Academics Academics (general), biology, ecology, environmental science, geography.
Special Interest Areas Community service, cross-cultural education, nature study, touring.
Sports Scuba diving, snorkeling, swimming.
Wilderness/Outdoors Backpacking, hiking.
Trips Cultural, day, overnight.
Program Information 1 session per year. Session length: 25–30 days in July. Ages: 16–19. 25 participants per session. Boarding program cost: 6395 Canadian dollars. Airfare from Toronto or New York included.
Application Deadline Continuous.
Jobs Positions for college students 25 and older.
Contact Blyth Education, 9 Sultan Street, Suite 300, Toronto, Ontario M5S 1L6, Canada. Phone: 416-960-3552. Fax: 416-960-9506. E-mail: info@blytheducation.com.
URL www.blytheducation.com

BROADREACH Academic Treks–Spanish Language Immersion in Ecuador

Broadreach
Ecuador

General Information Coed travel academic program, outdoor program, community service program, cultural program, and adventure program established in 1992. High school or college credit may be earned.
Program Focus Academic adventure program focusing on language study, cultural exchange, service learning, hiking in the Andes, homestay, and high school and college credit.
Academics Spanish language/literature, academics (general), area studies, intercultural studies.
Special Interest Areas Community service, conservation projects, cross-cultural education, homestays, leadership training.
Sports Horseback riding.
Wilderness/Outdoors Backpacking, hiking, wilderness camping.
Trips Cultural, day.
Program Information 2 sessions per year. Session length: 32 days in June, July, August. Ages: 16–20. 10–14 participants per session.
Application Deadline Continuous.
Contact Carlton Goldthwaite, Director, PO Box 27076, Raleigh, North Carolina 27611. Phone: 888-833-1907. Fax: 919-833-2129. E-mail: info@gobroadreach.com or info@academictreks.com.
URL www.academictreks.com
For more information, see page 1010.

BROADREACH Amazon and Galapagos Encounter

Broadreach
Ecuador

General Information Coed travel outdoor program, wilderness program, cultural program, and adventure program established in 1992.
Program Focus Coed program focusing on adventure travel, Amazon rainforest exploration, hiking in the Andes, and Galapagos ecosystem study with optional scuba.
Academics Botany, ecology, environmental science, intercultural studies, marine studies.
Arts Photography.
Special Interest Areas Community service, conservation projects, field research/expeditions, field trips (arts and culture), folklore, leadership training, nature study.
Sports Canoeing, horseback riding, sailing, scuba diving, snorkeling.

BROADREACH Amazon and Galapagos Encounter (continued)

Wilderness/Outdoors Canoe trips, hiking, pack animal trips, rafting, white-water trips, wilderness camping.
Trips Cultural.
Program Information 2 sessions per year. Session length: 22 days in June, July, August. Ages: 15–19. 10–12 participants per session. Cost: $5300.
Application Deadline Continuous.
Contact Carlton Goldthwaite, Director, PO Box 27076, Raleigh, North Carolina 27611-7076. Phone: 888-833-1907. Fax: 919-833-2129. E-mail: info@gobroadreach.com.
URL www.gobroadreach.com

For more information, see page 1010.

EARTHWATCH INSTITUTE–

Ecuador Forest Birds

Earthwatch Institute
Loma Alta Ecological Reserve
Ecuador

General Information Coed residential outdoor program, cultural program, and adventure program.
Program Focus Investigating the ecology of birds to save them and their dwindling tropical forest habitat.
Academics Biology, ecology, environmental science, ornithology, science (general).
Special Interest Areas Field research/expeditions, nature study.
Program Information 3 sessions per year. Session length: 2 weeks in January, June, December. Ages: 16+. 10 participants per session. Boarding program cost: $1795–$1895. Financial aid available. Financial aid for high school students and teachers.
Application Deadline Continuous.
Contact General Information Desk, PO Box 75, Maynard, Massachusetts 01754. Phone: 800-776-0188. Fax: 978-461-2332. E-mail: info@earthwatch.org.
URL www.earthwatch.org

EF International Language School–Quito

EF International Language Schools
Catalina Alda Z #263 y Avenida Portugal
Quito
Ecuador

General Information Coed travel academic program and cultural program established in 1996. High school or college credit may be earned.
Program Focus Language and cultural immersion.
Academics Spanish (Advanced Placement), Spanish language/literature.
Special Interest Areas Community service, field trips (arts and culture), touring.
Sports Horseback riding, sports (general).
Wilderness/Outdoors Wilderness/outdoors (general).
Trips Cultural, day, overnight.
Program Information Session length: 14–365 days in January, February, March, April, May, June, July, August, September, October, November, December. Ages: 16+. 100–150 participants per session. Call for costs.
Application Deadline Continuous.
Contact Ms. Katie Mahon, Director of Admissions, One Education Street, Cambridge, Massachusetts 02141. Phone: 800-992-1892. Fax: 800-590-1125. E-mail: ils@ef.com.
URL www.ef.com

For more information, see page 1102.

The Experiment in International Living–Ecuador Homestay

The Experiment in International Living
Ecuador

General Information Coed residential outdoor program, cultural program, and adventure program established in 1932.
Program Focus International youth travel, Galapagos trip/animal observation, homestay.
Academics Spanish language/literature, ecology.
Special Interest Areas Community service, homestays, nature study.
Sports Snorkeling, swimming.
Wilderness/Outdoors Hiking, rafting, white-water trips.
Trips Cultural, day, overnight.
Program Information 1 session per year. Session length: 5 weeks in July, August. Ages: 14–19. 10–15 participants per session. Boarding program cost: $4700. Financial aid available.
Application Deadline May 1.
Contact Annie Thompson, Enrollment Director, Summer Abroad, Kipling Road, PO Box 676, Brattleboro, Vermont 05302-0676. Phone: 800-345-2929. Fax: 802-258-3428. E-mail: eil@worldlearning.org.
URL www.usexperiment.org

For more information, see page 1116.

Global Teen–Spanish in Ecuador

Language Liaison
Quito
Ecuador

General Information Coed residential academic program. High school or college credit may be earned.
Program Focus Spanish language study and cultural immersion.
Academics Spanish language/literature, area studies, intercultural studies, reading, writing.
Arts Ceramics, dance, film.
Special Interest Areas Conservation projects, culinary arts, field trips (arts and culture), gardening, homestays, nature study, touring.
Sports Bowling, soccer, volleyball.
Trips Cultural, day, shopping.
Program Information Session length: 2–8 weeks in June, July, August. 2–4 participants per session. Application fee: $85. Financial aid available. Exit fee: $25.
Application Deadline Continuous.

Contact Nancy Forman, President, PO Box 1772, Pacific Palisades, California 90272. Phone: 800-284-4448. Fax: 310-454-1706. E-mail: learn@languageliaison.com.
URL www.languageliaison.com
For more information, see page 1184.

GLOBAL WORKS–Language Exposure-Ecuador and the Galapagos-4 weeks

GLOBAL WORKS
Ecuador

General Information Coed travel community service program, cultural program, and adventure program established in 1988. High school or college credit may be earned.
Program Focus Community service, cultural exchange, and outdoor adventure.
Academics Biology, ecology, environmental science, intercultural studies.
Arts Arts and crafts (general), dance (Latin), music.
Special Interest Areas Community service, conservation projects, construction, team building.
Sports Basketball, sea kayaking, snorkeling, swimming, volleyball.
Wilderness/Outdoors Hiking, outdoor adventure.
Trips Cultural, day, overnight.
Program Information 1–2 sessions per year. Session length: 28–31 days in June, July. Ages: 15–18. 16–20 participants per session. Cost: $4150–$4250. Application fee: $100. Financial aid available.
Application Deadline Continuous.
Jobs Positions for college students 23 and older.
Contact Mr. Erik Werner, Director, 1113 South Allen Street, State College, Pennsylvania 16801. Phone: 814-867-7000. Fax: 814-867-2717. E-mail: info@globalworksinc.com.
URL www.globalworksinc.com
For more information, see page 1136.

GLOBAL WORKS–Language Immersion-Ecuador and the Galapagos-4 weeks

GLOBAL WORKS
Ecuador

General Information Coed travel community service program, cultural program, and adventure program established in 1988. High school credit may be earned.
Program Focus Environmental and community service, language immersion, and cultural exchange.
Academics Spanish language/literature, intercultural studies.
Arts Arts and crafts (general), dance, music.
Special Interest Areas Community service, construction, field trips (arts and culture), homestays.
Sports Bicycling, snorkeling, soccer, sports (general), swimming, volleyball.
Wilderness/Outdoors Hiking.
Trips Cultural, day, overnight.
Program Information 1 session per year. Session length: 31 days in June, July. Ages: 15–18. 15–17 participants per session. Cost: $3950–$4000. Application fee: $100. Financial aid available. Airfare not included.
Application Deadline Continuous.
Jobs Positions for college students 23 and older.
Contact Erik Werner, Director, 1113 South Allen Street, State College, Pennsylvania 16801. Phone: 814-867-7000. Fax: 814-867-2717. E-mail: info@globalworksinc.com.
URL www.globalworksinc.com
For more information, see page 1136.

iBike Cultural Tours–Ecuador

International Bicycle Fund
Ecuador

General Information Coed travel outdoor program, cultural program, and adventure program established in 2001.
Program Focus Cross-cultural bicycle tour.
Academics Spanish language/literature, anthropology, architecture, area studies, art history/appreciation, botany, ecology, economics, environmental science, geography, geology/earth science, government and politics, history, intercultural studies, religion, social science, social studies.
Special Interest Areas Cross-cultural education, field trips (arts and culture), nature study.
Sports Bicycling.
Wilderness/Outdoors Bicycle trips, mountain biking.
Trips Cultural.
Program Information 1–2 sessions per year. Session length: 13–15 days in June, July, August. Ages: 16+. 6–12 participants per session. Cost: $1190–$1290. Financial aid available.
Application Deadline Continuous.
Contact David Mozer, Director, 4887 Columbia Drive South, Seattle, Washington 98108-1919. Phone: 206-767-0848. Fax: 206-767-0848. E-mail: ibike@ibike.org.
URL www.ibike.org/ibike

LIFEWORKS with the Galapagos Islands' National Parks

LIFEWORKS International
Ecuador

General Information Coed travel outdoor program, community service program, cultural program, and adventure program established in 1986. High school credit may be earned.
Program Focus Service-learning travel program with cultural immersion and outdoor adventure activities with a focus on the Galapagos ecosystem.
Academics Ecology.
Special Interest Areas Community service, nature study.
Sports Snorkeling.
Wilderness/Outdoors Hiking.
Trips Cultural, day, overnight.
Program Information 1 session per year. Session length: 22 days in July. Ages: 15–19. 8–15 participants per session. Cost: $3760. Financial aid available.

LIFEWORKS with the Galapagos Islands' National Parks (continued)

Application Deadline Continuous.
Contact James Stoll, Director, PO Box 5517, Sarasota, Florida 34277. Phone: 800-808-2115. Fax: 941-924-6075. E-mail: info@lifeworks-international.com.
URL www.lifeworks-international.com

For more information, see page 1196.

LSA Quito, Ecuador

Language Studies Abroad, Inc.
Quito
Ecuador

General Information Coed residential academic program and cultural program established in 1990. Formal opportunities for the artistically talented. High school or college credit may be earned.
Program Focus Language and culture.
Academics Spanish (Advanced Placement), Spanish language/literature, academics (general), intercultural studies.
Special Interest Areas Homestays.
Trips Cultural, day.
Program Information 1–26 sessions per year. Session length: 13–360 days in January, February, March, April, May, June, July, August, September, October, November, December. Ages: 14+. 15–60 participants per session. Boarding program cost: $575–$2100. Application fee: $100. Financial aid available.
Application Deadline Continuous.
Contact Director, 1801 Highway 50 East, Suite I, Carson City, Nevada 89701. Phone: 800-424-5522. Fax: 775-883-2266. E-mail: info@languagestudiesabroad.com.
URL www.languagestudiesabroad.com/

For more information, see page 1186.

PAX Abroad–Ecuador Rainforest Adventure

PAX Abroad
Ecuador

General Information Coed travel academic program, outdoor program, cultural program, and adventure program established in 1999.
Academics Ecology, environmental science, geology/earth science.
Sports Canoeing.
Wilderness/Outdoors Hiking.
Trips Cultural, day, overnight, shopping.
Program Information 1 session per year. Session length: 3 weeks in July. Ages: 15–18. 10–20 participants per session. Cost: $2900–$3400. Application fee: $100. Airfare from New York included.
Application Deadline April 15.
Contact Ms. Libby Cryer, Director, PAX Abroad, 71 Arch Street, Greenwich, Connecticut 06830. Phone: 800-555-6211. Fax: 203-629-0486. E-mail: academicexchange@pax.org.
URL www.pax.org

PAX Abroad–Ecuador–Spanish Language Immersion

PAX Abroad
Ecuador

General Information Coed travel academic program and cultural program established in 1999.
Academics Spanish (Advanced Placement), Spanish language/literature.
Special Interest Areas Touring.
Trips Cultural, day, overnight, shopping.
Program Information 1 session per year. Session length: 3 weeks in July. Ages: 15–18. 10–20 participants per session. Cost: $2900–$3400. Application fee: $100. Airfare included.
Application Deadline April 15.
Contact Ms. Libby Cryer, Director, PAX Abroad, 71 Arch Street, Greenwich, Connecticut 06830. Phone: 800-555-6211. Fax: 203-629-0486. E-mail: academicexchange@pax.org.
URL www.pax.org

Peace Works International–Ecuador

Peace Works International
Ecuador

General Information Coed travel community service program, cultural program, and adventure program established in 2003.
Academics Spanish language/literature, intercultural studies, peace education.
Special Interest Areas Community service, construction, cross-cultural education.
Sports Boating, snorkeling.
Wilderness/Outdoors Hiking.
Trips Cultural, overnight.
Program Information 1 session per year. Session length: 26 days in July. Ages: 15–18. 16–18 participants per session. Cost: $4395–$4495. Airfare included.
Application Deadline Continuous.
Jobs Positions for college students 22 and older.
Contact Mr. Christopher Kealey, Executive Director, PO Box 70905, Pasadena, California 91117. Phone: 626-798-5221. Fax: 626-798-2959. E-mail: info@peaceworksintl.org.
URL www.peaceworksintl.org

For more information, see page 1250.

Programs Abroad Travel Alternatives–Ecuador

Programs Abroad Travel Alternatives
Quito
Ecuador

General Information Coed travel academic program and cultural program established in 1996. Formal opportunities for the academically talented. College credit may be earned.
Program Focus Foreign language immersion for Spanish students.
Academics Spanish language/literature, art history/appreciation, history.

Special Interest Areas Community service, cross-cultural education.
Trips Cultural, day, overnight.
Program Information 2–3 sessions per year. Session length: 9–34 days in March, April, June, July. Ages: 15–19. 7–30 participants per session. Cost: $2300–$3800. Application fee: $90.
Application Deadline Continuous.
Contact Heather Kenley, Director, 6200 Adel Cove, Austin, Texas 78749. Phone: 512-282-2838. Fax: 512-282-7076. E-mail: studyabroad@gopata.com.
URL www.gopata.com
For more information, see page 1248.

Putney Student Travel–Community Service–Ecuador

Putney Student Travel
Ecuador

General Information Coed residential community service program and cultural program established in 1951.
Program Focus Community service, cultural exchange, and weekend excursions from a base in a small, rural community.
Academics Intercultural studies.
Special Interest Areas Community service, construction.
Sports Horseback riding, soccer.
Wilderness/Outdoors Hiking.
Trips Cultural, day.
Program Information 2 sessions per year. Session length: 28–30 days in June, July, August. Ages: 15–18. 16 participants per session. Boarding program cost: $5100. Financial aid available. Airfare from Miami included.
Application Deadline Continuous.
Contact Jeffrey Shumlin, Admissions Director, 345 Hickory Ridge Road, Putney, Vermont 05346. Phone: 802-387-5000. Fax: 802-387-4276. E-mail: info@goputney.com.
URL www.goputney.com
For more information, see page 1276.

Visions–Ecuador

Visions
Quito
Ecuador

General Information Coed travel community service program and cultural program established in 1989. High school credit may be earned.
Academics Spanish language/literature, intercultural studies, writing.
Arts Arts and crafts (general), basketry, creative writing, jewelry making.
Special Interest Areas Community service, construction, cross-cultural education, farming, field research/expeditions, homestays, leadership training, nature study.
Sports Bicycling, fishing, snorkeling, swimming.
Wilderness/Outdoors Hiking.
Trips Cultural, day, overnight.
Program Information 1 session per year. Session length: 4 weeks in July. Ages: 16–18. 15–17 participants per session. Cost: $3800. Financial aid available.
Application Deadline Continuous.
Jobs Positions for college students 22 and older.
Contact Joanne Pinaire, Director, PO Box 220, Newport, Pennsylvania 17074-0220. Phone: 717-567-7313. Fax: 717-567-7853. E-mail: info@visionsserviceadventures.com.
URL www.visionsserviceadventures.com
For more information, see page 1382.

Wilderness Ventures–Ecuador and Galapagos

Wilderness Ventures
Ecuador

General Information Coed travel outdoor program, wilderness program, cultural program, and adventure program established in 1973.
Program Focus Wilderness travel, cultural immersion, leadership skills.
Academics Environmental science.
Special Interest Areas Leadership training, touring.
Wilderness/Outdoors Backpacking, hiking, rafting, white-water trips, wilderness camping.
Trips Cultural, overnight.
Program Information 2 sessions per year. Session length: 3 weeks in June, July, August. Ages: 14–18. 12 participants per session. Cost: $4990. Financial aid available. Participants tour the Galapagos Islands.
Application Deadline Continuous.
Jobs Positions for college students 21 and older.
Contact Mike Cottingham, Director, PO Box 2768, Jackson Hole, Wyoming 83001. Phone: 800-533-2281. Fax: 307-739-1934. E-mail: info@wildernessventures.com.
URL www.wildernessventures.com
For more information, see page 1396.

Youth for Understanding USA–Ecuador

Youth for Understanding USA
Ecuador

General Information Coed residential academic program and cultural program established in 1951. High school or college credit may be earned.
Program Focus Living with a host family, learning about other cultures, and improving language skills.
Academics Spanish language/literature, anthropology, area studies, biology, ecology, intercultural studies, social studies.
Special Interest Areas Homestays.
Wilderness/Outdoors Hiking.
Trips Cultural, day, overnight.
Program Information 1 session per year. Session length: 35–45 days in June, July, August. Ages: 15–18. 10–50 participants per session. Boarding program cost:

Youth for Understanding USA–Ecuador (continued)
$4995. Application fee: $75. Financial aid available. Round-trip domestic and international airfare is included in the tuition.
Application Deadline Continuous.
Contact Admissions Counselor, 6400 Goldsboro Road, Suite 100, Bethesda, Maryland 20817. Phone: 800-TEENAGE (833-6243). Fax: 202-895-1104. E-mail: admissions@us.yfu.org.
URL www.yfu-usa.org
For more information, see page 1414.

EGYPT

BROADREACH Red Sea Scuba Adventure

Broadreach
Egypt

General Information Coed travel outdoor program, cultural program, and adventure program established in 1992.
Program Focus Coed program focusing on scuba diving, advanced and specialty dive training, marine biology, wilderness desert experience, cultural immersion and exploration.
Academics Area studies, environmental science, marine studies.
Arts Photography.
Special Interest Areas Community service, cross-cultural education, field research/expeditions, leadership training, nature study.
Sports Boating, fishing, scuba diving, snorkeling.
Wilderness/Outdoors Hiking, pack animal trips, safari, wilderness camping.
Trips Cultural, overnight.
Program Information 4 sessions per year. Session length: 3–4 weeks in June, July, August. Ages: 15–19. 12–14 participants per session. Cost: $4580.
Application Deadline Continuous.
Contact Carlton Goldthwaife, Director, PO Box 27076, Raleigh, North Carolina 27611-7076. Phone: 888-833-1907. Fax: 919-833-2129. E-mail: info@gobroadreach.com.
URL www.gobroadreach.com
For more information, see page 1010.

ESTONIA

EARTHWATCH INSTITUTE–Baltic Island Wetlands and Wildlife

Earthwatch Institute
Vormsi Island
Estonia

General Information Coed residential outdoor program, cultural program, and adventure program.
Program Focus Establishing the management needs of coastal wet grasslands to restore them.
Academics Ecology, environmental science, science (general).
Special Interest Areas Field research/expeditions, nature study.
Program Information 3 sessions per year. Session length: 12 days in June, July, August. Ages: 16+. 10 participants per session. Boarding program cost: $1995–$2095. Financial aid available. Financial aid for high school students and teachers.
Application Deadline Continuous.
Contact General Information Desk, PO Box 75, Maynard, Massachusetts 01754. Phone: 800-776-0188. Fax: 978-461-2332. E-mail: info@earthwatch.org.
URL www.earthwatch.org

Volunteers for Peace International Work Camp–Estonia

Volunteers for Peace International Work Camps
Tallin
Estonia

General Information Coed residential community service program established in 1981. Specific services available for the hearing impaired and physically challenged. College credit may be earned.
Program Focus International work camps.
Academics Intercultural studies, peace education.
Special Interest Areas Community service, farming, work camp programs.
Sports Swimming.
Trips Cultural, day, overnight.
Program Information Session length: 2–3 weeks in July, August. Ages: 15+. 12–20 participants per session. Boarding program cost: $250–$600.
Application Deadline Continuous.
Contact Peter Coldwell, Director, 1034 Tiffany Road, Belmont, Vermont 05730. Phone: 802-259-2759. Fax: 802-259-2922. E-mail: vfp@vfp.org.
URL www.vfp.org

FIJI

GLOBAL WORKS–CULTURAL EXCHANGE-FIJI ISLANDS-4 WEEKS

GLOBAL WORKS
Fiji

General Information Coed travel community service program, cultural program, and adventure program established in 1988. High school credit may be earned.
Program Focus Environmental and community service and cultural exchange.
Academics Intercultural studies.
Arts Arts and crafts (general), dance, music.
Special Interest Areas Community service, construction, field trips (arts and culture).
Sports Fishing, rugby, scuba diving, snorkeling, soccer, sports (general), swimming, volleyball.
Wilderness/Outdoors Hiking.
Trips Cultural, day, overnight.
Program Information 2 sessions per year. Session length: 28–30 days in June, July. Ages: 14–18. 15–17 participants per session. Cost: $3650. Application fee: $100. Financial aid available. Airfare not included.
Application Deadline Continuous.
Jobs Positions for college students 23 and older.
Contact Erik Werner, Director, 1113 South Allen Street, State College, Pennsylvania 16801. Phone: 814-867-7000. Fax: 814-867-2717. E-mail: info@globalworksinc.com.
URL www.globalworksinc.com

For more information, see page 1136.

RUSTIC PATHWAYS–BIG FIJI EXPLORER

Rustic Pathways
Fiji

General Information Coed travel community service program, cultural program, and adventure program established in 1994.
Special Interest Areas Community service, construction, cross-cultural education, touring.
Sports Bicycling, boating, fishing, kayaking, sailing, scuba diving, snorkeling, swimming.
Wilderness/Outdoors Hiking, outdoor adventure, white-water trips, wilderness camping.
Trips Cultural, day, overnight, shopping.
Program Information 4 sessions per year. Session length: 17 days in June, July, August. Ages: 14–18. 10–15 participants per session. Cost: $2495.
Application Deadline Continuous.
Jobs Positions for college students 18 and older.
Contact Mr. Evan Wells, President, 4121 Erie Street, Willoughby, Ohio 44094. Phone: 440-975-9691. Fax: 440-975-9694. E-mail: evan@rusticpathways.com.
URL www.rusticpathways.com

For more information, see page 1290.

RUSTIC PATHWAYS–DIVER'S DREAM IN THE FIJI ISLANDS

Rustic Pathways
Fiji

General Information Coed residential outdoor program, cultural program, and adventure program established in 1994.
Special Interest Areas Cross-cultural education.
Sports Scuba diving.
Trips Day, overnight, shopping.
Program Information 9 sessions per year. Session length: 10 days in June, July, August. Ages: 14–18. 5–10 participants per session. Boarding program cost: $1165.
Application Deadline Continuous.
Jobs Positions for college students 21 and older.
Contact Mr. Evan Wells, President, 4121 Erie Street, Willoughby, Ohio 44094. Phone: 440-975-9691. Fax: 440-975-9694. E-mail: evan@rusticpathways.com.
URL www.rusticpathways.com

For more information, see page 1290.

RUSTIC PATHWAYS–EXTENDED COMMUNITY SERVICE IN THE FIJI ISLANDS

Rustic Pathways
Fiji

General Information Coed residential community service program and cultural program established in 1994.
Arts Dance.
Special Interest Areas Community service, construction, cross-cultural education, farming, gardening, homestays, nature study.
Sports Boating, swimming.
Trips Cultural, day, overnight, shopping.
Program Information 7 sessions per year. Session length: 24 days in June, July, August. Ages: 14–18. 15–20 participants per session. Boarding program cost: $2485.
Application Deadline Continuous.
Jobs Positions for college students 21 and older.
Contact Mr. Evan Wells, President, 4121 Erie Street, Willoughby, Ohio 44094. Phone: 440-975-9691. Fax: 440-975-9694. E-mail: evan@rusticpathways.com.
URL www.rusticpathways.com

For more information, see page 1290.

RUSTIC PATHWAYS–HIGHLANDS COMMUNITY SERVICE IN FIJI

Rustic Pathways
Fiji

General Information Coed travel community service program and cultural program established in 1994.
Special Interest Areas Community service, construction, cross-cultural education, farming, gardening, homestays, nature study, touring.
Sports Boating, swimming.

RUSTIC PATHWAYS–HIGHLANDS COMMUNITY SERVICE IN FIJI (continued)

Trips Cultural, day, overnight, shopping.
Program Information 8 sessions per year. Session length: 17 days in June, July, August. Ages: 14–18. 10–15 participants per session. Cost: $1685.
Application Deadline Continuous.
Jobs Positions for college students 21 and older.
Contact Mr. Evan Wells, President, 4121 Erie Street, Willoughby, Ohio 44094. Phone: 440-975-9691. Fax: 440-975-9694. E-mail: evan@rusticpathways.com.
URL www.rusticpathways.com

For more information, see page 1290.

RUSTIC PATHWAYS–INTRO TO COMMUNITY SERVICE IN FIJI

Rustic Pathways
Fiji

General Information Coed residential community service program and cultural program established in 1994.
Arts Dance.
Special Interest Areas Community service, construction, cross-cultural education, farming, gardening, homestays, touring.
Sports Boating, swimming.
Wilderness/Outdoors Hiking.
Trips Cultural, day, overnight, shopping.
Program Information 9 sessions per year. Session length: 10 days in June, July, August. Ages: 14–18. 15–20 participants per session. Boarding program cost: $885.
Application Deadline Continuous.
Jobs Positions for college students 21 and older.
Contact Mr. Evan Wells, President, 4121 Erie Street, Willoughby, Ohio 44094. Phone: 440-975-9691. Fax: 440-975-9694. E-mail: evan@rusticpathways.com.
URL www.rusticpathways.com

For more information, see page 1290.

RUSTIC PATHWAYS–LEARN TO DIVE IN THE FIJI ISLANDS

Rustic Pathways
Fiji

General Information Coed travel outdoor program and adventure program established in 1994.
Special Interest Areas Cross-cultural education, touring.
Sports Boating, scuba diving.
Trips Day, overnight, shopping.
Program Information 9 sessions per year. Session length: 10 days in June, July, August. Ages: 14–18. 5–10 participants per session. Cost: $1165.
Application Deadline Continuous.
Jobs Positions for college students 21 and older.
Contact Mr. Evan Wells, President, 4121 Erie Street, Willoughby, Ohio 44094. Phone: 440-975-9691. Fax: 440-975-9694. E-mail: evan@rusticpathways.com.
URL www.rusticpathways.com

For more information, see page 1290.

RUSTIC PATHWAYS–SNAPSHOT OF FIJI

Rustic Pathways
Fiji

General Information Coed travel cultural program and adventure program established in 1994.
Special Interest Areas Cross-cultural education, touring.
Sports Boating, canoeing, fishing, kayaking, sailing, scuba diving, snorkeling, swimming.
Wilderness/Outdoors Outdoor adventure, white-water trips, wilderness camping.
Trips Cultural, day, overnight, shopping.
Program Information 4 sessions per year. Session length: 10 days in June, July, August. Ages: 15–18. 10–15 participants per session. Cost: $1295.
Application Deadline Continuous.
Jobs Positions for college students 21 and older.
Contact Mr. Evan Wells, President, 4121 Erie Street, Willoughby, Ohio 44094. Phone: 440-975-9691. Fax: 440-975-9694. E-mail: evan@rusticpathways.com.
URL www.rusticpathways.com

For more information, see page 1290.

RUSTIC PATHWAYS–SURF THE SUMMER–THE FIJI ISLANDS

Rustic Pathways
Fiji

General Information Coed residential sports camp established in 1994.
Special Interest Areas Cross-cultural education.
Sports Surfing.
Program Information 9 sessions per year. Session length: 10–17 days in June, July, August. Ages: 15–18. 10–15 participants per session. Boarding program cost: $985–$1885.
Application Deadline Continuous.
Jobs Positions for college students 21 and older.
Contact Mr. Evan Wells, President, 4121 Erie Street, Willoughby, Ohio 44094. Phone: 440-975-9691. Fax: 440-975-9694. E-mail: evan@rusticpathways.com.
URL www.rusticpathways.com

For more information, see page 1290.

WORLD HORIZONS INTERNATIONAL–FIJI

World Horizons International
Nokoru Kula
Fiji

General Information Coed residential community service program and cultural program established in 2003.

Program Focus Community service and cross-cultural education.
Special Interest Areas Community service, conservation projects, construction, cross-cultural education.
Sports Scuba diving, snorkeling, swimming.
Wilderness/Outdoors Hiking.
Trips Cultural, day, overnight.
Program Information 1 session per year. Session length: 3–5 weeks in June, July. Ages: 15–18. 10–12 participants per session. Boarding program cost: $4250–$5250. Application fee: $100. Financial aid available. Airfare from Los Angeles included.
Application Deadline Continuous.
Jobs Positions for college students 20 and older.
Contact Mr. Stuart L. Rabinowitz, Executive Director, PO Box 662, Bethlehem, Connecticut 06751. Phone: 800-262-5874. Fax: 203-266-6227. E-mail: worldhorizons@att.net.
URL www.world-horizons.com
For more information, see page 1406.

FINLAND

AFS-USA–Homestay–Finland

AFS-USA
Finland

General Information Coed residential cultural program.
Program Focus Living with a host family, taking part in activities with other teenagers, and a two-day cruise to Sweden.
Academics Finnish language/literature.
Special Interest Areas Homestays.
Trips Cultural, day, overnight.
Program Information 1 session per year. Session length: 6 weeks in June, July, August. Ages: 15–18. 15 participants per session. Boarding program cost: $3865–$4165. Application fee: $75. Financial aid available. International airfare and volunteer homestay support included.
Application Deadline Continuous.
Contact Manager, AFS Info Center, 506 Southwest 6th Avenue, 2nd Floor, Portland, Oregon 97204. Phone: 800-AFS-INFO. Fax: 503-248-4076. E-mail: afsinfo@afs.org.
URL www.afs.org/usa
For more information, see page 974.

FRANCE

AAVE–Bike France

AAVE–America's Adventure Ventures Everywhere
France

General Information Coed travel outdoor program, cultural program, and adventure program established in 1976. Accredited by American Camping Association.
Program Focus Adventure travel.
Academics Area studies, intercultural studies.
Special Interest Areas Leadership training, touring.
Sports Bicycling, swimming.
Wilderness/Outdoors Bicycle trips, canyoneering, mountain biking, rafting, white-water trips.
Trips Cultural, day, overnight.
Program Information 2–3 sessions per year. Session length: 2 weeks in June, July, August. Ages: 14–18. 15 participants per session. Cost: $2288. Financial aid available.
Application Deadline Continuous.
Jobs Positions for college students 21 and older.
Contact Mr. Abbott Wallis, Owner, 2245 Stonecrop Way, Golden, Colorado 80401. Phone: 800-222-3595. Fax: 303-526-0885. E-mail: info@aave.com.
URL www.aave.com
For more information, see page 952.

AAVE–Vivons le Français

AAVE–America's Adventure Ventures Everywhere
Nice
France

General Information Coed travel academic program, outdoor program, cultural program, and adventure program established in 1976. Accredited by American Camping Association.
Program Focus Language immersion and culture.
Academics French language/literature, area studies, intercultural studies.
Special Interest Areas Community service, leadership training, touring.
Sports Horseback riding, snorkeling, swimming.
Wilderness/Outdoors Backpacking, canyoneering, rafting, rock climbing, wilderness camping.
Trips Cultural, day, overnight.
Program Information 2–3 sessions per year. Session length: 30 days in July, August. Ages: 15–18. 13–16 participants per session. Cost: $4400. Financial aid available.
Application Deadline Continuous.
Jobs Positions for college students 21 and older.
Contact Mr. Abbott Wallis, Owner, 2245 Stonecrop Way, Golden, Colorado 80401. Phone: 800-222-3595. Fax: 303-526-0885. E-mail: info@aave.com.
URL www.aave.com
For more information, see page 952.

Abbey Road Overseas Programs–French Immersion and Homestay

Abbey Road Overseas Programs
Antibes
France

General Information Coed travel academic program, arts program, and cultural program established in 2000. Formal opportunities for the academically talented and artistically talented. High school or college credit may be earned.
Program Focus French language, immersion culture, arts and humanities.
Academics French (Advanced Placement), French language/literature, architecture, art history/ appreciation, history, humanities, intercultural studies, precollege program.
Arts Arts, arts and crafts (general), dance, drawing, film, graphic arts, music, theater/drama.
Special Interest Areas Homestays.
Sports Basketball, bicycling, boating, horseback riding, noncompetitive sports, sailing, soccer, swimming, tennis, volleyball, waterskiing, windsurfing.
Wilderness/Outdoors Backpacking, bicycle trips, canoe trips, hiking.
Trips Cultural, day, overnight, shopping.
Program Information 2 sessions per year. Session length: 28–34 days in June, July, August. Ages: 13–19. 30–50 participants per session. Cost: $4700–$5800.
Application Deadline Continuous.
Jobs Positions for college students 21 and older.
Contact Dr. Arthur Kian, Managing Director, 8904 Rangely Avenue, West Hollywood, California 90048. Phone: 888-462-2239. Fax: 866-488-4642. E-mail: info@goabbeyroad.com.
URL www.goabbeyroad.com/

Abbey Road Overseas Programs–French Study Abroad in Cannes

Abbey Road Overseas Programs
France

General Information Coed travel academic program, arts program, and cultural program established in 2000. Formal opportunities for the academically talented and artistically talented. High school or college credit may be earned.
Program Focus French language and culture.
Academics French (Advanced Placement), French language/literature, architecture, art history/ appreciation, intercultural studies.
Arts Music, theater/drama.
Special Interest Areas Cross-cultural education.
Sports Bicycling, boating, canoeing, horseback riding, soccer, swimming, tennis, volleyball, windsurfing.
Trips Cultural, day, overnight, shopping.
Program Information 1–2 sessions per year. Session length: 25–40 days in June, July, August. Ages: 15–19. 30–40 participants per session. Cost: $4900–$6000.
Application Deadline Continuous.
Jobs Positions for college students 21 and older.
Contact Dr. Arthur Kian, Managing Director, 8904 Rangely Avenue, West Hollywood, California 90048. Phone: 888-462-2239. E-mail: info@goabbeyroad.com.
URL www.goabbeyroad.com

Academic Study Associates–Nice

Academic Study Associates, Inc. (ASA)
Nice
France

General Information Coed residential academic program established in 1984. Formal opportunities for the academically talented. High school credit may be earned.
Program Focus Coed program focusing on academic enrichment, French language and culture, art history, literature, and European travel.
Academics French (Advanced Placement), French language/literature, academics (general), art history/ appreciation, history, intercultural studies, precollege program, writing.
Arts Film.
Special Interest Areas Culinary arts, touring.
Sports Basketball, canoeing, parasailing, soccer, swimming, tennis, volleyball.
Wilderness/Outdoors Hiking, white-water trips.
Trips Cultural, day, overnight.
Program Information 1 session per year. Session length: 27–31 days in July, August. Ages: 14–18. 50–75 participants per session. Boarding program cost: $5395. Paris extension: $850.
Application Deadline Continuous.
Jobs Positions for college students 21 and older.
Contact Marcia Evans, President, 10 New King Street, White Plains, New York 10604. Phone: 914-686-7730. Fax: 914-686-7740. E-mail: summer@asaprograms.com.
URL www.asaprograms.com

Academic Study Associates–Royan

Academic Study Associates, Inc. (ASA)
Royan
France

General Information Coed residential academic program established in 1998. Formal opportunities for the academically talented. High school credit may be earned.
Program Focus Cultural and linguistic immersion through daily language instruction and homestay.
Academics French (Advanced Placement), French language/literature, academics (general), intercultural studies, precollege program, writing.
Special Interest Areas Culinary arts, touring.
Sports Aerobics, archery, body boarding, horseback riding, sailing, surfing, swimming, tennis, volleyball, windsurfing.
Trips Cultural, day, overnight.
Program Information 1 session per year. Session length: 4 weeks in June, July. Ages: 14–18. 35–40 participants per session. Boarding program cost: $4995–$5295. Paris extension: $850.
Application Deadline Continuous.
Jobs Positions for college students 21 and older.

Contact Marcia Evans, President, 10 New King Street, White Plains, New York 10604. Phone: 914-686-7730. Fax: 914-686-7740. E-mail: summer@asaprograms.com.
URL www.asaprograms.com

L' Académie de Paris

Oxbridge Academic Programs
Lycée Notre-Dame de Sion
Paris
France

General Information Coed residential academic program and arts program established in 1989. Formal opportunities for the academically talented and artistically talented. High school credit may be earned.
Program Focus Academic and cultural enrichment.
Academics English language/literature, French (Advanced Placement), French language/literature, academics (general), art history/appreciation, business, government and politics, health sciences, history, humanities, law, medicine, philosophy, precollege program, writing.
Arts Arts, creative writing, drawing, painting, photography, theater/drama.
Special Interest Areas Field trips (arts and culture).
Sports Aerobics, basketball, cross-country, soccer, sports (general), tennis.
Trips Cultural, day.
Program Information 1 session per year. Session length: 31 days in July. Ages: 15–18. 150–160 participants per session. Boarding program cost: $5895. Financial aid available.
Application Deadline Continuous.
Contact Ms. Andrea Mardon, Executive Director, Oxbridge Academic Programs, 601 West 110th Street, Suite 7R, New York, New York 10025-2186. Phone: 800-828-8349. Fax: 212-663-8169. E-mail: info@oxbridgeprograms.com.
URL www.oxbridgeprograms.com

For more information, see page 1242.

AFS-USA–Homestay–France

AFS-USA
France

General Information Coed residential academic program and cultural program.
Program Focus 4-week homestay.
Academics French language/literature.
Special Interest Areas Homestays.
Trips Cultural, day, overnight.
Program Information 1 session per year. Session length: 6 weeks in June, July, August. Ages: 15–18. 70 participants per session. Boarding program cost: $5265. Application fee: $75. Financial aid available. International airfare and volunteer homestay support included.
Application Deadline Continuous.
Contact Manager, AFS Info Center, 506 Southwest 6th Avenue, 2nd Floor, Portland, Oregon 97204. Phone: 800-AFS-INFO. Fax: 503-248-4076. E-mail: afsinfo@afs.org.
URL www.afs.org/usa

For more information, see page 974.

Barat Foundation Summer Program in Provence and Paris

Barat Foundation
Provence and Paris
France

General Information Coed travel academic program, arts program, community service program, and cultural program established in 1997. Formal opportunities for the academically talented.

Barat Foundation Summer Program in Provence and Paris

Program Focus French language and cultural immersion.
Academics French (Advanced Placement), French language/literature, architecture, art history/appreciation, humanities, intercultural studies, music.
Arts Arts and crafts (general), film, graphic arts, music, photography, television/video, theater/drama.
Special Interest Areas Culinary arts, field trips (arts and culture).
Sports Aerobics, basketball, bicycling, canoeing, equestrian sports, horseback riding, kayaking, swimming, tennis, volleyball.
Wilderness/Outdoors Bicycle trips, canoe trips, hiking, mountain biking.
Trips Cultural, day, shopping.
Program Information 1–2 sessions per year. Session length: 4–6 weeks in July, August. Ages: 13–19. 30–35 participants per session. Cost: $3495–$9490. Application fee: $100. Financial aid available.
Application Deadline Continuous.
Jobs Positions for college students 21 and older.
Contact Chandri Barat, Executive Director, PO Box 609, Montville, New Jersey 07045. Phone: 973-263-1013. Fax: 973-263-2287. E-mail: info@baratfoundation.org.
URL www.baratfoundation.org

For more information, see page 988.

Blyth Education–Summer Study in Paris and the South of France

Blyth Education
France

General Information Coed travel academic program and cultural program established in 1977. High school credit may be earned.
Program Focus Experience the best of France.
Academics French (Advanced Placement), French language/literature, academics (general), art history/appreciation.
Special Interest Areas Touring.
Sports Swimming, tennis.
Trips Cultural, day, overnight.
Program Information 1 session per year. Session length: 25–30 days in July. Ages: 14–19. 50 participants per session. Cost: 4995 Canadian dollars. Airfare from Toronto or New York to Paris included.
Application Deadline Continuous.
Jobs Positions for college students 25 and older.
Contact Blyth Education, 9 Sultan Street, Suite 300, Toronto, Ontario M5S 1L6, Canada. Phone: 416-960-3552. Fax: 416-960-9506. E-mail: info@blytheducation.com.
URL www.blytheducation.com

Brighton in Cannes

Brighton
Cannes
France

General Information Coed residential academic program established in 2003. Formal opportunities for the academically talented. High school credit may be earned.
Program Focus Language and cultural immersion.
Academics French (Advanced Placement), French language/literature, art history/appreciation.
Special Interest Areas Cross-cultural education, culinary arts, touring.
Sports Basketball, diving, swimming, tennis, volleyball.
Trips Cultural, day, shopping.
Program Information 1 session per year. Session length: 3 weeks in July, August. Ages: 15–19. 30–35 participants per session. Boarding program cost: $4295.
Application Deadline Continuous.
Jobs Positions for college students 21 and older.
Contact David Allen, Executive Director, 101 East Green Street, Suite 14, Pasadena, California 91105. Phone: 626-795-2985. Fax: 626-795-5564. E-mail: info@brightonedge.org.
URL www.brightonedge.org
For more information, see page 1004.

Brighton in Paris

Brighton
Paris
France

General Information Coed residential academic program established in 2003. Formal opportunities for the academically talented. High school credit may be earned.

Brighton in Paris

Program Focus Language and cultural immersion.
Academics French (Advanced Placement), French language/literature, art history/appreciation.
Special Interest Areas Cross-cultural education, culinary arts, homestays, touring.
Sports Bicycling, swimming, tennis.
Trips Cultural, day, shopping.
Program Information 1 session per year. Session length: 23 days in June, July. Ages: 15–19. 30–35 participants per session. Boarding program cost: $4295.
Application Deadline Continuous.
Jobs Positions for college students 21 and older.

Contact David Allen, Executive Director, 101 East Green Street, Suite 14, Pasadena, California 91105. Phone: 626-795-2985. Fax: 626-795-5564. E-mail: info@brightonedge.org.
URL www.brightonedge.org
For more information, see page 1004.

Center for Cultural Interchange–France High School Abroad

Center for Cultural Interchange
France

General Information Coed residential academic program and cultural program established in 1985. High school credit may be earned.
Program Focus High school abroad.
Academics French language/literature, academics (general).
Special Interest Areas Cross-cultural education, homestays.
Trips Cultural, day.
Program Information 2 sessions per year. Session length: 90–300 days in January, February, March, April, May, June, July, August, September, October, November, December. Ages: 15–18. Boarding program cost: $5590–$6990. Financial aid available. Early Bird discount.
Application Deadline Continuous.
Contact Ms. Juliet Jones, Outbound Programs Director, 325 West Huron, Suite 706, Chicago, Illinois 60610. Phone: 866-684-9675. Fax: 312-944-2644. E-mail: info@cci-exchange.com.
URL www.cci-exchange.com
For more information, see page 1060.

Center for Cultural Interchange–France Independent Homestay

Center for Cultural Interchange
France

General Information Coed residential cultural program established in 1985.
Program Focus Independent homestay program.
Academics French language/literature, independent study.
Special Interest Areas Homestays.
Trips Cultural, day.
Program Information Session length: 1–4 weeks in January, February, March, April, May, June, July, August, September, October, November, December. Ages: 16+. Boarding program cost: $890–$1390. Financial aid available.
Application Deadline Continuous.
Contact Ms. Juliet Jones, Outbound Programs Director, 325 West Huron, Suite 706, Chicago, Illinois 60610. Phone: 866-684-9675. Fax: 312-944-2644. E-mail: info@cci-exchange.com.
URL www.cci-exchange.com
For more information, see page 1060.

Center for Cultural Interchange–France Language School

Center for Cultural Interchange
France

General Information Coed residential academic program and cultural program established in 1985. High school or college credit may be earned.
Program Focus Cultural immersion and language study.
Academics French language/literature.
Special Interest Areas Homestays.
Sports Swimming.
Trips Cultural, day.
Program Information 1–50 sessions per year. Session length: 14–90 days in January, February, March, April, May, June, July, August, September, October, November, December. Ages: 14+. Boarding program cost: $2250–$3190. Financial aid available.
Application Deadline Continuous.
Contact Ms. Juliet Jones, Outbound Programs Director, 325 West Huron, Suite 706, Chicago, Illinois 60610. Phone: 866-684-9675. Fax: 312-944-2644. E-mail: info@cci-exchange.com.
URL www.cci-exchange.com
For more information, see page 1060.

Choate Rosemary Hall Summer in Paris

Choate Rosemary Hall
Paris
France

General Information Coed residential academic program and cultural program established in 1975. High school credit may be earned.
Program Focus French language and culture immersion.
Academics French language/literature, art history/appreciation, history, social studies.
Special Interest Areas Cross-cultural education, homestays, touring.
Sports Swimming.
Trips Cultural, day, overnight.
Program Information 1 session per year. Session length: 36 days in June, July. Ages: 14–18. 28 participants per session. Boarding program cost: $6055. Application fee: $60. Financial aid available. Airfare from New York to Paris included.
Application Deadline Continuous.
Contact Mr. Carl Hermey, Co-Director, Summer Program in Paris, 333 Christian Street, Wallingford, Connecticut 06492. Phone: 203-697-2365. Fax: 203-697-2519. E-mail: chermey@choate.edu.
URL www.crhsummerabroad.org
For more information, see page 1070.

Concordia Language Villages–France

Concordia College
France

General Information Coed travel academic program and cultural program established in 1961. Accredited by American Camping Association. High school credit may be earned.
Program Focus French language and culture.
Academics French language/literature.
Arts Arts and crafts (general), music.
Special Interest Areas Cross-cultural education, field research/expeditions, field trips (arts and culture).
Sports Bicycling.
Wilderness/Outdoors Bicycle trips.
Trips Cultural, day, overnight, shopping.
Program Information 1 session per year. Session length: 30 days in June, July. Ages: 14–18. 25–30 participants per session. Cost: $5400. Airfare included.
Application Deadline Continuous.
Jobs Positions for college students 18 and older.
Contact Alex Loehrer, Assistant Director, Public Relations, 901 South Eighth Street, Moorhead, Minnesota 56562. Phone: 218-299-4544. Fax: 218-299-3807.
URL www.ConcordiaLanguageVillages.org

EF International Language School–Nice

EF International Language Schools
21, Rue Meyerbeer
Nice 06000
France

General Information Coed travel academic program and cultural program established in 1984. High school or college credit may be earned.
Program Focus Language and cultural immersion.
Academics French (Advanced Placement), French language/literature.
Special Interest Areas Field trips (arts and culture).
Sports Sports (general).
Wilderness/Outdoors Wilderness/outdoors (general).
Trips Cultural, day, overnight.
Program Information Session length: 2–12 weeks in January, February, March, April, May, June, July, August, September, October, November, December. Ages: 16+. 300–350 participants per session. Call for costs.
Application Deadline Continuous.
Contact Ms. Katie Mahon, Director of Admissions, One Education Street, Cambridge, Massachusetts 02141. Phone: 800-992-1892. Fax: 800-590-1125. E-mail: ils@ef.com.
URL www.ef.com
For more information, see page 1102.

EF International Language School–Nice

EF International Language School–Paris

EF International Language Schools
Paris
France

General Information Coed travel academic program and cultural program established in 1966. High school or college credit may be earned.
Program Focus Language and cultural immersion.
Academics French (Advanced Placement), French language/literature.
Special Interest Areas Field trips (arts and culture).
Trips Cultural, overnight.
Program Information Session length: 14–365 days in January, February, March, April, May, June, July, August, September, October, November, December. Ages: 16+. 200–250 participants per session. Call for costs.
Application Deadline Continuous.

Contact Ms. Katie Mahon, Director of Admissions, One Education Street, Cambridge, Massachusetts 02141. Phone: 800-992-1892. Fax: 800-590-1125. E-mail: ils@ef.com.
URL www.ef.com
For more information, see page 1102.

Encore! Ensemble Theatre Workshop

Learning Theatre, Inc.
Centre International de Valbonne
Sophia-Antipolis
France

General Information Coed residential arts program established in 1997.
Program Focus Study theatre arts, meet students from around the world, attend International Theatre Festival in Avignon, France.
Arts Acting, chorus, creative writing, dance, dance (jazz), dance (modern), graphic arts, music, music (vocal), musical productions, theater/drama.
Trips Cultural, day, overnight.
Program Information 1 session per year. Session length: 4 weeks in July. Ages: 14–18. 36 participants per session. Boarding program cost: $3800. Financial aid available.
Application Deadline April 15.
Contact Ms. Susan Burke, Program Administrator, 4661 Sweetmeadow Circle, Sarasota, Florida 34238. Phone: 941-926-3244. Fax: 941-926-3254. E-mail: susanb@learntheatre.org.
URL www.learntheatre.org

The Experiment in International Living–France, Biking and Homestay

The Experiment in International Living
France

General Information Coed residential outdoor program, cultural program, and adventure program established in 1932.
Program Focus International youth travel, homestay, biking in Brittany.
Academics French language/literature.
Special Interest Areas Homestays, touring.
Sports Bicycling.
Wilderness/Outdoors Bicycle trips.
Trips Cultural, day, overnight.
Program Information 1 session per year. Session length: 4 weeks in July, August. Ages: 14–19. 10–15 participants per session. Boarding program cost: $4500. Financial aid available.
Application Deadline May 1.
Contact Annie Thompson, Enrollment Director, Summer Abroad, Kipling Road, PO Box 676, Brattleboro, Vermont 05302-0676. Phone: 800-345-2929. Fax: 802-258-3428. E-mail: eil@worldlearning.org.
URL www.usexperiment.org
For more information, see page 1116.

The Experiment in International Living–France, Five-Week Art and Adventure in Provence

The Experiment in International Living
France

General Information Coed residential arts program and cultural program established in 1932.

The Experiment in International Living–France, Five-Week Art and Adventure in Provence

Program Focus International youth travel, homestay, exploration of Provence through the arts.
Academics French language/literature, art history/appreciation.
Arts Arts, painting.
Special Interest Areas Homestays, touring.
Trips Cultural, day, overnight.
Program Information 1 session per year. Session length: 5 weeks in July, August. Ages: 14–19. 10–15 participants per session. Boarding program cost: $4500. Financial aid available.
Application Deadline May 1.
Contact Annie Thompson, Enrollment Director, Summer Abroad, Kipling Road, PO Box 676, Brattleboro, Vermont 05302-0676. Phone: 800-345-2929. Fax: 802-258-3428. E-mail: eil@worldlearning.org.
URL www.usexperiment.org
For more information, see page 1116.

The Experiment in International Living–France, Four-Week Brittany Discovery

The Experiment in International Living
France

General Information Coed residential cultural program established in 1932.
Program Focus International youth travel, Brittany culture, homestay.
Academics French language/literature.
Special Interest Areas Homestays, touring.
Trips Cultural, day, overnight.

The Experiment in International Living–France, Four-Week Brittany Discovery (continued)

Program Information 1 session per year. Session length: 4 weeks in July, August. Ages: 14–19. 10–15 participants per session. Boarding program cost: $4000. Financial aid available.
Application Deadline May 1.
Contact Annie Thompson, Enrollment Director, Summer Abroad, Kipling Road, PO Box 676, Brattleboro, Vermont 05302-0676. Phone: 800-345-2929. Fax: 802-258-3428. E-mail: eil@worldlearning.org.
URL www.usexperiment.org

For more information, see page 1116.

The Experiment in International Living–France, Four-Week Homestay and Photography

The Experiment in International Living
France

General Information Coed residential arts program, cultural program, and adventure program established in 1932.
Program Focus International youth travel, homestay.
Academics French language/literature.
Arts Photography.
Special Interest Areas Homestays, touring.
Trips Cultural, day, overnight.
Program Information 1 session per year. Session length: 4 weeks in June, July, August. Ages: 14–17. 10–15 participants per session. Boarding program cost: $4100. Application fee: $75. Financial aid available.
Application Deadline May 1.
Contact Chris Frantz, Deputy Director, EIL–World Learning, PO Box 676, Kipling Road, Brattleboro, Vermont 05302-0676. Phone: 800-345-2929. Fax: 802-258-3428. E-mail: eil@worldlearning.org.
URL www.usexperiment.org

For more information, see page 1116.

The Experiment in International Living–France, Four-Week Homestay and Theatre

The Experiment in International Living
France

General Information Coed residential arts program, cultural program, and adventure program established in 1932.
Program Focus International youth travel, homestay.
Academics French language/literature.
Arts Theater/drama.
Special Interest Areas Homestays, touring.
Trips Cultural, day, overnight.
Program Information 1 session per year. Session length: 4 weeks in June, July, August. Ages: 14–19. 10–15 participants per session. Boarding program cost: $4100. Application fee: $75. Financial aid available.
Application Deadline May 1.
Contact Chris Frantz, Deputy Director, EIL–World Learning, PO Box 676, Kipling Road, Brattleboro, Vermont 05302-0676. Phone: 800-345-2929. Fax: 802-258-3428. E-mail: eil@worldlearning.org.
URL www.usexperiment.org

For more information, see page 1116.

The Experiment in International Living–France, Four-Week Homestay and Travel–Borders

The Experiment in International Living
France

General Information Coed residential outdoor program and cultural program established in 1932.
Program Focus International youth travel, homestay, travel in the Pyrenees.
Academics French language/literature.
Special Interest Areas Homestays, touring.
Wilderness/Outdoors Hiking.
Trips Cultural, day, overnight.
Program Information 1 session per year. Session length: 4 weeks in July, August. Ages: 14–19. 10–15 participants per session. Boarding program cost: $4000. Financial aid available.
Application Deadline May 1.
Contact Annie Thompson, Enrollment Director, Summer Abroad, Kipling Road, PO Box 676, Brattleboro, Vermont 05302-0676. Phone: 800-345-2929. Fax: 802-258-3428. E-mail: eil@worldlearning.org.
URL www.usexperiment.org

For more information, see page 1116.

The Experiment in International Living–France, Four-Week Homestay and Travel through Alps

The Experiment in International Living
France

General Information Coed residential outdoor program, cultural program, and adventure program established in 1932.
Program Focus International youth travel, homestay.
Academics French language/literature.
Special Interest Areas Homestays, touring.
Wilderness/Outdoors Hiking.
Trips Cultural, day, overnight.
Program Information 1 session per year. Session length: 4 weeks in June, July, August. Ages: 14–19. 10–15 participants per session. Boarding program cost: $4000. Application fee: $75. Financial aid available.
Application Deadline May 1.
Contact Chris Frantz, Deputy Director, EIL–World Learning, PO Box 676, Kipling Road, Brattleboro, Vermont 05302-0676. Phone: 800-345-2929. Fax: 802-258-3428. E-mail: eil@worldlearning.org.
URL www.usexperiment.org

For more information, see page 1116.

The Experiment in International Living–France, Homestay, Language Training, and Cooking

The Experiment in International Living
France

General Information Coed residential academic program and cultural program established in 1932.
Program Focus International youth travel, homestay, language classes, cooking.
Academics French language/literature.
Special Interest Areas Culinary arts, homestays, touring.
Trips Cultural, day, overnight.
Program Information 1 session per year. Session length: 5 weeks in July, August. Ages: 14–19. 10–15 participants per session. Boarding program cost: $4800. Financial aid available.
Application Deadline May 1.
Contact Annie Thompson, Enrollment Director, Summer Abroad, Kipling Road, PO Box 676, Brattleboro, Vermont 05302-0676. Phone: 800-345-2929. Fax: 802-258-3428. E-mail: eil@worldlearning.org.
URL www.usexperiment.org

For more information, see page 1116.

The Experiment in International Living–France, Three-Week Camargue Homestay

The Experiment in International Living
France

General Information Coed residential cultural program established in 1932.
Program Focus International youth travel, homestay, Camargue travel.
Academics French language/literature.
Special Interest Areas Homestays.
Trips Cultural, day, overnight.
Program Information 1 session per year. Session length: 3 weeks in July, August. Ages: 14–19. 10–15 participants per session. Boarding program cost: $3400. Financial aid available.
Application Deadline May 1.
Contact Annie Thompson, Enrollment Director, Summer Abroad, Kipling Road, PO Box 676, Brattleboro, Vermont 05302-0676. Phone: 800-345-2929. Fax: 802-258-3428. E-mail: eil@worldlearning.org.
URL www.usexperiment.org

For more information, see page 1116.

The Experiment in International Living–France, Three-Week Homestay and Travel–Borders

The Experiment in International Living
France

General Information Coed residential cultural program and adventure program established in 1932.
Program Focus International youth travel, homestay.
Academics French language/literature.
Special Interest Areas Homestays, touring.
Wilderness/Outdoors Hiking.
Trips Cultural, day, overnight.
Program Information 1 session per year. Session length: 3 weeks in June, July, August. Ages: 14–19. 10–15 participants per session. Boarding program cost: $3600. Application fee: $75. Financial aid available.
Application Deadline May 1.
Contact Chris Frantz, Deputy Director, EIL–World Learning, PO Box 676, Kipling Road, Brattleboro, Vermont 05302-0676. Phone: 800-345-2929. Fax: 802-258-3428. E-mail: eil@worldlearning.org.
URL www.usexperiment.org

For more information, see page 1116.

Global Teen–Learn French in Biarritz

Language Liaison
Biarritz
France

General Information Coed residential academic program. High school or college credit may be earned.
Program Focus French language study and cultural immersion.
Academics French language/literature, area studies, intercultural studies, reading, writing.
Special Interest Areas Field trips (arts and culture), homestays, touring.
Sports Basketball, canoeing, challenge course, golf, horseback riding, surfing, swimming, tennis, volleyball, water polo, waterskiing.
Wilderness/Outdoors Canyoneering, hiking, mountain biking, rafting.
Trips Cultural, day.
Program Information 5–12 sessions per year. Session length: 2–4 weeks in June, July, August. Ages: 13–17. 6–12 participants per session. Boarding program cost: $1877. Application fee: $85. Financial aid available. Additional week: $638.
Application Deadline Continuous.
Contact Nancy Forman, President, PO Box 1772, Pacific Palisades, California 90272. Phone: 800-284-4448. Fax: 310-454-1706. E-mail: learn@languageliaison.com.
URL www.languageliaison.com

For more information, see page 1184.

Global Teen–Learn French in Nice

Language Liaison
Nice
France

General Information Coed residential academic program. High school or college credit may be earned.
Program Focus French language study and cultural immersion.
Academics French language/literature, area studies, intercultural studies, reading, writing.
Special Interest Areas Field trips (arts and culture), homestays.

Global Teen–Learn French in Nice (continued)

Sports Bowling, kayaking, sailing, swimming, tennis, volleyball.
Program Information 8 sessions per year. Session length: 2–4 weeks in June, July, August. Ages: 15–18. 2–15 participants per session. Boarding program cost: $1644–$3246. Application fee: $100. Financial aid available.
Application Deadline Continuous.
Contact Nancy Forman, President, PO Box 1772, Pacific Palisades, California 90272. Phone: 800-284-4448. Fax: 310-454-1706. E-mail: learn@languageliaison.com.
URL www.languageliaison.com
For more information, see page 1184.

GLOBAL TEEN–LEARN FRENCH IN PARIS

Language Liaison
Paris
France

General Information Coed residential academic program. High school or college credit may be earned.
Program Focus French language study and cultural immersion.
Academics French language/literature, area studies, intercultural studies, reading, writing.
Arts Music (vocal), television/video, theater/drama.
Special Interest Areas Field trips (arts and culture).
Sports Archery, basketball, bicycling, volleyball.
Trips Cultural, day.
Program Information 2–8 sessions per year. Session length: 2–3 weeks in July, August. Ages: 15–18. 2–15 participants per session. Boarding program cost: $1904–$2975. Application fee: $85. Financial aid available.
Application Deadline Continuous.
Contact Ms. Nancy Forman, President, PO Box 1772, Pacific Palisades, California 90272. Phone: 800-284-4448. Fax: 310-454-1706. E-mail: learn@languageliaison.com.
URL www.languageliaison.com
For more information, see page 1184.

GLOBAL WORKS–LANGUAGE IMMERSION–FRANCE–4 WEEKS

GLOBAL WORKS
Carcassonne/Corsica
France

General Information Coed travel community service program, cultural program, and adventure program established in 1988. High school credit may be earned.
Program Focus Environmental and community service, language immersion, and cultural exchange.
Academics French language/literature, archaeology, intercultural studies.
Arts Arts and crafts (general).
Special Interest Areas Community service, construction, field trips (arts and culture), homestays.
Sports Bicycling, soccer, sports (general), swimming.
Wilderness/Outdoors Caving, hiking, rafting, rock climbing, white-water trips.
Trips Cultural, day, overnight.
Program Information 2 sessions per year. Session length: 28–30 days in June, July. Ages: 15–18. 15–16 participants per session. Cost: $4150–$4250. Application fee: $100. Financial aid available. Airfare not included.
Application Deadline Continuous.
Jobs Positions for college students 23 and older.
Contact Erik Werner, Director, 1113 South Allen Street, State College, Pennsylvania 16801. Phone: 814-867-7000. Fax: 814-867-2717. E-mail: info@globalworksinc.com.
URL www.globalworksinc.com
For more information, see page 1136.

INTERNATIONAL SUMMER CENTRE AT BIARRITZ

SILC
Biarritz
France

General Information Coed residential and day traditional camp and cultural program established in 1992.
Program Focus Language and culture.
Academics French (Advanced Placement), French language/literature.
Arts Arts and crafts (general), dance.
Special Interest Areas Culinary arts, homestays, nautical skills, touring.
Sports Archery, basketball, bicycling, bicycling (BMX), canoeing, fishing, football, kayaking, sailing, soccer, surfing, swimming, volleyball, windsurfing.
Wilderness/Outdoors Bicycle trips, canoe trips, rafting.
Trips College tours, cultural, day.
Program Information 1–6 sessions per year. Session length: 2–4 weeks in June, July, August. Ages: 12–18. 20–50 participants per session. Boarding program cost: 1000–2600 euros.
Application Deadline Continuous.
Contact Ms. Nathalie Deslande, 32 Rempart de L'Est, Angouleme 16022, France. Phone: 335-45974190. Fax: 335-45942063. E-mail: nathalie.d@silc.fr.
URL www.silc-france.com

INTERNATIONAL SUMMER CENTRE AT CHATEL

SILC
Chalet la Cascade
Thollon les Mémises
France

General Information Coed residential and day traditional camp and cultural program established in 2000.
Program Focus Language and sports activities.
Academics English as a second language, English language/literature, French (Advanced Placement), French language/literature, mathematics.
Arts Arts and crafts (general), dance, music, theater/drama.
Special Interest Areas Nature study, touring.

Sports Archery, bicycling, bicycling (BMX), climbing (wall), equestrian sports, football, horseback riding, soccer, swimming, tennis.
Wilderness/Outdoors Bicycle trips, climbing, hiking, mountain biking, rock climbing.
Trips College tours, cultural, day.
Program Information 1–8 sessions per year. Session length: 2–4 weeks in July, August. Ages: 11–18. 50–100 participants per session. Boarding program cost: 1250–2500 euros.
Application Deadline Continuous.
Contact Ms. Nathalie Deslande, 32 Rempart de L'Est, Angouleme 16022, France. Phone: 335-45974190. Fax: 335-45942063. E-mail: nathalie.d@silc.fr.
URL www.silc-france.com

International Summer Centre at Paris-Brétigny

SILC
Brétigny/Orge 91
France

General Information Coed residential and day traditional camp and cultural program established in 1992.
Program Focus Language and culture.
Academics French (Advanced Placement), French language/literature.
Arts Arts and crafts (general), dance, music, theater/drama.
Special Interest Areas Culinary arts, homestays, touring.
Sports Basketball, boating, football, swimming, tennis.
Trips College tours, cultural, day.
Program Information 1–4 sessions per year. Session length: 2–4 weeks in June, July. Ages: 13–18. 20–50 participants per session. Boarding program cost: 1100–2100 euros.
Application Deadline Continuous.
Contact Ms. Nathalie Deslande, 32 Rempart de L'Est, Angouleme 16022, France. Phone: 335-45974190. Fax: 335-45942063. E-mail: nathalie.d@silc.fr.
URL www.silc-france.com

The Loomis Chaffee Summer in France

The Loomis Chaffee School
Rennes
France

General Information Coed residential academic program and cultural program established in 1992.
Program Focus French language, French history and culture taught in French; daily excursions.
Academics French language/literature, art history/appreciation, history, social studies.
Special Interest Areas Field trips (arts and culture), homestays, touring.
Sports Bicycling, canoeing, kayaking, swimming, tennis.
Wilderness/Outdoors Bicycle trips, canoe trips, hiking.
Trips Cultural, day, overnight.
Program Information 1 session per year. Session length: 33–35 days in June, July. Ages: 14–18. 15–20 participants per session. Boarding program cost: $5200. Application fee: $25. Financial aid available. Airfare from New York included.
Application Deadline Continuous.
Contact Curtis M. Robison, Director, Summer Programs Abroad, The Loomis Chaffee School, 4 Batchelder Road, Windsor, Connecticut 06095. Phone: 860-687-6341. Fax: 860-687-6181. E-mail: curt_robison@loomis.org.
URL www.loomis.org

LSA Amboise, France

Language Studies Abroad, Inc.
Amboise
France

General Information Coed residential cultural program established in 2002. Formal opportunities for the academically talented. High school or college credit may be earned.
Program Focus Language and culture.
Academics French language/literature, intercultural studies, language study.
Special Interest Areas Homestays.
Trips Cultural, day.
Program Information 48 sessions per year. Session length: 13–336 days in January, February, March, April, May, June, July, August, September, October, November, December. Ages: 16+. 5–15 participants per session. Boarding program cost: $893–$2926. Application fee: $100. Financial aid available.
Application Deadline Continuous.
Contact Director, 1801 Highway 50 East, Suite I, Carson City, Nevada 89701. Phone: 800-424-5522. Fax: 775-883-2266. E-mail: info@languagestudiesabroad.com.
URL www.languagestudiesabroad.com

For more information, see page 1186.

LSA Antibes, France

Language Studies Abroad, Inc.
Antibes
France

General Information Coed residential academic program and cultural program established in 1985. Formal opportunities for the academically talented and artistically talented. High school or college credit may be earned.
Program Focus Learning language and culture.
Academics French language/literature, intercultural studies, reading, writing.
Special Interest Areas Homestays.
Sports Boating, sailing, skiing (downhill), swimming, waterskiing, windsurfing.
Wilderness/Outdoors Hiking.
Trips Cultural, day, overnight, shopping.
Program Information 19 sessions per year. Session length: 2–4 weeks in January, February, March, April, May, June, July, August, September, October, November,

LSA Antibes, France (continued)

LSA Antibes, France

December. Ages: 14+. 5–12 participants per session. Boarding program cost: $578–$2310. Application fee: $100. Financial aid available.
Application Deadline Continuous.
Jobs Positions for high school students and college students.
Contact Director, 1801 Highway 50 East, Suite I, Carson City, Nevada 89701. Phone: 800-424-5522. Fax: 775-849-2266. E-mail: info@languagestudiesabroad.com.
URL www.languagestudiesabroad.com
For more information, see page 1186.

LSA Argelés-Gazost, France

Language Studies Abroad, Inc.
France

General Information Coed residential academic program, outdoor program, and cultural program established in 2004. Formal opportunities for the academically talented. High school credit may be earned.
Program Focus Language and culture.
Academics French (Advanced Placement), French language/literature, academics (general), intercultural studies.
Arts Arts and crafts (general).
Sports Swimming, tennis.
Wilderness/Outdoors Mountain biking, rafting.
Trips Cultural, day.
Program Information 1–4 sessions per year. Session length: 2 weeks in July. Ages: 10–18. Boarding program cost: $2500–$5000. Application fee: $100. Financial aid available.
Application Deadline Continuous.
Contact Director, 1801 Highway 50 East, Suite I, Carson City, Nevada 89701. Phone: 800-424-5522. Fax: 775-883-2266. E-mail: info@languagestudiesabroad.com.
URL www.languagestudiesabroad.com
For more information, see page 1186.

LSA Biarritz, France

Language Studies Abroad, Inc.
Biarritz
France

General Information Coed residential academic program and cultural program established in 1995. Formal opportunities for the academically talented and artistically talented. High school or college credit may be earned.
Program Focus Learning language and culture.
Academics French language/literature, intercultural studies, language study.
Special Interest Areas Homestays.
Sports Bicycling, golf, horseback riding, surfing, swimming, waterskiing.
Wilderness/Outdoors Hiking, mountain biking.
Trips Cultural, day, overnight, shopping.
Program Information 1–8 sessions per year. Session length: 14–360 days in January, February, March, April, May, June, July, August, September, October, November, December. Ages: 13+. 4–12 participants per session. Boarding program cost: $1155–$2697. Application fee: $100.
Application Deadline Continuous.
Contact Director, 1801 Highway 50 East, Suite I, Carson City, Nevada 89701. Phone: 800-424-5522. Fax: 775-883-2266. E-mail: info@languagestudiesabroad.com.
URL www.languagestudiesabroad.com
For more information, see page 1186.

LSA Bordeaux, France

Language Studies Abroad, Inc.
Bordeaux
France

General Information Coed residential academic program and cultural program established in 1992. Formal opportunities for the academically talented and artistically talented. High school or college credit may be earned.
Program Focus Learning language and culture.
Academics French (Advanced Placement), French language/literature, intercultural studies, language study.
Special Interest Areas Homestays.
Trips Cultural, day, overnight, shopping.
Program Information 1–26 sessions per year. Session length: 14–360 days in January, February, March, April, May, June, July, August, September, October, November, December. Ages: 17+. 4–8 participants per session. Boarding program cost: $1008–$3687. Application fee: $100.
Application Deadline Continuous.
Jobs Positions for high school students and college students.
Contact Director, 1801 Highway 50 East, Suite I, Carson City, Nevada 89701. Phone: 800-424-5522. Fax: 775-883-2266. E-mail: info@languagestudiesabroad.com.
URL www.languagestudiesabroad.com
For more information, see page 1186.

LSA Cannes, France

Language Studies Abroad, Inc.
Cannes
France

General Information Coed residential academic program and cultural program established in 1931. Formal opportunities for the academically talented and artistically talented. High school or college credit may be earned.
Program Focus Learning language and culture.
Academics French language/literature, art history/appreciation, intercultural studies, reading, writing.
Arts Film.
Special Interest Areas Homestays.
Sports Bicycling (BMX), canoeing, diving, horseback riding, sailing, skiing (downhill), squash, tennis, volleyball, waterskiing, windsurfing.
Wilderness/Outdoors Hiking, mountain biking.
Trips Cultural, day, overnight, shopping.
Program Information 1–26 sessions per year. Session length: 7–360 days in January, February, March, April, May, June, July, August, September, October, November, December. Ages: 16+. 80–160 participants per session. Boarding program cost: $1111–$2885. Application fee: $100.
Application Deadline Continuous.
Contact Director, 1801 Highway 50 East, Suite I, Carson City, Nevada 89701. Phone: 800-424-5522. Fax: 775-883-2266. E-mail: info@languagestudiesabroad.com.
URL www.languagestudiesabroad.com

For more information, see page 1186.

LSA Hyères, France

Language Studies Abroad, Inc.
Hyères
France

General Information Coed residential academic program and cultural program established in 1975. Formal opportunities for the academically talented and artistically talented. High school or college credit may be earned.
Program Focus Learning language and culture.
Academics French (Advanced Placement), French language/literature, intercultural studies, language study.
Special Interest Areas Culinary arts, homestays.
Sports Bicycling, golf, horseback riding, swimming, tennis.
Trips Cultural, day, overnight, shopping.
Program Information 1–26 sessions per year. Session length: 14–360 days in January, February, March, April, May, June, July, August, September, October, November, December. Ages: 11–18. 100–125 participants per session. Boarding program cost: $979–$3476. Application fee: $100.
Application Deadline Continuous.
Contact Director, 1801 Highway 50 East, Suite I, Carson City, Nevada 89701. Phone: 800-424-5522. Fax: 775-883-2266. E-mail: info@languagestudiesabroad.com.
URL www.languagestudiesabroad.com

For more information, see page 1186.

LSA La Rochelle, France

Language Studies Abroad, Inc.
La Rochelle
France

General Information Coed residential cultural program established in 2002. Formal opportunities for the academically talented. High school or college credit may be earned.
Program Focus Language and culture.
Academics French language/literature, intercultural studies, language study.
Special Interest Areas Homestays.
Trips Cultural.
Program Information 1–24 sessions per year. Session length: 2–48 weeks in January, February, March, April, May, June, July, August, September, October, November, December. Ages: 16+. Boarding program cost: $1078–$3639. Application fee: $100. Financial aid available.
Application Deadline Continuous.
Contact Director, 1801 Highway 50 East, Suite I, Carson City, Nevada 89701. Phone: 800-424-5522. Fax: 775-883-2266. E-mail: info@languagestudiesabroad.com.
URL www.languagestudiesabroad.com

For more information, see page 1186.

LSA Nice, France

Language Studies Abroad, Inc.
Nice
France

General Information Coed residential academic program and cultural program established in 1987. Formal opportunities for the academically talented and artistically talented. High school or college credit may be earned.
Program Focus Learning language and culture.
Academics French (Advanced Placement), French language/literature, business, intercultural studies, language study.
Special Interest Areas Culinary arts, homestays.
Trips College tours, cultural, day, overnight, shopping.
Program Information 1–26 sessions per year. Session length: 14–360 days in January, February, March, April, May, June, July, August, September, October, November. Ages: 13+. 80–150 participants per session. Boarding program cost: $1045–$2090. Application fee: $100. Financial aid available.
Application Deadline Continuous.
Jobs Positions for high school students 17 and older and college students 17 and older.
Contact Director, 1801 Highway 50 East, Suite I, Carson City, Nevada 89701. Phone: 800-424-5522. Fax: 775-883-2266. E-mail: info@languagestudiesabroad.com.
URL www.languagestudiesabroad.com

For more information, see page 1186.

LSA Paris, France

Language Studies Abroad, Inc.
Paris
France

General Information Coed residential academic program and cultural program established in 1984. Formal opportunities for the academically talented and artistically talented. High school or college credit may be earned.
Program Focus Learning language and culture.
Academics French (Advanced Placement), French language/literature, business, intercultural studies, language study.
Special Interest Areas Culinary arts, homestays.
Trips College tours, cultural, day, overnight, shopping.
Program Information 1–26 sessions per year. Session length: 14–360 days in January, February, March, April, May, June, July, August, September, October, November, December. Ages: 16+. 50–60 participants per session. Boarding program cost: $825–$4879. Application fee: $100. Financial aid available.
Application Deadline Continuous.
Jobs Positions for high school students 17 and older and college students 17 and older.
Contact Director, 1801 Highway 50 East, Suite I, Carson City, Nevada 89701. Phone: 800-424-5522. Fax: 775-883-2266. E-mail: info@languagestudiesabroad.com.
URL www.languagestudiesabroad.com

For more information, see page 1186.

LSA Tours, France

Language Studies Abroad, Inc.
Tours
France

General Information Coed residential cultural program established in 1975. Formal opportunities for the academically talented. High school or college credit may be earned.
Program Focus Language and culture.
Academics French language/literature, intercultural studies, language study.
Special Interest Areas Homestays.
Trips Cultural.
Program Information 1–26 sessions per year. Session length: 2–36 weeks in January, February, March, April, May, June, July, August, September, October, November, December. Ages: 16+. Boarding program cost: $1089–$3889. Application fee: $100. Financial aid available.
Application Deadline Continuous.
Contact Director, 1801 Highway 50 East, Suite I, Carson City, Nevada 89701. Phone: 800-424-5522. Fax: 775-883-2266. E-mail: info@languagestudiesabroad.com.
URL www.languagestudiesabroad.com

For more information, see page 1186.

Mercersburg Academy Summer Study in France

Mercersburg Academy Summer and Extended Programs
France

General Information Coed travel academic program. High school credit may be earned.
Program Focus Youth enrichment.
Academics French language/literature, art history/appreciation, intercultural studies.
Special Interest Areas Homestays.
Trips Cultural, day, overnight, shopping.
Program Information 1 session per year. Session length: 3 weeks in June, July. Ages: 14–18. 10–15 participants per session. Cost: $3500. Airfare included.
Application Deadline April 30.
Contact Mr. Rick Hendrickson, Director of Summer and Extended Programs, 300 East Seminary Street, Mercersburg, Pennsylvania 17236. Phone: 717-328-6225. Fax: 717-328-9072. E-mail: summerprograms@mercersburg.edu.
URL www.mercersburg.edu

For more information, see page 1210.

The New York Film Academy in Paris

New York Film Academy
La Femis-The French National Film School
Paris
France

General Information Coed residential arts program established in 1992. College credit may be earned.
Program Focus "Total immersion" hands-on filmmaking workshop where students write, direct, shoot, and edit their own 16mm short films.
Arts Acting, creative writing, directing, film, film editing, film lighting, film production, screenwriting, sound design, television/video, theater/drama.
Trips Cultural.
Program Information 2–3 sessions per year. Session length: 1–6 weeks in June, July, August. Ages: 14–17. Boarding program cost: $1500–$6900.
Application Deadline Continuous.
Contact Admissions, 100 East 17th Street, New York, New York 10003. Phone: 212-674-4300. Fax: 212-477-1414. E-mail: film@nyfa.com.
URL www.nyfa.com

For more information, see page 1218.

Overland: Language Study Abroad in France

Overland Travel, Inc.
France

General Information Coed travel academic program and cultural program established in 1985. Accredited by American Camping Association. High school credit may be earned.
Program Focus French language program and cultural exploration of France.

Academics French language/literature.
Special Interest Areas Homestays.
Trips Cultural, day, overnight.
Program Information 2 sessions per year. Session length: 32 days in June, July, August. Ages: 14–18. 8–12 participants per session. Cost: $5995.
Application Deadline Continuous.
Jobs Positions for college students 20 and older.
Contact Ms. Brooks Follansbee, Director, PO Box 31, Williamstown, Massachusetts 01267. Phone: 800-458-0588. Fax: 413-458-5208. E-mail: overland@adelphia.net.
URL www.overlandsummers.com
For more information, see page 1240.

Overland: Paris to the Sea Bicycle Touring

Overland Travel, Inc.
Paris to Nice
France

General Information Coed travel outdoor program, cultural program, and adventure program established in 1985. Accredited by American Camping Association. High school credit may be earned.
Program Focus Exploration of the culture and countryside of France by bicycle.
Special Interest Areas Cross-cultural education, leadership training, touring.
Sports Bicycling.
Wilderness/Outdoors Bicycle trips, outdoor camping, rafting.
Trips Cultural, day.
Program Information 1–2 sessions per year. Session length: 30 days in June, July, August. Ages: 14–18. 8–12 participants per session. Cost: $4795.
Application Deadline Continuous.
Jobs Positions for college students 20 and older.
Contact Ms. Brooks Follansbee, Director, PO Box 31, Williamstown, Massachusetts 01267. Phone: 800-458-0588. Fax: 413-458-5208. E-mail: overland@adelphia.net.
URL www.overlandsummers.com
For more information, see page 1240.

Parsons Summer Intensive Studies–Paris

Parsons School of Design
Paris
France

General Information Coed residential and day arts program established in 1977. Formal opportunities for the artistically talented. College credit may be earned.
Program Focus Studio art and design courses.
Academics Architecture, precollege program.
Arts Drawing, fashion design/production, painting, photography.
Special Interest Areas Career exploration, college planning.
Trips Cultural, day.
Program Information 1 session per year. Session length: 4 weeks in July. Ages: 16+. 90–110 participants per session. Day program cost: $4300. Boarding program cost: $5200.
Application Deadline May 1.
Contact Mr. Roland Schneider, Program Coordinator, main address above. Phone: 212-229-8925. Fax: 212-229-8975. E-mail: summer@newschool.edu.
URL www.parsons.edu/summer

Phillips Exeter Academy French Study Tour

Phillips Exeter Academy
France

General Information Coed travel academic program and cultural program established in 1982.
Program Focus French language and culture.
Academics French language/literature, architecture, art history/appreciation.
Special Interest Areas Homestays.
Sports Bicycling, boating, canoeing, equestrian sports, kayaking, sailing, swimming, tennis, windsurfing.
Wilderness/Outdoors Caving, hiking.
Trips Cultural, day, overnight, shopping.
Program Information 1 session per year. Session length: 5 weeks in June, July, August. Ages: 15–18. 24 participants per session. Cost: $6495. Airfare from Boston included.
Application Deadline Continuous.
Contact Mr. Denis Brochu, Program Director, 20 Main Street, Exeter, New Hampshire 03833-2460. Phone: 603-777-3409. Fax: 603-777-4396.
URL www.exeter.edu

Programs Abroad Travel Alternatives–France

Programs Abroad Travel Alternatives
France

General Information Coed travel academic program and cultural program established in 1996. Formal opportunities for the academically talented. College credit may be earned.
Program Focus Immersion for foreign language students.
Academics French language/literature, art history/appreciation, history, intercultural studies.
Special Interest Areas Cross-cultural education, homestays, touring.
Trips Cultural, day, overnight.
Program Information 2–3 sessions per year. Session length: 9–34 days in March, June, July. Ages: 15+. 1–30 participants per session. Cost: $1500–$4500. Application fee: $90. Participant must be in high school.
Application Deadline Continuous.
Contact Rose Potter, Founder/CEO, 6200 Adel Cove, Austin, Texas 78749. Phone: 888-777-PATA. Fax: 512-282-7076. E-mail: immerse@gopata.com.
URL www.gopata.com
For more information, see page 1248.

Putney Student Travel–Language Learning–France

Putney Student Travel
France

General Information Coed residential academic program and cultural program established in 1951.

Putney Student Travel–Language Learning–France

Program Focus French language immersion. Participants housed in host-family homes and hotels. Enrollment limited to those who are studying French.
Academics French (Advanced Placement), French language/literature, area studies, art history/ appreciation, intercultural studies, linguistics.
Special Interest Areas Homestays.
Sports Bicycling, canoeing, fishing, horseback riding, kayaking, rappelling, skiing (downhill), snorkeling, soccer, swimming, tennis, windsurfing.
Wilderness/Outdoors Bicycle trips, hiking, mountaineering, rock climbing.
Trips Cultural, day, overnight.
Program Information 2–5 sessions per year. Session length: 35–45 days in June, July, August. Ages: 13–18. 16–18 participants per session. Boarding program cost: $7900–$8200. Financial aid available. Airfare from New York included.
Application Deadline Continuous.
Contact Jeffrey Shumlin, Admissions Director, 345 Hickory Ridge Road, Putney, Vermont 05346. Phone: 802-387-5000. Fax: 802-387-4276. E-mail: info@ goputney.com.
URL www.goputney.com
For more information, see page 1276.

Rassias Programs–Arles, France

Rassias Programs
Arles
France

General Information Coed travel academic program and cultural program established in 1985.
Program Focus French Language studies taught in the Rassias method, homestay, and travel in France.
Academics French (Advanced Placement), French language/literature.
Special Interest Areas Homestays, touring.
Sports Bicycling, kayaking, sailing, swimming, tennis.
Trips Cultural, overnight.
Program Information 1 session per year. Session length: 36 days in June, July. Ages: 14–17. 20–22 participants per session. Cost: $6000–$6500. Financial aid available. Airfare included.
Application Deadline Continuous.
Jobs Positions for college students 21 and older.
Contact Bill Miles, Director, PO Box 5456, Hanover, New Hampshire 03755. Phone: 603-643-3007. Fax: 603-643-4249. E-mail: rassias@sover.net.
URL www.rassias.com
For more information, see page 1280.

Rassias Programs–Tours, France

Rassias Programs
Tours
France

General Information Coed travel academic program and cultural program established in 1985.

Rassias Programs–Tours, France

Program Focus French language studies taught in the Rassias Method, homestay, and travel in France.
Academics French (Advanced Placement), French language/literature.
Special Interest Areas Homestays, touring.
Sports Bicycling, kayaking, sailing, swimming, tennis.
Trips Cultural, overnight.
Program Information 1 session per year. Session length: 30 days in June, July. Ages: 14–17. 20–22 participants per session. Cost: $5400–$6400. Financial aid available. Airfare included.

Application Deadline Continuous.
Jobs Positions for college students 21 and older.
Contact Bill Miles, Director, PO Box 5456, Hanover, New Hampshire 03755. Phone: 603-643-3007. Fax: 603-643-4249. E-mail: rassias@sover.net.
URL www.rassias.com
For more information, see page 1280.

SERVICE-LEARNING IN PARIS

International Seminar Series
Paris
France

General Information Coed residential academic program, community service program, and cultural program established in 1998. High school credit may be earned.

Service-Learning in Paris

Program Focus Participants fluent in French, or having strong competencies in French may complete their community service, academic course work, and cultural visits in the native language.
Academics French language/literature, architecture, art history/appreciation, government and politics, writing.
Arts Creative writing.
Special Interest Areas Community service, cross-cultural education, field trips (arts and culture).
Trips Cultural, day.
Program Information 1 session per year. Session length: 25–31 days in July. Ages: 16+. 25–40 participants per session. Boarding program cost: $6000. Financial aid available.
Application Deadline April 15.
Contact John Nissen, Director, PO Box 1212, Manchester, Vermont 05254-1212. Phone: 802-362-5855. Fax: 802-362-5855. E-mail: iss@study-serve.org.
URL www.study-serve.org
For more information, see page 1308.

SUMMER STUDY IN PARIS AT THE AMERICAN UNIVERSITY OF PARIS

Summer Study Programs
Paris
France

General Information Coed residential academic program and cultural program established in 1995. Formal opportunities for the academically talented. High school or college credit may be earned.
Program Focus Pre-college experience including college credits, enrichment classes, SAT preparation, daily cultural excursions and sightseeing in Paris, weekend excursions in France and London, French immersion (for interested students).
Academics American literature, English as a second language, English language/literature, French (Advanced Placement), French language/literature, SAT/ACT preparation, academics (general), architecture, art (Advanced Placement), art history/appreciation, business, communications, computers, ecology, economics, environmental science, government and politics, government and politics (Advanced Placement), history, humanities, journalism, mathematics, music, physics, precollege program, psychology, social science, study skills, writing.
Arts Creative writing, drawing, fabric arts, film, graphic arts, painting, photography, theater/drama.
Special Interest Areas Culinary arts, field trips (arts and culture), touring.
Sports Aerobics, baseball, basketball, bicycling, climbing (wall), football, lacrosse, racquetball, soccer, softball, sports (general), swimming, tennis, volleyball, weight training.
Trips Cultural, day, overnight, shopping.
Program Information 2 sessions per year. Session length: 3–5 weeks in July, August. Ages: 15–18. 150–300 participants per session. Boarding program cost: $4595–$6495. Application fee: $75. Financial aid available.
Application Deadline Continuous.
Jobs Positions for college students 21 and older.
Contact Mr. Bill Cooperman, Executive Director, 900 Walt Whitman Road, Melville, New York 11747. Phone: 800-666-2556. Fax: 631-424-0567. E-mail: precollegeprograms@summerstudy.com.
URL www.summerstudy.com
For more information, see page 1344.

TAFT SUMMER SCHOOL ABROAD–FRANCE

The Taft School
Aix-En-Provence
France

General Information Coed travel academic program established in 1982. Accredited by American Camping Association.
Program Focus The program is designed to completely immerse the student in the people, language, and culture of the country.
Academics French language/literature, art history/appreciation, history, intercultural studies.
Special Interest Areas Homestays, touring.
Trips Cultural, day, overnight, shopping.

Taft Summer School Abroad–France (continued)

Program Information 1 session per year. Session length: 35–40 days in June, July. Ages: 14–18. 10–20 participants per session. Cost: $5600. Application fee: $50. Airfare from New York to Nice included.
Application Deadline April 15.
Contact Ms. Jacqueline Fritzinger, Director, Taft Summer in France, 110 Woodbury Road, Watertown, Connecticut 06795. Phone: 860-945-7951. Fax: 860-945-7859. E-mail: jfritzinger@taftschool.org.
URL www.taftschool.org/summer
For more information, see page 1354.

TASIS Arts and Architecture in the South of France

TASIS The American School in England
Les Tapies, The Ardeche
France

General Information Coed residential arts program established in 2003. Formal opportunities for the artistically talented.
Program Focus Intense arts, photography, architecture.
Academics Architecture, art, art (Advanced Placement).
Arts Painting, photography, printmaking.
Sports Kayaking.
Trips Cultural, day.
Program Information 1 session per year. Session length: 3 weeks in June, July. Ages: 16–21. 16–20 participants per session. Boarding program cost: $3800.
Application Deadline Continuous.
Contact W. Thomas Fleming, US Director, 1640 Wisconsin Avenue NW, Washington, District of Columbia 20007. Phone: 202-965-5800. Fax: 202-965-5816. E-mail: usadmissions@tasis.com.
URL www.tasis.com

Tisch School of the Arts–International High School Program–Paris

New York University
Paris
France

General Information Coed residential academic program, arts program, and cultural program established in 2001. Formal opportunities for the artistically talented. College credit may be earned.
Program Focus Filmmaking, drama/theater, writing, art studies.
Academics French language/literature, intercultural studies.
Arts Acting, creative writing, film, music, theater/drama.
Trips Cultural, day.
Program Information 1 session per year. Session length: 28–30 days in July, August. Ages: 15+. 8–20 participants per session. Boarding program cost: $7645–$8645. Application fee: $50. Financial aid available.
Application Deadline March 7.
Contact Josh Murray, Assistant Director of Recruitment, Special Programs, 721 Broadway, 12th Floor, New York, New York 10003. Phone: 212-998-1500. Fax: 212-995-4610. E-mail: tisch.special.info@nyu.edu.
URL http://specialprograms.tisch.nyu.edu
For more information, see page 1220.

Tufts Summit

Tufts University
Tufts University European Center
Talloires 74290
France

General Information Coed residential academic program and cultural program established in 1993. Formal opportunities for the academically talented.
Program Focus International relations and French, supplemented by homestay with French host families; field trips to international organizations and hikes.
Academics French (Advanced Placement), French language/literature, international relations.
Special Interest Areas Homestays.
Sports Boating, horseback riding, swimming, tennis, volleyball, waterskiing.
Wilderness/Outdoors Hiking.
Trips Cultural, day, overnight.
Program Information 1 session per year. Session length: 28–31 days in July. Ages: 16–19. 25 participants per session. Boarding program cost: $4650–$4800. Application fee: $40. Financial aid available.
Application Deadline March 31.
Contact Christine Woodman, Office Coordinator, 108 Packard Avenue, Tufts European Center, Medford, Massachusetts 02155. Phone: 617-627-3290. Fax: 617-627-3457. E-mail: france@tufts.edu.
URL ase.tufts.edu/frenchalps

University of Chicago–ChicaGO! The Traveling Academy

University of Chicago
Paris
France

General Information Coed travel academic program and cultural program established in 1999. Formal opportunities for the academically talented. College credit may be earned.
Program Focus Interdisciplinary civilization studies.
Academics French language/literature, anthropology, archaeology, architecture, art history/appreciation, classical languages/literatures, geography, history, humanities, intercultural studies, philosophy, religion, social studies, writing.
Trips Cultural, day.
Program Information 1 session per year. Session length: 3 weeks in July. Ages: 15–18. 10–15 participants per session. Cost: $6895. Application fee: $40–$55. Financial aid available.
Application Deadline April 15.

Contact Ms. Valerie Huston, Secretary, Summer Session Office, Graham School of General Studies, The University of Chicago, 1427 East 60th Street, Chicago, Illinois 60637. Phone: 773-702-6033. Fax: 773-702-6814. E-mail: uc-summer@uchicago.edu.
URL summer.uchicago.edu/
For more information, see page 1360.

Village Camps–France

Village Camps
La Base du Cros
Salavas 07150
France

General Information Coed residential traditional camp and outdoor program established in 1972.
Program Focus Canoeing, kayak, caving, climbing, and French language.
Academics French language/literature, ecology, linguistics.
Arts Arts and crafts (general), drawing, jewelry making, painting.
Special Interest Areas Campcraft, nature study.
Sports Aerobics, basketball, bicycling, bicycling (BMX), canoeing, climbing (wall), kayaking, rappelling, soccer, softball, swimming, tennis, volleyball.
Wilderness/Outdoors Bicycle trips, canoe trips, caving, hiking, mountain biking, orienteering, outdoor adventure, rafting, rock climbing, white-water trips, wilderness camping.
Trips Cultural, day, overnight, shopping.
Program Information 2 sessions per year. Session length: 13 days in July, August. Ages: 10–16. 30–60 participants per session. Boarding program cost: $1680–$1875.
Application Deadline Continuous.
Jobs Positions for college students 21 and older.
Contact Roger Ratner, Director, 14 Rue de la Morâche, Nyon 1260, Switzerland. Phone: 41-22-990-9400. Fax: 41-22-990-9494. E-mail: camps@villagecamps.ch.
URL www.villagecamps.com
For more information, see page 1380.

Volunteers for Peace International Work Camp–France

Volunteers for Peace International Work Camps
Paris
France

General Information Coed residential community service program established in 1981. Specific services available for the hearing impaired and physically challenged. College credit may be earned.
Program Focus International work camps.
Academics Intercultural studies, peace education.
Special Interest Areas Community service, construction, gardening, work camp programs.
Trips Cultural, day, overnight.
Program Information Session length: 2–3 weeks in January, June, July, August, September, October, November, December. Ages: 15+. 12–20 participants per session. Boarding program cost: $250–$600.
Application Deadline Continuous.
Contact Peter Coldwell, Director, 1034 Tiffany Road, Belmont, Vermont 05730. Phone: 802-259-2759. Fax: 802-259-2922. E-mail: vfp@vfp.org.
URL www.vfp.org

Windsor Mountain: Crossroads France

Interlocken at Windsor Mountain
France

General Information Coed travel academic program, outdoor program, community service program, cultural program, and adventure program established in 1973. Accredited by American Camping Association.
Program Focus Live and travel with French students while exploring French culture and outdoors.
Academics French (Advanced Placement), French language/literature, intercultural studies.
Special Interest Areas Campcraft, community service, culinary arts, nature study.
Sports Bicycling, climbing (wall), rappelling, ropes course.
Wilderness/Outdoors Backpacking, bicycle trips, hiking, mountain biking, mountaineering, orienteering, outdoor adventure, rock climbing, wilderness camping.
Program Information 1 session per year. Session length: 3 weeks in July. Ages: 13–15. 12–15 participants per session. Cost: $3300–$3700. Financial aid available.
Application Deadline Continuous.
Jobs Positions for high school students 18 and older and college students 18 and older.
Contact Tom Herman, Marketing Director, 19 Interlocken Way, Windsor, New Hampshire 03244. Phone: 603-478-3166 Ext.20. Fax: 603-478-5260. E-mail: mail@windsormountain.org.
URL www.windsormountain.org/xrds
For more information, see page 1162.

Woodberry Forest Summer School–France

Woodberry Forest School
France

General Information Coed residential academic program established in 1922. Formal opportunities for the academically talented. High school credit may be earned.
Academics French language/literature, academics (general).
Sports Volleyball.
Trips Cultural, overnight.
Program Information 1 session per year. Session length: 6 weeks in July. Ages: 12–17. 5–20 participants per session. Boarding program cost: $5570. Financial aid available.
Application Deadline Continuous.

Woodberry Forest Summer School–France (continued)

Contact Dr. W. David McRae, Director of Summer Programs, 354 Woodberry Forest Street, Woodberry Forest, Virginia 22989. Phone: 540-672-6047. Fax: 540-672-9076. E-mail: wfs_summer@woodberry.org.
URL www.woodberry.org
For more information, see page 1402.

YOUTH FOR UNDERSTANDING USA–FRANCE

Youth for Understanding USA
France

General Information Coed residential academic program and cultural program established in 1951. High school or college credit may be earned.

Youth for Understanding USA–France

Program Focus Living with a host family, learning about other cultures, and improving French language skills.
Academics French language/literature, area studies, intercultural studies, social studies.
Special Interest Areas Field research/expeditions, homestays, touring.
Sports Bicycling, swimming, volleyball.
Trips Cultural, day, overnight, shopping.
Program Information 1 session per year. Session length: 35–45 days in June, July. Ages: 15–18. 10–50 participants per session. Boarding program cost: $7195. Application fee: $75. Financial aid available. Round-trip domestic and international airfare is included in the tuition.
Application Deadline Continuous.
Contact Admissions Counselor, 6400 Goldsboro Road, Suite 100, Bethesda, Maryland 20817. Phone: 800-TEENAGE (833-6243). Fax: 202-895-1104. E-mail: admissions@us.yfu.org.
URL www.yfu-usa.org
For more information, see page 1414.

FRENCH POLYNESIA

ACTIONQUEST: TAHITI AND FRENCH POLYNESIAN ISLAND VOYAGES

ActionQuest
French Polynesia

General Information Coed travel outdoor program, cultural program, and adventure program established in 1986.
Program Focus Sailing and land exploration of Tahiti and the surrounding French Polynesian Islands.
Academics Intercultural studies, marine studies.
Special Interest Areas Community service, leadership training, nature study, nautical skills, team building, touring.
Sports Bicycling, horseback riding, sailing, scuba diving, snorkeling.
Wilderness/Outdoors Hiking.
Trips Cultural, day, overnight.
Program Information 2 sessions per year. Session length: 3 weeks in June, July, August. Ages: 15–19. 10 participants per session. Cost: $4470.
Application Deadline Continuous.
Contact James Stoll, Director, PO Box 5517, Sarasota, Florida 34277. Phone: 800-317-6789. Fax: 941-924-6075. E-mail: info@actionquest.com.
URL www.actionquest.com
For more information, see page 964.

GERMANY

AMERICAN ASSOCIATION OF TEACHERS OF GERMAN, GERMAN SUMMER STUDY PROGRAM

American Association of Teachers of German, Inc.
Germany

General Information Coed residential academic program and cultural program established in 1970.
Program Focus German language and culture through homestays, academics, and travel.
Academics German language/literature.
Trips Cultural, day, overnight.
Program Information 10 sessions per year. Session length: 3 weeks in June, July. Ages: 15–18. 12–15 participants per session. Boarding program cost: $2500–$2700. Financial aid available. Airfare included.
Application Deadline March 1.
Contact Ms. Helene Zimmer-Loew, Executive Director, 112 Haddontowne Court, #104, Cherry Hill, New Jersey 08034. Phone: 856-795-5553. Fax: 856-795-9398. E-mail: headquarters@aatg.org.
URL www.aatg.org

Center for Cultural Interchange–Germany High School Abroad

Center for Cultural Interchange
Germany

General Information Coed residential academic program and cultural program established in 1985. High school credit may be earned.
Program Focus High school abroad in Germany, cultural immersion.
Academics German language/literature, academics (general), mathematics, music, philosophy, physics, science (general), social science.
Special Interest Areas Cross-cultural education, homestays.
Trips Cultural, day.
Program Information 2 sessions per year. Session length: 90–300 days in January, February, March, April, May, June, July, August, September, October, November, December. Ages: 15–18. Boarding program cost: $4490–$5690. Financial aid available. Early Bird discount.
Application Deadline Continuous.
Contact Ms. Juliet Jones, Outbound Programs Director, 325 West Huron, Suite 706, Chicago, Illinois 60610. Phone: 866-684-9675. Fax: 312-944-2644. E-mail: info@cci-exchange.com.
URL www.cci-exchange.com
For more information, see page 1060.

Center for Cultural Interchange–Germany Independent Homestay

Center for Cultural Interchange
Germany

General Information Coed residential cultural program established in 1985.
Program Focus Cultural immersion.
Academics German language/literature, independent study.
Special Interest Areas Homestays.
Trips Cultural, day.
Program Information Session length: 7–30 days in January, February, March, April, May, June, July, August, September, October, November, December. Ages: 16+. Boarding program cost: $890–$1350. Financial aid available.
Application Deadline Continuous.
Contact Ms. Juliet Jones, Outbound Programs Director, 325 West Huron, Suite 706, Chicago, Illinois 60610. Phone: 866-684-9675. Fax: 312-944-2644. E-mail: info@cci-exchange.com.
URL www.cci-exchange.com
For more information, see page 1060.

Center for Cultural Interchange–Germany Language School

Center for Cultural Interchange
Germany

General Information Coed residential academic program and cultural program established in 1985. High school or college credit may be earned.
Program Focus Cultural immersion and language study.
Academics German language/literature.
Special Interest Areas Homestays.
Trips Cultural, day.
Program Information 1–50 sessions per year. Session length: 14–90 days in January, February, March, April, May, June, July, August, September, October, November, December. Ages: 17+. Boarding program cost: $2090–$2590. Financial aid available.
Application Deadline Continuous.
Contact Ms. Juliet Jones, Outbound Programs Director, 325 West Huron, Suite 706, Chicago, Illinois 60610. Phone: 866-684-9675. Fax: 812-944-2644. E-mail: info@cci-exchange.com.
URL www.cci-exchange.com
For more information, see page 1060.

Concordia Language Villages–Germany

Concordia College
Germany

General Information Coed residential academic program and cultural program established in 1961. Accredited by American Camping Association. Formal opportunities for the academically talented. High school credit may be earned.
Program Focus German language and culture.
Academics German language/literature.
Arts Arts and crafts (general), music.
Special Interest Areas Cross-cultural education, field research/expeditions, field trips (arts and culture).
Sports Bicycling.
Wilderness/Outdoors Bicycle trips.
Trips Cultural, day, overnight, shopping.
Program Information 1 session per year. Session length: 30 days in July. Ages: 14–18. 25–30 participants per session. Boarding program cost: $5400. Airfare included.
Application Deadline Continuous.
Jobs Positions for college students 18 and older.
Contact Alex Loehrer, Assistant Director, Public Relations, 901 South Eighth Street, Moorhead, Minnesota 56562. Phone: 218-299-4544. Fax: 218-299-3807.
URL www.ConcordiaLanguageVillages.org

EF International Language School–Munich

EF International Language Schools
Herzogstrasse 36
Munich 80803
Germany

General Information Coed travel academic program and cultural program established in 1987. High school or college credit may be earned.
Program Focus Language and cultural immersion.
Academics German (Advanced Placement), German language/literature.
Special Interest Areas Field trips (arts and culture).
Sports Sports (general).
Wilderness/Outdoors Wilderness/outdoors (general).
Trips Cultural, day, overnight.
Program Information Session length: 14–365 days in January, February, March, April, May, June, July, August, September, October, November, December. Ages: 16+. 100–150 participants per session. Call for costs.
Application Deadline Continuous.
Contact Ms. Katie Mahon, Director of Admissions, One Education Street, Cambridge, Massachusetts 02141. Phone: 800-992-1892. Fax: 800-590-1125. E-mail: ils@ef.com.
URL www.ef.com

For more information, see page 1102.

The Experiment in International Living–Germany, Four-Week Homestay, Travel, Community Service

The Experiment in International Living
Germany

General Information Coed residential community service program, cultural program, and adventure program established in 1932.
Program Focus International youth travel, homestay.
Academics German language/literature.
Special Interest Areas Community service, homestays, touring.
Trips Cultural, day, overnight.
Program Information 1 session per year. Session length: 4 weeks in June, July, August. Ages: 14–19. 10–15 participants per session. Boarding program cost: $4000. Application fee: $75. Financial aid available.
Contact Mr. Chris Frantz, Deputy Director, EIL–World Learning, PO Box 676, Kipling Road, Brattleboro, Vermont 05302-0676. Phone: 800-345-2929. Fax: 802-258-3428. E-mail: eil@worldlearning.org.
URL www.usexperiment.org

For more information, see page 1116.

Global Teen–German in Bavaria

Language Liaison
Holtzkirchen, Bavaria
Germany

General Information Coed residential academic program. High school credit may be earned.
Program Focus German language study and cultural immersion.
Academics German language/literature, area studies, intercultural studies, reading, writing.
Arts Television/video.
Special Interest Areas Field trips (arts and culture), touring.
Sports Horseback riding, sailing, squash, swimming, tennis.
Trips Cultural, day, shopping.
Program Information 2–8 sessions per year. Session length: 2 weeks in June, July, August. Ages: 12–17. 12 participants per session. Boarding program cost: $1799–$2547. Application fee: $85. Financial aid available. Additional week: $745.
Application Deadline Continuous.
Contact Nancy Forman, President, PO Box 1772, Pacific Palisades, California 90272. Phone: 800-284-4448. Fax: 310-454-1706. E-mail: learn@languageliaison.com.
URL www.languageliaison.com

For more information, see page 1184.

Global Teen–German Plus Web Design, Video/Theatre in Berlin

Language Liaison
Loewenstein
Berlin
Germany

General Information Coed residential academic program and arts program. High school or college credit may be earned.
Program Focus German language study, web design, video and theatre.
Academics German language/literature, Web page design, area studies, intercultural studies, reading, writing.
Arts Film production, television/video, theater/drama.
Special Interest Areas Field trips (arts and culture).
Sports Badminton, tennis, volleyball.
Trips Cultural, day.
Program Information 2–12 sessions per year. Session length: 2–4 weeks in June, July, August. Ages: 12+. 12 participants per session. Boarding program cost: $1611–$2284. Application fee: $85. Financial aid available. Additional week: $679; cultural events: 25 euros.
Application Deadline Continuous.
Contact Ms. Nancy Forman, President, PO Box 1772, Pacific Palisades, California 90272. Phone: 800-284-4448. Fax: 310-454-1706. E-mail: learn@languageliaison.com.
URL www.languageliaison.com

For more information, see page 1184.

Global Teen–German Summer Camp in Potsdam

Language Liaison
Potsdam
Germany

General Information Coed residential academic program established in 1994.
Program Focus German language study and cultural immersion camp on Lake Schwielowsee.
Academics German language/literature, area studies, intercultural studies, reading, writing.
Special Interest Areas Field trips (arts and culture).
Trips Cultural, day, shopping.
Program Information 5 sessions per year. Session length: 2–3 weeks in July, August. Ages: 14–17. 2–12 participants per session. Boarding program cost: $1898–$2293. Application fee: $85. Financial aid available.
Application Deadline Continuous.
Contact Ms. Nancy Forman, Director, PO Box 1772, Pacific Palisades, California 90272. Phone: 800-284-4448. Fax: 310-454-1706. E-mail: learn@languageliaison.com.
URL www.languageliaison.com
For more information, see page 1184.

Global Teen–Learn German in Berlin, Ages 12-15 on Lake Schmockwitz

Language Liaison
Lake Schmockwitz
Berlin
Germany

General Information Coed residential academic program established in 1983. High school or college credit may be earned.
Program Focus German language study and cultural immersion.
Academics German language/literature, area studies, intercultural studies, reading, writing.
Arts Arts and crafts (general), dance, juggling, television/video, theater/drama.
Special Interest Areas Field trips (arts and culture), touring.
Sports Bicycling, football, rowing (crew/sculling), sailing, swimming, tennis, volleyball.
Trips Cultural.
Program Information 3 sessions per year. Session length: 2–3 weeks in June, July, August. Ages: 12–15. 2–12 participants per session. Boarding program cost: $1657–$2356. Application fee: $85. Financial aid available. Additional week: $699; sailing and tennis lessons extra.
Application Deadline Continuous.
Contact Nancy Forman, President, PO Box 1772, Pacific Palisades, California 90272. Phone: 800-284-4448. Fax: 310-454-1706. E-mail: learn@languageliaison.com.
URL www.languageliaison.com
For more information, see page 1184.

Global Teen–Learn German in Berlin-City Centre, Ages 16-19

Language Liaison
City Centre
Berlin
Germany

General Information Coed residential academic program established in 1983. High school or college credit may be earned.
Program Focus German language study and cultural immersion.
Academics German language/literature, area studies, intercultural studies, reading, writing.
Arts Dance, television/video.
Special Interest Areas Field trips (arts and culture), touring.
Sports Bowling, in-line skating, rowing (crew/sculling), swimming.
Trips Cultural.
Program Information 3 sessions per year. Session length: 2–3 weeks in June, July, August. Ages: 16–19. 2–12 participants per session. Boarding program cost: $1845–$2620. Application fee: $85. Financial aid available. Additional week: $782.
Application Deadline Continuous.
Contact Ms. Nancy Forman, President, PO Box 1772, Pacific Palisades, California 90272. Phone: 800-284-4448. Fax: 310-454-1706. E-mail: learn@languageliaison.com.
URL www.languageliaison.com
For more information, see page 1184.

Global Teen Summer Sports Camp in Berlin

Language Liaison
Blossin, Lake Wolzig
Berlin
Germany

General Information Coed residential traditional camp, academic program, and sports camp. High school or college credit may be earned.
Program Focus German language study, sports, and camp activities.
Academics German language/literature, area studies, intercultural studies, reading, writing.
Special Interest Areas Field trips (arts and culture).
Sports Badminton, bicycling, canoeing, sailing, soccer, sports (general), surfing, volleyball.
Wilderness/Outdoors Climbing.
Trips Cultural, day.
Program Information 9 sessions per year. Session length: 2 weeks in June, July, August. Ages: 12–17. 12 participants per session. Boarding program cost: $1980–$3821. Application fee: $85. Financial aid available. Additional night: $70; sailing course/license: $250; cultural activities: 25 euros.
Application Deadline Continuous.

Global Teen Summer Sports Camp in Berlin (continued)

Contact Nancy Forman, President, PO Box 1772, Pacific Palisades, California 90272. Phone: 800-284-4448. Fax: 310-454-1706. E-mail: learn@languageliaison.com.

URL www.languageliaison.com

For more information, see page 1184.

GLS Bavarian Summer School

GLS German Language School Berlin
c/o Sprachzentrum Sued–Marktplatz 20
Holzbirchen 83607
Germany

General Information Coed residential academic program established in 2000. High school credit may be earned.
Program Focus German language classes and excursions in Bavaria.
Academics German language/literature.
Special Interest Areas Touring.
Wilderness/Outdoors Hiking, outdoor adventure.
Trips Cultural, day, shopping.
Program Information 10 sessions per year. Session length: 10–20 days in June, July, August. Ages: 12–17. 100 participants per session. Boarding program cost: 1100 euros.
Application Deadline Continuous.
Contact Barbara Jaeschke, Managing Director, Kolonnenstrasse 26, Berlin 10829, Germany. Phone: 49-30-780089-24. Fax: 49-30-787-4192. E-mail: barbara.jaeschke@gls-berlin.com.
URL www.german-courses.com

GLS Berlin Summer School

GLS German Language School Berlin
Jugendbildungstaelte
Kaubstrasse 9-10
Berlin 10713
Germany

General Information Coed residential academic program established in 1998.
Program Focus German language classes and excursions.
Academics German language/literature.
Special Interest Areas Touring.
Trips Cultural, day, shopping.
Program Information 10 sessions per year. Session length: 10–20 days in July, August. Ages: 16–19. 60 participants per session. Boarding program cost: 1180 euros.
Application Deadline Continuous.
Contact Barbara Jaeschke, Managing Director, Kolonnenstrasse 26, Berlin 10829, Germany. Phone: 49-30-780089-24. Fax: 49-30-787-4192. E-mail: barbara.jaeschke@gls-berlin.com.
URL www.german-courses.com

GLS Potsdam Summer School

GLS German Language School Berlin
c/o Maerkisches Gildehaus
Schwielowsee Str. 58
Berlin-Potsdam 14584
Germany

General Information Coed residential academic program established in 2001.
Program Focus German language courses and excursions.
Academics German language/literature.
Special Interest Areas Touring.
Wilderness/Outdoors Bicycle trips, canoe trips, outdoor adventure.
Trips Cultural, day, shopping.
Program Information 10 sessions per year. Session length: 10–20 days in June, July, August. Ages: 14–17. 80 participants per session. Boarding program cost: 1250 euros.
Application Deadline Continuous.
Contact Barbara Jaeschke, Managing Director, Kolonnenstrasse 26, Berlin 10829, Germany. Phone: 49-30780089-24. Fax: 49-30-787 4192. E-mail: barbara.jaeschke@gls-berlin.com.
URL www.german-courses.com

GLS Sports and Language Camp Inzell

GLS German Language School Berlin
BLSV Jugendferiendorf
Holzen 4-6
Inzell, Bavaria 83334
Germany

General Information Coed residential academic program and sports camp established in 2002.
Program Focus German language classes and sport activities in Bavaria.
Academics German language/literature.
Sports Sports (general).
Wilderness/Outdoors Backpacking, bicycle trips, hiking, mountaineering, outdoor adventure, wilderness camping.
Trips Cultural, day, shopping.
Program Information 10 sessions per year. Session length: 2–4 weeks in July, August. Ages: 10–16. 100 participants per session. Boarding program cost: 1250 euros.
Application Deadline Continuous.
Contact Barbara Jaeschke, Managing Director, Kolonnenstrasse 26, Berlin 10829, Germany. Phone: 49-30-780-089-0. Fax: 49-30-787-4192. E-mail: barbara.jaeschke@gls-berlin.com.
URL www.german-courses.com

GLS Summer Camp Blossin

GLS German Language School Berlin
Jugenbildungszentrum Blossin e. V., Waldweg 10
Blossin, Brandenburg 15754
Germany

General Information Coed residential traditional camp and academic program established in 2003.
Program Focus German language classes and water sports.
Academics German language/literature.
Sports Canoeing, rowing (crew/sculling), sailing, sports (general), swimming, volleyball.
Wilderness/Outdoors Bicycle trips, canoe trips, outdoor adventure.
Trips Cultural, day, shopping.
Program Information 10 sessions per year. Session length: 10–20 days in June, July, August. Ages: 12–17. 80–100 participants per session. Boarding program cost: 1100–1400 euros.
Application Deadline Continuous.
Contact Ms. Marion Feuchtenberger, Director of Studies, Kolonnestrasse 26, Berlin 10829, Germany. Phone: 49-30-780089-0. Fax: 49-30-787-4192. E-mail: germancourses@gls-berlin.com.
URL www.german-courses.com

GLS Summer Camp Loewenstein

GLS German Language School Berlin
Jugenbildungsstaette Kurt Loewenstein
Freienwalder Chaussee 8-10
Werftpfuhl, Brandenburg 16356
Germany

General Information Coed residential traditional camp and academic program established in 2003.
Program Focus German language classes and arts.
Academics German language/literature.
Arts Arts, television/video, theater/drama.
Wilderness/Outdoors Backpacking, bicycle trips, canoe trips.
Trips Cultural, day, shopping.
Program Information 10 sessions per year. Session length: 10–20 days in June, July, August. Ages: 12–17. 60–80 participants per session. Boarding program cost: 900–1100 euros.
Application Deadline Continuous.
Contact Ms. Marion Feuchturberger, Director of Studies, Kolonnenstrasse 26, Berlin 10829, Germany. Phone: 49-30-780089-0. Fax: 49-30-787-4192. E-mail: germancourses@gls-berlin.com.
URL www.german-courses.com

GLS Summer Camp Schmoeckwitz

GLS German Language School Berlin
Teikyo University
Schmoeckwitzer Damm
Berlin-Schmoeckwitz 12527
Germany

General Information Coed residential traditional camp and academic program established in 1994.
Program Focus German language classes.
Academics German language/literature.
Sports Basketball, bicycling (BMX), boating, soccer, swimming, tennis.
Trips Cultural, day, shopping.
Program Information 10 sessions per year. Session length: 10–20 days in June, July, August. Ages: 8–15. 120 participants per session. Boarding program cost: 1030 euros.
Application Deadline Continuous.
Contact Ms. Gesine Schaefer, Director of Studies, Kolonnenstrasse 26, Berlin 10829, Germany. Phone: 49-30-780089-0. Fax: 49-30-7874192. E-mail: info@gls-berlin.com.
URL www.german-courses.com

LSA Berlin, Germany

Language Studies Abroad, Inc.
Berlin
Germany

General Information Coed residential academic program and cultural program established in 1983. Formal opportunities for the academically talented and artistically talented. High school or college credit may be earned.
Program Focus Learning language and culture.
Academics German language/literature, business, history, intercultural studies, journalism, language study.
Arts Arts and crafts (general), batiking, dance, dance (jazz), music, photography, theater/drama.
Special Interest Areas Homestays.
Sports Basketball, football, swimming, volleyball.
Trips College tours, cultural, day, overnight, shopping.
Program Information 4–26 sessions per year. Session length: 14–360 days in January, February, March, April, May, June, July, August, September, October, November, December. Ages: 8+. 90–150 participants per session. Boarding program cost: $1300–$2120. Application fee: $100. Financial aid available. Average of 8 students per course.
Application Deadline Continuous.
Jobs Positions for high school students 18 and older and college students 18 and older.
Contact Director, 1801 Highway 50 East, Suite I, Carson City, Nevada 89701. Phone: 800-424-5522. Fax: 775-883-2266. E-mail: info@langaugestudiesabroad.com.
URL www.languagestudiesabroad.com

For more information, see page 1186.

LSA Blossin, Germany

Language Studies Abroad, Inc.
Blossin
Germany

General Information Coed residential academic program and cultural program established in 2000. Formal opportunities for the academically talented. High school or college credit may be earned.
Program Focus Language and culture.
Academics German language/literature, academics (general), intercultural studies.
Wilderness/Outdoors Mountaineering.
Trips Cultural, day.

LSA Blossin, Germany (continued)
Program Information 1–3 sessions per year. Session length: 2–6 weeks in June, July, August. Ages: 12–17. Boarding program cost: $1600–$3200. Application fee: $100. Financial aid available.
Application Deadline Continuous.
Contact Director, 1801 Highway 50 East, Suite I, Carson City, Nevada 89701. Phone: 800-424-5522. Fax: 775-883-2266. E-mail: info@languagestudiesabroad.com.
URL www.languagestudiesabroad.com
For more information, see page 1186.

LSA Cologne, Germany

Language Studies Abroad, Inc.
Cologne
Germany

General Information Coed residential cultural program established in 2002. Formal opportunities for the academically talented. High school or college credit may be earned.
Program Focus Language and culture.
Academics German language/literature, intercultural studies, language study.
Special Interest Areas Homestays.
Trips Cultural, day.
Program Information 1–18 sessions per year. Session length: 2–36 weeks in January, February, March, April, May, June, July, August, September, October, November, December. Ages: 16+. Boarding program cost: $980–$3305. Application fee: $100. Financial aid available.
Application Deadline Continuous.
Contact Director, 1801 Highway 50 East, Suite I, Carson City, Nevada 89701. Phone: 800-424-5522. Fax: 775-883-2266. E-mail: info@languagestudiesabroad.com.
URL www.languagestudiesabroad.com
For more information, see page 1186.

LSA Hamburg, Germany

Language Studies Abroad, Inc.
Hamburg
Germany

General Information Coed residential academic program and cultural program established in 1952. Formal opportunities for the academically talented and artistically talented. High school or college credit may be earned.
Program Focus Learning language and culture.
Academics German language/literature, intercultural studies, language study.
Special Interest Areas Homestays.
Trips College tours, cultural, day, overnight, shopping.
Program Information 1–26 sessions per year. Session length: 7–360 days in January, February, March, April, May, June, July, August, September, October, November, December. Ages: 16+. 5–12 participants per session. Boarding program cost: $790–$3020. Application fee: $100. Financial aid available. Additional weeks available.
Application Deadline Continuous.
Jobs Positions for high school students and college students.
Contact Director, 1801 Highway 50 East, Suite I, Carson City, Nevada 89701. Phone: 800-424-5522. Fax: 775-883-2266. E-mail: info@languagestudiesabroad.com.
URL www.languagestudiesabroad.com
For more information, see page 1186.

LSA Holzkirchen, Germany

Language Studies Abroad, Inc.
Holzkirchen, Bavaria
Germany

General Information Coed residential academic program and cultural program established in 1983. Formal opportunities for the academically talented. High school or college credit may be earned.
Program Focus Language and culture.
Academics German language/literature, academics (general), intercultural studies.
Special Interest Areas Homestays.
Trips Cultural, day.
Program Information 1–3 sessions per year. Session length: 14–45 days in June, July, August. Ages: 12–17. Boarding program cost: $1500–$2700. Application fee: $100. Financial aid available.
Application Deadline Continuous.
Contact Director, 1801 Highway 50 East, Suite I, Carson City, Nevada 89701. Phone: 800-424-5522. Fax: 775-883-2266. E-mail: info@languagestudiesabroad.com.
URL www.languagestudiesabroad.com
For more information, see page 1186.

LSA Inzell, Germany

Language Studies Abroad, Inc.
Inzell, Bavaria
Germany

General Information Coed residential academic program and cultural program established in 1983. Formal opportunities for the academically talented. High school credit may be earned.
Program Focus Language and culture.
Academics German language/literature, academics (general), intercultural studies.
Wilderness/Outdoors Hiking.
Trips Cultural, day.
Program Information 1–3 sessions per year. Session length: 14–45 days in June, July, August. Ages: 10–16. Boarding program cost: $1600–$5000. Application fee: $100. Financial aid available.
Application Deadline Continuous.
Contact Director, 1801 Highway 50 East, Suite I, Carson City, Nevada 89701. Phone: 800-424-5522. Fax: 775-883-2266. E-mail: info@languagestudiesabroad.com.
URL www.languagestudiesabroad.com
For more information, see page 1186.

LSA Loewenstein, Germany

Language Studies Abroad, Inc.
Loewenstein
Germany

General Information Coed residential academic program, arts program, and cultural program established in 2000. Formal opportunities for the academically talented and artistically talented. High school or college credit may be earned.
Program Focus Language and culture.
Academics German language/literature, Web page design, academics (general), computers, intercultural studies.
Arts Acting, graphic arts, television/video, theater/drama.
Trips Cultural, day.
Program Information 1–3 sessions per year. Session length: 14–46 days in June, July, August. Ages: 12–17. Boarding program cost: $1250–$2350. Application fee: $100. Financial aid available.
Application Deadline Continuous.
Contact Director, 1801 Highway 50 East, Suite I, Carson City, Nevada 89701. Phone: 800-424-5522. Fax: 775-883-2266. E-mail: info@languagestudiesabroad.com.
URL www.languagestudiesabroad.com

For more information, see page 1186.

LSA Munich, Germany

Language Studies Abroad, Inc.
Munich
Germany

General Information Coed residential academic program and cultural program established in 1984. Formal opportunities for the academically talented and artistically talented. High school or college credit may be earned.
Program Focus Learning language, culture, music, and dance.
Academics German language/literature, business, intercultural studies, language study, music, music (Advanced Placement).
Arts Arts and crafts (general), dance, dance (ballet), dance (jazz), dance (modern), music, painting, sculpture.
Special Interest Areas Homestays.
Trips College tours, cultural, day, overnight, shopping.
Program Information 1–26 sessions per year. Session length: 14–360 days in January, February, March, April, May, June, July, August, September, October, November, December. Ages: 16+. 40–180 participants per session. Boarding program cost: $740–$2850. Application fee: $100. Financial aid available.
Application Deadline Continuous.
Jobs Positions for high school students 17 and older and college students 17 and older.
Contact Director, 1801 Highway 50 East, Suite I, Carson City, Nevada 89701. Phone: 800-424-5522. Fax: 775-883-2266. E-mail: info@langaugestudiesabroad.com.
URL www.languagestudiesabroad.com

For more information, see page 1186.

LSA Potsdam, Germany

Language Studies Abroad, Inc.
Potsdam
Germany

General Information Coed residential academic program and cultural program established in 1983. Formal opportunities for the academically talented. High school credit may be earned.
Program Focus Language and culture.
Academics German language/literature, academics (general), intercultural studies.
Trips Cultural, day.
Program Information 1–2 sessions per year. Session length: 14–45 days in July, August. Ages: 14–17. Boarding program cost: $1620–$2300. Application fee: $100. Financial aid available.
Application Deadline Continuous.
Contact Director, 1801 Highway 50 East, Suite I, Carson City, Nevada 89701. Phone: 800-424-5522. Fax: 775-883-2266. E-mail: info@languagestudiesabroad.com.
URL www.languagestudiesabroad.com

For more information, see page 1186.

LSA Schmoeckwitz, Germany

Language Studies Abroad, Inc.
Schmoeckwitz
Germany

General Information Coed residential academic program and cultural program established in 2000. Formal opportunities for the academically talented. High school credit may be earned.
Program Focus Language and culture.
Academics German language/literature, academics (general), intercultural studies.
Trips Cultural, day.
Program Information 1–9 sessions per year. Session length: 2–9 weeks in June, July, August. Ages: 8–15. Boarding program cost: $1680–$2400. Application fee: $100. Financial aid available.
Contact Director, 1801 Highway 50 East, Suite I, Carson City, Nevada 89701. Phone: 800-424-5522. Fax: 775-883-2266. E-mail: info@languagestudiesabroad.com.
URL www.languagestudiesabroad.com

For more information, see page 1186.

LSA Stuttgart, Germany

Language Studies Abroad, Inc.
Stuttgart
Germany

General Information Coed residential academic program and cultural program established in 1972. Formal opportunities for the academically talented and artistically talented. High school or college credit may be earned.
Program Focus Learning language and culture.
Academics German language/literature, architecture, business, engineering, intercultural studies, language study.
Special Interest Areas Homestays.
Trips Cultural, day, overnight, shopping.

LSA Stuttgart, Germany (continued)
Program Information 1–26 sessions per year. Session length: 14–360 days in January, March, April, May, June, July, August, September, October, November. Ages: 16+. 40–70 participants per session. Boarding program cost: $715–$2520. Application fee: $100.
Application Deadline Continuous.
Jobs Positions for high school students and college students.
Contact Director, 1801 Highway 50 East, Suite I, Carson City, Nevada 89701. Phone: 800-424-5522. Fax: 775-883-2266. E-mail: info@languagestudiesabroad.com.
URL www.languagestudiesabroad.com
For more information, see page 1186.

Programs Abroad Travel Alternatives–Germany

Programs Abroad Travel Alternatives
Germany

General Information Coed travel academic program and cultural program established in 1996. College credit may be earned.
Program Focus Immersion for foreign language students.
Academics German language/literature, art history/appreciation, history, intercultural studies.
Special Interest Areas Cross-cultural education, homestays, touring.
Trips Cultural, overnight.
Program Information 2–3 sessions per year. Session length: 9–34 days in March, June, July. Ages: 15+. 3–30 participants per session. Cost: $1500–$4500. Application fee: $90. Participant must be in high school.
Application Deadline Continuous.
Contact Rose Potter, Founder/CEO, 6200 Adel Cove, Austin, Texas 78749. Phone: 888-777-PATA. Fax: 512-282-7076. E-mail: immerse@gopata.com.
URL www.gopata.com
For more information, see page 1248.

Volunteers for Peace International Work Camp–Germany

Volunteers for Peace International Work Camps
Berlin
Germany

General Information Coed residential community service program established in 1981. Specific services available for the hearing impaired and physically challenged. College credit may be earned.
Program Focus International work camps.
Academics History, intercultural studies, peace education.
Arts Film, theater/drama.
Special Interest Areas Community service, construction, work camp programs.
Sports Swimming.
Wilderness/Outdoors Hiking.
Trips Cultural, day, overnight.
Program Information Session length: 2–3 weeks in May, June, July, August, September, October. Ages: 16+. 12–20 participants per session. Boarding program cost: $250–$600.
Application Deadline Continuous.
Contact Peter Coldwell, Director, 1034 Tiffany Road, Belmont, Vermont 05730. Phone: 802-259-2759. Fax: 802-259-2922. E-mail: vfp@vfp.org.
URL www.vfp.org

Youth for Understanding USA–Germany

Youth for Understanding USA
Germany

General Information Coed residential academic program and cultural program established in 1951. High school or college credit may be earned.
Program Focus Living with a host family, learning about other cultures, and improving language skills.
Academics German language/literature, area studies, intercultural studies, social studies.
Special Interest Areas Homestays.
Trips Cultural, day, overnight.
Program Information 1 session per year. Session length: 45–50 days in June, July, August. Ages: 15–18. 50–100 participants per session. Boarding program cost: $4595–$4995. Application fee: $75. Financial aid available. Round-trip domestic and international airfare is included in the tuition.
Application Deadline Continuous.
Contact Admissions Counselor, 6400 Goldsboro Road, Suite 100, Bethesda, Maryland 20817. Phone: 800-TEENAGE (833-6243). Fax: 202-895-1104. E-mail: admissions@us.yfu.org.
URL www.yfu-usa.org
For more information, see page 1414.

GHANA

AFS-USA–Team Mission–Ghana

AFS-USA
Ghana

General Information Coed residential community service program and cultural program established in 1995. High school credit may be earned.
Program Focus Learn about Ghanaian history, tribal culture and modern life. Sightsee in Accra, visit a tribal village, take language lessons and stay with a host family. Participants may also work in a Ghanaian foster home or be involved with a community service program with an adult team leader.
Academics Intercultural studies.
Arts Dance (folk), music.
Special Interest Areas Community service, cross-cultural education, homestays.
Trips Cultural, day, overnight.

Program Information 1 session per year. Session length: 4 weeks in July. Ages: 15–18. 15 participants per session. Boarding program cost: $4565–$5065. Application fee: $75. Financial aid available. International airfare and volunteer homestay support included.
Application Deadline Continuous.
Contact Manager, AFS Info Center, 506 Southwest 6th Avenue, 2nd Floor, Portland, Oregon 97204. Phone: 800-AFS-INFO. Fax: 503-248-4076. E-mail: afsinfo@afs.org.
URL www.afs.org/usa
For more information, see page 974.

EARTHWATCH INSTITUTE–WILDLIFE CONSERVATION IN WEST AFRICA

Earthwatch Institute
Wechiau Community Hippo Sanctuary
Ghana

General Information Coed residential outdoor program, cultural program, and adventure program.
Program Focus Monitoring wildlife ecology to develop a community reserve for hippos.
Academics Biology, ecology, environmental science, science (general).
Special Interest Areas Field research/expeditions, nature study.
Sports Canoeing.
Wilderness/Outdoors Hiking.
Program Information 2 sessions per year. Session length: 15 days in June, November. Ages: 16+. 13 participants per session. Boarding program cost: $2395–$2495. Financial aid available. Financial aid for high school students and teachers.
Application Deadline Continuous.
Contact General Information Desk, PO Box 75, Maynard, Massachusetts 01754. Phone: 800-776-0188. Fax: 978-461-2332. E-mail: info@earthwatch.org.
URL www.earthwatch.org

THE EXPERIMENT IN INTERNATIONAL LIVING–GHANA HOMESTAY

The Experiment in International Living
Ghana

General Information Coed residential community service program and cultural program established in 1932.
Program Focus International youth travel, homestay, community service.
Academics Language study, music.
Arts Dance (folk).
Special Interest Areas Community service, homestays, touring.
Trips Cultural, day, overnight.
Program Information 1 session per year. Session length: 5 weeks in July, August. Ages: 14–19. 10–15 participants per session. Boarding program cost: $4700. Financial aid available.
Application Deadline May 1.
Contact Annie Thompson, Enrollment Director, Summer Abroad, Kipling Road, PO Box 676, Brattleboro, Vermont 05302-0676. Phone: 800-345-2929. Fax: 802-258-3428. E-mail: eil@worldlearning.org.
URL www.usexperiment.org
For more information, see page 1116.

YOUTH FOR UNDERSTANDING USA–GHANA

Youth for Understanding USA
Ghana

General Information Coed residential academic program, community service program, and cultural program. High school credit may be earned.
Special Interest Areas Community service, cross-cultural education, homestays.
Trips Cultural, day, overnight.
Program Information 1 session per year. Session length: 40–45 days in June, July, August. Ages: 15–18. Boarding program cost: $4595–$6495. Application fee: $75. Financial aid available. Round-trip domestic and international airfare is included in the tuition.
Application Deadline Continuous.
Contact Admissions Counselor, 6400 Goldsboro Road, Suite 100, Bethesda, Maryland 20817. Phone: 800-TEENAGE (833-6243). Fax: 202-895-1104. E-mail: admissions@us.yfu.org.
URL www.yfu-usa.org
For more information, see page 1414.

GREECE

GREEK SUMMER

American Farm School
Greece

General Information Coed travel community service program and cultural program established in 1970.

Greek Summer

Greek Summer (continued)

Program Focus A Greek village homestay, community service, and travel.
Academics Greek language/literature, classical languages/literatures.
Arts Ceramics, dance (folk), woodworking.
Special Interest Areas Community service, construction, farming, homestays, team building, touring.
Wilderness/Outdoors Hiking.
Trips Cultural, day, overnight.
Program Information 1 session per year. Session length: 40–42 days in June, July, August. Ages: 15–18. 25–35 participants per session. Cost: $4300. Financial aid available. Airfare not included.
Application Deadline Continuous.
Contact Ms. Hilary Goldstein, Program Coordinator, 1133 Broadway, Suite 1625, New York, New York 10010. Phone: 212-463-8434. Fax: 212-463-8208. E-mail: info@greeksummer.org.
URL www.greeksummer.org
For more information, see page 1144.

Youth for Understanding USA–Greece

Youth for Understanding USA
Greece

General Information Coed residential academic program and cultural program established in 1951. High school or college credit may be earned.
Program Focus Living with a host family, learning about other cultures, and improving language skills.
Academics Greek language/literature, archaeology, area studies, intercultural studies, social studies.
Special Interest Areas Homestays.
Trips Cultural, day, overnight.
Program Information 1 session per year. Session length: 35–45 days in June, July, August. Ages: 15–18. 10–50 participants per session. Boarding program cost: $3375. Application fee: $75. Financial aid available. Round-trip domestic and international airfare is included in the tuition.
Application Deadline Continuous.
Contact Admissions Counselor, 6400 Goldsboro Road, Suite 100, Bethesda, Maryland 20817. Phone: 800-TEENAGE (833-6243). Fax: 202-895-1104. E-mail: admissions@us.yfu.org.
URL www.yfu-usa.org
For more information, see page 1414.

GRENADA

EARTHWATCH INSTITUTE–Biodiversity of the Grenadines

Earthwatch Institute
Grenada

General Information Coed residential outdoor program.
Program Focus Surveying the ecological resources of underdeveloped Caribbean islands to plan for sustainable tourism.
Academics Ecology.
Special Interest Areas Conservation projects, field research/expeditions, nature study.
Program Information 2 sessions per year. Session length: 11 days in June. Ages: 16+. 10 participants per session. Boarding program cost: $2195–$2295. Financial aid available. Financial aid for high school students and teachers.
Application Deadline Continuous.
Contact General Information Desk, PO Box 75, Maynard, Massachusetts 01754. Phone: 800-776-0188. Fax: 978-461-2332. E-mail: info@earthwatch.org.
URL www.earthwatch.org

GUADELOUPE

Visions–Guadeloupe

Visions
Guadeloupe

General Information Coed travel outdoor program, community service program, and cultural program established in 1989. High school credit may be earned.
Program Focus Community service, cross-cultural experience, and outdoor adventure activities, language immersion.
Academics French language/literature, intercultural studies, language study.
Arts Carpentry, painting.
Special Interest Areas Community service, construction, cross-cultural education, field research/expeditions, field trips (arts and culture), leadership training, nature study.
Sports Scuba diving, snorkeling, swimming.
Wilderness/Outdoors Backpacking, hiking.
Trips Cultural, day, overnight.
Program Information 1 session per year. Session length: 4 weeks in June, July. Ages: 14–18. 20–25 participants per session. Cost: $3850. Financial aid available.
Application Deadline Continuous.
Jobs Positions for college students 22 and older.
Contact Joanne Pinaire, Director, PO Box 220, Newport, Pennsylvania 17074. Phone: 717-567-7313. Fax: 717-567-7853. E-mail: info@visionsserviceadventures.com.
URL www.visionsserviceadventures.com
For more information, see page 1382.

GUATEMALA

EARTHWATCH INSTITUTE–GUATEMALA'S ANCIENT MAYA

Earthwatch Institute
Chocola
Guatemala

General Information Coed residential outdoor program and cultural program.
Program Focus Surveying an unexplored Maya site to reveal its role in regional cultural development.
Academics Archaeology, cartography, intercultural studies.
Special Interest Areas Mayan studies, field research/expeditions.
Trips Day, shopping.
Program Information 6 sessions per year. Session length: 2 weeks in May, June, July, August. Ages: 16+. 12 participants per session. Boarding program cost: $2095–$2195. Financial aid available. Financial aid for high school students and teachers.
Application Deadline Continuous.
Contact General Information Desk, PO Box 75, Maynard, Massachusetts 01754. Phone: 800-776-0188. Fax: 978-461-2332. E-mail: info@earthwatch.org.
URL www.earthwatch.org

LSA ANTIGUA, GUATEMALA

Language Studies Abroad, Inc.
Antigua
Guatemala

General Information Coed residential academic program and cultural program established in 2002. Formal opportunities for the academically talented. High school or college credit may be earned.
Program Focus Language and culture.
Academics Spanish (Advanced Placement), Spanish language/literature, academics (general), intercultural studies.
Special Interest Areas Homestays.
Trips Cultural, day.
Program Information 1–26 sessions per year. Session length: 13–360 days in January, February, March, April, May, June, July, August, September, October, November, December. Ages: 15+. 30–60 participants per session. Boarding program cost: $455–$1625. Application fee: $100. Financial aid available.
Application Deadline Continuous.
Contact Director, 1801 Highway 50 East, Suite I, Carson City, Nevada 89701. Phone: 800-424-5522. Fax: 775-883-2266. E-mail: info@languagestudiesabroad.com.
URL www.languagestudiesabroad.com/
For more information, see page 1186.

PROGRAMS ABROAD TRAVEL ALTERNATIVES–GUATEMALA

Programs Abroad Travel Alternatives
La Antigua
Guatemala

General Information Coed travel academic program established in 1996. Formal opportunities for the academically talented. College credit may be earned.
Program Focus Immersion for foreign language students.
Academics Spanish language/literature, art history/appreciation, history, intercultural studies.
Special Interest Areas Cross-cultural education, homestays, touring.
Trips Cultural, overnight.
Program Information 2–3 sessions per year. Session length: 9–34 days in March, June, July. Ages: 15–19. 1–30 participants per session. Cost: $1500–$4500. Application fee: $90.
Application Deadline Continuous.
Contact Heather Kenley, Director of Operations, 6200 Adel Cove, Austin, Texas 78749. Phone: 888-777-PATA. Fax: 512-282-7076. E-mail: immerse@gopata.com.
URL www.gopata.com
For more information, see page 1248.

WHERE THERE BE DRAGONS: GUATEMALA

Where There Be Dragons
Guatemala

General Information Coed travel academic program, outdoor program, community service program, wilderness program, cultural program, and adventure program established in 1993. High school or college credit may be earned.
Program Focus Spanish language study, remote homestays, cultural studies with sustainable development internships.
Academics Spanish (Advanced Placement), Spanish language/literature, anthropology, archaeology, area studies, art history/appreciation, government and politics, health sciences, history, humanities, intercultural studies, music, peace education, reading, social science, social studies, writing.
Arts Creative writing, dance (folk), music.
Special Interest Areas Native American culture, community service, field research/expeditions, homestays, nature study.
Sports Bicycling, soccer, swimming.
Wilderness/Outdoors Backpacking, canoe trips, hiking, rafting.
Trips Cultural, overnight.
Program Information 1 session per year. Session length: 6 weeks in July, August. Ages: 16–19. 10 participants per session. Cost: $4650. Financial aid available.
Application Deadline Continuous.

Where There Be Dragons: Guatemala (continued)

Contact Mr. Chris Yager, Director, PO Box 4651, Boulder, Colorado 80306. Phone: 800-982-9203. Fax: 303-413-0857. E-mail: info@wheretherebedragons.com.
URL www.wheretherebedragons.com
For more information, see page 1394.

GUYANA

IBIKE CULTURAL TOURS–GUYANA

International Bicycle Fund
Guyana

General Information Coed travel outdoor program and cultural program established in 2004.
Program Focus Cross-cultural bicycle tour.
Academics Anthropology, architecture, area studies, botany, ecology, economics, environmental science, geography, geology/earth science, government and politics, history, intercultural studies, social science, social studies.
Special Interest Areas Cross-cultural education, nature study.
Sports Bicycling.
Wilderness/Outdoors Bicycle trips, mountain biking.
Trips Cultural.
Program Information 1 session per year. Session length: 13–14 days in June. Ages: 16+. 6–12 participants per session. Cost: $1190–$1290.
Application Deadline Continuous.
Contact David Mozer, Director, 4887 Columbia Drive South, Seattle, Washington 98108-1919. Phone: 206-767-0848. Fax: 206-767-0848. E-mail: ibike@ibike.org.
URL www.ibike.org/ibike

HONDURAS

BROADREACH HONDURAS ECO-ADVENTURE

Broadreach
Honduras

General Information Coed travel academic program, outdoor program, wilderness program, and adventure program established in 1992.
Program Focus Coed program focusing on adventure travel, marine biology, scuba diving, dolphin studies, whitewater rafting, and rainforest ecology.
Academics Botany, ecology, environmental science, marine studies, oceanography.
Arts Photography.
Special Interest Areas Mayan studies, community service, conservation projects, field research/expeditions, nature study.
Sports Boating, horseback riding, scuba diving, sea kayaking, snorkeling, waterskiing, windsurfing.
Wilderness/Outdoors Backpacking, canoe trips, hiking, rafting, white-water trips, wilderness camping.
Trips Cultural.
Program Information 2 sessions per year. Session length: 3 weeks in June, July, August. Ages: 15–19. 12–14 participants per session. Cost: $3980.
Application Deadline Continuous.
Contact Carlton Goldthwaite, Director, PO Box 27076, Raleigh, North Carolina 27611-7076. Phone: 888-833-1907. Fax: 919-833-2129. E-mail: info@gobroadreach.com.
URL www.gobroadreach.com
For more information, see page 1008.

HONG KONG

SUPERCAMP–HONG KONG

SuperCamp
United World College
Stanley
Hong Kong

General Information Coed residential academic program established in 1993.
Program Focus Academic enrichment and personal development, tour of mainland China.
Academics SAT/ACT preparation, academics (general), communications, reading, study skills, writing.
Special Interest Areas Leadership training.
Sports Ropes course, soccer, swimming, volleyball.
Program Information 2–3 sessions per year. Session length: 7–10 days in July. Ages: 9–18. 84–112 participants per session. Boarding program cost: $1600–$1900. Application fee: $100. Financial aid available.
Application Deadline Continuous.
Jobs Positions for college students 18 and older.
Contact Enrollments Department, 1725 South Coast Highway, Oceanside, California 92054. Phone: 800-285-3276. Fax: 760-722-3507. E-mail: info@supercamp.com.
URL www.supercamp.com
For more information, see page 1348.

HUNGARY

AFS-USA–HOMESTAY PLUS–HUNGARY

AFS-USA
Hungary

General Information Coed residential arts program and cultural program established in 1995.
Program Focus Traditional crafts from local artisans, multiple day trips to cultural and historical sites.

Academics Hungarian language/literature, history, intercultural studies.
Arts Art (folk), arts and crafts (general), ceramics, dance (folk), fabric arts, jewelry making, leather working, music, pottery, weaving, woodworking.
Special Interest Areas Cross-cultural education, homestays.
Sports Fencing.
Wilderness/Outdoors Hiking.
Trips Cultural, day, overnight.
Program Information 1 session per year. Session length: 4 weeks in July. Ages: 15–19. 15–20 participants per session. Boarding program cost: $4165–$4365. Application fee: $75. Financial aid available. International airfare and volunteer homestay support included.
Application Deadline Continuous.
Contact Manager, AFS Info Center, 506 Southwest 6th Avenue, 2nd Floor, Portland, Oregon 97204. Phone: 800-AFS-INFO. Fax: 503-248-4076. E-mail: afsinfo@afs.org.
URL www.afs.org/usa

For more information, see page 974.

EARTHWATCH INSTITUTE–EUROPE–AFRICA SONGBIRD MIGRATIONS–HUNGARY

Earthwatch Institute
Ocsa Wetland
Hungary

General Information Coed residential outdoor program, cultural program, and adventure program.
Program Focus Monitoring bird migration on two continents to help restore declining populations and manage habitat change.
Academics Ecology, environmental science, ornithology, science (general).
Special Interest Areas Field research/expeditions, nature study.
Program Information 6 sessions per year. Session length: 7–12 days in August, September. Ages: 16+. 9 participants per session. Boarding program cost: $995–$1795. Financial aid available. Financial aid for high school students and teachers.
Application Deadline Continuous.
Contact General Information Desk, PO Box 75, Maynard, Massachusetts 01754. Phone: 800-776-0188. Fax: 978-461-2332. E-mail: info@earthwatch.org.
URL www.earthwatch.org

YOUTH FOR UNDERSTANDING USA–HUNGARY

Youth for Understanding USA
Hungary

General Information Coed residential academic program and cultural program established in 1951. High school or college credit may be earned.
Program Focus Living with a host family, learning about other cultures.
Academics Hungarian language/literature, area studies, intercultural studies, social studies.
Special Interest Areas Homestays.
Sports Horseback riding, sailing.
Trips Cultural, day, overnight.
Program Information 1 session per year. Session length: 35–45 days in July, August. Ages: 15–18. 10–50 participants per session. Boarding program cost: $4995. Application fee: $75. Financial aid available. Round-trip domestic and international airfare is included in the tuition.
Application Deadline May 1.
Contact Admissions Counselor, 6400 Goldsboro Road, Suite 100, Bethesda, Maryland 20817. Phone: 800-TEENAGE (833-6243). Fax: 202-895-1104. E-mail: admissions@us.yfu.org.
URL www.yfu-usa.org

For more information, see page 1414.

ICELAND

EARTHWATCH INSTITUTE–ICELANDIC AND ALASKAN GLACIERS

Earthwatch Institute
Iceland

General Information Coed residential outdoor program, cultural program, and adventure program.
Program Focus Predicting the impact of floods, surges and sediment transfer from active glaciers.
Academics Environmental science, geology/earth science, science (general).
Special Interest Areas Field research/expeditions, nature study.
Program Information 3 sessions per year. Session length: 15 days in June, July, August. Ages: 16+. 15 participants per session. Boarding program cost: $2295–$2395. Financial aid available. Financial aid for high school students and teachers.
Application Deadline Continuous.
Contact General Information Desk, PO Box 75, Maynard, Massachusetts 01754. Phone: 800-776-0188. Fax: 978-461-2332. E-mail: info@earthwatch.org.
URL www.earthwatch.org

LONGACRE EXPEDITIONS, ICELAND

Longacre Expeditions
Iceland

General Information Coed travel outdoor program, wilderness program, and adventure program established in 2002. Accredited by American Camping Association.
Program Focus Effective communication skills, responsibility, confidence building.
Academics Geology/earth science.
Sports Horseback riding, sea kayaking.
Wilderness/Outdoors Backpacking, hiking, wilderness camping.
Trips Cultural.

Longacre Expeditions, Iceland (continued)
Program Information 1 session per year. Session length: 24 days in July. Ages: 15–18. 10–16 participants per session. Cost: $4695.
Application Deadline Continuous.
Jobs Positions for college students 21 and older.
Contact Meredith Schuler, Director, 4030 Middle Ridge Road, Newport, Pennsylvania 17074. Phone: 717-567-6790. Fax: 717-567-3955. E-mail: longacre@longacreexpeditions.com.
URL www.longacreexpeditions.com
For more information, see page 1200.

World Horizons International–Iceland

World Horizons International
Reykjavik
Iceland

General Information Coed residential outdoor program, community service program, and cultural program established in 2001.
Program Focus Reforestation project with the government of Iceland.
Academics Environmental science.
Special Interest Areas Community service, conservation projects, cross-cultural education, work camp programs.
Sports Horseback riding.
Trips Cultural, day, overnight.
Program Information 1 session per year. Session length: 4 weeks in June, July. Ages: 14–18. 10–12 participants per session. Boarding program cost: $5250. Application fee: $100. Financial aid available. Airfare from New York included.
Application Deadline Continuous.
Jobs Positions for college students 20 and older.
Contact Mr. Stuart L. Rabinowitz, Executive Director, PO Box 662, Bethlehem, Connecticut 06751. Phone: 800-262-5874. Fax: 203-266-6227. E-mail: worldhorizons@att.net.
URL www.world-horizons.com
For more information, see page 1406.

INDIA

Earthwatch Institute–India's Sacred Groves

Earthwatch Institute
Keri and Surla Villages
India

General Information Coed residential outdoor program.
Program Focus Surveying sacred groves to restore these valuable forest resources and the biodiversity they protect.
Academics Ecology, intercultural studies.
Special Interest Areas Conservation projects, field research/expeditions, nature study.
Program Information 5 sessions per year. Session length: 12 days in January, March, May, July, November. Ages: 16+. 6 participants per session. Boarding program cost: $1995–$2095. Financial aid available. Financial aid for high school students and teachers.
Application Deadline Continuous.
Contact General Information Desk, PO Box 75, Maynard, Massachusetts 01754. Phone: 800-776-0188. Fax: 978-461-2332. E-mail: info@earthwatch.org.
URL www.earthwatch.org

Earthwatch Institute–Maternal and Child Healthcare in India

Earthwatch Institute
Tamil Nadu
India

General Information Coed residential community service program and cultural program.
Program Focus Using nutrition education to improve the health of pregnant and nursing women.
Academics Health sciences.
Arts Theater/drama.
Special Interest Areas Community service, field research/expeditions, nutrition.
Program Information 4 sessions per year. Session length: 2 weeks in January, February, August, September. Ages: 16+. 7 participants per session. Boarding program cost: $2295–$2395. Financial aid available. Financial aid for high school students and teachers.
Application Deadline Continuous.
Contact General Information Desk, PO Box 75, Maynard, Massachusetts 01754. Phone: 800-776-0188. Fax: 978-461-2332. E-mail: info@earthwatch.org.
URL www.earthwatch.org

Ladakh Summer Passage

Passage: Project for International Education
India

General Information Coed travel academic program, outdoor program, cultural program, and adventure program established in 2002.
Academics Anthropology, area studies, botany, ecology, geology/earth science, health sciences, history, medicine, peace education, philosophy, religion, social science.
Special Interest Areas Cross-cultural education, field research/expeditions, gardening, nature study.
Wilderness/Outdoors Backpacking, hiking.
Trips Cultural, overnight.
Program Information 1 session per year. Session length: 6 weeks in July, August. Ages: 16+. 16 participants per session. Cost: $3300. Financial aid available.
Application Deadline Continuous.
Jobs Positions for college students 21 and older.

Contact Vidhea Shrestha, Director of Programs, GPO Box 8974, CPC373, Kathmandu, Nepal. Phone: 866-840-9197. E-mail: programs@passageproject.org.
URL www.passageproject.org

Putney Student Travel–Community Service-India

Putney Student Travel
Rajasthan
India

General Information Coed residential community service program and cultural program established in 1951.
Program Focus Community service, cultural exchange, and weekend excursions from a base in a small, rural village.
Academics Intercultural studies.
Special Interest Areas Community service, construction, team building.
Wilderness/Outdoors Hiking, pack animal trips.
Trips Cultural, day, overnight.
Program Information 1 session per year. Session length: 28–30 days in June, July. Ages: 14–18. 16 participants per session. Boarding program cost: $6300. Financial aid available.
Application Deadline Continuous.
Jobs Positions for college students 21 and older.
Contact Jeffrey Shumlin, Director, 345 Hickory Ridge Road, Putney, Vermont 05346. Phone: 802-387-5000. Fax: 802-387-4276. E-mail: info@goputney.com.
URL www.goputney.com

For more information, see page 1276.

The Sikkim Cultural Immersion Experience

International Cultural Adventures
Darjeeling, Gangtok
India

General Information Coed travel community service program, cultural program, and adventure program established in 2004. Formal opportunities for the academically talented and artistically talented. High school or college credit may be earned.
Program Focus A unique volunteer service program that provides participants with an intimate cross-cultural immersion experience..
Academics English as a second language, Nepali, archaeology, area studies, art history/appreciation, geography, geology/earth science, government and politics, history, intercultural studies, music, religion.
Arts Ceramics, music, music (folk).
Special Interest Areas Community service, cross-cultural education, field trips (arts and culture), homestays, touring.
Sports Soccer.
Wilderness/Outdoors Hiking.
Trips Cultural, day, overnight.
Program Information 1–3 sessions per year. Session length: 44–90 days in February, July, August, September. Ages: 15+. 3–10 participants per session. Cost: $3150–$3950.
Application Deadline Continuous.
Contact David B. Pruskin, Program Director, 35 Suprenant Circle, Brunswick, Maine 04011-7142. Phone: 888-339-0460. E-mail: info@ICAdventures.com.
URL www.ICAdventures.com

Tibetan Culture of Northern India

Pacific Village Institute
India

General Information Coed residential community service program and cultural program established in 2003. High school or college credit may be earned.
Program Focus Travel to northern India, Varanasi, Bodh Gaya, Darjeeling, and Dharamsala.
Academics Academics (general), anthropology, art history/appreciation, ecology, environmental science, humanities, intercultural studies, peace education, pre-college program, religion, writing.
Arts Arts and crafts (general), creative writing, dance, music, painting, photography, sculpture.
Special Interest Areas Community service, homestays, leadership training, team building.
Wilderness/Outdoors Backpacking, hiking, pack animal trips, wilderness camping.
Trips Cultural, day, overnight.
Program Information 1–2 sessions per year. Session length: 30–40 days in June, July, August. Ages: 17–20. 10–14 participants per session. Boarding program cost: $3000–$5000. Financial aid available.
Application Deadline Continuous.
Contact Mr. Brad Choyt, Program Director, 325 Pleasant Street, Concord, New Hampshire 03301. Phone: 603-229-5551. E-mail: bradchoyt@yahoo.com.
URL www.pacificvillage.org

Where There Be Dragons: India Culture and Philosophy

Where There Be Dragons
India

General Information Coed travel academic program, outdoor program, community service program, cultural program, and adventure program established in 1993. Formal opportunities for the academically talented and gifted.
Program Focus Rugged and off the beaten path travel introduces a wide range of development issues.
Academics Anthropology, area studies, art history/appreciation, ecology, geography, government and politics (Advanced Placement), history, intercultural studies, peace education, philosophy, religion.
Arts Ceramics, jewelry making, leather working, metalworking, painting, photography, pottery, printmaking, weaving, woodworking.
Special Interest Areas Community service, field research/expeditions, homestays, leadership training, nature study.

Where There Be Dragons: India Culture and Philosophy (continued)

Wilderness/Outdoors Backpacking, hiking, mountaineering, orienteering, pack animal trips, wilderness camping.
Trips Cultural, overnight.
Program Information 1 session per year. Session length: 6 weeks in June, July, August. Ages: 16–20. 11 participants per session. Cost: $6000. Financial aid available. Airfare included.
Application Deadline Continuous.
Contact Chris Yager, Director, PO Box 4651, Boulder, Colorado 80306. Phone: 800-982-9203. Fax: 303-413-0857. E-mail: info@wheretherebedragons.com.
URL www.wheretherebedragons.com

For more information, see page 1394.

Where There Be Dragons: India Zanskar Trek

Where There Be Dragons
India

General Information Coed travel academic program, outdoor program, community service program, wilderness program, cultural program, and adventure program established in 1993. Formal opportunities for the academically talented.
Program Focus Rugged and off the beaten path travel introduces a wide range of development issues.
Academics Anthropology, area studies, ecology, government and politics, history, intercultural studies, peace education, philosophy.
Special Interest Areas Farming, homestays, leadership training.
Wilderness/Outdoors Backpacking, hiking, mountaineering, orienteering, pack animal trips, wilderness camping.
Trips Cultural, overnight.
Program Information 2 sessions per year. Session length: 6 weeks in June, July, August. Ages: 16–20. 10–12 participants per session. Cost: $5900. Financial aid available. Airfare included.
Application Deadline Continuous.
Contact Chris Yager, Director, PO Box 4651, Boulder, Colorado 80306. Phone: 800-982-9203. Fax: 303-413-0857. E-mail: info@wheretherebedragons.com.
URL www.wheretherebedragons.com

For more information, see page 1394.

INDONESIA

Putney Student Travel–Community Service–Nusa Penida and Bali

Putney Student Travel
Indonesia

General Information Coed residential community service program established in 1951.
Program Focus Community service, cultural exchange, and excursions (including to Bali) from a base in a small, rural community on the remote, unspoiled island of Nusa Penida.
Academics Intercultural studies.
Special Interest Areas Community service, construction, team building.
Sports Scuba diving, snorkeling, swimming.
Wilderness/Outdoors Bicycle trips, hiking.
Trips Cultural, day, overnight.
Program Information 1 session per year. Session length: 30–32 days in June, July, August. Ages: 14–18. 16 participants per session. Boarding program cost: $6000. Financial aid available.
Application Deadline Continuous.
Jobs Positions for college students 21 and older.
Contact Jeffrey Shumlin, Director, 345 Hickory Ridge Road, Putney, Vermont 05346. Phone: 802-387-5000. Fax: 802-387-4276. E-mail: info@goputney.com.
URL www.goputney.com

For more information, see page 1276.

IRELAND

Adventure Ireland–English Learning Option

Adventure Ireland
Donegal Adventure Centre
Bundoran, Co. Donegal
Ireland

General Information Coed residential academic program, cultural program, and adventure program established in 1977. Accredited by American Camping Association. High school credit may be earned.
Program Focus English as a second language combined with outdoor adventure.
Academics English as a second language, English language/literature, Irish studies, anthropology, archaeology, architecture, geography, history, peace education, social science, speech/debate.
Arts Arts and crafts (general), dance (folk), dance (modern), jewelry making, music, music (instrumental), theater/drama.
Special Interest Areas Cross-cultural education, touring.
Sports Aerobics, archery, basketball, canoeing, climbing (wall), football, gymnastics, horseback riding, kayaking, rappelling, rowing (crew/sculling), sailing, soccer, surfing, swimming, tennis, waterskiing, windsurfing.
Wilderness/Outdoors Backpacking, bicycle trips, canoe trips, mountaineering, orienteering, outdoor adventure, rafting, rock climbing, wilderness/outdoors (general).
Trips Cultural, day, overnight.
Program Information 3 sessions per year. Session length: 7–20 days in July, August. Ages: 12–18. 48 participants per session. Boarding program cost: 990–2500 euros.

Application Deadline Continuous.
Contact Niamh Hamill, Director, Donegal Adventure Centre, Bundoran, Co. Donegal, Ireland. Phone: 353-7198-42418. Fax: 353-7198-42429. E-mail: info@adventure-ireland.com.
URL www.adventure-ireland.com
For more information, see page 968.

Adventure Ireland–Irish Studies

Adventure Ireland
Donegal Adventure Centre
Bundoran, Co. Donegal
Ireland

General Information Coed residential cultural program.
Program Focus Total immersion in Irish culture.
Academics English as a second language, English language/literature, Irish language/literature, Irish studies, anthropology, archaeology, architecture, geography, history, intercultural studies, music, peace education, social science, speech/debate.
Arts Arts and crafts (general), dance (folk), dance (modern), jewelry making, music, music (instrumental), theater/drama.
Special Interest Areas Touring.
Sports Gaelic football, archery, canoeing, kayaking, snorkeling, sports (general), surfing.
Wilderness/Outdoors Hiking.
Trips Cultural, day, overnight.
Program Information 3 sessions per year. Session length: 7–20 days in July, August. Ages: 12–18. 48 participants per session. Boarding program cost: 990–2500 euros.
Application Deadline Continuous.
Contact Niamh Hamill, Director, Donegal Adventure Centre, Bundoran, Co. Donegal, Ireland. Phone: 353-7198-42418. Fax: 353-7198-42429. E-mail: info@adventure-ireland.com.
URL www.adventure-ireland.com
For more information, see page 968.

Adventure Ireland–Surf Camp/Activity Camp

Adventure Ireland
Donegal Adventure Centre
Bundoran, Co. Donegal
Ireland

General Information Coed residential outdoor program, cultural program, and adventure program.
Program Focus Surfing and outdoor activity.
Special Interest Areas Cross-cultural education, touring.
Sports Archery, body boarding, canoeing, horseback riding, kayaking, sailing, snorkeling, surfing, swimming.
Wilderness/Outdoors Orienteering, outdoor adventure, rock climbing.
Trips Cultural, day, overnight.

Adventure Ireland–Surf Camp/Activity Camp

Program Information 3 sessions per year. Session length: 7–20 days in July, August. Ages: 12–18. 48 participants per session. Boarding program cost: 990–2500 euros.
Application Deadline Continuous.
Contact Niamh Hamill, Director, Donegal Adventure Centre, Bundoran, Co. Donegal, Ireland. Phone: 353-7198-42418. Fax: 353-7198-42429. E-mail: info@adventure-ireland.com.
URL www.adventure-ireland.com
For more information, see page 968.

Celtic Learning and Travel Services–Summer in Ireland

Celtic Learning and Travel Services
Ireland

General Information Coed travel academic program, arts program, and cultural program established in 1996. Formal opportunities for the academically talented. High school credit may be earned.
Program Focus Experience Celtic culture in Galway, Cork and Dublin.
Academics English language/literature, Irish studies, geography, geology/earth science, government and politics, history, intercultural studies, music, reading, social science, social studies, speech/debate.
Arts Creative writing, dance, theater/drama.
Special Interest Areas Field trips (arts and culture), homestays, leadership training, touring.
Sports Basketball, golf, horseback riding, rugby, soccer, tennis.
Trips College tours, cultural, day, overnight, shopping.
Program Information Session length: 28–31 days in June, July, August. Ages: 14–21. 100–150 participants per session. Cost: $3195–$3710. Financial aid available.
Application Deadline Continuous.
Jobs Positions for college students 19 and older.
Summer Contact Mark Burke, Program Director, 17 Carysfort Road, Dalkey County, Dublin, Ireland. E-mail: info@celticsummer.com.
Winter Contact Mark Burke, Program Director, 189 Humbercrest Boulevard, Toronto, Ontario M6S 4L5, Canada. Phone: 888-220-2358. Fax: 416-762-2517. E-mail: info@celticsummer.com.
URL www.celticsummer.com

Center for Cultural Interchange–Ireland High School Abroad

Center for Cultural Interchange
Ireland

General Information Coed residential academic program and cultural program established in 1985. High school credit may be earned.
Program Focus Cultural immersion, high school in Ireland.
Academics Irish studies, academics (general).
Special Interest Areas Cross-cultural education, homestays.
Trips Cultural, day.
Program Information 3 sessions per year. Session length: 90–300 days in January, February, March, April, May, June, July, August, September, October, November, December. Ages: 15–18. Boarding program cost: $5900–$10,290. Financial aid available. Early Bird discount.
Application Deadline Continuous.
Contact Ms. Juliet Jones, Outbound Programs Director, 325 West Huron, Suite 706, Chicago, Illinois 60610. Phone: 866-684-9675. Fax: 312-944-2644. E-mail: info@cci-exchange.com.
URL www.cci-exchange.com
For more information, see page 1060.

Center for Cultural Interchange–Ireland Independent Homestay Program

Center for Cultural Interchange
Ireland

General Information Coed residential cultural program established in 1985.
Program Focus Cultural immersion; independent homestay.
Academics Irish studies, independent study.
Special Interest Areas Homestays.
Trips Cultural, day.
Program Information Session length: 7–90 days in January, February, March, April, May, June, July, August, September, October, November, December. Ages: 17+. Boarding program cost: $850–$1650. Financial aid available.
Application Deadline Continuous.
Contact Ms. Juliet Jones, Outbound Programs Director, 325 West Huron, Suite 706, Chicago, Illinois 60610. Phone: 866-684-9675. Fax: 312-944-2644. E-mail: info@cci-exchange.com.
URL www.cci-exchange.com
For more information, see page 1060.

The Experiment in International Living–Ireland/Northern Ireland Homestay and Peace Studies

The Experiment in International Living
Ireland

General Information Coed residential community service program, cultural program, and adventure program established in 1932.
Program Focus International youth travel, homestay, peace studies, community service.
Academics Peace education.
Special Interest Areas Community service, homestays, touring.
Trips Cultural, day, overnight.
Program Information 1 session per year. Session length: 5 weeks in July, August. Ages: 14–19. 10–15 participants per session. Boarding program cost: $4400. Financial aid available.
Application Deadline May 1.
Contact Annie Thompson, Enrollment Director, Summer Abroad, Kipling Road, PO Box 676, Brattleboro, Vermont 05302-0676. Phone: 800-345-2929. Fax: 802-258-3428. E-mail: eil@worldlearning.org.
URL www.usexperiment.org
For more information, see page 1116.

GLOBAL WORKS–Cultural Exchange-Ireland-4 weeks

GLOBAL WORKS
Ireland

General Information Coed travel community service program, cultural program, and adventure program established in 1988. High school credit may be earned.
Program Focus Environmental and community service and cultural exchange.
Academics Intercultural studies, peace education.
Arts Arts and crafts (general), creative writing, dance, music, theater/drama.
Special Interest Areas Community service, construction, cross-cultural education, field trips (arts and culture).
Sports Gaelic football, ropes course, rugby, sea kayaking, sports (general), ultimate frisbee, volleyball.
Wilderness/Outdoors Hiking, outdoor adventure.
Trips Cultural, day, overnight.
Program Information 1–2 sessions per year. Session length: 4 weeks in June, July. Ages: 14–18. 15–17 participants per session. Cost: $4050–$4150. Application fee: $100. Financial aid available. Airfare not included.
Application Deadline Continuous.
Jobs Positions for college students 23 and older.
Contact Erik Werner, Director, 1113 South Allen Street, State College, Pennsylvania 16801. Phone: 814-867-7000. Fax: 814-867-2717. E-mail: info@globalworksinc.com.
URL www.globalworksinc.com
For more information, see page 1136.

GLOBAL WORKS–Cultural Exchange-Ireland-4 weeks

Irish Way

Irish American Cultural Institute
Ireland

General Information Coed travel academic program, arts program, cultural program, and adventure program established in 1976. High school credit may be earned.
Program Focus History and culture of Ireland are taught in structured classroom sessions and workshops. Participants experience cities and countryside through touring and homestay.
Academics Irish language/literature, Irish studies, history, intercultural studies, music.
Arts Arts and crafts (general), dance, music, painting, theater/drama.
Special Interest Areas Community service, cross-cultural education, field trips (arts and culture), homestays.
Sports Gaelic football, basketball, bicycling, hurling, rugby, soccer, swimming, tennis.
Wilderness/Outdoors Bicycle trips, hiking.
Trips Cultural, day, shopping.
Program Information 1 session per year. Session length: 32 days in July. Ages: 15+. 75–100 participants per session. Cost: $3500. Application fee: $25. Financial aid available. Airfare from New York to Dublin included.
Application Deadline April 1.
Jobs Positions for college students 21 and older.
Contact Taryn Harrison, Irish Way Director, 1 Lackawanna Place, Morristown, New Jersey 07960. Phone: 973-605-1991. Fax: 973-605-8875. E-mail: tharrison@iaci-usa.org.
URL www.iaci-usa.org

Programs Abroad Travel Alternatives–Ireland

Programs Abroad Travel Alternatives
Ireland

General Information Coed travel academic program established in 1996. Formal opportunities for the academically talented. College credit may be earned.
Program Focus Immersion for foreign language students.
Academics Spanish language/literature, art history/appreciation, history, intercultural studies.
Special Interest Areas Cross-cultural education, homestays, touring.
Trips Cultural, overnight.
Program Information 2–3 sessions per year. Session length: 9–34 days in March, June, July. Ages: 15–19. 1–30 participants per session. Cost: $1500–$4500. Application fee: $90.
Application Deadline Continuous.
Contact Heather Kenley, Director of Operations, 6200 Adel Cove, Austin, Texas 78749. Phone: 888-777-PATA. Fax: 512-282-7076. E-mail: immerse@gopata.com.
URL www.gopata.com

For more information, see page 1248.

Tisch School of the Arts–International High School Program–Dublin

New York University
Dublin
Ireland

General Information Coed residential academic program, arts program, and cultural program established in 2001. Formal opportunities for the artistically talented. College credit may be earned.
Program Focus Filmmaking, drama/theater, writing, art studies.
Academics Irish language/literature, Irish studies, intercultural studies.
Arts Acting, creative writing, film, music, theater/drama.
Trips Cultural, day.
Program Information 1 session per year. Session length: 28–30 days in July, August. Ages: 15+. 8–20 participants per session. Boarding program cost: $7645–$8645. Application fee: $50. Financial aid available.
Application Deadline March 7.
Contact Mr. Josh Murray, Assistant Director of Recruitment, Special Programs, 721 Broadway, 12th

Tisch School of the Arts–International High School Program–Dublin (continued)

Floor, New York, New York 10003. Phone: 212-998-1500. Fax: 212-995-4610. E-mail: tisch.special.info@nyu.edu.
URL http://specialprograms.tisch.nyu.edu
For more information, see page 1220.

Youth for Understanding USA–Ireland

Youth for Understanding USA
Ireland

General Information Coed residential academic program, community service program, and cultural program established in 1951. High school or college credit may be earned.
Program Focus Living with a host family, learning about other cultures, and community service. Emphasis on forestry conservation and working with children with special needs.
Academics Area studies, ecology, environmental science, intercultural studies, social studies.
Special Interest Areas Community service, counselor-in-training program, homestays.
Trips Cultural, day, overnight.
Program Information 1 session per year. Session length: 4–5 weeks in June, July. Ages: 15–18. 10–50 participants per session. Boarding program cost: $5995. Application fee: $75. Financial aid available. Round-trip domestic and international airfare is included in the tuition.
Application Deadline Continuous.
Contact Admissions Counselor, 6400 Goldsboro Road, Suite 100, Bethesda, Maryland 20817. Phone: 800-TEENAGE (833-6243). Fax: 202-895-1104. E-mail: admissions@us.yfu.org.
URL www.yfu-usa.org
For more information, see page 1414.

ISRAEL

Alexander Muss High School in Israel

Hod Ha'Sharon
Israel

General Information Coed travel academic program and cultural program established in 1972. Religious affiliation: Jewish. Formal opportunities for the academically talented. High school or college credit may be earned.
Program Focus Israel learning experiences and encounters with the living history of Israel.
Academics American literature, Bible study, English language/literature, French language/literature, German language/literature, Hebrew language, Jewish studies, Latin language, SAT/ACT preparation, Spanish language/literature, anthropology, archaeology, biology, chemistry, computers, ecology, economics, environmental science, geography, government and politics, history, humanities, mathematics, peace education, physics, precollege program, reading, science (general), social studies, study skills, writing.
Special Interest Areas Field trips (arts and culture), homestays.
Sports Basketball, boating, climbing (wall), kayaking, rappelling, snorkeling, sports (general), swimming, tennis, weight training, windsurfing.
Wilderness/Outdoors Backpacking, caving, hiking, mountain biking, orienteering, rafting, rock climbing, survival training.
Trips Cultural, day, overnight, shopping.
Program Information 1 session per year. Session length: 7 weeks in June, July, August. Ages: 16–18. 120–300 participants per session. Cost: $5902. Application fee: $100. Financial aid available. AMHSI National Scholarship and local financial assistance available.
Application Deadline Continuous.
Jobs Positions for college students.
Contact Judy Dunner, National Director of Admissions, 12550 Biscayne Boulevard, Suite 604, North Miami, Florida 33181. Phone: 800-327-5980. Fax: 305-891-8806. E-mail: amhsi1@aol.com.
URL www.amhsi.com

ITALY

Abbey Road Overseas Programs–Italy Study Abroad: Language and Culture

Abbey Road Overseas Programs
Florence
Italy

General Information Coed travel academic program, arts program, and cultural program established in 2001. Formal opportunities for the artistically talented. High school or college credit may be earned.
Program Focus Italian language, culture, art, architecture, design, and fashion.
Academics Italian language/literature, Latin language, architecture, art history/appreciation, classical languages/literatures, history, humanities, precollege program.
Arts Arts, arts and crafts (general), dance, film, graphic arts, music, music (jazz), sculpture.
Special Interest Areas Culinary arts.
Sports Bicycling, boating, horseback riding, sailing, soccer, swimming, tennis, volleyball, waterskiing, windsurfing.
Wilderness/Outdoors Backpacking, bicycle trips, canoe trips, hiking.
Trips Cultural, day, overnight, shopping.
Program Information 1–2 sessions per year. Session length: 28–32 days in June, July, August. Ages: 15–19. 30–40 participants per session. Cost: $5000–$6000.
Application Deadline Continuous.

Jobs Positions for college students 21 and older.
Contact Dr. Arthur Kian, Managing Director, 8904 Rangely Avenue, West Hollywood, California 90048. Phone: 888-462-2239. Fax: 866-488-4642. E-mail: info@goabbeyroad.com.
URL www.goabbeyroad.com/

Academic Study Associates–Florence

Academic Study Associates, Inc. (ASA)
Florence
Italy

General Information Coed residential academic program established in 2004. Formal opportunities for the academically talented and artistically talented. High school credit may be earned.
Program Focus Academic enrichment, study abroad in the Arts, Humanities, cultural studies. Daily activities and weekend excursions.
Academics Italian language/literature, academics (general), archaeology, architecture, art (Advanced Placement), art history/appreciation, government and politics, history, humanities, intercultural studies, pre-college program, writing.
Arts Arts and crafts (general), creative writing, drawing, painting, photography.
Special Interest Areas Culinary arts, touring.
Sports Aerobics, basketball, soccer, swimming, tennis, volleyball.
Trips Cultural, day, shopping.
Program Information 1 session per year. Session length: 30 days in July. Ages: 15–18. 50 participants per session. Boarding program cost: $5795. Financial aid available.
Application Deadline Continuous.
Jobs Positions for college students 21 and older.
Contact Mr. David Evans, Vice President, 10 New King Street, White Plains, New York 10604. Phone: 914-686-7730. Fax: 914-686-7740. E-mail: summer@asaprograms.com.
URL www.asaprograms.com

AFS-USA–Homestay Plus–Italy

AFS-USA
Italy

General Information Coed residential cultural program.
Program Focus Week-long Italian language and culture camp, followed by a four-week homestay.
Academics Italian language/literature.
Arts Arts and crafts (general), music.
Special Interest Areas Culinary arts, homestays.
Trips Cultural, day.
Program Information 1 session per year. Session length: 38 days in July, August. Ages: 15–18. 50 participants per session. Boarding program cost: $4765–$5265. Application fee: $75. Financial aid available. International airfare and volunteer homestay support included.
Application Deadline Continuous.
Contact Manager, AFS Info Center, 506 Southwest 6th Avenue, 2nd Floor, Portland, Oregon 97204. Phone: 800-AFS-INFO. Fax: 503-248-4076. E-mail: afsinfo@afs.org.
URL www.afs.org/usa
For more information, see page 974.

American Collegiate Adventures–Italy

American Collegiate Adventures
Florence
Italy

General Information Coed residential academic program established in 2004. Accredited by American Camping Association. High school or college credit may be earned.
Academics Italian language/literature, Jewish studies, SAT/ACT preparation, academics (general), architecture, art history/appreciation, business, history, humanities, intercultural studies, music.
Arts Ceramics, desktop publishing, drawing, fashion design/production, music, music (vocal), music composition/arrangement, painting, photography, pottery, screenwriting, sculpture.
Special Interest Areas Cross-cultural education, culinary arts, touring, weight reduction.
Sports Aerobics, basketball, golf, mountain boarding, soccer, tennis, weight training.
Trips College tours, cultural, day, overnight, shopping.
Program Information 1 session per year. Session length: 30 days in June, July. Ages: 14–18. 50–100 participants per session. Boarding program cost: $5995–$6595. Application fee: $75.
Application Deadline Continuous.
Jobs Positions for college students 21 and older.
Contact Jason Lubar, Director of Summer Programs, 1811 W. North Avenue, Suite 201, Chicago, Illinois 60422. Phone: 800-509-SUMR. Fax: 773-342-0246. E-mail: info@acasummer.com.
URL www.acasummer.com

Blyth Education–Summer Study in Rome and Siena

Blyth Education
Italy

General Information Coed residential academic program and cultural program established in 1995. High school credit may be earned.
Program Focus Experience Rome and Siena.
Academics Academics (general), anthropology, archaeology, architecture, art history/appreciation, classical civilizations, classical languages/literatures, philosophy, social science.
Special Interest Areas Touring.
Sports Soccer, swimming, volleyball.
Trips Cultural, day, overnight.
Program Information 1 session per year. Session length: 25–30 days in July. Ages: 14–19. 70 participants per session. Boarding program cost: 5195 Canadian dollars. Airfare from Toronto or New York to Rome included.

Blyth Education–Summer Study in Rome and Siena (continued)

Application Deadline Continuous.
Jobs Positions for college students 25 and older.
Contact Blyth Education, 9 Sultan Street, Suite 300, Toronto, Ontario M5S 1L6, Canada. Phone: 416-960-3552. Fax: 416-960-9506. E-mail: info@blytheducation.com.
URL www.blytheducation.com

BRIGHTON IN TUSCANY

Brighton
Viareggio
Italy

General Information Coed residential academic program established in 2003. Formal opportunities for the academically talented.
Program Focus Language and cultural immersion.
Academics Italian language/literature, art history/appreciation.
Special Interest Areas Cross-cultural education, touring.
Sports Bicycling, horseback riding, swimming, volleyball.
Trips Cultural, day, shopping.
Program Information 3 sessions per year. Session length: 2 weeks in June, July, August. Ages: 14–18. 30–35 participants per session. Boarding program cost: $1700.
Application Deadline Continuous.
Contact David Allen, Executive Director, 101 East Green Street, Suite 14, Pasadena, California 91105. Phone: 626-795-2985. Fax: 626-795-5564. E-mail: info@brightonedge.org.
URL www.brightonedge.org

For more information, see page 1004.

CANADIAN COLLEGE ITALY/THE RENAISSANCE SCHOOL SUMMER ACADEMY

Canadian College Italy
Via Cavour 13
Lanciano, Chieti 66034
Italy

General Information Coed residential academic program established in 1998. High school credit may be earned.
Academics English language/literature, Italian language/literature, academics (general), art history/appreciation, biology, classical civilizations, history, mathematics.
Arts Drawing, painting, photography, printmaking.
Special Interest Areas Touring.
Sports Aerobics, bicycling, swimming, volleyball, weight training.
Wilderness/Outdoors Hiking.
Trips Cultural, day, overnight.
Program Information 1 session per year. Session length: 4 weeks in July, August. Ages: 15–18. 120 participants per session. Boarding program cost: $4595. Airfare included.

Canadian College Italy / The Renaissance School Summer Academy

Application Deadline Continuous.
Summer Contact Ms. Jocelyn Manchee, Admissions Officer, 59 Macamo Court, Maple, Ontario L6A 1G1, Canada. Phone: 800-422-0548. Fax: 905-508-5480. E-mail: cciren@rogers.com.
Winter Contact Ms. Jocelyn Manchee, Admissions Officer, 59 Macamo Court, Maple, Ontario L6A 1G1, Canada. Phone: 905-508-7108. Fax: 905-508-5480. E-mail: cciren@rogers.com.
URL www.ccilanciano.com

For more information, see page 1056.

CENTER FOR CULTURAL INTERCHANGE–ITALY LANGUAGE SCHOOL

Center for Cultural Interchange
Florence
Italy

General Information Coed residential academic program and cultural program established in 1985. High school or college credit may be earned.

Center for Cultural Interchange–Italy Language School

Program Focus Cultural immersion and language study.
Academics Italian language/literature.

Special Interest Areas Homestays.
Trips Cultural, day.
Program Information Session length: 3–4 weeks in January, February, March, April, May, June, July, August, September, October, November, December. Ages: 17+. Boarding program cost: $2150–$2590. Financial aid available.
Application Deadline Continuous.
Contact Ms. Juliet Jones, Outbound Programs Director, 325 West Huron, Suite 706, Chicago, Illinois 60610. Phone: 866-684-9675. Fax: 312-944-2644. E-mail: info@cci-exchange.com.
URL www.cci-exchange.com
For more information, see page 1060.

EARTHWATCH INSTITUTE–EUROPE–AFRICA SONGBIRD MIGRATIONS–ITALY

Earthwatch Institute
Roccolo de Ganda
Italy

General Information Coed residential outdoor program, cultural program, and adventure program.
Program Focus Monitoring bird migration on two continents to help restore declining populations and manage habitat change.
Academics Ecology, environmental science, ornithology, science (general).
Special Interest Areas Field research/expeditions, nature study.
Program Information 6 sessions per year. Session length: 7–12 days in August, September. Ages: 16+. 9 participants per session. Boarding program cost: $995–$1795. Financial aid available. Financial aid for high school students and teachers.
Application Deadline Continuous.
Contact General Information Desk, PO Box 75, Maynard, Massachusetts 01754. Phone: 800-776-0188. Fax: 978-461-2332. E-mail: info@earthwatch.org.
URL www.earthwatch.org

EARTHWATCH INSTITUTE–MEDICINAL PLANTS OF ANTIQUITY

Earthwatch Institute
Rome
Italy

General Information Coed residential academic program.
Program Focus Reconstructing the therapeutic use of plants in the ancient Mediterranean.
Academics Latin language, archaeology, botany, history, medicine, reading, research skills.
Special Interest Areas Field research/expeditions.
Program Information 5 sessions per year. Session length: 15 days in June, July, September, October. Ages: 16+. 10 participants per session. Boarding program cost: $2995–$3095. Financial aid available. Financial aid for high school students and teachers.
Application Deadline Continuous.
Contact General Information Desk, PO Box 75, Maynard, Massachusetts 01754. Phone: 800-776-0188. Fax: 978-461-2332. E-mail: info@earthwatch.org.
URL www.earthwatch.org

EF INTERNATIONAL LANGUAGE SCHOOL–ROME

EF International Language Schools
EF International School of Italian in Rome (DILIT)
Via Marghera, 22
Rome 00105
Italy

General Information Coed travel academic program and cultural program established in 1974. High school or college credit may be earned.
Program Focus Language and cultural immersion.
Academics Italian language/literature.
Special Interest Areas Field trips (arts and culture).
Trips Cultural, day, overnight.
Program Information Session length: 14–365 days in January, February, March, April, May, June, July, August, September, October, November, December. Ages: 16+. 200–250 participants per session. Call for costs.
Application Deadline Continuous.
Contact Ms. Katie Mahon, Director of Admissions, One Education Street, Cambridge, Massachusetts 02141. Phone: 800-992-1892. Fax: 800-590-1125. E-mail: ils@ef.com.
URL www.ef.com
For more information, see page 1102.

THE EXPERIMENT IN INTERNATIONAL LIVING–ITALY HOMESTAY

The Experiment in International Living
Italy

General Information Coed residential cultural program established in 1932.
Program Focus International youth travel, homestay, Italian language, travel.
Academics Italian language/literature.
Special Interest Areas Homestays, touring.
Trips Cultural, day, overnight.
Program Information 1 session per year. Session length: 5 weeks in July, August. Ages: 14–19. 10–15 participants per session. Boarding program cost: $4500. Financial aid available.
Application Deadline May 1.
Contact Annie Thompson, Enrollment Director, Summer Abroad, Kipling Road, PO Box 676, Brattleboro, Vermont 05302-0676. Phone: 800-345-2929. Fax: 802-258-3428. E-mail: eil@worldlearning.org.
URL www.usexperiment.org
For more information, see page 1116.

Global Teen–Italian and Soccer in Rome

Language Liaison
Rome
Italy

General Information Coed residential academic program and sports camp established in 1985.
Program Focus Italian language study and soccer.
Academics Italian language/literature, area studies, intercultural studies, reading, writing.
Special Interest Areas Homestays.
Sports Horseback riding, soccer.
Trips Cultural, day, shopping.
Program Information 3 sessions per year. Session length: 2 weeks in June, July, August. Ages: 16–25. Boarding program cost: $2692. Application fee: $150. Financial aid available.
Application Deadline Continuous.
Contact Ms. Nancy Forman, Director, PO Box 1772, Pacific Palisades, California 90272. Phone: 800-284-4448. Fax: 310-454-1706. E-mail: learn@languageliaison.com.
URL www.languageliaison.com

For more information, see page 1184.

Global Teen–Learn Italian in Italy

Language Liaison
Lignano
Italy

General Information Coed residential academic program established in 1976. High school or college credit may be earned.
Program Focus Italian language study and cultural immersion.
Academics Italian language/literature, area studies, intercultural studies, reading, writing.
Arts Arts and crafts (general), music (vocal), television/video.
Special Interest Areas Field trips (arts and culture), touring.
Sports Aerobics, basketball, bicycling, bowling, canoeing, football, horseback riding, in-line skating, miniature golf, soccer, swimming, tennis, volleyball, windsurfing.
Trips Cultural, day.
Program Information 8 sessions per year. Session length: 2–4 weeks in June, July, August. Ages: 10–16. 2–12 participants per session. Boarding program cost: $1855–$3614. Application fee: $75. Financial aid available.
Application Deadline Continuous.
Contact Ms. Nancy Forman, President, PO Box 1772, Pacific Palisades, California 90272. Phone: 800-284-4448. Fax: 310-454-1706. E-mail: learn@languageliaison.com.
URL www.languageliaison.com

For more information, see page 1184.

Humanities Spring in Assisi

Humanities Spring in Assisi
Santa Maria di Lignano, 2
Assisi 06081
Italy

General Information Coed travel academic program, arts program, and cultural program established in 1991. Formal opportunities for the academically talented and artistically talented. High school credit may be earned.
Program Focus To learn to use great Classical and Italian Renaissance literature and art as an inspiration for students' lives and creative work.
Academics English language/literature, Greek language/literature, Italian language/literature, Latin language, archaeology, architecture, art history/appreciation, classical languages/literatures, humanities, intercultural studies.
Arts Arts, creative writing, drawing, painting, photography.
Special Interest Areas Culinary arts, gardening, nature study.
Sports Bicycling, horseback riding, swimming.
Trips Cultural, day, overnight.
Program Information 1 session per year. Session length: 28–32 days in June, July. Ages: 15–22. 8–12 participants per session. Cost: $2650–$3200. Application fee: $25. Financial aid available. Includes trips to Venice, Rome, Florence, Amalfi coast and Spoleto Festival.
Application Deadline Continuous.
Jobs Positions for high school students 15 and older and college students 18 and older.
Contact Ms. Jane R. Oliensis, Director, main address above. Phone: 39-075-802400. Fax: 39-075-802400. E-mail: info@humanitiesspring.com.
URL www.humanitiesspring.com

Special Note
HSIA is a travel-study program in Assisi for students interested in poetry and art, ice cream, the Umbrian Hills, and the Italian language and culture. Students learn to use great Classical and Italian Renaissance literature and art as a springboard for journals, poems, sketches, paintings, collages, and their general development—in morning classes and related afternoon study trips. Students make day-trips to Florence, Ravenna, and Venice and a four-day trip to Pompeii/Paestum/Naples and attend operas, ballets, puppet shows, and concerts (classical and jazz). The staff includes art historians and painters, poets, and archaeologists. As a community, HSIA fosters the spirit of collaboration.

Humanities Spring on the Road

Humanities Spring in Assisi
Santa Maria di Lignano, 2
Assisi 06081
Italy

General Information Coed travel academic program, arts program, and cultural program established in 1998. Formal opportunities for the academically talented and artistically talented.
Program Focus Travel program; to teach students to respond creatively and individually to art and architecture from classical to contemporary.
Academics English language/literature, Italian language/literature, Latin language, archaeology, architecture, art history/appreciation, classical languages/literatures, history, humanities, writing.
Arts Creative writing, drawing, painting, photography.
Special Interest Areas Culinary arts, gardening, nature study, touring.
Trips Cultural, day, overnight.
Program Information 1 session per year. Session length: 4–5 weeks in June, July. Ages: 15–21. 8–12 participants per session. Cost: $2800–$3600. Financial aid available. Airfare not included.
Application Deadline Continuous.
Jobs Positions for high school students 15 and older and college students 18 and older.
Contact Ms. Jane R. Oliensis, Director, main address above. Phone: 39-075-802400. Fax: 39-075-802400. E-mail: info@humanitiesspring.com.
URL www.humanitiesspring.com

Knowledge Exchange Institute–Artist Abroad Program in Italy

Knowledge Exchange Institute
Scuola Internazionale Di Grafica
Venice
Italy

General Information Coed residential academic program and arts program established in 2000. Formal opportunities for the artistically talented. College credit may be earned.
Academics Italian language/literature, Web page design, art, art (Advanced Placement), art history/appreciation, precollege program.
Arts Arts, bookbinding, desktop publishing, drawing, graphic arts, painting, photography, printing, printmaking.
Special Interest Areas Field trips (arts and culture).
Trips Cultural, day, overnight.
Program Information 2 sessions per year. Session length: 2–6 weeks in June, July, August. Ages: 15–19. 4–12 participants per session. Boarding program cost: $2850–$5850. Application fee: $50. Financial aid available.
Application Deadline March 20.
Contact Kei Program Manager, 111 John Street, Suite 800, New York, New York 10038. Phone: 800-831-5095. E-mail: info@knowledgeexchange.org.
URL www.KnowledgeExchange.org

LSA Ascoli, Italy

Language Studies Abroad, Inc.
Ascoli
Italy

General Information Coed residential academic program, arts program, and cultural program established in 2001. Formal opportunities for the academically talented and artistically talented. High school or college credit may be earned.
Program Focus Learning language and culture.
Academics Italian language/literature, art (Advanced Placement), art history/appreciation, intercultural studies, language study.
Arts Graphic arts, painting, pottery, printmaking, weaving.
Special Interest Areas Homestays.
Trips Cultural, day.
Program Information 1–24 sessions per year. Session length: 14–360 days in January, February, March, April, May, June, July, August, September, October, November, December. Ages: 16+. 3–6 participants per session. Boarding program cost: $945–$3345. Application fee: $100. Financial aid available.
Application Deadline Continuous.
Contact Director, 1801 Highway 50 East, Suite I, Carson City, Nevada 89701. Phone: 800-424-5522. Fax: 775-883-2266. E-mail: info@languagestudiesabroad.com.
URL www.languagestudiesabroad.com

For more information, see page 1186.

LSA Florence, Italy

Language Studies Abroad, Inc.
Florence
Italy

General Information Coed residential academic program and cultural program established in 1975. Formal opportunities for the academically talented and artistically talented. High school or college credit may be earned.
Program Focus Learning language, culture, and art.
Academics Italian language/literature, business, computers, intercultural studies, language study.
Arts Antique trade, art restoration, arts, arts and crafts (general), design, graphic arts, painting, photography.
Special Interest Areas Culinary arts, gardening, homestays.
Trips College tours, cultural, day, overnight, shopping.
Program Information 1–25 sessions per year. Session length: 14–360 days in January, February, March, April, May, June, July, August, September, October, November, December. Ages: 16+. 90–160 participants per session. Boarding program cost: $603–$3212. Application fee: $100. Financial aid available.
Application Deadline Continuous.
Contact Director, 1801 Highway 50 East, Suite I, Carson City, Nevada 89701. Phone: 800-424-5522. Fax: 775-883-2266. E-mail: info@languagestudiesabroad.com.
URL www.languagestudiesabroad.com

For more information, see page 1186.

LSA Lignano, Italy–Active Junior Italian Summer Program

Language Studies Abroad, Inc.
Lignano
Italy

General Information Coed residential academic program, outdoor program, and cultural program established in 1976. Formal opportunities for the academically talented and artistically talented.
Program Focus Learning language and culture.
Academics Italian language/literature, language study, reading, writing.
Arts Creative writing, film, television/video.
Special Interest Areas Homestays.
Sports Football, golf, horseback riding, soccer, swimming, tennis, volleyball, water polo, windsurfing.
Trips Cultural, day.
Program Information 1–4 sessions per year. Session length: 2–8 weeks in June, July, August. Ages: 12–16. 40–60 participants per session. Boarding program cost: $1221–$2442. Application fee: $100. Financial aid available.
Application Deadline Continuous.
Contact Director, 1801 Highway 50 East, Suite I, Carson City, Nevada 89701. Phone: 800-424-5522. Fax: 775-883-2266. E-mail: info@languagestudiesabroad.com.
URL www.languagestudiesabroad.com

For more information, see page 1186.

LSA Livorno, Italy

Language Studies Abroad, Inc.
Livorno
Italy

General Information Coed residential academic program and cultural program established in 1995. Formal opportunities for the academically talented and artistically talented. High school or college credit may be earned.
Program Focus Learning language and culture.
Academics Italian language/literature, art history/appreciation, business, intercultural studies, language study, music.
Arts Arts and crafts (general), film, music (vocal).
Special Interest Areas Culinary arts, farming, homestays.
Sports Sailing, scuba diving, swimming, windsurfing.
Trips Cultural, day, overnight, shopping.
Program Information 1–26 sessions per year. Session length: 14–360 days in January, February, March, April, May, June, July, August, September, October, November, December. Ages: 16+. Boarding program cost: $597–$2142. Application fee: $100. Financial aid available. Additional weeks available.
Application Deadline Continuous.
Contact Director, 1801 Highway 50 East, Suite I, Carson City, Nevada 89701. Phone: 800-424-5522. Fax: 775-883-2266. E-mail: info@languagestudiesabroad.com.
URL www.languagestudiesabroad.com

For more information, see page 1186.

LSA Milan, Italy

Language Studies Abroad, Inc.
Milan
Italy

General Information Coed residential academic program and cultural program established in 1990. Formal opportunities for the academically talented. High school or college credit may be earned.
Program Focus Learn Italian language and culture.
Academics Italian language/literature, business, intercultural studies, language study.
Special Interest Areas Homestays.
Trips Cultural, day.
Program Information 1–26 sessions per year. Session length: 14–360 days in January, February, March, April, May, June, July, August, September, October, November, December. Ages: 16+. 6–12 participants per session. Boarding program cost: $880–$3838. Application fee: $100. Financial aid available.
Application Deadline Continuous.
Contact Director, 1801 Highway 50 East, Suite I, Carson City, Nevada 89701. Phone: 800-424-5522. Fax: 775-883-2266. E-mail: info@languagestudiesabroad.com.
URL www.languagestudiesabroad.com

For more information, see page 1186.

LSA Orvieto, Italy

Language Studies Abroad, Inc.
Orvieto
Italy

General Information Coed residential academic program and cultural program established in 1998. Formal opportunities for the academically talented. High school or college credit may be earned.
Program Focus Language and culture.
Academics Italian language/literature, academics (general), intercultural studies.
Special Interest Areas Homestays.
Trips Cultural, day.
Program Information 1–26 sessions per year. Session length: 13–360 days in January, February, March, April, May, June, July, August, September, October, November, December. Ages: 16+. 3–30 participants per session. Boarding program cost: $850–$2500. Application fee: $100. Financial aid available.
Application Deadline Continuous.
Contact Director, 1801 Highway 50 East, Suite I, Carson City, Nevada 89701. Phone: 800-424-5522. Fax: 775-883-2266. E-mail: info@languagestudiesabroad.com.
URL www.languagestudiesabroad.com

For more information, see page 1186.

LSA Rimini, Italy

Language Studies Abroad, Inc.
Rimini
Italy

General Information Coed residential academic program and cultural program established in 1976.

Formal opportunities for the academically talented and artistically talented. High school or college credit may be earned.
Program Focus Learning language and culture.
Academics Italian language/literature, art history/ appreciation, history, intercultural studies, language study.
Arts Arts and crafts (general), dance, music (vocal).
Special Interest Areas Culinary arts, homestays.
Sports Bicycling, equestrian sports, horseback riding, sailing, windsurfing.
Trips Cultural, day, overnight, shopping.
Program Information 1–26 sessions per year. Session length: 14–360 days in January, February, March, April, May, June, July, August, September, October, November, December. Ages: 14+. 23–25 participants per session. Boarding program cost: $656–$2240. Application fee: $100.
Application Deadline Continuous.
Contact Director, 1801 Highway 50 East, Suite I, Carson City, Nevada 89701. Phone: 800-424-5522. Fax: 775-883-2266. E-mail: info@languagestudiesabroad.com.
URL www.languagestudiesabroad.com

For more information, see page 1186.

LSA Rome, Italy

Language Studies Abroad, Inc.
Rome
Italy

General Information Coed residential academic program, arts program, and cultural program established in 1984. Formal opportunities for the academically talented. High school or college credit may be earned.
Program Focus Learn Italian language and culture.
Academics Italian language/literature, art history/ appreciation, business, intercultural studies, language study.
Special Interest Areas Homestays, opera.
Trips Cultural, day.
Program Information 1–24 sessions per year. Session length: 14–360 days in January, February, March, April, May, June, July, August, September, October, November, December. Ages: 16+. 30–160 participants per session. Boarding program cost: $603–$2728. Application fee: $100. Financial aid available.
Application Deadline Continuous.
Contact Director, 1801 Highway 50 East, Suite I, Carson City, Nevada 89701. Phone: 800-424-5522. Fax: 775-883-2266. E-mail: info@languagestudiesabroad.com.
URL www.languagestudiesabroad.com

For more information, see page 1186.

LSA Siena, Italy

Language Studies Abroad, Inc.
Siena
Italy

General Information Coed residential academic program and cultural program established in 1979. Formal opportunities for the academically talented and artistically talented. High school or college credit may be earned.
Program Focus Learning language and culture.
Academics Italian language/literature, intercultural studies, language study.
Arts Arts and crafts (general), drawing, painting, theater/drama.
Special Interest Areas Culinary arts, homestays.
Trips Cultural, day, overnight, shopping.
Program Information 1–26 sessions per year. Session length: 14–360 days in January, February, March, April, May, June, July, August, September, October, November, December. Ages: 16+. 15–200 participants per session. Boarding program cost: $603–$2844. Application fee: $100. Financial aid available.
Application Deadline Continuous.
Contact Director, 1801 Highway 50 East, Suite I, Carson City, Nevada 89701. Phone: 800-424-5522. Fax: 775-883-2266. E-mail: info@languagestudiesabroad.com.
URL www.languagestudiesabroad.com

For more information, see page 1186.

LSA Taormina, Italy

Language Studies Abroad, Inc.
Taormina
Italy

General Information Coed residential cultural program established in 1993. Formal opportunities for the academically talented. High school or college credit may be earned.
Program Focus Language and culture.
Academics Italian language/literature, intercultural studies, language study.
Special Interest Areas Homestays.
Trips Cultural.
Program Information 1–24 sessions per year. Session length: 14–360 days in January, February, March, April, May, June, July, August, September, October, November, December. Ages: 16+. Boarding program cost: $791–$2993. Application fee: $100. Financial aid available.
Application Deadline Continuous.
Contact Director, 1801 Highway 50 East, Suite I, Carson City, Nevada 89701. Phone: 800-424-5522. Fax: 775-883-2266. E-mail: info@languagestudiesabroad.com.
URL www.languagestudiesabroad.com

For more information, see page 1186.

LSA Treviso, Italy

Language Studies Abroad, Inc.
Treviso
Italy

General Information Coed residential academic program, outdoor program, arts program, and cultural program established in 1996. Formal opportunities for the academically talented and artistically talented. High school or college credit may be earned.
Program Focus Learning language and culture, Benetton Camp.
Academics Italian language/literature, computers, intercultural studies, language study, reading, writing.

LSA Treviso, Italy (continued)

Arts Arts and crafts (general), ceramics, dance, painting, stained glass, theater/drama, weaving.
Special Interest Areas Culinary arts, general camp activities, homestays.
Sports Basketball, canoeing, golf, lacrosse, skiing (downhill), soccer, swimming, volleyball.
Wilderness/Outdoors Backpacking, canoe trips, hiking, mountaineering, wilderness camping.
Trips Cultural, day, overnight, shopping.
Program Information 1–26 sessions per year. Session length: 14–360 days in January, February, March, April, May, June, July, August, September, October, November, December. Ages: 6–12. 5–10 participants per session. Boarding program cost: $624–$2261. Application fee: $100.
Application Deadline Continuous.
Contact Director, 1801 Highway 50 East, Suite I, Carson City, Nevada 89701. Phone: 800-424-5522. Fax: 775-883-2266. E-mail: info@languagestudiesabroad.com.
URL www.languagestudiesabroad.com
For more information, see page 1186.

The New York Film Academy in Florence, Italy

New York Film Academy
Studio Arts Center International
Florence
Italy

General Information Coed residential arts program established in 1992. College credit may be earned.
Program Focus "Total immersion" hands-on filmmaking workshop where students write, direct, shoot, and edit their own 16mm short films.
Arts Acting, creative writing, directing, film, film editing, film production, screenwriting, sound design, television/video, theater/drama.
Trips Cultural.
Program Information 2–3 sessions per year. Session length: 1–6 weeks in June, July, August. Ages: 14–17. 20 participants per session. Boarding program cost: $1500–$6900.
Application Deadline Continuous.
Contact Admissions, 100 East 17th Street, New York, New York 10003. Phone: 212-674-4300. Fax: 212-477-1414. E-mail: film@nyfa.com.
URL www.nyfa.com
For more information, see page 1218.

Operafestival di Roma

Operafestival Roma, Inc.
Rome
Italy

General Information Coed residential arts program established in 1994. Formal opportunities for the artistically talented.
Program Focus Opera and vocal performance.
Academics Italian language/literature, music.

Operafestival di Roma

Arts Chorus, music (chamber), music (classical), music (ensemble), music (instrumental), music (orchestral), music (vocal), musical performance/recitals, theater/drama.
Special Interest Areas Opera.
Trips Cultural, day.
Program Information 1 session per year. Session length: 4 weeks in June, July. Ages: 16+. 50–75 participants per session. Boarding program cost: $5500. Application fee: $50. Participants will perform in Rome.
Application Deadline Continuous.
Jobs Positions for high school students and college students.
Contact Dr. Louisa Panou, Artistic Director, 1445 Willow Lake Drive, Charlottesville, Virginia 22902. Phone: 434-984-4945. Fax: 434-984-5220. E-mail: operafest@aol.com.
URL www.operafest.com
For more information, see page 1238.

Programs Abroad Travel Alternatives–Italy

Programs Abroad Travel Alternatives
Italy

General Information Coed travel academic program and cultural program established in 1996. Formal opportunities for the academically talented. College credit may be earned.
Program Focus Immersion for foreign language students.
Academics Italian language/literature, Latin language, art history/appreciation, history.
Special Interest Areas Cross-cultural education, homestays, touring.
Trips Cultural, overnight.
Program Information 2–3 sessions per year. Session length: 9–34 days in March, June, July. Ages: 15+. 1–30 participants per session. Cost: $1500–$4800. Application fee: $90. Participant must be in high school.
Application Deadline Continuous.
Contact Rose Potter, Founder/CEO, 6200 Adel Cove, Austin, Texas 78749. Phone: 888-777-PATA. Fax: 512-282-7076. E-mail: immerse@gopata.com.
URL www.gopata.com

For more information, see page 1248.

Spoleto Study Abroad

Spoleto Study Abroad
Spoleto, Umbria
Italy

General Information Coed residential academic program, arts program, and cultural program established in 1997. Formal opportunities for the artistically talented.

Spoleto Study Abroad

Program Focus An intensive interdisciplinary program focusing on the arts and the humanities.
Academics Italian language/literature, architecture, art history/appreciation, history, humanities, music, writing.
Arts Acting, chorus, creative writing, drawing, music, music (chamber), music (classical), music (ensemble), music (instrumental), music (jazz), music (orchestral), music (vocal), painting, photography, theater/drama, visual arts.
Special Interest Areas Touring.
Sports Soccer, swimming, tennis.
Trips Cultural, day.
Program Information 1 session per year. Session length: 27–29 days in July, August. Ages: 15–19. 50–70 participants per session. Boarding program cost: $5600–$5800. Application fee: $75. Participants housed in renovated 15th-century Italian convents.
Application Deadline Continuous.
Jobs Positions for college students 21 and older.
Contact Jill Muti, Director, PO Box 99147, Raleigh, North Carolina 27624-9147. Phone: 919-384-0031. E-mail: spoleto@mindspring.com.
URL www.spoletostudyabroad.com

For more information, see page 1328.

TASIS Tuscan Academy of Art and Culture

TASIS The American School in Switzerland
Borgo San Lorenzo
Italy

General Information Coed residential arts program and cultural program established in 2002.
Program Focus Art and art history.
Academics Art history/appreciation.
Arts Arts, arts and crafts (general), drawing, painting.
Sports Basketball, swimming, tennis.
Wilderness/Outdoors Hiking.
Trips Cultural, day.
Program Information 1 session per year. Session length: 3 weeks in July, August. Ages: 15–19. 25 participants per session. Boarding program cost: $3800.
Application Deadline Continuous.
Contact Mrs. Toni Soule, US TASIS Representative, 1640 Wisconsin Avenue, NW, Washington, District of Columbia 20007. Phone: 202-965-5800. Fax: 202-965-5816. E-mail: usadmissions@tasis.com.
URL www.tasis.ch

For more information, see page 1358.

Volunteers for Peace International Work Camp–Italy

Volunteers for Peace International Work Camps
Rome
Italy

General Information Coed residential community service program established in 1999. Specific services available for the hearing impaired and physically challenged. College credit may be earned.
Academics Intercultural studies, peace education.

Volunteers for Peace International Work Camp–Italy (continued)

Special Interest Areas Community service, work camp programs.
Trips Cultural, day, overnight.
Program Information Session length: 2–3 weeks in July, August. Ages: 15+. 12–20 participants per session. Boarding program cost: $250–$600.
Application Deadline Continuous.
Contact Peter Coldwell, Director, 1034 Tiffany Road, Belmont, Vermont 05730. Phone: 802-259-2759. Fax: 802-259-2922. E-mail: vfp@vfp.org.
URL www.vfp.org

Youth for Understanding USA–Italy

Youth for Understanding USA
Italy

General Information Coed residential academic program and cultural program established in 1951. High school or college credit may be earned.
Program Focus Living with a host family, learning about other cultures, and improving Italian language skills.
Academics Italian language/literature, architecture, area studies, art history/appreciation, intercultural studies, social studies.
Arts Music.
Special Interest Areas Homestays, touring.
Trips Cultural, day, overnight, shopping.
Program Information 1 session per year. Session length: 25–35 days in June, July. Ages: 15–18. 10–50 participants per session. Boarding program cost: $6195. Application fee: $75. Financial aid available. Round-trip domestic and international airfare is included in the tuition.
Application Deadline Continuous.
Contact Admissions Counselor, 6400 Goldsboro Road, Suite 100, Bethesda, Maryland 20817. Phone: 800-TEENAGE (833-6243). Fax: 202-895-1104. E-mail: admissions@us.yfu.org.
URL www.yfu-usa.org

For more information, see page 1414.

JAMAICA

EARTHWATCH INSTITUTE–JAMAICA'S CORAL REEFS

Earthwatch Institute
Jamaica

General Information Coed residential outdoor program.
Program Focus Establishing models of coral reef recruitment and growth to predict their response to future environmental change.
Academics Ecology, environmental science, marine studies.
Special Interest Areas Conservation projects, field research/expeditions, nature study.
Program Information 3 sessions per year. Session length: 10 days in July, August. Ages: 16+. 8 participants per session. Boarding program cost: $2395–$2495. Financial aid available. Financial aid for high school students and teachers.
Application Deadline Continuous.
Contact General Information Desk, PO Box 75, Maynard, Massachusetts 01754. Phone: 800-776-0188. Fax: 978-461-2332. E-mail: info@earthwatch.org.
URL www.earthwatch.org

JAPAN

AFS-USA–Homestay Language Study–Japan

AFS-USA
Japan

General Information Coed residential cultural program.
Program Focus Living with a host family and attending language school in either Tokyo, Nagoya, or Osaka.
Academics Japanese language/literature.
Special Interest Areas Homestays.
Trips Cultural, day, overnight.
Program Information 1 session per year. Session length: 6 weeks in June, July, August. Ages: 15–18. 40–45 participants per session. Boarding program cost: $4965–$5495. Application fee: $75. Financial aid available. International airfare and volunteer homestay support included.
Application Deadline Continuous.
Contact Manager, AFS Info Center, 506 Southwest 6th Avenue, 2nd Floor, Portland, Oregon 97204. Phone: 800-AFS-INFO. Fax: 503-248-4076. E-mail: afsinfo@afs.org.
URL www.afs.org/usa

For more information, see page 974.

Center for Cultural Interchange–Japan High School Abroad

Center for Cultural Interchange
Japan

General Information Coed residential academic program and cultural program established in 1985. High school credit may be earned.
Program Focus High school abroad, homestay program, cultural immersion.
Academics Japanese language/literature, academics (general), precollege program.
Special Interest Areas Cross-cultural education, homestays.
Trips Cultural, day.
Program Information 2 sessions per year. Session length: 150–300 days in January, February, March, April, May, June, July, August, September, October,

November, December. Ages: 15–18. Boarding program cost: $4150–$4990. Financial aid available.
Application Deadline Continuous.
Contact Ms. Juliet Jones, Outbound Programs Director, 325 West Huron, Suite 706, Chicago, Illinois 60610. Phone: 866-684-9675. Fax: 312-944-2644. E-mail: info@cci-exchange.com.
URL www.cci-exchange.com
For more information, see page 1060.

Concordia Language Villages–Japan

Concordia College
Japan

General Information Coed residential academic program and cultural program established in 1961. Accredited by American Camping Association. Formal opportunities for the academically talented. High school credit may be earned.
Program Focus Japanese language and culture.
Academics Japanese language/literature.
Arts Arts and crafts (general), dance, music.
Special Interest Areas Cross-cultural education, field research/expeditions, field trips (arts and culture).
Trips Cultural, day, shopping.
Program Information 1 session per year. Session length: 30 days in June, July. Ages: 14–18. 10–15 participants per session. Boarding program cost: $5600. Financial aid available.
Application Deadline Continuous.
Jobs Positions for college students 18 and older.
Contact Alex Loehrer, Assistant Director, Public Relations, 901 South Eighth Street, Moorhead, Minnesota 56562. Phone: 218-299-4544. Fax: 218-299-3807. E-mail: clv@cord.edu.
URL www.ConcordiaLanguageVillages.org

The Experiment in International Living–Japan Homestay

The Experiment in International Living
Japan

General Information Coed residential cultural program established in 1932.
Program Focus International youth travel, homestay, Japanese language.
Academics Japanese language/literature.
Special Interest Areas Homestays.
Trips Cultural, day, overnight.
Program Information 1 session per year. Session length: 4 weeks in July, August. Ages: 14–19. 10–15 participants per session. Boarding program cost: $4300. Financial aid available.
Application Deadline May 1.
Contact Annie Thompson, Enrollment Director, Summer Abroad, Kipling Road, PO Box 676, Brattleboro, Vermont 05302-0676. Phone: 800-345-2929. Fax: 802-258-3428. E-mail: eil@worldlearning.org.
URL www.usexperiment.org
For more information, see page 1116.

LSA Kanazawa, Japan

Language Studies Abroad, Inc.
Kanazawa
Japan

General Information Coed residential academic program and cultural program established in 2002. Formal opportunities for the academically talented. High school or college credit may be earned.
Program Focus Language and culture.
Academics Japanese language/literature, academics (general), intercultural studies.
Special Interest Areas Homestays.
Trips Cultural, day.
Program Information 1–26 sessions per year. Session length: 6–360 days in January, February, March, April, May, June, July, August, September, October, November, December. Ages: 16+. Boarding program cost: $1770–$6800. Application fee: $100. Financial aid available.
Application Deadline Continuous.
Contact Director, 1801 Highway 50 East, Suite I, Carson City, Nevada 89701. Phone: 800-424-5522. Fax: 775-883-2266. E-mail: info@languagestudiesabroad.com.
URL www.languagestudiesabroad.com
For more information, see page 1186.

Woodberry Forest Summer School–Japan

Woodberry Forest School
Japan

General Information Coed residential academic program established in 1922. Formal opportunities for the academically talented. High school credit may be earned.
Academics Japanese language/literature, academics (general).
Sports Sports (general), weight training.
Trips Cultural, overnight.
Program Information 1 session per year. Session length: 27 days in June, July, August. Ages: 12–17. 5–20 participants per session. Boarding program cost: $4914. Financial aid available.
Application Deadline Continuous.
Contact Dr. W. David McRae, Director of Summer Programs, 354 Woodberry Forest Station, Woodberry Forest, Virginia 22989. Phone: 540-672-6047. Fax: 540-672-9076. E-mail: wfs_summer@woodberry.org.
URL www.woodberry.org
For more information, see page 1402.

Youth for Understanding USA–Japan

Youth for Understanding USA
Japan

General Information Coed residential academic program and cultural program established in 1951. High school or college credit may be earned.
Program Focus Living with a host family, learning about other cultures, and improving language skills.

Youth for Understanding USA–Japan (continued)

Academics Japanese language/literature, area studies, intercultural studies, social studies.
Special Interest Areas Homestays.
Trips Cultural, day, overnight.
Program Information 1 session per year. Session length: 35–45 days in June, July, August. Ages: 15–18. 200–300 participants per session. Boarding program cost: $5195. Application fee: $75. Financial aid available. Round-trip domestic and international airfare is included in the tuition.
Application Deadline March 15.
Contact Admissions Counselor, 6400 Goldsboro Road, Suite 100, Bethesda, Maryland 20817. Phone: 800-TEENAGE (833-6243). Fax: 202-895-1104. E-mail: admissions@us.yfu.org.
URL www.yfu-usa.org
For more information, see page 1414.

KAZAKHSTAN

Youth for Understanding USA–Kazakhstan

Youth for Understanding USA
Kazakhstan

General Information Coed residential academic program and cultural program. High school or college credit may be earned.
Special Interest Areas Community service, cross-cultural education, homestays.
Trips Cultural.
Program Information 1 session per year. Session length: 6–7 weeks in June, July, August. Ages: 15–18. 10 participants per session. Boarding program cost: $4595–$6495. Application fee: $75. Financial aid available. Round-trip domestic and international airfare is included in the tuition.
Application Deadline Continuous.
Contact Admissions Counselor, 6400 Goldsboro Road, Suite 100, Bethesda, Maryland 20817. Phone: 800-TEENAGE (933-6243). Fax: 202-895-1104. E-mail: admissions@us.yfu.org.
URL www.yfu-usa.org
For more information, see page 1414.

KENYA

Eagle Lake Camp Jaunts–Kenya Mission Adventure

The Navigators
Kenya

General Information Coed travel community service program, bible camp, and cultural program established in 1998. Religious affiliation: Christian. Accredited by American Camping Association. College credit may be earned.
Program Focus Team building, missions, Bible study.
Academics Bible study.
Special Interest Areas Construction, work camp programs.
Program Information 1 session per year. Session length: 19 days in July, August. Ages: 16+. 20 participants per session. Cost: $3500. Financial aid available. Airfare from Denver included; participants are housed with host-families.
Application Deadline Continuous.
Jobs Positions for college students 19 and older.
Summer Contact Office Manager, PO Box 6000, Colorado Springs, Colorado 80934. Phone: 719-472-1260. Fax: 719-623-0148. E-mail: registrar_el@navigators.org.
Winter Contact Mr. John Rogers, Director of Excursion Ministries, main address above. E-mail: john_rogers@navigators.org.
URL www.eaglelake.org

EARTHWATCH INSTITUTE–Conservation Research Initiative–Samburu: Communities and Water Resources

Earthwatch Institute
Northern Laikipia-Samburu
Kenya

General Information Coed residential outdoor program and cultural program.
Program Focus Mapping water resources and assessing human and wildlife use to avoid potential conflicts.
Academics Ecology.
Special Interest Areas Conservation projects, field research/expeditions, nature study.
Program Information 8 sessions per year. Session length: 2 weeks in January, February, March, May, June, July, August, October, November, December. Ages: 16+. 8 participants per session. Boarding program cost: $2395–$2495. Financial aid available. Financial aid for high school students and teachers.
Application Deadline Continuous.
Contact General Information Desk, PO Box 75, Maynard, Massachusetts 01754. Phone: 800-776-0188. Fax: 978-461-2332. E-mail: info@earthwatch.org.
URL www.earthwatch.org

EARTHWATCH INSTITUTE–CONSERVATION RESEARCH INITIATIVE–SAMBURU: COMMUNITIES AND WILDLIFE HABITAT

Earthwatch Institute
Samburu District
Kenya

General Information Coed residential outdoor program and cultural program.
Program Focus Comparing crucial wildlife habitats both within and outside protected areas to improve conservation efforts.
Special Interest Areas Conservation projects, field research/expeditions, nature study.
Program Information 8 sessions per year. Session length: 2 weeks in January, February, March, May, June, July, August, October. Ages: 16+. 8 participants per session. Boarding program cost: $2395–$2495. Financial aid available. Financial aid for high school students and teachers.
Application Deadline Continuous.
Contact General Information Desk, PO Box 75, Maynard, Massachusetts 01754. Phone: 800-776-0188. Fax: 978-461-2332. E-mail: info@earthwatch.org.
URL www.earthwatch.org

EARTHWATCH INSTITUTE–CONSERVATION RESEARCH INITIATIVE–SAMBURU: ZEBRAS

Earthwatch Institute
Samburu District
Kenya

General Information Coed residential.
Academics Ecology.
Special Interest Areas Conservation projects, field research/expeditions, nature study.
Program Information 9 sessions per year. Session length: 13 days in February, March, May, June, July, August, September. Ages: 16+. 10 participants per session. Boarding program cost: $2595–$2695. Financial aid available. Financial aid for high school students and teachers.
Application Deadline Continuous.
Contact General Information Desk, PO Box 75, Maynard, Massachusetts 01754. Phone: 800-776-0188. Fax: 978-461-2332. E-mail: info@earthwatch.org.
URL www.earthwatch.org

EARTHWATCH INSTITUTE–KENYA'S BLACK RHINO

Earthwatch Institute
Sweetwaters Black Rhino Reserve
Nanyuki
Kenya

General Information Coed residential outdoor program, cultural program, and adventure program.
Program Focus Making a black rhinoceros sanctuary work.
Academics Ecology, environmental science, science (general).
Special Interest Areas Field research/expeditions, nature study.
Program Information 5 sessions per year. Session length: 15 days in January, February, August, September, October. Ages: 16+. 10 participants per session. Boarding program cost: $2595–$2695. Financial aid available. Financial aid for high school students and teachers.
Application Deadline Continuous.
Contact General Information Desk, PO Box 75, Maynard, Massachusetts 01754. Phone: 800-776-0188. Fax: 978-461-2332. E-mail: info@earthwatch.org.
URL www.earthwatch.org

EARTHWATCH INSTITUTE–LAKES OF THE RIFT VALLEY

Earthwatch Institute
Kenya

General Information Coed residential outdoor program, cultural program, and adventure program.
Program Focus Tracking down vital data to protect unique natural and economic resources.
Academics Ecology, environmental science, science (general).
Special Interest Areas Field research/expeditions, nature study.
Program Information 8 sessions per year. Session length: 16 days in February, April, June, July, August, September, October, November, December. Ages: 16+. 12 participants per session. Boarding program cost: $2295–$2395. Financial aid available. Financial aid for high school students and teachers.
Application Deadline Continuous.
Contact General Information Desk, PO Box 75, Maynard, Massachusetts 01754. Phone: 800-776-0188. Fax: 978-461-2332. E-mail: info@earthwatch.org.
URL www.earthwatch.org

EARTHWATCH INSTITUTE–LIONS OF TSAVO

Earthwatch Institute
Taita/Rukinga Wildlife Conservancy
Kenya

General Information Coed residential outdoor program, cultural program, and adventure program.
Program Focus Observing the behavior and ecology of Greater Tsavo's unique maneless lions to mitigate conflicts with people.
Academics Biology, ecology, science (general).
Special Interest Areas Field research/expeditions, nature study.
Program Information 10 sessions per year. Session length: 13 days in January, February, March, April, June, August, September, December. Ages: 16+. 10

EARTHWATCH INSTITUTE–Lions of Tsavo (continued)

participants per session. Boarding program cost: $2895–$2995. Financial aid available. Financial aid for high school students and teachers.
Application Deadline Continuous.
Contact General Information Desk, PO Box 75, Maynard, Massachusetts 01754. Phone: 800-776-0188. Fax: 978-461-2332. E-mail: info@earthwatch.org.
URL www.earthwatch.org

EARTHWATCH INSTITUTE–Mangroves of the Kenyan Coast

Earthwatch Institute
Gazi Bay
Kenya

General Information Coed residential outdoor program.
Program Focus Determining how to restore ecosystems dynamics through mangrove reforestation.
Academics Ecology, environmental science, forestry.
Special Interest Areas Field research/expeditions, nature study.
Wilderness/Outdoors Wilderness/outdoors (general).
Trips Day.
Program Information 2 sessions per year. Session length: 9 days in August. Ages: 16+. 12 participants per session. Boarding program cost: $1995–$2095. Financial aid available. Financial aid for high school students and teachers.
Application Deadline Continuous.
Contact General Information Desk, PO Box 75, Maynard, Massachusetts 01754. Phone: 800-776-0188. Fax: 978-461-2332. E-mail: info@earthwatch.org.
URL www.earthwatch.org

EARTHWATCH INSTITUTE–Rare Plants of Kenya

Earthwatch Institute
Taita Hills
Kenya

General Information Coed residential outdoor program, cultural program, and adventure program.
Program Focus Recording the botanical diversity of one of Kenya's most-threatened ecosystems to ensure its conservation.
Academics Botany, ecology, science (general).
Special Interest Areas Field research/expeditions, nature study.
Wilderness/Outdoors Hiking.
Program Information 2 sessions per year. Session length: 15–16 days in July, November, December. Ages: 16+. 15 participants per session. Boarding program cost: $1995–$2095. Financial aid available. Financial aid for high school students and teachers.
Application Deadline Continuous.
Contact General Information Desk, PO Box 75, Maynard, Massachusetts 01754. Phone: 800-776-0188. Fax: 978-461-2332. E-mail: info@earthwatch.org.
URL www.earthwatch.org

Knowledge Exchange Institute–African Safari Program

Knowledge Exchange Institute
Kenya

General Information Coed travel outdoor program, cultural program, and adventure program established in 2004. College credit may be earned.
Program Focus Wildlife management and environment on safari.
Academics Area studies, biology, ecology, environmental science, natural resource management, precollege program, science (general).
Special Interest Areas Field research/expeditions, touring.
Wilderness/Outdoors Outdoor adventure, safari, wilderness camping, wilderness/outdoors (general).
Trips Cultural, day, overnight.
Program Information 1 session per year. Session length: 32 days in June, July, August. Ages: 15–19. 5–15 participants per session. Cost: $5350. Application fee: $50. Financial aid available.
Application Deadline March 20.
Contact Kei Program Manager, 111 John Street, Suite 800, New York, New York 10038. Phone: 800-831-5095. E-mail: info@knowledgeexchange.org.
URL www.KnowledgeExchange.org

SFS: Community Wildlife Management

The School for Field Studies
Center for Wildlife Management Studies
Nairobi
Kenya

General Information Coed residential academic program, outdoor program, and community service program established in 1980. Formal opportunities for the academically talented. College credit may be earned.
Program Focus Environmental field research and environmental problem solving.
Academics Anthropology, area studies, biology, botany, ecology, economics, environmental science, geography, geology/earth science, intercultural studies, science (general), social science, social studies, writing.
Special Interest Areas Community service, field research/expeditions, homestays, nature study.
Sports Baseball, basketball, soccer, volleyball.
Wilderness/Outdoors Backpacking, hiking, wilderness camping.
Trips Cultural, day, overnight.
Program Information 2 sessions per year. Session length: 30 days in June, July, August. Ages: 16–25. 32 participants per session. Boarding program cost: $3180–$3995. Application fee: $45. Financial aid available.
Application Deadline Continuous.
Contact Lili Folsom, Director of Admissions and Alumni Services, 10 Federal Street, Salem, Massachusetts 01970-3853. Phone: 800-989-4418. Fax: 978-741-3551. E-mail: admissions@fieldstudies.org.
URL www.fieldstudies.org

Youth for Understanding USA–Kenya

Youth for Understanding USA
Kenya

General Information Coed travel cultural program and adventure program established in 1951. High school or college credit may be earned.
Program Focus Living with a host family, participating in activities such as boat riding and hiking, and traveling throughout Kenya.
Academics Area studies, intercultural studies, social science.
Special Interest Areas Field research/expeditions, homestays, touring.
Sports Soccer.
Wilderness/Outdoors Hiking.
Trips Cultural, day, overnight, shopping.
Program Information 1 session per year. Session length: 20–25 days in July. Ages: 15–18. 10–50 participants per session. Cost: $4275. Application fee: $75. Financial aid available. Round-trip domestic and international airfare is included in the tuition.
Application Deadline Continuous.
Contact Admissions Counselor, 6400 Goldsboro Road, Suite 100, Bethesda, Maryland 20817. Phone: 800-TEENAGE. Fax: 202-895-1104. E-mail: admissions@us.yfu.org.
URL www.yfu-usa.org

For more information, see page 1414.

LATVIA

AFS-USA–Homestay Language Study–Latvia

AFS-USA
Latvia

General Information Coed residential academic program and cultural program.
Program Focus Living with a host family and studying Russian.
Academics Russian language/literature.
Special Interest Areas Homestays.
Trips Cultural, day, overnight.
Program Information 2 sessions per year. Session length: 6 weeks in June, July, August. Ages: 15–18. 12–24 participants per session. Boarding program cost: $5775–$6775. Application fee: $75. Financial aid available. International airfare and volunteer homestay support included.
Application Deadline Continuous.
Contact Manager, AFS Info Center, 506 Southwest 6th Avenue, 2nd Floor, Portland, Oregon 97204. Phone: 800-AFS-INFO. Fax: 503-248-4076. E-mail: afsinfo@afs.org.
URL www.afs.org/usa

For more information, see page 974.

LITHUANIA

Volunteers for Peace International Work Camp–Lithuania

Volunteers for Peace International Work Camps
Vilnius
Lithuania

General Information Coed residential community service program established in 1981. Specific services available for the hearing impaired and physically challenged. College credit may be earned.
Program Focus International work camps.
Academics Intercultural studies, peace education.
Arts Music.
Special Interest Areas Community service, construction, work camp programs.
Trips Cultural, day, overnight.
Program Information Session length: 2–3 weeks in July, August. Ages: 15+. 12–20 participants per session. Boarding program cost: $250–$600.
Application Deadline Continuous.
Contact Peter Coldwell, Director, 1034 Tiffany Road, Belmont, Vermont 05730. Phone: 802-259-2759. Fax: 802-259-2922. E-mail: vfp@vfp.org.
URL www.vfp.org

MADAGASCAR

Earthwatch Institute–Carnivores of Madagascar

Earthwatch Institute
Ankarafantsika National Park
Madagascar

General Information Coed residential outdoor program, cultural program, and adventure program.
Program Focus Tracking the habits of rare and little-known species to assure their survival.
Academics Ecology, environmental science, science (general).
Special Interest Areas Field research/expeditions, nature study.
Program Information 3 sessions per year. Session length: 13 days in July, August. Ages: 16+. 16 participants per session. Boarding program cost: $2095–$2195. Financial aid available. Financial aid for high school students and teachers.
Application Deadline Continuous.
Contact General Information Desk, PO Box 75, Maynard, Massachusetts 01754. Phone: 800-776-0188. Fax: 978-461-2332. E-mail: info@earthwatch.org.
URL www.earthwatch.org

MALAYSIA

EARTHWATCH INSTITUTE–MALAYSIAN BAT CONSERVATION

Earthwatch Institute
Krau Wildlife Reserve
Malaysia

General Information Coed residential outdoor program and wilderness program.
Program Focus Documenting bat diversity to help save a 30-million-year-old rainforest.
Academics Ecology, environmental science.
Special Interest Areas Field research/expeditions, nature study.
Wilderness/Outdoors Hiking, wilderness camping, wilderness/outdoors (general).
Trips Day.
Program Information 6 sessions per year. Session length: 2 weeks in March, April, July, August, September. Ages: 16+. 10 participants per session. Boarding program cost: $1995–$2095. Financial aid available. Financial aid for high school students and teachers.
Application Deadline Continuous.
Contact General Information Desk, PO Box 75, Maynard, Massachusetts 01754. Phone: 800-776-0188. Fax: 978-461-2332. E-mail: info@earthwatch.org.
URL www.earthwatch.org

MEXICO

ARTES EN MEXICO

Interamerican University Studies Institute
Querétaro
Mexico

General Information Coed travel academic program, arts program, and cultural program established in 2003. Formal opportunities for the artistically talented.
Academics Spanish language/literature, art.
Arts Acting, arts, ceramics, drawing, music, photography.
Special Interest Areas Homestays.
Trips Cultural, day, overnight.
Program Information 1 session per year. Session length: 30 days in July, August. Ages: 15–17. 16 participants per session. Cost: $2800–$3000. Financial aid available.
Application Deadline February 18.
Contact Ms. Amber Thacher, Program Assistant, PO Box 10958, Eugene, Oregon 97440. Phone: 800-345-4874. Fax: 541-686-5947. E-mail: office@iusi.org.
URL www.iusi.org

BLYTH EDUCATION–SUMMER STUDY IN COZUMEL

Blyth Education
Mexico

General Information Coed residential academic program established in 2004. High school credit may be earned.
Academics English language/literature, academics (general), biology, geography, mathematics, science (general), social science.
Special Interest Areas Community service, touring.
Sports Diving, scuba diving, snorkeling, swimming.
Trips Cultural, day, overnight.
Program Information 1 session per year. Session length: 25–30 days in July. Ages: 14–19. 80–100 participants per session. Boarding program cost: 2995 Canadian dollars.
Application Deadline Continuous.
Jobs Positions for college students 23 and older.
Contact Blyth Education, 9 Sultan Street, Suite 300, Toronto, Ontario M5S 1L6, Canada. Phone: 416-960-3552. Fax: 416-960-9506. E-mail: info@blytheducation.com.
URL www.blytheducation.com

BROADREACH ACADEMIC TREKS–SPANISH IMMERSION IN MEXICO

Broadreach
Mexico

General Information Coed travel academic program, outdoor program, cultural program, and adventure program established in 1992. High school or college credit may be earned.
Program Focus Academic adventure program focusing on Spanish language immersion, adventure travel, cultural exchange, hiking, camping, 5-day homestay, college credit, no pre-requisites.
Academics Spanish language/literature, academics (general), area studies, intercultural studies.
Special Interest Areas Community service, cross-cultural education, leadership training.
Wilderness/Outdoors Hiking, wilderness camping.
Trips Cultural.
Program Information 2 sessions per year. Session length: 3 weeks in June, July, August. Ages: 15–19. 10–14 participants per session. Cost: $3700–$4800.
Application Deadline Continuous.
Contact Carlton Goldthwaite, Director, PO Box 27076, Raleigh, North Carolina 27611-7076. Phone: 888-833-1907. Fax: 919-833-2129. E-mail: info@gobroadreach.com.
URL www.academictreks.com

For more information, see page 1010.

BROADREACH BAJA EXTREME–SCUBA ADVENTURE

Broadreach
Baja California Sur
Mexico

General Information Coed travel outdoor program and adventure program established in 1992.
Program Focus Coed program focusing on intensive scuba diving, advanced and specialty dive training, marine ecology, sea kayaking, surfing, adventure travel and exploration.
Academics Area studies, environmental science, marine studies.
Arts Photography.
Special Interest Areas Community service, leadership training, nature study.
Sports Boating, fishing, scuba diving, sea kayaking, snorkeling, surfing.
Wilderness/Outdoors Hiking, outdoor camping.
Trips Cultural, overnight.
Program Information 2 sessions per year. Session length: 20 days in June, July, August. Ages: 15–19. 12–14 participants per session. Cost: $4380. Financial aid available.
Application Deadline Continuous.
Contact Carlton Goldthwaite, Founder and Director, PO Box 27076, Raleigh, North Carolina 27611. Phone: 888-833-1907. Fax: 919-833-2129. E-mail: info@gobroadreach.com.
URL www.gobroadreach.com

For more information, see page 1010.

CENTER FOR CULTURAL INTERCHANGE–MEXICO HIGH SCHOOL ABROAD

Center for Cultural Interchange
Mexico

General Information Coed residential academic program and cultural program established in 1985. High school credit may be earned.
Program Focus High school abroad, homestay program, cultural immersion.
Academics Spanish language/literature, academics (general), precollege program.
Special Interest Areas Cross-cultural education, homestays.
Trips Cultural, day.
Program Information 2 sessions per year. Session length: 150–300 days in January, February, March, April, May, June, July, August, September, October, November, December. Ages: 14–17. Boarding program cost: $7260–$9080. Financial aid available.
Application Deadline Continuous.
Contact Ms. Juliet Jones, Outbound Programs Director, 325 West Huron, Suite 706, Chicago, Illinois 60610. Phone: 866-684-9675. Fax: 312-944-2644. E-mail: info@cci-exchange.com.
URL www.cci-exchange.com

For more information, see page 1060.

CENTER FOR CULTURAL INTERCHANGE–MEXICO LANGUAGE SCHOOL

Center for Cultural Interchange
Cuernavaca
Mexico

General Information Coed residential academic program and cultural program established in 1985. High school or college credit may be earned.
Program Focus Cultural immersion and language study.
Academics Spanish language/literature.
Special Interest Areas Homestays.
Trips Cultural, day.
Program Information 1–50 sessions per year. Session length: 14–90 days in January, February, March, April, May, June, July, August, September, October, November, December. Ages: 13+. Boarding program cost: $1600–$1900. Financial aid available.
Application Deadline Continuous.
Contact Ms. Juliet Jones, Outbound Programs Director, 325 West Huron, Suite 706, Chicago, Illinois 60610. Phone: 866-684-9675. Fax: 312-944-2644. E-mail: info@cci-exchange.com.
URL www.cci-exchange.com

For more information, see page 1060.

CUERNAVACA SUMMER PROGRAM FOR TEENS

AuLangue Idiomas & Culturas
Cuernavaca, Morelos 62520
Mexico

General Information Coed residential and day traditional camp, academic program, and cultural program established in 2000. Formal opportunities for the academically talented. Specific services available for the physically challenged and visually impaired. High school or college credit may be earned.
Academics Spanish (Advanced Placement), academics (general), intercultural studies.
Arts Arts and crafts (general), dance (Latin), painting.
Special Interest Areas Community service, cross-cultural education, homestays.
Sports Running/jogging, soccer, swimming.
Trips Cultural, day, shopping.
Program Information 5–15 sessions per year. Session length: 15–90 days in March, April, May, June, July, August, December. Ages: 13–18. 2–8 participants per session. Day program cost: $30–$75. Boarding program cost: $435–$7525. Application fee: $65.
Application Deadline March 3.
Jobs Positions for high school students 17 and older and college students 18 and older.
Contact Mr. Eugenio Palomares-Gonzalez, Director and General Coordinator, Allende #106, Colonia El Empleado, Cuernavaca, Morelos 62520, Mexico. Phone: 52-777-148-6193. Fax: 52-777-317-7958. E-mail: aulangue@yahoo.com.mx.
URL www.spanishlanguageschools.net/aulangue/pag/cuernavsummer.htm

Dickinson College Spanish Language and Cultural Immersion Program

Dickinson College Summer Programs
Queretaro
Mexico

General Information Coed travel academic program and cultural program established in 2001. High school or college credit may be earned.
Program Focus Spanish language and cultural immersion in Querétaro Mexico.
Academics Spanish language/literature, precollege program.
Special Interest Areas College planning, cross-cultural education, homestays, team building.
Sports Basketball, canoeing, climbing (wall), kayaking, racquetball, ropes course, swimming, tennis, weight training.
Wilderness/Outdoors Canoe trips, hiking.
Trips Cultural, day, overnight, shopping.
Program Information 1 session per year. Session length: 5 weeks in July, August. Ages: 16–18. 8–15 participants per session. Cost: $5400–$6000; including airfare. Application fee: $35. Financial aid available. Weeks 1 and 5 are spent in intensive language classes at Dickinson College.
Application Deadline Continuous.
Jobs Positions for college students 18 and older.
Contact Ms. Jennifer Howland, Office of Summer Programs, PO Box 1773, Carlisle, Pennsylvania 17013. Phone: 717-254-8782. Fax: 717-245-1972. E-mail: summer@dickinson.edu.
URL www.dickinson.edu/summer

EARTHWATCH INSTITUTE–Cacti and Orchids of the Yucatan

Earthwatch Institute
Mexico

General Information Coed residential outdoor program, cultural program, and adventure program.
Program Focus Surveying the dynamics of an arid coastal ecosystem to speed its regeneration.
Academics Biology, ecology, environmental science, science (general).
Special Interest Areas Field research/expeditions, nature study.
Program Information 5 sessions per year. Session length: 8 days in July, August, September, October, December. Ages: 16+. 6 participants per session. Boarding program cost: $1295–$1395. Financial aid available. Financial aid for high school students and teachers.
Application Deadline Continuous.
Contact General Information Desk, PO Box 75, Maynard, Massachusetts 01754. Phone: 800-776-0188. Fax: 978-461-2332. E-mail: info@earthwatch.org.
URL www.earthwatch.org

EARTHWATCH INSTITUTE–Mexican Mangroves and Wildlife

Earthwatch Institute
La Manzanilla
Mexico

General Information Coed residential outdoor program.
Program Focus Restoring and conserving mangrove ecosystems to benefit wildlife and local communities.
Academics Ecology.
Special Interest Areas Conservation projects, field research/expeditions, nature study.
Sports Fishing, kayaking, surfing.
Program Information 6 sessions per year. Session length: 12 days in February, March, April, July, August. Ages: 16+. 15 participants per session. Boarding program cost: $1495–$1595. Financial aid available. Financial aid for high school students and teachers.
Application Deadline Continuous.
Contact General Information Desk, PO Box 75, Maynard, Massachusetts 01754. Phone: 800-776-0188. Fax: 978-461-2332. E-mail: info@earthwatch.org.
URL www.earthwatch.org

EARTHWATCH INSTITUTE–Mexican Megafauna

Earthwatch Institute
Guanajuato
Mexico

General Information Coed residential outdoor program.
Program Focus Unearthing the fossil histories of animals to study the effects of climate change on evolution.
Academics Paleontology.
Arts Drawing, photography.
Special Interest Areas Field research/expeditions.
Trips Cultural, day.
Program Information 4 sessions per year. Session length: 1 week in June, July. Ages: 16+. 10 participants per session. Boarding program cost: $1295–$1395. Financial aid available. Financial aid for high school students and teachers.
Application Deadline Continuous.
Contact General Information Desk, PO Box 75, Maynard, Massachusetts 01754. Phone: 800-776-0188. Fax: 978-461-2332. E-mail: info@earthwatch.org.
URL www.earthwatch.org

EARTHWATCH INSTITUTE–Sea Turtles of Baja

Earthwatch Institute
Baja
Mexico

General Information Coed residential outdoor program, cultural program, and adventure program.
Program Focus Tracking the habits of Baja, California's black sea turtles to save them from local extinction.

Academics Ecology, marine studies, science (general).
Special Interest Areas Field research/expeditions, nature study.
Program Information 3 sessions per year. Session length: 2 weeks in June, July. Ages: 16+. 11 participants per session. Boarding program cost: $2095–$2195. Financial aid available. Financial aid for high school students and teachers.
Application Deadline Continuous.
Contact General Information Desk, PO Box 75, Maynard, Massachusetts 01754. Phone: 800-776-0188. Fax: 978-461-2332. E-mail: info@earthwatch.org.
URL www.earthwatch.org

The Experiment in International Living–Mexico, Community Service, Travel, and Homestay

The Experiment in International Living
Mexico

General Information Coed residential community service program and cultural program established in 1932.
Program Focus International youth travel, homestay, Spanish language, community service.
Academics Spanish language/literature.
Special Interest Areas Community service, homestays, touring.
Trips Cultural, day, overnight.
Program Information 1 session per year. Session length: 5 weeks in July, August. Ages: 14–19. 10–15 participants per session. Boarding program cost: $2650. Financial aid available.
Application Deadline May 1.
Contact Annie Thompson, Enrollment Director, Summer Abroad, Kipling Road, PO Box 676, Brattleboro, Vermont 05302-0676. Phone: 800-345-2929. Fax: 802-258-3428. E-mail: eil@worldlearning.org.
URL www.usexperiment.org
For more information, see page 1116.

The Experiment in International Living–Mexico Homestay and Travel

The Experiment in International Living
Mexico

General Information Coed residential cultural program established in 1932.
Program Focus International youth travel, homestay, Spanish language.
Academics Spanish language/literature.
Special Interest Areas Homestays, touring.
Wilderness/Outdoors Hiking.
Trips Cultural, day, overnight.
Program Information 1 session per year. Session length: 5 weeks in July, August. Ages: 14–19. 10–15 participants per session. Boarding program cost: $2650. Financial aid available.
Application Deadline May 1.
Contact Annie Thompson, Enrollment Director, Summer Abroad, Kipling Road, PO Box 676, Brattleboro, Vermont 05302-0676. Phone: 800-345-2929. Fax: 802-258-3428. E-mail: eil@worldlearning.org.
URL www.usexperiment.org
For more information, see page 1116.

Global Teen–Learn Spanish in Mexico

Language Liaison
Cuernavaca
Mexico

General Information Coed residential academic program established in 1980. High school or college credit may be earned.
Program Focus Spanish language study, cultural trips, and expeditions.
Academics Spanish language/literature, archaeology, area studies, intercultural studies, reading, writing.
Arts Dance, pottery, weaving.
Sports Aerobics, swimming, tennis.
Trips Cultural, day.
Program Information 2–25 sessions per year. Session length: 2 weeks in January, February, March, April, May, June, July, August, September, October, November, December. Ages: 13–17. 2–5 participants per session. Application fee: $125. Financial aid available. Cost: from $292 per week; lodging separate.
Application Deadline Continuous.
Contact Nancy Forman, President, PO Box 1772, Pacific Palisades, California 90272. Phone: 800-284-4448. Fax: 310-454-1706. E-mail: learn@languageliaison.com.
URL www.languageliaison.com
For more information, see page 1184.

GLOBAL WORKS–Language Exposure-Yucatan Peninsula, Mexico-4 weeks

GLOBAL WORKS
Mexico

General Information Coed travel community service program, cultural program, and adventure program established in 1988. High school credit may be earned.
Program Focus Environmental and community service, language exposure and cultural exchange.
Academics Spanish language/literature, archaeology, intercultural studies, language study.
Arts Arts and crafts (general), dance.
Special Interest Areas Community service, construction, cross-cultural education, field trips (arts and culture), team building.
Sports Snorkeling, soccer, sports (general), swimming.
Wilderness/Outdoors Hiking.
Trips Cultural, day, overnight.
Program Information 1 session per year. Session length: 4 weeks in June, July. Ages: 14–18. 16 participants per session. Cost: $3650–$3750. Application fee: $100. Financial aid available.

GLOBAL WORKS–Language Exposure-Yucatan Peninsula, Mexico-4 weeks (continued)

Application Deadline Continuous.
Jobs Positions for college students 23 and older.
Contact Erik Werner, Director, 1113 South Allen Street, State College, Pennsylvania 16801. Phone: 814-867-7000. Fax: 814-867-2717. E-mail: info@globalworksinc.com.
URL www.globalworksinc.com
For more information, see page 1136.

GLOBAL WORKS–Language Immersion-Yucatan Peninsula, Mexico-4 weeks

GLOBAL WORKS
Mexico

General Information Coed travel community service program, cultural program, and adventure program established in 1988. High school credit may be earned.
Program Focus Community service, language learning and travel.
Academics Latin language, Spanish (Advanced Placement), archaeology, intercultural studies, language study.
Arts Arts and crafts (general), dance (Latin), painting.
Special Interest Areas Community service, construction, homestays.
Sports Basketball, snorkeling, swimming, ultimate frisbee.
Wilderness/Outdoors Hiking, outdoor adventure.
Trips Cultural, day, overnight.
Program Information 1 session per year. Session length: 28–30 days in June, July. Ages: 15–18. 16–17 participants per session. Cost: $4150–$4250. Application fee: $100. Financial aid available. Airfare not included.
Application Deadline Continuous.
Jobs Positions for college students 23 and older.
Contact Erik Werner, Director, 1113 South Allen Street, State College, Pennsylvania 16801. Phone: 814-867-7000. Fax: 814-867-2717. E-mail: info@globalworksinc.com.
URL www.globalworksinc.com
For more information, see page 1136.

Knowledge Exchange Institute–Spanish on the Road in Mexico Program

Knowledge Exchange Institute
Mexico

General Information Coed travel academic program and cultural program established in 2003. College credit may be earned.
Program Focus Latin American studies and Spanish language.
Academics Spanish (Advanced Placement), Spanish language/literature, archaeology, area studies, government and politics, history, humanities, precollege program, social studies.
Special Interest Areas Touring.
Sports Swimming.
Trips Cultural, day, overnight.
Program Information 1 session per year. Session length: 30 days in June, July, August. Ages: 15–19. 5–15 participants per session. Cost: $5995. Application fee: $50. Financial aid available.
Application Deadline March 20.
Contact Kei Program Manager, 111 John Street, Suite 800, New York, New York 10038. Phone: 800-831-5095. E-mail: info@knowledgeexchange.org.
URL www.KnowledgeExchange.org

Learning Programs International–Mexico

Learning Programs International
Guanajuato
Mexico

General Information Coed residential academic program and cultural program established in 1990. Formal opportunities for the academically talented. High school or college credit may be earned.
Program Focus Language acquisition.
Academics Spanish (Advanced Placement), Spanish language/literature.
Arts Dance.
Special Interest Areas Community service, homestays.
Trips Cultural, day, overnight.
Program Information 4 sessions per year. Session length: 2–4 weeks in June, July. Ages: 14–18. 10–30 participants per session. Boarding program cost: $1100–$2900. Airfare not included.
Application Deadline Continuous.
Contact Michelle McRaney, Program Director, 901 West 24th Street, Austin, Texas 78705. Phone: 800-259-4439. Fax: 512-480-8866. E-mail: lpi@studiesabroad.com.
URL www.lpiabroad.com
For more information, see page 1190.

LSA Cuernavaca, Mexico

Language Studies Abroad, Inc.
Cuernavaca
Mexico

General Information Coed residential academic program and cultural program established in 1972. Formal opportunities for the academically talented and artistically talented. High school or college credit may be earned.
Program Focus Learning language and culture.
Academics Spanish (Advanced Placement), Spanish language/literature, business, intercultural studies, language study, law, medicine.
Special Interest Areas Homestays.
Trips Cultural, day, overnight, shopping.
Program Information 4–50 sessions per year. Session length: 2 weeks in January, February, March, April, May, June, July, August, September, October, November, December. Ages: 8–17. 45–80 participants per session.

Boarding program cost: $492–$980. Application fee: $100. Financial aid available. Additional weeks available.
Application Deadline Continuous.
Contact Director, 1801 Highway 50 East, Suite I, Carson City, Nevada 89701. Phone: 800-424-5522. Fax: 775-883-2266. E-mail: info@languagestudiesabroad.com.
URL www.languagestudiesabroad.com
For more information, see page 1186.

LSA Ensenada, Mexico

Language Studies Abroad, Inc.
Ensenada
Mexico

General Information Coed residential cultural program established in 1991. Formal opportunities for the academically talented. High school or college credit may be earned.
Program Focus Language and culture.
Academics Spanish language/literature, intercultural studies, language study.
Special Interest Areas Homestays.
Trips Cultural.
Program Information 1–52 sessions per year. Session length: 14–365 days in January, February, March, April, May, June, July, August, September, October, November, December. Ages: 16+. 6–50 participants per session. Boarding program cost: $798–$3192. Application fee: $100. Financial aid available.
Application Deadline Continuous.
Contact Director, 1801 Highway 50 East, Suite I, Carson City, Nevada 89701. Phone: 800-424-5522. Fax: 775-883-2266. E-mail: info@languagestudiesabroad.com.
URL www.languagestudiesabroad.com
For more information, see page 1186.

LSA Mérida, Mexico

Language Studies Abroad, Inc.
Mérida
Mexico

General Information Coed residential academic program and cultural program established in 1974. Formal opportunities for the academically talented and artistically talented. High school or college credit may be earned.
Program Focus Learning language and culture.
Academics Spanish (Advanced Placement), Spanish language/literature, intercultural studies, language study.
Special Interest Areas Homestays.
Trips Cultural, day, overnight, shopping.
Program Information 1–25 sessions per year. Session length: 14–360 days in January, February, March, April, May, June, July, August, September, October, November, December. Ages: 17+. 45–80 participants per session. Boarding program cost: $725–$2435. Application fee: $100. Financial aid available. Additional weeks available.
Application Deadline Continuous.
Contact Director, 1801 Highway 50 East, Suite I, Carson City, Nevada 89701. Phone: 800-424-5522. Fax: 775-883-2266. E-mail: info@languagestudiesabroad.com.
URL www.languagestudiesabroad.com
For more information, see page 1186.

LSA Oaxaca, Mexico

Language Studies Abroad, Inc.
Oaxaca
Mexico

General Information Coed residential academic program and cultural program established in 1984.
Program Focus Learn Spanish language and culture.
Academics Spanish language/literature, intercultural studies, language study.
Arts Arts and crafts (general).
Special Interest Areas Homestays.
Trips Cultural.
Program Information 1–26 sessions per year. Session length: 14–360 days in January, February, March, April, May, June, July, August, September, October, November, December. Ages: 6–14. 14 participants per session. Boarding program cost: $234–$510. Application fee: $100. Financial aid available.
Application Deadline Continuous.
Contact Director, 1801 Highway 50 East, Suite I, Carson City, Nevada 89701. Phone: 800-424-5522. Fax: 775-883-2266. E-mail: info@languagestudiesabroad.com.
URL www.languagesutdiesabroad.com/
For more information, see page 1186.

LSA Playa Del Carmen, Mexico

Language Studies Abroad, Inc.
Playa Del Carmen
Mexico

General Information Coed residential academic program and cultural program established in 1997. Formal opportunities for the academically talented. High school or college credit may be earned.
Academics Spanish (Advanced Placement), Spanish language/literature, academics (general), intercultural studies.
Special Interest Areas Homestays.
Sports Sea kayaking.
Trips Cultural, day.
Program Information 1–26 sessions per year. Session length: 13–300 days in January, February, March, April, May, June, July, August, September, October, November, December. Ages: 16+. 15–30 participants per session. Boarding program cost: $590–$2210. Application fee: $100. Financial aid available.
Application Deadline Continuous.
Contact Director, 1801 Highway 50 East, Suite I, Carson City, Nevada 89701. Phone: 800-424-5522. Fax: 775-883-2266. E-mail: info@languagestudiesabroad.com.
URL www.languagestudiesabroad.com/
For more information, see page 1186.

LSA Puebla, Mexico

Language Studies Abroad, Inc.
Puebla
Mexico

General Information Coed residential academic program and cultural program established in 1984. Formal opportunities for the academically talented and artistically talented. High school or college credit may be earned.
Program Focus Learning language and culture.
Academics Spanish (Advanced Placement), Spanish language/literature, intercultural studies, language study.
Special Interest Areas Homestays.
Trips Cultural, day, overnight, shopping.
Program Information 1–12 sessions per year. Session length: 28–360 days in January, February, March, April, May, June, July, August, September, October, November, December. Ages: 16+. 20–75 participants per session. Boarding program cost: $1695–$3195. Application fee: $100. Financial aid available.
Contact Director, 1801 Highway 50 East, Suite I, Carson City, Nevada 89701. Phone: 800-424-5522. Fax: 775-883-2266. E-mail: info@languagestudiesabroad.com.
URL www.languagestudiesabroad.com

For more information, see page 1186.

LSA Puerto Vallarta, Mexico

Language Studies Abroad, Inc.
Puerta Vallarta
Mexico

General Information Coed residential academic program and cultural program established in 1994. High school or college credit may be earned.
Program Focus Learn Spanish language and culture.
Academics Spanish (Advanced Placement), Spanish language/literature, intercultural studies, language study.
Special Interest Areas Homestays.
Trips Cultural, day.
Program Information 1–26 sessions per year. Session length: 14–360 days in January, February, March, April, May, June, July, August, September, October, November, December. Ages: 16+. 5–15 participants per session. Boarding program cost: $909–$3336. Application fee: $100. Financial aid available.
Application Deadline Continuous.
Contact Director, 1801 Highway 50 East, Suite I, Carson City, Nevada 89701. Phone: 800-424-5522. Fax: 775-8833-2266. E-mail: info@languagestudiesabroad.com.
URL www.languagestudiesabroad.com

For more information, see page 1186.

MexArt: Art and Spanish

MexArt
Calzada de la Aurora #48
San Miguel de Allende, 37700
Mexico

General Information Coed residential academic program, arts program, and cultural program established in 2001. Formal opportunities for the academically talented and artistically talented.
Program Focus Art, Spanish, and cultural immersion.
Academics Spanish language/literature, art history/appreciation, writing.
Arts Arts, arts and crafts (general), ceramics, creative writing, dance, drawing, metalworking, painting, photography, pottery, printmaking, sculpture.
Special Interest Areas Community service.
Sports Bicycling, horseback riding.
Wilderness/Outdoors Bicycle trips, hiking, mountain biking.
Trips Cultural, day, shopping.
Program Information 2 sessions per year. Session length: 4 weeks in June, July, August. Ages: 13–18. 20–30 participants per session. Boarding program cost: $3495.
Application Deadline Continuous.
Jobs Positions for college students 22 and older.
Contact Ms. Carly Cross, Director/Owner, 413 Inter America, BC-2323, Laredo, Texas 78045. Phone: 52-415-152-8900. Fax: 52-415-152-0624. E-mail: carly@gomexart.com.
URL www.gomexart.com

MexArt Dance: Dance and Spanish

MexArt
Calzada de la Aurora #48
San Miguel de Allende, 37700
Mexico

General Information Coed residential academic program, arts program, and cultural program established in 2001. Formal opportunities for the academically talented and artistically talented.
Program Focus Dance, Spanish, and cultural immersion.
Academics Spanish language/literature, writing.
Arts Dance, dance (ballet), dance (folk), dance (jazz), dance (modern).
Special Interest Areas Community service.
Sports Bicycling, horseback riding, swimming.
Wilderness/Outdoors Bicycle trips, hiking, mountain biking.
Trips Cultural, day, shopping.
Program Information 2 sessions per year. Session length: 4 weeks in June, July, August. Ages: 13–18. 20–30 participants per session. Boarding program cost: $3495.
Application Deadline Continuous.
Jobs Positions for college students 22 and older.
Contact Ms. Carly Cross, Director/Owner, 413 Inter America, BC-2323, Laredo, Texas 78045. Phone: 52-415-152-8900. Fax: 52-415-152-0624. E-mail: carly@gomexart.com.
URL www.gomexart.com

Outpost Wilderness Adventure–Copper Canyon Project

Outpost Wilderness Adventure
Creel
Mexico

General Information Coed travel outdoor program, community service program, wilderness program, cultural program, and adventure program established in 1979. Accredited by Association for Experiential Education.
Program Focus Adventure skills and expeditions.
Academics Ecology.
Special Interest Areas Community service, field research/expeditions, nature study, trail maintenance.
Sports Bicycling, rappelling.
Wilderness/Outdoors Bicycle trips, canyoneering, hiking, mountain biking, rock climbing.
Trips Overnight.
Program Information 1 session per year. Session length: 3 weeks in July. Ages: 14–18. Cost: $2700. Financial aid available.
Application Deadline Continuous.
Summer Contact Quentin Keith, Director, 20859 County Road 77, Lake George, Colorado 80827. Phone: 719-748-3080. Fax: 719-748-3046. E-mail: q@owa.com.
Winter Contact Quentin Keith, Director, 2107 Shovel Mountain Road, Cypress Mill, Texas 78663. Phone: 830-825-3015. Fax: 830-825-3116. E-mail: q@owa.com.
URL www.owa.com

Programs Abroad Travel Alternatives–Mexico

Programs Abroad Travel Alternatives
Mexico

General Information Coed travel academic program and cultural program established in 1996. Formal opportunities for the academically talented. College credit may be earned.
Program Focus Immersion for foreign language students.
Academics Spanish language/literature, art history/appreciation, history, intercultural studies.
Special Interest Areas Cross-cultural education, homestays, touring.
Trips Cultural, overnight.
Program Information 2–3 sessions per year. Session length: 9–34 days in March, June, July. Ages: 13–19. 1–30 participants per session. Cost: $1500–$4500. Application fee: $90. Participant must be in high school.
Application Deadline Continuous.
Contact Rose Potter, Founder/CEO, 6200 Adel Cove, Austin, Texas 78749. Phone: 888-777-PATA. Fax: 512-282-7076. E-mail: immerse@gopata.com.
URL www.gopata.com
For more information, see page 1248.

SFS: Conserving Coastal Diversity

The School for Field Studies
Center for Coastal Studies
Puerto San Carlos
Mexico

General Information Coed residential academic program, outdoor program, and community service program established in 1980. Formal opportunities for the academically talented. College credit may be earned.
Program Focus Environmental field research and environmental problem solving.
Academics Spanish language/literature, anthropology, biology, botany, ecology, economics, environmental science, geography, geology/earth science, intercultural studies, marine studies, oceanography, science (general), social science, social studies, writing.
Special Interest Areas Community service, field research/expeditions, homestays, nature study.
Sports Baseball, basketball, snorkeling, soccer, volleyball.
Wilderness/Outdoors Backpacking, hiking, wilderness camping.
Trips Cultural, day, overnight.
Program Information 2 sessions per year. Session length: 30 days in June, July, August. Ages: 16–25. 32 participants per session. Boarding program cost: $3180. Application fee: $45. Financial aid available. Airfare not included.
Application Deadline Continuous.
Contact Lili Folsom, Director of Admissions and Alumni Services, 10 Federal Street, Salem, Massachusetts 01970-3853. Phone: 800-989-4418. Fax: 978-741-3551. E-mail: admissions@fieldstudies.org.
URL www.fieldstudies.org

SuperCamp–Mexico

SuperCamp
Hacienda, Sta. Maria Pipioltepec
Mexico

General Information Coed residential academic program established in 2000.
Academics SAT/ACT preparation, academics (general), communications, reading, study skills, writing.
Special Interest Areas Leadership training.
Sports Ropes course, soccer, swimming, volleyball.
Program Information 1–2 sessions per year. Session length: 10 days in April, July, August. Ages: 13–18. 50–80 participants per session. Boarding program cost: $2095. Application fee: $100.
Application Deadline Continuous.
Jobs Positions for college students 18 and older.
Contact Enrollments Department, 1725 South Coast Highway, Oceanside, California 92054. Phone: 800-285-3276. Fax: 760-722-3507. E-mail: info@supercamp.com.
URL www.supercamp.com
For more information, see page 1348.

Where There Be Dragons: Mexico

Where There Be Dragons
Mexico

General Information Coed travel academic program, outdoor program, community service program, wilderness program, cultural program, and adventure program established in 1993. High school credit may be earned.
Program Focus Spanish language, geology and service program with art, cultural studies and artist internships.
Academics Spanish language/literature, anthropology, archaeology, area studies, geography, history, humanities, intercultural studies, music, reading, social science.
Arts Arts, arts and crafts (general), ceramics, creative writing, dance (folk), fabric arts, jewelry making, leather working, metalworking, music, weaving, woodworking.
Special Interest Areas Native American culture, community service, field research/expeditions, homestays, nature study.
Sports Bicycling, canoeing, fishing, snorkeling, soccer.
Wilderness/Outdoors Backpacking, canoe trips, hiking, rafting.
Trips Cultural, overnight.
Program Information 1 session per year. Session length: 6 weeks in June, July, August. Ages: 15–19. 12 participants per session. Cost: $4900. Financial aid available.
Application Deadline Continuous.
Contact Mr. Chris Yager, Director, PO Box 4651, Boulder, Colorado 80306. Phone: 800-982-9203. Fax: 303-413-0857. E-mail: info@wheretherebedragons.com.
URL www.wheretherebedragons.com

For more information, see page 1394.

Windsor Mountain: Mexico Community Service

Interlocken at Windsor Mountain
Mexico

General Information Coed travel community service program and cultural program established in 1967.
Program Focus Cross-cultural education, language study, community development.
Academics Spanish language/literature, intercultural studies.
Special Interest Areas Community service, conservation projects, cross-cultural education, homestays.
Wilderness/Outdoors Backpacking, hiking.
Program Information 1 session per year. Session length: 24 days in July, August. Ages: 13–18. Cost: $3595. Financial aid available.
Application Deadline Continuous.
Contact Tom Herman, Marketing Director, 19 Interlocken Way, Windsor, New Hampshire 03244. Phone: 603-478-3166 Ext.20. Fax: 603-478-5260. E-mail: mail@windsormountain.org.
URL www.windsormountain.org

For more information, see page 1162.

World Horizons International–Mexico

World Horizons International
Mexico

General Information Coed residential outdoor program, community service program, and cultural program established in 2004.
Academics Environmental science.
Special Interest Areas Community service, conservation projects.
Wilderness/Outdoors Hiking.
Trips Cultural, day, overnight.
Program Information 1 session per year. Session length: 4 weeks in July, August. Ages: 14–18. 10–12 participants per session. Boarding program cost: $4450. Application fee: $100. Financial aid available. Airfare from Los Angeles included.
Application Deadline Continuous.
Jobs Positions for college students.
Contact Mr. Stuart L. Rabinowitz, Executive Director, PO Box 662, Bethlehem, Connecticut 06751. Phone: 800-262-5874. Fax: 203-266-6227. E-mail: worldhorizons@att.net.
URL www.world-horizons.com

For more information, see page 1406.

MONACO

Global Teen–French Summer Camp in Monte Carlo

Language Liaison
Monte Carlo
Monaco

General Information Coed residential academic program established in 2002.
Program Focus French language study and cultural immersion.
Academics French language/literature, area studies, intercultural studies, reading, writing.
Arts Theater/drama.
Special Interest Areas Field trips (arts and culture), homestays, touring.
Sports Rowing (crew/sculling), sailing, scuba diving, swimming, table tennis/ping-pong, tennis.
Trips Cultural, day, shopping.
Program Information 8 sessions per year. Session length: 2–4 weeks in July, August. Ages: 13–17. 2–8 participants per session. Boarding program cost: $2649–$5193. Application fee: $85. Financial aid available.
Application Deadline Continuous.
Contact Ms. Nancy Forman, Director, PO Box 1772, Pacific Palisades, California 90272. Phone: 800-284-4448. Fax: 310-454-1706. E-mail: learn@languageliaison.com.
URL www.languageliaison.com

For more information, see page 1184.

MONGOLIA

EARTHWATCH INSTITUTE–MONGOLIAN ARGALI

Earthwatch Institute
Ikh Nartiin Chuluu Nature Reserve
Mongolia

General Information Coed residential outdoor program.
Program Focus Documenting the behavior and ecology of threatened wild sheep to stem their population decline.
Academics Ecology.
Special Interest Areas Conservation projects, field research/expeditions, nature study.
Program Information 4 sessions per year. Session length: 15 days in April, September. Ages: 16+. 10 participants per session. Boarding program cost: $2195–$2295. Financial aid available. Financial aid for high school students and teachers.
Application Deadline Continuous.
Contact General Information Desk, PO Box 75, Maynard, Massachusetts 01754. Phone: 800-776-0188. Fax: 978-461-2332. E-mail: info@earthwatch.org.
URL www.earthwatch.org

WHERE THERE BE DRAGONS: MONGOLIA

Where There Be Dragons
Mongolia

General Information Coed travel academic program, outdoor program, community service program, wilderness program, cultural program, and adventure program established in 1993. Formal opportunities for the academically talented.
Program Focus Rugged and off the beaten path travel introduces a wide range of development issues.
Academics Anthropology, area studies, art history/appreciation, ecology, economics, geography, government and politics, government and politics (Advanced Placement), history, intercultural studies, peace education, philosophy, religion, social studies.
Special Interest Areas Animal care, community service, field research/expeditions, homestays, leadership training, nature study.
Sports Horseback riding.
Wilderness/Outdoors Backpacking, hiking, mountaineering, orienteering, outdoor adventure, pack animal trips, wilderness camping.
Trips Cultural, overnight.
Program Information 1 session per year. Session length: 38 days in June, July, August. Ages: 17–20. 12 participants per session. Cost: $5900. Financial aid available. Airfare included.
Application Deadline Continuous.
Contact Chris Yager, Director, PO Box 4651, Boulder, Colorado 80306. Phone: 800-982-9203. Fax: 303-413-0857. E-mail: info@wheretherebedragons.com.
URL www.wheretherebedragons.com

For more information, see page 1394.

MOROCCO

THE EXPERIMENT IN INTERNATIONAL LIVING–MOROCCO FOUR-WEEK ARTS AND CULTURE PROGRAM

The Experiment in International Living
Morocco

General Information Coed residential arts program, community service program, cultural program, and adventure program established in 1932.
Program Focus International youth travel, homestay, community service, arts.
Academics Arabic, language study.
Arts Arts, ceramics, dance (folk), fabric arts, weaving.
Special Interest Areas Community service, homestays, nature study, touring.
Trips Cultural, day, overnight.
Program Information 1 session per year. Session length: 4 weeks in July, August. Ages: 14–19. 15–20 participants per session. Boarding program cost: $4950. Financial aid available.
Application Deadline May 1.
Contact Annie Thompson, Enrollment Director, Summer Abroad, Kipling Road, PO Box 676, Brattleboro, Vermont 05302-0676. Phone: 800-345-2929. Fax: 802-258-3428. E-mail: eil@worldlearning.org.
URL www.usexperiment.org

For more information, see page 1116.

NAMIBIA

EARTHWATCH INSTITUTE–CHEETAH

Earthwatch Institute
Namibia

General Information Coed residential outdoor program, cultural program, and adventure program.
Program Focus Finding common ground for cheetahs and ranchers.
Academics Biology, ecology, science (general).
Special Interest Areas Field research/expeditions, nature study.
Program Information 10 sessions per year. Session length: 15 days in March, April, May, June, July, August, September, October, November, December. Ages: 16+. 4 participants per session. Boarding program cost: $3095–$3195. Financial aid available. Financial aid for high school students and teachers.
Application Deadline Continuous.
Contact General Information Desk, PO Box 75, Maynard, Massachusetts 01754. Phone: 800-776-0188. Fax: 978-461-2332. E-mail: info@earthwatch.org.
URL www.earthwatch.org

EARTHWATCH INSTITUTE–DESERT ELEPHANTS OF NAMIBIA

Earthwatch Institute
Hoanib and Hoarusib River Catchments
Namibia

General Information Coed residential outdoor program.
Program Focus Defining the ecology and social structure of desert-dwelling elephant herds for effective management.
Academics Ecology.
Special Interest Areas Conservation projects, field research/expeditions, nature study.
Trips Day.
Program Information 5 sessions per year. Session length: 15 days in May, June, July, August, September. Ages: 16+. 6 participants per session. Boarding program cost: $2795–$2895. Financial aid available. Financial aid for high school students and teachers.
Contact General Information Desk, PO Box 75, Maynard, Massachusetts 01754. Phone: 800-776-0188. Fax: 978-461-2332. E-mail: info@earthwatch.org.
URL www.earthwatch.org

EARTHWATCH INSTITUTE–NAMIBIAN BLACK RHINOS

Earthwatch Institute
Waterberg Plateau National Park
Namibia

General Information Coed residential outdoor program.
Program Focus Assessing the nutritional status of endangered rhinos to improve their reproductive potential.
Academics Botany, ecology, environmental science.
Special Interest Areas Conservation projects, field research/expeditions, nature study.
Program Information 6 sessions per year. Session length: 15 days in May, July, August, September, October, November. Ages: 16+. 6 participants per session. Boarding program cost: $2795–$2895. Financial aid available. Financial aid for high school students and teachers.
Application Deadline Continuous.
Contact General Information Desk, PO Box 75, Maynard, Massachusetts 01754. Phone: 800-776-0188. Fax: 978-461-2332. E-mail: info@earthwatch.org.
URL www.earthwatch.org

EARTHWATCH INSTITUTE–NAMIBIAN WILDLIFE SURVEY

Earthwatch Institute
Namibia

General Information Coed residential outdoor program.
Program Focus Assessing wildlife diversity to ensure healthy prey populations for cheetahs and other predators.
Academics Ecology, environmental science.
Special Interest Areas Field research/expeditions, nature study.
Program Information 2 sessions per year. Session length: 9 days in July, August. Ages: 16+. 20 participants per session. Boarding program cost: $2395–$2495. Financial aid available. Financial aid for high school students and teachers.
Application Deadline Continuous.
Contact General Information Desk, PO Box 75, Maynard, Massachusetts 01754. Phone: 800-776-0188. Fax: 978-461-2332. E-mail: info@earthwatch.org.
URL www.earthwatch.org

NEPAL

LOWER MUSTANG SUMMER PASSAGE

Passage: Project for International Education
Nepal

General Information Coed travel academic program, outdoor program, cultural program, and adventure program established in 2002.
Academics Academics (general), architecture, area studies, art (Advanced Placement), art history/appreciation, botany, ecology, environmental science, geography, geology/earth science.
Arts Arts and crafts (general), batiking, ceramics, dance, dance (folk), drawing, fabric arts, film, jewelry making, leather working, metalworking, music, music (vocal), painting, photography, pottery, printmaking, sculpture, television/video, weaving, woodworking.
Special Interest Areas Animal care, community service, cross-cultural education, culinary arts, farming, field research/expeditions, gardening, homestays, leadership training, nature study, touring.
Sports Canoeing.
Wilderness/Outdoors Backpacking, hiking, rafting, wilderness camping.
Trips Cultural, day, overnight.
Program Information 1 session per year. Session length: 6 weeks in June, July. Ages: 16+. 16 participants per session. Cost: $3000–$4000. Financial aid available.
Application Deadline Continuous.
Jobs Positions for college students 21 and older.
Contact Ms. Vidhea Shrestha, Director of Programs, GPO Box 8974, CPC373, Kathmandu, Nepal. Phone: 866-840-9197. E-mail: programs@passageproject.org.
URL www.passageproject.org

THE NEPAL CULTURAL IMMERSION EXPERIENCE

International Cultural Adventures
Kathmandu
Nepal

General Information Coed travel community service program, cultural program, and adventure program

established in 1992. Formal opportunities for the academically talented and artistically talented. High school or college credit may be earned.
Program Focus A unique volunteer service program that provides participants with an intimate cross-cultural immersion experience.
Academics English as a second language, Nepali, archaeology, area studies, art history/appreciation, geography, geology/earth science, government and politics, history, intercultural studies, music, religion.
Arts Ceramics, dance, dance (folk), music, music (folk).
Special Interest Areas Community service, cross-cultural education, field trips (arts and culture), homestays, touring.
Sports Martial arts.
Wilderness/Outdoors Hiking, mountain biking, safari, white-water trips, wilderness/outdoors (general).
Trips Cultural, day, overnight.
Program Information 1–3 sessions per year. Session length: 44–90 days in February, July, August, September. Ages: 15+. 3–10 participants per session. Cost: $2250–$2950.
Application Deadline Continuous.
Contact David B. Pruskin, Program Director, 35 Suprenant Circle, Brunswick, Maine 04011-7142. Phone: 888-339-0460. Fax: 208-728-7338. E-mail: info@ICAdventures.com.
URL www.ICAdventures.com

Personal Passage

Passage: Project for International Education
Kathmandu
Nepal

General Information Coed travel academic program and cultural program established in 2002.
Academics Nepali, anthropology, area studies, art (Advanced Placement), art history/appreciation, botany, geology/earth science, health sciences, history, humanities, intercultural studies, journalism, language study, music, music (Advanced Placement), peace education, philosophy, religion, social science, social studies.
Arts Arts and crafts (general), ceramics, creative writing, dance, dance (folk), drawing, film, jewelry making, leather working, metalworking, music, music (vocal), painting, photography, pottery, printmaking, sculpture, television/video, weaving, woodworking.
Special Interest Areas Career exploration, community service, cross-cultural education, field research/expeditions, gardening, homestays, internships, nature study, touring.
Trips Cultural, day.
Program Information Session length: 30–150 days in January, February, March, April, May, June, July, August, September, October, November, December. Ages: 16+. Cost: $1250–$3000. Financial aid available.
Application Deadline Continuous.
Jobs Positions for college students 21 and older.
Contact Ms. Vidhea Shrestha, Director of Programs, GPO Box 8974, CPC373, Kathmandu, Nepal. Phone: 866-840-9197. E-mail: programs@passageproject.org.
URL www.passageproject.org

NETHERLANDS

AFS-USA–Homestay Plus–Netherlands

AFS-USA
Netherlands

General Information Coed residential cultural program.
Program Focus Living with a host family and taking part in activities with other teenagers, followed by a one-week bicycle trip.
Academics Dutch language.
Special Interest Areas Homestays.
Sports Bicycling.
Wilderness/Outdoors Bicycle trips.
Trips Cultural, day, overnight.
Program Information 1 session per year. Session length: 6 weeks in June, July, August. Ages: 15–17. Boarding program cost: $4065–$4365. Application fee: $75. Financial aid available. International airfare and volunteer homestay support included.
Application Deadline Continuous.
Contact Manager, AFS Info Center, 506 Southwest 6th Avenue, 2nd Floor, Portland, Oregon 97204. Phone: 800-AFS-INFO. Fax: 503-248-4076. E-mail: afsinfo@afs.org.
URL www.afs.org/usa

For more information, see page 974.

Center for Cultural Interchange–Netherlands High School Abroad

Center for Cultural Interchange
Netherlands

General Information Coed residential academic program and cultural program established in 1985. High school credit may be earned.
Program Focus Cultural immersion, high school in Holland.
Academics Dutch language, academics (general), independent study.
Special Interest Areas Cross-cultural education, homestays.
Trips Cultural, day.
Program Information 2 sessions per year. Session length: 150–300 days in January, February, March, April, May, June, August, September, October, November, December. Ages: 15–18. Boarding program cost: $5390–$6190. Financial aid available.
Application Deadline Continuous.
Contact Ms. Juliet Jones, Outbound Programs Director, 325 West Huron, Suite 706, Chicago, Illinois 60610. Phone: 866-684-9675. Fax: 312-944-2644. E-mail: info@cci-exchange.com.
URL www.cci-exchange.com

For more information, see page 1060.

NEW ZEALAND

AFS-USA–Homestay Plus–New Zealand

AFS-USA
New Zealand

General Information Coed residential outdoor program and cultural program.
Program Focus Living with a host family and participating in outdoor activities such as rafting, rock climbing, and wilderness camping. During the homestay students will also be involved in a community service project such as visiting schools or working at a public library.
Special Interest Areas Animal care, career exploration, community service, construction, culinary arts, farming, gardening, homestays.
Sports Kayaking.
Wilderness/Outdoors Backpacking, canoe trips, caving, hiking, mountaineering, orienteering, outdoor adventure, rafting, rock climbing, wilderness camping.
Trips Cultural, day, overnight.
Program Information 1 session per year. Session length: 7 weeks in June, July, August. Ages: 15–18. 40–60 participants per session. Boarding program cost: $4665–$5165. Application fee: $75. Financial aid available. International airfare and volunteer homestay support included.
Application Deadline Continuous.
Contact Manager, AFS Info Center, 506 Southwest 6th Avenue, 2nd Floor, Portland, Oregon 97204. Phone: 800-AFS-INFO. Fax: 503-248-4076. E-mail: afsinfo@afs.org.
URL www.afs.org/usa

For more information, see page 974.

EARTHWATCH INSTITUTE–New Zealand Dolphins

Earthwatch Institute
Kaikoura Peninsula
New Zealand

General Information Coed residential outdoor program, cultural program, and adventure program.
Program Focus Learning the basics of dusky dolphin society to manage fisheries and tourism for the benefit of both dolphins and humans.
Academics Marine studies, science (general).
Special Interest Areas Field research/expeditions, nature study.
Program Information 12 sessions per year. Session length: 13 days in January, February, March, April, May, June, July. Ages: 16+. 8 participants per session. Boarding program cost: $1995–$2095. Financial aid available. Financial aid for high school students and teachers.
Application Deadline Continuous.
Contact General Information Desk, PO Box 75, Maynard, Massachusetts 01754. Phone: 800-776-0188. Fax: 978-461-2332. E-mail: info@earthwatch.org.
URL www.earthwatch.org

The Experiment in International Living–New Zealand Homestay

The Experiment in International Living
New Zealand

General Information Coed residential outdoor program, community service program, and cultural program established in 1932.
Program Focus International youth travel, homestay, community service.
Academics Ecology, intercultural studies.
Special Interest Areas Community service, homestays, nature study, touring.
Wilderness/Outdoors Backpacking, hiking.
Trips Cultural, day, overnight.
Program Information 1 session per year. Session length: 5 weeks in July, August. Ages: 14–19. 10–15 participants per session. Boarding program cost: $4400. Financial aid available.
Application Deadline May 1.
Contact Annie Thompson, Enrollment Director, Summer Abroad, Kipling Road, PO Box 676, Brattleboro, Vermont 05302-0676. Phone: 800-345-2929. Fax: 802-258-3428. E-mail: eil@worldlearning.org.
URL www.usexperiment.org

For more information, see page 1116.

Poulter Colorado Camps: Adventures Planet Earth–New Zealand

Poulter Colorado Camps
New Zealand

General Information Coed travel outdoor program, cultural program, and adventure program established in 1966. Accredited by American Camping Association.
Program Focus Exciting international experiences combining adventure travel with cultural immersion.
Academics Intercultural studies.
Special Interest Areas Community service, homestays, leadership training, nature study, touring.
Sports Sea kayaking, skiing (downhill).
Wilderness/Outdoors Backpacking, bicycle trips, hiking.
Trips Cultural, day, overnight, shopping.
Program Information 2–4 sessions per year. Session length: 17–30 days in June, July, August, September, October. Ages: 13+. 6–10 participants per session. Cost: $1950–$3500. Financial aid available.
Application Deadline Continuous.
Jobs Positions for college students 21 and older.
Contact Mr. Jay B. Poulter, Director, PO Box 772947, Steamboat Springs, Colorado 80477. Phone: 888-879-4816. Fax: 800-860-3587. E-mail: poulter@poultercamps.com.
URL www.poultercamps.com

RUSTIC PATHWAYS–SKI AND SNOWBOARD ADVENTURE IN NEW ZEALAND

Rustic Pathways
New Zealand

General Information Coed travel adventure program established in 1994.
Sports Bungee jumping, skiing (downhill), snowboarding.
Wilderness/Outdoors Glacier travel, hiking.
Trips Day.
Program Information 6 sessions per year. Session length: 10–24 days in July, August. Ages: 15–18. 15–20 participants per session. Cost: $1295–$3695.
Application Deadline Continuous.
Jobs Positions for college students 21 and older.
Contact Ms. Tanya Ranaldi, Director, New Zealand Programs, 4121 Erie Street, Willoughby, Ohio 44094. Phone: 440-975-9691. Fax: 440-975-9694. E-mail: tanya@rusticpathways.com.
URL www.rusticpathways.com

For more information, see page 1290.

NICARAGUA

PUTNEY STUDENT TRAVEL–COMMUNITY SERVICE-NICARAGUA

Putney Student Travel
Ometepe
Nicaragua

General Information Coed residential community service program established in 1951.
Program Focus Community service, cultural exchange, and weekend excursions from a base in a small, rural community.
Academics Intercultural studies.
Special Interest Areas Community service, construction, team building.
Sports Snorkeling, swimming.
Wilderness/Outdoors Hiking, mountain biking.
Trips Cultural, day, overnight.
Program Information 1 session per year. Session length: 28–30 days in June, July. Ages: 14–18. 16 participants per session. Boarding program cost: $5100. Financial aid available.
Application Deadline Continuous.
Jobs Positions for college students 21 and older.
Contact Jeffrey Shumlin, Director, 345 Hickory Ridge Road, Putney, Vermont 05346. Phone: 802-387-5000. Fax: 802-387-4276. E-mail: info@goputney.com.
URL www.goputney.com

For more information, see page 1276.

SPANISH THROUGH LEADERSHIP–NICARAGUA

Nicaragua/Costa Rica High School Summer Exchange
Granada
Nicaragua

General Information Coed travel community service program and cultural program established in 1997. High school credit may be earned.

Spanish Through Leadership–Nicaragua

Program Focus Spanish immersion through community and culture.
Academics Spanish language/literature.
Arts Ceramics, dance, dance (Latin), music (instrumental), pottery.
Special Interest Areas Community service, homestays, leadership training.
Sports Basketball, ropes course, soccer, surfing, volleyball.
Wilderness/Outdoors Hiking, zip line.
Trips Cultural, day, overnight.
Program Information 2–3 sessions per year. Session length: 3–4 weeks in June, July, August. Ages: 14–18. 15–20 participants per session. Cost: $2650–$2850. Application fee: $250.
Application Deadline Continuous.
Contact Ms. Ilba Prego, Director, 1650 Monroe Street, Madison, Wisconsin 53711. Phone: 608-255-1426. E-mail: nica@terracom.net.
URL www.highschoolspanish.org

For more information, see page 1326.

SUMMER DELEGATION TO LEÓN, NICARAGUA

New Haven/León Sister City Project
León
Nicaragua

General Information Coed travel community service program and cultural program established in 1984.
Program Focus Social justice and sustainable development.

Summer Delegation to León, Nicaragua (continued)
Special Interest Areas Community service, cross-cultural education, homestays.
Trips Cultural, day.
Program Information 2–5 sessions per year. Session length: 10–15 days in March, July, August. Ages: 16+. 5–15 participants per session. Cost: $700–$1000. Financial aid available.
Contact Program Director, 608 Whitney Avenue, New Haven, Connecticut 06511. Phone: 203-562-1607. Fax: 203-624-1683. E-mail: nh@newhavenleon.org.
URL www.newhavenleon.org

NORWAY

Eagle Lake Camp Jaunts–Norway Mission Adventure

The Navigators
Norway

General Information Coed travel community service program and bible camp established in 2001. Religious affiliation: Christian. Accredited by American Camping Association.
Program Focus Missions, team building, group and individual Bible study.
Academics Bible study.
Special Interest Areas Community service, construction, work camp programs.
Wilderness/Outdoors Hiking, mountaineering, orienteering.
Program Information 1 session per year. Session length: 19 days in June, July, August. Ages: 16+. 20 participants per session. Cost: $3700. Financial aid available. Airfare from Denver included; participants are housed with host-families.
Application Deadline Continuous.
Jobs Positions for college students 19 and older.
Summer Contact Office Manager, PO Box 6000, Colorado Springs, Colorado 80934. Phone: 719-472-1260. Fax: 719-623-0148. E-mail: registrar_el@navigators.org.
Winter Contact John Rogers, Director of Excursion Ministries, main address above. E-mail: john_rogers@navigators.org.
URL www.eaglelake.org

Environmental Studies and Solutions

Scandinavian Seminar
Norway

General Information Coed travel outdoor program and cultural program established in 1999. Formal opportunities for the academically talented. High school or college credit may be earned.
Program Focus Interdisciplinary, cross-cultural approach to the environment and culture.
Academics Academics (general), architecture, area studies, biology, botany, business, ecology, environmental science, geography, geology/earth science, government and politics, history, humanities, intercultural studies, marine studies, peace education, philosophy, precollege program, psychology, science (general), social science, social studies, writing.
Arts Art (folk), arts and crafts (general), creative writing, dance (folk), drawing, fabric arts, photography, weaving, woodworking.
Special Interest Areas Animal care, campcraft, career exploration, culinary arts, farming, field research/expeditions, homestays, leadership training, nature study, nautical skills, touring.
Sports Boating, canoeing, fishing, sailing, swimming, volleyball.
Wilderness/Outdoors Backpacking, canoe trips, hiking, orienteering, wilderness camping.
Trips Cultural, day, overnight, shopping.
Program Information 1 session per year. Session length: 19 days in July. Ages: 15+. 15–30 participants per session. Cost: $2875. Financial aid available.
Application Deadline February 1.
Jobs Positions for college students 20 and older.
Contact Ms. Leslie Evans, Program Coordinator, 24 Dickinson Street, Amherst, Massachusetts 01002. Phone: 413-253-9736. Fax: 413-253-5282. E-mail: study@scandinavianseminar.org.
URL www.scandinavianseminar.org

PANAMA

AFS-USA–Community Service–Panama

AFS-USA
Panama

General Information Coed residential community service program and cultural program. High school credit may be earned.
Program Focus Stay in Puerto Belo in the Caribbean and work to protect coral reefs. Visit mountain community to work on reforestation, and live with host families in cities of David and Panama City.
Academics Spanish language/literature, geology/earth science.
Special Interest Areas Community service, field research/expeditions, nature study.
Wilderness/Outdoors Backpacking, hiking, mountaineering.
Trips Cultural, day, overnight.
Program Information 1 session per year. Session length: 4 weeks in July. Ages: 15–18. 20–30 participants per session. Boarding program cost: $3965–$4265. Application fee: $75. Financial aid available. International airfare and volunteer homestay support included.
Application Deadline Continuous.

Contact Manager, AFS Info Center, 506 Southwest 6th Avenue, 2nd Floor, Portland, Oregon 97204. Phone: 800-AFS-INFO. Fax: 503-248-4076. E-mail: afsinfo@afs.org.
URL www.afs.org/usa
For more information, see page 974.

Contact Manager, AFS Info Center, 506 Southwest 6th Avenue, 2nd Floor, Portland, Oregon 97204. Phone: 800-AFS-INFO. Fax: 503-248-4076. E-mail: afsinfo@afs.org.
URL www.afs.org/usa
For more information, see page 974.

PARAGUAY

AFS-USA–Community Service–Paraguay

AFS-USA
Paraguay

General Information Coed residential community service program and cultural program established in 1995. High school credit may be earned.
Program Focus Volunteer in a nature preserve or with indigenous people.
Academics Spanish language/literature, ecology, intercultural studies.
Special Interest Areas Community service, homestays.
Trips Cultural, day, overnight.
Program Information 1 session per year. Session length: 45 days in July, August. Ages: 16+. 10–25 participants per session. Boarding program cost: $3765–$4065. Application fee: $75. Financial aid available. International airfare and volunteer homestay support included.
Application Deadline Continuous.
Contact Manager, AFS Info Center, 506 Southwest 6th Avenue, 2nd Floor, Portland, Oregon 97204. Phone: 800-AFS-INFO. Fax: 503-248-4076. E-mail: afsinfo@afs.org.
URL www.afs.org/usa
For more information, see page 974.

AFS-USA–Homestay–Paraguay

AFS-USA
Paraguay

General Information Coed residential academic program and cultural program.
Program Focus Living with a host family, taking part in activities with other teenagers, and attending high school in Paraguay.
Academics Spanish language/literature, academics (general), social studies.
Special Interest Areas Homestays, touring.
Trips Cultural, day, overnight.
Program Information 1 session per year. Session length: 6 weeks in June, July, August. Ages: 15–18. 10–20 participants per session. Boarding program cost: $3665–$3965. Application fee: $75. Financial aid available. International airfare and volunteer homestay support included.
Application Deadline Continuous.

PERU

AAVE–Peru and Machu Picchu

AAVE–America's Adventure Ventures Everywhere
Peru

General Information Coed travel outdoor program, wilderness program, cultural program, and adventure program established in 1976. Accredited by American Camping Association.
Program Focus Cultural and outdoor experience.
Academics Area studies, intercultural studies.
Special Interest Areas Community service, cross-cultural education, leadership training, touring.
Wilderness/Outdoors Backpacking, hiking, rafting.
Trips Cultural, day, overnight.
Program Information 2–4 sessions per year. Session length: 3 weeks in June, July, August. Ages: 14–18. 12 participants per session. Cost: $4088. Financial aid available.
Jobs Positions for college students 21 and older.
Contact Mr. Abbott Wallis, Owner, America's Adventure, 2245 Stonecrop Way, Golden, Colorado 80401. Phone: 800-222-3595. Fax: 303-526-0885. E-mail: info@aave.com.
URL www.aave.com
For more information, see page 952.

EARTHWATCH INSTITUTE–Rivers of the Peruvian Amazon

Earthwatch Institute
Madre de Dios
Peru

General Information Coed residential outdoor program, wilderness program, cultural program, and adventure program.
Program Focus Documenting Amazon river biology and hydrology as part of an international program to protect these waters.
Academics Biology, ecology, science (general).
Special Interest Areas Field research/expeditions, nature study.
Program Information 4 sessions per year. Session length: 12 days in July, August. Ages: 16+. 7 participants per session. Boarding program cost: $1795–$1895. Financial aid available. Financial aid for high school students and teachers.
Application Deadline Continuous.

EARTHWATCH INSTITUTE–Rivers of the Peruvian Amazon (continued)
Contact General Information Desk, PO Box 75, Maynard, Massachusetts 01754. Phone: 800-776-0188. Fax: 978-461-2332. E-mail: info@earthwatch.org.
URL www.earthwatch.org

LSA Cuzco, Peru

Language Studies Abroad, Inc.
Cuzco
Peru

General Information Coed residential academic program and cultural program. Formal opportunities for the academically talented. High school or college credit may be earned.
Program Focus Language and culture.
Academics Spanish (Advanced Placement), Spanish language/literature, academics (general), archaeology, intercultural studies.
Special Interest Areas Homestays.
Wilderness/Outdoors Backpacking, hiking, mountaineering.
Trips Cultural, day, overnight.
Program Information 2–26 sessions per year. Session length: 13–300 days in January, February, March, April, May, June, July, August, September, October, November, December. Ages: 16+. 1–5 participants per session. Boarding program cost: $575–$2100. Application fee: $100. Financial aid available.
Application Deadline Continuous.
Contact Director, 1801 Highway 50 East, Suite I, Carson City, Nevada 89701. Phone: 800-424-5522. Fax: 775-883-2266. E-mail: info@languagestudiesabroad.com.
URL www.languagestudiesabroad.com/

For more information, see page 1186.

Peace Works International–Peru

Peace Works International
Peru

General Information Coed travel community service program, cultural program, and adventure program established in 1999.
Academics Spanish language/literature, intercultural studies, peace education.
Special Interest Areas Community service, construction, cross-cultural education.
Sports Volleyball.
Wilderness/Outdoors Backpacking, hiking.
Trips Cultural, overnight.
Program Information 1 session per year. Session length: 26 days in July. Ages: 15–18. 16–18 participants per session. Cost: $3895–$3995. Airfare included.
Application Deadline Continuous.
Contact Mr. Christopher Kealey, Executive Director, PO Box 70905, Pasadena, California 91117. Phone: 626-798-5221. Fax: 626-798-2959. E-mail: info@peaceworksintl.org.
URL www.peaceworksintl.org

For more information, see page 1250.

The Peru Cultural Immersion Experience

International Cultural Adventures
Cuzco
Peru

General Information Coed travel community service program, cultural program, and adventure program established in 2000. Formal opportunities for the academically talented and artistically talented. High school or college credit may be earned.
Program Focus A unique volunteer service program that provides participants with an intimate cross-cultural immersion experience.
Academics English as a second language, Spanish (Advanced Placement), Spanish language/literature, archaeology, area studies, art history/appreciation, geography, geology/earth science, government and politics, history, intercultural studies, music, religion.
Arts Ceramics, music, music (folk).
Special Interest Areas Community service, cross-cultural education, field trips (arts and culture), homestays, touring.
Sports Soccer.
Wilderness/Outdoors Hiking.
Trips Cultural, day, overnight.
Program Information 1–3 sessions per year. Session length: 44–90 days in March, July, August, September. Ages: 15+. 3–10 participants per session. Cost: $3050–$3850.
Application Deadline Continuous.
Contact David B. Pruskin, Program Director, 35 Suprenant Circle, Brunswick, Maine 04011-7142. Phone: 888-339-0460. Fax: 208-728-7338. E-mail: info@ICAdventures.com.

Programs Abroad Travel Alternatives–Peru

Programs Abroad Travel Alternatives
Peru

General Information Coed travel academic program, community service program, and cultural program established in 1996. Formal opportunities for the academically talented. College credit may be earned.
Program Focus Immersion for foreign language students.
Academics Spanish language/literature, art history/appreciation, history, intercultural studies.
Special Interest Areas Cross-cultural education, homestays, touring.
Trips Cultural, overnight.
Program Information 2–3 sessions per year. Session length: 9–34 days in March, June, July. Ages: 15–19. 1–30 participants per session. Cost: $1500–$4500. Application fee: $90.
Application Deadline Continuous.
Contact Heather Kenley, Director of Operations, 6200 Adel Cove, Austin, Texas 78749. Phone: 888-777-PATA. Fax: 512-282-7076. E-mail: immerse@gopata.com.
URL www.gopata.com

For more information, see page 1248.

Visions–Peru
Visions
Peru

General Information Coed travel outdoor program, community service program, and cultural program established in 1989. High school credit may be earned.
Program Focus Community service, cross-cultural experience, language immersion, and outdoor adventure activities.
Academics Spanish language/literature, intercultural studies, language study.
Arts Carpentry, painting, pottery.
Special Interest Areas Community service, construction, cross-cultural education, field trips (arts and culture), leadership training, nature study.
Wilderness/Outdoors Backpacking, hiking, rafting.
Trips Cultural, day, overnight.
Program Information 1–2 sessions per year. Session length: 3–4 weeks in June, July, August. Ages: 14–18. 20–25 participants per session. Cost: $2975–$3980. Financial aid available.
Application Deadline Continuous.
Jobs Positions for college students 22 and older.
Contact Joanne Pinaire, Director, PO Box 220, Newport, Pennsylvania 17074. Phone: 717-567-7313. Fax: 717-567-7853. E-mail: info@visionsserviceadventures.com.
URL www.visionsserviceadventures.com

For more information, see page 1382.

Where There Be Dragons: Peru
Where There Be Dragons
Peru

General Information Coed travel academic program, outdoor program, community service program, wilderness program, cultural program, and adventure program established in 1993. High school credit may be earned.
Program Focus Spanish language study, health-care and ecological restoration focus cultural studies with sustainable development internships.
Academics Spanish language/literature, anthropology, archaeology, area studies, art history/appreciation, geography, government and politics, health sciences, history, humanities, intercultural studies, music, peace education, reading, social science, social studies, writing.
Arts Ceramics, creative writing, dance (folk), music.
Special Interest Areas Native American culture, community service, field research/expeditions, homestays, nature study.
Sports Bicycling, canoeing, fishing, soccer.
Wilderness/Outdoors Backpacking, canoe trips, hiking, rafting.
Trips Cultural, overnight.
Program Information 1 session per year. Session length: 6 weeks in July, August. Ages: 15–19. 10–12 participants per session. Cost: $6250. Financial aid available.
Application Deadline Continuous.
Contact Mr. Chris Yager, Director, PO Box 4651, Boulder, Colorado 80306. Phone: 800-982-9203. Fax: 303-413-0857. E-mail: info@wheretherebedragons.com.
URL www.wheretherebedragons.com

For more information, see page 1394.

POLAND

Earthwatch Institute–Poland's Ancient Burials
Earthwatch Institute
Poland

General Information Coed residential outdoor program.
Program Focus Excavating the largest burial ground in Poland to reveal 2,000 years of cultural history.
Academics Archaeology.
Special Interest Areas Field research/expeditions.
Trips Cultural, day.
Program Information 3 sessions per year. Session length: 10 days in August, September. Ages: 16+. 12 participants per session. Boarding program cost: $1795–$1895. Financial aid available. Financial aid for high school students and teachers.
Application Deadline Continuous.
Contact General Information Desk, PO Box 75, Maynard, Massachusetts 01754. Phone: 800-776-0188. Fax: 978-461-2332. E-mail: info@earthwatch.org.
URL www.earthwatch.org

The Experiment in International Living–Poland, Homestay, Community Service, and Travel
The Experiment in International Living
Poland

General Information Coed residential community service program, cultural program, and adventure program established in 1932.
Program Focus International youth travel, homestay, public policy.
Academics Polish language/literature, government and politics.
Special Interest Areas Community service, homestays, touring.
Wilderness/Outdoors Hiking.
Trips Cultural, day, overnight.
Program Information 1 session per year. Session length: 5 weeks in July, August. Ages: 14–19. 10–15 participants per session. Boarding program cost: $4800. Application fee: $75. Financial aid available.
Application Deadline May 1.

The Experiment in International Living–Poland, Homestay, Community Service, and Travel (continued)

Contact Ms. Annie Thompson, Enrollment Director, Summer Abroad, Kipling Road, PO Box 676, Brattleboro, Vermont 05302-0676. Phone: 800-345-2929. Fax: 802-258-3428. E-mail: eil@worldlearning.org.
URL www.usexperiment.org

For more information, see page 1116.

YOUTH FOR UNDERSTANDING USA–POLAND

Youth for Understanding USA
Poland

General Information Coed residential academic program and cultural program established in 1951. High school or college credit may be earned.
Program Focus Living with a host family, learning about other cultures, and improving language skills.
Academics Polish language/literature, area studies, intercultural studies, social studies.
Special Interest Areas Homestays.
Trips Cultural, day, overnight.
Program Information 1 session per year. Session length: 35–45 days in June, July, August. Ages: 15–18. 10–50 participants per session. Boarding program cost: $4995. Application fee: $75. Financial aid available. Round-trip domestic and international airfare is included in the tuition.
Application Deadline Continuous.
Contact Admissions Counselor, 6400 Goldsboro Road, Suite 100, Bethesda, Maryland 20817. Phone: 800-TEENAGE (833-6243). Fax: 202-895-1104. E-mail: admissions@us.yfu.org.
URL www.yfu-usa.org

For more information, see page 1414.

PORTUGAL

LSA LISBON, PORTUGAL

Language Studies Abroad, Inc.
Lisbon
Portugal

General Information Coed residential academic program and cultural program established in 1959. Formal opportunities for the academically talented and artistically talented. High school or college credit may be earned.
Program Focus Learning language and culture.
Academics Portuguese language/literature, business, computer science (Advanced Placement), intercultural studies, language study.
Arts Ceramics.
Special Interest Areas Culinary arts, homestays.
Trips College tours, cultural, day, overnight, shopping.
Program Information 1–26 sessions per year. Session length: 2–4 weeks in January, February, March, April, May, June, July, August, September, October, November, December. Ages: 16+. 40–100 participants per session. Boarding program cost: $780–$1425. Application fee: $100. Financial aid available.
Application Deadline Continuous.
Contact Director, 1801 Highway 50 East, Suite I, Carson City, Nevada 89701. Phone: 800-424-5522. Fax: 775-883-2266. E-mail: info@languagestudiesabroad.com.
URL www.languagestudiesabroad.com

For more information, see page 1186.

PUERTO RICO

EARTHWATCH INSTITUTE–PUERTO RICO'S RAINFOREST

Earthwatch Institute
Las Casas de la Selva
Patillas
Puerto Rico

General Information Coed residential outdoor program, wilderness program, and adventure program.
Program Focus Testing the effectiveness of a new forestry method that could provide local income while conserving the rainforest.
Academics Botany, ecology, environmental science, forestry, science (general).
Special Interest Areas Field research/expeditions, nature study.
Wilderness/Outdoors Hiking.
Program Information 4 sessions per year. Session length: 10 days in January, March, June, July, December. Ages: 16+. 12 participants per session. Boarding program cost: $1495–$1595. Financial aid available. Financial aid for high school students and teachers.
Application Deadline Continuous.
Contact General Information Desk, PO Box 75, Maynard, Massachusetts 01754. Phone: 800-776-0188. Fax: 978-461-2332. E-mail: info@earthwatch.org.
URL www.earthwatch.org

GLOBAL WORKS–LANGUAGE EXPOSURE–PUERTO RICO–3 WEEKS

GLOBAL WORKS
Puerto Rico

General Information Coed travel community service program, cultural program, and adventure program established in 1988. High school credit may be earned.
Academics Spanish language/literature, intercultural studies, language study.
Arts Arts and crafts (general), dance (Latin).
Special Interest Areas Community service, construction, team building.
Sports Basketball, scuba diving, snorkeling, soccer, swimming, volleyball.
Wilderness/Outdoors Hiking, outdoor adventure.
Trips Cultural, day, overnight.

Program Information 2 sessions per year. Session length: 23 days in June, July, August. Ages: 14–18. 23–25 participants per session. Cost: $3250–$3350. Application fee: $100. Financial aid available. Airfare not included.
Application Deadline Continuous.
Jobs Positions for college students 23 and older.
Contact Erik Werner, Director, 1113 South Allen Street, State College, Pennsylvania 16801. Phone: 814-867-7000. Fax: 814-867-2717. E-mail: info@globalworksinc.com.
URL www.globalworksinc.com
For more information, see page 1136.

GLOBAL WORKS–Language Immersion-Puerto Rico-4 weeks

GLOBAL WORKS
Puerto Rico

General Information Coed travel community service program, cultural program, and adventure program established in 1988. High school credit may be earned.
Program Focus Environmental and community service, language learning, and cultural exchange.
Academics Spanish language/literature, intercultural studies.
Arts Arts and crafts (general), creative writing, dance.
Special Interest Areas Community service, construction, field trips (arts and culture), homestays.
Sports Basketball, scuba diving, snorkeling, soccer, sports (general), swimming, volleyball.
Wilderness/Outdoors Hiking.
Trips Cultural, day, overnight.
Program Information 1 session per year. Session length: 23 days in June, July, August. Ages: 15–18. 15–16 participants per session. Cost: $3750–$3850. Application fee: $100. Financial aid available. Airfare not included.
Application Deadline Continuous.
Jobs Positions for college students 23 and older.
Contact Erik Werner, Director, 1113 South Allen Street, State College, Pennsylvania 16801. Phone: 814-867-7000. Fax: 814-867-2717. E-mail: info@globalworksinc.com.
URL www.globalworksinc.com
For more information, see page 1136.

Windsor Mountain: Puerto Rico

Interlocken at Windsor Mountain
Puerto Rico

General Information Coed travel community service program, cultural program, and adventure program established in 1967.
Program Focus Cross-cultural exploration, family stays, language training.
Academics Spanish language/literature, intercultural studies.
Special Interest Areas Conservation projects, homestays, team building.
Sports Snorkeling.
Wilderness/Outdoors Caving.
Program Information 1 session per year. Session length: 23 days in July, August. Ages: 13–16. 12–15 participants per session. Cost: $3495. Financial aid available.
Application Deadline Continuous.
Contact Tom Herman, Marketing Director, 19 Interlocken Way, Windsor, New Hampshire 03244. Phone: 603-478-3166 Ext.20. Fax: 603-478-5260. E-mail: mail@windsormountain.org.
URL www.windsormountain.org/xrds/PR.html
For more information, see page 1162.

World Horizons International–Puerto Rico

World Horizons International
San Juan and Island of Culebra
Puerto Rico

General Information Coed residential outdoor program, community service program, and cultural program established in 2002.
Program Focus Community service and cross-cultural education.
Special Interest Areas Community service, conservation projects, cross-cultural education, field research/expeditions, work camp programs.
Sports Snorkeling, swimming.
Wilderness/Outdoors Hiking.
Trips Cultural, day, overnight.
Program Information 1–2 sessions per year. Session length: 2–4 weeks in June, July. Ages: 14–18. 10–12 participants per session. Boarding program cost: $3250–$4500. Application fee: $100. Financial aid available. Program cost includes airfare from Miami.
Application Deadline Continuous.
Jobs Positions for college students 20 and older.
Contact Mr. Stuart L. Rabinowitz, Executive Director, PO Box 662, Bethlehem, Connecticut 06751. Phone: 800-262-5874. Fax: 203-266-6227. E-mail: worldhorizons@att.net.
URL www.world-horizons.com
For more information, see page 1406.

REPUBLIC OF KOREA

Elite Educational Institute Elementary Enrichment–Korea

Elite Educational Institute
Republic of Korea

General Information Coed day academic program established in 1987. Formal opportunities for the academically talented.
Program Focus Elementary education: 2nd-6th grade.
Academics English as a second language, English language/literature, SAT/ACT preparation, mathematics, precollege program, reading, social studies, study skills, writing.

Elite Educational Institute Elementary Enrichment–Korea (continued)

Program Information 3 sessions per year. 10–40 participants per session. Day program cost: $280–$320. Financial aid available.
Application Deadline Continuous.
Contact Mr. Min, Director, Kongnam-gu Shinsa dong 634-4, Kwakyung Building 3F, Seoul, Republic of Korea. Phone: 02-3444-6886. Fax: 02-3444-6887.
URL www.eliteprep.com

For more information, see page 1104.

ELITE EDUCATIONAL INSTITUTE JUNIOR HIGH/PSAT PROGRAM–KOREA

Elite Educational Institute
Republic of Korea

General Information Coed day academic program established in 1987. Formal opportunities for the academically talented.
Academics English as a second language, English language/literature, SAT/ACT preparation, mathematics, reading, study skills, writing.
Special Interest Areas College planning.
Program Information 3–4 sessions per year. 40–80 participants per session. Day program cost: $240–$320. Financial aid available.
Application Deadline Continuous.
Contact Mr. Min, Director, Kongnam-gu Shinsa dong 634-4, Hwakyung Building 3F, Seoul, Republic of Korea. Phone: 02-3444-6886. Fax: 02-3444-6887.
URL www.eliteprep.com

For more information, see page 1104.

ELITE EDUCATIONAL INSTITUTE SAT BOOTCAMP–KOREA

Elite Educational Institute
Republic of Korea

General Information Coed day academic program established in 1987. Formal opportunities for the academically talented.
Program Focus Intensive SAT preparation program.
Academics English language/literature, SAT/ACT preparation, mathematics, precollege program, reading, writing.
Special Interest Areas College planning.
Program Information 1 session per year. Session length: 10 weeks in June, July, August. 20–60 participants per session. Day program cost: $2200. Financial aid available.
Application Deadline June 15.
Contact Mr. Min, Director, Kongnam-gu Shinsa dong 634-4, Kwakyung Building 3F, Seoul, Republic of Korea. Phone: 02-3444-6886. Fax: 02-3444-6887.
URL www.eliteprep.com

For more information, see page 1104.

ELITE EDUCATIONAL INSTITUTE SAT PREPARATION–KOREA

Elite Educational Institute
Republic of Korea

General Information Coed day academic program established in 1987. Formal opportunities for the academically talented.
Program Focus SAT I and SAT II preparation.
Academics SAT/ACT preparation, mathematics, precollege program, writing.
Program Information 3 sessions per year. Session length: 100–350 days in January, February, March, April, May, June, July, August, September, October, November, December. Day program cost: $340–$440. Financial aid available.
Application Deadline Continuous.
Contact Mr. Min, Director, Kongnam-gu Shinsa dong 634-4, Kwakyung Building 3F, Seoul, Republic of Korea. Phone: 02-3444-6886. Fax: 02-3444-6887.
URL www.eliteprep.com

For more information, see page 1104.

YOUTH FOR UNDERSTANDING USA–SOUTH KOREA

Youth for Understanding USA
Republic of Korea

General Information Coed residential academic program and cultural program established in 1951. High school or college credit may be earned.
Program Focus Living with a host family, learning about other cultures, and improving language skills.
Academics Korean, area studies, intercultural studies, social studies.
Special Interest Areas Cross-cultural education, homestays.
Trips Cultural, day, overnight.
Program Information 1 session per year. Session length: 35–45 days in June, July, August. Ages: 15–18. 10–50 participants per session. Boarding program cost: $4995. Application fee: $75. Financial aid available. Round-trip domestic and international airfare is included in the tuition.
Application Deadline Continuous.
Contact Admissions Counselor, 6400 Goldsboro Road, Suite 100, Bethesda, Maryland 20817. Phone: 800-TEENAGE (833-6243). Fax: 202-895-1104. E-mail: admissions@us.yfu.org.
URL www.yfu-usa.org

For more information, see page 1414.

ROMANIA

EARTHWATCH INSTITUTE–ROMAN FORT ON THE DANUBE

Earthwatch Institute
Halmyris
Romania

General Information Coed residential outdoor program, cultural program, and adventure program.
Program Focus Unearthing a major Roman fort and military supply depot to clarify the two-way street of acculturation.
Academics Archaeology, classical civilizations, history, intercultural studies, science (general).
Arts Drawing.
Special Interest Areas Field research/expeditions, nature study.
Program Information 5 sessions per year. Session length: 2 weeks in June, July, August. Ages: 16+. 8 participants per session. Boarding program cost: $1895–$1995. Financial aid available. Financial aid for high school students and teachers.
Application Deadline Continuous.
Contact General Information Desk, PO Box 75, Maynard, Massachusetts 01754. Phone: 800-776-0188. Fax: 978-461-2332. E-mail: info@earthwatch.org.
URL www.earthwatch.org

RUSSIAN FEDERATION

AFS-USA–TEAM MISSION–RUSSIA

AFS-USA
Russian Federation

General Information Coed residential outdoor program, community service program, and cultural program established in 1995. High school credit may be earned.
Program Focus Community service and outdoor education program in Russia with an adult team leader.
Academics Russian language/literature, intercultural studies.
Special Interest Areas Campcraft, community service, cross-cultural education, field research/expeditions, homestays, nature study.
Sports Canoeing.
Wilderness/Outdoors Backpacking, canoe trips, caving, hiking.
Trips Cultural, day, overnight.
Program Information 1 session per year. Session length: 8 weeks in June, July. Ages: 14–19. 15 participants per session. Boarding program cost: $4365–$4865. Application fee: $75. Financial aid available. International airfare and volunteer homestay support included.
Application Deadline Continuous.
Contact Manager, AFS Info Center, 506 Southwest 6th Avenue, 2nd Floor, Portland, Oregon 97204. Phone: 800-AFS-INFO. Fax: 503-248-4076. E-mail: afsinfo@afs.org.
URL www.afs.org/usa
For more information, see page 974.

EARTHWATCH INSTITUTE–SINGING RUSSIA

Earthwatch Institute
Russian Federation

General Information Coed residential arts program and cultural program.
Program Focus Exploring the process of integrating folk music traditions into modern Russian culture.
Academics History, intercultural studies, music.
Arts Dance (folk), music, music (folk), photography.
Special Interest Areas Cross-cultural education, field research/expeditions, folklore.
Program Information 6 sessions per year. Session length: 12 days in February, May, June, July, August. Ages: 16+. 6 participants per session. Boarding program cost: $1995–$2095. Financial aid available. Financial aid for high school students and teachers.
Application Deadline Continuous.
Contact General Information Desk, PO Box 75, Maynard, Massachusetts 01754. Phone: 800-776-0188. Fax: 978-461-2332. E-mail: info@earthwatch.org.
URL www.earthwatch.org

EF INTERNATIONAL LANGUAGE SCHOOL–ST. PETERSBURG

EF International Language Schools
Nevsky Prospekt 44
St. Petersburg 191011
Russian Federation

General Information Coed travel academic program and cultural program established in 2002.
Program Focus Language and cultural immersion.
Academics Russian language/literature.
Special Interest Areas Field trips (arts and culture), touring.
Sports Sports (general).
Wilderness/Outdoors Wilderness/outdoors (general).
Trips Cultural, day.
Program Information Session length: 14–365 days in January, February, March, April, May, June, July, August, September, October, November, December. Ages: 16+. 50–100 participants per session. Call for costs.
Application Deadline Continuous.
Contact Ms. Katie Mahon, Director of Admissions, One Education Street, Cambridge, Massachusetts 02141. Phone: 800-922-1892. Fax: 800-590-1125. E-mail: ils@ef.com.
URL www.ef.com
For more information, see page 1102.

Knowledge Exchange Institute–Research Abroad in Russia

Knowledge Exchange Institute
Puschino Science Center
Puschino
Russian Federation

General Information Coed residential academic program established in 1993. Formal opportunities for the academically talented. College credit may be earned.
Program Focus Science research.
Academics Aerospace science, astronomy, biology, biology (Advanced Placement), botany, chemistry, computer programming, computer science (Advanced Placement), computers, engineering, environmental science, geography, geology/earth science, health sciences, mathematics, mathematics (Advanced Placement), meteorology, physics, physiology, precollege program, research skills, science (general), writing.
Special Interest Areas Field research/expeditions, field trips (arts and culture).
Trips Cultural, day, overnight.
Program Information 1 session per year. Ages: 15–19. 5–15 participants per session. Boarding program cost: $5705. Application fee: $50. Financial aid available.
Application Deadline March 20.
Contact Kei Program Manager, 111 John Street, Suite 800, New York, New York 10038. Phone: 800-831-5095. E-mail: info@knowledgeexchange.org.
URL www.KnowledgeExchange.org

LSA Moscow, Russia

Language Studies Abroad, Inc.
Moscow
Russian Federation

General Information Coed residential academic program and cultural program established in 1989. Formal opportunities for the academically talented and artistically talented. High school or college credit may be earned.
Program Focus Learning language and culture.
Academics Russian language/literature, art history/appreciation, business, intercultural studies, language study.
Special Interest Areas Homestays, hotel management.
Trips College tours, cultural, day, overnight, shopping.
Program Information 1–26 sessions per year. Session length: 14–360 days in January, February, March, April, May, June, July, August, September, October, November, December. Ages: 16+. 100–250 participants per session. Boarding program cost: $986–$3640. Application fee: $100. Financial aid available.
Application Deadline Continuous.
Contact Director, 1801 Highway 50 East, Suite I, Carson City, Nevada 89701. Phone: 800-424-5522. Fax: 775-883-2266. E-mail: info@languagestudiesabroad.com.
URL www.languagestudiesabroad.com

For more information, see page 1186.

LSA St. Petersburg, Russia

Language Studies Abroad, Inc.
St. Petersburg
Russian Federation

General Information Coed residential academic program and cultural program established in 1992. Formal opportunities for the academically talented and artistically talented. High school or college credit may be earned.
Program Focus Learning language and culture.
Academics Russian language/literature, banking/finance, intercultural studies, language study.
Special Interest Areas Homestays, hotel management.
Trips College tours, cultural, day, overnight, shopping.
Program Information 1–24 sessions per year. Session length: 14–360 days in January, February, March, April, May, June, July, August, September, October, November, December. Ages: 16+. 25–50 participants per session. Boarding program cost: $890–$3242. Application fee: $100. Financial aid available.
Application Deadline Continuous.
Contact Director, 1801 Highway 50 East, Suite I, Carson City, Nevada 89701. Phone: 800-424-5522. Fax: 775-883-2266. E-mail: info@languagestudiesabroad.com.
URL www.languagestudiesabroad.com

For more information, see page 1186.

Programs Abroad Travel Alternatives–Russia

Programs Abroad Travel Alternatives
Russian Federation

General Information Coed travel academic program and cultural program established in 1996. Formal opportunities for the academically talented. College credit may be earned.
Program Focus Immersion for foreign language students.
Academics Russian language/literature, art history/appreciation.
Special Interest Areas Cross-cultural education, homestays, touring.
Trips Cultural, overnight.
Program Information 2–3 sessions per year. Session length: 9–34 days in March, June, July. Ages: 15+. 10–30 participants per session. Cost: $1500–$4500. Application fee: $90. Participant must be in high school.
Application Deadline Continuous.
Contact Rose Potter, Founder/CEO, 6200 Adel Cove, Austin, Texas 78749. Phone: 888-777-PATA. Fax: 512-282-7076. E-mail: immerse@gopata.com.
URL www.gopata.com

For more information, see page 1248.

Volunteers for Peace International Work Camp–Russia

Volunteers for Peace International Work Camps
Russian Federation

General Information Coed residential community service program established in 1981. Specific services available for the hearing impaired and physically challenged. College credit may be earned.
Program Focus International work camps.
Academics Intercultural studies, peace education.
Special Interest Areas Community service, construction, work camp programs.
Trips Cultural, day, overnight.
Program Information Session length: 2–3 weeks in May, June, July. Ages: 17+. 12–20 participants per session. Boarding program cost: $250–$600.
Application Deadline Continuous.
Contact Peter Coldwell, Director, 1034 Tiffany Road, Belmont, Vermont 05730. Phone: 802-259-2759. Fax: 802-259-2922. E-mail: vfp@vfp.org.
URL www.vfp.org

Youth for Understanding USA–Russia

Youth for Understanding USA
Russian Federation

General Information Coed residential academic program and cultural program established in 1951. High school or college credit may be earned.
Program Focus Living with a host family, learning about other cultures, and improving Russian language skills.
Academics Russian language/literature, area studies, intercultural studies, social studies.
Special Interest Areas Homestays.
Trips Cultural, day, overnight.
Program Information 1 session per year. Session length: 4–5 weeks in June, July. Ages: 15–18. 10–50 participants per session. Boarding program cost: $4995. Application fee: $75. Financial aid available. Round-trip domestic and international airfare is included in the tuition.
Application Deadline Continuous.
Contact Admissions Counselor, 6400 Goldsboro Road, Suite 100, Bethesda, Maryland 20817. Phone: 800-TEENAGE (833-6243). Fax: 202-895-1104. E-mail: admissions@us.yfu.org.
URL www.yfu-usa.org
For more information, see page 1414.

SAINT VINCENT AND THE GRENADINES

BROADREACH Adventures in the Grenadines–Advanced Scuba

Broadreach
Saint Vincent and The Grenadines

General Information Coed travel outdoor program and adventure program established in 1992.
Program Focus Coed program focusing on advanced PADI scuba certification, PADI rescue certification, sail training, marine biology, island exploration.
Academics Ecology, environmental science, marine studies.
Arts Photography.
Special Interest Areas Community service, field research/expeditions, leadership training, nature study.
Sports Boating, fishing, sailing, scuba diving, snorkeling, waterskiing.
Wilderness/Outdoors Hiking.
Trips Cultural.
Program Information 2 sessions per year. Session length: 3 weeks in June, July, August. Ages: 14–19. 10–12 participants per session. Cost: $4580. Financial aid available.
Application Deadline Continuous.
Contact Carlton Goldthwaite, Director, PO Box 27076, Raleigh, North Carolina 27611-7076. Phone: 888-833-1907. Fax: 919-833-2129. E-mail: info@gobroadreach.com.
URL www.gobroadreach.com
For more information, see page 1008.

Windsor Mountain: Adventures in Filmmaking

Interlocken at Windsor Mountain
Saint Vincent and The Grenadines

General Information Coed travel arts program and cultural program established in 1967.
Program Focus Documentary film production.
Academics Intercultural studies.
Arts Film, film production.
Sports Scuba diving, snorkeling, swimming.
Trips Cultural, day.
Program Information 1 session per year. Session length: 4 weeks in July, August. Ages: 15–18. 12–16 participants per session. Cost: $4500. Financial aid available.
Application Deadline Continuous.
Contact Tom Herman, Marketing Director, 19 Interlocken Way, Windsor, New Hampshire 03244. Phone: 603-478-3166 Ext.20. Fax: 603-478-5260. E-mail: mail@windsormountain.org.
URL www.windsormountain.org/xrds
For more information, see page 1162.

SINGAPORE

SUPERCAMP–SINGAPORE

SuperCamp
Julia Gabriel Centre
Singapore

General Information Coed residential academic program established in 1990.
Academics SAT/ACT preparation, academics (general), communications, reading, study skills, writing.
Sports Ropes course, soccer, swimming.
Program Information 2–4 sessions per year. Session length: 7–10 days in December. Ages: 9–18. 50–100 participants per session. Boarding program cost: $1100–$1300. Application fee: $100. Financial aid available.
Application Deadline Continuous.
Jobs Positions for college students 18 and older.
Contact Enrollment Department, 1725 South Coast Highway, Oceanside, California 92054. Phone: 800-285-3276. Fax: 760-722-3507. E-mail: info@supercamp.com.
URL www.supercamp.com

For more information, see page 1348.

SLOVAKIA

VOLUNTEERS FOR PEACE INTERNATIONAL WORK CAMP–SLOVAKIA

Volunteers for Peace International Work Camps
Bratislava
Slovakia

General Information Coed residential community service program established in 1981. Specific services available for the hearing impaired and physically challenged. College credit may be earned.
Program Focus International work camps.
Academics Archaeology, intercultural studies, peace education.
Special Interest Areas Community service, construction, work camp programs.
Sports Swimming.
Wilderness/Outdoors Hiking.
Trips Cultural, day, overnight.
Program Information Session length: 2–3 weeks in June, July, August, September. Ages: 15+. 12–20 participants per session. Boarding program cost: $250–$600. Financial aid available.
Application Deadline Continuous.
Contact Peter Coldwell, Director, 1034 Tiffany Road, Belmont, Vermont 05730. Phone: 802-259-2759. Fax: 802-259-2922. E-mail: vfp@vfp.org.
URL www.vfp.org

SOUTH AFRICA

CENTER FOR CULTURAL INTERCHANGE–SOUTH AFRICA HIGH SCHOOL ABROAD

Center for Cultural Interchange
South Africa

General Information Coed residential academic program and cultural program established in 1985. High school credit may be earned.
Program Focus High school abroad, homestay program, cultural immersion.
Academics Academics (general), precollege program.
Special Interest Areas Cross-cultural education, homestays.
Trips Cultural, day.
Program Information 2 sessions per year. Session length: 90–300 days in January, February, March, April, May, June, July, August, September, October, November, December. Ages: 15–18. Boarding program cost: $5190–$7490. Financial aid available.
Application Deadline Continuous.
Contact Ms. Juliet Jones, Outbound Programs Director, 325 West Huron, Suite 706, Chicago, Illinois 60610. Phone: 866-684-9675. Fax: 312-944-2644. E-mail: info@cci-exchange.com.
URL www.cci-exchange.com

For more information, see page 1060.

EARTHWATCH INSTITUTE–MEERKATS OF THE KALAHARI

Earthwatch Institute
Kuruman River Reserve
South Africa

General Information Coed residential outdoor program.
Program Focus Investigating the evolutionary causes and ecological consequences of cooperative behavior.
Academics Ecology, environmental science.
Special Interest Areas Animal care, birdwatching, conservation projects, field research/expeditions, nature study.
Program Information 12 sessions per year. Session length: 2 weeks in March, April, May, June, July. Ages: 16+. 5 participants per session. Boarding program cost: $2795–$2895. Financial aid available. Financial aid for high school students and teachers.
Application Deadline Continuous.
Contact General Information Desk, PO Box 75, Maynard, Massachusetts 01754. Phone: 800-776-0188. Fax: 978-461-2332. E-mail: info@earthwatch.org.
URL www.earthwatch.org

EARTHWATCH INSTITUTE–SOUTH AFRICAN PENGUINS

Earthwatch Institute
Robben Island
South Africa

General Information Coed residential outdoor program, cultural program, and adventure program.
Program Focus Using technology to aid penguin conservation.
Academics Biology, science (general), zoology.
Special Interest Areas Field research/expeditions, nature study.
Program Information 7 sessions per year. Session length: 12 days in March, April, May, June, July, August, September. Ages: 16+. 4 participants per session. Boarding program cost: $1995–$2095. Financial aid available. Financial aid for high school students and teachers.
Application Deadline Continuous.
Contact General Information Desk, PO Box 75, Maynard, Massachusetts 01754. Phone: 800-776-0188. Fax: 978-461-2332. E-mail: info@earthwatch.org.
URL www.earthwatch.org

EARTHWATCH INSTITUTE–SOUTH AFRICAN WILDLIFE

Earthwatch Institute
Hluhluwe-Imfolozi National Park
South Africa

General Information Coed residential outdoor program, cultural program, and adventure program.
Program Focus Monitoring large herbivores to manage their impact on a world-class park.
Academics Ecology, science (general).
Special Interest Areas Conservation projects, field research/expeditions, nature study.
Wilderness/Outdoors Hiking.
Program Information 4 sessions per year. Session length: 16 days in July, August, September. Ages: 16+. 11 participants per session. Boarding program cost: $2395–$2495. Financial aid available. Financial aid for high school students and teachers.
Application Deadline Continuous.
Contact General Information Desk, PO Box 75, Maynard, Massachusetts 01754. Phone: 800-776-0188. Fax: 978-461-2332.
URL www.earthwatch.org

THE EXPERIMENT IN INTERNATIONAL LIVING–SOUTH AFRICA HOMESTAY AND COMMUNITY SERVICE

The Experiment in International Living
South Africa

General Information Coed residential outdoor program, arts program, community service program, cultural program, and adventure program established in 1932.
Program Focus International youth travel, homestays, community service, arts.
Arts Arts, arts and crafts (general), dance, theater/drama.
Special Interest Areas Community service, homestays, touring.
Trips Cultural, day, overnight.
Program Information 1 session per year. Session length: 5 weeks in July, August. Ages: 14–19. 10–20 participants per session. Boarding program cost: $4800. Application fee: $75. Financial aid available.
Application Deadline May 1.
Contact Annie Thompson, Enrollment Director, Summer Abroad, Kipling Road, PO Box 676, Brattleboro, Vermont 05302-0676. Phone: 800-345-2929. Fax: 802-258-3428. E-mail: eil@worldlearning.org.
URL www.usexperiment.org

For more information, see page 1116.

YOUTH FOR UNDERSTANDING USA–SOUTH AFRICA

Youth for Understanding USA
South Africa

General Information Coed residential academic program and cultural program. High school credit may be earned.
Special Interest Areas Community service, cross-cultural education, homestays.
Trips Cultural.
Program Information 1 session per year. Session length: 40 days in July, August. Ages: 15–18. 4 participants per session. Boarding program cost: $4595–$6495. Application fee: $75. Financial aid available. Round-trip domestic and international airfare is included in the tuition.
Application Deadline Continuous.
Contact Admissions Counselor, 6400 Goldsboro Road, Suite 100, Bethesda, Maryland 20817. Phone: 800-TEENAGE (833-6243). Fax: 202-895-1104. E-mail: admissions@us.yfu.org.
URL www.yfu-usa.org

For more information, see page 1414.

SPAIN

AAVE–INMERSIÓN EN ESPAÑA

AAVE–America's Adventure Ventures Everywhere
Spain

General Information Coed travel academic program, outdoor program, wilderness program, cultural program, and adventure program established in 1976. Accredited by American Camping Association.
Program Focus Language immersion and adventure travel.
Academics Spanish language/literature, intercultural studies.

AAVE–Inmersión en España (continued)

Special Interest Areas Community service, cross-cultural education, homestays, leadership training, touring.
Sports Bicycling, horseback riding, sailing, surfing, swimming.
Wilderness/Outdoors Backpacking, bicycle trips, hiking, rafting, rock climbing, white-water trips.
Trips Cultural, day, overnight.
Program Information 2–4 sessions per year. Session length: 30 days in June, July, August. Ages: 14–18. 13–15 participants per session. Cost: $4688. Financial aid available.
Application Deadline Continuous.
Jobs Positions for college students 21 and older.
Contact Mr. Abbott Wallis, Owner, 2245 Stonecrop Way, Golden, Colorado 80401. Phone: 800-222-3595. Fax: 303-526-0885. E-mail: info@aave.com.
URL www.aave.com

For more information, see page 952.

Abbey Road Overseas Programs–Spanish Immersion and Homestay

Abbey Road Overseas Programs
Cádiz
Spain

General Information Coed travel academic program, arts program, and cultural program established in 2001. Formal opportunities for the artistically talented. High school or college credit may be earned.
Program Focus Spanish language immersion, culture, arts and humanities.
Academics Spanish (Advanced Placement), Spanish language/literature, architecture, art history/appreciation, history, humanities, intercultural studies, precollege program.
Arts Arts and crafts (general), dance, drawing, graphic arts, music, theater/drama.
Special Interest Areas Culinary arts, homestays.
Sports Basketball, bicycling, boating, horseback riding, noncompetitive sports, sailing, soccer, swimming, tennis, volleyball.
Wilderness/Outdoors Backpacking, bicycle trips, hiking.
Trips Cultural, day, overnight, shopping.
Program Information 1–2 sessions per year. Session length: 28–34 days in June, July, August. Ages: 13–19. 30–50 participants per session. Cost: $4500–$5800.
Application Deadline Continuous.
Jobs Positions for college students 21 and older.
Contact Dr. Arthur Kian, Managing Director, 8904 Rangely Avenue, West Hollywood, California 90048. Phone: 888-462-2239. Fax: 866-488-4642. E-mail: info@goabbeyroad.com.
URL www.goabbeyroad.com/

Academic Study Associates–Barcelona

Academic Study Associates, Inc. (ASA)
Barcelona
Spain

General Information Coed residential academic program established in 2001. Formal opportunities for the academically talented. High school credit may be earned.
Program Focus Language and cultural immersion program combining language, activities, and excursions.
Academics Spanish (Advanced Placement), Spanish language/literature, architecture, intercultural studies, precollege program, writing.
Arts Film.
Special Interest Areas Touring.
Sports Basketball, soccer, swimming, tennis, volleyball.
Trips Cultural, day.
Program Information 1 session per year. Session length: 4 weeks in July. Ages: 15–18. 50–75 participants per session. Boarding program cost: $5395. Financial aid available.
Application Deadline Continuous.
Jobs Positions for college students 21 and older.
Contact Marcia Evans, President, 10 New King Street, White Plains, New York 10604. Phone: 914-686-7730. E-mail: summer@asaprograms.com.
URL www.asaprograms.com

Academic Study Associates–Spanish in España

Academic Study Associates, Inc. (ASA)
Spain

General Information Coed residential academic program established in 1984. Formal opportunities for the academically talented. High school credit may be earned.
Program Focus Spanish language, art history, culture.
Academics Spanish language/literature, academics (general), art history/appreciation, history, intercultural studies.
Arts Dance, dance (folk), drawing, painting, photography, pottery.
Special Interest Areas Culinary arts, field trips (arts and culture), homestays, touring.
Sports Basketball, boating, canoeing, equestrian sports, horseback riding, sailing, scuba diving, soccer, sports (general), swimming, tennis, volleyball.
Wilderness/Outdoors Wilderness camping.
Trips Cultural, day.
Program Information 1 session per year. Session length: 32 days in June, July. Ages: 15–18. 130–150 participants per session. Boarding program cost: $5395. Participant may study in Cadiz, Conil, Tarifa or Nerja.
Application Deadline Continuous.
Jobs Positions for college students 21 and older.
Contact Marcia E. Evans, President, 10 New King Street, White Plains, New York 10604. Phone: 914-686-7730. Fax: 914-686-7740. E-mail: summer@asaprograms.com.
URL www.asaprograms.com

AFS-USA–Homestay–Spain

AFS-USA
Spain

General Information Coed residential cultural program.
Program Focus Living with a host family and taking part in a language/culture camp.
Academics Spanish language/literature.
Special Interest Areas Homestays.
Trips Cultural, day, overnight.
Program Information 1 session per year. Session length: 4 weeks in July. Ages: 15–18. 35 participants per session. Boarding program cost: $4465–$4965. Application fee: $75. Financial aid available. International airfare and volunteer homestay support included.
Application Deadline Continuous.
Contact Manager, AFS Info Center, 506 Southwest 6th Avenue, 2nd Floor, Portland, Oregon 97204. Phone: 800-AFS-INFO. Fax: 503-248-4076. E-mail: afsinfo@afs.org.
URL www.afs.org/usa

For more information, see page 974.

American Collegiate Adventures–Spain

American Collegiate Adventures
Seville
Spain

General Information Coed travel academic program and cultural program established in 2001. Accredited by American Camping Association. High school or college credit may be earned.
Academics Jewish studies, SAT/ACT preparation, Spanish language/literature, academics (general), architecture, area studies, art history/appreciation, history, humanities, intercultural studies, precollege program.
Arts Drawing, painting, photography.
Special Interest Areas Cross-cultural education, culinary arts, touring.
Sports Aerobics, basketball, boating, soccer, tennis, weight training.
Trips College tours, cultural, day, overnight, shopping.
Program Information 1 session per year. Session length: 30 days in June, July, August. Ages: 14–18. 75–125 participants per session. Cost: $5195–$6490. Application fee: $75. Financial aid available. Optional trip to London and Paris.
Application Deadline Continuous.
Jobs Positions for college students 21 and older.
Contact Jason Lubar, Director of Summer Programs, 1811 W. North Avenue, Suite 201, Chicago, Illinois 60622. Phone: 800-509-SUMR. Fax: 773-342-0246. E-mail: info@acasummer.com.
URL www.acasummer.com

Bravo Spain–Barcelona

Bravo Spain International Student Exchange
Barcelona
Spain

General Information Coed travel academic program and cultural program established in 2000. High school or college credit may be earned.
Program Focus Culture and language immersion program in Spain.
Academics Spanish language/literature, architecture, art history/appreciation, intercultural studies.
Special Interest Areas Homestays, touring.
Sports Bicycling, kayaking, swimming.
Trips Cultural, day, overnight.
Program Information 1 session per year. Session length: 30 days in June, July. Ages: 16–19. 8–20 participants per session. Cost: $4495.
Application Deadline March 15.
Contact Mr. John Kohler, Director, PO Box 641656, Los Angeles, California 90064. Phone: 310-479-5500. E-mail: bravospain@yahoo.com.
URL www.bravospain.net

Center for Cultural Interchange–Spain High School Abroad

Center for Cultural Interchange
Spain

General Information Coed residential academic program and cultural program established in 1985. High school credit may be earned.
Program Focus High school in Spain, cultural immersion.
Academics Spanish language/literature, academics (general).
Special Interest Areas Cross-cultural education, homestays.
Trips Cultural, day, overnight.
Program Information 2 sessions per year. Session length: 90–300 days in January, February, March, April, May, June, July, August, September, October, November, December. Ages: 15–18. Boarding program cost: $6790–$8390. Financial aid available.
Application Deadline Continuous.
Contact Ms. Juliet Jones, Outbound Programs Director, 325 West Huron, Suite 706, Chicago, Illinois 60610. Phone: 866-684-9675. Fax: 312-944-2644. E-mail: info@cci-exchange.com.
URL www.cci-exchange.com

For more information, see page 1060.

Center for Cultural Interchange–Spain Independent Homestay

Center for Cultural Interchange
Spain

General Information Coed residential cultural program established in 1985.
Program Focus Cultural immersion, homestay in Spain.

Center for Cultural Interchange–Spain Independent Homestay (continued)

Academics Spanish language/literature, independent study.
Special Interest Areas Homestays.
Trips Cultural, day.
Program Information Session length: 14–90 days in January, February, March, April, May, June, July, August, September, October, November, December. Ages: 14+. Boarding program cost: $1500–$1895. Financial aid available.
Application Deadline Continuous.
Contact Ms. Juliet Jones, Outbound Programs Director, 325 West Huron, Suite 706, Chicago, Illinois 60610. Phone: 866-684-9675. Fax: 312-944-2644. E-mail: info@cci-exchange.com.
URL www.cci-exchange.com
For more information, see page 1060.

Center for Cultural Interchange–Spain Language School

Center for Cultural Interchange
Spain

General Information Coed residential academic program and cultural program established in 1985. High school or college credit may be earned.
Program Focus Cultural immersion; language study.
Academics Spanish language/literature.
Arts Arts and crafts (general), dance (folk).
Special Interest Areas Homestays.
Trips Cultural, day.
Program Information 1–50 sessions per year. Session length: 2–6 weeks in January, February, March, April, May, June, July, August, September, October, November, December. Ages: 14+. Boarding program cost: $1790–$2690. Financial aid available.
Application Deadline Continuous.
Contact Ms. Juliet Jones, Outbound Programs Director, 325 West Huron, Suite 706, Chicago, Illinois 60610. Phone: 866-684-9675. Fax: 312-944-2644. E-mail: info@cci-exchange.com.
URL www.cci-exchange.com
For more information, see page 1060.

Center for Cultural Interchange–Spain Sports and Language Camp

Center for Cultural Interchange
Granada
Spain

General Information Coed residential academic program, outdoor program, sports camp, and cultural program established in 1985.
Program Focus Language and sports camp.
Academics Spanish language/literature.
Arts Arts and crafts (general).
Special Interest Areas Cross-cultural education.
Sports Archery, basketball, canoeing, equestrian sports, horseback riding, soccer, swimming, tennis, volleyball.
Wilderness/Outdoors Hiking, mountain biking, outdoor adventure.
Trips Cultural, day.
Program Information 1 session per year. Session length: 3 weeks in July. Ages: 10–17. Boarding program cost: $2590. Financial aid available.
Application Deadline Continuous.
Contact Ms. Juliet Jones, Outbound Programs Director, 325 West Huron, Suite 706, Chicago, Illinois 60610. Phone: 866-684-9675. Fax: 312-944-2644. E-mail: info@cci-exchange.com.
URL www.cci-exchange.com
For more information, see page 1060.

Choate Rosemary Hall Summer in Spain

Choate Rosemary Hall
Santander/La Coruña
Spain

General Information Coed travel academic program and cultural program established in 1973. High school credit may be earned.

Choate Rosemary Hall Summer in Spain

Program Focus Spanish language and culture immersion.
Academics Spanish language/literature, art history/appreciation, history, social studies.
Special Interest Areas Cross-cultural education, homestays, touring.
Sports Swimming.
Trips Cultural, day, overnight.
Program Information 1 session per year. Session length: 40 days in June, July. Ages: 14–18. 45–52 participants per session. Cost: $6055. Application fee: $60. Financial aid available. Airfare from New York to Madrid included.
Application Deadline Continuous.
Contact Mr. Thomas McRae, Director, Summer Programs in Spain, 333 Christian Street, Wallingford, Connecticut 06492. Phone: 203-697-2365. Fax: 203-697-2519. E-mail: tmcrae@choate.edu.
URL www.crhsummerabroad.org
For more information, see page 1066.

Columbia University Continuing Education–The Barcelona Experience

Columbia University Continuing Education
University of Barcelona
Barcelona
Spain

General Information Coed residential academic program and cultural program established in 2002. Formal opportunities for the academically talented.
Program Focus History, art, and urban development of Barcelona.
Academics Spanish language/literature, architecture, art history/appreciation, government and politics, history, intercultural studies.
Trips Cultural, day.
Program Information 1 session per year. Session length: 4 weeks in July. Ages: 16–18. 20–36 participants per session. Boarding program cost: $7825. Application fee: $35.
Application Deadline Continuous.
Jobs Positions for college students 18 and older.
Contact Ms. Darlene Giraitis, Director of Secondary School Programs, Columbia University, School of Continuing Education, 2970 Broadway Mail Code 4110, New York, New York 10027. Phone: 212-854-3771. Fax: 212-854-5861. E-mail: hsp@columbia.edu.
URL www.ce.columbia.edu/hsprogrambarcelona.cfm

Concordia Language Villages–Spain

Concordia College
Spain

General Information Coed travel academic program and cultural program established in 1961. Accredited by American Camping Association. Formal opportunities for the academically talented. High school credit may be earned.
Program Focus Spanish language and culture.
Academics Spanish language/literature.
Arts Arts and crafts (general), dance.
Special Interest Areas Cross-cultural education, field research/expeditions, field trips (arts and culture).
Wilderness/Outdoors Bicycle trips.
Trips Cultural, day, overnight, shopping.
Program Information 1 session per year. Session length: 30 days in June, July. Ages: 14–18. 25–35 participants per session. Cost: $5400; including airfare. Airfare included.
Application Deadline Continuous.
Jobs Positions for college students 18 and older.
Contact Alex Loehrer, Assistant Director, Public Relations, 901 South Eighth Street, Moorhead, Minnesota 56562. Phone: 218-299-4544. Fax: 218-299-3807.
URL www.ConcordiaLanguageVillages.org

EARTHWATCH INSTITUTE–Butterflies and Orchids of Spain

Earthwatch Institute
Picos de Europa
Spain

General Information Coed residential outdoor program.
Program Focus Assessing the impact of land-use changes to conserve local biodiversity.
Academics Botany, ecology, environmental science.
Special Interest Areas Animal care, field research/expeditions, nature study.
Sports Swimming.
Program Information 4 sessions per year. Session length: 2 weeks in June, July. Ages: 16+. 10 participants per session. Boarding program cost: $1695–$1795. Financial aid available. Financial aid for high school students and teachers.
Application Deadline Continuous.
Contact General Information Desk, PO Box 75, Maynard, Massachusetts 01754. Phone: 800-776-0188. Fax: 978-461-2332. E-mail: info@earthwatch.org.
URL www.earthwatch.org

EARTHWATCH INSTITUTE–Early Man in Spain

Earthwatch Institute
Orce, Andalusia
Spain

General Information Coed residential outdoor program, cultural program, and adventure program.
Program Focus Excavating a particularly rich site in Andalusia to establish when and how humans first came to Europe.
Academics Archaeology, science (general).
Special Interest Areas Field research/expeditions.
Program Information 5 sessions per year. Session length: 2 weeks in July, August, September. Ages: 16+. 15 participants per session. Boarding program cost: $1995–$2095. Financial aid available. Financial aid for high school students and teachers.
Application Deadline Continuous.
Contact General Information Desk, PO Box 75, Maynard, Massachusetts 01754. Phone: 800-776-0188. Fax: 978-461-2332. E-mail: info@earthwatch.org.
URL www.earthwatch.org

EARTHWATCH INSTITUTE–Mallorca's Copper Age

Earthwatch Institute
Mallorca
Spain

General Information Coed residential outdoor program, cultural program, and adventure program.
Program Focus Sifting through the prehistory of settlement and cultural evolution on Mallorca.
Academics Archaeology, history, science (general).
Special Interest Areas Field research/expeditions, nature study.

EARTHWATCH INSTITUTE–Mallorca's Copper Age (continued)

Program Information 7 sessions per year. Session length: 15 days in June, July, August, September, October, December. Ages: 16+. 15 participants per session. Boarding program cost: $2095–$2195. Financial aid available. Financial aid for high school students and teachers.
Application Deadline Continuous.
Contact General Information Desk, PO Box 75, Maynard, Massachusetts 01754. Phone: 800-776-0188. Fax: 978-461-2332. E-mail: info@earthwatch.org.
URL www.earthwatch.org

EARTHWATCH INSTITUTE–SPANISH DOLPHINS

Earthwatch Institute
Alboran Sea
Spain

General Information Coed residential outdoor program, cultural program, and adventure program.
Program Focus Designing marine protected areas to stem the decline of Mediterranean marine life.
Academics Ecology, environmental science, marine studies, science (general).
Special Interest Areas Field research/expeditions, nature study.
Program Information 10 sessions per year. Session length: 12 days in January, March, June, July, August, September, November. Ages: 16+. 7 participants per session. Boarding program cost: $2295–$2395. Financial aid available. Financial aid for high school students and teachers.
Application Deadline Continuous.
Contact General Information Desk, PO Box 75, Maynard, Massachusetts 01754. Phone: 800-776-0188. Fax: 978-461-2332. E-mail: info@earthwatch.org.
URL www.earthwatch.org

EF INTERNATIONAL LANGUAGE SCHOOL–BARCELONA

EF International Language Schools
Calle Calvet 68-70
2nd Floor
Barcelona 08021
Spain

General Information Coed travel academic program and cultural program established in 1988. High school or college credit may be earned.
Program Focus Language and cultural immersion.
Academics Spanish (Advanced Placement), Spanish language/literature.
Special Interest Areas Field trips (arts and culture).
Sports Sports (general).
Wilderness/Outdoors Outdoor adventure.
Trips Cultural, day, overnight.
Program Information Session length: 14–365 days in January, February, March, April, May, June, July, August, September, October, November, December. Ages: 16+. 200–250 participants per session. Call for costs.
Application Deadline Continuous.
Contact Ms. Katie Mahon, Director of Admissions, One Education Street, Cambridge, Massachusetts 02141. Phone: 800-992-1892. Fax: 800-590-1125. E-mail: ils@ef.com.
URL www.ef.com
For more information, see page 1102.

EF INTERNATIONAL LANGUAGE SCHOOL–MALAGA

EF International Language Schools
Malaga
Spain

General Information Coed travel academic program and cultural program established in 2004.
Program Focus Language and cultural immersion.
Academics Spanish (Advanced Placement), Spanish language/literature.
Special Interest Areas Field trips (arts and culture).
Sports Sports (general).
Wilderness/Outdoors Wilderness/outdoors (general).
Trips Cultural, day, overnight.
Program Information Session length: 14–365 days in January, February, March, April, May, June, July, August, September, October, November, December. Ages: 16+. 100–150 participants per session. Call for costs.
Application Deadline Continuous.
Contact Ms. Katie Mahon, Director of Admissions, One Education Street, Cambridge, Massachusetts 02141. Phone: 800-992-1892. Fax: 800-590-1125. E-mail: ils@ef.com.
URL www.ef.com
For more information, see page 1102.

ENFOREX–GENERAL SPANISH–ALMUÑECAR

Enforex Spanish in the Spanish World
Almuñecar
Spain

General Information Coed residential academic program established in 1989. High school or college credit may be earned.
Program Focus Language program with optional cultural and sport activities. Course offerings include part-time, intensive, super-intensive, and one-to-one.
Academics Spanish (Advanced Placement), Spanish language/literature, business, classical languages/literatures, computers, intercultural studies.
Special Interest Areas Homestays, nautical skills.
Sports Archery, baseball, canoeing, climbing (wall), cross-country, football, golf, gymnastics, horseback riding, sailing, soccer, swimming, volleyball, waterskiing.
Trips College tours, cultural, day, overnight, shopping.
Program Information 48 sessions per year. Session length: 2–52 weeks in January, February, March, April, May, June, July, August, September, October, November, December. Ages: 16+. 4–128 participants per session. Boarding program cost: 440 euros. Application fee: 65 euros. Financial aid available.
Application Deadline Continuous.

Contact Spanish Department, Alberto Aguilera 26, Madrid 28015, Spain. Phone: 34-91-594-3776. Fax: 34-91-594-5159. E-mail: registration@enforex.es.
URL www.enforex.com
For more information, see page 1110.

ENFOREX–GENERAL SPANISH–BARCELONA

Enforex Spanish in the Spanish World
Diputacion 92
Barcelona
Spain

General Information Coed residential academic program established in 1989. High school or college credit may be earned.
Program Focus Language program with optional cultural and sport activities. Course offerings include part-time, intensive, super-intensive, and one-to one.
Academics Spanish (Advanced Placement), Spanish language/literature, business, classical languages/ literatures, computers, intercultural studies.
Special Interest Areas Homestays, nautical skills.
Sports Archery, baseball, canoeing, climbing (wall), cross-country, football, golf, gymnastics, horseback riding, sailing, soccer, swimming, volleyball, waterskiing.
Trips College tours, cultural, day, overnight, shopping.
Program Information 48 sessions per year. Session length: 2–52 weeks in January, February, March, April, May, June, July, August, September, October, November, December. Ages: 16+. 4–128 participants per session. Boarding program cost: 440 euros. Application fee: 65 euros. Financial aid available.
Application Deadline Continuous.
Contact Spanish Department, Alberto Aguilera 26, Madrid 28015, Spain. Phone: 34-91-594-3776. Fax: 34-91-594-5159. E-mail: registration@enforex.es.
URL www.enforex.com
For more information, see page 1110.

ENFOREX–GENERAL SPANISH–GRANADA

Enforex Spanish in the Spanish World
Santa Teresa 20
Granada 18002
Spain

General Information Coed residential academic program established in 1989. High school or college credit may be earned.
Program Focus Language program with optional cultural and sport activities. Course offerings include part-time, intensive, super-intensive, and one-to-one.
Academics Spanish (Advanced Placement), Spanish language/literature, business, classical languages/ literatures, computers, intercultural studies.
Special Interest Areas Homestays, nautical skills.
Sports Archery, baseball, canoeing, climbing (wall), cross-country, football, golf, gymnastics, horseback riding, sailing, soccer, swimming, volleyball, waterskiing.
Trips College tours, cultural, day, overnight, shopping.
Program Information 48 sessions per year. Session length: 2–52 weeks in January, February, March, April, May, June, July, August, September, October, November, December. Ages: 16+. 4–128 participants per session. Boarding program cost: 440 euros. Application fee: 65 euros. Financial aid available.
Application Deadline Continuous.
Contact Spanish Department, Alberto Aguilera 26, Madrid 28015, Spain. Phone: 34-91-594-3776. Fax: 34-91-594-5159. E-mail: registration@enforex.es.
URL www.enforex.com
For more information, see page 1110.

ENFOREX–GENERAL SPANISH–MADRID

Enforex Spanish in the Spanish World
Alberto Aguilera 26
Madrid 28015
Spain

General Information Coed residential academic program established in 1989. High school or college credit may be earned.

Enforex–General Spanish–Madrid

Program Focus Language program with optional cultural and sport activities. Course offerings include part-time, intensive, super-intensive, and one-to-one.
Academics Spanish (Advanced Placement), Spanish language/literature, business, classical languages/ literatures, computers, intercultural studies.
Special Interest Areas Homestays, nautical skills.
Sports Archery, baseball, canoeing, climbing (wall), cross-country, football, golf, gymnastics, horseback riding, sailing, soccer, swimming, volleyball, waterskiing.
Trips College tours, cultural, day, overnight, shopping.
Program Information 48 sessions per year. Session length: 2–52 weeks in January, February, March, April, May, June, July, August, September, October, November, December. Ages: 16+. 4–128 participants per session. Boarding program cost: 440 euros. Application fee: 65 euros. Financial aid available.
Application Deadline Continuous.
Contact Spanish Department, main address above. Phone: 34-91-594-3776. Fax: 34-91-594-5159. E-mail: registration@enforex.es.
URL www.enforex.com
For more information, see page 1110.

Enforex–General Spanish–Marbella

Enforex Spanish in the Spanish World
Avenida Ricardo Soriano 43
Marbella 29600
Spain

General Information Coed residential academic program established in 1989. High school or college credit may be earned.
Program Focus Language program with optional cultural and sport activities. Course offerings include part-time, intensive, super-intensive, and one-to-one.
Academics Spanish (Advanced Placement), Spanish language/literature, business, classical languages/ literatures, computers, intercultural studies.
Special Interest Areas Homestays, nautical skills.
Sports Archery, baseball, climbing (wall), cross-country, football, golf, gymnastics, horseback riding, sailing, soccer, swimming, volleyball, waterskiing.
Trips College tours, cultural, day, overnight, shopping.
Program Information 48 sessions per year. Session length: 2–52 weeks in January, February, March, April, May, June, July, August, September, October, November, December. Ages: 16+. 4–128 participants per session. Boarding program cost: 440 euros. Application fee: 65 euros. Financial aid available.
Application Deadline Continuous.
Contact Spanish Department, Alberto Aguilera 26, Madrid 28015, Spain. Phone: 34-91-594-3776. Fax: 34-91-594-5159. E-mail: registration@enforex.es.
URL www.enforex.com
For more information, see page 1110.

Enforex–General Spanish–Salamanca

Enforex Spanish in the Spanish World
Marquesa de Almarza 1
Salamanca
Spain

General Information Coed residential academic program established in 1989. High school or college credit may be earned.
Program Focus Language program with optional cultural and sport activities. Course offerings include part-time, intensive, super-intensive, and one-to-one.
Academics Spanish (Advanced Placement), Spanish language/literature, business, classical languages/ literatures, computers, intercultural studies.
Special Interest Areas Homestays, nautical skills.
Sports Archery, baseball, canoeing, climbing (wall), cross-country, football, golf, gymnastics, horseback riding, sailing, soccer, swimming, volleyball, waterskiing.
Trips College tours, cultural, day, overnight, shopping.
Program Information 48 sessions per year. Session length: 2–52 weeks in January, February, March, April, May, June, July, August, September, October, November, December. Ages: 16+. 4–128 participants per session. Boarding program cost: 440 euros. Application fee: 65 euros. Financial aid available.
Application Deadline Continuous.
Contact Spanish Department, Alberto Aguilera 26, Madrid 28015, Spain. Phone: 34-91-594-3776. Fax: 34-91-594-5159. E-mail: registration@enforex.es.
URL www.enforex.com
For more information, see page 1110.

Enforex–General Spanish–Valencia

Enforex Spanish in the Spanish World
Valencia
Spain

General Information Coed residential academic program. High school or college credit may be earned.
Program Focus Language program with optional cultural and sports activities. Course offerings include part-time, intensive, super-intensive, and one-to-one.
Academics Spanish (Advanced Placement), Spanish language/literature, business, classical languages/ literatures, computers, intercultural studies.
Special Interest Areas Homestays, nautical skills.
Sports Archery, baseball, canoeing, climbing (wall), cross-country, football, golf, gymnastics, horseback riding, sailing, soccer, swimming, volleyball, waterskiing.
Trips College tours, cultural, day, overnight, shopping.
Program Information 48 sessions per year. Session length: 2–52 weeks in January, February, March, April, May, June, July, August, September, October, November, December. Ages: 16+. 4–128 participants per session. Boarding program cost: 440 euros. Application fee: 65 euros. Financial aid available.
Application Deadline Continuous.
Contact Spanish Department, Alberto Aguilera 26, Madrid 28015, Spain. Phone: 34-91-594-3776. Fax: 34-91-594-5159. E-mail: registration@enforex.es.
URL www.enforex.com
For more information, see page 1110.

Enforex Hispanic Culture: Civilization, History, Art, and Literature–Barcelona

Enforex Spanish in the Spanish World
Diputacion 92
Barcelona
Spain

General Information Coed residential and day academic program established in 1989. High school or college credit may be earned.
Program Focus Language program with special focus on Spanish history, art and literature.
Academics Spanish (Advanced Placement), Spanish language/literature, architecture, area studies, art (Advanced Placement), art history/appreciation, business, classical languages/literatures, computers, history, history (Advanced Placement), humanities, intercultural studies.
Arts Film.
Special Interest Areas Field trips (arts and culture), homestays, nautical skills.
Sports Aerobics, archery, baseball, basketball, canoeing, climbing (wall), cross-country, football, golf,

gymnastics, horseback riding, sailing, soccer, sports (general), swimming, volleyball, waterskiing.
Trips College tours, cultural, day, overnight, shopping.
Program Information 12 sessions per year. Session length: 4 weeks in January, February, March, April, May, June, July, August, September, October, November, December. Ages: 15+. 250 participants per session. Boarding program cost: 850 euros. Application fee: 65 euros.
Application Deadline Continuous.
Contact Spanish Department, Alberto Aguilera 26, Madrid 28015, Spain. Phone: 34-91-594-3776. Fax: 34-91-594-5159. E-mail: info@enforex.es.
URL www.enforex.com

For more information, see page 1110.

Enforex Hispanic Culture: Civilization, History, Art, and Literature–Granada

Enforex Spanish in the Spanish World
Santa Teresa 20
Granada 18002
Spain

General Information Coed residential and day academic program established in 1989. High school or college credit may be earned.
Program Focus Language program with optional sport and cultural activities.
Academics Spanish (Advanced Placement), Spanish language/literature, architecture, area studies, art (Advanced Placement), art history/appreciation, business, classical languages/literatures, computers, history, history (Advanced Placement), humanities, intercultural studies.
Special Interest Areas Field trips (arts and culture), homestays, nautical skills.
Sports Aerobics, archery, baseball, basketball, canoeing, climbing (wall), cross-country, football, golf, gymnastics, horseback riding, sailing, soccer, sports (general), swimming, volleyball, waterskiing.
Trips College tours, cultural, day, overnight, shopping.
Program Information 12 sessions per year. Session length: 4 weeks in January, February, March, April, May, June, July, August, September, October, November, December. Ages: 15+. 250 participants per session. Boarding program cost: 850 euros. Application fee: 65 euros.
Application Deadline Continuous.
Contact Spanish Department, Alberto Aguilera 26, Madrid 28015, Spain. Phone: 34-91-594-3776. Fax: 34-91-594-5159. E-mail: info@enforex.es.
URL www.enforex.com

For more information, see page 1110.

Enforex Hispanic Culture: Civilization, History, Art, and Literature–Madrid

Enforex Spanish in the Spanish World
Alberto Aguilera 26
Madrid 28015
Spain

General Information Coed residential and day academic program established in 1989. High school or college credit may be earned.
Program Focus Language program with optional sport and cultural activities.
Academics Spanish (Advanced Placement), Spanish language/literature, architecture, area studies, art (Advanced Placement), art history/appreciation, business, classical languages/literatures, computers, history, history (Advanced Placement), humanities, intercultural studies.
Special Interest Areas Field trips (arts and culture), homestays, nautical skills.
Sports Aerobics, archery, baseball, basketball, canoeing, climbing (wall), cross-country, football, golf, gymnastics, horseback riding, sailing, soccer, sports (general), swimming, volleyball, waterskiing.
Trips College tours, cultural, day, overnight, shopping.
Program Information 12 sessions per year. Session length: 4 weeks in January, April, May, July, October. Ages: 15+. 250 participants per session. Boarding program cost: 850 euros. Application fee: 65 euros.
Application Deadline Continuous.
Contact Spanish Department, main address above. Phone: 34-91-594-3776. Fax: 34-91-594-5159. E-mail: info@enforex.es.
URL www.enforex.com

For more information, see page 1110.

Enforex Homestay Program–Almuñecar

Enforex Spanish in the Spanish World
Almuñecar
Spain

General Information Coed residential academic program established in 1989. High school or college credit may be earned.
Program Focus Experience of living with Spanish family.
Academics Spanish (Advanced Placement), Spanish language/literature.
Special Interest Areas Homestays, nautical skills.
Sports Aerobics, archery, baseball, basketball, canoeing, climbing (wall), cross-country, football, golf, gymnastics, horseback riding, sailing, soccer, tennis, volleyball.
Trips College tours, cultural, day, overnight, shopping.
Program Information 48 sessions per year. Session length: 2–52 weeks in January, February, March, April, May, June, July, August, September, October, November, December. Ages: 13+. 250 participants per session. Boarding program cost: 340–810 euros. Application fee: 65 euros.

Enforex Homestay Program–Almuñecar (continued)

Application Deadline Continuous.
Contact Mr. Antonio Anadon, Director, Alberto Aguilera 26, Madrid 28015, Spain. Phone: 34-91-594-3776. Fax: 34-91-594-5159. E-mail: registration@enforex.es.
URL www.enforex.com

For more information, see page 1110.

Enforex Homestay Program–Barcelona

Enforex Spanish in the Spanish World
Diputacion 92
Barcelona
Spain

General Information Coed residential and day academic program established in 1989. High school or college credit may be earned.
Program Focus Experience of living with a Spanish family.
Academics Spanish (Advanced Placement), Spanish language/literature.
Special Interest Areas Homestays, nautical skills.
Sports Aerobics, archery, baseball, basketball, canoeing, climbing (wall), cross-country, football, golf, gymnastics, horseback riding, sailing, soccer, swimming, tennis, volleyball.
Trips College tours, cultural, day, overnight, shopping.
Program Information 48 sessions per year. Session length: 2–52 weeks in January, February, March, April, May, June, July, August, September, October, November, December. Ages: 13+. 250 participants per session. Boarding program cost: 340–810 euros. Application fee: 65 euros. Minimum age for participants is 15 in non-summer months, 13 during summer sessions.
Application Deadline Continuous.
Contact Antonio Anadon, Director, Alberto Aguilera 26, Madrid 28015, Spain. Phone: 34-91-594-3776. Fax: 34-91-594-5159. E-mail: registration@enforex.es.
URL www.enforex.com

For more information, see page 1110.

Enforex Homestay Program–Granada

Enforex Spanish in the Spanish World
Santa Teresa 20
Granada 18002
Spain

General Information Coed residential academic program established in 1989. High school or college credit may be earned.
Program Focus Experience of living with a Spanish family.
Academics Spanish (Advanced Placement), Spanish language/literature.
Special Interest Areas Homestays, nautical skills.
Sports Aerobics, archery, baseball, basketball, canoeing, climbing (wall), cross-country, football, golf, gymnastics, horseback riding, sailing, soccer, swimming, tennis, volleyball.
Trips College tours, cultural, day, overnight, shopping.
Program Information 48 sessions per year. Session length: 2–52 weeks in January, February, March, April, May, June, July, August, September, October, November, December. Ages: 13+. 250 participants per session. Boarding program cost: 340–810 euros. Application fee: 65 euros. Minimum age for participants is 15 in non-summer months, 13 during summer sessions.
Application Deadline Continuous.
Contact Antonio Anadon, Director, Alberto Aguilera 26, Madrid 28015, Spain. Phone: 34-91-594-3776. Fax: 34-91-594-5159. E-mail: registration@enforex.es.
URL www.enforex.com

For more information, see page 1110.

Enforex Homestay Program–Madrid

Enforex Spanish in the Spanish World
Alberto Aguilera 26
Madrid 28015
Spain

General Information Coed residential academic program established in 1989. High school or college credit may be earned.
Program Focus Experience of living with a Spanish family.
Academics Spanish (Advanced Placement), Spanish language/literature.
Special Interest Areas Homestays, nautical skills.
Sports Aerobics, archery, baseball, basketball, canoeing, climbing (wall), cross-country, football, golf, gymnastics, horseback riding, sailing, soccer, swimming, tennis, volleyball, waterskiing.
Trips College tours, cultural, day, overnight, shopping.
Program Information 48 sessions per year. Session length: 2–52 weeks in January, February, March, April, May, June, July, August, September, October, November, December. Ages: 13+. 250 participants per session. Boarding program cost: 340–810 euros. Application fee: 60 euros. Minimum age for participants is 15 in non-summer months, 13 during summer sessions.
Application Deadline Continuous.
Contact Antonio Anadon, Director, Alberto Aguilera 26, Madrid 28015, Spain. Phone: 34-91 594-3776. Fax: 34-91-594-5159. E-mail: registration@enforex.es.
URL www.enforex.com

For more information, see page 1110.

Enforex Homestay Program–Marbella

Enforex Spanish in the Spanish World
Avenida Ricardo Soriano 43
Marbella 29600
Spain

General Information Coed residential academic program established in 1989. High school or college credit may be earned.
Program Focus Experience of living with a Spanish family.
Academics Spanish (Advanced Placement), Spanish language/literature.

Special Interest Areas Homestays, nautical skills.
Sports Aerobics, archery, baseball, basketball, canoeing, climbing (wall), cross-country, football, golf, gymnastics, horseback riding, sailing, soccer, swimming, tennis, volleyball.
Trips College tours, cultural, day, overnight, shopping.
Program Information 48 sessions per year. Session length: 2–52 weeks in January, February, March, April, May, June, July, August, September, October, November, December. Ages: 13+. 250 participants per session. Boarding program cost: 340–810 euros. Application fee: 65 euros. Financial aid available. Minimum age for participants is 15 in non-summer months, 13 during summer sessions.
Application Deadline Continuous.
Contact Antonio Anadon, Director, Alberto Aguilera 26, Madrid 28015, Spain. Phone: 34-91-594-3776. Fax: 34-91-594-5159. E-mail: registration@enforex.es.
URL www.enforex.com

For more information, see page 1110.

Enforex Homestay Program–Salamanca

Enforex Spanish in the Spanish World
Marquesa de Almarza 1
Salamanca 37001
Spain

General Information Coed residential academic program established in 1989. High school or college credit may be earned.
Program Focus Experience of living with a Spanish family.
Academics Spanish (Advanced Placement), Spanish language/literature.
Special Interest Areas Homestays, nautical skills.
Sports Aerobics, archery, baseball, basketball, canoeing, climbing (wall), cross-country, football, golf, gymnastics, horseback riding, soccer, swimming, tennis, volleyball.
Trips College tours, cultural, day, overnight, shopping.
Program Information 48 sessions per year. Session length: 2–52 weeks in January, February, March, April, May, June, July, August, September, October, November, December. Ages: 13+. 250 participants per session. Boarding program cost: 340–810 euros. Application fee: 65 euros. Minimum age for participants is 15 in non-summer months, 13 during summer sessions.
Application Deadline Continuous.
Contact Antonio Anadon, Director, Alberto Aguilera 26, Madrid 28015, Spain. Phone: 34-91-594-3776. Fax: 34-91-594-5159. E-mail: registration@enforex.es.
URL www.enforex.com

For more information, see page 1110.

Enforex Residential Youth Summer Camp–Madrid

Enforex Spanish in the Spanish World
Madrid
Spain

General Information Coed residential traditional camp established in 1989.
Program Focus Sports, horseback riding, and trips to the beach and farms.
Academics Spanish language/literature.
Arts Arts and crafts (general), dance (jazz), drawing, leather working, music, radio broadcasting, television/video.
Special Interest Areas Farming, field research/expeditions, field trips (arts and culture).
Sports Aerobics, baseball, basketball, football, golf, horseback riding, soccer, swimming, tennis, waterskiing.
Wilderness/Outdoors Canoe trips.
Trips Cultural, day, overnight, shopping.
Program Information 4 sessions per year. Session length: 2–8 weeks in June, July, August. Ages: 6–18. 120 participants per session. Boarding program cost: 900–3160 euros. Application fee: 65 euros.
Application Deadline Continuous.
Contact Antonio Anadon, Spanish Department, Alberto Aguilera 26, Madrid 28015, Spain. Phone: 34-91-594-3776. Fax: 34-91-594-5159. E-mail: info@enforex.es.
URL www.enforex.com

For more information, see page 1110.

Enforex Residential Youth Summer Camp–Marbella

Enforex Spanish in the Spanish World
Marbella
Spain

General Information Coed residential traditional camp established in 1989.
Program Focus Sports, horseback riding, and trips to the beach and farms.
Academics Spanish language/literature.
Arts Arts and crafts (general), dance (jazz), drawing, leather working, music, painting, radio broadcasting, television/video.
Special Interest Areas Farming, field research/expeditions.
Sports Aerobics, archery, baseball, basketball, football, golf, horseback riding, snorkeling, soccer, swimming, tennis, waterskiing.
Wilderness/Outdoors Canoe trips.
Trips Cultural, day, overnight, shopping.
Program Information 4 sessions per year. Session length: 2–8 weeks in June, July, August. Ages: 6–18. 250 participants per session. Boarding program cost: 900–3160 euros. Application fee: 65 euros.
Application Deadline Continuous.
Contact Spanish Department, Alberto Aguilera 26, Madrid 28015, Spain. Phone: 34-91-594-3776. Fax: 34-91-594-5159. E-mail: info@enforex.es.
URL www.enforex.com

For more information, see page 1110.

Enforex Residential Youth Summer Camp–Salamanca

Enforex Spanish in the Spanish World
Salamanca
Spain

General Information Coed residential traditional camp.
Program Focus Sports, horseback riding, and trips to the beach and farms.
Academics Spanish (Advanced Placement), Spanish language/literature.
Arts Arts and crafts (general), dance (jazz), drawing, leather working, music, painting, radio broadcasting, television/video.
Sports Aerobics, archery, baseball, basketball, football, golf, horseback riding, snorkeling, soccer, swimming, tennis, waterskiing.
Wilderness/Outdoors Canoe trips.
Program Information 4 sessions per year. Session length: 2–8 weeks in June, July, August. Ages: 12–18. 250 participants per session. Boarding program cost: 850–3160 euros.
Application Deadline Continuous.
Contact Antonio Anadon, Head Office, Alberto Aguilera 26, Madrid 28015, Spain. Phone: 34-91-594-3776. Fax: 34-91-594-5159. E-mail: info@enforex.es.
URL www.enforex.com

For more information, see page 1110.

Enforex Spanish and Golf

Enforex Spanish in the Spanish World
Avenida Ricardo Soriano 43
Marbella 29600
Spain

General Information Coed residential academic program. High school or college credit may be earned.
Program Focus Course includes 20 classes of Spanish and 8 classes of golf.
Academics Spanish (Advanced Placement), Spanish language/literature.
Sports Football, golf, horseback riding, sailing, scuba diving, snorkeling, swimming, tennis, volleyball.
Trips Cultural, day, overnight, shopping.
Program Information 48 sessions per year. Session length: 2–3 weeks in January, February, March, April, May, June, July, August, September, October, November, December. Ages: 15+. 250 participants per session. Boarding program cost: 600–900 euros. Application fee: 65 euros. Minimum age for participants is 15 in non-summer months, exceptions made during summer sessions.
Application Deadline Continuous.
Contact Antonio Anadon, Spanish Department, Alberto Aguilera 26, Madrid 28015, Spain. Phone: 34-91-594-3776. Fax: 34-91-594-5159. E-mail: info@enforex.es.
URL www.enforex.com

For more information, see page 1110.

Enforex Spanish and Tennis

Enforex Spanish in the Spanish World
Avenida Ricardo Soriano 43
Marbella 29600
Spain

General Information Coed residential academic program. High school or college credit may be earned.
Program Focus Course offers 20 classes of Spanish and 8 classes of tennis.
Academics Spanish (Advanced Placement), Spanish language/literature.
Sports Football, golf, horseback riding, sailing, scuba diving, snorkeling, swimming, tennis, volleyball.
Trips Cultural, day, overnight, shopping.
Program Information 48 sessions per year. Session length: 2–3 weeks in January, February, March, April, May, June, July, August, September, October, November, December. Ages: 15+. 250 participants per session. Boarding program cost: 600–900 euros. Application fee: 65 euros. Minimum age for participants is 15 in non-summer months, exceptions made during summer sessions.
Application Deadline Continuous.
Contact Antonio Anadon, Spanish Department, Alberto Aguilera 26, Madrid 28015, Spain. Phone: 34-91-594-3776. Fax: 34-91-594-5159. E-mail: registration@enforex.es.
URL www.enforex.com

For more information, see page 1110.

Enforex Study Tour Vacational Program–Madrid

Enforex Spanish in the Spanish World
Alberto Aguilera 26
Madrid 28015
Spain

General Information Coed residential academic program established in 1989. High school or college credit may be earned.
Program Focus Language program with optional cultural activities.
Academics Spanish (Advanced Placement), Spanish language/literature, art history/appreciation, history, intercultural studies.
Special Interest Areas Field trips (arts and culture), homestays, touring.
Sports Football, gymnastics, soccer, swimming, volleyball.
Trips College tours, cultural, day, overnight, shopping.
Program Information 12 sessions per year. Session length: 2 weeks in January, February, March, April, May, June, July, August, September, October, November, December. Ages: 15+. 120 participants per session. Boarding program cost: 440 euros. Application fee: 65 euros. Financial aid available.
Application Deadline Continuous.
Contact Antonio Anadon, Spanish Department, main address above. Phone: 34-91-594-3776. Fax: 34-91-594-5159. E-mail: registration@enforex.es.
URL www.enforex.com

For more information, see page 1110.

Excel at Madrid/Barcelona

Putney Student Travel
Spain

General Information Coed residential academic program and cultural program established in 1951. Formal opportunities for the academically talented and artistically talented.
Program Focus EXCEL is an innovative precollege program that emphasizes small classes, creative interactions among student and faculty, and cultural exchange.
Academics Spanish language/literature, academics (general), architecture, area studies, art history/appreciation, government and politics, history, humanities, intercultural studies, precollege program, writing.
Arts Creative writing, drawing, film, music, painting, theater/drama.
Special Interest Areas Field research/expeditions, touring.
Sports Basketball, bicycling, soccer, swimming.
Wilderness/Outdoors Hiking.
Trips Cultural, day.
Program Information 1 session per year. Session length: 4 weeks in July, August. Ages: 15–18. 60–70 participants per session. Boarding program cost: $6000. Financial aid available.
Application Deadline Continuous.
Contact Tim Weed, Director, 345 Hickory Ridge Road, Putney, Vermont 05346. Phone: 802-387-5000. Fax: 802-387-4276. E-mail: info@goputney.com.
URL www.goputney.com

For more information, see page 1114.

The Experiment in International Living–Spain, Five-Week Homestay, Travel, Ecology

The Experiment in International Living
Spain

General Information Coed residential outdoor program, cultural program, and adventure program established in 1932.
Program Focus International youth travel, homestay.
Academics Spanish language/literature, ecology.
Special Interest Areas Homestays, touring.
Trips Cultural, day, overnight.
Program Information 1 session per year. Session length: 5 weeks in June, July, August. Ages: 14–19. 10–15 participants per session. Boarding program cost: $4400. Application fee: $75. Financial aid available.
Application Deadline May 1.
Contact Chris Frantz, Deputy Director, EIL–World Learning, PO Box 676, Kipling Road, Brattleboro, Vermont 05302-0676. Phone: 800-345-2929. Fax: 802-258-3428. E-mail: eil@worldlearning.org.
URL www.usexperiment.org

For more information, see page 1116.

The Experiment in International Living–Spain, Five-Week Language Training, Travel, and Homestay

The Experiment in International Living
Spain

General Information Coed residential academic program and cultural program established in 1932.
Program Focus International youth travel, homestay, language training.
Academics Spanish language/literature.
Special Interest Areas Homestays, touring.
Trips Cultural, day, overnight.
Program Information 1 session per year. Session length: 5 weeks in July, August. Ages: 14–19. 10–15 participants per session. Boarding program cost: $4500. Financial aid available.
Application Deadline May 1.
Contact Annie Thompson, Enrollment Director, Summer Abroad, Kipling Road, PO Box 676, Brattleboro, Vermont 05302-0676. Phone: 800-345-2929. Fax: 802-258-3428. E-mail: eil@worldlearning.org.
URL www.usexperiment.org

For more information, see page 1116.

The Experiment in International Living–Spain, Four-Week Homestay and Trekking Program

The Experiment in International Living
Spain

General Information Coed residential outdoor program, cultural program, and adventure program established in 1932.
Program Focus International youth travel, homestay, pilgrimage to Santiago de Compostela.
Academics Spanish language/literature.
Special Interest Areas Homestays, touring.
Wilderness/Outdoors Hiking.
Trips Cultural, day, overnight.
Program Information 1 session per year. Session length: 4 weeks in July, August. Ages: 14–19. 10–15 participants per session. Boarding program cost: $3800. Application fee: $75. Financial aid available.
Application Deadline May 1.
Contact Ms. Annie Thompson, Enrollment Director, Summer Abroad, Kipling Road, PO Box 676, Brattleboro, Vermont 05302-0676. Phone: 800-345-2929. Fax: 802-258-3428. E-mail: eil@worldlearning.org.
URL www.usexperiment.org

For more information, see page 1116.

The Experiment in International Living–Spain, Four-Week Language Study and Homestay

The Experiment in International Living
Spain

General Information Coed residential academic program and cultural program established in 1932.

The Experiment in International Living–Spain, Four-Week Language Study and Homestay (continued)

Program Focus International youth travel, homestay, Spanish language study.
Academics Spanish language/literature.
Special Interest Areas Homestays, touring.
Trips Cultural, day, overnight.
Program Information 1 session per year. Session length: 4 weeks in July, August. Ages: 14–19. 10–15 participants per session. Boarding program cost: $3700. Financial aid available.
Application Deadline May 1.
Contact Annie Thompson, Enrollment Director, Summer Abroad, Kipling Road, PO Box 676, Brattleboro, Vermont 05302-0676. Phone: 800-345-2929. Fax: 802-258-3428. E-mail: eil@worldlearning.org.
URL www.usexperiment.org
For more information, see page 1116.

The Experiment in International Living–Spain–Spanish Culture and Folklore

The Experiment in International Living
Spain

General Information Coed residential cultural program established in 1932.
Program Focus International youth travel, gypsy culture study.
Academics Spanish language/literature, intercultural studies.
Arts Dance (folk).
Special Interest Areas Homestays, touring.
Trips Cultural, day, overnight.
Program Information 1 session per year. Session length: 5 weeks in July, August. Ages: 14–19. 10–15 participants per session. Boarding program cost: $4300. Financial aid available.
Application Deadline May 1.
Contact Annie Thompson, Enrollment Director, Summer Abroad, Kipling Road, PO Box 676, Brattleboro, Vermont 05302-0676. Phone: 800-345-2929. Fax: 802-258-3428. E-mail: eil@worldlearning.org.
URL www.usexperiment.org
For more information, see page 1116.

The Experiment in International Living–Spain, Three-Week Homestay

The Experiment in International Living
Spain

General Information Coed residential cultural program established in 1932.
Program Focus International youth travel, homestay, Spanish language.
Academics Spanish language/literature.
Special Interest Areas Homestays.
Trips Cultural, day, overnight.
Program Information 1 session per year. Session length: 3 weeks in July. Ages: 14–19. 10–15 participants per session. Boarding program cost: $3100. Financial aid available.
Application Deadline May 1.
Contact Annie Thompson, Enrollment Director, Summer Abroad, Kipling Road, PO Box 676, Brattleboro, Vermont 05302-0676. Phone: 800-345-2929. Fax: 802-258-3428. E-mail: eil@worldlearning.org.
URL www.usexperiment.org
For more information, see page 1116.

Global Teen–Learn Spanish in Andalusia

Language Liaison
Malaga
Spain

General Information Coed residential academic program established in 1970. High school or college credit may be earned.
Program Focus Spanish language study and cultural immersion.
Academics Spanish language/literature.
Arts Dance.
Special Interest Areas Field trips (arts and culture).
Sports Badminton, basketball, bowling, swimming, table tennis/ping-pong, tennis, volleyball.
Trips Cultural, day, shopping.
Program Information 8 sessions per year. Session length: 2–4 weeks in June, July, August. Ages: 14–18. 10 participants per session. Boarding program cost: $1297–$2249. Application fee: $85. Financial aid available.
Application Deadline Continuous.
Contact Nancy Forman, President, PO Box 1772, Pacific Palisades, California 90272. Phone: 800-284-4448. Fax: 310-454-1706. E-mail: learn@languageliaison.com.
URL www.languageliaison.com
For more information, see page 1184.

Global Teen–Learn Spanish in Marbella, Ages 6-14

Language Liaison
Marbella
Spain

General Information Coed residential academic program. High school or college credit may be earned.
Program Focus Spanish language study and cultural immersion.
Academics Spanish language/literature, area studies, intercultural studies, journalism, reading, writing.
Arts Dance, guitar, juggling, music (instrumental).
Special Interest Areas Animal care, culinary arts, field trips (arts and culture), homestays, nature study.
Sports Horseback riding, swimming, tennis.
Trips Cultural, day.
Program Information 5–10 sessions per year. Session length: 2–8 weeks in June, July, August. Ages: 6–14. Boarding program cost: $1394–$3845. Application fee:

$80. Financial aid available. Extra week: $895; horseback riding, tennis, swimming, and paddleball lessons extra.
Application Deadline Continuous.
Contact Ms. Nancy Forman, President, PO Box 1772, Pacific Palisades, California 90272. Phone: 800-284-4448. Fax: 310-454-1706. E-mail: learn@languageliaison.com.
URL www.languageliaison.com
For more information, see page 1184.

Global Teen–Learn Spanish in Marbella-Young Adult

Language Liaison
Marbella
Spain

General Information Coed residential academic program. High school or college credit may be earned.
Program Focus Spanish language study and cultural immersion.
Academics Spanish language/literature, area studies, intercultural studies, journalism, reading, writing.
Arts Dance, guitar, juggling, music (instrumental).
Special Interest Areas Animal care, culinary arts, field trips (arts and culture), homestays, nature study.
Sports Horseback riding, swimming, tennis.
Trips Cultural, day.
Program Information 5–10 sessions per year. Session length: 2–8 weeks in June, July, August. Ages: 15–18. Boarding program cost: $895–$3845. Application fee: $80. Financial aid available. Horseback riding, tennis, swimming, and paddleball lessons extra.
Application Deadline Continuous.
Contact Ms. Nancy Forman, President, PO Box 1772, Pacific Palisades, California 90272. Phone: 800-284-4448. Fax: 310-454-1706. E-mail: learn@languageliaison.com.
URL www.languageliaison.com
For more information, see page 1184.

Global Teen–Learn Spanish in Salamanca, Ages 11-18

Language Liaison
University of Salamanca
Salamanca
Spain

General Information Coed residential academic program. High school or college credit may be earned.
Program Focus Spanish language study and cultural immersion.
Academics Spanish language/literature, architecture, area studies, intercultural studies, reading, writing.
Arts Arts and crafts (general).
Special Interest Areas Field trips (arts and culture).
Sports Swimming.
Trips Cultural, day.
Program Information 5 sessions per year. Session length: 1–5 weeks in June, July, August. Ages: 11–18. Boarding program cost: $1389–$3845. Application fee: $80. Financial aid available. Additional week: $899.
Application Deadline Continuous.
Contact Ms. Nancy Forman, President, PO Box 1772, Pacific Palisades, California 90272. Phone: 800-284-4448. Fax: 310-454-1706. E-mail: learn@languageliaison.com.
URL www.languageliaison.com
For more information, see page 1184.

Global Teen–Learn Spanish in Salamanca, Ages 13-16

Language Liaison
Salamanca
Spain

General Information Coed residential academic program established in 1956. High school or college credit may be earned.
Program Focus Spanish language study and cultural immersion.
Academics Spanish language/literature, area studies, intercultural studies, reading, writing.
Arts Arts and crafts (general).
Special Interest Areas Field trips (arts and culture), homestays.
Sports Gymnastics, swimming.
Trips Cultural, day.
Program Information 3–12 sessions per year. Session length: 2–4 weeks in June, July. Ages: 13–16. 12 participants per session. Boarding program cost: $1393–$2389. Application fee: $85. Financial aid available.
Application Deadline Continuous.
Contact Nancy Forman, President, PO Box 1772, Pacific Palisades, California 90272. Phone: 800-284-4448. Fax: 310-454-1706. E-mail: learn@languageliaison.com.
URL www.languageliaison.com
For more information, see page 1184.

Global Teen–Learn Spanish in Sevilla

Language Liaison
Sevilla
Spain

General Information Coed residential academic program established in 1956. High school or college credit may be earned.
Program Focus Spanish language study and cultural immersion.
Academics Spanish language/literature, area studies, art history/appreciation, intercultural studies.
Arts Dance, dance (Latin).
Special Interest Areas Culinary arts, field trips (arts and culture).
Sports Swimming, tennis, volleyball.
Trips Cultural, day.
Program Information 3–12 sessions per year. Session length: 2–4 weeks in June, July, August. Ages: 14–17. 2–6 participants per session. Boarding program cost: $1357–$2222. Application fee: $85. Financial aid available. Additional week: $529.
Application Deadline Continuous.

Global Teen–Learn Spanish in Sevilla (continued)
Contact Nancy Forman, President, PO Box 1772, Pacific Palisades, California 90272. Phone: 800-284-4448. Fax: 310-454-1706. E-mail: learn@languageliaison.com.
URL www.languageliaison.com
For more information, see page 1184.

Global Teen–Spanish in Madrid, Ages 6-14

Language Liaison
Madrid
Spain

General Information Coed residential academic program. High school or college credit may be earned.
Program Focus Spanish language and cultural immersion.
Academics Spanish language/literature, area studies, intercultural studies, reading, writing.
Arts Dance, guitar, juggling, music (instrumental).
Special Interest Areas Animal care, culinary arts, field trips (arts and culture).
Sports Basketball, handball, horseback riding, soccer, tennis.
Program Information 3–7 sessions per year. Session length: 2–4 weeks in July, August. Ages: 6–14. 2–12 participants per session. Boarding program cost: $1394–$2745. Application fee: $80. Financial aid available. Horseback riding and tennis lessons extra.
Application Deadline Continuous.
Contact Nancy Forman, President, PO Box 1772, Pacific Palisades, California 90272. Phone: 800-284-4448. Fax: 310-454-1706. E-mail: learn@languageliaison.com.
URL www.languageliaison.com
For more information, see page 1184.

Global Teen–Spanish in Malaga-Young Adult, Ages 16-20

Language Liaison
Malaga
Spain

General Information Coed residential academic program. High school or college credit may be earned.
Program Focus Spanish language study and cultural immersion.
Academics Spanish language/literature, area studies, intercultural studies, reading, writing.
Arts Dance (Latin).
Special Interest Areas Culinary arts, field trips (arts and culture), homestays.
Sports Golf, gymnastics, hang gliding, horseback riding, scuba diving, swimming, tennis, track and field, windsurfing.
Wilderness/Outdoors Bicycle trips.
Trips Cultural, day.
Program Information 3–5 sessions per year. Session length: 2–6 weeks in June, July, August. Ages: 16–20. 8–12 participants per session. Boarding program cost: $1389–$3697. Application fee: $90. Financial aid available. Homestays or school residence housing option.
Application Deadline Continuous.
Contact Ms. Nancy Forman, President, PO Box 1772, Pacific Palisades, California 90272. Phone: 800-284-4448. Fax: 310-454-1706. E-mail: learn@languageliaison.com.
URL www.languageliaison.com
For more information, see page 1184.

Global Teen–Spanish in Palma de Mallorca

Language Liaison
Palma de Mallorca
Spain

General Information Coed residential academic program. High school or college credit may be earned.
Program Focus Spanish language study and cultural immersion.
Academics Spanish language/literature, area studies, intercultural studies, reading, writing.
Arts Television/video.
Special Interest Areas Field trips (arts and culture).
Trips Cultural, day.
Program Information 2–12 sessions per year. Session length: 2 weeks in June, July, August. Ages: 16–19. 2–12 participants per session. Boarding program cost: $517. Application fee: $85. Financial aid available. Additional week: $259; accommodations: $215–$283 for two weeks; extra night: $38–$45; meals extra.
Application Deadline Continuous.
Contact Ms. Nancy Forman, President, PO Box 1772, Pacific Palisades, California 90272. Phone: 800-284-4448. Fax: 310-454-1706. E-mail: learn@languageliaison.com.
URL www.languageliaison.com
For more information, see page 1184.

Global Teen–Spanish Summer Camp in San Sebastian

Language Liaison
San Sebastian
Spain

General Information Coed residential academic program established in 1988.
Program Focus Spanish language study and cultural immersion.
Academics Spanish language/literature.
Special Interest Areas Field trips (arts and culture), homestays.
Sports Bicycling, kayaking, volleyball.
Trips Cultural, day.
Program Information 8 sessions per year. Session length: 2–4 weeks in June, July, August. Ages: 14–16. 2–12 participants per session. Boarding program cost: $1112–$1251. Application fee: $125. Financial aid available. Airport transfers extra.
Application Deadline Continuous.

Contact Ms. Nancy Forman, Director, PO Box 1772, Pacific Palisades, California 90272. Phone: 800-284-4448. Fax: 310-454-1706. E-mail: learn@languageliaison.com.
URL www.languageliaison.com
For more information, see page 1184.

Global Teen–Summer Camp in Barcelona

Language Liaison
Tarragona
Spain

General Information Academic program. High school or college credit may be earned.
Program Focus Spanish language study and cultural immersion.
Academics Spanish language/literature, area studies, intercultural studies, reading, writing.
Special Interest Areas Field trips (arts and culture), homestays, touring.
Sports Golf, horseback riding, tennis.
Trips Cultural, day.
Program Information 8 sessions per year. Session length: 2 weeks. Ages: 13–17. 2–12 participants per session. Boarding program cost: $1536–$1899. Application fee: $85. Financial aid available. Additional week: $698–$889.
Contact Ms. Nancy Forman, President, PO Box 1772, Pacific Palisades, California 90272. Phone: 800-286-4448. Fax: 310-454-1706. E-mail: learn@languageliaison.com.
URL www.languageliaison.com
For more information, see page 1184.

Global Teen–Summer Camp in Marbella, Ages 14-18

Language Liaison
Marbella
Spain

General Information Coed residential academic program. High school or college credit may be earned.
Program Focus Spanish language study and cultural immersion.
Academics Spanish language/literature, area studies, intercultural studies, journalism, reading, writing.
Arts Dance, guitar, juggling, music (instrumental).
Special Interest Areas Animal care, culinary arts, field trips (arts and culture), homestays, nature study.
Sports Horseback riding, swimming, tennis.
Trips Cultural, day.
Program Information 5–10 sessions per year. Session length: 2–8 weeks in June, July, August. Ages: 14–18. Boarding program cost: $1394–$3845. Application fee: $80. Financial aid available. Additional week: $895; horseback riding, tennis, swimming, and paddleball lessons extra.
Application Deadline Continuous.
Contact Ms. Nancy Forman, President, PO Box 1772, Pacific Palisades, California 90272. Phone: 800-284-4448. Fax: 310-454-1706. E-mail: learn@languageliaison.com.
URL www.languageliaison.com
For more information, see page 1184.

Global Teen–Vejer Beach Spectacular in Spain

Language Liaison
Vejer Beach
Spain

General Information Coed residential academic program and cultural program. High school or college credit may be earned.
Program Focus Spanish language study plus cultural immersion and beach/summer fun.
Academics Spanish language/literature, area studies, intercultural studies, reading, writing.
Special Interest Areas Culinary arts, field trips (arts and culture), homestays, nature study.
Sports Sports (general), windsurfing.
Trips Cultural, day.
Program Information 5 sessions per year. Session length: 2–4 weeks in June, July, August. Ages: 13–17. 3–10 participants per session. Boarding program cost: $1357–$2223. Application fee: $85. Financial aid available. Additional week: $529.
Application Deadline Continuous.
Contact Ms. Nancy Forman, President, PO Box 1772, Pacific Palisades, California 90272. Phone: 800-284-4448. Fax: 310-454-1706. E-mail: learn@languageliaison.com.
URL www.languageliaison.com
For more information, see page 1184.

Global Teen–Young Adult Summer Camp in Madrid, Ages 14-18

Language Liaison
Madrid
Spain

General Information Coed residential academic program. High school or college credit may be earned.
Program Focus Spanish language study and cultural immersion.
Academics Spanish language/literature, area studies, intercultural studies, reading, writing.
Arts Dance, guitar, juggling, music (instrumental).
Special Interest Areas Field trips (arts and culture).
Sports Basketball, horseback riding, soccer, tennis.
Program Information 3–4 sessions per year. Session length: 2–4 weeks in July, August. Ages: 14–18. 2–12 participants per session. Boarding program cost: $1394–$2745. Application fee: $80. Financial aid available. Tennis lessons extra.
Application Deadline Continuous.

Global Teen–Young Adult Summer Camp in Madrid, Ages 14-18 (continued)

Contact Ms. Nancy Forman, President, PO Box 1772, Pacific Palisades, California 90272. Phone: 800-284-4448. Fax: 310-454-1706. E-mail: learn@languageliaison.com.
URL www.languageliaison.com
For more information, see page 1184.

Global Teen–Young Adult Summer Program in Malaga, Ages 16-20

Language Liaison
Malaga
Spain

General Information Coed residential academic program established in 1983. High school or college credit may be earned.

Global Teen–Young Adult Summer Program in Malaga, Ages 16-20

Program Focus Spanish language study and cultural immersion at Malaga Beach.
Academics Spanish language/literature, area studies, intercultural studies, reading, writing.
Arts Dance (Latin), television/video.
Special Interest Areas Culinary arts, field trips (arts and culture), homestays, touring.
Sports Golf, hang gliding, horseback riding, scuba diving, swimming, tennis, track and field, waterskiing, windsurfing.
Wilderness/Outdoors Bicycle trips.
Trips Cultural, day.
Program Information 3 sessions per year. Session length: 2–3 weeks in June, July, August. Ages: 16–20. 8–12 participants per session. Boarding program cost: $956–$1492. Application fee: $85. Financial aid available.
Application Deadline Continuous.
Contact Nancy Forman, President, PO Box 1772, Pacific Palisades, California 90272. Phone: 800-284-4448. Fax: 310-454-1706. E-mail: learn@languageliaison.com.
URL www.languageliaison.com
For more information, see page 1184.

GLOBAL WORKS–Language Immersion–Spain–4 weeks

GLOBAL WORKS
Spain

General Information Coed travel community service program, cultural program, and adventure program established in 1988. High school credit may be earned.
Program Focus Environmental and community service, language immersion, and cultural exchange.
Academics Spanish language/literature, intercultural studies.
Arts Arts and crafts (general), dance (Latin).
Special Interest Areas Community service, construction, field trips (arts and culture), homestays.
Sports Basketball, soccer, sports (general), swimming, volleyball.
Wilderness/Outdoors Hiking, rafting.
Trips Cultural, day, overnight.
Program Information 1–2 sessions per year. Session length: 28–30 days in June, July. Ages: 15–18. 15–17 participants per session. Cost: $4150–$4250. Application fee: $100. Financial aid available.
Application Deadline Continuous.
Jobs Positions for college students 23 and older.
Contact Erik Werner, Director, 1113 South Allen Street, State College, Pennsylvania 16801. Phone: 814-867-7000. Fax: 814-867-2717. E-mail: info@globalworksinc.com.
URL www.globalworksinc.com
For more information, see page 1136.

iD Tech Camps–Documentary Filmmaking and Cultural Immersion at the University of Cádiz, Spain

iD Tech Camps
University of Cádiz
Cádiz
Spain

General Information Coed travel academic program and cultural program established in 2003. Accredited by American Camping Association. Formal opportunities for the academically talented and artistically talented.
Program Focus Documentary filmmaking and cultural immersion.
Academics Spanish (Advanced Placement), Spanish language/literature, computers, precollege program.
Arts Digital media, television/video.
Special Interest Areas Career exploration, homestays, leadership training, team building, touring.
Sports Frisbee, soccer, swimming, volleyball.
Trips Cultural, day, overnight.
Program Information 1 session per year. Session length: 14–20 days in July. Ages: 14–17. 20–50 participants per session. Cost: $3499. Application fee: $400.
Application Deadline Continuous.
Jobs Positions for college students 18 and older.
Contact Kendra Merrill, Spain Program Coordinator, 1885 Winchester Boulevard, Suite 201, Campbell,

California 95008. Phone: 408-871-2227 Ext.117. Fax: 408-871-2228. E-mail: kendra@internaldrive.com.
URL www.internaldrive.com
For more information, see page 1156.

Instituto de Idiomas Geos–Granada, Spain

Instituto de Idiomas Geos
Calle Puentezuelas, 3, 2B
Granada 18002
Spain

General Information Coed residential and day traditional camp, academic program, and cultural program established in 2002.
Academics Spanish (Advanced Placement), Spanish language/literature.
Arts Dance, dance (folk), dance (jazz), dance (modern), film, music, television/video, theater/drama.
Special Interest Areas Culinary arts, homestays, nature study.
Sports Aerobics, bicycling, boating, canoeing, climbing (wall), cross-country, diving, equestrian sports, golf, horseback riding, skiing (cross-country), skiing (downhill), soccer, squash, swimming, tennis, volleyball.
Wilderness/Outdoors Adventure racing, bicycle trips, canoe trips, hiking, mountain biking, mountaineering, rafting, rock climbing, wilderness camping.
Trips College tours, cultural, day, overnight, shopping.
Program Information 2–5 sessions per year. Session length: 1–4 weeks in January, February, March, April, May, June, July, August, September, October. Ages: 10–18. 5–30 participants per session. Boarding program cost: 480–2425 euros.
Application Deadline Continuous.
Jobs Positions for college students.
Contact Ms. Erika Hjelm, Admissions, Grenada 18002, Spain. Phone: 34-958-523100. Fax: 34-958-866337. E-mail: granada@geos-spain.com.
URL www.geos-spain.com

Instituto de Idiomas Geos–Marbella, Spain

Instituto de Idiomas Geos
Calle Valentunaña #4, Edificio AMI
Marbella 29600
Spain

General Information Coed residential and day academic program and cultural program established in 2000.
Academics English as a second language, Spanish (Advanced Placement), Spanish language/literature.
Arts Dance, dance (folk), dance (jazz), dance (modern), film, music, television/video.
Special Interest Areas Culinary arts, homestays.
Sports Aerobics, bicycling, boating, canoeing, diving, equestrian sports, fishing, golf, gymnastics, horseback riding, martial arts, sailing, scuba diving, sea kayaking, snorkeling, soccer, squash, swimming, tennis, volleyball, waterskiing, windsurfing.
Wilderness/Outdoors Bicycle trips, canoe trips, hiking, mountain biking, pack animal trips, rafting.
Trips College tours, cultural, day, overnight, shopping.
Program Information 4–8 sessions per year. Session length: 1–4 weeks in April, May, June, July, August, September, October, December. Ages: 10–18. 5–30 participants per session. Boarding program cost: 480–2425 euros.
Application Deadline Continuous.
Jobs Positions for college students.
Contact Ms. Carmen Illanes, Admissions, main address above. Phone: 34-952-867601. Fax: 34-952-824294. E-mail: info@geos-marbella.com.
URL www.geos-spain.com

Lacunza Junior Summer Spanish Course

Lacunza–ih-San Sebastian
Camino de Mundiaz 8
San Sebastian 20012
Spain

General Information Coed residential and day academic program and cultural program established in 1993. Formal opportunities for the academically talented. College credit may be earned.
Program Focus Learn Spanish and improve communicative skills. Live the Spanish language and culture.
Academics SAT/ACT preparation, Spanish (Advanced Placement), Spanish language/literature, intercultural studies.
Arts Dance.
Special Interest Areas Cross-cultural education, homestays, touring.
Sports Bicycling, sea kayaking, soccer, volleyball.
Trips Cultural, day, shopping.
Program Information 1 session per year. Session length: 13–55 days in June, July, August. Ages: 14–17. 15–50 participants per session. Boarding program cost: 920–3680 euros. Application fee: 50 euros.
Application Deadline Continuous.
Contact Marta Asensio, Admissions Officer, main address above. Phone: 34-943-326988. Fax: 34-943-326822. E-mail: info@lacunza.com.
URL www.lacunza.com

Learning Programs International–Spain

Learning Programs International
Spain

General Information Coed residential academic program and cultural program established in 1990. Formal opportunities for the academically talented. High school or college credit may be earned.
Program Focus Language acquisition.
Academics Spanish (Advanced Placement), Spanish language/literature.
Arts Dance.
Special Interest Areas Homestays.
Trips Cultural, day, overnight.

Learning Programs International–Spain (continued)

Learning Programs International–Spain

Program Information 1–2 sessions per year. Session length: 28–30 days in June, July. Ages: 16–18. 10–40 participants per session. Boarding program cost: $3550–$3950. Airfare not included.
Application Deadline Continuous.
Contact Michelle McRaney, Program Director, 901 West 24th Street, Austin, Texas 78705. Phone: 800-259-4439. Fax: 512-480-8866. E-mail: lpi@studiesabroad.com.
URL www.lpiabroad.com
For more information, see page 1190.

The Loomis Chaffee Summer in Spain

The Loomis Chaffee School
Barcelona
Spain

General Information Coed residential academic program and cultural program established in 1990.
Program Focus Study, homestays, and travel.
Academics Spanish language/literature, art history/appreciation.
Special Interest Areas Field trips (arts and culture), homestays, touring.
Trips Cultural, day, overnight.
Program Information 1 session per year. Session length: 33–35 days in June, July. Ages: 14–18. 16–20 participants per session. Boarding program cost: $5150. Application fee: $25. Financial aid available. Airfare from New York included.
Application Deadline Continuous.
Contact Curtis M. Robison, Director, Summer Programs Abroad, The Loomis Chaffee School, 4 Batchelder Road, Windsor, Connecticut 06095. Phone: 860-687-6341. Fax: 860-687-6181. E-mail: curt_robison@loomis.org.
URL www.loomis.org

LSA Alicante, Spain

Language Studies Abroad, Inc.
Alicante
Spain

General Information Coed residential academic program and cultural program established in 2000. Formal opportunities for the academically talented. High school or college credit may be earned.
Program Focus Learning languages and culture.
Academics Spanish (Advanced Placement), Spanish language/literature, intercultural studies, language study.
Special Interest Areas Homestays.
Trips Cultural, day.
Program Information 1–26 sessions per year. Session length: 13–26 days in January, February, March, April, May, June, July, August, September, October, November, December. Ages: 17+. 5–9 participants per session. Boarding program cost: $658–$2411. Application fee: $100. Financial aid available.
Application Deadline Continuous.
Contact Director, 1801 Highway 50 East, Suite I, Carson City, Nevada 89701. Phone: 800-424-5522. Fax: 775-883-2266. E-mail: info@languagestudiesabroad.com.
URL www.languagestudiesabroad.com
For more information, see page 1186.

LSA Almuñecar, Spain

Language Studies Abroad, Inc.
Almuñecar
Spain

General Information Coed residential academic program and cultural program established in 2001. Formal opportunities for the academically talented and artistically talented. Specific services available for the physically challenged. High school or college credit may be earned.
Program Focus Language and culture.
Academics Spanish (Advanced Placement), Spanish language/literature.
Arts Arts and crafts (general).
Trips Cultural, day, overnight, shopping.
Program Information 1–12 sessions per year. Session length: 13–360 days in January, February, March, April, May, June, July, August, September, October, November, December. Ages: 15+. 200–300 participants per session. Boarding program cost: $665–$2448. Application fee: $100. Financial aid available.
Application Deadline Continuous.
Contact Director, 1801 Highway 50 East, Suite I, Carson City, Nevada 89701. Phone: 800-424-5522. Fax: 775-883-2266. E-mail: info@languagestudiesabroad.com.
URL www.languagestudiesabroad.com
For more information, see page 1186.

LSA Barcelona, Spain

Language Studies Abroad, Inc.
Barcelona
Spain

General Information Coed residential academic program and cultural program established in 1999. Formal opportunities for the academically talented. High school or college credit may be earned.
Program Focus Learning language and culture.
Academics Spanish (Advanced Placement), Spanish language/literature, intercultural studies, language study.
Special Interest Areas Homestays.
Sports Swimming.
Trips Cultural, day, overnight, shopping.
Program Information 1–26 sessions per year. Session length: 14–360 days in January, February, March, April, May, June, July, August, September, October, November, December. Ages: 16+. Boarding program cost: $665–$2448. Application fee: $100. Financial aid available. Additional weeks available.
Application Deadline Continuous.
Contact Director, 1801 Highway 50 East, Suite I, Carson City, Nevada 89701. Phone: 800-424-5522. Fax: 775-883-2266. E-mail: info@languagestudiesabroad.com.
URL www.languagestudiesabroad.com

For more information, see page 1186.

LSA El Puerto de Santa Maria, Spain

Language Studies Abroad, Inc.
El Puerto de Santa Maria
Spain

General Information Coed residential academic program and cultural program established in 1956. High school or college credit may be earned.
Program Focus Learning language and culture with option to combine studies in Madrid, Salamanca, El Puerto, and Alicante.
Academics Spanish (Advanced Placement), Spanish language/literature, intercultural studies.
Arts Dance.
Special Interest Areas Culinary arts, homestays.
Trips Cultural, day, overnight, shopping.
Program Information 3–25 sessions per year. Session length: 2–16 weeks in January, February, March, April, May, June, July, August, September, October, November, December. Ages: 17+. 45–80 participants per session. Boarding program cost: $658–$2411. Application fee: $100. Financial aid available.
Application Deadline Continuous.
Contact Director, 1801 Highway 50 East, Suite I, Carson City, Nevada 89701. Phone: 800-424-5522. Fax: 775-883-2266. E-mail: info@languagestudiesabroad.com.
URL www.languagestudiesabroad.com

For more information, see page 1186.

LSA Granada, Spain

Language Studies Abroad, Inc.
Granada
Spain

General Information Coed residential academic program and cultural program established in 1993. Formal opportunities for the academically talented. High school or college credit may be earned.
Program Focus Language and culture.
Academics Spanish (Advanced Placement), Spanish language/literature, academics (general), intercultural studies.
Special Interest Areas Homestays.
Trips Cultural, day.
Program Information 1–26 sessions per year. Session length: 14–360 days in January, February, March, April, May, June, July, August, September, October, November, December. Ages: 16+. 130–180 participants per session. Boarding program cost: $780–$2900. Application fee: $100. Financial aid available.
Application Deadline Continuous.
Contact Director, 1801 Highway 50 East, Suite 1, Carson City, Nevada 89701. Phone: 800-424-5522. Fax: 775-883-2266. E-mail: info@languagestudiesabroad.com.
URL www.languagestudiesabroad.com

For more information, see page 1186.

LSA Madrid, Spain

Language Studies Abroad, Inc.
Madrid
Spain

General Information Coed residential academic program and cultural program established in 1956. Formal opportunities for the academically talented and artistically talented. High school or college credit may be earned.
Program Focus Learning language and culture.
Academics Spanish (Advanced Placement), Spanish language/literature, history, intercultural studies, language study, writing.
Special Interest Areas Field trips (arts and culture), homestays, touring.
Sports Golf, horseback riding, swimming, tennis.
Trips College tours, cultural, day, overnight, shopping.
Program Information 1–26 sessions per year. Session length: 14–360 days in January, February, March, April, May, June, July, August, September, October, November, December. Ages: 6+. 100–170 participants per session. Boarding program cost: $1062–$3768. Application fee: $100.
Application Deadline Continuous.
Contact Director, 1801 Highway 50 East, Suite I, Carson City, Nevada 89701. Phone: 800-424-5522. Fax: 775-883-2266. E-mail: info@languagestudiesabroad.com.
URL www.languagestudiesabroad.com

For more information, see page 1186.

LSA Màlaga, Spain

Language Studies Abroad, Inc.
Màlaga
Spain

General Information Coed residential academic program and cultural program established in 1994. Formal opportunities for the academically talented and artistically talented. High school or college credit may be earned.
Program Focus Learning language and culture.
Academics Spanish (Advanced Placement), Spanish language/literature, business, geography, history, intercultural studies, language study.
Arts Arts and crafts (general), cinematography.
Special Interest Areas Homestays, touring.
Sports Golf, swimming, tennis.
Trips College tours, cultural, day, overnight, shopping.
Program Information 1–26 sessions per year. Session length: 14–360 days in January, February, March, April, May, June, July, August, September, October, November, December. Ages: 16+. 170–300 participants per session. Boarding program cost: $831–$2420. Application fee: $100. Financial aid available.
Application Deadline Continuous.
Contact Director, 1801 Highway 50 East, Suite I, Carson City, Nevada 89701. Phone: 800-424-5522. Fax: 775-883-2266. E-mail: info@languagestudiesabroad.com.
URL www.languagestudiesabroad.com

For more information, see page 1186.

LSA Marbella, Spain

Language Studies Abroad, Inc.
Marbella
Spain

General Information Coed residential academic program, outdoor program, and cultural program established in 1999. Formal opportunities for the academically talented and artistically talented. High school or college credit may be earned.
Program Focus Learning language and culture.
Academics Spanish (Advanced Placement), Spanish language/literature, communications, history, intercultural studies, language study, reading, writing.
Arts Arts and crafts (general), photography, radio broadcasting.
Special Interest Areas Homestays, nautical skills, weight reduction.
Sports Archery, boating, equestrian sports, golf, horseback riding, sailing, soccer, swimming, tennis.
Trips Cultural, day, overnight, shopping.
Program Information 1–26 sessions per year. Session length: 14–360 days in January, February, March, April, May, June, July, August, September, October, November, December. Ages: 6+. 25–150 participants per session. Boarding program cost: $1062–$3768. Application fee: $100. Financial aid available.
Application Deadline Continuous.
Contact Director, 1801 Highway 50 East, Suite I, Carson City, Nevada 89701. Phone: 800-424-5522. Fax: 775-883-7651. E-mail: info@languagestudiesabroad.com.
URL www.languagestudiesabroad.com

For more information, see page 1186.

LSA Nerja, Spain

Language Studies Abroad, Inc.
Nerja
Spain

General Information Coed residential academic program and cultural program established in 1980. Formal opportunities for the academically talented and artistically talented. High school or college credit may be earned.
Program Focus Learning language and culture.
Academics Spanish (Advanced Placement), Spanish language/literature, business, intercultural studies, language study.
Special Interest Areas Homestays.
Sports Swimming.
Trips Cultural, day, overnight, shopping.
Program Information 1–26 sessions per year. Session length: 14–360 days in January, February, March, April, May, June, July, August, September, October, November, December. Ages: 16+. 60–100 participants per session. Boarding program cost: $649–$2218. Application fee: $100. Financial aid available. Additional weeks available.
Application Deadline Continuous.
Contact Director, 1801 Highway 50 East, Suite I, Carson City, Nevada 89701. Phone: 800-424-5522. Fax: 775-883-2266. E-mail: info@languagestudiesabroad.com.
URL www.languagestudiesabroad.com

For more information, see page 1186.

LSA Salamanca, Spain

Language Studies Abroad, Inc.
Salamanca
Spain

General Information Coed residential academic program and cultural program established in 1956. Formal opportunities for the academically talented and artistically talented. High school or college credit may be earned.
Program Focus Learning language and culture.
Academics Spanish (Advanced Placement), Spanish language/literature, intercultural studies, language study.
Arts Dance.
Special Interest Areas Homestays.
Sports Bicycling, swimming.
Trips College tours, cultural, day, overnight, shopping.
Program Information 1–25 sessions per year. Session length: 14–360 days in January, February, March, April, May, June, July, August, September, October, November, December. Ages: 14+. 40–75 participants per session. Boarding program cost: $1062–$3768. Application fee: $100.
Application Deadline Continuous.
Contact Director, 1801 Highway 50 East, Suite I, Carson City, Nevada 89701. Phone: 800-424-5522. Fax: 775-883-2266. E-mail: info@languagestudiesabroad.com.
URL www.languagestudiesabroad.com

For more information, see page 1186.

LSA San Sebastian, Spain

Language Studies Abroad, Inc.
San Sebastian
Spain

General Information Coed residential academic program and cultural program established in 1989. Formal opportunities for the academically talented and artistically talented. High school or college credit may be earned.
Program Focus Learning language and culture.
Academics Spanish language/literature, reading, writing.
Special Interest Areas Homestays.
Sports Canoeing, football, horseback riding, racquetball, skiing (downhill), volleyball.
Wilderness/Outdoors Mountain biking, rafting.
Trips Cultural, day, overnight, shopping.
Program Information 1–26 sessions per year. Session length: 14–360 days in January, February, March, April, May, June, July, August, September, October, November, December. Ages: 17+. 9–12 participants per session. Boarding program cost: $1815. Application fee: $100. Financial aid available.
Application Deadline Continuous.
Contact Director, 1801 Highway 50 East, Suite I, Carson City, Nevada 89701. Phone: 800-424-5522. Fax: 775-883-2266. E-mail: info@languagestudiesabroad.com.
URL www.languagestudiesabroad.com

For more information, see page 1186.

LSA Sevilla, Spain

Language Studies Abroad, Inc.
Seville
Spain

General Information Coed residential academic program and cultural program established in 1980. Formal opportunities for the academically talented and artistically talented. High school or college credit may be earned.
Program Focus Learning language and culture.
Academics Spanish (Advanced Placement), Spanish language/literature, business, intercultural studies, language study.
Arts Film.
Special Interest Areas Homestays.
Sports Swimming.
Trips College tours, cultural, day, overnight, shopping.
Program Information 1–26 sessions per year. Session length: 14–360 days in January, February, March, April, May, June, July, August, September, October, November, December. Ages: 15+. 15–100 participants per session. Boarding program cost: $917–$1562. Application fee: $100.
Application Deadline Continuous.
Contact Director, 1801 Highway 50 East, Suite I, Carson City, Nevada 89701. Phone: 800-424-5522. Fax: 775-883-2266. E-mail: info@languagestudiesabroad.com.
URL www.languagestudiesabroad.com

For more information, see page 1186.

LSA Tenerife, Spain

Language Studies Abroad, Inc.
Tenerife
Spain

General Information Coed residential cultural program established in 2000. Formal opportunities for the academically talented. High school or college credit may be earned.
Program Focus Language and culture.
Academics Spanish language/literature, intercultural studies, language study.
Special Interest Areas Homestays.
Trips Cultural.
Program Information 1–26 sessions per year. Session length: 14–360 days in January, February, March, April, May, June, July, August, September, October, November, December. Ages: 16+. Boarding program cost: $792–$2600. Application fee: $100. Financial aid available.
Application Deadline Continuous.
Contact Director, 1801 Highway 50 East, Suite I, Carson City, Nevada 89701. Phone: 800-424-5522. Fax: 775-883-2266. E-mail: info@languagestudiesabroad.com.
URL www.languagestudiesabroad.com

For more information, see page 1186.

LSA Valencia, Spain

Language Studies Abroad, Inc.
Valencia
Spain

General Information Coed residential academic program and cultural program established in 1975. Formal opportunities for the academically talented and artistically talented. High school or college credit may be earned.
Program Focus Learning language and culture.
Academics Spanish (Advanced Placement), Spanish language/literature, intercultural studies, language study.
Special Interest Areas Homestays.
Sports Sailing.
Trips College tours, cultural, day, overnight, shopping.
Program Information 1–26 sessions per year. Session length: 14–360 days in January, February, March, April, May, June, July, August, September, October, November, December. Ages: 17+. 40–100 participants per session. Boarding program cost: $703–$2380. Application fee: $100.
Application Deadline Continuous.
Contact Director, 1801 Highway 50 East, Suite I, Carson City, Nevada 89701. Phone: 800-424-5522. Fax: 775-883-2266. E-mail: info@languagestudiesabroad.com.
URL www.languagestudiesabroad.com

For more information, see page 1186.

Mercersburg Academy Summer Study in Spain

Mercersburg Academy Summer and Extended Programs
Spain

General Information Coed travel academic program established in 1998. High school credit may be earned.
Program Focus Youth enrichment.
Academics Spanish language/literature, art history/appreciation, intercultural studies.
Special Interest Areas Homestays.
Trips Cultural, day, overnight, shopping.
Program Information 1 session per year. Session length: 3 weeks in June, July. Ages: 14–18. 10–15 participants per session. Cost: $2650. Financial aid available. Airfare from Washington D.C. to Madrid included.
Application Deadline April 30.
Contact Mr. Rick Hendrickson, Director of Summer and Extended Programs, 300 East Seminary Street, Mercersburg, Pennsylvania 17236. Phone: 717-328-6225. Fax: 717-328-9072. E-mail: summerprograms@mercersburg.edu.
URL www.mercersburg.edu

For more information, see page 1210.

Overland: Language Study Abroad in Spain

Overland Travel, Inc.
Spain

General Information Coed travel academic program and cultural program established in 1985. Accredited by American Camping Association. High school credit may be earned.
Program Focus Spanish language program and cultural exploration of Spain.
Academics Spanish language/literature.
Special Interest Areas Homestays.
Trips Cultural, day, overnight.
Program Information 2 sessions per year. Session length: 32 days in June, July, August. Ages: 14–18. 8–12 participants per session. Cost: $5995.
Application Deadline Continuous.
Jobs Positions for college students 20 and older.
Contact Ms. Brooks Follansbee, Director, PO Box 31, Williamstown, Massachusetts 01267. Phone: 800-458-0588. Fax: 413-458-5208. E-mail: overland@adelphia.net.
URL www.overlandsummers.com

For more information, see page 1240.

PAX Abroad–Summer Spain

PAX Abroad
Cadiz
Spain

General Information Coed travel academic program and cultural program established in 2000.
Academics Spanish language/literature.
Trips Cultural, day, overnight, shopping.
Program Information 1 session per year. Session length: 3 weeks in July. Ages: 14–18. Cost: $3700–$4100. Application fee: $100. Airfare from New York included.
Application Deadline April 15.
Contact Ms. Libby Cryer, Director, PAX Abroad, 71 Arch Street, Greenwich, Connecticut 06830. Phone: 800-555-6211. Fax: 203-629-0486. E-mail: academicexchange@pax.org.
URL www.pax.org

Poulter Colorado Camps: Adventures Planet Earth–Spain

Poulter Colorado Camps
Spain

General Information Coed travel outdoor program, cultural program, and adventure program established in 1966. Accredited by American Camping Association.
Program Focus Exciting international experiences combining adventure travel with cultural immersion.
Academics Intercultural studies.
Special Interest Areas Community service, homestays, leadership training, nature study, touring.
Wilderness/Outdoors Backpacking, bicycle trips, hiking.
Trips Cultural, day, overnight, shopping.
Program Information 2–4 sessions per year. Session length: 17–30 days in June, July, August, September, October. Ages: 13+. 6–10 participants per session. Cost: $1950–$3500. Financial aid available.
Application Deadline Continuous.
Jobs Positions for college students 21 and older.
Contact Mr. Jay B. Poulter, Director, PO Box 772947, Steamboat Springs, Colorado 80477. Phone: 888-879-4816. Fax: 800-860-3587. E-mail: poulter@poultercamps.com.
URL www.poultercamps.com

Programs Abroad Travel Alternatives–Spain

Programs Abroad Travel Alternatives
Spain

General Information Coed travel academic program and cultural program established in 1996. Formal opportunities for the academically talented. College credit may be earned.
Program Focus Immersion for foreign language students.
Academics Spanish language/literature, art history/appreciation, history, intercultural studies.
Special Interest Areas Cross-cultural education, homestays, touring.
Trips Cultural, overnight.
Program Information 2–3 sessions per year. Session length: 9–34 days in March, June, July. Ages: 15+. 1–30 participants per session. Cost: $1500–$4500. Application fee: $90. Participant must be in high school.
Application Deadline Continuous.

Contact Ms. Rose Potter, Founder/CEO, 6200 Adel Cove, Austin, Texas 78749. Phone: 888-777-PATA. Fax: 512-282-7076. E-mail: immerse@gopata.com.
URL www.gopata.com

Special Note
As a participant in the PATA program, one student knew her trip to Santander wouldn't raise her AP score. But, after earning four semesters of credit in Spanish through CLEP testing, she was excited to learn that her PATA credit did earn her one more additional credit. With those five credits and only one college-level course, she earned a minor in Spanish. An impressed Spanish department then granted her their $1000 annual scholarship and a free semester abroad in Spain. Her PATA evaluation form noted, "I'd never met such amazing people. My outlook on life completely changed and I'm a better person because of it."

For more information, see page 1248.

Putney Student Travel–Language Learning–Spain

Putney Student Travel
Spain

General Information Coed residential academic program and cultural program established in 1951.
Program Focus Spanish language immersion. Participants housed in host-family homes and hotels. Enrollment limited to those who are studying Spanish.
Academics Spanish (Advanced Placement), Spanish language/literature, art history/appreciation, intercultural studies.
Special Interest Areas Homestays.
Sports Horseback riding, rappelling, sailing, soccer, swimming, windsurfing.
Wilderness/Outdoors Bicycle trips, hiking, mountaineering, rock climbing.
Trips Cultural, day, overnight.
Program Information 3–6 sessions per year. Session length: 38–40 days in June, July, August. Ages: 13–18. 16–18 participants per session. Boarding program cost: $8090. Financial aid available. Airfare from New York included.
Application Deadline Continuous.
Contact Jeffrey Shumlin, Admissions Director, 345 Hickory Ridge Road, Putney, Vermont 05346. Phone: 802-387-5000. Fax: 802-387-4276. E-mail: info@goputney.com.
URL www.goputney.com

For more information, see page 1276.

Rassias Programs–Gijón, Spain

Rassias Programs
Gijón
Spain

General Information Coed travel academic program and cultural program established in 1985.
Program Focus Spanish language studies taught in the Rassias method, homestays and travel in Spain.
Academics Spanish (Advanced Placement), Spanish language/literature.
Special Interest Areas Homestays, touring.
Sports Aerobics, basketball, kayaking, squash, swimming, tennis, weight training.
Wilderness/Outdoors Hiking.
Trips Cultural, overnight.
Program Information 1 session per year. Session length: 30 days in June, July. Ages: 14–17. 20–22 participants per session. Cost: $5800–$6000. Financial aid available. Airfare included.
Application Deadline Continuous.
Jobs Positions for college students 21 and older.
Contact Bill Miles, Director, PO Box 5456, Hanover, New Hampshire 03755. Phone: 603-643-3007. Fax: 603-643-4249. E-mail: rassias@sover.net.
URL www.rassias.com

For more information, see page 1280.

Rassias Programs–Pontevedra, Spain

Rassias Programs
Pontevedra
Spain

General Information Coed travel academic program and cultural program established in 1985.
Program Focus Spanish language studies taught in the Rassias method, homestays and travel in Spain.
Academics Spanish (Advanced Placement), Spanish language/literature.
Special Interest Areas Homestays, touring.
Sports Basketball, swimming, tennis.
Wilderness/Outdoors Hiking.
Trips Cultural, overnight.
Program Information 1 session per year. Session length: 30 days in June, July. Ages: 14–17. 20–22 participants per session. Cost: $5800–$6000. Financial aid available. Airfare included.
Application Deadline Continuous.
Jobs Positions for college students 21 and older.
Contact Bill Miles, Director, PO Box 5456, Hanover, New Hampshire 03755. Phone: 603-643-3007. Fax: 603-643-4249. E-mail: rassais@sover.net.
URL www.rassias.com

For more information, see page 1280.

Rassias Programs–Segovia, Spain

Rassias Programs
Segovia
Spain

General Information Coed travel academic program and cultural program established in 1985.
Program Focus Spanish language studies taught in the Rassias method, homestays and travel in Spain.
Academics Spanish (Advanced Placement), Spanish language/literature.
Special Interest Areas Homestays, touring.
Sports Basketball, kayaking, swimming, tennis, weight training.
Wilderness/Outdoors Hiking.
Trips Cultural, overnight.

Rassias Programs–Segovia, Spain (continued)

Program Information 1 session per year. Session length: 30 days in June, July. Ages: 14–17. 20–22 participants per session. Cost: $5800–$6000. Financial aid available. Airfare included.
Application Deadline Continuous.
Jobs Positions for college students 21 and older.
Contact Bill Miles, Director, PO Box 5456, Hanover, New Hampshire 03755. Phone: 603-643-3007. Fax: 603-643-4249. E-mail: rassias@sover.net.
URL www.rassias.com

For more information, see page 1280.

Spanish Language and Flamenco Enforex–Granada

Enforex Spanish in the Spanish World
Santa Teresa 20
Granada 18002
Spain

General Information Coed residential academic program. High school or college credit may be earned.
Program Focus Language program with optional cultural activities.
Academics Spanish (Advanced Placement), Spanish language/literature, business, computers, intercultural studies.
Arts Dance (folk), flamenco.
Special Interest Areas Homestays.
Sports Football, gymnastics, soccer, swimming, volleyball.
Trips College tours, cultural, day, overnight, shopping.
Program Information 48 sessions per year. Session length: 2–3 weeks in January, February, March, April, May, June, July, August, September, October, November, December. Ages: 15+. 50 participants per session. Boarding program cost: 600–900 euros. Application fee: 65 euros.
Application Deadline Continuous.
Contact Spanish Department, Alberto Aguilera 26, Madrid 28015, Spain. Phone: 34-91-594-3776. Fax: 34-91-594-5159. E-mail: registration@enforex.es.
URL www.enforex.com

For more information, see page 1110.

Spanish Language and Flamenco Enforex–Madrid

Enforex Spanish in the Spanish World
Alberto Aguilera 26
Madrid 28015
Spain

General Information Coed residential academic program. High school or college credit may be earned.
Program Focus Language program with optional cultural activities.
Academics Spanish (Advanced Placement), Spanish language/literature, business, computers, intercultural studies.
Arts Dance (folk), flamenco.
Special Interest Areas Homestays.
Sports Football, gymnastics, soccer, swimming, volleyball.
Trips College tours, cultural, day, overnight, shopping.
Program Information 48 sessions per year. Session length: 2–3 weeks in January, February, March, April, May, June, July, August, September, October, November, December. Ages: 15+. 50 participants per session. Boarding program cost: 600–900 euros. Application fee: 65 euros. Financial aid available. Extra weeks available.
Application Deadline Continuous.
Contact Spanish Department, main address above. Phone: 34-91-594-3776. Fax: 34-91-594-5159. E-mail: registration@enforex.es.
URL www.enforex.com

For more information, see page 1110.

Spanish Language and Flamenco Enforex–Marbella

Enforex Spanish in the Spanish World
Avenida Ricardo Soriano 43
Marbella 29600
Spain

General Information Coed residential academic program. High school or college credit may be earned.
Program Focus Language program with optional cultural activities.
Academics Spanish (Advanced Placement), Spanish language/literature, business, computers, intercultural studies.
Arts Dance (folk), flamenco.
Special Interest Areas Homestays.
Sports Football, gymnastics, soccer, swimming, volleyball.
Trips College tours, cultural, day, overnight, shopping.
Program Information 48 sessions per year. Session length: 2–3 weeks in January, February, March, April, May, June, July, August, September, October, November, December. 25 participants per session. Boarding program cost: 600–900 euros. Application fee: 65 euros. Financial aid available.
Application Deadline Continuous.
Contact Spanish Department, Alberto Aguilera 26, Madrid 28015, Spain. Phone: 34-91-594-3776. Fax: 34-91-594-5159. E-mail: registration@enforex.es.
URL www.enforex.com

For more information, see page 1110.

Study Tour Vacational Program Enforex–Barcelona

Enforex Spanish in the Spanish World
Diputacion 92
Barcelona
Spain

General Information Coed residential academic program. High school or college credit may be earned.
Program Focus Language program with optional cultural activities.
Academics Spanish (Advanced Placement), Spanish language/literature, art history/appreciation, history, intercultural studies.

Special Interest Areas Field trips (arts and culture), homestays, touring.
Sports Football, gymnastics, soccer, swimming, tennis, volleyball.
Trips College tours, cultural, day, overnight, shopping.
Program Information 12 sessions per year. Session length: 2 weeks in January, February, March, April, May, June, July, August, September, October, November, December. Ages: 15+. 250 participants per session. Boarding program cost: 440 euros. Application fee: 65 euros. Financial aid available.
Application Deadline Continuous.
Contact Spanish Department, Alberto Aguilera 26, Madrid 28015, Spain. Phone: 34-91-594-3776. Fax: 34-91-594-5159. E-mail: info@enforex.es.
URL www.enforex.com

For more information, see page 1110.

Taft Summer School Abroad–Spain

The Taft School
Madrid
Spain

General Information Coed travel academic program established in 1982. Accredited by American Camping Association.
Program Focus The program is designed to completely immerse the student in the people, language, and culture of the country.
Academics Spanish language/literature, art history/appreciation, history, intercultural studies.
Special Interest Areas Homestays, touring.
Trips Cultural, day, overnight, shopping.
Program Information 1 session per year. Session length: 35–40 days in June, July. Ages: 14–18. 10–20 participants per session. Cost: $5600. Application fee: $50. Airfare from New York to Madrid included.
Application Deadline April 15.
Contact Juan Ortiz, Director, Taft Summer in Spain, 110 Woodbury Road, Watertown, Connecticut 06795. Phone: 860-945-5926. Fax: 860-945-7859. E-mail: jortiz@taftschool.org.
URL www.taftschool.org/summer

For more information, see page 1354.

TASIS Spanish Summer Program

TASIS The American School in England
Colegio Internacional
Salamanca
Spain

General Information Coed residential academic program and cultural program established in 1993. High school credit may be earned.
Program Focus Intensive Spanish instruction combined with cultural experiences. The city of Salamanca is the School's classroom, with the last week of the program spent on the Costa del Sol.
Academics Spanish language/literature.
Sports Aerobics, basketball, gymnastics, soccer, swimming, tennis, weight training.
Trips Cultural, day, overnight, shopping.
Program Information 1 session per year. Session length: 30 days in July. Ages: 13–17. 75–100 participants per session. Boarding program cost: $4700.
Application Deadline Continuous.
Jobs Positions for college students.
Contact W. Thomas Fleming, US Director, 1640 Wisconsin Avenue, NW, Washington, District of Columbia 20007. Phone: 202-965-5800. Fax: 202-965-5816. E-mail: usadmissions@tasis.com.
URL www.tasis.com

For more information, see page 1356.

Wilderness Ventures–Spanish Pyrenees

Wilderness Ventures
Spain

General Information Coed travel outdoor program, wilderness program, cultural program, and adventure program established in 1973.
Program Focus Wilderness travel, cultural immersion, leadership skills.
Special Interest Areas Leadership training.
Sports Sea kayaking.
Wilderness/Outdoors Backpacking, rafting, white-water trips, wilderness camping.
Trips Cultural, overnight.
Program Information 2 sessions per year. Session length: 3 weeks in June, July, August. Ages: 14–18. 13 participants per session. Cost: $4090. Financial aid available.
Application Deadline Continuous.
Jobs Positions for college students 21 and older.
Contact Mike Cottingham, Director, PO Box 2768, Jackson Hole, Wyoming 83001. Phone: 800-533-2281. Fax: 307-739-1934. E-mail: info@wildernessventures.com.
URL www.wildernessventures.com

For more information, see page 1396.

Woodberry Forest Summer School–Spain

Woodberry Forest School
Spain

General Information Coed residential academic program established in 1922. Formal opportunities for the academically talented. High school credit may be earned.
Academics Spanish language/literature, academics (general).
Sports Sports (general), weight training.
Trips Cultural, overnight.
Program Information 1 session per year. Session length: 6 weeks in June, July, August. Ages: 12–17. 5–20 participants per session. Boarding program cost: $4753. Financial aid available.
Application Deadline Continuous.
Contact Dr. W. David McRae, Director of Summer Programs, 354 Woodberry Forest Station, Woodberry

Woodberry Forest Summer School–Spain (continued)
Forest, Virginia 22989. Phone: 540-672-6047. Fax: 540-672-9076. E-mail: wfs_summer@woodberry.org.
URL www.woodberry.org
For more information, see page 1402.

YOUTH FOR UNDERSTANDING USA–SPAIN

Youth for Understanding USA
Spain

General Information Coed residential academic program and cultural program established in 1951. High school or college credit may be earned.
Program Focus Living with a host family, learning about other cultures, and improving Spanish language skills.
Academics Spanish language/literature, area studies, intercultural studies, social studies.
Special Interest Areas Homestays.
Trips Cultural, day, overnight.
Program Information 2 sessions per year. Session length: 25–45 days in June, July. Ages: 15–18. 10–50 participants per session. Boarding program cost: $5195–$5995. Application fee: $75. Financial aid available. Round-trip domestic and international airfare is included in the tuition.
Application Deadline Continuous.
Contact Admissions Counselor, 6400 Goldsboro Road, Suite 100, Bethesda, Maryland 20817. Phone: 800-TEENAGE (833-6243). Fax: 202-895-1104. E-mail: admissions@us.yfu.org.
URL www.yfu-usa.org
For more information, see page 1414.

YOUTH PROGRAM IN SPAIN

Don Quijote
Calle Azuma 5
Granada, 18005
Spain

General Information Coed travel academic program and cultural program.
Program Focus Learn Spanish in Spain.
Academics Spanish (Advanced Placement), Spanish language/literature, intercultural studies.
Arts Dance, music.
Sports Aerobics, basketball, soccer, swimming, volleyball.
Trips Cultural, day.
Program Information 1–18 sessions per year. Session length: 5 days in June, July, August. Ages: 15–18. 1–120 participants per session. Cost: 551–3500 euros. Application fee: 35 euros.
Application Deadline Continuous.
Contact Mr. Manne Arranz, Area Manager, Plaza San Marcos 7, Salamanca, 37002, Spain. Phone: 34-923-26-88-60. Fax: 34-923-26-88-15. E-mail: manuel.arranz@donquijote.org.
URL www.donquijote.org

SRI LANKA

EARTHWATCH INSTITUTE–SRI LANKA'S TEMPLE MONKEYS

Earthwatch Institute
Polonnaruwa
Sri Lanka

General Information Coed residential outdoor program, cultural program, and adventure program.
Program Focus Documenting macaque society to understand primate social evolution.
Academics Ecology, environmental science, science (general).
Special Interest Areas Field research/expeditions, nature study.
Program Information 6 sessions per year. Session length: 13 days in March, June, July, August, September. Ages: 16+. 12 participants per session. Boarding program cost: $2195–$2295. Financial aid available. Financial aid for high school students and teachers.
Application Deadline Continuous.
Contact General Information Desk, PO Box 75, Maynard, Massachusetts 01754. Phone: 800-776-0188. Fax: 978-461-2332. E-mail: info@earthwatch.org.
URL www.earthwatch.org

SWEDEN

YOUTH FOR UNDERSTANDING USA–SWEDEN

Youth for Understanding USA
Sweden

General Information Coed residential academic program and cultural program established in 1951. High school or college credit may be earned.
Program Focus Living with a host family, learning about other cultures, and improving language skills.
Academics Swedish language/literature, area studies, intercultural studies, social studies.
Special Interest Areas Homestays.
Trips Cultural, day, overnight.
Program Information 1 session per year. Session length: 35–45 days in June, July, August. Ages: 15–18. 10–50 participants per session. Boarding program cost: $4595. Application fee: $75. Financial aid available. Round-trip domestic and international airfare is included in the tuition.
Application Deadline Continuous.
Contact Admissions Counselor, 6400 Goldsboro Road, Suite 100, Bethesda, Maryland 20817. Phone: 800-TEENAGE (833-6243). Fax: 202-895-1104. E-mail: admissions@us.yfu.org.
URL www.yfu-usa.org
For more information, see page 1414.

SWITZERLAND

Atelier des Arts

Atelier des Arts
La-Chaux-de-Fonds
Switzerland

General Information Coed residential arts program established in 1995. Formal opportunities for the artistically talented. High school or college credit may be earned.
Program Focus Jazz, fine arts, dance, studio work, travel, exhibitions, and concerts.
Academics Art history/appreciation, music.
Arts Dance, dance (jazz), dance (modern), drawing, music (ensemble), music (jazz), painting, photography, printmaking, sculpture, visual arts.
Wilderness/Outdoors Hiking.
Trips Cultural, day.
Program Information 1 session per year. Session length: 17 days in July, August. Ages: 16+. 20–30 participants per session. Boarding program cost: $2950. Application fee: $50.
Application Deadline Continuous.
Contact Bruce Smith, Director, 55 Bethune Street, B645, New York, New York 10014. Phone: 212-727-1756. Fax: 212-691-0631. E-mail: info@atelierdesarts.org.
URL www.atelierdesarts.org

Center for Cultural Interchange–Switzerland Language Camp

Center for Cultural Interchange
Leysin
Switzerland

General Information Coed residential traditional camp, academic program, outdoor program, and cultural program established in 1985. Accredited by American Camping Association.
Program Focus Swiss language and sports camp.
Academics French language/literature.
Arts Arts and crafts (general), dance, music, painting.
Special Interest Areas Cross-cultural education, culinary arts.
Sports Aerobics, archery, baseball, bicycling, canoeing, climbing (wall), equestrian sports, figure skating, golf, horseback riding, rappelling, skiing (downhill), soccer, sports (general), squash, swimming, tennis, volleyball, waterskiing.
Wilderness/Outdoors Canoe trips, hiking, mountain biking, orienteering, outdoor adventure, wilderness/outdoors (general).
Trips Cultural, day.
Program Information 3 sessions per year. Session length: 2–3 weeks in July, August. Ages: 10–15. Boarding program cost: $2700–$3500. Financial aid available.
Application Deadline Continuous.
Contact Ms. Juliet Jones, Outbound Programs Director, 325 West Huron, Suite 706, Chicago, Illinois 60610. Phone: 866-684-9675. Fax: 312-944-2644. E-mail: info@cci-exchange.com.
URL www.cci-exchange.com
For more information, see page 1060.

Collège du Léman Summer School

College du Leman International School
74 Route de Sauverny
1290 Versoix
Geneva
Switzerland

General Information Coed residential academic program established in 1964. High school credit may be earned.

Collège du Léman Summer School

Program Focus Choice of language program (French, English, German), or academic program, as well as recreation, sports, and historical, cultural and natural attractions of the region.
Academics English as a second language, English language/literature, French language/literature, German language/literature, biology, chemistry, computers, language study, mathematics, physics.
Arts Arts, arts and crafts (general), drawing, music, painting, pottery.
Special Interest Areas Touring.
Sports Aerobics, archery, badminton, basketball, bicycling, canoeing, cross-country, equestrian sports, fishing, golf, gymnastics, horseback riding, soccer, softball, sports (general), swimming, tennis, track and field, volleyball, water polo, waterskiing, weight training, windsurfing.
Wilderness/Outdoors Bicycle trips, hiking, rafting.

Collège du Léman Summer School (continued)

Trips Cultural, day, overnight, shopping.
Program Information 2 sessions per year. Session length: 3 weeks in July, August. Ages: 8–18. 300 participants per session. Boarding program cost: 4500–5400 Swiss francs.
Application Deadline Continuous.
Jobs Positions for high school students 17 and older and college students 19 and older.
Contact Mr. Francis Clivaz, Director, main address above. Phone: 41-22-775-5555. Fax: 41-22-775-5559. E-mail: info@cdl.ch or summerschool@cdl.ch.
URL www.cdl.ch

For more information, see page 1078.

The Experiment in International Living–Switzerland French Language Immersion, Homestay, and Alpine Adventure

The Experiment in International Living
Switzerland

General Information Coed residential outdoor program, cultural program, and adventure program established in 1932.
Program Focus International youth travel, homestay, French language, outdoor adventure.
Academics French language/literature.
Special Interest Areas Homestays, touring.
Wilderness/Outdoors Backpacking, hiking.
Trips Cultural, day, overnight.
Program Information 1 session per year. Session length: 4 weeks in July, August. Ages: 14–19. 10–15 participants per session. Boarding program cost: $4200. Financial aid available.
Application Deadline May 1.
Contact Annie Thompson, Enrollment Director, Summer Abroad, Kipling Road, PO Box 676, Brattleboro, Vermont 05302-9676. Phone: 800-345-2929. Fax: 802-258-3428. E-mail: eil@worldlearning.org.
URL www.usexperiment.org

For more information, see page 1116.

Institut auf dem Rosenberg

Institut auf dem Rosenberg
Hoehenweg 60
St. Gallen 9000
Switzerland

General Information Coed residential academic program.
Program Focus College counseling.
Academics English as a second language, French language/literature, German language/literature.
Sports Golf, horseback riding, soccer, swimming, tennis, volleyball, waterskiing.
Wilderness/Outdoors Hiking.
Trips Cultural, day, shopping.
Program Information 1 session per year. Session length: 3–4 weeks in July, August. Ages: 14–20. 30 participants per session. Boarding program cost: 4200–5600 Swiss francs.
Application Deadline Continuous.
Jobs Positions for college students 20 and older.
Contact Ms. M. Schmid, Director, main address above. Phone: 41-71-277-7777. Fax: 41-71-277-9827. E-mail: info@instrosenberg.ch.
URL www.instrosenberg.ch

International Summer Camp Montana, Switzerland

International Summer Camp Montana, Switzerland
La Moubra
Crans-Montana (Canton) Valais CH-3963
Switzerland

General Information Coed residential outdoor program and cultural program established in 1960.

International Summer Camp Montana, Switzerland

Program Focus All outdoor sports including horseback riding. Language courses.
Academics English as a second language, French language/literature, German language/literature.
Arts Arts and crafts (general), ceramics, dance (folk), drawing, jewelry making, leather working, macramé, modeling, musical productions, painting, performance art, photography, pottery, sculpture, weaving.
Special Interest Areas Nature study.
Sports Aerobics, archery, baseball, basketball, bicycling, boating, canoeing, climbing (wall), equestrian sports, fencing, field hockey, golf, gymnastics, horseback riding, ice hockey, physical fitness, sailing, skiing (downhill), snowboarding, soccer, softball, swimming, tennis, track and field, trampolining, volleyball.
Wilderness/Outdoors Hiking, mountain biking, mountaineering, rafting, rock climbing.
Trips Day, overnight, shopping.

Program Information 3 sessions per year. Session length: 3 weeks in July, August. Ages: 8–17. 280 participants per session. Boarding program cost: 4600 Swiss francs.
Application Deadline Continuous.
Jobs Positions for college students 20 and older.
Contact Philippe Studer, Director, La Moubra, CH-3963, Crans-Montana 1, Switzerland. Phone: 412-7481-5663. Fax: 412-7481-5631. E-mail: info@campmontana.ch.
URL www.campmontana.ch
For more information, see page 1166.

Les Elfes–International Summer/Winter Camp

Les Elfes International Summer/Winter Camp
Verbier 1936
Switzerland

General Information Coed residential and day traditional camp, academic program, and outdoor program established in 1987.

Les Elfes–International Summer/Winter Camp

Program Focus Language training: English, French, German, Spanish.
Academics English as a second language, English language/literature, French language/literature, German language/literature, Spanish language/literature, computers.
Arts Arts and crafts (general).
Special Interest Areas Counselor-in-training program, leadership training, team building.
Sports Basketball, bicycling, boating, climbing (wall), equestrian sports, figure skating, football, golf, horseback riding, ice hockey, ropes course, skiing (downhill), soccer, sports (general), squash, swimming, tennis, volleyball, waterskiing.
Wilderness/Outdoors Bicycle trips, hiking, mountain biking, mountaineering, rock climbing.
Trips Cultural, day, overnight.
Program Information 18–20 sessions per year. Session length: 7–20 days in January, February, March, April, May, June, July, August, December. Ages: 8–18. 120–130 participants per session. Boarding program cost: 2920–4490 Swiss francs.
Application Deadline Continuous.
Jobs Positions for college students 21 and older.
Contact Mr. Philippe Stettler, Director, PO Box 174, 1936 Verbier, Switzerland. Phone: 41-27-775-35-90. Fax: 41-27-775-35-99. E-mail: leselfes@axiom.ch.
URL www.leselfes.com
For more information, see page 1192.

LSA Lausanne, Switzerland

Language Studies Abroad, Inc.
Lausanne
Switzerland

General Information Coed residential academic program and cultural program established in 1967. Formal opportunities for the academically talented. High school or college credit may be earned.
Program Focus Learn French language and culture.
Academics French (Advanced Placement), French language/literature, intercultural studies, language study.
Special Interest Areas Homestays.
Trips Cultural, day.
Program Information 1–12 sessions per year. Session length: 14–360 days in January, February, March, April, May, June, July, August, September, October, November, December. Ages: 16+. 4–12 participants per session. Boarding program cost: $1455–$5095. Application fee: $100. Financial aid available.
Application Deadline Continuous.
Contact Director, 1801 Highway 50 East, Suite I, Carson City, Nevada 89701. Phone: 800-424-5522. Fax: 775-883-2266. E-mail: info@languagestudiesabroad.com.
URL www.languagestudiesabroad.com
For more information, see page 1186.

Sprachkurse Ariana, Arosa

Sprachkurse Ariana AG
Arosa 7050
Switzerland

General Information Coed residential academic program established in 1982.
Academics English as a second language, French language/literature, German language/literature, Italian language/literature.
Sports Basketball, golf, gymnastics, horseback riding, in-line skating, soccer, sports (general), swimming, tennis, volleyball, waterskiing.
Wilderness/Outdoors Hiking.
Trips Cultural, day.
Program Information 1 session per year. Session length: 2–7 weeks in June, July, August. Ages: 7–17. 150 participants per session. Boarding program cost: 2380–8330 Swiss francs.
Application Deadline Continuous.
Jobs Positions for college students 20 and older.
Contact Ms. M. Schmid, Director, Hoehenweg 60, St. Gallen 9000, Switzerland. Phone: 41-71-277-9291. Fax: 41-71-277-7253. E-mail: info@ariana.ch.
URL www.ariana.ch

Sprachkurse Ariana, Lenk

Sprachkurse Ariana AG
Lenk 3775
Switzerland

General Information Coed residential academic program established in 1986.
Academics English as a second language, French language/literature, German language/literature.
Sports Basketball, soccer, tennis, volleyball.
Wilderness/Outdoors Hiking, mountain biking.
Trips Cultural, day, overnight.
Program Information 1 session per year. Session length: 2–4 weeks in July, August. Ages: 12–18. 35 participants per session. Boarding program cost: 2040–4080 Swiss francs.
Application Deadline Continuous.
Jobs Positions for college students 20 and older.
Contact Ms. M. Schmid, Director, Hoehenweg 60, St. Gallen 9000, Switzerland. Phone: 41-71-277-9291. Fax: 41-71-277-7253. E-mail: info@ariana.ch.
URL www.ariana.ch

Summer in Switzerland

Leysin American School in Switzerland
Leysin 1854
Switzerland

General Information Coed residential traditional camp, academic program, outdoor program, arts program, and cultural program established in 1982. High school credit may be earned.

Summer in Switzerland

Program Focus Academic enrichment, ESL, theater, leadership, sports and recreation, travel, language study.
Academics American literature, English as a second language, English language/literature, French language/literature, SAT/ACT preparation, Spanish language/literature, TOEFL/TOEIC preparation, academics (general), art history/appreciation, computers, intercultural studies, journalism, mathematics, music, speech/debate, writing.
Arts Acting, arts and crafts (general), ceramics, chorus, creative writing, dance, drawing, music, music (instrumental), music (vocal), musical productions, photography, pottery, stage managing, theater/drama.
Special Interest Areas Field trips (arts and culture), general camp activities, leadership training.
Sports Aerobics, basketball, bicycling, climbing (wall), equestrian sports, golf, horseback riding, ice hockey, paragliding, rappelling, ropes course, skiing (downhill), snowboarding, soccer, squash, street/roller hockey, swimming, tennis, volleyball, weight training.
Wilderness/Outdoors Hiking, mountain biking, mountaineering, orienteering, rafting, rock climbing, white-water trips.
Trips Cultural, day, overnight, shopping.
Program Information 2 sessions per year. Session length: 3 weeks in June, July, August. Ages: 9–19. 200 participants per session. Boarding program cost: $3200–$6150. Financial aid available. Airfare not included.
Application Deadline Continuous.
Jobs Positions for college students 22 and older.
Contact Mr. Paul E. Dyer, US Director of Admissions, PO Box 7154, Portsmouth, New Hampshire 03802. Phone: 603-431-7654. Fax: 603-431-1280. E-mail: usadmissions@las.ch.
URL www.las.ch/summer
For more information, see page 1194.

SuperCamp–Switzerland

SuperCamp
Leysin
Switzerland

General Information Coed residential academic program established in 1990. Accredited by American Camping Association. High school credit may be earned.
Program Focus Academic enrichment and personal development, tour of Geneva and alpine villages.
Academics SAT/ACT preparation, academics (general), communications, reading, study skills, writing.
Arts Knitting.
Special Interest Areas Leadership training.
Sports Ropes course, swimming, volleyball.
Trips Cultural, day.
Program Information 2–4 sessions per year. Session length: 7–10 days in June, December. Ages: 14–18. 75–112 participants per session. Boarding program cost: $2095.
Application Deadline Continuous.
Contact Enrollments Department, 1725 South Coast Highway, Oceanside, California 92054. Phone: 800-285-3276. Fax: 760-722-3507. E-mail: info@supercamp.com.
URL www.supercamp.com
For more information, see page 1348.

Swiss Challenge

Swiss Challenge
Zermatt
Switzerland

General Information Coed travel sports camp established in 1970.
Program Focus Summer snow skiing, snowboarding, European travel, and mountain sports.
Special Interest Areas Field trips (arts and culture), touring.
Sports Bicycling, climbing (wall), rappelling, sailing, skiing (downhill), snowboarding, soccer, swimming, tennis, windsurfing.
Wilderness/Outdoors Backpacking, bicycle trips, hiking, ice climbing, mountaineering, rock climbing.
Trips Cultural, day, overnight.
Program Information 1 session per year. Session length: 2–3 weeks in June, July. Ages: 14–18. 15–75 participants per session. Cost: $2500–$4000. Application fee: $100. Extended travel programs available.
Application Deadline Continuous.
Jobs Positions for college students 21 and older.
Contact Eric Rohr, Director, Recruiting and Marketing, Wheeler Professional Park, Suite 10B, 1 Oak Ridge Road, West Lebanon, New Hampshire 03784. Phone: 800-762-0023. Fax: 603-643-1927. E-mail: swisschallenge@hotmail.com.
URL www.swisschallenge.com

TASIS French Language Program in Château-d'Oex, Switzerland

TASIS The American School in Switzerland
Le Vieux Chalet
Château–d'Oex 1660
Switzerland

General Information Coed residential academic program and outdoor program established in 1986. High school credit may be earned.
Program Focus Intensive French language study.
Academics French (Advanced Placement), French language/literature.
Sports Bicycling, soccer, swimming, tennis, volleyball.
Wilderness/Outdoors Hiking, mountain biking, rafting, rock climbing, white-water trips.
Trips Cultural, day, overnight.
Program Information 1 session per year. Session length: 4–5 weeks in June, July. Ages: 13–17. 60 participants per session. Boarding program cost: $4650–$5650.
Application Deadline Continuous.
Contact Mrs. Toni Soule, US TASIS Representative, 1640 Wisconsin Avenue, NW, Washington, District of Columbia 20007. Phone: 202-965-5800. Fax: 202-965-5816. E-mail: usadmissions@tasis.com.
URL www.tasis.ch

For more information, see page 1358.

TASIS Le Château des Enfants

TASIS The American School in Switzerland
Montagnola-Lugano, Ticino 6926
Switzerland

General Information Coed residential and day traditional camp, academic program, and cultural program established in 1969.
Program Focus Bilingual experiences. The program offers many excursions and field trips in neighboring northern Italy as well as southern Switzerland.
Academics English as a second language, French language/literature.
Arts Arts and crafts (general), chorus, drawing, mime, music, music (vocal), musical productions, painting, puppetry, theater/drama.
Special Interest Areas Campcraft, cross-cultural education, nature study.
Sports Basketball, bicycling, soccer, softball, swimming, tennis, volleyball.
Wilderness/Outdoors Hiking.
Trips Cultural, day, overnight.
Program Information 2 sessions per year. Session length: 3–4 weeks in June, July, August. Ages: 6–10. 50–55 participants per session. Day program cost: $1900–$2325. Boarding program cost: $3800–$4650. Application fee: $1000.
Application Deadline Continuous.
Jobs Positions for college students.
Contact Mrs. Toni Soule, US TASIS Representative, 1640 Wisconsin Avenue, NW, Washington, District of Columbia 20007. Phone: 202-965-5800. Fax: 202-965-5816. E-mail: usadmissions@tasis.com.
URL www.tasis.ch

For more information, see page 1358.

TASIS Middle School Program

TASIS The American School in Switzerland
Montagnola-Lugano, Ticino 6926
Switzerland

General Information Coed residential and day traditional camp, academic program, and cultural program established in 1976.
Program Focus Language study combined with local excursion and travel to places of interest.
Academics English as a second language, French language/literature.
Arts Acting, arts and crafts (general), chorus, graphic arts, jewelry making, music (vocal), musical productions, painting, puppetry, theater/drama.
Special Interest Areas Cross-cultural education.
Sports Basketball, bicycling, bicycling (BMX), soccer, swimming, tennis, volleyball.
Wilderness/Outdoors Hiking, mountain biking.
Trips Cultural, day, overnight.
Program Information 2 sessions per year. Session length: 3–4 weeks in June, July, August. Ages: 11–13. 80 participants per session. Day program cost: $1900–$2425. Boarding program cost: $3800–$4850. Application fee: $1000.
Application Deadline Continuous.
Jobs Positions for college students.

TASIS Middle School Program (continued)

Contact Mrs. Toni Soule, US TASIS Representative, 1640 Wisconsin Avenue, NW, Washington, District of Columbia 20007. Phone: 202-965-5800. Fax: 202-965-5816. E-mail: usadmissions@tasis.com.
URL www.tasis.ch
For more information, see page 1358.

TASIS Summer Program for Languages, Arts, and Outdoor Pursuits

TASIS The American School in Switzerland
Montagnola-Lugano, Ticino 6926
Switzerland

General Information Coed residential and day academic program and cultural program established in 1955. High school credit may be earned.

TASIS Summer Program for Languages, Arts, and Outdoor Pursuits

Program Focus Language study, photography, or architecture. Frequent trips to visit French- and German-speaking Switzerland and northern Italian cities.
Academics English as a second language, French language/literature, Italian language/literature, Spanish language/literature, architecture, writing.
Arts Arts and crafts (general), drawing, film, music (vocal), photography.
Special Interest Areas Touring.
Sports Aerobics, basketball, bicycling, sailing, soccer, swimming, tennis, volleyball, windsurfing.
Wilderness/Outdoors Bicycle trips, canyoneering, hiking, mountain biking, rafting, rock climbing.
Trips Cultural, day, overnight.
Program Information 2 sessions per year. Session length: 3–4 weeks in June, July, August. Ages: 14–18. 150–160 participants per session. Day program cost: $1900–$2325. Boarding program cost: $3800–$4650. Application fee: $1000.
Application Deadline Continuous.
Jobs Positions for college students 21 and older.
Contact Mrs. Toni Soule, US TASIS Representative, 1640 Wisconsin Avenue, NW, Washington, District of Columbia 20007. Phone: 202-965-5800. Fax: 202-965-5816. E-mail: usadmissions@tasis.com.
URL www.tasis.ch
For more information, see page 1358.

Village Camps–Switzerland

Village Camps
Grand Hotel
Leysin 1854
Switzerland

General Information Coed residential traditional camp and academic program established in 1972.

Village Camps–Switzerland

Program Focus Languages, leadership, computers, tennis, multi-activity.
Academics English as a second language, French language/literature, language study, linguistics.
Arts Arts and crafts (general), dance, drawing, film, jewelry making, music, photography, television/video, theater/drama.
Special Interest Areas Campcraft, culinary arts, leadership training, nature study.
Sports Aerobics, archery, baseball, basketball, bicycling, bicycling (BMX), climbing (wall), field hockey, figure skating, fishing, football, golf, gymnastics, ice

skating, martial arts, racquetball, rappelling, skiing (downhill), soccer, softball, sports (general), squash, swimming, tennis, volleyball, windsurfing.
Wilderness/Outdoors Bicycle trips, hiking, mountain biking, mountaineering, orienteering, rafting, rock climbing, survival training, white-water trips.
Trips Cultural, day, overnight, shopping.
Program Information 3 sessions per year. Session length: 2 weeks in June, July, August. Ages: 7–18. 150–180 participants per session. Boarding program cost: $2000–$3230. Financial aid available.
Application Deadline Continuous.
Jobs Positions for college students 21 and older.
Contact Roger Ratner, Director, 14 Rue de la Morâche, Nyon CH-1260, Switzerland. Phone: 41-22-990-9400. Fax: 41-990-9494. E-mail: camps@villagecamps.ch.
URL www.villagecamps.com
For more information, see page 1380.

THAILAND

AAVE–Thailand

AAVE–America's Adventure Ventures Everywhere
Thailand

General Information Coed travel outdoor program, cultural program, and adventure program established in 1976. Accredited by American Camping Association.
Program Focus Cultural and outdoor experience.
Special Interest Areas Cross-cultural education, culinary arts, leadership training, touring.
Sports Bicycling, kayaking, sea kayaking, snorkeling.
Wilderness/Outdoors Bicycle trips, hiking, rafting.
Trips Cultural, day, overnight.
Program Information 2–4 sessions per year. Session length: 3 weeks in June, July, August. Ages: 15–18. 12 participants per session. Cost: $3888. Financial aid available.
Application Deadline Continuous.
Jobs Positions for college students 21 and older.
Contact Mr. Abbott Wallis, Owner, 2245 Stonecrop Way, Golden, Colorado 80401. Phone: 800-222-3595. Fax: 303-526-0885. E-mail: info@aave.com.
URL www.aave.com
For more information, see page 952.

Adventures Cross-Country, Thailand Adventure

Adventures Cross-Country
Thailand

General Information Coed residential outdoor program and adventure program established in 1983.
Program Focus Exploring Thailand.
Special Interest Areas Campcraft, community service, cross-cultural education, field trips (arts and culture).
Sports Scuba diving, sea kayaking, snorkeling, swimming.
Wilderness/Outdoors Hiking, rafting, white-water trips, wilderness camping.
Program Information 1 session per year. Session length: 30 days in June, July. Ages: 13–18. 8–15 participants per session. Boarding program cost: $5995. Financial aid available.
Application Deadline Continuous.
Jobs Positions for college students 21 and older.
Contact Scott von Eschen, Director, 242 Redwood Highway, Mill Valley, California 94941. Phone: 415-332-5075. Fax: 415-332-2130. E-mail: arcc@adventurescrosscountry.com.
URL www.adventurescrosscountry.com
For more information, see page 972.

AFS-USA–Community Service–Thailand

AFS-USA
Thailand

General Information Coed residential community service program and cultural program. High school credit may be earned.

AFS-USA–Community Service–Thailand

AFS-USA–Community Service–Thailand (continued)
Program Focus Community service activities centered around the teaching of English as a second language.
Academics English as a second language, Thai language.
Arts Arts and crafts (general), dance (folk).
Special Interest Areas Community service, homestays, meditation.
Sports Martial arts.
Trips Cultural, day, overnight.
Program Information 1 session per year. Session length: 4 weeks in July, August. Ages: 16–19. Boarding program cost: $4065–$4365. Application fee: $75. Financial aid available. International airfare and volunteer homestay support included.
Application Deadline Continuous.
Contact Manager, AFS Info Center, 506 Southwest 6th Avenue, 2nd Floor, Portland, Oregon 97204. Phone: 800-AFS-INFO. Fax: 503-248-4076. E-mail: afsinfo@afs.org.
URL www.afs.org/usa
For more information, see page 974.

AFS-USA–Homestay–Thailand

AFS-USA
Thailand

General Information Coed residential academic program and cultural program.
Program Focus Living with a host family while attending school.
Academics English as a second language, Thai language.
Arts Arts and crafts (general), dance (folk).
Special Interest Areas Homestays, meditation.
Trips Cultural, day, overnight.
Program Information 1 session per year. Session length: 6 weeks in June, July, August. Ages: 15–17. Boarding program cost: $3965–$4465. Application fee: $75. Financial aid available. International airfare and volunteer homestay support included.
Application Deadline Continuous.
Contact Manager, AFS Info Center, 506 Southwest 6th Avenue, 2nd Floor, Portland, Oregon 97204. Phone: 800-AFS-INFO. Fax: 503-248-4076. E-mail: afsinfo@afs.org.
URL www.afs.org/usa
For more information, see page 974.

The Experiment in International Living–Thailand Homestay

The Experiment in International Living
Thailand

General Information Coed residential outdoor program, community service program, cultural program, and adventure program established in 1932.
Program Focus International youth travel, homestay, community service.
Academics Thai language, intercultural studies.
Special Interest Areas Community service, homestays, touring.
Wilderness/Outdoors Backpacking, hiking, rafting.
Trips Cultural, day, overnight.
Program Information 1 session per year. Session length: 5 weeks in July, August. Ages: 14–19. 10–15 participants per session. Boarding program cost: $3800. Financial aid available.
Application Deadline May 1.
Contact Annie Thompson, Enrollment Director, Summer Abroad, Kipling Road, PO Box 676, Brattleboro, Vermont 05302-0676. Phone: 800-345-2929. Fax: 802-258-3428. E-mail: eil@worldlearning.org.
URL www.usexperiment.org
For more information, see page 1116.

LIFEWORKS with the DPF Foundation in Thailand

LIFEWORKS International
Thailand

General Information Coed travel community service program, cultural program, and adventure program established in 1986. High school credit may be earned.
Program Focus Service-learning travel program with cultural immersion working with underprivileged children associated with the DPF Foundation.
Academics Thai language, intercultural studies.
Special Interest Areas Community service, touring.
Trips Cultural, day, overnight.
Program Information 2 sessions per year. Session length: 3 weeks in June, July. Ages: 15–19. 8–15 participants per session. Cost: $3560. Financial aid available.
Application Deadline Continuous.
Contact Mr. James Stoll, Director, PO Box 5517, Sarasota, Florida 34277. Phone: 800-808-2115. Fax: 941-924-6075. E-mail: info@lifeworks-international.com.
URL www.lifeworks-international.com
For more information, see page 1196.

Rustic Pathways–Elephants & Amazing Thailand

Rustic Pathways
Thailand

General Information Coed travel community service program, cultural program, and adventure program established in 1998.
Special Interest Areas Animal care, community service, construction, cross-cultural education, homestays, nature study, touring.
Sports Boating, soccer, swimming.
Wilderness/Outdoors Hiking, outdoor adventure.
Trips Cultural, day, overnight, shopping.
Program Information 4 sessions per year. Session length: 17 days in June, July, August. Ages: 15–18. 10–15 participants per session. Cost: $1965.
Application Deadline Continuous.
Jobs Positions for college students 21 and older.
Contact Mr. David Venning, Founder and Chairman, 4121 Erie Street, Willoughby, Ohio 44094. Phone: 440-975-9691. Fax: 440-975-9694. E-mail: david@rusticpathways.com.
URL www.rusticpathways.com
For more information, see page 1290.

RUSTIC PATHWAYS–INTRO TO COMMUNITY SERVICE IN THAILAND

Rustic Pathways
Udon Thani
Thailand

General Information Coed residential community service program and cultural program established in 1998.
Arts Arts and crafts (general), painting.
Special Interest Areas Community service, construction, cross-cultural education, farming, gardening, homestays, touring.
Sports Swimming.
Trips Cultural, day, overnight, shopping.
Program Information 9 sessions per year. Session length: 10 days in June, July, August. Ages: 14–18. 15–20 participants per session. Boarding program cost: $785.
Application Deadline Continuous.
Jobs Positions for college students 21 and older.
Contact Mr. David Venning, Founder and Chairman, 4121 Erie Street, Willoughby, Ohio 44094. Phone: 440-975-9691. Fax: 440-975-9694. E-mail: david@rusticpathways.com.
URL www.rusticpathways.com

For more information, see page 1290.

RUSTIC PATHWAYS–PHOTOGRAPHY & ADVENTURE IN THAILAND

Rustic Pathways
Thailand

General Information Coed travel arts program, cultural program, and adventure program established in 1998.
Arts Photography.
Special Interest Areas Cross-cultural education, touring.
Wilderness/Outdoors Hiking.
Trips Cultural, day, overnight, shopping.
Program Information 2 sessions per year. Session length: 17 days in June, July, August. Ages: 16–18. 10–15 participants per session. Cost: $2865.
Application Deadline Continuous.
Jobs Positions for college students 21 and older.
Contact Mr. David Venning, Founder and Chairman, 4121 Erie Street, Willoughby, Ohio 44049. Phone: 440-975-9691. Fax: 440-975-9694. E-mail: david@rusticpathways.com.
URL www.rusticpathways.com

For more information, see page 1290.

RUSTIC PATHWAYS–RHYTHM IN THE RICEFIELDS

Rustic Pathways
Udon Thani
Thailand

General Information Coed residential community service program and cultural program established in 1998.
Academics Music.
Arts Music.
Special Interest Areas Community service, cross-cultural education, homestays, touring.
Sports Swimming.
Wilderness/Outdoors Hiking.
Trips Cultural, day, overnight, shopping.
Program Information 9 sessions per year. Session length: 10–17 days in June, July, August. Ages: 14–18. 10–15 participants per session. Boarding program cost: $835–$1625.
Application Deadline Continuous.
Jobs Positions for college students 21 and older.
Contact Mr. David Venning, Founder and Chairman, 4121 Erie Street, Willoughby, Ohio 44094. Phone: 440-975-9691. Fax: 440-975-9694. E-mail: david@rusticpathways.com.
URL www.rusticpathways.com

For more information, see page 1290.

RUSTIC PATHWAYS–RICEFIELDS, MONKS & SMILING CHILDREN

Rustic Pathways
Udon Thani
Thailand

General Information Coed residential community service program and cultural program established in 1998.
Arts Arts and crafts (general), painting.
Special Interest Areas Community service, construction, cross-cultural education, farming, gardening, homestays, touring.
Sports Swimming.
Trips Cultural, day, overnight, shopping.
Program Information 8 sessions per year. Session length: 17 days in June, July, August. Ages: 14–18. 15–20 participants per session. Boarding program cost: $1525.
Application Deadline Continuous.
Jobs Positions for college students 21 and older.
Contact Mr. David Venning, Founder and Chairman, 4121 Erie Street, Willoughby, Ohio 44094. Phone: 440-975-9691. Fax: 440-975-9694. E-mail: david@rusticpathways.com.
URL www.rusticpathways.com

For more information, see page 1290.

RUSTIC PATHWAYS–THE AMAZING THAILAND ADVENTURE

Rustic Pathways
Thailand

General Information Coed travel cultural program and adventure program established in 2003.
Arts Arts and crafts (general).
Special Interest Areas Cross-cultural education, touring.
Sports Boating.
Wilderness/Outdoors Outdoor adventure.
Trips Cultural, day, overnight, shopping.
Program Information 5 sessions per year. Session length: 10 days in June, July, August. Ages: 15–18. 10–15 participants per session. Cost: $1095.
Application Deadline Continuous.
Jobs Positions for college students 21 and older.
Contact Mr. David Venning, Founder and Chairman, 4121 Erie Street, Willoughby, Ohio 44094. Phone: 440-975-9691. Fax: 440-975-9694. E-mail: david@rusticpathways.com.
URL www.rusticpathways.com
For more information, see page 1290.

RUSTIC PATHWAYS–THE THAI ELEPHANT CONSERVATION PROJECT

Rustic Pathways
Royal Thai Elephant Reserve
Chiang Mai
Thailand

General Information Coed residential community service program and cultural program established in 2003.
Special Interest Areas Animal care, community service, nature study, touring.
Wilderness/Outdoors Hiking.
Trips Cultural, day.
Program Information 4 sessions per year. Session length: 10 days in June, July, August. Ages: 15–18. 10–15 participants per session. Boarding program cost: $895.
Application Deadline Continuous.
Jobs Positions for college students 21 and older.
Contact Mr. David Venning, Founder and Chairman, 4121 Erie Street, Willoughby, Ohio 44094. Phone: 440-975-9691. Fax: 440-975-9694. E-mail: david@rusticpathways.com.
URL www.rusticpathways.com
For more information, see page 1290.

RUSTIC PATHWAYS–THE WONDERS & RICHES OF THAILAND

Rustic Pathways
Thailand

General Information Coed travel cultural program and adventure program established in 2003.
Special Interest Areas Cross-cultural education, culinary arts, massage therapy training, touring.
Sports Boating.
Wilderness/Outdoors Outdoor adventure.
Trips Cultural, day, overnight, shopping.
Program Information 1 session per year. Session length: 17 days in July. Ages: 14–18. 10–15 participants per session. Cost: $3695.
Application Deadline Continuous.
Jobs Positions for college students 21 and older.
Contact Mr. David Venning, Founder and Chairman, 4121 Erie Street, Willoughby, Ohio 44094. Phone: 440-975-9691. Fax: 440-975-9694. E-mail: david@rusticpathways.com.
URL www.rusticpathways.com
For more information, see page 1290.

SUPERCAMP–THAILAND

SuperCamp
Prem Tinsulanonda Center for International Education
Thailand

General Information Coed residential academic program established in 2002.
Program Focus Academic enrichment and personal development.
Academics SAT/ACT preparation, academics (general), communications, reading, study skills, writing.
Sports Ropes course, soccer, swimming, volleyball.
Program Information 2–4 sessions per year. Session length: 8–12 days in July, August. Ages: 9–18. 50–100 participants per session. Boarding program cost: $1100–$1300. Application fee: $100.
Application Deadline Continuous.
Jobs Positions for college students 18 and older.
Contact Enrollments Department, 1725 South Coast Highway, Oceanside, California 92054. Phone: 800-285-3276. Fax: 760-722-3507. E-mail: info@supercamp.com.
URL www.supercamp.com
For more information, see page 1348.

WHERE THERE BE DRAGONS: THAILAND

Where There Be Dragons
Thailand

General Information Coed travel academic program, outdoor program, community service program, cultural program, and adventure program established in 1993. Formal opportunities for the academically talented and gifted.
Program Focus Rugged and off the beaten path travel introduces a wide range of development issues.
Academics Anthropology, area studies, business, ecology, economics, geography, government and politics

(Advanced Placement), history, intercultural studies, linguistics, philosophy, religion, social studies.
Arts Photography, weaving.
Special Interest Areas Community service, field research/expeditions, homestays, nature study.
Sports Bicycling, snorkeling.
Wilderness/Outdoors Backpacking, hiking, outdoor adventure.
Trips Cultural, overnight.
Program Information 1 session per year. Session length: 38 days in June, July, August. Ages: 15–20. 10–12 participants per session. Cost: $5350. Financial aid available. Airfare included.
Application Deadline Continuous.
Contact Chris Yager, Director, PO Box 4651, Boulder, Colorado 80306. Phone: 800-982-9203. Fax: 303-413-0857. E-mail: info@wheretherebedragons.com.
URL www.wheretherebedragons.com
For more information, see page 1394.

YOUTH FOR UNDERSTANDING USA–THAILAND

Youth for Understanding USA
Thailand

General Information Coed residential academic program and cultural program established in 1951. High school or college credit may be earned.
Program Focus Living with a host family, participating in activities such as a camp and safari, dancing and music, traveling throughout Thailand, and improving Thai language skills.
Academics Thai language, area studies, intercultural studies, social studies.
Arts Dance, music.
Special Interest Areas Field research/expeditions, homestays, touring.
Sports Fencing, martial arts.
Trips Cultural, day, overnight, shopping.
Program Information 1 session per year. Session length: 35–45 days in June, July, August. Ages: 15–18. 10–50 participants per session. Boarding program cost: $4995. Application fee: $75. Financial aid available. Round-trip domestic and international airfare is included in the tuition.
Application Deadline Continuous.
Contact Admissions Counselor, 6400 Goldsboro Road, Suite 100, Bethesda, Maryland 20817. Phone: 800-TEENAGE (833-6243). Fax: 202-895-1104. E-mail: admissions@us.yfu.org.
URL www.yfu-usa.org
For more information, see page 1414.

TRINIDAD AND TOBAGO

EARTHWATCH INSTITUTE–TRINIDAD'S LEATHERBACK SEA TURTLES

Earthwatch Institute
Trinidad and Tobago

General Information Coed residential outdoor program.
Program Focus Aiding a massive sea turtle protection effort that serves as a model for combining community-based conservation and ecotourism.
Academics Ecology, environmental science, marine studies.
Special Interest Areas Animal care, conservation projects, field research/expeditions, nature study.
Trips Cultural, day.
Program Information 8 sessions per year. Session length: 12 days in April, May, June, July. Ages: 16+. 12 participants per session. Boarding program cost: $1995–$2095. Financial aid available. Financial aid for high school students and teachers.
Application Deadline Continuous.
Contact General Information Desk, PO Box 75, Maynard, Massachusetts 01754. Phone: 800-776-0188. Fax: 978-461-2332. E-mail: info@earthwatch.org.
URL www.earthwatch.org

VISIONS–TRINIDAD

Visions
Trinidad and Tobago

General Information Coed travel outdoor program, community service program, and cultural program established in 1989. High school credit may be earned.
Program Focus Community service, cross-cultural learning, nature exploration.
Academics Ecology, intercultural studies.
Arts Painting, radio broadcasting.
Special Interest Areas Community service, construction, cross-cultural education, field research/expeditions, field trips (arts and culture), leadership training.
Sports Kayaking, snorkeling, swimming.
Wilderness/Outdoors Backpacking, hiking, outdoor adventure.
Trips Cultural, day.
Program Information 1 session per year. Session length: 4 weeks in June, July. Ages: 16–18. 12–17 participants per session. Cost: $3800. Financial aid available.
Application Deadline Continuous.
Jobs Positions for college students 22 and older.
Contact Ms. Joanne Pinaire, Director, PO Box 220, Newport, Pennsylvania 17074. Phone: 717-567-7313. Fax: 717-567-7853. E-mail: info@visionsserviceadventures.com.
URL www.visionsserviceadventures.com
For more information, see page 1382.

TURKEY

AFS-USA–Homestay–Turkey

AFS-USA
Turkey

General Information Coed residential cultural program.
Program Focus Living with a host family and taking part in activities with other teenagers.
Academics Turkish language/literature.
Special Interest Areas Homestays.
Trips Cultural, day, overnight.
Program Information 1 session per year. Session length: 6 weeks in June, July, August. Ages: 15–18. Boarding program cost: $3965–$4465. Application fee: $75. Financial aid available. International airfare and volunteer homestay support included.
Application Deadline Continuous.
Contact Manager, AFS Info Center, 506 Southwest 6th Avenue, 2nd Floor, Portland, Oregon 97204. Phone: 800-AFS-INFO. Fax: 503-248-4076. E-mail: afsinfo@afs.org.
URL www.afs.org/usa
For more information, see page 974.

The Experiment in International Living–Turkey Homestay, Community Service, and Travel

The Experiment in International Living
Turkey

General Information Coed residential community service program and cultural program established in 1932.
Program Focus International youth travel, homestay, community service.
Academics Turkish language/literature.
Special Interest Areas Community service, homestays, touring.
Trips Cultural, day, overnight.
Program Information 1 session per year. Session length: 5 weeks in July, August. Ages: 14–19. 10–15 participants per session. Boarding program cost: $4100. Financial aid available.
Application Deadline May 1.
Contact Annie Thompson, Enrollment Director, Summer Abroad, Kipling Road, PO Box 676, Brattleboro, Vermont 05302-0676. Phone: 800-345-2929. Fax: 802-258-3426. E-mail: eil@worldlearning.org.
URL www.usexperiment.org
For more information, see page 1116.

Space Camp Turkey 6-Day International Program

Space Camp Turkey
ESBAS-Aegean Free Zone
Gaziemir
Izmir 35410
Turkey

General Information Coed residential academic program and cultural program established in 2000.
Academics English as a second language, aerospace science, science (general).
Trips Cultural.
Program Information 10–30 sessions per year. Session length: 6 days in January, February, March, April, May, June, July, August, September, October, November, December. Ages: 9–16. 12–180 participants per session. Boarding program cost: $400.
Application Deadline Continuous.
Jobs Positions for college students 20 and older.
Contact Ms. Beth Mitchell, Program Advisor, main address above. Phone: 90-232-252-3500. Fax: 90-232-252-3600. E-mail: beth@spacecampturkey.com.
URL www.spacecampturkey.com

Volunteers for Peace International Work Camp–Turkey

Volunteers for Peace International Work Camps
Istanbul
Turkey

General Information Coed residential community service program established in 1981. Specific services available for the hearing impaired and physically challenged. College credit may be earned.
Program Focus International work camp.
Academics Intercultural studies, peace education.
Special Interest Areas Community service, construction, work camp programs.
Sports Basketball, swimming, volleyball.
Wilderness/Outdoors Hiking.
Trips Cultural, day, overnight.
Program Information Session length: 2–3 weeks in June, July, August, September. Ages: 15+. 12–20 participants per session. Boarding program cost: $250–$600.
Contact Peter Coldwell, Director, 1034 Tiffany Road, Belmont, Vermont 05730. Phone: 802-259-2759. Fax: 802-259-2922. E-mail: vfp@vfp.org.
URL www.vfp.org

TURKS AND CAICOS ISLANDS

SFS: Marine Parks Management Studies

The School for Field Studies
Center for Marine Resource Studies
Turks and Caicos Islands

General Information Coed residential academic program, outdoor program, and community service program established in 1980. Formal opportunities for the academically talented. College credit may be earned.
Program Focus Environmental field research and environmental problem solving.
Academics Anthropology, biology, botany, ecology, economics, environmental science, geography, geology/earth science, intercultural studies, marine studies, oceanography, science (general), social science, social studies, writing.
Special Interest Areas Community service, field research/expeditions, nature study.
Sports Baseball, basketball, scuba diving, snorkeling, soccer, volleyball.
Wilderness/Outdoors Backpacking, hiking, wilderness camping.
Trips Cultural, day, overnight.
Program Information 2 sessions per year. Session length: 30 days in June, July, August. Ages: 16–25. 32 participants per session. Boarding program cost: $3560. Application fee: $45. Financial aid available. Airfare not included.
Application Deadline Continuous.
Contact Lili Folsom, Director of Admissions and Alumni Services, 10 Federal Street, Salem, Massachusetts 01970-3853. Phone: 800-989-4418. Fax: 978-741-3551. E-mail: admissions@fieldstudies.org.
URL www.fieldstudies.org

U.S. VIRGIN ISLANDS

EARTHWATCH INSTITUTE–Coral Reefs of the Virgin Islands

Earthwatch Institute
U.S. Virgin Islands

General Information Coed residential outdoor program.
Program Focus Monitoring critical species on coral reefs and nearby habitats to assess the impact of coastal development.
Academics Ecology, environmental science, marine studies.
Arts Television/video.
Special Interest Areas Field research/expeditions, nature study.
Sports Snorkeling, swimming.
Program Information 2 sessions per year. Session length: 8 days in August. Ages: 16+. 8 participants per session. Boarding program cost: $2395–$2495. Financial aid available. Financial aid for high school students and teachers.
Application Deadline Continuous.
Contact General Information Desk, PO Box 75, Maynard, Massachusetts 01754. Phone: 800-776-0188. Fax: 978-461-2332. E-mail: info@earthwatch.org.
URL www.earthwatch.org

EARTHWATCH INSTITUTE–Saving the Leatherback Turtle

Earthwatch Institute
St. Croix
U.S. Virgin Islands

General Information Coed residential outdoor program, cultural program, and adventure program.
Program Focus Delivering the largest population of leatherbacks in the U.S. from extinction.
Academics Biology, ecology, environmental science, marine studies, science (general).
Special Interest Areas Field research/expeditions, nature study.
Program Information 9 sessions per year. Session length: 11 days in April, May, June, July. Ages: 16+. 10 participants per session. Boarding program cost: $2095–$2195. Financial aid available. Financial aid for high school students and teachers.
Application Deadline Continuous.
Contact General Information Desk, PO Box 75, Maynard, Massachusetts 01754. Phone: 800-776-0188. Fax: 978-461-2332. E-mail: info@earthwatch.org.
URL www.earthwatch.org

UNITED KINGDOM

AFS-USA–Community Service–United Kingdom

AFS-USA
United Kingdom

General Information Coed residential community service program and cultural program. High school credit may be earned.
Program Focus Environmental conservation and restoration projects.
Special Interest Areas Campcraft, community service, homestays, work camp programs.
Trips Cultural, day, overnight.
Program Information 1 session per year. Session length: 5 weeks in July, August. Ages: 17–21. 15–40 participants per session. Boarding program cost: $4265–$4765. Application fee: $75. Financial aid available. International airfare and volunteer homestay support included.

AFS-USA–Community Service–United Kingdom (continued)

Application Deadline Continuous.
Jobs Positions for high school students.
Contact Manager, AFS Info Center, 506 Southwest 6th Avenue, 2nd Floor, Portland, Oregon 97204. Phone: 800-AFS-INFO. Fax: 503-248-4076. E-mail: afsinfo@afs.org.
URL www.afs.org/usa
For more information, see page 974.

Blyth Education–Summer Study in London and Oxford University

Blyth Education
United Kingdom

General Information Coed residential academic program and cultural program established in 1977. High school credit may be earned.
Academics English (Advanced Placement), English language/literature, academics (general).
Arts Theater/drama.
Special Interest Areas Touring.
Sports Tennis.
Trips Cultural, day, overnight.
Program Information 1 session per year. Session length: 25–30 days in July. Ages: 14–19. 100 participants per session. Boarding program cost: 5295 Canadian dollars. Airfare from Toronto or New York to London included.
Application Deadline Continuous.
Jobs Positions for college students 25 and older.
Contact Blyth Education, 9 Sultan Street, Suite 300, Toronto, Ontario M5S 1L6, Canada. Phone: 416-960-3552. Fax: 416-960-9506. E-mail: info@blytheducation.com.
URL www.blytheducation.com

Buckswood: English Language (ESL) and Activities–Bradfield, England

Buckswood Summer Programs
Bradfield College
Theale, Reading
Berkshire
United Kingdom

General Information Coed residential traditional camp, academic program, and cultural program established in 1978.
Program Focus Buckswood classic EFL offers English language tuition with activity program.
Academics English as a second language.
Arts Arts and crafts (general), dance.
Sports Aerobics, archery, basketball, boating, equestrian sports, football, golf, horseback riding, soccer, swimming, tennis, volleyball.
Trips Cultural, day, shopping.
Program Information 2–6 sessions per year. Session length: 1 week in July, August. Ages: 7–16. 50–100 participants per session. Boarding program cost: 535 British pounds.
Application Deadline Continuous.
Jobs Positions for college students 18 and older.
Contact Ms. Katie Bleck, Buckswood Summer Programmes, Belle Vue House, 259 Greenwich High Road, London SE10 8NB, United Kingdom. Phone: 44-(0)208-269-0044. Fax: 44-(0)208-293-1199. E-mail: info@buckswood.com.
URL www.buckswood.com

Buckswood: English Language (ESL) and Activities–Plumpton, England

Buckswood Summer Programs
Plumpton College
Lewes, North Brighton
East Sussex
United Kingdom

General Information Coed residential traditional camp, academic program, and cultural program established in 1978.
Program Focus Buckswood classic EFL offers English language tuition with activity program.
Academics English as a second language.
Arts Arts and crafts (general), dance.
Sports Aerobics, archery, basketball, boating, equestrian sports, football, golf, horseback riding, soccer, swimming, tennis, volleyball.
Trips Cultural, day, shopping.
Program Information 2–8 sessions per year. Session length: 1 week in July, August. Ages: 7–16. 50–100 participants per session. Boarding program cost: 495 British pounds.
Application Deadline Continuous.
Jobs Positions for college students 20 and older.
Contact Ms. Katie Black, Buckswood Summer Programs, Belle Vue House, 259 Greenwich High Road, London SE10 8NB, United Kingdom. Phone: 44-(0) 208-269-0044. Fax: 44-(0) 208-293-1199. E-mail: info@buckswood.com.
URL www.buckswood.com

Cambridge College Programme

Cambridge College Programme
Cambridge University
Cambridge
United Kingdom

General Information Coed travel academic program and cultural program established in 1986. Formal opportunities for the academically talented. High school or college credit may be earned.
Program Focus Academic and cultural enrichment in England. Optional one-week trip to Paris.
Academics Bible study, English language/literature, French language/literature, Jewish studies, Latin language, SAT/ACT preparation, academics (general), anthropology, archaeology, architecture, area studies, art history/appreciation, astronomy, biology, business, chemistry, computer programming, computers, ecology, economics, environmental science, geology/earth science, government and politics, history, journalism, marine studies, mathematics, medicine, meteorology, music, oceanography, philosophy, physics, physiology, precollege program, psychology, religion, science (general), social science, social studies, speech/debate, writing.

Cambridge College Programme

Arts Acting, chorus, creative writing, dance, drawing, film, music, music (ensemble), music (orchestral), music (vocal), painting, photography, theater/drama.
Special Interest Areas Field trips (arts and culture).
Sports Aerobics, baseball, basketball, boating, cricket, croquet, cross-country, equestrian sports, fencing, golf, gymnastics, lacrosse, rowing (crew/sculling), rugby, soccer, squash, swimming, tennis, volleyball, water polo, weight training.
Trips College tours, cultural, day, shopping.
Program Information 1 session per year. Session length: 3 weeks in July, August. Ages: 14–19. Cost: $5395. Application fee: $95.
Application Deadline Continuous.
Contact Ms. Taryn Edwards, Director, John Hancock Building, 175 East Delaware Place, Suite 5518, Chicago, Illinois 60611. Phone: 800-922-3552. Fax: 312-988-7268.

For more information, see page 1020.

The Cambridge Prep Experience

Oxbridge Academic Programs
Cambridge University
Cambridge
United Kingdom

General Information Coed residential academic program and arts program established in 1995. Formal opportunities for the academically talented and artistically talented.
Program Focus Academic and cultural enrichment.
Academics English language/literature, academics (general), criminal justice, history, humanities, law, mathematics, medicine, philosophy, psychology, science (general), speech/debate, writing.

The Cambridge Prep Experience

Arts Arts, creative writing, drawing, painting, theater/drama.
Special Interest Areas Field trips (arts and culture).
Sports Aerobics, baseball, basketball, rowing (crew/sculling), soccer, sports (general), tennis.
Trips Cultural, day.
Program Information 1 session per year. Session length: 30 days in July. Ages: 14–15. 170 participants per session. Boarding program cost: $5195. Financial aid available. Airfare not included.
Application Deadline Continuous.
Contact Ms. Andrea Mardon, Executive Director, Oxbridge Academic Programs, 601 West 110th Street, Suite 7R, New York, New York 10025-2186. Phone: 800-828-8349. Fax: 212-663-8169. E-mail: info@oxbridgeprograms.com.
URL www.oxbridgeprograms.com

For more information, see page 1242.

The Cambridge Tradition

Oxbridge Academic Programs
Cambridge University
Cambridge
United Kingdom

General Information Coed residential academic program and arts program established in 1999. Formal opportunities for the academically talented and artistically talented. High school credit may be earned.
Program Focus Academic and cultural enrichment.
Academics English language/literature, Latin language, academics (general), architecture, art history/appreciation, classical languages/literatures, computers, criminal justice, economics, government and politics, history, humanities, journalism, medicine, music, philosophy, precollege program, psychology, religion, social science, social studies.
Arts Arts, creative writing, drawing, music, music (ensemble), painting, photography, television/video, theater/drama.
Special Interest Areas Field trips (arts and culture).
Sports Aerobics, basketball, cross-country, soccer, sports (general), squash, tennis.
Trips Cultural, day.

The Cambridge Tradition (continued)

Program Information 1 session per year. Session length: 30 days in July. Ages: 15–18. 225 participants per session. Boarding program cost: $5895. Financial aid available.
Application Deadline Continuous.
Contact Ms. Andrea Mardon, Executive Director, Oxbridge Academic Programs, 601 West 110th Street, Suite 7R, New York, New York 10025-2186. Phone: 800-828-8349. Fax: 212-663-8169. E-mail: info@oxbridgeprograms.com.
URL www.oxbridgeprograms.com

For more information, see page 1242.

Center for Cultural Interchange–United Kingdom Independent Homestay

Center for Cultural Interchange
United Kingdom

General Information Coed residential cultural program established in 1985.
Program Focus Independent homestay in the United Kingdom.
Academics Independent study.
Special Interest Areas Cross-cultural education, homestays.
Trips Cultural, day.
Program Information Session length: 1–4 weeks in January, February, March, April, May, June, July, August, September, October, November, December. Ages: 16+. Boarding program cost: $950–$1590. Financial aid available.
Application Deadline Continuous.
Contact Ms. Juliet Jones, Outbound Programs Director, 325 West Huron, Suite 706, Chicago, Illinois 60610. Phone: 866-684-9675. Fax: 312-944-2644. E-mail: info@cci-exchange.com.
URL www.cci-exchange.com

For more information, see page 1060.

Cross Keys

Cross Keys
48 Fitzalan Road
Finchley
London N3 3PE
United Kingdom

General Information Coed day traditional camp established in 1989.
Program Focus Drama, art, sports.
Arts Arts and crafts (general), batiking, ceramics, dance, drawing, fabric arts, mask making, mime, music (vocal), painting, pottery, theater/drama.
Sports Archery, basketball, football, gymnastics, martial arts, soccer, swimming, tennis.
Program Information 10 sessions per year. Session length: 4–5 days in February, April, May, June, July, August, October, December. Ages: 4–12. 60–80 participants per session. Day program cost: 105 British pounds.
Application Deadline Continuous.
Jobs Positions for high school students 18 and older and college students 18 and older.
Contact Richard Bernstein, Managing Director, main address above. Phone: 020-8371-9686. Fax: 020-8343-0625. E-mail: richard@xkeys.co.uk.
URL www.campsforkids.co.uk

Earthwatch Institute–England's Hidden Kingdom

Earthwatch Institute
Yorkshire
United Kingdom

General Information Coed residential outdoor program, cultural program, and adventure program.
Program Focus Laying the groundwork for excavating an area that may prove to be a previously unknown independent kingdom in early England.
Academics Archaeology, geography, science (general).
Special Interest Areas Field research/expeditions.
Program Information 2 sessions per year. Session length: 15 days in June, July. Ages: 16+. 14 participants per session. Boarding program cost: $1995–$2095. Financial aid available. Financial aid for high school students and teachers.
Application Deadline Continuous.
Contact General Information Desk, PO Box 75, Maynard, Massachusetts 01754. Phone: 800-776-0188. Fax: 978-461-2332. E-mail: info@earthwatch.org.
URL www.earthwatch.org

Earthwatch Institute–Roman Fort on Tyne

Earthwatch Institute
South Shields
United Kingdom

General Information Coed residential outdoor program, cultural program, and adventure program.
Program Focus Furthering the largest investigation of a Roman military site to reveal the extent of cultural interchange.
Academics Archaeology, classical civilizations, history, intercultural studies, science (general).
Special Interest Areas Field research/expeditions, nature study.
Program Information 6 sessions per year. Session length: 2 weeks in June, July, August, September. Ages: 16+. 20 participants per session. Boarding program cost: $2095–$2195. Financial aid available. Financial aid for high school students and teachers.
Application Deadline Continuous.
Contact General Information Desk, PO Box 75, Maynard, Massachusetts 01754. Phone: 800-776-0188. Fax: 978-461-2332. E-mail: info@earthwatch.org.
URL www.earthwatch.org

The Experiment in International Living–The United Kingdom Celtic Odyssey

The Experiment in International Living
United Kingdom

General Information Coed residential cultural program and adventure program established in 1932.
Program Focus International youth travel, Celtic culture.
Academics Intercultural studies, language study.
Special Interest Areas Homestays, touring.
Trips Cultural, day, overnight.
Program Information 1 session per year. Session length: 4 weeks in July, August. Ages: 14–19. 10–15 participants per session. Boarding program cost: $4800. Financial aid available.
Application Deadline May 1.
Contact Annie Thompson, Enrollment Director, Summer Abroad, Kipling Road, PO Box 676, Brattleboro, Vermont 05302-0676. Phone: 800-345-2929. Fax: 802-258-3428. E-mail: eil@worldlearning.org.
URL www.usexperiment.org

For more information, see page 1116.

The Experiment in International Living–United Kingdom Filmmaking Program and Homestay

The Experiment in International Living
United Kingdom

General Information Coed residential arts program, cultural program, and adventure program established in 1932.
Program Focus International youth travel, homestays, film-making, travel.
Arts Film.
Special Interest Areas Homestays, touring.
Trips Cultural, day, overnight.
Program Information 1 session per year. Session length: 4 weeks in July, August. Ages: 14–19. 10–15 participants per session. Boarding program cost: $5000. Financial aid available.
Application Deadline May 1.
Contact Annie Thompson, Enrollment Director, Summer Abroad, Kipling Road, PO Box 676, Brattleboro, Vermont 05302-0676. Phone: 800-345-2929. Fax: 802-258-3428. E-mail: eil@worldlearning.org.
URL www.usexperiment.org

For more information, see page 1116.

The Experiment in International Living–United Kingdom Theatre Program

The Experiment in International Living
United Kingdom

General Information Coed residential arts program and cultural program established in 1932.
Program Focus International youth travel, homestay, theatre.
Academics Intercultural studies.
Arts Theater/drama.
Special Interest Areas Homestays, touring.
Trips Cultural, day, overnight.
Program Information 1 session per year. Session length: 4 weeks in July, August. Ages: 14–19. 10–15 participants per session. Boarding program cost: $4700. Financial aid available.
Application Deadline May 1.
Contact Annie Thompson, Enrollment Director, Summer Abroad, Kipling Road, PO Box 676, Brattleboro, Vermont 05302-0676. Phone: 800-345-2929. Fax: 802-258-3428. E-mail: eil@worldlearning.org.
URL www.usexperiment.org

For more information, see page 1116.

IEI–Digital Media Plus Programme

Intern Exchange International, Ltd.
London
United Kingdom

General Information Coed residential arts program established in 1987. High school credit may be earned.
Program Focus To give students first-hand knowledge of video production, TV graphics and Web site design.
Academics Web page design, computers, music, writing.
Arts Film, film editing, film production, graphic arts, television/video.
Special Interest Areas Computer graphics, field trips (arts and culture).
Sports Squash, tennis.
Trips Cultural, day.
Program Information 1 session per year. Session length: 31 days in June, July. Ages: 16–18. 30–40 participants per session. Boarding program cost: $5795. Application fee: $60.
Application Deadline Continuous.
Jobs Positions for college students 20 and older.
Contact Nina Miller Glickman, Director, 1858 Mallard Lane, Villanova, Pennsylvania 19085. Phone: 610-527-6066. Fax: 610-527-5499. E-mail: info@internexchange.com.
URL www.internexchange.com

For more information, see page 1168.

IEI–Fashion and Design Plus Programme

Intern Exchange International, Ltd.
London
United Kingdom

General Information Coed residential arts program established in 1987. High school credit may be earned.
Program Focus Fashion theory, fashion drawing, and production of a fashion design project.
Academics Business, marketing.
Arts Drawing, fabric arts, fashion design/production, illustration.
Special Interest Areas Field trips (arts and culture).

IEI–Fashion and Design Plus Programme (continued)
Sports Squash, tennis.
Trips Cultural, day.
Program Information 1 session per year. Session length: 31 days in June, July. Ages: 16–18. 20–30 participants per session. Boarding program cost: $5795. Application fee: $60.
Application Deadline Continuous.
Jobs Positions for college students 20 and older.
Contact Nina Miller Glickman, Director, 1858 Mallard Lane, Villanova, Pennsylvania 19085. Phone: 610-527-6066. Fax: 610-527-5499. E-mail: info@internexchange.com.
URL www.internexchange.com
For more information, see page 1168.

IEI–Fine Arts Plus Programme

Intern Exchange International, Ltd.
London
United Kingdom

General Information Coed residential arts program established in 1987. High school credit may be earned.
Program Focus Designed for students interested in developing their artistic vision including drawing, painting, printmaking and sculpture.
Arts Drawing, painting, printmaking, sculpture.
Special Interest Areas Field trips (arts and culture).
Sports Squash, tennis.
Trips Cultural, day.
Program Information 1 session per year. Session length: 31 days in June, July. Ages: 16–18. 8–10 participants per session. Boarding program cost: $5795. Application fee: $60.
Application Deadline Continuous.
Jobs Positions for college students 20 and older.
Contact Nina Miller Glickman, Director, 1858 Mallard Lane, Villanova, Pennsylvania 19085. Phone: 610-527-6066. Fax: 610-527-5499. E-mail: info@internexchange.com.
URL www.internexchange.com
For more information, see page 1168.

IEI–Photography Plus Programme

Intern Exchange International, Ltd.
London
United Kingdom

General Information Coed residential arts program established in 1987. High school credit may be earned.
Program Focus Documentary photography, special processes and experimental imaging photography, and digital photography.
Academics Computers.
Arts Photography.
Special Interest Areas Field trips (arts and culture).
Sports Squash, tennis.
Trips Cultural, day.
Program Information 1 session per year. Session length: 31 days in June, July. Ages: 16–18. 15–36 participants per session. Boarding program cost: $5795. Application fee: $60.
Application Deadline Continuous.
Jobs Positions for college students 20 and older.
Contact Nina Miller Glickman, Director, 1858 Mallard Lane, Villanova, Pennsylvania 19085. Phone: 610-527-6066. Fax: 610-527-5499. E-mail: info@internexchange.com.
URL www.internexchange.com
For more information, see page 1168.

IEI–Print and Broadcast Journalism

Intern Exchange International, Ltd.
London
United Kingdom

General Information Coed residential academic program established in 1987. High school credit may be earned.
Program Focus To learn and sharpen journalistic skills, cover and report on politics, art, music, sports and current events while creating a publication.
Academics Computers, journalism, writing.
Arts Design.
Special Interest Areas Computer graphics, field trips (arts and culture).
Sports Squash, tennis.
Trips Cultural, day.
Program Information 1 session per year. Session length: 31 days in June, July. Ages: 16–18. 10–20 participants per session. Boarding program cost: $5795. Application fee: $60.
Application Deadline Continuous.
Jobs Positions for college students 20 and older.
Contact Nina Miller Glickman, Director, 1858 Mallard Lane, Villanova, Pennsylvania 19085. Phone: 610-527-6066. Fax: 610-527-5499. E-mail: info@internexchange.com.
URL www.internexchange.com
For more information, see page 1168.

IEI Student Travel–Internship Program in London

Intern Exchange International, Ltd.
London
United Kingdom

General Information Coed residential academic program established in 1987. High school credit may be earned.
Program Focus Career internships in archaeology, art gallery and auction house, business/finance, community service, hotel management, law, medical research, public relations, publishing, retail sales and management, strategic studies, and veterinary medicine.
Academics Advertising, archaeology, art history/appreciation, banking/finance, business, communications, computers, government and politics, health sciences, journalism, marketing, prelaw, premed, psychology, social services, writing.
Arts Acting, drawing, fabric arts, fashion design/production, film, music (vocal), painting, photography, printmaking, sculpture, television/video, theater/drama.

IEI Student Travel–Internship Program in London

Special Interest Areas Career exploration, community service, field trips (arts and culture), internships.
Sports Squash, tennis.
Trips Cultural, day.
Program Information 1 session per year. Session length: 31 days in June, July. Ages: 16–18. 180–200 participants per session. Boarding program cost: $5795. Application fee: $60.
Application Deadline Continuous.
Jobs Positions for college students 20 and older.
Contact Nina Miller Glickman, Director, 1858 Mallard Lane, Villanova, Pennsylvania 19085. Phone: 610-527-6066. Fax: 610-527-5499. E-mail: info@internexchange.com.
URL www.internexchange.com
For more information, see page 1168.

IEI–Theatre Plus Programme

Intern Exchange International, Ltd.
London
United Kingdom

General Information Coed residential arts program established in 1987. High school credit may be earned.
Program Focus Designed for students interested in theatre and in exploring the nature of the acting process.
Arts Acting, dance, theater/drama, voice and speech.
Special Interest Areas Career exploration, field trips (arts and culture).
Sports Squash, tennis.
Trips Cultural, day.
Program Information 1 session per year. Session length: 31 days in June, July. Ages: 16–18. 10–18 participants per session. Boarding program cost: $5795. Application fee: $60.
Application Deadline Continuous.
Jobs Positions for college students 20 and older.
Contact Nina Miller Glickman, Director, 1858 Mallard Lane, Villanova, Pennsylvania 19085. Phone: 610-527-6066. Fax: 610-527-5499. E-mail: info@internexchange.com.
URL www.internexchange.com
For more information, see page 1168.

Longacre Expeditions, British Isles

Longacre Expeditions
United Kingdom

General Information Coed travel outdoor program and adventure program established in 1981. Accredited by American Camping Association.
Program Focus Effective communication skills, responsibility, confidence building.
Special Interest Areas Leadership training, nautical skills.
Sports Sea kayaking.
Wilderness/Outdoors Bicycle trips, hiking, rock climbing.
Program Information 1 session per year. Session length: 3 weeks in July. Ages: 13–17. 10–15 participants per session. Cost: $3195.
Application Deadline Continuous.
Jobs Positions for college students 21 and older.
Summer Contact Matthew Schuler, Director, 4030 Middle Ridge Road, Newport, Pennsylvania 17074. Phone: 717-567-6790. Fax: 717-567-3955. E-mail: matthew@longacreexpeditions.com.
Winter Contact Roger Smith, Director, main address above. Phone: 717-567-6790. Fax: 717-567-3955. E-mail: longacre@longacreexpeditions.com.
URL www.longacreexpeditions.com
For more information, see page 1200.

Midsummer in London

British American Drama Academy (BADA)
14 Gloucester Gate
London NW1 4HG
United Kingdom

General Information Coed residential arts program established in 2002. Formal opportunities for the artistically talented. College credit may be earned.
Program Focus Classical acting.
Academics English language/literature, study skills, writing.
Arts Acting, chorus, creative writing, dance, make up, mime, playwriting, stage combat, stage movement, theater/drama, voice and speech.
Special Interest Areas Career exploration.
Trips College tours, cultural, day.

Midsummer in London (continued)

Midsummer in London

Program Information 1 session per year. Session length: 30 days in July, August. Ages: 16–18. 30–45 participants per session. Boarding program cost: 4000–5000 British pounds. Application fee: 50 British pounds. Financial aid available.
Application Deadline March 25.
Jobs Positions for college students 21 and older.
Contact Ms. Frances Mayhew, Program Coordinator, main address above. Phone: 44-207-487-0730. Fax: 44-207-487-0731. E-mail: info@badaonline.com.
URL www.badaonline.com

For more information, see page 1006.

Mini Minors

Cross Keys
Brooklands School
Hampstead Garden Suburb NW 11
United Kingdom

General Information Coed day traditional camp established in 1989.
Program Focus Fun, fulfillment, variety.
Arts Arts and crafts (general), batiking, ceramics, dance, drawing, fabric arts, jewelry making, music, music (vocal), musical productions, painting, pottery, theater/drama, woodworking.
Sports Archery, basketball, football, gymnastics, martial arts, soccer, swimming, tennis.
Trips Day.
Program Information 6 sessions per year. Session length: 4–5 days in April, July, August. Ages: 3–12. 100–200 participants per session. Day program cost: 105 British pounds.
Application Deadline Continuous.
Jobs Positions for high school students 18 and older and college students 18 and older.
Contact Richard Bernstein, Managing Director, 48 Fitzalan Road, Finchley, London N3 3PE, United Kingdom. Phone: 020-8371-9686. Fax: 020-8343-0625. E-mail: richard@xkeys.co.uk.
URL www.campsforkids.co.uk

NBC Camps–Basketball Individual Training–Isle of Man

NBC Camps
King William's College
Isle of Man
United Kingdom

General Information Coed residential sports camp.
Program Focus Well-rounded skill development.
Sports Basketball.
Program Information 1 session per year. Session length: 5 days in August. Ages: 9–18. Boarding program cost: 225 British pounds. Financial aid available.
Application Deadline Continuous.
Jobs Positions for high school students 16 and older and college students.
Contact Ms. Bonnie Tucker, Office Manager, 10003 North Milan Road, #100, Spokane, Washington 99218. Phone: 509-466-4690. Fax: 509 467-6289. E-mail: bonnie@nbccamps.com.
URL www.nbccamps.com

The New York Film Academy in London

New York Film Academy
King's College
London
United Kingdom

General Information Coed residential arts program established in 1992. College credit may be earned.
Program Focus "Total immersion" hands-on filmmaking workshop where students write, direct, shoot, and edit their own 16mm short films.
Arts Acting, creative writing, directing, film, film editing, film lighting, film production, screenwriting, sound design, television/video.
Trips Cultural.
Program Information 2 sessions per year. Session length: 4–6 weeks in June, July, August. Ages: 14–17. Boarding program cost: $1500–$6900.
Application Deadline Continuous.
Contact Admissions, 100 East 17th Street, New York, New York 10003. Phone: 212-674-4300. Fax: 212-477-1414. E-mail: film@nyfa.com.
URL www.nyfa.com

For more information, see page 1218.

Oxford Advanced Seminars Programme

Albion International Study Centre, Oxford
Bocardo House, St. Michael's Street
Oxford OX1 2EB
United Kingdom

General Information Coed residential and day academic program and cultural program established in 1999. Formal opportunities for the academically talented. High school or college credit may be earned.
Program Focus For senior high and college students.

Academics American literature, Bible study, English as a second language, English language/literature, French (Advanced Placement), French language/literature, German language/literature, Greek language/literature, Italian language/literature, Latin language, Russian language/literature, SAT/ACT preparation, Spanish (Advanced Placement), Spanish language/literature, academics (general), architecture, art history/appreciation, biology, biology (Advanced Placement), botany, business, chemistry, classical languages/literatures, economics, environmental science, geography, government and politics, history, humanities, intercultural studies, linguistics, mathematics, mathematics (Advanced Placement), philosophy, physics, physiology, precollege program, psychology, reading, religion, science (general), social science, social studies, study skills, writing.
Arts Creative writing, drawing.
Sports Bicycling, boating, cricket, croquet, swimming, tennis.
Trips College tours, cultural, day.
Program Information 5–9 sessions per year. Session length: 10–84 days in January, February, March, April, May, June, July, August, September, October, November. Ages: 16+. 3–20 participants per session. Day program cost: 650–3900 British pounds. Boarding program cost: 980–5880 British pounds.
Application Deadline Continuous.
Contact Ms. Carolyn Llewelyn, Principal, main address above. Phone: 44-1865244470. Fax: 44-1865244112. E-mail: info@albionschools.co.uk.
URL www.albionschools.co.uk

Oxford Advanced Studies Program

Oxford Tutorial College
Magdalen College
Oxford OX1 4AU
United Kingdom

General Information Coed residential and day academic program and cultural program established in 1984. Formal opportunities for the academically talented and gifted. High school credit may be earned.

Oxford Advanced Studies Program

Program Focus Academic courses and cultural visits.
Academics English as a second language, English language/literature, French (Advanced Placement), French language/literature, German language/literature, Italian language/literature, Russian language/literature, SAT/ACT preparation, Spanish (Advanced Placement), Spanish language/literature, academics (general), architecture, art history/appreciation, biology, biology (Advanced Placement), business, chemistry, communications, economics, government and politics, government and politics (Advanced Placement), history, humanities, intercultural studies, journalism, mathematics, mathematics (Advanced Placement), philosophy, physics, precollege program, psychology, science (general), social science, speech/debate, writing.
Arts Acting, band, clowning, creative writing, dance, dance (modern), film, mime, music (instrumental), photography, theater/drama.
Special Interest Areas Community service, field trips (arts and culture).
Sports Aerobics, baseball, basketball, football, gymnastics, rowing (crew/sculling), soccer, softball, squash, swimming, tennis, ultimate frisbee, volleyball, weight training.
Trips College tours, cultural, day, shopping.
Program Information 1 session per year. Session length: 25 days in July. Ages: 15–18. 80–100 participants per session. Day program cost: $5200–$6000. Boarding program cost: $6200–$7000. Application fee: $300. Airfare not included.
Application Deadline June 1.
Summer Contact Ms. Joan Ives, Program Registrar, PO Box 2043, Darien, Connecticut 06820. Phone: 203-966-2886. Fax: 203-972-3083. E-mail: oxedge@aol.com.
Winter Contact Mr. Joel Roderick, Academic Registrar, 12 King Edward Street, Oxford, Oxon OX1 4HT, United Kingdom. Phone: 44-1865-793333. Fax: 44-1865-793233. E-mail: joel.roderick@oasp.ac.uk.
URL www.oasp.ac.uk

Special Note
Each year in July, a group of academically talented young people gather at Magdalen College, Oxford, to take part in a unique experience that combines the Oxbridge mode of tutorial-style learning with a wide range of cultural activities and visits. This is a stimulating and maturing 4 weeks, both academically and personally, which many previous participants have described as the most wonderful and rewarding experience of their lives. The course is intended for high school sophomores, juniors, and seniors who have an academic curiosity and ability well above average.

For more information, see page 1244.

The Oxford Experience

Academic Study Associates, Inc. (ASA)
Lady Margaret Hall College
Oxford University
Oxford
United Kingdom

General Information Coed residential academic program established in 1984. Formal opportunities for the academically talented. High school credit may be earned.
Program Focus Academic enrichment in humanities, arts, social sciences, and SAT preparation. Optional travel extension to Paris.
Academics Chinese languages/literature, English language/literature, SAT/ACT preparation, academics (general), anthropology, archaeology, architecture, art history/appreciation, biology, business, communications, economics, government and politics, history, humanities, journalism, mathematics, music, philosophy, physics, precollege program, psychology, social science, writing.
Arts Arts and crafts (general), creative writing, dance (modern), drawing, film, painting, photography, screenwriting, theater/drama.
Special Interest Areas Touring.
Sports Aerobics, basketball, boating, soccer, softball, sports (general), tennis, volleyball.
Trips Cultural, day, overnight, shopping.
Program Information 1 session per year. Session length: 28–32 days in June, July. Ages: 15–18. 250–300 participants per session. Boarding program cost: $5895.
Application Deadline Continuous.
Jobs Positions for college students 21 and older.
Contact Marcia Evans, President, 10 New King Street, White Plains, New York 10604. Phone: 914-686-7730. Fax: 914-686-7740. E-mail: summer@asaprograms.com.
URL www.asaprograms.com

For more information, see page 956.

Oxford Media School–Film

Oxford Media School–Film

Oxford Media School
New College, Oxford University
Oxford OX1 3BN
United Kingdom

General Information Coed residential academic program and arts program established in 1992. Formal opportunities for the artistically talented.
Program Focus Film, drama, and video.
Academics English language/literature, communications, history, journalism, reading, writing.
Arts Acting, cinematography, creative writing, film, film editing, film lighting, film production, radio broadcasting, screenwriting, sound design, television/video, theater/drama.
Special Interest Areas Field research/expeditions, touring.
Sports Boating, soccer, sports (general), tennis, ultimate frisbee.
Trips College tours, cultural, day, shopping.
Program Information 1 session per year. Session length: 4 weeks in July. Ages: 14–18. 20–35 participants per session. Boarding program cost: $5395–$6845.
Application Deadline Continuous.
Contact Mr. Desmond Smith, Director, 110 Pricefield Road, Toronto, Ontario M4W 1Z9, Canada. Phone: 416-964-0746. Fax: 416-929-4230. E-mail: newsco@sympatico.ca.
URL www.oxfordmediaschool.com

For more information, see page 1246.

Oxford Media School–Film Master Class

Oxford Media School
New College, Oxford University
Oxford OX1 3BN
United Kingdom

General Information Coed residential academic program and arts program. Formal opportunities for the artistically talented.
Program Focus Advanced film production.
Academics English language/literature, communications, history, journalism, reading, writing.

Arts Acting, cinematography, creative writing, film, film editing, film lighting, film production, radio broadcasting, screenwriting, sound design, television/video, theater/drama.
Special Interest Areas Field research/expeditions, touring.
Sports Boating, soccer, sports (general), tennis, ultimate frisbee.
Trips College tours, cultural, day, shopping.
Program Information 1 session per year. Session length: 4 weeks in July. Ages: 14–18. 20–35 participants per session. Boarding program cost: $5595–$7045. Financial aid available.
Application Deadline Continuous.
Contact Mr. Desmond Smith, Director, 110 Pricefield Road, Toronto, Ontario M4W 1Z9, Canada. Phone: 416-964-0746. Fax: 416-929-4230. E-mail: newsco@sympatico.ca.
URL www.oxfordmediaschool.com
For more information, see page 1246.

OXFORD MEDIA SCHOOL–NEWSROOM IN EUROPE

Oxford Media School
New College, Oxford University
Oxford OX1 3BN
United Kingdom

General Information Coed residential academic program and arts program. Formal opportunities for the artistically talented.
Program Focus Introduction to the basics of documentary making and television journalism.
Academics English language/literature, communications, history, journalism, reading, writing.
Arts Acting, creative writing, film, film editing, film production, radio broadcasting, television/video, theater/drama.
Special Interest Areas Field research/expeditions, touring.
Sports Boating, soccer, sports (general), tennis, ultimate frisbee.
Trips College tours, cultural, day, shopping.
Program Information 1 session per year. Session length: 4 weeks in July. Ages: 14–18. 20–35 participants per session. Boarding program cost: $5395–$6845. Financial aid available.
Application Deadline Continuous.
Contact Mr. Desmond Smith, Director, 110 Pricefield Road, Toronto, Ontario M4W 1Z9, Canada. Phone: 416-964-0746. Fax: 416-929-4230. E-mail: newsco@sympatico.ca.
URL www.oxfordmediaschool.com
For more information, see page 1246.

OXFORD MEDIA SCHOOL–NEWSROOM IN EUROPE, MASTER CLASS

Oxford Media School
New College, Oxford University
Oxford OX1 3BN
United Kingdom

General Information Coed residential academic program and arts program. Formal opportunities for the artistically talented.
Program Focus Advanced documentary making and television journalism.
Academics English language/literature, communications, history, journalism, reading, writing.
Arts Creative writing, film, film editing, film production, radio broadcasting, television/video, theater/drama.
Special Interest Areas Field research/expeditions, touring.
Sports Boating, soccer, sports (general), tennis, ultimate frisbee.
Trips College tours, cultural, day, shopping.
Program Information 1 session per year. Session length: 4 weeks in July. Ages: 14–18. 20–35 participants per session. Boarding program cost: $5595–$7045. Financial aid available.
Application Deadline Continuous.
Contact Mr. Desmond Smith, Director, 110 Pricefield Road, Toronto, Ontario M4W 1Z9, Canada. Phone: 416-964-0746. Fax: 416-929-4230. E-mail: newsco@sympatico.ca.
URL www.oxfordmediaschool.com
For more information, see page 1246.

THE OXFORD PREP EXPERIENCE

Oxbridge Academic Programs
Oxford University
Oxford
United Kingdom

General Information Coed residential academic program and arts program established in 2004. Formal opportunities for the academically talented and artistically talented.
Program Focus Academic and cultural enrichment.
Academics English language/literature, academics (general), art history/appreciation, government and politics, health sciences, history, humanities, precollege program, social science, social studies, speech/debate, writing.
Arts Acting, arts, creative writing, painting, theater/drama.
Special Interest Areas Field trips (arts and culture).
Sports Aerobics, basketball, cross-country, soccer, sports (general), tennis.
Trips Cultural, day.
Program Information 1 session per year. Session length: 24 days in July. Ages: 13–15. 125 participants per session. Boarding program cost: $5195. Financial aid available.
Application Deadline Continuous.
Contact Ms. Andrea Mardon, Executive Director, Oxbridge Academic Programs, 601 West 110th Street,

The Oxford Prep Experience (continued)

Suite 7R, New York, New York 10025-2186. Phone: 800-828-8349. Fax: 212-663-8169. E-mail: info@oxbridgeprograms.com.
URL www.oxbridgeprograms.com
For more information, see page 1242.

The Oxford Tradition

Oxbridge Academic Programs
Oxford University
Oxford
United Kingdom

General Information Coed residential academic program and arts program established in 1983. Formal opportunities for the academically talented and artistically talented. High school credit may be earned.

The Oxford Tradition

Program Focus Academic and cultural enrichment.
Academics English language/literature, academics (general), anthropology, archaeology, architecture, art history/appreciation, classical languages/literatures, economics, environmental science, government and politics, history, humanities, international relations, journalism, law, medicine, music, philosophy, precollege program, psychology, social science, social studies, speech/debate, writing.
Arts Acting, arts, creative writing, drawing, film, music, painting, photography, theater/drama.
Special Interest Areas Field trips (arts and culture).
Sports Aerobics, basketball, cross-country, soccer, sports (general), tennis.
Trips Cultural, day.
Program Information 1 session per year. Session length: 31 days in July. Ages: 15–18. 370 participants per session. Boarding program cost: $5895. Financial aid available. Airfare not included.
Application Deadline Continuous.
Contact Ms. Andrea Mardon, Executive Director, Oxbridge Academic Programs, 601 West 110th Street, Suite 7R, New York, New York 10025-2186. Phone: 800-828-8349. Fax: 212-663-8169. E-mail: info@oxbridgeprograms.com.
URL www.oxbridgeprograms.com
For more information, see page 1242.

Putney Student Travel–Cultural Exploration–Theatre in Britain

Putney Student Travel
United Kingdom

General Information Coed residential arts program established in 1951.
Program Focus Working in a small group, students create a theatrical production and perform it at the Edinburgh Fringe Festival.
Arts Theater/drama.
Special Interest Areas Team building.
Trips Cultural, day, overnight.
Program Information 1 session per year. Session length: 28–30 days in July, August. Ages: 15–18. 16 participants per session. Boarding program cost: $7900. Financial aid available.
Application Deadline Continuous.
Jobs Positions for college students 21 and older.
Contact Jeffrey Shumlin, Director, 345 Hickory Ridge Road, Putney, Vermont 05346. Phone: 802-387-5000. Fax: 802-387-4276. E-mail: info@goputney.com.
URL www.goputney.com
For more information, see page 1276.

Sprachkurse Ariana, Aldenham

Sprachkurse Ariana AG
Aldenham School
Elstree
United Kingdom

General Information Coed residential academic program established in 1995.
Academics English as a second language.
Sports Badminton, basketball, gymnastics, rugby, soccer, sports (general), tennis, volleyball.
Trips Cultural, day, shopping.
Program Information 1 session per year. Session length: 2–4 weeks in July, August. Ages: 14–19. 50 participants per session. Boarding program cost: 2040–3060 Swiss francs.
Application Deadline Continuous.
Jobs Positions for college students 20 and older.
Contact Ms. M. Schmid, Director, Hoehenweg 60, St. Gallen 9000, Switzerland. Phone: 41-71-277-9291. Fax: 41-71-277-7253. E-mail: info@ariana.ch.
URL www.ariana.ch

Summer Discovery at Cambridge

Summer Discovery
New Hall College
Cambridge University
Cambridge
United Kingdom

General Information Coed residential academic program established in 1987. High school or college credit may be earned.
Program Focus Pre-college enrichment.
Academics English as a second language, English language/literature, French language/literature, SAT/ACT preparation, academics (general), archaeology, architecture, art history/appreciation, business, communications, government and politics, humanities, journalism, philosophy, precollege program, psychology, science (general), speech/debate.
Arts Creative writing, painting, photography, theater/drama.
Special Interest Areas Community service.
Sports Aerobics, basketball, bicycling, golf, rowing (crew/sculling), soccer, softball, tennis, volleyball, weight training.
Trips Cultural, overnight.
Program Information 1 session per year. Session length: 4 weeks in June, July. 200 participants per session. Boarding program cost: $5699–$5899. Application fee: $60–$70. Open to participants completing grades 10–12.
Application Deadline Continuous.
Jobs Positions for college students 21 and older.
Contact The Musiker Family, Director, 1326 Old Northern Boulevard, Roslyn Village, New York 11576. Phone: 888-878-6637. Fax: 516-625-3438. E-mail: discovery@summerfun.com.
URL www.summerfun.com

For more information, see page 1338.

TASIS England Summer Program

TASIS The American School in England
Coldharbour Lane
Thorpe, Surrey TW20 8TE
United Kingdom

General Information Coed residential and day academic program established in 1976. High school credit may be earned.
Program Focus Enrichment, theatre, acting, and academic summer school courses for credit.
Academics English as a second language, English language/literature, SAT/ACT preparation, TOEFL/TOEIC preparation, academics (general), archaeology, architecture, art (Advanced Placement), art history/appreciation, biology, chemistry, communications, computers, history, journalism, mathematics, music, study skills, writing.
Arts Arts and crafts (general), creative writing, dance, dance (jazz), dance (modern), drawing, film, graphic arts, music, music (instrumental), painting, photography, theater/drama.
Sports Aerobics, baseball, basketball, bicycling, golf, horseback riding, soccer, softball, swimming, tennis, waterskiing, weight training.
Trips Cultural, day, overnight, shopping.
Program Information 2 sessions per year. Session length: 3–6 weeks in June, July, August. Ages: 12–18. 150–220 participants per session. Boarding program cost: $3200–$5350. Airfare not included.
Application Deadline Continuous.
Jobs Positions for college students 21 and older.
Contact W. Thomas Fleming, US Director, 1640 Wisconsin Avenue, NW, Washington, District of Columbia 20007. Phone: 202-965-5800. Fax: 202-965-5816. E-mail: usadmissions@tasis.com.
URL www.tasis.com

For more information, see page 1356.

University of St. Andrews Creative Writing Summer Program

University of St. Andrews Summer Studies
66 North Street
St. Andrews, Fife KY16 9AH
United Kingdom

General Information Coed residential academic program and cultural program established in 2003. Formal opportunities for the academically talented. High school credit may be earned.
Program Focus Creative writing.
Academics Academics (general), precollege program.
Arts Creative writing.
Sports Golf.
Wilderness/Outdoors Hiking.
Trips Cultural, day, overnight, shopping.
Program Information 1 session per year. Session length: 4 weeks in June, July. Ages: 15–18. 10–40 participants per session. Boarding program cost: 2600 British pounds. Application fee: 20 British pounds.
Application Deadline Continuous.
Contact Dr. M. Ian S. Hunter, Director, main address above. Phone: 44-1334-462238. Fax: 44-1334-462208. E-mail: mish@st-and.ac.uk.
URL www.st-andrews.ac.uk/services/admissions/CWSPweb.htm

University of St. Andrews Scottish Studies Summer Program

University of St. Andrews Summer Studies
66 North Street
St. Andrews, Fife KY16 9AH
United Kingdom

General Information Coed residential academic program and cultural program established in 1999. Formal opportunities for the academically talented. High school credit may be earned.
Program Focus Scottish culture: history, literature, music, art, architecture, environment.
Academics English language/literature, academics (general), archaeology, architecture, art history/appreciation, government and politics, history, intercultural studies, music, precollege program.
Sports Golf.
Wilderness/Outdoors Hiking.
Trips Cultural, day, overnight, shopping.

University of St. Andrews Scottish Studies Summer Program (continued)

Program Information 1 session per year. Session length: 4 weeks in June, July. Ages: 15–18. 40–70 participants per session. Boarding program cost: 2500 British pounds. Application fee: 20 British pounds.
Application Deadline Continuous.
Contact Dr. M. Ian S. Hunter, Director, main address above. Phone: 44-1334-462238. Fax: 44-1334-462208. E-mail: mish@st-and.ac.uk.
URL www.st-andrews.ac.uk/services/admissions/sssprog.htm

Village Camps–England

Village Camps
Hurstpierpoint College
Hassocks BN6 9JS
United Kingdom

General Information Coed residential traditional camp and academic program established in 1972.
Program Focus Languages, English, tennis, soccer, golf, and Web site design and construction.
Academics English as a second language, English language/literature, Web page design, computers, language study, linguistics, music.
Arts Arts and crafts (general), dance, dance (modern), drawing, fabric arts, film, jewelry making, music, painting, photography, puppetry, radio broadcasting, television/video, theater/drama.
Special Interest Areas Campcraft, culinary arts, field trips (arts and culture), leadership training.
Sports Aerobics, archery, baseball, basketball, bicycling, bicycling (BMX), climbing (wall), field hockey, golf, sailing, skiing (downhill), soccer, softball, sports (general), squash, swimming, tennis, volleyball.
Wilderness/Outdoors Hiking, mountain biking, orienteering.
Trips Cultural, day, shopping.
Program Information 2 sessions per year. Session length: 13–20 days in July, August. Ages: 7–15. 150–180 participants per session. Boarding program cost: $1680–$2770.
Application Deadline Continuous.
Jobs Positions for college students 21 and older.
Contact Roger Ratner, Director, 14 Rue de la Morâche, Nyon CH-1260, Switzerland. Phone: 41-22-990-9400. Fax: 41-22-990-9494. E-mail: camps@villagecamps.ch.
URL www.villagecamps.com

For more information, see page 1380.

Woodberry Forest Summer School–England

Woodberry Forest School
Oxford
United Kingdom

General Information Coed residential academic program established in 1922. Formal opportunities for the academically talented. High school credit may be earned.
Academics English language/literature, French language/literature, academics (general), art history/appreciation, biology, history, music.
Sports Football, sports (general), swimming, weight training.
Wilderness/Outdoors Backpacking, canoe trips, hiking.
Trips Cultural, day, overnight, shopping.
Program Information 1 session per year. Session length: 23 days in June, July. Ages: 12–17. 5–20 participants per session. Boarding program cost: $4696. Financial aid available.
Application Deadline Continuous.
Contact Dr. W. David McRae, Director of Summer Programs, 354 Woodberry Forest Station, Woodberry Forest, Virginia 22989. Phone: 540-672-6047. Fax: 540-672-9076. E-mail: wfs_summer@woodberry.org.
URL www.woodberry.org

For more information, see page 1402.

Woodberry Forest Summer School–Scotland

Woodberry Forest School
Glasgow and Inverness, Scotland
United Kingdom

General Information Coed residential academic program established in 1998. Formal opportunities for the academically talented. High school credit may be earned.
Academics English language/literature, French language/literature, academics (general), art history/appreciation, biology, history, music.
Sports Football, golf, sports (general), swimming, weight training.
Wilderness/Outdoors Backpacking, canoe trips, hiking.
Trips Cultural, day, overnight, shopping.
Program Information 1 session per year. Session length: 23 days in June, July. Ages: 12–17. 5–20 participants per session. Boarding program cost: $4259. Financial aid available.
Application Deadline Continuous.
Contact Dr. W. David McRae, Director of Summer Programs, 354 Woodberry Forest Station, Woodberry Forest, Virginia 22989. Phone: 540-672-6047. Fax: 540-672-9076. E-mail: wfs_summer@woodberry.org.
URL www.woodberry.org

For more information, see page 1402.

XUK

Cross Keys
Riddlesworth Hall
Norfolk
United Kingdom

General Information Coed residential traditional camp established in 1989. Specific services available for the emotionally challenged, developmentally challenged, and learning disabled.
Program Focus Residential camp in the beautiful English countryside.

Academics Computers.
Arts Arts and crafts (general), batiking, ceramics, dance, drawing, fabric arts, jewelry making, music, music (vocal), musical productions, painting, pottery, puppetry, television/video, theater/drama, woodworking.
Special Interest Areas Culinary arts.
Sports Archery, basketball, climbing (wall), football, golf, gymnastics, martial arts, soccer, swimming, tennis.
Trips Cultural, day, shopping.
Program Information 4 sessions per year. Session length: 1 week in July, August. Ages: 6–17. 100–150 participants per session. Boarding program cost: 259–420 British pounds.
Application Deadline Continuous.
Jobs Positions for high school students 18 and older and college students 18 and older.
Contact Richard Bernstein, Managing Director, main address above. Phone: 020-8371-9686. Fax: 020-8343-0625. E-mail: richard@xkeys.co.uk.
URL www.campsforkids.co.uk

UNITED REPUBLIC OF TANZANIA

EARTHWATCH INSTITUTE–EARLY MAN AT OLDUVAI GORGE

Earthwatch Institute
Olduvai Gorge
United Republic of Tanzania

General Information Coed residential outdoor program, cultural program, and adventure program.
Program Focus Rescuing the heritage of a world-renowned site.
Academics Anthropology, archaeology, paleontology, science (general).
Special Interest Areas Field research/expeditions.
Program Information 4 sessions per year. Session length: 3 weeks in June, July, August, September. Ages: 16+. 14 participants per session. Boarding program cost: $2995–$3095. Financial aid available. Financial aid for high school students and teachers.
Application Deadline Continuous.
Contact General Information Desk, PO Box 75, Maynard, Massachusetts 01754. Phone: 800-776-0188. Fax: 978-461-2332. E-mail: info@earthwatch.org.
URL www.earthwatch.org

FLINT HILL SCHOOL–"SUMMER ON THE HILL"–TRIPS FROM THE HILL–TANZANIA SAFARI

Flint Hill School
United Republic of Tanzania

General Information Coed travel outdoor program.
Program Focus Photo-safari in Tarangire, Ngorongoro Crater and the Serengeti.
Academics Area studies, intercultural studies.
Special Interest Areas Field research/expeditions, nature study.
Wilderness/Outdoors Outdoor adventure, outdoor camping, safari.
Trips Cultural, day, overnight.
Program Information 1 session per year. Session length: 2 weeks in June, July. Ages: 6+. 2–20 participants per session. Cost: $5950. Under age 14 must be accompanied by a parent.
Application Deadline Continuous.
Jobs Positions for high school students 16 and older and college students 18 and older.
Contact Ms. Peggy Laurent, Director of Special and Summer Programs, 3320 Jermantown Road, Oakton, Virginia 22124. Phone: 703-584-2315. Fax: 703-242-0718. E-mail: plaurent@flinthill.org.
URL www.flinthill.org

PUTNEY STUDENT TRAVEL–COMMUNITY SERVICE–TANZANIA

Putney Student Travel
United Republic of Tanzania

General Information Coed residential community service program and cultural program established in 1951.
Program Focus Community service, cultural exchange, and weekend excursions from a base in a small, rural community, and a week-long safari.
Academics Intercultural studies.
Special Interest Areas Community service, construction, farming.
Sports Soccer.
Wilderness/Outdoors Hiking, safari.
Trips Cultural, day.
Program Information 1 session per year. Session length: 4 weeks in June, July. Ages: 15–18. 16 participants per session. Boarding program cost: $6900. Financial aid available. Airfare from New York included.
Application Deadline Continuous.
Contact Jeffrey Shumlin, Admissions Director, 345 Hickory Ridge Road, Putney, Vermont 05346. Phone: 802-387-5000. Fax: 802-387-4276. E-mail: info@goputney.com.
URL www.goputney.com
For more information, see page 1276.

URUGUAY

YOUTH FOR UNDERSTANDING USA–URUGUAY

Youth for Understanding USA
Uruguay

General Information Coed residential academic program and cultural program established in 1951. High school or college credit may be earned.

Youth for Understanding USA–Uruguay (continued)
Program Focus Living with a host family, learning about other cultures, and improving language skills.
Academics Spanish language/literature, area studies, intercultural studies, social studies.
Special Interest Areas Homestays.
Trips Cultural, day, overnight.
Program Information 1 session per year. Session length: 35–45 days in June, July, August. Ages: 15–18. 10–50 participants per session. Boarding program cost: $4595. Application fee: $75. Financial aid available. Round-trip domestic and international airfare is included in the tuition.
Application Deadline Continuous.
Contact Admissions Counselor, 6400 Goldsboro Road, Suite 100, Bethesda, Maryland 20817. Phone: 800-TEENAGE (833-6243). Fax: 202-895-1104. E-mail: admissions@us.yfu.org.
URL www.yfu-usa.org
For more information, see page 1414.

VENEZUELA

Youth for Understanding USA–Venezuela

Youth for Understanding USA
Venezuela

General Information Coed residential academic program and cultural program established in 1951. High school or college credit may be earned.
Program Focus Living with a host family, learning about other cultures, and improving language skills.
Academics Spanish language/literature, area studies, intercultural studies, social studies.
Special Interest Areas Homestays.
Trips Cultural, day, overnight.
Program Information 1 session per year. Session length: 35–45 days in June, July, August. Ages: 15–18. 10–50 participants per session. Boarding program cost: $4595. Application fee: $75. Financial aid available. Round-trip domestic and international airfare is included in the tuition.
Application Deadline Continuous.
Contact Admissions Counselor, 6400 Goldsboro Road, Suite 100, Bethesda, Maryland 20817. Phone: 800-TEENAGE (833-6243). Fax: 202-895-1104. E-mail: admissions@us.yfu.org.
URL www.yfu-usa.org
For more information, see page 1414.

VIETNAM

AAVE–Vietnam

AAVE–America's Adventure Ventures Everywhere
Vietnam

General Information Coed travel outdoor program, cultural program, and adventure program established in 1976. Accredited by American Camping Association.
Program Focus Adventure travel.
Special Interest Areas Community service, cross-cultural education, culinary arts, leadership training, touring.
Sports Bicycling, boating, sailing, sea kayaking, snorkeling.
Wilderness/Outdoors Bicycle trips, hiking.
Trips Cultural, day, overnight.
Program Information 2–4 sessions per year. Session length: 3 weeks in June, July, August. Ages: 15–18. 15 participants per session. Cost: $3250. Financial aid available.
Application Deadline Continuous.
Jobs Positions for college students 21 and older.
Contact Mr. Abbott Wallis, Owner, 2245 Stonecrop Way, Golden, Colorado 80401. Phone: 800-222-3595. Fax: 303-526-0885. E-mail: info@aave.com.
URL www.aave.com
For more information, see page 952.

Earthwatch Institute–Butterflies of Vietnam

Earthwatch Institute
Tam Dao National Park
Vietnam

General Information Coed residential outdoor program, cultural program, and adventure program.
Program Focus Surveying butterfly diversity as an indicator of habitat disturbance.
Academics Biology, ecology, science (general).
Special Interest Areas Field research/expeditions, nature study.
Program Information 6 sessions per year. Session length: 9 days in May, June, July, August, September, October. Ages: 16+. 7 participants per session. Boarding program cost: $1795–$1895. Financial aid available. Financial aid for high school students and teachers.
Application Deadline Continuous.
Contact General Information Desk, PO Box 75, Maynard, Massachusetts 01754. Phone: 800-776-0188. Fax: 978-461-2332. E-mail: info@earthwatch.org.
URL www.earthwatch.org

EARTHWATCH INSTITUTE–MEDICINAL PLANTS OF VIETNAM

Earthwatch Institute
Ba Vi National Park
Vietnam

General Information Coed residential outdoor program.
Program Focus Establishing a monitoring program for endangered medicinal plants to conserve these valuable tropical forest resources.
Academics Botany, ecology.
Special Interest Areas Conservation projects, field research/expeditions, nature study.
Program Information 4 sessions per year. Session length: 15 days in April, June, October, December. Ages: 16+. 8 participants per session. Boarding program cost: $1795–$1895. Financial aid available. Financial aid for high school students and teachers.
Application Deadline Continuous.
Contact General Information Desk, PO Box 75, Maynard, Massachusetts 01754. Phone: 800-776-0188. Fax: 978-461-2332. E-mail: info@earthwatch.org.
URL www.earthwatch.org

EARTHWATCH INSTITUTE–RESTORING VIETNAM'S FORESTS

Earthwatch Institute
Cuc Phuong National Park
Vietnam

General Information Coed residential outdoor program.
Program Focus Gathering baseline data on forest ecology to restore native tree species.
Academics Ecology, environmental science, forestry.
Arts Photography.
Special Interest Areas Field research/expeditions, nature study.
Wilderness/Outdoors Wilderness/outdoors (general).
Program Information 8 sessions per year. Session length: 9 days in April, May, June, July, August. Ages: 16+. 5 participants per session. Boarding program cost: $1795–$1895. Financial aid available. Financial aid for high school students and teachers.
Application Deadline Continuous.
Contact General Information Desk, PO Box 75, Maynard, Massachusetts 01754. Phone: 800-776-0188. Fax: 978-461-2332. E-mail: info@earthwatch.org.
URL www.earthwatch.org

WHERE THERE BE DRAGONS: VIETNAM

Where There Be Dragons
Vietnam

General Information Coed travel academic program, outdoor program, community service program, and cultural program established in 1993. Formal opportunities for the academically talented.
Program Focus Rugged and off the beaten path travel introduces a wide range of development issues.
Academics Anthropology, area studies, art history/appreciation, business, ecology, economics, geography, government and politics (Advanced Placement), history, intercultural studies, journalism, peace education, philosophy, religion, social studies.
Arts Ceramics, fabric arts, jewelry making, leather working, metalworking, painting, photography, pottery, printmaking, weaving, woodworking.
Special Interest Areas Community service, field research/expeditions, homestays, leadership training, nature study, touring.
Sports Snorkeling.
Wilderness/Outdoors Backpacking, hiking, wilderness camping.
Trips Cultural, overnight.
Program Information 1 session per year. Session length: 6 weeks in June, July, August. Ages: 15–20. 12 participants per session. Cost: $5550. Financial aid available. Airfare included.
Application Deadline Continuous.
Contact Chris Yager, Director, PO Box 4651, Boulder, Colorado 80306. Phone: 800-982-9203. Fax: 303-413-0857. E-mail: info@wheretherebedragons.com.
URL www.wheretherebedragons.com

For more information, see page 1394.

YOUTH FOR UNDERSTANDING USA–VIETNAM

Youth for Understanding USA
Vietnam

General Information Coed residential academic program and cultural program. High school credit may be earned.
Special Interest Areas Community service, cross-cultural education, homestays.
Trips Cultural.
Program Information 1 session per year. Session length: 6 weeks in June, July, August. Ages: 15–18. Boarding program cost: $4595–$6495. Application fee: $75. Financial aid available. Round-trip domestic and international airfare is included in the tuition.
Application Deadline Continuous.
Contact Admissions Counselor, 6400 Goldsboro Road, Suite 100, Bethesda, Maryland 20817. Phone: 800-TEENAGE (833-6243). Fax: 202-895-1104. E-mail: admissions@us.yfu.org.
URL www.yfu-usa.org

For more information, see page 1414.

TRAVEL PROGRAMS IN THE UNITED STATES

AAVE–Bold West

AAVE–America's Adventure Ventures Everywhere
Locations California, Nevada, Utah.

General Information Coed travel outdoor program, wilderness program, and adventure program established in 1976. Accredited by American Camping Association.
Program Focus Adventure travel.
Special Interest Areas Community service, leadership training, touring.
Sports Rappelling, surfing, swimming.
Wilderness/Outdoors Hiking, mountaineering, orienteering, rafting, rock climbing, white-water trips, wilderness camping.
Excursions Overnight.
Program Information 3–6 sessions per year. Session length: 4 weeks in June, July, August. Ages: 14–18. 13 participants per session. Cost: $3688. Financial aid available.
Housing Tents and youth hostels.
Application Deadline Continuous.
Jobs Positions for college students 21 and older.
Contact Mr. Abbott Wallis, Owner, 2245 Stonecrop Way, Golden, Colorado 80401. Phone: 800-222-3595. Fax: 303-526-0885. E-mail: info@aave.com.
URL www.aave.com

For more information, see page 952.

AAVE–Boot/Saddle/Paddle

AAVE–America's Adventure Ventures Everywhere
Locations Arizona, Colorado, Utah.

General Information Coed travel outdoor program, wilderness program, and adventure program established in 1976. Accredited by American Camping Association.
Program Focus Adventure travel.
Academics Intercultural studies.
Special Interest Areas Native American culture, campcraft, community service, leadership training, touring.
Sports Horseback riding, swimming.
Wilderness/Outdoors Backpacking, hiking, mountain biking, mountaineering, orienteering, pack animal trips, rafting, white-water trips, wilderness camping.
Excursions Cultural, overnight.
Program Information 4 sessions per year. Session length: 4 weeks in June, July, August. Ages: 14–18. 13 participants per session. Cost: $3688. Financial aid available.
Housing Tents.
Application Deadline Continuous.
Jobs Positions for college students 21 and older.
Contact Mr. Abbott Wallis, Owner, 2245 Stonecrop Way, Golden, Colorado 80401. Phone: 800-222-3595. Fax: 303-526-0885. E-mail: info@aave.com.
URL www.aave.com

For more information, see page 952.

AAVE–Border Cross

AAVE–America's Adventure Ventures Everywhere
Locations Canada, Washington.

General Information Coed travel outdoor program, community service program, wilderness program, and adventure program established in 1976. Accredited by American Camping Association.
Program Focus Adventure travel.
Special Interest Areas Community service, leadership training, nautical skills, touring.
Sports Bicycling, rappelling, sea kayaking, skiing (downhill), snowboarding, swimming.

AAVE–Boot / Saddle / Paddle

Wilderness/Outdoors Backpacking, bicycle trips, hiking, mountain biking, mountaineering, orienteering, rock climbing, wilderness camping.
Excursions Overnight.
Program Information 3–4 sessions per year. Session length: 3 weeks in June, July, August. Ages: 13–14. 13 participants per session. Cost: $2588. Financial aid available.
Housing Tents.
Application Deadline Continuous.
Jobs Positions for college students 21 and older.
Contact Mr. Abbott Wallis, Owner, 2245 Stonecrop Way, Golden, Colorado 80401. Phone: 800-222-3595. Fax: 303-526-0885. E-mail: info@aave.com.
URL www.aave.com

For more information, see page 952.

AAVE–Rock & River

AAVE–America's Adventure Ventures Everywhere
Locations Colorado, Utah.

General Information Coed travel outdoor program, wilderness program, and adventure program established in 1976. Accredited by American Camping Association.
Program Focus Adventure travel.
Special Interest Areas Campcraft, community service, leadership training.
Sports Rappelling, swimming.
Wilderness/Outdoors Backpacking, hiking, orienteering, rafting, rock climbing, white-water trips, wilderness camping.
Excursions Cultural, day, overnight.
Program Information 5–8 sessions per year. Session length: 3 weeks in June, July, August. Ages: 14–18. 13 participants per session. Cost: $2588. Financial aid available.
Housing Tents.
Application Deadline Continuous.
Jobs Positions for college students 21 and older.
Contact Mr. Abbott Wallis, Owner, 2245 Stonecrop Way, Golden, Colorado 80401. Phone: 800-222-3595. Fax: 303-526-0885. E-mail: info@aave.com.
URL www.aave.com

For more information, see page 952.

AAVE–X–Five

AAVE–America's Adventure Ventures Everywhere
Locations Colorado, Utah.

General Information Coed travel outdoor program, wilderness program, and adventure program established in 1976. Accredited by American Camping Association.
Program Focus Adventure travel.
Special Interest Areas Campcraft, community service, leadership training, team building.
Sports Rappelling, swimming.
Wilderness/Outdoors Backpacking, bicycle trips, hiking, mountain biking, orienteering, rafting, rock climbing, white-water trips, wilderness camping.
Excursions Overnight.
Program Information 4–6 sessions per year. Session length: 26 days in June, July, August. Ages: 14–18. 13 participants per session. Cost: $3288. Financial aid available.
Housing Tents.
Application Deadline Continuous.
Jobs Positions for college students 21 and older.
Contact Mr. Abbott Wallis, Owner, 2245 Stonecrop Way, Golden, Colorado 80401. Phone: 800-222-3595. Fax: 303-526-0885. E-mail: info@aave.com.
URL www.aave.com

For more information, see page 952.

Adventure Links

Adventure Links
Locations North Carolina, Pennsylvania, Virginia, West Virginia.

General Information Coed travel outdoor program, wilderness program, and adventure program established in 1994. Accredited by American Camping Association.
Special Interest Areas Campcraft, field research/expeditions.
Sports Canoeing, climbing (wall), kayaking, rappelling, ropes course, sea kayaking.

Adventure Links (continued)

Wilderness/Outdoors Backpacking, canoe trips, caving, hiking, mountain biking, orienteering, rafting, rock climbing, white-water trips, wilderness camping.
Excursions Day, overnight.
Program Information 8–24 sessions per year. Session length: 5–18 days in June, July, August. Ages: 8–17. 15 participants per session. Cost: $650–$2750.
Housing Tents.
Application Deadline Continuous.
Jobs Positions for high school students 18 and older and college students 18 and older.
Summer Contact Elena Gonzalez, Summer Camp Director, 21498 Blue Ridge Mountain Road, Paris, Virginia 20130. Phone: 540-592-3682. Fax: 540-592-3316. E-mail: elena@adventurelinks.net.
Winter Contact Austin Birch, Co-Owner, 21498 Blue Ridge Mountain Road, Paris, Virginia 20130. Phone: 800-877-0954. Fax: 540-592-3316. E-mail: info@adventurelinks.net.
URL www.adventurelinks.net

Adventure Links–Appalachian Odyssey

Adventure Links
Locations Virginia, West Virginia.

General Information Coed travel outdoor program, wilderness program, and adventure program established in 2002. Accredited by American Camping Association.
Special Interest Areas Campcraft.
Sports Climbing (wall), rappelling, ropes course.
Wilderness/Outdoors Backpacking, hiking, mountain biking, rock climbing, wilderness camping.
Excursions Day, overnight.
Program Information 1 session per year. Session length: 2 weeks in August. Ages: 14–17. 15–20 participants per session. Cost: $1395.
Housing Tents.
Application Deadline Continuous.
Jobs Positions for high school students 17 and older and college students 17 and older.
Summer Contact Elena Gonzalez, Summer Camps Director, 21498 Blue Ridge Mountain Road, Paris, Virginia 20130. Phone: 540-592-3682. Fax: 540-592-3316. E-mail: elena@adventurelinks.net.
Winter Contact Austin Birch, Owner, 31498 Blue Ridge Mountain Road, Paris, Virginia 20130. Phone: 800-877-0954. Fax: 540-592-3316. E-mail: programs@adventurelinks.net.
URL www.adventurelinks.com

Adventures Cross-Country, Western Adventure

Adventures Cross-Country
Locations Arizona, California, Colorado.

General Information Coed travel outdoor program, wilderness program, and adventure program established in 1983.
Program Focus Wilderness adventures in California, Arizona and Colorado.
Sports Kayaking.
Wilderness/Outdoors Backpacking, hiking, orienteering, rafting, white-water trips, wilderness camping.
Program Information 2 sessions per year. Session length: 27 days in June, July, August. Ages: 13–18. 8–15 participants per session. Cost: $3695. Financial aid available.
Housing Tents.
Application Deadline Continuous.
Jobs Positions for college students 21 and older.
Contact Scott von Eschen, Owner, 242 Redwood Highway, Mill Valley, California 94941. Phone: 415-332-5075. Fax: 415-332-2130. E-mail: arcc@adventurescrosscountry.com.
URL www.adventurescrosscountry.com
For more information, see page 972.

Adventure Treks–California Challenge Adventures

Adventure Treks, Inc.
Locations California, Oregon.

General Information Coed travel outdoor program, wilderness program, and adventure program established in 1978.
Program Focus Multi-activity outdoor adventures with focus on fun, personal growth, teamwork, leadership, building self-confidence, outdoor skills, and community living; visits to Shasta-Trinity and Lost Coast.
Sports Swimming.
Wilderness/Outdoors Backpacking, mountain biking, mountaineering, orienteering, rafting, rock climbing, survival training, white-water trips, wilderness camping.
Program Information 3–4 sessions per year. Session length: 25 days in June, July, August. Ages: 15–17. 24 participants per session. Cost: $3095. Financial aid available.
Housing Tents.
Application Deadline Continuous.
Contact John Dockendorf, Director, PO Box 1321, Flat Rock, North Carolina 28731. Phone: 888-954-5555. Fax: 828-696-1663. E-mail: info@advtreks.com.
URL www.adventuretreks.com

Adventure Treks–Summit Fever

Adventure Treks, Inc.
Locations California, Oregon, Washington.

General Information Coed travel outdoor program, wilderness program, and adventure program established in 1978.
Program Focus Multi-activity outdoor adventure program with an emphasis on fun, personal growth, leadership, teamwork and outdoor skills.
Sports Sea kayaking.
Wilderness/Outdoors Backpacking, hiking, mountain biking, mountaineering, orienteering, rafting, rock climbing, white-water trips, wilderness camping.
Program Information 1–2 sessions per year. Session length: 20 days in June, July. Ages: 17–18. 10 participants per session. Cost: $3895. Financial aid available.

Housing Tents.
Application Deadline Continuous.
Contact John Dockendorf, Director, PO Box 1321, Flat Rock, North Carolina 28731. Phone: 888-954-5555. Fax: 828-696-1663. E-mail: info@advtreks.com.
URL www.adventuretreks.com

Adventure Treks–Ultimate Northwest Adventures

Adventure Treks, Inc.
Locations Oregon, Washington.

General Information Coed travel outdoor program, wilderness program, and adventure program established in 1978.
Program Focus Multi-activity adventure programs with a focus on fun, personal growth, leadership, outdoor skills, and teamwork.
Wilderness/Outdoors Backpacking, hiking, mountain biking, mountaineering, orienteering, rafting, rock climbing, survival training, white-water trips, wilderness camping.
Program Information 1–2 sessions per year. Session length: 24 days in June, July, August. Ages: 15–17. 24 participants per session. Cost: $3095. Financial aid available.
Housing Tents.
Application Deadline Continuous.
Contact John Dockendorf, Director, PO Box 1321, Flat Rock, North Carolina 28731. Phone: 888-954-5555. Fax: 828-696-1663. E-mail: info@advtreks.com.
URL www.adventuretreks.com

Alien Adventure Overnight Camp

KidsMakeADifference.org
Locations Arizona, California, Nevada, New Mexico.

General Information Coed travel outdoor program, wilderness program, and cultural program established in 1994.
Program Focus Space, science, UFO's, aliens, Native American Villages, national parks, ghost towns.
Academics Aerospace science, astronomy, botany, ecology, environmental science, geology/earth science, journalism, meteorology, music, peace education, writing.
Arts Drawing, music, music (vocal), photography, television/video.
Special Interest Areas Native American culture, campcraft, culinary arts, nature study, team building, touring.
Sports Frisbee, swimming.
Wilderness/Outdoors Caving, hiking, mountaineering, orienteering, outdoor adventure.
Excursions Cultural, day, overnight, shopping.
Program Information 1 session per year. Session length: 13 days in June, July. Ages: 8–13. 8 participants per session. Cost: $1395. Financial aid available.
Housing Cabins, hotels, and tents.
Application Deadline Continuous.
Jobs Positions for college students 18 and older.
Contact Dr. Andy Mars, Director, PO Box 24922, West Los Angeles, California 90024-0922. Phone: 818-344-7838.
URL www.kidsmakeadifference.org

Alpengirl–Montana Art

Alpengirl, Inc.
Locations Idaho, Montana, Wyoming.

General Information Girls' travel outdoor program, arts program, wilderness program, and adventure program. Accredited by American Camping Association.
Program Focus Photojournalism camp, multi-adventure, creative writing, camp gourmet, Yellowstone and Grand Teton National Parks.
Academics Area studies, ecology, geology/earth science, science (general).
Arts Creative writing, photography.
Sports Canoeing, horseback riding, swimming.
Wilderness/Outdoors Canoe trips, hiking, pack animal trips, rafting, white-water trips, wilderness camping.
Excursions Cultural, day, overnight, shopping.
Program Information 1 session per year. Session length: 2 weeks in June. Ages: 12–14. 10–12 participants per session. Cost: $1820. Financial aid available.
Housing Tents.
Application Deadline Continuous.
Jobs Positions for college students 21 and older.
Contact Alissa Farley, Camp Owner, PO Box 1138, Manhattan, Montana 59741. Phone: 800-585-7476. Fax: 406-284-9036. E-mail: alissa@alpengirl.com.
URL www.alpengirl.com

Apogee Outdoor Adventures–Burlington to Boston

Apogee Outdoor Adventures
Locations Maine, Massachusetts, New Hampshire, Vermont.

General Information Coed travel outdoor program, community service program, wilderness program, and adventure program established in 2001.
Special Interest Areas Community service, touring.
Sports Bicycling.
Wilderness/Outdoors Backpacking, bicycle trips, hiking.
Program Information 1–2 sessions per year. Session length: 14–16 days in June, July, August. Ages: 14–17. 5–12 participants per session. Cost: $2395–$2495. Financial aid available.
Housing Tents and youth hostels.
Application Deadline Continuous.
Jobs Positions for college students.
Contact Mr. Kevin Cashman, Director, 40 Bowker Street, Brunswick, Maine 04011. Phone: 207-725-7025. Fax: 509-693-8868. E-mail: info@apogeeadventures.com.
URL www.apogeeadventures.com

Apogee Outdoor Adventures–Coast to Quebec

Apogee Outdoor Adventures
Locations Canada, Maine.

General Information Coed travel community service program, wilderness program, and adventure program established in 2001.
Program Focus Teamwork, character building, and fun.
Special Interest Areas Community service, touring.
Sports Bicycling.
Wilderness/Outdoors Bicycle trips, rafting, white-water trips.
Program Information 1–3 sessions per year. Session length: 15 days in June, July, August. Ages: 14–17. 6–12 participants per session. Cost: $2395–$2495. Financial aid available.
Housing Tents and youth hostels.
Application Deadline Continuous.
Jobs Positions for college students 21 and older.
Contact Mr. Kevin Cashman, Director, 40 Bowker Street, Brunswick, Maine 04011. Phone: 207-725-7025. Fax: 509-693-8868. E-mail: info@apogeeadventures.com.
URL www.apogeeadventures.com

Apogee Outdoor Adventures–New England Mountains and Coast

Apogee Outdoor Adventures
Locations Maine, Massachusetts, New Hampshire.

General Information Coed travel wilderness program and adventure program established in 2001.
Sports Climbing (wall), sea kayaking.
Wilderness/Outdoors Backpacking, hiking, wilderness camping.
Program Information 2 sessions per year. Session length: 1 week in June, July, August. Ages: 11–13. 7–12 participants per session. Cost: $895–$995. Financial aid available.
Housing Tents.
Application Deadline Continuous.
Jobs Positions for college students 21 and older.
Contact Mr. Kevin Cashman, Director, 40 Bowker Street, Brunswick, Maine 04011. Phone: 207-725-7025. Fax: 509-693-8868. E-mail: info@apogeeadventures.com.
URL www.apogeeadventures.com

ATW: Action America West

American Trails West
Locations Alabama, Arizona, California, Nevada, Utah, Wyoming.

General Information Coed travel adventure program established in 1966.
Special Interest Areas Touring.
Sports Bicycling, boating, horseback riding, in-line skating, swimming, tennis, waterskiing.
Wilderness/Outdoors Hiking, mountain biking, rafting.
Excursions College tours.
Program Information 1–2 sessions per year. Session length: 25 days in July, August. Ages: 13–17. 40–45 participants per session. Cost: $4695.
Housing College dormitories, hotels, and tents.
Application Deadline Continuous.
Jobs Positions for college students 20 and older.
Contact Director, 92 Middle Neck Road, Great Neck, New York 11021. Phone: 800-645-6260. Fax: 516-487-2855. E-mail: info@americantrailswest.com.
URL www.americantrailswest.com
For more information, see page 982.

ATW: Adventure Roads

American Trails West
Locations Canada, District of Columbia, Florida, Georgia, Louisiana, Massachusetts, Pennsylvania, South Carolina, Virginia.

General Information Coed travel adventure program established in 1966.
Special Interest Areas Touring.
Sports Bicycling, boating, horseback riding, in-line skating, swimming, tennis.
Wilderness/Outdoors Hiking, mountain biking, rafting.
Excursions College tours.
Program Information 1–2 sessions per year. Session length: 30 days in July, August. Ages: 13–15. 40–45 participants per session. Cost: $5595.
Housing Hotels.
Application Deadline Continuous.
Jobs Positions for college students 20 and older.
Contact Director, 92 Middle Neck Road, Great Neck, New York 11021. Phone: 800-645-6260. Fax: 516-487-2855. E-mail: info@americantrailswest.com.
URL www.americantrailswest.com
For more information, see page 982.

ATW: American Horizons

American Trails West
Locations Arizona, California, Canada, Colorado, Illinois, Michigan, Minnesota, Nevada, New York, Ohio, Pennsylvania, South Dakota, Utah, Wyoming.

General Information Coed travel adventure program established in 1966.
Special Interest Areas Touring.
Sports Bicycling, boating, horseback riding, in-line skating, swimming, tennis, waterskiing.
Wilderness/Outdoors Hiking, mountain biking, rafting.
Excursions College tours.
Program Information 2–3 sessions per year. Session length: 45 days in July, August. Ages: 13–17. 40–45 participants per session. Cost: $7095.
Housing College dormitories, hotels, and tents.
Application Deadline Continuous.
Jobs Positions for college students 20 and older.
Contact Director, 92 Middle Neck Road, Great Neck, New York 11021. Phone: 800-645-6260. Fax: 516-487-2855. E-mail: info@americantrailswest.com.
URL www.americantrailswest.com
For more information, see page 982.

ATW: California Sunset

American Trails West
Locations Arizona, California, Nevada.

General Information Coed travel adventure program established in 1966.
Special Interest Areas Touring.
Sports Bicycling, boating, horseback riding, in-line skating, swimming, tennis, waterskiing.
Wilderness/Outdoors Hiking, mountain biking, rafting.
Excursions College tours.
Program Information 1–3 sessions per year. Session length: 3 weeks in July, August. Ages: 13–17. 40–45 participants per session. Cost: $5095.
Housing College dormitories and hotels.
Application Deadline Continuous.
Jobs Positions for college students 20 and older.
Contact Director, 92 Middle Neck Road, Great Neck, New York 11021. Phone: 800-645-6260. Fax: 516-487-2855. E-mail: info@americantrailswest.com.
URL www.americantrailswest.com

For more information, see page 982.

ATW: Camp Inn 42

American Trails West
Locations Arizona, California, Canada, Hawaii, Montana, Nevada, Utah, Washington, Wyoming.

General Information Coed travel adventure program established in 1966.
Special Interest Areas Touring.
Sports Bicycling, boating, horseback riding, in-line skating, skiing (downhill), snorkeling, swimming, tennis, waterskiing.
Wilderness/Outdoors Hiking, mountain biking, rafting.
Excursions College tours.
Program Information 3–4 sessions per year. Session length: 6 weeks in July, August. Ages: 13–18. 40–45 participants per session. Cost: $7695.
Housing College dormitories, hotels, and tents.
Application Deadline Continuous.
Jobs Positions for college students 20 and older.
Contact Director, 92 Middle Neck Road, Great Neck, New York 11021. Phone: 800-645-6260. Fax: 516-487-2855. E-mail: info@americantrailswest.com.
URL www.americantrailswest.com

For more information, see page 982.

ATW: Discoverer

American Trails West
Locations Arizona, California, Colorado, Nevada, South Dakota, Utah, Wyoming.

General Information Coed travel adventure program established in 1966.
Special Interest Areas Touring.
Sports Bicycling, boating, horseback riding, in-line skating, swimming, tennis, waterskiing.
Wilderness/Outdoors Hiking, mountain biking, rafting.
Excursions College tours.

ATW: Discoverer

Program Information 2–3 sessions per year. Session length: 30 days in July, August. Ages: 13–17. 40–45 participants per session. Cost: $5995.
Housing College dormitories, hotels, and tents.
Application Deadline Continuous.
Jobs Positions for college students 20 and older.
Contact Director, 92 Middle Neck Road, Great Neck, New York 11021. Phone: 800-645-6260. Fax: 516-487-2855. E-mail: info@americantrailswest.com.
URL www.americantrailswest.com

For more information, see page 982.

ATW: Fire and Ice

American Trails West
Locations Alaska, California, Canada, Hawaii, Washington.

General Information Coed travel adventure program established in 1966.
Special Interest Areas Touring.
Sports Bicycling, boating, horseback riding, in-line skating, skiing (downhill), snorkeling, swimming, tennis, waterskiing.
Wilderness/Outdoors Rafting.
Excursions College tours.
Program Information 1–2 sessions per year. Session length: 5 weeks in July, August. Ages: 14–17. 40–45 participants per session. Cost: $7995.
Housing Hotels.
Application Deadline Continuous.
Jobs Positions for college students 20 and older.
Contact Director, 92 Middle Neck Road, Great Neck, New York 11021. Phone: 800-645-6260. Fax: 516-487-2855. E-mail: info@americantrailswest.com.
URL www.americantrailswest.com

For more information, see page 982.

ATW: Mini Tours

American Trails West
Locations Canada, Florida, Maine, Maryland, Massachusetts, New Hampshire, New York, Pennsylvania, Virginia.

ATW: Mini Tours (continued)

General Information Coed travel cultural program and adventure program established in 1966.
Program Focus Travel Monday through Friday, home on the weekends.
Special Interest Areas Touring.
Sports Bicycling, boating, horseback riding, in-line skating, swimming, tennis, waterskiing.
Wilderness/Outdoors Hiking, mountain biking, rafting.
Program Information 4–6 sessions per year. Session length: 3–7 weeks in July, August. Ages: 12–15. 40–45 participants per session. Cost: $2895–$6990.
Housing Hotels.
Application Deadline Continuous.
Jobs Positions for college students 20 and older.
Contact Director, 92 Middle Neck Road, Great Neck, New York 11021. Phone: 800-645-6260. Fax: 516-487-2855. E-mail: info@americantrailswest.com.
URL www.americantrailswest.com

For more information, see page 982.

ATW: Pacific Paradise

American Trails West
Locations Arizona, California, Canada, Montana, Nevada, Utah, Washington, Wyoming.

General Information Coed travel adventure program established in 1966.
Special Interest Areas Touring.
Sports Bicycling, boating, horseback riding, in-line skating, swimming, tennis, waterskiing.
Wilderness/Outdoors Hiking, mountain biking, rafting.
Excursions College tours.
Program Information 1–2 sessions per year. Session length: 40 days in July, August. Ages: 13–17. 40–45 participants per session. Cost: $8195.
Housing College dormitories and hotels.
Application Deadline Continuous.
Jobs Positions for college students 20 and older.
Contact Director, 92 Middle Neck Road, Great Neck, New York 11021. Phone: 800-645-6260. Fax: 516-487-2855. E-mail: info@americantrailswest.com.
URL www.americantrailswest.com

For more information, see page 982.

ATW: Skyblazer

American Trails West
Locations Arizona, California, Canada, Colorado, Montana, Nevada, Oregon, South Dakota, Utah, Washington, Wyoming.

General Information Coed travel adventure program established in 1966.
Special Interest Areas Touring.
Sports Bicycling, boating, horseback riding, in-line skating, skiing (downhill), swimming, tennis, waterskiing.
Wilderness/Outdoors Hiking, mountain biking, rafting.
Excursions College tours.
Program Information 1–2 sessions per year. Session length: 6 weeks in July, August. Ages: 14–17. 40–45 participants per session. Cost: $7195.
Housing College dormitories, hotels, and tents.
Application Deadline Continuous.
Jobs Positions for college students 20 and older.
Contact Director, 92 Middle Neck Road, Great Neck, New York 11021. Phone: 800-645-6260. Fax: 516-487-2855. E-mail: info@americantrailswest.com.
URL www.americantrailswest.com

For more information, see page 982.

ATW: Sunblazer

American Trails West
Locations Arizona, California, Nevada, Utah.

General Information Coed travel adventure program established in 1966.
Special Interest Areas Touring.
Sports Bicycling, boating, horseback riding, in-line skating, swimming, tennis, waterskiing.
Wilderness/Outdoors Hiking, mountain biking, rafting.
Excursions College tours.
Program Information 2–3 sessions per year. Session length: 3 weeks in July, August. Ages: 13–17. 40–45 participants per session. Cost: $4595.
Housing College dormitories, hotels, and tents.
Application Deadline Continuous.
Jobs Positions for college students 20 and older.
Contact Director, 92 Middle Neck Road, Great Neck, New York 11021. Phone: 800-645-6260. Fax: 516-487-2855. E-mail: info@americantrailswest.com.
URL www.americantrailswest.com

For more information, see page 982.

ATW: Wayfarer

American Trails West
Locations Arizona, California, Canada, Colorado, Illinois, Michigan, Minnesota, Nevada, New York, South Dakota, Utah, Wyoming.

General Information Coed travel adventure program established in 1966.
Special Interest Areas Touring.
Sports Bicycling, boating, horseback riding, in-line skating, swimming, tennis, waterskiing.
Wilderness/Outdoors Hiking, mountain biking, rafting.
Excursions College tours.
Program Information 5–6 sessions per year. Session length: 6 weeks in July, August. Ages: 13–18. 40–45 participants per session. Cost: $6795.
Housing College dormitories, hotels, and tents.
Application Deadline Continuous.
Jobs Positions for college students 20 and older.
Contact Director, 92 Middle Neck Road, Great Neck, New York 11021. Phone: 800-645-6260. Fax: 516-487-2855. E-mail: info@americantrailswest.com.
URL www.americantrailswest.com

For more information, see page 982.

Barton Adventure Camp

The Barton Center for Diabetes Education, Inc.
Locations Maine, Massachusetts, New Hampshire, New York.

General Information Coed travel outdoor program, wilderness program, and special needs program established in 1994. Accredited by American Camping Association. Specific services available for the diabetic.
Program Focus Outdoor adventure for teens with diabetes.
Academics Environmental science.
Special Interest Areas Campcraft, diabetic education, leadership training, nature study.
Sports Bicycling, canoeing, kayaking, rappelling, ropes course, sea kayaking.
Wilderness/Outdoors Backpacking, canoe trips, hiking, mountain biking, mountaineering, orienteering, rafting, rock climbing, survival training, white-water trips, wilderness camping.
Excursions Day, overnight.
Program Information 2 sessions per year. Session length: 2 weeks in June, July, August. Ages: 13–19. 7 participants per session. Cost: $2000. Application fee: $50.
Housing Tents.
Application Deadline Continuous.
Jobs Positions for college students 21 and older.
Contact Gaylen McCann, Resident Camps Director, PO Box 356, 30 Ennis Road, North Oxford, Massachusetts 01537. Phone: 508-987-3856. Fax: 508-987-2002. E-mail: gaylen.mccann@bartoncenter.org.
URL www.bartoncenter.org

BICYCLE TRAVEL ADVENTURES–Student Hosteling Program–A Thousand Miles: Massachusetts to Nova Scotia

BICYCLE TRAVEL ADVENTURES–Student Hosteling Program
Locations Canada, Maine, Massachusetts, New Hampshire, Vermont.

General Information Coed travel outdoor program and adventure program established in 1970. Accredited by American Camping Association. Formal opportunities for the academically talented. Specific services available for the emotionally challenged and learning disabled. High school credit may be earned.
Program Focus A moderate-to-challenging 25-day bicycling/camping trip starting at SHP headquarters in Massachusetts and cycling a thousand miles to Nova Scotia.
Special Interest Areas Campcraft, field trips (arts and culture), touring.
Sports Bicycling, boating, canoeing, fishing, sailing, swimming.
Wilderness/Outdoors Bicycle trips, canoe trips, hiking, mountain biking, wilderness camping.
Excursions Day, overnight, shopping.
Program Information 1–2 sessions per year. Session length: 25 days in June, July, August. Ages: 15–18. 8–12 participants per session. Cost: $2495.
Housing Tents and youth hostels.
Application Deadline Continuous.
Jobs Positions for high school students 16 and older and college students 18 and older.
Contact Ted Lefkowitz, Director, 1356 Ashfield Road, PO Box 419, Conway, Massachusetts 01341. Phone: 800-343-6132. Fax: 413-369-4257. E-mail: shpbike@aol.com.
URL www.bicycletrips.com

For more information, see page 994.

BICYCLE TRAVEL ADVENTURES–Student Hosteling Program–Canadian Rockies to California

BICYCLE TRAVEL ADVENTURES–Student Hosteling Program
Locations California, Canada, Oregon, Washington.

General Information Coed travel outdoor program and adventure program established in 1970. Accredited by American Camping Association. Formal opportunities for the academically talented. Specific services available for the emotionally challenged and learning disabled. High school credit may be earned.
Program Focus A moderate-to-challenging 39-day trip traveling through the Canadian Rockies, Washington state, Oregon, and ending with a 3-day stay in San Francisco.
Special Interest Areas Campcraft, field trips (arts and culture), touring.
Sports Bicycling, boating, canoeing, fishing, sailing, swimming.
Wilderness/Outdoors Bicycle trips, canoe trips, hiking, mountain biking, wilderness camping.
Excursions Cultural, day, overnight, shopping.
Program Information 1 session per year. Session length: 39 days in June, July, August. Ages: 15–18. 8–12 participants per session. Cost: $4320; including airfare from Boston, MA to Edmonton, Alberta, Canada.
Housing Tents and youth hostels.
Application Deadline Continuous.
Jobs Positions for high school students 16 and older and college students 18 and older.
Contact Ted Lefkowitz, Director, 1356 Ashfield Road, PO Box 419, Conway, Massachusetts 01341. Phone: 800-343-6132. Fax: 413-369-4257. E-mail: shpbike@aol.com.
URL www.bicycletrips.com

For more information, see page 994.

BICYCLE TRAVEL ADVENTURES–Student Hosteling Program–Cross-Country America

BICYCLE TRAVEL ADVENTURES–Student Hosteling Program
Locations Colorado, Idaho, Illinois, Indiana, Kansas, Kentucky, Massachusetts, Missouri, Montana, New Jersey, Ohio, Pennsylvania, Washington, West Virginia, Wyoming.

General Information Coed travel outdoor program and adventure program established in 1970. Accredited by American Camping Association. Formal opportunities

BICYCLE TRAVEL ADVENTURES–Student Hosteling Program–Cross-Country America (continued)

for the academically talented. Specific services available for the emotionally challenged and learning disabled. High school credit may be earned.
Program Focus A 60-day challenging bicycling/camping tour starting in Seattle, Washington and crossing America, ending at the New Jersey coast.
Special Interest Areas Campcraft, field trips (arts and culture), touring.
Sports Bicycling, boating, canoeing, fishing, sailing, swimming.
Wilderness/Outdoors Bicycle trips, canoe trips, hiking, mountain biking, wilderness camping.
Excursions Day, overnight, shopping.
Program Information 1 session per year. Session length: 60 days in June, July, August. Ages: 15–18. 8–12 participants per session. Cost: $4325; including airfare from Boston, MA to Seattle, WA.
Housing Tents and youth hostels.
Application Deadline Continuous.
Jobs Positions for high school students 16 and older and college students 18 and older.
Contact Ted Lefkowitz, Director, 1356 Ashfield Road, PO Box 419, Conway, Massachusetts 01341. Phone: 800-343-6132. Fax: 413-369-4257. E-mail: shpbike@aol.com.
URL www.bicycletrips.com

For more information, see page 994.

BICYCLE TRAVEL ADVENTURES–Student Hosteling Program–Maine-Nova Scotia Coast Loop

BICYCLE TRAVEL ADVENTURES–Student Hosteling Program
Locations Canada, Maine, Massachusetts.

General Information Coed travel outdoor program and adventure program established in 1970. Accredited by American Camping Association. Formal opportunities for the academically talented. Specific services available for the emotionally challenged and learning disabled. High school credit may be earned.
Program Focus A moderate 25-day bicycling/camping tour that begins in Bar Harbor, Maine and ends in Nova Scotia, Canada.
Special Interest Areas Campcraft, field trips (arts and culture), touring.
Sports Bicycling, boating, canoeing, fishing, sailing, swimming.
Wilderness/Outdoors Bicycle trips, canoe trips, hiking, mountain biking, wilderness camping.
Excursions Day, overnight, shopping.
Program Information 1–2 sessions per year. Session length: 25 days in June, July, August. Ages: 13–16. 8–12 participants per session. Cost: $2395.
Housing Tents and youth hostels.
Application Deadline Continuous.
Jobs Positions for high school students 16 and older and college students 18 and older.
Contact Ted Lefkowitz, Director, 1356 Ashfield Road, PO Box 419, Conway, Massachusetts 01341. Phone: 800-343-6132. Fax: 413-369-4257. E-mail: shpbike@aol.com.
URL www.bicycletrips.com

For more information, see page 994.

BICYCLE TRAVEL ADVENTURES–Student Hosteling Program–Niagara Falls to Montreal

BICYCLE TRAVEL ADVENTURES–Student Hosteling Program
Locations Canada, Massachusetts, New York.

General Information Coed travel outdoor program and adventure program established in 1970. Accredited by American Camping Association. Formal opportunities for the academically talented. Specific services available for the emotionally challenged and learning disabled. High school credit may be earned.

BICYCLE TRAVEL ADVENTURES–Student Hosteling Program–Niagara Falls to Montreal

Program Focus A moderate 25-day bicycling/camping/hosteling tour that begins at spectacular Niagara Falls and ends with a stay in French-speaking Montreal.
Special Interest Areas Campcraft, field trips (arts and culture), touring.
Sports Bicycling, boating, canoeing, fishing, sailing, swimming.
Wilderness/Outdoors Bicycle trips, canoe trips, hiking, mountain biking, wilderness camping.
Excursions Cultural, day, overnight, shopping.
Program Information 1–2 sessions per year. Session length: 25 days in June, July, August. Ages: 13–16. 8–12 participants per session. Cost: $2360.
Housing College dormitories, tents, and youth hostels.
Application Deadline Continuous.
Jobs Positions for high school students 16 and older and college students 18 and older.
Contact Ted Lefkowitz, Director, 1356 Ashfield Road, PO Box 419, Conway, Massachusetts 01341. Phone: 800-343-6132. Fax: 413-369-4257. E-mail: shpbike@aol.com.
URL www.bicycletrips.com

For more information, see page 994.

BICYCLE TRAVEL ADVENTURES–STUDENT HOSTELING PROGRAM–OFF-ROAD VERMONT

BICYCLE TRAVEL ADVENTURES–Student Hosteling Program
Locations Massachusetts, New York, Vermont.

General Information Coed travel outdoor program and adventure program established in 1970. Accredited by American Camping Association. Formal opportunities for the academically talented. Specific services available for the emotionally challenged and learning disabled. High school credit may be earned.
Program Focus An 18-day off-road biking trip utilizing the trails of major Vermont ski areas such as Mount Snow and Killington.
Special Interest Areas Campcraft, field trips (arts and culture), touring.
Sports Bicycling, boating, canoeing, fishing, sailing, swimming.
Wilderness/Outdoors Bicycle trips, canoe trips, hiking, mountain biking, wilderness camping.
Excursions Overnight.
Program Information 1–2 sessions per year. Session length: 18 days in June, July, August. Ages: 13–16. 8–12 participants per session. Cost: $2235.
Housing Tents.
Application Deadline Continuous.
Jobs Positions for high school students 16 and older and college students 18 and older.
Contact Ted Lefkowitz, Director, 1356 Ashfield Road, PO Box 419, Conway, Massachusetts 01341. Phone: 800-343-6132. Fax: 413-369-4257. E-mail: shpbike@aol.com.
URL www.bicycletrips.com

For more information, see page 994.

BICYCLE TRAVEL ADVENTURES–STUDENT HOSTELING PROGRAM–PACIFIC COAST ADVENTURE: WASHINGTON, OREGON, AND CALIFORNIA

BICYCLE TRAVEL ADVENTURES–Student Hosteling Program
Locations California, Oregon, Washington.

General Information Coed travel outdoor program and adventure program established in 1970. Accredited by American Camping Association. Formal opportunities for the academically talented. Specific services available for the emotionally challenged and learning disabled. High school credit may be earned.
Program Focus A moderate 30-day bicycling/camping/hosteling tour cycling from Washington state through Oregon and ending with a 3-day stay in San Francisco.
Special Interest Areas Campcraft, field trips (arts and culture), touring.
Sports Bicycling, boating, canoeing, fishing, sailing, swimming.
Wilderness/Outdoors Bicycle trips, canoe trips, hiking, mountain biking, wilderness camping.
Excursions Cultural, day, overnight, shopping.
Program Information 1–2 sessions per year. Session length: 30 days in June, July, August. Ages: 14–18. 8–12 participants per session. Cost: $3610; including airfare from Boston, MA to Seattle, WA.
Housing Tents and youth hostels.
Application Deadline Continuous.
Jobs Positions for high school students 16 and older and college students 18 and older.
Contact Ted Lefkowitz, Director, 1356 Ashfield Road, PO Box 419, Conway, Massachusetts 01341. Phone: 800-343-6132. Fax: 413-369-4257. E-mail: shpbike@aol.com.
URL www.bicycletrips.com

For more information, see page 994.

BICYCLE TRAVEL ADVENTURES–STUDENT HOSTELING PROGRAM–VERMONT

BICYCLE TRAVEL ADVENTURES–Student Hosteling Program
Locations Massachusetts, New Hampshire, Vermont.

General Information Coed travel outdoor program and adventure program established in 1970. Accredited by American Camping Association. Formal opportunities for the academically talented. Specific services available for the emotionally challenged and learning disabled. High school credit may be earned.
Program Focus A 16-day moderate bicycling/camping tour through the valleys of the Green Mountains and the Connecticut River Valley of Vermont.
Special Interest Areas Campcraft, field trips (arts and culture), touring.
Sports Bicycling, boating, canoeing, fishing, sailing, swimming.
Wilderness/Outdoors Bicycle trips, canoe trips, hiking, mountain biking, wilderness camping.
Excursions Day, overnight, shopping.
Program Information 1–5 sessions per year. Session length: 16 days in June, July, August. Ages: 13–18. 8–12 participants per session. Cost: $1475.
Housing Tents and youth hostels.
Application Deadline Continuous.
Jobs Positions for high school students 16 and older and college students 18 and older.
Contact Ted Lefkowitz, Director, 1356 Ashfield Road, PO Box 419, Conway, Massachusetts 01341. Phone: 800-343-6132. Fax: 413-369-4257. E-mail: shpbike@aol.com.
URL www.bicycletrips.com

For more information, see page 994.

BICYCLE TRAVEL ADVENTURES–STUDENT HOSTELING PROGRAM–VERMONT TO THE ATLANTIC OCEAN

BICYCLE TRAVEL ADVENTURES–Student Hosteling Program
Locations Canada, Maine, Massachusetts, New Hampshire, Vermont.

General Information Coed travel outdoor program and adventure program established in 1970. Accredited by American Camping Association. Formal opportunities

BICYCLE TRAVEL ADVENTURES–Student Hosteling Program–Vermont to the Atlantic Ocean (continued)

for the academically talented. Specific services available for the emotionally challenged and learning disabled. High school credit may be earned.
Program Focus A 21-day moderate bicycling/camping tour that crosses Vermont and New Hampshire's White Mountains to the coast of Maine.
Special Interest Areas Campcraft, field trips (arts and culture), touring.
Sports Bicycling, boating, canoeing, fishing, sailing, swimming.
Wilderness/Outdoors Bicycle trips, canoe trips, hiking, mountain biking, wilderness camping.
Excursions Day, overnight, shopping.
Program Information 1–4 sessions per year. Session length: 3 weeks in June, July, August. Ages: 13–18. 8–12 participants per session. Cost: $2040.
Housing Tents and youth hostels.
Application Deadline Continuous.
Jobs Positions for high school students 16 and older and college students 18 and older.
Contact Ted Lefkowitz, Director, 1356 Ashfield Road, PO Box 419, Conway, Massachusetts 01341. Phone: 800-343-6132. Fax: 413-369-4257. E-mail: shpbike@aol.com.
URL www.bicycletrips.com

For more information, see page 994.

Camp Chi Teenage Adventure Trips

Camp Chi/Jewish Community Center of Chicago
Locations Canada, Minnesota, Montana, South Dakota, Washington, Wisconsin.

General Information Coed travel adventure program established in 1975. Religious affiliation: Jewish. Accredited by American Camping Association.
Special Interest Areas Personal development.
Sports Bicycling, kayaking.
Wilderness/Outdoors Backpacking, bicycle trips, canoe trips, hiking, mountain biking, orienteering, outdoor adventure, rafting.
Excursions Day.
Program Information 2 sessions per year. Session length: 34 days in July, August. Ages: 13+. 24 participants per session. Cost: $3200. Financial aid available. Open to participants entering grades 9–11.
Housing Tents.
Application Deadline Continuous.
Jobs Positions for college students.
Summer Contact Mr. Brad Finkel, Assistant Director, PO Box 104, Lake Delton, Wisconsin 53940. Phone: 608-253-1681. Fax: 608-253-4302. E-mail: info@campchi.com.
Winter Contact Mr. Brad Finkel, Assistant Director, 3050 Woodridge, Northbrook, Illinois 60062. Phone: 847-272-2301. Fax: 847-272-5357. E-mail: info@campchi.com.
URL www.campchi.com

Camp Friendship Challenge Program

Camp Friendship
Locations Maine, North Carolina, Virginia, West Virginia.

General Information Coed travel wilderness program established in 1981. Accredited by American Camping Association.
Special Interest Areas Campcraft.
Sports Bicycling, canoeing, climbing (wall), fishing, hang gliding, horseback riding, kayaking, rappelling, ropes course, scuba diving, waterskiing.
Wilderness/Outdoors Backpacking, bicycle trips, canoe trips, caving, hiking, mountain biking, mountaineering, orienteering, outdoor adventure, rafting, rock climbing, white-water trips, wilderness camping.
Program Information Session length: 1–2 weeks in June, July, August. Ages: 11–16. 12 participants per session. Cost: $675–$1350. Financial aid available.
Housing Tents.
Application Deadline Continuous.
Jobs Positions for college students 21 and older.
Contact Ray Ackenbom, Co-Director, PO Box 145, Palmyra, Virginia 22963. Phone: 434-589-8950. Fax: 434-589-5880. E-mail: info@campfriendship.com.
URL www.campfriendship.com

Camp Tawonga–Teen Quest: Northwest

Camp Tawonga (Tawonga Jewish Community Corp.)
Locations California, Oregon.

General Information Coed travel wilderness program and adventure program established in 1926. Religious affiliation: Jewish. Accredited by American Camping Association.
Arts Theater/drama.
Special Interest Areas Touring.
Wilderness/Outdoors Backpacking, hiking, mountain biking, outdoor adventure, rafting, white-water trips.
Program Information 2 sessions per year. Session length: 3 weeks in July. 10–11 participants per session. Cost: $2840. Financial aid available. Open to participants entering grades 8–10.
Application Deadline Continuous.
Jobs Positions for college students 18 and older.
Contact Sara Rubinett, Office Manager, 131 Steuart Street, San Francisco, California 94105. Phone: 415-543-2267. Fax: 415-543-5417. E-mail: info@tawonga.org.
URL www.tawonga.org

Camp Tawonga–Teen Quest: Southwest

Camp Tawonga (Tawonga Jewish Community Corp.)
Locations Arizona, Nevada, Utah.

General Information Coed travel wilderness program and adventure program established in 1926. Religious affiliation: Jewish. Accredited by American Camping Association.
Academics Ecology.
Special Interest Areas Native American culture, touring.
Wilderness/Outdoors Backpacking, caving, hiking, outdoor adventure, rafting, white-water trips.

Program Information 1 session per year. Session length: 3 weeks in July. 10–11 participants per session. Cost: $2840. Financial aid available. Open to participants entering grades 9–11.
Application Deadline Continuous.
Jobs Positions for college students 18 and older.
Contact Sara Rubinett, Office Manager, 131 Steuart Street, San Francisco, California 94105. Phone: 415-543-2267. Fax: 415-543-5417. E-mail: info@tawonga.org.
URL www.tawonga.org

Cheerio Adventures–5 Rivers in 5 Days

YMCA of Greater High Point, North Carolina, Inc.
Locations Georgia, North Carolina, South Carolina, Tennessee.

General Information Coed travel wilderness program and adventure program established in 1982. Religious affiliation: Christian. Accredited by American Camping Association.
Wilderness/Outdoors Rafting, white-water trips, wilderness camping.
Excursions Day, overnight.
Program Information 2 sessions per year. Session length: 1 week in July. Ages: 14–17. 10 participants per session. Cost: $885. Financial aid available.
Housing Tents.
Application Deadline Continuous.
Jobs Positions for college students 19 and older.
Contact Keith Russell, Director, 1430 Camp Cheerio Road, Glade Valley, North Carolina 28627. Phone: 336-363-2604. Fax: 336-363-3671. E-mail: krussell@campcheerio.org.
URL www.cheerioadventures.com

College Impressions

College Impressions
Locations Connecticut, Maine, Massachusetts, New Hampshire, New Jersey, New York, Pennsylvania, Rhode Island, Vermont.

General Information Coed travel academic program established in 1980. Formal opportunities for the academically talented and gifted.
Program Focus Precollege orientation and motivational experiences designed to demystify the college admission process.
Academics College tours, writing.
Special Interest Areas College planning, touring.
Sports Basketball, running/jogging, swimming, volleyball.
Excursions College tours, overnight.
Program Information 10 sessions per year. Session length: 1 week in June, July. Ages: 15–18. 8 participants per session. Cost: $2000. Financial aid available.
Housing College dormitories.
Application Deadline Continuous.
Contact Arthur P. Mullaney, President, 64 Shore Drive, Kingston, Massachusetts 02364. Phone: 781-585-4070. Fax: 781-585-4070. E-mail: collegeimp@cape.com.

Discovery Works New England Community Service Experience

Musiker Tours
Locations Maine, Massachusetts, New Hampshire, Rhode Island, Vermont.

General Information Coed travel outdoor program, community service program, and adventure program established in 1966. High school credit may be earned.
Special Interest Areas Animal care, community service, conservation projects, touring.
Wilderness/Outdoors Rafting, white-water trips.
Excursions College tours, day.
Program Information 1 session per year. Session length: 4 weeks in June, July. Ages: 13–15. 30–45 participants per session. Cost: $4299.
Housing College dormitories and youth hostels.
Application Deadline Continuous.
Jobs Positions for college students 21 and older.
Contact James Musiker, Owner/Director, 1326 Old Northern Boulevard, Roslyn, New York 11576. Phone: 888-878-6637. Fax: 516-625-3438. E-mail: musiker@summerfun.com.
URL www.summerfun.com

For more information, see page 1214.

East Coast College Tour by Education Unlimited

Education Unlimited
Locations Connecticut, District of Columbia, Maryland, Massachusetts, New York, Pennsylvania, Rhode Island.

General Information Coed travel academic program established in 1999.
Program Focus Exploration of colleges on the east coast.
Academics College tours.
Special Interest Areas Career exploration, field trips (arts and culture), touring.
Excursions College tours, cultural, day, overnight, shopping.
Program Information 1 session per year. Session length: 1 week in July. Ages: 15–19. 12–36 participants per session. Cost: $1895. Financial aid available.
Housing College dormitories and hotels.
Application Deadline Continuous.
Contact Mr. Matthew Fraser, Executive Director, 1700 Shattuck Avenue, #305, Berkeley, California 94709. Phone: 510-548-6612. Fax: 510-548-0212. E-mail: camps@educationunlimited.com.
URL www.educationunlimited.com

ExploraMar: Marine Biology Sailing Expeditions–Sea of Cortez, Baja, Mexico

ExploraMar
Locations California, Mexico.

General Information Coed travel outdoor program and adventure program established in 1997.

ExploraMar: Marine Biology Sailing Expeditions–Sea of Cortez, Baja, Mexico (continued)

Program Focus Co-ed sailing, marine biology, island exploration.
Academics Spanish language/literature, biology, ecology, marine studies, oceanography.
Arts Arts and crafts (general), drawing.
Special Interest Areas Field research/expeditions, leadership training, nature study, nautical skills.
Sports Boating, fishing, sailing, snorkeling, swimming.
Wilderness/Outdoors Hiking.
Excursions Day, overnight.
Program Information 4–6 sessions per year. Session length: 8 days in June, July, August. Ages: 13–17. 9–18 participants per session. Cost: $1850–$2350.
Housing Yachts.
Application Deadline Continuous.
Jobs Positions for college students 21 and older.
Contact Mr. Tom Funkhouser, Director/Owner, 3 Fern Lane, Mill Valley, California 94941. Phone: 415-389-6644. Fax: 415-389-6644. E-mail: tom@exploramar.com.
URL www.exploramar.com

FLINT HILL SCHOOL–"SUMMER ON THE HILL"–ENRICHMENT ON THE HILL–WOMEN WRITERS' ADVENTURE

Flint Hill School
Locations Arizona, Colorado, New Mexico, Utah.

General Information Girls' travel arts program. High school credit may be earned.
Program Focus A writer's adventure.
Academics English language/literature, geology/earth science, intercultural studies, reading, writing.
Arts Arts and crafts (general), creative writing, drawing, photography.
Special Interest Areas Field research/expeditions, touring.
Wilderness/Outdoors Hiking, outdoor camping, rafting.
Excursions Cultural, day, overnight.
Program Information 1 session per year. Session length: 2 weeks in June, July. Ages: 14+. 2–40 participants per session. Cost: $1700. Mothers welcome, space permitting, priority given to girls enrolled.
Housing College dormitories and hotels.
Application Deadline Continuous.
Jobs Positions for high school students 16 and older and college students 18 and older.
Contact Ms. Peggy Laurent, Director of Special and Summer Programs, 3320 Jermantown Road, Oakton, Virginia 22124. Phone: 703-584-2315. Fax: 703-242-0718. E-mail: plaurent@flinthill.org.
URL www.flinthill.org

FOUR CORNERS SCHOOL OF OUTDOOR EDUCATION: SOUTHWEST ED-VENTURE

Prescott College
Locations Arizona, Colorado, New Mexico, Utah.

General Information Coed travel outdoor program, family program, community service program, wilderness program, cultural program, and adventure program established in 1984. Formal opportunities for the academically talented, artistically talented, and gifted. College credit may be earned.
Program Focus Outdoor education.
Academics Anthropology, archaeology, botany, ecology, environmental science, geology/earth science.
Arts Pottery, weaving.
Special Interest Areas Native American culture, community service, leadership training, team building, work camp programs.
Sports Sea kayaking, skiing (cross-country).
Wilderness/Outdoors Backpacking, canoe trips, hiking, outdoor adventure, rafting, wilderness camping.
Excursions Cultural, overnight.
Program Information 35–50 sessions per year. Session length: 3–14 days in January, February, March, April, May, June, July, August, September, October, November, December. Ages: 16+. 8–25 participants per session. Cost: $525–$2095. Financial aid available.
Housing Navajo hogans, college dormitories, host-family homes, hotels, and tents.
Application Deadline Continuous.
Jobs Positions for college students 18 and older.
Contact David Bragg, SW Ed-Ventures Program Manager, PO Box 1029, Monticello, Utah 84535. Phone: 435-587-2156. Fax: 435-587-2193. E-mail: dbragg@fourcornersschool.org.
URL www.sw-adventures.org

GERONIMO PROGRAM

Geronimo Program
Locations Bahamas, Bermuda, Maine, Massachusetts, Rhode Island.

General Information Coed travel academic program, outdoor program, and adventure program established in 1974.
Program Focus Sailing and marine science, working with sea turtles and sharks.
Academics Area studies, biology, ecology, environmental science, marine studies, oceanography.
Special Interest Areas Field research/expeditions, field trips (arts and culture), nature study, navigation.
Sports Fishing, sailing, snorkeling, swimming.
Wilderness/Outdoors Sailing trips.
Excursions Overnight.
Program Information 2–3 sessions per year. Session length: 7–18 days in June, July, August. Ages: 15–19. 8 participants per session. Cost: $1400–$3800.
Housing Sailboats.
Application Deadline Continuous.
Contact Betsy Leslie, Program Coordinator, PO Box 1910, Newport, Rhode Island 02840-0190. Phone: 401-842-6702. Fax: 401-842-6696. E-mail: betsy_leslie@stgeorges.edu.
URL www.sailgeronimo.org

GREAT ESCAPES (ADVENTURE TRIPS FOR TEENS)–CANADIAN ADVENTURE

South Shore YMCA Camps
Locations Canada, New Hampshire.

General Information Coed travel outdoor program and adventure program established in 1989. Religious affiliation: Christian. Accredited by American Camping Association.
Program Focus Whitewater, group travel, cross-cultural experiences.
Special Interest Areas Cross-cultural education.
Sports Horseback riding.
Wilderness/Outdoors Mountain biking, outdoor adventure, rafting, white-water trips.
Program Information 1 session per year. Session length: 13 days in August. Ages: 14–17. 10–12 participants per session. Cost: $1195. Financial aid available.
Housing Tents and youth hostels.
Application Deadline Continuous.
Jobs Positions for college students 21 and older.
Contact Joseph O'Keefe, Great Escapes Director, 75 Stowe Road, Sandwich, Massachusetts 02563. Phone: 508-428-2571 Ext.110. Fax: 508-420-3545. E-mail: joeokeefe@ssymca.org.
URL www.ssymca.org/camps/great_escapes.asp

Great Escapes (Adventure Trips for Teens)–Colorado River and Canyons Adventure

South Shore YMCA Camps
Locations Colorado, Utah.

General Information Coed travel outdoor program and adventure program established in 1989. Religious affiliation: Christian. Accredited by American Camping Association.
Program Focus Multi-day river rafting/kayaking, mountain biking, canyoneering.
Special Interest Areas Native American culture, nature study.
Sports Kayaking.
Wilderness/Outdoors Hiking, mountain biking, rafting, wilderness camping, wilderness/outdoors (general).
Program Information 1 session per year. Session length: 13 days in June, July. Ages: 14–17. 10–12 participants per session. Cost: $1995; including airfare from Boston, MA to Salt Lake City, UT. Financial aid available.
Housing Tents.
Application Deadline Continuous.
Jobs Positions for college students 21 and older.
Contact Joseph O'Keefe, Great Escapes Director, 75 Stowe Road, Sandwich, Massachusetts 02563. Phone: 508-428-2571 Ext.110. Fax: 508-420-3545. E-mail: joeokeefe@ssymca.org.
URL www.ssymca.org/camps/great_escapes.asp

Great Escapes (Adventure Trips for Teens)–Rock and Rapids

South Shore YMCA Camps
Locations Massachusetts, Pennsylvania, West Virginia.

General Information Coed travel outdoor program and adventure program established in 1989. Religious affiliation: Christian. Accredited by American Camping Association.
Program Focus Rock climbing, white-water rafting, kayaking, caving.
Sports Kayaking, rappelling.
Wilderness/Outdoors Caving, hiking, mountain biking, rafting, rock climbing, white-water trips, wilderness/outdoors (general).
Program Information 1 session per year. Session length: 13 days in July, August. Ages: 14–17. 10–12 participants per session. Cost: $1095. Financial aid available.
Application Deadline Continuous.
Jobs Positions for college students 21 and older.
Contact Joseph O'Keefe, Great Escapes Director, 75 Stowe Road, Sandwich, Massachusetts 02563. Phone: 508-428-2571 Ext.110. Fax: 508-420-3545. E-mail: joeokeefe@ssymca.org.
URL www.ssymca.org/camps/great_escapes.asp

Great Escapes (Adventure Trips for Teens)–Saddle and Sail

South Shore YMCA Camps
Locations Massachusetts, New York, Vermont.

General Information Coed travel outdoor program and adventure program established in 1989. Religious affiliation: Christian. Accredited by American Camping Association.
Program Focus Sailing, horseback riding.
Special Interest Areas Animal care, leadership training, nature study, navigation.
Sports Boating, equestrian sports, horseback riding, sailing.
Wilderness/Outdoors Sailing trips.
Program Information 1 session per year. Session length: 13 days in July. Ages: 13–16. 10–12 participants per session. Cost: $1195; including airfare. Financial aid available.
Housing Tents.
Application Deadline Continuous.
Jobs Positions for college students 21 and older.
Contact Joseph O'Keefe, Great Escapes Director, 75 Stowe Road, Sandwich, Massachusetts 02563. Phone: 508-428-2571 Ext.110. Fax: 508-420-3545. E-mail: joeokeefe@ssymca.org.
URL www.ssymca.org

Hiker's Heaven Overnight Camp

KidsMakeADifference.org
Locations California, Nevada, Utah.

General Information Coed travel outdoor program and wilderness program established in 1994.
Program Focus Hiking.
Academics Botany, ecology, environmental science, geology/earth science, journalism, music, peace education, writing.
Arts Drawing, music, music (vocal), photography, television/video.

Hiker's Heaven Overnight Camp (continued)

Special Interest Areas Native American culture, campcraft, culinary arts, nature study, team building.
Sports Frisbee, swimming.
Wilderness/Outdoors Hiking, mountaineering, orienteering.
Excursions Day, overnight.
Program Information 1 session per year. Session length: 1 week in August. Ages: 7–13. 8 participants per session. Cost: $695. Financial aid available.
Housing Cabins, hotels, and tents.
Application Deadline Continuous.
Jobs Positions for college students 18 and older.
Contact Dr. Andy Mars, Director, PO Box 24922, West Los Angeles, California 90024-0922. Phone: 818-344-7838.
URL www.kidsmakeadifference.org

HULBERT VOYAGEURS YOUTH WILDERNESS TRIPS

Aloha Foundation, Inc.
Locations Canada, Maine, New Hampshire, New York, Vermont.

General Information Coed travel outdoor program, wilderness program, and adventure program established in 1996. Accredited by American Camping Association.
Program Focus Team building, environmental awareness, confidence.
Arts Music (vocal).
Special Interest Areas Campcraft, conservation projects, field research/expeditions, leadership training, nature study, team building.
Sports Canoeing, climbing (wall), fishing, kayaking, rappelling, ropes course, sea kayaking, swimming.
Wilderness/Outdoors Backpacking, canoe trips, hiking, orienteering, rafting, rock climbing, survival training, white-water trips, wilderness camping, wilderness/outdoors (general).
Excursions Cultural, overnight.
Program Information 15–20 sessions per year. Session length: 7–26 days in June, July, August. Ages: 10–17. 8–12 participants per session. Cost: $790–$3200. Financial aid available.
Housing Tents.
Application Deadline Continuous.
Jobs Positions for high school students 16 and older and college students 18 and older.
Contact Greg Auch, Director, Hulbert Voyageurs, 2968 Lake Morey Road, Fairlee, Vermont 05045-9400. Phone: 802-333-3405. Fax: 802-333-3404. E-mail: greg_auch@alohafoundation.org.
URL www.alohafoundation.org/hulbert

HURRICANE ISLAND OUTWARD BOUND–MID-ATLANTIC CANOEING, BACKPACKING, AND ROCK CLIMBING

Hurricane Island Outward Bound/Outward Bound, USA
Locations District of Columbia, Maryland, Pennsylvania.

General Information Coed travel wilderness program and adventure program established in 1964. College credit may be earned.
Program Focus Teamwork and leadership wilderness adventure.
Academics Environmental science, history.
Special Interest Areas Campcraft, communication skills, community service, first aid, leadership training, nature study, outdoor cooking, personal development, team building.
Sports Canoeing, rappelling.
Wilderness/Outdoors Backpacking, canoe trips, hiking, outdoor adventure, rock climbing, wilderness camping.
Excursions Overnight.
Program Information 3–9 sessions per year. Session length: 2 weeks in June, July, August. Ages: 14–20. Cost: $2095–$2295. Application fee: $95. Financial aid available.
Application Deadline Continuous.
Jobs Positions for college students 21 and older.
Contact Admissions Advisor, 75 Mechanic Street, Rockland, Maine 04841. Phone: 866-746-9771. Fax: 207-594-8202. E-mail: admissions@hurricaneisland.org.
URL www.hurricaneisland.org

HURRICANE ISLAND OUTWARD BOUND–OCEAN BOUND: TALL SHIP SAILING AND SEA KAYAKING SEMESTER

Hurricane Island Outward Bound/Outward Bound, USA
Locations Canada, Maine, Massachusetts.

General Information Coed travel wilderness program and adventure program established in 1964. College credit may be earned.
Program Focus Teamwork and leadership sailing adventure.
Academics Astronomy, biology, environmental science, history, marine studies, meteorology, oceanography.
Special Interest Areas Campcraft, community service, field research/expeditions, first aid, leadership training, nature study, nautical skills, navigation, personal development, team building, whale watching.
Sports Sailing, sea kayaking.
Wilderness/Outdoors Outdoor adventure, wilderness camping.
Excursions Overnight.
Program Information 1 session per year. Session length: 40 days in June, July, August. Ages: 16–18. 24 participants per session. Cost: $5995. Application fee: $95. Financial aid available.
Housing Sailboats.
Application Deadline Continuous.
Jobs Positions for college students 21 and older.
Contact Admissions Advisor, 75 Mechanic Street, Rockland, Maine 04841. Phone: 866-746-9771. Fax: 207-594-8202. E-mail: admissions@hurricaneisland.org.
URL www.hurricaneisland.org

Hurricane Island Outward Bound–Western Maine and New Hampshire Canoeing and Backpacking

Hurricane Island Outward Bound/Outward Bound, USA
Locations Maine, New Hampshire.

General Information Coed travel wilderness program and adventure program established in 1964. College credit may be earned.
Program Focus Teamwork and leadership wilderness adventure.
Academics Area studies, environmental science.
Special Interest Areas Native American culture, campcraft, community service, conservation projects, leadership training, nature study, outdoor cooking, personal development, team building.
Sports Canoeing.
Wilderness/Outdoors Backpacking, canoe trips, hiking, outdoor adventure, wilderness camping.
Excursions Overnight.
Program Information 2 sessions per year. Session length: 2 weeks in June, July, August. Ages: 15–17. Cost: $2095. Application fee: $95. Financial aid available.
Application Deadline Continuous.
Jobs Positions for college students 21 and older.
Contact Admissions Advisor, 75 Mechanic Street, Rockland, Maine 04841. Phone: 866-746-9771. Fax: 207-594-8202. E-mail: admissions@hurricaneisland.org.
URL www.hurricaneisland.org

Ibike Cultural Tours–Washington/British Columbia

International Bicycle Fund
Locations Canada, Washington.

General Information Coed travel outdoor program, cultural program, and adventure program established in 2000.
Program Focus Cross-cultural bicycle tour.
Academics Anthropology, architecture, area studies, art history/appreciation, botany, ecology, economics, environmental science, geography, geology/earth science, government and politics, history, intercultural studies, religion, social science, social studies.
Special Interest Areas Cross-cultural education, field trips (arts and culture), nature study.
Sports Bicycling, sea kayaking.
Wilderness/Outdoors Bicycle trips.
Excursions Cultural.
Program Information 1–2 sessions per year. Session length: 13–15 days in July, August. Ages: 16+. 6–12 participants per session. Cost: $1290–$1490. Financial aid available.
Housing Hotels and youth hostels.
Application Deadline Continuous.
Contact David Mozer, Director, 4887 Columbia Drive South, Seattle, Washington 98108-1919. Phone: 206-767-0848. Fax: 206-767-0848. E-mail: ibike@ibike.org.
URL www.ibike.org/ibike

Julian Krinsky Golf Tours

Julian Krinsky Camps and Programs
Locations District of Columbia, Maryland, Pennsylvania.

General Information Boys' travel sports camp established in 1986.
Program Focus High-quality golf instruction.
Sports Golf.
Excursions Cultural, day, overnight.
Program Information 1 session per year. Session length: 3 weeks in June, July, August. Ages: 13–17. 25 participants per session. Cost: $4145. Financial aid available.
Housing Hotels.
Application Deadline Continuous.
Jobs Positions for college students 21 and older.
Contact Julian Krinsky, Owner/Director, PO Box 333, Haverford, Pennsylvania 19041-0333. Phone: 800-TRY-JKST. Fax: 610-265-3678. E-mail: info@jkcp.com.
URL www.jkcp.com

For more information, see page 1172.

Kroka Expeditions–Advanced Rock Climbing

Kroka Expeditions of Vermont
Locations New Hampshire, New York.

General Information Coed travel outdoor program and wilderness program established in 1996.
Program Focus Intermediate to advanced level rock climbing.
Special Interest Areas Campcraft, community service.
Sports Climbing (wall), rappelling, swimming.
Wilderness/Outdoors Backpacking, hiking, mountaineering, orienteering, rock climbing, wilderness camping.
Excursions Day, overnight.
Program Information 1 session per year. Session length: 2 weeks in July, August. Ages: 14–18. 8–12 participants per session. Cost: $350–$1850. Financial aid available.
Housing Tents.
Application Deadline Continuous.
Jobs Positions for college students 18 and older.
Contact Misha Golfman, Executive Director, 659 West Hill Road, Putney, Vermont 05346. Phone: 802-387-5397. Fax: 802-387-4536. E-mail: kroka@sover.net.
URL www.kroka.org

Kroka Expeditions–Paddlers Journey Up North

Kroka Expeditions of Vermont
Locations Maine, Vermont.

General Information Coed travel outdoor program, wilderness program, and adventure program established in 1996. Specific services available for the learning disabled and physically challenged.
Program Focus Intermediate to advanced level whitewater paddling.
Academics Ecology, environmental science, geography, geology/earth science, marine studies.

Kroka Expeditions–Paddlers Journey Up North (continued)

Special Interest Areas Campcraft, community service, field research/expeditions, leadership training, nature study, nautical skills.
Sports Boating, canoeing, kayaking, rappelling, sea kayaking, swimming.
Wilderness/Outdoors Backpacking, canoe trips, climbing, hiking, mountaineering, orienteering, rafting, rock climbing, survival training, white-water trips, wilderness camping.
Excursions Day, overnight.
Program Information 1 session per year. Session length: 2 weeks in July. Ages: 12–18. 8–12 participants per session. Cost: $1750. Financial aid available.
Application Deadline Continuous.
Jobs Positions for college students 18 and older.
Contact Misha Golfman, Executive Director, 659 West Hill Road, Putney, Vermont 05346. Phone: 802-387-5397. Fax: 802-387-4536. E-mail: kroka@sover.net.
URL www.kroka.org

Longacre Expeditions, Adventure 28

Longacre Expeditions
Locations Canada, Maine.

General Information Coed travel outdoor program, wilderness program, and adventure program established in 1981. Accredited by American Camping Association.
Program Focus Effective communication skills, responsibility, and confidence building.
Sports Bicycling, sailing, sea kayaking.
Wilderness/Outdoors Bicycle trips, hiking, rock climbing, white-water trips, wilderness camping.
Program Information 1 session per year. Session length: 4 weeks in July. Ages: 13–17. 10–16 participants per session. Cost: $4595. Financial aid available.
Housing Sailboats and tents.
Application Deadline Continuous.
Jobs Positions for college students 21 and older.
Contact Meredith Schuler, Director, 4030 Middle Ridge Road, Newport, Pennsylvania 17074. Phone: 717-567-6790. Fax: 717-567-3955. E-mail: longacre@longacreexpeditions.com.
URL www.longacreexpeditions.com
For more information, see page 1200.

Longacre Expeditions, British Columbia

Longacre Expeditions
Locations Canada, Washington.

General Information Coed travel outdoor program, wilderness program, and adventure program established in 1981. Accredited by American Camping Association.
Program Focus Effective communication skills, responsibility, confidence building.
Sports Sea kayaking, skiing (glacial), snowboarding.
Wilderness/Outdoors Backpacking, hiking, rock climbing, wilderness camping.
Program Information 2 sessions per year. Session length: 15 days in July, August. Ages: 14–17. 13 participants per session. Cost: $2395.
Housing Tents.
Application Deadline Continuous.
Jobs Positions for college students 21 and older.
Contact Meredith Schuler, Director, 4030 Middle Ridge Road, Newport, Pennsylvania 17074. Phone: 717-567-6790. Fax: 717-567-3955. E-mail: longacre@longacreexpeditions.com.
URL www.longacreexpeditions.com
For more information, see page 1200.

Longacre Expeditions, New England/Canada

Longacre Expeditions
Locations Canada, Maine.

General Information Coed travel outdoor program, wilderness program, and adventure program established in 1981. Accredited by American Camping Association.
Program Focus Effective communication skills, responsibility, confidence building.
Sports Bicycling, sea kayaking, swimming.
Wilderness/Outdoors Backpacking, bicycle trips, rock climbing, white-water trips, wilderness camping.
Program Information 3 sessions per year. Session length: 18 days in June, July, August. Ages: 13–17. 10–16 participants per session. Cost: $2795.
Housing Tents.
Application Deadline Continuous.
Jobs Positions for college students 21 and older.
Contact Meredith Schuler, Director, 4030 Middle Ridge Road, Newport, Pennsylvania 17074. Phone: 717-567-6790. Fax: 717-567-3955. E-mail: longacre@longacreexpeditions.com.
URL www.longacreexpeditions.com
For more information, see page 1200.

Longacre Expeditions, Pacific Coast and Inlands

Longacre Expeditions
Locations Canada, Washington.

General Information Coed travel outdoor program, wilderness program, and adventure program established in 1981. Accredited by American Camping Association.
Program Focus Effective communication skills, responsibility, confidence building.
Special Interest Areas Nautical skills, whale watching.
Sports Bicycling, sailing, sea kayaking, skiing (downhill), snowboarding.
Wilderness/Outdoors Bicycle trips, hiking, rock climbing.
Program Information 2 sessions per year. Session length: 22 days in July, August. Ages: 13–17. 10–15 participants per session. Cost: $3495.
Housing Tents.
Application Deadline Continuous.
Jobs Positions for college students 21 and older.

Contact Meredith Schuler, Director, 4030 Middle Ridge Road, Newport, Pennsylvania 17074. Phone: 717-567-6790. Fax: 717-567-3955. E-mail: longacre@longacreexpeditions.com.
URL www.longacreexpeditions.com
For more information, see page 1200.

Longacre Expeditions, Volcanoes

Longacre Expeditions
Locations Oregon, Washington.

General Information Coed travel outdoor program, wilderness program, and adventure program established in 1981. Accredited by American Camping Association.
Program Focus Effective communication skills, responsibility, confidence building.
Academics Environmental science.
Sports Snowboarding, swimming.
Wilderness/Outdoors Bicycle trips, hiking, rafting, rock climbing, white-water trips, wilderness camping.
Program Information 2 sessions per year. Session length: 15 days in July, August. Ages: 13–15. 10–16 participants per session. Cost: $2595.
Housing Tents.
Application Deadline Continuous.
Jobs Positions for college students 21 and older.
Contact Meredith Schuler, Director, 4030 Middle Ridge Road, Newport, Pennsylvania 17074. Phone: 717-567-6790. Fax: 717-567-3955. E-mail: longacre@longacreexpeditions.com.
URL www.longacreexpeditions.com
For more information, see page 1200.

Longacre Expeditions, Western Challenge

Longacre Expeditions
Locations Canada, Oregon, Washington.

General Information Coed travel outdoor program, wilderness program, and adventure program established in 1981. Accredited by American Camping Association.
Program Focus Travel and wilderness adventure.
Sports Kayaking, sandboarding, skiing (downhill), snowboarding, surfing, swimming.
Wilderness/Outdoors Hiking, rafting, rock climbing, wilderness camping.
Program Information 2 sessions per year. Session length: 17 days in July. Ages: 14–17. 10–16 participants per session. Cost: $4795.
Housing Tents.
Application Deadline Continuous.
Jobs Positions for college students 21 and older.
Contact Meredith Schuler, Director, 4030 Middle Ridge Road, Newport, Pennsylvania 17074. Phone: 717-567-6790. Fax: 717-567-3955. E-mail: longacre@longacreexpeditions.com.
URL www.longacreexpeditions.com
For more information, see page 1200.

Luna Adventures with AAG SummerSkills

Albany Academy for Girls
Locations Maine, Vermont.

General Information Girls' travel outdoor program and adventure program established in 2004.
Sports Bicycling, canoeing, kayaking, sea kayaking.
Wilderness/Outdoors Hiking, mountain biking, rafting, rock climbing, white-water trips.
Excursions Overnight.
Program Information 3 sessions per year. Session length: 5 days in June, July. Ages: 10–15. 10 participants per session. Cost: $410–$475.
Application Deadline Continuous.
Contact Ms. Donna Keegan, Program Coordinator, 140 Academy Road, Albany, New York 12208. Phone: 518-463-2201. Fax: 518-463-5096.
URL www.albanyacademyforgirls.org

Mountain Workshop/Dirt Camp: Dirt Camp Junior Killington

Mountain Workshop
Locations Connecticut, Vermont.

General Information Coed travel outdoor program established in 2001.
Program Focus Off-road riding for strong, skilled mountain bikers.
Sports Bicycling.
Wilderness/Outdoors Mountain biking.
Excursions Overnight.
Program Information 1–3 sessions per year. Session length: 1 week in July, August. Ages: 12–17. 13–26 participants per session. Cost: $1100.
Application Deadline Continuous.
Jobs Positions for college students 21 and older.
Contact J. J. Jameson, Director, Dirt Camp, 9 Brookside Place, West Redding, Connecticut 06896. Phone: 203-544-0555. Fax: 203-544-0333. E-mail: jj@dirtcamp.com.
URL www.mountainworkshop.com

Musiker Tours: Action USA

Musiker Tours
Locations Arizona, California, Colorado, Idaho, Montana, Nevada, Utah, Wyoming.

General Information Coed travel outdoor program and adventure program established in 1966.
Special Interest Areas Touring.
Sports Basketball, bicycling, in-line skating, snorkeling, swimming, tennis, volleyball, waterskiing.
Wilderness/Outdoors Backpacking, bicycle trips, canoe trips, hiking, mountain biking, outdoor adventure, white-water trips.
Excursions College tours, day, shopping.
Program Information 1–3 sessions per year. Session length: 30 days in June, July. Ages: 13–17. 40–48 participants per session. Cost: $5599–$5899.
Housing College dormitories, hotels, and tents.
Application Deadline Continuous.

Musiker Tours: Action USA (continued)
Jobs Positions for college students 21 and older.
Contact James Musiker, Owner/Director, 1326 Old Northern Boulevard, Roslyn, New York 11576. Phone: 888-878-6637. Fax: 516-625-3438. E-mail: musiker@summerfun.com.
URL www.summerfun.com
For more information, see page 1214.

Musiker Tours: Alaska Aloha

Musiker Tours
Locations Alaska, California, Canada, Hawaii, Oregon, Washington.
General Information Coed travel adventure program established in 1966.
Special Interest Areas Touring.
Sports Basketball, bicycling, climbing (wall), skiing (downhill), snorkeling, swimming, tennis, volleyball, waterskiing.
Excursions College tours, cultural, day.
Program Information 1–3 sessions per year. Session length: 30 days in June, July. Ages: 15–18. 40–45 participants per session. Cost: $6899–$7199.
Housing Hotels.
Application Deadline Continuous.
Jobs Positions for college students 21 and older.
Contact James Musiker, Owner/Director, 1326 Old Northern Boulevard, Roslyn, New York 11576. Phone: 888-878-6637. Fax: 516-625-3438. E-mail: musiker@summerfun.com.
URL www.summerfun.com
For more information, see page 1214.

Musiker Tours: America Coast to Coast

Musiker Tours
Locations Arizona, California, Canada, Colorado, Idaho, Illinois, Michigan, Minnesota, Montana, Nevada, New York, South Dakota, Utah, Wisconsin, Wyoming.
General Information Coed travel outdoor program and adventure program established in 1966.
Special Interest Areas Touring.
Sports Basketball, bicycling, climbing (wall), in-line skating, sailing, sea kayaking, snorkeling, soccer, swimming, tennis, volleyball, waterskiing.
Wilderness/Outdoors Backpacking, bicycle trips, hiking, mountain biking, outdoor adventure, rafting, white-water trips.
Excursions College tours, day.
Program Information 1–3 sessions per year. Session length: 40 days in June, July. Ages: 13–17. 40–48 participants per session. Cost: $6299–$6599.
Housing College dormitories, hotels, and tents.
Application Deadline Continuous.
Jobs Positions for college students 21 and older.
Contact James Musiker, Owner/Director, 1326 Old Northern Boulevard, Roslyn, New York 11576. Phone: 888-878-6637. Fax: 516-625-3438. E-mail: musiker@summerfun.com.
URL www.summerfun.com
For more information, see page 1214.

Musiker Tours: Cali-Pacific Passport

Musiker Tours
Locations California, Canada, Nevada, Washington.
General Information Coed travel outdoor program and adventure program established in 1966.
Special Interest Areas Touring.
Sports Basketball, bicycling, climbing (wall), in-line skating, snorkeling, swimming, tennis, volleyball, waterskiing.
Wilderness/Outdoors Bicycle trips, hiking, outdoor adventure, rafting, white-water trips.
Excursions College tours, day.
Program Information 1–2 sessions per year. Session length: 3 weeks in June, July. Ages: 13–17. 40–48 participants per session. Cost: $4899–$5099.
Housing Hotels.
Application Deadline Continuous.
Jobs Positions for college students 21 and older.
Contact James Musiker, Owner/Director, 1326 Old Northern Boulevard, Roslyn, New York 11576. Phone: 888-878-6637. Fax: 516-625-3438. E-mail: musiker@summerfun.com.
URL www.summerfun.com
For more information, see page 1214.

Musiker Tours: ComboCamp America

Musiker Tours
Locations Arizona, California, Canada, Hawaii, Idaho, Montana, Nevada, Utah, Washington, Wyoming.
General Information Coed travel outdoor program and adventure program established in 1966.
Special Interest Areas Touring.
Sports Basketball, bicycling, canoeing, climbing (wall), in-line skating, rappelling, sea kayaking, skiing (downhill), snorkeling, swimming, tennis, volleyball, waterskiing.
Wilderness/Outdoors Backpacking, bicycle trips, canoe trips, hiking, mountain biking, outdoor adventure, rafting, rock climbing, white-water trips.
Excursions College tours, day.
Program Information 1–5 sessions per year. Session length: 6 weeks in June, July, August. Ages: 13–17. 40–48 participants per session. Cost: $7399–$7699.
Housing College dormitories, hotels, and tents.
Application Deadline Continuous.
Jobs Positions for college students 21 and older.
Contact James Musiker, Owner/Director, 1326 Old Northern Boulevard, Roslyn, New York 11576. Phone: 888-878-6637. Fax: 516-625-3438. E-mail: musiker@summerfun.com.
URL www.summerfun.com
For more information, see page 1214.

MUSIKER TOURS: DISCOVER AMERICA

Musiker Tours
Locations Arizona, California, Canada, Idaho, Montana, Nevada, Utah, Washington, Wyoming.

General Information Coed travel outdoor program and adventure program established in 1966.
Special Interest Areas Touring.
Sports Basketball, bicycling, boating, canoeing, climbing (wall), in-line skating, skiing (downhill), snorkeling, soccer, swimming, tennis, volleyball, waterskiing.
Wilderness/Outdoors Backpacking, bicycle trips, canoe trips, hiking, mountain biking, outdoor adventure, rafting, white-water trips.
Excursions College tours, day.
Program Information 1–2 sessions per year. Session length: 5 weeks in June, July, August. Ages: 13–17. 40–48 participants per session. Cost: $7099–$7499.
Housing Hotels.
Application Deadline Continuous.
Jobs Positions for college students 21 and older.
Contact James Musiker, Owner/Director, 1326 Old Northern Boulevard, Roslyn, New York 11576. Phone: 888-878-6637. Fax: 516-625-3438. E-mail: musiker@summerfun.com.
URL www.summerfun.com

For more information, see page 1214.

MUSIKER TOURS: EASTCOASTER

Musiker Tours
Locations Canada, District of Columbia, Florida, Massachusetts, New Hampshire, New York, Pennsylvania, South Carolina, Virginia.

General Information Coed travel outdoor program and adventure program established in 1966.
Special Interest Areas Touring.
Sports Basketball, bicycling, boating, canoeing, climbing (wall), in-line skating, skiing (downhill), street/roller hockey, swimming, tennis, volleyball, waterskiing.
Wilderness/Outdoors Backpacking, bicycle trips, hiking, mountain biking, outdoor adventure, rafting, rock climbing, white-water trips.
Excursions College tours, day.
Program Information 1–2 sessions per year. Session length: 30 days in June, July. Ages: 12–14. 40–48 participants per session. Cost: $4999–$5199.
Housing College dormitories, hotels, and tents.
Application Deadline Continuous.
Jobs Positions for college students 21 and older.
Contact James Musiker, Owner/Director, 1326 Old Northern Boulevard, Roslyn, New York 11576. Phone: 888-878-6637. Fax: 516-625-3438. E-mail: musiker@summerfun.com.
URL www.summerfun.com

For more information, see page 1214.

MUSIKER TOURS: WESTCOASTER

Musiker Tours
Locations Arizona, California, Nevada, Utah.

General Information Coed travel outdoor program and adventure program established in 1966.
Special Interest Areas Touring.
Sports Basketball, bicycling, in-line skating, sea kayaking, snorkeling, swimming, tennis, volleyball, waterskiing.
Wilderness/Outdoors Backpacking, bicycle trips, hiking, outdoor adventure, rafting, white-water trips.
Excursions College tours, day.
Program Information 1–4 sessions per year. Session length: 3 weeks in June, July. Ages: 13–17. 40–48 participants per session. Cost: $4399–$4599.
Housing College dormitories, hotels, and tents.
Application Deadline Continuous.
Jobs Positions for college students 21 and older.
Contact James Musiker, Owner/Director, 1326 Old Northern Boulevard, Roslyn, New York 11576. Phone: 888-878-6637. Fax: 516-625-3438. E-mail: musiker@summerfun.com.
URL www.summerfun.com

For more information, see page 1214.

92ND STREET Y CAMPS–THE TIYUL

92nd Street YM–YWHA
Locations Connecticut, Georgia, Maine, Massachusetts, New York, West Virginia.

General Information Coed travel community service program and bible camp established in 1955. Religious affiliation: Jewish. Accredited by American Camping Association.
Program Focus Informal Jewish education.
Academics Jewish studies, environmental science.
Special Interest Areas Community service, farming, gardening, leadership training, nature study, touring.
Program Information 1 session per year. Session length: 6 weeks in July, August. Ages: 15–18. 30–40 participants per session. Cost: $5000. Financial aid available.
Housing College dormitories, host-family homes, and hotels.
Application Deadline Continuous.
Jobs Positions for college students 21 and older.
Contact Mr. Alan Saltz, Director of Camp Programs, 1395 Lexington Avenue, New York, New York 10128. Phone: 212-415-5613. Fax: 212-415-5637. E-mail: camps@92y.org.
URL www.92y.org/camps

OUTWARD BOUND WEST–CATARACT CANYON RAFTING

Outward Bound West/Outward Bound, USA
Locations Colorado, Utah.

General Information Coed travel outdoor program and wilderness program established in 1965. College credit may be earned.
Program Focus Teamwork and leadership wilderness adventure.
Academics Environmental science.
Special Interest Areas Leadership training, outdoor cooking, personal development, team building.
Sports Swimming.
Wilderness/Outdoors Hiking, outdoor adventure, rafting, white-water trips, wilderness camping.

Outward Bound West–Cataract Canyon Rafting (continued)

Excursions Overnight.
Program Information 5 sessions per year. Session length: 1 week in July, August. Ages: 16+. Cost: $1295. Application fee: $95. Financial aid available.
Application Deadline Continuous.
Jobs Positions for college students 21 and older.
Contact Admissions Advisor, 910 Jackson Street, Golden, Colorado 80401. Phone: 866-746-9777. Fax: 720-497-2421. E-mail: info@obwest.org.
URL www.outwardboundwest.org

OVERLAND: ACADIA AND PRINCE EDWARD ISLAND BICYCLE TOURING AND SEA-KAYAKING

Overland Travel, Inc.
Locations Canada, Maine.

General Information Coed travel outdoor program and adventure program established in 1985. Accredited by American Camping Association. High school credit may be earned.
Program Focus Bicycle touring, camping, and sea-kayaking.
Special Interest Areas Leadership training, team building.
Sports Bicycling, canoeing, kayaking, sea kayaking.
Wilderness/Outdoors Bicycle trips, canoe trips.
Program Information 2–4 sessions per year. Session length: 3 weeks in June, July, August. Ages: 14–18. 8–12 participants per session. Cost: $2895.
Housing Tents.
Application Deadline Continuous.
Jobs Positions for college students 20 and older.
Contact Ms. Brooks Follansbee, Director, PO Box 31, Williamstown, Massachusetts 01267. Phone: 800-458-0588. Fax: 413-458-5208. E-mail: overland@adelphia.net.
URL www.overlandsummers.com

For more information, see page 1240.

OVERLAND: AMERICAN CHALLENGE COAST-TO-COAST BICYCLE TOURING

Overland Travel, Inc.
Locations Alabama, Arizona, Arkansas, California, Georgia, Mississippi, New Mexico, Oklahoma.

General Information Coed travel outdoor program and adventure program established in 1985. Accredited by American Camping Association. High school credit may be earned.
Program Focus Explore America by bicycle from coast-to-coast.
Special Interest Areas Leadership training, touring.
Sports Bicycling.
Wilderness/Outdoors Bicycle trips.
Program Information 3 sessions per year. Session length: 6 weeks in June, July, August. Ages: 15–19. 8–12 participants per session. Cost: $4795.
Housing Tents.
Application Deadline Continuous.
Jobs Positions for college students 20 and older.
Contact Ms. Brooks Follansbee, Director, PO Box 31, Williamstown, Massachusetts 01267. Phone: 800-458-0588. Fax: 413-458-5208. E-mail: overland@adelphia.net.
URL www.overlandsummers.com

For more information, see page 1240.

OVERLAND: AMERICAN COMMUNITY SERVICE, NEW ENGLAND

Overland Travel, Inc.
Locations Massachusetts, Vermont.

General Information Coed travel community service program established in 1985. Accredited by American Camping Association. High school credit may be earned.
Program Focus Community service.
Special Interest Areas Community service, conservation projects, construction, farming, leadership training, nature study, team building.
Sports Bicycling.
Wilderness/Outdoors Hiking.
Excursions Cultural, day, overnight.
Program Information 2 sessions per year. Session length: 2 weeks in June, July, August. Ages: 15–18. 10–12 participants per session. Cost: $2495.
Housing College dormitories.
Application Deadline Continuous.
Jobs Positions for college students 20 and older.
Contact Ms. Brooks Follansbee, Director, PO Box 31, Williamstown, Massachusetts 01267. Phone: 800-458-0588. Fax: 413-458-5208. E-mail: overland@adelphia.net.
URL www.overlandsummers.com

For more information, see page 1240.

OVERLAND: APPALACHIAN TRAIL CHALLENGE HIKING

Overland Travel, Inc.
Locations Massachusetts, New Hampshire, Vermont.

General Information Coed travel outdoor program, wilderness program, and adventure program established in 1985. Accredited by American Camping Association. High school credit may be earned.
Program Focus Challenge hiking on the Appalachian Trail.
Special Interest Areas Leadership training, team building.
Wilderness/Outdoors Backpacking, hiking, wilderness camping.
Program Information 1 session per year. Session length: 32 days in June, July, August. Ages: 15–19. 8 participants per session. Cost: $2995.
Housing Tents and youth hostels.
Application Deadline Continuous.
Jobs Positions for college students 20 and older.
Contact Ms. Brooks Follansbee, Director, PO Box 31, Williamstown, Massachusetts 01267. Phone: 800-458-0588. Fax: 413-458-5208. E-mail: overland@adelphia.net.
URL www.overlandsummers.com

For more information, see page 1240.

OVERLAND: COLORADO AND UTAH MOUNTAIN BIKING AND RAFTING

Overland Travel, Inc.
Locations Colorado, Utah.

General Information Coed travel outdoor program, wilderness program, and adventure program established in 1985. Accredited by American Camping Association. High school credit may be earned.
Program Focus Mountain biking and white-water rafting in Colorado and Utah, leadership skills.
Special Interest Areas Leadership training.
Sports Bicycling, kayaking.
Wilderness/Outdoors Bicycle trips, hiking, mountain biking, mountaineering, outdoor camping, rafting, rock climbing, white-water trips, wilderness camping.
Program Information 3 sessions per year. Session length: 2 weeks in June, July, August. Ages: 13–18. 8–21 participants per session. Cost: $2895.
Housing Tents.
Application Deadline Continuous.
Jobs Positions for college students 20 and older.
Contact Ms. Brooks Follansbee, Director, PO Box 31, Williamstown, Massachusetts 01267. Phone: 800-458-0588. Fax: 413-458-5208. E-mail: overland@adelphia.net.
URL www.overlandsummers.com

For more information, see page 1240.

OVERLAND: NEW ENGLAND EXPLORER HIKING, MOUNTAIN BIKING, AND RAFTING

Overland Travel, Inc.
Locations Maine, Massachusetts, New Hampshire, Vermont.

General Information Coed travel outdoor program, wilderness program, and adventure program established in 1985. Accredited by American Camping Association. High school credit may be earned.
Program Focus Explore New England by foot, bike and raft.
Special Interest Areas Leadership training, team building.
Sports Bicycling.
Wilderness/Outdoors Backpacking, bicycle trips, hiking, mountain biking, rafting, white-water trips, wilderness camping.
Program Information 3–6 sessions per year. Session length: 2 weeks in June, July, August. Ages: 13–16. 8–12 participants per session. Cost: $2495.
Housing Tents and youth hostels.
Application Deadline Continuous.
Jobs Positions for college students 20 and older.
Contact Ms. Brooks Follansbee, Director, PO Box 31, Williamstown, Massachusetts 01267. Phone: 800-458-0588. Fax: 413-458-5208. E-mail: overland@adelphia.net.
URL www.overlandsummers.com

For more information, see page 1240.

OVERLAND: PACIFIC COAST BICYCLE TOURING AND RAFTING

Overland Travel, Inc.
Locations California, Oregon.

General Information Coed travel outdoor program and adventure program established in 1985. Accredited by American Camping Association. High school credit may be earned.
Program Focus Exploration of the Pacific Coast from Portland to San Francisco by bicycle.
Special Interest Areas Leadership training, touring.
Sports Bicycling.
Wilderness/Outdoors Bicycle trips, outdoor camping, rafting, white-water trips.
Program Information 3–4 sessions per year. Session length: 4 weeks in June, July, August. Ages: 14–18. 8–12 participants per session. Cost: $3895.
Housing Tents and youth hostels.
Application Deadline Continuous.
Jobs Positions for college students 20 and older.
Contact Ms. Brooks Follansbee, Director, PO Box 31, Williamstown, Massachusetts 01267. Phone: 800-458-0588. Fax: 413-458-5208. E-mail: overland@adelphia.net.
URL www.overlandsummers.com

For more information, see page 1240.

OVERLAND: ROCKY MOUNTAIN EXPLORER HIKING, MOUNTAIN BIKING, AND RAFTING

Overland Travel, Inc.
Locations Colorado, Utah, Wyoming.

General Information Coed travel outdoor program, wilderness program, and adventure program established in 1985. Accredited by American Camping Association. High school credit may be earned.
Program Focus Explore the Rockies by foot, bicycle, and raft.
Special Interest Areas Leadership training, team building.
Sports Bicycling, kayaking.
Wilderness/Outdoors Backpacking, hiking, mountain biking, rafting, white-water trips, wilderness camping.
Program Information 3–6 sessions per year. Session length: 2 weeks in June, July, August. Ages: 13–16. 8–12 participants per session. Cost: $2895.
Housing Tents.
Application Deadline Continuous.
Jobs Positions for college students 20 and older.
Contact Ms. Brooks Follansbee, Director, PO Box 31, Williamstown, Massachusetts 01267. Phone: 800-458-0588. Fax: 413-458-5208. E-mail: overland@adelphia.net.
URL www.overlandsummers.com

For more information, see page 1240.

OVERLAND: SHASTA & THE SIERRAS BACKPACKING, CLIMBING AND RAFTING

Overland Travel, Inc.
Locations California, Oregon.

Overland: Shasta & the Sierras Backpacking, Climbing and Rafting (continued)

General Information Coed travel outdoor program, wilderness program, and adventure program established in 1985. Accredited by American Camping Association. High school credit may be earned.

Overland: Shasta & the Sierras Backpacking, Climbing and Rafting

Program Focus Backpacking, mountaineering, alpine leadership, and rafting.
Special Interest Areas Leadership training, team building, touring.
Sports Kayaking.
Wilderness/Outdoors Backpacking, hiking, mountaineering, rafting, rock climbing, white-water trips, wilderness camping.
Program Information 2 sessions per year. Session length: 27 days in June, July, August. Ages: 14–18. 8–12 participants per session. Cost: $3895.
Housing Tents.
Application Deadline Continuous.
Jobs Positions for college students 20 and older.
Contact Ms. Brooks Follansbee, Director, PO Box 31, Williamstown, Massachusetts 01267. Phone: 800-458-0588. Fax: 413-458-5208. E-mail: overland@adelphia.net.
URL www.overlandsummers.com

For more information, see page 1240.

Overland: Vermont & Montreal Bicycle Touring

Overland Travel, Inc.
Locations Canada, Massachusetts, Vermont.

General Information Coed travel outdoor program, cultural program, and adventure program established in 1985. Accredited by American Camping Association. High school credit may be earned.
Program Focus Beginning in Williamstown, Massachusetts, bike the length of beautiful Vermont, plus sightsee in Montreal.
Special Interest Areas Leadership training, touring.
Sports Bicycling.
Wilderness/Outdoors Bicycle trips, outdoor camping.
Excursions Cultural.
Program Information 3–6 sessions per year. Session length: 2 weeks in June, July, August. Ages: 13–18. 8–12 participants per session. Cost: $2495.
Housing Tents and youth hostels.
Application Deadline Continuous.
Jobs Positions for college students 20 and older.
Contact Ms. Brooks Follansbee, Director, PO Box 31, Williamstown, Massachusetts 01267. Phone: 800-458-0588. Fax: 413-458-5208. E-mail: overland@adelphia.net.
URL www.overlandsummers.com

For more information, see page 1240.

Overland: Yellowstone Explorer Backpacking, Rock Climbing, and Rafting

Overland Travel, Inc.
Locations Idaho, Montana, Wyoming.

General Information Coed travel outdoor program, wilderness program, and adventure program established in 1985. Accredited by American Camping Association. High school credit may be earned.
Program Focus Outdoor leadership training, backpacking, climbing, rafting, kayaking.
Special Interest Areas Community service, leadership training, team building, touring.
Sports Kayaking.
Wilderness/Outdoors Backpacking, hiking, mountaineering, rafting, rock climbing, white-water trips, wilderness camping.
Program Information 1–2 sessions per year. Session length: 3 weeks in June, July, August. Ages: 14–18. 8–12 participants per session. Cost: $3595.
Housing Tents.
Application Deadline Continuous.
Jobs Positions for college students 20 and older.
Contact Ms. Brooks Follansbee, Director, PO Box 31, Williamstown, Massachusetts 01267. Phone: 800-458-0588. Fax: 413-458-5208. E-mail: overland@adelphia.net.
URL www.overlandsummers.com

For more information, see page 1240.

The Ranch–Lake Placid Teen Travel Camp

The Ranch–Lake Placid Academy
Locations Canada, Connecticut, New York, Vermont.

General Information Coed travel outdoor program established in 1998.
Program Focus Horseback riding.
Special Interest Areas Animal care, campcraft, leadership training.
Sports Canoeing, equestrian sports, horseback riding, swimming, tennis, waterskiing.

Wilderness/Outdoors Canoe trips, hiking, pack animal trips, rafting, white-water trips, wilderness camping.
Excursions Overnight.
Program Information 4 sessions per year. Session length: 2 weeks in June, July, August. 20–40 participants per session. Cost: $1000–$2000; including airfare. Open to participants entering grades 8–12.
Housing Hotels and tents.
Application Deadline Continuous.
Jobs Positions for college students 18 and older.
Contact Marleen Goodman, Admissions, 4 Yankee Glen, Madison, Connecticut 06443. Phone: 518-891-5684. Fax: 518-891-6350. E-mail: marleengoodman@hotmail.com.
URL www.childrenscamps.com

REIN TEEN TOURS–AMERICAN ADVENTURE

Rein Teen Tours
Locations Arizona, California, Canada, Illinois, Kansas, Michigan, Minnesota, Missouri, Nevada, New York, Ohio, Pennsylvania, South Dakota, Utah, Wyoming.

General Information Coed travel outdoor program and adventure program established in 1985.
Program Focus Travel in the United States.
Special Interest Areas Touring.
Sports Basketball, bicycling, canoeing, climbing (wall), in-line skating, ropes course, sea kayaking, snorkeling, softball, swimming, tennis, waterskiing, windsurfing.
Wilderness/Outdoors Canoe trips, hiking, mountain biking, outdoor adventure, rafting, rock climbing, white-water trips, wilderness camping.
Program Information 4 sessions per year. Session length: 45 days in June, July, August. Ages: 13–17. 40 participants per session. Cost: $6500–$7000.
Housing College dormitories, hotels, and tents.
Application Deadline Continuous.
Jobs Positions for college students 21 and older.
Contact Norman Rein, President, 30 Galesi Drive, Wayne, New Jersey 07470. Phone: 800-831-1313. Fax: 973-785-4268. E-mail: summer@reinteentours.com.
URL www.reinteentours.com

For more information, see page 1282.

REIN TEEN TOURS–CALIFORNIA CAPER

Rein Teen Tours
Locations Arizona, California, Nevada, Utah.

General Information Coed travel outdoor program and adventure program established in 1985.
Program Focus Travel in the United States.
Special Interest Areas Touring.
Sports Basketball, bicycling, canoeing, climbing (wall), in-line skating, ropes course, sea kayaking, snorkeling, softball, swimming, tennis, waterskiing, windsurfing.
Wilderness/Outdoors Canoe trips, mountain biking, outdoor adventure, rafting, rock climbing, white-water trips, wilderness camping.
Program Information 3 sessions per year. Session length: 3 weeks in June, July, August. Ages: 13–17. 40 participants per session. Cost: $4500–$5000.
Housing College dormitories, hotels, and tents.
Application Deadline Continuous.
Jobs Positions for college students 21 and older.
Contact Norman Rein, President, 30 Galesi Drive, Wayne, New Jersey 07470. Phone: 800-831-1313. Fax: 973-785-4268. E-mail: summer@reinteentours.com.
URL www.reinteentours.com

For more information, see page 1282.

REIN TEEN TOURS–CROSSROADS

Rein Teen Tours
Locations Arizona, California, Canada, Illinois, Michigan, Minnesota, Nevada, New York, Ohio, South Dakota, Utah, Wyoming.

General Information Coed travel outdoor program and adventure program established in 1985.
Program Focus Travel in the United States and Canada.
Special Interest Areas Touring.
Sports Basketball, bicycling, canoeing, climbing (wall), in-line skating, ropes course, sea kayaking, snorkeling, softball, swimming, tennis, waterskiing, windsurfing.
Wilderness/Outdoors Canoe trips, hiking, mountain biking, outdoor adventure, rafting, rock climbing, white-water trips, wilderness camping.
Program Information 4 sessions per year. Session length: 40 days in June, July, August. Ages: 13–17. 40 participants per session. Cost: $6500–$7000.
Housing College dormitories, hotels, and tents.
Application Deadline Continuous.
Jobs Positions for college students 21 and older.
Contact Norman Rein, President, 30 Galesi Drive, Wayne, New Jersey 07470. Phone: 800-831-1313. Fax: 973-785-4268. E-mail: summer@reinteentours.com.
URL www.reinteentours.com

For more information, see page 1282.

REIN TEEN TOURS–EASTERN ADVENTURE

Rein Teen Tours
Locations Canada, Florida, Maine, Massachusetts, New Hampshire, New York, Pennsylvania, South Carolina, Virginia.

General Information Coed travel outdoor program and adventure program established in 1985.
Program Focus Travel in the United States and Canada.
Special Interest Areas Touring.
Sports Basketball, bicycling, canoeing, climbing (wall), in-line skating, ropes course, sea kayaking, snorkeling, softball, swimming, tennis, waterskiing, windsurfing.
Wilderness/Outdoors Canoe trips, hiking, mountain biking, outdoor adventure, rafting, rock climbing, white-water trips, wilderness camping.
Program Information 1–2 sessions per year. Session length: 30 days in June, July, August. Ages: 13–15. 40 participants per session. Cost: $4500–$5000.
Housing College dormitories, hotels, and tents.
Application Deadline Continuous.

Rein Teen Tours–Eastern Adventure (continued)
Jobs Positions for college students 21 and older.
Contact Norman Rein, President, 30 Galesi Drive, Wayne, New Jersey 07470. Phone: 800-831-1313. Fax: 973-785-4268. E-mail: summer@reinteentours.com.
URL www.reinteentours.com
For more information, see page 1282.

REIN TEEN TOURS–GRAND ADVENTURE

Rein Teen Tours
Locations Arizona, California, Canada, Montana, Nevada, South Dakota, Utah, Washington, Wyoming.
General Information Coed travel outdoor program and adventure program established in 1985.

Rein Teen Tours–Grand Adventure

Program Focus Travel in the United States and Canada.
Special Interest Areas Touring.
Sports Basketball, bicycling, canoeing, climbing (wall), in-line skating, ropes course, sea kayaking, skiing (downhill), snorkeling, softball, swimming, tennis, waterskiing, windsurfing.
Wilderness/Outdoors Canoe trips, hiking, mountain biking, outdoor adventure, rafting, rock climbing, white-water trips, wilderness camping.
Program Information 6 sessions per year. Session length: 6 weeks in June, July, August. Ages: 13–17. 40 participants per session. Cost: $7500–$8000.
Housing College dormitories, hotels, and tents.
Application Deadline Continuous.
Jobs Positions for college students 21 and older.
Contact Norman Rein, President, 30 Galesi Drive, Wayne, New Jersey 07470. Phone: 800-831-1313. Fax: 973-785-4268. E-mail: summer@reinteentours.com.
URL www.reinteentours.com
For more information, see page 1282.

REIN TEEN TOURS–HAWAIIAN/ALASKAN ADVENTURE

Rein Teen Tours
Locations Alaska, California, Canada, Hawaii, Oregon, Washington.
General Information Coed travel outdoor program and adventure program established in 1985.
Program Focus Travel in the United States and Canada.
Special Interest Areas Touring.
Sports Basketball, bicycling, canoeing, climbing (wall), in-line skating, ropes course, sea kayaking, skiing (downhill), snorkeling, softball, swimming, tennis, waterskiing, windsurfing.
Wilderness/Outdoors Canoe trips, hiking, mountain biking, outdoor adventure, rafting, rock climbing, white-water trips, wilderness camping.
Program Information 4 sessions per year. Session length: 34 days in June, July, August. Ages: 13–17. 40 participants per session. Cost: $7500–$8000.
Housing College dormitories and hotels.
Application Deadline Continuous.
Jobs Positions for college students 24 and older.
Contact Norman Rein, President, 30 Galesi Drive, Wayne, New Jersey 07470. Phone: 800-831-1313. Fax: 973-785-4268. E-mail: summer@reinteentours.com.
URL www.reinteentours.com
For more information, see page 1282.

REIN TEEN TOURS–WESTERN ADVENTURE

Rein Teen Tours
Locations Arizona, California, Nevada, South Dakota, Utah, Wyoming.
General Information Coed travel outdoor program and adventure program established in 1985.
Program Focus Travel in the United States.
Special Interest Areas Touring.
Sports Basketball, bicycling, canoeing, climbing (wall), in-line skating, ropes course, sea kayaking, snorkeling, softball, swimming, tennis, waterskiing, windsurfing.
Wilderness/Outdoors Canoe trips, hiking, mountain biking, outdoor adventure, rafting, rock climbing, white-water trips, wilderness camping.
Program Information 4 sessions per year. Session length: 30 days in June, July, August. Ages: 13–17. 40 participants per session. Cost: $5500–$6000.
Housing College dormitories, hotels, and tents.
Application Deadline Continuous.
Jobs Positions for college students 21 and older.
Contact Norman Rein, President, 30 Galesi Drive, Wayne, New Jersey 07470. Phone: 800-831-1313. Fax: 973-785-4268. E-mail: summer@reinteentours.com.
URL www.reinteentours.com
For more information, see page 1282.

RUSTIC PATHWAYS–ADVENTURE IN AMERICA'S SOUTHWEST

Rustic Pathways
Locations Arizona, Colorado, New Mexico, Utah.
General Information Coed travel cultural program and adventure program established in 2003.
Arts Arts and crafts (general).
Special Interest Areas Community service, touring.
Sports Bicycling, horseback riding.

Wilderness/Outdoors Outdoor adventure, white-water trips.
Excursions Cultural, day, overnight, shopping.
Program Information 2 sessions per year. Session length: 17 days in June, July. Ages: 13–18. 10–15 participants per session. Cost: $2695.
Housing Hotels.
Application Deadline Continuous.
Jobs Positions for college students 21 and older.
Contact Mr. Travis Owens, Director, North America Programs, 4121 Erie Street, Willoughby, Ohio 44094. Phone: 440-975-9691. Fax: 440-975-9694. E-mail: travis@rusticpathways.com.
URL www.rusticpathways.com
For more information, see page 1290.

Summer Conservation Corps

Northwest Youth Corps
Locations California, Idaho, Oregon, Washington.

General Information Coed travel outdoor program established in 1984. High school credit may be earned.
Program Focus Outdoor education and travel throughout the Northwest.
Academics Environmental science, science (general).
Special Interest Areas Career exploration, field research/expeditions, nature study, trail maintenance, work camp programs.
Sports Fishing, swimming.
Wilderness/Outdoors Backpacking, hiking, rafting, wilderness camping.
Excursions Day.
Program Information 4 sessions per year. Session length: 5–6 weeks in June, July, August. Ages: 16–19. 10 participants per session. Financial aid available. Cost: program fee/tuition $200.
Housing Tents.
Application Deadline Continuous.
Jobs Positions for high school students 16 and older and college students 16 and older.
Contact Elizabeth Wartluft, Youth Services Coordinator, 2621 Augusta Street, Eugene, Oregon 97403. Phone: 541-349-5055 Ext.236. Fax: 541-349-5060. E-mail: nyc@nwyouthcorps.org.
URL www.nwyouthcorps.org

Summit Travel Program

Summit Camp
Locations Arizona, California, Canada, Colorado, Utah, Wyoming.

General Information Coed travel outdoor program and special needs program established in 1972. Specific services available for the emotionally challenged, learning disabled, participant with ADD, and participant with Aspergers Syndrome.
Program Focus Coed program focusing on travel for older adolescents and young adults with non-verbal learning disabilities, social difficulties, ADD, or Asperger's Syndrome.
Special Interest Areas Touring.
Wilderness/Outdoors Hiking.
Program Information 1 session per year. Session length: 21–25 days in July, August. Ages: 16–20. 40–50 participants per session. Cost: $5495; including airfare from New York or Newark to Denver, CO.
Housing College dormitories and hotels.
Application Deadline Continuous.
Jobs Positions for college students 21 and older.
Contact Mr. Mayer Stiskin, Director, 18 East 41st Street, # 402, NY, New York 10017. Phone: 800-323-9908. Fax: 212-689-4347. E-mail: summitcamp@aol.com.
URL www.summitcamp.com

Swift Nature Camp–Canadian Canoe Trip

Swift Nature Camp
Locations Canada, Minnesota.

General Information Coed travel outdoor program and wilderness program established in 1996. Specific services available for the learning disabled.
Program Focus Explore the Boundary Waters area of Canada and northern Minnesota.
Academics Astronomy, biology, ecology, marine studies.
Arts Arts and crafts (general), ceramics.
Special Interest Areas Nature study.
Sports Canoeing.
Wilderness/Outdoors Canoe trips.
Excursions Day, overnight.
Program Information 1 session per year. Session length: 5 days in August. Ages: 14–17. 9 participants per session. Cost: $375. Financial aid available.
Application Deadline Continuous.
Jobs Positions for college students 18 and older.
Summer Contact Jeff Lorenz, Director, W7471 Ernie Swift Road, Minong, Wisconsin 54859. Phone: 630-654-8036. Fax: 630-654-8036. E-mail: swiftcamp@aol.com.
Winter Contact Jeff Lorenz, Director, 25 Baybrook Lane, Oak Brook, Illinois 60523. Phone: 630-654-8036. Fax: 630-654-8036. E-mail: swiftcamp@aol.com.
URL www.swiftnaturecamp.com

Teen Tours of America–Alaskan Expedition

Teen Tours of America
Locations Alaska, California, Canada, Oregon, Washington.

General Information Coed travel outdoor program and adventure program established in 1994.
Special Interest Areas Touring.
Sports Basketball, bicycling, boating, canoeing, climbing (wall), figure skating, football, horseback riding, kayaking, ropes course, sea kayaking, soccer, softball, swimming, tennis, volleyball, waterskiing, weight training.
Wilderness/Outdoors Bicycle trips, canoe trips, hiking, mountain biking, rafting, white-water trips.
Program Information 1–3 sessions per year. Session length: 26 days in July, August. Ages: 13–17. 40–44 participants per session. Cost: $5095–$5495.
Housing College dormitories, hotels, and yachts.
Application Deadline Continuous.

Teen Tours of America–Alaskan Expedition (continued)
Jobs Positions for college students 23 and older.
Contact Mr. Ira Solomon, Director, 318 Indian Trace #336, Weston, Florida 33326. Phone: 888-868-7882. Fax: 954-888-9781. E-mail: tourtta@teentoursofamerica.com.
URL www.teentoursofamerica.com

TEEN TOURS OF AMERICA–ALOHA HAWAII

Teen Tours of America
Locations California, Hawaii, Oregon, Washington.

General Information Coed travel outdoor program and adventure program established in 1994.
Special Interest Areas Touring.
Sports Baseball, basketball, bicycling, boating, canoeing, climbing (wall), equestrian sports, fishing, football, golf, horseback riding, in-line skating, kayaking, ropes course, sailing, sea kayaking, skiing (downhill), snorkeling, soccer, softball, swimming, tennis, volleyball, waterskiing, weight training.
Wilderness/Outdoors Bicycle trips, canoe trips, hiking, mountain biking, outdoor adventure, rafting, white-water trips.
Program Information 1–4 sessions per year. Session length: 3 weeks in June, July, August. Ages: 13+. 30–44 participants per session. Cost: $4495–$4995.
Housing College dormitories, hotels, and yachts.
Application Deadline Continuous.
Jobs Positions for college students 23 and older.
Summer Contact Ira Solomon, Director, 318 Indian Trace #336, Weston, Florida 33326. Phone: 888-868-7882. Fax: 954-888-9781. E-mail: tourtta@teentoursofamerica.com.
Winter Contact Ira Solomon, Director, main address above. E-mail: tourtta@teentoursofamerica.com.
URL www.teentoursofamerica.com

TEEN TOURS OF AMERICA–NEW ENGLAND JOURNEY

Teen Tours of America
Locations Canada, Connecticut, Maine, Massachusetts, New Hampshire, New York, Vermont.

General Information Coed travel outdoor program and adventure program established in 1994.
Special Interest Areas Touring.
Sports Basketball, bicycling, boating, canoeing, climbing (wall), football, horseback riding, ropes course, sea kayaking, soccer, swimming, tennis, volleyball, waterskiing, weight training.
Wilderness/Outdoors Backpacking, bicycle trips, hiking, mountain biking, white-water trips.
Program Information 2 sessions per year. Session length: 3 weeks in July, August. Ages: 13–17. 40 participants per session. Cost: $3995–$4295.
Housing College dormitories and hotels.
Application Deadline Continuous.
Jobs Positions for college students 23 and older.
Contact Mr. Ira Solomon, Director, 318 Indian Trace #336, Weston, Florida 33326. Phone: 888-868-7882. Fax: 954-888-9781. E-mail: tourtta@teentoursofamerica.com.
URL www.teentoursofamerica.com

TEEN TOURS OF AMERICA–WESTERN ADVENTURE

Teen Tours of America
Locations Arizona, California, Canada, Montana, Nevada, South Dakota, Utah, Washington, Wyoming.

General Information Coed travel outdoor program and adventure program established in 1994.
Special Interest Areas Touring.
Sports Basketball, bicycling, boating, canoeing, climbing (wall), diving, equestrian sports, football, golf, horseback riding, in-line skating, ropes course, sea kayaking, soccer, softball, swimming, tennis, volleyball, waterskiing, weight training.
Wilderness/Outdoors Backpacking, bicycle trips, canoe trips, hiking, mountain biking, rafting, white-water trips.
Program Information 1–3 sessions per year. Session length: 6 weeks in June, July, August. Ages: 12–17. 40–44 participants per session. Cost: $6095–$6595. Financial aid available.
Housing College dormitories, hotels, and tents.
Application Deadline Continuous.
Jobs Positions for college students 23 and older.
Contact Mr. Ira Solomon, Director, 318 Indian Trace #336, Weston, Florida 33326. Phone: 888-868-7882. Fax: 954-888-9781. E-mail: tourtta@teentoursofamerica.com.
URL www.teentoursofamerica.com

TEEN TOURS OF AMERICA–WESTERN SPRINT

Teen Tours of America
Locations Arizona, Canada, Nevada, Utah.

General Information Coed travel outdoor program and adventure program established in 1994.
Special Interest Areas Touring.
Sports Basketball, bicycling, boating, canoeing, climbing (wall), equestrian sports, football, golf, horseback riding, in-line skating, kayaking, ropes course, sea kayaking, soccer, softball, swimming, tennis, volleyball, waterskiing, weight training.
Wilderness/Outdoors Bicycle trips, canoe trips, hiking, mountain biking, rafting, white-water trips.
Program Information 1–5 sessions per year. Session length: 3 weeks in June, July, August. Ages: 12–17. 40–44 participants per session. Cost: $3895–$4095.
Housing College dormitories, hotels, and tents.
Application Deadline Continuous.
Jobs Positions for college students 23 and older.
Contact Mr. Ira Solomon, Director, 318 Indian Trace #336, Weston, Florida 33326. Phone: 888-868-7882. Fax: 954-888-9781. E-mail: tourtta@teentoursofamerica.com.
URL www.teentoursofamerica.com

TEEN TOUR USA AND CANADA

New England Vacation Tours Inc.
Locations Canada, Connecticut, District of Columbia, Maine, Maryland, Massachusetts, New Hampshire, New Jersey, New York, Pennsylvania, Vermont, Virginia.

General Information Coed travel academic program and cultural program established in 1998.
Program Focus Learning through travel.
Academics American literature, aerospace science, architecture, art history/appreciation, government and politics, government and politics (Advanced Placement), history, social studies.
Arts Arts and crafts (general), ceramics, music (orchestral), musical productions, theater/drama.
Special Interest Areas Community service, leadership training, touring.
Sports Archery, baseball, basketball, bicycling, bicycling (BMX), boating, canoeing, climbing (wall), cross-country, football, golf, gymnastics, horseback riding, kayaking, racquetball, sailing, sea kayaking, snorkeling, soccer, softball, swimming, tennis, volleyball, waterskiing, windsurfing.
Wilderness/Outdoors Backpacking, bicycle trips, canoe trips, caving, hiking, mountain biking, rafting, rock climbing, white-water trips.
Excursions College tours, cultural, day, overnight, shopping.
Program Information 1 session per year. Session length: 36 days in June, July, August. Ages: 13–17. Cost: $6000–$7000.
Housing College dormitories, hotels, and youth hostels.
Application Deadline Continuous.
Jobs Positions for college students 21 and older.
Contact Mr. William A. Buswell, President and CEO, PO Box 560, West Dover, Vermont 05356-0560. Phone: 802-464-2076. Fax: 802-464-2629. E-mail: nevt@sover.net.
URL www.sover.net/~nevt

TENNIS: EUROPE & MORE–NORTH AMERICAN TEAMS

TENNIS: EUROPE
Locations California, Canada, Colorado, Idaho, Utah, Washington, Wyoming.

General Information Coed travel sports camp established in 1973.
Program Focus Tournament competition.
Academics College tours.
Special Interest Areas Career exploration, college planning.
Sports Aerobics, basketball, bicycling, boating, canoeing, fishing, golf, horseback riding, in-line skating, sailing, skiing (downhill), snorkeling, soccer, swimming, tennis, volleyball, waterskiing, weight training, windsurfing.
Wilderness/Outdoors Hiking, rafting, white-water trips.
Excursions College tours, cultural.
Program Information 3–6 sessions per year. Session length: 17–30 days in June, July, August. Ages: 14–18. 18–20 participants per session. Cost: $3400–$5500. Financial aid available. Financial aid for European teams only. Airfare to first destination and return is not included; only flights between tournaments.
Housing Hotels.
Application Deadline Continuous.
Jobs Positions for college students 21 and older.
Contact Dr. Martin Vinokur, Co-Director, 73 Rockridge Lane, Stamford, Connecticut 06905. Phone: 800-253-7486. Fax: 203-322-0089. E-mail: tenniseuro@aol.com.
URL www.tenniseurope.com

TRAILMARK OUTDOOR ADVENTURES–NEW ENGLAND–ACADIA

Trailmark Outdoor Adventures
Locations Maine, New Hampshire.

General Information Coed travel outdoor program, wilderness program, and adventure program established in 1985. Accredited by American Camping Association.
Program Focus Coed outdoor adventure.
Sports Bicycling, climbing (wall), kayaking, rappelling, ropes course, swimming.
Wilderness/Outdoors Bicycle trips, climbing, hiking, mountain biking, rafting, rock climbing, white-water trips, wilderness camping.
Program Information 4–6 sessions per year. Session length: 15 days in June, July, August. Ages: 12–16. 12–16 participants per session. Cost: $2295. Financial aid available.
Housing Tents.
Application Deadline Continuous.
Jobs Positions for college students 21 and older.
Contact Mr. Rusty Pedersen, Director, 16 Schuyler Road, Nyack, New York 10960. Phone: 845-358-0262. Fax: 845-348-0437. E-mail: info@trailmark.com.
URL www.trailmark.com

TRAILMARK OUTDOOR ADVENTURES–NEW ENGLAND–CAMDEN

Trailmark Outdoor Adventures
Locations Maine, New Hampshire.

General Information Coed travel outdoor program, wilderness program, and adventure program established in 1985. Accredited by American Camping Association.
Program Focus Coed outdoor adventure.
Special Interest Areas Community service.
Sports Climbing (wall), rappelling, ropes course, sailing, sea kayaking, swimming.
Wilderness/Outdoors Hiking, rafting, rock climbing, white-water trips, wilderness camping.
Program Information 3 sessions per year. Session length: 15 days in July, August. Ages: 13–16. 12–18 participants per session. Cost: $2395. Financial aid available.
Housing Tents.
Application Deadline Continuous.
Jobs Positions for college students 21 and older.
Contact Mr. Rusty Pedersen, Director, 16 Schuyler Road, Nyack, New York 10960. Phone: 845-358-0262. Fax: 845-348-0437. E-mail: info@trailmark.com.
URL www.trailmark.com

Trailmark Outdoor Adventures–New England–Downeast

Trailmark Outdoor Adventures
Locations Maine, New Hampshire.

General Information Coed travel outdoor program, wilderness program, and adventure program established in 1985. Accredited by American Camping Association.
Program Focus Coed outdoor adventure.
Sports Climbing (wall), rappelling, ropes course, sea kayaking, swimming.
Wilderness/Outdoors Hiking, rafting, rock climbing, white-water trips, wilderness camping.
Program Information 3 sessions per year. Session length: 15 days in July, August. Ages: 13–16. 12–18 participants per session. Cost: $2395. Financial aid available.
Housing Tents.
Application Deadline Continuous.
Jobs Positions for college students 21 and older.
Contact Mr. Rusty Pedersen, Director, 16 Schuyler Road, Nyack, New York 10960. Phone: 845-358-0262. Fax: 845-348-0437. E-mail: info@trailmark.com.
URL www.trailmark.com

Trailmark Outdoor Adventures–New England–Jr. Acadia

Trailmark Outdoor Adventures
Locations Maine, New Hampshire.

General Information Coed travel outdoor program and adventure program established in 1985. Accredited by American Camping Association.
Program Focus Coed outdoor adventure.
Sports Bicycling, climbing (wall), in-line skating, rappelling, ropes course.
Wilderness/Outdoors Hiking, mountain biking, rafting, rock climbing, white-water trips.
Program Information 1 session per year. Session length: 15 days in July, August. Ages: 11–12. 12–18 participants per session. Cost: $2295. Financial aid available.
Housing Tents.
Application Deadline Continuous.
Jobs Positions for college students.
Contact Mr. Rusty Pedersen, Director/Owner, 16 Schuyler Road, Nyack, New York 10960. Phone: 845-358-0262. Fax: 845-348-0437. E-mail: info@trailmark.com.
URL www.trailmark.com

Trailmark Outdoor Adventures–New England–Mahoosoc

Trailmark Outdoor Adventures
Locations Maine, New Hampshire.

General Information Coed travel outdoor program, wilderness program, and adventure program established in 1985. Accredited by American Camping Association.
Program Focus Coed outdoor adventure.
Special Interest Areas Leadership training.
Sports Climbing (wall), in-line skating, rappelling, ropes course, sea kayaking, swimming.
Wilderness/Outdoors Backpacking, hiking, rafting, rock climbing, white-water trips, wilderness camping.
Program Information 1 session per year. Session length: 3 weeks in July. Ages: 14–16. 12–14 participants per session. Cost: $3395. Financial aid available.
Housing Tents.
Application Deadline Continuous.
Jobs Positions for college students 21 and older.
Contact Mr. Rusty Pedersen, Director, 16 Schuyler Road, Nyack, New York 10960. Phone: 845-358-0262. Fax: 845-348-0437. E-mail: info@trailmark.com.
URL www.trailmark.com

Trailmark Outdoor Adventures–New England–Moose River

Trailmark Outdoor Adventures
Locations Maine, New Hampshire.

General Information Coed travel outdoor program, wilderness program, and adventure program established in 1985. Accredited by American Camping Association.
Program Focus Coed outdoor adventure.
Sports Bicycling, canoeing, in-line skating, kayaking, rappelling, ropes course, swimming.
Wilderness/Outdoors Canoe trips, hiking, mountain biking, outdoor adventure, rafting, rock climbing, white-water trips, wilderness camping.
Program Information 1 session per year. Session length: 3 weeks in July. Ages: 13–14. 12–18 participants per session. Cost: $3395. Financial aid available.
Housing Tents.
Application Deadline Continuous.
Jobs Positions for college students 21 and older.
Contact Mr. Rusty Pedersen, Director, 16 Schuyler Road, Nyack, New York 10960. Phone: 845-358-0262. Fax: 845-348-0437. E-mail: info@trailmark.com.
URL www.trailmark.com

Trailmark Outdoor Adventures–New England–Mt. Desert

Trailmark Outdoor Adventures
Locations Maine, New Hampshire.

General Information Coed travel outdoor program, wilderness program, and adventure program established in 1985. Accredited by American Camping Association.
Program Focus Coed outdoor adventure.
Sports Bicycling, rappelling, sea kayaking.
Wilderness/Outdoors Mountain biking, rafting, rock climbing, white-water trips, wilderness camping.
Program Information 2 sessions per year. Session length: 15 days in July, August. Ages: 14–16. 12–18 participants per session. Cost: $2395. Financial aid available.
Housing Tents.
Application Deadline Continuous.
Jobs Positions for college students.

Contact Mr. Rusty Pedersen, Director/Owner, 16 Schuyler Road, Nyack, New York 10960. Phone: 845-358-0262. Fax: 845-348-0437. E-mail: info@trailmark.com.
URL www.trailmark.com

Trailmark Outdoor Adventures–New England–Rangeley Coed

Trailmark Outdoor Adventures
Locations Maine, New Hampshire.

General Information Girls' travel outdoor program, wilderness program, and adventure program established in 1985. Accredited by American Camping Association.
Program Focus Coed outdoor adventure.
Sports Horseback riding, rappelling.
Wilderness/Outdoors Hiking, rafting, rock climbing, white-water trips.
Program Information 1 session per year. Session length: 15 days in July. Ages: 12–14. 12–18 participants per session. Cost: $2495. Financial aid available.
Housing Tents.
Application Deadline Continuous.
Jobs Positions for college students.
Contact Mr. Rusty Pedersen, Director/Owner, 16 Schuyler Road, Nyack, New York 10960. Phone: 845-358-0262. Fax: 845-348-0437. E-mail: info@trailmark.com.
URL www.trailmark.com

Trailmark Outdoor Adventures–Northern Rockies–Tetons with Backpack

Trailmark Outdoor Adventures
Locations Utah, Wyoming.

General Information Coed travel outdoor program, wilderness program, and adventure program established in 1985. Accredited by American Camping Association.
Program Focus Coed outdoor adventure.
Sports Bicycling, rappelling.
Wilderness/Outdoors Backpacking, hiking, mountain biking, mountaineering, outdoor adventure, rafting, rock climbing, white-water trips, wilderness camping.
Program Information 1 session per year. Session length: 15 days in July. Ages: 13–16. 12–18 participants per session. Cost: $2395. Financial aid available.
Housing Tents.
Application Deadline Continuous.
Jobs Positions for college students 21 and older.
Contact Mr. Rusty Pedersen, Director, 16 Schuyler Road, Nyack, New York 10960. Phone: 845-358-0262. Fax: 845-348-0437. E-mail: info@trailmark.com.
URL www.trailmark.com

Trailmark Outdoor Adventures–Northern Rockies–Tetons with Horseback

Trailmark Outdoor Adventures
Locations Utah, Wyoming.

General Information Coed travel outdoor program, wilderness program, and adventure program established in 1985. Accredited by American Camping Association.
Program Focus Coed outdoor adventure.
Sports Bicycling, horseback riding, rappelling.
Wilderness/Outdoors Hiking, mountain biking, pack animal trips, rafting, rock climbing, white-water trips, wilderness camping.
Program Information 1–2 sessions per year. Session length: 15 days in July. Ages: 13–16. 12–18 participants per session. Cost: $2495. Financial aid available.
Housing Tents.
Application Deadline Continuous.
Jobs Positions for college students 21 and older.
Contact Mr. Rusty Pedersen, Director, 16 Schuyler Road, Nyack, New York 10960. Phone: 845-358-0262. Fax: 845-348-0437. E-mail: info@trailmark.com.
URL www.trailmark.com

Trailridge Mountain Camp

Trailridge Mountain Camp, Inc.
Locations District of Columbia, Florida, Georgia, Kentucky, Maryland, North Carolina, South Carolina, Tennessee, Virginia.

General Information Boys' travel adventure program established in 1982.
Special Interest Areas Campcraft, nature study, touring.
Sports Bicycling, canoeing, climbing (wall), snorkeling.
Wilderness/Outdoors Backpacking, bicycle trips, canoe trips, hiking, mountain biking, mountaineering, rafting, rock climbing, white-water trips, wilderness camping.
Excursions Overnight.
Program Information 3–5 sessions per year. Session length: 4–7 days in June, July. Ages: 9–16. 1–16 participants per session. Cost: $700–$850. Application fee: $50.
Housing Cabins and tents.
Application Deadline Continuous.
Contact David Broshar, Director, 198 Holland Drive, Black Mountain, North Carolina 28711. Phone: 828-669-5636. E-mail: broshar@aol.com.

Voyageur Outward Bound–Lake Superior Freshwater Kayaking and Backpacking

Voyageur Outward Bound/Outward Bound, USA
Locations Canada, Minnesota.

General Information Coed travel outdoor program, wilderness program, and adventure program established in 1964. High school or college credit may be earned.
Program Focus Teamwork and leadership development while kayaking in Ontario's Black Bay and hiking on Superior Hiking trail in Minnesota.
Academics Environmental science.
Special Interest Areas Campcraft, community service, leadership training, nature study, personal development, team building.
Sports Rappelling, sea kayaking.

Voyageur Outward Bound–Lake Superior Freshwater Kayaking and Backpacking (continued)
Wilderness/Outdoors Backpacking, hiking, outdoor adventure, rock climbing, survival training, wilderness camping.
Excursions Overnight.
Program Information 2 sessions per year. Session length: 22 days in July, August. Ages: 16+. Cost: $2995. Application fee: $95. Financial aid available. Deadline 30 days prior to course start date.
Housing Tents.
Jobs Positions for college students 21 and older.
Contact Anne DesLauriers, Admissions Advisor, 101 East Chapman Street, Ely, Minnesota 55731. Phone: 800-328-2943. Fax: 218-365-7079. E-mail: info@vobs.org.
URL www.vobs.org

Voyageur Outward Bound–Manitoba to Montana Summer Semester

Voyageur Outward Bound/Outward Bound, USA
Locations Canada, Montana.

General Information Coed travel outdoor program and wilderness program established in 1964. High school or college credit may be earned.
Program Focus Teamwork and leadership development while canoeing in Atikaky Provincial Wilderness Park and backpacking through the Continental Divide Mountains.
Academics Ecology, environmental science.
Special Interest Areas Campcraft, community service, field research/expeditions, leadership training, nature study, personal development, team building.
Sports Canoeing, climbing (wall).
Wilderness/Outdoors Backpacking, canoe trips, mountaineering, outdoor adventure, rock climbing, survival training, white-water trips, wilderness camping.
Excursions Overnight.
Program Information 1 session per year. Session length: 55 days in June, July, August. Ages: 16+. Cost: $5995. Application fee: $95. Financial aid available. Deadline 30 days prior to course start date.
Housing Tents.
Jobs Positions for college students 21 and older.
Contact Ms. Anne DesLauriers, Admissions Advisor, 101 East Chapman Street, Ely, Minnesota 55731. Phone: 800-328-2943. Fax: 218-365-7079. E-mail: info@vobs.org.
URL www.vobs.org

Weissman Teen Tours–"Aloha–Welcome to Hawaiian Paradise"

Weissman Teen Tours
Locations California, Hawaii, Mexico.

General Information Coed travel outdoor program and cultural program established in 1974.
Program Focus Owner-escorted, personally-supervised, action-packed, culturally-oriented, upscale student travel—no camping or dormitory accommodations.
Special Interest Areas Native American culture, nature study, team building, touring.
Sports Aerobics, basketball, bicycling, bicycling (BMX), boating, body boarding, diving, football, golf, horseback riding, in-line skating, kayaking, scuba diving, sea kayaking, snorkeling, soccer, sports (general), surfing, swimming, tennis, volleyball, waterskiing, weight training.
Wilderness/Outdoors Hiking, mountain biking.
Excursions College tours, cultural, day, overnight, shopping.
Program Information 1 session per year. Session length: 3 weeks in July, August. Ages: 14–18. 30–40 participants per session. Cost: $5999.
Housing Hotels.
Application Deadline Continuous.
Jobs Positions for college students 21 and older.
Contact Ms. Ronee Weissman, Owner/Director, 517 Almena Avenue, Ardsley, New York 10502. Phone: 800-942-8005. Fax: 914-693-4807. E-mail: wtt@cloud9.net.
URL www.weissmantours.com
For more information, see page 1388.

Weissman Teen Tours–U.S. and Western Canada, 4 Weeks

Weissman Teen Tours
Locations California, Canada, Colorado, Mexico, Montana, Utah, Washington, Wyoming.

General Information Coed travel outdoor program and cultural program established in 1974.
Program Focus Owner-escorted, personally-supervised, action-packed, sports-oriented, upscale travel program in the U.S. and Western Canada. No camping or dormitory accommodations.
Academics Architecture, art history/appreciation, history, intercultural studies.
Special Interest Areas Native American culture, field trips (arts and culture), nature study, nautical skills, touring.
Sports Aerobics, basketball, bicycling, bicycling (BMX), boating, climbing (wall), cross-country, football, golf, horseback riding, in-line skating, kayaking, parasailing, sailing, skiing (downhill), snorkeling, snowboarding, soccer, sports (general), swimming, tennis, volleyball, waterskiing, weight training.
Wilderness/Outdoors Hiking, mountain biking, outdoor adventure, rafting, rock climbing, white-water trips.
Excursions College tours, day, overnight.
Program Information 1 session per year. Session length: 30 days in July, August. Ages: 13–17. 40 participants per session. Financial aid available.
Housing Hotels.
Application Deadline Continuous.
Jobs Positions for college students 21 and older.
Contact Mr. Eugene Weissman, Owner / Director, 517 Almena Ave, Ardsley, New York 10502. Phone: 800-942-8005. Fax: 914-693-4807. E-mail: wtt@cloud9.net.
URL www.weissmantours.com
For more information, see page 1388.

Weissman Teen Tours–U.S. and Western Canada, 6 Weeks

Weissman Teen Tours
Locations Arizona, California, Canada, Colorado, Mexico, Montana, Nevada, Utah, Washington, Wyoming.

General Information Coed travel outdoor program established in 1974.

Weissman Teen Tours–U.S. and Western Canada, 6 Weeks

Program Focus Owner-escorted, personally-supervised, action-packed, sports-oriented, upscale travel program in the U.S. and western Canada. No camping or dormitory accommodations.
Special Interest Areas Native American culture, field trips (arts and culture), nature study, nautical skills, touring.
Sports Aerobics, basketball, bicycling, bicycling (BMX), boating, climbing (wall), cross-country, football, golf, horseback riding, in-line skating, kayaking, parasailing, sailing, skiing (downhill), snorkeling, snowboarding, soccer, sports (general), swimming, tennis, volleyball, waterskiing, weight training.
Wilderness/Outdoors Hiking, mountain biking, outdoor adventure, rafting, rock climbing, white-water trips.
Excursions College tours, day, overnight.
Program Information 2 sessions per year. Session length: 40 days in July, August. Ages: 13–17. 40–45 participants per session. Cost: $8399.
Housing National Park lodges and resorts and hotels.
Application Deadline Continuous.
Jobs Positions for college students 21 and older.
Contact Mr. Eugene Weissman, Owner/Director, 517 Almena Avenue, Ardsley, New York 10502. Phone: 800-942-8005. Fax: 914-693-4807. E-mail: wtt@cloud9.net.
URL www.weissmantours.com

For more information, see page 1388.

Westcoast Connection–American Voyageur

Westcoast Connection
Locations Arizona, California, Canada, Montana, Nevada, Oregon, Utah, Washington, Wyoming.

General Information Coed travel outdoor program and adventure program established in 1982. Accredited by Ontario Camping Association.
Program Focus A balance of daytime activities, the sights and sounds of cities, exciting nightly entertainment, and natural wonders of the great outdoors.
Special Interest Areas Touring.
Sports Bicycling, boating, canoeing, golf, horseback riding, in-line skating, kayaking, ropes course, sea kayaking, skiing (downhill), snorkeling, snowboarding, swimming, tennis, waterskiing.
Wilderness/Outdoors Hiking, mountain biking, outdoor adventure, rafting, white-water trips, wilderness/outdoors (general).
Program Information 3–4 sessions per year. Session length: 6 weeks in July, August. Ages: 13–17. 40–50 participants per session. Cost: $6699. Financial aid available.
Housing College dormitories, hotels, and tents.
Application Deadline Continuous.
Jobs Positions for college students 21 and older.
Contact Mr. Mark Segal, Director, 154 East Boston Post Road, Mamaroneck, New York 10543. Phone: 800-767-0227. Fax: 914-835-0798. E-mail: usa@westcoastconnection.com.
URL www.westcoastconnection.com

For more information, see page 1392.

Westcoast Connection–Californian Extravaganza

Westcoast Connection
Locations Arizona, California, Colorado, Nevada, Utah, Wyoming.

General Information Coed travel outdoor program and adventure program established in 1982. Accredited by Ontario Camping Association.
Program Focus A balance of daytime activities, the sights and sounds of cities, exciting nightly entertainment, and the natural wonders of the great outdoors.
Special Interest Areas Touring.
Sports Bicycling, boating, golf, horseback riding, in-line skating, kayaking, ropes course, sea kayaking, snorkeling, swimming, tennis, volleyball, waterskiing.
Wilderness/Outdoors Hiking, mountain biking, outdoor adventure, rafting, white-water trips, wilderness/outdoors (general).
Program Information 2–4 sessions per year. Session length: 30 days in July, August. Ages: 13–17. 40–50 participants per session. Cost: $5699.
Housing College dormitories, hotels, and tents.
Application Deadline Continuous.
Jobs Positions for college students 21 and older.
Contact Mr. Mark Segal, Director, 154 East Boston Post Road, Mamaroneck, New York 10543. Phone: 800-767-0227. Fax: 914-835-0798. E-mail: usa@westcoastconnection.com.
URL www.westcoastconnection.com

For more information, see page 1392.

WESTCOAST CONNECTION–HAWAIIAN SPIRIT

Westcoast Connection
Locations California, Hawaii, Oregon, Washington.

General Information Coed travel adventure program established in 1982. Accredited by Ontario Camping Association.
Program Focus Touring and recreational activities on the Pacific coast and the Hawaiian Islands.
Special Interest Areas Touring.
Sports Bicycling, boating, ropes course, sea kayaking, skiing (downhill), snorkeling, snowboarding.
Wilderness/Outdoors Hiking, mountain biking, outdoor adventure, rafting, white-water trips.
Program Information 1–2 sessions per year. Session length: 23 days in July. Ages: 14–17. 25–45 participants per session. Cost: $5699.
Housing College dormitories and hotels.
Application Deadline Continuous.
Jobs Positions for college students 21 and older.
Contact Mr. Mark Segal, Director, 154 East Boston Post Road, Mamaroneck, New York 10543. Phone: 800-767-0227. Fax: 914-835-0798. E-mail: usa@westcoastconnection.com.
URL www.westcoastconnection.com

For more information, see page 1392.

WESTCOAST CONNECTION TRAVEL/ON TOUR–NORTHWESTERN ODYSSEY

Westcoast Connection
Locations Canada, Montana, Oregon, Utah, Washington, Wyoming.

General Information Coed travel outdoor program and adventure program established in 1982. Accredited by Ontario Camping Association.
Program Focus A balanced variety of daytime activities, the sights and sounds of cities, exciting nightly entertainment, and the natural wonders of the great outdoors.
Special Interest Areas Touring.
Sports Bicycling, boating, canoeing, golf, horseback riding, in-line skating, ropes course, skiing (downhill), snowboarding, swimming, tennis.
Wilderness/Outdoors Hiking, mountain biking, outdoor adventure, rafting, white-water trips.
Program Information 1–2 sessions per year. Session length: 25 days in July. Ages: 17–19. 20–40 participants per session. Cost: $4199.
Housing College dormitories, hotels, and tents.
Application Deadline Continuous.
Contact Mr. Mark Segal, Director, 154 East Boston Post Road, Mamaroneck, New York 10543. Phone: 800-767-0227. Fax: 914-835-0798. E-mail: usa@westcoastconnection.com.
URL www.westcoastconnection.com

For more information, see page 1392.

WESTCOAST CONNECTION TRAVEL–CALIFORNIA AND THE CANYONS

Westcoast Connection
Locations Arizona, California, Nevada, Utah.

General Information Coed travel outdoor program and adventure program established in 1982. Accredited by Ontario Camping Association.
Program Focus A balance of daytime activities, the sights and sounds of cities, exciting nightly entertainment, and the natural wonders of the great outdoors.
Special Interest Areas Touring.
Sports Bicycling, boating, golf, horseback riding, in-line skating, kayaking, ropes course, sea kayaking, snorkeling, swimming, tennis, volleyball, waterskiing.
Wilderness/Outdoors Hiking, mountain biking, outdoor adventure, rafting, white-water trips, wilderness/outdoors (general).
Program Information 2–4 sessions per year. Session length: 3 weeks in July, August. Ages: 13–17. 40–50 participants per session. Cost: $4399.
Housing College dormitories, hotels, and tents.
Application Deadline Continuous.
Jobs Positions for college students 21 and older.
Contact Mr. Mark Segal, Director, 154 East Boston Post Road, Mamaroneck, New York 10543. Phone: 800-767-0227. Fax: 914-835-0798. E-mail: usa@westcoastconnection.com.
URL www.westcoastconnection.com

For more information, see page 1392.

WESTCOAST CONNECTION TRAVEL–CANADIAN MOUNTAIN MAGIC

Westcoast Connection
Locations Canada, Washington.

General Information Coed travel outdoor program and adventure program established in 1982. Accredited by Ontario Camping Association.
Program Focus A challenging outdoor adventure in Whistler and the Canadian Rockies with visits to Vancouver and Calgary.
Special Interest Areas Community service.
Sports Bicycling, canoeing, kayaking, rappelling, ropes course, sea kayaking, skiing (downhill), snowboarding, swimming.
Wilderness/Outdoors Caving, hiking, mountain biking, outdoor adventure, rafting, rock climbing, white-water trips.
Program Information 6–8 sessions per year. Session length: 18–27 days in July. Ages: 13–17. 12–25 participants per session. Cost: $2799–$3799.
Housing College dormitories and tents.
Application Deadline Continuous.
Jobs Positions for college students 21 and older.
Contact Mr. Mark Segal, Director, 154 East Boston Post Road, Mamaroneck, New York 10543. Phone: 800-767-0227. Fax: 914-835-0798. E-mail: usa@westcoastconnection.com.
URL www.westcoastconnection.com

For more information, see page 1392.

Westcoast Connection Travel–Eastcoast Encounter

Westcoast Connection
Locations Canada, District of Columbia, Florida, Maine, Massachusetts, New Hampshire, New York, Virginia.

General Information Coed travel outdoor program and adventure program established in 1982. Accredited by Ontario Camping Association.
Program Focus A balance of daytime activities, the sights and sounds of cities, exciting nightly entertainment, and the natural wonders of the great outdoors.
Special Interest Areas Touring.
Sports Bicycling, boating, horseback riding, in-line skating, rappelling, ropes course, sea kayaking, snorkeling, swimming, tennis, windsurfing.
Wilderness/Outdoors Hiking, mountain biking, outdoor adventure, rafting, white-water trips.
Program Information 1–2 sessions per year. Session length: 23–28 days in July. Ages: 13–16. 30–50 participants per session. Cost: $3999–$4999.
Housing College dormitories, hotels, and tents.
Application Deadline Continuous.
Jobs Positions for college students 21 and older.
Contact Mr. Mark Segal, Director, 154 East Boston Post Road, Mamaroneck, New York 10543. Phone: 800-767-0227. Fax: 914-835-0798. E-mail: usa@westcoastconnection.com.
URL www.westcoastconnection.com

For more information, see page 1392.

Westcoast Connection Travel–Great West Challenge

Westcoast Connection
Locations California, Canada, Oregon, Washington.

General Information Coed travel outdoor program and adventure program established in 1982. Accredited by Ontario Camping Association.
Program Focus A challenging outdoor adventure in Whistler, the Canadian Rockies, Mt. Rainier, the San Juan Islands and Mt. Hood.
Special Interest Areas Community service.
Sports Bicycling, canoeing, kayaking, rappelling, ropes course, sailing, sea kayaking, skiing (downhill), snowboarding, swimming.
Wilderness/Outdoors Caving, hiking, mountain biking, outdoor adventure, rafting, rock climbing, white-water trips, wilderness camping, wilderness/outdoors (general).
Program Information 2–3 sessions per year. Session length: 40 days in July, August. Ages: 13–17. 10–25 participants per session. Cost: $5399.
Housing College dormitories and tents.
Application Deadline Continuous.
Jobs Positions for college students 21 and older.
Contact Mr. Mark Segal, Director, 154 East Boston Post Road, Mamaroneck, New York 10543. Phone: 800-767-0227. Fax: 914-835-0798. E-mail: usa@westcoastconnection.com.
URL www.westcoastconnection.com

For more information, see page 1392.

Westcoast Connection Travel–Northwestern Odyssey

Westcoast Connection
Locations Canada, Montana, Oregon, Washington, Wyoming.

General Information Coed travel outdoor program and adventure program established in 1982. Accredited by Ontario Camping Association.
Program Focus A balanced variety of daytime activities, the sights and sounds of cities, exciting nightly entertainment, and the natural wonders of the great outdoors.
Special Interest Areas Touring.
Sports Bicycling, boating, canoeing, horseback riding, in-line skating, ropes course, skiing (downhill), snowboarding, swimming, tennis.
Wilderness/Outdoors Hiking, outdoor adventure, rafting, white-water trips.
Program Information 2–3 sessions per year. Session length: 25 days in July, August. Ages: 13–17. 40–50 participants per session. Cost: $4399. Financial aid available.
Housing College dormitories, hotels, and tents.
Application Deadline Continuous.
Jobs Positions for college students 21 and older.
Contact Mr. Mark Segal, Director, 154 East Boston Post Road, Mamaroneck, New York 10543. Phone: 800-767-0227. Fax: 914-835-0798. E-mail: usa@westcoastconnection.com.
URL www.westcoastconnection.com

For more information, see page 1392.

Westcoast Connection Travel/On Tour–Canadian Adventure

Westcoast Connection
Locations Canada, Washington.

General Information Coed travel outdoor program and adventure program established in 1982. Accredited by Ontario Camping Association.
Program Focus This program is designed for greater independence for ages 17-19. An outdoor adventure in Whistler and the Canadian Rockies, with visits to Vancouver and Calgary.
Sports Bicycling, canoeing, in-line skating, rappelling, ropes course, skiing (downhill), snowboarding, swimming.
Wilderness/Outdoors Caving, hiking, mountain biking, outdoor adventure, rafting, rock climbing, white-water trips, wilderness/outdoors (general).
Program Information 1–2 sessions per year. Session length: 27 days in July, August. Ages: 17–19. 15–25 participants per session. Cost: $3699.
Housing College dormitories and tents.
Application Deadline Continuous.
Jobs Positions for college students 22 and older.
Contact Mr. Mark Segal, Director, 154 East Boston Post Road, Mamaroneck, New York 10543. Phone: 800-767-0227. Fax: 914-835-0798. E-mail: usa@westcoastconnection.com.
URL www.westcoastconnection.com

For more information, see page 1392.

Westcoast Connection Travel–Ski and Snowboard Sensation

Westcoast Connection
Locations Canada, Oregon, Washington.

General Information Coed travel sports camp established in 1982. Accredited by Ontario Camping Association.
Program Focus Participants receive professional instruction in skiing and/or snowboarding combined with other recreational activities and touring Western USA and Canada.
Special Interest Areas Touring.
Sports Skiing (downhill), snowboarding, swimming.
Wilderness/Outdoors Mountain biking, rafting.
Program Information 1–2 sessions per year. Session length: 20 days in July. Ages: 13–17. 13–25 participants per session. Cost: $4499; including airfare. Financial aid available.
Housing College dormitories and hotels.
Application Deadline Continuous.
Jobs Positions for college students 21 and older.
Contact Mr. Mark Segal, Director, 154 East Boston Post Road, Mamaroneck, New York 10543. Phone: 800-767-0227. Fax: 914-835-0798. E-mail: usa@westcoastconnection.com.
URL www.westcoastconnection.com
For more information, see page 1392.

Westcoast Connection Travel–Southwesterner

Westcoast Connection
Locations Arizona, Colorado, Nevada, Utah.

General Information Coed travel outdoor program and adventure program established in 1982. Accredited by Ontario Camping Association.
Program Focus A challenging outdoor adventure in the Southwest, with a focus on Canyonlands, Arches, Mesa Verde, Monument Valley, Grand Canyon, Bryce, and Zion National Parks.
Special Interest Areas Community service.
Sports Bicycling, horseback riding, rappelling, ropes course.
Wilderness/Outdoors Bicycle trips, caving, hiking, mountain biking, outdoor adventure, pack animal trips, rafting, rock climbing, survival training, white-water trips, wilderness camping, wilderness/outdoors (general).
Program Information 1–2 sessions per year. Session length: 18 days in July. Ages: 13–17. 12–25 participants per session. Cost: $3299. Financial aid available.
Housing Tents.
Application Deadline Continuous.
Jobs Positions for college students 21 and older.
Contact Mr. Mark Segal, Director, 154 East Boston Post Road, Mamaroneck, New York 10543. Phone: 800-767-0227. Fax: 914-835-0798. E-mail: usa@westcoastconnection.com.
URL www.westcoastconnection.com
For more information, see page 1392.

Westcoast Connection–U.S. Explorer

Westcoast Connection
Locations Arizona, California, Canada, Illinois, Michigan, Minnesota, Nevada, New York, South Dakota, Utah, Wyoming.

General Information Coed travel outdoor program and adventure program established in 1982. Accredited by Ontario Camping Association.
Program Focus A balance of daytime activities, the sights and sounds of cities, exciting nightly entertainment, and the natural wonders of the great outdoors.
Special Interest Areas Touring.
Sports Bicycling, boating, golf, horseback riding, in-line skating, kayaking, ropes course, sea kayaking, snorkeling, swimming, tennis, volleyball, waterskiing.
Wilderness/Outdoors Hiking, mountain biking, outdoor adventure, rafting, white-water trips, wilderness/outdoors (general).
Program Information 1–2 sessions per year. Session length: 41 days in July, August. Ages: 13–17. 40–50 participants per session. Cost: $6199. Financial aid available.
Housing College dormitories, hotels, and tents.
Application Deadline Continuous.
Jobs Positions for college students 21 and older.
Contact Mr. Mark Segal, Director, 154 East Boston Post Road, Mamaroneck, New York 10543. Phone: 800-767-0227. Fax: 914-835-0798. E-mail: usa@westcoastconnection.com.
URL www.westcoastconnection.com
For more information, see page 1392.

Wilderness Ventures–Colorado/Utah Mountain Bike

Wilderness Ventures
Locations Colorado, Utah.

General Information Coed travel outdoor program, wilderness program, and adventure program established in 1973.
Program Focus Bike program, leadership training.
Sports Bicycling.
Wilderness/Outdoors Bicycle trips, mountain biking, rafting, white-water trips.
Excursions Overnight.
Program Information 3 sessions per year. Session length: 16 days in June, July, August. Ages: 14–18. 13 participants per session. Cost: $2990. Financial aid available.
Application Deadline Continuous.
Jobs Positions for college students 21 and older.
Contact Mike Cottingham, Director, PO Box 2768, Jackson Hole, Wyoming 83001. Phone: 800-533-2281. Fax: 307-739-1934. E-mail: info@wildernessventures.com.
URL www.wildernessventures.com
For more information, see page 1396.

Wilderness Ventures–Great Divide

Wilderness Ventures
Locations Idaho, Montana, Oregon, Wyoming.

General Information Coed travel outdoor program, wilderness program, and adventure program established in 1973.
Program Focus Wilderness travel, wilderness skills, leadership skills.
Special Interest Areas Leadership training.
Sports Sea kayaking.
Wilderness/Outdoors Backpacking, hiking, mountaineering, rafting, rock climbing, white-water trips, wilderness camping.
Excursions Overnight.
Program Information 2 sessions per year. Session length: 27 days in June, July, August. Ages: 14–18. 10 participants per session. Cost: $4290. Financial aid available.
Housing Tents.
Application Deadline Continuous.
Jobs Positions for college students 21 and older.
Contact Mike Cottingham, Director, PO Box 2768, Jackson Hole, Wyoming 83001. Phone: 800-533-2281. Fax: 307-739-1934. E-mail: info@wildernessventures.com.
URL www.wildernessventures.com
For more information, see page 1396.

Wilderness Ventures–Great Divide Bike

Wilderness Ventures
Locations Idaho, Montana, Wyoming.

General Information Coed travel outdoor program, wilderness program, and adventure program established in 1973.
Program Focus Bike touring, leadership training.
Sports Bicycling, sea kayaking.
Wilderness/Outdoors Bicycle trips, mountain biking, rafting, white-water trips.
Excursions Overnight.
Program Information 1 session per year. Session length: 3 weeks in July, August. Ages: 14–18. 12 participants per session. Cost: $3290. Financial aid available.
Application Deadline Continuous.
Jobs Positions for college students 21 and older.
Contact Mike Cottingham, Director, PO Box 2768, Jackson Hole, Wyoming 83001. Phone: 800-533-2281. Fax: 307-739-1934. E-mail: info@wildernessventures.com.
URL www.wildernessventures.com
For more information, see page 1396.

Wilderness Ventures–Northwest

Wilderness Ventures
Locations Oregon, Washington.

General Information Coed travel outdoor program, wilderness program, and adventure program established in 1973.
Program Focus Wilderness travel, wilderness skills, leadership skills.
Special Interest Areas Leadership training.
Sports Sea kayaking.
Wilderness/Outdoors Backpacking, hiking, mountaineering, rafting, rock climbing, wilderness camping.
Excursions Overnight.
Program Information 1 session per year. Session length: 40 days in June, July, August. Ages: 14–18. 10 participants per session. Cost: $4890.
Housing Tents.
Application Deadline Continuous.
Jobs Positions for college students 21 and older.
Contact Mike Cottingham, Director, PO Box 2768, Jackson Hole, Wyoming 83001. Phone: 800-533-2281. Fax: 307-739-1934. E-mail: info@wildernessventures.com.
URL www.wildernessventures.com
For more information, see page 1396.

Wilderness Ventures–Pacific Coast Bike

Wilderness Ventures
Locations California, Oregon, Washington.

General Information Coed travel outdoor program, wilderness program, and adventure program established in 1973.
Program Focus Bike touring and leadership training.
Sports Bicycling.
Wilderness/Outdoors Bicycle trips, hiking, rafting, white-water trips.
Excursions Overnight.
Program Information 1 session per year. Session length: 31 days in June, July, August. Ages: 14–18. 12 participants per session. Cost: $3890. Financial aid available.
Application Deadline Continuous.
Jobs Positions for college students 21 and older.
Contact Mike Cottingham, Director, PO Box 2768, Jackson Hole, Wyoming 83001. Phone: 800-533-2281. Fax: 307-739-1934. E-mail: info@wildernessventures.com.
URL www.wildernessventures.com
For more information, see page 1396.

Wilderness Ventures–Pacific Northwest

Wilderness Ventures
Locations Oregon, Washington.

General Information Coed travel outdoor program, wilderness program, and adventure program established in 1973.
Program Focus Wilderness travel, wilderness skills, leadership skills.
Special Interest Areas Leadership training.
Sports Sea kayaking.
Wilderness/Outdoors Backpacking, hiking, rafting, rock climbing, white-water trips, wilderness camping.
Excursions Overnight.
Program Information 2 sessions per year. Session length: 3 weeks in June, July, August. Ages: 14–18. 10 participants per session. Cost: $3290. Financial aid available.
Housing Tents.

Wilderness Ventures–Pacific Northwest (continued)
Application Deadline Continuous.
Jobs Positions for college students 21 and older.
Contact Mike Cottingham, Director, PO Box 2768, Jackson Hole, Wyoming 83001. Phone: 800-533-2281. Fax: 307-739-1934. E-mail: info@wildernessventures.com.
URL www.wildernessventures.com
For more information, see page 1396.

Wilderness Ventures–Rocky Mountain

Wilderness Ventures
Locations Idaho, Montana, Wyoming.

General Information Coed travel outdoor program, wilderness program, and adventure program established in 1973.
Program Focus Wilderness travel, wilderness skills, leadership skills.
Special Interest Areas Leadership training.
Sports Sea kayaking.
Wilderness/Outdoors Backpacking, hiking, mountain biking, rafting, white-water trips, wilderness camping.
Excursions Overnight.
Program Information 2 sessions per year. Session length: 22 days in June, July, August. Ages: 14–18. 13 participants per session. Cost: $3490. Financial aid available.
Housing Tents.
Application Deadline Continuous.
Jobs Positions for college students 21 and older.
Contact Mike Cottingham, Director, PO Box 2768, Jackson Hole, Wyoming 83001. Phone: 800-533-2281. Fax: 307-739-1934. E-mail: info@wildernessventures.com.
URL www.wildernessventures.com
For more information, see page 1396.

Wilderness Ventures–Yellowstone Fly Fishing

Wilderness Ventures
Locations Idaho, Montana, Wyoming.

General Information Coed travel outdoor program, wilderness program, and adventure program established in 1973.
Program Focus Wilderness travel, wilderness skills, leadership skills.
Special Interest Areas Leadership training.
Sports Fishing.
Wilderness/Outdoors Backpacking, fly fishing, rafting, white-water trips.
Excursions Overnight.
Program Information 3 sessions per year. Session length: 16 days in June, July, August. Ages: 14–18. 10 participants per session. Cost: $2490. Financial aid available.
Application Deadline Continuous.
Jobs Positions for college students 21 and older.
Contact Mike Cottingham, Director, PO Box 2768, Jackson Hole, Wyoming 83001. Phone: 800-533-2281. Fax: 307-739-1934. E-mail: info@wildernessventures.com.
URL www.wildernessventures.com
For more information, see page 1396.

Williwaw Adventures–Maine Wilderness

Williwaw Adventures
Locations Maine, Massachusetts, New Hampshire.

General Information Coed travel outdoor program and wilderness program established in 1999.
Program Focus Multi-activity wilderness travel.
Academics Marine studies, meteorology, oceanography.
Special Interest Areas Leadership training, nautical skills, navigation.
Sports Boating, canoeing, sailing, sea kayaking.
Wilderness/Outdoors Backpacking, canoe trips, hiking, mountaineering, rafting, white-water trips, wilderness camping.
Program Information 2–3 sessions per year. Session length: 24 days in June, July, August. Ages: 14–18. 10–12 participants per session. Cost: $2600–$3000. Financial aid available.
Housing Sailboats and tents.
Application Deadline Continuous.
Jobs Positions for college students 21 and older.
Contact Mr. Mike Dawson, Director, PO Box 166, Kingston, Massachusetts 02364. Phone: 800-585-2523. Fax: 801-720-4378. E-mail: info@williwawadventures.com.
URL www.williwawadventures.com

Williwaw Adventures–Pacific Northwest Expedition

Williwaw Adventures
Locations Oregon, Washington.

General Information Coed travel outdoor program and wilderness program established in 1999.
Program Focus Multi-activity wilderness travel.
Special Interest Areas Leadership training, nautical skills, navigation.
Sports Sailing.
Wilderness/Outdoors Backpacking, hiking, mountaineering, rafting, white-water trips, wilderness camping.
Program Information 2–3 sessions per year. Session length: 26 days in June, July, August. Ages: 14–18. 10–12 participants per session. Cost: $2800–$3200. Financial aid available.
Housing Tents.
Application Deadline Continuous.
Jobs Positions for college students 21 and older.
Contact Mr. Mike Dawson, Director, PO Box 166, Kingston, Massachusetts 02364. Phone: 781-585-3459. Fax: 801-720-4378. E-mail: info@williwawadventures.com.
URL www.williwawadventures.com

Windsor Mountain: Experiential Summer School

Interlocken at Windsor Mountain
Locations Maine, New Hampshire, Vermont.

General Information Coed travel academic program, outdoor program, and adventure program established in 2005. High school credit may be earned.
Program Focus Offers credit to high school students in English or math.
Academics American literature, English language/literature, academics (general), humanities, mathematics, reading, study skills, writing.
Special Interest Areas Leadership training, team building, touring.
Wilderness/Outdoors Backpacking, bicycle trips, canoe trips, hiking, rock climbing.
Program Information 1 session per year. Session length: 5 weeks in June, July, August. Ages: 13–17. 14–18 participants per session. Cost: $3800. Financial aid available.
Housing Tents.
Application Deadline Continuous.
Contact Tom Herman, Marketing Director, 19 Interlocken Way, Windsor, New Hampshire 03244. Phone: 603-478-3166 Ext.20. Fax: 603-478-5260. E-mail: mail@windsormountain.org.
URL www.windsormountain.org/xrds
For more information, see page 1162.

Windsor Mountain: New England Adventure

Interlocken at Windsor Mountain
Locations Maine, New Hampshire, Vermont.

General Information Coed travel outdoor program and adventure program established in 1967.
Program Focus Wilderness adventure.
Special Interest Areas Community service, leadership training, team building.
Sports Ropes course, sea kayaking.
Wilderness/Outdoors Backpacking, canoe trips, hiking, mountain biking, rock climbing, wilderness camping.
Program Information 2–3 sessions per year. Session length: 2–3 weeks in July, August. Ages: 11–13. 13 participants per session. Cost: $1995–$2495. Financial aid available.
Housing Tents.
Application Deadline Continuous.
Jobs Positions for college students 23 and older.
Contact Richard Herman, Director, 19 Interlocken Way, Windsor, New Hampshire 03244. Phone: 800-862-7760. Fax: 603-478-5260. E-mail: mail@windsormountain.org.
URL www.windsormountain.org/xrds
For more information, see page 1162.

Windsor Mountain: New England Traveling Minstrels

Interlocken at Windsor Mountain
Locations Maine, Massachusetts, New Hampshire, Vermont.

General Information Coed travel arts program established in 1967.
Program Focus Creative traveling theater for beginning or experienced students.
Arts Acting, clowning, creative writing, dance, mime, music, theater/drama.
Special Interest Areas Leadership training, team building.
Sports Swimming.
Excursions Cultural, day.
Program Information 1 session per year. Session length: 5 weeks in July, August. Ages: 13–15. 13 participants per session. Cost: $3895. Financial aid available.
Housing Tents.
Application Deadline Continuous.
Contact Richard Herman, Director, 19 Interlocken Way, Windsor, New Hampshire 03244. Phone: 800-862-7760. Fax: 603-478-5260. E-mail: mail@windsormountain.org.
URL www.windsormountain.org/xrds
For more information, see page 1162.

Windsor Mountain: Random Acts of Kindness

Interlocken at Windsor Mountain
Locations Maine, Massachusetts, New Hampshire, Vermont.

General Information Coed travel outdoor program, community service program, and cultural program established in 1967.
Academics Intercultural studies, peace education.
Special Interest Areas Native American culture, community service, leadership training, team building.
Sports Sea kayaking.
Wilderness/Outdoors Hiking, white-water trips.
Program Information 1 session per year. Session length: 27 days in July. Ages: 13–15. 13 participants per session. Cost: $3195. Financial aid available.
Application Deadline Continuous.
Jobs Positions for college students 23 and older.
Contact Richard Herman, Director, 19 Interlocken Way, Windsor, New Hampshire 03244. Phone: 800-862-7760. Fax: 603-478-5260. E-mail: mail@windsormountain.org.
URL www.windsormountain.org/xrds
For more information, see page 1162.

TRAVEL PROGRAMS ABROAD

AAVE–AFRICA

AAVE–America's Adventure Ventures Everywhere
Locations Namibia, South Africa.

General Information Coed travel outdoor program, wilderness program, cultural program, and adventure program established in 1976. Accredited by American Camping Association.
Program Focus Adventure travel, including wildlife viewing and service project monitoring elephant watering holes.
Academics Area studies, intercultural studies.
Special Interest Areas Campcraft, community service, cross-cultural education, leadership training, nature study, touring.
Sports Bicycling, boating, kayaking, sandboarding.
Wilderness/Outdoors Hiking, pack animal trips, rafting, safari, white-water trips, wilderness camping.
Excursions Cultural, day, overnight.
Program Information 2–4 sessions per year. Session length: 3 weeks in June, July, August. Ages: 15–18. 15 participants per session. Cost: $3650. Financial aid available.
Housing Cabins and tents.
Application Deadline Continuous.
Jobs Positions for college students 21 and older.
Contact Mr. Abbott Wallis, Owner, 2245 Stonecrop Way, Golden, Colorado 80401. Phone: 800-222-3595. Fax: 303-526-0885. E-mail: info@aave.com.
URL www.aave.com
For more information, see page 952.

AAVE–ALPS RIDER

AAVE–America's Adventure Ventures Everywhere
Locations France, Italy, Switzerland.

General Information Coed travel outdoor program, wilderness program, cultural program, and adventure program established in 1976. Accredited by American Camping Association.
Program Focus Adventure travel.
Special Interest Areas Campcraft, community service, leadership training.
Sports Bicycling, rappelling, skiing (downhill), snowboarding, swimming, waterskiing.
Wilderness/Outdoors Backpacking, hiking, mountain biking, mountaineering, orienteering, rock climbing, wilderness camping.
Program Information 4–6 sessions per year. Session length: 3 weeks in June, July, August. Ages: 14–18. 13–15 participants per session. Cost: $4288. Financial aid available.
Housing Cabins and tents.
Application Deadline Continuous.
Jobs Positions for college students 21 and older.
Contact Mr. Abbot Wallis, Owner, 2245 Stonecrop Way, Golden, Colorado 80401. Phone: 800-222-3595. Fax: 303-526-0885. E-mail: info@aave.com.
URL www.aave.com
For more information, see page 952.

AAVE–BOLD EUROPE

AAVE–America's Adventure Ventures Everywhere
Locations France, Italy, Spain.

General Information Coed travel outdoor program, wilderness program, cultural program, and adventure program established in 1976. Accredited by American Camping Association.
Program Focus Adventure travel.
Special Interest Areas Community service, cross-cultural education, leadership training, touring.

AAVE–Bold Europe

Sports Bicycling, climbing (wall), rappelling, ropes course, snorkeling, swimming.
Wilderness/Outdoors Bicycle trips, hiking, mountain biking, mountaineering, orienteering, outdoor adventure, outdoor camping, rafting, rock climbing, white-water trips.
Excursions Cultural, day, overnight.
Program Information 4–6 sessions per year. Session length: 4 weeks in June, July, August. Ages: 14–18. 13–15 participants per session. Cost: $4188. Financial aid available.
Housing Tents and youth hostels.
Application Deadline Continuous.
Jobs Positions for college students 21 and older.
Contact Mr. Abbott Wallis, Owner, 2245 Stonecrop Way, Golden, Colorado 80401. Phone: 800-222-3595. Fax: 303-526-0885. E-mail: info@aave.com.
URL www.aave.com

For more information, see page 952.

AAVE–Wild Isles

AAVE–America's Adventure Ventures Everywhere
Locations Ireland, United Kingdom.

General Information Coed travel outdoor program, wilderness program, cultural program, and adventure program established in 1976. Accredited by American Camping Association.
Program Focus Adventure travel.
Special Interest Areas Campcraft, cross-cultural education, leadership training, touring.
Sports Bicycling, horseback riding, kayaking, rappelling, sea kayaking, surfing, swimming.
Wilderness/Outdoors Bicycle trips, hiking, mountain biking, outdoor adventure, rock climbing.
Excursions Cultural, day, overnight.
Program Information 2–4 sessions per year. Session length: 3 weeks in June, July, August. Ages: 14–18. 16 participants per session. Cost: $4188. Financial aid available.
Housing Tents and youth hostels.
Application Deadline Continuous.
Jobs Positions for college students 21 and older.
Contact Mr. Abbott Wallis, Owner, 2245 Stonecrop Way, Golden, Colorado 80401. Phone: 800-222-3595. Fax: 303-526-0885. E-mail: info@aave.com.
URL www.aave.com

For more information, see page 952.

ActionQuest: Leeward and French Caribbean Island Voyages

ActionQuest
Locations Antigua and Barbuda, British Virgin Islands, Guadeloupe, Netherlands Antilles, Saint Kitts and Nevis.

General Information Coed travel outdoor program, cultural program, and adventure program established in 1970.
Program Focus Sailing voyage throughout the Leeward Islands, with emphasis on seamanship, sailing certifications, water sports, and island exploration.
Academics Astronomy, intercultural studies.
Special Interest Areas Leadership training, nature study, nautical skills, team building, touring.
Sports Sailing, scuba diving, snorkeling, waterskiing, windsurfing.
Wilderness/Outdoors Hiking.
Excursions Cultural, day.
Program Information 2 sessions per year. Session length: 3 weeks in June, July. Ages: 14–19. 10–20 participants per session. Cost: $4170.
Housing Yachts.
Application Deadline Continuous.
Contact James Stoll, Director, PO Box 5517, Sarasota, Florida 34277. Phone: 800-317-6789. Fax: 941-924-6075. E-mail: info@actionquest.com.
URL www.actionquest.com

For more information, see page 964.

ActionQuest: Mediterranean Sailing Voyage

ActionQuest
Locations France, Italy, Monaco.

ACTIONQUEST: Mediterranean Sailing Voyage (continued)

General Information Coed travel outdoor program, cultural program, and adventure program established in 1986.

ACTIONQUEST: Mediterranean Sailing Voyage

Program Focus Live-aboard voyage throughout French and Italian Rivieras. Ports of call include Rome, Corsica, Sardinia, Elba, and Monaco. Emphasis on sailing certifications, history, and culture, with numerous shore excursions.
Academics Astronomy, geography, history, intercultural studies.
Special Interest Areas Field trips (arts and culture), leadership training, nautical skills, team building, touring.
Sports Sailing, swimming.
Wilderness/Outdoors Hiking.
Excursions Cultural, day.
Program Information 1 session per year. Session length: 3 weeks in June, July. Ages: 15–19. 10 participants per session. Cost: $4470.
Housing Yachts.
Application Deadline Continuous.
Contact James Stoll, Director, PO Box 5517, Sarasota, Florida 34277. Phone: 800-317-6789. Fax: 941-924-6075. E-mail: info@actionquest.com.
URL www.actionquest.com
For more information, see page 964.

!ADVENTURES–AFLOAT: ADVANCED SCUBA ADVENTURE VOYAGES–CARIBBEAN ISLANDS

!Adventures–Afloat/Odyssey Expeditions
Locations Grenada, Saint Lucia, Saint Vincent and The Grenadines.

General Information Coed travel outdoor program and adventure program established in 1995. High school or college credit may be earned.
Program Focus Coed underwater adventure program featuring PADI advanced, rescue, and specialty scuba certifications, sailing, and marine biology.
Academics Biology, ecology, geology/earth science, marine studies, oceanography.
Arts Photography, television/video.
Special Interest Areas Career exploration, community service, field research/expeditions, leadership training, nature study, nautical skills.
Sports Boating, diving, fishing, sailing, scuba diving, sea kayaking, snorkeling, waterskiing, windsurfing.
Wilderness/Outdoors Hiking.
Excursions Cultural.
Program Information 3 sessions per year. Session length: 3 weeks in June, July, August. Ages: 13–19. 10 participants per session. Cost: $4390.
Housing Yachts.
Application Deadline Continuous.
Jobs Positions for college students 21 and older.
Contact Jason Buchheim, Director, 650 Southeast Paradise Point Road, #100, Crystal River, Florida 34429. Phone: 800-929-7749. E-mail: odyssey@usa.net.
URL www.odysseyexpeditions.org
For more information, see page 970.

!ADVENTURES–AFLOAT: SCUBA AND SAILING DISCOVERY VOYAGES–CARIBBEAN ISLANDS

!Adventures–Afloat/Odyssey Expeditions
Locations Grenada, Saint Lucia, Saint Vincent and The Grenadines.

General Information Coed travel outdoor program and adventure program established in 1995. High school or college credit may be earned.
Program Focus PADI scuba certification, sail training, island exploration, and watersports.
Academics Biology, ecology, marine studies, oceanography.
Arts Photography, television/video.
Special Interest Areas Community service, field research/expeditions, leadership training, nature study, nautical skills.
Sports Boating, fishing, sailing, scuba diving, sea kayaking, snorkeling, waterskiing, windsurfing.
Wilderness/Outdoors Hiking.
Excursions Cultural.
Program Information 3 sessions per year. Session length: 3 weeks in June, July, August. Ages: 13–19. 10 participants per session. Cost: $4390.
Housing Yachts.
Application Deadline Continuous.
Jobs Positions for college students 21 and older.
Contact Jason Buchheim, Director, 650 Southeast Paradise Point Road, #100, Crystal River, Florida 34429. Phone: 800-929-7749. E-mail: odyssey@usa.net.
URL www.odysseyexpeditions.org
For more information, see page 970.

ADVENTURES CROSS-COUNTRY, AUSTRALIA/FIJI ADVENTURE

Adventures Cross-Country
Locations Australia, Fiji.

!ADVENTURES–AFLOAT: Scuba and Sailing Discovery Voyages–Caribbean Islands

General Information Coed travel outdoor program, wilderness program, and adventure program established in 1983.
Program Focus Exploring Australia's and Fiji's beaches, reefs, rainforest, and rivers.
Sports Scuba diving, snorkeling.
Wilderness/Outdoors Backpacking, hiking, orienteering, rafting, white-water trips, wilderness camping.
Program Information 1 session per year. Session length: 34 days in June, July, August. Ages: 14–18. 8–15 participants per session. Cost: $6295; including airfare from Los Angeles, CA to all trip destinations in Australia and Fiji.
Housing Tents and youth hostels.
Application Deadline Continuous.
Jobs Positions for college students 21 and older.
Contact Scott von Eschen, Director, 242 Redwood Highway, Mill Valley, California 94941. Phone: 415-332-5075. Fax: 415-332-2130. E-mail: arcc@adventurescrosscountry.com.
URL www.adventurescrosscountry.com
For more information, see page 972.

Adventures Cross-Country, Caribbean Adventure

Adventures Cross-Country
Locations British Virgin Islands, U.S. Virgin Islands.

General Information Coed travel outdoor program and adventure program established in 1983.
Program Focus Exploring St. John's and the Caribbean.
Special Interest Areas Conservation projects.
Sports Sailing, scuba diving, sea kayaking, snorkeling, swimming.
Wilderness/Outdoors Hiking, outdoor adventure.
Program Information 1 session per year. Session length: 22 days in July. Ages: 13–18. 8–15 participants per session. Cost: $3995. Financial aid available.
Application Deadline Continuous.
Jobs Positions for college students 21 and older.
Contact Scott von Eschen, Director, 242 Redwood Highway, Mill Valley, California 94941. Phone: 415-332-5075. Fax: 415-332-2130. E-mail: arcc@adventurescrosscountry.com.
URL www.adventurescrosscountry.com
For more information, see page 972.

Adventures Cross-Country, Southern Europe Adventure

Adventures Cross-Country
Locations France, Italy, Switzerland.

General Information Coed travel outdoor program, wilderness program, and adventure program established in 1983.
Program Focus Outdoor adventures in France, Switzerland, Italy and Europe's Alps.
Sports Sea kayaking.
Wilderness/Outdoors Backpacking, glacier travel, hiking, mountaineering, orienteering, rafting, white-water trips, wilderness camping.
Program Information 1 session per year. Session length: 4 weeks in July. Ages: 14–18. 8–15 participants per session. Cost: $4695. Financial aid available.
Housing Tents and youth hostels.
Application Deadline Continuous.
Jobs Positions for college students 21 and older.
Contact Scott von Eschen, Owner, 242 Redwood Highway, Mill Valley, California 94941. Phone: 415-332-5075. Fax: 415-332-2130. E-mail: arcc@adventurescrosscountry.com.
URL www.adventurescrosscountry.com
For more information, see page 972.

Alpengirl–Scandinavia

Alpengirl, Inc.
Locations Norway, Sweden.

General Information Girls' travel wilderness program, cultural program, and adventure program.
Special Interest Areas Cross-cultural education.
Sports Fishing, physical fitness, sea kayaking, yoga.
Wilderness/Outdoors Backpacking, hiking, rock climbing, wilderness camping.
Excursions Cultural, day, overnight, shopping.
Program Information 1 session per year. Session length: 3 weeks in July. Ages: 14–16. 10–12 participants per session. Cost: $3100. Financial aid available.
Housing Hotels and tents.

Alpengirl–Scandinavia (continued)
Application Deadline Continuous.
Contact Alissa Farley, Camp Director, PO Box 1138, Manhattan, Montana 59741. Phone: 800-585-7476. E-mail: alissa@alpengirl.com.
URL www.alpengirl.com

ATW: European Adventures

American Trails West
Locations Belgium, France, Italy, Switzerland, United Kingdom.

General Information Coed travel cultural program and adventure program established in 1966.
Special Interest Areas Touring.
Sports Bicycling, boating, horseback riding, in-line skating, skiing (downhill), snorkeling, swimming, tennis, waterskiing.
Wilderness/Outdoors Hiking, mountain biking, rafting.
Excursions College tours, cultural.
Program Information 1–2 sessions per year. Session length: 4 weeks in July, August. Ages: 15–18. 40–45 participants per session. Cost: $7695.
Housing Hotels.
Application Deadline Continuous.
Jobs Positions for college students 20 and older.
Contact Director, 92 Middle Neck Road, Great Neck, New York 11021. Phone: 800-645-6260. Fax: 516-487-2855. E-mail: info@americantrailswest.com.
URL www.americantrailswest.com

For more information, see page 982.

Bicycle Africa Tours

International Bicycle Fund
Locations Benin, Cameroon, Eritrea, Ethiopia, Gambia, Ghana, Guinea, Kenya, Malawi, Mali, Senegal, South Africa, Togo, Tunisia, Uganda, United Republic of Tanzania, Zimbabwe.

General Information Coed travel outdoor program, cultural program, and adventure program established in 1983.
Program Focus Cross-cultural bicycle tour.
Academics African languages, anthropology, archaeology, architecture, area studies, botany, ecology, economics, geography, geology/earth science, government and politics, health sciences, history, intercultural studies, peace education, religion, social science, social studies.
Special Interest Areas Cross-cultural education, field trips (arts and culture), homestays, nature study.
Sports Bicycling, canoeing.
Wilderness/Outdoors Bicycle trips, hiking, mountain biking.
Excursions Cultural.
Program Information 8–14 sessions per year. Session length: 12–16 days in January, February, April, June, July, August, September, October, November, December. Ages: 16+. 6–12 participants per session. Cost: $990–$1490. Financial aid available.
Housing Host-family homes and hotels.
Application Deadline Continuous.
Contact David Mozer, Director, 4887 Columbia Drive South, Seattle, Washington 98108-1919. Phone: 206-767-0848. Fax: 206-767-0848. E-mail: ibike@ibike.org.
URL www.ibike.org/bikeafrica

BICYCLE TRAVEL ADVENTURES–Student Hosteling Program–Amsterdam to Paris

BICYCLE TRAVEL ADVENTURES–Student Hosteling Program
Locations Belgium, France, Netherlands.

General Information Coed travel outdoor program, cultural program, and adventure program established in 1970. Accredited by American Camping Association. Formal opportunities for the academically talented. Specific services available for the emotionally challenged and learning disabled. High school credit may be earned.
Program Focus A moderate 28-day bicycling/camping/hosteling tour through Holland, Belgium, and France, ending with 4 days in Paris.
Special Interest Areas Campcraft, field trips (arts and culture), touring.
Sports Bicycling, boating, canoeing, fishing, sailing, swimming.
Wilderness/Outdoors Bicycle trips, canoe trips, hiking, mountain biking, wilderness camping.
Excursions Cultural, day, overnight, shopping.
Program Information 1–3 sessions per year. Session length: 4 weeks in June, July, August. Ages: 14–18. 8–12 participants per session. Cost: $4500; including airfare from Boston, MA to Amsterdam, Netherlands.
Housing Tents and youth hostels.
Application Deadline Continuous.
Jobs Positions for high school students 16 and older and college students 18 and older.
Contact Ted Lefkowitz, Director, 1356 Ashfield Road, PO Box 419, Conway, Massachusetts 01341. Phone: 800-343-6132. Fax: 413-369-4257. E-mail: shpbike@aol.com.
URL www.bicycletrips.com

For more information, see page 994.

BICYCLE TRAVEL ADVENTURES–Student Hosteling Program–France and Italy

BICYCLE TRAVEL ADVENTURES–Student Hosteling Program
Locations France, Italy.

General Information Coed travel outdoor program, cultural program, and adventure program established in 1970. Accredited by American Camping Association. Formal opportunities for the academically talented. Specific services available for the emotionally challenged and learning disabled. High school credit may be earned.
Program Focus A moderate 30-day bicycling/camping/hosteling tour cycling through France's beautiful Loire Valley and spending 3 days in Paris before touring Italy, by public transportation, from Venice to Rome.

Special Interest Areas Campcraft, field trips (arts and culture), touring.
Sports Bicycling, boating, canoeing, fishing, sailing, swimming.
Wilderness/Outdoors Bicycle trips, canoe trips, hiking, mountain biking, wilderness camping.
Excursions Cultural, day, overnight, shopping.
Program Information 1 session per year. Session length: 30 days in June, July, August. Ages: 16–18. 8–12 participants per session. Cost: $5120; including airfare from Boston, MA to Paris, France.
Housing College dormitories, hotels, tents, and youth hostels.
Application Deadline Continuous.
Jobs Positions for high school students 16 and older and college students 18 and older.
Contact Ted Lefkowitz, Director, 1356 Ashfield Road, PO Box 419, Conway, Massachusetts 01341. Phone: 800-343-6132. Fax: 413-369-4257. E-mail: shpbike@aol.com.
URL www.bicycletrips.com

For more information, see page 994.

BICYCLE TRAVEL ADVENTURES–STUDENT HOSTELING PROGRAM–IRELAND AND ENGLAND

BICYCLE TRAVEL ADVENTURES–Student Hosteling Program
Locations Ireland, United Kingdom.

General Information Coed travel outdoor program, cultural program, and adventure program established in 1970. Accredited by American Camping Association. Formal opportunities for the academically talented. Specific services available for the emotionally challenged and learning disabled. High school credit may be earned.
Program Focus A moderate 30-day camping/hosteling trip cycling through magical Ireland and touring England by public transportation, ending in a 3-day stay in London.
Special Interest Areas Campcraft, field trips (arts and culture), touring.
Sports Bicycling, boating, canoeing, fishing, sailing, swimming.
Wilderness/Outdoors Bicycle trips, canoe trips, hiking, mountain biking, wilderness camping.
Excursions Cultural, day, overnight, shopping.
Program Information 1–2 sessions per year. Session length: 30 days in June, July, August. Ages: 13–18. 8–12 participants per session. Cost: $4600; including airfare from Boston, MA to Shannon, Ireland.
Housing Hotels, tents, and youth hostels.
Application Deadline Continuous.
Jobs Positions for high school students 16 and older and college students 18 and older.
Contact Ted Lefkowitz, Director, 1356 Ashfield Road, PO Box 419, Conway, Massachusetts 01341. Phone: 800-343-6132. Fax: 413-369-4257. E-mail: shpbike@aol.com.
URL www.bicycletrips.com

For more information, see page 994.

BICYCLE TRAVEL ADVENTURES–STUDENT HOSTELING PROGRAM–SPAIN AND FRANCE

BICYCLE TRAVEL ADVENTURES–Student Hosteling Program
Locations France, Portugal, Spain.

General Information Coed travel outdoor program, cultural program, and adventure program established in 1970. Accredited by American Camping Association. Formal opportunities for the academically talented. Specific services available for the emotionally challenged and learning disabled. High school credit may be earned.
Program Focus A moderate 40-day bicycling/camping/hosteling tour through Spain, Portugal, and France, ending with 4 days in Paris.
Special Interest Areas Campcraft, field trips (arts and culture), touring.
Sports Bicycling, boating, canoeing, fishing, sailing, swimming.
Wilderness/Outdoors Bicycle trips, canoe trips, hiking, mountain biking, wilderness camping.
Excursions Day, overnight, shopping.
Program Information 1 session per year. Session length: 40 days in June, July, August. Ages: 15–18. 8–12 participants per session. Cost: $5500; including airfare from Boston, MA to Madrid, Spain. Financial aid available.
Housing Hotels, tents, and youth hostels.
Application Deadline Continuous.
Jobs Positions for high school students 16 and older and college students 18 and older.
Contact Ted Lefkowitz, Director, 1356 Ashfield Road, PO Box 419, Conway, Massachusetts 01341. Phone: 800-343-6132. Fax: 413-369-4257. E-mail: shpbike@aol.com.
URL www.bicycletrips.com

For more information, see page 994.

BLUE LAKE INTERNATIONAL EXCHANGE PROGRAM

Blue Lake Fine Arts Camp, Inc.
Locations Austria, Belgium, Denmark, France, Germany, Italy.

General Information Coed travel arts program and cultural program established in 1970. Formal opportunities for the artistically talented.
Program Focus Cultural exchange through youth concert tours.
Arts Band, chorus, dance, dance (ballet), music (jazz), music (orchestral), musical performance/recitals.
Special Interest Areas Cross-cultural education, homestays, touring.
Excursions Cultural, day, shopping.
Program Information 6 sessions per year. Session length: 3 weeks in June, July, August. Ages: 12–18. 350 participants per session. Cost: $3250–$3600; including airfare from Chicago, IL to Frankfurt, Germany. Financial aid available.
Housing Host-family homes.
Application Deadline Continuous.
Jobs Positions for college students 18 and older.

Blue Lake International Exchange Program (continued)

Contact Admissions, International Exchange Program, 300 East Crystal Lake Road, Twin Lake, Michigan 49457. Phone: 800-221-3796. Fax: 231-893-5120. E-mail: international@bluelake.org.
URL www.bluelake.org

BROADREACH Academic Treks–Marine Park Management

Broadreach
Locations Guadeloupe, Netherlands Antilles, Saint Kitts and Nevis.

General Information Coed travel academic program, outdoor program, and adventure program established in 1992. High school or college credit may be earned.
Program Focus Academic adventure program focusing on the design and management of underwater marine parks, scuba diving, community service, island exploration and school credit. Travel to Saba, Statia, St. Kitts, and St. Barts.
Academics Academics (general), ecology, environmental science, marine studies.
Special Interest Areas Community service, conservation projects, field research/expeditions, leadership training.
Sports Sailing, scuba diving, snorkeling, swimming.
Wilderness/Outdoors Hiking.
Program Information 2 sessions per year. Session length: 22 days in June, July, August. Ages: 15–19. 10–14 participants per session. Cost: $4400; including airfare. Financial aid available.
Housing Hotels and yachts.
Application Deadline Continuous.
Contact Carlton Goldthwaite, Director, PO Box 27076, Raleigh, North Carolina 27611-7076. Phone: 888-833-1907. Fax: 919-833-1907. E-mail: info@gobroadreach.com or info@academictreks.com.
URL www.academictreks.com

For more information, see page 1010.

BROADREACH Adventures in Scuba and Sailing–Underwater Discoveries

Broadreach
Locations Antigua and Barbuda, Guadeloupe, Netherlands Antilles, Saint Kitts and Nevis.

General Information Coed travel outdoor program and adventure program established in 1992.
Program Focus Coed program focusing on PADI scuba certification, sail training, marine biology, island exploration, and travel to St. Barts and St. Marten and throughout the Leeward Islands.
Academics Environmental science, marine studies.
Arts Photography.
Special Interest Areas Community service, conservation projects, field research/expeditions, leadership training, nature study.
Sports Boating, fishing, sailing, scuba diving, snorkeling, waterskiing.
Wilderness/Outdoors Hiking.
Excursions Cultural.
Program Information 3 sessions per year. Session length: 17–21 days in June, July, August. Ages: 13–19. 10–12 participants per session. Cost: $3500–$4300.
Housing Yachts.
Application Deadline Continuous.
Contact Carlton Goldthwaite, Director, PO Box 27076, Raleigh, North Carolina 27611-7076. Phone: 888-833-1907. Fax: 919-833-2129. E-mail: info@gobroadreach.com.
URL www.gobroadreach.com

For more information, see page 1008.

BROADREACH Adventures in the Windward Islands–Advanced Scuba

Broadreach
Locations Grenada, Saint Lucia, Saint Vincent and The Grenadines.

General Information Coed travel outdoor program and adventure program established in 1992.
Program Focus Coed program focusing on advanced PADI scuba certification, PADI specialty and rescue certifications, sail training and certification, and island exploration.
Academics Ecology, marine studies.
Arts Photography.
Special Interest Areas Community service, conservation projects, field research/expeditions, leadership training, nature study.
Sports Boating, fishing, sailing, scuba diving, snorkeling, waterskiing.
Wilderness/Outdoors Hiking.
Excursions Cultural, day.
Program Information 2 sessions per year. Session length: 3 weeks in June, July, August. Ages: 15–19. 10–12 participants per session. Cost: $4500. Financial aid available.
Housing Yachts.
Application Deadline Continuous.
Contact Carlton Goldthwaite, Founder/Program Director, PO Box 27076, Raleigh, North Carolina 27611. Phone: 888-833-1907. Fax: 919-833-2129. E-mail: info@gobroadreach.com.
URL www.gobroadreach.com

For more information, see page 1008.

BROADREACH Adventures Underwater–Advanced Scuba

Broadreach
Locations Antigua and Barbuda, Guadeloupe, Netherlands Antilles, Saint Kitts and Nevis.

General Information Coed travel outdoor program and adventure program established in 1992.
Program Focus Coed program focusing on advanced PADI scuba certification, PADI rescue certification, sail training, marine biology, underwater community service and island exploration, travel to St. Barts and St. Marten and throughout the Leeward Islands.

BROADREACH Adventures Underwater–Advanced Scuba

Academics Ecology, environmental science, marine studies.
Arts Photography.
Special Interest Areas Community service, conservation projects, field research/expeditions, leadership training, nature study.
Sports Boating, fishing, sailing, scuba diving, snorkeling, waterskiing.
Wilderness/Outdoors Hiking.
Excursions Cultural.
Program Information 3 sessions per year. Session length: 16–21 days in June, July, August. Ages: 13–19. 10–12 participants per session. Cost: $3500–$4300.
Housing Yachts.
Application Deadline Continuous.
Contact Carlton Goldthwaite, Director, PO Box 27076, Raleigh, North Carolina 27611-7076. Phone: 888-833-1907. Fax: 919-833-2129. E-mail: info@gobroadreach.com.
URL www.gobroadreach.com
For more information, see page 1008.

BROADREACH Arc of the Caribbean Sailing Adventure

Broadreach
Locations Antigua and Barbuda, Dominica, Guadeloupe, Martinique, Netherlands Antilles, Saint Kitts and Nevis, Saint Lucia, Saint Vincent and The Grenadines, Trinidad and Tobago.

General Information Coed travel outdoor program, cultural program, and adventure program established in 1992.

BROADREACH Arc of the Caribbean Sailing Adventure

Program Focus 31-day sailing voyage focusing on intensive sail training, ASA sailing certification, seamanship, island exploration, optional scuba, and leadership course.
Academics Ecology, environmental science, intercultural studies, marine studies.
Arts Photography.
Special Interest Areas Community service, conservation projects, leadership training.
Sports Boating, fishing, sailing, scuba diving, snorkeling, waterskiing.
Wilderness/Outdoors Hiking, wilderness camping.
Excursions Cultural.
Program Information 3 sessions per year. Session length: 32 days in June, July, August. Ages: 15–19. 8–10 participants per session. Cost: $5300.
Housing Yachts.
Application Deadline Continuous.

BROADREACH Arc of the Caribbean Sailing Adventure (continued)

Contact Carlton Goldthwaite, Director, PO Box 27076, Raleigh, North Carolina 27611-7076. Phone: 888-833-1907. Fax: 919-833-2129. E-mail: info@gobroadreach.com.
URL www.gobroadreach.com
For more information, see page 1008.

BROADREACH Fiji Solomon Quest

Broadreach
Locations Fiji, Solomon Islands, Vanuatu.

General Information Coed travel outdoor program, cultural program, and adventure program established in 1992.
Program Focus Coed program focusing on scuba diving, cultural immersion, adventure travel, and exploration in Fiji, Vanuatu, and the Solomon Islands in the South Pacific.
Academics Area studies, environmental science, history, marine studies.
Arts Photography.
Special Interest Areas Community service, cross-cultural education, field research/expeditions, leadership training, nature study.
Sports Fishing, scuba diving, sea kayaking, snorkeling, swimming.
Wilderness/Outdoors Hiking, wilderness camping.
Excursions Cultural.
Program Information 2 sessions per year. Session length: 24 days in June, July, August. Ages: 15–19. 10–12 participants per session. Cost: $4480.
Housing Tents and youth hostels.
Application Deadline Continuous.
Contact Carlton Goldthwaite, Director, PO Box 27076, Raleigh, North Carolina 27611-7076. Phone: 888-833-1907. Fax: 919-833-2129. E-mail: info@gobroadreach.com.
URL www.gobroadreach.com
For more information, see page 1010.

Burklyn Ballet Edinburgh Connection

Burklyn Ballet Theatre, Inc.
Locations United Kingdom, Vermont.

General Information Coed travel arts program established in 1994. Formal opportunities for the artistically talented. Specific services available for the hearing impaired. College credit may be earned.
Program Focus Classical ballet training and performance opportunities, including participation at Edinburgh Fringe Festival.
Arts Dance, dance (ballet), dance (folk), dance (jazz), dance (modern), music, music (jazz), music (orchestral), music (vocal), theater/drama.
Special Interest Areas Career exploration, field trips (arts and culture).
Excursions Cultural, day, shopping.
Program Information 1 session per year. Session length: 8 weeks in July, August. Ages: 14–25. 20–25 participants per session. Cost: $3000–$6500; including airfare from Boston, MA to Edinburgh, Scotland. Application fee: $25. Financial aid available.
Housing College dormitories.
Application Deadline March 30.
Jobs Positions for college students 20 and older.
Summer Contact Joanne Whitehill, Artistic Director, PO Box 302, Johnson, Vermont 05656-0302. Phone: 802-635-1390.
Winter Contact Joanne Whitehill, Artistic Director, PO Box 907, Island Heights, New Jersey 08732-0907. Phone: 732-288-2660. Fax: 732-288-2663. E-mail: burklyn@aol.com.
URL www.burklynballet.com

Celtic Learning and Travel Services–Edinburgh and Dublin

Celtic Learning and Travel Services
Locations Ireland, United Kingdom.

General Information Coed travel academic program, arts program, and cultural program. Formal opportunities for the academically talented. High school credit may be earned.
Program Focus Experience Celtic culture in Scotland and Ireland.
Academics English language/literature, Irish studies, geography, geology/earth science, government and politics, history, intercultural studies, music, reading, social science, social studies, speech/debate.
Arts Creative writing, dance, television/video, theater/drama.
Special Interest Areas Field trips (arts and culture), homestays, leadership training, touring.
Sports Basketball, golf, horseback riding, rugby, soccer, tennis.
Excursions College tours, cultural, day, overnight, shopping.
Program Information Session length: 28–31 days in June, July, August. Ages: 14–21. 85–90 participants per session. Cost: $3795–$4140; including airfare from Toronto, Canada or New York, NY to Dublin, Ireland. Local transit included in cost.
Housing College dormitories and host-family homes.
Application Deadline Continuous.
Jobs Positions for college students 19 and older.
Summer Contact Mark Burke, Program Director, 17 Carysfort Road, Dalkey County, Dublin, Ireland. E-mail: info@celticsummer.com.
Winter Contact Mark Burke, Program Director, 189 Humbercrest Boulevard, Toronto, Ontario M6S 4L5, Canada. Phone: 888-220-2358. Fax: 416-762-2517. E-mail: info@celticsummer.com.
URL www.celticsummer.com

Celtic Learning and Travel Services–London and Dublin

Celtic Learning and Travel Services
Locations Ireland, United Kingdom.

General Information Coed travel academic program, arts program, and cultural program. Formal opportunities for the academically talented. High school credit may be earned.
Program Focus Experience the Celtic culture in Dublin and visit London.
Academics English language/literature, Irish studies, geography, geology/earth science, government and politics, history, intercultural studies, music, reading, social science, social studies, speech/debate.
Arts Creative writing, dance, television/video, theater/drama.
Special Interest Areas Field trips (arts and culture), homestays, leadership training, touring.
Sports Basketball, golf, horseback riding, rugby, soccer, tennis.
Excursions College tours, cultural, day, overnight, shopping.
Program Information Session length: 28–31 days in June, July, August. Ages: 14–21. 85–90 participants per session. Cost: $4195–$4330; including airfare from New York or Toronto to London, England.
Housing College dormitories.
Application Deadline Continuous.
Jobs Positions for college students 19 and older.
Summer Contact Mark Burke, Program Director, 17 Carysfort Road, Dalkey County, Dublin, Ireland. E-mail: info@celticsummer.com.
Winter Contact Mark Burke, Program Director, 189 Humbercrest Boulevard, Toronto, Ontario M6S 4L5, Canada. Phone: 888-220-2358. Fax: 416-762-2517. E-mail: info@celticsummer.com.
URL www.celticsummer.com

Costa Rica Rainforest Outward Bound School–Tri-Country/Tri-Mester

Costa Rica Rainforest Outward Bound School
Locations Costa Rica, Nicaragua, Panama.

General Information Coed travel outdoor program, wilderness program, cultural program, and adventure program established in 1994. High school or college credit may be earned.
Program Focus Leadership skills, teamwork and personal development.
Academics Spanish language/literature, anthropology, biology, botany, ecology, environmental science, geography, intercultural studies, oceanography, science (general).
Special Interest Areas Campcraft, community service, homestays, leadership training, nature study.
Sports Climbing (wall), kayaking, rappelling, scuba diving, sea kayaking, snorkeling, surfing, swimming.
Wilderness/Outdoors Backpacking, caving, hiking, mountain biking, mountaineering, rafting, white-water trips, wilderness camping.
Excursions Cultural, day, overnight.
Program Information 1 session per year. Session length: 85 days in April, May, June. Ages: 17+. 8–12 participants per session. Cost: $7995. Application fee: $60. Financial aid available.
Housing College dormitories, host-family homes, hotels, tents, and youth hostels.
Application Deadline Continuous.
Jobs Positions for college students 21 and older.
Contact Student Administrator, Box 1817-2050, San Pedro-San Jose, Costa Rica. Phone: 011-506-278-6058. Fax: 011-506-278-6059. E-mail: info@crrobs.org.
URL www.crrobs.org

Excel at Oxford/Tuscany

Putney Student Travel
Locations France, Italy, United Kingdom.

General Information Coed travel academic program and cultural program established in 1951. Formal opportunities for the academically talented and artistically talented.
Program Focus Two weeks at Oxford University, two weeks in Tuscany, and a weekend in France.
Academics Italian language/literature, academics (general), archaeology, architecture, art history/appreciation, government and politics, history, intercultural studies, international relations, precollege program, social science, writing.
Arts Creative writing, drawing, painting, television/video, theater/drama.
Special Interest Areas Field research/expeditions.
Sports Basketball, bicycling, boating, soccer, swimming, tennis.
Wilderness/Outdoors Hiking.
Excursions Cultural, day, overnight.
Program Information 1 session per year. Session length: 29–32 days in July, August. Ages: 16–18. 70 participants per session. Cost: $6500. Financial aid available.
Housing College dormitories.
Application Deadline Continuous.
Contact Tim Weed, Director, 345 Hickory Ridge Road, Putney, Vermont 05346. Phone: 802-387-5000. Fax: 802-387-4276. E-mail: excel@goputney.com.
URL www.goputney.com
For more information, see page 1114.

GLOBAL WORKS–Cultural Exchange-New Zealand and Fiji Islands-4 weeks

GLOBAL WORKS
Locations Fiji, New Zealand.

General Information Coed travel community service program, cultural program, and adventure program established in 1988. High school credit may be earned.
Program Focus Environmental service and cultural exchange.
Academics Intercultural studies.
Arts Arts and crafts (general), dance, music (instrumental), music (vocal), weaving.
Special Interest Areas Community service, construction, field trips (arts and culture), homestays, nature study.
Sports Kayaking, rappelling, rugby, scuba diving, sea kayaking, snorkeling, soccer, swimming, volleyball.

GLOBAL WORKS–Cultural Exchange-New Zealand and Fiji Islands-4 weeks (continued)
Wilderness/Outdoors Hiking.
Excursions Cultural, day, overnight.
Program Information 1–2 sessions per year. Session length: 28–30 days in June, July. Ages: 14–18. 15–17 participants per session. Cost: $3750–$3850. Application fee: $100. Financial aid available.
Housing Host-family homes and youth hostels.
Application Deadline Continuous.
Jobs Positions for college students 23 and older.
Contact Erik Werner, Director, 1113 South Allen Street, State College, Pennsylvania 16801. Phone: 814-867-7000. Fax: 814-867-2717. E-mail: info@globalworksinc.com.
URL www.globalworksinc.com
For more information, see page 1136.

Israel Discovery

Young Judea
Locations Israel, Italy, Spain.

General Information Coed travel outdoor program, community service program, bible camp, cultural program, and adventure program established in 1951. Religious affiliation: Jewish. High school or college credit may be earned.
Academics Bible study, Hebrew language, Jewish studies, archaeology, geography, geology/earth science, government and politics, history, intercultural studies, peace education, religion.
Special Interest Areas Community service, nature study, team building, touring.
Sports Boating, canoeing, kayaking, swimming, waterskiing.
Wilderness/Outdoors Backpacking, canoe trips, hiking, rafting.
Program Information 1 session per year. Session length: 37–42 days in June, July, August. Ages: 14–18. 250–400 participants per session. Cost: $5000–$5500; including airfare from New York, NY to Tel Aviv, Israel. Financial aid available.
Housing Hotels and youth hostels.
Application Deadline Continuous.
Jobs Positions for college students 21 and older.
Contact Mr. Benji Lovitt, Assistant Director, Short-term Israel Programs, 50 West 58th Street, New York, New York 10019. Phone: 212-303-4577. Fax: 212-303-7411. E-mail: blovitt@youngjudea.org.
URL www.youngjudaea.org/html/summer_for_teens.html

Kayak Adventures Unlimited

Wilderness Experiences Unlimited, Inc.
Locations Dominica, Netherlands Antilles.

General Information Coed travel outdoor program and wilderness program established in 1981.
Program Focus Flat water, moving water, and white-water kayaking.
Special Interest Areas Native American culture, campcraft, leadership training, nature study, touring.
Sports Canoeing, climbing (wall), kayaking, rappelling, ropes course, scuba diving, sea kayaking, snorkeling, swimming.
Wilderness/Outdoors Backpacking, bicycle trips, canoe trips, caving, hiking, mountain biking, mountaineering, orienteering, rafting, rock climbing, survival training, white-water trips, wilderness camping.
Excursions Overnight.
Program Information 9 sessions per year. Session length: 5–14 days in May, June, July, August, September. Ages: 12–17. 10–30 participants per session. Cost: $1550–$2000; including airfare from Hartford, CT to Marigot, Dominica or Curacao, Netherlands Antilles.
Application Deadline Continuous.
Jobs Positions for college students 18 and older.
Contact Taylor Cook, Executive Director, 499 Loomis Street, Westfield, Massachusetts 01085. Phone: 413-562-7431. Fax: 413-562-7431. E-mail: adventures@weu.com.
URL www.weu.com

Knowledge Exchange Institute–Discover Spain and Portugal Program

Knowledge Exchange Institute
Locations Portugal, Spain.

General Information Coed travel cultural program established in 2003. College credit may be earned.
Program Focus Spanish studies and language.
Academics Spanish language/literature, economics, government and politics, history, intercultural studies, precollege program, social studies.
Special Interest Areas Field trips (arts and culture), touring.
Sports Swimming.
Wilderness/Outdoors Hiking.
Excursions Cultural, day, overnight.
Program Information 1 session per year. Session length: 30 days in June, July, August. Ages: 15–19. 5–15 participants per session. Cost: $6350. Application fee: $50. Financial aid available.
Housing Hotels and youth hostels.
Application Deadline March 20.
Contact Kei Program Manager, 111 John Street, Suite 800, New York, New York 10038. Phone: 800-831-5095. E-mail: info@knowledgeexchange.org.
URL www.KnowledgeExchange.org

Knowledge Exchange Institute–European Capitals Program

Knowledge Exchange Institute
Locations Austria, Belgium, Czech Republic, France, Germany, Luxembourg, Netherlands, Switzerland, United Kingdom.

General Information Coed travel cultural program established in 2001. College credit may be earned.
Program Focus European studies, language study.
Academics Dutch language, French language/literature, German language/literature, Italian language/literature, Spanish language/literature, area studies, economics, government and politics, government

and politics (Advanced Placement), history, humanities, language study, precollege program, social studies.
Special Interest Areas Cross-cultural education, field trips (arts and culture), touring.
Excursions Cultural, day, overnight.
Program Information 1 session per year. Session length: 32 days in June, July, August. Ages: 15–19. 4–15 participants per session. Cost: $6350. Application fee: $50. Financial aid available.
Housing Hotels and youth hostels.
Application Deadline March 20.
Contact Kei Program Manager, 111 John Street, Suite 800, New York, New York 10038. Phone: 800-831-5095. E-mail: info@knowledgeexchange.org.
URL www.KnowledgeExchange.org

Longacre Expeditions, Virgin Islands

Longacre Expeditions
Locations British Virgin Islands, U.S. Virgin Islands.

General Information Coed travel outdoor program, wilderness program, and adventure program established in 1981. Accredited by American Camping Association.
Program Focus Effective communication skills, responsibility, confidence building.
Academics Ecology, marine studies.
Special Interest Areas Community service, leadership training.
Sports Scuba diving, sea kayaking, snorkeling, swimming.
Wilderness/Outdoors Hiking, wilderness camping.
Excursions Cultural.
Program Information 3 sessions per year. Session length: 20 days in July. Ages: 14–17. 10 participants per session. Cost: $3750.
Housing Tents.
Application Deadline Continuous.
Jobs Positions for college students 21 and older.
Contact Meredith Schuler, Director, 4030 Middle Ridge Road, Newport, Pennsylvania 17074. Phone: 717-567-6790. Fax: 717-567-3955. E-mail: longacre@longacreexpeditions.com.
URL www.longacreexpeditions.com

For more information, see page 1200.

Musiker Tours: Action Europe

Musiker Tours
Locations Belgium, France, Italy, Netherlands, Switzerland, United Kingdom.

General Information Coed travel cultural program and adventure program established in 1966.
Special Interest Areas Touring.
Sports Bicycling, canoeing, skiing (downhill), tennis.
Excursions Cultural, day.
Program Information 1–2 sessions per year. Session length: 30 days in June, July. Ages: 15–18. 40–48 participants per session. Cost: $7999–$8399.
Housing Hotels.
Application Deadline Continuous.
Jobs Positions for college students 21 and older.

Musiker Tours: Action Europe

Contact James Musiker, Owner/Director, 1326 Old Northern Boulevard, Roslyn, New York 11576. Phone: 888-878-6637. Fax: 516-625-3438. E-mail: musiker@summerfun.com.
URL www.summerfun.com

For more information, see page 1214.

ODYSSEY EXPEDITIONS: Tropical Marine Biology Voyages–Caribbean Islands

!Adventures–Afloat/Odyssey Expeditions
Locations Grenada, Saint Lucia, Saint Vincent and The Grenadines.

General Information Coed travel outdoor program and adventure program established in 1995. High school or college credit may be earned.
Program Focus Coed marine biology field studies program featuring underwater research, scuba certifications, sailing, and island exploration.
Academics Biology, ecology, environmental science, geology/earth science, marine studies, oceanography.
Arts Photography, television/video.
Special Interest Areas Career exploration, community service, field research/expeditions, leadership training, nature study, nautical skills.
Sports Boating, diving, fishing, sailing, scuba diving, sea kayaking, snorkeling, waterskiing, windsurfing.
Wilderness/Outdoors Hiking.
Excursions Cultural.
Program Information 3 sessions per year. Session length: 3 weeks in June, July, August. Ages: 13–19. 10 participants per session. Cost: $4390.
Housing Yachts.
Application Deadline Continuous.
Jobs Positions for college students 21 and older.
Contact Jason Buchheim, Director, 650 Southeast Paradise Point Road, #100, Crystal River, Florida 34429. Phone: 800-929-7749. E-mail: odyssey@usa.net.
URL www.odysseyexpeditions.org

For more information, see page 970.

Overland: European Challenge Bicycle Touring from Paris to Rome

Overland Travel, Inc.
Locations France, Italy, Switzerland.

General Information Coed travel outdoor program, cultural program, and adventure program established in 1985. Accredited by American Camping Association. High school credit may be earned.
Program Focus Bicycle across Europe from Paris to Rome.
Special Interest Areas Leadership training, touring.
Sports Bicycling.
Wilderness/Outdoors Bicycle trips, outdoor camping.
Excursions Cultural.
Program Information 2–3 sessions per year. Session length: 30 days in June, July, August. Ages: 15–19. 8–12 participants per session. Cost: $4795.
Housing Tents and youth hostels.
Application Deadline Continuous.
Jobs Positions for college students 20 and older.
Contact Ms. Brooks Follansbee, Director, PO Box 31, Williamstown, Massachusetts 01267. Phone: 800-458-0588. Fax: 413-458-5208. E-mail: overland@adelphia.net.
URL www.overlandsummers.com

For more information, see page 1240.

Overland: European Explorer Hiking, Rafting, and Sea Kayaking

Overland Travel, Inc.
Locations France, Spain, Switzerland.

General Information Coed travel outdoor program, wilderness program, and adventure program established in 1985. Accredited by American Camping Association. High school credit may be earned.
Program Focus Explore the beauty of Europe by foot, kayak and raft.
Special Interest Areas Leadership training, team building.
Sports Sea kayaking.
Wilderness/Outdoors Backpacking, hiking, rafting, white-water trips, wilderness camping.
Excursions Cultural.
Program Information 1–2 sessions per year. Session length: 30 days in June, July, August. Ages: 14–18. 8–12 participants per session. Cost: $4795.
Housing Tents and youth hostels.
Application Deadline Continuous.
Jobs Positions for college students 20 and older.
Contact Ms. Brooks Follansbee, Director, PO Box 31, Williamstown, Massachusetts 01267. Phone: 800-458-0588. Fax: 413-458-5208. E-mail: overland@adelphia.net.
URL www.overlandsummers.com

For more information, see page 1240.

Overland: The Alpine Challenge Leadership Course Backpacking and Hiking

Overland Travel, Inc.
Locations France, Italy, Switzerland.

General Information Coed travel outdoor program, wilderness program, cultural program, and adventure program established in 1985. Accredited by American Camping Association. High school credit may be earned.
Program Focus Alpine leadership skills.
Special Interest Areas Leadership training, team building, touring.
Wilderness/Outdoors Backpacking, hiking, mountaineering, rock climbing, wilderness camping.
Excursions Cultural.
Program Information 1 session per year. Session length: 4 weeks in June, July, August. Ages: 15–18. 8–12 participants per session. Cost: $4795.
Housing Tents and youth hostels.
Application Deadline Continuous.
Jobs Positions for college students 20 and older.
Contact Ms. Brooks Follansbee, Director, PO Box 31, Williamstown, Massachusetts 01267. Phone: 800-458-0588. Fax: 413-458-5208. E-mail: overland@adelphia.net.
URL www.overlandsummers.com

For more information, see page 1240.

Phillips Exeter Academy Taiwan and Beijing Summer Study Tour

Phillips Exeter Academy
Locations China, Taiwan.

General Information Coed travel academic program and cultural program established in 1996.
Program Focus Chinese language and culture.
Academics Chinese languages/literature.
Arts Calligraphy, painting.
Special Interest Areas Cross-cultural education, homestays, touring.
Sports Basketball, martial arts, swimming, tennis.
Excursions Cultural, day, overnight, shopping.
Program Information 1 session per year. Session length: 5 weeks in June, July, August. Ages: 13+. 12–24 participants per session. Application fee: $50.
Application Deadline March 30.
Contact Ms. Ming Fontaine, Program Director, 20 Main Street, Exeter, New Hampshire 03833. Phone: 603-772-7708. Fax: 603-777-4384. E-mail: mfontaine@exeter.edu.
URL www.exeter.edu

Poulter Colorado Camps: Adventures Planet Earth–Austria

Poulter Colorado Camps
Locations Austria, Germany.

General Information Coed travel outdoor program, cultural program, and adventure program established in 1966. Accredited by American Camping Association.
Program Focus Exciting international experiences combining adventure travel with cultural immersion.
Academics Intercultural studies.
Special Interest Areas Community service, homestays, leadership training, nature study, touring.
Wilderness/Outdoors Backpacking, bicycle trips, hiking.
Excursions Cultural, day, overnight, shopping.

Program Information 2–4 sessions per year. Session length: 10–30 days in June, July, August, September, October. Ages: 14+. 6–10 participants per session. Cost: $2450–$3500. Financial aid available.
Housing Host-family homes and hotels.
Application Deadline Continuous.
Jobs Positions for college students 21 and older.
Contact Mr. Jay B. Poulter, Director, PO Box 772947, Steamboat Springs, Colorado 80477. Phone: 888-879-4816. Fax: 800-860-3587. E-mail: poulter@poultercamps.com.
URL www.poultercamps.com

Putney Student Travel–Cultural Exploration–Australia, New Zealand, and Fiji

Putney Student Travel
Locations Australia, Fiji, New Zealand.

General Information Coed travel cultural program and adventure program established in 1951.
Program Focus Active exploration of the cultures and landscapes of the region through direct interaction with local people, and sailing and skiing adventures.
Academics Intercultural studies.
Special Interest Areas Homestays.
Sports Canoeing, rappelling, sailing, scuba diving, skiing (downhill), snorkeling, swimming.
Wilderness/Outdoors Hiking, outdoor adventure, rock climbing.
Excursions Cultural, day.
Program Information 1–2 sessions per year. Session length: 5–6 weeks in June, July. Ages: 16–18. 16–18 participants per session. Cost: $9000; including airfare. Financial aid available. Airfare from Los Angeles included.
Housing Host-family homes, hotels, and yachts.
Application Deadline Continuous.
Contact Jeffrey Shumlin, Admissions Director, 345 Hickory Ridge Road, Putney, Vermont 05346. Phone: 802-387-5000. Fax: 802-387-4276. E-mail: info@goputney.com.
URL www.goputney.com

For more information, see page 1276.

Putney Student Travel–Cultural Exploration–Eastern European Heritage

Putney Student Travel
Locations Czech Republic, Hungary, Poland, Slovakia.

General Information Coed residential cultural program established in 1951.
Program Focus Exploration of Jewish cultural heritage, and the transition from communism to capitalism in Krakow, Budapest, Prague, and adjacent rural areas.
Academics Jewish studies, government and politics, intercultural studies.
Special Interest Areas Cross-cultural education.
Sports Bicycling, canoeing, sailing, swimming.
Wilderness/Outdoors Hiking.
Excursions Cultural, day, overnight.
Program Information 1 session per year. Session length: 28–30 days in July. Ages: 14–18. 16 participants per session. Cost: $6000; including airfare from New York. Financial aid available.
Housing College dormitories and hotels.
Application Deadline Continuous.
Jobs Positions for college students 21 and older.
Contact Jeffrey Shumlin, Director, 345 Hickory Ridge Road, Putney, Vermont 05346. Phone: 802-387-5000. Fax: 802-387-4276. E-mail: info@goputney.com.
URL www.goputney.com

For more information, see page 1276.

Putney Student Travel–Cultural Exploration–France, Holland, and England

Putney Student Travel
Locations France, Netherlands, United Kingdom.

General Information Coed travel cultural program and adventure program established in 1951.
Program Focus An active exploration program of Europe's cultures and landscapes designed for younger teenagers.
Academics Intercultural studies.
Sports Bicycling, canoeing, sailing, skiing (downhill), swimming, tennis, windsurfing.
Wilderness/Outdoors Bicycle trips, hiking, mountaineering, rock climbing.
Excursions Cultural, day.
Program Information 1 session per year. Session length: 5–6 weeks in June, July, August. Ages: 14–15. 16 participants per session. Cost: $8190; including airfare from New York to Paris or Geneva. Financial aid available.
Housing Hotels and youth hostels.
Application Deadline Continuous.
Contact Jeffrey Shumlin, Admissions Director, 345 Hickory Ridge Road, Putney, Vermont 05346. Phone: 802-387-5000. Fax: 802-387-4276. E-mail: info@goputney.com.
URL www.goputney.com

For more information, see page 1276.

Putney Student Travel–Cultural Exploration–Switzerland, Italy, France, and Holland

Putney Student Travel
Locations France, Italy, Netherlands, Switzerland.

General Information Coed travel cultural program and adventure program established in 1951.
Program Focus Active exploration of the cultures and landscapes of Europe in both major cities and rural areas.
Academics Art history/appreciation, intercultural studies.
Special Interest Areas Homestays.

Putney Student Travel–Cultural Exploration–Switzerland, Italy, France, and Holland (continued)

Sports Bicycling, horseback riding, skiing (downhill), soccer, swimming.
Wilderness/Outdoors Bicycle trips, hiking, mountaineering, outdoor adventure.
Excursions Cultural, day.
Program Information 2 sessions per year. Session length: 5–6 weeks in June, July, August. Ages: 16–18. 16 participants per session. Cost: $8190; including airfare from New York to Geneva. Financial aid available.
Housing Host-family homes and hotels.
Application Deadline Continuous.
Contact Jeffrey Shumlin, Admissions Director, 345 Hickory Ridge Road, Putney, Vermont 05346. Phone: 802-387-5000. Fax: 802-387-4276. E-mail: info@goputney.com.
URL www.goputney.com
For more information, see page 1276.

PUTNEY STUDENT TRAVEL–CULTURAL EXPLORATION–THAILAND AND CAMBODIA

Putney Student Travel
Locations Cambodia, Thailand.

General Information Coed residential cultural program established in 1951.
Program Focus Active exploration of the culture and history of Thailand and Cambodia through direct contact with local people.
Academics Intercultural studies.
Special Interest Areas Community service, cross-cultural education.
Wilderness/Outdoors Hiking, pack animal trips.
Excursions Cultural, day, overnight.
Program Information 1 session per year. Session length: 28–30 days in June, July. Ages: 15–18. 16 participants per session. Cost: $6500; including airfare from Los Angeles. Financial aid available.
Housing Hotels.
Application Deadline Continuous.
Jobs Positions for college students 21 and older.
Contact Jeffrey Shumlin, Director, 345 Hickory Ridge Road, Putney, Vermont 05346. Phone: 802-387-5000. Fax: 802-387-4276. E-mail: info@goputney.com.
URL www.goputney.com
For more information, see page 1276.

RUST COLLEGE STUDY ABROAD IN AFRICA

Rust College
Locations Gambia, Ghana, Senegal.

General Information Coed travel academic program established in 1992. Formal opportunities for the academically talented. College credit may be earned.
Academics English language/literature, anthropology, area studies, art history/appreciation, business, communications, economics, engineering, environmental science, geography, government and politics (Advanced Placement), history, intercultural studies, social studies.
Arts Arts and crafts (general), dance, music, television/video.
Sports Basketball, bicycling, soccer, swimming, tennis.
Excursions College tours, cultural, day, overnight, shopping.
Program Information 1 session per year. Session length: 5 weeks in May, June. Ages: 15+. 30–40 participants per session. Cost: $2900–$3500; including airfare from Memphis or participant's local airports to Dakar, General ACCRA, Ghana. Application fee: $100. Financial aid available.
Housing College dormitories, host-family homes, and hotels.
Application Deadline April 15.
Contact A. J. Stovall, Director, International Studies, 150 Rust Avenue, Holly Springs, Mississippi 38635. Phone: 662-252-8000 Ext.4311. Fax: 662-252-6107. E-mail: astovall@rustcollege.edu.
URL www.naaslc.org

RUSTIC PATHWAYS–BUDDHIST LIFE & ANGKOR WAT

Rustic Pathways
Locations Cambodia, Thailand.

General Information Coed travel community service program and cultural program established in 1998. Religious affiliation: Buddhist faith.
Academics Anthropology.
Special Interest Areas Community service, construction, cross-cultural education, touring.
Excursions Cultural, day, overnight, shopping.
Program Information 1 session per year. Session length: 17 days in July. Ages: 15–18. 10–15 participants per session. Cost: $2685.
Housing Host-family homes and hotels.
Application Deadline Continuous.
Jobs Positions for college students 21 and older.
Contact Mr. David Venning, Founder and Chairman, 4121 Erie Street, Willoughby, Ohio 44094. Phone: 440-975-9691. Fax: 440-975-9694. E-mail: david@rusticpathways.com.
URL www.rusticpathways.com
For more information, see page 1290.

RUSTIC PATHWAYS–EXTREME PLANET

Rustic Pathways
Locations Australia, Costa Rica, Fiji, New Zealand, Thailand.

General Information Coed travel community service program, cultural program, and adventure program established in 1994.
Special Interest Areas Aboriginal studies, community service, construction, cross-cultural education, homestays, touring.
Sports Boating, climbing (wall), fishing, horseback riding, kayaking, rappelling, sailing, scuba diving, sea kayaking, skiing (cross-country), skiing (downhill), snorkeling, soccer, surfing, swimming.
Wilderness/Outdoors Backpacking, bicycle trips, hiking, mountain biking, outdoor adventure, rafting, white-water trips, wilderness camping.

RUSTIC PATHWAYS–EXTREME PLANET

Excursions Cultural, day, overnight, shopping.
Program Information 2 sessions per year. Session length: 59–66 days in June, July, August. Ages: 16–18. 10–15 participants per session. Cost: $9500–$10,750.
Housing Host-family homes, hotels, tents, and youth hostels.
Application Deadline Continuous.
Jobs Positions for college students 21 and older.
Contact Mr. David Venning, Founder and Chairman, 4121 Erie Street, Willoughby, Ohio 44094. Phone: 440-975-9691. Fax: 440-975-9694. E-mail: david@rusticpathways.com.
URL www.rusticpathways.com
For more information, see page 1290.

SAIL CARIBBEAN–LEEWARD ISLANDS

Sail Caribbean
Locations Anguilla, Netherlands Antilles, Saint Kitts and Nevis.

General Information Coed travel outdoor program, cultural program, and adventure program established in 1979. High school credit may be earned.
Program Focus Teaching sailing, racing, and seamanship.
Academics Marine studies, oceanography.
Special Interest Areas Leadership training, team building.
Sports Boating, diving, kayaking, sailing, scuba diving, swimming, volleyball, waterskiing, windsurfing.
Wilderness/Outdoors Hiking.
Excursions Cultural, shopping.
Program Information 3 sessions per year. Session length: 17 days in June, July, August. Ages: 13–18. 50 participants per session. Cost: $3925. Financial aid available.
Housing Yachts.
Application Deadline Continuous.
Jobs Positions for college students 20 and older.
Contact Michael Liese, Director, 79 Church Street, Northport, New York 11768. Phone: 800-321-0994. Fax: 631-754-3362. E-mail: info@sailcaribbean.com.
URL www.sailcaribbean.com
For more information, see page 1292.

SPANISH THROUGH LEADERSHIP–NICARAGUA/COSTA RICA

Nicaragua/Costa Rica High School Summer Exchange
Locations Costa Rica, Nicaragua.

General Information Coed travel community service program and cultural program established in 1997. High school credit may be earned.
Program Focus Spanish immersion through community and culture.
Academics Spanish language/literature.
Arts Ceramics, dance, music (instrumental), pottery.
Special Interest Areas Community service, homestays, leadership training.
Sports Basketball, ropes course, soccer, surfing, volleyball.
Wilderness/Outdoors Hiking, zip line.
Excursions Cultural, day, overnight.
Program Information 2–3 sessions per year. Session length: 3–4 weeks in June, July, August. Ages: 14–18. 15–20 participants per session. Cost: $2650–$2850; including airfare from Major U.S. cities to Managua, Nicaragua or San Jose, Costa Rica. Application fee: $250.
Housing Host-family homes.
Application Deadline Continuous.
Contact Mrs. Ilba Prego, Director, 1650 Monroe Street, Madison, Wisconsin 53711. Phone: 608-255-1426. E-mail: nica@terracom.net.
URL www.highschoolspanish.org
For more information, see page 1326.

TENNIS: EUROPE

TENNIS: EUROPE
Locations Austria, Denmark, France, Germany, Greece, Italy, Netherlands, Portugal, Spain, Sweden, Switzerland, United Kingdom.

General Information Coed travel sports camp and cultural program established in 1973.
Program Focus Coed program focusing on tennis competition at major international tournaments in 3-6 countries, for junior tennis players (high school varsity level or better).
Academics French language/literature, German language/literature, Spanish language/literature.
Special Interest Areas Career exploration.
Sports Aerobics, basketball, bicycling, boating, canoeing, fishing, golf, horseback riding, in-line skating, sailing, skiing (downhill), soccer, swimming, tennis, volleyball, waterskiing, weight training, windsurfing.
Wilderness/Outdoors Hiking, rafting, white-water trips.
Excursions College tours, cultural.
Program Information 12–15 sessions per year. Session length: 16–35 days in June, July, August. Ages: 14–18. 14–15 participants per session. Cost: $3400–$7200. Application fee: $375. Financial aid available. Airfare not included.
Housing Host-family homes and hotels.
Application Deadline Continuous.
Jobs Positions for college students 21 and older.

TENNIS: EUROPE (continued)

Contact Dr. Martin Vinokur, Co-Director, 73 Rockridge Lane, Stamford, Connecticut 06903. Phone: 800-253-7486. Fax: 203-322-0089. E-mail: tenniseuro@aol.com.
URL www.tenniseurope.com

TIBETAN SUMMER PASSAGE

Passage: Project for International Education
Locations China, India, Nepal.

General Information Coed travel academic program, outdoor program, cultural program, and adventure program established in 2002.
Academics Anthropology, architecture, area studies, art (Advanced Placement), art history/appreciation, botany, ecology, geology/earth science, health sciences, history, humanities, intercultural studies, journalism, music, music (Advanced Placement), peace education, philosophy, religion, social science, social studies.
Arts Arts and crafts (general), ceramics, dance, dance (folk), drawing, film, jewelry making, leather working, metalworking, music, music (vocal), painting, photography, pottery, printmaking, television/video, weaving, woodworking.
Special Interest Areas Animal care, community service, cross-cultural education, culinary arts, farming, field research/expeditions, gardening, homestays, touring.
Wilderness/Outdoors Backpacking, hiking, rafting, wilderness camping.
Excursions Cultural, day, overnight.
Program Information 1 session per year. Session length: 6 weeks in June, July. Ages: 16+. 16 participants per session. Cost: $3950. Financial aid available.
Housing Host-family homes and hotels.
Application Deadline Continuous.
Jobs Positions for college students 21 and older.
Contact Ms. Vidhea Shrestha, Director of Programs, GPO Box 8974, CPC373, Kathmandu, Nepal. Phone: 866-840-9197. E-mail: programs@passageproject.org.
URL www.passageproject.org

WEISSMAN TEEN TOURS–EUROPEAN EXPERIENCE

Weissman Teen Tours
Locations Belgium, France, Italy, Netherlands, Switzerland, United Kingdom.

General Information Coed travel outdoor program and cultural program established in 1974.
Program Focus Owner-escorted, action-packed, culturally-oriented, upscale European travel program. No camping or dormitory accommodations.
Academics Architecture, art history/appreciation, college tours, history, intercultural studies.
Arts Theater/drama.
Special Interest Areas Touring.
Sports Aerobics, bicycling, boating, parasailing, skiing (downhill), snowboarding, swimming, tennis, weight training.
Wilderness/Outdoors Bicycle trips, hiking, white-water trips.
Excursions College tours, cultural, day, overnight, shopping.
Program Information 2 sessions per year. Session length: 34 days in June, July, August. Ages: 14–18. 45 participants per session. Cost: $9599.
Housing Hotels.
Application Deadline Continuous.
Jobs Positions for college students 21 and older.
Contact Ms. Ronee Weissman, Owner/Director, 517 Almena Avenue, Ardsley, New York 10502. Phone: 800-942-8005. Fax: 914-693-4807. E-mail: wtt@cloud9.net.
URL www.weissmantours.com
For more information, see page 1388.

WESTCOAST CONNECTION–AUSTRALIAN OUTBACK PLUS HAWAII

Westcoast Connection
Locations Australia, Hawaii.

General Information Coed travel outdoor program and adventure program established in 1982. Accredited by Ontario Camping Association.

Westcoast Connection–Australian Outback Plus Hawaii

Program Focus A balance of touring, recreation, and adventure.
Special Interest Areas Touring.
Sports Kayaking, scuba diving, sea kayaking, snorkeling, surfing, swimming.
Wilderness/Outdoors Hiking, rafting, white-water trips.
Program Information 2–3 sessions per year. Session length: 30 days in July. Ages: 14–19. 30–50 participants per session. Cost: $6999. Financial aid available.
Housing Hotels.
Application Deadline Continuous.
Contact Mr. Mark Segal, Director, 154 East Boston Post Road, Mamaroneck, New York 10543. Phone: 800-767-0227. Fax: 914-835-0798. E-mail: usa@westcoastconnection.com.
URL www.westcoastconnection.com
For more information, see page 1392.

Westcoast Connection Travel–European Discovery

Westcoast Connection
Locations Belgium, France, Italy, Monaco, Netherlands, Switzerland, United Kingdom.

General Information Coed travel cultural program and adventure program established in 1982. Accredited by Ontario Camping Association.
Program Focus A six-country tour balancing big city highlights and nightlife with adventure in the French and Swiss Alps and recreation on the French and Adriatic Rivieras.
Special Interest Areas Touring.
Sports Bicycling, boating, skiing (downhill), snowboarding, swimming, windsurfing.
Wilderness/Outdoors Mountain biking, rafting, whitewater trips.
Program Information 1–2 sessions per year. Session length: 34 days in July, August. Ages: 14–17. 40–50 participants per session. Cost: $7799.
Housing Hotels.
Application Deadline Continuous.
Jobs Positions for college students 21 and older.
Contact Mr. Mark Segal, Director, 154 East Boston Post Road, Mamaroneck, New York 10543. Phone: 800-767-0227. Fax: 914-835-0798. E-mail: usa@westcoastconnection.com.
URL www.westcoastconnection.com
For more information, see page 1392.

Westcoast Connection Travel–European Escape

Westcoast Connection
Locations France, Italy, Switzerland.

General Information Coed travel cultural program and adventure program established in 1982. Accredited by Ontario Camping Association.
Program Focus A three-country tour balancing big city (Paris, Rome, Geneva and others) highlights and nightlife, with adventure in the Swiss Alps and recreation on the French and Adriatic Rivieras.
Special Interest Areas Touring.
Sports Boating, skiing (downhill), snowboarding, swimming, windsurfing.
Wilderness/Outdoors Mountain biking, rafting, whitewater trips.
Program Information 1–2 sessions per year. Session length: 25 days in July. Ages: 14–17. 20–45 participants per session. Cost: $6699.
Housing Hotels.
Application Deadline Continuous.
Jobs Positions for college students 21 and older.
Contact Mr. Mark Segal, Director, 154 East Boston Post Road, Mamaroneck, New York 10543. Phone: 800-767-0227. Fax: 914-835-0798. E-mail: usa@westcoastconnection.com.
URL www.westcoastconnection.com
For more information, see page 1392.

Westcoast Connection Travel/On Tour–European Experience

Westcoast Connection
Locations France, Italy, Monaco, Switzerland, United Kingdom.

General Information Coed travel cultural program and adventure program established in 1982. Accredited by Ontario Camping Association.
Program Focus This program is designed for greater independence for ages 17 to 19. A three- or four-country tour balancing big city highlights and nightlife with adventure in the French and Swiss Alps, and recreation on the French and Adriatic Rivieras.
Special Interest Areas Touring.
Sports Bicycling, skiing (downhill), snowboarding, swimming, windsurfing.
Wilderness/Outdoors Mountain biking, rafting, whitewater trips.
Program Information 3–5 sessions per year. Session length: 25–30 days in July, August. Ages: 17–19. 40–50 participants per session. Cost: $5199–$5899.
Housing Hotels.
Application Deadline Continuous.
Contact Mr. Mark Segal, Director, 154 East Boston Post Road, Mamaroneck, New York 10543. Phone: 800-767-0227. Fax: 914-835-0798. E-mail: usa@westcoastconnection.com.
URL www.westcoastconnection.com
For more information, see page 1392.

Wilderness Ventures–European Alps

Wilderness Ventures
Locations France, Italy, Switzerland.

General Information Coed travel outdoor program, wilderness program, cultural program, and adventure program established in 1973.
Program Focus Wilderness travel, cultural immersion, leadership skills.
Academics Intercultural studies.
Special Interest Areas Leadership training.
Wilderness/Outdoors Backpacking, hiking, mountaineering.
Excursions Cultural, overnight.
Program Information 1 session per year. Session length: 29 days in June, July, August. Ages: 14–18. 15 participants per session. Cost: $4590. Financial aid available.
Housing Youth hostels.
Application Deadline Continuous.
Jobs Positions for college students 21 and older.
Contact Mike Cottingham, Director, PO Box 2768, Jackson Hole, Wyoming 83001. Phone: 800-533-2281. Fax: 307-739-1934. E-mail: info@wildernessventures.com.
URL www.wildernessventures.com
For more information, see page 1396.

Windsor Mountain: European Traveling Minstrels

Interlocken at Windsor Mountain
Locations France, Italy.

General Information Coed travel arts program and cultural program established in 1967. College credit may be earned.
Program Focus Creative traveling theater and commedia dell'Arte.
Academics French language/literature, Italian language/literature, Spanish language/literature.
Arts Acting, clowning, creative writing, mask making, mime, music, theater/drama.
Special Interest Areas Leadership training, team building.
Excursions Cultural, day.
Program Information 1 session per year. Session length: 5 weeks in July, August. Ages: 14–18. 15 participants per session. Cost: $4650. Financial aid available.
Housing Tents and youth hostels.
Application Deadline Continuous.
Contact Richard Herman, Director, 19 Interlocken Way, Windsor, New Hampshire 03244. Phone: 800-862-7760. Fax: 603-478-5260. E-mail: mail@windsormountain.org.
URL www.windsormountain.org/xrds
For more information, see page 1162.

Youth for Understanding USA–Estonia/Latvia-Baltic Summer

Youth for Understanding USA
Locations Estonia, Latvia.

General Information Coed travel academic program and cultural program established in 1951. High school credit may be earned.
Program Focus Living with a host family, learning about other cultures, and improving language skills.
Academics Estonian language/literature, Latvian language/literature, area studies, intercultural studies, social studies.
Special Interest Areas Cross-cultural education, homestays.
Excursions Cultural, day.
Program Information 1 session per year. Session length: 43 days in June, July, August. Ages: 15–18. 5–10 participants per session. Cost: $4995; including airfare from East Coast, USA to Estonia. Application fee: $75. Financial aid available. Round-trip domestic and international airfare is included in the tuition.
Housing Host-family homes.
Application Deadline Continuous.
Contact Admissions Counselor, 6400 Goldsboro Road, Suite 100, Bethesda, Maryland 20817. Phone: 800-TEENAGE (833-6243). Fax: 202-895-1104. E-mail: admissions@us.yfu.org.
URL www.yfu-usa.org
For more information, see page 1414.

In-Depth Descriptions

AAVE TEEN ADVENTURES

WORLDWIDE TEEN ADVENTURE PROGRAMS SINCE 1976

GOLDEN, COLORADO

Type of Program: Adventure, wilderness, community service and culture, travel, and French and Spanish language immersion
Participants: Coeducational and international; grades 6–12, ages 11–18 separated by age
Enrollment: 800 participants per summer in independent groups of 13 teenagers
Program Dates: Two-, three-, four-, and six-week trips from June through August
Head of Program: Abbott Wallis, Owner

LOCATION

AAVE Teen Adventures has its year-round bases in Colorado. Trips include adventure travel in Colorado, Utah, Arizona, Alaska, Washington, California, Belize, Vietnam, Africa, Hawaii, Costa Rica, Australia, Thailand, Canada, South America, and Europe with no base facility.

BACKGROUND AND PHILOSOPHY

Since 1976, AAVE Teen Adventures has been about feeling alive, competent, and part of a highly motivated team of teenagers having fun. The hallmark of AAVE has been to combine inspirational leaders, innovative adventures, and a high level of individual responsibility and commitment. An interview and two references are required prior to acceptance. All groups include 13 teenagers and 2 adults; the small group size results in an honest experience in which each participant's contribution makes a difference. AAVE Teen Adventures is accredited by the American Camping Association.

PROGRAM OFFERINGS

Australia (twenty-three days, Australia) Beach activities down under include scuba certification, diving the Great Barrier Reef, sailing, surfing, the Great Northern Walk, and sightseeing in Sydney.

Thailand (twenty-one days, Thailand) Thailand is the ultimate adventure off the beaten tourist path. Participants learn about Asian culture as they go elephant trekking and exploring.

Hawaii (twenty-one days, Hawaii) Hawaii is a rugged adventure, including tropical backpacking, one day of surfing, seven days of mountain biking around Hawaii's Volcano National Park and coastal trails, and a five-day water sport and Pacific sailing experience, including instruction in navigation and sea kayaking.

Boot•Saddle•Paddle (twenty-eight days, Colorado, Utah, and Arizona) Boot·Saddle·Paddle, in the southwestern United States, includes three backpacking trips, including the southern rim of the Grand Canyon, a horseback riding adventure in Colorado, Native American intercultural experiences and community service projects, and a class III–IV white-water rafting trip.

Bold Europe (twenty-eight days, Spain, France, and Italy) Bold Europe is an exploration of three distinct European regions. Activities include hiking, mountain biking, rafting, canyoning, rock climbing, Mediterranean beaches, museums, Barcelona, Florence, Siena, and Paris.

X-Five (twenty-six days, Colorado and Utah) X-Five is a fast-paced, athletic trip that includes two backpacking trips, 14,000-foot peak ascents, a technical rock-climbing school in Aspen, five days of mountain biking, five days of white-water rafting on class III and IV rapids in Utah, and a service project in Colorado's high country.

Bold West (twenty-eight days, Utah, Nevada, and California) Bold West is an active way to explore the western United States. Itineraries include hiking in National Parks; rafting; rock climbing; surfing; and exploring western towns and cities.

Rock and River (twenty-one days, Colorado and Utah) Rock and River is skill packed and includes five days of white-water rafting, rock climbing in Rocky Mountain National Park, and two backpacking trips in the high country of Colorado and Utah.

Rocky Mountain Adventure (eighteen days, Colorado) Rocky Mountain Adventure is designed exclusively for 12- and 13-year-olds and is a challenging, introductory sampler of wilderness sports, including backpacking, white-water rafting, mountain biking, rock climbing, horseback riding, and adventure camping.

Alaska (twenty-six days, Alaska) Alaska requires previous backcountry experience. This rugged Alaskan adventure includes a five-day backpacking trip in the Chugach Mountain Range, a four-day sea kayaking trip in Prince William Sound's Blackstone Bay, a five-day technical glacier climbing school on the Matanuska Glacier, a three-day river trip on the Matanuska River, and a final backpacking trip in Denali State Park.

Alps Rider (twenty-one days, France, Italy, and Switzerland) Alps Rider is an exciting adventure in the alpine center of Europe. Summer snow sports, white-water rafting, klettersteig, canyoning, mountain biking, and backpacking complete this high-powered international mountaineering trip.

Costa Rica (twenty-one days, Costa Rica) Costa Rica combines Spanish language, adventure, and community service in a wondrous, friendly, and safe Central American country.

Vivons le Français (twenty-eight days, France) Vivons le Français is an aggressive French language immersion program that combines University study, cultural excursions, and outdoor adventure. Basic knowledge of French (a minimum of one year) is required.

Immersión en España (twenty-eight days, Spain) Immersión en España is an aggressive Spanish language immersion program combining University study, homestays, and outdoor adventure in Madrid and Santander. Basic knowledge of Spanish (a minimum of one year) is required.

Border Cross (twenty-one days, Washington and British Columbia, Canada) Border Cross is designed for teens 13 and 14 years old and explores Washington and British Columbia. It features two days of skiing or snowboarding, sea kayaking on Puget Sound, biking on San Juan Island, rock climbing in Canada, and backpacking trips in the Olympic and Cascade Mountains.

Wild Isles (twenty-two days, Ireland, Wales, and England) Wild Isles takes place in the wilderness and culture of Ireland, Wales, and England. Activities include two days of horseback riding, two days of surfing, two days of mountain biking, and plenty of sightseeing.

Belize (twenty-one days, Belize) Belize is a travel, culture, adventure, and sport experience that is uncrowded, adventurous, English speaking, and populated by an easy-going, friendly mixture of Mayan, Creole, Latin, and European people. This amazing adventure allows teens to snorkel, jungle hike, kayak, cave, visit Mayan ceremonial sights, and enjoy mountain streams and waterfalls.

Peru and Machu Pichu (twenty-one days, Peru) Students explore the legacy of the Incas high up in the Peruvian Andes. They explore ancient cities, hike the famous Inca Trail, and visit Machu Pichu, the most beautiful and mysterious of all the Inca ruins. This trip also includes rafting class III rapids, visiting the largest lake in the world, and enjoying the wonders of the Amazon.

Ecuador and Galapagos Islands (twenty-one days, Ecuador and Galapagos) This trip gives students the best of mainland Ecuador, a trip to the Galapagos Islands, and a rare glimpse of the cloud forest. A naturalist teaches students about the surrounding ecosystems. Participants explore, snorkel, hike, swim, bike, and work with local school children.

Africa (twenty-one days, South Africa and Namibia) This program is a combination of high-adrenaline activities in some of the world's largest desert sand dunes, first-rate rapids, and rugged trails, with unique exposure to diverse cultures and wildlife.

Vietnam (twenty-one days, Vietnam) Teens discover some of the country's many treasures, such as stunning beaches, hilltribes, Hanoi markets, tropical rain forests, and the Mekong Delta. Exploration is done by foot, biking, kayaking, boating, snorkeling, and cooking.

Bike France (fourteen days, Switzerland, France) Bike France is a short but unforgettable mountain bike adventure from the alpine center of France to the blue Mediterranean. Challenging downhills, technical short track, and off-road days guarantee a unique experience to biking fanatics.

ENROLLMENT

Each coed group of 13 participants and 2 trip leaders is carefully grouped by age. Participants from forty-two states and twenty-six countries have joined AAVE. The small group size promotes strong friendships and one-on-one instruction and responsibility. AAVE trips feature service projects and intercultural exchanges with an international staff, group, and locale. No previous experience is needed for most trips.

DAILY SCHEDULE

Each day, participants have a variety of responsibilities that may include leadership, grocery shopping, cooking, cleaning, environmental service projects, and orienteering.

STAFF

AAVE Teen Adventures requires staff members to have Wilderness First Responder, Adult CPR, and Lifeguard Training certification; extensive experience with teenagers; backcountry travel knowledge; and proven leadership skills. The minimum age of staff members is 21, and the average age is 26. Each trip includes a female leader and a male leader.

COSTS

Tuition ranges from $1988 to $4688. AAVE recommends $45 per week for personal expenses.

FINANCIAL AID

Scholarships are based on financial need. Interested participants should call for an application.

TRANSPORTATION

Round-trip airfare to all trip locations is the participant's responsibility. All participants are met at the airline gate for arrival and departure.

APPLICATION TIMETABLE

Interested participants should call for more information. Applications are processed in the order in which they are received.

For more information, contact:

AAVE Teen Adventures
2245 Stonecrop Way
Golden, Colorado 80401
303-526-0806
800-222-3595 (toll-free)
Fax: 303-526-0885
E-mail: info@aave.com
World Wide Web: http://www.aave.com

PARTICIPANT/FAMILY COMMENTS

"I saw my first shooting star, slept on beaches, planned and cooked meals, had plenty of water fights, and climbed a 14,000-foot peak."

"Not only do I recommend AAVE, I think it should be required for all!"

ACADEMIC CAMPS AT GETTYSBURG COLLEGE

SUMMER ACADEMIC CAMPS

GETTYSBURG, PENNSYLVANIA

Type of Program: Academic enrichment
Participants: Coeducational, students entering grades 9–12
Enrollment: 50–100 students each session
Program Dates: Multiple two-week sessions in June and July
Heads of Program: Doug Murphy, Executive Director; Traci Hudson, Program Services

LOCATION

Academic Camps at Gettysburg College is located in Gettysburg, Pennsylvania, on the campus of the nationally recognized, coeducational residential college of liberal arts and sciences. Just 80 minutes by car from Washington, D.C., the campus lies on 200 acres in a historic town that is home to an array of stores, restaurants, and cultural and historical attractions, including Gettysburg National Military Park.

BACKGROUND AND PHILOSOPHY

The Camp Gettysburg experience is a two-week-long immersion in a stimulating and fun on-campus academic environment. Designed to further its participants' scholastic aptitude and broaden their academic interests within a dynamic, structured environment, the program's unique curricular approach was developed specifically to pique the students' interests and challenge their abilities. Academic Camps at Gettysburg combines rigorous yet interesting academic endeavors during the day with great evening and weekend activities.

PROGRAM OFFERINGS

Astronomy Gettysburg's summer astronomy students have full use of all of the college's state-of-the-art facilities, including the Hayden Planetarium, a radio telescope, 8-inch Celestron and Meade telescopes, computer labs, and bright night skies. Program activities include charting stars and solar systems, observing solar flares, and building spectroscopes and sundials. In addition, all students visit the National Air and Space Museum, the Naval Observatory, and the Maryland Science Center.

College Prep and Preview Camp Gettysburg's College Prep and Preview gives high school students a head start on the college admission process. By the end of the session, each student has developed her or his own college plan. Classes include SAT Prep; Writing for College–Applications and Essays; Writing for College–Academic Papers, Clubs, and Volunteerism; Choosing a College; The College Admissions Process; and Social Life at College. Off-campus field trips might include visits to local colleges for tours and visits with admissions officers.

Community Service In this program, students learn to set service-oriented goals for improving the well-being of a population, an environment, or a way of life. The satisfaction that comes from guiding a plan through to fruition is deeply rewarding. Throughout this two-week workshop, students develop their leadership skills and the ability to work effectively in teams. They engage in hands-on projects and off-campus mini-internship experiences. All instruction is geared toward the creation of new skills to effect change, both interpersonally and within the local community. Gettysburg College's proximity to Washington, D.C., is invaluable in learning about and addressing service issues.

Foreign Language Study (Spanish) The program is designed for any ability level and is based not on rote memorization, but rather on conversation. Offering a unique linguistic learning environment, the program provides students with the opportunity to speak their selected language in a real-life setting. Cultural awareness is taught through learning traditional geographic areas, traditions, customs, and foods. In addition, campers enjoy an exploration of cultures, which might include learning folk dances, cooking dishes from specific regions, or taking a field trip to Manhattan for foreign language–themed productions on or off Broadway.

U.S. Civil War This program takes advantage of the amazing resources offered by the college, including teachers and teachings from the Civil War Institute (CWI) and its surroundings. Whether students are Civil War buffs or they simply have an interest in history, this program enhances their understanding of the Civil War and how it shaped the nation. Topics include the events that led to war (a broad introduction that explores the issues of slavery, economics, and the cultural clash between North and South in the antebellum period and the decade of crisis that began in 1850), the conflict (an examination of the lives of soldiers, civilians, and leaders as well as the details and consequences of military operations), and Reconstruction (a study of the Civil War's aftermath from social, economic, and political perspectives).

Writer's Workshops Students who love to write and students who want to improve their writing abilities get the opportunity to work in intensive writing workshops of limited size. Discussion and ideas abound. This program is a comprehensive education in the craft of writing, and it outlines the lessons student need in order to be good writers. Main topics covered by the students include an introduction to writing, the mechanics of creative writing, journaling, poetry, and fiction writing. Off-campus field trips might include a visit to a major publishing house and talks with writers, editors, and others in the field.

ENROLLMENT

To allow for small classes with individual attention, Camp Gettysburg enrolls a maximum of 100 campers each session.

DAILY SCHEDULE

Though actual schedules may vary, the following is a typical schedule for program participants.

7:30	Rise and shine
8:00	Breakfast
9:00	Announcements
9:15–10:30	Classroom session I
10:30–10:45	Morning break
10:45–12:00	Classroom session II
12:00–1:00	Lunch
1:15–2:30	Classroom session III
2:30–2:45	Afternoon break
2:45–4:00	Classroom session IV
4:00–5:30	Sports, activities, free time
5:30–6:30	Dinner
7:00–8:00	Special events
8:00–11:00	Movies, games, free time
11:00	Students in rooms (most nights)

EXTRA OPPORTUNITIES AND ACTIVITIES

Each academic camp goes on unique and exciting field trip adventures. Depending on the program, participants might visit a major college or university in the area, science centers or planetariums, Spanish-themed events or restaurants, or a major publishing house to meet authors and editors.

Each two-week session incorporates a Saturday excursion, known as SuperSaturday, to local diversions and cultural attractions. Buses depart early Saturday morning for a variety of exciting, popular destinations, such as amusement parks, beaches, aquariums, music festivals, shopping malls, and Manhattan.

FACILITIES

All students stay overnight in the college's spectacular dormitory facilities and enjoy the first-rate services and amenities that full-time Gettysburg students experience during the school year. Campers are supervised by adult and junior counselors who live in the dorms with them.

STAFF

Intelligent and energetic, the staff is the heart of the Camp Gettysburg experience. From professional teachers to talented graduate and undergraduate students, all staff members participate in safety and training sessions. The maximum student-teacher ratio is 8:1.

MEDICAL CARE

Medical care is available 24 hours a day at nearby hospital facilities. All participants must submit comprehensive medical forms and proof of insurance.

COSTS

The tuition for each two-week session is $2395. This includes all instruction; instructional materials; breakfast, lunch, and dinner each day; a dorm room with linens; self-service laundry facilities; all sports and recreational activities; transportation for sponsored trips; admission tickets to excursion destinations; and total 24-hour supervision for the duration of each camp session. Students may wish to bring spending money for snacks, shopping, and incidentals.

FINANCIAL AID

No financial aid is available at this time.

TRANSPORTATION

Airport pick-up and drop-off are available for an additional fee.

APPLICATION TIMETABLE

Inquiries are welcome at any time. Applications are accepted on a rolling basis. After June 1, acceptance to the program is based on availability, and applications must include a late fee of $100.

For more information, contact:

Academic Camps at Gettysburg College
300 North Washington Street, Box 2994
Gettysburg, Pennsylvania 17325
800-289-7029 (toll-free)
World Wide Web:
http://www.gettysburg.edu/homepage/academiccamps/

ACADEMIC STUDY ASSOCIATES PRE-COLLEGE PROGRAMS

AT UMASS–AMHERST, UC–BERKELEY, AND OXFORD UNIVERSITY

SUMMER PRE-COLLEGE ENRICHMENT PROGRAMS

AMHERST, MASSACHUSETTS; BERKELEY, CALIFORNIA; OXFORD, ENGLAND

Type of Program: Academic enrichment
Participants: Coeducational, students completing grades 9–12 (UMass–Amherst and Oxford) and 10–12 (UC–Berkeley)
Enrollment: UMass: five-week program, 200; three-week program, 100; UC–Berkeley: 150; Oxford: 250
Program Dates: UMass: June 27 to July 30 or August 2 to August 21; UC–Berkeley: July 6 to August 15; Oxford: July 2 to July 28
Head of Program: Marcia E. Evans, Director

LOCATION

Academic Study Associates (ASA) uses three of the world's most magnificent college campuses as locations for its enrichment programs: UMass–Amherst, located in the picturesque college town of Amherst in the foothills of the Berkshire Mountains of western Massachusetts; UC–Berkeley, overlooking the San Francisco Bay; and Oxford University in Oxford, England, Great Britain's most beautiful and famous university city located some 60 miles northwest of London.

BACKGROUND AND PHILOSOPHY

Since 1984, ASA has been offering the finest educational opportunities for students in both the United States and Europe. Over the past sixteen years, ASA's academic enrichment programs have gained an excellent reputation for providing students with an exciting and challenging educational experience as well as an environment in which they can sample the academic, social, and recreational aspects of college life.

PROGRAM OFFERINGS

ASA's programs at the University of Massachusetts Amherst and UC–Berkeley offer students the opportunity to take either college credit or enrichment courses. The Oxford Experience at Oxford University consists of enrichment courses taught by Oxford faculty members. College credit courses are taught by faculty members and are open only to ASA students. At most campuses, students select one major and one elective from a large variety of courses in many academic disciplines. Enrichment courses are held in the format of a college seminar and incorporate a great deal of exchange between teachers and students. Major courses meet Monday through Friday from 9 to noon, electives from 1:30 to 3 p.m. In addition to enrichment courses, students at all ASA campuses have the opportunity to take SAT Preparation, designed and taught by the Princeton Review. SAT classes are small and are tailored to students' individual needs.

College credit courses are offered in the humanities, social sciences, mathematics, natural sciences, and computer science. Enrichment courses are offered in expository and creative writing, literature, journalism and broadcast journalism, history, economics and business, law, philosophy, psychology, mathematics, chemistry, physics, environmental science, international relations, politics and government, French, Spanish, speech and debate, music, video production and film criticism, theater and musical theater, art, art history, sculpture, and photography.

ENROLLMENT

The ASA program at UMass–Amherst enrolls approximately 200 students in the five-week program and approximately 100 students in the three-week program; ASA at Oxford enrolls approximately 250 students; UC–Berkeley enrolls approximately 150 students. Participating students have completed grades 9–12. UC–Berkeley is limited to students completing grades 10–12.

EXTRA OPPORTUNITIES AND ACTIVITIES

In the ASA program at Amherst, students have the opportunity to receive daily professional instruction in either tennis, soccer, or golf. Tennis instruction is provided by UMass varsity tennis coach Judy Dixon. Golf and soccer instruction is provided by ASA's professional coaches.

In all programs, a wide range of optional recreational and social activities are organized in the afternoon and evening. These include team sports such as soccer, softball, basketball, and volleyball; intramural competitions; working on the newspaper or yearbook; tie-dyeing; debating; or working on a community service project. Evening activities include

dances, movies, theater performances, ice skating, bowling, concerts, talent shows, and games.

On weekends, fully supervised excursions offer students the opportunity to visit places in the area. Excursions from Amherst include Boston, Tanglewood, Williamstown, a white-water rafting trip on the Deerfield River, an optional weekend trip to Cape Cod, and an optional college extension trip. Students in the UC–Berkeley program have weekend trips to Yosemite National Park, Monterey, and Carmel and several day trips to San Francisco. In the Oxford Experience there are visits to London, Bath, Stonehenge, Stratford-upon-Avon, Cambridge, and Brighton as well as an optional four-day trip to Paris.

DAILY SCHEDULE

7:30–8:30	Breakfast
9:00–12:00	Major course
12:15–1:15	Lunch
1:30–3:00	Elective
3:30–5:30	Recreation and activities
6:00–7:00	Dinner
7:30–10:30	Evening activities
11:00	Students in dormitories

FACILITIES

All students are housed in residence halls at each campus. In Oxford students are accommodated at Lady Margaret Hall, one of the colleges that constitutes Oxford University. Students have access at each college to such facilities as libraries, art rooms, athletic facilities, swimming pools, and coffee bars. Staff members live on each floor, and the dorms are the hub of many activities. Meals are provided in the dining rooms of the colleges.

STAFF

The President of ASA is Marcia Evans. Mrs. Evans has a noteworthy educational background and wide professional experience as a teacher and educational consultant in England and the United States. The administrative and supervisory staff members are all professional educators and graduate students from the finest schools in the United States and abroad. The program's academic courses are taught by professors, teachers, and teaching assistants from leading colleges and schools. The residential and recreational components of the program are under the supervision of carefully selected college students who attend an extensive training program before the summer begins.

MEDICAL CARE

There are medical facilities within easy reach of all the program sites. Each student submits a medical form and release form before joining the program. Staff members accompany students to medical facilities.

COSTS

The 2004 tuition costs were as follows: UMass–Amherst five-week program, $5295; UMass–Amherst three-week program, $3995; UC–Berkeley program: $5995; and Oxford Experience, $5795.

Fees include tuition, accommodations, three meals daily (two meals a day at Oxford), use of most college facilities, all scheduled excursions (except optional trips), the scheduled afternoon and evening recreational program, and transportation from and to the local airports. There are supplemental fees for some of the courses, including SAT Preparation by the Princeton Review; tennis and golf instruction; art, photographic, and video supplies; and college credit courses at UMass–Amherst and UC–Berkeley.

APPLICATION TIMETABLE

Initial inquiries are welcome at any time. A brochure describing the program and containing an application form is available. Applications are accepted on a rolling basis starting in September, and students are advised to apply early to ensure that they get their first choice of courses. ASA requires a teacher recommendation before acceptance can be confirmed. Students are notified of acceptance within fourteen days of receipt of all application materials.

FOR MORE INFORMATION, CONTACT:

Academic Study Associates
10 New King Street
White Plains, New York 10604
914-686-7730
800-752-2250 (toll-free outside New York State)
Fax: 914-686-7740
E-mail: summer@asaprograms.com
World Wide Web: http://www.asaprograms.com

PARTICIPANT/FAMILY COMMENTS

"This program was fun, exciting, and challenging. I took great classes and made friends from all over the world. Thank you ASA!"

"I got a great taste of college life and feel better prepared academically and socially for when I go to college."

ACADEMY BY THE SEA/ CAMP PACIFIC

SUMMER PROGRAMS

CARLSBAD, CALIFORNIA

Type of Program: Academic program (grades 7–10), recreational camp (ages 8–16), and surf and bodyboard camp (ages 8–16)
Participants: All programs are coeducational
Enrollment: Academic program: 150, Camp Pacific: 60, surf and bodyboard camp: 60
Program Dates: Academic program: five weeks in July and August; Camp Pacific: three-week session in July; surf and bodyboard camp: one-week sessions, June–August
Head of Program: Mr. Jeffrey Barton, Director of Summer Programs

LOCATION

The Academy by the Sea/Camp Pacific is held on the Army and Navy Academy campus in beautiful Carlsbad, California. Carlsbad is a quaint seaside town. The campus is located on 16 acres of prime oceanfront property. The average temperature in Carlsbad from June to August is 75 degrees. Students and campers stay in dormitories (2–3 per room) and eat at the on-campus dining facility.

BACKGROUND AND PHILOSOPHY

The Camp Pacific program was founded in 1943 as an all-boys' surfing camp. Since then, the program has grown to offer a wide variety of sessions for both boys and girls. The camp's philosophy is to provide a safe and fun environment in which young people can learn and grow.

PROGRAM OFFERINGS

Five-week academic program The Academy by the Sea's five-week summer session offers a coeducational program that balances academics and recreation for a fulfilling educational experience. The Academy offers a variety of class subjects, and students are expected to pick the four classes to comprise their summer schedules. Students have the option of being boarding or day students. Boarding is encouraged, as the dormitory experience is an important part of a student's overall learning and enjoyment. Boarding students also have the benefit of participating in a mandatory evening study hall and afternoon activities. The summer academic session classes are small (generally 6–10 students), and individual participation is required. Subjects offered include math, English, science, oceanography, creative writing, computers, history, Spanish, English as a second language, and various electives. Designated courses may be taken for a semester of high school credit. Afternoon activities, special events, and weekend excursions allow each student the opportunity to take a break from scholastic responsibilities and experience lasting friendships and fun.
Camp Pacific—three-week session Founded in 1943, Camp Pacific is a recreation- and sports-based camp that continues to provide a safe and fun summer experience for kids ages 8–16. During the three-week Camp Pacific session, the focus is on teamwork, sportsmanship, and fun. Campers can choose to participate in a wide variety of exciting activities. At Camp Pacific, campers learn new skills, gain self-confidence, and are encouraged to work with their peers. In the morning, campers are divided into weekly interest groups and are led by a counselor through an activity. In the afternoon, campers participate in daily free-choice recreational activities or sports. Trips to area attractions are offered on a weekly basis. Typical activities include arts and crafts, baseball, basketball, bodyboarding, camp radio broadcasting, capture the flag, clay sculpting, cricket, drama, flag football, Frisbee golf, jewelry making, kayaking, mask making, painting, riflery, rugby, sand castle contests, scavenger hunts, snorkeling, soccer, surfing, swimming, tennis, tie-dye, Ultimate Frisbee, water polo, and much more.
Camp Pacific's Surf and Bodyboard Camp—one-week sessions At Camp Pacific's Surf and Bodyboard Camp, the goal is to provide each camper with an unforgettable experience. The surf and bodyboard camp is designed for all skill levels, from beginner to intermediate. Each session is one week long and is full of activities. Group beach instruction, classroom instruction, independent practice, and field trips all combine for a very exciting week of learning. Campers are taught skills in equipment options, wave selection, and basic surf techniques. All activities are supervised by counselors, certified lifeguards, and experienced surfing and bodyboarding instructors. In the afternoons, campers can continue their practice at the beach or participate in the variety of activities enjoyed by participants in the three-week Camp Pacific, listed above. Surfers and bodyboarders ages 8–16 are eligible.

ENROLLMENT

The academic program enrolls between 120 and 160 students. Camp Pacific enrolls between 40 and 60

campers. The surf and bodyboard camp enrolls between 40 and 60 campers.

EXTRA OPPORTUNITIES AND ACTIVITIES

Each program offers a wide variety of fun and educational activities. On weekends, the five-week and three-week groups participate in outings to popular southern California destinations such as theme parks, sporting events, museums, and beaches.

FACILITIES

Boarding students and campers live in dormitories that house 2–3 people per room. Dormitories are important centers of activity where friendships with peers and counselors are formed. Each dormitory is supervised by resident faculty members and counselors who serve as advisers to students and campers, ensuring that an adult is always available for assistance and guidance. Boys and girls are housed in separate dormitories. Rooms are furnished with beds, desks, and bureaus. Each student or camper is responsible for the condition of his or her room. Although the basic organization of the dormitories is informal, constant faculty presence is essential to develop an atmosphere of learning and safety. Students and campers receive three meals each day, served at the dining hall. Security personnel are on campus 24 hours a day. Campus facilities include tennis courts, private beach access, a swimming pool, athletic fields, an on-campus dining facility, an oceanfront recreation hall, a chapel, a library, a radio station, health center, and an indoor gymnasium and weight room.

STAFF

For the academic Academy by the Sea session, experienced teachers and administrators provide classroom instruction and overall supervision of academics, dormitories, and campus life. For Camp Pacific sessions, college and university students, selected for their demonstrated responsibility and experience, live in the dormitories and serve as counselors and resident assistants. All staff members successfully complete a thorough background check and drug test.

MEDICAL CARE

Medical personnel are on campus, and a physician is on call 24 hours a day. Due to the high cost of hospitalization, it is required that all students enroll in a medical insurance program prior to arriving at The Academy by the Sea/Camp Pacific. All international campers must have a temporary U.S. medical insurance policy, for which an additional fee is charged.

COSTS

Costs vary according to the program. Costs are as follows for boarding students and campers: five-week academic session, $4330; three-week Camp Pacific session, $2230; and one-week surf and bodyboard camp, $810. Costs are reduced for day students and day campers. An incidental account of between $200 to $400 is recommended for the three- and five-week sessions.

TRANSPORTATION

With advance notice, students and campers can be transported to and from San Diego International Airport, Los Angeles International Airport, Carlsbad Airport, or Oceanside Amtrak Train Station for a nominal fee.

APPLICATION TIMETABLE

Applications are preferred before May 15; however, they are accepted until enrollment is full.

For more information, contact:

Academy by the Sea/Camp Pacific
P.O. Box 3000
Carlsbad, California 92018-3000
760-434-7564
877-581-9283 (toll-free)
Fax: 760-729-1574
E-mail: info@abts.com
World Wide Web: http://www.abts.com

ACADIA INSTITUTE OF OCEANOGRAPHY

MARINE SCIENCE PROGRAM

MOUNT DESERT ISLAND, MAINE

Type of Program: Educational camping program in marine science and oceanography
Participants: Coeducational, ages 12–18
Enrollment: 45 students per session
Program Dates: Four sessions per summer, mid-June to mid-August
Head of Program: Sheryl Christy Gilmore, Executive Director

LOCATION

The Acadia Institute of Oceanography (AIO) is based in the picturesque village of Seal Harbor on the southern end of Mount Desert Island, Maine, approximately 5 hours north of Boston along one of the most beautiful coastlines in the United States. Located adjacent to Acadia National Park, the program is housed three blocks from the harbor in a vintage schoolhouse that serves as the base of operations for this field-oriented program.

BACKGROUND AND PHILOSOPHY

The Acadia Institute of Oceanography is a one-of-a-kind educational experience for students ages 12 to 18. Since 1975, AIO has introduced young people to the world of marine science through a curriculum that combines the basic elements of biological, physical, and chemical oceanography with field, classroom, offshore, and laboratory work.

AIO seeks highly motivated students for participation in the program. All are expected to arrive with a curious mind and a commitment to learn. A science teacher's recommendation is required for admission.

PROGRAM OFFERINGS

Mount Desert Island is the perfect location to study marine ecology. Waters are rich in plankton, and there are many species of fish. Rocky tidal pools shelter invertebrates, rivers and estuaries serve as ocean nurseries, and offshore dredges yield sediments full of benthic life. The AIO program makes full use of the natural environment. Sample activities include tidal pool study; beach profiles; coastal transects; geologic profiles; algal study; seabirds, seals, and cetacean observations; chemical study of a fjord (Somes Sound); island ecology; plankton collection and study; dissections; developmental biology; fishing; navigation; and whale watching.

Collecting water samples and mud in Somes Sound.

Over the course of a summer, AIO offers four 2-week sessions. Two of these are basic sessions and two are advanced.

The basic sessions are designed for students, age 12–15. These courses present a solid natural-history approach to oceanography and introduce students to marine concepts and laboratory procedures. Many students who attend a basic session return another year for an advanced session.

The advanced sessions are precollege courses offered to students age 15–18 who have completed a minimum of high school–level biology or chemistry. These students are expected to prepare laboratory reports and do analysis of their field work.

ENROLLMENT

Each summer, students come to AIO from all over North America and around the world. Individual sessions are limited to 45 students.

DAILY SCHEDULE

The edge of the sea is AIO's classroom, and academic activities follow the tides. While one group of student oceanographers might finish a transect of the beach, another group collects specimens for the cold water tanks in the wet lab. Others may have focused their binoculars on the seabirds and cetaceans that swim offshore.

Mini-seminars are offered before dinner for those students interested in pursuing more specialized topics. For early risers, AIO offers optional morning laboratory activities. Evenings are devoted to more traditional classroom academics. Each night, students attend a lecture to provide background information and prepare them for upcoming field activities. All students design and maintain a saltwater aquarium.

Despite the busy academic schedule, AIO leaves a block of time each day for recreational activities, such as hiking, swimming, group games, and visits to local laboratories and museums. There is plenty of free time for students to read, write letters, and relax.

EXTRA OPPORTUNITIES AND ACTIVITIES

Graduates of advanced sessions are eligible to apply for one of the programs offered by AIO during the school vacations. A Marine Biology Career Seminar will take place in Florida for nine days in December of 2004. Students go behind the scenes to meet and work with rangers, scientists, and marine mammal trainers to explore potential careers in the field. AIO's seventh trip to the Hofstra University Marine Lab in St. Ann's Bay, Jamaica, is planned for Thanksgiving week of 2005. Students are chosen for these programs based on the quality of their past work and social maturity. Information is available during summer orientation meetings.

FACILITIES

The program is housed in the vintage Dunham Schoolhouse, built in 1931 by John D. Rockefeller. The building was acquired by AIO in 1976 and has been carefully restored. Accommodations are clean and comfortable. Three of the large classrooms have been converted into dormitories, and students sleep on bunk beds. The facility includes a lecture hall, a recreation room, a research wet laboratory, a library, a nurse's office, a dining room, bathrooms, and showers.

STAFF

At the heart of the program is an experienced and qualified core of educators trained in the field of oceanography. These are classroom teachers, practicing scientists, and researchers, many with advanced graduate degrees. Each faculty member brings his or her own unique background to the program. The student-instructor ratio is approximately 4:1.

Other staff members include a nurse, a professional chef, and interns. Internships are offered to college students who have attended AIO previously and are seriously considering a career in marine studies and education.

MEDICAL CARE

A full-time registered nurse is on staff and lives in the building with the students. There is a fully equipped hospital 8 miles away in Bar Harbor, and Eastern Maine Medical Center, a regional state-of-the-art medical facility, is located 1 hour away in the city of Bangor.

All students must have a health form completed by a physician before final acceptance into the program.

COSTS

For 2005, the cost is $1800 per two-week session. The price includes tuition, room, board, and all program costs except for transportation to the site.

A small amount of spending money ($50–$60) is recommended for trips into Bar Harbor.

FINANCIAL AID

A limited number of partial scholarships are available at the discretion of the executive director. Students are asked for additional references and to provide written material in support of their application.

TRANSPORTATION

Transportation is available from the Bar Harbor-Hancock County Regional Airport or the Vermont/Greyhound terminal in Bar Harbor. Students can also be picked up at the Bangor International Airport for an additional fee.

APPLICATION TIMETABLE

Student registration begins in the fall and continues until all available slots are filled. Sessions typically begin filling by March, and most slots are filled by Memorial Day.

A $200 deposit and completed registration form are required at the time of application. Health and teacher recommendation forms are sent upon receipt of deposit. Notification of acceptance is given upon the return of a satisfactory recommendation.

For more information, contact:

Sheryl Christy Gilmore, Executive Director
Acadia Institute of Oceanography
P.O. Box 2220
St. Augustine, Florida 32085
904-829-1112
207-276-9825 (June 10–September 1 only)
E-mail: info@acadiainstitute.com
World Wide Web: http://www.acadiainstitute.com

PARTICIPANT/FAMILY COMMENTS

"There is a wealth of knowledge to be gained at AIO; in the field, in the lecture hall and in discussions with other students and faculty."—Michael Harmon, student, Baltimore, Maryland

"Heather spent two great summers (at AIO) and was motivated beyond all expectations. She is very excited about her future in the Marine Sciences and AIO was the catalyst for sure."—Steve and Mary McRae, parents, Temple, New Hampshire

ACTEEN

ACTING FOR TEENS

SUMMER PROGRAMS

NEW YORK, NEW YORK

Type of Program: Acting conservatory with a film and television concentration
Participants: Coeducational, ages 13–20
Enrollment: Limited to 60 students per session
Program Dates: June 20 to June 30, July 5 to 28, August 1 to 17, or July 9 to August 13 (Saturdays)
Head of Program: Rita Litton, Director

LOCATION

ACTeen is located in New York City's Broadway theater district, near Rockefeller Center and Radio City Music Hall. ACTeen shares studios with the Weist-Barron School of Television, which is the oldest on-camera acting school in the U.S. and the home of Weist-Barron Casting. ACTeen occupies the entire sixth floor of a midtown office building.

BACKGROUND AND PHILOSOPHY

ACTeen was created in 1978 by successful theater and commercial actress Rita Litton, who was approached by the Weist-Barron School to develop a special film/commercial acting curriculum for teenagers. Weist-Barron, the first on-camera acting school in the U.S., was established in 1958 by Dwight Weist (former president of the Screen Actor's Guild) and Robert Barron. Stories about Weist-Barron and ACTeen have appeared in the *New York Times, New York Magazine, Cosmopolitan,* and the *Wall Street Journal;* on television and news broadcasts; and in various acting books, including praise in *How to Be a Working Actor* by Mari Lyn Henry (former head of East Coast casting for ABC-TV) and *Acting Like a Pro* by Mary McTigue. ACTeen is consistently recommended to clients and prospective clients by more than 30 New York City talent agents and managers. Hundreds of ACTeen graduates have achieved successful careers in film, television, and the theater, including China Shavers *(Boston Public),* Jamie Lynn DiScala *(The Sopranos,* Broadway's *Beauty and the Beast),* Jordana Brewster *(The Fast and the Furious, The Faculty),* Danny Masterson *(That 70's Show),* Jon Seda (*Homicide, Seleena*), and Emmy-winner Dana Barron *(Beverly Hills 90210).* Many acquired their first representation through ACTeen's industry showcases.

The ACTeen Summer Academy accepts dedicated preprofessionals and attempts to develop them into technically proficient, versatile, marketable actors. By combining a theatrical discipline with spontaneous, effective on-camera acting techniques, students learn to successfully navigate both film and theater media with skill and professionalism. ACTeen believes that acting is action oriented and that emotions are the result of intentions successfully or unsuccessfully achieved. Various acting techniques are incorporated, therefore, to offer more than one path to characterization. Students learn to function among diverse directors and actors, with varying acting approaches. In addition, students benefit enormously from the video playbacks (the "one picture is worth a thousand words" theory), which are an integral part of the on-camera acting classes and may be utilized in elective courses.

PROGRAM OFFERINGS

While ACTeen offers courses during the fall and spring, its summer academies are more extensive. ACTeen offers six different courses in the June academy, fifteen in the four-week July academy, and nine in the three-week August academy. Students may attend full-time or part-time. There is also a four-course, six-week Saturday-only summer session. A typical 29-hour week for students who attend ACTeen's July full-time summer academy includes 8 hours of on-camera acting technique and scene study, 4 hours of commercial audition skills, 3 hours of speech and voice, 3 hours of movement, 3 hours of improvisation, 4 hours of auditioning skills, and 4 hours of musical theater or Shakespeare. Various electives include directing and script writing. Students may choose from several course offerings, including those listed below.

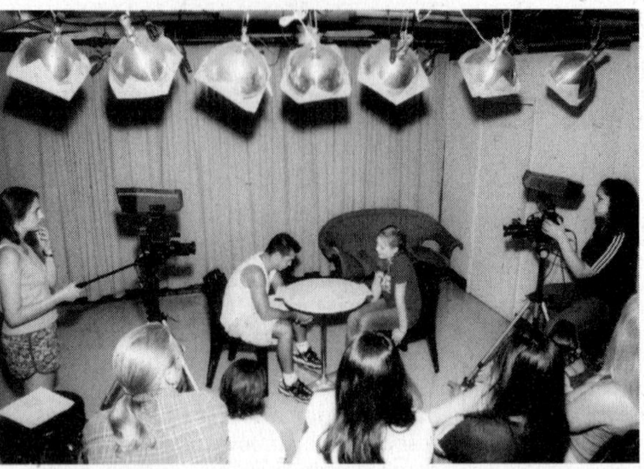

Film/Film Acting Technique Theater terminology (intention, motivation, relationship, obstacles, actions) is explored through various individual and ensemble moment-to-moment exercises. Student exercises are hinged to assigned film and television scripts to better relate process with result. All exercises and scenes are videotaped in a two-camera setup, and playback critiques are an essential part of class time.
Film/Film Scene Study In multicamera studios students explore the technique and emotional depth required for successful film acting. Emphasis is on creating characters common or unique to television and film—situation comedy, episodic TV, feature films, soap operas. Class discussion defines particular problems, themes, and audition problems inherent in a variety of on-camera material.
Commercial Audition Technique To successfully audition for TV commercials, actors must please the sponsor by effectively relaying his sales message and creatively compete against other competent actors of similar type. To this end, ACTeen trains students in on-camera public speaking techniques but encourages a natural delivery that utilizes an actor's unique personality. Students perform all work on videotape to improve skills and will audition privately for a guest casting director. Copyrighted course text includes valuable information on agents, unions, photos, and getting started professionally.
Improvisation Improvisation attempts to develop creative, collaborative actors who accept and expand upon impulses. Using the wonderful theater games of Viola Spolin and Keith Johnstone, actors learn to listen, work creatively and physically, and channel fears into actions.
Speech and Voice A workshop to develop the flexibility and musicality of the actor's speaking voice.

Speech exercises on phonetics develop standardized American speech, while voice work deals with breath control, relaxation, resonance, and tone.

ENROLLMENT

Previous students (ages 13–20) have come to ACTeen from all over the world. Class size for each workshop is extremely limited—6 to 12 students maximum—for utmost personal attention. ACTeen seeks bright, dedicated teens who love to act. Prior experience is recommended but not required. Students requiring housing must be 17 years old by the summer to qualify for suggested off-site housing.

DAILY SCHEDULE

Classes meet Monday through Thursday from 9 to 5 and Friday 10 to 3 (June) or Monday through Thursday from 10 to 6 (July) or Monday through Friday from 9:30 to 5:30 (August), with appropriate lunch breaks. Students have the option of attending part-time. Beyond the classroom, students must devote time to homework preparation.

EXTRA OPPORTUNITIES AND ACTIVITIES

ACTeen has a special VIP guest series on selected evenings during which visiting professionals share their insights and expertise. In addition, students enrolled in the Audition Workshop work closely with New York City industry guests, including a Broadway director, a film/theater casting director, a commercial casting director, a monologue coach, and guest professional actors.

FACILITIES

ACTeen has seven air-conditioned on-camera video studios. Three studios are equipped with double cameras and simultaneous editing equipment. There are three lounges and office space.

STAFF

The staff is exemplary and includes adults from professional acting, directing, and casting backgrounds. Many also teach in colleges, universities, and other acting conservatories, and the majority hold advanced degrees. Full-time academy students work with 6 to 8 different experienced instructors as well as special guest artists. The small class size enables a close personal relationship between students and faculty members. Teachers work creatively to tailor scenes and exercises to best stimulate each student.

COSTS

Tuition for full-time programs ranges from $1250 to $1350 for the June academy, $1675 to $2350 in July, and $1075 to $1925 in August. Individual courses cost $275 to $300, with discounts for multiple course selection. No financial aid is available. ACTeen does not maintain housing or off-studio supervision for its out-of-state academy participants. However, affordable dormitory or apartment-style rooms are available at discounted rates for accepted ACTeen registrants (over age 17 only) through April 1. Fees range from $800 to $2000 per month. Students may request a housing list when they submit their applications.

TRANSPORTATION

ACTeen's midtown location is ideally situated so that all public transportation is accessible. ACTeen is within walking distance of all the suburban transportation hubs, including Grand Central Station, Penn Station, and the Port Authority Bus Terminal.

APPLICATION TIMETABLE

ACTeen prefers on-site audition and interviews if possible. Long-distance applicants should request a registration packet. Completed applications (including recommendation, questionnaire, fee, and optional video) are accepted January through June, but Summer Academy students are advised to apply early, preferably by April 1, for the best housing opportunities. Summer housing is not available for students younger than 17 years old. Tuition discounts are typically available through April 15.

FOR MORE INFORMATION, CONTACT:

Rita Litton, ACTeen Director
ACTeen
35 West 45th Street, 6th floor
New York, New York 10036
212-391-5915
Fax: 212-768-8918
E-mail: rita@acteen.com
World Wide Web: http://www.acteen.com

PARTICIPANT/FAMILY COMMENTS

"My first on-camera acting experience took place at ACTeen. I still use the techniques I acquired in my classes."—Jamie Lynn DiScala *(The Sopranos,* Broadway's *Beauty and the Beast)*

"The school is a must experience for the committed acting student"—China Shavers *(Boston Public, Sabrina)*

"I will always be grateful to ACTeen for helping my daughter, China, achieve her dreams. "—Angela Shavers

ACTIONQUEST

WORLDWIDE ADVENTURES IN SAILING, SCUBA DIVING, AND MARINE SCIENCE

SUMMER PROGRAMS

CARIBBEAN, MEDITERRANEAN, GALAPAGOS, AUSTRALIA, AND TAHITI VOYAGES

Type of Program: Live-aboard sailing and diving adventures: beginner and advanced sail training, all levels of scuba diving certifications, marine science, cultural and historical shore exploration, leadership training programs, and life skills. No previous experience necessary.

Participants: Coed, ages 13–19, grouped by grade

Enrollment: More than 400 shipmates in seventeen different voyage programs grouped by age and grade. Group size ranges from 10 to 60.

Program Dates: Two-, three-, five-, and six-week programs from June through August.

Heads of Program: James Stoll, Master Mariner; Mike Meighan, B.Sc.

LOCATION

ActionQuest offers programs for students of all levels, beginner through advanced, in the British Virgin Islands, the Leeward Islands, the Mediterranean, Galapagos, Australia, and Tahiti. Participants in all programs live aboard 50-foot sailing yachts and catamarans while voyaging from island to island.

BACKGROUND AND PHILOSOPHY

Unique in the world and backed by more than thirty years of dependability, ActionQuest offers sailing and scuba diving live-aboard adventures for teenagers. Safety, a dedicated staff, and close interaction make adventuring with ActionQuest extraordinary. Programs are noncompetitive and centered around dynamic small-group support and self-reliance.

ActionQuest gives young adults the excitement of yachting while living aboard, making new friends through teamwork, and acquiring valuable, lifelong leadership skills.

ActionQuest annually attracts more than 400 teens from the United States, the Far East, South America, and Europe—people whose interests are as diverse as their geographical backgrounds.

PROGRAM OFFERINGS

British Virgin Islands Voyage itineraries and specific activities are described fully in the brochure and at the ActionQuest Web site. The Vega and Quest voyages are designed for shipmates with little or no previous experience and offer the broadest range of activities. Shipmates earn sailing and diving certifications through the American Sailing Association (ASA), the American Red Cross, and the Professional Association of Diving Instructors (PADI). Water skiing, windsurfing, small-boat sailing, and nautical training round out the program. For the more seasoned sailor or diver, programs are available for shipmates to build on their skills and earn ASA sailing certifications up to and including BareBoat Charter and PADI Advanced and Specialty certifications. ActionQuest is the only fully accredited PADI International Five-Star Gold Palm Facility dedicated entirely to teenagers. For those already dive-certified, distinctive voyages offer participants multiple certifications while living aboard sailing yachts and diving to explore the rich coral reefs of the British Virgin Islands. Students receive training in safe diving practices from Advanced levels through to professional Divemaster level. These voyages are designed for teens ages 13–19 who have already been certified by any organization. Program offerings include PADI Advanced and Junior Advanced Open Water, Rescue Diver, Master Scuba Diver, and Divemaster as well as ten different PADI specialties.

Tropical Marine Biology voyages, conducted by staff marine biologists, are live-aboard programs combining diving and field studies with marine sciences. This program is designed for participants interested in studying the coral reefs and participating in underwater research to build knowledge in this growing area of environmental science. High school credit documentation is available on request.

The Leeward Islands Voyages sail longer distances, challenging both the novice and advanced shipmates. The travel/adventure focus offers intriguing shore exploration from the British Virgin Islands to Antigua. Depending on previous experience, shipmates may earn ASA sailing certifications from Basic Keelboat to BareBoat Charter. Hiking the hand-carved steps to Mt. Scenery at Saba, exploring the rain forest and volcanic terrain of Nevis, and snorkeling the reefs of Ile Forche are some of the highlights.

The Mediterranean Voyage follows the wake of Ulysses to ports of call, including Nice, Cannes, Corsica, Sardinia, Rome, Elba, Portofino, and Monte Carlo. This voyage combines offshore sailing skills with cultural and historical exploration.

The Galapagos Archipelago Experience combines snorkeling and hiking the main islands of the Galapagos with an expedition to Ecuador. Nature study, rain-forest trekking, white-water rafting, and cultural exploration are part of the voyage.

The Australia and Great Barrier Adventure encompasses exploration of Sydney, live-aboard sailing, and diving in the Whitsunday Islands and action-packed touring in Queensland—an incredible way to experience the land down under.

The Tahiti Voyage offers the opportunity to experience the exotic setting of the tropical South Seas. These volcanic islands offer lush rain forests, blue lagoons, and dazzling reefs and have a history rich with tradition. Activities include interisland sailing, snorkeling, trekking, and community service.

ENROLLMENT

Every year, more than 400 shipmates and staff members from at least thirty-three different states and fifteen other countries participate. Coed crew members are grouped according to age. Shipmates live together on yachts while sailing in a fleet. Small groups and close working relationships help build lasting friendships and allow for a strongly beneficial experience in teamwork.

DAILY SCHEDULE

About the only thing typical of the ActionQuest day is that there is no such thing as a typical day. The days are as varied as the activities pursued. A rotation of positions aboard allows shipmates to develop diverse skills—whether as skipper of the day or chef. Regardless of prior experience, the first time the yachts sail from the dock, it is a shipmate who takes the helm under the guidance of licensed sailing masters. Whether participants are sailing, scuba diving, trekking, or simply taking in the local sights and sounds, each day is another opportunity to make life extraordinary.

EXTRA OPPORTUNITIES AND ACTIVITIES

Although all shipmates participate in most of the core certification programs, the optional Action Credit program is designed to quantify what is learned and accomplished during the voyage. The program encompasses forty-five skills useful both on and off the water. ActionQuest also offers Sea-mester programs (live-aboard college semester voyages), Argo Academy (a high school semester afloat), and Lifeworks international service-learning programs (http://www.lifeworks-international.com).

FACILITIES

All shipmates live aboard modern, fully equipped 50-foot sailing yachts or catamarans, each containing five cabins with four bathrooms and showers. Ninety sets of dive gear are carried with more than 120 tanks and nine ski boats. Laser sailboats, Mistral windsurfers, wake boards, water skis, and all other training equipment are provided.

STAFF

Sailing and diving instructors are fully licensed and certified men and women eager to share their areas of expertise. They come from a variety of backgrounds. Many have been with ActionQuest for years. Among the 30 staff members are 12 USCG-licensed Sailing Masters, 12 PADI-certified dive instructors, and those assisting in other activities. No other U.S.-based program can offer their combined level of certification and experience. The staff-shipmate ratio is 1:4, the average staff age is 27.

COSTS

Program costs for two- and three-week voyages in 2004 ranged from $3470 to $4470. Five- and six-week program costs vary depending upon courses chosen.

TRANSPORTATION

Shipmates fly in small groups, and staff assistance is available at arrival airports.

APPLICATION TIMETABLE

Applications are accepted at any time. Some programs fill up faster in certain age groups than in others. Some fill up in February, but most are full by April. Students should call for information on availability if applying late.

For more information, contact:

ActionQuest
P.O. Box 5517
Sarasota, Florida 34277
941-924-6789
800-317-6789 (toll-free)
Fax: 941-924-6075
E-mail: info@actionquest.com
World Wide Web: http://www.actionquest.com

PARTICIPANT/FAMILY COMMENTS

"In three weeks, I made the best of friends, had the best times, and learned things I will never ever forget. Thank you for everything you taught me."

"We had high expectations and they were exceeded. The increase in self-confidence and the motivation and skills learned were most valuable."

ADIRONDACK CAMP

SUMMER CAMP

PUTNAM STATION, NEW YORK

Type of Program: Traditional camping with an emphasis on the waterfront, wilderness, athletics, and arts
Participants: Boys and girls, ages 7–16, from around the world
Enrollment: 185 per session
Program Dates: One 8-week session and two 4-week sessions, from June 22 to August 16; two 2-week sessions available for first-time campers only, ages 8–9
Head of Program: Matt Basinet, Director

LOCATION

Adirondack Camp is located on the northern end of 36-mile-long Lake George on its own peninsula. The water in the lake is pure enough to drink. The camp is within a short distance of outdoor adventures in the Adirondack High Peaks, Vermont's Green Mountains, and countless lakes, rivers, and wilderness areas. It is a 4-hour drive from Boston, Montreal, and New York City.

BACKGROUND AND PHILOSOPHY

Founded on traditional values in 1904, Adirondack was first established as a base camp to explore the dramatic, wild countryside and waterfront surrounding it. Throughout the camp's history and today, campers are part of a coherent, open community in which diverse individuals come to value, support, and cheer each other on. For 100 years at Adirondack, youngsters from around the world have gained the skills of self-reliance, leadership, and teamwork and have developed greater self-confidence and respect for each other in the spectacular outdoor setting. Friendship, respect for the great outdoors, lifelong sports and outdoor adventure and wilderness skills are the memories and core values that old-time campers carry with them to this day. This corner of the world remains as beautiful as ever, and Adirondack's commitment to tradition endures. With an emphasis on self-esteem through personal achievement, Adirondack provides a wealth of fun, friends, and memories to last a lifetime.

PROGRAM OFFERINGS

Campers design their own programs each week with guidance from activity leaders and their cabin counselors. Activities focus on the four main attributes of the camp: waterfront, wilderness adventure, land sports, and the creative arts. Since the camp sits on a peninsula surrounded by almost 2 miles of waterfront, instructional swimming is the one required activity. Many campers of all ages sign up for long-distance swimming. Their reward is the ability to swim 2 miles across the lake and back without breaking stroke. Other water-related activities, which originate from different parts of the waterfront, include waterskiing, sailing, windsurfing, canoeing, kayaking, snorkeling, fishing, and boating. Land sports include golf, baseball, softball, basketball, volleyball, archery, tennis, and even fencing. The creative arts program includes traditional camp crafts, and also focuses on drawing, painting, ceramics, wood carving, and acting. The wilderness excursions program offers both long and short overnight wilderness trips and features rock climbing, mountain biking, white-water rafting, kayaking, and hiking along naturalist trails. Campers prepare for these adventures on the camp's climbing wall and on its low-elements ropes course that is used in small groups to help develop leadership, teamwork, and cooperation. A fifth aspect to Adirondack's program includes activities such as culinary fun, magic, star gazing, a carnival, backwards day, and other surprise events.

ENROLLMENT

Campers and counselors come from throughout the United States and several other countries. More than 75 percent of campers return year after year. Enrollment is limited to 175 campers per session. In 2002, campers came from twenty-two states and ten other countries. Many campers stay in touch with each other through the winter and often become lifelong friends.

DAILY SCHEDULE

7:30	Wake-up
8:00	Breakfast
9:15	Inspection
9:30	Activity A
10:45	Activity B
11:30	General swim/free time
12:30	Lunch
1:15	Rest hour
2:30	Activity C
3:45	Activity D
4:45	General swim
5:00	Adventure period
6:30	Dinner
7:30	Evening activity

There are two visiting days during the season, and parents may choose to visit during one of them. The camp encourages parents to visit on these days and to enjoy the magnificent setting with their children.

FACILITIES

Adirondack has open-air cabins, several activity buildings, a magnificent dining hall, a low-elements ropes course, a playing field, a volleyball court, a basketball court, and three tennis courts. Adirondack's infirmary is fully equipped and staffed by a registered nurse 24 hours a day. There are four separate waterfronts for swimming and five dock areas for boating, sailing, kayaking, canoeing, waterskiing, fishing, windsurfing, and snorkeling.

STAFF

Adirondack maintains a 1:3 staff member-camper ratio. Many of the staff members were once campers at Adirondack, and many are teachers. The mature and nurturing staff members are hired for their ability to teach and to instill in campers the fine ideals that have made Adirondack's program so successful.

COSTS

In 2004, the cost for both four-week sessions was $3750. An eight-week program was $6500. The two-week sessions for young, first-time campers was $2350. Those wishing to extend their stay to four weeks pay only the difference. Sibling discounts are available. A $500 deposit, which is applied to tuition, must accompany the registration. There is limited financial aid available.

TRANSPORTATION

Counselors accompany campers from New York and Westchester on a chartered bus. Airports close to camp are Albany and Burlington. Arrangements for pickup at Montreal can be made. Many campers arrive by car. A handbook that includes complete travel details is sent to parents in April.

For more information, contact:

Linda Goodwin, Owner
Matt Basinet, Director
P.O. Box 97
Putnam Station, New York 12861
518-547-8261
Fax: 518-547-8973
E-mail: linda@adirondackcamp.com
World Wide Web: http://www.adirondackcamp.com

PARTICIPANT/FAMILY COMMENTS

"Everything I love to do, I learned to do at Adirondack."—Mitch Mitchell

"It was the best camp I ever went to and hope to come again."—Lee Johnson

"We were so impressed by the counselors and thrilled by our children's new skills."—Jim and Nancy Holland

ADVENTURE IRELAND

ADVENTURE CENTRE AND SURF SCHOOL

BUNDORAN, COUNTY DONEGAL, REPUBLIC OF IRELAND

Type of Program: Irish cultural studies, scenic outdoor activities, and teenage fun.
Participants: Coed, ages 12–18
Enrollment: 50
Program Dates: July 3–22 and August 7–26
Head of Program: Mrs. Niamh Hamill, Director

LOCATION

Adventure Ireland Summer Programmes is located in Bundoran Village, County Donegal. Bundoran, a small, Irish town right on the Atlantic coast, is famous for its surfing waves and its stunningly scenic location in the west of Ireland. Sligo town is 30 minutes away, and Dublin City is 3½ hours by coach. The location is a very safe, friendly Irish town deeply immersed in the thriving Irish culture.

BACKGROUND AND PHILOSOPHY

The programme was founded by teacher Niamh (pronounced "Neeve") Hamill after a visit to the United States in 1995. Niamh attended a popular Irish festival and was amazed at the strong interest in Irish culture among young people who had ancestral links with Ireland but had never visited the country. She discovered that although many teenagers paid cultural visits to mainland Europe, there seemed to be no opportunity for a trip to Ireland. She and her brother, Collie, designed the kind of programme they thought would give the full Ireland experience. Originally from Dublin, they moved to County Donegal, the most beautiful location for the Irish experience.

Ireland, renowned as a place where kindness, humor, and friendliness are championed as values, is traditionally known as the land of "a hundred thousand welcomes." The goal of the programme is to communicate that sense of welcome through an experiential three-week stay that includes education, activity, and fun.

The Adventure Ireland programme has been running since 1996, and hundreds of American teens have enjoyed Collie and Niamh's unique hospitality.

There are classes on Irish history, literature, music, and sociology. Participants surf, kayak, and hike in scenic and beautiful locations. Tours take the campers to places of interest, such as Donegal Castle, Dublin City, and Sligo town. There is a combination of the ancient and the modern Ireland in everything. Adventure Ireland is not a sports camp or an academic camp; it is a mix of many different things glued together with a spirit of tolerance and friendliness so that every child feels at home.

PROGRAM OFFERINGS

The full Adventure Ireland session is nearly three weeks long. Shorter stays are an option, but it is recommended that first-time visitors stay for the duration. The programme is based at the Donegal Adventure Centre, but teens travel to other parts of Ireland, including Dublin City, during their stay. All students are encouraged to try all of the activities and options, but there is no academic or physical pressure to perform. There are no prerequisites. A sense of humor is the only official requirement.

The programme has three main strands. A cultural focus on the history, literature, customs, traditions, arts, and music of Ireland is delivered through workshops, classes, field trips, and site visits. The second part of the programme involves the fantastic natural resources in the area—surfing, hiking, canoeing, snorkelling, and more. There is a huge range of activities available, all suitable for beginners, and all equipment and instruction is provided. The third part of the programme is designed to ensure fun and entertainment: talent shows, competitions, games, quizzes, and overnight camps. The teens mix with other teens from Ireland and Europe in a friendly and fun atmosphere and make friends from all over the world.

ENROLLMENT

The summer programme is designed for teenagers, ages 12 to 18, who want to sample the best aspects of Irish culture in a rural and peaceful location. It is of special interest to students who have an Irish background. The small and family-run programme, which won the Irish Tourist Board's hospitality award in 2003, is renowned for its friendliness and care of young American teenagers. Typically, about 50 percent of each session's enrolled teens are from the U.S. and Canada, 30 percent from mainland Europe, and 20 percent from Ireland.

DAILY SCHEDULE

9:00	Breakfast
10:00	Workshop on Irish history—the Celts
11:00	Introduction to Celtic arts and crafts
12:00	Irish ballad session
1:00	Lunch
2:00–5:00	Afternoon outing
5:00	Evening meal
6:00	Tullan Strand
8:00	Evening activity
11:30	Bed time

During the afternoon outings, campers visit Ballyshannon, Ireland's oldest town, or experience the beautiful Mill Walk, complete with Mass Rock and Cave, which go back to the times of the penal laws. They also visit the lonely Port Na Marbh (Port of the Dead), so named for the number of ships that left for the U.S. during the famine. There is also time to visit the local record shop, where they can hear the music of Rory Gallagher, Ballyshannon's famous rock guitarist.

After the evening meal, campers enjoy a leisurely surf on Tullan Strand. Only 5 minutes from the centre, this 3-mile stretch of golden sand offers perfect waves for the beginner surfers.

EXTRA OPPORTUNITIES AND ACTIVITIES

The programme includes an overnight camping expedition (weather permitting), a visit to an Gaelic inter-county football match, the July 4 barbeque, a Spanish evening, and a

French evening. Participants also visit a traditional Irish pub (under strict supervision) and Leo's Tavern, the homeplace of Enya.

FACILITIES

The Donegal Adventure Centre is a residential centre with en-suite, twin-room accommodations; large activity area; shop; reception; TV room; large game room; laundry; kitchen and dining room; shower suites; and garden. The centre is 2 minutes from the town and the beach. Stores, pharmacies, the doctor's surgery, library, cinema, and other amenities are adjacent to the centre. Students have access to e-mail, Internet, phone, and fax. The Adventure Ireland Web Diary, a day-by-day account of the programme, is posted on the Adventure Ireland Web site each day, with digiphotos to keep parents up to date with all the news. Parents are welcome to travel over and vacation nearby. There are hotels and holiday cottages in the immediate area to accommodate families and younger children.

STAFF

The director of the programme is Niamh Hamill, a qualified and experienced schoolteacher. The curriculum director is (Jolly) Collie Mac Phaidin, also an experienced teacher. Cathal Bennett is the director of outdoor activities, and all staff members involved in outdoor activities are fully qualified in their disciplines. All outdoor activities are run according to the strict guidelines of the Governing Bodies. Donegal Adventure Centre is a full-time, year-round residential centre, and all staff members are full-time and fully qualified.

MEDICAL CARE

All staff are fully trained in first aid and child protection. The local medical practice is 5 minutes from the centre, with emergency treatment facilities and a staff of five doctors. The local hospital is in Sligo town, 30 minutes from the centre. All participating students must have full holiday insurance before travelling. Parents must provide emergency contact numbers in the application forms.

RELIGIOUS LIFE

Daily and Sunday services are available locally for students who wish to attend.

COSTS

Fees, except for airfare, are inclusive of transfer from Dublin Airport, all meals, activities, tours, accommodations, entertainments, classes, workshops, and supervision. The fees for 2005, payable in euro dollars, are: three-week programme, €1995; two-week programme, €1600; and one-week programme,€900. Bookings, with the €500 deposit, are taken on a rolling basis until the programme fills. Very little pocket money is required, although students generally like to return with gifts.

TRANSPORTATION

Staff members meet all students on arrival at Dublin Airport. The transfer time from Dublin to the programme is approximately 3½ hours, and students are transferred by coach. The transfer fees are included in the overall fees unless students arrive outside of designated dates.

APPLICATION TIMETABLE

Inquiries are welcome any time. There is a comprehensive application form which must be completed and sent with the deposit. Application forms can be downloaded from the Web site.

For more information, contact:

Mrs. Niamh Hamill
Adventure Ireland
Donegal Adventure Centre
Bay View Avenue, Bundoran
County Donegal
Republic of Ireland
011-353-7198-42418
888-677-2652 (toll-free)
Fax: 011 353 7198 42429
World Wide Web: http://www.adventure-ireland.com

PARTICIPANT/FAMILY COMMENTS

"Adventure Ireland is a parent's dream. Although it's an overseas trip, it's like sending our son to a home away from home."—Bill Guinan, Connecticut

"Our daughter has fallen in love with Ireland. She has not stopped raving about how beautiful it is, how friendly everyone was, and how much she discovered about her Irish background. Although the family is Irish, she is the first to return to the old country, and she's brought back wonderful stories, songs, and smiles that we haven't seen in our teenager for some time! Adventure Ireland says that their values are humor and tolerance, and our daughter certainly seems to have returned with a happier and more positive attitude. Next year, we're all going!"—Sue McGrath, Marin County, California

!ADVENTURES-AFLOAT/ ODYSSEY EXPEDITIONS

LIVE-ABOARD SAIL AND SCUBA PROGRAMS/TROPICAL MARINE BIOLOGY VOYAGES

CARIBBEAN: BRITISH VIRGIN ISLANDS, SANTA LUCIA, SAINT VINCENT, THE GRENADINES, MARTINIQUE, GRENADA

Type of Program: Educational adventure programs exploring sailing, SCUBA diving, and tropical marine biology while living and sailing aboard catamarans in the Caribbean. SCUBA certifications, sailing, marine biology and oceanography instruction, island exploration, sea kayaking, waterskiing, and leadership training. No experience is necessary.
Participants: Coed, ages 13–19
Enrollment: 10 participants per trip
Program Dates: Three-week programs in June, July, and August

LOCATION

Participants explore the extraordinary islands of the eastern Caribbean with !Adventures Afloat/Odyssey Expeditions, including the coral reefs, volcanoes, rainforests, waterfalls, towering mountains, and friendly villages along a 200-mile area of island stepping stones. Participants visit either the Windward Islands, including Saint Lucia, St. Vincent and the Grenadines, Martinique, and Grenada, or the British Virgin Islands. They dive some of the world's best underwater locations, with diverse coral reefs and marine life, crystal clear waters, and spectacular topography. The islands' marine resources are conserved by national marine park systems and remain healthy and vibrant. Sailing is the means of transport and discovery as participants enjoy the steady trade winds and calm protected waters aboard comfortable sailing catamarans. Ashore, students hike to the rim of volcanoes, bathe in hot spring-fed waterfalls, and enjoy miles of relaxing beaches. The British Virgin Islands are the wreck-diving capital of the world and feature the *HMS Rhone* and six other shipwrecks for exploration. St. Vincent has the Caribbean's clearest waters, wildest marine life, and most spectacular underwater pinnacles and sheer coral walls. The friendly English-speaking peoples of these safe, democratic countries welcome participants as they enjoy their islands. With all the spectacular natural resources, there is guaranteed an exciting adventure of live-aboard diving and sailing.

BACKGROUND AND PHILOSOPHY

!Adventures are designed around discovery, accomplishment, and exploration to challenge young adults in developing and broadening their personal abilities and gaining insight into themselves and the natural wonders of the world. A motivated staff of sailing instructors, SCUBA professionals, and marine biologists provide opportunities for young adults to learn sailing and seamanship, earn PADI SCUBA certifications, and discover marine science while living aboard high-quality sailing yachts, making new friends, exploring diverse cultures and islands, diving spectacular coral reefs, and developing valuable leadership abilities. Programs are full of participatory experiences dedicated to discovering the surrounding world in a safe and stimulating environment that is full of challenges but without competition. Itineraries are carefully designed to maximize cultural and educational opportunities and take advantage of what is unique in each region visited. Whether it's navigating to the next island, taking the helm, trimming the sails, exploring a shipwreck, meeting face-to-face with a loggerhead turtle, climbing to the top of a volcano, getting up on water skis, or triangulating the boat's location on the chart, participants can be sure their adventure will be extraordinary. !ADVENTURES-AFLOAT programs offer leadership and skill building activities in sailing and SCUBA diving during an extraordinary adventure of above-and-below-the-waterline island exploration combined with the excitement of yachting under sail. Living aboard and making new friends while participating in a diverse array of activities and water sports provides discovery, challenge, and exceptional personal growth experiences. ODYSSEY EXPEDITIONS is a unique educational adventure program dedicated to providing a foundation in biological understanding, underwater exploration skills, and personal talents that enable participants to become "Ambassadors of the World's Oceans" during a marine science sailing expedition.

PROGRAM OFFERINGS

!ADVENTURES-AFLOAT Discovery Voyages offer sailing and PADI Open Water and Advanced SCUBA certifications. No prior sailing or SCUBA experience is necessary; experienced instructors teach the course one step at a time at the participants' own pace. Participants are taught island exploration, windsurfing, waterskiing, wakeboarding, and seamanship and receive introductory instruction in marine biology and oceanography. **!ADVENTURES-AFLOAT Adventure Voyages** are for certified divers and continuing diver education, with PADI

Advanced and Rescue Diver courses as well as a broad spectrum of PADI specialty certifications, including Night Diver, Wreck Diver, Underwater Photography, Underwater Navigation, Computer Diver, and Drift Diver. Participants live and sail aboard 45-foot catamarans while exploring the rich and colorful reefs, rain forests, mangroves, mountains, volcanoes, and beaches of these exotic Caribbean islands. No prior sailing experience is required, but opportunities abound to develop personal seamanship and navigation abilities as participants learn to take command of the vessel. Marine biology and underwater photography instruction further enhance the experience.

ODYSSEY EXPEDITIONS Tropical Marine Biology Voyages dive deep into biology and oceanography, allowing motivated students the opportunity to interact with dedicated marine biologists on voyages of marine science discovery. Participants in exciting underwater research activities learn the scientific approach to understanding the marine environment. Using the reefs, mangroves, and rain forests as living laboratories, participants have an incredible opportunity for career exploration. Participants should be certified divers, but no prior marine science or sailing experience is necessary for this adventure. PADI Advanced Open Water, Research Diver, and two specialty certifications are included. High school and college credit documentation and recommendations are available.

ENROLLMENT

In order to maintain a flexible, noncompetitive, and highly supportive atmosphere, !ADVENTURES-AFLOAT/ODYSSEY EXPEDITIONS limits the enrollment of any trip to a small group size of 10 participants of similar ages. The small group size allows each trip to be a personal experience, with an emphasis on developing communication, teamwork, and leadership skills in a dynamic and safe environment.

DAILY SCHEDULE

Although each trip has specific objectives and goals, the small group size allows for personal input on every aspect of an adventure. The daily itinerary and schedule are flexible and not limited by the constraints of a flotilla of vessels traveling together. Each day is action packed and exciting, filled with two to three SCUBA dives, sailing, island exploration, and educational activities.

FACILITIES

!ADVENTURES-AFLOAT/ODYSSEY EXPEDITIONS sails aboard new 45-foot catamarans of the highest quality, each fully equipped for diving, adventure, and educational activities. These sailing vessels have comfortable cabins with private facilities and include an air compressor, top-quality dive gear with integrated dive computers, digital underwater photography and video equipment, a science lab with microscopes and research tools, underwater communications equipment, a computer, a windsurfer, a sea kayak, all yacht safety equipment, and a water-ski boat in tow.

STAFF

!ADVENTURES-AFLOAT/ODYSSEY EXPEDITIONS staff members are a select group of highly trained leaders and educators with a commitment to safety and the individual success and growth of each participant. Sailing masters are U.S. Coast Guard licensed. Professional PADI SCUBA instructors supervise all training and diving activities. Science instructors have advanced degrees or are active graduate students, all with ongoing tropical research projects. Staff members are trained in first aid and CPR and include Emergency Medical Technicians. A staff member–student ratio of 1:4 is maintained, with both male and female leaders. All staff members are friendly and eager to share their particular area of expertise. Professionalism, maturity, enthusiasm, and a love of working with young people are the most important character traits the Director looks for when hiring staff members.

COSTS

Programs cost $4290 all-inclusive (except airfare). All course tuitions, SCUBA training certifications, diving, equipment rental, meals, lodging, tours, and local transportation are included.

FOR MORE INFORMATION, CONTACT:

!ADVENTURES-AFLOAT
ODYSSEY EXPEDITIONS
#100
650 Southeast Paradise Point Road
Crystal River, Florida 34429
352-527-3366
800-929-7749 (toll-free)
E-mail: odyssey@usa.net
World Wide Web: http://www.adventures-afloat.com
http://www.odysseyexpeditions.org

PARTICIPANT/FAMILY COMMENTS

"I learned so much about myself and the marine environment and made some very good friends. The staff were great and treated me as an equal. Thanks for everything you have taught us!"

"I had an incredible time sailing and diving in the islands, and am sure that I learned many things that will guide me through my life. I learned a lot about trust and to conquer challenges, my biggest challenge now is waiting to come back."

ADVENTURES CROSS-COUNTRY

ADVENTURE PROGRAMS

MILL VALLEY, CALIFORNIA

Type of Program: Multiactivity wilderness adventure programs
Participants: Coeducational, ages 13–18
Enrollment: 8–15 participants in each of fifteen adventures, grouped by age
Program Dates: Fifteen to forty days in June, July, and August
Heads of Program: Scott von Eschen and Lisa Halsted, Directors

LOCATION

Adventures Cross-Country (ARCC) offers adventure programs in a wide range of wilderness settings. Students participate in multi-activity wilderness adventures (backpacking, mountaineering, white-water rafting, sea kayaking, rock climbing, scuba diving, and others) in national parks and forests throughout the western United States, Alaska, Hawaii, British Columbia, Costa Rica, Europe, Fiji, Australia, the Caribbean, and Thailand.

BACKGROUND AND PHILOSOPHY

Established in 1982, ARCC strives to teach participants wilderness living and travel skills by having them experience a diverse range of outdoor activities and environments. No previous experience is necessary. Backpacking and backcountry travel form the core of an ARCC adventure. Students participate in at least two and sometimes four backpacking expeditions lasting between three and nine days, depending on the program. Between backpacking excursions, ARCC students experience a variety of other wilderness activities, including white-water rafting, sea kayaking, mountain biking, sailing, rock and ice climbing, and mountaineering. Individual growth and personal experience are a critical part of each ARCC wilderness experience. ARCC's small group size allows each student to receive individualized attention and be an active participant in team decisions.

By the end of an ARCC adventure, participants have gained many valuable wilderness skills such as minimum-impact camping, trip planning, backcountry travel, outdoor cooking, and group leadership. Along the way, other personal goals are invariably achieved, from mastering a white-water rafting technique to forming a special friendship. ARCC students return home with a willingness to face new challenges, a greater sense of responsibility, a deep love and respect for the outdoors, and, most importantly, confidence in themselves.

PROGRAM OFFERINGS

Alaska Adventure The thirty-nine-day Alaska Adventure travels through some of Alaska's most breathtaking and rugged wilderness areas and sharpens wilderness skills through three backpacking trips, a white-water rafting expedition, ice climbing, glacier travel, and sea kayaking in spectacular but demanding environments.
Western Adventure The twenty-eight-day Adventure takes participants across five western states, from backpacking and rafting in the Colorado Rockies to backpacking in Yosemite. Along the way participants backpack in four different environments, have a chance to mountain bike to scenic mountain lakes, and swim in waterfalls in the Grand Canyon.
Thailand Adventure In a magical land of Buddhist temples, white sand beaches, and the world's friendliest people, participants spend thirty days here beginning with a language and cultural orientation. During this exotic adventure, participants scuba dive on spectacular multicolored coral reefs, white-water raft tropical river rapids, trek the hilltribe country, and trace the wilderness corners of the Land of Smiles. A highlight of this adventures is a community service project at a local elementary school.
Colorado Adventure For students with limited time who seek the same fun-filled challenges of the longer trips, the fifteen-day Colorado Adventure offers an excellent opportunity to experience a range of outdoor wilderness activities while traveling through Colorado's varying terrain. The adventure includes two spectacular backpacking trips, a rafting adventure, and an amazing mountain-biking trip.
Caribbean Adventure The sunny beaches and lush forests of the U.S. and British Virgin Islands are the setting for the Caribbean Adventure. Participants hike, snorkel, ocean kayak, swim, and explore the highlands of several islands, while learning fundamental wilderness skills and soaking in the island culture. A highlight of this trip is a six-day island-hopping sail on a chartered boat.
Hawaii Adventure Gorgeous black sand beaches, red-hot lava, and rugged inland peaks are just a few of the highlights of the twenty-two-day Hawaiian Adventure. This adventure offers an excellent opportunity to experience a wide range of outdoor activities such as snorkeling, ocean kayaking, sailing, and backpacking while traveling to the islands of Kauai and the Big Island of Hawaii.
Costa Rica Adventure From sea kayaking along sun-drenched beaches to hiking through dense jungle, from white-water rafting through tropical rain forest to climbing Costa Rica's highest peak, participants experience it all in the Costa Rica Adventure. This is a chance to combine adventure travel with a unique cultural experience in this fascinating and peaceful country.
Australia/Fiji Adventure The spectacular Australia/Fiji Adventure blends wilderness travel with international excitement. While traveling through sun-drenched Queensland, participants snorkel and scuba dive in the crystal clear waters of the Great Barrier Reef, backpack in the desert Outback, and white-water raft for days through the dense rain forest

of the magnificent Johnstone River, providing a unique view of this wonderful nation. While in Fiji, the group backpacks through the amazing Fijian Highlands and camps on deserted tropical islands.

Extreme British Columbia This is a twenty-day, action-packed journey through British Columbia's extremes—from the slopes of Blackcomb Glacier to paddling the swirling waters of the Lillooet River and climbing the rock faces of the Squamish peaks. Situated in Canada's western wilderness, this adventure is the perfect choice for students who want adrenaline-inducing activities in a pristine backcountry environment.

Southern Europe Adventure From Rome and Italy's dazzling beaches to the mountaintops of the Swiss Alps, from the Mediterranean islands to Paris' Eiffel Tower, the Southern Europe Adventure explores the quintessential European landscape and a wilder side of Europe. Students sea kayak the Italian coast, backpack in Tuscany, explore the exquisite Cinque Terre, and white-water raft the tumbling waters of the Alps. A highlight of this trip is hiking into three different countries on the tour de Mont Blanc.

ENROLLMENT

All ARCC groups are coed and have 8–15 participants per trip. All students are grouped by age. Two leaders (a man and a woman) accompany each ARCC trip. ARCC's small group size is a unique and important part of the overall ARCC experience. No previous outdoor experience is necessary for any ARCC trip.

DAILY SCHEDULE

With very few exceptions, every night is spent camping in tents or under the stars. Days are spent learning wilderness skills such as outdoor cooking and map reading and participating in wilderness activities such as rafting, sea kayaking, and rock climbing. Due to the special permits ARCC has long held, participants are able to hike areas like Waipio Valley in Hawaii, the Trinity Alps in California, and Telluride in Colorado that are inaccessible to other companies. Students travel between wilderness areas in new minivans, and driving time is kept to a minimum.

STAFF

ARCC takes great care in choosing its leaders each summer. They are all mature adults ranging in age from 21 to 33. They enjoy working with young adults and have had extensive treaining in wilderness living and team-leading skills. All are trained and certified as Wilderness First Responders or EMTs. ARCC was one of the first companies of its kind to require this high level of wilderness medical training. Leaders bring first-aid kits, emergency cell phones, and emergency evacuation plans out on trips. Each year, ARCC has at least a 50 percent return rate for staff members.

COSTS

Costs vary depending on the location and duration of the trip. Prices range from $2595 to $6295. Tuition covers all trip expenses except for airfare to and from the trip's departure location.

FINANCIAL AID

Financial aid is available on an as-needed basis.

TRANSPORTATION

ARCC staff members meet each student upon arrival at the airport. ARCC provides all the necessary transportation during the adventures. A staff member accompanies each student to their plane on the day of departure and remains with them until they have departed.

APPLICATION TIMETABLE

Initial inquiries are welcome at any time. Applications are processed on a first-come, first-served basis. There is no final deadline for submitting applications, although many trips fill by February.

For more information, contact:

Adventures Cross-Country
242 Redwood Highway
Mill Valley, California 94941
800-767-2722 (toll-free)
Fax: 415-332-2130

PARTICIPANT/FAMILY COMMENTS

"Thank you for one of the best—no, the best experience of my life! ARCC has opened my eyes to a world I knew little about before this trip and has taught me so much. I learned independence, self-reliance, compassion, appreciation for nature, appreciation for my blessings, and respect for others, as well as the willingness to help others for the benefit of the group."

AFS INTERCULTURAL PROGRAMS/USA

SUMMER PROGRAMS

AFRICA, ASIA AND THE PACIFIC, EUROPE, AND LATIN AMERICA

Type of Program: Summer Homestay: Language study, plus, community service, and team mission
Participants: Coeducational, ages 15–18
Enrollment: Varies, depending on program
Program Dates: Four- to eight-week sessions

LOCATION

AFS offers summer exchange programs for young people, ages 15–18 in twenty-three countries: Argentina, Australia, Bolivia, Brazil, Canada, Chile, China, Costa Rica, Ecuador, Finland, Ghana, Hungary, Italy, Japan, the Netherlands, New Zealand, Panama, Paraguay, Russia, Spain, Thailand, Turkey, and the United Kingdom.

BACKGROUND AND PHILOSOPHY

With more than fifty-five years of proven success, AFS Intercultural Programs/USA is a nonprofit, volunteer-based organization with international partners in more than forty countries. Its mission is to provide international and intercultural learning experiences to individuals, families, schools, and communities through a global volunteer partnership that works toward a more just and peaceful world. AFS has made this dream possible for more than 300,000 students from 103 countries.

The international exchange program was founded in 1947 by volunteer ambulance drivers from World Wars I and II, who fervently believed that the way to ensure future peace among nations was to educate a generation of enlightened world leaders through international student exchanges.

More than 350 leading colleges and universities recognize the value of the AFS experience by awarding AFS alumni preferential admission and, often, scholarship consideration. A life-changing overseas experience may also prepare young people to consider many career opportunities.

PROGRAM OFFERINGS

Nothing compares to the life-changing experience of living and studying abroad with AFS. Students discover a world of new experiences and gain self-confidence, resourcefulness, and self-reliance. AFS programs are, above all, about learning through active participation in the host family, school, and community. Previous foreign language experience is not required. Many AFS programs offer some language training as part of orientation.

Summer Homestay As members of AFS host families and communities, participants, ages 15–18, discover what it really means to learn about another culture. They make new friends, gain or improve language skills, and get more out of life than they may have ever imagined while in Argentina, Chile, Ecuador, Finland, Paraguay, Spain, Thailand, and Turkey.

Summer Homestay: Language Study This program offers students, ages 15–18, at all language levels, a total immersion experience through formal instruction and daily informal conversation with the host family or dorm mates. Students are placed in small classes according to their proficiency. Programs last four to eight weeks and are offered in Canada, Costa Rica, and Japan.

Summer Homestay Plus Participants, ages 15–18, enjoy all the benefits of a homestay. In addition, they participate in group activities, such as studying the arts in Hungary, mountain hiking in New Zealand, biking through the Netherlands, or studying the environment in Brazil. Programs are offered in Australia, Brazil, Costa Rica, Hungary, Italy, the Netherlands, and New Zealand.

Summer Community Service and Team Mission Participants make a difference and learn new skills through four weeks of volunteer work that might include helping physically challenged children in Argentina or working in an orphanage and learning about tribal culture in Ghana. Community Service programs are for students aged 15–21. Team Mission students, in China, Ghana, and Russia, travel in groups with adult leaders for three to four weeks. Community Service programs are available in Argentina, Bolivia, Costa Rica, Panama, Paraguay, Thailand, and the United Kingdom.

ENROLLMENT

Students ages 15–18 (15–21 for Community Service) are eligible to enroll. Previous foreign language experience is desirable but not required for all programs.

STAFF

The AFS network of experienced, international volunteers serves more than 10,000 students in more than forty countries each year. More than 100,000 volunteers work with AFS worldwide, making it one of the largest community-based volunteer organizations in the world. Local members recruit and screen host families and student candidates. They also provide orientation, counseling, and enrichment for AFS students and their natural and host families.

COSTS

Program fees range from $3895 to $5495. All fees include international travel with the AFS group and transportation to and from the host family, placement with a carefully selected family who provides room and board, predeparture and postarrival orientations, 24-hour worldwide emergency numbers, a tuition waiver from the host school, and visa information.

MEDICAL CARE

Secondary medical coverage is required so that immediate assistance can be provided.

FINANCIAL AID

AFS is actively committed to making its programs available to all qualified students, irrespective of their financial situation, with many need-based and merit-based scholarships available. Examples of some of the financial aid and scholarships awarded nationally are Local AFS Chapter Awards, DeWitt Scholars Diversity Award, Awards for Excellence, and Global Scholars.

To qualify for financial aid, candidates must demonstrate strong financial need, a willingness to allow AFS to help select country placements, interest in community service, and/or a strong academic record. Financial aid is limited; applicants are advised to apply early. Merit scholarships are awarded to applicants who exemplify the qualities promoted and valued by AFS. These include, but are not limited to, academic excellence, strong community involvement, and an interest in intercultural learning.

AFS staff members and volunteers can help participants with financial planning for study abroad. Ways to raise funds to cover remaining program costs are described in *Financing Your AFS Experience,* a free booklet.

TRANSPORTATION

International transportation is provided with the participation fee, and students fly together through a gateway city. Transportation to and from the host community is also provided. AFS volunteers and staff members meet students at the airport upon arrival in the host country and upon their return to the U.S. Assistance in arranging affordable domestic flights to gateway cities is available from AFS Travel.

APPLICATION TIMETABLE

AFS has a rolling admissions policy. Because popular programs fill quickly, students are advised to apply early.

FOR MORE INFORMATION, CONTACT:

AFS Info Center
506 SW Sixth Avenue, Second Floor
Portland, Oregon 97204
800-AFS-INFO (toll-free)
Fax: 503-229-0753
E-mail: afsinfo@afs.org
World Wide Web: http://www.afs.org/usa

PARTICIPANT/FAMILY COMMENTS

"I was placed with a great host family and our local volunteers were good teachers. The program included much traveling. I saw more of Russia than most Americans ever will."—Jason LaBouyer, Russia, 2002

"In just six weeks, I made friends—both Dutch and American—bonded with my host family, and traversed some of the most amazing places on the face of the earth.—Dinah Winnick, Netherlands, 2002

"Everyone in Chile is so nice. My mother and I had a wonderful relationship. We joked around with each other and I enjoyed spending time with her."—Shadell Noel, Chile, 2002

ALFORD LAKE CAMP

SUMMER PROGRAMS

HOPE, MAINE

Type of Program: Multi-activity camping, lifetime sports, arts, and wilderness trips, as well as challenge trips for teens

Participants: Seven-week resident camp and 3½-week resident camp: girls, grades 2–9; counselor training: girls completing grades 10–12; 7-week backpacking trip: coed, grades 8–10; 7-week trip to Great Britain: girls, grades 8–10; 7-week trip to Italy: girls, grade 9; 7-week sailing trip to Nova Scotia, coed, grades 8–9; 5-week trip to Mexico: coed, grades 8–9

Enrollment: In-camp, 180; counselor trainees, 20; extended trips, 35

Program Dates: Resident camp: June 28 to August 15 (full season), June 28 to July 22 or July 24 to August 15 (half season); other program dates vary

Heads of Program: Suzanne McMullan, Director, and Jean McMullan, Consulting Director

LOCATION

Located 10 miles inland from the picturesque seacoast towns of Camden and Rockport, Maine, Alford Lake has extensive freshwater lake frontage and 400 acres of woods and blueberry fields. The camp area is beautiful and secluded. It is close to Maine's Penobscot Bay and is only a 2-hour trip from Bar Harbor and Acadia National Park.

BACKGROUND AND PHILOSOPHY

Alford Lake Camp was founded in 1907 and is in its ninth decade, making it one of the oldest girls' camps in the world. Three generations of McMullans are involved with the camp.

Alford Lake believes that campers should experience challenge and adventure through a largely elective program, that they should be relaxed and able to enjoy any activity without self-consciousness or fear, and that they should feel warmly accepted and be steadily encouraged.

The simple outdoor setting gives campers the opportunity to enjoy their natural surroundings and to gain awareness of the importance of environmental responsibility. The community also practices and promotes responsibility in health and nutrition.

Challenge trips are offered to capable and deserving campers, grades 7–10, by invitation. These trips include a coed backpacking/hiking trip on the Appalachian Trail, a coed sailing trip to Nova Scotia, a coed trip to Mexico, and trips for girls to Great Britain and Italy.

One of the camp goals is to nurture international friendships and to foster attitudes of greater global understanding.

PROGRAM OFFERINGS

Resident Camp Lifetime sports, arts, and outdoor living skills are offered to 180 campers. Activities chosen daily may include swimming, sailing, tennis, kayaking, sailboarding, field sports, archery, climbing wall, gymnastics, and riding (2–3 times a week). Creative arts choices are art and ceramics, dance, drama, and a library program. Music and singing are also a part of camp life. A variety of traditional and original camp songs are sung throughout the day. The outdoor camping skills portion of the program encompasses campcraft skills (including environmental and nature exploration), canoeing, overnight trips, trips geared toward community service, and two- to five-day trips on Maine's rivers, mountains, lakes, and islands. These trips are arranged according to age and skill.

Junior Counselor Training Program
Approximately 15 girls completing grades 10 and 11 are invited to join this program, which includes courses in American Red Cross first aid and lifeguard training, camping philosophy, advanced wilderness skills, camper development, and communication skills. The program includes a six- to seven-day canoe or mountain trip. Junior trainees join the teaching staff for five days of orientation before campers arrive.

Leadership Training Internship Three to 6 girls completing grades 11 and 12 are invited to join this program. Senior trainees assist in two activities throughout the summer and have counselor privileges, including days off each week. Senior trainees join the teaching staff for six days of orientation before campers arrive.

Appalachian Mountain Trail Trip A highly challenging backpacking trip, from Maine's Mount Katahdin to the New Hampshire border, is provided for 10 coed campers (grades 8–10) and 2 leaders. (June 28–August 15)

Alford Lake Abroad Ten girls (grades 8–10) and 2 leaders explore Great Britain, staying in prearranged youth hostels. The group visits sites and explores the countryside of England (including London), Scotland, Wales, and perhaps Ireland. (June 28–August 15)

Alford Lake Camp/Nova Scotia Coeds (grades 8 and 9) experience seven weeks of travel, sailing, and wilderness adventure in Nova Scotia. (Dates are yet to be determined.)

Exchange Trip to Mexico A coed group (grades 8–9) travels to Camp Pipiol in Valle de Bravo for five weeks. (Dates are yet to be determined.)

Alford Lake Camp/Italy Eight girls (grade 9) experience backpacking and cultural immersion throughout the Italian countryside for seven weeks.

Family Camp After the resident camp ends, Family Camp begins. ALC leaders facilitate activities for adults and children of all ages. This is a wonderful

way to introduce children to camping or for adults and families to enjoy a low-cost vacation. (August 17–21)

ENROLLMENT

Alford Lake enrolls approximately 180 resident campers at any one time, about 35 in the extended trip programs, and about 20 counselor-trainees.

Although the number varies from year to year, the total camp community may represent upwards of twenty-five states and twenty countries in a season.

FACILITIES

There are fifteen small cabins for activities and staff living quarters as well as seven large buildings that house the dining hall, kitchen, offices, and a large recreational area; the Camp House, which is a meeting hall and theater building; a large stable with stalls for fourteen horses and jodhpur and boot storage; a health center; a library; an art complex of three buildings with five studio areas; and a staff recreation building. The campers, counselor-trainees, and tent counselors live in forty-one large platform tents with double roofs, permanent superstructures, and floors. Toilet buildings are located at each end of the tent line, with one containing shower facilities. Four hardtop tennis courts, a nature building, thirty canoes, ten sailboats, six sailboards, twelve kayaks, archery facilities, gymnastics equipment, a 26-foot climbing wall, and an activities building are also extensively used. With more than a mile of lakefront, Alford Lakers are blessed with privacy and a clear, sandy-bottomed swim area on a 550-acre lake.

STAFF

The teaching staff, including the directors, key staff members, and 2 nurses, numbers about 60 women and a few men, not including the counselor-trainees. The maintenance, office, and kitchen staff add another 15 persons to the community. The leader-camper ratio is 1:3. Teaching staff members are college students or older. They are selected for their interest and experience in teaching children, their enthusiasm and energy, and their ability to be positive role models for campers. Alford Lake employs only nonsmokers.

MEDICAL CARE

There are 2 registered nurses in residence. Within 10 miles of camp are excellent physicians, specialists, and the Pen Bay Medical Center. The camp doctor visits camp on a regular basis.

RELIGIOUS LIFE

Sunday-in-the-Pines is a weekly gathering of the entire camp that celebrates its community values. The gathering is coordinated by counselors with camper/counselor participation.

COSTS

For the seven-week resident camp, the all-inclusive 2005 tuition is $5750; the shorter sessions, lasting 3½ weeks, cost $3950. Costs for the Junior Counselor

Training Program are $4950, with suggested spending money being $300. The Appalachian Mountain Trail Trip is $6500. Alford Lake Abroad and trips to Mexico and Italy cost $6500, including airfare; the Nova Scotia sailing trip is $6500. Additional spending money is suggested for each of the international trips. Cost information on Family Camp will be supplied upon request.

TRANSPORTATION

On June 28, transportation is available from New York City; Greenwich, Connecticut; Boston, Massachusetts (airport); and Portland, Maine (airport). Similar arrangements for the trip home are provided on August 15. Campers leaving on July 22 or arriving on July 24 may travel by car or plane with service only to the Portland airport.

APPLICATION TIMETABLE

Early enrollment is encouraged as most camp registrations are received before November for the following June. No cost reduction is given for late arrival or early departure of a camper. In the event a camper must withdraw before camp opens, half of the tuition deposit is refundable until February 1; after February 1, the full tuition deposit will be retained.

FOR MORE INFORMATION, CONTACT:

Suzanne McMullan
winter
5 Salt Marsh Way
Cape Elizabeth, Maine 04107
207-799-3005
Fax: 207-799-5044
E-mail: alc@alfordlake.com
summer
258 Alford Lake Road
Hope, Maine 04847
207-785-2400
Fax: 207-785-5290
E-mail: alc@alfordlake.com

ALFRED UNIVERSITY

ALFRED UNIVERSITY SUMMER PROGRAMS

ALFRED, NEW YORK

Type of Program: Academic enrichment
Participants: Boys and girls entering their sophomore, junior, or senior year of high school
Enrollment: 15–30
Program Dates: Late June to mid-July
Head of Program: Melody McLay, Director of Summer Programs

LOCATION

Alfred University (AU) is located in the village of Alfred. Situated in the Finger Lakes region of upstate New York, about 70 miles south of Rochester, the campus spans 232 acres in a peaceful, parklike setting and offers glorious views of the surrounding countryside. AU is a small university made up of the privately endowed Colleges of Business, Liberal Arts and Sciences, and Engineering and the publicly supported New York State College of Ceramics.

BACKGROUND AND PHILOSOPHY

Institutes in astronomy and entrepreneurial leadership were established in 1998, and, in 2000, the institute in creative writing was added. Each offers students the opportunity to sample life on a college campus, to learn more about the subject that most appeals to them, and to meet other students with similar interests and academic ability.

PROGRAM OFFERINGS

High school institutes are held each summer in astronomy, entrepreneurial leadership, and creative writing.

The **Astronomy Institutes** are conducted at AU's Stull Observatory, one of the best teaching observatories in the country. The observatory is equipped with telescopes ranging from 8 to 32 inches in diameter, electronic detectors, and support computers. Areas of study include astronomical basics; variable star photometry; asteroid astrometry and photometry; astronomical imaging of nebulae, clusters, and galaxies; observation/analysis of solar activity; lunar and planetary science; solar flares; stellar evolution; CCD imaging; galactic structure; cosmology; and spectroscopy.

Students attending the **Entrepreneurial Leadership Institute** learn how to be successful in business. Workshops cover a variety of topics, including entrepreneurial leadership, electronic commerce, financial planning, marketing, and creating and living a business plan.

The **Creative Writing Institutes** are for students who wish to become better writers, better readers, and better thinkers. Using lecture, small-group, and workshop strategies, instructors offer an introduction to creative and critical writing, encouraging students to produce and revise work that will prove successful in high school and college. The programs promote a process approach to writing, focusing on the skills that are essential to effective, eloquent writing.

ENROLLMENT

Enrollment for each of the institutes ranges from 15 to 30 students each year. Participants come from all over the United States and from other countries.

DAILY SCHEDULE

Schedules vary, depending on the institute. Each day includes three meals, 5–6 hours of class time, 2–3 hours of organized recreational/social activity, and time for relaxation and conversation.

FACILITIES

Students are housed in University residence halls and take meals in the Powell Campus Center. Students attend classes in state-of-the-art classrooms in the Olin building, Science Center, Seidlin Hall, Kanakadea Hall, and Stull Observatory. Other activities are held in Nevins Theater, McLane Physical Education Center, and various outdoor locations on campus.

STAFF

AU summer programs are directed by 2 full-time professional administrators. Classes are taught by distinguished members of the Alfred University faculty. When not in class or participating in orga-

TRANSPORTATION

The Alfred University campus, which is a 7-hour drive from New York City, is easily accessible by car or bus and is just 5 miles south of Interstate 86. The nearest large airport is the Rochester International Airport (about 65 miles north). Transportation to and from the Rochester airport can be provided by the University for an additional charge if the student's request and flight information are received at least two weeks prior to the start of the institute.

APPLICATION TIMETABLE

Brochures and application forms are available in February. The application deadline is May 20. Students receive an acceptance decision within a week of the deadline.

FOR MORE INFORMATION, CONTACT:

Melody McLay, Director of Summer Programs
Alfred University
Saxon Drive
Alfred, New York 14802-1205
607-871-2612
Fax: 607-871-2045
E-mail: summerpro@alfred.edu
World Wide Web: http://www.alfred.edu/summer/html/hs_inst_.html

nized activities, students are supervised by a professional resident director and college-aged counselors who are selected and trained for this responsibility.

MEDICAL CARE

Twenty-four-hour health care is provided by a residential registered nurse and EMTs. The Alfred area is served by Jones Memorial Hospital, in Wellsville, and St. James Mercy Hospital, in Hornell. Medical forms must be completed and returned, along with proof of current immunizations and medical insurance, before students are allowed to participate.

COSTS

Fees, including room, board, tuition, and instructional materials, range from $500 to $600, depending on the institute.

Full payment must be received prior to the start of each institute.

FINANCIAL AID

No financial aid is available.

AMERICAN ACADEMY OF DRAMATIC ARTS

SUMMER PROGRAM

NEW YORK CITY, NEW YORK, AND HOLLYWOOD, CALIFORNIA

Type of Program: Dramatic arts conservatory
Participants: Coeducational; teenagers (ages 14 and older), college students, and adults
Enrollment: Approximately 120 students at each campus
Program Dates: Six weeks in July and August
Heads of Program: Roger Croucher, President; New York City: Thelma Carter, Director; Hollywood: Madonna Young, Director

LOCATION

The Academy's New York home, an outstanding example of the architecture of Stanford White, is an official New York City Landmark and is on the National Register of Historic Places. The six-story building is centrally located in midtown Manhattan.

The Academy's West Coast home is set on a 2.5 acre campus in the heart of Hollywood.

BACKGROUND AND PHILOSOPHY

Founded in New York in 1884, the Academy was the first school in America to provide professional education for actors. Now in its second century, the Academy remains dedicated to that single purpose: training actors. The love of acting, as an art and as an occupation, is the motivating spirit of the school. The soundness of the Academy's approach is reflected in the achievements of its alumni, a body of professionals unmatched by any other institution of actor training.

In 1974, a west coast campus was established in the Los Angeles area.

The six-week Summer Program was established for those who want to test their interest and ability in an environment of professional training. It provides an opportunity to evaluate educational goals and to assist the student in choosing a profession. Academy training involves the student intellectually, physically, and emotionally, stressing self-discovery and self-discipline and cherishing individuality.

The Academy is accredited in New York by the Middle States Association of Colleges and Schools and in California by the Western Association of Schools and Colleges. The Academy is accredited at both locations by the National Association of Schools of Theatre.

PROGRAM OFFERINGS

Summer students take classes in acting, voice and speech, vocal production, and movement.

Acting Through exercises, improvisations, and scene study, students learn the importance of relaxation, concentration, involvement, contact, sense memory, and gain a sense of truthful behavior.

Voice and speech Starting with basic principles of vocal production, placement, and control, students develop the speaking voice as an instrument of better communication both on and off the stage.

Vocal production This course augments the Academy's emphasis on the development of an expressive and flexible speaking voice through singing.

Movement Students are exposed to a variety of dance and movement techniques for the development of the imagination, coordination, and body awareness necessary to an actor.

At the conclusion of the six-week program, each student performs in a presentation of scenes.

ENROLLMENT

Students attending the Academy come from all over the world, united by their shared commitment to acting and the challenge of working to become the best actors they can be. Students are grouped in sections that are carefully selected to ensure as much similarity of background, maturity, and objectives as possible. Teenagers are grouped separately.

DAILY SCHEDULE

At both schools, summer classes take place Monday through Thursday, from 9 to 1 for morning students and from 2 to 6 for afternoon students. Electives are scheduled between 1 and 2 Monday through Thursday and all day on Friday.

EXTRA OPPORTUNITIES AND ACTIVITIES

Depending on the interests expressed by applicants, electives such as Fencing, Mime, Improvisation, Acting for the Camera, Swing Dancing, and Musical Theatre may be offered.

FACILITIES

The Academy's New York building includes classrooms, rehearsal halls, dance studios, a student lounge, locker areas, dressing rooms, a prop department/production workshop, a costume department, a library/audiovisual learning center, and three theaters.

The Hollywood campus has similar facilities, including classrooms, dance studios, two theaters, a library, full production facilities, and ample parking.

The Academy does not maintain living quarters for students at either campus but housing options are available.

STAFF

Most of the Summer Program faculty members also staff the full-time two-year program. Others are distinguished professionals who are available to the Academy only in the summer. The Academy's faculty comprises alumni of the most esteemed acting schools in the world. Their professional experience encompasses Broadway, off-Broadway, stock, regional theater, film, and television in a variety of positions. In both New York and Hollywood, the Summer Program is staffed by faculties of 12 instructors.

COSTS

The 2004 Summer Program fee was $1900 for six weeks. A nonrefundable $50 application fee was also required. Each elective cost an additional $90. No refunds are granted after classes have begun. There is no financial aid available for the Summer Program.

TRANSPORTATION

Students at the New York school generally travel to and from classes by public transportation. The Academy is a short distance from the Port Authority Bus Terminal and both Grand Central and Pennsylvania stations and is within walking distance of PATH trains to New Jersey.

California students generally rely on cars to get them to and from class every day, although some use bicycles or public transportation.

APPLICATION TIMETABLE

Applications are accepted year-round on a rolling timetable, but applicants should confirm their plans well before the program begins in early July. All applicants must audition. An audition is scheduled after the completed application, health forms, and $50 application fee have been received. An audition consists of the delivery from memory of two contrasting monologues (one comic, one serious) of up to 2 minutes each from published plays. Auditions can take place at either the New York or California school for acceptance at either school; the audition, however, must be scheduled through the school to which the student is applying. For those students unable to get to New York or Hollywood for an audition, a regional audition may be arranged.

For more information, contact:

Ms. Karen Higginbotham, Director of Admissions
AADA/New York
120 Madison Avenue
New York, New York 10016
212-686-0620
800-463-8990 (toll-free)

Mr. Dan Justin, Director of Admissions
AADA/Hollywood
1336 North La Brea Avenue
Hollywood, California 90028
323-464-2777
800-222-2867 (toll-free)

PARTICIPANT/FAMILY COMMENTS

"Through the professional atmosphere at AADA, I learned about the hard work and creative rewards that are the life of the actor. Whether you are an actor-in-training or a student testing your curiosity further, I can honestly say that the summer program won't let you down. For me personally, it was one of the best and most positive choices I have ever made. (P.S.—It was a lot of fun!)"

"The experience I had over the summer was so amazing. The teachers were excellent, and I grew tremendously."

"I was astounded by how much I learned in only six weeks."

AMERICAN TRAILS WEST

SUMMER TRAVEL PROGRAMS

UNITED STATES, CANADA, HAWAII, ALASKA, AND EUROPE

Type of Program: Active student travel
Participants: Coeducational, ages 12–18, grouped by age
Enrollment: Approximately 40 per group
Program Dates: End of June through August, twenty-one to forty-two days
Heads of Program: Howie Fox, Jeff Gass, Howard Gorchov, and Will Thompson, directors

BACKGROUND AND PHILOSOPHY

Since 1965, the American Trails West (ATW) family has been the originator and innovator in the field of student travel. From the first camping trip to the first combination trip to the exciting itineraries for the summer of 2004, American Trails West has led the way. ATW's years of experience in working with young people, as well as their expertise in the field of travel, can be seen in every aspect of their program. Student travel is a specialized field, and the ATW family devotes its full-time efforts year-round solely to the preparation of their summer programs.

A summer of travel with American Trails West is a broadening experience in discovering new places and an opportunity to make friends with fellow travelers from across the United States, Canada, and Europe. Many teenagers come on their own, and compatible age groupings and a wide geographic mix assure that each one feels comfortable. Traveling on an American Trails West trip means being part of the group, a member of the ATW family. ATW's philosophy, staff, and activities make that goal a reality.

PROGRAM OFFERINGS

North, South, East and West, American Trails West takes students to the most exciting destinations. ATW is the only student travel program that features so many great itineraries. Across the **U.S.**, through **Canada**, north to **Alaska**, west to **Hawaii**, or around **Europe**, travelers experience the best that each has to offer. From the natural beauty of National Parks to the high energy of great cities, students are always in the very center of the action on American Trails West.

Students may choose exciting combination camping/hotel/dorm trips or hotel/dorm trips. Each one offers a skillful blend of outdoor adventures, sightseeing, sports, and evening entertainment. During the day campers raft the best rivers, hike the most exciting canyon trails, or ski down awesome Alpine mountains. Campers do everything from in-line skating, mountain biking, and horseback riding to dog-sledding, inner tubing, and waterskiing, depending on the itinerary. At night, it's comedy clubs and campfires, rock concerts and dance clubs, go-carts, theme parks, and much more.

ATW is the only student travel program whose itineraries have no one-night stops. Every location visited is for two nights or more. No one-night stops means more time for activities, more time for nightlife, and more time to make friends. It provides more time for breaking the ice, learning the ropes, and feeling at home. Everyone can use a little help during the first few days of a new experience. Meeting new people, adjusting to new routines, and being in new locations can be overwhelming if the itinerary rushes from place to place. All ATW camping and dorm trips start with a special two-day group orientation. Travelers learn all they need to know, meet the staff, and begin to make those "friends for a lifetime" in a relaxed, unpressured atmosphere.

For families located in the New York metropolitan area, ATW offers its unique **MINI TOURS**. Specially designed for middle school students, MINI TOURS feature travel from Monday to Friday, with weekends at home. Destinations range from Virginia Beach to Niagara Falls and from Maine to Orlando. Pick-ups and drop-offs each week are conveniently located around the Greater New York metropolitan area.

ENROLLMENT

Each summer, American Trails West attracts students from across the United States and from around the world. Through the years, campers from forty states and more than a dozen countries have traveled with American Trails West. Living together, learning from each other, and having fun with students from all over is what makes an American Trails West summer so special.

EXTRA OPPORTUNITIES AND ACTIVITIES

The Princeton Review is an American Trails West exclusive. Only ATW offers Word Smart, Princeton Review's excellent SAT vocabulary-building program. Word Smart is featured on selected itineraries with age-appropriate groups at no additional charge.

American Trails West itineraries are planned to maximize action, fun, and excitement, while minimizing bus riding. ATW's unique blend of great activities, both day and night, guarantees each traveler the greatest summer ever. These include everything from waterskiing to snow skiing, London theater to laser tag, jet boating to river rafting, and Planet Hollywood to the Hard Rock Café. Nonetheless, ATW directors have the flexibility, as well as the experience, to find new and exciting, up-to-the-minute surprises while traveling, and to incorporate them into the itinerary.

FACILITIES

American Trails West pioneered cross-country camping in 1965. Over the next three decades, continual innovation and improvement have culminated in ATW's Five-Star Camping. Personally selected National Park and private campgrounds, custom-designed walk-in cabin tents, comfortable cots with mattresses, three delicious and nutritious meals each day plus snacks, and meticulous year-round maintenance of all camping equipment are hallmarks of ATW's commitment to the comfort and safety of its travelers. Each trip travels with everything it needs, right down to its own spotless picnic tables, so it never has to depend on equipment used by the general public.

All dorms, hotels, and resorts are chosen for security, comfort, and outstanding facilities. Every camper sleeps in an individual bed each night. Whether it's shooting hoops at UCLA, playing tennis at the Hyatt Regency, or working out in the state-of-the-art fitness center at a mountain resort, American Trails West campers enjoy the finest accommodations and facilities.

STAFF

Each American Trails West trip is personally supervised by an experienced director returning for another summer of leadership. These directors and their specially selected staff, all college graduates over the age of 21, offer youthful participation in all facets of the ATW program. The ratio of campers to staff members is 6:1. All senior staff members (directors, co-directors, and returning counselors) are CPR and first aid certified. Every staff member takes part in ongoing training sessions at the American Trails West office over the winter months. In the spring, these culminate in the five-day orientation program of workshops, seminars, and hands-on training.

Each trip staff combines many summers of ATW experience with the unique ability to understand and relate to their campers. This combination guarantees each trip the finest in responsible supervision. The ATW family is very proud of the large number of past campers who return as staff members each year.

MEDICAL CARE

The health, safety, and security of each trip member is the number one priority of the ATW family. The senior staff of each trip is certified in CPR and first aid. Over the years, American Trails West has developed a wide network of doctors, hospitals, and 24-hour emergency facilities in every part of the country to whom the staff turns should medical attention be necessary. A sick traveler is accompanied by an ATW staff member at all times, and parents are always contacted when a traveler sees a doctor.

COSTS

Costs vary by program depending on length, location, and accommodations. For 2004, prices ranged from \$2895 to \$8195. Three meals daily and all entertainment, recreation, lodging, gratuities, and taxes are included. Airfare to and from home is not included.

TRANSPORTATION

All air travel on American Trails West is by regularly scheduled jet. American Trails West arranges round-trip transportation for all travelers. Each camper is met at the airport upon arrival and accompanied to their flight on the day of departure.

ATW's deluxe motorcoach and professional driver remain with each trip for the entire summer. ATW's ultramodern motorcoaches are air conditioned and restroom equipped. They feature reclining seats, video and stereo sound systems, and panoramic windows for the greatest view on the road.

APPLICATION TIMETABLE

Inquiries are welcomed year-round. Admissions are on a rolling basis starting in the fall. Because the number of seats is limited, early enrollment is encouraged. A deposit of \$300 is required (fully refundable until February 1).

For more information, contact:

American Trails West
92 Middle Neck Road
Great Neck, New York 11021-1243
516-487-2800 (in New York State)
800-645-6260 (toll-free)
Fax: 516-487-2855
E-mail: info@americantrailswest.com
World Wide Web: http://www.americantrailswest.com

PARTICIPANT/FAMILY COMMENTS

"Alex had an unbelievably fantastic summer. She has not stopped talking about the trip, and especially about Doug, the director, and his staff. It sounds like they really put everything into making it a fun and one-of-a-kind experience. Thank you for providing the wonderful staff, director, bus driver and summer experience."—Debbie and Owen Kassimir, East Hills, New York

"Ask Abbie how her trip was and she'll answer 'amazing.' Her description of the staff: caring, really nice, enthusiastic, respectful . . . let's just say 'amazing.' She has not stopped talking about all the places she saw and all the activities, from the majesty of the National Parks to the glitz of Las Vegas, the food, the bus rides . . . in short, it was all 'amazing.' You have truly provided her with an unforgettable experience. So ATW, 'Amazing Trails West,' thank you . . . you are indeed 'amazing.'"—Rebecca and Art Strichman, Orange, Connecticut

APPEL FARM ARTS & MUSIC CENTER

SUMMER ARTS CAMP

ELMER, NEW JERSEY

Type of Program: Arts camp emphasizing music, theater, dance, media arts, fine arts, and sports
Participants: Coeducational, ages 9–17
Enrollment: Limited to 210 per session
Program Dates: Four- and eight-week programs
Head of Program: Matt Sisson and Jennie Quinn, Camp Directors; Mark Packer, Executive Director

LOCATION

Appel Farm's 176-acre site is nestled in the fields and woods of Salem County in southern New Jersey. The New Jersey shore, Philadelphia, New York City, and Washington, D.C., are all close by.

BACKGROUND AND PHILOSOPHY

Founded in 1960 by Albert and Clare Appel, Appel Farm is now in its fifth decade of providing a nurturing, supportive environment where all children—regardless of ability—can explore the arts. Creative abilities are cultivated and encouraged in a noncompetitive atmosphere where the arts are taken seriously, but budding artists are not overwhelmed by the pressure to produce. At Appel Farm, campers gain confidence in themselves and make lifelong friendships while receiving instruction from professional artists and educators, broadening their horizons, and discovering hidden abilities and talents.

PROGRAM OFFERINGS

Campers choose their own program of one major and two minors based on their interests and experience. Majors are offered in theater, music, dance, fine arts, photography, and video. Minors include all major areas as well as sports, swimming, creative writing, journalism, and interdisciplinary areas such as mask and movement or theater for television.

Theater Majors choose either a performance or a technical theater program. Performance campers are cast in one of several productions (comedies, dramas, musicals, classics, original scripts, and improvs), where ensemble work is emphasized. Majors include rehearsal as well as class time, where instruction in theater craft and technique is given.

Technical theater majors learn the fundamentals of lighting and sound, set and costume design, and stage management. Majors act as the technical staff for theatrical performances.

Theater minors include acting, directing, improv, playwriting, musical theater, mime, and technical theater.

Music The music program emphasizes ensemble work but also includes theory, ear training, and practice time. Every music student receives individual lessons in his or her instrument. Majors have a personal schedule based on their skills, experience, and interests. Many performance opportunities are available.

Major and minor areas of instruction include violin, viola, cello, bass, flute, clarinet, saxophone, trumpet, trombone, French horn, acoustic and electric guitar, percussion, piano and keyboards, electronic music, voice, and composition. Ensembles include rock, jazz, and big bands; orchestra; chorus; chamber orchestra; duets; and trios.

Fine arts Majors and minors may concentrate in one or more areas. Campers create from their own ideas while receiving guidance to help develop projects. Group projects include outdoor murals and sculptures. Exhibitions of camper work occur at camp and in the community.

Classes include painting, drawing, illustration, ceramics, printmaking, sculpture (including welding), fiber arts, and handicrafts (jewelry making and beading).

Media arts Majors choose either photography or video. Photography students learn techniques of shooting, processing, and developing 35-mm film; both artistic and commercial photography are explored.

Video students work with digital video in numerous styles, including documentary, science fiction, and film noir, following an idea through inception, storyboard, shooting, directing, and editing.

Media minors are offered in photography, video, journalism, and creative writing. Journalism minors edit and write the camp newsletter, the *Appel Core.*

Dance Majors and minors are offered a program in ballet, jazz, modern, and choreography. Creative expression and experimentation are stressed, and all are encouraged to perform. Campers have choreographed pieces to poetry, prose, and various musical compositions.

Sports and swim Recreational sports include soccer, basketball, volleyball, softball, tennis, Ultimate Frisbee, kickball, street hockey, and new games. Red Cross swim instruction, tennis instruction, and afternoon games are offered during minor periods. All athletic programs are noncompetitive, emphasizing skill development, cooperative play, and fun.

ENROLLMENT

Each year, campers ages 9–17 come from all over the world to participate in Appel's four- and eight-week sessions. Sessions are limited to 210 participants.

DAILY SCHEDULE

Major classes are held for 2½ hours each morning, and minors, each 1 hour long, are held in the afternoon.

Instructional time is complemented by free time, workshops, performances, games, trips, recreational sports, and activities.

EXTRA OPPORTUNITIES AND ACTIVITIES

Hour-long workshops in such diverse areas as drum making, water ballet, rocketry, and kitemaking are offered on Sundays and on Tuesday evenings. Campers are also treated to performances and workshops offered by visiting artists.

Participants often plan evening activities together; these include campfires, noncompetitive games, and pool parties. Trips to off-site locations such as the Philadelphia Art Museum, professional theater performances, and television stations, as well as day trips to the New Jersey shore, are offered.

Campers and staff members perform and exhibit both at camp and in the community. Friday Night Concerts are a long-standing tradition. The last week of each four-week session is for performance, when campers share with the community what they've worked on during the session. Campers and staff members may also share their art with neighboring schools, hospitals, and nursing homes.

FACILITIES

Campers live in wooden, screened-in bunks; each bunk has electricity, hot and cold water, and a bathroom with shower. Housing is based on age and gender; 2 counselors and 8 to 10 campers live in each bunk.

Instruction, exhibit, and performance spaces feature a fully equipped, air-conditioned, 300-seat theater; an outdoor performance stage; seven air-conditioned rehearsal spaces and six practice rooms; a costume shop; a music library; the large, new Art Building; three fully equipped, air-conditioned photo labs; the Media Center, with three editing and production rooms; and an air-conditioned dance studio.

Athletic areas include three fields, two tennis courts, a volleyball court, a basketball court, a 25-meter pool, and a recreational pool.

STAFF

Appel Farm's camper-staff ratio is 3:1. The 85-member staff hails from across the United States and around the world. Ninety-five percent are over 21 and hold bachelor's degrees in the arts or education; many have advanced degrees and are arts educators or professional artists. Only those who are committed to developing each child's creativity and who are sensitive to children's needs are chosen to be staff members.

MEDICAL CARE

Appel Farm has a multiroom, air-conditioned Health Center, and a registered nurse is on site at all times. A licensed physician, on call 24 hours a day, visits daily; a fully accredited hospital is less than 1 mile away.

COSTS

Tuition for the four-week program is around $3700 and for the eight-week program, $5300, with discounts for early registration. Tuition is all-inclusive. Payment plans are available.

FINANCIAL AID

Appel Farm awards $40,000 in partial tuition assistance each year, based primarily on financial need and the potential for growth through the camp program. Full scholarships may also be available through the corporate, foundation, and private scholarship programs.

TRANSPORTATION

Appel Farm is easily accessible from the New Jersey Turnpike, Interstate 95, and Routes 40 and 76 and is just 30 minutes from the Philadelphia Airport, 2 hours from the Newark Airport, and 3 hours from New York City airports. Appel Farm staff members pick up campers from the Philadelphia airport, train station, or bus station for no additional fee. Bus service from New York City is provided for $40 each way.

APPLICATION TIMETABLE

Campers are accepted on a first-come, first-served basis; no auditions are required. An $800 deposit must be received at the time of application. There is no application deadline, but prospective campers are encouraged to apply early. Open Houses are held throughout the fall, winter, and spring.

FOR MORE INFORMATION, CONTACT:

Matt Sisson and Jennie Quinn, Camp Directors
Appel Farm Arts & Music Center
P.O. Box 888
Elmer, New Jersey 08318-0888
800-394-8478 (toll-free)
Fax: 856-358-6513
E-mail: appelcamp@aol.com
World Wide Web: http://www.appelfarm.org

PARTICIPANT/FAMILY COMMENTS

"It's a place where our hearts can sing, our minds can dance. Wherever you come from, this is a good place to make music, art, theater, and most especially, a place to make good friends."

ASHEVILLE SCHOOL SUMMER ACADEMIC ADVENTURES

SUMMER ACADEMIC ADVENTURES

ASHEVILLE, NORTH CAROLINA

Type of Program: Experiential academics and outdoor adventure
Participants: Coed; residential students entering grades 7–10
Enrollment: 80 students per session
Program Dates: First session, June 19–July 9; second session, July 10–July 30
Head of Program: Elysia Versen, Director of Summer Academic Adventures

LOCATION

Situated on nearly 300 wooded acres at Asheville's city limits, Asheville School is minutes from downtown, yet a stone's throw from the surrounding Blue Ridge Mountains. Such a setting offers many resources: Pisgah National Forest, the Pigeon and French Broad Rivers, and Blue Ridge Parkway.

BACKGROUND AND PHILOSOPHY

Summer opportunities were introduced at the School in the early 1900s, but it was not until 1954 that its first summer school was established, offering only two courses. By 2000, a "new" summer program was under way, offering a wider variety of courses and activities. Summer Academic Adventures' (SAA) mission is to provide an atmosphere in which all members of the community appreciate and strive for excellence of mind, body, and spirit. SAA has grown to include new programs and goals that serve academically gifted and high-achieving students who want to get ahead or who consider themselves aspiring writers, artists, scientists, historians, and leaders. SAA also serves students desiring instruction in English as a Second Language (ESL). Students who would like to experience boarding school life have the perfect short-term opportunity to do so.

PROGRAM OFFERINGS

The Summer Academic Adventures curriculum offers courses in art, drama, English, mathematics, science, and technology. Students choose three academic courses each session. The average class size is 9 students. Instead of a traditional exam, students produce a final project, paper, experiment, or portfolio on a subject of interest.

The program embraces Dewey's concept that experience and education are one and also touches on Grant Wiggins' writings on project-based assessment. Students study literature, science, math, art, drama, or technology in an academic setting and then go out into the field to find or make connections. For example, students from the forensic science, mysteries, and real life logic courses work together to solve a "murder mystery," gathering evidence, interviewing witnesses, and holding a mock trial.

International students are immersed in the English language through course work and social interaction. Outside the ESL classroom, students join their English-speaking peers in two additional course of their choosing. They participate in all afternoon and weekend activities and live in the dormitories with the other students. This is a very special opportunity for developing conversational English and creating lasting friendships.

ENROLLMENT

Summer Academic Adventures draws participants from all around the country and the globe. Last year, participants represented twenty-one states and five countries.

DAILY SCHEDULE

After breakfast, participants gather for a brief morning assembly or chapel. Morning classes follow, and all summer participants spend three 70-minute periods in class each morning. Students also attend a Conference Period in order to get additional help from teachers or to begin the day's assignments. Despite its demanding academic schedule, Asheville School realizes the importance of allowing time for recreation and friendly competition. In the afternoon, students participate in a wide variety of athletic activities of their choosing. Each Monday, students sign up for a different sport or activity for the week. Mountaineering, which takes full advantage of Asheville's unique location, is especially popular among the students, who learn basic rock-climbing and kayaking skills. Students return to the dining hall for dinner before settling in for study hall. After study hall, students enjoy some free time in the dorms or the student center before lights-out.

EXTRA OPPORTUNITIES AND ACTIVITIES

Wednesday and Saturday afternoons and Sundays allow for extensive activities both on and off campus. These are organized by a full-time activities director, interns, and the director of mountaineering. Included in the tuition are activities such as white-water rafting, a day at Paramount's Carowinds, a local dramatic performance, and many mountaineering opportunities (equipment is provided) such as hiking, camping, backpacking, rock climbing, kayaking, and use of the campus ropes course and alpine tower. Greater understanding of teamwork and trust, the development of new friendships, and a renewed appreciation for the environment are just some of the benefits of participating in the mountaineering program.

FACILITIES

Campus facilities for academic work and social interaction are superior. Many buildings are nearly a century old, while others are quite modern, providing a mix of historical value and up-to-date amenities. Traditional classrooms, a state-of-the-art media center, and computer labs complement each other. The student center includes a game room, snack bar, post office, TV room, and art gallery. Campus activities abound, with tennis courts, an Olympic-size pool, a gymnasium, a wooded trail for hiking, an alpine tower, a ropes course, and several playing fields. Students reside in Anderson Hall and meals are served in Sharp Dining Hall.

STAFF

Learning is interactive, so there is a friendly spirit of give-and-take between teachers and students. With a student-faculty ratio of 3:1 and an average class size of 9 students, every student receives individual attention. Each is assigned a faculty adviser who serves as a mentor and friend. Interns are college students who have demonstrated leadership skills, responsibility, and an eagerness to teach. Interns live in the residence halls with the students and provide support and guidance. Mountaineering is led by skilled outdoor enthusiasts who are part of the year-round mountaineering staff. An Activities Director coordinates all school-wide activities and supports interns in planning and leading activities.

The Summer Academic Adventures Director works throughout the year to prepare for the summer, ensuring first-rate faculty and staff members, high quality in programming, and a well-rounded campus life.

MEDICAL CARE

A full-time nurse lives on campus and is available 24 hours a day. The campus infirmary is located in the dormitory, and an urgent-care center is within 2 miles of the School. In emergencies, students are transported to one of two excellent Asheville hospitals, both only minutes away. Participants are required to have a complete physical examination within one year prior to registration; they must also have health insurance against major illnesses and accidents. Students who do not have such coverage with an American carrier may purchase temporary insurance.

RELIGIOUS LIFE

Asheville School embraces a Judeo-Christian heritage, and chapel services are designed to be a time for all students of many faiths to feel comfortable and spiritually uplifted. Chapel "talks" are values-based and are typically given by the interns and faculty members. Twice weekly, students, faculty members, and interns gather in the chapel for these brief services.

COSTS

In 2005, the application fee is $30 and tuition is $2550 for one 3-week session and $4895 for a 6-week term. Tuition includes fees for all courses, textbooks, room, board, and activities.

There are merit scholarships that cover either full or partial tuition. A limited amount of need-based financial aid is available.

TRANSPORTATION

The Asheville Regional Airport (AVL) is located approximately 9 miles from the School. Transportation to Asheville is not included in tuition; however, students are transported to and from the airport at no charge.

APPLICATION TIMETABLE

Inquires are welcome at any time throughout the year. Campus visits are available but are not required for admission. Applicants are selected on the basis of teacher recommendations and school transcripts. Admission decisions are made on a rolling basis until the program fills. Notification of acceptance takes place within two weeks of receipt of all application materials. It is advisable to begin the application process early.

FOR MORE INFORMATION, CONTACT:

Director of Summer Academic Adventures
Asheville School
Asheville, North Carolina 28806
828-254-6345
Fax: 828-252-8666
E-mail: saa@ashevilleschool.org
World Wide Web: http://www.ashevilleschool.org

PARTICIPANT/FAMILY COMMENTS

"In math we covered material that was useful and challenging; we did things that had never occurred to me in school at home."

"He has enjoyed all the great outdoor activities and trips (I expected he would). What excites his dad and me so is his enthusiasm for his schoolwork...I feel this is just the boost he needs, and the greatest thing is—he does too."

BARAT FOUNDATION

SUMMER PROGRAM

PROVENCE AND PARIS, FRANCE

Type of Program: Precollege enrichment with total immersion in French language and culture
Participants: Coeducational; rising ninth graders through rising college freshmen
Enrollment: 30–35 per group
Program Dates: Four to six weeks in July and August
Head of Program: Chandri Barat, Executive Director

LOCATION

Located amidst fields of sunflowers and lavender in the famous region of Provence, the Barat Summer Program provides the ideal setting for a French language and culture immersion program. The sun-drenched region of Provence has inspired artists and writers throughout the centuries and continues to lure travelers to its dreamlike cities of Avignon, Aix en Provence, and Arles, located between the white sand beaches of the Mediterranean and the gentle mountains of the Vaucluse and Alpes de Haute Provence.

BACKGROUND AND PHILOSOPHY

The Barat Foundation Summer Program in Provence and Paris combines academics with real-life experience to bring learning alive. The program is designed to help participants develop skills that will prepare them for life in the global marketplace of the twenty-first century, in which national borders will cease to separate one people from another and knowledge and understanding will be the international currency. Classes, grouped according to language proficiency, offer students the opportunity to learn French at a rate they never thought possible, as the classroom is extended to all aspects of daily life.

PROGRAM OFFERINGS

The program is a total language learning experience, combining morning academic study with exciting nonclassroom afternoon, evening, and weekend activities and excursions.

Up to 15 hours of structured classes are provided each week, including 1½ hours per day of French language study and 1½ hours per day of enrichment studies in art history, history, literature, architecture, theater, cinema, music, cuisine, fashion, photography, and culture. The French language curriculum is individually tailored to each student's needs and abilities. Enrichment classes are designed to deepen participants' understanding and enjoyment of France.

Throughout the program, emphasis is placed on everyday practical dialogue and speech, with intensive practice focusing on conversation and everyday needs.

A "Buddy System" has been established to bring French students of similar age from neighboring areas to meet and socialize with program members in order to exchange ideas and form lasting friendships.

ENROLLMENT

The program accepts students at all levels of French language proficiency, from beginners with no foreign language experience to fluent speakers.

EXTRA OPPORTUNITIES AND ACTIVITIES

Students enjoy frequent excursions to explore and enjoy the wonders of the region. While in Provence, students attend the spectacular summer music and theater festivals in Avignon and Aix-en-Provence, visit Van Gogh's city of Arles, and go horseback riding at the Camarague wetlands nature preserve on the Rhone Delta. Participants shop at colorful open-air markets, travel through spectacular vineyards and orchards, enjoy the beaches and shores of the Mediterranean, go hiking and canoeing, and linger at day's end at outdoor cafes with new French friends. In Paris, students stroll along the Seine, visit Notre Dame Cathedral and the Eiffel Tower, and tour the Sorbonne, the Luxembourg gardens, the Louvre, and the Musée d'Orsay, where they see the paintings they studied during their stay in Provence. Day trips include visits to Versailles and Monet's Gardens at Giverny.

FACILITIES

Accommodations in Provence are at a beautiful, centrally located country estate. Surrounded by spectacular gardens, the facility also features an outdoor swimming pool. Meals are provided by a French chef, who creates wonderful French meals prepared with delectable local produce. Linens are provided, and laundry is sent out at the student's expense. While in Paris, students stay at a centrally located hotel that is equipped with kitchenettes. Two meals per day are provided.

STAFF

Teachers are young French nationals with advanced graduate degrees in teaching French as a foreign

language and teaching experience in both France and the U.S. Their goal is not only to instruct participants in the language and customs of the country but also to make each student feel comfortable and at home. Each instructor has specific expertise in one of the academic areas studied. Class size is limited.

Mrs. Barat has been a successful businesswoman and entrepreneur for the past eighteen years. After recently selling her natural foods business, she decided to return to her roots as an academic to develop a unique French language and culture immersion program for secondary school students. The mother of 2 teenage girls, she was eager to create a program that would provide an opportunity for organic learning by immersing the student in a welcoming, enriching, and completely French environment. Mrs. Barat spent her junior year in college in France at Reid Hall in Paris, an experience that forever changed her life and world view. Her goal is to inspire her students as she was inspired by immersing them in an environment so rich and wonderful that it has inspired artists on both sides of the ocean for centuries. Students will never be quite the same after they have experienced France from this insider's perspective.

MEDICAL CARE

France has one of the most sophisticated health-care systems in the world. In case of emergency, students are treated at a nearby state-of-the-art hospital facility. Students are encouraged to carry a supplemental international health insurance policy provided by a major insurance carrier through the foundation.

COSTS

Program tuition in 2004 was $5995 for four weeks in Provence, which included lodging and three meals daily, and $3495 for two weeks in Paris, which included lodging and two meals per day. Both programs included all classes and all excursions, all planned evening and weekend activities, and all local transportation in France. Not included in the tuition were transportation to and from Paris from students' home cities, round-trip transportation from Paris to Marseilles, intensive horseback riding and tennis lessons, medical expenses, personal spending money, laundry, textbooks/instructional materials, and one meal per day in Paris.

FINANCIAL AID

Merit-based financial aid is available to those outstanding students who are financially in need.

TRANSPORTATION

To ensure the lowest group airfare rate for flights to and from Paris and New York, Barat makes all travel arrangements. Barat also helps to coordinate flights to New York from students' home cities. Staff members meet the students at the New York airport, travel with them to Paris and Provence, and remain with them for the rest of the trip. The foundation also secures round-trip air transportation between Paris and Marseilles.

APPLICATION TIMETABLE

A $1000 deposit plus a $100 application fee must accompany the application to ensure enrollment. The $1000 deposit is refundable if the student is not accepted or withdraws from the program prior to April 1. As enrollment is limited, early application is advised. U.S. citizens must possess a valid passport. A visa is not required. International students must be responsible for securing passports and for any required special visas to enter France; such students should contact the French Embassy or Consulate to obtain accurate information and forms.

FOR MORE INFORMATION, CONTACT:

Chandri Barat, Executive Director
Barat Foundation
P.O. Box 609
Montville, New Jersey 07045
973-263-1013
Fax: 973-263-2287
E-mail: info@baratfoundation.org
World Wide Web: http://www.baratfoundation.org

BARNARD'S SUMMER IN NEW YORK CITY

PRE-COLLEGE PROGRAM

NEW YORK, NEW YORK

Type of Program: College-level academic enrichment and leadership development
Participants: Coeducational, students who have completed grade 10 or 11
Enrollment: 170
Program Dates: Five-week session: June 19–July 23; one-week mini-course: June 19–25; Young Women's Leadership Institute: July 10–16
Head of Program: Director of Pre-College Programs

LOCATION

The 4-acre Barnard College campus on Morningside Heights in Manhattan is adjacent to the Columbia University campus. Barnard's Summer in New York City makes full use of New York City's exceptional educational, cultural, and recreational resources.

BACKGROUND AND PHILOSOPHY

The Barnard Pre-College Program was established in 1985 as a program for high school students with substantial academic commitment and interest as well as the ability to handle college-level work. As a selective liberal arts college affiliated with Columbia University, Barnard offers an unusual educational opportunity for coeducational life on a university campus, enriched by the unparalleled offerings of New York City. The city often becomes an extension of the classroom. The Metropolitan Museum of Art and Broadway are used extensively, for example. Each week, students have the opportunity to shadow professionals at some of the city's major businesses and organizations. Evening and weekend programs provide students with additional exposure to New York City's cultural, historical, and international attractions.

PROGRAM OFFERINGS

Course offerings are varied, and classes are limited in size so that students can receive individual attention, engage in lively discussion, and work on independent projects.

The city plays an important role in the design of courses. Resources such as the Bronx Zoo, the Museum of Television and Radio, Ellis Island, the Hayden Planetarium, the Cathedral of St. John the Divine, and the Museum of Modern Art are used extensively. Guest lecturers, artists, and performers are invited to participate. Students are graded on a pass/fail basis and receive reports from each of their professors, who evaluate their participation, performance, and academic promise. Official course credit is not granted.

The Young Women's Leadership Institute combines academic learning, skill-building workshops, and student-run sessions to train young women leaders in an intensive weeklong program.

ENROLLMENT

Approximately 170 young men and women attend each summer, coming from more than thirty states and several other countries. More than 80 percent are residential, but students whose families live within the New York metropolitan area may choose to commute.

DAILY SCHEDULE

Students in the five-week program attend morning and afternoon classes four days per week, while students in the one-week program take a morning course in writing or theater and complete intensive assignments each afternoon. Young Women's Leadership Institute students learn from college staff members, alumnae, and professional facilitators in a series of workshops, discussions, and seminars. On Wednesdays, students in the five-week program participate in the Life After College career exploration series. Organized evening and weekend programs include supervised trips to famous New York City attractions as well as to lesser-known venues. Coffeehouses featuring local entertainers, talent shows, dances, parties, sports activities, and workshops on current issues are available on campus. Students may also volunteer for community service programs.

Students are expected to observe sign-out procedures and curfews and to comply with regulations designed to protect the health and safety of all participants. The social policy is sent to each admitted applicant and is available on request.

EXTRA OPPORTUNITIES AND ACTIVITIES

The Life After College series gives students a taste of both the occupational and the neighborhood diversity that makes New York such an exciting place. Each week, small escorted groups visit leading institutions and businesses, meet with professionals, take "inside" tours, and learn about career opportunities. Elective workshops on applying to college, interviewing strategies, and study skills are also offered.

FACILITIES

Residential students live in an air-conditioned residence hall and eat in the student cafeteria. Classes meet in air-conditioned classrooms, and students have access to all the modern campus facilities, including Wollman Library, the Academic Computer Center, and the campus gym.

STAFF

Courses are taught by graduate students and Barnard faculty members who have adapted their undergraduate courses for the program. Students are supervised by the professional staff, including 12 specially selected and trained undergraduate assistants and 2 graduate assistants. The entire staff offers support and guidance to all.

MEDICAL CARE

The Columbia University Health Service provides medical care, low-cost prescriptions, and routine lab tests. St. Luke's–Roosevelt Hospital, three blocks from campus, is available for emergency medical care. All students must provide themselves with health insurance coverage, including benefits for emergency care and hospitalization.

RELIGIOUS LIFE

Barnard College has no religious affiliation. Religious services for all denominations are available close to the campus. The meal plan accommodates religious dietary restrictions.

COSTS

The 2004 comprehensive charge for the five-week program was $3600 for residential students, including tuition, fees, room and board, and some evening and weekend programs. For commuting students, the charge was $2400 for tuition, weekday lunches, and fees. The one-week mini-course session fees was $1500 for residential students and $900 for commuting students. The Young Women's Leadership Institute is a residential program only, and the fee was $1200. Transportation, books, course supplies, weekend dinners, optional trips, personal laundry, and incidentals are not included.

FINANCIAL AID

A limited number of partial financial grants are available.

TRANSPORTATION

Barnard is accessible from all area airports and train and bus stations as well as by car. Buses and subways make campus stops.

APPLICATION TIMETABLE

Admission is selective and based upon receipt of the completed application, including the $35 application fee. For those living outside the United States, the application fee is $65. Applicants must be completing grade 10 or 11 and must demonstrate academic strength. High motivation, emotional stability, and social maturity are expected. Admission decisions are made on a rolling basis beginning March 1. Course enrollment and housing are limited, so early application is advised.

For more information, contact:

Director of Pre-College Programs
Barnard College
Columbia University
3009 Broadway
New York, New York 10027-6598
212-854-8866
Fax: 212-854-8867
E-mail: pcp@barnard.edu
World Wide Web: http://www.barnard.edu/pcp

BELVOIR TERRACE

SUMMER PROGRAMS

LENOX, MASSACHUSETTS

Type of Program: Educational program focusing on fine and performing arts and individual sports
Participants: Girls, ages 8–16
Enrollment: 180
Program Dates: June 24 to August 12, 2004
Head of Program: Nancy S. Goldberg, Director

LOCATION

Belvoir Terrace is a historic Lenox cottage built in 1896. The 40-acre estate is in Lenox, 2 hours west of Boston and 3 hours from New York City. The site has been maintained by preserving the great lawn, wooded paths, and imported trees and carefully developed into a camp with eighteen clustered buildings.

BACKGROUND AND PHILOSOPHY

Belvoir Terrace was founded in 1954 by Edna Schwartz. It continues to be a family-operated business, with three generations currently involved. Emphasis is placed on individual development, program excellence, and camper fun. The opportunity for an individual program in art, dance, music, theater, and sports attracts motivated young women.

PROGRAM OFFERINGS

Each camper is interviewed to develop her individual program. It is possible to elect ten activities from a comprehensive syllabus in the arts or individual sports, but most campers define one or two major areas. All activities are graded by age and skill level, and every program activity is available to each age group. Skill development and creativity are emphasized in all activities.

Fine arts and crafts Girls interested in art can elect drawing, painting, graphics, sculpture, ceramics, crafts, fashion design, jewelry, photography, and video taught by 15 staff members. The campers enjoy the outcome of their work in completed pieces, art openings, and special exhibitions. Frequent trips to local and major art galleries enrich the program. However, it is the close relationship between student and artist/teacher that is the program's core and strength.

Dance Daily ballet classes are offered at all levels, and pointe and repertoire classes are offered for advanced students. The modern, jazz, and tap programs are equally strong and popular. Six teachers, 3 dance accompanists, and four professionally equipped dance spaces are available. Advanced students perform at the Koussevitsky Memorial Theater.

Music The music program offers excellent practice facilities, high-quality instruction from a staff of 22, and frequent performance opportunities. Private lessons are offered in piano, voice, and all instruments. Classes in orchestra, theory, opera workshop, and chamber music are also available. Proximity to Tanglewood allows campers to attend many excellent concerts and to benefit from master classes and guest teachers.

Theater Fourteen teacher/directors work in five fully equipped theaters, teaching spaces, and shops. Major classes include acting, Shakespearean acting, and musical theater. The department offers electives in mime, speech, directing, technical theater, production, film, costuming, and makeup. Most acting students elect voice and movement to complete their training. Thirty high-quality productions develop each season from class work.

Tennis, swimming, and riding Each of the individual sports classes develops skills for recreational enjoyment as well as technique and strategy for intercamp competition. Seven staff members provide specific tutoring within the various United States Tennis Association proficiency levels. Swimming offerings, in a heated Olympic-size pool, include competitive swimming, synchronized swimming, and all levels of the American Red Cross award scheme. Riding is at nearby UnderMountain Farm, which offers indoor and outdoor rings, a jumping field, trails, and horse shows. Outdoor education, soccer, basketball, golf, and running/fitness are also offered.

DAILY SCHEDULE

The program at Belvoir operates six days a week. The schedule alternates between a Monday-Wednesday-Friday and Tuesday-Thursday-Saturday rotation, but girls may elect major activities that meet daily. A typical day includes five 1-hour activities, a rest period, general swimming, and an organized evening activity. The planned evening program generally reflects the camp's fine and performing arts emphasis. The campers enjoy performances at cultural attractions in the area, guests in the arts, art openings, and camper performances. Traditional camping activities are also part of the evening program and include hikes, games, socials, and campfires. Sunday is an unstructured day beginning with a leisurely buffet brunch followed by optional activities and trips, work on individual projects, or relaxation. Excellent food is served family-style in one sitting, and five salad bars offer variety at each meal.

FACILITIES

At Belvoir Terrace, campers grouped by school grade level share comfortable living spaces with their counselors. The original mansion provides accommodations for the younger girls, dining and living rooms for the camp, and rooms for chamber music. Girls who have completed grade 7, 8, or 9 are housed in three modern chalet-style dorms with adjoining baths and counselors' rooms. The senior campers enjoy a modern six-bedroom house with a living room, kitchen, and two tiled baths. Four dance studios, five theaters, ten art studios, twenty-four music studios, two pools, and six tennis courts complete the facilities.

STAFF

All 90 staff members at Belvoir are professionals with teaching experience in their area of expertise. In addition to their teaching responsibility, staff members from the music and sports departments perform the role of bunk counselors. The art, dance, and theater staff members teach and assist as counselors. The staff at Belvoir is selected for its competence, interest in working with the campers, and commitment to the life of the camp community.

MEDICAL CARE

Two nurses in a modern five-room infirmary handle all health-care needs under the direction of a pediatric group in Lee. Belvoir Terrace has an excellent association with local specialists at the Berkshire Medical Center.

RELIGIOUS LIFE

There is no formal religious activity at camp, but all religions are respected, and trips to local churches are supervised.

COSTS

The tuition for 2004 was $8100 for the seven-week period. Additional costs included a canteen account of $350 for spending money and tickets; art studio classes cost $50 or $100, depending on the course. Payment is generally spread between January and June. Limited scholarships are available.

TRANSPORTATION

Chartered buses leaving from Lincoln Center for the 3-hour trip to camp cost $100 round-trip. Belvoir staff members meet campers who fly to Hartford.

APPLICATION TIMETABLE

Enrollment begins in October and is generally complete by January. Because a few spaces in particular groups may remain open in the spring, all interested candidates should apply.

FOR MORE INFORMATION, CONTACT:

Nancy S. Goldberg, Director
101 West 79th Street, #15 B
New York, New York 10024
212-580-3398
Fax: 212-579-7282
E-mail: info@belvoirterrace.com
World Wide Web: http://www.belvoirterrace.com

PARTICIPANT/FAMILY COMMENTS

"Belvoir is the perfect place to work on your artistic interests while finding out who you really are. Belvoir is a way of learning, making friends, working, and growing."

BICYCLE TRAVEL ADVENTURES STUDENT HOSTELING PROGRAM

BICYCLING TRIPS

CONWAY, MASSACHUSETTS

Type of Program: Bicycle travel camp
Participants: Coeducational, ages 12–18
Enrollment: 8–12 per trip
Program Dates: Vary, depending on trip
Heads of Program: Ted and Barbara Lefkowitz, Directors

LOCATION

Bicycle Travel Adventures (BTA), a part of the Student Hosteling Program (SHP), offers one- to eight-week road- and off-road programs through the countrysides and cultural centers of the world. In 2004, the schedule included trips to Vermont, New Hampshire, the Maine coast, Cape Cod, New York, Washington, Oregon, California, the Canadian Rockies, Alberta, British Columbia, Quebec, New Brunswick, Nova Scotia, and across the United States, as well as trips to England, southern Ireland, France, Belgium, Holland, Spain, and Italy.

BACKGROUND AND PHILOSOPHY

Founded in 1970, the Student Hosteling Program is the premier private teenage bicycling program in the United States and the only fully accredited American Camping Association bicycle travel camp. Trips provide adventure, fun, outdoor education, and the opportunity for emotional growth while at the same time offering one of the safest, most wholesome youth environments available. SHP places the physical and psychological well-being of participants above all else.

It is the view of the Student Hosteling Program that one of the primary functions of an organization responsible for the well-being of teenagers is the elimination of as many potential problems as possible before a trip even begins. Safety is a prime example. Twenty-five years ago, SHP became the first bicycling organization to require the use of protective headgear at all times when cycling. Since that time, concussions, the most common potentially serious accident, have virtually been eliminated.

BTA groups are small, usually consisting of 8 to 12 trippers and 2 leaders (grade 7 trips have 3 leaders), which makes a very close, rewarding group experience possible. Participants are also expected to do their share of the work and day-to-day chores.

A BTA trip is well-rounded. Not only do groups bike in the countryside, but they also tour the major cultural areas and cities along the route. The group follows an unhurried itinerary, which gives them an excellent opportunity to learn about an area and its people. Biking is on country roads, and all city touring is done on foot or by public transportation.

Alcohol, drugs, and tobacco are not permitted on BTA trips. Possession or use of any of these will result in immediate dismissal from the trip.

PROGRAM OFFERINGS

Programs range in length from a one-week trip in Vermont to an eight-week trip across America. A range of cycling levels is offered, from a relatively easy fifteen-day Cape Cod trip to the major challenge of the cross-America trip.

A person does not have to be an experienced cycle tourer to participate on a trip but must be in good shape and not mind putting out physical effort. In fact, all trips, even the most challenging, have people who have never been involved in cycle touring.

Mountain bikes, road bikes, and touring bikes are acceptable on all trips. Both camping and noncamping trips are offered. Bike rentals are available for all trips except the cross-America trip.

ENROLLMENT

Approximately 400 students from all over the United States and Canada (and some from abroad) participate in Student Hosteling biking programs. Trip offerings are available for seventh- through twelfth-graders, and each trip groups by age and grade.

DAILY SCHEDULE

Groups generally cycle for two or three days and then have a nontravel day in a town or area where there are numerous opportunities for exploring, sightseeing, and fun activities.

Groups usually get up around 7 on travel days and 8 on nontravel days. After breakfast, the group goes over the plans for the day using the notes and guides provided by BTA.

The group has flexibility, as a group, to decide what to see and do along the way each day. The group chooses checkstops, such as picnic spots, swimming holes, or crossroads, along the route. At each checkstop the group stops, and leaders make sure that everyone is OK, take care of any bike problems, and give slower riders a chance to rest.

Groups usually cycle 24–45 miles each travel day. This amounts to 3–5 hours of cycling, leaving plenty of time for frequent stops. On nontravel days, the group decides on the distance to be covered, depending on the activities the group chooses for that day.

At lunchtime the group stops to buy supplies for a picnic on a nearby village green, riverbank, or field. After lunch there are more checkstops for whatever activities the group decides upon. Late in the afternoon the group stops to buy food before going on to the campsite or hostel for dinner.

After-dinner activities are usually available at the campsite or near the hostel. Groups can also take advantage of local events accessible by foot or public transportation, such as town fairs, movies, or plays. Groups usually go to sleep around 10:30 or 11.

STAFF

All BTA trips have at least 2 leaders—a senior leader and 1 or 2 co-leaders or assistant leaders. The average age of senior leaders is about 23. (The minimum age is 21.) Senior leaders are typically graduating college seniors, graduate students, or teachers.

Each senior leadership applicant goes through a lengthy application process, a personal interview with the directors, and a five-day training course.

Many BTA assistant leaders are drawn from within the program as former trippers. The assistant leader positions provide an excellent opportunity for former BTA trippers to develop leadership skills and job responsibility. In fact, a tripper who receives a recommendation from his or her leader can look forward to many years of involvement with BTA/SHP.

MEDICAL CARE

All leaders and assistants must hold a valid Red Cross First Aid Certificate, and many leaders have advanced and other first aid training as well.

If a tripper needs medical attention due to illness or accident, he or she is taken to the nearest hospital or doctor. Whenever this happens, the leader is required to call BTA/SHP, and every effort is made to reach the parents. Most illnesses are brief and mild and do not require that the tripper go home. The tripper can be sent ahead with the assistant leader, by cab or private car, to the next one or two accommodations to rest. Trippers in the New England area can be brought back to BTA/SHP headquarters for a few days before rejoining the group.

RELIGIOUS LIFE

BTA/SHP is not affiliated with any religious organization.

COSTS

Trip costs vary widely depending on location and duration. In 2004, prices ranged from $875 to $5700. Trip costs included food, accommodations, transportation during the trip, scheduled activities, laundry, leadership, hostel membership if needed, use of group equipment (cooking equipment, tents, bike repair equipment, and first aid supplies), insurance, an equipment package (described below), and a $25 refundable contingency fund. Only personal expenses were not covered.

Bicycles are usually supplied by the tripper; however, BTA/SHP offers a bike-rental program for those who do not have or are not able to purchase a bike of the type required. Rental rates vary from $110 to $150, depending on the length of the trip. Bike rental is not available for trips more than six weeks in length.

BTA/SHP gives trippers an equipment package of excellent quality as part of the trip cost, including panniers, a front handlebar bag, and a sleeping bag. For those who already have good equipment, the cost of the package is reduced.

TRANSPORTATION

BTA bus transportation is provided from Boston's Logan Airport, from Hartford's Bradley Airport, from Framingham, Massachusetts, from Morristown, New Jersey, and from Rye, New York, to the headquarters in Conway, Massachusetts.

APPLICATION TIMETABLE

Initial inquiries are welcome at any time. Applications are accepted up to the trip departure date. There is no cutoff date for applying. A free video is available by contacting the address below.

Some trips fill earlier than others—sometimes as early as mid-January. If a participant is looking at a specific trip or has tight date requirements, it is recommended that application be made as early as possible. However, there are usually spaces left on several trips even as late as July and August.

For more information, contact:

Bicycle Travel Adventures or
Student Hosteling Program
P.O. Box 419
Ashfield Road
Conway, Massachusetts 01341
413-369-4275
800-343-6132 (toll-free in the United States and Canada)
E-mail: shpbike@aol.com
World Wide Web: http://www.bicycletrips.com

PARTICIPANT/FAMILY COMMENTS

"As I hoped, this was about a lot more than bike riding. It's about learning how to deal with new situations, meeting and cooperating with people. It's about self-confidence. Mission accomplished."

"I wouldn't trade this summer for anything. It was the best of my life! If I were to sum up my SHP trip, I would have to say that I learned the most in those weeks than anytime else in my life."

BISHOP'S COLLEGE SCHOOL

SUMMER SCHOOL

LENNOXVILLE, QUEBEC, CANADA

Type of Program: Residential language enrichment in either French as a second language or English as a second language
Participants: Coeducational, ages 11–16
Enrollment: 180
Program Dates: June 26 to July 23, 2005
Head of Program: Jeff Bray, Director

LOCATION

The Bishop's College School Summer School is situated on a 350-acre campus in Lennoxville, in the Eastern Townships of Quebec, Canada.

BACKGROUND AND PHILOSOPHY

The programme has been in existence for forty-three years and offers to its students a sound academic training combined with full extracurricular activities. Academically, the school appeals to two types of students: those who wish to accelerate or enrich their progress at their current school and those who need remediation before returning to school in the fall. One of the keystones at Bishop's is that, while it is a school, it must be remembered that it is summer, and students should therefore have fun. It is for this reason that there is an equal mixture of classes and out-of-class activities and excursions.

PROGRAMME OFFERINGS

Courses are offered in both English as a second language and French as a second language. In both areas, the emphasis is placed on the "communicative approach." Students work on their comprehension as well as their written and oral skills, with a strong emphasis placed on the latter. At the beginning of the session, students are given a placement test and are put in a class according to their ability. Student placement is carefully monitored, and students may be moved to a different class if the placement is judged to be incorrect. Course levels run from complete beginners to advanced. The average class size is 10–12. There is an exam every Saturday, and at the end of the session students are given a full report with a written comment as well as a mark out of 100. In addition, teachers are available to meet parents on the closing day. In order to foster academic excellence, scholarships worth $250 are awarded to 4 students (2 in English and 2 in French) at the end of the month. Each week one student in each class is awarded a "Spirit Pin" for his or her effort in class that week.

ENROLLMENT

The school accepts 180 students for the monthlong session. Whenever possible, students are placed in their rooms with a native speaker of the language they are learning. The majority of students come from Quebec; however, the school has a large international population from countries such as the United States, Columbia, Bermuda, Japan, Taiwan, Spain, the Bahamas, Mexico, and France.

DAILY SCHEDULE

A typical day starts at 7:30 with breakfast. Class runs from 8:30 to 10, when there is a 30-minute break. During this time there is an assembly, where announcements for the day are made and the students receive their mail. Classes continue from 10:30 until noon. After lunch (usually at 1:30), activities and sports start. Sports days take place on the campus and consist of such activities as volleyball, tennis, touch football, rock climbing (on the school's own wall), and softball. Activity days are twice a week, when the students leave the campus and go bowling, swimming, fishing, and horseback riding, among other things. Following dinner on Monday to Thursday, there is an evening study period in the classrooms from 6:30 to 8. During this time, students review the work done that day, have individual help, or play language-based games. Following this, students are free until their bedtimes, which vary from 9:30 to 10:15 depending upon their age.

Rules and regulations are based upon the welfare of the whole community and are simple and easy to follow. Smoking, drinking, and the use of illegal drugs are not tolerated and will result in the expulsion of the student. Before attending the school, all students must sign a form stating that they have read the school rules and agree to abide by them.

EXTRA OPPORTUNITIES AND ACTIVITIES

Besides the activities previously mentioned, there are major excursions every Sunday. During the course of the month, students attend a game of the Montreal Expos, spend a day at LaRonde (a major entertainment park in Montreal), and visit a local waterslide. In addition, all classes have one major academic excursion. Students studying French visit Quebec City for a day, and those in the English programme visit Ottawa, the nation's capital.

FACILITIES

The 350-acre campus of Bishop's College has all the modern facilities that a school of its stature would be expected to have. Classes take place in the main school building in cheerful and welcoming classrooms. There is a new $5-million gymnasium, which is available for use during free time as well as on days when the weather does not permit outdoor sports. Students live 2 per room in residences that are supervised by a houseparent who is available 24 hours a day. In addition, there are eight playing fields, three all-weather tennis courts, and a well-equipped kitchen and dining room.

STAFF

The school has a staff of 30. All teachers have a degree (many in second language teaching), and a number of the teachers have been at the school for several years. In addition to a teaching staff, there is also an activities/sports staff of 8 that is run by the codirector. Regular teaching staff members are expected to help in the afternoon sports and activities as well as in residence supervision.

MEDICAL CARE

The school has a fully equipped infirmary, and there is a nurse on duty 24 hours a day. Local doctors are on call, and more serious cases are dealt with at a local hospital that is ten minutes from the school. All students must have a medical form completed by a doctor before attending. Students from outside of Quebec are required to have medical insurance (approximately Can$80).

COSTS

Fees for the month are Can$2600. This cost covers room, board, and activities. A deposit of Can$400 is required at the time of application, with the balance due by June 1.

TRANSPORTATION

The school provides transportation to and from the two Montreal airports (Dorval and Mirabel) for a charge of Can$55 in each direction. The students are accompanied by a staff member. Students can also be met at the bus station in either Montreal or Sherbrooke.

APPLICATION TIMETABLE

Enquiries are welcome at any time; however, applications are not processed until February. Prospective students and parents may visit the school whenever they wish and can make an appointment by calling the director; however, this is not a required part of the application procedure. Once a student's file is complete with a recent report card, application, and deposit, the parents will receive notice of acceptance.

FOR MORE INFORMATION, CONTACT:

Bishop's College School Summer School
80 Moulton Hill Road
Lennoxville, Quebec J1M 1Z8
Canada
819-566-0227 Ext. 319
Fax: 819-822-8917
E-mail: summer@bishopscollegeschool.com

PARTICIPANT/FAMILY COMMENTS

"Bishop's College School Summer School programme is a most rewarding experience for young people. The opportunity of spending a month in Quebec with young people from around the world, traveling the province, and learning another language is an exciting and worthwhile way of spending part of the summer. Our children have attended several summers."—Victor and Elizabeth Vere, Sudbury, Ontario, Canada

BOSTON UNIVERSITY

COLLEGE OF COMMUNICATION INSTITUTE FOR TELEVISION, FILM & RADIO PRODUCTION

BOSTON, MASSACHUSETTS

Type of Program: Training in communication-related fields
Participants: Coeducational, students in grades 9–12
Program Dates: July 12 to August 13
Head of Program: Christophor Cavalieri, Academic Director

LOCATION

The Institute for Television, Film & Radio Production (ITRP) is held at Boston University's College of Communication, located in the heart of Boston along the Charles River.

BACKGROUND AND PHILOSOPHY

ITRP began its summer program in 1989. Its purpose is to offer high school students interested in a career in communication the opportunity to gain valuable experience in the areas of television, film, radio, and multimedia production.

ITRP provides a broad-based yet intensive five-week program specializing in hands-on workshop instruction. Students explore all areas of broadcast media.

PROGRAM OFFERINGS

Students participate in three of five workshops:
TV Field The TV Field Workshop focuses on disciplines and techniques of Electronic Field Production (EFP) and Electronic News Gathering (ENG) style of productions. Instruction covers story development, writing, producing, directing, shooting, sound recording, and editing. Project work includes news features, documentary profiles, interviews, and commercials. Selected workshop projects are incorporated into an edition of *Commonwealth Connections,* a half-hour news magazine program.
TV Studio The TV Studio Workshop incorporates the theory and practical application of studio production with an emphasis on multicamera production. Instruction includes creative development as well as technical training in both the studio and control room environments. Each student directs a live-to-tape episode of *Studio East,* an interview program, as his or her classmate's crew out the production. The students then produce a short drama or sitcom as well as a commercial spot or public service announcement.
Film The Film Workshop introduces students to the study and processes of single camera film production, concentrating on the traditional "Hollywood" film style. Students are encouraged to experience the creativity of script development combined with technical variables of focus, exposure, lighting, composition, and editing. Students create and produce two 16-mm black and white, nonsynchronous film projects.
Radio The Radio Workshop experience allows students to create and operate their own station, culminating in a live 2-hour Web cast with students performing every role necessary in this broadcasting environment. Format programming, field and studio production, postproduction, and talent performance are all areas of instruction covered in the workshop.
Nonlinear Editing The Nonlinear Editing Workshop presents the robust dynamics of digital postproduction. Working in the state-of-the-art media labs, students learn how to edit video and audio using Final Cut Pro with After Effects and Flash animation. Students have the ability to use previously created media as well as acquiring new material for their workshop projects.

ENROLLMENT

The summer program is open to students who have completed one year of high school. In 2003, 60 participants came from all over the United States and from several other countries.

DAILY SCHEDULE

Students spend sixteen sessions (eight days) in each workshop. Classes are held from 9 a.m. to 4 p.m. Monday through Thursday and on Friday morning. Friday afternoon is spent with senior faculty members, who give lectures on producing, directing, writing, and multimedia. A weekly lecture series held in the evening introduces students to other areas of communication.

EXTRA OPPORTUNITIES AND ACTIVITIES

ITRP sponsors many special activities on the weekends, which participants are encouraged to attend. Past events have included trips to the New England Aquarium, the Museum of Science and Omni Theatre, and a Red Sox game as well as a whale watch, a talent show, plays, and many others.

FACILITIES

The College of Communication has fully equipped modern studios. Facilities include editing suites and two studios, one of which houses the permanent set of the news program, *Neighborhood Network News.*

Room and board are available to ITRP participants in a Boston University dormitory. All participants are under the supervision of resident assistants in the dormitory and are expected to comply with Boston University dormitory regulations.

STAFF

The ITRP staff includes Christophor Cavalieri, Academic Director of the Institute; professionals in the field; and former and present students at Boston University.

MEDICAL CARE

Participants have use of the Boston University infirmary, and several hospitals are nearby for serious medical cases.

RELIGIOUS LIFE

Students may attend nondenominational services at Marsh Chapel on the Boston University campus if they wish.

COSTS

Tuition for the 2003 program was $2700, which included a materials and activities fee. Housing rates were approximately $1300. The nonrefundable application fee was $25.

TRANSPORTATION

Arrangements can be made for students to be met at the Boston train station, bus terminal, or airport.

APPLICATION TIMETABLE

To be considered for admission to ITRP, students must submit a complete application, which includes the application form, a one-page essay explaining why the student wants to attend ITRP, a transcript, and a letter of recommendation from a guidance counselor or teacher. The Institute encourages all interested students to apply, regardless of whether or not they have communication-related experience.

No admission decision is made until all portions of the application have been returned. Admission decisions are based on students' overall application packages. The essay is a critical component of the application. The application deadline is March 30.

FOR MORE INFORMATION, CONTACT:

Institute for Television, Film & Radio Production
College of Communication
Boston University
640 Commonwealth Avenue
Boston, Massachusetts 02215
617-353-5015
E-mail: itrp@bu.edu
World Wide Web: http://www.bu.edu/com/itrp

BRANT LAKE DANCE CENTRE

SUMMER PROGRAMS

BRANT LAKE, NEW YORK

Type of Program: Dance for girls in a coeducational setting
Participants: Girls, ages 12–16
Enrollment: 60
Program Dates: June 27–August 8
Heads of Program: Kirstin Been Spielman, Director

LOCATION

The Dance Centre is located adjacent to Brant Lake Camp for Boys, with which it is affiliated. The campus is on Brant Lake, a 6-mile-long, crystal-clear lake in the foothills of the Adirondack Mountains, within the Adirondack Park.

BACKGROUND AND PHILOSOPHY

The goal is to provide a high-quality experience for girls with an interest in dance. The Dance Centre helps the girls plan a fun program while ensuring that they can improve their ability in dance. When they are not dancing, there are many activities, often coed, from which campers may choose. The staff is well aware that teenagers need freedom of choice coupled with close, warm guidance and supervision. Brant Lake is a wonderful place for an active teenage girl. She does not have to be headed for a lifelong pursuit of dance, although Brant Lake does have some noted alumni, and superb instruction is offered at all levels.

The girls are asked to set goals for their stay at camp. Kirstin Been Spielman, the program director, helps guide each girl to achieve those goals as needed. Brant Lake's experienced and mature staff members provide guidance that leads to a safe, healthy, rewarding, and memorable summer.

Brant Lake Camp for Boys, part of one family since 1917, has enjoyed an outstanding reputation, not just for its beauty and fine facilities but also because of its guidance and fine supervision. The same high standards have been upheld for the Dance Centre since its inception in 1980.

PROGRAM OFFERINGS

Dance There are ballet, modern, tap, and jazz teachers who offer beginner through advanced classes. Girls can take up to 5 hours of dance a day if they wish, with a required minimum of 1 hour a day.

Sharon Gersten Luckman, founder of Brant Lake's Dance Centre, has created an intensive, professional dance program where teens get guidance, have lots of fun, and socialize in a healthy atmosphere. Sharon is currently the Executive Director of the Alvin Ailey American Dance Theater and was formerly the Director of Dance at the 92nd Street Y.

Brant Lake hires dance teachers who not only are wonderful professional dancers but also know how to teach dance, especially to teenagers.

Tennis All lessons are ability grouped. There are clinics (some coed), group lessons (with a maximum of 4 per court), and intensives (with 1 pro per 2 girls). Court time and matches are available throughout the day and evening.

Brant Lake has more than 20 tennis instructors (varsity players with teaching experience) and 5 tennis pros. The thirteen clay and three hard courts are beautifully maintained in picturesque settings.

Waterfront Swimming, waterskiing, windsurfing, sailing, canoeing, and kayaking are done on Brant Lake, which is crystal clear with a lovely sand bottom and ideally suited to learning and participating in these water sports.

Fine arts There is a choice of wood crafts, papermaking, leathercraft, weaving, painting, drawing, sculpture, jewelry, photography, and video in the arts facility.

Performing arts There are Wednesday and Saturday variety shows that include singing, dancing, and drama. There is a "works-in-progress" performance at the end of each session. This performance is a culmination of the work that has taken place in the various dance classes.

Sports The sports program provides both instruction and games to those interested. Land sports include tennis, basketball, aerobics, volleyball, jogging, and fitness training. Water sports include swimming, waterskiing, windsurfing, sailing, canoeing, and boating. Brant Lake Camp's wonderful boys' instructors and fields enrich and facilitate the sports program. There is an opportunity for activities with boys of appropriate ability.

ENROLLMENT

Girls ages 12–16 come from all over the country and all around the world. Sessions are three or six weeks.

EXTRA OPPORTUNITIES AND ACTIVITIES

Evening activities vary daily. Once a week, the group travels to the Saratoga Performing Arts Center to enjoy a rock concert, dance performance, or a play. On other evenings, girls may choose from mixed doubles tennis, movies, coed activities, dance, or art electives, or they may rehearse for the weekly musical or cabaret night. On certain evenings, bunks have campfires or run an activity. Many evenings end with the senior boys—they are casual, supervised, and fun.

The Sunday program provides for a change of pace, a time for relaxation after a busy week. Brunch is followed by many choices. The late afternoon offers coed waterfront and other activities, a barbecue, and a movie.

Trip day is one day each week. Girls may go to such local attractions as Lake George, Saratoga, Lake Placid, or Great Escape theme park. They may also choose a bicycling trip through the countryside, a mountain hike, a daylong canoe trip, or an overnight camping trip on a private mountain nearby.

FACILITIES

The Centre's dance and lodging facilities are beautifully designed to fit the special needs of its campers. The upper level of the Dance Lodge contains a spacious, professional studio overlooking peaceful woods. A second studio for tap and aerobics is housed in a beautifully restored barn. A third dance studio in the field house has a professional vinyl floor. On the main level of the lodge is a lovely living room that serves as a communal lounge for the girls, two large dormitory-style bunks, and two bathrooms (each with sinks, showers, and toilets). Four other bunks provide the same homey atmosphere and facilities. Here the girls live with others their own age and 2 counselors per bunk. They eat breakfast and lunch in the relaxed atmosphere of the Field House dining room. Healthy snacks and juice are available throughout the day. Dinner is served in the dining hall on the boys' campus.

In addition to this, the Dance Centre shares many of the numerous outstanding indoor and outdoor facilities with Brant Lake Camp for Boys.

STAFF

In addition to the professional dance staff, the camp hires experienced, mature counselor staff members. Because the program is small (60 girls), the staff is "the cream of the crop." Each staff member is personally interviewed; the average age of the staff is 22. Brant Lake looks for experienced women who can guide teenage girls in making appropriate decisions in a fun, safe, and compassionate way. At all times, the girls are supervised by these mature counselors, who understand that teenagers are ready to make many of their own decisions and able to set their own goals.

MEDICAL CARE

The Health Center is fully equipped and has 4 nurses and 1 doctor in residence throughout the season. In addition, most counselors are certified in first aid and CPR.

COSTS

Tuition in 2004 was approximately $3500 for three weeks and $6000 for six weeks. Extra costs are incurred for transportation and spending money.

TRANSPORTATION

Girls may take the chartered bus (from New York City) or fly to the Albany airport, where they are met by a staff member, or parents may drive them to camp.

FOR MORE INFORMATION, A TAPE, AND AN APPLICATION, CONTACT:

Kirsten Been Spielman
Brant Lake's Dance Centre
7586 State Route 8
Brant Lake, New York 12815
518-494-2406
Fax: 518-494-7372
E-mail: brantlakec@aol.com

PARTICIPANT/FAMILY COMMENTS

"I learned different techniques; that's fun. I think it makes you a stronger dancer."—Debra (age 16), Barcelona, Spain

"The counselors and advisers are great. They're really friendly. If you ever have a problem, you would immediately go to them because they're more your friends than your advisers."—Dana (age 15), New Jersey

BREWSTER ACADEMY SUMMER SESSION

THE PERFECT SUMMER

WOLFEBORO, NEW HAMPSHIRE

Type of Program: Academics, instructional support, English as a second language (ESL), adventure education, and technology enrichment
Participants: Coeducational, ages 12–17
Program Dates: Six weeks in July and August
Head of Program: Bill Lee, Director

LOCATION

Brewster Academy, on Lake Winnipesaukee, is located where the lakes meet the mountains in one of New England's most picturesque areas. The campus, adjacent to the safe and quaint village of Wolfeboro, is on 75 acres of playing fields and rolling hillside overlooking one half mile of waterfront on New Hampshire's largest lake.

BACKGROUND AND PHILOSOPHY

The Brewster Academy Summer Session provides summer fun while teaching important skills that serve students well in school and in life. Brewster takes full advantage of its beautiful site and the extraordinary resources that serve both academics and athletics on its campus. In the outdoor adventure program, participants climb, hike, paddle, and play in one of the most spectacular geographic regions of New Hampshire. Brewster has high expectations concerning the amount of academic material that can be covered in a six-week summer program. There are similarly high expectations for having fun in the beautiful New Hampshire summer. So everyone works hard when they work, and plays hard when they play.

Brewster's Summer Session is designed with the belief that there are things that every successful and happy person needs to know and be able to do. In addition to the skills of reading and writing and/or mathematics, there is an emphasis on study, organization, and time-management skills. There are three other skill areas that are essential for success in secondary school, college, the workplace, and life: the skills of critical thinking and problem-solving, the skills of collaborative teamwork, and the skills that lead to technological literacy and fluency. The first two are taught both indoors and outdoors; the third is taught on Brewster's technologically sophisticated campus, where students are able to access the network from anywhere on the campus using laptop computers that are provided as part of the program.

PROGRAM OFFERINGS

Core Courses Everyone takes one core course: English (reading and writing), math (pre-algebra, algebra I, or geometry), or English as a second language (ESL), level one or two. These courses meet for two hours each morning, Monday through Friday, supported by daily 90-minute study sessions conducted by qualified teaching assistants who work collaboratively with the core classroom teachers. These courses can be taken either as accelerated classes or as make-up for those seeking or requiring remedial work. Up to a full year's academic credit can be granted to those who demonstrate mastery. These courses are intensive; the primary purpose is not issuing credit, but rather to teach important concepts and to meaningfully advance student knowledge in the six short weeks available.

Photo courtesy of Eric Poggenpohl

English Brewster uses the advantage of small classes and an intentional curriculum to focus on the relevance of reading and writing to the lives of the students. A student is met where he or she is in terms of reading or writing skills and is helped to achieve proficiency in those skills through a sequential skill-building program.

Mathematics The summer math courses are pre-algebra, algebra I, or geometry. The classes are intensive, but they have an individualized tutorial aspect as well. A great deal of material is covered and no one gets left behind. Instructors change the pace, the approaches, and the perspective often to keep things interesting and make sure that everyone really understands what are, sometimes, abstract principles.

English as a Second Language The summer ESL program is an integrated system of learning where students participate in various classes and activities that are intricately connected. An unusually rich and intensive set of daily offerings is provided, resulting in as many as 4 to 6 hours a day of directed English learning as well as a full immersion in English-only classes, recreational activities, and dorm life for the remainder of each day. The ESL academic program includes three courses: the ESL language, ESL

communication, and an innovative ESL video-editing course. Each student also takes an elective class with native English speakers.

Non-Core Courses Everyone takes two elective courses, choosing from computer graphic art and design, experiential science, video production, and/or instructional support (IS). IS, a program for which Brewster is renown, offers one-on-one instruction that focuses on the learning needs of each student (see details below). These courses meet for one hour each morning.

Instructional Support A very popular option, instructional support employs a tutorial approach to guide students to better understand how they best learn and to develop improved study, organization, and time-management skills. The IS program is directly linked to the student's core curriculum (reading/writing or math skills) as a collaboration between the teacher, the IS teacher, and the student.

Science This course, taken for enrichment and enjoyment, provides students with a refreshing new way to approach the discipline of science. There are no boring "stand-and-deliver" lectures. It is a get-involved, hands-on, experiential class in which the basic principles of scientific investigation are learned by doing.

Computer Graphics Led by an energetic, popular, and experienced teacher, the computer graphics program consists of three sections: Adobe Photoshop, an award-winning digital imaging program; iMovie, devoted to making short movies; and Dreamweaver, the current leader of Web site programs.

Adventure Education These courses are fun, but they are also purposeful and important and are not just for recreation. Adventure education courses are designed to build skills. Confidence, critical thinking, judgment, precision, teamwork, and leadership skills are just some of the benefits derived from engaging in outdoor adventure. The courses include rock and wall climbing, rappelling, flat and white-water canoeing, kayaking, hiking/camping, and a few surprises.

Technology Enrichment "Brewster is probably the most innovative and successful school using (information technology) on this planet... The success of their students has been enormous," says Steve Kessell of Curtin University of Technology. Summer session students use laptops, provided by Brewster, in every class and learn firsthand how powerful technology can be when purposefully integrated into the curriculum.

ENROLLMENT

Students from throughout the United States and many other countries attend Summer Session. Brewster does not discriminate on the basis of race, color, or national or ethnic origin in administering its programs. Demonstrations of motivation are criteria for inclusion.

DAILY SCHEDULE

Classes and study halls meet five days per week until 2:30 p.m. Adventure recreation lasts until 5:30 p.m. Adventure trips, with some overnight stays beginning on Friday, are scheduled on Saturdays.

EXTRA OPPORTUNITIES AND ACTIVITIES

Three nights a week, everyone goes to the spectacular Athletics and Wellness Center for games and to learn fitness regimens. Sundays are set aside for trips that take advantage of New England's scenic and cultural opportunities, including the mountains, seacoast, and Boston.

FACILITIES

Brewster enjoys modern dormitory and dining facilities, innovative classrooms, a campus-wide network that provides network and Internet access from every dorm room, a multipurpose boathouse, and a modern fitness center.

STAFF

All classes are taught by teachers who have many years of experience. Teacher interns, recruited from America's top universities, oversee study halls, adventure activities, and dorms. All are American Red Cross-certified in CPR and first aid and in basic water safety and rescue. Rock climbing instructors are qualified, certified, and experienced.

MEDICAL CARE

There is an on-campus infirmary, and a hospital is ¼ mile from the campus.

COSTS

The 2004 tuition was $5795. Instructional support fees are additional.

TRANSPORTATION

Transportation from air and rail centers is included.

APPLICATION TIMETABLE

The admissions process is rolling and ongoing.

For more information, contact:

Brewster Academy Summer Session
80 Academy Drive
Wolfeboro, New Hampshire 03894
Telephone: 603-569-7155
Fax: 603-569-7050
E-mail: summer@brewsteracademy.org
World Wide Web: http://www.brewsteracademy.org

BRIGHTON FOUNDATION

COLLEGE ADMISSIONS PREP CAMPS AND LANGUAGE AND CULTURAL IMMERSION PROGRAMS

BOSTON AND LOS ANGELES; COSTA RICA, FRANCE, ITALY, AND SPAIN

Type of Program: College admissions prep camps with campus tours; Language and cultural immersion programs (campus and homestay options) in French, German, Italian, and Spanish
Participants: Coeducational, grades 9–12
Enrollment: 25–50 per session
Program Dates: College admissions prep: 9-day sessions in late June and early August; language and cultural immersion: 3½ week sessions, June through August
Head of Program: David Allen, Executive Director

LOCATION

Based in Pasadena, California, Brighton offers college admissions prep camps at University of California in Los Angeles (UCLA) and at Tufts University in Boston. Language immersion programs are held in Costa Rica, France, Italy, Spain, and Switzerland.

BACKGROUND AND PHILOSOPHY

Brighton's admissions-prep and language immersion programs share the common purpose of preparing teenage students for successful, fulfilling, and exciting adult lives. Three words guide the design of every Brighton summer experience: explore, learn, excel. These words represent Brighton's belief that as teenage students prepare for college, summers represent an invaluable opportunity to explore independently, to learn actively beyond the classroom, and to discover the potential to excel as thoughtful and engaged young adults.

Brighton's college admissions prep camps at UCLA and Tufts University focus on developing a thorough understanding of the college admissions process; methodically preparing each facet of the college admissions applications, with the guidance of experienced counselors and writing instructors; and visiting campuses in the Los Angeles and Boston areas. Perhaps most importantly, tackling college applications while experiencing college life with students from around the country transforms what can be a dreary and intimidating task into a fun and memorable experience. Students find that every element of their application, from the personal statement to selecting schools, comes into focus as they take possession of the process and experience the independence and excitement of life as a college student.

Brighton's language immersion programs offer high school students opportunities for travel that go beyond tourism—travel that provides opportunities for profound contact with local people and their history, language, and culture. Believing that the development of an appreciation for cultural subtleties requires time and familiarity, Brighton students, whether lodged with families or in campus dormitories, are always based in one location for the length of their stay in a country. A foundation of daily language instruction is complemented by active cultural workshops, a wide variety of sport and leisure activities, and extensive travel excursions on afternoons and weekends. The overarching goal is not simply to improve language skills, but to develop a passion for travel and international exchange that students continue to nurture throughout their lives.

PROGRAM OFFERINGS

College Admissions Prep Camps–UCLA and Tufts University These 9-day campus-based programs are held in late June and early August so that students can participate without altering their other summer vacation plans. Admission is limited to sophomores and juniors rising into their junior or senior years. Participants live in campus dormitories, take meals in campus dining halls, and enjoy full access to campus facilities. Each day, Brighton's guidance counselors, writing instructors, and admissions professionals help the students understand how college admissions decisions are made. They work with students individually and in small groups to prepare excellent application portfolios. The programs include a series of visits to major campuses in the Los Angeles and Boston areas.

French Language and Cultural Immersion–Cannes and Paris (ages 15–18) Brighton offers two 3½-week options in France: a campus-based program in Cannes and a homestay program in St. Germain-en-Laye, in suburban Paris. Both programs focus on language immersion, with daily French courses at various levels, supplemented by a program of afternoon and weekend cultural workshops, leisure activities, and travel excursions.

Italian, Spanish, and German Language and Cultural Immersion–Tuscany, Costa Rica, Spain, and Switzerland (ages 14–18) Through its network of partner schools in Europe and Central America, Brighton offers a wide variety of language, culture, sport, and travel opportunities. Because these programs can be tailored to individual needs, students can define the length of their stay, the focus of their studies, and how they would like to structure their leisure time, cultural study, and travel. Interested students should contact a Brighton representative to discuss the ideal location and program design that matches their summer goals.

ENROLLMENT

Brighton programs are restricted to fewer than 50 participants in each session. The small-sized groups allow for individualized counseling, writing instruction, and language instruction and make it possible to offer an active schedule of campus visits and travel excursions. Both language immersion and college admissions prep programs attract students from diverse ethnic backgrounds, from public and private schools, and from various regions of the United States and other nations. Brighton does not discriminate on the basis of race, religion, or ethnicity and seeks out applicants with a wide range of interests, backgrounds,and perspectives.

DAILY SCHEDULE

College Admissions Prep Camps After breakfast in the campus dining hall, students take part in a rotating morning schedule of group counseling workshops, individual counseling appointments, and SAT practice sessions. Students who have already taken the SAT may select an independent study project. After lunch, students attend a course in writing a personal statement. Early evenings are scheduled for individual counseling or writing appointments, open study periods, and activities in town or on the campus.

Language Immersion Programs Language courses are held each weekday morning between 9 a.m. and noon. Several afternoons each week are reserved for cultural workshops and for outings to nearby attractions, such as museums, historical sites, and wilderness areas. The leisure schedule includes beaches, water sports, athletics, excursions to neighboring towns, movies, concerts, and free time for independent exploration with friends.

EXTRA OPPORTUNITIES AND ACTIVITIES

College Admissions Prep Camps The program includes a series of guided campus visits to major universities in Los Angeles or Boston. These visits provide an opportunity for students to develop a strong sense of what is important to them in narrowing their college list. They also provide a unique way to visit two of America's greatest cities. Campuses visited during the programs include USC, Pepperdine, and the Claremont Colleges (Los Angeles program) and Boston College, Boston University, Northeastern, and Harvard (Boston program). In addition to organized outings to local attractions such as Faneuil Hall and Harvard Square in Boston and the Santa Monica Promenade in Los Angeles, students also have free time in the evenings to enjoy movies, restaurants, and cafés around Westwood and Medford/Somerville.

Language Immersion Programs Each of Brighton's language immersion locations offers an exciting program of outdoor activities and travel excursions each weekend. Trips range from active outdoor adventures, such as whitewater rafting and parasailing to visits to many of the most celebrated destinations in the world, such as Nice, Versailles, Florence, and the Costa Rican rainforest. For detailed descriptions of the activity and excursion schedules for each location, students should visit Brighton online at http://www.brightonedge.org.

FACILITIES

Students at UCLA and Tufts live in double rooms in on-campus dormitories, with shared bathroom facilities. Brighton's college admissions prep students receive three meals each day in the campus dining hall and enjoy full access to the university's facilities.

Students in language immersion programs in Paris and Costa Rica live with local families. Students enrolled in language and culture programs in Cannes, Switzerland, and Tuscany are lodged and take courses on college campuses or in private residence halls.

STAFF

Brighton's faculty/staff/administrative team is composed of licensed college guidance counselors; admissions officers, writing instructors, and graduate students from top universities; native language teachers; and program directors with many years of experience in international education and travel. Members of both the faculty and residential staff live with students in the dormitory to provide constant supervision and support. In Paris, the program staff lives in St. Germain-en-Laye with local families and is on-call by portable phone 24 hours a day. Brighton's partner programs in Costa Rica, Switzerland, and Italy are staffed by native instructors, local guides, and year-round school administrators.

MEDICAL CARE

Prior to the program, all students are required to submit a detailed medical form. At Tufts and UCLA, urgent care is available on the campus at the Student Health Center. Brighton's language immersion programs are affiliated with local general practitioners who speak English and have agreed to admit Brighton students on a priority basis during their stay. In the case of health problems or injury, the program staff immediately arranges qualified and appropriate medical care. It is Brighton's policy that a staff member accompany students to all medical appointments. All Brighton programs are drug and alcohol free.

COSTS

In 2004, the comprehensive fees for Brighton's college admissions prep camps at UCLA and Tufts were $2,295 for residential students and $775 for day students.

For the language immersion programs, the comprehensive fee for Paris (homestay) was $4295; Cannes (campus), $4295; Costa Rica (homestay), $1100 to $3200 for 2 to 6 weeks; Switzerland (campus), $4100; and Tuscany (campus), $1700 to $3300 for 2 to 4 weeks.

These fees include lodging and all meals, tuition for formal instruction, all required books, use of campus facilities (where applicable), scheduled guest lectures, guides, field trips, campus tours, excursions, activities and performances, airport transfers, and linens. Fees do not include transportation to and from the program; taxis, bike rentals, or other discretionary transportation; activities and excursions outside the scheduled itinerary; snacks, souvenirs, and personal expenses; meals eaten in lieu of provided cafeteria or homestay meals; phone charges; and medical or travel insurance.

A deposit of $300 should accompany the application. This deposit is fully credited toward the program fee and is entirely refundable until 120 days prior to the program's start date.

APPLICATION TIMETABLE

Applications are reviewed using a rolling admissions system. The program application and a fully-refundable $300 deposit hold an applicant's place in the program pending completion of the application process and acceptance. To ensure a place in the program and priority for special housing requests, students are encouraged to apply before February 1 for homestay programs and before March 1 for dormitory programs.

FOR MORE INFORMATION, CONTACT:

The Brighton Foundation
101 E. Green Street, Suite 14
Pasadena, California 91105
626-795-2985
Fax: 626-795-5564
E-mail: info@brightonedge.org
World Wide Web: www.brightonedge.org

BRITISH AMERICAN DRAMA ACADEMY

MIDSUMMER IN LONDON PRE-COLLEGE PROGRAM

LONDON, UNITED KINGDOM

Type of Program: Intensive classical acting training
Participants: Coeducational; ages 16–18
Enrollment: 32 students (two groups of 16)
Program Dates: July 3 –August 1, 2004
Heads of Program: Nick Hutchison, Dean, and Frances Mayhew, Program Manager

LOCATION

The British American Drama Academy (BADA) is located in regency-style crown buildings overlooking Regents Park in central London. Regents Park is close to the bustling West End, trendy Camden Lock shopping, coffee shops, and, of course, acres of beautiful park land. Accommodations are a short walk away in the University of London's halls of residence.

BACKGROUND AND PHILOSOPHY

The British American Drama Academy was founded in 1983 to enable students from around the world to study classical theatre with leading actors and directors of the British theatre. The Midsummer in London Program is designed for serious acting students at the precollege level and concentrates on classical acting. The main objective of the program is to help students improve their acting skills so they are better able to meet the challenges that confront them at college, drama school, and university. Participation in this program serves as excellent training for those who plan to study theatre elsewhere. Students leave with a firm knowledge of British plays and theatre and a profound understanding of acting styles and techniques.

PROGRAM OFFERINGS

The program is acccredited by the University of Southern California and students may claim 3 credits upon successful completion. This is available at an extra cost to the student. All classes are compulsory:

Acting Shakespeare (core subject) This offering is a practical class in comedy, history, and tragedy. Particular attention is given to textual analysis and verse speaking.

High Comedy (core subject) This is a practical class devoted to work from the Restoration and later periods. Playwrights include Wilde, Sheridan, Vanbrugh, Congreve, Coward, and Shaw.

Modern and Contemporary Playwrights (core subject) This is a practical class covering playwrights such as Brecht, Berkoff, Osborne, McDonagh, and Pinter.

Movement This class is directed to general movement exercises involving muscular coordination and control.

Voice Structured exercises are combined with guided vocal discovery to add strength, creativity, and emotional range to the student's natural voice as well as the development of self-awareness in personal voice usage.

Dramatic Criticism Students see professional theatre productions twice a week. Plays are discussed in class and students must submit short critiques on the required productions.

Audition Technique This class helps students develop their audition technique and learn about how to approach a monologue for an audition.

Tutorials Students have one-to-one tutorials with a professional actor to discuss and practice any work of their choice.

Master Classes These classes are weekly sessions taught by some of Britain's finest actors and directors, depending on availability.

Workshops These are weekly sessions on other aspects of theatre, such as stage fighting and set design.

ENROLLMENT

BADA accepts students of all nationalities, but entry is strictly by audition only. The course lasts for four weeks and must be completed in full. The audition consists of two contrasting monologues; one must be from Shakespeare, and the other is the student's own choice. Speeches must not total more than five minutes.

DAILY SCHEDULE

Breakfast is served in hall from about 7 to 9. Classes start at 9:30 a.m., and students are walked to class from hall with the Program Counsellors. Time is scheduled before dinner to learn lines and group scenes before class the next day. Dinner is taken between 5:30 and 7 p.m.

EXTRA OPPORTUNITIES AND ACTIVITIES

Students visit the theatre twice weekly and take part in excursions outside of London every weekend. These trips include visiting Stratford-upon-Avon to see a production by the Royal Shakespeare Company, visiting Oxford, and having opportunities to discover London in more depth. During the week, there are extra activities organised that include an entertainment evening, cinema nights, and in-hall pizza evenings. There is an Open Day at the end of the course when students perform scenes and work in progress.

FACILITIES

In hall, there is a dining hall that provides a range of foods for breakfast and dinner. The hall provides single rooms with sinks and phones, computer access, a TV room, tennis courts, and a laundry. BADA's classic buildings offer large classrooms, a library, a greenroom for quiet study, a canteen, a computer and Internet access, and a private garden.

STAFF

The Dean and the Program Manager are full-time in the program. The faculty members are freelance professionals who have a long history of working with BADA, returning regularly for specific classes. A member of the faculty of the University of Southern California also teaches in the program. The Dean takes responsibility for disciplinary matters, and the Program Manager manages pastoral matters concerning students.

To ensure maximum safety and to minimise risk, BADA's staff members are assisted by a number of Program Counsellors who have experience with BADA's programs and of living in London. They live with the students and accompany them at all times. Students must adhere to BADA's Code of Conduct, which has been devised to reduce the chance of any mishap in what is a large and, for many students, bewildering city. BADA realises that this is the first trip abroad on their own for many students, so every effort is made to make the students feel at home and at ease.

MEDICAL CARE

A qualified first-aider is on-site all the time. BADA and the hall of residence are close to many hospitals. BADA can arrange for a doctor to come and see a student in person, or BADA can arrange for a student to be taken to a clinic. It is vital that students have adequate insurance. BADA does not provide insurance of any kind. After acceptance, there is a medical form that students have to fill in with information about their own insurance.

COSTS

Full fees for summer 2003 are £3025: £1805 for tuition and £1220 for accommodation and food. Students are required to bring a set of the complete works of Shakespeare with them. After being accepted, students secure their place with a £250 deposit. The rest of the fee can be paid in three stages, but the full fees must be paid at least two weeks before the start of the program if the students wishes to attend. Scholarships are available. The fees do not cover airfares.

TRANSPORTATION

BADA arranges group transportation from Heathrow Airport to the accommodation on the day of arrival. Students arriving at other airports must make their own way to BADA, but full transport details are sent to make this journey as easy as possible. It is recommended that students fly to Heathrow and take advantage of the transport provided by BADA.

APPLICATION TIMETABLE

The application deadline is March 31. Auditions take place during March and April. Students are notified within twenty-eight days of their audition as to whether or not they have been accepted. The deadline for the final fee payment is June 20.

FOR MORE INFORMATION, CONTACT:

Enquiries from the U.S.:

Jennifer Rockwood
900 West End Avenue, #15F
New York, New York 10025
Phone: 212-749-0120
Fax: 212-749-0120
E-mail: jrockwood@badaonline.com
World Wide Web: http://www.badaonline.com

Non-U.S. enquiries:

Frances Mayhew
Program Manager
14 Gloucester Gate
London
NW1 7HG, United Kingdom
Phone: 44-020-7487-0730
Fax: 44-020-7487-0731
E-mail: info@badaonline.com
World Wide Web: www.badaonline.com

PARTICIPANT/FAMILY COMMENTS

"Andrea's calls and e-mails are full of the wonderful time she is having with BADA! Thank you so much for making her experience so comfortable and memorable. Last night she told us some things about Shakespeare that she learned from Nick. They were fascinating. She is enjoying her classes and teachers very much. Thanks again for everything you are doing."—Maria Spillman, mother.

"I would like to thank everyone involved with BADA for the most incredible summer of my life. Not only did I grow as an artist, but I also grew as a person. Everyone that I met has and will continue to have a vast impact on me for the rest of my life. I loved London and miss England terribly. I cannot wait until I can return. Hope all is well! Thank you, thank you, thank you!"—Carla Maye, 2003 participant

BROADREACH

CARIBBEAN SCUBA DIVING, SAILING, AND MARINE BIOLOGY ADVENTURES

LEEWARD ISLANDS: ST. MARTIN, ST. BARTS, ST. KITTS, NEVIS, STATIA, AND SABA; WINDWARD ISLANDS: ST. LUCIA, ST. VINCENT, AND THE GRENADINES; BAHAMAS: CAPE ELEUTHERA; HONDURAS: BAY ISLANDS

Type of Program: Hands-on educational adventures, including marine studies, SCUBA diving, sailing, and leadership training. Marine science programs focus on marine ecology, aquaculture, dolphin studies, reef formation, and SCUBA certification (beginner and advanced). Activities include sea kayaking, snorkeling, hiking, and community service. Live-aboard sailing and diving voyages focus on SCUBA certification (beginner to advanced), sail training, island exploration, waterskiing, and marine ecology. No experience is necessary.

Participants: Coed, grouped by ages 13–19.

Enrollment: 10–14 participants per trip

Program Dates: Two-, three-, and four-week programs, June through August

LOCATION

Selection of each program location is carefully evaluated and chosen to best fit BROADREACH's activities and goals. Live-aboard sail and dive programs in the Leeward and Windward Islands take advantage of top Caribbean dive sites, ideal sail training grounds, lush rain forests, and islands with diverse European and cultural influences. Cape Eleuthera in the Bahamas offers one of the most biologically diverse and pristine marine environments in the world. Honduras's rich ecological diversity makes it ideal for both marine and environmental studies.

BACKGROUND AND PHILOSOPHY

BROADREACH provides opportunities for teens to learn new skills and explore the world in an active, hands-on environment that fully immerses the participant in the adventure experience. Unlike traditional camps or other programs with large groups or flotillas, Broadreach limits the trip size to just 10–14 participants. Living in a small group promotes teamwork, leadership, compromise, and consideration, teaching important lessons that will last long after the program is over. The flexibility of a small group allows staff and students to come together as a team to make the adventure happen. Staff members can give participants individual attention and shape the trip around the goals and abilities of the group. Trips are age appropriate, without socially mixing 13 and 18 year olds. Teens can relax and be themselves in a supportive, noncompetitive atmosphere in which participants make close friendships with people with diverse interests and backgrounds. No experience is necessary on most programs, only a desire to have a blast, try new things, and broaden experiences.

PROGRAM OFFERINGS

Adventures in SCUBA and Sailing/Underwater Discoveries (Leeward Islands) No experience is required for this incredible live-aboard voyage that offers SCUBA instruction, sail training, and island exploration. Discover the magic of the underwater world, feel the freedom of life aboard a yacht, hike through lush rain forests, and water ski at sunset in a paradise cove. Explore beautiful reefs on more than seventeen dives, earning both PADI Open Water and Advanced certifications. Small groups allow participants to learn one step at a time at their own pace. On board the yacht, participants take the helm, trim the sails and navigate by celestial and GPS techniques as they rotate responsibilities of skipper, Divemaster, chef, and crew. With gentle tradewinds, the Leewards provide perfect conditions for hands-on sailing training and certification. These islands have rich French, Dutch, and English colonial histories.

Adventures Underwater–Advanced SCUBA (Leewards) and **Adventures in the Grenadines–Advanced SCUBA** (Windwards) Designed for certified divers, these SCUBA-intensive programs take Underwater Discoveries to the next level. Dive right into Advanced and Specialty certification training with PADI dive instructors, earning C-cards in Night, Wreck, Drift, Marine Biology, and U/W Photography. With small groups, participants learn and do more, earning Rescue and possibly Master Diver certifications on more than twenty-eight dives. The diving is exceptional with flourishing coral gardens, mysterious wrecks, dramatic pinnacles, and world-renowned marine parks. Above the waterline, participants have a blast with new friends enjoying life aboard, exploring beautiful islands, hiking, water skiing and working on seamanship skills.

Arc of the Caribbean (Leeward and Windward Islands) This is a thirty-one-day sailing voyage of a lifetime from St. Martin to the coast of South America. Participants crew a 50-foot sailing yacht on this comprehensive sail training, adventure travel, and educational experience. Long-distance sailing, spectacular snorkeling, rain forest exploration, and swimming in mountain waterfalls simply hint at the overall adventure. Participants discover islands few have heard of, in ways ordinary tourists cannot, on their way to becoming accomplished and confident sailors.

Marine Biology Accredited (Cape Eleuthera, Bahamas) This is an outstanding program for anyone fascinated with the underwater world or interested in marine biology. Based at the Island School in the Bahamas, the thriving reef system of Cape Eleuthera is the classroom. Under the instruction of professional marine biologists, the program anchors traditional learning with real-world application and hands-on experience. The combination of dive training, field excursions, lab work, lectures, and aquaculture research qualifies this course for high school and/or college credit. Participants SCUBA dive each day, and PADI instructors teach those with no prior experience one step at a time. Open Water and Advanced certification are offered along with specialty cards in Underwater Naturalist and Marine Ecology. Participants also explore the island, sea kayak, bike ride, and hike.

Honduras Marine Studies This unique ecological adventure combines SCUBA diving, marine biology, rain forest ecology, and field studies. Participants dive and study the Bay Islands' thriving reef, the world's second largest, and participate in dolphin research with marine mammal scientists. Then, they travel to the mainland to visit Mayan ruins, raft the Rio Congrejal, and explore lush rain forests.

Those interested in learning more should see the **BROADREACH Worldwide Scuba, Wilderness and Sailing Adventures** in-depth description in this edition of *Peterson's Summer Opportunities for Kids and Teenagers.*

ENROLLMENT

A small group size of 10 to 14 participants is one of the defining characteristics of BROADREACH programs. Limited enrollment gives flexibility to the trip and responsibility to Broadreachers, enhancing communication, teamwork, and leadership skills. With small groups, participants don't have to wait their turn to dive, water-ski, or try something new.

FACILITIES

On sail and SCUBA voyages, participants live aboard fully equipped yachts. Each yacht includes dive gear, an air compressor, a water ski boat, communication and safety equipment. The Island School boasts an aquaculture station, dive boats, dorm-style facilities, a full kitchen, kayaks, and beach cruiser bikes. In Honduras, participants live in huts on a palm-fringed beach or in tents under a rainforest canopy. Broadreach is a fully accredited PADI International Five Star Gold Palm Facility.

COSTS

Tuition is between $3600 and $5400, depending on the program and the duration of the trip. Tuition is all-inclusive, except for airfare. Sibling discounts are available.

FOR MORE INFORMATION, CONTACT:

BROADREACH
P.O. Box 27076
Raleigh, North Carolina 27611
919-833-1907
888-833-1907 (toll-free)
Fax: 919-833-2129
E-mail: info@gobroadreach.com
World Wide Web: http://www.gobroadreach.com

PARTICIPANT/FAMILY COMMENTS

"I loved the staff; they let us be individuals and treated the entire team as equals. The program was not like a camp; I felt I was important to the group and the experience."

"I had an incredible time in the islands: diving, kayaking, exploring, sleeping under the stars. I made great friends and the staff was totally committed. But since I've returned home, I've been able to look at the trip in its entirety. I realized I learned about trust, working with other people, meeting challenges, and accomplishing the goals I set."

BROADREACH

WORLDWIDE SCUBA, WILDERNESS, SAILING, AND ACADEMIC ADVENTURES

CARIBBEAN, AUSTRALIA, EGYPT–RED SEA, COSTA RICA, HONDURAS, ECUADOR–GALAPAGOS, BRITISH COLUMBIA, BAJA–MEXICO, FIJI, THE SOLOMON ISLANDS, AND CAPE ELEUTHERA–BAHAMAS

Type of Program: International educational adventure programs, including scuba diving and dive training from beginner to advanced, wilderness expeditions, sail training voyages, and academic expeditions. Hands-on skill building, cultural immersion, leadership training, and exploration. No experience is necessary for many trips.

Participants: Coed, grouped by ages 13–19

Enrollment: 10–14 participants per trip

Program Dates: Two-, three-, four-, and six-week programs, June through August

LOCATION

Each BROADREACH location offers its own special blend of discovery and challenge. Destinations are selected to maximize cultural and educational opportunities and provide participants with exceptional personal growth experiences. The Caribbean islands (St. Martin, St. Barts, Saba, Nevis, Antigua, St. Vincent and the Grenadines, and the Bahamas), Australia, the Red Sea, Ecuador, the Galapagos Islands, Honduras, Costa Rica, Fiji, British Columbia, Baja, and the Solomon Islands are primary BROADREACH locales.

BACKGROUND AND PHILOSOPHY

BROADREACH goes beyond the traditional structure of other summer programs. Each BROADREACH program is designed to take advantage of the unique opportunities in regions traveled by combining the thrill of discovery, the pride of accomplishment, and the excitement of exploring the wilderness and sea. BROADREACH offers a unique opportunity for young adults to learn and grow together in an active, hands-on environment that is both fun and educational. Whether the activity is sailing, sea kayaking, or scuba diving, expertise is built sensibly through a step-by-step, learn-by-doing approach. Every program meets BROADREACH's foremost objective: to challenge young adults to discover their own abilities, to overcome self-imposed limitations, to develop greater responsibility, and to gain further insight into themselves and the world around them. Trips are challenging, noncompetitive, and adventurous and incorporate an experiential education approach. Participation, cooperation, and leadership help the entire group grow and achieve. One of the key ingredients in BROADREACH's ability to offer the highest caliber summer experience is the small group size. Limiting the group size to 10 to 14 participants encourages strong friendships and esprit de corps in an atmosphere of teamwork, support, and accomplishment. The small group permits individual attention, preserves the sense of discovery, and allows the BROADREACH staff to cater to the specific dynamics of each group.

PROGRAM OFFERINGS

Australia Discover the "World Down Under!" On this action-packed adventure, participants scuba dive the spectacular Great Barrier Reef and explore Australia's diverse terrain—beautiful beaches, lush rain forest, thrilling white water, and the Outback.

Costa Rica Experience This trip is for those with a spirit for adventure travel. Costa Rica is an ecological treasure chest and an explorer's dream. From lush rain forests to fantastic white-water rivers descending volcanic peaks to pristine tropical waters, Broadreachers experience the ultimate adventure by backpacking, rafting, horseback riding, surfing, and sea kayaking in this wilderness wonderland.

Baja Extreme Participants experience amazing diving, countless opportunities for adventure, and a festive culture on this journey to the Sea of Cortez. They swim and dive alongside sea lions, huge schools of jacks, and giant manta rays with 15-foot wingspans. Participants see pods of pilot whales and dolphins as they sea kayak along rugged coastline. Scuba training, surfing, beach camping, hiking, and cultural exploration round out this incredible expedition.

Academic Treks (Caribbean, Costa Rica, Ecuador, Belize, Mexico, British Columbia) BROADREACH's academic adventures combine experiential learning, service learning, and traditional classroom learning with wilderness adventure, international travel, and cultural exchange to create extraordinary expeditions. Programs focus on marine science, language learning, or environmental studies.

The Galapagos and Amazon Encounter (Ecuador) On this extraordinary wilderness and naturalist expedition, participants trek the snowcapped Andes Mountains and raft, hike, and canoe through the mysterious Amazon jungle. Then they travel to Darwin's Galapagos to explore the world's most unique ecosystem and discover an abundance of biodiversity both above and below the waterline. This trip is offered both with and without scuba diving.

Fiji Solomon Quest Participants on this quest to the South Pacific encounter the magnificent scuba diving, beautiful islands, lush rain forests, rich history, and unique cultures of Fiji and the Solomon Islands.

Red Sea (Sinai Peninsula, Egypt) Looking for the ultimate in underwater adventure? The Red Sea is hypnotic. What Jacques Cousteau rated as the best diving in the world is the heart of this trip—a spectacular odyssey combining scuba training, cultural immersion, and a desert camel safari.

Adventures in Scuba and Sailing/Underwater Discoveries, Adventures Underwater–Advanced Scuba (St. Martin, St. Barts, Saba, Nevis, and Statia), and **Adventures in the Grenadines–Advanced Scuba** (St. Lucia, St. Vincent, and the Grenadines) are extraordinary dive-training and sail-training adventures in the Caribbean. Participants live aboard and crew fully equipped yachts while working toward multiple scuba and sailing certifications. **Arc of the Caribbean** is an intensive thirty-one-day sail-training voyage from St. Martin to the coast of South America. Those interested in learning more about these trips to the Caribbean should see the **BROADREACH Caribbean Scuba Diving, Sailing, and Marine Biology Adventures** in-depth description in this edition of *Peterson's Summer Opportunities for Kids and Teenagers.*

ENROLLMENT

The limited group size of 10 to 14 participants allows Broadreachers to do more, see more, and have more fun. Small groups promote a sense of adventure and discovery that is unattainable when traveling in a larger group. The flexibility created permits the BROADREACH staff members to cater the program to the dynamics and goals of each group and to work with the students as a team to create the experience.

DAILY SCHEDULE

Days are energizing, challenging, and fun, with participants fully involved in all aspects of the trip. There are goals for each day, but the schedule is flexible, and the group decides how the adventure will unfold.

FACILITIES

Depending on the program, participants may stay in youth hostels, tents, and open-air dorms and/or on yachts or marine research vessels. BROADREACH is a fully accredited PADI International Five Star Gold Palm Facility.

STAFF

BROADREACH staff members are as diverse as its programs. Program leaders include experiential education professionals, PADI professional scuba instructors, marine biologists, Coast Guard–licensed sailing masters, teachers, and graduate students. At various points in the programs, marine scientists, naturalists, and native culturalists join the group to enhance the educational experience.

COSTS

Tuition is between $3600 and $5400, depending on the program and the duration of the trip. Tuition is all-inclusive except for airfare. Sibling discounts are available.

For more information, contact:

BROADREACH
P.O. Box 27076
Raleigh, North Carolina 27611
919-833-1907
888-833-1907 (toll-free)
E-mail: info@gobroadreach.com
World Wide Web: http://www.gobroadreach.com

PARTICIPANT/FAMILY COMMENTS

"I learned more, did more, and had more fun than on any other summer program I've done. I made best friends, saw new places, and learned more about myself ... Having only ten people in the group was the best. I took more responsibility and gained confidence."

"An outstanding experience! The teaching was of the highest caliber and beyond our expectations. My daughter's adventure was unforgettable ... Enriching ... Broadreaching. You live up to your name."

BUCK'S ROCK PERFORMING AND CREATIVE ARTS CAMP

SUMMER CAMP

NEW MILFORD, CONNECTICUT

Type of Program: Creative and performing arts
Participants: Coeducational, ages 11–16
Enrollment: 350–400
Program Dates: June 30 to August 21, 2004
Heads of Program: Mickey and Laura Morris

LOCATION

Situated on 125 acres of deeply wooded forest, only 85 miles from New York City (1½ hours by car), Buck's Rock is located in the heart of many cultural facilities.

BACKGROUND AND PHILOSOPHY

The challenge to create, to strive, and to know the triumph of achievement: this is the challenge that Buck's Rock offers teens. Buck's Rock provides campers with the freedom of choice—the ability to choose their own activities and spend as much time at them as they need. Campers are thus able to commit themselves wholeheartedly to their chosen activities, gaining self-confidence and, in the process, develop a better sense of purpose and direction.

Buck's Rock was founded in 1942 by Ernst and Ilse Bulova, European educators who studied under Maria Montessori. Dr. and Mrs. Bulova left Nazi Germany for England and then came to the United States. They chose a camp setting to apply their convictions about how young people learn. At a time when camps were highly regimented, their approach was daring. In its early years, Buck's Rock emphasized farming, crafts, music, and drama. Gradually, fine arts and additional crafts were introduced, and studios and workshops were built to house them. The performing arts—music, drama, dance, clowning, and improvisation—flourished, as did programs in science, technology, sports, and creative and journalistic writing.

PROGRAM OFFERINGS

Buck's Rock is especially proud of its performing arts program. The Theater Department produces eight to twelve fully mounted plays each summer at one of many stages. Campers may choose to participate not only as actors, but also as stage lighting, sound system, costume, and set design crew members. At the Actor's Studio, daily classes in improvisation, movement, scene study, and characterization are also offered. Clowning workshops include improvisation, pantomime, slapstick, and juggling. The Music Shed houses an orchestra, chorus, a cappella chorus, jazz band, and chamber ensembles. Private lessons are available for most instruments. A full guitar program, folk music, rock bands, and a madrigal group are also part of camp life. Buck's Rock's own recording studio has state-of-the-art professional recording and mixing equipment, a full music-sequencing keyboard workstation, a digital keyboard and drum kit, a sound booth, a band room, and a vocal/drum room. Dance classes are provided at all levels in modern, jazz, tap, ballet, hip-hop, and swing.

The high level of instruction in studio arts includes painting and drawing using various techniques and paints; printmaking, in which students may create posters, cards, hand-printed fabrics for clothing, quilts, or three-dimensional pieces using silkscreen, intaglio, monotype, etching, linoleum, and woodcuts; and sculpture, in which campers use plaster, wood, steel, aluminum, and various combinations of these materials, in addition to casting in bronze. Campers interested in photography are encouraged to explore Buck's Rock's beautiful surroundings using a 35-mm format and are taught developing and printing techniques; studio photography and photojournalism workshops are also available. Other fine arts include woodworking, ceramics, metalsmithing, and glass: blowing, casting, beading, fusion, and slumping. The fiber arts feature batik, sewing, weaving and bargello, and a book arts and papermaking studio, where campers may also use letter presses to make stationery, business cards, announcements, and notepads.

Superb opportunities in communications are offered. The publications shop produces newspapers, literary art magazines, a yearbook, programs for productions, and many other items using word processors, commercial art facilities, offset presses, and digital photography. Creative writing groups, journalism workshops, and poetry and short story seminars meet regularly to produce materials for publication. Campers work on the layout, design, graphics, and art for all projects. WBBC, the camp's radio voice, broadcasts news, reviews, talk shows, radio plays, forums, documentaries, and music seven days a week on its own FM frequency; campers are announcers, performers, DJs, script writers, commentators, and panelists. The digital video program is used as a teaching device, as a recorder of special programs and events, and as an opportunity for creative endeavors in acting and cinematography.

The computer program provides instruction in using IBM and Mac equipment. Campers may work on a variety of projects, including the design and implementation of personal programs, HTML, graphics, animation, and games.

Campers may also enjoy working on the vegetable and animal farms. The animal farm offers an alternative experience to many of the other shops. Campers may choose to adopt an animal, which then becomes their responsibility and playmate during their stay. Opportunities are available to milk a goat, bottle feed a calf, and learn much about basic biology and animal care. The vegetable farm is a well-organized farm project. The ground is plowed and harrowed, and campers are taught how to hoe, weed, and harvest the produce.

Augmenting these excellent programs is a noncompetitive yet comprehensive sports program in which fun and recreation are emphasized. Sports include tennis, fencing, martial arts, basketball, swimming, softball, archery, horseback riding, volleyball, pioneering, and spelunking.

ENROLLMENT

Many talented children attend camp each summer, but talent is not a prerequisite, since it is at Buck's Rock that many first discover their talents and potential.

DAILY SCHEDULE

7:30	Wake-up (8:30 on Sundays)
8	Breakfast (9 on Sundays)
9	Open shop time, morning activities begin
12	Lunch
2	Open shop time, afternoon activities begin
6	Dinner
After dinner	Team sports/early evening activities
7:30	Shops and studios reopen on an alternating schedule
8:30	Evening activities
10:30	Bedtime (lights-out 20–30 minutes later)

EXTRA OPPORTUNITIES AND ACTIVITIES

Evenings are for relaxation, recreation, and entertainment. Campers may engage in team sports, and a choice of activities is offered. Each evening includes a featured activity, and a movie is shown outdoors on the lawn every week.

Buck's Rock holds many seminars throughout the summer, visiting artists lecture and demonstrate their own methods, and trips are taken to nearby museums and galleries. Because the camp believes that an appreciation of the performing arts enriches the lives of young people, trips are made to the Shakespeare Theater, the Berkshire Music Festival at Tanglewood, the Caramoor Festival, and Jacob's Pillow. Concerts by professional musicians are also performed during the summer.

The main event of the summer is Buck's Rock's Festival, when parents, friends, alumni, and neighbors are invited to see what campers have accomplished. Displays of fine arts and crafts, demonstrations in the shops, a parade of farm animals, a fencing exhibition, a fashion show, and performances by the orchestra, chorus, jazz band, Actor's Studio, clowns, and dancers are enjoyed by all.

Campers who have reached the age of 15½ are eligible to apply for the Counselor-in-Training (CIT) program, in which they serve an apprentice internship in a specialty area of their choice.

FACILITIES

Dormitory rooms, most occupied by 4 campers, are well planned, practical, and comfortable. Each dormitory and annex contains bathrooms with running hot and cold water and showers. Bathroom facilities are cleaned daily by the housekeeping staff; campers are responsible for cleaning their own living areas.

Many large buildings house workshops and studios. Buck's Rock's Summer Theater compares favorably with professional theaters in both size and equipment; the music shed and dance studio permit camper concerts, and the recreation hall provides ample room for an actor's studio. The dining hall includes a thoroughly modern kitchen, a bakery, and a large dining room, where meals are served buffet-style. The camp also has a fully stocked canteen, which is open daily.

STAFF

The camper-staff ratio is 2:1, ensuring individualized attention in every area of interest. The large number of staff members who return to the program year after year ensures the stability and continuity of camp programs. Staff members are all college trained and are either teachers in leading schools or universities or talented young artists. All are selected based on their proven abilities in working successfully with teens.

Each living area is supervised by guidance counselors who live and work with campers, providing leadership, stimulating initiative, and encouraging participation in camp activities.

MEDICAL CARE

Every effort is made to protect the health and safety of campers. Buck's Rock is equipped with an infirmary/dispensary. Medical care is supervised by the camp physicians. Three nurses and a nurse's aide are in residence throughout the summer.

COSTS

For 2004, tuition is $7340 for the full season and $5240 for the half season. Fees include laundry, short trips, and most shop materials. Fees do not include optional items such as horseback riding, the canteen, long trips, and some shop materials. CITs receive a $500 reduction in tuition for the full season.

TRANSPORTATION

Campers arriving at New York City airports and local bus and rail terminals can be met and picked up by Buck's Rock staff members.

APPLICATION TIMETABLE

Initial inquiry is welcome year-round. An open house is held in the spring. Tours are available during the summer. There is no application deadline or fee, space permitting.

For more information, contact:

Mickey and Laura Morris, Directors
Buck's Rock Camp
59 Buck's Rock Road
New Milford, Connecticut 06776
860-354-5030
Fax: 860-354-1355
E-mail: bucksrock@mindspring.com
World Wide Web: http://bucksrockcamp.com

BUSCH GARDENS ADVENTURE CAMP

SEAWORLD/BUSCHGARDENS ADVENTURE CAMPS

BUSCH GARDENS ADVENTURE CAMP

TAMPA BAY, FLORIDA

Type of Program: Resident camps
Participants: Coeducational, grades 4 through adult
Enrollment: Varies with the program
Program Dates: Summer (select dates throughout spring and fall)
Heads of Program: Hollis Gillespie, Director of Education; Rebecca Amy, Camp Manager; Linda Burdick, Camp Director

LOCATION

Set amid one of the country's most beautiful zoological parks, this camp is located in Tampa, Florida. The adventure park is known for its innovative approach to habitat design, groundbreaking veterinary techniques, participation in species survival programs, and award-winning educational programs.

BACKGROUND AND PHILOSOPHY

Playing host to more than 35,000 youth from across the U.S. and around the word, SeaWorld/Busch Gardens Adventure Camps provide up-close, behind-the-scenes, hands-on experiences with amazing animals, including many that are threatened or endangered. Alongside veterinarians, trainers, and other animal-care experts, campers have the opportunity to feed, interact with, and care for animals ranging from dolphins and manatees to giraffes and great apes. But it is not all about animals—it is about having fun, exploring the great outdoors, enjoying the world-class roller coasters and spectatular shows of the park, and making lifelong friends and memories. For campers of all ages, it is about putting their passion for wildlife to work and learning how they can make the world a better place.

PROGRAM OFFERINGS

Young Explorers (Grades 4–5) Young Adventure Campers discover new possibilities and make new friends as they journey through Busch Gardens' 335-acre park in this five-day program. Campers visit a variety of fascinating wild animals, explore their habitats, and meet some very special animal ambassadors face to face.

Zooventures (Grades 6–8) Campers should be ready to be up to their elbows in animals, with a celebrity sloth, gigantic gorillas, and rare reptiles. Campers focus on different animal areas and interactions each day and make some new best friends—of both the two- and four-legged kind in this six-day program. In addition, participants visit Busch Gardens' Adventure Island water park and SeaWorld Orlando.
Animal Adventures (Grades 9–12) Participants can not get any closer to animals than this. They work alongside professional zookeepers while caring for some of the world's most exotic and endangered animals. Campers go behind the scenes and observe animal-care sessions, carry out behavioral studies, and experience up-close encounters of the wild kind. Participants also experience Adventure Island and Busch Gardens' world-class rides. Seven-day and ten-day sessions are available. Returning campers enroll in the Advanced Animal Adventures.
Advanced Animal Adventures (Grades 10–12; returning Animal Adventure and Zoo Careers campers) This program builds on the Animal Adventures camp. Two extended sessions are available, including a trip to SeaWorld Orlando.
Zoo Careers (Grades 11–college; returning Advanced Animal Adventurers and Advanced Zoo Careers campers) Campers dreaming of

working in an animal-care field pick their area of focus, dig in, and hold on, because this seven-day camp crosses over into the exciting world of zoological career exploration. They experience the daily life of a zookeeper in a world-class zoological facility in an intense, hands-on experience in animal behavior, zoo nutrition, animal health, and wildlife conservation. Participants explore Discovery Cove at Busch SeaWorld in Orlando on a field trip.

Combo (Grades 6–12) Campers can double their fun by combining two Adventure Camp programs. For grades 6–8, the two programs are Summer Splash at SeaWorld Orlando and Busch Gardens Tampa Bay Zooventures; for grades 10–12, Animal Adventures or Advanced Animal Adventures at Tampa Bay and a program at SeaWorld Orlando; and for grades 11–12, Advanced Animal Adventures or Zoo Careers at Tampa Bay and a program at SeaWorld Orlando. Combo camp fees include transportation between the two parks.

Family Fun Family campers (parents and children ages 8 and older) meet the Busch Gardens family in this three-day program. Participants go behind the scenes with some of the animals that call Busch Gardens home. The family enjoys up-close animal encounters, animal habitats, live shows, rides, and attractions, while making memories to last a lifetime.

Animal Quest (Grades 4–8) Participants learn about the fascinating animals and the habitats they call home in this four-day group program. One day includes the Serengeti Safari truck tour. Campers voyage through Busch Gardens and Adventure Island (in season), learning more about the animals and experiencing exciting rides and spectacular shows.

Zany Zoo Days (Grades 3–12) Participants take a break at the zoo. Whether it is winter break, spring break, or teacher workdays, Busch Gardens has an adventure waiting. During this two-day group camp, participants have an in-depth look at the zoo, meet exotic animals, and have fun.

Zoo Journeys (Grades 3–12) Students join the Adventure Camp for three days of behind-the-scenes zoo excursions, up-close animal encounters, wild rides, and more. This camp includes environmental and wildlife conservation curriculum that adheres to National Science Education Standards and is designed for school groups.

Eco-Educators Educators who are wild about exotic animals and their habitats can work alongside professional zookeepers and meet endangered species face to face. Participants network with educators from around the country while examining interdisciplinary teaching guides and benchmarked environmental curriculum. There is even time left over to enjoy world-class shows and a few of the Southeast's most spectacular roller coasters. Three- and five-day sessions are available.

FACILITIES

Campers stay in Busch Gardens' Mzinga Lodge. This modern facility, located on the property, includes a multipurpose room and a classroom. For certain sessions, campers spend a night in an animal attraction. During field study camps, campers stay in approved dorms, hotels, or motels.

STAFF

The camp staff includes Busch Gardens education instructors and experienced summer intern counselors with CPR, water safety, and first-aid training. Counselors undergo in-depth interviews to assess their skills in communication, organization, behavior management, and safety. They are also background-checked and drug-tested. All camp, staff, and counselor-camper ratios exceed American Camping Association accreditation requirements.

MEDICAL CARE

There is a Health Services Team on site, and each counselor is trained in first aid and CPR. Transportation is provided to the nearest hospital, if necessary.

COSTS

Fees for 2004–05 were Young Explorers, $675; Zooventures, $800; Animal Adventures, $900/$1200; Advanced Animal Adventures, $900; Zoo Careers, $1050; Combo, $1675–$1900; Family Fun, $600 for 1 adult and 1 child; Animal Quest, $480; Zany Zoo Days, $190; Zoo Journeys, $320; and Eco-Educators, $500. Camp fees include transportation between Busch Gardens Tampa Bay and the airport, field trips, lodging, meals and snacks, equipment and materials, camp t-shirt, water bottle, and transportation between camps (Combo Camp).

Southwest Airlines offers Adventure Campers a 10 percent discount. Details about the discount are on the Web site.

APPLICATION TIMETABLE

All registrations must be accompanied by a nonrefundable deposit. Space is limited and registration before February is recommended. Students should visit the Web site to learn more about program options and to download a registration packet.

For more information, contact:

Education Department
Resident Camp
P.O. Box 9157
Tampa Bay, Florida 33674-9157
877-BGT-CAMP (toll-free)
813-987-5252 (international visitors)
Fax: 813-987-5878
E-mail: education@buschgardens.org
World Wide Web: http://www.swbg-adventurecamps.org

BUSCH GARDENS ADVENTURE CAMP

SEAWORLD/BUSCHGARDENS ADVENTURE CAMPS

SEAWORLD ADVENTURE CAMP

SAN ANTONIO, TEXAS

Type of Program: Resident camps
Participants: Coeducational, grades 4 through adult
Enrollment: Varies with the program
Program Dates: Summer (select dates throughout spring and fall)
Heads of Program: Ann Quinn, Director of Education; Chris David Lambert, Camp Manager

LOCATION

Set amid one of the country's most beautiful marine life parks, this camp is located in the Texas Hill Country in San Antonio, Texas.

BACKGROUND AND PHILOSOPHY

Playing host to more than 35,000 youth from across the U.S. and around the word, SeaWorld/Busch Gardens Adventure Camps provide up-close, behind-the-scenes, hands-on experiences with amazing animals, including many that are threatened or endangered. Alongside veterinarians, trainers, and other animal-care experts, campers have the opportunity to feed, interact with, and care for animals ranging from dolphins and manatees to giraffes and great apes. But it is not all about animals—it is about having fun, exploring the great outdoors, enjoying the world-class roller coasters and spectatular shows of the park, and making lifelong friends and memories. For campers of all ages, it is about putting their passion for wildlife to work and learning how they can make the world a better place.

PROGRAM OFFERINGS

Junior Expedition (Grades 4–5) and Expedition Camp (Grades 6–8) Campers discover the magic and beauty of killer whales, penguins, sharks, and more through the awesome camp activities and behind-the-scenes action of this seven-day program. Campers travel to the Texas Gulf Coast to explore wetlands, beaches, and native coastal animals. And it would not be a SeaWorld adventure without SeaWorld's entertaining shows and thrilling roller coasters.
Eco-OdysSea Camp (Grades 7–9) In this eleven-day program, campers explore the depths of marine sciences. After getting their feet wet at SeaWorld, they depart for an extended voyage to study the diverse ecosystems of Galveston Bay and the Trinity River Delta. Participants discover the intricate balance of history, economy, recreation, and science that influence this region. Upon their return, students who have chosen the extended session experience an introduction to Career Camp by participating in hands-on experiences with the zoological team.

Career Camp (Grades 9–12) For campers dreaming of working closely with animals, this seven-day camp provides a rare opportunity to gain first-hand experience in this field. Participants work side by side with the zoological team, learning to monitor animal health, record behavior, and prepare food for all the SeaWorld animals. Campers discover fascinating facts about the animals and learn from SeaWorld professionals in the fields of veterinary science, animal training, and conservation.
Advanced Career Camp (Grades 10–college) Students explore the depths of zoological careers at SeaWorld. As a SeaWorld apprentice, campers have unforgettable encounters with dolphins, penguins, beluga whales, and sharks. The eligibility requirement for this seven- or eleven-day camp is previous attendance at Career Camp.
Counselor-In-Training (CIT) (Grades 11–12) This program is for campers who are enthusiastic about interacting with children in the SeaWorld camp environment and are willing to assist with all aspects

of camp. As a CIT, campers learn leadership skills, make new friends, and assist younger campers in camp activities. To attend this eleven-day camp, students must have previously attended a resident-camp program at SeaWorld San Antonio.

Marine Zoological Careers Camp (College) College students in this program discover whether a career in animal training, marine mammal care, aviculture, or aquarium sciences is the right choice for them. Practical experiences include exposure to animal care and nutrition, anatomy and physiology, and animal behavior and training. Lectures focus on specific topics related to animal rehabilitation, research, husbandry, laboratory procedures, and veterinary sciences.

Parent/Child Adventure A parent or grandparent brings their child or grandchild for a wild weekend of fun and animal adventure. Together they marvel at the beauty of SeaWorld's magnificent marine animals and the excitement of up-close animal adventures. Participants stay at the SeaWorld dorms and experience all the fun SeaWorld has to offer.

FACILITIES

Campers stay in lodging on the property of SeaWorld San Antonio. Camp facilities include meeting, play, and eating areas and a classroom. During field study camps, campers stay in approved dorms, hotels, or motels.

STAFF

The camp staff includes SeaWorld education instructors and experienced summer intern counselors with CPR, water safety, and first-aid training. Counselors undergo in-depth interviews to assess their skills in communication, organization, behavior management, and safety. They are also background-checked and drug-tested. All camps, staff, and counselor-to-camper ratios exceed American Camping Association accreditation requirements.

MEDICAL CARE

There is a Health Services Team on site, and each counselor is trained in first aid and CPR. Transportation is provided to the nearest hospital, if necessary.

COSTS

Fees for 2004–05 were Junior Expedition and Expedition Camps, $825; Eco-OdysSea Camp, $1225; Career Camp, $800; Advanced Career Camp, $850–$1375; Counselor-In-Training, $1250; Marine Zoological Careers Camp, $850; and Parent/Child Adventure, $600 for 1 adult and 1 child. Camp fees include transportation between SeaWorld San Antonio and the nearest major airport, field trips, lodging, meals and snacks, equipment and materials, camp t-shirt, and water bottle.

APPLICATION TIMETABLE

All registrations must be accompanied by a nonrefundable deposit. Space is limited and registration before February is recommended. Students should visit the Web site to learn more about program options and to download a registration packet.

For more information, contact:

Education Department
Resident Camp
10500 SeaWorld Drive
San Antonio, Texas 78251-3002
800-700-7786 (toll-free)
210-523-3608
Fax: 210-523-3898
E-mail: education@buschgardens.org
World Wide Web: http://www.swbg-adventurecamps.org

CALIFORNIA STATE SUMMER SCHOOL FOR THE ARTS–INNERSPARK

SUMMER PROGRAM

VALENCIA, CALIFORNIA

Type of Program: Arts program
Participants: Coeducational, grades 9–12
Enrollment: More than 520
Program Dates: July 9 through August 6
Head of Program: Robert M. Jaffe, Director

LOCATION

The California State Summer School for the Arts–InnerSpark is held at the California Institute of the Arts (CalArts), a fully accredited degree-granting institution of higher learning for students of the visual, cinematic, and performing arts. Established through the vision and generosity of Walt Disney in 1961, CalArts is located in Valencia, a residential community situated 25 miles north of Hollywood in the Santa Clarita Valley.

BACKGROUND AND PHILOSOPHY

The California State Summer School for the Arts–InnerSpark is a rigorous preprofessional training program in the visual and performing arts, creative writing, animation, and film for talented artists of high school age. InnerSpark provides a supportive environment in which students hone acquired skills and explore new techniques and ideas for an intense and exciting learning experience. The School was created by the California Legislature and held its first session in 1987. Its purpose is to provide a training ground for future artists who wish to pursue careers in the arts and entertainment industries in California. The California State Summer School for the Arts–InnerSpark is a state agency funded through a unique public-private partnership.

PROGRAM OFFERINGS

Students apply for the opportunity to study in one of the School's seven departments. They receive 3 units of California State University elective credit for successful participation.

Animation students explore the theories and techniques of animation in studio workshops conducted by leading artists in the field. Course work in two-dimensional animation, figure drawing, and conceptual issues in art is augmented by visits from guest animators and tours of Hollywood animation studios. Students attend screenings of animations that demonstrate the history and breadth of the art form.

Students in the **Creative Writing** Program receive individualized instruction in poetry, fiction, and scriptwriting. They work with an award-winning faculty in small groups and have opportunities to learn from visiting writers, literary agents, journalists, and poets. Students and faculty members share their work with the School community in weekly open readings and publish an anthology at the end of the session.

InnerSpark's **Dance** Program provides a rigorous course of dance instruction. The curriculum includes intensive training in ballet, modern, and body conditioning mat technique; choreography; dance history; and jazz. Students have the option of taking classes in improvisation and modern repertory or pointe and ballet repertory.

Film and Video students receive instruction and experience in film and video production techniques. They work with Super-8 and 16-mm film and a variety of video media to create short works individually and in collaboration with other students. They attend film screenings, meet filmmakers and producers, and go on field trips to film studios and locations of interest in the Los Angeles area.

InnerSpark's **Music** Program for vocalists, instrumentalists, and composers is designed to develop each student's creativity, fundamental musicianship, and understanding of contemporary musical history and styles. Courses include musicianship and theory, twentieth-century musical styles, improvisation, world music, composition, electro-acoustic computer music, piano, and voice. Students receive private lessons and participate in student ensembles. The School presents leading professionals in concerts and master classes.

The **Theatre** Program is an intensive acting course that emphasizes the development of physical and vocal awareness and control as essential elements of the actor's craft. Classes are held in tai chi chu'an, acting, movement, voice, story, stage combat, physical comedy, stage acrobatics, and musical theater. There are special forums, workshops, and guest lecturers. Students perform works-in-progress throughout the summer.

InnerSpark's **Visual Arts** Program offers studio classes in figure drawing, design, painting, computer graphics, printmaking, sculpture, ceramics, and photography. Lectures on topics of importance to visual artists are given by guest artists and others. Workshops are conducted by visiting artists, and students go on field trips to local museums and galleries.

ENROLLMENT

California residents enrolled in grades 9 through 12 may attend InnerSpark. Students from outside of California may also apply; a limited number are admitted each year. Participants are selected in the spring on the basis of their talent and creativity as demonstrated through assignments and teacher

recommendations. InnerSpark's student body is representative of the ethnic and socioeconomic diversity of the state. The admissions process is highly competitive; in 2002 approximately 1 in 3 applicants were accepted. Students invited to the School are named California Arts Scholars and receive the California Arts Scholar Medallion in local ceremonies.

DAILY SCHEDULE

On Monday through Saturday, breakfast is available in the cafeteria beginning at 7 a.m. Regular classes are held between 8 a.m. and 4 p.m. and generally last about 3½ hours each. One hour is set aside for lunch. Students have opportunities to participate in special interdisciplinary classes and other activities from 4 to 6 p.m. Dinner is served from 5 to 7 p.m. Evenings are devoted to rehearsals, self-paced studio work, film screenings, collaborative projects, concerts, lectures, sports activities, and informal student performances and poetry readings in the student coffeehouse.

EXTRA OPPORTUNITIES AND ACTIVITIES

There is a full schedule of recreational opportunities available on weekdays and Saturdays after classes and all day on Sundays. Optional field trips to California attractions such as Six Flags Magic Mountain, the Los Angeles Music Center, and the Getty Museum are offered on Sundays at cost.

FACILITIES

The main building on the 60-acre campus is a five-level multiwinged structure of 500,000 square feet that houses art and electronic music studios, classrooms, dance spaces, rehearsal rooms, theaters, galleries, film editing laboratories, sound and video stages, animation studios, libraries, the bookstore, and the cafeteria. All students reside in Chouinard Hall, the student dormitory. Tennis courts and a large swimming pool are located adjacent to the facility. Spacious lawns with shade trees, open fields, and large hillside areas provide room for sports and relaxation.

STAFF

InnerSpark faculty members are accomplished practicing professional artists, musicians, writers, dancers, actors, and filmmakers. Many are distinguished college and university instructors. The teacher-student ratio is roughly 1:9. The School employs a registered nurse and assistants, a licensed counselor, and a recreation director. The CalArts Residential Life staff, supervised by an experienced professional director, includes 16 graduate student resident assistants. CalArts security personnel are on campus at all times.

MEDICAL CARE

A registered nurse is on duty Monday through Friday from 8:30 a.m. to 4:30 p.m. and on Saturdays and Sundays from 11 a.m. to 3:30 p.m. Emergency and after-hours care and medical referrals are available through Santa Clarita Valley Quality Care (medical walk-in center), Kaiser-Permanente (HMO), and the Henry Mayo Newhall Memorial Hospital, all of which are located within 4 miles of the campus.

RELIGIOUS LIFE

InnerSpark is a nonsectarian institution. Students with parental permission and prearranged transportation may leave campus to attend religious services.

COSTS

The comprehensive fee covering room, board, and tuition for California residents is $2185; for out-of-state attendees it is $3800. Students must pay a $45 credit registration fee if they wish to receive California State University credit. Animation, Film and Video, and Visual Arts students pay additional materials fees of $120. The nonrefundable application fee is $20. A small amount of pocket money for laundry, postage, and souvenirs is recommended. Optional Sunday field trips are offered at cost. A nonrefundable deposit of 30 percent of the comprehensive fee is required upon acceptance. Payment plans are available.

FINANCIAL AID

InnerSpark provides financial aid for applicants based on demonstrated need. Nearly half of the students who have attended InnerSpark have had from 20 percent to 90 percent of their tuition paid by the California State Summer School for the Arts (CSSS) Foundation. A financial aid request form is included in the InnerSpark application flyer. A request for financial aid does not affect a student's chances of being accepted. Financial aid is available only to California residents.

TRANSPORTATION

The Hollywood/Burbank airport is located 20 miles south of CalArts and is served by major domestic airlines. InnerSpark provides transportation to and from this airport on the first and last day with prior reservation. Those who come by car should take Interstate 5 to the McBean Parkway exit and head east. The campus entrance is on the immediate right.

APPLICATION TIMETABLE

Inquiries are welcome throughout the year. The application postmark deadline is February 28, 2005. Letters of acceptance are sent out by the first week in May. The application assignments require careful preparation, so interested students should request the application forms as early as possible.

For more information, contact:

California State Summer School for the Arts–InnerSpark
916-227-9320
Fax: 916-227-9455
E-mail: cynthia@csssa.org
World Wide Web: http://www.csssa.org/

CAMBRIDGE COLLEGE PROGRAMME

PRECOLLEGE SUMMER PROGRAMME AT UNIVERSITY OF CAMBRIDGE, ENGLAND

CAMBRIDGE, ENGLAND

Type of Program: Precollege academic and cultural enrichment
Participants: Coeducational, high school ages
Enrollment: Limited
Program Dates: Three-week session during July and August; optional one-week Paris trip afterward
Head of Program: Ms. Taryn Edwards, Director

LOCATION

The University of Cambridge is made up of more than thirty colleges located in the city centre and its environs. The programme is held at several of these colleges. Headquarters is at Queens' College, one of the most beautiful of all the colleges, which is located on the banks of the River Cam in the historic centre of Cambridge.

BACKGROUND AND PHILOSOPHY

This Programme is the oldest established teen program at Cambridge. It is the *only* program at either Oxford or Cambridge where students are lectured *only* by faculty members associated with the University of Cambridge. Founded in 1986, the Programme provides a stimulating and rigorous course of study for qualified and well-motivated students. It stresses the needs of the individual student and provides an opportunity to explore subjects on the skill-building level where no prerequisites are required.

Faculty members guide students to master skills, to acquire knowledge, and to think critically, creatively, and independently. The Programme's structure fosters close association between staff and students for personal, social, and intellectual development.

The director and staff live at the colleges with the students to supervise and ensure their safety and well-being. Academics are enriched with both field trips and day trips to historic sites, plus trips to London, Bath, Stratford-upon-Avon, and Stonehenge. Cultural enrichment is achieved through visits to London museums, a workshop for Shakespeare and Drama classes at Shakespeare's Globe Theatre in London, and theatre performances in the West End.

PROGRAM OFFERINGS

The programme offers a choice of academic study in courses. Last year they included History of Chemistry, Criminal Law, English Literary Villains, Veterinary Medicine, Philosophy of Mind, The British Monarchy, History of Calculus, Tibetan Buddhism, Jane Austen, Marine Biology, Special Relativity, Superstrings, A Hitchhiker's Guide to 20th-Century Physics, Comparative Law, Psychology of War, Sociology, International Relations and Terrorism, Astrophysics, British Intelligence and the Art of Espionage, War and Chivalry, Biomedical Ethics, Photography, Scriptwriting, Moot Court, Archaeology, Philosophy, Shakespeare, *Hamlet,* Cambridge Scientific Discoveries, Studio Art, Saxons, Saints and Scholars, Psychology, Creative Writing, Debate, History of Art, Latin, Quantum Physics, Major World Religions, DNA Fingerprinting, Evolutionary Biology, Economics,

Alfred Hitchcock, Journalism, Psychology and Law, World War II, Egyptology, Drama, Architecture and History, and Political Theory. In addition, there are daily group lectures and field trips on British cultural history. Supplemental lectures by distinguished professors enrich the curriculum on a variety of subjects, such as Roman Britain, the mysteries of Stonehenge, and much more. The large variety of evening activities includes tennis, punting, rowing, volleyball, croquet, basketball, lacrosse, squash, soccer, rugby, cricket, aerobics, swimming, field hockey, golf, running, chess, movies, salsa dancing, concerts, choir, plays on the College lawns, polo, fencing, ice skating, a James Bond party, and barbeques.

Most students participate in the programme to broaden their knowledge and strengthen their skills rather than to gain academic credits. Each student receives an evaluation of performance for classwork, including detailed comments by their instructor, a syllabus of each course, and a certificate of attendance. Many students include these in their applications to colleges and universities, and many high schools and colleges give credit to students on the basis of these reports.

ENROLLMENT

One of the most pleasant and beneficial experiences of the Cambridge College Programme is living and working with other students who represent diverse geographic locations, religions, races, and economic circumstances.

DAILY SCHEDULE

The day begins with a self-service breakfast, followed by the first course, freely elected, which meets from 9 to 10:30 a.m. Field trips are scheduled in conjunction with the lectures. The second course, British Cultural History, meets from 11 to 12:30 p.m. and is structured for the whole group, with lectures and field trips planned to enrich students' knowledge of England. The afternoon course, also elected, meets from 2 to 3:30 and is followed by free time for exploring Cambridge or studying. Or students may use this time to rehearse for a play, orchestra, or choir, or take golf lessons or an SAT Review. Dinner is taken between 4:30 and 7:15

p.m., with 2 hours reserved afterward for the evening activities described above. Study hours are from 9 to 11 p.m.

EXTRA OPPORTUNITIES AND ACTIVITIES

Excursions are supervised by the director and staff members. Four trips are taken to London for museums, sightseeing, shopping, and two plays, such as *The Lion King* or *My Fair Lady,* in the West End. Sites visited in London include the British Museum, the Tower of London, the National Gallery and Portrait Gallery, the new Tate Modern, Churchill's War Rooms, Covent Garden, and Harrod's. Sites viewed on day trips are Big Ben, the Houses of Parliament, Trafalgar Square, St. Paul's Cathedral, Hyde Park, Buckingham Palace, Westminister Abbey, and 10 Downing Street. Day trips are to Warwick Castle, Stonehenge, Bath, Ely Cathedral, and Stratford-upon-Avon for a Royal Shakespeare Company play such as *Richard III.*

Though the daily schedule is a full one, there is ample free time to walk into town for lunch, relax with friends, play tennis, or punt on the River Cam. Cambridge is one of the most beautiful cities in England. Its college quadrangles of ancient stone buildings along the river surround gardens of trees, flowers, and manicured lawns. The city has an active cultural life during the summer, including concerts, plays, and special events during the Cambridge Festival, the annual historic fair, and the annual Shakespeare Festival. Museums, theatres, and shops are within a short walk of the colleges.

All students have the option to participate in sports, which are scheduled in the early evening. The programme aims to provide practical experience in traditional British sports. Each year an exhibition and opportunity to play real tennis are offered, and the programme also offers daily supervised use of the weight and fitness gym at Queens' College.

There is an optional 10-hour workshop to coach students in how to mentally prepare for the PSAT/SAT exams, how to approach each section, and how to manage time during the test. Practice tests are taken, timed, and results discussed.

There is also an optional one-week trip to Paris with the director and staff after the regular program, for a cultural feast of French history. This includes visits to the Eiffel Tower, the Louvre, the Arc de Triomphe, the Tuileries Garden, the Sacré Coeur, Notre Dame, Versailles, Claude Monet's home, Vincent Van Gogh's village, Rodin's studio, a boat tour on the Seine, shopping, and more.

FACILITIES

Students have a private room in a college dormitory with daily maid service. The sexes are segregated, and all supervision and curfew enforcement is undertaken by the live-in director and staff.

STAFF

The founder and director, Ms. Taryn Edwards, is Fmr. Honorary Senior Member of Staff at a college of the university, and a member of the College Board of Appeals. She has served on the Board of Trustees at the Putney School of Vermont and on the Board of Directors at the Chicago Academy. Ms. Edwards and staff are present throughout the programme.

The faculty members are British lecturers and educators distinguished in their fields. The motivating faculty members care about their students and are available to them both in and out of class, creating an atmosphere in which learning is a positive experience.

MEDICAL CARE

Addenbrooke's Hospital is available for emergencies on a 24-hour basis. Students are accompanied to these facilities by the director or a member of the staff.

RELIGIOUS LIFE

The Programme is nondenominational, but schedules of church and synagogue services are made available.

COSTS

The 2003 resident-student charge, which included a private room in a college dormitory, breakfast and dinners while on campus (vegetarian meals available), theatre, excursions, scheduled transportation to and from London airports, entrance fees, linen, and daily maid service, was $5295. This fee excluded airfare, lunches, any dinners off campus, and tickets for some optional evening activities. A fee of $595 was required with each application. Optional costs: golf lessons, $250; Cambridge SAT Review fee, $450; Paris trip, $1700. The latter included all fees and excursions, room and breakfast, and transportation to Paris and to the airport for departure. It did not include lunch, dinner, or airfare home. Enrollment was limited to 75 students and the fee must have been paid in full immediately upon acceptance. Students can write or call the programme for a brochure that reflects 2004 costs.

TRANSPORTATION

The director organizes a group for departure with her from Chicago to London. All students departing from other cities will be met by staff and private coaches at both London's Heathrow and Gatwick Airports.

APPLICATION TIMETABLE

Enrollment is limited, and there is a rolling admission policy.

For more information, contact:

Ms. Taryn Edwards, Director
Cambridge College Programme, U.S. Office
175 East Delaware Place, Suite 5518
Chicago, Illinois 60611
312-787-7477
800-922-3552 (toll-free)
Fax: 312-988-7268

CAMP BALLIBAY

SUMMER CAMP

CAMPTOWN, PENNSYLVANIA

Type of Program: Fine and performing arts summer camp with an individual choice, noncompetitive program
Participants: Coeducational, ages 6–16
Enrollment: Regular sessions, 150; Theatre Workshop, 50 or more
Program Dates: Seven weeks, June 27 to August 14; five weeks (three weeks plus two-week Theatre Workshop), July 25 to August 28; four weeks, June 27 to July 24; three weeks, July 25 to August 14; two-week Theatre Workshop, August 15 to August 28
Heads of Program: Gerard, Dorothy, and John J. Jannone, Owners/Directors

LOCATION

Camp Ballibay is located in Camptown, in the "Endless Mountains" of northeastern Pennsylvania. Ballibay is about 40 miles northwest of Scranton, Pennsylvania, on Route 6 (which parallels the Susquehanna River). By car, camp is 3 hours from the Tappan Zee Bridge, the George Washington Bridge, and Philadelphia. Ballibay is 2½ hours from Harrisburg and a little more than 5 hours from Baltimore and Washington, D.C. Camptown is the place where Stephen Foster wrote the famous song "Camptown Races."

BACKGROUND AND PHILOSOPHY

Camp Ballibay was established in 1964 by its current owners, Gerard and Dorothy Jannone. The Jannones left teaching in New Jersey in 1967 to operate the camp full time. Their son, John J. A. Jannone, currently Assistant Professor of Radio and TV at Brooklyn College, has become a partner in the operation of the camp.

Camp Ballibay's philosophy centers on love for, and excitement about, the fine and performing arts. Camp's belief is that "The Arts are for a Lifetime," and, at Ballibay, an environment that fosters a lasting interest in art, theater, music, and dance is created. Programs are creative and noncompetitive and always emphasize "the journey, not the product." The well-rounded camp program embraces the philosophy that individual choice and a low-key, noncompetitive approach will yield genuine participation and learning among campers. Campers must participate during activity times, but they may focus their activities according to their interests.

PROGRAM OFFERINGS

Ballibay offers a unique individual-choice, noncompetitive program focusing on the fine and performing arts and including many traditional camping activities. Major program areas include all aspects of theater, two- and three-dimensional studio art, instrumental and vocal music, ballet/jazz/tap/modern dance, and creative video. Other camping areas include horseback riding (except during the Theatre Workshop), tennis, creative writing, radio, technical theater, photography, swimming, and outdoor camping.

Campers participate in a complete orientation at the beginning of each session, during which they meet all of the staff members and are introduced to all of the programs offered at camp. During this orientation, campers express their interest in one, several, or many areas of camp activity. Campers interested in theater also have the opportunity to audition for plays, readings, and musicals during this time. Through this orientation, every camper develops a personalized, flexible schedule that includes rehearsals for the theatrical productions in which he or she has been cast and lessons and classes in the other areas in which he or she has expressed interest.

Ballibay's theater program offers campers the opportunity to participate in many types of performances and productions, including script-in-hand Readers' Theatre productions, puppet theater, one-act plays, full-length plays and musicals, classic dramatic literature, and large-scale music and dance revues. Ballibay produces more than twenty staged productions each summer. Almost all campers elect some participation in the theater program, and any camper wanting to participate in a production will.

The theater staff also offers numerous classes and workshops in all aspects of theater. Like all camp activity areas, the Ballibay theater program is focused on "the journey"—the process of putting on a theatrical production—rather than on "the product" only. Theater staff members concentrate on creating a strong learning environment during the production process while working intensely with campers to put on a good show, too!

The art program is based around an "open studio" concept, where many campers have one or several projects always in process and come to the studios to work on these projects at their leisure. Instructors are always in the studios to offer guidance and make sure that safe and responsible studio practices are maintained. In addition to the "open studio," many small-group classes are offered, including drawing, painting, pottery, sculpture, mask making, puppet making, and many more.

Ballibay's music program includes individual and group instruction in instrumental music, vocal music, and rock & roll. Instructors teach a full range of styles and techniques, from traditional individual instruction to solo and group improvisation, composition, and songwriting.

Video is Ballibay's newest and fastest-growing major program area. Campers interested in video can explore many areas, including shooting and editing their own music videos, short narratives, "video letters," abstract video, and more. With access to and instruction on digital, VHS, and SVHS camcorders and editing equipment, video effects, computer graphics, audio effects, and more, campers have the materials and assistance they need to create any video they can imagine. Campers also have the opportunity to learn professional camera operation and two-camera documentation skills through the documentation of all of Ballibay's staged theater productions.

DAILY SCHEDULE

7:30	Wake-up, cabin clean-up
8:30	Breakfast, followed by a meeting announcing daily activities
9:30–12:00	Morning activities (individual choice)
12:00	Cabin time
12:30	Lunch, followed by rest period
2:45	Hillside meeting
3:00–5:00	Afternoon activities (individual choice)
5:00	Cabin time
5:30	Supper, followed by free time
7:00–8:15	Evening activities (individual choice)
8:15	Back to cabin to dress for evening activities
8:45	Evening program: talent shows, plays, musicals, readings, bonfires, special game night, or Saturday evening movies

Ballibay's Sunday schedule includes breakfast in bed, cabin clean-up, and a special Sunday smorgasbord.

FACILITIES

Camp Ballibay's spacious, wooded campus is situated on 400 acres in beautiful northeastern Pennsylvania. Campus facilities include thirteen cabins with running water and electricity; a dining hall and camp store; a music building with piano practice rooms and rehearsal space; a video/radio building housing rock & roll rehearsal/recording space, a radio station, and a video studio; art studios with painting and drawing, ceramics, jewelry, printmaking, and photography studios; two 1,600-square-foot indoor dance studios; three main theaters with full costume, lighting, sound, and set facilities; four environmental theater spaces; horseback riding facilities; an overnight camping area; a swimming pool; a sports field; a lake for canoeing, kayaking, and fishing; a summer office; and the directors' year-round home. New dance studios opened in 2002.

STAFF

Ballibay's 43-member staff comprises college juniors and seniors, graduate students, and teachers. Ballibay looks for staff members who are working toward a career in education or are currently teaching. Most staff members are from the United States. A great deal of time is spent recruiting the staff through "face-to-face" interviews and careful attention to references and qualifications. More than half of the staff members are returns or referrals from previous summers.

MEDICAL CARE

An infirmary and a resident medical assistant or nurse are on campus. Matters of any medical relevance are treated by a local physician 5 miles from camp. Memorial Hospital is 7 miles from camp in Towanda, Pennsylvania. Guthrie Clinic, The Robert Packard Hospital (a teaching hospital), is 45 minutes from camp. A camper medical form completed by a physician and including family or camper medical insurance information is required prior to attending camp.

COSTS

Tuition for the 2005 season is as follows: seven weeks, \$5525; four weeks, \$3475; three weeks, \$2675; two-week Theatre Workshop, \$1750; five weeks (three weeks plus Theatre Workshop), \$4250; junior Counselor-in-Training program (age 16), \$5175; and seven-week Counselor-in-Training program (for previous campers only, minimum age 17), \$5075. Extras include camp store purchases (about \$8 per week of stay), transportation to and from airports, and camp-chartered buses (from New York and New Jersey). Camp shirts are available, but no uniform is required.

Families with multiple children attending and campers attending five or more years receive a discount. No financial aid is available.

TRANSPORTATION

Camp-chartered buses are available at the beginning and end of camp to and from New York City and Saddle River, New Jersey. Campers from all over the United States and abroad fly into Wilkes-Barre/Scranton Airport and are met by camp personnel.

APPLICATION TIMETABLE

Ballibay recruits campers year round. Early enrollment discounts are available before November 1 and January 1.

For more information, contact:

Gerard, Dorothy, or John Jannone
Camp Ballibay
Box P, Ballibay Road
Camptown, Pennsylvania 18815-0001
570-746-3223
Fax: 570-746-3691
E-mail: jannone@ballibay.com
World Wide Web: http://www.ballibay.com

CAMP CAYUGA IN THE POCONO MOUNTAINS

SUMMER PROGRAM

HONESDALE, PENNSYLVANIA

Type of Program: Traditional residential private camp
Participants: Coeducational, ages 5–15
Enrollment: 390
Program Dates: Full season: June 27 to August 19; Options: two-, four-, six-, and eight-week sessions available.
Heads of Program: Brian Buynak and family

LOCATION

Camp Cayuga is located on 350 secluded acres in the Pocono Mountains of northeast Pennsylvania, approximately 3 hours from New York City and Philadelphia. Cayuga features two separate campuses on the same estate: Junior Campus (ages 5 to 13) and Teen Campus (ages 13 to 15). The camp occupies hundreds of acres of unspoiled hardwood and evergreen forestland, embellished with expansive fields and a natural stream-fed lake. The high elevation provides low humidity, warm days, and cool evenings.

BACKGROUND AND PHILOSOPHY

Camp Cayuga was founded in 1957 by Arline and Mike Buynak. Continuing the tradition of caring for the needs of each and every camper, Brian, their son, now owns and directs Cayuga.

PROGRAM OFFERINGS

Aquatics Cayuga features two swimming pools and a private natural stream-fed lake. Campers receive American Red Cross instruction by certified instructors in swimming, water ballet, water polo, water basketball, sailing, canoeing, rowboating, windsurfing, kayaking, and fishing. Special activities and events include the rolling log, a 20-foot lake trampoline with slide, Delaware River canoe trips, evening pool parties, swim meets, beach bash parties, a boating regatta, and a water carnival.
Land Sports Cayuga provides high-quality instruction in all team sports and individual sports, including archery, badminton, baseball, basketball, dodgeball, exercise/fitness, field hockey, flag football, gaga, golf, gymnastics, in-line skating, kickball, kickboxing, lacrosse, martial arts, newcomb, Ping-Pong, riflery, roller hockey, skateboarding, soccer, softball, tennis, tetherball, track, Ultimate Frisbee, volleyball, weight training, and wrestling. Campers who wish to compete can participate in Cayuga's popular Intercamp Tournament Program, which features more than 120 tournaments throughout the summer.

Horsemanship Program Cayuga features equitation classes in English and Western styles from beginner to advanced levels, intercamp horse shows, horseback overnights, evening trail rides, jumping, and animal-care instruction. Cayuga's Equestrian Center includes twenty-five horses, two instructional riding rings, a stable, a tack room, jumps, and more than 5 miles of scenic horse trails. Horseback riding is offered every day at no extra charge.
Arts Program Cayuga's Creative Arts Program is a favorite among many Cayuga campers and includes instruction in basket weaving, ceramics, sculpting, potter's wheel, painting, sketching, leather work, silk screening, tie-dyeing, wood projects, model rocketry, stained glass, copper enameling, mask making, macramé, jewelry making, papier-mache, block printing, beading, puppetry, and nature crafts. Cayuga's Performing Arts Program features drama productions, improvisation, mime, set construction, costuming, makeup, dance recitals, musical instruments, chorus/singing, and aerobics. Cayuga's Art Programs are directed by 2 Art Directors, who are assisted by 12 specialists.
Wilderness and Adventure Program Cayuga's exciting Wilderness and Adventure Program includes challenging activities and professional instruction at the ropes course (205-foot zip line, 20-foot climbing wall, rappelling, and more), mountain biking, nature hikes, overnights, compass reading, cabin cookouts, nature studies, and backpacking on the Appalachian Trail.
Flying Trapeze and Circus Program Cayuga's Flying Trapeze and Circus Program is instructed by qualified professional circus performers. Campers of all ages can learn to "fly through the air on the flying trapeze" every day. Cayuga's popular Circus Program features unicycling, juggling, magic tricks, diabolo, devil sticks, acrobatics, plate spinning, clowning, and two big circus performances each summer.
Additional Programs Additional activities include ATV four-wheelers, radio broadcasting, chess, cooking, video camera filming, photography/darkroom, camp newspaper, tutoring, foreign language instruction, ESL, and the petting zoo (goats, sheep, ducks, bunnies, and more).

DAILY SCHEDULE

Cayuga's schedule includes seven activity periods. The activity program stresses self-improvement, with emphasis on instruction and fun rather than competition.
Cabin-Group Activity Program Campers entering fourth grade and younger travel to activities with

their cabin group and counselors. Most activities are structured, though some are free choice.
Free-Choice Elective Program Campers entering fifth grade and older design their own activity schedule by selecting from more than sixty activities.

EXTRA OPPORTUNITIES AND ACTIVITIES

Evening Activities Many campers report that the evening activities are the best part of camp. They are different every night of the summer. Evening activities include campfires, skits, socials, recitals, drama productions, and much more.
Weekly Special Events Cayuga's popular Special Events include some of the wackiest activities of the summer, such as the Big Beach Bash, Cayuga Carnival, Boating Regatta, Wacky Water Carnival, Camper Counselor Day, Backwards Day, and the Annual Camp Olympics, to name a few.
Trips Program This summer includes two big day trips: DorneyPark & Wild Water Kingdom, Hersheypark, and Chocolate World. These trips are included in the camp tuition. Cayuga also offers three-day trips to Niagara Falls/Canada and Busch Gardens/Colonial Williamsburg in Virginia. Other trips include AAA baseball games, paintball, golf courses, backpacking, theater, and canoe trips. Cayuga also sponsors a three-day Winter Ski Reunion, a great way to renew camp friendships and to learn to ski.

FACILITIES

Cayuga is proud to feature some of the most comprehensive facilities available in camping today, including two separate campuses, modern cabins with bathrooms, two dining halls, two pools, a private lake, an equestrian center with twenty-five horses, two large gymnasiums, ten tennis courts, two art pavilions, four basketball courts, a hockey rink, skateboard park, dance studio, weight room, martial arts building, game room, petting zoo, two Honda ATV tracks, two riflery ranges, two archery ranges, two radio broadcasting stations, five golf cages, a ropes course, and activity sites for sixty daily activities.

STAFF

Since their beginning in camping in 1957, the Buynak family has maintained that a camp staff is the most important ingredient to ensuring a positive and enjoyable experience for each and every camper. Special emphasis is placed on interviewing individuals who have demonstrated competency in working with children and the capacity to provide warm, mature guidance. The youngest counselor is entering the sophomore year of college; the average age is 21. Cayuga's senior staff members are adults who have experience as teachers and coaches. These individuals direct the various activity programs and oversee the instructors. The staff member–camper ratio is better than 1:4.

MEDICAL CARE

Cayuga's infirmary is staffed by 5 full-time registered nurses. A doctor is on call within 10 minutes, and the county hospital is only 6 miles from camp.

RELIGIOUS LIFE

Camp Cayuga is nondenominational. Campers may voluntarily attend religious services.

COSTS

Tuition ranges from $1300 to $6600, depending on the session and grade of the camper. Sibling credits and tuition discounts are available.

TRANSPORTATION

Bus transportation is available from New York, New Jersey, Philadelphia, and Maryland. Airport transfers to and from Newark International Airport in New Jersey are also available.

APPLICATION TIMETABLE

Cayuga accepts applications until spaces are filled. Tours of the facility are available throughout the year.

FOR MORE INFORMATION, CONTACT:

Camp Cayuga Business Office
P.O. Box 151, Suite PETG
Peapack, New Jersey 07977
908-470-1224 (winter)
800-422-9842 (winter, toll-free)
570-253-3133 (summer)
Fax: 908-470-1228 (winter)
570-253-3194 (summer)
E-mail: info@campcayuga.com
World Wide Web: http://www.campcayuga.com

CAMP DUDLEY

SUMMER PROGRAM

WESTPORT, NEW YORK

Type of Program: Traditional camping
Participants: Boys, ages 11–15
Enrollment: 320 per session
Program Dates: Full season, June 22 to August 15, and two 4-week half sessions, June 22 to July 18 and July 20 to August 15
Head of Program: Andrew P. Bisselle

LOCATION

Camp Dudley is located in the Adirondack Wilderness Park, 3 miles south of Westport, New York, on the western shore of Lake Champlain and the eastern edge of the Adirondack High Peaks. The camp's principal property comprises about 500 acres at two locations: the main 250-acre campus on Lake Champlain, which features more than 2 miles of shore frontage, and the camp's 250-acre facility, used for hiking and overnight camping, located 3 miles from the main campus in the Adirondack foothills.

BACKGROUND AND PHILOSOPHY

Founded in 1885 by Sumner F. Dudley, Camp Dudley is the nation's oldest camp for boys. Dudley, a nonprofit institution affiliated with the YMCA of the United States, offers boys a place to learn, grow physically and spiritually, and have the best summer of their lives in the atmosphere of placing others ahead of themselves. Dudley's motto—"The other fellow first"—is acted out in all aspects of daily life at camp. In its 119-year history, the camp's facilities and diverse programs have grown far beyond Mr. Dudley's expectations. Extensive programs in sports, dramatics, art, hiking, and music are now provided each summer for hundreds of Dudley campers.

One of the most unique characteristics of Dudley is the loyalty and support of its alumni. For most campers, their relationship with Dudley does not end with the close of the camping season. Rather, it endures, as former campers return as leaders. Alumni and parents contribute to Dudley through their financial support and attendance at alumni gatherings. Each year at the end of the regular camp, Dudley holds an alumni reunion/family camp. More than thirty alumni gatherings are held during the year throughout the country.

Dudley is operated as an independent YMCA-chartered corporation by a board of managers that is elected from the camp's constituency. The board sets camp policy, oversees its finances and physical plant, and appoints the camp director.

PROGRAM OFFERINGS

Camp Dudley offers a broad and diverse program of activities, adjusted for camper age, which focuses on participation and instruction. The program rests on four interrelated activities: athletics, arts, outdoors, and the cabin unit. Success in each area is valued equally, helping the camper gain self-confidence. Athletics are important at Dudley, but so are programs in vocal and instrumental music, dramatics, arts and crafts, mountain hiking, canoe trips, nature study, photography, and publications. Variety underpins the Dudley program. Among the athletic offerings are archery, baseball, basketball, canoeing, fishing, flag football, golf, kayaking, lacrosse, lifesaving, riflery, rock climbing, sailing, snorkeling, soccer, softball, swimming and diving, tennis, track and field, volleyball, water polo, and weight lifting. In all athletic competitive programs, leaders and coaches emphasize fair play, teamwork, generosity to one's opponent, good conduct, and decent language.

Each camper sets personal goals and reflects on progress and issues weekly with trained leaders. By doing so, the camp aims to develop lifelong values and leadership qualities in its campers. The director and leaders give camp awards to those who achieve personal goals; practice the camp motto, "The other fellow first"; and gain the respect of their fellow campers and leaders.

ENROLLMENT

Each year, campers come from approximately thirty-five states and fifteen other countries to join in the Dudley experience. The camp is organized into four divisions and boys are assigned to specific divisions based upon age and school grade. The Director and Admissions Committee use their knowledge of each boy and the camp's program to make the final assignment. Most Cubs are entering the sixth grade and are 11 years old; Plebes, entering the seventh grade and 12 years old; Juniors, entering the eighth grade and 13 years old; and Seniors, entering the ninth grade and 14 years old. Each boy is assigned to a team that competes and plays with other teams in his division each morning and afternoon.

DAILY SCHEDULE

7:20	First whistle
7:30	Second whistle
7:33	Cannon and flag raising
8	Chapel talk and breakfast
8:30	Cabin inspection
9	First period of team activities/arts time
10:30	Second period of team activities/arts time
12	Choice time
1	Lunch
1:45	Rest period
2:45	Rest period ends
3	Afternoon team activities
4:30	Choice time
6	Dinner
7:30	Night activity
8:45	First whistle—campers ready for bed
9:00	Second whistle—vespers by cabin
9:30	Taps—all lights out

EXTRA OPPORTUNITIES AND ACTIVITIES

Dudley's evening programs feature an excellent theater program, all-camp meetings, divisional cabin games, movies, campfires, storytelling, and special events.

Cabin groups often organize their own evening programs. Older boys take three-day canoeing and hiking trips into the Adirondacks throughout the session. Shorter overnight hiking trips are also taken to nearby Stacy Brook camping sites by cabin groups. Other highlights include aquatic meets, sailing regattas, treasure hunts, Parents' Visitation, orchestras, Friday night Council Rings, Saturday night shows, and excellent dramatic productions.

FACILITIES

Campers are housed in forty cabins located on the perimeter of the main campus and along the lake shore. Most cabins have fireplaces, and each cabin has fixed bunks and individual closets. Separate facilities are used for showers and toilets.

Among the impressive facilities at Dudley are a dining hall with modern kitchens, an auditorium-theater, a gymnasium, a weight room, an arts and crafts building, a boat house, an infirmary, an outdoor chapel, Maclean Alumni Lodge, and numerous service buildings. Witherbee Hall is the theater and concert hall and a hub of artistic activity. The Hike Hut is yet another hub, teaching self-reliance, concern for nature, outdoor skills, and inspiring awe for the physical environment. Extensive playing fields feature four baseball diamonds, eight basketball courts (six outdoor, two indoor), four soccer fields, three lacrosse fields, eight tennis courts, an archery range, a rifle range, an all-weather 200-meter track, and a swimming and diving area with racing lanes.

STAFF

More than 150 leaders and staff members assist the director in the day-to-day operations of the camp. The camper-counselor ratio averages 3:1. Leaders, who coach teams and are in charge of cabin life, are college students or graduates who have been at Dudley for a number of years and have progressed through the camp's leadership program. In each cabin, the leader is assisted by an assistant or junior leader and an aide, young men in training to be a leader.

Staff members support the activities of the camp program. They are trained professionals, many of whom work in the field of education. The majority of the staff members have served at Dudley for more than five years, and several members have been at camp for twenty-five years or more.

Dudley's director, Andrew P. Bisselle, was appointed in April 2000. He has been connected with Dudley for 25 years as a camper, leader, and staff member. Mr. Bisselle has dedicated his professional life to education, most recently as a master teacher of history, a class dean, and athletic coach at the Taft School in Connecticut.

MEDICAL CARE

Dudley's well-equipped infirmary is staffed by 3 registered nurses and a resident doctor. All boys must have a completed health information card on file before the beginning of camp. The well-being of each camper—body, mind, and spirit—is of prime importance to Camp Dudley.

RELIGIOUS LIFE

Dudley's heritage is Christian and as part of their schedule, they have chapel talks, vespers, and a Sunday service. However, they welcome boys of all faiths into their community; the diversity of their camper body fosters an appreciation of difference. Every camper and staff member is asked to attend all camp activities and to respect Dudley's traditions. Each person can expect that his own religious faith will be likewise respected and honored.

COSTS

Fees for the 2005 season are approximately $6200 for the full season and $3700 for the half season. Fees are all-inclusive.

FINANCIAL AID

Camp Dudley is committed to the principle of making camp affordable for boys from all socioeconomic levels. To ensure this, the camp has a strong scholarship program. Scholarships are awarded on the basis of financial need, and a vigorous effort is made to seek out deserving boys whose families are economically in need. The camp director works with the YMCA, schools, and with other nonprofit organizations to recruit scholarship campers. This year, $400,000 in scholarship aid was available for campers.

TRANSPORTATION

Westport is just 120 miles north of Albany, New York, and 95 miles south of Montreal. Amtrak trains from New York City to Montreal stop in Westport. The nearest airport is in Burlington, Vermont (1 hour and 15 minutes away). Staff members pick up boys at the Westport Train Station for free or from the Burlington Airport for a nominal fee (usually $40, depending on arrival time).

APPLICATION TIMETABLE

Applicants are encouraged to attend Camp Dudley for the full eight weeks. Half-season placements are available and meet the needs of boys with other commitments. The camp believes that it is important for new applicants and their parents to meet the director. Reunions are held throughout the country to provide an opportunity to do so. A $300 deposit or full tuition payment is due with the application. The application deadline for new campers is February 1. The deadline for scholarship applications is March 1.

For more information, contact:

Andrew P. Bisselle, Director
Camp Dudley
126 Dudley Road
Westport, New York 12993
518-962-4720
Fax: 518-962-4320
E-mail: dudley@campdudley.org

CAMP LA JOLLA

FITNESS AND WEIGHT-LOSS VACATION

LA JOLLA, CALIFORNIA

Type of Program: Weight-loss, exercise, nutrition, behavior modification, and field trips
Participants: Separate girls' and boys' programs; girls, ages 8–12, 13–16, and 17–29; boys, ages 8–18; exclusive adult ladies' program, ages 30 and older
Enrollment: 200 per summer
Program Dates: Two- through nine-week programs, late June through August
Head of Program: Nancy Lenhart, Founder/Director

LOCATION

Camp La Jolla's programs are held on the beautiful campus of the University of California at San Diego in La Jolla, California. Just a short walk from the sandy beaches of the Pacific Ocean, Camp La Jolla's site offers campers boundless recreational and educational opportunities. The weather in La Jolla, known as "the jewel city of the Pacific Ocean," is sublime, stimulating campers to get active in an adventurous setting.

BACKGROUND AND PHILOSOPHY

Camp La Jolla was founded for the camper who really wants to lose weight. The program's goal-oriented, positive, fun atmosphere teaches campers how to stay thin and motivates them to always want to look and feel their best. Nutrition, exercise, and behavior modification are combined in this home-away-from-home environment, where individualized attention and communication are emphasized. The goal of Camp La Jolla is for campers to take home a feeling of confidence, success, and positivity that will encourage them to always strive for a healthy mind and body.

Camp La Jolla is accredited by the American Camping Association (ACA).

PROGRAM OFFERINGS

As featured on the *Oprah Winfrey* show, Camp La Jolla follows a three-step program that encourages a positive attitude toward changing poor eating habits into healthy ones, instructs campers on choosing the most nutritionally sound foods, incorporates physical fitness into a lifelong routine, and teaches each camper how to maintain his or her desired weight. Private weekly weight-ins provide positive reinforcement and motivation to give campers complete self-confidence and pride.

Campers attend classes in La Jolla's behavior modification program, Slimdown, where they are motivated to lose weight the right way. Topics covered in Slimdown's open discussion forum include building self-esteem, controlling food intake, obtaining family and peer support, how to be assertive, and becoming your own best friend.

An integral part of the program covers food preparation; campers observe meals being prepared by the Camp La Jolla staff members and participate on the serving line. These firsthand experiences teach campers about the importance of portion control, food variations, and exchange groups.

The extensive exercise program includes bicycling, swimming, step aerobics, firm-n-tone, power walking, volleyball, basketball, hiking, tennis, water exercises, hiking, softball, kickball, soccer, weight training, aerobics, tae kwon do, dance, cheerleading, snorkeling, boogie boarding, kayaking, and indoor rock climbing.

Campers are grouped by age for all activities and have the opportunity to choose for themselves in which sports they'd like to participate.

Campers also have the option of participating in Camp La Jolla's Theatre Arts Program and arts and crafts.

ENROLLMENT

Each year, Camp La Jolla enrolls hundreds of young men and women who want to turn their lives around and become thinner and more active—campers who want to finally start living the lives they were meant to live!

EXTRA OPPORTUNITIES AND ACTIVITIES

Weekly field trips include visits to Disneyland, Sea World, the San Diego Zoo, Hollywood game shows and sitcoms, water parks, ice-skating rinks, arcades, and professional baseball games. Outings are made for day hikes, sightseeing, miniature golf, bowling, the movies, and shopping for campers' graduation outfits at the International Horton Plaza. Evening activities include skit nights, bonfires, arts and crafts, and special clubs. The Talent Show, staged at the Parent's Weekend Seminar, is a camp highlight.

FACILITIES

Campers live in spacious, suite-style collegiate accommodations. Residences feature a private lounge and bathroom, and campers enjoy oceanview dining in La Casa, Camp La Jolla's exclusive indoor/outdoor dining room. The University of California's indoor pool, jacuzzi, sports fields, gymnasiums, track, and hiking and biking trails are all open for camper use.

STAFF

Camp La Jolla's counselors are chosen for their enthusiasm, caring personality, motivation, and previous experience in health education, nutrition, and sports. Staff members are totally dedicated to helping each camper attain his or her personal goals.

Nancy Lenhart, the founder and director of Camp La Jolla, is an ACA-certified Camp Director and nationally recognized authority on adolescent weight loss with more than twenty years of experience in the field. Nancy communicates on a personal level with each participant before, during, and after camp. Nancy holds membership in the International Association of Eating Disorder Professionals, the Adolescent Obesity Center, and the California Parenting Institute. Her expertise includes teaching, private and group counseling, school guidance administration and crisis intervention, motivational speaking, and behavior modification.

MEDICAL CARE

Camp La Jolla has an experienced registered nurse in residence, a medical doctor on call, and a nutritionist, a behavior modification specialist, ACE-certified specialists, a registered dietician, and a medical consultant on staff. The world-renowned Scripps Hospital is just minutes away for emergency treatment.

COSTS

In 2003, program fees were as follows: three weeks, $4595; four weeks, $5495; five weeks, $6095; six weeks, $6595; seven weeks, $7095; eight weeks, $7595; and nine weeks, $7995. Special end-of-summer three- and four-week programs are offered at lower rates. Camp tuition includes room and board, the entire instructional program, all equipment and supplies, pre- and post-camp counseling, and all scheduled activities. It does not include transportation to and from the program, laundry, and optional off-campus activities.

An additional $100 is deducted from the tuition for referrals that result in enrollments. Credit card payment is accepted.

TRANSPORTATION

San Diego International Airport is just minutes away from camp, and there is no charge for meeting campers' incoming flights. For those who would like to drive, Camp La Jolla is accessible from Interstate 5 .

APPLICATION TIMETABLE

A reservation fee of $100 must be received with the application. Admissions are accepted on a first-come, first-served basis until the programs fill.

For more information, contact:

Nancy Lenhart
Camp La Jolla
176 C Avenue
Coronado, California 92118
800-825-8746 (toll-free)
Fax: 619-435-8188
E-mail: camp@camplajolla.com
World Wide Web: http://www.camplajolla.com

PARTICIPANT/FAMILY COMMENTS

"Not only did I lose a lot of weight, but I learned to change my eating habits and attitude about food. Camp La Jolla changed my life, and it can change yours, too!"

"We feel Camp La Jolla is the very best thing we've ever done for our son and daughter—and wish every child could experience the wonderful environment La Jolla offers."

CAMP LOHIKAN IN THE POCONO MOUNTAINS

SUMMER PROGRAM

LAKE COMO, PENNSYLVANIA

Type of Program: Traditional residential private camp
Participants: Coeducational, ages 6–15
Program Dates: Full session, June 27 to August 19; first half session, June 27 to July 23; second half session, July 24 to August 19; limited two-week program available for youngest campers; one-week mini-camp, August 19 to August 26
Head of Program: Mark Buynak, C.C.D.

LOCATION

Camp Lohikan is located on 1,200 acres in the Pocono Mountains of Pennsylvania, approximately 2½ hours from New York City. The camp is situated on a hilltop with gorgeous views of the camp's private lake and hundreds of acres of Pocono Mountain landscape. The area's elevation of 1,700 feet ensures low humidity, warm days, cool nights, and few mosquitoes.

BACKGROUND AND PHILOSOPHY

Camp Lohikan was founded in 1957 by Arline and Mike Buynak. In 1983, the full-time directorship of Lohikan was turned over to their eldest son, Mark, who now continues the Camp Lohikan tradition of excellence.

PROGRAM OFFERINGS

Water Sports Lohikan's private lake and heated swimming pool are the most popular sites in the camp. Campers receive professional instruction in swimming, waterskiing, jet skiing, knee boarding, sailing, windsurfing, canoeing, kayaking, rowing, paddle boating, banana boating, and fishing. Free swims, swim meets, pool parties, water trampoline, beach parties, Delaware River canoe trips, and a fleet of more than fifty boats ensure there's never a lack of excitement in the water sports department.
Team Sports Sports are the best part of camp for many Lohikan campers. Professional instruction, fun recreational play, and exciting intercamp games are featured in nine team sports and twelve individual sports activities. The team sports program features lacrosse, baseball, softball, soccer, football, roller hockey, basketball, volleyball, and newcombe.
Individual Sports Each sports activity is organized with a department head who is a professional in the sport. Staff instructors are specialists who are handpicked for their sports knowledge and their ability to relate this knowledge to children. Lohikan's individual sports program features tennis, gymnastics, bungee trampoline, archery, riflery, golf, martial arts (karate and judo), skateboarding, wrestling, weightlifting/training, track, tetherball, and in-line skating.
Horsemanship Program English and Western instruction is provided by a staff of 10 instructors and headed by expert rider Gill Cessaro, Lohikan's horseback riding director. The comprehensive program features dressage, jumping, trail rides, horse care, four horse shows, and weekly horseback overnights.
Circus Arts Everyone knows that the circus is fun, so Lohikan's circus program produces two major public performances every summer. Circus professionals provide instruction in flying trapeze, juggling, clowning, rolling globe, tight wire, Spanish web, mini-trampoline, acrobatics, fire eating, circus bike, unicycle, and magic tricks.

Creative Arts Three professional artists head Lohikan's comprehensive creative arts activity department. They are assisted by a staff of 14 specialists. Instruction is provided in painting (acrylic, watercolors), drawing, leather work, silk screening, tie-dyeing, batiking, woodworking, ceramics, potter's wheel, sculpting, model rocketry, basket weaving, stained glass, enameling, mask making, papier mâché, paper making, block printing, fimo jewelry, puppetry, and nature crafts. Weekly art gallery shows are scheduled to showcase Lohikan's camper artists.
Performing Arts Program Broadway professional Bob Johnenne heads the program, which includes musicals, dramas, scripting, improvisation, mime, voice, set design, set construction, costuming, makeup, stage lighting, sound engineering, dance recitals, modern dance, jazz, ballet, tap, choreography, movement, aerobics, music, guitar, keyboards, drums, singing, and songwriting. It's a complete program.
Media Arts Lohikan's wide-ranging arts program is rounded out with the media arts department, which features classes in photography, radio broadcasting, video production, computers, and a daily newspaper.
Outdoor Adventure Program Adventure activities add a lot of excitement to the camp program. Expert instruction is provided in rock climbing, rappelling, mountain cycling, ropes course, zip line, hiking, and orienteering. Three-day backpacking trips are scheduled for interested campers on the Appalachian Trail and in the Catskill Mountains.
Special Programs Additional activity choices include paintball, ATV four-wheelers, spy camp, chess, billiards, cooking, academic tutoring, and ESL studies.
First-Time–Camper Program Since 1957, Camp Lohikan has earned a reputation for its success with First-Time Campers. It's a comprehensive program that provides advice and support before, during, and even after camp ends. It's also backed up by Camp Lohikan's exclusive Great Camp Guarantee.

DAILY SCHEDULE

Lohikan's program features more than sixty activities on a daily basis. The camp's teaching approach is based upon the philosophy that learning with fun is the best way to learn. Activity instruction covers the fundamentals and from there progresses to the more advanced skill levels. From beginner to advanced, campers learn at their own pace in a fun, relaxed, noncompetitive, stress-free environment.

Elective Program Campers 10–11 years of age choose all of their activities on a weekly basis. What is unique about Lohikan's elective program is that campers are guaranteed to receive every activity selected for the exact number of periods requested every day.

Cabin-Structured, Counselor-Supervised Program Junior campers aged 6 to 10 years old travel as a cabin group with their counselors to a schedule of activities designed for their age. While maintaining cabin supervision, Lohikan is able to provide even younger campers with elective choices at certain activity sites, including the waterfront, field sports, creative arts, performing arts, and arena sports.

EXTRA OPPORTUNITIES AND ACTIVITIES

While the daily activity program is the backbone of the camp program, the highlight of each day is the evening activity. Whether it be the Superstars Competition, Mad Mike's Mimic Mania, the Camp Gold Rush, or Sadie Hawkins Night, this is the time when the entire camp coalesces and camper enthusiasm peaks. A different entertaining evening activity is scheduled every night of the summer.

Weekly special events like the Camp Carnival, the Wild Water War, the Boating Regatta, Camper-Counselor Day, the Summer Fest, and the Camp Olympics are scheduled to add diversity to the summer program and are very popular with the campers. Camp trips to Hersheypark, Dorney Park, and other local amusements lend excitement to the camp's dynamic summer program. For interested campers, there's also an extensive intercamp games program that involves more than twenty local camps. For older campers, Lohikan sponsors an optional three-day trip to a site of educational and entertaining interest. This summer, the three-day trip is scheduled to visit Niagara Falls, Canada's Wonderland, and the Ontario Science Center. In late December, Camp Lohikan sponsors a three-day ski reunion that is attended by campers, parents, staff members, and alumni.

FACILITIES

Designed to compliment the natural beauty of the setting are more than fifty buildings, more than 40,000 square feet of indoor activity facilities, a heated swimming pool, private lake, four regulation sports fields, performing arts center, gymnasium, indoor roller hockey rink, sports center, indoor and outdoor basketball courts, an outdoor amphitheater, eleven tennis courts with lights, on-premises stables with two riding rings, 7 miles of trails, a large skate park, a 40-foot climbing tower, three zip lines, and separate activity sites to accommodate more than sixty-five daily activities. Campers are housed in modern, wood-paneled, insulated cabins complete with electrical outlets, smoke alarms, windows with screens, lighted front porches, and bathroom facilities equipped with private stall showers, toilets, sinks, and hot and cold water.

STAFF

More than anything else, the staff members of a camp make the difference between a good summer and a great summer. For that reason, Camp Lohikan spares no expense nor time in recruiting staff members who are warm, caring individuals experienced in working with children and who will make strong, positive role models for children in the camp setting. Specialty counselors meet the additional criteria of having strong personal skills and teaching experience in the area of their expertise. A stringent screening process is personally managed by the Camp Director, who has forty-three years of camp experience. The minimum age of in-cabin staff members is 19, and the camp averages a staff return rate of better than 50 percent.

Senior staff members are camp professionals with coaching and teaching experience, and 1 senior staff member heads each activity department, each division/cabin group, and each special program area. More than 90 percent of the camp's 50 senior staff members return each summer.

MEDICAL CARE

Lohikan's infirmary is staffed by 5 full-time registered nurses and a licensed physician, all of whom live on the camp grounds. A local ambulance service is less than 3 miles away, and the local hospital is a 25-minute drive. All staff members are CPR- and first aid–trained in a weeklong precamp orientation session.

RELIGIOUS LIFE

Camp Lohikan is nondenominational. Campers may attend religious services nearby. Sabbath services are offered on Friday nights, with voluntary attendance.

COSTS

Tuition for first-time junior campers in 2004 was $5200 for the full session, $3100 for the first half session, and $3000 for the second half session.

TRANSPORTATION

Camp-chartered bus transportation is available from the New York, New Jersey, Philadelphia, and Baltimore areas. International campers are met at Newark Airport in New Jersey.

APPLICATION TIMETABLE

Lohikan accepts applications until spaces are filled.

For more information, contact:

Camp Lohikan in the Pocono Mountains
P. O. Box 189, Suite PETG
Gladstone, New Jersey 07934
800-488-4321 (toll-free)
Fax: 908-470-9319
World Wide Web: http://www.lohikan.com

CAMP MONDAMIN CAMP GREEN COVE

BOYS' AND GIRLS' SUMMER CAMPS

TUXEDO, NORTH CAROLINA

Type of Program: Traditional camping and wilderness expeditions
Participants: Boys and girls in separate camps, ages 6–16
Enrollment: 190 in each camp
Program Dates: Early June Camp: June 1 to June 5; June Camp, ages 7–13: June 7 to June 26; Main Camp, ages 8–16: July 1 to August 8; August Camp, ages 6–10: August 10 to August 15
Heads of Program: Frank Bell Jr., Director (boys); Nancy Bell, Director (girls)

LOCATION

Eight miles south of Hendersonville, North Carolina, at an elevation of 2,050 feet, the camps are located on Lake Summit, a 350-acre lake in the Blue Ridge Mountains. Mondamin (for boys) and Green Cove (for girls) own about 800 acres of woodland and have easy access to hundreds of square miles of the Pisgah National Forest and the Great Smoky Mountains National Park for longer hiking, climbing, white-water canoeing and kayaking, biking, and riding trips.

BACKGROUND AND PHILOSOPHY

Mondamin was founded in 1922, Green Cove in 1945. Their approach to camping has evolved over the years into a nonregimented program that de-emphasizes competition and encourages goal setting, initiative, and self-direction. The goal is to educate through adventure. The camps provide, through staff, facilities, and program, an atmosphere conducive to the development of habits, attitudes, and values that can last a lifetime. The de-emphasis of competition encourages campers to try new activities and develop new skills rather than stay with the familiar.

PROGRAM OFFERINGS

Activities at both camps center around water (canoeing and kayaking, sailing, and swimming), woods (hiking, rock climbing, and mountain biking), and horses and include the opportunity for many wilderness trips. Some campers choose to spend half or more of their camp experience out on trails and rivers. Each camp has its own location and facilities, about a mile apart but they share activities such as sailing, one-day trips, and weekly social events. The camps own an excellent string of horses and offer systematic instruction in horseback riding. Facilities include rings of varying sizes, fields equipped for intermediate to advanced instruction, and many trails. Overnight to four-day trips are part of the riding program.

A nature program aims to teach awareness and appreciation of the environment. Backpacking, rock-climbing, and mountain-biking trips range over local property and beyond to the Great Smokies, the Pisgah National Forest, and other national parkland and forestland. A ropes course helps develop self-confidence and helps groups learn to work together. A 45-foot climbing tower offers beginning- and advanced-level climbing challenges.

Water activities include beginning, intermediate, and advanced instruction in swimming, canoeing, and sailing. The sailing fleet includes a wide variety of boats, so campers learn how to manage different rigs and different handling characteristics. Capable sailors have the opportunity to take boats to other, larger lakes for three- or four-day trips.

The camps are especially well known in white-water circles for their excellent white-water canoeing program, which includes kayaks and C-1's. Campers work hard on basic lake skills and then begin a progression of river trips that build on skills previously learned and culminate in multiday trips on Class III/IV rivers. The program is not a "quick course," but it produces many highly competent paddlers, including some current Olympic competitors.

Tennis is offered on a daily basis at both camps. Both also offer crafts; other activities, including photography, riflery, and archery are available, though on a much less ambitious scale.

Each camper can choose from many opportunities. At night, cabin counselors go over what each camper did that day and help plan for the next day. They emphasize setting goals and working toward them—offering encouragement where needed. They strive for productive use of time but recognize that time for relaxation and play are important, too. The most advanced levels of skill are normally attainable only in the longer session and may require more than one summer. Skill level, not age, determines eligibility for trips. Each camper progresses at his or her own rate and is not tied to a cabin or age group.

ENROLLMENT

Last year, campers from thirty-three states as well as a small percentage from other countries were enrolled.

EXTRA OPPORTUNITIES AND ACTIVITIES

An important part of the camps' experience is the out-of-camp tripping program. Campers work up to some of the most exciting trips offered by any camp. Some examples include five-day white-water canoeing trips; three-day mountain-biking adventures; four-day sailing trips on Lake Jocassee, an 8,000-acre wilderness body of water; five-day horseback-riding trips in the Pisgah National Forest; and three- to seven-day hiking and rock-climbing trips into the Great Smoky Mountains National Park or the Linville Gorge. There is no extra charge for any activity or trip.

FACILITIES

In-camp facilities at both camps include tennis courts, barns and riding rings, craft shops, and ball fields as well as the waterfront. Mondamin also has an indoor rifle range and a gymnasium.

STAFF

Mondamin and Green Cove are fortunate to have a highly experienced group of counselors, many of whom return year after year. (The average counselor has been there four to five years.) The youngest is 18 and has completed a year of college. The average age is about 25. Most young counselors have been campers in previous years. Most counselors live in a cabin with 4 to 6 campers and teach an activity during activity periods. The camp experience allows adults to spend ample time with youngsters. The overall camper-to-counselor ratio is less than 4:1, allowing superb opportunity for individual attention. All staff members have current Red Cross first aid and CPR training, waterfront staff members have lifeguard training, and trip leaders have wilderness first aid training. A listing of staff, including qualifications and a brief biography, is available upon request.

MEDICAL CARE

Each camp has consistently held a grade "A" rating from the North Carolina State Board of Health. There is an infirmary in each camp with 2 nurses in residence, a doctor serves both camps, and a hospital is 6 miles away. Health checks are made daily; parents receive weekly letters from counselors and a telephone call in case of any unusual problems.

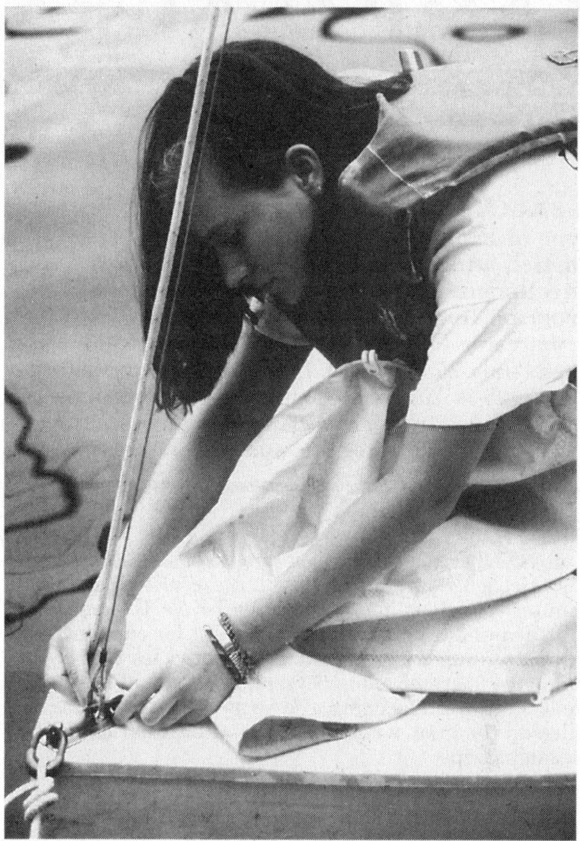

COSTS

Total fees for the Main Session are $4375, with a $200 discount for registration before December 1. Fees for Early June Camp are $790; for June Camp, $2700; and for August Camp, $850. There is no extra charge for any trip or activity.

APPLICATION TIMETABLE

The camps accept registrations beginning in August. The June session fills quickly; the Main Session fills in mid-spring. An early enrollment discount is available for the Main Session.

For more information and a video, contact:

Frank Bell Jr., Mondamin Director
Nancy Bell, Green Cove Director
P.O. Box 8
Tuxedo, North Carolina 28784
800-688-5789 (toll-free)
E-mail: mondamin@mondamin.com
greencove@greencove.com
World Wide Web: http://www.mondamin.com
http://www.greencove.com

PARTICIPANT/FAMILY COMMENTS

"The best thing about camp was that both children came home feeling great about themselves. Your 'out-of-doors' classroom taught lessons of life that will never be forgotten and will always be treasured. We chose Mondamin and Green Cove because we thought they would offer truly unique experiences—you didn't let us down, and, in fact, you surpassed our expectations!"

CAMP O-AT-KA

SUMMER CAMP

SEBAGO, MAINE

Type of Program: Traditional camping
Participants: Boys, ages 7–16
Enrollment: 150 per session
Program Dates (2004): Two-week starter programs, June 27 to July 10, July 11 to July 24, and July 25 to August 7; three-week program, July 25 to August 14; four-week program, June 27 to July 20; seven-week program, June 27 to August 14; CIT program, June 23 to August 7

LOCATION

Camp O-AT-KA is situated on ½ mile of shorefront on Lake Sebago, southern Maine's largest lake. Just 40 minutes from Portland, Maine, O-AT-KA's 100 acres and surrounding woodlands are perfect for camping, hiking, sailing, cookouts, and other activities that build adventurous young boys' appreciation of the great outdoors. The camp also owns a small island 2 miles up the lake, which is a popular destination for overnight trips.

BACKGROUND AND PHILOSOPHY

One of the oldest overnight camps in the country, O-AT-KA was founded in 1906 and incorporated in 1942 as a nonprofit educational institution. First and foremost, Camp O-AT-KA focuses on building character and good citizenship through a structured program of safe and wholesome activities. The supportive, family environment instills confidence and traditional values through group living, daily camp gatherings, and superb staff members who help campers build a solid foundation for life that stresses values, skills, fun, and the opportunity to create lifelong friendships.

PROGRAM OFFERINGS

O-AT-KA's program offers limitless opportunities for boys to develop their abilities and discover new horizons. A variety of competitive and noncompetitive activities cover a broad spectrum of interests. O-AT-KA's "All-Around CO" award recognizes boys who become proficient in a variety of disciplines and who display good citizenship consistently. Daily offerings include swimming, sailing, waterskiing, steel drums, tubing, windsurfing, archery, campcraft, lacrosse, baseball, basketball, tennis, soccer, riflery, nature/environment courses, rocketry, woodworking, dramatics, fly tying, rod building, and photography. Art activities include drawing, silkscreening, tie-dyeing, copper enameling, stained glass, pottery, and rocket building. All campers are required to participate in daily swimming instruction. Up to six other activities are chosen to round out each boy's program.

Boys are encouraged to participate in team competitions in baseball, basketball, soccer, archery, riflery, tennis, swimming, and sailing with other area camps. Teams are organized by age and ability. Teams compete with area camps.

All campers participate in the camp's rope course. Each cabin and its counselors are presented with a variety of challenges that they need to solve. The solution to all challenges comes through support of each other and team work. This is an ideal way to integrate the campers into a cohesive cabin unit. It is also an effective way for campers to develop self-confidence.

O-AT-KA teaches respect and appreciation for the outdoors through a variety of camping experiences. Boys have opportunities for canoeing, map reading, and fire building in a safe, controlled environment. Proficiency and confidence are developed through day trips and short overnights. Older boys may participate in more rigorous trips. Extended trips for boys 11 and older consist of multiday backpacking, canoeing, river rafting, kayaking, and mountain biking trips led by experienced, licensed trip leaders. There are also the opportunities for day and overnight fishing trips.

The Junior Maine Guide Program, a joint venture of the Maine Youth Camping Association and the State Department of Inland Fisheries and Wildlife, promotes understanding of and respect for the outdoors through skills training, wilderness experience, and responsible recreation. The program, open to boys and girls attending Maine camps, comprises written and practical tests; candidates live in groups and demonstrate their mastery of skills to professional examiners.

The CIT program, open to 16-year-olds, provides extensive training in first aid, safety, leadership, and conflict mediation. Every two weeks, CITs select new activities, crafts, and sports in which they'd like to be apprentice instructors. CITs help plan a group overnight and assist in cabin supervision.

ENROLLMENT

O-AT-KA campers come primarily from the eastern United States, but many southern and western states are represented. In addition, O-AT-KA has campers from many countries, including Spain, Mexico, France, Germany, England, Russia, Canada, and Brazil. Typically, more than thirty states and twelve countries are represented each summer.

EXTRA OPPORTUNITIES AND ACTIVITIES

In their leisure time, boys enjoy horseshoes, Frisbee golf, tetherball, Ping-Pong, volleyball, capture the flag, and much more. Planned extra activities include hiking area mountains, outings to Portland Sea Dog baseball games, trips to the beaches, overnight camping, appearances by visiting artists and coaches, optional day trips, community service projects, King's Day, the July 4th Carnival, the Medieval Banquet, sailing regattas, Green and Gray Day, and the Awards Banquet, to name but a few.

Intramural competitions include cabin-to-cabin challenges in athletics and all-camp games, such as scavenger hunts and relays.

DAILY SCHEDULE

7:15	Reveille
7:40	Colors
7:45	Password
8	Breakfast
8:30	Cabin clean-up
9–12	Morning activities
12	Free swim
12:30	Lunch
1:30	Siesta
2:30–4:30	Afternoon activities
4:30	Team practices, rehearsals, leisure activities
5	Free swim, Camp Store open
6	Dinner
6:45	Colors
7	Evening activities
9–9:30	Taps

FACILITIES

O-AT-KA's 100 acres feature more than sixty buildings, including screened camper cabins, dining and assembly buildings, athletic facilities, and staff and guest housing. The ½ mile of shore line includes an E-shaped swimming dock with two 25-yard enclosed swimming areas and a 50-yard outer area, a separate diving platform, and areas for waterskiing, windsurfing, and canoeing.

Campers are grouped by age and grade into three units, each supervised by a Unit Head Counselor. The cabins house 6–10 campers and 2 staff members. Showers, toilets, and sinks are in separate washhouses near the cabins. Thanks to generous alumni donors, Camp O-AT-KA has recently completed eight new art studios that create the Goff Art Center; a newly constructed Keeler Athletic Center, housing basketball courts; and the Wheeler Tennis Center, with five new courts. The facilities are well maintained and designed to serve the campers by providing a safe place to develop new skills.

STAFF

O-AT-KA staff members are chosen for their sensitivity with children, sound judgment, skills, and maturity; many have attended O-AT-KA as campers themselves. A professional staff of teachers and college-age students oversee the camp program. All staff members undergo one week of training prior to the opening of camp and participate in more specialized activity training and clinics and training camps. The camper-staff member ratio is 3:1. Generally, more than 70 percent of staff members return from the previous year.

MEDICAL CARE

Two registered nurses and a medical assistant oversee the infirmary. Camp also maintains relationships with nearby Bridgton Hospital and the Maine Medical Center. Parents must provide proof of camper insurance on a completed health history form.

COSTS

In 2004, tuition is as follows: two-week starter program (for boys new to overnight camping), $2150; three-week program, $3000; four-week program, $3700; seven-week program, $5250; CIT program, $2700. Tuition must be paid in full by June 1.

TRANSPORTATION

O-AT-KA is just 25 miles northwest of Portland on Route 114 and is easily accessible from the Maine Turnpike (Interstate 95). Boys arriving by bus or plane are met by staff members in Portland and in Boston.

APPLICATION TIMETABLE

Camp begins accepting applications on July 15 for the following season; admission is rolling until the programs fill. Applications must be accompanied by a $350 nonrefundable fee. There is an early registration discount for applications received by November 1.

FOR MORE INFORMATION, CONTACT:

Camp O-AT-KA
593 Sebago Road
Sebago, Maine 04029
207-787-3401
800-818-8455 (toll-free)
Fax: 207-787-3930
E-mail: info@campoatka.com
World Wide Web: http://www.campoatka.com

CAMP REGIS–APPLEJACK

SUMMER CAMP

PAUL SMITHS, NEW YORK

Type of Program: Traditional camping, land sports, water sports, and wilderness experiences
Participants: Coeducational, ages 6–16
Enrollment: 280
Program Dates: Late June through August: one 8-week and two 4-week sessions (two-week sessions available for younger, first-time campers)
Head of Program: Michael P. Humes

LOCATION

Camp Regis-Applejack occupies its own protected cove with a ¾-mile shoreline on one of the most treasured lakes in the pristine Adirondack Park, Upper St. Regis Lake. Access to wilderness canoeing and hiking are at the camp's doorstep. Within the 6-million-acre park are forty-six high peaks and thousands of lakes, streams, and rivers. Regis-Applejack is 2½ hours south of Montreal, 5 hours from New York City, and 1½ hours from Burlington, Vermont.

BACKGROUND AND PHILOSOPHY

Much of the feeling and spirit at Regis-Applejack can be attributed to its location and philosophy. Upper St. Regis Lake puts campers in touch with the wild every day. They see, hear, and touch nature, whether watching a sunset across the water, listening to the call of loons, or feeling the wind in their faces while sailing. This closeness to nature is a profound counterpoint to an often crowded urban environment and to the pressures of today's busy lifestyle. Here campers learn about nature and themselves by observing and by doing—a refreshing change from the academic climate of a student's school year.

The camp philosophy has been established through the years by the Humes family, who founded Regis-Applejack in 1946. The family's background is in education. The Humes believe that camping is best when it strives for excellence and brings together a variety of religions and races, as is the tradition in the Society of Friends (Quakers), of which the Humes are members. Each camper is made to feel accepted as an individual. To help implement this philosophy, a mature staff is employed, including many couples who are skilled in making campers feel at home and at ease.

Because the boys' and girls' sections are on the same campus, meals and many activities are routinely shared, creating a comfortable climate and avoiding the often forced situations where boys and girls meet only on formal occasions. Both sexes are encouraged to try all the activities at camp without preconceptions about what they "should" enjoy.

PROGRAM OFFERINGS

Regis-Applejack offers an extensive water sports program. Three separate docks support the small-craft and waterskiing programs; a fourth Olympic-regulation dock and sand beach support the swimming program. One of the highlights of a Regis-Applejack summer is sailing the length of the lake aboard a variety of boats, from small craft to full-size sloops. Campers can waterski, windsurf, sail, fish, dive, earn American Red Cross swim certificates, canoe, and kayak.

Land sport facilities include seven all-weather tennis courts, handball and basketball courts, and four large playing fields. Regis-Applejack offers a wide range of land sports, including basketball, field hockey, street hockey, football, lacrosse, soccer, softball, tennis, volleyball, and track and field. Instruction in all athletics is patient and thorough; emphasis is put on learning the proper technique through individual instruction from experienced coaches who know how to focus on the special abilities of each camper. Thus the shy beginner and the natural athlete can both learn and have fun.

The Adirondack Park offers splendid opportunities to explore the natural world. All campers participate in outings, which vary in length from overnight to a week, depending on age, experience, and interest. Campers study campcraft and pioneering in a setting that lends substance to what is taught. Camp Applejack, the teen division, makes optional weeklong canoeing and hiking trips in the wilderness as well as "teen tour" excursions to such places as Montreal, Cape Cod, and Maine.

ENROLLMENT

Campers come from different racial and ethnic backgrounds as well as from other countries.

EXTRA OPPORTUNITIES AND ACTIVITIES

The athletics and outing programs are balanced by a wide choice of arts and crafts, performing arts, special interest activities, hobbies, and field trips. During the summer, every group in camp puts on a play or musical and takes part in theater workshops, including ones on stagecraft, lighting, and makeup. The arts and crafts building offers classes in everything from batik to woodworking. Special interests include club nights, the small farm and animal center, photography, the yearbook, and cooking. For those interested in more sports, there are active competitive programs.

FACILITIES

Regis-Applejack, on 70 acres, was originally a private estate, and many of the "Adirondack rustic" buildings have been carefully restored to keep their original spirit. The camp's forty-five buildings include the playhouse and recreation and dining halls. Campers are housed approximately 12–16 to a cabin. All cabins have their own inside bathrooms, three or four bedrooms, and rustic recreation rooms with fireplaces.

Girls' cabins are near the boating area and boys' are near the swimming dock; most have views of the lake.

DAILY SCHEDULE

8:00	Breakfast
9:15	Free-choice activities
10:30	Group activities or swim
11:45	Free-choice activities
1:00	Lunch
2:00	Quiet time
2:45	Free-choice activities
4:00	Group activities
5:15	General swim or free time
6:00	Dinner
7:00	Evening activities
8:30	Special teen programs

Thursday is set aside for field trips in the Lake George–Lake Placid area or for occasional trips to Montreal. On Saturday, there are picnics in the afternoon and skits and plays in the evening. Sunday afternoon is devoted to all-camp activities and programs, and Sunday evening is Buffet Night in the dining hall.

STAFF

The highly qualified and mature counselors include many married couples. Bunk counselors and program leaders do not double as athletics coaches; coaches are specialists and teachers. All staff members spend a week on campus familiarizing themselves with camp philosophy and programs and learning about each camper in their group.

MEDICAL CARE

The infirmary is staffed by 2 nurses. A doctor is on call, and a hospital is 12 miles away in Saranac Lake.

RELIGIOUS LIFE

The camp has always been nonsectarian, although its origins are loosely tied with the Society of Friends and Unitarians. Catholic campers have the option of attending Mass nearby. There is a nondenominational Sunday meeting on campus at which topics relating to ethics and values are discussed.

COSTS

The 2004 costs were $2800 to $5100. A registration deposit of $600 is required.

FINANCIAL AID

A limited number of scholarships are available based on need. Work-study positions for college students ages 19 and older are available.

TRANSPORTATION

Staff members escort campers from the New York tristate area aboard the camp's chartered overland bus, and group flights are arranged out of the Philadelphia, Baltimore/Washington, Atlanta, and Miami airports. Campers may also be met at the Plattsburgh, Albany, and Montreal, Canada airports. Travel details are worked out with each camper.

APPLICATION TIMETABLE

Applications are accepted beginning in early October. The director visits prospective campers in their homes in fall and winter. Parents are welcome to visit camp during summer.

FOR MORE INFORMATION, CONTACT:

summer
Michael Humes
Camp Regis-Applejack
P.O. Box 245
Paul Smiths, New York 12970
518-327-3117
Fax: 518-327-3193

fall, winter, spring
Michael Humes
Camp Regis-Applejack
60 Lafayette Road West
Princeton, New Jersey 08540
609-688-0368
Fax: 609-688-0369
E-mail: campregis@001.com
World Wide Web: http://www.campregis-applejack.com

PARTICIPANT/FAMILY COMMENTS

"Yesterday I climbed a nearby mountain and sat on the top for a couple of hours. As I sat there, I thought about all the fun times I have had at camp. I have so many memories from the last six summers. . . . many of the happiest days of my life took place at Camp Regis-Applejack. Within only two months a year, I made some of my closest friends—both campers and staff. The conditions at camp force people to learn to live together, accept each other, and understand each other. I think I owe a lot of my good qualities to the summers at Camp Regis."

"Hank and I want to thank you for providing another successful summer for our daughter Katherine. Each summer we have seen a big leap in her independence and development of social skills. Thanks for your diligence in providing a safe atmosphere in which learning and childhood joys appear to be intertwined and flourish."

CAMP ST. JOHN'S NORTHWESTERN

SUMMER PROGRAM

DELAFIELD, WISCONSIN

Type of Program: Military and adventure skills
Participants: Boys: ages 12–16 (boarding), entering grades 6–8 (day)
Enrollment: 40–100, depending on the session
Program Dates: One- and two-week day and boarding camps in July
Head of Program: Lt. Col. James Kebisek, Camp Director

LOCATION

Camp St. John's Northwestern is located in Delafield, Wisconsin, approximately 25 miles west of Milwaukee. It is situated on 150 wooded acres near the beautiful Kettle Moraine Forest Preserve and across the street from Lake Nagawicka.

BACKGROUND AND PHILOSOPHY

St. John's Military Academy was founded in 1884 by Dr. Sidney T. Smythe. Dr. Smythe saw a need for a strong preparatory school for boys in grades 7–12 to prepare them for college and life. In 1995, St. John's merged with Northwestern Military and Naval Academy in Lake Geneva, Wisconsin, and formed St. John's Northwestern Military Academy.

Camp St. John's Northwestern, a summer camp for boys, was designed to motivate campers to better understand their potential through a semimilitary-structured program. The camp combines military- and adventure-skills training with physical activities and general fun.

PROGRAM OFFERINGS

The mission of Camp St. John's Northwestern is to promote growth in the areas of leadership, physical training, and self-confidence. This is obtained through a daily schedule of fun and challenging activities.

One- and two-week day and boarding sessions are available. Daily activities include fitness training, adventure skills, survival skills, and athletic/recreation activities. Some of the activities boys experience include rappelling, paintballing, canoeing, marksmanship, rope bridging, fishing, and sailing.

ENROLLMENT

Camp St. John's Northwestern can accommodate 40–100 boys, depending on the session. Boarding camp is open to boys ages 12–16. Day camp is open to boys entering grades 6–8. In 2003, campers came from sixteen states and five different countries.

DAILY SCHEDULE

A typical morning begins at 6:30 a.m. with physical training and breakfast followed by activities that include rappelling, paintball battles, archery, rope bridging, orienteering, marksmanship, and water survival techniques. Lunch is served at noon, and the schedule from 1:30 to 4 p.m. may include such recreational activities as self-defense techniques, PADI skin diving/Discover SCUBA, fishing, sailing, and golf. Dinner is served at 5 p.m. After dinner, campers participate in organized athletics and activities. Off-campus movies are scheduled once a week. Lights-out is at 10 p.m.

EXTRA OPPORTUNITIES AND ACTIVITIES

Additional camp activities may include island survival training on St. John's Island, a 10-mile canoe trip, and a ropes and challenge course. A 1-mile open lake swim challenge is optional. At the end of camp, the Camp Challenge tests each camper and his platoon's ability to successfully complete missions covering skills learned at camp. Camp awards are distributed at a closing ceremony at the end of each session.

FACILITIES

Camp St. John's Northwestern uses the same Academy facilities as the fall program. For housing, the campers occupy one of the three barracks on campus, where most live 2 to a room. For athletics and recreation, a nine-hole golf course is located adjacent to the soccer, track, baseball, and football fields. A full-size gymnasium includes a basketball court, weight training and tae kwon do rooms, a swimming pool, and a barbershop. Mouso Hall, the student recreation center, offers a snack bar, an HDTV home theater system, Ping-Pong tables, billiard tables, video games, and an indoor rifle range.

Campers enjoy three meals per day in Welles Dining Hall.

STAFF
The staff is drawn from the regular school faculty and TAC (Train, Advise, Counsel) instructors, all who have military training. The campers are divided into four platoons. Two adults and one cadet are assigned to a platoon of campers.

MEDICAL CARE
Nurses run the nine-bed infirmary on campus. All prescribed medication is administered by the nursing staff. The school's nurse practitioner is on call as needed. A physical exam, health history form (provided by the camp), and health insurance are required.

RELIGIOUS LIFE
Campers attend a nondenominational service on Sunday.

COSTS
Camp fees vary from $475 to $1400, depending on the session. Camp fees include the uniform (camouflage uniform, athletic shirts and shorts, and one pair of jungle-style boots), paintball equipment, all camp transportation fees, off-campus entrance fees, and breakfast and lunch for day campers or room, board, and laundry service for those boarding.

TRANSPORTATION
The campus is located approximately 25 miles west of Milwaukee, Wisconsin, off Interstate 94, an hour from Madison, Wisconsin, and approximately 2 hours from Chicago, Illinois. Campers traveling great distances may fly into Mitchell International Airport located in Milwaukee, Wisconsin. Arrangements to pick up a camper from the Milwaukee airport may be made through the Academy for a fee.

APPLICATION TIMETABLE
Applications are accepted until sessions are full. Early application is advised as camp space is limited. Campus tours may be scheduled throughout the year. There is a nonrefundable application fee of $75. All eligible campers may be tested and interviewed during camp for possible enrollment at St. John's Northwestern Military Academy.

FOR MORE INFORMATION, CONTACT:
Director of Camp Enrollment
Camp St. John's Northwestern
1101 North Genesee Street
Delafield, Wisconsin 53018
262-646-7115
800-752-2338 (toll-free)
Fax: 262-646-7128
E-mail: admissions@sjnma.org
World Wide Web: http://www.sjnma.org

PARTICIPANT/FAMILY COMMENTS

"My son not only had a good time, he learned what it takes to become a leader."—Mrs. S. Johnson

"My son's attitude changed for the better, he even keeps his bedroom clean and orderly, and that would have never happened a year ago!"—Mrs. J. Hughs

CAMP SANGAMON CAMP BETSEY COX

SUMMER CAMPS

PITTSFORD, VERMONT

Type of Program: Traditional camping
Participants: Boys and girls in separate camps, ages 9–15
Enrollment: 85 in each camp
Program Dates: Two-, three-, and five-week sessions
Heads of Program: Mike Byrom and Lorrie Byrom, Directors

LOCATION

Six miles north of Rutland, the setting for Camp Sangamon and Camp Betsey Cox is pure Vermont. The camps are located on two old farms in the foothills of the Green Mountains on more than 200 acres of woods and pastures and a 25-acre spring-fed lake.

BACKGROUND AND PHILOSOPHY

The camps have more than 100 years of experience between them, and the program has been innovative from the beginning. One of the camps' guiding principles is that children can be good decision-makers and benefit greatly from taking charge of their own lives. Campers choose individually each day from a wide range of activities and trips to create a unique, personal program centered on their own interests.

PROGRAM OFFERINGS

The elective nature of the program helps nurture self-confidence, independence, and creative decision making. Instruction covers a wide range of skills and activities, with a strong emphasis on creative arts, hobbies, and lifetime individual sports and team sports. Instructional activities include riding, tennis, archery, sailing, canoeing, kayaking, ropes course, and swimming. Creative arts include photography, drama, arts and crafts, pottery, rocketry, weaving, and woodshop. Campers play a variety of team sports, including soccer, basketball, and softball. Canoeing, kayaking, cycling, sailing, and hiking are offered as day trips and overnights. A small working farm has a milk cow, chickens, ducks, pigs, lambs, goats, and kittens, providing children with the chance to enhance their understanding of animals and their connection to the natural world. Campers tend and harvest summer vegetables from a community garden.

The eight-week season offers a variety of session lengths and is divided into two-, three-, five-, and eight-week sessions.

ENROLLMENT

Each camp has a total enrollment of 85 campers ages 9–15. There is an eight-week counselor-in-training program for graduates of grades 9 and 10. Forty-five staff members complete the camp community. The camper population hails mostly from New England, with a strong contingent from New York, New Jersey, and the Washington, D.C., area. Alumni and friends from all over the United States provide campers from such places as Wyoming, Texas, Arizona, Florida, California, and Louisiana. Campers also represent France, England, Canada, Mexico, Japan, and Venezuela.

DAILY SCHEDULE

A typical day starts with breakfast at 8. The morning consists of two instructional activity periods, followed by a short free recreational period and lunch. After rest hour, one or two activity periods and a free swim/free time period fill the time until dinner. After dinner, there is an all-camp program or several activity choices. Bedtime varies and includes a half-hour story or reading aloud in front of the fireplace.

EXTRA OPPORTUNITIES AND ACTIVITIES

There are trips taken out of camp every day of the week. These include a wide variety of day and overnight hiking, backpacking, canoeing, bicycling, sailing, kayaking, and horseback-riding trips. Campers seek out Vermont's special hidden wonders—caves, mountains, swimming holes, and snorkeling and tire-tubing spots.

Saturday is a special day at the camps. Old Vermont Day has been featured in several newspapers for its special attention to old-time crafts, skills, and games. The camps put on their own circuses, country fairs, dramatic productions, and a musical.

Sunday is another special day, with a late wake-up time, a buffet breakfast, special morning and afternoon events, and parent visits. The afternoon ends with a community meeting, cookout supper, and Cabin Night.

FACILITIES

The farm heritage of the camps is evident in the buildings. Cabins, each with 2 staff members and 8–10 campers, are simple native pine buildings lit with kerosene lanterns and warmed by a fieldstone fireplace. Washhouses have flush toilets and plenty of hot water for showers. On the 200 acres are several barns, crafts buildings, riding rings and trails, and lots of woods, meadows, and pastures in which to play and learn. The waterfronts occupy an entire side of a private, spring-fed lake.

STAFF

The camps employ a staff with an older average age than do most summer camps; half are over 23. Many are teachers, graduate students, or self-employed persons who love camp and the kind of learning that goes on in the summer. The annual staff return rate is 70–80 percent, and many staff members have been with the camps for four or five years. The staff represents a diverse group of nationalities, races, and religions. The British staff members are a popular and long-standing contingent. Austria, Belgium, Germany, Australia, New Zealand, Mexico, Canada, and a variety of Eastern European countries are also represented. Junior-level staff members work as assistants to the senior-level staff in the cabins and activities.

MEDICAL CARE

A resident nurse lives at the camps and supervises the medical care and infirmary staff. Rutland Hospital is 15 minutes away, and the camps are linked with several pediatricians and general practitioners in town. Medical forms and an inexpensive health and accident insurance plan are required for all those attending camp.

RELIGIOUS LIFE

The camps are not affiliated with any religious denomination but acknowledge a Creator and a positive approach to life. Virtually all religions usually are represented in the diverse camp community.

COSTS

The 2004 costs were as follows: two weeks, $1425; three weeks, $2130; and five weeks, $3550.

TRANSPORTATION

Public transportation is available by bus and train to Rutland and by plane to Burlington International Airport. The camps arrange to meet campers at both locations. There is good train service from New York City to Rutland.

APPLICATION TIMETABLE

New applications are accepted beginning in November. Sibling discounts are available.

For more information, contact:

Mike Byrom
Executive Director
P.O. Box 886
Key Largo, Florida 33037
888-345-9193 (toll-free)
E-mail: sangamonvt@aol.com
betcoxvt@aol.com
World Wide Web: http://www.campbetseycox.com
http://www.campsangamon.com

PARTICIPANT/FAMILY COMMENTS

"Our children hadn't been home a day and they were talking about going to camp again next year. Our thanks for the wonderful job you did with our children."

"As you know, we did an absolutely exhaustive study of camps for children when we considered where our son could best grow, learn, and most of all, have fun. The unique qualities of your program made your camp a very attractive option. We have yet to come across any other summer camp with such a wonderful outlook or with a similar philosophy."

CAMP SHANE

WEIGHT LOSS AND NUTRITION PROGRAMS

FERNDALE, NEW YORK

Type of Program: Weight loss and nutrition
Participants: Girls ages 7–25 and boys ages 7–17
Enrollment: 450
Program Dates: 3–9 weeks, late June to mid-August
Heads of Program: David Ettenberg, Certified Camp Director; Simon Greenwood, BCD

LOCATION

Located in the rural, magnificent Catskill Mountains in New York State, Camp Shane is run exactly as a traditional camp. Shane's warm, comfortable, and homelike atmosphere is devoted entirely to campers with weight problems.

BACKGROUND AND PHILOSOPHY

Camp Shane was founded in 1968 and is still run by the Ettenberg family. The camp does not unduly focus on or become obsessed with weight loss. It is founded on a "Commitment to Care" program, where every camper and counselor agrees to help create a camp where everyone is included in all activities, kids are congratulated for simply trying (not for how good they are), and there is no name-calling or stiff competition. Camp is a very supervised setting, with many counselors and adults on staff.

PROGRAM OFFERINGS

Campers are on a healthy, portioned, controlled meal plan. The camp serves foods that kids love, and the program is easy to continue when returning home. The menus are prepared by the staff's registered dietitian and follow American Dietetic Association guidelines. The camp also provides nutrition education, cooking classes, and meetings with guidance counselors to build self-esteem. Recreational activities include a wide variety of sports, twelve art shops, computers, video games, dune buggies, paintball, mini speed boats, waterskiing, tae-bo, aerobics, and much more. Evening activities include a DJ party, talent show, movie, and professional entertainment.

ENROLLMENT

Camp Shane has about 450 campers. They come from all over the U.S. and other countries. Daytime activities are grouped by the same age and gender. Campers are from varied socioeconomic backgrounds.

DAILY SCHEDULE

8:00	Wake up
8:30	Breakfast
9:45	Morning stretch
10:15	First period
11:00	Second period
11:45	Third period
12:30	Lunch
1:30	Rest hour
2:30	Fourth period
3:15	Afternoon snack
3:30	Fifth period
4:15	Sixth period
5:00	Shower hour
6:00	Dinner
7:30	Evening activity
9:00	Evening snack
9:30–11:30	Bedtime (by age group)

EXTRA OPPORTUNITIES AND ACTIVITIES

Camp Shane has a significant theater program, running three complete shows each summer. Off-camp activities include river rafting, amusement parks, and water parks. Optional opportunities at an additional cost include horseback riding, scuba diving, and trips to New York City; Boston; Philadelphia; Washington, D.C.; and Toronto.

FACILITIES

The camp is beautiful and well-maintained. Campers live in cheerful cabins that have paneled walls, modern lighting, and private bathrooms with private showers. Three staff members live in the bunks with the campers, ensuring safety and supervision at all times.

STAFF

Camp Shane's staff members are at least second-year college students. The head staff consists of adults who are teachers and parents themselves. The Director is designated a Certified Camp Director by the American Camping Association. There is an excellent guidance staff at Camp Shane.

MEDICAL CARE

Camp Shane has a fully equipped Health Center with 3 full-time nurses on staff 24 hours a day. A doctor comes to camp every day, and the community hospital is only 10 minutes from camp.

RELIGIOUS LIFE

Camp Shane offers campers the opportunity to attend services of most faiths.

COSTS

Tuition for the 2004 season for three weeks was $2900; six weeks, $4900; and nine weeks, $6400. No spending money is necessary. Fees are inclusive for all in-camp activities and the nutrition follow-up program after camp. The follow-up program includes monthly newsletters with nutrition information, exercise tips, and menus, and provides access to the Internet so campers may continue contact with the staff's registered dietician.

TRANSPORTATION

Camp Shane provides bus transportation from various points around metropolitan New York. Campers arriving by airplane are met by Camp Shane staff members at their arrival gates and are escorted to camp on chartered buses.

APPLICATION TIMETABLE

Inquiries are welcome year-round. Applicants must fill out a contract of enrollment and include an initial deposit of $500. Parents and campers are invited to attend an open house at the end of May.

FOR MORE INFORMATION, CONTACT:

David Ettenberg, Director
Simon Greenwood, Assistant Director
134 Teatown Road
Croton-on-Hudson, New York 10520
914-271-4141
877-914-4141 (toll-free)
Fax: 914-271-2103
E-mail: office@campshane.com
World Wide Web: http://www.campshane.com

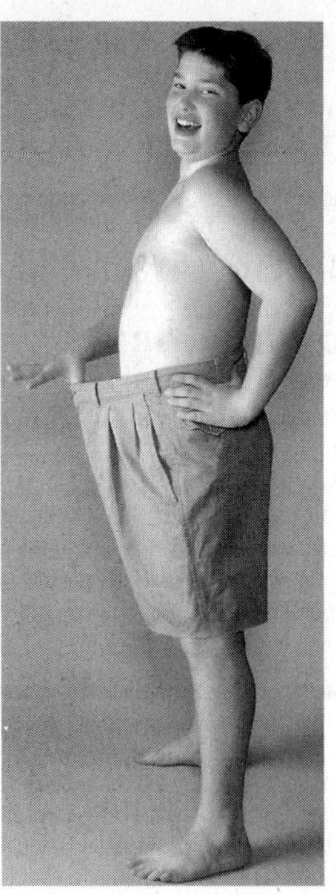

PARTICIPANT/FAMILY COMMENTS

"As eager as we were to help our son lose weight, we also wanted him to have an opportunity to make special friends and feel like a super star. Camp Shane made us believe that could happen...and you delivered. Thank you again."

"Camp Shane goes way beyond weight loss. The good feelings, the incredible friendships...they care about you."

"I love this place. I would definitely tell anyone to go. When I have kids, I'm sending them to Shane."

CAMP TREETOPS

SUMMER PROGRAM

LAKE PLACID, NEW YORK

Type of Program: Traditional camp, farm and garden programs, arts and crafts, overnight wilderness trips
Participants: Coeducational, ages 8–14: junior division, ages 8–11; senior division, ages 12–14
Enrollment: Junior Camp, 60; Senior Camp, 90; all children attend the full seven-week session
Program Dates: June 30 to August 17
Head of Program: Karen Culpepper, Director

LOCATION

Camp Treetops is just outside the village of Lake Placid, home of the 1980 Winter Olympics. The 200 acres, shared with North Country School, border Round Lake and are in the center of the "high peak" region of the Adirondack Mountains.

BACKGROUND AND PHILOSOPHY

When Treetops was established in 1920, it was one of the few coeducational camps for young children. It was founded by the educator Donald Slesinger.

The camp provides a rich, noncompetitive environment through programs in swimming, canoeing, sailing, horseback riding, music, creative and performing arts, camping skills, athletics, nature study, and farmwork. The children take many day and overnight camping trips by foot, horse, and canoe. Children may plan most of their own activities beyond the required swimming and riding classes. A work program, in which all participate, emphasizes community needs. Group life is made as meaningful as possible through the enrollment of staff and children from various racial, religious, national, economic, and geographic backgrounds.

PROGRAM OFFERINGS

The waterfront Round Lake is relatively small, shallow, and warm (for a mountain lake). Skills are taught for their intrinsic value as well as for preparing children for longer trips or more challenging conditions.

Swimming Each child is placed in an appropriate American Red Cross swim class, each of which is taught with an emphasis on "safety first." In addition to instructional classes, general swims are part of the daily schedule.

Canoeing and kayaking Most children avail themselves of paddling and Canoe Safety instruction. Basic skills are taught on the lake and are tested on the bigger lakes and rivers of the Adirondacks later in the summer.

Sailing Expert instruction is available. Many of the sailboats are moved to the Saranac Lakes in midsummer to provide greater challenges for the sailors.

English riding Treetops has its own horses. In addition to the required weekly lesson, many children choose to ride more often. The horses are ridden in the two riding rings, on the camp's own trails, and at Clifford Falls, where Treetops has the use of another barn, corral, and trails that lead into the backwoods. When campers have learned to saddle, bridle, and care for their mounts and have demonstrated adequate ability on the trails, they are eligible for an overnight riding trip to Clifford Falls.

Hiking and climbing Treetops is closer to the High Peaks of the Adirondacks than any other camp. There are easy hikes for beginners and mountains, trails, and rock formations for the most rugged and adventurous.

Overnight trips Overnight trips last from two to five days. They vary widely in difficulty in order to accommodate beginners, seasoned veterans, and all those in between. In addition to the hiking and climbing and riding trips, children paddle or sail in nearby lakes and rivers, swim in little-known prime swimming holes, explore, or gather flora and fauna for the science rooms.

Crafts and the arts Both divisions of the camp have a well-equipped ceramics studio, a woodshop, and a weaving room. Children participate in batik, photography and darkroom use, painting, drawing, and other crafts. Campers make their own music, whether by singing before mealtimes, practicing instruments, or performing in informal concerts. They enjoy participating in plays and practicing their own dance and gymnastics routines.

Work program Treetops depends on group sharing and individual contributions in order to foster responsibility. An extensive work program involves all the children in daily chores and in the physical care of the gardens and animals. Barn chores, although the most arduous and demanding assignments, are the most popular jobs.

The farm and gardens The barn provides the chance not only to watch the ways of horses, ponies, cows, pigs, chickens, sheep, and goats but also to care for them. The 3½ acres of camp gardens do far more than contribute fresh lettuce, beans, and strawberries to the camp table. The gardens help children see how every bit of food they eat derives from soil, sun, and water and demands planting, cultivating, weeding, and harvesting.

ENROLLMENT

Campers come from throughout the United States and represent a range of economic, racial, religious, and social backgrounds. Routinely, children attend from such countries as France, Spain, Italy, England, and Colombia. In 2002, Treetops was fully enrolled, with 60 children in the junior division and 90 children in the senior division.

DAILY SCHEDULE

7:00	Barn chores
8:00	Breakfast
8:45	Clean-up and morning council
9:45	Morning activities
12:00	Lunch
1:00	Afternoon council and rest hour
2:45	Afternoon activities
5:00	Work jobs
6:00	Dinner
7:00	Evening activities

One evening each week is set aside for square dancing, and, on a second evening, campers gather to sing, watch drama productions, or listen to musical pieces on which children have been working.

EXTRA OPPORTUNITIES AND ACTIVITIES

The camp program is complemented by field trips to such places as the Lake Placid Horse Show, the Essex County Fair (where Treetops shows its own animals), the nearby fish hatchery, the fort at Crown Point, and the Onchiota Indian Museum. Professional artists and crafts people are brought in as "artists in residence." For children ages 14–16 who are alumni of Camp Treetops or North Country School, there are small-group wilderness programs (8–12 children). These groups have spent past summers canoeing and backpacking in the Adirondacks, climbing out West, canoeing in Canada, and backpacking in Ecuador, Scotland, and France.

FACILITIES

Treetops has access to the North Country School's facilities, including its library. Children live in large platform tents, lean-tos, or small cabins.

STAFF

Camp Treetops' counselor-camper ratio is 1:3. The youngest staff members tend to have at least a year of college behind them, and many of the others are professional teachers. Many older, married couples are on the staff. Generally, two thirds of the staff return each summer. In 2002, the staff numbered 75.

MEDICAL CARE

Treetops employs 2 full-time nurses, 1 in each division. The camp doctor has offices 7 miles away at the Lake Placid Hospital. Because Lake Placid—one of two Olympic Training Centers in the United States—attracts world-class athletes, the medical facilities are excellent. There is a strong emphasis on nutrition at Treetops. The camp grows much of its own food and bakes its own bread. No soda, candy, or junk food is served. Care packages from home are carefully screened.

RELIGIOUS LIFE

Treetops is nondenominational. The camp tries to arrange for children who wish to attend services to be taken into Lake Placid.

COSTS

The camp fee for the 2005 season was $5700. A $1000 deposit is required with registration and is applied to tuition. The fee is all-inclusive, with the exception of transportation to and from camp and incidentals. No spending money is needed; incidentals are billed to the child's account.

FINANCIAL AID

To provide a diverse community, Treetops awards need-based scholarships; applications are available on request. About one sixth of the campers received varying levels of financial aid in 2001, amounting to 18 percent of total tuition income.

TRANSPORTATION

Counselors accompany children on buses from Manhattan. Children are also picked up at the Albany Airport and the Saranac Lake Airport. Driving time from New York City is approximately 5½ hours.

APPLICATION TIMETABLE

Although applications are accepted beginning in September, there is often a waiting list until all of the returning campers have been heard from. The return rate is routinely more than 80 percent, which limits openings, especially for the older age groups.

For more information, contact:

Karen Culpepper, Director
Camp Treetops
P.O. Box 187
Lake Placid, New York 12946
518-523-9329 Ext. 112
Fax: 518-523-4858
E-mail: karenc@nct.org
World Wide Web: http://www.nct.org

PARTICIPANT/FAMILY COMMENTS

"I would like to take this opportunity to tell you what a successful stay Ted had at Treetops. I recognize a great deal of personal growth in him and the proud acquisition of many new skills and areas of interest."

CAMP WAZIYATAH

SUMMER CAMP

WATERFORD, MAINE

Type of Program: ACA-accredited traditional family-oriented camp for fun, friendship, and excitement

Participants: Coed, ages 9–15; Leadership Training Program, ages 16–17.

Enrollment: 200

Program Dates: Four weeks, June 26 to July 22; three weeks, July 26 to August 12; 9–12-year olds, two weeks, June 26 to July 9 or July 24 to August 6

Heads of Program: The Kerns Family, Owners and Directors

LOCATION

Site of the original 1998 Disney TV series "Bug Juice," Waziyatah is among the beautiful lakes and mountains region of southern Maine. The 150 acres encompass open meadows, riding and hiking trails, woods, a lakefront beach, and playing fields.

BACKGROUND AND PHILOSOPHY

In a family-based environment of fun, friendship, and tradition, Camp Waziyatah encourages campers to develop the physical and social skills that will enable them to make courageous, mindful choices throughout their lives. The camp experience teaches children through the practical, everyday events of living together. When campers face choices, determine cabin chore lists, plan an event, play on a team, or talk out an issue instead of fighting, they are learning and practicing the real-life skills of compromise, leadership, cooperation, teamwork, and confrontation.

The Pines (ages 9 to 12) provides special attention to the younger, and often first-time, campers to help them enjoy familiar activities and discover new talents.

The Grove and The Hill (ages 12 to 15) help campers develop an even greater sense of fun and responsibility. Individualized program choices provide the opportunity to concentrate on certain areas or to explore widely in many areas. Teen campers often help plan evening programs for the entire division.

PROGRAM OFFERINGS

The instructional program embraces and encourages the beginner; challenges the experienced, confident camper; and helps advanced participants master many skills. Waziyatah emphasizes developing self-esteem through true competence. Campers choose from more than fifty activity options for each five-day cycle.

The program director takes a personal interest in helping each participant create a unique schedule filled with fun, variety, and the potential for learning new skills and making new friends.

Team and Individual Sports emphasize skill acquisition and development, expert coaching, and the chance to practice skills in intercamp and intramural games. Wazi builds a love of playing the game with caring adult support and lots of encouragement. Many campers find that the superb instruction they receive at camp advances their status on teams at home, while they increase self-confidence and have fun.

Performing Arts and Media offer the fun of participating in a dance or acting class, creating sets or costumes, learning to belt out a song, or being cast in a major musical in camp.

Visual Arts explores two- and three-dimensional media, including woodwork; drawing, painting, and sculpture; copper; and metalwork. Two electric wheels and hand-built pottery give free rein to the imagination. Photography teaches campers to process and print their photos while they develop an eye for composition. The art studio is an atelier of creative collaboration.

Riding offers both English and Western instruction at all levels. Advanced riders enjoy trail rides, develop jumping skills, join the mounted drill team, and go on riding overnights. Horse shows and special equestrian events are highlights of each session.

Waterfront activities include waterskiing, sailing, canoeing, sailboarding, kayaking, and rowing. All campers take Red Cross swimming to attain at least Level III proficiency. Accomplished swimmers may choose higher-level Red Cross classes, the swim team, or competitive training and conditioning.

ENROLLMENT

Approximately 200 spirited, energetic, and fun-loving campers from all over the world enjoy the friendships, fun, and excitement of Camp Waziyatah each summer.

DAILY SCHEDULE

7:30–8:15	Breakfast
9:30–12:30	Two activity periods
12:30	Lunch
1:30	Rest period
2:30–5:30	Three activity periods
6:00	Dinner
7:30	Evening activity (coed)
9:00–10:00	Bedtime (depending on age)

EXTRA OPPORTUNITIES AND ACTIVITIES

ESL instruction during activity periods provides support to campers not yet fluent in English. Instructors focus on conversational English, with an empahsis on language that will be of use during the camp experience.

Adventure Bound Trips on lakes and rivers or in the mountains are available for all ages and are designed for all abilities. Campouts and training in outdoor-living skills also play an important role. Fifteen-year-old campers enjoy the special thrill of a challenging white-water rafting trip.

Adventure Challenge operates a 50-foot climbing tower offering four very different faces, each with more than 2,000 possibilities for creative, challenging routes to the top.

FACILITIES

Twenty-six sturdy, spacious, and screened cabins, all with electricity, sinks, and toilets. and many with showers, each house 6–12 campers and 2 counselors. The large, lodge-style dining room overlooking Lake McWain offers several wholesome choices at each meal. The Waziyatah Playhouse—a gem of a barn theater—is part of the arts complex, which includes a video studio, photography lab, dance studio, art studio, and woodshop.

The Lakeside Gymnasium is home to gymnastics, martial arts, and an open-air amphitheatre for large performances. The Waziyatah Stables are near the two school rings, with easy access to miles of trails for riding. Stable management activities ensure the understanding of proper animal care, thorough grooming, familiarity with tack, and equipment maintenance.

A beautiful beach waterfront welcomes swimmers, water skiers, canoeists, sailors, and windsurfers. Closer to the woods, the Great Wazi Climbing Tower soars 50 feet into the treetops, inviting campers of all ages and sizes to an appropriate challenge with expert instruction and close supervision. Tennis courts, street hockey, volleyball and basketball courts, archery and rifle ranges, tetherball areas, a fencing court, two soccer fields, and softball/baseball fields round out the sports facilities.

STAFF

The directors choose an energetic, highly motivated, competent cadre of women and men to lead spirited, imaginative, and involved campers. The camper-staff member ratio is nearly 2:1. Extensive staff training and development produces counselors who are caregivers, excellent role models, and professional and effective activity leaders who make each camper's summer happy and productive.

MEDICAL CARE

Two licensed nurses are on 24-hour duty in the well-equipped health center. Doctors and hospital support are on call night and day and are 20 minutes from camp. Many on-site staff members are qualified first-aiders and wilderness first responders.

COSTS

Fees, policies, and payment schedules arrive with the enrollment packet.

TRANSPORTATION

Waziyatah staff members meet each arriving camper at the Portland airport. Many families drive to camp, spending a minivacation at the Maine coast. Families may opt to use Waziyatah's chartered bus service from the Boston area.

APPLICATION TIMETABLE

Initial inquiries are welcome year-round; early enrollment is advised. Prospective families may phone ahead to visit between May 30 and October 10.

FOR MORE INFORMATION, CONTACT:

The Kerns Family, Owners and Directors
Camp Waziyatah

June to September
530 Mill Hill Road
Waterford, Maine 04088
207-583-6781

October to May
19 Vose Lane
East Walpole, Massachusetts 02032
508-668-9758

E-mail: info@wazi.com
World Wide Web: http://www.wazi.com

CAMP WEKEELA

COEDUCATIONAL SUMMER CAMP

CANTON, MAINE

Type of Program: Traditional camping
Participants: Coeducational, ages 6–16
Enrollment: 300
Program Dates: Last week in June to third week in August
Heads of Program: Eric Scoblionko, Director; Ephram Caflun, Assistant Director

LOCATION

Camp Wekeela lies nestled among woods that have been timbered since Colonial times in south-central Maine. Abundant recreational facilities, rustic cabins, and a scenic nature preserve span more than 150 acres next to Little Bear Pond, a gorgeous natural lake connected to Big Bear Pond. Wekeela is about 3 hours from Boston, 1 hour from Portland, Maine, and ½ hour from Lewiston/Auburn, Maine.

BACKGROUND AND PHILOSOPHY

Wekeela draws from a unique history that binds campers to the pioneers of the past. Camping first came here three quarters of a century ago when Emma Graumann founded a girls' summer camp called We-You-Wega. Eric and Lauren Scoblionko took up the mantel in 1981 to establish one of America's premier coed camp experiences. Wekeela challenges every camper to experiment, learn, and grow. Flexible four-, six-, and eight-week camp session options accommodate family needs, and, no matter the length of the visit, every camper enjoys a complete, well-rounded experience of self-discovery, friendship, and challenge. Staff members are exceptionally well qualified, offering specialty instruction in team and individual athletics, water sports, tennis, wilderness and outdoor adventure programs, and creative and performing arts. Finally, campers explore every inch of Wekeela, from serpentine hiking trails and vertical rock climbs to the expansive waterfront and outdoor adventure zone. Outside the camp's borders, exciting destinations beckon campers, from the rocky Maine shores and the White Mountains of New Hampshire to historic Boston's North Shore, Montreal, and more.

PROGRAM OFFERINGS

The Wekeela program is divided into six developmental areas (athletics, water sports, tennis, wilderness/outdoor adventure programs, and creative and performing arts), each staffed by skilled professionals. All campers participate in required and elective programs; older campers have more freedom to choose areas of interest. Campers establish their schedules prior to camp based on an A-, B-, and C-day rotation. Every fifth day is a "Wekeela Day," during which half the camp goes on an out-of-camp trip while the other half participates in special camp events.

Athletics The athletics included in each camper's schedule provide competition, challenges, discipline, skills, and loads of fun. Younger campers receive instruction in the fundamental skills of major sports, including baseball, basketball, and soccer. Offerings include archery, baseball (two fields), softball, basketball, soccer (three regulation fields), beach volleyball, field hockey, football, Frisbee, golf, gymnastics, horseback riding, lacrosse, a multistation fitness studio, weight training, and track and field.

Water Sports Wekeela's expansive, picturesque waterfront provides campers with a wide variety of nonstop summer fun. Every child in Kids Camp receives American Red Cross swimming instruction, and all campers can elect to participate in the enormously popular water-ski program. Canoeing, competitive swimming, fishing, kayaking, sailing, snorkeling, swimming, water polo, waterskiing, and windsurfing round out the comprehensive waterfront offerings.

Tennis Wekeela has earned the unofficial title of "Wimbledon Down East" for its top-caliber instruction and abundant tennis facilities, even drawing young people who are interested principally in specialty tennis camps. The program provides USTA-certified instruction, a miniclubhouse, ten all-weather courts (six lighted), and two grass courts.

Wilderness/Outdoors Wekeela offers traditional wilderness activities with a twist—contemporary, extreme outdoor challenges that push the envelope on excitement and fun. Offerings include backpacking, bicycle trips, canoe trips, caving, mountaineering, orienteering, rafting, rock climbing, a fifteen-station ropes course, white-water rafting, wilderness camping, and a three-sided, 40-foot climbing tower.

Creative Arts In the hands of the camp's skilled staff, campers can tap the creative talent that is deep within them. Activities include batik, ceramics, woodworking, pottery, sculpture, drawing, fabric arts, film, graphic arts, jewelry making, painting, printmaking, leather working, metalworking, photography, and radio/video production.

Performing Arts At Wekeela, expert coaching and instruction help campers hone their unique performance skills in aerobics, dance (ballet, folk, jazz, modern, and tap), mime, musical productions, music (piano, guitar, and vocal), and puppetry.

Wekeela offers flexibility to families with four-, six-, and eight-week sessions. Each has its own unique ingredients, with specific program highlights. Campwide, there is no sense of coming and going, due to consistent cabin groupings. Younger campers break loose from camp for regular, supervised day and evening events. Teen campers have additional options, including multiday trips outside Wekeela. Special events culminate in the season finale—a three-day Color War where teams match their skills, strength, and wits in a multidisciplinary battle for top honors.

ENROLLMENT

Young people flock to Wekeela from across the United States and around the globe. This rich diversity of ex-

periences and cultures serves as a wonderful springboard, introducing campers to the wider world around them. There are approximately 300 campers in attendance at any one time, with 425 enrolled during the season.

DAILY SCHEDULE

Each day begins with reveille at 7:30 a.m., followed by breakfast and then Kids Camp and Teen Camp meetings. Next come three 1-hour periods of action-packed play and/or instruction. A buffet-style lunch alfresco features multiple entrees, fresh fruits and vegetables, and mouth-watering desserts. An after-lunch rest hour is followed by three more activity periods. A nutritious and delicious evening meal in the dining hall is followed by an evening activity. In addition to daily activities, there are regular trips to points of interest as well as intercamp athletic contests.

FACILITIES

State-of-the-art facilities include lighted all-weather regulation tennis courts with a miniclubhouse; an expansive floating dock system for swimming; four tournament water-ski boats and a marina; lighted basketball courts; a fully equipped gymnastics center with a tumbling strip, a vault, uneven parallel bars, and more; a fitness studio; multiple regulation, groomed playing fields; a three-sided climbing tower; a fifteen-station ropes adventure course; an air-conditioned darkroom; a camp radio station and video lab; a fully equipped ceramics and woodworking studio; an art center with a two-story deck; a game room; an outdoor theater; sturdy wood cabins; a General Store with a post office; on-site laundry; and a 350-seat dining hall and main lodge.

STAFF

Providing an outstanding camp experience requires outstanding staff members. The camp's 150 counselors and program specialists offer top-of-the-line specialty instruction, coaching, and cabin supervision. Wekeela's staff maintains a high level of licensing, certification, experience, and professional affiliations. At a minimum, counselors have attended one year of college. Numerous college-level coaches from a variety of sports are on staff.

Camp staff members participate in a ten-day precamp orientation, during which they receive intensive preparation in camp curricula, lesson plan development, behavioral and psychological counseling, and teaching specializations. Wekeela is kept in prime condition by 5 full-time groundskeepers, while an office staff of 7 oversees administrative functions. Wekeela has an excellent camper-staff ratio of 3:1.

MEDICAL CARE

Campers are assured of expert, on-site medical attention. Three full-time registered nurses staff the on-campus infirmary, and doctors located within 10 minutes are on call. The Central Maine Medical Center in Lewiston, Maine, is within easy reach. The camp is 911 accessible in the event of an emergency. Campers must submit a medical history and should provide their own medical insurance.

COSTS

Enrollment fees for 2005 are $4975 for four weeks, $7800 for six weeks, and $8200 for eight weeks. Each camper maintains a nonrefundable personal expense account of $175 to $275, depending upon session length. Additional fees include charges for golf, horseback riding, scuba diving, and transportation. An initial deposit is required upon enrollment, with a second payment due in January and the balance due by May 1.

TRANSPORTATION

Wekeela has a designated travel agent with specifically recommended flights, a number of which include chaperones. Campers can use a camp bus service from Boston (3 hours away) or Portland (1 hour away), or parents can arrange to drop off and pick up their children.

APPLICATION TIMETABLE

Applications are welcome at any time. Families are encouraged to visit the campus for a personal tour. Appointments are necessary and should be made in advance by calling the camp office. A significant percentage of campers re-enroll by November 1, with most fully enrolled by January 1.

FOR MORE INFORMATION REGARDING PROSPECTIVE CAMPERS, CONTACT:

Eric Scoblionko, Director

FOR MORE INFORMATION REGARDING PROSPECTIVE STAFF, CONTACT:

Ephram Caflun, Assistant Director

September 1–May 31	*June 1–August 31*
2807C Delmar Drive	1750 Bear Pond Road
Columbus, Ohio 43209	Hartford, Maine 04220
614-253-3177	207-224-7878
800-959-3177 (toll-free)	Fax: 207-224-7999
Fax: 614-253-3661	

E-mail: wekeela1@aol.com
World Wide Web: http://www.campwekeela.com

PARTICIPANT/FAMILY COMMENTS

"Out of the five camp experiences I've had, this summer at Wekeela was definitely the best."—Camper

CARDIGAN MOUNTAIN SCHOOL

SUMMER SESSION

CANAAN, NEW HAMPSHIRE

Type of Program: Academic review, enrichment, and recreation
Participants: Coeducational, grades 4–8
Program Dates: A six-week program from the third week in June to the first week in August
Head of Program: Thomas S. Pastore, Director

LOCATION

Cardigan Mountain School is located approximately 18 miles from Dartmouth College on Canaan Street Lake in Canaan, New Hampshire. Situated on a 500-acre campus, Cardigan is easily accessible by car or plane.

BACKGROUND AND PHILOSOPHY

The Summer Session was instituted in 1951 to meet the needs of four groups of students—those who require work in basic skills, those who desire review, those who desire enrichment, and those who are candidates for entrance to Cardigan Mountain School in the fall. The program also serves a limited number of international students for whom English is not their first language. Finally, recognizing that for most children summer traditionally means recreation, Cardigan provides sports and activities along with its academic offerings, creating an exciting blend of camp and school.

PROGRAM OFFERINGS

The main purpose of the academic program is to assist students in strengthening basic skills in the core areas of English, mathematics, and reading; developing effective study techniques; and becoming involved in the process of his or her own education. An enrichment curriculum offers students opportunities to challenge themselves in topics of interest outside of the traditional model. Much is accomplished by means of small classes (maximum class size is 7 students), individualized instruction, and close supervision of study time. As part of the application, Cardigan requests information from the parent, the present school, individual teachers, guidance counselors, and educational consultants.

Traditional class offerings include English, mathematics, foreign languages (French, Spanish, and Latin), and computers. A course in reading and study skills, providing students with the strategies to further develop those important skills, emphasizes four areas: reading flexibility, comprehension, vocabulary development, and study skills. The Language Learning Lab is a tutorial to aid students who need remediation in reading and/or writing. Tutorial groups are limited to no more than 3 students.

The Bronfman science and arts facility provides space for the enrichment curriculum. Environmental science courses, an enhanced computer science program, and courses in the fine arts (painting, ceramics, drawing, and chorus) have been introduced to the morning academic curriculum. Other enrichment electives include writers' workshops, literary surveys, and an SSAT/SAT preparation course.

Teachers create an individualized plan for instruction. Students participate in the formulation and daily implementation of that plan. Evaluation of the student is based upon effort. Performance reports are sent to parents at midsession and at the end of the program. Also included in these mailings are dormitory and faculty adviser comments.

ENROLLMENT

Approximately 180 boys and girls attend, with the majority enrolling as boarders. Students are eligible to attend if they are presently in grades 4 through 8. Students come from about twenty-five states and ten other countries.

DAILY SCHEDULE

Students enjoy a balance between an academic morning and camplike activities in the afternoon. Monday through Saturday, students rise at 7 a.m. After breakfast, students begin their academic day, which consists of five 40-minute periods. A sit-down lunch is served after classes. After lunch, students participate in recreational activities, including swimming, baseball, tennis, sailing, soccer, lacrosse, basketball, windsurfing, trapshooting, archery, rock climbing, golf, rocketry, art, and music. A family style dinner is followed by a supervised study hall. Younger students are in bed by 9:15 p.m., and older students by 10 p.m. On Sundays, students select on- and off-campus activities, attend Chapel, and enjoy free time.

EXTRA OPPORTUNITIES AND ACTIVITIES

On weekends, students may elect to take part in a variety of off-campus activities. Taking advantage of Cardigan's proximity to the Green and White Mountains of Vermont and New Hampshire, students leave campus regularly on hiking and canoe trips. Sunday overnights at Cardigan's Clark Pond cabin are also offered. Trips to nearby Hanover; Burlington, Vermont; and the coast are also included.

Cardigan's intramural Green and White competitions, capped by the exciting Great Race during the final week, are a student favorite. Some evenings are reserved for visiting performers or educational/cultural presentations.

FACILITIES

Cardigan's science and art facility offers nearly 14,000 square feet of classroom, studio, and laboratory (science and computer) space. The Kirk Library is a well-equipped multimedia resource center.

Students reside in traditional boarding school dormitories and are supervised by the faculty. A health center is located on campus. While students take advantage of the good weather and have some picnics, the majority of meals are taken family style in the dining room.

Acres of athletic fields, six tennis courts, and the sandy beach of Canaan Street Lake allow students to play on sunny days, while the Cardigan hockey arena, featuring indoor tennis courts and space for volleyball and street hockey, keeps them dry when it rains. The waterfront is the hub of summer fun, and students may be found sailing in the fleet of boats, swimming off the docks, or casting for trout.

STAFF

The Summer Session has approximately 55 experienced educators on the faculty. Teachers come from Cardigan Mountain School and from other independent and public schools.

The director of the Summer Session is Thomas S. Pastore, who holds a B.A. degree from Hamilton College and a M.A. degree from Trinity College. Mr. Pastore was appointed to the directorship in 2003.

MEDICAL CARE

The Morrison Health Center is an on-campus facility. Supplementary services are provided by the Dartmouth-Hitchcock Medical Center or its satellite clinic in Canaan.

RELIGIOUS LIFE

Cardigan Mountain School is nondenominational in the Judeo-Christian tradition. Students are required to attend the Sunday evening chapel service. These inclusive services give students the opportunity to have a quiet moment of reflection or to participate by reading a poem, singing a song, or playing an instrument.

COSTS

Tuition for 2003 was $6400. Day tuition was $3400. The application fee was $35 for U.S. residents and $125 for non-U.S. residents.

FINANCIAL AID

Need-based financial aid is available.

TRANSPORTATION

Transportation is provided to and from Boston. Air service is also available to Manchester and Lebanon, New Hampshire.

APPLICATION TIMETABLE

Inquiries may be made at any time. Applications are reviewed on a rolling basis. An interview is not a requirement, but visitors are welcome.

For more information, contact:

Thomas S. Pastore, Summer Session Director
Cardigan Mountain School Summer Session
62 Alumni Drive
Canaan, New Hampshire 03741-9307
603-523-3528
Fax: 603-523-3565
World Wide Web: http://www.cardigan.org

CAREER EXPLORATIONS

IN RESIDENCE AT THE SAMUEL B. AND DAVID ROSE BUILDING, JUILLIARD SCHOOL

SUMMER INTERNSHIP PROGRAM

NEW YORK CITY, NEW YORK

Type of Program: Residential internship program for high school students
Participants: Coeducational, ages 16–18
Enrollment: 40–50
Program Dates: One 4-week session, late June through July
Heads of Program: Margot Jackler, M.Ed, and Josh Flowerman, Directors

LOCATION

Based in New York City, Career Explorations makes full use of the diverse cultural, educational, and recreational resources that make New York City one of the most exciting cities in the world. Students and staff members reside on the campus of the Juilliard School in the midst of Lincoln Center, the world-renowned home of the New York Philharmonic, the Metropolitan Opera, and the New York City Ballet.

BACKGROUND AND PHILOSOPHY

Founded in 2003 by the Flowerman family, Career Explorations is designed to provide opportunities for highly motivated high school students to gain valuable insight into possible career goals and courses of study in a nurturing and supervised environment. Career Explorations makes available a healthy balance of work, culture, social life, and entertainment as participants embrace the transition from high school to college.

PROGRAM OFFERINGS

Career Explorations presents a unique opportunity for high school students to sample the professional world thorough monthlong hands-on internships. Interns receive practical experience working alongside professional mentors at top firms and organizations throughout Manhattan. Career Explorations offers internships in a variety of fields including cooking, fashion, finance, journalism, law, media, medicine, music/recording industry, professional sports, psychology, real estate, social service, veterinary medicine, and others.

ENROLLMENT

Enrollment is competitive and based upon merit, application, and recommendations.

EXTRA OPPORTUNITIES AND ACTIVITIES

In addition to a glimpse into a professional field, Career Explorations offers a fun, activity-packed summer that includes supervised activities and opportunities to explore New York City. Students experience live theater, concerts, sporting events, museums, shopping, restaurants, and everything else that the city has to offer. Career Explorations also offers seminars on the college admissions process with alumni of Harvard and Princeton and optional tours of college campuses in the area. A community service project and a career night complement the experience.

FACILITIES

Students and staff members live in an air-conditioned residence hall at the Juilliard School. The building provides 24-hour security and includes amenities such as a cafeteria, a lounge area with television, a pool table, a computer center, and a card-operated laundry.

Juilliard provides dining options for program participants in its modern cafeteria. On weekdays, students and staff members have breakfast and dinner at Juilliard, while taking responsibility for their own lunches. Juilliard's food services provide brunch and dinner on Saturday and Sunday.

STAFF

Career Explorations summer staff is comprised of a diverse team of qualified and caring college graduates and graduate students who have extensive experience working with adolescents. Staffers function as dorm parents, mentors, and liaisons between student and internship provider. Resident advisers live in the dorm with students, supervise their activities, and maintain their overall welfare and safety. The ratio of students to staff members is approximately 6:1. Directors also live in the residence hall.

MEDICAL CARE

All participants are required to have health insurance including benefits for emergency care and hospitalization. Emergency and urgent care is available at St. Luke's Hospital, seven blocks away from Juilliard on 59th Street and Amsterdam Avenue.

COSTS

Tuition for the full four-week residential program is $5495 and includes tuition, housing, breakfast and dinner, a MetroCard for transportation within New York City, group activities, special events, and weekend excursions. Transportation to and from New York City, lunch during the week, optional trips, personal laundry, and incidentals are not included.

Early enrollment discounts are available.

TRANSPORTATION

Juilliard is accessible by all area airports, trains and bus stations, as well as by car. Students arriving at local airports, Penn Station, Grand Central Terminal, and Port Authority are met by staff members.

Each intern receives a prepaid MetroCard good for one-month travel on buses and subways in Manhattan. During orientation, students participate in activities in order to learn their way around the city and to be prepared to travel independently to and from their internships.

APPLICATION TIMETABLE

Initial inquiry is welcome year-round. Career Explorations encourages students to apply early, as internships are selective and spaces are limited. Applications are carefully considered, and students are notified of their admission decision within two weeks of receipt of all application materials. Applications and schedules are available online at the Career Explorations Web address.

For more information, contact:

Margot Jackler and Josh Flowerman, Directors
Career Explorations
119 Headquarters Plaza
Morristown, New Jersey 07960
973-455-1478
Fax: 973-984-5666
E-mail: info@careerexplorations.com
World Wide Web: http://www.ceinternships.com

PARTICIPANT/FAMILY COMMENTS

"This summer has really helped me grow, not only in the workplace, but also as a person. This was one month I will never forget."

"I learned more than I thought I ever could."

CARNEGIE MELLON PRE-COLLEGE

SUMMER PROGRAMS

PITTSBURGH, PENNSYLVANIA

Type of Program: Intensive academic and fine arts program
Participants: Coeducational, ages 16–18
Enrollment: 400–500
Program Dates: One six-week session: early July to mid-August
Head of Program: Director of Pre-College Programs

LOCATION

Carnegie Mellon Pre-College is held on Carnegie Mellon University's 105-acre campus 5 miles east of downtown Pittsburgh, Pennsylvania. The campus is bordered by two residential neighborhoods and a 500-acre city park, providing students with a quiet setting for study, but easy access to shopping, dining, and entertainment.

BACKGROUND AND PHILOSOPHY

Carnegie Mellon has offered pre-college programs for more than fifty years. The purpose of the Pre-Programs is to recruit qualified prospective students to the Carnegie Mellon community with the eventual goal of enrolling them into the undergraduate population. Each program has its own course work and requirements that allow students a summer of exploration in their chosen area of study. Academic credit is available in Advanced Placement/ Early Admission (APEA). All programs are intensive experiences designed to challenge and stretch students' intellect and artistic talents.

PROGRAM OFFERINGS

Carnegie Mellon offers six distinct pre-college programs, allowing high school students the opportunity to learn and grow in a university setting with peers from across the country and abroad. To closely approximate the college experience, the programs combine hard work, independence, the pleasure of accomplishment, interaction, and cultural diversity.

The APEA program enables students to take challenging, freshmen-level courses for college credit in a variety of subjects, including biology, calculus, chemistry, computing, economics, engineering, history, humanities, math, philosophy, physics, and writing. Additional courses may be offered each summer. APEA students may elect to receive No Grade for a course they don't want reported on their transcript. Typically, APEA students choose two courses for study, with special permission granted to those students requesting three courses. Traditional classroom instruction, along with creative hands-on projects, allow students to apply concepts and ideas. The fine arts programs offer non-credit experience in architecture, art, design, drama (acting, musical theater, and technical design), and music. All fine arts programs simulate the freshman year in Carnegie Mellon's fine arts conservatory programs.

ENROLLMENT

Each year, between 400 and 500 students from across the United States and around the world enroll in the six Pre-College Programs. APEA and the Drama program are the largest, with annual enrollments of up to 150 students. The Architecture, Art, Design, and Music programs have annual enrollments ranging from 16 (Design) to 50 or more. In 2002, students enrolled from more than thirty states and seven countries. Approximately 15 percent of enrolled students are from African-American, Hispanic, or Asian backgrounds.

DAILY SCHEDULE

The daily schedule for Pre-College students differs slightly depending on the program into which they enroll. Advanced Placement/Early Admission (APEA) students typically have two classes per day; the first morning classes begin at 9 a.m., and the last afternoon class ends at 4:30 p.m. If students are studying a lab science or engineering course, they most likely have a 3-hour lab section one afternoon a week from 1:30 to 4:30. Fine arts students in the architecture, art, design, drama, or music programs follow an intensive schedule that requires significant studio and rehearsal time as well as frequent evening hours.

All Pre-College students are required to abide by a series of regulations designed to ensure students' safety and well-being. Residential students have an 11 p.m. curfew Sunday through Thursday and a 12 midnight curfew on Friday and Saturday nights. No overnight guests are allowed in residence halls, and students must receive written permission from parents/guardians to leave campus. Students are allowed to explore Pittsburgh by public transportation, but no car travel is allowed unless approved by Student Life counselors.

EXTRA OPPORTUNITIES AND ACTIVITIES

While Pre-College students work hard in their respective programs, they are expected to have fun. After all, it is their summer vacation. The Student Life staff plans a series of educational and social activities, including trips to area museums, a Fourth of July party, a river cruise and dance, and more. In addition, faculty members in the various programs have coordinated trips to Washington, D.C.; Baltimore; and other nearby cities. Weekend activities consist of movies in the park, field trips, and free time for individual activities. During the third week of the program, families are invited to attend the Family Weekend, during which antique trolley tours of Pittsburgh are offered. Other Family Weekend activities have included Pittsburgh Pirates baseball games, trips to the Carnegie Science Center, a talent show, and art and design project showings.

FACILITIES

All residential Pre-College students live in three on-campus residence halls. Most students share a double room with a roommate. Each room has full Internet access and is completely furnished. Students have complete access to all campus facilities, including the recreation center, library, computer labs, dining establishments, and academic buildings. Students are not allowed to enter residence halls not affiliated with Pre-College and are forewarned about all summer construction sites.

STAFF

The summer staff consists of 20 Student Life counselors selected from the Carnegie Mellon undergraduate population. All counselors are supervised by two professional Student Life staff members. Counselors serve as mentors, confidantes, disciplinarians, and friends to Pre-College students and work diligently to ensure a positive experience.

MEDICAL CARE

Pre-College students enjoy access to Carnegie Mellon's medical and psychiatric care facilities. If necessary, students can receive routine medication, such as allergy shots, from the Health Center. There are several nearby hospitals, including the renowned University of Pittsburgh Medical Center, in case of emergency. At least three hospitals are within 10 minutes of Carnegie Mellon's campus. All students must submit medical forms prior to enrolling in Pre-College; health insurance must be provided through family or individual policies.

RELIGIOUS LIFE

The Carnegie Mellon Pre-College Program is not religiously affiliated. No services are offered on campus during the summer; however, several nearby churches and temples are within easy walking distance for students interested in continuing their worship. Student Life staff members can help direct students to appropriate sites of worship.

COSTS

In summer 2003, program costs for the six Pre-College programs varied, depending on whether students received academic credit for their program. For the APEA program, tuition was $3965, housing was $750, dining fees were $820, and the activity fee was $350, for a total estimated cost of $5885, with books and supplies costing an additional $175. In architecture, art, design, and music, the total estimated costs amounted to $4785 (tuition, $2865; housing, $750; dining fees, $820; and activity fee, $350). Books and supplies were $375 for art and $300 for architecture and design. For the drama program, total estimated expenses were $4985 (tuition, $3065; housing, $750; dining fees, $820; and activity fee, $350). Books and supplies were an additional $475–$525 for drama. All costs are for residential students; students commuting from the surrounding area have reduced charges.

In addition to the above fees, all applicants must pay a $25 application fee. All students must submit their payments before enrolling in the program; no payment plans are offered. Although most organized activities are free of charge, in some cases students are expected to purchase tickets at a reduced cost. Most students find they can successfully participate in all activities for no more than $150–$200.

TRANSPORTATION

Carnegie Mellon's campus is located 5 miles east of downtown Pittsburgh. The city is accessible by all major airlines, trains, and buses. The airport shuttle stops at Carnegie Mellon; trips to and from the airport cost $2.25 and take between 45 and 60 minutes. Students arriving by train or bus can catch a number of buses ($1.75 fare), which stop at Carnegie Mellon, or take a cab from directly outside the stations. Travel time from the downtown stations to Carnegie Mellon is about 20 minutes. All Pre-College students arriving on their own are met at the airport shuttle drop-off and assisted with their luggage by Student Life counselors.

APPLICATION TIMETABLE

Pre-College applications are available in early January. Interested students may contact the Office of Admission at Carnegie Mellon at any time during the year; all sophomore and junior students in the admission database are sent Pre-College applications. Interviews and campus tours are not required for Pre-College applicants, although all interested students are invited to visit campus prior to enrolling in the summer program.

Students may submit applications via mail or over the Internet with a nonrefundable $25 application fee. The suggested application deadline is May 1, although applications are typically accepted until June 1, if space is available. Applicants are typically notified of their admission decision within two to three weeks of receipt of their completed application, beginning in April. All fees and forms must be postmarked by early June (a date is set each year) to ensure enrollment in the program.

FOR MORE INFORMATION, CONTACT:

Pre-College Programs
Office of Admission
Carnegie Mellon University
5000 Forbes Avenue
Pittsburgh, Pennsylvania 15213-3890
412-268-2082
Fax: 412-268-7838
E-mail: precollege@andrew.cmu.edu
World Wide Web: http://www.cmu.edu/enrollment/pre-college/

CCI THE RENAISSANCE SCHOOL, ITALY

CCI SUMMER ACADEMY ITALY

LANCIANO, ITALY

Type of Program: Academic
Participants: Coed, ages 15–18
Enrollment: 120
Program Dates: Four weeks in July/August
Head of Program: Marisa DiCarlo D'Alessandro

LOCATION

Located minutes from the Adriatic coast, Lanciano is beautifully situated between the ocean and the Apennine Mountains and provides a safe, friendly, and charming environment. The air is clean and fresh, and this small city of 40,000 people is alive with musical concerts all summer long. The streets are lined with cafés and restaurants, and the historical town center is 2,300 years old. Local trains are available for day excursions to nearby magnificent towns, and the beach at San Vito Marino is just a 15-minute drive from Lanciano.

BACKGROUND AND PHILOSOPHY

CCI The Renaissance School, Canadian College Italy, offers a high-quality academic curriculum that leads to admission in North American and international universities. CCI offers a summer program of academic-credit courses. Courses conform to the accreditation guidelines of the Ontario, Canada, Ministry of Education, and credits may be applied toward a high school diploma at institutions throughout North America and abroad. Upon successful completion of the program, a copy of course results and a transcript are sent to each student and his or her school. At CCI, the combination of the students' desire to learn, the teachers' dedication to teaching, and community involvement create a highly effective learning experience.

PROGRAM OFFERINGS

English The Grade 11 course emphasizes development of literacy, critical thinking, and communication skills. Students analyze challenging texts from various periods; conduct research and analyze the information they gather; write persuasive and literary essays; and analyze the relationships among media forms, audiences, and media-industry practices. The development of the English language is also studied. The Grade 12 course emphasizes consolidation of literacy, critical thinking, and communication skills. Students spend time analyzing a range of challenging texts from various periods, countries, and cultures; writing analytical and argumentative essays and a major paper for an independent literary research project; and applying key concepts to analyze media works. Time is spent focusing on understanding academic language and using it coherently and confidently in discussion and argument.

Classical Civilization In this Grade 12 course, students explore the beliefs and achievements of the classical world that have shaped Western thought and civilization. Students investigate classical culture's mythology, art, literature, and philosophy, as well as elements of ancient Greek and Latin, through a variety of activities such as dramatization, audiovisual presentations, and discussions. They read classical authors in English and examine archeological evidence to enhance their skills in communication and critical and creative thinking.

Visual Arts Students in the Grade 11 course develop skills and knowledge in the visual arts, explore a range of subject matter through studio activities, and consolidate practical skills. They also analyze art works and study aspects of Western art history and art forms from Canada and various other parts of the world. In the Grade 12 course, students analyze art form; use theories of art in analyzing and producing art; increase their understanding of stylistic changes in modern and contemporary Western art, Canadian (including Native Canadian) art, and art forms from various parts of the world; and produce a body of work demonstrating a personal approach.

Italian The courses in Italian are offered on three levels. Level 2, the first course, provides students with the language-learning experiences that enable them to communicate in Italy. Students develop and apply speaking skills in a variety of contexts, participating in activities that improve their reading comprehension and writing skills. They also explore Italy's cultural aspects by taking part in community-sponsored events and activities involving both print and technological resources. The Level 3 course offers review and further development of the students' knowledge of Italian and communication skills. Students learn to speak and write with clarity and accuracy through a variety of activities. Thinking skills are enhanced through a critical study of literature, and a variety of print and technological resources enable continued exploration of Italy's culture. At Level 4, students are prepared for university studies in Italian. Clear and precise language usage is enhanced, and the students develop the skills needed to engage in sustained conversations and discussions, understand and evaluate information, read diverse materials for both study and pleasure, and write clearly and effectively. Community resources and computer technology are used to add to the students' knowledge of the culture of Italy.

Biology The Grade 11 course furthers students' understanding of the processes involved in biological systems. Students study cellular functions, genetic continuity, internal systems and regulation, the diversity of living things, and the anatomy, growth, and functions of plants. The course focuses on the theoretical aspects of the topics under study and helps students refine skills related to

scientific investigation. In the Grade 12 course, students look more deeply into the concepts and processes associated with biological systems. They study theory and conduct investigations in the areas of metabolic processes, molecular genetics, homeostatis, evolution, and population dynamics. Emphasis is placed on gaining the detailed knowledge and refined skills needed for further study in various branches of the life sciences and related fields.

Mathematics, Functions, and Relations This Grade 11 course introduces some financial applications of mathematics, extends students' experiences with functions, and introduces second-degree relations. Students solve problems in personal finance involving applications of sequences and series; investigate properties and applications of trigonometric functions; develop facility in operating with polynomials, rational, and exponential expressions; develop an understanding of inverses and transformation of functions; and develop facility in using function notation and in communicating mathematical reasoning. They also investigate loci and the properties and applications of conics.

World History to the Sixteenth Century This Grade 12 course investigates the history of humanity from the earliest times to the sixteenth century. Students analyze diverse societies from around the world, with particular regard to the political, cultural, and economic structures and historical forces that form the foundation of the modern world. Students also examine the influence of selected individuals, groups, and innovations. They develop skills in historical inquiry, organization analysis, and communication.

World History: The West and the World In this Grade 12 course, students investigate the major trends in Western civilization and world history from the sixteenth century to the present. Student learn about the interactions between the emerging West and other regions of the world and about the development of modern social, political, and economic systems. The skills and knowledge developed in this course enable students to understand and appreciate both the character of historical change and the historical roots of contemporary issues.

The Writer's Craft With an emphasis on the knowledge and skills related to the craft of writing, students analyze models of effective writing; use a workshop approach to produce a range of works, identify and use techniques required for specialized forms of writing, and identify effective ways to improve the quality of their writing. They also complete a major paper as part of a creative or analytical independent study project and investigate opportunities for publication and for writing careers.

ENROLLMENT

Students from across Canada, the United States, and Europe attend CCI to enhance their high school education in a culturally rich environment. Enrollment has grown steadily over six years as students have discovered this academically rewarding and personally enriching program.

DAILY SCHEDULE

Classes are held from 8:30 a.m. to 3:30 p.m., Monday through Friday, with a one-hour break for lunch.

EXTRA OPPORTUNITIES AND ACTIVITIES

An overnight trip to Florence and day excursions to Rome are an integral part of the program. Extracurricular sports include cycling, hiking, swimming, aerobics, and weight lifting.

FACILITIES

The school residences are located just minutes from the main school building. Each of the student buildings has laundry facilities and a common room where students socialize and watch movies. Faculty members live in the same residences as students and monitor their academic progress as well as extracurricular activities. Students take their meals at the Allegria, the School Inn, which also features a student lounge and coffeehouse.

STAFF

Courses are taught by certified teachers who are enthusiastic about their subject and teach it with passion and pride. Faculty members are available after class time for extra tutoring.

MEDICAL CARE

There is a local medical doctor on call, and the hospital is within walking distance of the school.

COSTS

Costs for the summer session are $4595, which includes return airfare from Toronto, tuition, accommodations, excursions, lunch and dinner daily, and departure taxes. Additional fees are incurred for art supplies, insurance, health club membership, and breakfast.

TRANSPORTATION

Round-trip air transportation from Toronto to CCI is included in the program cost.

APPLICATION TIMETABLE

Students should consult with the guidance office at their current school before registering with the program to ensure that the course selected is appropriate and that the student has the required prerequisites for that level of study. A $500 deposit must accompany the completed application for admission. Applications are reviewed by an advisory committee as they are received.

For more information, contact:

CCI Summer Academy Italy

North America Office:	*Italy Office:*
59 Macamo Court	Via Cavour 13
Maple, Ontario L6A 1G1	66034 Lanciano (CH)
Canada	Italy
905-508-7108	011-39-0872-714969
800-422-0548 (toll-free)	Fax: 011-39-0872-45028
Fax: 905-508-5480	E-mail: cciren@tin.it

E-mail: cciren@rogers.com
World Wide Web: http://www.ccilanciano.com

CENTER FOR CREATIVE YOUTH

INTENSIVE ARTS EXPERIENCE

MIDDLETOWN, CONNECTICUT

Type of Program: Intensive precollege experience in the arts
Participants: Coeducational, students going into grades 10–12
Enrollment: Up to 200
Program Dates: June 26 to July 30, 2005
Heads of Program: Nancy Wolfe, Director; Herbert L. Sheppard, Ed.D., General Director

LOCATION

The Center for Creative Youth (CCY), a program of the Capitol Region Education Council, is housed on the campus of Wesleyan University in Middletown, Connecticut, about midway between Hartford and New Haven and approximately 2 hours from Boston and New York. The campus itself is green and spacious and is in a classic New England setting. It is a perfect environment in which to study, relax, and take advantage of all of the summer concert activities. Middletown is a small, friendly city with a few stores, restaurants, churches, banks, and other facilities within walking distance.

BACKGROUND AND PHILOSOPHY

Founded in 1977, CCY has become a national model of a public and independent school/university partnership. Its philosophy is to provide high-quality arts education in a precollege setting with an emphasis on intercultural and interdisciplinary learning, critical thinking, and leadership. CCY is committed to making this opportunity available to qualified students from a variety of economic and cultural backgrounds. The program is endorsed by the Connecticut State Department of Education and is a member of the International Network of Performing and Visual Arts Schools and the Connecticut Association of Independent Schools.

PROGRAM OFFERINGS

Students participate daily in morning intensive major art form and afternoon interdisciplinary classes. Each class is designed to enhance students' exposure and skills in problem solving in various art forms. Students exhibit their work and perform for the public at two Share Days, in class, and during the final Critique Week. Classes use all the facilities at Wesleyan's Center for the Arts. A complete evaluation of each student is prepared for college recommendations.

Creative Writing Emphasis is on increasing skills in both fiction and nonfiction prose and poetry. Artists-in-residence, a visiting poet, a playwright, and a novelist work closely with students. A CCY literary magazine is produced at the end of the summer.
Dance Students work daily on ballet and modern dance technique, stressing classical body placement, clarity of line, and strong energetic movement. They also work daily to develop performance skills through improvisation and composition, and a historical perspective is provided through study of major figures in dance. Final class compositions are performed in the Center for the Arts Theater.
Music (Instrumental or Vocal) This program focuses on extensive experience in vocal and instrumental chamber and jazz ensemble performance. Small group instruction is provided in music theory (including jazz), ear training, music history, and composition. Group sessions in classical music, jazz, opera, and madrigal singing as well as master-classes with musicians-in-summer-residence at Wesleyan are also featured. Private lessons may be arranged.
Technical Theater Students study lighting, sound, costume, and set design in Wesleyan's Center for the Arts facilities using state-of-the-art equipment. Students also travel to Goodspeed Opera House and Hartford Stage Company, which are both Tony-award-winning regional theaters located 20 miles from the Wesleyan campus, for workshops and hands-on activities.
Theater Students learn advanced acting skills, with an emphasis on physical approaches to creating a character. Monologue and scene work are performed. The final project develops polished audition material for future use.
Musical Theater Students may major in musical theater, which integrates concentrated actor and dance training with voice work. Classes begin each morning with movement and warm-ups, followed by solo and duet song work and large-group numbers as well.
Visual Arts Emphases are on problem solving and on drawing using a variety of media: pencil, charcoal, watercolor, brush and ink, and acrylic. Figure drawing, sculpture, printmaking, and architectural design are offered in rotation each summer.
Filmmaking Using video and digital equipment, students are taught filmmaking techniques, including story line, screenplay, photography, editing, and scoring. The group produces two or three short films.
Photography Students gain mastery of photographic equipment, materials, and processes, learning qualities of light and shadow, sense of motion, and relationship of subject to frame. Practicing methods of film development prepares students to exhibit their work. They learn to jury and hang their original photographs.

As per Connecticut state statute, "High school or college credit pursuant to C.G.S. 10-221a must be awarded for successful completion of the program." Many districts in Connecticut have agreed to provide from ½ to 1½ academic credits for students who attend and complete the CCY program.

ENROLLMENT

Nearly 200 students enroll in CCY each summer. Approximately 83 percent are from public and independent schools in Connecticut, 14 percent are from other states, and 3 percent are from overseas. CCY strives to maintain economic and cultural diversity in the student body.

Students agree to live by the residence rules and regulations as outlined in the CCY *Student Handbook* and are expected to be courteous and respectful to other community members as well as committed to their classes. Driving a car is not permitted at CCY. Drugs and alcohol are forbidden. Students must be on their halls by 10:30 each evening for hall meetings and socializing. Dormitories are not coed.

EXTRA OPPORTUNITIES AND ACTIVITIES

Students attend Wesleyan's Summer at the Center events, which include noon world music concerts, afternoon films, dance lectures, and evening performances by world-class artists. In addition, many classes schedule guest speakers or field trips to performances or exhibits in Connecticut or nearby New England locations.

FACILITIES

Students have full use of campus facilities, including the eleven-building Center for the Arts complex (classrooms, studios, workshops, performance spaces, and galleries), the extensive libraries, pool, athletic and sports field facilities, and modern residence and dining halls.

STAFF

Students benefit from three levels of mentoring and role models. Professional artists serve as teachers, nationally renowned artists perform and conduct workshops, and former CCY students who are now in college or postgraduates serve as residential advisers.

MEDICAL CARE

A nurse practitioner and a psychologist are on duty on weekday mornings and can handle most routine matters. If a student needs to be seen at another time, he or she is escorted by a counselor to the Community Health Center approximately ½ mile away. For emergency medical care, Middlesex Memorial Hospital is also only ½ mile from the campus.

RELIGIOUS LIFE

Numerous places of worship are within walking distance of campus.

COSTS

In 2004, the tuition fee was $1950, and the room and board fee was $1850. Students must also pay materials fees of $40 for visual arts and photography.

FINANCIAL AID

Some financial aid is available based on talent and need. Although most of the funds are earmarked for in-state students, some monies are set aside for deserving out-of-state students and any student may apply by filling out the back of the application form. In Connecticut, students may inquire if the local school

district will pay all or part of the tuition cost. All students with financial need are urged to seek out other sources of scholarship, such as the local PTA, Rotary Club, Women's League, art or music clubs, local businesses, and other organizations.

TRANSPORTATION

Bus service to Middletown is available via Peter Pan Bus Lines from Boston and New York and points in between. Amtrak runs to nearby Meriden; taxi service is available from there to Middletown. Limousine service from Bradley International Airport in Hartford (about 40 minutes from Middletown) runs to Cromwell. Taxi service from there to Middletown is available. In 2005, Wesleyan van service will be available.

APPLICATION TIMETABLE

Brochures and application forms are available beginning in January. Completed applications—consisting of an application form, two teacher recommendations, and an autobiographical statement—should be submitted by the deadline, which is March 8. After the application materials have been received at the CCY office, in-state applicants are scheduled to attend a required interview/audition session at Wesleyan University. Out-of-state applicants are asked to submit further appropriate documentation of their work through the mail or are welcomed at the Wesleyan audition. Letters of acceptance are mailed by mid- to late April, although in cases where school districts are providing tuition scholarships, notification may be handled by the school. Students who wish to attend CCY should confirm by May 15 by sending in a $350 nonrefundable deposit. The balance of the room and board and tuition fees is due by early June. Informational handbooks are mailed to incoming students during the first week of June.

For more information, contact:

Nancy Wolfe, Director
Center for Creative Youth
Wesleyan University
350 High Street
Middletown, Connecticut 06459
860-685-3307
Fax: 860-685-3311
E-mail: ccy@wesleyan.edu
World Wide Web: http://www.crec.org/ccy
http://www.wesleyan.edu/CCY

CENTER FOR CULTURAL INTERCHANGE

DISCOVERY ABROAD

DESTINATIONS THROUGHOUT EUROPE, ASIA, AFRICA, SOUTH AMERICA, AUSTRALIA, AND MEXICO

Type of Program: Language-School Programs (homestay), International Youth Camps, Independent Homestay Programs, and High School Abroad (homestay)

Participants: Coeducational, ages 10–18

Enrollment: Approximately 150 outbound students in 2003

Program Dates: Two-, three-, and four-week programs available year-round; three-, five-, and ten-month programs available beginning in the fall and winter

Head of Program: Jacqui Metcalf, Outbound Programs Director

LOCATION

The Center for Cultural Interchange (CCI) offers American youth the chance to experience the life and language of many countries around the world. Eligible participants can take part in homestay or camp programs in Argentina, Australia, Brazil, Chile, England, France, Germany, Ireland, Italy, Japan, Mexico, Poland, Spain, and Switzerland.

BACKGROUND AND PHILOSOPHY

The Center for Cultural Interchange is a nonprofit student exchange organization founded in 1985. CCI's goals are to promote cultural understanding, academic development, and world peace. CCI focuses primarily on the homestay experience, as it is by far the best way for participants to get a firsthand understanding of another culture. By becoming a member of a family in another country, participants are given the opportunity to share in meals, conversation, and the daily life and traditions of the country visited.

CCI organizes academic-year, semester, and short-term homestay programs for Americans abroad as well as academic-year, semester, and short-term homestay programs for international students in the United States. More than 1,300 American students and host families participate in CCI programs each year. CCI welcomes participants and hosts of every race, nationality, creed, and religion.

CCI is listed by the Council on Standards for International Educational Travel (CSIET) and is designated by the USIA as a J-1 Exchange Visitor Program Sponsor. CCI is also a member of the Federation of International Youth Travel Organizations (FIYTO).

PROGRAM OFFERINGS

CCI offers a wide range of summer, semester, and academic-year programs in Europe, Asia, Africa, South America, Australia, and Mexico. CCI provides each student with comprehensive orientation materials, full medical insurance coverage, and a well-structured network of support in the U.S. and abroad.

Students may choose from Language-School Programs, International Youth Camps, Independent Homestay Programs, or High School Abroad in many parts of the world.

Language-School Programs For students who want to live with a host family while participating in fun language classes and activities, CCI offers a variety of Language-School Programs. All Language-School Programs emphasize language study and provide the opportunity to participate in planned cultural/sport activities while sharing in the daily life of a host family. Junior Language-School Programs in Spain and France cater specifically to students ages 14–16.

International Youth Camps CCI International Youth Camps offer a wonderful opportunity to young travelers who want to participate in exciting sports and camp activities, learn a foreign language, and meet like-minded international friends. CCI Camps offer many activities and high-quality supervision, which make them perfect for the younger student. Several destinations throughout Europe are available.

Independent Homestay Programs CCI's Independent Homestay Programs focus exclusively on the homestay experience. Welcoming host families provide room and board and consider participants full members of the family. This program is perfect for the mature student who desires full immersion in the culture and language.

Summer Group Programs CCI also coordinates group homestay and camp programs to exciting destinations around the globe. Students may travel with a group organized from their own school or can join a CCI group with other students from around the

United States. Group programs are escorted by a trained adult American leader and vary in length from ten days to four weeks.

High School Abroad CCI's High School Abroad focuses on the importance of complete linguistic and cultural immersion. Participants attend high schools abroad, make new international friends, share time with host families, and learn a great deal about themselves during this three-, five-, or ten-month program.

ENROLLMENT

More than 1,300 American and international students participate in CCI programs each year. Language requirements vary by destination and program length; in some cases, there is no language requirement.

EXTRA OPPORTUNITIES AND ACTIVITIES

Many of CCI's programs offer optional activities that the student can choose to participate in for an extra fee. These activities may be weekend excursions to historical sites, sports activities, or local cultural events.

STAFF

The CCI National Office is located near Chicago in St. Charles, Illinois. The national office staff is composed of caring individuals with extensive experience in student exchange, many of whom are former homestay participants themselves. CCI also maintains a network of nine regional offices across the United States. These regional offices are responsible for the screening, recruitment, and orientation of American students and host families and provide ongoing support. The CCI Board of Directors is composed of volunteer educational professionals who maintain the direction for CCI's mission of global cross-cultural understanding.

MEDICAL CARE

All programs include comprehensive medical insurance for the duration of the program.

COSTS

The 2004 program fees for CCI short-term programs (two weeks to three months) began at $820 and varied depending on the length of stay, country, and type of program. The 2004 program fees for long-term programs (three, five, or ten months) began at $5000.

All CCI programs include orientation materials, the support of the CCI U.S. National Office and partner offices abroad, support of a local representative while abroad, housing, airport transfers, and comprehensive medical insurance. Program fees do not include international airfare, optional activities, passport/visa fees, or spending money.

FINANCIAL AID

The Center for Cultural Interchange prides itself on providing interesting and affordable opportunities to all American students interested in cultural exchange. To that end, CCI offers several possibilities for students to offset the cost of participating in a cultural exchange program.

Applicants for the High School Abroad program may apply for a $1000 scholarship.

CCI also encourages U.S. host family members to expand on their cultural experience by participating in the Host Family Circle, a program that provides partial scholarships to host family members interested in studying abroad.

CCI also offers an annual essay contest to its academic-year or semester host brothers and sisters (14–17 years) through which they can win a free program abroad.

TRANSPORTATION

International airfare arrangements are generally the responsibility of the participants, but CCI is happy to provide assistance, if necessary. Transfers to and from the major airport nearest the host family are included in most teen program fees.

APPLICATION TIMETABLE

U.S. students interested in applying are required to submit a complete application with a $250 deposit for short-term programs and a $500 deposit for High School Abroad programs. Applications for short-term programs are due no later than six weeks prior to departure. High School Abroad applications are due no later than April 15 for the fall semester and September 15 for the spring semester.

FOR MORE INFORMATION, CONTACT:

Outbound Department
Center for Cultural Interchange
325 West Huron, Suite 706
Chicago, Illinois 60610
312-944-2544 (in Chicago area)
866-684-9675 (toll-free)
Fax: 312-944-2644
E-mail: info@cci-exchange.com
World Wide Web: http://www.cci-exchange.com

PARTICIPANT/FAMILY COMMENTS

"I am really happy I decided to take this year to be here in Spain. I love it! I am really glad I am here with CCI. I am so pleased with the amount of support I'm getting. I never want (it) to end!"—Eve Pulver, former CCI student to Spain

"Our experience was perfect!"—Julie Vedvick, Spanish teacher and CCI group leader to Mexico

CHESHIRE ACADEMY

SUMMER PROGRAMS

CHESHIRE, CONNECTICUT

Type of Program: English as a second language (ESL); writing, reading, and study skills (WRSS); select college prep courses; and International Ocean Shipping Summer Advantage
Participants: Coeducational, grades 7–12
Enrollment: Approximately 150
Program Dates: Five weeks, from the first week of July until the first week of August
Head of Program: Matthew Kallas, Director

LOCATION

The 100-acre wooded campus is located in the center of an attractive New England town of 30,000 residents. The Academy is 2 hours from New York City and Boston. The surrounding cities, such as the state capital, Hartford (22 miles away), and the home of Yale University, New Haven (14 miles away)—along with Boston and New York City—offer a wide range of cultural opportunities for Summer Programs students.

BACKGROUND AND PHILOSOPHY

Founded in 1794, Cheshire Academy is a highly regarded coeducational college-preparatory school with an academic tradition of preparing young men and women for rewarding college experiences, careers, and personal lives. Graduates from around the world include many highly respected and successful people in all fields of endeavor.

Summer Programs, now more than ninety years old, takes great pride in offering a challenging academic program that meets the educational interests of a variety of students. This is accomplished in a structured, stimulating, and supportive family-like environment, created by small classes (an average of 7 students) and a close, personal working relationship between teachers and students.

Academic courses are monitored weekly by the individual teachers and the Director of the Summer Programs. The student receives a progress report each week which, with a comment from the classroom teacher, is sent to the parents or guardian. This allows the teachers, students, and parents to remain informed of the student's progress throughout the summer.

PROGRAM OFFERINGS

Writing, Reading, and Study Skills Program The WRSS Program is designed to help students improve their academic skills, independence, self-confidence, and achievement in a classroom setting. Students learn to develop healthy habits and strategies that support learning and that have a direct bearing on the students' success in all academic disciplines. Students are placed in the appropriate level of the program after taking diagnostic tests to assess their verbal and study skills.

English as a Second Language Program Cheshire Academy's English as a Second Language Program has served the Academy since 1911. The program is practically oriented and challenging, providing ESL classes that increase English proficiency for beginning, intermediate, and advanced students. The ESL curriculum stresses writing, vocabulary, grammar, speaking, and reading. Students take a placement test and are assigned according to their levels in each of the basic skills. Small classes and the sensitivity of our highly committed, caring, experienced faculty members make it possible for students to develop their new found English skills and knowledge quite rapidly.

College Prep The College Prep program is designed for high school students who are seeking academic enrichment in one or two specific areas of study. The students can concentrate on one or two courses and really focus on the subject matter for five weeks. It is hoped that the students are able to embrace a subject and be rewarded by a real sense of accomplishment at the end of the summer. Course offerings, subject to enrollment, are Algebra I, Algebra II, Geometry, Precalculus, Chemistry, Biology, Physics, Spanish I, and U.S. History.

International Ocean Shipping Summer Advantage A recent, one-of-a-kind addition to the program, International Ocean Shipping Summer Advantage familiarizes students with the basics of ocean shipping, international trade, and ship finance. From classroom instruction to field trips, this unique opportunity introduces students to the top professionals in the field. This class can be taken with other courses, such as ESL or College Prep, and students also participate in all the afternoon activities.

ENROLLMENT

The average enrollment is 150 students, with close to a 1:1 ratio of girls to boys. Most students board, and twenty different countries and ten states are represented in the student body.

DAILY SCHEDULE

8:00–12:30	Classes
12:00–1:30	Lunch
2:30–4:30	Afternoon activities
5:45–6:15	Dinner
7:00	Study hall
9:00	Break
9:45	Check into dormitories

On Saturday and Sunday, brunch is served from 10:30 to 12. Dinner is served from 5:45 to 6:30. Students are expected to follow all of the rules and regulations outlined in the *Student Handbook*. Stealing, possession or use of alcohol or illegal drugs, visiting the rooms of students of the opposite sex, or any activity that compromises the good name of Cheshire Academy will result in dismissal from Summer Programs.

EXTRA OPPORTUNITIES AND ACTIVITIES

Afternoon Activities The Afternoon Activities Program offers a variety of athletic activities designed to encourage a healthy balance between the student's academic goals and athletic goals. All students in Summer Programs must participate in afternoon activities. Because each student's interest in athletic activities varies, they may select from a variety of afternoon activities on a daily basis. The athletic activities are designed for athletes and nonathletes of all abilities and levels to participate in, providing fun and a proper foundation to excel to a higher level. Cheshire Academy athletic facilities accommodate swimming in its six-lane pool, basketball on two full-size courts, five playing fields for soccer, two baseball diamonds, an outdoor track, and a weight training room for strength, endurance, and aerobic conditioning.

Saturday Morning Enrichment Program The objective of the Saturday Morning Enrichment Program is to promote supportive and challenging courses that extend beyond the classroom and have a specific interest for the student. All students are required to sign up for one of the Saturday morning enrichment courses that are offered. The enrichment courses offer the student effective learning strategies and skills to improve specific areas of weaknesses that are essential for personal and academic success. In addition, other courses of student interest are offered subject to enrollment demands. The Scholastic Assessment Test (SAT) enrichment course helps students prepare for the College Entrance Examination Board's SAT, and is normally taken by American students in the eleventh and twelfth grades. The Test of English as a Foreign Language (TOEFL) Prep enrichment course provides international students with effective techniques and skills in taking the TOEFL. Math and Writing Labs are enrichment courses in which students work on areas of mathematical weakness and on key points essential for writing. The Saturday Morning Enrichment Programs also offer, in combination, Computers and Discovering the Internet, Performing Arts, Fine Arts, and Creative Writing/Journalism, with the end product being one or more issues of a Summer Programs newspaper or literary magazine.

Weekend Recreation Program The Weekend Recreation Program is chaperoned by faculty members and designed to involve students in a variety of social and recreational activities on and off campus. On-campus activities typically include student dances, swimming, recreational sports, and hot air balloon rides. Examples of off-campus trips include a discovery trip to Washington, D.C.; white-water rafting; Boston's Quincy Market; Broadway plays; major amusement parks; movies; and malls. The weekend program culminates with graduation exercises and a dinner dance on the last evening.

FACILITIES

Bowden Hall (1796), the original school building, now houses various administrative offices. Bronson Hall, which also dates to the beginning of the school, contains offices, a meeting room, and the miniauditorium. Hurley Hall (1940) houses the library, college center, and girls' dormitory. Woodbury Hall (1976) contains classrooms and a student lounge. Horton Hall (1946) is a residence hall for girls and von der Porten Hall (1959) is a residence hall for boys. The Student Health Center is located on campus in the Richmond Building. Two additional houses, Walters and Skilton, are smaller residences. The John J. White Science Center provides science facilities. Music classes are conducted in the Charles Harwood Student Center (1988). The student center houses recreational rooms and lounges, a snack bar, and the Academy's bookstore. Art classes are held in the Beardsley House located across from the Middle School Building. The Arthur N. Sheriff Field House provides extensive athletic facilities and additional classrooms. The Gideon Welles Dining Commons provides excellent dining facilities. The newest residence hall opened in fall 2001, complete with air conditioning. A new humanities building and library were added to the campus in 2003.

The 100-acre campus includes eight athletic fields, eight tennis courts, a quarter-mile track, woodlands, and a stream. The indoor athletic facilities includes two basketball courts, exercise room and a swimming pool.

STAFF

The majority of the Summer Programs teaching staff are members of the Academy's school year program.

MEDICAL CARE

The Student Health Center is a recently renovated state-of-the-art facility. It is located in the Richmond Building in the center of campus. The nursing staff collaborates with a multispecialty physician group within walking distance of campus. The nursing staff is on-site or on call 24 hours a day. The Academy is conveniently located approximately 20 minutes from both Yale–New Haven Hospital and Midstate Medical Center.

RELIGIOUS LIFE

Cheshire Academy is not affiliated with any religion, but it is within walking distance of churches of several denominations and a synagogue.

COSTS

The boarding tuition for the 2003 five-week program was $4700; day tuition is $2600.

TRANSPORTATION

Cheshire Academy is 45 minutes from Bradley International Airport in Hartford, 20 minutes from Tweed–New Haven Airport, and 1½ hours from New York City airports. All are easily reached by Connecticut Limousine service, which has a terminal in New Haven. Private limousine service is also available.

APPLICATION TIMETABLE

Cheshire Academy's Summer Programs have a rolling admissions policy. Students are urged to submit their application as early as possible, due to limited boarding space.

For more information, contact:

Matthew Kallas, Director
Summer Programs
Cheshire Academy
10 Main Street
Cheshire, Connecticut 06410
203-272-5396
Fax: 203-250-7209
E-mail: summer@cheshireacademy.org
World Wide Web: http://www.cheshireacademy.org

PARTICIPANT/FAMILY COMMENTS

"I would like the person in charge of last summer's program to see the enclosed report from my son's middle school principal and from his skills teacher, both commenting on the positive effects of the Cheshire Academy summer program. I spoke to the parents of his friend who attended last summer and they were also thrilled with the program. My son has attended some academic-oriented programs every summer, but this is the only one that had a noticeable effect. I certainly intend to send him to the summer program this year, regardless of where he attends high school."
—Parent of a Summer Programs student

CHOATE ROSEMARY HALL

SUMMER ARTS CONSERVATORY

WALLINGFORD, CONNECTICUT

Type of Program: Intensive arts conservatory, emphasizing performance and exhibitions
Participants: Coeducational, entering grades 7–12
Enrollment: 90
Program Dates: June 29 to July 30
Head of Program: Paul J. Tines, Executive Director

LOCATION

The 400-acre campus of Choate Rosemary Hall is located in the center of Wallingford, a town 12 miles north of New Haven and 20 miles south of Hartford. It is a 2-hour drive from Boston and New York City.

BACKGROUND AND PHILOSOPHY

Students come to celebrate the arts. The five-week Arts Conservatory offers programs in theater, playwriting, choral music, stringed instruments, and the visual arts. Arts Conservatory students create together, live together, and play together. Each morning begins as students gather in the Experimental Theater for physical warm-ups and the day's announcements.

Several characteristics make the Arts Conservatory unique. It offers a truly interdisciplinary approach to arts education. The Conservatory embraces the philosophy that the student must first understand the process of creating art. Students are given the tools to understand how to create. In all five programs, they consistently work on the techniques and skills of painting, drawing, singing, dancing, acting, playing an instrument, or playwriting.

PROGRAM OFFERINGS

Theater In this program, 40 students explore and experience all phases of theatrical expression. The curriculum consists of classes in acting, acting style, stage movement, and musical theater—voice and dance. Students perform in new works and previously published plays.

Playwriting The Student Playwriting Program is developed to nurture 12 young writers and to provide a solid foundation for both stage plays and film. The curriculum consists of classes in elements of scriptwriting, film analysis, screenplay development, and film and play labs. Students have public readings of their works.

Visual Arts The Visual Arts Program is a rare opportunity for 20 students to explore the creative process and challenge their artistic potential under the instruction of professional artists who are also teachers. The curriculum consists of painting, ceramics, drawing, photography, portfolio discussions, and open studio time.

Digital Video The Digital Video Program takes 12 students through the preproduction, production, and postproduction process of creating digital videos. The facility is state of the art and includes four beautifully designed workstations. Students work in Final Cut software and will learn all methods of filmmaking associated with this program. The Digital Video Program includes the use of Power Mac G4 computers, digital video cameras, lighting, and related equipment. The curriculum also covers the history of cinema, film analysis, and screenwriting.

ENROLLMENT

Each summer, 90 students from all over the country participate in the Arts Conservatory.

DAILY SCHEDULE

During the day, students attend classes, open studio sessions, and play, choral, and string rehearsals. Students take field trips to museums, theaters, outdoor musical concerts, and art openings.

EXTRA OPPORTUNITIES AND ACTIVITIES

Time is set aside for leisure activities, including swimming, tennis, volleyball, or relaxing in the Student Activities Center. Students spend one weekend (optional trip) during the program in New York City, where they attend Broadway and off-

Broadway shows, visit museums and galleries, explore Shubert Alley, and shop in SoHo and Greenwich Village.

FACILITIES

The Paul Mellon Arts Center, designed by world-renowned architect I. M. Pei, houses two theaters, a recital hall, music classrooms and practice rooms, art studios, dance facilities, and a large art gallery/lounge area. Students live in campus dormitories and have access to Choate Rosemary Hall's recreational and athletic facilities.

STAFF

Classes are taught by experienced arts educators from Choate Rosemary Hall's faculty and from other private and public schools around the country. Faculty members also serve as dormitory advisers.

Paul Tines, Director of the Paul Mellon Arts Center, is chair of the arts department at Choate Rosemary Hall. Mr. Tines, who received his master's degree from Johns Hopkins University and a Certificate of Advanced Studies from Wesleyan University, has studied at the American Academy of Dramatic Arts in New York and the Royal Academy of Dramatic Arts in London. He was a member of Choate's theater department from 1982 to 1992 and served as the Director of the Ward Center for the Arts and Chair of the Arts Department at the St. Paul's Schools in Baltimore.

MEDICAL CARE

The Pratt Health Center is staffed 24 hours a day. Overnight care in the health center is provided when necessary, but there is an additional charge. Each student is required to submit health forms before registration. All students must have proper immunizations and provide complete medical information on these forms. By Connecticut law, failure to submit the proper medical forms or to have immunizations (or to get them immediately upon arrival at Choate) obligates the school to dismiss the student. Each student is also required to submit proof of medical insurance before registration. Failure to submit proof of medical insurance upon arrival at Choate obligates the school to dismiss the student.

RELIGIOUS LIFE

A synagogue and various denominational churches (Congregational, Baptist, Roman Catholic, and Episcopalian) are within walking distance of the campus.

COSTS

The charge for resident students, including room, board, and field trips, is $4200. Linen service is available at an additional fee. The fee for day students is $3200. The fee for the optional weekend trip to New York City is $500.

TRANSPORTATION

Transportation is provided to students. Ground transportation upon arrival to and departure from the program is an additional fee.

APPLICATION TIMETABLE

A $50 nonrefundable application fee payable to Choate Rosemary Hall is required. The Summer Arts Conservatory's application deadline is May 10, 2004.

For more information, contact:

Randi Joseph Brandt, Admissions Director
Choate Rosemary Hall Summer Arts Conservatory
Paul Mellon Arts Center
333 Christian Street
Wallingford, Connecticut 06492
203-697-2423
Fax: 203-697-2396
E-mail: rbrandt@choate.edu
World Wide Web: http://www.choate.edu/pmac

PARTICIPANT/FAMILY COMMENTS

"I learned more in five weeks than I did in two years of drama classes back home. I will always look back and remember Choate as a very special and wonderful time in my life."

CHOATE ROSEMARY HALL

SUMMER PROGRAM IN SPAIN

LA CORUÑA AND SANTANDER, SPAIN

Type of Program: Academic and cultural enrichment
Participants: Coeducational, grades 9–11
Enrollment: 51
Program Dates: Six weeks, traditionally from the third Monday in June through the first weekend in August
Head of Program: Thomas K. McRae Jr., Director

LOCATION

The program begins on the Choate Rosemary Hall campus in Wallingford, Connecticut, with the required 2½-day orientation session. After transfer to Kennedy Airport via air-conditioned coaches, the group travels on a regularly scheduled flight to Madrid. There, half of the students travel to La Coruña and the other half to Santander, both of which are important port cities with fine beaches on the north coast of Spain. For one month, the students live in private homes and attend classes every weekday morning. A week's excursion brings the students back to Madrid.

BACKGROUND AND PHILOSOPHY

The current program was founded in 1974 by Mr. Juan López, assisted by Mr. McRae, so that students might have an opportunity to develop fluency in Spanish by experiencing the culture first-hand in a structured, caring environment. The thrust of the program is academic, but the seaside locations ensure access to summertime recreational activities, and excursions provide exposure to many of the jewels of Spain's historic past.

PROGRAM OFFERINGS

After enrollment is complete, students take a placement test, which is used to establish three distinct class levels: primary, intermediate, and advanced. Students at the first two levels study grammar; the history of Spanish art and architecture, taught through slides; and the history and civilization of Spain. Instead of grammar, the advanced students take an introduction to literature, in which they read and discuss short stories and plays. All classes are conducted entirely in Spanish and include final examinations.

Fluency in Spanish is developed primarily through contact with the host family members, with whom all three meals are taken during the homestay. Students gain confidence and improve their skills through their regular dealings with bank tellers, store owners, and other vendors. By the end of the month, students who approach the experience with eagerness to learn are quite surprised by their progress, as are their former teachers. At the end of the program, parents receive written summaries of student performance in the program.

One or two afternoons a week, the group visits local points of interest, such as a maritime museum, lighthouse, planetarium, castle, newspaper, or government assembly. On Saturdays, there are day trips to more distant attractions, such as the medieval town of Santillana del Mar or La Toja. After a picnic lunch and an afternoon at the beach, the group wends its way back to its Spanish hometown.

At the end of the homestay, the group from Santander joins the students from La Coruña, and the larger group travels from the northwest back to Madrid. Stops include Santiago de Compostela (full day), Salamanca (full day), Ávila, Segovia (afternoon and evening), Toledo, and Madrid (two nights). Unlike typical tourists from abroad, the students find that the art class has prepared them well for this excursion; the students understand the guided visits more readily and discover that they can enhance their appreciation by asking intelligent questions during their tour.

Returning to school in the fall, many students find that they are able to accelerate in their Spanish curricula. With their enhanced skills and new-found appreciation for the Hispanic world, many determine to continue their studies at the collegiate level, and some may eventually make use of Spanish in their careers. Upon request, the director is pleased to write a letter of recommendation, based on performance in the program, in support of a participant's college application.

ENROLLMENT

The Summer Program in Spain has a capacity of 51 high school students—25 in one town and 26 in the other. Candidates are expected to have completed the equivalent of at least two years of high school Spanish. There are four classes, two in each town. Every student has regular contact with at least 1 teacher from Choate Rosemary Hall and 2 native Spaniards.

EXTRA OPPORTUNITIES AND ACTIVITIES

The student's day is usually quite busy, with morning classes, homework assignments for the next day, lengthy midday meals at home, and occasional required afternoon programs. Because of the maritime location of both campuses, there is ample opportunity to participate in recreational activities at the shore. The walk home from the beach inevitably brings contact with alluring stores, tempting pastry shops, and the ubiquitous sidewalk café. The intellectually curious student can find numerous galleries, museums, and architectural gems to explore in

addition to those included in the program. Sunday is the only unscheduled day. Fortunate students—usually as a matter of chance—may then find themselves bustled off to a wedding, country fair, or similar weekend outing with their host families, contingent upon the director's permission.

During the final weeklong excursion, there is a busy schedule of travel and participation in guided tours, during which free time is at a premium. Highlights include the cathedral at Santiago, the University of Salamanca, the fortified walls of Ávila, the aqueduct of Segovia, the house of El Greco and the Synagogue in Toledo, and the Prado Museum and the Royal Palace in Madrid. The last Sunday afternoon in Madrid provides an optional opportunity to see a bullfight, and the final dinner that evening, a memorable occasion, provides a chance for that special last snapshot of a new friend.

DAILY SCHEDULE

8	Continental breakfast and travel to class
9	Grammar or literature class
10:15	Break
10:25	History and Civilization class
11:15	History of Art and Architecture
12	End of morning classes
1:30	Main meal
3:30	Students typically leave for the beach
4–6:30	Afternoon activity (as scheduled)
9	Students return to homestays
10:30	Curfew and supper (Sunday–Friday)

Students are expected to be on time to all scheduled activities as a courtesy to the responsible adults and to the other group members. They are expected to respect the instructions of their families and teachers, to submit assignments punctually, and to avoid activities capable of bringing disrepute to the individual, the adults, the group, the program, or Choate Rosemary Hall. The use or possession of controlled substances is cause for dismissal from the program. The abuse of alcohol, violation of parietal rules, failure to observe curfew, dishonesty, stealing, and behavior endangering one's own safety or that of another are all serious offenses that could result in dismissal.

FACILITIES

The Summer Program in Spain rents space in modern, private schools located close to the beach. In each school, there are spacious classrooms, appropriate for slide presentations and standard classes, as well as clean restroom facilities. Some students live close enough to class to arrive on foot. Others use public transportation and are reimbursed for their expense.

Students are placed in families that are selected by local coordinators for their appropriateness. Most families live in apartments. The local coordinator visits each family and evaluates each living situation with careful consideration of the neighborhood, the availability of public transportation, the condition of the building and apartment, the sleeping arrangements for the student, and the general atmosphere in the home, as well as the level of Castilian Spanish used in the household. Students are placed 1 to a family, and each home has at least 1 Spanish child of the same sex and similar age as the student guest. There is a telephone in every home.

During the main excursion, students stay in three- and/or four-star hotels, all of which may be found in any recent travel guide. Excursion travel is by air-conditioned coaches, which are operated by experienced drivers.

STAFF

In each city, the staff is composed of 2 American teachers, 1 of whom is a codirector or associate director of the program; the other codirector; and 2 Spaniards, both of whom teach each student in one of two 45-minute periods each day. A codirector is in regular contact with each family. Thomas McRae, the codirector of the program, is a full-time Spanish teacher at Choate Rosemary Hall, where he has taught since 1964.

MEDICAL CARE

Both cities have modern hospitals, and every family has a doctor to call in the event of illness. Students are never far from competent medical attention. Medical insurance in the United States that covers the student while in Spain is required of every participant.

COSTS

The tuition, which is approximately $6055, covers all expenses between the arrival of the student on campus for orientation and the return to Kennedy Airport. It does not include the required health insurance, dry cleaning, writing materials, or personal spending money.

APPLICATION TIMETABLE

Choate Rosemary Hall's summer programs have a rolling admission policy beginning in the fall; as soon as an applicant's folder is complete, a decision is made on the candidacy. No interview is required. When all places have been filled, a waiting list is formed. Although the date varies, it is worth noting that a waiting list has occasionally been formed as early as midwinter.

The application fee is $60. After an acceptance has been issued, there are three weeks before the enrollment contract and deposit are due. Staff members are available to answer questions from 8 a.m. until 4 p.m. EST, Monday through Friday.

For more information, contact:

Thomas McRae
Choate Rosemary Hall Summer in Spain
333 Christian Street
Wallingford, Connecticut 06492
203-697-2365
Fax: 203-697-2519
E-mail: tmcrae@choate.edu
World Wide Web: http://crhsummerabroad.org

CHOATE ROSEMARY HALL

SUMMER PROGRAMS

WALLINGFORD, CONNECTICUT

Type of Program: College-preparatory academic enrichment/credit for residential and day students
Participants: Coeducational, students who have completed grades 6–8 and 9–12
Enrollment: 500
Program Dates: June 26 to July 29, 2005
Head of Program: James Irzyk, Director

LOCATION

The 400-acre campus of Choate Rosemary Hall is in the center of Wallingford, a town 12 miles north of New Haven and 20 miles south of Hartford. It is a 2-hour drive from Boston and New York City.

BACKGROUND AND PHILOSOPHY

The Choate Rosemary Hall Summer Programs were established in 1916. The goal of the programs is for students to leave with a sense of accomplishment and pride in their work and to return to their home schools with new friends and an awareness of different cultures.

PROGRAM OFFERINGS

Students in each program are fully integrated into all athletic, extracurricular, and social activities on campus.

Summer Session (for students completing grades 9–12) More than eighty course offerings in ten departments give students the opportunity for advancement, credit, academic adventure, or preparation for courses for the next school year. All courses stress skills in reading, writing, computation, and analytical thought.

The average class size is 12; many classes have a teaching intern as well as a teacher, increasing the individual attention each student receives.

English Language Institute (for students completing grades 9–12) The English Language Institute (ELI) is a program designed to help students improve their English in a supportive yet challenging academic environment. Students develop their ability in language skills, including writing, speaking, listening, and reading.

John F. Kennedy Institute in Government (for students completing grades 9–12) Students take three courses on the formation of political ideas, the foundation and workings of the American government, and current domestic issues. A trip to Washington, D.C., is a highlight of the program, as students meet members of Congress, lobbyists, and journalists.

The Writing Project (for students completing grades 9–12) In this intensive two-week program (offered in two different sessions), students receive daily writing and reading assignments and an introduction to computer-assisted writing and gain confidence in their writing skill.

Immersion Courses (for students completing grades 8–12) During the five-week summer session, students may enroll in one of the following courses: first-year French, Latin, or Spanish; algebra I; geometry; trigonometry/precalculus; or physics. Credit is granted by the student's school.

Math/Science Institute for Girls (CONNECT) (for students completing grades 6–8) Advanced knowledge of mathematics and science is not necessary, but motivation, curiosity, inventiveness, and the desire to explore topics in physics, biology, chemistry, and mathematics are essential. Doing experiments, building models, developing and testing hypotheses, and using technology are integral components of the curriculum. This four-week program is an opportunity for students to discover the natural and logical relationship between math and science. Enrollment is limited to 30 girls.

Young Writers Workshop (for students completing grades 6–8) These two-week workshops use both the critical and creative writing methods to instill confidence, develop understanding, and suggest strategies to improve writing skills. Class discussions, exercises, and individual conferences develop a supportive, cohesive group in which students can produce their best writing.

FOCUS Program (for students completing grades 6–8) This four-week program parallels the Summer Session but stresses cooperative learning, the use of technology in the classroom, problem-solving skills, effective communication, hands-on projects, and research skills. Small classes and experienced dorm advisers encourage personal growth and self-awareness. Enrollment is limited to 75 students.

FOCUS English Language Institute (for students who have completed grades 6–8) Similar to the ELI program, this four-week program is open to students who have studied English for at least two years in their home school. Social activities are planned with the other grade 6–8 program. Enrollment is limited to 30 students.

ENROLLMENT

Each summer, 500 students from nearly thirty-five states and countries attend the summer programs. Students come from such countries as France, Japan, Spain, Switzerland, Germany, Korea, Turkey, and Argentina. Adding strength to the student body are 30 highly motivated students (Connecticut Scholars) from Connecticut's urban public school systems.

DAILY SCHEDULE

Classes meet Monday, Tuesday, Thursday, and Friday from 8:15 a.m. to 2:40 p.m. and Wednesday and Saturday from 8:15 a.m. to 12:45 p.m. Athletics are held from 3:30 to 5:30 p.m. All programs have 2 hours of evening study.

EXTRA OPPORTUNITIES AND ACTIVITIES

A variety of activities are offered on campus: a college fair, pool and pizza parties, a student talent show, International Festival, and weekend dances. Trips are scheduled on Wednesday afternoons and on weekends and usually include visits to Boston, New York City, shopping malls, movie theaters, professional sporting events, and nearby college campuses.

FACILITIES

Choate's academic and athletic facilities are among the best in the country. The campus resembles those of many small liberal arts colleges. The Science Center includes twenty-two air-conditioned classrooms and laboratories and a 150-seat auditorium. The Humanities Center houses thirty air-conditioned classrooms, an audiovisual viewing room, a computer center, and photographic studios. The dining hall is air conditioned.

The Andrew Mellon Library has more than 60,000 volumes, 6,700 reels of microfilm, more than 2,000 CDs, English and foreign language periodicals and newspapers, and the latest library research technology, as well as wireless Internet access. The Archives hold school memorabilia, including the papers of such distinguished alumni as John F. Kennedy '35, Adlai Stevenson '18, Alan Jay Lerner '36, Glenn Close '65, Jamie Lee Curtis '76, and Michael Douglas '63.

The International Learning Center includes a thirty-two-station language laboratory and allows for individual instruction and practice for the English Language Institute and foreign language classes. The Paul Mellon Arts Center houses two theaters, a recital hall, music classrooms and practice rooms, art studios, dance and film facilities, and an art gallery. The renovated Johnson Athletic Center houses three basketball and three volleyball courts and weight-training and Nautilus rooms. There are twenty-seven outdoor tennis courts, thirteen athletic fields, and a 25-meter, eight-lane indoor swimming pool with an electronic timing system. The social hub is the John Joseph Activities Center, which has games, a snack shop, and several televisions with VCRs.

STAFF

Many of the faculty members are teachers in Choate Rosemary Hall's regular session. Additional faculty members come from other independent secondary and public schools and from colleges and universities. Thirty teaching interns from select colleges and universities complement the program.

MEDICAL CARE

The infirmary is open daily, and overnight care is available. The school physician is in residence and can be paged for emergencies. Parents must have some form of insurance for their child. Each student is required by Connecticut law to submit a health form before enrolling.

COSTS

In 2004, tuition, room, and board for the summer session were $4900. Day student costs ranged from $760 to $3600. Costs for the Kennedy Institute were $4800, with an additional $450 for the Washington, D.C., trip. Costs for the English Language Institute were $5200, with an additional $385 for the long weekend trip. Boarding students in the two-week Writing Project paid $1970, and day students paid $1500. Boarding students in the CONNECT program paid $4000, and day students paid $2870. For the Young Writers Workshop, boarding students paid $1970, and day students paid $1500. Boarding students in the Immersion Courses paid $4900, and day students paid $3600.

FINANCIAL AID

Need-based financial aid is available; applications should be submitted by March 15. Candidates are notified of their acceptance and financial aid awards by April 1.

APPLICATION TIMETABLE

Early application is encouraged. Students are strongly encouraged to apply by May 15. Admission is on a rolling basis. Acceptance decisions are made within two weeks of receiving a completed application.

For more information, contact:

Mariann Arnold, Director of Admissions
Choate Rosemary Hall Summer Programs
Wallingford, Connecticut 06492
203-697-2365
Fax: 203-697-2519
E-mail: marnold@choate.edu
World Wide Web: http://www.choate.edu/summer

CHOATE ROSEMARY HALL

SUMMER PROGRAMS ABROAD

PARIS, FRANCE AND BEIJING, CHINA

Type of Program: Academic and cultural enrichment
Participants: Coed; students must have completed grade 9
Program Dates: Five weeks, typically beginning the third Monday in June
Heads of Program: Carl Hermey and Elizabeth Jannot, Paris; Carol Chen-Lin, Beijing

LOCATION

Choate Rosemary Hall Summer Programs Abroad offer students the opportunity to spend and exciting summer in a faraway place, immersed in the language and culture of either Paris, France or Beijing, China.

BACKGROUND AND PHILOSOPHY

Students supercharge their language skills for school and standardized tests and get to visit some of the places they've seen only in the movies. The goal of the programs is to help students develop fluency in written and spoken French or Chinese, in a secure and caring environment.

PROGRAM OFFERINGS

Students are required to attend the two-day orientation program on the Choate Rosemary Hall campus, where language instruction begins and where they are introduced to the culture that is soon to become part of their lives.

Choate's Summer in Paris is modeled after the school's term-long academic program in France. The Summer in China program, located in the capital city of Beijing, consists of the study of spoken and written Chinese at the Beijing Language Institute. Both programs immerse students in the culture of the host country, helping them to dramatically improve fluency and four essential skills: listening, speaking, reading and writing.

Students who clearly demonstrate progress and proficiency in the major language skills at the close of summer programs abroad may be eligible for higher placement in their home schools. A written report will be sent to the student's school upon request and is always sent to parents. Choate Rosemary Hall students have the opportunity to accelerate as much as a year in language study, as determined by their degree of improvement.

ENROLLMENT

Participants must have completed grade 9 before the start of the program. Two years study of the French language is the usual requirement for the Paris program, but exceptions may be made for strong students who have completed only one year. Students who would like to begin the study of Chinese are welcome in that program. All participants are expected to show sufficient maturity and the self-discipline to avoid inappropriate behavior. The program director has the right to send home (at the parents' expense) any student whose behavior jeopardizes the safety or viability of the group. Possession or use of controlled substances at any point in the program is strictly forbidden and will result in immediate dismissal.

DAILY SCHEDULE

In the Summer in Paris program, students take 3 hours of classes each morning. Four courses—French language, French literature, art history, and French history—comprise the academic program, along with an independent research project on an artistic or cultural topic, which each student carries out using the libraries, galleries, or museums of Paris. Afternoons are devoted to exploring the historic and artistic treasures of the city. These visits are thematically linked to the morning art history class and are led by two Parisian teachers. Free time in the city precedes dinner with the French family; homework for the next day follows dinner.

In the Summer in China program, students attend 4-hour classes at the Beijing Language Institute each weekday. Twice each week, in the afternoon, students participate in a variety of activities, such as calligraphy, painting, and dancing, and have an opportunity to attend selected cultural events, such as the Beijing Opera.

EXTRA OPPORTUNITIES AND ACTIVITIES

After the Wallingford orientation and the overnight flight to Paris, students spend three days in the Loire Valley. They tour well-known châteaux, explore the city of Tours, and, en route to Paris, take a guided tour of Chartres cathedral. Additional excursions have included Versailles, Vaux-le-Vicomte and Monet's house and gardens at Giverny.

On weekends, Summer in China students visit historical sites and local points of interest such as the Great Wall, the Ming Tomb, the Forbidden City, and the Summer Palace. The highlight of this program, at the end of the academic session, is a nine-day excursion which takes students to Shanghai, Nanjing, Suzhou, Hangzhou, and Xi'an. This is an experience of a lifetime for students who are eager to explore the Chinese language and culture.

FACILITIES

The homestay, the heart of the Summer in Paris program, allows students to live with and become part of a Parisian family. Students are placed individually or in pairs with carefully selected families, many of whom have enrolled their own children in Choate's Summer Programs.

Students in the China program live in a dormitory community under the supervision of Choate faculty members.

STAFF

Carl W. Hermey, a senior member of Choate's Language Department, administers the Summer in Paris program in the U.S. and Elizabeth Jannot, a longtime resident of Paris, leads the program in Paris. At least one other member of the French department accompanies the group to Paris. All classes are taught in French by a team of native speakers whose combined experience with Choate students totals more than 40 years.

The Summer in China program is organized, led, and directed by Dr. Carol S. Chen-Lin, a Choate Rosemary Hall faculty member and experienced teacher of Chinese. Classes are taught by experienced, native speakers who are trained to teach Chinese as a second language.

COSTS

Programs cost approximately $6055. This includes airfare, transportation abroad, tuition, all meals and lodging, books, and entrance fees for group activities. Expenses not included in the fee are a passport, transportation to the Choate campus, transportation after return to the U.S., and personal expenses such as telephone calls and spending money. Expenses are based on the exchange rate effective September 1, 2003. Prices are subject to equitable adjustment should there be a significant change in the rate of exchange or in the airfare prior to the start of the program.

FINANCIAL AID

A limited amount of need-based financial aid is allocated for each program.

APPLICATION TIMETABLE

All candidates must submit an application, the $60 application fee, an official transcript, and teacher recommendations. Since the number of candidates for these programs exceeds the available spaces, early applications are recommended. Some applications are received in early fall before the desired summer of entry. Last minute applicants, if accepted, are placed in families and classes in accordance with availability.

FOR MORE INFORMATION, CONTACT:

Summer Programs Abroad
Choate Rosemary Hall
333 Christian Street
Wallingford, Connecticut 06492
203-697-2365
E-mail: chermey@choate.edu (Summer in Paris)
cchen-lin@choate.eud (Summer in China)
World Wide Web: http://www.crhsummerabroad.org

CHRISTCHURCH SCHOOL

SUMMER CAMPS ON THE RIVER

CHRISTCHURCH, VIRGINIA

Type of Program: Sailing, crew/rowing, marine science, and skills in math, writing, and studying
Participants: Coeducational, ages 9–17
Enrollment: 18–35 participants (varies by camp)
Program Dates: One- to four-week sessions of camper's choice, June 26–July 23
Heads of Program: Dan Hayes, Ann Roebuck, Steve Fluhr, Chris Carrillo, Henry Selby

LOCATION

Summer Camps on the River is located on a 125-acre open and wooded waterfront campus 45 miles north of Williamsburg, Virginia; 60 miles east of Richmond, Virginia; 135 miles south of Washington, D.C.; 3 miles east of Saluda, Virginia; and 2 miles from the historic fishing village of Urbanna, Virginia.

BACKGROUND AND PHILOSOPHY

Summer Camps on the River employs the same philosophy the school follows during the regular school year. All camps are opportunities offered in a recreational setting. The overall goal of the camps is to provide positive reinforcement and recreational camps that beginners to intermediate campers can experience and enjoy for one to four weeks.

PROGRAM OFFERINGS

Sailing Camp (one to four weeks, ages 9–17) is limited to 35 campers. Sailing techniques, rigging, points of sail, terminology, and safety are studied in this exciting camp which provides basic- through intermediate-level training. In addition to lectures and onshore and offshore instruction, the program includes plenty of practical experience with sailing on the Rappahannock River. The program has more than thirty sailboats which, in part, are updated yearly. The boats used included Resolute, Quantum, Fillippi, and Empacher. The core curriculum follows Chesapeake Bay Yacht Racing Association standards. Campers are encouraged to stay two or more weeks to finish all instruction and have the opportunity to use all of the boats.

Crew/Rowing Camp (one to four weeks, ages 12–17) is limited to 35 campers. Crew camp is for novice to experienced youths who want to learn or improve the quality of their rowing. This unique camp provides a rower with the opportunity to enjoy the unhurried atmosphere of a rural and pristine tributary of the Chesapeake Bay.

Areas of instruction include but are not limited to sculling and sweep rowing, coxswain training, technique improvements, video analysis, weight- and strength-training techniques, basic planning for aerobic conditioning, rigging fundamentals, drills for refining skills, intergroup racing, racing tips, and ergometer sessions. The following equipment is used in the program: singles, double/pairs, 4-man shells, 8-man shells, and ergometers (rowing stations). Campers are encouraged to stay more than one week to finish all instruction and to utilize all skills.

Marine Sciences Camps Situated on the Rappahannock River, 10 nautical miles from the Chesapeake Bay, the camp's ideal location and its own marine science boats provide students with a hands-on opportunity to learn about the bay and its tributaries through two marine science programs.

Marine Science I—Explore the Mysteries of the Chesapeake (two weeks, ages 11–14) This program is limited to 18 campers, whose mornings are spent at the waterfront or in the lab, setting up aquaria, preparing for afternoon field studies, and conducting laboratory experiments. Afternoons are spent in the field examining the different habitats and animals as well as conducting field experiments.

Each day brings new experiences, building on the day before. Students first learn about the history of the bay and visit a geological site to examine 2-million-year-old fossils. They gain an understanding of what makes up the bay ecosystem by canoeing, boating, or walking through a variety of habitats, all within 25 minutes of camp. Campers also examine threats to the health of the bay, such as pollution and overharvesting.

Campers explore basic questions of marine science and learn about wetlands, the tides, and waves and how they affect coastal areas. Through field trips to salt marshes, swamps, and mudflats and through lab experiences, students explore the Chesapeake Bay and its mysteries. Students fish with crab pots, trawl the Rappahannock River, and collect specimens for marine aquaria they set up. The program's goal is to have participants leave with a better understanding and appreciation of the Chesapeake Bay and its history, waters, shores, and wildlife.

Marine Science II—The Chesapeake Bay Region "A Closer Look" (two weeks, ages 14–17) This program is limited to 18 campers. It is designed for participants who are most interested in science and have a special interest in marine science. The most important part of this program is the daily, hands-on experience campers gain. Participants explore on land and water and gather information that furthers their interest in marine studies, the Chesapeake Bay, and its tributaries. Projects range from water chemistry testing to wetland plant identification. Participants learn how to record and disseminate information in standard scientific research formats. The program also allows them to be a part of a broad-based effort to save the bay. The equipment used in the projects is the same caliber as that being used by professionals.

In addition to field studies done in the program's research boats and canoes, visits are made to local watermen's harvesting operations, the Virginia Mariners Museum, the Virginia Marine Science Museum, and other task-oriented locations.

Skill Building Programs (four-week program) The School offers three courses designed to reinforce material and/or prepare students for upcoming course work in the next school year.

The math skills course is designed to strengthen math performance in future math courses, such as algebra and geometry, and on standardized tests. Materials from middle school and high school texts are used to review or introduce math skills that students will require in future academic courses.

The how-to-study skills course is designed to cover the areas of organization, work habits, note-taking, and test-taking skills. Equal time is devoted to helping students review or be introduced to skills that ensure academic success, including identifying their own unique learning styles and using them in the classroom and in studying for tests.

The writing skills course is designed to cover writing mechanics, sentence construction, paragraph development, and the use of outline formats to help students develop skills that will strengthen writing performance in their academic English courses in grades 7 through 10 and on standardized tests. Students gain experience in a variety of writing genres, including the five-paragraph essay, research papers, personal narratives, and other creative writing opportunities.

In the evening, counselors conduct activities that make use of the many facilities of Christchurch School. On weekends, boarding campers have one on-campus event and one off-campus event scheduled; the cost of these events is included in tuition.

ENROLLMENT

Most campers come from the mid-Atlantic states of Virginia, North Carolina, Maryland, South Carolina, Georgia, and Pennsylvania. However, other regions of the country and other countries are represented as well. Each camp has an enrollment limit as stated in the program listings above. The overall camper-to-staff member ratio is 4:1. The camper-to-staff member ratio for individual programs is between 4:1 and 6:1.

DAILY SCHEDULE

On Monday through Saturday, the daily schedule is consistent throughout all programs:

Breakfast	7:15–7:55
Program	8:00–11:45
Lunch	12:00–12:45
Rest period	12:45–1:45
Program	2:00–5:00
Pool/free time	5:00–5:45
Dinner	5:30–6:15
Evening activities	7:00–8:30
Free time	8:30–9:45
In-dorm (ages 9–13)	9:00
Lights out (ages 9–13)	9:45
In dorm (ages 14–17)	9:45
Lights out (ages 14–17)	10:30

FACILITIES

Its 125-acre riverfront campus enables the Camp to offer an abundance of water-related activities, including sailing, crew/rowing, marine science, study skills, and swimming. Three fully air-conditioned dormitories provide comfortable housing. Additional campus facilities include a recently renovated academic building, a new 22,000-square-foot field house/practice facility, and a newly renovated fine arts center. In addition to a cross-country course, a weight-training room, boat house and dock, all-weather track, outdoor swimming pool, lighted tennis courts, and field hockey, soccer, lacrosse, football, and baseball fields make up the athletic facilities.

STAFF

Dan Hayes, Director, has been running camps for eleven years and serves as the year-round camp director. Ann Roebuck, Associate Director and Director of the Skills Program, has been at Christchurch for twenty years as a learning skills/math teacher, dorm parent, Director of Student Activities, and administrative assistant to the Headmaster. Steve Fluhr has been a crew coach for more than thirteen years. He serves Christchurch as a coach, math teacher, and dorm parent. Henry Selby, Director of Sailing, has been at the School for three years as a

Spanish/music/drama teacher and waterfront director. Dr. Chris Carrillo (Marine Sciences director) is the chairman of the science department in addition to serving as a dorm parent and coach. Merridee Michelsen has been at Christchurch for four years and serves as learning skills teacher, Director of ESL, and dorm parent. All other staff members are experienced in their program areas. More than 90 percent of the Summer Camps staff members are either teachers, graduates of Christchurch School, or past campers; they help to establish a family-like feel for the program.

MEDICAL CARE

The on-campus Health Services Center is staffed by a nurse 24 hours per day. Any campers who require medical attention may report to the center at any time. Each camper must be covered by his or her family's medical and hospital insurance plan. In the event of an emergency, transportation is provided to either of the two local hospitals. The School physician is also available for campers.

COSTS

In the summer of 2003, fees for Summer Camps on the River vary because of the number of choices that are offered. There are savings for campers who choose multiple weeks. The range of tuition for boarding campers is $630–$3660. For day campers, the tuition range is $380–$1900. Campers should call or write for more detailed prices. Applications can be downloaded from the Web site listed below.

APPLICATION TIMETABLE

Summer Camps has an open policy for applications. A deposit is required to reserve a space for each camper. In 2003, Summer Camps was full on or about March 20. Early application is suggested.

For more information, contact:

Admissions at Christchurch School
49 Seahorse Lane
Christchurch, Virginia 23031
800-296-2306 (toll-free)
Fax: 804-758-0721
E-mail: admissions@christchurchschool.org
World Wide Web: http://www.christchurchschool.org

CLEARWATER CAMP FOR GIRLS

SUMMER CAMP

MINOCQUA, WISCONSIN

Type of Program: Traditional camping, sailing, waterskiing, aquatic sports and horseback-riding programs, overnight wilderness trips, extended trips
Participants: Girls, ages 8–16
Enrollment: 120 per session
Program Dates: Two 3½-week sessions, June 22 to July 16 and July 18 to August 11, or a full seven-week session, 2005
Head of Program: Sunny Moore, Director; Laurie and Perry Smith, Co-directors

LOCATION

Clearwater Camp is located in north central Wisconsin on Tomahawk Lake, 3 miles south of Minocqua off U.S. 51. It is about 340 miles northwest of Chicago, 220 miles northeast of Minneapolis, and 200 miles north of Madison.

BACKGROUND AND PHILOSOPHY

Clearwater was founded in 1933 by Mrs. John P. Sprague, who owned and directed the camp for thirty-eight years. One of the campers during this period was the current director. Sunny Moore, who has directed Clearwater since 1970, became the principal owner in 1975.

The camp is dedicated to providing an environment that will stimulate the most healthy and purposeful growth toward maturity possible. It is a place where a camper may learn to interact with her peers, to develop new skills, to venture into the unknown, and to succeed in her pursuit of new goals. Considerable effort goes into structuring the program to ensure a proper balance between scheduled activity instruction and the free use of time to enjoy the beauty of the Northwoods with new friends. The wonders of a summer at Clearwater are many and varied, but perhaps the greatest of all is the joy of learning to know one's self.

PROGRAM OFFERINGS

Campers participate in 18 hours of instruction per week in the following camp activities: archery, arts and crafts, campcraft, canoeing and canoe trips, drama, English riding, kayaking, nature lore, pioneer camping, photography, sailing, swimming, tennis, tumbling, waterskiing, and windsurfing. Each week, every girl receives a new schedule of activities. Each girl's program, built upon activity preferences and parent requests, makes the best use of staff members' skills and available equipment.

The activity program at Clearwater is designed to allow for the growth of the camper not only at the activity level but also in her relationships with others and with herself. Weeks in camp are a time to explore, to develop new hobbies, to have fun, and to learn the satisfying use of nonscheduled time.

Clearwater does not have awards for achievement in activities. Instead, if competition is to develop among campers, it is the decision of the campers to compete. Clearwater relies on a camper's natural enthusiasm, on its staff, and on its flexible yet determined program to provide the initiative that leads to success in and mastery of activities.

Each activity is governed by rules and procedures designed for the safety of the campers and for the proper learning of the activity. Water safety is a very important element in the camp's many water-oriented activities. Each camper must pass a swimming safety test before she may go out in any boat without a counselor or participate in sailing or waterskiing activities.

ENROLLMENT

Recent campers represent more than twenty states and four other countries. Enrollment is open to any girl who meets the age requirements.

DAILY SCHEDULE

Clearwater Camp's daily schedule features four instructional periods as well as scheduled portions of free-choice time. Three times per week, larger blocks of time are left unscheduled; these time blocks may be used to pursue individual nonscheduled interests, to clean cabins, or to spend extra time perfecting skills in the principal activities.

EXTRA OPPORTUNITIES AND ACTIVITIES

The out-of-camp trip program fulfills an important and unique role in the total Clearwater experience. Trip groups are small, usually consisting of 8 girls and 2 counselors. Trips are unhurried, as it sometimes takes a slower pace to respond to the beauty of nature and to realize that a person can cope and be comfortable in an environment markedly different from any encountered before. Such discoveries build self-confidence and expand a girl's knowledge of herself.

The type of trip, its destination, and its length are determined by camper desire, skill, and previous expe-

rience. Some trips are by canoe for two or three days along one of the many northern Wisconsin waterways.

For the skilled, older campers, trips of up to ten days are taken with backpacks or by canoe to Isle Royale or the B.W.C.A.

FACILITIES

Campers live in three main cabin units: Harbor, Cape, and Point. These are organized according to age. Many cabins are enclosed, while many, especially for the older girls, have 3½-foot canvas flaps over screens on four sides. For younger campers, each cabin is equipped with bathroom facilities. The two older units have central toilet and shower facilities.

The three units are geographically separate from one another. The youngest girls live near main camp buildings such as the dining room, the office area, and general meeting areas; the Cape and Point girls live out on the 5-acre island, which is reached by a footbridge and walk along wooded trails from which the lake is always visible.

For the sailing program, Clearwater has ten boats—six C-scows, three X-boats, and two Sunfish. The latter are excellent training boats because of their small size, while the X's and C's can accommodate larger classes for teaching and require greater skill from the sailors.

STAFF

Each member of the Clearwater staff is selected not only for her maturity and skills in an activity area but also for her commitment to young people and her belief in the value of a camp experience. On the staff are counselors who have previously been campers at Clearwater as well as returning and new counselors. Each summer a few staff members are 19 years old; the majority are older, with all having completed college work. The ratio of campers to staff members is 4:1.

A registered nurse is a full-time member of the staff. She determines when it would be in the best interest of a camper to be in the infirmary or to be seen by one of the physicians in Minocqua, 10 minutes away.

COSTS

Clearwater's tuition for the 2004 season was $5000 for the full seven-week season and $2800 for one 3½-week session. When 2 or more children from the same family register, a reduction of $100 is allowed for each full-season registration, $75 for each single session. Tuition includes all phases of the camp program in which a camper is able to participate, including living expenses, laundry, out-of-camp trips in Wisconsin, sailing and basic riding instruction, and use of all equipment. Not included are transportation to and from camp, strictly personal expenses, and extended trips.

For campers who enjoy more riding and want to perfect horsemanship, an extended program is offered with more riding hours, more advanced instruction, and trail rides. The charge is $250 per session. An extended waterskiing program for campers in grades 7–10 is also available for $250 per session.

APPLICATION TIMETABLE

Inquiries and enrollment applications are welcome year-round.

FOR MORE INFORMATION, CONTACT:

Sunny Moore
Clearwater Camp
7490 Clearwater Road
Minocqua, Wisconsin 54548
winter
800-399-5030 (toll-free)
715-356-5030
summer
715-356-5030
Fax: 715-356-3124
E-mail: clearwatercamp@newnorth.net
World Wide Web: http://www.clearwatercamp.com

PARTICIPANT/FAMILY COMMENTS

"My daughter and I think of camp often. She is quick to tell a camp story or sing a favorite song. Without doubt, her experience at Clearwater will be with her forever. She tells everyone it was the best summer of her life. Words just can't explain all the wonderful feelings and experiences that she gained at camp."

"She has a confidence I've never seen before—she is still radiating! Please save a place for her next year."

COLLEGE ADMISSION PREP CAMP BY EDUCATION UNLIMITED

SUMMER CAMP FOR COLLEGE ADMISSION

BERKELEY, LOS ANGELES, SAN DIEGO, AND STANFORD, CALIFORNIA, AND BOSTON, MASSACHUSETTS

Type of Program: College admission
Participants: Coeducational, students entering grades 11–12
Enrollment: 60 students per session
Program Dates: Ten-day sessions in June, July, and August
Head of Program: Byron Arthur, Director

LOCATION

Education Unlimited's College Admission Prep Camp programs are independent offerings held at top-ranked academic institutions in the United States. The camps provide a safe and secure environment while participants experience some of the nation's most dynamic universities. Students live in the residence halls on campus and eat in meal facilities.

BACKGROUND AND PHILOSOPHY

Education Unlimited has run college-admission prep programs for older high school students for more than ten years. The programs were founded to address the concerns of students and parents about the increasingly competitive and often mystifying college admission process.

The College Admission Prep Camp (CAPC) is a ten-day program that prepares entering juniors and seniors for one of the most important processes of their lives. Its exclusive curriculum demystifies the college application process by helping students craft a personal statement ready or nearly ready for submission, guiding them throughout the college selection process, improving their test-taking strategies, readying them for the SAT, and providing a taste of college life. The program curriculum has been fully updated to reflect the changes made to the SAT.

PROGRAM OFFERINGS

The focus of the CAPC is on SAT preparation, personal statement instruction, and one-on-one college counseling. The CAPC gives SAT students intensive SAT preparation, including 40 hours of SAT instruction, three practice tests, and plenty of individual attention. Experienced instructors employ the exclusive Test Scholars SAT curriculum, which familiarizes students with all aspects of the SAT exam. The focus is to provide students with test-taking strategies and reasoning skills rather than training students to rely primarily on tricks. Test Scholars students have historically scored average increases of more than 150 points.

Personalized writing instruction is all too elusive at most high schools. The CAPC offers every student hours of one-on-one consulting with expert writing instructors. From the conception of a topic to the final revised piece, the writing program teaches students how to write the kind of essay that presents them in the best light during the college admission process.

College counselors at the CAPC meet with students individually to identify excellent colleges that are appropriate for each student's interests and academic background. Students leave the CAPC program with a list of potential schools that have been reviewed and discussed with their counselor. In addition, the CAPC offers supplementary seminars and lectures on interview skills and time management, two areas overlooked by many high schools.

ENROLLMENT

Students from across the nation attend CAPC summer sessions. Admission is limited at each site and is open to any students who are entering their junior and senior years of high school.

EXTRA OPPORTUNITIES AND ACTIVITIES

Throughout the camp, recreational and fun activities, as well as other study breaks, are planned for. Planned recreational excursions allow students to experience the wonderful attractions of the Bay Area, southern California, and Boston.

DAILY SCHEDULE

8:00	Breakfast
9:00	SAT verbal preparation
11:30	Lunch
1:00	Personal statement instruction
3:00	SAT math preparation
5:00	Dinner
6:30	Counseling lecture
7:30	Recreation time
10:00	Floor check

This is a typical day's schedule. Specific class subjects change from day to day in the time allotted. Students rotate through electives in small groups.

FACILITIES

Students live in residence halls on campus and are supervised by adult counselors who share in dormitory life. Meals are included in the program cost and are served at the dormitory meal complex or elsewhere on campus.

STAFF

Each member of the faculty is a carefully chosen professional with years of experience in his or her field. Many staff members are guidance counselors or educators at prestigious prep schools and have specific experience working with students in this age range. Experienced directors and staff members continue with CAPC.

MEDICAL CARE

Medical care is available 24 hours a day at local and campus clinics and hospitals. All participants must submit comprehensive medical forms and proof of insurance.

COSTS

Camp fees for CAPC ten-day sessions in 2004 ranged from $1830 to $2225, depending on the campus. Room, board, tuition, and all materials necessary for the program are included in the cost. A $525 fee (applied toward tuition) is required upon application. Fees cover tuition for all classes, including SAT preparation and scored full-length exams, all required workbooks and materials, access to recreational and athletic facilities, planned recreational and evening activities, and camp memorabilia. Fees do not cover transportation to and from the program site, spending and laundry money, bath and bed linens, or additional nights' lodging for any students arriving before the program begins or staying after the conclusion of the program.

FINANCIAL AID

A limited amount of need-based financial aid is available. To be considered, relevant tax returns for the current and previous year are required. The total amount of aid awarded is based upon the applicant pool and total enrollment at the sessions. Financial aid awards are usually for tuition only, with applicants paying room and board costs.

TRANSPORTATION

The campuses are accessible from major airports. Most of these airports service international flights. Education Unlimited offers an optional airport pickup service for a round-trip fee of $45. This service provides transportation from the airport to the dorms at the beginning of the program and return transportation to the airport at the conclusion of the program.

APPLICATION TIMETABLE

Beginning in November, enquiries regarding programs for the coming summer are welcome. Office hours are from 9 to 6 (Pacific Standard Time) year round, and messages can be left 24 hours a day. The application deadline is usually May 15. Late applications are considered on a rolling basis.

FOR MORE INFORMATION, CONTACT:

Education Unlimited
1700 Shattuck Avenue, #305
Berkeley, California 94709
510-548-6612
800-548-6612 (toll-free)
E-mail: camps@educationunlimited.com
World Wide Web:
http://www.educationunlimited.com

PARTICIPANT/FAMILY COMMENTS

"I learned so much in a mere ten days. Without this camp, I would not be half as prepared or sure about my future."—CAPC participant

COLLÈGE DU LÉMAN

SUMMER SCHOOL

VERSOIX-GENEVA, SWITZERLAND

Type of Program: Academic enrichment
Participants: Coeducational, ages 8–18
Enrollment: 300
Program Dates: Two sessions of three weeks each, June 27 to July 17 and July 18 to August 7, 2004
Head of Program: Mr. Francis A. Clivaz, Director

LOCATION

Collège du Léman International School is located on an 18-acre campus in Versoix, a city about 5 miles from the center of Geneva. Geneva, one of the leading international cities of Europe, offers easy access not only to the surrounding Alps, but also to other sites of historic and cultural interest in Switzerland and neighboring France. It is the site of the European headquarters of the United Nations and of hundreds of other organizations and businesses. While its "Old Town," gardens, and parks endow it with a typical Old-World charm, its natural surroundings provide a multitude of recreational and outdoor activities, such as hiking, waterskiing, lake cruises, mountain climbing, and windsurfing. The mild summer climate of the area makes a stay relaxing and invigorating.

BACKGROUND AND PHILOSOPHY

The school was founded in 1960 by Francis A. Clivaz to help serve the needs of the enlarging diplomatic and international business community in the Geneva area. The school has always strived to take advantage of its location to implement the philosophy of the school: to provide a stimulating and effective college-preparatory education enriched by the wealth of cultural experiences offered by its international community. In so doing, the school hopes to develop internationally minded young people who can appreciate both the differences and the basic oneness of all peoples and who understand and respect the earth's many cultures and their interdependence in the world.

PROGRAM OFFERINGS

In the summer, Collège du Léman offers two programs. Students are given the choice between a language program (French, English, or German) or the academic program (revision or credit award). English, French, and computer studies are taught as noncredit courses. Language classes are offered for beginning, intermediate, and advanced students. A placement test is given in order to identify ability and skill levels in the language chosen. Depending on the level of instruction, classes comprise grammar, vocabulary, text analysis, and conversation courses. These classes, taught by native speakers, are supplemented by the use of language labs, films, games, and other informal activities. At the successful completion of the program, all students are awarded a Certificate of the Collège du Léman Summer School.

Collège du Léman, being accredited by both the Council of International Schools (CIS) and the New England Association of Schools and Colleges (NEASC), allows credits to be transferred from one institution to another and to become part of the official school report.

ENROLLMENT

Students ages 8–18 come to the Collège du Léman Summer School from all over the world. They are all motivated by a desire to take intensive classes in French or English. They may enroll for three- or six-week sessions.

DAILY SCHEDULE

Language classes are held six days a week from 9 until noon. Afternoons are devoted to recreation and sports such as tennis, volleyball, badminton, basketball, soccer, aerobics, cycling, and swimming in the college's own pool. All sports activities are closely supervised by the Collège du Léman's athletics staff.

EXTRA OPPORTUNITIES AND ACTIVITIES

A comprehensive program of excursions and visits is an integral part of the Collège du Léman Summer School. Students discover many of the historical, cultural, and natural attractions of the region: Zermatt, Chamonix, Interlaken, Gruyere, Bern, and Montreux are just some of the sites visited. Visits to some of the principal international organizations in Geneva, such as the United Nations, complete the program.

FACILITIES

Girls and boys are housed separately in school buildings, or villas, in comfortable bedrooms with three or four beds each. Students have access to reading rooms, a television, pianos, and a library containing more than 25,000 volumes and periodicals. Balanced and varied meals are served three times a day in the school's dining room. Students can use the college's own pool and weight room.

STAFF

Many of the college's 156 full-time and 28 part-time faculty members teach in the summer school as well. Although most teachers are from Switzerland, Great Britain, and the United States, nearly 30 nationalities are represented on the staff. Because of a very small annual turnover, teachers average nine years' experience at Collège du Léman and twelve years' experience overall.

MEDICAL CARE

There are separate infirmaries for boys and girls. A male and female nurse are on duty, and a doctor with

a residence and office facilities adjacent to the campus is on call. Medical and pharmaceutical expenses are not included in the tuition fee.

COSTS

In 2004, the price of a three-week language course was SwFr 4500, and the price of a three-week academic program session was SwFr 5400. These amounts included tuition, full board and lodging, laundry costs, use of all of the college's sports facilities, day trips and excursions, and transfer to and from Geneva Airport. Personal expenses, medical expenses, pocket money, and private sports instruction are not included. There is a compulsory medical deposit of SwFr 300, which is reimbursed, if unused, upon the departure of the student. The first week's fee must accompany all applications; the remaining balance must be paid by the day of the student's arrival.

APPLICATION TIMETABLE

Interested students should send the completed application form, one teacher's letter of recommendation, two photographs, and a medical certificate to the address below. When registration is complete, parents receive written confirmation of admission.

FOR MORE INFORMATION, CONTACT:

Mr. Francis A. Clivaz, Director
Collège du Léman International School
1290 Versoix (Geneva), Switzerland
41-22-775-5555
Fax: 41-22-775-5559
E-mail: info@cdl.ch
summerschool@cdl.ch
World Wide Web: http://www.cdl.ch

CORNELL UNIVERSITY SUMMER COLLEGE

SUMMER PROGRAM

ITHACA, NEW YORK

Type of Program: Academic course work
Participants: Coeducational, students who have completed the sophomore, junior, or senior year of high school
Enrollment: 600 juniors and seniors; 150 sophomores
Program Dates: June 26 to August 10, 2004, for juniors and seniors; June 26 to July 17, 2004, for sophomores
Head of Program: Abby H. Eller, Director

LOCATION

Cornell University is located at the heart of the Finger Lakes region of central New York State, one of the Northeast's most spectacular summer vacation areas. The 740-acre campus overlooks Cayuga Lake and is surrounded by rolling hills. Some of the most breathtaking waterfalls and state parks in New York are a short bike or bus ride away.

Ithaca is a small, cosmopolitan city with a population of 30,000. Ithaca can be reached by car from Boston in 7 hours, from Buffalo in 3 hours, from Cleveland in 7 hours, from Manhattan in under 5 hours, from Philadelphia in 4 hours, and from Washington, D.C., in 7 hours; Syracuse and Binghamton are within 1 hour's drive.

BACKGROUND AND PHILOSOPHY

Now in its forty-third year, Cornell University Summer College provides academically talented high school students with the opportunity to experience a rigorous college-level program in an optimally supportive environment. Summer College offers six- and three-week programs for juniors and seniors and three-week programs for sophomores. Students enroll in regular Cornell University courses. Grades are recorded on a university transcript, and course credits can generally be applied toward an undergraduate degree.

PROGRAM OFFERINGS

Juniors and seniors enrolled in the six-week Summer College choose from more than sixty Cornell courses that are offered in a full range of subjects. They may earn an average of 6 college credits. Juniors and seniors enrolled in the three-week session may take one or both 3-credit courses, either Democracy and its Discontents: Political Traditions in the U.S. and/or Introduction to Psychology: Personality and Social Behavior. These courses may be taken individually or sequentially. Juniors and seniors also participate in a noncredit seminar to explore an academic or career field of special interest. Exploration seminars are offered in the following: architecture, art world, biological research and the health professions, business, CollegeSuccess, communication, engineering, the humanities and sciences, law and the legal profession, psychology, and veterinary medicine.

Sophomores have three 3-week options: Freedom and Justice in the Western Tradition: Introduction to Political Philosophy; Leadership Through Managerial Communication: Introduction to Managerial Communication; or Body, Mind, and Health. These programs are designed to develop both critical thinking and the writing skills essential to success in college. Students who choose the Freedom and Justice program examine some of the most fundamental questions facing democratic society as they learn more advanced approaches to critical analysis and discussion. Students who enroll in Leadership Through Managerial Communication expand on their business, communication, and leadership skills while exploring their interest in hospitality management.

ENROLLMENT

Summer College students are part of an international, multicultural community, with members coming from all over the United States and the world.

DAILY SCHEDULE

Juniors and seniors spend mornings in classes (roughly 2½ hours each weekday, with laboratory courses requiring an additional 2 to 3 hours a day). Most afternoons are devoted to career exploration activities such as field trips, experiments, simulations, lectures, or discussions. The academic course work is rigorous; students should plan to spend 2 hours a day in preparation for every hour in class. The nightly check-in is midnight, Sunday through Thursday, and 1 a.m., Friday and Saturday.

Sophomores spend weekday mornings in class (roughly 2½ hours each day) and afternoons in a seminar and in meetings with teaching assistants and the faculty director. The nightly check-in is 11 p.m., Sunday through Thursday, and midnight, Friday and Saturday.

EXTRA OPPORTUNITIES AND ACTIVITIES

Sessions about the college application process are offered throughout the summer, with information on the art of filling out applications, the value of campus visits, and the nitty-gritty of college interviews. Cornell's Undergraduate Admissions staff answers questions about applying to selective colleges. Juniors and seniors may also take part in a half-day crash

course in college study skills before classes begin and in math, study skills, and writing workshops throughout the summer.

Students enjoy theater parties; athletic activities, including sailboarding, basketball, volleyball, aerobics, yoga, and intramural sports; weekend dances; a student-organized show; and get-togethers with faculty members to discuss current topics. They also produce Summer College's weekly newspaper and its literary supplement. Free concerts and lectures are offered throughout the summer.

FACILITIES

Students are housed in residence halls and eat and relax together in on-campus dining halls and student community centers. They have full access to Cornell's academic facilities, including the Cornell library system (which holds more than 6 million volumes), numerous computer laboratories (with Internet access), an astronomical observatory, an extensive botanical garden, and an art museum. Students may also use the athletics facilities on campus, including tennis courts, swimming pools, gyms, and an eighteen-hole golf course. Cornell University is famed for the spacious beauty of its campus. Students enjoy hiking in the gorges that cut through the campus and exploring the spectacular waterfalls and geologic formations.

STAFF

Most courses are taught by Cornell University faculty members. The residence halls are staffed by head residents, residential community advisers, and program assistants, all of whom work to ensure that the students' experiences in the residence halls are good ones. In addition to the residence staff, teaching assistants live in the residence halls with sophomore participants.

MEDICAL CARE

Gannett Health Center is open for general and emergency health care. Students complete both the Proof of Compliance with Medical Requirements and Authorization to Treat and Health Information Forms prior to registration.

RELIGIOUS LIFE

Cornell University is a secular institution. Cornell United Religious Work coordinates religious activities on campus, and services for many religious groups are held during the summer.

COSTS

The cost for the 2004 six-week Summer College program for high school juniors and seniors was $6910; the cost for the three-week programs for sophomores and Summer College three-week sessions was $4150. Both amounts covered tuition, room, board, and all fees, including those for courses and activities at Cornell. They did not include the cost of books, supplies, or travel.

FINANCIAL AID

For juniors and seniors, Summer College's limited financial aid is awarded to students whose academic performance has been outstanding and who demonstrate financial need. The deadline for financial aid applications in 2004 is April 2. Summer College offers several full and partial Dean's Scholarships to gifted students who could not otherwise attend. The program also awards several Jerome H. Holland Memorial Scholarships, full scholarships for minority high school students who demonstrate outstanding academic ability in addition to financial need. The Jerry M. Rivers Summer College Scholarships are set aside specifically for Native American high school students. Limited financial aid is available for sophomores who apply to the Leadership Through Managerial Communication program.

TRANSPORTATION

The Ithaca Tompkins Regional Airport (10 minutes from the campus) is served by US Airways. Syracuse (Hancock International) is served by most major airlines, including American, Continental, Delta, United, and US Airways.

APPLICATION TIMETABLE

Inquiries are welcome throughout the year. The admissions application deadline is May 3. Admissions are made on a rolling basis, so it is to the student's advantage to apply early.

FOR MORE INFORMATION, CONTACT:

Cornell University Summer College
B20 Day Hall
Ithaca, New York 14853-2801
607-255-6203
Fax: 607-255-6665
E-mail: summer_college@cornell.edu
World Wide Web: http://www.summercollege.cornell.edu

SUMMER PROGRAMS

CULVER, INDIANA

Type of Program: Boarding, with more than sixty-five recreational and academic opportunities
Participants: Coeducational, ages 9–17
Enrollment: 1,300 in six-week programs, 400 in Specialty Camps
Program Dates: Six-week Woodcraft Camp and Upper Camp, late June to early August; two-week Specialty Camps, early August to mid-August
Head of Program: Anthony Mayfield, Director

LOCATION

The campus of the Culver Academies occupies 1,800 wooded acres along the north shore of Indiana's second-largest lake.

BACKGROUND AND PHILOSOPHY

For the 101st year, 1,700 young people from more than forty states and twenty countries will develop worldwide friendships through sailing on a tall ship; riding a horse; snorkeling; flying an airplane; taking dance, band, or hockey; playing tennis; learning to dive forward, backward, and upside down; waterskiing; playing soccer; improving their golf game; and fencing. Every program offers fun with a purpose and emphasizes leadership training and character development. Culver only offers progressive, or graduated, instruction, so that campers are actually taught activities rather than just practicing skills they bring from home. The number of campers allows for each camp to offer beginner, intermediate, and

advanced instruction to meet the needs of each camper. The highlight of each camp is the Sunday Parade, to which parents are invited to see their youngsters progress through the presentation of patches and awards signifying achievement.

PROGRAM OFFERINGS

Woodcraft Camp for boys and girls ages 9–13
Woodcrafters have a campus all their own. The wide-open spaces and wooded setting of this beautiful, rustic, multimillion-dollar facility are ideal for filling every hour of a six-week camp with experiences that will last a lifetime. On the north shore of 1,900-acre Lake Maxinkuckee, which means "clear, deep blue water," campers live with 9 other youngsters and a counselor in one of sixty-four cabins beside a museum, library, two authentic pioneer log cabins, classroom cabins, an observatory, and a dining hall. Like the older campers in the Upper Camp, Woodcrafters select their instruction from more than sixty-five options, including waterskiing, hockey, soccer, Indian lore and dancing, leadership, scuba diving, a variety of academic programs, fencing, and other options ranging from traditional campcraft to rocketry.

Upper Camp for boys and girls ages 13–17
During six activity periods every day, Upper Campers are offered more than sixty-five elective courses that allow room for experimenting, practicing, and succeeding. Campers may find themselves fencing with someone who has never fenced before, swimming with someone who has swum competitively since the age of 8, or cheering for someone who has just gotten up on his first try at waterskiing.

What matters at Culver isn't the winning but the way the game is played. A girl or boy may be one of the best tennis players at Culver and win every match or perhaps never be on the winning polo team. The true value of the experience is developing a positive attitude.

Upper Campers can learn to fly at the camp's own airport, with six Piper Cherokee aircraft and FAA-certified flight instructors. Culver offers the opportunity to fly solo when campers turn 16 and obtain a private pilot license at 17. They can learn or improve on their scuba diving skills, sharpen their skills on the golf links, learn modern dance, or develop an appreciation of fine art.

With a stable of nearly 100 horses, the country's largest indoor riding hall, 600 acres of riding trails, and facilities that are considered to be among the best in the nation, campers can receive basic horse riding instruction. They can also develop or sharpen their skills in polo, combined training, or dressage working with Culver's full-time equestrian instructors.

The fleet of boats includes a 54-foot square rigger—the largest on any U.S. inland lake—and 120 sailboats and power boats of all sizes. Campers can take courses in boats, sailing, seamanship, and navigation.

There's a marching band whose members perform on- and off-campus at parades and other events. Reading, mathematics, computer programming, and English are important supplements to a Culver summer as well. Campers may want to explore computers or to study art or English. And the pressure is off—there are no grades, so campers know the thrill of learning for learning's sake.

Throughout the entire camp there is a strong emphasis on leadership training, responsibility, reliability, organization, self-confidence, and self-discipline. Culver also provides many opportunities to practice and hone these skills.

Specialty Camps for boys and girls ages 11–16
Specialty Camps are two-week camps for youths from 11 to 16 years old who want specialized instruction in one of ten offerings: sailing, waterskiing, aviation, fencing, scuba diving, hockey, soccer, tennis, golf, or equestrian arts. Campers receive 5 hours of instruction daily from outstanding teachers and coaches, and, because of the quality of instruction, candidates are encouraged to apply as early as possible. Specialty Campers are offered participation in a variety of evening recreational and social activities that take advantage of Culver's excellent facilities. Dances, movies, hayrides, boat rides, hockey games, bowling, video and board games, and skating are just a few of the options offered to this select group of campers.

ENROLLMENT
Young people from all over the world attend Culver. Last summer's enrollment included campers from forty-two states and twenty-eight countries.

DAILY SCHEDULE
Six instructional periods begin each day and are followed by a competitive intramural sports program and social activities. Culver's military framework provides unusual opportunities for leadership, character training, interpersonal skills development, and responsibility.

FACILITIES
The Culver campus includes an airport, a parade ground, athletic fields, seventeen tennis courts, a track, a nine-hole golf course, 2 miles of lakefront, bridle paths, and nature trails. The thirty-six buildings include a $10-million library with 75,000 volumes, three gymnasiums, an indoor swimming pool, two ice arenas for hockey and figure skating, a rifle range, a dance studio, a beautiful chapel, a 1,500-seat auditorium, dormitories, and classroom buildings.

STAFF
Culver offers an outstanding staff of carefully selected college students, college graduates, and adults. The vast majority of the staff are certified teachers and counselors, and all camps offer a 5:1 camper-staff ratio. All staff members are dedicated to providing each child with excellent instruction, supervision, guidance, and individual attention.

MEDICAL CARE
Culver has a sixty-bed infirmary, which is staffed around the clock by registered nurses and 2 resident physicians.

RELIGIOUS LIFE
Although Culver is nondenominational, religion is an important part of the summer, and all faiths are respected. Weekly religious observance is required.

COSTS
Costs for the Woodcraft Camp and the Upper Camp programs for 2003 were $3750. The Specialty Camps for 2003 were $1200.

FINANCIAL AID
Need-based financial aid is available for the six-week Woodcraft and Upper camps. About 10 percent of Culver's campers receive assistance; the average award is one half of tuition.

TRANSPORTATION
Culver is easily accessible by car. Students flying into Chicago's O'Hare Airport and South Bend's Michiana Regional Airport are met by Culver staff members.

For more information, contact:

Culver Summer Camps
1300 Academy Road, CEF Box 138
Culver, Indiana 46511-1291
574-842-8300
800-221-2020 (toll-free)
Fax: 574-842-8462
E-mail: summer@culver.org
World Wide Web: http://www.culver.org

CUSHING ACADEMY

SUMMER SESSION

ASHBURNHAM, MASSACHUSETTS

Type of Program: Academic enrichment
Participants: Coeducational, ages 12–18
Enrollment: 300
Program Dates: July 3 to August 12
Head of Program: Dan Frank, Director of Summer Session

LOCATION

Located in the hills of north-central Massachusetts, 60 miles from Boston, Cushing Academy's 100-acre campus offers a rural atmosphere with the cultural advantages of a major city only an hour's drive away. The school is situated in and overlooks the picturesque New England town of Ashburnham.

BACKGROUND AND PHILOSOPHY

Established in 1865, Cushing Academy is an accredited boarding school for boys and girls in grades 9 through 12. The Summer Session, offering programs for boys and girls ages 12 to 18, continues the school's approach to education into the summer. The mission of the Summer Session is to allow young people to grow and learn by facing challenges in a secure and supportive environment, thereby successfully developing self-esteem. Cushing strives to develop happy, fair-minded, and productive human beings, and all of its programs are directed toward this goal. The focus is always on the potential of the adolescent, and Cushing helps students discover, develop, and appreciate their own uniqueness and value.

PROGRAM OFFERINGS

Each student is enrolled in one of six major programs: College Prep–Secondary School Level; Critical Skills Across the Curriculum in English, Mathematics, Study Techniques, and Technology; English as a Second Language; the Prep for Success Program; Studio Art; or Community Service. The average class contains 8–12 students, with a purposeful yet friendly atmosphere that encourages questions and discussion. Faculty members prepare two formal evaluations on each student, one in the middle and one at the end of the summer. Written evaluations highlight the progress made by the individual student relative to his or her own needs and placement, and a grade of honors, pass, or fail is given.

College Prep–Secondary School Level For students ages 14–18, this program offers a choice of Critical and Creative Writing, A Literary Tour of New England, Research and Technology, Geometry, Algebra I and II, Precalculus, AB Calculus, U.S. History, Biology, Chemistry, Physics, and Theater Workshop. The courses taught in this program prepare students to meet the challenge of a college-level curriculum confidently and successfully. Each of these courses is the equivalent of a year of secondary school course work, and Cushing awards a full year of secondary school academic credit upon successful completion of the program.

Critical Skills Across the Curriculum in English, Mathematics, Study Techniques, and Technology This program is for students ages 14–18. It encompasses four key components: English, Mathematics, Study Techniques, and Technology. Each student is given placement tests to assess skills and learning styles and an individualized learning program is developed. Students are assigned to classes structured to meet their specific learning needs. Each student learns at his or her own pace, mastering progressively higher levels of skills. The schedule is flexible enough to allow a focus on either English or mathematics development or both. Study Techniques and Technology are taught within the context of the subject matter.

English as a Second Language (ESL) is offered for students ages 14–18. Within the ESL program, classes enhance skills in reading, writing, speaking, and listening. Students can dramatically increase their proficiency in English through this three- or six-week immersion experience. Students are tested at the beginning of the program and placed in a class appropriate to their skill level. Up to fourteen levels ensure that each student's needs are met. Preparation for the Test of English as a Foreign Language (TOEFL) is offered, and the opportunity to take the official TOEFL is offered to students of advanced and high intermediate levels during the final weeks of the program.

Prep for Success For students ages 12–13, this program offers a choice of science, English, mathematics, study skills, and ESL. The courses taught in this program prepare students for the academic experiences that lie ahead in secondary school. Featuring hands-on learning, each course has a dual focus on the subject matter and on the skills needed for academic success, including reading comprehension strategies, vocabulary development, word analogies, time management, organizational techniques, and test-taking strategies.

Studio Art This program, for students ages 12–18, is taught in Cushing's state-of-the-art Emily Fisher Landau Center for the Visual Arts, a beautiful facility with five advanced studios and a gallery. Both experienced and beginning art students are provided with opportunities to explore a variety of media, including painting and drawing, pottery, silversmithing, and photography.

Community Service Summer Session provides community service trips locally and to Chile. Each includes a classroom component, while the trip to Chile also includes adventure travel.

ENROLLMENT

Approximately 300 students, representing more than thirty countries and as many states, attend the session.

DAILY SCHEDULE

Classes in the major programs take place for 4 hours, Monday through Friday, beginning at 8:15 a.m. Each afternoon, students participate in academic, athletic, and fine arts electives, of which Cushing offers a wide variety. Writing workshop, SAT preparation, computer design, and Algebra I are just a few academic electives offered. Fine arts electives include painting and drawing, photography, silversmithing, pottery, dance, theater, and videomaking, while athletic activities include soccer, basketball, tennis, volleyball, aerobics, golf, and swimming.

EXTRA OPPORTUNITIES AND ACTIVITIES

Each week brings a variety of activities to campus, including dances, sports events, and performances by musical groups and entertainers. Optional excursions are scheduled every Saturday and Sunday to shopping centers, amusement parks, beaches, Red Sox games, local community service opportunities, and other activities that take advantage of recreational and cultural offerings in the Boston area and throughout New England.

On Wednesdays, a variety of class field trips to sites such as Plimoth Plantation, the New England Aquarium, and Mystic Seaport are organized. These excursions are included in the comprehensive fee and are chaperoned by faculty members. College counseling and secondary school placement counseling are available for students who want assistance with educational planning.

During each week, Cushing offers a special all-school activity, including a trip to High Meadow resort and a dinner/dance cruise around Boston Harbor. Among the special events is International Evening, a celebration of the rich cultural diversity present at the Summer Session. In preparation the students bring from home traditional clothing, flags, posters, and recipes. Cushing's dining hall is transformed into an international bazaar, where students view displays and sample foods from other cultures. The evening concludes with student-created performances of songs, dances, and skits representative of their culture. The Cushing Cabaret, a night dedicated to short programs and entertainment by the Cushing community, has also become a well-loved summer tradition. Students and faculty members show off their talent through comedy, music, poetry, skits, and more.

FACILITIES

The campus combines the charm of nineteenth-century buildings with the graceful contemporary style of Cushing's award-winning library. Boys and girls live in separate dormitories with roommates, supervised by members of the faculty. Two or three students are assigned to each room. The spacious dining hall accommodates the entire Cushing community for relaxed and congenial mealtimes. The Student Center, part of the student commons complex, houses the student post office, student bank, bookstore, snack bar, and lounge. Athletic facilities include playing fields, tennis courts, a gymnasium with weight room, and a world-class ice arena.

STAFF

Teachers are experienced professionals educated in the theories and methods of teaching. They are also supportive, insightful, caring, good-humored, and kind. A diverse group, they share a willingness to spend their lives with young people. Most have master's degrees, and some have doctorates; all have experience teaching in this country or abroad. The faculty-student ratio is approximately 1:8. In their roles as dorm parents, athletic coaches, and chaperones, Cushing teachers are in an excellent position to know when to offer support, enforce discipline, mediate a dispute, or let students work things out among themselves.

MEDICAL CARE

The Health Center is fully equipped to handle all routine medical needs. Nurses and doctors are available at all times. Cushing uses the Henry Heywood Hospital in nearby Gardner for nonroutine needs.

COSTS

Program tuitions vary, but the six-week fee of $5450 covers the following: tuition for all courses, academic electives, and athletic activities; meals and dormitory housing; required trips and excursions; special all-school activities; books and supplies; weekly linen and laundry services; athletic uniform; on-campus social activities; dormitory-room supplies; institution and limited accident insurance; and TOEFL and pre-TOEFL preparation materials. In addition, students have use of the Academy's communications system, which includes a private telephone, voice mail, and Internet access for each student.

TRANSPORTATION

The staff meets flights and provides free transportation between Cushing and Logan International Airport (Boston) on scheduled arrival and departure dates. Parents may also wish to secure personalized transportation assistance through Concierge Services for Students LTD, at 617-523-8686.

APPLICATION TIMETABLE

The application form should be completed and mailed with the nonrefundable processing fee of $50 as early as possible. Admissions decisions are made as soon as these materials are in hand. Within four weeks of acceptance, a nonrefundable enrollment deposit of $500 is due. The remainder of the tuition is due on or before May 15.

For more information, contact:

G. Daniel Frank, Director
Cushing Academy
Ashburnham, Massachusetts 01430-8000
978-827-7700
Fax: 978-827-6927
World Wide Web: http://www.cushing.org

DARLINGTON SUMMER CAMPS

SUMMER PROGRAMS

ROME, GEORGIA

Type of Program: One-week overnight experiences in sports and science or two-week overnight sessions emphasizing outdoor eco-adventure activities

Participants: Boys and girls entering sixth through ninth grades

Enrollment: Varies by program

Program Dates: One- and two-week sessions, June through July

Head of Program: Ballard Betz, Director of Summer Programs

LOCATION

Darlington Summer Camps nestles around a small lake in the foothills of the Lookout Mountain Range. Located in Rome, Georgia, the Darlington Summer Camps program is held on Darlington School's 500-acre main campus. Rome, a community of 30,000, is home to Berry, Floyd, and Shorter Colleges, is the medical hub of northwest Georgia, and is just a little more than an hour's drive from Atlanta and Chattanooga.

BACKGROUND AND PHILOSOPHY

Darlington Summer Camps, begun in 2003, give middle schoolers the opportunity to enjoy Darlington School's campus, its facilities, and the surrounding area. The camps provide unique learning and playing environments; passionate, caring teachers and counselors; well-trained and experienced staff members; and jam-packed schedules—all to help campers grow intellectually, physically, socially, culturally, morally, and spiritually, in keeping with Darlington School's mission statement.

PROGRAM OFFERINGS

Eco-Adventure Darlington, Darlington Summer Camps' signature camp, offers campers two sessions, each two weeks long, of outdoor fun and nature exploration. Eco-Adventure takes full advantage of Darlington's 500-acre campus by canoeing and kayaking on Silver Lake, hiking and biking on the School's miles of mountain trails, and observing flora and fauna both on the campus and in the laboratory.

In addition to the many activities available on campus, campers take full advantage of the myriad of outdoor activities and cultural offerings in the area, such as whitewater rafting on the Ocoee and Nantahala Rivers, snorkeling and observing the diverse fishes of the pristine Conasauga River, and kayaking and canoeing on the Hiawassee River and Big Cedar Creek. They rock climb and rappel at Desoto Falls and Little River Canyon, go spelunking in Pigeon Mountain and Sinking Cove Cave, and experience mountain biking on Lavender Mountain. Time is spent hiking, backpacking, and camping on the Appalachian Trail. Campers explore marshlands and wetlands, monitor the water quality of the Coosa River, and embark on trips to the Huntsville Space Center, Arrowhead Environmental Education Center, and Chattanooga Aquarium. Some pursue Boy and Girl Scout merit badge criteria.

ENROLLMENT

Middle school students entering sixth through ninth grades enjoy Darlington's 500 acres with woodlands and a small lake. Nearly 1,000 campers participated in the 2003 season's offerings of Adventure Darlington and the wide variety of sport, science, and cultural offerings.

DAILY SCHEDULE

Camp Darlington gives campers a sense of adventure while providing a variety of safe and wholesome activities to intrigue every kind of camper.

Each morning, after a complete breakfast in Darlington's Dodd Dining Room, campers go to two activities, chosen from among a host of possibilities, and a break between them. After lunch in the dining room, rest, and mail call, campers enjoy afternoon activities, a break, and supervised free play. After dinner each evening, campers enjoy another activity before returning to the dormitories for bunk time at 9:30 and lights out at 10 p.m.

EXTRA OPPORTUNITIES AND ACTIVITIES

A variety of science and sports are also offered during the summer. Camps offered in 2004 include:

Rockets and Robotics Camp Campers receive hands-on educational experiences in two cutting-edge technology fields, robotics and rocketry. Campers design, conduct, and report experimental investigations in areas such as robot construction, using Lego Mindstorms robotics kits; Robot Rodeo; model rocket construction; weather prediction for launches; rocket launches; and brain "stims" (stimulating, hands-on mini scientific seminars on, for example, lasers, holograms, and electronics).

Fast-Pitch Softball Camp Campers are taught the fundamentals of pitching, hitting, and fielding, along with the importance of player positioning on the field, through drills, play, and lots of individual instruction. Players improve their skills by learning the mechanics of proper hitting and pitching.

Golf Camp Campers receive instruction in course management, strategy, rules, and etiquette. Each camper receives a golf fitness assessment and a videotaped swing analysis. They compete in daily tournaments at Rome's Stonebridge Golf Course, an 18-hole, 72-par course, which is ranked as one of the top 10 public courses in the state.

Tennis Camp Campers play on twelve outdoor hard courts and take full advantage of Darlington's three-year old, $16-million athletic facility. They learn stroke techniques and tactics; develop topspin and backspin, serve, and volley shot tactics; and train for mental and physical toughness. In addition, they practice patterns of play, match play each day, set personal-best goals, and learn about nutrition and the science of tennis. Each camper receives a videotaped performance analysis.

FACILITIES

Campers use Darlington School's many facilities, including the Kawamura Science Center, with classroom and laboratory facilities; Porter Hall, containing the dining room; Syndenham Hall, with administrative offices, bookstore, and post office; Zelle Fine Arts Building, which houses art, drama, and music studios; six residential houses; the Old Gym; a climbing wall; the A. J. Huffman '67 Memorial Athletic Center, with a natatorium, performance gym, three basketball practice courts, indoor track, large wrestling and weight room, and extensive locker space; the stadium for football and track; soccer field complex; baseball, softball, lacrosse, and football practice fields; cross-country courses; and a 12-court tennis complex.

Campers live in one of Darlington's six student houses, the housing used by resident students during the academic year. These houses are fully air-conditioned and are complete with all the modern amenities of home. Campers eat in Darlington School's Dodd Dining Room, enjoying three meals and two snacks each day.

Girls and boys are separated by floor in all of the houses. Two campers of similar age are assigned a room, which is furnished with two single beds, two chest of drawers, and two storage closets. Each house floor has its own bathroom and shower area. Staff members reside with the campers in the houses and are available at all times. A counselor-to-camper ratio of 1:5 ensures proper supervision in the houses.

STAFF

The director of summer programs and each camp's directors, counselors, and coaches are devoted, professional, well trained, and fun-loving. Nearly all have Darlington connections and many have a long-standing history with the school as instructors, parents, and/or alumni. Guest directors, speakers, and coaches, who are experts in their fields, also participate.

Darlington School has 24-hour campus security and many of Darlington's faculty members reside on campus.

MEDICAL CARE

Darlington Summer Camps employs a full-time camp nurse who works in the School's infirmary during camp hours. Campers check any medication they bring into the camp infirmary on opening day. Darlington also retains two local physicians on call for further medical attention, as needed. Floyd Medical Center and Redmond Regional Hospital are located in Rome, only a short distance from the campus. All campers must have a completed health form on file in the infirmary.

COSTS

The average cost for one-week overnight camps is $540. Each two-week session of Eco-Adventure Darlington costs $1350, or $2500 for both sessions.

APPLICATION TIMETABLE

Campers can apply online.

For more information, contact:

Ballard Betz, Director of Summer Programs
1014 Cave Spring Road S.W.
Rome, Georgia 30161-4700
800-368-4437 (toll-free)
Fax: 706-232-3600
E-mail: bbetz@darlingtonschool.org
World Wide Web: http://www.darlingtonschool.org

DIGIPEN INSTITUTE OF TECHNOLOGY

DIGIPEN SUMMER WORKSHOPS

REDMOND, WASHINGTON

Type of Program: Video game programming, video game development, 3-D animation, and robotics
Participants: Coeducational; Junior Game Developer Workshop, grades 5–7; Summer Workshops, grades 8–college
Enrollment: 20–25 students per workshop
Program Dates: Two-week sessions, beginning June 21, July 5, July 19, August 2, and August 16
Head of Program: Raymond Yan

LOCATION

DigiPen Institute of Technology is located 15 miles east of Seattle at the intersection of the cities of Redmond and Bellevue. The area offers urban conveniences and easy access to the rugged beauty of Washington. Family entertainment and outdoor recreation, including parks, ball fields, bicycling, rock climbing, and movie theaters, are easy to reach.

BACKGROUND AND PHILOSOPHY

In their tenth year, the summer workshops at DigiPen Institute of Technology present a series of workshops designed to introduce participants of all experience levels to the fundamentals of game programming and 3-D computer animation. Beginning students learn basic concepts in each discipline and then produce a small project through implementation. The two-week workshops are also ideal for students considering a serious career as a video game programmer or as a 3-D artist.

PROGRAM OFFERINGS

Video Game Programming Workshop–Level One This workshop introduces the fundamentals of C/C++ programming, computer hardware theory, and the essential elements of creating a video game. Students then create their own computer/video game. Topics include an overview of the video game production process, an introduction to the C/C++ programming languages, game loop concepts, mouse and keyboard input, animation, object behaviors, sound effects and music, and special effects. The workshop is for students grade 8 and above. No previous programming or computer experience is required.

Video Game Programming Workshop–Level Two This program covers more-advanced programming concepts and gives the students training on additional game element implementation. Students then complete a game project. The workshop gives an overview of video game production and of the C programming language, including expressions, statements, functions, pointers, and structures. Students also learn how to handle game events, write game events, and link components. The program is for students entering grade 9 and above who have previously completed Video Game Programming Workshop–Level 1.

Video Game Programming Workshop–Level Three This most-advanced video game programming workshop covers the general 3-D graphics pipeline found in many 3-D video games. Practical work is focused on building a game utilizing a 3-D ray-casting engine. The workshop is an intensive programming experience. Topics include review of C/C++ coding concepts, pointers, general 3-D pipeline, and 3-D ray-casting. This program is for students who are entering grade 9 and above and have previously completed Video Game Programming Workshop–Level 2.

3-D Computer Animation Workshop–Level One The process of creating 3-D computer animation is introduced in this workshop. Students are taught the importance of strong traditional art skills. Topics include an overview of the 3-D computer animation industry, basic modeling techniques, creation of materials and texture maps, basic lighting techniques, basic camera manipulation, hierarchy linking, basic keyframing techniques, and rendering. The program is for students in grade 8 and above.

3-D Computer Animation Workshop–Level Two This program provides an appreciation for the technical and creative skills needed to create animation. Program topics include an overview of the 3-D computer animation industry, a review of basic principles of computer animation, character design, basic anatomy, advanced modeling techniques for creating characters, use of bone systems, facial animation, and inverse kinematics. The workshop is for students entering grade 9 and above who have completed Level 1 of the 3-D Animation Workshop.

Robotics–Level One The fundamentals behind autonomous robot action and interaction are introduced. Students learn the basics of robot mechanics, electronics, and software. Students reinforce lessons with increasingly difficult robot missions and can compete in competitions that culminate in the Iron Robot Challenge. Topics include an overview of robotics, introduction to robot locomotion, application of sensors, introduction to circuits and logic, and the GUI interface for robot control. The program is open to students entering grade 8 and above.

Junior Game Developer Workshop Game programming gives young students an understanding of the creative and technical issues in creating a video game and the importance of core academic subjects such as math, science, and art. This fun program provides a unique opportunity for middle school students to learn about the game development process. It is a hands-on workshop leading to an understanding of some of the creative and technical issues involved with creating a video game. This workshop is open to students registered for grades 5 through 7.

Off-site Summer Workshops Various programs are held at college and high school facilities around the U.S. Students who enroll in these programs study the same material as those who attend the workshops offered in Washington.

ENROLLMENT

U.S. and international students are welcome to apply. Each workshop is two weeks in length. All workshop levels are offered in each session, with five start dates for all workshops. Each workshop of 20–25 students is led by two teachers, providing a very favorable student-teacher ratio.

DAILY SCHEDULE

Workshops run Monday through Friday, 10 to 5, except the Junior Game Developer Workshop, which meets from 10 to 2, Monday through Friday.

EXTRA OPPORTUNITIES AND ACTIVITIES

All workshop attendees can tour portions of Nintendo of America. Workshop participants also have the opportunity to participate in monitored, on-site activities between 5 and 8 p.m. These voluntary activities are designed to provide the students with some fun away from the computers. Planned activities include such events as a barbecue, movie nights (held in DigiPen's auditorium), video game tournament nights, and an R/C Car Grand Prix.

FACILITIES

Summer workshops are held at the DigiPen campus in Redmond, Washington. Each student works on his or her individual computer. The DigiPen campus has a library, lunchroom, and auditorium.

DigiPen does not provide housing for summer workshop students. However, there are many alternatives for short-term housing. Hotels, motels, bed and breakfasts, and other short-term housing options are available near the campus. Information about housing is available at the Web site listed below.

If they so choose, enrolled students can access a special DigiPen database to identify possible roommates who can share their temporary accommodations.

STAFF

The workshops are taught by knowledgeable instructors who strive not only to teach the relevant material but also to provide an engaging experience for every student.

COSTS

Each summer workshop costs $845, including a nonrefundable $50 application fee. The Junior Game Developer Workshop costs $600, including a nonrefundable $50 application fee.

There is a meal plan for summer workshop attendees. An additional $65 includes lunch Monday through Friday during each workshop but does not include dinner.

TRANSPORTATION

DigiPen and its surrounding areas are easily accessible by automobile or public transportation. The nearest airport is Sea-Tac, approximately an hour's drive from the Institute. Shuttle buses, taxis, Metro buses, and Sound Transit express buses service the airport. Additional information about transportation in the area is available on the Web site listed below.

FINANCIAL AID

Financial aid is not available for summer workshop students.

APPLICATION TIMETABLE

To be sure of a place in the desired workshop, students should apply as early as possible. Applications, available online, are accepted until seven days prior to the start date of the workshop session, provided seats are still available. A nonrefundable $50 application fee and a $195 deposit (refundable if the desired session is full or canceled) must accompany all applications. Applications received after April 30, 2004, must be accompanied by the full workshop fee in order to secure a seat. There is no refund of tuition for voluntary withdrawal or cancellation. Students who wish to withdraw and request a partial tuition refund due to medical emergencies must submit the request in writing. A physician's note must accompany the request.

For more information, contact:

Masayo Arakawa
DigiPen Institute of Technology
5001 150th Avenue, NE
Redmond, Washington 98052
425-558-0299
Fax: 425-558-0378
E-mail: workshops@digipen.edu
World Wide Web: http://workshops.digipen.edu

DUKE YOUTH PROGRAMS

SUMMER ENRICHMENT PROGRAMS

DURHAM, NORTH CAROLINA

Type of Program: Summer enrichment programs for academically motivated students in the areas of writing, science, drama, fine arts, and college selection/admissions

Participants: Middle school and high school students

Enrollment: 40–150 participants per program; varies by program

Program Dates: Duke Young Writers' Camp: three 2-week sessions June through July; Duke Action Science Camp for Young Women: one 2-week session in June; Duke Drama Workshop: one 2-week session in July; Duke Creative Writers' Workshop: one 2-week session in June or July; Duke Constructing Your College Experience: one 1-week session in July or August.

LOCATION

Duke University is located in Durham, North Carolina. Duke is a 20-minute drive from Raleigh-Durham International Airport and about 15 minutes from the University of North Carolina at Chapel Hill.

BACKGROUND AND PHILOSOPHY

Duke Youth Programs is a part of Duke University Continuing Studies and has offered summer enrichment programs for more than twenty years. Young people from around the country attend to engage in interactive, innovative, and transformative learning experiences. Programs are designed to meet the needs of motivated students who desire intellectual experiences beyond the traditional academic setting. The programs provide a supportive atmosphere of active learning. Cocurricular social and recreational activities are planned to complement the instructional day. Participants also experience life in a college setting and the responsibilities of independent living with supervision.

PROGRAM OFFERINGS

Duke Young Writers' Camp (grades 6–11 in 2004–05 school year) The Duke Young Writers' Camp provides participants the opportunity to explore and refine writing skills through a diverse curriculum of short story, poetry, journalism, playwriting, mystery writing,

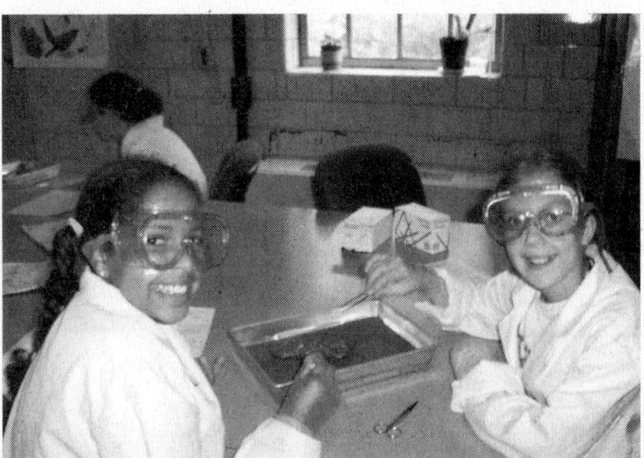

and more. Students develop creative and analytical processes of writing in self-selected courses under the guidance of professional educators and published writers. Classes are small and the learning environment is supportive yet challenging. Each instructional day begins with a morning gathering period, a time for large group instruction and guest speakers, followed by classes and concludes with a readers' forum, a time for students to share their work with their peers.

Duke Action Science Camp for Young Women (grades 5–7 in 2004–05 school year) Duke Action promotes scientific discovery through field and laboratory experiences in a forest environment. Participants examine ecological and biological principles through explorations of terrestrial and aquatic life, chemical and physical properties of the environment, and the impact of human activities on ecosystems. Learning activities include trips to outdoor field sites, educational games and simulations, and laboratory experiments. Opportunities are provided for students to interact with women in careers in the physical, biological, and environmental sciences. Applicants should have a genuine enthusiasm for science and a willingness to engage in outdoor exploration of scientific concepts through hands-on activities.

Duke Drama Workshop (grades 9–11 in 2004–05 school year) The Duke Drama Workshop offers high school students an intense drama experience, which culminates with a final performance. The workshop provides a supportive environment for students who are committed to refining their skills and building a community of actors. Participants attend daily acting classes to learn the creative and technical processes of acting. They also attend rehearsal periods of selected scenes from plays under the direction of professional educators, actors, and artists. Based on their individual areas of interest, students select from several acting classes and rehearsal periods representing drama, musical theater, and comedy.

Duke Creative Writers' Workshop (grades 10–11 in 2004–05 school year) The Duke Creative Writers' Workshop provides advanced writers, who are committed to refining their skills and building a community of writers, an intensive creative writing experience. Instructors and peers work collaboratively to assist participants in reaching their self-defined workshop goals. The interactive format allows participants to share work in small groups and receive constructive written and verbal feedback in a supportive environment. Students select a primary instructor based on the genre in which they wish to work for the duration of the camp. Other learning experiences include participation in mini-lessons, individual conferences, forums, writing exercises, and readings.

Duke Constructing Your College Experience (grades 10–11 in 2004–05 school year) Constructing Your College Experience is designed to empower college-bound students in their exploration of college options and navigation of the college application process. Participants learn to evaluate colleges relative to their needs and interests, understand the multidimensional application process, and discover the challenges and opportunities of university life. In addition to small group instruction, each student receives individualized guidance from an experienced college admissions counselor. Students sample college life by living, eating, and attending class on the Duke campus.

ENROLLMENT

Enrollment varies by program and ranges from 40 to 150 participants per program.

DAILY SCHEDULE

Specific program schedules vary. The average instructional day is from 9 a.m. to 4 p.m.

EXTRA OPPORTUNITIES AND ACTIVITIES

A variety of cocurricular social and recreational activities are offered afternoons, evenings, and weekends. Each afternoon, students participate in elective activities, such as arts and crafts, sports and games, drama, or community service. Additional evening and weekend activities include dances, talent shows, karaoke, movies, and more.

FACILITIES

All participants live, dine, and attend class on Duke University's East Campus. Some programs have class on West Campus. All participants have an opportunity to visit West Campus during their stay.

STAFF

The instructional staff includes professional educators, published writers, and talented artists. Each camp has an academic director, who coordinates the academic life and advises instructional staff members. The residential staff members are mature, talented, and enthusiastic graduate and undergraduate students, who supervise campers in the residential hall and at other out-of-class times, such as meals, free times, and special events. The residential counselors also plan and lead a variety of social and recreational activities. A professional educator directly supervises the residential staff members and their activities.

MEDICAL CARE

Medical care is available at Duke University Medical Center.

RELIGIOUS LIFE

The Duke University Chapel offers nondenominational services on Sunday mornings. Residential staff members are available to escort participants to these services as well as Friday evening temple services. Requests for other services are handled individually and are accommodated if possible.

COSTS

Tuition for 2004 was $775 to $865 for day participants, $900 to $1025 for extended day participants, and $1150 to $1655 for residential participants.

Residential tuition covers instruction, instructional supplies, room, board, recreational activities, a camp T-shirt, and a notebook. Day and extended day camper tuition covers Monday-through-Friday instruction, instructional supplies, lunch, a camp T-shirt, and a notebook. Extended day camper tuition also includes Monday-through-Friday dinner and afternoon/evening academic and recreational activities until 9 p.m. Students are encouraged to bring spending money for optional activities and souvenirs.

FINANCIAL AID

Limited need-based financial assistance is available. The financial aid application is available on the Youth Programs Web site or by calling the program. Contact information is listed below. Applications are due by March 15.

TRANSPORTATION

Duke University is 20 minutes from Raleigh-Durham International Airport and 10 minutes from the Durham Amtrak Station. Duke Youth Programs transports students to and from the airport and train station during designated times. The program cannot meet and escort unaccompanied minors from the gates. Only participants who meet airline requirements to travel alone and are comfortable making their way to the baggage area should plan to fly and use the shuttle provided.

APPLICATION TIMETABLE

Inquiries are always welcome. Registrations are accepted on a first-come, first-served basis. Registration begins in January and remains open as space is available. A $300 nonrefundable deposit is required at the time of registration. All balances must be paid by May 15, 2005.

FOR MORE INFORMATION, CONTACT:

Duke Continuing Studies
Duke Youth Program
Box 90700
201 Bishop's House
Durham, North Carolina 27708
919-684-6259
Fax: 919–681–8235
E-mail: youth@duke.edu
World Wide Web: http://www.learnmore.duke.edu/youth

PARTICIPANT/FAMILY COMMENTS

"You make so many awesome friends and you have such a good time that you don't even realize that you're learning as much as you are."

DUNNABECK AT KILDONAN

LANGUAGE TRAINING PROGRAM

AMENIA, NEW YORK

Type of Program: Residential program focusing on language training for students with dyslexia or language-based learning difficulties
Participants: Coeducational, ages 8–16
Enrollment: 85
Program Dates: End of June through the middle of August
Heads of Program: Ronald A. Wilson, Headmaster; Kevin Pendergast, Camp Director

LOCATION

Located on a hillside of woodlands, fields, and a pond, the 450-acre campus of Kildonan School, which includes school facilities and athletic fields, is in a spacious rural setting 90 miles north of New York City.

BACKGROUND AND PHILOSOPHY

Dunnabeck At Kildonan was established in 1955 by Diana Hanbury King to meet the needs of normal, intelligent boys and girls failing or underachieving in their academic work because of specific difficulties in reading, writing, and spelling. The Orton-Gillingham approach is used throughout the program. Standardized diagnostic tests are given at the beginning of the season to plan the student's program and at the end to assess progress. Keyboarding and word processing form an integral part of the program. The recreational program is designed to supplement rather than compete with the academic program.

PROGRAM OFFERINGS

During the six-week summer program, all tutoring is done on an individual basis. Each student receives a 1-hour lesson daily. In addition, students are taught to study independently and to make the best possible use of group study periods. From the tutor, the student learns to set high standards, to work confidently, and to take pride in achievement. Considerable emphasis is placed on the student's writing. Stimulating and interesting material is provided for leisure reading. Math tutoring is available on a limited basis for an additional cost. Word processing classes are taught using an alphabetical keyboarding approach developed by the tutor.

ENROLLMENT

Dunnabeck can accommodate 85 boys and girls ranging in age from 8 to 16. Students are admitted to the program without regard to race, creed, or color. Enrollment is for the full six weeks.

DAILY SCHEDULE

A typical day of activities may include:

8:00	Breakfast
9:00	Swimming
10:00	One-on-one tutorial
11:00	Horseback riding
12:00	Art/woodshop
1:00	Lunch
2:00	Study hall/word processing
3:00	General swim/waterskiing
4:30	Study hall
6:00	Dinner
7:00	Group activities
9:00	Lights out

EXTRA OPPORTUNITIES AND ACTIVITIES

Ceramics, crafts, woodworking, horseback riding, waterskiing, swimming, sailing, hiking, tennis, archery, painting, photography, multimedia, camping, soccer, softball, and canoeing are all offered.

FACILITIES

Kildonan's campus features a schoolhouse with a computer center and gymnasium, The Francis St. John Library, Simon Art Studios, two stables, a woodworking facility, and an elementary building with a computer center. There are also three dormitories.

STAFF

Ronald A. Wilson, Headmaster, was educated in New York and Connecticut. He holds a B.S. in psychology from SUNY at Brockport and an M.S. in counselor education from Western Connecticut State University.

The Camp Director, Kevin Pendergast, conducted his undergraduate work in English at SUNY at Albany and his master's work in English at Fordham University in New York City. He has taught at Kildonan for a total of five years. He also tutored at Durango Mountain Camp in Colorado. In the last few years, he cofounded and directed Shoshone Summer Camp in Cody, Wyoming.

Diana Hanbury King, Founder and Director Emeritus, was educated in England and Canada. She holds a B.A.Hons. degree from the University of London and an M.A. from George Washington University. Mrs. King was the 1990 recipient of the Samuel T. Orton Award, the highest honor bestowed by the International Dyslexia Association.

The Academic Dean is Dr. Robert A. Lane. Dr. Lane received his doctorate in learning disabilities from Teachers College, Columbia University. As an instructor in Columbia's Department of Curriculum and Teaching, he taught graduate-level courses in the Learning dis/Abilities Program, coordinated the student-teaching program, and was Clinical Supervisor at the Center for Educational and Psychological Services. His career in education began at Kildonan, where he taught literature and language training and supervised from 1992 to 1995. Before returning to Kidonan, Dr. Lane was also a diagnostic clinician at a private clinic in Connecticut.

William Van Cleave is Assistant Head of School and Outreach Coordinator at Kildonan. A tutor and literature teacher at the school since 1991, he chaired the technology department for seven years and currently chairs the literature department. He earned his B.A. is English and women's studies from the College of Wooster and his M.A. in English from SUNY at New Paltz. He is a Fellow of the Academy of Orton-Gillingham Practitioners and Educators.

Theresa L. Collins, Director of Language Training at the Kildonan School, completed a B.A. in psychology at Colgate University and holds an M.S. in educational psychology from SUNY at Albany. She has been involved with Camp Dunnabeck since 1986 and with the Kildonan School since 1987. A Fellow of the Academy of Orton-Gillingham Practitioners and Educators, she plays a major role in training and supervising teachers at both Dunnabeck and Kildonan.

Karen Leopold holds a Master of Science in Education degree and New York State permanent certifications in reading, special education, and English 7–12. She is also a certified member and Fellow-in-Training in the Academy of Orton-Gillingham Practitioners and Educators. For the past eight years, Karen has taught in one-on-one and small group settings. In addition to acting as the K–12 Multisensory Language Consultant for various public school districts, she has been evaluating Kildonan tutors and helping them meet the individual needs of their students for the past two years.

All tutors are trained in the Orton-Gillingham method by Fellows in the Orton Gillinham Academy. Many of the tutors come to Dunnabeck and the Kildonan Language Training Department and, therefore, have extensive experience in this specialized tutoring.

Since the success of the program is dependent on staff, great care is taken in selecting mature and imaginative men and women who enjoy working with young people. Most of the counselors come from Europe, Australia, New Zealand, and England through the Camp America program.

The Dunnabeck staff-camper ratio is 1:2. A number of tutors also work at Kildonan during the school year.

MEDICAL CARE

There is a fully equipped infirmary on campus with full-time nursing coverage, and local physicians serve as the school doctors. Sharon (Connecticut) Hospital is approximately 5 miles away.

COSTS

Tuition for the 2004 session was $7300 for residential students, $5725 for day students, and $3725 for half-day students. Additional expenses include fees for transportation, laundry, and special trips. Financial aid is available. Students should contact Admissions for the appropriate form.

TRANSPORTATION

Arrangements can be made for students to be transported from LaGuardia and Kennedy International airports in New York or Bradley Airport in Hartford. Harlem Valley Line train service is available from Grand Central Station in New York City to Wassaic.

APPLICATION TIMETABLE

Applications should be received by March 1. A $30 fee should accompany the initial application. A $1000 deposit is due upon acceptance.

For more information, contact:

Director of Admissions
Dunnabeck At Kildonan
425 Morse Hill Road
Amenia, New York 12501
845-373-8111
Fax: 845-373-2004
E-mail: admissions@kildonan.org
World Wide Web: http://www.Kildonan.org

EASTERN U.S. MUSIC CAMP

AT COLGATE UNIVERSITY

SUMMER CAMP

HAMILTON, NEW YORK

Type of Program: Music performance and instruction
Participants: Coeducational, ages 10–19
Enrollment: 200
Program Dates: Two-, three-, and four-week sessions, July 3 through July 30, 2005
Heads of Program: Thomas and Grace Brown, Directors

LOCATION

Eastern U.S. Music Camp, Inc., established in 1976, is conducted at Colgate University in Hamilton, New York. The University is ideally situated on a 1,100-acre hillside campus. This magnificent campus shares a valley with the quaint village of Hamilton. The peaceful countryside surrounding Hamilton has gently rolling hills in a tranquil rural setting.

Hamilton is a village of 2,500 people. Shops, homes, and the Colgate Inn front a green in the center of this friendly town. The campus adjoins the village, and the shops and services are within easy walking distance.

BACKGROUND AND PHILOSOPHY

For thirty years, Thomas and Grace Brown have designed and directed a program to provide students with opportunities and enrichment in all areas of music. Each summer, students who attend are happy to be an integral part of the music program and exciting campus life. They are offered a professional, well-balanced music program of high standards and an opportunity to pursue musical studies through class, individual, and group instruction; to perform a wide range of instrumental and choral works in ensemble and concert; and to participate in supervised sports (optional) and other informal recreational activities. The program is designed to complement the growth and development of young people. Such musical training teaches concentration, offers social opportunities, and helps develop sensitivity to, and pride in, the beautiful things in life. Careers in music are not necessarily the goals of students attending the Camp; the experience is one that is remembered and valued throughout life in any career. The total musical and social experience has made the Camp one of the most highly regarded music programs in the country.

Enrollment is limited to ensure ample opportunity for both individual and group instruction. Highly individualized instruction in a friendly atmosphere is stressed by the professional, nationally known staff, including college faculty members.

PROGRAM OFFERINGS

Performing Groups Each student may participate in several groups and on more than one instrument and/or voice. Original compositions by students studying composition are developed and rehearsed for possible performance. Music ranges from classical to modern and traditional to rock.

Each of the following thirteen groups performs in a public concert on campus every week:

Concert Band is open to all competent wind, brass, and percussion players. Major works of all periods are performed.

Symphony Orchestra Symphonic works of all periods are performed.

Concert Choir includes all students. Choral works from all periods of composition are presented.

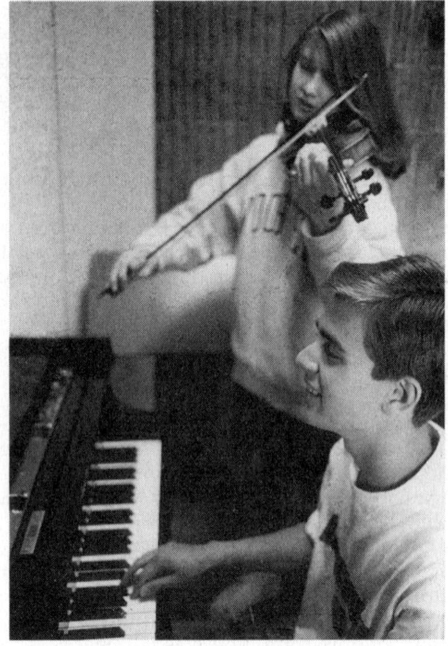

Jazz Ensembles are open to all competent players.

Jazz-Rock Combos are open to all jazz players.

Vocal Jazz (admission by audition) features modern choral arrangements accompanied by a complete rhythm section.

Chamber Orchestra is open to all string players.

Studio Orchestra is open to all competent string players, who perform special arrangements with Jazz Ensemble.

Wind Ensemble is a select ensemble open to all competent players.

Madrigal Choir is a select voice ensemble.

Women's Choir, Men's Choir, and **Chamber Choir** are also offered.

Ensembles and Workshops Opportunities are available in ensemble performances that emphasize individualized instruction. Rehearsals are daily. Ensembles and workshops are available in Piano, Brass, Improvisation, Percussion, Guitar, String, Woodwind, Harp, Flute, Jazz Combos, Composition and Arranging, Vocal Techniques/Repertoire, Vocal Jazz, Piano Techniques/Repertoire, Madrigal Choir, Women's Choir, Men's Choir, Chamber Choir, and Electronic Music.

Classes Each student selects one of the following daily classes: Beginning Theory, Theory, Harmony, Composition and Arranging, and Conducting (credit).

Private Instruction Private lessons are offered weekly on all instruments, plus voice, piano, guitar, harp, and pipe organ, and can be arranged for a nominal fee.

Concerts are held Saturdays at 8 p.m. and Sundays at 3 p.m. Recitals are held Wednesdays at 8 p.m. All concerts and recitals are open to the public and take place in the air-conditioned Dana Arts Center on the Colgate University campus.

ENROLLMENT

Eastern U.S. Music Camp offers two-, three-, and four-week sessions from July 3 to July 30, 2005.

Students can select from the following sessions: July 3 to July 30 (four weeks), July 3 to July 24 (three weeks), July 10 to July 30 (three weeks), July 3 to July 17 (two weeks), July 10 to July 24 (two weeks), and July 17 to July 30 (two weeks).

Students, encouraged to stay for the full four weeks, may enroll for the two- or three-week sessions. Musical and social benefits are greater with longer sessions. Tape auditions are not required but are encouraged. Students may earn high school credit when enrolled for the full four weeks.

EXTRA OPPORTUNITIES AND ACTIVITIES

Students enjoy numerous recreational and sports facilities such as an indoor/outdoor Olympic-size pool, a gym, a golf course, tennis courts, a track, and a new fully equipped fitness center. There are also picnics on the Student Union patio; movies; a trip to nearby Cooperstown, New York; games; softball; volleyball; golf; basketball; and a pizza party Saturday evenings after the concert. There are informal workshops, lectures, and opportunities to question faculty members and instructors. Colgate-sponsored performances are also held. This is a wonderful opportunity to meet talented and interesting people from around the country and other countries. The friendly faculty and staff members coach the students daily and are always available to share their talents with the students. This is an ideal place to grow.

FACILITIES

The campus is accented by a spring-fed lake with swans, wild and domestic ducks, and tree-lined walks and drives. Several buildings date to the nineteenth century. The quad on the hill includes modern residence halls, Memorial Chapel, O'Connor Campus Center, and a blend of old and new academic buildings. Also on the hill and overlooking scenic mountains are the Observatory, Cultural Center, and dining hall. Down from the hill are Case Library, Dana Arts Center, Sanford Field House, and well-manicured athletic fields.

Rehearsals, classes, concerts, private lessons, and recitals are held in the air-conditioned Dana Arts Center. Resident students live in modern boys' and girls' dorms, 2 per room by age, that include laundry facilities, lounges, and TVs. Three well-balanced meals, including a full and varied salad bar, are served daily by the Marriott Corporation in a modern stone facility with an intimate atmosphere. Wooden tables next to the windows overlook the beautiful valley and hills below.

STAFF

Faculty and staff members are carefully selected professional certified educators, solo artists, composers, and conductors, including members of the Colgate Music Department, area college music faculties, and symphony orchestras. Nationally renowned guest artists and clinicians are on campus for master classes and concerts. The counseling staff, including carefully selected and qualified counselors plus 2 dorm directors who are certified teachers, reside in the same living areas with the students, an approximate 1:5 ratio.

COSTS

The resident student cost for instruction, room, and board for 2005 is as follows: two weeks, $1459; three weeks, $2188; and four weeks, $2859. The day student cost for instruction and complete program (lunch included) is as follows: two weeks, $569; three weeks, $853; and four weeks, $1138. Costs cover lodging, meals, ensembles, workshops, class, participation in organizations, sports, recreational activities, personal guidance, recitals, special programs, and campus concerts. Weekly private music lessons offered by professional artists-instructors are optional at $23 per half-hour or $46 per hour. A class workbook costs about $5. Use of the dorm washers and dryers costs $1 for each.

FINANCIAL AID

A financial aid form is available. Funds are limited.

TRANSPORTATION

Colgate University is about 45 miles southeast of Hancock International Airport in Syracuse, New York, and 25 miles from the Utica, New York, train station. Regular bus services stop on campus each day. By car, the campus is 1½ hours west of Albany, New York.

APPLICATION TIMETABLE

To provide the highest quality music program, enrollment is limited. Admission is on a rolling basis, and the application should be mailed as soon as possible with a $295 nonrefundable deposit. Applications are available on the Web site or in the brochure. The balance is due June 17, 2005. All applications, deposits, balances, and inquiries should be directed to the address below.

FOR MORE INFORMATION, CONTACT:

Before July 1, 2005
Thomas or Grace Brown
Eastern U.S. Music Camp
7 Brook Hollow Road
Ballston Lake, NY 12019
518-877-5121
866-777-7841 (toll-free)
Fax: 518-877-4943
E-mail: summer@easternusmusiccamp.com

After July 1 and until July 30
Eastern U.S. Music Camp
Colgate University
Hamilton, NY 13346
315-228-7041
Fax: 315-228-7557
E-mail: mleone@mail.colgate.edu
World Wide Web: http://easternusmusiccamp.com
http://www.colgate.edu

EDUCATION UNLIMITED ACTOR'S WORKSHOP

THEATER ARTS PROGRAM

BERKELEY, CALIFORNIA

Type of Program: Theater
Participants: Coeducational, students in grades 6–12
Enrollment: Up to 100
Program Dates: Two- and three-week programs in July and August
Head of Program: Andy Spear, Director

LOCATION

The program is held in the residence halls adjacent to the University of California, Berkeley, campus in a college-town environment. Numerous walking and hiking trails, museums, theaters, cafés, shops, and parks are nearby.

BACKGROUND AND PHILOSOPHY

The Actor's Workshop is an independent program founded in 1998 and sponsored and conducted exclusively by Education Unlimited. The program is divided into three sessions, one for participants entering grades 9–12 and one for participants entering grades 7–8. The third program is an advanced workshop. The program is designed to give young actors training in several different acting skills, including basic acting technique, voice, movement, and improvisation. The workshop emphasis is on the process of acting rather than on staging a major production, though the students in the advanced program do participate in more fully staged final productions. Students have performance opportunities and the workshop culminates in the presentation of final projects, but the primary emphasis is on developing the tools to enable students to develop a character and to expand the way they use their voice and body on stage. The goal of the program is to get young actors thinking about acting from a number of different perspectives and to help develop and polish the many skills that make up the varied work of an actor.

PROGRAM OFFERINGS

Students work with one primary instructor every morning for duration of the program. In the second half of the program, students work with their primary instructor to develop a final acting project for presentation at the end of the program. In addition to the work completed with the primary instructor, each student also rotates through afternoon workshops with the other instructors. These secondary workshops ensure that each student gets a chance to learn skills from all instructors' areas of expertise. In a secondary class with the movement instructor, for example, students concentrate more specifically on the movement aspects of their performance and fill out their characters from that perspective.

Four areas that make up the camp's core curriculum are acting technique, improvisational acting, voice, and movement. Acting technique is approached through the morning class, and focuses on building a character through work with monologues, scenes, and non-script-based exercises. The improvisational acting class includes work on nonscripted scenes developed from spur-of-the-moment suggestions from classmates, the audience, or the instructor. Improv comedy is the major focus, but attention is also given to more serious situations. The voice class includes experimenting with ranges of vocal expression and vocal character, caring for the voice, and increasing vocal versatility. The movement class focuses on using the body to communicate and developing a range of physical expression for the actor; equally important is simply helping the actor discover his or her body and its strengths and weaknesses.

The daily class schedule is supplemented by guest speakers, discussions of directing techniques, and several trips to local theaters to see a variety of performances. Class size is around 15 students. No grades are given. A variety of different teaching techniques are used, and the students primarily learn by doing, guided by instructor critiques and demonstrations.

DAILY SCHEDULE

8:00–9:00	Breakfast
9:00–9:30	Warm-ups
9:30–12:00	Workshop with primary instructor (includes break time)
12:00–1:00	Lunch
1:00–3:00	Workshop with secondary teacher
3:00–5:00	Workshop with secondary teacher
5:00–6:30	Dinner
6:30–10:00	Combination of rehearsal time and recreation

A code of conduct designed to ensure participants' safety and to foster a friendly environment where all students feel comfortable is enforced.

ENROLLMENT

The program is designed to accommodate up to 100 participants, and the boy-girl ratio is approximately

1:1. Students are tracked by experience level. No prior acting experience is necessary for enrollment in the program, except in the case of the advanced program, where admission is based on evidence of experience in acting technique and performance. Approximately 50 percent of students are from California, 45 percent are from the rest of the United States, and 5 percent are international students. Students from all ethnic and socioeconomic backgrounds are welcome to attend the program.

EXTRA OPPORTUNITIES AND ACTIVITIES

Regular excursions to local theaters to see a variety of plays are an integral part of the program. Other possible recreational opportunities include visits to Strawberry Canyon, Tilden Park, Lawrence Hall of Science, the Exploritorium, the Berkeley Rose Garden, the Oakland Zoo, the Oakland Coliseum for an Oakland A's game, Golden Gate Park in San Francisco, Fisherman's Wharf, the California Shakespeare Festival in Orinda, and other local features. Trips depend on student interest and time constraints. Free time and local recreational opportunities occur daily.

FACILITIES

The program is held in the University of California, Berkeley, residence halls. All classes are held in these facilities. Use of a theater is scheduled for final projects.

STAFF

The faculty is composed of experienced theater pros, all of whom are college graduates and all of whom have previous teaching experience. Andy Spear, the director, taught drama, English, and history at the Head-Royce school in Oakland, California, for six years. He has also taught several drama workshops in the Bay Area and has worked with a number of small theater companies as a director, actor, and playwright. Other faculty members include stage, screen, and television actors and professional stage managers.

MEDICAL CARE

All students with medical needs are taken to one of the area medical centers. Medical release and information forms are required for participation.

COSTS

Tuition, room, and board for the advanced program are $3250, for the high school program, $2528, and for the middle school program, $1796. Of these amounts, $525 is required as a deposit upon application. Spending money of $75 to $150 is recommended. Fees do not cover transportation to and from the program, spending and laundry money, or additional nights lodging if required.

FINANCIAL AID

Need-based financial aid is available. A financial aid form and copies of parent/guardian tax forms must be submitted for consideration. Last year, about 20 percent of Education Unlimited participants received partial financial aid.

TRANSPORTATION

The program is located about 15 miles from the Oakland International Airport. For an additional $45 round trip, students are met at and returned to the airport.

APPLICATION TIMETABLE

Initial inquiries are welcome beginning November 15. The application deadline is May 15; $525 is due upon application. Notification of acceptance is sent within two weeks of application.

For more information, contact:

Andy Spear, Program Director
Actor's Workshop
1700 Shattuck Avenue, #305
Berkeley, California 94709
510-548-6612
Fax: 510-548-0212
World Wide Web:
http://www.educationunlimited.com

PARTICIPANT/FAMILY COMMENTS

"The instructors were excellent, educated, and caring (and) very knowledgeable in theater and acting technique (and I'm a drama and theater teacher myself)."—Holly Henle, parent of participant

"I would definitely recommend this camp to anyone who has a passion for the performing arts. I had never realized how much I love performing until I was around instructors who are so dedicated to performing. I learned so much!"—Julia Martin, Actor's Workshop participant

EDUCATION UNLIMITED COMPUTER CAMP

COMPUTER CAMP

BERKELEY, STANFORD, AND LOS ANGELES, CALIFORNIA

Type of Program: Academic enrichment
Participants: Coeducational, grades 4–12
Enrollment: 46 per session
Program Dates: One-week sessions, June through August
Head of Program: Matthew Fraser, Executive Director

LOCATION

Education Unlimited Computer Camps are independent programs that are held at well-respected academic institutions in the United States. All locations provide a safe and secure environment while allowing participants to experience vibrant college campuses. Campuses include Stanford University; University of California, Berkeley; and UCLA.

BACKGROUND AND PHILOSOPHY

The program was founded by Education Unlimited, Inc.® to provide the hands-on instruction that is normally unavailable in schools and to teach students creative and practical computer skills in a top-ranked university setting. The Computer Camp teaches students to use the computer technologies that are related to academic success in high school, college, and business. In addition, the program helps students learn to use computers artistically and creatively.

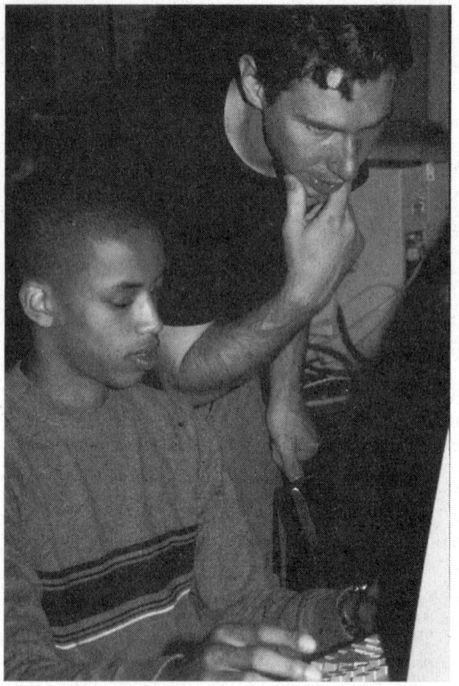

The detailed curriculum uses many teaching approaches, including large-group lectures, small-group exercises, team projects, and individual consultations. All classroom activities are designed to maximize each student's sense of camaraderie, enjoyment, and accomplishment.

The program accepts students of all levels of experience. Academically motivated and talented students are best served by the program.

PROGRAM OFFERINGS

Classes focus on learning new software applications, Internet and multimedia projects, programming, and games. The program is divided into one-week sessions. Students may enroll for one- or two-week sessions. Students also have the option of combining Computer Camp sessions with those of the Public Speaking Institute.

Students participate in a group multimedia project and design and post their own Web page. Multimedia projects include creating text fields, using graphic design tools, importing clip art and photos, creating and saving stacks, and adding sound/animation and video to cards. Students apply these skills by producing a weekly camp newsletter using cutting-edge graphic design software. Programming students use Java programming language and gain in-depth coverage of programming elements such as looping, conditional statements, and logic. Students write programs that solve simple math problems and design input-output programs and code breakers. More advanced students write interactive user-friendly programs. Game nights are also a popular feature. Students get to play newly released games as well as classics.

The program is structured as a series of classes, seminars, practicums, and simulations. Classes are tracked based upon previous experience. No entrance exam is required for admission. The average class has about 10 to 12 students. No grades or exams are given.

ENROLLMENT

The program is designed to accommodate 46 participants; the boy-girl ratio is usually 50:50. No previous course work or experience is required. Classes are tracked by experience level. Students are allowed to enroll in both sessions to create a comprehensive two-week program or cross-register in the Education Unlimited Public Speaking Institute for a two- or four-week mixed computer/speech option. Sessions may be added as needed. Education Unlimited also offers special advanced sessions exclusively for students who exhibit exceptional talent and passion for computers. These sessions focus on more complex Web-design and programming projects.

Approximately 65 percent of the students attending the program are from California, and 25 percent are from out of state. Another 10 percent are international students.

DAILY SCHEDULE

A typical day might be as follows:

8:00–9:00	Breakfast
9:00–12:00	Internet/Web-design class
12:00–1:00	Lunch
1:00–3:00	Afternoon recreation and open lab time
3:00–5:00	Programming class
5:00–6:15	Dinner
6:15–8:00	Layout and graphics class
8:00–10:00	Evening recreation time
11:00	Room check/curfew

EXTRA OPPORTUNITIES AND ACTIVITIES

Depending on which location the student attends, he or she has the opportunity to take advantage of the unique activities that are available in that part of the country. The schedule includes casual recreational activities each day, including hikes and walking tours. In addition, chaperoned recreational excursions include possible visits to area parks, science centers, zoos, baseball games, Golden Gate Park in San Francisco, Fisherman's Wharf, the California Shakespeare Festival in Orinda, and Universal Studios in Los Angeles. Selection of excursions depends on student interest. The program includes guest speakers and a talent and skills exhibition at the conclusion of the camp.

FACILITIES

Students live in dormitories on college campuses. Students are supervised by adult residence counselors who share in dormitory life. Meals are included in the program cost and are served on campus. The computer lab includes a ratio of one PC per student. Computer labs are equipped with Ethernet connections, the same lightning-fast Internet access that university faculty members and students use. New computers are purchased each summer for student use.

STAFF

The faculty is composed of computer educators with experience in high schools, colleges, and summer camps. These educators are supplemented with industry professionals and computer science graduate students, ensuring students exposure to the most contemporary and relevant technology skills. In order to offer the most personalized attention possible, a student-to-staff ration of 10:1 is maintained. Most teachers live in the dorms as supervisors so students have access to faculty members anytime day or night. Each student works with each staff member during the academic session.

MEDICAL CARE

Students with medical needs are taken to nearby medical centers. No on-site medical care is provided. Medical release and information forms are required for program participation.

COSTS

Programs cost $1050 to $1140 per week, depending on location. One- and two-week sessions are available. Fees cover tuition, all lodging for the duration of the program, a full meal program, all required workbooks and materials, access to athletic and recreational facilities, planned recreational and evening activities, and camp memorabilia. Costs for day students are approximately 25 percent less and include meals. A deposit of $325 is required upon application and is applied toward the tuition, and all fees must be paid at least thirty days before the start of the program. Fees do not include transportation to and from the program site, spending and laundry money, or additional night's lodging before or after the program. About $75 to $150 for spending money per week is recommended.

FINANCIAL AID

Need-based financial aid is available. A financial aid form and copies of parent/guardian tax forms must be submitted for consideration. Last year, about 20 percent of participants in Education Unlimited summer programs were awarded partial financial aid.

TRANSPORTATION

Students can be picked up and returned to the airport for an additional fee of $45 round-trip.

APPLICATION TIMETABLE

Initial inquiries are welcome November 15. The application deadline is May 15.

For more information, contact:

Education Unlimited
Summer Programs
1700 Shattuck Avenue, #305
Berkeley, California 94709
510-548-6612
Fax: 510-548-0212
World Wide Web:
http://www.educationunlimited.com

PARTICIPANT/FAMILY COMMENTS

"(The program) builds self-confidence, introduces new skills in a safe and supportive environment, and allows for new friendships to form with kids from all over the earth."—Mary Kundert, parent of participant

EDUCATION UNLIMITED PUBLIC SPEAKING INSTITUTE

PUBLIC SPEAKING, LEADERSHIP, AND MOCK TRIAL PROGRAM

BERKELEY, STANFORD, AND LOS ANGELES, CALIFORNIA, AND BOSTON, MASSACHUSETTS

Type of Program: Academic enrichment
Participants: Coeducational, grades 4–12
Enrollment: 48
Program Dates: One- and two-week sessions in June, July, and August
Head of Program: Matthew Fraser, Executive Director

LOCATION

Education Unlimited's Public Speaking Institutes are independent programs that are held at well-respected academic institutions in the United States. All locations a provide safe and secure environment while allowing participants to experience vibrant college campuses. Campuses include UC Berkeley, Stanford University, UCLA, and Tufts University in Boston.

BACKGROUND AND PHILOSOPHY

The Public Speaking Institute is an independent program founded in 1995 and sponsored and conducted exclusively by Education Unlimited, Inc.® The purpose of the program is to provide students with practical instruction in public speaking, rhetoric, and logic in a top-ranked university setting, training them in public speaking and communication skills that are generally not taught in standard secondary education. The program seeks to instill in its students a strong sense of confidence, articulation, research skills, organization, clear and effective writing abilities, exemplary classroom participation skills, and the ability to give well-delivered and crafted presentations in and outside of the classroom. The Institute also seeks to provide foundational training for academic, scholarship, and job-related interviews. Ultimately, the program seeks to provide participants with a distinct verbal advantage over students who have not had such training.

PROGRAM OFFERINGS

The program is structured as a series of classes, seminars, practicums, and simulations offered in one-week programs that can be taken as a one- or two-week course or can be combined with the Education Unlimited Computer Camp. One week at selected locations is a special session that offers a unique opportunity for students to immerse themselves in the American legal system by working with attorneys and arguing legal cases. All academic offerings are provided to all students. Classes are tracked based upon previous experience, and no entrance exam is required for admission. Placement activities occur on the first day of the program to ensure that all students are placed in classes that will maximize both their comfort and enjoyment. Average class size is about 12. No grades or exams are given. The program is highly practical in orientation, and only academically motivated students should apply.

Methods used include small classes, hands-on learning through regular practice, an emphasis on student involvement and activity, and small teacher-student ratios to guarantee one-on-one instruction. The program instructors use simulations that demonstrate that public speaking is fun, challenging, and exciting. Various curricular strategies are used, including mock classroom presentations, impromptu speech competitions, congressional-style speech competitions, written oratory competitions, professionally critiqued debates, and leadership simulations. All classroom activities are designed to maximize each student's sense of camaraderie, enjoyment, and accomplishment.

DAILY SCHEDULE

8:00–9:00	Breakfast
9:00–11:45	Oratorical speaking
11:45–1:00	Lunch
1:00–4:00	Debates
4:00–5:00	Afternoon recreation
5:00–6:15	Dinner
6:15–9:00	Electives
9:00–11:00	Free time
11:00	Floor check
12:00	Room check/curfew

Students must observe the program rules and all rules and conduct codes of the university at which the program is being held. They must act in a manner that respects the rights of others at all times.

ENROLLMENT
The program is designed to accommodate approximately 45 participants, and the ratio of boys to girls is approximately 1:1. Classes are tracked by grade level. Simultaneous sessions may be added as enrollment necessitates. No previously required courses or experience are necessary, but a minimum 3.0 GPA is recommended. Approximately 5 percent of students are from California, 40 percent are from other states, and 10 percent are international. Students from all ethnic and socioeconomic backgrounds are welcome to attend the program. The program accepts students of all levels of natural speaking ability and experience. Academically motivated and talented students are best served by the program.

EXTRA OPPORTUNITIES AND ACTIVITIES
Depending on which location students attend, they have the opportunity to take advantage of the activities available in that part of the country. The schedule includes at least 1½ hours of casual recreational activities per day, including hikes, walking tours, and impromptu sports events. In addition, chaperoned recreational excursions include possible visits to area parks, science centers, zoos, baseball games, Fisherman's Wharf and Golden Gate Park in San Francisco, the California Shakespeare Festival in Orinda, Universal Studios in Los Angeles, and others. Selection depends upon student interest. The program includes guest speakers and a talent and skills exhibition at the conclusion of the camp.

FACILITIES
Students live in dormitories on college campuses. Students are supervised by adult residence counselors who share in dormitory life. Meals are included in the program cost and are served on campus or at the dormitory meal complex.

STAFF
The faculty is composed of experienced high school, collegiate, and summer camp educators, including attorneys, experienced summer camp counselors, and guest lecturers.

MEDICAL CARE
All students with medical needs are taken to one of the various area medical centers. No on-site medical care is provided. Medical release and information forms are required for program participation.

RELIGIOUS LIFE
Religious services of most types are available within a few blocks of the campus residence hall facilities, and, with parental permission, students are permitted to attend any services that the family feels are appropriate. The program is nondenominational.

COSTS
Programs cost $940 to $1030 per week. One- and two-week sessions are available. Fees cover tuition, all lodging for the duration of the program, a full meal program, all required workbooks and materials, access to athletic and recreational facilities, planned recreational and evening activities, and camp memorabilia. Costs for day students are approximately 25 percent less. A deposit of $325 toward tuition is required upon application, and all fees must be paid at least thirty days before the start of the program. Spending money of $75 to $150 is recommended. Fees do not cover transportation to and from the program site, spending and laundry money, or additional nights' lodging before or after the program.

FINANCIAL AID
Need-based financial aid is available. A financial aid form and copies of parent/guardian tax forms must be submitted for consideration. Last year, about 20 percent of participants in Education Unlimited summer programs were awarded partial financial aid, with maximum aid awards of $600 for extreme need.

TRANSPORTATION
For an additional fee of $45 round-trip, students can be met at and returned to the airport.

APPLICATION TIMETABLE
Initial inquiries are welcome as of November 15. The application deadline is May 15, and $325 is due upon application. Notification of acceptance is sent within two weeks.

FOR MORE INFORMATION, CONTACT:

Education Unlimited Summer Programs
1700 Shattuck Avenue, #305
Berkeley, California 94709
510-548-6612
Fax: 510-548-0212
World Wide Web: http://www.educationunlimited.com

PARTICIPANT/FAMILY COMMENTS

"The instructors were excellent! Not only would they give their all during the scheduled activities, but they were eager to sit down with you and discuss anything from how to start your own debate team to an entertaining explanation of their own public speaking experiences, all on their own free time. I was truly impressed and inspired. Yes . . . I would definitely recommend this camp without hesitation. It wasn't too intense nor too relaxed. I was able to get everything out of it that I wanted. I actually did not mind spending a week of my summer vacation here."—Kim Wolf, Program Participant

EF INTERNATIONAL LANGUAGE SCHOOLS

LANGUAGE STUDY

SPAIN, ECUADOR, FRANCE, ITALY, GERMANY, CHINA, AND RUSSIA

Type of Program: Language immersion courses
Participants: Coeducational, open to students and professionals 16 years of age and older
Enrollment: Approximately 16 students per class (average)
Program Dates: Two- to fifty-two-week sessions every other Monday year-round. Semester courses and Academic Year Abroad courses are also available.

LOCATION

EF International Language Schools offers courses in France, Spain, Ecuador, Italy, Germany, Russia, and China.

BACKGROUND AND PHILOSOPHY

EF International Language Schools believes that the most effective way to learn a language is by living it. With forty years of experience as a leader in language education, EF offers students a variety of programs to match their academic and professional needs while studying in an international environment and living among native speakers. Whether students are looking for a short intensive course to boost their language skills, an enriching summer-study vacation, or a full year of living and studying abroad, EF has a course that is right for them. Social, athletic, and cultural activities are available in addition to classroom instruction. Courses are taught by native speakers, and students have the opportunity to make friends from all over the world right in an internationally diverse classroom. Teachers focus on grammar and conversation in their instruction, with the aid of textbooks and language laboratory sessions. EF courses are suitable for students and professionals of all ability levels, from beginner to advanced.

PROGRAM OFFERINGS

Spain
Barcelona Students can study in Spain's most dynamic city. The School is located on Calle Calvet, a short walk from the city's most fashionable cafés and shops. Students have the choice of enjoying Spanish hospitality in a homestay or living in the University of Barcelona's student residence in the summer. Classes are held for 3 to 4 hours per day, Monday through Friday. Excursions to Madrid, Seville, and the Pyrenees are among the many activities that may be offered by the School.

Ecuador
Quito Quito has become one of the most popular destinations in which to learn Spanish. The EF Escuela Internacional de Espanol in Quito is a charming building in one of the city's best residential areas, just 5 minutes from the city center. Course instruction is given five days a week, 3 to 4 hours per day, in modern educational facilities complete with a great computer lab. EF trips take students to visit and explore the Amazon, the equator, the foothills of the Andes, beautiful protected rain forests, and even the Galápagos Islands.

France
Nice Students study in sunny southern France. EF Ecole Internationale de Français stands just 100 yards from the beach and the famous Promenade des Anglais. Students can live in a homestay year-round or choose nearby residence accommodation during the summer. Course instruction is given five days a week, 3 to 4 hours per day, followed by endless opportunities for sports and outdoor activities. Popular excursions include day trips to Monaco and Cannes, visits to famous museums, and weekend trips to Paris and the Alps.
Paris There's little that can't be found in Paris, France's largest and capital city. Students focus on conversation in French, with the option of taking special interest courses (e.g., literature, film, business language, etc.). The course includes accomodation in a local Parisian homestay. Frequent excursions include visits to the Palace of Versailles, the Louvre, Chartres, and Fontainebleau.

Italy
Rome If students are looking for a city full of cultural and historical treasures, Rome is the perfect destination. The language school is located in an elegant building in the center of the city, convenient to the central rail station and many cultural attractions. Learning facilities include a modern language laboratory, as well as a study center equipped with computers, video booths, and worksheets to help students practice their language skills. Students may choose homestay or apartment accommodations. Classes are held for 3 to 4 hours per day, Monday through Friday. Weekend excursions include other Italian cities such as Siena, Naples, Venice, and Florence.

Germany
Munich The EF Internationale Sprachschule is located in the lively Schwabing district of Munich, a favorite meeting place for students and artists. Occupying a four-story building in a quiet courtyard on Herzogstrasse, the EF School provides a stimulating international environment in which to study. Classes are held for 3 to 4 hours per day, Monday through Friday. In their homestay, students have the chance to learn about the German way of life from inside its culture as their language ability naturally develops. The school staff organizes a variety of social activities for students' stays. Excursion destinations include Prague, Innsbruck, Salzburg, the majestic castles of Füssen, or an Austrian alpine resort for weekend skiing.

China
Shanghai EF's Mandarin Chinese program is located in Shanghai, known as the Pearl of the Orient. The city has transformed into a thriving metropolis with

the perfect combination of modern development and old traditions. EF's language school is within walking distance of the premier shopping and entertainment districts, where a number of shopping malls, restaurants, bookstores, and banks are situated. The city hosts the Shanghai International Arts Festival in September, The International Film Festival in June, and many other cultural and sporting events.

Russia

St. Petersburg EF's International Language School is located in a quiet area in the historical center of St. Petersburg and offers modern teaching facilities, a newly installed language laboratory, and a student lounge for meeting with international friends. Visits include trips to the Hermitage, the Mariinsky Opera and Ballet Theater, St. Isaac's Cathedral, and the Imperial Palace. Host family accommodations are available.

College Credit Students can work toward completion of an undergraduate degree while improving their language skills and experiencing a new culture. Through EF's unique partnership with Eastern Washington University, eligible students may earn up to 6 quarter language credits (equivalent to 4 semester credits) on the university level by advancing from one EF proficiency level to the next with a minimum grade. Credit is available on the 100 and 200 levels. More information is available by contacting the EF Admissions Office.

DAILY SCHEDULE

The following is a typical day at the EF Ecole Internationale de Français in Nice, France:

9:00–10:20	Grammar
10:45–12:05	Reading and writing
12:30–1:40	Special interest class: Business Communications
2:00	Excursion to the Musée Chagall
7:00	Mediterranean dinner and game of boules at local outdoor café

ENROLLMENT

EF programs are open to students and adults. Students must be at least 16 years of age at the start of their course. No previous language study experience is required to attend a short-term course, EF Academic Year Abroad, or Multi-Language Year Abroad. Students enroll all parts of North America and countries all over the world, including Germany, Sweden, France, Spain, Japan, Korea, and Italy. Average class size is approximately 16 students.

STAFF

EF teachers are native speakers qualified to teach their own language to nonnative speakers. EF's experience over the past forty years has demonstrated that the selection and training of qualified teachers must be the first priority of any language school. EF teachers have access to an extensive range of classroom material and equipment, including the latest in language-teaching technology.

COSTS

The cost of each program depends on length of stay and course location. Those interested should contact the EF Admissions Office for specific program fees by telephone or e-mail.

TRANSPORTATION

Students enrolling in EF International Language School courses have the option of booking their international travel through EF. In addition, all course centers offer the security and convenience of an EF-organized transfer to their accommodation.

APPLICATION TIMETABLE

Applications are accepted at any time, however, students are advised that courses are extremely popular and can fill up quickly. Applications are processed upon their receipt, and it is therefore recommended that students apply as early as possible in order to avoid disappointments in availability.

For more information, contact:

EF International Language Schools
EF Center Boston
One Education Street
Cambridge, Massachusetts 02141
800-992-1892 (toll-free)
Fax: 800-590-1125 (toll-free)
E-mail: ils@ef.com
World Wide Web: http://www.ef.com

ELITE EDUCATIONAL INSTITUTE

SUMMER PROGRAM

SOUTHERN CALIFORNIA; NEW JERSEY; VANCOUVER, CANADA; AND SEOUL, SOUTH KOREA

Type of Program: Academic enrichment and test preparation
Participants: Coeducational, grades 3 through 12
Enrollment: Varies according to individual centers
Program Dates: Most programs are eight-week sessions from late June to late August. The 2100 Guarantee Program runs from late June until the national SAT testing date in October
Head of Program: Ms. Wonna Kim, Program Director

LOCATION

Elite has sixteen educational centers—seven in southern California; two in New Jersey; two in Vancouver, Canada; and five in Seoul, South Korea—and is continuing to grow. All of the School's centers are in suburbs convenient to major cities. The southern California centers are in Anaheim Hills, Arcadia, Cerritos, Irvine, Los Angeles, Northridge, and Rowland Heights. The New Jersey centers are in East Brunswick and Middletown.

BACKGROUND AND PHILOSOPHY

Founded in 1987, Elite has built its reputation by offering academic enrichment to motivated, goal-oriented students of all ability levels. The School's flagship programs prepare students for successful performance on the SAT through a variety of course offerings and schedules. Younger students benefit from the disciplined, results-oriented environment and get a head start on the fundamental language and math skills they need for success in middle school, junior high, and high school.

Elite distinguishes itself in the field of SAT preparation by taking the test very seriously. The School avoids the use of gimmicky shortcuts and misleading, get-smart-quick promises, focusing instead on developing those underlying skills actually measured by the SAT and other standardized tests: verbal, math, and writing proficiency, critical thinking, and sound reasoning. As a result, Elite's students are prepared not just for higher test scores but also for continued academic success in college and beyond.

In the last few years, more than a dozen Elite students have scored a perfect 1600 on the SAT, and countless others have scored in the high 1500s. Elite's younger students sign up to improve their performance in grade school, prepare for admission to private primary and secondary schools, or just to get an advance look at the subjects ahead.

Through the Elite Total Learning Commitment (ETLC), Elite's directors provide extensive one-on-one counseling with students at all grade levels. Furthermore, Elite encourages parents to stay involved by issuing status reports every few weeks, providing students with computer-analyzed score reports on practice tests, and offering an accessible, open environment that encourages questions and participation.

PROGRAM OFFERINGS

Elementary Enrichment classes, intended for students about to enter grades 3 through 6, are kept small to foster confidence and participation. The academic emphasis is on reading, writing, and mathematics, with some initial work on critical thinking and analysis. Teachers emphasize the process of discovery, learning, and understanding so that all students finish the summer better prepared for the school year ahead, regardless of their present ability level.

Students can enroll in general classes for writing, vocabulary, reading, and math. Some centers also offer classes for specific middle school admissions tests.

Junior High Enrichment courses, recommended for the summer before grades 7 through 9, are intended to give students a head start on high school. Some students want a "preview" of the specific math class ahead, like geometry, so they know what to expect. Others may have finished a math or English class with an acceptable grade but still feel unprepared for the next year's class.

Almost all of the Junior High Enrichment students are about to enter competitive high schools where enrollment in honors and AP classes is limited and want to get a head start on admission to the best courses their high schools offer.

The core of the Junior High Enrichment program is critical writing, an essential skill for success in high school. All subjects are taught at a variety of ability and pacing levels to maximize their usefulness for both remedial and advanced students.

Elite SAT Boot Camp is an eight-week program designed for high school students who want to commit most of their summer to raising their SAT scores. Students attend 5 hours of class each day, Monday through Friday, mastering the definitions of thousands of common SAT words and sharpening their other critical reading skills by reading and analyzing hundreds of short stories, critical essays, books, and magazine articles. Classes are kept varied and interesting, with a variety of instructors and class materials throughout each day.

The Boot Camp program puts the summer to good use for students of all ability levels. The program is particularly useful for students whose critical reading skills lag behind their math skills. The Boot Camp program can be taken on its own, or in combination with Elite's more traditional SAT prep classes, as a powerful boost on the critical reading side.

Elite Basic SAT Classes offers students a basic package of four interlocking classes: a critical reading class, a math class, a writing class, and a practice test session. Students enrolled in the Basic SAT Classes meet for a total of 8½ hours per week—each of the weekly classes meets for 2 hours, and the practice test lasts for 2½ hours.

A majority of the students who live near Elite's educational centers continue with the program after the summer. Enrollment in the Basic SAT Classes is on a rolling basis, with students signing up for four-week blocks. The curriculum is intentionally designed to be useful for long-term students, with materials that are never exactly the same twice. Even the vocabulary is constantly updated and revised.

The 2100 Guarantee and Accelerated Programs are extremely intensive and demanding SAT test-preparation programs that require many hours of out-of-class work and preparation. The aims of the 2100 Programs are college-level reading and writing and a thorough mastery of high school mathematics, resulting in truly outstanding test scores in high school and academic success thereafter.

These programs are designed for high school students at the top of their game who successfully take AP and honors classes at their high schools and want to round out their college applications with truly outstanding test scores.

The fifteen-week Guarantee Program is for students who can stay enrolled until the national SAT testing date in October. For this program, Elite offers an unusual guarantee: those students who do not score at least 2100 on the SAT get their tuition refunded.

The eight-week Accelerated Program is identical to the first eight weeks of the Guarantee Program. Students typically enroll in the eight-week program when they cannot commit to the full fifteen weeks, either because they face an unusually difficult class load in September or because they live too far from one of Elite's centers. Since this program is shorter than the Guarantee Program, no guarantee applies. Students who are successful in the eight-week Accelerated Program are permitted to switch to the fifteen-week Guarantee version of the program.

Admission to either version of the 2100 Programs is very selective; students have to achieve minimum scores on Elite's diagnostic tests, have high GPAs, and demonstrate the maturity and commitment the program demands. Acceptance to the 2100 Program is always at the discretion of the center directors. Students should contact the directors of the center they plan to attend to determine eligibility.

ENROLLMENT

The maximum number of students in each class at Elite is 15. Elite Summer Program attracts students from all over the United States and Canada, though the majority come from California, New Jersey, and Vancouver. Elite does not offer room or board, so students from other states and provinces typically spend the summer with relatives or family friends. The School's students reflect a range of academic abilities and ethnic backgrounds.

Students who want to register are required to take a diagnostic test prior to registration and undergo a personal interview.

DAILY SCHEDULE

Classes in elementary enrichment, junior high enrichment, basic SAT preparation, and the 2100 Guarantee and Accelerated Programs meet for 2 hours each. Practice SAT tests, required of students in the Basic SAT and 2100 Programs, last for 2½ hours each week. Each class is held at a variety of times and days to make it easy for students to fit their SAT work around their other plans for the summer. Schedules vary from center to center. At every center, Elite Boot Camp starts at 8:30 a.m. and ends at 2:30 p.m., with a half-hour break for lunch.

Students of all ages and abilities are expected to preserve the School's productive, academically focused atmosphere. The School has zero tolerance for academic dishonesty, truancy, or possession of any tobacco, alcohol, or drugs. Elite immediately expels students who violate its rules of conduct.

EXTRA OPPORTUNITIES AND ACTIVITIES

Elite does not sponsor activities outside of its core classroom offerings. However, because the School's summer offerings are so rigorous and attract students with shared goals for success, satisfying and lasting friendships are formed each year.

FACILITIES

There are seven education centers in southern California, two in New Jersey, two in Vancouver, Canada, and five in Seoul, South Korea.

STAFF

Elite's faculty is composed primarily of professional teachers carefully selected from the most prestigious local public and private schools and universities. They have years of experience in sharing their expertise and enthusiasm with Elite's students in a presentation that is clear, reliable, and easy to remember.

Even though the atmosphere is informal, and many of the teachers are on a first-name basis with students, the focus is on work and making students smarter.

MEDICAL CARE

Elite does not provide on-site medical care.

RELIGIOUS LIFE

Elite is not affiliated with any religious organization.

COSTS

Tuition for Elite programs is as follows: Elementary Enrichment, $740–$880 for eight weeks; Junior High Enrichment, $960–$1200 for eight weeks; Basic SAT Program, $880 for eight weeks; Elite SAT Boot Camp, $2200 for eight weeks; and 2100 Guarantee Program, $1750 for fifteen weeks.

FINANCIAL AID

Financial aid is not available.

TRANSPORTATION

Transportation options vary according to individual centers. Most centers can help make arrangements for students enrolled in the Elementary and Junior High Enrichment programs.

APPLICATION TIMETABLE

The School encourages inquiries from both students and parents at any time. Students are accepted in order of applications received. Early registration is advised, as space is limited. Registration cannot be considered unless accompanied by a diagnostic test report.

For more information, contact:

Ms. Wonna Kim
Program Director
Elite Educational Institute
4009 Wilshire Boulevard, Suite 200
Los Angeles, California 90010
213-365-8008
Fax: 213-365-1253
World Wide Web: http://www.ElitePrep.com

EMAGINATION COMPUTER CAMPS

SUMMER CAMP

ATLANTA, GEORGIA; LAKE FOREST, ILLINOIS; AND WALTHAM, MASSACHUSETTS

Type of Program: Computer technology in a traditional summer camp setting
Participants: Boys and girls, ages 8–17
Program Dates: Four 2-week sessions, late June through mid-August. Overnight, day, extended-day, and full-day programs offered
Head of Program: Michael Currence, Camps Director

LOCATION

Emagination's newest camp is located on the campus of the prestigious Georgia Institute of Technology (Georgia Tech) in Atlanta. Georgia Tech is a national and international leader in scientific and technological education and research. The beautiful campus occupies more than 300 acres in Atlanta and has a distinctly suburban feel with green space and tree-lined roads. At Georgia Tech, Emagination has its own parklike "campus within a campus."

The Lake Forest Academy, in Lake Forest, Illinois, is situated on 160 parklike suburban acres, providing an idyllic location for summer camp. The campus occupies the former J. Ogden Armour estate, which was built in the early 1900s, and is located 30 miles from Chicago on the North Shore of Lake Michigan.

The Bentley College campus is Waltham, Massachusetts, is suburban, beautiful, and impeccably maintained. Bentley is a business university and is a leader in integrating education and information technology. The Princeton Review recently named Bentley third among the nation's most connected campuses. Bentley is less than 10 miles from the heart of historic Boston.

Overnight campers at all three locations live in dorm rooms, grouped by age and gender, with counselors providing 24-hour supervision. Athletic facilities include a pool, playing fields, and a gymnasium.

BACKGROUND AND PHILOSOPHY

Emagination's mission is to provide boys and girls interested in computers and digital technologies with a fun, challenging, and enriching camp experience in a safe and nurturing environment. New and updated technology workshops delight campers and provide the benefits of a high-quality traditional summer camp.

Emagination is a family-owned company with an experienced staff. The camps are about having fun—both in tech workshops and in recreation. Celebrating twenty-three years, Emagination was founded in 1982 with the opening of a camp in Connecticut. From 1992 to 2003, camps have operated at Lasell College in Newton, Massachusetts, and, since 1999, at Lake Forest Academy in Lake Forest, Illinois. In 2004, the Massachusetts camp began operations at Bentley College, and the prestigious Georgia Tech became the newest location of Emagination Computer Camps. Emagination understands kids who love computers and are proud that so many campers return year after year, many of them even becoming counselors.

PROGRAM OFFERINGS

At Emagination, campers can build a PC and go for a swim, design a Web page and kick a soccer ball. They advance their computer skills, make friends, learn independence, and develop self-confidence. Campers from all across America and around the world come together in a community of kids like themselves. They explore in more than twenty-five workshops and have fun doing things that interest them. Plus, they gain the social and emotional benefits of the traditional summer camp experience in a structured environment.

Two-week sessions enable campers to unleash creativity in Web design, video game design, animation, and digital photography. They discover building skills in Build a PC, robotics, rockets, and RC cars. They explore programming in programming BASICs, C, C++, Java, and PERL. Workshops range in size from 6 to 12 campers. In addition, everyone needs a tech break. Emagination's Fun and Games program emphasizes participation and combines games including kickball and capture the flag with indoor activities, such as arts and crafts.

DAILY SCHEDULE
A typical day at Emagination begins when the overnight and full-day campers and counselors come together in the dining hall for an all-you-can-eat breakfast at 8 a.m. From 9 until noon, all campers participate in two 90-minute workshops that thrill and challenge them. At noon, campers and counselors enjoy another nutritious, all-you-can-eat meal while hanging out with friends. From 1 until 4, campers head into two more 90-minute workshops. After that, full- and extended-day campers head for the computer labs to work on projects or do some gaming with friends. Overnight campers head to their dorms for some rest and relaxation before dinner, where overnight, full-, and extended-day campers come together for a hearty, all-you-can-eat meal. Campers talk about projects and activities, making the meal a great time to develop friendships. From 6 to 9, overnight campers (and full-day campers until 7:30) tech the night away in network gaming tournaments, Internet scavenger hunts, open-lab time, or console gaming contests. Other activities can include games of capture the flag, arts and crafts, board games, or time in the camp's swimming pool. At 9, campers are free to read, relax, talk with friends and counselors, or get ready for bed before lights out at 10.

EXTRA OPPORTUNITIES AND ACTIVITIES
Evening activities vary and include workshops, field trips, the talent show, movies, sports, and much more. Residential campers are also offered day trips each weekend. Destinations have included Boston's Quincy Market, the New England Aquarium, the Museum of Science, the Computer Museum, Alcatraz National Park, professional baseball and soccer games, Six Flags Amusement Parks, and other exciting places.

FACILITIES
Residential campers are housed in college dorm rooms by age and gender. Rooms accommodate 2–3 campers. On-site, mature residential counselors are available 24 hours a day to supervise campers. Air-conditioned computer rooms feature multiple bays of PCs and a bay of systems for games classes as well as computers for "Build and Repair" PC courses. Emagination Computer Camps has access to athletic fields, tennis courts, and gymnasiums for a variety of indoor sports. An array of nutritious foods are offered at the cafeterias.

STAFF
Emagination carefully selects counselors who embrace technology, enjoy being with kids, and want to teach, lead, and have fun. Many counselors started out as campers, so they understand the important role computers play in growing up. College students, graduate students, and schoolteachers—these technology-savvy staff members are wonderful teachers, leaders, and mentors, and the majority of them stay with the camps for at least two summers. All counselors are adults and they complete a comprehensive training program developed over twenty-three years.

MEDICAL CARE
Emagination Computer Camps are located within 3 miles of a hospital, with a health supervisor on premises. Staff members are certified in Red Cross First Aid and CPR. Parents and the camper's physician provide important information so that staff members know about the camper's medical conditions and needs as well as any dietary, activity, and other restrictions and limitations. Parents are encouraged to call or e-mail to ask questions or discuss any health-care-related issues.

COSTS
Total tuition for day campers in 2004 was $1195 per session. Tuition for the extended-day option (Monday to Friday from 8 a.m. to 6:15 p.m.) was $1245 per session. Tuition for the full-day (7:30 a.m. to 7:45 p.m.) session was $1495. Tuition for the overnight session was $1995. Students should visit the camp's Web site, listed below, for available discounts.

TRANSPORTATION
For overnight campers, transportation may be arranged to and from nearby airports, railroad stations, and bus terminals. The staff members help parents make arrangements and contacts for car pooling or shuttle services for day campers. In Illinois, daily pick-up and drop-off at both Lake Forest train stations is available.

APPLICATION TIMETABLE
Applications are available beginning in November. As courses are filled on a first-come, first-served basis, early application is highly recommended. Due to complexities in scheduling, Emagination Computer Camps cannot guarantee a camper's course choices or special requests. Reservations are confirmed by mail and are accompanied by an information/orientation packet.

FOR MORE INFORMATION, CONTACT:

Emagination Computer Camps
110 Winn Street, Suite 207
Woburn, Massachusetts 01801
781-933-8795
888-226-6733 (toll-free)
Fax: 781-933-0749
E-mail: camp@computercamps.com
World Wide Web: http://www.computercamps.com

EMMA WILLARD SCHOOL

GIRLSUMMER

TROY, NEW YORK

Type of Program: Academic enrichment
Participants: Girls entering grades 7 through 12
Enrollment: 50–100 girls each session
Program Dates: Multiple two-week sessions in June, July, and August
Heads of Program: Doug Murphy, Executive Director; Traci Hudson, Program Services

LOCATION

GirlSummer is located on 137 extraordinary acres atop Mount Ida amid the natural beauty of Troy, New York. The school is listed in the National Register of Historic Places and offers inspiring architecture and a state-of-the-art setting for learning and living. Just a little more than 2 hours by car from Manhattan, New York's historic Capital Region is the pride of the Hudson Valley and has been designated a National Heritage Area.

BACKGROUND AND PHILOSOPHY

Since 1814, Emma Willard School has been one of the nation's leading college-preparatory boarding and day schools for young women. As an extension of its successful and long-standing summer day program for elementary school–age girls, Emma Willard developed GirlSummer for middle and high school girls who want a taste of residential campus life in an all-girls environment.

The GirlSummer experience is a two-week-long immersion in a stimulating and fun on-campus academic environment. Designed to further scholastic aptitude and broaden academic interests within a dynamic, structured environment, GirlSummer's unique curriculum approach was developed specifically to pique each student's interests and challenge her abilities. GirlSummer combines rigorous yet interesting academic endeavors during the day with great evening and weekend activities.

PROGRAM OFFERINGS

College Prep & Preview GirlSummer College Prep & Preview gives high school girls a head start on the college admission process. By the end of the session, each girl will have developed her own College Plan. Classes include SAT Prep, Writing for College—Applications and Essays, Writing for College—Academic Papers, Clubs and Volunteerism, Choosing a College, the College Admissions Process, and Social Life at College. Off-campus field trips might include visits to local colleges for college tours and visits with college admissions officers.

Computers, Science, and Technology This program offers hands-on classes in a variety of cutting-edge academic environments and topics. It gives girls an opportunity to learn all about the world of science, computers, robotics, and other disciplines of the future. Classes include programming, Web design, Java, LEGO robotics, and hands-on science labs. There are also visits from college-level science professors and sneak peeks at undergraduate majors such as applied physics, bioinformatics, biochemistry, biology, premedicine, astronomy, computer science, environmental science, oceanography, and geology. Field trips might include visits to the Henry Hudson Planetarium and the science facilities at nearby Rensselaer Polytechnic Institute.

Foreign Language Study (Spanish or French) The program is designed for any ability level and is based not on rote memorization but rather on conversation. It offers a unique linguistic learning environment that provides students the opportunity to speak their selected language in a real-life setting. Cultural awareness is taught through learning traditional geographic areas, traditions, customs, and foods. In addition, campers enjoy an exploration of cultures, which might include learning folk dances, cooking dishes from specific regions, or even taking a field trip to Manhattan for foreign language–themed productions on or off Broadway.

Fine Arts GirlSummer offers a dynamic program, investigating many fields and media of the fine arts. Moving from drawing and mixed media through painting and photography, fine arts students gain a broad view of modern working art. The program offers a review of the basics of proportion, lines, and shading, using charcoal, pencil, pastels, and markers to create an array of graphic presentations. Campers then move on to painting, implementing much of what has already been learned to focus on subject matter, use of color, and application of paint and style. The final topic of the session is digital photography. Students learn how to frame compositions and balance style, colors, and contrast.

Performing Arts Beginning with the building blocks of acting, students learn the tools professional actors use to create believable performances by working on scenes, monologues, and speeches. GirlSummer builds on this by allowing campers to study improv and musical theater. Girls are asked if they are comfortable in front of an audience, if they can be put on the spot, and what improv games they have tried. The weeks are then rounded out with dramatic acting, when everything the girls have learned is brought together. They can practice dialogue, monologue, emotional expression, voice, and more.

Writer's Workshops This program offers students who love to write and students who want to improve their writing abilities the opportunity to work in intensive writing workshops of limited size. Discussion and ideas abound. It is a comprehensive education in the craft of writing, and the program outlines the lessons needed to be a good writer. Main topics covered include introduction to writing, the mechanics of creative writing, journaling, poetry, and fiction writing. Off-campus field trips might include a visit to a major publishing house and talks with writers, editors, and others in the field.
AP U.S. History This program gives students a jump on the AP course for the fall. The curriculum is designed by the chair of Emma Willard's history and social sciences division. Summer students learn the facts in easy-to-remember ways, discuss current events and historical accounts, examine questions, and practice writing document-based questions. GirlSummer utilizes local field trips, history labs, and film study. The course includes timed practice tests, document-based questions, test-taking skills, essay writing, discussions, critical dates, and turning points.
AP English Language or Literature These programs are designed for any girls who are thinking about taking an AP English class or either AP English exam. It's also a great program for those who simply want to improve their reading, analytical, and composition skills. Campers learn how to write effective essays and analyze and interpret historical accounts, plays, journals, newspapers, and more.

ENROLLMENT
To allow for small classes with individual attention, GirlSummer enrolls a maximum of 100 campers each session.

EXTRA OPPORTUNITIES AND ACTIVITIES
Each academic camp goes on unique and exciting field trip adventures. Depending on the program, field trips might include visiting a major college or university in the area, science centers or planetariums, French- or Spanish-themed events or restaurants, or a major publishing house to meet authors and editors.

Each two-week session incorporates a Saturday excursion, known as Super Saturday, to local diversions and cultural attractions. Buses depart early Saturday morning for a variety of exciting destinations. Popular destinations include amusement parks, beaches, aquariums, music festivals, shopping malls, and Manhattan.

FACILITIES
All students stay overnight in the spectacular dormitory facilities located on campus and enjoy the first-rate services and amenities that full-time Emma Willard School students do during the school year. Campers are supervised by adult and junior counselors who live in the dorms with them.

STAFF
Intelligent and energetic, the staff is the heart of the GirlSummer experience. From professional teachers to talented graduate and undergraduate students, all staff members participate in safety and training sessions. The maximum student-teacher ratio is 8:1.

MEDICAL CARE
Medical care is available 24 hours a day at nearby hospital facilities. All participants must submit comprehensive medical forms and proof of insurance.

COSTS
The tuition for each two-week session is $2295. This includes all instruction; instructional materials; a breakfast, lunch, and dinner each day; a dorm room with linens; self-service laundry facilities; all sports and recreational activities; transportation for sponsored trips; admission tickets to excursion destinations; and total 24-hour supervision for the duration of each camp session. Students may wish to bring spending money for snacks, shopping, and incidentals.

FINANCIAL AID
Very limited financial aid is available at this time.

TRANSPORTATION
Airport pick-up and drop-off are available for an additional fee.

APPLICATION TIMETABLE
Inquiries are welcome at any time. Applications are accepted on a rolling basis. After June 1, acceptance to the program is based on availability, and applications must include a late fee of $100.

For more information, contact:

GirlSummer at Emma Willard School
285 Pawling Avenue
Troy, New York 12180
866-EWS-CAMP (397-2267, toll-free)
World Wide Web: http://www.emmawillard.org/summer

ENFOREX INTERNATIONAL SUMMER SCHOOLS IN SPAIN

Enforex

ENFOREX SUMMER PROGRAM

MARBELLA, SALAMANCA, AND MADRID, SPAIN

Type of Program: Spanish-language, educational, activities, sports, and cultural camp
Participants: Coeducational, ages 5–18
Enrollment: 230 per session, in each school
Program Dates: Two-, four-, six-, and eight-week sessions starting June 27, July 4, July 18, August 1, and August 15
Head of Program: Antonio Anadon, Director

LOCATION

Marbella Summer Camp (La Costa del Sol) Marbella (Málaga) is a beach resort located south of Spain, 20 minutes from Málaga and 1½ hours from Granada and Seville, the capital of Andalusia. Marbella is one of the most attractive cities on the famous Mediterranean Costa del Sol. An old town that still preserves most of its character, it has its own microclimate, white Mediterranean-style houses, and luxurious beaches. Marbella and the sophisticated marina of Puerto Banús are the playgrounds of international stars, Spanish high society, and worldwide personalities. The residential school complex is 18 square miles, located in the midst of an extensive pine area. It is situated between the prestigious Hotel Don Carlos and Marbella's General Hospital, a 5-minute walk from the beach and surrounded by nature. Nearby sites of special interest include Nerja Caves, Granada, Gibraltar, and Seville.

Madrid Summer Camp Madrid, capital city of Spain, is located in the very center of the country. Its geographic location allows visits to representative cities such as Barcelona, Seville, and Granada in less than 4 hours and other closer cities such as Toledo, El Escorial, Salamanca, and Segovia in less than 1 hour. The Summer Campus is located in one of the most prestigious colleges and is surrounded by a marvelous landscape. It is only 20 minutes from the city center and is well equipped for sports such as football, basketball, tennis, and swimming. Students practice horseback riding and golf at a nearby club.

Salamanca Summer Camp The School is located in a five-floor, sixteenth-century Renaissance building, recognized by UNESCO as a World Heritage Complex. Located in the old walled city center, the complex also has a classic cloister patio and an attached fifteenth-century church, one of the best examples of plateresque architecture in Salamanca. The walled sports facilities include a soccer field, an in-line skating rink, a jailai frontón, and basketball, handball, and volleyball courts. Students are transported to a nearby swim club.

Camp for Families A new opportunity exists for families to come to camp together. Parents stay in an apartment or with host families and study Spanish in the adult school while their children go to camp.

BACKGROUND AND PHILOSOPHY

The Marbella, Salamanca, and Madrid International Summer Schools were founded in 1989 by ENFOREX, Spanish in the Spanish World. In the program, designed and elaborated by professional educators, Spanish (60 percent) and international (40 percent from all over the world) teenagers enjoy an educational holiday at three of the top Spanish residential schools in Spain. The program's main goals are to learn Spanish in an attractive environment and inculcate the basis of teamwork and individual responsibility in common tasks, to study and play in direct contact with nature, and to build social relationships and make new friends. To enhance students' ability to handle daily tasks without the support and protection of their families and to facilitate through sports and cultural activities, a wide range of opportunities that enrich the character are offered. The Summer Camp is also designed for Spanish students. This creates an international atmosphere suitable for the development of languages and exchange of cultures. The School is CEELE certified by the University of Alcala and is also accredited by Instituto Cervantes.

PROGRAM OFFERINGS

The program also offers facilities for families and is designed for students between 5 and 18 years of age. At the School, they are divided into three different groups: 5–9, 10–13, and 14–18.

Students receive four lessons of Spanish language and culture per day. Class size averages 5 students and is a maximum of 12. Each lesson is 45 minutes long. On the first day of school, a placement test is administered to determine the student's level of Spanish. There are six different levels in Spanish, from complete beginners to proficiency.

Classes are designed specifically for each level and age group. The following language skills are taught at all levels: speaking, listening, writing, grammar, Spanish culture, and Spanish history. All students receive a certificate diploma at the end of the course.

Recreational sports are one the camp's most joyful activities. Sports activities may be practiced individually or in groups and include swimming, horseback riding, archery, paddleball, tennis, water sports, jet skiing, camping, golf, basketball, aerobics, soccer, baseball, handball, and volleyball.

Day camp is offered to external students, who take part from 9 a.m. until 9 p.m. and do not need accommodation at the residential school. The student attends the academic program, Spanish classes, and cultural and sports program with the rest of the students.

EXTRA OPPORTUNITIES AND ACTIVITIES

The School offers a wide range of activities, including an open-air workshop, handcrafts, theater, photography, computers and the Internet, radio, press, mural, and dance (jazz and flamenco "Sevillanas" workshops), which are available for all students who wish to experience one or more of the above cultural activities. Students also have the option of staying with host families.

A wide range of fun social activities are organized in the afternoon or after dinner, indoors and outdoors, and include parties, concerts, entertaining games, competitions, picnics and camping, movies, camp dances, or talent shows. Students enjoy two half-day and two day trips every week to nearby sites of special interest, such as Marbella (Granada, Nerja Caves, Banús Yatch Harbor, Gibraltar, and Seville), Madrid (El Prado, Toledo, El Escorial, Salamanca, Plaza Mayor, and Barcelona), and Salamanca.

DAILY SCHEDULE

8:00–9:00	Wake up and breakfast
9:00–10:45	Spanish lessons
10:45–11:15	Break
11:15–1:00	Spanish lessons
1:00–2:15	Sport and cultural activities and swimming
2:15–3:00	Lunch
3:00–4:30	Workshops
4:30–8:30	Sports, activities, afternoon snack, and games
8:30–9:30	Dinner
10:30–11:00	To bed

FACILITIES

The School's main building has a dining room, classrooms, dormitories, a computer room, and a library. The campuses have a swimming pool, golf, archery, soccer fields, and a sports complex with a gymnasium and paddleball, tennis, basketball, and volleyball courts. The School has its own farm, and there is a horseback riding school with more than 14 horses at the Marbella School.

STAFF

Spanish lessons are taught by native Spanish teachers holding five-year college degrees in Spanish linguistics and teaching Spanish as a foreign language, plus the CAP (teachers' aptitude test). Some have master's degrees and doctorates in Spanish.

The School Director, the maximum authority in the program, supervises both a Coordinator for Social Activities and a team of group leaders, who also work under the direction of the Coordinator for Social

Activities. There is approximately 1 group leader for every 8 students. ENFOREX offers a free group leader placement for minimum groups of 8 students. If a teacher or educational leader sends a group of 8 students and wishes to accompany them, ENFOREX provides him or her with a scholarship.

MEDICAL CARE

Medical personnel are on 24-hour call at the School. The School has arrangements with Marbella's General Hospital, which is 5 minutes away, for emergency treatment. All students are covered with medical insurance; however, it is recommended that students take out a private insurance that covers repatriation.

COSTS

International School fees are as follows: full board with accommodation, €900 for two weeks, €1800 for four weeks, €2520 for six weeks, and €3360 for eight weeks; and day camp, €510 for two weeks, €1020 for four weeks, €1530 for six weeks, and €2040 for eight weeks. These fees include twenty Spanish lessons per week, accommodation in the camp's dormitory, four meals a day, course material, two afternoon excursions every fortnight, one full-day excursion every fortnight, activities described, assistance of group leaders, health insurance, application and enrollment fees, and laundry service once a week. There is a homestay option. Optional fees include horseback riding classes (5 hours a week), €120; tennis classes (6 hours a week), €120; and golf (6 hours a week), €170.

TRANSPORTATION

Marbella International School is located 20 minutes from Málaga airport and 6 hours from Madrid's (capital city) airport, Barajas. Transfers are available from both airports for all students. Madrid and Salamanca International Schools are located 15 minutes and 2 hours from the Madrid airport, respectively. ENFOREX can arrange packages for international students to arrive from New York, Miami, Los Angeles, or other cities.

FOR MORE INFORMATION, CONTACT:

ENFOREX Spanish in the Spanish World
c/o Alberto Aguilera, 26
28015 Madrid
Spain
34-91-594-3776
Fax: 34-91-594-5159
E-mail: info@enforex.es
World Wide Web: http://www.enforex.com

PARTICIPANT/FAMILY COMMENTS

"This year, I told mom I want to go back. I can't forget the good times we had, the friends I met, the fun activities we did and all I learned. It's going to be another great summer!"—Carlos Martí, Barcelona, Spain

ENVIRONMENTAL STUDIES SUMMER YOUTH INSTITUTE

AT HOBART AND WILLIAM SMITH COLLEGES

GENEVA, NEW YORK

Type of Program: Academic and outdoors environmental studies
Participants: High school students entering their junior or senior year
Enrollment: 36–40 students
Program Dates: Two-week program, last two weeks in July
Head of Program: Professor D. Brooks McKinney, Director

LOCATION

Hobart and William Smith Colleges have a campus of more than 200 acres in Geneva, New York. The campus is located on Seneca Lake, the largest lake in western New York's Finger Lakes region. The program includes fieldwork throughout the Finger Lakes region and a four-day camping-research trip in the Adirondack Mountains.

BACKGROUND AND PHILOSOPHY

Founded in 1993 by an interdisciplinary team of college professors working on environmental issues, the Environmental Studies Summer Youth Institute offers a two-week program each summer for talented high school students. Institute faculty members are nationally and internationally known in biology, chemistry, geoscience, public policy, social philosophy, literature, and art.

Students conduct research aboard the *HWS Scandling,* a fully equipped oceanographic vessel on Seneca Lake; in streams, fields, and nature preserves; and in state-of-the-art laboratory facilities. Other local resources include the New York State Agricultural Experiment Station, a world-renowned research facility at which some of the Summer Institute's faculty members hold adjunct appointments.

Working in the field, on the water, in laboratories, in seminars, and on a four-day camping trip, students explore a variety of interrelated topics in environmental policy, economics, and ethics and come to see the natural world through the eyes of artists, historians, philosophers, policy analysts, and scientists. There is an opportunity to work closely with college professors and with students from all over the country who share an interest in the environment. While the curriculum is challenging, the atmosphere is cooperative. College credit is awarded upon successful completion of the course.

Fieldwork sessions include work in the Hanley Nature Preserve and at the Cayuga Nature Center; Seneca Lake research aboard the *HWS Scandling;* analysis of water in streams, lakes, and bogs; geological study of mountains and shoreline erosion and earth history; and environmental assessment and preservation of biodiversity. Other sessions include nature photography, art history, environmental literature, and discussions of public policy and environmental philosophy. Four days are spent conducting research while camping, hiking, and canoeing in the Adirondack region.

Examples of sessions include Acid Rain and Global Change; Topographical Mapping; Watersheds and Streamflow Analysis; Water Quality, Geology, and Plant Ecology in the Adirondacks; Ecology and Conservation in a Quaking Bog; The Geology of Chimney Bluffs; Ecology and Our Relationship to the Rest of Nature; Biodiversity and the Endangered Species Act; Environmental Law; The Environment and the Economy; and Environmental Justice and Social Justice.

DAILY SCHEDULE

A typical day begins with breakfast at 8 a.m., followed by a 3-hour fieldwork session, lunch at noon, another fieldwork session or class, dinner at 5:30, and a short seminar.

FACILITIES

The Environmental Studies Summer Youth Institute is located in the heart of the Finger Lakes region, on the picturesque campus of Hobart and William Smith Colleges. Students live in a college residence hall and have access to Hobart and William Smith Colleges' computer laboratories, library, and academic, athletic, and recreational facilities.

STAFF

Four residential staff members live with the 36–40 students. The instructional staff consists of 15 to 20 college professors and the staff members of a number of consulting organizations.

MEDICAL CARE

Participants must fill out the program's health form. Medical facilities, including a hospital, are nearby.

COSTS

The fee of $1700 includes tuition, room, board, instructional materials, and all other program costs. There is a $500 initial deposit. The remaining $1200 is due July 1.

FINANCIAL AID

A limited number of 50 percent and 25 percent scholarships, based on need and merit, are awarded each year.

TRANSPORTATION

Bus service directly to Geneva and train service to Rochester or Syracuse is available. Airports are located in Rochester, Syracuse, and Ithaca, each about an hour away. Airport pick-up and drop-off can be arranged by the program for $50 each way.

APPLICATION TIMETABLE

Inquiries are welcome year-round. Applications are reviewed on a rolling basis. There is a $25 application fee. Notification of acceptance is made within three weeks of the completed application. The reply date is two to three weeks following acceptance.

For more information, contact:

Professor Brooks McKinney, Director
Environmental Studies Summer Youth Institute
Hobart and William Smith Colleges
Geneva, New York 14456-3397
315-781-4401
Fax: 315-781-4400
E-mail: essyi@hws.edu
World Wide Web: http://academic.hws.edu/enviro

EXCEL

AT AMHERST COLLEGE; WILLIAMS COLLEGE; BENNINGTON COLLEGE; UNIVERSITY OF CALIFORNIA, SANTA CRUZ; OXFORD/TUSCANY; MADRID/BARCELONA; AND CUBA

SUMMER PROGRAMS

AMHERST AND WILLIAMSTOWN, MASSACHUSETTS; BENNINGTON, VERMONT; SANTA CRUZ, CALIFORNIA; OXFORD, ENGLAND; FLORENCE, ITALY; MADRID AND BARCELONA, SPAIN; AND CUBA

Type of Program: Precollege academic enrichment
Participants: Coeducational, students completing grades 9–12
Enrollment: 100–150 per session, U.S.; 70, Europe and Cuba
Program Dates: Three-, four-, and seven-week programs in June, July, and August
Heads of Program: Jeffrey Shumlin and Tim Weed, Directors

LOCATION

Excel at Amherst College is based on the campus of Amherst College, Amherst, Massachusetts. Located in the heart of the Pioneer Valley, Amherst College and the town of Amherst offer a picturesque setting for learning and adventure. The college campus and adjacent town common form the heart of the "Five-College Area."

Excel at Williams College is based on the campus of Williams College, Williamstown, Massachusetts. Nestled in the picturesque Berkshire Mountains of western Massachusetts, and just a few miles from the New York and Vermont borders, Williams College and the surrounding area provide an outstanding balance of natural splendor and cultural vitality.

Excel at Bennington College takes full advantage of the extraordinary arts facilities of this scenic campus in southern Vermont. The program has full and exclusive access to the theaters, art, dance and ceramic studios, and other venues that make Bennington College an ideal location for a summer program with an emphasis on the arts.

Excel at Oxford/Tuscany is located at St. Hilda's College in Oxford, England, and at a sixteenth-century villa outside Florence, Italy. Each location serves as an ideal base for active, focused study of the history, archeology, literary traditions, and politics of the region. Excel at Madrid/Barcelona students explore the rich and varied culture of Spain from the modern campuses of universities. Located in architecturally and culturally rich Havana, Excel Cuba allows participants to take advantage of the historic opportunity to learn about Cuban life and culture through active seminars that emphasize independent field-based projects and close contact with the Cuban people.

BACKGROUND AND PHILOSOPHY

The Excel programs are sponsored by Putney Student Travel (Web site: http://www.goputney.com), now in its fifth decade of offering educational programs for high school students. Excel emphasizes growth and education through the challenges of hands-on learning by doing, exploring and adapting to new experiences, working cooperatively in small groups, and setting and achieving high personal expectations. Students select two areas of study and work in small seminars, undertaking extensive field trips and projects related to their subject areas. Each course culminates in a final project; a theatrical production, a student newspaper, an art and photography exhibit, a mock trial, a video, and a debate forum are among the possibilities, depending on the course. Course work is intellectually challenging, but credit is not offered and grades are not given since Excel students typically attend high-pressure schools during the academic year and want to focus in a more informal context during the summer on subjects that genuinely interest them. Outside the classroom, Excel offers a variety of athletic and cultural activities, many are organized by students themselves. Students best suited for the program are those who are motivated to stretch themselves intellectually, artistically, and physically and, in so doing, have fun!

PROGRAM OFFERINGS

Courses are divided into five categories: Arts (drawing and painting, photography, architectural design, writing, theater production, music composition, fashion design, dance, ceramics, and video production); Humanities (ethics, film studies, history, and philosophy); Languages and Rhetoric (journalism, French, and Spanish); Social and Natural Sciences (field biology, archaeology, international relations, criminal justice, and behavioral and social psychology); and Specialized Courses (SAT Preparation and Structured Writing, which are offered on the domestic campuses only). There is also a program at Excel Amherst, Williams, Santa Cruz, and Bennington, featuring college visits and small workshops to introduce students to the college admissions process.

ENROLLMENT

Enrollment at each domestic session ranges from 100 to 150 students, who are selected from across the country and around the world. European and Cuban programs are limited to 70 students.

EXTRA OPPORTUNITIES AND ACTIVITIES

During afternoons and evenings, students choose from a wide variety of organized activities ranging from swimming and Ultimate Frisbee to community service (during the afternoons) and from on-campus coffee houses to off-campus visits to arts productions in the local area (during the evenings). Instructional sports clinics in soccer, tennis, and golf are offered three late-afternoons a week at Amherst and Williams; and clinics in soccer, tennis, and surfing are offered at Santa Cruz. On weekends, all students and staff participate in excursions to areas of local and regional interest, including Cape Cod, Montreal, Vermont, and San Francisco. Excel at Oxford/Tuscany allows students to explore the rich heritage of Europe with frequent day trips and a weekend interlude in Paris. Excel at Madrid/Barcelona includes day trips and small-group weekend excursions to Se-

govia, Toledo, and Salamanca, among others. Excel Cuba offers daily opportunities for exploration and weekends with the group at the colonial city of Trinidad and the scenic rural region of Pinar del Rio.

FACILITIES

Students are housed in residence halls of each campus. Meals are provided in one of each college's dining halls. In addition, students at each campus have access to college athletic facilities, libraries, art studios, computer rooms, and language labs.

STAFF

Excel faculty members are among the finest in their fields, drawn from some of the world's best colleges and universities. They are chosen for their extensive knowledge of and enthusiasm for the course material as well as for their dynamic teaching methods and their willingness and ability to work closely with their students. A complete set of biographies of Excel instructors from the summer of 2004 is available at http://www.goputney.com/about/excel_staff.htm.

DAILY SCHEDULE

The daily schedules at Excel Oxford/Tuscany, Madrid/Barcelona, and Cuba are flexible, allowing for frequent field trips and in-depth exploration of the surrounding regions. The community meeting is a crucial part of the daily schedule of all programs.

MEDICAL CARE

There are excellent medical facilities within easy reach of each campus. All students must provide a medical form completed by their physician and a medical treatment release form prior to the beginning of the program.

RELIGIOUS LIFE

Excel is nondenominational. Students may attend area religious services if they wish.

COSTS

The tuition fees in 2004 were as follows: Excel at Amherst College, $4890 for the four-week (July) program and $4090 for the three-week (August) program. The tuition fees for Excel at Williams College was $4890 for the four-week program. The tuition for Excel at Oxford/Tuscany was $6790. Tuition for the Madrid/Barcelona program was $5990, and tuition for Excel Cuba was $6190. Tuition includes instructional programs, all regularly scheduled activities, room, board (two meals on the European program), overnight excursions that are a part of the Excel program (including lodging, meals, and transportation), use of college facilities, afternoon and evening activities, and transportation to and from the local airport.

TRANSPORTATION

Amherst, Williams, and Bennington College are within a 3 hours' drive of New York City and Boston. The airports in Hartford, Connecticut, and Albany, New York, are nearby. UC Santa Cruz is 1½ hours south of San Francisco and is easily accessible to the airport there and in San Jose. Staff members pick up students at these airports and at nearby train and bus stations on the first day of the program and drop them off on the last.

Excel organizes group flights for its Oxford/Tuscany and Madrid/Barcelona programs, in which students can participate if they choose. A flight from Miami to Havana is included in the fee for the Cuba program.

APPLICATION TIMETABLE

Admission to Excel is selective. Applications, which must be accompanied by a personal statement and two teacher references, are carefully considered by the Admissions Committee. Maturity, intellectual curiosity, integrity, and a cooperative spirit are all important admissions criteria. Students should apply early, as limited spaces in small classes are granted on a first-come, first-served basis.

FOR MORE INFORMATION, CONTACT:

Tim Weed, Director
345 Hickory Ridge Road
Putney, Vermont 05346
Telephone: 802-387-5000
Fax: 802-387-4276
E-mail: excel@goputney.com
World Wide Web: http://www.goputney.com

PARTICIPANT/FAMILY COMMENTS

"This was, by far, the best summer of my entire life. The people I met were amazing. The places I went and the things I was exposed to made this experience one I will never forget. Thank you so much for letting me be part of Excel for my second year!"

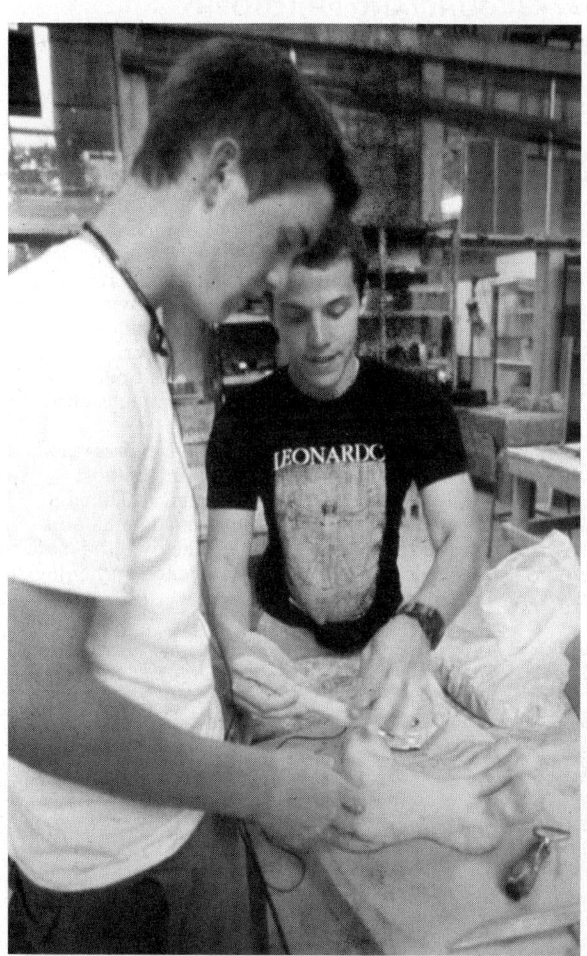

THE EXPERIMENT IN INTERNATIONAL LIVING

OFFERED BY WORLD LEARNING

EXPERIMENT IN INTERNATIONAL LIVING

BRATTLEBORO, VERMONT

Type of Program: International youth travel
Participants: Coeducational, high school students
Enrollment: 800–1,000
Program Dates: Three to five weeks in the summer
Head of Program: Tony Allen, Director of The Experiment in International Living

LOCATION

The Experiment in International Living is offered by World Learning, which is located in southern Vermont, and by affiliated offices on six continents. These offices provide Experiment in International Living programs with full-time international support and up-to-the-minute information on local events in program countries.

BACKGROUND AND PHILOSOPHY

World Learning was founded in 1932 as The Experiment in International Living, a pioneer in people-to-people exchange. It is one of the oldest private nonprofit international educational services organizations in the world. For more than seventy-two years, it has sustained its founding concept—learning the culture and language of another country by living as a member of one of its families—while also pioneering new initiatives in response to a changing world.

The range of Experiment in International Living programs includes snorkeling with seals in lava grottoes while observing the ecology of Ecuador's Galapagos Islands, wandering through Samurai villages after language classes in Japan, and biking along the coast of Brittany while immersing oneself in French culture and history.

Each Experiment in International Living program begins with a cross-cultural orientation in the host country, usually in the capital of the country. During orientation, participants learn about the customs and characteristics of the society in which they will be living in order to help them fully experience and enjoy their new environment.

Experiment in International Living programs are especially suited to students who are inquisitive and highly motivated to learn about cultures other than their own. Essential personality traits are adaptability, responsibility, a spirit of cooperation, and a sense of humor.

PROGRAM OFFERINGS

Students can choose from extraordinarily diverse programs in any of twenty-six countries from Australia to South Africa. Some programs provide intense immersion in the language and culture of a single place and people; some engage students in a culture through community service; and others develop the global perspective necessary to tackle international ecological problems. Choices are based on participant preference and on the special program opportunities made available by the Experiment's overseas contacts. Traditional Homestay and Travel programs in such countries as Brazil, Chile, China, France, Ghana, Ireland, Italy, Mexico, New Zealand, Northern Ireland, Poland, Spain, Switzerland, Thailand, Turkey, and the United Kingdom are popular. Ecological Adventure programs in places like Argentina, Australia, Belize, Botswana, Brazil, Chile, Costa Rica, Ecuador, Mexico, the Navajo Nation, New Zealand, Spain, and Switzerland offer exciting learning opportunities. Community Service programs in Argentina, Belize, Botswana, Brazil, Chile, Costa Rica, Germany, Ghana, Ireland, Mexico, the Navajo Nation, Northern Ireland, Poland, South Africa, Thailand, and Turkey attract students who want to make personal contributions to the well-being of the world community. Language Training programs are available in France, Japan, Italy, and Spain.

The following programs were offered in 2004; students should contact the Vermont office for more details.

Homestay By living with a family, students absorb and experience not just the language but also the values, customs, and traditions of a new country. They participate in the everyday life of the host family and engage in regular, fun activities with the U.S. leader, other group members, and host families. Traveling with the group and leader, students journey to another part of the country, trying out communication and exploration skills. The group visits three or four places, taking in the main sights while still having time to interact with local people.

Ecological Adventure Students examine rich natural and cultural resources through an adventurous travel program that is sensitive to environmental needs. As they tour historic, cultural, and scenic areas, the students explore ecological diversity firsthand, with the leader keeping the focus on the extraordinary balance of nature in the host country. Through camping, canoeing, snorkeling, or sailing, students embark on adventurous exploration into rural areas to appreciate a culture's spiritual and economic relationships to its environment. Students learn the value of being a global citizen and understanding the impact of ecological issues from a local and global perspective.

Community Service Students can make a peaceful, personal contribution to the well-being of the common planet by working on a Community Service program. Students gain invaluable hands-on experience in the process and discover how community service lets them learn from, as well as about, people in another culture. Students gain an understanding of how much can be accomplished with very few resources and of the cultural variations in approaches to problem solving. Students travel with their group and leader during the last part of the program to explore other parts of the country.

Language Training Focusing on verbal communications skills, students benefit from the highly skilled, experienced teachers and the community-based interactive learning of the Language Training programs. Participants work hard, but the rewards are extraordinary. Students can apply their lessons every minute of every day and can learn with an astonishing speed and ease. The Language Training programs require one year of French and one year of Spanish for the France and Spain programs, respectively. The Japan and Italy Language Training programs have no language prerequisites.

Travel Participants discover famous cultural and historical sights, interpreting them from the enriched perspective gained by living with a local family and taking part in the daily life of a community. They may journey to bustling port cities; hike through animal sanctuaries; travel by horse; sail, swim, and snorkel; or visit native markets.

The Arts Students explore theater, film, photography, or folklore to enrich the understanding of the host culture. Whether engaging in a photography project in the streets of Paris, flamenco dance lessons in southern Spain, or performing theater in the land of Shakespeare, a participant's creativity and talent provide a palette for a remarkable summer.

ENROLLMENT

Experiment in International Living programs are open to high school students. The majority are sophomores, juniors, and recently graduated seniors. Previous study of the host country language is required for some programs. Each participant is part of a group of travel companions for the duration of the Experiment in International Living program. Groups represent a broad spectrum of interests and personalities, encouraging the development of warm and lasting friendships.

STAFF

Leaders provide the support each participant needs to learn and to discover what international understanding means. The Experiment in International Living chooses its group leaders for their language fluency, maturity, emotional balance, experience in group leadership, and skill in working with young people. From the in-country orientation to the return to the United States, both the group and the leader serve as valuable resources for personal support, idea exchange, and activity planning.

COSTS

Fees for Experiment in International Living programs are determined by the chosen program's components, length of stay, and host country. Prices ranged from about $3000 to $5300 in 2004. These all-inclusive fees cover round-trip international transportation; orientation and language training; meals, lodging, and transportation throughout the program; admission to the program's scheduled events; costs related to the group leader; and health and accident insurance. Not included in the program fees are round-trip transportation to and from the program's U.S. starting point, personal spending money (usually $350 to $500), and costs of required travel documents and immunizations.

A $75 nonrefundable application fee must accompany the initial application, along with a $225 space reservation deposit, which is applied to the program fee. Full payment is required before the program start date. VISA and MasterCard are accepted.

FINANCIAL AID

Some awards are based on merit, most on need, and some on a combination of the two. Annually, more than 35 percent of Experiment in International Living participants receive scholarships from The Experience. Awards range from 10 to 75 percent of the individual's program fee. Scholarships are awarded on a rolling first-come, first-served basis. Program applicants are sent financial aid information and applications upon request.

APPLICATION TIMETABLE

Initial inquiries are welcome throughout the year. Detailed information and application forms are available early in the fall. May 1 is the deadline for the initial application. World Learning's Admission Committee reviews an individual's application as soon as all of the application materials have been received. The candidate is contacted in writing soon after the committee has reached a decision. Students are accepted into Experiment in International Living programs on a rolling basis beginning in the fall. Applicants may choose any program for which they meet the minimum age and language study requirements.

FOR MORE INFORMATION, CONTACT:

The Experiment in International Living
Kipling Road
Brattleboro, Vermont 05302-0676
802-257-7751
800-345-2929 (toll-free)
Fax: 802-258-3428
E-mail: eil@worldlearning.org
World Wide Web: http://www.usexperiment.org

EXPLORATION INTERMEDIATE PROGRAM

AN INDEPENDENT PROGRAM AT WELLESLEY COLLEGE

COEDUCATIONAL ENRICHMENT

WELLESLEY, MASSACHUSETTS

Type of Program: Enrichment, including academic enrichment courses; athletic, artistic, and recreational activities; and weekday and weekend educational and recreational trips

Participants: Coeducational; students entering grades 8–9

Enrollment: Each session: 450 residential and 200 day students

Program Dates: Two 3-week sessions. Students may stay for one or two sessions. First session: June 26 to July 16, 2005; second session: July 17 to August 6, 2005

Heads of Program: Mary-Ann Sullivan, B.A., Ed.M., M.A., Head of Program. Arnie Singal, B.A., S.M., J.D., and Ann Singal, B.A., M.Ed., Executive Directors

LOCATION

Nestled on the picturesque shores of Lake Waban, Wellesley College is located on a nationally acclaimed 500-acre campus only 12 miles from the heart of Boston. Featuring outstanding academic and athletic facilities, grassy quads with large shade trees, acres of woodlands, an arboretum, and several ponds, Wellesley College offers students the perfect place for a summer of exploration. Only a 5-minute walk from campus, the town center of Wellesley is a vibrant New England college town full of exciting restaurants, music shops, fashion boutiques, and bookstores.

BACKGROUND AND PHILOSOPHY

Founded in 1984, the Intermediate Program prepares middle school students for the challenges of high school life by encouraging them to explore a breadth of academic, recreational, and social opportunities. Exploration features an ungraded, pressure-free environment where students not only participate in innovative academic courses and mini-courses, but also take part in a variety of athletics, trips, and extracurricular activities. By emphasizing student choice and positive decision making in all aspects of program life, the Intermediate Program encourages students to develop self-confidence and self-esteem. While pursuing their passions and interests with a talented, diverse, and international student body, students gain valuable life experiences and a lifelong love of learning.

PROGRAM OFFERINGS

Enrichment Courses Students sign up for two 3-week courses each session. Exploration offers noncredit courses in subject areas that are not usually part of a middle school or high school curriculum. Courses are hands-on and student-centered, culminating in a final project or performance that gives students a tangible sense of accomplishment. Last year, more than eighty courses were offered, including acting and directing, drawing and painting, architecture, physics, marketing and advertising, natural sciences, anatomy, design and engineering, musical theater, dance, a cappella singing, math and problem solving, mock trials, and comparative government.

Mini-courses Each session, students enroll in two mini-courses, which meet Wednesday morning and afternoon. Mini-courses are designed to help students develop new skills and interests in academic, athletic, or artistic areas. Approximately 35 mini-courses are offered each session. Last year's mini-courses included Latin music and dance, basketball, calligraphy, outdoor skills, snorkeling, soccer, Italian cooking, poetry writing, sailing and canoeing, Shakespearean acting, community service, and tennis.

International Student Program Exploration welcomes international students with an intermediate-level of English proficiency. Many international students with strong English language skills enroll in regular Exploration courses. Other students choose English as a second language (ESL) instruction for one course period.

ENROLLMENT

One of the great strengths of the Intermediate Program is that its students come from all over the world and from a variety of racial, ethnic, and socioeconomic backgrounds. A typical summer includes students from more than forty states and forty countries.

EXTRA OPPORTUNITIES AND ACTIVITIES

Activities In addition to courses and mini-courses, more than thirty organized activities are offered at the Intermediate Program every afternoon and evening. Activity offerings include hobbies such as hiking, martial arts, chess, cooking, and role-playing games; crafts such as papier mâché, tie-dyeing, and batik; performance arts such as theater, dance, music composition, and improvisational comedy; and discussions and debates on social issues, global problems, the environment, and politics.

Athletics Both formal and informal athletics are available every day as part of the daily activity options. In addition, weekly mini-courses offer beginning, intermediate, and advanced levels of sports instruction, and students and staff members often organize pick-up games and program-wide tournaments. Regular sports offerings include tennis, basketball, soccer, softball, swimming, sailing and canoeing, ultimate frisbee, touch football, volleyball, track and field, and lacrosse.

Sports Clinics Each session, students may participate in daylong sports clinics with experienced college coaches at their home facilities. Last year's options for both boys and girls included basketball at Stonehill College, tennis at Tufts University, and soccer at Harvard University.

Trips Each session, students may choose from more than fifty organized trips to many of New England's favorite destinations. Last summer's trips included Cape Cod; historic downtown Boston; Fenway Park, home of the Boston Red Sox; the mansions in Newport, Rhode Island; L. L. Bean in Freeport, Maine; the Boston Science Museum; Harvard Square and the Harvard College Yard; historic Quincy Market; Six Flags New England; local beaches; the Federal Reserve Bank; Water Country Amusement Park; a cruise on Boston Harbor; the New England Aquarium; and the Wang Center for the Performing Arts. An overnight trip to New York City is also offered for rising ninth graders.

Main Events Each evening, the Intermediate Program sponsors one or more main events. Main events can feature anything from professional performers and guest speakers to staff-led events and student dances. Past main events have included staff improv night, a tae kwan do demonstration, movie night, a lip-synch contest, a cruise of Boston Harbor, student-faculty talent nights, a capella groups, and more.

FACILITIES

Intermediate Program students live on a centrally located residence hall on the Wellesley College campus. The dormitory complex houses student living quarters, the dining halls, and spaces for activities and performances. While living on the campus of Wellesley College, students have access to fantastic academic and athletic facilities, including classrooms in Wellesley's academic quad, dance studios, Alumnae Hall for performances and main events, Lake Waban for swimming and sailing, an arboretum and botanical gardens for biological study, the Davis Museum, a number of athletic playing fields, tennis courts, an outdoor track, and the multimillion-dollar Keohane Sports Center, with its indoor track, basketball and volleyball courts, pool table, squash and racquetball courts, and swimming pool.

STAFF

Each year, Exploration interviews several hundred individuals from the nation's top colleges and graduate programs. Faculty members are exceptionally talented, creative, and responsible. They are superb role models. Supporting the summer faculty is a team of highly experienced professional educators who work year-round on program planning, curriculum development, and faculty training. The faculty-to-student ratio is approximately 1:7.

MEDICAL CARE

Registered nurses are on duty on the campus 24 hours a day. Physician care is provided by a local medical practice and a university teaching hospital.

COSTS

Program costs for 2004 were $3450 (one session, residential) and $6595 (two sessions, residential). These prices covered tuition, room, full board, books and supplies, weekday trips, and transportation to and from Logan Airport. Day student costs were $1675 (one session) and $3195 (two sessions).

FINANCIAL AID

A limited number of partial- to full-tuition merit scholarships are available for those with financial need.

TRANSPORTATION

Exploration meets students at Logan International Airport in Boston and transports them to and from the program at the beginning and end of each session. Students are also met and transported to and from the Route 128 train station. Bus transportation is provided for day students through much of the greater Boston area for an additional charge.

APPLICATION TIMETABLE

Admission is on a rolling basis. Early application is encouraged. There is no application fee; however, a deposit (refundable until March 1) is required with the application to hold a student's space.

FOR MORE INFORMATION, CONTACT:

Exploration Intermediate Program
470 Washington Street
P.O. Box 368
Norwood, Massachusetts 02062
Phone: 781-762-7400
Fax: 781-762-7425
World Wide Web: http://www.explo.org

PARTICIPANT/FAMILY COMMENTS

"We think your amazing program—the diversity of activities and how well designed they were for the 14-year-old kid—really opened our son's eyes to how interesting the world can be."

"This is the best thing that has ever happened to me. It completely changed the way I appreciate things."

EXPLORATION JUNIOR PROGRAM

AN INDEPENDENT PROGRAM AT ST. MARK'S SCHOOL

ACADEMIC ENRICHMENT

SOUTHBOROUGH, MASSACHUSETTS

Type of Program: Academic enrichment

Participants: Coeducational and nondenominational; two divisions—Pioneers entering grades 4 and 5, and Voyagers entering grades 6 and 7

Enrollment: Each session: 200 residential and 240 day students

Program Dates: Two 3-week sessions. Students may stay for one or two sessions. First session: June 26 to July 16, 2005; second session: July 17 to August 6, 2005

Heads of Program: Moira Kelly, B.A., J.D., Head of Program. David Torcoletti, B.F.A., M.F.A., Head of Program. Arnie Singal, B.A., S.M., J.D., and Ann Singal, B.A., M.Ed., Executive Directors.

LOCATION

Set amidst 250 acres of picturesque woodlands, ponds, and fields, St. Mark's School is located in the small New England village of Southborough, 26 miles west of Boston. St. Mark's proximity to Boston, Worcester, Providence, and the New England seacoast allows students to take full advantage of the many cultural and recreational opportunities in the area. St. Mark's is one of the country's oldest and most prominent coeducational college-preparatory schools. There are superb classroom facilities, music practice rooms, art studios, a computer lab, and a superb science center. Complementing the school's academic facilities are an extensive sports complex, eight playing fields, eight tennis courts, and a large outdoor pool. Just down the road from the Junior Program is Hopkinton State Park, which offers many opportunities for hiking, swimming, canoeing, and fishing. St. Mark's is only 20 minutes from Wellesley College, making it easy for Junior Program students to visit brothers and sisters at the Exploration Intermediate Program.

BACKGROUND AND PHILOSOPHY

The Junior Program was founded to provide an opportunity for young people to explore academic, artistic, and athletic interests in a relaxed and creative environment that encourages a lifelong love of learning. Though not a camp, the Junior Program combines the best aspects of traditional camps—close friendships, activities, the outdoors, and adventure—with intellectual inquiry and exploration. The Junior Program is based on the belief that children can be good decision makers and that making choices about their daily schedules helps build self-confidence, independence, and maturity.

PROGRAM OFFERINGS

Academic Enrichment Courses Exploration offers "hands-on" noncredit courses on a variety of subjects not traditionally part of elementary or junior high school curriculum. Courses do not include tests or homework; they are designed to be fun, stimulate curiosity and discussion, and encourage a love for learning. Fourth and fifth graders take their courses together, and sixth and seventh graders take their courses together. Each student takes two courses each session, and each course meets four days a week. Last summer, students enrolled in more than fifty courses, including entomology, multimedia, chemistry and physics, math and architecture, painting and drama, civil engineering, woodworking, journalism, conflict resolution, constitutional law, automotive design, astronomy, creative writing, animation, improvisational theater, soapbox derby design and building, elections and debate, video production, and medieval history.

Mini-courses Each session, students enroll in two mini-courses, which meet each Wednesday morning and afternoon. Mini-courses offer skill-based instruction in a variety of areas. Last summer, students chose from forty mini-courses, including swimming, soccer, lacrosse, tennis, basketball, pottery, improv, poetry, wilderness survival, archery, canoeing, fencing, dance, Indian cooking, Japanese cooking, chess, physics, and model rocketry.

International Student Program Exploration welcomes international students who have attained an intermediate level of English proficiency. International students with strong English skills enroll in regular Exploration courses. Other students choose English as a second language (ESL) instruction for one or both course periods.

ENROLLMENT

One of the great strengths of the Junior Program is that students come from all over the world and from a variety of racial, cultural, and socioeconomic backgrounds. A typical summer includes students from thirty states and a dozen countries.

DAILY SCHEDULE

Students eat breakfast between 8 and 9. Pioneers (students entering grades 4 and 5) spend most mornings in two courses. Voyagers (students entering grades 6 and 7) spend most mornings doing two different organized activities. Lunch is served between noon and 1 and then the schedule is reversed: Voyagers go to their courses and Pioneers do activities. Halfway through the afternoon, a snack is served. Four o'clock is quiet time or free swim time. Dinner is followed by an activity period and then the main event, a performance or demonstration in the school's indoor theater or in an outdoor performance space. The main event is followed by a snack, socializing time, and then check-in and lights out.

The Wednesday schedule is slightly different. Students attend mini-courses in the morning and another mini-course in the afternoon.

Both weekend days are spent going on trips, followed by evening activities.

EXTRA OPPORTUNITIES AND ACTIVITIES

Activities Each day, more than forty organized activities are offered, including swimming, water polo, basketball, street hockey, volleyball, soccer, tennis, cooking, science experiments, hiking, canoeing, dance, acting, juggling, singing, creative writing, painting, papier mâché, and beading.

Trips Saturday and Sunday are trip days. Each trip day, students choose from six to eight different trips, and each session, more than twenty-five different trips are offered. Saturday trips are educational and include options such as farms, the New England Aquarium, Salem, the Rocky Shore Science Center, the Higgins Armory, whale watches in Boston Harbor, Plimouth Plantation, and the Museum of Fine Arts. Sundays include a mix of recreational and educational options, such as hiking Mount Monadnock, canoeing on the Concord River, water parks, amusement parks, and the Museum of Science. Recent trips have also included professional soccer games, Boston Red Sox games, and plays such as *Beauty and the Beast* and *42nd Street*.

Main Events Five times per week, the Junior Program hosts on-campus performances, presentations, and demonstrations by professional actors, musicians, storytellers, and dancers, as well as naturalists, scientists, and journalists.

FACILITIES

The "Living Group" is Exploration's version of the bunkhouse. Each Living Group is composed of approximately 8 to 12 students and two residential advisers. Students live in homelike double rooms. Each student has a roommate and his or her own bed, dresser, and closet/wardrobe. Bathrooms are located down the hall from student rooms.

Meals are served cafeteria-style in a dining room with large decorative windows and magnificent woodwork. St. Mark's has a reputation for outstanding food. Salad and deli bars, several main entrees at each meal, and fresh fruits are some of the options.

STAFF

Each fall, Exploration interviews more than 600 individuals from the nation's top colleges and graduate programs. The staff application process is rigorous, and it results in an exceptionally talented, experienced, and creative staff. They are superb role models. Each year more than 50 percent of the Junior Program staff return, and many individuals have been with the Program for several years. Supporting these summer staff members is a team of highly experienced professional educators who work year-round on planning, curriculum development, and staff training. The staff member–student ratio is 1:5.

MEDICAL CARE

Registered nurses are on duty in the St. Mark's health center 24 hours a day. Physician care is provided by a pediatrics practice minutes from campus and two nearby university teaching hospitals.

COSTS

Program costs for 2004 were $3350 (three-week, residential) and $6395 (six-week, residential). These prices covered tuition, room, full board, books and supplies, and transportation to and from Logan Airport. Day student costs were $1625 (three weeks) and $2995 (six weeks).

FINANCIAL AID

A limited number of partial- to full-tuition merit scholarships are available for those with financial need.

TRANSPORTATION

Exploration meets students at and escorts them to the Logan International Airport in Boston at the beginning and end of each session. There is extensive bus and van transportation provided for day students throughout much of the greater Boston area.

APPLICATION TIMETABLE

Admission is on a rolling basis.

For more information, contact:

Exploration Junior Program
470 Washington Street
P.O. Box 368
Norwood, Massachusetts 02062
781-762-7400
Fax: 781-762-7425
World Wide Web: http://www.explo.org

PARTICIPANT/FAMILY COMMENTS

"I'm not sure where to begin to thank you. Not only did my child learn a lot about the world (the whale watch, Phantom of the Opera, *the courses she attended, etc.), but she came back with so much more confidence and happiness....For the few activities I saw while my daughter was there, the staff seemed to be unbelievably wacky, dedicated, and extremely gifted, which I know helped Jennifer grow."*

EXPLORATION SENIOR PROGRAM

AN INDEPENDENT PROGRAM AT YALE UNIVERSITY

COEDUCATIONAL PRECOLLEGE ENRICHMENT

NEW HAVEN, CONNECTICUT

Type of Program: Academic enrichment
Participants: Coeducational; students entering grades 10–12
Enrollment: Each session: 600 residential and 50 day students
Program Dates: Two 3-week sessions. Students may stay for one or two sessions. First session: June 26 to July 16, 2005; second session: July 17 to August 6, 2005
Heads of Program: Bill Clough, M.A., M.Ed., Head of Program. Arnie Singal, B.A., S.M., J.D., and Ann Singal, B.A., M.Ed., Executive Directors

LOCATION

With Yale at its center and five additional colleges and universities, New Haven, Connecticut, is a vibrant college town. Yale's Old Campus is located in the heart of the "Elm City," nestled between tree-lined rows of boutiques, restaurants, theaters, and museums. As the cultural capital of Connecticut, New Haven combines the richness of a small city with the comforts of a college town. Its location between New York City and Boston makes New Haven the perfect departure point for trips into New York and throughout New England.

BACKGROUND AND PHILOSOPHY

Founded in 1975, the Senior Program prepares high school students for the challenges of college life by giving students the opportunity to explore innovative academic courses and extracurricular activities on the campus of one of the nation's finest universities. Students at the Senior Program learn to live as a part of a talented, diverse, and international student body as they explore their unique interests and passions. Because academics at Exploration are ungraded, students are free to take risks and are encouraged to explore subjects not typically offered in a high school environment. Outside the classroom, students participate in a number of engaging activities, athletics, special events, and trips that help frame a total summer experience of learning and exploration.

PROGRAM OFFERINGS

Academic The Senior Program allows students to tailor their academic experience to best fit their needs. For the mornings, students may choose to enroll in two enrichment courses or one college seminar. The enrichment courses are free of grades and competitive pressures and aim to maximize student involvement through discussion and debate as well as small group and independent work. More than eighty courses are offered, including architecture, acting and directing, model U.N., public speaking, neuroscience, environmental science, creative writing, modern dance, constitutional law, sports marketing, international politics, and abnormal psychology. Enrichment courses are open to students entering grades 10, 11, and 12.

Students entering grades 11 and 12 have the option of challenging themselves with a three-week college seminar. Taught by a college or university faculty member, the seminars give students the opportunity to engage academic material in more depth and offer the students a college-level experience. Seminar subjects range from psychology and civil rights to college writing.

In the afternoon, students may pursue a range of interests by taking 3 one-week mini-courses, featuring everything from athletic clinics, such as field hockey and crew, to academic explorations, such as engineering and photography. Students interested in preparing for academic testing may use the afternoon to enroll in a three-week Princeton Review course.

College Preparation Program Beyond the invaluable experience of living on a college campus, the Senior Program offers a variety of options for students looking for help with the college selection and admissions process. Exploration hosts a college fair, and many organized activities and discussions are focused on the college experience. Students can tour colleges in the Northeast with staff members who can provide an insider's perspective about campus life. College seminars let students challenge themselves with college-level work taught by visiting faculty members, and Princeton Review classes can help students prepare for PSAT and SAT I exams. In addition, the Senior Program offers an all-day workshop to help students prepare for college admissions. Senior Program staff members—who are current students and graduates of schools such as Yale, Brown, NYU, Stanford, Harvard, Amherst, and Oberlin—are also excellent resources for students with questions about the college experience.

International Student Program Exploration welcomes international students with an intermediate-level of English proficiency. Many international students with strong English skills enroll in regular Exploration courses. Other students choose English as a second language (ESL) instruction for one or both course periods.

ENROLLMENT

One of the great strengths of the Senior Program is that its students come from all over the world and from a variety of racial, ethnic, and socioeconomic backgrounds. A typical summer includes students from more than forty states and forty countries; 15–20 percent of the Senior Program's participants are international students.

EXTRA OPPORTUNITIES AND ACTIVITIES

Extracurricular Activities and Athletics In addition to academic courses, many organized activities and athletics are offered each day, including theater, soccer, basketball, poetry readings, community service, printmaking, Ultimate Frisbee, fitness workouts, painting, debates, squash, improvisational comedy, drawing, discussions, volleyball, and swimming.

Sports Clinics Sports clinics provide an opportunity for Senior Program students to receive personalized, skills-based instruction from some of Yale University's top coaches. Taught in Yale's premier athletic facilities, all sports clinics are coed and are designed to accommodate students of varying ability levels. Sports clinic offerings include basketball, crew, field hockey, tennis, volleyball, softball, and squash.

Trips Because Yale is centrally located between Boston and New York City, students have the opportunity to explore much of New England and the Northeastern Seaboard. Each session, students may choose from more than fifty organized trips. Destinations have included Broadway shows; white-water rafting; Mets and Yankees baseball; Boston Symphony Orchestra at Tanglewood; NBC Studios Tour; the mansions of Newport, Rhode Island; college tours; the Guggenheim Museum; Greenwich Village and SoHo; and more. The Senior Program also offers special overnight trips to Boston, Philadelphia, and Washington, D.C.

Guest Speakers The Senior Program Speaker Series is an entertaining and intimate opportunity for students to converse with extraordinary guests from a broad spectrum of disciplines and backgrounds. Past speakers have included Ralph Elliott, a former counsel to the Republican Party and current First Amendment lawyer; Jean Kilbourne, an internationally renowned lecturer on issues in advertising, including alcohol and tobacco advertising and the image of women; Travis Roy, a former star athlete and current quadriplegic, who talks and writes about living with a disability; Lisa Gossels, an Emmy Award-winning documentarian; and Mark Synnott, an adventurer and author who has climbed many of the world's highest peaks.

Main Events Each evening, the Senior Program sponsors a main event. Main events feature anything from professional performers and special off-campus trips to staff-led events and student dances. Past main events have included the ska band Skavoovie, the dance troupe Phunk Phenomenon, student open mike night, theater performances *Mask Man* and *Mother/Son,* carnival nights, lip-synchs, and dance club night at Toad's Place.

FACILITIES

Senior Program students live in the same Old Campus dormitories as first-year students at Yale University. The Old Campus features computer labs with T1 Internet connections and a spacious lawn for studying, playing Frisbee, and enjoying evening concerts. Students eat in Commons, the dining hall used by Yale freshmen, and have access to Yale's many world-class academic and athletic facilities. Highlights include Sterling Memorial Library's undergraduate reading and research areas; Yale drama, law, and art school facilities; science laboratories; the Peabody Museum, Yale Art Gallery, and British Art Center; more than 100 acres of outdoor playing fields; the Yale tennis complex; and Payne Whitney gym, the largest indoor athletic center in the world, featuring air-conditioned basketball and volleyball courts, swimming pools, and a state-of-the-art fitness center.

STAFF

Each year, Exploration interviews several hundred individuals from the nation's top colleges and graduate programs. Faculty and staff members are exceptionally talented, creative, and responsible. They are superb role models. Supporting the summer staff is a team of highly experienced professional educators who work year-round on program planning, curriculum development, and staff training. Exploration is proud of the fact that college seminar professors live on campus so that students see them not only in the classroom but also get to know them at meals and other times. The student-to-staff ratio is approximately 7:1.

MEDICAL CARE

Registered nurses are on duty in the residential quad from 8 a.m. to 11 p.m. Monday through Friday and 8 a.m. to 8 p.m. Saturday and Sunday, after which students are referred to the nurses and physicians at Yale University Health Services.

COSTS

Residential student costs for 2004 were $3550 (one session) and $6795 (two sessions). These prices covered tuition, room, full board, books, supplies, and some trips. Day student costs were $1725 (one session) and $3195 (two sessions).

FINANCIAL AID

A limited number of partial to full tuition merit scholarships are available for those with financial need.

TRANSPORTATION

Exploration meets students at, and escorts them to, Bradley International Airport in Hartford, Connecticut, at the beginning and end of each session. The Senior Program also provides a free shuttle bus to and from Union Station in New Haven each morning and early evening.

APPLICATION TIMETABLE

Admission is on a rolling basis. Early application is encouraged. There is no application fee; however, a deposit (refundable until March 1) is required with the application to hold a student's space.

FOR MORE INFORMATION, CONTACT:

Exploration Senior Program
470 Washington Street
P.O. Box 368
Norwood, Massachusetts 02062
781-762-7400
Fax: 781-762-7425
World Wide Web: http://www.explo.org

THE FESSENDEN SCHOOL

ESL SUMMER PROGRAM

WEST NEWTON, MASSACHUSETTS

Type of Program: Total immersion English as a second language, international residential living
Participants: Coeducational, ages 10–15
Enrollment: 45
Program Dates: June 26 to July 30

LOCATION

The Fessenden School, established in 1903, is located on a beautiful 41-acre campus just 12 miles from the historic and cultural center of Boston.

BACKGROUND AND PHILOSOPHY

The five-week Fessenden English as a Second Language (ESL) Summer Program has had more than twenty-five countries represented since its inception in 1992. What makes the Fessenden ESL Summer Program so special is its small size, personal attention, blend of academics, cultural interactions, language projects, travel experiences, summer camp activities, and total language immersion. Students attend academic classes, use the English language in a variety of projects and enrichment classes, play together in the pool and on the athletic fields, travel to New York City, camp in the woods of Maine, and learn how to work and live in a global society. Students use their English language skills while learning to work as a team. The School places a strong emphasis upon respect for the individual and cultural differences that each student brings to the community.

Community life at the Fessenden ESL Summer Program is also an integral part of the Fessenden experience. Children of the same gender and similar age groups but different nationalities live together in the same dormitory. Great friendships develop from living in a multinational, multilingual environment using English as a common language. Family-style dining encourages English language development, while students sample American and international cuisine.

PROGRAM OFFERINGS

The Language Classroom All morning classes emphasize the four basic skills of listening, speaking, reading, and writing. Classes taught by Fessenden's team of language specialists are small enough to offer consistent individual attention to each student. The student to teacher ratio is 5:1. The Summer ESL Program's multilevel curriculum serves to enhance the students' understanding of cultural events, excursions, and weekend trips while helping them to demonstrate progressively greater competence in English.

The academic objective of Fessenden's Summer ESL Program is to make learning English language skills a positive and valuable experience for each student regardless of his or her prior knowledge of English. Students are placed in small classes based on the results of comprehensive language assessments. Fessenden offers many levels of language instruction ranging from beginning to advanced. Teachers take into consideration each student's linguistic needs when planning lessons. The girls and boys leave the program with greatly improved skills in speaking, listening, writing, and reading English.

Afternoon Enrichment Program Students also gain English skills while participating in less formal but carefully planned afternoon activities. These activities include computer skills, language lab, arts and crafts, hands-on science, video production, and International Day.

The purpose of the enrichment program is to integrate English language learning into real-life situations as well as to have fun in a relaxing and creative setting. Teachers provide situations that require students to use English while gaining knowledge and skill in diverse activities.

EXTRA OPPORTUNITIES AND ACTIVITIES

The Summer ESL Program offers a wide variety of experiences through field trips and weekend excursions. Two of the biggest "traveling classrooms" are the four-day trip to New York City and the four-day camping trip in the woods of Maine. Other events include trips to historic downtown Boston, a July 4 Independence Day celebration, barbecues, fireworks, a Boston Red Sox baseball game, the Big Apple Circus, a whale watch, a trip to the beach, and International Day presentations.

COSTS

For 2005, the total cost of the five-week program is $5600. The cost of the program includes all class and material fees, weekend and evening trips, meals, transportation, laundry service, and required health insurance. Personal spending money is not included in the cost of the program. The School recommends $300 in personal spending money be kept in an account for each student by the director.

APPLICATION TIMETABLE

Interested applicants and their families should contact the Fessenden School Summer ESL Program at the address, phone numbers, or Web site listed in the Contact section of this description. Applicants who access the School's Web site should select "summer."

For more information, contact:

Mark Hansen
Director of the Fessenden ESL Summer Program
250 Waltham Street
West Newton, Massachusetts 02465
617-928-8887 or 617-630-2300
Fax: 617-928-8888
E-mail: esl@fessenden.org
World Wide Web: http://www.fessenden.org

FISHBURNE MILITARY SCHOOL

SUMMER SESSION

WAYNESBORO, VIRGINIA

Type of Program: Academic, nonmilitary
Participants: Boys boarding and day, grades 7–12
Enrollment: 100
Program Dates: June 27 to July 31
Head of Program: Colonel William Alexander.

LOCATION

The Fishburne Military School campus overlooks the city of Waynesboro in the Shenandoah Valley of Virginia. Waynesboro is located between Staunton and Charlottesville, just off Interstate Highways 64 and 81. It is approximately 2½ hours southwest of Washington, D.C., by automobile and a 1½-hour drive west of Richmond, Virginia. The scenic Skyline Drive and Blue Ridge Parkway are only minutes away, as are many points of historical and cultural interest such as Monticello, the University of Virginia at Charlottesville, and sites of Civil War encounters.

BACKGROUND AND PHILOSOPHY

The nonmilitary academic Summer Session is designed to provide each student with a high-quality education in an atmosphere that offers a high degree of individual attention and a well-rounded program of extracurricular activities. Both new and repeat work are offered to students in grades 7–12. Students who anticipate difficult academic requirements for which they feel unprepared or students who failed academic work and wish to make up the work for credit attend the five-week session. Students who want to broaden their education by taking enrichment work in new areas or seniors who need 2 additional credits for graduation also attend.

Most students enroll in two courses. Students may take one or two repeat subjects, one repeat and one new subject, or one new subject. Every student has at least 2 hours of supervised study each evening. Supervision is provided by the same instructors who teach classes during the regular school day. Therefore, instruction carries over into evening lesson preparation.

PROGRAM OFFERINGS

Fishburne offers new or repeat summer work in four subject areas: English, mathematics, science, and social studies. As demand warrants, a noncredit SAT I preparation course for sophomores and juniors and repeat-only courses in Spanish I and chemistry are offered. Because the School's goal is to provide each student with high-quality educational instruction in an environment that provides individual attention and participation, classes are limited in size. The Fishburne Summer Session achieves this goal with a 7:1 student-teacher ratio.

All summer students receive instruction in fundamental study techniques at the beginning of the session. Instruction covers test taking, note taking, writing, critical thinking, and time management. To assist in time management and general organizational skills, each student is required to keep an assignment notebook, which is subject to random checks by the classroom teacher or by the study hall monitor. Learning skills and proper study habits are reinforced in all academic activities.

A faculty adviser system ensures the success of each summer student. Each adviser is expected to establish a close rapport with his student and to assist in everything from adjusting to the new program and being away from home to developing proper study skills. Parents receive communication every other week from their child's adviser, and communication from the parent is always welcome.

DAILY SCHEDULE

7:00	Wake-up
7:30	Breakfast
8:45	First period
9:50	Second period
10:55	Third period
12:00	Fourth period
1:05	Lunch
2:00	Fifth period
3:05	Sixth period
4:30	Mandatory activities
6:00	Dinner
7:30–8:20	Study hall
8:30–9:20	Study hall
10:30	Lights-out

EXTRA OPPORTUNITIES AND ACTIVITIES

Ample time is scheduled during the daily academic schedule and on weekends for free time. Even though Fishburne's Summer Session has a limited enrollment, all School facilities are open to students. These facilities include the library and computer center, the student store, the student lounge, the rifle range (with supervision), the gymnasium and weight room, and all outdoor athletic facilities. Supervised activities follow classes each day. These may include basketball, lacrosse, soccer, swimming, volleyball, weight training, or tennis. Martial arts and golf clinics, as well as drivers' education, are available at an additional cost. Weekend chaperoned trips to Kings Dominion, Busch Gardens, and Water Country are scheduled, and the cost is included in the boarding student fee.

ENROLLMENT

The Fishburne Summer Session enrollment is limited to 100 students. While most are boarding students, there is traditionally a small day-student population. Students come from as many as twenty-four states and twelve different countries.

FACILITIES

Fishburne Military School is situated on a hill overlooking the town of Waynesboro, Virginia. The 10-acre campus includes an Administration Building, containing five classrooms, a cadet store, the gymnasium, and faculty offices; the Barracks Building, housing student rooms, an infirmary, a cadet lounge, two science laboratories, and air-conditioned classrooms; a library offering numerous publications and serving as the School's student-accessible computer center, where, under the supervision of library personnel, students may access the Internet or check their personal e-mail messages from family and friends; and a weight training and athletic facility. A dining facility and auditorium complete the indoor facilities. Outdoor facilities include an athletic field and tennis, volleyball, and basketball courts. The Fishburne Military School campus is listed on the Virginia Register of Historic Landmarks and the National Register of Historic Places.

STAFF

Classes during the Summer Session are taught by the same instructors who comprise the faculty for the School's regular session. Each instructor is a professional who meets the requirements of the Southern Association of Schools and Colleges and the Virginia Association of Independent Schools. Under the guidance of the Headmaster and Commandant, all students are expected to show proper respect to School personnel and conduct themselves in a respectable manner.

MEDICAL CARE

The School's infirmary is staffed by 3 qualified medical professionals, one of whom is on campus between 7 a.m. and 7 p.m. and on call at other times. The newly constructed Augusta Medical Center is within 15 minutes of the School, and the Waynesboro First Aide Crew is located only 5 minutes away.

Students must have up-to-date medical and exam records on file prior to the opening of the session. Family insurance forms should be given to the medical staff before or during registration.

RELIGIOUS LIFE

Although Fishburne is nonsectarian, it does expect its students to attend the church of their choice during the regular weekly worship service. The city of Waynesboro and its environs provide more than fifty churches of various faiths.

COSTS

The 2004 fee for boarding students was $2950. This fee included academic instruction, books, laboratory fees, weekend trips, normal medical care in the School infirmary, living quarters, meals, laundry, and use of all School facilities. The fee did not include the student's weekly allowance, professional services of doctors (if required), the cost of transportation to and from the School, or the cost of pens, pencils, paper, and notebooks. There is an application fee of $50 for new students. Fees must be paid in full on the opening day of the Summer Session.

TRANSPORTATION

The closest airports are the Shenandoah Valley Airport and the Charlottesville-Albemarle Airport. Amtrak offers service to Charlottesville and Staunton.

APPLICATION TIMETABLE

Applications to the Fishburne Military School Summer Session are welcome at any time throughout the year. The applicant should submit the completed application and its fee and complete academic and testing records. Two letters of recommendation, one of which should be from a school official, are required. A visit prior to the opening of the Summer Session is recommended. It is the policy of Fishburne Military School to review and act on applications for admission on a nondiscriminatory basis without regard to race, creed, national origin, or sex.

For more information, contact:

Captain Carl V. Lambert, FMS '90
Fishburne Military School
P.O. Box 988E
Waynesboro, Virginia 22980
540-946-7703
800-946-7773 (toll-free)
Fax: 540-946-7738
E-mail: lambert@fishburne.org
World Wide Web: http://www.fishburne.org

FLS INTERNATIONAL

FLS LANGUAGE CENTERS STUDY TOURS

PASADENA, CALIFORNIA

Type of Program: ESL/TOEFL preparation
Participants: International students
Enrollment: More than 2,000
Program Dates: Year-round; sessions begin every four weeks
Head of Program: Francine Forman-Swain, President

LOCATION

FLS has six year-round language centers located in southern California, Nevada, Massachusetts, and Pennsylvania. The centers are near some of the most popular destinations in the world for students and tourists alike. FLS locations are housed on college campuses, allowing students access to such facilities as language labs, computer labs, libraries, and athletic facilities. In addition, each program is filled with optional excursions to dozens of exciting local attractions, offering countless opportunities for educational and cultural enrichment.

Located in the foothills of the San Gabriel Mountains, Citrus College offers a great combination of suburban comfort and safety along with access to all of the attractions and cultural life of the Los Angeles area. Lock Haven University is located in the all-American small town of Lock Haven, Pennsylvania, on the historic East Coast of the United States. Located 30 minutes north of San Diego, California, MiraCosta College is near the beautiful southern California coastline. Dean College is located in Franklin, Massachusetts, a short train ride from Boston. Oxnard College sits on the beautiful southern California coastline. Swimming, surfing, horseback riding, and tanning are popular after-school activities. Located in the thriving community of Las Vegas, the College of Southern Nevada reflects the optimistic urban spirit of this quickly growing city.

Study tours are also offered through California State University at Northridge and California Polytechnic University at Pomona.

BACKGROUND AND PHILOSOPHY

FLS International was founded in 1987 as FLS Language Centers. In the beginning, FLS opened and operated only two classrooms in a small neighborhood school for English instruction. From these modest beginnings, FLS has experienced tremendous and steady growth, now teaching students and operating programs on many campuses. FLS also has special programs in California and New York. Since its inception, FLS has taught more than 10,000 students. Its expansion and wider scope of program offerings are now reflected in its new name—FLS International.

PROGRAM OFFERINGS

FLS specializes in providing English-language programs to nonnative speakers. The FLS program teaches students to speak English in the same way they learned to speak their native language—through listening, speaking, and doing. Professional language specialists have designed courses at FLS to meet the needs of students at every level of proficiency. FLS International Centers have met the educational needs of Japanese stockbrokers, Russian educators, Colombian physicians, international lawyers, Indonesian basketball players, Taiwanese real estate brokers, Brazilian hotel managers, and TV and film professionals.

Study tours are a great opportunity for students to enjoy themselves and learn something as well. Field trips allow students to practice English with native speakers in relaxed, everyday situations. All study tour programs include exciting escorted trips to famous museums, theaters, restaurants, and amusement parks. In addition to these excursions, all participants are able to join other optional outings at an additional price.

FLS also offers university study tours at beautiful locations. At prestigious college campuses across the United States, students study together in safe, suburban environments. Programs include 17.5 hours of English class per week, excursions, and either a homestay with an American family or accommodations in a comfortable college dormitory. Full access to all campus facilities allows participants to live like a typical American university student.

ENROLLMENT

FLS International has more than 2,000 students enrolled across seven campuses.

FACILITIES

Citrus College offers students a language lab, a computer lab, a library, the Robert D. Hough Performing Arts Center, a TV and radio technology center, a cafeteria, a swimming pool, a gymnasium, tennis courts, a golf driving range, and a child-care center. Citrus College has just added a new state-of-the-art video and audio recording studio. At Dean College, students have access to a language lab, computer labs, a library, a performing arts center, the radio station WGAO, a fitness center, a pool, and tennis courts. Lock Haven University houses the Robinson Hall Learning Center, an FM radio station, a TV studio, a computing center, a psychology lab, the Model United Nations auditorium, the Stevenson Library, and the John Sloan Fine Arts Center. MiraCosta College includes a language lab, a computer lab, a library, a cafeteria, a medical center, and a recreational center. At Oxnard College, students have a library, a learning center, a listening lab, a computer lab, a media center, a child development center, and a television station.

STAFF

FLS provides full-time student advisers who are available to help students with academic and personal concerns. The FLS student adviser assists students in making their adjustment to the United States as quickly, easily, and pleasantly as possible. The student adviser also helps students select and apply to colleges and universities that best fit their academic goals.

COSTS

Interested students should contact FLS directly for specific study tour fees.

TRANSPORTATION

Many apartment complexes are located within walking distance of FLS language centers. Hotels located near the FLS centers offer convenient housing for those who are staying only a short time.

APPLICATION TIMETABLE

FLS offers starting dates every four weeks. Students should submit their applications at least two weeks before the desired starting date (three weeks if a letter of conditional acceptance is required). To apply, students should fill out the application form online or print it out and mail it to the FLS Admissions Office (same address as the FLS International Administrative Offices listed in the Contact section). Applicants should include the proper payment and arrange to have a financial statement—an affidavit or financial guarantee from a financial institution, government, or sponsor that shows sufficient financial resources for the intended term from the applicant or parent—sent to FLS.

For more information, contact:

FLS International Administrative Offices
101 East Green Street, Suite 14
Pasadena, California 91105
626-795-2912
Fax: 626-795-5564
E-mail: info@fls.net
World Wide Web: http://www.fls.net

FUTURE LEADER CAMP AT NORWICH UNIVERSITY

CHALLENGE—TEAMWORK—ADVENTURE

NORTHFIELD, VERMONT

Type of Program: Leadership development
Participants: Coeducational, students who have completed grades 9, 10, and 11 and are in good academic standing
Enrollment: Limited to 80 per session
Program Dates: Two 2-week sessions in July
Head of Program: Lieutenant Colonel "Skip" Davison, Director of Future Leader Camp

LOCATION

Future Leader Camp (FLC) is conducted at Norwich University, which is located in the heart of the Green Mountains of Vermont right in the middle of ski country. The campus is located in the small town of Northfield, 10 miles south of the state capital of Montpelier and 50 miles from Burlington, the largest city in Vermont. Both Montpelier and Burlington are cultural centers for the arts and the Burlington International Airport is within an hour's drive. Vermont is world-renowned as one of America's most beautiful states, and some of the nation's most popular ski resorts, such as Stowe, Sugarbush, and Killington, are located within an hour's drive. Vermont is an outdoor paradise for those who like rock climbing, hiking, camping, mountain biking, swimming, canoeing, kayaking, fishing, and more. In addition, the cities of Boston and Montreal are only a 3-hour drive from the campus.

BACKGROUND AND PHILOSOPHY

FLC is designed for students who wish to develop leadership skills or are already serving in leadership positions within their school, community, or place of employment. The camp staff members take participants to the next level of leadership development while providing a fun and worthwhile camp experience.

Using a combination of adventure training, group discussions, and hands-on training, the goal of FLC is to instill the basic principles of small-group leadership techniques, ethics, effective communications, problem solving, and teamwork, while developing in each participant a sense of confidence, self-respect, and self-discipline. The leadership philosophy emanates from Director of Recruitment Lt. Col. "Skip" Davison, who believes that "leadership is an art...acquired over time...by those with the strength of character...to master its form."

Training includes physical fitness, rappelling, high ropes, climbing wall, rifle range, land navigation, leadership reaction course, wilderness and water survival, paintball, rock climbing, hiking, rope bridging, and a three-day overnight Challenge Course.

Camp participants are issued uniforms as part of the program to facilitate training and create an atmosphere of camaraderie. FLC is not a military boot-camp and only those with demonstrated leadership potential and proven academic success need apply. The professional staff members are trained and qualified to instruct all courses taught.

PROGRAM OFFERINGS

The first phase of Future Leader Camp begins with daily instruction in rappelling, rope bridging, climbing and survival techniques, paintball, rifle range, water survival, and physical fitness training. Physical fitness training is conducted by ability groups and instructs participants in how to properly exercise. Each evening, group discussion are held. Topics include effective communications and its use in the fine art of making peanut butter and jelly sandwiches, examining leadership by film, how to conduct briefings and coordinate events, and becoming CPR certified. The next phase requires participants to face two physical challenges, which are hiking to the top of Camels Hump, one of Vermont's many mountains, and then climbing and rappelling at Dear Leap Rock, one of Vermont's many cliff faces. Phase three finds participants on a three-day "in the woods" overnight field exercise, in which the team's individual and collective skills are put to the test. The exercise includes extensive wilderness survival skills training and land navigation.

All participants are required to hold the position of Team Leader at least once during the camp. The position is rotated daily and each participant receives a performance evaluation as Team Leader from his or her counselor. From the beginning, teams are assigned unscheduled training requirements. Teams are required to make a team guidon (flag) and prepare themselves for a drill competition and team skit. There is no time on the training schedule to prepare for these events. Teams have to work together, find the time, and take the initiative.

Finally, the camp ends with a drill competition and Team Olympics. The drill competition measures the team's ability to work together as a unit and define the group as participants of FLC. The Team Olympics includes such events as the Tired Relay, the Litter Press, the Run-Dodge and Jump, and Log Toss. The last day is one of rest and relaxation at Lake Elmore, one of Vermont's most beautiful lakes for a day of swimming, canoeing, kayaking, hiking, and some really good chow.

ENROLLMENT

Camp is conducted in two sessions. Enrollment is limited to the first 80 qualified applicants. Interested individuals must submit an application, a letter of recommendation, and a medical form to be considered. The camp is open to both boys and girls who have completed grades 9, 10, or 11 and are in good academic standing.

DAILY SCHEDULE

First call is at 5:30 a.m., followed by physical fitness training the first week from 6 to 7. During the first week, there are morning, afternoon, and evening train-

ing sessions. Evenings are generally reserved for group discussions or recreational activities. The training schedule is full and participants are kept busy from sunup to sundown. Midweek and week two are filled with training events that last all day and the schedule changes from day to day. Lights go out by 10 p.m. except during the overnight field exercise.

EXTRA OPPORTUNITIES AND ACTIVITIES

During the course, all participants earn their CPR certification. Those who arrive already certified are asked to assist the instructor and receive appropriate recognition for their assistance.

FACILITIES

Participants stay in dorm rooms on campus and dine in the university's dining facility. Participants must supply their own linen and washing machines are available in the dorms. The dining facility is operated by SODEXHO food service and meals are served cafeteria style, offering a wide variety of choices. The university campus consists of 1,200 acres and has numerous athletic and classroom facilities.

STAFF

The director is a full-time employee of Norwich University and is retired from the military with more than thirty years of experience working with young people. The camp training officer is also a full-time employee and a graduate of Norwich University. The training officer is a certified CPR instructor and is qualified to oversee all training events. Camp counselors are junior and senior cadets who attend Norwich University. They must apply and be interviewed for the counselor positions. Physical fitness instructors are active duty Marine sergeants attending the university to earn their degree and become commissioned officers. In addition, a number of faculty and staff members from the university contribute to training and classes.

MEDICAL CARE

All staff members and counselors are CPR certified. An EMT first responder is on call during all training. Green Mountain Medical Clinic is located across the street from the university and provides basic health care. Central Vermont Hospital is located less than 10 miles from the campus.

RELIGIOUS LIFE

Due to a tightly packed training schedule, times to attend services during the two-week camp cannot be provided.

COSTS

The camp costs $1325. This includes room, meals, uniforms, and all camp activities.

FINANCIAL AID

Financial aid is available for need-based families. Applicants should contact the Future Leader Camp office for additional information.

TRANSPORTATION

Participants provide their own transportation to the camp. Included with every information packet is a travel brochure outlining how to get to Vermont by air, train, bus, or privately owned vehicle. The Burlington International Airport (BTV) is located an hour from the campus in Burlington, Vermont. The bus and train station are located in Montpelier, Vermont, only 10 miles from the campus. Arrangements will be made to have participants who arrive by air, train, or bus picked up and dropped off. Participants who arrive by privately owned vehicle will be provided with a parking pass.

APPLICATION TIMETABLE

The office begins accepting applications January 1. Applications are submitted with a letter of recommendation, medical form, and $25 nonrefundable application fee. A $250 nonrefundable deposit must be received upon acceptance to guarantee the applicants seat in the camp and order their uniforms. The entire cost of the camp is due by June 1, unless the family has made other arrangements with the camp director.

FOR MORE INFORMATION, CONTACT:

Future Leader Camp at Norwich University
27 I. D. White Avenue
Northfield, Vermont 05663
802-485-2531
Fax: 802-485-2739
E-mail: flc@norwich.edu
World Wide Web: http://www.norwich.edu/flc

GEORGETOWN UNIVERSITY

HIGH SCHOOL PROGRAMS

WASHINGTON, D.C.

Type of Program: Academic enrichment and college preparation
Participants: Coeducational, grades 10–12, depending upon program
Enrollment: 125–150
Program Dates: College Prep Program, one 5-week session in June and July; Summer College for High School Juniors, two 5-week sessions, June to July and July to August; International Relations Program, one week in July
Head of Programs: Emma Harrington, Director, Special Programs

LOCATION

The programs take place on the Georgetown University campus in Washington, D.C. Participants take advantage of the cultural, recreational, and educational opportunities abounding in the nation's capital.

PROGRAM OFFERINGS

College Prep Program This program offers a series of classes for students wishing to prepare for college-level study. Targeted for students who have completed their sophomore year in high school, these courses are designed to promote concrete improvement in the basic subject areas of English, math, and college research/study skills (sections for students whose first language is not English are offered). In all aspects of instruction the importance of critical thinking is underscored.

Course work is intensive both in and out of class. Students can expect 45 minutes to an hour of homework daily per hour of class instruction. At the start of the program diagnostic tests are administered to determine the course level best suited to the needs of the student. On Fridays, students get a chance to experience and master college-level note-taking skills. Guest professors from departments such as English, philosophy, history, or government deliver lectures and conduct question-and-answer dialogues with the students. Study skills teachers provide feedback on students' lecture notes. Friday morning seminars end with presentations and workshops on college applications and admissions.

Summer College for High School Juniors Outstanding high school students are offered the opportunity to expand their studies with college courses taken in an intensive yet supportive college environment. Juniors live on campus and attend classes with undergraduate Georgetown students. A limited number of students are accepted for each session.

A student enrolls in one or two courses appropriate to his or her interests, background, and previous academic achievement. Courses include business administration, biology, computer science, economics, English, fine arts, government, history, languages, math, philosophy, physics, psychology, sociology, and theology. A typical full-time course load for a five-week session is 6 credits. This requires the student to spend about 3 hours every day in class and several more hours studying outside the classroom. Students may enroll for both sessions with the approval of the director.

To be admitted into the program, students must have completed their junior year by June 2004 with a B average or better. Nonnative speakers of English must send evidence of sufficient English language ability (TOEFL, CELT, ALIGU, or other standardized test scores).

International Relations Program This program provides an opportunity for high school students to acquire intercultural awareness through an exploration of the complex nature of international relations and the ethical implications of foreign-policy decisions. The program is designed to take advantage of Georgetown University's resources as a leading center of international studies located in the nation's capital. This brief but intensive program combines lectures by members of Georgetown's faculty and distinguished guest speakers; visits to governmental departments, agencies, or international organizations; small-group discussions; and an international crisis simulation. This approach does not offer simple answers to the complex issues but rather develops conceptual tools for understanding them.

ENROLLMENT

Georgetown University's summer programs enroll students from across the United States and from several other countries.

EXTRA OPPORTUNITIES AND ACTIVITIES

Many trips and activities are organized by program counselors, including area sightseeing and cultural and sports events. Students are also encouraged to explore Washington, D.C., independently.

FACILITIES

In addition to the university dormitories for residential participants, all students have access to the university library and to the sports/gym complex.

STAFF

Courses are taught by Georgetown University summer sessions faculty members, and there is a full-time staff of trained counselors (university undergraduates), who live in the dormitories.

COSTS

For the 2004 College Prep Program, tuition is $2165. Housing costs $1540 for an air-conditioned double room, and food is estimated at $625. Pay-as-you-go dining is also available. Provisions should be made for approximately $75 per course for books.

For the Summer College for High School Juniors, tuition in 2004 is $780 per credit. Housing costs $1290 for an air-conditioned double room, and food is estimated at $625, available on either a board plan or a pay-as-you-go basis. Books and personal expenses are not included.

Tuition, room, board, and selected recreational activities for the International Relations Program in 2004 costs $1255 for resident students; commuting students pay $850.

FINANCIAL AID

A limited number of partial tuition scholarships are available for the College Prep Program and the Summer College for High School Juniors.

APPLICATION TIMETABLE

Inquiries are welcome in the fall for the following summer; applications are available in January. Interested students may request a catalog by sending an e-mail to sscespecialprograms@georgetown.edu.

For more information, contact:

Special Programs
School for Summer and Continuing Education
Georgetown University
Box 571010
Washington, D.C. 20057-1010
202-687-5832 or 5719
Fax: 202-687-8954
E-mail: harringe@georgetown.edu
World Wide Web: http://www.georgetown.edu/ssce/

THE GEORGE WASHINGTON UNIVERSITY SUMMER SCHOLARS PRECOLLEGE PROGRAM

THE GEORGE WASHINGTON UNIVERSITY WASHINGTON DC

EXPERIENCE GW! DISCOVER D.C.!

WASHINGTON, D.C.

Type of Program: Academic courses and precollege enrichment program
Participants: Coeducational, rising seniors
Enrollment: 60 students
Program Dates: Six weeks, early July to mid-August
Head of Program: Georgette Edmondson-Wright, Director

LOCATION

Participants in The George Washington University (GW) Summer Scholars Precollege Program experience two distinctly different collegiate environments during their stay in the nation's capital. Classes are held at the Foggy Bottom campus, located in the heart of the city and surrounded by a wealth of cultural and educational resources. Situated among abundant examples of important American architecture, from grand monuments and historical row houses to commanding federal buildings, the Foggy Bottom campus is an ideal place to study and explore the nation's history and the inner workings of government organizations that shape national and international policy.

Participants reside 3 miles from the Foggy Bottom campus at GW's Mount Vernon campus in northwest Washington, D.C., nestled in a peaceful, wooded, residential neighborhood and in proximity to parks and biking and hiking trails. A 15-minute shuttle ride links the two campuses and offers a view of the Potomac waterfront and the historic Watergate Hotel. Both campuses are a short distance from Washington, D.C.'s world-class attractions and historical sites, allowing for a variety of exciting excursions to area shops, cafes, restaurants, and monuments.

BACKGROUND AND PHILOSOPHY

The GW Summer Scholars Program enables high school juniors (who are approaching their senior year) to preview an authentic college experience. The six-week residential program offers a unique opportunity for participants to accelerate their college career and earn credit in a college-level course at a top-ranked university. In addition to complete integration in an intensive course with undergraduate students, Summer Scholars participate in the Academic Exploration and Beyond Admissions seminars as well as the Exploring D.C. Through Writing program.

The GW Summer Scholars Program draws upon the wealth of cultural and educational opportunities unique to Washington, D.C., and the greater metropolitan area to expand upon the range of enrichment and recreational activities available to participants. The program introduces students to the experience of independent living, while offering important educational resources and programs that enhance their understanding of college life.

PROGRAM OFFERINGS

The GW Summer Scholars Program is composed of an academic and an enrichment component. The academic component consists of enrollment in one 3-credit hour course that meets four days per week. Course offerings are specially selected from a wide variety of academic disciplines and are taught by University faculty members.

Exploring D.C. Through Writing integrates cultural exploration with the process of writing a college-level paper—developing critical writing and research skills that are applicable to any area of study. Academic Exploration seminars encourage students to explore the range of their academic interests and the variety of specialized learning communities within the university setting.

A practical focus on college readiness is addressed through weekly seminars that range from the college admissions process to career paths, study skills, and research strategies, promoting confidence and self-sufficiency in balancing the academic and social demands of college life. Enrichment opportunities extend beyond the classroom to include the cultural and educational resources of the Washington, D.C., area.

ENROLLMENT

The Summer Scholars Program is a coeducational program that draws upon a diverse group of students from across the nation. Admission is open to high school juniors with a B average or better.

DAILY SCHEDULE

A typical weekday in the Summer Scholars Program begins with breakfast in Ames Dining Hall. After breakfast, students participate in the Exploring D.C. Through Writing program. The remainder of the day is occupied by the course for credit, study time, and a variety of talks and activities offered by the academic departments and learning communities. College study seminars provide students with a forum to reflect on their academic experiences and implement new learning strategies.

On Fridays, students attend Beyond Admissions and learn how to access and evaluate colleges and programs of interest. Students have the option of visiting an area college or exploring the sites. Saturdays include recreational activities, such as touring Baltimore Harbor, paddling the Potomac, or visiting the Kennedy Center of the Performing Arts. On Sundays, students are free to relax, socialize, and study. The schedule is designed so that students have sufficient time for study and recreation.

EXTRA OPPORTUNITIES AND ACTIVITIES

The program's location in Washington, D.C., provides students with a unique opportunity to enjoy the vibrant international and multicultural community of the nation's capital. Students discover that life in Washington, D.C., appeals to every possible interest, such as history, government, the arts, and entertainment. Summer Scholars have the opportunity to go shopping in Georgetown or to enjoy ethnic cuisine in Adams Morgan. Summer Scholars also participate in organized outings to a variety of destinations, such as national and historic sites, the Smithsonian, the Library of Congress, the U.S. Capitol, area universities, and recreational parks.

FACILITIES

Summer Scholars reside on the beautiful grounds of the Mount Vernon campus. Students have access to the campus facilities, including the library, computer labs, swimming pool, tennis courts, and top notch recreational facilities. Students share double rooms on floors that are staffed by a resident adviser. Each room is furnished with beds, dressers, desks, and a microfrige. Rooms are also cable ready and come equipped with phone jacks and Internet access. A community lounge, complete with a kitchen, a TV, and vending machines is available in the residence hall. A computer lab and laundry facilities are also located inside the building. Entrance to the resident hall is secure, and the Mount Vernon campus is gated and staffed with on-site security 24 hours a day.

STAFF

A dedicated, on-site team coordinates the Summer Scholars Program, emphasizing a high degree of individual attention for every student. A full-time director manages the day-to-day activities. Highly trained, live-in resident advisers staff the residence halls and are available to assist students 24 hours a day. Staff members also accompany all planned group activities. The courses are taught by GW faculty members with years of experience teaching students at all levels of learning.

MEDICAL CARE

Although a very safe and healthy summer is anticipated, the GW Summer Scholars staff is prepared to handle emergencies. In the event of an illness or a medical emergency, Student Health Services is staffed and equipped to deal with most routine situations that require medical attention. If a situation requires hospital treatment, program staff members accompany the student to the nearest hospital and parents are immediately contacted.

COSTS

Program costs in 2004 were approximately $5600. This included tuition for a 3-credit hour course, Exploring D.C. Through Writing, Academic Exploration, Beyond Admissions, room, and partial board. Textbooks, notebooks, and supplies are additional costs. Participants should plan to bring spending money for laundry and recreational and incidental expenses.

FINANCIAL AID

Limited need-based scholarship assistance is available for qualified applicants. Students who are applying for need-based scholarship assistance are required to fill out the Summer Scholars Financial Aid Form, detailing the basis for the request, and submit it with their application.

TRANSPORTATION

Leaving on the half hour and operating until 7 p.m., the GW Shuttle links the two campuses with a scenic 15-minute ride down the hill to Foggy Bottom. The Foggy Bottom campus also has its own stop on the D.C. Metro, and both campuses are on Metro bus lines. The Mount Vernon campus is conveniently located near Washington-Dulles International Airport, Reagan National Airport, and Union Station. The Summer Scholars Program is able to provide detailed information about transportation to and from these locations.

APPLICATION TIMETABLE

Applications are accepted on a rolling basis up until late May. Priority consideration is given to early applicants.

For more information, contact:

GW Summer Scholars Program
The George Washington University
2100 Foxhall Road NW
Washington, D.C. 20007
202-242-6802
E-mail: scholars@gwu.edu
World Wide Web: http://www.gwu.edu/summer/scholars

GLOBAL WORKS

SUMMER PROGRAMS

COSTA RICA, FRANCE, ECUADOR AND THE GALAPAGOS ISLANDS, PUERTO RICO, IRELAND, SPAIN, FIJI ISLANDS/ NEW ZEALAND, YUCATAN/MEXICO, PACIFIC NORTHWEST

Type of Program: International travel combining environmental and community service, cultural and language immersion, and outdoor adventure activities
Participants: Coeducational, high school students
Enrollment: 15–25 (depending on program)
Program Dates: Two to four weeks in the summer
Head of Program: Erik Werner, Director/Owner

LOCATION

Global Works summer programs are located all over the world. Students live in places that range from small village homes in the mountains of Fiji to dormitories located just outside of the French Alps. Several Global Works programs offer homestays with families in order to increase language learning and cultural exchange. The Global Works home office is located in State College, Pennsylvania.

BACKGROUND AND PHILOSOPHY

Today's community- and service-minded youths make a difference in the global community as they live with and touch the lives of the people they serve. Days filled with meaningful projects, travel, and exposure to different cultures are rounded out with just the right amount of adventure, fun, and play.

PROGRAM OFFERINGS

Costa Rica: Global Works offers seven 28-day trips to Costa Rica with 15 participants and 3 leaders on each. All seven trips uncover the country's many treasures, from 12,000-foot mountain peaks to lush cloud forests and beautiful, pristine beaches. Service projects represent 60 percent of the experience. In cooperation with local community members, participants build health centers, community centers, school playgrounds, and bridges. They may assist in reforestation, help with conservation projects, or perform similar service. Non-project time is spent white-water rafting, hiking through the cloud forests of Monteverde, swimming at the beach, playing soccer, or visiting new friends. Each trip includes a ten- to twelve-day homestay with a village family. Homestays are carefully arranged, allowing participants to experience different customs, traditions, foods, and to practice their language skills. All but one of these trips is a serious language learning program. All staff members are bilingual.

Fiji Islands: This trip captures the magic of these exotic South Pacific Islands. From the welcoming ceremonies of each village to the environmental- and community-service projects, participants are treated to sun-filled days reminiscent of another time. Traditional Fijian hospitality is unsurpassed. Projects include constructing *bures* (thatched huts), building a tree nursery, developing reforestation zones, and restoring community buildings. Participants truly feel as if they are part of each community. Adventure activities include scuba diving, hiking into dormant volcano craters, and snorkeling through beautiful reefs. Participants experience "island time" and a beautifully different culture.

Puerto Rico: Global Works offers three trips to Puerto Rico. All are focused on service and adventure. One of the trips has an additional focus of language learning and includes a homestay. Projects always meet a community need. Adventure activities include scuba diving, hikes in the rain forest, snorkeling, sea kayaking, swimming, and visits to Old San Juan and Spanish forts.

France: This journey takes students to three different regions of France for service projects and adventure activities. This is also a language program—there are ten- to twelve-day homestays and French is spoken 80 percent of the time. Projects such as castle restoration, construction of educational centers, reforestation, and interpretive trail blazing are cooperatively worked upon by both the local community and Global Works members. When the group is not working on projects, time is spent rock climbing, biking, rafting, hiking, and visiting museums, chateaux, medieval fortresses, and more.

Ireland: The warm hospitality of Irish culture opens its doors to students through community projects. Projects include reforestation, building playgrounds for elementary schools and working with Seeds of Hope. Students participate in kayaking, ropes courses, gaelic football, sightseeing, and numerous other activities centered on outdoor pursuits, all with professional guides. Irish culture is filled with music, writers, warm hospitality, and wit. Western Ireland (where groups spend 90 percent of the trip), quenches the eyes with dramatic landscapes, seaside cliffs, lush green farms, and beautiful mountains.

Ecuador: In geographic and cultural diversity, few countries compare to Ecuador. The Andean highlands, mountain villages, dormant volcanoes, thermal baths, and cloud forest biospheres provide majestic settings for community projects, nature preserve construction, adventure activities, and friendly homestays. Homestays with village friends last ten days and provide a unique opportunity for serious language learning and cultural immersion. Students travel to the Galapagos Islands to see incredible wildlife and help at Parque Nacional and Darwin Stations, which are isolated biological preserves with numerous unique and threatened species. Participants contribute to projects assisting the giant turtles and developing responsible ecotourism.

Mexico-Yucatan: This is a journey through the Yucatan peninsula that most tourists never encounter. Participants sleep in a seventeenth-century Spanish hacienda, work alongside archaeologists on a private excavation, swim in an underground pool or cenote, live and interact with Mayan families, eat home-cooked Mexican meals, learn traditional dances, release sea turtles on the beach, and snorkel on a small rustic island. They also work on meaningful service projects such as building trails and signs in the archaeological reserve Yaxunah, repairing homes damaged by Hurricane Isidore, helping out in a soup kitchen for the elderly, assisting teachers in a camp for Mexican youth, and aiding conservationists in the flamingo and turtle preserve Ria Lagarto.

Pacific Northwest: Participants visit Bellingham, Washington; the San Juan Islands; the Cascade Mountains; and the vibrant city of Seattle. The program is a wonderful blend of environmental service, community service, and adventure activities. The group works with Wolf Hollow Rehabilitation Center in the San Juan Islands. Past activities have included building avian flight cages, holding tanks for baby waterfowl, and rabbit hutches. Participants also work with a day-care group and children of migrant farm workers just outside Bellingham. Activities include rock climbing, hiking, sightseeing, whale watching, and a three-day sea kayaking trip in the San Juan Islands.

Spain: Students are invited on a journey through Spain that combines old world charm; visits to renowned sites; homestays with warm, friendly families; and cultural and language immersion. Projects include working with a self-sustaining community on construction and greenhouse needs. Activities blend water sports, day excursions to the mountains, soccer, sightseeing in Madrid, and day hikes.

ENROLLMENT

Global Works programs are open to participants who are 14 to 18 years old. Some trips require two years of secondary language study in French or Spanish. No special construction skills are needed—just a desire to have fun, participate, and be part of a community.

EXTRA OPPORTUNITIES AND ACTIVITIES

Serious language learning is available on the trips to France, Costa Rica, Puerto Rico, Ecuador, Spain, and Mexico. Global Works also provides certificates of participation after the completion of the program that describe and reflect the service work completed. Students generally receive 40–70 hours of service credit.

FACILITIES

Depending on the day and the trip, students may stay in hostels, university dormitories, lodges in the wilderness, local villagers' homes, or tents on the beach.

STAFF

Skilled, knowledgeable, friendly, mature, and detail-oriented staff members are hired for Global Works programs. Leaders are chosen for their language skills, experience working with youth, flexibility, responsibility, organization, and ability to have fun. The staff-student ratio is 1:5 and each program has an on-site director who works closely with the home base in Pennsylvania.

COSTS

In 2004, tuition ranged from $2950 to $4150 for three to four weeks, depending on the destination. Airfare is additional; a group fare is offered when possible.

TRANSPORTATION

Students are met and returned to designated airports on the opening and closing days of each program. Staff members travel with students on all international trips.

APPLICATION TIMETABLE

A $600 deposit (nonrefundable after March 15, and credited towards tuition) is due at the time of application. Applications are accepted on a rolling basis until programs fill. Most participants apply during the months of January, February, and March.

For more information, contact:

Global Works, Home Office
1113 South Allen Street
State College, Pennsylvania 16801
814-867-7000
Fax: 814-867-2717
E-mail: info@globalworksinc.com
World Wide Web: http://www.globalworksinc.com

GORDON KENT'S NEW ENGLAND TENNIS CAMP 2005

SUMMER CAMP

PAWLING, NEW YORK

Type of Program: Tennis and recreational camp
Participants: Coeducational, ages 9–17
Enrollment: 75 per session
Program Dates: Four 2-week sessions, late June through mid-August
Head of Program: Gordon Kent, Owner/Director

LOCATION

New England Tennis Camp (NETC) takes place on the beautiful campus of the Trinity–Pawling School in Pawling, New York. One of the finest college-prep schools in the eastern United States, Trinity–Pawling—just 70 miles north of New York City—features 165 acres of rolling countryside and picturesque woodlands.

BACKGROUND AND PHILOSOPHY

Campers who enroll in NETC's summer camp receive specialized instruction in tennis from professional and college players while enjoying a wide range of fun-filled activities and social events. Complete and well-designed, the NETC program not only provides comprehensive tennis lessons for each camper but also instills above all a genuine love for the game and respect for the ideals of good sportsmanship. With more than thirty years of experience working with campers in a completely supervised program that offers each student a rewarding and fun-filled summer, NETC enjoys a reputation as one of the finest tennis camps in the United States.

PROGRAM OFFERINGS

Tennis programs are designed to develop and challenge players of all levels and ages. NETC's curriculum includes work on fundamentals in group and private lessons, drills, videotape analysis, games, competition, and sport psychology. All campers participate in individual and team competition. The director carefully groups campers by skill and age. At the end of the session, each camper receives an individualized videotape providing direction for postcamp development.

Beginners and advanced beginners receive extensive instruction in fundamental stroke production and basic strategies. A thorough understanding of the basics is reinforced through drills, games, and singles and doubles competition.

Intermediate players make stroke corrections necessary to develop more reliable and effective shots. Serve, net play, and consistency at the baseline are also emphasized. Intermediate campers' skills are further tested in singles and doubles tournaments and in team competition.

High school and beginning tournament players further refine stroke production, with the emphasis on improving match play skills necessary to advance team standing or individual ranking.

Tournament players hone existing skills and drill extensively in weak areas with the goal of adding new dimensions to their game. The mental aspect of the game is emphasized, as is improving physical conditioning. Matches further challenge tournament players' skills.

ENROLLMENT

Most campers are from the New York City area; however, campers come from the Boston, Philadelphia, and Washington, D.C., areas as well as from other areas of the United States. Campers from other countries, including France, Germany, Italy, Spain, Canada, Bermuda, Turkey, the Philippines, Indonesia, Austria, and Japan, also attend. Sectionally and nationally ranked players attend the NETC program each summer.

DAILY SCHEDULE

7:30	Wake-up
8:00–9:00	Breakfast and room check
9:00–12:00	Tennis instruction, drills, play
12:00–1:00	Lunch, mail call
1:00–2:30	Swimming, private lessons, relaxation
2:30–5:00	Tennis instruction, drills, and/or match play
5:00–6:30	Dinner, relaxation
6:30	Evening activities
10:30	Lights-out

EXTRA OPPORTUNITIES AND ACTIVITIES

Evening sports activities include soccer, basketball, softball, volleyball, Ping-Pong, pool, and baseball. Social activities include movies, games, lip-sync contests, dances and parties, bowling, and trips to a nearby water park.

Camper achievements are celebrated at an end-of-session awards ceremony at which prizes are given for

individual tennis accomplishments, team winners, and winners of special events and tournaments.

FACILITIES

NETC campers enjoy exclusive use of sixteen all-weather tennis courts; nearby indoor facilities are used in bad weather. Participants may also take advantage of all of Trinity–Pawling's athletic facilities, which include volleyball and basketball courts and softball and soccer fields. Daily swimming takes place at the nearby "Holiday Hills" lakefront. Cluett Hall, the camp gathering area that is equipped with a color television and Ping-Pong tables, is the site for numerous social activities.

STAFF

Gordon Kent, the owner of NETC, directs the tennis program and all camp activities. Gordon brings twenty-six years of teaching experience with every level of junior player—from beginner through tournament competitor—to camp. Gordon Kent has established a reputation as one of the finest coaches in the East, where his programs at Stadium Tennis Center have attracted hundreds of New York–area juniors. Past president of the USPTA Eastern Division, Gordon has served on the Executive Committee of the USPTA, has received the "Pro of the Year" award from both the USPTA Eastern Division in 1992 and the USPTR Eastern Division in 1989, and was honored with the USTA/USPTR Public Service Award for Outstanding Contributions to Tennis Development. He is also a past chairman of the Junior Competitions Committee for the Eastern Section of the USTA and served on the Management Committee of the ETA.

The NETC staff, carefully selected and trained by Gordon Kent, includes teaching professionals and college players who are friendly, enthusiastic, and committed to the development of each and every camper.

MEDICAL CARE

The camp nurse supervises the campus infirmary and sees to the daily health needs of each camper. A camp doctor, less than 1 mile away, is on call 24 hours a day. NETC carries medical insurance secondary to parent coverage.

COSTS

Costs in 2004 were $1700 for boarders per two-week session; day campers may also attend from 9 a.m. to 5 p.m. at a cost of $1150 per two-week session. Fees for boarding campers include all tennis instruction, meals, and lodging. Day camper fees do not include breakfast, dinner, and lodging. The balance of fees (after the deposit) is due May 15.

TRANSPORTATION

Staff members meet campers at New York City airports and at Westchester County Airport for a small fee. Campers can also be met at the Pawling train station at no charge. Most campers come to camp by car.

APPLICATION TIMETABLE

Those interested should submit the NETC application with a $500 per-session deposit. Applications mailed after May 15 should be accompanied by full payment. Confirmation packages, sent upon receipt of application, include travel information; roommate request, health, and personal information forms; complete information on arrival and departure; directions to camp; and information on what to bring to camp.

FOR MORE INFORMATION AND A CAMP VIDEO, CONTACT:

Gordon Kent
Gordon Kent's New England Tennis Camp
winter
P.O. Box 212
New York, New York 10044
212-750-3810
800-528-2752 (toll-free)
Fax: 212-750-3704
summer
P.O. Box 840
Pawling, New York 12564
845-855-9650
800-528-2752 (toll-free)
Fax: 845-855-9661

THE GOW SCHOOL SUMMER PROGRAM

CAMPING, ACADEMICS, AND WEEKEND OVERNIGHT TRIPS

SOUTH WALES, NEW YORK

Type of Program: Academics, traditional camping activities, and weekend trips
Participants: Coeducational, ages 8–16
Enrollment: 85
Program Dates: June 27 to July 31, 2004
Head of Program: Brett Marcoux, Director

LOCATION

South Wales is a rural community in the western part of New York State, approximately 25 miles southeast of Buffalo and a short drive from Niagara Falls and Toronto.

BACKGROUND AND PHILOSOPHY

The Gow School Summer Program was created for girls and boys who have experienced past academic difficulties and have learning differences but possess the potential for success. The programs are composed of a carefully considered balance between academics, traditional camp activities, and weekend overnight trips. At summer's end, camper-students go home confident, relaxed, and prepared for the coming school year.

The academic program provides young people with an opportunity to improve their academic skills and achieve personal victories over those things that stand in the way of their success. A summer at Gow provides not only remediation and enrichment in the academic program but also allows for a fun and engaging summer full of new experiences, opportunities, and friendships. The Gow School's dedication to providing camper-students with a balance between academics and camp is demonstrated in its dual certification from the New York State Association of Independent Schools and membership in the American Camping Association.

PROGRAM OFFERINGS

The program is one of balance—solid academics and strong athletic, social, cultural, and recreational activities. The weekly program combines structure and focus with flexibility and choice. Gow strives to develop the skills and natural abilities of each person while encouraging a sense of enthusiasm and positive self-image. Campers should go home feeling confident, relaxed, and ready for the coming school year.

Academic program Since all the students have experienced past academic difficulties or learning differences, the democracy of common problems begins to erase self-consciousness, and self-esteem increases. Classes have an average enrollment of 3 to 6 students and meet five days per week. An optional postlunch tutorial supervised by faculty members, many focus programs, a word processing/computer literacy course, and a comprehensive language course are offered.

Daily drills and written work are stressed, and all classes focus on motivation, positive mental attitude, organization, study skills, social growth, confidence, and self-esteem.

Traditional camp and tripping program
Camping can contribute to a young person's life in a way that few other experiences can. The program goals are for each camper to have a pleasant, fun-filled summer; improve skills; and develop confidence, self-control, inner discipline, good sportsmanship, and self-esteem. Campers unskilled in particular activities are channeled into special instruction so that they may become more proficient and develop a feeling of adequacy. As they continue to grow in confidence, they are able to take their place with their peers and contribute successfully. Character development and citizenship are stressed at all times.

Activity Instruction Clinics (AICs) are one-week individually chosen options that offer more focus, skill, and individual attention. Optional Period activities include creative arts and individual and team sports, with an emphasis on playing sports over instruction in the sport.

In addition to daily activities, campers take advantage of the rich geographical setting with overnight trips on weekends, including educational, cultural, pioneering, and canoe trips.

ENROLLMENT

Campers come from all over the United States and the world and are generally language disabled, underachieving, and/or experiencing academic difficulty.

DAILY SCHEDULE

7:30	Wake-up
8:00	Breakfast and cleanup
8:45–12:45	Four academic periods
12:45	Lunch and rest period
2:00–5:30	Three camp activity periods
6:00	Group meetings and camp lineup
6:10	Dinner
7:15	Evening activity
8:30	In dorms
8:45–9:45	Late-night activity
10:00–11:00	Lights-out

EXTRA OPPORTUNITIES AND ACTIVITIES

Special events include a carnival, Icky Olympics, a softball league World Series, casino night, big/little-brother and big/little-sister activities, campfires, talent shows, and the last night banquet and rock ceremony. There is also a counselor-in-training (CIT) program for older campers.

FACILITIES

The buildings include the Main Building (1926), which houses classrooms, the infirmary, and the Govian Book Store. The library contains a reading room, book stacks capable of storing 10,000 volumes, classrooms, an audiovisual room, and a well-equipped darkroom. Orton Hall contains classrooms, a science laboratory, a spacious study hall, and a state-of-the-art computer resource center. There are six comfortable dormitories on campus. The Thompson Building contains a stage, two classrooms, and two metal shops. In 2002, the Gow Center opened. It contains three squash courts, a basketball court, an indoor tennis/lacrosse facility, a 3,000-square-foot weight room, locker rooms, and a social/recreation area. The physical plant is valued at more than $7 million. The school has facilities for tennis, basketball, volleyball, baseball, softball, soccer, lacrosse, weight lifting, archery, golf, wrestling, floor hockey, ceramics, painting, arts and crafts, trail hiking, horseback riding, a ropes course, and fishing. The swimming program makes use of a nearby natatorium.

STAFF

Most of the camp's academic instructors come from The Gow School's regular faculty. The dorm counselors and coaches are college students, graduate students, and teachers, some of whom are alumni of The Gow School and Summer Programs. The staff members are selected on the basis of character, stability, interest in working with young people, warmth, personality, education, and the ability to teach a skill. An extensive orientation period is held. Emphasis is given to the development of friendships, regard for others, and a sense of community.

MEDICAL CARE

The resident camp nurse works with the local physician. There is a 24-hour ambulatory center about 15 minutes away, and Buffalo hospitals are about 30 minutes away.

COSTS

Tuition for the 2004 program is $5800 (for those who register before April 1, the cost is $5650). This charge is comprehensive and includes the cost of instruction, lodging in dormitories, all meals, course materials, and transportation to and from the airport. It also includes day trips and all weekend excursions and tours. The tuition should be paid in full by June 1.

FINANCIAL AID

Tuition loans and scholarships are also available on a limited basis.

TRANSPORTATION

Campers are met by counselors at either the Buffalo International Airport, the Greyhound station, or the Amtrak station on opening day and dropped off accordingly on the final day.

APPLICATION TIMETABLE

The Summer Programs have a rolling admission policy. Students should submit their application with a guidance counselor reference, teacher evaluations, an official transcript, and a handwritten letter from the camper. Personal interviews and tours of the campus are encouraged and available year-round. The application form should be completed and returned as soon as possible.

FOR MORE INFORMATION, CONTACT:

Brett Marcoux, Director
The Gow Summer Programs
South Wales, New York 14139
716-652-3450
Fax: 716-687-2003
E-mail: summer@gow.org

THE GRAND RIVER ACADEMY

SUMMER ACADEMY

AUSTINBURG, OHIO

Type of Program: Residential academic program, enrichment and credit, and English as a second language
Participants: Coeducational; ages 14–18, grades 9–12
Enrollment: Maximum of 100
Program Dates: June 27 to August 6, 2004
Head of Program: Bill Thomas, Dean of Students

LOCATION

The Grand River Academy is located on a 200-acre campus in the rural town of Austinburg, in northeastern Ohio's Western Reserve. The campus is 1 hour east of Cleveland and 2 hours west of Pittsburgh.

BACKGROUND AND PHILOSOPHY

The Academy is nationally recognized as one of the few remaining nonmilitary, nonsectarian boys' boarding schools in the United States. Although the Grand River Academy is committed to single-sex education, in response to parents' requests that their daughters also have an opportunity to benefit from the Academy's unique program, the six-week summer academy is a coeducational boarding program.

The summer program is fundamentally designed as an extension of the Academy's winter school. The goal is to prepare students, including those not working to their potential, for a successful college education. During summer, as in the winter session, attention is paid to physical, emotional, and social growth in a community where concern for each individual's needs is emphasized. Each day is structured in order to provide students with a harmonious blend of academics and fun activities.

PROGRAM OFFERINGS

During the six-week summer academy, a student can strengthen an academic area or investigate a new subject. The program emphasizes small classes (2–5 students per class) and individual attention.

The Academy typically offers most college-preparatory courses each summer. Students may complete only 1 credit each summer. Written reports from teachers, with percentage grades, summarize individual student progress every week.

Students attend class for 4 hours each morning; several activity options are available each afternoon. As in the regular school year, all teachers live on campus and are available for extra help in the afternoon and during a supervised evening study period.

ENROLLMENT

Students enroll from throughout the United States and several other countries. The Academy offers a diverse population with roughly an equal number of boys and girls. Applicants of any race, color, or national or ethnic origin are welcome.

DAILY SCHEDULE

7:00–7:30	Breakfast
8:00–10:00	Class
10:00–10:30	Morning break
10:30–12:30	Class
12:30–1:15	Lunch
1:30–5:00	Recreational activities
5:00–6:00	Free time
6:15–7:00	Family-style dinner
7:00–8:45	Free time
8:45–10:45	Study period
11:00	Lights-out

All accepted students receive a handbook that includes the Academy's discipline code. The structure that is a cornerstone of the Academy's educational program throughout the year continues in the summer.

EXTRA OPPORTUNITIES AND ACTIVITIES

The Academy's North Coast location offers an impressive array of social and cultural options. Students may enjoy professional baseball games, paintball games, local amusement parks, concerts, Lake Erie beaches, regular Friday night dances, and Saturday night movies at a local theater. All activities and field trips are carefully scheduled and supervised by a faculty member.

FACILITIES

Everyone makes use of the Academy's abundant facilities, which include classroom buildings, five dormitories, an air-conditioned library, a fine arts area, the student union, a gymnasium, a weight room, tennis courts, soccer, baseball, and paintball fields, and a beach volleyball court. An excellent golf course is also available nearby for recreation.

STAFF

The summer faculty comprises members of the winter school staff.

MEDICAL CARE

A licensed nurse and a doctor are on staff and on call at all times to respond to student health needs from the Academy's well-equipped infirmary.

COSTS

Tuition, room, and board for the 2004 summer academy were $3500 for seven-day boarding students and $3300 for five-day boarding students. In addition, parents should plan on approximately $400 for such things as laundry, books, and entertainment. An allowance account can be set up at the parents' request.

TRANSPORTATION

The Academy is easily accessible by car or bus. Students flying into Cleveland's Hopkins International Airport are met by staff members. There is an extra charge for this service.

APPLICATION TIMETABLE

Applications should be accompanied by a nonrefundable $25 processing fee. Upon notification of acceptance, a nonrefundable $500 deposit is due to hold a place in the program. Upon receipt of the deposit, an I-20 Certificate of Eligibility is sent to foreign nationals for U.S. immigration purposes.

A visit to campus is not required but may be arranged with the admissions office.

For more information, contact:

Office of Admission
The Grand River Academy
3042 College Street, P.O. Box 222
Austinburg, Ohio 44010
440-275-2811
Fax: 440-275-3275
E-mail: academy@grandriver.org
World Wide Web: http://www.grandriver.org

PARTICIPANT/FAMILY COMMENTS

"I have made ties with people all over the world...an unforgettable experience."—Rachel Kroner, Geneva, Ohio

"GRA not only helped me pass a class, but I also learned about different cultures."—Will Modic, Cleveland, Ohio

"GRA Summer School is even better than Burger King"—Sergei Timofeev, Moscow, Russia

"Summer School was great...but I like the food better in Puerto Rico."—Jose Luis "Bubba" Morales, San Juan, Puerto Rico

"I learned how to have fun and get my work done."—Jackson Robb, Charleston, South Carolina

GREEK SUMMER

SUMMER PROGRAM

THESSALONIKI, GREECE

Type of Program: Greek village homestay, community service project, and travel
Participants: Coeducational, grades 10–12
Enrollment: 35 (maximum)
Program Dates: Six-week session from the end of June to the beginning of August
Head of Program: Greek Summer Coordinator

LOCATION

Greek Summer is based at the American Farm School's campus in Thessaloniki, Greece. The chosen village for the 2½-week community service project and homestay changes yearly but is always in the vicinity of Thessaloniki. In addition to the village stay, the group tours the country for ten days, visiting several ancient historical sites, including Meteora, Delphi, and Athens, among others, as well as the beautiful Aegean islands. The program concludes with a two-day climb to the summit of Mount Olympus.

BACKGROUND AND PHILOSOPHY

Since 1970, Greek Summer has promoted intercultural exchange between Americans and Greeks, under the sponsorship of the American Farm School. It serves young people who are enthusiastic about immersing themselves in another culture, contributing to the quality of life in a rural Greek village, and having the opportunity to make great new friends. Through the years, the American Farm School has built a tradition of helping Greek villagers meet their evolving needs through a coordinated community service project. During Greek Summer, young Americans undergo their own metamorphosis of thought and spirit as they work to accomplish set goals. The intensity of the experience leads participants to realize new potential and discover resources within themselves and each other. Of the more than 1,000 alumni who have participated in Greek Summer, most consider it one of the most important growth experiences of their lives.

PROGRAM OFFERINGS

A short group orientation introduces participants to the Greek language, folk traditions, and modern society. Orientation activities include time for Greek folk dancing, singing, some Aegean sun and surf, and getting to know fellow participants.

Most of the participants spend approximately twenty-one days and nights in a rural Greek village, working on a community service project for about 7 hours a day. Participants spend the evenings with their Greek host families. Time with the family is spent in as many ways as there are host families; every participant has a different experience.

At the Farm School, the focus is on group activities related to the village project, sightseeing in Thessaloniki, and learning about the workings and teachings of the American Farm School. At the end of the summer, participants celebrate a completed project and newfound friendships at the festive, poignant Village Farewell.

A ten-day excursion by boat, hydrofoil, and private bus highlights the middle of the program. The trip exposes participants to ancient sites, including Delphi, Dion, Meteora, and the Acropolis in Athens; some days are spent exploring the archaeological sites and natural beauty of the Aegean islands. An unforgettable two-day ascent of Mount Olympus, the highest peak in the Balkans, is the culmination of the group's Greek experience.

ENROLLMENT

Greek Summer enrolls a maximum of 35 participants. Applicants must interview with the Program Coordinator or a designated representative and provide biographical information, essays, and a school recommendation form. Students completing grades 10–12 are eligible.

DAILY SCHEDULE

No two days are the same. Usually, participants rise at 7 a.m., have breakfast, and commence village work, expeditions, or farm activities at 8. Lunch is at 1 p.m. (if it is hot, there may be frequent impromptu breaks before then), and the afternoon shift begins at 2:30. At 4, participants go to their homes for a shower and "siesta." Greek social hours are late, and participants find that the siesta is important. At the Farm School, the afternoons are filled with sports or farm activities, depending on individual inclination. Dinners at the Farm School take place at staff homes or in the school dining hall, while in the village, participants eat with their respective families. The school dorm curfew is midnight on most nights.

Participants must understand that they are ambassadors to another culture, and they need to aspire to exemplary behavior among Greeks and Americans alike. The program depends upon mutual respect.

STAFF

Six full-time staff members are with the group 24 hours a day. They concentrate on counseling and leading by example. Most staff members are former participants. In addition, many resident American Farm School staff and faculty members work with participants at the school and in the village.

MEDICAL CARE

The school has 24-hour access to well-equipped health centers. In emergencies, the area of Thessaloniki, Greece's second-largest city, provides access to modern hospitals and specialists. Participants must submit a medical report by their doctor before participation, and insurance must be provided by the parents. No special inoculations are necessary, though a tetanus booster is encouraged.

RELIGIOUS LIFE

Participants of all faiths are welcome and comfortable in the program. Since Greek Orthodox Christianity is central to Greek culture, participants have some exposure to its practice and services.

COSTS

A $1000 fee accompanies the application materials to guarantee space in the program, pending the review and interview of each applicant. This fee is fully refundable if the applicant is not chosen. The remaining program balance of $3300 includes a $1000 tax-deductible contribution to the American Farm School. Airfare is additional. Participants usually spend between $300 and $500 in pocket money.

FINANCIAL AID

A scholarship fund supported by past participants is used to provide financial aid to a few applicants each year. The amount of financial aid is dependent on family need and the applicant's potential for contributing to and benefiting from Greek Summer.

TRANSPORTATION

Every year, the round-trip international air travel is arranged in a group package between New York's JFK Airport, where the program begins, and the Thessaloniki Airport.

APPLICATION TIMETABLE

Requests for applications are welcome anytime. Greek Summer uses a rolling admissions process. Because the program tends to fill by March, early application is strongly recommended.

For more information, contact:

Program Coordinator
Greek Summer
American Farm School
1133 Broadway, Suite 1625
New York, New York 10010-7903
212-463-8434
Fax: 212-463-8208
E-mail: info@greeksummer.org
World Wide Web: http://www.greeksummer.org

PARTICIPANT/FAMILY COMMENTS

"(My son) is my third child to have been through this program and each one has come back a better person. They have all had life-changing experiences and cherish the memories. . . . Thank you."

"I really feel like Greek Summer has allowed me to proceed in the search for myself. Now I understand more of what interests me. Also, I have really learned to look inside myself and really see what I want."

"A summer of unique experiences with unique friends and people. I still live in my memories of Greek Summer and always will."

HARVARD SECONDARY SCHOOL PROGRAM

SUMMER SCHOOL

CAMBRIDGE, MASSACHUSETTS

Type of Program: College-level academic
Participants: Coed residential or commuter students who are completing grade 10, 11, or 12 and are fluent in English
Enrollment: 1,000
Program Dates: June 27–August 19, 2005

LOCATION

Harvard University Summer School is in Cambridge, Massachusetts. By subway, Harvard is only minutes from downtown Boston. Cambridge is popular with young people and is considered the ultimate college town. There are bookstores, music stores, sidewalk cafés, shops, and ethnic restaurants.

BACKGROUND AND PHILOSOPHY

The Harvard Summer School, the oldest summer session in the United States, was founded in 1871. The Harvard Secondary School Program was developed to offer academically talented high school students a college experience, enabling them to make better-informed decisions about their academic future.

PROGRAM OFFERINGS

Secondary school students take college courses along with college students, and they earn college credit. During the eight-week summer session, Harvard offers nearly 200 courses in more than forty liberal arts fields. Areas of study include anthropology, computer science, foreign languages, astronomy, natural sciences, classics, expository and creative writing, drama, economics, fine arts, studio arts, government, history, linguistics, literature, mathematics, and music, among others. Most Summer School faculty members have Harvard affiliations during the academic year, but instructors also are recruited from other universities.

ENROLLMENT

Harvard's academic resources and distinguished reputation attract people of all ages, backgrounds, and nationalities. Last year, more than 5,000 students from all areas of the United States and ninety other countries attended Harvard Summer School. Selected on the basis of their high school grades, school recommendations, and College Board scores, secondary school men and women who have finished the tenth, eleventh, or twelfth grade make up one fifth of the Summer School population. Approximately 90 percent of the secondary school participants live in dormitories on campus; the remaining 10 percent commute.

DAILY SCHEDULE

Secondary school resident students must enroll in eight units of credit; 4- and 8-unit courses are offered. Sophomores must take a writing or math class; they choose a second class from a selected list. Four-unit courses meet either daily for 1 hour or twice weekly for 2½ hours. Eight-unit courses meet for 2 or more hours per day. Commuting students take either 4 or 8 units of study. Summer school students eat meals together in a campus dining hall three times a day, seven days a week. Students are given freedom and responsibility to establish their own priorities and manage their own time.

EXTRA OPPORTUNITIES AND ACTIVITIES

Harvard Summer School, Cambridge, Boston, and the New England region offer a multitude of summer activities. The Summer School sponsors movies, concerts, dances, social gatherings, and day trips in Boston and around New England. The College Choices Program offers tours of other New England colleges, a workshop on writing college applications, and a college fair attended by thirty colleges. Students may audition to join the Summer School Chorus, or Orchestra; all students may join the Pops Band. Students can join intramural sports teams, learn to row, attend professional sports events, perform in the talent show or the trivial bowl, or volunteer for community service projects in the area.

FACILITIES

Harvard University's resources are exceptional. A distinguished faculty, well-equipped laboratories, fine museums, many athletic facilities, and the largest university library system in the world are available to Summer School students.

Secondary school students live with other secondary school students in dormitories in and near Harvard Yard. Several of the dormitories are more than a century old, and the furnishings are simple.

STAFF

A carefully chosen resident proctor (a Harvard College undergraduate) serves as an adviser during the summer to provide support and guidance—suggesting activities, helping students find their way around

Cambridge and Boston, and inviting students to weekly study breaks. Proctors are assigned an average of 20 students each.

Each proctor serves under the guidance of an assistant dean. Assistant deans live in dormitories and work with their proctors to develop a sense of community and to guarantee appropriate conditions for study.

The director of the Secondary School Program, along with her staff and 3 assistant deans, is responsible for the campus life and academic welfare of Secondary School Program students. There is always a Secondary School Program dean on call.

MEDICAL CARE

All Summer School students are required to have health insurance against major illnesses and accidents. Students who do not have such coverage with an American carrier must buy it through the Summer School. The outpatient facilities of the University Health Services are available 24 hours a day for urgent care needs. The Stillman Infirmary, an on-campus hospital facility, is available for acute inpatient care.

RELIGIOUS LIFE

Harvard University has no religious affiliation, but opportunities for worship are available on or near campus for members of many faiths.

COSTS

In 2004, costs per 4-unit course are as follows: application fee, $50; tuition, $2025 ($4050 for 8 units); room and board, $3550; health insurance, $110. Late fees also apply after payment deadlines.

TRANSPORTATION

Harvard University is located approximately 6 miles from Logan International Airport in Boston. Transportation to and from the airport is available by taxi or public transportation.

APPLICATION TIMETABLE

Applicants are admitted to the Secondary School Program and notified on a rolling basis until the program fills—i.e., there is no specific application deadline. The Secondary School Program welcomes inquiries at any time throughout the year.

For more information, call or write:

Harvard Secondary School Program
51 Brattle Street
Cambridge, Massachusetts 02138-3722
617-495-3192
E-mail: ssp@hudce.harvard.edu
World Wide Web: http://www.ssp.harvard.edu

HAWAII PREPARATORY ACADEMY

Summer@hpa

SUMMER SESSION

WAIMEA, HAWAII (BIG ISLAND)

Type of Program: Academic enrichment, boarding and day
Participants: Boys and girls entering grades 6–12
Enrollment: 150
Program Dates: Mid- to late June to mid- to late July
Head of Program: Shirley Ann K. Fukumoto

LOCATION

Hawaii Preparatory Academy (HPA) is one of the premier college-preparatory boarding and day schools in the Pacific region. The school has two campuses on the island of Hawaii. The Upper Campus, which hosts the Summer Session program, is located on 120 acres at the foot of the Kohala Mountains, in the heart of Hawaii's ranching country. The Lower and Middle Schools are housed on a separate 6-acre campus in the nearby village of Waimea, which recently was recognized as one of the top 10 best places to live in the United States.

HPA programs take advantage of Hawaii's unique geographical and social setting. Through many courses and activities, the school gives students a strong sense of Hawaii and its culture.

HPA is a 45-minute drive from the Kona International Airport. There are many daily, direct flights to Kona from the Honolulu International Airport. Flight time is about 40 minutes.

BACKGROUND AND PHILOSOPHY

The HPA Summer Session, established in 1974, offers enrichment and unique study opportunities in English, science, and culture for boarding students and a limited number of day students entering grades 6–12. The program, which enrolls boys and girls from throughout the world, runs for four weeks from late-June to late-July.

Summer Session offers new and prospective HPA students an excellent introduction to the school's program and instructors. Many students return every summer to take advantage of the outstanding program and staff and to meet students from around the world.

PROGRAM OFFERINGS

Upper School students can select from the following 2-hour academic and elective courses: algebra I, algebra II, analytical college reading, art explorations, astronomy, ceramics, college planning, computer graphics, creative writing, culture of Hawaii, environmental art, geometry, marine biology, pre-algebra, reading/study skills, SAT preparation (math and verbal), video production, and Web design. ESL courses include discussion through film, grammar (beginning, intermediate, and advanced), introduction to science, and writing (intermediate and advanced).

Middle School offerings include algebra I, algebra II, art explorations, astronomy, ceramics, computer graphics, creative writing, culture of Hawaii, environmental art, exploring the Big Island, geometry, hands on Hawaii, marine biology, music appreciation, pre-algebra, problem solving in math, reading/study skills, video production, and Web design. ESL courses include art/writing, grammar (beginning, intermediate, and advanced), performing arts, and writing (intermediate and advanced).

These courses are predominately for enrichment and do not offer credit. Many courses—particularly in the sciences—include field trips as part of the curriculum.

ENROLLMENT

HPA's diverse students come predominantly from the Hawaiian Islands, the U.S. mainland, and the Pacific Rim nations.

DAILY SCHEDULE

On Monday through Friday, students attend three courses (two 2-hour morning courses and one 2-hour afternoon course). There are afternoon sports until 5:30 p.m. A 1-hour study hall follows the buffet dinner and ends with a social period, and then lights out. Weekend excursions include trips to state and national parks, such as Volcanoes National Park, and cultural sites.

EXTRA OPPORTUNITIES AND ACTIVITIES

Optional sports include instruction in horseback riding, scuba certification, swimming, and tennis. On

Saturday, buses take students to the beach and shopping areas. Students can also go to the movies or on camping excursions.

During the last few afternoons of the Summer Session sports program, students participate in the "mini Olympics," which includes many nonathletic and athletic team events. The final summer and Olympics event is the talent show, presented on the last evening of the Summer Session program. Parents are encouraged to come to campus a day early to join their children at this event.

FACILITIES

Ten buildings on the Upper Campus house multiple classrooms. Other facilities include the Gates Performing Arts Center, the Dyer Memorial Library, the Gerry Clark Art Center, Davies Memorial Chapel, the award-winning Rutgers Tennis Center, Castle Gymnasium, the Nakamaru Fitness Center, Dowsett Swimming Pool, a cross-country course, a track, tack room, and football, baseball, soccer, and polo fields.

Three Upper School residence halls house students in double rooms. Each building has a central lounge and laundry facilities. Faculty members and residential assistants provide supervision.

All rooms have beds and built-in closets, shelves, desks, and dressers. Rooms are equipped with telephone connections and computer access to the campuswide computer network and the Internet. Students may bring computers and stereos (with headphones).

Students can use their own computers in their rooms or work in Macintosh-based learning labs. A 350-node fiber-optic network system interconnects computer workstations and servers to provide Academy users with word processing, spreadsheet, database, graphics, and Internet services. An e-mail system connects the staff and faculty members and students. Internet service is available on all networked computers throughout both campuses. Access to the network is available in dormitory rooms on the Upper Campus.

Dining facilities are located in the Taylor Commons. Also located in this building are the Development Office, Special Programs, Accounting, and Business Office; an infirmary and wellness center; and a videography laboratory.

STAFF

The teaching staff consists of regular school faculty members as well as teachers from Hawaii and around the world. Teachers take a personal interest in every student and often serve as advisers and dorm parents.

Faculty and staff members, most of whom are regular school faculty members or college students who are HPA alumni, supervise the dormitories and excursions.

MEDICAL CARE

Students must have a physical examination and a TB test prior to arrival. HPA has a fully equipped infirmary/dispensary, and a nurse is on duty or on call at all times. For more serious emergencies, the North Hawaii Community Hospital is located 3 miles from campus.

COSTS

Tuition covers instruction, room, board, books, most group activities, and excursions. Airfare and ground transportation, optional sports, and personal expenses are extra. Costs in 2004 include an application fee ($25), tuition ($3800), an equestrian program ($450), swimming lessons ($300), tennis instruction ($375), and SCUBA certification ($375).

TRANSPORTATION

Participants fly directly into Kona International Airport from Honolulu, the U.S. mainland, or Japan. For students flying into Honolulu first, the school can assist with travel arrangements to Kona (additional fees apply). The school also can arrange for transportation to and from Kona International Airport at the beginning and end of the summer session (additional fees apply).

APPLICATION TIMETABLE

Applications are accepted from January 1 until April 15. Late applications are considered on a space-available basis. Notification of acceptance starts March 15. Upon acceptance, students are required to pay a $500 nonrefundable reservation deposit and return the registration materials with course selections.

For more information, contact:

Shirley Ann Fukumoto
Special Programs Office
Hawaii Preparatory Academy
65-1692 Kohala Mountain Road
Kamuela, Hawaii 96743
808-881-4088
Fax: 808-881-4071
E-mail: summer@hpa.edu
World Wide Web: http://www.hpa.edu

HIDDEN VALLEY CAMP

SUMMER CAMP

FREEDOM, MAINE

Type of Program: Noncompetitive camp with many elective specialties
Participants: Coeducational, ages 8–13
Enrollment: 275 per session
Program Dates: Two 4-week sessions, June 25 to July 21 and July 23 to August 18; one 8-week session, June 25 to August 18
Heads of Program: Peter and Meg Kassen, Directors/Owners

LOCATION

Located near the beautiful coastal villages of Belfast and Camden on Maine's historic Penobscot Bay, Hidden Valley is secluded in a 300-acre wooded glen with a mile-long private lake. Entering the valley, a visitor's first impression might be of a farm. The meadows, pine trees, animal corrals, and sprawling red farmhouse with attached barn all create a friendly, homelike atmosphere.

BACKGROUND AND PHILOSOPHY

Hidden Valley is not a traditional camp. For more than twenty years, it has served as a noncompetitive, nonsectarian community that encourages camper choices, spontaneity, friendship, and personal growth. Throughout its history, Hidden Valley has pioneered international youth exchanges and has become known for its distinctive instructional programs and innovative offerings in the arts.

Hidden Valley's programs provide individualized attention in a wholesome and structured—yet unpressured—atmosphere. It is the directors' hope that the summer experience at Hidden Valley enhances self-esteem, fosters a feeling of independence, and nurtures young people's capacity to live happily and work constructively with others.

The camp is accredited by the American Camping Association.

PROGRAM OFFERINGS

At the Hidden Valley lakefront, campers may elect to go kayaking, learn to canoe or windsurf, fish for bass and perch, or take American Red Cross swimming lessons. A pool provides a secondary location for swimming lessons and cabin parties. Land sports include soccer, basketball, tennis, softball, volleyball, and floor hockey. The instruction is top-notch, and the noncompetitive atmosphere means that everybody wins.

Crafts programs feature pottery, stained glass, clothesmaking, woodworking, batik, printmaking, musical instrument making, drawing, painting, jewelry, and photography. Workshops are taught by professionals and encourage children to explore at their own pace. The accompanying photograph was taken by a Hidden Valley camper.

In the performing arts, workshops in jazz, ballet, tap, and ethnic and modern dance are available at all levels of proficiency. Campers may also choose from such theater classes as improvisation, mime, stagecraft, sound and lighting, clowning, and musical theater. Three monthly camp shows (requiring no auditions) are also available. Energetic gymnastics classes involve floor exercises and use the low balance beam and other equipment. Campers participate in weekly gymnastics exhibitions.

Other special programs include English riding, which allows campers to practice in two spacious rings and to ride through the camp's forested trails; animal care, a program featuring Hidden Valley's herd of magnificent llamas and many farm animals; mountain biking; and the ropes course and climbing wall, an exciting and challenging set of adventurous, growth-filled activities.

Hidden Valley's elective program allows campers to specialize in any of these areas or to explore a range of interests. Workshop choices are guided by Hidden Valley staff. The camper's life outside class is also considered important. Counselors are sensitive to individual needs and are available to speak with parents about family concerns. Meals are nutritious and highly varied; most special diets can be accommodated.

ENROLLMENT

More than 200 boys and girls, ages 8–13, come from far and wide to attend each of Hidden Valley's four-week sessions. Through the years, the camp has hosted children from more than fifty countries and throughout the United States.

DAILY SCHEDULE

Every fourth day is unusual and exciting as campers go on trips or attend special in-camp events. Other days follow the schedule below.

7:45	Wake-up
8:00	Breakfast with cabin group
9:00	Classes (three periods)
12:30	Picnic lunch
1:30	Rest period
2:30	Fourth class
3:30	Interest-group meetings, free swim, special workshops
5:30	Camp meeting
6:00	Dinner
7:15	Evening programs
9:30	Bedtime

EXTRA OPPORTUNITIES AND ACTIVITIES

Hidden Valley offers three optional outdoor-oriented programs. The Brumby group is designed for young people particularly interested and experienced in horseback riding. These campers live with the riding staff near the stables and manage their "own" horses. Special features of the program include horse shows and long trail rides in the afternoon.

Another group of campers lives in tepees atop a hill at Hidden Valley's Tipi Village. Developed for young people who like to live outdoors, Indian Village emphasizes crafts, cooking on open fires, and the exploration of Maine's environment.

Community service is available through Outreach-Outdoors, a program that takes a small group of 11- to 13-year-olds into the local community each afternoon to help at a recycling center, assist rangers at state parks, or pitch in with local farmers.

Out-of-camp trips for all campers include visits to Maine beaches and ferry rides to coastal islands. In addition, Hidden Valley's informal atmosphere allows for many unscheduled activities. Small groups of campers may find themselves helping Meg pick salad vegetables in her organic garden or hiking with Peter to a lookout tower for a view of nearby mountains.

FACILITIES

Nestled in Hidden Valley's woods and fields are 40 buildings—all recently built or renovated—providing living accommodations and space for creative activities. All cabins have electricity, lavatories, and hot-water showers; they house approximately 12 campers and 3 counselors, who sleep in the cabins. There are three dance studios, a large recreation hall, and many crafts buildings. The traditional red farmhouse/barn houses a piano room, a stone fireplace, a large-screen video monitor, and a kitchen for the camp's cooking class. Next door is a bright, heated dining hall and kitchen.

Hidden Valley has a fine soccer field, three hardtop tennis courts, a basketball court, and a swimming pool. Of outstanding interest are a pine grove amphitheater, an organic vegetable garden, and an adventure/ropes course and climbing wall set in a stand of maples and oaks. A pavilion, wood-heated sauna, water slide, and dock, from which trained staff members provide supervision and instruction, are found lakeside.

STAFF

The staff consists of 90 members, whose age averages 24; many return year after year, ensuring continuity of programs and atmosphere. Hidden Valley seeks warm, bright, responsive, energetic, child-centered individuals for its staff. In interviewing candidates, the directors look for extensive personal resources and accomplishments, camp program skills, self-awareness, and a sense of humor. All counselors arrive at camp twelve days before campers for a professional training session.

Peter and Meg Kassen, director and owners, have been organizing children's programs for more than twenty years. They live at camp year-round and devote their full-time energies to the direction of Hidden Valley.

MEDICAL CARE

Hidden Valley possesses a large infirmary staffed by 4 nurses. A hospital and a pediatrician's office are only 15 miles away in Belfast. Counselor orientation includes first-aid classes as well as training in accident and illness prevention.

COSTS

In 2004, tuition is $3790 for four weeks and $6190 for eight weeks. These fees cover insurance, laundry charges (done weekly in camp), trips, and supplies. Sibling discounts are offered. There are no additional charges except for horseriding.

TRANSPORTATION

The camp arranges travel on chaperoned, air-conditioned buses from New Jersey, New York, Connecticut, and Boston and flights from such cities as Baltimore, Miami, and Chicago to the Jetport in Portland, Maine. All flights are met at the gate. Luggage travels with children on buses and planes. Some parents drive children to camp; they may visit campers at any time during the summer.

APPLICATION TIMETABLE

Since some groups fill early in the winter, timely inquiries are encouraged. Families then have an opportunity to view the camp's video, consult written materials, ask questions of parents whose children are current campers, and meet with the directors.

FOR MORE INFORMATION, CONTACT:

Peter and Meg Kassen
Hidden Valley Camp
161 Hidden Valley Road
Freedom, Maine 04941
800-922-6737 (toll-free)
207-342-5177
Fax: 207-342-5685
E-mail: summer@hiddenvalleycamp.com
World Wide Web: http://www.hiddenvalleycamp.com

PARTICIPANT/FAMILY COMMENTS

"I can't begin to tell you how much we appreciate being able to let the children go away, knowing they are safe, happy, and enriched. You do a lot of creative things and offer activities and ideas to the children that are so expansive and ingenious. They've come home thinking, creating, cooperative, happy, proud, and communicating directly. Thank you."

THE HUN SCHOOL OF PRINCETON

SUMMER ACADEMIC SESSION/AMERICAN CULTURE AND LANGUAGE INSTITUTE (ACLI)/SUMMER THEATRE CLASSICS

PRINCETON, NEW JERSEY

Type of Program: Academic enrichment classes and/or full-credit classes in a variety of subjects, including intensive English language courses in grammar and reading and opportunities for American cultural and historical enrichment/classical theater

Participants: Coeducational, ages 12 to 18 (12-year-olds may be accepted into enrichment courses). Must be 13 to board. Theatre accepts ages 13 to 18.

Enrollment: Approximately 180 students in the Summer Academic Session; maximum of 30 in ACLI; 15 in Theatre

Program Dates: One 5-week session, June 27 to July 29

Heads of Program: Mr. William McQuade, The Hun School Upper School Head; Mrs. Donna O'Sullivan, Coordinator of Summer Programs; Ms. LeRhonda Greats, Director of Summer Academic Session; Ms. Dianne Somers, Director, ESL Program

LOCATION

The Hun School of Princeton, located in historical Princeton, New Jersey, is a private coeducational school for grades 6–12. The five-week summer session complements and follows the curriculum, standards, and philosophy of the Hun School. The greater Princeton area is available to students with its many resources. Resident students frequently take trips into town for ice cream or shopping or to enjoy the sights of Princeton University.

BACKGROUND AND PHILOSOPHY

The Hun School Summer Session offers students an ideal setting to explore new areas of learning while building on basic foundations of knowledge. At Hun, a dedicated and experienced faculty helps students to gain confidence in their scholastic abilities as they guide them to appreciate their talents. Students' efforts are supported by programs that adhere to the highest standards of excellence while helping them achieve their specific goals. The incorporation of innovative learning technologies within the summer curriculum completes what can be the road map to success. Summer at Hun represents a special time when friendships are made and horizons are expanded. During its summer session, Hun welcomes students from surrounding communities and from around the world.

PROGRAM OFFERINGS

There are three main programs offered at Hun:

The Summer Academic Session serves students in grades 6–12. Some enrichment courses are appropriate for students entering sixth, seventh, or eighth grade. Small-group instruction, traditional grading standards, and individual attention are hallmarks of the Summer Academic Session at Hun. Students may choose 2½-hour courses or full-credit (comprehensive) courses, which meet 5 hours per day. There are two class periods. Comprehensive course work is for students wishing to accelerate their curriculum, enhance their high school transcripts for college admission, or make up a class. Enrollment in one comprehensive course, 120 hours, constitutes a full academic load for the five-week session. Preview/review classes or other 2½-hour classes are designed for students wishing to make up incomplete problems in a particular subject. Students may choose a course that reviews work they have previously taken in order to reinforce material covered, or they may select a course that prepares them for work they will undertake in the fall. Students may select one or two courses from this category. Each course is 60 hours.

Comprehensive courses offered include Algebra I, Algebra II, Geometry, Precalculus, and Chemistry. Enrichment courses are Algebra I Preview or Review, Algebra II Preview or Review, Calculus, Precalculus, Geometry, Competence and Confidence in Reading and Writing, Middle School English Prep, Middle School Math, English Literature, American Literature, Biology, Physics, Chemistry, and SAT Prep. Additional courses may be added if there is sufficient student interest. Courses are subject to cancellation due to lack of enrollment. Students may be day students or board on campus (must be 13 years of age to reside at the School).

The American Culture and Language Institute (ESL) is designed specifically for international students who wish to study English at an American school. Students from the Princeton area may also attend as day students; however, most students in the program board at the School and are from outside the United States. Balancing academic classroom work with cultural enrichment, the program offers students an ideal environment in which to improve their English language skills while learning more about the history of the United States and American customs and society. International students interested in making the transition from schools in their home country to college-preparatory study in America find the ACLI program to be ideally suited to their needs (must be 13 years of age to reside at the School).

Summer Theatre Classics is an intensive four-week drama workshop that culminates in a fully executed production. Participants develop performance skills and assist with all aspects involved in producing a play. Participants must be between the ages of 13 and 18. Some experience is required, along with a genuine desire for theater. An audition is required.

ENROLLMENT

There are approximately 180 students in the Summer Academic Session, both boarding and day, and about 25 students in the American Culture and Language Institute. Students come from all over the United States and the world and, in 2004, represented the countries of Japan, Turkey, Korea, Taiwan, China, Italy, Lithuania, and Russia.

DAILY SCHEDULE

Resident Students

7:00–7:45	Breakfast
8:00–10:30	Period 1
10:30–10:50	Break
10:50–12:20	Period 2
12:20–1:00	Lunch
1:00–2:00	Period 2 (continued)
2:00–2:45	Extra Help
3:00–5:00	Intramurals/Activities
5:30–6:00	Dinner
6:00–7:15	Free Time
7:30–9:30	Study Hall
9:45	On Corridor
10:30	Lights Out

(Day students follow the same schedule from Period 1 through Extra Help)

EXTRA OPPORTUNITIES AND ACTIVITIES

The Student Activities Center and Game Room are open to all summer students for enjoyment. A Snack Bar opens after classes and remains open into the evening. The Game Room houses pool and Ping-Pong tables and air hockey and Foosball tables. Boarding students participate in weekday activities from 3 to 5 p.m. They include miniature golf, bowling, swimming, shopping, ice skating, and other activities. During that time, the computer lab is open, as is the Game Room and Fitness Center. Weekend activities for boarders include trips to amusement parks, the New Jersey shore, Philadelphia, white-water rafting, movies off campus and in the Student Activities Center, and other organized trips. Hun also organizes tournaments in Ping-Pong, pool, and volleyball. The students in the American Culture and Language Institute follow a trip schedule that includes outings each Wednesday and a weekend trip to Washington, D.C.

FACILITIES

Classes are held in air-conditioned classrooms in two buildings: the Buck Activities Center and the Chesebro Academic Center. The Bookstore, Snack Bar, Game Room, and Summer Programs Office are located in the Buck Activities Center. Students who choose to reside on campus live in dormitory-style housing. Students may use the gymnasium, tennis courts, basketball courts, and weight room facility. Students eat meals in the School's air-conditioned dining hall. Boarding students have access to the Internet in their dorm rooms.

STAFF

Instructors are chosen for their ability to motivate and communicate with students and for their love of teaching. A core of Hun School faculty members is the heart of the program, in addition to local teachers who come highly recommended. The residential staff consists of Hun School alumni and faculty and staff members.

MEDICAL CARE

The Hun School Clinic is staffed by a nurse who is available from 8 a.m. to 2 p.m. on school days. A nurse is on call 24 hours a day, including weekends and evenings. In addition, the Medical Center of Princeton is approximately 2 miles from the Hun campus. Resident students who become seriously ill are sent home to be cared for by their parents or guardian.

RELIGIOUS LIFE

The Hun School welcomes students from all faiths and religions. Students may attend nearby religious services on weekends.

COSTS

In 2004, the cost for the Summer Academic Program was $4785 for boarding students, $1120 for a 2½-hour course as a day student, $1975 for a comprehensive course, and $1975 for two 2½-hour courses. For the American Culture and Language Institute, boarding students' tuition was $5870 and day students paid $2650. The Summer Theatre Classics tuition was $805 for day students and $3825 for boarding students.

TRANSPORTATION

Parents or guardians must arrange transportation from nearby airports (Kennedy International Airport and Newark International Airport) to the Hun School on the day of registration, Sunday, June 26, 2005. Other students arrive by car or train.

APPLICATION TIMETABLE

The School accepts students on a rolling admission basis beginning in December and continuing until the start of the summer session. Applicants are urged to apply by May 1 in order to ensure a placement in the resident program or to maximize their placement possibilities in a popular class. Hun cannot guarantee space availability in all classes. Applications are available on the School's Web site.

For more information, contact:

Mrs. Donna O'Sullivan
Coordinator of Summer Programs
The Hun School of Princeton
176 Edgerstoune Road
Princeton, New Jersey 08540
609-921-7600 Ext. 2265
Fax: 609-924-2170
E-mail: summer@hunschool.org
World Wide Web: http://www.hunschool.org

PARTICIPANT/FAMILY COMMENTS

"Thank you once again for providing another year of summer learning and fun for my son. I continue to feel that spending part of his summer at Hun is part of the reason he is growing up and maturing into a caring and refined young man."

HYDE SCHOOL

HYDE SUMMER CHALLENGE 2004

WOODSTOCK, CONNECTICUT, AND BATH, MAINE

Type of Program: Residential summer program of academics, athletics, performing arts, wilderness trips, and family education

Participants: Coeducational, ages 14–18 (grades 9–12)

Enrollment: Bath campus, 120; Woodstock campus, 120

Program Dates: Five-week session, July 5–August 8

LOCATION

Hyde–Woodstock is located in a town that was founded in 1686. Woodstock is south of the Massachusetts state line, along Highway 169 near the Quinebaug River. Set in the rolling farmland of northeastern Connecticut, Woodstock is a haven of open fields and peaceful woodlands.

Hyde–Bath is located near the Kennebec River in midcoast Maine. Bath is a classic example of Maine's seagoing heritage. All midcoast Maine communities are easily accessible to Bath via the Route 1/I-95 corridor, as well as many other primary state route systems.

BACKGROUND AND PHILOSOPHY

At the Hyde Summer Challenge, teens learn about what it takes to build their confidence: hard work, taking learning risks, and a willingness to take a deep look at their attitudes. Academics, athletics, performing arts, wilderness exploration, and community service are all part of the Hyde Summer Challenge experience, where teens discover the best in themselves and what it takes to be a leader in today's world. The Hyde Summer Challenge blends thrilling outdoor experiences with a fully integrated character curriculum in which teens have the opportunity to connect with the positive influences that will drive them toward reaching their highest potential. This residential experience is designed for teens who want to experience what it feels like to be a leader and who want a genuine understanding of what they can accomplish in college and beyond.

PROGRAM OFFERINGS

Sports Hyde's sports programs offer physical challenges in a character-building culture. Attitude and effort are emphasized during Hyde's summer athletics, where students master team-playing and fitness skills in soccer, basketball, cross-country running, wrestling, and track and field. Recreational swimming and tennis are also offered.

Performing Arts Programs in performing arts provide a test of courage and leadership. Students present a solo audition to the school and work closely throughout the summer with the faculty members to produce, direct, and perform in a full-scale production featuring song, dance, and drama.

Wilderness Trips Wilderness trips present students with obstacles that become opportunities as they face outdoor physical and mental challenges. Hyde's spectacular 600-acre wilderness preserve in Eustis, Maine, overlooking Flagstaff Lake and the Bigelow mountain range, provides a stimulating outdoor classroom for students. Working with Hyde's well-trained wilderness faculty, students test their ability to lead and make decisions that significantly impact their exploration teams. They learn the importance of identifying their attitudes—attitudes that will either help or hinder personal growth and ultimately their success.

Academics Hyde's summer academic program blends character development with a creative approach to inspiring students as they develop reading, writing, math, art, and study skills. Courses are taught on a noncredit basis.

Family Education The Family Education Program makes a Hyde education unique from all other schools. Hyde believes that whatever it asks students to do in developing their character, it also must ask of the adults in their lives, including parents and teachers. Parents are their children's primary teachers, and they have the ability to inspire their children to be productive, good leaders in the world. At Hyde, parents participate in Family Weekend, regional meetings, and seminars, which offer them the unique opportunity to contribute to their student's future success.

ENROLLMENT

Summer Challenge students, who come from many states and from abroad, often enroll to "test drive" Hyde's educational approach before starting school in the fall. Many also enroll for the experience itself—a one-time summer challenge that gives them a renewed sense of purpose and deepens their understanding of themselves and their families.

DAILY SCHEDULE

6:30–7:30	Breakfast, student jobs
8:00–12:00	Academics
12:15–1:00	Lunch
1:00–3:00	Discovery groups, performing arts
3:00–5:00	Sports, wilderness
6:00	Dinner
8:00–10:00	Study hall
10:30	Lights out

EXTRA OPPORTUNITIES AND ACTIVITIES

The summer session culminates with Family Weekend, which brings the entire family to the Hyde campus for an artistic performance by students and for a program involving parents, siblings, faculty members, and students.

FACILITIES

Hyde–Woodstock The Hyde–Woodstock campus is situated on the grounds of a former Catholic women's college. The 120-acre campus includes spacious classroom buildings, a student union with a dining hall, 200-room dormitory facilities, two playing fields, and a practice field. A gymnasium, built in 1998, includes weight and wrestling rooms and basketball courts.

One of the unique features of the Woodstock campus is a state-of-the-art 1,017-seat theater, home to the Opera New England and Theatre of Northeastern Connecticut. The Performing Arts Program benefits from the theater's sophistication.

Hyde–Bath The Hyde–Bath campus extends more than 145 acres and includes three playing fields, an all-weather track, indoor tennis courts, basketball courts, and a gymnasium–field house. The historic mansion and carriage house consist of classrooms and offices. New dormitories, the Renewal Center, the Student Union, and the field house are scattered around the former of estate of John S. Hyde.

Visiting parents can be accommodated at the Renewal Center, an on-campus conference center and dormitory. The Spiritual Center, overlooking the duck pond, offers a quiet place for meditation.

STAFF

A Hyde faculty member's primary responsibility is to help students catch glimpses of themselves at their best in a variety of settings: the classroom, the athletic field, the stage, and the wilderness. All faculty members are meaningfully involved in the lives of students and their families. The demands of the job, as well as the rewards that follow, are extraordinary. The opportunities to teach and to inspire, whether through a classroom lesson, a personal conversation, or an invigorating hike, abound for anyone willing to be both a teacher and a learner in this one-of-a-kind educational process.

COSTS

The total cost for the program is $6000.

TRANSPORTATION

Both campuses are easily accessible to major airports. Bath is less than a 45-minute drive from the Portland International Jetport. Woodstock is within an hour's drive of Hartford and Providence airports. Transportation can be conveniently arranged to these airports, as well as to Boston, from both schools.

APPLICATION TIMETABLE

Hyde does not use grades or test scores to determine admission. The school is interested in enrolling students with the courage and desire to uncover the very best they can be. Students selected possess the willingness to accept responsibility for their personal growth and a family that is sufficiently strong to help them do it.

During the admissions process, families meet with an interviewer for an intensive, confidential discussion of past family history and dynamics. Admissions interviews are a critical first step in the process—a chance for the school, student, and family to sit together and make an honest assessment of some basic family issues. After the interview, both parents and students write a paper describing personal goals.

For more information, contact:

Admissions
Hyde–Woodstock
P.O. Box 237
Woodstock, Connecticut 06281
860-963-4736
Fax: 860-929-0612
E-mail: mtingley@hyde.edu
World Wide Web: http://www.hyde.edu

Admissions
Hyde–Bath
616 High Street
Bath, Maine 04530
207-443-7101
Fax: 207-442-9346
E-mail: krush@hyde.edu
World Wide Web: http://www.hyde.edu

iD TECH CAMPS HANDS-ON TECHNOLOGY FUN!

HIGH-TECH COMPUTER CAMPS FOR THE DIGITAL GENERATION

LOCATED AT MORE THAN THIRTY-FIVE UNIVERSITIES NATIONWIDE

Type of Program: Summer technology and computer camps
Participants: Coeducational, ages 7–17
Program Dates: Weeklong and multiweek day and overnight programs, June to August

LOCATION

iD tech Camps provides day and overnight hands-on technology summer camps at more than thirty-five prestigious universities nationwide. Overnight students reside in college dormitories with adult supervision.

Camp locations in California include Stanford; Berkeley; UCLA; Santa Clara (day only); California, San Diego; California Lutheran (day only); Pepperdine; California, Irvine (day only); and Notre Dame de Namur (day only).

Other locations are Colorado: Colorado College and the University of Denver; Connecticut: Sacred Heart; Florida: Miami; Georgia: Emory; Illinois: Lake Forest and Northwestern; Massachusetts: MIT (day only); Michigan: University of Michigan; Minnesota: University of Minnesota, Minneapolis; New Jersey: Princeton; New York: Vassar; North Carolina: North Carolina at Chapel Hill; Pennsylvania: Carnegie Mellon and Villanova; South Carolina: Clemson; Texas: SMU and Texas at Austin; Virginia: University of Virginia; Washington: University of Washington; Washington, D.C.: Georgetown; and Spain: University of Cadiz (special two-week program).

BACKGROUND AND PHILOSOPHY

iD Tech Camp's summer technology programs are sophisticated, yet personalized, for beginner to advanced-skill levels. The collegiate atmosphere ensures a well-rounded camp experience. While most of the day is spent on the computer, iD staff members actively promote other activities, including chess, capture the flag, and campus scavenger hunts.

iD Tech Camps has teamed with Microsoft, Apple, Adobe, Canon, HP, and Macromedia to deliver a one-of-a-kind technology experience. At iD Tech Camps, students learn more because they are doing, not just watching. By developing the philosophy of "one computer for each student, and an average of 6 students per instructor," iD Tech Camps promotes hands-on learning.

PROGRAM OFFERINGS

Web Design and Graphic Arts, ages 10–17. Students create their own Web site, incorporating Web animation and graphic design. They begin by hand-coding raw HTML then graduate to an industrial-strength Web editor. Students launch into producing professional Web sites complete with graphics, Flash animation, and sound.

Video Game Creation, ages 10–17. Students create their own animated story or video games that other students test and play. This course takes them through the creative game-making process. It is user friendly, exciting, and challenging. Students make their very own videogame.

Programming and Robotics, ages 11–17. This program is for students who like to solve mathematical equations and to make things work. They learn the fundamentals of the programming languages C++ and/or Java and use a program compiler to write and test programs for everything from calculators to simple games. Students also explore the interactive world of Robotics using ROBIX kits and LEGO Mindstorms.

Digital Video and Movie Production, ages 10–17. Instructors take their "crew," through the entire production process from the creation of a storyboard to the completion of a video short. Students use state-of-the-art software and equipment including Apple Final Cut Pro, iMovie, Adobe After Effects, and Canon digital video cameras. Students gain valuable team-building skills as they write, produce, direct, shoot, edit, and star in their own short film.

Multimedia Adventures, ages 7–10. Ideal for younger campers, this course takes students on a journey that mixes game making, the creation of digital photography, and an introduction to graphic design. Students are introduced to basic priciples of game making using the user friendly software, Stagecast Creator. Switching gears, students also use Canon digital still cameras, Adobe Photoshop Elements, and Adobe Photo Album to capture images that they can twist, warp, and stretch. Students create slide shows, greeting cards, and more.

3D Game Design and Animation, ages 13–17. This awesome 3D game design and animation computer camp course offers the chance for students to immerse themselves in a 3D world. Using Conitec's state-of-the-art *3D Game Studio* software, aspiring game designers create complex virtual 3D landscapes, create models, design levels, assign character actions,

develop customizable skins, and create lighting and shadow effects. This truly interactive 3D gaming and animation experience takes campers' imaginations to a whole new realm (only at select locations).

Programming—College Prep, ages 13–17. Students prepare for higher-level computer science classes through an intensive week in college-prep programming. Students learn to design and implement computer-based solutions and code in C++ and/or Java (only at select locations).

Cinematography and Special Effects, ages 13–17. For students with previous digital video experience who are interested in pursuing the art of professional cinematography, this course provides an in-depth perspective of the technical aspects of postproduction. Students focus primarily on special effects and cinematic composition in their short films (only at select locations).

Digital Music Editing, ages 12–17. For students captivated by music, this course offers an introduction to the latest technology for digital music editing that is used by the music industry of the twenty-first century. Students compose, mix, and edit their own songs or soundtracks from scratch (only at select locations).

Sports and Tech with Stanford or UC Berkeley Athletics, for ages 11–14. Students exercise both body and mind in this unique hybrid camp, spending half the time in the tech lab and the other half improving their athletic prowess (only at Stanford University and UC Berkeley).

Documentary Filmmaking and Cultural Immersion in Spain, for ages 14–17. Students live with a Spanish family, go to a Spanish class each morning, then learn how to storyboard, film, and edit their very own documentary film of their experience in Spain. This is a two-week program from July 8 to July 25 at a cost of $3499, airfare not included.

EXTRA OPPORTUNITIES AND ACTIVITIES

During Family Night, iD cordially invites family and friends to tour its labs and meet with iD staff members. Evening activities play a prominent role at the camp. The campus boarding experience promotes new friendships and more time with instructors. Campers join in evening sessions that include chess, campus scavenger hunts, and short programs (animation, tech support, robotics, and networking).

STAFF

The blend of spirit, energy, dedication, and desire to work with kids and teens is something that the iD Tech Camp staff members all share. Each instructor is personally interviewed and carefully selected. Because the camp tries to hire the best, they also pay the best, which means that the instructors are enthusiastic, energetic, and tech-knowledgeable.

MEDICAL CARE

iD Tech Camps' directors and instructors are trained in first aid and CPR and have gone through company training sessions. All students have 24-hour access to on-campus emergency health facilities as well as to local hospitals and emergency centers.

COSTS

Tuition is $639 for day students and $989 for boarding students per weekly session. There are multiweek and sibling discounts available (promo code 45WD).

APPLICATION TIMETABLE

Applications are accepted on a rolling basis, starting in November. Since courses are filled on a first-come, first-served basis, early and multiple-week applications are highly recommended. A parent-orientation packet is provided in May.

FOR MORE INFORMATION, CONTACT:

iD Tech Camps
1885 Winchester Boulevard, Suite 201
Campbell, California 95008
888-709-TECH (8324) (toll-free)
Fax: 408-871-2228
World Wide Web: http://www.internalDrive.com

PARTICIPANT/FAMILY COMMENTS

"Working with the kids and seeing that flicker in their eyes when they learned something new was amazing and incredibly exciting."—Janny Chang, Instructor

"Besides having a fun summer, enrolling Eeman at iD Tech Camps was a worthy investment for her future. As a result of attending iD Tech Camps, she is highly motivated to excel and now is a leader in her school."—Rayda Edding

"After just three days at iD Tech Camps, I've never seen my 9-year-old so excited about learning!"—Nadine Hoffman

IDYLLWILD ARTS SUMMER PROGRAM

SUMMER ARTS PROGRAM

IDYLLWILD, CALIFORNIA

Type of Program: Summer arts program
Participants: Coeducational, ages 5–adult
Enrollment: 1,850
Program Dates: July 3–August 22, 2004
Head of Program: Steven Fraider, Director

LOCATION

Nestled at the mile-high level in the San Jacinto Mountains of southern California, the 205-acre Idyllwild Arts campus is located in one of the most spectacular natural settings in the western U.S. This tranquil site is far removed from urban distractions and offers students a unique learning environment. The campus is surrounded by 20,000 acres of protected woodland, making it a gateway for wilderness activities. Idyllwild is approximately 110 miles southeast of Los Angeles and northeast of San Diego. The village of Idyllwild supports a year-round population of approximately 2,500 in addition to many weekend and holiday visitors. The towns nearest to Idyllwild are Palm Springs, Hemet, and Banning.

BACKGROUND AND PHILOSOPHY

The Idyllwild Arts Foundation was incorporated in 1946 "for the purpose of promoting and advancing artistic and cultural development in Southern California and primarily for the advancement of instruction in music and the arts." Founder Dr. Max Krone, then Dean of the Institute of the Arts at the University of Southern California, and his wife, Beatrice, envisioned a beautiful and harmonious atmosphere that would provide opportunities for a wide variety of artistic experiences to students of all ages and levels of ability. In 1950, the first students enrolled in the Idyllwild School of Music and the Arts (ISOMATA) Summer Program. Today, the mission of the Idyllwild Arts Summer Program—the name was updated by the Board of Trustees in 1995—is to provide for students of all ages and abilities the opportunity to benefit from arts instruction of the highest caliber.

Students enrolled in the Idyllwild Arts Summer Program receive intensive, hands-on arts experience in a competition-free environment that emphasizes individual growth. Students enroll in one course per session that becomes the primary focus of their participation in the Summer Program. Students are expected to attend every class meeting or rehearsal. If a student is unable or unwilling to participate fully in the program, he or she may be asked to leave the program. Students should be prepared to work hard and learn a great deal. Although many optional recreational activities are scheduled, the requirements of a student's chosen course, whether a rehearsal, class, or lecture, always take first priority. If a student feels the need for additional help or instruction, he or she can feel comfortable about asking an instructor for more time and attention.

PROGRAM OFFERINGS

The Summer Program consists of courses in dance, music, theater, visual arts, creative writing, and Native American arts. Specific course offerings are organized into art centers according to age. Courses are available to both boarding and day students.

Children's Center (ages 5–12): The minimum boarding age is 9. Courses include Multi-Arts, a one-week day program for students ages 5–8. For students ages 9–12, there are one- and two-week programs in dance, music (piano), theater, visual arts, and creative writing. Professional artist-educators use age-appropriate materials and methods to convey the excitement and discipline necessary for accomplishment in the arts. Small classes and a low student-teacher ratio, approximately 9:1, ensure that students receive a great deal of individual attention and support. An important goal of the Children's Center is for students to gain an enthusiasm and excitement for the arts and a basic foundation of technical knowledge.

Junior Artist's Center (ages 11–13): Workshops include one- and two-week offerings in theater, visual arts, and creative writing. In addition, students in this age range may participate in selected Youth Arts Center music and dance courses based on experience and ability.

Youth Arts Center (ages 13–18): Courses are two weeks in length with the exception of the Summer Theatre Festival, which is offered in two 3-week sessions. The Youth Arts Center comprises the largest segment of the Summer Program, with forty-eight weeks of course offerings in all of the visual and performing arts. Courses include art exploration, two bands, ceramics, chamber music, choir, computer animation, dance, fiction writing, filmmaking, guitar, jazz, jewelry making, musical theater, two orchestras, painting and drawing, photography, piano, playwriting, poetry, and theater.

Family Week: A one-week session is offered. Families live together and have the opportunity to explore the visual and performing arts in a relaxed setting. Adults and children choose from a variety of arts and outdoor activities. Evening events are for the whole family.

ENROLLMENT

The Idyllwild Arts Summer Program enrolls approximately 1,850 students per summer, consisting of 350 children, 900 teenagers, 450 adult and college students, and 150 family campers. About 75 percent of students are from California, with the remaining 25 percent from the rest of the U.S. and abroad. Approximately 60 percent of summer students are female.

DAILY SCHEDULE

In general, Youth and Junior Artist students can expect to be involved in course-related activities a minimum of 6 hours per day, six days per week. Individual course schedules vary according to the needs and requirements of each discipline. Instruction begins at 9 a.m. and may continue into the evening in some programs. Children's Center courses meet Monday through Friday, with recreational activities for boarding students on the weekends.

Fostering respect for individuals, for the arts, and for education are the foundations upon which expectations of student behavior are based. A few policies pertaining to safe and cooperative communal living and adherence to state and federal laws, including student use of tobacco, drugs, and alcohol, along with vandalism, violence, and leaving campus without permission, are enforced rigorously.

EXTRA OPPORTUNITIES AND ACTIVITIES

A variety of evening and weekend activities, including dances, game nights, art playgrounds, pool parties, talent shows, and field games, are organized by the counseling staff and offered to students. In the Children's Center, all boarding students participate in an extensive program of recreational activities offered each evening from 7 to 9 p.m. On weekends, longer and more extensive activities, including art projects, informal drama productions, and field games, are scheduled.

FACILITIES

The Idyllwild Arts campus has more than one hundred buildings, including an air-conditioned concert hall, a modern library, an exhibition center, a sound stage, two recital halls, three outdoor theaters, numerous art studios, classrooms and practice rooms, a dining hall, a health center, a swimming pool, residence halls for faculty members and adult students, three large college-style dormitories for Youth students, and four small dormitories for Children's Center and Junior Artist students. Students are housed with 3 or 4 roommates per room. Each room has a private bathroom with a shower.

STAFF

Faculty members are dedicated artist-teachers who look forward to the challenge of working with a diverse student body. The Summer Program provides students with the opportunity to work directly with professional artists, dancers, directors, musicians, and writers who are committed to the process of arts education and to their own arts discipline. Approximately 225 faculty members participate in the Summer Program. The summer staff of 55 consists of deans, counselors, teaching assistants, lifeguards, and nurses. Students are supervised in the dormitories by resident counselors. Most counselors are college students or recent graduates with a major or strong interest in the arts. Counselor applicants are rigorously screened and interviewed.

MEDICAL CARE

Health services are administered by 2 resident nurses and a certified emergency medical technician. There is a medical clinic in the village of Idyllwild that treats students who require the services of a physician. Idyllwild also has a pharmacy and fire department paramedics. The nearest hospital is located in Hemet, approximately 25 miles from the campus.

COSTS

Fees vary by art center and by course. In 2003, the cost of a two-week Youth, Junior Artist, or Children's Center program, including tuition, meals, housing, application fee, and lab fee, ranged from $1650 to $1950, depending on the course. The all-inclusive cost of a one-week Family Camp program ranged from $1580 for 2 people to $3300 for a group of 6. An initial deposit of $250 is required with all applications. All fees are payable in full thirty days before a program begins. Students who pay in full by March 15 receive a 10 percent discount. It is recommended that boarding students keep $25 per week in the student bank to pay for snacks, art supplies, and postcards.

FINANCIAL AID

A significant part of the school's mission is to provide financial aid where needed for talented young artists from diverse backgrounds. In 2003, nearly 250 students received financial aid totaling more than $185,000. All financial aid is in the form of scholarships. Scholarships are awarded based on the financial need of the student, the talent of the student in a specific discipline, and the enrollment needs of the school.

TRANSPORTATION

Idyllwild is approximately 2½ hours by car from Los Angeles or San Diego. Students flying to southern California should arrange a flight to the Ontario International Airport, 75 miles from Idyllwild, or the Palm Springs Airport, 60 miles from the campus. The school offers van pick-up service to and from either airport for a fee of $100 each way. There is no public transportation to Idyllwild.

APPLICATION TIMETABLE

Enrollment begins in early February. Inquiries are welcome anytime. Families interested in touring the campus may do so by contacting the school at the address listed below. Most courses maintain open enrollment. Visual arts classes are small, so early enrollment is encouraged.

FOR MORE INFORMATION, CONTACT:

Idyllwild Arts Summer Program
P.O. Box 38
Idyllwild, California 92549
909-659-2171 Ext. 365
Fax: 909-659-5463
E-mail: summer@idyllwildarts.org
World Wide Web: http://www.idyllwildarts.org

INTERLOCHEN

INTERLOCHEN ARTS CAMP

INTERLOCHEN, MICHIGAN

Type of Program: Coeducational summer arts program
Participants: Girls and boys, ages 8–18
Enrollment: More than 2,500
Program Dates: June to August
Head of Program: Jeffrey S. Kimpton, President

LOCATION

Interlochen Arts Camp is located on a wooded 1,200-acre campus situated between Duck Lake and Green Lake in rural northwest lower Michigan. It is approximately 4 hours from the Detroit area and 6 hours from Chicago. It is close to Lake Michigan, the Sleeping Bear Dunes National Lakeshore, and Traverse City, a popular year-round tourist destination.

BACKGROUND AND PHILOSOPHY

The mission of Interlochen Center for the Arts, of which the camp is a part, is to offer gifted and talented young people the opportunity to develop their creative abilities in a wholesome community under the guidance of an exemplary faculty of artists and educators. Founded in 1928, the camp provides arts education at its highest level, not just for the young artist, but for the growth of the complete individual, preparing them well for today's demanding and changing society. High school, intermediate, and junior campers learn as much about themselves as they do about their art, meeting young people from different environments, backgrounds, and cultures. Through individualized attention from counselors and instructors and exposure to famous conductors and guest artists, students are encouraged to explore and reach for their dreams.

PROGRAM OFFERINGS

Specific class offerings vary in each of the three divisions: junior (grades 3–6), intermediate (grades 6–9), and high school (grades 9–12). Each student's schedule is determined individually.
Music Offerings include band, orchestra, jazz ensemble, piano and organ, beginning through advanced instrument instruction, chorus, music theory, chamber music, computer music, jazz improvisation, vocal technique, classical guitar, and composition. Four-week Advanced High School String Quartet and Advanced Vocal Institutes are also offered.
Dance Offerings include beginning through advanced levels in both ballet and modern dance technique.
Theatre Arts Courses include theatre production, theatre workshop, acting studio, early musical theatre, modern musical theatre, Shakespeare, and playwriting.
Visual Arts Courses include art exploration, drawing, painting, ceramics, fiber arts, metalsmithing, printmaking, sculpture, photography, and more.
Creative Writing Offered for high school students through the Creative Writing Institute, a special intensive course is offered in each four-week session. Students work under the apprenticeship of professional writers and teachers on an individual basis. A creative writing class is also offered at the intermediate level.

ENROLLMENT

Interlochen Arts Camp enrolls more than 2,100 campers each summer. Minorities and international students represent 15 percent of the population. Students come from all fifty states and more than forty other countries.

DAILY SCHEDULE

Arts instructional classes are held Tuesday through Saturday from approximately 8:30 a.m. to 4:30 p.m. Sunday's schedule includes religious services and concerts. Rehearsals and recreational and divisional activities take place on Mondays.

EXTRA OPPORTUNITIES AND ACTIVITIES

Extracurricular activities include recreation, picnics, campfires, dances, arts and crafts, off-campus trips, and other planned activities.

FACILITIES

Campers live with a counselor and 10–18 other campers in one of the 120 rustic cabins located in each division. There are 450 buildings on the Interlochen campus, including the cabins, fourteen performance sites, and seventeen practice studios, which hold more than 275 individual practice rooms. The camp can seat more than 12,500 in its performance venues. Performance sites include Corson Auditorium (1,000), Kresge Auditorium (4,000), and the historic Interlochen Bowl (6,000). Michael P. Dendrinos Chapel/Recital Hall, Hildegarde Lewis Dance Building, Harvey Theatre, and Phoenix Theatre each seat up to 200 people comfortably.

STAFF

Faculty members at Interlochen Arts Camp include distinguished artists and educators from colleges,

universities, and secondary schools around the world. Guest artists also enhance instruction by providing master classes.

MEDICAL CARE

A team of doctors and nurses is on staff throughout the summer. There is an infirmary for each division. Interlochen is within minutes of a large regional medical center in Traverse City.

RELIGIOUS LIFE

Interlochen is not affiliated with any particular religion. The camp provides campers with the opportunity to attend a variety of religious services on campus.

COSTS

The cost for the eight-week session in 2004 was $5250. The four-week sessions were $3495. The Advanced String Quartet Institute (high school only) was $3700 (including 60-minute lessons) and the Advanced Vocal Institute was $3736 (including 60-minute lessons).

The fees include general expenses such as room, board, most classes and group instruction, camp uniform, all recreational facilities, and admission to faculty and student performances. Any additional fees for supplies or laboratory costs are listed within the camp schedule. Students should contact Interlochen for rates for 2005.

High school division students are accepted only for the full eight-week session with the exception of the four-week Dance, String Quartet, Drawing, Vocal, and Creative Writing Institutes. Junior and intermediate division students may attend either one or both of the four-week sessions.

Private lessons are available for an additional fee.

It is recommended that students maintain a personal account of $400 for the eight-week session and $250 for the four-week sessions to cover miscellaneous expenses.

A $1000 deposit is required at the time of acceptance. Full payment is due by June 1.

FINANCIAL AID

The purpose of Interlochen's financial aid program is to help provide outstanding young performers the means to further their artistic development. Interlochen is able to provide some degree of assistance to approximately 25 percent of its campers. Financial aid is based on one or a combination of three criteria: financial need of the family, the artistic ability of the student, and the enrollment needs of the camp.

In addition, the Emerson Scholars Program provides a full music scholarship for 52 students from across the United States.

TRANSPORTATION

Interlochen is approximately 16 miles southwest of Traverse City and is easily accessible by any mode of transportation. The camp is served by Cherry Capital Airport in Traverse City via direct flights from Chicago, Detroit, Milwaukee, and Minneapolis. Interlochen staff members pick up campers at the airport.

APPLICATION TIMETABLE

The priority review application deadline is February 15. Notification of acceptance is made by April 15. Early applications for non-audition-based areas are highly recommended. The application fee is $35.

FOR MORE INFORMATION, CONTACT:

Interlochen Center for the Arts
Office of Admissions
P.O. Box 199
Interlochen, Michigan 49643–0199
Telephone: 231-276-7472
E-mail: admissions@interlochen.org
World Wide Web: http://www.interlochen.org

INTERLOCKEN AT WINDSOR MOUNTAIN

(NAME IS BEING CHANGED TO WINDSOR MOUNTAIN INTERNATIONAL) LANGUAGE IMMERSION, FRIENDSHIP EXCHANGES, COMMUNITY SERVICE, THEATER, WILDERNESS ADVENTURE, AND INTERNATIONAL SUMMER CAMP

UNITED STATES, LATIN AMERICA, EUROPE, ASIA, AFRICA, AND THE CARIBBEAN

Type of Program: Friendship Exchanges, wilderness and adventure travel, traveling theater, leadership development, community service, international residential summer camp

Participants: Coeducational for students completing grades 3–12 (travel programs) and students completing grades 3–8 (summer camp)

Enrollment: 10–16 per travel or community service program; summer camp, 175

Program Dates: One to six weeks in July and August, travel and community service programs; four or eight weeks in July and August, summer camp

Head of Program: Richard Herman, Director

LOCATION

Each destination for Interlocken's travel and community service programs is carefully chosen to provide a safe, challenging, and personalized learning environment for students. Since 1967, when the first travel group took off for Scandinavia, Windsor Mountain students have explored more than thirty countries. Some programs have withstood the test of time: New England Traveling Minstrels and New England Adventure have been running for more than twenty years.

The International Summer Camp is situated on a 1,000-acre lakeside wilderness preserve, 2 hours from Boston. The rustic, architect-designed facilities feature an enormous deck—the center of camp activity and community life—and a dining hall complete with a three-story bell tower and a giant fieldstone fireplace. Windsor Mountain's base camp also houses the central offices of the travel programs and other year-round programs.

BACKGROUND AND PHILOSOPHY

Windsor Mountain International was founded in 1961 by Richard Herman as the first United Nations–inspired residential summer camp dedicated to bringing together campers from different ethnic, religious, socioeconomic, and national backgrounds.

Crossroads Travel programs were introduced in 1967 and grew out of Windsor Mountain's desire to expand the opportunity for cross-cultural exploration beyond the boundaries of the international summer camp.

The first community service program was offered in 1986, a response to the increased desire among young people to contribute to the well-being of others while being able to explore an interesting part of the world.

Beyond a shared international and cross-cultural basis, all Windsor Mountain programs are bound together by the core values of community building and learning through active, hands-on participation. Participants are expected to have fun, to give generously of themselves, to help in the planning of activities, to accept occasional disappointments, to respect others, and to bring enthusiasm to their chosen program.

PROGRAM OFFERINGS

Cuba Friendship Camp In its fourth year, the Cuba Friendship Camp offers students a change to learn about Cuban culture and politics, as well as to study Spanish and learn to dance salsa.

Friendship Exchange In addition to Cuba, Windsor Mountain offers friendship exchange and language immersion programs in Burma, France, Mexico, Puerto Rico, and Quebec and four friendship exchange programs with communities ranging from Alaska to Hawaii. Friendship Exhanges are cross-cultural programs that provide the opportunity for students to gain powerful new understandings. Students often stay with families, learn some of the local language, and spend time interacting with local youth groups.

Traveling Theater Now in its thirty-fourth season, the Traveling Minstrels programs enable participants to design and produce an original theater piece and take their show on the road to perform throughout New England or California (five weeks) or Western Europe (six weeks). This program is open to students finishing grades 8–12.

Leadership Development Two distinct programs are offered under the Leadership Development umbrella: Random Acts of Kindness and Leaders in Action. Random Acts of Kindness is a New England-based community service program. Students travel throughout the region doing real work, assisting and improving the lives of people and their communities. This four-week program is open to students finishing grades 8–12. Leaders in Action is a unique opportunity for students to develop leadership skills that prepare them to be camp counselors. After an initial period of training and certification, students travel to the Bequia to teach activities at the summer camp. Volunteer service work and fun outdoor adventures are also included in this four-week program, open to students finishing grades 10–11.

Horseback Riding Camp At the Driftwood Ranch Camp, students finishing grades 7–8 are given their own horse to care for and ride through the forests and lake country of New Hampshire. Students also help out at a rodeo and work at a therapeutic riding center. The camp culminates in a three-day horse packing trip.

Wilderness and Adventure Students develop skills in low-impact camping, hiking and backpacking, rock climbing or mountain biking, white-water rafting, or sea kayaking. One-, 2-, or 3-week novice programs in New England, a 4-week intermediate program in California, and a 4-week program in Australia are open to students finishing grades 7–11.

Community Service Students live and work like Peace Corps volunteers in small, rural villages and begin to understand and appreciate the problems and joys of living in a developing country. Every program also includes adventure: Amazon canoeing, elephant trekking, African safaris, Mayan ruin explorations, and more. This program is open to students finishing grades 9–12.

International Summer Camp The residential camp is a caring, creative community of 175 boys and girls, ages 9–14, and 70 staff members from all over the world. All campers take an active part in choosing and carrying out their own activity programs, sharing their summer with people from a multitude of different backgrounds.

A wide range of activities is offered, including creative theater and dance, noncompetitive and team sports, Red Cross swimming and water sports, music, applied arts, mountain biking, environmental explorations, community service projects, and wilderness/adventure expeditions.

ENROLLMENT

Each travel and community service program enrolls 10–18 participants; the summer camp enrolls 175 campers per session. Since 1961 more than 10,000 young people have explored the world with Windsor Mountain.

FACILITIES

Windsor Mountain travelers live simply, either camping or living with families and/or in hostel-like accommodations. Most groups prepare their own meals. Summer campers live in cabins or tents and enjoy healthy meals served cafeteria-style.

STAFF

Experienced, competent leadership is undeniably one of the most important sources of strength and success of Windsor Mountain programs. Travel leaders range in age from 23 to 40 and have substantial experience working with high school–age students. Enthusiasm, creativity, maturity, compassion, sound judgment, first aid/CPR, lifeguard training, and excellent teaching skills are required

staff qualifications. Each travel program has 2 or 3 leaders; 60 staff members from around the world infuse the camp with spirited fun and adventure.

COSTS

Tuition ranges from $999 to $5350, depending on the location and duration of the program. Tuition is all inclusive, except for airfare and personal spending money.

FINANCIAL AID

Since its inception, Windsor Mountain has been committed to providing an enriching educational summer experience to the widest spectrum of students possible. Approximately 25 percent of the participants receive some form of financial assistance, ranging from 10 to 50 percent of the program's tuition.

TRANSPORTATION

Bus transportation from New York City, Westchester, Hartford, and Boston is available for the camp and for programs originating in New Hampshire.

APPLICATION TIMETABLE

Applications are accepted on a rolling basis. Students are encouraged to apply early.

For more information, contact:

Admissions Department/PG
Windsor Mountain International
19 Interlocken Way
Hillsboro, New Hampshire 03244
603-478-3166
Fax: 603-478-5260
E-mail: mail@windsormountain.org
World Wide Web: http://www.WindsorMountain.org

PARTICIPANT/FAMILY COMMENTS

"Dan's socialization skills improve every year with Windsor Mountain's programs. You can't put a price on that facet of education."

"I gave of myself 100% and received back ten times that amount."

"I wasn't a tourist, but a student. I didn't observe another culture, but lived in it."

"This trip introduced me to a new people whose lifestyle is everything but similar to mine. They are content with what they have and ask for nothing more than what they need. My eyes have opened to new angles on life."

INTERNATIONAL SCHOOL OF BEIJING

ISB CHINESE LANGUAGE CAMP

BEIJING, CHINA

Type of Program: Language immersion with teacher support
Participants: Students between the ages of 9 and 18 who have completed at least one year of Chinese classes or the equivalent
Enrollment: 5–10 students per language class
Program Dates: June 20–July 8, 2005
Head of Program: Theresa Chao, Director

LOCATION

The ISB Chinese Language Camp is located in the ISB International School of Beijing (ISB) in Beijing, the capital of the People's Republic of China and China's political and cultural center. Beijing and its surroundings are interwoven with the history and cultures of the Ming and Qing dynasties and attractions such as the Forbidden City, the Great Wall, the Ming Tombs, the Summer Palace, the Temple of Heaven, and many other sites.

BACKGROUND AND PHILOSOPHY

In 1980, existing U.S., British, Australian, Canadian, and New Zealand embassy schools in Beijing merged to form the International School of Beijing on the grounds of the U.S. Embassy. In 1988, it relocated and was officially registered as a school for diplomatic children under the auspices of China's Ministry of Foreign Affairs. In 2002, ISB was restructured as an independent school for international children under the auspices of the Beijing Municipal Education Bureau. The school has grown to become a leading international school.

In 2002, the four-week ISB Chinese Language Camp language-immersion program was created with the main goal of helping students learn to function successfully in a Chinese-speaking environment. Campers improve their language skills and pursue self-challenges while developing an appreciation of Chinese culture.

PROGRAM OFFERINGS

Participants are grouped according to their language level for daily morning language classes. All instruction is conducted in Chinese, based on a thematic curriculum. Students choose an afternoon elective, such as line dance, martial arts, calligraphy, brush painting, or Peking opera. Field trips around Beijing are integrated into the curriculum. In addition to visiting historical sites, museums, and performances, students also experience everyday life by shopping in traditional markets, visiting a farming village, and ordering food in local restaurants.

ENROLLMENT

Participants in the ISB Chinese Language Camp are all international students. Students in language classes are grouped according to level, but class size is limited so that each student receives helpful individual attention as needed.

DAILY SCHEDULE

The Chinese Language Camp begins with a two-day orientation and a Beijing tour, including the Forbidden City, the Summer Palace, the Temple of Heaven, the Ming Tombs, and the Great Wall. Language classes are held in the morning, which leaves the afternoon open for elective cultural events in and around Beijing.

EXTRA OPPORTUNITIES AND ACTIVITIES

Cultural electives and other fun experiences include everything from camping out on the Great Wall and flying kites on Tiananmen Square to visiting the Temple of Heaven after a traditional Chinese breakfast. Students also can enjoy a tea ceremony at a royal garden or ride in a pedicab to tour the Hutongs of Beijing, visit the Bell Temple, and enjoy a bell concert. For an overnight experience, students take a trip to Chengde Summer Palace.

FACILITIES

The ISB Chinese Language Camp is held in the facilities of the International School of Beijing, which is nestled in the countryside setting of the Shunyi District of Beijing. The campus has excellent views of the mountain range northwest of Beijing and overlooks fields of corn in the Shunyi District. Students are accommodated in the air-conditioned dorm of the Limai School near the campus. Buses bring students to the campus each day and take them on excursions around the city. Meals are served on the ISB campus and in Beijing restaurants. Some features of the campus include dedicated state-of-the-art technology labs, art exhibition space, a 600-seat theater, a 25-meter pool and natatorium, three gymnasiums, and extensive grass and turf outdoor facilities with lighting for night use.

STAFF

Professional language teachers create a fun and exciting atmosphere for students to learn and improve their language skills.

COSTS

A $350 nonrefundable registration fee reserves a participant's place in the program. After applications are processed, the balance of $2150 must be paid. Late payments are assessed a late fee. Payment methods include checks (U.S. dollars) drawn on a U.S. bank only and made payable to the International School of Beijing–Shunyi. Wire transfers are accepted in the account name of the International School of Beijing–Shunyi, account number 2401142210000208, China Construction Bank Beijing Anhua Branch, No. 35 Anding Road, Chayang District, Beijing 100029, The People's Republic of China.

TRANSPORTATION

The ISB Chinese Language Camp is located in the northeast section of the city, 15 minutes from Beijing's international airport, with direct access to an efficient road network and the airport expressway.

FINANCIAL AID

An ISB discount is available.

APPLICATION TIMETABLE

Payment must be made by April 30. Final payments received (postmarked) between May 1 and May 31 must include an additional $50 late fee. If payment is not received by June 1, applicants lose their place in the program.

For more information, contact:

ISB Chinese Language Camp
No. 10 An Hua Street
Shunyi District, Beijing 101300
The People's Republic of China
8610-8149-2345
Fax: 8610-8046-2004
E-mail: ISBchinese@isb.bj.edu.cn
World Wide Web: http://chinese.isb.bj.edu.cn

INTERNATIONAL SUMMER CAMP MONTANA, SWITZERLAND

SUMMER PROGRAMS

CRANS-MONTANA (VALAIS), SWITZERLAND

Type of Program: Sports and language camp
Participants: Coeducational, ages 8–17
Enrollment: 280 (maximum)
Program Dates: June 26 to July 16, July 17 to August 6, and August 7 to August 27
Heads of Program: Philippe Studer, Erica Studer-Mathieu, and Erwin Mathieu, Camp Directors

LOCATION

Crans-Montana, an internationally known health and sports resort area in the heart of the Swiss Alps, is located 1,500 meters above sea level in the French-speaking part of Switzerland. Known as "The Sun Terrace of Switzerland," Crans-Montana is situated on a sun-drenched plateau that enjoys an average of 13 hours of sunshine every day in the summer. Rising above the vineyards and orchards of the Rhone Valley, the camp is surrounded by magnificent pine tree forests and is protected from wind by a snow-peaked mountain range. Campers enjoy miles of beautiful trails that traverse meadows of alpine flowers, leading to majestic views of forests, lakes, mountains, and glaciers.

BACKGROUND AND PHILOSOPHY

For more than forty years, International Summer Camp Montana (ISCM) has strived to develop in its campers physical and intellectual achievement through an American-style camping experience employing European traditions. The camp's fundamental philosophy is to provide a healthy outdoor-living experience through sports and fellowship in a creative and wholesome environment. Campers develop both their minds and their bodies through a myriad of activities, broadening their outlook and enriching their lives through the opportunity to meet people of different backgrounds from all over the world. Through its combination of cooperative living with recreational, educational, and social activities, ISCM enables each young man and woman to acquire the maturity and independence essential to his or her well-being. Respect for others' views, understanding of democratic ideals, and responsible citizenship are stressed in this unique program, which provides an unforgettable opportunity for campers to gain self-understanding while interacting with others in a surrounding of beauty, joy, and learning. At ISCM, the emphasis is on cooperation, not competition; creativity, not conformity.

International Summer Camp Montana is a member of the Crans-Montana and Valais Tourist Offices, the Swiss Hotel Association, the Swiss Ski Federation, and the Association for Horsemanship Safety and Education.

PROGRAM OFFERINGS

Just a sampling of the numerous activities offered at ISCM include sailing, rafting, swimming, English riding instruction, dressage, jumping and vaulting, trail riding, tennis, summer skiing and snowboarding in Saas Fee and Zermatt, fencing, mountain hiking, campcraft, overnight hikes, rock climbing, golf, circus skills, mountain biking, basketball, volleyball, softball, soccer, touch football, cricket, table tennis, floor hockey, fitness training, performing arts, drawing, painting, screen printing, creative nature crafts, weaving, macrame, modelling, nature collecting, scrapbook making, aerobics, archery, badminton, billiards, Frisbee, a fitness course, gymnastics, minigolf, trampolining, track and field, outdoor games, and various educational talks and videos covering Swiss history and culture, classical and modern music, and nature study.

Activities are directed toward both personal and group development, and, while enjoyable and interesting, they challenge each camper to exercise his or her intelligence and promote the emergence of abilities and insight. Campers may participate in the activities of their choice during free time and are always under the supervision and guidance of the staff.

Campers are divided into three groups: Juniors, ages 8–10; Pioneers, ages 11–13; and Seniors, ages 14–17. Programs for each section are commensurate with the ability, endurance, and resourcefulness of its age level. The average Junior group size is 6 campers; the average Pioneer and Senior group size is 8.

Although ISCM is a coeducational camp, boys and girls generally pursue programs separately; experience has shown that wholesome contact during selected activities—excursions, hikes, games, and entertainment—is beneficial to all.

English is the main language spoken at camp, although French, Italian, and German are also spoken. Upon request, campers may be grouped with others who speak a specific language.

ENROLLMENT

Since 1961, boys and girls from all over the world have come to ISCM. Each year campers represent more than fifty countries in North America, South America, Europe, North Africa, and Asia, with the majority coming from the United States, Canada, Mexico, Italy, France, Great Britain, The Netherlands, Scandinavia, Germany, Belgium, Spain, and the Middle East. Only boys and girls of outstanding moral character are accepted; for this reason, a letter of recommendation from each camper's teacher is required.

DAILY SCHEDULE

Because of the great deal of individual choice, particularly for older campers, no day at ISCM is exactly the same as any other. Meal times, evening program schedules, and lights-out are determined by age group.

EXTRA OPPORTUNITIES AND ACTIVITIES

In addition to exploring neighboring mountain areas through day and overnight hikes, campers participate in two excursions, included in the camp fee, during each period. One excursion visits places of interest in the Central Valais: Zermatt, the mountain village at the foot of the Matterhorn; Saas Fee, the village of the glaciers; the St. Bernard Pass; the Rhone Glacier; and Sierre with its manor, art exhibitions, and various museums. The second excursion is to other parts of Switzerland such as the Lake Geneva area, with the towns of Geneva, Lausanne, and Montreux and the castles of Chillon and Gruyère; Bern, the medieval town and capital of Switzerland; the Bernese Oberland; Thun; and Interlaken.

ISCM also features traditional activities such as campfires, sing-a-longs, stunt nights, theater groups, folk dancing, shopping trips, a camp horse show, storytelling, and birthday parties.

An optional language program is offered in English, French, Spanish, and German at beginner, intermediate, and advanced levels. Five 50-minute lessons are taught each week in the native language of the instructors.

FACILITIES

ISCM's main building is the solidstone Moubra House, which overlooks spacious playing fields, forests, a lake, and the Rhone Valley and includes camper and staff living quarters, a dining room, a rec room, a living room, a theater, a game room, and six classrooms. Camp also features four additional buildings, including a large chalet. Campers are housed by gender on separate floors of Moubra House or in the chalet. Rooms are sunny and well-equipped with all modern conveniences; most have wide balconies. Each floor has a large number of bathrooms.

STAFF

The camp staff comprises 3 camp directors, each in charge of his or her own sector (programming and educational supervision, administration, and catering); 3 head counselors, each responsible for one of the age groups; counselors; sports instructors; language teachers; and office staff members. A trained dietitian supervises the preparation of excellent French-style food with an international flavor. The program staff consists of approximately 80 multilingual members.

Each member of the International Summer Camp Montana staff is carefully chosen on the basis of age, education, camping experience, emotional maturity, and the ability to work with growing children. Experienced counselors from previous seasons provide stability to the counseling group. All counselors have experience in American or European camps.

MEDICAL CARE

The health, safety, and general welfare of each camper are meticulously guarded. Two resident nurses and an on-call physician are responsible for the good health of campers and staff members. There is a fully equipped hospital nearby in Sierre.

COSTS

The camp fee for each three-week session is 4900 Swiss francs (US$3630). This fee includes all living expenses, excursions and overnight hikes, activities and sports, infirmary service, laundry service, and instruction in riding, tennis, swimming, and other activities. Not included in this cost are travel to and from camp, personal allowances, medical treatment and medical prescriptions, the optional language program (250 Swiss francs), and fees for ski lifts and transportation during skiing trips. All fees are payable in Swiss francs.

TRANSPORTATION

ISCM representatives meet and escort campers traveling by air to and from Geneva Airport on arrival and departure days and facilitate check-in and customs formalities. The fee for this service is 80 Swiss francs one-way and 160 Swiss francs for a round-trip; transportation is provided by deluxe bus and includes a snack or meal as well as confirmation of return flight. Arrangements for this service must be made at least two weeks before the camper's arrival.

APPLICATION TIMETABLE

The number of places is limited; parents, particularly those who wish to enroll their children in the second session, are advised to make reservations early. Campers may enroll for one, two, or all three sessions. Extensions of camp sessions are accepted only on a space-available basis.

A nonrefundable deposit of 1000 Swiss francs is required with registration. The balance of tuition is payable in full before May 31. Various cancellation policies apply.

A camp DVD is available free of charge.

FOR ENROLLMENT, DVD, OR MORE INFORMATION, CONTACT:

Philippe Studer, Erica Studer, and Erwin Mathieu, Directors
International Summer Camp Montana
La Moubra
CH-3963 Crans-Montana 1
Switzerland
41 27 481 56 63
Fax: 41 27 481 56 31
E-mail: info@campmontana.ch
World Wide Web: http://www.campmontana.ch

INTERN EXCHANGE INTERNATIONAL

SUMMER INTERNSHIP/TRAVEL PROGRAM

LONDON, ENGLAND

Type of Program: Residential career internship program
Participants: Coeducational, ages 16–18
Enrollment: 180–220 participants per session
Program Dates: One session per year, thirty days in June and July
Heads of Program: Nina Miller Glickman, M.Ed., and Lynn Ann Weinstein, Directors

LOCATION

Intern Exchange International (IEI) participants live in London, a dynamic, safe, world-class city without language barriers. Students reside in the University of London residence halls in the heart of Bloomsbury, the historic literary district where Virginia Woolf and Charles Dickens once lived. The British Museum, Soho, Oxford Street, and the West End theatres are just minutes away.

BACKGROUND AND PHILOSOPHY

Nina Glickman and Lynn Weinstein established Intern Exchange International in 1987 as a way to encourage high school students to make an informed career choice. IEI's exciting summer internships in London offer students a hands-on experience in a profession that interests them. In addition to career exposure and the opportunity to obtain prestigious references for college, this monthlong peek into the day-to-day rhythms of the working world provides a wonderful growth experience. Day trips, weekend excursions, and special touring events are an integral part of the summer.

IEI is a bridge between high school and college, where students experience tremendous social, academic, and personal growth; their newfound sense of independence will serve them well in college. Because of the unique nature of this program, the interns experience freedom as young, responsible adults within established boundaries. IEI students are self-directed, responsible individuals who enjoy learning in a real-world environment and who are excited by this outstanding opportunity to learn and live in London for the summer.

PROGRAM OFFERINGS

In this program, students gain exposure to a promising career at the side of a practicing professional. Work is combined with interesting and fun evening and weekend activities and excursions.

Internships give students a chance to participate firsthand in a field of interest by doing meaningful work with a preceptor. They might help prepare cases for trial with prominent barristers and solicitors, conduct research in the clinics of well-known physicians, or unearth underground ruins with archaeologists. Internship programs include Archaeology, Architecture, Art Gallery and Auction House, Community Service/Social Services, Genealogy, Hotel Management, Law, Medicine (Medical Research, Veterinary Medicine), Public Relations, Publishing, Retail Sales and Marketing, and Strategic Studies. New internships are always being developed.

Career Plus-Programmes take students into the real world, where they get the background and skills they need to pursue their chosen path. Accomplished professionals serve as mentors and tutors in a variety of project-based workshops. Video Production students work with professionals to create their own documentaries, Journalism interns team up with journalists to publish their own newspaper, and those in the Theatre programme study The Method with experienced actors and then test their skills on scenes and improvisation. Plus-Programmes include Fine Arts, Digital Media, Fashion and Design, Journalism, Photography, and Theatre.

Interns maintain a weekly journal in which they reflect on a subject of their own choice or pick from a wide range of suggested topics. The journal can be used as a valuable resource for writing high school essays and preparing for college entrance essays.

ENROLLMENT

The program accepts high school students, including graduating seniors, ages 16 to 18. Between 180 and 220 students are enrolled each session.

EXTRA OPPORTUNITIES AND ACTIVITIES

After a full week of internships, theatre, concerts, and special dinners out on the town, weekends are split between "pick and choose" days in London and daylong excursions into the country. Interns enjoy exploring the historic sites of Stonehenge, Bath, the Cotswolds, and Cambridge. London itself has much to offer, including afternoon tea with scones and cream, Madame Tussaud's, Picadilly, and the street musicians in Leicester Square. Past interns have seen Good Charlotte, Tina Turner, Green Day, and Oasis in concert. Opportunities abound for the free evenings.

FACILITIES

Interns live in two comfortable, secure, University of London residence halls—Hughes Parry Hall and Commonwealth Hall. These adjacent modern dormitories, with single rooms, shared baths, common rooms, and TV lounges, face an elegant Georgian

crescent with lovely gardens. Tennis and squash courts, pool, and darts are available for the interns' use. Reception desks are manned 24 hours a day; public telephones and laundry facilities are available. A full English breakfast and a three-course evening meal (with vegetarian options) are provided in the spacious, self-service dining rooms. The surrounding Russell Square neighborhood, friendly and cozy, offers all the conveniences of home—cleaners, a supermarket, a chemist, a movie theatre, and a health food store. Three tube stations are within easy walking distance.

STAFF

The program staff includes Directors Nina M. Glickman and Lynn Ann Weinstein, who founded Intern Exchange International seventeen years ago and have personally supervised its growth and development ever since. Summer staff members include the Assistant to the Directors, an experienced teacher whose duties include overseeing the Career Plus-Programmes. The Career Plus Administrator works with staff members in the day-to-day operations of these programs. The Dorm Leaders, all of whom have experience working with teens, serve as liaisons between the students, Resident Assistants (RAs), and the Directors. The RAs are college and graduate students, many of whom were once interns themselves. Resident Assistants also work as Teaching Assistants (TAs) in the Career Plus-Programmes, where they serve as assistant tutors in their field of expertise. IEI is privileged to have many of its alumni on its staff. The IEI staff members live in the dorms with the interns and are available at all times.

MEDICAL CARE

IEI is affiliated with experienced physicians who are available to see the interns and on call 24 hours a day in the event of an emergency.

COSTS

Program tuition in 2004 was $5795 plus group airfare and included tuition, housing, breakfast and dinner daily, linens and towels, and housekeeping services. Also included were special dinner events, group activities (scheduled theatre, weekend trips, and excursions), a Tube Pass, a group photo, and luggage tags. Not included in the fee were transportation to and from London from the students' home cities, lunches, laundry, souvenirs, personal spending money, optional day trip to Paris, and optional trip cancellation and medical insurance.

TRANSPORTATION

IEI interns are routed to London from major airports convenient to their homes. All flights are on regularly scheduled commercial airlines. Interns on IEI group flights are met at London's Heathrow Airport and transferred to IEI's housing in London. To facilitate well-organized departures and arrivals, all travel is arranged by IEI's Travel Coordinator. Students need a valid passport to enter the United Kingdom; visas are not required for holders of U.S. passports.

APPLICATION TIMETABLE

Admission to the internship program is on a rolling basis and is extremely limited in certain programs. There is no final date for registration; the final date depends on the availability of internships and housing. Students who apply after April 15 should telephone the IEI office to confirm availability of places in the program. Completed applications are reviewed promptly. After acceptance, Interns receive a BritKit (IEI's summer guide), travel information, medical forms, and other important information.

FOR MORE INFORMATION, CONTACT:

Nina Miller Glickman, M.Ed., and Lynn Ann Weinstein, Directors
Intern Exchange International
130 Harold Road
Woodmere, New York 11598
516-374-3939
Fax: 516-374-2104
E-mail: info@internexchange.com
World Wide Web: http://www.internexchange.com

PARTICIPANT/FAMILY COMMENTS

"Thank you for another fabulous summer! I had so much fun in London. I really got a taste of behind-the-scenes gallery work."

"I've had a great time on this program with the friends I've made as well as at my medical internship. I wish I could do this every summer!"

JOHNS HOPKINS UNIVERSITY PRE-COLLEGE PROGRAM

SUMMER ACADEMIC ENRICHMENT

BALTIMORE, MARYLAND

Type of Program: Academic enrichment, residential and commuter
Participants: Coeducational, high school students finishing their junior or senior year
Program Dates: Term I (commuters only), June; Term II, July

LOCATION

The Johns Hopkins University (JHU) Homewood Campus is home to 4,000 undergraduates, 1,400 graduate students, and 400 faculty members. Not all stay for the summer, but many do, making the campus a lively place for summer study and exploration. The 140-acre campus, located in a residential area north of downtown Baltimore, is closed to automobiles. Students walk along brick paths, study under trees, and meet friends on the park benches around campus.

BACKGROUND AND PHILOSOPHY

Johns Hopkins University offers a wide range of undergraduate credit courses, and the Pre-college Program opens many of them to outstanding high school students. The program gives students the opportunity to sample the University's offerings as they decide on an undergraduate education. Rigorous courses challenge students academically, while a speakers series and field trips expose them to career areas.

PROGRAM OFFERINGS

The Johns Hopkins Pre-college Program offers a variety of academic credit options and an introduction to the faculty members and resources that make Hopkins a world-renowned research center. Students may choose to explore varied interests by selecting any two courses of interest, or they may concentrate their study by selecting two courses that direct them toward an academic area. Extracurricular activities allow exploration into the depth and breadth of Hopkins and individual interests. Participants may follow a student at the medical school, listen to computer music at the Peabody Conservatory, observe astronomers at work on Hubble and FUSE, or enjoy a reading by an award-winning author.

Participants try a subject of interest, complete a course most colleges require, or fill in areas not reached by high school curricula. The schedule could include Calculus III, Understanding Beethoven, or Modern Medicine. Students may take tours of Hopkins centers and research facilities, talk to physicians and specialists at the Bloomberg School of Public Health, get advice from the Hopkins prelaw adviser, see the latest data from the Space Telescope Science Institute, or visit an embassy.

ENROLLMENT

Students who are finishing their sophomore, junior, or senior year of high school with a minimum grade point average of 3.0 are eligible to apply for admission.

DAILY SCHEDULE

The resident program allows participants to spend five weeks of their summer as a Hopkins student. They live in on-campus dorms, join their friends in the dining halls, work late in the computer labs, and relax in the social lounges—all while earning college credit in actual JHU undergraduate courses. As residential students, they make the 140-acre Homewood Campus their home.

EXTRA OPPORTUNITIES AND ACTIVITIES

Activities are abundant at Johns Hopkins University. Participants can choose to join a field trip to Baltimore's Inner Harbor, Gettysburg, or Washington, D.C.; swim or work out at the athletic center; tour Hopkins Lacrosse Hall of Fame; share traditions and customs at Culturefest; visit the Baltimore Museum of Art; kick a soccer ball, return a tennis serve, or run three miles around the track; play the piano in an arts center practice room; show off at the Pre-college Talent Show; make a difference in the Community Service Club; stargaze through the Hopkins telescope; relax with friends at a coffee house; or hang out on the quad.

FACILITIES

Facilities open to Pre-college Program students include state-of-the-art classrooms and language, science, and computer laboratories; a comprehensive research library; an athletic center with a climbing wall, indoor and outdoor tracks, courts, fields, and pool; residence and dining halls; and a health center.

STAFF

Residential staff members are present to assist students in learning about outside activities and social events. They also direct students to the best resources for academic assistance.

MEDICAL CARE

The campus Health Center is open from 8:30 a.m. until 5 p.m., Monday through Friday, and through Campus Security on weekends for emergencies and referrals. Residential advisers aid students in obtaining health services. Students needing special medication should arrive with a five-week supply. The Health Center requires several immunizations for students living in campus housing.

RELIGIOUS LIFE

The Office of the Chaplain publishes a Faith Community Directory that is included in each orientation packet. The directory lists more than twenty-five different religious denominations that hold services in Baltimore, many within walking distance of the residence halls. Every reasonable attempt is made to assist students with transportation to and from religious services.

COSTS

The residential program (Term II) fee includes tuition for two courses and the costs of room and board; admissions, college-living, time-management, and diversity workshops; field trips; and other scheduled activities. Books, independent activities, and miscellaneous pocket expenses are not included in the program fee. About $50 per week is recommended for pocket expenses. The cost for the program is $5500.

Students living with a parent or legal guardian in the Baltimore area may commute to classes during Term I or II. The tuition is $540 per credit. Note: The full Pre-college Program is available in Term II only. The program fee for Term II is $100. The program fee covers administrative services, use of university facilities, and special program activities. Books are not covered in the cost of tuition.

TRANSPORTATION

Residential students spend five weeks of their summer as Hopkins students, living in on-campus dorms. Commuter students need to provide their own transportation to and from class.

APPLICATION TIMETABLE

The early admission deadline is March 15. Applications accompanied by financial aid forms are due by April 5. Applications for the Term II residential program are due by April 22. Term II commuter applications and online applications are due by June 14.

For more information, contact:

Hopkins Summer Programs
Johns Hopkins University
Wyman Park Building/Suite G1
3400 North Charles Street
Baltimore, Maryland 21218-9985
410-516-4548
800-548-0548 (toll-free)
E-mail: summer@jhu.edu
World Wide Web: http://www.jhu.edu/summer

JULIAN KRINSKY CAMPS & PROGRAMS

TENNIS, GOLF, ENRICHMENT, BUSINESS, COOKING, TEEN TOURS, FITNESS, COLLEGE EXPLORATION, AND JEWISH LIFE

PENNSYLVANIA AND CALIFORNIA

Type of Program: Tennis, golf, enrichment (including art, business, cooking, drama, music, or discovery tracks), teen tours, fitness, precollege, and Jewish life

Participants: Coeducational. Tennis and Golf: ages 7–17, depending on program. Enrichment: ages 11–17. Leadership in the Business World at the Wharton School at the University of Pennsylvania: grades 11–12. California Teen Tours: ages 13–16. Canyon Ranch Young Adult Summer Program: ages 13–17. Yesh Shabbat Summer Camp: ages 10–17. Yesh Shabbat California Teen Tours: ages 14–16. Exploring the Majors at the University of Pennsylvania: grades 10–12.

Enrollment: Tennis and Golf: 200 maximum per session; Enrichment: 150 maximum per session; California Teen Tours: 80 maximum per tour; Canyon Ranch Young Adult Summer Program: 80 maximum per session; Yesh Shabbat: 125 maximum per session; Yesh Teen Tours: 45; Exploring the Majors: 150; Leadership in the Business World: 65.

Program Dates: Early June to August, depending on the program

Heads of Program: Julian Krinsky and Adrian Castelli

LOCATION

Julian Krinsky Camps & Programs (JKC&P) are conducted in Pennsylvania and California. In Pennsylvania, they are held at Haverford, Cabrini, and Bryn Mawr Colleges and the University of Pennsylvania and Arcadia University, all within 30 minutes of Philadelphia and 2 hours of New York City and Washington, D.C. In California, tours travel between San Francisco and San Diego.

BACKGROUND AND PHILOSOPHY

Julian Krinsky Camps & Programs offers campers the opportunity to learn sports and academic subjects in a relaxed summer camp setting. Whether campers are trying something for the first time, or want to seriously improve their level of ability, Julian Krinsky's experienced teachers and coaches can help achieve those goals. At the same time, campers build self-confidence and maturity—positive qualities that carry over and help them in all areas of life.

At JKC&P, each camper's needs are addressed on an individual basis, and instruction is tailored accordingly. Sports camps combine work on fundamental techniques with match play in a competitive environment. Enrichment camps feature small class size and expert instructors drawn from the professional ranks. All camps have separate residential and counseling staffs, with members carefully selected for their credentials, experience, and enthusiasm.

PROGRAM OFFERINGS

Prospective participants should use the site visit link at the JKCP Web site listed below to check for program news.

Tennis Players receive a minimum of 5 hours of on-court teaching and training, reinforced with competitive play and up to two private half-hour lessons each week at no extra charge. For advanced players, the renowned ATS, PTS, and Challenge programs provide special tournament training. Squash instruction is available to all campers. Junior Camp for grades 5 through 8 is at Cabrini College; Senior Camp for grades 9 through 12 is at Haverford College.

Golf Featuring a favorable student-teacher ratio of 4:1, the program consists of up to 5 hours of golf instruction daily, covering every aspect of the modern game from putting and driving to course management and etiquette. In addition, each student receives at least one private lesson per week at no extra charge. Classes are conducted at courses and driving ranges convenient to the camps. Junior Campers grades 5 through 8 reside at Cabrini College; Senior Campers grades 9 through 12 reside at Haverford College.

Leadership in the Business World (LBW) Sponsored by the Wharton School of the University of Pennsylvania, LBW exposes students entering the twelfth grade to major factors impacting business leadership in the twenty-first century. Students live on the campus of the University of Pennsylvania, attend classes and other learning activities at Wharton, and enjoy recreational activities provided by Julian Krinsky Camps & Programs.

Enrichment Julian Krinsky Enrichment Camps offer an outstanding opportunity to sample the excitement and challenge of college life. Junior Enrichment Camps for grades 5 through 8 take place at Cabrini College. Senior Enrichment Camp for grades 9 through 12 is at Haverford College. Campers chose one of the six major tracks listed below or can use the Discovery track to sample as many as four areas of interest. Classes range in size from single-student tutorials to up to 10 students. Each afternoon, campers have the option of participating in sports programs, enrolling in dozens of special workshops, or joining trips to local college campuses and other places of interest.

Art The art track heightens new senses and awakens creative instincts. Beginners and experienced artists alike learn the basics of drawing and painting in various media. Expert instruction is combined with field trips to the Philadelphia Museum of Art, the Barnes Foundation, and the Academy of Fine Arts.

Business Classes cover subjects ranging from personal finance and investing to entrepreneurship and business law. Topics include personal credit, career planning, business start-ups, incorporation, leadership, real estate, equity, loans, advertising, and multinational corporations.

Cooking The program covers a wide variety of food types and preparation skills, with an emphasis on technique, fresh ingredients, and presentation. Students learn about ethnic and regional cuisines as well as fashioning their own culi-

nary styles. The program features guest demonstrations from expert chefs and field trips to acclaimed restaurants and markets.

Drama Students are introduced to many aspects of theater. The curriculum covers areas such as performance, voice and text, movement, dance, singing, stage management, camera technique, costume, and makeup. Guest speakers and actors, trips to local TV and radio stations, and theater performances round out the program.

Music Participants choose a specialized track in rock or jazz and are arranged in groups according to their instruments and music choice. Students learn studio and recording techniques, take part in vocal ensembles, and rehearse as a band. Each band has the opportunity to record and produce a CD.

Photography Students cover all aspects of this exciting art form from camera basics to special effects, portraiture techniques, digital photography, and audiovisual presentations. This program is a fast-paced mix of classroom instruction, multiple field trips, hands-on photography, and critiques of shooting and developing.

Discovery Students may chose up to four classes, each lasting the entire session. Drawn from the arts, humanities, and sciences, more than forty topics are offered, including fashion design, drawing, computer animation, Web page design, videography, theater performance, yoga, and SAT preparation.

Exploring the Majors JKC&P presents this summer experience at the University of Pennsylvania for high-achieving students entering grades 10–12 who want to find out what it's all about at top Ivy League universities. They explore fields of study and undergraduate life as they sample a different major and minor every week from a typical Ivy League curriculum. During their three-week stay, they live in the University's dorms (the Quad) and enjoy all that the University has to offer as well as evening activities and weekend trips to local attractions.

California Teen Tours Campers explore California the Julian Krinsky way, traveling from San Diego to Los Angeles to San Francisco. They travel in luxury vans and tour buses and stay in four-star hotels. The tour visits thirty attractions, including sightseeing, shopping, beaches, theme parks, movie studios, sports activities, and recreational stops. There are two 3-week tours, starting in late June.

Julian Krinsky/Canyon Ranch Young Adult Summer Staff members from the world-famous Canyon Ranch facilities join with Julian Krinsky instructors to create a one-of-kind experience "for smarter minds and bodies." The program focuses on strength training, fitness, mountain biking, yoga, Tai Chi, kickboxing, tennis, golf, journal writing, spa activities, and more.

Yesh Shabbat Summer Camp A coed summer camp for observant Jews, with an emphasis on golf, tennis, basketball, soccer, and enrichment programs. Campers spend two or three weeks living, learning, and playing in a comfortable Jewish setting under the supervision of two Modern Orthodox rabbis. Yesh Shabbat offers a growing knowledge and understanding of traditional Judaism, along with a unique and memorable Shabbat experience.

Yesh Shabbat California Teen Tour Like the JKC&P Yesh Shabbat camp, this teen tour of the California coast is a Modern Orthodox program for young observant Jews ages 14 through 16. Campers travel from San Diego to San Francisco in luxury vans and tour buses, stay in four-star hotels, and visit all of the must-see attractions. Campers also participate in projects throughout the towns and cities they visit to strengthen their connection and responsibility to the Jewish community. This seventeen-day tour begins in late July.

COSTS

Tennis and Golf Camps Tennis Overnight Camp is $995 for one week or $945 per week for two or more weeks. Eleven 1-week tennis sessions are available. Golf Overnight Camp is $1145 for one week or $1045 per week for two or more weeks. Eleven 1-week sessions are available. Rates include tuition, room, board, and all private lessons and evening trips. Weekend trips are an additional $130 per weekend.

Leadership in the Business World The cost for the four-week program is $4950.

Enrichment Camp Junior and Senior Enrichment Camps are $2300 for the overnight two-week session and $3450 for the overnight three-week session. There is an additional charge of $130 per weekend for weekend trips and $150 for course materials and lab fees.

Exploring the Majors The three-week program is $3450. There is an additional cost of $260 for weekend and weekday trips off campus.

Teen Tours The price of this three-week tour is $4150. Optional golf and tennis instruction are additional.

Julian Krinsky/Canyon Ranch This two-week residential program is $2750 plus an additional $130 per weekend for weekend trips and $100 for course material.

Yesh Shabbat Summer Camp Overnight tuition for session one (thirteen days) is $1755; session two, (twenty-two days), $2970; and session three (fourteen days), $1890. There is an additional charge of $130 per week for all off-campus trips.

Yesh Shabbat California Teen Tour The price of this seventeen-day tour is $3300.

Day camp opportunities for most camps are available for those living within commuting distance.

FOR MORE INFORMATION, CONTACT:

Julian Krinsky Camps & Programs
610 South Henderson Road
King of Prussia, Pennsylvania 19406
610-265-9401
866-TRY-JKCP (879-5527) (toll-free)
Fax: 610-265-3678
E-mail: julian@jkcp.com
World Wide Web: http://www.jkcp.com

THE JUNIOR STATESMEN SUMMER SCHOOL

SUMMER PROGRAMS

PRINCETON, STANFORD, YALE, NORTHWESTERN, AND GEORGETOWN UNIVERSITIES

Type of Program: Political education and leadership training
Participants: Coeducational, ages 14–18, entering grades 10–12
Enrollment: Varies by session
Program Dates: Princeton, Yale, and Northwestern, June 28 to July 23; Stanford, June 27 to July 22; Georgetown Session I, June 13–July 4; Georgetown Session II, July 11–August 1
Head of Program: Matthew Randazzo, National Summer School Director

LOCATION

There are six sessions of The Junior Statesmen Summer School: Session I is held in the San Francisco Bay Area at Stanford University; Session II is held at Yale University in Connecticut; Sessions III and IV are held in Washington, D.C., at Georgetown University; Session V is held at Northwestern University near Chicago; and Session VI is held at Princeton University in New Jersey. Each locale is within minutes of famous historical and cultural attractions.

BACKGROUND AND PHILOSOPHY

For seventy years, the Junior Statesmen Summer School has prepared students for responsible leadership in a democratic society. The goals of the Summer School are to develop an appreciation and understanding of American democratic government; to encourage the natural idealism of youth while confronting them with the realities of practical politics and helping them learn that a just and democratic society requires adherence to certain ethical principles; to help create an atmosphere, a challenge, and a stimulus for the intellectual awakening of high school students; to help students develop leadership skills; to teach students techniques of oral communication, argumentation, and persuasion; to confront a diverse group of young people with the challenge of living together in an independent environment; to encourage logical and critical thinking; to help students discover the joy and excitement of independent research; to develop students' self-confidence, which is essential to effective leadership; to develop an appreciation of freedom of speech; and to help students develop time-management skills and a sense of personal responsibility.

PROGRAM OFFERINGS

The Junior Statesmen Summer School offers a rigorous academic challenge to outstanding high school students. The curriculum at all sessions includes an Advanced Placement course in U.S. government and politics, an honors course in speech communication, an exciting high-level political speakers program, and debates on current issues. Students at the Junior Statesmen Stanford Summer School may take AP Economics, Constitutional Law, or AP Comparative Government instead of AP American Government. Students at the Yale session may take Constitutional Law. Students at the Washington session may take U.S. Foreign Policy, The Presidency, or Constitutional Law. Princeton University students may take AP Comparative Government or U.S. Foreign Policy.

Students may obtain high school credit for their course work at the Summer School. These courses are offered as Advanced Placement and/or Honors classes. If high school credit is desired, students must make preliminary arrangements with their school prior to the session.

Speakers Program The Summer School is enriched by a high-level, nonpartisan speakers program that is closely integrated with classroom instruction. Free-wheeling question-and-answer sessions allow students to examine the institutions and processes of American government with controversial policy makers.

Students at the Georgetown session question national leaders in the Capitol Building, the Pentagon, the State Department, the White House, and the Supreme Court Chambers. Yale and Princeton session students question ambassadors in the United Nations building. During the Stanford Summer School speakers program, students question outstanding scholars on campus as well as national and state leaders who join the students for in-depth examinations of politics in the "Golden State." Northwestern session students quiz headline figures from the 6 o'clock news in the exciting city of Chicago.

ENROLLMENT

About 1,400 outstanding high school students attend the five Summer School sessions. Enrollment at Yale is 250 students; at Stanford, 300 students; at Georgetown, 250 students; at Northwestern, 100 students; and at Princeton, 250 students. At the Georgetown session, most students are entering their senior or junior year in high school. At the other sessions, incoming high school sophomores may also participate. The age range is from 14 to 18.

DAILY SCHEDULE

At the Stanford, Yale, Princeton, and Northwestern sessions, government classes are held in the morning, speech classes in the afternoon, and student debates in the evening. At the Georgetown session there is no set schedule owing to an extensive speakers program.

Classes are held six days a week at various times during the day and evening. No classes are held on Sunday. There is a curfew, at which time students must be in the dorm. High school field trip rules apply. Expulsion, without refund, is the penalty for serious rule violations.

EXTRA OPPORTUNITIES AND ACTIVITIES

At each session, university admissions officials discuss their institution's admission policies, financial aid, housing, student life, and academic offerings.

Parties and dances are held on Saturday. A talent show is held during each session. On Sunday, students and faculty may visit nearby cultural and historical attractions. In Washington, trips to the Smithsonian museums and other landmarks are encouraged. Stanford session students go to San Francisco; Yale and Princeton students enjoy attractions in New York City. Northwestern students travel to Chicago for recreational and cultural activities. Students may take advantage of recreational facilities on each campus; some incur a fee. Recreation includes swimming, tennis, basketball, racquetball, and volleyball.

FACILITIES

Students use university classrooms, libraries, and recreational facilities and live in residence halls.

STAFF

The Junior Statesmen Summer School faculty members, resident assistants, and staff members are drawn from universities around the country. Government professors are political scientists who hold a doctorate. Speech instructors have at least a master's degree and are dedicated to excellence in their own classroom teaching and in the oral and written work of their students. Resident Assistants are college students (or recent college graduates) who have attended a previous session of the Summer School.

Faculty and staff members and resident assistants live in the university residence near the students and are responsible around the clock for student supervision and academic and personal counseling.

COSTS

Tuition, room, and board for the 2004 sessions was about $3500, which included transportation to the speakers program. Not covered were school supplies, souvenirs, access to recreational facilities (if the university charges a fee), laundry, and some meals off campus on speaker program days. Up to $250 is recommended for spending money. A $200 refundable deposit is required upon acceptance. The tuition balance is due one month before the program. All tuition paid by the student's parents is refundable until one week before the start of the Summer School.

FINANCIAL AID

The Junior Statesmen Foundation has a $350,000 scholarship fund to assist students who find tuition to be a barrier. Scholarships ranging from $50 to $1900 are awarded on the basis of academic merit and financial need. More than half of the students receive a scholarship. Parents fill out a financial aid form, which can be requested from The Junior Statesmen Foundation. Staff members assist students who want to try to raise funds in their community.

APPLICATION TIMETABLE

Students may request a Summer School catalog from the Junior Statesmen Foundation. Applicants submit an application form, a three-page essay, a high school transcript, and one teacher recommendation. Students are accepted on a rolling basis. The admission season begins in February and ends in June. There is no application fee.

FOR MORE INFORMATION, CONTACT:

Admissions Director
The Junior Statesmen Summer School
60 East Third Avenue, Suite 320
San Mateo, California 94401
650-347-1600
800-334-5353 (toll-free)
Fax: 650-347-7200
World Wide Web: http://www.jsa.org

KILLOOLEET

SUMMER PROGRAM

HANCOCK, VERMONT

Type of Program: Traditional summer camp
Participants: Coeducational, ages 9–14
Enrollment: 100 campers per summer
Program Dates: June 29 to August 21
Heads of Program: Kate Seeger and Dean Spencer, Directors

LOCATION

Located on the edge of the Green Mountain National Forest—which extends for hundreds of square miles to the north, west, and south—Killooleet's 300 acres feature woods, meadows, rolling hills, and a private lake. Most campers bring or rent bicycles to explore Killooleet's expansive ½-mile campus. Camp is just 35 miles northeast of Rutland, in the center of Vermont.

BACKGROUND AND PHILOSOPHY

Killooleet is run by educators who believe that a supportive environment emphasizing community, group dynamics, and respect for individual freedom promotes happiness and helps everyone achieve more. Killooleet campers find an atmosphere in which they can invest their energy in growth, learning as they explore new challenges. They come to value their contributions, believe in themselves, enjoy life, develop close friendships, and, ultimately, stand on their own two feet. Self-confidence blossoms as campers acquire skills and discipline in activities in which they are personally interested. Through its noncompetitive program, Killooleet removes winning as a motivation and replaces it with the pleasures of participation, challenge, and accomplishment. Killooleet has little need for hierarchy and has only a few educational rules: scapegoating, rudeness, put-downs, and breaking group concentration are not allowed.

Killooleet is coeducational, understanding that, in childhood, youths need to define their own masculinity or femininity. Realistic relationships between the sexes, rather than segregation, are nurtured at all ages in camp. While cabin groups are assigned by age and gender, girls and boys share meals, hikes, and activities.

There is respect for the value of work. Days begin with cabin cleanup, and periods include time for getting out and putting away materials. On overnight trips, campers do everything to make a campsite livable. During Crew Time, campers work in the kitchen, garden, and horse barn or bike to town for the mail. The oldest campers assist the staff and run tables, games, and activities.

Founded in 1927, Killooleet has been under the direction and ownership of the Seeger family—John, Eleanor, and Kate—since 1949. The camp is accredited by the American Camping Association.

PROGRAM OFFERINGS

Killooleet believes in the value of a full camp season, which enables children to face issues and work through them. Summers at Killooleet begin slowly, as each child becomes a respected member of his or her cabin group. During the first ten days, each group is scheduled for every activity. Middle weeks find campers developing individual interests through afternoon choice periods or "checking in" to a favorite activity. The final week is full of performances and closing activities.

Visual Arts The camp provides facilities for woodwork, stained glass, jewelry, silversmithing, batik, drawing, painting, silk screen, sculpture, sewing, weaving, knitting, and ceramics.
Performing Arts The dramatics program is based on improvisation and creative dramatics, and each summer features a musical and several cabin productions. Campers use Killooleet's video studio, cameras, and editing equipment to produce essays, skits, parodies, and short movies. Music is an integral part of camp. Singing and lessons on guitar, five-string banjo, bass, drums, and harmonica are offered. The R&B band and various music ensembles practice regularly.
Sports and Skills Killooleet offers horseback riding, soccer, tennis, basketball, bicycling, swimming, canoeing, sailing, archery, riflery, Ultimate Frisbee, volleyball, and softball. Dance, gymnastics, windsurfing, fencing, karate, lacrosse, and track are often available. The nature room has an array of tools for collecting and examining finds. Electronics and rockets are also available.
Outdoor Exploration Campers explore the beauty of Vermont during day hikes and overnight trips. On these days, everyone is out of camp, climbing a mountain and enjoying the view, bicycling, caving, canoeing, horseback riding, rock climbing, exploring a local brook, or strolling with frequent stops to sketch and photograph the scenery.

ENROLLMENT

Children of every faith, race, and nationality are welcome. Although the majority of campers come from metropolitan New York and Boston, campers and counselors represent many parts of the United States and, normally, six to eight other nations. Killooleet works to dispel prejudices, as every camper finds respected leaders and friends among people of different backgrounds.

DAILY SCHEDULE

Killooleet features four hour-long activity periods each day. Half-hour "recalls" between periods help keep the pace slow and allow campers to learn to use their free time wisely—swimming in the lake on a hot day, finishing a ceramics project, taking a guitar lesson, or just having time to get ready for the next scheduled period.

Ending times for evening programs vary with the activity. Bedtime includes time for winding down, chatting, independent reading, and reading aloud or singing.

Killooleet punctuates the week twice, with hikes on Wednesday and a Town Meeting on Sunday. The season features two 3-day camping trips.

EXTRA OPPORTUNITIES AND ACTIVITIES

Cabins take turns planning Sunday afternoon's all-camp game or special event. Evening activities include sings, campfires, cabin evenings, and one or two evenings a week for special interest clubs such as cooking, dance, cartooning, and juggling.

FACILITIES

Killooleet's grounds include a private lake, tennis courts, softball and soccer fields, a basketball court, archery and riflery ranges, a garden, barns, and a horseback riding ring as well as a theater, band room, the Main House, and five arts buildings. The center room of the Main House features a library filled with books and music. Campers live in wooden cabins with screened, shuttered windows and doors. Groups of 8 to 12 live with 2 or 3 counselors. Campers eat in groups of 4 (with 1 counselor) on the screened porch of the Main House.

STAFF

Counselors run their cabins and activities in a manner consistent with their individual personalities and beliefs. From this, campers learn the value of individuality. Teachers anchor the staff; most staff members are in college or are recent college graduates (the minimum counselor age is 18). Each summer, about one half of the staff members return. Counselors are equally divided between men and women, and the camper-counselor ratio is 3:1.

MEDICAL CARE

A registered nurse oversees health care and a doctor is on call. The nearest hospital is just 25 miles away. The state of Vermont inspects and licenses Killooleet and approves sources of water and food.

RELIGIOUS LIFE

Killooleet's philosophy is partially based on Quaker principles, which teach that each person has an inner light and balance. Everyone is encouraged to speak specifically of their own faith and philosophy freely as occasion arises. There is no all-camp devotion.

COSTS

Camp costs in 2004 were $5900 for the full season. This fee covers all camp expenses except travel to and from camp. After the deposit, which is due upon enrollment, two payments are usually made to cover the remaining balance; other payment plans are available.

FINANCIAL AID

Some scholarships, based on need, are available. On average, 22 percent of campers do not pay full tuition.

APPLICATION TIMETABLE

Killooleet is glad to answer questions about camp over the phone and will arrange a personal interview with parents if possible. Applications are accepted until the program is full.

FOR MORE INFORMATION, CONTACT:

winter
Kate Seeger
Killooleet
70 Trull Street
Somerville, Massachusetts 02145
617-666-1484
800-395-2221 (toll-free)
Fax: 617-666-0378
E-mail: kseeger@killooleet.com
World Wide Web: http://www.killooleet.com

summer
Kate Seeger
Killooleet
Hancock, Vermont 05748
802-767-3152

PARTICIPANT/FAMILY COMMENTS

"Thanks for the two best summers of my life. I learned so much and grew so much as a person. I learned about kindness, respect for others, and human nature, not to mention many other things. More importantly I learned about confidence and believing in myself. The values that Killooleet has taught me will stay with me for the rest of my life....it is truly a special place."

KIPPEWA FOR GIRLS

SUMMER CAMPS

MONMOUTH, MAINE

Type of Program: Traditional residential camping in seven specialty areas
Participants: Girls, ages 6½–16
Enrollment: 165
Program Dates: Eight-week season, June 25–August 20, 2005; half-season available
Heads of Program: Marty, Sylvia, Jon, and Paul Silverman, owners and directors

LOCATION

Kippewa is secluded directly on the shore of 10-mile-long Lake Cobbosseecontee in south central Maine, close to the Atlantic Ocean and the remote lakes and mountains of the Great North Woods. Towering pines and glistening white birches frame panoramic views of the lake beyond Kippewa's gentle hillside.

BACKGROUND AND PHILOSOPHY

Kippewa believes that every girl needs a safe, fun place to make friends with other girls and women, to learn social, artistic, and athletic skills, and to take childhood's steps toward the independence of adulthood. Recent research in coeducation has begun to catch up with what Kippewa has known for decades: that girls make closer friendships, build greater confidence, demonstrate greater ability, and feel a heightened sense of well-being in a place of their own.

Founding directors Marty and Sylvia Silverman have owned and operated Kippewa For Girls since 1957, making Kippewa among the oldest camps still being run by its founders. Like fewer than 20 percent of their eligible colleagues nationwide, Marty and Sylvia Silverman are American Camping Association Certified Camp Directors. Marty is also a member of the Academy of Certified Social Workers. The founders have been joined by their sons, Jon and Paul Silverman, in the last decade.

Small groupings in both the cabins and the activities allow the campers to feel nurtured and the counselors to be attentive and successful. The cabins are of various sizes and house an average of 6 girls each, along with at least 2 counselors. At night, a counselor remains in every cabin with the children. Campers live in cabins and attend individually scheduled activities with girls of their own age and grade in school.

PROGRAM OFFERINGS

To bring growing summer friends together for many years, the camp's activities must grow with the girls' interests and abilities. Toward this end, Kippewa teaches the nearly 100 activities that are listed in the profile section of *Peterson's Summer Opportunities for Kids and Teenagers,* encompassing horseback riding and stable management, studio and performing arts, land and water sports, gymnastics, tennis, wilderness camping, white-water rafting, and ocean sailing trips.

Kippewa can advance the most sophisticated student in every activity, yet the focus is on individually teaching each girl to learn in her own way and to her highest level, regardless of her ability. This is especially important in group activities such as

athletics, dance, and theater, where careful attention to each girl's place in the whole allows girls at various stages of development in their skills to enjoy working together. In this flexible setting, friendships grow between girls of diverse interests.

ENROLLMENT

Girls ages 6½ through 16 attend for all or half of the eight-week season. Enrollment is limited to 165 campers from all over the United States and the world. Kippewa is large enough to have plenty of girls in every age group and to support an extensive activities program and small enough that everyone in camp gets to know everyone else. At this workable size, the camp's many opportunities are readily available to every girl, and the directors can personally give individualized attention to the campers and their families at home. This knowledge of how each camper's separation from home affects her entire family, and of how she responds to her perception of her family's feelings, allows the directors to guide each girl in her adjustment to camp.

DAILY SCHEDULE

Individualized scheduling allows every camper to follow her interests in her own unique way. There are five scheduled activity periods each day, one of which is an assigned swimming lesson. The other four are electives selected from carefully arranged sets of choices, giving the freedom children desire and the structure they need. In addition, several free choice periods each day and an evening activity add to the variety and give girls of different ages time to get to know each other. New electives are chosen weekly, and favorites may be repeated.

EXTRA OPPORTUNITIES AND ACTIVITIES

Four decades of expanding opportunities have created seven camps-within-camps at Kippewa For Girls: Horseback Riding, Studio and Performing Arts, Gymnastics, Tennis, Field Sports, Water Sports, and Wilderness Camping Trips. A chief advantage is having full access to the vast offerings of these seven specialty programs in one setting, with the flexibility to broaden or change focus even after arrival at Kippewa.

FACILITIES

Kippewa is a greatly expanded, classic, turn-of-the-century sporting camp. Eighteen hundred feet of prime lake frontage, one hundred secluded lakeside acres, seventy boats, and sixty buildings serve the 165 girls of Kippewa. Highlights include skylit lakeside cabins, a natural beach with a gently sloping sand bottom, a 25-acre on-site horse farm, three water-ski boats, six tennis courts, twelve art studios in three buildings, a gymnasium with gymnastics apparatus, a theater, and an island outpost campsite. Every cabin has electricity, screened glass windows, and a full bathroom with hot water. Maintenance on the entire property is flawless.

STAFF

The relationships that the girls form with their caregivers are vital to their comfort, so for its cabin counselors, Kippewa carefully selects women whom the campers' parents would want their daughters to emulate. Love of children, warmth of personality, calmness, independence, quiet strength, inner confidence, and a solid work ethic are essential, along with teaching ability in several specialized activities. Two years of college are required to ensure the maturity that is vital to focusing one's self on caring for children.

Senior staff members are in charge of each of the many activity areas. They bring the additional maturity and management experience needed to guide the counselors into reaching their potential as exceptional teachers and caregivers. Some senior staff members have been with Kippewa for more than twenty and even thirty years. With at least 1 counselor for every 3 girls, and a senior staff member for every 4 counselors, supervision and guidance are abundant.

MEDICAL CARE

Medical care at Kippewa's infirmary is overseen by a local medical practice and is supervised round-the-clock by 2 resident nurses. A sophisticated ambulance can arrive within minutes, and the major hospitals of central Maine are only 25 minutes away. Personal hygiene is carefully monitored.

COSTS

Costs for the 2004 season/half-season were tuition, \$7230/\$4325; horseback riding, \$1475/\$775 (or \$425 for two weeks); average camp bank deposit, \$350; medical insurance, \$90; and transportation at additional cost.

TRANSPORTATION

Kippewa chaperones chartered buses via the Boston, Massachusetts, and New York City metropolitan areas, including the middle of the summer to accommodate half-season campers. Some parents prefer to drive the 3 hours from Boston or 7 from New York. Kippewa meets flights from all over the world at airports 20 minutes, 1 hour, and 3 hours from camp.

APPLICATION TIMETABLE

Kippewa accepts applications as space permits.

For more information, contact:

Marty Silverman, A.C.S.W., C.C.D.
Sylvia Silverman, C.C.D.
Jon Silverman
Paul Silverman
Kippewa For Girls

winter
60 Mill Street
P. O. Box 340
Westwood, Massachusetts 02090-0340
781-762-8291
800-KIPPEWA (800-547-7392, toll-free)
Fax: 781-255-7167
E-mail: info@kippewa.com
World Wide Web: http://www.kippewa.com

summer
1 Kippewa Drive
Monmouth, Maine 04259-6700
207-933-2993
Fax: 207-933-2996
E-mail: info@kippewa.com
World Wide Web: http://www.kippewa.com

LANDMARK SCHOOL

SUMMER PROGRAMS

PRIDES CROSSING, MASSACHUSETTS

Type of Program: Academic remediation and study skills for students with language-based learning disabilities or dyslexia
Participants: Coeducational, ages 7–20
Enrollment: 175
Program Dates: Six-week session, from early July to mid-August
Head of Program: Robert J. Broudo, M.Ed., Headmaster

LOCATION

Landmark School has two beautiful campuses on the Atlantic coast just 25 miles north of Boston and close to beaches, fishing ports, and sailing centers. The location is ideal for educational, cultural, and recreational activities, and the school takes full advantage of its setting to make each student's summer productive, both in and out of the classroom.

BACKGROUND AND PHILOSOPHY

Landmark's Summer Programs are designed to help youngsters ages 7–20, in grades 2–12, who have been diagnosed as having a language-based learning disability or dyslexia, who are of average to above-average intelligence, and who are emotionally healthy, socially adept, and behaviorally sound. Landmark individualizes instruction and provides a structured learning environment for students who are failing in regular classrooms because their reading, writing, spelling, and study skills have not caught up with their problem-solving capabilities.

The present Landmark School began in 1971 but traces its beginnings as far back as 1956 to the Reading Research Institute of Berea, Kentucky. It is the purpose of the school to provide a summer of educational services, enabling students to master the skills of literacy and become academic achievers. Academics are augmented by a well-rounded recreation program as well as frequent trips to beaches, state parks, overnight camping areas, and cultural centers.

PROGRAM OFFERINGS

Full Academic Program This program concentrates on mastering the skills of reading, writing, spelling, and composition by providing two daily periods of one-on-one tutorial instruction. These fundamental skills are reinforced and developed in small language arts classes of 6–8 students in which writing skills and literature are emphasized. Mathematics is also taught in small classes in which students progress at their own rate.

In addition, students can choose an elective class in art, physical education, woodworking, or computer science. A student-faculty ratio of 3:1 allows Landmark to provide a program specific to the needs of each student.

Preparatory Summer Program This program is designed for students in grades 9–12 who do not require intensive language remediation but need further training and development in organizational and study skills. Students are taught specific strategies and coping mechanisms to help them apply

individual skills to higher-level content areas. Classes in the preparatory program are larger than those in the regular remedial program, consisting of 7–12 students. A daily one-to-one tutorial is also available.

Courses offered include social science, math, grammar and composition, literature, and study skills. Each content area provides the process and necessary skills for students to learn how to study.

Summer Seamanship Program The Seamanship Program combines academics with seamanship skills for students ages 10 and older. Students attend an individual language tutorial, a math class, and a language arts class for half the day. The other half is spent on the water studying seamanship in both small and large sailboats and rowboats. The sense of community, the necessity for discipline, the spirit of cooperation, and the demand for independent action inherent in sailing give the student a new sense of personal worth.

Marine Science Program Marine science education is offered to students ages 11 and older who are comfortable around water and interested in the environment. Students spend half the day exploring local coastal and ocean ecosystems, working on research teams, and collecting data. The other half of the day is spent in classes in which students develop their language skills through a one-on-one tutorial and in language arts and math classes. This program provides experience in the field, the laboratory, and the classroom and includes overnight and weekend expeditions.

Adventure Ropes Program The Adventure Ropes Program offers students ages 10 and older an opportunity to spend part of their summer experience in an outdoor adventure-based program. Students attend a one-on-one language arts tutorial, a math class, and a language arts class for half of the day. The remainder of the day is spent on the ropes course in small groups, where students develop their vocabulary, establish trust relationships, learn to understand group dynamics, and recapture their self-esteem.

Half-Day Option for Younger Day Students As an alternative to the full-day academic program, day students may choose a morning-only academic program (ages 7–13). The academic half day includes a one-to-one language tutorial, a language arts class, and a math class.

ENROLLMENT

Landmark Summer Programs attract students from across the United States and from many other countries. The student body is made up of 54 percent boarding students and 46 percent day students. Girls make up 32 percent of enrollment, and minority students about 7 percent. Students with language-based learning disabilities or dyslexia, average to above-average intelligence, and emotional stability are eligible.

DAILY SCHEDULE

The day is divided into two parts from 8 to 11 a.m. and from 12:30 to 3 p.m. Academics are scheduled into one part and the program activity (sailing, marine, or ropes) is scheduled into the other part. (Students in the full academic or Prep programs have classes in the morning and the afternoon.) During the midday period (11–12:30), high school students have a study period and lunch, while younger students are involved in age-appropriate recreational activities and lunch. At 3 p.m., recreational activities are planned for boarding students, which include dinner followed by a quiet hour. Bedtimes vary according to student's age.

EXTRA OPPORTUNITIES AND ACTIVITIES

Afternoons and weekends offer opportunities for outdoor activities and trips (both day and overnight) to local points of interest, historic sites, and cultural programs. Free time, movies, and social events on campus complement these activities.

FACILITIES

The oceanside campuses were created out of four former estates along Boston's "Gold Coast" and are a mixture of the original buildings and modern additions for academics, sports, and living. Students are housed in dormitories on and near the campuses.

STAFF

Summer staff members are highly trained teachers and supervisors from the regular school year staff. The student-teacher ratio is 3:1.

MEDICAL CARE

The Landmark School infirmary attends to the medical needs of both students and staff members. The infirmary is available on school days from 7 a.m. to 11 p.m.; the duty staff is in charge at other times.

Student medications are dispensed from the infirmary. The school physician and other specialists are available for scheduled appointments or emergencies, and the Beverly Hospital Emergency Room is nearby. The state requires that immunization history forms be submitted at enrollment. In addition, counselors are available if necessary.

RELIGIOUS LIFE

Students who wish to attend religious services are provided with transportation.

COSTS

Tuition varies according to the program; 2004 tuition was as follows: full academic program—$7600 for residents and $5500 for day students; preparatory, seamanship, marine science, or ropes programs—$7200 for residents and $5100 for day students; and elementary programs—$3600 for half-day students.

TRANSPORTATION

Landmark is located about 25 miles from Boston's Logan Airport and within walking distance of the train from Boston. Scheduled transportation to and from Logan Airport is available.

APPLICATION TIMETABLE

Students are accepted in order of applications received. Early application is advised, as space is limited. Applicants cannot be considered without a full diagnostic report; the school is happy to answer questions about testing and to help guide parents or school counselors to diagnostic sources. A fee of $100 must accompany the application.

FOR MORE INFORMATION, CONTACT:

Director of Admission
Landmark School
P.O. Box 227
Prides Crossing, Massachusetts 01965-0227
978-236-3000
Fax: 978-927-7268
E-mail: jtruslow@landmarkschool.org
World Wide Web: http://www.landmarkschool.org

LANDMARK VOLUNTEERS

SUMMER VOLUNTEER PROGRAMS

ACROSS THE UNITED STATES

Type of Program: Two-week nonprofit summer service opportunities for high school students
Participants: Coeducational: rising sophomores, juniors, and seniors
Enrollment: 800
Program Dates: Two-week summer programs from June 15 to August 15; One-week spring programs: mid-March and mid-April

LOCATION

Volunteers serve at one of sixty-four important historical, cultural, environmental, or social service institutions in twenty-one states. Recent locations have included Strawbery Banke Museum, New Hampshire; Glacier Institute, Montana; Shakespeare & Company, Massachusetts; Maine Coast Heritage Trust, Maine; Rocky Mountain Village; Colorado; Pathfinder Village, New York; Boys and Girls Harbor, New York; the Acadia National Park, Maine; Gould Farm, Massachusetts; Sawtooth National Recreation Area, Idaho; the Boston Symphony at Tanglewood, Massachusetts; the Hole in the Wall Gang Camp, Connecticut; Calvin Coolidge Homestead, Vermont; Morgan Horse Farm–UVM, Vermont; Norman Rockwell Museum, Massachusetts; National Elk Refuge, Wyoming; and many others.

BACKGROUND AND PHILOSOPHY

Landmark Volunteers was founded in 1990 by a board of prominent educators and community leaders to provide teenagers, with their quickened sense of social conscience, an opportunity to enjoy the rewards of volunteer service and to meet the needs of the participating institutions.

PROGRAM OFFERINGS

Volunteers serve in teams of 13 students under the full-time supervision of an adult team leader. In order to accomplish as much as possible, teams work six days during the first week and five days during the second week, with a day off in between for rest and recreation. They earn credit for 80 hours of community service.

The work is primarily manual labor: painting, trail building, brush clearing, and bridge construction and maintenance, augmented by tasks related to the mission of the institution, such as bird banding, inventorying species, serving as guides and ushers, preparing displays, or assisting handicapped children. The purpose is to deliver maximum value to the host institution.

Landmark Volunteers offers two 1-week spring service opportunities. At the Hole in the Wall Gang Camp, the volunteers help open up the facility and prepare it for the summer camp program for seriously ill children. At the Cumberland Trail in Tennessee, volunteers are part of a network of groups building a statewide hiking trail.

ENROLLMENT

Enrollment in 2004 was approximately 750. Teams are usually coeducational and are approximately 13 in number. Volunteers come from public, private, and parochial schools from more than thirty-six states and five other countries. The cooperative nature of team life engenders strong bonds of friendship. Students are permitted to enroll in more than one program.

Students are admitted to Landmark Volunteers through a competitive process. Purpose, diligence, and responsibility weigh more importantly than academic standing. Although location preferences may be indicated and generally can be met, volunteers are presumed to be willing to serve where needed. Assignments are made in order of receipt of completed applications. Letters of recommendation are provided to those whose performance warrants them.

DAILY SCHEDULE

Landmark teams work a full day and generally adhere to the normal hours of the staff members at their particular location. After-work recreation, at the discretion of the team leader, may include a swim, a movie, or other activities within the limits of the spending money that each volunteer is asked to bring. Teams that are doing their own cooking divide up the cooking and shopping duties. Typically, there is one trip to the Laundromat. At some locations, community members may provide cookouts, pool parties, or other after-work entertainment.

EXTRA OPPORTUNITIES AND ACTIVITIES

Every Landmark location offers its own particular attractions, and there are always opportunities to explore and take advantage of. In particular, the day off in the middle of the session is an occasion for an extended activity. Examples have included taking canoe trips, climbing mountains, visiting the Ben & Jerry's ice cream factory, and touring nearby colleges. A party on the final evening is traditional.

FACILITIES

Volunteers are usually housed as a group with their leader in facilities that are provided by their institution or cooperating schools, colleges, or camps. In some instances, food is provided and, in others, the team does its own cooking. When food and lodging is provided by neighboring organizations, it is usual for the team to divert one or two days of its labor in exchange.

At most locations, teams are provided with a van that may be driven only by the team leader or another

authorized adult. Volunteers may not operate any vehicle or power equipment during their session. Landmark reserves the right to ask any volunteer who is acting to the detriment of the organization or to the individuals within it to leave. Neither drugs nor alcohol are tolerated at any time.

STAFF

Team leaders are usually schoolteachers or graduate students. They live and work as members of the team and are responsible for their activities 24 hours a day. In each community, the Overseer, a local Landmark representative, serves as a backup to the team leader, assists with volunteer travel plans, and provides access to local resources.

MEDICAL CARE

Each team leader is required to know how to reach the local emergency room, to identify a local physician, and to have read the Red Cross first aid manual that is provided to them with their first aid kit. Parents must complete a medical form that advises of any relevant condition or medication and permits Landmark to authorize treatment in the event of an emergency.

COSTS

The tax-deductible contribution for the two-week period is $875 for those applications postmarked before March 31 and $925 for those applications postmarked after that date. Landmark is a nonprofit organization that is made possible by the generosity of others. Volunteer contributions only partially cover the cost of each student's service to their institution. Of this amount, $100 is due with the application. This deposit is nonrefundable if the volunteer is accepted at one of his or her first six choices of location or accepts an alternative. Otherwise, it is returned. For a place to be held, the balance is due no later than May 1.

TRANSPORTATION

Soon after acceptance to a specific team, volunteers receive an information packet about their location, specifying directions to the meeting point and arrival times and identifying the nearest airport. Travel arrangements are the responsibility of each volunteer, and the local Overseer acts as a resource.

For more information, contact:

Landmark Volunteers
P.O. Box 455
800 North Main Street
Sheffield, Massachusetts 01257
800-955-1178 (toll-free for brochure)
Fax: 413-229-2050
E-mail: landmark@volunteers.com
World Wide Web: http://www.volunteers.com

PARTICIPANT/FAMILY COMMENTS

"I learned about nature, teamwork, friendship....I couldn't have asked for a more exciting, challenging, or fun experience."

"My son had a fabulous time... his self assurance grew a hundredfold."

"Our team leader was outstanding. He was there for us 24 hours a day with help, caring, and leadership."

LANGUAGE LIAISON GLOBAL TEEN™

A DIVISION OF LANGUAGE LIAISON, INC.®

EUROPE, ASIA, AND CENTRAL AND SOUTH AMERICA

Type of Program: Language and cultural immersion
Participants: Coeducational, ages 13–17
Enrollment: Varies by program
Program Dates: Two to eight weeks, June–August
Head of Program: Nancy Forman, Director

LOCATION

Language Liaison (LL) offers exciting teen summer language camps throughout Europe and Central and South America. The programs described are some of Language Liaison Global Teen's top picks from Italy, Spain, France, Canada, Mexico, and Costa Rica.

BACKGROUND AND PHILOSOPHY

Language Liaison, Inc., was founded in 1988 by Nancy Forman after having undertaken the challenges of organizing her own lengthy study-abroad adventure. Language Liaison's Global Teen was formed in response to the many requests from members of the American Council on the Teaching of Foreign Languages (ACTFL) for similar programs for their students, ages 13 to 17.

Language Liaison believes learning while living in a diverse multicultural environment can be particularly enriching for young adults. It is an opportunity to meet other students from all over the world with the same goals, each bringing a unique point of view and their own collection of cultural and life experiences. While experiencing a new culture, students learn more about themselves.

Language Liaison Global Teen's top picks share this philosophy. Courses are available for learners between the ages of 13 and 17 at all ability levels. Courses are taught by highly qualified native speakers who are sensitive to the needs of the younger learner. After morning classes, afternoons are filled with exciting cultural, social, and sports activities that enable students to practice their newly learned language skills. Depending on the program, lodging is provided in a residence at the school or with a welcoming native host family, where students experience support and interaction.

SAFE™ (Study Abroad Federation of Educators) was founded by Language Liaison to help ensure the safety of their young learners. It is dedicated to enhancing the safety and comfort of each student through an annual recertification program undertaken by LL.

PROGRAM OFFERINGS

The following are some of Language Liaison's favorite summer programs:

Spanish in Malaga This program is available for young adults in either the dynamic city center or on the beach in Malaga. Classes take place in either the mornings or afternoons, leaving plenty of time for sunbathing, beach volleyball, table tennis, self-defense classes, basketball, and more. Other activities include tennis, horseback riding, and fitness training. A wide variety of excursions are available in Cordoba, Granada, Seville, Ronda, Nerja, and Frigilana. Students can choose accommodations either with a host family or at the school residence. There is occasional homework involving projects for students to discover information about Malaga and the Spanish way of life.

Spanish in Salamanca Salamanca is a charming university town where everything lies within walking distance, including beautiful old Spanish churches and streets with years of history. The school has a cozy, personal feel, and the teachers know each other. Nearby towns include Segovia, Burgos, Santiago de Compostela, Leon, and Madrid. Organized activities include visits to the museums, monuments, cathedrals, and cloisters of Salamanca as well as sporting events. Optional full-day excursions to bullfights, La Albeerca, and Candelario are also offered. Full board accommodations are provided with specially selected Spanish host families.

Spanish in Costa Rica Costa Rica is a beautiful country, has the highest standard of living, and is known as the Switzerland of Central America. It is exceptional in its many environments—rain forests, cloud forests, unspoiled beaches, coral reefs, white-water rivers, and volcanoes. The school is located in a safe, quiet area, and learning Spanish at the school is exciting, quick, efficient, and relaxed, with lots of personal attention. Accommodations are with specially selected native host families. Afternoons are filled with art classes, dance and cooking classes, and visits to Los Chorros Waterfall, Irazu Volcano, Tortuga Island, and much more.

French in Paris Students live about 30 minutes Paris on the edge of the famous Fontainebleau Forest. An open environment offers terrific outdoor activities, including basketball, soccer, and volleyball. Lessons take place in the residence and are fun, relaxed, and adapted to the age of the students. Activities include theater, mask making, special-effects makeup, and dance. Instructors and workshop leaders are qualified personnel who speak French at all times, reinforcing the work that is done in class. There are one full-day and three half-day excursions per week; students are accompanied by teachers and often by guides to discover important sites of Paris and the surrounding area, such as Notre Dame, the Palace of Versailles, the Museum of Science and Industry, and La Villette.
French in Antibes and Paris Students get the best of both worlds by combining the culture of Paris with the beach on the French Riviera. After class, participants spend afternoons taking wine and cooking classes, studying art, or simply getting to know the customs and colors of Antibes on the French Riviera or the culture (or couture) of Paris.
French in Nice Nice, the capital of the French Riviera, is a town filled with flowers, examples of which can be seen in the Place Massena, the famous Flower Market, the Castle park, and the famous gardens of Cimiez. Old Town is just a few steps from the sea and is the historic center of the city. This program for young adults includes excursions and recreational activities ranging from beach volleyball to visits to Old Nice, St. Tropez, Monaco, Eze Village, and St. Paul de Vence. The school was opened in 1984 and occupies the second floor of a fine old bourgeois building. A communicative approach is emphasized within the guidance of native-language speaking teachers who have undergone additional training in French as a foreign language and regularly participate in ongoing internal training.
French in Montreal Students who want an alternative to France can try this outstanding summer program in Montreal. Teenagers from around the globe come to this bilingual, bicultural city to learn French. They meet other teenagers in classes, then spend the afternoons cycling, swimming, canoeing, and participating in cultural outings. Learning takes place in an entertaining and meaningful context in which speaking and listening take priority. Accommodation is provided with a warm and welcoming host family that has an active interest in hosting younger students.
Europe, Central and South America With the customized features of this program, students live and study in the home of a certified teacher. This type of intense immersion is the ultimate way to learn another language. Participants are isolated from his or her native language. Global Teen develops a personalized program based on the specific locale and date desired. Parents and students decide the number of hours of instruction needed; the rest of the time the student is treated as a member of the host family he or she is living with, further enhancing the cultural immersion. This program is especially appealing to parents who are looking for personal supervision of their children while they are studying away from home and for students who want to learn more privately.

ENROLLMENT

Hundreds of young learners ages 13–17 from around the world participate in these summer programs. No prior language experience is required. Classes are small, with a maximum of 12 students.

MEDICAL CARE

All schools have health-care establishments or hospitals nearby that are readily available in the event of an emergency. Some schools have medical assistance on staff. Most schools provide emergency medical insurance for students enrolled in one of their programs. LL strongly recommends supplemental international medical evacuation insurance with 24-hour multilingual assistance.

COSTS

Prices vary according to the country and length of stay. All programs include tuition, lodging, full board, course materials, activities, and airport transfers.

TRANSPORTATION

Each school offers transfer service to and from the airport or train station to their accommodation. This service is often included in the price.

APPLICATION TIMETABLE

Applications are accepted at any time. The application fee of $175 is nonrefundable but is valid for one year in the event of cancellation.

For more information, contact:

Nancy Forman, Director
P.O. Box 1772
Pacific Palisades, California 90272
310-454-1701
800-284-4448 (toll-free)
Fax: 310-454-1706
E-mail: learn@languageliaison.com
World Wide Web: http://www.languageliaison.com

LANGUAGE STUDIES ABROAD

LSA YEAR-ROUND AND SUMMER LANGUAGE AND CULTURE PROGRAMS

AUSTRIA, ARGENTINA, BOLIVIA, BRAZIL, CANADA, CHINA, COSTA RICA, DOMINICAN REPUBLIC, ECUADOR, FRANCE, GERMANY, GUATEMALA, ITALY, JAPAN, MEXICO, PERU, PORTUGAL, RUSSIA, SPAIN, SWITZERLAND, AND VENEZUELA.

Type of Program: Language and culture total-immersion through classes, workshops, sports, and cultural activities

Participants: International students ages 3–19 (in age-appropriate groups) with target-language proficiency from absolute beginner to advanced

Enrollment: Varies by site from 20 or fewer to as many as 300 students per site. Most classes have 8–12 students per class

Program Dates: Most programs begin any Monday if the student knows some of the language; otherwise, they usually begin every other week or at the beginning of each month. Year-round programs last for two weeks to a year; summer programs from two weeks to two months

LOCATION

More than 100 schools are located throughout much of Europe, Asia, and the Americas in outstanding, culturally rich settings. For more detailed information regarding the programs, refer to the LSA listings for the specific country in the Opportunities Abroad section of this book.

BACKGROUND AND PHILOSOPHY

Language and cultural total-immersion are used along with workshops, sports, and activities to promote cultural understanding, respect, and friendship through a fun and stimulating educational experience. Travel abroad is a growing experience that university admissions offices and employers recognize as a valuable indication of character and accomplishment.

The mission of Language Studies Abroad (LSA) is to provide an opportunity for young minds to learn foreign languages and cultures during the formative years when minds are most capable of developing good skills and attitudes. LSA provides a glance into the cultural treasures of a foreign country and its people that introduces young people to a lifetime of fascinating possibilities on this incredible planet where all people need to work together for the common benefit of all mankind. The program's philosophy lies in the promotion of respect, friendship, and fellowship in an atmosphere that strives for a memorable learning experience by combining sports, fun, and culture through the target language.

PROGRAM OFFERINGS

LSA offers both "youth programs" and "adult programs". The main difference between the two is the amount of supervision. Supervision ranges from total 24-hour supervision to supervision only during classes and activities to no supervision, depending on the site and program. Some youth programs are only offered in the summertime, others all year. The cultural activities in most youth programs are required, whereas they are optional in adult programs. Most youth programs have 3–5 hours of classroom lessons per day while adult programs have choices ranging from 2–8 hours of class per day. LSA offers many kinds of accommodations, including residential "camps" where 8–13 students live together, residences with 1–4 students per room, and homestays where students stay with local families.

The programs feature flexible start dates, flexible duration of most programs, small classes for all ages, credit or no-credit options at universities and high schools, excursions, and a variety of optional courses, including sports, the arts, business, cooking, etc.

CHINESE

China *Summer Youth Program* is for ages 18 and older and may be private lessons if there are no other students at the same level.

FRENCH

Canada *Summer Youth Program* in Montreal is for ages 13–17 in homestays. *Year-Round Programs* in Montreal and Quebec are for ages 18 and older.

France *Summer Youth Programs* in Antibes, Biarritz, Cannes, Hyéres, Melun, and Nice are offered for ages 13–17 with supervision ranging from total 24-hour supervision to very little supervision in either on-site residences or homestays. *Year-Round Programs* in Aix-en-Provence, Amboise, Antibes, Bordeaux, Cannes, Hyéres, Paris, Nice, and Tours are for ages 17 and older.

GERMAN

Austria *Summer Youth Program* is held in Vienna for ages 15–18 in on-site residences. *Year-Round Programs* for ages 16 and older are offered in Vienna.

Germany *Summer Youth Programs* in Berlin, Bavaria, Iznell, Potsdam, and Schmöckwitz are offered for ages 11–18 with supervision ranging from total 24-hour supervision to very little supervision in either on-site residences or homestays. *Year-Round Programs* are offered in Berlin, Cologne, Hamburg, Munich, and Stuttgart for ages 16 and older.

ITALIAN

Italy *Summer Youth Programs* in Lignano and Treviso are for ages 6–18 with supervision ranging from total 24-hour supervision to very little in either

on-site residences or homestays. *Year-Round Programs* are offered in Ascoli, Florence, Livorno, Milan, Orvieto, Rimini, Rome, Siena, Taoramina, Treviso, and Venice for ages 16 and older.

JAPANESE
Japan *Year-Round Programs* in Kanazawa and Tokyo are for ages 18 and older.

PORTUGUESE
Brazil *Year-Round Programs* are offered in Maceio for ages 18 and older.
Portugal *Year-Round Programs* in Lisbon and Faro are for ages 16 and older.

RUSSIAN
Russia *Year-Round Programs* in Moscow and St. Petersburg are for ages 16 and older.

SPANISH
Central and South America—Argentina, Bolivia, Costa Rica, Dominican Republic, Ecuador, Guatemala, Perú, Venezuela *Summer Youth Programs* are offered in Costa Rica for ages 13–18 with moderate supervision in homestays. *Year-Round Programs* are held in Cordoba, Argentina; Sucre, Bolivia; Flamingo Beach, Manuel Antonio, and San José, Costa Rica; Santo Domingo, Dominican Republic; Cuenca and Quito, Ecuador; Antigua, Guatemala; Cuzco, Perú; and Caracus, Venezuela for ages 15 and older.
Mexico *Summer Youth Programs* in Cuernavaca and Oaxaca offer childcare for ages 1 and 2 and homestays for ages 3–18. *Year-Round Programs* in Cuernavaca, Guadalajara, Guanajuato, Merida, Morelia, Oaxaca, Puerto Vallarta, and San Miguel de Allende are offered for ages 1 and 2 (childcare) and 3–18.
Spain *Summer Youth Programs* are held in Almuñecar, Madrid, Málaga, Marbella, Salamanca, San Sebastian, and Sevilla for ages 3–19 with supervision ranging from total 24-hour supervision in the Madrid, Marbella, and Salamanca camps to no supervision in Almuñecar. *Year-Round Programs* in Alicante, Barcelona, El Puerto de Santa Maria, Granada, Madrid, Málaga, Marbella, Nerja, Salamanca, San Sebastian, Sevilla, Tenerife, and Valencia are for students ages 15 and older.

EXTRA OPPORTUNITIES AND ACTIVITIES

Residential programs offer optional workshops in which the students can participate for an additional fee. Year-Round programs offer specialized programs, including private, business, dance, history, art, literature, and internships.

STAFF

All schools are staffed by native professional educators who specialize in teaching their native language as a second language.

MEDICAL CARE

All schools have health-care establishments and/or hospitals nearby that are readily available in the event of any emergency. Some schools have staff members trained for medical emergencies. International medical coverage is offered at an additional cost.

COSTS

All program costs include tuition, accommodations (in a residence or a homestay), course material, and activities. There are also day camps and classes available without accommodations so a student can stay with parents or friends or find his/her own accommodations. Actual costs vary by locations and length of stay.

TRANSPORTATION

Students arrange their own transportation to the program's location. Airport pickup is usually included in the cost for youth programs and can be arranged to most schools for an additional fee.

APPLICATION TIMETABLE

Applications are accepted all year, however there is a late fee for applications received less than four weeks before the program starts. There is a nonrefundable $100 application fee. The nonrefundable $100 deposit will be credited toward tuition.

For more information, contact:

Language Studies Abroad, Inc.
1801 Highway 50 East, Suite I
Carson City, Nevada 89701
775-883-6554
800-424-5522 (toll-free)
Fax: 775-883-2266
E-mail: info@languagestudiesabroad.com
World Wide Web: http://www.languagestudiesabroad.com

LEADERSHIP ADVENTURE IN BOSTON

PINE MANOR COLLEGE LEADERSHIP CAMP

CHESTNUT HILL, MASSACHUSETTS

Type of Program: Support of leadership development through outdoor activities and creative exploration, boarding camp
Participants: Girls, ages 11 to 14
Enrollment: Approximately 30 girls per session
Program Dates: One- and two-week sessions, beginning in July
Head of Program: Whitney Retallic, Director of Youth and Student Programs

LOCATION

Pine Manor College (PMC) is located in Chestnut Hill, Massachusetts, a suburb of Boston located 5 miles from the heart of the city. Pine Manor's beautiful campus is a former New England estate that was converted to accommodate student living and learning. The classic buildings are situated among 60 acres of wooded landscape.

BACKGROUND AND PHILOSOPHY

Leadership Adventure was developed in 1994 by President Gloria Nemerowicz. This is the seventh year that the program is running on the campus. The Pine Manor College Leadership Camp is a reflection of the values and the principles that are the foundation for the undergraduate programs. At Pine Manor College, it is believed that through collaboration, creativity, and common good thinking, girls and women can help shape a new kind of leadership. In the camp program, PMC students and staff members work and play alongside younger girls to build confidence while building the skills of leadership. Staff members demonstrate that building leadership skills can be fun as well as worthwhile.

The Center for Inclusive Leadership and Social Responsibility at Pine Manor College is committed to fostering leadership that is inclusive of all people and many styles and is directed toward a common good. It seeks to promote new models of leadership for women and men that are required for a new millennium, to facilitate the participation of women in leadership and organizational change, to build community partnerships, and to extend Pine Manor College's mission of preparing women for socially responsible leadership beyond the campus.

PROGRAM OFFERINGS

Campers participate in various activities that support leadership. Each activity is designed to foster the girls' creativity, growth, teamwork, success, and fun. The camping trip is a perfect example of an activity that promotes such ideals. There are also day trips into Boston that allow the girls to explore the city and the women who made a difference. Each camper also has the opportunity to choose activities during their free-choice time, including arts and crafts, photography, computers, and sports.

ENROLLMENT

The Leadership Adventure is a multicultural, diverse camp that appreciates and supports differences in campers. Approximately 30 girls, ages 11–14, come for one- or two-week sessions. About 90 percent of the campers come for a two-week session. Campers come from many places in the United States. Since 2000, the Leadership Adventure has been fortunate to partner with a school in Japan. That school plans to send 15 campers to Leadership Adventure in 2005, again providing a wonderful opportunity to explore cultural differences, make friends around the world, and possibly learn words in a new language.

DAILY SCHEDULE

The daily schedules for the Leadership Adventure vary, depending on the nature of each day's activities. The typical wake-up time is 8 a.m., and the morning usually involves a leadership activity or community service. Lunch, at noon, is followed by an off-campus activity or Free Choice Time. Dinner is at 5:30, and the evening includes a fun program on-campus or a trip to a Boston-area attraction, such as a professional sporting event or a museum.

EXTRA OPPORTUNITIES AND ACTIVITIES

Days at camp are filled with excursions, learning through discovery, and challenging new adventures. All of the activities support growth through team building, collaboration, and modeling new ways of leadership.

Throughout the camp adventure, participants make trips into downtown Boston, where they explore the historical, social, and cultural environment of this spectacular city. Each day consists of workshops and activities, with opportunities for free time. During Free Choice Time, campers choose among activities at the Computer Center, Arts and Crafts Center, Recreation Room, and PMC Athletics Facilities. Some of the daily adventures may include hiking at the nearby Blue Hills Reservation; watching a professional women's soccer game; canoeing down the Charles River; taking field trips to the beach, the Boston Harbor Islands, or the Museum of Fine Arts; or participating in a talent show, a wacky Olympics field day, or a "drive-in" movie night.

FACILITIES

The 60-acre campus includes dormitories in which girls are housed 2 to a spacious room, a full-service dining hall, classroom buildings, a computer lab, an auditorium, a new student center with a pool table, a fitness center, a gymnasium, basketball courts, tennis courts, soccer and softball fields, and an arts and crafts center.

STAFF

The staff includes 1 full-time director and 7 full-time, live-in counselors. The staff-camper ratio is 1:4. In addition, College faculty and staff members are brought into the program for their areas of expertise.

MEDICAL CARE

The College is located just 3 miles from Boston's most prestigious hospitals: Children's Hospital, Beth Israel Deaconess Medical Center, and Brigham and Women's Hospital. Arrangements have been made with medical facilities for emergency treatment. All staff members are trained in CPR and first aid. A physical exam and immunization records are required.

RELIGIOUS LIFE

Transportation and supervision are provided for those students who wish to attend any religious service.

COSTS

Tuition, room, board, and all excursions are included in a fee of $600 for a one-week session and $1100 for a two-week session. Recommended spending money is $70 for two weeks. Payment plans are available; prospective participants may phone for more information.

FINANCIAL AID

Need-based financial aid is available. A financial aid application is required.

TRANSPORTATION

Pine Manor College is located 15 minutes from downtown Boston, approximately 15 miles from Logan International Airport and 1 mile from the local train stop. Transportation is provided for the campers from either location at no extra charge.

APPLICATION TIMETABLE

Applications should be accompanied by a $100 deposit. A visit is welcomed and encouraged. Students may phone the center's office to set up a time for a tour.

FOR MORE INFORMATION, CONTACT:

Whitney Retallic, Director
Center for Inclusive Leadership and Social Responsibility
400 Heath Street
Chestnut Hill, Massachusetts 02467
617-731-7620
Fax: 617-731-7185
E-mail: leadcamp@pmc.edu
World Wide Web: http://www.pmc.edu

PARTICIPANT/FAMILY COMMENTS

"Since last summer, I have seen my daughter grow tremendously in her self-confidence and independence. She made so many new friends and can't wait to come back. Thank you again for giving her such a wonderful experience."

"I now feel I can make a difference in the world."

"I found out that the leader doesn't always have to be the most ambitious and loudest person."

LEARNING PROGRAMS INTERNATIONAL

LANGUAGE IMMERSION IN SPAIN, MEXICO, AND COSTA RICA

AUSTIN, TEXAS

Type of Program: Language acquisition and travel
Participants: Coeducational, students ages 15–18
Enrollment: 10–20 students per program
Program Dates: Four to five weeks, June and July
Head of Program: Gustavo J. Artaza, Executive Director

LOCATION

Learning Programs International (LPI) programs are located in Granada, Salamanca, Santander, and Sevilla, Spain; Guanajuato, Mexico; and San José, Costa Rica. All academic classes are taught by local university faculty members at the host university.

Granada, Spain (population 250,000) lies at the foot of the majestic Sierra Nevada Mountain Range. With almost 500 years of history, the University of Granada has increased its influence on the social and cultural environment to become one of the major intellectual centers of Spain. The university is particularly proud of its Centro de Lenguas Modernas, which has the unique characteristic of being the only center within Spain where international students share the same premises as Spanish students who are interested in other languages and cultures.

Salamanca, Spain (population 180,000) was the Cultural Capital of Europe for the year 2002. Salamanca's Plaza Mayor is one of the most beautiful plazas in Europe. The plaza is a place where friends gather in charming cafés and on stone benches to enjoy Salamanca's quintessential Spanish atmosphere. However, it is Salamanca's famous university that gives much of the passion and color to life in Salamanca. For 700 years, the University of Salamanca has attracted students from all over the world to study. It is widely known and considered the Oxford of Spain.

Santander, Spain (population 220,000) is the capital of the Cantabria region located in the north of Spain. The city enjoys an extraordinary landscape mainly due to its coastal location on the shores of the Bay of Biscay. This large natural port has been used since before the Roman Empire. The beaches of Santander have received the European Union Blue Flag, and the city was designated Spain's most elegant city.

Sevilla, Spain (population 600,000), capital city of the region of Andalucía, lies along the Guadalquivir River in southern Spain. This great city was built as a shelter from the heat of the Andalucían summers by the Romans, who appreciated its beautiful location. Barrio Santa Cruz, the old part of Sevilla, is a labyrinth of passages, small squares, and narrow streets, characterized by quaint, lime-washed houses with flowering plants draping the balconies or patios. Sevilla has an astonishing number of palaces, towers, historic hospitals, and churches, such as the Cathedral, which claims to contain the remains of Columbus.

Guanajuato, Mexico (population 120,000) remains one of Mexico's best-preserved colonial cities. Its buildings still appear relatively untouched by modern construction, lending the town a distinctive European air. Streets turned into tunnels contribute to the town's timeless appearance and eliminate many of the cars that would otherwise crowd the center of town. The University of Guanajuato has undergone three centuries of institutional transformation. By placing the values of truth, knowledge, and human decency at the core of its mission statement, the university commits itself to promoting the educational, social, and cultural well-being of its students and surrounding community.

San José, Costa Rica (population 3.5 million) lies approximately 10 degrees north of the equator and is quite mountainous. It is located in a country rich in many things, among which are lush tropical rain forests and beautiful Atlantic and Pacific coast beaches. The Collegiums Veritas, created in 1976, was one of the four founding schools of the first private university in Costa Rica. After demonstrating an exceptionally high level of academics for eighteen years, the Universidad de Veritas is now an independent institution, accredited by the authorities of the country and highly regarded by the intellectual community.

BACKGROUND AND PHILOSOPHY

LPI sent its first group of high school students to Salamanca, Spain, during the summer of 1990. Over the past thirteen years, the program has grown to include five additional locations. LPI hopes that students gain a cultural understanding and personal independence that can only be achieved by living and studying in another country. During a study-abroad program, students encounter people from all walks of life with whom they are able to make a connection, whether through similar interests, a shared laugh, or a long bus-ride. Moreover, LPI hopes that students continue to reap the benefits of study abroad by encouraging cultural understanding in their own communities. This enlightening experience is an increasingly precious asset as America's youth are encouraged to become credible and sensitive members of today's expanding global community.

PROGRAM OFFERINGS

Each academic program is four to five weeks long. Students earn a minimum of 60 contact hours of college credit. An official transcript is issued by the foreign university upon successful completion of the program. Students are required to take a language placement exam upon arrival in the program city. Once the language level is determined, students attend 3–4 hours of Spanish language instruction each day, Monday through Friday. The language instruction always includes grammar, conversation, and culture. Course descriptions are available on LPI's Web page. The average class size is 15 students. In Mexico and Costa Rica students take class with other LPI students. In Spain, students take class with other international students, mostly college level, at the foreign university's language school. Final exams are administered during the last two days of the program.

ENROLLMENT

Each LPI program accepts from 10 to 30 students. LPI students come from all across the United States and Canada. LPI requires a transcript and one letter of recommendation, preferably written by a foreign language teacher. Also, LPI prefers that students have at least two years of foreign language background. Students applying for the Spain and Costa Rica programs must be 16 years of age by the program start date in order to be accepted into a program; however, students participating on the Guanajuato, Mexico, program may apply at age 15.

DAILY SCHEDULE

Students either have class from 9 a.m. to 1 p.m. or from 4 to 8 p.m., Monday through Friday. The schedule is determined on the basis of the language level placement exam. Afternoon activities include visiting museums, playing sports, dancing, and cooking. LPI also arranges "intercambios" (exchanges) with local high school students.

EXTRA OPPORTUNITIES AND ACTIVITIES

Most weekends consist of one overnight excursion or two daytime excursions. The weekend activities are designed to allow each student to observe and learn about the culture and history of a surrounding area. Each tour is accompanied by an official guide that has an educated knowledge of the site visited. All students are placed with a host family where they are provided three meals a day. Laundry is taken care of once a week. Unless requested otherwise, there are two LPI students per family. All of the families are personally interviewed by LPI's full-time, on-site staff, and the family database is continually updated, based on the students' evaluations of their host families.

COSTS

The program prices are as follows: Mexico, $2400; Costa Rica, $2500; and Spain, $3100. The cost includes room and board with a host family, tuition and books at the host university, tutorial assistance, medical insurance, overnight cultural excursions, entrance fees and ground transportation for all organized excursions, airport transfers, an on-site office with Internet access, and LPI's full-time on-site director. LPI can arrange individual flights for an additional charge.

APPLICATION TIMETABLE

Applications are accepted on a rolling basis. As spaces fill quickly, students are encouraged to apply before March. Students must turn in the application, a copy of their high school transcript, an academic letter of recommendation, and a $350 deposit toward the total program cost. If students meet the eligibility requirements, they are notified of acceptance within two weeks.

FOR MORE INFORMATION, CONTACT:

LPI, Learning Programs International
901 West 24th Street
Austin, Texas 78705
512-474-1041
800-259-4439 (toll-free outside of Austin)
Fax: 512-480-8866
E-mail: lpi@studiesabroad.com
World Wide Web: http://www.lpiabroad.com/lpi

PARTICIPANT/FAMILY COMMENTS

"I would definitely recommend studying with LPI. Both of my children have participated on this program over the last three years and they have benefited tremendously. Santander is a great town!"—Helen Hutchings, Santander, Spain

"The LPI staff was very responsive and helpful, and the program itself couldn't have been better. It exceeded all of our and our daughter's expectations. Do this for your child—it will change them in wonderful ways!"—Debby and Gerry de Junco, Salamanca, Spain

"Learning to live in a college-like environment and in a foreign country has served our son well as he finishes high school and begins college. We thought that our son had a great experience and we would recommend the program."—Bill and Linda Earle, Granada, Spain

"My daughter felt very welcome and comfortable with her host family. She loved them! We were thrilled with the positive outcomes—the learning, the Spanish immersion, the cultural experience and the trips."—Jean and Stanley Estrin, Guanajuato, Mexico

"I had the time of my life in Santander. I met new people, sat on the beach, went shopping, lived with an AMAZING host family, and tried food I probably would never have tried at home. It was a life-changing experience."—Julia Pratt, Santander, Spain

"I had a great time in Salamanca! I think LPI is very organized and well-structured."—Joanna Tong, Salamanca, Spain

"Don't miss an opportunity like this. You'll have the time of your life, so long as you have an open mind and a love of Spanish."—Laurie Hathaway, Guanajuato, Mexico

LES ELFES–INTERNATIONAL SUMMER/WINTER CAMP

SPORTS, LANGUAGES, AND CULTURAL AND PERSONAL ENRICHMENT

VERBIER, SWITZERLAND

Type of Program: Wide variety of sports (including summer skiing), language study (French, Spanish, German, and English), cultural activities, and personal development
Participants: Coeducational, ages 8 to 18
Enrollment: Maximum of 140 students per session
Program Dates: Summer: early June through end of August; winter: December through April
Head of Program: Philippe and Nicole Stettler, Associate Directors

LOCATION

In the heart of the Swiss Alps, Verbier, the home of Les Elfes–International Summer/Winter Camp, is a cosmopolitan resort. As the camp is located on a mountain meadow overlooking Verbier, the panorama from the camp is breathtaking. Verbier offers exceptional conditions for summer skiing on the Mont Fort glacier. With more than 250 miles of connected trails, skiers in winter are served by ultramodern equipment and more than 100 ski lifts. The area provides all kinds of summer sports, including horseback riding, golf, swimming, tennis, rock climbing, paragliding, a ropes course, and mountain bike treks. Near Les Elfes is a new sports center with an Olympic-size indoor swimming pool, an ice rink, and tennis and squash courts. A stable for horseback riding is nearby. Many cultural and historic sites are in the area. Campers enjoy the nearby streams, mountain meadows, and a lake with a private beach and waterskiing.

BACKGROUND AND PHILOSOPHY

Since 1987, Les Elfes–International Summer/Winter Camp has provided children and teens from around the world with holidays that combine the discovery and practice of new exciting sports with learning and perfecting languages (French, Spanish, German, and English). Children and teens discover other cultures and make new friends. Activities are designed to promote leadership and teamwork and to challenge students toward excellence in a way that maximizes both personal and group development and enhances self-confidence and interpersonal skills. Each child's program of activities reflects his or her personal aptitudes and choices. Children return home with the best of memories of their holidays, whether in summer or winter.

PROGRAM OFFERINGS

The summer camp experiences are organized into three-week sessions. When participants arrive (usually on a Sunday), they are introduced to the camp and are shown the sports installations and the town. The following day, the newcomers choose their various activities with the counselors.

Sports, Culture, and Activities The camp is focused mainly on outdoor sports activities. To complete their program, the students have the opportunity to discover sites outside Verbier and to waterski. Youngsters are encouraged to try new activities with optimum safety and to make progress in those they already know. The International Summer Camp's program is extremely varied. Sports include football, volleyball, table tennis, basketball, squash, tennis, badminton, and miniature golf. There is also an eighteen-hole golf course in magnificent surroundings. Students enjoy hikes and mountain bike treks surrounded by alpine flora and fauna, rock climbing, figure skating, ice hockey, curling, swimming, and waterskiing. Cultural activities include weekly excursions to a town or an interesting and entertaining site and concert outings (classical, blues, jazz, or rock).

Language Study The language program includes 8 hours per week of language courses (French, German, Spanish, or English), which are optionally expandable to 15 hours per week for an intensive course. The teachers are young, enthusiastic, and helpful college graduates. During their stay, the youngsters have a chance to practice the languages with their friends.

ENROLLMENT

The program serves groups of 140 students from more than forty-five nations. This international setting allows children and teens to experience and value other cultures and to make new worldwide friends.

DAILY SCHEDULE

The day begins at 7:45 a.m. with rising, washing, and the cleaning of rooms. A full breakfast is served at 8:15 with juice, hot and cold cereal, bread with ham and cheese, and fruit. At 9, students engage in their language activities, ski or snowboard, or take a tour depending on the day and individual program. At noon, campers enjoy a picnic lunch. Sports activities at 1 p.m. are followed by a snack at 4 p.m. At 4:30, the campers enjoy games and recreational activities, sports, or individual courses. Dinner prepared by the chef is served to students at the table beginning at 6:30. The menu includes American and European dishes and international foods. At 8 p.m., students participate in organized activities, play games, watch a video, or enjoy quiet time. Bedtime is at 10 p.m.

EXTRA OPPORTUNITIES AND ACTIVITIES

As extra-cost options, the students can take a beginner course in paragliding, enjoy horseback riding, or go summer skiing or snowboarding with instructors from the Swiss Ski School for three days per stay. A more intensive language study program is also available for an additional charge. After sessions 4 and 5, a fully supervised one-week trip to Paris is offered at a supplementary cost of $1000.

In addition to the activities program, it is possible to have private lessons in golf ($40 per hour), tennis ($40 per hour), and horseback riding ($40 per hour).

FACILITIES

Students live in two recently constructed (1995) chalets of wood and stone in the Swiss alpine tradition that offer charm and elegant comfort. Both chalets are situated in green, calm surroundings and are only 5 minutes from the center of Verbier. The chalets are completely equipped with a professionally equipped kitchen and a vast and sunny dining room, which opens onto a sitting room with a fireplace. There are classrooms, conference rooms, a library, a game hall, a film theater, a music hall (or discotheque), and a fitness room. The camp is fully equipped with all the equipment and accessories for indoor and outdoor games and sports. Campers live in large rooms with two to four beds, a bathroom including a shower, and a radio and telephone. Maid service in the rooms is provided daily.

The menus are well balanced and adapted to the youngsters' needs and activities. The dietary needs of each individual are taken into consideration.

STAFF

A sports director and her assistant manage the instructors, the programs, and the smooth running of the camp. Three group leaders, their "second-in-command," and their assistants accompany the youngsters during activities organized into three independent age groups. All of the staff members (counselors, instructors, teachers, cooks, and camp and sports administrators) are dedicated young people trained for this kind of work. Most of the staff members are college graduates; they come from many nations and are fluent in both English and French. They are extremely enthusiastic and entirely committed. They give careful and effective supervision in order to direct the youngsters' energy and make their stay safe and enjoyable.

MEDICAL CARE

To avoid injury, the participants are trained by professional instructors or sports masters in all of their sports activities. Weather conditions are monitored by experienced mountain guides, and summer skiing and snowboarding, rock climbing, mountain biking treks, and hiking are only allowed under good weather conditions. In the event of a medical necessity other than the basic first aid, the camp offers around-the-clock nurses and doctors, an up-to-date clinic ¼-mile from the camp, three drugstores, and a regional hospital. By car, two University hospitals are 40 minutes and 1 hour and 15 minutes away, respectively (10 minutes away by helicopter). These advantages and the reputation of Swiss medical treatment guarantee the best care in all situations. Parents are encouraged to provide their own health and accident insurance; otherwise, health and accident insurance provided by the camp is required at an additional cost of Sw fr 80 ($55) per week.

RELIGIOUS LIFE

Arrangements for attendance at church can be made on an individual basis.

COSTS

Costs for this extraordinary sports and educational program, including all living expenses, 8 hours per week of language study (in French, German, Spanish, or English), cultural excursions, and activities, are as follows: three-week summer sessions, Sw fr 4715 ($3145); two-week winter sessions, Sw fr 3065 ($2045); and one-week school-group ski camps, Sw fr 1050–1400 ($700–$935). These group programs include a minimum of 20 students and a maximum of 140 students. A deposit of $800 holds a student reservation; the balance must be paid prior to arrival. An additional health and accident insurance fee of Sw fr 80 ($55) per week is required. An additional 7 hours of language study are available for ($70) per week. Round-trip transportation by private bus is available to Geneva for ($90) and to Martigny for Sw fr 70 ($50). Personal expenses are not included. Full details are in the camp agreement, which can be obtained by request.

During the summer, optional sports expenses for skiing or snowboarding, including equipment and instructors (for six half-days per twenty-one-day session) are ($250); horseback riding, including equipment, is six half-days for ($160) per hour; and paragliding tandem flights ($100) per flight.

During the winter, optional sports expenses include full skiing plus equipment at ($90) per week, full snowboarding plus equipment at ($95) per week, and paragliding tandem flights at ($100) per flight.

TRANSPORTATION

The camp is located 105 miles from Geneva, 60 miles from Lausanne, 20 miles from Martigny, and 165 miles from Milan. Transportation by private bus to airports, bus stations, and trains in Geneva, Martigny, and other locations can be arranged.

APPLICATION TIMETABLE

Applications are accepted year-round as long as session openings are available. A brochure is available from the address below.

FOR MORE INFORMATION, CONTACT:

Philippe and Nicole Stettler
Les Elfes International Summer and Winter Camps
P.O. Box 174
1936 Verbier
Switzerland
41-27-775-35-90
Fax: 41-27-775-35-99
E-mail: leselfes@axiom.ch
World Wide Web: http://www.leselfes.com

PARTICIPANT/FAMILY COMMENTS

"During six weeks with new friends from all the world, the children gained a new understanding of other people...enjoying beauty and freedom that only the Swiss Alps can provide."—Mr. Alexander W. K., Florida

LEYSIN AMERICAN SCHOOL IN SWITZERLAND

SUMMER IN SWITZERLAND

LEYSIN, SWITZERLAND

Type of Program: Academic enrichment, language studies, SAT prep, I.B. prep, performing and visual arts, travel, leadership, sports, and recreation
Participants: Coeducational; Alpine Adventure (ages 9–12), Alpine Exploration (ages 13–15), Alpine Challenge (ages 16–19)
Enrollment: 200 each session
Program Dates: First Session: June 25 to July 15; Recreation and Culture Week: July 16 to July 22; Second Session: July 23 to August 12
Head of Program: Tim Sloman

LOCATION

Summer in Switzerland (SIS) is located in the picturesque town of Leysin, overlooking the Rhone Valley 1,000 meters (3,000 feet) below and facing the majestic panorama of the southern Alps.

BACKGROUND AND PHILOSOPHY

SIS provides a special summer experience of academic enrichment, foreign language study, performing and visual arts, travel, leadership, sports, and recreation. The global community at SIS is warm and friendly, and all the students, from more than forty different countries, are appreciated for their uniqueness. SIS is a program of the Leysin American School in Switzerland (LAS) and takes place on the LAS campus. LAS is a coeducational, college-preparatory boarding school for American and non-American students in grades 9–12, with postgraduate and year abroad programs.

PROGRAM OFFERINGS

The program is organized as follows: First Session (three weeks), Recreation and Culture Week, and Second Session (three weeks). There are three student groups: Alpine Adventure (AA), ages 9–12; Alpine Exploration (AE), ages 13–15; and Alpine Challenge (AC), ages 16–19. There are differences in activities among age groups in each program. AA has a student-faculty ratio of 4:1 and is more of a camp setting. Activities are generally by group and are closely supervised. AE is a program designed for middle schoolers, and AC is for high schoolers. Students in both AE and AC take 4 hours of morning classes and all participate in afternoon activities. Their student-faculty ratio is 5:1. Curfews vary depending on age group. AE and AC students have more independence and may also sign up for the following special programs and opportunities: Leadership Adventure, Theater International, intensive ESL, weekend excursions to Paris and Milan, and Highlight Tours to France and Italy.

Enrichment and Academic Courses Students participate on weekday mornings in four periods of enrichment and academic courses. SIS offers high school credit classes for those enrolled for both the first and second sessions. Courses for AE and AC students include French, Spanish, algebra, geometry, computer science, English, TOEFL, International Baccalaureate (I.B.) prep (math, science, creative writing, and extended essay), SAT prep, photography, chorus, piano, acting, 2-D art, 3-D art (including ceramics), and visual and performing arts. Art students participate in a schoolwide exhibit of painting, sculpture, writing, and photography. Many nonnative English speakers choose to enroll in comprehensive English as a second language (ESL) courses. The courses cover conversation, grammar, and written communication at all levels. The AA class schedule is organized differently. AA students have the choice of taking either beginning French or English as a second language. They also take the following classes together: environmental education, computer proficiency, arts and crafts, and theater.

Recreation and Sports In the afternoon, students take part in various recreational, sports, and leadership activities. Recreation and sports include basketball, volleyball, soccer, Frisbee, hiking, open tennis and tennis lessons, ice-skating, swimming, paragliding, white-water rafting, mountain biking, and horseback riding. Glacier snowboarding and skiing are located 30 minutes away from the campus and are offered as a weekend alternative. Activities may vary depending on the age of the student. AA participants typically do activities as a group.

Theater International This program is for students who wish to add international credits to their resume while dedicating three to six weeks to skill development. Theater International students train in the mornings, improving skills in acting, improvisation, costuming, writing, directing, stage combat, and acting for film. In the afternoons, Theater International students prepare, publicize, rehearse, and stage a number of shows to the whole SIS community. Productions have included *A Midsummer Night's Dream, Our Town, West Side Story, Annie Get Your Gun,* and *The Sound of Music*. Whenever possible, Theater International takes advantage of Leysin's central European location by offering students special excursions to theater productions.

Leadership Adventure This program is for students who want to challenge themselves with alpine activities, such as climbing, rappelling, white-water rafting, hydrospeeding, alpine hiking, ropes courses, and other outdoor activities. An important goal of this program is the development of leadership skills. During school mornings, students participate in outdoor education and leadership classes, such as a first-aid and CPR class. They also learn to develop their leadership styles, map-reading techniques, nature and conservation skills, and outdoor skills, such as climbing. Students do more than simply climb; they also learn to lead a climbing activity and what different types of equipment are and how they are used. Students also learn how to prepare an activity that they will lead with some of the younger students at SIS. Activities include overnight and longer trips out of Leysin. The program staff members are experienced, skilled, and certified outdoors instructors.

Excursions Students visit Swiss cities and cultural centers on weekend day trips. Outings are also taken to tourist attractions in the mountains and the countryside. Faculty guides accompany each trip. Students are given information and an orientation before the trips begin. Typically excursions are to Lausanne, Geneva, Berne, Lucerne, and Zermatt. Depending on interest, students in AE and AC can participate on extended weekend trips to Paris and Milan during the sessions.

Evening Activities and Special Events Evening recreation includes watching theater productions, excursions to the Montreux Jazz Festival, talent shows, ice skating parties, casino night, eating special dinners like Swiss fondue, dancing at the disco, campfires, night hikes, and sports tournaments. Most of these activities take place on campus, but some special events take place in Leysin and are chaperoned by faculty members.

DAILY SCHEDULE

8:00	Breakfast
9:00	Morning classes
12:10	Lunch for AA
12:25	Lunch for AE and AC
1:30	Quiet time and study hour
2:45	First activity period
4:15	Second activity period
5:30	Dinner, AC allowed off campus in Leysin village
6:30	Free time, AC/AE allowed off campus in Leysin
8:00	Evening activities
9:30	AA lights-out, Red Frog/on-campus open time
10:45	AE lights-out
11:15	AC lights-out

EXTRA OPPORTUNITIES AND ACTIVITIES

Recreation and Culture Week This exciting, fun-filled week is between the first and second sessions. It may be attended by students in either session and any age group. Days consist of half- and full-day trips, recreational opportunities, and cultural activities. Special emphasis is placed on teaching students about the host country, Switzerland, and having SIS international students share the beauty of their own cultures with one another.

Highlight Tours Optional weeklong tours to France and/or Italy are offered for students in the AE and AC programs. The tour to France takes place before the first session and the tour to Italy at the end of the second session. Both tours depart from Leysin. The French Highlight Tour includes Paris, Versailles, Blois, Orléans, and the Loire Valley. The Italian Highlight Tour offers visits to Florence, Venice, and Pisa. Faculty members supervise the coach bus tours.

FACILITIES

SIS uses the boarding facilities of the Leysin American School in Switzerland (LAS). Boys and girls are housed in different dormitories according to age group. The dormitories are safe, clean, and fully staffed by resident faculty members. Every effort is made to make the dorm a home away from home. Resources of LAS available to SIS students include music practice rooms, an art studio, and computer science labs. A well-equipped black box theater is available for the dramatic arts. On-campus sports take place in the LAS gymnasium, which has a basketball court, fitness center, and a squash court. Students also use the two sports centers in Leysin that contain an indoor swimming pool, squash and tennis courts, an ice skating rink, a soccer field, and climbing walls.

STAFF

Faculty members are primarily from schools in the United States and Canada. Teachers are certified. Professional theater people with teaching experience supervise the theater department.

MEDICAL CARE

The school provides accident and health insurance coverage for students. A medical clinic is available in Leysin, and there are regional hospitals in Aigle and Lausanne. The school has a complete infirmary, and two full-time nurses are on staff.

RELIGIOUS LIFE

The school is nonsectarian, but provisions are made for students to attend Protestant and Roman Catholic services in Leysin on Sunday mornings.

COSTS

Fees are all-inclusive and cover room, board, tuition, books, activities, and excursions. Costs in 2004 were as follows: three-week session, $3200; six-week session, $6150; and optional Highlight Tour, $1400. A surcharge of $100 per week applies to the specialized theater, leadership, and ESL programs. The anticipated cost of the Recreation and Culture Week, a new program component for 2005, is $1200.

FINANCIAL AID

Up to four scholarships are awarded each session. Two are based on financial need, and the other two are merit-based awards, one for theater and one for leadership. Each scholarship is for $1350.

TRANSPORTATION

The school provides all SIS participants with transportation on official arrival and departure dates to and from the airport in Geneva at no additional cost.

APPLICATION TIMETABLE

Students of all nationalities, ages 9–19, are eligible for admission to SIS. All specific information regarding tuition, fees, application forms, and supplementary data is provided in an annually updated flyer. Applications are accepted on a rolling basis.

FOR MORE INFORMATION, CONTACT:

For families in North and South America:

U.S. Admissions Office
P.O. Box 7154
Portsmouth, New Hampshire 03802
U.S.A.
603-431-7654
888-642-4142 (toll-free in the U.S.)
Fax: 603-431-1280
E-mail: usadmissions@las.ch
World Wide Web: http://www.las.ch/summer

For families outside of North and South America:

Leysin American School
1854 Leysin
Switzerland
41-24-493-3777
Fax: 41-24-494-1585
E-mail: admissions@las.ch
World Wide Web: http://www.las.ch/summer

LIFEWORKS INTERNATIONAL

GLOBAL SERVICE-LEARNING PROGRAMS

BRITISH VIRGIN ISLANDS, THAILAND, GALAPAGOS, AND AUSTRALIA

Type of Program: Cultural, experiential, and adventure-based community-service programs. Students qualify for high school community-service credits.
Participants: Coeducational, ages 15–19
Enrollment: Up to 15 students per group
Program Dates: Two- to four-week programs from June through August
Head of Program: James Stoll

LOCATION

Lifeworks offers community-service programs in the British Virgin Islands (land- and sea-based voyage), Thailand (outskirts of Bangkok and in the provinces), Galapagos (based on Santa Cruz island, with day and overnight trips to neighboring islands), and Australia (Sydney, Queensland, and Northern Territories).

BACKGROUND AND PHILOSOPHY

Backed by thirty years of offering experiential education for youth, Lifeworks has been developed as a service-learning opportunity. Based on the premise that every participant has something unique to offer, students are provided the opportunity to make their own ripple in this world through their involvement with Lifeworks. At the core of Lifeworks is the mission statement "...to come to know that even one life has breathed easier because we were given the opportunity to walk the planet."

Students work in collaboration with established local, national, and international service organizations. The symbiosis of such an arrangement enables students to share in knowledge specific to the region in which they are living and undertake significant local assignments. Skills and learning are fostered through hands-on participation in service projects. Each program location offers a distinctive focus so that students may gain insight into a new field of study or further develop an existing interest. Team-building, leadership, and self-reliance development are a natural part of living and working in a close community with a common goal.

At the completion of the program, a direct donation is made to the service organizations with which students have worked. This donation is included in the tuition cost and helps to fund ongoing projects. All participating students are enrolled in the President's Student Service Award—an initiative that recognizes young Americans for outstanding community service. This award scheme is also sponsored by the Corporation for National and Community Service.

Lifeworks programs are designed to focus on three levels of support: human, community, and global, each intrinsically linked. Service on the human level aims to transcend cultures and beliefs, working toward a broader common goal. Lifeworks looks for effective ways to reach individuals through their community using health, education, environmental, or safety-based projects. It is the hope of Lifeworks that individual involvement will have an impact at the global level.

PROGRAM OFFERINGS

In the British Virgin Islands, Lifeworks participants assist with the BVI College and local schools, the Red Cross, the Conservation and Fisheries Department, the National Parks Trust, and the Marine Parks service organizations of the British Virgin Islands. This is a mobile, live-aboard service program based on a sailing yacht to enable multiple projects and marine-related work. Ongoing projects include the repropagation of mangrove systems and the monitoring of turtle populations and nesting. As part of a worldwide effort, students participate in the Darwin Initiative, which includes the tagging and monitoring of turtles and their nests, along with sea grass, water-quality, and beach monitoring around the islands. At intervals, Lifeworkers visit local schools and community centers to develop full days of activities and programming. Outside of project work, students also snorkel, hike, and sail throughout this island group.

In Thailand, Lifeworks teams up with the DPF Foundation for underprivileged children. DPF's Founder and Senator, Ms. Prateep Ungsongtham Hata, was awarded the prestigious 2004 World Children's Prize for the Rights of the Child in recognition of her work with Bangkok's disadvantaged children. Students work in the kindergartens and schools created by the foundation, with a focus on enhancing the children's self-esteem through team-building games, art projects, and teaching English.

In Galapagos, Lifeworks students work with the national parks on Santa Cruz and San Cristobal islands, assisting with maintenance of the giant tortoise hatchery facility and activities, signage, and general upkeep within the parks. Other projects are involved with local schools, cultural exchange, and ranger patrol programs. In addition, there are trips to St. Bartholomew, to the Plazas to snorkel with sea lions, and for a long weekend of exploring and horseback riding on the high volcanic island of Isabella.

In Australia, working with the Australian Red Cross, Lifeworks students participate primarily in aboriginal community projects. Beginning in Sydney, students have a cultural orientation as well as explore

the city. Participants take an active role in learning about aboriginal history and customs, with a unique and rare opportunity to experience their culture firsthand. Students live within the aboriginal community of the Tiwi Islands offshore from Darwin, designing local youth projects and putting them into action. Students learn how aboriginals live with the land, use bush medicines, and preserve their ancient traditions and, in turn, offer the local children summer program activities. Students' interaction and education is furthered with travel to the National Parks of the Northern Territories and then to Queensland, where the reef and rain forest meet.

ENROLLMENT

Enrollment is limited to 15 students per group, with participants from all over the United States. International students are also encouraged to participate. All programs are coed.

EXTRA OPPORTUNITIES AND ACTIVITIES

Unique to Lifeworks is the Lifeworks Forum, which takes place at intervals throughout the program. Students take time to participate in a variety of discussions, focusing on assisting each student in identifying and moving toward making their own individual contribution to the world. The Lifeworks Forum focuses on that goal as well as discussing related subjects, including integrity dilemmas, goals and affirmations, and other life choices people make.

STAFF

The average age of staff members is 27 and up. A staff-to-student ratio of 1:6 is maintained throughout the programs. Lifeworks selects staff members who have good organizational skills, demonstrate ingenuity, have mature decision-making abilities, are responsible, and have experience working with teens. Desirable staff qualities include adaptability and an adventurous spirit.

COSTS

Program costs for 2004 ranged from $3060 to $3760, depending upon location and duration chosen. Each program tuition includes a direct donation to be made by the students to the service organizations with which they work.

TRANSPORTATION

Students fly in small groups and staff assistance is available at arrival airports.

APPLICATION TIMETABLE

Applications are accepted at any time. Some programs are filled faster than others. Some fill in February, and most are full by April. Students should call for information on availability if applying late.

FOR MORE INFORMATION, CONTACT:

Lifeworks International
P.O. Box 5517
Sarasota, Florida 34277
941-924-2115
800-808-2115 (toll-free)
Fax: 941-924-6075
E-mail: info@lifeworks-international.com
World Wide Web: http://www.lifeworks-international.com

LINDEN HILL SUMMER PROGRAM

MORNING ACADEMICS, TRADITIONAL CAMP ACTIVITIES, AND WEEKEND OVERNIGHTS

NORTHFIELD, MASSACHUSETTS

Type of Program: Morning academics with afternoon/evening traditional camp activities and weekend overnight trips
Participants: Coeducational, ages 7–15
Enrollment: 60
Program Dates: July 1 to August 1
Head of Program: James A. McDaniel, Summer Director and Headmaster

LOCATION

Linden Hill's rural campus is set on the side of a mountain overlooking the Connecticut River Valley, near the town of Northfield. The rural setting, with breathtaking scenery and a peaceful environment, is ideal for exploring on foot, mountain bike, or horseback. The surrounding towns offer many diverse and exciting cultural and historical opportunities for all ages.

BACKGROUND AND PHILOSOPHY

Since 1961, Linden Hill School has served the needs of boys ages 9–18 with language-based learning differences in a traditional boarding school with a family setting. Linden Hill has developed a highly successful multisensory teaching program, which utilizes a child's senses to reinforce learning. Building upon the school's successful year-round formula, the Linden Hill Summer Program combines challenging, stimulating academic classes with exciting and extensive recreational opportunities. In a structured, supportive environment, participants are encouraged to grow in confidence and self-esteem, to make lasting friendships, and to develop as individuals. Linden Hill is accredited by the New England Association of Schools and Colleges. It holds membership in the National Association of Independent Schools, the Independent School Association of Massachusetts, and the Pioneer Valley Independent Schools Association.

PROGRAM OFFERINGS

A balanced program offers students solid academics and strong athletic, social, cultural, and recreational activities. The weekly program combines structure and focus with flexibility and choice. Linden Hill develops the skills and natural abilities of each person while encouraging a sense of enthusiasm and positive self-image. Campers go home feeling confident, relaxed, and ready for the coming school year.

Academic Program Since all of the students have experienced past academic difficulties or learning differences, the democracy of common problems begins to erase self-consciousness, and self-esteem increases. Classes have an enrollment of 1 to 6 students and meet five days per week. Daily drills and written work are stressed, and all classes focus on motivation, a positive mental attitude, organization, study skills, social growth, confidence, and self-esteem.

Traditional Camp and Tripping Program Camping can contribute to a young person's life in a way that few other experiences can. The program goals are for each camper to have a pleasant, fun-filled summer; improve skills; and develop confidence, self-control, inner discipline, good sportsmanship, and self-esteem. Campers who are unskilled in particular activities are channeled into special instruction so that they may become more proficient and develop a feeling of self-confidence. As they continue to grow in confidence, they are able to take their place with their peers and contribute successfully. Character development and citizenship are stressed at all times. In addition to daily activities, campers take advantage of the rich geographical setting with overnight trips on weekends, including educational, cultural, pioneering, and canoe trips.

ENROLLMENT

The Linden Hill Summer Program attracts campers from across the United States and from many other countries. Generally, the campers are underachieving and experiencing some academic difficulty, although they have average to above-average intelligence.

EXTRA OPPORTUNITIES AND ACTIVITIES

Weekend trips have included a Red Sox baseball game, Boston's Faneuil Hall and Quincy Market, and overnight camp trips. Talent shows, plays, and special guests are just a few of the many exciting events. There is also a counselor-in-training (CIT) program for older campers.

FACILITIES

The buildings include Bennett House, Haskell Hall, Hayes Hillside Dormitory, Duplex Dormitory, and the gymnasium. The newly renovated Bennett House, originally a farmhouse, accommodates the kitchen,

dining room, reception room, spacious dorm rooms, and student center. Haskell Hall (1964) houses the classrooms, art studio, science laboratory, comprehensive library, computer center, and spacious study hall. Hayes Hillside Dormitory (1961) sleeps 30 students. The new, full-sized gym, finished in 1998, is a multipurpose facility housing a full-sized basketball court. The school overlooks the Connecticut River and some of the most beautiful landscape in New England. There are nature walks and hikes on-site and at the nearby Northfield Mountain facility; these trails are also great for mountain bikes. A large pond provides entertainment for students. Linden Hill also has its own athletic field. Nearby, Northfield Mount Hermon School has many facilities that are made available to Linden Hill, including a swimming pool and tennis courts.

DAILY SCHEDULE

7:30	Wake-up
8	Flagpole honors assembly
8:10	Breakfast, followed by room inspection
9	Focus period one
10	Circle of Friendship with snack
10:30	Focus period two
11:30	Focus period three
12:30	Lunch and rest period
2–3	First activity instruction clinic
3	Juice Break
3:10–4:10	Second activity instruction clinic
4:15–5	Optional period (hobby, creative arts, technology, special activity)
5–6	Showers and relaxation
6	Flagpole honors assembly, followed by dinner
7:15	Special evening activity
8:30	Snack, return to dorm

STAFF

The majority of the program's academic instructors, along with the dorm parents and athletic director, are part of Linden Hill's regular faculty. Staff members are carefully chosen for their ability to relate to the student body, exceptional talents, warmth, personality, and ability to inspire. The staff-camper ratio is about 1:3. James A. McDaniel is the Headmaster and Summer Program Director.

MEDICAL CARE

Students are provided with medical services as required. The nurse resides on campus. In case of emergency, Linden Hill is just 25 minutes from the Northfield Mount Hermon Health Clinic, and 20 minutes from Franklin Medical Center. Staff members are trained in first aid and CPR.

COSTS

Tuition for the 2004 season was $4750. This charge was comprehensive and included the cost of instruction, lodging in dormitories, all meals, course materials, and transportation to and from the airport. It also included day trips and all weekend excursions and tours. The tuition should be paid in full by June 15.

FINANCIAL AID

Tuition loans and scholarships are available on a limited basis. Early payment discounts are available.

TRANSPORTATION

Linden Hill is located approximately 75 miles from Bradley International Airport in Hartford, Connecticut. Transportation can be provided to the airport.

APPLICATION TIMETABLE

The Linden Hill Summer Program has a rolling admissions policy. Students should submit their application with teacher evaluations, an official transcript, and a handwritten letter from the camper. Personal interviews and tours of the campus are encouraged and available year-round. The application form should be completed and returned as soon as possible.

For more information, contact:

James A. McDaniel, Headmaster and Summer Program Director
Linden Hill Summer Program
154 South Mountain Road
Northfield, Massachusetts 01360
413-498-2906
888-254-6336 (toll-free)
Fax: 413-498-2908
E-mail: admissions@lindenhs.org
World Wide Web: http://www.lindenhs.org

LONGACRE EXPEDITIONS

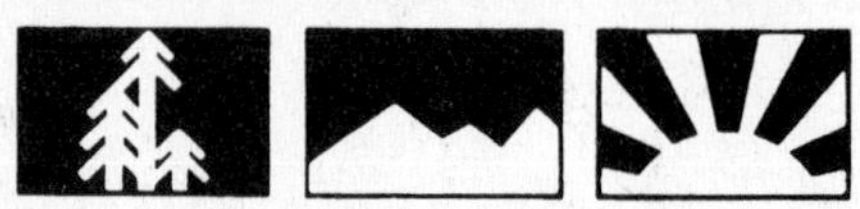

WILDERNESS/ADVENTURE TRAVEL

NORTH AND CENTRAL AMERICA, HAWAII, THE VIRGIN ISLANDS, AND EUROPE

Type of Program: Wilderness/adventure travel
Participants: Ages 11–19 in small coed groups by age
Enrollment: 10–16 participants in more than twenty different expeditions
Program Dates: Fourteen- to twenty-eight-day expeditions from late June to mid-August
Heads of Program: Meredith and Matthew Schuler and Roger Smith

LOCATION

Longacre Expeditions operates adventure travel programs in Alaska, British Columbia, Washington, Oregon, Colorado, Pennsylvania, Maine, Nova Scotia, Belize, Hawaii, the Virgin Islands, Iceland, Ireland, and the United Kingdom.

BACKGROUND AND PHILOSOPHY

Longacre Expeditions was established in 1981. The goal of each Longacre expedition is to provide teenagers the opportunity to grow by successfully accepting challenge.

These goals are approached uniquely, however, by broadening the forum in which the challenges occur. The great outdoors, of course, is the most apparent backdrop. Kids grow in confidence when they realize that they can, in fact, achieve age-appropriate physical goals, such as scaling a 30-foot rock face, biking a 50-mile day, or kayaking down Class II white water. Yet the physical aspect of an expedition is only half of the Longacre Experience.

Group meetings held four evenings a week under the guidance and participation of the trip leaders are the other half. Kids take time out to say "thank you" for kindnesses that occurred during the day or to iron out problems while they are small. Everyone is encouraged to identify and express their feelings and hear the concerns of others. Longacre kids learn to speak from the heart and to listen with respect.

Verbalizing feelings in front of a group can feel risky—not unlike shooting Class III white water in a raft or climbing a wall of ice with crampons and ice axes. The benefits are as significant. Kids gain confidence in the power of their own feelings, in their ability to communicate, and in the process that bonds individuals into a large comfortable group.

PROGRAM OFFERINGS

Each expedition takes advantage of the unique aspects of the environments that are visited and offers a different mix of activities.

Western U.S. and Canada (ages 13–19) In Alaska, participants sea kayak amid whales and glaciers in Prince William Sound. In Oregon, participants backpack near Crater Lake, raft on multiday excursions, and snowboard on 11,000-foot Mount Hood. In British Columbia, participants backpack in the remote backcountry of Garibaldi Provincial Park, sea kayak in the Straits of Georgia, and rock climb in the shadow of 1,800-foot walls at Squamish. In

Washington, participants are transported via the famous Washington State Ferry System to bike on four islands with distinctly different ecologies in the San Juan archipelago, backpack in the alpine meadows of North Cascades National Park, climb Mount St. Helens, and snow mountaineer on Mount Baker. In Colorado, Longacre's Leadership Training expedition attracts kids who have been hooked by the Longacre experience and want to hone their leadership skills in a wilderness environment. Leadership Training, in turn, becomes the launch pad for internship with Longacre in subsequent summers.

Eastern U.S. and Canada (ages 11–17) The Ridge and Valley Section of Pennsylvania provides a wealth of bicycle touring loops. Longacre's rural routes pass by isolated Amish farms, through old covered bridges and still offer time enough in the afternoon for a swim. In the Laurel Highlands, participants backpack amidst lush mountain laurel or raft and kayak down the Youghiogheny River. Maine and Nova Scotia are an outdoor enthusiast's dream. Participants hike, sea kayak, climb, bike, and raft through magnificent scenery and famous locales. The Penobscot Bay, dotted with uninhabited islands, offers unforgettable sea kayaking and schooner sailing expeditions. Nova Scotia is ideal for bicycle touring. The terrain is gently rolling, the culture is engaging, and the sea is a constant companion.

Tropical and North Atlantic Expeditions (ages 14–18) Longacre offers expeditions in five tropical and international settings—Hawaii, the Virgin Islands, Belize, Iceland, and Ireland and the United Kingdom. Each activity takes advantage of the unique flavor of the areas visited. Participants scuba dive and snorkel amidst unspoiled coral reefs; backpack in lush backcountry; get up close and personal with glaciers,

geysers, and icebergs; bike through centuries-old villages; and get an untouristy view of magnificent islands by sea kayak.

ENROLLMENT

All programs are coed and grouped by age. Enrollment varies from 10 to 16, with 2 to 4 leaders per group. Longacre believes that with the right attitude and a moderate degree of physical fitness, kids can be extremely successful in any of the programs. All expeditions are structured to offer age-appropriate challenges, regardless of the participant's level of experience. Some of the most successful kids have been older first-timers; their attitudes won out over experience.

DAILY SCHEDULE

A typical day finds the group breaking camp by 9 a.m.; hiking, biking, or paddling for most of the day (with a break for lunch and some rest in early afternoon); and at a new campsite by 4 or 5 p.m. After chores are done, kids often find time for swimming, writing letters, or a game of Frisbee—about as competitive as it gets at Longacre. A cooking crew of 2 or 3 kids and a leader are responsible for meal prep. In the evening, Group Meetings last until 9 or so. Other evening fare includes group campfires or taking advantage of local events.

FACILITIES

Base Camp accommodations vary in each course area. While in the field, participants sleep in backpacking tents. When in state parks or private campsites, there are often showers, toilets, and places to swim.

STAFF

The most important element in Longacre Expeditions' excellent reputation is its competent, caring staff. Staff members come from all over the country. They are often teachers who see the summer as an opportunity to be with kids in a nonclassroom setting. Others join Longacre each year from seasonal positions at ski resorts, environmental centers, and other wilderness programs.

The minimum age for staff members is 21. Each year, 40–50 percent return. Many others are former campers. Valued qualities are the ability to communicate and be comfortable with teenagers, competence in a variety of outdoor activities, very good physical condition, and the ability to embrace Longacre's trip-leading philosophy and commitment to Group.

MEDICAL CARE

Each Longacre staff member is certified with a minimum of Wilderness First Aid, CPR, and water safety. The first aid kit that goes out with each trip contains a list of all phone numbers for each ambulance service, hospital, and clinic in every area visited.

COSTS

Tuition ranges from $2000 to $4800. Families should assume that there will be additional expenses for appropriate personal gear and equipment, transportation to and from Base Camp, and spending money.

TRANSPORTATION

There is van transportation for eastern programs, with stops near Boston, Hartford, and New York. In addition, participants are picked up at Logan Airport in Boston; Baltimore-Washington International; Harrisburg (Pennsylvania) International; Seatac in Seattle; Portland (Oregon) International; Anchorage, Alaska; St. Thomas, Virgin Islands; Kauai, Hawaii; Belize City, Belize; Reykjavik, Iceland; and London.

APPLICATION TIMETABLE

Applications are received from mid-September on. Many trips are filled by mid-January. Interested individuals are encouraged to call about availability after this time.

For more information, contact:

Matthew and Meredith Schuler or Roger Smith
Longacre Expeditions
4030 Middle Ridge Road
Newport, Pennsylvania 17074
800-433-0127 (toll-free)
717-567-6790
Fax: 717-567-3955
E-mail: Longacre@LongacreExpeditions.com
World Wide Web: http://www.LongacreExpeditions.com

MAINE TEEN CAMP

SUMMER CAMP

PORTER, MAINE

Type of Program: Residential camp
Participants: Coeducational, ages 13–17
Enrollment: Approximately 275 per session
Program Dates: Two-, four-, six-, and eight-week sessions
Head of Program: Robert Briskin, Owner/Director

LOCATION

Maine Teen Camp is situated in southwestern Maine between two lakes. With more than 4,000 feet of shorefront, the camp is almost surrounded by water and has two sand beaches. Camp buildings are carefully integrated into the landscape of green fields and tall pines. Maine Teen is located on a private isthmus with no through traffic and is less than 1 hour from the Maine coast and the spectacular White Mountains and just 2½ hours by car to Boston, Massachusetts.

BACKGROUND AND PHILOSOPHY

In 1920, Camp Hiawatha was founded on the site of the present-day Maine Teen Camp. Over the years, Hiawatha enjoyed affiliation with several of New England's finest camps, including Wigwam and Robin Hood. In 1984, Kris Kamys and Jay Stager (Owner/Director of Hidden Valley Camp from 1969 to 1988) purchased Camp Hiawatha, and Maine Teen Camp came into being. In 1989, Kris and Jay were joined by Bob Briskin, who took over as owner and director.

The directors of Maine Teen are educators and professional camp people, and many of the staff members are teachers and students. The program reflects Maine Teen's conviction that summer camp is not just a recreational experience but is also an important extension of the educational process. When a camper joins Maine Teen Camp, he or she becomes part of a dynamic community of enthusiastic teenagers and adults from throughout the United States and around the world. Maine Teen's common goal is the creation of a supportive environment where living, learning, growing, and fun are a part of every day.

PROGRAM OFFERINGS

The elective format allows each Maine Teen camper to custom design his or her own schedule, choosing from the more than forty activities that are offered.

The waterfront offers instruction in waterskiing, wakeboarding, windsurfing, canoeing, swimming, sailing, fishing, lifeguard training, and more. Sports include mountain biking, soccer, volleyball, softball, basketball, professional instruction in tennis, and informal games of all kinds. Creative arts programs include stained glass, jewelry, pottery, silk screen, fabric arts, cartooning, drawing, sketching, and painting. The performing arts program offers instruction in dance (modern, jazz, and ballet), theater (acting, script writing, stage combat, and set and costume design), guitar, keyboards, drums, and voice, as well as a fully equipped music recording studio. Additionally, campers may choose to participate in instruction in video production and photography.

Maine Teen Camp also offers academic tutoring and English as a Second Language (ESL) programs.

The elective program encourages combining quality academic enrichment programs with professional coaching and instruction in sports, adventure programs in ropes course and climbing wall, waterfront activities, and arts and crafts activities. This balanced approach allows campers to gain and improve skills in one or two areas of known interest while still having an opportunity to explore a variety of new activities.

Evening programs are also an important part of life at Maine Teen. A fun event for the entire community is planned every evening of the summer. Examples include things like social dances, campfires, beach parties, cookouts, Casino Night, the MTC Film Festival, intracamp sports, cabin parties, International Night, and special programs and presentations by performers, artists, and a variety of other interesting people.

ENROLLMENT

Each session enrolls approximately 275 boys and girls, ages 13–17. Campers come from throughout the United States and abroad. The camp begins anew each session, so long-term cliques do not develop. Teens are a dynamic group, so approximately 70 percent of the campers are new each year.

DAILY SCHEDULE

8	Wake up
8:30	Breakfast
9	Morning announcements
9:30	Period one
11:45	Period two
12:00	Period three
1:00	Lunch
2:15	Period four
3:30	Period five
4:30	Period six
6	Dinner
7	Cabin clean-up and chores
8 *(approximate time)*	Evening program
11	Lights-out

EXTRA OPPORTUNITIES AND ACTIVITIES

Special programs at Maine Teen Camp include hiking in the White Mountains; white-water rafting trips; canoeing down the Saco River; and trips to Freeport, Maine beaches, and Quebec City. Golf, deep-sea fishing, windsurfing, and whale-watching trips are also offered.

FACILITIES

The spacious, modern lodge overlooks Stanley Lake. With two levels of open interior space and a massive stone fireplace, this dramatic building is the center of much camp activity. The lodge also houses the campers' e-mail center.

Living accommodations for boys and girls are at opposite ends of camp and include a large contemporary lakeside bunkhouse, as well as both modern and rustic cabins, all with indoor bathrooms and electricity.

Maine Teen also has a theater; a recreation building and weight-training room; five tennis courts; a basketball court; a sand volleyball court; a darkroom; a camp store; a well-equipped and staffed infirmary; numerous studios for crafts and creative and performing arts, including a state-of-the-art recording studio for camp musicians, language study, and academic tutorials; and a sports field used for soccer, softball, rugby, and football.

MEDICAL CARE

Maine Teen has a modern infirmary, an experienced and qualified nursing staff, and staff EMTs. Family medical insurance coverage is required, however, if the incident goes beyond the ordinary limits of the camp's coverage. The costs of all other preexisting medical problems are the responsibility of the family.

RELIGIOUS LIFE

Maine Teen Camp is nonsectarian. Teens from all faiths and cultures are fully integrated.

COSTS

The 2003 camp tuition fee was $3495 for the first session, $3495 for the second session, $4495 for the six-week session, and $5495 for the full season. A deposit of $500 is required with the registration form. An additional "personal account" fee of $175 or more is charged to provide all campers with the necessary spending money for use on trips and for e-mail service, toiletries, laundry, and purchases at the camp store. Any outstanding balance in this account is refunded in cash to the camper before he or she leaves the camp. Campers may also elect to participate in a number of extra-cost trip options such as a four-day trip to the historic city of Quebec, Canada ($400); an exciting guided white-water rafting trip on Maine's scenic Kennebec River ($200); or a day spent ocean fishing or whale watching off Maine's coast ($100, includes a lobster dinner). Prices are subject to change and are available by telephone.

APPLICATION TIMETABLE

Initial inquiries are welcome at any time. Registrations are accepted at any time, subject to the availability of space. References are sent upon request.

FOR MORE INFORMATION, CONTACT:

Bob Briskin (Director) or Monique Rafuse-Pines (Assistant Director)

winter
Maine Teen Camp
190 Upper Gulph Road
Radnor, Pennsylvania 19087
610-527-6759
800-752-2267 (toll-free)
Fax: 610-520-0182
E-mail: mtc@teencamp.com
World Wide Web: http://www.teencamp.com

summer
Maine Teen Camp
481 Brownfield Road
Porter, Maine 04068
207-625-8581
Fax: 207-625-8738
E-mail: mtc@teencamp.com
World Wide Web: http://www.teencamp.com

THE MARVELWOOD SUMMER

ACADEMIC PROGRAM

KENT, CONNECTICUT

Type of Program: Academic remediation, enrichment, and skills building
Participants: Coeducational, students entering grades 7–11
Enrollment: A maximum of 40
Program Dates: Late June to early August

LOCATION

The Marvelwood School is located on a 75-acre campus in the historic village of Kent, amidst the foothills of the Berkshire Hills in Litchfield County. This delightful country setting provides an ideal environment for purposeful academic work and recreational activity.

BACKGROUND AND PHILOSOPHY

Begun by Marvelwood's founder, Robert A. Bodkin, who adopted the successful methods of the Salisbury Summer School, The Marvelwood Summer has provided instruction in reading, English, and study skills to students of widely varied backgrounds and abilities since 1964. During Mr. Bodkin's tenure as Marvelwood headmaster and summer school director, the Marvelwood name became synonymous with caring and effective developmental education. For the many students who have been genuinely motivated to improve their academic work, The Marvelwood Summer has been an academic turning point. The ungraded curriculum, which emphasizes skill building and confidence building, enables young people to manage their schoolwork more effectively; to apply their newly developed skills to reading, writing, and mathematics; and to think of themselves as capable and successful learners.

PROGRAM OFFERINGS

Academic Courses All students take six classes, which average 8 members. Courses include:

Study Skills The objective is to ensure structured practice in efficient study methods and the various comprehension techniques required for effective reading.

Word Attack and Spelling Students develop strong word-recognition skills and improve spelling and vocabulary through increased familiarity with the structure of words.

Composition Students strengthen their basic writing skills through intensive practice and study of essay structure and style, mechanics, and grammar.

Vocabulary Using programmed texts, etymology exercises, and structured cards, students expand their working vocabulary.

Optional courses also offer skill-building work in basic math, prealgebra, algebra I, geometry, word processing, critical reading, studio art, filmmaking, drama, journalism, SAT/SSAT review, and English as a second language (ESL). Remedial English 9, remedial English 10, or algebra I credit is available to students who qualify. Parents should alert the admissions staff if their child needs make up one of these courses, as special arrangements are necessary. Interested students should contact the Admission Office for further information.

Sports and Activities Each afternoon, students choose from a wide variety of sports and activities, including sailing, swimming, softball, soccer, basketball, volleyball, touch football, lacrosse, tennis, Ultimate Frisbee, mountain biking, horseback riding, golf, nature hikes along the Appalachian Trail, arts and crafts, filmmaking, and photography. Qualified instructors are available for swimming and sailing lessons.

ENROLLMENT

A maximum of 40 students from across the country and overseas who have just completed the sixth through the tenth grades are admitted to the program each summer. Typically, students are well-motivated boys and girls with deficits in the verbal area and in study discipline who need an intensive, structured experience. For international students who need a working knowledge of English, Marvelwood Summer provides ESL instruction. Students with learning disabilities and ADD should have received enough compensatory education so that they can function in a mainstreamed classroom. The small size of the program permits the personal attention and warm, familial atmosphere that are so important to its success.

EXTRA OPPORTUNITIES AND ACTIVITIES

Weekend activities include supervised trips to malls, movie theaters, restaurants, museums, playhouses, local fairs, and nearby amusement parks; picnics at state forests; pizza parties; dances; a lip-sync competition; and an all-school Olympics. According to student interest, special excursions are planned to

Boston, New York City, Mystic Seaport and Aquarium, Tanglewood, and Old Sturbridge Village.

DAILY SCHEDULE

7:45–8:15	Breakfast
8:30–10:10	Classes
10:10–10:25	Break
10:25–12:25	Classes
12:30–1	Lunch
1:10–1:20	Jobs
1:30–2	Free reading
2:15–5	Sports and activities
5–5:30	Dorm jobs
5:30–6:15	Study hall
6:30–7	Dinner
7:30–9:15	Study hall
9:15–9:30	Study break
10	Lights out

STAFF

Most faculty members in the Summer School are members of the Marvelwood School faculty. The staff is made up of at least one teacher for each five students. Specialists in study skills, remedial reading, English composition, mathematics, and literature form part of the faculty each year.

MEDICAL CARE

A registered nurse holds infirmary hours each morning, and an experienced school physician is on call and regularly on duty at the Sharon Hospital in Sharon. All students must submit a standard health form before matriculating. Enrollment in a student accident insurance policy is required to cover the full cost of any potential injury while participating in Marvelwood activities.

RELIGIOUS LIFE

There are weekly opportunities to attend Roman Catholic, Protestant, and Jewish services in the area, but attendance is not required.

COSTS

The boarding tuition for 2004 is $5300; tuition for day students was $4000. This charge is comprehensive and covers such costs as room and board, classes, books, and supplies. There is an additional fee for field trips and special activities as well as laundry service and transportation. Spending money can be deposited at the Business Office. Marvelwood recommends $15–$20 per week. Any unused portion is refunded at the end of the summer.

A $1500 deposit is required upon acceptance. Tuition must be paid in full prior to the beginning of the program in June.

TRANSPORTATION

Staff members meet flights at Bradley International Airport (Hartford/Springfield), JFK and La Guardia airports in New York, trains and buses in Hartford, and the New York bus at Kent. Travel information is sent upon acceptance.

APPLICATION TIMETABLE

As space is limited, students are admitted on a first-come, first-served basis. Families seriously interested in securing a place in the summer program should complete the application process as soon as possible. Applications are accepted up to the end of June or as long as spaces are available. Inquiries and campus visits are welcome at any time.

In addition to the application, Marvelwood also requires a current school transcript and any pertinent testing results as well as two teacher recommendations.

For more information, contact:

The Admissions Office
The Marvelwood School
476 Skiff Mountain Road
P.O. Box 3001
Kent, Connecticut 06757
860-927-0047 Ext. 27
Fax: 860-927-0021
E-mail: marvelwood.school@snet.net
World Wide Web: http://www.themarvelwoodschool.com/summer.html

PARTICIPANT/FAMILY COMMENTS

"I have proven to myself that I can do well . . . It gives me great satisfaction knowing that some hard work and a little extra push can go a long way. Marvelwood has taught me something valuable which will stay with me the rest of my life."

"We were so pleased with the program and what it did for our son. He continues to exhibit greatly improved study habits. Perhaps even more important, his attitude toward his schoolwork and learning responsibilities has become noticeably more serious and mature."

MASSACHUSETTS COLLEGE OF ART

mass | art

SUMMER STUDIOS

BOSTON, MASSACHUSETTS

Type of Program: Visual arts
Participants: Coeducational, students entering grades 11 and 12
Enrollment: Approximately 90 (about 25 residential)
Program Dates: Four weeks in July and August, 2005
Head of Program: Liz Rudnick, K–12 Outreach Coordinator

LOCATION

On the Avenue of the Arts, Massachusetts College of Art (MassArt) is situated in the heart of Boston's cultural district. The Emerald Necklace weaves its way by, with the Museum of Fine Arts and the Isabella Stewart Gardner Museums each within one walking block. The Institute for Contemporary Art, the Museum of the National Center of Afro-American Artists, the Photographic Resource Center, and more than sixty other museums and art galleries make Boston a thriving urban cultural center.

Outside the city, Massachusetts offers the beautiful rocky coastline of the North Shore and the sweeping beaches that extend down through the South Shore toward Cape Cod. Inland, Massachusetts' rolling hills, mountains, and farmland extend out to the west toward Mass MOCA and the Berkshires.

BACKGROUND AND PHILOSOPHY

MassArt's precollege summer program is an intensive experience in artmaking and viewing designed specifically for students entering their junior and senior years in high school. Students develop work for their portfolios and develop work habits that encourage excellence in their artistic endeavors. Through the structured curriculum that combines foundation courses with electives, students are able to experience the rigors of higher education in the visual arts. Students attending MassArt's Summer Studios are well prepared to make decisions about their future education, whether it is a liberal arts education or an education focused on fine arts and design.

Summer Studios takes advantage of MassArt's extraordinary facilities. Printmaking, metal sculpting, photography, fashion, ceramics, filmmaking, and computer animation are some of the areas students can select to study. MassArt faculty members, graduate students, undergraduate students, and alumni return to the campus for the summer months to teach and share their knowledge with the students of Summer Studios.

Established in 1873, Massachusetts College of Art was the first and remains the only four-year independent public art college in the U.S. The College is nationally known for offering broad access to a high-quality professional arts education, accompanied by a strong general education in the liberal arts. A major cultural force in Boston, MassArt offers public programs of innovative exhibitions, lectures, and events.

PROGRAM OFFERINGS

There are four components to the Summer Studios program: the two morning foundation classes, electives, and Sneak Preview College Day. The morning foundation classes are 2D and 3D Fundamentals and Issues and Images.

2D and 3D Fundamentals All students study the fundamentals of design and composition while building a strong foundation in two- and three-dimensional work. Students develop their ability to observe through the practice of drawing and sculpting from the figure. Students receive a written evaluation from the faculty at the conclusion of the program.

Issues and Images Students study various questions concerning art, including what it is, why people look at and make it, and what the role of the artist is in society. This class emphasizes critical-thinking skills through the study of contemporary art, art history, and current events. Students receive a written evaluation from the faculty at the conclusion of the program. Issues and Images enables students to experience arts in the community through weekly field trips to artists' studios, galleries, and museums.

Electives All students attend two elective studios. Students receive a written evaluation from the faculty at the conclusion of the program. The Monday/Thursday choices are Surreal Painting: Myth and Metaphor, Painting from the Figure, Metalworking, Design and Composition, and Fashion Design. The Tuesday/Friday choices are Ceramics, Printmaking, Jewelry and Metals, Computer Animation, Comic Book Art, and Fundamentals in Filmmaking.

Sneak Preview College Day College Day is a full-day event that addresses the needs of students who are trying to understand college admissions policies and procedures. This event focuses on portfolio reviews, resume writing, artists' statements, and admission applications. A panel discussion of artists from a variety of fields addresses Summer Studios participants, talking about how they got to where they are.

ENROLLMENT

In past years, Summer Studios has had approximately 25 percent of its student body come from Boston and the surrounding area. Fifty-eight percent of the student body has come from western and central Massachusetts. Seventeen percent of the students have come from out of state and from other countries.

DAILY SCHEDULE

Monday, Tuesday, Thursday, and Friday:

8:30–11:20	2D and 3D Fundamentals
11:30–12:30	Issues and Images
12:30–1:30	Lunch
1:30–4:30	Electives

Wednesday (except for Sneak Preview College Day):

8:30–12	Electives
1:30–4:30	Issues and Images field trips

In addition to program activities, the staff of the residence hall plans additional activities for resident students on evenings and weekends. The following is a sampling of past activities and destinations that residents have visited: Arnold Arboretum, bookbinding workshop, Castle Island, Crane Beach Sand Castle Competition, DeCordova Museum and Sculpture Park, flea markets, George's Island, gym/team sports, hiking, Institute of Contemporary Art, MIT Science Park, Museum of African American Art, Museum of Fine Arts, New England Aquarium, Newburyport, Omni Theater at the Science Museum, open mike at the Student Center, outdoor picnics and barbecues, papermaking workshop, planetarium, poetry readings, Quincy Market and Faneuil Hall, running, science museum, sketching trips, and whale watching.

COSTS

Tuition for the 2004 Summer Studios was $1890. The residence fee, which includes room and board, was $2125. The program fee and residential fee were $4015. A $100 nonrefundable program deposit is required with all applications. Residential students must submit a $100 residence hall deposit.

FOR MORE INFORMATION, CONTACT:

Liz Rudnick
Massachusetts College of Art
621 Huntington Avenue
Boston, Massachusetts 02115
617-879-7174
E-mail: lizrudnick@massart.edu
World Wide Web: http://www.massartplus.org

MED-O-LARK CAMP

SUMMER CAMP

WASHINGTON, MAINE

Type of Program: Focus on the visual and performing arts. Med-O-Lark is a nontraditional, noncompetitive camp.
Participants: Coed, ages 11–15
Enrollment: 275
Program Dates: Two 4-week sessions from June 26 to July 22, 2004, and July 24 to August 19, 2004; eight-week option from June 26 to August 19, 2004; two-week session from July 24 to August 5, 2004
Head of Program: Jay R. Stager, Director

LOCATION

Med-O-Lark Camp is situated in the small town of Washington, Maine. A short drive to Camden, Maine, takes visitors to one of Maine's most popular communities and the midcoastal Penobscot Bay region. The camp is 20 minutes from the ocean and an hour north of Portland. Med-O-Lark is located on 4-mile, crystal-clear Washington Lake.

BACKGROUND AND PHILOSOPHY

Med-O-Lark has been a camp for sixty-eight years. From 1946 to 1965, it was the girls' camp associated with one of America's oldest boys' camps (Camp Medomak) across the lake. In 1967, Jay Stager established it as an independent camp and it became an alternative to the traditional camps of that time. He opted for a coed camp when most camps were single-sex and he banned color wars, guns, archery, uniforms, junk food, and strict regimentation. Med-O-Lark was an instant success and has continued to evolve as a child-centered camp ever since under the direction of Jay R. Stager.

The program centers upon the arts, crafts, dance, music, theater, an extensive waterfront, and gymnastics. An all-elective schedule enables campers to choose their own daily instructional activities. Campers choose five 2-week workshops from more than fifty workshop opportunities taught by counselors and professionals. Activities in the visual and performing arts and at the waterfront offer a wealth of instructional depth and continuity over the two-week period. Evening programs involve the whole community and provide an opportunity for guest artist performances. On other evenings, campers and staff members perform for each other or participate in dances and games.

Med-O-Lark offers a supportive environment in which campers can explore their artistic side and have fun. There is a strong emphasis on self-expression, human values, and understanding in a pressure-free context. The staff receives an intense twelve-day orientation and training period. Counselors and professional staff members have teachable skills and are open, giving, patient, sensitive, and fun.

The menu at camp is diverse, and most importantly, edible! Vegetarian options are abundantly available, and a wide array of choices for each person's tastes can be found at the large buffet meals.

PROGRAM OFFERINGS

All campers discuss their program choices with their counselors, and then they select activities for two weeks (five class periods) at a time.

Visual Arts This is not a typical arts and crafts program. Med-O-Lark has more than twenty craft studios for such activities as fabric arts, painting, pottery, silver jewelry, candle making, batik, tie-dying, stone carving, enameling, woodworking/carving, stained glass, weaving, silkscreening, and more. The farmhouse highlights the popular culinary arts program. Med-O-Lark feels the day-to-day process of creating is just as important as the finished product. Beginner and advanced courses are available for all activities. Trying new forms of expression is encouraged.

Performing Arts Classes in varying dance styles are offered in ballet, tap, jazz, modern, hip hop, and aerobics. Each summer there are additional nontraditional forms of dance, such as African dance, Indian dance, and Irish folk dance. Theater is another of the camp's strongest areas. Campers can perform in the play or musical produced each session or simply take classes in performance, improvisation, monologue, Shakespeare, or stand-up comedy. This area of camp is exciting and stimulating for the novice or the experienced performer. English horseback riding, a high art form requiring diligent practice, is also available, as are fencing and martial arts.

Waterfront Located on a 4-mile lake, Med-O-Lark Camp is ideal for water sports. With a fleet of more than thirty boats, campers enjoy sailing, canoeing, crew/rowing, sea kayaking, windsurfing, aquacycling, waterskiing, and kneeboarding. The large swim area is great for swim lessons, endurance swimming, water ballet, or just taking an afternoon dip. Four speedboats are used for waterskiing.

Sports While this is a noncompetitive camp with no leagues or intracamp contests, there is a wide range of physical activity and individual sports, including tennis, ropes course challenges, mountain biking, roller hockey, basketball, fencing, volleyball, soccer, weight lifting, softball, and martial arts.

ENROLLMENT

Med-O-Lark enrolls 275 boys and girls each month-long session. Up to one fourth of the campers remain

for both sessions. International campers help to diversify the camp. Campers and counselors hail from such countries as Russia, Venezuela, France, Italy, Japan, and Brazil.

DAILY SCHEDULE

7:30	Wake-up
8:00	Drift-in breakfast
9:00	All-camp meeting
9:30	First period activity
10:30	Second period activity
11:30	Third period activity
12:30	Lunch
1:15	Turtle time
2:00	Fourth period activity
3:00	Fifth period activity
4:00	Free time
5:30	All-camp meeting
6:00	Dinner
7:30	Evening program
10:15	Good night

The schedule is five days a week. Every Thursday and Sunday, campers sleep late, have a lazy day at camp, or go on a trip out of camp (i.e., the beach, roller skating, ocean trips, hiking, or sea kayaking).

EXTRA OPPORTUNITIES AND ACTIVITIES

The camp offers optional trips to Quebec, Canada, for three days and an overnight white-water rafting experience. Weekly trips are normal for all campers. These day trips include a visit to Bar Harbor, ocean beaches, roller rinks, Camden Hills, miniature golf, or sea kayaking. Language arts classes are also available. Spanish, French, Hebrew, and ESL are offered.

FACILITIES

The twenty-three cabins all have bathrooms and showers. The dance studios are inspiring and charming. A large recreation hall for group programs, a newly renovated dining hall, and more than twenty craft studios are a vital part of the property. A new farm has been added to the premises. The farm house is the hub of the culinary arts program. The horses and a herd of llamas live on the farm. The ropes course is large and nestled in the adjacent forest. With some thirty-five watercraft and a sandy beach, Med-O-Lark provides a very popular swim, sail, and ski program. The camp sits on 40 acres with a half-mile lakefront.

STAFF

Counselors are undergraduate and graduate students and performing and visual arts professionals. Three or 4 counselors live in each bunk with 10 to 15 campers. At least one counselor goes to sleep with the campers, so campers are always supervised, even at night. An extensive twelve-day orientation period effectively develops staff members. Usually up to a third of the staff members are returning counselors, and a third are also international, from such places as Australia, New Zealand, Ukraine, Germany, and Ireland.

MEDICAL CARE

There is a fully equipped, 24-hour infirmary staffed by 3 nurses. Camp doctors are on call 24 hours a day, and the Pen Bay Medical Center is in nearby Camden, Maine. Other medical specialists nearby are also always available.

RELIGIOUS LIFE

Med-O-Lark is nonsectarian. Those who wish are transported to nearby services.

COSTS

Med-O-Lark has an all-inclusive fee. Additional fees are applied for the Canada trip, white-water rafting, linen rental, and the store account. There is a no-tipping policy and no need for extra camper spending money. The fee is $3495 for a four-week session and $5995 for an eight-week session. The fee for a two-week session is $1795.

TRANSPORTATION

All transportation for campers within the United States may be arranged by the camp. Charter buses are provided with chaperones from New York City, Boston, Montreal, and points in Connecticut and Massachusetts. Campers from further away travel by air. Camper flights arrive at Logan Airport in Boston or Portland Jetport in Maine, where campers are met by Med-O-Lark staff members.

FOR MORE INFORMATION AND A VIDEO, CONTACT:

Med-O-Lark Camp
214 Atlantic Highway
Northport, Maine 04849
800-292-7757 (toll-free)
Fax: 207-338-0848
E-mail: medolark@acadia.net
World Wide Web: http://www.medolark.com

MERCERSBURG ACADEMY SUMMER AND EXTENDED PROGRAMS

ADVENTURE CAMPS, ESLPLUS, ACADEMIC ENRICHMENT, THE ARTS, SPORTS CAMPS

MERCERSBURG, PENNSYLVANIA

Type of Program: Adventure camps, ESL*Plus*, academic enrichment, performing arts, sports camps
Participants: Coeducational; ages vary with each program
Enrollment: Varies with each program
Program Dates: Varies with each program
Head of Program: Rick Hendrickson, Director of Summer and Extended Programs

LOCATION

Mercersburg Academy's beautiful campus is located in south-central Pennsylvania, about 90 minutes from the Baltimore, Washington, and Harrisburg metropolitan areas. Pittsburgh and Philadelphia are approximately 2½ hours away.

BACKGROUND AND PHILOSOPHY

Nationally recognized as one of the top prep schools in the country, Mercersburg is a private, coed boarding school with a reputation for excellence that attracts young men and women from across the country and around the world during the school year.

The school's summer and extended programs reflect that standard of excellence as well as its diversity. More than 3,000 participants from twenty-one states and fifteen countries gain from the Mercersburg experience each summer.

Mercersburg's diverse programs focus on challenging participants to excel in their interests and to try new ideas. This is accomplished by providing participants with the chance to learn, experience, and succeed. Limited enrollments ensure the quality of attention and instruction that makes the Mercersburg experience unique.

PROGRAM OFFERINGS

Adventure Camp Series (Junior Adventure Camp, ages 7–8; Adventure Camp, ages 8–14; Teen Adventure Camp, ages 14–16) The Academy's Mercersburg Adventure Camps blend a traditional summer camp atmosphere with a modern school setting, enhancing the development of every camper's mind, body, and spirit. Featuring two-week sessions (one week for Junior Adventure Camp) throughout the summer and a 3:1 camper-counselor ratio, the Adventure Camps' diverse programs offers a great blend of enrichment, sports, outdoor activities, and fun trips. Adventure Camps challenge campers to grow and explore various opportunities, starting with their choice of the activities from the Academy's contemporary schedule. Every camper builds friendships, learns teamwork, and develops independence and leadership.

Young Writer's Camp (grades 6–9) Young Writer's Camp draws a diverse enrollment, but the common thread running among the participants is an expectation for more than just classrooms and keyboarding. This is an experience that builds writing skills in the real world. The young writers hike nature trails, explore Civil War battlefields, interview interesting people, study the news, and watch movies. Then they write about their experiences. Poems, stories, articles, essays, journal entries, and letters—these writers utilize the full spectrum of writing.

ESL*Plus* (international students, grades 6–12) ESLPlus provides international students with the opportunity for three to five weeks of summer study and cultural enrichment at a premier private boarding school in the United States. A comprehensive and stimulating curriculum improves communication skills in English speaking, listening, writing, and reading. Studies also feature U.S. history and culture and TOEFL preparation, along with recreational trips and enriching weekend excursions to Washington, D.C.; New York; and other areas.

ESL*Plus* draws many types of students, including those who are making the transition to North American boarding schools. The program also draws students who want intensive summer work with the English language and the U.S. culture before returning to their home countries. The program typically includes students from Asia, Western Europe, Eastern Europe, and the Middle East.

Other Offerings (varied ages) The school also offers programs in sports, the arts, and professional development. Mercersburg's sports camps feature coaches and collegiate athletes who have achieved success at the highest levels while keeping the proper perspective on sportsmanship. Arts programs focus on performance- oriented workshops for youths in both middle school and high school, while professional development institutes encompass theater, digital arts, and technology in the classroom.

ENROLLMENT

Program enrollments vary, but typically range from 10 (professional development workshops) to 75

(Mercersburg Adventure Camp). Summer 2004 brought participants from around the United States as well as from Bermuda, China, Costa Rica, France, Germany, Great Britain, Japan, Korea, Russia, Spain, Switzerland, Taiwan, and Thailand.

DAILY SCHEDULE

The daily schedule varies with each program.

EXTRA OPPORTUNITIES AND ACTIVITIES

Extracurricular opportunities vary with each program, but can include trips that feature whitewater rafting, amusement parks, professional baseball and soccer games, challenge courses, professonal theater, and Civil War battlefields.

FACILITIES

Mercersburg Academy's summer programs utilize the school's contemporary academic facilities that include a 55,000-volume library, full computer networking and Internet access across campus, extensive science labs, audio and video production areas, and outstanding fine arts studios. Mercersburg's athletic facilities rival any in the nation with a 10,000-square-foot main arena, a 6,000-square-foot fitness center, a 3,600-square-foot wrestling/multipurpose room, a nine-lane swimming and diving pool, eight outdoor athletic fields, outdoor tennis courts, and indoor and outdoor tracks.

Residential participants are housed in one of the school's modern, air-conditioned dormitories, with 24-hour supervision by program staff members. Programs gather at Ford Dining Hall for all-you-can-eat buffet meals that are tasty, nutritious, and consistently rated as excellent each summer by program participants.

Rolling hills encompass the 300-acre campus that includes the expansive athletic facilities, farmland, and wildlife habitat areas. The surrounding area includes tributary streams of the Potomac River watershed, as well as thousands of acres of nearby state forests in the heart of the Appalachian Mountains.

STAFF

Camps, workshops, and institutes feature quality staff members with excellent reputations and credentials. Caring, professional teachers and energetic, well-trained counselors share the common bonds of enthusiasm, experience, and a commitment to working with people.

MEDICAL CARE

The safety and care of participants is a priority at all times. An on-campus health center is staffed with licensed nurses to provide medical services. Mercersburg also has access to a primary care doctor, and local hospitals are close by, should emergencies arise.

COSTS

Tuition and fees vary with each program. Tuition for each program is comprehensive and includes all costs for instruction, activities, lodging, meals, and materials.

TRANSPORTATION

Shuttles are available that service regional airports, train stations, and bus stations in the Washington, D.C. area.

APPLICATION TIMETABLE

Early application is encouraged, as some programs fill by early February; most are filled by the middle of May. Admission to most programs is on a rolling basis and notification of acceptance is made within two weeks of receiving all application materials.

For more information, contact:

Rick Hendrickson, Director
Office of Summer and Extended Programs
Mercersburg Academy
300 East Seminary Street
Mercersburg, Pennsylvania 17236
717-328-6225
Fax: 717-328-9072
E-mail: summerprograms@mercersburg.edu
World Wide Web: http://www.mercersburg.edu

PARTICIPANT/FAMILY COMMENTS

"This was awesome! It's been the best two weeks of my life."—Adventure Camper

"The personal attention given to each child was extraordinary."—Parent

MOUNT HOLYOKE COLLEGE

SUMMERMATH AND SEARCH PROGRAMS

SOUTH HADLEY, MASSACHUSETTS

Type of Program: Academic enrichment
Participants: Young women, grades 8–12
Enrollment: Approximately 60 students
Program Dates: Four weeks, June 26–July 23, 2005
Heads of Program: Dr. Charlene Morrow, Psychology Department, and Dr. James Morrow, Mathematics Department

LOCATION

SummerMath and SEARCH take place concurrently on the campus of Mount Holyoke College in western Massachusetts. The area is known for its natural beauty, institutions of higher learning, and cultural offerings.

BACKGROUND AND PHILOSOPHY

SummerMath was initiated in 1982 with an emphasis on teaching and learning mathematics in a more conceptual and participatory manner. SummerMath works to increase the participation of women and minorities in science, mathematics, engineering, and technology.

SummerMath focuses on understanding rather than just memorizing, on learning to be an independent learner without being isolated, and on doing mathematics in context. The program is neither competitive nor remedial; rather, it uses a problem-solving format in which students work on challenging problems, devise their own approaches for solving problems, and then give detailed explanations of their solutions. There are frequent interactions with teachers as the students learn to become more self-motivated and better able to direct their own learning.

The SEARCH program was initiated in 2004 to offer young women the opportunity to experience a mathematics research environment. This is an in-depth and intensive program for students who want to know about mathematics that is beyond what is seen in high school.

PROGRAM OFFERINGS

The SummerMath Program Students take three classes, each involving student activity, questioning, discussion, and discovery. Each class has the goal of helping students become powerful and effective problem solvers.

The three classes are: Fundamental Mathematical Concepts, where students work and discuss ideas in pairs, with an instructor and an undergraduate assistant circulating about the classroom asking probing questions and leading small-group discussions; Computer Programming, where students work in pairs at a computer using Logo to solve problems of geometric design, learning to plan, organize, and revise their ideas by working on projects such as transformational geometry, tangram puzzles, patchwork quilt designs, and group murals; and Workshops, consisting of two 2-week workshops, with choices including robotics, statistics, architecture, economics, and geometric origami. Workshops are intended to give students a hands-on experience with ways in which mathematics can be applied.

The SEARCH Program This program is designed for students who have developed some confidence in mathematics but who have not seen mathematics beyond the high school curriculum. Students are given the opportunity for in-depth exploration guided by mathematics faculty members and in collaboration with other students. The environment is hands-on and lively, with an emphasis on students formulating and answering their own questions. Students are introduced to several pieces of software that are useful tools for mathematical explorations. There are several evening collaborative problem solving sessions, as well as field trips.

DAILY SCHEDULE

A typical day at SummerMath:

8:00	Breakfast
8:30	Mathematics
10:00	Break
10:15	Computer Programming
11:45	Lunch
12:45–2:15	Workshop
3:00	Recreation
4:30	Floor meeting with RA
5:30	Dinner, free time
7:00	College student panel
8:00	Social events, free time
11:00	Room Check-In

A typical day at SEARCH:

8:30	Breakfast
9:00–11:45	Classes and Problem Sessions (including a break)
11:45	Lunch
1:00–2:45	Technology Workshop
3:00	Recreation
4:30	Floor meeting
5:30	Dinner, free time
6:30	Problem Solving Session
8:00	Social events, free time
11:00	Room Check-In

ENROLLMENT

The SummerMath student body of around 50 students is academically, geographically, and racially diverse. Some students excel in math and some do not, but

many experience a lack of confidence in their mathematical abilities that is still far too prevalent in young women. Virtually all past SummerMath students have expressed an increase in self-confidence upon completion of the program. SummerMath seeks students who are highly motivated and open to trying new methods of learning.

SEARCH is a small program of about a dozen students, equally as diverse as SummerMath and housed in the same dormitory. The two programs share many activities.

EXTRA OPPORTUNITIES AND ACTIVITIES

Most students live in the dormitory, and the residential program is designed to give students a taste of college life. There are offerings from workshops on personal growth to colleges and careers to SAT preparation to jewelry making. Each afternoon there are recreational choices including swimming, team sports, weight training, and aerobic dance. Weekends include day trips to such places as the Boston Museum of Science or Shakespeare & Co. in the Berkshires.

FACILITIES

Students have full access to the library, art museum, hiking and biking trails, and athletic facilities on the 800-acre campus of Mount Holyoke. Classes take place on campus. One dormitory is used exclusively for SummerMath and SEARCH students. All meals are served at the newly renovated campus center overlooking Lower Lake.

STAFF

SummerMath staff members are drawn from Mount Holyoke and other colleges throughout the United States. SEARCH classes are taught by college mathematics faculty members. Resident assistants and teaching assistants are undergraduate students from Mount Holyoke and other colleges.

MEDICAL CARE

Free emergency and one-time medical coverage is provided through the University of Massachusetts Health Service.

COSTS

The fee for SummerMath 2004 was $3900, which included room, board, all program materials, event tickets, and local transportation. For day students, the fee was $3100. The fee for SEARCH 2004 was $3600.

FINANCIAL AID

Need-based scholarships of up to $1500 are available.

TRANSPORTATION

The campus is located 45 minutes from Bradley International Airport (Hartford/Springfield) and 30 minutes from the Springfield Amtrak station. Transportation is provided to and from Bradley Airport and the Springfield bus and train stations.

APPLICATION TIMETABLE

Applications are due by May 1, with late acceptance on a space-available basis. Financial aid is awarded on a rolling basis, so early application is strongly advised.

FOR MORE INFORMATION, CONTACT:

Charlene and James Morrow, Directors
SummerMath and SEARCH
Mount Holyoke College
South Hadley, Massachusetts 01075-1441
413-538-2608
Fax: 413-538-2002
E-mail: summermath@mtholyoke.edu
World Wide Web: http://www.mtholyoke.edu/proj/summermath
http://www.mtholyoke.edu/proj/search

PARTICIPANT/FAMILY COMMENTS

"I met so many wonderful and diverse people...most importantly, SummerMath improved my self-confidence in all areas tremendously! It's definitely an experience I will always carry with me." —SummerMath student

"I think our teachers have been keeping secrets from us...you will never see mathematics like this in high school! Now I can make connections between the real world and mathematics."—SEARCH student

"Of all the experiences that [our daughter] has had, SummerMath at Mount Holyoke was the most singular and the most influential in her development." —Parent

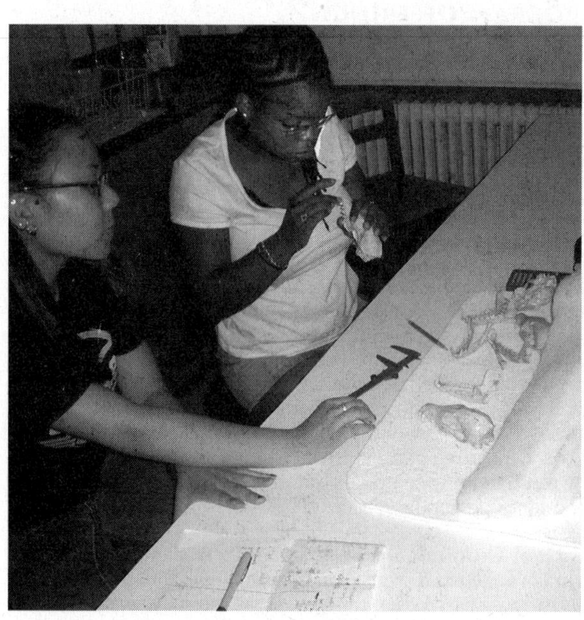

MUSIKER TOURS

SUMMER PROGRAMS

UNITED STATES (INCLUDING ALASKA AND HAWAII), CANADA, AND EUROPE

Type of Program: Active touring, combination camping/hotel/dorm tours, all-hotel tours, and special golf tour
Participants: Coeducational, ages 12–18
Enrollment: 40–50 per group
Program Dates: Vary depending on tour, from twenty-one to forty-four days
Heads of Program: Musiker family, founders and directors

BACKGROUND AND PHILOSOPHY

The roots of Musiker Tours are in camping and education. Judy and Mike Musiker, both educators, founded Musiker Tours in 1966 after owning a successful coed summer camp. Today, eight Musiker family members work together year-round, creating and coordinating the summer programs. As owners, the family travels all summer to meet and spend time with every group of teens and staff members as they tour. This direct involvement with all programs at all levels ensures high quality and consistency. Each year, many of the participants are referred to Musiker by positive word of mouth.

A Musiker Tour is not just a trip, it is an experience. The tour directors and staff members help participants develop an appreciation and understanding of the things the group sees and does. Musiker does more than just show the world to students. The leaders explain what is seen, helping participants to experience it more fully.

For close to forty years, the Musiker family has been committed to the safety, security, and health of all tour and staff members. The quality and consistency of the staff, accommodations, communications, activities, and medical facilities ensure this.

PROGRAM OFFERINGS

For almost forty years, the Musiker family has offered a wide variety of Active Travel and programs in the United States, Canada, and Europe.

As the innovative leader in active student travel, Musiker's programs are action packed with a great variety of day and evening activities, balanced out with sports (play by choice), touring, and time to relax with new friends. Leaders and professional outfitters and instructors help group members unfamiliar with any activity.

Most U.S./Canada trips include quality camping combined with hotels, activity-oriented resorts, and fun college dorms; there are also tours that are all indoors. Students choosing a camping combination tour find camping the Musiker way to be one of the most enjoyable ways to experience North America's unparalleled natural beauty. It is also one of the best ways for participants to get to know themselves and others. Camping responsibilities are a shared experience between tour members and the staff, helping to prevent cliques and create closer, long-lasting friendships. No prior camping experience is necessary.

Cool Combo-Camping Teen Tours These programs range from twenty-one- to forty-two-day tours that feature visits to national parks, recreation areas, and cities, with a combination of campground, hotel, resort, and college dormitory accommodations. These programs, featuring coed, age compatible groups, are open to current seventh through eleventh graders, except where noted.

Current seventh and eighth graders can travel on the *Eastcoaster,* a thirty-day tour through New England, Quebec, Ontario, the Mid-Atlantic, and the Southeast.

Current eighth through eleventh graders can choose from several tours. The *Westcoaster* twenty-one-day tour travels throughout the Southwest Canyon areas and California. The *Action USA* thirty-day tour explores the western United States. The *America Coast-to-Coast* forty-day tour travels across the United States and Canada from east to west by bus, beginning in New York. The *American Adventure* forty-two-day tour travels throughout the western United States, Pacific Northwest, and Canadian Rockies. The *Combocamp America* forty-two-day tour travels throughout the western United States, Pacific Northwest, and Canadian Rockies and features a finale on two Hawaiian Islands—Oahu and Maui.

Fun Hotel and Resort Tours These tours, ranging from twenty-one to thirty-five days, feature visits to national parks, recreation areas, and cities with a combination of hotel and resort accommodations. These programs are open to current eighth through eleventh graders, placed in coed, age compatible groups. The *Cali-Pacific Passport* is a twenty-one-day tour that travels throughout the Pacific Northwest (U.S. and Canada) and California and features a Las Vegas finale. The *Discover America* thirty-five-day tour explores the western United States, Pacific Northwest, and Canadian Rockies. The incredible thirty-day *Alaska Aloha* tour, bookended by the beautiful forty-ninth and fiftieth states, features the Pacific Northwest and northern California. Teens experience a glacier cruise, visit Denali National Park, ride a dune buggy at the Great Sand Dune National Monument, whitewater raft, and, in Hawaii, snorkel, visit Pearl Harbor and the world's best beaches, learn how to surf, and more, over thirteen days on four islands.

Special Golf America Tour This twenty-one-day program, with an optional six-day extension, enables golfers of all abilities to improve their golf game through an intensive five-day golf school, combined with additional clinics, and play at some of the West Coast's most spectacular golf courses. Developed in association with the Collegiate Golf Alliance, this program includes play at resort and private courses, including Pumpkin Ridge, Torrey Pines, Rancho San Marcos, Edgewood, Lost Canyons, and Sandpiper. In addition to golf, this tour features amazing hotels and resorts, fun college dorm stays, and a full range of daytime and evening activities, such as a major-league baseball game, a comedy club, waterskiing, and sports.

Active European Program The thirty-day *Action Europe* tour (for current ninth through twelfth graders) travels through Italy, Switzerland, France, Belgium, the Netherlands, and England. Accommodations are at top-quality, centrally located hotels and resorts. The program features a balance of sightseeing with English-speaking native guides in major cities, culture, and recreation, including summer snow skiing, mountain biking, and hiking.

ENROLLMENT

Musiker Tours attracts students from all over the United States and the world. Past participants have come from forty-one states and twenty-one other countries.

EXTRA OPPORTUNITIES AND ACTIVITIES

Musiker Tours are extremely well organized and carefully planned and are led by experienced, youthful professionals. There is always room, however, for exciting surprises. If a worthwhile activity suddenly becomes available, the group does it, with no extra charges to participants.

FACILITIES

Musiker Tours feature a well-balanced combination of outdoor natural beauty, recreational opportunity, and urban excitement. Tours use the finest hotels, resort activity centers, college dorms, and campgrounds in the safest areas. Accommodations are chosen for location, safety, service, and facilities. For added security, all college dorms and hotels have single lobby entrances. All rooms are located on the same floor or wing, and each student is provided with an individual bed.

Tours that include camp outs use North America's premier national park and recreation areas. The Musiker family personally selects the campgrounds, all of which are privately owned and operated, reservation-only, family-oriented campgrounds. Some are located on waterfronts. All campgrounds have private-stall, hot shower facilities; flush toilets; large recreation areas; and dozens of clean, comfortable redwood picnic tables for healthy dining. Whether camping or staying indoors, three meals are provided daily. During the camping portions of a Musiker Tour, a Camp Chef/Food Manager orchestrates food preparation. On the hotel/resort/dorm portions, participants eat in restaurants with complete choice off the menu and the most generous food allowances in student travel. Staff members and students often have the opportunity to divide into smaller groups for a wider selection of restaurants and menus.

Resort activity centers are featured on all tours. They offer a combination of magnificent natural beauty and a wide variety of recreational activities. All resorts are four-season, year-round, activity-oriented, hotel and/or camping resorts.

STAFF

Superb, caring, and consistent leadership is a Musiker hallmark. Tour directors are not just summer employees, but experienced, youthful professionals who return summer after summer. The Musiker family personally interviews and selects all staff members. Every staff member attends an intensive Safety Leadership Training Orientation. Combined with enthusiasm and an average of seven years of Musiker Tour experience, this training program makes the leadership team the most skilled, experienced, and well liked in student travel.

Each tour has a leadership team. The directors average seven years of on-tour experience, are trained in first aid and CPR, and are educators who meet and work year-round planning the summer tours. The Camp Chef/Food Managers are experienced, returning staff members who coordinate the purchasing, storage, and preparation of food (in accordance with the group's eating habits and any individual health needs), and maintain the group's camping equipment and camping supply vehicle. All staff members are adult college graduates, over the age of 21 (directors are over the age of 25), nonsmokers, and on duty 24-hours a day for the duration of the tour. Many staff members went on Musiker tours as teenagers. The staff-student ratio is approximately 1:7 on camping combination tours and 1:9 on all indoor tours.

MEDICAL CARE

The Musiker family is committed to the safety, security, and health of all tour and staff members. When necessary, tours use an extensive network of medical facilities and doctors in every city, town, resort, and national park area visited.

COSTS

Trips range in cost from $4599 to $8399. The charge includes all food, activities, and accommodations. Airfare to/from the starting/ending point is not included.

APPLICATION TIMETABLE

Admission is on a rolling basis. Early application is recommended. A $350 deposit is required with enrollment and is fully refundable until February 1.

For more information, contact:

Musiker Tours
1326 Old Northern Boulevard
Roslyn, New York 11576
516-621-3939
888-8-SUMMER (toll-free outside New York State)
Fax: 516-625-3438
E-mail: musiker@summerfun.com
World Wide Web: http://www.summerfun.com

PARTICIPANT/FAMILY COMMENTS

"After years of camp, I was ready for something new. This summer was such an incredible experience for me. I made closer friends in a few weeks than I was ever able to make anywhere else. The staff was incredible, so helpful, and considerate."—Berkeley Heights, New Jersey

"This trip has helped me to open my mind to new experiences and people. Thanks, Musiker!"—Baltimore, Maryland

"I met tons of new people. These new friendships and memories will last a lifetime."—Bloomfield Hills, Michigan

"This was by far the most amazing experience of my life. My world grew larger. My expectations of the summer were met and elevated way beyond what can be written on paper. It was absolutely perfect."—Los Angeles, California

NATIONAL STUDENT LEADERSHIP CONFERENCE

LEADERSHIP PROGRAMS FOR OUTSTANDING HIGH SCHOOL STUDENTS

STANFORD UNIVERSITY, PALO ALTO, CALIFORNIA; AMERICAN UNIVERSITY, WASHINGTON, D.C.; UNIVERSITY OF MARYLAND; SAN DIEGO STATE UNIVERSITY; EUROPE; AND CHICAGO

Type of Program: Develop key leadership skills while exploring careers in law, diplomacy, medicine, engineering, business, national security, or the arts

Participants: Coeducational, ages 14–18

Enrollment: Limited to approximately 200 to 250 per program session

Program Dates: Six- and eleven-day programs in the winter, spring, and summer

Head of Program: Dr. Paul M. Lisnek, J.D., Ph.D.; Executive Director/Director of Academics

LOCATION

National Student Leadership Conference (NSLC) programs take place at many of the nation's outstanding educational institutions, including Stanford and San Diego State Universities in California, the University of Maryland in College Park, Maryland, and American University in Washington, D.C., where students visit historical landmarks and monuments in our nation's capital. Inside the Arts is offered in downtown Chicago, steps from the city's main cultural institutions.

BACKGROUND AND PHILOSOPHY

Since 1989, the National Student Leadership Conference has been preparing outstanding high school students for leadership roles in high school, college, and beyond. In these unique and exciting programs, young leaders from across the country and around the world do more than just explore exciting careers—they live them. Student involvement is at the core of the academic environment. Participants learn by doing as they immerse themselves in the area they are studying and develop their abilities to think, analyze, and effectively make decisions. Because the NSLC believes that students can learn and have fun at the same time, these outstanding programs are highlighted with interesting activities, exciting field trips, and enriching social experiences.

PROGRAM OFFERINGS

Programs are offered in the winter/spring (February–April) and summer (June–August) and emphasize leadership in different academic areas. In all programs, students learn communication skills and negotiation strategies through interactive workshops taught by a distinguished faculty. Special guest speaker programs allow students to meet and learn from national and world leaders. Students also gain the added advantage of experiencing college life while living on beautiful university campuses.

The NSLC on Law & Advocacy (eleven days) is offered at Stanford University in Palo Alto, California, and in Washington, D.C. This program provides students with the opportunity to study and experience the American judicial system, from the earliest stages of an investigation through a comprehensive mock trial simulation.

The NSLC on International Diplomacy (eleven days) is offered at American University in Washington, D.C. This program immerses participants in the study of world politics, government, and international relations. In a Model United Nations simulation, students serve as delegates to the United Nations and debate controversial world issues.

The NSLC on Medicine & Health Care (eleven days) is offered at the University of Maryland and San Diego State University. Students explore the fascinating world of medicine and health care through discussions with practicing physicians, their patients, and leading medical researchers; site visits; and various simulations designed to examine some of the most controversial issues facing the medical community.

The NSLC on Mastering Leadership (six days) is offered in Washington, D.C. Students experience the excitement of the nation's capital while studying and living the principles and qualities of the world's greatest leaders. Special workshops and simulations help students unlock their own hidden leadership potential and further develop the leadership skills they already possess.

The NSLC on Entrepreneurship & Business, offered at American University in Washington, D.C., presents students with a firsthand look at the intricacies and challenges of modern business and the opportunity to learn from prominent business leaders and experts.

At the NSLC on U.S. Policy & Politics, students visit the halls of government, discuss current issues with leading political advisers, politicians, and government experts, and return home with a real-world understanding of the roles played by the public, press, and leaders of our nation. A presidential campaign simulation and mock senate are highlights of the program.

The world is a student's classroom at the NSLC Diplomacy Abroad program. NSLC scholars travel to Paris, Brussels, Geneva, and the Hague. Students explore the world of international relations with visits to the European Union, the United Nations, the International Court of Justice, and the International Red Cross.

The NSLC on Engineering immerses students in the ever-changing world of aircraft, robotics, space stations, computer animation, bridges, and biological and chemical engineering. The NSLC partnership with the Junior Engineering Technical Society and the University of Maryland A. James Clark School of Engineering makes this conference an extraordinary opportunity the puts the student on the path to becoming a leading engineer.

At the end of each program, students receive a Certificate of Achievement and an official program transcript verifying their participation in the program. Work completed may be used for high school credit and/or may be submitted to colleges as part of the admissions process. The NSLC is sponsored and endorsed by the American University School of International Service. Students participating in all programs have the option of earning college credit through the American University, which is transferable to most institutions. This credit-bearing curriculum, which links theory to practice, recognizes the increasing importance of global approaches to leadership and to preparing leaders for the complexities and challenges of an increasingly interconnected world.

ENROLLMENT

The NSLC is open to students who have demonstrated academic excellence (B average or better), leadership potential, and a commitment to improving themselves and the world in which they live. Students must either be nominated by their school or make a merit application to NSLC; nominated students are preapproved for admission. Last year, young men and women from throughout the United States and more than forty different countries participated in NSLC programs.

DAILY SCHEDULE

7:30–8:30	Breakfast
9–10:15	Workshop
10:30–12	Lecture/discussion
12–1:30	Lunch
1:30–3:30	Field trip
3:30–5	Leadership exercise
5–6:30	Dinner
7–9	Simulations: Mock trial/United Nations/ leadership in action (depending on program)
9–11	Social activity

EXTRA OPPORTUNITIES AND ACTIVITIES

Stanford students enjoy numerous educational and recreational off-campus trips to the San Francisco Bay Area, which include visits to the courthouse, a crime lab, Pier 39, and Ghiradelli Square. In Washington, D.C., special tours, field trips, and briefings take students "inside" Washington. These have included foreign embassies, Capitol Hill, the Supreme Court, the Pentagon, the Smithsonian Institution, the FBI, the World Health Organization, the National Institutes of Health, and much more.

FACILITIES

Students reside 2–4 to a room in university dormitories or hotel conference facilities. Experienced residential advisers and counselors live in halls with the students and are always available to answer questions and solve problems. Participants have full use of university classrooms, libraries, and recreational facilities. All on-campus meals are taken in university or hotel dining rooms.

STAFF

Teaching faculty members include law professors, deans, judges, Ph.D.s, graduate school professors, and respected academic scholars. Faculty and staff members reside on-site. The faculty/staff–student ratio is approximately 1:15.

MEDICAL CARE

Students have access to 24-hour medical care; each university has a hospital on campus or nearby. Students must have medical insurance to enroll and are responsible for all medical expenses incurred during the program.

COSTS

Tuition is $1950 for eleven-day programs and $1250 for six-day programs. This includes housing, all on-campus meals, course materials, miscellaneous academic expenses, and activities. It also includes off-campus field trips, chartered bus transportation for educational tours, counselor supervision, and 24-hour access to medical treatment. Students are held responsible for damage to rooms or lost room keys.

FINANCIAL AID

Partial academic scholarships and financial assistance are available to qualified students. Scholarships are based on need and academic merit. A scholarship application must be requested from the NSLC office. Scholarships are awarded on a rolling basis, so students should apply early.

TRANSPORTATION

Students are responsible for transportation to and from the programs. Airport pick-up and drop-off can be arranged through the NSLC for a $25 fee (each way).

APPLICATION TIMETABLE

Admission to NSLC is highly selective, and the programs fill quickly, so early application is encouraged. Students nominated by their schools receive an invitation to apply for preapproved admission, based on space availability. A student making a merit application must complete an enrollment application and submit it with a teacher/counselor recommendation form. A tuition deposit is required with all applications. Admission is granted on the bases of academic merit, extracurricular accomplishment, and leadership potential. Merit applications are reviewed immediately by the Admissions Committee, and acceptance is offered on a rolling basis.

For more information, contact:

National Student Leadership Conference
111 West Jackson Boulevard, 7th Floor
Chicago, Illinois 60604
312-322-9999
800-994-NSLC (6752) (toll-free)
Fax: 312-765-0081
E-mail: info@nslcleaders.org
World Wide Web: http://www.nslcleaders.org

PARTICIPANT/FAMILY COMMENTS

"This conference gave me more than an insight into law and leadership. It gave me the opportunity to discover myself."

NEW YORK FILM ACADEMY

FILM AND ACTING CAMP

NEW YORK, NEW YORK

Type of Program: Arts program
Participants: Coeducational, ages 14–17
Enrollment: Varies depending upon location
Program Dates: One-, four-, and six-week filmmaking workshops in July and August; four-week acting for film workshop in July; a one-year filmmaking program began in July 2003.

LOCATION

The New York Film Academy (NYFA) high school filmmaking workshops are held in locales in the United States and Europe. In the United States, students can choose from Universal Studios in Los Angeles, California; Disney–MGM Studios in Florida; Princeton University in New Jersey; Harvard University in Cambridge, Massachusetts; Savannah College of Art and Design in Georgia, and the Dalton School in New York City (Dalton is a nonresidential program). In Europe, students can attend the New York Film Academy workshop at Kings College in London, England; FEMIS (The French National Film School) in Paris, France; and locations in Florence, Italy, and Amsterdam, The Netherlands.

BACKGROUND AND PHILOSOPHY

It is the belief of the New York Film Academy that film is the art form that defines the present. Through the medium of film, individuals, communities, and nations express their most profound visions of humanity to the world. The Academy's high school filmmaking workshop was designed for people 14 to 17 years old who wish to learn the art of film through a hands-on program.

The Academy provides students with the opportunity to learn directing by doing just that—directing. From day one, the students get behind a 16-mm camera. Learning by doing means each student must make a series of short films. This takes them through the entire filmmaking process. Each student writes, produces, directs, and edits his/her own films. In addition, they assist other members of the crew in the roles of director of photography and assistant cameraperson, providing each student with extensive set experience.

PROGRAM OFFERINGS

Filmmaking Workshop In the creation of the curriculum, the Academy worked with students and faculty members from around the world. The best ideas and elements from the leading film degree programs were integrated to provide a thorough grounding in filmmaking; the program is also flexible in meeting the diverse needs of students. It is undergraduate-level training in filmmaking, using the same equipment as the nation's leading undergraduate film programs. Participants have been able to skip prerequisites in college or receive college credit for taking the New York Film Academy Film Workshop.

During the program, each weekday is split between in-class instruction and on-set production. Weekends are reserved for writing, relaxation, and supervised group activities. Students cover the art of visual storytelling in their directing classes, the organization of film and sound material in their editing classes, and how to use the Arriflex 16-S camera and other equipment in their hands-on camera and lighting classes.

The Academy strives to create an environment that promotes personal development and learning over competition. In keeping with this philosophy, the New York Film Academy takes pride in its open-door policy of admission. Students from diverse backgrounds, from all countries, and from all walks of life are welcome. This nurtures a supportive, positive atmosphere conducive to the level of collaboration required to make a great film.

Acting for Film Workshop The New York Film Academy also offers the acting for film workshop in acknowledgment of the importance of the film actor's job and in support of the skills required to do the job brilliantly. Unlike other acting workshops, the program is integrated with the Academy's film school. This has many advantages for the acting student interested in work in front of the camera. Students are able to get invaluable experience in front of the camera by being cast in student productions.

Classes emphasize the theory and practice of the basic elements of the acting craft, using Stanislavsky's method and scene and monologue work as starting points. In conjunction with these classes, students participate in courses aimed specifically at training the actor for the arduous requirements of acting on a film set.

The curriculum of the acting workshop consists of courses in method (Stanislavsky) acting for film and television, film craft, scene and monologue work, voice and singing, yoga for actors, movement and dance, audition techniques, master classes, Shakespeare's method, the Alexander technique, and comedy.

ENROLLMENT

Students ages 14–17 are eligible to apply. Younger students with a demonstrated level of maturity may apply.

DAILY SCHEDULE

Students stay busy with class and film production Monday through Friday from 9 a.m. to 6 p.m. During the evening and on weekends, students take part in planned activities and field trips. These include screenings and trips for cultural enrichment.

FACILITIES

At the New York Film Academy's workshops at Princeton University, Harvard University, and Savannah College of Art and Design, students live in fully furnished college dormitories. Two or three meals a day are served in the dining halls. At Universal Studios, Disney–MGM Studios, the FEMIS film school in Paris, and in Florence and Amsterdam, students live in group residences with NYFA staff members and supervisors. Meal plans are also available for these programs. Students enrolled in the Dalton School program in New York City must have parents or guardians in the New York City area.

STAFF

The faculty is composed of award-winning professional filmmakers who studied film and completed their undergraduate and graduate work at Harvard University, Columbia University, NYU's Tisch School of the Arts, and USC. Their films have screened and won awards internationally at festivals such as Cannes, Berlin, Venice, and Sundance, in addition to winning Academy Awards.

MEDICAL CARE

The Academy's choice of locations is meant to ensure the student's safety, which is of primary concern. Each campus location has a 24-hour public safety service that includes security escorts during the evening and emergency medical help.

COSTS

Program fees range from $1500 to $6900. These fees do not include travel or housing.

TRANSPORTATION

For those arriving by plane, NYFA staff members meet students at their gates, if requested, and transport students between the airport and the program campus at additional cost.

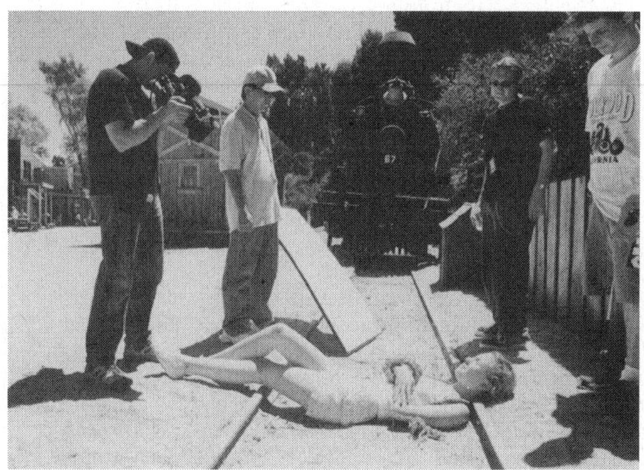

APPLICATION TIMETABLE

The New York Film Academy has a rolling admissions policy. Since popular programs fill up first, students are advised to apply early.

For more information, contact:

New York Film Academy
100 East 17th Street
New York, New York 10003
212-674-4300
Fax: 212-477-1414
E-mail: film@nyfa.com
World Wide Web: http://www.nyfa.com or http://www.nyfa.com/hs

PARTICIPANT/FAMILY COMMENTS

"It was a wonderful experience. If you are interested in film, you should absolutely take this course! I have made videos before, but this was my first time using real film and film equipment. I look at movies in such a different way now, and appreciate what filmmakers have to do. Even though we had long days, we had a lot of fun! This workshop made me even more sure that I want to continue with film, at least in college."—Andre Anglade, 17, Puerto Rico

"The instructors were great! I learned so much from every one of them. They respected our ideas and didn't treat us like children. I've taken video classes before but I wanted to get a taste of real filmmaking. Now I have a good idea of what's in store for me when I study film in college! If you are ready to work hard and put in a lot of effort, this workshop is for you!"—Becky Goldberg, 16, Omaha, Nebraska

NEW YORK UNIVERSITY

TISCH SCHOOL OF THE ARTS

SUMMER HIGH SCHOOL PROGRAMS IN ACTING, MUSICAL THEATRE PERFORMANCE, VIDEO NARRATIVE, ANIMATION, DRAMATIC WRITING, AND MUSICAL THEATRE WRITING IN NEW YORK, DUBLIN, AND PARIS

NEW YORK, NEW YORK

Type of Program: College-level training for high school students
Participants: Rising high school seniors and rising juniors of exceptional maturity
Enrollment: 16–26 per program/course
Program Dates: Four weeks, July and August

LOCATION

Tisch School of the Arts at New York University is located in the heart of New York City, surrounded by the neighborhoods of Greenwich Village and SoHo, centers for the visual arts, contemporary music, poetry, and avant-garde theater. Within walking distance, one will find productions at nearby off-Broadway and experimental theaters such as Joseph Papp's Public Theater and La MaMa Experimental Theatre Club or at the performance spaces of TriBeCa and SoHo. Just a bus ride away are the Museum of Television and Radio, the Metropolitan and Whitney museums and the Museum of Modern Art, the Shakespeare Festival in Central Park, and Lincoln Center. In the summer, the city becomes a festival of street fairs, alfresco concerts, and impromptu street performances.

Students may also choose to participate in one of the study-abroad opportunities and experience the rich cultural offerings of Dublin or Paris.

BACKGROUND AND PHILOSOPHY

The Tisch School is internationally recognized as a premier center for the study of the performing and media arts, with programs in acting, cinema studies, dance, design, dramatic writing, film and television, interactive telecommunications, musical theater, performance studies, and photography. The School has a faculty of more than 300 artist-teachers whose professional careers lend depth and insight to their teaching. Merging the artistic training of a professional school with the academic resources of a major university, the Tisch School provides young artists and scholars with a humanistic education, rigorous training in their discipline, and an invaluable opportunity to pursue their development as an artist.

Within the Tisch School of the Arts, the Department of Drama offers an undergraduate program that leads to the B.F.A. degree. Training the professionally focused actor is the Department of Drama's principal concern. The department offers one of the most prestigious and unique theater training programs in the country, combining rigorous studio classes offered at select professional New York City studios with academic course work at the NYU campus.

The Department of Film and Television offers an undergraduate program leadomg to the B.F.A. degree and provides a comprehensive education that includes the liberal arts as well as professional training. The program is designed to offer a broad range of exposure—from creative experiences in conceiving and producing works in film, television, and radio to theoretical studies that provide a historical frame of reference.

The Musical Theatre Writing Program is a master's degree program designed in a nontraditional format, with a major emphasis on collaboration in the creation of new musical theater and opera. The program's overall aim is to give students the skills to wed form to content in original ways that best fulfill their unique artistic visions. Students participate in ongoing writing workshops that emphasize craft, the art of collaboration, rewriting, developing the student's original voice, storytelling, and content (putting the ideas on stage). Students collaborate on an impressive volume of new material to give them experience with a variety of styles, genres, and approaches—from the book musical to opera to new alternative forms of musical theater.

The summer programs in acting, musical theater performance, musical theater writing, dramatic writing, video narrative, and animation are direct outgrowths of the professional training offered to B.F.A. and M.F.A. students and reflect the same standards of excellence that characterize Tisch's degree programs. These are precollege training programs. Students earn 6 college credits. Each program enrolls 16 to 26 students of top quality.

The Tisch summer programs help high school students learn more about themselves, about their talent, and about the standards of college training programs. Participants gain an enriching and enlightening experience as well as a sense of what a professional training program can offer them and their suitability for such study.

PROGRAM OFFERINGS

All programs are for high school students entering their senior year. (Rising juniors of exceptional maturity may be considered.)

Acting (Strasberg) is an intensive introduction to college-level professional actor training. Training includes 28 hours of class work each week conducted at the Lee Strasberg Theatre Institute. The Strasberg Institute practices the acting technique commonly known as the "Method," one of the most renowned techniques in the world. The Method focuses on the connection between the actor's personal experience and emotions (called the "sense memory") and the experiences and emotions of the character. It is this personal spark that turns a skilled technician into a true artist. Classes include acting technique, scene study, tap, jazz, speech, movement, production rehearsal, acting for the camera, and singing. Students present a special workshop performance at the end of the session.

Musical Theatre Performance is an intense introduction to college-level professional musical theater performance training. The program strives for proficiency in acting, dance, and voice to produce a complete and well-rounded musical theater performer. All classes are aimed at developing the strength, stamina, discipline, and professionalism needed to compete and succeed as a professional. Students attend classes in tap, ballet, jazz, modern dance, acting, vocal technique, and vocal performance.

The **Experimental Theatre Workshop** (ETW) at the Experimental Theatre Wing has gained, since its inception in 1975, an international reputation as a hotbed for the creation of new theater artists and cutting-edge theater art. Based on the work of Jerzy Grotoski and Konstantin Stanislavski, the primary curriculum combines physically based acting, postmodern dance (including Viewpoints), extended vocal technique, and various approaches to improvisation and creating individual theater, with rigorous training in realistic acting, speech, and singing. Seeking playfulness, the goal of all classroom work is spontaneity inside of a disciplined approach in order for each student to discover and shape his or her own artistic vision. The faculty of ETW consists of professionals in contemporary theater, dance, and music. Studio training is composed of physically based acting and improvisation, speech, and vocal performance with a focus on freeing the voice and finding the uniqueness of each voice. Movement classes focus on heightening body awareness, with additional training in contact improvisation, postmodern dance, and hip-hop. There are also classes in self-scripting, giving the student an opportunity to explore his or her own artistic vision while creating original work.

Filmmakers Workshop: Video Narrative is designed to introduce students to the techniques and theory of developing and producing short-story ideas that they shoot on video and edit digitally on computer. As most students enter the program with little or no experience in film or video, early assignments are designed to familiarize them with equipment and to introduce documentary, experimental, and narrative approaches. Working in teams in the digital video medium, students learn directing, shooting, and editing skills as they produce pieces that are 3–5 minutes in length. Special emphasis is placed on visual language; early projects are produced entirely without sound. In addition, screenings of significant works and discussions with industry professionals and Tisch faculty members are held. Daily sessions are divided into lecture, lab, and screening periods.

The **Animation Filmmaker's Workshop** is an exciting and intensive course focusing on the basic techniques of animation. In each class, students explore a sampling of animation methods and view a variety of animated films from all over the world. Techniques include 2-D drawings, stop-motion puppets, pixilation, collage, paint-on-film, and 3-D computers. The course demonstrates how drawing and moving graphics relate, but students do not have to know how to draw in order to take this course. At the end of the course, students compile their animation exercises on DVD, digital video, or video reel.

Dramatic Writing provides an intensive introduction to writing for film and stage, using core classes taught in the bachelor's degree curriculum of the Department of Dramatic Writing. Students learn the fundamentals of dramatic structure in lecture and discussion sessions, develop their own scripts in writing workshop, and present their work in an afternoon colloquium. Theater games, improvisation, and writing exercises are employed to help students develop their writing and presentation skills.

Musical Theatre Writing is for students who are interested in writing and composing for musical theater. Students participate in a team-taught workshop on the art and craft of collaboration. The workshop offers study in theater songwriting and the principles of playwriting (bookwriting) for the musical theater, stressing plot, character, and action. Students work in rotating teams on a series of projects that culminate in a 10-minute musical. Students also attend theatrical performances, watch films and tapes of major productions, and participate in discussions with industry professionals and Tisch faculty members.

International High School Programs in acting and film offer students the opportunity to immerse themselves in the rich cultural and artistic offerings of Dublin and Paris, while participating in the same curriculum as the programs listed for New York.

ENROLLMENT

The person who best benefits from and contributes to the programs is disciplined and prepared to focus on the work at hand and brings an abiding respect for his or her fellow human beings. Prior accomplishment as an artist is not as important as an openness to the training and ideas being presented.

Tisch School of the Arts attempts to judge the suitability of applicants from their academic records, essays, résumés, and recommendations from teachers, counselors, and/or drama directors. Tisch seeks a culturally diverse student body.

FACILITIES

Students in all programs reside together in New York University housing located within walking distance of the classes. NYU housing includes front desk service and 24-hour security. Residential advisers share living space with the students and supervise activities outside of the studio. Evening and weekend time is scheduled to include a variety of group outings as well as class preparation and rehearsal time.

MEDICAL CARE

All students enrolled in the Tisch School of the Arts high school programs are considered to be officially enrolled New York University students and thus have access to NYU Health Services.

COSTS

The comprehensive fee for tuition, room, and board was $6465–$7645 for the 2004 program. This included tuition for 6 college credits, meals Monday through Friday and weekend dinners, accommodations, activities, and a fee for health services. Students in the Filmmakers Workshops were also assessed a lab and equipment insurance fee of approximately $400. Interested students should visit the Web site, listed below, for the current fees.

FINANCIAL AID

Accepted students may apply for limited need-based scholarships. However, students in need of financial aid are urged to speak to their guidance counselors about community sources of funding.

APPLICATION TIMETABLE

Tisch School of the Arts encourages students to apply early. Applications and related materials (personal statements, recommendations of guidance counselors and drama directors, and transcripts) should be received no later than March 7. (This date may be subject to change. Interested students should call for updated information.) Applications received after that date are not reviewed. The application fee is $50.

For more information, contact:

Summer High School Programs
Tisch School of the Arts
New York University
721 Broadway, 12th Floor
New York, New York 10003-6807
212-998-1500
Fax: 212-995-4578
E-mail: tisch.special.info@nyu.edu
World Wide Web:
http://www.tisch.nyu.edu/sphsinfo04

When inquiring for more information, students should specify which program(s) they are interested in and clearly state that they are interested in **high school programs.**

PARTICIPANT/FAMILY COMMENTS

"There was a unique environment of trust and experimentation amongst teenagers of diverse personalities and backgrounds . . . an environment in which each of us could grow as both social and artistic beings and, through our own individual growth and interaction with professionals and the city itself, encourage and shape the growth of the group."

NORTHFIELD MOUNT HERMON SCHOOL

NMH SUMMER SESSION

NORTHFIELD, MASSACHUSETTS

Type of Program: Academic credit and enrichment
Participants: Coeducational, students entering grades 7–13
Enrollment: 350
Program Dates: July 3 to August 7
Head of Program: Thomas P. Pratt, Director

LOCATION

The 300-acre campus is located at the edge of the town of Northfield, overlooking the Connecticut River, in western Massachusetts. Although the setting is rural, field trips take students to nearby New England locales, such as Boston and Hampton Beach.

BACKGROUND AND PHILOSOPHY

In a supportive residential setting, NMH Summer Session provides a strong program to students from a wide variety of backgrounds and cultures.

PROGRAM OFFERINGS

NMH Summer Session offers several distinct programs, both on and off campus.

On-campus:
College Prep—students entering grades 10–13
Junior High Program—students entering grades 7–9

Off-campus:
Chinese Language and Culture—students entering grades 10–13

College Prep This program is for capable, motivated high school students. Course offerings include Expository Writing, Academic Writing, Creative Writing, Literature and Composition, Images of the Self, Moral Philosophy, American History, Algebra I and II, Geometry, Precalculus, Calculus, Chemistry, Biology, and English as a Second Language.

The average class size is 10 students. Academic classes meet in the morning six days a week. Each student chooses one class. Some classes may qualify for academic-year credit if students make prior arrangements with their own schools. In addition, there are afternoon sports and minor courses in art, music, drama, SAT preparation, TOEFL preparation, and various other subjects.

Junior High This program is designed to provide students with a taste of serious academic work in a boarding school setting. Each participant takes two courses that are intended to help prepare him or her for the academic year. Offerings include Writing, Skills in Literature, Communication Through Drama, Prealgebra, Algebra I, Field Biology, Beginning Spanish, and English as a Second Language.

There are two 75-minute morning sessions each day, six days a week, and afternoon sports and minor courses.

Chinese Language and Culture Participants take intensive language and culture instruction at No. 4 Middle School in Beijing, with additional travel in China.

ENROLLMENT

On campus, there are about 350 students. Approximately 40 percent come from abroad, most notably from Europe, Latin America, and East Asia. In addition, the summer population includes minority students and students from all parts of the United States.

The off-campus program in China enrolls 12 students.

DAILY SCHEDULE

The following schedule is for on-campus programs:

7:30–8:15	Breakfast
8:30–11:45	Classes
11:45–1	Lunch
1:30–3	College Prep minors and labs, Junior High sports
3:30–5	College Prep sports, Junior High minors
5:15–6:30	Dinner
6:30–8	Open
8–10	Study
10:30	Junior High students lights-out
11	College Prep students in rooms

EXTRA OPPORTUNITIES AND ACTIVITIES

NMH Summer Session regularly provides trips that range from seeing a Red Sox game to visiting the Boston Aquarium and historic sites to fun excursions to Hampton Beach or amusement parks.

FACILITIES

The school's facilities include phone and computer network connections in student rooms; online access to a library and more than 100,000 volumes; computer and multimedia labs; specialty studios for painting, photography, and dance; and a music building with pianos and practice rooms. Athletic facilities include a gym with an indoor pool and a fitness center and outdoor playing fields and tennis courts.

STAFF

Teachers are drawn from Northfield Mount Hermon's school-year teaching staff and from other schools and colleges. In addition, 30 teaching interns from top colleges and universities assist with the on-campus program.

MEDICAL CARE

A resident physician and nurse are on call 24 hours a day.

COSTS

Tuition, room, and board for on-campus programs are $4600 in 2004. Some courses have special fees. About $400 should be enough for personal spending money.

For the program in China, the 2004 charge is $5000. The fee includes everything except the passport, transportation after returning to the United States, and personal expenses.

For all programs, there is a $1500 nonrefundable deposit at the time of enrollment, which is applied to the tuition charge.

FINANCIAL AID

A financial aid program makes it possible for students from all economic levels to attend. Financial aid is based on demonstrated financial need.

APPLICATION TIMETABLE

Inquiries are welcome anytime. Although there is no application deadline (unless a student is applying for financial aid), students are encouraged to apply early, as some courses fill quickly. Financial aid applications should be submitted by March 15. Admission decisions are made as files are completed.

FOR MORE INFORMATION, CONTACT:

Northfield Mount Hermon Summer Session
206 Main Street
Northfield, Massachusetts 01360-1089
413-498-3290
Fax: 413-498-3112
E-mail: summer_school@nmhschool.org
World Wide Web: http://www.nmhschool.org

NORTHWESTERN UNIVERSITY

CENTER *for* TALENT DEVELOPMENT

CENTER FOR TALENT DEVELOPMENT

EVANSTON, ILLINOIS

Type of Program: Residential academic summer program for academically talented youth
Participants: Coeducational, grades pre-K–12
Enrollment: 1,000 per session
Head of Program: Joe Salvatore, Summer Program Coordinator

LOCATION

Northwestern University (NU) is located in Evanston, Illinois, approximately 12 miles north of downtown Chicago. On the shores of Lake Michigan, Northwestern University's 240-acre campus includes beaches, tennis courts, a lagoon, and a sports and aquatics center. The parklike campus also offers a dramatic view of the Chicago skyline, hinting at the city's famous architecture, vibrant cultural life, and bustling metropolitan atmosphere. However, Northwestern is more than another pretty campus. Established in 1851, it is considered one of the premier universities in the United States, well known for its top-notch academic programs, world-class faculty members, and superbly qualified student body.

The Center for Talent Development (CTD) also offers two other sites. They are the Civic Leadership Institute, on NU's Chicago campus, and Equinox, at Case Western Reserve University (CWRU), as a joint program of Northwestern University's Center for Talent Development and Case Western Reserve University. CWRU, located in Cleveland, Ohio, is one of the nation's leading independent research universities. It occupies 550 acres in University Circle, a park-like concentration of approximately fifty cultural, medical, educational, religious, and social service institutions located at the eastern edge of the city center. University Circle attracts visitors from throughout the region to its concerts, theater performances, athletic events, art shows, public lectures, exhibits, and restaurants. Housing, shopping, and recreational facilities are all located in the area. Equinox students also have the opportunity to study at Northwestern University's Chicago campus in the Civic Leadership Institute. Northwestern's Chicago campus was opened in 1927 to centralize its professional schools. Today the campus provides its students with immediate access to Chicago's lakefront, cultural institutions, and more.

BACKGROUND AND PHILOSOPHY

Celebrating twenty years of summer programming, the Center has continued to expand its scope to provide high-quality academic enrichment and acceleration for gifted precollegiate students. The success of these CTD programs stems from the Center's unique commitment to research on the psychology, sociology, and education of gifted and talented learners; the staff's experience of working with academically able students on a year-round basis; and the program's ability to attract innovative master teachers.

While academics come first, CTD summer programs also provide a rich, supervised setting for the social interactions and friendships so important to a student's developing self-concept. An added distinction of the Center is its accreditation by the North Central Association of Colleges and Schools. It is the only center for gifted education in the country to receive this distinction.

CTD's high academic standards and diverse student body ensure that students learn not only from their teachers but also from one another. While students share a passion for learning and discovering and the intellectual capacity for advanced academic work, they also possess unique backgrounds and experiences. In 2003, CTD students came to Northwestern from urban, suburban, and rural settings in forty-one states and thirteen other countries. About one third of the students return for a second year, and about 70 percent choose to reside on campus for their three-week class.

DAILY SCHEDULE

7:30–8:15	Breakfast
8:30–12	Class
12–1	Lunch
1–2:30	Class
3–5	Afternoon activities
5–7	Dinner/relax
7–9	Evening activity or study session
9–10	Free time
10	Room check
11	Lights out

PROGRAM OFFERINGS

The Center for Talent Development offers four academic programs: Leapfrog (pre-K–grade 3), Apogee (grades 4–6), Spectrum (grades 7–9), and Equinox (grades 10–12). Leapfrog is a commuter-only, one-week program that is held for three sessions.

Apogee, Spectrum, and Equinox students at CTD enroll in one class for the three-week program. CTD offers more than ninety classes in the sciences, literature, humanities, writing, history, and language. Classes meet for 5 to 6 hours a day, depending on the program, and are divided into morning and afternoon components. Classes are not held on weekends, but some study sessions for residential students are scheduled on Saturdays and Sundays. In order to maximize personal attention to the learner, CTD

summer courses are limited to 18 students per class, and each class has both a master teacher and a teaching assistant.

Participants have opportunities to interact with intellectual peers and develop friendships, engage in recreational activities, and enjoy local events and resources, ranging from swimming in Lake Michigan to Chicago Symphony Orchestra concerts under the stars.

FACILITIES

Students have access to many of Northwestern's facilities, including recreational sites, the University Library, and the Norris University Center. CTD students have access to computer facilities owned by both the CTD and the University, but hours are somewhat limited. In 2001, 24 percent of enrolled students reported that they brought their own computers to the campus. Students who own portable computers, especially those enrolled in writing-intensive classes, may find it convenient to have their computers with them while attending the CTD. Students should note that the CTD, Northwestern University, and Case Western Reserve University cannot provide technical support for personal computers.

Residential students live in dormitories under the supervision of specially trained residential staff members. Male and female students may share a floor but have separate bathrooms. Students eat with residential staff members and other members of the University community in a dormitory dining room and, on weekends, enjoy a broad range of activities, such as off- and on-campus theater, concerts, movies, sports events, dances, and talent shows.

STAFF

Teaching staff members for the CTD summer programs are drawn from premier schools in the Chicago and Cleveland areas. Teachers are chosen for their mastery of subject matter, enthusiasm, ability to individualize their teaching, and skill in providing interesting, thought-provoking, and varied classroom experiences. Each class has a teaching assistant selected from students at university campuses across the United States. The residential staff is drawn from undergraduate campuses from around the country and consists of mature, responsible, well-trained undergraduates who exhibit both academic achievement and a love of learning.

MEDICAL CARE

The summer program fee covers basic health services at each of the campuses' fully staffed and equipped health centers. Students who require more extensive assistance are taken to nearby hospitals. The residential fee covers clinic services; it does not provide medical insurance coverage. All summer program participants must be covered by a major medical insurance policy.

COSTS

Tuition for residents in 2004 was $2300 and for commuters was $1200. Leapfrog tuition is $200. A nonrefundable $50 application fee is required. Financial aid is available.

APPLICATION TIMETABLE

Summer brochures are available in January. Students should call or e-mail the Center to request a brochure. Space is limited, and applicants are encouraged to apply early. Applications must be received by May 1 2004.

For more information, contact:

Center for Talent Development
617 Dartmouth Place
Evanston, Illinois 60208
847-491-3782
E-mail: ctd@northwestern.edu
World Wide Web: http://www.ctd.northwestern.edu

NORTHWESTERN UNIVERSITY

COLLEGE PREPARATION PROGRAM

EVANSTON, ILLINOIS

Type of Program: College preparation
Participants: Coeducational; residential and commuter high school students between their junior and senior years
Enrollment: Approximately 80
Program Dates: June 19 to July 30 (six-week courses), June 19 to August 13 (eight-week and intensive course sequences)
Head of Program: Stephanie Teterycz, Associate Director of Summer Session

LOCATION

Northwestern University is located along the shores of Lake Michigan, 12 miles from the heart of Chicago. The 240-acre Evanston campus boasts a private beach, lakefront jogging paths, sailing facilities, and playing fields. The quiet atmosphere of the surrounding neighborhood is truly conducive to study, while the proximity to the city of Chicago offers students access to cultural events, museums, and world-famous architecture.

BACKGROUND AND PHILOSOPHY

The College Preparation Program (CPP) offers high school students entering their senior year a truly unique college experience. The CPP combines Northwestern courses and a rigorous college-level writing tutorial with many opportunities for summertime fun. Combined, these elements provide students with the knowledge and experience they need for a successful college career. The program is founded on the premise that college life is not simply an academic experience but a social and cultural one as well. CPP participants are encouraged to take full advantage of Northwestern University's diverse community of students by building mature social relationships as they explore new intellectual avenues. Although newfound freedoms can be liberating, they can also be distracting and even frightening. This is why the College Preparation Program employs college-age resident advisers who help students learn to manage time, focus energies, and balance academic and social commitments.

PROGRAM OFFERINGS

College Preparation Program students may enroll in almost any of the freshman- and sophomore-level courses that Northwestern offers during the summer. Virtually every academic discipline is represented, from anthropology and French to physics and biology. Students may register for up to three courses with many CPP participants choosing to take one of the popular three-course foreign language or science sequences. Summer Session staff members are always available for consultation during course selection.

In addition to those courses, an essential part of the College Prep experience is the mandatory College Writing Tutorial. This is a noncredit course taught by a high school English teacher and consists of weekly lectures, group activities, and instructor-led discussions about advanced writing techniques. Careful reading, textual analysis, and skills building are emphasized in an atmosphere of open interaction as students are introduced to strategies for building a focused argument, supporting a thesis, and constructing an annotated bibliography. The Tutorial and related, individual sessions that are staffed by teaching assistants meet each week during the first six weeks of the program.

College is, however, far more than a purely academic enterprise. It is with this fact in mind that the College Preparation Program offers access to numerous social and cultural activities in Evanston and Chicago. Every summer, students visit some of Chicago's most famous cultural attractions, including the Art Institute and the Museum of Science and Industry. The Program also organizes outings to ball games at Wrigley Field and live performances at a variety of venues. Students may participate in any activities that interest them, with the understanding that their studies take precedence.

Campus life at Northwestern is rich and diverse. There are plays on campus, concerts, sporting events, and picnics. The College Prep residence hall is a true home away from home, where students share ideas, study, chat, relax, play games, and enjoy movie nights.

ENROLLMENT

Students who are between their junior and senior years in high school and who have a minimum 3.0 GPA (on a 4.0 scale) are eligible to apply. Admission is competitive and all admitted students are academically gifted, demonstrating exceptional talents in a variety of subjects. Approximately 65 students enroll as residents in the program, while another 15 enroll as commuters. Students who live in Evanston or the surrounding city and suburbs, or those who plan to live with relatives in the area during the summer, may apply as CPP Commuting Scholars. Both residential and commuting students enjoy the same program benefits and everyone participates in the Writing Tutorial. The College Preparation Program embraces ethnic and cultural diversity, and encourages students of all backgrounds to apply.

DAILY SCHEDULE

A College Prep student's daily schedule is very much like that of any other college student. A typical morning might consist of breakfast with a roommate

and a 9 a.m. class. After lunch, students might spend their time researching a paper in the library, working in the lab, or attending the Writing Tutorial. A CPP participant might finish off the day with a jog along the lakefront, dinner and a movie with friends, or an evening of quiet study.

FACILITIES

Residential College Prep students share double rooms in a University residence hall and take their meals in a nearby dining hall. Students have access to Northwestern's sports and aquatics center, which includes an Olympic-size swimming pool; tennis, basketball, racquetball, and squash courts; an exercise room; and a large gym. There are also several other sports facilities on campus, including a sailing center. In the Norris Student Center, students can enjoy a crafts studio, a game room, a browsing library, a snack bar, an ice cream parlor, shops, and an art gallery. Students also have access to any of the state-of-the-art labs, studios, and theaters that are part of their course work.

MEDICAL CARE

Residential staff members have first aid and CPR training, and a student health service is located on campus. Evanston Hospital is located approximately 1 mile from campus.

RELIGIOUS LIFE

The College Prep Program is secular and nonaffiliated. There are, however, a number of places of worship located on or near campus.

COSTS

Students are encouraged to take 2 six- or eight-week courses or one intensive sequence. The projected cost per course is $2400. The cost for the six-week program in 2004 was $4265, which included room, board, the program fee, and tuition for one course. The cost for the intensive sequence was $9270, which included room, board, the program fee, and tuition for three courses. Use of University health services and athletic facilities is included in the program fee. Students are responsible for paying for their own books and transportation.

FINANCIAL AID

A limited amount of financial aid is available. Those interested in applying for financial aid should visit the Northwestern University College Preparation Program Web site listed below.

TRANSPORTATION

The city of Evanston is a suburb of Chicago and, as such, is easily accessible. Travel time to the campus is about 30 minutes from O'Hare International Airport and about 1 hour from Midway Airport. Shuttle buses run from both airports to Northwestern on the first day of the program. All students are responsible for arranging their own transportation home at the end of the program.

APPLICATION TIMETABLE

The early and international application deadline is March 11, 2005. The regular application deadline is April 15, 2005. Along with the application, students must submit one essay, an official high school transcript, a letter of recommendation from a teacher or counselor, and an application fee. Students are advised to apply as early as possible to ensure that all of their materials are received by the deadline.

FOR MORE INFORMATION, CONTACT:

Stephanie Teterycz
Associate Director of the Summer Session
Northwestern University
405 Church Street
Evanston, Illinois 60201-4558
847-491-4358
Fax: 847-491-3660
E-mail: cpp@northwestern.edu
World Wide Web: http://www.northwestern.edu/collegeprep/

NORTHWESTERN UNIVERSITY

NATIONAL HIGH SCHOOL INSTITUTE

EVANSTON, ILLINOIS

Type of Program: Summer enrichment and college preparation
Participants: Coeducational, high school students
Enrollment: Approximately 700 students enrolled in seven programs
Program Dates: Approximately June 26 to July 31, 2005 for theater arts, digital media, journalism, and music. Approximately July 5 to August 7, 2005 for debate and July 5 to July 26, 2005 for forensics.
Director: Barbara Reeder, Administrative Director

LOCATION

Northwestern University is located 12 miles north of downtown Chicago on Lake Michigan.

BACKGROUND AND PHILOSOPHY

Since 1931, the National High School Institute (NHSI) has brought outstanding students to Northwestern University's Evanston campus for an intense educational experience in one of several programs. The oldest and largest university-based program of its kind, the NHSI allows students to experience aspects of college life while submerged in study. Students are affectionately known as "cherubs," a name given to them in the 1930s by Northwestern Dean Ralph Dennis whose goal, "to bring together gifted young people and superior teachers in an atmosphere of affection, knowledge, and trust," is still upheld today.

PROGRAM OFFERINGS

Each of the six divisions has its own curricular goals and objectives, but all are united in their educational philosophy to challenge and develop the potential of every student. Programs are enrichment-based and students are neither graded nor do they receive high school or college credit. An intense schedule of academics is accented with many of the opportunities that Evanston and Chicago have to offer.

Coon-Hardy Debate Program for High School Students Modeled after the national championship Northwestern Debate Society, this program investigates how to apply argumentation, communication, and research skills to the study of the next year's national debate proposition. The curriculum is designed to teach principles that can be abstracted to many debating situations well beyond the study of this year's topic. Coon-Hardy is based on three complementary principles: interactive learning, teamwork, and curricular integration. An amazing faculty, led by Northwestern Professor and Director of Debate Scott Deatherage, completes an aggressive learning experience. The program runs for four weeks and is open to current high school freshman, sophomores, and juniors with debate experience.

Forensics This program offers complete curricula in four areas of high school speech: limited preparation events, oral interpretation of literature, original oratory, and Lincoln-Douglas debate. Programs are available in two- and three-week sessions and are open to current high school freshman, sophomores, and juniors.

Journalism This program is designed to sharpen journalistic skills of writers and editors for print or broadcast. In intensive lab sessions, students learn how to write news, feature, and editorial stories and television news; edit stories others have written; write headlines; design newspaper pages; and report the news. College professors and practitioners evaluate writing assignments in one-on-one sessions. Workshops expose students to a variety of subjects such as freelance writing, sports reporting, and journalistic ethics. The program runs for five weeks and is open to current high school juniors with a special interest in journalism.

Music As a Music Division participant, students may choose from among eight programs: composition, jazz studies, music education, piano, strings, voice, winds/ percussion, and guitar. All include private practice sessions and weekly seminars. The programs runs for five weeks (guitar for two weeks) and are open to current eighth graders and high school freshmen, sophomores, and juniors.

Digital Media Arts: Students are introduced to the art and science of television, digital imagery, and writing through courses in camera, digital design, cinema history, and critical theory. The Media Arts Division simulates this process through two intensive concentrations: production and writing. The program runs for five weeks and is open to current high school juniors.

Writing: Daily writing labs and intensive instruction in story structure, dialog, and visual storytelling are supplemented by a wide range of electives that provide students with thorough knowledge and practice in creating scripts.

Production: College-level instruction gives students the skills necessary to produce original projects in documentary video, narrative video, animated short, and interactive video (Web). NHSI students have access to the same new equipment as the Northwestern undergraduates.

Theater Arts By experimenting with the medium and its multitude of crafts and disciplines, students discover that theater is a collaborative art and an emotionally, physically, and intellectually rigorous one. Two programs are offered within this division. The programs run for five weeks and are open to current high school juniors. The estimated program size is 150 general theater students and 10 design and technical students.

General Theater Curriculum: Designed for students with a serious interest in theater, this program immerses students in the theater experience by delving into the essential concern of theater process—the human condition. The student performs in one of ten production companies and studies with professional directors, choreographers, acting coaches, and designers. Core classes include acting, voice and movement, aesthetics of theater, text analysis, and production crew. Electives, guest lectures, and field trips to relevant productions supplement core classes.

Design/Technical Concentration: In addition to the core classes, students take special courses in the design process, enroll in a stage management workshop, and concentrate a portion of their time in the study of theater design and production.

Musical Theater: This program builds upon the instruction in the Theater Arts program, furthering the study in acting and voice and movement, while adding relevant course work in musical theater scene study, dance, and voice master classes. Students must be accepted to and complete the full Theater Arts Division curriculum before proceeding to the musical theater extension. The program runs two weeks following theater arts and is open to high school juniors only. The estimated program size is fewer than 40 students.

ENROLLMENT

Criteria for acceptance into the programs include grades, letters of recommendation, PSAT (or SAT) scores, personal essays, and experience in the student's chosen concentration.

COSTS

The 2004 program costs were as follows: Coon-Hardy debate, $3600; forensics, $1500; musical theater (includes theater), $6200; journalism, music, digital/media arts, and theater arts, $3650; and classical guitar, $1750. All programs are residential. In addition to tuition, the fees include housing, meals, and tickets to all events and field trips. Additional costs are at the discretion of the student.

FINANCIAL AID

Each year, a large number of students receive scholarships and financial assistance. Awards are given based on academic achievement and financial need. Financial aid requests are included with the division applications.

APPLICATION TIMETABLE

Applications are usually due by mid-April; however, deadlines vary slightly, so students should verify dates with the current brochures. An early deadline date is usually available a few weeks prior to the regular deadline, usually in March. This deadline serves as a planning opportunity for families and students and does not increase admission chances. There is a $35 application fee.

For more information, contact:

Nick Kanel
National High School Institute
617 Noyes Street
Evanston, Illinois 60208
800-662-NHSI (toll-free)
Fax: 847-467-1057
E-mail: nhsi@nwu.edu
World Wide Web: http://www.nwu.edu/nhsi

OAK CREEK RANCH SCHOOL

SUMMER SESSIONS

SEDONA, ARIZONA

Type of Program: Traditional summer school and intensive ESL (English as a second language) for international students
Participants: Coeducational, grades 6–12
Enrollment: 50 per session
Program Dates: Contact the Admissions Office
Head of Program: Nadine O'Brien, Principal

LOCATION

The 20-acre campus of the Oak Creek Ranch School adjoins the Coconino National Forest in the central mountains, 100 miles north of Phoenix, 45 miles from Flagstaff, and 15 miles from the beautiful Red Rock Country of Sedona. Both the campus and the national forest are used by summer campers for horseback riding and camping.

BACKGROUND AND PHILOSOPHY

Oak Creek Ranch School, founded in 1972 by David Wick, the School's director, provides a structured, safe environment for boys and girls from around the world. The program develops self-discipline, intellectual growth, strong character, loyalty, responsibility, and consideration for others. Oak Creek's philosophy of education may be called traditional, with a great deal of experiential, hands-on, high-quality classroom and laboratory learning opportunities. Self-esteem is developed through improved motivation, achievement of exemplary results, and recognition of work well done.

PROGRAM OFFERINGS

A fully accredited academic program is available.

For students in grades 6–8, morning classes include choices of language arts (writing, spelling, vocabulary, and reading), math, geography, computer science, and study skills.

For students in grades 9–12, 1 semester credit for each of two subjects may be earned during a four-week session. Subjects offered are basic English skills, English literature and composition, creative writing, basic math, algebra I, algebra II, geometry, general science, earth science, geology, world history, American studies, government, and reading. For students taking 2 four-week sessions, 2 full credits may be granted for any combination of the above subjects. Students may take (with principal's approval) a supervised independent-study course each four-week session for additional credits.

Especially popular is Oak Creek's computer program. The computing technology at the School is used in two ways: in the instruction of the tools of computing and through the integration of computers in all curriculum areas. The School's intention is to provide students with solid grounding in the skills they will need academically and vocationally. The School accomplishes this through instruction in productivity software, presentation software, desktop publishing, Web site design, and management. Strong emphasis is also placed on learning in a networked environment, including the use of LANs, e-mail, and information retrieval on the Internet as well as content creation for the Internet. The computer labs are completely refurbished every three years so that the students use the most modern technology available, including scanners, Web cams, digital cameras, a variety of display systems, and laser and color printers.

During the summer, the School offers special courses designed to teach traditional curricula in completely nontraditional ways. Among the courses offered in the past are the ones below. This summer's special course offerings can be found on the School's Web site (listed below) or by calling the School.

Wilderness literature This course combines the study of great outdoor authors with hiking through the places the authors wrote about and writing about the experience. The students hike through some of the most spectacular areas in the Southwest, including the Grand Canyon and Yosemite National Park.

Geometry through geology This fascinating course allows students to study the geology of Arizona and at the same time study mathematics. Geometric principles are applied and problem-solving strategies are developed to address practical interpretations of the environment.

Math in building Students of all ability levels learn new math skills while they apply those skills to building objects. From the most elementary Lego and Lincoln Log constructions to the most sophisticated building and road construction operations, the students learn to solve problems and apply their knowledge as they acquire the math skills they need.

English through drama This course allows students to study English at all levels through the study of dramatic productions (writing, staging, etc.). Students read and attend dramatic productions. The class culminates in the creation of the students' own digital video production.

Reading through heroes Students of all ability levels enjoy improving their skills while reading about heroes of their own choice. Students choose heroes that range from the mythical to the real. This is a very enjoyable way to improve basic through advanced reading skills.

ENROLLMENT

During each four-week session, approximately 30–50 students may be accommodated, including international students enrolled in the ESL program. The classes are small, with a maximum student-teacher ratio of 8:1, allowing an individualized work environment to meet the specific needs of a wide range of student capabilities.

Oak Creek Ranch School is not structured to work with students who have emotional or behavioral problems.

A student handbook that sets forth rules and regulations that must be observed to make the Oak Creek Ranch School experience enjoyable and beneficial for all is available.

EXTRA OPPORTUNITIES AND ACTIVITIES

Recreational activities include fishing, water polo, swimming, golf, camping, trips to Phoenix water parks, mountain biking, volleyball, horseback riding, overnight horsepack trips, shopping trips, movies on campus or in town, rock climbing, paintball games, trips to the Grand Canyon, Sedona Slide Rock, Jerome, Meteor Crater, and more.

Field trips and excursions throughout Arizona, including the Grand Canyon, are also offered. The Fourth of July Prescott Rodeo is a favorite for students to attend.

DAILY SCHEDULE

Classes rotate daily.

7:00–7:50	Breakfast
8:00–11:00	Class A
11:00–11:15	Break
11:15–12:15	Class B
12:15–1:00	Lunch
1:00–3:00	Class B
3:00–5:00	Activities
5:00–6:00	Dinner
6:30–9:30	Study/activities

FACILITIES

All of the facilities of Oak Creek Ranch School are used for the summer program. The main building houses eight classrooms that are modern, well lighted, temperature-controlled, and well equipped with visual aids and media equipment. Science and crafts buildings are spaced around the campus. Other facilities include a library, three computer labs, a photography studio, an art studio, a student recreation center, residence halls, the health center, the dining room, a swimming pool, a playing field, a volleyball court, and staff living quarters.

STAFF

The teaching and supervisory staff comprises members of the Oak Creek Ranch School's regular school-year faculty and staff. Each dormitory is supervised by a caring and supportive dorm adviser.

MEDICAL CARE

A registered nurse is on campus five days each week at the Wellness Center. The Verde Valley Medical Center is in nearby Cottonwood, and emergency care is only minutes from the School any time of the day or night. A student health record, emergency medical release, medical history, immunization record, physical examination, and medical insurance must be completed before the first day of the program.

RELIGIOUS LIFE

Oak Creek Ranch School is nonsectarian, and students are invited to attend the church of their choice when they wish.

COSTS

The 2003 tuition was $3950 for each four-week session. This fee included room, board, and all classes.

TRANSPORTATION

Students should arrive at the School by 3 p.m. on the opening day of each session. Students can be met at Phoenix Sky Harbor Airport by staff members and driven to the campus. They are returned to Phoenix by staff members at the close of each session.

APPLICATION TIMETABLE

Inquiries are welcome all year. The most current brochure is mailed upon request, and students are accepted from April through the summer, as space allows. The completed application form should be returned with the health report to ensure a reservation. A $500 deposit is required for allowances, books, supplies, transportation, and other incidentals. A video about the program is available upon request.

For more information, contact:

David Wick Jr., Headmaster
Oak Creek Ranch School
P.O. Box 4329
West Sedona, Arizona 86340
928-634-5571
Fax: 928-634-4915
E-mail: admissions@ocrs.com
World Wide Web: http://www.ocrs.com

OAK RIDGE MILITARY ACADEMY

ACADEMIC SUMMER SCHOOL/LEADERSHIP ADVENTURE CAMP

OAK RIDGE, NORTH CAROLINA

Type of Program: Two separate summer programs: Academic Summer School consists of academic courses for credit, acceleration, enhancement, and enrichment; Leadership Adventure Camp involves leadership training, athletics, and recreational activities. Both programs are presented in a residential and day format.
Participants: Coeducational; students who are in grades 6–12
Enrollment: 350
Program Dates: Session 1, June; Session 2, July
Head of Program: Academic Dean/Commandant of Cadets

LOCATION

Oak Ridge is a national and state historic district located in the picturesque rural area of the Piedmont Plateau. The 101-acre campus is 15 miles from Greensboro, High Point, and Winston-Salem. The Academy is 6 miles north of the Piedmont Triad International Airport and lies at the crossroads of North Carolina Routes 68 and 150, which lead to Interstates 40 and 85.

BACKGROUND AND PHILOSOPHY

Oak Ridge Military Academy (ORMA) was founded in 1852 by community leaders dedicated to offering a superior college-preparatory education to students in the Piedmont area, throughout North Carolina, and in nearby southern states. Oak Ridge Military Academy built an early reputation for excellence and, in 1899, was the first school in North Carolina accredited by the Southern Association of Colleges and Schools (SACS).

The Leadership Adventure Camp was established in 1980 to teach leadership skills to young men and women through classroom instruction and practical application. Organizational skills, communication skills, arbitration, mediation, and conflict resolution are part of the instructional program. Teamwork and practical application of classroom knowledge develop self-esteem as students learn to be responsible for themselves and others. In 1991, Oak Ridge Military Academy was designated the official military school of North Carolina by the state's General Assembly.

PROGRAM OFFERINGS

The Oak Ridge Summer program is designed to serve capable students that include the gifted and talented and students whose academic potential has not yet been realized. The formal, structured environment allows students to develop the habits of success required for the classroom and life. All courses are taught by certified teachers. Academic records, transcripts, and standardized test scores are required for all students. Students who are identified with learning differences are required to submit a complete copy of their most recent evaluation.

Academic Summer School The Academic Summer School at ORMA is a program of total immersion into one field of study. Six hours of classroom time and 2 evening hours of supervised study hall are required. Five days per week and on weekends, students participate in leadership training activities such as rappelling, confidence course, and athletics.

Courses are offered in algebra I and II and geometry; English I, II, III, and IV; U.S. history; world history; American government; and chemistry. English as a second language is offered to international students. For middle school students, language arts, math, science, and study skills are offered as remedial subjects.

All Academic Summer School courses are taught by distinguished faculty members; all are certified in their fields of study. Dr. David Price, Academic Dean of Oak Ridge Military Academy, serves as the Director of the Academic Summer School.

Leadership Adventure Camp The mission of the Leadership Adventure Camp is to afford all participants an opportunity to develop their leadership skills while enjoying their summer vacation. This program combines leadership training, athletic/recreational activities, and adventure training. All activities and events are supervised and taught by subject-matter experts. Individual skills are developed, and teamwork is promoted in a structured environment, thus providing the right atmosphere of competitiveness, sportsmanship, and responsibility; in this way, a young man or woman's leadership and life skills can be developed. Leadership and life skills are taught through a system of rotating leadership positions in which close supervision and mentorship is exercised by Oak Ridge Military Academy TAC Officers.

Leadership Training Leadership training is taught through classroom instruction and a system of rotating leadership positions. Each student has an opportunity to learn leadership principles and to practice leadership techniques in a formal, supervised environment. The uniform structure of the program teaches the value of organization as well as setting and accomplishing goals. Organizational skills, communication skills, arbitration, mediation, and conflict resolution are part of the instructional program. Teamwork and practical application of classroom knowledge develop self-esteem as students learn to be responsible not only for themselves, but also for others. Confidence, self-esteem, respect, teamwork, and responsibility are the hallmarks of effective leadership. All students are required as part of the program to participate in Leadership Training.

Athletic Competition The well-organized competitive athletic program includes many traditional team sports as well as swimming, marksmanship, and rappelling. These activities are supervised by knowledgeable coaches who focus on developing team play, good sportsmanship, and a competitive attitude.

Recreational Activities Although the Leadership Adventure Camp is designed to provide a worthwhile growth experience, it is never forgotten that it is summer vacation. Having a good time is a key element of every activity. Students take chaperoned field trips that are carefully planned and closely supervised to ensure the safety of every student. Students participate in other activities that include paintball, movies, cookouts, and field days.

FACILITIES

Classes are conducted in a new, state-of-the-art classroom building. The library is equipped with IBM computer workstations. The system is networked to the computer lab (which has additional workstations) and offers a CD-ROM stack for access to reference materials. The library also contains the school's computer laboratory, which is used to enhance reading, math, and science skills. The system was developed by Computer Curriculum Corporation and has become a valuable asset in the educational development of Oak Ridge students.

Of the four dormitories—Holt Hall, Caesar Cone Hall, Armfield Hall, and Whitaker Hall—three are for males and one is for females. Residential students live two to a large room. Rooms are inspected daily and must meet standardized requirements. Each dorm has an apartment in which a staff or faculty member resides.

Students eat in White Dining Hall, which is adjacent to the student lounge and store. The dining facility is run by an independent professional food service.

The Bonner Field House is the primary athletic facility. King Gymnasium houses the indoor swimming pool and indoor marksmanship range.

STAFF

Full-time faculty members teach during the Academic Summer School. In addition, full-time staff members are employed as counselors and activity supervisors. Cadets who attend the Academy during the school year are offered the opportunity to act as junior leaders and counselors during the camp.

MEDICAL CARE

The modern infirmary is staffed by qualified medical personnel, who are in attendance at all activities, including field trips. Full medical services are available at hospitals in Greensboro and Winston-Salem. All faculty members receive instruction in CPR and first aid.

COSTS

Costs associated with the Academic Summer School are $2300 for boarding participants. The Leadership Adventure Camp costs $2300 for boarding cadets. The tuition fees for both camps cover all costs, including deposits, uniforms, books, laundry service, meals, and haircuts for boys. Three daily meals are provided for boarding participants.

APPLICATION TIMETABLE

Acceptance is dependent on the applicant's qualifications and space availability. Following receipt of the registration form and a $100 nonrefundable deposit, other enrollment documents are mailed to parents for completion.

Oak Ridge Military Academy admits students of any race, color, creed, and national and ethnic origin to all the rights, privileges, programs, and activities generally accorded or made available to cadets at the Academy. The Academy does not discriminate in the administration of its educational policies, admission policies, or any other administered programs.

FOR MORE INFORMATION, CONTACT:

Admissions Office
Oak Ridge Military Academy
P.O. Box 498
Oak Ridge, North Carolina 27310
Telephone: 336-643-4131 Ext. 148
Fax: 336-643-1797
E-mail: rwilson@oakridgemilitary.com
World Wide Web: http://www.oakridgemilitary.com

OJAI VALLEY SCHOOL

SUMMER PROGRAMS

OJAI, CALIFORNIA

Type of Program: Academic enrichment, English as a second language (ESL), activities, and camping
Participants: Coeducational, ages 8–18
Enrollment: 350 on two campuses
Program Dates: Two-, four-, and six-week sessions from mid-June to July; four-week ESL session for international students in August
Heads of Program: Eleanora Burright, Director of Summer Programs, Lower School; David Edwards, Director of Summer Programs, Upper School

LOCATION

The Ojai Valley School Summer Programs use the facilities on two campuses of the Ojai Valley School (OVS) in Ojai, California. The beautiful rural resort town of Ojai is bordered by 600,000 acres of the Los Padres National Forest, which campers use for backpacking, hiking, biking, and horseback riding. The Pacific Ocean, which is located 15 minutes west of Ojai, provides ideal opportunities for swimming, surfing, and camping. The town of Ojai (population 8,600) is located 90 minutes north of Los Angeles, 40 minutes southeast of Santa Barbara, and 15 miles inland from the coastal city of Ventura.

BACKGROUND AND PHILOSOPHY

The Ojai Valley School originated in 1911 as the Bristol School. In 1923, Headmaster Edward Yeomans changed the name to Ojai Valley School. The Summer Programs were established in 1943.

The philosophy of the school and camp is contained in the motto "Integer Vitae"—wholeness of life, symmetry of life, soundness of life. The camp has as its objective the development of each student's character through the advantageous use of Ojai's natural surroundings and stresses a well-rounded experience that encompasses academic enrichment, athletics, horsemanship, camping, computers, art, music, and wilderness skills in a safe and supportive environment.

Ojai Summer Programs offer a special and diverse experience. Special accommodations are made for many international students learning English as a second language.

The camp is accredited by the American Camping Association and is a member of the Western Association for Independent Camps.

PROGRAM OFFERINGS

One of the few boarding schools in the West to operate year-round, Ojai Valley School hosts a variety of safe, purposeful, and fun summer programs.

Ojai Valley Summer School and Camp In operation since 1943, Ojai Valley Summer School and Camp offers programs to students in prekindergarten through grade 12. Students may enroll for two, four, or six weeks. The six-week session is geared to students who want to preview difficult classes, take enrichment courses, earn credit toward high school graduation requirements, and take advantage of the wide range of recreational and camping opportunities. Afternoon and evening enrichment activities are part of the program. Many OVS faculty members are part of the summer staff. A student-faculty ratio of less than 5:1 makes a tutorial approach to enhance student motivation possible. Study for Success, a course on study skills and the psychology of self-esteem, is one of the more popular courses. English as a second language is available.

Britannia Soccer Camp, with coaches from Great Britain, is held during the first week of August at the Lower School.

English Language Camp Many international students ages 8–18 attend the August English Language Camp. This four-week program offers intensive English instruction with teachers and peer tutors in the morning, recreational activities in the afternoon, and many day and weekend trips to southern California attractions. Group programs are also available.

Equestrian Programs A competitive program, vaulting program, and horse camp program are available to campers who are interested in riding or showing. The competitive program is designed for a limited number of riders who would like to participate in a concentrated English training and showing program within the structure of the Ojai Valley Summer School and Camp.

ENROLLMENT

Enrollment numbers 260 at the Lower School and 75 at the Upper School during any one session. The August English Language Camp accommodates 70 international students. Students come from eight different states and ten countries. The camp does not discriminate on the basis of race, color, or national or ethnic origin. All applicants are expected to contribute in a positive and reasonable manner at all times during the summer sessions.

EXTRA OPPORTUNITIES AND ACTIVITIES

Trips to Santa Barbara beaches, along with dances, hiking, rock climbing and rappelling, and overnight camping, contribute to a balanced, varied, and exciting program. All students go on an overnight campout to a beach, lakeside, or mountain site. Backpacking and horseback trail riding are part of the camping program. Older students may take driver's education, or English as a second language.

DAILY SCHEDULE

The following is a typical Summer Program schedule:

6:45	Wake up
7	Dorm clean-up
7:30	High-energy breakfast
8:15	Class 1
9:05	Class 2
9:50	Morning break
10:10	Class 3
11	Class 4
11:45	Lunch/announcements
12:50	Activity 1
2	Activity 2
3:10	Activity 3
4	Free time
5:45	Dinner
7	Evening camp activities
9:30–11:30	Lights-out (depending on age)

FACILITIES

The Lower School campus offers boarding facilities for both girls and boys. Reed Hall houses boarding girls. Frost Hall has accommodations for boarding boys. It also houses the kitchen, the dining hall, and administrative offices. In addition, Lower School facilities include 5 acres devoted to the equestrian program, 2 acres of playing fields, a 25-meter pool and locker rooms, tennis and basketball courts, a baseball and soccer field, a technology center, and an art and ceramics studio.

Upper School boys are housed in three dormitories. Grace Hobson Smith House provides air-conditioned living quarters for boarding girls. The girls' dormitory provides a large living room with a fireplace and a kitchen area. All Upper School dorms have laundry facilities. Students and faculty members eat their meals together in the dining hall.

A large outdoor amphitheater is used for school assemblies, drama productions, and ceremonies. A high- and low-elements ropes course, a swimming pool, a student center, an art and ceramics studio, a photo lab, tennis courts, an equestrian center, playing fields, and a basketball court are also available.

STAFF

The staff consists of 60 people divided between two programs. Many of the staff members are full-time

teachers at the Ojai Valley School during the fall. The Upper and Lower School camp directors are full-time faculty members. Many teachers live on campus in the dorms or in nearby housing. Each dorm is staffed by caring, experienced, and supportive dorm counselors.

MEDICAL CARE

The Ojai Valley School campus houses an infirmary staffed by a registered nurse 24 hours per day, with a school physician on call. The nearby Ojai Valley Community Hospital (located 1 mile from the school) is available for emergency care. A student health record, emergency medical release, medical history, immunization history, physical examination, and medical insurance are required. When medical insurance is not provided, a $200 refundable medical deposit is required.

RELIGIOUS LIFE

Ojai Valley School is not affiliated with any religious organization.

COSTS

An appropriate fee must accompany the application. The fees in 2004 ranged from $2170 for a two-week resident to $5930 for a six-week resident. There are extra fees for ESL and driver's education classes. A full fee schedule is enclosed in the catalog.

TRANSPORTATION

The Ojai Valley School is located 90 miles from the Los Angeles International Airport (LAX). All campers arriving by plane are met by certified OVS bus drivers and staff members. Campers are bused to camp in OVS buses. Campers are returned to LAX at the end of their respective sessions.

APPLICATION TIMETABLE

Inquiries are welcome throughout the year. Catalogs and application forms are available in January and mailed to all who have inquired by that time. A visit to the campus is welcome and may be scheduled by contacting the Admission Office.

For more information, contact:

John H. Williamson, Director of Admission
Ojai Valley School
723 El Paseo Road
Ojai, California 93023
805-646-1423
Fax: 805-646-0362
E-mail: jhw@ovs.org
World Wide Web: http://www.ovs.org

OMNI CAMP

SUMMER CAMP

POLAND SPRING, MAINE

Type of Program: Elective choices in arts, theater, outdoor challenge, trips, waterfront activities, and sports
Participants: Coeducational, ages 9–15
Enrollment: 225
Program Dates: Late June to August; two-, four-, six-, or eight-week sessions
Heads of Program: Betsy and Gar Roper, Owners/Directors

LOCATION

OMNI Camp is located in Poland Spring, Maine, home of the famous "Poland Spring" bottled water. It is 45 minutes north of Portland and 2½ hours from Boston. The 280-acre property is privately situated on a clear, spring-fed lake, surrounded by tall, stately pine trees and dramatic rock outcroppings.

BACKGROUND AND PHILOSOPHY

Owner-directors Betsy and Gar Roper have been involved with camping since the late 1960s. OMNI Camp creates a supportive, accepting community that promotes the understanding of people from diverse backgrounds and cultures. These values are a part of daily interaction in workshops and the many recreational activities at OMNI Camp.

OMNI is a coed, nonsectarian camp where campers are challenged and encouraged to advance the skills they already have and explore activities that are entirely new. Campers choose their activities on a weekly basis from more than fifty electives. The fun and interaction in activities and workshops help campers to discover a new awareness of themselves in relation to the people around them, the environment, and the world. They work, play, and create in a caring and noncompetitive environment. OMNI emphasizes participation, team effort, and independence, as well as fun and friendship. Structure and freedom are balanced for maximum success, safety, and enjoyment.

OMNI Camp is accredited by the American Camping Association.

PROGRAM OFFERINGS

Campers choose their activities from a wide variety of options. Classes are limited in size and, where appropriate, are grouped according to age and ability.

Outdoor Challenge Through activities such as rock climbing, using the high ropes challenge course, hiking, and canoeing, the program emphasizes personal growth, teamwork, and a sense of accomplishment. OMNI offers a wide selection of canoeing, hiking, and backpacking trips that explore the rivers and mountains of Maine. All trips are led by certified trip leaders.

Sports programs develop skills and provide lots of fun and action. Offerings include soccer, volleyball, archery, basketball, softball, tennis, golf, mountain biking, horseback riding, martial arts, and Ultimate Frisbee. The emphasis is on good sportsmanship and teamwork, not competition.

Creative and performing arts An extensive theater program allows campers to be involved at many levels, from exploring basic theater techniques to participating in a full-scale production. Music opportunities include singing, guitar, keyboard, and drum instruction. A mirrored dance studio provides space for jazz, ballet, modern, and tap dance, as well as aerobics and African dance.

Communication skills are learned and practiced through video and computer classes. ESL is offered to international campers. A camp newspaper is published by campers.

Arts and crafts Drawing and painting, fabric arts, silk-screening, stained glass, basketry, tie-dyeing, sewing, sculpture, jewelry making, and ceramics are taught by skilled instructors. A fully equipped darkroom houses the photography program, which complements the visual arts, creative writing, and journalism.

The waterfront features a clear spring-fed lake entirely surrounded by camp land. Campers can opt to improve swimming skills with help from certified instructors or go windsurfing, sailing, canoeing, kayaking, fishing, or waterskiing.

Community service and environmental projects Campers can do volunteer work in area nursing homes, food banks, and shelters. Participants can also learn about forest and lake habitats and how they are impacted by humans. Campers are busy with hands-on projects, animal care, and recycling.

ENROLLMENT

OMNI is a coed camp that accommodates up to 225 campers (ages 9 to 15) who come from all over the United States and many other countries. CIT (campers in transition/counselors in training) positions are available for ages 16 to 17. Acceptance and friendship for all is a key element in OMNI's diverse nonsectarian community.

EXTRA OPPORTUNITIES AND ACTIVITIES

Campers may specialize in theater through a series of workshops and performance classes. The last days of camp feature dance and theater productions, which are sometimes taken on tour. Other special opportunities include optional flight instruction, backpacking and hiking trips, and canoeing and white-water rafting, plus weekly out-of-camp trips to ocean beaches, roller skating, baseball games, and other special events. Evening programs include guest performing artists, theme nights, dances, talent shows, campfires, group games, and cabin nights.

FACILITIES

Campers live in attractively situated cabins that overlook the lake and are equipped with full bathrooms and electricity. Each cabin houses 10–12 campers grouped by age and 2 counselors. There are program buildings for arts and music, a spacious dining hall, a recreation hall with a stage and huge stone fireplace, a mirrored dance studio, field house, playing fields, basketball court, tennis courts, climbing cliffs, an animal barn, riding stables, and acres of woods and trails. In 2004, a beautiful 10,000-square-foot Arts and Conference Center was built to house the arts programs.

DAILY SCHEDULE

7:15	Wake-up
8	Breakfast
8:45	Cabin and camp cleanup
9:15	Period 1: awareness workshops
10:20	Period 2: elective activity
11:30	Period 3: elective activity
12:30	Lunch
1	Down-time to relax, read, and write
2	Period 4: elective activity
3	Period 5: elective activity
4	Special options, free time
5:30	Camp meeting
6	Dinner
7:30	Evening program
9:30–10:30	Bedtime

STAFF

The warm, talented, and energetic staff is carefully chosen based on experience and ability to relate to children and teens. Most are at least 20 years old, and many are teachers or professionals in the arts or other fields. The staff-camper ratio is 1:3. A precamp training week thoroughly prepares staff members.

Co-founders and directors Betsy and Gar Roper each have more than twenty-five years of experience in camping. Betsy, who holds a B.S. degree in education, has served in a variety of leadership roles at Hidden Valley and Med-O-Lark camps, including program director and hiking trip leader. Gar, who holds a Ph.D. in psychology, has worked in family counseling, creativity education, and children's marketing.

MEDICAL CARE

A complete health center is on site, with resident nurses available at all times. The camp doctor is on call, and a full-service hospital is located in Lewiston,

12 minutes away. Many staff members are certified in CPR and first aid. During staff orientation, staff members are trained to deal with medical emergencies and safety procedures.

COSTS

The tuition in 2004 ranged from $1850 to $6000 for two to eight weeks and covered room, board, and all regular camp programs. A "store account" of $25 per week is recommended to cover spending money for trips and other incidentals. There are additional costs for transportation and optional programs.

TRANSPORTATION

Chaperoned buses and vans meet campers in New York City, Connecticut, and Massachusetts. Campers who travel by plane are met at Logan Airport in Boston, Portland Jetport in Maine, or Manchester Airport in New Hampshire. Many families choose to drive their children to camp.

APPLICATION TIMETABLE

Applications are received starting in the fall. In recent years, camp has filled early. Families may request written materials, the camp video or DVD, and references. When possible, home visits are made to prospective campers. Upon registration, a $500 nonrefundable deposit is required. Siblings receive a 10 percent discount. Tours of the camp during camp season are available.

FOR MORE INFORMATION, CONTACT:

winter
Betsy and Gar Roper
15 Merganser Way
Freeport, Maine 04032-6366
888-417-6664 (toll-free)
207-865-2266
Fax: 207-865-3894

summer
OMNI Camp
200 Verrill Road
Poland Spring, Maine 04274-5318
207-998-4777
Fax: 207-998-4722
E-mail: info@omnicamp.com
World Wide Web: http://www.omnicamp.com

OPERAFESTIVAL DI ROMA

SUMMER OPERA PROGRAM

ROME, ITALY

Type of Program: Opera and vocal training and performance
Participants: Coeducational, age 16+
Enrollment: 60
Program Dates: Four weeks in July
Head of Program: Dr. Louisa Panou, Artistic Director

LOCATION

Each summer, Operafestival di Roma brings 60 musicians, from high school age to young professionals, to Italy to study and perform opera. Participants rehearse and reside in a residential hotel in Rome and perform in the courtyard of S. Ivo alla Sapienza in central Rome.

BACKGROUND AND PHILOSOPHY

Founded in 1994 by Dr. Louisa Panou, this program provides a unique experience in voice training and opera performance for young singers. Younger students are accepted for the ensemble program, which provides a training regimen consisting of individual voice lessons, master classes, an opera scenes experience, an Italian diction class, a conversational Italian class, and recital coaching. Ensemble members participate in the opera and in the Broadway/operetta program as members of the chorus and also sing individually in public recitals and in opera scenes performances. Ensemble applicants should have some classical vocal training and a desire to participate in a serious musical training experience. Unlike many summer programs, Operafestival di Roma is not a summer camp experience.

Past productions have included *Don Giovanni, Die Zauberflote, L'elisir d'amore, Le nozze di Figaro, I Pagliacci, Suor Angelica, Cosi fan tutte, Die lustige Witwe, and Il barbiere di Siviglia.* All productions are sung in the original language.

PROGRAM OFFERINGS

Ensemble members participate in the following learning experiences on a regular basis: music and staging rehearsal for opera chorus, music and staging rehearsal for Broadway/operetta concert, individual voice lessons, conversational Italian class, Italian diction class, opera scenes class, individual recital coaching, and master classes on a variety of subjects.

Ensemble members appear in each performance of the opera as members of the chorus and also perform individually in a vocal recital. In addition, the opera scenes class culminates in a public presentation.

ENROLLMENT

Enrollment for the 2004 season is limited to 60 participants, 30 of whom will be in the ensemble program and 10 of whom will be under the age of 18.

EXTRA OPPORTUNITIES AND ACTIVITIES

Participants are encouraged to take advantage of the enormous cultural and recreational opportunities offered by Rome. Students visit museums, historical sites, and productions by other opera and classical music companies. The world-famous Teatro di Opera performs throughout the course of the program.

DAILY SCHEDULE

A typical day for the ensemble program is as follows:

7:30	Breakfast in hotel
8:30	Chorus music rehearsal
10:00	Individual voice lessons, Italian diction class, conversational Italian class, recital coaching
1:00	Lunch in hotel
2:30	Opera scenes program, Broadway/operetta concert rehearsal, master classes
5:30	Opera staging rehearsal, individual voice lessons, free time
7:00	Dinner on own
8:30	Vans leave for performance space
9:00	Performance
11:45	Vans return to hotel

FACILITIES

The Hotel Domus Pacis has been Operafestival's "home away from home" since the program began. Located just 10 minutes from St. Peter's, the hotel is a large yet warm and friendly place and combines spacious indoor and outdoor public spaces with a staff who treat each guest like a member of the family. Program tuition includes housing in a double, air-conditioned room with private bath and breakfast and lunch served each day. Rehearsals, master classes, voice lessons, and other activities are held in the hotel.

Operafestival di Roma performs its operas in the magnificent courtyard of the Palazzo della Sapienza, located in the heart of Rome, just a 2-minute walk from Piazza Navona. Built in the fifteenth century and for nearly 500 years the seat of the University of Rome, the building now houses the library of the Senate of the Republic. The famous Borromini-designed church, S. Ivo alla Sapienza, built inside the courtyard, is considered one of the architectural masterpieces of Rome. The facade of the church provides an ideal scenic background for the opera, and the four-sided courtyard, which seats up to 600 people, becomes a vibrant acoustical space.

Opera productions are fully staged with original costumes and lighting and are accompanied by a full professional orchestra.

STAFF

Operafestival di Roma has a staff of 25 American and Italian professionals and university teachers, including voice teachers, accompanists, coaches, costumers, and stage technicians, and is led by Dr. Louisa Panou, Artistic Director and founder of Operafestival di Roma. Dr. Panou studied voice in Italy, graduating from the Conservatorio di S. Cecilia. She performed and taught in Italy, Germany, and Greece before settling in the United States. Dr. Panou is also Director of the Opera program at the University of Virginia.

Productions in Rome are accompanied by the Orchestra Sinfonica dell' International Chamber Ensemble, founded in 1980 by its Artistic Director and Conductor, Francesco Carotenuto.

COSTS

Tuition for the complete program is $5500, which includes an air-conditioned double room with private bath, breakfast and lunch each day, and a transportation pass. Tuition does not include airfare.

Fifteen days after acceptance into the program, participants are required to pay a nonrefundable registration deposit of $1500 to hold their place. Tuition must be paid in full by May 15. No financial aid is awarded, but the company can help individuals raise money, and work-study opportunities are available in Italy.

TRANSPORTATION

Operafestival di Roma vans meet all participants upon arrival at the Fiumicino (Leonardo da Vinci) airport in Rome. Participants are given Roman metropolitan transportation passes.

APPLICATION TIMETABLE

Applications are accepted beginning in September 2004 and continue to be accepted until all positions are filled. Applicants must attend either a live audition or submit an audition tape/CD along with a $50 application fee. Acceptance decisions are rendered one week after the audition. Students can access the program's Web site to apply online and find specific information about audition repertoire, dates and locations of live auditions, and exact festival dates.

For more information, contact:

William M. Welty, Executive Director
Operafestival di Roma
1445 Willow Lake Drive
Charlottesville, Virginia 22902
434-984-4945
Fax: 434-984-5220
E-mail: operafest@aol.com
World Wide Web: http://www.operafest.com

OVERLAND ADVENTURE TRAVEL

SUMMER PROGRAMS

WILLIAMSTOWN, MASSACHUSETTS

Type of Program: Overland offers outdoor adventures, community service, and language study abroad. Overland's outdoor adventures include bicycle touring, hiking, backpacking, rock and mountain climbing, mountain biking, rafting, and sea and river kayaking in beautiful places all over the U.S. and abroad. Overland's American Community Service and World Service programs reach out to disadvantaged communities in New England, the American Southwest, Alaska, Hawaii, and Costa Rica. Overland's Language Study Abroad programs offer rigorous language instruction, and intensive cultural explorations in France, Spain, and Costa Rica.

Participants: Coeducational, ages 10–18

Enrollment: 8 to 12 participants on each trip

Program Dates: Two-, three-, four-, and six-week programs, late June through the first week of August

Heads of Program: Tom Costley and Brooks Follansbee

LOCATION

Overland offers programs in New England's mountains, on Cape Cod and the Islands, in the Blue Ridge Mountains of North Carolina, the Rockies, the American Southwest, the Sierras of California, along the northern Pacific Coast, across the southern United States, in Alaska, and in Hawaii. Overland also travels abroad to Costa Rica, France, Italy, Spain, and Switzerland.

BACKGROUND AND PHILOSOPHY

Overland offers carefully crafted programs with clearly defined goals, such as hiking to the summit of a mountain peak, reaching out to a community in need, or mastering another language. By providing exceptional leaders and small, supportive groups, the result is an experience of unsurpassed quality for Overland's students.

Whether the setting is a mountaintop in the Rockies, an impoverished neighborhood in the Southwest, or a classroom in the chateaux country of France, Overland's students thrive in an environment of friendship and fun as they learn from caring leaders and discover their own strengths through their accomplishments.

Carefully selected and thoroughly prepared, Overland's leaders are bright, dynamic, and accomplished individuals whose commitment to their students' safety and well-being is foremost on their list of priorities. Serving as powerful role models for their students, Overland's leaders guide and motivate while providing 24-hours-a-day leadership of an unfailingly high standard.

Overland's groups are small. No Overland program has more than 12 students or fewer than 2 leaders. This means there is 1 leader for every 6 students, and sometimes the ratio is 1:4. Overland's small groups encourage strong friendships and create spirited, close-working teams. At its heart, this is what the

Overland experience is all about: a small group with inspiring leadership engaged in a challenge that captures students' imaginations, stretches their abilities, and strengthens their bonds with each other. Overland places a premium on fun, friendship, teamwork, and determination. In doing so, they catalyze in their students an understanding of the world beyond themselves, beyond their own needs and wants—and they do this while showing students how beautiful and exciting and how full of promise the world is. And they have a lot of fun!

PROGRAM OFFERINGS

Overland's Adventure Camp for Fifth & Sixth Grade Boys and Girls is the ideal introduction to outdoor adventures for 10, 11, and 12 year olds. With simple, rustic housing and full days of hiking, biking, swimming, and games, Overland's youngest participants enjoy the pleasures of outdoor adventures at a pace and intensity that matches their abilities and desires.

Overland's Outdoor Adventures include the following bicycling trips: **Cape Cod and the Islands** (two weeks on Cape Cod, Martha's Vineyard, and Nantucket, with a whale watch and sightseeing in Boston); **Vermont and Montréal** (two weeks exploring the length of Vermont, crossing into Canada at the end of the trip for a day exploring Montréal); **Prince Edward Island and Acadia** (a three-week bicycle tour of Prince Edward Island, Nova Scotia, and Acadia National Park); **Pacific Coast** (four weeks from Portland to San Francisco); **Paris to the Sea** (Paris, the Loire chateaux, rafting, Provence's hilltop villages, and the beaches of the Côte d'Azur on a four week bicycle tour); **The European Challenge** (a challenging ride across Europe for four weeks, exploring Paris, the heart of France, the mountains of Switzerland, and Tuscany and Rome); **The American Challenge** (six weeks on bicycle across America from Savannah, Georgia, to Santa Monica, California. Groups visit Taos, New Mexico, and the Grand Canyon); and **Colorado and Utah** (a two-week mountain biking trip that explores Park City, Moab, Steamboat, and Breckenridge. The trip ends with rafting on the Colorado River).

Outdoor Adventures on foot include: **New England Explorer** (two weeks of hiking, backpacking, mountain biking, and white-water rafting in Massachusetts, Vermont, New Hampshire, and Maine); **Blue Ridge Explorer** (backpacking, climbing, white-water rafting, and kayaking for two weeks in the mountains of North Carolina); **Rocky Mountain Explorer** (two weeks in Colorado, Utah, and Wyoming that includes hiking, backpacking, climbing a 14,000-foot peak, mountain biking, and white-water rafting); **Yellowstone Explorer** (a three-week trip featuring backpacking in Yellowstone, kayaking, and rock climbing in Grand Teton National Park); **Shasta Explorer** (four weeks of hiking, backpacking, and rock climbing in California's Sierra Nevada Mountains and Yosemite, with a climb of Mount Shasta (14,162 feet) and white-water rafting); **Alaskan Expedition** (backpacking, sea-kayaking, and white-water rafting in the heart of Alaska for three weeks); **Hawaii Explorer** (a three-week trip offering hiking, sea-kayaking, sailing, surfing, and snorkeling on Kauai and the Big Island); **Costa Rica Explorer** (three weeks of exploration by foot, kayak, and raft as groups discover the mountains, beaches, rain forests, and culture of Costa Rica); **European Explorer** (a four-week journey exploring the mountains, beaches, rivers, and cultures of Spain, France, Italy, and Switzerland by foot, kayak, and raft); **Alpine Challenge** (challenge hiking, high-altitude climbing, and leadership training for four weeks in the Alps); **AT Challenge** (a four-week, 300-mile hike of the world-famous Appalachian Trail from the top of Mount Greylock in Massachusetts to Mount Washington in New Hampshire); **Teton Challenge** (three weeks in Yellowstone and the Tetons for backpacking, kayaking the Snake River, and a climb of the Grand Teton).

Overland's American Community Service and **World Service** programs in **New England**, the American **Southwest, Hawaii, Alaska,** and **Costa Rica** reach out to disadvantaged communities through youth work, building projects, conservation efforts, and other volunteer opportunities.

Overland's Language Study Abroad Programs in **France, Spain,** and **Costa Rica** give students the chance to improve language skills by being fully immersed in the culture and language of the country; all programs include 80 hours of native-speaker instruction, weekly excursions, and a homestay.

ENROLLMENT

Participants come from all over the United States and several other countries. Three references are required for admission, as is a phone interview.

FACILITIES

Overland's outdoors participants sleep in lightweight tents, staying in campgrounds ranging from organized, full-facility campgrounds to the backcountry. Community service and language program participants live indoors in dormitory accommodations and/or with home-stay families.

STAFF

The combined twenty-five years of experience of Overland's directors, Tom Costley and Brooks Follansbee, assure excellent leadership and a clear vision for Overland. A staff of 9 year-round professionals helps to run Overland in Williamstown, Massachusetts.

Finding and training caring, competent, and dynamic leaders is Overland's most important task. Overland leaders have distinguished themselves in academics, athletics, or community service. In any given year, more than half of Overland's leaders are returning from previous years. All leaders complete lifesaving, CPR, basic or wilderness first aid training, and Overland's training program. The staff-student ratio averages 1:5.

COSTS

Tuition ranges from $2250 to $6500, depending on the length and location of the program.

TRANSPORTATION

Programs begin and end at a variety of locations. Group leaders always meet incoming students at the airport and are there to send off participants at trip's end.

APPLICATION TIMETABLE

Applications are accepted anytime after September 1; many programs fill by mid-February. Waiting lists are maintained from mid-February until June. Students should always call first about program availability.

For more information, contact:

Tom Costley and Brooks Follansbee
Overland
P.O. Box 31
Williamstown, Massachusetts 01267
413-458-9672
800-458-0588 (toll-free)
Fax: 413-458-5208
E-mail: overland@adelphia.net
World Wide Web: www.overlandsummers.com

PARTICIPANT/FAMILY COMMENTS

"I've never had so much fun and challenge, so many laughs and memories." —Courtney Blethen, Seattle, Washington

OXBRIDGE ACADEMIC PROGRAMS

OXBRIDGE ACADEMIC PROGRAMS

THE OXFORD TRADITION, THE CAMBRIDGE TRADITION, L'ACADÉMIE DE PARIS, THE OXFORD PREP EXPERIENCE, AND THE CAMBRIDGE PREP EXPERIENCE

OXFORD AND CAMBRIDGE, ENGLAND; PARIS, FRANCE

Type of Program: Academic and cultural enrichment
Participants: Coeducational; grades 8–12
Enrollment: The Oxford Tradition, 370; the Cambridge Tradition, 200; L'Académie de Paris, 155; the Oxford Prep Experience, 100; the Cambridge Prep Experience, 170
Program Dates: The month of July; optional week in Paris in early August
Head of Program: Professor James G. Basker, Director

LOCATION

Established more than twenty years ago, Oxbridge Academic Programs offers academic summer programs at Oxford and Cambridge Universities in England and in the heart of Paris in France.

BACKGROUND AND PHILOSOPHY

Each program is designed to immerse students in two academic subjects or creative arts while taking advantage of the enormous cultural resources of Oxford, Cambridge, or Paris. All five programs combine rigorous classroom activity with day trips, eminent guest speakers, cultural enrichment, and the experience of studying in one of the world's great centers of learning and history. The emphasis is on small classes, individual attention, and innovative teaching methods. Through the use of dynamic, caring, and imaginative teachers drawn from Oxford and Cambridge Universities, the Sorbonne, and other leading global institutions, coupled with a hands-on approach that creates an immediacy and excitement about learning, students are inspired to new levels of performance. The challenging academic program, a rich array of extracurricular activities, and a mixture of independence and structured living help students develop the best in themselves while building a foundation for their college years and beyond.

PROGRAM OFFERINGS

Oxbridge Academic Programs offers a wide range of courses in the sciences, humanities, social sciences, and creative arts. In Oxford, Cambridge, and Paris, each student selects two subjects, one as a Major and one as a Minor. Major courses meet five or six mornings a week and include in-class time for fieldwork, labs, workshops, writing, guest speakers, group discussion, and one-on-one attention. Major courses require homework and project and preparation time in the afternoons and evenings. Minor courses meet three afternoons a week, with all work contained within the class session.

All of the programs aim to provide the student with a unique and tangible interaction with his or her subject in a way that cannot be reproduced in any other location. Using the extensive history and cultural resources of their immediate surroundings, teachers create an environment in which the students learn not only through traditional class instruction but also from firsthand interaction with the famous landmarks, museums, sites, and research facilities that surround them. From molecular medicine and quantum physics to creative writing, drama, and English literature to war in world history, each of more than 100 courses is designed to combine the expertise of the faculty member with the enthusiasm and energy of the students. Combine this with the ancient and stimulating surroundings of Oxford, Cambridge, or Paris, and it creates an unforgettable and often life-changing experience. At the end of each program, every student receives a grade, a report from their teacher, and a formal description of their course, which can be used to apply for high school and college credit and supplement college applications.

ENROLLMENT

The Oxford Tradition, the Cambridge Tradition, and L'Académie de Paris are for students who have completed grades 10–12 and enroll 370, 200, and 155 students, respectively. The Oxford Prep Experience and the Cambridge Prep Experience are exclusively for students completing grades 8 and 9 and enroll 100 and 170 students, respectively. The 2004 student body included participants from forty states, five provinces of Canada, and twenty countries, including South Africa, Russia, Japan, Saudi Arabia, Kuwait, Venezuela, South Korea, Austria, Hungary, and Germany. Students come from diverse ethnic backgrounds, from public and private schools, and from cities and rural areas. Participants represent an exceptional range of interests, ideas, and perspectives.

DAILY SCHEDULE

Days begin with breakfast in the college or school dining hall, followed by Major classes. After a lunch break, afternoons include Minor classes, museum and gallery visits, guest lectures, sports, walking tours, and time for private study. In the afternoons, students are offered a wide variety of elective options by a full-time activities staff, allowing them to pursue activities of particular interest to them either individually or in groups with their friends. Dinner is served at approximately 6. Evening activities include social events, concerts, films, literary talks, theater, and more. Students are required to sign in at their colleges by 11 p.m. (10 p.m. in the Oxford Prep Experience and the Cambridge Prep Experience).

EXTRA OPPORTUNITIES AND ACTIVITIES

Each program offers group field trips, theater and concert outings, and guest lectures. These include poetry readings by the Poet Laureate of England, Andrew Metion; a private tour of Broughton Castle by Lord Saye and Sele; and wathcing a play at Shakespeare's Globe Theatre in London. In addition, each class features outings and cultural activities appropriate to its course of study. There is also a daily program of sports and recreational activities.

Students enrolled in the Oxford and Cambridge Traditions have the opportunity to extend their experience by one week by participating in the Paris Connection. In the Paris Connection, students are introduced to major elements of French culture, to prominent features of Parisian society, and, of course, to the wonders of the City of Lights. While there are no formal class sessions, the participants are led through Paris by expert scholars and art historians, who give in-depth and informative presentations at many of the main historical and cultural sites.

FACILITIES

Students in the Oxford Tradition live in Pembroke, St. Peter's, and Corpus Christi Colleges of Oxford University. Students in the Oxford Prep Experience live in Corpus Christi College, Oxford but separately from their Oxford Tradition counterparts. Students in the Cambridge Tradition live in Jesus College, and Cambridge Prep Experience students live in Magdalene College, Cambridge University. The Lycée Notre Dame de Sion, one of the most prestigious girls' schools in the center of Paris, is the host of L'Académie de Paris. All the students live in college rooms—singles and doubles—with shared bathroom facilities. Each facility has its own dining hall and communal recreation areas.

STAFF

The program faculties contain distinguished scholars from Oxford, Cambridge, the Sorbonne, and other leading universities from around the world as well as writers, artists, and other professionals in their fields. Each year, these select groups include Rhodes, Marshall, Fulbright, and Gates Scholars as well as university professors, senior research fellows, published writers, professional actors, and internationally recognized artists. Oxford Academic Programs employs teaching faculty members who not only have the highest academic credentials but the personalities and passion to teach teenagers. Each program also has a full administrative staff of experienced deans (all with extensive secondary school experience), assistants, and activities coordinators. The programs are fully residential, and members of the administration and faculty live among the students to provide around-the-clock supervision and support.

All programs were founded by Professor James G. Basker. Still the Director of Oxbridge Academic Programs, he was educated at Harvard (A.B.), Cambridge (M.A.), and, as a Rhodes Scholar, Oxford (D.Phil.). He is currently the Ann Whitney Olin Professor of English at Barnard College, Columbia University, and President of the Gilder Lehrman Institute of American History in New York City.

MEDICAL CARE

Each program is affiliated with a local general practitioner who is available to see students who require care. Prior to the program, attendees submit information regarding allergies to food and medication and other health issues that the administration closely monitors and refers to.

The policy of Oxbridge Academic Programs is to forbid any behavior that is illegal, antisocial, or dangerous either to the student or to the group. All programs are nonsmoking and strictly forbid the use or possession of drugs or alcohol.

RELIGIOUS LIFE

The programs are nondenominational. Students interested in attending religious services may consult the staff in each program for information regarding local places of worship.

COSTS

The comprehensive fees for the programs in 2004 were as follows: the Oxford Tradition, $5395; the Cambridge Tradition, $5395; L'Académie de Paris, $5395; the Oxford Prep Experience, $4795; and the Cambridge Prep Experience, $4795. These fees included all tuition and instruction, accommodation, breakfast and dinner daily, transportation to and from the airports, all books and course materials, guest lectures, workshops, field trips, sports and activities, theater tickets, museum and gallery admissions, and social events. Fees did not include airfare, lunch daily, unscheduled (elective) activities, lab fees (specific courses only), or personal expenses such as snacks, laundry, and souvenirs. The fee in 2004 for the optional Paris Connection was $1395.

A deposit of $750 ($825 with cancellation insurance) should accompany the application and is fully refundable until March 3. Families are invoiced for the balance, which is due by April 16.

FINANCIAL AID

A limited number of full scholarships are available based on financial need, academic excellence, and the ability to contribute to the program in the broadest sense. Those interested should call the office for the separate application forms and information about the process that accompanies the scholarship application. The deadline for scholarships is usually around the first week of March.

TRANSPORTATION

Students are met by staff members at the London and Paris airports and transported on buses to their program. At the end of each program, they are chaperoned back to the airport and are supervised right up to the security gate that leads to the passenger departure area.

APPLICATION TIMETABLE

Inquiries are welcome all year. Students whose applications are postmarked by January 12, 2005 (the Oxford Tradition) or February 1, 2005 (both Cambridge programs, the Oxford Prep Experience, and Paris), are guaranteed a place in their program and first choice of courses (subject to being admitted and to enrollment minimums). The programs fill quickly, so early application is recommended. Office hours are 9 a.m. to 6:30 p.m. EST, Monday through Friday, and 10 a.m. to 4 p.m. on weekends.

For more information, contact:

Oxbridge Academic Programs
601 Cathedral Parkway, Suite 7R
New York, New York 10025-2186
800-828-8349 (toll-free in the U.S. and Canada)
212-932-3049
Fax: 212-663-8169
E-mail: info@oxbridgeprograms.com
World Wide Web: http://www.oxbridgeprograms.com

PARTICIPANT/FAMILY COMMENTS

"I enjoyed it so much. I would feel that I was cheating people of the opportunity if I didn't tell anybody else about it. Thank everyone for the summer of my lifetime!"

OXFORD ADVANCED STUDIES PROGRAM

SUMMER IN OXFORD, ENGLAND

OXFORD, ENGLAND

Type of Program: Academic enrichment and acceleration, high school credit, cultural visits, recreation, and theater
Participants: Coeducational, ages 15–18
Enrollment: 100
Program Dates: July 4–29, 2005
Head of Program: Ralph Dennison, B.A., PGCE, Director, Oxford Tutorial College

LOCATION

The program takes place in the medieval city of Oxford, England, 60 miles northwest of London. Oxford is the oldest university in the United Kingdom and is renowned throughout the world as a center of learning and education. Oxford Advanced Studies uses the facilities of Magdalen College, a fourteenth-century foundation and one of the oldest, largest, and most beautiful colleges in the university.

BACKGROUND AND PHILOSOPHY

The Oxford Advanced Studies Program is in its twenty-second year. It offers American and other international students the opportunity to combine an in-depth and challenging educational experience with an exciting and stimulating range of social and cultural activities. Because accredited high school courses are offered, work undertaken during the summer has relevance to education at home. Experienced British university graduates teach students in small seminar groups, and an outstanding feature of the course is the weekly individual tutorial in each subject. Students are set challenging academic assignments and are encouraged to develop tutorial-style relationships with their teachers, the hallmark of the educational system at Oxford and Cambridge. The academic experience is balanced with trips around England and a full and varied sports and social itinerary, which enables everyone to have a recreational, as well as intellectually enriching, vacation. The goals of the program are achieved through close individual attention and interaction.

PROGRAM OFFERINGS

The program combines academic study and cultural visits and experiences. Students choose two major subjects and may select an optional third subject. The course offerings are broken down into six areas: Creative Arts (Practical Drama, Film Studies, and Creative Writing), Humanities (Art and Architecture, Shakespeare, The Modern Novel, The Ancient World, and The Dictatorships in Europe), Social Sciences (Introduction to Economics, International Relations, Comparative Government, Psychology, and International Business Management), Languages (French, Spanish, German, Russian, and Italian at levels III, IV, and V), Mathematics (Algebra, Trigonometry, Pre-Calculus, Calculus AB, Calculus BC, and Probability and Statistics), and Sciences (Medical Biology, Physics, and Chemistry).

Courses are offered in other subjects as requested. Recently, students have followed specially designed curricula in Russian History, Greek and Latin, Romantic Poetry, and Meteorology.

Two course assignments are set in each subject, and final grades and reports are based both on those and on all-round classroom performance. Students are recommended to receive half credit for work completed in each of their academic subjects and are requested to check with their school guidance counselor regarding the transferability of credits earned during the course.

ENROLLMENT

Oxford Advanced Studies students are enrolled from all over the United States and from international schools worldwide. The program is limited to students from public and independent high schools who have just completed their sophomore, junior, or senior year.

DAILY SCHEDULE

After breakfast, students attend classes from 9 to 1. For each subject studied, there are daily seminars in small groups and tutorials on a one-to-one basis. Afternoons are devoted to visits, sports, cultural activities, and study sessions, and there is some free time. Dinner is at 6:30; evening activities usually last from 7 to 11. Students are required to be back in college by 11.

EXTRA OPPORTUNITIES AND ACTIVITIES

Afternoons and evenings are kept free for various cultural and social activities, some of which take place in Oxford itself, including visits to other colleges, galleries and museums, and theatrical and musical events. In addition, students are taken to visit historic and cultural sites, such as Stratford-upon-Avon (to see a play at the Shakespeare Memorial Theatre), Blenheim Palace, Warwick Castle, and London. Several guided tours are offered on weekends. There are additional opportunities to travel to London for cultural, recreational, and shopping visits. Students are given a personal introduction to the British Houses of Parliament, where they are escorted through this seat of democracy.

Sports are not neglected, and, if they wish, students can participate in soccer, basketball, baseball, tennis, swimming, and squash. The traditional river pastime of punting is popular with many students, and the mysteries of the noble English sport of cricket are explained, culminating in a staff-student cricket match.

FACILITIES

The Oxford Advanced Studies Program takes place in Magdalen College, Oxford. Founded in 1483, it is one of the University's oldest constituent colleges. Students live in a modern student residence where they are supervised by residential staff members. Teaching takes place within the college, and many of the rooms used date from Magdalen's foundation. Students take breakfast and evening meals in the college dining hall, with its impressive beamed ceiling and imposing portraits of illustrious alumni looking down on the dining tables. The accommodations are individual study bedrooms with a common room area for social gatherings and small group activities. Laundry facilities are available. The college buttery is open for lunches, and students have access to the college sports ground, squash courts, and croquet lawns.

STAFF

The course is supervised by Ralph Dennison, Director of Oxford Tutorial College, one of Oxford's leading independent further education colleges. A gifted educationalist with more than thirty years' teaching experience, he has brought together an excellent team of tutors, all of whom are highly qualified academics and natural communicators. The majority of course tutors are Oxbridge graduates and many are still actively engaged in academic research. Most have taught in the program for a number of years and are familiar with U.S. and international high school curricula and aware of the needs of students from the U.S. They offer a dynamic and enthusiastic approach, which engages students' interest and invites active participation and discussion. The staff-student ratio of 1:4 allows for close attention to each individual student and allows for a less formal teaching approach. The residential staff members work closely with students to create a vibrant, sympathetic community and keep a careful eye on student welfare.

MEDICAL CARE

The college physician is available to students as required. The renowned John Radcliffe Hospital is just over a mile away. Because of the English National Health Service, all medical treatments are available at a reasonable cost. However, it is required that students take out a comprehensive medical policy before traveling to England.

RELIGIOUS LIFE

Oxford Advanced Studies Program is nondenominational, but provisions can be made for students to attend places of worship in the Oxford area. Special dietary needs can be catered for when requested in advance.

COSTS

The all-inclusive course fee for the four-week program is $6500, payable by June 1. This covers all the program costs, including room, board, tuition, extracurricular activities, transportation, and entrances. It does not cover airfare, lunches, and personal expenditure.

TRANSPORTATION

The program organizes chaperoned round-trip flights from both New York and Los Angeles to London at a cost of approximately $850. This includes transportation from the airport to Oxford. Students who wish to make their own travel arrangements may, of course, do so, and the college advises students of transportation arrangements between the airport and Oxford.

APPLICATION TIMETABLE

The program is open to all students who have completed tenth grade. Students should apply early in order to increase their chances of being accepted. Applications are received from December 1 through May 31. In addition to an application, students must submit a high school transcript and a letter of recommendation from a teacher. There is a registration fee of $350. Applicants are notified of their acceptance immediately upon evaluation by the Course Director in Oxford, and a formal acceptance is then issued.

For more information, contact:

The Registrar
Oxford Advanced Studies Program
P.O. Box 2043
Darien, Connecticut 06820
203-966-2886

PARTICIPANT/FAMILY COMMENTS

"Looking back on the summer, I can only say that I absolutely loved it. I truly enjoyed the program. I felt there was a great balance between study, sports, visits, and fun. I would just like to thank everyone involved. Words could hardly describe the absolutely fabulous time I had with the Oxford Advanced Studies Program."—Sam Giller, Florida

OXFORD FILM AND MEDIA SCHOOL

FILM SCHOOL/MASTER FILM CLASS/VIDEO JOURNALISM/ DOCUMENTARY/INWARD BOUND ADVENTURE LEARNING

OXFORD, ENGLAND

Type of Program: Educational enrichment, individual expression, and creative experiences
Participants: Coeducational, ages 14–18
Enrollment: 10–20 participants per program
Program Dates: Four-week program in July
Head of Program: Desmond Smith; Nick Smith, Assistant Head

LOCATION

The Oxford Media School (OMS) is located at New College in Oxford, England. It is 44 miles (70 kilometers) from Heathrow Airport and 50 miles (80 kilometers) from London.

BACKGROUND AND PHILOSOPHY

The Oxford Media School program was developed to offer a creative introduction to the worlds of film, television journalism, documentary production, and the dramatic arts.

The School brings together a film school, a "newsroom in Europe: for young journalists, a basic course in how to make one's own documentaries, and drama as a second subject for all students. Young people work in a friendly environment where fun is part of the learning philosophy.

The course welcomes inventive spirits, prepared for team effort and hard, stimulating work, in an atmosphere that develops strong friendships and personal achievement.

PROGRAM OFFERINGS

The Film School The School's main requirements are enthusiasm, dedication, and an ability to spend long hours on the set or at the editing table. Filmmaking is fun, but it's also teamwork. Students should be adaptable in group situations in order to take this course.

Introduction to Film In Week One, the team works in film and video exactly as Hollywood does today. Students shoot both film and digital video cameras and edit on Final Cut Pro Software. The basics include how to write, direct, and shoot a script. Preproduction commences during Week Two. Movies are cast. Locations are scouted and costumes are arranged. Instructions are given on location shooting. Students work as part of the film crew, rotating key jobs. Camera and sound test rolls shot during the first week are checked. During Week Three, students learn the process of digital nonlinear editing for the final edits. Everyone works late during this week. In Week Four, the most hectic period, postproduction means adding music, sound effects, and preparation for the all-important screen credits.

Film Making: The Master Class (maximum of 10 students) This advanced film class is for film students who have already attended a first-year film school such as Oxford and wish to make films in a small unit, with a focus on script writing, filmmaking, and in-depth writing. During the course, work is divided between hands-on learning, writing, shooting, and screening and discussing films with faculty members for their visual and narrative content.

The Documentary School The program teaches the basics of documentary film making and television journalism. Subjects can be serious or light hearted. Film deals with fiction; documentary makers find their material in the reality around them.

Introduction to the Documentary In this course, students get the basics of handling camera and sound alongside the film-school students. By the week two, students are researching and shooting segments for the school documentary. Students work in teams of two, one directing and the other shooting, then swap roles as they move through their stories. Together, the class makes a documentary about Oxford and how the city is changing in the 21st century. The group also goes to London to visit the foreign news bureaus of CBS News and the New York Times.

Documentary Making: The Master Class This program is designed for students who have already taken the first-year documentary or film course. This is a senior class that enhances the skills already gained in a first-year course. Students not attending OMS previously should send a reference and a copy of their previous work. This one-month workshop gives students more editing and shooting time and the ability to write and produce a longer documentary. In addition to advanced camera and editing workshops, students learn how to set up and use lights, how to make a budget, and ways to finance their first documentary.

The Television Documentary While a news story runs less than 3 minutes, a documentary can be as short as 6 minutes or as long as 6 hours. What makes documentaries different from daily news is the point of view of the director. Passion, intensity, and a sense of justice underscore the best documentary making. In this course, students get the basics of how to find a subject, how to write the outline, and how to then work as part of a team that actually makes a documentary in Oxford. In week one, the topic of the documentary is chosen along with learning the basics of camera and sound recording. In week two, shooting of the documentary begins. In weeks three and four, students write, record, and edit.

Field work is an essential component of all courses, and related excursions include visits to the news bureaus of ABC News, CBS News, and the Canadian Broadcasting

Corporation. Additional visits to the BBC and Independent Television allow students to watch television programs in the making.

ENROLLMENT

Oxford Media School sessions are limited to 40 students or fewer. The small group size (limited to 10–20 students) encourages friendly, noncompetitive teamwork.

The media revolution involves the world. Oxford Media School wants to attract people of different backgrounds, cultures, and nationalities. Past experience suggests that students are equally divided between girls and boys.

DAILY SCHEDULE

The School runs by Oxford rules. Students go to the Great Hall for breakfast between 8 and 9 a.m. Classes start at 9 a.m. Students meet in the Common Room for coffee or tea at 10 a.m. Classes then resume until noon.

After a break for lunch, students return to their assignments for 3 to 4 hours in the afternoon. Participants spend 5 to 6 hours each day working with faculty members. Dinner is at 6 p.m., followed by tea or coffee in the Common Room. Most nights, students watch some of the world's best movies in the projection room.

EXTRA OPPORTUNITIES AND ACTIVITIES

The School arranges weekend picnics and, of course, that most Oxford of all activities—punting on the Cherwell. On weekends, there are trips to London, both to see the sights and to sample the British capital's incomparable shopping. Included in the School fee is a unique, supervised London and Stratford theater program that takes students each weekend to some of the best new plays of the London season and often features stagedoor visits. Everyone enjoys a staff versus summer students barbecue and sports night on the New College sports grounds.

Students can enjoy Shakespeare on the college lawn most evenings and at many colleges. The Sheldonian—where Handel played—offers classical music most summer nights. Tennis with both grass and Har-Tru surfaces is available. On a glorious midsummer's eve, there is the Farewell Dinner and Graduation Ceremony to which all parents are invited.

FACILITIES

The Oxford Media program shares New College, Oxford with several other summer schools, including Duke University, during the month of July. Founded in the fifteenth century, it is one of Oxford's founding colleges. Students live in single rooms with individual showers. Most rooms have computer-ready connections. Linen is supplied, and there is daily maid service, except on weekends.

STAFF

Desmond Smith, the School's founder and director, has been a writer, teacher, and television producer all his working life. He spent nearly twenty years working for three of the American networks. Oxford Media's teachers consist of skilled film, drama, and journalism teachers and have been members of the summer faculty for many years. The School maintains a 5:1 ratio of students to staff members.

MEDICAL CARE

New College has both a nurse and a medical doctor on call. In case of an emergency, the nearest hospital is less than 1 mile away. Students are requested to bring medical insurance with them.

RELIGIOUS LIFE

Within easy walking distance of student accommodations are opportunities for worship for members of many faiths.

COSTS

The comprehensive fees for 2004, including room, board, tuition, a London theater program each weekend, and transportation to and from Heathrow airport, were $6845 for four weeks. The fees do not cover airfare, lunches, and personal expenditures.

FINANCIAL AID

Financial aid is not offered.

TRANSPORTATION

Transportation to and from the airport is provided.

APPLICATION TIMETABLE

There is no application deadline.

For more information, contact:

Desmond Smith, Director
Oxford Media School
110 Pricefield Road
Toronto, Ontario M4W 1Z9
Canada
416-964-0746
Fax: 416-929-4230
E-mail: newsco@sympatico.ca
World Wide Web: http://www.oxfordmediaschool.com

PARTICIPANT/FAMILY COMMENTS

"I learned so much over the four weeks, and now I can't watch television or a movie without looking critically at the technical aspects, such as lighting and editing, as well as the story. Your staff were some of the best teachers I've ever had, guiding me and letting me discover things for myself, rather than telling me what's right and wrong."—Martha Jack

"Walter learned an incredible amount about the entire film making process. When I came to the 'graduation' night festivities, I was so impressed by the quality of his and his fellow students' work. When I asked Walter what the best part of the entire experience was, he said, 'The teachers, the teachers, the teachers!'"—Julie Haas

PATA STUDY ABROAD

COLLEGE CREDIT STUDY ABROAD FOR HIGH SCHOOL STUDENTS

AUSTIN, TEXAS

Type of Program: Intensive foreign language programs, intercultural studies, creative writing programs, and adventure travel
Participants: Coeducational middle school and high school students, ages 12–14 and 15–18, respectively
Enrollment: 4–30
Program Dates: June, July, and August; custom program dates are available year-round
Head of Program: Rose Potter, Executive Director

LOCATION

Based in Austin, Texas, Programs Abroad–Travel Alternatives (PATA) offers foreign language study-abroad programs in Spain, Mexico, Costa Rica, Peru, France, Canada, Germany, Italy, and Russia and creative writing in Ireland and/or England.

BACKGROUND AND PHILOSOPHY

Founded in 1996, PATA's roots extend to 1984 when master Spanish teacher Rose Potter established educational travel programs for her Advanced Placement (AP) Spanish students. With the goal of providing an in-depth experience similar to her master's program, the six essential components of those first trips became the basis for the PATA experience. Those components include exclusive use of the language of study by group leaders and participants, classes offering transferable college credit, room and board with a local family, high-quality excursions supporting U.S. curriculum, mature leadership by a certified teacher, and a limited group size of 30 participants.

PATA participants' increased language skills raise their AP, I.B. (International Baccalaureate), and CLEP scores. With PATA credit and credit by exam, students can earn a year of college credit. Many complete a minor with one course. Most PATA participants graduate in three years. Participants who develop fluency in their language of study during high school have an opportunity to pursue a third language during their university years, allowing them to enter the adult world as trilingual, tricultural citizens.

PROGRAM OFFERINGS

High School and Middle School Summer Study Abroad Summer study abroad programs run three to four weeks. Four hours of class each weekday include language, culture, and conversation. Back-to-back programs offer students six to eight weeks of immersion. Upon completion, students who attend a PATA program at an accredited university receive a university or language institute transcript. PATA holds and facilitates the transfer of credit. The decision to grant credit is based on university guidelines and degree plans. Students generally receive 1 hour of credit for every 15 hours of class contact.

PATA develops foreign language and cross-curricular middle school programs according to demand. Interested students can visit PATA's Web site listed below to determine if a program is offered in a specific language area.

School Break Abroad PATA organizes custom trips for any school or independent group. The group does not need to consist of students from the same school, nor does it require the participants' teachers to travel with them. PATA encourages the spring-break immersion experience to students who plan to take AP or I.B. exams at the end of the academic year.

Custom and Individual Programs PATA designs custom programs for public and private schools, clubs, families, home-schooled students who wish to travel as a group, and for individual students aged 17 and older.

ENROLLMENT

Students must meet prerequisites, as described in the PATA brochure. PATA requires parent, teacher, and counselor recommendations. Because PATA programs attract mature, motivated, responsible students, incidences of poor decision making are rare.

DAILY SCHEDULE

Participants take 4 hours of class each day. Directors offer optional afternoon excursions based on the homestay communities' cultural activities and events calendar. On weekends, participants take overnight and/or day excursions.

Participants' safety is the foremost concern. Students and parents sign a guideline contract that outlines inappropriate behavior. Because parents have the greatest impact on their child's decision making, PATA involves parents when a concern arises. The on-site team first counsels the student, then informs PATA. PATA then contacts the parents and asks that they counsel their child. If a second guideline infraction occurs, the student is dismissed.

FACILITIES

Students take course work at selected universities and language institutes abroad. Students fill out a personality questionnaire before departure, allowing PATA to carefully select and match each student with an appropriate, compatible host family as well as a roommate. Participants have the option to live alone for an additional charge.

Custom payment plans are also available. Applications are accepted on a first-come, first-served basis. Late fees are applied to applications received after the deadline.

For more information, contact:

PATA Study Abroad–Client Services
888-777-PATA (7282, toll-free)
E-mail: studyabroad@gopata.com
World Wide Web: http://www.gopata.com

PARTICIPANT/FAMILY COMMENTS

"My PATA trip to Jena, Germany, opened my mind to new ideas and new people...and gave me the confidence that I could do anything. After the trip, I applied for and won a scholarship to spend an entire year there. I know it wouldn't have been possible without the experience I gained with PATA."—Heather Hooks, PATA Participant

"Take advantage of this opportunity to open your child's mind."—PATA Parent, Jamestown, North Carolina

"The total immersion made a difference! His confidence in speaking Spanish soared! As a dyslexic, this made a huge difference to him."—PATA Parent, Colorado Springs, Colorado

STAFF

Certified foreign language teachers design, direct, and lead PATA programs. Local certified native speakers teach classes.

MEDICAL CARE

PATA provides students with medical and repatriation insurance. Emergency centers and hospitals are located in homestay cities.

RELIGIOUS LIFE

PATA directors are available to help students find the location of the service of their choice.

COSTS

Program fees range from $3390 to $4890 and include round-trip airfare from the gateway city, room and meals, tuition and books, tutorial assistance, on-site language assistance, hotel accommodations, medical insurance for the duration of the program, day and overnight excursions (including entrance fees), ground transportation, predeparture orientation, and newsletters. Upon enrollment, a $500 deposit to be applied toward the program price is due. Discounts are available for students who arrange their own flight.

TRANSPORTATION

PATA groups travel by air, private coach, train, and boat.

APPLICATION TIMETABLE

PATA accepts year-round applications; however, because of limited enrollment, early application is encouraged. Final payment for Spring Break Abroad is January 1 and for Summer Study Abroad is March 1.

PEACE WORKS INTERNATIONAL

EDUCATIONAL SERVICE AND LANGUAGE TOURS

COSTA RICA, ECUADOR, PERU

Type of Program: Service projects, homestay living, language immersion, and adventure travel to develop responsible leadership and global awareness
Participants: Coeducational, high school students at all levels of the Spanish language
Enrollment: Students ages 15–18; Spanish-language skills recommended, but not required
Program Dates: Costa Rica, Ecuador, and Peru: Twenty-six days in the summer
Head of Program: Christopher Kealey, CEO

LOCATION

Trip destinations are in Costa Rica, Peru, and Ecuador. Peace Works International's (PWI) offices are located in Pasadena, California.

BACKGROUND AND PHILOSOPHY

Peace Works International specializes in educational tours incorporating volunteer service, Spanish study, and adventure. PWI challenges students with opportunities for personal growth through cross-cultural experiences and volunteer service. Participants volunteer in South American communities that match the students' resources and potential. Students improve foreign language skills and interests through daily lessons, experiential learning projects, and homestay family experiences.

PWI was developed by Christopher and Heather Kealey and Christopher and Kathleen Bertrand. Together with Randy Haley, they spent 2½ years in the Peace Corps in Costa Rica, during which time they learned Spanish through the experiential learning method. They returned to the U.S. with the desire to start Peace Works International. In July 1994, they embarked on an investigatory trip to Costa Rica, and they successfully launched its first summer program in 1995.

The idea for PWI came from the experiences the founders had in the Peace Corps, but PWI is not associated with either the Peace Corps or the U.S. government.

PROGRAM OFFERINGS

Service Learning Students work side by side with a South American community, exchanging ideas and building new friendships while making the world a better place. Working with local leaders, PWI identifies projects based on a community's assets and resources. During a project, PWI finds tasks for students, regardless of their technical backgrounds; teaches them the skills they need; and lets them put those skills to work helping the people around them. Past projects have included building playgrounds, multiuse courts, and school walkways; renovating high schools; and repairing roads.

Spanish Study Living in another country is the best way to learn that country's language. With PWI, students are immersed in a Spanish-speaking environment to develop their conversational skills. Part of the immersion is living with a host family while becoming a confident and comfortable second-language speaker. PWI is designed for high school students of all Spanish language levels and has beginning and advanced classes. Students find themselves talking to local teens about dating traditions or poplar music, learning grammar through group scavenger hunts, or practicing verb forms while playing charades.

Homestay The best way to learn about the culture, customs, and values of a country is to live with a host family. Upon arrival in their new community, PWI students are paired up and welcomed into carefully selected homes. By participating in a family's everyday life, the student becomes part of that family and experiences cultural education through direct interaction with the family and the surrounding community.

Adventure So students can explore the beautiful mountains, jungles, and valleys of their chosen countries, PWI offers an exciting range of adventure treks during each tour. Students experience a variety of outings that depend on the trip they have chosen. Students in Costa Rica spend two nights in an open-air cave while learning to rappel from tropical waterfalls. In Peru, students take multiple-day adventures in the Sacred Valley, including a dramatic hike along the Inca Trail to Machu Picchu. The Galapagos Islands and its resident sea lions await students in Ecuador.

ENROLLMENT

Regardless of their Spanish-speaking skills, all high school students are welcome to apply.

DAILY SCHEDULE

Costa Rica PWI's homestay program in Costa Rica revolves around three rural communities in the San Isidro region. Mornings are spent with local people on a cooperative service project. Afternoons are a mix of Spanish-language games, hikes to waterfalls, dips in the

river, and other personal growth activities. Every group goes on two unique adventure treks.

The first adventure is a strenuous day hike into a rain forest and to an open-air cave that becomes their home for two nights. While there, PWI students are treated to twelve waterfalls, four swimming holes, and more than 15 miles of hiking trails on 200 acres of pristine rain forest. All PWI students learn to rappel under the guidance of trained professionals. Students are provided safety gear and assistance to safely rappel down two waterfalls.

Toward the end of the trip, students travel by private bus to one of the last untouched preserves in Costa Rica, the Osa Peninsula. This trip to the southern coastal zone includes mangrove kayaking, river hiking, surfing, and evening bonfires on the beach. Students spend four nights at the beach, sleeping in grass-hut cabanas and surrounded by the wild sounds of the jungle.

Ecuador Beginning in Quito, students head off for 15 days in their homestay community. The work project is a combined effort of the PWI group, the community, and an on-site Peace Corps volunteer. Students might mix cement for use at the local school or build a playground for the town's children.

In the middle of the trip, students visit Intag Cloudforest Reserve, a paradise of virgin forest, to spend two days hiking and exploring the spectacular surroundings.

At the end of the trip, students fly to the Galapagos Islands. They see sea lions and curious iguanas basking in the sun. They visit with biologists who are studying at the Research Station and learn how these islands are unique. Traveling by boat throughout the islands, students explore the rich diversity of the Galapagos archipelago.

Peru Starting out in Cusco, students descend into the Sacred Valley of Urubamba to begin a volunteer service project at Casa de Milagros, a children's home. The PWI group helps develop the children's home facility and provide the hands needed for ongoing projects. Students can explore the surrounding area as they visit ruins and archeological sites, such as Ollantaytambo and Pisac, and discover the history and hear the personal stories of the Inca culture and its people.

After acclimating to the high elevations, students take a train to the Inca Trail and begin their journey. To reach their destination, students pass through the breathtaking Intipunku, the Doorway of the Sun, and explore the ruins of Machu Picchu, including the mystical hidden Temple of the Moon. Toward the middle of the trip, students take another adventure to Manu National Park, a virgin cloudforest reserve, to see a variety of monkeys and macaws.

FACILITIES

Participants use facilities that range from the homes of carefully selected host families to an open-air cave and grass-covered beach cabanas.

STAFF

Christopher Kealey, CEO and cofounder of Peace Works International, served two years as a Peace Corps volunteer in a rural Costa Rican community where he headed up various community service programs.

Randy Haley served two years as a Peace Corps volunteer in Costa Rica. He organized a youth group that developed projects in education, recreation, and community service. He has coordinated PWI's language program and presently supervises study-abroad programs.

Steve Risser has worked with PWI since 1998 and served as a Peace Corps volunteer in Costa Rica as an environmental education instructor for local children and students, from 1995 to 1997. He is an ESL (English as a second language) teaching assistant with the Santa Barbara School District.

Heather Kealey served as the Project Manager of Cultural Studies for PWI since 1995. She is currently a department chair and art teacher in Pasadena. She has traveled throughout Europe and Latin America and spent more than six months in rural Costa Rica assisting with English classes and learning Spanish.

Other staff members include Melissa Hall, Jen Gamez, Jennifer Werle, Nancy Maupin, Michael Bates, and Maria Jessop.

COSTS

The Costa Rica trip costs $3695; Peru, $3895; and Ecuador, $4395. The costs for all trips include transportation, food, lodging, entrance to national parks, the adventure tours, 15 hours of Spanish training, PWI and local-country staff members, project materials and supplies, and a donation to the community.

A $600 deposit must be sent with the application. PWI accepts checks with mailed applications. Credit card transactions for faxed and e-mailed applications must be completed by telephone.

TRANSPORTATION

The cost of each trip includes airfare from Los Angeles, California (or a prior-arranged city), to the airport in the country of destination; in-country transportation via train or private bus; in-country air flights; and, for those in Ecuador, a boat trip.

APPLICATION TIMETABLE

Applications can be downloaded from Peace Works International's Web site (listed below). Completed applications, along with a student's self-description (written on a separate paper), can be submitted via e-mail, fax, or mail to the contact points listed below. Applications without a self-description are not accepted.

Applications are accepted on a rolling basis. Most programs fill up by early March and April, and early applications receive priority consideration.

All participants must complete a medical form and have a valid U.S. passport.

FOR MORE INFORMATION, CONTACT:

Peace Works International
P.O. Box 70905
Pasadena, California 91117
626-798-5221
Fax: 626-798-2959
E-mail: info@peaceworksintl.org
World Wide Web: http://peaceworksintl.org

PEPPERDINE UNIVERSITY

SUMMER COLLEGE FOR HIGH SCHOOL STUDENTS

MALIBU, CALIFORNIA

Type of Program: Academic enrichment
Participants: High school juniors and seniors, coeducational
Enrollment: 50
Program Dates: July 5–July 31, 2004
Head of Program: Dana Dudley, Director of Summer School

LOCATION

Pepperdine is an independent, private university located on 830 acres in the Santa Monica Mountains overlooking the Pacific Ocean in Malibu, California. The University is recognized nationally for its excellent academic programs and enrolls approximately 8,000 full-time and part-time students in its five colleges and schools. Seaver College, the University's undergraduate college of letters, arts, and sciences, enrolls approximately 3,000 students, who reflect the highest standards of academic excellence and personal conduct.

BACKGROUND AND PHILOSOPHY

Pepperdine's Summer College for High School Students gives participants the opportunity to experience the academic challenge and social interaction of university life. Students enroll in undergraduate courses, receive college credit, live in undergraduate residences, and interact with Seaver College faculty members and students. The program emphasizes college preparation through enrichment curriculum, guest lectures from admissions counselors, and assistance with college applications and essays.

PROGRAM OFFERINGS

All Summer College program students enroll in a 3-unit course entitled Turning Points: Colleges, Careers, and Self-Assessment. This course begins in mid-June in an online format and is completed in a traditional classroom setting when students arrive at Pepperdine. Students examine the role of psychological assessments in decision making. They also complete several assessments and use the results to examine decisions regarding colleges, major selection, and, ultimately, career choices.

In addition to the Turning Points class, students enroll in a second course and may choose from any undergraduate course that does not require a prerequisite. Subjects include art, astronomy, business, communication, French, geology, history, humanities, math, nutrition, religion, Spanish, speech, and statistics. These courses are regular undergraduate offerings, and Summer College program students are in class with undergraduates.

Students also participate in an enrichment seminar, High School to 101: The Road to College. This is a noncredit seminar, which features presentations from admissions counselors, writing tutors, and other professionals. The goal of the seminar is to demystify the admissions process and to assist students in making tangible progress on college applications and essays.

ENROLLMENT

Summer College program students come from all over the United States as well as other countries. Motivated students of character who have completed their junior or senior year of high school are invited to apply. Admission is competitive, and application for early decision is encouraged.

DAILY SCHEDULE

Schedules vary, depending on course selection. Courses that begin at either 8 a.m. or 11:30 a.m. meet five days a week, and courses that begin after 2:30 p.m. meet Monday through Thursday. Friday afternoons are reserved for field trips, the High School to 101 seminar, and other activities. Students eat meals together in the dining hall. Students are given the freedom and responsibility to establish their own priorities and manage their own time.

EXTRA OPPORTUNITIES AND ACTIVITIES

Students are encouraged to attend activities planned for the undergraduate students by the Student Activities Office and the Student Government Association. In addition, field trips are planned specifically for Summer College program students. Possible field trips include the J. Paul Getty Museum, the Museum of Tolerance, Santa Monica Pier, Six Flags Magic Mountain, or Disney Land. In support of

Pepperdine's long tradition of service and volunteerism, students participate in one service project. Possible service sites include Food Share, Habitat for Humanity, or Union Rescue Mission.

FACILITIES

Students live together in undergraduate residence halls and are assigned by gender. They have access to all undergraduate facilities, including Payson Library, computer labs, tennis facilities, the swimming pool, the weight room, and the newly remodeled Sandbar student center.

STAFF

Courses are taught by Seaver College faculty members as well as distinguished visiting scholars from other universities. Trained resident advisers (RAs) live in the residence hall with Summer College program students. RAs are Seaver undergraduate students and are responsible for fostering a comfortable and supportive residential environment for all students. They are available to provide advice and guidance to students as they acclimate to college living. RAs are supported by the Office of Housing and Community Living and have a team of resident directors, resident director assistants, and an associate dean, who are all committed to providing a safe and supportive living environment.

MEDICAL CARE

The Health Center on the campus is available to all students for any routine medical needs. The Health Center includes board-certified physicians and physician assistants as well as registered nurses, who are on call 24 hours a day. Any nonroutine needs or emergencies are handled by nearby facilities, such as the St. John's Urgent Care in Malibu and the Santa Monica/UCLA Medical Center.

RELIGIOUS LIFE

Pepperdine University is affiliated with the Churches of Christ and maintains a dual commitment to academic excellence and Christian values. Faculty members, administrators, and members of the University's governing Board of Regents represent many religious backgrounds, and students of all faiths are welcome. Students may attend religious services at any nearby church, synagogue, or Islamic center.

COSTS

The 2004 program fee of $6100 includes two academic courses, room, board, and program-sponsored activities. The program fee for commuter students is $5130 and includes all of the services available to residential students except room and board. Books are not included in the program fee.

TRANSPORTATION

Los Angeles International Airport is the closest of the L.A. airports to Pepperdine. Students can take a shuttle directly to the campus.

APPLICATION TIMETABLE

The application deadline is April 15. For early decision, the application deadline is March 15. Inquiries are welcome at any time. Summer College program course schedules and applications are available in January. Because admission is selective and space is limited, students are encouraged to apply for early decision. Early decision applications are evaluated as soon as they are received, and students are notified of the committee's decision within two to three weeks.

For more information, contact:

Dana Dudley, Director
Pepperdine University
Seaver Dean's Office/Summer School
24255 Pacific Coast Highway
Malibu, California 90263-4280
310-506-6079
Fax: 310-506-4816
E-mail: Leslie.Seah@pepperdine.edu
World Wide Web: http://seaver.pepperdine.edu/summerschool/summercollege.htm

PERFORMANCE PLUS

POSITIVE LEARNING USING THE STAGE/STUDIO/SCREEN

NEW HAMPTON SCHOOL

NEW HAMPTON, NEW HAMPSHIRE

Type of Program: Performing arts training program
Participants: Coed, ages 13–18, boarding
Enrollment: 70–80 students
Program Dates: Three weeks in July
Heads of Program: Morgan Murphy, Artistic Director; Lori Ann Murphy, Producing Director

LOCATION

The 300-acre New Hampton School campus is nestled in the midst of the Lakes Region and the White Mountains. The 185-year-old private campus comprises traditional ivy-covered academic buildings, a fishing pond, and a new Arts and Athletics Center. McEvoy Theater contains state-of-the-art sound and lighting equipment, and the music facility features a professional recording studio. Other facilities include a dance studio and the radio station WNHS. The New Hampton campus is off I-93 at exit 23, 30 miles north of Concord, New Hampshire, and 100 miles north of Boston, Massachusetts.

BACKGROUND AND PHILOSOPHY

Morgan Murphy, founder and Artistic Director of Performance PLUS, served as the Arts Director at New Hampton School from 1992–2001. Performance PLUS is the culmination of twelve years of his exploration into the celebration of the arts as a path for adolescent development. Mr. Murphy and his professional staff utilize the performing arts as a guide for positive artistic growth with respect, responsibility, and relationships as their founding principles. Performance PLUS offers hands-on professional training in the performing arts and related fields of interest for the ambitious, experienced artist as well as the novice artistic explorer. Through knowing the participants and creating art together, the Performance PLUS staff assists participants in making connections that allow artistic success to filter into all aspects of life.

PROGRAM OFFERINGS

Performance PLUS offers five disciplines on which to focus. Participants must choose one area of focus.

Theater Arts and Contemporary Performance Students focused on theater arts are challenged to explore and discover their potential as theater artists and to perform in various styles of theater and related disciplines while studying the masters. Through the use of in-class activities, various texts, guest artists, and selected adventures/exercises, students enhance their performance and presentation skills, gain appreciation for the craft of theater and the necessary disciplines, and discover what they can bring to any role and to their futures—themselves. Different aspects of theater arts include contemporary drama and comedy, improvisation, screen acting, musical theater, performance art, scene study, physical character, classical theater, writing, mask, and stage combat.

Music Production and Recording Participants in the music program perform in their own band while exploring the sound recording and engineering processes and cutting a CD in a state-of-the-art recording studio. Students may realize their potential studying voice or any instrument. Participants explore digital multitrack recording, song writing, and sound engineering.

Dance The dance program allows students to condition their bodies, skills, and minds for a lifetime. Program offerings include technique, choreography, alignment, character movement, and modern, jazz, classical, and hip-hop dance.

Film The film program allows students to bring their imagination to all production aspects of an original film. Students work with an established independent film writer, producer, and director. Different aspects of film include producing, directing, writing, camera manipulation, lighting, sound, location and studio shoots, and digital editing.

Technical Production Through the use of imagination, technology, the body, and creative spirit, participants challenge themselves in all areas of technical design and production. These different areas of focus include scenic design, lighting design, sound design, technical direction, stage management, computer-aided design, film and TV production, scenic artistry, costume design, and scenic construction.

DAILY SCHEDULE

The following is a typical day's schedule. There are also activities throughout the day on Sundays.

Monday–Saturday

7:30–8:30	Breakfast
8:30–9:30	Meeting and warm-up
9:30–12:00	Rehearsal
12:00–1:00	Lunch
1:00–3:00	Rehearsal
3:00–5:00	Workshops/activities
5:00–6:00	Dinner
6:00–10:00	Studio/evening activities
10:00	Dorm check-in

EXTRA OPPORTUNITIES AND ACTIVITIES

Students produce their own original Performance PLUS SHOWCASE, CD presentation, dance concert, or film presentation, highlighting the accomplishments of each participant, at the end of the three-week session. This event takes place on the final day of the

program. Also included are several outings, including professional productions and Sunday recreational activity trips. Numerous workshops are held by staff members and visiting professional artists.

FACILITIES

Performance PLUS members stay in dormitories on the New Hampton School campus and have access to state-of-the-art athletic and arts facilities, the Academic Research Center, computer labs, and, of course, the White Mountains.

STAFF

The Performance PLUS staff is made up of a coed team of full-time and part-time teachers and several college apprentices who serve as their assistants. This diverse group of performing artists lives, eats, and works with participants on a daily basis. All staff members are current professionals in the industry or have professional backgrounds. Full-time staff members serve as dorm parents and weekend activity leaders. The participant-staff ratio is 6:1.

MEDICAL CARE

New Hampton offers an on-campus health center and doctor's office. Lakes Region General Hospital is only 20 minutes away. Medical insurance is required for participation.

COSTS

Tuition for Performance PLUS is $3600 for boarding students. There is an additional $400 equipment fee for film participants. Included in this cost are three meals a day, field trips, guest artists, professional production outings, and planned activities. Participants must bring extra money for personal items or souvenirs. A recommended amount of spending money ranges from $50 to $150, which must be deposited in an allowance account and distributed through the bookstore on the New Hampton School campus.

FINANCIAL AID

Financial aid is available for those who qualify. Financial aid awards are based on financial need and a sense of commitment to the program.

TRANSPORTATION

The airport in Manchester, New Hampshire, is located less than 1 hour from New Hampton, and Logan International Airport in Boston, Massachusetts, is located less than 2 hours away. Rental cars and taxis are available at both locations. Special arrangements may be made. Performance PLUS offers transportation to and from Manchester Airport for an additional charge.

APPLICATION TIMETABLE

There is open enrollment for Performance PLUS until all spaces fill. A registration form, personal statement, and nonrefundable $500 deposit are required for admission. A complete welcome packet is mailed upon receipt of the registration form, which assists participants in preparation for the program.

For more information, contact:

Morgan and Lori Murphy
Performance PLUS
New Hampton School
70 Main Street
P.O. Box 579
New Hampton, New Hampshire 03256
603-677-3403
Fax: 603-677-3481
E-mail: lmurphy@performanceplus.org
World Wide Web: http://www.performanceplus.org

PERFORMING ARTS INSTITUTE OF WYOMING SEMINARY

PERFORMING ARTS PROGRAM

KINGSTON, PENNSYLVANIA

Type of Program: Coeducational residential and day summer performing arts program
Participants: Girls and boys, ages 12–18; dance, ages 10–18
Enrollment: 200 per session
Program Dates: Six-week session, June 26 to August 7, 2005; first 3-week session, June 26 to July 16, 2005; second 3-week session, July 17 to August 7, 2005; dance program, June 26 to July 24, 2005
Head of Program: Nancy Sanderson, Director

LOCATION

The Performing Arts Institute is located on the 18-acre campus of Wyoming Seminary in a small-town residential setting that adjoins the recreation areas of the Pocono and Endless Mountains, lakes, and state parks. Nearby cultural resources include professional performing arts venues, museums, and historic sites. Movie theaters, shopping, and restaurants are within walking distance. Kingston is approximately 2 hours from Philadelphia and New York City.

BACKGROUND AND PHILOSOPHY

The Performing Arts Institute is part of the Summer at Sem program established in 1991 at Wyoming Seminary College Preparatory School (founded 1844). Rigorous programs in instrumental music, musical theater, and dance aim to serve serious artists who seek to master their craft as either avocation or career. As a preprofessional program, the Institute prepares students for conservatory entrance auditions by providing academic training and performance experience at the highest level. Students work closely with an international faculty, gaining exposure to individual visions and styles in performing major works from the standard repertory. Resident conductors and teachers perform with students, coach them, and conduct master classes, serving as both mentors and friends.

PROGRAM OFFERINGS

Music Offerings follow individualized tracks. String musicians participate in large and small ensembles (symphony orchestra, string orchestra, and chamber groups), as do wind musicians (wind ensemble; symphony orchestra; jazz band; and mixed, woodwind, and brass chamber groups). Orchestral and wind tracks also include daily theory and master classes as well as an Institute-wide choral program that emphasizes solfeggio and sight-reading. Vocalists participate in two choruses as well as theory classes; they may take musical theater or piano skills, opera, and master classes. Pianists, guitarists, and percussionists participate in large and small ensembles, master classes, and chorus, as do jazz musicians, who apply improvisation skills in small combos and big bands. Every ensemble rehearses 1 to 2 hours each day; students devote 2 hours daily to individual practice. All students take at least one private lesson a week; instruction is offered in all instruments, voice, composition, and conducting. Public concerts are held each Friday, Saturday, and Sunday; student solo recitals are held each Wednesday.

Musical Theater This program combines music, theory, acting while singing, and dance to give participants full exposure to the Broadway musical. Daily rehearsals focus on stage direction, dance, and vocal technique. The program culminates in a full-scale, faculty-choreographed and -directed production featuring the students. Past productions include *Into the Woods, Dear World, The Mystery of Edwin Drood, Cabaret, West Side Story,* and *Les Misérables,* high school edition.

Dance Offerings include classical ballet, modern dance, jazz, and improvisation and encompass standard dance methodologies from Vaganova to Paul Taylor. All dancers take intermediate- or advanced-level classes in technique and in pointe, partnering, variations, or modern and jazz. Rehearsals are held daily for a full dance production. Dancers may remain for the final two weeks to participate in the musical theater production.

ENROLLMENT

The Performing Arts Institute enrolls a total of 180 students per session, according to ensemble needs and residence hall capacity. Music applicants must submit an application form, references from a music teacher and a school teacher, a musical resume, and an audiotape demonstrating technical and expressive ability in a variety of musical styles. Live auditions are optional.

DAILY SCHEDULE
Following breakfast, classes and rehearsals are scheduled from 9 to noon and from 1 to 6. Lunch is from noon to 1, and dinner is from 6 to 7. Recreation and evening performances begin at 8. Boarding students must check into their dormitories by 10.

EXTRA OPPORTUNITIES AND ACTIVITIES
Students may utilize campus athletic fields, tennis courts, gymnasiums with fitness rooms and an Olympic-size swimming pool, and the student center with lounges, game rooms, and a wide-screen television. Extracurricular activities include sports, picnics, dances, films, and off-campus trips. Students socialize with the entire Summer at Sem community, including many international students who are attracted to the renowned English as a second language program.

FACILITIES
Performance sites include a 400-seat concert hall/ theater, with dance studios, a scene shop, and rehearsal and practice rooms; a flexible-space recital hall; a church with pipe organ; and several outdoor settings. Residence halls are designated men- or women-only. The dining hall, library, studio art rooms, computer labs, athletic center, and student center are open to summer students. Administrative offices are on campus.

STAFF
Performing Arts Institute faculty members include distinguished conductors, performers, coaches, and teachers from conservatories, colleges and universities, and schools worldwide. The string quartet in residence program and famous guest artists enhance instruction with workshops and master classes. A full-time Performing Arts faculty of approximately 50 members is supplemented by 24 university music students who serve as counselors and resident assistants under the Director of Residential Life.

MEDICAL CARE
Medical personnel are on staff throughout the summer. Wilkes-Barre General Hospital is located less than 10 minutes from the Wyoming Seminary campus.

RELIGIOUS LIFE
Churches and synagogues are within walking distance of campus. Students may participate in religious services of their choice.

COSTS
In 2004, the cost for the six-week day program (music, musical theater) was $1600; the six-week residential fee was $4200. Three-week costs (music only) were $800 for day students and $2200 for residential

students. 2004 fees for the dance program were $1100 for day students and $3050 for residential students. Students are also charged $40 per 1-hour private lesson. Spending money is discretionary.

FINANCIAL AID
Performance grants are allocated according to financial and ensemble needs.

TRANSPORTATION
The Wilkes-Barre/Scranton Airport is served by major commercial airlines that offer direct or connecting flights from U.S. metropolitan centers. Limousine service is available for the 20-minute ride to Wyoming Seminary. The school is 1 mile from central Wilkes-Barre, which is served by national bus lines and is easily accessible from Interstates 80 and 81 and the Pennsylvania Turnpike.

APPLICATION TIMETABLE
Applications are available in early January and are accepted until ensemble requirements are met. Application by April 15 is strongly advised. An application fee of $25 is required, and a deposit is required upon acceptance.

For more information, contact:

Nancy Sanderson, Director
Performing Arts Institute of Wyoming Seminary
201 North Sprague Avenue
Kingston, Pennsylvania 18704-3593
570-270-2186
Fax: 570-270-2198
E-mail: onstage@wyomingseminary.org
World Wide Web: http://www.wyomingseminary.org/pai

PERRY-MANSFIELD PERFORMING ARTS SCHOOL & CAMP

SUMMER PROGRAM

STEAMBOAT SPRINGS, COLORADO

Type of Program: An intensive performing arts summer school. Classes are offered in theater, musical theater, dance, and dramatic writing, with electives in visual arts and equitation.

Participants: Coeducational, age 8–senior in college

Enrollment: 350

Program Dates: Two 4-week Junior/Intermediate Programs (entering grades 5–9), June to August. High School/College Program (entering grade 10–college), June to July. Two 1-week Discovery Programs (ages 8–11), June to August. Two 1-week Equestrian Programs, week one (ages 10–12) and week two (ages 13–16), June to August.

Head of Program: June Lindenmayer, Executive Director

LOCATION

Perry-Mansfield is located in Steamboat Springs, Colorado, 150 miles northwest of Denver. Steamboat Springs, a small Rocky Mountain community of 10,000, is rich with Western charm and natural beauty, making it a popular vacation destination.

Nestled in the hills of beautiful Strawberry Park, Perry-Mansfield's rustic 75-acre campus provides students with a safe, nurturing environment in which to learn. Students spend their days in open-air studios, which are naturally landscaped with grassy meadows, aspen groves, and alpine ponds.

BACKGROUND AND PHILOSOPHY

In 1913, Charlotte Perry and Portia Mansfield fulfilled their dreams of creating a theater and dance camp in the mountains. Now, ninety years later, Perry-Mansfield is recognized as the oldest continuously operating performing arts school and camp in the nation. Throughout the years, a number of distinguished alumni, faculty members, and guest artists have passed through the doors of Perry-Mansfield. The list includes Robert Battle, Sammy Bayes, Jessica Biel, Ruthanna Boris, John Cage, Wally Cardona, Martha Clarke, Merce Cunningham, Harriette Ann Gray, Julie Harris, Dustin Hoffman, Hanya Holm, Lee Horsley, Doris Humphrey, José Limon, Agnes de Mille, Daniel Nagrin, Jason Raize, Lee Remick, Amala Shankar, Ton Simons, Frances Sternhagen, Helen Tamiris, Joan Van Ark, and Charles Weidman.

Today, students from all over the world take classes from a select group of accomplished and internationally renowned faculty members. The tradition of Perry-Mansfield remains unsurpassed as the camp continues to prepare emerging young artists for the stage. Recent alumni are performing with Ballet Hispanico, Munich Ballet, Paul Taylor, Nederlands Dans Theatre, and on Broadway and television. Students are invited to share in the magic of Perry-Mansfield.

PROGRAM OFFERINGS

At the high school/college level, the Theater Program offers classes in acting, advanced acting, scene study, voice and movement, acting Shakespeare, directing, production, stage combat, and audition workshop. The Musical Theater Program offers classes in musicianship, explorations in ear training, and rhythmic foundations. Core studies are offered in musical scene study and audition technique, original works (cabaret and song writing), great shows, and great performers (learning the repertoire and movement for the singing actor). The Dance Program offers classes in ballet, modern, jazz, repertory, dance composition, pointe, tap, and trapeze. Students have the opportunity to learn to perform repertory from both faculty members and guest artists.

At the junior (grades 5–7) and intermediate (grades 8–9) levels, the Theater Program offers classes in creative dramatics for the juniors and intermediate acting for the intermediates. An accelerated class is available to the advanced intermediate by audition only. The Musical Theater Program offers classes in foundations in musical theater, performance skills for the young singing actor, and musical theater workshop. The Dance Program offers classes in ballet, modern, jazz, dance composition, tap, and trapeze.

Discovery Camp is for students ages 8–11. Discovery Camp serves as an introduction to performing arts. Children spend their mornings taking classes in theater, dance, music, creative writing, and visual arts. Discovery students have a preset curriculum and do not register for classes. Each afternoon, students participate in traditional camp activities such as horseback riding, hiking, and local field trips. At the end of each week, campers present a final showcase, to which all parents are invited.

Equestrian Camp is for students ages 10–12 (session one) and ages 13–16 (session two). The Equestrian Program teaches students horsemanship and riding instruction. Riders learn the fundamentals of horse care, training, dressage, and jumping. Students choose from either English or Western styles of riding.

ENROLLMENT
This community provides a safe, nurturing atmosphere for approximately 350 residential and day students.

EXTRA OPPORTUNITIES AND ACTIVITIES
Students can take private voice, piano, flute, and riding lessons. Students also have the opportunity to enjoy the Rocky Mountains with planned hiking and rafting trips and trips to the hot springs and pool. Local events, including the Balloon Rodeo, Art in the Park, and the Fourth of July Parade, are all a part of the summer experience at Perry-Mansfield.

FACILITIES
There are four dance studios, two theaters, two art studios, rehearsal spaces, a dramatic writing studio, a music composition lab, an infirmary, a dining hall, a scene shop, a cantina, a camp store, stables, a barn, and riding arenas. All buildings are equipped with fire extinguishers and smoke alarms. Students and staff members are informed of fire evacuation plans and a fire drill is conducted at the beginning of each camp session.

STAFF
Perry-Mansfield prides itself on its renowned faculty members who come from all over the United States and abroad. Counselors are selected based on their experience with children and must participate in a weeklong training program. Both faculty and staff members must pass a background check before being hired. The staff-camper ratio is 1:2.

MEDICAL CARE
Two registered nurses reside on campus and are available 24 hours a day. Perry-Mansfield has an infirmary where all medication is stored and administered. Students are insured by Perry-Mansfield while at camp for accidents and illnesses; however, preexisting conditions are not covered. Yampa Valley Medical Center is located 7 miles from the campus.

COSTS
Tuition for the High School/College Program is $3755. For the Junior/Intermediate Program, tuition is $3055. For a one-week session in the Discovery Program, tuition is $800. The Equestrian Program tuition is $875 for either session. Day-student rates vary, based on the number of classes taken. For the High School/College Program, the rate ranges from $495 to $1195. For the Junior/Intermediate Program, the rate ranges from $350 to $830. The Discovery Camp day-student tuition is $450 for a one-week session. The Equestrian day-student tuition is $500.

FINANCIAL AID
Scholarships are awarded in the areas of theater, musical theater and dance. Scholarships are merit based. Those interested in applying for a scholarship can participate in a live audition or submit a video to be viewed by the appropriate departmental faculty members and directors.

Work-study is awarded based on need. Positions available are studio host, dining hall attendant, camp beautification, and equestrian wrangler. The equestrian wrangler positions are filled strictly with students having a strong background in equitation. For more information, prospective students should call the Perry-Mansfield office at the toll-free number listed below.

TRANSPORTATION
Arrangements for transportation from Denver International Airport can be arranged through Alpine Taxi, a Steamboat company providing shuttle service from the airport to Perry-Mansfield. Alpine Taxi's toll-free number is 800-343-7433. Students flying into Yampa Valley Regional Airport in Hayden (the closest airport to the camp) are picked up by a Perry-Mansfield staff member. United Airlines is the official airlines of Perry-Mansfield Performing Arts School and Camp and provides special discounts to campers and staff members flying into Denver and Hayden.

APPLICATION TIMETABLE
Inquiries are welcome throughout the year. Registrations are accepted on a first-come, first-served basis beginning in September until all available spaces are filled. Tuition is due in full no later than April 1. Enrollments after April 1 must be paid in full.

FOR MORE INFORMATION, CONTACT:
Perry-Mansfield Performing Arts School and Camp
40755 RCR 36
Steamboat Springs, Colorado 80487
800-430-2787 (toll-free)
Fax: 970-879-5823
E-mail: p-m@perry-mansfield.org
World Wide Web: http://www.perry-mansfield.org

THE PHILLIPS ACADEMY SUMMER SESSION

SUMMER SCHOOL

ANDOVER, MASSACHUSETTS

Type of Program: Academic enrichment, precollege
Participants: Coeducational, boarding and day, rising grades 9–12
Enrollment: 500
Program Dates: June 28 to August 3
Head of Program: Ralph C. Bledsoe, Director

LOCATION

The buildings and facilities of the Academy are located on 500 acres of landscaped campus. Andover, Massachusetts, incorporated in 1646, is an attractive elm-shaded community 25 miles north of Boston and close to historical sites, the mountains, and the seacoast locations of New England.

BACKGROUND AND PHILOSOPHY

Fostering a passion for lifelong learning, the Summer Session combines a full boarding (precollege) experience with small classes in a multicultural community. Innovative pedagogy complements traditional areas. The Summer Session offers its students five weeks of intensive academic and personal growth—growth that can certainly make a difference beyond the limits of this program and this campus.

The Summer Session program encompasses demanding classes, recreational afternoon activities, engaging trips to colleges, social and cultural opportunities, and welcoming dormitories that prepare students for collegiate residential life in an environment designed for their age group.

Here for five weeks, students with impressive academic goals prepare for the rigors of the best colleges and for the rigors of thriving and serving in this complex world.

PROGRAM OFFERINGS

There are more than sixty course and program offerings in Literature and Writing, Computer Programming, Computer Animation, Mathematics, the Natural Sciences, Philosophy, the Social Sciences, Languages, Speech and Debate, English as a Second Language, and SAT Prep, as well as an Intensive Writing Workshop specifically for day students. In addition, there is a Music Performance program and courses in the visual and performing arts. The average class size is 14.

The Summer Session has an organized recreational activities program. Sports such as basketball, tennis, swimming, soccer, softball, volleyball, aerobics, dance, physical fitness, and squash are offered. All activities are coed. The numerous Academy music studios, playing fields and tennis courts, the gymnasium, and the six-lane swimming pool provide excellent facilities for both scheduled and informal activities.

Of additional interest are a number of activities, such as Outdoor Adventure, that are not always available in secondary schools.

ENROLLMENT

Summer Session students represent an extraordinary diversity of geography, religion, race, and economic circumstances. They represent approximately forty-five states, the District of Columbia, and Puerto Rico and more than thirty other countries; approximately 15 percent are granted financial aid.

The Admission Committee looks for evidence that the applicant has the intellectual ability, the industry, and the character to make the most of the Summer Session opportunity. The Committee expects the applicant to have a strong school record and a serious desire to spend the summer in challenging, disciplined study.

DAILY SCHEDULE

Classes meet Monday through Saturday, and the daily schedule depends on the courses or program selected. Students minimally spend 18 hours per week in class. It is assumed that at least 1½ hours are spent preparing for each class meeting.

College workshops are held Monday, Tuesday, Thursday, and Friday afternoons. Academic resource areas, including the Math Center, Writing Center, library, photo lab, art studio, music studios, and all computer labs, are available for use by all students. Study hours are kept in dormitories and academic resource areas.

EXTRA OPPORTUNITIES AND ACTIVITIES

Special trips and tours offer travel to museums, Red Sox games, the beach, a whale-watching expedition,

Tanglewood concerts, and other activities. There are also trips to nearby colleges in addition to the regularly scheduled college counseling workshops.

Weekly colloquia provide the opportunity to hear and discuss ideas on a range of contemporary topics with scholars, artists, activists, and other speakers. The diversity of the community is highlighted in international celebrations, and students share their talents in self-initiated shows.

FACILITIES

In addition to six classroom buildings, the campus encompasses a 120,000-volume library, an impressive athletic complex, the Addison Gallery of American Art, the newly constructed Gelb Science Center, the Peabody Museum of Archaeology, the Moncrieff Cochran Sanctuary, the Elson Art Center, Isham Health Center, a computer center, a theater complex, and forty-three dormitories.

STAFF

The teaching faculty members, teachers from private and public schools and colleges as well as Phillips Academy, are selected for their excellence in the classroom and their understanding of young people. The senior teaching staff is augmented by a corps of some 20 teaching assistants, recent college graduates whose enthusiasm for learning serves as a model for serious but joyful intellectual inquiry.

MEDICAL CARE

The Isham Health Center is licensed as a hospital by the Commonwealth of Massachusetts. Registered nurses are on duty at all times, and, in addition to having usual office hours, a physician is always on call.

RELIGIOUS LIFE

In the town of Andover, there are Protestant churches of several denominations, a Roman-Catholic church, and a Jewish Reform temple, all of which welcome students of the Summer Session for worship.

COSTS

In 2004, the $5000 charge for boarding students included tuition, board, room, linens, and supplemental medical insurance. The day-student charge of $3500 covered tuition, supplemental medical insurance, and all meals. The nonrefundable application fee ($50 for U.S. students, $80 for international students) must accompany the application. Within two weeks of acceptance, the student must pay a nonrefundable $1000 deposit, which is credited toward the tuition charge.

Expenditures for books, trips, tours, and extras (such as spending money) should be approximately $500–$700.

FINANCIAL AID

Financial aid is awarded according to financial need. The Summer Session Financial Aid Form must be requested, completed as directed, and postmarked no later than March 1.

TRANSPORTATION

The Academy provides transportation upon arrival and departure to and from Boston's Logan International Airport and the Manchester, New Hampshire, airport at specified times. Train and bus access is available.

APPLICATION TIMETABLE

Catalogs containing application forms may be obtained in November. Courses often fill quickly; it is therefore advantageous to apply as early as possible. The suggested deadline is April 7.

All application materials—the recommendations, transcript, autobiographical statement, other required forms, and fee—should be placed in the envelope provided and mailed to the Phillips Academy Summer Session.

FOR MORE INFORMATION, CONTACT:

Maxine S. Grogan, Dean of Admission
The Phillips Academy Summer Session
Phillips Academy
180 Main Street
Andover, Massachusetts 01810-4166
978-749-4400
Fax: 978-749-4414
E-mail: summersession@andover.edu
World Wide Web: http://www.andover.edu

PARTICIPANT/FAMILY COMMENTS

"The experience of living with her peers from other parts of the world helped our daughter immeasurably to assess her priorities as she enters high school and looks towards college."

"He loved his teachers and especially his class discussions. . . . The Session helped him to develop independence, social maturity and the ability to relate to students from diverse backgrounds."

"It gave me the opportunity to meet new and invigorating people, to overcome the various challenges that came with dorm life, and to excel in an intellectual and stimulating environment. It will forever be a special summer in my mind."

PHILLIPS EXETER ACADEMY

SUMMER SCHOOL

EXETER, NEW HAMPSHIRE

Type of Program: Academic enrichment
Participants: Coeducational, grades 8–12 and postgraduate year
Enrollment: 590
Program Dates: Five-week program; July 4–August 7, 2004
Head of Program: Douglas G. Rogers, Director

LOCATION

The 400-acre Phillips Exeter Academy campus is located in the town of Exeter, Colonial capital of New Hampshire, which is in the heart of the state's seacoast area. Boston, Newburyport, Portsmouth, and the White Mountains are all within easy access for excursions.

BACKGROUND AND PHILOSOPHY

Every summer, Phillips Exeter Academy welcomes to the campus some 590 students for five weeks of academic study, athletics, and exploration that carry participants far beyond the classrooms and the playing fields. Typically, students come from more than forty states; Puerto Rico; Washington, D.C.; and several dozen foreign nations. Most reside in campus dormitories; others travel daily from their homes in the New Hampshire seacoast area. Together they embody a rich diversity of language, culture, religion, and race. They come to Exeter with that particular mix of intellectual curiosity and adventurous spirit that holds the promise of glimpsing new horizons and making new discoveries.

PROGRAM OFFERINGS

Exeter's Upper School offers programs of study for high school students entering grades 10 and beyond. Students create their own academic programs by selecting three courses from the more than 100 offered in a wide range of disciplines. Students may choose to concentrate on a specific academic area, taking science courses such as Introduction to Physics, Marine Biology, and Animal Behavior, or arts courses such as Photography, Sculpture, and Architecture. More often, however, they elect to balance the arts and sciences, enrolling in Creative Writing, American Government, and Problem-Solving in Algebra, or Shakespeare Unplugged, Ancient Egypt, and Introduction to Chemistry. Whatever their academic choices, students find themselves working in small classes with highly experienced, dedicated teachers. During the five-week term, they have full access to the Academy's exceptional facilities, including the state-of-the-art Phelps Science Center and the Class of 1945 Library, the largest secondary school library in the world.

Younger students, those entering grades 8 and 9, may apply for the Access Exeter program, which offers accelerated studies in five different academic clusters. Each cluster consists of three courses organized around a central theme: The American Experience in War, The Land and the Sea, Problem-Solving: An Odyssey of the Mind, A Global Community, and The Creative Arts. Each cluster emphasizes hands-on learning, or participatory education, both in and beyond the classroom. Students in The Land and the Sea program, for example, venture out to Appledore Island on the Isles of Shoals and go whale-watching along Jeffreys Ledge off the coast of Massachusetts. At midterm, all Access Exeter students and their teachers depart campus for a two-night/three-day excursion; students in A Global Community program travel to Quebec, where they immerse themselves in the French-speaking Canadian culture.

Complementing the academic curriculum, the Summer School offers a physical education program that is an essential part of the student's Exeter experience. For two 12-day sessions, students participate in a variety of physical activities that include tennis, soccer, softball, basketball, track and field, lacrosse, aerobics, weight training, and water polo. Upper School students may also apply for the crew program, an option in physical education that provides rowing instruction for both experienced and novice rowers and coxswains.

ENROLLMENT

Students come to the Summer School from about thirty countries and more than forty states. Students of all racial, religious, and social backgrounds are welcome.

DAILY SCHEDULE

Academic and athletics classes are required appointments. When students do not have required appointments, they are expected to use their time productively. Dormitory check-in is at 9 p.m. (11 p.m. on Saturday), and the dorm is expected to be conducive to study after this time. Students should be mature enough to regulate their behavior; antisocial behavior may result in disciplinary action. Disciplinary procedures are designed to teach the student the value of integrity. The daily schedule for students enrolled in Access Exeter varies slightly from the schedule observed by older students.

EXTRA OPPORTUNITIES AND ACTIVITIES

Educational and recreational excursions are a regular feature of Wednesday afternoons and weekends, when there are no required appointments. Such excursions are optional and may consist of a hike in the White Mountains, tours of New England colleges, a Boston museum visit, or a whale watch. Extracurricular activities include theater, music, and various sports. Students are encouraged to enjoy the cultural and ethnic diversity that is at the heart of the Exeter Summer School experience.

On Beyond Exeter At the conclusion of Summer School, five small groups of students travel with Academy instructors for an additional week of exploration and discovery. The On Beyond Exeter programs afford students exciting opportunities to travel to sites beyond the

Exeter campus, to live with a small number of like-minded peers, and to continue the hands-on education of the Summer School experience. Exeter's Summer Session 2004 offered five different courses of study for Upper School students: Art Along the Coast of Maine, Marine Biology in the Warm Waters of the Bahamas, The Heart of Shakespeare's England, Community Service: Giving Something Back, and Aboard the Spirit of Massachusetts: Sailing with the Whales. The courses have limited enrollment and require an additional tuition that covers all expenses: transportation, lodging, meals, and entertainment. All On Beyond Exeter programs begin after the conclusion of the main Summer School schedule. Limited financial assistance is available for this program.

FACILITIES

Exeter is proud of its outstanding academic and athletic facilities. The centerpiece of the campus is Louis Kahn's architectural landmark, the Phillips Exeter Library, which has a capacity of 250,000 volumes and can seat 400 students. The collection currently consists of 150,000 volumes in addition to an extensive collection of tapes, albums, and compact discs. The library houses one of the academy's six computer labs. Equally imposing is the Love Gymnasium, with its five basketball floors, two ice rinks, two pools, fifteen squash courts, a weight-training room, a dance room, and a training room. Outside there are acres of baseball diamonds, soccer fields, tennis courts, an all-weather 400-meter track, and a cross-country course through the nature preserve.

The Forrestal-Bowld Music Center is a state-of-the-art facility with more than 24,000 square feet of space dedicated to the study of music. In addition to three large rehearsal rooms, there are eleven teacher studios, eight of them equipped with grand pianos, and sixteen practice rooms with upright pianos. New to the campus in fall 2001 was the Phelps Science Center, a $38-million complex that offers students and teachers outstanding facilities for scientific investigation and study. Other highlights of the campus are the two-stage Fisher Theater, the Frederick R. Mayer Art Center and Lamont Gallery, and the Grainger Observatory.

STAFF

The majority of the Summer School's instructors are Phillips Exeter Academy faculty members. Additional qualified instructors are recruited from other schools and universities, and many have made long-term commitments to teaching Summer School.

MEDICAL CARE

The infirmary is staffed 24 hours a day. Exeter Hospital, just minutes away, offers emergency medical service. Enrollment in the Summer School Group Insurance Plan is included in the tuition.

RELIGIOUS LIFE

The Summer School is nondenominational; students may attend religious services at nearby churches and synagogues if they wish.

COSTS

Boarding tuition for the 2004 Summer School was $5295 for Upper School students. The Access Exeter boarding tuition was $5595 (including required excursion fee). A nonrefundable $1500 deposit is due at the time of enrollment, with the balance due on May 15. The 2004 tuition for day students was $995 per course. It was $3395, including the required excursion fee, for Access Exeter day students. Courses of study and travel offered in the On Beyond Exeter program require a separate tuition.

FINANCIAL AID

Limited financial aid is available. The deadline for financial aid application is March 1.

APPLICATION TIMETABLE

Admission to the Phillips Exeter Academy Summer School is competitive and is based on academic achievement and motivation. There is a rolling admission procedure, and only completed applications can be considered. Since many courses fill up rapidly, it is in the candidate's best interest to complete the application as early as possible. Application and teacher reference forms are to be found in the Summer School catalog. A separate application form is required for those students who wish to participate in Access Exeter.

For more information, contact:

Douglas G. Rogers, Director
Phillips Exeter Summer School
20 Main Street
Exeter, New Hampshire 03833-2460
603-777-3488
800-828-4325 Ext. 3488 (toll-free)
Fax: 603-777-4385
E-mail: summer@exeter.edu
World Wide Web: http://www.exeter.edu/summer

PINE RIDGE SCHOOL

SUMMER PROGRAM

WILLISTON, VERMONT

Type of Program: Intensive six-week academic, social, and personal enrichment program for learning disabled students with specific language-based learning disabilities and nonverbal learning disabilities
Participants: Coeducational, ages 9–18
Enrollment: 45 students
Program Dates: July 4 to August 14, 2004
Head of Program: Anne DeVos, Director

LOCATION

Nestled at the foot of rural Vermont's Green Mountains, the Pine Ridge campus encompasses more than 100 acres, yet is only 8 miles from Burlington, Vermont's largest city and home to the University of Vermont. Recent studies have ranked Vermont as one of the two safest states and Burlington as one of America's best places to live.

BACKGROUND AND PHILOSOPHY

Founded in 1968, the Pine Ridge School characterizes itself and its mission as "an educational community committed to assisting adolescents with learning disabilities to define and achieve success throughout their lives." The staff understands the frustrations and needs, as well as the rich potential, of learning disabled students. Pine Ridge addresses students as unique individuals, with strengths, weaknesses, talents, gifts, and abilities to be recognized and developed. Realizing that students have individual learning styles and needs, Pine Ridge provides a highly structured and individualized program in a success-oriented environment where students live, learn, grow, and have fun together in coordinated academic and social activities.

PROGRAM OFFERINGS

The Summer Program utilizes a highly structured approach to language learning, including such components as word attack, spelling, handwriting, comprehension, and composition. For two periods daily, five days a week, each student meets with his or her own tutor. Some tutors are enrolled in the Pine Ridge Summer Internship in Learning Disabilities, a closely supervised course of study, for which they earn college credit in programs designed to train teachers of learning disabled students. The Orton-Gillingham approach, an alphabetic, multisensory method, is used extensively whenever appropriate. Since the needs of each student are varied, the tutoring is tailored to the specific strengths and weaknesses of the individual student. Basic to the program is a return to the beginning of each student's formal language learning, followed by quick movement to the point in which language skills are no longer secure and remediation can begin. In this way, success is built into the remediation and students who have previously encountered frustration and failure find that they can learn and build on their day-to-day successes. As they acquire skills and build self-esteem, students, in fact, find their own voices and learn to speak confidently as they begin to take responsibility for their learning and performance. In addition to the remedial program, students also have classes in four of the following: remedial mathematics or composition, art, social communication, physical education, study skills, and computers.

DAILY SCHEDULE

6:45	Wake-up
7:20	Gather in dorm lounge
7:25	Flag raising
7:30	Breakfast
8:00	Morning announcements
8:10	Warning bell for classes
8:15–9:05	First period
9:10–10:00	Second period
10:00–10:20	Break
10:20–11:10	Third period
11:15–12:05	Fourth period
12:10	Staff to lunch
12:15	Students to lunch
12:35	Announcements
	Swim
2:25	Warning bell for classes
2:30–3:20	Fifth period
3:20–4:15	Sixth period
4:15	After school activities
5:40	Flag lowering
5:45	Dinner
6:30	Evening activities
9:00	All students in dorm
9:30	In bed; lights out for younger students

ENROLLMENT

Because of the specific nature of the remedial process used at Pine Ridge, every student must have a proper diagnostic battery of tests before he or she can be accepted. Parents or the sponsoring agency must make arrangements for the testing, which must include a Wechsler intelligence test (WISC-R or WAIS) that has been administered within the past three years, and all recent educational testing (such as the WRAT or PIAT), along with all subtest scores. Testing should also include auditory and visual-motor function tests, projective tests and language arts achievements tests, as well as a thorough medical examination. A test

battery given by a hospital language clinic or a qualified psychologist is acceptable to Pine Ridge.

EXTRA OPPORTUNITIES AND ACTIVITIES

While the Summer Program is tightly structured, adequate time has been allotted for experiential learning through nonacademic activities. It is here that students build confidence and friendships as they learn to negotiate with each other in a group setting. The residential staff plans and implements an extensive recreation program each evening and on weekends. Current plans call for activities such as hiking, camping, swimming, folk dancing, dramatics, and mountain climbing, as well as the usual sports. Every opportunity is taken to participate in the many special activities offered in the surrounding area of Vermont and New York, including trips to the Great Escape and Fort Ticonderoga. The program is configured to emphasize skill development, team spirit, and cooperation, as well as personal respect, satisfaction, and success.

FACILITIES

There are ten individual buildings that form the main facilities of the campus. One building is devoted to tutorial teaching. A large academic building with ten classrooms, a computer lab, and offices was built in 1985. The Duerr Activity Center offers numerous physical education opportunities as well as space for social events and interactions. Students are housed in single-sex dormitories, 2 in each room and 16 in each building. Care is taken to see that students are paired for good companionship and growth. The Main Building, an old inn, contains dormitory space, the kitchen, dining room, and administrative offices.

STAFF

With a student-staff ratio of 1:1, the Pine Ridge staff maintains a high standard of professionalism, in which a disciplined competence is combined with a warm concern for the well-being and individual rights of each student entrusted to their care. The Summer Program has an average of 25 teachers and tutors, 8 residential staff members, and additional support staff members. Experienced supervisors of teachers, tutors, and residential staff members closely manage the activities. The Director of the Summer Program is responsible for teacher training, and consults with parents and school districts while monitoring and maintaining the students' academic programs.

MEDICAL CARE

Burlington's Fletcher-Allen Medical Center is only 10 minutes away from the campus.

COSTS

Tuition and room and board for the 2003 session was $6700. Day tuition is $5100. A nonrefundable deposit of $500 is required upon acceptance to reserve a place in the program. The balance is due on or before May 31, 2004. An activity fee of $300 covers all special activities and trips. It also includes money for laundry and a small weekly allowance. The activity fee is also nonrefundable and is due on or before opening day. Day students who participate in extra activities are expected to pay on a per activity basis.

TRANSPORTATION

Pine Ridge is located in the town of Williston, Vermont, which is 7 miles east of Burlington. Open fields and pine forest surround the school property, yet it is conveniently adjacent to U.S. Route 7 and Interstate 89. Continental, US Airways, United Airlines, Northwest Airlink, and Delta service Burlington International Airport. Vermont Transit and Greyhound bus systems also service Burlington. The school will provide transportation to and from buses and planes if given adequate notice.

FOR MORE INFORMATION, CONTACT:

Joshua C. Doyle
Director of Admissions
Pine Ridge School
9505 Williston Road
Williston, Vermont 05495
802-434-6915
Fax: 802-434-5512
E-mail: jdoyle@pineridgeschool.com
World Wide Web: http://www.pineridgeschool.com

POK-O-MACCREADY CAMPS

SUMMER CAMPS

WILLSBORO, NEW YORK

Type of Program: Traditional summer camping
Participants: Boys and girls, ages 6 to 16
Enrollment: 235 campers
Program Dates: Last week of June to mid-August
Heads of Program: John Sharp Swan and Margaret Swan Reinckens

LOCATION

Pok-O-MacCready Camps are brother and sister camps with separate campuses but shared facilities and coordinated programs in traditional camp activities. The camps are located on nearly 300 acres of forest, meadow, and lakefront on beautiful Adirondack Lake in New York's Adirondack Park. Willsboro is approximately 2 hours north of Albany and 1 hour south of Montreal, Canada. Burlington, Vermont is less than an hour away. The Olympic Village of Lake Placid, pristine lakes and ponds, and the high peaks of the Adirondacks are nearby. Only 1 mile from camp is the Adirondack's newest cultural resource, the 1812 Homestead, a living history museum where campers can practice blacksmithing; tend the gardens; split shingles and rails; learn to spin and weave; make candles and soap; feed the sheep, pig, oxen, turkeys, and chickens; and attend and conduct lessons in the one-room schoolhouse.

BACKGROUND AND PHILOSOPHY

The Pok-O-MacCready Camps began with the establishment of Pok-O-Moonshine for boys by Dr. Charles Robinson in 1905. His grandson, the present owner, Jack Swan, opened Camp MacCready for girls in 1967. Pok-O-MacCready became a camp where all campers learn and practice new skills under experts, meet and live with other children of diverse cultural backgrounds, and spend joyous summers while developing skills and interests that will stay with them through life. Pok-O-MacCready campers—who come from throughout the United States, Europe, South America, Asia, Africa, Mexico, and Canada—gain outstanding instruction from mature counselors in the numerous activities and classes offered. They also enjoy an expanded program that includes athletic competitions within the camps and with other camps, hiking and camping in the high peaks, sailing on Lake Champlain, canoe trips along Adirondack Lake and river routes, horse shows, trail rides, rock climbing, and mountain biking. The goals that Pok-O-MacCready has for each of its campers are simple ones: to learn, to grow, to experience, to master skills, to expand horizons, to be safe, and to have fun.

PROGRAM OFFERINGS

During their second day of camp, Pok-O-MacCready boys and girls attend an activity fair at which they meet the instructing counselors and learn about their offerings. They may choose major activities, which meet every day, and minor activities, which meet every other day, as they create their own individual activity schedules. The choices are numerous. Included in the arts are ceramics and pottery, creative writing, drawing, drama and musical productions, photography, and spinning and weaving. Sports include archery, baseball, basketball, boating, canoeing, fishing, football, gymnastics, horseback riding, in-line skating, kayaking, rock climbing, sailboarding, sailing, snorkeling, soccer, softball, street hockey, swimming, tennis, volleyball, and weight training. Other specialties include campcraft, farming, gardening, leadership training, Native American crafts and lore, and nature study. The general program for all campers also features participation on camp sports teams, backpacking and camping trips, canoe trips, science trips, sailing trips, mountain biking, fishing trips, kayak trips, and numerous horse shows. The riding program is one of the best in the Adirondacks; a camper can take care of a horse, ride daily, participate in a stable management class, and go to outside horse shows each Sunday with one of the twenty-four horses.

Pok-O-MacCready's basic program is offered through the full camp season, but a four-week session is also available. A new, innovative offering is a special three-week program (from the end of July to mid-August) that focuses on programs in horseback riding, wilderness excursions, sailing trips, and mountain biking. One such trip is a mountain biking expedition in the Laurentian Mountains of Canada.

DAILY SCHEDULE

A typical day, beginning with reveille at 7 a.m., starts with a morning dip and Horse Masters tending to their horses at the girls' camp. The boys eat breakfast while the girls clean their cabins and undergo morning inspection before they head to the dining hall and the boys go to their sections to prepare for inspection. The morning's coeducational activities, in two periods, begin at 9. The boys have a third morning session and a general swimming period before heading to lunch and a brief rest hour. The girls also have lunch and rest hour, followed by two afternoon activity periods. The boys have afternoon section activities: baseball or soccer practice, sports competitions, capture the flag, boating and fishing, tennis matches, street hockey, etc. The girls have a late-afternoon swimming period followed by supper. The boys end their activities around 5 p.m. and head to the swimming area with its diving boards, rafts, slide, and rope swing before their supper. Evening activities for both boys and girls may include section games and competitions, campfires, and coed activities, including skit nights, dances, and Indian Council fire. Bedtime is geared to age levels:

the youngest campers turn in around 8 p.m. and the older campers have lights out between 9 and 9:45.

EXTRA OPPORTUNITIES AND ACTIVITIES

Pok-O-MacCready's special summer events include several activities that involve the entire camp. Each Fourth of July, campers and counselors reconduct the American Revolution with battles on land and at sea, on Long Pond, with the colonies at stake. Throughout the first few weeks of camp and culminating in three days of events, campers in five Iroquois tribes test their Indian skills through games and contests that close with an impressive campfire ceremony. Later, the girls at Camp MacCready conduct both an in-camp horse show and an all-day show that is open to the public. Special hiking, canoeing, and mountain biking expeditions are conducted during Trip Week in August, when campers go out on three- and five-day trips to climb many of the forty-six high peaks of the Adirondacks and to paddle some of the major canoe routes. On weekends in July the camp has overnight wilderness trips. Campers participate in hiking, rock climbing, kayaking, canoeing, and mountain biking expeditions.

STAFF

Pok-O-MacCready's staff includes college-age and older counselors from all over the United States and from England and other countries. In each section of camp, there are counselors for every cabin. Additional staff members include mature section heads, a program director for each division, a nurse for each division, a medical supervisor, the camp chef and his assistants, and a specialist in the areas of swimming, boating, riding, wilderness trips, rock climbing, and biking. Many of the staff members were Pok-O-MacCready campers themselves, and more than a few have been involved with camp for more than twenty-five years. All are professional, eager, and devoted to the concept that camp is a special place where campers develop skills and acquire friendships that will carry through life. The counselor-camper ratio is 1:4.

MEDICAL CARE

Two infirmaries, one on each campus, serve the campers and counselors at Pok-O-MacCready. Each is managed by a full-time nurse, and a medical supervisor oversees the health and safety of all campers and staff members. Additional medical support is provided at a health-care center in nearby Willsboro and through excellent hospital facilities in Plattsburgh, 30 minutes from camp. The local emergency squad can be summoned to answer the call of any medical emergency at camp, and all supervisory staff members at the camps are trained in first aid.

RELIGIOUS LIFE

Pok-O-MacCready welcomes campers and counselors of all religious faiths and backgrounds and conducts a nondenominational devotional meeting on Sunday evenings. A town meeting follows in which the Camp Director recognizes individuals and groups for their accomplishments of the past week. The Camper Council also meets with Jack Swan. Arrangements to escort Catholic campers to masses are made each week.

COSTS

For the year 2005, tuition for the full camp season is $4850. For the four-week session, the fee is $3350. The special three-week session (from the end of July to the middle of August) is $2000. Tuition includes laundry, sheets, a pillow and blankets, plus wilderness trips and all regular camp programs and activities, with the exception of riding and tutoring. Campers who ride every day pay an extra $375 (seven-week session). Those who ride every other day pay an extra $275. Tutoring fees (for English and math) are $175 for every day and $100 for every other day during the first four weeks of the camp season only.

FINANCIAL AID

Financial aid is available to qualified applicants through the Adirondack Scholarship Foundation, P.O. Box 97, Willsboro, New York 12996.

TRANSPORTATION

Camp buses depart from and return to Elmsford in Westchester County and New York City. Campers from great distances fly to Burlington, Vermont, or Montreal, where they are picked up and escorted to camp. The cost of transportation to and from camp is additional.

APPLICATION TIMETABLE

Parents wishing to contact Pok-O-MacCready may do so at any time. Most inquires are made between November and May.

For more information, contact:

Margaret Swan Reinckens or John Sharp Swan
Pok-O-MacCready Camps

winter

P.O. Box 397
Willsboro, New York 12996
518-963-POKO (7656)
800-982-3538 (toll-free, out of state)
Fax: 518-963-4165
E-mail: pokomac@aol.com
World Wide Web: http://www.pokomac.com

summer

100 Mountain Road
Willsboro, New York 12996
518-963-8366
Fax: 518-963-1128
World Wide Web: http://www.pokomac.com

PORTSMOUTH ABBEY SUMMER SCHOOL

SUMMER PROGRAM

PORTSMOUTH, RHODE ISLAND

Type of Program: Academic enrichment
Participants: Coeducational, grades 8–11, ages 13–17
Enrollment: 70
Program Dates: Five weeks, beginning fourth Sunday in June
Head of Program: Robert Sahms, Director

LOCATION

The Portsmouth Abbey School is located on 500 acres on the shores of Narragansett Bay in Portsmouth, Rhode Island. It is several miles north of Newport, Rhode Island; 25 miles from Providence, Rhode Island; 65 miles from Boston, Massachusetts; and 190 miles from New York, New York.

BACKGROUND AND PHILOSOPHY

The Summer Session, established in 1943, provides each student with a talented and dedicated faculty, excellent facilities, and a sound program of studies that is faithful to the moral and intellectual ideals that Benedictine communities have been passing on to youths for 1,500 years.

PROGRAM OFFERINGS

The academic program of the Summer School provides a focus on basic subjects and offers enrichment courses. Most students usually choose to take courses for review or enrichment, but intensive courses (meeting three to four periods each day) are also available in English as a second language and drama. In addition to the intensive programs, courses are offered in literature, English composition, creative writing, public speaking, history, algebra 1, geometry, algebra 2, trigonometry, Latin, Spanish, French, marine biology, human anatomy and physiology, genetic engineering, Web page design, studio art, study skills, geology, and digital photography.

There are four periods per day and an evening study hall. Most courses meet one period per day. Classes are very small, and a faculty-student ratio of 1:5 ensures personal attention.

Afternoons are set aside for recreational athletics, including basketball, tennis, volleyball, soccer, and weight training. A sailing program, an equestrian program, and squash are also available for an extra fee.

ENROLLMENT

About 70 boys and girls from the United States and other countries attend the Summer Session.

DAILY SCHEDULE

Classes meet Monday through Saturday from 8:30 a.m. to 12:45 p.m. The athletic and recreational programs are reserved for 2 to 5. The evening study period is from 7:30 to 9:30 p.m.

EXTRA OPPORTUNITIES AND ACTIVITIES

Afternoon excursions to Newport are scheduled several times during the summer. Each Saturday night, the students are taken to the movies. On Sundays, the School goes on day trips. Trips in past summers have included the Boston Aquarium, Faneuil Hall/Quincy Market, Martha's Vinyard, and amusement parks.

FACILITIES

All Summer School participants have access to the modern facilities of the School, including Internet access, the St. Thomas More Library, audiovisual facilities, complete indoor and outdoor athletic facilities for tennis, soccer, basketball, volleyball, and weight training, and an all-weather track. Students are housed in three houses. Resident faculty and staff members supervise each house.

STAFF

The Summer Session is fortunate to have a loyal staff, many of whom have been returning for ten years or more. The staff includes both regular faculty members from the Portsmouth Abbey School and dedicated teachers from other independent and public schools.

MEDICAL CARE

The School Infirmary is open each day at specific and published times, and a registered nurse is on duty. At times when the infirmary is closed, a registered nurse is always on call. The School physician has daily clinic hours at the School as needed. For emergency cases, Newport Hospital is a few minutes away.

The School physician must have a complete health history of every student. The forms for the health history are mailed to parents when the student is enrolled.

RELIGIOUS LIFE

Portsmouth Abbey School is a Catholic school in the Benedictine tradition. All boarding students attend Mass weekly in the School church.

COSTS

The fee for boarding students in 2005 is $4400, which includes tuition, room, board, textbooks, and all weekend activities. For day students, the fee is $2300.

FINANCIAL AID

Financial aid is both limited and competitive. Requests for financial aid should be submitted by April 15.

TRANSPORTATION

Arriving students are met at T. F. Green Airport in Providence and Logan Airport in Boston. Students are also transported to these airports at the end of the Summer School.

APPLICATION TIMETABLE

Inquiries are welcome at any time; interested students should contact the Director. Applications are processed on a rolling basis but some programs fill early, so the Summer School recommends filing materials as soon as possible. The application fee is $55.

FOR MORE INFORMATION, CONTACT:

Robert Sahms, Director
Portsmouth Abbey Summer School
285 Cory's Lane
Portsmouth, Rhode Island 02871
401-683-2000 Ext. 225
Fax: 401-683-5888
E-mail: summer@portsmouthabbey.org
World Wide Web: http://www.portsmouthabbey.org

PRATT INSTITUTE

SUMMER PRE-COLLEGE PROGRAM

BROOKLYN/MANHATTAN, NEW YORK

Type of Program: College-credit bearing Pre-College Program in art, design, and architecture
Participants: Coeducational; students who have completed grades 10–12
Enrollment: 300
Program Dates: Four weeks: July 6 to July 30
Head of Program: Special Programs Administrator

LOCATION

Pratt Institute, one of the world's leading schools of art, design, and architecture, has campuses in Brooklyn and Manhattan. Each site is located in the heart of museums, theaters, cultural centers, galleries, and design centers. Pratt Brooklyn's university setting provides ample space for student enrichment and the pursuit of artistic endeavors.

BACKGROUND AND PHILOSOPHY

Founded in 1887 by industrialist and philanthropist Charles Pratt, Pratt Institute offers precollege programs in art, design, architecture, and creative writing for high school students considering careers in those fields. The Pre-College Program is an intense learning experience; 4 college credits are earned upon successful completion. Students develop their creative talents and skills and build an effective portfolio for college admission.

PROGRAM OFFERINGS

The Brooklyn campus accommodates residential and commuter students. The Manhattan campus is for commuter students only. The curriculum is comprised of six mandatory courses or activities: an elective, a Foundation course, an art history appreciation course, a portfolio development course, a lecture series, and cultural insights activities.

Elective Courses Students may choose one course from the following fifteen majors: architecture, creative writing, fashion design, fine arts/painting and drawing, graphic design, illustration (digital), illustration (traditional), industrial design, interior design, photography, and sculpture as well as the following new 2-credit electives: art and design discovery, art history, cultural studies, and media arts/video.

Architecture New York City, with its wealth of architectural treasures, provides the ideal setting for this intensive hands-on workshop. Students learn to think about an architectural problem, develop a solution, produce sketches, draft plans, and build models.

*Art and Design Discovery** (Brooklyn only) This new course allows students to experience different disciplines in art, design, and architecture. Through hands-on projects and lectures, students sample areas of study such as fine arts/painting and drawing, illustration, graphic design, interior design, industrial design, and architecture.

*Art History** This new course offers an introductory historical survey of Western art and examines the major artistic movements of the last 600 years within their social, political, and cultural contexts. Students can develop their skills in both visual analysis and critical thinking. They learn to recognize the distinct hands of individual artists as well as to understand fundamental concepts. Painting, sculpture, architecture, and graphic art are explored.

Creative Writing This elective offers opportunities to develop writing skills in one or more genres and helps students prepare for college. Students begin with an examination of written language, the composing process, and voice, followed by exposure to various genres, including poetry, essay, fiction, writing for film, magazine writing, and text for Web sites.

*Cultural Studies** This new course draws its inspiration from the social sciences and humanities. This elective is an introduction to the relation between cultural practices and their various social contexts in the contemporary world. Through their explorations, students begin to develop the skills necessary to intervene in the production of culture. At the final precollege Art Exhibit, students present their critical analysis of a chosen aspect of culture.

Fashion Design (Brooklyn only) New York, a leading fashion capital, is the ideal setting to study fashion design. Students learn key aspects of the design process, including sketching, pattern making, and clothing construction. Participants apply real-world knowledge to their work after visiting successful designers' studios. Students are exposed to the industry's many career options.

Fine Arts / Painting and Drawing This studio course enhances perceptual and aesthetic awareness through the creation of fine art. Instruction in drawing and painting incorporates various techniques, media, and subject matter. On-site work is an essential element of this course.

Graphic Design This course shows how and when to use photography, illustration, typography, and computer graphics to design logos, Web pages, books, video spots, exhibits, posters, and packaging. Field trips to great graphic design showcases and studios around New York City are included.

Illustration (Digital) In this elective, students analyze the style trends used in today's illustration field and explore the trends of the future. Participants incorporate and develop their illustration skills while experimenting with scanning, digital photography, and software such as PhotoShop and Illustrator. Study combines technology and traditional illustration. Students are expected to produce professional-level work. The only deviation from established illustration is that the final outcome is digital.

Illustration (Traditional) In this course, participants explore ways to create pictures that communicate new ideas. Students develop their technical and artistic skills in drawing and painting and learn how photographic and digital media can enhance their art.

Industrial Design (Brooklyn only) Industrial design is the thoughtful creation of forms to find solutions needed in everyday life. This course examines how embracing today's social, physical, and ecological needs presents opportunities for creative design. Through drawing and model making, students explore and redefine society's forms and inventions.

Interior Design (Brooklyn only) New York City is the world center for interior design and is the perfect setting for this course, where space is shaped, planned, and furnished. There is emphasis on the impact of the interior space on the individual as well as various groups. Students work with the classic elements of light, color, form, and space in this exciting studio course. Students visit some of New York's outstanding interior spaces and commercial showrooms.

*Media Arts / Video** (Brooklyn only) This new elective is an introduction to the craft and aesthetic of video. Students explore perception, motion, composition, and sequence in order to develop the language and grammar of video, before engaging in actual video-making exercises and creative projects. The course utilizes lightweight cameras. Preproduction planning and postproduction digital editing are introduced.

Photography Participants achieve a broad-based knowledge of black and white photography by studying 35mm camera operations, lighting techniques, and darkroom procedures. Making contact prints, enlarging and finishing photographs, and techniques of shooting are explored. Introduction to color and digital photography is included. Students must have access to a 35mm camera. This studio course entails extensive fieldwork.

Sculpture (Brooklyn only) This course concentrates on the creation of three-dimensional art. It offers an in-depth examination of the materials and processes used in sculpture. It explores subtractive methods, such as carving stone, and additive methods, such as construction with wire.

Foundation Courses Students enrolling in an art, design, or architecture elective automatically are enrolled in Foundation of Art and Design. Students enrolling in the creative writing elective are automatically enrolled in Foundation Writing Studio. Students enrolling in the cultural studies elective are automatically enrolled in Foundation–Cultural Studies. Each Foundation course is worth 2 credits.

Foundation of Art and Design Students develop their skills in using color, shape, and other formal concepts basic to professional study of art and design. Modeled after Pratt's first-year Foundation program and taught by professional artists and designers, this course expands participants' visual thinking, strengthens their portfolio, and provides a basis for further study.

Foundation Writing Studio This course introduces students to the three traditional forms of creative writing, offers them opportunities to develop their writing skills in each of the genres, and helps them prepare for college. Through reading assignments, writing exercises, workshops, and critical analysis of readings, students develop basic skills in expository and creative writing. Genres covered include poetry, fiction, and plays.

*Foundation–Cultural Studies** (Brooklyn only) This new course introduces essential skills and methods of the analysis of culture. Students draw examples of concrete objects of study from specific design, media, arts, communications, and popular culture sources for class exercises. Students gain familiarity with computer applications of data analysis and use of video for data collection.

Art History Appreciation (noncredit) Mostly through guided visits at New York's museums, students gain appreciation of a wide range of chronological and geographic periods, media, and disciplines. Students explore the many functions of art and the stylistic differences and similarities across historical periods. The course also serves as a complement to studio classes.

Portfolio Development (noncredit) In this course, students learn how to select what to include in their portfolio, based on standards set by top colleges, as well as develop the basic technical skills for creating a professional portfolio. Upon conclusion, students can have their portfolios reviewed by a Pratt admissions counselor to help them gain first-hand understanding of what might be expected by colleges.

Lecture Series (noncredit; Brooklyn only) The Pre-College lecture series invites successful artists, industrial design professionals, and architects to share their individual perspectives on the path they have chosen. Presenters speak for 20 minutes then answer students' questions.

Cultural Insights (noncredit; Brooklyn only) Cultural insights are activities that allow students to explore the many offerings available in New York City. Students participate in social and cultural activities such as plays, museums, and studio visits. The activities are chaperoned, typically last 3 to 4 hours, and take place on the weekend.

*pending Academic Senate approval

DAILY SCHEDULE

There are about 30 hours of class per week. Weekends consist mostly of free, unsupervised time during the day, except for Sunday afternoon, and Friday and Saturday evenings, which include a mandatory cultural insights activity. The following is the daily schedule, Monday through Friday:

9:00–12:15	Class (mandatory)
12:15–1:30	Lunch break
1:30–4:45	Class (mandatory)
5:00–6:00	Dinner
6:00–10:30	Homework space available (optional) or evening activity on Friday (mandatory)
11:00	Curfew

ENROLLMENT

American and international high school students enroll in Pratt's Summer Pre-College Program. Some students have extensive backgrounds; others have had less training. Students who have completed grades 10–12 may apply. Generally, students who demonstrate the ability to benefit from the program are admitted.

EXTRA OPPORTUNITIES AND ACTIVITIES

Weekend social and cultural activities are open to all Pre-College Program students and are mandatory for Brooklyn resident students. These activities offer further opportunities to explore art and New York City.

FACILITIES

The Pratt Brooklyn campus has twenty-three buildings, including an athletics center with a track, tennis courts, a sauna, and a weight room. The campus has centrally located air-conditioned residence halls, dining rooms, spacious studios, an extensive library, and art galleries. Both campuses have numerous state-of-the-art computer labs.

STAFF

Pratt's Center for Continuing and Professional Studies provides the leadership for the program. The faculty members for the Pre-College Foundation Program and electives are recognized writers, architects, artists, and designers. Expert guest lecturers and critics are also an essential part of the program. The Office of Residential Life oversees the residential portion of the program; a director and several advisers live in the residence halls. The staff members check curfews, organize small social activities, and monitor the living environment. All residents are expected to follow curfew.

MEDICAL CARE

All students must fill out health forms included in their Pre-College package. Staffed by a full-time nurse and counselor, Pratt's on-campus Office of Counseling and Health Services is available to Pre-College students.

COSTS

Tuition for the program is $1850. Other costs are as follows: photo lab fee, $125; graphic design fee, $40; digital illustration fee, $20; sculpture fee, $385; video, $176; student activities fee, $75 (optional for commuters); health insurance, $45; housing, $621; meal plan for residents, $595; local transportation for residents, $63; and optional commuter board plan, $150. Spending money of $300 for the purchase of art supplies is suggested. Prices are subject to change. The campus residence package includes breakfast, lunch, and dinner during the week and brunch and supper on weekends. Residence halls are available only in Brooklyn.

FINANCIAL AID

Merit-based scholarships are available for qualified students. The deadline for applications and slides is April 1 (postmark). Late applications are not accepted. All scholarships are for tuition only; they do not cover supplies, room, or board. The Black Alumni at Pratt sponsors a full scholarship program (for New York State resident students of minority groups only). Interested students should call 718-636-3479 for further information. Scholarship applications and instructions for submitting slides of work can either be sent upon request or downloaded from the Web site listed below.

APPLICATION TIMETABLE

The registration deadline is April 1. Full payment deadline is May 15, by which time all tuition and fees are due. Applications are accepted as early as October. Since many classes fill quickly, students should apply early. A campus tour or overnight stay as a Pratt guest can be arranged through the Admissions Office (telephone: 718-636-3514). All applications must be accompanied by a $200 deposit, a $25 application fee, and a letter of recommendation from the student's guidance counselor or art teacher. International students are required to submit a letter from their English teacher that states their level of spoken and written comprehension.

For more information, contact:

Center for Continuing and Professional Studies
Summer Pre-College Program, Pratt Institute
200 Willoughby Avenue, ISC 205
Brooklyn, New York 11205
Telephone: 718-636-3453
Fax: 718-399-4410
E-mail: precollege@pratt.edu
World Wide Web: http://www.pratt.edu/precollege/pres/index.html

PREP CAMP EXCEL BY EDUCATION UNLIMITED

SUMMER CAMPS FOR HIGH SCHOOL PREP

BERKELEY, DAVIS, LOS ANGELES, AND STANFORD, CALIFORNIA

Type of Program: High School Prep
Participants: Coeducational, students entering grades 9–10
Enrollment: 60 students per session
Program Dates: Eight-day sessions in June, July, and August
Head of Program: Jenny Herbert, Director

LOCATION

Education Unlimited's Prep Camp Excel programs are independent offerings held at top-ranked academic institutions in the United States. The camps provide a safe and secure environment while participants experience some of the nation's most dynamic universities. Students live in the residence halls on campus and eat in meal facilities.

BACKGROUND AND PHILOSOPHY

Education Unlimited has run college-admission prep programs for older high school students for more than ten years. The programs were founded to address the concerns of students and parents about the increasingly competitive and often mystifying college admission process. Increasingly, parents of high school freshmen, or those just entering high school, have contacted Education Unlimited for information regarding programs aimed at their children's needs. Many students and parents want a program that shows how to get the most out of high school and how to begin early preparation for college and includes preparation for the PSAT.

In 2000, Education Unlimited launched Prep Camp Excel to meet these needs. Students who have completed the program are far more comfortable with the high school experience and have a long-range view on how to aim their high school career toward college admission.

PROGRAM OFFERINGS

The focus of the Prep Camp Excel programs is on PSAT preparation, essay writing instruction, and study skills training.

The PSAT is a crucial test for college recruiting as well as for the National Merit Scholarship competition; yet, most students go into the exam with little or no preparation. Prep Camp Excel offers the same type of strategy and preparation for this test as is usually reserved for the SAT. Its exclusive curriculum teaches math skills and vocabulary building in order to prepare students for the PSAT and math and English classes in high school.

Writing competent essays is not only critical to getting good grades, it is also one of the most important skills a student can take away from high school. Unfortunately, the kind of one-on-one instruction necessary to learn to excel in writing is rare in school. Students work individually with writing faculty members. Each student brings home one of the best essays he or she has ever written and, more importantly, the skills to continue to write in that fashion.

Students receive expert guidance on topics ranging from high school course selection and extracurricular activities to career exploration. This portion of the program seeks to instill the motivation and direction that students need to make high school count.

ENROLLMENT

Students from across the nation attend Prep Camp Excel summer sessions. Admission is limited at each site and is open to any students who are entering their freshman and sophomore years of high school.

EXTRA OPPORTUNITIES AND ACTIVITIES

Throughout the camp, recreational and fun activities, as well as other study breaks, are planned for. Planned recreational excursions allow students to experience the wonderful attractions of the Bay Area and southern California.

DAILY SCHEDULE

8:00	Breakfast
9:00	PSAT preparation
11:30	Lunch
1:00	Essay writing seminar
3:00	PSAT preparation
5:00	Dinner
6:30	Study skills seminar
7:30	Recreation time
10:00	Floor check

This is a typical day's schedule. Specific class subjects change from day to day in the time allotted. Students rotate through electives in small groups.

FACILITIES

Students live in residence halls on campus and are supervised by adult counselors who share in dormitory life. Meals are included in the program cost and are served at the dormitory meal complex or elsewhere on campus.

STAFF

Each member of the faculty is a carefully chosen professional with years of experience in his or her field. Many staff members are guidance counselors or educators at prestigious prep schools and have specific experience working with students in this age range.

MEDICAL CARE

Medical care is available 24 hours a day at local and campus clinics and hospitals. All participants must submit comprehensive medical forms and proof of insurance.

COSTS

Camp fees for Excel seven-day sessions in 2004 ranged from $1275 to $1400, depending on the campus. Room, board, tuition, and all materials necessary for the program are included in the cost. A $525 fee (applied toward tuition) is required upon application. Fees cover tuition for all classes, including PSAT preparation and scored full-length exams, all required workbooks and materials, access to recreational and athletic facilities, planned recreational and evening activities, and camp memorabilia. Fees do not cover transportation to and from the program site, spending and laundry money, bath and bed linens, or additional nights' lodging for any students arriving before the program begins or staying after the conclusion of the program.

FINANCIAL AID

A limited amount of need-based financial aid is available. To be considered, relevant tax returns for the current and previous year are required. The total amount of aid awarded is based upon the applicant pool and total enrollment at the sessions. Financial aid awards are usually for tuition only, with applicants paying room and board costs.

TRANSPORTATION

The campuses are accessible from major airports. Most of these airports service international flights. Education Unlimited offers an optional airport pickup service for a round-trip fee of $45. This service provides transportation from the airport to the dorms at the beginning of the program and return transportation to the airport at the conclusion of the program.

APPLICATION TIMETABLE

Beginning in November, inquiries regarding programs for the coming summer are welcome. Office hours are from 9 to 6 (Pacific Standard Time) year round, and messages can be left 24 hours a day. The application deadline is usually May 15. Late applications are considered on a rolling basis.

For more information, contact:

Education Unlimited
1700 Shattuck Avenue, #305
Berkeley, California 94709
510-548-6612
800-548-6612 (toll-free)
E-mail: camps@educationunlimited.com
World Wide Web:
http://www.educationunlimited.com

PARTICIPANT/FAMILY COMMENTS

"Before attending Prep Camp Excel, I had given little thought to college ... now I know how to best prepare for the SATs and what to look for in a college."

"I learned a lot of helpful tips for the PSAT. The writing class helped me develop my creativity. I think I will do better in school because of this program."

THE PUTNEY SCHOOL

SUMMER PROGRAMS

PUTNEY, VERMONT

Type of Program: Visual and Performing Arts, Creative Writing, and EFL/ESL
Participants: Coeducational, ages 14–17
Enrollment: 160 boarding and 15 day students
Program Dates: Session I: Sunday, June 26, through Friday, July 15; Session II: Sunday, July 17, through Friday, August 5
Head of Program: Thomas D. Howe, Director

LOCATION

The Putney School campus is located in southeastern Vermont on a 500-acre hilltop farm near the Connecticut River. The campus offers beautiful views, miles of trails, a pond, a nature preserve, and a working dairy and animal farm.

BACKGROUND AND PHILOSOPHY

The Putney School Summer Programs offer students the opportunity for in-depth exploration in areas of special interest while learning the value and responsibility of working in a community and living close to the land. The Summer Programs highlight successful academic-year programs at The Putney School in the arts, writing, and international education and share the school's emphasis on self-discovery and inner growth, independent inquiry and initiative, and community exchange.

PROGRAM OFFERINGS

Summer Arts Workshops Designed for students seriously interested in the arts, these workshops offer students the opportunity to work in depth with professional artists, writers, and performers in two chosen areas. Offerings include drawing, painting, sculpture, ceramics, stained glass, dance, playwriting, book arts, chamber music, chamber orchestra, songwriting, music composition, drama, filmmaking, printmaking, theater tech, fiction writing, poetry writing, photography, weaving, woodworking, jewelry, theater intensive, and other fields.

The Program for International Education (EFL/ESL) This program is designed for international students who wish to build confidence in using English as a living language in academic and social situations as well as increase their awareness of other cultures.

The Writing Program This program offers students guidance and instruction in all aspects of the written word. The Writing Program looks at writing as a craft and a tool for self-expression, heightened observation, analytic thinking, problem solving, and reflection.

Each program provides 6 hours of hands-on instruction a day. All programs share community, residential, and recreational activities.

ENROLLMENT

The enrollment figures for each session are as follows: Summer Arts Workshops, 135; The Writing Program, 15; and the Program for International Education, 25.

Students attend the summer programs from all areas of the United States and from countries in Eastern and Western Europe, Asia, Latin America, and Africa.

DAILY SCHEDULE

7:45	Breakfast
8:45	Morning workshops
11:45	Lunch
12:20	Assembly
1:00	Afternoon workshops
4:00	Outdoor activities
5:45	Dinner
7:15	Evening workshops
9:00	Visiting hour
10:00	In dorms

The goal of the program is for students to grow through enjoyable, productive, and safe experiences. Students are asked to agree to certain expectations to ensure the safety of the community and mutual respect of all individuals. The use of alcohol or illegal drugs is strictly prohibited and results in dismissal.

EXTRA OPPORTUNITIES AND ACTIVITIES

Afternoon outdoor activities include community service, supervised swimming, basketball, biking, hiking, soccer, ultimate Frisbee, softball, gardening, and work on the farm. Organized evening activities in the arts and off-campus cultural excursions are offered. Weekends are devoted to camping trips, recreational activities, and local trips to flea markets, the town of Brattleboro, and state parks.

FACILITIES

Putney has superb facilities for the arts, including fully equipped studios for printmaking, welding, woodworking, photography, weaving, painting, ceramics, dance, and theater; a 250-seat concert hall; and art galleries. The computer lab provides support for writing programs and Internet access. The campus includes the 70-acre Garland Pond Nature Preserve, a protected wildlife area. The school library contains more than 25,000 volumes. Dormitories are small (10–25 students), and each is supervised by 2 to 3 adult dorm heads. Outdoor facilities include miles of riding and biking trails, an outdoor basketball court, extensive playing fields, and a working farm.

STAFF

The staff consists of 30 faculty members, some of whom are members of the academic-year faculty and all of whom are highly qualified instructors, equally

experienced in teaching and the practice of their field. Sixteen college-age resident staff members assist in the program. Staff members are caring, supportive, and deeply involved in the welfare and growth of participants.

MEDICAL CARE

A registered nurse is on staff and available for office hours during the week and on-call during the evenings and weekends. A pediatric medical clinic and a fully equipped hospital are twenty minutes away. Residential staff members are trained in emergency first aid. Each student submits a medical examination and release form before arriving on campus. The program requires family medical insurance for all participants and provides supplemental insurance for a small fee.

RELIGIOUS LIFE

The program has no religious affiliation but provides transportation for students who wish to attend local services.

COSTS

Tuition, room, and board are $2750 for each three-week session; two sessions are $5300. Tuition, room, and board for international students is $3000 for one session, which includes health insurance; two sessions are $5600. Tuition for day students is $950 for one session; two sessions are $1650. There is an additional materials fee for some workshops. Students should bring no more than $150 for spending money.

FINANCIAL AID

Financial aid is offered based on need, as assessed from a family financial statement. Most qualified applicants receive some financial assistance. Financial aid applications are due March 1.

TRANSPORTATION

Putney is about 2½ hours from Boston and 4 hours from New York City, just off Exit 4 of Interstate 91 in southeastern Vermont. The nearest airport is Bradley International Airport in Hartford, Connecticut. The program provides transportation to and from Bradley International Airport (BDL) and Manchester Airport (MHT) in New Hampshire on arrival and departure days, for an additional fee.

APPLICATION TIMETABLE

Inquiries and visits to campus are welcome throughout the year. Students are accepted to the programs on a rolling basis beginning in December. Early application is encouraged; applications completed by February 15 receive a 5 percent tuition discount.

FOR MORE INFORMATION, CONTACT:

Thomas D. Howe
Director of Summer Programs
The Putney School
Elm Lea Farm
Putney, Vermont 05346
802-387-6297
Fax: 802-387-6216
E-mail: summer@putneyschool.org
World Wide Web: http://www.putneyschool.org/summer

PARTICIPANT/FAMILY COMMENTS

"She returned happier than we have ever seen her. She found kindred spirits at Putney and an atmosphere that was respectful, supportive, and full of the joy of creativity. She came home clearer in her identity and more confident: she found resonance that validated her person as an artist and as a human being of aesthetic and kindly nature."

"He is so happy, clearly comfortable and confidant, and seems to be growing in every way. Clearly, the community at Putney both suits and stimulates him, and for us, it is thrilling to observe."

"After three summers at Putney, we are as impressed as we were at the beginning. The program has been great for our daughter—it is her home away from home!"

"Perhaps more impressive than the variety of offerings is the happiness the students seem to derive from classes. Every class was filled with engaged, smiling, and animated students."—New England Association of Schools and Colleges report

PUTNEY STUDENT TRAVEL

SUMMER PROGRAMS

PUTNEY, VERMONT

Type of Program: Community service, language learning, cultural exploration, and campus-based precollege enrichment—Excel. (For more details regarding the Excel programs, students should see the separate listing in this guide.)

Participants: Coeducational, students completing grades 8–12

Enrollment: 16–18 per group except Excel programs that range from 70–150

Program Dates: Programs of three to seven weeks in June, July, and August

Heads of Program: Jeffrey and Peter Shumlin and Tim Weed, Directors

LOCATION

Putney Student Travel offers **Community Service** programs in Alaska, Bali, Brazil, Costa Rica, Dominica, Dominican Republic, Ecuador, Hawaii, India, Montana, Nicaragua, Tanzania, and Vermont. **Language Learning** programs are offered in Costa Rica, France, and Spain. **Cultural Exploration** programs visit Australia/New Zealand, Cambodia/Thailand, and Europe. **Excel** campus-based programs are held at Amherst, Williams, and Bennington Colleges, and at University of California, Santa Cruz; Oxford/Tuscany; Madrid/Barcelona; and Cuba. Putney Student Travel's year-round home is a converted barn, surrounded by the rolling hills of Putney, Vermont.

BACKGROUND AND PHILOSOPHY

Putney Student Travel was founded in 1952 by George and Kitty Shumlin, devoted educators and parents of the present Directors, Peter and Jeffrey Shumlin. Over the course of five decades, the mission has remained unchanged—to enable young people to learn firsthand about the lives and cultures of people in the United States and other nations, to establish communication and friendship with them, to learn other languages, to pursue academic interests in an active and fun environment, to give of themselves, and, through these experiences, to enhance their confidence, skills, perspectives, and values.

Putney Student Travel programs are special. They emphasize doing, having fun, getting off the beaten track, making friends, and being involved with people rather than just touring, sightseeing, or studying. Participants are encouraged to take responsibility and to help develop group spirit. All programs are designed for motivated, inquisitive students who are mature and responsible. Admission is selective.

PROGRAM OFFERINGS

Community Service Programs Students in these programs give of themselves to people in need. They spend four weeks living as a group in small, rural communities where they join local people to work on small-scale construction projects, teach local children, and help villagers with maintenance, farming, and environmental projects. Each group of 16 students and 2 leaders has the opportunity to provide useful help to communities in need and to understand another culture at a level far beyond what tourists or short-term visitors experience. On weekends, there is time to relax on the beaches, make wilderness and cultural excursions, and join in community life. One need not be a skilled laborer to apply. Students must possess sensitivity toward others, a sense of humor and adventure, and a desire to work hard and make the most of simple living conditions.

Language Learning Programs The Putney way of learning a language emphasizes having fun in France, Spain, or Costa Rica while speaking French or Spanish in natural, everyday living situations. Over the past half century, Putney has learned that sitting passively in a classroom with other Americans does not enhance language learning. Putney's dramatic oral/conversational exercises and games are combined with carefully planned itineraries that allow students to immerse themselves in the local life and culture, encouraging students to discard their inhibitions and speak freely. The atmosphere in each language group is noncompetitive. These five- to six-week programs explore out-of-the-way regions of France, Spain, and Costa Rica; cultural sites in cities; and skiing, hiking, fishing, and work projects in rural areas. Each program includes a one-week, carefully selected homestay.

Cultural Exploration Programs The best way to understand another culture is to get off the tourist track and engage with local people on a personal level. On Putney Cultural Exploration programs, students aren't passive observers—they explore the bush of Queensland with a longtime resident as their guide, learn about Cambodian traditional culture from an artist who survived the Khmer Rouge regime, follow Wordsworth's footsteps in the English Lake District, or explore Renaissance treasures in Florence's less-frequented museums. These programs include a mix of high culture in cities, direct involvement with local people, and physically active adventures.

Excel at Amherst, Williams, and Bennington Colleges; and at University of California, Santa Cruz; Oxford/Tuscany; Madrid/Barcelona; and Cuba These three-, four-, and seven-week programs provide students with an experience that is very different from traditional summer school. In small, seminar-style classes, without the pressure of grades, students interact with outstanding instructors and motivated peers, participate in hands-on activities,

and incorporate local resources in their learning. Interested students should see the separate listing for Excel in this guide.

ENROLLMENT

Putney groups (other than Excel) are limited to 16 to 18 students, depending on the program. Students completing grade 8 are eligible for some Cultural Exploration and Language Learning Programs. Students completing grades 9–12 are eligible for all programs.

FACILITIES

Putney accommodations are simple, but comfortable and safe. In the Language Learning and Cultural Exploration Programs, students stay in small inns and chalets and at student centers, where they have a chance to make friends with young people from other countries. Putney trips are not camping trips, unless specified in the brochure. Meals are taken in small restaurants, inns, and residences. On Community Service projects, students live in small, rural villages in a school or other community building that is not in use during the summer. There is separate space for boys and girls and simple bathroom facilities with running water. Helpers from the community take primary responsibility for meals, but students assist with preparation and cleanup.

STAFF

Putney Student Travel leaders are selected on the basis of their maturity, enthusiasm, patience, judgment, and ability to win the trust and respect of participants. Many are graduate students or instructors who have lived, studied, and traveled abroad and who speak foreign languages. Leaders are given extensive preparation and training in Putney before departure. Brief bios of each of Putney's leaders from 2004 are available on the Web site at http://www.goputney.com/about/bios/allPST.htm.

COSTS

Tuition fees of $4000 to $8000, depending upon the program, cover all regular expenses including meals, accommodations, excursions, and entertainment. Most tuition fees also include roundtrip airfare from New York, Miami, or Los Angeles, depending on the destination. There are no hidden expenses. A $500 deposit must be submitted with the application; this fee is credited to the total tuition fee and is refunded in full if the application is not accepted.

TRANSPORTATION

Putney groups travel by air, train, bus, boat, and bicycle and on foot.

APPLICATION TIMETABLE

In forming each group, attention is given to the age and school year of applicants. Applications are carefully considered by the Admissions Committee, and participants are selected on the basis of their readiness for the Putney experience. Each year Putney receives more applications than it is able to accept, so early application is encouraged. Admission is on a rolling basis.

For more information, contact:

Jeffrey Shumlin, Admissions Director
Putney Student Travel
345 Hickory Ridge Road
Putney, Vermont 05346
802-387-5000
Fax: 802-387-4276
E-mail: info@goputney.com
World Wide Web: http://www.goputney.com

PARTICIPANT/FAMILY COMMENTS

"This was an outstanding summer for Max. He fell in love with France, speaks 100 percent better than before he left, and he's come home with a tremendous sense of confidence and maturity."

RANDOLPH-MACON ACADEMY

SUMMER PROGRAMS

FRONT ROYAL, VIRGINIA

Type of Program: Academic enrichment
Participants: Coeducational, grades 6–12
Enrollment: 200 students
Program Dates: End of June to end of July (4 weeks)
Head of Program: Maj. Gen. Henry M. Hobgood, USAF (Ret.), President

LOCATION

Randolph-Macon Academy's 135-acre campus is located 70 miles west of Washington, D.C., in picturesque Front Royal, Virginia. The town is nestled along the banks of the south fork of the Shenandoah River, at the head of the beautiful Skyline Drive.

BACKGROUND AND PHILOSOPHY

Founded in 1892, Randolph-Macon Academy (R-MA) is affiliated with the United Methodist Church and has separate Middle and Upper School campuses. R-MA's summer program provides a nonmilitary, structured environment in which students are inspired to become lifelong learners.

Throughout the four weeks of the program, students from around the United States and the world immerse themselves in academics while participating in athletic and learning activities that contribute to their development and growth. At the high school level, students choose between one new course and two repeat courses. Students who have the desire to improve their grades or to get ahead for the coming school year benefit most from this program.

R-MA is fully accredited by the Virginia Association of Independent Schools and the Southern Association of Colleges and Schools. R-MA is also a member of the National Association of Independent Schools and The Association of Boarding Schools.

PROGRAM OFFERINGS

R-MA's Summer School Program offers a low student-teacher ratio, supervised study periods, Saturday classes, air-conditioned facilities, a full sports complex, and outstanding afternoon and weekend activities.

The Middle School program offers advancing sixth through eighth grade students the opportunity to focus on three key academic areas, choosing from math, English, computer applications, and study skills. Classes are held in the morning. In the afternoons, students participate in mentoring groups and then have the opportunity to go on short recreational trips or participate in various sports and games. Academic field trips are taken on Wednesdays.

The Upper School program offers English (grades 8–12), pre-algebra; algebra I; algebra II; geometry; Spanish I and II; computer applications; biology, chemistry, and physics (which include laboratory work); U.S. government; U.S. history; world history; and study skills. Students may take one new course or two repeat courses.

The average class size for both the Middle School and the Upper School is 12 students. Students are graded on the following scale: A (90–100 percent), B (80–89 percent), C (70–79 percent), D (60–69 percent), and F (0–59 percent).

R-MA also offers a unique summer flight-training program that provides the aspiring aviator with ground school, approximately 15 hours of aircraft time, an FAA medical examination, and transportation to and from the airport. Flight time is logged in one of the Academy's single-engine Cessna 152 airplanes. Students who already have a single-engine private pilot rating may work toward their instrument rating. Students must turn 16 during or before the summer program in order to participate in the flight program.

The Independent Student Summer Program provides the non-English-speaking student with practical instruction in English as a Second Language (ESL). The course combines classroom group sessions, cultural experiences, and other activities to provide a total-immersion program. The program includes Beginner ESL, Intermediate ESL, Advanced ESL, and TOEFL Prep.

ENROLLMENT

Approximately 200 students enroll in R-MA's Summer Program each year—140 at the Upper School, 50 at the Middle School, and 10 in the flight program. More than 50 percent of the students are from Virginia and Maryland, 10–15 percent are from outside the U.S., and the rest of the students come from approximately twenty states all over the country.

DAILY SCHEDULE

A typical day at the Upper School may include the following:

6:30	Wake-up
7:15	Breakfast
8:00–9:00	First period
9:00–9:15	Break
9:15–10:15	First period
10:15–10:30	Break
10:30–11:30	Second period
11:30–11:45	Break
11:45–12:45	Second period
12:55–1:45	Lunch
2:00–3:00	First period lab
3:00–3:15	Break
3:15–4:15	Second period lab
4:30–5:45	Study hall
6:15–7:00	Dinner
7:30–9:00	Activity period
9:00–10:00	Free time
10:00–10:30	CQ'd to room
10:30	Lights-out

A typical day at the Middle School may include:

6:45	Wake-up
7:45–8:15	Breakfast
8:20	Flag ceremony/announcements
8:30–9:45	First period
9:50–11:05	Second period
11:10–12:25	Third period
12:40–1:20	Lunch
1:25–2:10	Mentoring
2:15	Afternoon announcements
2:20–3:20	Intramurals/homework lab
3:20–4:40	Free time
4:45–5:30	Study hall
5:50–6:30	Dinner
7:00–9:00	Recreational activities
9:30	Prepare for bed
9:45	Lights-out

EXTRA OPPORTUNITIES AND ACTIVITIES

Weekend activities may include trips to King's Dominion, Busch Gardens, Hershey Park, Half Moon Beach, Splashdown Water Park, white-water rafting, golf and batting cages, local movie theaters, bowling, swimming, and paintball competitions.

The Middle School academic trips on Wednesdays may include trips to the White House, Arlington National Cemetery, Luray Caverns, Frontier Culture Museum, Manassas Battlefield Park, Antietam Battlefield Park/Harpers Ferry, or Shenandoah National Park.

FACILITIES

All classes and dorm rooms are air conditioned and wired for Internet capability. Two students share a room; roommates are determined by grade and/or age. Each floor is supervised by a dorm counselor.

The R-MA pool is open to students during free time, as are the gymnasium and the weight room. Two soccer fields, five tennis courts, a football field, lacrosse field, softball field, baseball field, and an outdoor basketball court are available for student use.

The Middle School students are housed on a separate campus from the Upper School, with their own classrooms, spacious dorm rooms, cafeteria, and gymnasium. They share the Upper School weight room, pool, and chapel throughout the week.

MEDICAL CARE

Registered nurses are on staff. Students requiring additional medical care may go to Warren County Hospital, located less than a mile away from the campus. Each student is required to submit immunization records and a copy of their last physical before registration day.

COSTS

Tuition, room, and board costs for 2004 were $2278, plus a recommended personal account of $700 and an application fee of $75. Tuition, room, and board for international students was $2688, plus a recommended personal account of $800, an ESL lab fee of $250, and an application fee of $200. For day students, costs were $610 per new Upper School course and $285 for repeat Upper School courses. The cost of the Middle School day program was $830.

Lunch for the entire four weeks was $93.75 for Upper School day students taking repeat courses. The cost of lunch is included in the tuition for all other students.

Miscellaneous charges included $15 for telephone rental and $100 in lab fees. Cost for the flight program was $2278 plus flying time per hour and $700 for the personal account.

APPLICATION TIMETABLE

Inquiries into the summer programs are welcomed year-round; updated information is published in December of each year. Tours of the campus are available Monday through Saturday. Interviews are not required for the summer program. Applications are accepted until classes are full, but should be turned in no later than one week before the summer program begins. Application fee is $75. Applicants are notified of the admissions decision a few days after the admissions office has received all the required paperwork.

For more information, contact:

Admissions Office
200 Academy Drive
Front Royal, Virginia 22630
800-272-1172 (toll-free)
Fax: 540-636-5419
E-mail: admissions@rma.edu
World Wide Web: http://www.rma.edu

RASSIAS
STUDENT PROGRAMS

RASSIAS PROGRAMS

FRANCE AND SPAIN

Type of Program: French and Spanish language studies, family-stays, and travel
Participants: Coeducational, grades 9–11
Enrollment: 100 students in groups of 20 to 25
Program Dates: Four to five weeks from late June through early August
Heads of Program: Bill Miles and Helene Rassias-Miles, Directors

LOCATION

Rassias Programs offers language studies, family-stays, and travel in France and Spain.

BACKGROUND AND PHILOSOPHY

Rassias has been offering European experiences to students since 1985.

The Rassias Programs sprang from Helene Rassias' childhood experiences in France. There she accompanied her father, a renowned professor at Dartmouth College and developer of the Rassias Method® of language instruction. All Rassias language programs use the Rassias Method—an approach that provides a dynamic, uninhibited cultural and linguistic immersion. The approach is widely used at Dartmouth and 600 other institutions worldwide.

The European family-stay programs benefit from the directors' personal contacts, which they have developed over twenty-five years of traveling and studying abroad. Working closely with local sources who are friends of the directors, Rassias carefully selects families for the homestay program. Students continue to speak, write, and read in the foreign language even after departing for the travel portion of their trip.

PROGRAM OFFERINGS

Rassias Programs—France (grades 9–11) Rassias French language programs, offered in Tours and Arles, combine French language studies with travel and cultural immersion. Courses are taught by a master teacher and 2 or 3 assistants. Group size varies from 20 to 25 participants, with orientation taking place in Amboise (Tours) or the Pyrenees (Arles).

Tours (four weeks) Students with two or more years of French can expand their language skills while living with host families in Tours, a town located on

the banks of the Loire River. Once in Tours, students attend French language classes in the morning. Afternoons, evenings, and weekends are devoted to planned group activities or excursions with host families. Visits to a Brittany coastal town, Normandy beaches, and Paris round out the experience.

Arles (five weeks) Students with one or more years of French study the language while living with host families in Arles, a town located in the beautiful region of Provence. Classes are held in the morning. Students spend the afternoons and evenings traveling to local sites or with their host families. During the final weeks of the program, students tour the Riviera, the Loire Valley, and Paris.

Rassias Programs—Spain (grades 9–11) These three 4-week Spanish language and family-stay programs are designed for students with two or more years of Spanish. They are based in Gijón, Segovia, and Pontevedra and are taught by a master teacher and 2 or 3 assistants. Group size varies from 20 to 25 students.

Gijón (four weeks) The family-stay and classes unfold in Gijón, a beach resort city of 250,000 inhabitants, which lies on Spain's North Atlantic coast. Classes are held in Gijón's famous sports club where afterwards students can play basketball and volleyball, swim, or take an aerobics class—all in Spanish. Orientation and a bit of tourism start the program in Segovia and Madrid. The final weeks are spent on a day kayak near the Pikos Mountains and then end with exploration of fabulous Barcelona.

Segovia (four weeks) The ancient city of Segovia is the core of this program, where classes, excursions both in Segovia and to the castle towns that surround it, visits with local artists and politicians, and the family-stay all take place. The program starts with orientation in Toledo, where students not only explore this city, which is entirely on Spain's national historical register, but also spend time getting acquainted and moving away from English to Spanish. Following the home stay, the group travels through Andalusia (while continuing to speak Spanish) to amazing Granada, the classic beaches of the south, ancient Cordoba, lively Sevilla, and, finally, Madrid.

Pontevedra (four weeks) The program begins with orientation at a historical thirteenth-century monastery perched high in the mountains of Ourense Province. Here, students relax, hike, explore the local aldeas (small villages), and start practicing Spanish by talking with real Spaniards. The home stay and classes take place in coastal Pontevedra. With a name dating back to time of the Roman Empire (Pontus Veteri), Pontevedra has been a central point of travel for pilgrims along the southern leg of the Camino de Santiago since medieval times. Located in Galicia, in a region known as Rías Bajas, Pontevedra is off the beaten track of foreign tourists, offering an advantage to those students who wish to speak only Spanish. While in Pontevedra, students visit beach resorts, small fishing villages, inland medieval sites, and the protected islands just off the coast, as well as more well-known places such as Santiago de Compostela, Bayone, and Tuy. Students then travel to musical Oporto, vibrant Sevilla, and Extremadura, the land of the conquistadors. Here, students visit Mérida, Cáceres, the Yuste Monastery, and the beautiful valley of the Jerte River. Student travels end in Madrid, the capital and heart of Castillian Spain. The sights, sounds, and overall urban quality of the city make this a favorite stop among students and staff members.

STAFF

The language programs are taught by a master teacher and teaching assistants. Many have had prior teaching experience using the Rassias Method. All attend Rassias Foundation teacher workshops.

All staff members have studied and have usually lived in the region that they will tour with students; many possess a near native understanding of a country's language and culture.

COSTS

The fees, including airfare, range from $5500 to $6500 for the language programs.

APPLICATION TIMETABLE

Starting with November 30 of each year, all completed applications are reviewed during the first fifteen days of the following month. Programs are usually full following the February 28 deadline.

For more information, contact:

Bill Miles
Rassias Programs
P.O. Box 5456
Hanover, New Hampshire 03755
603-643-3007 or 603-643-3323
Fax: 603-643-4249
E-mail: rassias@sover.net
World Wide Web: http://www.sover.net/~rassias

REIN TEEN TOURS

SUMMER TRAVEL PROGRAMS

UNITED STATES, CANADA, HAWAII, AND ALASKA

Type of Program: Active travel
Participants: Coeducational, ages 12–17
Enrollment: 40 per group
Program Dates: End of June through August; tours vary from twenty-one to forty-two days
Head of Program: Norman Rein, Owner

BACKGROUND AND PHILOSOPHY

Rein Teen Tours was founded in 1986 with the objective of offering teenagers activity-oriented, supervised travel in places throughout North America. The Rein Teen Tour staff, with more than thirty years of experience in organizing teen travel, works diligently throughout the year to promote creativity in its tour planning and to guarantee a safe, educational, productive summer for its participants. Since its inception, Rein Teen Tours has shown a commitment to supervision, safety, and worthwhile programming.

Believing that the composition of the group is crucial to the success of the tour, great energy is invested in assembling the tour groups, emphasizing age compatibility and geographic diversity among the members of each group. Many teenagers choose to join on their own, as the program is specifically designed to promote interaction and to keep social pressure to a minimum. The professional tour staff specializes in promoting socialization and minimizing "cliqueness" among tour members. Teenagers come to Rein Teen Tours with positive attitudes, anxious to make many new friends, visit many great places, and participate in a variety of activities that ultimately exceed their greatest expectations.

A Rein Teen Tour summer is appropriate for any teenager with a desire to participate in a variety of unforgettable activities while enjoying the excitement of traveling throughout North America. When teenagers outgrow traditional camp, the ever-changing daily events on a Rein Teen Tour hold their interest while maintaining their enthusiasm throughout the trip.

PROGRAM OFFERINGS

Rein Teen Tours offers a wide variety of tour itineraries for travel throughout North America.

A variety of tours that visit the western United States and western Canada are offered. Western options include three-week, thirty-day, and six-week tours. Three-week tours begin in Salt Lake City and travel to Bryce Canyon and Zion Canyon National Parks, Grand Canyon National Park, Las Vegas, San Diego, Los Angeles, Lake Tahoe, and San Francisco. Thirty-day trips add to the excitement with visits to the Black Hills of South Dakota, Mount Rushmore, and the Badlands, Yellowstone, and Grand Teton National Parks. Six-week tours visit all the same great spots in the western United States and add the thrill of visiting western Canada and the Pacific Northwest. This includes the excitement of Calgary and the Calgary Stampede, the beauty of Banff and Jasper National Parks, and the majesty of Lake Louise, Vancouver, Whistler, British Columbia, and Seattle.

The Eastern Adventure, limited to junior high school–age teenagers, visits many beautiful scenic

areas, including Niagara Falls, the White Mountains of New Hampshire, and Acadia and Shenandoah National Parks. Action-packed city stops include Toronto, Montreal, Quebec City, Boston, and Washington, D.C. The tour also includes two sun-drenched days at a resort in Myrtle Beach and five days of nonstop excitement in Orlando. This thirty-day trip is a great first tour for young teenagers who are anxious to travel.

The Hawaiian/Alaskan Adventure allows teenagers to visit the farthest and most exotic reaches of the United States. Alaskan highlights include a seven-day Inside Passage luxury liner cruise. Three of the Hawaiian Islands—Oahu, the "Big Island of Hawaii," and Maui—are visited and allow for fun activities, including snorkel cruises, submarine trips, and a memorable journey to Hawaii Volcanoes National Park. The tour also visits Vancouver, Whistler, British Columbia, Seattle, Portland, Mount Hood National Park, Lake Tahoe, and San Francisco. In these areas, participants enjoy summer snow skiing, jet boating, whale watching, and sea kayaking.

ENROLLMENT

Rein Teen Tours attracts teenagers from all over the United States, Canada, and the world. Over the past several summers, international participants from Europe, South America, and Asia have added to the geographic diversity of the tour groups.

EXTRA OPPORTUNITIES AND ACTIVITIES

Each teenager is treated as an individual, as the flexibility of the programs allows participants to choose from a variety of activities in the areas visited. In scenic areas and national parks, teenagers are encouraged to try new activities and benefit from professional instruction. Examples include snorkeling at Catalina Island, waterskiing on Lake Tahoe, and summer snow skiing in Whistler, British Columbia. While visiting major cities, such as Los Angeles and San Francisco, tours attend live theater, comedy clubs, teen dance clubs, major league baseball games, laseriums, and theme parks. Past travelers have remarked that there is never a dull moment on a Rein Teen Tour. They compliment Rein Teen Tours on its innovative, up-to-date activities, citing examples such as high energy dragster racing, summer snow skiing, off-road Jeep trips, and jet boating.

FACILITIES

Rein Teen Tours believes that tour members should enjoy the most convenient accommodations in all areas visited. Safety and security are top priorities when choosing facilities. A variety of facilities, chosen because of their proximity to many local activities, vary between scenic campgrounds, fun college dorms, and exciting resort hotels. Camping highlights include waterfront resort campgrounds in California, tranquil campground settings in the mountains of the Canadian Rockies, and picturesque camping near the rim of the Grand Canyon. All campgrounds feature modern bathroom facilities with hot water, private showers, flush toilets, and electricity. When camping, a great night's sleep is certain on a self-inflating Thermorest camping mattress and cot inside a custom-designed cabin tent, all provided by Rein Teen Tours. Three nutritious meals featuring a wide variety of food, as well as fun snacks, are provided when camping.

Fun campus stays at popular universities include UCLA, University of Michigan, University of Alaska, the University of Utah, University of Toronto, and University of Minnesota. Dynamic hotels include the Hyatt at Fisherman's Wharf in San Francisco, the Monte Carlo Resort in Las Vegas, the Doubletree Guest Quarters Suite Resort in Orlando, the Hilton Waikoloa Village in Hawaii, and the Loews Coronado Beach Resort in San Diego. Tour members are always provided individual beds in university dormitories and hotels. On hotel and dormitory days, three meals are provided at varied restaurants, with teenagers ordering directly from regular menus. Dining accommodations include fun dinner parties at trendy Hard Rock Cafes and Planet Hollywood restaurants in various cities.

STAFF

The summer tour staff comprises teachers, graduate students, and college graduates who are experienced campers and travelers. Each tour operates with a ratio of 1 adult for every 7 teenagers. The tour directors, all certified by the American Red Cross for basic first aid training and CPR, are among the most experienced in the teen tour industry. Staff members receive extensive training prior to the tour, as their leadership qualities consistently play a major role in the success of the summer tours. Rein Teen Tours summer staff members are frequently commended for their mature and responsible attitude as well as their sense of humor and compassion for the needs of the teenagers.

MEDICAL CARE

The safety and health of the tour members are the most important aspect of the operation of the tours. To promote tour wellness, tours are planned to allow time for leisure, relaxation, nutritious meals, and adequate sleep. In the event that medical services are needed, Rein Teen Tours has established relationships with an extensive network of medical facilities, including hospitals, 24-hour emergency medical clinics, and local physicians, who are available to treat teenagers requiring medical attention at any time or place during the tour.

COSTS

Trips range in price from $4499 to $7499 and include all lodging, three meals daily, all recreation and entertainment admissions, gratuities, and taxes.

TRANSPORTATION

Travel arrangements for all teenagers are made by the Rein Teen Tour travel staff and provide for getting teenagers from their home area to tour start points and back home upon completion of the tour.

APPLICATION TIMETABLE

Tour enrollment is on a rolling basis, and early inquiry is suggested as tour spaces are limited. A $350 deposit is required with the enrollment application.

FOR MORE INFORMATION, CONTACT:

Rein Teen Tours
30 Galesi Drive
Wayne, New Jersey 07470
800-831-1313 (toll-free)
Fax: 973-785-4268
E-mail: summer@reinteentours.com
World Wide Web: http//www.reinteentours.com

PARTICIPANT/FAMILY COMMENTS

"My parents and I investigated many summer options and decided Rein Teen Tours offered the most. Boy, did we make the right decision! Not only did I visit the most amazing American sights, but also in a relatively short period of time, I made wonderful and lasting friendships. Highest marks to the Rein Teen Tour staff for providing me with the best accommodations, an incredible itinerary (full of activity everyday!), and a dynamic staff who made me their number one priority. Everyone was terrific! Thank you for giving me a summer of excellent memories!"

"My husband and I just want to thank you for the wonderful experience you have given our son. Jayson went on this trip not knowing anyone, and came home with wonderful friends and lifetime relationships! He has not stopped raving about the marvelous things that he was exposed to. Each and every place was an 'awesome' adventure for him. The trip was well organized and relevant to the interests of teens. All of the pre-planning was obvious in the smooth manner in which the trip ran. We highly recommend Rein Teen Tours!"

RHODE ISLAND SCHOOL OF DESIGN

PRE-COLLEGE PROGRAM

PROVIDENCE, RHODE ISLAND

Type of Program: Visual arts study
Participants: Coeducational, students between ages 16 and 18 (born between July 31, 1985, and June 19, 1988)
Enrollment: About 500
Program Dates: June 19–July 31, 2004

LOCATION

Rhode Island offers some of New England's most scenic coastline, beautifully preserved colonial villages, and the cultural richness of Providence and Newport. Rhode Island School of Design's (RISD) main campus is on College Hill, on Providence's East Side, home to both RISD and Brown University. Additional facilities are located in downtown Providence's up-and-coming arts enclave. The elegantly restored homes and gardens of College Hill offer students the relaxed ambience of neighborhood life, while Providence Place Mall, Thayer and Wickenden Streets, and the historic downtown area provide easy access to numerous restaurants, bookstores, specialty shops, and cultural activities. In addition, Waterplace Park, adjacent to RISD's campus, is home to the acclaimed waterfront festival WaterFire.

BACKGROUND AND PHILOSOPHY

The Pre-College Program accepts high school students into an intensive six-week college-like art and design program. In the setting of an internationally renowned design school, a structured curriculum gives each student a strong foundation of skills and understanding in the visual arts. The intensity and focus of the program provide students with the opportunity to experience art as a major academic priority before investing in a college program. Many students create a portfolio for college admissions, while others explore art and design to complement their liberal arts background. Although a previous background in art or design is not necessary, all students should be strongly motivated and ready to commit to a rigorous schedule of study. Students should be prepared to undertake and complete a considerable amount of out-of-class work.

PROGRAM OFFERINGS

All students are required to take three foundation courses: Foundation Drawing, Basic Design, and Art History. In addition, students may choose a major area of concentration: architecture, ceramics, computer animation, drawing, fashion design, furniture design, graphic design, illustration, industrial design, interior design, jewelry, painting, photography (digital), photography (traditional), printmaking, sculpture, or textile design.

The required Foundation Drawing and Basic Design courses each meet one full day per week. Another two days each week are spent working intensively in the major area. Two hours of the fifth weekday are devoted to art history, with the remaining time available for completion of homework assignments.

ENROLLMENT

High school students who have reached their sixteenth birthday as of June 19, 2004, and have enrolled as a junior or senior by September 2004 may apply for admission to the 2004 Pre-College Program. Graduating seniors are welcome, as long as they do not turn 19 before July 31, 2004. Other than these age restrictions, all applicants who show promise of being able to benefit from the program are admitted. The approximately 500 students enrolled in the program usually represent thirty to forty states and more than ten countries.

DAILY SCHEDULE

7:30–8:30	Breakfast
9:00	Classes begin
12:00–1:00	Lunch
4:00	Classes end
5:00–6:00	Dinner
7:00–10:00	Open studio, social and recreational activities
11:00	Curfew (Sunday–Thursday)
12:00	Curfew (Friday and Saturday)

Students should know all of the regulations of the Pre-College Program. A handbook, which clearly describes these and other rules, is sent to all student and their parents. Violation of Pre-College Program policies or regulations is taken seriously by the college administration; students may be subject to various sanctions or dismissal if they disregard them.

For example, students are required to be in the dormitories by curfew. They are not permitted to sign out from their dormitory overnight unless written permission from a parent or guardian is on file in the office of the resident director. Resident students are not allowed to possess or drive motor vehicles, including motor scooters and motorcycles.

EXTRA OPPORTUNITIES AND ACTIVITIES

Students in the program may take part in a full schedule of evening and weekend activities. Trips are planned to popular Rhode Island landmarks, including Newport and Narragansett beaches. At RISD's Tillinghast Farm, a 33-acre expanse on Narragansett

Bay, students may enjoy sailing, sunbathing, kite flying, picnicking, and relaxing in the outdoors. At least one trip to Boston and/or a prominent New England museum of art is organized. Excellent theater productions are sponsored by nearby Brown University. There are also school-sponsored concerts, films, dances, and other social events. In the evenings, students can work in open studios.

FACILITIES

The RISD campus is one of this country's largest and best-equipped centers for the study of art and design. Its forty-one restored campus buildings house studios, classrooms, a library, an auditorium, an excellent museum, galleries, and book and supply stores. The school's dining and residence facilities are near the center of campus. College housing has quiet study areas, recreational facilities, and work areas.

STAFF

Members of the faculty are drawn from RISD's regular academic-year faculty, RISD alumni, professionals in the field, and instructors from colleges and universities throughout the country.

The residence staff is made up of RISD's year-round professional staff members and resident assistants—RISD students who are carefully selected, trained, and supervised. RISD's Public Safety Department also monitors dormitories.

MEDICAL CARE

RISD's on-campus Health Services is staffed by a registered nurse and on-call physicians. If students have emergency medical problems requiring treatment at the local hospital, they are escorted there and their parents are notified. Health forms are included in the application package. Medical insurance is required.

COSTS

The 2004 tuition and fees were as follows: a $4535 program fee for boarding students (includes tuition, housing, and dining) and a $3075 program fee for commuting students (tuition only). Boarding students are required to pay a nonrefundable deposit of $300, and commuting students pay a nonrefundable deposit of $200. These deposits are applied to the total program fee. The meal contract is mandatory for all residential students. Students may need to spend as much as $700 for art supplies, depending on their major. In addition, there are equipment rental fees in certain majors.

For the 2004 summer session, applications submitted on or before April 14 must be accompanied by a nonrefundable deposit or payment in full. The deadline for full payment is April 30. Applications submitted after April 14 must include payment in full of all tuition and fees. If the application is not accepted or registration is closed, tuition and fees are refunded promptly.

APPLICATION TIMETABLE

Early application is highly recommended. All of the major courses have a limited number of spaces, and students are assigned to each on a first-come, first-served basis.

To apply, students must return a completed Pre-College Program Application Form, a short statement of interest, and one letter of recommendation from either an art instructor or a guidance counselor.

Non-U.S. citizens must submit special paperwork by April 1. RISD holds a Pre-College Open House in early March for students and their families.

FOR MORE INFORMATION, CONTACT:

Pre-College Program
Rhode Island School of Design
Two College Street
Providence, Rhode Island 02903-2787
401-454-6200
Fax: 401-454-6218
World Wide Web: http://www.risd.edu/precollege.cfm

ROCKBROOK CAMP

SUMMER CAMP

BREVARD, NORTH CAROLINA

Type of Program: Traditional camping
Participants: Girls, ages 6–16
Enrollment: 190 per session
Program Dates: One-, two-, three-, and four-week sessions from mid-June to mid-August
Head of Program: Jerry Stone, Director

LOCATION

Rockbrook is located 4 miles from Brevard, North Carolina. Camp is situated "in the heart of a wooded mountain" (the appropriate name of a popular camp song). The 200-acre site is replete with beautiful forests and waterfalls, which are accessible by numerous hiking trails. Rockbrook campers also have access to the Camp's outpost system that borders the Pisgah National Forest. The new 100-acre Pisgah Outpost is minutes from camp. Lakes, trails, and a playing field make it a great destination for day and overnight trips. Campers take full advantage of the neighboring national forest with rock-climbing and backpacking trips. Rockbrook borders the French Broad River, which is perfect for beginning flat-water river instruction. Also, for more advanced instruction, several whitewater rivers, including the Green, Tuckasegee, and the Nantahala, are nearby. Rockbrook is a licensed outfitter on the Nantahala River, located near the Camp's Nantahla Outpost. The outpost is conveniently located near the Appalachian Trail and the Great Smoky Mountains.

BACKGROUND AND PHILOSOPHY

Since 1921, Rockbrook Camp has been a place where girls ages 6–16 can enjoy a summer away from home. Here, in a noncompetitive environment, campers gain experience in making their own decisions, since many opportunities are available daily. Campers from many geographic regions live with others their age in small cabin groups of 8 campers and 2 counselors. Campers receive instruction with others at their age and skill level and progress according to individual ability. Activities are structured so that, as campers return for successive seasons, new challenges and opportunities are always available.

PROGRAM OFFERINGS

Many activities are offered during morning and afternoon instructional periods. Campers choose their five daily classes once a week. The choices include target sports, athletics, several crafts, and outdoor instruction. The program concentrates on a half-dozen specialties that provide a good balance between sports, such as gymnastics and horseback riding; creative outlets, such as pottery and drama; and several outdoor specialties, including white-water canoeing, mountain biking, rafting, kayaking, backpacking, and rock climbing.

Rockbrook has a commercial pottery operation that is devoted entirely to campers during the summer. And the horses that are used to teach all levels of hunter-jumper instruction are also used for riding instruction throughout the year.

Outdoor specialists teach white-water activities, backpacking, and rock climbing year-round. These activities offer many challenges to campers as they return each summer. Rockbrook has excellent in-camp rock-climbing facilities. These include an indoor climbing wall, a 50-foot alpine tower, and several on-site climbs. Several outdoor trips involving these activities are offered daily both on and off the camp property. These optional challenging activities are excellent vehicles for promoting self-confidence.

ENROLLMENT

Rockbrook can accommodate 190 campers per session. The campers are organized into three age groups, each with a program of activities administered in terms of age, ability, and interests of the campers. Although campers come primarily from the southeastern United States, many other states and countries are also represented.

DAILY SCHEDULE

8	Rising bell
8:30	Breakfast
9:30	Morning activities
1:15	Lunch
2	Rest hour
3	Afternoon activities
6:15	Supper and free time
8	Evening programs
9:30	Lights-out (later for older campers)

Wednesday afternoons are set aside for cabin activities. On Sunday, there is a late wake-up time. In addition, special morning and afternoon programs are followed by a picnic dinner.

EXTRA OPPORTUNITIES AND ACTIVITIES

Trips are taken out of camp almost every day. These include a wide variety of day and overnight hiking, backpacking, canoeing, kayaking, expeditionary sea kayaking, white-water rafting, and mountain-biking trips. Campers who have completed at least the fifth grade enjoy the white-water rafting trips offered on the Nantahala River.

There are many special events and traditional programs throughout the summer. Campers participate in evening and Sunday programs consisting of skits, treasure hunts, campfire programs, carnivals, and dances. A camper-planned banquet is a highlight at the end of the June and July sessions.

FACILITIES

Campers live in screened cabins accommodating 8 campers and 2 counselors. Bath houses are located near the cabins. The main buildings include a dining hall, gym, three stone lodges, barn, two log cabins, and a pottery studio. There are three tennis courts, a rifle range, an archery range, a lake, an alpine tower, an indoor climbing wall, and an in-camp climbing area.

Rockbrook also has an outpost with sleeping cabins, a tepee, bathrooms, and eating facilities near the Nantahala River.

STAFF

Rockbrook's counselor-camper ratio is approximately 1:4. The staff includes professional instructors, teachers, and former campers. Most cabin counselors are college students who are selected for their understanding of youth as well as their qualities of leadership and character and teaching skills. Key staff members plan and supervise the instructional program, trips, daily activities, and cabin activities.

MEDICAL CARE

A full-time registered nurse is on duty in the health lodge. All staff members are trained in CPR and first aid. A doctor is on call, and a medical clinic and hospital are located 4 miles from camp.

RELIGIOUS LIFE

Rockbrook enrolls campers of all faiths. Sunday chapel services are nondenominational and focus on friendship, respect, and appreciation of nature. Catholic campers may attend Sunday Mass in Brevard.

COSTS

The fees for the 2005 season are $900 for one week, $1750 for two weeks, $2475 for three weeks, and $3000 for four weeks. A $350 deposit is due with the application form and is applied to the tuition. A $750 payment is due March 1, and the balance is due May 1. The fees are all-inclusive except for incidental spending money for the camp store and other personal items.

TRANSPORTATION

Many campers travel to Rockbrook by car; others fly into the Asheville, North Carolina, airport, where they are met by camp staff members and transported to camp.

APPLICATION TIMETABLE

Returning campers are guaranteed their spaces at camp until October 1. After October 1, applications are accepted as they are received until sessions are filled. Group presentations are made in many southeastern cities, and a list of Rockbrook representatives is available as references. A color brochure and video are available upon request. The office is open year-round, from 9 a.m. to 5 p.m., Monday through Friday. An answering machine collects messages after regular business hours.

FOR MORE INFORMATION, CONTACT:

Rockbrook Camp
P.O. Box 792
Brevard, North Carolina 28712
828-884-6151
Fax: 828-884-6459
E-mail: office@rockbrookcamp.com
World Wide Web: http://www.rockbrookcamp.com

PARTICIPANT/FAMILY COMMENTS

"Our daughter's camp experience was positive in all respects. The setting of the camp is beautiful, of course, but what pleased and impressed us most was the genuine caring of each and every staff member. Our daughter pushed herself to do new things and loved them. She thought mountain biking was the BEST experience; her sense of pride was tremendous. She can't wait to come back next year. She has been writing friends and has already visited two. A great summer!"

"Rockbrook is a place to retreat to, a land of beauty and peace, a place of friends and fun and people who love and care, a place where dreams come true."

RUMSEY HALL SCHOOL

SUMMER SESSION

WASHINGTON DEPOT, CONNECTICUT

Type of Program: Academic enrichment or review
Participants: Coeducational; boarding, grades 5–9; day, grades 3–9
Enrollment: 65 students
Program Dates: Five-week program, June 29 to August 2
Head of Program: Dave Whiting, Director

LOCATION

Situated in the southern foothills of northwestern Connecticut's Berkshire Mountains, Rumsey Hall is 43 miles from Hartford, Connecticut, and 80 miles northeast of New York City. The 147-acre campus is surrounded by beautiful wooded hills and the scenic Bantam River.

BACKGROUND AND PHILOSOPHY

Rumsey Hall School was established in 1900 and is noted for high academic standards and individual attention. Since its inception, the School has retained its original philosophy, "to help each child develop to his or her maximum stature as an individual, as a family member, and as a contributing member of society." Students are constantly exposed to the idea that success comes through the application of steady effort. The Summer Session is an extension of the Rumsey philosophy. Working with a limited enrollment in a relaxed, sensibly structured, and informal atmosphere, experienced Rumsey faculty members provide intensive academic review or give students a head start for the coming year.

PROGRAM OFFERINGS

Normal class size ranges from 8 to 10 students, and individual attention and help are available. Special emphasis is placed on English, mathematics, study skills, and computer skills. Students who need language skills or developmental reading help are given individual attention from trained specialists. English as a second language (ESL) is offered to international students. Rumsey Hall students have access to state-of-the-art personal computers and software. Each classroom is equipped with at least one station, and there are sixteen terminals in the computer lab. All terminals are linked to a schoolwide information system, and students have appropriate access to the Internet. Each student has an e-mail address for easy communication with home and friends.

The close relationship between teachers and students is a special part of boarding school. Opportunities for support and encouragement are abundant, and renewed self-confidence is often the most outstanding product of a summer at Rumsey. Most students have roommates, and life in a dormitory teaches valuable lessons about getting along with others and being part of a community. All meals are family-style, with faculty members and their families in attendance.

Report cards are mailed at midterm and at the end of the term. Written reports, which include grades for each subject and teacher comments regarding academic and social progress, are provided at the end of the session. Each student is discussed individually at weekly faculty meetings. Parental input is encouraged.

ENROLLMENT

Students come from a variety of states, countries, and local communities.

DAILY SCHEDULE

7:45	Wake up
8:00–8:30	Breakfast
8:45–10:30	Classes
10:30–11:00	Recess and snack
11:00–1:10	Classes
1:15	Lunch
2:00–4:30	Activities/recreation
5:00–6:00	Reading period
6:00	Dinner
7:00–8:00	Study hall
8:00–9:30	Free time
9:30–10:00	Lights out

EXTRA OPPORTUNITIES AND ACTIVITIES

Great emphasis is placed on providing a variety of recreational and enrichment activities to ensure a balanced, happy, and productive Summer Session. Every afternoon, students select from a variety of activities, such as swimming, hiking, tennis, fishing, horseback riding, baseball, soccer, lacrosse, and basketball. Occasional off-campus school trips are planned to museums, concerts, amusement parks, and sporting events. A considerable effort is made to cultivate students' interests and to expose them to new experiences.

Weekends begin on Friday after classes. Livery service to and from train stations, bus depots, and airports is easily arranged if enough notice is given to the School office. Students are free to leave with parental permission but must return by 7 p.m. Sunday evening. For students who choose to remain on campus, there is a range of on- and off-campus activities available with close faculty supervision at all times. Students may attend church service in Washington and nearby towns.

FACILITIES

Buildings include a new art room, music room, and science lab. Traditional-style classrooms, a library, and a study hall encompass the academic setting. Boys' and girls' dorms allow for both single and double rooms. Two beautiful on-campus ponds supply fishing and nature activities. There are three newly renovated indoor tennis courts, a large gym for basketball and volleyball, and a spacious dining hall that allows for family-style meals.

STAFF

Both full- and part-time staff members make up the Rumsey Hall Summer Session faculty. The faculty members instruct classes, supervise afternoon activities, and are dorm parents for the boarding students. Students live with supportive dorm parents and become a part of their dorm parents' families.

COSTS

Tuition, room, and board totaled $4600 for boarding students, $1500 for day students, and $1060 for half-day students for the 2004 summer session. A deposit of $500 for boarders and $200 for day students is required to secure a space for the summer and is used as a drawing account for student expenses. Any money remaining in the drawing account is returned at the end of the summer session. There is an additional fee of $525 for individual tutoring in language skills and an additional $650 for enrollment in ESL.

FINANCIAL AID

Financial aid is available through the School's financial aid office and is based on need. A copy of the previous year's tax return is required.

TRANSPORTATION

Livery service to and from train stations, bus depots, and airports can be easily arranged with advance notice.

APPLICATION TIMETABLE

Inquiries are welcome at any time of the year, with most families beginning the admissions process in the winter or early spring in anticipation of summer enrollment. Admissions interviews and tours are scheduled throughout the year. Applications are accepted on a rolling basis, and decisions are made within two weeks of receiving the completed application package. Families are asked to respond to an offer of acceptance in a similar time frame due to the limited space available.

FOR MORE INFORMATION, PLEASE CONTACT:

Matthew S. Hoeniger, Director of Admission
Rumsey Hall School
201 Romford Road
Washington Depot, Connecticut 06794
860-868-0535
Fax: 860-868-7907
E-mail: admiss@rumseyhall.org

PARTICIPANT/FAMILY COMMENTS

"One of the things I enjoy most about summer life at Rumsey is the range of experiences available to students. We are not watchers, we are doers. The question is not whether we'll participate. The question is which activity we will participate in."

"The faculty and students are very close at Rumsey. That should be a given at any boarding school for children this age, but there is something special about this community that surpasses your expectations."

RUSTIC PATHWAYS

INTERNATIONAL COMMUNITY SERVICE, ADVENTURE TRAVEL, AND FOREIGN LANGUAGE

AUSTRALIA, NEW ZEALAND, THE FIJI ISLANDS, THAILAND, COSTA RICA, AND THE UNITED STATES

Type of Program: International community service, adventure travel, and foreign language
Participants: High school students, 13–18 years old
Enrollment: Differs from program to program, but generally 14–16 students per program departure
Heads of Program: David Venning, Chairman; Evan Wells, President

LOCATION

Rustic Pathways serves Australia, New Zealand, the Fiji Islands, Thailand, Costa Rica, Hawaii, and the American Southwest. Programs operate in a variety of locations within each country. The specific locations of various programs depend on program focus, experience levels of student participants, weather conditions, and local conditions.

BACKGROUND AND PHILOSOPHY

Rustic Pathways is an international travel organization with year-round operations in many of the countries it serves. Focused in safe, clean, friendly, and culturally diverse destinations, its high school programs offer students an array of overseas travel opportunities. Rustic Pathways also offers interesting and economical college programs as well as customized excursions for families, teacher-led groups, and special interest groups throughout the year.

Rustic Pathways began operations twenty-one years ago. David Venning initially set the tone for the company by taking small groups of high school students into the outback of Australia via four-wheel-drive vehicles. Over the years, the list of destinations and programs has expanded, while the personal attention and emphasis on safety, learning, and growing has continued. David still leads trips himself, but he now has a fantastic team of well-traveled, highly respected, intelligent individuals who continue to promote the ideals of Rustic Pathways through their own program leadership. Adventure travel is still an integral part of the company's offerings, but community service and foreign language instruction have also taken on a vital role within the company's ideals and future development. Rustic Pathways offers exciting and worthwhile community service projects that help students explore the local flavor and unique lifestyles of remote village communities in several countries. Among other objectives, these community service and language programs seek to bridge cultural gaps by allowing students to donate time, energy, and resources to helping others while experiencing life in a different cultural environment firsthand.

PROGRAM OFFERINGS

More than forty diverse and unique programs make up the list of choices for students and parents interested in traveling with Rustic Pathways. Each program generally has several departure dates throughout the summer, and programs are designed to easily interconnect, allowing a student to customize the summer of their dreams.

Australia Programs offered in Australia include the Sunshine Coast and Sydney (ten days), High Adrenaline Aussie Adventure (ten days), Outback 4-Wheel-Drive Safari (ten days), Tropical Aussie Adventure (seventeen days), Totally DownUnder (seventeen days), Awesome Aussie Explorer (seventeen days), Ultimate Aussie Adventure (twenty-four days), and Study in Australia (various lengths of stay).
New Zealand In New Zealand, Rustic Pathways offers the Ski and Snowboard Adventures program, which lasts ten, seventeen, or twenty-four days.
The Fiji Islands Programs offered in the Fiji Islands include Introduction to Community Service (ten days), Highlands Community Service (seventeen days), Extended Community Service (twenty-four days), Snapshot of Fiji (ten days), Big Fiji Explorer (seventeen days), Learn to Dive in Fiji (ten days), Scuba Divers Dream (ten days), and Surf the Summer in Fiji (ten or seventeen days).
Thailand Rustic Pathways' Thailand-based programs include Introduction to Community Service (ten days); Ricefields, Monks and Smiling Children (seventeen days); Rhythm in the Ricefields Music Project (ten or seventeen days); the Elephant Conservation Project (ten days); Amazing Thailand Adventure (ten days); Elephants and Amazing Thailand (seventeen days); Buddhist Life and Angkor Wat (seventeen days); Photography and Adventure in Thailand (seventeen days); and the Wonders and Riches of Thailand (seventeen days).
Costa Rica Programs offered in Costa Rica include the Caño Negro Project (eight or fifteen days), the Turtle Conservation Project (eight days), Volcanoes and Rainforests (eight or fifteen days), Costa Rica Adventurer (fifteen days), Costa Rica Extreme (twenty-two days), Costa Rica Natural Wonders (eight days), Surf the Summer in Costa Rica (eight or fifteen days), Ramp Up Your Spanish (eight days), Spanish Language Immersion (fifteen days), and Accelerated Spanish Immersion (fifteen days).
The United States Rustic Pathways offers two programs in the United States: Hawaiian Islands Adventure (fifteen days) and Adventure in America's Southwest (seventeen days).

ENROLLMENT

Rustic Pathways draws students from nearly all fifty states as well as from many countries around the world, creating groups that learn from each other while growing together. Rustic Pathways seeks students who have enthusiastic dispositions and are cooperative and seeking adventure.

FACILITIES

Because of the diverse nature of Rustic Pathways programs, facilities may differ considerably from program to program and country to country. Students may find themselves sleeping in a thatched hut in a remote village, aboard a large sailing boat in the south Pacific, camping beneath the Southern Cross in the middle of the Australian Outback, or tucked in the warm bed of a luxurious five-star hotel. Rustic Pathways utilizes local facilities and resources in an effort to provide culturally unique and diverse travel experiences. Program participants regularly have the opportunity to avail themselves of local customs, foods, and facilities as they travel.

STAFF

In an organization like Rustic Pathways, having wonderful, dedicated staff members with caring hearts and strong backgrounds is essential. Rustic Pathways is a rich and diverse company full of sincere, committed professionals with wide-ranging experience in their various fields. Taken together, team members speak more than twenty languages, have traveled across more than 130 countries, and have led countless groups of students and adult clients across some of the world's most interesting, exotic places. In terms of diversity, the full-time staff includes international sportsmen and sportswomen, champion snowboarders, accomplished musicians, teachers, authors, published songwriters, competitive surfers, and former Buddhist monks.

MEDICAL CARE

Student safety is a top priority for Rustic Pathways. Its staff commonly includes wilderness first responders, registered nurses, wilderness EMTs, surf lifeguards, staff members with St. Johns certificates, those with first aid certification, and those with Red Cross first aid and CPR training.

APPLICATION TIMETABLE

Admission to Rustic Pathways programs is by application only. Students and their parents must file an application through Rustic Pathways' Web site or by mail. Applications are accepted as early as November and are accepted up to two weeks prior to a scheduled trip departure if there is space available on the requested program. Applications are processed on a first-come, first-served basis. There is a $100 nonrefundable application fee for each participant ($200 after April 15), which is returned to students who are not accepted into the program. This is a one-time fee regardless of the number of programs participants join. There is no application fee for returning students. Programs are popular, and participants are encouraged to apply as early as possible to ensure a departure date that suits their summer schedule.

Between January and April, Rustic Pathways staffing teams tour the United States, visiting schools, summer camp fairs, and interested parents and students. Staff members enjoy and appreciate the opportunity to meet with parents and prospective students during this time. Students should contact Rustic Pathways' office to schedule a home visit while staff members are in their area.

For more information, contact:

Rustic Pathways
P.O. Box 1150
Willoughby, Ohio 44096
440-975-9691
800-321-4353 (toll-free)
Fax: 440-975-9694
E-mail: rustic@rusticpathways.com
World Wide Web: http://www.rusticpathways.com

SAIL CARIBBEAN

SUMMER PROGRAM

BRITISH VIRGIN ISLANDS, LEEWARD ISLANDS, AND WINDWARD ISLANDS

Type of Program: Sailing, scuba certifications, community service, lifeguard training, marine biology, water sports, island exploration, and instructor training (graduating seniors–college)
Participants: Coeducational, grades 7–12
Enrollment: 50–80 per session
Program Dates: Fourteen, seventeen, and twenty-one day programs or combined programs from early June to late August
Head of Program: Mike Liese, Founder Director

LOCATION

Sail Caribbean's sailing programs visit more than twenty islands in the British Virgin and Leeward Islands. According to many experts, the waters surrounding the islands offer the best sailing in the world as well as astounding underwater sights. Steady trade winds and crystal-clear waters create exceptional venues for island exploration.

The islands vary in topography (caves to volcanic boulders), vegetation (cactus to rain forest), and civilization (deserted islands to islands rich in African, Dutch, British, Spanish, Scandinavian, and Caribe Indian influences).

BACKGROUND AND PHILOSOPHY

Mike Liese has directed Sail Caribbean for twenty-five years. The living environment on board the yachts provides the foundation and is the key ingredient for the program's success. Students are challenged through programs that promote personal growth, leadership skills, self-reliance, and self-confidence. Hands-on experience and daily lessons motivate students to gain valuable knowledge and develop life skills such as teamwork, problem solving, feedback, and trust. Daily students assume various roles on board such as skipper, mate, and navigator. Students are given the freedom and responsibility of working together to accomplish tasks as simple as cleaning up after breakfast or as complex as docking the boat. Environmental awareness programs encourage students to minimize impact on the environment while learning to respect and care for the habitats they live and play in every day.

Participants should have a strong interest in learning how to sail or dive, a love of the water, and the desire to take on new and challenging responsibilities and experiences.

PROGRAM OFFERINGS

Summer programs have a variety of focuses to meet different needs and interests. Some programs focus primarily on sailing. While aboard the sailboats, students develop living skills by creating and fitting into the group dynamic. For students who want to get a taste of the underwater world, an introductory scuba experience (Discover Scuba Diving) is available, however, participation is limited. One program offers a focus on scuba diving. No prior scuba experience is necessary. PADI instructors offer certifications from entry level (open water scuba diver) to professional levels (Divemaster). Another program challenges older students interested in becoming sailing instructors to develop leadership techniques and skills through practical experience and learning seminars.

All programs offer water sports. Students water-ski and tube from rigid inflatable ski boats. Snorkeling, kayaking, and windsurfing are popular afternoon or early morning activities. Many students are able to enjoy newly found sailing skills aboard smaller boats such as 14-foot Lasers and 15-foot Hobies.

Days are full of exciting exploration and many evenings are spent listening to steel-drum bands and Caribbean music.

ENROLLMENT

Each program session has fleet of three to eight boats with 30 to 80 participants. Boats are coed, with 10 or 12 high school students (grades 7–12) grouped by age. More than forty states and fourteen countries are represented each year.

DAILY SCHEDULE

On a typical day, participants wake at 7 and have the opportunity to take a refreshing swim or windsurf while crewmates fix breakfast. The day's sail is usually 2 to 4 hours long. Instruction takes place en route. If the program includes scuba, 4 to 5 hours are set aside either in the morning or the afternoon for certifications and recreational diving.

All students unite at an anchorage in the late afternoon to share in the day's events. After an evening shower, some students relax on board listening to quiet music while others prepare dinner.

Every second or third day after dinner cleanup, students dress up for an evening of enjoyment ashore with friends while listening to the sounds of the islands provided by local steel drum bands and DJ's.

EXTRA OPPORTUNITIES AND ACTIVITIES

The lifeguard training course complies with the strict standards of the American Red Cross, with well-defined measures of accomplishment at each level of proficiency.

Basic Keel Boating is for experienced sailors who wish to receive a national certificate. During practice, the students sail on Rhode 19 or J 24 sailboats. The course includes seminars, practical instruction on the boats, and a written exam.

Students can earn community service hours through Sail Caribbean's marine biology course.

FACILITIES

Yachts are chartered from one of the foremost charter companies in the world, Sunsail. The boats are 50 feet with five cabins (shared by 2 or 3 students per cabin) and five heads (bathrooms). Most students choose to sleep on deck under the stars. All boats have a full galley (kitchen) and salon (sitting area).

STAFF

Whether sailors or divers, staff members at Sail Caribbean have very high credentials. Staff members play a critical role in the program's success and are hand picked from a large group of potential candidates. All staff members are hired for their sailing or driving skills. However, most importantly, they are selected for their professionalism, maturity, enthusiasm, and a love of working with people. A comprehensive week of staff training helps to enable newer members. To perform to Sail Caribbean's high standards, captains must perform well in the role of a mate prior to taking charge of a student boat. All dive staff members are PADI instructors or Divemasters in good standing.

MEDICAL CARE

The British Virgin Islands have good doctors and medical facilities. All staff members are certified in first aid and CPR. Each program has an EMT or Wilderness First Responder (WFR) acting as its safety officer. The safety and well-being of the students are the highest priority and are never compromised.

COSTS

The price range is from $3375 to $4575 which includes everything except airfare, departure taxes ($10), and dive insurance. Costs include three meals each day, and all rentals, activities, equipment, and instruction. Students who are interested in diving must obtain diving insurance. A minimal amount of spending money is needed for ice cream, soda, souvenirs, and the like.

TRANSPORTATION

Staff members are present in the island airports to meet and greet all students as they arrive. They are there to ensure that students complete the final leg of their journey safely. Sail Caribbean has a travel agent. Although it is not necessary, applicants may wish to contact them to compare prices. Traveler's insurance is strongly recommended for all students.

APPLICATION TIMETABLE

Enrollment is limited in all sessions, with some filling as early as February. Candidates are strongly encouraged to speak with former participants and their parents to get impressions of the program. Applicants are required to provide the name and address of a character reference.

For more information, contact:

Mike Liese, Founder Director
Sail Caribbean
79 Church Street
Northport, New York 11768
631-754-2202
800-321-0994 (toll-free)
Fax: 631-754-3362
E-mail: info@sailcaribbean.com
World Wide Web: http://www.sailcaribbean.com

ST. GEORGE'S SCHOOL

SUMMER PROGRAM

NEWPORT, RHODE ISLAND

Type of Program: Academic enrichment in residential and day formats
Participants: Coeducational; grades 8–12, ages 13–18
Enrollment: 150
Program Dates: Five weeks, late June to August
Head of Program: Richard K. Dempsey, Director

LOCATION

The 200-acre campus of St. George's School overlooks the Atlantic Ocean in Newport, Rhode Island. It is 45 minutes from Providence, Rhode Island; 70 miles from Boston, Massachusetts; and 180 miles from New York City.

BACKGROUND AND PHILOSOPHY

Established in 1944, the Summer Session is committed to providing an academic enrichment program in a caring, supportive environment.

PROGRAM OFFERINGS

The Summer Session offers college-preparatory courses, review classes, and enrichment electives in all major disciplines, as well as a comprehensive English as a foreign language (EFL) program. The elective offers may vary from summer to summer but usually include computer workshops, marine biology, creative writing, speech, acting, and SAT I and TOEFL preparation. The EFL program is offered on both an intermediate and advanced level and includes classes in reading and writing, grammar, and American culture.

Another exciting opportunity for students is study aboard St. George's sailing vessel, the *Geronimo.* Students enrolled in the Summer Session course FOCUS Marine Biology pursue genuine laboratory experience on Newport's famous beaches as well as on a weeklong journey aboard the *Geronimo.*

A low student-teacher ratio (6:1) ensures close supervision and the development of sound study techniques, while the adviser system offers strong support to each student, particularly to the younger ones. Resident faculty members monitor evening study hours (8–10 p.m., Sunday through Friday) to provide the appropriate environment for studying and to encourage students to use their time wisely and efficiently.

Each boarding student is required to take three courses (six times a week). Classes meet Monday through Saturday, and homework is assigned for each class meeting. A student's winter school determines whether academic credit is granted for a St. George's Summer Session course.

St. George's also offers a strong support program for younger students and those taking foundation courses.

Athletics are an integral part of the St. George's Summer Session. Underlying the sports program is the philosophy that an active, healthy body is an important aspect of the complete person; most students take part in at least one organized athletic activity for an hour each afternoon, Monday through Friday. The on-campus sports include sailing, soccer, tennis, basketball, weight training, and running.

ENROLLMENT

Each summer, more than 150 students from nearly twenty states and fifteen countries attend program offerings on campus. Slightly less than half reside outside the United States, coming from such countries as Japan, Spain, Italy, the Dominican Republic, China, Thailand, Germany, Peru, England, Korea, France, Turkey, Singapore, and Saudi Arabia.

DAILY SCHEDULE

Classes meet Monday through Saturday. The academic day runs from 8 a.m. to 1 p.m. Athletics are held from 2 to 3 p.m. On academic nights, study hours are from 8 to 10 p.m. in the dormitories.

EXTRA OPPORTUNITIES AND ACTIVITIES

A variety of activities is offered on campus, including dances, concerts, movies, and the annual Newport harbor cruise. Students also take field trips to museums and amusement parks in Rhode Island and Massachusetts.

FACILITIES

The well-equipped academic facilities include the newly constructed William H. Drury and Richard Grosvenor Center for the Arts. This building contains

art and music classrooms, a photo lab, a computer lab, a drama lab, and a spacious 400-seat auditorium, used in the summer for movies, lectures, and drama productions. In addition to the art center, the newly renovated duPont Science Center, which has a state-of-the-art laptop computer center, is also available to students. The Nathaniel Hill Memorial Library has a circulating book collection of 23,500 volumes, a reference section of 2,170 volumes, CD-ROM workstations, and nearly 150 periodicals.

The Dorrance Field House contains four indoor tennis courts, three basketball courts, two volleyball courts, and an indoor track. The campus encompasses five soccer fields, two field hockey fields, a cross-country running course, four lacrosse fields, football game and practice fields, two baseball diamonds, a softball diamond, an outdoor track, and twelve tennis courts.

STAFF

The summer faculty is an experienced and dedicated group of educators from both independent and public schools.

MEDICAL CARE

The School Health Center is open throughout the Summer Session; a registered nurse is on duty at all times. The school physician visits daily Monday through Saturday and is on call on Sunday. For emergencies, Newport Hospital is located 2 miles away.

COSTS

The overall fee for boarding students in the 2004 Summer Session was $4800; for day students, it was $2400 for two or more courses.

FINANCIAL AID

A limited amount of financial aid is available. Those interested should contact the Director of the Summer Session.

APPLICATION TIMETABLE

Application should be made as early as possible. A nonrefundable fee of $50 must accompany the application for the on-campus session.

FOR MORE INFORMATION, CONTACT:

Richard K. Dempsey, Director
St. George's Summer Session
P.O. Box 1910
Newport, Rhode Island 02840-0190
401-842-6712
Fax: 401-842-6763
E-mail: richard_dempsey@stgeorges.edu
World Wide Web:
http://www.stgeorges.edu/summerschool

SAINT THOMAS MORE SCHOOL

SUMMER ACADEMIC CAMP

OAKDALE, CONNECTICUT

Type of Program: Summer academic camp
Participants: Boys, grades 7–12
Enrollment: 90
Program Dates: Five-week session, July 3 to August 5
Head of Program: James F. Hanrahan Jr.

LOCATION

Saint Thomas More School is located in the Oakdale section of Montville, Connecticut, which is midway between Boston and New York, about 10 miles north of the Long Island Sound. The 100-acre campus is situated along 4,000 feet of waterfront on Gardner Lake, the largest lake in eastern Connecticut.

BACKGROUND AND PHILOSOPHY

Saint Thomas More School was founded in 1962 by Headmaster James F. Hanrahan to assist the underachiever, the young person with no social, emotional, or behavioral problems who is not living up to his academic potential. The Saint Thomas More School way of life is based on the belief that young people need structure, order, clear expectations, close personal attention, and consequences appropriate to their behavior.

Boys attend the summer program for a combination of summer fun and academic improvement. Some students come for make-up credit; others seek academic enrichment. International students at the beginner and intermediate level attend to improve their English fluency.

The average class size in the summer is 8. Students are given close personal attention by dedicated teachers drawn from the regular School faculty.

PROGRAM OFFERINGS

There are four class periods from 8 a.m. to noon, Monday through Saturday. Students typically take three courses and one study hall. Courses include English I, II, and III; world history; U.S. history; arithmetic; pre-algebra; algebra I and II; geometry; general science; physical science; biology; chemistry; Spanish I and II; computer science; art; reading I and II; ESL reading and writing I and II; and SAT preparation.

ENROLLMENT

About 90 boys attend the five-week session. The program is open to boys entering grades 7–12. Students come from many states and from all over the world.

DAILY SCHEDULE

All students attend classes from 8 a.m. to noon from Monday through Saturday. From lunch until 8 p.m., the School transforms into a summer camp. After lunch, there is a structured activity period, during which campers play in an organized intramural program. This is followed by a period in which the boys can choose their own recreation. Options include tennis, swimming, boating, basketball, and weight lifting. On rainy days, the indoor pool is available. After dinner, there is a mail call, then free time until study hall begins at 8 p.m. At that time, all students return to their rooms for a 2-hour, teacher-supervised study period. At 10:30 p.m., lights go out.

EXTRA OPPORTUNITIES AND ACTIVITIES

There are eleven field trips over the five weeks. Every Wednesday, after lunch, campers go by bus to one of the nearby attractions, including museums, beaches, roller-skating arenas, and the Mystic Aquarium. On Sunday, there are full-day trips to amusement parks, ocean beaches, Mystic Seaport, and the Boston Museum of Science. Also, there is a trip every Saturday night, usually to a movie theater.

FACILITIES

The summer program has the use of all facilities of Saint Thomas More School. For academic use, this includes three classroom buildings, science laboratories, a language laboratory, a computer room, and a library. For housing, boys live 1 or 2 to a room, in three modern dormitories. Teachers live in the boys' dorms to monitor and supervise their lives. All dorms are carpeted and oak-paneled. For athletics, a full-size gymnasium includes a basketball court and a large, twenty-station weight room equipped with cardiovascular machines and free weights. The student recreation area includes pool, Ping-Pong, and a TV room. The School's 100 acres include 4,000 feet of waterfront on Gardner Lake. The boathouse holds numerous canoes, sailboats, windsurfers, paddle boats, and rowboats for recreational use. Many campers enjoy the high-quality fishing in the lake, which is stocked with game fish. Other outdoor facilities include a running track, two soccer fields, two baseball fields, a lacrosse practice field, four outdoor tennis courts, and six outdoor basketball courts.

STAFF

The staff is drawn from the regular School faculty. Every teacher has a minimum of a bachelor's degree; many have their master's. With 15 teachers for 90 student campers, there is a great amount of close personal attention for each student.

MEDICAL CARE

A nurse is a member of the staff and is available for regular office hours from Monday to Saturday. In addition, a second nurse is on call for health-related needs. The School physician is on call as needed. There is a local ambulance service 5 minutes away, and a modern hospital is 12 miles from the campus.

Students are required to have had a recent physical examination and to have medical insurance.

RELIGIOUS LIFE

Saint Thomas More School is Catholic in philosophy. All students attend mass once each week at a nearby church.

COSTS

Tuition, room, and board cost for the five-week session in 2004 totaled $5495 for domestic campers and $5995 for international campers. This cost also covered books, fees, laundry, and trips. Extra costs include travel to and from the camp and a weekly spending allowance of $20 per week.

TRANSPORTATION

The campus is approximately midway between Boston and New York, about 10 miles north of New London, and less than 10 minutes from Exit 80 of I-395 in Norwich. Students traveling from great distances can fly into Bradley (Hartford-Springfield) Airport or JFK International Airport.

Arrangements for a driver service to pick up a camper at an airport can be made through the School. The School can also arrange for campers to be escorted back to the airport for return flights at the end of the program.

APPLICATION TIMETABLE

Applications are accepted until the session is full. To ensure the availability of courses, early application is encouraged. Interviews and campus tours can be arranged throughout the year. The application fee is $50 for domestic campers and $75 for international campers. An admission decision will be made within one week of the School's receiving the required forms and application.

For more information, contact:

Timothy Riordan
Office of Admissions
Saint Thomas More School
45 Cottage Road
Oakdale, Connecticut 06370
860-823-3861
Fax: 860-823-3863
E-mail: stmadmit@stthomasmoreschool.com
World Wide Web: http://stthomasmoreschool.com

PARTICIPANT/FAMILY COMMENTS

"Colin has already asked me if he can come back next year. How can a parent say 'No' to a child who wants to go to summer school?"

"It was more fun than I expected, and it felt good to finally start getting good grades."

SALISBURY SUMMER SCHOOL

ACADEMIC ENRICHMENT PROGRAM

SALISBURY, CONNECTICUT

Type of Program: Study skills development
Participants: Coeducational, ages 12–18
Enrollment: 105
Program Dates: June 26 to July 31
Head of Program: Ralph J. Menconi, Director

LOCATION

Salisbury School is set on a hilltop surrounded by 725 acres of extensive woodlands, fields, streams, and lakefront in the foothills of the Berkshire Mountains. The campus is bordered by the Appalachian Trail to the west and the Twin Lakes to the north. While seemingly rural, Salisbury is only 1 hour from Hartford, 2 hours from New York City, and 3 hours from Boston.

BACKGROUND AND PHILOSOPHY

Founded in 1946 as a unique program for students in need of academic remediation, the Salisbury Summer School continues to be recognized by educational consultants and educators from the United States and abroad as one of the finest resources for helping students whose lack of interest, language skills, and/or self-confidence have prevented them from achieving their full potential.

The Salisbury Summer School provides the comfortable environment needed to learn the most important lesson in all of schooling: how to learn. In a nongraded setting, the teachers at Salisbury Summer School are trained to make young people become better students or true students for the first time. Skills training focuses on the study of English through reading and writing, but the skills learned also transfer easily to other disciplines.

PROGRAM OFFERINGS

While many summer schools offer reading and study skills courses, only Salisbury immerses students in a curriculum and academic environment structured exclusively to promote better organization and improved reading and writing. Minimizing distractions and maximizing student-teacher contact (a ratio of 4:1), Salisbury employs experienced teachers who also serve as dorm monitors and advisers. Students become part of a five-week summer boarding school in which teachers get to know students in all facets of their lives.

All students are required to take the three core courses: reading and study skills, composition, and word skills. In addition, students may choose from electives in creative writing or mathematics review.

Reading and Study Skills The core of the Summer School program, the skills course integrates proven reading comprehension techniques and study methods that are designed to help students work more accurately and efficiently in their winter school courses. All students are trained to use a plan book to take assignments, to maintain an organized notebook, and to use a study schedule to plan their time. Outlining provides essential training for the development of skills of logic, discrimination, and orderly thought. Since reading must have lasting value, strategies to reinforce recall and improve memory are presented together with a variety of study systems, in order to synthesize the total study process. The double-period course also emphasizes application of the various comprehension techniques. Sentences, paragraphs, and longer articles are analyzed for their underlying structure. Common paragraph patterns such as cause-and-effect, comparisons, examples, and analysis are studied. Other exercises seek to develop discrimination between main ideas and supporting details. The course concludes with instruction in how to prepare for and take examinations. Developmental reading classes are given three days per week to all students, with the aim of significantly improving each student's reading rate and comprehension.

Composition This class seeks to give students the writing skills necessary to perform well on the kinds of academic essays and tests they encounter during the school year. Writing practice is given every day, with assignments structured along the lines of English papers, history essays, or even science laboratory reports. Other composition assignments include book reports or book reviews, dramatic criticism, and, for older students, timed writings required for the SAT II. Peer evaluation, in the form of oral readings, forms part of each class, and most papers are revised and rewritten to correct errors. This class also stresses grammatical accuracy and proofreading skills. In coordination with the study skills class, composition class reinforces note taking, outlining, and other organizational skills. Class texts include a book of writing models, a grammar exercise workbook, and other basic writing sourcebooks. Every composition class has two instructors and meets for two periods each day.

Word Skills Diagnostic tests determine the placement of each student in different sections of this course, each of which includes varying amounts of vocabulary, spelling, and word analysis, depending on individual needs. In word analysis, the student examines the structure of language from a phonetic and structural viewpoint; those in need of more remedial instruction focus on decoding the encoding skills. In spelling, rules and generalizations are presented in a systematic manner and commonly misspelled words are routinely examined. Vocabulary study is based upon the study of affixes, roots, word families, word histories, and words in context. Emphasis is placed not only on the acquisition of a

larger vocabulary over the course of the program, but also on the fostering of the student's curiosity about words and their definitions. SAT preparation for the upper-level students is also a main focus.

ENROLLMENT
Students come from a number of states as well as countries such as Mexico, Korea, Turkey, China, Argentina, Germany, and Spain.

DAILY SCHEDULE

8–8:30	Breakfast
8:45–12:55	Classes
1	Lunch
1:30	Adviser/advisee conferences, reading time, town trips
2:30	Sports/activity program
5	Reading hour
6	Dinner
7:30–9	Study hall
10–11	Quiet hour

EXTRA OPPORTUNITIES AND ACTIVITIES
As part of the boarding school experience, the School offers a number of options for the afternoon portion of the day. Students sign up for an activity elective prior to the start of each week. On Monday, Wednesday, and Friday of each week, every student is required to attend an athletic commitment. Additional weekend activities include sports events, videos (shown on campus), bike and hiking trips, and off-campus visits to museums, theaters, and concerts.

FACILITIES
The School teaches all classes in the new, 40,000-square-foot Humanities Center that is located on campus. The new building is a state-of-the-art facility, which also houses the library. Students are separated into six dorms by age and gender. Access to numerous athletic facilities contributes to a diverse afternoon schedule.

STAFF
Faculty members enjoy returning to the Berkshire Mountains in the summer. Two thirds of the faculty members returned for the 2003 summer, and new additions brought a great deal of experience to the programs. A small number of interns also have the opportunity to work with master teachers.

MEDICAL CARE
Medical services are available to all students on a 24-hour basis and under the supervision of the School physician. The doctor sees emergency cases at the School's Health Center, at his office, or at Sharon Hospital, located in Sharon, Connecticut. The hospital is a well-equipped community hospital with a full complement of board-certified specialists. Students are referred to the emergency room or to a medical specialist when necessary. For severe cases, there is an emergency helicopter evacuation service to Hartford Hospital Trauma Center. Salisbury's Health Center maintains a licensed five-bed infirmary. Students may come for evaluation and treatment of illness and injuries, as well as for dispensing of medications.

COSTS
Tuition for the 2004 session was $6750, which included the cost of books, entertainment, and town trips. A nonrefundable tuition deposit of $500, payable upon acceptance, is required. The balance of the tuition and a $250 incidental deposit for international students was due before June 1, 2004.

FINANCIAL AID
Financial aid is available on a limited basis. Inquiries should be addressed to the Summer School Office.

APPLICATION TIMETABLE
Applications, accompanied by a $25 application fee, are accepted on a rolling basis. Interviews and tours are given beginning in January. Acceptances are also sent out on a rolling basis, usually within two weeks of receipt of a completed application, which includes an interview, recommendations, transcripts, and testing.

FOR MORE INFORMATION, CONTACT:

Summer School Office
Salisbury Summer School
251 Canaan Road
Salisbury, Connecticut 06068
860-435-5700

THE SCHOOL FOR FILM & TELEVISION

SUMMER IN THE CITY

NEW YORK, NEW YORK

Type of Program: Advanced-placement college program
Participants: Coeducational, ages 16–25
Enrollment: 100 students
Program Dates: June 27 to August 7
Heads of Program: Joan See, Artistic Director; Steven Chinni, Director of Admission

LOCATION

The School for Film & Television (SFT) is located in Chelsea, a vibrant historic section of New York City. Within Chelsea's borders are the historic Ladies Mile, Gramercy Park, and plenty of boutiques and restaurants. Chelsea is adjacent to the beautiful West Village and is only a short bus or subway ride from world-famous museums and the New York Theater District.

BACKGROUND AND PHILOSOPHY

The School for Film & Television was founded in 1980 and has grown to become a unique film-acting program accredited by the National Association of Schools of Theatre. It offers the film actor-in-training skills for careers in film, television, theater, and new media.

Based philosophically on the Meisner Technique, a proven method for teaching acting, The School for Film & Televison has created an environment for artistic growth based on personal attention and experiential learning. Classes are kept intentionally small to give the students the maximum number of opportunities to test new skills and take artistic risks. SFT faculty members, who continue to work as professional film and television actors, are dedicated to giving student actors the individual attention they need to grow as artists and professionals. Through audition experiences and meetings with industry professionals, SFT also exposes students to the business of show business.

The Summer in the City program is a perfect vehicle for students who might be interested in a conservatory education as well as for actors anxious to augment their stage and on-camera performance skills.

PROGRAM OFFERINGS

Designed specifically for high school and college students, Summer in the City allows students to earn college credits while learning cutting-edge on-camera performance techniques. Because SFT is accredited by the National Association of Schools of Theatre and its college credit recommendations are supported by the National Program on Non-Collegiate Sponsored Instruction, credit for the summer program may be available upon successful completion of the program.

Located in New York City, an international center for the performing arts, The School for Film & Television offers young talent a challenging opportunity to learn acting techniques and camera performance from a dedicated faculty of working actors and directors through an intense six-week program. Two levels are offered.

The Technique Level At the Technique Level, novice performers explore the physical, emotional, and vocal life necessary for energized, focused, and creative camera performance. The curriculum includes workshops in acting technique, voice and speech, movement, improvisation, and comedy as well as on-camera scene and script work. The program culminates in a performance day.

The Performance Level More-experienced actors receive a vigorous workout as they make the transition from stage to screen. The curriculum emphasizes on-camera techniques in both single camera and multicamera performance. Topics include advanced acting, voice and speech, mask work, movement, scene study for film and TV, on-camera commercials and voice-overs, monologues, audition techniques, and industry presentation.

ENROLLMENT

The majority of applicants are between the ages of 16 and 22. The average age of the summer student actor is 18. There are as many as 100 students each summer, divided into study sections of 12 or 14. Class size is limited so that maximum attention is spent on the individual development of each actor.

No prior training is required for admission to the Technique Level. The Performance Level requires prior acting training, including skills with scenes, monologues, and improvisation.

Generally, acceptance is based on the recommendation letters that are returned with the application, together with a personal interview, usually conducted by phone. Applicants must audition if they wish to be considered for scholarships. Audition dates and sites can be found at SFT's Web site (listed below). All students must perform a placement audition (a single, memorized, 1- to 2-minute contemporary monologue) at the orientation session the night before the program begins. Placement for the two programs is determined by the monologue performance and the student's level of experience.

DAILY SCHEDULE

Each program is six weeks long and consists of 180 contact hours. Workshops meet from 10 a.m. to 5 p.m., five days a week, with appropriate breaks. No classes meet during the Fourth of July holiday.

EXTRA OPPORTUNITIES AND ACTIVITIES

Because of the program's rigorous nature, students often use evenings and weekends to rehearse and practice for their classes. Guest lectures, field trips, and movies are offered on either Wednesday or Thursday evenings from 6:30 until 9 p.m. Guest lectures involve talks by New York agents and casting directors about the business of the business and the realities of acting. Time is also provided to address the students' questions and concerns.

Students also receive information about free or low-cost performances in the area. Students in both levels also participate in a variety of extracurricular activities that only New York City can offer, including a double-decker bus tour of the city and a graduation cruise around the Statue of Liberty and Lower Manhattan.

FACILITIES

In addition to classrooms, SFT's facilities include studios for movement, on-camera studies, and acting classes; two state-of-the-art two-camera studios; and a library stocked with hundreds of plays, screenplays, and videos. The school's campus serves as the largest casting facility on the East Coast, giving students a taste of the real world of film and television.

Throughout the curriculum, the camera is used as a teaching tool. Exercises and scenes are taped for review and home study. Students in film and television classes practice all techniques and perform in scenes from film, daytime drama, and episodic television.

SFT also offers safe and secure housing. The School's residential facilities are located at the George Washington Student Residence at Lexington and 23rd Street, in the historic Flatiron district of Manhattan. The residence is approximately four blocks from the studio spaces in which classes are held. Formerly a classic New York hotel, the building has been renovated into a dormitory for the School for Visual Arts. Each air-conditioned room has a private bath, a cable-TV jack, a refrigerator, and a microwave oven. A phone jack is available for those students who wish to have a private phone. Students provide linens, dishes, coffee makers, and other simple cooking implements and should plan an adequate food budget for their stay.

A 24-hour concierge desk monitors all entries. No one can visit a residential floor without proper identification and/or the permission of the person being visited. The living floors are patrolled by uniformed security guards overnight.

STAFF

The faculty consists of professional actors, directors, and producers in film and television who provide students with the most current information available in the industry. The techniques and skills the students learn are the same ones that are employed by the faculty members as they continue to audition and pursue work in the New York market.

COSTS

Tuition is $3690 for the summer program. Housing costs are $1995, which includes a $150 refundable damage deposit. Students who register by March 1 receive a 10 percent early-registration tuition discount.

FINANCIAL AID

For the summer programs, alternative funding is available by contacting the school. In addition, advanced-placement college credit may be available upon successful completion of the course work.

APPLICATION TIMETABLE

Applicants should mail a completed application (available online) and a nonrefundable application fee of $30 to the Summer Admission Office. Space is limited in each section. A current picture and resume, a letter of interest, and two letters of recommendation are also required. Early registration ends May 1; late registration is considered as space allows.

For more information, contact:

Summer Admission Office
The School for Film and Television
39 West 19th Street, 12th Floor
New York, New York 10011
212-645-0030 (in state)
888-645-0030 Ext. 772 (toll-free outside New York)
World Wide Web: http://www.sft.edu

PARTICIPANT/FAMILY COMMENTS

"Teachers here really know what they're doing. If you are open to their suggestions, you'll see a big improvement in your acting work."—Ryan Hoffman *(The Sopranos)*

"The summer program at SFT introduced me to the world of film and television. After developing my technique for a full summer, I felt competent enough to look for representation. I landed a guest role on Ed, and it turned into a regular gig."—Robin Paul *(Ed)*

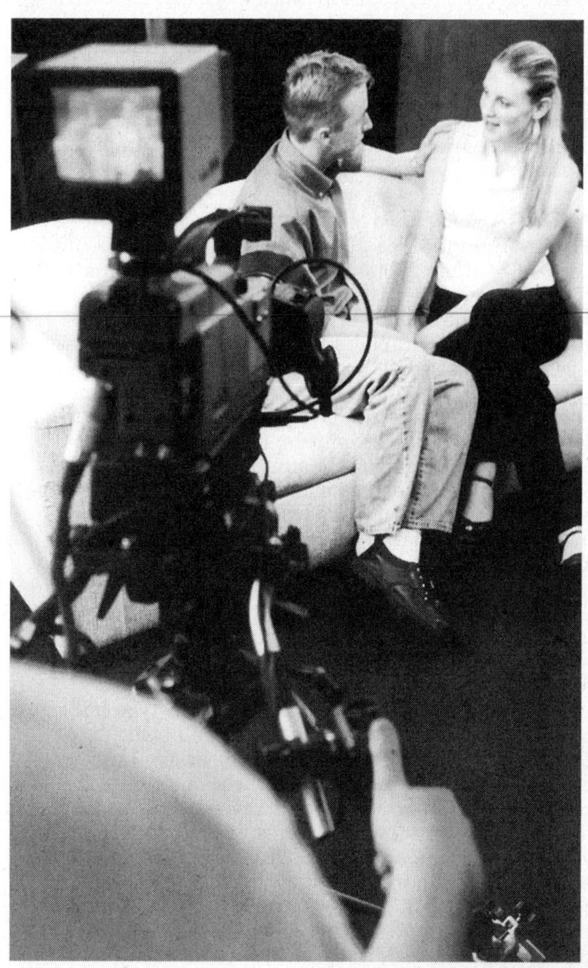

SEACAMP

SUMMER PROGRAM

BIG PINE KEY, FLORIDA

Type of Program: Marine science, scuba, sailing, environmental, and recreational program
Participants: Coeducational, ages 12–17
Enrollment: 140–160 per session
Program Dates: June 24 to July 11, July 14 to July 31, and August 3 to August 20
Heads of Program: Irene Hooper, Executive Director; Grace Upshaw, Camp Director; David Mallory, Assistant Camp Director

LOCATION

Seacamp's tropical location on Newfound Harbor in the lower Florida Keys, just minutes from the only living coral reef in the United States and only 30 miles east of Key West, enables campers to participate in a truly one-of-a-kind marine studies program. Campers investigate the Atlantic Ocean, the Gulf of Mexico, and Florida Keys National Marine Sanctuary, moving among clear blue waters, coral canyons, sandy and grassy areas, mud flats, and natural tide pools—all teeming with invertebrates, fish, and mammals.

BACKGROUND AND PHILOSOPHY

Founded in 1966, Seacamp, the first program dedicated to the education of youth in marine sciences, is the result of a cooperative effort of parents, scientists, businessmen, and camp leaders. Conservation practices and a respect for the marine environment are at the core of the Seacamp philosophy. "For all the sea has to teach us and all the fun of learning it."

Seacamp is accredited by the American Camping Association.

PROGRAM OFFERINGS

Marine Science The Marine Science Program is the heart of Seacamp. Young scientists participate in a variety of courses under the guidance of academically trained marine science instructors, biologists, geologists, and oceanographers. Campers work at their own level of interest while learning basic ecological principles that are pertinent both to the study of marine science and to the future of our natural resources. Designed to appeal to all campers, this comprehensive program is coordinated in a number of 21-hour course offerings selected each summer based on responses elicited from the current year's participants. Courses may include general marine sciences, marine communities, animal behavior, marine invertebrates, marine botany, marine vertebrates, marine geology, and marine aquaria. Advanced studies are offered in reef fish ecology, coral reef ecology, independent studies, and underwater field research using scuba. All science activities include studies in both the field and the laboratory. Boat trips take place on 10' x 25' trimaran-type hulls that accommodate 12–15 participants; all boats carry Coast Guard-approved safety equipment. On-board radios are constantly monitored by Seacamp's base station. During boat trips, campers investigate various marine environments and species, including 400 varieties of algae, coral, and fishes. On-shore trips vary, depending upon the weather, the tide, and areas of camper interest. In the past, such trips have included a geological survey of the keys, visits to the Key Deer Refuge, zonation studies of the intertidal areas, and investigations of canals and the mangrove fringe area.

Upon completion, campers receive a Seacamp Certification describing courses taken.

Independent Research Projects Campers may pursue an independent research project of their choice through arrangements with the science staff, the culmination of which may be published in *The Seacamp Journal of Research*.

Scuba Seacamp offers several courses in scuba diving to qualified participants. Scuba courses are designed to give the camper the appropriate skills for safely using scuba as an underwater research tool. In order to participate in scuba, campers should have no history of heart, lung (including asthma), sinus, or ear troubles. Seacamp's Scuba I course is a National Association of Underwater Instructors (NAUI) basic certification class offered to campers 13 and older. Satisfactory course completion earns the camper a nationally recognized certificate issued through NAUI. Marine investigation courses (Scuba II) using scuba techniques for certified divers are offered at introductory, intermediate, and advanced levels. Scuba III is offered to campers 15 and older. Successful completion of Scuba III earns the camper a NAUI Master Diver Certification. Scuba IV is an ongoing research class that publishes a paper in *The Seacamp Journal of Research*.

Aquatic Programs Winds, tides, and currents guide campers' exploration of the ocean's surface. Beginning sailing classes familiarize campers with the winds, tides, and currents. The windsurfing course starts campers on a dry-land simulator; they learn the basic aspects of rigging, tacking, jibing, rules of the road, board control, and more and progress to racing and freestyle techniques. Canoeing and kayaking classes explore the natural resources of the Coupon Bight Aquatic Preserve. Certification in ARC lifeguarding is also offered.

ENROLLMENT

Each session, 140 to 160 campers come to Seacamp, mostly from the U.S., but also from across the world. There are about 30 international campers each summer from an average of twelve countries. Many Seacamp program graduates have gone on to prominent careers as environmental educators and marine scientists.

DAILY SCHEDULE

One of Seacamp's unique aspects is that campers create their schedules. In addition to science and scuba classes, campers choose from a variety of programs to ensure that there is something interesting and exciting for everyone. Typically, the day starts at 7 a.m., with breakfast at 7:30. Campers enjoy free time before the morning program, which runs from 9 until noon. Lunch is at 12:30, after which campers rest or explore the area. The afternoon program runs from 2:15 until 5:20, after which there is just enough time to dry off and get ready for dinner at 6. After dinner there is free time until 8:30, during which campers enjoy a swim, volleyball, or basketball and talk about the day's excitement. The evening program begins at 8:30 and comprises anything from dancing with friends to the latest music to hearing a visiting scientist talk about current international scientific issues to playing blackjack at Seacamp's version of a Caribbean casino to sitting by the campfire next to the open ocean, singing and laughing. Lights-out is at 10:30, by which time campers can hardly wait for the next exciting day.

EXTRA OPPORTUNITIES AND ACTIVITIES

Campers with journalism experience may work on the camp newspaper, *SEASCOPE*, which is published periodically during camp sessions. Arts and crafts activities include ceramics, copper enameling, stone carving, tie-dyeing, driftwood art, macramé, and painting. Photography allows campers to take home memories of friends, wildlife, and underwater experiences.

Activities are planned to incorporate the needs of all of the campers, so no one is ever left out. Seacamp's enthusiastic and gregarious staff members go out of their way to include everyone in the fun.

FACILITIES

Campers and staff members are housed by age in dormitories. Seacamp honors cabinmate requests, if possible, when both families are in agreement.

Seacamp's lab facilities include a running seawater circulation system that serves two 250-gallon display tanks, two 50-gallon aquaria, twenty 20-gallon aquaria, and two 600-gallon tanks, which campers and science staff members use for research and observation. A preparation room is stocked with charts, illustrations, stereo and compound microscopes, preserving jars and solutions, water analysis kits, seines, and oceanographic equipment. A man-made lagoon serves as a temporary habitat for larger live specimens.

Other camp facilities include a dining hall, a kitchen, a recreation hall, an arts and crafts building, a health center, a sailing shelter, several teaching shelters, a staff lounge, and administration offices.

STAFF

Seacamp receives more than 1,000 requests for applications, from all over the world, for 55 program staff positions. Staff members are chosen for their expertise as program directors, marine science instructors, nationally certified scuba instructors, Red Cross-certified water safety instructors, and their overall ability. Before campers arrive, program staff members go through an intensive three-week training session in which they are certified in American Red Cross lifeguarding, first aid, CPR, and NAUI skin diving instruction. If arriving staff members are scuba certified, Seacamp also certifies them as NAUI rescue divers. In addition to all of these certifications, staff members are also trained extensively in boat-handling skills through Seacamp's Captain's Workshop, and in consistent leadership skills. Most staff members come from across the U.S.; however, there have been staff members from places as far away as New Zealand, England, South Africa, Scotland, and Russia. The overall resident camper-staff member ratio is 3:1. The close relationships developed between staff members and campers because of this small ratio encourages individuality and provides for small group instruction.

MEDICAL CARE

An in-residence registered nurse manages the health center. A camp physician from Big Pine Key is on call, and ambulance service is available around the clock. Complete hospital facilities are in nearby Marathon and Key West. First aid equipment and supplies are kept on all motor boats.

A general health certificate form and a scuba health certificate must be submitted at least three weeks prior to each camper's arrival. All campers are covered by Seacamp's health insurance while at camp; this policy is limited, however, and parents are encouraged to carry their own insurance for their children.

COSTS

Costs for the 2004 program were $2750. Extra fees for scuba were $375 per course. All campers must have masks, fins, and snorkels to participate in Seacamp's programs; these can be bought in the camp's Ships Store. Other optional equipment, T-shirts, candy, and toiletries are also available at the Ships Store.

Campers enrolled for more than one session stay at camp between sessions at no extra charge. During this time, they participate in a variety of supervised programs, get a chance to do their laundry, and take advantage of opportunities to visit historic Key West. About $75 spending money is suggested for this time.

TRANSPORTATION

Parents may bring campers by car to Big Pine Key. Counselors also meet participants at the Miami International Airport on the opening day of camp and escort them to Big Pine Key on a chartered bus (about 120 miles). The fee for round-trip service is $75.

APPLICATION TIMETABLE

To join the Seacamp adventure, contact Seacamp for an application. Off-season tours of the facilities are available, and all are welcome to visit. Completed applications must include a $350 deposit (refundable until May 1) and a letter of recommendation from the camper's science teacher or principal. Parents and campers receive a Seacamp information packet, with articles on transportation, what to bring, camp store credit, permission forms, and health forms.

For more information, contact:

Seacamp
1300 Big Pine Avenue
Big Pine Key, Florida 33043-3336
Telephone: 305-872-2331
Fax: 305-872-2555
E-mail: snorkel+scuba@seacamp.org
World Wide Web: http://www.seacamp.org

SEAWORLD ADVENTURE CAMP SAN DIEGO

SEAWORLD/BUSCHGARDENS ADVENTURE CAMPS

MARINE SCIENCE EDUCATION CAMP

SAN DIEGO, CALIFORNIA

Type of Program: Residential camps
Participants: Coeducational, grades 4 through adult
Enrollment: Varies by program
Program Dates: Year-round (with select dates throughout spring and fall)
Heads of Program: Joy Wolf, Director of Education; Karen I, Resident Camp Manager

LOCATION

SeaWorld Adventure Camp San Diego is uniquely located in a protected cove right on the water on Fiesta Island in Mission Bay, San Diego, California.

BACKGROUND AND PHILOSOPHY

Playing host to more than 35,000 youth from across the U.S. and around the word, SeaWorld/Busch Gardens Adventure Camps provide up-close, behind-the-scenes, hands-on experiences with amazing animals, including many that are threatened or endangered. Working alongside veterinarians, trainers, and other animal-care experts, campers have the opportunity to feed, interact with, and care for animals ranging from dolphins and manatees to giraffes and great apes.

But it's not all about animals—it's about having fun, exploring the great outdoors, riding world-class coasters, and making lifelong friends and memories. For campers of all ages, it's about putting their passion for wildlife to work and learning how they can make the world a better place.

PROGRAM OFFERINGS

Ocean Adventure (Grades 4–6) Campers get to know bottlenose dolphins, penguins, sharks, and more. They even go behind the scenes and learn how these amazing animals are cared for.

Out-of-park excursions are also part of the adventure. Campers spend a lazy afternoon on one of San Diego's beautiful beaches and have an exciting kayaking adventure on Mission Bay.

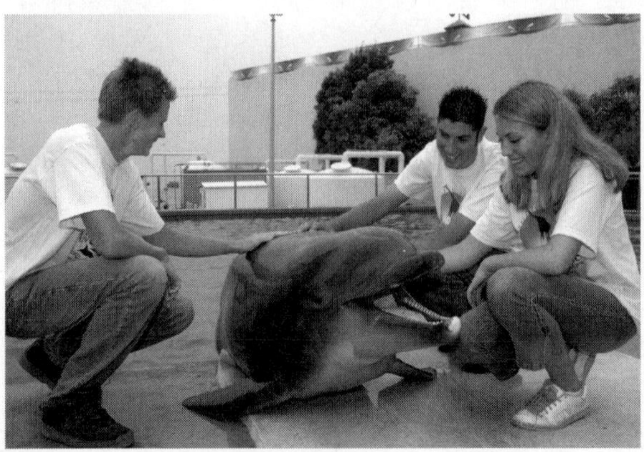

Campers also have plenty of time to enjoy all the awesome shows, rides, and attractions. There are five nights to explore the park after dark and enjoy the thrilling night attractions at SeaWorld San Diego.

Ocean Animals (Grades 7–8) Campers feel like real animal keepers when they immerse themselves in this adventure, spending five nights and six days at SeaWorld San Diego. During this time, they meet SeaWorld's animal experts and discover the real world of animal care. Campers visit a working animal-care facility and laboratory, and their animal knowledge is put to the test as they plunge into Mission Bay and snorkel with Southern California sea creatures. And of course, they enjoy the many thrilling shows, rides, and attractions of SeaWorld San Diego.

Career Camp (Grades 9–12) These one-week sessions are designed for students interested in pursuing careers in an animal-care field. The program gives students a realistic and hands-on look at what animal-care positions at SeaWorld involve, including food preparation, cleaning, animal interaction (when available), and some long hours.

Students visit several animal areas throughout the week and learn in-depth information about many of the animals at the park. A typical day involves waking up early, spending the morning and early afternoon learning about an animal area, and spending the late afternoon and evening enjoying all that SeaWorld has to offer. Students must come prepared to do heavy lifting, work hard, learn, and, of course, have fun.

Counselor-In-Training (Grades 9–10) These two-week sessions give students the opportunity to learn the leadership skills needed to become a counselor. The first week is split between leadership training and learning crafts and activities while observing and assisting day camp. The second week is spent shadowing resident camp counselors as they lead a group of campers in the established curriculum. Counselors-in-training (CITs) have ample opportunity to enjoy all that SeaWorld has to offer. Students must be enthusiastic about interacting with children and willing to assist with all aspects of camp, including cleaning.

FACILITIES

Campers are lodged right at SeaWorld. Camp facilities include meeting, play, and eating areas as well as separate boys' and girls' sleeping quarters and showers. For certain sessions, campers spend a night in an animal attraction.

STAFF

The camp staff includes SeaWorld education instructors and experienced summer intern counselors with CPR, water safety, and first aid training. Members of the camp staff work 24 hours a day to monitor the camper's safety and to respond to camper needs.

Counselors undergo in-depth interviews to assess their skills in communication, organization, behavior management and safety. They also undergo background checks and drug testing. All camps, staff members, and counselor-to-camper ratios meet and exceed American Camping Association accreditation requirements.

COSTS

For 2004–05, the fee for Ocean Adventure is $895; Ocean Animals, $895; Career Camp, $950; and Counselor-In-Training, $1600. Camp fees include transportation between SeaWorld San Diego and the nearest major airport, field trips, lodging, meals and snacks, equipment and materials, camp t-shirt, and water bottle.

APPLICATION TIMETABLE

Students may register by mail, fax, or telephone. All registrations must be accompanied by a nonrefundable deposit. Space is limited and registrations before February are recommended.

Confirmation materials are sent to students after their registration materials and deposit have been received. These materials include the confirmed dates of the camp session(s); a program schedule, packing list, health history form, medical release, liability release, general camp guidelines; and a coupon for a discount on Southwest airlines.

Interested students should visit the Web site to learn more about program options and to download a registration packet.

FOR MORE INFORMATION, CONTACT:

Education Department
Adventure Camp
SeaWorld San Diego
500 SeaWorld Drive
San Diego, California 92109-7904
800-23-SHAMU (toll-free)
Fax: 619-226-3634
E-mail: swc.education@seaworld.com
World Wide Web: http://www.swbg-adventurecamps.org

SEAWORLD/BUSCH GARDENS ADVENTURE CAMPS

SEAWORLD/BUSCHGARDENS ADVENTURE CAMPS

SUMMER CAMPS

ORLANDO, FLORIDA

Type of Program: Residential camps
Participants: Coeducational, grades 6 through adult
Enrollment: Varies with the program
Program Dates: Year-round (with select dates throughout spring and fall)
Heads of Program: John Lowe, Director of Education; Josh Kennedy, Education Manager

LOCATION

Set amid one of the country's most beautiful marine life and zoological parks, this SeaWorld is located in Orlando, Florida.

BACKGROUND AND PHILOSOPHY

Playing host to more than 35,000 youth from across the U.S. and around the word, SeaWorld/ Busch Gardens Adventure Camps provide up-close, behind-the-scenes, hands-on experiences with amazing animals, including many that are threatened or endangered. Alongside veterinarians, trainers, and other animal-care experts, campers have the opportunity to feed, interact with, and care for animals ranging from dolphins and manatees to giraffes and great apes.

But it's not all about animals—it's about having fun, exploring the great outdoors, riding world-class coasters and making lifelong friends and memories. For campers of all ages, it's about putting their passion for wildlife to work and learning how they can make the world a better place.

PROGRAM OFFERINGS

Careers Camp (Grades 7–9) and **Advanced Careers Camp (Grades 10–12)** Campers dive into a dream-come-true experience as they discover the rewards and challenges of working in a zoological park. They encounter everything from animal enrichment and training to animal rescue and rehabilitation as they become SeaWorld's newest animal experts. Their final

day provides a lifetime of memories as they swim with dolphins, rays, and tropical fish and interact with a variety of exotic birds at Discovery Cove.

Ultimate Florida Adventure (Grades 7–12) Campers experience the best of Florida's unique wildlife as they travel to the nation's oldest city, St. Augustine, and visit some of the city's most famous sites. They explore the beauty and wildlife of Florida's beaches, wetlands, and lagoons; canoe down a scenic Florida waterway in search of endangered manatees, stingrays, dolphins, and other native animals; and travel through the Everglades on an exciting airboat ride looking for alligators.

Then they journey to the Florida Keys for unforgettable snorkeling in the beautiful waters of the Florida Keys National Marine Sanctuary and visit the southernmost point in the continental U.S. to tour historic Key West.

Finally, they return to SeaWorld and discover what goes on behind the scenes, learning about SeaWorld's rescue and rehabilitation program for Florida's endangered manatees, sea turtles, and native birds. Their final full day of adventure is at Discovery Cove. Here, they swim with dolphins, stingrays, and tropical fishes and interact with a variety of exotic birds for memories that truly last a lifetime.

Teacher Camp This four-day program is designed with professional development in mind. Participants work side-by-side with SeaWorld animal experts, gather multidisciplinary tools for their classrooms, and even have a chance to swim with the dolphins and snorkel with the rays at Discovery Cove.

The program includes visits to several SeaWorld attractions, instructive seminars, interactive activities, and one night sleeping next to sharks, dolphins, manatees, or beluga whales. (The other nights are spent at a nearby hotel.)

FACILITIES

All camp sessions that take place in the Florida Keys stay at Ocean Pointe Suites in Key Largo. Ocean Pointe Suites feature a full-size pool, tennis courts, a volleyball court, and a beach.

STAFF

The camp staff includes SeaWorld education instructors and experienced summer intern counselors with CPR, water safety, and first aid training. Counselors undergo in-depth interviews to assess their skills in communication, organization, behavior management, and safety. They also undergo background checks and drug testing.

All camps, staff members, and counselor-to-camper ratios meet and exceed American Camping Association accreditation requirements.

COSTS

Fees in 2004–05 for Summer Splash were $925. The cost for the Florida Keys Adventure was $975 and the Ultimate Florida Adventure was $1975. Teacher Camp was $695. Camp fees include transportation between SeaWorld Orlando and the nearest major airport, field trips, lodging, meals and snacks, equipment and materials, camp t-shirt, and water bottle.

APPLICATION TIMETABLE

Students may register by mail, fax, or telephone. All registrations must be accompanied by a nonrefundable deposit. Space is limited and registrations before February are recommended.

Confirmation materials are sent to students after their registration materials and deposit have been received. These materials include the confirmed dates of the camp session(s); a program schedule, packing list, health history form, medical release, liability release, general camp guidelines; and a coupon for a discount on Southwest airlines.

Interested students should visit the Web site to learn more about program options and to download a registration packet.

FOR MORE INFORMATION, CONTACT:

Education Department
Resident Camp
SeaWorld Orlando
7007 SeaWorld Drive
Orlando, Florida 32821-8097
866-4SW-CAMP (toll-free)
Fax: 407-363-2399
E-mail: education@seaworld.org
World Wide Web: http://www.swbg-adventurecamps.org

SERVICE LEARNING IN PARIS

CULTURAL IMMERSION THROUGH COMMUNITY SERVICE

PARIS, FRANCE

Type of Program: Community service, academic study, and language intensive
Participants: Coeducational, international, from age 16
Enrollment: 30+
Program Dates: July 2–28, 2005
Head of Program: John Nissen, Director

LOCATION

The 2005 site for the International Seminar Series' seventh Service Learning program is once again Paris. The program is based in the 15th arrondissement.

BACKGROUND AND PHILOSOPHY

International Seminar Series' vision is to give thoughtful and accomplished young people an opportunity for immersion in another culture through active participation in community service work and focused study. Daily, on-going service projects distinguish this program from the more usual study-and-travel approach to summer programs. From this engagement, each participant can derive richness of experience, depth of understanding, and reflective interaction with a greater world.

PROGRAM OFFERINGS

Community Service Participation in Community Service is at the core of the program. For the entire month students explore the everyday aspects of contemporary French culture through direct participation in it, offering assistance to a specific community outside their own and carefully considering what the offering and receipt of such assistance can mean. Students work three to four hours a day, five days a week, during their month in Paris. Assignments with established organizations are made according to the student's interest and experience, the skills required by the organization, and the student's ability in French. Specific activities vary according to the needs of the organization.

The Academic Seminar The Seminar is the academic complement to community service work. It gives grounding to the students' daily experience as they work and go about Paris. The goal is to understand the city and its people through study, observation, and interaction. For their seminar class, students choose one class from Art and Architecture (in English or French), French Politics and History, or Writing and Literature.

French Language Use and Instruction Students speak and study French from the first day. They are tested and grouped into four sections, from beginners (no previous experience in French) to advanced (mostly students who have taken or will be taking Advanced Placement French). Class size does not exceed ten. The emphasis of the work is oral expression. Speaking French outside academic classes is the norm—at meals, in the office, and in daily conversation.

Study Travel and Cultural Explorations During the month, a significant amount of time is devoted to visiting traditional places such as Chartres, Versailles, Vaux-le-Vicomte, and sites more closely related to the work done in Community Service and the Seminar. Modern Paris is defined as much by its new towns and ethnic suburbs as by the Champs Elysées.

FACILITIES

Students and staff are housed in a Foyer, a residence hall complex in the 15th arrondissement, with dining facilities and classrooms. Breakfast and dinner are provided each day. Students are responsible for their own lunches. Many will share a meal with people at the Community Service site. Others may buy the quintessential baguette and cheese sandwich at a patisserie, or meet friends for an inexpensive plat du jour at local restaurants. Students are also able and encouraged to use the kitchen at the Foyer.

STAFF

Faculty and staff members are thoughtful, experienced teachers drawn from Paris and elsewhere. They teach individual courses, oversee community service work, and conduct study travel, but they also act as mentors to the students and links to the community beyond. Faculty and staff members work hard in helping students become thoughtful observers and active participants in the larger host culture. During the winter, they work collaboratively to develop the content of the program.

COSTS

The program fee for 2005 is $5800, which includes a $50 application fee and a $250 enrollment deposit. Additional expenses to be anticipated are transportation to and from Paris, lunch costs, and personal expenses for laundry, individual purchases, and other incidentals.

FINANCIAL AID

A modest amount of need-based financial aid is available. A separate application will be sent on request.

TRANSPORTATION

Students are responsible for making their own travel arrangements to and from Paris. They are met at their point-of-arrival airport, train station, or bus terminal and accompanied to the Seminar housing site. The procedure is reversed on departure.

APPLICATION TIMETABLE

Students must complete a formal application (either on paper or through the ISS Web site), and submit transcripts and teacher or counselor recommendations. Admission is selective and places are limited. The recommended deadline is April 15, and students are encouraged to apply early.

For more information, contact:

John Nissen, Director
P.O. Box 1212
Manchester, Vermont 05254-1212
802-362-5855 (telephone and fax)
800-353-5534 (when asked for PIN, 01; toll-free in North America)
E-mail: iss@study-serve.org
World Wide Web: http://www.study-serve.org

SHATTUCK–ST. MARY'S SCHOOL

SUMMER PROGRAM

FARIBAULT, MINNESOTA

Type of Program: Academic enrichment and review (and language instruction for international students) in residential formats
Participants: Coeducational, grades 6–11, ages 11–17
Enrollment: 75
Program Dates: Summer Discovery: July 3–July 22; English Language Institute: July 24–August 12
Head of Program: Mike Frankenfield

LOCATION

Shattuck–St. Mary's School's 250-acre campus is located in Faribault, Minnesota, a community of 20,000 people 50 miles south of the twin cities of Minneapolis and St. Paul and 50 miles north of Rochester.

A national poll conducted in 1990 ranked Faribault in the top twenty small towns in the United States. Minneapolis–St. Paul International Airport is 50 minutes from campus.

BACKGROUND AND PHILOSOPHY

Shattuck–St. Mary's has been providing summer learning opportunities since 1915. Taking full advantage of the campus and all of its facilities, as well as lakefront properties in Faribault and in northern Minnesota, the summer program allows young people to gain an understanding about what currently does, or potentially could, interest them in a safe, relaxed setting. The breadth of course offerings engages a child's curiosity, challenges his or her assumptions, and encourages explorations of the unknown. By the end of the program, each participant will have assembled a portfolio of his or her work or will have maintained a daily journal.

PROGRAM OFFERINGS

Students participating in Summer Discovery select two academic courses from such areas as English, mathematics, computer, or history for morning class work. The two courses are accompanied by an afternoon enrichment course such as art, outdoor discovery, or sports.

Mathematics Discovery Students are provided with an intensive review of math as well as preparation for the following year's work. In the classroom students discover the excitement of mathematical problem solving. Topics in various levels of algebra are presented, and problems solved.

English Discovery Composition, grammar, and vocabulary are reviewed and drilled. This practice serves as the basis for creative writing and poetry workshops where various styles are examined. Participants are asked to compose their own essays, short stories, and poems.

Writing Discovery Writing Discovery is designed to refine basic writing skills and foster an interest in writing. Students begin with a review of grammar and syntax. They then progress to a variety of paragraph and essay styles, including descriptive, persuasive, narrative, and informative. Students work also on basic interview and dialogue writing. In the process of writing, basic word processing skills are also enhanced. The course culminates in the production of a Summer Discovery Newsletter.

Computer Discovery Computer Discovery aims to provide the skills to enhance learning abilities through the use of today's technology. In addition to familiarity with the Macintosh operating system, students acquire basic competence in word processing, spreadsheets, databases, and desktop publishing. Computer Discovery incorporates innovative techniques and procedures to keep pace with advances in the field; for instance, Shattuck–St. Mary's connection to the Internet allows students to explore the World Wide Web and communicate via electronic mail. Other elements of the course include an overview of the development and history of computers.

Art Discovery This course has been designed for the student with serious interest in the visual arts. Participants receive instruction in painting, sculpture, drawing, and pottery. In addition to a rich studio experience, opportunities to visit museums, galleries, and studios locally and in the Twin Cities are integrated into the program.

Outdoor Discovery This course examines the various gifts and mysteries of our environment. While in the field, the bulk of the program emphasizes the ecology of woodlands, lakes, and rivers in the area and in northern Minnesota as well as the wildlife that inhabits these regions.

Sports Discovery This program encourages aspiring athletes to become exposed to and learn new skills through an array of sports and sports-related experiences. The object of this experience is not to train would-be professionals, but rather to encourage experimentations through a variety of physical skills and challenges in a nonthreatening manner.

English Language Institute The English Language Institute is designed to provide international students with the opportunity to develop the skills necessary to communicate in English and to gain a more intimate understanding of American life and traditions. Writing, reading, listening, and speaking are the four major skills taught during the summer. Students enrolled in the English Language Institute participate in one enrichment course such as art, outdoor discovery, or sports along with participants in the academic enrichment program.

DAILY SCHEDULE

Classes meet Monday through Friday from 8:30 to 11:45 a.m. The enrichment courses (Art, Outdoor, Sports) run from 1 to 4:30 p.m. On academic nights, study and review hours are 7 to 8:30 p.m.

FACILITIES

Many of the buildings, constructed in the 1800s, are on the National Register of Historic Places, and the entire campus has been designated a National Historic District. Four academic buildings house classrooms, a computer center (linked to the Internet), an art studio, a dance studio, a music studio and practice rooms, and a library with 20,000 volumes. Student productions are staged in the Newhall Performing Arts Auditorium.

Shattuck–St. Mary's School has one of the most complete athletic complexes in Minnesota, which includes an eighteen-hole regulation golf course, ice arena, weight room, all-weather track, gymnasium, ten tennis courts, two football fields, three soccer fields, and an indoor pool.

STAFF

The summer faculty is an experienced and dedicated group of educators from both Shattuck–St. Mary's and other public and independent schools. The faculty–student ratio of 1:7 ensures an environment of close supervision and frequent opportunity for academic and personal guidance.

MEDICAL CARE

The school's Health Service Center is open through the summer session; a registered nurse is available on campus. The District One Hospital is a 5-minute drive from campus.

COSTS

Students in Summer Discovery are charged $2250 for three weeks. English Language Institute students are charged $2400 for three weeks.

APPLICATION TIMETABLE

To provide the best possible experience, Shattuck–St. Mary's School is committed to small classes of no more than 15 participants. There is a rolling admissions procedure, and the application should be mailed as soon as possible with a nonrefundable $50 processing fee. Once a student is accepted into the program, a $700 nonrefundable deposit must be paid within two weeks in order to hold a spot. The $700 deposit is credited to the tuition account. Any balance of tuition is due ten working days prior to the first day of the session.

FOR MORE INFORMATION, CONTACT:

Mike Frankenfield, Summer Program Director
P.O. Box 218
Faribault, Minnesota 55021
507-333-1674
800-617-8469 (toll-free)
Fax: 507-333-1591
E-mail: mfrankenfield@s-sm.org
World Wide Web: http://www.s-sm.org/summ_progs.asp

SIMON'S ROCK COLLEGE OF BARD

YOUNG WRITERS WORKSHOP

GREAT BARRINGTON, MASSACHUSETTS

Type of Program: Academic and cultural enrichment
Participants: Coeducational; ages 14–18, grades 9–12
Enrollment: 70–80
Program Dates: Last week in June and first two weeks in July
Head of Program: Dr. Jamie Hutchinson, Director

LOCATION

The Young Writers Workshop is held on the 275-acre campus of Simon's Rock College of Bard, the nation's only four-year college of liberal arts and sciences devoted exclusively to early admissions. The college is located in the Berkshire Hills of rural southwestern Massachusetts, an area rich in summer cultural activities, ranging from Tanglewood, the summer home of the Boston Symphony Orchestra, to Shakespeare and Company, one of the country's premier summer Shakespearean groups.

BACKGROUND AND PHILOSOPHY

The Young Writers Workshop is intended for intellectually curious and motivated students whose academic interests range across the disciplines. Based on the work of the nationally recognized Bard Institute for Writing and Thinking, which was established in 1982 as a result of Bard's success in developing an intensive three-week workshop for its entering freshmen, the summer workshop introduces students to a writing process that emphasizes the intimate relationship between language and thought.

Unlike more traditional programs, the Simon's Rock Workshop emphasizes informal, playful, expressive writing as a way to strengthen skills of language and thinking. The subjects range from stories and poems the group has read to personal experience, natural phenomena, and works of art. Out of this informal writing, using techniques of peer response, students develop more polished pieces, from poems and stories to exploratory essays.

Writing is seen as integral to learning, and throughout the program students practice using writing as a tool for exploring the meaning and significance of personal experience and observation, as well as what they read. Continuous practice in writing, reading, and responding to writing helps students learn to trust their own voices as writers and to express themselves in engaging and lively language.

The value of collaborative work with one's peers is also emphasized, whether the task is revising a piece of writing or furthering one's inquiry into a subject. These activities help students develop the writing and learning skills appropriate to high school and college.

Former students are enrolled in such colleges as Amherst, Bard, Carleton, Harvard, Haverford, Kenyon, Princeton, Smith, Williams, and Yale.

PROGRAM OFFERINGS

Participants are divided into sections of approximately 13 students. Each section meets for three 90-minute sessions every weekday. Activities range from in-class writing (fiction, poetry, personal narratives, imaginative responses to assigned readings) to discussions of writing techniques to work in small inquiry or peer writing groups. The small-group work helps to create a feeling of supportive community that enhances the writing and learning process. The workshop is run as a writing seminar, with the workshop leader participating in most of the activities. Weekly conferences allow students to explore issues specific to their growth as writers.

ENROLLMENT

The program normally enrolls 70–80 students. Admission is selective, based on the applicant's personal narrative and a teacher's recommendation. Although most students are from the East Coast, all regions of the United States are typically represented each summer.

DAILY SCHEDULE

There are three 90-minute workshops each day, beginning at 9 and ending at 3, with a break at 10:30 and lunch from 12:15 to 1:30. After 3, various social, recreational, and cultural activities are available to students. There is some reading, journal writing, or revision assigned each evening as preparation for the next day's workshop. An 11 o'clock curfew is enforced on weeknights, and there is a midnight curfew on weekends. The use of alcohol or illegal drugs is strictly prohibited and results in dismissal.

EXTRA OPPORTUNITIES AND ACTIVITIES

A varied program of informal and supervised activities is available to students, from student-organized talent shows to listening to music in the student union snack bar. Other recreational and social activities include swimming, tennis, weekend dances, films, student readings and performances, basketball, hiking, table tennis, pool, softball, running, biking, canoeing, swimming, and volleyball. During the three weeks students may also attend Boston Symphony Orchestra concerts at Tanglewood, outdoor productions of Shakespeare, modern dance performances at Jacob's Pillow, and minor-league baseball games. Trips to local sites, museums, and galleries such as the Norman Rockwell Museum, the Massachusetts Museum of Contemporary Art (MASS MoCA), and Hancock Shaker Village, as well as a Saturday trip to Northampton, are also offered. Most students participate in the organized weekend activities, but they may leave campus with parental permission.

FACILITIES

Most of the college's buildings were constructed in the 1960s, including the dormitories, the library, classrooms, the lecture center, the dining commons, faculty and administrative offices, and the student union. A science center opened in 1998, and an athletic center opened in 2000. During the summer, students have access to the art galleries, the theater, the bookstore, a small computer center, music practice rooms, laundry facilities, tennis courts, hiking trails, the athletic center, and soccer, volleyball, and softball fields. An indoor pool is available for supervised swimming.

STAFF

All workshop faculty members are experienced teachers and writers as well as associates of the Bard College Institute for Writing and Thinking. Dormitory and recreational supervision is provided by adult members of the college's student life staff as well as by Simon's Rock students hired to serve as summer counselors.

MEDICAL CARE

A fully equipped hospital is in the immediate vicinity of the campus. Minor medical needs are handled by the student health service nurse.

RELIGIOUS LIFE

The college provides transportation for students who wish to attend local religious services.

COSTS

The cost of room, board, and tuition for 2004 is $1925. Tickets for off-campus performances, museums, and the like are normally available at group discount rates. Students are responsible for buying some of their classroom supplies, such as notebooks and pens. Total spending money for supplies, snacks, and cultural excursions varies according to individual needs, but $175 to $200 is normally adequate.

FINANCIAL AID

Approximately one third of the students in the program receive partial financial aid. A financial aid form should be submitted with the student's application. Funds are limited.

Minority students with demonstrated financial need are eligible to apply for the Dorothy West Scholarship. This scholarship covers the full cost of tuition and room and board. The deadline for applying is April 16. For more information, students should contact the program director. A number of runner-ups are chosen and are eligible for lesser financial-aid awards. Information about how to apply is sent to all students who request application materials.

TRANSPORTATION

The nearest airports are in Albany, New York, and Hartford, Connecticut. The college can provide transportation to students flying into Hartford.

APPLICATION TIMETABLE

The admissions process begins in January and runs through May. Files are reviewed as they become complete. Students should apply as early as possible. A personal narrative and a teacher's recommendation are the primary application materials.

For more information, contact:

Dr. Jamie Hutchinson, Director
Summer Young Writers Workshop
Simon's Rock College of Bard
84 Alford Road
Great Barrington, Massachusetts 01230
413-528-7231
E-mail: jamieh@simons-rock.edu
World Wide Web: http://www.simons-rock.edu/young_writers

PARTICIPANT/FAMILY COMMENTS

"After discussing the experience with my daughter, I can say that the workshop was not what I expected, but it was even better than what I had hoped."

"At this workshop I have done the kind of writing I have always wanted to do, and I leave here with an excitement and curiosity that I didn't have before. My writing has been set free and is enjoying itself immensely."

SKIDMORE COLLEGE AP/ART (ACCELERATION PROGRAM IN ART)

SUMMER ARTS PROGRAM

SARATOGA SPRINGS, NEW YORK

Type of Program: Pre-college program in studio art, credit and noncredit courses
Participants: Coeducational, grades 10–12
Enrollment: 100
Program Dates: Five-week program, July 2 to August 5, 2005
Head of Program: Marianne Needham, Coordinator

LOCATION

Acceleration Program in Art (APA) takes place on the campus of Skidmore College, an independent, residential college hailed by *Newsweek* magazine as an "all-around gem." The 850-acre campus is located in Saratoga Springs, New York, a city rich in history, architectural beauty, and cultural traditions. Saratoga Springs is equidistant from Boston, New York City, and Montreal; each city is about 180 miles away.

BACKGROUND AND PHILOSOPHY

Skidmore's APA Program is designed for highly motivated and talented high school students who want to augment their studio art experiences in a rigorous college environment. APA is sponsored by Skidmore's Summer SIX Art Program, which has been distinguished as a special summer learning opportunity for more than thirty years. Students can explore and develop artistic talents; work alongside college students in small, individualized classes; and benefit from the stimulating learning environment created by excellent resident faculty members, nationally reputed visiting artists, a diverse student body, and outstanding facilities. Students leave the program enriched and invigorated, with warm memories of an exciting summer, new friends, and challenges faced and met. APA students have gone on to study at top colleges and universities across the country.

PROGRAM OFFERINGS

Residential students must enroll in two courses. The program works with students to decide which combination of courses is most appropriate for their skill levels and goals. APA offers both college credit foundation courses and noncredit Advanced Placement workshops. Credit courses provide students with the same intensive curriculum that a Skidmore College freshman would encounter. Noncredit Advanced Placement workshops offer a similar experience without the pressure of grades.

Students may choose from three possible combinations of college credit courses and Advanced Placement workshops. They are two college-credit courses, one credit course and one Advanced Placement workshop, or two Advanced Placement workshops. The combination chosen is based on present skill level, degree of motivation, and class year. All courses, both credit and noncredit, focus on course work that builds strong fundamental skills. Upon completion of a credit course, students may request that the transcript of the course be sent to the college of his or her choice. Credit courses include Introduction to Painting, Drawing, Basic Ceramics, Form and Space, 3-D Design, Introduction to Fiber Arts, Watercolor, and Sculpture. Noncredit courses are Drawing, Computer Design, Videography, Life Drawing and Painting, Sculpture, Fiber Arts, and Painting.

Students with an interest in an academic class may supplement their studio art courses by cross-registering in the Pre-College Program in the Liberal Arts.

ENROLLMENT

Approximately 70 residential and 20 commuter students enroll in the program each year.

DAILY SCHEDULE

Students enroll in one morning and one afternoon class. Morning courses are scheduled from 9 a.m. to 12:15 p.m.; afternoon classes are from 1:15 to 4:30 p.m.

EXTRA OPPORTUNITIES AND ACTIVITIES

Evening seminars help APA students prepare for the college admission process. Workshops examine topics such as choosing the right college, submitting a portfolio to colleges and to the College Board for AP credit, and photographing artwork for submission of slides. In addition, visiting artists, art historians, and critics with national and international reputations present exciting and informative lectures that give insight into their work and the larger context of contemporary art.

Weekly events organized by the dorm staff members include picnics, movie nights, volleyball games, and weekend trips. Weekend events off campus include hiking in the Adirondack State Park,

swimming at Lake George, exploring downtown Saratoga Springs, trips to the New York City Ballet, rock concerts at the Saratoga Performing Arts Center, and Great Escape Amusement Park.

FACILITIES
Students reside in a Skidmore dormitory with other high school students. Accommodations are suites with adjoining bathrooms. Small lounges throughout the dormitory and a large ground-floor lounge provide ample space for socializing. An adult residence hall director and a group of Skidmore students who serve as resident assistants also live in the dorm. Dining halls are cafeteria-style, with small tables for 10. Hot and cold entrees and a full salad bar are always available for lunch and dinner. The campus snack bar is open between dining hall hours.

The theater, gallery, and recital and lecture halls on campus showcase the talents of participants in various programs at Skidmore. Jazz Institute faculty members and visiting artists perform in Bernhard Theater. Writer's Institute faculty members offer readings and discussions of the work in lecture halls. The Schick Art Gallery houses shows and talks by artists of world acclaim. The Lucy Scribner Library features 380,000 volumes, subscriptions to 1,600 journals and periodicals, 80,000 art and art history slides, more than 1,000 videotapes, computer access to the Web, and more than 6,600 records, tapes, and CDs.

The Sports and Recreation Center provides weight rooms, a competition-size swimming pool, an all-weather outdoor track and artificial turf field, and tennis, racquetball, squash, and basketball courts. A running path winds its way around campus, and numerous hiking trails go through the woods north of campus. The Tang Teaching Museum and Art Gallery features world-renowned artists.

STAFF
Professors are faculty members and visiting faculty members of Skidmore College. All have advanced degrees in the fine arts and have studied at schools and universities around the country and the world.

MEDICAL CARE
The College provides basic medical services for minor injuries or illnesses between the hours of 9 a.m. and 3 p.m., Monday through Friday. For more serious injuries and illness after hours, students are referred to Saratoga Hospital. All APA students must have a medical form on file at the Health Services Office.

COSTS
In 2004, fees for APA were as follows: $1350 to $1450 per credit course, $780 per Advanced Placement workshop, $1505 room and board, and a $185 activity fee. Studio lab fees range from $50 to $100 per course, depending on the course chosen. Most students also bring $200 to $250 for spending money.

FINANCIAL AID
Scholarships are awarded on the basis of financial need and artistic merit. To be considered for a scholarship, a student must enclose copies of his or her family's IRS 1040 form, including any pertinent explanations of his or her financial status, along with the application materials. A special scholarship, the High School Art Teachers Fellowship Award, is made possible by art teachers across the country who have participated in Summer SIX at Skidmore.

TRANSPORTATION
Skidmore College is 30 minutes from the Albany County airport, 45 minutes from the Albany-Rensselaer Amtrak station, and 5 minutes from the Saratoga Amtrak station.

APPLICATION TIMETABLE
Acceptance is on a rolling basis. Prospective students must submit the following: the application form with a $30 nonrefundable fee, a personal statement describing the student's interests in art and reasons for applying to the APA program, a letter of recommendation from an art teacher, high school transcripts, and five to ten color slides or photos of recent art work. For scholarship consideration, materials must be received by May 6, 2005. All applications are reviewed by the director and coordinator of the program and are processed as received. Although there is no formal deadline, students should apply by June 10, 2005 to ensure preferred course selections.

For more information, students should contact:

Regis Brodie, Director
Marianne Needham, Coordinator
APA and Summer SIX
Skidmore College
815 North Broadway
Saratoga Springs, New York 12866-1632
518-580-5052
Fax: 518-580-5029
E-mail: mneedham@skidmore.edu

PARTICIPANT/FAMILY COMMENTS
"I will be going on for the rest of my life about how this program is the best thing I have ever done."

SKIDMORE COLLEGE PRE-COLLEGE PROGRAM FOR HIGH SCHOOL STUDENTS

SUMMER PROGRAM

SARATOGA SPRINGS, NEW YORK

Type of Program: Credit-bearing, first-year college courses in the liberal arts
Participants: Coeducational, grades 11–12
Enrollment: 40–50
Program Dates: Five weeks, July to early August
Head of Program: Dr. James Chansky, Director of Summer Special Programs

LOCATION

Saratoga Springs is a small, cosmopolitan town in upstate New York, well known as a summer resort town and for its Victorian heritage, famed spas, and thoroughbred racing. The lively summer season at Skidmore College receives national recognition for the rich diversity of its programs in the liberal, fine, creative, and performing arts and for the public offerings that fill Skidmore's theater, gallery, and recital and lecture halls.

BACKGROUND AND PHILOSOPHY

Since the late 1970s, Skidmore has been bringing bright high school students to campus for a summer experience of college life and learning. Through the combination of first-year college-level courses, dormitory living, and the rich and varied intellectual, cultural, artistic, and social life of the summer campus, the program is designed to offer high school students a true college experience.

PROGRAM OFFERINGS

Pre-College students enroll in two credit bearing courses selected from among a range of offerings in the humanities, social sciences, natural sciences, and mathematics. Students with a particular interest in the studio arts may also cross-register in a studio art course or workshop offered through AP/Art, the Acceleration Program in the Arts. All courses are taught primarily by full-time Skidmore faculty members, known for their attention to students and to student learning. In addition to faculty support, the Academic Coordinator assists students in their course work, managing their time, and acclimating to the pace of college life. Special sessions help Pre-College students think about what they want to study in college, what sort of college they want to attend, and how to negotiate the college application process. The evening lectures, readings, recitals, and performances offered by the concurrently running summer programs further enhance students' intellectual and cultural life, and the extracurricular activities put together by the residence hall staff inject an element of pure fun into the program.

ENROLLMENT

Students are drawn from all over the United States, the majority coming from the Northeast and mid-Atlantic states, and reflect a very wide diversity of social, economic, ethnic, and racial backgrounds.

DAILY SCHEDULE

Pre-College students enroll in two courses, each of which meets for approximately 90 minutes daily, five days per week. Preparation time averages about 2 hours daily for each class. Free time is spent engaging in the more relaxing and fun program-sponsored events, swimming, playing or working out in the gym, walking downtown to a coffee house and socializing with new friends on campus and in the dormitory, and attending the many performances, films, lectures, and other events happening across campus.

EXTRA OPPORTUNITIES AND ACTIVITIES

Among the larger challenges facing Pre-College students is finding the time to take advantage of all the activities and events on campus: jazz concerts offered by the nationally known Jazz Institute faculty members and visiting artists; fiction, nonfiction, and poetry readings and discussions by the prize-winning writers in the New York State Summer Writer's Institute; great movies shown in the International Film Festival; lecture-demonstrations and art openings through the Summer SIX Art Program; and more.

Events organized by the dorm staff specifically for high school students include regular get-togethers following evening events, movie nights, volleyball games, study breaks, and other activities. Weekend off-campus events include attending rock concerts and a performance of the New York City Ballet at the Saratoga Performing Arts Center, spending a day at the Great Escape Amusement Park (among the largest in the U.S.), taking a day trip to New York City, swimming in Lake George in the Adirondacks, and exploring downtown.

FACILITIES

Students are housed in a dormitory and dine in the College's dining hall. The library provides lots of space for study and group work, a substantial collection of books and journals, and state-of-the-art computers. The sports and recreation center includes weight rooms; racquetball, squash, and basketball courts; a competition-sized swimming pool; an all-weather outdoor track and artificial turf field; and several tennis courts. A running path winds its way around the perimeter of the campus, and numerous hiking trails zigzag through the woods to the north of the campus.

STAFF

The Pre-College Program is one among the many summer academic programs administered by Skidmore's Office of the Dean of Special Programs, the office bearing responsibility for all summer programs. The teaching faculty members and the academic coordinator are members of the Skidmore faculty and community and are all seasoned educators selected on the basis of their ability to teach first-year level courses. The residential staff consists of an adult professional Residential Director and a staff of well-trained and experienced college students who serve as residential assistants.

MEDICAL CARE

Emergency and critical care for program participants is available through the College's Office of Health Services and the Saratoga Hospital, which is 5 minutes from campus. All students are required to submit a medical and release form prior to their arrival.

COSTS

The total program cost for a residential student is approximately $4300 and includes tuition for two courses, room, board, and an activity fee. Books and supplies carry additional charges.

FINANCIAL AID

Some full and partial scholarships are awarded annually on the basis of need and merit. As aid is limited, early application is advisable.

TRANSPORTATION

Skidmore College is ½-hour from the Albany County Airport and 45 minutes from the Albany-Rensselaer Amtrak station. Major bus lines also deliver service directly to Saratoga Springs. Taxi and limousine service is available to take students to campus.

APPLICATION TIMETABLE

Students are encouraged to make their inquiries in the late fall and to apply as soon as they receive application materials. Admission decisions are made on a rolling basis, usually within a week of receipt of a completed application. To ensure a place in the program, applications are best received by May 1, though applications are reviewed up to mid-June on a space-available basis.

For more information, contact:

Dr. James Chansky, Director of Summer Special Programs
Pre-College Program for High School Students
Office of the Dean of Special Programs
Skidmore College
815 North Broadway
Saratoga Springs, New York 12866
518-580-5590
Fax: 518-580-5548
E-mail: jchansky@skidmore.edu
World Wide Web: http://www.skidmore.edu/summer

PARTICIPANT/FAMILY COMMENTS

"This was one of my greatest summers ... Skidmore had so much to offer me, from friends in the dorm, a big and comfortable library, great trips, college life, friendly professors ... an overall great place away from home."

SMITH COLLEGE

SMITH SUMMER SCIENCE AND ENGINEERING PROGRAM

NORTHAMPTON, MASSACHUSETTS

Type of Program: Enrichment programming in science and engineering for girls
Enrollment: 100
Participants: Girls, grades 9–12
Program Dates: July 3 to July 30
Head of Program: Dr. Gail E. Scordilis, Director

LOCATION

Smith College is located in Northampton, Massachusetts, in the scenic Pioneer Valley of western New England. The 125-acre Smith campus is situated a short walk from downtown Northampton (population 31,000), and it is bordered by the natural beauty of the Connecticut River, the Holyoke Mountain Range, and the foothills of the Berkshire Mountains.

BACKGROUND AND PHILOSOPHY

Girls in high school with dreams of pursuing a career in science, engineering, or medicine should make the 2005 Smith College Summer Science and Engineering Program (SSEP) part of their plan. A month in the summer at Smith gives students an exceptional opportunity to do science and engineering, enhance their skills, boost their confidence, and connect them with professionals who support their efforts. Students also make great new friends from all over the world who share their interests. Since its initiation in 1990, more than 1000 high school girls from across America and abroad have participated in this innovative program. After the program, participants report that they return to high school better prepared to tackle tough science courses and better informed about what to expect in college.

Smith College is one of the top-rated liberal arts colleges in the U.S. and the nation's largest college dedicated solely to the education of women. Housed in the multi-building Clark Science Center, the Smith science faculty includes some of the finest researchers and teachers in the country. Smith undergraduates don't just hear and read about scientific research, they are active participants. As a result, for more than seventy-five years, Smith has ranked in the top 3 percent of 519 private colleges in the number of graduates who have gone on to earn Ph.D.'s in science. In 1999, Smith became the first women's college in the nation to establish its own program in engineering science, the Picker Program in Engineering. Beginning in 2000, the Ford Foundation granted four full scholarships annually for outstanding applicants to the Picker Program.

Students don't have to wait until college to experience the benefits of a Smith education. The summer of 2005 marks the sixteenth year of the Smith College Summer Science and Engineering Program. The SSEP extends the benefits of Smith's strong traditions to girls still in high school. Participants in the summer program are taught by Smith faculty members, live in a college house alongside Smith undergraduate interns, and have access to all campus facilities. Central to the program is a learning community that is rich in role models, cooperative, hands-on, minds-on, investigative, and challenging—where girls get all of the faculty's attention, all of the opportunities, and all of the encouragement to achieve their best.

PROGRAM OFFERINGS

The 2005 SSEP runs from Sunday, July 3, through Saturday, July 30. All SSEP participants give two oral presentations of their work, one at the midpoint of the program (Saturday, July 16) and a second presentation at the conclusion of the program (Saturday, July 30). At the conclusion of the program, parents and family members arriving to pick up their daughters attend the final student presentations and share in their accomplishments. The presentations are followed by a family/student/faculty lunch that concludes the summer program.

Unlike regular school classes, SSEP research courses emphasize asking questions and learning by doing, not listening and watching. During their monthlong stay on campus, students choose to take either two 2-week-long courses or one 4-week-long course. A maximum of 16 students work alongside a Smith faculty member who is assisted by an undergraduate intern. Informal lectures in the laboratory and field provide students with the basis for asking experimental questions; then they learn how to do real experiments. Most of the work is carried out as a cooperative team effort, with ample opportunities for individual contributions. SSEP participants learn how scientists and engineers formulate questions, work on some amazingly sophisticated scientific instruments, and develop valuable critical-thinking and analytical skills.

Research courses for the 2005 program include investigations in astronomy, biology, biochemistry, chemistry, computer engineering, engineering and design, women's health, and writing. SSEP courses are designed to be relevant and interesting. In courses such as Your Genes, Your Chromosomes: A Laboratory Course in Human Genetics, Designing Intelligent Robots, and Rare and Endangered Species, SSEP participants explore their world in new and intriguing ways. In addition, Experiment and Exploration: A Laboratory for Writers is an intensive SSEP course that offers students individualized instruction to strengthen their writing skills. Participants in the 2005 SSEP may also choose to join a group of researchers from Smith, the YWCA, and Mt. Sinai Adolescent Health Center who are investigating young women's health issues. These student researchers will contribute to the Web site ByGirlsForGirls.org and help to disseminate important information about teen health to girls around the world.

ENROLLMENT

Enrollment in the program is limited to 100 to ensure the quality of the academic experience offered. Eligible candidates are academically talented girls who will be entering grades 9–12 in fall 2005. In all of its programming, Smith is committed to reaching a diverse student body. In the 2004 SSEP, 50 percent of participants identified themselves as students of color.

DAILY SCHEDULE

On a typical weekday, students eat breakfast from 7:30 to 8:30 a.m., are involved in 2 to 3 hours of investigation in the morning, break for lunch at noon, and then return to their research for 2 to 3 hours in the afternoon. On average, participants spend 120 contact hours working with faculty members.

Dinner each evening is scheduled from 5:30 to 7 p.m. Throughout the program, evening discussion sessions are given on exploring career opportunities in science, engineering, and medicine. In addition, the Smith Office of Admission sponsors workshops that support students at different stages of the college planning process.

EXTRA OPPORTUNITIES AND ACTIVITIES

In addition to doing great science, the SSEP is about making new friends and getting a taste of college life. Smith's 125-acre campus is beautiful, with traditional ivy-covered buildings, magnificent gardens, and a pond named Paradise. SSEP participants live together in one college house along with SSEP interns, who serve as supervisors, advisers, and teaching/research assistants, and SSEP residence coordinators, who are in charge of all aspects of students' residential life. All meals are served in the house dining room. During free time, participants can choose from organized sport, recreational, and cultural activities or be on their own with friends from the program. Smith's superb athletic facilities include two gymnasiums, an indoor pool, indoor and outdoor track and tennis facilities, squash courts, horseback riding arena, dance studio, croquet court, and weight rooms. Weekend field trips journey to local arts festivals, museums, and theatrical performances throughout the Pioneer Valley. Participants enjoy hikes to local nature preserves, rollerblading, movie nights, and the annual SSEP talent show. Also located within an easy walking distance of campus in downtown Northampton are a varied selection of shops, restaurants, and movies. The program fee covers the costs of all organized program activities and field trips.

STAFF

The Program Director is Dr. Gail E. Scordilis, an alumna of Smith and a member of the Department of Biological Sciences. Dr. Leslie Jaffe, Director of Smith College Health Services, is the SSEP Health Consultant. Smith College faculty and academic staff members instruct participants in the SSEP. For every 7–8 students enrolled, there is a Smith undergraduate intern who serves as a residential counselor and research/teaching assistant to the faculty. Two residence coordinators, who are trained in residential life management, supervise the undergraduate staff.

MEDICAL CARE

Upon acceptance, all SSEP participants are required to submit a prescription medication form and a medical information form detailing their relevant medical histories, insurance information, and parental consent for care. Medical care is provided for program participants by a group of 6 local physicians who specialize in pediatric and adolescent medicine. In addition, Smith is only a few miles from Northampton's Cooley Dickinson Hospital and convenient to Springfield's extensive Bay State Medical Center.

COSTS

The fee for participation in the 2005 Smith Summer Science and Engineering Program is $3950 and covers the cost of all program materials and activities.

FINANCIAL AID

Partial to full financial aid is available to a limited number of participants and is awarded solely on the basis of demonstrated financial need. The SSEP is supported in part by grants to Smith College from the GE Foundation; the Howard Hughes Medical Institute, a medical research organization; and the Metropolitan Life Foundation. More than 50 percent of 2004 participants received financial aid. Students requesting financial aid must complete the financial aid application, found on the reverse side of the SSEP application.

TRANSPORTATION

Smith College is located in Northampton in the Connecticut River valley of western Massachusetts. From I-91, students should take Exit 18 and follow the signs to Route 9, which leads directly to campus. Bradley International Airport, 33 miles south of Northampton on I-91, is the nearest airport. Major train and bus lines also serve the area.

APPLICATION TIMETABLE

The 2005 SSEP is open to academically talented girls who will enter grades 9–12 in the fall of 2005. Enrollment in the program is limited to ensure the quality of the academic experience. Admission to the SSEP is selective and is based on academic performance in middle and/or high school, teacher recommendation, and a written essay. Applications from students with all levels of previous science training are welcome. Students need not have taken advanced science courses, but they must have a strong record of academic achievement, a high level of motivation, and willingness to explore. There are two deadlines for application, an early admission date of March 1 and a regular admission date of May 1. The program fills quickly so early application is strongly encouraged. All applications received prior to these dates are promptly evaluated.

For more information, contact:

Gail E. Scordilis, Ph.D., Director
Educational Outreach
Clark Hall
Smith College
Northampton, Massachusetts 01063
Telephone: 413-585-3060
Fax 413-585-3068
E-mail: gscordil@smith.edu
World Wide Web:
http://www.smith.edu/summerprograms/ssep/

SNOW FARM: THE NEW ENGLAND CRAFT PROGRAM

SUMMER HIGH SCHOOL PROGRAM

WILLIAMSBURG, MASSACHUSETTS

Type of Program: Intensive craft program
Participants: Coeducational, teens
Enrollment: Approximately 60 students per session
Program Dates: Two sessions or one full month session in July; 10-day Accelerated Art Studies Program, August 1–10
Head of Program: Mary Colwell, Executive Director

LOCATION

Snow Farm is located off Route 9 in Williamsburg, Massachusetts, in the heart of the Pioneer Valley, home to a large number of the country's most prominent master craftspeople. Also part of the five-college community of Northampton and Amherst in western Massachusetts, it is just 15 minutes from Northampton and 30 minutes from Amherst.

BACKGROUND AND PHILOSOPHY

In January 2001, Snow Farm took over the beautiful, historic 50-acre farm and school that was formerly the site of Horizons: The New England Craft Program. Nestled among hills and pastures in the Berkshire foothills, it runs a wide range of craft programs for teens and adults of all ages. Snow Farm features workshops on glassblowing, flameworking, welded sculpture, jewelry making, ceramics, metalsmithing, fiber arts, woodworking, photography (digital, black and white), painting, and drawing.

The staff at Snow Farm embraces the creative magic that is the heart of the New England Craft Program. Most important is the artistic foundation and spirit of community that make Snow Farm a unique learning experience. Snow Farm looks forward to its future with great excitement and bountiful energy as it continues to provide the highest quality of instruction in an inspiring New England setting.

PROGRAM OFFERINGS

The Summer High School Program offers three sessions in 2005: session I, July 2–July 16; session II, July 17–July 31; and full summer, July 2–July 31. Studio choices include ceramics, drawing and color, photography, textile art (session I only), metalsmithing and jewelry construction, glassblowing, flameworking, and welding (session II only). New for 2005 is the 10-day Accelerated Art Studies Program, which is for students ages 16–18 and is based on Snow Farm's Adult Intensives model. Students choose one of two mediums (glassblowing and lampworking or digital and traditional photography) and receive 7 hours of advanced instruction as well as participate in evening activities. Some experience is required for the accelerated program. After a student evaluation, certificates are awarded.

Snow Farm's programs allow students the opportunity to be part of a small community of people joined by a common interest in creativity and in each other. The programs have an excellent faculty-student ratio, enabling each person to work at their own pace and level. A diversity of backgrounds and interests and a wide geographical area are represented both in staff members and in students. The pervasive spirit of learning from and helping each other makes Snow Farm not just an intense creative experience but also a significant personal experience nurtured by developing close friendships and discovering new ways of perceiving the world and one's own capabilities.

ENROLLMENT

Enrollment in the Summer High School Program is about 60 students per session and 48 for the Accelerated Art Studies program.

DAILY SCHEDULE

The student's morning is devoted to a 3-hour studio, and most of the afternoon is devoted to a second 3-hour studio. Open studio time is scheduled in late afternoons and evenings, giving students an opportunity to continue work on pieces begun earlier in the day and to work and explore on their own. Considerable independence is given to all students in managing time, with the foundation of the program resting on each student's strong sense of commitment to themselves and their work.

The school's small size creates an atmosphere that is flexible and spontaneous. Students are encouraged to voice their ideas and opinions. Each person, student as well as faculty member, has the opportunity to influence the flow of day-to-day life and activities. Late afternoons offer free time in the studio or the spontaneity of group swims, Frisbee games, or volleyball. Hot nights may see a group going swimming; cool nights lend themselves to a bonfire with singing and conversation.

EXTRA OPPORTUNITIES AND ACTIVITIES

Friday nights bring the special Guest Artist Program, in which established and successful artists of varied mediums join Snow Farm for dinner and present their work to students, showing slides and samples. On Saturday, students work with the artist of their choice for a day of new and exciting explorations, giving a unique opportunity to interact with master crafts artists. Saturday evenings are highlighted with a special Big Event night, a community gathering with the emphasis on fun. Sundays are nonstudio days and give students a chance to see more of Massachusetts and New England. There are frequent trips to craft-related settings, such as MASS MoCA in North Adams, artists' studios, and galleries.

FACILITIES

Snow Farm's four living modules are designed as a series of double rooms, each of which opens out onto a large, covered outdoor deck. The kitchen is the focal point of Snow Farm, with wholesome food prepared from fresh ingredients. Formal and informal participation in the kitchen by Snow Farm students helps create a real sense of community.

STAFF

The High School Director, Brian Brown, has been involved with Snow Farm in many capacities over the past eleven years. Brian has directed Snow Farm's very successful Summer High School Program for the past two years, and the program is delighted to have him return for this season. The program artist-instructors come from across the United States and often from other countries, too. Heads of Studio are required to have an M.F.A. or equivalent experience in their medium. Assistant Heads of Studio must have a B.F.A. in their medium. Snow Farm looks for individuals who have experience and an enthusiasm for working with high school students as well as a passion for their own art mediums.

MEDICAL CARE

A registered nurse is available for consultation and visits. The program physician is located a mile from Snow Farm, and the local hospital is 15 minutes away. Safety and prevention standards are emphasized in each studio and throughout the campus.

COSTS

For the Summer High School Program, tuition for 2005, including room and board, studio fees, field trips, and laundry fees, is $2500 for sessions I and II and $4800 for the full summer. Additional studio fees (per session) are glassblowing, $140; flameworking $135; welding, $135; photography, $80; and metals/jewelry, $75. A refundable physical plant deposit fee is $50. High school credit is also available and must be coordinated with the student's art and/or guidance office. Tuition for the Accelerated Art Studies Program is $1900, which includes room and meals as well as studio fees.

FINANCIAL AID

Scholarships are available through the Snow Farm program and may be applied for by contacting the Executive Director, Mary Colwell, or the Program Director, Karen Totman, at the Snow Farm office. Every year throughout November, Snow Farm runs an extensive sale of the work of leading craftspeople from across the country. Proceeds from the sale benefit both the participating artists and the scholarship fund for the Summer High School Program.

TRANSPORTATION

Students can be transported by van before and after each session to or from Bradley International Airport in Hartford, Connecticut, for a fee of $35.

APPLICATION TIMETABLE

Applicants to the Summer High School Program must submit an application form indicating choices for studios, a personal statement that tells something about the applicant, two reference letters, and a deposit of $400, $320 of which is applied toward tuition, the $80 balance being a nonrefundable registration fee. The application is reviewed for acceptance after all items have been completed and submitted. Applications are considered on a first come, first served basis, with no application deadline.

FOR MORE INFORMATION, CONTACT:

Snow Farm
5 Clary Road
Williamsburg, Massachusetts 01096
413-268-3101
Fax: 413-268-3163
E-mail: info@snowfarm-art.org
World Wide Web: http://www.snowfarm.org/

SOUTHERN METHODIST UNIVERSITY

SUMMER PROGRAMS

DALLAS, TEXAS

Type of Program: Academic enrichment and acceleration
Participants: Coeducational, students who have completed grades 7–11
Enrollment: Approximately 200 per program
Program Dates: Two sessions: Talented and Gifted, July 11–30, 2004; College Experience, July 5–August 6, 2004
Head of Program: Dr. Kathy Hargrove, Director of Pre-College Programs, Division of Evening and Summer Studies

LOCATION

The programs are held on the campus of Southern Methodist University (SMU), a private coeducational institution located in University Park, a district surrounded by the city of Dallas. The 164-acre campus, replete with Georgian architecture, is home to numerous theaters, concert halls, and a library collection of more than 2 million volumes.

BACKGROUND AND PHILOSOPHY

SMU programs began in 1978 and are designed to provide students with intellectual challenges and exciting learning experiences. Many students establish mentor relationships and develop friendships that last a lifetime. Programs encourage students to mature socially as well as intellectually and foster the development of maturity and self-confidence.

PROGRAM OFFERINGS

Southern Methodist University offers two summer residential programs. The Talented and Gifted Program (TAG) is for academically talented and gifted youths completing grades seven, eight, and nine. College Experience (CE) is planned for rising high school juniors and seniors who are motivated and capable of successfully completing college-credit courses. In all programs, small classes ensure that students develop strong relationships with faculty members, and residence hall life provides a warm, supportive environment. In addition, a variety of educational and recreational experiences are offered.

Talented and Gifted TAG is open to students entering grades 8–10 in 2004–05. During this three-week residential program, students participate in two stimulating classes chosen from a wide selection of SMU credit and noncredit courses. Cultural enrichment activities are provided for all TAG students. Three-hour credit courses include mathematical sciences, economics, political science, mechanical engineering, psychology, philosophy, and ethics. Noncredit courses include poetry writing, engineering, Shakespeare, theater arts, film, public discourse, mathematics, photography, physics, geography, rocketry, and paleontology.

College Experience Academically talented high school students can get a head start on college and a taste of campus life during this exciting five-week summer program at SMU. The selection of college-credit subjects for morning classes includes philosophy, English, math, psychology, history, and government. In the afternoon, all College Experience students participate in a "core" class or humanities overview class for 3 hours of college credit. Students who elect to live in the CE residence hall participate in special cultural, educational, and recreational activities.

ENROLLMENT

Enrollment for the College Experience program is limited to 60 students. Applicants must have completed the tenth or eleventh grade. Enrollment for TAG is limited to 150 students. Applicants must have completed the seventh, eighth, or ninth grade.

Participants are selected on the basis of academic ability and motivation as demonstrated by grades, SAT I or ACT test scores, teacher recommendations, and other application requirements.

SMU does not discriminate on the basis of race, color, national or ethnic origin, sex, or disability.

DAILY SCHEDULE

Students attend morning and afternoon classes. Evenings are spent in study and recreation.

EXTRA OPPORTUNITIES AND ACTIVITIES

In addition to challenging course work, students take advantage of campus libraries, museums, the student center, and computer labs. Both programs offer planned activities both for individuals and small and large groups. Activities include evening seminars, movies, musical and dramatic performances, picnics, athletics events, talent shows, guest lectures, special programs, and parties and dances. During free time, students decide individually whether to study or just to relax with their friends.

FACILITIES

Students for both programs live in air-conditioned residence halls near the center of campus. For both programs, the hall is reserved exclusively for program students, their hall director, and resident advisers (RAs). Students are housed 2 to a room with adjoining or hall bathrooms. Boys and girls are separated. Meals are served cafeteria-style and feature a salad bar, sandwich bar, hot entrees and vegetables, and a variety of desserts.

STAFF

TAG students are supervised in every activity by the faculty and staff. College Experience students experience life as college students. The residence hall staff is carefully selected and qualified to provide academic and nonacademic guidance. College Experience faculty members are SMU professors. TAG teachers are both SMU faculty members and secondary school teachers with training and an interest in working with gifted students.

MEDICAL CARE

Students in both programs are covered by group medical insurance while enrolled. They are treated for illness or injury at the SMU Health Center or at a local hospital, if necessary, during their program participation.

RELIGIOUS LIFE

Religious services are held on campus.

COSTS

Tuition for College Experience is $1794. Cost for CE room and board is $1250. The total cost for TAG is $2450. All costs are estimated.

FINANCIAL AID

Limited financial aid is available and is awarded on the basis of need. Early application is highly recommended.

TRANSPORTATION

Students are responsible for their own transportation to and from the programs, but students who arrive in Dallas by air, bus, or train can make arrangements to be picked up by program staff members.

APPLICATION TIMETABLE

Application forms are available in January and are accepted on a rolling basis until all available spaces are filled. SAT I or ACT scores are highly recommended. College Experience and TAG applicants complete an application that includes recommendations, a brief essay, transcripts, and test scores.

For more information, contact:

Marilyn Swanson, Assistant Director
Gifted Students Institute–College Experience
Gifted Students Institute–TAG
Southern Methodist University
P.O. Box 750383
Dallas, Texas 75275-0383
214-768-5437
E-mail: gifted@smu.edu
World Wide Web: http://tag.smu.edu
http://collegeexperience.smu.edu

PARTICIPANT/FAMILY COMMENTS

"A day of TAG is equivalent to a week of life outside the world of TAG. My two summers gave birth to new knowledge and new friendships; I finally found my 'niche.'"

"Her time at TAG has been the most positive educational experience she has ever had."

SOUTHWESTERN ADVENTURES

SUMMER PROGRAM

RIMROCK, ARIZONA

Type of Program: Academic enrichment, outdoor and environmental education, field trips, and recreation
Participants: Coeducational, ages 11–18
Enrollment: 45
Program Dates: Two-, three-, and six-week sessions, June 28 to August 6
Head of Program: Dr. Marshall Whitmire, Campus Dean

LOCATION

Southwestern Academy's Beaver Creek Ranch Campus, at an elevation of 4,000 feet, is 15 miles from Sedona, 45 miles south of Flagstaff, and 100 miles north of Phoenix, Arizona, in a secluded red sandstone canyon that was carved by the creek.. The Coconino National Forest surrounds the 180-acre campus.

BACKGROUND AND PHILOSOPHY

The summer program offers intensive morning studies for high school credit, make-up, or academic enrichment. Course offerings include electives that support the outdoor/environmental education focus at Beaver Creek Ranch Campus. Students study in a relaxed, supportive, and informal environment with afternoon and evening activities, field strip, and travel.

PROGRAM OFFERINGS

The Summer Program curriculum includes a core program with comprehensive courses in English, history, computer instruction, science, math, Spanish, and art. Courses are selected individually to meet each student's academic needs. Classes are held Monday through Friday mornings and are taught by Southwestern faculty members. Small class sizes and one-to-one instruction help students build self-confidence and study skills. Afternoons are left open for study time, enrichment through arts and crafts, field trips, elective course work, and travel. Electives include Outdoor and Wilderness Skills, Writing Skills, Art: Southwestern Flora, and History of the Old West.

Weekend activities include overnight travel to Sunset Crater, Grand Canyon, Lake Powell, Navajo and Hopi reservations, Petrified Forest, and Canyon de Chelly. Camping skills are learned and applied during these trips. In addition, there are organized studies at each site that provide hands-on learning in history, archaeology, geology, ecology, economics, and geography. Recreational activities include camping, water sports, hiking, mountain climbing, mountain hiking, and more.

High school course credit and lower school letters of achievement can be earned to make up credits for deficiencies, or students can gain a head start on the coming year. Southwestern is accredited by the Western Association of Schools and Colleges.

ENROLLMENT

Campers and counselors generally come from the Southwest, with a few boys and girls coming from other states and from overseas. (A separate session at Southwestern's California campus offers intensive English as a second language programs for international students.) The Southwestern Adventures Summer Program is for students with English as a native language or with strong English-speaking abilities. Southwestern's programs are open to all qualified students without regard to race or national origin.

DAILY SCHEDULE

7:00–7:30	Breakfast
7:30–9:00	Period 1
9:10–10:40	Period 2
10:50–12:20	Period 3
12:20–1:00	Lunch
1:30–2:30	Study hall
3:00–6:00	Activities
6:00–6:30	Dinner
7:00–10:00	Programs

EXTRA OPPORTUNITIES AND ACTIVITIES

The canyon setting of Beaver Creek Ranch Campus provides creek and pool swimming, archaeological and geological field trips, backpacking, rock climbing, and the exploration of nearby caves containing prehistoric remains. There is trout fishing in the creek or fly casting for bass in the pond. The nights are clear for star watching.

Recreational activities include basketball, softball, waterskiing, swimming, volleyball, horseback riding, hiking, billiards, table tennis, horseshoes, mountain biking, weight training, and indoor games. A golf course is nearby. There is a full gymnasium on campus. Computers and computer instruction are available to all students.

FACILITIES

Campus buildings include modern dorms with double and triple rooms; river stone cottages for faculty members; new classrooms; a new science lab; a library; recreation halls; natural and man-made swimming pools; indoor tennis, basketball, and volleyball courts; weight and fitness rooms; art buildings; and sports fields. Surrounded by large sycamores and cottonwoods, two ponds and a trout stream are on campus.

STAFF

Southwestern Academy is an accredited college-preparatory school with a noncompetitive program in

which students are grouped by ability. Teachers from the school's winter term instruct the summer program classes.

Resident teachers supervise afternoon and evening travel and activities.

COSTS

In 2004, tuition, room, and board totaled $4800 for the six-week session, $2500 for the three-week session, and $1700 for the two-week session. A deposit of $500 is required for personal expenses.

FINANCIAL AID

Financial aid is available through the school's nonprofit scholarship fund. Special grants are based on financial need.

TRANSPORTATION

Beaver Creek Ranch Campus is seven hours from Los Angeles by car and 1½ hours from Phoenix. A private airstrip is nearby. Unless other arrangements are made, summer campers fly into Phoenix Sky Harbor Airport and take a shuttle to Camp Verde, where they are picked up by a Southwestern Academy staff or faculty member.

APPLICATION TIMETABLE

Southwestern's year-round campuses are always open for tours, interviews, and/or admission information. Applications are accepted until June. However, most applications are made in April, and space is limited.

FOR MORE INFORMATION, CONTACT:

Admissions Office
Southwestern Academy
San Marino Campus
2800 Monterey Road
San Marino, California 91108
626-799-5010
Fax: 626-799-0407
E-mail: admissions@southwesternacademy.edu
World Wide Web:
http://www.SouthwesternAcadcmy.edu

Southwestern Academy
Beaver Creek Ranch Campus
Rimrock, Arizona 86335
928-567-4581

PARTICIPANT/FAMILY COMMENTS

"It was a good summer—the best of my life. The studying was difficult, but I'm so glad my parents sent me, or I never would have had this experience. You work for the teachers and counselors, and they work for you. There's not anything in the world they wouldn't do for us. They're just fantastic."

"Everybody works together as a unit. You know the teachers personally and respect their knowledge. But they're more than teachers, they're people who care. They teach you more than lessons—they teach you about life."

SPANISH THROUGH LEADERSHIP

NICARAGUA/COSTA RICA SUMMER EXCHANGE

NICARAGUA AND COSTA RICA

Type of Program: Spanish immersion, community service, cultural enrichment, Latin dance
Participants: Coeducational, high school age
Enrollment: 10–20 per session
Program Dates: Three 4-week sessions during June, July, and August
Head of Program: Ilba Prego, Director

LOCATION

The Spanish Through Leadership Program is based in Central America's oldest Spanish-colonial community, Granada, Nicaragua. In few places in Latin America does the Spanish language resonate with more passion and color than along the Nicaragua-Costa Rica isthmus. Connected by history, culture, volcanoes, rainforests, and two oceans, this dynamic region provides endless opportunities to celebrate Spanish in the warm embrace of Central America's remarkable people and vibrant pueblos.

BACKGROUND AND PHILOSOPHY

"An incredible life-changing experience," "a greater appreciation," "a new outlook"—these are words parents use to describe how the Spanish Through Leadership Program impacted their children's lives. The program was created in 1998, with the purpose of linking high school Spanish study to the dynamics of community life in Central America. The Spanish through Leadership Program is part of the Wisconsin Public Schools International Programs and is considered to be Latin America's most authentic and empowering high school language experience. The program's profound connection to local culture, families, schools, and youth makes it a role model for immersion programs. Students literally feel adopted into the local community. Whether making homemade tortillas, leading a youth soccer practice, or joining a high school dance fiesta, each day in the community reveals a new adventure. Students quickly discover that building language confidence is easy and rewarding when it is connected to a meaningful purpose. With more than 60 percent of the local population under the age of 16, it's no wonder that the most enduring part of the trip is the friendships that continue long after summer is over. In the spirit of local community, students discover that Spanish is just the beginning. They return home with more than new Spanish skills; they return with a positive vision of themselves in a changing America.

PROGRAM OFFERINGS

The community immersion programs are held in the historic community of Granada, Nicaragua, June 20 through July 17 and July 18 through August 16. The Teo community immersion program combines isthmus communities in Nicaragua and Costa Rica and is offered July 10 through August 7.

The highlights of each program include a focus on Spanish in the community, homestays, youth exchange, Latin dance, and unforgettable excursions. Each program provides the perfect balance between cultural immersion, community interaction, and adventure activities. To learn more about the programs, interested students should request the free program video.

ENROLLMENT

The program is open to high school Spanish students who have an interest in Latin America at the community level. Each session has a maximum of 20 and a minimum of 10 students.

DAILY SCHEDULE

All students live close to each other, near the Central Plaza, in comfortable, friendly homestays that include healthy meals, fresh squeezed fruit drinks, private rooms, and laundry service. In small groups, students meet with their language teacher each morning at the cultural center. Language sessions take students out into the community, where they develop speaking skills in a fun, relaxed, nonthreatening environment that encourages mistakes. The morning language sessions prepare students for enjoyable afternoon encounters with local youth programs and children's centers. Students round out their evenings exploring Latin music and dance and attending live cultural events. Students enjoy the relaxed tropical traditions, siestas, colorful vendors, playful parrots, and friendly neighborhoods.

EXTRA OPPORTUNITIES AND ACTIVITIES

Included in the journey are exciting local excursions that, in themselves, are worth the price of admission. Students can hike the trail of the jaguar in Chocoyero rainforest, search for a new species in the Mombacho cloudforest, glide through the longest canopy tour in Central America, swim in blue lagoon, take an island-to-island tour, enjoy a Pacific beach retreat, surf, view indigenous art, visit villages and coffee and butterfly farms, hear marimba music, and folk dance and *cumbia* in the plaza.

STAFF

Supervision is high-school-age appropriate. Program coordinators have decades of experience leading programs in the United States and Central America. All parents are contacted personally by the program leader who can be reached 24 hours a day during the program.

The strength of the programs lies in the strong community ties provided by a talented staff of respected local teachers, community leaders, and school directors. All members of the teaching staff are

native Central Americans who offer unique insights into local history, culture, and daily family life. The small teacher-student ratio of 1:4 is ideal for integrating students into local culture.

MEDICAL CARE

The program fee includes overseas health insurance and an on-call program doctor. Bilingual staff members accompany all student health visits.

COSTS

Program tuition is $2850 for the four week programs and $2650 for the three week programs. The program fee includes round-trip airfare from major U.S. cities, overseas health insurance, program doctor, land transports, bilingual support staff, host family lodging, all meals, Spanish sessions and tutors, youth-to-youth exchange, Latin music and dance enrichment, and all excursions and cultural events.

TRANSPORTATION

The program provides round trip airfare and coordinates all in-country land transportation (including meeting students at the airport) and all excursions.

APPLICATION TIMETABLE

Interested students should request the free program video. Because of limited enrollment, students are encouraged to apply early. Applications are accepted on a first come, first served basis until late April.

FOR MORE INFORMATION, CONTACT:

Nicaragua/Costa Rica Summer Exchange Program
1650 Monroe Street
Madison, Wisconsin 53711
608-255-1426
E-mail: nica@terracom.net
World Wide Web: http://www.highschoolspanish.org

FAMILY/PARTICIPANT COMMENTS

"This is the most comprehensive program of its kind available to students that I have ever known."—Becky Garcia, Spanish teacher

"We would like to thank you for offering a wonderful experience to our daughter. She learned more Spanish in four weeks than in four years of high school."—Nancy Sloan, parent

SPOLETO STUDY ABROAD

SUMMER ARTS AND HUMANITIES PROGRAM

SPOLETO, ITALY

Type of Program: Instrumental and vocal music, visual arts, photography, drama, and creative writing programs
Participants: Coeducational, ages 15–19
Enrollment: 65
Program Dates: Four weeks, mid-July to mid-August
Heads of Program: Jill and Lorenzo Muti, Co-Directors

LOCATION

Spoleto is an ideal starting point for students interested in an in-depth exploration of the visual and historical heritage of Italy. Cities like Assisi, Siena, Arezzo, or Orvieto, all filled with incredible artistic treasures, are easily reached by car or by train, and major centers like Rome or Florence are less than 2 hours away. Spoleto is emblematic of central Italy, both historically and artistically.

BACKGROUND AND PHILOSOPHY

The Spoleto Study Abroad summer session is an intensive interdisciplinary program focusing on the arts and humanities for high school students, ages 15–19, interested in instrumental or vocal music, visual arts, photography, creative writing, or drama. Students are given the opportunity to explore their academic and artistic interests through exposure to an integrated style of learning in a unique European setting. The mission of the program is to provide a challenging and innovative experience for students who have the desire to expand their knowledge while immersed in a diverse and vibrant culture.

PROGRAM OFFERINGS

Music Students are immersed in a wealth of musical offerings emphasizing artistic and technical growth. The program offers private lessons with leading musicians in the field, chamber music sessions, and orchestral and vocal experiences. Several concerts are given throughout the session, both in Spoleto and in neighboring towns.
Visual Arts Students explore the philosophical, intellectual, and mechanical aspects of art through art history, studio classes, and hands-on field trips. Courses include instruction and practice in drawing, painting, and two-dimensional design. The theoretical aspects of the course are then illustrated with visits to and examinations of works of art found throughout the town and the region. Final projects are exhibited at the art show.
Photography Students study a selection of historical and contemporary photographers while developing a personal style of their own. The course focuses on a variety of photographic techniques, such as portraiture, landscape, night photography, documentary photography, and hand-coloring Polaroid dye transfers. Final projects are exhibited at the art show.
Creative Writing Through an intensive curriculum, students develop writing skills while learning more advanced techniques of language and expression. Students participate in selected exercises designed to strengthen specific elements of writing. Journaling, a cornerstone of the course, serves as a foundation for an exploration of poetry, prose, prose-poems, and lyrics. Contributions from class are published in a literary magazine as the final project of the program.
Drama Students explore acting through vocal and physical techniques, character analysis, pantomime techniques, and improvisation skills. They apply these skills to selecting, rehearsing, and performing monologues and scenes during the course of their study. The final project is a 40–60 minute performance.

ENROLLMENT

Students must have finished the ninth grade and demonstrate marked proficiency in either instrumental/vocal music or drama through an audition process or through submission of a portfolio. There is no language requirement.

DAILY SCHEDULE

Classes are scheduled four days a week and follow a typical Italian pace of life.

8:00	Breakfast
9:00	Classes
1:15	Lunch
2:30–5:00	Free time/organized activities
5:00	Studio workshops and rehearsals
8:00	Dinner

EXTRA OPPORTUNITIES AND ACTIVITIES

Throughout the session, the faculty team plans interdisciplinary units of study that are enriched by twice-a-week excursions to such cultural centers as Rome, Urbino, Florence, Siena, Assisi, and other medieval hill towns throughout Umbria and Tuscany.

Recreational activities are planned throughout the session. The city also offers facilities for swimming, soccer, basketball, and tennis.

FACILITIES

Classes take place in a beautiful building called the Terrazza Frau. Its name is derived from its location on the slopes of a hill overlooking the lower part of the town of Spoleto and the contiguous valley. In addition to the breathtaking view, there is abundant, luminous space for art and music classes. One of the most charming aspects of the Terrazza Frau is the deconsecrated chapel that has been converted into a small auditorium.

Students live together European collegial style in the Convento di Sant' Angelo, a gorgeous fifteenth-century convent in the medieval section of Spoleto that has been renovated to combine the traditions of the past with all the modern conveniences of today. It is only a short walk from the convent to school and to the main piazzas of town and the restaurants where meals are eaten.

STAFF

Faculty members at Spoleto Study Abroad are distinguished artists and educators from colleges, universities, and secondary schools from the United States and Italy. They are chosen for their extensive knowledge and enthusiasm, their dynamic teaching methods, and their willingness and ability to work closely with students.

MEDICAL CARE

Spoleto Study Abroad is affiliated with a medical staff that is available to see students who require care. Students needing emergency attention are taken to the closest hospital.

COSTS

The comprehensive fee for Spoleto Study Abroad is $5800. This fee includes tuition, all meals, lodging, books, materials, entrance fees for group activities, and all transportation in Italy. Expenses not included are round-trip airfare to Rome, passport fees, travel insurance, and personal expenses, such as laundry, snacks, telephone calls, and spending money.

TRANSPORTATION

Specific flights are announced at the time of acceptance into the program. Staff members meet all participants to escort them to Rome on the same international flight. Students are met at Fiumicino Airport in Rome by Spoleto Study Abroad staff members for transportation to Spoleto. At the end of the program, students are chaperoned back to the program's gateway city.

APPLICATION TIMETABLE

Inquiries about the program are welcome anytime. Applications can also be downloaded from the Web site listed below. Consortium School applications are due February 1 and all other applications are due on February 15. Spoleto Study Abroad accepts late applications as long as space remains available.

FOR MORE INFORMATION, CONTACT:

Spoleto Study Abroad
P.O. Box 99147
Raleigh, North Carolina 27624-9147
919-384-0031
E-mail: spoleto@mindspring.com
World Wide Web: http://www.spoletostudyabroad.com

PARTICIPANT/FAMILY COMMENTS

"Traveling to Italy to pursue my passion for art while working in an atmosphere where everyone is also striving to fulfill their insatiable hunger for learning is truly ideal. What an opportunity!"—Whitner Belk, Charlotte, North Carolina

"The classes and teachers are amazing! Such dedication! Such skill and talent do these wonderful people possess that I don't feel as if I am in school ... no, I truly love waking up and going to class."—Alex Metelitsa, Princeton Junction, New Jersey.

"I have learned more about being an actor throughout the summer session than I would in a semester course at home. The faculty is intense, demanding, and fun."—Zoe Savitsky, San Francisco, California

STAGEDOOR MANOR PERFORMING ARTS CENTER

SUMMER THEATER/DANCE CAMP

LOCH SHELDRAKE IN THE CATSKILL MOUNTAINS, NEW YORK

Type of Program: Theater, dance camp
Participants: Boys and girls, ages 8–18
Enrollment: 265
Program Dates: Three-, six-, or nine-week sessions; June 20–July 10, July 11–31, and August 1–21
Heads of Program: Cynthia Samuelson, Owner and Producer; Barbara Fine Martin, Director

LOCATION

Located in the heart of the famous "Catskills on Broadway" vacation area, Stagedoor Manor is in a woodland setting just 95 miles northwest of New York City. Twenty-nine years ago, the Samuelson family bought and converted a small resort hotel into a multispace theater complex.

BACKGROUND AND PHILOSOPHY

Stagedoor Manor combines all the excitement of theater with all the fun of a great summer camp.

Stagedoor Manor is the only camp of its kind in the world, a complete community where all of the kids and staff members are in love with the theater, dance, and the performing arts. Stagedoor believes that each boy and girl should be guided to choose his or her own schedule, with a flexibility that encourages them to stretch and grow and discover new capabilities.

No previous experience is required. Many of the campers are beginners or have been in school plays. Others have already appeared on Broadway, in films, or on television. Each camper is given the opportunity at his or her experience level to study and grow at his or her own pace.

Stagedoor Manor teaches theater, dance, and voice extremely well, but much more important is its goal to nurture and care for its campers.

PROGRAM OFFERINGS

At Stagedoor Manor, time is divided in thirds.

Classes: Taught in almost every aspect of performance, classes include theater, dance, voice, and technical arts; technique and improvisation; acting for film and television; comedy; movie making; Shakespeare; modeling and make up; speech and diction; costuming, lights, and technical theater; ballet (all levels), tap, jazz, and modern dance; and choreography and styles. Advanced master classes are available for those ready to go beyond the beginner levels. Guest workshops on all subjects are taught by working leaders in the industry. More than fifty different classes are offered in all skill levels. Each camper chooses an individual class program with faculty guidance and mentoring.

Performances: Every camper is in a show at all times. Nobody is left out. Stagedoor produces eight musicals and five dramas in every session. To ensure individual attention and coaching, musicals are cast of 24 to 26 campers per show; dramas with 10 to 15 campers per show. Many agents, managers, and casting directors attend rehearsals and performances searching for fresh talent.

Stagedoor alumni include film star Natalie Portman, singer/actress Mandy Moore, *Scrubs* star Zach Braff, Robert Downey Jr., *2½ Men* star Josh Charles, Jon Cryer, Helen Slater, Mary Stuart Masterson, *The Village* star Bryce Dallas Howard, and writer/director Todd Graff, who created the movie *CAMP* based on his memories of Stagedoor Manor and filmed it at the camp in 2003. Many famous alumni return each summer to share their experiences with current campers.

Recreation: Activities include swimming (outdoor pool for hot summer days and a heated indoor pool for rainy days and evenings), tennis (coach on staff), volleyball, horseback riding, basketball, dee-jay dances, open microphone coffee house and canteen, game nights, trips off camp to movies and dinner, camper-organized showcases, and themed parties every session. All sports are noncompetitive for those who want to join in.

ENROLLMENT

Boys and girls, ages 8–18, come to Stagedoor Manor from every state and all over the world. They attend for three weeks, six weeks, or nine weeks. No audition is required, but Stagedoor seeks campers who love performance and want to be totally immersed in the world of theater.

FACILITIES

At Stagedoor Manor's private former resort hotel, campers live (4–6 in a room) dormitory style in regular hotel rooms with private bathrooms. All rooms are fully carpeted with bunks, full-size clothing chests, and closets. Landscaped grounds and cozy walkways give the camp a campus atmosphere. Adding on through the years, the site now houses seven theaters, twenty-two classrooms, video studios, outdoor and indoor heated pools, an air-

conditioned dining room, and dance and rehearsal studios. Two major theaters are also air conditioned.

STAFF

Teachers at Stagedoor Manor are mature professionals who are active in the theatrical industry and teach at leading universities. A separate counseling staff (all age 21 or over), with no junior counselors or counselors in training, provides close supervision and support. The staff numbers 160 members for 265 campers.

Guest workshop and Master Class visitors include Broadway, movie, and television stars, along with agents, casting directors, and behind-the-scene creative talent. Recent guests include Broadway duo Richard Maltby and David Shire, CBS series star Yancy Arias, Rockette dance captain Kim Calore, commercial actor and author Aaron Marcus, Broadway musical director and conductor Kim Grigsby, Tony-nominated actor Gavin Creel, Tony award-winning Broadway composer Jeanine Tesori, *Wicked* star Michelle Federer, and multiple Tony costume designer Ann Hould-Ward. Representatives from Nickelodeon, Disney, Wilhelmina, Brookside Artists, Carson Adler, Warner Brothers, MTV, and many others visit looking for tomorrow's stars. Former Stagedoor alumni, now working on film, TV, and stage join the camp on show weekends to share their experiences and give advice to current campers.

MEDICAL CARE

Stagedoor provides a health center staffed by registered nurses, paramedics, and emergency medical technicians 24 hours a day. There are separate rooms, with television and air conditioning, for those who require isolation and rest. A nearby medical group is on call with Catskill Medical Center, only 10 minutes away.

RELIGIOUS LIFE

Stagedoor Manor is nonsectarian. Campers who wish may attend services at nearby churches and temples. Escort and transportation are provided.

COSTS

Sessions at Stagedoor are three weeks. Tuition starts at $4195 for on session, with consideration for additional sessions. This tuition includes room and board, use of all facilities, rental of scripts and costumes, and any technical support required for productions. A full preview of fees is listed on the enrollment contract.

TRANSPORTATION

Campers fly into Newark Airport, just outside New York, where they are met by Stagedoor staff members and taken to the camp in large air-conditioned coaches. Return to the airport is provided if required.

APPLICATION TIMETABLE

Rolling enrollment begins in September and continues to late spring the next year. Some sessions and age groups fill up faster than others and early registration is advised.

FOR MORE INFORMATION, CONTACT:

Cynthia Samuelson and Barbara Fine Martin
8 Wingate Road
Lexington, Massachusetts 02421
888-STAGE-88 (toll-free)
E-mail: stagedoormanor@aol.com
World Wide Web: http://www.stagedoormanor.com/

PARTICIPANT/FAMILY COMMENTS

"Stagedoor Manor was a wonderful way to be introduced to the world of acting. It was great groundwork into musical theater, dance, and most importantly, acting."—Actress Helen Slater (as quoted in the *New York Times*)

"I was born at Stagedoor Manor. The camp is like Oz. Your real life is in black and white, but the minute you step off the bus, everything is in color."—Writer/director Todd Graff *(CAMP)*

"We will never be able to tell you what your camp has meant to us and our son . . . he has carried the pride and new found confidence with him all year long!"—Stagedoor parent

"Solid educational and administrative foundation, a history of success, and an overriding concern for the character development of the children entrusted to them."—Town and Country magazine

"Thank you so very much for a summer filled with wonderful memories and so much joy. I learned so much about myself as an artist, in an environment filled with unconditional love and support. Stagedoor made me who I am."—Stagedoor camper

"The only thing wrong with Stagedoor Manor is it's only for kids. This truly ticks me off. Every time I go, I want to stay!"—Actor Richard Dreyfuss

STANFORD UNIVERSITY

SUMMER COLLEGE FOR HIGH SCHOOL STUDENTS

STANFORD, CALIFORNIA

Type of Program: College preparation
Participants: Coeducational; for students who have completed their junior or senior year of high school
Enrollment: 350 students
Program Dates: One eight-week session during July and August
Head of Program: Patricia Brandt, Associate Dean for Summer Session

LOCATION

Stanford University is located approximately 35 miles south of San Francisco, California.

BACKGROUND AND PHILOSOPHY

Stanford admits to the summer session exceptional high school students who are ready to explore a challenging university environment. This includes enrolling in regular Stanford courses, living together in Stanford student residences, and interacting with members of the Stanford faculty and student community. Students gain an inside perspective on life at a major university and begin to shape the college study skills that will prepare them for their freshman year.

PROGRAM OFFERINGS

All Stanford undergraduate courses for which the student has met the prerequisites are open to Summer College students. Subjects include anthropology, art, astronomy, athletics, biological sciences, chemistry, classics, communications, comparative literature, computer science, drama, economics, English, French, German, history, industrial engineering, Japanese, mathematics, music, philosophy, political science, psychology, sociology, Spanish, statistics, and urban studies. The recommended course load for Summer College students is 8 units, which consists of two or three elective courses. The maximum course load is 12 units. As is to be expected at a preeminent university, course work expectations are demanding and grading is far more difficult than in high school. All summer course work completed by high school students in the Stanford Summer College may be applied toward a Stanford degree should the student subsequently be admitted to a regular degree program. Credit for work at Stanford may also be transferred to other universities.

A special program has been developed for participants in the Summer College for High School Students. "College Admission 101: A Seminar Series" is an 8-hour series of seminars designed to assist students in identifying, selecting, and applying to colleges and universities that are appropriate for them. Students gain an inside perspective on the college admission process through the workshops and through the knowledge and experience of the instructors, all of whom are former selective college and university admission officers. Discussion topics include understanding the culture of college campuses, exploring different types of institutions, reading college literature with a critical eye, examining admission applications, practicing techniques for writing essays, interviewing, and talking about issues on college campuses today. This seminar is free of charge and available to all Summer College participants.

While it is recommended that all high school students take part in the residential program, students from the Bay Area who live within manageable commuting distance may participate in the program as commuter students. Commuter students are required to take a minimum of 3 units of course work. They are assigned to a residence counselor, who serves as an adviser and liaison between the commuter students and the residential students, and are welcomed and encouraged to join in all the activities of the program.

The University also offers three-week Discovery Institutes for students who have completed their sophomore year of high school and are looking for a program of shorter duration. Students choose from a variety of topics and earn Stanford University credit for their course work. For more information, students should refer to *Stanford Discovery Institutes* in the Summer Program Profiles for California.

ENROLLMENT

Approximately 350 high school students from all around the world participate in the Summer College.

EXTRA OPPORTUNITIES AND ACTIVITIES

While it is true that students spend a large portion of their free time studying, there are many opportunities for out-of-classroom learning and fun. Some activities are organized by the program staff, while others are initiated and planned by the students themselves. Activities include intramural sports teams, dorm yearbook, talent show, house discussions with Stanford professors and undergraduate admission staff members, visits to San Francisco and Monterey, and public service projects.

FACILITIES

Located on a stunning 8,100-acre campus, Stanford University is renowned for its dedication to scholarly pursuits. All Summer College students live together in historic Lagunita Court, which is located within 5 minutes' walking or biking distance of most classrooms and is equipped with computer lounges and quiet areas perfect for late-night studying. In addition, students have access to Stanford Libraries' more than 2.4 million volumes in the humanities and social sciences collections, as well as Stanford's extensive athletic facilities, including two fully equipped gymnasiums, a recently renovated Olympic-size pool, and an eighteen-hole golf course.

STAFF

An experienced and carefully chosen group of Stanford students serve as Resident Counselors in the dorm, providing students with advice on how to make the most of a quarter at Stanford. An adult program director is also in residence to provide supervision. Students are trained to be their own educational advocates, forming a house government, and organizing house programs, debates, and activities.

MEDICAL CARE

Vaden Student Health Center has a full-time staff of physicians, nurses, and mental health professionals. Students must have health insurance to register at Stanford University. They may purchase insurance from the University, if necessary.

COSTS

The cost for 8 units, room, board, and program fee was approximately $8355 for the eight-week session in 2004.

FINANCIAL AID

A limited amount of financial aid is available.

TRANSPORTATION

The San Francisco Bay Area is served by three international airports in San Francisco, San Jose, and Oakland. Students can take a shuttle directly from any of the airports to the Stanford campus.

APPLICATION TIMETABLE

Summer catalogs and applications are available beginning in early February; applications are due in mid-April. Admission is selective but is designed to be more open than the Stanford undergraduate admission process. Students are encouraged to apply as early as possible, as enrollment is limited. Students who wish to be admitted as commuters submit the same application as the residential students and are evaluated by the same standards as residential applicants. Admission decisions are made on a rolling basis to accommodate early applications.

A completed application consists of the application form; an official high school transcript, including SAT I/PSAT scores; an essay; two letters of recommendation from a high school teacher or counselor; and a $50 application fee. Admission to the Stanford Summer College for High School Students does not imply later admission to one of Stanford's regular degree programs.

FOR MORE INFORMATION, CONTACT:

Stanford Summer Session
Building 590, Room 103
Stanford, California 94305-3005
650-723-3109
Fax: 650-725-6080
E-mail: summersession@stanford.edu
World Wide Web: http://summersession.stanford.edu

STONELEIGH-BURNHAM SCHOOL SUMMER CAMPS

SUMMER OPPORTUNITIES FOR GIRLS

GREENFIELD, MASSACHUSETTS

Type of Program: Riding camp, dance camp, debate and public speaking camp, and softball camp
Participants: Girls, ages 9–16
Enrollment: 20 to 50 participants (varies by camp)
Program Dates: Bonnie Castle Riding Camp: Three 2-week sessions starting in July. Dance Camp: Two 1-week sessions starting in July. Debate and Public Speaking Camp: Five days starting mid-August. Softball Camp: Six days running from the end of July through the beginning of August. Camp $tart-Up®: One 5-day session. For program dates and brochures, those interested can call the number below (using extension 274) or e-mail the address below.
Heads of Programs: Mina Cooper, Riding; Dr. Paul Bassett, Debate and Public Speaking and Softball; Ann Sorvino, Dance

LOCATION

Stoneleigh-Burnham School (SBS) is located on 100 acres of open and wooded country 2 miles outside of the town of Greenfield, a residential community of 20,000 in the historic Pioneer Valley of northwestern Massachusetts. The School is a 1-hour drive from Hartford, Connecticut; a 2-hour drive from Boston; and a 3-hour drive from New York City and is located at the junction of Interstate 91 and Route 2 East.

BACKGROUND AND PHILOSOPHY

Stoneleigh-Burnham School summer programs reflect the same philosophy that the School itself embraces and promotes—that of offering interesting opportunities for girls that enable them to both enhance existing skills and develop new skills within a small, all-girl setting. The tone of the summer programs is focused as well as fun.

PROGRAM OFFERINGS

Bonnie Castle Riding Camp (ages 9–16) Bonnie Castle Riding Camp was established in 1982 and is named after Stoneleigh-Burnham School's most famous and beloved horse, Bonnie Castle, Grand Hunter Champion in 1978 at the Grand National Horse Show at Madison Square Garden. The Bonnie Castle Riding Camp philosophy emphasizes the basic techniques of riding and builds a firm foundation that proves useful to the serious rider. Bonnie Castle campers ride twice each day and have a private or semiprivate lesson each week with one of the Camp's experienced instructors. The goal is to help girls develop and improve their riding skills with instruction, practice, and competition that are appropriate for the beginning rider as well as for the more experienced young horsewoman. The Riding Team members from Stoneleigh-Burnham School are current National Champions in Interscholastic Equestrian Association Hunt Seat and Interscholastic National Dressage. The School has one of the finest and most impressive equestrian facilities in the Northeast. Stabling for sixty-six horses is available in two separate barns, and one of the two indoor riding arenas features a heated viewing lounge that seats 200 spectators. Outside are two sand rings; a derby field with permanent European-style derby jumps; a cross-country course for novice, training, and preliminary levels; and an extensive bridle path that rings the picturesque campus. Two wash stalls, two tack rooms, laundry facilities, and lockers are available for participants to use. Bonnie Castle Riding Camp features instruction at all levels in hunters, jumpers, equitation, dressage, combined training, and equine studies. Session I focuses on combined training. Campers learn fundamental dressage and jumping techniques, while equitation is stressed throughout. At the end of Session I, all campers participate in dressage and jumping tests that are appropriate for their level. Experienced competitive riders who would like to compete in the SBS-recognized Horse Trials (novice, training, and preliminary) may have their schedule modified to accommodate this goal. The Horse Trials take place at SBS the first weekend of Session I. For incoming campers, Session II is similar to the first, with stronger emphasis placed in hunt seat equitation. Continuing campers progress to more complicated work on the flat and over fences. At the end of Session II, a show with equitation and hunter classes is held, with all campers participating. In addition to the intensive riding program, electives are offered in art, dance, and drama. Academic tutoring is also available.

Stoneleigh-Burnham School Debate and Public Speaking Camp (ages 12–17) Through its continued commitment to the education of young women, Stoneleigh-Burnham School presents A Voice of Her Own, a residential debate and public speaking camp. The School has always believed that for a girl, finding her voice and using it with confidence are important lifetime skills and goals. The debate and public speaking camp features instruction in Lincoln-Douglas debating, cross-examination debating, parliamentary extemporaneous debating, interpretive reading, dramatic interpretation, impromptu speaking, after-dinner speaking, and persuasive speaking.

Stoneleigh-Burnham School Dance Camp (ages 11–16) The Stoneleigh-Burnham School Dance Camp presents an opportunity for 20 participants to improve their skills as dancers in an intensive and nurturing environment. Experienced teachers offer instruction through two daily technique classes in ballet, modern dance, and jazz. Repertory, improvisation, and choreography sessions are also offered each day in preparation for the end-of-camp performance. Small, personal classes stress improvement of technical skills, flexibility, strength, and alignment. On Tuesday afternoon, participants attend the International Dance Festival at Jacob's Pillow in Lee, Massachusetts, to watch workshop classes and a presentation on the Inside/Out stage. On Saturday afternoon, there is a final showing of dances prepared during the week.

Stoneleigh-Burnham School Softball Camp (ages 12–15) The Stoneleigh-Burnham School Softball Camp presents an opportunity for participants to improve their skills as hitters, fielders, and pitchers. Experienced coaches offer instruction to participants during the three daily sessions, Monday through Friday. With a player-coach ratio of 6:1 and camp being limited to 50 players, instruction stresses fundamentals and techniques to augment players' skills. Two complete softball diamonds are available at all times throughout the camp session. Hitting, bunting, fielding, and base-running skills are addressed, as are the psychological aspects of the game. Defensive and hitting (including bunting) techniques are videotaped for diagnostic assessment. Pitchers may enroll in the windmill pitching or catching program at no extra cost. Campers play a competitive schedule of night games.

Camp $tart-Up (ages 13–18) At Camp $tart-Up, girls discover how their interests and dreams translate into enterprise and independence. The goal of Camp $tart-Up is to put teen women in control of their future by teaching them the basic components of business and how the components fit together in a successful organization. Campers are taught to understand the language and culture of business to increase their confidence in interviews and on the job. Sessions include working with a team to originate an idea for a business and develop a business plan. The team then learns how to translate ideas into action through research, planning, marketing, and networking. Professional faculty members teach classes in presenting, Internet and library research with the latest technology, and networking to get the information needed to build a business or an investment portfolio. The faculty members also teach the girls how to find their dream job or college opportunity. At Camp $tart-Up, the approach is creative, sometimes messy, unpredictable, and fun. Games, role playing, and laughter are an integral part of the learning activities. In addition, Camp $tart-Up balances the business curriculum with an afternoon recreational program. With full access to the school's facilities, participants enjoy swimming and other activities.

ENROLLMENT

Most campers are from New England and the northeastern states; however, other regions of the country and other countries are represented as well. Bonnie Castle Riding Camp is limited to 48 girls per session (campers may attend any or all of the three two-week sessions). The dance camp is limited to 20 girls per weeklong session (campers may attend one or both sessions). The debate and public speaking camp is limited to 40 girls (the pupil-teacher ratio is 8:1). The softball camp is limited to 50 girls.

DAILY SCHEDULE

The daily schedule varies for each camp. In general, there are morning and afternoon instructional sessions, followed by free time and evening activities.

FACILITIES

The 100-acre Stoneleigh-Burnham School campus includes an outdoor swimming pool; tennis courts; a weight room; a dance studio; art studios for painting, ceramics, weaving, and photography; a gymnasium; a stage; computer laboratories; a media room (for viewing movies); dining facilities; and a library (the debate camp is held in part in the library). Residence halls are located in the Main Building, which also houses student lounges, the Health Care Center, and the School's dining room, whose staff provides excellent food for the School's camps.

STAFF

The Director of Riding, Mina Cooper, has been at Stoneleigh-Burnham School since 1979. She has a diverse competitive background in hunters, jumpers, eventing, and dressage. She is an active member of the AHSA, USCTA, and USDF. She is also the regional representative for the Interscholastic Team Competitions Committee. She has been a licensed riding instructor since 1980 and has coached many riders to national recognition. Mina is assisted by a summer staff of experienced instructors; the residential component of the camp is staffed by trained camp counselors. Other camp activities, such as dance, fine arts, and tutoring, are offered. Ann Sorvino, who founded the dance camp, is a graduate of the Juilliard School and a former member of the Merce Cunningham Dance Company and has performed professionally in New York City. Two other teachers who are professionally experienced and have performed and taught throughout the New England area work with Ms. Sorvino. They enjoy working with adolescents and have an interest in encouraging and training young women who are interested in continuing their dance careers at the college and professional levels. The debate camp was founded by Dr. Paul Bassett, Debate Coach and teacher at SBS, who also coached the American Debate and Public Speaking Team at the World Championship in Nicosia, Cyprus. Other staff members include drama teachers and North American and World Championship debaters who are graduates of SBS. The softball camp is staffed by experienced coaches, each with a particular expertise in the sport. Each instructor has been involved with high school or collegiate championship seasons at either the state or New England level. The program and curriculum for Camp $tart-Up are through Independent Means, Inc., leaders in teaching young women about business.

MEDICAL CARE

The on-campus Health Care Center is staffed by a health care provider who oversees any medical attention that may be required by campers. Each camper must be covered by her family's medical and hospital insurance plan. In case of an emergency, transportation is provided to Franklin Medical Center, which is 5 minutes away. The School physician is also available for campers.

COSTS

In summer 2004, the Bonnie Castle Riding Camp cost $1800 per session (including room and board), with additional fees charged for academic tutoring; boarding a horse cost $275 per session. The dance camp cost $575 per session, the debate and public speaking camp cost $295 for four nights and five days, and the softball camp cost $295 for the session.

APPLICATION TIMETABLE

For the Bonnie Castle Riding Camp, the registration deadline is June 15; for the dance camp and for Camp $tart-Up, the registration deadline is June 1. Students must register for the debate and public speaking camp by August 1 and for the softball camp by July 15.

FOR MORE INFORMATION, CONTACT:

Mina Cooper, Director of Riding (Bonnie Castle Riding Camp)
Dr. Paul Bassett (debate and public speaking camp and softball camp)
Ann Sorvino (dance camp)
Stoneleigh-Burnham School
574 Bernardston Road
Greenfield, Massachusetts 01301
413-774-2711
E-mail: summerprograms@sbschool.org
World Wide Web: http://www.sbschool.org

SUMMER AT DELPHI™

THE DELPHIAN SCHOOL

SHERIDAN, OREGON

Type of Program: Residential private academic camp with personalized student programs, challenging activities, weekend trips, and traditional camping; also an English as a second language (ESL) program
Participants: Coeducational; day, ages 5–18; boarding, ages 8–18)
Enrollment: 300 students
Program Dates: June 27 to August 5
Head of Program: Rosemary Didear, Headmistress

LOCATION

The Delphian School's 700-acre campus is set among rolling hills in the Oregon Coast Range. The expanses of meadows and forestland support many outdoor activities. The recreational resources of the city of Portland, Mount Hood, and the Pacific Coast are nearby.

BACKGROUND AND PHILOSOPHY

Delphi was founded in 1976 by a group of educators and parents concerned about the decline that they perceived in the standards of American education. Delphi uses innovative study methods developed by American philosopher and educator L. Ron Hubbard. These methods are recognized worldwide as a breakthrough in education, and with them, students develop the confidence and know-how to tackle even the most challenging subjects. Students become increasingly able to take responsibility for their own education. The Delphian School is licensed to use Applied Scholastics International™ educational services.

PROGRAM OFFERINGS

Delphi's unique approach to academics provides an individually tailored program for each student as well as one-on-one assistance. Students can brush up in weak areas (at any level), tackle advanced subjects, or simply explore new interests. Individual progress is not tied to the speed of others in the class. Students who have mastered the basics are free to advance quickly into new areas.

Delphi is one of the only summer camps to give students instruction in the subject of how to study. This vital instruction—missing in many school systems today—can greatly increase any student's enthusiasm for learning. As they learn these study methods, students find they are able to fully understand and apply the data they are studying in school. The result is that many students realize they can succeed in today's competitive environment and their enthusiasm for learning soars.

Delphi's summer program also includes the arts, science, horseback riding, computers, and a wealth of challenging outdoor activities, as well as soccer, volleyball, and tennis camps, and exciting weekend trips.

ENROLLMENT

Delphi enrolls 300 boys and girls, ages 5–18, for the Summer Session. Students who are 8 years or older may board. The Summer Session is an international experience—students come from across the United States and from various other countries. Delphi admits students of any race, color, and national or ethnic origin.

DAILY SCHEDULE

In the Upper School, mornings and evenings are devoted to classroom academics. Afternoons are spent on sports, special activities, and projects, such as swimming, horseback riding, ceramics, and computer studies.

Middle School students spend their mornings and late afternoons on academic subjects. Afternoons include such activities as art, ceramics, music, horseback riding, swimming, computer studies, and a variety of sports. Evenings are reserved for group activities such as crafts and games.

In the Lower School, there is even greater emphasis on the outdoors and on recreational activities that have educational value. Students go on field trips and other outings. In general, the mornings are devoted to basic reading and math studies.

All students who are 11 or older participate in the school's Student Services program. Through the program, students contribute 50 minutes a day to the operation and maintenance of the school, gaining a greater appreciation and responsibility for the workings of a large organization.

EXTRA OPPORTUNITIES AND ACTIVITIES

Regular weekend excursions can include anything from white-water rafting to exploring Seattle. There is a swimming and/or bowling trip one afternoon a week, and several off-campus full weekend excursions, including at least one camping trip. Upper School students can travel to Ashland for the world-renowned Shakespearean Festival. On-campus activities include dances, movies, cookouts, a model rocket launch, and sports tournaments. Older Middle School and Upper School students may also participate in a weeklong (part-time) computer camp. Fluent English is required for participation in computer camp. There is also a weeklong (part-time) horse camp offered.

All students should bring camping gear, including backpacks or knapsacks, a sleeping bag, and hiking boots.

FACILITIES

All academic facilities are located in the large main building. There is a chemistry/biology lab as well as an audio/visual lab. There are more than 100

computers with Internet access available throughout the school; a library with more than 10,000 volumes; a theater; music practice rooms; art, ceramics, and photography studios; a career center; and a woodshop. There is also a student lounge, a recreation room, a snack bar, and a bookstore.

Student dormitories are also located in the main building, and a girls' dormitory, with a panoramic view of the Willamette Valley, is a short walk away.

Athletics facilities include a 13,500-square-foot gymnasium with basketball, volleyball, and racquetball courts and a room for weight lifting and gymnastics. There are athletics fields for soccer, baseball, and softball and four outdoor lighted tennis courts.

STAFF

Rosemary Didear became the third Head of School in 2000. She is a graduate of Columbia University's Barnard College and, before her appointment, she served as the School's Dean. Mrs. Didear is married and has two children.

The faculty is composed of 55 experienced educators and 45 additional staff members who instruct, provide dorm supervision, coach, and generally advise students outside of the classroom in the afternoons and evenings. Faculty members have a broad range of practical and professional experience, and many have been at the Delphian School for more than ten years. All faculty and staff members are chosen to work closely with students, and most live on campus with their families.

MEDICAL CARE

A Medical Liaison on campus is able to give immediate first aid for injuries and accidents and arrange for emergency or specialized medical care when necessary.

Not all injuries and illnesses call for treatment by a physician, and care may be carried out at Delphi following guidelines developed with the school's consulting physician.

Doctors are on call in the nearby towns of Sheridan, McMinnville, and Willamina; the nearest hospital is 30 minutes away.

RELIGIOUS LIFE

The neighboring towns have religious services for most major faiths; the school arranges for transportation so that students may attend.

COSTS

In 2004, the four-week Summer Session cost from $4522 to $4866, depending on the age of the student. A six-week session ranged from $5290 to $5806. Participants should call the Office of Admissions for specifics and ESL prices. All Lower School and Middle School students who are boarding pay a personal teacher fee (a personal teacher is a faculty member who acts as a parent away from home for the student). Upon enrollment, parents fill out a miscellaneous expense form, which details minor expenses such as the recommended weekly allowance of $15 to $25. The school also requires that $140 be set aside in case the child needs to see a doctor.

TRANSPORTATION

Transportation between the school and the Portland airport is provided on certain days of the week and is also available for students arriving by train.

APPLICATION TIMETABLE

An initial inquiry is welcome at any time. On-campus interviews are conducted from 9 a.m. to 5 p.m. Monday through Friday. Because space is limited, the Summer Application form should be completed and returned to the school as soon as possible. There is a nonrefundable $50 application fee.

For more information, contact:

Donetta Phelps, Director of Admissions
The Delphian School
Department 18
20950 Southwest Rock Creek Road
Sheridan, Oregon 97378
503-843-3521
800-626-6610 (toll-free)
E-mail: info@delphian.org
World Wide Web: http://www.delphian.org

PARTICIPANT/FAMILY COMMENTS

"I've learned more about responsibility and integrity, and I've gained more confidence in myself. The wholesome learning environment has made me enthusiastic about education again."

SUMMER DISCOVERY

AT UCLA, UC SANTA BARBARA, U. OF VERMONT, U. OF MICHIGAN, GEORGETOWN U., UC SAN DIEGO, CAMBRIDGE UNIVERSITY, AND U. OF SYDNEY

SUMMER PROGRAMS

UCLA, UC SANTA BARBARA, U. OF VERMONT, U. OF MICHIGAN, GEORGETOWN U., UC SAN DIEGO, CAMBRIDGE UNIVERSITY, AND U. OF SYDNEY

Type of Program: Precollege enrichment and preparation

Participants: Coeducational; grades 9–12, depending on program

Enrollment: 450 at UCLA, 125 at UC Santa Barbara, 200 at UVM, 400 at Michigan, 200 at Georgetown, 100 at UC San Diego, and 200 at Cambridge

Program Dates: UCLA: six weeks, June 22 to August 2, and three weeks, July 28 to August 16; UC Santa Barbara: six weeks, June 22 to August 2; UVM: five weeks, July 6 to August 8; Michigan: two 3-week sessions or one 6-week session, June 29 to August 8; Georgetown: five weeks, June 29 to August 1; UC San Diego: five weeks, June 29 to August 2; Cambridge: four weeks, June 28 to July 26

Heads of Program: The Musiker and Waldman families

LOCATION

The 411-acre campus of the University of California at Los Angeles (UCLA) is nestled between the residential communities of Bel Aire and Beverly Hills, with the Santa Monica Mountains to the north and the bustling college town of Westwood Village to the south. Only minutes from the beaches of the Pacific Ocean, UCLA offers extensive cultural activities, with some of the nation's most outstanding athletic and recreational complexes.

The University of California at Santa Barbara (UCSB) has a breathtaking 989-acre campus located approximately 100 miles north of Los Angeles, beautifully situated on a promontory that is bordered by the Pacific Ocean and the Channel Islands to the west, and the Santa Ynez Mountains to the east.

The University of California at San Diego is situated on a bluff overlooking the Pacific Ocean by the costal town of La Jolla. This awe-inspiring 1,976-acre campus is one of America's premier research universities, featuring an outstanding faculty and a big, beautiful campus with a friendly, small-campus environment—perfect for a summer of discovery.

The University of Vermont's (UVM) historic campus is located in northern Vermont, overlooking Lake Champlain and the Green Mountains. Nestled on a sloping hillside in Burlington, the campus is centrally located to outdoor pursuits and famous New England sights.

The University of Michigan's commitment to academic, athletic, recreational, and cultural excellence make it an ideal setting. The 2,600-acre Ann Arbor campus, 225 acres of which are dedicated to world-class recreation facilities, has twenty-three libraries and nine museums. The campus has been selected by Rand McNally as providing the best cultural environment of any American university.

Established in 1789 and perched on a hilltop overlooking the Potomac, Georgetown University is located only 1.8 miles from the White House in the quaint, famous village of Georgetown. The campus's location gives students exceptional access to countless historic, political, and cultural sites in Washington, D.C.

Cambridge University in England is one of the world's great academic and cultural centers and is approximately 1 hour from London in the East Anglican countryside. The town is renowned for its architectural heritage and surrounding natural beauty. Students live in New Hall College, one of thirty-one colleges that collectively constitute Cambridge University.

The University of Sydney was founded in 1850 as Australia's first university. Summer Discovery Australia immerses students in the culture, academics, adventure, and fun that defines Australia. This program offers three weeks of precollege experience at the University of Sydney and two weeks of Australian travel.

BACKGROUND AND PHILOSOPHY

The Musiker family has directed summer programs for high school students for more than thirty years. Summer Discovery introduces high school students to the college experience in an environment that is intellectually stimulating, socially enriching, and fun. A team of program directors, academic advisers, and resident counselors help program participants succeed.

PROGRAM OFFERINGS

College Credit Courses Five of the Summer Discovery programs offer advanced college credit opportunities for students completing grades 10–12. Courses are offered in a wide range of fields, including the arts, sciences, humanities, mathematics, theater, communications, and the environment. An Early Start Program, an intensive Research Mentorship Program, and an Academic Connections Research Program are also offered.

Enrichment Courses All eight Summer Discovery programs offer noncredit preparatory courses that include subjects not often found in the regular high school curriculum. They include skill-building courses such as the Princeton Review PSAT/SAT I prep, reading comprehension, expository writing, and creative writing. In addition, courses are available in ESL, TOEFL prep, journalism, debating, painting, photography, video production, acting, and computers.

Summer Discovery "Preparing for College and Life" Workshops This informal discussion course meets in the evening and aims to prepare students for college life. Guest speakers include college admissions officers, educational counselors, and current and recently graduated college students.

Community Service Students have an opportunity, through community service work, to become actively involved in the betterment of their college community.

ESL Program This program is of special interest to the international student who wants to improve English language communication skills. Students are tested and assigned a personalized program based on their ability and cultural background. The majority of Summer Discovery students are American, so interaction with fellow students outside of class is particularly effective in improving language skills.

ENROLLMENT

Last year, participants came from forty-four states and forty-two countries.

DAILY SCHEDULE

The following schedule is for Monday through Friday; weekends are filled with excursions and activities. The time by which students must be in dorm rooms varies according to the activity scheduled.

7:30–9:00	Breakfast
9	Morning class
11:30–1	Lunch
1:30	Afternoon class
3:30	Recreation and activities
6–7	Dinner
8	Study, activities, speakers

EXTRA OPPORTUNITIES AND ACTIVITIES

Students at UCLA take extensive excursions to sites around the Los Angeles area, including Universal Studios, Dodgers games, Disneyland, rock concerts, movie screenings, and visits to colleges throughout the Los Angeles area. World-class recreational activities are provided in numerous sports from weight training to basketball to tennis. An optional excursion to San Francisco is available. Students at UC Santa Barbara take advantage of the Santa Barbara beaches, the Museum of Natural History, the Historical Society Museum, and the Old Mission. Special excursions included are to Disneyland, Six Flags Magic Mountain, Universal Studios, Hollywood Walk of Fame, major league baseball games, whale watches, and the Channel Islands National Park. Students at the campus of University of California, San Diego, participate in numerous activities in the San Diego area. Destinations include the San Diego Zoo, Sea World, White Water Canyon Water Park, Point Loma/Cabrillo National Monument, and Los Angeles. Optional excursions to Las Vegas and Catalina Island are available.

For those in the UVM program, excursions throughout New England include trips to Lake Placid, Saratoga, white-water rafting and sailing, Ben & Jerry's Ice Cream factory, and visits to several New England colleges. Excellent athletic and recreational facilities include those for tennis, soccer, golf, horseback riding, water sports, basketball, softball, football, and aerobics. Michigan's students enjoy trips to Chicago, Detroit Tigers baseball games, the Gerald Ford Presidential Library, the Henry Ford Museum, and the Omnimax Theater. There are canoe trips and comedy and dance clubs. Georgetown students take advantage the Washington, D.C., monuments; the White House; the Smithsonian Institute; the National Archives; the U.S. Holocaust Memorial Museum; and much more. Trips include college tours and visits to Baltimore, Philadelphia, and the Maryland shore. Also included are concerts, theater, and extensive athletic and recreational activities.

Excursions in and around Cambridge include Stratford-upon-Avon, Warwick Castle, Windsor Castle, Duxford Air Force Base, and theater performances. London offers Parliament, Big Ben, the Tower of London, the Hard Rock Café, Madame Tussaud's Wax Museum, and other sites. Recreational sports include soccer, tennis, punting on the River Cam, basketball, volleyball, aerobics, and swimming. An optional excursion to Paris is available. Excursions in and around Sydney include the Ledge Climbing Centre, Darling Harbour, downtown Sydney, and theater performances and museums. Two-week travel includes trips to Ayers Rock, Kings Canyon, the Great Barrier Reef, Brisbane, and Surfers Paradise.

FACILITIES

Students are securely housed in the same residence hall at each campus; the halls are under 24-hour supervision controlled by university and Summer Discovery staff. Students have complete access to all cultural, recreational, athletic, and computer facilities.

STAFF

Administrative and supervisory staff members are professional educators and graduate students from the finest schools in the United States and abroad. Many are Summer Discovery alumni. College credit courses are taught by university professors. Enrichment courses are taught by university professors, graduate teaching assistants, and top secondary school teachers. All staff members are over 21 years of age and are nonsmokers. The staff member–student ratio is approximately 1:10.

MEDICAL CARE

Staff members always accompany students to medical facilities. Private physicians and excellent university hospitals are used for medical care.

COSTS

Depending on the program, the estimated tuition for 2004 was between $3499 and $6499. Tuition included term fees, the full academic and enrichment program, room, meals, campus activities, most excursions, recreational facilities, linen, and transfers. Not included were textbooks, laundry, and transportation.

TRANSPORTATION

Transfers are provided to and from all airports to campus. Parents may also drive students to the campuses. All international students are met at the airport by Summer Discovery staff members.

APPLICATION TIMETABLE

Admission is on a rolling basis. Early application is encouraged. The application fee is $65.

For more information, contact:

Summer Discovery Educational Programs
1326 Old Northern Boulevard
Roslyn, New York 11576
516-621-3939
888-8-SUMMER (888-878-6637; toll-free)
Fax: 516-625-3438
E-mail: discovery@summerfun.com
World Wide Web: http://www.summerfun.com

SUMMER FOCUS AT BERKELEY

SUMMER STUDY AT UNIVERSITY OF CALIFORNIA AT BERKELEY FOR COLLEGE CREDIT

BERKELEY, CALIFORNIA

Type of Program: Academic enrichment
Participants: Coeducational, grades 11–12
Enrollment: 20–60
Program Dates: Six weeks in July and August
Head of Program: Lexy Green, Director

LOCATION

The program is held at the University of California (UC) at Berkeley. Berkeley is an exciting college town with numerous cafés, bookstores, shops, museums, and recreational opportunities. The University is world-famous for its academic excellence.

BACKGROUND AND PHILOSOPHY

Summer Focus, run in partnership with Berkeley Summer Sessions, was founded in 1998. The program is sponsored and conducted by Education Unlimited. The goal of the program is to offer high school students a varied college academic experience on a dynamic university campus while providing supervision and a supportive learning environment. The comprehensive program includes supervised residential living, courses at UC Berkeley for college credit, tutoring sessions with degreed professionals who audit the same classes students attend, supplemental classes taught by the faculty, and weekend trips to take advantage of the many cultural offerings of the Bay Area.

PROGRAM OFFERINGS

Participants enroll in a UC Berkeley summer session course that is taught by a member of the University's faculty, graduate student instructor, or distinguished visitor. These classes are offered through the University. Expert Summer Focus instructors provide tutoring for these University classes most evenings and also teach special electives available only through Summer Focus. The Summer Focus instructors design the curricula for these electives to convey their own specialized knowledge of a variety of fields. Students experience large lecture classes at the University but also learn through small classes and one-on-one instruction in the tutoring sessions and elective classes. There are approximately twenty-five UC classes recommended by the University for high school summer students, so a large variety of courses are available. It is possible to arrange to take a class not on the recommended list. Normally, it is recommended that students take one UC Berkeley class and two supplemental electives. With the permission of the University, it may be possible to take more than one UC class. Electives (in addition to the UC classes) to choose from may include College Level Writing, Film History: California in the Movies, The History of American Social Protest in the 20th Century, Public Speaking and Debate, Survey of 19th and 20th Century Art and Architecture, Political Scandals of the 20th Century, Journalism and Newspaper, and Test Scholars SAT Preparation Course. More classes may be added, and these courses are subject to change. UC Berkeley classes are for college credit, and students are graded in these classes. Electives are for academic enrichment only, and no grades are given.

ENROLLMENT

The program is designed to accommodate up to 60 students. The boy-girl ratio is usually 1:1. No previously required courses or experience is necessary, but students must have at least a 3.0 GPA and need a teacher's recommendation. Approximately 45 percent of students are from California, 45 percent are from the rest of the United States, and 10 percent are international students. Students from all socioeconomic and ethnic backgrounds are welcome. The program accepts international students of at least a moderate level of English proficiency. Academically motivated and talented students are served best by the program.

DAILY SCHEDULE

7:15–8:45	Breakfast
9:00–10:30	UC Summer Session class
10:30–11:30	Study time/break
11:45–1:00	Lunch
2:00–3:30	Enrichment course
3:30–5:00	Free time
5:15–6:30	Dinner
7:00–8:30	Tutoring/study
9:30	Dorm check

A code of conduct designed to ensure participants' safety and to foster a friendly environment where all students are comfortable is strictly enforced.

EXTRA OPPORTUNITIES AND ACTIVITIES

Ample free time is scheduled throughout the program, so students should have plenty of opportunity to relax. Students dine out in Berkeley occasionally, enjoy films in the dorm and around town, and visit local cultural attractions. Each weekend there is the opportunity to travel to a popular recreation site. Possible day trips include Great America Amusement Park, Pier 39 in San Francisco, Oakland A's or San Francisco Giants baseball, the California Shakespeare Festival in Orinda, or the beautiful Pacific Ocean beaches. Many parks, hiking trails, shops, and cafés can be enjoyed in Berkeley.

FACILITIES

The program is held in the UC Berkeley residence halls. University classes are held in a variety of locations on campus.

STAFF

All staff members have at least a bachelor's degree, and many have advanced degrees in the field they are teaching or tutoring. The faculty is composed of experienced high school, college, and summer camp educators. Staff members are chosen to cover a wide variety of specialized areas of expertise.

MEDICAL CARE

All students with medical needs are taken to one of the area medical centers. No on-site medical care is provided. Medical release and information forms are required for participation.

RELIGIOUS LIFE

The program is nondenominational. Religious services of most types are available near campus.

COSTS

The 2004 cost, including tuition, meals, housing, one UC Berkeley summer class, two supplemental electives, and all materials for electives, was $5425. Access to athletic and recreational facilities, most planned recreational and evening activities, and camp memorabilia are also included. Fees do not cover transportation to and from the program site, spending and laundry money, additional nights of lodging if necessary, UC classes above 4 units, and books for UC classes. A $950 deposit applied toward the total tuition cost is required upon application. Students not accepted into the program receive full refunds of their deposits. Spending money of $150 per week is recommended.

FINANCIAL AID

Need-based financial aid is available. A financial aid form and copies of parent/guardian tax forms are required. Participants and their parents or guardians should contact Summer Focus officers for more information.

TRANSPORTATION

The program is located about 15 miles from the Oakland International Airport, and for an additional fee of $45 round-trip, students can be met at and returned to the airport.

APPLICATION TIMETABLE

Initial inquiries are welcome as early as December 15. The application deadline is May 15, and $950 is due upon application. Notification of acceptance is sent within two weeks.

For more information, contact:

Summer Focus
1700 Shattuck Avenue, #305
Berkeley, California 94709
510-548-6612
Fax: 510-548-0212
World Wide Web:
http://www.educationunlimited.com

PARTICIPANT/FAMILY COMMENTS

"The greatest strength of this program was the assistance the staff provided to my son on how to negotiate the college system, how to get help during office hours, and how to request pass/fail grades, etc. The staff gave them support as they learned 'the ropes' of campus life . . ." —Wendy Baird, parent of 2003 participant

SUMMER INSTITUTE FOR THE GIFTED

PARSIPPANY, NEW JERSEY

Type of Program: A three-week coeducational, residential summer program for academically gifted students in grades 1–11. Combines a challenging academic program with traditional summer camp activities
Participants: Gifted students in grades 1–11
Enrollment: 1,800, each session has approximately 175–275 students
Program Dates: June 26 to July 15, July 17 to August 6, July 24 to August 13, July 31 to August 20
Head of Program: Dr. Stephen Gessner, Ph.D.

LOCATION

The Summer Institute for the Gifted (SIG) is held at some of the most beautiful campuses in the United States, including the University of California at Berkeley and Los Angeles, Vassar College (Poughkeepsie, New York), Amherst College (Amherst, Massachusetts), Drew University (Madison, New Jersey), Oberlin College (Oberlin, Ohio), and Bryn Mawr College (Bryn Mawr, Pennsylvania). Day campuses include Fairfield University (Fairfield, Connecticut), Hofstra University (Hempstead, New York), Purchase College (Purchase, New York), and Moorestown Friends School (Moorestown, New Jersey).

BACKGROUND AND PHILOSOPHY

Since its founding in 1984, the Summer Institute for the Gifted has provided academically talented young people with an important enrichment supplement to their regular education. The Summer Institute blends a strong academic program of introductory and college-level courses, an opportunity for cultural exposure, social growth, and traditional summer camp activities. Although the program is held at several different locations, the sessions at each site are identical in purpose and structure.

The Summer Institute for the Gifted enables enthusiastic and capable students to become involved in a challenging academic program that is designed to engage students at a level commensurate with their abilities. The academic program is central to the spirit of SIG. Students are expected to perform at the upper level of their capabilities.

Varied cultural opportunities, educational evening entertainment performances, weekend off-campus trips, a full recreational program, and social activities address all the needs of the academically talented student.

This mixture of offerings allows the participants to be in a stimulating intellectual atmosphere, as well as an enjoyable social setting. Most importantly, it provides them the opportunity to engage with their intellectual peers, students who have similar interests and abilities.

PROGRAM OFFERINGS

Academic offerings The curriculum combines traditional subjects with courses that are meant to introduce new topics to students. There is a wide range of course offerings geared for highly motivated students of all ages. Course offerings for younger students range from Foundations of Mathematics, to Introduction to Robotics, to The Wonders and Mysteries of Ancient Egypt. Classes available to students in grades 7–9 include selections such as Introduction to Veterinary Medicine, Mock Trials and the Justice System, and Psychology. Older students may choose anything from an Introduction to Genetics to the Art of Debate.

PSAT/SAT mathematics and verbal preparatory courses are available to prepare students for standardized exams. High school students may take some courses for college credit. The courses are taught by selected college professors and experts in the fields in which they teach. Counselors are regularly available to assist and tutor students. A final grade report is sent to each student's home at the conclusion of the program and, upon written request, a grade report is sent to the student's school.

Cultural offerings There are a number of cultural courses available to students, regardless of age. The classes are meant to introduce areas of study that may not be available in the student's current local school. Architecture, Modern Dance, Painting and Drawing, Photography, Sculpture, and Theater and Drama are just a few of the cultural courses that a student can choose from at the Summer Institute for the Gifted.

Recreational offerings SIG offers a wide range of recreational courses. Tennis, squash, fencing, chess, lacrosse, soccer, swimming, archery, and other recreational courses are available to be learned and enjoyed. Each course is taught by an experienced professional who will work with the beginners as well as the more advanced. A free recreational hour each day gives the SIG student a chance to participate in sports and recreation in a noninstructional environment.

EXTRA OPPORTUNITIES AND ACTIVITIES

In the Residential Program, special off-campus trips are planned for Saturdays (Saturday Get-Away Trips). Some of the previous years' trips included hiking the Appalachian Trail; canoeing or rafting down the Delaware River; a relaxing day at the lake; historical trips to New York City and Philadelphia; trips to the South Street Seaport; Radio City Music Hall; the Museum of Broadcasting; the Intrepid Air-Sea-Space Museum; Franklin Museum; an archaeological expedition; Hershey Park; Renaissance Faires caving; the Kutztown Folk Festival; Washington, D.C.; Baltimore's Inner Harbor; the Rock and Roll Hall of Fame/Playhouse Square Center; Sea World; the Cleveland Museum of Art; the Cleveland Museum of Natural History; the Great Lakes Science Center; and Dover Lake Waterpark.

FACILITIES

Sites for SIG include some of the country's most prestigious academic institutions. Each campus is carefully selected on the basis of its academic facility, its outstanding reputation, and its capability to assist with the accomplishment of SIG goals and purposes. Complete use of the academic and research facilities on all campuses is available to all students.

STAFF

SIG's faculty and staff members are carefully chosen to ensure that only the most qualified people work with the students. They are selected not only on the basis of their credentials, but also on their enthusiasm and interest in working with younger students. All staff members, counselors, faculty members, and directors, are well-trained, highly motivated, and responsible individuals who demonstrate a genuine interest in the educational and social growth of young people.

COSTS

The cost of the Summer Institute for the Gifted three-week residential program for 2004 was $3350. This amount included tuition for the academic program; all room and board charges, including three meals each day; recreational program costs; evening entertainment program expenses; Saturday Get-Away Trip costs, including transportation and admission fees; and all special program costs. An additional nonrefundable application processing fee of $75 is due with the application. Some financial aid is offered to students on a need basis. The deadline for financial aid applications is April 1.

APPLICATION TIMETABLE

Inquiries are always welcome. The admissions office is open Monday through Friday from 8 a.m. to 6 p.m., Eastern time.

Students who meet one of the following criteria are invited to apply to SIG programs: all participants in recognized talent searches, students who score in the 95th percentile or higher on standardized tests (administered locally or by their schools), students who have been identified as gifted and/or who have participated successfully in a local or school gifted program, and students providing strong letters of recommendation from teachers or counselors citing their academic gifted ability and performance.

Students should apply as early as possible as only a limited number of students can be accepted and accommodated by each session of the Summer Institute for the Gifted. In past seasons, qualified applicants have been turned away due to space limitations. Applications are accepted at any time, but should be postmarked no later than May 15. Qualified applicants are accepted and enrolled on a first-come, first-served basis, according to the postmarked date on the application envelope.

For more information, contact:

Summer Institute for the Gifted
River Plaza
9 West Broad Street
Stamford, Connecticut 06902-3788
866-303-4744 (toll-free)
Fax: 203-399-5598
E-mail: sig.info@aifs.com
World Wide Web: http://www.giftedstudy.com

SUMMER STUDY PROGRAMS

COLLEGE CREDIT/PRE-COLLEGE ENRICHMENT PROGRAMS

UNIVERSITY PARK, PENNSYLVANIA; BOULDER, COLORADO; AND PARIS, FRANCE

Type of Program: College credit and/or enrichment courses; Kaplan SAT review; athletic, recreational, outdoor, and cultural activities; and weekend trips

Participants: Coeducational, students completing grades 9–12

Enrollment: 125 to 400 students, depending on the location

Program Dates: Three to 6½ weeks, late June through mid-August

Heads of Program: Bill Cooperman, Executive Director; Mike Sirowitz, David Wolk, Roland Hulme, Joe Dostilio, and Lina Dee Yacovelli, Directors

LOCATION

Penn State Situated in the center of Pennsylvania and surrounded by the Appalachian Mountains, Penn State's University Park campus is located in what has been called the "ultimate college town" and is one of the nation's most beautiful campuses. The campus includes two golf courses, forty-eight tennis courts, and a 72-acre lake, as well as Beaver Stadium, a 108,500-seat football complex that is home to the Nittany Lions. Participants in Summer Study at Penn State find themselves immersed in the quaint, yet upscale, atmosphere of State College. The town revolves around the university and caters to the needs of its student population. There are restaurants, shops, fashion boutiques, bookstores, playhouses, movie theaters, video arcades, and dance clubs across the street.

University of Colorado Recently rated the number one Recreation and Outdoor Town in America by *Outdoor Magazine,* Boulder, Colorado, offers students 200 miles of biking and hiking trails and 30,000 acres of open space. The university's location at the base of the majestic Rocky Mountains means white-water rafting, backpacking, hiking, and rock climbing are easily accessible to students. Summer Study students at CU-Boulder find themselves immersed in a beautiful Western college town featuring concert halls, restaurants, art galleries, shops, dance clubs and bookstores.

American University of Paris Located in the center of Paris on the fashionable Left Bank, the American University of Paris lies in the shadow of the Eiffel Tower, a few blocks from the Seine. The university's central location permits Paris to be an extension of the classroom and the city itself to be the campus. The buildings on the university's campus are all within a short walk of one another. The central city location puts the Eiffel Tower, Place de la Concorde, the Champs-Elysees, the Arc de Triomphe, Napoleon's Tomb, and many other major points of interest within a short walking distance. All the other sights and sounds of Paris are visited on daily excursions.

BACKGROUND AND PHILOSOPHY

Summer Study programs offer high school students completing grades 9–12 the opportunity to experience college life in a relaxed summertime atmosphere. With the pressure off, summer academic life permits time for personal growth and maturation and the successful development of study, time management, and community living skills; motivation; and independence. Students enjoy a unique summer filled with stimulating academic challenges and fun.

PROGRAM OFFERINGS

Students opting to join the 6½-week program at Penn State, the five-week program in Boulder, or the five-week program in Paris attend freshman-level college courses with college students. At each location, the distinguished university faculty members teach all college-credit classes. Most courses offered to Summer Study students award 3 college credits. Participants may choose a summer curriculum of college credits, an enrichment class, or the Kaplan SAT review.

Students opting to join the 3½-week program at Penn State, the three-week program in Boulder, or the three-week program in Paris attend two or three enrichment courses or the Kaplan SAT review, which prepares all students for the newly reformatted SAT. Enrichment classes are taught by Summer Study instructors and are designed to assist precollege students by offering opportunities not generally given as part of the regular high school curriculum. Students should call Summer Study's office or visit its Web site for a complete listing of college and enrichment courses that are offered. College credits earned at the American University of Paris transfer to most institutions worldwide.

DAILY SCHEDULE

Weekdays start with breakfast, followed by a morning class. College-credit courses (if applicable) and enrichment classes are held after lunch. The balance of the afternoon permits plenty of time for organized events, excursions, sports, outdoor activities, individual exploration, art, theater, and music. Dinner is followed by exciting planned evening activities at all campus locations.

EXTRA OPPORTUNITIES AND ACTIVITIES

Penn State Summer Study's College Counseling Center is a professional advisory service offered to all students. Students electing this option are scheduled for a series of seven private half-hour sessions, matching the students' academic abilities, social maturity, and career aspirations with the college that best suits those interests. Private instruction in tennis and golf are also available, as are driver education and speed-reading. Intensive soccer, basketball, volleyball, and wrestling clinics are offered for students wanting to improve their skills and techniques. Students may also join Body Works Fitness Center, a 20,000-square-foot, state-of-

the-art fitness facility. Evenings include rock concerts, shows, dance clubs, ice skating, movies, broomball, skit night, video game night, Arts Festival concerts, and a banquet/awards night. Three weekends are spent visiting universities in nearby cities, including Cornell, Syracuse, the University of Maryland, and Johns Hopkins. First-class hotels and major attractions are featured during these weekends, including Hersheypark, Harbor Place in Baltimore, and water slides in upstate New York.

University of Colorado Amid the splendor of the Rocky Mountains, University of Colorado at Boulder students may enroll in instructional sports clinics in tennis, basketball, soccer, or volleyball. Specialty clinics in rock climbing, pottery, and yoga are also available. Evening activities include rock concerts, movies, shows, dance clubs, street fairs, amusement parks, a Colorado Rockies baseball game, theater productions, and skit nights. Exciting weekend trips include action-packed adventure trips, white-water rafting, hiking, horseback riding, and visits to Vail, Breckinridge, Colorado Springs, Pikes Peak, and Rocky Mountain National Park.

American University of Paris Cultural excursions and recreational outings are the special features of the five- and three-week Paris programs. Excursions include visits to many famous sites in Paris and hot-air balloon rides. Students also enjoy browsing through high-fashion Parisian boutiques, people-watching at Parisian cafés, and shopping at open-air markets. Nightly planned events include going to dance clubs, Bastille Day fireworks, movies, the Latin Quarter, the Gardens of Tuileries, the Fireman's Ball, the opera, and Planet Hollywood and taking a Seine cruise. Weekend excursions include visits to the Palace of Versailles, the Loire Valley chateau country, and Disneyland Paris. Students interested in learning French can enroll in the French Immersion portion of the program, featuring speak-only-French roommates and groups for day/night excursions and French classes. As English is the working language of American University, Summer Study students do not need to have any working knowledge of French to join the program.

FACILITIES

All Summer Study participants fill out a roommate survey form for careful roommate matching according to students' ages and interests.

At Penn State and CU-Boulder, students live in one residence hall, 2 students per room. A telephone, refrigerator, freezer, microwave oven, and Internet access are available in each room. Television and laundry facilities are available in the residence. Students have full use of all athletic facilities and computer/word processing labs.

Participants in Paris are housed in an all-suites hotel, with 3 or 4 students sharing a two-bedroom, private-bath suite (including a kitchen with a refrigerator, freezer, and microwave; cable television; and telephone service). Breakfast is served at the hotel. Dinner is served at six local restaurants that cooperate in the program's unique dine-around plan. Students have full access to a computer and word processing center, e-mail, and the Internet.

STAFF

All of the campuses are rated among the top universities in the world. Professors, graduate students, and upper-level undergraduate students teach enrichment courses. All staff members are dedicated professionals who live in the residence halls with the students. They are available at all times to facilitate activities and help with student guidance.

COSTS

Program tuition for the 2004 summer was as follows: 6½-week program at Penn State, $5995; 3½-week program at Penn State, $3795; five-week program in Colorado, $5795; three-week program in Colorado, $3495; five-week program in Paris, $6495; and three-week program in Paris, $4595.

FINANCIAL AID

Limited partial tuition scholarships are available for those who are academically qualified but financially needy.

TRANSPORTATION

Summer Study provides round-trip motorcoach transportation from centrally located points ($65 each way) for the Penn State programs. For full coordination, Creative Travel International, Inc., an affiliate of Summer Study, arranges all air-travel arrangements and transfers for out-of-town and international students. Students flying to Denver or Paris or connecting in New York are met by Summer Study staff members upon arrival.

APPLICATION TIMETABLE

Enrollment is limited, and applications are reviewed on a rolling admissions basis.

For more information, contact:

Bill Cooperman, Executive Director
Summer Study Programs
900 Walt Whitman Road
Melville, New York 11747
631-424-1000
800-666-2556 (toll-free)
Fax: 631-424-0567
E-mail: info@summerstudy.com
World Wide Web: http://www.summerstudy.com

SUMMER THEATRE INSTITUTE–2005

YOUTH THEATRE OF NEW JERSEY'S SUMMER TEEN THEATRE TRAINING PROGRAM

IN RESIDENCE AT ALFRED LERNER HALL, COLUMBIA UNIVERSITY, NEW YORK

NEW YORK, NEW YORK

Type of Program: Professional theater training program for actors, dancer-actors, musical-theater actors, directors, and playwrights

Participants: Coeducational, ages 14 (or entering their freshman year in fall 2005) to 19 years

Enrollment: 40–45 students for the full four-week residential program

Program Dates: Four-week residential theater training program: June 26 to July 22, 2005

Head of Program: Allyn Sitjar, Artistic Director

LOCATION

Summer Theatre Institute is in residence at Columbia University. This beautiful campus is located in the heart of one of the greatest cultural cities in the world—New York City. The campus is located in the Morningside Heights area of the city and is a beehive of exciting activity for hundreds of high school students. In addition to the intense theater training program, students have an opportunity to experience a variety of shows and concerts, museums, and the creatively inspiring energy of New York City.

BACKGROUND AND PHILOSOPHY

Summer Theatre Institute is Youth Theatre of New Jersey's preprofessional summer theater training program for teens. Now in its twenty-first year, this nonprofit arts organization, based in Sparta, New Jersey, specializes in training kids, teens, and young adults in a broad range of theater skills. Students of all levels are taught by professional theater artists. The Institute auditions students of all levels from across the country and overseas. Youth Theatre of New Jersey continuously trains young artists year-round and also produces new American plays and musicals. It is a member of the American Alliance for Theatre & Education and Artpride.

The Summer Theatre Institute program offers an exciting total theater experience for young aspiring theater artists. It is a chance for teens and young adults to learn new physical theater skills, explore their creativity, expand their imaginations, and celebrate the performing artist in themselves.

The main goal of the preprofessional program at Summer Theatre Institute is to create an atmosphere in which young theater artists can explore, experience, and process a variety of theater skills without pressure or competition. For the beginning student, it is a chance to learn, explore, and create a dynamic and accessible repertoire of theater skills. For students who have had some exposure to doing shows or taking some classes, it is a chance to discover new methods and techniques, and to strengthen, deepen, and explore their artistic muse as well as their physical skills. The program is also designed to reinforce personal confidence, performance technique, and ensemble work. Ensemble work is emphasized to develop a sense of total group cooperation while still maintaining a sensitivity to individual needs. Through the ensemble work, the young artists discover the true meaning of theater as a collaborative art form. In addition to the theater training and creative process, social and communication skills are nurtured and the development of strong friendships are common.

PROGRAM OFFERINGS

The Summer Theatre Institute program offers a full process experience in multidisciplinary performance skills. With enthusiastic and experienced professional theater artists, young actors, dancer-actors, musical-theater actors, directors, and playwrights immerse themselves in their particular craft, developing both the physical/mental sharpness and fluidity that only comes with intensive process work. They are then given the practical experience of making their work come alive through several final projects and showcases.

The program exposes the young theater artist to the inner workings of a true conservatory program and prepares precollege and college students for the rigors and joys of the top theater conservatory programs in the country. Having this experience in their portfolio has proven to be a big plus for many alumni, who have gone on to professional theater careers and top college programs, such as Boston University, Carnegie Mellon University, New York University's Tisch School of the Arts, Syracuse University, the University of Southern California, and others. For young artists who are new to the experience, it is a chance to discover the joys of true process work in classes that challenge their physical prowess, explode their imagination, focus their creative energy, and are just plain fun.

The four-week residential program of the Summer Theatre Institute is designed to offer the maximum experience of being part of a theater company of young artists who are completely immersed in honing their craft and working on process. Students enrolled in the full four-week residential program can take advantage of the full training program, performance opportunities, campus life, and field trips. The residential experience is also an opportunity to experience living on a college campus, make friends with fellow artists, and experience the mentoring of professional theater artists and teachers who all share a love of theater.

Core Classes Core ensemble classes are taught in acting, improvisation, mime/theater movement, dance, voice, and speech. In addition to core classes and specialized workshops, informational guests give practical advice on show business.

Actors The acting program consists of a wide variety of skills, including scene study, improvisation, theater movement, mime, mask improvisation, audition technique, stage combat, monologue and scene projects, showcase collaborations, and more.

Dancer-Actors and Musical-Theater Actors Special workshops for young performers who have been busy honing their dance and song skills help to focus, integrate their training, and stretch their imagination in such classes as acting, dance/theater improvisation, choreography, movement styles, styling the song, musical theater movement, audition technique, and more.

Playwrights Writers are able to stretch their skills and challenge their imaginations in workshops such as writing through theater games, elements of playwriting, dramatic structure, the playwright's voice, staged readings, and more.

Directors Directors hone their craft through script analysis, open scenes, the director's tools, language and imagery, the collaborative imperative, performance projects, and more.

ENROLLMENT

Summer Theatre Institute currently accepts 45 students between the ages of 14 and 19 from across the country and overseas for the full four-week residential program. It is important to fill out the application and set audition appointments early. Auditions are held in New York and New Jersey between February and May. Out-of-town and overseas students may submit their auditions on videotape and then have their interview by telephone after their tape has been received and viewed.

EXTRA OPPORTUNITIES AND ACTIVITIES

Enhancing the training at Summer Theatre Institute is the experience of living in one of the greatest cultural cities in the world. Students are a part of the pulse, energy, and variety of New York City. Included in the program are field trips to the Metropolitan Museum of Art and a variety of theatergoing experiences, from dance, comedy, and cabaret to Broadway and Off-Broadway. In addition to the various field trips, the campus of Columbia University is a beehive of activity, including concerts on the lawn, weekly movies, lectures, and exhibitions.

FACILITIES

The dorms at Columbia University are air conditioned and recently renovated. Students are housed at Carman Hall, which has a 24-hour guard on duty at the main entrance; Columbia University ID must be shown to gain entry. A full meal plan is included with the housing.

Complete information on Carman Hall at Columbia University can be found on the World Wide Web (http://www.columbia.edu/cu/reshalls).

STAFF

Summer Theatre Institute's staff consists of 3 full-time faculty members available and living on campus with the students and 2 full-time graduate student teaching assistants. Professional theater teachers from the New York and New Jersey area come in every day for classes and workshops. All teaching theater artists are professionally involved in theater projects all over the country. Most of the teachers are part-time faculty members of Youth Theatre of New Jersey's extensive year-round theater program. Newer teachers are put through several interview/reference screenings, as well as several demonstration workshops.

MEDICAL CARE

An infirmary and medical care are available on campus during the summer. St. Luke's Hospital, the closest hospital, is located on 114th and Amsterdam, approximately 3 to 5 minutes from the campus.

COSTS

Tuition for the full four-week residential program is $4995 for students applying before May 20. Tuition increases after the May 20 deadline.

TRANSPORTATION

Students arrange their own airport transportation from the three major airports to Columbia University. Students can choose from a variety of transportation options, including buses, cabs, or reservations made with limousine companies or airport shuttle companies. The Summer Theatre Institute is happy to provide more detailed information. Students fly into either Newark International Airport in New Jersey or La Guardia Airport in New York. Students flying from outside of the United States fly into either JFK Airport in New York or Newark International Airport.

APPLICATION TIMETABLE

Initial inquiries from students of all levels can be made in mid-October for the following year. Students should apply and schedule their audition early. Staff members are happy to answer any questions students may have regarding audition requirements.

Priority consideration is given to students who complete the application and audition process by April 25. Auditions are required, and they are held in New York and New Jersey between February and May. Students from out of town or overseas who cannot audition in person can send a videotaped audition; once their tapes have been received and viewed, they are interviewed by telephone. The deadline for videotaped auditions is May 20. The final application/audition deadline is June 5.

The application fee is $60. An early enrollment discount is available until May 20.

An Open House at Columbia University is scheduled in May. At that time, prospective students can audition, meet some of the faculty members, take a sample class, and tour the campus.

Interested students should call or e-mail their mailing address to Summer Theatre Institute at the address listed below to receive the complete 2005 application packet. The Web site is being revised and may not be available.

For more information, contact:

Allyn Sitjar, Artistic Director
Summer Theatre Institute
Youth Theatre of New Jersey
23 Tomahawk Trail
Sparta, New Jersey 07871
201-415-5329 (cell)
212-258-2110 (weekday evenings)
973-729-6026 (weekends)
Fax: 973-729-3654
E-mail: youththeatreallyn@yahoo.com
asitjar@yahoo.com

SUPERCAMP

LEARNING FORUM

OCEANSIDE, CALIFORNIA

Type of Program: Academic enrichment
Participants: Coeducational, ages 9–24, grades 4–12 and college level
Enrollment: 112 per camp
Program Dates: Ten-day junior high and senior high, and nine-day college sessions in June through August; eight-day pre-teen sessions in July
Head of Program: Bobbi DePorter, President

LOCATION

In 2004, U.S. camps will be held from June through August on the campuses of Stanford University, California; Claremont Colleges, California; Colorado College, Colorado; University of Wisconsin–Parkside, Wisconsin; Hampshire College, Massachusetts; and Wake Forest University, North Carolina.

International sites include Bermuda, Brunei, China, Dominican Republic, Hong Kong, Malaysia, Mexico, Puerto Rico, Singapore, Switzerland, and Thailand.

BACKGROUND AND PHILOSOPHY

SuperCamp is an exciting eight- to ten-day summer program of nonstop work and play, learning and growing, and classes and outdoor challenges. Founded in 1981, it is based on accelerated learning techniques, positive peer support, and carefully orchestrated environmental factors that make the learning process fun and easy.

Students are seldom taught learning skills in a classroom, and it is often this deficiency that leads to poor grades and low self-worth. The SuperCamp philosophy stresses that every person is capable of learning if given the proper tools and that varying teaching methods are needed to reach different types of learners.

Students are given the tools and strategies that can be used to learn any subject rather than instructed in specific subjects. They learn how to read with greatly improved speed and comprehension, memorize long lists of new terms or facts with ease, develop a flow of ideas for writing assignments, and speak in front of groups with self-assurance. The classes have an "I can do it" atmosphere in which learning occurs without stress and frustrations. Music, games, and an attitude of celebration are all used to help students reach beyond the boundaries set by themselves or others.

The program is as concerned with personal development as it is with academics. Self-worth and confidence may well be the most important factors in a young person's life. Much that is worth pursuing in life entails taking risks—whether it's trying out for sports while in school or meeting a new person. To do well, people need self-confidence. One of the program's goals is to have the students learn to live life to the fullest and reach their full potential. During SuperCamp, students stretch themselves to their limits, experiencing the satisfaction of fully applying their mental and physical energies and the joy of succeeding.

SuperCamp is a member of the American Camping Association.

PROGRAM OFFERINGS

SuperCamp provides a diverse range of academic enrichment and personal development courses. The academic offerings focus on reading, comprehension and memory techniques; test preparation; study skills; writing; and problem solving. The classes are designed to help students rediscover the fun of learning. They learn how to break through "writer's block" and write with ease. The test preparation course is designed to improve performance on both regular school tests and standardized college admission tests and also includes an SAT preview course at the senior forum level; it helps students avoid "freezing" on tests or overstudying yet scoring poorly. Students also learn how to memorize unfamiliar information, such as foreign words or chemistry terms, in a way that is fast, fun, and easy.

Personal development activities concentrate on building confidence and self-esteem, increasing motivation, and enhancing skills for communicating with parents, peers, and teachers. Self-esteem and confidence are fostered not only by providing constant encouragement, but also by enabling students to master physical challenges. A typical activity of this type is walking on a steel cable tightrope strung high in the air between two trees; the student, wearing a safety harness, jumps down into the arms of friends below. Students also learn how to speak in front of others with self-assurance and learn how to listen. Listening is regarded as a valuable skill, one that provides a sure way to gain another person's understanding, respect, and trust.

A follow-up study of former students found they improved their performance in schoolwork and on the SAT and ACT, enhanced their motivation and self-worth, and raised scores by as much as 200 points. Some students have undertaken more challenging curricula on returning to school in the fall. Others who were already excellent students have focused their energies on cutting study time and lessening stress. Many have found the time and confidence to become

more involved in outside activities and improve their relationships with family members, peers, and teachers.

ENROLLMENT

The enrollment in each camp is approximately 112 students ages 9–24. Separate sessions are held for preteen, junior high, high school, and college-age students. All academic ability levels are welcome. Participants have come from all fifty states and more than seventy countries.

DAILY SCHEDULE

7:15	Wake-up
7:45	Breakfast
8:30	Opening session
10:00	Class session
12:30	Lunch
1:30	Class session
4:00	Free time or recreation
5:30–6:15	Dinner
6:30–8:45	Class session
9:00	Closing session

FACILITIES

The sessions are conducted on some of the country's most prominent academic college campuses. Participants live in the dormitories, and meals are prepared by a catering staff at the schools.

STAFF

Staff members are professionals carefully chosen and well trained. Every teacher in the program is enthusiastic, respectful, caring toward students, and expert in his or her field. Knowing that students learn differently—that one might learn best by watching, another by hearing, and another by doing—the teachers are flexible in their approach. They are highly committed to every student's success. The ratio of students to staff is 4:1, ensuring that students receive personal attention and appropriate supervision.

MEDICAL CARE

Each camp is staffed by a registered nurse or a fully trained emergency medical technician. Participants are asked to provide basic health information on a form included in the enrollment package. Medical insurance is strongly recommended.

COSTS

Tuition for the eight- to ten-day programs in 2004 was between $1895 and $2395. This charge is comprehensive and includes instructions, lodging in dorm rooms, all meals, course materials, notebooks, pens, and a courtesy airport pickup. The tuition must be paid in full by May 1.

TRANSPORTATION

SuperCamp meets participants at nearby airports and drives them to and from the campuses.

APPLICATION TIMETABLE

Since space is limited, early application and enrollment are recommended; a $700-down payment is due with the application to reserve space. The balance is due on May 1. Applications are taken until the camp is full or the first day of camp. Call for availability. A free brochure or CD can be requested for review. SuperCamp is accredited by the American Camping Association (ACA).

FOR MORE INFORMATION, CONTACT:

SuperCamp
1725 South Coast Highway
Oceanside, California 92054
760-722-0072
800-28-LEARN (285-3276) (toll-free)
Fax: 760-722-3507
E-mail: info@supercamp.com
World Wide Web: http://www.supercamp.com

PARTICIPANT/FAMILY COMMENTS

"Because he was having fun, he was receptive and absorbed skills while gaining self-confidence and raising his self-esteem. It's a motivational and 'how-to-succeed-in-life' camp. Teens learn different skills (like how to interface with teachers, speed reading, relationships, etc.) while having fun. My teen loved it and was glad he went!"—Michael and Carol Hadjinian, New Berlin, Wisconsin

"I improved my grades and self-esteem while I made tons of new friends that I'm still in touch with."—Melanie Dackman, Randallstown, Maryland

SYRACUSE UNIVERSITY SUMMER COLLEGE

SUMMER PROGRAM

SYRACUSE, NEW YORK

Type of Program: Academic programs
Participants: Coeducational; high school juniors and seniors
Enrollment: 225 to 250
Program Dates: July 3 to August 13, 2005
Head of Program: Director of Syracuse University's Summer College for High School Students

LOCATION

The program takes place on the Syracuse University (SU) campus, with offices at 111 Waverly Avenue, Suite 240. The University is on a hill on the east side of downtown Syracuse, at the crossroads of upstate New York. Syracuse is in the western foothills of the Adirondack Mountains and at the eastern edge of the Finger Lakes region, renowned for its scenic lakes, vineyards, and vacation areas. It is within a 5-hour drive of New York City, Toronto, Philadelphia, and Boston.

BACKGROUND AND PHILOSOPHY

Syracuse University began its Summer College for academically talented high school students in 1961 to offer teenagers the opportunity to start college study early and to test career interests firsthand before making crucial decisions about the future. Summer College students choose one of eleven programs and attend college-level, credit-bearing, preprofessional courses. They live the life of a college student—on campus in a regular residence hall, sharing experiences and living space with other high school students from a variety of backgrounds.

PROGRAM OFFERINGS

The 2005 curriculum options include acting and musical theater, architecture, art and design, engineering and computer science, fashion and textile design, forensic science, law, liberal arts, management, public communications, and theater production. Many programs include a liberal arts course; students choose two classes from a wide variety of course offerings and earn 6 or 7 credits. Credits earned through Summer College are accepted at Syracuse University and most other colleges and universities upon matriculation and credit-transfer request. It is the student's college of matriculation that determines credit transfer. The typical class meets for six weeks, Monday through Thursday (plus Friday in some programs) for four to six hours per day, depending on the program. Students participate in field trips and campus activities. Supervised residence hall living includes special weekend events. The residence hall staff is trained for supervising, not only in the residence hall but also outside the classroom as tutors and mentors.

ENROLLMENT

There are between 225 and 250 participants in Summer College, with an average of 25 students per program. Many are from New York State, Pennsylvania, New Jersey, and New England. Some come from as far as Florida, Texas, California, and Puerto Rico or internationally from St. Croix, Turkey, and Ukraine. Students come from all socioeconomic levels and ethnic backgrounds. Successful applicants are in good academic standing and demonstrate maturity and self-discipline. Eligibility is determined by completed applications, which include high school transcripts, national test scores, and letters of recommendation. The acting and musical theater and art and design programs may have additional eligibility requirements.

DAILY SCHEDULE

A typical day in Summer College at Syracuse University mirrors a day in the life of a college first-year student; breakfast in a residence dining hall in time to get to class, a class schedule that varies according to the academic program, and lunch and dinner with fellow students in the dining hall. In the evening, there are often meetings for the weekly student newsletter, a memory CD project, and planning for special events. Special activities typically include an ice cream social, a outdoor carnival, a talent show, a semiformal dance, a fashion show, casino nights, field trips to amusement parks and beaches, and picnics. In addition to planned group activities, Summer College students have access to the University's swimming pools, tennis courts, computer clusters, gyms, game rooms, and an ice rink.

EXTRA OPPORTUNITIES AND ACTIVITIES

Extra opportunities vary by academic program. Acting and musical theatre students perform in at least two public presentations. Architecture students travel to

study buildings designed by prominent architects such as Frank Lloyd Wright, Louis Kahn, and I. M. Pei. Their course projects are critiqued by professors from SU's School of Architecture. Art and design students present an exhibition and host a reception at an art facility on the campus. Law students participate in mock trials.

The University's faculty, staff, and summer student population enjoy traditional summer weekday events that take advantage of fine weather and the beautiful campus location. Such events may include a movie on the quad and a strawberry festival.

FACILITIES

Summer College students live in an undergraduate residence hall on the Syracuse campus. Athletic facilities on the campus include the well-known Carrier Dome. The Schine Student Center is centrally located near the residence halls, dining centers, and classroom buildings and next door to the Byrd Library. The Summer College Office is located diagonally across from the Science Student Center.

STAFF

The Summer College Office is staffed year-round. In the summer, Syracuse University professors and instructors teach all credit courses. The Summer College residential staff lives in the residence hall and includes a director, 2 assistant directors, and an average of 12 resident advisers (RAs). RAs are mature, trained graduate and undergraduate students who supervise, tutor, and plan activities.

MEDICAL CARE

In addition to its Health Services Center, the University shares its "hill" with University Hospital and Crouse-Irving Memorial Hospital. As part of the application process, students supply complete medical information, and a parent or guardian signs an authorization form for medical treatment and provides insurance information.

RELIGIOUS LIFE

Summer College students have the option of attending religious services within walking distance from the campus. There are no services that are a part of Summer College.

COSTS

In 2004, the cost of tuition, room, board, activities, and insurance was between $5050 and $5750, depending on the program of study. Textbooks and supplies are not included in the cost of the program. A $500 RSVP deposit is required and is applied to the cost of the program. There is a $50 application fee and a $50 refundable room-damage deposit.

FINANCIAL AID

A limited number of partial scholarships are awarded based solely on financial need. No full scholarships are available.

TRANSPORTATION

Syracuse University is 15 minutes from Hancock International Airport, 10 minutes from the east-west Amtrak interstate railway, and adjacent to north-south Route 81, which connects with the New York State Thruway about 6 miles north of the campus.

APPLICATION TIMETABLE

Inquiries are welcome at any time, and applications are accepted throughout the year. Tours and interviews may be arranged at the student's convenience. Offices are open from 8:30 a.m. to 5 p.m. September through mid-May and from 8 a.m. to 4:30 p.m. in the summer. The application deadline is June 7.

FOR MORE INFORMATION, CONTACT:

Syracuse University Summer College
for High School Students
111 Waverly Avenue, Suite 240
Syracuse University
Syracuse, New York 13244-2320
315-443-5297
Fax: 315-443-3976
E-mail: sumcoll@syr.edu
World Wide Web: http://www.summercollege.syr.edu

PARTICIPANT/FAMILY COMMENTS

"I have made lots of new friends, learned to set up my own schedule, and have become more self-reliant."

"We put in a lot of hours on projects, but the work was interesting and the time flew by."

"Summer College is a respectful, mature environment in which everyone comes together for the same reason—to learn."

"I like the Syracuse campus. The buildings are beautiful, and, while the campus is very big, it's fairly compact and almost everything is convenient."

"My son enjoyed the summer program tremendously. It has had a profound and lasting impression on him."

TABOR ACADEMY

SUMMER PROGRAM

MARION, MASSACHUSETTS

Type of Program: Sports and arts instruction, academic enrichment
Participants: Coeducational, ages 9–15
Enrollment: 165 boarding, 250 day camp
Program Dates: June 26–July 24 or August 7
Head of Program: William A. Hrasky, Director

LOCATION

Situated directly on the shore of Sippican Harbor, Buzzards Bay, in Marion, Massachusetts, the Tabor Academy Summer Program makes full use of the residential, academic, and athletic facilities of Tabor Academy, an independent, coeducational boarding school founded in 1876.

BACKGROUND AND PHILOSOPHY

Established in 1917, the Tabor Academy Summer Program gives young people the opportunity to develop to their full potential as athletes, students, and individuals. Under the guidance of highly qualified counselors, coaches, and teachers, the program encourages young people to take pride in their personal achievements in the classroom, on the playing fields, and on the waterfront. Tabor provides the option of doing summer schoolwork without losing any of the joys of summer camp.

PROGRAM OFFERINGS

Each of the activities offered in the program is carefully supervised, with special attention to the individual. Instruction is a major part of each activity, and emphasis is placed on personal achievement, rather than competitive "success." Each camper creates his or her own recreational program by choosing among these activities: art, baseball, basketball, ceramics, dance/aerobics, drama, field hockey, golf, lacrosse, sailing, soccer, softball, swimming, tennis, and volleyball.

Because of Tabor's oceanfront location and extensive waterfront facilities, sailing is among the most popular activities. Tabor's fleet includes Capris, Lasers, Optimists, and several larger boats. Sailing lessons are provided by certified instructors who offer basic lessons for beginners and more challenging opportunities for experienced sailors.

Campers may also take advantage of academic offerings. Although academic courses are not required, most participants in the program choose to take one or two of the following classes: computers, creative writing, developmental reading, English, French, Latin, mathematics (including algebra and geometry), oceanography, planet Earth, Spanish, and study skills. Whether the course is taken for purposes of review or enrichment, classes are kept small so that teachers may work closely with individual students. Classes meet five times a week and do not require homework, as both instruction and practice exercises are completed during the 70-minute class periods.

Tabor's waterfront oceanography laboratory is a state-of-the-art facility for the study of marine biology, and oceanography is the most popular course selection in the summer program. Field trips to local beaches and wetlands, as well as to the New England Aquarium and the Woods Hole Oceanographic Institute, complement the hands-on experience in Tabor's oceanography lab.

DAILY SCHEDULE

7–8:30	Rising, breakfast, and room inspection
8:30–12:15	Periods A, B, and C for academics and activities
12:15–12:45	Buffet lunch
12:45–2:20	Rest period
2:20–2:30	Afternoon meeting
2:30–5	Periods D and E for activities
5–6	Showers and clean-up
6–6:45	Family-style dinner
6:45–7	Evening meeting
7–9	Evening activities
9–10	Lights out

Sundays are reserved for special programs and trips to local attractions in Boston, Providence, and Cape Cod.

ENROLLMENT

While the vast majority of campers come to Tabor from the New England and mid-Atlantic states, others come from around the nation and the world. In a typical summer, 20 or 30 international students, representing twelve or thirteen different countries, join the 120–130 American participants in the program.

FACILITIES

Tabor Academy provides first-class facilities for academics, the fine and performing arts, and outdoor sports (with nine playing fields, seven all-weather tennis courts, and access to a golf course). The athletic center offers an indoor skating rink, a gymnasium, a multipurpose field house, a fitness center, and nine squash courts. Campers live in the well-equipped dormitories of the Academy, and they enjoy the full services of the school's health center and dining hall.

STAFF

The program's staff includes more than eighty teachers, coaches, and counselors, many of whom are faculty members at Tabor Academy or similar schools. In a typical summer, several staff members are Tabor Academy graduates or former participants in the Summer Program.

MEDICAL CARE

Basic medical care is provided by Tabor Academy's Baxter Health Center, which is supplemented by local community health and hospital services. Campers are required to have medical insurance, and parents are asked to submit a detailed medical form before registration day.

COSTS

Tuition for the four-week session (including two academic courses) is $4500; tuition for the six-week session (including two academic courses) is $5800. There are no other fees, and laundry service is included in the tuition. The program recommends establishing a $200 "bank account" for a camper's spending money; campers may make withdrawals from this account only with the Director's permission, and the balance is returned to the parents at the end of the session.

TRANSPORTATION

On opening and closing days, the program provides transportation to Marion from Boston.

APPLICATION TIMETABLE

Applications are welcome throughout the year and can be accepted late in the spring, if spaces still remain in the program. Tours of Tabor's campus and meetings with summer program administrators are also available throughout the year.

For more information, contact:

William A. Hrasky, Director, or
Richard DaSilva Jr., Program Director (winter contact)
Tabor Academy Summer Program
Tabor Academy
Marion, Massachusetts 02738
508-748-2000 Ext. 2242
World Wide Web: http://www.taborsummer.org

TAFT SUMMER SCHOOL

ON-CAMPUS PROGRAM

WATERTOWN, CONNECTICUT

Type of Program: Academic enrichment
Participants: Coeducational, grades 7–12
Enrollment: 150
Head of Program: Stephen J. McCabe Jr., Director

LOCATION

The Taft School, founded in 1890 by Horace Taft, is located in Watertown, Connecticut, a community of 20,000 residents close to the city of Waterbury. Watertown is 45 minutes from Hartford, 1½ hours from New York City, and 2½ hours from Boston.

BACKGROUND AND PHILOSOPHY

The Taft Summer School, established in 1982, provides an opportunity for motivated students entering grades 7–12 to review course material, prepare for future courses, or enrich their academic experience by taking courses not normally available to them. The school offers intensive study in a residential, independent school environment—one in which boys and girls can learn how best to realize their potential as students. Teachers from Taft's faculty join teachers from other fine public and private schools to provide an exciting and varied academic program. While the Summer School's primary focus is academic, an extensive athletic program and a varied schedule of weekend activities round out the residential experience.

PROGRAM OFFERINGS

Young Scholars Program Aimed at younger men and women (those completing the sixth through eighth grades) who intend to take on the challenges of rigorous public and private secondary schools, this program focuses on building essential skills and instilling students with greater confidence as they look ahead to seventh, eighth, and ninth grades and further down the road, to the demands of college preparatory program.

Liberal Studies Program This program offers major courses and electives in a variety of disciplines to students entering the tenth, eleventh, and twelfth grades. Each student is required to take four courses: two 100-level majors and two 200-level electives.

Major course offerings include English, mathematics, biology, environmental science, physical science, French, Spanish, ESL, history, and studio art. Elective course offerings include creative writing, photography, acting, drawing and painting, art history, testing, reading and study skills, current events, public speaking, keyboarding and computers, SAT verbal and math prep, and SSAT prep.

DAILY SCHEDULE

7:00–8:15	Breakfast
8:30–10:00	First period
10:00–10:30	Break or assembly
10:30–12:00	Second period
12:00–1:00	Lunch
1:00–1:40	Third period
1:45–2:25	Fourth period
3:15–4:30	Sports
5:00–6:30	Dinner
6:30–7:30	Freetime/Extracurricular activities
7:30–9:30	Supervised evening study hall
10:15	Students in dormitories
10:30	Lights out

EXTRA OPPORTUNITIES AND ACTIVITIES

On weekends and certain Wednesdays, activities are organized in school or trips off campus are available to students. In the past, students have visited Mystic Seaport; Washington, D.C.; Boston; and New York City. Dances, shopping, barbecues, Broadway shows, and a trip to an amusement park are common outings. Optional trips include beaches, Tanglewood, and the ballpark.

All Summer School students are encouraged to try out for the Summer School play. Art students' work is exhibited at the end of the program.

FACILITIES

Taft's 220-acre campus includes six separate dormitories, the 53,000-volume Hulbert Taft, Jr. Library, the Ivy Kwok Wu Science and Mathematics Center, a modern infirmary, and the Bingham Auditorium. The Modern Language Learning and Resource Center uses a sophisticated combination of computer hardware and software to facilitate learning a foreign language. The Arts and Humanities Center contains classrooms, faculty offices, the Student Union, spacious art rooms, and a black-box experimental theater. The Cruiskshank Athletic Center contains a field house for basketball and volleyball and indoor tennis and squash courts. In addition to Taft's athletic fields, twelve tennis courts and a running track are available to Summer School students.

STAFF

Faculty members at Taft are selected on the basis of their excellence in teaching, their commitment to young people, and their desire to instill enthusiasm for learning. The Summer School faculty is chosen primarily from the regular school-year faculty and from other independent and public schools. In addition, Taft selects several outstanding college seniors and recent graduates who are interested in education to assist faculty members. Interns work in the classroom with a senior teacher, live in the dormitories, assist in the afternoon sports, and serve as advisers to Summer School students.

MEDICAL CARE

The Martin Infirmary is a fully equipped facility with a registered nurse on duty at all times. A physician visits the school on a regular basis and is on call throughout the day. Local hospitals are nearby for medical service.

RELIGIOUS LIFE

While Taft is a nonsectarian school, students are encouraged to attend the religious institution of their choice. Churches of various denominations are within walking distance to campus. Students with special needs can be accommodated.

COSTS

The charge for all boarding students in the on-campus program is $4950. For 2004, this covers tuition, room and board, and all trips and activities. Tuition for a full-time day student living in Watertown or the immediate vicinity is $2950. The tuition for part-time day students is $900 per course. An additional fee to cover books, supplies, incidentals, and spending money is placed in each student's bank account—$400 for boarding students and $200 for day students. An independent laundry service is available.

FINANCIAL AID

Limited financial aid is available to deserving boarding and day students.

TRANSPORTATION

Taft provides transportation, free of charge, to and from Bradley International Airport in Windsor Locks, Connecticut, and JFK Airport in New York. Additional fees are charged to arrange pick-up at other locations. There is train and bus transportation into Waterbury.

APPLICATION TIMETABLE

Applications are accepted beginning December 1. As there is a rolling admissions process and applications are reviewed as soon as they are received, it is wise to submit an application early to secure a boarding space and classroom choices before they fill. An application fee must accompany the application. Upon enrollment, which secures a place, a nonrefundable deposit of $1000 is required. The balance of tuition is due by June 10. The application may be downloaded from the Web site listed below.

For more information, contact:

Taft Summer School
110 Woodbury Road
Watertown, Connecticut 06795
860-945-7961
Fax: 860-945-7859
E-mail: summerschool@taftschool.org
World Wide Web: http://www.taftschool.org/summer

TASIS–THE AMERICAN SCHOOL IN ENGLAND/THE TASIS SPANISH SUMMER SCHOOL IN SPAIN

ENGLAND: SUMMER SCHOOL
SPAIN: SUMMER LANGUAGE PROGRAM

THORPE, SURREY, ENGLAND
SALAMANCA AND COSTA DEL SOL, SPAIN

Type of Program: *England:* Academic enrichment courses, theater workshops, sports, and travel; *Spain:* Intensive immersion in Spanish language
Participants: *England:* coeducational, ages 12–18; *Spain:* coeducational, ages 13–17
Enrollment: *England:* 220; *Spain:* 110
Program Dates: *England:* Four weeks in July, three weeks in August; *Spain:* July 3–August 1
Heads of Program: David West and Chris Tragas, Directors

LOCATION

England The School's beautiful 35-acre rural campus, set in the heart of a beautiful English country village, is only 8 miles from Royal Windsor, 18 miles from the city of London, and 6 miles from Heathrow International Airport. Rich in natural leisure and cultural resources, this prime residential area is also a popular tourist destination. King John sealed the Magna Carta here in the fields of Runnymede, and the Royal Shakespeare Theatre and Stratford-upon-Avon attract classical drama lovers the world over.
Spain The TASIS Spanish Summer Language Program offers students a means to broaden their linguistic and cultural horizons by bringing them to the ancient learning center of Salamanca, 2 hours from Madrid. Students reside in a beautifully restored fourteenth-century building, which is just a 5-minute walk from the famous Plaza Mayor. For the final week of the program, students relocate to a luxury resort on the Costa del Sol, with faculty and student housing, classrooms, a swimming pool, and immediate access to the beach.

BACKGROUND AND PHILOSOPHY

England The American School in England was founded twenty-seven years ago, and the Summer School was inaugurated that same year to offer an intensive credit-based learning experience for students new to Europe or for those seeking to strengthen skills or knowledge in one particular area.

PROGRAM OFFERINGS

England Each course provides a minimum of 4 hours of classroom work every day, small classes, and individualized instruction. Students choose an elective course in addition to one major course. Major courses are English Literature and Composition, High School Skills, Middle School Skills, Archaeology and Architecture, Shakespeare and British History, Ensemble Theatre, Theatre in London, Biology, Chemistry, Algebra I and II, Geometry, Precalculus, Computer Graphic Design, Lights Camera Action, Art Portfolio in London, SAT Review, English-as-a-Second Language, and TOEFL Review.

Theatre in London With a focus on reading and analysing plays, this course's major objective is to enjoy as many productions as possible in London and Stratford-upon-Avon. Recent plays and musicals seen include *Phantom of the Opera, Les Misérables, The Lion King,* and *Chicago.*

Shakespeare and British History Designed to enrich a student's understanding and appreciation of both drama and history, this course integrates literary and historical approaches to the study of selected Shakespearean plays while examining his historic settings and characters. Numerous excursions to theaters and sites of historical interest are included.

Ensemble Theatre This course teaches the full range of theater skills.

English Language Program ESL courses are offered in four- and three-week sessions, as are TOEFL preparation classes.

Spain The daily schedule includes four language classes and one Language in Life activity, using Salamanca as the classroom. There is an average of 12 students in each class and six levels, ranging from beginning to advanced. All classes are conducted entirely in Spanish. Students may earn one academic credit upon completion of the course.

ENROLLMENT

In **England,** 220 students enroll each summer, with approximately 30 percent originating from the United States. Students enrolled in intensive English as a second language classes represent thirty different countries.
In **Spain,** 100 to 120 students enroll each summer, with approximately 80 percent from the United States.

EXTRA OPPORTUNITIES AND ACTIVITIES

England On-campus extracurricular activities include photography, drama, music, journalism, and art as well as social activities such as picnics, barbecues, discos, videos, and films. All students participate in the off-campus travel program each weekend by choosing from the wide variety of overnight and day trips available. These include trips to Oxford, Cambridge, Brighton, and Bath and frequent trips to Windsor and London. Optional weekend trips are offered to destinations such as Edinburgh, Wales, and Paris at extra cost. Students aged 14 to 18 attending a three-week course also have the option to spend an extra week at the Edinburgh Festival in August, which is one of the world's greatest celebrations of art and culture.

Sports such as horseback riding, waterskiing, basketball, tennis, golf, and baseball are all included in the schedule each day.
Spain Students explore the Spanish heritage by visiting the towns of Granda, La Alberca, Toledo, Segovia, and Madrid as well as the famous El Prado Museum. Students participate in sports during the afternoon, including swimming, aerobics classes, soccer, and tennis.

FACILITIES

England The American School in England is a coeducational boarding and country day school for 750 students. The programs draw on the full facilities of the year-round boarding program, which includes two late-Georgian mansions that serve as the main student residences and house dining rooms and a 20,000-volume library. Other facilities include a computer center, an art/music complex, a modern gymnasium, a fitness center, and a 350-seat theater. There are also outdoor tennis and basketball courts, three athletics fields, and a regulation baseball diamond. Off-campus facilities are used for swimming, horseback riding, golf, and waterskiing.

STAFF

England The faculty consists of 40 qualified and experienced members. A 6:1 student-faculty ratio allows for personalized instruction and individual attention for each student.

COSTS

England The all-inclusive 2004 cost for four-week enrichment courses was $4350; for three-week enrichment courses, $3350; and for the six-week academic courses, $5750.
Spain The all-inclusive 2004 cost for one month was $4700.

FOR MORE INFORMATION, CONTACT:

The TASIS Schools, U.S. Office
1640 Wisconsin Avenue, NW
Washington, D.C. 20007
202-965-5800
800-442-6005 (toll-free)
Fax: 202-965-5816
E-mail: usadmissions@tasis.com
World Wide Web: http://www.tasis.com

TASIS–THE AMERICAN SCHOOL IN SWITZERLAND AND THE TASIS TUSCAN ACADEMY OF ART AND CULTURE IN ITALY

SWITZERLAND: LANGUAGE, ARCHITECTURE AND DESIGN, ART, PHOTOGRAPHY, COMPOSITION WORKSHOP, AND TOEFL REVIEW ITALY: ART HISTORY AND STUDIO ART

LUGANO AND CHÂTEAU D'OEX, SWITZERLAND
CAPITIGNANO, TUSCANY, ITALY

Type of Program: *Switzerland—Lugano*: Intensive foreign language study, architecture and design, photography, expository writing, and TOEFL review; *Switzerland—Chateau-d'Oex:* Intensive French language instruction; *Italy—Capitignano, Tuscany:* Art history and studio art

Participants: *Switzerland:* Coeducational, ages 6–18; *Italy:* Coeducational, ages 15–19

Enrollment: *Switzerland:* 300; *Italy:* 25

Program Dates: *Switzerland:* Four weeks June–July; three weeks July–August; *Italy:* three weeks July–August

Program Directors: Switzerland: Betsy Newell, Dean Topodas, Berkley Latimer, David Damico; *Italy:* John Smalley, Melissa Eichner

LOCATION

Lugano, Switzerland Nestled in the foothills of the southern Swiss Alps, with spectacular views, the TASIS campus is a compact cluster of historic buildings and new facilities. It overlooks the attractive resort town of Lugano and is 2 miles from Agno International Airport and less than an hour's drive from Milan (Malpensa) International Airport in Italy. The idyllic setting allows for a wide range of enjoyable activities, including windsurfing, pleasure cruises to lakeside hamlets, picnics, and hiking to picturesque villages.

Château d'Oex, Switzerland Located in the French-speaking canton of Vaud, the area offers outstanding opportunities for French language learning and an appreciation of the area's natural beauty.

Capitignano, Tuscany, Italy The campus is located in the Mugello area, an undiscovered treasure in the heart of Tuscany. The campus is ideally located one hour outside of Florence, and the other principal towns of Tuscany are easily within reach.

BACKGROUND AND PHILOSOPHY

Founded in 1956 by Mrs. M. Crist Fleming, TASIS is a coed college-preparatory American boarding school for students in grades 6–12 and postgraduates.

The Summer Programs began thirty-two years ago and were designed to offer American and international students an opportunity to study abroad and a chance to live in a truly international environment. The French Language Program, located in Château d'Oex, was founded thirteen years ago. The Tuscan Academy of Art is the latest addition to the summer course offerings.

PROGRAM OFFERINGS

Four- and three-week courses in English as a second language, French, Italian, and German are offered during the months of June, July, and August. Expository writing and architecture and design are offered during the first session; photography and TOEFL review are offered during the second session only. The age range is 14–18, and the average class size is 11. Courses such as drama, video making, art, and computer language learning programs complement intensive classroom work, offering creative options for the practice of oral communication skills. Progress reports are mailed home to parents at the end of the session.

Le Château des Enfants (CDE) An international summer camp for students ages 6–10, Le Château des Enfants offers English and French instruction. Emphasis is placed on acquiring oral skills in the target language through music, drama, games, excursions, and activities as well as classroom study.

Middle School Program (MSP) This program is specifically designed to cater to the needs of preadolescents, ages 11–13. The program offers intensive French and English as a second language.

TASIS French Language Program (TFLP) This program in Château d'Oex offers intensive language instruction for 13- to 17-year-olds and an optional six days at the end of the four weeks in the south of France.

Tuscan Academy of Art and Culture This program is ideal for students who intend to enroll in an AP art history course as well as for those who simply wish to obtain knowledge of Italian Renaissance art and to develop their artistic talents. The program offers art history and studio art courses to students between the ages of 15 and 19 during the second summer session.

ENROLLMENT

In Lugano, 300 students represent as many as forty different countries. In Château d'Oex, approximately

70 students enroll from all over the world, including the Americas, Europe, and Asia.

EXTRA OPPORTUNITIES AND ACTIVITIES

Lugano All students participate in afternoon sports and activities. Students choose from a variety of sports, including swimming, aerobic dance, basketball, cross-country running, soccer, softball, tennis, and volleyball. The afternoon activities include art, photography, and computer club. Weekend excursions provide ample opportunity for students to explore local areas of interest. Full-day excursions to Como and Milan, Lucerne, and Valley Verzasca and half-day excursions to nearby places of interest, such as Swiss Miniature in Melide and the antique street markets in Como, are organized. Optional weekend travel destinations (at an extra cost) include such cities as Florence, Nice, Paris, Venice, and Verona.
Château d'Oex Hiking, rock climbing, tennis, swimming, basketball, and soccer are offered. Weekend destinations include Geneva, Interlaken, Zermatt, and Gstaad.
Capitignano Swimming, tennis, basketball, and hiking are offered. The program also includes workshops by local visiting artists and frequent excursions to Florence and cultural excursions to renaissance towns such as Lucca, Pisa, and San Gimignano.

FACILITIES

Lugano The program uses all of the boarding school facilities of The American School in Switzerland. The historic Villa de Nobili houses the administrative offices, dining rooms/terraces, classrooms, and dormitory areas. Villa Monticello contains classrooms, a computer center, and dormitories. Hadsall House houses an audiovisual lab, a recreation center, and a snack bar, as well as dormitory accommodations. The art and photography studios are adjacent. The new M. Crist Fleming Library holds 20,000 volumes. On-campus sports facilities include a new gymnasium, an outdoor pool, a fitness center, and two multipurpose hard courts.
Château d'Oex The historic wood-carved chalets, set in the heart of the village, are home to TASIS students. They house dormitories, classrooms, a dining room, and recreation areas. There is a tennis/basketball court and ping-pong tables in the garden the main chalet. Nearby facilities include a swimming pool, soccer field, and beach-volley.
Capitignano The estate has art studios, a swimming pool and two tennis courts. Dormitories are in restored Tuscan farm houses.

STAFF

There are 60 full-time summer staff members (the staff-student ratio is 1:5). Qualified classroom teachers also undertake supervisory responsibilities, including coaching sports, chaperoning trips, dormitory coverage, and the "in loco parentis" role. Counselors work alongside teachers in the dorms, on excursions, on the sports fields, and in recreational activities to help provide a caring environment for students.

Many of the staff members are current or former TASIS faculty members, and counselors are alumni from all TASIS programs.

COSTS

For Lugano and Château d'Oex, Switzerland, the all-inclusive cost for a four-week session in 2004 was $4650. The cost for the three-week session and the Tuscan Academy of Art and Culture Program was $3800. The TASIS French Language Program, with the additional optional week to Nice, South of France, amounts to $5650. There are no additional fees, with the exception of long-haul airfare, the optional European weekend travel costs, personal spending money, and health insurance and medical expenses.

For more information, contact:

The TASIS Schools, U.S. Office
1640 Wisconsin Avenue, NW
Washington, D.C. 20007
202-965-5800
800-442-6005 (toll-free)
Fax: 202-965-5816
E-mail: usadmissions@tasis.com
World Wide Web: http://www.tasis.ch

UNIVERSITY OF CHICAGO

GRAHAM SCHOOL OF GENERAL STUDIES

SUMMER PROGRAMS FOR HIGH SCHOOL STUDENTS

CHICAGO, ILLINOIS

Type of Program: Academic enrichment, college credit
Participants: Coeducational, sophomores and juniors in high school
Enrollment: 175
Program Dates: Begins June 20, end dates vary
Head of Program: Jeffrey Rosen, Associate Dean

LOCATION

The University of Chicago is located in the historic Hyde Park neighborhood of Chicago, 7 miles south of the Loop, as the city's downtown center is called. Hyde Park has been home to artists and writers throughout the last century, and 60 percent of the University's faculty members live in the neighborhood. Diverse and vibrant, Hyde Park offers all the amenities of a small college town—bookstores, restaurants, cafés, and shops—but is only a quick train, bus, or bike ride from the treasures of downtown Chicago, America's third-largest city. The beaches and biking and jogging paths of Lake Michigan are a short walk away.

BACKGROUND AND PHILOSOPHY

The University of Chicago was founded in 1892 to inspire excellence in liberal arts education as well as in a variety of professions. A leader in higher education since its inception, the University College (for undergraduates) focuses on a broad liberal education in the humanities, the sciences, the social sciences, and the arts. The University's Summer Programs for High School Students, offered through the Graham School of General Studies, reflect the University's overall emphasis on a commitment to intellectual challenge, critical thinking, and personal discovery. The programs also offer a college-preparatory environment in which students can test their intellectual limits and learn to make thoughtful and informed decisions about their academic future. All courses are offered for college credit.

PROGRAM OFFERINGS

High school students have four program options.

Summer College for High School Students
Students take courses with University of Chicago students and may take two, three, or four courses that are three to ten weeks in length, depending on the schedule they choose.

Insight This program consists of three-week, intensive courses in which students can explore their personal intellectual passion in depth and in a hands-on environment. Topics include law writing, Egyptology, and animal behavior, and new offerings are added annually.

Research in the Biological Sciences This program offers intensive theoretical and practical experience with current research techniques, in and out of the laboratory, in the biological sciences.

Stones and Bones This program provides students with an opportunity to join undergraduate and graduate students on a paleontological expedition. After two weeks of training in geology and evolutionary biology on campus, students apply their knowledge for two weeks at an expedition site in Wyoming. In summer 2001, students discovered a complete dinosaur skeleton that may be a smaller cousin of Tyrannosaurus Rex. Students are invited to join the dig and find out for themselves what will be uncovered this summer!

ChicaGO!—The Traveling Academy
Interdisciplinary courses in Western civilization are offered overseas. Overseas locations change annually.

ENROLLMENT

Students are drawn from throughout the United States. Students who complete their sophomore or junior year before the summer are welcome to apply. Admission is competitive and administered on a rolling basis. The University is committed to a diverse student body, and that commitment is reflected in the summer programs.

DAILY SCHEDULE

Students in the Summer Quarter for High School Students program take two courses simultaneously. Weekly classroom and lab hours vary depending on the length of the course—the shorter the course, the more intensive the work. Courses are offered on the Hyde Park main campus. Courses are scheduled from 8 a.m. to 8:30 p.m., and students choose their own course schedule. There are a variety of possible course combinations; courses are three to ten weeks in length, and students take a total of two to four courses in a summer.

Students in the Insight and Research in the Biological Sciences programs can expect to be in class-related activities—whether in the classroom, the lab, the field, tutorials, or small-group work—all day.

Residential students take their meals together in the dormitory dining hall three times a day, and there are many other cafés, coffee shops, and cafeterias on campus.

EXTRA OPPORTUNITIES AND ACTIVITIES

In the evening and on weekends, a full program of social and recreational events is available, and students can participate as they have interest. Dances, concerts, movies on the quads, lectures, a fine arts festival, DOC Films (the oldest student-run film organization in the country), barbecues, study breaks, and more are normally planned. Excursions to Great

America Amusement Park, Ravinia Music Festival, Chicago Cubs or Chicago Fire (soccer) games, and behind-the-scenes visits to Chicago's world-class museums are also part of the extracurricular schedule. Students are encouraged to organize their own events with the help of the Resident Advisers who live in the dormitory with students.

The Reynolds Club is the hub of student activity in the summer. Students play pool, discuss current events with friends, get a snack, study, read, or just relax among the Gothic gargoyles.

Each summer, a series of college-preparatory workshops are offered. They cover many topics of interest to the college-bound student, including preparing the college admission application and essay, making the most of the admission interview, and honing study skills for college-level work.

The city of Chicago offers something for everyone and is especially attractive and active in the summer. Summer participants explore ethnic neighborhoods, discover the wonders of the Shedd Aquarium or the Adler Planetarium, admire the Impressionists' works at the Art Institute, shop along the Magnificent Mile, take a Ferris-wheel ride on Navy Pier, cruise the Chicago River on an architectural tour, hear outstanding jazz and blues, or savor the many cuisines of the city's restaurants.

FACILITIES

The University's facilities are open to all summer students. Computing clusters (including one in the dormitory), e-mail and Internet access, the libraries, the laboratories (if related to a student's course work), and athletic facilities are among the resources available for study, research, and recreation.

On campus, Robie House, considered Frank Lloyd Wright's finest creation, is open for tours; the Smart Museum of Art houses the University's collection of fine arts that span a period of 5,000 years; the Oriental Institute museum is home to the University's collection of ancient Near Eastern artifacts; and the gallery of the Renaissance Society fosters an understanding of contemporary art and introduces international artists to Chicago audiences.

Residential students live in a University dormitory in a double room with a roommate.

STAFF

Courses are taught by University faculty members and advanced graduate students, many of whom are nationally and internationally recognized in their fields. Insight courses may be taught by other professionals from the University or the Chicago area because of their recognized expertise in a particular discipline.

A staff of trained Resident Advisers (RAs), normally University of Chicago undergraduates, live in the dormitory with summer students. They are available to provide advice and guidance as students acclimate themselves to college living, the campus, and the city. They are responsible for fostering a comfortable and supportive residential environment for all students. In addition, they plan, implement, and attend all of the social and recreational activities. The RA staff is supervised by a Residential Program Director and an Assistant Director, who are graduate students or other adults. They, in turn, report to the Associate Dean.

MEDICAL CARE

All students are required to have adequate health insurance coverage for injury, accident, or major illness. Students who are not covered are required to purchase health insurance, which is available through the University. In addition, all students pay a health services fee that entitles them to care through the Primary Care Group at the University of Chicago Hospitals. A physician and a therapist are on call 24 hours a day. Students must have required immunizations (including two vaccinations against measles, consistent with state of Illinois law) before classes begin.

RELIGIOUS LIFE

The University maintains no religious affiliation. Rockefeller Chapel is the center of religious life at the University, and weekly ecumenical services are held there in the summer. Centers for a number of other faiths are available to students.

FINANCIAL AID

Financial aid, which is awarded on the basis of need and academic merit, is available. Awards are made on a rolling basis, and early application is encouraged. A completed Financial Aid Form as well as the parents' most recent tax return are required for consideration. Financial aid is awarded for tuition costs only; there is no aid available for room and board.

COSTS

Tuition costs vary from program to program. In 2004, the Summer College for High School Students cost $2075 per course. Insight students paid between $2075 and $2750 per course. Research in the Biological Sciences cost $4767. Room and board for all these programs cost $425 per week. Stones and Bones cost $4150 plus $2800 for room, board, and transportation. ChicaGO—The Traveling Academy was $6895, all costs included.

TRANSPORTATION

The city of Chicago is served by Chicago–O'Hare International Airport and Midway Airport (closer to the University). Students are advised of airport shuttle services upon their acceptance to the program, and students must make their own transportation arrangements to and from the airport at both the beginning and the conclusion of the program.

APPLICATION TIMETABLE

Applications are accepted through mid May and students should access the Web site below for the specific date. Admission decisions are made on a rolling basis. Because admission is selective and limited, early application is encouraged. In addition to the application form, students must submit a personal essay, two letters of recommendation from teachers, and a current transcript.

For more information, contact:

Valerie Huston, Secretary
Summer Session Office
Graham School of General Studies
University of Chicago
1427 East 60th Street
Chicago, Illinois 60637
773-702-6033
Fax: 773-702-6814
E-mail: uc-summer@uchicago.edu
World Wide Web: http://summer.uchicago.edu

UNIVERSITY OF CONNECTICUT

UCONN MENTOR CONNECTION

STORRS, CONNECTICUT

Type of Program: Mentorship program; provides students with academic enrichment in a focused interest area
Participants: Coeducational, students currently in grades 10–11
Enrollment: 85
Program Dates: July 11–July 29, 2005
Head of Program: Dr. Joseph Renzulli, Director, Neag Center for Gifted Education and Talent Development

LOCATION

UCONN Mentor Connection is located in the heart of New England on the University of Connecticut's campus. Storrs is approximately 40 minutes southeast of Hartford, 2 hours southwest of Boston, and 2½ hours northeast of New York City. UCONN is less than an hour from historic Mystic Seaport and the Connecticut shoreline and less than 2 hours from Newport, Rhode Island.

BACKGROUND AND PHILOSOPHY

UCONN Mentor Connection was founded on the belief that it is essential for students to have the opportunity to manifest their talents in high levels of creative productivity. The program's goals are to recruit highly motivated, academically talented teenagers from throughout the nation who can benefit from a stimulating summer program; to allow students to achieve their highest potential by participating in unique, real-world mentorship experiences; to increase students' awareness of their personal strengths and options; and to nurture their talents.

Creative productivity results from the interaction of above-average ability, creativity, and task commitment (motivation), and each of these can be developed and nurtured through authentic opportunities to conduct real research. The university setting provides an especially promising context for creative productivity, because firsthand inquiry is the core of almost all daily work. The purpose of Mentor Connection is to allow students to participate in real-life experiential research projects.

PROGRAM OFFERINGS

UCONN Mentor Connection offers approximately thirty different mentorship sites in all areas of the arts and sciences. Each site provides direct, apprentice-based involvement with faculty members and advanced graduate students at the University. Sites include advertising, archaeology, astronomy, biological research, biotechnology, chemistry, communications, creative writing, education, engineering, environmental research, mathematics, molecular and cell biology, music, pharmacy research, physics, plant science, puppetry, statistics, and Web page design.

Participants in the UCONN Mentor Connection program take on the role of a practicing professional, experience real-world problem solving, and develop a collaborative relationship with a researcher in their area of interest. Participants also have the opportunity to earn 3 college credits through the University of Connecticut, provided certain requirements are met.

ENROLLMENT

UCONN Mentor Connection welcomes applications from a wide variety of students. Motivated, creative, resourceful, enthusiastic, inquisitive, and academically inclined are only a few of the adjectives that describe UCONN Mentor Connection students. Students must be willing to engage in exciting challenges, learn how to conduct investigations in an area of interest, and sustain a long-term commitment to a project.

Roughly half of the students are Connecticut residents, and the rest come from out of state. Participants have the opportunity to make friends with other students who share similar interests, but who come from very different backgrounds than they do.

DAILY SCHEDULE

9–4	Mentorship
5	Dinner
6	Group meeting
6:30–10	Evening activities

Optional hands-on workshops in college and career planning are offered in the evening.

EXTRA OPPORTUNITIES AND ACTIVITIES

There are optional group activities every evening and organized field trips every weekend. UCONN Mentor Connection celebrates students' projects with a large, formal banquet at the end of the program.

FACILITIES

Students are housed in dormitories at the University of Connecticut, and they receive three meals a day in a University dining hall. While at UCONN Mentor Connection, students can take advantage of some of the University's intramural athletic facilities, the University library, and the University computer center.

COSTS

Tuition is $3000 and includes room, board, field trips, activities, and the option to earn 3 credits. Students should not bring more than $50–$100 spending money for the three-week program. Tuition is due June 24, 2005.

APPLICATION TIMETABLE

Initial inquiries are welcome after January 3, 2005. The application deadline is May 2, 2005. The application packet must include essays, teacher recommendations, and a school transcript.

FINANCIAL AID

A limited number of full and partial tuition scholarships are available for qualified applicants from the state of Connecticut who demonstrate financial need.

FOR MORE INFORMATION, CONTACT:

Heather Spottiswoode or Betsy McCoach
University Mentor Connection
University of Connecticut
2131 Hillside Road, U-7
Storrs, Connecticut 06269-3007
860-486-0283
Fax: 860-486-2900
E-mail: heather.spottiswoode@uconn.edu
World Wide Web: http://www.gifted.uconn.edu

PARTICIPANT/FAMILY COMMENTS

"This program is not summer school. It doesn't teach basic, boring stuff over and over again. This program is hands-on. It is an experience in life. Students get to actively participate in a project or in research in which they choose to be involved. The people at the program are unbelievable. The mentors are fascinating and interesting. Everyone has a different background and a different life story. . . .This program has changed my life. I know what college will be like, I have decided on my future major, I have broadened my interests, and I have made 80 new friends."

UNIVERSITY OF MARYLAND

YOUNG SCHOLARS PROGRAM AND THE ARTS! AT MARYLAND

COLLEGE PARK, MARYLAND

Type of Program: College preparation
Participants: Coeducational; Young Scholars Program, rising high school juniors and seniors; The Arts! at Maryland; rising high school juniors and seniors and college freshmen and sophomores
Enrollment: Approximately 200 students per program
Program Dates: The Arts! at Maryland, June 20–July 10, 2004; Young Scholars Program, July 11–30, 2004
Heads of Program: Terrie Hruzd, Program Manager, Summer and Special Programs

LOCATION

Programs are held at the University of Maryland, College Park. The University is the leading public research institution in the mid-Atlantic region and ranks seventeenth nationwide among public universities in the 2003 *U.S. News & World Report* "America's Best Colleges." This year's incoming freshmen have an average GPA of 3.9 and SAT score of 1290. The University's location allows students to be a mere Metro ride away from the sights and culture of Washington, D.C., and a 45 minute trip—either by rail or car—from Baltimore, Maryland.

BACKGROUND AND PHILOSOPHY

The University of Maryland's Summer and Special Programs offers two pre-college programs. The Young Scholars Program allows rising high school juniors and seniors and college freshmen and sophomores to test their academic interests, gain exposure to campus life, and jump-start their college experience. Students choose from academic courses that are designed to be an introduction to a particular field of study. Moreover, students explore career options through field trips and guest speakers. Upon successful completion of the three-week program, students earn 3 academic credits. Participants should possess a deep commitment to learning, thrive in a competitive environment, and have an open mind that includes a spirit of adventure.

The Arts! at Maryland targets highly motivated high school juniors and seniors who are passionate about the arts and thrive in an energetic environment. The program is a collaborative, interdisciplinary experience that offers college credit as well as opportunities to meet and work with major artists in the Washington, D.C., area. The Arts! includes a culminating, collaborative performance and exhibition where students showcase their work. All students participate in a series of workshops, performances, and events as an introduction to interrelated disciplines while expanding their artistic horizons.

PROGRAM OFFERINGS

The 2004 **Young Scholars Program** offers twelve 3-credit courses: 21st-Century Learning Environments-Students, Learning, and Technology; American History as Viewed Through American Music; Classical Foundations-Diversity in the Ancient World; International Political Relations (ICONS); Introduction to Architecture-Discovering Architecture; Introduction to Astronomy; Introduction to Engineering Design; Introduction to Kinesiology-Discover Kinesiology; Modern Biology-The Science Behind the Headlines; Shakespeare in the Renaissance; Technology, Satellites, and Global Change; and The Interplay of Math and Games.

In 2004, **The Arts! at Maryland** offers seven 3-credit courses: Drawing I; Fiction Writing Across Cultures-Rising Originality; Multiples and Monoprints-Contemporary Printmaking Techniques; Musical Theatre Workshop; Poetry Writing Across Cultures-Renaissance Reverberations; Practicum in Choreography, Production and Performance I; and The Jazz Experience.

ENROLLMENT

Each course has an enrollment limit ranging from 15 to 40 students.

DAILY SCHEDULE

Participants begin their day with breakfast between 7:30 and 8:30 a.m. Classes and workshops meet Monday–Friday, 9 a.m.–4 p.m., with variations in the schedule depending on the particular course requirements. Lunch is held from noon–1:30 p.m. and varies depending on class schedules. Dinner takes place around 6 p.m. Students in The Arts! at Maryland attend workshops from 7:30–9 p.m.

EXTRA OPPORTUNITIES AND ACTIVITIES

Young Scholars Program participants enjoy scheduled weekend and evening activities designed to expose them to different facets of campus life. Activities include trips to nearby Washington, D.C., and Six Flags America in Largo, Maryland, as well as movie and bowling nights, Campus Recreation Center night, a pizza party, and an ice cream social.

Students participating in The Arts! at Maryland organize a cabaret coffee house that includes poetry, music, displays of artwork, and scene excerpts. Students also attend workshops, performances, and events in the Washington, D.C., area.

FACILITIES

Young scholars reside in on-campus housing or commute to the campus. The residence halls are air-conditioned, dormitory or suite-style accommodations. Residential particpants have the use of in-room telephones. For research and writing needs, all participants have access to the University's 1,700 computers in thirty-seven separate computing labs.

Students enjoy meals in two dining halls offering a selection of entrées at every meal. All residential students receive a meal card that provides for breakfast, lunch, and dinner; commuter students receive a meal card that provides for daily lunches.

STAFF

Students benefit from the wide range of impressive learning experience provided to them through all the courses. The highly qualified faculty members have both teaching expertise and experience and are published in their fields, with many being recipients of prestigious teaching awards.

MEDICAL CARE

If a student becomes ill or injured, she or he is taken to the Campus Health Center, a nationally accredited ambulatory health-care facility, located on campus, or to the nearest hospital, depending on the severity of the injury or illness.

RELIGIOUS LIFE

The University has fourteen chaplaincies. Many are housed in Memorial Chapel, and some provide services at off-campus houses of worship.

COSTS

The Young Scholars Program's course fee is $1249, which includes tuition for 3 credits, the use of campus facilities, and other course-related costs. In addition, students pay either $1299 for the residential package (room, board, linen service, social activities, scheduled seminars on college and scholarship preparation, and parking) or $349 for the commuter package (fourteen lunches, social activities, and scheduled seminars on college and scholarship preparation). Commuters must also obtain a parking permit.

Fees for The Arts! at Maryland include the course fee of $1299 (tuition for 3 credits, the use of campus facilities, and other course-related costs) and either the residential package fee of $1369 (room, board, linen service, social activies, and parking) or the commuter package of $425 (fifteen lunches and social and scheduled activities). Commuters must also obtain a parking permit.

The course fee includes most course expenses, but students should expect to purchase books, class packets, and classroom supplies. Approximately $50–$75 per week should cover most miscellaneous expenses, including gifts, snacks, film, meals, and other items. Additional information on fees and costs is available at the Web site listed below.

TRANSPORTATION

The University of Maryland is located between two major airports, BWI and Reagan International. Subway and train stations are connected to the University by the Shuttle-UM bus service. The Shuttle-UM service route also offers transportation services throughout the vicinity at predetermined locations, five days a week.

APPLICATION TIMETABLE

Applications must be accompanied by the nonrefundable $50 processing fee. Because the programs have limited enrollment, early application is encouraged. The application process begins February 16, 2004, and course registration begins February 24. The deadline for application with best consideration is May 7. Student are notified approximately ten days after the application, transcript, and recommendation forms have been received.

The entire course fee and residential- or commuter-package fee are due by May 20 for The Arts! at Maryland Program and June 21 for the Young Scholars Program.

For more information, contact:

Terrie Hruzd, Program Manager
Summer and Special Programs
Office of Continuing and Extended Education
4321 Hartwick Road, Suite 208
College Park, Maryland 20740
301-405-8588
E-mail: hruzd@umd.edu
World Wide Web: http://www.summer.umd.edu

PARTICIPANT/FAMILY COMMENTS

"The program was fabulous. Maryland was my only choice for college. This was a great way to learn about campus life and get acquainted."—Natalie Adams, student, Young Scholars Program

"This was a life altering experience. I was exposed to new ideologies, cultures, and people. No one should pass up this amazing opportunity."—Student, Young Scholars Program

UNIVERSITY OF MIAMI

SUMMER SCHOLAR PROGRAMS

CORAL GABLES, FLORIDA

Type of Program: Academic enrichment, college credit
Participants: Coeducational, grades 11 and 12
Enrollment: Approximately 100
Program Dates: June 26 through July 15
Head of Program: Brian L. Blythe, Director of High School Programs, Division of Continuing Studies

LOCATION

The University of Miami (UM) undergraduate campus is nestled in the heart of Coral Gables, a picturesque suburb that blends tropical splendor with Mediterranean-inspired architecture. Walkways link the flora-filled campus courtyard, plazas, arboretums, and quadrangles. Lake Osceola, located in the center of the campus, is surrounded by a red brick sidewalk and feeds into the canals that wander through the lush grounds. Enjoyment of nature, sports, water, and outdoor life are possible year-round in south Florida.

BACKGROUND AND PHILOSOPHY

The University of Miami is the largest private research university in the Southeast. Established in 1925, UM is known for its outstanding faculty, groundbreaking research, diverse student body, and history of excellence in athletics. The University's Summer Scholar Programs (SSP) were established in 1991. Taught by outstanding University of Miami faculty members, these programs present a unique opportunity for students to earn college credit in specific areas of concentration. The programs offer intensive three-week studies. Students learn firsthand what college is like by living and studying on campus. Students also take laboratory classes and have the opportunity to learn about their particular interests by visiting local sites that are relevant to their fields of study.

PROGRAM OFFERINGS

High school students have the opportunity to choose from a variety of programs to meet their interests and should contact the University for specific program offerings. Fieldwork and laboratory research enhance the academic teachings and help students explore potential careers. Previous summer scholars studying broadcast journalism have visited local television studios and produced their own segments; marine science students have completed oceanic studies on the coral reefs of south Florida; film students have produced their own films; and health and medicine students have visited the medical campus and talked with medical experts. Programs currently scheduled for 2005 include Art, Broadcast Journalism, Filmmaking, Global Politics, Health and Medicine, Marine Science, Sports Management, and Young Writers.

ENROLLMENT

Students are drawn from areas throughout the United States. Admission is competitive and administered on a rolling basis. Any student who has completed their sophomore or junior year of high school is welcome to apply. To be accepted, students must demonstrate high academic standards, with a minimum B average. In order to participate in the health and medicine program, students must also have completed two science courses, one of which must be a biology course, with a competitive grade point average. The rich cultural diversity of the University of Miami is reflected in all of the Summer Scholar Programs.

DAILY SCHEDULE

Summer scholars enroll in two courses that meet daily. The length of each class varies depending on lab work, field trips, and lectures; however, summer scholars are in class-related activities all day. All students live in campus residential housing, which is supervised by trained staff members. Three meals each day during the week and two meals each day during the weekend are provided. All programs have evening curfews. With the exception of students walking to shops across the street from the campus, students are not to leave the campus on their own during their stay. Several evening and weekend activities are planned, and anyone may participate.

EXTRA OPPORTUNITIES AND ACTIVITIES

Though the Summer Scholar Programs are challenging academic programs for students, evening and weekend activities are also scheduled, which allow students the time to enjoy the camaraderie of fellow scholars and experience the tropical flavor of the region. Excursions to local hot spots, a snorkeling trip, and the opportunity to take advantage of the University's facilities, such as the wellness/fitness center, are available during the students' free time.

FACILITIES

The University of Miami's facilities, including the Richter Library and the Smathers Wellness Center, are available for student use during the program. During free time, students have access to the University's billiards tables, fitness room, and tennis, volleyball, and basketball courts. Computer facilities are accessible when required for class projects, and the residence hall rooms also have Internet access for those who bring their own computer. Students share an air-conditioned room with another scholar in on-campus residence halls that are staffed with program resident assistants.

STAFF

Classes are taught by UM faculty members who engage students in discovery through discussion, debate, lab experiments, and field trips as appropriate to the program. They are available for questions, addressing concerns, or assistance.

University of Miami undergraduate and graduate students, as well as recent graduates, live in the residential halls and serve as teaching assistants in the classroom. Many have served as UM resident advisers during the academic year and are available to promote a comfortable learning environment for the scholars.

MEDICAL CARE

All students are required to have adequate health insurance coverage for injury, accident, or major illness. There is a health center on campus that can handle injuries, illnesses, and prescriptions. In addition, Health South Hospital is directly across from the University, in case of serious injury or medical emergency.

RELIGIOUS LIFE

The University has no religious affiliation; however, opportunities for worship are available on campus for members of a variety of faiths.

COSTS

The cost of attending the Summer Scholar Programs in 2004 was $3850, which included tuition, textbooks, instructional supplies, residence hall lodging, the meal plan, field trips, access to the Student Health Center and the Smathers Wellness Center, all planned excursions, and some extracurricular activities. A nonrefundable application fee of $100 and deposit of $500 (due within two weeks of acceptance into the program) are applied toward the final cost of the program.

FINANCIAL AID

A limited number of partial scholarships may be available for students who demonstrate financial need and high academic performance. Parents' personal income and tax return information are required. Students who apply for assistance must have all applications and documentation postmarked by March 15, 2005.

TRANSPORTATION

For those who plan to arrive by air, Miami International Airport is near the University. Upon arrival at the airport, students are met by a resident assistant, who directs students to the baggage claim and guides them to transportation that will deliver them directly to the residence hall on campus. Flight arrangements are the responsibility of the student, and transportation costs are not included in the cost of the program.

APPLICATION TIMETABLE

Application for admission to the Summer Scholar Programs required materials: a current transcript, letter of introduction and interest, and letter of recommendation from a teacher, and a nonrefundable $100 application fee are accepted through the middle of May. Because admission is selective and space is limited, applicants are encouraged to apply early. When a particular program becomes full, applicants are considered for their second choice if they desire or are placed on a waiting list. A deposit of $500 must be received within two weeks of acceptance. Students who withdraw from the program after May 20, 2005, forfeit their $500 deposit. The University reserves the right to cancel any program due to insufficient enrollment or events beyond its control. In such cases, applicants are considered for their program of second choice or given a refund of all fees and deposits. All programs are subject to change without notice.

FOR MORE INFORMATION, CONTACT:

Mr. Brian Blythe, Director of High School Programs
Summer Scholar Programs
Division of Continuing Studies
P.O. Box 248005
Coral Gables, Florida 33124-1610
305-284-6107
800-STUDY-UM (toll-free)
Fax: 305-284-2620
E-mail: ssp.cstudies@miami.edu
World Wide Web: http://www.miami.edu/summerscholar

UNIVERSITY OF PENNSYLVANIA

PENN PRECOLLEGE PROGRAM, PENN SUMMER SCIENCE ACADEMY, AND PENN SUMMER ART STUDIOS

PHILADELPHIA, PENNSYLVANIA

Type of Program: Credit and noncredit summer programs for academically talented high school students

Participants: Coeducational, students completing grades 10–11

Enrollment: Approximately 400 students

Program Dates: (2005) Penn Precollege Program: June 25 to August 6; Penn Summer Science Academy and Penn Summer Arts Studio: June 25 to July 23

Head of Program: Dr. Rosalie Guzofsky, Director of Professional Programs and Summer Sessions

LOCATION

The University of Pennsylvania's Summer High School Programs take place on its historic, tree-lined, 260-acre campus. One of the oldest universities in the United States, Penn's campus is a wonderful combination of ivy-covered structures in the 19th-century tradition and architecturally unique facilities designed by such contemporaries as Louis Kahn and Eero Saarinen. All undergraduate and graduate buildings are integrated into a largely pedestrian campus, which includes the largest open-stack library in the nation, state-of-the-art laboratories, a leading museum of archeology and anthropology, the Hospital of the University of Pennsylvania, and the Annenberg Center for the Performing Arts.

Summer months in Philadelphia are always exciting and eventful. A brief trolley ride from campus leads to the site of the First Continental Congress, the Liberty Bell, the home of Betsy Ross, or the new National Constitution Center. Walk across South Street Bridge and visit fashionable Rittenhouse Square and its boutiques and cafés. Philadelphia is known for its diverse restaurants, theaters, museums, shops, and most of all, its many neighborhoods—from Center City's urban sophistication and South Street's funkiness to bustling Chinatown, the Italian market, and the historic charms of Society Hill and Old City.

BACKGROUND AND PHILOSOPHY

Founded by Benjamin Franklin in 1740, Penn was the fourth college of the colonies. Among the ten largest research complexes in the U.S., the University of Pennsylvania is now one of the world's leading educational, research, and health services institutions. A private university and member of the Ivy League, Penn is known for its academic excellence.

PROGRAM OFFERINGS

Penn's summer programs are intended for academically talented, committed students. Each program provides many academic, cultural, and recreational activities for residential and day students. The goal is to provide a rewarding, rigorous, and pleasurable introduction to university life. Penn wants its students to be ahead of the curve, enthusiastically prepared for all the challenges of their freshman year of college.

Penn Precollege Program Students in the Penn Precollege Program get a head start on college life by earning undergraduate credit for the courses they take alongside Penn undergraduates. The credits earned may be applied to a Penn degree if the participant is later accepted as an undergraduate student and are generally transferable to other colleges and universities. Comprehensive course offerings range from Acting, Arabic, and Archeology, to Creative Writing, History, Biology, Jazz Styles, Psychology, Microeconomics, Ethics, Alternative Medicine, International Relations, Psychology, and Law and Society. Precollege students are carefully selected to insure that they have the most enriching and positive experience possible. Courses are intense, demanding, and fast-paced. Students are encouraged to enroll in two courses, a full-time summer course load. Numerous social, intellectual, and cultural activities are available to precollege students.

Successful applicants to this program must have completed their sophomore or junior year of high school by June. They must have an outstanding record of achievement and demonstrate maturity, discipline, and the ability to undertake course work at Penn. College Board scores (PSAT, SAT, or ACT) are required, along with a letter of recommendation, official high school transcripts, and a writing sample.

Penn Summer Science Academy (PSSA) The Penn Summer Science Academy offers the opportunity for high-achieving high school students to pursue in-depth study in one of two areas: biomedical research or physics. This noncredit program consists of both guided and independent lab and field projects, lectures and workshops, and computer labs and seminars, all of which are taught by Penn scientists. The pace is rapid, the work is hard, and students are constantly challenged to go beyond their studies to experience what research and practice are really like in these areas. Intensive study and lab work (9 a.m. to 4 p.m. every day) is supplemented by a wide range of additional academic opportunities.

Applicants must have completed their sophomore or junior year in high school by June. All applicants must have outstanding records and demonstrate ability to do creative work. A teacher recommendation, a transcript, and an essay are required.

Penn Summer Arts Studios (PSAS) In spring 2001, Penn's nationally ranked fine arts department moved into Addams Hall, a new high-tech, state-of-the-art facility. It is the hub for the Penn Summer Art Studios. PSAS is an intensive, noncredit program consisting of studios in the following areas of concentration: animation, architecture, ceramics, digital video, drawing and painting studio, and photography. Instruction by Penn faculty members is both technical and conceptual. Studios take place from 9 a.m. to 4:30 p.m., Mondays through Fridays.

Applicants must have completed their sophomore or junior year in high school by June. Depending on the program, prerequisites may be necessary. All applicants must have strong academic records and show evidence of ability to do creative work. A high school transcript and teacher recommendations are required. It is recommended that students submit a portfolio in any format (CD, slides, Web site, or the actual work) with their applications.

ENROLLMENT

Penn Precollege, Penn Summer Science Academy, and Penn Summer Arts Studio students comprise a talented, international, and multicultural group. While the majority of students come from throughout the U.S., about 15 percent are international students.

DAILY SCHEDULE

The daily schedule is varied. Breakfast, lunch, and dinner are served in the Commons. Before and after classes, students may avail themselves of a variety of recreational and social activities that are offered each day. The coursework is very rigorous, so students should expect to spend approximately 4 to 6 hours each day in study and class preparation. There are evening chat sessions, student groups, and floor and program activities each evening. Curfew during the week is 10:30 p.m., and on weekends, midnight. Students are able to leave campus with written permission from their parents.

EXTRA OPPORTUNITIES AND ACTIVITIES

All programs are designed to provide social and intellectual enrichment. Students enjoy an extraordinary range of activities, including trips to the beach; the mountains; New York City; Washington, D.C.; Six Flags Great Adventure; restaurants; museums; theaters; and concerts. Community service opportunities are available and encouraged. Penn has two indoor pools and gymnasiums, track and football fields, and tennis and basketball courts. Residence Counselors organize daily jogs, in-line skating, biking, and Ultimate Frisbee, basketball, baseball, and volleyball games.

Students also participate in a series of college study skills and preprofessional workshops, including the College Survival Skills series, SAT preparation series, and the Future in Focus professional forums. They also enjoy field trips and guided tours of professional and other sites, such as the Children's Hospital of the University of Penn and Penn's Veterinary Hospital. Students are also invited to write for the *Summer Pennsylvanian,* which is widely regarded as one of the best college papers in the nation.

FACILITIES

Residential students are housed in the Quad, the tradidtional first-year student residence. All rooms are air-conditioned and wired for Internet service, telephone, and cable television. The residents are supervised seven days a week by a trained residence hall staff. The dorm also has pool and Ping-Pong tables, vending machines, study and television lounges, and a computer lab. Academic support services are also available, on campus.

STAFF

Each program is staffed by Resident Counselors (RCs). RCs are outstanding Penn undergraduates who take an active role in working with the students, from helping them adjust to dormitory life to acting as counselors, tutors, and guides around the campus and the city. The ratio of RCs to students is about 1 to 15. The College House Dean and Penn residential staff and counselors are also in residence.

MEDICAL CARE

All summer school students are required to participate in the University's health insurance program. Emergency or urgent care is provided by the Childrens' Hospital of Philadelphia or by the Hospital of the University of Pennsylvania Emergency Room, and routine care is provided through Student Health Services.

RELIGIOUS LIFE

University of Pennsylvania is a secular institution. Its chaplain coordinates many programs and is available to all students at any time. Numerous religious centers are also available to students on and around the campus.

COSTS

Precollege Program costs are estimated at $4900 to $6800 for residential students and $2900 to $4900 for day students (depending on the number of courses taken). PSSA and PSAS costs are estimated at $2700 for day students and $4600 for residential students. Residential costs include housing, dining, program fees, and tuition.

TRANSPORTATION

A variety of transportation options are available in Philadelphia and from the Philadelphia Airport to the campus.

APPLICATION TIMETABLE

Applications are welcome throughout the year. The application deadline is April 30. Completed applications are evaluated within one week of receipt.

FOR MORE INFORMATION, CONTACT:

Summer High School Programs
University of Pennsylvania
3440 Market Street, Suite 100
Philadelphia, Pennsylvania 19104-3335
215-746-6900
Fax: 215-573-2053
World Wide Web: http://www.upenn.edu/summer

UNIVERSITY OF SOUTH CAROLINA SUMMER PROGRAMS

CAROLINA MASTERS SCHOLARS ADVENTURES SERIES

COLUMBIA, SOUTH CAROLINA

Type of Program: Summer enrichment programs in art, business, computer arts, criminology, engineering, filmmaking, forensics, law, medicine, music, testing, writing, and more.
Participants: Academically talented middle and high school students.
Enrollment: 10–20 participants per program.
Program Dates: Weeklong programs open to both residential and commuter students.
Heads of Program: Cynthia Steele, Director.

LOCATION

Chartered in 1801 as South Carolina College, the University of South Carolina still resides on its original site in Columbia, the state capital. The campus has grown from it origins of one building on the historic Horseshoe to 175 facilities on 330 acres. The University offers more than 350 undergraduate and graduate courses of study. Programs range from liberal arts and sciences to business, law, medicine, and other professional studies, many of which have been widely recognized for their academic excellence. The Carolina Masters Scholars (CMS) Adventures Series residential students live in an honors dorm, located in the historic Horseshoe area of the University. The honors dorm houses only summer academic youth programs during the summer.

BACKGROUND AND PHILOSOPHY

Students are encouraged to embark on the journey to become a Carolina Master Scholar by attending the invigorating, academically challenging CMS Adventures Program. A Carolina Master Scholar is any student who participated in three adventures programs over a six-year period. The program runs in three-year cycles, grades 6–12. CMS students receive special admission tracking to the University and special alumni status.

The CMS Adventures Series is designed to be academically challenging, socially interactive, and culturally simulating. A small group of students in grades 6–12 gathers on campus for a weeklong academic exploration of the arts and sciences.

Serving students in the Southeast as well as local students, the program exposes them in greater depth to a given subject and encourages independent thinking. Students enroll in a one-week course taught by a University faculty member, a community educator, or a professional in the field. Course content ranges from the arts and humanities to the sciences to professional schools. Classes are lecture and interactive, often with field trips included. The program accepts both residential and day students.

PROGRAM OFFERINGS

Adventures in Advancement (Testing skills) SAT/ACT testing plus career counseling.
Adventures in America: Patriotic Trips Visit the historical sites of South Carolina.
Adventures in Business: Investment Learn what and how to invest personal monies.
Adventures in Digital Film Making Write and produce a digital film.
Adventures in Forensic Science Scientific exploration of solving a crime.
Adventures in Information Technology and Expert Systems Learn how to develop an Expert System.
Adventures in Law and Criminology From crime to trial, explore the law.
Adventures in Medicine Exploration in gross anatomy.
Adventures in Science Experiment with a multitude of sciences.
Adventures in the Visual Arts Hands-on art production.
Adventures in Writing Anthology of writing styles.

ENROLLMENT

Students from across Canada, the U.S., Mexico, and Europe are eligible to attend this series. Students can attend from one week to six weeks of programs. Weekend stays are available. The programs are designed by age group and activities and studies reflect that fact.

DAILY SCHEDULE

Day students attend from 8:20 a.m. to 5 p.m., Monday through Friday, with a Sunday orientation. Residential students attend from 2 p.m. Sunday through 4 p.m. on Friday. Weekend stayovers are available. Students attend classes from 9 a.m. to 3:15 p.m. In the afternoon, residential staff members lead students in recreational activities. Each evening, residential students enjoy activities such as swimming, craft workshops, movies, barbecues, and field trips to local events. At the end of the week, students participate in a closing ceremony and make short presentations to parents, staff members, teachers, and friends, which reflect on the events of the previous week.

EXTRA OPPORTUNITIES AND ACTIVITIES

The Adventures Series combines academic, physical, and social outlets. Outdoor games, swimming, scavenger hunts, or other physical activities take place in the late afternoon. Evenings are a special time at the University, with events that help build friendships, create memories, and bond the community. Events include going to a minor-league baseball game, bowling, board game frenzy night, and the weekly pizza party. Each Friday afternoon, the students make a presentation to parents and faculty members on the week's studies. A light reception is included in this event.

FACILITIES

The University campus features federalist architecture with the latest in high-technology classrooms that blends the old with the new. All classes are taught in the College of Study, which has the best facilities the College has to offer for that discipline.

The Sol Blatt Physical Education Center has two indoor Olympic-size swimming pools with an outdoor deck. The center features indoor courts, outdoor tennis courts, and gymnasiums. A supply of equipment, such as basketballs or volleyballs, is available.

Residential students live in the Honors College dorm. Living in an honors dorm is a community experience. Students have the opportunity to interact socially and academically with other summer academic youth. While living in an honors dorm, participants are expected to be a contributing member of the community as well to make responsible decisions on their health and safety, time management, and behavior. All residents of an honors dorm are held to the trends of the Carolinian Creed, which can be found on the Web at http://www.sa.sc.edu/creed/index. Honors dorms are suite-style residence halls.

STAFF

The Department of Continuing Education at the University of South Carolina has 2 professional staff members dedicated to summer academic programs. In addition, there is a registration coordinator and business manager.

Faculty members are selected by each academic department to ensure the best instructor for the subject and the age group. A lead faculty member coordinates other faculty members from his or her discipline to allow a full ensemble of expert knowledge on the Adventures topic. In the field, professionals are selected for the Adventures Series that can benefit most from the on-the-front-line personnel. This is especially true in the professional schools, such as law, medicine, and criminal justice.

Professionals in the fields of risk management, safety, and first aid extensively train all counselors. Further, to ensure the safety of the program's youth, all counselors working with a youth group are subject to a South Carolina Law Enforcement (SLED) background check.

The University's Summer Academic Programs division selects the best and brightest from its academic-year students to be counselors for CMS programs. Typically, the CMS Adventures staff counselor–student ratio is 1:10. In addition, there is a graduate student who acts as the programmed hall live-in manager. Counselors are typically hired in February. With registration confirmation materials, participants receive a complete listing of the counselors working with the CMS Adventures Series.

MEDICAL CARE

The Thomson Student Health Center (open 8:30–4:30, Monday through Friday) is located on campus and provides a variety of ambulatory primary-care services for students attending the CMS Adventures Series. For after-hours or emergency care, the Palmetto Baptist Hospital is less than 1 mile from campus.

COSTS

The fee structure for 2004 was as follows: early-bird residential, $700; residential, $800; early-bird day, $450; day, $500; and travel programs, $1050. This included food, accommodations, certification, instruction, recreational and social activities, transportation, all materials, laundry, and snacks. Parents are advised to call to check program availability as some of the programs fill fast.

TRANSPORTATION

The University is a 15-minute drive from Columbia Metropolitan Airport and less than 5 minutes from Amtrak or bus service. If requested, staff members are glad to meet and/or return students at the designated public transit area and provide transportation to and from campus. Students are transported in state-approved vehicles only. Parents who drive their students to the University may receive a tour of the facility and an opportunity to meet the staff. On the final day of each session, there is a reception/presentation from 2 to 4 p.m., which parents are encouraged to attend.

APPLICATION TIMETABLE

To register, applicants should complete the CMS Adventures Series registration form (available at the Web site listed below) and send it with payment to CMS 2004 at the address listed below. Applications may also be submitted via fax or online; payment for these applications must be made by credit card. In addition to the application, a teacher/counselor recommendation letter should be submitted, as well as GPA, PSAT, SAT, or ACT scores (if applicable).

Applications postmarked prior to mid-May receive a special early-bird discount (see program selection). For convenience, VISA, MasterCard, and Discover Card are accepted. Credit card payments may be sent to the fax number listed below. The cardholder's signature is required to process credit card transactions. All methods of payments should be made payable to the University of South Carolina. The University's Federal Tax I.D. number is 57-6001153.

Parents of applicants should note that the CMS registration fee includes a $200 nonrefundable portion. This advance fee is only refunded if the applicant is not accepted into the program. Full refunds are processed only if the University of South Carolina cancels a program. No refunds are made after thirty days prior to the start of the program, and the date is determined by postmark. There are no exceptions. Applicants should send withdrawal or refund requests to CMA at the address listed below. For convenience, withdrawal or refund requests may be faxed to the number listed below. Refunds are in the form of a check only. Allowable refunds are mailed from the University within three to four weeks of accepted refund requests and/or program cancellation.

FOR MORE INFORMATION, CONTACT:

Carolina Master Scholars
Continuing Education
University of South Carolina
1600 Hampton Street Annex, Suite 203
Columbia, South Carolina 29208
803-777-9444
Fax: 803-777-2663
E-mail: confs@gwm.sc.edu
World Wide Web: http://www.ced.sc.edu/adventures

UNIVERSITY OF SOUTHERN CALIFORNIA

EXPLORATION OF ARCHITECTURE

LOS ANGELES, CALIFORNIA

Type of Program: Intensive academic introduction
Participants: Coeducational; ages 15–18, grades 10–12
Enrollment: 100
Program Dates: One-, two-, or three-week programs beginning in July.
Head of Program: Paul R. Tang, AIA, School of Architecture Instructor

LOCATION

The University of Southern California (USC) is located in downtown Los Angeles, which is situated between the southern California mountain ranges and the Pacific Ocean. The campus is located just north of the Museum of Natural History, near where the I-10 and I-110 freeways meet. Hollywood, Los Angeles International Airport (LAX), and the Pacific coast are no more than 20–30 minutes from campus. The University currently occupies 155 acres. The wide variety of urban and environmental conditions in the area make Los Angeles an excellent laboratory for the study of architecture, from hillside housing in Hollywood to high-rise office towers and recreational centers such as the newly constructed Staples Center. USC is close to the various cultural and historical districts of Los Angeles such as Chinatown, Olivera Street, Koreatown, and Old Pasadena. Students can visit film studios, hear music at the Hollywood Bowl, or visit world-class museums such as the Los Angeles County Museum of Art and the Norton Simon Museum. Through joint programs with the University's neighbors and campus safety programs, USC has become one of the safest urban campuses in the United States. In fact, USC's Department of Public Safety is one of the largest private security forces in the world today.

BACKGROUND AND PHILOSOPHY

One of the most comprehensive and rewarding programs of its kind in the country, USC's Exploration of Architecture high school program was begun in 1985. Today, students can choose to participate in the one-, two-, or three-week programs. The programs are intended to provide high school students from across the country and around the world with an intensive, in-depth, and "hands-on" introduction to the design of the built environment and the experience of architectural studies at the university level. The ultimate goal is to help students make a highly informed decision regarding their college and career direction while at the same time exposing them to the ethnic, cultural, and artistic diversity of one of the country's largest metropolitan centers.

Previous architectural study is not a requirement for admission; all students need is their enthusiasm and an interest in architecture. Participants benefit from the involvement of several full- and part-time faculty members, teaching assistants, and resident advisers. Participating students experience firsthand what it is like to tackle design projects in a real studio setting.

Outside of the classroom, students tour various architectural points of interest including construction sites, firm offices, important historical and contemporary structures, and museums. Students have the opportunity to explore the full spectrum of Los Angeles' built environment, from downtown high-rises to the houses of Frank Lloyd Wright.

PROGRAM OFFERINGS

The design studio experience is the focus of the program, emphasizing the basic skills of drawing and model building. Studio projects explore the design of cities, furniture, landscapes, and buildings. At the end of each week, students present their projects to faculty members and visitors for a discussion of their ideas, intentions, and execution. Each week builds upon the lessons and projects of the previous week. Students participating for three weeks are advised on how to use their work from the program to produce a portfolio for college admission. In addition, students have the chance to use the school's computer design labs to explore applications such as AutoCAD and FormZ. Students also learn about the restoration of historic architecture by visiting structures like Frank Lloyd Wright's Freeman House and the Gamble House by Greene & Greene. Participants attend lectures and studios with USC architecture faculty members and get assistance from upper-division architecture students. Finally, while living at a USC residence hall, students receive an important introduction to college life. Furthermore, participants have the chance to meet and make friends with other students from around the country and around the world.

ENROLLMENT

The Exploration of Architecture program can accommodate up to 100 students. Students from nearly all cultural and socioeconomic backgrounds have participated in this program. Typically, about 5 percent of students are international, while approximately 20–30 percent of domestic students are from outside California.

DAILY SCHEDULE

After breakfast, the day's activities begin at 9 a.m. and continue until 9 p.m. No two days follow the same schedule; one day may begin with studio time or lecture, while another may begin right away with a

tour. Lunch and dinner breaks are typically taken at noon and 5 p.m., respectively. Students must observe a strict curfew of 10:30 p.m.

FACILITIES

Studios and lectures take place in Watt and Harris Halls. In 2004, students were housed in Marks Tower on the USC campus. Students are able to purchase some supplies at the Pertusati Bookstore. Health and fitness facilities are open to students over 16 years of age.

MEDICAL CARE

Exploration of Architecture requires that all students pay the weekly student health fee, which was $12 per week for summer 2004. This fee is subject to change.

COSTS

Costs for the 2004 program were $1075 for one week, $1850 for two weeks, and $2450 for three weeks. The cost covered meals, housing, transportation, and a studio fee. Prices are subject to change. Approximate cost of supplies is $75. Students should consider bringing a minimum of $40 to $50 per week for personal spending money.

FINANCIAL AID

Financial aid is offered to students on the basis of financial need. Students who wish to be considered for financial aid must also submit copies of their parents' tax returns along with a copy of their high school transcripts.

TRANSPORTATION

Transportation is provided for all field trips and off-campus activities. Students arriving at LAX are provided with shuttle service to and from the campus.

APPLICATION TIMETABLE

Applications are processed beginning April 1. Applications received after the deadline are reviewed on a space-available basis.

For more information, contact:

Director of Admissions
USC School of Architecture
Watt Hall 204
Los Angeles, California 90089-0291
213-740-2420
Fax: 213-740-8884
E-mail: uscarch@usc.edu
World Wide Web: http://www.usc.edu/dept/architecture/explor

THE UNIVERSITY OF THE ARTS

PRE-COLLEGE SUMMER INSTITUTE

PHILADELPHIA, PENNSYLVANIA

Type of Program: Visual and performing arts; media and communications
Participants: Students entering their sophomore, junior, or senior year of high school, as well as recent graduates, ages 16–19
Enrollment: Approximately 250
Program Dates: July 10 through August 5, 2005
Head of Program: Erin Elman, Director of Pre-College Programs; Melissa DiGiacomo, Assistant Director of Pre-College Programs

LOCATION

The University of the Arts (UArts) is unlike any other university. It is the only university in the nation teaching a broad range of visual, performing, and communication arts and focusing exclusively on the arts. The University comprises three colleges and a liberal arts division. Summer program courses are offered in each college of the University: College of Art and Design, College of Media and Communication, and College of Performing Arts.

UArts is located in the heart of Center City Philadelphia on the Avenue of the Arts (South Broad Street). It is in the center of the arts and culture district and within walking distance of museums, galleries, theaters, and the cultural life of the city.

BACKGROUND AND PHILOSOPHY

The Pre-College Summer Institute was created as an opportunity for students who have had varying interests and backgrounds in the visual and performing arts to study together in a university environment. Some participants enroll to discover their individual talents. Others want to build on their education. Still others seek to learn about specific careers in the arts. The programs are flexible enough to address all of these various needs.

PROGRAM OFFERINGS

Visual arts programs include PREP and ArtsSmart. The PREP program is modeled after the Freshman Foundation year at the University of the Arts and provides serious high school seniors and recent graduates with study in drawing and two- and three-dimensional design.

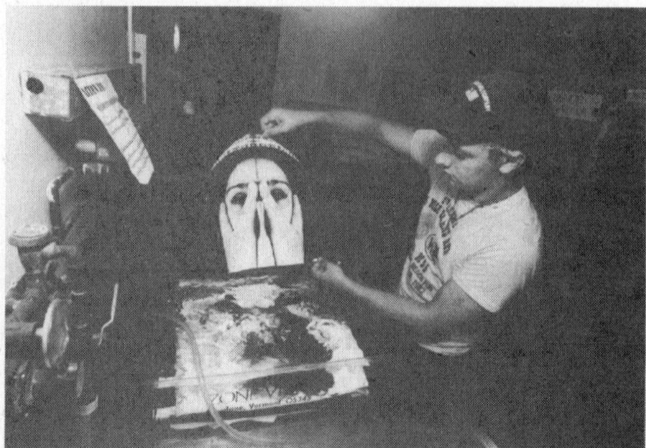

The ArtsSmart program allows high school students to explore their individual talents and interests, learn new art and design skills, and develop a better, more comprehensive portfolio. The program provides students with an arts education experience comparable to one at the college level. It is also a great opportunity for young artists to experiment with new materials and arts forms as they develop their portfolios. Students in the ArtsSmart program choose two concentrations as well as two electives.

The media workshops provide students with intensive study in animation, computer game design, screen directing, video production, or writing for film and television, using state-of-the-art equipment and facilities.

Performing arts programs include the four-week process-oriented drama and musical theater programs, as well as a two-week intensive jazz performance program for instrumentalists and/or vocalists.

Interested students should visit the UArts Web site (http://www.uarts.edu/precollege) for the complete list of concentrations and electives that are offered.

ENROLLMENT

The Pre-College Summer Institute enrolls students from all over the world. A letter of recommendation from an art instructor or guidance counselor and a portfolio or audition tape are required for a scholarship.

DAILY SCHEDULE

9:00	Classes begin
12:00–1:00	Lunch
5:00	Classes end
7:00	Social activities
10:00	Curfew (Sunday–Thursday)
11:00	Curfew (Friday and Saturday)

EXTRA OPPORTUNITIES AND ACTIVITIES

Activities include museum visits, concerts, films, sports events, trips to the New Jersey shore, barbecues, and other social events. At the end of the program, there are a reception and an exhibition of works created by the visual arts students and a showcase presentation by the performing arts students.

FACILITIES

The University of the Arts campus comprises ten buildings with classrooms, studios, theaters, galleries, lounges, residential apartments, and administrative offices.

Visual arts students work in recently renovated studios with fully equipped shops for working in ceramics and jewelry/metals, photography labs, and state-of-the-art multimedia labs.

The facilities used by performing arts students reflect the growing range of tools available to professional composers, artists, and performers. They include a music technology studio, a recording studio, editing suites, practice rooms, and light-filled dance studios with mirrors and resilient floors with 4-inch suspension for safety and comfort.

STAFF

The staff includes a year-round Director, Erin Elman, and Assistant Director, Melissa DiGiacomo.

Faculty members are expert, practicing professionals in the visual and performing arts. They provide instruction and direction to developing student artists who are serious about academic study. The faculty members understand the demands of their respective professions and are expert at imparting knowledge, technique, energy, and discipline.

MEDICAL CARE

The University's Health Services Office is open weekdays, 8 a.m. to 7 p.m., and is professionally staffed. In instances of medical emergencies, students are taken to Graduate Hospital or Thomas Jefferson Hospital for care.

COSTS

For 2005 tuition and housing pricing information, students should contact the precollege department directly. Information is also available on the Web at http://www.uarts.edu/precollege.

FINANCIAL AID

A limited number of partial-tuition scholarships are available for visual and performing arts students. Interested students should apply early. The deadline is in May.

TRANSPORTATION

The University is easily accessible by public transportation from New Jersey and suburban Philadelphia via the regional rail lines of PATCO and SEPTA, respectively. UArts is also convenient to Amtrak and Greyhound stations and to the Philadelphia International Airport.

APPLICATION TIMETABLE

Scholarship and registration deadlines are in May.

For more information, contact:

Pre-College Programs
The University of the Arts
320 South Broad Street
Philadelphia, Pennsylvania 19102
215-717-6430
800-616-ARTS (toll-free outside Pennsylvania)
Fax: 215-717-6433
E-mail: precollege@uarts.edu
World Wide Web: http://www.uarts.edu

USDAN CENTER FOR THE ARTS

SUMMER PROGRAM

SOUTH HUNTINGTON, NEW YORK

Type of Program: Study in music, art, theater, dance, creative writing, and chess
Participants: Coeducational, ages 6–18
Enrollment: 1,750
Program Dates: Two sessions, June 28 to August 13 (seven weeks); June 28 to July 23 (four weeks)
Head of Program: Dale Lewis, Executive Director

LOCATION

Usdan Center for the Creative and Performing Arts is situated on 200 acres of rolling woodland in Huntington, Long Island, just 1 hour from Manhattan.

BACKGROUND AND PHILOSOPHY

Usdan Center is a nonprofit summer arts camp chartered by the New York Board of Regents. Usdan was developed in the mid-1960s to become the New York area's "mini-Lincoln Center" on Long Island. At Usdan, young people realize artistic potential and personal growth in an atmosphere that inspires lifetime friendships with others who share their love of the arts. Usdan's award-winning campus features seventy theaters, studios, galleries, and rehearsal halls incorporating fine architectural, acoustical, and natural details in which learning is fun and productive.

Usdan's program offers intensive four- and seven-week courses of study in one specific area of its six major departments: music, art, theater, dance, writing, and chess. Instruction takes place in groups determined by age and experience. Students enroll on the basis of interest, except in the piano, jazz ensemble, ballet theater, jazz and tap, and repertory theater programs, which require auditions.

PROGRAM OFFERINGS

Students select a major class in musical theater, drama, repertory theater, technical theater, or theater workshop offered by the Theater Department; photography, ceramics, cartooning, computer graphics, jewelry, painting, sculpture, or video, offered by the Art Department; ballet or jazz and tap, offered by the Dance Department; and piano, orchestra, band, jazz ensemble, or chorus, offered by the Music Department. In band and orchestra, the 2-hour major class is split into a 1-hour group lesson on the student's individual instrument and a 1-hour band or orchestra rehearsal. Other major programs include chess, creative writing, and nature, ecology and design.

After choosing a major, each student chooses a minor interest activity. Available minor classes are creative writing, painting, ballet, modern, tap, band, orchestra, chamber music, folk guitar, chorus, chess, and recreation.

Each student swims for one period a day in the Center's Olympic-size pools. Instruction is offered from beginning to advanced levels in American Red Cross certificate programs.

Two hours of advance credit for college are available for high school students through New York University.

ENROLLMENT

One of the largest summer arts camps in the United States, Usdan enrolls 1,750 students each summer. In many courses, students may study as beginners. Classes for advanced students are also offered.

Usdan Center is not a residential program, so most students live in the New York metropolitan area. Each year, however, about 100 students from other parts of the nation and from other countries study at Usdan while living with friends or relatives in the New York metropolitan area.

DAILY SCHEDULE

9:30	Arrival
10–11:55	Major class
12:05–12:25	Lunch
12:35–12:55	Festival concert
1:10–2	Swimming
2:15–3:05	Minor class
3:05–3:15	Ice cream break
3:30	Departure

This is the schedule for Senior Division students (grades 7–12). Students in the Junior Division (grades 2–6) have their swimming period and minor class in the morning and their major class in the afternoon. All students are expected to attend class each day. The Center does not permit smoking on its grounds.

EXTRA OPPORTUNITIES AND ACTIVITIES

A highlight of Usdan Center is the daily concert series, known as the Festival Concerts. Every day in July, this series presents a performance by an artist of international renown. In August, Usdan students present daily music, dance, and theater performances. Among the artists who have appeared at the Festival Concerts are The Canadian Brass, Yo-Yo Ma, Emanuel Ax, Eliot Fisk, The Tokyo String Quartet, Paula Robison, James Galway, Jane Monheit, Savion Glover, The Dance Theater of Harlem, Ana Sokolow's Player's Project, and stars of the Broadway stage.

Usdan's visual arts students show their work in the Center's Goetz Exhibition Gallery. Video students produce segments for New York–area television stations in the Center's Block Television and Video Arts Center, and theater students present dramatic productions in the Lemberg Drama Center.

FACILITIES

The Center's 200-acre campus has seventy award-winning studios, theaters, art galleries, and television studios. The buildings are spread out for acoustic isolation and are grouped by department. Among the

outstanding structures is the Lemberg Drama Center, a complex of five buildings for teaching and performing plays and musicals. Usdan has eight large dance studios with sprung floors and a 1,000-seat amphitheater where large-scale productions take place. The Art Department, in addition to its Goetz Gallery and Hexter Museum, features the Block Television and Video Arts Center. The Block Center has control rooms, studios, and editing suites with broadcast-quality equipment for television productions. Usdan has two modern swimming pools, including an Olympic-size pool for bathing and diving.

STAFF

Usdan Center's faculty is composed of artist-teachers from New York's foremost professional arts companies and schools. One hundred master teachers are assisted by assistant teachers who are conservatory-trained professionals in the arts. A complete faculty roster is available from the Center.

MEDICAL CARE

The services of a registered nurse are available at Usdan's infirmary. The Center is located a short distance from Long Island's major teaching hospitals.

RELIGIOUS LIFE

Students of all faiths are warmly welcomed at the Center, a beneficiary of UJA-Federation of New York. The Center does not conduct religious programs.

COSTS

Tuition for the seven-week season is $2500; tuition for four weeks is $2100. An additional fee for daily bus transportation varies by location; the range is $600–$850 for the seven-week season. There are no fees for materials and books, although photography students supply their own film and video students may need extra videotapes. Total fees for tuition, registration, transportation, and medical insurance generally amount to $3000 to $3700.

FINANCIAL AID

For each of the past five seasons, at least $100,000 has been raised to provide scholarships, which are awarded on the basis of family need.

TRANSPORTATION

Usdan Center is in Huntington, Long Island, within the postal designation of Wheatley Heights, New York. The Center is 1 hour by car from New York City and is also accessible by train. It is 10 minutes from Republic Airport in Farmingdale. All students commute to the Center daily on chartered buses leaving from hundreds of pickup points in Manhattan, Brooklyn, Queens, Westchester, Nassau, Suffolk, and New Jersey.

APPLICATION TIMETABLE

The Center maintains a New York City office from September to June, and inquiries are welcome at any time. Applications are accepted from October through June.

FOR MORE INFORMATION, CONTACT:

Admissions Office
Usdan Center for the Creative and Performing Arts
420 East 79th Street
New York, New York 10021
212-772-6060
World Wide Web: http://www.usdan.com

or

Long Island Admissions/Summer
Usdan Center for the Creative and Performing Arts
185 Colonial Springs Road
Wheatley Heights, Long Island, New York 11798
631-643-7900

VALLEY FORGE MILITARY ACADEMY

SUMMER CAMP

WAYNE, PENNSYLVANIA

Type of Program: Traditional outdoor challenge
Participants: Boys, ages 8–16
Enrollment: 320
2004 program dates: Saturday, June 19, to Friday, July 16
Heads of Program: COL Thomas A. DeBlois, Commandant of Cadets, and MAJ Jeff Bond, Director of Summer Camp

LOCATION

Valley Forge is located on 120 acres of beautifully maintained grounds in Wayne, Pennsylvania, just 15 miles west of Philadelphia and minutes from Valley Forge National Park.

BACKGROUND AND PHILOSOPHY

The Valley Forge Summer Camp is operated by the Valley Forge Military Academy (VFMA) Foundation and maintains the same high standards that have made that institution internationally famous. They are part of the foundation's comprehensive program for providing boys with the very best in recreational and educational opportunities. At Valley Forge, boys become men as they learn the ingredients of a successful and happy life.

PROGRAM OFFERINGS

There are several options for a fantastic camp experience. Four different camps are offered: a four-week overnight camp for boys, a coed six-week day camp, a coed tennis camp, and an overnight or day coed band camp.

The camps are divided into age-appropriate groups consisting of Pathfinders (ages 6–7), Pioneers (ages 8–9), Junior Rangers (ages 10–11), Raiders (ages 12–13), and Senior Rangers (ages 14–16). Each camp has several activity periods each day to challenge and build self-confidence in the campers' lives. The camp's uniqueness lies in its ability to enhance the lives of the campers through team building, esteem building, and helping all the campers realize their own innate ability to succeed. During these periods, campers participate in sports, swimming, go-carts, low ropes and high ropes courses, rappelling tower, wall climbing, drill, marching, orienteering, night patrols, and more. A Boy Scout can attend and earn merit badge requirements. There are at least five trips during the four-week stay that all campers participate in, depending on their ages. Some of these trips include Six Flags Great Adventure, Dorney Park, Paintball Skirmish, canoeing, an army base, and a Philadelphia Phillies baseball game.

There are several special activities to enhance the camping experience. For an extra fee, the academic program provides each camper with the opportunity to improve his skills in reading, English, or math on the elementary and middle school levels. The faculty of VFMA conducts classes in a relaxed and informal atmosphere. Class size varies between four and ten campers. Sessions are held five mornings each week for two weeks and are scheduled so as not to interfere with afternoon camp activities. There are other optional activities available on a first come, first served basis. Space is limited and an additional fee is charged. These programs include Competitive Marksmanship Training, Karate, and a horsemanship program. The Band Camp offers an excellent program through individual lessons, theory classes, concert band techniques, and camper/staff recitals for youths with one or more years of instrumental experience. Afternoons and evenings are rounded out with fun activities, such as sports, canoeing, swimming, and trips.

The day campers participate in all the activities of the overnight camp as well as the trips available on the week of attendance. The tennis camp offers professional instruction as well as the added dimension of mental training from a certified sports psychologist. Tennis and day campers begin their day at 9 a.m. and conclude at 4 p.m.

ENROLLMENT

Approximate numbers are as follows: 40 each in Band and Pioneers, and 100 each in Junior Rangers, Raiders, and Senior Rangers. Participants in Band Camp must already play a concert band instrument at the middle school level or better with a minimum of two years' experience. Valley Forge Military Academy summer campers represent more than twenty-two states and fourteen other countries.

DAILY SCHEDULE

7:00	Reveille
8:00	1st mess (Breakfast)
9:00-10:15	1st activity
10:15-10:30	Break to next challenge
10:30-11:45	2nd activity
11:45-12:15	Break to 2nd mess
12:15	2nd mess (Lunch)
13:15-14:30	3rd activity
14:30-14:45	Break to next challenge
14:45-16:00	4th activity
16:00-16:15	Break to next challenge
16:15-17:30	5th activity
17:30-18:15	Break to 3rd mess
18:15	3rd mess (Supper)
19:15-20:15	6th activity
20:15-20:30	Break to next challenge
20:30-21:30	7th activity
21:30	Back to barracks
22:15	Taps

The schedule varies on weekends and during field trips. Campers are required to follow the school rules, which include a code of conduct. Counselors receive conflict resolution training and work individually with their campers to resolve individual problems. The Director of Summer Camp will handle special circumstances.

FACILITIES

Campers stay on campus in one of five cadet barracks. Senior Rangers camp in a tent for several nights while at a local army base. The 120-acre campus has every facility necessary to ensure that each camper has an enjoyable and safe place to live and have fun.

STAFF

The staff of 160 men and women consists of approximately 45 counselors, 12 Assistant Camp Commandants, 6 Camp Commandants, food service staff, medical staff, teaching faculty, sports coordinators, and other personnel. The camp maintains an 8:1 camper-counselor ratio. All counselors and other professional staff desire to work with school-age children and receive special training to enhance the experience for each of the campers.

MEDICAL CARE

The Academy Health Center is staffed during camp. Minor ailments are treated promptly. Local hospitals are used for medical support beyond the capabilities of the Health Center.

RELIGIOUS LIFE

The Valley Forge Military Academy Summer Camp Chapel service is held every Sunday and is a nondenominational service that campers are required to attend. It is an essential part of their character development at Valley Forge. Arrangements can be made for campers of particular faiths to attend services locally.

COSTS

Charges for 2004 were as follows: Pioneer Camp, $3100; Raider/Ranger Camp, $3200; and Band Camp, $2900. Fees include the cost of room and board; use of all athletic facilities; instruction in athletics, leadership, campcrafts, and basic scouting skills; and camp uniforms. There is an additional fee of $175 for each camper's spending and activities allowance. The additional fees for specialty programs range from $250 to $400 and are available on a first come, first served limited basis until June 1.

TRANSPORTATION

Valley Forge Military Academy is approximately 40 minutes from both the Philadelphia International Airport and 30th Street Station. Valley Forge provides pickup and drop-off services for the start and end of camp.

APPLICATION TIMETABLE

Initial inquiries are welcome at anytime. Appointments to visit the campus are made on a daily basis. Invitations are sent for special campus visitation programs. It is recommended that parents and prospective campers schedule a visit at their earliest convenience. Camp applications are accepted starting in January and must include a nonrefundable $125 deposit. Character and medical references are required and acceptance letters are sent promptly. The balance of the fees is due on or before the reporting date to camp.

FOR MORE INFORMATION, CONTACT:

MAJ Jeff Bond, Director of Summer Camp
Valley Forge Military Academy & College
1001 Eagle Road
Wayne, Pennsylvania 19087
610-989-1253
Fax: 610-989-1260
E-mail: jbond@vfmac.edu
admissions@vfmac.edu

VILLAGE CAMPS

INTERNATIONAL SUMMER CAMPS

SWITZERLAND, AUSTRIA, ENGLAND, FRANCE

Type of Program: Academic, language (English, French, German), leadership, and sports
Participants: Coeducational, ages 7–18
Enrollment: Leysin, Switzerland: 180 (maximum); Zell am See, Austria: 80 (maximum); Hurstpierpoint, UK: 180 (maximum); Ardèche, France: 50 (maximum)
Program Dates: 2 to 2½ weeks, June 29 through August 21
Head of Program: Ed Ivy and Roger Ratner, Directors

LOCATION

With twelve camps in four countries, Village Camps offers the ultimate European camp experience. Participants can enjoy the spectacular mountain setting of Leysin, Switzerland, with an awe-inspiring panoramic view across the beautiful Rhône valley to the distant French Alps, or the traditional English boarding-school setting in Hurstpierpoint, England. Camps in Zell am See, Austria, are ideal for campers who appreciate a choice of lake and mountain activities. One day, campers sail and windsurf on Lake Zell, and the next they hike through mountains at almost 2500 m. Camps in the Ardèche, France, are ideal for campers with a taste for action and adventure and those wanting to improve their French in a natural environment. Campers might find themselves navigating rapids on the Ardèche River in the morning and then crawling through some of the world's most beautiful caves that afternoon.

BACKGROUND AND PHILOSOPHY

More than 150,000 young people from every corner of the world have relished their sports, language, and academic experiences at Village Camps. The raison d'etre of each camp is to provide the distinctive challenge and utmost benefit of "education through recreation." Every event, activity, and experience is crafted so as to entertain and educate in a way that contributes to the well-being and personal development of each individual camper. The goal is to provide campers with all the tools needed to reach their full potential as they mature into young adults. To this end, a unique combination of peer support and camaraderie is encouraged so that campers feel comfortable within new environments as they face new challenges and engage in the kinds of character-building experiences that enrich their lives. Whether learning a new language or sport, developing leadership and communication skills, or strengthening academic knowledge to improve school performance, the result of time spent at Village Camps is a youngster who has grown in character and stature—while having had the time of his or her life. Thanks to the international flavor and *joie de vivre* at Village Camps, campers not only make lasting new friendships but also learn of and better understand new cultures and traditions. Each child leaves camp with new friends, new experiences, and memories that are to last a lifetime.

PROGRAM OFFERINGS

Village Camps is unique in offering campers such a wide variety of choice. There are twelve camps available in four countries to accommodate the varying needs of today's diverse youth.

Golf Camp-England This camp provides instruction and supervised play every weekday with PGA pros for all ability levels.

Junior Camp-Switzerland, England A perfect introduction to residential camp for children 7–9, this camp (with a supervision ratio of 1:5 or less) is specifically designed for younger campers and those away from home for the first time.

Language Camp (English/French/German)-Austria, France, Switzerland, England Each weekday, these camps provide three hours of practical instruction with qualified teachers. The focus is on gaining confidence in the spoken language through class-based activities and visits to local places.

Leadership Training Course-Switzerland This award-winning program provides active challenges and interactive workshop presentations for young people wishing to develop effective leadership skills.

Multiactivity Camp-Austria, France, Switzerland, England In the mornings, campers follow an action-packed schedule sampling a range of activities that are available. In the afternoons, campers have the opportunity to choose their favourite activities and to focus on improving in them.

Outdoor Adventure Camp-France In this program, campers follow an action-packed schedule that includes learning a range of outdoor activities, such as canoeing, rock climbing, and caving. The highlight of the trip is a two day 30 km descent of the Ardèche River in Canadian canoes.

Senior Camp-Switzerland A programme specifically designed for young adults, this camp develops their independence and encourages them to take responsibility for the success of their camp experience.

Soccer Camp-England Under the guidance of experienced coaches, campers experience 3 hours of drills and competition each weekday. The program is for all ability levels.

Tennis Camp-Austria, Switzerland, England All ability levels receive 3 hours of coaching and supervised play per weekday.

Video Making Camp-Austria Lights, camera, action. Participants learn all about making videos and video clips, from script writing to filming and from editing and directing to sound and lighting. The program comprises ten 3-hour periods with a specialist working on projects to be presented to the camp.

Village Super Camp-Switzerland Campers learn to learn more effectively—raising their grades, motivation, and confidence.

Web Design Camp-England The camp emphasises Microsoft FrontPage 2003, JavaScript, and writing in a "Flash-like" environment and each weekday offers 3 hours of Web site design and construction.

Once their specific camp activity is completed for the day, campers participate in their choice of exciting activities offered on-location and instructed by professionals. Camps are run in English and the language of the host country, but Village Camps' international staff can often speak an additional five languages, which generally include Spanish, Italian, Arabic, Russian, and Japanese.

Cultural excursions to local areas of interest are also an integral part of every camp. Campers in England visit the historic sites of London and the amusements of Brighton, while campers in Switzerland visit the Olympic museum, among other places. Overnight trips to mountain huts are popular at the camps in Austria, and the trip to a medieval castle in France is always a memorable time.

ENROLLMENT

Campers come to Village Camps from every corner of the world each year, ensuring a culturally diverse and enriching experience. All young people aged 7–18 are welcome at Village Camps. The maximum enrollment varies by camp.

EXTRA OPPORTUNITIES AND ACTIVITIES

Village Camps offers a multitude of activities that stimulate campers both mentally and physically. Day activities include aerobics, archery, arts and crafts, badminton, banana boat, basketball, canoeing, canyoning, caving, cookery, cricket, dance, drama, horseback riding, ice skating, kayaking, lacrosse, mini golf, mountain biking, mountain hut overnight, music, netball, photography, orienteering, rafting, rappelling, rugby, rock climbing, Rollerblading, ropes course, sailing, soccer, softball, squash, summer sledding, swimming, table tennis, tennis, trekking, beach volleyball, weight training, and wind surfing. Evening activities include camp fires, imaginative games, and spectacular events designed to stir the imagination and reinforce the bonds between campers.

Campers participate in activities according to their age and skill levels and often have the opportunity to choose their favourites. Village Camps offers a unique and popular award system at all camps: When a camper has successfully completed a certain number of selected activities—judged against a set of participation and skill criteria—he or she is presented with a special Village Camps coloured bandanna. The more activities completed, the more bandannas collected; a prestigious black bandanna is awarded for 21 activities. Credits from one summer are not forgotten—they are carried forward to the next camp as each child gains skills and confidence as well as a sense of achievement.

FACILITIES

At each location, Village Camps has one facility that houses all campers at that location. Except for in the Ardèche which, true to its outdoor adventure theme, has tents, all facilities include living quarters for campers and staff, a dining room, recreation areas, classrooms, a common room, and site-specific special features, such as a video editing room in Austria, a theatre in England, and a panoramic deck in Switzerland.

STAFF

Every year Village Camps provides some of the best international camp directors, educators, sports coaches, and counsellors in Europe. The staff goes through a meticulous selection process and many are recommended by previous staff members. Counsellors are chosen for their character, leadership qualities, language skills, and demonstrated ability to interact well with children. All of Village Camps' counsellors are at least 21 years old and most are older. In addition, each one of them has prior experience in childcare, either with Village Camps or elsewhere. The ratio of campers to counsellors averages 6:1 and is often less.

MEDICAL CARE

The well-being of all the campers is of paramount importance. All camp locations have a health care manager or nurse with extensive knowledge of first aid and are close to a hospital or medical center.

COSTS

The costs of the camps vary by their duration and type and range from Sw Fr 2,275 to Sw Fr 3,800. Included in the costs are room and board, excursions, and instruction in the available activities. Laundry service, transport services, and certain activities are not included but can be purchased for an additional fee. Pocket money and medical treatment costs are the parents' responsibility.

TRANSPORTATION

Village Camps is pleased to offer an escorted travel service to and from its programmes for children arriving at designated airports and train stations. Prices vary by location, ranging Sw Fr 60–250 for two way service.

APPLICATION TIMETABLE

There are no deadlines for application. However, in order to ensure a place at the camp of their choice, campers are encouraged to book before March, as camps become fully booked after that time. To receive a special "Early Bird" discount, the application and payment must be made before February 29, 2004. A deposit of Sw Fr 1,000 per child per session is payable at the time of booking. Final payment of camp fees, including any extra items, must be received by May 15. Bookings received after May 15 must be accompanied by full payment.

FOR MORE INFORMATION, CONTACT:

Ed Ivy and Roger Ratner, Directors
Village Camps
14 Rue de la Morache
1260 Nyon
Switzerland
41 22 990 9400
Fax: 41 22 990 9494
E-mail: camps@villagecamps.ch
World Wide Web: http://www.villagecamps.com

VISIONS

COMMUNITY SERVICE, CROSS-CULTURAL LEARNING, AND OUTDOOR ADVENTURE

NORTH AMERICA, SOUTH AMERICA, AUSTRALIA, AND THE EASTERN CARIBBEAN

Type of Program: Community service, outdoor adventure, and cross-cultural experiences
Participants: Coeducational, ages 14–18 (grades 9–12)
Enrollment: 350 total in twelve locations
Program Dates: Four weeks in July; three weeks in August
Heads of Program: Joanne Pinaire and Teena Beutel

LOCATION

VISIONS offers summer residential experiences based in Alaska, Montana, the South Carolina Sea Islands, Australia, the British Virgin Islands, Dominica, the Dominican Republic, Ecuador, Guadeloupe, and Peru. Housing is in a school or community building or in local homes at some sites in the heart of each community.

BACKGROUND AND PHILOSOPHY

Established in 1988, VISIONS offers uniquely integrated summer experiences for teenagers. Community service work is the focus of the programs, which feature an intentional blend of cross-cultural experiences and outdoor adventure. Students and staff members live and work together as a team. VISIONS emphasizes cooperative living in a supportive setting. Weekly circle meetings are a deliberate process for improving communication through reflection and focused listening. Under staff guidance, participants play the central role in building the trusting foundation of their program environment.

At every VISIONS site, projects encompass construction and other service such as tutoring or volunteering with children, the elderly, or the handicapped; environmental work in national parks and wilderness areas; or agricultural work. Participants learn carpentry skills from staff carpenters. Past projects include ground-up construction of low-income housing, schools, medical clinics, youth centers, and playground structures, and rehabilitation of housing and community buildings.

Time is always set aside for exploring surroundings. Depending on the location, outdoor activities include rock climbing, ice climbing, backpacking, rafting, snorkeling, sea kayaking, scuba diving, horseback riding, and sight seeing. Participants work and socialize with residents and attend ceremonies and cultural festivities. Relationships with local people provide the important contexts for understanding and learning about other cultures.

PROGRAM OFFERINGS

Alaska VISIONS has sites on the northern boundary of south-central Alaska, roughly 5 hours from Anchorage, near Wrangell St. Elias National Park. Projects in native villages include building playgrounds and recreation facilities, renovating and upgrading community buildings, and supervising children's activity programs. Alaska participants learn about Athabascan native culture and this state's unique frontier heritage. Recreation includes day hikes and extended backpacking trips in the Wrangell Mountains, an ice-climbing adventure that begins in a historic ghost town, trips to neighboring towns, and wildlife viewing.

Montana Participants live and work on Plains Indian reservations surrounded by abundant natural resources and stunning landscapes. Projects include renovating tribal buildings and elders' homes, constructing ceremonial structures, building playgrounds for schools and communities, tutoring or organizing day camp activities for children, and working on trails in primitive wilderness.

Renowned for its natural beauty, the "Last Best Place" offers recreation that includes backpacking, rock climbing, horseback riding, rafting, attending powwows, and sharing a sweat lodge with native friends. Participants learn firsthand about native traditions and history that has shaped Native American life on and off the reservations.

South Carolina Sea Islands Along the southeast U.S. shoreline are nearly 1,000 islands separated from the mainland by an intricate maze of waterways. These sea islands are a wondrous natural environment for wild birds and other water species. The isolation of the islands helped preserve a unique way of life that has endured for two centuries. Many island residents, the descendants of slaves, have retained a distinct black culture and language called Gullah, which is authentic English-derived Creole that mixes English words and syntax with Caribbean and West African dialects.

VISIONS groups partner with local organizations on needed projects such as renovation of low-income housing, construction of buildings and playgrounds, and tutoring in Head Start preschool programs. Recreation includes sea kayaking, swimming off the white sand beaches, overnight hiking, and sightseeing in and around historic Charleston.

The Dominican Republic This program offers service work and language immersion in a Spanish-speaking Third-World country. VISIONS works in a poor section of Santo Domingo. Past participants have built a medical clinic, schools, and housing. Every summer, VISIONS organizes an extensive day camp for Dominican children.

During free time, students experience the vibrant culture and beauty in and around Santo Domingo. Swimming, snorkeling, an overnight hike into the interior, and evenings of merengue dancing are some of the recreation activities offered. This program has a minimum requirement of two years of high school Spanish.

British Virgin Islands In the Caribbean British Virgin Island (BVI), VISIONS groups work on community projects in collaboration with the Ministry of Health and Welfare, National Parks Trust, Red Cross, Disaster Relief Services, and BVI Services. One group lives on Tortola, the largest of the British Virgin Islands; a second group lives on Virgin Gorda, a smaller neighboring island. Construction is the focus—housing from the ground up, public buildings, structures, and trails for the National Parks Trust. VISIONS also works with public school summer programs, the elderly, and subsistence farmers.

The BVI offers classic Caribbean beaches and coves that are perfect for snorkeling and scuba diving.

Trinidad Trinidad lies between the Caribbean Sea and the North Atlantic Ocean, northeast of Venezuela. Among its marvels are hundreds of species of birds, butterflies, reptiles, and many mammals, including anteaters, armadillos, and red howler monkeys. Trinidad is more prosperous than most Caribbean islands due to its petroleum and natural gas production and asphalt reserves. Nevertheless, high unemployment is persistent; at least 20 percent live in poverty.

VISIONS works in the Ward of Toco along the northern rainforest range on Trinidad's northeast tip. Toco's coastal communities are small, rural, and rustic, comprised mostly of fishermen and subsistence farmers. Toco's undeveloped beaches are major nesting grounds for leatherback turtles from March to August.

VISIONS service work encompasses assistance to community-based ecotourism initiatives such as construction of guesthouses, preservation of turtle and other wildlife habitats, and collaborations with the Trinidad Youth Council.

Guadeloupe Guadeloupe is a French language immersion experience on a Caribbean island that is unique for its blend of French and Caribbean cultures. VISIONS works on Basse Terre, one of the two main islands, in collaboration with the Ministry of Youth and Culture. With teenage Guadeloupeans, VISIONS participants undertake joint renovation projects designated by the government, and volunteer in public school programs.

Besides swimming and snorkeling, the group explores the numerous smaller islands of Guadeloupe; the colorful, fragrant open-air markets; and the exquisite countryside. This program has a minimum requirement of two years of high school French.

Dominica The "Nature Island" of the Lesser Antilles, with its lush, unspoiled beauty, stands apart from other Caribbean islands. A rainforest mountain range, which forms the north-south spine of Dominica, is alive with rare tropical birds and flowers. Whales and dolphins inhabit the coastal waters. The volcanic island soil is rich, rainfall is abundant, and hundreds of rivers and streams drain the island. Despite its natural beauty, Dominica's economy is strictly Third World.

VISIONS participants live and work on the Carib Reserve, home to the sole surviving original inhabitants of the Caribbean Islands. Work projects focus on pressing needs in Carib Territory, such as reforestation, supervising enrichment activities for children, renovating housing and community buildings, and constructing schools, cisterns, roads, and shelters.

Peru VISIONS Peru combines service work in a southeastern Andean village with discovery of ancient Inca and colonial Spanish cultures. Participants live in a highland community while accomplishing adobe construction projects, environmental work, and volunteering in the Pintacha School.

Students explore Peru's majestic landscapes by hiking the Inca Trail, rafting river gorges, and traveling to centuries-old marketplaces and resplendent historic sites. Groups learn local customs and sometimes participate in cultural traditions. They also work with and meet Andean farmers, educators, politicians, musicians, and artisans. This program has a minimum requirement of two years of high school Spanish.

Ecuador Ecuador, Mitad del Mundo, offers Spanish language and indigenous culture immersion in two communities: the rarely glimpsed indigenous *Tsachila* community of Chiguilpe toward the coast and Pijal in the highlands near Otavalo, just north of the equator, where a homestay experience is available. Participants explore Ecuador's jungle, coast, and the highlands of Quito.

Activities include hikes to waterfalls; farming, fishing, and living with the host families; ceremonies led by *Tsachila* shamans; visiting marketplaces and thermal baths; learning about folkloric music, arts, and dancing. VISIONS Ecuador pushes beyond the classroom to a fully dynamic learning process. This program has a minimum requirement of two years of high school Spanish.

Australia The Butchella Aboriginal community in Hervey Bay is host to VISIONS groups. The home base is located on land that Korrawinga Corporation has transformed into a fertile farm and information and education center. Participants undertake work such as building kiosks for displaying Aboriginal art, shade arbors, or agricultural processing facilities; assisting with perma-culture farming; and working with elders and young children.

North of Brisbane, at the southern tip of the Great Barrier Reef, there is endless outdoor recreation. Regular beach excursions, an island snorkeling expedition, and hiking Noosa National Park and Fraser Island (a World Heritage site and home to the world's purest strain of dingoes) are some pastime activities. Participants learn about Aboriginal history and beliefs, and about contemporary issues facing Aboriginal people. They also explore the spectacular Great Sandy Region of Australia.

ENROLLMENT

There is a maximum of 25 students and 6 staff members and a minimum of 16 students in any program. All programs are coed. The age range of participants is from 14 to 18.

STAFF

The backbone of a safe, high-quality experience is the staff. VISIONS maintains a staff-student ratio of 1:4. The average age of leaders is in the mid-20s and upward. Roughly 50 percent of staff members return from the previous year. They are returned Peace Corps volunteers, outdoor wilderness experts, graduate students, teachers, and other educators. Experienced carpenters teach building skills. Program directors have proven leadership abilities and are almost always veterans of previous VISIONS summers. All staff members are, at minimum, first aid and CPR certified; some sites require higher certification (Lifeguard Training, WFR, WEMT) and most staff hold advanced certifications.

COSTS

Tuition ranges from $2800 to $4000, depending on location and length of the program.

FINANCIAL AID

VISIONS offers partial and full scholarships. Applications for financial assistance are accepted until March 15.

APPLICATION TIMETABLE

VISIONS accepts applications starting in October. Because enrollment in each program is limited, students are advised to inquire and apply early.

For more information, contact:

VISIONS
P.O. Box 220
Newport, Pennsylvania 17074
717-567-7313
800-813-9283 (toll-free)
Fax: 717-567-7853
E-mail: info@visionsserviceadventures.com
World Wide Web: http://www.VisionsServiceAdventures.com

WASHINGTON UNIVERSITY

HIGH SCHOOL SUMMER SCHOLARS PROGRAM

ST. LOUIS, MISSOURI

Type of Program: Intensive academic program awarding college credit
Participants: Coeducational, rising high school seniors ages 16 and older
Enrollment: 70–80 per session
Program Dates: Two five-week sessions, June 13 to July 17 and July 18 to August 20, 2004
Head of Program: Marsha Hussung, Director

LOCATION

Washington University is located in a quiet, tree-lined suburban neighborhood 7 miles west of downtown St. Louis and the St. Louis Cardinals. It is circled by the city's Central West End and the suburban communities of University City and Clayton. Directly across the street is Forest Park, one of the largest urban parks in the country and home to the St. Louis Art Museum, the St. Louis Zoo, the Science Center, and more.

BACKGROUND AND PHILOSOPHY

Founded in 1988, Washington University's High School Summer Scholars Program (SSP) provides academically talented rising seniors with a rare and special experience—five weeks of a rewarding academic challenge, serious fun, and the excitement of living and bonding with fellow students from around the globe. The best possible introduction to college life and a chance to earn college credit are offered in an atmosphere that values excellence in teaching and personal attention to each student. Participants get a head start on college courses (and learn the study skills required to do well), garner helpful hints on college admissions and financial aid, and experience the independence of college life through residence hall living.

PROGRAM OFFERINGS

In this small, selective program, participants can earn up to 7 semester units of college credit. Nearly sixty stimulating introductory college courses from two dozen departments are offered, ranging from the arts and humanities to science and social science. Courses include French, German, Italian, Spanish, Russian, dance, fiction writing, music, biology, chemistry, earth and planetary science, mathematics, physics, art history, English literature and composition, history, philosophy, archaeology, economics, political science, psychology, and religious studies. Most courses carry 3 credits, and participants usually take two courses during a session. Participants study with undergraduates from Washington University and other colleges and universities.

Weekly Exploratory Seminars provide information on college life and financial and career planning. Sessions are led by University staff members and representatives of the Schools of Architecture, Art, Arts and Sciences, Business, and Engineering.

ENROLLMENT

In 2003, 140 students came to SSP from every part of the United States and from around the world, including Turkey, Bulgaria, and Hong Kong. All applicants should be dedicated and willing to meet the challenges of the program. To be eligible, participants must be at least 16 years old, must have completed their junior year (but not begun their senior year) in high school by the beginning of the program, should have at least a B+ average and a combined SAT I score of at least 1200, a PSAT score (combined verbal and math) of at least 120, or an ACT or PLAN composite score of at least 25.

EXTRA OPPORTUNITIES AND ACTIVITIES

Weekly meetings, trips, and social events are planned, but plenty of unscheduled time is also allotted for participants to get to know Washington University and the other students who are there for the summer. Ozark float trips and visits to Six Flags and a St. Louis Cardinals baseball game are especially popular with Summer Scholars. On campus, the Holmes Lounge provides jazz, blues, and folk music throughout the summer. The Gateway Festival Orchestra presents free concerts on several Sunday evenings in the Washington University Quadrangle. A free international and American film series is offered throughout the summer sessions.

FACILITIES

Students live in a modern, air-conditioned campus residence hall occupied only by other members of the program and are supervised by experienced resident advisers (RAs) who hold weekly meetings to share concerns and help plan the social life and outings. The residence hall is equipped with computers, laundry facilities, study and lounge areas, and additional amenities.

Summer students may use the University's general library, or any of the twelve department and school libraries located on campus. All libraries offer a wide variety of electronic resources, including access to the Internet. The Washington University Computing and

Communications Center provides a variety of computer resources and services; public terminal areas are equipped with Macintoshes and personal computers.

The Athletic Complex provides a variety of recreational opportunities such as racquetball, squash, tennis, track, weight training, and swimming. The Campus Y also sponsors exercise classes and programs.

STAFF

The Program Director oversees all logistical and residential aspects of the Summer Scholars Program, providing informal academic counseling and enrollment assistance and also working closely with the residential staff. Living in the residence hall with the Summer Scholars are a Residential Program Supervisor and specially selected and trained Resident Advisers (RAs) who are Washington University students or recent graduates.

Washington University faculty members, graduate students, and subject specialists teach the regular college courses in which Summer Scholars enroll. On average, the summer instructor to student ratio is 1:10.

MEDICAL CARE

The University Health Services Center is staffed with a physician and a nurse Monday through Friday. Emergency care is available through Barnes-Jewish Hospital, part of the Washington University Medical Center. All participants must be covered by medical insurance and must complete medical forms prior to enrollment.

COSTS

Program fees in 2004 were $4565, which covered tuition, housing, meals, use of the Athletic Complex, and participation in special workshops and social activities. Books, supplies, travel, and personal and incidental expenses are not covered by the program fees. All program fees are due three weeks prior to the start of the desired session.

FINANCIAL AID

Scholarship aid, based on financial need and academic performance, ranges from $500 to $3500. Financial aid applications must be included with program application forms.

TRANSPORTATION

Washington University is centrally located in the St. Louis metropolitan area and is readily accessible by major highways (I-44, I-55, I-64, I-70), bus (Greyhound), rail (Amtrak), and air (Lambert–St. Louis International Airport). Within the city, there is extensive public transportation by bus and light rail. Students should contact their travel agency for advice on travel arrangements.

APPLICATION TIMETABLE

The program is limited in size and admission is competitive, so early application is encouraged. Admissions are made on a rolling basis. The application deadline for session I is May 7; the deadline for session II is June 11. For international applicants, the deadline for session I is April 2, and the deadline for session II is May 7. Applications must include a $35 application fee ($70 for international applicants), recommendations from a school guidance counselor and a teacher, an essay, and the applicant's official high school transcript. The application fee is waived for applications received by March 1. Applications are available in late January. Learn more by visiting the program at the Web site listed below.

FOR MORE INFORMATION, CONTACT:

Marsha Hussung, Director
High School Summer Scholars Program
Campus Box 1145
One Brookings Drive
Washington University
St. Louis, Missouri 63130-4899
Telephone: 314-935-6834
Fax: 314-935-4847
E-mail: mhussung@artsci.wustl.edu
World Wide Web: http://ucollege.wustl.edu/hssp

PARTICIPANT/FAMILY COMMENTS

"The High School Scholars Summer Residence Program was a really great experience—it introduced us to college life while allowing us to make friends with other juniors from all over the world."

WASHINGTON UNIVERSITY IN ST. LOUIS

SCHOOL OF ART–PORTFOLIO PLUS

ST. LOUIS, MISSOURI

Type of Program: Credit and noncredit art classes
Participants: High school students
Enrollment: Limited
Program Dates: June 12–July 16
Heads of Program: Cris Baldwin and Belinda Lee

LOCATION

Set amid a thriving metropolitan region of 2.6 million residents, Washington University in St. Louis benefits from the vast array of social, cultural, and recreational opportunities offered by the St. Louis area. Bordered on the east by St. Louis's famed Forest Park and on the north, west, and south by well-established suburbs, the 169-acre Hilltop Campus features predominantly Collegiate Gothic architecture, including a number of buildings on the National Register of Historic Places.

BACKGROUND AND PHILOSOPHY

Washington University in St. Louis is among the world's leaders in teaching and research. The School of Art was established in 1879, the first in the nation to become a part of a university. In 125 years, the Washington University School of Art has gone from 30 students in a cramped attic to a well-respected professional school whose faculty comprises practicing artists, whose talented students are drawn from all over the world, and whose alumni star in every area of art. The School of Art is strongly committed to the development and success of young artists.

Students are constantly reminded that the study of art is on a broader plane than may at first be supposed. The mind, as well as the eye and hand, must be trained. The broader the general education of the student, the more likely the success of the student in later years.

PROGRAM OFFERINGS

Portfolio Plus is the School of Art's new summer program, established in summer 2004. This curriculum is open to students who have completed their sophomore, junior, or senior years of high school students. It offers portfolio preparation in the studios of one of the top universities in the country, the opportunity to earn college credit (4 hours for the full-day session and 2 hours for the morning or afternoon sessions), the documentation of work in slide form, and letters of recommendation for college admission upon successful completion of the program.

The morning session includes a drawing class that emphasizes both observational drawing and the figure and a class that explores both 2-dimensional and 3-dimensional design. During the afternoon session, students may choose from watercolor painting, ceramics, photography, printmaking, computer graphics, fashion design, and sculpture. Field trips to local museums are also scheduled.

The School of Art also offers seven art electives. Students may receive 3 hours of college credit. In-service credit is available.

Drawing: Students learn to recognize and manipulate fundamental elements of line, tone, texture, volume, and plane with relation to representational drawing. Students work in a wide variety of media and techniques (charcoal, pencil, pastels, and wet media) from the figure, still life, and the environment.

2-D/3-D Design: This course is an introduction to basic design principles and their applications on the 2-dimensional surface and in 3-dimensional form.

Ceramics: This course is an introduction to the design and making of functional pottery as well as sculptural objects. Students learn the basic forming processes of the wheel, coil, and slab construction.

Computer Graphics: Students explore digital image creation, photo restoration, animation, and digital programming as well as fine art applications of computer and video technology. All work is done on Macintosh computers.

Fashion Design: This course familiarizes students with techniques and materials used in drawing illustrations for fashion designs. Problems associated with designing groups, collections, and lines of apparel for popular and selected consumption are included.

Painting/Watercolor Techniques: Students explore traditional and nontraditional techniques both on-site as well as in the studio. Students look at examples from art history as well as from contemporary artists.

Photography: This course in basic black-and-white photography includes technical skills from camera handling and film exposure to development and printing. Student-directed assignments emphasize visual expression and the formal qualities of photography. Students supply their own 35mm camera, film, and paper.

Printmaking: Students explore various mixed media approaches to printmaking, including collagraph, pronto plate lithography, etching, and other contemporary processes. There is a focus on making editions as well as one-of-a-kind prints.

Sculpture: Students explore contemporary sculptural concepts and processes in various media, including plaster, wax, plastics, metal, and wood fabrication, with an emphasis on the development of technical skills.

ENROLLMENT

Studio sizes are limited. Minimum enrollment is required for all classes. Students must be at least 16 years of age and have completed their sophomore year of high school to be eligible for the program.

DAILY SCHEDULE

Portfolio Plus classes meet both in the morning from 9 a.m. to noon and in the afternoon from 1 to 4 p.m. All classes run Monday through Friday.

FACILITIES

The Sam Fox Arts Center at Washington University, a new $56.8-million complex, serves as a campuswide umbrella organization for the study and promotion of visual culture. The center allows for greater collaboration between the participating units and the development of new and interdisciplinary programs, while also preserving the integrity of the distinct disciplines of architecture, art, and art history and archaeology. In addition, it brings students and faculty members in the School of Art, now studying and working in three separate buildings—one of them a renovated former junior high school located one mile from campus—together in two adjacent buildings on the Hilltop Campus.

Students live in one of the secure, modern residence halls on the South Forty (the undergraduate residential area) with other members of the program and the residential staff. In addition, there are students from other precollege programs at the University living in the dormitories. The dormitories are secure and are kept locked 24 hours a day. Resident Advisers (RAs) living in the halls provide advice, information, social planning, and assurance that the rules and regulations of the program are maintained. There are planned activities for the evenings.

STAFF

All classes are taught by School of Art faculty members.

MEDICAL CARE

All students attending the program have access to the health-care facility, which is on campus. In addition, major medical centers are located throughout the St. Louis area.

COSTS

The estimated cost for the program in 2005 is $4565. This includes tuition and lab fees for 6 hours of college credit, housing, meals, access to student health services, student ID, use of library facilities, use of the Athletic Complex, and an e-mail account. Individual art supplies as well as personal and other items are not included. The tuition for commuting students is estimated at $2282 for the program.

FINANCIAL AID

At least one full scholarship is offered. Students wishing to be considered for this award must submit with their application materials five slides and a high school transcript showing a minimum B average. The deadline to apply for the scholarship is April 1, 2005.

TRANSPORTATION

Students need to provide their own transportation to the University. Those students traveling by air should contact Belinda Lee at the phone number or e-mail address provided in the Contact section regarding shuttles to and from the airport.

APPLICATION TIMETABLE

To apply, students must submit an application form, which can be found online, along with a one-page essay on why he or she would like to study art, a letter of recommendation from a high school teacher, and a check for $225 before May 1. $25 is an application fee and is not applied toward tuition.

For more information, contact:

Belinda Lee
School of Art
Washington University in St. Louis
Campus Box 1031
One Brookings Drive
St. Louis, Missouri 63130-4899
314-935-4643
E-mail: bslee@art.wustl.edu
World Wide Web: http://art.wustl.edu

WEISSMAN TEEN TOURS

SUMMER PROGRAMS

UNITED STATES/WESTERN CANADA, HAWAII, AND EUROPE

Type of Program: Activity-oriented travel
Participants: Coeducational, ages 13–18 (grouped compatibly by age)
Enrollment: Europe, 40 per group; United States/ Western Canada, 40 per group; Hawaii, 40 per group
Program Dates: Europe, late June through early August; United States/Western Canada, early July through mid-August; Hawaii, late July through mid-August
Heads of Program: Eugene, Ronee, and Adam Weissman, Founders/Owners/Directors

BACKGROUND AND PHILOSOPHY

"We're family . . . not just another teen tour" clearly defines the degree of warmth and caring that best describes the "Weissman Experience." Each tour is personally escorted by Ronee, Adam, or Eugene Weissman and their experienced staff. From the inception of their program thirty years ago, the Weissmans have devoted themselves to providing tours that are among the most personalized in the student travel field. The Weissmans stress quality, not quantity, allowing them to direct their attention to each teen as an individual and to guarantee a personally customized experience for everyone. Despite a waiting list every year, the program is limited to two European tour groups, two United States/Western Canadian tour groups, and one Hawaiian tour group.

Students develop friendships and a genuine respect for themselves, their natural surroundings, and the people they come in contact with wherever they go. Ronee, Adam, and Eugene have given the Weissman Student Tour its unique, family-oriented style and unusual togetherness that all its members share.

PROGRAM OFFERINGS

Weissman Tours offers one United States, one Hawaiian, and one European itinerary, which provide high-quality, action-packed—yet leisurely—experiences that are among the best in student travel. The domestic program focuses on the national parks, big cities, and resort activity centers located in the far western portion of the United States and Canada. The Aloha Hawaii tour includes a magnificent Carnival cruise to Ensenada, Mexico (also included as part of the U.S./Western Canadian tour), in addition to beautiful Hawaiian oceanfront resorts. The European Experience encompasses England, Holland, Belgium, France, Switzerland, and Italy, combining the exploration of the culture and history of the cities with the recreation and outdoor adventure found in some of the most magnificent resorts in Europe.

The Weissman Tours are incredibly active, with planned activities every day and evening. Since they are not wasting time setting up and taking down tents, everyone has more time to explore the cities and to enjoy all of the fabulous adventures travel has to offer. The Weissmans personally lead their groups on hikes, bicycling adventures, white-water rafting, kayaking, sailing, parasailing and waterskiing, horseback riding, skiing, snowboarding, snorkeling, scuba diving, surfing, golfing, and organized sports. The resorts also provide health clubs and fitness centers with the most up-to-date equipment and classes in aerobics and calisthenics. Every evening, teens enjoy discos, TV tapings, concerts, shows, cruises, skating, campfires, comedy clubs, and much more. Since the program's jet flights are longer and the bus rides are shorter than those on other student tours, students on a Weissman Teen Tour have more time to experience, appreciate, and enjoy the cities and parks and all they have to offer.

ENROLLMENT

Weissman Teen Tours attracts students from the United States, Canada, Latin America, Europe, and Asia. Teens who travel with the Weissmans live together, work together, share responsibilities, and learn while having fun, enabling each tour member to develop lasting friendships within a warm family atmosphere.

EXTRA OPPORTUNITIES AND ACTIVITIES

Having the owner lead the tours fosters spontaneity and affords the group special opportunities that they would never have otherwise experienced. The Weissman Tour has often dined at restaurants that are "off the beaten trail" in Europe, where English is not spoken but the food and ambience are local and incredible. If a meaningful adventure should suddenly present itself, the Weissmans will jump at the chance to participate. Groups have, for example, joined the North American Indian Council meeting in Montana, witnessing the tribal dances as well as making new pen pals. In addition, the European group has dined at a magnificent villa overlooking the Tuscan countryside as guests of friends of the Weissmans, joined a "Sweet 16" party at an Italian dance club by invitation of the owner of an exquisite European hotel, challenged some Swiss friends to a game of tennis in Zermatt, and participated in a special presentation at the Anne Frank House in Amsterdam planned especially for the Weissman group.

FACILITIES

The Weissmans prepare throughout the year, personally visiting hotels, restaurants, and activities prior to booking groups. Teens are welcomed warmly, as if part of the hotel "family," upon their arrival. The U.S./Western Canadian and Hawaiian itineraries feature a well-balanced combination of centrally located first-class hotels in the major cities, such as Hiltons, Marriotts, Hyatts, and Sheratons; a four-night Carnival Ecstasy Cruise; national park lodges; and resort activity centers. In addition, the Aloha Hawaii tour includes magnificent, activity-oriented, deluxe oceanfront resorts. In Europe, the superior four- and five-star hotels are all selected for their location, strictly European ambience, excellent facilities, and safety regulations. Students awaken each morning to all the city has to offer. There is definitely an advantage to sleeping in a dry, safe, and beautiful hotel with plenty of great facilities, including pools, jacuzzis, health clubs, and tennis courts—all waiting for the Weissman group to relax in after a busy day of activity.

STAFF

Weissman Tours is the only student travel program personally escorted in the United States and Europe by both the owner/directors and leaders who are experienced, well-trained, and committed to providing a safe and fun environment. All staff members are over 21, college graduates, nonsmokers, and certified in CPR and first aid. European staff members are fluent in French and/or Italian and have backgrounds in art history. They are required to live and work at the home/office of the Weissmans and to participate in extensive training sessions prior to the departure of the tours. Since many of the staff members are Weissman Teen Tour alumni, they understand the significance of the bond that is established between the teens and their leaders. The Weissmans believe that when teens travel so far from home, they should be with people with whom they can communicate, feel secure, and have fun.

Eugene Weissman has a master's degree in mathematics and has completed postgraduate work in administration, group dynamics, and child guidance. He has extensive experience as a high school educator, College Bound coordinator and administrator, teacher/consultant for the College Board SAT, camp director, and youth director. Ronee Weissman graduated Phi Beta Kappa, magna cum laude, and holds a master's degree in speech pathology. She has been elected to *Who's Who of American Women, Who's Who in the World,* and *Who's Who of Emerging Leaders in America,* as well as other biographical publications, for her outstanding achievement as a teen tour director and New York state–licensed, ASHA-certified speech pathologist. Adam Weissman, a graduate of the University of Pennsylvania, is pursuing a career in adolescent psychology. In preparation for his admission to a Ph.D. program in clinical psychology, Adam is spending his second year doing research for the Treatment and Research Institute at Penn. As an undergraduate, he spent the spring semester of his junior year studying art history and French language and literature in Aix-en-Provence. With their diversified and well-rounded backgrounds, Eugene, Ronee, and Adam are able to provide leadership that combines knowledge, warmth, and genuine concern with all aspects of the development of a healthy, well-rounded teenager.

MEDICAL CARE

The Weissman family is committed to the health, safety, and security of all of its tour members. They have an extensive network of medical facilities and doctors in every city, both in the United States and abroad. In Europe, the

list includes many American hospitals as well as U.S. trained doctors. Parents are always contacted when a student receives medical treatment. All staff members are certified in CPR and first aid.

COSTS

The U.S./Western Canadian tour is $8399, the Hawaiian tour is $5999, and the European tour is $9599. All first-class, deluxe accommodations; three healthy and nutritious meals daily; and extensive day and evening activities are included in the price. The lowest available scheduled APEX airfare is extra.

APPLICATION TIMETABLE

Students are welcome to inquire at any time. Enrollment is on a rolling basis. The brochure and United States or European DVD/video may be requested. Due to the limited number of openings each season, early registration is recommended. Ronee and Eugene Weissman are available to speak to all interested students and their families.

For more information, contact:

Ronee and Eugene Weissman
Weissman Teen Tours
517 Almena Avenue
Ardsley, New York 10502
914-693-7575
800-942-8005 (toll-free outside New York state)
Fax: 914-693-4807
E-mail: wtt@cloud9.net
World Wide Web: http://www.weissmantours.com

PARTICIPANT/FAMILY COMMENTS

"Perhaps the most unique quality of the Weissman Teen Tour is the caring found there. Through your caring, you encouraged others to give of themselves. Never before had I met 2 people interested in whatever I had to say. It's very difficult to achieve such a special relationship between tour members and leaders, but you have more than succeeded! Maybe that's why we say, 'We're family. . . not just another teen tour!'"

"When Evan went to Europe three years ago with your group, I thought I had heard every superlative in the world, but Erica found a few new ones. Not only did she have a fantastic time meeting new people, but the reuniting with her former counselor and your continuing care and concern made this the premiere event of her life."

WENTWORTH MILITARY ACADEMY AND JUNIOR COLLEGE

ACADEMIC SUMMER SCHOOL AND PATHFINDER ADVENTURE CAMP

LEXINGTON, MISSOURI

Type of Program: Academic enrichment and leadership development
Participants: Coeducational: boys, grades 7–12; girls, grades 9–12
Program Dates: Summer School: June 20 to July 30, 2004; Pathfinder Camp: June 28 to July 3, 2004
Head of Program: Maj. Gen. John Little, USA (Ret.), Superintendent and President

LOCATION

Wentworth is located 40 miles east of Kansas City in historic Lexington, Missouri. Situated adjacent to a Civil War battlefield on the bluffs of the Missouri River, the 137-acre campus is listed in the National Register of Historic Places.

BACKGROUND AND PHILOSOPHY

Wentworth is one of the nation's oldest and most respected military schools. For nearly 125 years, Wentworth has been guided by three principles: to stimulate academic and intellectual growth, to provide strong values and moral development, and to ensure physical maturity and well-being.

Success at Wentworth encompasses more than test scores or graduation statistics. It involves social and moral values and ethics, learning to live daily by the Golden Rule, developing self-discipline, and building self-confidence. The goal of Wentworth's summer programs is to provide participants with a solid foundation for academic progress and life success.

In the Academic Summer School program, the low student-teacher ratio allows each student to obtain the individual attention necessary for personal success. This is further enabled through regular supervised evening study periods, a structured boarding school environment, and positive peer influences. Wentworth's unique military structure also offers valid educational advantages. Regimentation and organization promote the formation of good habits such as study skills, time management, and self-discipline.

Pathfinder Adventure Camp is intended to provide participants with an introduction to the exciting challenges that military life and military school have to offer. The emphasis is on completing fun and exciting activities that stretch personal boundaries and instill basic discipline and focus.

Wentworth is fully accredited by the North Central Association Commission on Accreditation and School Improvement.

PROGRAM OFFERINGS

The **Academic Summer School** academic program is designed to establish the habits of excellence in students that will contribute to their success in life. Students are offered a variety of classes to improve their knowledge in the areas of prealgebra, algebra, plane geometry, biology, geography, English, and world history. Intensive preview or review courses are also offered for grades 7–8. Classes are held in the mornings. In the afternoon, students may participate in a variety of activities, including basketball, canoeing, ceramics, lifesaving, golf, rocketry, model airplane making, volleyball, skydiving, and scouting. Each activity is held in two-week increments, allowing students to receive the benefits of three separate programs.

The Summer School also offers an English as a Second Language Program, which is designed to improve vocabulary and pronunciation. The instructor tailors the program to meet the individual needs of each student based on his or her fluency level.

Classroom progress in all facets of the Summer School program is enhanced through supervised evening study periods and adult mentorship. Students receive 1 unit of credit or enroll in two courses and receive ½ unit of credit per course. Grade reports are sent to parents every three weeks and at the conclusion of the program.

Pathfinder Adventure Camp is a weeklong program designed to introduce campers to the fundamental tenets of the military while also enjoying summer vacation. In the spirit of Lewis and Clark, whose bicentennial has been celebrated this past year and who encamped nearby, campers test their limits while experiencing extreme fun. Activities include rappelling, paintball, scuba, camping, canoeing, and rock-wall climbing. All activities and events are supervised and taught by subject-matter experts, while the overall camp is under the supervision and mentorship of Wentworth Military Academy camp staff and cadet cadre.

EXTRA OPPORTUNITIES AND ACTIVITIES

For Academic Summer School students, daylong trips to regional recreational and educational facilities are scheduled every weekend. Students have an opportunity to experience many of the Kansas City area attractions, including the Worlds of Fun and Oceans of Fun Amusement Parks, the Kansas City Zoo, Kansas City Royals Major League Baseball, and a

professional rodeo. They also attend local festivities, such as the Lexington Heritage Day Festival and Fourth of July celebration.

DAILY SCHEDULE

0700	First call/Wake up
0720	BRC formation
0720–0745	BRC
0745–0755	Sick call/meds/details
0755	Classes form
0800–1000	Classes
1000–1015	Break
1015–1200	Classes
1200–1210	DRC formation (inspection)
1200–1255	DRC
1300–1500	Classes
1515–1645	Physical education
1645–1730	Drill (Monday, Wednesday, Friday)
1730–1800	Personal hygiene
1800–1815	SRC formation
1815–1915	SRC
1930–2020	1st CQ
2020–2030	Break
2030–2120	2nd CQ
2120–2145	Personal time (in company area or snack bar)
2145–2200	Personal hygiene (must be in barracks)
2230	Taps (lights out)

FACILITIES

The campus features thirteen buildings, including the Administration Building, the Sellers-Wikoff Scholastic Building, Groendyke Hall, a field house, a chapel, three dormitories, a student infirmary, the Quartermaster Store, the dining facility, and a student snack bar. The new Tillotson Barracks has the capacity to house an additional 106 cadets.

The Scholastic Building houses the classrooms, a new computer laboratory, science laboratories, and the Sellers-Coombs Library, which contains 17,000 volumes, more than 4,000 microforms of periodicals, and 170 magazine and newspaper titles in subscription. The library offers a large reading room for research or study purposes. Microfilm and microfiche readers are available for research. Computer workstations meet students' needs for word processing, graphics production, and computer-assisted instruction. The Academy also houses an extensive Civil War collection of books, weapons, and military equipment.

The field house contains three basketball courts, a Laykold-type indoor track, a racquetball court, a modern weight room, a wrestling room, a sauna, and an Olympic-size swimming pool. The campus also provides athletic and drill fields, tennis courts, a nine-hole golf course, and natural woodlands used for military exercises and outdoor recreation.

Students reside with a roommate in 2-person rooms. They may individualize their rooms within allowable limits and may keep stereos with headphones and computers in their rooms.

MEDICAL CARE

The Academy maintains a nineteen-bed infirmary under the direction of a registered professional nurse and a nursing staff to provide daily health services. The staff works closely with physicians, dentists, and psychologists in the immediate area, who provide on-call service. Hospital facilities are within easy access in Lexington and the surrounding communities.

COSTS

The Academic Summer School tuition, room and board, and fees total $4800. Fees include the registration fee, room deposit, pocket money, and fees for books, cadet store charges, personal needs, and other miscellaneous expenses. Pathfinder Adventure Camp costs $695, inclusive of application fee, boarding, camp clothing, and activities fees. This cost does not include spending money, which parents can provide if they so chose (limit is $50). There is a $100 nonrefundable application fee for the Academic Summer School and a $50 nonrefundable application fee for Pathfinder Camp, both of which contribute to the total cost.

TRANSPORTATION

A travel hostess is available to assist students with travel arrangements. Academy staff members transport students to and from the Kansas City International Airport.

APPLICATION TIMETABLE

Students must complete and return an application obtained through the Wentworth Military Academy Admissions Office. Interviews are conducted when advised by the Admissions Committee. Campus tours may be arranged by contacting the Wentworth Admissions Office. A video of the Wentworth campus and educational experience is also available for applicants. The deadline for applications for both programs is May 31. Applications received by May 15 have the application fee waived.

For more information, contact:

Director of Admissions
Wentworth Military Academy and Junior College
1880 Washington Avenue
Lexington, Missouri 64067
800-962-7682
Fax: 660-259-2677
E-mail: admissions@wma1880.org
World Wide Web: http://www.wma1880.org

WESTCOAST CONNECTION TRAVEL

SUMMER TRAVEL PROGRAMS

UNITED STATES, CANADA, EUROPE, AND AUSTRALIA

Type of Program: Four types of activity-oriented travel: outdoor adventures, touring groups, sports programs (golf, skiing, or snowboarding), and community service

Participants: Coeducational, ages 13–18 (grouped compatibly by age); separate group for those 17 and older

Enrollment: Adventure, sports, and service groups are 12–24 students; touring groups are 35–50 students

Program Dates: Vary from eighteen to forty-two days from the end of June to August

Heads of Program: Mark Segal, Stan Browman, Fran Grundman, Mitch Lerner, Ira Solomon, and Jason Tanner, Directors

BACKGROUND AND PHILOSOPHY

Westcoast Connection was founded in 1982. Programs give students the opportunity to discover new and exciting places; to develop greater self-confidence, a respect for others, and new skills; and to make new friends. Through travel and a wide variety of activities, each student develops self-reliance and becomes an integral member of a tight-knit group. Students learn something about themselves while also enjoying an unlimited amount of fun and excitement.

No prior experience is necessary, just a willingness and a desire to participate. On all adventures, the experienced and qualified staff ensures that everyone is equally comfortable and welcome right from day one.

PROGRAM OFFERINGS

Programs explore many regions of the United States, Canada, Europe, and Australia and generally run for three, four, or six weeks.

On the East Coast, programs are in New England, Florida, the Mid-Atlantic, Quebec, and Ontario. In the southwestern United States, participants travel to California, Arizona, Nevada, and Utah. In the Pacific Northwest, locations offered are in Washington and Oregon, along with the Canadian Rockies and Whistler. Other locations include Colorado, Wyoming, Montana, Hawaii, and Alaska.

Trip settings encompass many of the most naturally beautiful locations in the world. Some of the spectacular national parks visited include Yellowstone, Grand Canyon, Bryce, Zion, Banff, and Jasper. Other natural settings are in the San Juan Islands and overseas in the Swiss Alps or at Australia's Great Barrier Reef.

Outdoor Adventure For students seeking greater physical activity, there is an increased emphasis on challenging oneself, developing skills, and gaining a sense of accomplishment. Programs offer activities that include surfing, white-water rafting, snow skiing, snowboarding, rock climbing, mountain biking, sea kayaking, canoeing, ropes courses, caving, and hiking. Smaller groups enable students to form a unique trust and a tight bond with their peers. Professional guides are there to instruct and lead specialty activities.

Active Tours Trips combine the natural wonders of the great outdoors with the attractions of major cities, including Los Angeles, San Francisco, San Diego, Las Vegas, Vancouver, and Seattle in North America. Students participate in recreational activities, including white-water rafting, snowboarding, snow skiing, horseback riding, mountain biking, and hiking. Evening activities include baseball games, concerts, comedy clubs, miniature golf, roller skating, campfires, and more. These trips combine stays at hotels, resorts, college dorms, and campsites. Some of the tours are all indoors.

European Programs Countries visited include France, Italy, Switzerland, Belgium, Holland, and England. Trips balance sightseeing and touring in major cities, along with recreation and entertainment as well as outdoor activities such as rafting, skiing/snowboarding, and biking in the French and Swiss Alps. Restful stays on the French and Adriatic Rivieras help relax the pace and enable students to enjoy a truly special experience in Europe.

On Tour These programs are for students 17 and older and provide participants with more independence. Programs are in western Canada, Europe, and Australia. Although encouraged to join daily group activities, students may explore and discover the ultimate bistro or café on their own.

Florida Swing Junior Touring Golf Camp This features PGA instruction while touring top-rated courses.

Skiing and Snowboarding at Mt. Hood and Whistler This offers professional skiing or snowboarding instruction, a variety of recreational activities, and touring in the Pacific Northwest.

Community Service Teens combine volunteering and touring highlights in Washington State or Alaska.

Australia This action-packed trip includes scuba diving at the Great Barrier Reef, hiking with aborigines in the outback, surfing lessons, touring Sydney, hiking in the rain forest, petting koala bears and kangaroos, and a fantastic finale stop in Hawaii.

ENROLLMENT

One outstanding aspect of Westcoast Connection's enrollment is its international flavor and geographic diversity. Approximately 85 percent of the students come from different regions of the United States, and 15 percent are from Canada. International participants have come from Aruba, Austria, Belgium, Brazil, Colombia, England, France, Honduras, India, Israel, Italy, Japan, Peru, Russia, South Africa, and Venezuela. Westcoast Connection is nondenominational. This diversity ensures a well-balanced geographic mix and helps prevent cliques.

FACILITIES

All accommodations are preselected for safety, cleanliness, facilities, and location. They include campsites, college dorms, hotels, chalets, and inns. On Outdoor Adventures, most nights are spent camping. On most Active Tours, 30 to 50 percent of the nights are spent camping; the balance are spent in dorms, resorts, and hotels. The Hawaiian, European, and Australian tours and the sports programs feature all-indoor stays. Private campsites all have indoor washrooms with hot water, private showers, flush toilets, and electricity and an array of recreational facilities. Camping is on mattresses in spacious tents. On the Active Tours, camping cots are also provided. On indoor stays, every student has an individual bed. Special dietary requests (including vegetarian and religious) are accommodated.

STAFF

Experienced, fun, exciting, patient, and sensitive leaders are selected for their ability to relate to, care for, and support teenagers. Directors and staff members complete CPR and first aid training and are committed first and foremost to the health and safety of their students. All staff members are personally interviewed. Leaders participate in several pretrip orientation sessions and workshops to ensure the highest level of preparation in student travel.

Directors are generally teachers, social workers, coaches, or graduate students. All directors and staff members are nonsmokers.

MEDICAL CARE

Westcoast Connection's number one priority is the health and safety of every participant. Each trip director is equipped with an extensive listing of local hospitals, clinics, and physicians to visit as needed. A sick or injured tour member is accompanied by a staff member at all times.

COSTS

Tuition ranges from $2799 to $7999; most trips range from $2800 to $5000. Fees include all activities, meals, accommodations, gratuities, and taxes. Airfare is not included.

APPLICATION TIMETABLE

Enrollment is on a rolling basis; initial inquiries are welcome at any time. Brochures and videos are available in October. Early enrollment is advised to secure trip preference. Discounts are available for early enrollment.

For more information, contact:

United States
Westcoast Connection
154 East Boston Post Road
Mamaroneck, New York 10543
914-835-0699
800-767-0227 (toll-free outside New York State)
Fax: 914-835-0798
E-mail: usa@westcoastconnection.com
World Wide Web: http://www.westcoastconnection.com

Canada
5585 Monkland, Suite 140
Montreal, Quebec, Canada H4A 1E1
514-488-8920

WHERE THERE BE DRAGONS: ASIA/LATIN AMERICA

SUMMER AND SEMESTER TRAVEL PROGRAMS

CHINA, THAILAND, VIETNAM, TIBET, INDIA, MONGOLIA, PERU, MEXICO, AND GUATEMALA

Type of Program: Rugged travel, cultural studies, language, service work, backpacking and wilderness exploration, homestays; midyear semester programs in India, China, the Tibetan Plateau, and Guatemala

Participants: Coeducational, students entering grades 10 and older

Enrollment: 12 students per program

Program Dates: Four to six weeks in June, July, and August; semester programs are three months in fall and spring

Head of Program: Chris Yager, Director

LOCATION

DRAGONS runs programs in the majestic, culturally rich areas of developing Asian and Latin American nations. Combining a rich mixture of wilderness exploration, homestays, apprenticeships, service work, and off-the-beaten-path travel, DRAGONS offers intimate and comprehensive introductions to the developing world.

Programs involve extensive exploration of rural towns and villages, enabling students to witness ancient traditions that remain largely unaffected by Western culture. Programs also include visits to key urban centers, where students explore monuments of great cultural achievement and meet with leaders in commerce, politics, traditional religion, and development.

BACKGROUND AND PHILOSOPHY

Since 1992, DRAGONS has offered honest, dynamic, and personal educational adventures—unique programs that introduce the beauty and challenges of life in Asia and Latin America through rugged, off-the-beaten-path experiences.

Far from being "tours," DRAGONS programs are active and engaging small-group odysseys. Students travel by foot, bus, train, tractor, and horse-drawn cart to small and remote villages where traditions run deep and the Earth's natural beauty is breathtaking.

Small group size and a 4:1 student-leader ratio create a casual, flexible, and fun traveling environment. Trip leaders work closely with students to define student goals, and itineraries are kept flexible so that changes

can be made to better address student needs and interests. Leaders facilitate dynamic, experiential learning opportunities, such as apprenticeships with traditional craftsmen, tutorials with Buddhist monks, and meetings with herbal doctors. With a low student-leader ratio, program staff members can work closely with students, teaching valuable language skills and ensuring that students are comfortable in their new cultures.

PROGRAM OFFERINGS

China A comprehensive survey of modern China, DRAGONS' China program includes visits to rural villages and urban cultural centers, exploration of stunning wilderness, and a survey of both Han and minority cultures. Highlights include trekking on the Great Wall; visits to Tibetan monastic towns; bike rides through terraced rice paddies; and meetings with Chinese doctors, Taoist alchemists, artists, authors, and community leaders. Program leaders facilitate language study and cover topics in political and economic studies. A sometimes gritty program that includes travel on trains, tractors, and horse-drawn carts, DRAGONS' China program provides an honest perspective on the beauty and drama of modern China.

Thailand An ecology, cultural studies, and service program, the Thailand sojourn offers a broad survey of development issues. Students participate in rain forest research, enjoy remote jungle trekking, assist with rural health-care projects, homestay in a small village, and learn fundamental principles in Buddhist philosophy. Beginning with a stay at a Buddhist monastery, students move on to trek the lush jungle of northern Thailand. With an extended trip into Laos, homestays and service work in northeastern Thailand, and time spent along Thailand's magical coast, students visiting the Land of Smiles delight in Thai hospitality while enjoying the beauty of a stunning landscape.

Vietnam A service-oriented program, the Vietnam sojourn offers students profound opportunities to engage in humanitarian aid while introducing them to the ancient traditions, epic history, and changing economy of Indochina. Service-learning projects, such as work in health clinics and assistance with environmental protection, are combined with jungle trekking, open-water kayaking, meetings with development professionals, visits with diplomats and community leaders, and an introduction to Buddhist philosophy. Students interested in politics, peace studies, and modern American history will enjoy learning about the history of America's involvement in Indochina, as well as efforts at reconciliation.

Tibet DRAGONS runs three different programs in Tibet, each providing a rich introduction to the area's cultural traditions, philosophies, and wilderness. The *Rugged Himalayan Adventure* features incredible hiking and includes exploration of the northern base of Mt. Everest. The *Cultural Odyssey* offers intimate cultural experiences through homestays, internships, independent study projects, and meetings with high Lamas. The *Pilgrimage to Mt. Kailas* offers students the remarkable opportunity to trek alongside pilgrims around one of Asia's most sacred and remote natural monuments.

North India Emphasizing comparative religion and philosophy studies, DRAGONS' North India program introduces students to the foundations of India's principal belief systems, including Buddhism, Islam, and Hinduism. The North India program combines extended homestay and service work with an introduction to the philosophical traditions of Tibetan, Indian, and Ladakhi people. Self-starting students are afforded unique opportunities to participate in internships and to design independent study projects. Participants meet with high Lamas and saddhus; explore traditional crafts, dance, and music; and work with local aid agencies on service projects. The program concludes with an extraordinary hike to remote villages deep in the Himalayas.

Mongolia An intern- and guide-training program for students who are 18 years or older, DRAGONS' Mongolia program combines trekking, homestays, and service-learning with leadership seminars, emergency medical training, and a foundation in overseas guiding. Only open to foreigners since 1990, Mongolia offers a rare and extraordinary opportunity to witness traditional nomadic life and to explore remarkable unspoiled wilderness; it is an ideal setting to challenge and engage older students who are looking to hone their outdoor leadership and guiding skills.

Guatemala, Mexico, and Peru DRAGONS offers three unique programs in Latin America, each providing intimate cultural immersion with language study, homestays, service work, and wilderness exploration. DRAGONS' Mexico course is specifically designed for students 15 to 16 years old who are looking for a service-intensive program that combines elements of wilderness adventure and language study. The Guatemala course is for students 17 and older and offers rich cultural immersion with rigorous language study, including professional one-on-one Spanish instruction during three of the course's six weeks. In Peru, students enjoy extensive wilderness exploration, with high-mountain trekking in the Andes and foot and boat travel through protected rain forest and a jungle biosphere preserve.

Semester Programs For students deferring college, taking a "gap year," DRAGONS offers four unique fall and spring semester programs. The *India Semester* is based in Varanasi, the holiest city in India. It combines homestays and service work with a profound introduction to the depth of India's sacred traditions. The *China Semester* introduces students to China's political history and ancient culture through rural homestays, work projects, travel across the country, intensive language instruction, and internships with accomplished professionals. The *Himalayan Studies* program offers students intimate cultural exposure to the peoples of the Himalayas while also exploring the peaks, valleys, and immense plateaus of the largest mountains on earth. The *Guatemala Semester* combines intensive Spanish-language training with opportunities to live in a small, rural village; partake in the daily lives of Maya's indigenous people; and work on a number of community aid and development projects.

ENROLLMENT

To ensure an intimate and dynamic learning experience, DRAGONS limits each program's enrollment to 12 students who have completed grade 9 or higher.

FACILITIES

Students stay in small guest houses, school dormitories, family homes, Buddhist monasteries, tents, and village common houses.

STAFF

Each program is run by 3 adult leaders, whose average age is 29. Trip leaders take on much of the responsibility for planning each program's special elements—meetings with political leaders and intellectuals, homestays, service projects, and work internships. Leaders are teachers, returned Peace Corps volunteers, doctoral candidates, development professionals, and professional guides.

COSTS

Tuition fees range from $4650 to $6600 and include round-trip international airfare from Los Angeles.

APPLICATION TIMETABLE

Applications are accepted at any time. Early application is advised.

For more information, contact:

Chris Yager, Director
P.O. Box 4651
Boulder, Colorado 80306
800-982-9203 (toll-free)
E-mail: dragons@earthnet.net
World Wide Web:
http://www.WhereThereBeDragons.com

PARTICIPANT/FAMILY COMMENTS

"I learned far more than I ever expected, though my expectations were quite high. Coming away from this trip, I'm realizing more and more how much my understanding of people and of life has increased in the past month. The combination of traveling with new people, being taught by three leaders for whom I have tremendous respect, and being exposed to a whole new culture and accompanying way of thinking has helped me to resolve a lot in my own mind. I understand a lot better now myself and my life, and how I want to live."

WILDERNESS VENTURES

WILDERNESS EDUCATION AND EXPEDITIONS

THE AMERICAS, CANADA, AUSTRALIA, AND EUROPE

Type of Program: Wilderness expeditions, leadership training, and community service
Participants: Coeducational, ages 13–20, grouped by age
Enrollment: More than thirty different expeditions with 10 to 15 participants each. Multiple sections grouped by age are offered for each expedition.
Program Dates: Sixteen to forty-two day expeditions in June, July, and August
Heads of Program: Mike and Helen Cottingham

LOCATION

Wilderness Ventures offers expeditions throughout the western United States, Hawaii, Alaska, Canada, Europe, Australia, Central America, and South America. The expeditions are multienvironmental, enabling the participants to experience a variety of some of the most beautiful wilderness areas in the world.

BACKGROUND AND PHILOSOPHY

Established in 1973, Wilderness Ventures has become the most recognized and experienced multienvironmental wilderness program for young adults.

Each summer, a variety of expeditions embark upon sixteen- to forty-two-day programs designed to teach the acquisition of wilderness skills, leadership techniques, and respect for the natural landscape. These goals are accomplished within a noncompetitive, nurturing, and fun environment in which students gain self-confidence through challenging activities, learn about themselves and others, and attain a lifelong appreciation for the spectacular beauty of wilderness.

Wilderness Skills All Wilderness Ventures expeditions teach a variety of wilderness skills, including, but not limited to, expedition planning; backcountry safety; meal planning, purchasing, and preparation; navigation; minimum-impact camping; and landscape and natural history interpretation. Specific programs also include instruction in sea kayaking, rock climbing, mountaineering, snow and ice climbing, canoeing, surfing, whitewater rafting, whitewater kayaking, mountain biking, road biking, sailing, snorkeling, surfing, and scuba diving. The acquisition of these skills develops self-confidence and prepares young adults for a lifetime of enjoyment in the outdoors.

Leadership Wilderness Ventures believes that leadership involves much more than leading a group safely through a wilderness or to the summit of a peak. All Wilderness Ventures expeditions emphasize the importance of learning how to make decisions and solve problems within a group. These skills are useful throughout life and well beyond the wilderness environment. The small-group format and the emphasis on the group experience require that all expedition members learn to place their personal needs behind the needs of the group. This group focus creates intimate bonding among expedition members and provides each individual with a valuable understanding of group cooperation that enhances social skills for success in life.

Wilderness Appreciation In 1973, access to the most spectacular wilderness environments was still available. It is a privilege for Wilderness Ventures expeditions to visit these natural treasures. Travel through these wilderness areas instills in students a responsibility for their future survival. On the expeditions, students not only learn the methods of minimum-impact camping, but also gain a love for these places and a burning desire to see them saved so that future generations might someday have a similar experience.

PROGRAM OFFERINGS

Students may choose an expedition based upon age appropriateness, level of prior experience, degree of physical challenge desired, and geographical areas of interest. The expeditions are divided into five distinct categories: Domestic Wilderness Adventures, International Adventures, Advanced Leadership Programs, Bicycle Adventures, and Service Adventures.

Domestic Wilderness Adventures Conducted for the past thirty years, these classic adventures range from two to six weeks and offer varying degrees of challenge in a variety of outdoor environments. Participants do not need prior experience for any program. Those who do have experience still find challenging offerings. Backcountry trips range from four to eight days, depending on the program.

International Adventures These exciting adventures range from three to four weeks, offering varying degrees of challenge in a variety of exotic wilderness and outdoor environments around the globe. They are excellent choices for both beginners and experienced students who thrive on outdoor adventure and cultural immersion.

Advanced Outdoor Leadership Programs Ranging from three to four weeks in length, these wonderful programs offer the highest degree of challenge and are conducted in only one or two environments. The programs are open to both beginning and experienced students seeking extended wilderness travel with a thorough focus on outdoor skills.

Bicycle Adventures Conducted in and around some of the most spectacular natural environments, these programs offer varying degrees of challenge. Either on road or mountain bikes, these adventures range from two to four weeks and are offered to both beginning and experienced students seeking an outdoor adventure without a backpack. Wilderness Ventures supplies all biking equipment.

Service Adventures Students can fulfill high school community service requirements by working with Native Americans and assisting in environmental projects while adventuring in some of the most spectacular outdoor settings found in North America and several international destinations. Service trips to Costa Rica are also offered.

ENROLLMENT

Participants enroll from almost every state and several countries each year, with an even distribution of students coming from the Eastern Seaboard, the Midwest, the South, and the West. All expeditions are coeducational. A thorough screening process allows students to travel with others who are highly motivated to succeed and who will contribute positively to the group experience. Each expedition offers multiple sections which are grouped by age and experience compatibility.

DAILY SCHEDULE

The majority of time is spent in the backcountry. Because Wilderness Ventures holds so many wilderness permits throughout the United States and several other countries, expeditions are able to offer a variety of backcountry experiences and activities with minimal travel between areas. The daily schedule is flexible and varied, depending upon the expedition. Besides learning a wide variety of outdoor skills, participants have opportunities to relax by cooling off in a refreshing lake, soaking in a natural hot spring, basking in the mountain sunlight, or photographing or sketching wildlife.

EXTRA OPPORTUNITIES AND ACTIVITIES

Each expedition is conducted in a specific geographical region. During the brief travel between wilderness areas within each region, itineraries are planned to take advantage of worthwhile scenic, cultural, and historic sites. The leaders' knowledge of the areas traveled through prompts frequent informal discussions dealing with each region's particular history, economy, and geography. These discussions, together with the evening campfire programs and the comprehensive mobile libraries, enable students to gain a better understanding of local regions and instill within them a sense of place.

FACILITIES

When not sleeping under the stars, participants use lightweight mountaineering tents.

STAFF

Wilderness Ventures staff members average 26 years of age, with a minimum age of 21. All are experienced leaders and educators. When not working with Wilderness Ventures, many teach at the secondary school or university level or pursue full-time careers in other environmental or outdoor occupations. All staff members are certified Wilderness First Responders or EMTs. All expeditions operate with low student-to-staff ratios, allowing for the highest level of personal attention. A man and a woman accompany each trip. Every summer, Wilderness Ventures averages a 60 percent return rate for staff members.

COSTS

Tuition ranges from $2600 to $6300, depending on the length and location of the expedition, the activities engaged in, and the geographical region. Tuition covers all expenses for the entire expedition except airfare to and from staging cities.

TRANSPORTATION

All expeditions begin or end in Anchorage, Alaska; Juneau, Alaska; Los Angeles, California; San Francisco, California; Denver, Colorado; Honolulu, Hawaii; Boise, Idaho; Portland, Oregon; Salt Lake City, Utah; Seattle, Washington; Spokane, Washington; Jackson, Wyoming; San Jose, Costa Rica; Quito, Ecuador; and several European cities. Staff members meet participants at a central location in the airport on arrival day and accompany them back to the airport and remain with them until their flights depart.

APPLICATION TIMETABLE

Applications are accepted after September 1. Expeditions fill at varying rates, depending on the number of spaces available; many fill by January 1 and most are full by March 1. Students should call for information on program availability, especially if applying late. To receive an extensive catalog describing all of the adventures, interested students can contact the address below.

FOR MORE INFORMATION, CONTACT:

Mike and Helen Cottingham, Directors
Wilderness Ventures
P.O. Box 2768
Jackson Hole, Wyoming 83001
800-533-2281 (toll-free)
E-mail: info@wildernessventures.com
World Wide Web: http://www.wildernessventures.com

PARTICIPANT/FAMILY COMMENTS

"Carson had an amazing trip this summer with Wilderness Ventures. We developed his photos immediately and he dove into remarkable detail about each day and what the group accomplished together and personally. He enjoyed his leaders and appreciated their expertise and leadership. We feel this trip was a real passage for him and definitely a highlight of his life."

THE WINCHENDON SCHOOL

SUMMER SESSION

WINCHENDON, MASSACHUSETTS

Type of Program: Academic remediation, makeup, and enrichment
Participants: Coeducational, grades 8–12
Enrollment: 60
Program Dates: June 27 to August 7, 2004
Head of Program: Elliot C. Harvey, Director

LOCATION

The Winchendon School is located in north central Massachusetts just 65 miles west of Boston. Its rural setting in the foothills of Mt. Monadnock is peaceful and secure. Situated advantageously, the School is able to offer wide-ranging field trips to museums, historic locations, mountains, and the seashore.

BACKGROUND AND PHILOSOPHY

Throughout its existence The Winchendon School Summer Session has provided students with an opportunity to make up lost credits, improve study skills, and generally strengthen their academic standing in a caring, structured setting. A multisensory, multiactivity approach characterizes the small classes (averaging 5 students), which place emphasis on individual needs.

PROGRAM OFFERINGS

Winchendon offers two distinct programs during its summer session. The first is a skills-based program for English-speaking college-bound students who need to make up courses. English, mathematics, and U.S. history courses are regularly available, as are courses in SAT preparation (both verbal and math sections). During the six-week summer session, students receive 13 hours of weekly instruction in each course. Credit can be given if the student has made arrangements before starting the summer program.

Winchendon also offers an ESL program for international students who wish to familiarize themselves with the language, life, and customs of our country. In the formal ESL classes, emphasis is placed on spoken English, listening comprehension, reading, and writing. Three levels of instruction are available: beginning, intermediate, and advanced. Preparation for the TOEFL is a major objective of the intermediate and advanced levels.

Also available to ESL students is an American Culture course, which gives international students an opportunity to learn about American history and society in a hands-on field trip–oriented program that is highly conducive to a successful understanding and appreciation of the history and culture of the United States.

Of advantage to all students are the integrated afternoon sports/activities offerings. Students engage daily in such sports as golf, tennis, swimming, horseback riding, basketball, baseball, and soccer. Professional golf lessons are available at a small fee.

ENROLLMENT

Of the approximately 60 students on campus during the six-week summer experience, the session seeks to enroll 30 students from abroad and 30 from various parts of the United States. Class size averages 5 students per class.

DAILY SCHEDULE

7–7:30	Breakfast
7:35	Room inspection
7:40–8:40	Class
8:45–9:45	Class
9:45–10	Break
10:05–10:45	Study hall/special help
10:50–11:50	Class
11:50–12:15	Lunch
12:20–1:20	Class
1:30–3	Sports/activities
5–5:30	Work program
5:30–6:15	Dinner
7–7:30	Dorm cleanup
7:30–9	Dorm study hours
10	In room
10:30	Lights-out

All students are expected to meet all School appointments and to follow rules of acceptable behavior.

EXTRA OPPORTUNITIES AND ACTIVITIES

Field trips to historic, cultural, and recreational areas are regularly available. On weekends, a variety of activities designed to enhance the students' learning experience are also scheduled.

FACILITIES

All School facilities, including an 18-hole golf course, are available to students on a daily basis. Other facilities located on the 250-acre campus are a swimming pool, tennis courts, a gymnasium, an arts studio, several dormitories, a library, and three classroom buildings.

STAFF

Most teachers in the summer session are members of The Winchendon School faculty. When necessary, the staff is supplemented by qualified teachers from other private and public schools. The director of the program is a Winchendon School administrator during the regular academic year.

MEDICAL CARE

A nurse is available throughout the session. Less than five minutes from campus is a medical clinic that is fully staffed throughout the day and into the evening. The Henry Heywood Hospital is in Gardner, which is less than 10 minutes away.

RELIGIOUS LIFE

The Winchendon School is nondenominational. A variety of local churches are within easy reach of the campus.

COSTS

The cost for the 2004 summer session is $5600, including all field trips, books, and other expenses. Students need approximately $25 a week in spending money. Golf instruction is available for an extra fee.

APPLICATION TIMETABLE

Applications are accepted throughout the year, but it is recommended that they be forwarded by early May. Students wishing to visit the campus before enrolling are encouraged to do so. Appointments can be arranged by calling the Admissions Office.

For more information, contact:

Richard J. Plank
Admissions
The Winchendon School Summer Session
172 Ash Street
Winchendon, Massachusetts 01475
800-622-1119 (toll-free)
Fax: 508-297-0911
E-mail: admissions@winchendon.org
World Wide Web: http://www.winchendon.org

WOLFEBORO

THE SUMMER BOARDING SCHOOL

WOLFEBORO, NEW HAMPSHIRE

Type of Program: Academic
Participants: Coeducational, ages 11–18
Enrollment: 200
Program Dates: Last week of June to second week of August
Head of Program: William A. Cooper, Head of School

LOCATION

The School is situated about 3 miles from the center of Wolfeboro, a charming town in central New Hampshire. The school's 128 acres include a quarter mile of shoreline on Rust Pond. The pond is approximately 2 miles long.

BACKGROUND AND PHILOSOPHY

Since 1910, the school has provided a valuable educational experience for young people. It first served as a tutoring school for boys in need of summer study and offered the opportunity to earn credit and to prepare for college entrance exams. In 1977, the school was reorganized, became coed, and expanded its mission. Today, the School plays a unique role in education and provides a strong model for both students and staff members to learn from within as well as from without.

PROGRAM OFFERINGS

The primary purpose of Wolfeboro is to provide constructive scholastic work for girls and boys, ages 11–18, in an atmosphere of healthy outdoor living combined with summer recreation.

The program emphasizes effective and efficient study skills, organization, motivation, and confidence. The program is individualized to meet each student's needs. All courses may be taken for credit. Students may make up failures; review or preview work in specific academic subjects; strengthen skills in English, grammar, writing, vocabulary, reading, mathematics, science, history, study skills, and foreign language; and take new courses for credit by special arrangement with the student's school. All students attend three academic periods six days per week.

The School serves as a valuable transitional experience for students who are about to enter a boarding school for the first time. Individual goals and a "Goals Document" are established for each student prior to arrival, after discussions with parents, schools, and counselors and a review of available standardized test scores, transcripts, and teachers' reports.

Classes are small (2–6 students per class), so student programs can be individualized within a given section. Credit courses are adjusted to satisfy the requirements of the student's school.

Weekly written teacher reports are made to the Head of School and to the student. Parents receive comprehensive reports after the first three weeks and at the end of the session. The Head of School also writes a final summary report.

An examination is given in each course. In most cases, students are expected to take the program's examination. For schools requiring their own examination, a complete course outline must be submitted before the opening of the summer school.

ENROLLMENT

There are 200 students who come from nearly all of the fifty states and several other countries. Wolfeboro does not discriminate on the basis of race, color, and national and ethnic origin in the administration of its educational policies, admission policies, financial assistance, and athletics and other school-administrated programs.

DAILY SCHEDULE

6:45	Rising bell
7:15	Breakfast
7:45	Daily chores and inspection
8:05	Class bell
8:10	First period
9	Second period
9:50	Third period
10:40	Recess—morning snacks
10:50	Fourth period
11:40	Fifth period
12:30	Short swim
1	Dinner
2–5	Programmed activities and sports
5:15	Mail call
6	Supper
6:40	Intramural league play
7:20	Prepare for study period
7:30	Study period
8:30	Study break
8:45	Study period
9:30	End of evening study
9:45	Prepare for lights-out
10	Lights-out

Sunday

7:30	Rising bell
8	Breakfast
9	Tent inspection
9:45	Trips depart
10	Recreation
1	Dinner
2:15	Recreation
6	Picnic supper
6:40–10	Same as daily schedule

Transportation is available on weekends to attend religious services.

Wolfeboro provides a structured, no-nonsense approach to both scholastic work and to the quality of student life. The school believes that a student functions best in an environment in which all expectations are clearly understood. For this reason, the school has a detailed statement of required student conduct and methods of operation, which is mailed to each individual requesting information about the school.

Attendance at the school implies a sincerity of purpose and a sense of responsibility and cooperation. Students are assigned daily chores necessary to maintain a neat and clean school. Work assignments change every nine days.

EXTRA OPPORTUNITIES AND ACTIVITIES

Many trips are made to the White Mountains and to Maine beaches. There are overnight camping trips each weekend as well as numerous other weekend trips to places of special interest.

FACILITIES

The administrative core of the campus is located near the entrance. The Gertrude Johnson Center accommodates offices and the central reception area. Jousson Lodge, with an excellent view of the main campus, the lake, surrounding woodland, and neighboring mountains, contains the dining room, kitchen, and dispensary. Near Jousson Lodge is The Barn, site of many student functions and activities and the campus store and weight-training room.

The academic core occupies the north periphery of the central campus and includes thirty-six classrooms. Complementing the academic area are two study halls and the faculty center.

The boys' residential area is between the administrative core and the lakefront. Middle School boys enjoy a separate, newly built campus. Waterfront facilities include a sandy beach, two large docks, six swimming lanes, sailboats, rowboats, patrol boats, lifeguard apparatus, and related safety equipment. The girls' residential area is beyond the playing fields at the opposite end of the campus.

Students live in sturdy 7-foot-high tents with screen doors mounted on 10-foot by 12-foot permanent wooden platform bases. Most tents are shared by 2 students. All are equipped with electric lighting, outlets, beds, shelves, and desks. Residential areas include modern bathroom and shower facilities. Each residential area is under the direction of a residential division head. Students are grouped by age into five-tent clusters, each of which is supervised by a faculty member living in an adjacent cottage. Dotted

along the shoreline and periphery of the campus are cottages that house other faculty and staff members and their families.

The dining hall is more than a facility in which good food is served. By intent, mealtimes provide an opportunity to gather the whole community together in an atmosphere that reflects and affirms the very essence of the Wolfeboro experience. All meals, except Sunday's picnic supper, are served family-style at tables of 10 that include students, faculty members, and faculty families. Seating assignments and student-waiter assignments are rotated, which provides enriching and supportive social interaction for all. Each table is headed by a faculty member who ensures the observation of good eating habits and gracious social manners. All meals in the dining room begin with a blessing.

MEDICAL CARE

The ratio of students to staff members enables Wolfeboro to place top priority on health and safety. The school is fortunate to have a large, fully equipped hospital 2 miles away. Students are under the direct supervision of a local physician. A registered nurse is always on duty and routinely attends to students in the dispensary.

COSTS

A $2000 fee must accompany the application. If the applicant is accepted, then the $2000 deposit is credited toward the fee for room, board, and tuition. The fee in 2003 was $8400. Fees are not refundable for early withdrawal or dismissal.

FINANCIAL AID

Limited financial assistance is available. Grants are made on a case-by-case basis.

TRANSPORTATION

Travel to Wolfeboro is quite simple. Staff members meet planes at the airport on opening day and transport students to Wolfeboro by chartered bus. The process is reversed on closing day.

APPLICATION TIMETABLE

Inquiries concerning Wolfeboro may be made at any time, and an opportunity to tour the facilities may be made with the Head of School.

FOR MORE INFORMATION, CONTACT:

William A. Cooper, Head of School
Wolfeboro Camp School
Box 390
Wolfeboro, New Hampshire 03894-0390
603-569-3451
Fax: 603-569-4080
World Wide Web: http://www.wolfeboro.org

WOODBERRY FOREST SCHOOL

SUMMER ADVENTURE

WOODBERRY FOREST, VIRGINIA

Type of Program: Academic enrichment and credit and study abroad
Participants: Coeducational, rising students in grades 7–12
Enrollment: 150
Program Dates: Senior Adventure: June 19 to July 17 (four weeks); Junior Adventure: June 19 to July 9 (three weeks)

LOCATION

Woodberry Forest School is located just north of Charlottesville in the rolling farmland of the Virginia Piedmont. The dormitories and academic buildings are set among shaded lawns, offering a beautiful view of the countryside and the Blue Ridge Mountains.

BACKGROUND AND PHILOSOPHY

The Woodberry Forest Summer Programs, in continuous operation since 1921, incorporate in a coeducational boarding school summer experience the same qualities of excellence in faculty, facilities, and programs that have characterized Woodberry Forest School since its founding in 1889.

Woodberry Forest's 1,200-acre campus provides a safe, secluded environment that allows the School and its faculty to concentrate on developing qualities of honor, decency, and integrity among students. The entire community operates under a system of mutual trust and respect based on Woodberry's honor system.

PROGRAM OFFERINGS

Woodberry Forest Summer Programs offer the Senior Adventure and Junior Adventure. The Senior Adventure is designed for students who will be in high school in the fall of 2005. Each student has the opportunity to focus on one major academic course. The courses are designed to supplement the material studied in a winter course, develop specific study or testing skills, or expose the student to an exciting new topic. Each student also chooses two enrichment classes designed to provide an exciting exploration in personal development and intellect. The afternoons afford each student a variety of options, including sports, art, driver's ed, or community service. During the second week, students in some of these afternoon courses are given the opportunity to try a different option for the last half of the session.

The Junior Adventure combines all of the fun of summer with the thrill of intellectual challenge. Participants immerse themselves in two of eight courses, each of which meets for 2 hours per day and places a tremendous emphasis on creativity and hands-on learning. Students are not only asked to learn new skills and new material but to apply their knowledge immediately. Young computer scientists, for example, build Web sites and write simple programs; history scholars explore battlefields and nineteenth-century documents; and artists assemble their own portfolios. Talented and motivated students delight in the opportunity to focus on a subject that interests them, and the diverse offerings in art, literature, music, computers, math, science, history, and drama appeal to any rising seventh or eighth grader.

ENROLLMENT

In 2003, 87 boys and girls from twenty-two states and five other countries attended the summer session.

DAILY SCHEDULE

7:15–8:00	Breakfast
8:15–9:45	Academic course
10:00–11:00	Short course (alternating days between two courses)
11:15–12:45	Academic course (continued)
12:45–1:30	Lunch
1:30	Assembly (Monday, Tuesday, Thursday, Friday)
2:00–3:30	Nonacademic course (Monday, Tuesday, Thursday, Friday)
4:00–5:30	Recreation
5:45–6:15	Dinner
7:30–9:45	Two study periods (with 15-minute break)
10:45	Lights-out

EXTRA OPPORTUNITIES AND ACTIVITIES

Woodberry Forest Summer Adventure takes full advantage of its proximity to natural, cultural, and recreational resources. Four afternoons a week, students participate in a full range of activities—recreational athletics, community service, and personal enrichment activities. The Alpine Tower and Ropes Program is an adventure-based program that provides participants with opportunities for individual challenge and group development.

Weekends are filled with attractive options, including trips to Washington, D.C.; hiking in the Blue Ridge Mountains; rafting in West Virginia; and excursions to Williamsburg, Kings Dominion, and Busch Gardens.

FACILITIES

The School's facilities include new classroom buildings, an expansive library and audiovisual center, a state-of-the-art campus computer network, an indoor athletics center, and six dormitories. A nine-hole golf course; swimming pools; tennis, squash, and basketball courts; and a variety of playing fields and hiking trails allow a wide range of recreational activities.

STAFF

The summer session staff is made up primarily of Woodberry Forest teachers. College students, many of whom are alumni of the School, serve as interns in the summer session.

The ratio of 1 faculty member for every 5 students ensures that each student receives personal attention. Small classes and daily consultation periods give students easy access to faculty members who are committed to helping students achieve their goals.

MEDICAL CARE

The Summer School employs 2 registered nurses and a doctor who are on call at all times to respond to student health needs. The campus infirmary, equipped to care for 20 patients, keeps a medical record on file for each student.

RELIGIOUS LIFE

Students attend a nondenominational Sunday evening worship service. Students from many denominations attend the School, and all are encouraged to attend services in the nearby churches of their choice.

COSTS

Tuition for the 2004 four-week Senior Adventure was $3675. Tuition for the three-week Junior Adventure was $2730. Tuition and other fees for specific courses are outlined in the Summer Programs catalog.

FINANCIAL AID

A limited amount of scholarship aid is available and is awarded based on need. Students wishing to apply for financial aid should request the appropriate application form from the Woodberry Forest Financial Aid Office.

TRANSPORTATION

The School provides transportation to and from Dulles and National airports in Washington, D.C., and the nearby Charlottesville Airport at the opening and closing of the session.

APPLICATION TIMETABLE

Applicants should request the Woodberry Forest 2004 Summer Adventure Catalog, which contains the necessary application forms and outlines the application procedure. Students are admitted on a rolling basis starting February 1 and are encouraged to apply before May 1 in order to have the best chance of being admitted. Applications may be submitted until June 1.

For more information, contact:

Dr. David McRae, Director
Woodberry Forest Summer Adventure
Woodberry Forest, Virginia 22989
540-672-6047
Fax: 540-672-9076
E-mail: wfs_summer@woodberry.org
World Wide Web: http://www.woodberry.org/campus/summer

WORCESTER POLYTECHNIC INSTITUTE

WPI FRONTIERS PROGRAM

WORCESTER, MASSACHUSETTS

Type of Program: Academic enrichment
Participants: Coeducational, students entering grades 11 and 12
Enrollment: 115–135
Program Dates: July 10–22, 2005
Head of Program: Julie Chapman, Assistant Director of Admissions

LOCATION

WPI is situated on 88 acres in Worcester, Massachusetts, New England's second-largest city. The campus, surrounded by parks and residential neighborhoods, is located 1 mile from downtown. Students have full access to WPI's facilities, including the Gordon Library, state-of-the-art laboratories and equipment, athletic facilities, and the university computer system.

BACKGROUND AND PHILOSOPHY

WPI Frontiers was founded twenty-two years ago to allow high school students to further explore their interests in science, mathematics, technology, and engineering. WPI Frontiers exposes students to current research problems and methods and encourages pursuit of careers in science and technology.

PROGRAM OFFERINGS

Aerospace Engineering Students explore the science of flight and learn how wings and aircraft create lift to fly. Basic concepts in aerodynamics—including drag, streamlining, airfoil stall, and aircraft design—are studied. They conduct wind and water tunnel experiments to visualize the flow over aircraft, then run simulations on laptop computers. Using what they have learned, students design and build a simple model aircraft, test it in the wind tunnel, and see it soar in free flight.
Biology and Biotechnology This program allows students to explore this science, from molecules and cells to ecology and evolution. They cut, splice, and insert DNA to enginneer new bacteria; eavesdrop on their own nerves and muscles with computer-based technology; prepare and view cells in an electron microscope; meet a tiny roundworm that is the new favorite of geneticists; use DNA fingerprinting and antibodies to track genes and the proteins they code for; and study reproduction, ecology, anatomy, and scientific contributions (including a Nobel Prize) of the ancient horseshoe crab.
Computer Science Students journey into the world of object-oriented and Web programming. They explore at their own pace the world of programming as it is used in the World Wide Web and object-oriented languages, such as Java. Students have the opportunity to incorporate the work as part of effective multimedia interfaces for content of interest to them. In addition, special topics in computer science are discussed according to student interest.
Electrical and Computer Engineering Students discover the fascinating world of analog and digital electronics through classroom exercises and laboratory hands-on activities. They learn to use lab equipment, including power supplies, function generators, and oscilloscopes to test circuits that they build. Students apply this knowledge to a design project that they are working on throughout the course. Topics include audio amplification, light-wave transmission, analog signal processing, and digital circuitry. The prerequisites for students are a good attitude, an open mind, a desire to learn.
Mathematics Students in this program learn how a mix of classical mathematics and modern technology can be used to solve current problems and open new areas. They use this background to examine encryption of numbers on the Internet via the RSA Algorithm and analysis of human voice patterns and musical instruments through Fourier methods. Specific problems of current information technology that these address include the need for secure transmission of data such as credit card numbers over the Internet, voice-print technology, and storage and use of music in digital format (WAV vs. MP3 files, for example).
Mechanical Engineering Mechanical engineering is a broad discipline that includes many areas of interest, such as energy production and transfer, mechanical design, materials science, biomechanics, and fluid flow. Students explore the breadth of this discipline through a mixture of fundamental concepts and experimentation. Their focus is on the design of a device and the integration of mechanics and thermofluids.
Physics Students investigate selected fields and tools of modern physics—such as interplanetary travel, atomic spectroscopy, MRI (magnetic resonance imaging) and black holes—through a combination of lectures, audio-visual presentations, hands-on laboratory experiments, and visits to research facilities.
Robotics Students discover the science and technology of recreational robot design and operation. (This session is particularly useful in preparing participants for entry or leadership within the FIRST robotics team in their high schools.) Students learn about driveline design, sensor operations, programming, pneumatics, and manufacturing techniques. They use this information to solve a challenging robotics problem. Each subgroup in the session brainstorms, designs, builds, and tests its own creation. The chance for each subgroup to show its

team's design superiority comes when robots meet for the climatic end-of-session tournament.

In addition to the major areas of study, students also participate in a communication workshop of their choosing. These workshops include speech, creative writing, music, theater, and elements of writing.

ENROLLMENT

WPI Frontiers seeks students who have demonstrated superior ability and interest in science and mathematics. It is recommended that applicants be enrolled in a college-preparatory curriculum where they have completed, or will complete, 4 units of English, 4 units of mathematics (including trigonometry and analytical geometry), and 2 units of a lab science. A letter of recommendation from a science or mathematics teacher or guidance counselor is also required.

DAILY SCHEDULE

Breakfast	7:00–8:00
Academic programs	8:00–10:30
Communication workshops	10:30–12:30
Lunch	12:30–1:30
Academic programs	1:30–4:30
Dinner	5:00–6:00
Extracurricular activities	6:30–10:30
Check in	11:00
Lights out	12:00

EXTRA OPPORTUNITIES AND ACTIVITIES

In addition to attending the academic programs and workshops, participants enjoy a full schedule of activities. Field trips, movies, performances, and tournaments enable participants to interact with each other and help develop leadership skills and friendships.

FACILITIES

Students are housed in one of WPI's supervised residence halls and attend classes in modern facilities. Students have access to the athletic facilities, including a fitness center, gymnasium, softball diamond, and tennis courts, and computer labs.

STAFF

Each course and workshop is taught by a WPI faculty member. In addition, residence halls and program activities are supervised by WPI upperclass students as well as members of the WPI administrative staff. Student staff members are selected based on leadership skills, academic achievement, enthusiasm, and demonstrated responsible behavior.

MEDICAL CARE

WPI's Health Center is open Monday through Friday, 8 a.m. to 4 p.m. After regular hours and on weekends, campus police and Frontiers staff members, in cooperation with local hospitals, handle any medical emergencies that may arise.

COSTS

The tuition cost for the 2004 Frontiers program was $1900. This covered tuition, books, meals, housing, field trips, and activities.

TRANSPORTATION

Worcester is centrally located in New England, with access to four airports within an hour of the city: Logan Airport (Boston, Massachusetts), T.F. Green (Providence, Rhode Island), Bradley International (Hartford, Connecticut), and Manchester Airport (Manchester, New Hampshire). Worcester also has an airport and Amtrak station located within 10 miles of campus. Students traveling from outside of Worcester are given information on traveling and transportation to the campus.

APPLICATION TIMETABLE

The application deadline is May 15. Students are notified of acceptance on a rolling basis.

FOR MORE INFORMATION, CONTACT:

WPI Frontiers Program
100 Institute Road
Worcester, Massachusetts 01609-2280
508-831-5286 or 5060
Fax: 508-831-5875
E-mail: frontiers@wpi.edu
World Wide Web: http://www.wpi.edu/+frontiers

WORLD HORIZONS INTERNATIONAL

SUMMER PROGRAMS

COSTA RICA; PUERTO RICO; MEXICO; ENGLISH-SPEAKING CARIBBEAN ISLAND OF DOMINICA; HAWAIIAN ISLAND OF OAHU; ISLAND OF FIJI; ICELAND; KANAB, UTAH (IN CONJUNCTION WITH BEST FRIENDS ANIMAL SANCTUARY AND ZION NATIONAL PARK) AND THE NAVAJO NATION; CANADA; AND MAINE

Type of Program: Community service, cross-cultural exchange, and intercultural language and learning
Participants: Coeducational programs for high school students
Enrollment: 10–12 students per group, under the supervision of 2 adult leaders
Program Dates: Two-, three-, four-, and five-week sessions beginning in early June
Head of Program: Stuart L. Rabinowitz, Executive Director

LOCATION

World Horizons International (WHI), LLC, offers programs for Spanish-speaking students in Costa Rica, Puerto Rico, and Mexico. WHI also has a French-speaking program in Canada. In addition, there are also intercultural-travel learning programs in small village settings in Fiji, in the village of Nokoru-Kula on the island of Viti Levu; in Hawaii on the island of Oahu; in Dominica, an English-speaking island in the Caribbean; in a program in Kanab, Utah, working with Best Friends Animal Sanctuary; in Maine at Camp Sunshine; and at an environmental program in Iceland.

BACKGROUND AND PHILOSOPHY

World Horizons International is an organization founded in 1987 to sponsor programs for students interested in cross-cultural community service. World Horizons has established, developed, and run summer programs in the Caribbean and Central America that have provided volunteer opportunities for thousands of high school students. World Horizons started in 1988 with projects on English-speaking islands in the Caribbean, Alaska, and Central America. Now, after seventeen years, WHI's strong presence has continued in these areas and also in Hawaii, Puerto Rico, South America, Iceland, and additional locations around the U.S.

World Horizons, under the leadership of Stuart Rabinowitz since 2001, continues to offer cross-cultural community service opportunities for teenage participants who wish to expand their knowledge of themselves and the world in which they live.

Every aspect of the World Horizons program is designed to enable each participant to enter into the life and culture of the local community. The immediate rewards of a summer with World Horizons come from the relationships that students build with people from the local community and members of their WHI group and from the success of community service involvement. One student on the program to Central America described her experience as "having assisted me in redirecting my academic concentrations, and also helping me to transform my thoughts and feelings on life in general. World Horizons allows one to see what is really important in life." Another student who went on a program to Ecuador remarked, "I returned with a different perspective of myself and the American society. I brought home the knowledge that happiness does not rely on material possessions as our society seems to indicate, but rather it relies on the love we share with friends and families."

PROGRAM OFFERINGS

World Horizons volunteers live, work, and travel in groups of 10–12 students led by 2 highly qualified staff members. Local representatives arrange housing for the group to live together in a local home, school, or community facility. During the week, participants spend part of each day on a group project identified by the local host organization. These involvements might find the student painting and repairing homes of senior citizens; teaching arts and crafts, dance, music, or sports to children in a day-camp setting; or building a school, medical clinic, or community hall. Continuing the concept of community service, a portion of the afternoon is devoted to an individual internship program selected by the student. These are unique involvements that are focused on learning more about the local people and their culture. Past individual internships have included tutoring children; participating in an environmental awareness program; assisting a local physician; hosting a call-in radio show; helping in a dairy; and working in a fishery that cultivates giant clams and exotic fish.

Spanish Language Programs There are two World Horizons programs in **Costa Rica**; both are designed to facilitate Spanish-speaking skills and cultural immersion. One site is near the city of San Isidro, about 3 hours south of San Jose, while the other is located west of the capital city. These sites have been very popular with WHI volunteers who want to participate in community service and use their Spanish skills within the total immersion of a small Central American town. Participants work alongside local counterparts in painting senior citizens' homes and refurbishing community facilities. In addition, they establish a day camp for children and teach activities such as sports, arts and crafts, dance, and music. Afternoon internships are unique and diversified and may include picking coffee beans on a coffee plantation, assisting at the local health center, tutoring at an orphanage, working with the elderly, writing for the local newspaper, or learning the art of Costa Rican cooking in a local restaurant.

In **Mexico,** the group stays at an eco-village called Huehuecoyotl, located near Tepotzion, about 1½ hours south of Mexico City. The students work with an orphanage and a women's cooperative, and they are involved with numerous ecological projects. Weekends are spent

exploring the scenery and historic sites, such as the Pyramids, the Frieda Kahlo Museum, and much more.

In **Puerto Rico,** participants work with a senior citizens' home, run a day camp, and assist with environmental projects on the island of Culebra. Participants also work on community development and beautification projects, such as painting classrooms, sprucing up homes of elderly residents, and repairing playground equipment. Internships may include working in a health clinic, visiting needy communities with the director of community development, and tutoring children. Highlights for participants include daylong excursions to El Yunque (the rain forest), Old San Juan, and caving in central Puerto Rico.

In **Fiji**, the program works in conjunction with the senior education officer on the island of Viti Levu, near the city of RakiRaki. Located in the village of Nokoru Kula, students tutor and run day camp activities for local children. Volunteers also paint and build projects for the village and help senior citizens. Weekends are used to see the sights of Fiji and for activities such as snorkeling and swimming.

In the **Caribbean**, community service offerings on the island of Dominica, in the eastern Caribbean, involve painting and repairing senior citizens' homes, working with preschools and daycare centers painting and fixing facilities as well as creating activities for the children, and assisting with local environmental issues. Individual internships are varied and may involve working with a health clinic, daycare centers, and with orphans through "Operation Youthquake." Weekends are set aside for expeditions to nearby islands, hiking in the countryside, enjoying local beaches, sightseeing, or taking part in festivals, such as Carnival or the regatta boat races.

The island of Oahu in **Hawaii** is an incredibly beautiful spot with high mountain peaks, aqua-blue bays, and valleys dotted with pineapple fields. The group is located in Honolulu and on the northeast coast in Kaneohe Bay. Students work with groups called HUGS and Kama'aini Kids and with children at the YWCA and YMCA. Individual internships focus on the indigenous culture of the people of this area. There are opportunities to assist with the farming and harvesting of crops, to work in botanic gardens, and to restore hiking trails through the Division of Forestry and Wildlife. Weekends are set aside to explore the many historic sites on Oahu as well as to participate in some of the best swimming, hiking, and photographic possibilities on the Hawaiian Islands. The trip culminates with a 2½ day Coast Guard-certified sailing course to the island of Molokai.

The **Maine** trip goes to Camp Sunshine located in Casco, Maine. Camp Sunshine was established to support critically ill children and their families by addressing the impact of a critical illness on every member of the immediate family. The families involved have children diagnosed with cancer, kidney disease, lupus, diabetes, solid organ transplants, and other life-threatening illnesses. World Horizons students help with the daily activities and services needed to keep the camp running. They are involved in recreational leadership, childcare, food service, and whatever else needs to be done. WHI students also help with games and events designed to foster family involvement.

In **Iceland**, the Land of the Midnight Sun, summers are light, promoting a fun nightlife and recreational opportunities that include whale watching and the "swimming pool and steam bath culture" of the high north. The group is based partially in the capital city of Reykjavik and participants plant trees in the government-sponsored reforestation project. The area is famous for its geothermals and accompanying horticulture. Internships may include working at the horticultural college and with horticultural businesses in the region. The highlight of this trip is a two-to-three-day pony trek into the interior to see the beautiful and unusual scenery.

In **Utah**, working in conjunction with the Best Friends Animal Sanctuary, participants work alongside staff members in the daily care of the animals, many of which have been abused or abandoned. The group helps to feed, exercise, observe behavior, and work with animals with special needs. At any given time, there are more than 1,500 dogs, cats, birds, rabbits, goats, horses, and burros who have to be nursed back to health. Weekend trips may include hiking, backpacking, canoeing, and visits to the Grand Canyon and Bryce Canyon. The second half of this trip consists of participants camping at Zion National Park and assisting the rangers with trail maintenance, or it may involve working with the Navajo Nation on projects in Utah and Arizona.

In **Canada**, the group works in conjunction with Horizons Cosmopolite. Located 90 minutes from Montreal in the small town of Victoriaville, students work with children on local recycling projects and are also involved in fix-up projects for daycare centers and elderly homes. Students have the opportunity to improve their French while working alongside the local residents of the town.

STAFF

Leaders are college graduates with extensive experience working with students as teachers or in teenage-related programs. Many have worked, lived, and traveled abroad as Peace Corps volunteers. Assistant leaders are at least juniors in college. In addition, a facilitator from the local community assists with World Horizons programs.

COSTS

The all-inclusive fees for the 2004 programs, including roundtrip airfare from the departure point, ranged from $2850 to $5250.

FINANCIAL AID

World Horizons offers limited scholarship assistance to students with financial need. Individual fund-raising information is available upon request.

TRANSPORTATION

Programs begin with students departing from New York, Miami, and Los Angeles area airports on regularly scheduled commercial airline flights.

APPLICATION TIMETABLE

World Horizons accepts applications on a year-round basis. Enrollment is limited and participants are encouraged to apply as early as possible to secure a spot in the program of their choice. Students are required to complete an application form and supply the name of at least two references. A decision is made within two weeks of receiving the completed application.

For more information, contact:

World Horizons International, LLC.
P.O. Box 662
Bethlehem, Connecticut 06751
203-266-5874
800-262-5874 (toll-free)
Fax: 203-266-6227
E-mail: worldhorizons@att.net
World Wide Web: http://www.world-horizons.com

WRITING FOR COLLEGE AT BRYN MAWR COLLEGE

SUMMER PROGRAM

BRYN MAWR, PENNSYLVANIA

Type of Program: Residential writing program and pre-college experience
Participants: Young women completing their sophomore, junior, or senior year
Enrollment: Up to 50
Program Dates: Three weeks, late June to mid-July, with optional fourth-week program
Head of Program: Ann Brown, Coordinator

LOCATION

The College's 135-acre campus is located 11 miles west of Philadelphia, in a suburban town with a population of 9,000. The town is an easy 5-minute walk from the campus and offers a movie theater, several cafés and restaurants, and a drugstore, a bookstore, and a variety of other stores.

BACKGROUND AND PHILOSOPHY

Since 1993, Bryn Mawr's Writing for College program has prepared high school–aged young women to write well for college in a program that is intensive, supportive, and fun. The academic, recreational, and college-preparatory dimensions are interwoven to create an integrated experience whose aim is to build a community of writers. All experiences, including seminars, workshops, tutorials, student readings, field trips, college visits, guest writers/speakers, and personal interactions together challenge and stimulate the community.

In addition to participating in the three-week academic program, students are invited to participate in a fourth-week program, Women of Distinction: College Admissions Preparation. This program is designed to assist students in navigating the college admissions process.

PROGRAM OFFERINGS

Students apply to participate in one of the writing-intensive strands. For up-to-date information on the 2005 program, students should request a brochure or visit the program Web site listed below. The 2004 summer program offered the following classes.

Creative Writing Modeled on undergraduate creative writing programs, the creative writing strand helps participants balance the solitary act of writing with the artistic, academic, and peer interaction that nourishes and supports it. This strand links study of the art and craft of literature to a workshop approach to creative writing that offers a range of experiences from free writing to radical revision in a supportive, encouraging community. As readers and writers, participants explore approaches to three genres—poetry, short fiction, and creative nonfiction—as well as cross-genre writing, literary essay, and portfolio preparation. Readings in contemporary and period literature, primarily by women, inspire creative writing, and the creative writing stimulates brief essays responding to literature.

Environmental Studies Participants explore their relationship with the natural world in the context of significant environmental issues. They address such questions as, How do our connections with natural places influence our daily practices and long-term choices, how does our culture derive from our landscape, and, conversely, how does our landscape change in relation to our culture? Participants draw on the rich resources of history, literature, folklore, art, and ecology to inform and shape their own writing, which includes autobiographical, analytical, and creative pieces.

Urban Studies Participants investigate life in the contemporary city. What makes urban life so compelling and also so complex? How do diverse people experience and express their experiences of the city? What can we learn from investigating the uses of space, the diversity of culture, and urban education as dimensions of life in the city? Participants look at how life in cities is represented in literature, photography, music, and film. They also spend time together in the city of Philadelphia exploring, writing about, and in other ways representing this city from its cultural and political centers to its residential neighborhoods. Participants write descriptively, creatively, and analytically.

Women of Distinction: College Admissions Preparation Students may also apply to the weeklong Women of Distinction program. This program is designed to assist students in navigating the college admissions process. Through interactive workshops and personality assessment tools such as the Myers Briggs Type Indicator, students gain a better understanding of themselves and what is important to them in selecting a college. Students spend time learning about their motives and styles and what makes them unique. They receive coaching on how to express their unique story effectively in an essay and in an interview. Finally, armed with more information about themselves, students learn what distinguishes one college from another as well as what to expect in their first year.

ENROLLMENT

Writing frequently and receiving detailed one-on-one instruction are the best ways to learn to write. Therefore, program size is limited so that each student receives helpful attention in small-group workshops and individual conferences.

DAILY SCHEDULE

8:30	Breakfast
9:30–11	Seminars
11–12:30	Workshop
12:30	Lunch
2–4:00	Lab
4:00	Sports
6:00	Dinner
7–10:00	Work time, entertainment activities

During the week, students also take field trips related to their academic work or visit area colleges. Outings and other activities are scheduled for weekends.

FACILITIES

Students reside in a Bryn Mawr College residence hall with their resident advisers. Participants can take advantage of all of Bryn Mawr's facilities, including the campus center, the computing center, libraries, gymnasium, tennis courts, and playing fields.

STAFF

The program staff includes a coordinator, an academic director, instructors for each strand, teaching assistants, and resident advisers who are Bryn Mawr College seniors or recent graduates. The faculty-student ratio is typically 1:10, as is the resident adviser-student ratio.

COSTS

The all-inclusive cost for tuition, dormitory, meals, activities, and materials is $2700 for three weeks and an additional $800 for the fourth-week Women of Distinction program. Students can also apply only to the Women of Distinction program, either as a day student ($900) or as a residential student ($1100).

FINANCIAL AID

A limited amount of need-based financial aid is available.

TRANSPORTATION

The Bryn Mawr College campus is only 30 minutes by car from the Philadelphia International Airport. It is also accessible by commuter train.

APPLICATION TIMETABLE

Applications are accepted on a rolling basis until May 1.

For more information, contact:

Ann Brown, Coordinator
Writing for College
Bryn Mawr College
101 North Merion Avenue
Bryn Mawr, Pennsylvania 19010-2899
610-526-5376 (year-round)
E-mail: writingforcollege@brynmawr.edu
World Wide Web: http://www.brynmawr.edu/writingforcollege

PARTICIPANT/FAMILY COMMENTS

"Writing for College was absolutely wonderful. I feel that I have truly grown as a writer. I am eager to use my new techniques at school. The people here were all so enthusiastic (especially the professors)—there was just an absolutely wonderful atmosphere pervading the program."

WYOMING SEMINARY

SEM SUMMER 2005

KINGSTON, PENNSYLVANIA

Type of Program: Academic enrichment, science discovery, English as a second language, performing arts, and sports camps
Participants: Coeducational, grades PK–12
Enrollment: 700
Program Dates: July and August; length of each program varies
Head of Program: John R. Eidam, Director

LOCATION

Wyoming Seminary, founded in 1844, is one of the nation's oldest continuously coeducational college-preparatory schools. During the regular school year, it enrolls more than 400 students in pre-kindergarten through grade 8 on the Lower School campus in Forty Fort and 443 students in grade 9 through the postgraduate year on the Upper School campus in Kingston. Summer programs attract more than 700 students each year.

Summer programs are held on the 18-acre Kingston campus, set in a small-town residential area of northeastern Pennsylvania. Campus activities include concerts, films, picnics, and sports. The school is close to the recreational advantages of the Pocono region: mountains, lakes, and open space. Movie theaters, shopping, and restaurants are within walking distance.

BACKGROUND AND PHILOSOPHY

Summer at Sem 2005 offers a seven-day boarding program for high school students. English as a second language is offered for international students. The Performing Arts Institute attracts extraordinarily talented students who work with world-renowned faculty members and conductors.

The school's faculty, recreational facilities, library resources, and small-town setting provide outstanding opportunities for growth in a safe and supportive environment.

PROGRAM OFFERINGS

Students can combine courses to meet their own interests; they can register for either one or two half-day courses. Although most courses are 2½ hours, five days each week for four weeks, several are two weeks in length.

Primary and Middle School Music Programs Designed for young musicians between the ages of 7–9, the *Music Makers* program includes fun activities, such as musical games, recorder, solfeggio-singing, movement, chorus, and mallet percussion. The *Young Artists* program is for students between the ages of 10–13 who have a love of singing and musical theater. *Junior PAI* is for students in grades 5–8 who seek a positive instrumental music experience.

Secondary School Programs A wide range of enrichment and credit courses are offered for students entering grades 9–12, including computer science, languages, music and art, mathematics and science, English literature and writing, and theater arts.

Sports Camps The Girls' Clinic's goal is to improve basic skills and strategies. The Girls' Field Hockey Clinic is designed for girls entering grades 4–12. The Girls' Basketball Clinic is designed for girls entering grades 5–9. The Girls' Lacrosse Clinic is for girls entering grades 5–8.The Blue Knights Sports Camp offers coed recreation and sports activities for participants ages 8–14.

English as a Second Language Program Now in its twelfth year, this program attracts students from Asia, South America, and Europe. Students may enroll for four, five, or nine weeks depending upon their own school's calendar. Along with intensive study of the English language, students travel with teachers to New York City, Philadelphia, and New Hampshire. Exposure to American culture is an important part of Sem Summer ESL.

College Prep Institute Under the guidance of members of Sem's seasoned teaching staff, the College Prep Institute offers students a summer of enrichment and academic challenge in courses ranging from American History on Film to Public Speaking to The Creation of Music.

Performing Arts Institute (PAI) Students, teachers, and conductors from all over the world are attracted to this program. Intended for especially gifted musicians and dancers, PAI of Wyoming Seminary is a haven for young performing artists who are serious about developing their talents and who seek a truly enriching summer experience. Institute Director Nancy Sanderson brings twenty-three years of experience, talented faculty members, and professional associates to this creative endeavor.

ENROLLMENT

Summer programs enroll more than 700 boarding and day students: day students in grades PK–4 and boarding and day students in grades 9–12, including U.S. and international students. Students of all ethnic, racial, religious, and social backgrounds are welcome.

EXTRA OPPORTUNITIES AND ACTIVITIES

Field trips and travel opportunities using the resources of the Wyoming Valley and northeastern Pennsylvania—parks, museums, recreational facilities, and historical sites—are important to the summer program. Campus cookouts, films, dances, sports, and the many concerts and shows of the Performing Arts Institute play a key role in campus life.

FACILITIES

Campus facilities include four residence halls; fully equipped Macintosh computer labs; a performing arts center, including music practice rooms, a 400-seat theater, a concert hall, and a scene shop; a science center with five laboratories; a 21,000-volume library that provides access to many Pennsylvania libraries; two gymnasiums with a fitness room and pool; a stadium, athletic fields, and tennis courts; studio art rooms and dance facilities; and a student center with lounges, games, and a wide-screen television.

STAFF

Regular Wyoming Seminary faculty members are joined by adjunct faculty members from regional and international schools, colleges, and universities. More than 30 faculty members live on campus year-round in residence halls and school housing; they provide a 24-hour presence on campus. Dormitories are supervised by the Director of Residence. College students, most of them Seminary graduates, serve as resident assistants and tutors.

MEDICAL CARE

The school is served by an on-staff nurse and school physician and is less than 10 minutes away from a fully accredited medical center. Students must complete health and health insurance forms prior to enrollment.

RELIGIOUS LIFE

Wyoming Seminary, affiliated with the United Methodist Church, welcomes students of all denominations. During the summer session, no religious services are scheduled; churches and synagogues are, however, within walking distance of campus. The school's chaplain is in residence during the summer.

COSTS

In 2004, the application fee for middle and secondary school academic programs was $25; the application fee for English as a second language was $50. Instructional fees were $300 for a two-week academic course and $525 for a four-week academic course. Boarding fees for four weeks were $1900 (seven days per week).

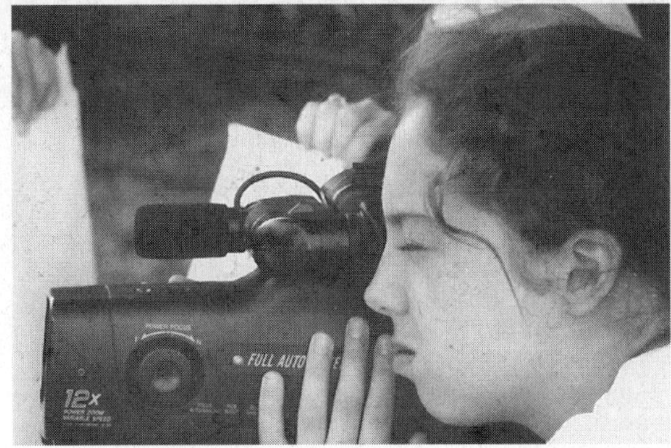

English as a second language course fees were as follows: Session I (four weeks), $3400, and Session II (five weeks, including one week of travel), $5200. The Blue Knights Sports Camp was $120 per week, the Lady Blue Knights Basketball Clinic was $140, and the Lady Blue Knights Field Hockey Clinic was $85.

Primary program costs in 2004 were $70 per weekly session, with one to three sessions available daily. Tutorials in reading and math were available at $150 per week, with a two-week minimum.

FINANCIAL AID

Financial aid is available on a limited basis for summer school programs.

TRANSPORTATION

The Wilkes-Barre/Scranton International Airport (AVP) at Avoca is served by USAir, United, Delta, TWExpress, and Continental airlines. Limousine service is available for the 20-minute ride to Wyoming Seminary. The school is 1 mile from downtown Wilkes-Barre, which is served by national bus lines and is easily accessible from Interstates 80 and 81 and the Pennsylvania Turnpike.

APPLICATION TIMETABLE

Applications are available in early February, and applications are accepted until registration in June.

FOR MORE INFORMATION, CONTACT:

John R. Eidam
Dean of Admission and Director
of Summer and International Programs
Wyoming Seminary
201 North Sprague Avenue
Kingston, Pennsylvania 18704-3593
570-270-2187
Fax: 570-270-2198
E-mail: semsum@wyomingseminary.org
World Wide Web: http://www.wyomingseminary.org/summer

YOUNG ACTORS CAMP

YOUNG ACTORS CAMP

LOS ANGELES, CALIFORNIA

Type of Program: Acting for film and televison
Participants: Coeducational, ages 12–19
Enrollment: 60
Program Dates: Los Angeles, first two weeks in August; London and Paris, third week in August
Head of Program: Samanthia Sierakowski

LOCATION

The Young Actors Camp is based at the University of California, Los Angeles (UCLA) campus, which is located on the west side of Los Angeles at the foot of the Santa Monica Mountains, a few miles from the Pacific Ocean and adjacent to the residential communities of Bel Air and Beverly Hills. Its location in the midst of the star-powered entertainment industry in and around Hollywood and Los Angeles makes it an extraordinary setting for exposure to the film and TV industries.

The third week of the program is an optional excursion trip to London and Paris.

BACKGROUND AND PHILOSOPHY

Los Angeles is known as the world center of the film industry. Young Actors Camp was founded in 1999 by Nichelle and Rene Rodriguez as a place for young actors to experience the film and television industry firsthand. Talented young students come from across the country and around the world to experience the intensive program and meet other teens who share their acting passion. They learn acting, marketing, and career development techniques; have the opportunity to be signed by an agent; and are taken to auditions if signed. Whether the campers are accomplished professional young actors or have only had local acting experience, they are challenged by some of the best instructors in Hollywood and in some of the most prestigious training centers available to an actor.

PROGRAM OFFERINGS

Young Actors Camp has an intermediate program as well as an advanced/professional program and an optional week in London and Paris.

Intermediate Program Participants must be between the ages of 12 and 18 during the camp dates and have at least one year of basic acting experience. This program is limited to 30 students and includes several workshops and classes.

In Acting for Film Technique/Scene Study, presented Universal Studios, campers learn technical terms, the differences between acting on stage and screen, and how to develop and deliver a performance for the screen.

Improv and Theatre Games, presented by The Second City, teaches the art form of improvisation through games, exercises, and scenes.

Cold Reading Technique, presented by TVI Actors Studio, instructs campers on techniques for cold reading (auditioning without having access to the script in advance).

Career Assessment and Development, presented by Hollywood Headshots Studio, gives instructions on resume and photo session preparation.

How to Market You, presented by an actor from Actors Consultation Services, instructs campers how to secure an agent and sell themselves.

There are also the Commercial Workshop and various field trips to learn about other aspects of the industry.

Advanced/Professional Program This program is by audition and invitation only and is limited to 30 students. Campers must be between the ages of 12 and 19 during camp dates, have at least two years of basic acting instruction, submit a 3-minute monologue audition or two letters of recommendation from acting teachers, have reasonable parent support for future work offers/auditions, and either bring an entertainment work permit to camp or open a Coogan-Minor Blocked Account with the First Entertainment Credit Union in Hollywood before arriving. The program includes the same workshops and classes as the Intermediate Program, with the addition of Agents Panel, in which campers perform a monologue in front of several Hollywood agents who are scouting for new actors to represent. Campers who sign with an agent are accompanied to film and TV auditions by Young Actors Camp staff members.

London/Paris Excursion A weeklong excursion to London and Paris gives campers an in-depth view of the international film/television industry. Campers can participate in this program either as session two of their Young Actors Camp experience or as a stand-alone session. Students visit film studios and top acting schools and talk to actors and agents about opportunities abroad. The group leaves from Los Angeles International Airport and spends three nights in London and five nights in Paris, experiencing acting intensives, lectures, meetings, Disneyland Paris, and several tours.

ENROLLMENT

Each summer, students come to the Young Actors Camp from all over North America and around the world. Individual sessions are limited to 30 students for each program.

DAILY SCHEDULE

The film industry of Hollywood and Los Angeles is the classroom for the Young Actors Camp. Campers participate in a rigorous 8-hour day, two- to three-week intensive training program of learning experiences, field trips, screenings, and fun. At the Young Actors Camp, participants meet with agents, watch a sitcom being made, visit world-renowned agencies, tour movie studios, and complete their own resume and photo shoot. Most evenings are spent touring the Hollywood/Los Angeles area.

EXTRA OPPORTUNITIES AND ACTIVITIES

Participants have their evenings and weekends full of fun things to do. There are touring, group activities, amusement parks, museums, and celebrity and industry executive question-and-answer sessions. They tour Hollywood and Los Angeles, visit Universal Studios, and have a cookout on the beach. In addition, various industry-related field trips are planned every summer. Several outings throughout Hollywood open up new options for those wishing to pursue other career avenues in the industry.

FACILITIES

Campers are housed on the UCLA campus. Campers stay in double, triple, or quad accommodations. Roommates are chosen at the discretion of Young Actors Camp but are always age and gender appropriate. Students should contact the office if special arrangements are needed. Campers are bused daily to the Hollywood training centers where the various classes are held. Breakfast and lunch are included, but campers purchase most evening meals when touring Los Angeles/Hollywood in the evening. Campers have access to the pool, a gym, and movie theaters at UCLA.

STAFF

The diverse camp counseling staff is made up of professional actors, acting students from top acting schools and universities, and teachers. Most of them are in Hollywood acting or looking for acting work. All of them are hired through the National Camp Association and have been rigorously screened by the Employment Background Investigations company (EBI). Young Actors Camp's first concern is the safety of its campers.

MEDICAL CARE

Campers have access to the Student Health and Wellness Center on the UCLA campus.

COSTS

In 2004, tuition costs were Intermediate Program, $2640; combination Intermediate and London/Paris Excursion, $4340; Advanced/Professional Program, $3080; combination Advanced/Professional Program and London/Paris Excursion, $4780; and London/Paris Excursion only, $2040. Additional money is needed for laundry, bus driver tips, optional excursions, personal expenses, unscheduled activities, and some meals.

Parents may send checks directly to Young Actors Camp at the address listed below or may register and pay online through the National Camp Directory service for camp registrations, payments, and installment billing. For more information about online registration and payment, students should visit the camp's Web site listed below or contact the camp.

TRANSPORTATION

All campers' flights must arrive at Los Angeles International Airport (LAX) for pickup between 10 a.m. and 3 p.m. on the first day of the camp, and departure flights must be scheduled between 7 a.m. and 1 p.m. on the last day of camp. Special arrangements for transportation can be made if these hours are not possible, but students should discuss options with the Young Actors Camp office before purchasing the ticket.

APPLICATION TIMETABLE

Initial inquiries are welcome at any time. To reserve a space at Young Actors Camp, students you must submit an application, available on the Web site or at the address listed below, along with a nonrefundable deposit of $500. A $100 discount can be applied if full payment is made by March 1. Applications and/or balance of fees received forty-five days or less before the beginning camp date are subject to a $25 late fee. Late applicants may be placed on a waiting list pending space availability.

Applicants to the Advanced/Professional program are notified of acceptance within two weeks of their completed application.

For more information, contact:

Young Actors Camp
305 North 2nd Avenue #118
Upland, California 91786
909-982-8059
Fax: 909-982-5328
E-mail: educationsvc@msn.com
World Wide Web: http://www.youngactorscamp.com

PARTICIPANT/FAMILY COMMENTS

"We thought we knew a lot about the industry. We were wrong. Thank you for such an informative program."

"This was a dream come true for my daughter. Two weeks of the Hollywood film industry in the palm of her hands."

YOUTH FOR UNDERSTANDING USA

SUMMER PROGRAMS

LOCATIONS AROUND THE WORLD

Type of Program: International exchange
Participants: Coeducational, ages 15–18
Enrollment: 750
Program Dates: Three- to eight-week programs, late June through mid-August
Head of Program: Michael Finnell, President

LOCATION

Youth for Understanding USA offers programs in more than thirty-five countries around the globe. Participants enjoy unparalleled opportunities to learn about and live with people in Argentina, Australia, Brazil, Chile, China, Denmark, Ecuador, Estonia, Finland, France, Germany, Greece, Hungary, Ireland, Italy, Japan, Kenya, Latvia, Norway, Poland, Russia, South Africa, South Korea, Spain, Sweden, Thailand, Uruguay, and Venezuela.

BACKGROUND AND PHILOSOPHY

Youth for Understanding USA (YFU), which is an educational nonprofit organization, prepares young people for their opportunities and responsibilities in a changing, interdependent world. With YFU, students can choose a year, semester, or summer program in one of more than thirty-five countries worldwide. More than 200,000 young people from more than fifty nations in Asia, Europe, North and South America, Africa, and the Pacific have participated in YFU exchanges. Each exchange is coordinated by a worldwide network of national YFU organizations and supported by more than 3,500 trained and dedicated volunteers.

Established in 1951, YFU is one of the oldest, largest, and most respected exchange organizations in the world, with the staff, the experience, and the international network needed to send participants on once-in-a-lifetime adventures that can change their lives forever. Participation in these extraordinary experiences creates benefits that endure well beyond the program's end: more than 100 colleges and universities in the United States offer scholarships to program alumni, and the ability to speak more than one language and to understand other cultures helps many alumni establish successful international careers.

PROGRAM OFFERINGS

Overseas exchange students live with volunteer host families. The students develop a real understanding of their host country and its culture, make new friends, see new sights—and have lots of fun in the process. Because participants visit countries as more than just tourists, they learn the language faster than they ever thought possible. All programs are family based; participants are involved in their host families' day-to-day lives—their outings, their activities, and their holiday celebrations—and come to feel that they are "one of the family" in the truest sense. Cross-cultural orientation and counseling are provided for program participants.

EXTRA OPPORTUNITIES AND ACTIVITIES

YFU summer programs fall into three basic categories, all providing a homestay experience and full cultural immersion. The first category offers intensive language study, such as those programs in Argentina, Spain, and Italy. The second offers action, adventure, and travel (for example, those in Australia). The third offers study in a specific area of interest, such as environmental programs in Brazil and the Ireland community service program. Students can receive more information about YFU special summer programs by visiting the Web site (listed below) or calling 800-TEENAGE (toll-free).

ENROLLMENT

Every year, more than 6,000 students from all around the world participate in YFU summer, semester, and academic year programs. In most cases, students need not speak the language of the country in which they'd like to stay, although a few countries do ask for previous language study. The summer programs require that applicants have a 2.0 or better GPA.

STAFF

The worldwide network of professional staff members and volunteers includes 2,600 volunteers in the United States alone. Volunteers assist in recruiting and screening students and host families, act as liaisons with schools, implement orientation programs, support students during their exchange experience, work with the media, and train other volunteers. Prominent business and government leaders as well as international educators serve as volunteer board and committee members, donating their time, energy, and expertise to guide and support the programs.

MEDICAL CARE

Families should confirm that their health coverage extends to out-of-country situations. A valid insurance policy is required, and all participants must be able to complete an insurance claim form independently should the need arise. YFU has made arrangements for a private company to offer insurance to participants, if necessary, at an extremely competitive rate.

COSTS

Tuition for YFU summer programs starts at $3875 and varies depending on the country chosen. Tuition includes round-trip domestic and international travel from YFU-designated departure points, assistance from international gateways for all flights leaving the United States, cultural and educational activities for students at home and abroad (where available), placement with a host family, careful screening and interviewing of host families, professional orientations and handbooks at all phases of the program, 24-hour worldwide professional counseling and emergency assistance, and information on and assistance with acquiring visas. Tuition does not include medical and dental fees or insurance coverage overseas, spending money, passport and visa fees, excess luggage tariffs, or any applicable international airport taxes.

FINANCIAL AID

YFU administers several scholarship programs funded by the governments of Finland and Japan as well as one of the largest international corporate scholarship programs in the world. Currently, YFU administers more than 400 full and partial scholarships. Deadlines for submission of scholarship applications fall between November and February.

YFU also advises interested students on how to raise money to offset program costs through part-time jobs or fund-raising.

Those interested in more information should contact the Admissions Office at 800-TEENAGE (toll-free).

TRANSPORTATION

YFU tuition includes round-trip domestic and international travel, as well as transportation to the host family from the arrival airport. Domestic travel includes round-trip tickets to YFU-designated international gateway cities. Some scholarship programs exclude domestic travel.

APPLICATION TIMETABLE

The final deadline to apply for summer programs is May 1. However, some programs fill early in the year, so students are encouraged to apply as early as possible. Once an application is received, each student is assigned a personal admissions counselor to answer questions and facilitate further steps in the enrollment process, which include a personal interview with a YFU volunteer. Applications are processed on a first-come, first-served basis.

FOR MORE INFORMATION, CONTACT:

Youth for Understanding USA
6400 Goldsboro Road, Suite 100
Bethesda, Maryland 20817
800-TEENAGE (toll-free)
Fax: 240-235-2104
E-mail: admissions@yfu.org
World Wide Web: http://www.yfu-usa.org

PARTICIPANT/FAMILY COMMENTS

"Our host family was perfectly chosen and we could trust them absolutely. They not only took care of our daughter, but had common interests and views."—Konstantin Tolskiy and Maria Tolskaya

"I wanted to meet new people and learn about a totally cool culture and at the same time learn how it feels to be independent and on my own. I loved it!"—Tatiana Pizonero

"One of the greatest things I learned is that if we live in one place all of our lives, we begin to think that the culture and way of thinking around us is all that exists and we sometimes forget about the different social realities of other nations."—Derek Garcia

INDEXES

A bold page number indicates an In-Depth Description.

▶ ABORIGINAL STUDIES

Aboriginal Studies

LIFEWORKS with the Australian Red Cross, Australia

Academics (General)

Academic Study Associates–ASA at the University of California, Berkeley, CA
Academic Study Associates–ASA at the University of Massachusetts Amherst, MA
Academic Study Associates–Florence, Italy
Academic Study Associates–Nice, France
Academic Study Associates–Pathways Program at Amherst College, MA
Academic Study Associates–Royan, France
Academic Study Associates–Spanish in España, Spain
L' Académie de Paris, France
Academy, OR
Academy by the Sea, CA
Adventures in Learning, OR
Adventures in Science and Arts, WA
All Arts and Sciences Camp–George Mason University, VA
All Arts and Sciences Camp–North Carolina State University, NC
All Arts and Sciences Camp–The College of William and Mary, VA
All Arts and Sciences Camp–The University of North Carolina at Greensboro, NC
All Arts and Sciences Camp–Virginia Tech, VA
American Collegiate Adventures–Wisconsin, WI
Appleby College Summer Academy, Canada
Asheville School Summer Academic Adventures, NC
Beekman School Summer Session, NY
Blyth Education–Summer Study in Cozumel, Mexico
Boston University High School Honors Program, MA
Bridge to the Future, NJ
Brown University Summer Programs–Pre-College Program, RI
Cambridge College Programme, United Kingdom
The Cambridge Prep Experience, United Kingdom
The Cambridge Tradition, United Kingdom
Camden Military Academy Summer Session/Camp, SC
Camp College–Institute for Arts and Sciences, NJ
Camp Kodiak, Canada
Camp Lee Mar, PA
Camp Pocono Ridge, PA
Camp Watonka, PA
Canadian College Italy/The Renaissance School Summer Academy, Italy
The Cardigan Mountain School Summer Session, NH
Carnegie Mellon University Advanced Placement Early Admission, PA
Carolina Master Scholars Adventure Series, SC
Carson-Newman College–EXCEL Program, TN
Catholic University College Courses for High School Students, DC
Center for Cultural Interchange–Australia High School Abroad, Australia
Center for Cultural Interchange–Brazil High School Abroad, Brazil
Center for Cultural Interchange–France High School Abroad, France
Center for Cultural Interchange–Germany High School Abroad, Germany
Center for Cultural Interchange–Ireland High School Abroad, Ireland
Center for Cultural Interchange–Japan High School Abroad, Japan
Center for Cultural Interchange–Mexico High School Abroad, Mexico
Center for Cultural Interchange–Netherlands High School Abroad, Netherlands
Center for Cultural Interchange–South Africa High School Abroad, South Africa
Center for Cultural Interchange–Spain High School Abroad, Spain
Center for Talent Development Summer Academic Program, IL
Cheshire Academy Summer Program, CT
Children's Creative and Performing Arts Academy Summer Middle School Program, CA
Children's Creative and Performing Arts Academy Summer Program for Preschool/Prekindergarten, CA
Children's Creative and Performing Arts Academy Summer Programs for High School Students, CA
Choate Rosemary Hall Focus Program, CT
Choate Rosemary Hall Summer Session, CT
Clark Scholars Program, TX
Collegiate Summer Program for High School Students, NH
Colorado Academy Summer Programs, CO
Columbia College Chicago's High School Summer Institute, IL
Columbia University Summer Program for High School Students, NY
Cornell University Summer College Programs for High School Students, NY
Crossroads School–Summer Educational Journey, CA
Cushing Academy Summer Session, MA
Davidson College July Experience, NC
Delphi's Summer Session, OR
Denver Academy Summer Program, CO
Dickinson Summer College Program, PA
Dunnabeck at Kildonan, NY
Dwight-Englewood Summer Academic Session, NJ
Dwight-Englewood Weekly Enrichment, NJ
Eaglebrook Summer Semester, MA
Eagle Hill School Summer Session, MA
Environmental Studies and Solutions, Norway
Episcopal High School Academic Camp, FL
Excel at Amherst College and Williams College, MA
Excel at Madrid/Barcelona, Spain
Excel at Oxford/Tuscany
Excel Cuba, Cuba
Expeditions, OR
Exploration Intermediate Program at Wellesley College, MA
Exploration Junior Program at St. Mark's School, MA
Exploration Senior Program at Yale University, CT
Fairfax Collegiate School Summer Enrichment Program, VA
Fay Summer School, MA
The Festival of Creative Youth, ME
Fishburne Summer Session, VA
4 Star Academics Junior Camp at the University of Virginia, VA
4 Star Academics Scholars at the University of Virginia, VA
4 Star Academics Senior Camp at the University of Virginia, VA
Furman University Summer Scholars Program, SC
Georgetown University Summer College for High School Juniors, DC
George Washington University Summer Scholars Pre-college Program, DC
GirlSummer at Emma Willard School, NY
The Governor's Program for Gifted Children, LA
The Gow School Summer Program, NY
The Grand River Summer Academy, OH
Grinnell Summer Institute, IA
Hamilton Learning Centre Summer School, Canada
Hargrave Summer Program, VA
The Harker Summer Institute, CA
Harker Summer Programs, CA
Harvard University Summer School: Secondary School Program, MA
Hawaii Preparatory Academy Summer Session, HI
High School Scholars (Summer Courses), PA
The Hockaday School Summer Session, TX
The Hun School of Princeton–Summer Academic Session, NJ
Hyde School Summer Challenge Program–Bath, ME, ME
Hyde School Summer Challenge Program–Woodstock, CT, CT
International Junior Golf Academy, SC
JHS/HS Academic Summer School Program, NY
The John Cooper School Academic Camps, TX
Johns Hopkins University Zanvyl Krieger School of Arts and Sciences Summer Programs, MD
Julian Krinsky Junior Enrichment Camp at Cabrini College, PA
Julian Krinsky Senior Enrichment Camp at Haverford College, PA
Kids on Campus, MD
Linden Hill Summer Program, MA
Louisiana College Center for Academically Talented Students (CATS), LA
Louisiana College Summer Superior Program, LA
Maplebrook School's Summer Program, NY
Marvelwood Summer, CT
Massanutten Military Academy Summer Cadet Program, VA
McCallie Academic Camp, TN
Miami University Junior Scholars Program, OH
Mississippi Governor's School, MS
The Monarch School Summer Course, TX
Montclair State University Hi Jump Program, NJ
Montclair State University Summer Camp for Academically Gifted and Talented Youth, NJ
Montgomery Bell Academy–Summer School, TN
Montgomery College WDCE–FIT Summer Camp, MD
Montverde Academy Summer School, FL
Newgrange Summer Program, NJ
Newgrange Summer Tutoring Program, NJ

New York Military Academy–JROTC Summer Program, NY
Northfield Mount Hermon Summer Session, MA
Northwestern University's College Preparation Program, IL
Northwestern University's National High School Institute, IL
The Northwest School Summer Program, WA
Oak Creek Ranch Summer School, AZ
Oak Hill Academy Summer Program, VA
Oak Ridge Academic Summer Camp, NC
OES–Challenge Workshops, OR
Ojai Valley School Summer Programs, CA
The Oxford Academy Summer Program, CT
Oxford Advanced Studies Program, United Kingdom
The Oxford Experience, United Kingdom
The Oxford Prep Experience, United Kingdom
The Oxford Tradition, United Kingdom
Pathways at Marywood University, PA
The Peddie School Summer Day School, NJ
Pepperdine University Summer College for High School Students, CA
Phillips Academy Summer Session, MA
Phillips Exeter Academy Summer School, NH
Pingry Academic Camps, NJ
Pingry Summer Enrichment Experience, NJ
Plato College–English/French Intensive Courses, Canada
Portsmouth Abbey Summer School, RI
Purcell Marian High School Summer School, OH
Randolph-Macon Academy Summer Programs, VA
Rectory School Summer Session, CT
Rhodes Summer Writing Institute, TN
Rider University Opportunity for Academically Gifted and Talented High School Students, NJ
Riverside Military Academy Summer Opportunity and Academic Review, GA
St. George's Summer Session, RI
St. John's Northwestern Academic Camp, WI
St. John's University Scholars Program, NY
St. Paul's Preparatory Academy Summer Program, AZ
Saint Thomas More School–Summer Academic Camp, CT
Saint Vincent College Challenge Program, PA
Shattuck-St. Mary's Summer Discovery and English Language Institute, MN
Sidwell Friends Summer Studies, DC
Skidmore College–Pre-College Program in the Liberal Arts for High School Students, NY
Southern Methodist University–College Experience, TX
Southern Methodist University TAG (Talented and Gifted), TX
Southwestern Adventures, AZ
Squirrel Hollow Learning Camp, GA
Stanford University Summer College for High School Students, CA
Star Ranch Summer Camp, TX
Stevenson School Summer Camp, CA
Stony Book University–Summer Camp at Stony Brook, NY
Stony Brook University Summer Sessions College Program, NY
The Summer Academy at Suffield, CT
Summer Academy of Mathematics and Sciences, PA
Summer at Altamont, AL
Summer Discovery at Australia, Australia
Summer Discovery at Cambridge, United Kingdom
Summer Discovery at Georgetown, DC
Summer Discovery at Michigan, MI
Summer Discovery at UCLA, CA
Summer Discovery at UC San Diego, CA
Summer Discovery at UC Santa Barbara, CA
Summer Discovery at Vermont, VT
Summer Focus at Berkeley, CA
The Summer Institute for the Gifted at Amherst College, MA
The Summer Institute for the Gifted at Bryn Mawr College, PA
The Summer Institute for the Gifted at Drew University, NJ
The Summer Institute for the Gifted at Fairfield University, CT
The Summer Institute for the Gifted at Hofstra University, NY
The Summer Institute for the Gifted at Moorestown Friends School, NJ
The Summer Institute for the Gifted at Oberlin College, OH
The Summer Institute for the Gifted at Princeton University, NJ
The Summer Institute for the Gifted at Purchase College, NY
The Summer Institute for the Gifted at UCLA, CA
The Summer Institute for the Gifted at University of California, Berkeley, CA
The Summer Institute for the Gifted at Vassar College, NY
Summer in Switzerland, Switzerland
Summer School at New York Military Academy, NY
Summer Science Program at the South Carolina Governor's School for Science and Math, SC
Summer Study at Penn State, PA
Summer Study at The University of Colorado at Boulder, CO
Summer Study in Paris at The American University of Paris, France
SuperCamp–Claremont Colleges, CA
SuperCamp–Colorado College, CO
SuperCamp–Dominican Republic, Dominican Republic
SuperCamp–Hampshire College, MA
SuperCamp–Hong Kong, Hong Kong
SuperCamp–Mexico, Mexico
SuperCamp–Singapore, Singapore
SuperCamp–Stanford University, CA
SuperCamp–Switzerland, Switzerland
SuperCamp–Thailand, Thailand
SuperCamp–University of Wisconsin at Parkside, WI
SuperCamp–Wake Forest University, NC
Syracuse University Summer College, NY
Tabor Academy Summer Program, MA
Taft Summer School, CT
Talisman–Academics, NC
Tampa Prep–Academic Credit and Enrichment Courses, FL
TASIS England Summer Program, United Kingdom
Teen Challenge, PA
Time Travelers Program, PA
Tufts Summer Study, MA
UC San Diego Academic Connections, CA
University of Connecticut Mentor Connection, CT
University of Delaware Summer College, DE
University of Kansas–Duke University Talent Identification Program, KS
University of Kansas–Natural History Museum Summer Workshops, KS
University of Maryland Young Scholars Program, MD
University of Southern California Summer Seminars, CA
University of Wisconsin–Green Bay Summer Discovery, WI
Washington and Lee University Summer Scholars, VA
Wentworth Military Academy Summer School, MO
Wolfeboro: The Summer Boarding School, NH
Woodberry Forest Junior Adventure, VA
Woodberry Forest Senior Adventure, VA
Woodberry Forest Summer School–England, United Kingdom
Woodberry Forest Summer School–France, France
Woodberry Forest Summer School–Japan, Japan
Woodberry Forest Summer School–Scotland, United Kingdom
Woodberry Forest Summer School–Spain, Spain
Wright State University Residential Camps and Institutes, OH
Wyoming Seminary–Sem Summer 2005, PA

Acting

Acteen August Academy, NY
Acteen July Academy, NY
Acteen June Academy, NY
Acteen Summer Saturday Academy, NY
Acting Academy at Pali Overnight Adventures, CA
The Actor's Workshop by Education Unlimited, CA
American Academy of Dramatic Arts Summer Program at Hollywood, California, CA
American Academy of Dramatic Arts Summer Program at New York, NY
Boston University Summer Theatre Institute, MA
Choate Rosemary Hall Summer Arts Conservatory–Theater, CT
Duke Drama Workshop, NC
Encore! Ensemble Theatre Workshop, France
Ensemble Theatre Community School, PA
Hollywood Stunt Camp at Pali Overnight Adventures, CA
IEI–Theatre Plus Programme, United Kingdom
Mercersburg Onstage! Young Actors Workshop, PA
Mercersburg The World's A Stage Theatre Workshop, PA
Midsummer in London, United Kingdom
The New York Film Academy, Disney-MGM Studios, FL, FL
The New York Film Academy, Harvard University, Cambridge, MA, MA
The New York Film Academy in Florence, Italy, Italy
The New York Film Academy in London, United Kingdom
The New York Film Academy in Paris, France
The New York Film Academy, Princeton University, Princeton, NJ, NJ

Acting

The New York Film Academy, The Dalton School, New York, NY, NY
The New York Film Academy, Universal Studios, Hollywood, Ca, CA
Shippensburg University Academic Camps–Acting & Theatre Arts, PA
Sidwell Friends Drama and Dance Workshops with BAPA, DC
"Summer in the City", NY
Summer Theatre Institute–2005, NY
Traveling Players Ensemble Camp, MD
Vermont Arts Filmmaking Institute, VT
Vermont Arts Theatre Camp Institute, VT
Vermont Arts Theatre Institute, VT
Young Actors Camp, CA

Aerospace Science

Aerospace Camp Experience, WA
Embry-Riddle Aeronautical University–Aerospace Summer Camp, FL
Future Astronaut Training Program, KS
Mars Academy, KS
Montgomery College WDCE–Science Adventures, MD
Space Camp Turkey 6-Day International Program, Turkey
University of Wisconsin–Green Bay Space Trek Camp, WI

Agricultural Sciences

Organic Farm Camp, CO

All-Terrain Vehicles

Mini-Camp in the Pocono Mountains, PA

Animal Care

Camp Catherine Capers, VT
Camp Hitaga–Stirrups and Saddles, IA
Camp Winding Gap, NC
The Country School Farm, OH
Farm and Wilderness Camps–Indian Brook, VT
Farm and Wilderness Camps–Timberlake, VT
Hidden Villa Summer Camp, CA
Horseback Riding Academy at Pali Overnight Adventures, CA
Road's End Farm Horsemanship Camp, NH
RUSTIC PATHWAYS–THE THAI ELEPHANT CONSERVATION PROJECT, Thailand
RUSTIC PATHWAYS–THE TURTLE CONSERVATION PROJECT, Costa Rica
SeaWorld/Busch Gardens Tampa Bay Adventure Camp, FL
SeaWorld San Diego Adventure Camp, CA
SJ Ranch Riding Camp, CT
Sprucelands Camp, NY
Tuskegee University Vet Step I, AL
Tuskegee University Vet Step II, AL
Windsor Mountain: Driftwood Stables Ranch Camp, NH
World Horizons International–Kanab, Utah, UT
YMCA Camp Lincoln–Specialty Camps: Horse Camp, NH

Animation

Cleveland Institute of Art Pre-College Program–Special Effects and Animation, OH
DigiPen Institute of Technology 3D Computer Animation Workshop, WA
Flint Hill School–"Summer on the Hill"–Creative Arts on the Hill–Art Camp, VA
PixelNation, NJ
Ringling School of Art and Design Pre-College Perspective, FL
University of Pennsylvania–Penn Summer Art Studio, PA
Vermont Arts Animation Institute, VT

Anthropology

Bicycle Africa Tours

Archaeology

Alabama Museum of Natural History Summer Expedition, AL
Center for American Archeology/Archeology Field School, IL
Center for American Archeology/Past Lifeways Program, IL
Children's Creative and Performing Arts Academy Archaeology Adventure Camp, CA
Crow Canyon Archaeological Center High School Excavation Program, CO
Crow Canyon Archaeological Center High School Field School, CO
Crow Canyon Archaeological Center Middle School Archaeology Program, CO
EARTHWATCH INSTITUTE–Archaeology at West Point Foundry, NY
EARTHWATCH INSTITUTE–Chilean Coastal Archaeology, Chile
EARTHWATCH INSTITUTE–Conservation Research Initiative–Traditions of Cedar, Salmon, and Gold, WA
EARTHWATCH INSTITUTE–Early Man at Olduvai Gorge, United Republic of Tanzania
EARTHWATCH INSTITUTE–Early Man in Spain, Spain
EARTHWATCH INSTITUTE–England's Hidden Kingdom, United Kingdom
EARTHWATCH INSTITUTE–Frontier Fort in Virginia, VA
EARTHWATCH INSTITUTE–Guatemala's Ancient Maya, Guatemala
EARTHWATCH INSTITUTE–Hopi Ancestors, AZ
EARTHWATCH INSTITUTE–Jackson Hole Bison Dig, WY
EARTHWATCH INSTITUTE–Mallorca's Copper Age, Spain
EARTHWATCH INSTITUTE–Moundbuilders on the Mississippi, IL
EARTHWATCH INSTITUTE–Poland's Ancient Burials, Poland
EARTHWATCH INSTITUTE–Prehistoric Pueblos of the American Southwest, NM
YMCA Camp Lincoln–Specialty Camps: Archaeology Camp, NH

Archery

Haycock Camping Ministries–Battalion Program, PA
Haycock Camping Ministries–Stockade Program, PA
Haycock Camping Ministries–Trailbuilders Program, PA

Architecture

Architecture Summer Camp, AL
Catholic University Experiences in Architecture, DC
Center Summer Academy, MA
Cleveland Institute of Art Pre-College Program–Architecture, OH
EARTHWATCH INSTITUTE–China's Ancestral Temples, China
Exploration of Architecture, CA
Pratt Institute Summer Pre-College Program for High School Students, NY

Area Studies

World Affairs Seminar, WI

Art

Knowledge Exchange Institute–Artist Abroad Program in Italy, Italy
Montgomery College WDCE–Joy of Art, MD
TASIS Arts and Architecture in the South of France, France

Art (Advanced Placement)

Corcoran College of Art and Design–Pre-College Summer Portfolio Workshop, DC

Art (Folk)

AFS-USA–Homestay Plus–Hungary, Hungary

Art History/Appreciation

Abbey Road Overseas Programs–French Study Abroad in Cannes, France
Abbey Road Overseas Programs–Italy Study Abroad: Language and Culture, Italy
Academic Study Associates–Florence, Italy
Blyth Education–Summer Study in Paris and the South of France, France
Bravo Spain–Barcelona, Spain
Humanities Spring in Assisi, Italy
Humanities Spring on the Road, Italy
Programs Abroad Travel Alternatives–Ireland, Ireland
Taft Summer School Abroad–France, France
Taft Summer School Abroad–Spain, Spain
University of St. Andrews Scottish Studies Summer Program, United Kingdom

Arts

L' Académie de Paris, France
Adventures in Science and Arts, WA
All Arts and Sciences Camp–George Mason University, VA
All Arts and Sciences Camp–North Carolina State University, NC
All Arts and Sciences Camp–The College of William and Mary, VA
All Arts and Sciences Camp–The University of North Carolina at Greensboro, NC
All Arts and Sciences Camp–Virginia Tech, VA
Appel Farm Summer Arts Camp, NJ
Arrowsmith Academy Arts and Academics, CA
Art Center College of Design Art Center for Kids, CA
Artes en Mexico, Mexico
The Art Institute of Boston Pre-College Program, MA
Arts Unite, PA
Atlanta College of Art–Pre-College Program, GA
Belvoir Terrace, MA
California College of the Arts Pre-College Program, CA

California State Summer School for the Arts/Inner Spark, CA
The Cambridge Prep Experience, United Kingdom
The Cambridge Tradition, United Kingdom
Camp Ballibay for the Fine and Performing Arts, PA
Camp College–Institute for Arts and Sciences, NJ
Camp Horizons Explorer, VA
Camp Horizons Specialty Camp, VA
Camp Pocono Ridge, PA
Camp Rim Rock–Arts Camp, WV
Camp Togowoods, AK
Carnegie Mellon University Pre-College Program in the Fine Arts, PA
Carolina Master Scholars Adventure Series, SC
Centauri Summer Arts Camp, Canada
Center for Creative Youth, CT
The Children's Art Institute, CA
Children's Creative and Performing Arts Academy Summer Middle School Program, CA
Children's Creative and Performing Arts Academy Summer Program for Preschool/Prekindergarten, CA
Choate Rosemary Hall Summer Arts Conservatory–Visual Arts Program, CT
Cleveland Institute of Art Portfolio Preparation/Young Artist Programs, OH
Collège du Léman Summer School, Switzerland
Columbia College Chicago's High School Summer Institute, IL
Corcoran College of Art and Design–Camp Creativity, DC
Cottonwood Gulch Family Trek, NM
Cottonwood Gulch Mountain Desert Challenge, NM
Cottonwood Gulch Outfit Expedition, NM
Cottonwood Gulch Prairie Trek Expedition, NM
Cottonwood Gulch Turquoise Trail Expedition, NM
Eagle's Nest Camp, NC
Episcopal High School Eagle Arts Camp, FL
Excel at Amherst College and Williams College, MA
Excel at UC Santa Cruz, CA
Excel Cuba, Cuba
The Experiment in International Living–France, Five-Week Art and Adventure in Provence, France
The Experiment in International Living–Morocco Four-Week Arts and Culture Program, Morocco
The Experiment in International Living–South Africa Homestay and Community Service, South Africa
EXPRESSIONS! Duke Fine Arts Camp, NC
Fenn School Summer Day Camp, MA
The Festival of Creative Youth, ME
Flint Hill School–"Summer on the Hill"–Creative Arts on the Hill–Art Camp, VA
GirlSummer at Emma Willard School, NY
GLS Summer Camp Loewenstein, Germany
The Governor's Program for Gifted Children, LA
Hidden Valley Camp, ME
Interlochen Arts Camp, MI
International Music Camp, ND
JCC Houston: Art Camp, TX
Julian Krinsky Creative and Performing Arts Camp at The Shipley School/Bryn Mawr, PA
Jumonville Creative and Performing Arts Camps, PA
Knowledge Exchange Institute–Artist Abroad Program in Italy, Italy
Massachusetts College of Art/Creative Vacation, MA
Massachusetts College of Art/Summer Studios, MA
MexArt: Art and Spanish, Mexico
MidSummer Macon, GA
Miss Porter's School Arts Alive!, CT
Montclair State University Summer Camp for Academically Gifted and Talented Youth, NJ
92nd Street Y Camps–Camp Yaffa for the Arts, NY
North Carolina School of the Arts Summer Session, NC
Northwestern University's National High School Institute, IL
The Northwest School Summer Program, WA
The Oxford Prep Experience, United Kingdom
The Oxford Tradition, United Kingdom
Perry-Mansfield Performing Arts School and Camp, CO
Pratt Institute Summer Pre-College Program for High School Students, NY
Rhode Island School of Design Pre-College Program, RI
Ringling School of Art and Design Pre-College Perspective, FL
Ringling School of Art and Design's Teen Studio, FL
Saturday High at Art Center College of Design, CA
Sports and Arts Center at Island Lake, PA
The Summer Academy at Suffield, CT
TASIS Tuscan Academy of Art and Culture, Italy
University of Wisconsin–Green Bay Summer Art Studio, WI
Washington International School Passport to Summer, DC
Where There Be Dragons: Mexico, Mexico
YMCA Camp Lincoln–Specialty Camps: Arts & Drama, NH

Astronomy

Academic Camps at Gettysburg College–Astronomy, PA
Aerospace Camp Experience, WA
Alfred University Summer Institute in Astronomy, NY
Hancock Field Station, OR
The Summer Science Program–California Campus, CA
The Summer Science Program–New Mexico Campus, NM

Athletic Training

Montgomery College WDCE–FIT Summer Camp, MD
Springfield College Athletic Trainer Workshop, MA

Audition Technique

Young Actors Camp, CA

Aviation

Culver Summer Camps/Culver Specialty Camp– Aviation, IN
Embry-Riddle Aeronautical University–Aviation Career Exploration, FL
Embry-Riddle Aeronautical University–Flight Exploration, FL
Embry-Riddle Aeronautical University–Generations, FL
Embry-Riddle Aeronautical University–Sun Flight, FL

Backpacking

AAVE–Alaska, AK
AAVE–Alps Rider
AAVE–Boot/Saddle/Paddle
AAVE–Border Cross
AAVE–Rock & River
Adventure Camps, PA
Adventure Links–Appalachian Odyssey
Adventure Links–North Carolina Expeditions, NC
Adventure Links–The Costa Rica Experience, Costa Rica
Adventures Cross-Country, Alaska Adventure, AK
Adventures Cross-Country, Australia/Fiji Adventure
Adventures Cross-Country, Colorado Adventure, CO
Adventures Cross-Country, Costa Rica Adventure, Costa Rica
Adventures Cross-Country, Extreme British Columbia Adventure, Canada
Adventures Cross-Country, Hawaii Adventure, HI
Adventures Cross-Country,Southern Europe Adventure
Adventures Cross-Country, Western Adventure
Adventure Treks–Alaska Adventures, AK
Adventure Treks–California Challenge Adventures
Adventure Treks–California 19 Adventures, CA
Adventure Treks–Canadian Rockies Adventures, Canada
Adventure Treks–Montana Adventures, MT
Adventure Treks–Pacific Northwest Adventures, WA
Adventure Treks–PAC 16, OR
Adventure Treks–Ultimate Northwest Adventures
Alpengirl–Alaska, AK
Alpengirl–Montana, MT
Alpengirl–Scandinavia
Alpengirl–Washington, WA
Alpengirl–Washington Alpenguide Training, WA
Alpengirl–Washington Lil' Alpengirl, WA
American Youth Foundation–Camp Merrowvista, NH
Apogee Outdoor Adventures–Burlington to Boston
Camp Henry Offsite: Teen Challenge, MI
Camp Tawonga–Summer Camp, CA
Camp Tawonga–Teen Quest: Northwest
Camp Tawonga–Teen Quest: Southwest
Camp Tawonga–Teen Quest: Yosemite, CA
Canadian Rockies Adventurer Camp, Canada
Christikon, MT
Costa Rica Rainforest Outward Bound School–Multi-Element, Costa Rica

▶ Backpacking

Costa Rica Rainforest Outward Bound School–Summer Semester, Costa Rica
Costa Rica Rainforest Outward Bound School–Tri-Country/Tri-Mester
Darrow Youth Backpacking, ME
The Experiment in International Living–Thailand Homestay, Thailand
Farm and Wilderness Camps–Saltash Mountain, VT
Flying Moose Lodge, ME
Girl Scouts of Mid-Continent–Camp Oakledge, MO
High Sierra Wilderness Camps, CA
Hurricane Island Outward Bound–Maine Coast and Western Maine Sailing and Backpacking, ME
Hurricane Island Outward Bound–Maine Coast and Western Maine Sea Kayaking and Backpacking, ME
Hurricane Island Outward Bound–North Woods Maine Allagash and Appalachian Trail Canoeing and Backpacking, ME
Hurricane Island Outward Bound–North Woods Maine Canoeing and Backpacking, ME
Hurricane Island Outward Bound–Western Maine and New Hampshire Canoeing and Backpacking
Keystone Science Adventures, CO
Kooch-I-Ching, MN
Lifeschool Wilderness Adventures–Summer Adventures, CA
Longacre Expeditions, Alaska, AK
Longacre Expeditions, Belize, Belize
Longacre Expeditions, British Columbia
Longacre Expeditions, Iceland, Iceland
Longacre Expeditions, Laurel Highlands, PA
Longacre Expeditions, Peak to Peak, OR
Mountain Adventure Guides: Summer Adventure Camp–Blue Ridge Expedition I, NC
Mountain Adventure Guides: Summer Adventure Camp–Blue Ridge Expedition II, NC
Mountain Adventure Guides: Summer Adventure Camp–Jr. Adventure Camp, NC
Mountain Workshop–Awesome 6: Quebec, Canada
Mountain Workshop–Awesome 2: Vermont, VT
Outpost Wilderness Adventure–Adventure Skills, CO
Outpost Wilderness Adventure–Wind River Expedition, WY
Outward Bound–Connecting with Courage, MA
Outward Bound–Passages, MA
Outward Bound West–Backpacking and Whitewater Rafting, Oregon, OR
Outward Bound West–Backpacking, Climbing, and Rafting–Boys, CO
Outward Bound West–Backpacking, Climbing, and Rafting–Colorado, CO
Outward Bound West–Colorado Rockies Lightweight Backpacking, CO
Outward Bound West–Sierra Nevada Mountaineering, CA
Overland: Alaskan Expedition Hiking, Sea-Kayaking, and Rafting, AK
Overland: Appalachian Trail Challenge Hiking
Overland: Blue Ridge Explorer Hiking, Rafting and Kayaking, NC
Overland: Costa Rica Explorer Hiking, Rafting, and Sea-Kayaking, Costa Rica
Overland: European Explorer Hiking, Rafting, and Sea Kayaking
Overland: New England Explorer Hiking, Mountain Biking, and Rafting
Overland: Rocky Mountain Explorer Hiking, Mountain Biking, and Rafting
Overland: Shasta & the Sierras Backpacking, Climbing and Rafting
Overland: The Alpine Challenge Leadership Course Backpacking and Hiking
Overland: Yellowstone Explorer Backpacking, Rock Climbing, and Rafting
Poulter Colorado Camps, CO
Sanborn Western Camps: Big Spring Ranch for Boys, CO
Sanborn Western Camps: High Trails Ranch for Girls, CO
Streamside Pathfinder Adventure Camp, PA
Talisman–Trek Hiking Program, NC
Talisman–Tri-Adventures, NC
Trailmark Outdoor Adventures–Colorado–West Elks with Backpack, CO
Trailmark Outdoor Adventures–New England–Mahoosoc
Trailmark Outdoor Adventures–Northern Rockies–Tetons with Backpack
Traveling Players Ensemble Camp, MD
Voyageur Outward Bound–Boundary Waters Wilderness Canoeing, MN
Voyageur Outward Bound–Greater Yellowstone Whitewater and Backpacking, MT
Voyageur Outward Bound–Lake Superior Freshwater Kayaking and Backpacking
Voyageur Outward Bound–Lewis and Clark Alpine Backpacking, MT
Voyageur Outward Bound–Lewis and Clark Alpine Backpacking-Girls, MT
Voyageur Outward Bound–Montana High Alpine Backpacking, MT
Voyageur Outward Bound–Northern Rockies Backpacking Family Adventure, MT
Voyageur Outward Bound–Northwoods Wilderness Canoeing and Backpacking, MN
Where There Be Dragons: India Zanskar Trek, India
Wilderness Adventure, CO
Wilderness Ventures–Alaska Leadership, AK
Wilderness Ventures–Alaska Southcentral, AK
Wilderness Ventures–Alaska Southeast, AK
Wilderness Ventures–Australia, Australia
Wilderness Ventures–California, CA
Wilderness Ventures–Cascade-Olympic, WA
Wilderness Ventures–Costa Rica, Costa Rica
Wilderness Ventures–Ecuador and Galapagos, Ecuador
Wilderness Ventures–European Alps
Wilderness Ventures–Grand Teton, WY
Wilderness Ventures–Great Divide
Wilderness Ventures–Hawaii, HI
Wilderness Ventures–High Sierra, CA
Wilderness Ventures–Jackson Hole, WY
Wilderness Ventures–Northwest
Wilderness Ventures–Oregon, OR
Wilderness Ventures–Pacific Northwest
Wilderness Ventures–Puget Sound, WA
Wilderness Ventures–Rocky Mountain
Wilderness Ventures–Spanish Pyrenees, Spain
Wilderness Ventures–Teton Adventure, WY
Wilderness Ventures–Washington Alpine, WA
Wilderness Ventures–Washington Mountaineering, WA
Wilderness Ventures–Wyoming Mountaineering, WY
Wilderness Ventures–Yellowstone Fly Fishing
Williwaw Adventures–Maine Mountains and Coast, ME
Williwaw Adventures–Maine Wilderness
Williwaw Adventures–Pacific Northwest Expedition
Windsor Mountain: Alaska, AK
Windsor Mountain: California Community Service, CA
Windsor Mountain: New England Adventure
YMCA Camp Lincoln–Outdoor Adventure Camp: Backpacking, NH
YMCA Camp Widjiwagan, MN
YMCA Wilderness Camp Menogyn, MN
Yosemite Backpacking Adventures, CA

Band

Longhorn Music Camp: High School Band Camp, TX
Longhorn Music Camp: Middle School Band Camp, TX
Signature Music Teen Camp, NY
Valley Forge Military Academy Summer Band Camp, PA

Baseball

Davidson Academy–Sports Camps, TN
Dwight-Englewood Summer Sports Clinics, NJ
Flint Hill School–"Summer on the Hill"–Sports on the Hill–Coed, VA
JCC Houston: Sports Camp, TX
Jumonville Baseball/Softball Camp, PA
Professional Sports Camps–Big League Baseball Camp, NJ
Shippensburg University Sports Camps–Baseball–Regular Camp, PA
Shippensburg University Sports Camps–Baseball–Specialist Camp, PA
University of Kansas–Jayhawk Baseball Camps–Little League, Super Skills, and All-Star, KS
University of San Diego Sports Camps–Baseball Camp, CA
University of San Diego Sports Camps–Boys High School Elite Baseball Camp, CA

Basketball

Bill Self Kansas Summer Basketball Camp, KS
Cage Scope/High Potential "Blue-Chip" Basketball Camp, KY
Camp All-Star, ME
Crossroads School– Basketball Camps, CA
Davidson Academy–Sports Camps, TN
Dwight-Englewood Summer Sports Clinics, NJ
Flint Hill School–"Summer on the Hill"–Sports on the Hill for Boys, VA
Flint Hill School–"Summer on the Hill"–Sports on the Hill for Girls, VA
FUN-damental Basketball Camp–Morrisville, New York, NY
FUN-damental Basketball Camp–The Sports Mall, FL
The Hun School of Princeton Boys' Basketball Camp, NJ
The Hun School of Princeton Girls' Basketball Camp, NJ
JCC Houston: Sports Camp, TX

Julian Krinsky Super Sports Camp at The Shipley School, PA
Julian Krinsky Yesh Shabbat Summer Camp, PA
Jumonville Basketball Camp, PA
Lady Wildcat Basketball Camp, LA
Mercersburg Academy Blue Storm Boys Basketball School, PA
NBC Camps–Basketball–Adult & Child Hoops–Spokane, WA, WA
NBC Camps–Basketball–Crowell's Intensity–Spokane, WA, WA
NBC Camps–Basketball Individual Training–Alaska, AK
NBC Camps–Basketball Individual Training (Boys)–Auburn, WA, WA
NBC Camps–Basketball Individual Training–CA, CA
NBC Camps–Basketball Individual Training (Girls)–Auburn, WA, WA
NBC Camps–Basketball Individual Training–La Grande, OR, OR
NBC Camps–Basketball Individual Training–Montana, MT
NBC Camps–Basketball Individual Training–Newberg, OR, OR
NBC Camps–Basketball Individual Training–Olds, AB Canada, Canada
NBC Camps–Basketball Individual Training–Spangle, WA, WA
NBC Camps–Basketball Individual Training–Spokane, WA, WA
NBC Camps–Basketball Individual Training–Three Hills, AB Canada, Canada
NBC Camps–Basketball Point Guard Play–Spangle, WA, WA
NBC Camps–Basketball Post & Shooting–Spokane, WA, WA
NBC Camps–Basketball Speed–Alaska, AK
NBC Camps–Basketball Speed Explosion–California, CA
NBC Camps–Basketball Speed Explosion–Spokane, WA, WA
NBC Camps–Basketball–Team–Billings, MT, MT
NBC Camps–Basketball–Team (Boys)–Alaska, AK
NBC Camps–Basketball–Team (Girls)–Alaska, AK
NBC Camps–Basketball–Team (Girls)–Spangle, WA, WA
NBC Camps–Basketball–Team–La Grande, OR, OR
NBC Camps–Basketball Individual Training–Isle of Man, United Kingdom
Padua Franciscan High School Sports Camps, OH
Paul Hogan's Shooter's Gold Basketball Camp–Alton, NH
Paul Hogan's Shooter's Gold Basketball Camp–Gilford, NH
Paul Hogan's Shooter's Gold Basketball Camp–Laconia, NH
Paul Hogan's Shooter's Gold Basketball Camp–Lancaster, NH
Paul Hogan's Shooter's Gold Basketball Camp–Littleton, NH
Paul Hogan's Shooter's Gold Basketball Camp–Manchester, NH
Paul Hogan's Shooter's Gold Basketball Camp–Meredith, NH
Paul Hogan's Shooter's Gold Basketball Camp–Tilton, NH
Paul Hogan's Shooter's Gold Basketball Camp–Woodsville, NH
Paul Hogan's Specialty Basketball Camp, NH
Professional Sports Camps–Hall of Fame Basketball Camp, NJ
ProShot Basketball Camp–Boys Camp, PA
ProShot Basketball Camp–Girls Camp, PA
Purcell Marian High School Cavalier Basketball Camp, OH
76ers Basketball Camp, PA
Shippensburg University Sports Camps–Boys Basketball, PA
Shippensburg University Sports Camps–Father/Son Basketball Camp, PA
Shippensburg University Sports Camps–Girls Basketball, PA
Sidwell Friends Basketball Camp, DC
University of San Diego Sports Camps–Boys Basketball High School Team Camp, CA
University of San Diego Sports Camps–Boys High School Basketball Camp, CA
University of San Diego Sports Camps–Boys Junior Basketball Camp, CA
University of San Diego Sports Camps–Girls Basketball Fundamentals Camp, CA
University of San Diego Sports Camps–Girls Basketball High School Elite Camp, CA
University of San Diego Sports Camps–Girls Basketball High School Team Camp, CA
Vassar College Coed Basketball Camp, NY
Wildcat Basketball Camp, LA
Woodberry Forest Basketball Camp, VA

Bible Study

Abilene Christian University–Cross Training, NM
Abilene Christian University–Kadesh Life Camp, TX
Abilene Christian University–Learning to Lead, TX
Abilene Christian University–MPulse, TX
Abiliene Christian University–KidQuest Day Camp, TX
Camp Canonicus, RI
Camp Echoing Hills, OH
Camp Ganadaoweh, Canada
Camp Geneva, MI
Camp Mt. Luther, PA
Camp Roger, MI
Camp Sandy Cove, WV
Camp Streamside, PA
Eagle Lake Bike Camp, CO
Eagle Lake Camp Crew Program, CO
Eagle Lake Camp–East, NC
Eagle Lake Camp Jaunts–Kenya Mission Adventure, Kenya
Eagle Lake Camp Jaunts–Minnesota Boundary Waters, MN
Eagle Lake Camp Jaunts–Norway Mission Adventure, Norway
Eagle Lake Horse Camp, CO
Eagle Lake Wilderness Program, CO
Freed-Hardeman Horizons for Ages 12-18, TN
Haycock Camping Ministries–Adventure Trails, PA
Haycock Camping Ministries–Battalion Program, PA
Haycock Camping Ministries–Stockade Program, PA
Haycock Camping Ministries–Trailbuilders Program, PA
KidzZone Summer Camp, GA
Lake Ann Baptist Camp, MI
Makemie Woods Summer Camp, VA
The Marsh, MD
Star Ranch Summer Camp, TX
Streamside Camp and Conference Center, PA
Streamside Family Camp, PA
Summer Family Conference, MD
Timber-lee Horsemanship Camps, WI
Timber-lee Wilderness Trips, WI
Timber-lee Youth Camp, WI

Bicycle Trips

AAVE–Bike France, France
AAVE–Vietnam, Vietnam
Apogee Outdoor Adventures–Burlington to Boston
Apogee Outdoor Adventures–Coast to Quebec
Apogee Outdoor Adventures–Montana Service Adventure, MT
Apogee Outdoor Adventures–Cape Cod and the Islands, MA
Bicycle Africa Tours
BICYCLE TRAVEL ADVENTURES–Student Hosteling Program–Amsterdam to Paris
BICYCLE TRAVEL ADVENTURES–Student Hosteling Program–A Thousand Miles: Massachusetts to Nova Scotia
BICYCLE TRAVEL ADVENTURES–Student Hosteling Program–Canadian Rockies to California
BICYCLE TRAVEL ADVENTURES–Student Hosteling Program–Cape Cod, MA
BICYCLE TRAVEL ADVENTURES–Student Hosteling Program–Cross-Country America
BICYCLE TRAVEL ADVENTURES–Student Hosteling Program–France and Italy
BICYCLE TRAVEL ADVENTURES–Student Hosteling Program–Ireland and England
BICYCLE TRAVEL ADVENTURES–Student Hosteling Program–Maine Coast, ME
BICYCLE TRAVEL ADVENTURES–Student Hosteling Program–Maine-Nova Scotia Coast Loop
BICYCLE TRAVEL ADVENTURES–Student Hosteling Program–Niagara Falls to Montreal
BICYCLE TRAVEL ADVENTURES–Student Hosteling Program–Pacific Coast Adventure: Washington, Oregon, and California
BICYCLE TRAVEL ADVENTURES–Student Hosteling Program–Province du Québec, Canada
BICYCLE TRAVEL ADVENTURES–Student Hosteling Program–Province du Québec (short program), Canada
BICYCLE TRAVEL ADVENTURES–Student Hosteling Program–Spain and France
BICYCLE TRAVEL ADVENTURES–Student Hosteling Program–Vermont
BICYCLE TRAVEL ADVENTURES–Student Hosteling Program–Vermont to the Atlantic Ocean
The Experiment in International Living–France, Biking and Homestay, France
Flint Hill School–"Summer on the Hill"–A Biking Odyssey Day Camp, VA
Great Escapes (Adventure Trips for Teens)–Cape Escapes, MA
Ibike Cultural Tours–Ecuador, Ecuador
Ibike Cultural Tours–Guyana, Guyana
Ibike Cultural Tours–Washington/British Columbia
Longacre Expeditions, Adventure 28

▶ Bicycle Trips

Longacre Expeditions, Blue Ridge, PA
Longacre Expeditions, British Isles, United Kingdom
Longacre Expeditions, New England/Canada
Longacre Expeditions, Pacific Coast and Inlands
Longacre Expeditions, Surf Oregon, OR
Mountain Workshop–Bike 1: Martha's Vineyard and Nantucket, MA
Mountain Workshop–Bike Touring Days 1, CT
Mountain Workshop–Bike 2, MA
Overland: Acadia and Prince Edward Island Bicycle Touring and Sea-Kayaking
Overland: American Challenge Coast-to-Coast Bicycle Touring
Overland: Cape Cod and the Islands Bicycle Touring, MA
Overland: European Challenge Bicycle Touring from Paris to Rome
Overland: Pacific Coast Bicycle Touring and Rafting
Overland: Paris to the Sea Bicycle Touring, France
Overland: Vermont & Montreal Bicycle Touring
Putney Student Travel–Cultural Exploration–France, Holland, and England
Trailridge Mountain Camp
Wilderness Ventures–Great Divide Bike
Wilderness Ventures–Pacific Coast Bike

Bicycling

Craftsbury Running Camps, VT
Overland: Adventure Camp for 5th and 6th Grade Boys, MA
Overland: Adventure Camp for 5th and 6th Grade Girls, MA
Trailmark Outdoor Adventures–New England–Acadia
Trailmark Outdoor Adventures–New England–Jr. Acadia
Trailmark Outdoor Adventures–New England–Mt. Desert

Bicycling (BMX)

Woodward Freestyle BMX Bicycle, Inline Skate, Skateboarding Camp, PA

Biology

AFS-USA–Homestay, Outdoor Adventure Amazon–Brazil, Brazil
Blyth Education–Summer Study in the Amazon and the Galapagos Islands, Ecuador
Bugs to Biospheres, CO
Costa Rica ¡Pura Vida!, Costa Rica
EARTHWATCH INSTITUTE–Argentina's Pampas Carnivores, Argentina
Flint Hill School–"Summer on the Hill"–Enrichment on the Hill–Gee, Whiz!, VA
Flint Hill School–"Summer on the Hill"–Trips from the Hill–Ecological Study of Coral Reefs, Bahamas, Bahamas
Michigan Technological University American Indian Workshop, MI
Montgomery College WDCE–Young Scientist Academy, MD
On the Wing, CO
Science Quest, PA
Summer Biotechnology Institute for High School and Middle School Teachers and Students, OH
University of Chicago–Research in the Biological Sciences, IL
University of Chicago–Stones and Bones, WY
University of Pennsylvania–Penn Summer Science Academy, PA

Biotechnology

Montgomery College WDCE–Biotechnology and Diversity Camp, MD
Stony Brook University–Biotechnology Summer Camp, NY

Body Boarding

Camp Pacific's Recreational Camp, CA
Camp Pacific's Surf and Bodyboard Camp, CA
YMCA Camp Surf, CA

Botany

EARTHWATCH INSTITUTE–Butterflies and Orchids of Spain, Spain
EARTHWATCH INSTITUTE–Rare Plants of Kenya, Kenya

Business

Alfred University Summer Institute in Entrepreneurial Leadership, NY
Julian Krinsky Business School at Haverford College, PA
Julian Krinsky Business School at Wharton (Leadership in the Business World), PA
Julian Krinsky Senior Enrichment Camp at Haverford College, PA
Millennium Entrepreneurs Camp CEO, CA
Millennium Entrepreneurs "Training Tomorrow's Business Leaders Today", CA
Montgomery College WDCE–Entrepreneurship Camp 2005, MD
National Student Leadership Conference: Business and Commerce, DC
Stoneleigh–Burnham School: Camp $tart-Up, MA
University of Wisconsin–Green Bay Biz 4 Youth Camp, WI

Campcraft

BICYCLE TRAVEL ADVENTURES–Student Hosteling Program–A Thousand Miles: Massachusetts to Nova Scotia
BICYCLE TRAVEL ADVENTURES–Student Hosteling Program–Canadian Rockies to California
BICYCLE TRAVEL ADVENTURES–Student Hosteling Program–Cape Cod, MA
BICYCLE TRAVEL ADVENTURES–Student Hosteling Program–Cross-Country America
BICYCLE TRAVEL ADVENTURES–Student Hosteling Program–France and Italy
BICYCLE TRAVEL ADVENTURES–Student Hosteling Program–Maine Coast, ME
BICYCLE TRAVEL ADVENTURES–Student Hosteling Program–Maine-Nova Scotia Coast Loop
BICYCLE TRAVEL ADVENTURES–Student Hosteling Program–Niagara Falls to Montreal
BICYCLE TRAVEL ADVENTURES–Student Hosteling Program–Off-Road Vermont
BICYCLE TRAVEL ADVENTURES–Student Hosteling Program–Pacific Coast Adventure: Washington, Oregon, and California
BICYCLE TRAVEL ADVENTURES–Student Hosteling Program–Vermont
BICYCLE TRAVEL ADVENTURES–Student Hosteling Program–Vermont to the Atlantic Ocean
Camp Echo, MI
Camp Friendship Challenge Program
Camp Hitaga, IA
Camp Kirkwold, ME
Camp Niwana, TX
Camp Pondicherry, ME
Camp Scelkit, ME
Flint Hill School–"Summer on the Hill"–Boys Outdoor Adventures! Day Camp, VA
Flint Hill School–"Summer on the Hill"–Into the Woods Day Camp, VA
Girl Scouts of Genesee Valley Resident Camp, NY
Maine Conservation School Summer Camps, ME
Overland: Adventure Camp for 5th and 6th Grade Boys, MA
Overland: Adventure Camp for 5th and 6th Grade Girls, MA

Canoe Trips

Adventure Treks–Canadian Rockies Adventures, Canada
Audubon Journeys, VT
Camp Arowhon–Voyageur Canoe Trip Program, Canada
Camp Chewonki for Girls, ME
Camp Chippewa for Boys, MN
Camp Ganadaoweh, Canada
Camp Nominingue, Canada
Camp Roger, MI
Camp Wendigo, Canada
Darrow Wilderness Trips–Maine, ME
Darrow Wilderness Trips–Quebec: Mistassini, Canada
Darrow Wilderness Trips–St. Croix, ME
Darrow Wilderness Trips–Voyageurs, ME
Excalibur, Canada
Farm and Wilderness Camps–Saltash Mountain, VT
Great Escapes (Adventure Trips for Teens)–White Mountain Adventure, NH
Hurricane Island Outward Bound–Mid-Atlantic Canoeing, Backpacking, and Rock Climbing
Hurricane Island Outward Bound–North Woods Maine Expedition Canoeing, ME
Keewaydin Canoe Camp, Canada
Keewaydin Dunmore, VT
Keewaydin Temagami, Canada
Kooch-I-Ching, MN
Kroka Expeditions–Introduction to White Water, VT
Kroka Expeditions–Paddlers Journey Up North
Langskib Wilderness Programs, Canada
Maine Wilderness Adventure Trip, ME
Mountain Workshop–Awesome 5: North Woods of Maine, ME
Mountain Workshop–Awesome 1: Adirondacks, NY
Mountain Workshop–Awesome 3: Maine Coast, ME
Northern Lights, Canada
Northwaters Wilderness Programs, Canada
Songadeewin of Keewaydin, VT
Streamside Pathfinder Adventure Camp, PA
Swift Nature Camp–Canadian Canoe Trip

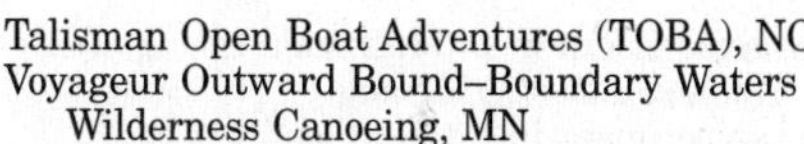

Talisman Open Boat Adventures (TOBA), NC
Voyageur Outward Bound–Boundary Waters Wilderness Canoeing, MN
Voyageur Outward Bound–Boundary Waters Wilderness Canoeing and Climbing XT, MN
YMCA Camp Widjiwagan, MN
YMCA Wilderness Camp Menogyn, MN

Canoeing

Adventure Links
Adventure Links–Ultimate Adventure Camps, VA
Camp Arowhon–Voyageur Canoe Trip Program, Canada
Camp Northway, Canada
Eagle Lake Camp Jaunts–Minnesota Boundary Waters, MN
Flying Moose Lodge, ME
Great Escapes (Adventure Trips for Teens)–Canadian Canoe and Kayak Adventure, Canada
Great Escapes (Adventure Trips for Teens)–Maine Waterways, ME
Hurricane Island Outward Bound–Maine Coast and Western Maine Canoeing and Sailing, ME
Hurricane Island Outward Bound–North Woods Maine Allagash and Appalachian Trail Canoeing and Backpacking, ME
Hurricane Island Outward Bound–North Woods Maine Canoeing and Backpacking, ME
Hurricane Island Outward Bound–North Woods Maine Expedition Canoeing, ME
Hurricane Island Outward Bound–Western Maine and New Hampshire Canoeing and Backpacking
Hurricane Island Outward Bound–Western Maine Woods Expedition Canoeing, ME
Kroka Expeditions–Wild Arts and Canoe Adventure, VT
Mad River Glen Naturalist Adventure Camp, VT
Outward Bound West–Climbing, Backpacking, and Canoeing–North Cascades, WA, WA
Swift Nature Camp–Canadian Canoe Trip
Tanager Lodge, NY
Voyageur Outward Bound–Manitoba to Montana Summer Semester
Voyageur Outward Bound–Northwoods Wilderness Canoeing and Backpacking, MN
Wentworth Military Academy Pathfinder Adventure Camp, MO

Canyoneering

Outward Bound West–Southwest Mountaineering, Rafting, and Canyoneering, UT
Outward Bound West–Utah Summer Semester, UT

Cardiac Education

Camp Bon Coeur, LA

Career Exploration

Adventures in Veterinary Medicine, MA
Barnard's Summer in New York City: Young Women's Leadership Institute, NY
Birmingham-Southern College Summer Scholar Program, AL
Career Explorations, NY
Carroll Center for the Blind–Real World Work Experience, MA
Central Wisconsin Environmental Station–Natural Resources Careers Camp, WI
ECOES: Exploring Career Options in Engineering and Science, NJ
IEI Student Travel–Internship Program in London, United Kingdom
Landmark Volunteers: Michigan, MI
Landmark Volunteers: Minnesota, MN
Landmark Volunteers: New Hampshire, NH
Landmark Volunteers: Ohio, OH
Landmark Volunteers: Rhode Island, RI
Landmark Volunteers: Vermont, VT
Landmark Volunteers: Washington, WA
Montgomery College WDCE–GURL Power, MD
Montgomery College WDCE–Summer Science Camp for Girls, MD
National Student Leadership Conference: Medicine and Health Care, MD
Pathways at Marywood University, PA
SeaWorld San Antonio Adventure Camp, TX
Stoneleigh–Burnham School: Camp $tart-Up, MA
Summer Summit on Leadership, MA
Summer Vet, CO
Tuskegee University Vet Step I, AL
Tuskegee University Vet Step II, AL
University of Kansas–School of Pharmacy Summer Camp, KS
University of Wisconsin–Superior Youthsummer 2005, WI

Cartography

EARTHWATCH INSTITUTE–Guatemala's Ancient Maya, Guatemala

Caving

Adventure Links
Cheerio Adventures–Cave/Raft, VA
Cheerio Adventures–Sampler, VA
Greenbrier River Outdoor Adventures, Adventure Camp, WV
Greenbrier River Outdoor Adventures, Wilderness Explorer, WV
Kroka Expeditions–Vermont Underground Trail, VT
NAWA Academy–Girls on the Go, CA
NAWA Academy–Great Challenge, CA
NAWA Academy–Lassen Expedition, CA
NAWA Academy–Trinity Challenge, CA
Village Camps–France, France

Ceramics

ClayCamp, CA
Cleveland Institute of Art Portfolio Preparation/Young Artist Programs, OH
JCC Houston: Art Camp, TX
Skidmore College–Acceleration Program in Art for High School Students, NY

Cheerleading

National Cheerleaders Association Cheerleader Camps, AL
Universal Cheerleaders Association and Universal Dance Association Camps, AL

Chemistry

Bugs to Biospheres, CO
Flint Hill School–"Summer on the Hill"–Enrichment on the Hill–Gee, Whiz!, VA
Science Quest, PA
University of Pennsylvania–Penn Summer Science Academy, PA

Chess

Flint Hill School–"Summer on the Hill"–Enrichment on the Hill–Summer Chess Camp, VA

Chinese Languages/Literature

AFS-USA–Team Mission–China, China
China Summer Learning Adventures, China
Choate Rosemary Hall Summer in China, China
Concordia Language Villages–Chinese, MN
EF International Language School–Shanghai, China
The Experiment in International Living–China North and East Homestay, China
The Experiment in International Living–China South and West Homestay, China
ISB Chinese Language Camp, China
Phillips Exeter Academy Taiwan and Beijing Summer Study Tour
Where There Be Dragons: China, China

Chorus

Longhorn Music Camp: All-State Choir Camp, TX
Signature Music Teen Camp, NY
Summer Sonatina International Piano Camp, VT

Cinematography

Montgomery College WDCE–Aspiring Filmmakers, MD

Circus Arts

Camp Curtain Call, VA
Camp Westmont, PA

Classical Civilizations

Blyth Education–Summer Study in Rome and Siena, Italy

Classical Languages/Literatures

Humanities Spring in Assisi, Italy

Climbing

Blue Ridge School–Adventure Camps, VA
Talisman–Tri-Adventures, NC
Trailmark Outdoor Adventures–New England–Acadia
YMCA Camp Fitch Summer Camp, PA

Climbing (Wall)

Apogee Outdoor Adventures–New England Mountains and Coast

College Planning

Academic Camps at Gettysburg College–College Prep & Preview, PA
California Campus Tours, CA
Cal Poly State University Young Scholars–Find the College for You!, CA
Carroll Center for the Blind–Computing for College: Computer and Communication Skills, MA

▶ College Planning

College Admission Prep Camp by Education Unlimited–San Diego, CA
College Admission Prep Camp by Education Unlimited–Stanford University, CA
College Admission Prep Camp by Education Unlimited–UC Berkeley, CA
College Admission Prep Camp by Education Unlimited–UCLA, CA
College Admission Prep Camp Choice by Education Unlimited–Stanford, CA
College Impressions
Constructing Your College Experience, NC
Elite Educational Institute SAT Bootcamp–Korea, Republic of Korea
Elite Educational Institute SAT Summer Bootcamp, CA
Pathways at Marywood University, PA
Prep Camp Excel by Education Unlimited–Stanford University, CA
Prep Camp Excel by Education Unlimited–UC Berkeley, CA
Stoneleigh–Burnham School: Camp $tart-Up, MA
University of Kansas–School of Pharmacy Summer Camp, KS

College Tours

Brighton College Admissions Prep at Tufts University, MA
Brighton College Admissions Prep at UCLA, CA
California Campus Tours, CA
College Admission Prep Camp by Education Unlimited–Boston, MA
College Impressions
East Coast College Tour by Education Unlimited
Summer Study at Penn State, PA

Color Guard/Flag

Half–Time USA, AL
KU Marching Band Camps, KS

Communication Skills

Carroll Center for the Blind–Computing for College: Computer and Communication Skills, MA
University of Kansas–Sertoma-Schiefelbush Communication Camp, KS

Communications

Carroll Center for the Blind–Youth in Transition, MA
Emerging Leaders 2005, SC
National Student Leadership Conference: Mastering Leadership, DC

Community Service

AAVE–Belize, Belize
AAVE–Costa Rica, Costa Rica
Abilene Christian University–Kadesh Life Camp, TX
Academic Camps at Gettysburg College–Community Service, PA
AFS-USA–Community Service–Argentina, Argentina
AFS-USA–Community Service–Bolivia, Bolivia
AFS-USA–Community Service–Costa Rica, Costa Rica
AFS-USA–Community Service–Panama, Panama
AFS-USA–Community Service–Paraguay, Paraguay
AFS-USA–Community Service–Thailand, Thailand
AFS-USA–Community Service–United Kingdom, United Kingdom
AFS-USA–Homestay Plus–New Zealand, New Zealand
AFS-USA–Team Mission–China, China
AFS-USA–Team Mission–Ghana, Ghana
AFS-USA–Team Mission–Russia, Russian Federation
Apogee Outdoor Adventures–Burlington to Boston
Apogee Outdoor Adventures–Coast to Quebec
Apogee Outdoor Adventures–Montana Service Adventure, MT
Apogee Outdoor Adventures–Cape Cod and the Islands, MA
Birmingham-Southern College Student Leaders in Service Program, AL
BROADREACH Academic Treks–Language Exposure and Service Learning, Chile
BROADREACH Academic Treks–Marine Mammal Studies, Canada
BROADREACH Academic Treks–Sea Turtle Studies, Costa Rica
BROADREACH Academic Treks–Spanish Language Immersion in Ecuador, Ecuador
BROADREACH Academic Treks–Wilderness Emergency Medicine, Belize
Camp Tawonga–Teen Service Learning to Alaska, AK
China's Frontiers: Diverse Landscapes and Peoples, China
Cottonwood Gulch Mountain Desert Challenge, NM
Cottonwood Gulch Outfit Expedition, NM
Cottonwood Gulch Prairie Trek Expedition, NM
Cottonwood Gulch Turquoise Trail Expedition, NM
Cottonwood Gulch Wild Country Trek, NM
Deer Hill Expeditions, Arizona, AZ
Deer Hill Expeditions, Colorado, CO
Deer Hill Expeditions, Costa Rica, Costa Rica
Deer Hill Expeditions, New Mexico, NM
Deer Hill Expeditions, Utah, UT
Discovery Works New England Community Service Experience
Eagle Lake Camp Jaunts–Norway Mission Adventure, Norway
EARTHWATCH INSTITUTE–Community Health in Cameroon, Cameroon
EARTHWATCH INSTITUTE–Maternal and Child Healthcare in India, India
The Experiment in International Living–Argentina Homestay, Community Service, and Outdoor Ecological Program, Argentina
The Experiment in International Living–Belize Homestay, Belize
The Experiment in International Living–Botswana Homestay, Botswana
The Experiment in International Living–Brazil Homestay and Community Service, Brazil
The Experiment in International Living–Costa Rica Homestay, Costa Rica
The Experiment in International Living–Germany, Four-Week Homestay, Travel, Community Service, Germany
The Experiment in International Living–Ghana Homestay, Ghana
The Experiment in International Living–Ireland/Northern Ireland Homestay and Peace Studies, Ireland
The Experiment in International Living–Mexico, Community Service, Travel, and Homestay, Mexico
The Experiment in International Living–Morocco Four-Week Arts and Culture Program, Morocco
The Experiment in International Living–Navajo Nation, NM
The Experiment in International Living–New Zealand Homestay, New Zealand
The Experiment in International Living–Poland, Homestay, Community Service, and Travel, Poland
The Experiment in International Living–South Africa Homestay and Community Service, South Africa
The Experiment in International Living–Thailand Homestay, Thailand
The Experiment in International Living–Turkey Homestay, Community Service, and Travel, Turkey
Farm and Wilderness Camps–Flying Cloud, VT
Farm and Wilderness Camps–Tamarack Farm, VT
Flint Hill School–"Summer on the Hill"–Enrichment on the Hill–Summer Service, VA
Four Corners School of Outdoor Education: Southwest Ed-Venture
GLOBAL WORKS–Adventure Travel-Pacific Northwest-3 weeks, WA
GLOBAL WORKS–Cultural Exchange-Fiji Islands-4 weeks, Fiji
GLOBAL WORKS–Cultural Exchange-Ireland-4 weeks, Ireland
GLOBAL WORKS–Cultural Exchange-New Zealand and Fiji Islands-4 weeks
GLOBAL WORKS–Language Exposure-Costa Rica-4 weeks, Costa Rica
GLOBAL WORKS–Language Exposure-Ecuador and the Galapagos-4 weeks, Ecuador
GLOBAL WORKS–Language Exposure-Puerto Rico-3 weeks, Puerto Rico
GLOBAL WORKS–Language Exposure-Yucatan Peninsula, Mexico-4 weeks, Mexico
GLOBAL WORKS–Language Immersion-Costa Rica-4 weeks, Costa Rica
GLOBAL WORKS–Language Immersion-Ecuador and the Galapagos-4 weeks, Ecuador
GLOBAL WORKS–Language Immersion-France-4 weeks, France
GLOBAL WORKS–Language Immersion-Puerto Rico-4 weeks, Puerto Rico
GLOBAL WORKS–Language Immersion-Spain-4 weeks, Spain
GLOBAL WORKS–Language Immersion-Yucatan Peninsula, Mexico-4 weeks, Mexico
Great Escapes (Adventure Trips for Teens)–Costa Rica Rainforest Adventure, Costa Rica
Greek Summer, Greece
Hurricane Island Outward Bound–Maine Woods High School Summer Semester, ME

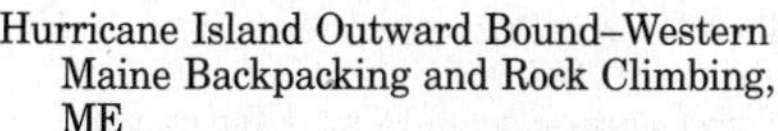

Hurricane Island Outward Bound–Western Maine Backpacking and Rock Climbing, ME
Landmark Volunteers: Arizona, AZ
Landmark Volunteers: California, CA
Landmark Volunteers: Colorado, CO
Landmark Volunteers: Connecticut, CT
Landmark Volunteers: Idaho, ID
Landmark Volunteers: Maine, ME
Landmark Volunteers: Massachusetts, MA
Landmark Volunteers: Michigan, MI
Landmark Volunteers: Minnesota, MN
Landmark Volunteers: Montana, MT
Landmark Volunteers: New Hampshire, NH
Landmark Volunteers: New Mexico, NM
Landmark Volunteers: New York, NY
Landmark Volunteers: North Carolina, NC
Landmark Volunteers: Ohio, OH
Landmark Volunteers: Rhode Island, RI
Landmark Volunteers: Vermont, VT
Landmark Volunteers: Virginia, VA
Landmark Volunteers: Washington, WA
Landmark Volunteers: Wyoming, WY
Leadership Adventure in Boston, MA
LIFEWORKS with the Australian Red Cross, Australia
LIFEWORKS with the British Virgin Islands Marine Parks and Conservation Department, British Virgin Islands
LIFEWORKS with the DPF Foundation in Thailand, Thailand
LIFEWORKS with the Galapagos Islands' National Parks, Ecuador
Longacre Expeditions, Belize, Belize
Longacre Leadership Program, PA
MexArt: Art and Spanish, Mexico
MexArt Dance: Dance and Spanish, Mexico
The Nepal Cultural Immersion Experience, Nepal
New Strides Day Camp, Canada
92nd Street Y Camps–The TIYUL
Outpost Wilderness Adventure–Copper Canyon Project, Mexico
Outward Bound West–Service Course–North Cascades, WA
Overland: American Community Service, Alaska, AK
Overland: American Community Service, Hawaii, HI
Overland: American Community Service, New England
Overland: American Community Service, Southwest, NM
Overland: World Service, Costa Rica, Costa Rica
Peace Works International–Costa Rica, Costa Rica
Peace Works International–Peru, Peru
Peace Works International–Ecuador, Ecuador
The Peru Cultural Immersion Experience, Peru
Poulter Colorado Camps: Adventures Planet Earth–Costa Rica, Costa Rica
Programs Abroad Travel Alternatives–Ecuador, Ecuador
Putney Student Travel–Community Service–Alaska, AK
Putney Student Travel–Community Service–Brazil, Brazil
Putney Student Travel–Community Service–Costa Rica, Costa Rica
Putney Student Travel–Community Service–Dominican Republic, Dominican Republic
Putney Student Travel–Community Service–Dominica, West Indies, Dominica
Putney Student Travel–Community Service–Ecuador, Ecuador
Putney Student Travel–Community Service–Hawaii, HI
Putney Student Travel–Community Service-India, India
Putney Student Travel–Community Service–Montana, MT
Putney Student Travel–Community Service-Nicaragua, Nicaragua
Putney Student Travel–Community Service–Nusa Penida and Bali, Indonesia
Putney Student Travel–Community Service–Tanzania, United Republic of Tanzania
Putney Student Travel–Cultural Exploration–Thailand and Cambodia
RUSTIC PATHWAYS–EXTENDED COMMUNITY SERVICE IN THE FIJI ISLANDS, Fiji
RUSTIC PATHWAYS–HIGHLANDS COMMUNITY SERVICE IN FIJI, Fiji
RUSTIC PATHWAYS–INTRO TO COMMUNITY SERVICE IN FIJI, Fiji
RUSTIC PATHWAYS–INTRO TO COMMUNITY SERVICE IN THAILAND, Thailand
RUSTIC PATHWAYS–RHYTHM IN THE RICEFIELDS, Thailand
RUSTIC PATHWAYS–RICEFIELDS, MONKS & SMILING CHILDREN, Thailand
RUSTIC PATHWAYS–THE CANO NEGRO SERVICE PROJECT, Costa Rica
RUSTIC PATHWAYS–THE THAI ELEPHANT CONSERVATION PROJECT, Thailand
RUSTIC PATHWAYS–THE TURTLE CONSERVATION PROJECT, Costa Rica
RUSTIC PATHWAYS–VOLCANOES AND RAINFORESTS, Costa Rica
Sail Caribbean–Community Service, British Virgin Islands
Service-Learning in Paris, France
SFS: Conserving Coastal Diversity, Mexico
SFS: Sustaining Tropical Ecosystems, Costa Rica
Sidwell Friends Service Expedition to Hawaii, HI
Sidwell Friends Summer Community Service Programs, DC
Sidwell Friends Summer Program: Costa Rica, Costa Rica
The Sikkim Cultural Immersion Experience, India
Spanish Through Leadership–Nicaragua, Nicaragua
Spanish Through Leadership–Nicaragua/Costa Rica
Student Conservation Association–Conservation Leadership Corps, Bay Area, CA
Student Conservation Association–Conservation Leadership Corps–Northwest, WA
Student Conservation Association–Conservation Leadership Corps–Washington, DC Metropolitan Area, VA
Summer Delegation to León, Nicaragua, Nicaragua
Summer JAM (Judaism, Activism, and Mitzvah Work), DC
Summer Summit on Leadership, MA
Tibetan Culture of Northern India, India
Visions–Alaska, AK
Visions–Australia, Australia
Visions–British Virgin Islands, British Virgin Islands
Visions–Dominica, Dominica
Visions–Dominican Republic, Dominican Republic
Visions–Ecuador, Ecuador
Visions–Guadeloupe, Guadeloupe
Visions–Montana, MT
Visions–Peru, Peru
Visions–South Carolina, SC
Visions–Trinidad, Trinidad and Tobago
Volunteers for Peace International Work Camp–Armenia, Armenia
Volunteers for Peace International Work Camp–Belarus, Belarus
Volunteers for Peace International Work Camp–Belgium, Belgium
Volunteers for Peace International Work Camp–Czech Republic, Czech Republic
Volunteers for Peace International Work Camp–Estonia, Estonia
Volunteers for Peace International Work Camp–France, France
Volunteers for Peace International Work Camp–Germany, Germany
Volunteers for Peace International Work Camp–Italy, Italy
Volunteers for Peace International Work Camp–Lithuania, Lithuania
Volunteers for Peace International Work Camp–Russia, Russian Federation
Volunteers for Peace International Work Camp–Slovakia, Slovakia
Volunteers for Peace International Work Camp–Turkey, Turkey
Voyageur Outward Bound–Manitoba to Montana Summer Semester
Westcoast Connection–Community Connections Alaska, AK
Westcoast Connection–Community Service, WA
Where There Be Dragons: Guatemala, Guatemala
Where There Be Dragons: Mexico, Mexico
Where There Be Dragons: Mongolia, Mongolia
Where There Be Dragons: Peru, Peru
Where There Be Dragons: Thailand, Thailand
Where There Be Dragons: Tibet, China
Where There Be Dragons: Vietnam, Vietnam
Wilderness Ventures–Alaska Service, AK
Windsor Mountain: Alaska, AK
Windsor Mountain: California Community Service, CA
Windsor Mountain: Cuba Friendship Exchange, Cuba
Windsor Mountain: Driftwood Stables Ranch Camp, NH
Windsor Mountain: Hawaii, HI
Windsor Mountain: Mexico Community Service, Mexico
Windsor Mountain: Random Acts of Kindness
Windsor Mountain: Voices of the Wind River, Wyoming, WY
World Horizons International–Costa Rica, Costa Rica
World Horizons International–Dominica, Dominica
World Horizons International–Fiji, Fiji
World Horizons International–Iceland, Iceland
World Horizons International–Kanab, Utah, UT

World Horizons International–Oahu, Hawaii, HI
World Horizons International–Puerto Rico, Puerto Rico
Youth for Understanding USA–Ireland, Ireland

Computer Game Design

DigiPen Institute of Technology Junior Game Developer Workshop, WA
DigiPen Institute of Technology Video Game Programming Workshop, WA
Technology Encounters–Video Encounter/Computer Encounter–California, CA
Technology Encounters–Video Encounter/Computer Encounter–Colorado, CO
Technology Encounters–Video Encounter/Computer Encounter–Florida, FL
Technology Encounters–Video Encounter/Computer Encounter–New York, NY
Technology Encounters–Video Encounter/Computer Encounter–Pennsylvania, PA

Computer Graphics

Montgomery College WDCE–GURL Power, MD
Montgomery College WDCE–Web Design Camp for Girls and Boys, MD

Computer Programming

Computer Camp by Education Unlimited–Stanford, CA
Computer Camp by Education Unlimited–UC Berkeley, CA
Computer Camp by Education Unlimited–UCLA, CA
DigiPen Institute of Technology Video Game Programming Workshop, WA
Montgomery College WDCE–Computer Programming Camp–Co-ed, MD
Montgomery College WDCE–Computer Programming Camp for Middle School Girls, MD
Mount Holyoke College SummerMath Program, MA
National Computer Camps at Fairfield University, CT
National Computer Camps at La Roche College, PA
National Computer Camps at Notre Dame College, OH
National Computer Camps at Oglethorpe University, GA
National Computer Camps at San Francisco State University, CA
The Summer Science Program–California Campus, CA
The Summer Science Program–New Mexico Campus, NM

Computer Science (Advanced Placement)

OPTIONS for Young Women, IN

Computer-Aided Drafting

Idaho Engineering Science Camp, ID

Computers

Brewster Academy Summer Session, NH
Carroll Center for the Blind–Computing for College: Computer and Communication Skills, MA
Computer Camp by Education Unlimited–Stanford, CA
Computer Camp by Education Unlimited–UC Berkeley, CA
Computer Camp by Education Unlimited–UCLA, CA
Cybercamps–Adelphi University, NY
Cybercamps–American University, DC
Cybercamps–Amherst College, MA
Cybercamps–Babson College, MA
Cybercamps–Benedictine University, IL
Cybercamps–Bentley College, MA
Cybercamps–Bryn Mawr College, PA
Cybercamps–College of St. Elizabeth, NJ
Cybercamps–Concordia University, IL
Cybercamps–DeAnza College, CA
Cybercamps–Duke University, NC
Cybercamps–FDU Metropolitan Campus, NJ
Cybercamps–George Mason University, VA
Cybercamps–Johns Hopkins University, MD
Cybercamps–Lewis and Clark College, OR
Cybercamps–Manhattanville College, NY
Cybercamps–Merrimack College, MA
Cybercamps–MIT, MA
Cybercamps–Princeton University, NJ
Cybercamps–Rollins College, FL
Cybercamps–Stanford University, CA
Cybercamps–UCLA, CA
Cybercamps–UC San Diego (UCSD), CA
Cybercamps–UNC, Chapel Hill, NC
Cybercamps–University of California at Berkeley, CA
Cybercamps–University of Hartford, CT
Cybercamps–University of Maryland, MD
Cybercamps–University of Michigan, MI
Cybercamps–University of Minnesota, MN
Cybercamps–University of Washington, WA
Cybercamps–University of Washington, Bothell, WA
Cybercamps–Washington University, MO
Emagination Computer Camps–Georgia, GA
Emagination Computer Camps–Illinois, IL
Emagination Computer Camps–Massachusetts, MA
Frontiers Program, MA
Future Astronaut Training Program, KS
iD Tech Camps–Cal Lutheran University, Thousand Oaks, CA, CA
iD Tech Camps–Carnegie Mellon University, Pittsburgh, PA, PA
iD Tech Camps–Colorado College, Colorado Springs, CO, CO
iD Tech Camps–Documentary Filmmaking and Cultural Immersion at the University of Cádiz, Spain, Spain
iD Tech Camps–Dominican University, San Rafael, CA, CA
iD Tech Camps–Emerson College, Boston, MA, MA
iD Tech Camps–Emory University, Atlanta, GA, GA
iD Tech Camps–Georgetown University, Washington, DC, DC
iD Tech Camps–Lake Forest College, Evanston, IL, IL
iD Tech Camps–Merrimack College, North Andover, MA, MA
iD Tech Camps–MIT, Cambridge, MA, MA
iD Tech Camps–Northwestern University, Chicago, IL, IL
iD Tech Camps–Pepperdine University, Malibu, CA, CA
iD Tech Camps–Princeton University, Princeton, NJ, NJ
iD Tech Camps–Sacred Heart University, Fairfield, CT, CT
iD Tech Camps–Santa Clara University, Santa Clara, CA, CA
iD Tech Camps–Smith College, Northampton, MA, MA
iD Tech Camps–Southern Methodist University, Dallas, TX, TX
iD Tech Camps–Stanford University, Palo Alto, CA, CA
iD Tech Camps–St. Mary's College, Moraga, CA, CA
iD Tech Camps–UC Berkeley, Berkeley, CA, CA
iD Tech Camps–UC Irvine, Irvine, CA, CA
iD Tech Camps–UCLA, Westwood, CA, CA
iD Tech Camps–UC San Diego, La Jolla, CA, CA
iD Tech Camps–UC Santa Cruz, Santa Cruz, CA, CA
iD Tech Camps–University of Denver, Denver, CO, CO
iD Tech Camps–University of Miami, Coral Gables, FL, FL
iD Tech Camps–University of Michigan, Ann Arbor, MI, MI
iD Tech Camps–University of Minnesota, Minneapolis, MN, MN
iD Tech Camps–University of North Carolina at Chapel Hill, Chapel Hill, NC, NC
iD Tech Camps–University of Virginia, Charlottesville, VA, VA
iD Tech Camps–University of Washington, Seattle, WA, WA
iD Tech Camps–UT Austin, Austin, TX, TX
iD Tech Camps–Vassar College, Poughkeepsie, NY, NY
iD Tech Camps–Villanova University, Villanova, PA, PA
IMACS–Full Day Summer Camp–Connecticut, CT
IMACS–Full Day Summer Camp–Florida, FL
IMACS–Full Day Summer Camp–Missouri, MO
IMACS–Full Day Summer Camp–North Carolina, NC
IMACS–Full Day Summer Camp–Pennsylvania, PA
IMACS–Full Day Summer Camp–South Carolina, SC
IMACS–Individual Summer Programs–Connecticut, CT
IMACS–Individual Summer Programs–Florida, FL
IMACS–Individual Summer Programs–Missouri, MO
IMACS–Individual Summer Programs–North Carolina, NC
IMACS–Individual Summer Programs–Pennsylvania, PA
IMACS–Individual Summer Programs–South Carolina, SC
Johns Hopkins University Zanvyl Krieger School of Arts and Sciences Summer Programs, MD
Learn English and Discover Canada, Canada
Michigan Technological University American Indian Workshop, MI
Michigan Technological University Summer Youth Program, MI

National Computer Camps at Fairfield University, CT
National Computer Camps at La Roche College, PA
National Computer Camps at Notre Dame College, OH
National Computer Camps at Oglethorpe University, GA
National Computer Camps at San Francisco State University, CA
Newman School Summer Session, MA
OES–Challenge Workshops, OR
Project SUCCEED, NC
Ringling School of Art and Design's Teen Studio, FL
University of Vermont Summer Institute for High School Students Discovering Engineering, Computers, and Mathematics, VT
University of Wisconsin–Green Bay Computer Camp, WI
Wesleyan Summer Gifted Program, WV

Conservation Projects

EARTHWATCH INSTITUTE–Biodiversity of the Grenadines, Grenada
EARTHWATCH INSTITUTE–Bogs of Belarus, Belarus
EARTHWATCH INSTITUTE–Brazil's Marine Wildlife, Brazil
EARTHWATCH INSTITUTE–Coastal Archaeology of Maine, ME
EARTHWATCH INSTITUTE–Conservation Research Initiative–Climate Change in the Rainforest, Australia
EARTHWATCH INSTITUTE–Conservation Research Initiative–Hawksbill Turtles of the Great Barrier Reef, Australia
EARTHWATCH INSTITUTE–Conservation Research Initiative–Queensland Tropical Fish Ecology, Australia
EARTHWATCH INSTITUTE–Conservation Research Initiative–Salmon of the Pacific Northwest, WA
EARTHWATCH INSTITUTE–Conservation Research Initiative–Samburu: Communities and Water Resources, Kenya
EARTHWATCH INSTITUTE–Conservation Research Initiative–Samburu: Communities and Wildlife Habitat, Kenya
EARTHWATCH INSTITUTE–Conservation Research Initiative–Samburu: Zebras, Kenya
EARTHWATCH INSTITUTE–Crocodiles of Cuba, Cuba
EARTHWATCH INSTITUTE–Desert Elephants of Namibia, Namibia
EARTHWATCH INSTITUTE–India's Sacred Groves, India
EARTHWATCH INSTITUTE–Jamaica's Coral Reefs, Jamaica
EARTHWATCH INSTITUTE–Medicinal Plants of Vietnam, Vietnam
EARTHWATCH INSTITUTE–Meerkats of the Kalahari, South Africa
EARTHWATCH INSTITUTE–Mexican Mangroves and Wildlife, Mexico
EARTHWATCH INSTITUTE–Mojave Desert Tortoises, CA
EARTHWATCH INSTITUTE–Mongolian Argali, Mongolia
EARTHWATCH INSTITUTE–Namibian Black Rhinos, Namibia
EARTHWATCH INSTITUTE–Restoring Costa Rica's Rainforest, Costa Rica
EARTHWATCH INSTITUTE–Trinidad's Leatherback Sea Turtles, Trinidad and Tobago
Groundwater University, NE
RUSTIC PATHWAYS–THE TURTLE CONSERVATION PROJECT, Costa Rica
RUSTIC PATHWAYS–VOLCANOES AND RAINFORESTS, Costa Rica
SeaWorld Orlando Adventure Camp, FL
SeaWorld San Antonio Adventure Camp, TX

Construction

Eagle Lake Camp Jaunts–Kenya Mission Adventure, Kenya
Eagle Lake Camp Jaunts–Norway Mission Adventure, Norway
Longacre Leadership Program, PA

Counselor-In-Training Program

Camp Berachah Ministries–Counselor-In-Training, WA
Flint Hill School–"Summer on the Hill"–Counselor-in-Training Day Camp, VA
Leadership Training at Pali Overnight Adventures, CA
Wilderness Experiences Unlimited–Leaders In Training Camp, MA
YMCA Camp Lincoln–Junior CIT Program, NH
YMCA Camp Lincoln–Senior CIT Program, NH
YMCA Camp Pendalouan–Counselor-in-Training, MI
YMCA Camp Tippecanoe–Jr. Counselor, OH

Creative Writing

Academic Camps at Gettysburg College–Writer's Workshops, PA
Alpengirl–Montana Art
The Arts! at Maryland, MD
Bryn Mawr College–Writing for College, PA
Choate Rosemary Hall Writing Project, CT
Choate Rosemary Hall Young Writers Workshop, CT
Dickinson College Young Writer's Workshop, PA
Duke Creative Writers' Workshop, NC
Flint Hill School–"Summer on the Hill"–Enrichment on the Hill–Women Writers' Adventure
Humanities Spring on the Road, Italy
Iowa Young Writers' Studio, IA
Kent School Summer Writers Camp, CT
The Putney School Summer Writing Program, VT
Putney Student Travel–Cultural Exploration-Creative Writing in Cuba, Cuba
Simon's Rock College of Bard Young Writers Workshop, MA
Stanford Discovery Institutes, CA
Susquehanna University Advanced Writers Workshop for High School Students, PA
Tisch School of the Arts–International High School Program–Dublin, Ireland
Tisch School of the Arts–International High School Program–Paris, France
University of St. Andrews Creative Writing Summer Program, United Kingdom
Visions–Ecuador, Ecuador
Young Actors and Playwrights Workshop, NY

Cross-Country

Shippensburg University Sports Camps–Cross Country, PA
University of Kansas–Jayhawk Track and Field/Cross Country Camps, KS

Cross-Cultural Education

AAC–Aloha Adventure Photo Camp, HI
AAC–Aloha Adventure Surf Camp, HI
AAVE–Bold Europe
AAVE–Thailand, Thailand
AAVE–Vietnam, Vietnam
Abbey Road Overseas Programs–French Study Abroad in Cannes, France
Academic Camps at Gettysburg College–Foreign Language Study (Spanish), PA
A.C.E. Intercultural Institute, WA
Adventure Ireland–English Learning Option, Ireland
Adventure Links–The Costa Rica Experience, Costa Rica
AFS-USA–Homestay Plus–Hungary, Hungary
AFS-USA–Team Mission–China, China
AFS-USA–Team Mission–Ghana, Ghana
AFS-USA–Team Mission–Russia, Russian Federation
American Collegiate Adventures–Italy, Italy
American Collegiate Adventures–Spain, Spain
American Youth Foundation Leadership Conference, MI
Blue Lake International Exchange Program
BROADREACH Academic Treks–Language Exposure and Service Learning, Chile
BROADREACH Academic Treks–Spanish Immersion in Mexico, Mexico
BROADREACH Academic Treks–Spanish Language Immersion in Ecuador, Ecuador
BROADREACH Academic Treks–Wilderness Emergency Medicine, Belize
BROADREACH Fiji Solomon Quest
BROADREACH Red Sea Scuba Adventure, Egypt
Center for Cultural Interchange–Australia High School Abroad, Australia
Center for Cultural Interchange–Brazil High School Abroad, Brazil
Center for Cultural Interchange–France High School Abroad, France
Center for Cultural Interchange–Germany High School Abroad, Germany
Center for Cultural Interchange–Ireland High School Abroad, Ireland
Center for Cultural Interchange–Japan High School Abroad, Japan
Center for Cultural Interchange–Mexico High School Abroad, Mexico
Center for Cultural Interchange–Netherlands High School Abroad, Netherlands
Center for Cultural Interchange–South Africa High School Abroad, South Africa
Center for Cultural Interchange–Spain High School Abroad, Spain
Center for Cultural Interchange–Spain Sports and Language Camp, Spain
Center for Cultural Interchange–Switzerland Language Camp, Switzerland
Choate Rosemary Hall Summer in China, China
Choate Rosemary Hall Summer in Paris, France

▶ Cross-Cultural Education

Choate Rosemary Hall Summer in Spain, Spain
Concordia Language Villages–Chinese, MN
Concordia Language Villages–Danish, MN
Concordia Language Villages–Finnish, MN
Concordia Language Villages–France, France
Concordia Language Villages–French–Bemidji, MN
Concordia Language Villages–French–Camp Holiday, MN
Concordia Language Villages–French–Fosston, MN
Concordia Language Villages–French–Savannah, GA, GA
Concordia Language Villages–French Voyageur, MN
Concordia Language Villages–German–Bemidji, MN
Concordia Language Villages–German–Camp Trowbridge, MN
Concordia Language Villages–Germany, Germany
Concordia Language Villages–Japan, Japan
Concordia Language Villages–Japanese, MN
Concordia Language Villages–Korean, MN
Concordia Language Villages–Russian, MN
Concordia Language Villages–Spain, Spain
Concordia Language Villages–Spanish–Maplelag, MN
Concordia Language Villages–Spanish–Wilder Forest, MN
Concordia Language Villages–Swedish, MN
Cuernavaca Summer Program for Teens, Mexico
Deer Hill Expeditions, Arizona, AZ
Deer Hill Expeditions, Costa Rica, Costa Rica
GLOBAL WORKS–Cultural Exchange-Ireland-4 weeks, Ireland
GLOBAL WORKS–Language Exposure-Costa Rica-4 weeks, Costa Rica
GLOBAL WORKS–Language Exposure-Yucatan Peninsula, Mexico-4 weeks, Mexico
Great Escapes (Adventure Trips for Teens)–Canadian Adventure
Great Escapes (Adventure Trips for Teens)–Costa Rica Rainforest Adventure, Costa Rica
Hawaii Preparatory Academy Summer Session, HI
Ibike Cultural Tours–Ecuador, Ecuador
Ibike Cultural Tours–Guyana, Guyana
Ibike Cultural Tours–Washington/British Columbia
Irish Way, Ireland
ISB Chinese Language Camp, China
Junior Institute, WA
Knowledge Exchange Institute–European Capitals Program
Lacunza Junior Summer Spanish Course, Spain
Ladakh Summer Passage, India
Lower Mustang Summer Passage, Nepal
Mercersburg ESL Plus Program, PA
The Nepal Cultural Immersion Experience, Nepal
Overland: Language Study Abroad in Costa Rica, Costa Rica
Overland: Paris to the Sea Bicycle Touring, France
Overland: World Service, Costa Rica, Costa Rica
Personal Passage, Nepal
The Peru Cultural Immersion Experience, Peru
Programs Abroad Travel Alternatives–Canada, Canada
Programs Abroad Travel Alternatives–Costa Rica, Costa Rica
Programs Abroad Travel Alternatives–Ecuador, Ecuador
Programs Abroad Travel Alternatives–France, France
Programs Abroad Travel Alternatives–Germany, Germany
Programs Abroad Travel Alternatives–Guatemala, Guatemala
Programs Abroad Travel Alternatives–Ireland, Ireland
Programs Abroad Travel Alternatives–Italy, Italy
Programs Abroad Travel Alternatives–Mexico, Mexico
Programs Abroad Travel Alternatives–Peru, Peru
Programs Abroad Travel Alternatives–Russia, Russian Federation
Programs Abroad Travel Alternatives–Spain, Spain
The Putney School Summer Program for International Education (ESL), VT
Putney Student Travel–Cultural Exploration-Creative Writing in Cuba, Cuba
Putney Student Travel–Cultural Exploration–Eastern European Heritage
Putney Student Travel–Cultural Exploration–Thailand and Cambodia
RUSTIC PATHWAYS–BUDDHIST LIFE & ANGKOR WAT
The Sikkim Cultural Immersion Experience, India
Summer Delegation to León, Nicaragua, Nicaragua
TASIS Le Château des Enfants, Switzerland
TASIS Middle School Program, Switzerland
Visions–Alaska, AK
Visions–Australia, Australia
Visions–British Virgin Islands, British Virgin Islands
Visions–Dominica, Dominica
Visions–Dominican Republic, Dominican Republic
Visions–Guadeloupe, Guadeloupe
Visions–Montana, MT
Visions–Peru, Peru
Visions–South Carolina, SC
Visions–Trinidad, Trinidad and Tobago
Wilderness Ventures–Alaska Service, AK
Windsor Mountain: Bonjour Quebec, Canada
Windsor Mountain: Cuba Friendship Exchange, Cuba
Windsor Mountain: Hawaii, HI
Windsor Mountain: International Summer Camp, NH
Windsor Mountain: Mexico Community Service, Mexico
World Horizons International–Costa Rica, Costa Rica
World Horizons International–Dominica, Dominica
World Horizons International–Fiji, Fiji
World Horizons International–Iceland, Iceland
World Horizons International–Oahu, Hawaii, HI
World Horizons International–Puerto Rico, Puerto Rico
Youth for Understanding USA–Argentina, Argentina
Youth for Understanding USA–Denmark, Denmark
Youth for Understanding USA–Estonia/Latvia-Baltic Summer
Youth for Understanding USA–Ghana, Ghana
Youth for Understanding USA–Kazakhstan, Kazakhstan
Youth for Understanding USA–South Africa, South Africa
Youth for Understanding USA–South Korea, Republic of Korea
Youth for Understanding USA–Vietnam, Vietnam

Culinary Arts

The Art Institute of Seattle–Studio 101, WA
Barat Foundation Summer Program in Provence and Paris, France
The Children's Art Institute, CA
Culinary Institute at Pali Overnight Adventures, CA
The Experiment in International Living–France, Homestay, Language Training, and Cooking, France
GIC Arg–Argentinian Cooking, Argentina
Julian Krinsky Senior Enrichment Camp at Haverford College, PA
Kendall College Culinary Camp, IL
Montgomery Bell Academy–Summer Cooking Camp, TN
Montgomery College WDCE–Culinary Arts–Kids Cook, MD

Current Events

Montgomery College WDCE–World Events 2005, MD

Daily Living Skills

Carroll Center for the Blind–Youth in Transition, MA
Marbridge Summer Camp, TX

Dance

American Allstar Dance Camp, AL
Arts on the Lake, TX
Atelier des Arts, Switzerland
Blue Lake Fine Arts Camp, MI
Brant Lake Camp's Dance Centre, NY
Camp Curtain Call, VA
Camp Rim Rock–Arts Camp, WV
Centauri Summer Arts Camp, Canada
Children's Creative and Performing Arts Academy Summer Elementary Program, CA
Children's Creative and Performing Arts Academy Summer Programs for High School Students, CA
Dance Magic, AL
Davidson Academy–Academy Arts, TN
Ensemble Theatre Community School, PA
EXPRESSIONS! Duke Fine Arts Camp, NC
GIC Arg–Tango, Argentina
Greenhouse: Litchfield Jazz Festival Summer Dance Institute, CT
Idyllwild Arts Summer Program–American Experience for International Students, CA
Idyllwild Arts Summer Program–Children's Center, CA
Idyllwild Arts Summer Program–Family Week, CA

Idyllwild Arts Summer Program–Junior Artists' Center, CA
Idyllwild Arts Summer Program–Youth Arts Center, CA
Julian Krinsky Creative and Performing Arts Camp at The Shipley School/Bryn Mawr, PA
Med-O-Lark Camp, ME
MexArt Dance: Dance and Spanish, Mexico
Music and Dance Summer Workshops, MO
92nd Street Y Camps–Camp Yaffa for the Arts, NY
Performance PLUS–Positive Learning Using the Stage+Studio+Screen, NH
The Performing Arts Institute of Wyoming Seminary, PA
Princeton Ballet School's Ballet Plus Junior, NJ
Princeton Ballet School's Ballet Plus Senior, NJ
Princeton Ballet School's Summer Intensive, NJ
Rock Star Camp at Pali Overnight Adventures, CA
Sidwell Friends DaVinci Days Art Studios, Young Artist Academy and Young Scientist Academy, DC
Sidwell Friends Drama and Dance Workshops with BAPA, DC
Stagedoor Manor Performing Arts Training Center/Theatre and Dance Camp, NY
Stoneleigh–Burnham School Summer Dance Camp, MA
Study Tours and Dance/Theater Camp in the USA–Dean College, MA
Universal Cheerleaders Association and Universal Dance Association Camps, AL
Vermont Arts Dance Institute, VT
Wilderness Dance Camp, MN

Dance (Ballet)
Burklyn Ballet Edinburgh Connection
Burklyn Ballet Theatre, VT
Burklyn Ballet Theatre II, The Intermediate Program, VT
Princeton Ballet School's Ballet Plus Junior, NJ
Princeton Ballet School's Ballet Plus Senior, NJ
Princeton Ballet School's Summer Intensive, NJ
Summer Dance '05, MA

Dance (Folk)
Cordova 4-H Bluegrass and Old Time Music and Dance Camp, AK

Dance (Latin)
Spanish Through Leadership–Nicaragua, Nicaragua

Dance (Modern)
Summer Dance '05, MA

Danish Language/Literature
Concordia Language Villages–Danish, MN
Youth for Understanding USA–Denmark, Denmark

Design
Art Center College of Design Art Center for Kids, CA
The Art Institute of Seattle–Studio 101, WA
Auburn University Design Workshop, AL
Center Summer Academy, MA
Cleveland Institute of Art Pre-College Program–Product and Auto Design, OH
Idaho Engineering Science Camp, ID
IEI–Print and Broadcast Journalism, United Kingdom
Massachusetts College of Art/Summer Studios, MA
Parsons Pre-College Academy, NY
Parsons Summer Intensive Studies–New York, NY
Pratt Institute Summer Pre-College Program for High School Students, NY
Rhode Island School of Design Pre-College Program, RI
Ringling School of Art and Design Pre-College Perspective, FL
Saturday High at Art Center College of Design, CA
Washington University in St. Louis, School of Art–Portfolio Plus, MO

Diabetic Education
Barton Adventure Camp
Barton Day Camp–New York, NY
Barton Day Camp–Worcester, MA
Clara Barton Camp, MA
Clara Barton Family Camp, MA
Lions Camp Merrick Diabetes Program, MD

Digital Media
Corcoran College of Art and Design–Focus on Photojournalism, DC
DigiPen Institute of Technology Junior Game Developer Workshop, WA

Digital Press Run
Graphic Media Experience, NY

Directing
Vermont Arts Filmmaking Institute, VT

Drawing
Cleveland Institute of Art Pre-College Program–Product and Auto Design, OH
IEI–Fine Arts Plus Programme, United Kingdom
Skidmore College–Acceleration Program in Art for High School Students, NY
University of Connecticut Community School of the Arts–World Arts Camps, CT
Vermont Arts Visual Arts Institute, VT
Washington University in St. Louis, School of Art–Portfolio Plus, MO

Drill Team
Riverside Military Academy Young Cadet Camp, GA

Driver's Education
SummerSkills at Albany Academy for Girls, NY

Drum Majoring
Half–Time USA, AL
KU Marching Band Camps, KS

Dutch Language
Center for Cultural Interchange–Netherlands High School Abroad, Netherlands

Ecology
AFS-USA–Community Service–Paraguay, Paraguay
AFS-USA–Homestay, Outdoor Adventure Amazon–Brazil, Brazil
Alton Jones Day Camp, RI
Alton Jones Earth Camp, RI
Blyth Education–Summer Study in the Amazon and the Galapagos Islands, Ecuador
BROADREACH Amazon and Galapagos Encounter, Ecuador
BROADREACH Honduras Eco-Adventure, Honduras
Cascade Science School, OR
EARTHWATCH INSTITUTE–Conservation Research Initiative–Conserving the Pantanal, Brazil
EARTHWATCH INSTITUTE–Conservation Research Initiative–Mountain Meadows of the North Cascades, WA
EARTHWATCH INSTITUTE–Conservation Research Initiative–Salmon Hotspots of the Skagit River, WA
EARTHWATCH INSTITUTE–Conservation Research Initiative–Samburu: Communities and Water Resources, Kenya
EARTHWATCH INSTITUTE–Coral Reefs of the Virgin Islands, U.S. Virgin Islands
EARTHWATCH INSTITUTE–Crocodiles of Cuba, Cuba
EARTHWATCH INSTITUTE–Dolphins of Costa Rica, Costa Rica
EARTHWATCH INSTITUTE–India's Sacred Groves, India
EARTHWATCH INSTITUTE–Lakes of the Rift Valley, Kenya
EARTHWATCH INSTITUTE–Maine's Island Ecology, ME
EARTHWATCH INSTITUTE–Malaysian Bat Conservation, Malaysia
EARTHWATCH INSTITUTE–Mangroves of the Kenyan Coast, Kenya
EARTHWATCH INSTITUTE–Meerkats of the Kalahari, South Africa
EARTHWATCH INSTITUTE–Mojave Desert Tortoises, CA
EARTHWATCH INSTITUTE–Namibian Wildlife Survey, Namibia
EARTHWATCH INSTITUTE–Restoring the Sagebrush Steppe, ID
EARTHWATCH INSTITUTE–Restoring Vietnam's Forests, Vietnam
EARTHWATCH INSTITUTE–Rivers of the Peruvian Amazon, Peru
EARTHWATCH INSTITUTE–Wildlife Trails of the American West, UT
The Experiment in International Living–Australia Homestay, Australia
The Experiment in International Living–Belize Homestay, Belize
The Experiment in International Living–Brazil–Ecological Preservation, Brazil
The Experiment in International Living–Costa Rica Homestay, Costa Rica
The Experiment in International Living–Ecuador Homestay, Ecuador

▶ Ecology

The Experiment in International Living–Spain, Five-Week Homestay, Travel, Ecology, Spain
From the Forest to the Sea, AK
Hancock Field Station, OR
LIFEWORKS with the Galapagos Islands' National Parks, Ecuador
Longacre Expeditions, Virgin Islands
Pacific Marine Science Camp, OR
Redwood National Park Camps, CA
Salmon Camp for Native Americans, OR
Salmon Camp Research Team for Native Americans–Oregon, OR
Salmon Camp Research Team for Native Americans–Redwoods, CA
Salmon Camp Research Team for Native Americans–San Juan Island, WA
Stony Brook University–Environmental Education Summer Camp, NY
Teen Expeditions, RI
Youth for Understanding USA–Chile, Chile
Youth for Understanding USA–Ireland, Ireland

Economics

Clemson University Economics Summer Camp, SC
Julian Krinsky Business School at Haverford College, PA
Julian Krinsky Business School at Wharton (Leadership in the Business World), PA
Junior Statesmen Summer School–Stanford University, CA

Electronics

IMACS–Full Day Summer Camp–Connecticut, CT
IMACS–Full Day Summer Camp–Florida, FL
IMACS–Full Day Summer Camp–Missouri, MO
IMACS–Full Day Summer Camp–North Carolina, NC
IMACS–Full Day Summer Camp–Pennsylvania, PA
IMACS–Full Day Summer Camp–South Carolina, SC
IMACS–Individual Summer Programs–Connecticut, CT
IMACS–Individual Summer Programs–Florida, FL
IMACS–Individual Summer Programs–Missouri, MO
IMACS–Individual Summer Programs–North Carolina, NC
IMACS–Individual Summer Programs–Pennsylvania, PA
IMACS–Individual Summer Programs–South Carolina, SC

Engineering

Baylor University High School Summer Science Research Program, TX
Catholic University Eye on Engineering, DC
ECOES: Exploring Career Options in Engineering and Science, NJ
Frontiers Program, MA
Gems: Girls in Engineering, Math and Science, MA
Idaho Engineering Science Camp, ID
Johns Hopkins University Zanvyl Krieger School of Arts and Sciences Summer Programs, MD
Michigan State University High School Engineering Institute, MI
Michigan Technological University Explorations in Engineering Workshop, MI
Michigan Technological University Summer Youth Program, MI
Michigan Technological University Women in Engineering Workshop, MI
Milwaukee School of Engineering (MSOE)–Discover the Possibilities, WI
Milwaukee School of Engineering (MSOE)–Focus on the Possibilities, WI
MIT MITE^{2}S (Minority Introduction to Engineering, Entrepreneurship and Science), MA
New Mexico Tech Summer Mini-Course, NM
OPTIONS for Young Women, IN
Preparatory Academics for Vanderbilt Engineers (PAVE), TN
Research Internship in Science and Engineering, MA
Robotics Camp, MI
Smith College Summer Science and Engineering Program, MA
Strive: Exploring Engineering, Math and Science, MA
University of Kansas–Project Discovery, KS
University of Vermont Summer Institute for High School Students Discovering Engineering, Computers, and Mathematics, VT
Women in Engineering Summer Camp, OH
Women in Science & Engineering Camp, PA
Women in Technology, MI
Young Investigators Program in Nuclear Science & Technology, NC

English as a Second Language

Adventure Ireland–English Learning Option, Ireland
Bark Lake Leadership Through Recreation Camp, Canada
Bishop's College School Summer School, Canada
Buckswood: English Language (ESL) and Activities–Bradfield, England, United Kingdom
Buckswood: English Language (ESL) and Activities–Plumpton, England, United Kingdom
Buckswood: English Language (ESL) and Activities–West Virginia, WV
EKOCAMP International, Canada
Fay Summer School, MA
The Fessenden School Summer ESL Program, MA
Georgetown Prep School Summer English Program, MD
Harker Summer English Language Institute, CA
Houghton Academy Summer ESL, NY
The Hun School of Princeton American Culture and Language Institute, NJ
Institut auf dem Rosenberg, Switzerland
Learn English and Discover Canada, Canada
Marine Military Academy English as a Second Language (ESL), TX
Mercersburg ESL Plus Program, PA
Monte Vista ESL Intensive Language Institute, CA
The Northwest School Summer Program, WA
Oxford School Summer Camp, CA
The Putney School Summer Program for International Education (ESL), VT
St. John's Northwestern ESL Camp, WI
St. Margaret's School International Summer ESL Programme, Canada
Southwestern Academy International Summer Semester, CA
Space Camp Turkey 6-Day International Program, Turkey
Sprachkurse Ariana, Aldenham, United Kingdom
Sprachkurse Ariana, Arosa, Switzerland
Sprachkurse Ariana, Lenk, Switzerland
Sprachkurse Ariana, Seefeld-Austria, Austria
Stanstead College–English as a Second Language, Canada
Study Tours and Cinema Program in the USA–Oxnard College, CA
Study Tours and Dance/Theater Camp in the USA–Dean College, MA
Study Tours and Hotel and Tourism Management in the USA–Southern Nevada College, NV
Study Tours and Leisure Sports in the USA–Citrus College, CA
Study Tours and Surf Program in the USA–Mira Costa College, CA
Study Tours in the USA–Citrus, CA
Study Tours in the USA–Dean College, MA
Study Tours in the USA–Lock Haven, PA
Study Tours in the USA–Mira Costa College, CA
Study Tours in the USA–Oxnard, CA
Study Tours in the USA–Southern Nevada, NV
UCAELI Summer Camp, CT
The Winchendon School Summer Session, MA
Wyoming Seminary–Sem Summer 2005, PA

English Language/Literature

Alexander-Smith Academy Summer School, TX
Blyth Education–Summer Study in London and Oxford University, United Kingdom
Carleton College Summer Writing Program, MN
Choate Rosemary Hall English Language Institute, CT
Choate Rosemary Hall English Language Institute/Focus Program, CT
Flint Hill School–"Summer on the Hill"–Enrichment on the Hill–Junior Great Books, VA
Flint Hill School–"Summer on the Hill"–Enrichment on the Hill–Women Writers' Adventure
Georgetown University College Prep Program, DC
Montgomery College WDCE–Super Sleuths–Meet the Challenge, MD
Oxford Advanced Seminars Programme, United Kingdom
Pine Ridge Summer Program, VT
Plato College–English/French Intensive Courses, Canada
Rumsey Hall School Summer Session, CT
University of St. Andrews Scottish Studies Summer Program, United Kingdom
Windsor Mountain: Experiential Summer School

Environmental Science

Audubon Journeys, VT
Audubon Vermont Youth Camp, VT
Austin Nature and Science Center, TX
Blyth Education–Summer Study in the Amazon and the Galapagos Islands, Ecuador
BROADREACH Academic Treks–Marine Park Management
Camp Greenkill–Conservation/Adventure, NY
Camp Ledgewood, OH
Camp Togowoods, AK
EARTHWATCH INSTITUTE–Dolphins of Costa Rica, Costa Rica
EARTHWATCH INSTITUTE–Mangroves of the Kenyan Coast, Kenya
EARTHWATCH INSTITUTE–Mountain Waters of Bohemia, Czech Republic
EARTHWATCH INSTITUTE–Restoring the Sagebrush Steppe, ID
Environmental Studies Summer Youth Institute, NY
Landmark Volunteers: Massachusetts, MA
Landmark Volunteers: Montana, MT
Landmark Volunteers: New York, NY
Landmark Volunteers: North Carolina, NC
Landmark Volunteers: Wyoming, WY
Longacre Expeditions, Whales, ME
Marine and Environmental Science Program, Canada
Maritime Camp, NJ
92nd Street Y Camps–The TIYUL
Organic Farm Camp, CO
PAX Abroad–Ecuador Rainforest Adventure, Ecuador
Quest Scholars Program at Stanford/ QuestLeadership, CA
SeaWorld/Busch Gardens Tampa Bay Adventure Camp, FL
SFS: Community Wildlife Management, Kenya
SFS: Conserving Coastal Diversity, Mexico
SFS: Marine Parks Management Studies, Turks and Caicos Islands
SFS: Sustaining Tropical Ecosystems, Costa Rica
SFS: Tropical Reforestation Studies, Australia
Stony Brook University–Environmental Education Summer Camp, NY
Student Conservation Association–Conservation Crew Program (Kentucky), KY
Student Conservation Association–Conservation Leadership Corps–Northwest, WA
University of Wisconsin–Green Bay Ecosystem Investigations, WI
WEI Leadership Training, CO
Wildlife Camp, CO
World Horizons International–Iceland, Iceland
Youth for Understanding USA–Brazil, Brazil

Equestrian Sports

Camp Carysbrook Equestrian, VA
Camp Skyline–Equestrian Program, AL
Eagle Lake Horse Camp, CO
Horseback Riding Academy at Pali Overnight Adventures, CA
International Riding Camp, NY
SJ Ranch Riding Camp, CT
Valley View Ranch Equestrian Camp, GA
YMCA Camp Lincoln–Specialty Camps: Horse Camp, NH

Farming

Alton Jones Day Camp, RI
Camp Treetops, NY
The Country School Farm, OH
Farm and Wilderness Camps–Tamarack Farm, VT
Hidden Villa Summer Camp, CA
Summer Days at the Morris Farm, ME

Fashion Design/Production

IEI–Fashion and Design Plus Programme, United Kingdom

Fencing

Culver Summer Camps/Culver Specialty Camp–Fencing, IN

Field Hockey

Shippensburg University Sports Camps–Field Hockey, PA
Vassar College Girl's Field Hockey Camp, NY

Field Research/Expeditions

AFS-USA–Team Mission–Russia, Russian Federation
Alabama Museum of Natural History Summer Expedition, AL
Asheville School Summer Academic Adventures, NC
BROADREACH Marine Biology Accredited, Bahamas
EARTHWATCH INSTITUTE–Archaeology at West Point Foundry, NY
EARTHWATCH INSTITUTE–Argentina's Pampas Carnivores, Argentina
EARTHWATCH INSTITUTE–Bahamian Reef Survey, Bahamas
EARTHWATCH INSTITUTE–Baltic Island Wetlands and Wildlife, Estonia
EARTHWATCH INSTITUTE–Biodiversity of the Grenadines, Grenada
EARTHWATCH INSTITUTE–Bogs of Belarus, Belarus
EARTHWATCH INSTITUTE–Brazil's Marine Wildlife, Brazil
EARTHWATCH INSTITUTE–Butterflies and Orchids of Spain, Spain
EARTHWATCH INSTITUTE–Butterflies of Vietnam, Vietnam
EARTHWATCH INSTITUTE–Cacti and Orchids of the Yucatan, Mexico
EARTHWATCH INSTITUTE–Canyonland Creek Ecology, UT
EARTHWATCH INSTITUTE–Caring for Chimpanzees, WA
EARTHWATCH INSTITUTE–Carnivores of Madagascar, Madagascar
EARTHWATCH INSTITUTE–Cheetah, Namibia
EARTHWATCH INSTITUTE–Chilean Coastal Archaeology, Chile
EARTHWATCH INSTITUTE–China's Ancestral Temples, China
EARTHWATCH INSTITUTE–Climate Change at Arctic's Edge, Canada
EARTHWATCH INSTITUTE–Coastal Archaeology of Maine, ME
EARTHWATCH INSTITUTE–Coastal Ecology of the Bahamas, Bahamas
EARTHWATCH INSTITUTE–Community Health in Cameroon, Cameroon
EARTHWATCH INSTITUTE–Conservation Research Initiative–Climate Change in the Rainforest, Australia
EARTHWATCH INSTITUTE–Conservation Research Initiative–Conserving the Pantanal, Brazil
EARTHWATCH INSTITUTE–Conservation Research Initiative–Hawksbill Turtles of the Great Barrier Reef, Australia
EARTHWATCH INSTITUTE–Conservation Research Initiative–Mountain Meadows of the North Cascades, WA
EARTHWATCH INSTITUTE–Conservation Research Initiative–Queensland Tropical Fish Ecology, Australia
EARTHWATCH INSTITUTE–Conservation Research Initiative–Restoring Wild Salmon, WA
EARTHWATCH INSTITUTE–Conservation Research Initiative–Salmon Hotspots of the Skagit River, WA
EARTHWATCH INSTITUTE–Conservation Research Initiative–Salmon of the Pacific Northwest, WA
EARTHWATCH INSTITUTE–Conservation Research Initiative–Samburu: Communities and Water Resources, Kenya
EARTHWATCH INSTITUTE–Conservation Research Initiative–Samburu: Communities and Wildlife Habitat, Kenya
EARTHWATCH INSTITUTE–Conservation Research Initiative–Samburu: Zebras, Kenya
EARTHWATCH INSTITUTE–Conservation Research Initiative–Traditions of Cedar, Salmon, and Gold, WA
EARTHWATCH INSTITUTE–Crocodiles of Cuba, Cuba
EARTHWATCH INSTITUTE–Crocodiles of the Okavango, Botswana
EARTHWATCH INSTITUTE–Desert Elephants of Namibia, Namibia
EARTHWATCH INSTITUTE–Dolphins and Whales of Abaco Island, Bahamas
EARTHWATCH INSTITUTE–Dolphins of Brazil, Brazil
EARTHWATCH INSTITUTE–Early Man at Olduvai Gorge, United Republic of Tanzania
EARTHWATCH INSTITUTE–Early Man in Spain, Spain
EARTHWATCH INSTITUTE–Echidnas and Goannas of Kangaroo Island, Australia
EARTHWATCH INSTITUTE–Ecuador Forest Birds, Ecuador
EARTHWATCH INSTITUTE–England's Hidden Kingdom, United Kingdom
EARTHWATCH INSTITUTE–Europe–Africa Songbird Migrations–Hungary, Hungary
EARTHWATCH INSTITUTE–Europe–Africa Songbird Migrations–Italy, Italy
EARTHWATCH INSTITUTE–Frontier Fort in Virginia, VA
EARTHWATCH INSTITUTE–Guatemala's Ancient Maya, Guatemala
EARTHWATCH INSTITUTE–Hawksbill Turtles of Barbados, Barbados
EARTHWATCH INSTITUTE–Health and Nutrition in Botswana, Botswana
EARTHWATCH INSTITUTE–Hopi Ancestors, AZ
EARTHWATCH INSTITUTE–Icelandic and Alaskan Glaciers, Iceland

▶ FIELD RESEARCH/EXPEDITIONS

EARTHWATCH INSTITUTE–India's Sacred Groves, India
EARTHWATCH INSTITUTE–Inner Mongolia's Lost Water, China
EARTHWATCH INSTITUTE–Itjaritjari: the Outback's Mysterious Marsupial, Australia
EARTHWATCH INSTITUTE–Jackson Hole Bison Dig, WY
EARTHWATCH INSTITUTE–Jamaica's Coral Reefs, Jamaica
EARTHWATCH INSTITUTE–Kenya's Black Rhino, Kenya
EARTHWATCH INSTITUTE–Koala Ecology, Australia
EARTHWATCH INSTITUTE–Lakes of the Rift Valley, Kenya
EARTHWATCH INSTITUTE–Lions of Tsavo, Kenya
EARTHWATCH INSTITUTE–Maine's Island Ecology, ME
EARTHWATCH INSTITUTE–Malaysian Bat Conservation, Malaysia
EARTHWATCH INSTITUTE–Mallorca's Copper Age, Spain
EARTHWATCH INSTITUTE–Mammoth Cave, KY
EARTHWATCH INSTITUTE–Mammoth Graveyard, SD
EARTHWATCH INSTITUTE–Manatees in Belize, Belize
EARTHWATCH INSTITUTE–Maternal and Child Healthcare in India, India
EARTHWATCH INSTITUTE–Medicinal Plants of Vietnam, Vietnam
EARTHWATCH INSTITUTE–Meerkats of the Kalahari, South Africa
EARTHWATCH INSTITUTE–Mexican Mangroves and Wildlife, Mexico
EARTHWATCH INSTITUTE–Mexican Megafauna, Mexico
EARTHWATCH INSTITUTE–Mojave Desert Tortoises, CA
EARTHWATCH INSTITUTE–Mongolian Argali, Mongolia
EARTHWATCH INSTITUTE–Moose and Wolves, MI
EARTHWATCH INSTITUTE–Moundbuilders on the Mississippi, IL
EARTHWATCH INSTITUTE–Mountain Waters of Bohemia, Czech Republic
EARTHWATCH INSTITUTE–Namibian Black Rhinos, Namibia
EARTHWATCH INSTITUTE–Namibian Wildlife Survey, Namibia
EARTHWATCH INSTITUTE–New Zealand Dolphins, New Zealand
EARTHWATCH INSTITUTE–Orca, WA
EARTHWATCH INSTITUTE–Pine Marten of the Ancient Forest, Canada
EARTHWATCH INSTITUTE–Poland's Ancient Burials, Poland
EARTHWATCH INSTITUTE–Prehistoric Pueblos of the American Southwest, NM
EARTHWATCH INSTITUTE–Puerto Rico's Rainforest, Puerto Rico
EARTHWATCH INSTITUTE–Rainforest Caterpillars–Costa Rica, Costa Rica
EARTHWATCH INSTITUTE–Rare Plants of Kenya, Kenya
EARTHWATCH INSTITUTE–Restoring Costa Rica's Rainforest, Costa Rica
EARTHWATCH INSTITUTE–Restoring the Sagebrush Steppe, ID
EARTHWATCH INSTITUTE–Restoring Vietnam's Forests, Vietnam
EARTHWATCH INSTITUTE–Rivers of the Peruvian Amazon, Peru
EARTHWATCH INSTITUTE–Roman Fort on the Danube, Romania
EARTHWATCH INSTITUTE–Roman Fort on Tyne, United Kingdom
EARTHWATCH INSTITUTE–Saving the Leatherback Turtle, U.S. Virgin Islands
EARTHWATCH INSTITUTE–Sea Otters of Alaska, AK
EARTHWATCH INSTITUTE–Sea Turtles of Baja, Mexico
EARTHWATCH INSTITUTE–Singing Russia, Russian Federation
EARTHWATCH INSTITUTE–South African Penguins, South Africa
EARTHWATCH INSTITUTE–South African Wildlife, South Africa
EARTHWATCH INSTITUTE–Spanish Dolphins, Spain
EARTHWATCH INSTITUTE–Sri Lanka's Temple Monkeys, Sri Lanka
EARTHWATCH INSTITUTE–Triassic Park, Argentina
EARTHWATCH INSTITUTE–Trinidad's Leatherback Sea Turtles, Trinidad and Tobago
EARTHWATCH INSTITUTE–Wild Dolphin Societies, FL
EARTHWATCH INSTITUTE–Wildlife Conservation in West Africa, Ghana
EARTHWATCH INSTITUTE–Wildlife Trails of the American West, UT
Environmental Studies Summer Youth Institute, NY
Flint Hill School–"Summer on the Hill"–Enrichment on the Hill–Investigating Where We Live, VA
Flint Hill School–"Summer on the Hill"–Enrichment on the Hill–Scientific Super Sleuths, VA
Groundwater University, NE
Landmark Volunteers: California, CA
LIFEWORKS with the British Virgin Islands Marine Parks and Conservation Department, British Virgin Islands
Montgomery College WDCE–GURL Power, MD
On the Wing, CO
Program of Audubon Research for Teens (Take P.A.R.T.), VT
Salmon Camp Research Team for Native Americans–Oregon, OR
Salmon Camp Research Team for Native Americans–Redwoods, CA
Salmon Camp Research Team for Native Americans–San Juan Island, WA
SFS: Community Wildlife Management, Kenya
SFS: Conserving Coastal Diversity, Mexico
SFS: Marine Parks Management Studies, Turks and Caicos Islands
SFS: Sustaining Tropical Ecosystems, Costa Rica
SFS: Tropical Reforestation Studies, Australia
University of Chicago–Insight, IL
University of Chicago–Stones and Bones, WY

Field Trips (Arts and Culture)

L' Académie de Paris, France
BICYCLE TRAVEL ADVENTURES–Student Hosteling Program–Amsterdam to Paris
BICYCLE TRAVEL ADVENTURES–Student Hosteling Program–Ireland and England
BICYCLE TRAVEL ADVENTURES–Student Hosteling Program–Province du Québec, Canada
BICYCLE TRAVEL ADVENTURES–Student Hosteling Program–Province du Québec (short program), Canada
BICYCLE TRAVEL ADVENTURES–Student Hosteling Program–Spain and France
Birmingham-Southern College Summer Scholar Program, AL
Cambridge College Programme, United Kingdom
The Cambridge Prep Experience, United Kingdom
The Cambridge Tradition, United Kingdom
Center Summer Academy, MA
East Coast College Tour by Education Unlimited
Flint Hill School–"Summer on the Hill"–Enrichment on the Hill–Investigating Where We Live, VA
Flint Hill School–"Summer on the Hill"–Enrichment on the Hill–Spanish Immersion Camp, VA
Flint Hill School–"Summer on the Hill"–Trips and Travel Day Camp, VA
Miss Porter's School Summer Challenge, CT
Oxford Advanced Studies Program, United Kingdom
The Oxford Prep Experience, United Kingdom
The Oxford Tradition, United Kingdom
Service-Learning in Paris, France
YMCA Camp Lincoln–On the Road, NH
YMCA Camp Lincoln–Travel Camp, NH

Film

Boston University Institute for Television, Film, and Radio Production, MA
Camp Hawthorne Creative Arts Camp, ME
The Experiment in International Living–United Kingdom Filmmaking Program and Homestay, United Kingdom
Film Institute at Pali Overnight Adventures, CA
Hollinsummer, VA
iD Tech Camps–Cal Lutheran University, Thousand Oaks, CA, CA
iD Tech Camps–Carnegie Mellon University, Pittsburgh, PA, PA
iD Tech Camps–Colorado College, Colorado Springs, CO, CO
iD Tech Camps–Dominican University, San Rafael, CA, CA
iD Tech Camps–Emerson College, Boston, MA, MA
iD Tech Camps–Emory University, Atlanta, GA, GA
iD Tech Camps–Georgetown University, Washington, DC, DC
iD Tech Camps–Lake Forest College, Evanston, IL, IL
iD Tech Camps–Merrimack College, North Andover, MA, MA
iD Tech Camps–MIT, Cambridge, MA, MA
iD Tech Camps–Northwestern University, Chicago, IL, IL
iD Tech Camps–Pepperdine University, Malibu, CA, CA

iD Tech Camps–Princeton University, Princeton, NJ, NJ
iD Tech Camps–Sacred Heart University, Fairfield, CT, CT
iD Tech Camps–Santa Clara University, Santa Clara, CA, CA
iD Tech Camps–Smith College, Northampton, MA, MA
iD Tech Camps–Southern Methodist University, Dallas, TX, TX
iD Tech Camps–Stanford University, Palo Alto, CA, CA
iD Tech Camps–St. Mary's College, Moraga, CA, CA
iD Tech Camps–UC Berkeley, Berkeley, CA, CA
iD Tech Camps–UC Irvine, Irvine, CA, CA
iD Tech Camps–UCLA, Westwood, CA, CA
iD Tech Camps–UC San Diego, La Jolla, CA, CA
iD Tech Camps–UC Santa Cruz, Santa Cruz, CA, CA
iD Tech Camps–University of Denver, Denver, CO, CO
iD Tech Camps–University of Miami, Coral Gables, FL, FL
iD Tech Camps–University of Michigan, Ann Arbor, MI, MI
iD Tech Camps–University of Minnesota, Minneapolis, MN, MN
iD Tech Camps–University of North Carolina at Chapel Hill, Chapel Hill, NC, NC
iD Tech Camps–University of Virginia, Charlottesville, VA, VA
iD Tech Camps–University of Washington, Seattle, WA, WA
iD Tech Camps–UT Austin, Austin, TX, TX
iD Tech Camps–Vassar College, Poughkeepsie, NY, NY
iD Tech Camps–Villanova University, Villanova, PA, PA
Montgomery College WDCE–Aspiring Filmmakers, MD
The New York Film Academy, Disney-MGM Studios, FL, FL
The New York Film Academy, Harvard University, Cambridge, MA, MA
The New York Film Academy in Florence, Italy, Italy
The New York Film Academy in London, United Kingdom
The New York Film Academy in Paris, France
The New York Film Academy, Princeton University, Princeton, NJ, NJ
The New York Film Academy, The Dalton School, New York, NY, NY
The New York Film Academy, Universal Studios, Hollywood, Ca, CA
Oxford Media School–Film, United Kingdom
Oxford Media School–Film Master Class, United Kingdom
Oxford Media School–Newsroom in Europe, United Kingdom
Oxford Media School–Newsroom in Europe, Master Class, United Kingdom
PixelNation, NJ
Stagedoor Manor Performing Arts Training Center/Theatre and Dance Camp, NY
Study Tours and Cinema Program in the USA–Oxnard College, CA
Technology Encounters–Video Encounter/ Computer Encounter–California, CA
Technology Encounters–Video Encounter/ Computer Encounter–Colorado, CO
Technology Encounters–Video Encounter/ Computer Encounter–Florida, FL
Technology Encounters–Video Encounter/ Computer Encounter–New York, NY
Technology Encounters–Video Encounter/ Computer Encounter–Pennsylvania, PA
Tisch School of the Arts–International High School Program–Dublin, Ireland
Tisch School of the Arts–International High School Program–Paris, France
Vermont Arts Filmmaking Institute, VT
Village Camps–Austria, Austria
Windsor Mountain: Adventures in Filmmaking, Saint Vincent and The Grenadines
Young Filmmakers at Purchase, NY

Finnish Language/Literature

Concordia Language Villages–Finnish, MN

First Aid

BROADREACH Academic Treks–Wilderness Emergency Medicine, Belize

Fishing

Camp Chippewa for Boys, MN
Camp Lincoln Fishing Camp, MN
Camp Stanislaus, MS
EARTHWATCH INSTITUTE–Conservation Research Initiative–Salmon Hotspots of the Skagit River, WA
Sea Kayak Expedition (English), Canada
TASC Canadian Wilderness Fishing Camps, Canada
Wediko Summer Program, NH

Flamenco

Spanish Language and Flamenco Enforex–Granada, Spain
Spanish Language and Flamenco Enforex–Madrid, Spain
Spanish Language and Flamenco Enforex–Marbella, Spain

Flight Instruction

Aerospace Camp Experience, WA
Camp Redwood, NY
Embry-Riddle Aeronautical University–Flight Exploration, FL
Embry-Riddle Aeronautical University–Sun Flight, FL
Florida Air Academy Summer Session, FL

Fly Fishing

Wilderness Ventures–Yellowstone Fly Fishing

Football

Alex Brown and Dustin Lyman Football Camp/Sports International, IL
Andy McCollum Football Camp, IL
Antwaan Randle Football Camp/Sports International, PA
Art Monk Football Camp/Sports International–Maryland, MD
Art Monk Football Camp/Sports International–Virginia, VA
Brad Hoover and Will Witherspoon Football Camp/Sports International, NC
Damon Huard and Matt Light Football Camp/Sports International, RI
Davidson Academy–Sports Camps, TN
Deuce McCallister Football Camp, LA
Dhani Jones Football Camp/Sports International, PA
Flint Hill School–"Summer on the Hill"–Sports on the Hill–Coed, VA
James Thrash and Hollis Thomas Football Camp/Sports International, PA
Jay Novacek Football Camp/Sports International, TX
Joe Krivak Quarterback Camp, Maryland/ Sports International, MD
Joe Krivak Quarterback Camp, North Carolina/Sports International, NC
Joe Krivak Quarterback Camp, Pennsylvania/ Sports International, PA
Joe Krivak Quarterback Camp, Rhode Island/Sports International, RI
Keenan McCardell and Jimmy Smith Football Camp/Sports International, FL
Keenan McCardell Football Camp, FL
Mercersburg Academy Blue Storm Football Camp, PA
Padua Franciscan High School Sports Camps, OH
Shippensburg University Sports Camps–Football, PA
Tice Brothers Football Camp, MN
William Henderson Football Camp/Sports International, WI

Forestry

EARTHWATCH INSTITUTE–Mangroves of the Kenyan Coast, Kenya
EARTHWATCH INSTITUTE–Puerto Rico's Rainforest, Puerto Rico
EARTHWATCH INSTITUTE–Restoring Vietnam's Forests, Vietnam

French Language/Literature

AAVE–Vivons le Français, France
Abbey Road Overseas Programs–French Immersion and Homestay, France
Abbey Road Overseas Programs–French Study Abroad in Cannes, France
Academic Study Associates–Nice, France
Academic Study Associates–Royan, France
AFS-USA–Homestay–France, France
AFS-USA–Homestay Language Study–Canada, Canada
Barat Foundation Summer Program in Provence and Paris, France
Bishop's College School Summer School, Canada
Blyth Education–Summer Study in Paris and the South of France, France
Brighton in Cannes, France
Brighton in Paris, France
Center for Cultural Interchange–France High School Abroad, France
Center for Cultural Interchange–France Language School, France
Center for Cultural Interchange–Switzerland Language Camp, Switzerland
Choate Rosemary Hall Summer in Paris, France
Concordia Language Villages–France, France
Concordia Language Villages–French–Bemidji, MN
Concordia Language Villages–French–Camp Holiday, MN
Concordia Language Villages–French–Fosston, MN

▶ French Language/Literature

Concordia Language Villages–French–Savannah, GA, GA
Concordia Language Villages–French Voyageur, MN
EF International Language School–Nice, France
EF International Language School–Paris, France
EKOCAMP International, Canada
The Experiment in International Living–France, Biking and Homestay, France
The Experiment in International Living–France, Five-Week Art and Adventure in Provence, France
The Experiment in International Living–France, Four-Week Brittany Discovery, France
The Experiment in International Living–France, Four-Week Homestay and Photography, France
The Experiment in International Living–France, Four-Week Homestay and Theatre, France
The Experiment in International Living–France, Four-Week Homestay and Travel–Borders, France
The Experiment in International Living–France, Four–Week Homestay and Travel through Alps, France
The Experiment in International Living–France, Homestay, Language Training, and Cooking, France
The Experiment in International Living–France, Three-Week Camargue Homestay, France
The Experiment in International Living–France, Three-Week Homestay and Travel–Borders, France
The Experiment in International Living–Switzerland French Language Immersion, Homestay, and Alpine Adventure, Switzerland
French Immersion Kayak Expedition, Canada
French Immersion Summer Camp, Canada
Global Teen–French Summer Camp in Monte Carlo, Monaco
Global Teen–Learn French in Biarritz, France
Global Teen–Learn French in Nice, France
Global Teen–Learn French in Paris, France
Global Teen–Summer Language Adventure in Montreal, Canada
GLOBAL WORKS–Language Immersion-France-4 weeks, France
Institut auf dem Rosenberg, Switzerland
International Summer Centre at Biarritz, France
International Summer Centre at Chatel, France
International Summer Centre at Paris-Brétigny, France
Les Elfes–International Summer/Winter Camp, Switzerland
The Loomis Chaffee Summer in France, France
LSA Amboise, France, France
LSA Antibes, France, France
LSA Argelés-Gazost, France, France
LSA Biarritz, France, France
LSA Bordeaux, France, France
LSA Cannes, France, France
LSA Hyères, France, France
LSA La Rochelle, France, France
LSA Lausanne, Switzerland, Switzerland
LSA Montreal, Canada–English/French, Canada
LSA Nice, France, France
LSA Paris, France, France
LSA Tours, France, France
Mercersburg Academy Summer Study in France, France
Millersville University of Pennsylvania–Summer Language Camps for High School Students, PA
Overland: Language Study Abroad in France, France
Phillips Exeter Academy French Study Tour, France
Plato College–English/French Intensive Courses, Canada
Programs Abroad Travel Alternatives–Canada, Canada
Programs Abroad Travel Alternatives–France, France
Putney Student Travel–Language Learning–France, France
Rassias Programs–Arles, France, France
Rassias Programs–Tours, France, France
Service-Learning in Paris, France
Sprachkurse Ariana, Arosa, Switzerland
Sprachkurse Ariana, Lenk, Switzerland
Sprachkurse Ariana, Seefeld-Austria, Austria
Stanstead College–English as a Second Language, Canada
Stanstead College–French as a Second Language, Canada
Summer Study in Paris at The American University of Paris, France
Taft Summer School Abroad–France, France
TASIS French Language Program in Château–d'Oex, Switzerland, Switzerland
Tufts Summit, France
Windsor Mountain: Bonjour Quebec, Canada
Windsor Mountain: Crossroads France, France
Woodberry Forest Summer School–France, France
Youth for Understanding USA–France, France

Gardening

The Country School Farm, OH
Farm and Wilderness Camps–Tamarack Farm, VT
St. Louis County 4-H Camp, MN

General Camp Activities

Abiliene Christian University–KidQuest Day Camp, TX
Ability First–Camp Joan Mier, CA
Ability First–Camp Paivika, CA
Adirondack Camp, NY
Agassiz Village, ME
Alford Lake Camp, ME
Alford Lake Family Camp, ME
Aloha Camp, VT
American Youth Foundation–Camp Merrowvista, NH
American Youth Foundation–Camp Miniwanca, MI
Anderson Camps' Colorado River Ranch for Boys/Hilltop Ranch for Girls, CO
Appleby College Summer Camps, Canada
Applejack Teen Camp, NY
Bar 717 Ranch/Camp Trinity, CA
Barton Day Camp–Long Island, NY
Barton Day Camp–New York, NY
Barton Day Camp–Worcester, MA
Birch Trail Camp for Girls, WI
Blue Star Camps, NC
Boulder Ridge Day Camp, CT
Breezy Point Day Camp, PA
Brewster Academy Summer Session, NH
Brown Ledge Camp, VT
Buckswood: English Language (ESL) and Activities–Bradfield, England, United Kingdom
Buckswood: English Language (ESL) and Activities–Plumpton, England, United Kingdom
Buckswood: English Language (ESL) and Activities–West Virginia, WV
Camden Military Academy Summer Session/Camp, SC
Camp Airy, MD
Camp AK-O-MAK, Canada
Camp Aldersgate–Kota Camp, AR
Camp Aldersgate–Med Camps, AR
Camp Aldersgate–Respite Care, AR
Camp Allen, NH
Camp Aloha Hive, VT
Camp Androscoggin, ME
Camp Arcadia, ME
Camp Arowhon–Boys and Girls Camp, Canada
Camp Atwater–Boys Session, MA
Camp Atwater–Girls Session, MA
Camp Avoda, MA
Camp Awosting, CT
Camp Barney Medintz, GA
Camp Berachah Ministries–Day Camp, WA
Camp Berachah Ministries–Junior Camp, WA
Camp Berachah Ministries–Legend Teen Camp, WA
Camp Berachah Ministries–Primary Camp, WA
Camp Berachah Ministries–Teen Leadership, WA
Camp Betsey Cox, VT
Camp Billings, VT
Camp Birch Trails, WI
Camp Bon Coeur, LA
Camp Brandon for Boys, NH
Camp Brookwoods and Deer Run, NH
Camp Burgess, MA
Camp Butterworth, OH
Camp Canadensis, PA
Camp Canonicus, RI
Camp Carysbrook, VA
Camp Catherine Capers, VT
Camp Cayuga, PA
Camp Cedar Point, IL
Camp Chateaugay, NY
Camp Chatuga, SC
Camp Cheerio YMCA, NC
Camp Chen-A-Wanda, PA
Camp Chewonki, ME
Camp Chi, WI
Camp Chinqueka, CT
Camp Chippewa for Boys, MN
Camp Chosatonga for Boys, NC
Camp Conrad Weiser, PA
Camp Courageous of Iowa, IA
Camp Craig Horse Residential Summer Camp, Canada
Camp Craig Sports and Recreation Summer Camp, Canada
Camp Crestridge for Girls, NC
Camp Discovery–Madison, NJ
Camp Discovery–Teaneck, NJ
Camp Dudley, NY
Camp Echo in Coleman High Country, NY

Camp Echoing Hills, OH
Camp Fire Camp Wi-Ta-Wentin, LA
Camp Fowler, MI
Camp Friendship, VA
Camp Geneva, MI
Camp Glen Arden for Girls, NC
Camp Glen Brook, NH
Camp Good News for Young People and Teens, MA
Camp Greenbrier for Boys, WV
Camp Green Cove, NC
Camp Greylock for Boys, MA
Camp Hawthorne, ME
Camp Hayward, MA
Camp Heartland Summer Camp–California, CA
Camp Heartland Summer Camp–Minnesota, MN
Camp Henry, MI
Camp Highlands for Boys, WI
Camp High Rocks, NC
Camp Hillside, MA
Camp Hilltop, NY
Camp Hitaga, IA
Camp Holiday Trails, VA
Camp Horizons Discover, VA
Camp Horizons Pathfinder, VA
Camp Horseshoe, WI
Camp Illahee for Girls, NC
Camp James Summer Day Camp, CA
Camp JCA Shalom, CA
Camp Jordan for Children with Diabetes, VA
Camp Joy, OH
Camp Kahdalea for Girls, NC
Camp Kawanhee for Boys, ME
Camp Kennybrook, NY
Camp Kingsmont, MA
Camp Kiniya, VT
Camp Kirkwold, ME
Camp Kodiak, Canada
Camp Kostopulos, UT
Camp La Junta, TX
Camp Lakeland, NY
Camp Lanakila, VT
Camp Laney for Boys, AL
Camp Laurel, ME
Camp Laurel South, ME
Camp Ledgewood, OH
Camp Lee Mar, PA
Camp Lincoln for Boys/Camp Lake Hubert for Girls, MN
Camp Lincoln for Boys/Camp Lake Hubert for Girls Family Camp, MN
Camp Lindenmere, PA
Camp Lohikan in the Pocono Mountains, PA
Camp Lookout, MI
Camp Louemma, NJ
Camp Lou Henry Hoover, NJ
Camp Louise, MD
Camp Maplehurst, MI
Camp Maromac, Canada
Camp Matoaka for Girls, ME
Camp McAlister, NY
Camp Menominee, WI
Camp Merrie-Woode, NC
Camp Mi-A-Kon-Da, Canada
Camp Mishawaka for Boys, MN
Camp Mishawaka for Girls, MN
Camp Modin, ME
Camp Mondamin, NC
Camp Monroe, NY
Camp Mt. Luther, PA
Camp Mowglis, School of the Open, NH
Camp Nakanawa, TN
Camp Nashoba North, ME
Camp Nawaka, MA
Camp Nock-A-Mixon, PA
Camp North Star for Boys, WI
Camp Northway, Canada
Camp Nor'wester, WA
Camp O-AT-KA, ME
Camp O'Bannon, OH
Camp Olympia, TX
Camp Onaway, NH
Camp Ouareau, Canada
Camp Oweki Summer Day Camp, MI
Camp Pacific's Recreational Camp, CA
Camp Pasquaney, NH
Camp Pinehurst, ME
Camp Pisgah, NC
Camp Ponacka, Canada
Camp Pondicherry, ME
Camp Quinebarge, NH
Camp Redwood, NY
Camp Regis, NY
Camp Ridgecrest for Boys, NC
Camp Rim Rock–General Camp, WV
Camp Rim Rock–Mini Camp, WV
Camp Rio Vista for Boys, TX
Camp Robin Hood for Boys and Girls, NH
Camp Rockmont for Boys, NC
Camp Runoia, ME
Camp Sabra, MO
Camp Saginaw, PA
Camp Sandy Cove, WV
Camp Sangamon for Boys, VT
Camp Scatico, NY
Camp Scelkit, ME
Camp Seagull for Girls, MI
Camp Shohola, PA
Camp Sierra Vista for Girls, TX
Camp Skylemar, ME
Camp Skyline, AL
Camp Sky Ranch, Inc., NC
Camp Starfish, NH
Camp Stonybrook, OH
Camp Streamside, PA
Camp Superkids–Camp Crosley, IN
Camp Superkids–Happy Hollow Children's Camp, IN
Camp Susquehannock for Boys, PA
Camp Susquehannock for Girls, PA
Camp Talcott, NY
Camp Tall Timbers, WV
Camp Tapawingo, ME
Camp Tawonga–Summer Camp, CA
Camp Tawonga–Summertime Family Camp, CA
Camp Timanous, ME
Camp Tioga, PA
Camp Tohkomeupog, NH
Camp Towanda, PA
Camp Treetops, NY
Campus Kids–CT, CT
Campus Kids–Minisink, NY
Campus Kids–NJ, NJ
Camp Veritans, NJ
Camp Wah-Nee, CT
Camp Walden, NY
Camp Walt Whitman, NH
Camp Watitoh, MA
Camp Watonka, PA
Camp Wawenock, ME
Camp Wayne for Boys, PA
Camp Wayne for Girls, PA
Camp Waziyatah, ME
Camp Wekeela for Boys and Girls, ME
Camp Westmont, PA
Camp Wicosuta, NH
Camp Wilvaken, Canada
Camp Wing, MA
Camp Wingate Kirkland, MA
Camp Wing Day Camp, MA
Camp Winnebago, ME
Camp WinShape for Boys, GA
Camp WinShape for Girls, GA
Cape Cod Sea Camps–Monomoy/Wono, MA
The Cardigan Mountain School Summer Session, NH
Carousel Day School, NY
Castilleja Summer Day Camp, CA
Catalina Island Camps, CA
Catholic Youth Camp, MN
Channel 3 Kids Camp, CT
Cheshire Academy Summer Program, CT
Chop Point Camp, ME
Circle Pines Center Summer Camp, MI
Clara Barton Camp, MA
Clara Barton Family Camp, MA
Clearwater Camp for Girls, WI
Cloverleaf Ranch Summer Camp, CA
Coleman Country Day Camp, NY
College for Kids, PA
College Settlement of Philadelphia, PA
Colorado Academy Summer Programs, CO
The Colorado Mountain Ranch, CO
The Community Center Going Places Camp, MD
Cordova 4-H Hawaiian Camp, AK
Cragged Mountain Farm, NH
Crane Lake Camp, MA
Cross Keys, United Kingdom
Crossroads School–Summer Educational Journey, CA
Crystalaire Camp, MI
Culver Summer Camps/Culver Specialty Camp– Aviation, IN
Culver Summer Camps/Culver Specialty Camp–Equestrian Arts, IN
Culver Summer Camps/Upper Camp–Boys, IN
Culver Summer Camps/Upper Camp–Girls, IN
Culver Summer Woodcraft Camp, IN
CYO Boys Camp, MI
CYO Girls Camp, MI
Darlington School Summer Camps, GA
Davidson Academy–Bear Country Day Camp, TN
Deerfoot Lodge, NY
Deerkill Day Camp, NY
Double "H" Hole in the Woods Ranch Summer Camp, NY
Douglas Ranch Camps, CA
Dwight-Englewood Summer Adventures, NJ
Dwight-Englewood Weekly Enrichment, NJ
Eagle Hill School Summer Session, MA
Eagle's Nest Camp, NC
Eden Wood Camp, MN
Enforex Residential Youth Summer Camp–Madrid, Spain
Enforex Residential Youth Summer Camp–Marbella, Spain
Enforex Residential Youth Summer Camp–Salamanca, Spain
Environmental Studies and Solutions, Norway
Exploration Intermediate Program at Wellesley College, MA
Exploration Junior Program at St. Mark's School, MA

GENERAL CAMP ACTIVITIES

Exploration Senior Program at Yale University, CT
Explorer Day Camp, OH
Falcon Camp, OH
Falcon Young Adventure Camp, OH
Falling Creek Camp, NC
Farm and Wilderness Camps–Barn Day Camp, VT
Fay School Day Camp, MA
Fenn School Summer Day Camp, MA
Fleur de Lis Camp, NH
Flint Hill School–"Summer on the Hill"–Junior Day/Day Camps, VA
Flying G Ranch, Tomahawk Ranch, CO
Forest Ridge Summer Program, WA
Forrestel Farm Riding and Sports Camp, NY
Four Winds * Westward Ho, WA
Friends Camp, ME
Geneva Glen Camp, CO
Girl Scouts of Genesee Valley Day Camp, NY
Girl Scouts of Mid-Continent–Camp Prairie Schooner, MO
Girl Scouts of Mid-Continent–Juliette Low Camp, MO
Girl Scouts of Mid-Continent–Winding River Camp and Ranch, MO
The Glen at Lake of the Woods, MI
Gold Arrow Camp, CA
The Gow School Summer Program, NY
Grandparents' and Grandchildren's Camp, NY
Greenbrier River Outdoor Adventures, Camp Snowshoe, WV
Greenwoods Camp for Boys, MI
Griffith Park Boys Camp, CA
The Grove at Greenwoods, MI
Harker Summer Programs, CA
Harmon's Pine View Camp, OH
Hidden Hollow Camp, OH
The Hollows Camp, Canada
Horizons for Youth, MA
The Hun School of Princeton Summer Day Camp, NJ
Indian Head Camp, PA
International Summer Camp Montana, Switzerland, Switzerland
Iroquois Springs, NY
JCC Houston: Camp Bami, TX
JCC Houston: Camp Kaleidoscope, TX
JCC Houston: Gordon Campsite, TX
JCC Houston: Kindercamp, TX
Jewish Community Center Day Camp, NJ
The John Cooper School Discovery Camps, TX
Jumonville Discovery Camp, PA
Jumonville Sampler Camps, PA
Junior Institute, WA
Kamp Kohut, ME
Kampus Kampers, FL
Kawkawa Summer Camps, Canada
Keewaydin Dunmore, VT
Keystone Camp, NC
Kickapoo Kamp, TX
KidzZone Summer Camp, GA
Killooleet, VT
Kingsley Pines Camp, ME
Kippewa for Girls, ME
Kiski Summer Camp–Junior Division-Boys Grades 5-8, PA
Kiski Summer Camp–Senior Division-Boys Grades 9-12, PA
Kiski Summer Camp–Senior Division-Girls Grades 9-12, PA
Kutsher's Sports Academy, NY
Lake Ann Baptist Camp, MI
Lake of the Woods Camp for Girls, MI
Leadership Adventure in Boston, MA
Ligonier Camp, PA
Linden Hill Summer Program, MA
Lindley G. Cook 4-H Camp, NJ
Lions Camp Merrick Deaf/HOH/KODA Program, MD
Lions Camp Merrick Diabetes Program, MD
Little Keswick School Summer Session, VA
Lochearn Camp for Girls, VT
Luna Adventures with AAG SummerSkills
Mah Meh Weh, MI
Maine Teen Camp, ME
The Marsh, MD
Marydale Resident Camp, LA
Medeba Summer Camp, Canada
Mercersburg Academy Junior Adventure Camp, PA
Mercersburg Adventure Camp, PA
Mercersburg Teen Adventure Camp, PA
Mini Minors, United Kingdom
Miracle Makers Summer Camp, CA
Missouri Children's Burn Camp, MO
Moose River Outpost, ME
Mountain Camp, CA
Mountain Meadow Ranch, CA
New Jersey YMHA–YWHA Camp Mountaintop, PA
New Jersey YMHA–YWHA Camp Nah-jee-wah, PA
New Jersey YMHA–YWHA Camp Nesher, PA
New Jersey YMHA–YWHA Cedar Lake Camp, PA
New Jersey YMHA–YWHA Round Lake Camp, PA
New Jersey YMHA–YWHA Teen Camp, PA
New Strides Day Camp, Canada
Next Level Camp, PA
92nd Street Y Camps–Camp Bari Tov, NY
92nd Street Y Camps–Camp Haverim, NY
92nd Street Y Camps–Camp Kesher, PA
92nd Street Y Camps–Camp Kesher Junior, PA
92nd Street Y Camps–Camp K'Ton Ton, NY
92nd Street Y Camps–Camp Tevah for Science and Nature, NY
92nd Street Y Camps–Camp Tova, NY
92nd Street Y Camps–Camp Yomi, NY
92nd Street Y Camps–Trailblazers, NY
North Country Camps—Camp Lincoln for Boys, NY
North Country Camps—Camp Whippoorwill for Girls, NY
North Woods Camp for Boys, NH
Oak Creek Ranch Summer School, AZ
OES–Summer Discovery, OR
OES–Summer Mini Camps, OR
OES–Summer Wonder, OR
OMNI Camp, ME
Padua Summer Experience, OH
Pali Overnight Adventures Camp, CA
Pine Island Camp, ME
Pine Tree Camps at Lynn University, FL
Pingry Day Camps, NJ
Pleasant Valley Camp for Girls, NH
Point O' Pines Camp for Girls, NY
Ponkapoag Outdoor Center Day Camps, MA
Potomac School Summer Programs, VA
Poulter Colorado Camps, CO
Presbyterian Clearwater Forest, MN
Pripstein's Camp, Canada
Rainbow Club–Greenwich, Connecticut, CT
Red Pine Camp for Girls, WI
River Way Ranch Camp, CA
Rockbrook Camp, NC
Rocky Mountain Village, CO
Rowe Camp, MA
St. Andrew's Summer Programs, MD
St. Johns Summer Camp, FL
Saint Thomas More School–Summer Academic Camp, CT
St. Louis County 4-H Camp, MN
Sandy Island Camp for Families, NH
Sidwell Friends Bethesda Day Camp, MD
Sidwell Friends Camp Corsica, MD
Sidwell Friends Explorer Day Camp, Explorer Voyagers and ExploreStar, DC
Skylake Yosemite Camp, CA
Skyland Camp for Girls, NC
Snowy Owl Camp for Girls, ME
Songadeewin of Keewaydin, VT
South Shore YMCA Specialty Camp, MA
Southwestern Adventures, AZ
Springfield Technical Community College–College for Kids, MA
Stevenson School Summer Camp, CA
Stony Book University–Summer Camp at Stony Brook, NY
Streamside Camp and Conference Center, PA
Streamside Family Camp, PA
Summer at Altamont, AL
Summer at the Academy, TX
Summer Horizons Day Camp, VT
SummerWorks, UT
Summit Camp, PA
Surprise Lake Camp, NY
Swift Nature Camp–Adventure Camp, WI
Swift Nature Camp–Discovery Camp, WI
Swift Nature Camp–Explorer Camp, WI
Tabor Academy Summer Program, MA
Talisman–Academics, NC
Talisman Mini-Camp, NC
Talisman–SIGHT, NC
Talisman Summer Camp, NC
Tampa Prep–Terrapin Day Camp, FL
TASIS Le Château des Enfants, Switzerland
TASIS Middle School Program, Switzerland
Thunderbird Ranch, CA
Timber-lee Youth Camp, WI
Towering Pines Camp, WI
UCSB Alumni Association Santa Barbara Family Vacation Center, CA
University of Wisconsin–Green Bay Summer Discovery, WI
University of Wisconsin–Superior Youthsummer 2005, WI
Valley Forge Military Academy Summer Camp for Boys, PA
Valley Forge Military Academy Summer Coed Day Camp, PA
Watersports Extravaganza at Pali Overnight Adventures, CA
West River United Methodist Center, MD
Wilderness Experiences Unlimited–Pathfinders Day Camp, MA
Windsor Mountain: Family Camp, NH
Windsor Mountain: International Summer Camp, NH
Winona Camp for Boys, ME
Wohelo-Luther Gulick Camps, ME
Woodland, WI
XUK, United Kingdom
YMCA Camp Abnaki, VT
YMCA Camp Abnaki–Counselor-in-Training Program, VT
YMCA Camp Abnaki–Family Camp, VT

YMCA Camp Abnaki–Mini Camp, VT
YMCA Camp Bernie, NJ
YMCA Camp Fitch Summer Camp, PA
YMCA Camp Icaghowan, WI
YMCA Camp Ihduhapi, MN
YMCA Camp Kanata, NC
YMCA Camp Lincoln–Traditional Day Camp, NH
YMCA Camp Matollionequay, NJ
YMCA Camp Michikamau, NY
YMCA Camp Minikani, WI
YMCA Camp Oakes Rangers, CA
YMCA Camp Ockanickon, NJ
YMCA Camp Pendalouan–Bugs and Bunks, MI
YMCA Camp Pendalouan–Counselor-in-Training, MI
YMCA Camp Pendalouan–Resident Camp, MI
YMCA Camp Pendalouan–Teen Xtreme, MI
YMCA Camp Seymour Summer Camp, WA
YMCA Camp Shand, PA
YMCA Camp Tippecanoe–Adventure Camp, OH
YMCA Camp Tippecanoe–Bike Camp, OH
YMCA Camp Tippecanoe–Equine Camp, OH
YMCA Camp Tippecanoe–Girl's & Guy's Corral, OH
YMCA Camp Tippecanoe–Horse Pals, OH
YMCA Camp Tippecanoe–Teen Camp, OH
YMCA Camp U-Nah-Li-Ya, WI
YMCA Camp Wabansi, WI
YMCA Camp Warren for Boys, MN
YMCA Camp Warren for Girls, MN
YMCA Lake Stockwell, NJ
YMCA Wanakita Summer Family Camp, Canada
YMCA Wanakita Summer Resident and Day Camp, Canada

Geology/Earth Science
Cascade Science School, OR
EARTHWATCH INSTITUTE–Moundbuilders on the Mississippi, IL
Hancock Field Station, OR
Stony Brook University–Environmental Education Summer Camp, NY
University of Chicago–Stones and Bones, WY

German Language/Literature
American Association of Teachers of German, German Summer Study Program, Germany
Center for Cultural Interchange–Germany High School Abroad, Germany
Center for Cultural Interchange–Germany Language School, Germany
Concordia Language Villages–German–Bemidji, MN
Concordia Language Villages–German–Camp Trowbridge, MN
Concordia Language Villages–Germany, Germany
EF International Language School–Munich, Germany
The Experiment in International Living–Germany, Four-Week Homestay, Travel, Community Service, Germany
Global Teen–German in Bavaria, Germany
Global Teen–German Plus Web Design, Video/Theatre in Berlin, Germany
Global Teen–German Summer Camp in Potsdam, Germany
Global Teen–Learn German in Berlin, Ages 12-15 on Lake Schmockwitz, Germany
Global Teen–Learn German in Berlin-City Centre, Ages 16-19, Germany
Global Teen–Learn German in Vienna, Summer Camp-Ages 12-18, Austria
Global Teen–Learn German in Vienna, Young Adult Summer Camp, Ages 16-18, Austria
Global Teen Summer Sports Camp in Berlin, Germany
GLS Bavarian Summer School, Germany
GLS Berlin Summer School, Germany
GLS Potsdam Summer School, Germany
GLS Sports and Language Camp Inzell, Germany
GLS Summer Camp Blossin, Germany
GLS Summer Camp Loewenstein, Germany
GLS Summer Camp Schmoeckwitz, Germany
Institut auf dem Rosenberg, Switzerland
LSA Berlin, Germany, Germany
LSA Blossin, Germany, Germany
LSA Cologne, Germany, Germany
LSA Hamburg, Germany, Germany
LSA Holzkirchen, Germany, Germany
LSA Inzell, Germany, Germany
LSA Loewenstein, Germany, Germany
LSA Munich, Germany, Germany
LSA Potsdam, Germany, Germany
LSA Schmoeckwitz, Germany, Germany
LSA Stuttgart, Germany, Germany
LSA Vienna, Austria, Austria
Millersville University of Pennsylvania–Summer Language Camps for High School Students, PA
Programs Abroad Travel Alternatives–Germany, Germany
Sprachkurse Ariana, Arosa, Switzerland
Sprachkurse Ariana, Lenk, Switzerland
Sprachkurse Ariana, Seefeld-Austria, Austria
Youth for Understanding USA–Germany, Germany

Glacier Travel
Adventures Cross-Country,Southern Europe Adventure

Go-Carts
Camp James Summer Day Camp, CA

Golf
Camp Lincoln for Boys/Camp Lake Hubert for Girls Golf Camp, MN
Camp Olympia Junior Golf Academy, TX
Culver Summer Camps/Culver Specialty Camp–Golf, IN
Enforex Spanish and Golf, Spain
4 Star Golf Camp at the University of Virginia, VA
4 Star Golf Plus All Sports Camp at the University of Virginia, VA
4 Star Tennis Plus Golf Camp at the University of Virginia, VA
International Junior Golf Academy, SC
Joel Ross Tennis & Sports Camp, CT
Julian Krinsky California Teen Tours, CA
Julian Krinsky Golf Camp at Cabrini College, PA
Julian Krinsky Golf Camp at Haverford College, PA
Julian Krinsky Golf Tours
Julian Krinsky Tennis Camp at Cabrini College, PA
Julian Krinsky Tennis Camp at Haverford College, PA
Julian Krinsky Yesh Shabbat California Teen Tour, CA
Julian Krinsky Yesh Shabbat Summer Camp, PA
Jumonville Golf Camp, PA
Maine Golf Academy–Family Camp, ME
Maine Golf Academy–Junior Golf Camp, ME
Maine Golf and Tennis Academy–Serve and Turf, ME
Maine Tennis Academy–Junior Tennis Camp, ME
Offense-Defense Golf Camp, Massachusetts, MA
Parent/Youth Golf School, TX
The Ranch–National Golf Camp–Lake Placid, NY
Study Tours and Leisure Sports in the USA–Citrus College, CA
Teen Tours of America–Golf Camp–Florida Swing, FL
University of Kansas–Girls Golf Camp, KS
University of Kansas–Jayhawk Golf Camp–Boys, KS
Westcoast Connection–Florida Swing Junior Touring Golf Camp, FL
Woodberry Forest Golf Camp, VA

Government and Politics
Choate Rosemary Hall John F. Kennedy Institute in Government, CT
The Congressional Seminar, DC
Diplomacy and Global Affairs Seminar, DC
The Experiment in International Living–Poland, Homestay, Community Service, and Travel, Poland
Junior Statesmen Symposium on California State Politics and Government, CA
Junior Statesmen Symposium on Los Angeles Politics and Government, CA
Junior Statesmen Symposium on New Jersey State Politics and Government, NJ
Junior Statesmen Symposium on Ohio State Politics and Government, OH
Junior Statesmen Symposium on Texas Politics and Leadership, TX
Junior Statesmen Symposium on Washington State Politics and Government, WA
National Debate Institute–DC, MD
Peace in the Modern World, Denmark
Stanford National Forensic Institute, CA
Teen Tour USA and Canada
Washington Internship Experience, DC
Where There Be Dragons: Silk Road, China
World Affairs Seminar, WI
World Affairs Youth Seminar, AL

Government and Politics (Advanced Placement)
Junior Statesmen Summer School–Georgetown University, DC
Junior Statesmen Summer School–Northwestern University, IL
Junior Statesmen Summer School–Princeton University, NJ
Junior Statesmen Summer School–Stanford University, CA
Junior Statesmen Summer School–Yale University, CT

▶ Graphic Arts

Graphic Arts
Architecture Summer Camp, AL
Auburn University Design Workshop, AL
Cleveland Institute of Art Pre-College Program–Special Effects and Animation, OH
Graphic Media Experience, NY
Knowledge Exchange Institute–Artist Abroad Program in Italy, Italy

Greek Language/Literature
Youth for Understanding USA–Greece, Greece

Guitar
National Guitar Workshop–Chicago, IL, IL

Gymnastics
Camp Greenkill–Gymnastics, NY
Gymnastics Academy at Pali Overnight Adventures, CA
Hollywood Stunt Camp at Pali Overnight Adventures, CA
JCC Houston: Gymnastics Camp, TX
92nd Street Y Camps–Fantastic Gymnastics, NY
Woodward Gymnastics Camp, PA

Health Education
Camp Jordan for Children with Diabetes, VA
Julian Krinsky/Canyon Ranch Young Adult Summer Program " for Smarter Minds and Bodies", PA

Health Sciences
EARTHWATCH INSTITUTE–Community Health in Cameroon, Cameroon
EARTHWATCH INSTITUTE–Health and Nutrition in Botswana, Botswana
EARTHWATCH INSTITUTE–Maternal and Child Healthcare in India, India
Milwaukee School of Engineering (MSOE)–Focus on Nursing, WI
Montgomery College WDCE–Young Scientist Academy, MD
Springfield College Allied Health Career Exploration Program, MA
Springfield College Athletic Trainer Workshop, MA
Tufts Summer Study, MA

Hearing Therapy
Meadowood Springs Speech and Hearing Camp, OR

Herpetology
Program of Audubon Research for Teens (Take P.A.R.T.), VT

Hiking
AAVE–Africa
AAVE–Ecuador and Galapagos, Ecuador
AAVE–Inmersión en España, Spain
AAVE–Peru and Machu Picchu, Peru
ACTIONQUEST: Galapagos Archipelago Expeditions, Ecuador
ACTIONQUEST: Leeward and French Caribbean Island Voyages
Adventure Links–Appalachian Odyssey
Adventure Links–Ultimate Adventure Camps, VA
Adventures Cross-Country, Caribbean Adventure
Adventures Cross-Country, Thailand Adventure, Thailand
Alpengirl–Hawaii, HI
Alpengirl–Washington Alpenguide Training, WA
Alpengirl–Washington Lil' Alpengirl, WA
Apogee Outdoor Adventures–New England Mountains and Coast
Barton Adventure Camp
BROADREACH Academic Treks–Spanish Immersion in Mexico, Mexico
BROADREACH Adventures Down Under, Australia
BROADREACH Amazon and Galapagos Encounter, Ecuador
BROADREACH Arc of the Caribbean Sailing Adventure
BROADREACH Baja Extreme–Scuba Adventure, Mexico
BROADREACH Costa Rica Experience, Costa Rica
BROADREACH Fiji Solomon Quest
Camp Exploration Travel Day Camp, CA
Camp Mowglis, School of the Open, NH
Camp Tawonga–Summer Camp, CA
Canadian Rockies Adventurer Camp, Canada
Cheley Colorado Camps, CO
Christikon, MT
Darrow Youth Backpacking, ME
Discovery Camp, CO
Eagle Lake Camp–East, NC
Eagle Lake Wilderness Program, CO
EARTHWATCH INSTITUTE–Wildlife Trails of the American West, UT
The Experiment in International Living–France, Four-Week Homestay and Travel–Borders, France
The Experiment in International Living–Spain, Four-Week Homestay and Trekking Program, Spain
The Experiment in International Living–Switzerland French Language Immersion, Homestay, and Alpine Adventure, Switzerland
Flint Hill School–"Summer on the Hill"–Into the Woods Day Camp, VA
Great Escapes (Adventure Trips for Teens)–Colorado River and Canyons Adventure
Great Escapes (Adventure Trips for Teens)–Rocky Mountain Horsepacking Adventure, CO
Green River Preserve, NC
Hidden Villa Summer Camp, CA
Hiker's Heaven Overnight Camp
Israel Discovery
Keewaydin Dunmore, VT
Landmark Volunteers: New Mexico, NM
Longacre Expeditions, Downeast, ME
Longacre Expeditions, Volcanoes
Lower Mustang Summer Passage, Nepal
LSA Inzell, Germany, Germany
Luna Adventures with AAG SummerSkills
Mountain Retreat Overnight Camp, CA
Overland: Adventure Camp for 5th and 6th Grade Boys, MA
Overland: Adventure Camp for 5th and 6th Grade Girls, MA
Overland: Appalachian Trail Challenge Hiking
Overland: European Explorer Hiking, Rafting, and Sea Kayaking
Overland: Hawaii Explorer Hiking, Kayaking, Sailing and Snorkeling, HI
Poulter Colorado Camps: Adventures Planet Earth–Austria
Poulter Colorado Camps: Adventures Planet Earth–New Zealand, New Zealand
Poulter Colorado Camps: Adventures Planet Earth–Spain, Spain
Songadeewin of Keewaydin, VT
Swiss Challenge, Switzerland
Talisman–SIGHT, NC
Tanager Lodge, NY
Tibetan Summer Passage
Trailmark Outdoor Adventures–New England–Acadia
Trailmark Outdoor Adventures–New England–Downeast
Trailmark Outdoor Adventures–New England–Jr. Acadia
Trailmark Outdoor Adventures–New England–Rangeley Coed
Where There Be Dragons: Guatemala, Guatemala
Where There Be Dragons: Peru, Peru
Where There Be Dragons: Silk Road, China
Where There Be Dragons: Tibet, China
Wilderness Ventures–Pacific Coast Bike
YMCA Camp Lincoln–Outdoor Adventure Camp: Canadian Adventure, Canada

History
Academic Camps at Gettysburg College–U.S. Civil War, PA
Alexander Muss High School in Israel, Israel
Columbia University Continuing Education–The Barcelona Experience, Spain
EARTHWATCH INSTITUTE–Archaeology at West Point Foundry, NY
EARTHWATCH INSTITUTE–Chilean Coastal Archaeology, Chile
EARTHWATCH INSTITUTE–China's Ancestral Temples, China
EARTHWATCH INSTITUTE–Conservation Research Initiative–Traditions of Cedar, Salmon, and Gold, WA
EARTHWATCH INSTITUTE–Medicinal Plants of Antiquity, Italy
EARTHWATCH INSTITUTE–Singing Russia, Russian Federation
Fort Union Civil War Camp, MN
Ibike Cultural Tours–Ecuador, Ecuador
Ibike Cultural Tours–Washington/British Columbia
Oxford Advanced Seminars Programme, United Kingdom
Programs Abroad Travel Alternatives–Ireland, Ireland
Programs Abroad Travel Alternatives–Italy, Italy
Rust College Study Abroad in Africa
University of St. Andrews Scottish Studies Summer Program, United Kingdom
Where There Be Dragons: China, China
Where There Be Dragons: Vietnam, Vietnam

Homestays
AAVE–Inmersión en España, Spain
Abbey Road Overseas Programs–French Immersion and Homestay, France
Abbey Road Overseas Programs–Spanish Immersion and Homestay, Spain
AFS-USA–Community Service–Argentina, Argentina

AFS-USA–Homestay–Argentina, Argentina
AFS-USA–Homestay–Chile, Chile
AFS-USA–Homestay–Ecuador, Ecuador
AFS-USA–Homestay–Finland, Finland
AFS-USA–Homestay–France, France
AFS-USA–Homestay Language Study–Canada, Canada
AFS-USA–Homestay Language Study–Costa Rica, Costa Rica
AFS-USA–Homestay Language Study–Japan, Japan
AFS-USA–Homestay Language Study–Latvia, Latvia
AFS-USA–Homestay, Outdoor Adventure Amazon–Brazil, Brazil
AFS-USA–Homestay–Paraguay, Paraguay
AFS-USA–Homestay Plus–Australia, Australia
AFS-USA–Homestay Plus–Brazil, Brazil
AFS-USA–Homestay Plus–Costa Rica, Costa Rica
AFS-USA–Homestay Plus–Hungary, Hungary
AFS-USA–Homestay Plus–Italy, Italy
AFS-USA–Homestay Plus–Netherlands, Netherlands
AFS-USA–Homestay Plus–New Zealand, New Zealand
AFS-USA–Homestay–Spain, Spain
AFS-USA–Homestay–Thailand, Thailand
AFS-USA–Homestay–Turkey, Turkey
AFS-USA–Team Mission–Ghana, Ghana
Bravo Spain–Barcelona, Spain
Brighton in Costa Rica, Costa Rica
Brighton in Paris, France
Center for Cultural Interchange–Argentina Independent Homestay, Argentina
Center for Cultural Interchange–Brazil High School Abroad, Brazil
Center for Cultural Interchange–Chile Independent Homestay, Chile
Center for Cultural Interchange–France Independent Homestay, France
Center for Cultural Interchange–Germany Independent Homestay, Germany
Center for Cultural Interchange–Ireland Independent Homestay Program, Ireland
Center for Cultural Interchange–Japan High School Abroad, Japan
Center for Cultural Interchange–Mexico High School Abroad, Mexico
Center for Cultural Interchange–South Africa High School Abroad, South Africa
Center for Cultural Interchange–Spain Independent Homestay, Spain
Center for Cultural Interchange–United Kingdom Independent Homestay, United Kingdom
China's Frontiers: Diverse Landscapes and Peoples, China
Choate Rosemary Hall Summer in Paris, France
Choate Rosemary Hall Summer in Spain, Spain
Enforex Homestay Program–Almuñecar, Spain
Enforex Homestay Program–Barcelona, Spain
Enforex Homestay Program–Granada, Spain
Enforex Homestay Program–Madrid, Spain
Enforex Homestay Program–Marbella, Spain
Enforex Homestay Program–Salamanca, Spain
The Experiment in International Living–Argentina Homestay, Community Service, and Outdoor Ecological Program, Argentina
The Experiment in International Living–Australia Homestay, Australia
The Experiment in International Living–Belize Homestay, Belize
The Experiment in International Living–Botswana Homestay, Botswana
The Experiment in International Living–Brazil–Ecological Preservation, Brazil
The Experiment in International Living–Brazil Homestay and Community Service, Brazil
The Experiment in International Living–Chile North Homestay, Community Service, Chile
The Experiment in International Living–Chile South Homestay, Chile
The Experiment in International Living–China North and East Homestay, China
The Experiment in International Living–China South and West Homestay, China
The Experiment in International Living–Costa Rica Homestay, Costa Rica
The Experiment in International Living–Ecuador Homestay, Ecuador
The Experiment in International Living–France, Biking and Homestay, France
The Experiment in International Living–France, Five-Week Art and Adventure in Provence, France
The Experiment in International Living–France, Four-Week Brittany Discovery, France
The Experiment in International Living–France, Four-Week Homestay and Photography, France
The Experiment in International Living–France, Four-Week Homestay and Theatre, France
The Experiment in International Living–France, Four-Week Homestay and Travel–Borders, France
The Experiment in International Living–France, Four–Week Homestay and Travel through Alps, France
The Experiment in International Living–France, Homestay, Language Training, and Cooking, France
The Experiment in International Living–France, Three-Week Camargue Homestay, France
The Experiment in International Living–France, Three-Week Homestay and Travel–Borders, France
The Experiment in International Living–Germany, Four-Week Homestay, Travel, Community Service, Germany
The Experiment in International Living–Ghana Homestay, Ghana
The Experiment in International Living–Ireland/Northern Ireland Homestay and Peace Studies, Ireland
The Experiment in International Living–Italy Homestay, Italy
The Experiment in International Living–Japan Homestay, Japan
The Experiment in International Living–Mexico, Community Service, Travel, and Homestay, Mexico
The Experiment in International Living–Mexico Homestay and Travel, Mexico
The Experiment in International Living–Morocco Four-Week Arts and Culture Program, Morocco
The Experiment in International Living–Navajo Nation, NM
The Experiment in International Living–New Zealand Homestay, New Zealand
The Experiment in International Living–Poland, Homestay, Community Service, and Travel, Poland
The Experiment in International Living–South Africa Homestay and Community Service, South Africa
The Experiment in International Living–Spain, Five-Week Homestay, Travel, Ecology, Spain
The Experiment in International Living–Spain, Five-Week Language Training, Travel, and Homestay, Spain
The Experiment in International Living–Spain, Four-Week Homestay and Trekking Program, Spain
The Experiment in International Living–Spain, Four-Week Language Study and Homestay, Spain
The Experiment in International Living–Spain–Spanish Culture and Folklore, Spain
The Experiment in International Living–Spain, Three-Week Homestay, Spain
The Experiment in International Living–Switzerland French Language Immersion, Homestay, and Alpine Adventure, Switzerland
The Experiment in International Living–Thailand Homestay, Thailand
The Experiment in International Living–The United Kingdom Celtic Odyssey, United Kingdom
The Experiment in International Living–Turkey Homestay, Community Service, and Travel, Turkey
The Experiment in International Living–United Kingdom Filmmaking Program and Homestay, United Kingdom
The Experiment in International Living–United Kingdom Theatre Program, United Kingdom
GLOBAL WORKS–Language Immersion-Ecuador and the Galapagos-4 weeks, Ecuador
GLOBAL WORKS–Language Immersion-France-4 weeks, France
GLOBAL WORKS–Language Immersion-Spain-4 weeks, Spain
Greek Summer, Greece
The Loomis Chaffee Summer in France, France
The Loomis Chaffee Summer in Spain, Spain
LSA Antibes, France, France
LSA Antigua, Guatemala, Guatemala
LSA Buenos Aires, Argentina, Argentina
LSA Cordoba, Argentina, Argentina
LSA Cuzco, Peru, Peru
LSA Flamingo Beach, Costa Rica, Costa Rica
LSA Granada, Spain, Spain
LSA Holzkirchen, Germany, Germany
LSA Kanazawa, Japan, Japan
LSA Madrid, Spain, Spain
LSA Màlaga, Spain, Spain
LSA Orvieto, Italy, Italy

▶ Homestays

LSA Playa Del Carmen, Mexico, Mexico
LSA Quito, Ecuador, Ecuador
LSA Sevilla, Spain, Spain
LSA Sucre, Bolivia, Bolivia
LSA Vienna, Austria, Austria
LSA Viña del Mar, Chile, Chile
The Nepal Cultural Immersion Experience, Nepal
Programs Abroad Travel Alternatives–Peru, Peru
Rassias Programs–Arles, France, France
Rassias Programs–Gijón, Spain, Spain
Rassias Programs–Pontevedra, Spain, Spain
Rassias Programs–Segovia, Spain, Spain
Rassias Programs–Tours, France, France
Study Tours and Cinema Program in the USA–Oxnard College, CA
Study Tours and Hotel and Tourism Management in the USA–Southern Nevada College, NV
Study Tours and Surf Program in the USA–Mira Costa College, CA
Study Tours in the USA–Citrus, CA
Study Tours in the USA–Dean College, MA
Study Tours in the USA–Lock Haven, PA
Study Tours in the USA–Mira Costa College, CA
Study Tours in the USA–Oxnard, CA
Study Tours in the USA–Southern Nevada, NV
Taft Summer School Abroad–France, France
Taft Summer School Abroad–Spain, Spain
Tibetan Culture of Northern India, India
Where There Be Dragons: India Culture and Philosophy, India
Youth for Understanding USA–Argentina, Argentina
Youth for Understanding USA–Australia, Australia
Youth for Understanding USA–Brazil, Brazil
Youth for Understanding USA–Chile, Chile
Youth for Understanding USA–China, China
Youth for Understanding USA–Denmark, Denmark
Youth for Understanding USA–Ecuador, Ecuador
Youth for Understanding USA–Estonia/Latvia-Baltic Summer
Youth for Understanding USA–France, France
Youth for Understanding USA–Germany, Germany
Youth for Understanding USA–Ghana, Ghana
Youth for Understanding USA–Greece, Greece
Youth for Understanding USA–Hungary, Hungary
Youth for Understanding USA–Ireland, Ireland
Youth for Understanding USA–Italy, Italy
Youth for Understanding USA–Japan, Japan
Youth for Understanding USA–Kazakhstan, Kazakhstan
Youth for Understanding USA–Kenya, Kenya
Youth for Understanding USA–Poland, Poland
Youth for Understanding USA–Russia, Russian Federation
Youth for Understanding USA–South Africa, South Africa
Youth for Understanding USA–South Korea, Republic of Korea
Youth for Understanding USA–Spain, Spain
Youth for Understanding USA–Sweden, Sweden
Youth for Understanding USA–Thailand, Thailand
Youth for Understanding USA–Uruguay, Uruguay
Youth for Understanding USA–Venezuela, Venezuela

Horseback Riding

AAVE–Boot/Saddle/Paddle
AAVE–Rocky Mountain Adventure, CO
Alpengirl–Montana Horse, MT
Black River Farm and Ranch, MI
Bonnie Castle Riding Camp, MA
Camp Berachah Ministries–Horse Day Camp, WA
Camp Berachah Ministries–Overnight Horse Camp, WA
Camp Berachah Ministries–Wrangler-In-Training, WA
Camp Carysbrook Equestrian, VA
Camp Catherine Capers, VT
Camp Craig Horse Residential Summer Camp, Canada
Camp Craig Sports and Recreation Summer Camp, Canada
Camp Echo, MI
Camp Hitaga–Stirrups and Saddles, IA
Camp Lohikan in the Pocono Mountains, PA
Camp Pok-O-MacCready, NY
Camp Rim Rock–Horseback Riding Camp, WV
Camps with Meaning–Advanced Horsemanship I & II, Canada
Camp Winding Gap, NC
Cedar Lodge, MI
Cheley Colorado Camps, CO
Culver Summer Camps/Culver Specialty Camp–Equestrian Arts, IN
Douglas Ranch Camps, CA
Eagle Lake Horse Camp, CO
Falcon Horse Lover Camp, OH
Falcon Horse Lover Camp for Girls, OH
Forrestel Farm Riding and Sports Camp, NY
Girl Scouts of Mid-Continent–Winding River Camp and Ranch, MO
Great Escapes (Adventure Trips for Teens)–Rocky Mountain Horsepacking Adventure, CO
Great Escapes (Adventure Trips for Teens)–Saddle and Sail
Greenwoods Camp for Boys, MI
Horseback Riding Academy at Pali Overnight Adventures, CA
International Riding Camp, NY
Lake of the Woods Camp for Girls, MI
Mah Meh Weh, MI
Mini-Camp in the Pocono Mountains, PA
Ramey Summer Riding Camps, IN
The Ranch–Lake Placid Academy, NY
The Ranch–Lake Placid Teen Travel Camp
Rawhide Ranch, CA
River Way Ranch Camp, CA
Road's End Farm Horsemanship Camp, NH
Sanborn Western Camps: Big Spring Ranch for Boys, CO
Sanborn Western Camps: High Trails Ranch for Girls, CO
Shwayder Camp, CO
Sprucelands Camp, NY
Talisman–SIGHT, NC
Teton Valley Ranch Camp–Boys Camp, WY
Teton Valley Ranch Camp–Girls Camp, WY
Timber-lee Horsemanship Camps, WI
Trailmark Outdoor Adventures–Colorado–West Elks with Horseback, CO
Trailmark Outdoor Adventures–New England–Rangeley Coed
Trailmark Outdoor Adventures–Northern Rockies–Tetons with Horseback
Valley View Ranch Equestrian Camp, GA
Willow Hill Farm Camp, NY
Windridge Tennis Camp at Teela-Wooket, Vermont, VT
Windsor Mountain: Driftwood Stables Ranch Camp, NH
YMCA Camp Lincoln–Specialty Camps: Horse Camp, NH
YMCA Camp Pendalouan–Ropers and Wranglers Horse Camp, MI
YMCA Camp Tippecanoe–Equine Camp, OH
YMCA Camp Tippecanoe–Girl's & Guy's Corral, OH

Hotel Management

Study Tours and Hotel and Tourism Management in the USA–Southern Nevada College, NV

Humanities

Explore-A-College, IN
Oxford Advanced Seminars Programme, United Kingdom
University of Chicago–Insight, IL

Hungarian Language/Literature

Youth for Understanding USA–Hungary, Hungary

Ice Climbing

AAVE–Alaska, AK
Adirondack Alpine Adventures, NY
Adventure Treks–Alaska Adventures, AK
Longacre Expeditions, Alaska, AK
Outpost Wilderness Adventure–Alpine Rock and Ice, CO

Ice Hockey

Camp All-Star, ME
Culver Summer Camps/Culver Specialty Camp–Ice Hockey, IN
Hockey Opportunity Camp, Canada
Shattuck–St. Mary's Girls Elite Hockey Camp, MN
Shattuck-St. Mary's Boys Elite Hockey Camp, MN

In-Line Skating

Woodward Freestyle BMX Bicycle, Inline Skate, Skateboarding Camp, PA

Independent Study

University of Connecticut Mentor Connection, CT

Intercultural Studies

AAVE–Vivons le Français, France
A.C.E. Intercultural Institute, WA
Barat Foundation Summer Program in Provence and Paris, France
Bicycle Africa Tours
China's Frontiers: Diverse Landscapes and Peoples, China
Circle Pines Center Summer Camp, MI

Columbia University Continuing Education–The Barcelona Experience, Spain
Cordova 4-H Hawaiian Camp, AK
Cuernavaca Summer Program for Teens, Mexico
Environmental Studies and Solutions, Norway
Excel at Oxford/Tuscany
Flint Hill School–"Summer on the Hill"–Enrichment on the Hill–Spanish Immersion Camp, VA
GLOBAL WORKS–Cultural Exchange-Fiji Islands-4 weeks, Fiji
GLOBAL WORKS–Cultural Exchange-New Zealand and Fiji Islands-4 weeks
Israel Discovery
Lacunza Junior Summer Spanish Course, Spain
LSA Alicante, Spain, Spain
LSA Antibes, France, France
LSA Antigua, Guatemala, Guatemala
LSA Argelés-Gazost, France, France
LSA Barcelona, Spain, Spain
LSA Berlin, Germany, Germany
LSA Biarritz, France, France
LSA Blossin, Germany, Germany
LSA Bordeaux, France, France
LSA Buenos Aires, Argentina, Argentina
LSA Cannes, France, France
LSA Cordoba, Argentina, Argentina
LSA Cuzco, Peru, Peru
LSA El Puerto de Santa Maria, Spain, Spain
LSA Flamingo Beach, Costa Rica, Costa Rica
LSA Granada, Spain, Spain
LSA Holzkirchen, Germany, Germany
LSA Inzell, Germany, Germany
LSA Kanazawa, Japan, Japan
LSA Livorno, Italy, Italy
LSA Oaxaca, Mexico, Mexico
LSA Orvieto, Italy, Italy
LSA Playa Del Carmen, Mexico, Mexico
LSA Potsdam, Germany, Germany
LSA Puebla, Mexico, Mexico
LSA Quito, Ecuador, Ecuador
LSA Salamanca, Spain, Spain
LSA Schmoeckwitz, Germany, Germany
LSA Siena, Italy, Italy
LSA Sucre, Bolivia, Bolivia
Mercersburg Academy Summer Study in France, France
Mercersburg Academy Summer Study in Spain, Spain
Peace in the Modern World, Denmark
Peace Works International–Costa Rica, Costa Rica
Peace Works International–Peru, Peru
Peace Works International–Ecuador, Ecuador
Personal Passage, Nepal
The Putney School Summer Program for International Education (ESL), VT
Putney Student Travel–Cultural Exploration–Eastern European Heritage
Rust College Study Abroad in Africa
Study Tours in the USA–Citrus, CA
Study Tours in the USA–Dean College, MA
Study Tours in the USA–Lock Haven, PA
Study Tours in the USA–Mira Costa College, CA
Study Tours in the USA–Oxnard, CA
Study Tours in the USA–Southern Nevada, NV
Tibetan Culture of Northern India, India
Tibetan Summer Passage
University of Chicago–ChicaGO! The Traveling Academy, France
Weissman Teen Tours–European Experience
Where There Be Dragons: China, China
Where There Be Dragons: India Culture and Philosophy, India
Where There Be Dragons: Mongolia, Mongolia
Where There Be Dragons: Silk Road, China
Where There Be Dragons: Thailand, Thailand
Where There Be Dragons: Tibet, China
Where There Be Dragons: Vietnam, Vietnam
Wilderness Ventures–European Alps
Windsor Mountain: Alaska, AK
Windsor Mountain: Puerto Rico, Puerto Rico
Windsor Mountain: Voices of the Wind River, Wyoming, WY
Youth for Understanding USA–Australia, Australia
Youth for Understanding USA–Brazil, Brazil
Youth for Understanding USA–Chile, Chile
Youth for Understanding USA–China, China
Youth for Understanding USA–Ecuador, Ecuador
Youth for Understanding USA–France, France
Youth for Understanding USA–Germany, Germany
Youth for Understanding USA–Greece, Greece
Youth for Understanding USA–Hungary, Hungary
Youth for Understanding USA–Italy, Italy
Youth for Understanding USA–Japan, Japan
Youth for Understanding USA–Kenya, Kenya
Youth for Understanding USA–Poland, Poland
Youth for Understanding USA–Russia, Russian Federation
Youth for Understanding USA–Spain, Spain
Youth for Understanding USA–Sweden, Sweden
Youth for Understanding USA–Thailand, Thailand
Youth for Understanding USA–Uruguay, Uruguay
Youth for Understanding USA–Venezuela, Venezuela

International Relations

Diplomacy and Global Affairs Seminar, DC
Georgetown University International Relations Program for High School Students, DC
National Student Leadership Conference: International Diplomacy, DC
Tufts Summit, France
World Affairs Youth Seminar, AL

Internships

Career Explorations, NY
IEI Student Travel–Internship Program in London, United Kingdom

Irish Studies

Adventure Ireland–English Learning Option, Ireland
Adventure Ireland–Irish Studies, Ireland
Celtic Learning and Travel Services–Edinburgh and Dublin
Celtic Learning and Travel Services–London and Dublin
Celtic Learning and Travel Services–Summer in Ireland, Ireland
Irish Way, Ireland

Italian Language/Literature

Abbey Road Overseas Programs–Italy Study Abroad: Language and Culture, Italy
American Collegiate Adventures–Italy, Italy
Brighton in Tuscany, Italy
Center for Cultural Interchange–Italy Language School, Italy
Concordia Language Villages–Italian, MN
EF International Language School–Rome, Italy
The Experiment in International Living–Italy Homestay, Italy
Global Teen–Italian and Soccer in Rome, Italy
Global Teen–Learn Italian in Italy, Italy
Humanities Spring in Assisi, Italy
Humanities Spring on the Road, Italy
LSA Ascoli, Italy, Italy
LSA Florence, Italy, Italy
LSA Lignano, Italy–Active Junior Italian Summer Program, Italy
LSA Livorno, Italy, Italy
LSA Milan, Italy, Italy
LSA Orvieto, Italy, Italy
LSA Rimini, Italy, Italy
LSA Rome, Italy, Italy
LSA Siena, Italy, Italy
LSA Taormina, Italy, Italy
LSA Treviso, Italy, Italy
Programs Abroad Travel Alternatives–Italy, Italy
Youth for Understanding USA–Italy, Italy

Japanese Language/Literature

AFS-USA–Homestay Language Study–Japan, Japan
Concordia Language Villages–Japan, Japan
Concordia Language Villages–Japanese, MN
The Experiment in International Living–Japan Homestay, Japan
LSA Kanazawa, Japan, Japan
Shizen Kyampu-Japanese Language Science Camp, OR
Woodberry Forest Summer School–Japan, Japan
Youth for Understanding USA–Japan, Japan

Jet Skiing

Mini-Camp in the Pocono Mountains, PA
Watersports Extravaganza at Pali Overnight Adventures, CA

Jewish Studies

Camp Tawonga–Teen Service Learning to Alaska, AK
Camp Veritans, NJ
Genesis at Brandeis University, MA
Israel Discovery
Jewish Community Center Day Camp, NJ
92nd Street Y Camps–The TIYUL
Putney Student Travel–Cultural Exploration–Eastern European Heritage
Shwayder Camp, CO
Summer JAM (Judaism, Activism, and Mitzvah Work), DC
Surprise Lake Camp, NY

Journalism

Ball State University Summer Journalism Workshops, IN
Corcoran College of Art and Design–Focus on Photojournalism, DC

Journalism

IEI–Print and Broadcast Journalism, United Kingdom
Junior Statesmen Symposium on Los Angeles Politics and Government, CA
Kansas Journalism Institute, KS
Oxford Media School–Newsroom in Europe, United Kingdom
Oxford Media School–Newsroom in Europe, Master Class, United Kingdom
Sidwell Friends Riverview Programs, VA

Kayaking
Adventure Links–North Carolina Expeditions, NC
Adventure Links–The Costa Rica Experience, Costa Rica
Adventures Cross-Country, Western Adventure
Camp Tawonga–Surf 'n Turf Quest, CA
French Immersion Kayak Expedition, Canada
GLOBAL WORKS–Adventure Travel-Pacific Northwest-3 weeks, WA
Great Escapes (Adventure Trips for Teens)–Canadian Canoe and Kayak Adventure, Canada
Great Escapes (Adventure Trips for Teens)–Colorado River and Canyons Adventure
Great Escapes (Adventure Trips for Teens)–Maine Waterways, ME
Greenbrier River Outdoor Adventures, Rock and River, WV
Kayak Adventures Unlimited
Kroka Expeditions–Introduction to White Water, VT
Kroka Expeditions–Paddlers Journey Up North
Kroka Expeditions–Wild World of White Water, VT
Longacre Expeditions, Laurel Highlands, PA
Longacre Expeditions, Leadership Training, CO
Longacre Expeditions, Western Challenge
Mountain Workshop–Awesome 4: Pennsylvania, PA
Mountain Workshop–Awesome 6: Quebec, Canada
Nantahala Outdoor Center–Kids Adventure Sports Camp, NC
Nantahala Outdoor Center–Kids Kayaking Courses, NC
Overland: Blue Ridge Explorer Hiking, Rafting and Kayaking, NC
Overland: Hawaii Explorer Hiking, Kayaking, Sailing and Snorkeling, HI
Overland: Yellowstone Explorer Backpacking, Rock Climbing, and Rafting
Voyageur Outward Bound–Lake Superior Freshwater Kayaking, Canada
Wediko Summer Program, NH
White Water Learning Center of Georgia Kids Kayaking Summer Day Camp, GA

Korean
Concordia Language Villages–Korean, MN
Youth for Understanding USA–South Korea, Republic of Korea

Lacrosse
Flint Hill School–"Summer on the Hill"–Sports on the Hill for Boys, VA
Flint Hill School–"Summer on the Hill"–Sports on the Hill for Girls, VA
McCallie Lacrosse Camp, TN
Pingry Lacrosse Camp–Martinsville Campus, NJ
Pingry Lacrosse Camp–Short Hills Campus, NJ
Woodberry Forest Lacrosse Camp, VA

Language Study
Camp Ouareau, Canada
Camp Wilvaken, Canada
Choate Rosemary Hall Immersion Program, CT
Collège du Léman Summer School, Switzerland
Concordia Language Villages–English, MN
Explore-A-College, IN
GLOBAL WORKS–Language Exposure-Yucatan Peninsula, Mexico-4 weeks, Mexico
GLOBAL WORKS–Language Immersion-Yucatan Peninsula, Mexico-4 weeks, Mexico
Knowledge Exchange Institute–European Capitals Program
LSA Alicante, Spain, Spain
LSA Ascoli, Italy, Italy
LSA Barcelona, Spain, Spain
LSA Berlin, Germany, Germany
LSA Biarritz, France, France
LSA Bordeaux, France, France
LSA Cuernavaca, Mexico, Mexico
LSA Florence, Italy, Italy
LSA Hamburg, Germany, Germany
LSA Hyères, France, France
LSA Lausanne, Switzerland, Switzerland
LSA Lignano, Italy–Active Junior Italian Summer Program, Italy
LSA Lisbon, Portugal, Portugal
LSA Livorno, Italy, Italy
LSA Madrid, Spain, Spain
LSA Màlaga, Spain, Spain
LSA Marbella, Spain, Spain
LSA Mérida, Mexico, Mexico
LSA Milan, Italy, Italy
LSA Montreal, Canada–English/French, Canada
LSA Moscow, Russia, Russian Federation
LSA Munich, Germany, Germany
LSA Nerja, Spain, Spain
LSA Nice, France, France
LSA Oaxaca, Mexico, Mexico
LSA Paris, France, France
LSA Puerto Vallarta, Mexico, Mexico
LSA Rimini, Italy, Italy
LSA Rome, Italy, Italy
LSA St. Petersburg, Russia, Russian Federation
LSA Salamanca, Spain, Spain
LSA San José, Costa Rica, Costa Rica
LSA Sevilla, Spain, Spain
LSA Siena, Italy, Italy
LSA Stuttgart, Germany, Germany
LSA Treviso, Italy, Italy
LSA Valencia, Spain, Spain
LSA Vienna, Austria, Austria
MIMC–Language Camp, Canada
Village Camps–Austria, Austria
Village Camps–England, United Kingdom
Village Camps–Switzerland, Switzerland
Visions–Dominican Republic, Dominican Republic
Visions–Guadeloupe, Guadeloupe
Visions–Peru, Peru
Washington International School Passport to Summer, DC

Latin Language
EARTHWATCH INSTITUTE–Medicinal Plants of Antiquity, Italy

Latvian Language/Literature
Youth for Understanding USA–Estonia/Latvia-Baltic Summer

Law
American Legal Experience by Education Unlimited–Berkeley, CA, CA
American Legal Experience by Education Unlimited–Stanford, CA, CA

Leadership Training
Abilene Christian University–Learning to Lead, TX
Abilene Christian University–MPulse, TX
Abiliene Christian University–KidQuest Day Camp, TX
Academic Camps at Gettysburg College–Community Service, PA
American Youth Foundation Leadership Conference, MI
Bark Lake Leadership Through Recreation Camp, Canada
Barnard's Summer in New York City: A Pre-College Program, NY
Barnard's Summer in New York City: One-Week Mini-Course, NY
Barnard's Summer in New York City: Young Women's Leadership Institute, NY
Birmingham-Southern College Student Leaders in Service Program, AL
Birmingham-Southern College Summer Scholar Program, AL
BROADREACH Arc of the Caribbean Sailing Adventure
Camp Berachah Ministries–Teen Leadership, WA
Camp Pisgah, NC
Camp Pondicherry, ME
Camp St. John's Northwestern, WI
Canadian Rockies Outdoor Leader Camp, Canada
Career Explorations, NY
Catholic Youth Camp, MN
Colvig Silver Camps, CO
Emerging Leaders 2005, SC
Freed-Hardeman Horizons for Ages 12-18, TN
Future Astronaut Training Program, KS
Future Leader Camp, VT
Hyde School Summer Challenge Program–Bath, ME, ME
Hyde School Summer Challenge Program–Woodstock, CT, CT
ISB Chinese Language Camp, China
JCC Houston: Counselor-In-Training, TX
Julian Krinsky Business School at Haverford College, PA
Julian Krinsky Business School at Wharton (Leadership in the Business World), PA
Junior Statesmen Summer School–Northwestern University, IL
Junior Statesmen Summer School–Princeton University, NJ
Junior Statesmen Symposium on California State Politics and Government, CA

Junior Statesmen Symposium on New Jersey State Politics and Government, NJ
Junior Statesmen Symposium on Ohio State Politics and Government, OH
Junior Statesmen Symposium on Texas Politics and Leadership, TX
Junior Statesmen Symposium on Washington State Politics and Government, WA
Keystone Counselor Assistant Program, CO
Kroka Expeditions–Coming of Age for Young Women, VT
Leadership Adventure in Boston, MA
Leadership Training at Pali Overnight Adventures, CA
Lead 2005, SC
Longacre Leadership Program, PA
Mars Academy, KS
Medeba Leader in Training Program, Canada
Montgomery Bell Academy–LEAD Program, TN
Montgomery College WDCE–Leadership Skills Camp, MD
Mountain Workshop–Graduate Plus Awesome Adventures, NY
Mountain Workshop–Leadership Through Adventure: Adirondacks, NY
National Student Leadership Conference: Business and Commerce, DC
National Student Leadership Conference: International Diplomacy, DC
National Student Leadership Conference: Law and Advocacy–California, CA
National Student Leadership Conference: Law and Advocacy–Washington, DC, DC
National Student Leadership Conference: Mastering Leadership, DC
National Student Leadership Conference: Medicine and Health Care, MD
New England Camping Adventures, ME
New York Military Academy–JROTC Summer Program, NY
North Carolina Outward Bound–Outer Banks, NC
North Carolina Outward Bound–Southern Appalachian Mountains, NC
Oak Ridge Summer Leadership Camp, NC
Outdoor Adventure, WA
Overland: American Challenge Coast-to-Coast Bicycle Touring
Overland: European Challenge Bicycle Touring from Paris to Rome
Overland: The Alpine Challenge Leadership Course Backpacking and Hiking
Poulter Colorado Camps: Adventures Planet Earth–Austria
Poulter Colorado Camps: Adventures Planet Earth–New Zealand, New Zealand
Poulter Colorado Camps: Adventures Planet Earth–Spain, Spain
Public Speaking Institute by Education Unlimited–Boston, MA
Public Speaking Institute by Education Unlimited–Stanford, CA
Public Speaking Institute by Education Unlimited–UC Berkeley, CA
Public Speaking Institute by Education Unlimited–UCLA, CA
Quest Scholars Program at Stanford/ QuestLeadership, CA
Riverside Military Academy Young Cadet Camp, GA
Sail Caribbean–Leeward Islands
The Sarah Porter Leadership Institute, CT
Sidwell Friends Women's Leadership–St. Margaret's School, VA
Sprucelands Camp, NY
Student Conservation Association–Conservation Leadership Corps, Bay Area, CA
Student Conservation Association–Conservation Leadership Corps–Northwest, WA
Summer in Switzerland, Switzerland
Summer Leadership Education and Training, VA
Summer Summit on Leadership, MA
Village Camps–Switzerland, Switzerland
WEI Leadership Training, CO
Wentworth Military Academy Summer School–Camp LEAD, MO
Wilderness Ventures–Washington Alpine, WA
Wilderness Ventures–Washington Mountaineering, WA
Wilderness Ventures–Wyoming Mountaineering, WY
Windsor Mountain: Leaders in Action, NH
YMCA Camp Abnaki–Counselor-in-Training Program, VT
YMCA Camp Oakes Teen Leadership, CA

Lecture Series

High Cascade Snowboard Camp Photography Workshop, OR

Linguistics

MIMC–Language Camp, Canada

Magic

Tannen's Summer Magic Camp, NY

Marine Studies

Acadia Institute of Oceanography, ME
ACTIONQUEST: Advanced PADI Scuba Certification and Specialty Voyages, British Virgin Islands
ACTIONQUEST: Junior Advanced Scuba with Marine Biology, British Virgin Islands
ACTIONQUEST: Tropical Marine Biology Voyages, British Virgin Islands
!ADVENTURES–AFLOAT: Advanced Scuba Adventure Voyages–British Virgin Islands, British Virgin Islands
!ADVENTURES–AFLOAT: Advanced Scuba Adventure Voyages–Caribbean Islands
!ADVENTURES–AFLOAT: Scuba and Sailing Discovery Voyages–British Virgin Islands, British Virgin Islands
BROADREACH Academic Treks–Marine Mammal Studies, Canada
BROADREACH Academic Treks–Marine Park Management
BROADREACH Academic Treks–Sea Turtle Studies, Costa Rica
BROADREACH Adventures in Scuba and Sailing–Underwater Discoveries
BROADREACH Adventures in the Grenadines–Advanced Scuba, Saint Vincent and The Grenadines
BROADREACH Adventures Underwater–Advanced Scuba
BROADREACH Honduras Eco-Adventure, Honduras
BROADREACH Marine Biology Accredited, Bahamas
EARTHWATCH INSTITUTE–Brazil's Marine Wildlife, Brazil
EARTHWATCH INSTITUTE–Coastal Ecology of the Bahamas, Bahamas
EARTHWATCH INSTITUTE–Coral Reefs of the Virgin Islands, U.S. Virgin Islands
EARTHWATCH INSTITUTE–Dolphins of Brazil, Brazil
EARTHWATCH INSTITUTE–Dolphins of Costa Rica, Costa Rica
EARTHWATCH INSTITUTE–Hawksbill Turtles of Barbados, Barbados
EARTHWATCH INSTITUTE–Jamaica's Coral Reefs, Jamaica
EARTHWATCH INSTITUTE–Manatees in Belize, Belize
ExploraMar: Marine Biology Sailing Expeditions–Sea of Cortez, Baja, Mexico
Flint Hill School–"Summer on the Hill"–Trips from the Hill–Ecological Study of Coral Reefs, Bahamas, Bahamas
Geronimo Program
Longacre Expeditions, Whales, ME
Marine and Environmental Science Program, Canada
ODYSSEY EXPEDITIONS: Tropical Marine Biology Voyages–British Virgin Islands, British Virgin Islands
ODYSSEY EXPEDITIONS: Tropical Marine Biology Voyages–Caribbean Islands
Outward Bound–Environmental Expeditions, MA
Pacific Marine Science Camp, OR
Sail Caribbean–All Levels of Scuba Certification with Sailing, British Virgin Islands
Sail Caribbean–Marine Biology, British Virgin Islands
Salmon Camp Research Team for Native Americans–San Juan Island, WA
San Juan Island Camps, WA
Santa Catalina School Summer Camp, CA
Sea Camp, TX
Seacamp, FL
SEACAMP San Diego, CA
SeaWorld Orlando Adventure Camp, FL
SeaWorld San Antonio Adventure Camp, TX
SeaWorld San Diego Adventure Camp, CA
SFS: Marine Parks Management Studies, Turks and Caicos Islands
Shizen Kyampu-Japanese Language Science Camp, OR
Sidwell Friends Riverview Programs, VA
Summer Programs on the River; Marine Science Camp, VA
The Whale Camp–Youth Programs, Canada

Martial Arts

Camp Greenkill–Judo, NY
China Summer Learning Adventures, China
Florida Air Academy Summer Session, FL

Mathematics

Access to Careers in the Sciences (ACES) Camps, TX
Alexander-Smith Academy Summer School, TX
Arrowsmith Academy Arts and Academics, CA
Baylor University High School Summer Science Research Program, TX
Boston University Promys Program, MA
Bridge to the Future, NJ

▶ Mathematics

Choate Rosemary Hall Math/Science Institute for Girls–CONNECT, CT
Elite Educational Institute Elementary Enrichment, CA
Elite Educational Institute Elementary Enrichment–Korea, Republic of Korea
Flint Hill School–"Summer on the Hill"–Academics on the Hill–English and Math Review, VA
Flint Hill School–"Summer on the Hill"–Academics on the Hill–Geometry for Credit, VA
Gems: Girls in Engineering, Math and Science, MA
Georgetown University College Prep Program, DC
IMACS–Full Day Summer Camp–Connecticut, CT
IMACS–Full Day Summer Camp–Florida, FL
IMACS–Full Day Summer Camp–Missouri, MO
IMACS–Full Day Summer Camp–North Carolina, NC
IMACS–Full Day Summer Camp–Pennsylvania, PA
IMACS–Full Day Summer Camp–South Carolina, SC
IMACS–Individual Summer Programs–Connecticut, CT
IMACS–Individual Summer Programs–Florida, FL
IMACS–Individual Summer Programs–Missouri, MO
IMACS–Individual Summer Programs–North Carolina, NC
IMACS–Individual Summer Programs–Pennsylvania, PA
IMACS–Individual Summer Programs–South Carolina, SC
Michigan Technological University American Indian Workshop, MI
Michigan Technological University Explorations in Engineering Workshop, MI
Michigan Technological University Women in Engineering Workshop, MI
Miss Porter's School Summer Challenge, CT
Montgomery College WDCE–Mathematics Enrichment Program, MD
Mount Holyoke College SEARCH (Summer Explorations and Research Collaborations for High School Girls) Program, MA
Mount Holyoke College SummerMath Program, MA
New Mexico Tech Summer Mini-Course, NM
Pine Ridge Summer Program, VT
Project SUCCEED, NC
Rumsey Hall School Summer Session, CT
Sciencescape, MO
Stoneleigh–Burnham School: Science Camp for Middle School Girls, MA
Strive: Exploring Engineering, Math and Science, MA
Summer Programs on the River; Skills Program, VA
The Summer Science Program–California Campus, CA
The Summer Science Program–New Mexico Campus, NM
University of Vermont Summer Institute for High School Students Discovering Engineering, Computers, and Mathematics, VT
Wesleyan Summer Gifted Program, WV
Windsor Mountain: Experiential Summer School
WRC Weather Camp, TX

Medicine

Ladakh Summer Passage, India
Milwaukee School of Engineering (MSOE)–Focus on Nursing, WI

Meteorology

WRC Weather Camp, TX

Microbiology

Stony Brook University–Biotechnology Summer Camp, NY

Military Program

Wentworth Military Academy Pathfinder Adventure Camp, MO

Mixed Media

Flint Hill School–"Summer on the Hill"–Creative Arts on the Hill–Art Camp, VA

Model Rocketry

Montgomery College WDCE–Science Adventures, MD
Stoneleigh–Burnham School: Science Camp for Middle School Girls, MA
University of Wisconsin–Green Bay Space Trek Camp, WI

Motocross

Secret Agent Camp at Pali Overnight Adventures, CA

Mountain Biking

AAVE–Bike France, France
AAVE–Hawaii, HI
AAVE–X–Five
Adventures Cross-Country, Colorado Adventure, CO
Adventure Treks–Montana Adventures, MT
Adventure Treks–Summit Fever
BICYCLE TRAVEL ADVENTURES–Student Hosteling Program–Off-Road Vermont
Camp Tawonga–Teen Quest: High Sierra, CA
Camp Tawonga–Teen Quest: Northwest
Camp Winding Gap, NC
Canadian Rockies Adventurer Camp, Canada
Eagle Lake Bike Camp, CO
Great Escapes (Adventure Trips for Teens)–Colorado River and Canyons Adventure
Horizon Adventures Inc., CO
Mountain Workshop/Dirt Camp: Dirt Camp Junior Killington
Mountain Workshop/Dirt Camp–Mountain Bike Days 1, CT
Mountain Workshop/Dirt Camp–Mountain Bike Days 3, CT
Mountain Workshop/Dirt Camp–Mountain Bike Days 2, CT
Nantahala Outdoor Center–Kids Adventure Sports Camp, NC
Outpost Wilderness Adventure–Adventure Skills, CO
Outpost Wilderness Adventure–Copper Canyon Project, Mexico
Outpost Wilderness Adventure–Mountain Bike/Rock Camp, CO
Overland: Colorado and Utah Mountain Biking and Rafting
Overland: New England Explorer Hiking, Mountain Biking, and Rafting
Overland: Rocky Mountain Explorer Hiking, Mountain Biking, and Rafting
Pleasant Valley Camp for Girls, NH
Shaffer's High Sierra Camp, CA
Wediko Summer Program, NH
Wilderness Ventures–Colorado/Utah Mountain Bike

Mountaineering

Adirondack Alpine Adventures, NY
Adventure Treks–California Challenge Adventures
Adventure Treks–Summit Fever
Adventure Treks–Ultimate Northwest Adventures
Anderson Camps' Wilderness Pioneer Camp, CO
Cheley Colorado Camps, CO
Longacre Expeditions, Leadership Training, CO
LSA Blossin, Germany, Germany
Outpost Wilderness Adventure–Alpine Rock and Ice, CO
Outpost Wilderness Adventure–Wind River Expedition, WY
Outward Bound West–Climbing and Backpacking–High Sierra, CA, CA
Outward Bound West–Colorado Rockies Lightweight Backpacking, CO
Outward Bound West–Mountaineering and Rafting, Oregon, OR
Outward Bound West–Mountaineering–Colorado, CO
Outward Bound West–Mountaineering–North Cascades, WA, WA
Outward Bound West–Mountaineering, Rafting, and Climbing-XT, Oregon, OR
Outward Bound West–Sea Kayaking and Mountaineering–Alaska, AK
Outward Bound West–Sea Kayaking, Backpacking, and Mountaineering–Washington, WA
Outward Bound West–Service Course–North Cascades, WA
Outward Bound West–Sierra Nevada Mountaineering, CA
Outward Bound West–Southwest Mountaineering, Rafting, and Canyoneering, UT
Outward Bound West–Utah Summer Semester, UT
Outward Bound West–Volcanoes Mountaineering–Oregon, OR
Overland: Shasta & the Sierras Backpacking, Climbing and Rafting
Overland: Teton Challenge Hiking, Climbing and Kayaking, WY
Overland: The Alpine Challenge Leadership Course Backpacking and Hiking
Putney Student Travel–Cultural Exploration–France, Holland, and England
Sanborn Western Camps: Big Spring Ranch for Boys, CO
Sanborn Western Camps: High Trails Ranch for Girls, CO
Voyageur Outward Bound–Lewis and Clark Alpine Backpacking, MT
Voyageur Outward Bound–Lewis and Clark Alpine Backpacking-Girls, MT

Voyageur Outward Bound–Montana High Alpine Backpacking, MT
Voyageur Outward Bound–Northern Rockies Backpacking Family Adventure, MT
Wilderness Ventures–Cascade-Olympic, WA
Wilderness Ventures–European Alps
Wilderness Ventures–Northwest
Wilderness Ventures–Washington Mountaineering, WA

Music

Belvoir Terrace, MA
Berklee Business of Music Program, MA
Berklee College of Music Summer Performance Program, MA
Berklee in L.A. Summer Performance Program, CA
Berklee Music Production Workshop, MA
Berklee Summer Basslines Program, MA
Berklee Summer Brass Weekend, MA
Berklee Summer Guitar Sessions, MA
Berklee Summer Saxophone Weekend, MA
Berklee Summer Songwriting Workshop, MA
Berklee Summer String Fling, MA
Berklee World Percussion Festival, MA
Blue Lake Fine Arts Camp, MI
Boston University Tanglewood Institute, MA
Brevard Music Center, NC
Bristol Hills Music Camp, NY
Buck's Rock Performing and Creative Arts Camp, CT
Camp Encore-Coda for a Great Summer of Music, Sports, and Friends, ME
Children's Creative and Performing Arts Academy Summer Elementary Program, CA
Davidson Academy–Academy Arts, TN
Drew Summer Music, NJ
Eastern U.S. Music Camp, Inc., NY
Flint Hill School–"Summer on the Hill"–Creative Arts on the Hill–Let the Drums Roll, VA
French Woods Festival of the Performing Arts, NY
Friends Music Camp, OH
Guitar Workshop Plus–Bass, Drums, Keyboards, Canada
Idyllwild Arts Summer Program–American Experience for International Students, CA
Idyllwild Arts Summer Program–Children's Center, CA
Idyllwild Arts Summer Program–Family Week, CA
Idyllwild Arts Summer Program–Junior Artists' Center, CA
Idyllwild Arts Summer Program–Youth Arts Center, CA
Indiana University School of Music College Audition Preparation Workshop, IN
Indiana University School of Music Piano Academy, IN
Indiana University School of Music Recorder Academy, IN
International Music Camp, ND
Irish Way, Ireland
Lebanon Valley College Summer Music Camp, PA
Longhorn Music Camp: Piano Performance Workshop, TX
Michigan Technological University Honors Orchestra Program, MI
MIMC–Intensive Music Camp, Canada
MIMC–Music and Sports Camp, Canada
Montgomery Bell Academy–Summer Music Camp, TN
Music and Dance Summer Workshops, MO
Oregon Summer Music Camps, OR
Performance PLUS–Positive Learning Using the Stage+Studio+Screen, NH
The Performing Arts Institute of Wyoming Seminary, PA
Point Arts Camp–Music, WI
Power Chord Academy–Chicago, IL
Power Chord Academy–Los Angeles, CA
Power Chord Academy–New York City, NY
Spoleto Study Abroad, Italy
Stony Brook Summer Music Festival, NY
Summer Music at The Hollows, Canada
Summer Music Clinic, WI
Summer Sonatina International Piano Camp, VT
Suzuki Family Camp, MI
University of Connecticut Community School of the Arts–Music Camps, CT
University of Kansas–Midwestern Music Camp–Junior and Senior Divisions, KS
University of Wisconsin–Green Bay Summer Music Camps, WI
Westminster Choir College Composition Week, NJ
Westminster Choir College High School Solo Vocal Artist: A Performance Workshop for Singers, NJ
Westminster Choir College Middle School Vocal Camp, NJ
Westminster Choir College Vocal Institute, NJ
Westminster Conservatory of Music–Musical Jamboree, NJ

Music (Chamber)

Drew Summer Music, NJ
Foster High School Strings Camp, KY
Foster Middle School Strings Camp, KY
Kinhaven Music School, VT
Longhorn Music Camp: Harp Solo and Ensemble Camp, TX
Point CounterPoint Chamber Music Camp, VT
Sequoia Chamber Music Workshop, CA

Music (Ensemble)

Berklee College of Music Summer Performance Program, MA
Berklee in L.A. Summer Performance Program, CA
Berklee Summer Basslines Program, MA
Berklee Summer Brass Weekend, MA
Berklee Summer Guitar Sessions, MA
Berklee Summer Saxophone Weekend, MA
Berklee Summer String Fling, MA
Berklee World Percussion Festival, MA
Kinhaven Music School, VT
Longhorn Music Camp: All-State Choir Camp, TX
Longhorn Music Camp: Harp Solo and Ensemble Camp, TX
Longhorn Music Camp: High School Band Camp, TX
Longhorn Music Camp: Middle School Band Camp, TX
Longhorn Music Camp: Middle School String Orchestra Camp, TX

Music (Folk)

Cordova 4-H Bluegrass and Old Time Music and Dance Camp, AK
EARTHWATCH INSTITUTE–Singing Russia, Russian Federation

Music (Instrumental)

Catholic University Benjamin T. Rome School of Music, DC
Cazadero Music Camp, CA
Foster Middle School Band Camp, KY
Indiana University School of Music String Academy, IN
Longhorn Music Camp: High School Band Camp, TX
Longhorn Music Camp: Middle School Band Camp, TX
Marrowstone-in-the-City, WA
Marrowstone Music Festival, WA
National Guitar Workshop–Austin, TX, TX
National Guitar Workshop–Los Angeles, CA, CA
National Guitar Workshop–Murfreesboro, TN, TN
National Guitar Workshop–New Milford, CT, CT
National Guitar Workshop–New Orleans, LA, LA
National Guitar Workshop–San Francisco, CA, CA
National Guitar Workshop–Seattle, WA, WA
Signature Music Youth Camp, NY
University of Connecticut Community School of the Arts–Music Camps, CT
Valley Forge Military Academy Summer Band Camp, PA
Westminster Conservatory of Music–Flute Camp, NJ
Westminster Conservatory of Music–Summer Ensemble, NJ
Westminster Conservatory of Music–Try It Out, NJ

Music (Jazz)

Atelier des Arts, Switzerland
Crossroads School–Jazz Workshop, CA
KU Jazz Workshop, KS
Litchfield Jazz Festival Summer Music School Program, CT
National Guitar Workshop–Austin, TX, TX
National Guitar Workshop–Los Angeles, CA, CA
National Guitar Workshop–Murfreesboro, TN, TN
National Guitar Workshop–New Milford, CT, CT
National Guitar Workshop–New Orleans, LA, LA
National Guitar Workshop–San Francisco, CA, CA
National Guitar Workshop–Seattle, WA, WA
Signature Music Teen Camp, NY
Signature Music Youth Camp, NY
Stanford Jazz Workshop, CA
Stanford Jazz Workshop: Jazz Camp, CA
Stanford Jazz Workshop: Jazz Residency, CA

Music (Orchestral)

Eastern Music Festival and School, NC
Foster High School Strings Camp, KY
Foster Middle School Band Camp, KY
Foster Middle School Strings Camp, KY
Kinhaven Music School, VT
Longhorn Music Camp: Middle School String Orchestra Camp, TX

▶ Music (Orchestral)

Michigan Technological University Honors Orchestra Program, MI
Young Musicians & Artists, OR

Music (Piano)
Ithaca College Summer Piano Institute, NY

Music (Recorder)
Indiana University School of Music Recorder Academy, IN

Music (Rock)
National Guitar Workshop–Austin, TX, TX
National Guitar Workshop–Los Angeles, CA, CA
National Guitar Workshop–Murfreesboro, TN, TN
National Guitar Workshop–New Milford, CT, CT
National Guitar Workshop–New Orleans, LA, LA
National Guitar Workshop–San Francisco, CA, CA
National Guitar Workshop–Seattle, WA, WA
The National Music Workshop Day Jams–Alexandria, VA, VA
The National Music Workshop Day Jams–Ann Arbor, MI, MI
The National Music Workshop Day Jams–Baltimore, MD, MD
The National Music Workshop Day Jams–Boston, MA, MA
The National Music Workshop Day Jams–Chicago, IL, IL
The National Music Workshop Day Jams–Long Island, NY, NY
The National Music Workshop Day Jams–Los Angeles, CA, CA
The National Music Workshop Day Jams–Manhattan, NY, NY
The National Music Workshop Day Jams–Purchase, NY, NY
The National Music Workshop Day Jams–Rockville, MD, MD
Rock Star Camp at Pali Overnight Adventures, CA

Music (Vocal)
Boston University Summer Theatre Institute, MA
Catholic University Benjamin T. Rome School of Music, DC
Foster Vocal Camp, KY
JCC Houston: Theater Camp, TX
Longhorn Music Camp: All-State Choir Camp, TX
Operafestival di Roma, Italy
Signature Music Youth Camp, NY
Summer Academy for the Visual and Performing Arts, NJ
Westminster Choir College High School Solo Vocal Artist: A Performance Workshop for Singers, NJ
Westminster Choir College Middle School Vocal Camp, NJ
Westminster Choir College Vocal Institute, NJ

Music Theory
Foster Guitar Camp, KY
Foster High School Band Camp, KY

Musical Performance/Recitals
Berklee College of Music Summer Performance Program, MA
Berklee in L.A. Summer Performance Program, CA
Berklee Summer Basslines Program, MA
Berklee Summer Brass Weekend, MA
Berklee Summer Guitar Sessions, MA
Berklee Summer Saxophone Weekend, MA
Berklee Summer String Fling, MA
Berklee World Percussion Festival, MA
Blue Lake International Exchange Program
Foster Guitar Camp, KY
Foster High School Band Camp, KY
Foster High School Strings Camp, KY
Foster Middle School Band Camp, KY
Foster Middle School Strings Camp, KY
Foster Piano Camp I, KY
Foster Piano Camp II, KY
Foster Vocal Camp, KY
Michigan Technological University Honors Orchestra Program, MI
Operafestival di Roma, Italy
Sequoia Chamber Music Workshop, CA
University of Connecticut Community School of the Arts–Music Camps, CT

Musical Theater
Camp Little Palm for the Performing Arts, FL
Montgomery College WDCE–Summer Dinner Theatre, MD
Purchase Youth Theatre, NY
Summer Academy for the Visual and Performing Arts, NJ
Summer Theatre Institute–2005, NY
Westminster Choir College Middle School Music Theater, NJ
Westminster Choir College Music Theater Workshop, NJ

Native American Culture
Alien Adventure Overnight Camp
Center for American Archeology/Past Lifeways Program, IL
Cottonwood Gulch Family Trek, NM
Deer Hill Expeditions, New Mexico, NM
EARTHWATCH INSTITUTE–Hopi Ancestors, AZ
The Experiment in International Living–Navajo Nation, NM
Four Corners School of Outdoor Education: Southwest Ed-Venture
Landmark Volunteers: Arizona, AZ
Roaring Brook Camp for Boys, VT

Natural Resource Management
Groundwater University, NE
Landmark Volunteers: Colorado, CO
Landmark Volunteers: Montana, MT
Salmon Camp for Native Americans, OR

Nature Study
AAVE–Africa
ACTIONQUEST: Galapagos Archipelago Expeditions, Ecuador
Alton Jones Day Camp, RI
Alton Jones Earth Camp, RI
Audubon Vermont Youth Camp, VT
Austin Nature and Science Center, TX
Burgundy Center for Wildlife Studies Summer Camp, WV
Camp Chewonki, ME
Camp Chewonki for Girls, ME
Camp Chewonki Wilderness Expeditions, ME
Camp Niwana, TX
Timber-lee Science Camp, WI
Central Wisconsin Environmental Station–Sunset Lake Adventures, WI
College Settlement of Philadelphia, PA
Colvig Silver Camps, CO
EARTHWATCH INSTITUTE–Bahamian Reef Survey, Bahamas
EARTHWATCH INSTITUTE–Baltic Island Wetlands and Wildlife, Estonia
EARTHWATCH INSTITUTE–Biodiversity of the Grenadines, Grenada
EARTHWATCH INSTITUTE–Bogs of Belarus, Belarus
EARTHWATCH INSTITUTE–Butterflies and Orchids of Spain, Spain
EARTHWATCH INSTITUTE–Butterflies of Vietnam, Vietnam
EARTHWATCH INSTITUTE–Cacti and Orchids of the Yucatan, Mexico
EARTHWATCH INSTITUTE–Canyonland Creek Ecology, UT
EARTHWATCH INSTITUTE–Caring for Chimpanzees, WA
EARTHWATCH INSTITUTE–Carnivores of Madagascar, Madagascar
EARTHWATCH INSTITUTE–Cheetah, Namibia
EARTHWATCH INSTITUTE–Climate Change at Arctic's Edge, Canada
EARTHWATCH INSTITUTE–Conservation Research Initiative–Climate Change in the Rainforest, Australia
EARTHWATCH INSTITUTE–Conservation Research Initiative–Conserving the Pantanal, Brazil
EARTHWATCH INSTITUTE–Conservation Research Initiative–Hawksbill Turtles of the Great Barrier Reef, Australia
EARTHWATCH INSTITUTE–Conservation Research Initiative–Mountain Meadows of the North Cascades, WA
EARTHWATCH INSTITUTE–Conservation Research Initiative–Queensland Tropical Fish Ecology, Australia
EARTHWATCH INSTITUTE–Conservation Research Initiative–Restoring Wild Salmon, WA
EARTHWATCH INSTITUTE–Conservation Research Initiative–Salmon of the Pacific Northwest, WA
EARTHWATCH INSTITUTE–Conservation Research Initiative–Samburu: Communities and Wildlife Habitat, Kenya
EARTHWATCH INSTITUTE–Conservation Research Initiative–Samburu: Zebras, Kenya
EARTHWATCH INSTITUTE–Crocodiles of the Okavango, Botswana
EARTHWATCH INSTITUTE–Desert Elephants of Namibia, Namibia
EARTHWATCH INSTITUTE–Dolphins and Whales of Abaco Island, Bahamas
EARTHWATCH INSTITUTE–Dolphins of Brazil, Brazil
EARTHWATCH INSTITUTE–Echidnas and Goannas of Kangaroo Island, Australia
EARTHWATCH INSTITUTE–Ecuador Forest Birds, Ecuador

EARTHWATCH INSTITUTE–Europe–Africa Songbird Migrations–Hungary, Hungary
EARTHWATCH INSTITUTE–Europe–Africa Songbird Migrations–Italy, Italy
EARTHWATCH INSTITUTE–Hawksbill Turtles of Barbados, Barbados
EARTHWATCH INSTITUTE–Icelandic and Alaskan Glaciers, Iceland
EARTHWATCH INSTITUTE–Inner Mongolia's Lost Water, China
EARTHWATCH INSTITUTE–Itjaritjari: the Outback's Mysterious Marsupial, Australia
EARTHWATCH INSTITUTE–Kenya's Black Rhino, Kenya
EARTHWATCH INSTITUTE–Koala Ecology, Australia
EARTHWATCH INSTITUTE–Lakes of the Rift Valley, Kenya
EARTHWATCH INSTITUTE–Lions of Tsavo, Kenya
EARTHWATCH INSTITUTE–Malaysian Bat Conservation, Malaysia
EARTHWATCH INSTITUTE–Mammoth Cave, KY
EARTHWATCH INSTITUTE–Mammoth Graveyard, SD
EARTHWATCH INSTITUTE–Manatees in Belize, Belize
EARTHWATCH INSTITUTE–Medicinal Plants of Vietnam, Vietnam
EARTHWATCH INSTITUTE–Mexican Mangroves and Wildlife, Mexico
EARTHWATCH INSTITUTE–Mongolian Argali, Mongolia
EARTHWATCH INSTITUTE–Moose and Wolves, MI
EARTHWATCH INSTITUTE–Namibian Black Rhinos, Namibia
EARTHWATCH INSTITUTE–Namibian Wildlife Survey, Namibia
EARTHWATCH INSTITUTE–New Zealand Dolphins, New Zealand
EARTHWATCH INSTITUTE–Orca, WA
EARTHWATCH INSTITUTE–Pine Marten of the Ancient Forest, Canada
EARTHWATCH INSTITUTE–Puerto Rico's Rainforest, Puerto Rico
EARTHWATCH INSTITUTE–Rainforest Caterpillars–Costa Rica, Costa Rica
EARTHWATCH INSTITUTE–Restoring Costa Rica's Rainforest, Costa Rica
EARTHWATCH INSTITUTE–Rivers of the Peruvian Amazon, Peru
EARTHWATCH INSTITUTE–Roman Fort on the Danube, Romania
EARTHWATCH INSTITUTE–Roman Fort on Tyne, United Kingdom
EARTHWATCH INSTITUTE–Saving the Leatherback Turtle, U.S. Virgin Islands
EARTHWATCH INSTITUTE–Sea Otters of Alaska, AK
EARTHWATCH INSTITUTE–Sea Turtles of Baja, Mexico
EARTHWATCH INSTITUTE–South African Penguins, South Africa
EARTHWATCH INSTITUTE–South African Wildlife, South Africa
EARTHWATCH INSTITUTE–Spanish Dolphins, Spain
EARTHWATCH INSTITUTE–Sri Lanka's Temple Monkeys, Sri Lanka
EARTHWATCH INSTITUTE–Trinidad's Leatherback Sea Turtles, Trinidad and Tobago
EARTHWATCH INSTITUTE–Wild Dolphin Societies, FL
EARTHWATCH INSTITUTE–Wildlife Conservation in West Africa, Ghana
The Experiment in International Living–New Zealand Homestay, New Zealand
From the Forest to the Sea, AK
Girl Scouts of Genesee Valley Resident Camp, NY
Great Escapes (Adventure Trips for Teens)–Costa Rica Rainforest Adventure, Costa Rica
Green River Preserve, NC
Hiker's Heaven Overnight Camp
Ibike Cultural Tours–Guyana, Guyana
Keystone Counselor Assistant Program, CO
Keystone Science Adventures, CO
Kroka Expeditions–Adventures for Small People, VT
Kroka Expeditions–Coastal Sea Kayaking, ME
Ladakh Summer Passage, India
Landmark Volunteers: Connecticut, CT
Landmark Volunteers: Virginia, VA
LIFEWORKS with the Galapagos Islands' National Parks, Ecuador
Mad River Glen Naturalist Adventure Camp, VT
Maine Conservation School Summer Camps, ME
The Marsh, MD
Mountain Retreat Overnight Camp, CA
92nd Street Y Camps–Camp Tevah for Science and Nature, NY
St. Louis County 4-H Camp, MN
SeaWorld/Busch Gardens Tampa Bay Adventure Camp, FL
SeaWorld Orlando Adventure Camp, FL
SeaWorld San Diego Adventure Camp, CA
SFS: Community Wildlife Management, Kenya
SFS: Tropical Reforestation Studies, Australia
Swift Nature Camp–Discovery Camp, WI
Swift Nature Camp–Explorer Camp, WI
Teen Expeditions, RI
Timber-lee Creation Camp, WI
Wilderness Adventure, CO
Wildlife Camp, CO
YMCA Camp Shand, PA
Yosemite Backpacking Adventures, CA

Nautical Skills

ACTIONQUEST: British Virgin Islands–Sailing and Scuba Voyages, British Virgin Islands
ACTIONQUEST: British Virgin Islands-Sailing Voyages, British Virgin Islands
ACTIONQUEST: Mediterranean Sailing Voyage
Hurricane Island Outward Bound–Maine Coast Schooner Sailing, ME
Hurricane Island Outward Bound–Ocean Bound: Tall Ship Sailing and Sea Kayaking Semester
Maritime Camp, NJ

Norwegian Language/Literature

Concordia Language Villages–Norwegian, MN

Nutrition

Camp Jordan for Children with Diabetes, VA
Camp La Jolla, CA
EARTHWATCH INSTITUTE–Health and Nutrition in Botswana, Botswana
Science Quest, PA
Shane (Trim-Down) Camp, NY

Oceanography

Science Program for High School Girls, CA
Science Program for Middle School Boys on Catalina, CA
Science Program for Middle School Girls on Catalina, CA

Opera

Operafestival di Roma, Italy
Westminster Conservatory of Music–Youth Opera Workshop, NJ

Organ

Westminster Choir College Organ Week, NJ

Orienteering

Flint Hill School–"Summer on the Hill"–Boys Outdoor Adventures! Day Camp, VA
Flint Hill School–"Summer on the Hill"–Into the Woods Day Camp, VA

Ornithology

Audubon Vermont Youth Camp, VT
EARTHWATCH INSTITUTE–Maine's Island Ecology, ME
On the Wing, CO
Program of Audubon Research for Teens (Take P.A.R.T.), VT

Outdoor Adventure

AAVE–Belize, Belize
AAVE–Bold Europe
AAVE–Wild Isles
Adventure Ireland–Surf Camp/Activity Camp, Ireland
AFS-USA–Homestay Plus–Australia, Australia
AFS-USA–Homestay Plus–Brazil, Brazil
AFS-USA–Homestay Plus–New Zealand, New Zealand
Alien Adventure Overnight Camp
Camp Berachah Ministries–Leadership Expedition Camp, WA
Camp Chi Teenage Adventure Trips
Camp Courageous of Iowa, IA
Camp Echo in Coleman High Country, NY
Camp Friendship Challenge Program
Camp Green Cove, NC
Camp Greenkill–Conservation/Adventure, NY
Camp Horizons Adventure, VA
Camp Horizons Explorer, VA
Camp Horizons Specialty Camp, VA
Camp Mondamin, NC
Camp Niwana, TX
Camp Roger, MI
Camp Tawonga–Call of the Wild, CA
Camp Tawonga–Surf 'n Turf Quest, CA
Camp Tawonga–Teen Quest: Canada, Canada
Camp Tawonga–Teen Quest: High Sierra, CA
Camp Tawonga–Teen Quest: Northwest
Camp Tawonga–Teen Quest: Southwest
Camp Tawonga–Teen Quest: Yosemite, CA
Timber-lee Science Camp, WI

▶ Outdoor Adventure

Center for Cultural Interchange–Spain Sports and Language Camp, Spain
Center for Cultural Interchange–Switzerland Language Camp, Switzerland
Cheerio Adventures–Sampler, VA
Cottonwood Gulch Family Trek, NM
Cottonwood Gulch Mountain Desert Challenge, NM
Cottonwood Gulch Outfit Expedition, NM
Cottonwood Gulch Prairie Trek Expedition, NM
Cottonwood Gulch Turquoise Trail Expedition, NM
Cottonwood Gulch Wild Country Trek, NM
Fenn School Summer Day Camp, MA
Flint Hill School–"Summer on the Hill"–Boys Outdoor Adventures! Day Camp, VA
Flint Hill School–"Summer on the Hill"–Trips and Travel Day Camp, VA
Forrestel Farm Riding and Sports Camp, NY
Four Corners School of Outdoor Education: Southwest Ed-Venture
Future Leader Camp, VT
GLOBAL WORKS–Adventure Travel-Pacific Northwest-3 weeks, WA
GLOBAL WORKS–Cultural Exchange-Ireland-4 weeks, Ireland
GLOBAL WORKS–Language Exposure-Costa Rica-4 weeks, Costa Rica
GLOBAL WORKS–Language Exposure-Ecuador and the Galapagos-4 weeks, Ecuador
GLOBAL WORKS–Language Exposure-Puerto Rico-3 weeks, Puerto Rico
GLOBAL WORKS–Language Immersion-Costa Rica-4 weeks, Costa Rica
GLOBAL WORKS–Language Immersion-Yucatan Peninsula, Mexico-4 weeks, Mexico
GLS Bavarian Summer School, Germany
GLS Potsdam Summer School, Germany
GLS Sports and Language Camp Inzell, Germany
GLS Summer Camp Blossin, Germany
Great Escapes (Adventure Trips for Teens)–Canadian Adventure
Hante School, NC
Haycock Camping Ministries–Adventure Trails, PA
Hurricane Island Outward Bound–Maine Coast Schooner Sailing, ME
Hurricane Island Outward Bound–Maine Woods High School Summer Semester, ME
Hurricane Island Outward Bound–Mid-Atlantic Canoeing, Backpacking, and Rock Climbing
Hurricane Island Outward Bound–Ocean Bound: Tall Ship Sailing and Sea Kayaking Semester
Hurricane Island Outward Bound–Western Maine and New Hampshire Canoeing and Backpacking
Hurricane Island Outward Bound–Western Maine Backpacking and Rock Climbing, ME
Hurricane Island Outward Bound–Western Maine Woods Expedition Canoeing, ME
Jumonville Adventure Camps, PA
Kroka Expeditions–Adventures for Small People, VT
Kroka Expeditions–Introduction to Adventure Day Camp, VT
Kroka Expeditions–Introduction to Adventure Residential Camp, VT
Longacre Expeditions, Wind and Waves, OR
Michigan Technological University Summer Youth Program, MI
Mountain Workshop–Awesome 4: Pennsylvania, PA
Mountain Workshop–Awesome 1: Adirondacks, NY
Mountain Workshop–Awesome 6: Quebec, Canada
Mountain Workshop–Awesome 3: Maine Coast, ME
Mountain Workshop–Awesome 2: Vermont, VT
Mountain Workshop–Graduate Awesome Adventures, CT
Mountain Workshop–Junior Awesome Adventures, CT
Mountain Workshop–Original Awesome Adventures, CT
Mountain Workshop–Trailblazer Awesome Adventures, CT
Musiker Tours: Action USA
Musiker Tours: America Coast to Coast
Musiker Tours: Cali-Pacific Passport
Musiker Tours: ComboCamp America
Musiker Tours: Discover America
Musiker Tours: Eastcoaster
Musiker Tours: Westcoaster
New England Camping Adventures, ME
Oak Creek Ranch Summer School, AZ
OES–Summer Adventure Camp, OR
Outpost Wilderness Adventure–Adventure Skills, CO
Outpost Wilderness Adventure–Alpine Rock and Ice, CO
Outpost Wilderness Adventure–Mountain Bike/Rock Camp, CO
Outpost Wilderness Adventure–Wind River Expedition, WY
Outward Bound–Connecting with Courage, MA
Outward Bound–Environmental Expeditions, MA
Outward Bound–Passages, MA
Outward Bound West–Backpacking and Whitewater Rafting, Oregon, OR
Outward Bound West–Cataract Canyon Rafting
Outward Bound West–Climbing and Backpacking–High Sierra, CA, CA
Outward Bound West–Climbing, Backpacking, and Canoeing–North Cascades, WA, WA
Outward Bound West–Mountaineering and Rafting, Oregon, OR
Outward Bound West–Mountaineering–Colorado, CO
Outward Bound West–Mountaineering–North Cascades, WA, WA
Outward Bound West–Mountaineering, Rafting, and Climbing-XT, Oregon, OR
Outward Bound West–Sea Kayaking and Mountaineering–Alaska, AK
Outward Bound West–Sea Kayaking, Backpacking, and Mountaineering–Washington, WA
Outward Bound West–Service Course–North Cascades, WA
Outward Bound West–Sierra Nevada Mountaineering, CA
Outward Bound West–Southwest Mystery Expedition, UT
Outward Bound West–Utah Summer Semester, UT
Outward Bound West–Volcanoes Mountaineering–Oregon, OR
Outward Bound West–Wyoming Rock Climbing, WY
Overland: Language Study Abroad in Costa Rica, Costa Rica
Putney Student Travel–Community Service–Alaska, AK
Putney Student Travel–Cultural Exploration–Australia, New Zealand, and Fiji
Putney Student Travel–Cultural Exploration–Switzerland, Italy, France, and Holland
Rein Teen Tours–American Adventure
Rein Teen Tours–California Caper
Rein Teen Tours–Crossroads
Rein Teen Tours–Eastern Adventure
Rein Teen Tours–Grand Adventure
Rein Teen Tours–Hawaiian/Alaskan Adventure
Rein Teen Tours–Western Adventure
Riverside Military Academy High Adventure Camp, GA
Riverside Military Academy Young Cadet Camp, GA
RUSTIC PATHWAYS–ADVENTURE IN AMERICA'S SOUTHWEST
RUSTIC PATHWAYS–AWESOME AUSSIE EXPLORER, Australia
RUSTIC PATHWAYS–BIG FIJI EXPLORER, Fiji
RUSTIC PATHWAYS–COSTA RICA ADVENTURER, Costa Rica
RUSTIC PATHWAYS–COSTA RICA EXTREME, Costa Rica
RUSTIC PATHWAYS–ELEPHANTS & AMAZING THAILAND, Thailand
RUSTIC PATHWAYS–EXTREME PLANET
RUSTIC PATHWAYS–HAWAIIAN ISLANDS ADVENTURE, HI
RUSTIC PATHWAYS–HIGH ADRENALINE AUSSIE, Australia
RUSTIC PATHWAYS–OUTBACK 4-WHEEL DRIVE SAFARI, Australia
RUSTIC PATHWAYS–SNAPSHOT OF FIJI, Fiji
RUSTIC PATHWAYS–THE AMAZING THAILAND ADVENTURE, Thailand
RUSTIC PATHWAYS–THE SUNSHINE COAST & SYDNEY, Australia
RUSTIC PATHWAYS–THE WONDERS & RICHES OF THAILAND, Thailand
RUSTIC PATHWAYS–TOTALLY DOWNUNDER ADVENTURE, Australia
RUSTIC PATHWAYS–TROPICAL AUSSIE ADVENTURE, Australia
RUSTIC PATHWAYS–ULTIMATE AUSTRALIAN ADVENTURE, Australia
Sargent Center Adventure Camp, NH
Teen Tours of America–Aloha Hawaii
Timber-lee Creation Camp, WI
Trailmark Outdoor Adventures–New England–Moose River
Trailmark Outdoor Adventures–Northern Rockies–Tetons with Backpack
Village Camps–France, France
Visions–Alaska, AK
Visions–Australia, Australia
Visions–British Virgin Islands, British Virgin Islands
Visions–Dominica, Dominica
Visions–Montana, MT

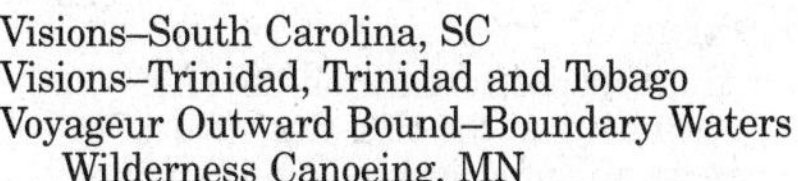

Visions–South Carolina, SC
Visions–Trinidad, Trinidad and Tobago
Voyageur Outward Bound–Boundary Waters Wilderness Canoeing, MN
Voyageur Outward Bound–Boundary Waters Wilderness Canoeing and Climbing XT, MN
Voyageur Outward Bound–Greater Yellowstone Whitewater and Backpacking, MT
Voyageur Outward Bound–Lake Superior Freshwater Kayaking, Canada
Voyageur Outward Bound–Lake Superior Freshwater Kayaking and Backpacking
Voyageur Outward Bound–Lewis and Clark Alpine Backpacking, MT
Voyageur Outward Bound–Lewis and Clark Alpine Backpacking-Girls, MT
Voyageur Outward Bound–Manitoba to Montana Summer Semester
Voyageur Outward Bound–Montana High Alpine Backpacking, MT
Voyageur Outward Bound–Montana Rock Climbing XT, MT
Voyageur Outward Bound–Northern Rockies Backpacking Family Adventure, MT
Voyageur Outward Bound–Northwoods Wilderness Canoeing and Backpacking, MN
Weissman Teen Tours–U.S. and Western Canada, 4 Weeks
Weissman Teen Tours–U.S. and Western Canada, 6 Weeks
Westcoast Connection–American Voyageur
Westcoast Connection–Californian Extravaganza
Westcoast Connection–Hawaiian Spirit
Westcoast Connection/On Tour– Australian Outback, Australia
Westcoast Connection Travel/On Tour–Northwestern Odyssey
Westcoast Connection Travel–Adventure California, CA
Westcoast Connection Travel–California and the Canyons
Westcoast Connection Travel–Canadian Mountain Magic
Westcoast Connection Travel–Eastcoast Encounter
Westcoast Connection Travel–Great West Challenge
Westcoast Connection Travel–Northwestern Odyssey
Westcoast Connection Travel/On Tour–Canadian Adventure
Westcoast Connection Travel–Quebec Adventure, Canada
Westcoast Connection Travel–Southwesterner
Westcoast Connection Travel–Western Canadian Adventure, Canada
Westcoast Connection–U.S. Explorer
Where There Be Dragons: Mongolia, Mongolia
Where There Be Dragons: Thailand, Thailand
Wilderness Experiences Unlimited–Explorers Camp, MA
Wilderness Experiences Unlimited–Leaders In Training Camp, MA
Wilderness Experiences Unlimited–Pathfinders Day Camp, MA
Wilderness Experiences Unlimited–Trailblazers Camp, MA
Windsor Mountain: Crossroads France, France
Windsor Mountain: Hawaii, HI
Windsor Mountain: Voices of the Wind River, Wyoming, WY
YMCA Camp Abnaki–Teen Adventure Trips, VT
YMCA Camp Lincoln–Outdoor Adventure Camp: Backpacking, NH
YMCA Camp Lincoln–Outdoor Adventure Camp: Canadian Adventure, Canada
YMCA Camp Lincoln–Outdoor Adventure Camp: Everything Outdoors, NH
YMCA Camp Lincoln–Outdoor Adventure Camp: River Runners, NH
YMCA Camp Minikani, WI

Outdoor Camping

Costa Rica Rainforest Outward Bound School–Surf Adventure, Costa Rica
Shwayder Camp, CO
Tanager Lodge, NY

Outdoor Living Skills

Austin Nature and Science Center, TX
Central Wisconsin Environmental Station–Sunset Lake Adventures, WI
Farm and Wilderness Camps–Flying Cloud, VT
From the Forest to the Sea, AK
Kroka Expeditions–Coming of Age for Young Women, VT
Student Conservation Association–Conservation Crew Program (Alabama), AL
Student Conservation Association–Conservation Crew Program (Alaska), AK
Student Conservation Association–Conservation Crew Program (Arizona), AZ
Student Conservation Association–Conservation Crew Program (Arkansas), AR
Student Conservation Association–Conservation Crew Program (California), CA
Student Conservation Association–Conservation Crew Program (Colorado), CO
Student Conservation Association–Conservation Crew Program (Connecticut), CT
Student Conservation Association–Conservation Crew Program (Delaware), DE
Student Conservation Association–Conservation Crew Program (Florida), FL
Student Conservation Association–Conservation Crew Program (Georgia), GA
Student Conservation Association–Conservation Crew Program (Hawaii), HI
Student Conservation Association–Conservation Crew Program (Idaho), ID
Student Conservation Association–Conservation Crew Program (Illinois), IL
Student Conservation Association–Conservation Crew Program (Indiana), IN
Student Conservation Association–Conservation Crew Program (Iowa), IA
Student Conservation Association–Conservation Crew Program (Kansas), KS
Student Conservation Association–Conservation Crew Program (Kentucky), KY
Student Conservation Association–Conservation Crew Program (Louisiana), LA
Student Conservation Association–Conservation Crew Program (Maine), ME
Student Conservation Association–Conservation Crew Program (Maryland), MD
Student Conservation Association–Conservation Crew Program (Massachusetts), MA
Student Conservation Association–Conservation Crew Program (Michigan), MI
Student Conservation Association–Conservation Crew Program (Minnesota), MN
Student Conservation Association–Conservation Crew Program (Mississippi), MS
Student Conservation Association–Conservation Crew Program (Missouri), MO
Student Conservation Association–Conservation Crew Program (Montana), MT
Student Conservation Association–Conservation Crew Program (Nebraska), NE
Student Conservation Association–Conservation Crew Program (Nevada), NV
Student Conservation Association–Conservation Crew Program (New Hampshire), NH
Student Conservation Association–Conservation Crew Program (New Jersey), NJ
Student Conservation Association–Conservation Crew Program (New Mexico), NM
Student Conservation Association–Conservation Crew Program (New York), NY
Student Conservation Association–Conservation Crew Program (North Carolina), NC
Student Conservation Association–Conservation Crew Program (North Dakota), ND
Student Conservation Association–Conservation Crew Program (Ohio), OH
Student Conservation Association–Conservation Crew Program (Oklahoma), OK
Student Conservation Association–Conservation Crew Program (Oregon), OR
Student Conservation Association–Conservation Crew Program (Pennsylvania), PA
Student Conservation Association–Conservation Crew Program (Rhode Island), RI
Student Conservation Association–Conservation Crew Program (South Carolina), SC
Student Conservation Association–Conservation Crew Program (South Dakota), SD
Student Conservation Association–Conservation Crew Program (Tennessee), TN
Student Conservation Association–Conservation Crew Program (Texas), TX
Student Conservation Association–Conservation Crew Program (Utah), UT

▶ Outdoor Living Skills

Student Conservation Association–Conservation Crew Program (Vermont), VT
Student Conservation Association–Conservation Crew Program (Virginia), VA
Student Conservation Association–Conservation Crew Program (Washington), WA
Student Conservation Association–Conservation Crew Program (West Virginia), WV
Student Conservation Association–Conservation Crew Program (Wisconsin), WI
Student Conservation Association–Conservation Crew Program (Wyoming), WY
Trail Blazers, NJ
YMCA Camp Lincoln–Outdoor Adventure Camp: Backpacking, NH
YMCA Camp Lincoln–Outdoor Adventure Camp: Everything Outdoors, NH
YMCA Camp Lincoln–Outdoor Adventure Camp: River Runners, NH

Pack Animal Trips

Great Escapes (Adventure Trips for Teens)–Rocky Mountain Horsepacking Adventure, CO
The Ranch–Lake Placid Teen Travel Camp
Success Oriented Achievement Realized (SOAR)–North Carolina, NC
Success Oriented Achievement Realized (SOAR)–Wyoming, WY
Teton Valley Ranch Camp–Boys Camp, WY
Teton Valley Ranch Camp–Girls Camp, WY

Paintball

Secret Agent Camp at Pali Overnight Adventures, CA

Painting

IEI–Fine Arts Plus Programme, United Kingdom
JCC Houston: Art Camp, TX
Montgomery College WDCE–Hands on Art, MD
Skidmore College–Acceleration Program in Art for High School Students, NY
University of Connecticut Community School of the Arts–World Arts Camps, CT
University of Pennsylvania–Penn Summer Art Studio, PA
Vermont Arts Visual Arts Institute, VT
Young Artists at Purchase, NY

Paleontology

Alabama Museum of Natural History Summer Expedition, AL
EARTHWATCH INSTITUTE–Early Man at Olduvai Gorge, United Republic of Tanzania
EARTHWATCH INSTITUTE–Mexican Megafauna, Mexico
EARTHWATCH INSTITUTE–Triassic Park, Argentina

Peace Education

Circle Pines Center Summer Camp, MI
The Experiment in International Living–Ireland/Northern Ireland Homestay and Peace Studies, Ireland
Peace in the Modern World, Denmark
World Affairs Seminar, WI

Performance Art

The Arts! at Maryland, MD
Camp Ballibay for the Fine and Performing Arts, PA
Eastern U.S. Music Camp, Inc., NY
The Putney School Summer Arts Program, VT

Personal Development

Hurricane Island Outward Bound–Maine Woods High School Summer Semester, ME
Hurricane Island Outward Bound–Western Maine Backpacking and Rock Climbing, ME
Outward Bound West–Mountaineering–North Cascades, WA, WA
Outward Bound West–Southwest Mystery Expedition, UT

Pharmacology

University of Kansas–School of Pharmacy Summer Camp, KS

Philosophy

National Debate Institute–DC, MD
Stanford Discovery Institutes, CA
Stanford National Forensic Institute, CA
Where There Be Dragons: India Zanskar Trek, India

Photography

AAC–Aloha Adventure Photo Camp, HI
Alpengirl–Montana Art
Ball State University Summer Journalism Workshops, IN
Cleveland Institute of Art Portfolio Preparation/Young Artist Programs, OH
Corcoran College of Art and Design–Focus on Photojournalism, DC
The Experiment in International Living–France, Four-Week Homestay and Photography, France
Flint Hill School–"Summer on the Hill"–Enrichment on the Hill–Investigating Where We Live, VA
Fotocamp, FL
High Cascade Snowboard Camp Photography Workshop, OR
IEI–Photography Plus Programme, United Kingdom
Longacre Expeditions, Photography, ME
Ringling School of Art and Design's Teen Studio, FL
RUSTIC PATHWAYS–PHOTOGRAPHY & ADVENTURE IN THAILAND, Thailand
University of Pennsylvania–Penn Summer Art Studio, PA
Young Photographers, NY

Physical Fitness

Alpengirl–Alaska, AK
Alpengirl–Montana, MT
Alpengirl–Montana Fitness, MT
Alpengirl–Montana Horse, MT
Alpengirl–Washington, WA
Camp Kingsmont, MA
Camp La Jolla, CA
Shane (Trim-Down) Camp, NY
University of Kansas–Sports Skills and Fitness Camp, KS

Physics

Flint Hill School–"Summer on the Hill"–Enrichment on the Hill–Gee, Whiz!, VA
University of Pennsylvania–Penn Summer Science Academy, PA
Wesleyan Summer Gifted Program, WV

Piano

Eastern Music Festival and School, NC
Foster Piano Camp I, KY
Foster Piano Camp II, KY
Indiana University School of Music Piano Academy, IN
Ithaca College Summer Piano Institute, NY
Longhorn Music Camp: Piano Performance Workshop, TX
Summer Sonatina International Piano Camp, VT
Westminster Choir College High School Solo Pianist, NJ
Westminster Choir College Middle School Piano Camp, NJ
Westminster Choir College Piano Camp, NJ

Planning Skills

Montgomery College WDCE–Entrepreneurship Camp 2005, MD

Playwriting

Choate Rosemary Hall Summer Arts Conservatory–Playwriting, CT
The Putney School Summer Writing Program, VT
Summer Theatre Institute–2005, NY
Young Actors and Playwrights Workshop, NY

Polish Language/Literature

Youth for Understanding USA–Poland, Poland

Portuguese Language/Literature

The Experiment in International Living–Brazil Homestay and Community Service, Brazil
LSA Lisbon, Portugal, Portugal

Precollege Program

Abbey Road Overseas Programs–French Immersion and Homestay, France
Abbey Road Overseas Programs–Spanish Immersion and Homestay, Spain
Academic Camps at Gettysburg College–College Prep & Preview, PA
American Collegiate Adventures–Wisconsin, WI
The Art Institute of Boston Pre-College Program, MA
Barnard's Summer in New York City: A Pre-College Program, NY
Barnard's Summer in New York City: One-Week Mini-Course, NY
Boston University Summer Challenge Program, MA
Brown University Summer Programs–Pre-College Program, RI
Bryn Mawr College–Writing for College, PA
Cambridge College Programme, United Kingdom
Carnegie Mellon University Advanced Placement Early Admission, PA

Carnegie Mellon University Pre-College Program in the Fine Arts, PA
College Quest, WA
Cornell University Summer College Programs for High School Students, NY
Embry-Riddle Aeronautical University–Aerospace Summer Camp, FL
Emerging Leaders 2005, SC
Ithaca College Summer College for High School Students: Session II, NY
Ithaca College Summer College for High School Students: Minicourses, NY
Maine College of Art Early College Program, ME
MIT MITE^{2}S (Minority Introduction to Engineering, Entrepreneurship and Science), MA
Northwestern University's College Preparation Program, IL
Pre-College Summer Institute, The University of the Arts, PA
Quest Scholars Program at Stanford/QuestLeadership, CA
Skidmore College–Pre-College Program in the Liberal Arts for High School Students, NY
Southwestern Academy International Summer Semester, CA
Springfield College Sports Management Career Exploration Program, MA
Stanford Discovery Institutes, CA
Stanford University Summer College for High School Students, CA
Summer Discovery at Australia, Australia
Summer Discovery at Cambridge, United Kingdom
Summer Discovery at Georgetown, DC
Summer Discovery at Michigan, MI
Summer Discovery at UCLA, CA
Summer Discovery at UC San Diego, CA
Summer Discovery at UC Santa Barbara, CA
Summer Discovery at Vermont, VT
The Summer Institute for the Gifted at Amherst College, MA
The Summer Institute for the Gifted at Bryn Mawr College, PA
The Summer Institute for the Gifted at Drew University, NJ
The Summer Institute for the Gifted at Fairfield University, CT
The Summer Institute for the Gifted at Hofstra University, NY
The Summer Institute for the Gifted at Moorestown Friends School, NJ
The Summer Institute for the Gifted at Oberlin College, OH
The Summer Institute for the Gifted at Princeton University, NJ
The Summer Institute for the Gifted at Purchase College, NY
The Summer Institute for the Gifted at UCLA, CA
The Summer Institute for the Gifted at University of California, Berkeley, CA
The Summer Institute for the Gifted at Vassar College, NY
Summer Study at Penn State, PA
Summer Study at The University of Colorado at Boulder, CO
Summer Study in Paris at The American University of Paris, France
Syracuse University Summer College, NY
University of Chicago–Research in the Biological Sciences, IL
University of Chicago–Summer Quarter for High School Students, IL
University of Delaware Summer College, DE
University of Maryland Young Scholars Program, MD
University of Miami Summer Scholar Programs, FL
University of Pennsylvania–Precollege Program, PA
Washington University High School Summer Scholars Program, MO
Wright State University Residential Camps and Institutes, OH

Prelaw

Junior Statesmen Summer School–Georgetown University, DC
Junior Statesmen Summer School–Yale University, CT
National Student Leadership Conference: Law and Advocacy–California, CA
National Student Leadership Conference: Law and Advocacy–Washington, DC, DC
Saint Vincent College Challenge Program, PA

Premed

Hollinsummer, VA
National Student Leadership Conference: Medicine and Health Care, MD

Preveterinary

Adventures in Veterinary Medicine, MA
Summer Vet, CO

Problem Solving

Montgomery College WDCE–Biotechnology and Diversity Camp, MD
Montgomery College WDCE–Inventor's Workshop, MD
Montgomery College WDCE–Super Sleuths–Meet the Challenge, MD
Stony Brook University–Science Exploration Camp, NY

Psychology

Explore-A-College, IN

Radio Broadcasting

Boston University Institute for Television, Film, and Radio Production, MA

Rafting

AAVE–Africa
AAVE–Bike France, France
AAVE–Bold West
AAVE–Boot/Saddle/Paddle
AAVE–Peru and Machu Picchu, Peru
AAVE–Rock & River
AAVE–Rocky Mountain Adventure, CO
AAVE–X–Five
Adventures Cross-Country, Alaska Adventure, AK
Adventures Cross-Country, Australia/Fiji Adventure
Adventures Cross-Country, Colorado Adventure, CO
Adventures Cross-Country, Costa Rica Adventure, Costa Rica
Adventures Cross-Country, Extreme British Columbia Adventure, Canada
Adventures Cross-Country,Southern Europe Adventure
Adventures Cross-Country, Western Adventure
Adventure Treks–PAC 16, OR
Apogee Outdoor Adventures–Coast to Quebec
Apogee Outdoor Adventures–Montana Service Adventure, MT
Camp Tawonga–Call of the Wild, CA
Camp Tawonga–Teen Quest: High Sierra, CA
Camp Tawonga–Teen Quest: Southwest
Cheerio Adventures–Cave/Raft, VA
Cheerio Adventures–5 Rivers in 5 Days
Cheerio Adventures–Rock Climb/Raft, VA
Discovery Camp, CO
Flint Hill School–"Summer on the Hill"–Enrichment on the Hill–Women Writers' Adventure
Kroka Expeditions–Introduction to Adventure Day Camp, VT
Longacre Expeditions, Downeast, ME
Longacre Expeditions, Peak to Peak, OR
Longacre Expeditions, Western Challenge
Outward Bound West–Backpacking, Climbing, and Rafting–Boys, CO
Outward Bound West–Backpacking, Climbing, and Rafting–Colorado, CO
Outward Bound West–Cataract Canyon Rafting
Outward Bound West–Southwest Mountaineering, Rafting, and Canyoneering, UT
Overland: Blue Ridge Explorer Hiking, Rafting and Kayaking, NC
Overland: Colorado and Utah Mountain Biking and Rafting
Overland: Costa Rica Explorer Hiking, Rafting, and Sea-Kayaking, Costa Rica
Overland: Pacific Coast Bicycle Touring and Rafting
Overland: Paris to the Sea Bicycle Touring, France
Overland: Rocky Mountain Explorer Hiking, Mountain Biking, and Rafting
Overland: Shasta & the Sierras Backpacking, Climbing and Rafting
Overland: Teton Challenge Hiking, Climbing and Kayaking, WY
Poulter Colorado Camps: Adventures Planet Earth–Costa Rica, Costa Rica
Wilderness Ventures–Alaska Southcentral, AK
Wilderness Ventures–Alaska Southeast, AK
Wilderness Ventures–Pacific Northwest
Williwaw Adventures–Pacific Northwest Expedition
YMCA Camp Lincoln–Outdoor Adventure Camp: Canadian Adventure, Canada

Rappelling

Voyageur Outward Bound–Montana Rock Climbing XT, MT
Wentworth Military Academy Pathfinder Adventure Camp, MO

Reading

Camp Buckskin, MN
Choate Rosemary Hall Beginning Writers Workshop, CT
Choate Rosemary Hall English Language Institute, CT
Choate Rosemary Hall English Language Institute/Focus Program, CT
Choate Rosemary Hall Writing Project, CT
Dunnabeck at Kildonan, NY

▶ Reading

Elite Educational Institute Elementary Enrichment, CA
Elite Educational Institute Elementary Enrichment–Korea, Republic of Korea
Elite Educational Institute Junior High/PSAT Program–Korea, Republic of Korea
Flint Hill School–"Summer on the Hill"–Academics on the Hill–English and Math Review, VA
Flint Hill School–"Summer on the Hill"–Academics on the Hill–The Reading Clinic, VA
Flint Hill School–"Summer on the Hill"–Enrichment on the Hill–Junior Great Books, VA
Flint Hill School–"Summer on the Hill"–Enrichment on the Hill–Study Skills for 9th Graders, VA
Landmark School Summer Academic Program, MA
Salisbury Summer School of Reading and English, CT

Religion
Catholic Youth Camp, MN
Where There Be Dragons: India Culture and Philosophy, India

Remedial Academics
Camp Buckskin, MN
Flint Hill School–"Summer on the Hill"–Academics on the Hill–English and Math Review, VA
Flint Hill School–"Summer on the Hill"–Academics on the Hill–The Reading Clinic, VA
Hamilton Learning Centre Summer Fun in the Sun Camp, Canada
Hill Top Summer Programs, PA
The Oxford Academy Summer Program, CT
The Phelps School Summer Program, PA

Research Skills
Deep River Science Academy–Deep River Campus, Canada
Deep River Science Academy–Whiteshell Campus, Canada
Dickinson College Research and Writing Workshop, PA
EARTHWATCH INSTITUTE–Medicinal Plants of Antiquity, Italy
Knowledge Exchange Institute–Research Abroad in Russia, Russian Federation
Montgomery College WDCE–Entrepreneurship Camp 2005, MD
Montgomery College WDCE–Young Scientist Academy, MD
Stony Brook University–Biotechnology Summer Camp, NY

Riflery
Haycock Camping Ministries–Adventure Trails, PA
Haycock Camping Ministries–Battalion Program, PA
Haycock Camping Ministries–Stockade Program, PA
Haycock Camping Ministries–Trailbuilders Program, PA

Robotics
Battlebot Mania at Pali Overnight Adventures, CA
DigiPen Institute of Technology Robotics Workshop, WA
Mars Academy, KS
Montgomery College WDCE–Science Adventures, MD
Robotics Camp, MI
SummerSkills at Albany Academy for Girls, NY
University of Wisconsin–Green Bay Space Trek Camp, WI
Women in Technology, MI

Rock Climbing
AAVE–Bold West
AAVE–Border Cross
AAVE–Rock & River
AAVE–Rocky Mountain Adventure, CO
AAVE–X–Five
Adirondack Alpine Adventures, NY
Adventure Camps, PA
Adventure Links
Adventure Links–Appalachian Odyssey
Adventure Links–North Carolina Expeditions, NC
Adventure Links–Ultimate Adventure Camps, VA
Adventure Treks–PAC 16, OR
Anderson Camps' Wilderness Pioneer Camp, CO
Blue Ridge School–Rock Climbing Camp, VA
Camp Henry Offsite: Teen Challenge, MI
Camp Tawonga–Call of the Wild, CA
Camp Tawonga–Teen Quest: Canada, Canada
Cheerio Adventures–Rock Climb/Raft, VA
Cheerio Adventures–Sampler, VA
Great Escapes (Adventure Trips for Teens)–Rock and Rapids
Great Escapes (Adventure Trips for Teens)–White Mountain Adventure, NH
Greenbrier River Outdoor Adventures, Adventure Camp, WV
Greenbrier River Outdoor Adventures, Rock and River, WV
Greenbrier River Outdoor Adventures, Wilderness Explorer, WV
Horizon Adventures Inc., CO
Hurricane Island Outward Bound–Maine Coast Sailing/Sailing and Rock Climbing, ME
Hurricane Island Outward Bound–Mid-Atlantic Canoeing, Backpacking, and Rock Climbing
Kooch-I-Ching, MN
Kroka Expeditions–Advanced Rock Climbing
Kroka Expeditions–Introduction to Adventure Day Camp, VT
Kroka Expeditions–Introduction to Rock Climbing, VT
Kroka Expeditions–Rock 'n Road, VT
Kroka Expeditions–Vermont Underground Trail, VT
Longacre Expeditions, Blue Ridge, PA
Longacre Expeditions, British Columbia
Longacre Expeditions, Laurel Highlands, PA
Longacre Expeditions, Leadership Training, CO
Longacre Expeditions, New England/Canada
Longacre Expeditions, Peak to Peak, OR
Longacre Expeditions, Volcanoes
Mad River Glen Naturalist Adventure Camp, VT
Mountain Adventure Guides: Summer Adventure Camp–Blue Ridge Expedition I, NC
Mountain Adventure Guides: Summer Adventure Camp–Blue Ridge Expedition II, NC
Mountain Adventure Guides: Summer Adventure Camp–Jr. Adventure Camp, NC
NAWA Academy–Girls on the Go, CA
NAWA Academy–Great Challenge, CA
NAWA Academy–Lassen Expedition, CA
NAWA Academy–Trinity Challenge, CA
New England Camping Adventures, ME
Outpost Wilderness Adventure–Copper Canyon Project, Mexico
Outpost Wilderness Adventure–Mountain Bike/Rock Camp, CO
Outward Bound West–Backpacking, Climbing, and Rafting–Boys, CO
Outward Bound West–Backpacking, Climbing, and Rafting–Colorado, CO
Outward Bound West–Climbing and Backpacking–High Sierra, CA, CA
Outward Bound West–Climbing, Backpacking, and Canoeing–North Cascades, WA, WA
Outward Bound West–Wyoming Rock Climbing, WY
Overland: Yellowstone Explorer Backpacking, Rock Climbing, and Rafting
Secret Agent Camp at Pali Overnight Adventures, CA
Success Oriented Achievement Realized (SOAR)–North Carolina, NC
Success Oriented Achievement Realized (SOAR)–Wyoming, WY
Trailmark Outdoor Adventures–New England–Mahoosoc
Voyageur Outward Bound–Boundary Waters Wilderness Canoeing and Climbing XT, MN
Voyageur Outward Bound–Montana Rock Climbing XT, MT
Wilderness Ventures–Grand Teton, WY
Wilderness Ventures–Great Divide
Wilderness Ventures–High Sierra, CA
Wilderness Ventures–Jackson Hole, WY
Wilderness Ventures–Oregon, OR
Wilderness Ventures–Wyoming Mountaineering, WY
Windsor Mountain: New England Adventure
Yo! Basecamp Rock Climbing Camps, CA

Ropes Course
Adventure Camps, PA
Alpine Camp for Boys, AL
Camp Tawonga–Teen Quest: Yosemite, CA
Nantahala Outdoor Center–Kids Adventure Sports Camp, NC
Pine Ridge Summer Program, VT
Shaffer's High Sierra Camp, CA
Sidwell Friends Women's Leadership–St. Margaret's School, VA

Rowing (Crew/Sculling)
Camp Mowglis, School of the Open, NH
Craftsbury Sculling Camps, VT
Summer Programs on the River; Crew/Rowing Camp, VA

Running/Jogging
Craftsbury Running Camps, VT

Russian Language/Literature

AFS-USA–Homestay Language Study–Latvia, Latvia
Concordia Language Villages–Russian, MN
EF International Language Schools–St. Petersburg, Russian Federation
LSA Moscow, Russia, Russian Federation
LSA St. Petersburg, Russia, Russian Federation
Programs Abroad Travel Alternatives–Russia, Russian Federation
Youth for Understanding USA–Russia, Russian Federation

Safari

BROADREACH Red Sea Scuba Adventure, Egypt
Flint Hill School–"Summer on the Hill"–Trips from the Hill–Tanzania Safari, United Republic of Tanzania
Knowledge Exchange Institute–African Safari Program, Kenya
RUSTIC PATHWAYS–OUTBACK 4-WHEEL DRIVE SAFARI, Australia

Sailing

AAVE–Australia, Australia
ACTIONQUEST: Advanced PADI Scuba Certification and Specialty Voyages, British Virgin Islands
ACTIONQUEST: Australian and Great Barrier Reef Adventures, Australia
ACTIONQUEST: British Virgin Islands–Sailing and Scuba Voyages, British Virgin Islands
ACTIONQUEST: British Virgin Islands-Sailing Voyages, British Virgin Islands
ACTIONQUEST: Junior Advanced Scuba with Marine Biology, British Virgin Islands
ACTIONQUEST: Leeward and French Caribbean Island Voyages
ACTIONQUEST: Mediterranean Sailing Voyage
ACTIONQUEST: Rescue Diving Voyages, British Virgin Islands
ACTIONQUEST: Tahiti and French Polynesian Island Voyages, French Polynesia
ACTIONQUEST: Tropical Marine Biology Voyages, British Virgin Islands
!ADVENTURES–AFLOAT: Advanced Scuba Adventure Voyages–British Virgin Islands, British Virgin Islands
!ADVENTURES–AFLOAT: Advanced Scuba Adventure Voyages–Caribbean Islands
!ADVENTURES–AFLOAT: Scuba and Sailing Discovery Voyages–British Virgin Islands, British Virgin Islands
!ADVENTURES–AFLOAT: Scuba and Sailing Discovery Voyages–Caribbean Islands
Adventures Cross-Country, Caribbean Adventure
Adventures Cross-Country, Hawaii Adventure, HI
American Youth Foundation–Camp Miniwanca, MI
BROADREACH Adventures in Scuba and Sailing–Underwater Discoveries
BROADREACH Adventures in the Grenadines–Advanced Scuba, Saint Vincent and The Grenadines
BROADREACH Adventures in the Windward Islands–Advanced Scuba
BROADREACH Adventures Underwater–Advanced Scuba
BROADREACH Arc of the Caribbean Sailing Adventure
Camp Chewonki, ME
Camp Matoaka for Girls, ME
Camp Mishawaka for Boys, MN
Camp Mishawaka for Girls, MN
Camp Northway, Canada
Camp Nor'wester, WA
Camp Stanislaus, MS
Cape Cod Sea Camps–Monomoy/Wono, MA
Cheerio Adventures–Mountains to the Sea, VA
Cheerio Adventures–Ocean Odyssey, VA
Community Sailing of Colorado–Advanced Sailing, CO
Community Sailing of Colorado–Learn to Sail, CO
Community Sailing of Colorado–Sailboat Racing Camp, CO
Culver Summer Camps/Culver Specialty Camp–Sailing, IN
ExploraMar: Marine Biology Sailing Expeditions–Sea of Cortez, Baja, Mexico
French Immersion Summer Camp, Canada
Geronimo Program
Girl Scouts of Mid-Continent–Camp Oakledge, MO
Great Escapes (Adventure Trips for Teens)–Cape Cod Sail Adventure, MA
Great Escapes (Adventure Trips for Teens)–Saddle and Sail
Hurricane Island Outward Bound–Maine Coast and Western Maine Canoeing and Sailing, ME
Hurricane Island Outward Bound–Maine Coast and Western Maine Sailing and Backpacking, ME
Hurricane Island Outward Bound–Maine Coast Sailing/Sailing and Rock Climbing, ME
Hurricane Island Outward Bound–Maine Coast Schooner Sailing, ME
Hurricane Island Outward Bound–Ocean Bound: Tall Ship Sailing and Sea Kayaking Semester
LIFEWORKS with the British Virgin Islands Marine Parks and Conservation Department, British Virgin Islands
Longacre Expeditions, Adventure 28
Longacre Expeditions, Downeast, ME
Longacre Expeditions, Pacific Coast and Inlands
Maritime Camp, NJ
ODYSSEY EXPEDITIONS: Tropical Marine Biology Voyages–British Virgin Islands, British Virgin Islands
ODYSSEY EXPEDITIONS: Tropical Marine Biology Voyages–Caribbean Islands
Outward Bound–Connecting with Courage, MA
Outward Bound–Environmental Expeditions, MA
Outward Bound–Passages, MA
Putney Student Travel–Cultural Exploration–Australia, New Zealand, and Fiji
Sail Caribbean–All Levels of Scuba Certification with Sailing, British Virgin Islands
Sail Caribbean–British Virgin Islands, British Virgin Islands
Sail Caribbean–Community Service, British Virgin Islands
Sail Caribbean–Leeward Islands
Sail Caribbean–Marine Biology, British Virgin Islands
Sailing Program at NE Camping Adventures, ME
Sidwell Friends Riverview Programs, VA
Summer Programs on the River; Sailing Camp, VA
Trailmark Outdoor Adventures–New England–Camden
Wilderness Ventures–Hawaii, HI
Williwaw Adventures–Maine Mountains and Coast, ME
Williwaw Adventures–Maine Wilderness
Williwaw Adventures–Pacific Northwest Expedition
Windsor Mountain: Coast of Australia, Australia

SAT/ACT Preparation

Academic Camps at Gettysburg College–College Prep & Preview, PA
Academic Study Associates–ASA at the University of California, Berkeley, CA
Academic Study Associates–ASA at the University of Massachusetts Amherst, MA
Academic Study Associates–Pathways Program at Amherst College, MA
Brighton College Admissions Prep at Tufts University, MA
Brighton College Admissions Prep at UCLA, CA
Cal Poly State University Young Scholars Prepare for the PSAT & SAT I, CA
College Admission Prep Camp by Education Unlimited–Boston, MA
College Admission Prep Camp by Education Unlimited–San Diego, CA
College Admission Prep Camp by Education Unlimited–Stanford University, CA
College Admission Prep Camp by Education Unlimited–UC Berkeley, CA
College Admission Prep Camp by Education Unlimited–UCLA, CA
College Admission Prep Camp Choice by Education Unlimited–Stanford, CA
Elite Educational Institute Junior High/PSAT Program, CA
Elite Educational Institute Junior High/PSAT Program–Korea, Republic of Korea
Elite Educational Institute SAT Bootcamp–Korea, Republic of Korea
Elite Educational Institute SAT I and II Preparation, CA
Elite Educational Institute SAT Preparation–Korea, Republic of Korea
Elite Educational Institute SAT Summer Bootcamp, CA
Montgomery College WDCE–Mathematics Enrichment Program, MD
The Oxford Experience, United Kingdom
Prep Camp Excel by Education Unlimited–Stanford University, CA
Prep Camp Excel by Education Unlimited–UC Berkeley, CA
Prep Camp Excel by Education Unlimited–UCLA, CA

Science (General)

Access to Careers in the Sciences (ACES) Camps, TX
Adventures in Science and Arts, WA

▶ Science (General)

Alexander-Smith Academy Summer School, TX
Baylor University High School Summer Science Research Program, TX
Blyth Education–Summer Study in Costa Rica, Costa Rica
Bugs to Biospheres, CO
Camp Discovery–Madison, NJ
Camp Discovery–Teaneck, NJ
Camp Middlesex, NJ
Timber-lee Science Camp, WI
Camp Watonka, PA
Carolina Master Scholars Adventure Series, SC
Choate Rosemary Hall Math/Science Institute for Girls–CONNECT, CT
Discovery Camp, CO
Duke Action: Science Camp for Young Women, NC
EARTHWATCH INSTITUTE–Argentina's Pampas Carnivores, Argentina
EARTHWATCH INSTITUTE–Bahamian Reef Survey, Bahamas
EARTHWATCH INSTITUTE–Baltic Island Wetlands and Wildlife, Estonia
EARTHWATCH INSTITUTE–Butterflies of Vietnam, Vietnam
EARTHWATCH INSTITUTE–Cacti and Orchids of the Yucatan, Mexico
EARTHWATCH INSTITUTE–Canyonland Creek Ecology, UT
EARTHWATCH INSTITUTE–Caring for Chimpanzees, WA
EARTHWATCH INSTITUTE–Carnivores of Madagascar, Madagascar
EARTHWATCH INSTITUTE–Cheetah, Namibia
EARTHWATCH INSTITUTE–Climate Change at Arctic's Edge, Canada
EARTHWATCH INSTITUTE–Coastal Ecology of the Bahamas, Bahamas
EARTHWATCH INSTITUTE–Conservation Research Initiative–Restoring Wild Salmon, WA
EARTHWATCH INSTITUTE–Crocodiles of the Okavango, Botswana
EARTHWATCH INSTITUTE–Dolphins and Whales of Abaco Island, Bahamas
EARTHWATCH INSTITUTE–Early Man in Spain, Spain
EARTHWATCH INSTITUTE–Echidnas and Goannas of Kangaroo Island, Australia
EARTHWATCH INSTITUTE–Ecuador Forest Birds, Ecuador
EARTHWATCH INSTITUTE–England's Hidden Kingdom, United Kingdom
EARTHWATCH INSTITUTE–Europe–Africa Songbird Migrations–Hungary, Hungary
EARTHWATCH INSTITUTE–Europe–Africa Songbird Migrations–Italy, Italy
EARTHWATCH INSTITUTE–Frontier Fort in Virginia, VA
EARTHWATCH INSTITUTE–Icelandic and Alaskan Glaciers, Iceland
EARTHWATCH INSTITUTE–Inner Mongolia's Lost Water, China
EARTHWATCH INSTITUTE–Itjaritjari: the Outback's Mysterious Marsupial, Australia
EARTHWATCH INSTITUTE–Jackson Hole Bison Dig, WY
EARTHWATCH INSTITUTE–Kenya's Black Rhino, Kenya
EARTHWATCH INSTITUTE–Koala Ecology, Australia
EARTHWATCH INSTITUTE–Lions of Tsavo, Kenya
EARTHWATCH INSTITUTE–Mallorca's Copper Age, Spain
EARTHWATCH INSTITUTE–Mammoth Cave, KY
EARTHWATCH INSTITUTE–Mammoth Graveyard, SD
EARTHWATCH INSTITUTE–Moose and Wolves, MI
EARTHWATCH INSTITUTE–Mountain Waters of Bohemia, Czech Republic
EARTHWATCH INSTITUTE–New Zealand Dolphins, New Zealand
EARTHWATCH INSTITUTE–Orca, WA
EARTHWATCH INSTITUTE–Pine Marten of the Ancient Forest, Canada
EARTHWATCH INSTITUTE–Prehistoric Pueblos of the American Southwest, NM
EARTHWATCH INSTITUTE–Rainforest Caterpillars–Costa Rica, Costa Rica
EARTHWATCH INSTITUTE–Rare Plants of Kenya, Kenya
EARTHWATCH INSTITUTE–Roman Fort on the Danube, Romania
EARTHWATCH INSTITUTE–Roman Fort on Tyne, United Kingdom
EARTHWATCH INSTITUTE–Saving the Leatherback Turtle, U.S. Virgin Islands
EARTHWATCH INSTITUTE–Sea Otters of Alaska, AK
EARTHWATCH INSTITUTE–Sea Turtles of Baja, Mexico
EARTHWATCH INSTITUTE–South African Penguins, South Africa
EARTHWATCH INSTITUTE–South African Wildlife, South Africa
EARTHWATCH INSTITUTE–Spanish Dolphins, Spain
EARTHWATCH INSTITUTE–Sri Lanka's Temple Monkeys, Sri Lanka
EARTHWATCH INSTITUTE–Wild Dolphin Societies, FL
EARTHWATCH INSTITUTE–Wildlife Conservation in West Africa, Ghana
ECOES: Exploring Career Options in Engineering and Science, NJ
Flint Hill School–"Summer on the Hill"–Enrichment on the Hill–Scientific Super Sleuths, VA
Frontiers Program, MA
Gems: Girls in Engineering, Math and Science, MA
The Governor's Program for Gifted Children, LA
Hillsdale College Summer Science Camps, MI
Ithaca College Summer College for High School Students: Session I, NY
Knowledge Exchange Institute–Research Abroad in Russia, Russian Federation
Learn English and Discover Canada, Canada
Michigan Technological University Explorations in Engineering Workshop, MI
Michigan Technological University Women in Engineering Workshop, MI
Miss Porter's School Summer Challenge, CT
MIT MITE^{2}S (Minority Introduction to Engineering, Entrepreneurship and Science), MA
Montgomery Bell Academy–Summer Science Experience, TN
Montgomery College WDCE–Inventor's Workshop, MD
Montgomery College WDCE–Summer Science Camp for Girls, MD
New Mexico Tech Summer Mini-Course, NM
92nd Street Y Camps–Camp Tevah for Science and Nature, NY
Project SUCCEED, NC
Research Internship in Science and Engineering, MA
Science Program for High School Girls, CA
Science Program for Middle School Boys on Catalina, CA
Science Program for Middle School Girls on Catalina, CA
Sciencescape, MO
Shippensburg University Academic Camps–Science Academy for Girls, PA
Smith College Summer Science and Engineering Program, MA
Space Camp Turkey 6-Day International Program, Turkey
Stoneleigh–Burnham School: Science Camp for Middle School Girls, MA
Stony Brook University–Science Exploration Camp, NY
Strive: Exploring Engineering, Math and Science, MA
University of Connecticut Mentor Connection, CT
University of Kansas–Project Discovery, KS
Women in Science & Engineering Camp, PA
WRC Weather Camp, TX
Young Investigators Program in Nuclear Science & Technology, NC

Screenwriting

Choate Rosemary Hall Summer Arts Conservatory–Playwriting, CT
Vermont Arts Screenwriting Institute, VT

Scuba Diving

AAVE–Australia, Australia
ACTIONQUEST: Advanced PADI Scuba Certification and Specialty Voyages, British Virgin Islands
ACTIONQUEST: Australian and Great Barrier Reef Adventures, Australia
ACTIONQUEST: British Virgin Islands–Sailing and Scuba Voyages, British Virgin Islands
ACTIONQUEST: Junior Advanced Scuba with Marine Biology, British Virgin Islands
ACTIONQUEST: Rescue Diving Voyages, British Virgin Islands
ACTIONQUEST: Tropical Marine Biology Voyages, British Virgin Islands
!ADVENTURES–AFLOAT: Advanced Scuba Adventure Voyages–British Virgin Islands, British Virgin Islands
!ADVENTURES–AFLOAT: Advanced Scuba Adventure Voyages–Caribbean Islands
!ADVENTURES–AFLOAT: Scuba and Sailing Discovery Voyages–British Virgin Islands, British Virgin Islands
!ADVENTURES–AFLOAT: Scuba and Sailing Discovery Voyages–Caribbean Islands
Adventures Cross-Country, Australia/Fiji Adventure
Adventures Cross-Country, Caribbean Adventure
Blyth Education–Summer Study in Cozumel, Mexico

BROADREACH Academic Treks–Marine Park Management
BROADREACH Academic Treks–Sea Turtle Studies, Costa Rica
BROADREACH Adventures Down Under, Australia
BROADREACH Adventures in Scuba and Sailing–Underwater Discoveries
BROADREACH Adventures in the Grenadines–Advanced Scuba, Saint Vincent and The Grenadines
BROADREACH Adventures in the Windward Islands–Advanced Scuba
BROADREACH Adventures Underwater–Advanced Scuba
BROADREACH Amazon and Galapagos Encounter, Ecuador
BROADREACH Baja Extreme–Scuba Adventure, Mexico
BROADREACH Fiji Solomon Quest
BROADREACH Honduras Eco-Adventure, Honduras
BROADREACH Marine Biology Accredited, Bahamas
BROADREACH Red Sea Scuba Adventure, Egypt
Culver Summer Camps/Culver Specialty Camp–Scuba, IN
Florida Air Academy Summer Session, FL
Great Escapes (Adventure Trips for Teens)–Cape Cod Underwater Adventure, MA
Hawaii Extreme Adventure Scuba Camp, HI
Longacre Expeditions, Belize, Belize
Longacre Expeditions, Hawaii, HI
Longacre Expeditions, Virgin Islands
Marine and Environmental Science Program, Canada
ODYSSEY EXPEDITIONS: Tropical Marine Biology Voyages–British Virgin Islands, British Virgin Islands
ODYSSEY EXPEDITIONS: Tropical Marine Biology Voyages–Caribbean Islands
RUSTIC PATHWAYS–DIVER'S DREAM IN THE FIJI ISLANDS, Fiji
RUSTIC PATHWAYS–LEARN TO DIVE IN THE FIJI ISLANDS, Fiji
Sail Caribbean–All Levels of Scuba Certification with Sailing, British Virgin Islands
Sail Caribbean–British Virgin Islands, British Virgin Islands
Sail Caribbean–Community Service, British Virgin Islands
Sail Caribbean–Leeward Islands
Sail Caribbean–Marine Biology, British Virgin Islands
Scuba Adventures at Pali Overnight Adventures, CA
Seacamp, FL
Wilderness Experiences Unlimited/Westfield Water Sports: Scuba Camp, MA
Wilderness Ventures–Australia, Australia
Windsor Mountain: Coast of Australia, Australia

Sculpture
IEI–Fine Arts Plus Programme, United Kingdom
University of Connecticut Community School of the Arts–World Arts Camps, CT
Young Artists at Purchase, NY

Sea Kayaking
AAVE–Alaska, AK
Adventures Cross-Country, Alaska Adventure, AK
Adventures Cross-Country, Costa Rica Adventure, Costa Rica
Adventures Cross-Country, Extreme British Columbia Adventure, Canada
Adventures Cross-Country, Hawaii Adventure, HI
Adventures Cross-Country, Thailand Adventure, Thailand
Adventure Treks–Alaska Adventures, AK
Adventure Treks–California 19 Adventures, CA
Adventure Treks–Pacific Northwest Adventures, WA
Alpengirl–Scandinavia
Apogee Outdoor Adventures–New England Mountains and Coast
BROADREACH Academic Treks–Marine Mammal Studies, Canada
BROADREACH Adventures Down Under, Australia
BROADREACH Baja Extreme–Scuba Adventure, Mexico
BROADREACH Costa Rica Experience, Costa Rica
Camp Chewonki Eco-Kayak Australia, Australia
Camp Tawonga–Teen Quest: Canada, Canada
Darrow Wilderness Trips–Kayak, ME
Hurricane Island Outward Bound–Maine Coast and Western Maine Sea Kayaking and Backpacking, ME
Hurricane Island Outward Bound–Maine Coast Sea Kayaking, ME
Kroka Expeditions–Coastal Sea Kayaking, ME
Lifeschool Wilderness Adventures–Summer Adventures, CA
Longacre Expeditions, Adventure 28
Longacre Expeditions, Alaska, AK
Longacre Expeditions, British Columbia
Longacre Expeditions, British Isles, United Kingdom
Longacre Expeditions, Hawaii, HI
Longacre Expeditions, Iceland, Iceland
Longacre Expeditions, New England/Canada
Longacre Expeditions, Pacific Coast and Inlands
Longacre Expeditions, Photography, ME
Longacre Expeditions, Virgin Islands
Longacre Expeditions, Whales, ME
Luna Adventures with AAG SummerSkills
Outward Bound West–Sea Kayaking and Mountaineering–Alaska, AK
Outward Bound West–Sea Kayaking, Backpacking, and Mountaineering–Washington, WA
Overland: Acadia and Prince Edward Island Bicycle Touring and Sea-Kayaking
Overland: Alaskan Expedition Hiking, Sea-Kayaking, and Rafting, AK
Overland: Costa Rica Explorer Hiking, Rafting, and Sea-Kayaking, Costa Rica
RUSTIC PATHWAYS–COSTA RICA NATURAL WONDERS, Costa Rica
Sea Kayak Expedition (English), Canada
Sidwell Friends Overnight Sea Kayaking Trip, MD
Trailmark Outdoor Adventures–New England–Downeast
Trailmark Outdoor Adventures–New England–Mahoosoc
Trailmark Outdoor Adventures–New England–Mt. Desert
Voyageur Outward Bound–Lake Superior Freshwater Kayaking and Backpacking
Wilderness Ventures–Alaska Leadership, AK
Wilderness Ventures–Alaska Southcentral, AK
Wilderness Ventures–Alaska Southeast, AK
Wilderness Ventures–Cascade-Olympic, WA
Wilderness Ventures–Costa Rica, Costa Rica
Wilderness Ventures–Grand Teton, WY
Wilderness Ventures–Great Divide Bike
Wilderness Ventures–Hawaii, HI
Wilderness Ventures–Northwest
Wilderness Ventures–Pacific Northwest
Wilderness Ventures–Puget Sound, WA
Wilderness Ventures–Rocky Mountain
Wilderness Ventures–Spanish Pyrenees, Spain
Wilderness Ventures–Teton Adventure, WY
Williwaw Adventures–Maine Mountains and Coast, ME
Williwaw Adventures–Maine Wilderness
Windsor Mountain: New England Adventure

Self-Defense
Sidwell Friends Women's Leadership–St. Margaret's School, VA

Skateboarding
High Cascade Snowboard Camp, OR
Skateboarding Academy at Pali Overnight Adventures, CA
Vans Skateboard Camp, OR
Woodward Freestyle BMX Bicycle, Inline Skate, Skateboarding Camp, PA

Skiing (Downhill)
AAVE–Alps Rider
AAVE–Border Cross
International Summer Camp Montana, Switzerland, Switzerland
RUSTIC PATHWAYS–SKI AND SNOWBOARD ADVENTURE IN NEW ZEALAND, New Zealand
Swiss Challenge, Switzerland
Westcoast Connection Travel–Ski and Snowboard Sensation

Skin Diving
Culver Summer Camps/Culver Specialty Camp–Scuba, IN

Snorkeling
AAVE–Belize, Belize
AAVE–Ecuador and Galapagos, Ecuador
AAVE–Hawaii, HI
AAVE–Vietnam, Vietnam
ACTIONQUEST: British Virgin Islands-Sailing Voyages, British Virgin Islands
ACTIONQUEST: Galapagos Archipelago Expeditions, Ecuador
ACTIONQUEST: Tahiti and French Polynesian Island Voyages, French Polynesia
Alpengirl–Hawaii, HI
EARTHWATCH INSTITUTE–Coral Reefs of the Virgin Islands, U.S. Virgin Islands
ExploraMar: Marine Biology Sailing Expeditions–Sea of Cortez, Baja, Mexico

▶ Snorkeling

Flint Hill School–"Summer on the Hill"–Trips from the Hill–Ecological Study of Coral Reefs, Bahamas, Bahamas
GLOBAL WORKS–Cultural Exchange-New Zealand and Fiji Islands-4 weeks
Great Escapes (Adventure Trips for Teens)–Cape Cod Underwater Adventure, MA
Longacre Expeditions, Hawaii, HI
Putney Student Travel–Cultural Exploration–Australia, New Zealand, and Fiji

Snowboarding

AAVE–Alps Rider
High Cascade Snowboard Camp, OR
High Cascade Snowboard Camp Photography Workshop, OR
Longacre Expeditions, Surf Oregon, OR
RUSTIC PATHWAYS–SKI AND SNOWBOARD ADVENTURE IN NEW ZEALAND, New Zealand
Swiss Challenge, Switzerland
Vans Skateboard Camp, OR
Westcoast Connection Travel–Ski and Snowboard Sensation

Soccer

Britannia Soccer Camp, CA
Camp All-Star, ME
Camp Berachah Ministries–Soccer Camp, WA
Camp Hillside Soccer Program, MA
Crossroads School–Soccer Camps, CA
Culver Summer Camps/Culver Specialty Camp–Soccer, IN
Dwight-Englewood Summer Sports Clinics, NJ
GIC Arg–Soccer, Argentina
Global Teen–Italian and Soccer in Rome, Italy
JCC Houston: Sports Camp, TX
Joe Machnik's No. 1 Academy One and Premier Programs–Aston, Pennsylvania, PA
Joe Machnik's No. 1 Academy One and Premier Programs–Brooklyn, Michigan, MI
Joe Machnik's No. 1 Academy One and Premier Programs–Claremont, California, CA
Joe Machnik's No. 1 Academy One and Premier Programs–Colorado Springs, Colorado, CO
Joe Machnik's No. 1 Academy One and Premier Programs–Columbus, Ohio, OH
Joe Machnik's No. 1 Academy One and Premier Programs–Dyke, Virginia, VA
Joe Machnik's No. 1 Academy One and Premier Programs–Fort Worth, Texas, TX
Joe Machnik's No. 1 Academy One and Premier Programs–Kenosha, Wisconsin, WI
Joe Machnik's No. 1 Academy One and Premier Programs–Newtown, Pennsylvania, PA
Joe Machnik's No. 1 Academy One and Premier Programs–Olympia, Washington, WA
Joe Machnik's No. 1 Academy One and Premier Programs–Rohnert Park, California, CA
Joe Machnik's No. 1 Academy One and Premier Programs–Rome, Georgia, GA
Joe Machnik's No. 1 Academy One and Premier Programs–Vero Beach, Florida, FL
Joe Machnik's No. 1 Academy One and Premier Programs–Windsor, Connecticut, CT
Joe Machnik's No. 1 College Prep Academy–Colorado Springs, Colorado, CO
Joe Machnik's No. 1 College Prep Academy–Fort Worth, Texas, TX
Joe Machnik's No. 1 College Prep Academy–Kenosha, Wisconsin, WI
Joe Machnik's No. 1 College Prep Academy–Newtown/Aston, Pennsylvania, PA
Joe Machnik's No. 1 College Prep Academy–Windsor, Connecticut, CT
Joe Machnik's No. 1 Mighty Mini, Goalkeeper and Striker Camp–Aston, Pennsylvania, PA
Joe Machnik's No. 1 Mighty Mini, Goalkeeper and Striker Camp–Brooklyn, Michigan, MI
Joe Machnik's No. 1 Mighty Mini, Goalkeeper and Striker Camp–Claremont, California, CA
Joe Machnik's No. 1 Mighty Mini, Goalkeeper and Striker Camp–Colorado Springs, Colorado, CO
Joe Machnik's No. 1 Mighty Mini, Goalkeeper and Striker Camp–Columbus, Ohio, OH
Joe Machnik's No. 1 Mighty Mini, Goalkeeper and Striker Camp–Dyke, Virginia, VA
Joe Machnik's No. 1 Mighty Mini, Goalkeeper and Striker Camp–Newtown, Pennsylvania, PA
Joe Machnik's No. 1 Mighty Mini, Goalkeeper and Striker Camp–Olympia, Washington, WA
Joe Machnik's No. 1 Mighty Mini, Goalkeeper and Striker Camp–Rohnert Park, California, CA
Joe Machnik's No. 1 Mighty Mini, Goalkeeper and Striker Camp–Rome, Georgia, GA
Joe Machnik's No. 1 Mighty Mini, Goalkeeper and Striker Camp–Vero Beach, Florida, FL
Joe Machnik's No. 1 Mighty Mini, Goalkeeper and Striker Camp–Windsor, Connecticut, CT
Joe Machnik's No. 1 Mighty Mini, Goalkeeper and Striker Camp–Fort Worth, Texas, TX
Joe Machnik's No. 1 Mighty Mini, Goalkeeper and Striker Camp–Kenosha, Wisconsin, WI
Jumonville Soccer Camp, PA
Jumonville Spirit and Sport Spectacular–Soccer Camp, PA
Lenny Armuth Soccer Academy, NJ
NBC Camps–Soccer–Spangle, WA, WA
NBC Camps–Soccer Speed Explosion–Spokane, WA, WA
PAX Abroad–Brazil, Brazil
Pingry Soccer Camp, NJ
Professional Sports Camps–Hall of Fame Soccer Camp, NJ
Shippensburg University Sports Camps–Soccer–Boys Camp, PA
Shippensburg University Sports Camps–Soccer–Day Camp, PA
Shippensburg University Sports Camps–Soccer–Girls Camp, PA
Sidwell Friends Soccer Program with American Soccer Academy, DC
SoccerPlus FieldPlayer Academy–Charleston, IL, IL
SoccerPlus FieldPlayer Academy–Easthampton, MA, MA
SoccerPlus FieldPlayer Academy–Hamilton, NY, NY
SoccerPlus FieldPlayer Academy–Kent, CT, CT
SoccerPlus FieldPlayer Academy–Pottstown, PA, PA
SoccerPlus FieldPlayer Academy–Rome, GA, GA
SoccerPlus FieldPlayer Academy–Slippery Rock, PA, PA
SoccerPlus Goalkeeper School–Advanced National Training Center–Connecticut, CT
SoccerPlus Goalkeeper School–Challenge Program–Brunswick, ME, ME
SoccerPlus Goalkeeper School–Challenge Program–Charleston, IL, IL
SoccerPlus Goalkeeper School–Challenge Program–Delaware, OH, OH
SoccerPlus Goalkeeper School–Challenge Program–Fayetteville, NC, NC
SoccerPlus Goalkeeper School–Challenge Program–Franklin, MA, MA
SoccerPlus Goalkeeper School–Challenge Program–Hamilton, NY, NY
SoccerPlus Goalkeeper School–Challenge Program–Kent, CT, CT
SoccerPlus Goalkeeper School–Challenge Program–Pottstown, PA, PA
SoccerPlus Goalkeeper School–Challenge Program–Rome, GA, GA
SoccerPlus Goalkeeper School–Challenge Program–San Diego, CA, CA
SoccerPlus Goalkeeper School–Challenge Program–Slippery Rock, PA, PA
SoccerPlus Goalkeeper School–Challenge Program–Stockton, CA, CA
SoccerPlus Goalkeeper School–Challenge Program–Suffield, CT, CT
SoccerPlus Goalkeeper School–Challenge Program–Waco, TX, TX
SoccerPlus Goalkeeper School–Competitive Program–Charleston, IL, IL
SoccerPlus Goalkeeper School–Competitive Program–Easthampton, MA, MA
SoccerPlus Goalkeeper School–Competitive Program–Hamilton, NY, NY
SoccerPlus Goalkeeper School–Competitive Program–Kent, CT, CT
SoccerPlus Goalkeeper School–Competitive Program–Pottstown, PA, PA
SoccerPlus Goalkeeper School–Competitive Program–Rome, GA, GA
SoccerPlus Goalkeeper School–Competitive Program–Slippery Rock, PA, PA
SoccerPlus Goalkeeper School–Competitive Program–Suffield, CT, CT
SoccerPlus Goalkeeper School–National Training Center–Brunswick, ME, ME
SoccerPlus Goalkeeper School–National Training Center–Charleston, IL, IL
SoccerPlus Goalkeeper School–National Training Center–Delaware, OH, OH
SoccerPlus Goalkeeper School–National Training Center–Fayetteville, NC, NC
SoccerPlus Goalkeeper School–National Training Center–Franklin, MA, MA
SoccerPlus Goalkeeper School–National Training Center–Hamilton, NY, NY
SoccerPlus Goalkeeper School–National Training Center–Kent, CT, CT
SoccerPlus Goalkeeper School–National Training Center–Pottstown, PA, PA

SoccerPlus Goalkeeper School–National Training Center–Rome, GA, GA
SoccerPlus Goalkeeper School–National Training Center–San Diego, CA, CA
SoccerPlus Goalkeeper School–National Training Center–Slippery Rock, PA, PA
SoccerPlus Goalkeeper School–National Training Center–Stockton, CA, CA
SoccerPlus Goalkeeper School–National Training Center–Waco, TX, TX
United Soccer Academy–Goal Keeping Training Camp, Connecticut, CT
United Soccer Academy–Goal Keeping Training Camp, Delaware, DE
United Soccer Academy–Goal Keeping Training Camp, Maryland, MD
United Soccer Academy–Goal Keeping Training Camp, New Jersey, NJ
United Soccer Academy–Goal Keeping Training Camp, New York, NY
United Soccer Academy–Goal Keeping Training Camp, Pennsylvania, PA
United Soccer Academy–Junior Soccer Squirts, Connecticut, CT
United Soccer Academy–Junior Soccer Squirts, Delaware, DE
United Soccer Academy–Junior Soccer Squirts, Maryland, MD
United Soccer Academy–Junior Soccer Squirts, New Jersey, NJ
United Soccer Academy–Junior Soccer Squirts, New York, NY
United Soccer Academy–Junior Soccer Squirts, Pennsylvania, PA
United Soccer Academy–Recreation Soccer Community Camp, Connecticut, CT
United Soccer Academy–Recreation Soccer Community Camp, Delaware, DE
United Soccer Academy–Recreation Soccer Community Camp, Maryland, MD
United Soccer Academy–Recreation Soccer Community Camp, New Jersey, NJ
United Soccer Academy–Recreation Soccer Community Camp, New York, NY
United Soccer Academy–Recreation Soccer Community Camp, Pennsylvania, PA
United Soccer Academy–Regional Academy Camp, New Jersey, NJ
United Soccer Academy–Regional Academy Camp, New York, NY
United Soccer Academy–Regional Academy Camp, Pennsylvania, PA
United Soccer Academy–Senior Soccer Squirts, Connecticut, CT
United Soccer Academy–Senior Soccer Squirts, Delaware, DE
United Soccer Academy–Senior Soccer Squirts, Maryland, MD
United Soccer Academy–Senior Soccer Squirts, New Jersey, NJ
United Soccer Academy–Senior Soccer Squirts, New York, NY
United Soccer Academy–Senior Soccer Squirts, Pennsylvania, PA
United Soccer Academy–Team Training Camp, Connecticut, CT
United Soccer Academy–Team Training Camp, Delaware, DE
United Soccer Academy–Team Training Camp, Maryland, MD
United Soccer Academy–Team Training Camp, New Jersey, NJ
United Soccer Academy–Team Training Camp, New York, NY
United Soccer Academy–Team Training Camp, Pennsylvania, PA
United Soccer Academy–Travel Soccer Community Camp, Connecticut, CT
United Soccer Academy–Travel Soccer Community Camp, Delaware, DE
United Soccer Academy–Travel Soccer Community Camp, Maryland, MD
United Soccer Academy–Travel Soccer Community Camp, New Jersey, NJ
United Soccer Academy–Travel Soccer Community Camp, New York, NY
United Soccer Academy–Travel Soccer Community Camp, Pennsylvania, PA
University of Kansas–Boys Soccer Camp, KS
University of Kansas–Girls Soccer Camp, KS
University of San Diego Sports Camps–Boys High School Soccer Camp, CA
University of San Diego Sports Camps–Coed Junior Soccer Camp, CA
University of San Diego Sports Camps–Girls Soccer Camp, CA
Vassar College Coed Soccer Camp, NY
Windridge Tennis Camp at Teela-Wooket, Vermont, VT

Social Science

University of Chicago–Insight, IL

Social Services

Landmark Volunteers: Colorado, CO
Landmark Volunteers: Maine, ME
Landmark Volunteers: Massachusetts, MA
Landmark Volunteers: Minnesota, MN
Landmark Volunteers: New York, NY
Landmark Volunteers: Ohio, OH

Social Skills Development

Camp Kodiak, Canada
Maplebrook School's Summer Program, NY
The Monarch School Summer Camp, TX
Summit Camp, PA
Talisman–Tri-Adventures, NC

Social Studies

Celtic Learning and Travel Services–Edinburgh and Dublin
Celtic Learning and Travel Services–London and Dublin
Celtic Learning and Travel Services–Summer in Ireland, Ireland
Rust College Study Abroad in Africa

Sociology

Montgomery College WDCE–World Events 2005, MD

Softball

Jumonville Baseball/Softball Camp, PA
Pingry Softball Camp, NJ
Shippensburg University Sports Camps–Fast Pitch Softball, PA
Stoneleigh-Burnham School Softball Camp, MA
University of Kansas–Softball–Teen and Advanced Camps, KS
University of San Diego Sports Camps–Girls Softball Advanced Camp, CA
University of San Diego Sports Camps–Girls Softball Beginner/Intermediate Camp, CA

Spanish (Advanced Placement)

Cuernavaca Summer Program for Teens, Mexico
Montgomery College WDCE–Language in Motion, MD
The Peru Cultural Immersion Experience, Peru

Spanish Language/Literature

AAVE–Costa Rica, Costa Rica
AAVE–Inmersión en España, Spain
Abbey Road Overseas Programs–Spanish Immersion and Homestay, Spain
Academic Camps at Gettysburg College–Foreign Language Study (Spanish), PA
Academic Study Associates–Barcelona, Spain
Academic Study Associates–Spanish in España, Spain
AFS-USA–Community Service–Argentina, Argentina
AFS-USA–Homestay Language Study–Costa Rica, Costa Rica
AFS-USA–Homestay–Paraguay, Paraguay
American Collegiate Adventures–Spain, Spain
Artes en Mexico, Mexico
Bravo Spain–Barcelona, Spain
Brighton in Costa Rica, Costa Rica
BROADREACH Academic Treks–Language Exposure and Service Learning, Chile
BROADREACH Academic Treks–Spanish Immersion in Mexico, Mexico
BROADREACH Academic Treks–Spanish Language Immersion in Ecuador, Ecuador
Center for Cultural Interchange–Mexico Language School, Mexico
Center for Cultural Interchange–Spain High School Abroad, Spain
Center for Cultural Interchange–Spain Language School, Spain
Center for Cultural Interchange–Spain Sports and Language Camp, Spain
Choate Rosemary Hall Summer in Spain, Spain
Concordia Language Villages–Spain, Spain
Concordia Language Villages–Spanish–Bemidji, MN
Concordia Language Villages–Spanish–Maplelag, MN
Concordia Language Villages–Spanish–Wilder Forest, MN
Costa Rica ¡Pura Vida!, Costa Rica
Dickinson College Spanish Language and Cultural Immersion Program, Mexico
EF International Language School–Barcelona, Spain
EF International Language School–Malaga, Spain
EF International Language School–Quito, Ecuador
Enforex–General Spanish–Almuñecar, Spain
Enforex–General Spanish–Barcelona, Spain
Enforex–General Spanish–Granada, Spain
Enforex–General Spanish–Madrid, Spain
Enforex–General Spanish–Marbella, Spain
Enforex–General Spanish–Salamanca, Spain
Enforex–General Spanish–Valencia, Spain
Enforex Hispanic Culture: Civilization, History, Art, and Literature–Barcelona, Spain

▶ Spanish Language/Literature

Enforex Hispanic Culture: Civilization, History, Art, and Literature–Granada, Spain
Enforex Hispanic Culture: Civilization, History, Art, and Literature–Madrid, Spain
Enforex Homestay Program–Almuñecar, Spain
Enforex Homestay Program–Barcelona, Spain
Enforex Homestay Program–Granada, Spain
Enforex Homestay Program–Madrid, Spain
Enforex Homestay Program–Marbella, Spain
Enforex Homestay Program–Salamanca, Spain
Enforex Residential Youth Summer Camp–Marbella, Spain
Enforex Residential Youth Summer Camp–Salamanca, Spain
Enforex Spanish and Golf, Spain
Enforex Spanish and Tennis, Spain
Enforex Study Tour Vacational Program–Madrid, Spain
Excel at Madrid/Barcelona, Spain
Excel Cuba, Cuba
The Experiment in International Living–Argentina Homestay, Community Service, and Outdoor Ecological Program, Argentina
The Experiment in International Living–Chile North Homestay, Community Service, Chile
The Experiment in International Living–Chile South Homestay, Chile
The Experiment in International Living–Ecuador Homestay, Ecuador
The Experiment in International Living–Mexico Homestay and Travel, Mexico
The Experiment in International Living–Spain, Five-Week Homestay, Travel, Ecology, Spain
The Experiment in International Living–Spain, Five-Week Language Training, Travel, and Homestay, Spain
The Experiment in International Living–Spain, Four-Week Homestay and Trekking Program, Spain
The Experiment in International Living–Spain, Four-Week Language Study and Homestay, Spain
The Experiment in International Living–Spain–Spanish Culture and Folklore, Spain
The Experiment in International Living–Spain, Three-Week Homestay, Spain
Flint Hill School–"Summer on the Hill"–Enrichment on the Hill–Spanish Immersion Camp, VA
GIC Arg–Spanish Language, Argentina
Global Teen–Learn Spanish in Andalusia, Spain
Global Teen–Learn Spanish in Costa Rica, Costa Rica
Global Teen–Learn Spanish in Marbella, Ages 6-14, Spain
Global Teen–Learn Spanish in Marbella-Young Adult, Spain
Global Teen–Learn Spanish in Mexico, Mexico
Global Teen–Learn Spanish in Salamanca, Ages 11-18, Spain
Global Teen–Learn Spanish in Salamanca, Ages 13-16, Spain
Global Teen–Learn Spanish in Sevilla, Spain
Global Teen–Spanish in Ecuador, Ecuador
Global Teen–Spanish in Madrid, Ages 6-14, Spain
Global Teen–Spanish in Malaga-Young Adult, Ages 16-20, Spain
Global Teen–Spanish in Palma de Mallorca, Spain
Global Teen–Spanish Summer Camp in San Sebastian, Spain
Global Teen–Summer Camp in Barcelona, Spain
Global Teen–Summer Camp in Marbella, Ages 14-18, Spain
Global Teen–Vejer Beach Spectacular in Spain, Spain
Global Teen–Young Adult Summer Camp in Madrid, Ages 14-18, Spain
Global Teen–Young Adult Summer Program in Malaga, Ages 16-20, Spain
GLOBAL WORKS–Language Immersion-Costa Rica-4 weeks, Costa Rica
GLOBAL WORKS–Language Immersion-Ecuador and the Galapagos-4 weeks, Ecuador
GLOBAL WORKS–Language Immersion-Puerto Rico-4 weeks, Puerto Rico
GLOBAL WORKS–Language Immersion-Spain-4 weeks, Spain
iD Tech Camps–Documentary Filmmaking and Cultural Immersion at the University of Cádiz, Spain, Spain
Instituto de Idiomas Geos–Costa Rica, Costa Rica
Instituto de Idiomas Geos–Granada, Spain, Spain
Instituto de Idiomas Geos–Marbella, Spain, Spain
Knowledge Exchange Institute–Discover Spain and Portugal Program
Knowledge Exchange Institute–Spanish on the Road in Mexico Program, Mexico
Lacunza Junior Summer Spanish Course, Spain
Learning Programs International–Argentina, Argentina
Learning Programs International–Chile, Chile
Learning Programs International–Costa Rica, Costa Rica
Learning Programs International–Mexico, Mexico
Learning Programs International–Spain, Spain
Les Elfes–International Summer/Winter Camp, Switzerland
The Loomis Chaffee Summer in Spain, Spain
LSA Alicante, Spain, Spain
LSA Almuñecar, Spain, Spain
LSA Antigua, Guatemala, Guatemala
LSA Barcelona, Spain, Spain
LSA Buenos Aires, Argentina, Argentina
LSA Cordoba, Argentina, Argentina
LSA Cuernavaca, Mexico, Mexico
LSA Cuzco, Peru, Peru
LSA El Puerto de Santa Maria, Spain, Spain
LSA Ensenada, Mexico, Mexico
LSA Flamingo Beach, Costa Rica, Costa Rica
LSA Granada, Spain, Spain
LSA Madrid, Spain, Spain
LSA Màlaga, Spain, Spain
LSA Marbella, Spain, Spain
LSA Mérida, Mexico, Mexico
LSA Nerja, Spain, Spain
LSA Playa Del Carmen, Mexico, Mexico
LSA Puerto Vallarta, Mexico, Mexico
LSA Quito, Ecuador, Ecuador
LSA Salamanca, Spain, Spain
LSA San José, Costa Rica, Costa Rica
LSA San Sebastian, Spain, Spain
LSA Sevilla, Spain, Spain
LSA Sucre, Bolivia, Bolivia
LSA Tenerife, Spain, Spain
LSA Valencia, Spain, Spain
LSA Viña del Mar, Chile, Chile
Mercersburg Academy Summer Study in Spain, Spain
MexArt: Art and Spanish, Mexico
MexArt Dance: Dance and Spanish, Mexico
Millersville University of Pennsylvania–Summer Language Camps for High School Students, PA
Montgomery College WDCE–Language in Motion, MD
Overland: Language Study Abroad in Costa Rica, Costa Rica
Overland: Language Study Abroad in Spain, Spain
PAX Abroad–Ecuador–Spanish Language Immersion, Ecuador
PAX Abroad–Summer Spain, Spain
Peace Works International–Costa Rica, Costa Rica
Peace Works International–Ecuador, Ecuador
Programs Abroad Travel Alternatives–Costa Rica, Costa Rica
Programs Abroad Travel Alternatives–Ecuador, Ecuador
Programs Abroad Travel Alternatives–Guatemala, Guatemala
Programs Abroad Travel Alternatives–Mexico, Mexico
Programs Abroad Travel Alternatives–Peru, Peru
Programs Abroad Travel Alternatives–Spain, Spain
Putney Student Travel–Language Learning–Costa Rica, Costa Rica
Putney Student Travel–Language Learning–Spain, Spain
Rassias Programs–Gijón, Spain, Spain
Rassias Programs–Pontevedra, Spain, Spain
Rassias Programs–Segovia, Spain, Spain
RUSTIC PATHWAYS–ACCELERATED SPANISH IMMERSION, Costa Rica
RUSTIC PATHWAYS–RAMP UP YOUR SPANISH, Costa Rica
RUSTIC PATHWAYS–SPANISH LANGUAGE IMMERSION, Costa Rica
Spanish Language and Flamenco Enforex–Granada, Spain
Spanish Language and Flamenco Enforex–Madrid, Spain
Spanish Language and Flamenco Enforex–Marbella, Spain
Spanish Through Leadership–Nicaragua, Nicaragua
Spanish Through Leadership–Nicaragua/Costa Rica
Study Tour Vacational Program Enforex–Barcelona, Spain
Taft Summer School Abroad–Spain, Spain
TASIS Spanish Summer Program, Spain
University of Wisconsin–Green Bay Summer Spanish Immersion, WI
Visions–Ecuador, Ecuador
Where There Be Dragons: Guatemala, Guatemala
Where There Be Dragons: Mexico, Mexico
Where There Be Dragons: Peru, Peru

Windsor Mountain: Cuba Friendship Exchange, Cuba
Windsor Mountain: Mexico Community Service, Mexico
Woodberry Forest Summer School–Spain, Spain
World Horizons International–Costa Rica, Costa Rica
Youth for Understanding USA–Argentina, Argentina
Youth for Understanding USA–Ecuador, Ecuador
Youth for Understanding USA–Spain, Spain
Youth for Understanding USA–Uruguay, Uruguay
Youth for Understanding USA–Venezuela, Venezuela
Youth Program in Spain, Spain

Speech Therapy

Camp Lee Mar, PA
Meadowood Springs Speech and Hearing Camp, OR
University of Kansas–Sertoma-Schiefelbush Communication Camp, KS

Speech/Debate

American Legal Experience by Education Unlimited–Berkeley, CA, CA
American Legal Experience by Education Unlimited–Stanford, CA, CA
California National Debate Institute, CA
Catholic University Capitol Classic Debate Institute, DC
Catholic University of America–Capitol Mock Trial Institute, DC
Catholic University of America–the Capitol Hill Lincoln-Douglas Debate Group, DC
Choate Rosemary Hall Beginning Writers Workshop, CT
Jayhawk Debate Institute, KS
Junior Statesmen Summer School–Georgetown University, DC
Junior Statesmen Summer School–Northwestern University, IL
Junior Statesmen Summer School–Princeton University, NJ
Junior Statesmen Summer School–Stanford University, CA
Junior Statesmen Summer School–Yale University, CT
Junior Statesmen Symposium on California State Politics and Government, CA
Junior Statesmen Symposium on Los Angeles Politics and Government, CA
Junior Statesmen Symposium on New Jersey State Politics and Government, NJ
Junior Statesmen Symposium on Ohio State Politics and Government, OH
Junior Statesmen Symposium on Texas Politics and Leadership, TX
Junior Statesmen Symposium on Washington State Politics and Government, WA
National Debate Institute–DC, MD
Public Speaking Institute by Education Unlimited–Boston, MA
Public Speaking Institute by Education Unlimited–Stanford, CA
Public Speaking Institute by Education Unlimited–UC Berkeley, CA
Public Speaking Institute by Education Unlimited–UCLA, CA
Stanford National Forensic Institute, CA
Stoneleigh–Burnham School: Summer Debate and Public Speaking Camp, MA
Whitman National Debate Institute, WA

Sports (General)

Camp Chikopi for Boys, Canada
Collège du Léman Summer School, Switzerland
Episcopal High School Sports Camp, FL
4 Star Golf Plus All Sports Camp at the University of Virginia, VA
4 Star Tennis Plus Camp at the University of Virginia, VA
Global Teen Summer Sports Camp in Berlin, Germany
GLS Sports and Language Camp Inzell, Germany
GLS Summer Camp Blossin, Germany
Hargrave Summer Program, VA
The John Cooper School Recreational Activities and Sports, TX
Julian Krinsky Super Sports Camp at The Shipley School, PA
Jumonville Sports Camp, PA
Kutsher's Sports Academy, NY
Les Elfes–International Summer/Winter Camp, Switzerland
Loras All-Sports Camp, IA
McCallie Sports Camp, TN
Miami University Summer Sports School, OH
MIMC–Music and Sports Camp, Canada
Miss Porter's School Athletic Experience, CT
Montgomery Bell Academy–All-Sports Camps, TN
Montgomery Bell Academy–Specialty Sports Camps, TN
Montgomery College WDCE–FIT Summer Camp, MD
Sports and Arts Center at Island Lake, PA
Tampa Prep–Boys Athletic Camps, FL
Tampa Prep–Girls Athletic Camps, FL
University of Kansas–Sports Skills and Fitness Camp, KS
University of San Diego Sports Camps–Sports–N–More All Sports Camp, CA
University of San Diego Sports Camps–Sports–N–More Team Sports Camp, CA
University of San Diego Sports Camps–Sports–N–More Wet & Wild Sports Camp, CA
Village Camps–England, United Kingdom
Weissman Teen Tours–U.S. and Western Canada, 6 Weeks
Woodberry Forest Sports Camp, VA
YMCA Camp Lincoln–Specialty Camps: Sports Camp, NH

Squash

Julian Krinsky Tennis Camp at Cabrini College, PA
Julian Krinsky Tennis Camp at Haverford College, PA

Stage Combat

Hollywood Stunt Camp at Pali Overnight Adventures, CA
Mercersburg The World's A Stage Theatre Workshop, PA

Stage Movement

Vermont Arts Theatre Institute, VT

Strategy Games

Fort Union Civil War Camp, MN

Studio Arts

Miss Porter's School Arts Alive!, CT
Parsons Pre-College Academy, NY
Parsons Summer Intensive Studies–New York, NY
Sidwell Friends DaVinci Days Art Studios, Young Artist Academy and Young Scientist Academy, DC
University of Wisconsin–Green Bay Summer Art Studio, WI

Study Skills

Brewster Academy Summer Session, NH
Delphi's Summer Session, OR
Eaglebrook Summer Semester, MA
Flint Hill School–"Summer on the Hill"–Enrichment on the Hill–Study Skills for 9th Graders, VA
Georgetown University College Prep Program, DC
Landmark School Summer Academic Program, MA
Marvelwood Summer, CT
Prep Camp Excel by Education Unlimited–Stanford University, CA
Prep Camp Excel by Education Unlimited–UC Berkeley, CA
Prep Camp Excel by Education Unlimited–UCLA, CA
Rectory School Summer Session, CT
Rumsey Hall School Summer Session, CT
Salisbury Summer School of Reading and English, CT
Squirrel Hollow Learning Camp, GA
The Summer Academy at Suffield, CT
Summer Programs on the River; Skills Program, VA
The Winchendon School Summer Session, MA

Surfing

AAC–Aloha Adventure Surf Camp, HI
AAVE–Australia, Australia
AAVE–Bold West
AAVE–Hawaii, HI
Adventure Ireland–Surf Camp/Activity Camp, Ireland
Camp Pacific's Recreational Camp, CA
Camp Pacific's Surf and Bodyboard Camp, CA
Camp Tawonga–Surf 'n Turf Quest, CA
Cheerio Adventures–Ocean Odyssey, VA
Costa Rica Rainforest Outward Bound School–Multi-Element, Costa Rica
Costa Rica Rainforest Outward Bound School–Summer Semester, Costa Rica
Costa Rica Rainforest Outward Bound School–Surf Adventure, Costa Rica
Costa Rica Rainforest Outward Bound School–Tri-Country/Tri-Mester
Great Escapes (Adventure Trips for Teens)–California Beach Escape, CA
Kroka Expeditions–Cape Cod Triple Surfing Bonanza, MA
Longacre Expeditions, Surf Oregon, OR
Longacre Expeditions, Western Challenge
Longacre Expeditions, Wind and Waves, OR
Maui Surfer Girls, HI
Maui Surfer Girls–Advanced Surf Camp on Kauai, HI
Maui Surfer Girls–Mother/Daughter, HI

▶ Surfing

RUSTIC PATHWAYS–SURF THE SUMMER–COSTA RICA, Costa Rica
RUSTIC PATHWAYS–SURF THE SUMMER–THE FIJI ISLANDS, Fiji
Study Tours and Surf Program in the USA–Mira Costa College, CA
Surf Quest, HI
Wilderness Ventures–California, CA
Windsor Mountain: Coast of Australia, Australia
YMCA Camp Surf, CA

Survival Training

Maine Conservation School Summer Camps, ME

Swedish Language/Literature

Concordia Language Villages–Swedish, MN
Youth for Understanding USA–Sweden, Sweden

Swimming

Camp AK-O-MAK, Canada
Craftsbury Running Camps, VT
Crossroads School–Aquatics, CA
Jumonville Spirit and Sport Spectacular–Swim Camp, PA
Shippensburg University Sports Camps–Swimming, PA
University of Kansas–Jayhawk Swim Camp, KS
University of San Diego Sports Camps–Competitive Swim Camp, CA
University of San Diego Sports Camps–Sports–N–More Wet & Wild Sports Camp, CA
Vassar College Coed Swim Camp, NY

Team Building

Abilene Christian University–Cross Training, NM
Blue Ridge School–Adventure Camps, VA
California Cruzin' Overnight Camp, CA
Camp Exploration Travel Day Camp, CA
Flint Hill School–"Summer on the Hill"–Sports on the Hill for Boys, VA
Future Leader Camp, VT
Hiker's Heaven Overnight Camp
Hulbert Voyageurs Youth Wilderness Trips
Keystone Counselor Assistant Program, CO
Landmark Volunteers: Idaho, ID
Mountain Retreat Overnight Camp, CA
Sail Caribbean–British Virgin Islands, British Virgin Islands

Technology

Access to Careers in the Sciences (ACES) Camps, TX
Emagination Computer Camps–Georgia, GA
Emagination Computer Camps–Illinois, IL
Emagination Computer Camps–Massachusetts, MA
Maplebrook School's Summer Program, NY
Robotics Camp, MI
Women in Technology, MI
Young Investigators Program in Nuclear Science & Technology, NC

Television/Video

Acteen August Academy, NY
Acteen July Academy, NY
Acteen June Academy, NY
Acteen Summer Saturday Academy, NY
The Art Institute of Seattle–Studio 101, WA
Boston University Institute for Television, Film, and Radio Production, MA
Catholic University Communication and Media Studies Workshops, DC
Global Teen–German Plus Web Design, Video/Theatre in Berlin, Germany
iD Tech Camps–Cal Lutheran University, Thousand Oaks, CA, CA
iD Tech Camps–Carnegie Mellon University, Pittsburgh, PA, PA
iD Tech Camps–Colorado College, Colorado Springs, CO, CO
iD Tech Camps–Documentary Filmmaking and Cultural Immersion at the University of Cádiz, Spain, Spain
iD Tech Camps–Dominican University, San Rafael, CA, CA
iD Tech Camps–Emerson College, Boston, MA, MA
iD Tech Camps–Emory University, Atlanta, GA, GA
iD Tech Camps–Georgetown University, Washington, DC, DC
iD Tech Camps–Lake Forest College, Evanston, IL, IL
iD Tech Camps–Merrimack College, North Andover, MA, MA
iD Tech Camps–MIT, Cambridge, MA, MA
iD Tech Camps–Northwestern University, Chicago, IL, IL
iD Tech Camps–Pepperdine University, Malibu, CA, CA
iD Tech Camps–Princeton University, Princeton, NJ, NJ
iD Tech Camps–Sacred Heart University, Fairfield, CT, CT
iD Tech Camps–Santa Clara University, Santa Clara, CA, CA
iD Tech Camps–Smith College, Northampton, MA, MA
iD Tech Camps–Southern Methodist University, Dallas, TX, TX
iD Tech Camps–Stanford University, Palo Alto, CA, CA
iD Tech Camps–St. Mary's College, Moraga, CA, CA
iD Tech Camps–UC Berkeley, Berkeley, CA, CA
iD Tech Camps–UC Irvine, Irvine, CA, CA
iD Tech Camps–UCLA, Westwood, CA, CA
iD Tech Camps–UC San Diego, La Jolla, CA, CA
iD Tech Camps–UC Santa Cruz, Santa Cruz, CA, CA
iD Tech Camps–University of Denver, Denver, CO, CO
iD Tech Camps–University of Miami, Coral Gables, FL, FL
iD Tech Camps–University of Michigan, Ann Arbor, MI, MI
iD Tech Camps–University of Minnesota, Minneapolis, MN, MN
iD Tech Camps–University of North Carolina at Chapel Hill, Chapel Hill, NC, NC
iD Tech Camps–University of Virginia, Charlottesville, VA, VA
iD Tech Camps–University of Washington, Seattle, WA, WA
iD Tech Camps–UT Austin, Austin, TX, TX
iD Tech Camps–Vassar College, Poughkeepsie, NY, NY
iD Tech Camps–Villanova University, Villanova, PA, PA
IEI–Digital Media Plus Programme, United Kingdom
Ithaca College Summer College for High School Students: Session II, NY
LSA Loewenstein, Germany, Germany
Montgomery College WDCE–Aspiring Filmmakers, MD
Oxford Media School–Newsroom in Europe, United Kingdom
Oxford Media School–Newsroom in Europe, Master Class, United Kingdom
PixelNation, NJ
Saint Vincent College Challenge Program, PA
Tisch School of the Arts–Summer High School Programs, NY
Village Camps–Austria, Austria
Young Actors Camp, CA

Tennis

Camp Lincoln for Boys/Camp Lake Hubert for Girls Tennis Camp, MN
Camp Lohikan in the Pocono Mountains, PA
Camp Matoaka for Girls, ME
Camp Rim Rock–Tennis Camp, WV
Carmel Valley Tennis Camp, CA
Culver Summer Camps/Culver Specialty Camp–Tennis, IN
Douglas Ranch Camps, CA
Enforex Spanish and Tennis, Spain
Flint Hill School–"Summer on the Hill"–Sports on the Hill–Coed, VA
4 Star College Prep Tennis at the University of Virginia, VA
4 Star Tennis Camp at the University of Virginia, VA
4 Star Tennis Plus Camp at the University of Virginia, VA
4 Star Tennis Plus Golf Camp at the University of Virginia, VA
Gordon Kent's New England Tennis Camp, NY
JCC Houston: Tennis Camp, TX
Joel Ross Tennis & Sports Camp, CT
Julian Krinsky California Teen Tours, CA
Julian Krinsky Super Sports Camp at The Shipley School, PA
Julian Krinsky Tennis Camp at Cabrini College, PA
Julian Krinsky Tennis Camp at Haverford College, PA
Julian Krinsky Yesh Shabbat California Teen Tour, CA
Julian Krinsky Yesh Shabbat Summer Camp, PA
Jumonville Spirit and Sport Spectacular–Tennis Camp, PA
Maine Golf Academy–Family Camp, ME
Maine Golf Academy–Junior Golf Camp, ME
Maine Golf and Tennis Academy–Serve and Turf, ME
Maine Tennis Academy–Junior Tennis Camp, ME
Nelson/Feller Tennis Camp–Lakeland College, WI
Nelson/Feller Tennis Camp–University of Wisconsin–Oshkosh, WI
Offense-Defense Tennis Camp, MA
Point O' Pines Camp for Girls, NY
Ramey Summer Riding Camps, IN

Ramey Summer Tennis Camps, KY
Shippensburg University Sports Camps–Tennis, PA
Sidwell Friends Tennis Camp, DC
Study Tours and Leisure Sports in the USA–Citrus College, CA
TENNIS: EUROPE
TENNIS: EUROPE & MORE–North American Teams
University of Kansas–Jayhawk Boys and Girls Tennis Camp, KS
University of San Diego Sports Camps–Sherri Stephens High School Tennis Camp, CA
University of San Diego Sports Camps–Sherri Stephens Junior Tennis Camp, CA
Valley Forge Military Academy Extreme Tennis Camp, PA
Windridge Tennis Camp at Craftsbury Common, VT
Windridge Tennis Camp at Teela-Wooket, Vermont, VT

Thai Language

LIFEWORKS with the DPF Foundation in Thailand, Thailand
Youth for Understanding USA–Thailand, Thailand

Theater/Drama

Acteen August Academy, NY
Acteen July Academy, NY
Acteen June Academy, NY
Acteen Summer Saturday Academy, NY
Acting Academy at Pali Overnight Adventures, CA
The Actor's Workshop by Education Unlimited, CA
Arts on the Lake, TX
Bay Area Shakespeare Camp, CA
Belvoir Terrace, MA
Blyth Education–Summer Study in London and Oxford University, United Kingdom
Boston University Summer Theatre Institute, MA
Buck's Rock Performing and Creative Arts Camp, CT
Camp Curtain Call, VA
Camp Hawthorne Creative Arts Camp, ME
Camp Little Palm for the Performing Arts, FL
Camp Middlesex, NJ
Camp Rim Rock–Arts Camp, WV
Camp Shakespeare, UT
Celtic Learning and Travel Services–Edinburgh and Dublin
Celtic Learning and Travel Services–London and Dublin
Celtic Learning and Travel Services–Summer in Ireland, Ireland
Centauri Summer Arts Camp, Canada
The Children's Art Institute, CA
Children's Creative and Performing Arts Academy Summer Elementary Program, CA
Children's Creative and Performing Arts Academy Summer Programs for High School Students, CA
Choate Rosemary Hall Summer Arts Conservatory–Theater, CT
Drama Kids International Summer FUN Camp, TX
Duke Drama Workshop, NC
Encore! Ensemble Theatre Workshop, France
Ensemble Theatre Community School, PA
The Experiment in International Living–France, Four-Week Homestay and Theatre, France
The Experiment in International Living–United Kingdom Theatre Program, United Kingdom
EXPRESSIONS! Duke Fine Arts Camp, NC
French Woods Festival of the Performing Arts, NY
Harand Camp of the Theatre Arts, WI
The Hun School of Princeton Summer Theatre Classics, NJ
Idyllwild Arts Summer Program–American Experience for International Students, CA
Idyllwild Arts Summer Program–Children's Center, CA
Idyllwild Arts Summer Program–Family Week, CA
Idyllwild Arts Summer Program–Junior Artists' Center, CA
Idyllwild Arts Summer Program–Youth Arts Center, CA
IEI–Theatre Plus Programme, United Kingdom
Ithaca College Summer College for High School Students: Session I, NY
Ithaca College Summer College for High School Students: Session II, NY
JCC Houston: Theater Camp, TX
Julian Krinsky Creative and Performing Arts Camp at The Shipley School/Bryn Mawr, PA
LSA Loewenstein, Germany, Germany
Med-O-Lark Camp, ME
Mercersburg Onstage! Young Actors Workshop, PA
Midsummer in London, United Kingdom
Montgomery Bell Academy–Summer Theater Camp, TN
Montgomery College WDCE–Summer Dinner Theatre, MD
92nd Street Y Camps–Camp Yaffa for the Arts, NY
Northwestern University's National High School Institute, IL
Oxford Media School–Film, United Kingdom
Oxford Media School–Film Master Class, United Kingdom
Performance PLUS–Positive Learning Using the Stage+Studio+Screen, NH
The Performing Arts Institute of Wyoming Seminary, PA
The Putney School Summer Arts Program, VT
Putney Student Travel–Cultural Exploration–Theatre in Britain, United Kingdom
Shakespeare at Purchase, NY
Shippensburg University Academic Camps–Acting & Theatre Arts, PA
Sidwell Friends Drama and Dance Workshops with BAPA, DC
Spoleto Study Abroad, Italy
Stagedoor Manor Performing Arts Training Center/Theatre and Dance Camp, NY
Study Tours and Dance/Theater Camp in the USA–Dean College, MA
Summer in Switzerland, Switzerland
TASIS England Summer Program, United Kingdom
Timber-lee Drama Camp, WI
Tisch School of the Arts–International High School Program–Dublin, Ireland
Tisch School of the Arts–International High School Program–Paris, France
Tisch School of the Arts–Summer High School Programs, NY
Traveling Players Ensemble Camp, MD
Vermont Arts Theatre Camp Institute, VT
Vermont Arts Theatre Institute, VT
Westminster Choir College Middle School Music Theater, NJ
Westminster Choir College Music Theater Workshop, NJ
Windsor Mountain: European Traveling Minstrels
Windsor Mountain: New England Traveling Minstrels
YMCA Camp Lincoln–Specialty Camps: Arts & Drama, NH
Young Musicians & Artists, OR

TOEFL/TOEIC Preparation

Academic Study Associates–ASA at the University of California, Berkeley, CA

Touring

AAC–Aloha Adventure Photo Camp, HI
AAC–Aloha Adventure Surf Camp, HI
AAVE–Bold Europe
AAVE–Ecuador and Galapagos, Ecuador
AAVE–Peru and Machu Picchu, Peru
AAVE–Thailand, Thailand
AAVE–Vivons le Français, France
AAVE–Wild Isles
Academic Study Associates–Barcelona, Spain
Academic Study Associates–Florence, Italy
Academic Study Associates–Nice, France
Academic Study Associates–Royan, France
Academic Study Associates–Spanish in España, Spain
ACTIONQUEST: Australian and Great Barrier Reef Adventures, Australia
ACTIONQUEST: Leeward and French Caribbean Island Voyages
ACTIONQUEST: Mediterranean Sailing Voyage
ACTIONQUEST: Tahiti and French Polynesian Island Voyages, French Polynesia
AFS-USA–Community Service–Costa Rica, Costa Rica
AFS-USA–Homestay–Ecuador, Ecuador
AFS-USA–Homestay Language Study–Costa Rica, Costa Rica
AFS-USA–Homestay–Paraguay, Paraguay
Alien Adventure Overnight Camp
American Collegiate Adventures–Italy, Italy
American Collegiate Adventures–Spain, Spain
Apogee Outdoor Adventures–Cape Cod and the Islands, MA
ATW: Action America West
ATW: Adventure Roads
ATW: American Horizons
ATW: California Sunset
ATW: Camp Inn 42
ATW: Discoverer
ATW: European Adventures
ATW: Fire and Ice
ATW: Mini Tours
ATW: Pacific Paradise
ATW: Skyblazer
ATW: Sunblazer
ATW: Wayfarer
BICYCLE TRAVEL ADVENTURES–Student Hosteling Program–Amsterdam to Paris

▶ Touring

BICYCLE TRAVEL ADVENTURES–Student Hosteling Program–A Thousand Miles: Massachusetts to Nova Scotia
BICYCLE TRAVEL ADVENTURES–Student Hosteling Program–Canadian Rockies to California
BICYCLE TRAVEL ADVENTURES–Student Hosteling Program–Cape Cod, MA
BICYCLE TRAVEL ADVENTURES–Student Hosteling Program–Cross-Country America
BICYCLE TRAVEL ADVENTURES–Student Hosteling Program–France and Italy
BICYCLE TRAVEL ADVENTURES–Student Hosteling Program–Ireland and England
BICYCLE TRAVEL ADVENTURES–Student Hosteling Program–Maine Coast, ME
BICYCLE TRAVEL ADVENTURES–Student Hosteling Program–Maine-Nova Scotia Coast Loop
BICYCLE TRAVEL ADVENTURES–Student Hosteling Program–Niagara Falls to Montreal
BICYCLE TRAVEL ADVENTURES–Student Hosteling Program–Pacific Coast Adventure: Washington, Oregon, and California
BICYCLE TRAVEL ADVENTURES–Student Hosteling Program–Province du Québec, Canada
BICYCLE TRAVEL ADVENTURES–Student Hosteling Program–Province du Québec (short program), Canada
BICYCLE TRAVEL ADVENTURES–Student Hosteling Program–Spain and France
BICYCLE TRAVEL ADVENTURES–Student Hosteling Program–Vermont
BICYCLE TRAVEL ADVENTURES–Student Hosteling Program–Vermont to the Atlantic Ocean
Blyth Education–Summer Study in Costa Rica, Costa Rica
Blyth Education–Summer Study in Cozumel, Mexico
Blyth Education–Summer Study in London and Oxford University, United Kingdom
Blyth Education–Summer Study in Paris and the South of France, France
Blyth Education–Summer Study in Rome and Siena, Italy
Brighton in Cannes, France
Brighton in Costa Rica, Costa Rica
Brighton in Paris, France
Brighton in Tuscany, Italy
California Cruzin' Overnight Camp, CA
Camp Exploration Travel Day Camp, CA
Canadian College Italy/The Renaissance School Summer Academy, Italy
China Summer Learning Adventures, China
Choate Rosemary Hall Summer in China, China
Discovery Works New England Community Service Experience
Enforex Study Tour Vacational Program–Madrid, Spain
The Experiment in International Living–Brazil–Ecological Preservation, Brazil
The Experiment in International Living–Chile North Homestay, Community Service, Chile
The Experiment in International Living–Chile South Homestay, Chile
The Experiment in International Living–China North and East Homestay, China
The Experiment in International Living–China South and West Homestay, China
The Experiment in International Living–France, Four-Week Brittany Discovery, France
The Experiment in International Living–France, Four–Week Homestay and Travel through Alps, France
The Experiment in International Living–France, Three-Week Homestay and Travel–Borders, France
The Experiment in International Living–Ghana Homestay, Ghana
The Experiment in International Living–Italy Homestay, Italy
The Experiment in International Living–Mexico, Community Service, Travel, and Homestay, Mexico
The Experiment in International Living–Mexico Homestay and Travel, Mexico
The Experiment in International Living–Spain, Five-Week Language Training, Travel, and Homestay, Spain
The Experiment in International Living–Spain–Spanish Culture and Folklore, Spain
The Experiment in International Living–The United Kingdom Celtic Odyssey, United Kingdom
The Experiment in International Living–Turkey Homestay, Community Service, and Travel, Turkey
The Experiment in International Living–United Kingdom Filmmaking Program and Homestay, United Kingdom
The Experiment in International Living–United Kingdom Theatre Program, United Kingdom
The Fessenden School Summer ESL Program, MA
Fort Union Civil War Camp, MN
GLS Bavarian Summer School, Germany
GLS Berlin Summer School, Germany
GLS Potsdam Summer School, Germany
Great Escapes (Adventure Trips for Teens)–Cape Escapes, MA
Greek Summer, Greece
JCC Houston: Teen Trek, TX
Julian Krinsky California Teen Tours, CA
Julian Krinsky Yesh Shabbat California Teen Tour, CA
Kayak Adventures Unlimited
LIFEWORKS with the Australian Red Cross, Australia
LIFEWORKS with the DPF Foundation in Thailand, Thailand
Linden Hill Summer Program, MA
The Loomis Chaffee Summer in France, France
The Loomis Chaffee Summer in Spain, Spain
Musiker Tours: Action Europe
Musiker Tours: Action USA
Musiker Tours: Alaska Aloha
Musiker Tours: America Coast to Coast
Musiker Tours: Cali-Pacific Passport
Musiker Tours: ComboCamp America
Musiker Tours: Discover America
Musiker Tours: Eastcoaster
Musiker Tours: Westcoaster
OES–Summer Adventure Camp, OR
Overland: American Challenge Coast-to-Coast Bicycle Touring
Overland: Cape Cod and the Islands Bicycle Touring, MA
Overland: European Challenge Bicycle Touring from Paris to Rome
Overland: Pacific Coast Bicycle Touring and Rafting
Overland: Vermont & Montreal Bicycle Touring
The Oxford Experience, United Kingdom
PAX Abroad to Australia, Australia
Poulter Colorado Camps: Adventures Planet Earth–Austria
Poulter Colorado Camps: Adventures Planet Earth–Costa Rica, Costa Rica
Poulter Colorado Camps: Adventures Planet Earth–New Zealand, New Zealand
Poulter Colorado Camps: Adventures Planet Earth–Spain, Spain
Rassias Programs–Arles, France, France
Rassias Programs–Gijón, Spain, Spain
Rassias Programs–Pontevedra, Spain, Spain
Rassias Programs–Segovia, Spain, Spain
Rassias Programs–Tours, France, France
Rein Teen Tours–American Adventure
Rein Teen Tours–California Caper
Rein Teen Tours–Crossroads
Rein Teen Tours–Eastern Adventure
Rein Teen Tours–Grand Adventure
Rein Teen Tours–Hawaiian/Alaskan Adventure
Rein Teen Tours–Western Adventure
RUSTIC PATHWAYS–ADVENTURE IN AMERICA'S SOUTHWEST
RUSTIC PATHWAYS–AWESOME AUSSIE EXPLORER, Australia
RUSTIC PATHWAYS–BIG FIJI EXPLORER, Fiji
RUSTIC PATHWAYS–BUDDHIST LIFE & ANGKOR WAT
RUSTIC PATHWAYS–COSTA RICA ADVENTURER, Costa Rica
RUSTIC PATHWAYS–COSTA RICA EXTREME, Costa Rica
RUSTIC PATHWAYS–ELEPHANTS & AMAZING THAILAND, Thailand
RUSTIC PATHWAYS–EXTREME PLANET
RUSTIC PATHWAYS–HAWAIIAN ISLANDS ADVENTURE, HI
RUSTIC PATHWAYS–HIGH ADRENALINE AUSSIE, Australia
RUSTIC PATHWAYS–OUTBACK 4-WHEEL DRIVE SAFARI, Australia
RUSTIC PATHWAYS–PHOTOGRAPHY & ADVENTURE IN THAILAND, Thailand
RUSTIC PATHWAYS–SNAPSHOT OF FIJI, Fiji
RUSTIC PATHWAYS–THE AMAZING THAILAND ADVENTURE, Thailand
RUSTIC PATHWAYS–THE SUNSHINE COAST & SYDNEY, Australia
RUSTIC PATHWAYS–THE WONDERS & RICHES OF THAILAND, Thailand
RUSTIC PATHWAYS–TOTALLY DOWNUNDER ADVENTURE, Australia
RUSTIC PATHWAYS–TROPICAL AUSSIE ADVENTURE, Australia
RUSTIC PATHWAYS–ULTIMATE AUSTRALIAN ADVENTURE, Australia
Sidwell Friends Service Expedition to Hawaii, HI
Sidwell Friends Summer Program: Costa Rica, Costa Rica

Study Tour Vacational Program Enforex–Barcelona, Spain
Summit Travel Program
TASIS Summer Program for Languages, Arts, and Outdoor Pursuits, Switzerland
Teen Tours of America–Alaskan Expedition
Teen Tours of America–Aloha Hawaii
Teen Tours of America–Golf Camp–Florida Swing, FL
Teen Tours of America–New England Journey
Teen Tours of America–Western Adventure
Teen Tours of America–Western Sprint
Teen Tour USA and Canada
Tibetan Summer Passage
UCAELI Summer Camp, CT
Ventures Travel Service–Arizona, AZ
Ventures Travel Service–California, CA
Ventures Travel Service–Florida, FL
Ventures Travel Service–Iowa, IA
Ventures Travel Service–Kentucky, KY
Ventures Travel Service–Minnesota, MN
Ventures Travel Service–Missouri, MO
Ventures Travel Service–New York, NY
Ventures Travel Service–North Dakota, ND
Ventures Travel Service–Oregon, OR
Ventures Travel Service–South Carolina, SC
Ventures Travel Service–South Dakota, SD
Ventures Travel Service–Tennessee, TN
Ventures Travel Service–Texas, TX
Ventures Travel Service–Washington, WA
Ventures Travel Service–Wisconsin, WI
Weissman Teen Tours–"Aloha–Welcome to Hawaiian Paradise"
Weissman Teen Tours–European Experience
Weissman Teen Tours–U.S. and Western Canada, 4 Weeks
Weissman Teen Tours–U.S. and Western Canada, 6 Weeks
Westcoast Connection–American Voyageur
Westcoast Connection–Australian Outback Plus Hawaii
Westcoast Connection–Californian Extravaganza
Westcoast Connection–Hawaiian Spirit
Westcoast Connection Travel–California and the Canyons
Westcoast Connection Travel–Eastcoast Encounter
Westcoast Connection Travel–European Discovery
Westcoast Connection Travel–European Escape
Westcoast Connection Travel–Northwestern Odyssey
Westcoast Connection Travel/On Tour–European Experience
Westcoast Connection–U.S. Explorer
Youth for Understanding USA–Australia, Australia
Youth for Understanding USA–China, China
Youth for Understanding USA–Kenya, Kenya

Track and Field

Shippensburg University Sports Camps–Jumps, PA
Shippensburg University Sports Camps–Throws Camp, PA
Shippensburg University Sports Camps–Track & Field, PA
University of Kansas–Jayhawk Track and Field/Cross Country Camps, KS

Trail Maintenance

Appalachian Mountain Club–Teen Crews–Alpine Trail, Berkshires, MA
Appalachian Mountain Club–Teen Crews–Mount Greylock, MA
Appalachian Mountain Club–Teen Crews–Pinkham Notch, NH
Appalachian Mountain Club–Teen Crews–Spike, NH
Appalachian Mountain Club–Teen Crews–Two-week Teen Spike, NH
Appalachian Mountain Club–Teen Stewardship Training, NH
Appalachian Mountain Club–Trail Crew–Berkshires, MA
Appalachian Mountain Club–Trail Crew–Mount Everett/Alpine Trail, MA
Appalachian Mountain Club–Trail Crew–White Mountains, NH
Appalachian Mountain Club–Volunteer Trail Crew–Alpine/Mount Washington, NH
Appalachian Mountain Club–Volunteer Trail Crew–Crawford Notch, NH
Appalachian Mountain Club–Volunteer Trail Crew–Grafton Loop, ME
Appalachian Mountain Club–Volunteer Trail Crew–Hut Crew, NH
Appalachian Mountain Club–Volunteer Trail Crew–Mount Greylock, MA
Appalachian Mountain Club–Wild New Hampshire Trail Crew, NH
Appalachian Mountain Club–Women's Trail Crew, NH
Landmark Volunteers: California, CA
Landmark Volunteers: Connecticut, CT
Landmark Volunteers: Idaho, ID
Landmark Volunteers: Michigan, MI
Landmark Volunteers: Vermont, VT
Landmark Volunteers: Virginia, VA
Landmark Volunteers: Washington, WA
Landmark Volunteers: Wyoming, WY
Student Conservation Association–Conservation Crew Program (Alabama), AL
Student Conservation Association–Conservation Crew Program (Alaska), AK
Student Conservation Association–Conservation Crew Program (Arizona), AZ
Student Conservation Association–Conservation Crew Program (Arkansas), AR
Student Conservation Association–Conservation Crew Program (California), CA
Student Conservation Association–Conservation Crew Program (Colorado), CO
Student Conservation Association–Conservation Crew Program (Connecticut), CT
Student Conservation Association–Conservation Crew Program (Delaware), DE
Student Conservation Association–Conservation Crew Program (Florida), FL
Student Conservation Association–Conservation Crew Program (Georgia), GA
Student Conservation Association–Conservation Crew Program (Hawaii), HI
Student Conservation Association–Conservation Crew Program (Idaho), ID
Student Conservation Association–Conservation Crew Program (Illinois), IL
Student Conservation Association–Conservation Crew Program (Indiana), IN
Student Conservation Association–Conservation Crew Program (Iowa), IA
Student Conservation Association–Conservation Crew Program (Kansas), KS
Student Conservation Association–Conservation Crew Program (Louisiana), LA
Student Conservation Association–Conservation Crew Program (Maine), ME
Student Conservation Association–Conservation Crew Program (Maryland), MD
Student Conservation Association–Conservation Crew Program (Massachusetts), MA
Student Conservation Association–Conservation Crew Program (Michigan), MI
Student Conservation Association–Conservation Crew Program (Minnesota), MN
Student Conservation Association–Conservation Crew Program (Mississippi), MS
Student Conservation Association–Conservation Crew Program (Missouri), MO
Student Conservation Association–Conservation Crew Program (Montana), MT
Student Conservation Association–Conservation Crew Program (Nebraska), NE
Student Conservation Association–Conservation Crew Program (Nevada), NV
Student Conservation Association–Conservation Crew Program (New Hampshire), NH
Student Conservation Association–Conservation Crew Program (New Jersey), NJ
Student Conservation Association–Conservation Crew Program (New Mexico), NM
Student Conservation Association–Conservation Crew Program (New York), NY
Student Conservation Association–Conservation Crew Program (North Carolina), NC
Student Conservation Association–Conservation Crew Program (North Dakota), ND
Student Conservation Association–Conservation Crew Program (Ohio), OH
Student Conservation Association–Conservation Crew Program (Oklahoma), OK
Student Conservation Association–Conservation Crew Program (Oregon), OR
Student Conservation Association–Conservation Crew Program (Pennsylvania), PA
Student Conservation Association–Conservation Crew Program (Rhode Island), RI
Student Conservation Association–Conservation Crew Program (South Carolina), SC

▶ Trail Maintenance

Student Conservation Association–Conservation Crew Program (South Dakota), SD
Student Conservation Association–Conservation Crew Program (Tennessee), TN
Student Conservation Association–Conservation Crew Program (Texas), TX
Student Conservation Association–Conservation Crew Program (Utah), UT
Student Conservation Association–Conservation Crew Program (Vermont), VT
Student Conservation Association–Conservation Crew Program (Virginia), VA
Student Conservation Association–Conservation Crew Program (Washington), WA
Student Conservation Association–Conservation Crew Program (West Virginia), WV
Student Conservation Association–Conservation Crew Program (Wisconsin), WI
Student Conservation Association–Conservation Crew Program (Wyoming), WY
Summer Conservation Corps
Teens-n-Trails, OR
World Horizons International–Kanab, Utah, UT
Youth Forest Camps, OR

Tutoring

Newgrange Summer Tutoring Program, NJ

Veterinary Science

Adventures in Veterinary Medicine, MA
Summer Vet, CO
Tuskegee University Vet Step I, AL
Tuskegee University Vet Step II, AL

Visual Arts

The Arts! at Maryland, MD
Arts on the Lake, TX
Atelier des Arts, Switzerland
Blue Lake Fine Arts Camp, MI
Buck's Rock Performing and Creative Arts Camp, CT
Camp Hawthorne Creative Arts Camp, ME
Choate Rosemary Hall Summer Arts Conservatory–Visual Arts Program, CT
Cleveland Institute of Art Pre-College Program, OH
French Woods Festival of the Performing Arts, NY
Maine College of Art Early College Program, ME
Med-O-Lark Camp, ME
The Putney School Summer Arts Program, VT
Snow Farm: The New England Craft Program, MA
Spoleto Study Abroad, Italy
Summer Academy for the Visual and Performing Arts, NJ
University of Wisconsin–Green Bay Summer Art Studio, WI
Vermont Arts Visual Arts Institute, VT
Visual Arts Institute for High School Students, NY
Washington University in St. Louis, School of Art–Portfolio Plus, MO
Young Musicians & Artists, OR

Volleyball

Big Island Volleyball Elite Camp, HI
Big Island Volleyball Player Camp, HI
Camp Greenkill–Volleyball, NY
Flint Hill School–"Summer on the Hill"–Sports on the Hill for Girls, VA
Jumonville Spirit and Sport Spectacular–Volleyball Camp, PA
NBC Camps–Volleyball–Alaska, AK
NBC Camps–Volleyball–California, CA
NBC Camps–Volleyball–Oregon, OR
NBC Camps–Volleyball Speed Explosion–California, CA
NBC Camps–Volleyball Speed Explosion–Spokane, WA, WA
Padua Franciscan High School Sports Camps, OH
Shippensburg University Sports Camps–Volleyball–Girls Camp, PA
University of Kansas–Jayhawk Volleyball Camp, KS
University of San Diego Sports Camps–Girls Volleyball Camp, CA

Wakeboarding

High Cascade Snowboard Camp, OR
Vans Skateboard Camp, OR
Watersports Extravaganza at Pali Overnight Adventures, CA

Water Polo

University of San Diego Sports Camps–Coed Water Polo Camp, CA

Waterskiing

ACTIONQUEST: Rescue Diving Voyages, British Virgin Islands
!ADVENTURES–AFLOAT: Scuba and Sailing Discovery Voyages–Caribbean Islands
Camp Echo, MI
Camp Stanislaus, MS
Culver Summer Camps/Culver Specialty Camp–Water Ski, IN
Greenwoods Camp for Boys, MI
Lake of the Woods Camp for Girls, MI
River Way Ranch Camp, CA

Web Page Design

Computer Camp by Education Unlimited–Stanford, CA
Computer Camp by Education Unlimited–UC Berkeley, CA
Computer Camp by Education Unlimited–UCLA, CA
Global Teen–German Plus Web Design, Video/Theatre in Berlin, Germany
IEI–Digital Media Plus Programme, United Kingdom
Montgomery College WDCE–Web Design Camp for Girls and Boys, MD
National Computer Camps at Fairfield University, CT
National Computer Camps at La Roche College, PA
National Computer Camps at Notre Dame College, OH
National Computer Camps at Oglethorpe University, GA
National Computer Camps at San Francisco State University, CA
University of Wisconsin–Green Bay Computer Camp, WI
Village Camps–England, United Kingdom

Weight Reduction

Alpengirl–Montana Fitness, MT
Camp Kingsmont, MA
Camp La Jolla, CA
Shane (Trim-Down) Camp, NY

Whale Watching

The Whale Camp–Youth Programs, Canada

White-Water Trips

AAVE–Costa Rica, Costa Rica
Adventures Cross-Country, Thailand Adventure, Thailand
Adventure Treks–California Challenge Adventures
Adventure Treks–California 19 Adventures, CA
Adventure Treks–Canadian Rockies Adventures, Canada
Adventure Treks–Montana Adventures, MT
Adventure Treks–Pacific Northwest Adventures, WA
Adventure Treks–Summit Fever
Adventure Treks–Ultimate Northwest Adventures
Anderson Camps' Wilderness Pioneer Camp, CO
BROADREACH Costa Rica Experience, Costa Rica
Camp Henry Offsite: Teen Challenge, MI
Cheerio Adventures–5 Rivers in 5 Days
Costa Rica Rainforest Outward Bound School–Multi-Element, Costa Rica
Costa Rica Rainforest Outward Bound School–Summer Semester, Costa Rica
Costa Rica Rainforest Outward Bound School–Tri-Country/Tri-Mester
Darrow Wilderness Trips–Maine, ME
Darrow Wilderness Trips–St. Croix, ME
Great Escapes (Adventure Trips for Teens)–Maine Waterways, ME
Great Escapes (Adventure Trips for Teens)–Rock and Rapids
Greenbrier River Outdoor Adventures, Adventure Camp, WV
Greenbrier River Outdoor Adventures, Rock and River, WV
Greenbrier River Outdoor Adventures, Wilderness Explorer, WV
Kayak Adventures Unlimited
Keewaydin Canoe Camp, Canada
Kroka Expeditions–Wild World of White Water, VT
Lifeschool Wilderness Adventures–Summer Adventures, CA
Longacre Expeditions, Volcanoes
Maine Wilderness Adventure Trip, ME
Mountain Adventure Guides: Summer Adventure Camp–Blue Ridge Expedition I, NC
Mountain Adventure Guides: Summer Adventure Camp–Blue Ridge Expedition II, NC
Mountain Adventure Guides: Summer Adventure Camp–Jr. Adventure Camp, NC
Mountain Workshop–Awesome 5: North Woods of Maine, ME
Mountain Workshop–Awesome 4: Pennsylvania, PA
NAWA Academy–Girls on the Go, CA
NAWA Academy–Great Challenge, CA

NAWA Academy–Lassen Expedition, CA
NAWA Academy–Trinity Challenge, CA
Outward Bound West–Backpacking and Whitewater Rafting, Oregon, OR
Outward Bound West–Cataract Canyon Rafting
Outward Bound West–Mountaineering and Rafting, Oregon, OR
Outward Bound West–Mountaineering, Rafting, and Climbing-XT, Oregon, OR
Overland: New England Explorer Hiking, Mountain Biking, and Rafting
Shaffer's High Sierra Camp, CA
Success Oriented Achievement Realized (SOAR)–North Carolina, NC
Success Oriented Achievement Realized (SOAR)–Wyoming, WY
Trailmark Outdoor Adventures–New England–Jr. Acadia
Trailmark Outdoor Adventures–New England–Mt. Desert
Trailmark Outdoor Adventures–New England–Rangeley Coed
Trailridge Mountain Camp
Voyageur Outward Bound–Greater Yellowstone Whitewater and Backpacking, MT
White Water Learning Center of Georgia Kids Kayaking Summer Day Camp, GA
Wilderness Ventures–Alaska Leadership, AK
Wilderness Ventures–Australia, Australia
Wilderness Ventures–California, CA
Wilderness Ventures–Colorado/Utah Mountain Bike
Wilderness Ventures–Costa Rica, Costa Rica
Wilderness Ventures–Ecuador and Galapagos, Ecuador
Wilderness Ventures–Great Divide
Wilderness Ventures–Great Divide Bike
Wilderness Ventures–High Sierra, CA
Wilderness Ventures–Oregon, OR
Wilderness Ventures–Pacific Coast Bike
Wilderness Ventures–Puget Sound, WA
Wilderness Ventures–Rocky Mountain
Wilderness Ventures–Spanish Pyrenees, Spain
Wilderness Ventures–Teton Adventure, WY
Wilderness Ventures–Washington Alpine, WA
Wilderness Ventures–Yellowstone Fly Fishing

Wilderness Camping

Alpengirl–Hawaii, HI
Alpengirl–Montana Art
Alpengirl–Scandinavia
Alpengirl–Washington Alpenguide Training, WA
Alpengirl–Washington Lil' Alpengirl, WA
Alton Jones Earth Camp, RI
American Youth Foundation–Camp Merrowvista, NH
American Youth Foundation–Camp Miniwanca, MI
Audubon Journeys, VT
Barton Adventure Camp
Blue Ridge School–Adventure Camps, VA
Camp Chewonki Adventure Camps, ME
Camp Chewonki for Girls, ME
Camp Chewonki Wilderness Expeditions, ME
Camp Chikopi for Boys, Canada
Camp Mishawaka for Boys, MN
Camp Mishawaka for Girls, MN
Camp Runoia, ME
Camp Wendigo, Canada
Darrow Wilderness Trips–Kayak, ME
Darrow Wilderness Trips–Maine, ME
Darrow Wilderness Trips–Quebec: Mistassini, Canada
Darrow Wilderness Trips–St. Croix, ME
Darrow Wilderness Trips–Voyageurs, ME
Darrow Youth Backpacking, ME
Deer Hill Expeditions, Arizona, AZ
Deer Hill Expeditions, Colorado, CO
Deer Hill Expeditions, Costa Rica, Costa Rica
Deer Hill Expeditions, New Mexico, NM
Deer Hill Expeditions, Utah, UT
Eagle Lake Camp–East, NC
Eagle Lake Wilderness Program, CO
Excalibur, Canada
Flying Moose Lodge, ME
French Immersion Kayak Expedition, Canada
Horizon Adventures Inc., CO
Hurricane Island Outward Bound–North Woods Maine Allagash and Appalachian Trail Canoeing and Backpacking, ME
Hurricane Island Outward Bound–North Woods Maine Canoeing and Backpacking, ME
Hurricane Island Outward Bound–North Woods Maine Expedition Canoeing, ME
Hurricane Island Outward Bound–Western Maine Woods Expedition Canoeing, ME
Keewaydin Canoe Camp, Canada
Keewaydin Temagami, Canada
Keystone Science Adventures, CO
Kroka Expeditions–Cape Cod Triple Surfing Bonanza, MA
Kroka Expeditions–Coastal Sea Kayaking, ME
Kroka Expeditions–Coming of Age for Young Women, VT
Kroka Expeditions–Expedition Pre-Columbus, VT
Kroka Expeditions–Introduction to Adventure Residential Camp, VT
Kroka Expeditions–Introduction to White Water, VT
Kroka Expeditions–Paddlers Journey Up North
Kroka Expeditions–Rock 'n Road, VT
Kroka Expeditions–Wild Arts and Canoe Adventure, VT
Kroka Expeditions–Wild World of White Water, VT
Langskib Wilderness Programs, Canada
Maine Wilderness Adventure Trip, ME
Next Level Camp, PA
North Country Camps—Camp Lincoln for Boys, NY
North Country Camps—Camp Whippoorwill for Girls, NY
Northern Lights, Canada
Northwaters Wilderness Programs, Canada
Outward Bound West–Colorado Rockies Lightweight Backpacking, CO
Outward Bound West–Mountaineering–Colorado, CO
Outward Bound West–Volcanoes Mountaineering–Oregon, OR
Overland: Alaskan Expedition Hiking, Sea-Kayaking, and Rafting, AK
Overland: Appalachian Trail Challenge Hiking
Overland: Teton Challenge Hiking, Climbing and Kayaking, WY
Poulter Colorado Camps, CO
RUSTIC PATHWAYS–COSTA RICA NATURAL WONDERS, Costa Rica
Sargent Center Adventure Camp, NH
Sea Kayak Expedition (English), Canada
Streamside Pathfinder Adventure Camp, PA
Student Conservation Association–Conservation Leadership Corps, Bay Area, CA
Talisman Open Boat Adventures (TOBA), NC
Talisman Summer Camp, NC
Talisman–Trek Hiking Program, NC
Teen Expeditions, RI
Teton Valley Ranch Camp–Boys Camp, WY
Teton Valley Ranch Camp–Girls Camp, WY
Timber-lee Wilderness Trips, WI
Where There Be Dragons: India Zanskar Trek, India
Wilderness Adventure at Eagle Landing, VA
Windsor Mountain: Bonjour Quebec, Canada
Windsor Mountain: California Community Service, CA
YMCA Camp Widjiwagan, MN
YMCA Wilderness Camp Menogyn, MN
Yosemite Backpacking Adventures, CA

Wilderness/Outdoors (General)

Alpengirl–Alaska, AK
Alpengirl–Montana, MT
Alpengirl–Montana Fitness, MT
Alpengirl–Montana Horse, MT
Alpengirl–Washington, WA
Anderson Camps' Colorado River Ranch for Boys/Hilltop Ranch for Girls, CO
Camp AK-O-MAK, Canada
Camp Pok-O-MacCready, NY
Camp Tawonga–Magical Mystery Tour, CA
Camp Togowoods, AK
Cascade Science School, OR
Cheerio Adventures–Appalachian Adventure, VA
Cheerio Adventures–Mountains to the Sea, VA
Cheerio Adventures–Seekers, VA
Cheerio Adventures–Standard, VA
Eagle's Nest Camp, NC
EDUCO Summer Adventure Programs, CO
EKOCAMP International, Canada
Elk Creek Ranch and Trek Program, WY
Farm and Wilderness Camps–Indian Brook, VT
Farm and Wilderness Camps–Saltash Mountain, VT
Farm and Wilderness Camps–Timberlake, VT
Hante School, NC
High Sierra Wilderness Camps, CA
Hulbert Voyageurs Youth Wilderness Trips
Hyde School Summer Challenge Program–Bath, ME, ME
Hyde School Summer Challenge Program–Woodstock, CT, CT
Ligonier Camp, PA
Mountain Workshop–Awesome 5: North Woods of Maine, ME
Next Level Camp, PA
North Carolina Outward Bound–Outer Banks, NC
North Carolina Outward Bound–Southern Appalachian Mountains, NC
Roaring Brook Camp for Boys, VT
Sidwell Friends Summer Program: Costa Rica, Costa Rica
Summer Study at The University of Colorado at Boulder, CO
Wilderness Ventures–Alaska Service, AK

Windsurfing

Cheerio Adventures–Ocean Odyssey, VA
French Immersion Summer Camp, Canada

▶ WINDSURFING

Great Escapes (Adventure Trips for Teens)–Cape Cod Sail Adventure, MA
Kroka Expeditions–Cape Cod Triple Surfing Bonanza, MA
Longacre Expeditions, Wind and Waves, OR

Work Camp Programs

Christikon, MT
Eagle Lake Camp Crew Program, CO
Landmark Volunteers: Arizona, AZ
Student Conservation Association–Conservation Crew Program (Alabama), AL
Student Conservation Association–Conservation Crew Program (Alaska), AK
Student Conservation Association–Conservation Crew Program (Arizona), AZ
Student Conservation Association–Conservation Crew Program (Arkansas), AR
Student Conservation Association–Conservation Crew Program (California), CA
Student Conservation Association–Conservation Crew Program (Colorado), CO
Student Conservation Association–Conservation Crew Program (Connecticut), CT
Student Conservation Association–Conservation Crew Program (Delaware), DE
Student Conservation Association–Conservation Crew Program (Florida), FL
Student Conservation Association–Conservation Crew Program (Georgia), GA
Student Conservation Association–Conservation Crew Program (Hawaii), HI
Student Conservation Association–Conservation Crew Program (Idaho), ID
Student Conservation Association–Conservation Crew Program (Illinois), IL
Student Conservation Association–Conservation Crew Program (Indiana), IN
Student Conservation Association–Conservation Crew Program (Iowa), IA
Student Conservation Association–Conservation Crew Program (Kansas), KS
Student Conservation Association–Conservation Crew Program (Kentucky), KY
Student Conservation Association–Conservation Crew Program (Louisiana), LA
Student Conservation Association–Conservation Crew Program (Maine), ME
Student Conservation Association–Conservation Crew Program (Maryland), MD
Student Conservation Association–Conservation Crew Program (Massachusetts), MA
Student Conservation Association–Conservation Crew Program (Michigan), MI
Student Conservation Association–Conservation Crew Program (Minnesota), MN
Student Conservation Association–Conservation Crew Program (Mississippi), MS
Student Conservation Association–Conservation Crew Program (Missouri), MO
Student Conservation Association–Conservation Crew Program (Montana), MT
Student Conservation Association–Conservation Crew Program (Nebraska), NE
Student Conservation Association–Conservation Crew Program (Nevada), NV
Student Conservation Association–Conservation Crew Program (New Hampshire), NH
Student Conservation Association–Conservation Crew Program (New Jersey), NJ
Student Conservation Association–Conservation Crew Program (New Mexico), NM
Student Conservation Association–Conservation Crew Program (New York), NY
Student Conservation Association–Conservation Crew Program (North Carolina), NC
Student Conservation Association–Conservation Crew Program (North Dakota), ND
Student Conservation Association–Conservation Crew Program (Ohio), OH
Student Conservation Association–Conservation Crew Program (Oklahoma), OK
Student Conservation Association–Conservation Crew Program (Oregon), OR
Student Conservation Association–Conservation Crew Program (Pennsylvania), PA
Student Conservation Association–Conservation Crew Program (Rhode Island), RI
Student Conservation Association–Conservation Crew Program (South Carolina), SC
Student Conservation Association–Conservation Crew Program (South Dakota), SD
Student Conservation Association–Conservation Crew Program (Tennessee), TN
Student Conservation Association–Conservation Crew Program (Texas), TX
Student Conservation Association–Conservation Crew Program (Utah), UT
Student Conservation Association–Conservation Crew Program (Vermont), VT
Student Conservation Association–Conservation Crew Program (Virginia), VA
Student Conservation Association–Conservation Crew Program (Washington), WA
Student Conservation Association–Conservation Crew Program (West Virginia), WV
Student Conservation Association–Conservation Crew Program (Wisconsin), WI
Student Conservation Association–Conservation Crew Program (Wyoming), WY
Student Conservation Association–Conservation Leadership Corps–Washington, DC Metropolitan Area, VA
Summer Conservation Corps
Teens-n-Trails, OR
Volunteers for Peace International Work Camp–Armenia, Armenia
Volunteers for Peace International Work Camp–Belarus, Belarus
Volunteers for Peace International Work Camp–Belgium, Belgium
Volunteers for Peace International Work Camp–Czech Republic, Czech Republic
Volunteers for Peace International Work Camp–Estonia, Estonia
Volunteers for Peace International Work Camp–France, France
Volunteers for Peace International Work Camp–Germany, Germany
Volunteers for Peace International Work Camp–Italy, Italy
Volunteers for Peace International Work Camp–Lithuania, Lithuania
Volunteers for Peace International Work Camp–Russia, Russian Federation
Volunteers for Peace International Work Camp–Slovakia, Slovakia
Volunteers for Peace International Work Camp–Turkey, Turkey
Youth Forest Camps, OR

Worship

Abilene Christian University–Cross Training, NM
Abilene Christian University–Kadesh Life Camp, TX
Abilene Christian University–Learning to Lead, TX
Abilene Christian University–MPulse, TX
Camp Good News for Young People and Teens, MA

Wrestling

Mercersburg All-American Wrestling Camp & Junior All-American Wrestling Camp, PA

Writing

Academic Camps at Gettysburg College–Writer's Workshops, PA
Alfred University Summer Institute in Writing, NY
Bridge to the Future, NJ
Brighton College Admissions Prep at Tufts University, MA
Brighton College Admissions Prep at UCLA, CA
Bryn Mawr College–Writing for College, PA
Camp Buckskin, MN
Carleton College Summer Writing Program, MN
Choate Rosemary Hall Beginning Writers Workshop, CT
Choate Rosemary Hall English Language Institute, CT
Choate Rosemary Hall English Language Institute/Focus Program, CT
Choate Rosemary Hall Writing Project, CT
Choate Rosemary Hall Young Writers Workshop, CT
College Admission Prep Camp by Education Unlimited–Boston, MA
College Admission Prep Camp by Education Unlimited–San Diego, CA

College Admission Prep Camp by Education Unlimited–Stanford University, CA
College Admission Prep Camp by Education Unlimited–UC Berkeley, CA
College Admission Prep Camp by Education Unlimited–UCLA, CA
College Admission Prep Camp Choice by Education Unlimited–Stanford, CA
Dickinson College Research and Writing Workshop, PA
Duke Young Writers Camp, NC
Dunnabeck at Kildonan, NY
Elite Educational Institute Elementary Enrichment, CA
Elite Educational Institute Elementary Enrichment–Korea, Republic of Korea
Elite Educational Institute Junior High/PSAT Program, CA
Elite Educational Institute Junior High/PSAT Program–Korea, Republic of Korea
Fir Acres Workshop in Writing and Thinking, OR
Flint Hill School–"Summer on the Hill"–Enrichment on the Hill–Junior Great Books, VA
Flint Hill School–"Summer on the Hill"–Enrichment on the Hill–Study Skills for 9th Graders, VA
Hollinsummer, VA
IEI–Print and Broadcast Journalism, United Kingdom
Ithaca College Summer College for High School Students: Session I, NY
Kenyon Review Young Writers, OH
Landmark School Summer Academic Program, MA
Miss Porter's School Arts Alive!, CT
Montgomery College WDCE–Summer Student Writing Institute, MD
Prep Camp Excel by Education Unlimited–UCLA, CA
Rhodes Summer Writing Institute, TN
Salisbury Summer School of Reading and English, CT
Simon's Rock College of Bard Young Writers Workshop, MA
Summer Programs on the River; Skills Program, VA
Tisch School of the Arts–Summer High School Programs, NY
Tufts Summer Study, MA

Yearbook Production

Josten Yearbook Summer Workshop, AL

AAC–Aloha Adventure Camps
AAC–Aloha Adventure Photo Camp
AAC–Aloha Adventure Surf Camp

AAVE–America's Adventure Ventures Everywhere
AAVE–Africa
AAVE–Alaska
AAVE–Alps Rider
AAVE–Australia
AAVE–Belize
AAVE–Bike France
AAVE–Bold Europe
AAVE–Bold West
AAVE–Boot/Saddle/Paddle
AAVE–Border Cross
AAVE–Costa Rica
AAVE–Ecuador and Galapagos
AAVE–Hawaii
AAVE–Inmersión en España
AAVE–Peru and Machu Picchu
AAVE–Rock & River
AAVE–Rocky Mountain Adventure
AAVE–Thailand
AAVE–Vietnam
AAVE–Vivons le Français
AAVE–Wild Isles
AAVE–X–Five

Abbey Road Overseas Programs
Abbey Road Overseas Programs–French Immersion and Homestay
Abbey Road Overseas Programs–French Study Abroad in Cannes
Abbey Road Overseas Programs–Italy Study Abroad: Language and Culture
Abbey Road Overseas Programs–Spanish Immersion and Homestay

Abilene Christian University
Abilene Christian University–Cross Training
Abilene Christian University–Kadesh Life Camp
Abilene Christian University–Learning to Lead
Abilene Christian University–MPulse
Abiliene Christian University–KidQuest Day Camp

Ability First
Ability First–Camp Joan Mier
Ability First–Camp Paivika

Academic Study Associates, Inc. (ASA)
Academic Study Associates–ASA at the University of California, Berkeley
Academic Study Associates–ASA at the University of Massachusetts Amherst
Academic Study Associates–Barcelona
Academic Study Associates–Florence
Academic Study Associates–Nice
Academic Study Associates–Pathways Program at Amherst College
Academic Study Associates–Royan
Academic Study Associates–Spanish in España
The Oxford Experience

The Academy by the Sea/Camp Pacific
Academy by the Sea
Camp Pacific's Recreational Camp
Camp Pacific's Surf and Bodyboard Camp

The Academy of Golf Dynamics
Parent/Youth Golf School

Acadia Institute of Oceanography

Acteen
Acteen August Academy
Acteen July Academy
Acteen June Academy
Acteen Summer Saturday Academy

ActionQuest
ACTIONQUEST: Advanced PADI Scuba Certification and Specialty Voyages
ACTIONQUEST: Australian and Great Barrier Reef Adventures
ACTIONQUEST: British Virgin Islands–Sailing and Scuba Voyages
ACTIONQUEST: British Virgin Islands-Sailing Voyages
ACTIONQUEST: Galapagos Archipelago Expeditions
ACTIONQUEST: Junior Advanced Scuba with Marine Biology
ACTIONQUEST: Leeward and French Caribbean Island Voyages
ACTIONQUEST: Mediterranean Sailing Voyage
ACTIONQUEST: Rescue Diving Voyages
ACTIONQUEST: Tahiti and French Polynesian Island Voyages
ACTIONQUEST: Tropical Marine Biology Voyages

Adirondack Camp

Adventure Ireland
Adventure Ireland–English Learning Option
Adventure Ireland–Irish Studies
Adventure Ireland–Surf Camp/Activity Camp

Adventure Links
Adventure Links
Adventure Links–Appalachian Odyssey
Adventure Links–North Carolina Expeditions
Adventure Links–The Costa Rica Experience
Adventure Links–Ultimate Adventure Camps

!Adventures–Afloat/Odyssey Expeditions
!ADVENTURES–AFLOAT: Advanced Scuba Adventure Voyages–British Virgin Islands
!ADVENTURES–AFLOAT: Advanced Scuba Adventure Voyages–Caribbean Islands
!ADVENTURES–AFLOAT: Scuba and Sailing Discovery Voyages–British Virgin Islands
!ADVENTURES–AFLOAT: Scuba and Sailing Discovery Voyages–Caribbean Islands
ODYSSEY EXPEDITIONS: Tropical Marine Biology Voyages–British Virgin Islands
ODYSSEY EXPEDITIONS: Tropical Marine Biology Voyages–Caribbean Islands

Adventures Cross-Country
Adventures Cross-Country, Alaska Adventure
Adventures Cross-Country, Australia/Fiji Adventure
Adventures Cross-Country, Caribbean Adventure
Adventures Cross-Country, Colorado Adventure
Adventures Cross-Country, Costa Rica Adventure
Adventures Cross-Country, Extreme British Columbia Adventure
Adventures Cross-Country, Hawaii Adventure
Adventures Cross-Country,Southern Europe Adventure
Adventures Cross-Country, Thailand Adventure
Adventures Cross-Country, Western Adventure

Adventure Treks, Inc.
Adventure Treks–Alaska Adventures
Adventure Treks–California Challenge Adventures
Adventure Treks–California 19 Adventures
Adventure Treks–Canadian Rockies Adventures
Adventure Treks–Montana Adventures
Adventure Treks–Pacific Northwest Adventures
Adventure Treks–PAC 16
Adventure Treks–Summit Fever
Adventure Treks–Ultimate Northwest Adventures

AFS-USA
AFS-USA–Community Service–Argentina
AFS-USA–Community Service–Bolivia
AFS-USA–Community Service–Costa Rica
AFS-USA–Community Service–Panama
AFS-USA–Community Service–Paraguay
AFS-USA–Community Service–Thailand
AFS-USA–Community Service–United Kingdom
AFS-USA–Homestay–Argentina
AFS-USA–Homestay–Chile
AFS-USA–Homestay–Ecuador
AFS-USA–Homestay–Finland
AFS-USA–Homestay–France
AFS-USA–Homestay Language Study–Canada
AFS-USA–Homestay Language Study–Costa Rica
AFS-USA–Homestay Language Study–Japan
AFS-USA–Homestay Language Study–Latvia
AFS-USA–Homestay, Outdoor Adventure Amazon–Brazil
AFS-USA–Homestay–Paraguay
AFS-USA–Homestay Plus–Australia
AFS-USA–Homestay Plus–Brazil
AFS-USA–Homestay Plus–Costa Rica
AFS-USA–Homestay Plus–Hungary
AFS-USA–Homestay Plus–Italy
AFS-USA–Homestay Plus–Netherlands
AFS-USA–Homestay Plus–New Zealand
AFS-USA–Homestay–Spain
AFS-USA–Homestay–Thailand
AFS-USA–Homestay–Turkey
AFS-USA–Team Mission–China
AFS-USA–Team Mission–Ghana
AFS-USA–Team Mission–Russia

Agassiz Village, Inc.
Agassiz Village

Albany Academy for Girls
Luna Adventures with AAG SummerSkills
SummerSkills at Albany Academy for Girls

Albion International Study Centre, Oxford
Oxford Advanced Seminars Programme

Alexander Muss High School in Israel

Alexander Smith Academy
Alexander-Smith Academy Summer School

Alford Lake Camp
Alford Lake Camp
Alford Lake Family Camp

Alfred University
Alfred University Summer Institute in Astronomy
Alfred University Summer Institute in Entrepreneurial Leadership
Alfred University Summer Institute in Writing

All Arts and Sciences Camp
All Arts and Sciences Camp–George Mason University
All Arts and Sciences Camp–North Carolina State University
All Arts and Sciences Camp–The College of William and Mary
All Arts and Sciences Camp–The University of North Carolina at Greensboro
All Arts and Sciences Camp–Virginia Tech

Almada Lodge-Times Farm Camp Corporation
Channel 3 Kids Camp

Aloha Foundation, Inc.
Aloha Camp
Camp Aloha Hive
Camp Lanakila
Hulbert Voyageurs Youth Wilderness Trips
Summer Horizons Day Camp

Alpengirl, Inc.
Alpengirl–Alaska
Alpengirl–Hawaii
Alpengirl–Montana
Alpengirl–Montana Art
Alpengirl–Montana Fitness
Alpengirl–Montana Horse
Alpengirl–Scandinavia
Alpengirl–Washington
Alpengirl–Washington Alpenguide Training
Alpengirl–Washington Lil' Alpengirl

Alpine Adventures, Inc.
Adirondack Alpine Adventures

Alpine Camp for Boys
Alpine Camp for Boys

The Altamont School
Summer at Altamont

American Academy of Dramatic Arts
American Academy of Dramatic Arts Summer Program at Hollywood, California
American Academy of Dramatic Arts Summer Program at New York

American Association of Teachers of German, Inc.
American Association of Teachers of German, German Summer Study Program

American Collegiate Adventures
American Collegiate Adventures–Italy
American Collegiate Adventures–Spain
American Collegiate Adventures–Wisconsin

American Cultural Exchange
A.C.E. Intercultural Institute
Junior Institute

American Farm School
Greek Summer

American Lung Association of Indiana
Camp Superkids–Camp Crosley
Camp Superkids–Happy Hollow Children's Camp

American Trails West
ATW: Action America West
ATW: Adventure Roads
ATW: American Horizons
ATW: California Sunset
ATW: Camp Inn 42
ATW: Discoverer
ATW: European Adventures
ATW: Fire and Ice
ATW: Mini Tours
ATW: Pacific Paradise
ATW: Skyblazer
ATW: Sunblazer
ATW: Wayfarer

American Youth Foundation
American Youth Foundation–Camp Merrowvista
American Youth Foundation–Camp Miniwanca
American Youth Foundation Leadership Conference

Anderson Western Colorado Camps, Ltd.
Anderson Camps' Colorado River Ranch for Boys/Hilltop Ranch for Girls
Anderson Camps' Wilderness Pioneer Camp

Apogee Outdoor Adventures
Apogee Outdoor Adventures–Burlington to Boston
Apogee Outdoor Adventures–Coast to Quebec
Apogee Outdoor Adventures–New England Mountains and Coast
Apogee Outdoor Adventures–Montana Service Adventure
Apogee Outdoor Adventures–Cape Cod and the Islands

Appalachian Mountain Club
Appalachian Mountain Club–Teen Crews–Alpine Trail, Berkshires
Appalachian Mountain Club–Teen Crews–Mount Greylock
Appalachian Mountain Club–Teen Crews–Pinkham Notch
Appalachian Mountain Club–Teen Crews–Spike
Appalachian Mountain Club–Teen Crews–Two-week Teen Spike
Appalachian Mountain Club–Teen Stewardship Training
Appalachian Mountain Club–Trail Crew–Berkshires
Appalachian Mountain Club–Trail Crew–Mount Everett/Alpine Trail
Appalachian Mountain Club–Trail Crew–White Mountains
Appalachian Mountain Club–Volunteer Trail Crew–Alpine/Mount Washington
Appalachian Mountain Club–Volunteer Trail Crew–Crawford Notch
Appalachian Mountain Club–Volunteer Trail Crew–Grafton Loop
Appalachian Mountain Club–Volunteer Trail Crew–Hut Crew
Appalachian Mountain Club–Volunteer Trail Crew–Mount Greylock
Appalachian Mountain Club–Wild New Hampshire Trail Crew
Appalachian Mountain Club–Women's Trail Crew

Appel Farm Arts and Music Center
Appel Farm Summer Arts Camp

Appleby College
Appleby College Summer Academy
Appleby College Summer Camps

Arrowsmith Academy
Arrowsmith Academy Arts and Academics

Art Center College of Design
Art Center College of Design Art Center for Kids
Saturday High at Art Center College of Design

The Art Institute of Boston at Lesley University
The Art Institute of Boston Pre-College Program

The Art Institute of Seattle
The Art Institute of Seattle–Studio 101

Asheville School
Asheville School Summer Academic Adventures

Atelier des Arts
Atelier des Arts

▶ Atlanta College of Art

Atlanta College of Art
Atlanta College of Art–Pre-College Program

Audubon Vermont
Audubon Journeys
Audubon Vermont Youth Camp
Program of Audubon Research for Teens (Take P.A.R.T.)

AuLangue Idiomas & Culturas
Cuernavaca Summer Program for Teens

Austin Nature and Science Center

Ball State University
Ball State University Summer Journalism Workshops

Barat Foundation
Barat Foundation Summer Program in Provence and Paris

Bark Lake Leadership Centre
Bark Lake Leadership Through Recreation Camp

Barnard College/Columbia University
Barnard's Summer in New York City: A Pre-College Program
Barnard's Summer in New York City: One-Week Mini-Course
Barnard's Summer in New York City: Young Women's Leadership Institute

Bar 717 Ranch/Camp Trinity
Bar 717 Ranch/Camp Trinity

The Barton Center for Diabetes Education, Inc.
Barton Adventure Camp
Barton Day Camp–Long Island
Barton Day Camp–New York
Barton Day Camp–Worcester
Clara Barton Camp
Clara Barton Family Camp
Rainbow Club–Greenwich, Connecticut

Baylor University
Baylor University High School Summer Science Research Program

Bayshore Discovery Project
Maritime Camp

The Bedford School
Squirrel Hollow Learning Camp

The Beekman School
Beekman School Summer Session

Belvoir Terrace

Berklee College of Music
Berklee Business of Music Program
Berklee College of Music Summer Performance Program
Berklee in L.A. Summer Performance Program
Berklee Music Production Workshop
Berklee Summer Basslines Program
Berklee Summer Brass Weekend
Berklee Summer Guitar Sessions
Berklee Summer Saxophone Weekend
Berklee Summer Songwriting Workshop
Berklee Summer String Fling
Berklee World Percussion Festival

BICYCLE TRAVEL ADVENTURES–Student Hosteling Program
BICYCLE TRAVEL ADVENTURES–Student Hosteling Program–Amsterdam to Paris
BICYCLE TRAVEL ADVENTURES–Student Hosteling Program–A Thousand Miles: Massachusetts to Nova Scotia
BICYCLE TRAVEL ADVENTURES–Student Hosteling Program–Canadian Rockies to California
BICYCLE TRAVEL ADVENTURES–Student Hosteling Program–Cape Cod
BICYCLE TRAVEL ADVENTURES–Student Hosteling Program–Cross-Country America
BICYCLE TRAVEL ADVENTURES–Student Hosteling Program–France and Italy
BICYCLE TRAVEL ADVENTURES–Student Hosteling Program–Ireland and England
BICYCLE TRAVEL ADVENTURES–Student Hosteling Program–Maine Coast
BICYCLE TRAVEL ADVENTURES–Student Hosteling Program–Maine-Nova Scotia Coast Loop
BICYCLE TRAVEL ADVENTURES–Student Hosteling Program–Niagara Falls to Montreal
BICYCLE TRAVEL ADVENTURES–Student Hosteling Program–Off-Road Vermont
BICYCLE TRAVEL ADVENTURES–Student Hosteling Program–Pacific Coast Adventure: Washington, Oregon, and California
BICYCLE TRAVEL ADVENTURES–Student Hosteling Program–Province du Québec
BICYCLE TRAVEL ADVENTURES–Student Hosteling Program–Province du Québec (short program)
BICYCLE TRAVEL ADVENTURES–Student Hosteling Program–Spain and France
BICYCLE TRAVEL ADVENTURES–Student Hosteling Program–Vermont
BICYCLE TRAVEL ADVENTURES–Student Hosteling Program–Vermont to the Atlantic Ocean

Birch Trail Camp for Girls

Birmingham-Southern College
Birmingham-Southern College Student Leaders in Service Program
Birmingham-Southern College Summer Scholar Program

Bishop's College School
Bishop's College School Summer School

Black River Farm and Ranch

Blue Lake Fine Arts Camp, Inc.
Blue Lake Fine Arts Camp
Blue Lake International Exchange Program
Suzuki Family Camp

The Blue Ridge School
Blue Ridge School–Adventure Camps
Blue Ridge School–Rock Climbing Camp

Blue Star Camps

Blyth Education
Blyth Education–Summer Study in Costa Rica
Blyth Education–Summer Study in Cozumel
Blyth Education–Summer Study in London and Oxford University
Blyth Education–Summer Study in Paris and the South of France
Blyth Education–Summer Study in Rome and Siena
Blyth Education–Summer Study in the Amazon and the Galapagos Islands

Boise State University, College of Engineering
Idaho Engineering Science Camp

Boston Architectural Center
Center Summer Academy

The Boston Conservatory
Summer Dance '05

Boston University Institute for Television, Film, and Radio Production

Boston University Promys Program

Boston University Summer Term
Boston University High School Honors Program
Boston University Summer Challenge Program
Research Internship in Science and Engineering

Boston University Summer Theatre Institute

Boston University Tanglewood Institute

Brant Lake Camp
Brant Lake Camp's Dance Centre

Bravo Spain International Student Exchange
Bravo Spain–Barcelona

Breezy Point
Breezy Point Day Camp

Brevard Music Center
Brevard Music Center

Brewster Academy
Brewster Academy Summer Session

Brighton
Brighton College Admissions Prep at Tufts University
Brighton College Admissions Prep at UCLA
Brighton in Cannes
Brighton in Costa Rica
Brighton in Paris
Brighton in Tuscany

Bristol Hills Music Camp, Inc.
Bristol Hills Music Camp

Britannia Soccer Camp

British American Drama Academy (BADA)
Midsummer in London

Broadreach
BROADREACH Academic Treks–Language Exposure and Service Learning
BROADREACH Academic Treks–Marine Mammal Studies
BROADREACH Academic Treks–Marine Park Management
BROADREACH Academic Treks–Sea Turtle Studies
BROADREACH Academic Treks–Spanish Immersion in Mexico
BROADREACH Academic Treks–Spanish Language Immersion in Ecuador
BROADREACH Academic Treks–Wilderness Emergency Medicine
BROADREACH Adventures Down Under
BROADREACH Adventures in Scuba and Sailing–Underwater Discoveries
BROADREACH Adventures in the Grenadines–Advanced Scuba
BROADREACH Adventures in the Windward Islands–Advanced Scuba
BROADREACH Adventures Underwater–Advanced Scuba
BROADREACH Amazon and Galapagos Encounter
BROADREACH Arc of the Caribbean Sailing Adventure
BROADREACH Baja Extreme–Scuba Adventure
BROADREACH Costa Rica Experience
BROADREACH Fiji Solomon Quest
BROADREACH Honduras Eco-Adventure
BROADREACH Marine Biology Accredited
BROADREACH Red Sea Scuba Adventure

Brown Ledge Camp

Brown University
Brown University Summer Programs–Pre-College Program

Bryn Mawr College
Bryn Mawr College–Writing for College

Buck's Rock, LLC
Buck's Rock Performing and Creative Arts Camp

Buckswood Summer Programs
Buckswood: English Language (ESL) and Activities–Bradfield, England
Buckswood: English Language (ESL) and Activities–Plumpton, England
Buckswood: English Language (ESL) and Activities–West Virginia

Burgundy Farm School
Burgundy Center for Wildlife Studies Summer Camp

Burklyn Ballet Theatre, Inc.
Burklyn Ballet Edinburgh Connection
Burklyn Ballet Theatre
Burklyn Ballet Theatre II, The Intermediate Program

Burns Recovered Support Group
Missouri Children's Burn Camp

Cage Scope/High Potential "Blue-Chip" Basketball Camp
Cage Scope/High Potential "Blue-Chip" Basketball Camp

California Campus Tours
California Campus Tours

California College of the Arts
California College of the Arts Pre-College Program

California Polytechnic State University, San Luis Obispo
Cal Poly State University Young Scholars–Find the College for You!
Cal Poly State University Young Scholars Prepare for the PSAT & SAT I

California State Summer School for the Arts/Inner Spark
California State Summer School for the Arts/Inner Spark

Cambridge College Programme
Cambridge College Programme

Camden Military Academy
Camden Military Academy Summer Session/Camp

Camp Airy and Camp Louise Foundation, Inc.
Camp Airy
Camp Louise

Camp AK-O-MAK
Camp AK-O-MAK

Camp Aldersgate
Camp Aldersgate–Kota Camp
Camp Aldersgate–Med Camps
Camp Aldersgate–Respite Care

Camp All-Star, Inc.
Camp All-Star

Camp Androscoggin

Camp Arcadia

Camp Arowhon, Ltd.
Camp Arowhon–Boys and Girls Camp
Camp Arowhon–Voyageur Canoe Trip Program

Camp Avoda, Inc.
Camp Avoda

Camp Ballibay for the Fine and Performing Arts

Camp Barney Medintz
Camp Barney Medintz

Camp Berachah Ministries Christian Camps and Conferences
Camp Berachah Ministries–Counselor-In-Training
Camp Berachah Ministries–Day Camp
Camp Berachah Ministries–Horse Day Camp
Camp Berachah Ministries–Junior Camp
Camp Berachah Ministries–Leadership Expedition Camp
Camp Berachah Ministries–Legend Teen Camp
Camp Berachah Ministries–Overnight Horse Camp
Camp Berachah Ministries–Primary Camp
Camp Berachah Ministries–Soccer Camp
Camp Berachah Ministries–Teen Leadership
Camp Berachah Ministries–Wrangler-In-Training

Camp Betsey Cox/Camp Sangamon for Boys, Inc.
Camp Betsey Cox
Camp Sangamon for Boys

Camp Billings

Camp Bon Coeur

Camp Buckskin

Camp Canadensis

Camp Carysbrook
Camp Carysbrook
Camp Carysbrook Equestrian

Camp Catherine Capers

Camp Cayuga

Camp Chateaugay

Camp Chatuga

Camp Chen-A-Wanda

Camp Chi/Jewish Community Center of Chicago
Camp Chi
Camp Chi Teenage Adventure Trips

Camp Chikopi
Camp Chikopi for Boys

Camp Chippewa Foundation
Camp Chippewa for Boys

Camp Courageous of Iowa

Camp Craig
Camp Craig Horse Residential Summer Camp
Camp Craig Sports and Recreation Summer Camp

Camp Curtain Call

Camp Dudley
Camp Dudley

Camp Echoing Hills

Camp Encore-Coda for a Great Summer of Music, Sports, and Friends

Camp Fire Council of Sowela
Camp Fire Camp Wi-Ta-Wentin

Camp Fire USA Eastern Massachusetts Council
Camp Nawaka

Camp Fire USA, Iowana Council
Camp Hitaga
Camp Hitaga–Stirrups and Saddles

Camp Fire USA North Oakland
Camp Oweki Summer Day Camp

Camp Fire USA Portland Metro Council
Camp Namanu

Camp Fire USA Southeast Texas Council, Inc.
Camp Niwana

Camp Friendship
Camp Friendship
Camp Friendship Challenge Program

Camp Ganadaoweh
Camp Ganadaoweh

Camp Glen Arden
Camp Glen Arden for Girls

Camp Glen Brook

Camp Greenbrier for Boys
Camp Greenbrier for Boys

Camp Greylock for Boys

Camp Hawthorne, Inc.
Camp Hawthorne
Camp Hawthorne Creative Arts Camp
New England Camping Adventures
Sailing Program at NE Camping Adventures

Camp Heartland
Camp Heartland Summer Camp–California
Camp Heartland Summer Camp–Minnesota

Camp Highlands for Boys

Camp High Rocks

Camp Hilltop

Camp Horizons
Camp Horizons Adventure
Camp Horizons Discover
Camp Horizons Explorer
Camp Horizons Pathfinder
Camp Horizons Specialty Camp

Camp Horseshoe
Camp Horseshoe

Camp Illahee for Girls

Camping and Education Foundation
Kooch-I-Ching

Camping and Retreat Ministries of Western Pennsylvania Conference of the United Methodist Church
Jumonville Adventure Camps
Jumonville Baseball/Softball Camp
Jumonville Basketball Camp
Jumonville Creative and Performing Arts Camps
Jumonville Discovery Camp
Jumonville Golf Camp
Jumonville Sampler Camps
Jumonville Soccer Camp
Jumonville Spirit and Sport Spectacular–Soccer Camp
Jumonville Spirit and Sport Spectacular–Swim Camp
Jumonville Spirit and Sport Spectacular–Tennis Camp
Jumonville Spirit and Sport Spectacular–Volleyball Camp
Jumonville Sports Camp
Jumonville Youth Mission Work Camp

Camp James Summer Day Camp

Camp JCA Shalom

Camp Kawanhee for Boys

Camp Kennybrook, Inc.
Camp Kennybrook

Camp Kingsmont
Camp Kingsmont

Camp Kiniya

Camp Kodiak

Camp La Jolla
Camp La Jolla

Camp La Junta
Camp La Junta

Camp Laney for Boys
Camp Laney for Boys

Camp Laurel

Camp Laurel South
Camp Laurel South

Camp Lee Mar

Camp Lincoln/Camp Lake Hubert
Camp Lincoln Fishing Camp
Camp Lincoln for Boys/Camp Lake Hubert for Girls
Camp Lincoln for Boys/Camp Lake Hubert for Girls Family Camp
Camp Lincoln for Boys/Camp Lake Hubert for Girls Golf Camp
Camp Lincoln for Boys/Camp Lake Hubert for Girls Tennis Camp

Camp Lindenmere

Camp Lohikan in the Pocono Mountains
Camp Lohikan in the Pocono Mountains
Mini-Camp in the Pocono Mountains

Camp Louemma, Inc.
Camp Louemma

Camp Maplehurst

Camp Maromac
Camp Maromac

Camp Matoaka for Girls

Camp Menominee

Camp Merrie-Woode

Camp Mi-A-Kon-Da

Camp Micah
Camp Micah

Camp Modin

Camp Monroe

Camp Mt. Luther

Camp Mowglis, School of the Open

Camp Nakanawa, Inc.
Camp Nakanawa

Camp Nashoba North

Camp Nock-A-Mixon

Camp Nominingue

Camp North Star for Boys

Camp Northway
Camp Northway
Camp Wendigo

Camp Nor'wester
Camp Nor'wester
Explore Nor'wester

Camp O-AT-KA, Inc.
Camp O-AT-KA

Camp O'Bannon
Camp O'Bannon

Camp Olympia
Camp Olympia
Camp Olympia Junior Golf Academy

Camp Ouareau
Camp Ouareau

Camp Pasquaney

Camp Pinehurst

Camp Pocono Ridge

Camp Pok-O-MacCready

Camp Ponacka

Camp Quinebarge

Camp Redwood

Camp Regis, Inc.
Applejack Teen Camp
Camp Regis

Camp Rim Rock
Camp Rim Rock–Arts Camp
Camp Rim Rock–General Camp
Camp Rim Rock–Horseback Riding Camp
Camp Rim Rock–Mini Camp
Camp Rim Rock–Tennis Camp

Camp Robin Hood for Boys and Girls

Camp Rockmont for Boys

Camp Roger
Camp Roger

Camp Runoia
Camp Runoia
Maine Wilderness Adventure Trip

Camp Saginaw

Camp Scatico, Inc
Camp Scatico

Camp Seagull
Camp Seagull for Girls

Camp Shohola
Camp Shohola

Camps Kahdalea for Girls and Chosatonga for Boys
Camp Chosatonga for Boys
Camp Kahdalea for Girls

Camp Skylemar

Camp Skyline
Camp Skyline
Camp Skyline–Equestrian Program

Camp Sky Ranch, Inc.

Camps Mondamin and Green Cove
Camp Green Cove
Camp Mondamin

Camp Stanislaus
Camp Stanislaus

Camp Starfish
Camp Starfish

Camp Susquehannock, Inc.
Camp Susquehannock for Boys
Camp Susquehannock for Girls

Camps with Meaning
Camps with Meaning–Advanced Horsemanship I & II
Camps with Meaning–Boys Camp
Camps with Meaning–Girls Camp
Camps with Meaning–Junior High/Junior Youth Camp
Camps with Meaning–PreJunior/Junior/Intermediate Camp
Camps with Meaning–Youth Camp

Camp Tall Timbers

Camp Tapawingo

Camp Tawonga (Tawonga Jewish Community Corp.)
Camp Tawonga–Call of the Wild
Camp Tawonga–Magical Mystery Tour
Camp Tawonga–Summer Camp
Camp Tawonga–Summertime Family Camp
Camp Tawonga–Surf 'n Turf Quest
Camp Tawonga–Teen Quest: Canada
Camp Tawonga–Teen Quest: High Sierra
Camp Tawonga–Teen Quest: Northwest
Camp Tawonga–Teen Quest: Southwest
Camp Tawonga–Teen Quest: Yosemite
Camp Tawonga–Teen Service Learning to Alaska

Camp Timanous

Camp Timber-lee
Timber-lee Science Camp
Timber-lee Creation Camp
Timber-lee Drama Camp
Timber-lee Horsemanship Camps
Timber-lee Wilderness Trips
Timber-lee Youth Camp

Camp Timberline–Kama'aina Kids, Inc.
Surf Quest

Camp Tioga
Camp Tioga

Camp Tohkomeupog

Camp Towanda
Camp Towanda

Camp Wah-Nee
Camp Wah-Nee

Camp Walden, LLC
Camp Walden

Camp Walt Whitman
Camp Walt Whitman

Camp Watitoh

Camp Watonka

Camp Wawenock

Camp Wayne
Camp Wayne for Boys
Camp Wayne for Girls

Camp Waziyatah

Camp Wekeela for Boys and Girls

Camp Westmont

Camp Wicosuta

Camp Wilvaken

Camp Winding Gap
Camp Winding Gap

Camp Wingate Kirkland

Camp Winnebago
Camp Winnebago

Camp WinShape/WinShape Foundation
Camp WinShape for Boys
Camp WinShape for Girls

Canadian College Italy
Canadian College Italy/The Renaissance School Summer Academy

Canonicus Camp and Conference Center
Camp Canonicus

Cape Cod Sea Camps, Inc.
Cape Cod Sea Camps–Monomoy/Wono

Capitol Region Education Council
Center for Creative Youth

Cardigan Mountain School
The Cardigan Mountain School Summer Session

Career Explorations, LLC
Career Explorations

Carleton College
Carleton College Summer Writing Program

Carmel Valley Tennis Camp

Carnegie Mellon University
Carnegie Mellon University Advanced Placement Early Admission
Carnegie Mellon University Pre-College Program in the Fine Arts
Summer Academy of Mathematics and Sciences

Carousel Day School

Carroll Center for the Blind
Carroll Center for the Blind–Computing for College: Computer and Communication Skills
Carroll Center for the Blind–Real World Work Experience
Carroll Center for the Blind–Youth in Transition

Carson-Newman College
Carson-Newman College–EXCEL Program

Case Western Reserve University and Howard Hughes Medical Institute
Summer Biotechnology Institute for High School and Middle School Teachers and Students

Castilleja School
Castilleja Summer Day Camp

Catalina Island Camps, Inc.
Catalina Island Camps

The Catholic University of America
Catholic University Benjamin T. Rome School of Music
Catholic University Capitol Classic Debate Institute
Catholic University College Courses for High School Students
Catholic University Communication and Media Studies Workshops
Catholic University Experiences in Architecture
Catholic University Eye on Engineering
Catholic University of America–Capitol Mock Trial Institute
Catholic University of America–the Capitol Hill Lincoln-Douglas Debate Group

Catholic Youth Camp
Catholic Youth Camp

Catholic Youth Organization
CYO Boys Camp
CYO Girls Camp

Cazadero Performing Arts Camp
Cazadero Family Camp
Cazadero Music Camp

Cedar Lodge

Celtic Learning and Travel Services
Celtic Learning and Travel Services–Edinburgh and Dublin
Celtic Learning and Travel Services–London and Dublin
Celtic Learning and Travel Services–Summer in Ireland

Centauri Summer Arts Camp
Centauri Summer Arts Camp

Center for American Archeology
Center for American Archeology/Archeology Field School
Center for American Archeology/Past Lifeways Program

Center for Cultural Interchange
Center for Cultural Interchange–Argentina Independent Homestay
Center for Cultural Interchange–Australia High School Abroad
Center for Cultural Interchange–Brazil High School Abroad
Center for Cultural Interchange–Chile Independent Homestay
Center for Cultural Interchange–France High School Abroad
Center for Cultural Interchange–France Independent Homestay
Center for Cultural Interchange–France Language School
Center for Cultural Interchange–Germany High School Abroad
Center for Cultural Interchange–Germany Independent Homestay
Center for Cultural Interchange–Germany Language School
Center for Cultural Interchange–Ireland High School Abroad
Center for Cultural Interchange–Ireland Independent Homestay Program
Center for Cultural Interchange–Italy Language School
Center for Cultural Interchange–Japan High School Abroad
Center for Cultural Interchange–Mexico High School Abroad
Center for Cultural Interchange–Mexico Language School
Center for Cultural Interchange–Netherlands High School Abroad
Center for Cultural Interchange–South Africa High School Abroad
Center for Cultural Interchange–Spain High School Abroad
Center for Cultural Interchange–Spain Independent Homestay
Center for Cultural Interchange–Spain Language School
Center for Cultural Interchange–Spain Sports and Language Camp
Center for Cultural Interchange–Switzerland Language Camp
Center for Cultural Interchange–United Kingdom Independent Homestay

Center for Science, Mathematics and Technology Education (CSMATE)
Bugs to Biospheres
Summer Vet

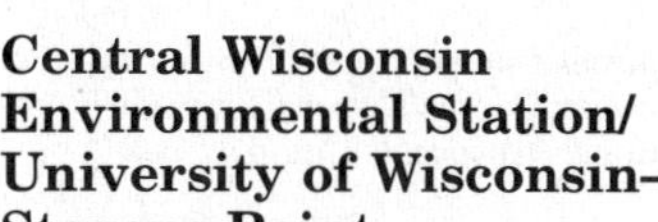

Central Wisconsin Environmental Station/ University of Wisconsin–Stevens Point
Central Wisconsin Environmental Station–Natural Resources Careers Camp
Central Wisconsin Environmental Station–Sunset Lake Adventures

Centre Nautique de L'Istorlet
French Immersion Kayak Expedition
French Immersion Summer Camp
Sea Kayak Expedition (English)

Cheley Colorado Camps

Cheshire Academy
Cheshire Academy Summer Program

Chewonki Foundation, Inc.
Camp Chewonki
Camp Chewonki Adventure Camps
Camp Chewonki Eco-Kayak Australia
Camp Chewonki for Girls
Camp Chewonki Wilderness Expeditions

The Children's Art Institute
The Children's Art Institute

Children's Creative and Performing Arts Academy of San Diego
Children's Creative and Performing Arts Academy Archaeology Adventure Camp
Children's Creative and Performing Arts Academy Summer Elementary Program
Children's Creative and Performing Arts Academy Summer Middle School Program
Children's Creative and Performing Arts Academy Summer Program for Preschool/ Prekindergarten
Children's Creative and Performing Arts Academy Summer Programs for High School Students

Choate Rosemary Hall
Choate Rosemary Hall Beginning Writers Workshop
Choate Rosemary Hall English Language Institute
Choate Rosemary Hall English Language Institute/Focus Program
Choate Rosemary Hall Focus Program
Choate Rosemary Hall Immersion Program
Choate Rosemary Hall John F. Kennedy Institute in Government
Choate Rosemary Hall Math/Science Institute for Girls–CONNECT
Choate Rosemary Hall Summer Arts Conservatory–Playwriting
Choate Rosemary Hall Summer Arts Conservatory–Theater
Choate Rosemary Hall Summer Arts Conservatory–Visual Arts Program
Choate Rosemary Hall Summer in China
Choate Rosemary Hall Summer in Paris
Choate Rosemary Hall Summer in Spain
Choate Rosemary Hall Summer Session
Choate Rosemary Hall Writing Project
Choate Rosemary Hall Young Writers Workshop

Chop Point Camp

Christchurch School
Summer Programs on the River; Crew/Rowing Camp
Summer Programs on the River; Marine Science Camp
Summer Programs on the River; Sailing Camp
Summer Programs on the River; Skills Program

Christian Camps and Conferences, Inc.
Camp Brookwoods and Deer Run
Moose River Outpost

Christian Camps, Inc.
Deerfoot Lodge

Christikon

Church In The Now
KidzZone Summer Camp

Circle Pines Center Summer Camp

City of Los Angeles Department of Recreation and Parks
Griffith Park Boys Camp

City of Toronto Parks and Recreation West District
New Strides Day Camp

CK Summer Camps, Inc.
Campus Kids–CT
Campus Kids–Minisink
Campus Kids–NJ

Clayworks Studio
ClayCamp

Clearwater Camp, Inc.
Clearwater Camp for Girls

Clemson University Department of Economics
Clemson University Economics Summer Camp

The Cleveland Institute of Art
Cleveland Institute of Art Portfolio Preparation/Young Artist Programs
Cleveland Institute of Art Pre-College Program
Cleveland Institute of Art Pre-College Program–Architecture
Cleveland Institute of Art Pre-College Program–Product and Auto Design
Cleveland Institute of Art Pre-College Program–Special Effects and Animation

Cloverleaf Ranch Summer Camp

Coleman Family Camps
Camp Echo in Coleman High Country
Coleman Country Day Camp

Colgate University
Eastern U.S. Music Camp, Inc.

College du Leman International School
Collège du Léman Summer School

College Impressions
College Impressions

College Settlement of Philadelphia

Colorado Academy
Colorado Academy Summer Programs

The Colorado Mountain Ranch

Columbia College Chicago
Columbia College Chicago's High School Summer Institute

Columbia College Leadership Institute
Emerging Leaders 2005
Lead 2005

Columbia International College of Canada
Learn English and Discover Canada

Columbia University Continuing Education
Columbia University Continuing Education–The Barcelona Experience
Columbia University Summer Program for High School Students

Colvig Silver Camps

The Community Center
The Community Center Going Places Camp

Community Sailing of Colorado, Ltd.
Community Sailing of Colorado–Advanced Sailing
Community Sailing of Colorado–Learn to Sail
Community Sailing of Colorado–Sailboat Racing Camp

Concordia College
Concordia Language Villages–Chinese
Concordia Language Villages–Danish
Concordia Language Villages–English
Concordia Language Villages–Finnish
Concordia Language Villages–France
Concordia Language Villages–French–Bemidji

Concordia Language Villages–French–Camp Holiday
Concordia Language Villages–French–Fosston
Concordia Language Villages–French–Savannah, GA
Concordia Language Villages–French Voyageur
Concordia Language Villages–German–Bemidji
Concordia Language Villages–German–Camp Trowbridge
Concordia Language Villages–Germany
Concordia Language Villages–Italian
Concordia Language Villages–Japan
Concordia Language Villages–Japanese
Concordia Language Villages–Korean
Concordia Language Villages–Norwegian
Concordia Language Villages–Russian
Concordia Language Villages–Spain
Concordia Language Villages–Spanish–Bemidji
Concordia Language Villages–Spanish–Maplelag
Concordia Language Villages–Spanish–Wilder Forest
Concordia Language Villages–Swedish

Congregation Emanuel
Shwayder Camp

Conservation Education Foundation of Maine
Maine Conservation School Summer Camps

Corcoran College of Art and Design
Corcoran College of Art and Design–Camp Creativity
Corcoran College of Art and Design–Focus on Photojournalism
Corcoran College of Art and Design–Pre-College Summer Portfolio Workshop

Cordova 4-H
Cordova 4-H Bluegrass and Old Time Music and Dance Camp
Cordova 4-H Hawaiian Camp

Cornell University
Cornell University Summer College Programs for High School Students

Costa Rica Rainforest Outward Bound School
Costa Rica Rainforest Outward Bound School–Multi-Element
Costa Rica Rainforest Outward Bound School–Summer Semester
Costa Rica Rainforest Outward Bound School–Surf Adventure
Costa Rica Rainforest Outward Bound School–Tri-Country/Tri-Mester

Cottey College
Music and Dance Summer Workshops
Sciencescape

Cottonwood Gulch Foundation
Cottonwood Gulch Family Trek
Cottonwood Gulch Mountain Desert Challenge
Cottonwood Gulch Outfit Expedition
Cottonwood Gulch Prairie Trek Expedition
Cottonwood Gulch Turquoise Trail Expedition
Cottonwood Gulch Wild Country Trek

The Country School Farm
The Country School Farm

Craftsbury Outdoor Center
Craftsbury Running Camps
Craftsbury Sculling Camps

Cragged Mountain Farm

Cross Keys
Cross Keys
Mini Minors
XUK

Crossroads for Kids
Camp Wing
Camp Wing Day Camp

Crossroads School for Arts and Sciences
Crossroads School–Aquatics
Crossroads School– Basketball Camps
Crossroads School–Jazz Workshop
Crossroads School–Soccer Camps
Crossroads School–Summer Educational Journey

Crow Canyon Archaeological Center
Crow Canyon Archaeological Center High School Excavation Program
Crow Canyon Archaeological Center High School Field School
Crow Canyon Archaeological Center Middle School Archaeology Program

Crystalaire Camp, Inc.
Camp Lookout
Crystalaire Camp

Culver Summer Camps
Culver Summer Camps/Culver Specialty Camp– Aviation
Culver Summer Camps/Culver Specialty Camp–Equestrian Arts
Culver Summer Camps/Culver Specialty Camp–Fencing
Culver Summer Camps/Culver Specialty Camp–Golf
Culver Summer Camps/Culver Specialty Camp–Ice Hockey
Culver Summer Camps/Culver Specialty Camp–Sailing
Culver Summer Camps/Culver Specialty Camp–Scuba
Culver Summer Camps/Culver Specialty Camp–Soccer
Culver Summer Camps/Culver Specialty Camp–Tennis
Culver Summer Camps/Culver Specialty Camp–Water Ski
Culver Summer Camps/Upper Camp–Boys
Culver Summer Camps/Upper Camp–Girls
Culver Summer Woodcraft Camp

Cushing Academy
Cushing Academy Summer Session

Cybercamps–Giant Campus, Inc.
Cybercamps–Adelphi University
Cybercamps–American University
Cybercamps–Amherst College
Cybercamps–Babson College
Cybercamps–Benedictine University
Cybercamps–Bentley College
Cybercamps–Bryn Mawr College
Cybercamps–College of St. Elizabeth
Cybercamps–Concordia University
Cybercamps–DeAnza College
Cybercamps–Duke University
Cybercamps–FDU Metropolitan Campus
Cybercamps–George Mason University
Cybercamps–Johns Hopkins University
Cybercamps–Lewis and Clark College
Cybercamps–Manhattanville College
Cybercamps–Merrimack College
Cybercamps–MIT
Cybercamps–Princeton University
Cybercamps–Rollins College
Cybercamps–Stanford University
Cybercamps–UCLA
Cybercamps–UC San Diego (UCSD)
Cybercamps–UNC, Chapel Hill
Cybercamps–University of California at Berkeley
Cybercamps–University of Hartford
Cybercamps–University of Maryland
Cybercamps–University of Michigan
Cybercamps–University of Minnesota
Cybercamps–University of Washington
Cybercamps–University of Washington, Bothell
Cybercamps–Washington University

Darlington School
Darlington School Summer Camps

Darrow Foundation
Darrow Wilderness Trips–Kayak
Darrow Wilderness Trips–Maine
Darrow Wilderness Trips–Quebec: Mistassini
Darrow Wilderness Trips–St. Croix
Darrow Wilderness Trips–Voyageurs
Darrow Youth Backpacking

Davidson Academy
Davidson Academy–Academy Arts
Davidson Academy–Bear Country Day Camp
Davidson Academy–Sports Camps

Davidson College
Davidson College July Experience

The Deep River Science Academy
Deep River Science Academy–Deep River Campus
Deep River Science Academy–Whiteshell Campus

Deer Hill Expeditions
Deer Hill Expeditions, Arizona
Deer Hill Expeditions, Colorado
Deer Hill Expeditions, Costa Rica
Deer Hill Expeditions, New Mexico
Deer Hill Expeditions, Utah

Deerkill Day Camp

The Delphian School
Delphi's Summer Session

Denver Academy
Denver Academy Summer Program

Dickinson College Summer Programs
Dickinson College Research and Writing Workshop
Dickinson College Spanish Language and Cultural Immersion Program
Dickinson College Young Writer's Workshop
Dickinson Summer College Program

DigiPen Institute of Technology
DigiPen Institute of Technology Junior Game Developer Workshop
DigiPen Institute of Technology Robotics Workshop
DigiPen Institute of Technology 3D Computer Animation Workshop
DigiPen Institute of Technology Video Game Programming Workshop

Don Quijote
Youth Program in Spain

Double "H" Hole in the Woods Ranch
Double "H" Hole in the Woods Ranch Summer Camp

Douglas Ranch Camps, Inc.
Douglas Ranch Camps

Drama Kids International–Houston Central
Drama Kids International Summer FUN Camp

Drew University
Lenny Armuth Soccer Academy

Drew University Music Department
Drew Summer Music

Ducks in a Row Foundation, Inc./Technology Encounters
Technology Encounters–Video Encounter/ Computer Encounter–California
Technology Encounters–Video Encounter/ Computer Encounter–Colorado
Technology Encounters–Video Encounter/ Computer Encounter–Florida
Technology Encounters–Video Encounter/ Computer Encounter–New York
Technology Encounters–Video Encounter/ Computer Encounter–Pennsylvania

Duke Youth Programs–Duke University Continuing Studies
Constructing Your College Experience
Duke Action: Science Camp for Young Women
Duke Creative Writers' Workshop
Duke Drama Workshop
Duke Young Writers Camp
EXPRESSIONS! Duke Fine Arts Camp

Dwight-Englewood School
Dwight-Englewood Summer Academic Session
Dwight-Englewood Summer Adventures
Dwight-Englewood Summer Sports Clinics
Dwight-Englewood Weekly Enrichment

Eaglebrook School
Eaglebrook Summer Semester

Eagle Hill School
Eagle Hill School Summer Session

Eagle's Nest Foundation
Eagle's Nest Camp
Hante School

Earlham College
Explore-A-College

Earthwatch Institute
EARTHWATCH INSTITUTE–Archaeology at West Point Foundry
EARTHWATCH INSTITUTE–Argentina's Pampas Carnivores
EARTHWATCH INSTITUTE–Bahamian Reef Survey
EARTHWATCH INSTITUTE–Baltic Island Wetlands and Wildlife
EARTHWATCH INSTITUTE–Biodiversity of the Grenadines
EARTHWATCH INSTITUTE–Bogs of Belarus
EARTHWATCH INSTITUTE–Brazil's Marine Wildlife
EARTHWATCH INSTITUTE–Butterflies and Orchids of Spain
EARTHWATCH INSTITUTE–Butterflies of Vietnam
EARTHWATCH INSTITUTE–Cacti and Orchids of the Yucatan
EARTHWATCH INSTITUTE–Canyonland Creek Ecology
EARTHWATCH INSTITUTE–Caring for Chimpanzees
EARTHWATCH INSTITUTE–Carnivores of Madagascar
EARTHWATCH INSTITUTE–Cheetah
EARTHWATCH INSTITUTE–Chilean Coastal Archaeology
EARTHWATCH INSTITUTE–China's Ancestral Temples
EARTHWATCH INSTITUTE–Climate Change at Arctic's Edge
EARTHWATCH INSTITUTE–Coastal Archaeology of Maine
EARTHWATCH INSTITUTE–Coastal Ecology of the Bahamas
EARTHWATCH INSTITUTE–Community Health in Cameroon
EARTHWATCH INSTITUTE–Conservation Research Initiative–Climate Change in the Rainforest
EARTHWATCH INSTITUTE–Conservation Research Initiative–Conserving the Pantanal
EARTHWATCH INSTITUTE–Conservation Research Initiative–Hawksbill Turtles of the Great Barrier Reef
EARTHWATCH INSTITUTE–Conservation Research Initiative–Mountain Meadows of the North Cascades
EARTHWATCH INSTITUTE–Conservation Research Initiative–Queensland Tropical Fish Ecology
EARTHWATCH INSTITUTE–Conservation Research Initiative–Restoring Wild Salmon
EARTHWATCH INSTITUTE–Conservation Research Initiative–Salmon Hotspots of the Skagit River
EARTHWATCH INSTITUTE–Conservation Research Initiative–Salmon of the Pacific Northwest
EARTHWATCH INSTITUTE–Conservation Research Initiative–Samburu: Communities and Water Resources
EARTHWATCH INSTITUTE–Conservation Research Initiative–Samburu: Communities and Wildlife Habitat
EARTHWATCH INSTITUTE–Conservation Research Initiative–Samburu: Zebras
EARTHWATCH INSTITUTE–Conservation Research Initiative–Traditions of Cedar, Salmon, and Gold
EARTHWATCH INSTITUTE–Coral Reefs of the Virgin Islands
EARTHWATCH INSTITUTE–Crocodiles of Cuba
EARTHWATCH INSTITUTE–Crocodiles of the Okavango
EARTHWATCH INSTITUTE–Desert Elephants of Namibia
EARTHWATCH INSTITUTE–Dolphins and Whales of Abaco Island
EARTHWATCH INSTITUTE–Dolphins of Brazil
EARTHWATCH INSTITUTE–Dolphins of Costa Rica
EARTHWATCH INSTITUTE–Early Man at Olduvai Gorge
EARTHWATCH INSTITUTE–Early Man in Spain
EARTHWATCH INSTITUTE–Echidnas and Goannas of Kangaroo Island
EARTHWATCH INSTITUTE–Ecuador Forest Birds
EARTHWATCH INSTITUTE–England's Hidden Kingdom
EARTHWATCH INSTITUTE–Europe–Africa Songbird Migrations–Hungary
EARTHWATCH INSTITUTE–Europe–Africa Songbird Migrations–Italy
EARTHWATCH INSTITUTE–Frontier Fort in Virginia
EARTHWATCH INSTITUTE–Guatemala's Ancient Maya
EARTHWATCH INSTITUTE–Hawksbill Turtles of Barbados
EARTHWATCH INSTITUTE–Health and Nutrition in Botswana
EARTHWATCH INSTITUTE–Hopi Ancestors
EARTHWATCH INSTITUTE–Icelandic and Alaskan Glaciers

▶ EARTHWATCH INSTITUTE

EARTHWATCH INSTITUTE–India's Sacred Groves
EARTHWATCH INSTITUTE–Inner Mongolia's Lost Water
EARTHWATCH INSTITUTE–Itjaritjari: the Outback's Mysterious Marsupial
EARTHWATCH INSTITUTE–Jackson Hole Bison Dig
EARTHWATCH INSTITUTE–Jamaica's Coral Reefs
EARTHWATCH INSTITUTE–Kenya's Black Rhino
EARTHWATCH INSTITUTE–Koala Ecology
EARTHWATCH INSTITUTE–Lakes of the Rift Valley
EARTHWATCH INSTITUTE–Lions of Tsavo
EARTHWATCH INSTITUTE–Maine's Island Ecology
EARTHWATCH INSTITUTE–Malaysian Bat Conservation
EARTHWATCH INSTITUTE–Mallorca's Copper Age
EARTHWATCH INSTITUTE–Mammoth Cave
EARTHWATCH INSTITUTE–Mammoth Graveyard
EARTHWATCH INSTITUTE–Manatees in Belize
EARTHWATCH INSTITUTE–Mangroves of the Kenyan Coast
EARTHWATCH INSTITUTE–Maternal and Child Healthcare in India
EARTHWATCH INSTITUTE–Medicinal Plants of Antiquity
EARTHWATCH INSTITUTE–Medicinal Plants of Vietnam
EARTHWATCH INSTITUTE–Meerkats of the Kalahari
EARTHWATCH INSTITUTE–Mexican Mangroves and Wildlife
EARTHWATCH INSTITUTE–Mexican Megafauna
EARTHWATCH INSTITUTE–Mojave Desert Tortoises
EARTHWATCH INSTITUTE–Mongolian Argali
EARTHWATCH INSTITUTE–Moose and Wolves
EARTHWATCH INSTITUTE–Moundbuilders on the Mississippi
EARTHWATCH INSTITUTE–Mountain Waters of Bohemia
EARTHWATCH INSTITUTE–Namibian Black Rhinos
EARTHWATCH INSTITUTE–Namibian Wildlife Survey
EARTHWATCH INSTITUTE–New Zealand Dolphins
EARTHWATCH INSTITUTE–Orca
EARTHWATCH INSTITUTE–Pine Marten of the Ancient Forest
EARTHWATCH INSTITUTE–Poland's Ancient Burials
EARTHWATCH INSTITUTE–Prehistoric Pueblos of the American Southwest
EARTHWATCH INSTITUTE–Puerto Rico's Rainforest
EARTHWATCH INSTITUTE–Rainforest Caterpillars–Costa Rica
EARTHWATCH INSTITUTE–Rare Plants of Kenya
EARTHWATCH INSTITUTE–Restoring Costa Rica's Rainforest
EARTHWATCH INSTITUTE–Restoring the Sagebrush Steppe
EARTHWATCH INSTITUTE–Restoring Vietnam's Forests
EARTHWATCH INSTITUTE–Rivers of the Peruvian Amazon
EARTHWATCH INSTITUTE–Roman Fort on the Danube
EARTHWATCH INSTITUTE–Roman Fort on Tyne
EARTHWATCH INSTITUTE–Saving the Leatherback Turtle
EARTHWATCH INSTITUTE–Sea Otters of Alaska
EARTHWATCH INSTITUTE–Sea Turtles of Baja
EARTHWATCH INSTITUTE–Singing Russia
EARTHWATCH INSTITUTE–South African Penguins
EARTHWATCH INSTITUTE–South African Wildlife
EARTHWATCH INSTITUTE–Spanish Dolphins
EARTHWATCH INSTITUTE–Sri Lanka's Temple Monkeys
EARTHWATCH INSTITUTE–Triassic Park
EARTHWATCH INSTITUTE–Trinidad's Leatherback Sea Turtles
EARTHWATCH INSTITUTE–Wild Dolphin Societies
EARTHWATCH INSTITUTE–Wildlife Conservation in West Africa
EARTHWATCH INSTITUTE–Wildlife Trails of the American West

Eastern Kentucky University Department of Music

Foster Guitar Camp
Foster High School Band Camp
Foster High School Strings Camp
Foster Middle School Band Camp
Foster Middle School Strings Camp
Foster Piano Camp I
Foster Piano Camp II
Foster Vocal Camp

Eastern Music Festival and School

Easter Seals Colorado

Rocky Mountain Village

Ebner Camps, Inc.

Boulder Ridge Day Camp
Camp Awosting
Camp Chinqueka

Education Unlimited

The Actor's Workshop by Education Unlimited
American Legal Experience by Education Unlimited–Berkeley, CA
American Legal Experience by Education Unlimited–Stanford, CA
California National Debate Institute
College Admission Prep Camp by Education Unlimited–Boston
College Admission Prep Camp by Education Unlimited–San Diego
College Admission Prep Camp by Education Unlimited–Stanford University
College Admission Prep Camp by Education Unlimited–UC Berkeley
College Admission Prep Camp by Education Unlimited–UCLA
College Admission Prep Camp Choice by Education Unlimited–Stanford
Computer Camp by Education Unlimited–Stanford
Computer Camp by Education Unlimited–UC Berkeley
Computer Camp by Education Unlimited–UCLA
East Coast College Tour by Education Unlimited
National Debate Institute–DC
Prep Camp Excel by Education Unlimited–Stanford University
Prep Camp Excel by Education Unlimited–UC Berkeley
Prep Camp Excel by Education Unlimited–UCLA
Public Speaking Institute by Education Unlimited–Boston
Public Speaking Institute by Education Unlimited–Stanford
Public Speaking Institute by Education Unlimited–UC Berkeley
Public Speaking Institute by Education Unlimited–UCLA
Summer Focus at Berkeley

EDUCO Colorado

EDUCO Summer Adventure Programs

EF International Language Schools

EF International Language School–Barcelona
EF International Language School–Malaga
EF International Language School–Munich
EF International Language School–Nice
EF International Language School–Paris
EF International Language School–Rome
EF International Language School–Quito
EF International Language School–St. Petersburg
EF International Language School–Shanghai

EKOCAMP

EKOCAMP International

Elite Educational Institute

Elite Educational Institute Elementary Enrichment
Elite Educational Institute Elementary Enrichment–Korea
Elite Educational Institute Junior High/PSAT Program
Elite Educational Institute Junior High/PSAT Program–Korea
Elite Educational Institute SAT Bootcamp–Korea
Elite Educational Institute SAT I and II Preparation
Elite Educational Institute SAT Preparation–Korea
Elite Educational Institute SAT Summer Bootcamp

Elk Creek Ranch and Trek Program

Emagination Computer Camps
Emagination Computer Camps–Georgia
Emagination Computer Camps–Illinois
Emagination Computer Camps–Massachusetts

Embry-Riddle Aeronautical University
Embry-Riddle Aeronautical University–Aerospace Summer Camp
Embry-Riddle Aeronautical University–Aviation Career Exploration
Embry-Riddle Aeronautical University–Flight Exploration
Embry-Riddle Aeronautical University–Generations
Embry-Riddle Aeronautical University–Sun Flight

Emma Willard School
GirlSummer at Emma Willard School

Enforex Spanish in the Spanish World
Enforex–General Spanish–Almuñecar
Enforex–General Spanish–Barcelona
Enforex–General Spanish–Granada
Enforex–General Spanish–Madrid
Enforex–General Spanish–Marbella
Enforex–General Spanish–Salamanca
Enforex–General Spanish–Valencia
Enforex Hispanic Culture: Civilization, History, Art, and Literature–Barcelona
Enforex Hispanic Culture: Civilization, History, Art, and Literature–Granada
Enforex Hispanic Culture: Civilization, History, Art, and Literature–Madrid
Enforex Homestay Program–Almuñecar
Enforex Homestay Program–Barcelona
Enforex Homestay Program–Granada
Enforex Homestay Program–Madrid
Enforex Homestay Program–Marbella
Enforex Homestay Program–Salamanca
Enforex Residential Youth Summer Camp–Madrid
Enforex Residential Youth Summer Camp–Marbella
Enforex Residential Youth Summer Camp–Salamanca
Enforex Spanish and Golf
Enforex Spanish and Tennis
Enforex Study Tour Vacational Program–Madrid
Spanish Language and Flamenco Enforex–Granada
Spanish Language and Flamenco Enforex–Madrid
Spanish Language and Flamenco Enforex–Marbella
Study Tour Vacational Program Enforex–Barcelona

Ensemble Theatre Community School

Episcopal High School of Jacksonville
Episcopal High School Academic Camp
Episcopal High School Eagle Arts Camp
Episcopal High School Sports Camp

The Experiment in International Living
The Experiment in International Living–Argentina Homestay, Community Service, and Outdoor Ecological Program
The Experiment in International Living–Australia Homestay
The Experiment in International Living–Belize Homestay
The Experiment in International Living–Botswana Homestay
The Experiment in International Living–Brazil–Ecological Preservation
The Experiment in International Living–Brazil Homestay and Community Service
The Experiment in International Living–Chile North Homestay, Community Service
The Experiment in International Living–Chile South Homestay
The Experiment in International Living–China North and East Homestay
The Experiment in International Living–China South and West Homestay
The Experiment in International Living–Costa Rica Homestay
The Experiment in International Living–Ecuador Homestay
The Experiment in International Living–France, Biking and Homestay
The Experiment in International Living–France, Five-Week Art and Adventure in Provence
The Experiment in International Living–France, Four-Week Brittany Discovery
The Experiment in International Living–France, Four-Week Homestay and Photography
The Experiment in International Living–France, Four-Week Homestay and Theatre
The Experiment in International Living–France, Four-Week Homestay and Travel–Borders
The Experiment in International Living–France, Four–Week Homestay and Travel through Alps
The Experiment in International Living–France, Homestay, Language Training, and Cooking
The Experiment in International Living–France, Three-Week Camargue Homestay
The Experiment in International Living–France, Three-Week Homestay and Travel–Borders
The Experiment in International Living–Germany, Four-Week Homestay, Travel, Community Service
The Experiment in International Living–Ghana Homestay
The Experiment in International Living–Ireland/Northern Ireland Homestay and Peace Studies
The Experiment in International Living–Italy Homestay
The Experiment in International Living–Japan Homestay
The Experiment in International Living–Mexico, Community Service, Travel, and Homestay
The Experiment in International Living–Mexico Homestay and Travel
The Experiment in International Living–Morocco Four-Week Arts and Culture Program
The Experiment in International Living–Navajo Nation
The Experiment in International Living–New Zealand Homestay
The Experiment in International Living–Poland, Homestay, Community Service, and Travel
The Experiment in International Living–South Africa Homestay and Community Service
The Experiment in International Living–Spain, Five-Week Homestay, Travel, Ecology
The Experiment in International Living–Spain, Five-Week Language Training, Travel, and Homestay
The Experiment in International Living–Spain, Four-Week Homestay and Trekking Program
The Experiment in International Living–Spain, Four-Week Language Study and Homestay
The Experiment in International Living–Spain–Spanish Culture and Folklore
The Experiment in International Living–Spain, Three-Week Homestay
The Experiment in International Living–Switzerland French Language Immersion, Homestay, and Alpine Adventure
The Experiment in International Living–Thailand Homestay
The Experiment in International Living–The United Kingdom Celtic Odyssey
The Experiment in International Living–Turkey Homestay, Community Service, and Travel
The Experiment in International Living–United Kingdom Filmmaking Program and Homestay
The Experiment in International Living–United Kingdom Theatre Program

ExploraMar
ExploraMar: Marine Biology Sailing Expeditions–Sea of Cortez, Baja, Mexico

Exploration School, Inc.
Exploration Intermediate Program at Wellesley College
Exploration Junior Program at St. Mark's School
Exploration Senior Program at Yale University

Fairfax Collegiate School
Fairfax Collegiate School Summer Enrichment Program

Fairleigh Dickinson University
Camp Discovery–Madison
Camp Discovery–Teaneck

Falcon Camp
Falcon Camp
Falcon Horse Lover Camp
Falcon Horse Lover Camp for Girls
Falcon Young Adventure Camp

Falling Creek Camp

Farm and Wilderness Camps
Farm and Wilderness Camps–Barn Day Camp
Farm and Wilderness Camps–Flying Cloud
Farm and Wilderness Camps–Indian Brook
Farm and Wilderness Camps–Saltash Mountain
Farm and Wilderness Camps–Tamarack Farm
Farm and Wilderness Camps–Timberlake

Fay School
Fay School Day Camp
Fay Summer School

The Fenn School
Fenn School Summer Day Camp

The Fessenden School
The Fessenden School Summer ESL Program

Fir Acres Writing Workshop
Fir Acres Workshop in Writing and Thinking

Fishburne Military School
Fishburne Summer Session

Fleur de Lis Camp, Inc.
Fleur de Lis Camp

Flint Hill School
Flint Hill School–"Summer on the Hill"–A Biking Odyssey Day Camp
Flint Hill School–"Summer on the Hill"–Academics on the Hill–English and Math Review
Flint Hill School–"Summer on the Hill"–Academics on the Hill–Geometry for Credit
Flint Hill School–"Summer on the Hill"–Academics on the Hill–The Reading Clinic
Flint Hill School–"Summer on the Hill"–Boys Outdoor Adventures! Day Camp
Flint Hill School–"Summer on the Hill"–Counselor-in-Training Day Camp
Flint Hill School–"Summer on the Hill"–Creative Arts on the Hill–Art Camp
Flint Hill School–"Summer on the Hill"–Creative Arts on the Hill–Let the Drums Roll
Flint Hill School–"Summer on the Hill"–Enrichment on the Hill–Gee, Whiz!
Flint Hill School–"Summer on the Hill"–Enrichment on the Hill–Investigating Where We Live
Flint Hill School–"Summer on the Hill"–Enrichment on the Hill–Junior Great Books
Flint Hill School–"Summer on the Hill"–Enrichment on the Hill–Scientific Super Sleuths
Flint Hill School–"Summer on the Hill"–Enrichment on the Hill–Spanish Immersion Camp
Flint Hill School–"Summer on the Hill"–Enrichment on the Hill–Study Skills for 9th Graders
Flint Hill School–"Summer on the Hill"–Enrichment on the Hill–Summer Chess Camp
Flint Hill School–"Summer on the Hill"–Enrichment on the Hill–Summer Service
Flint Hill School–"Summer on the Hill"–Enrichment on the Hill–Women Writers' Adventure
Flint Hill School–"Summer on the Hill"–Into the Woods Day Camp
Flint Hill School–"Summer on the Hill"–Junior Day/Day Camps
Flint Hill School–"Summer on the Hill"–Sports on the Hill–Coed
Flint Hill School–"Summer on the Hill"–Sports on the Hill for Boys
Flint Hill School–"Summer on the Hill"–Sports on the Hill for Girls
Flint Hill School–"Summer on the Hill"–Trips and Travel Day Camp
Flint Hill School–"Summer on the Hill"–Trips from the Hill–Ecological Study of Coral Reefs, Bahamas
Flint Hill School–"Summer on the Hill"–Trips from the Hill–Tanzania Safari

Florida Air Academy
Florida Air Academy Summer Session

FLS International
Study Tours and Cinema Program in the USA–Oxnard College
Study Tours and Dance/Theater Camp in the USA–Dean College
Study Tours and Hotel and Tourism Management in the USA–Southern Nevada College
Study Tours and Leisure Sports in the USA–Citrus College
Study Tours and Surf Program in the USA–Mira Costa College
Study Tours in the USA–Citrus
Study Tours in the USA–Dean College
Study Tours in the USA–Lock Haven
Study Tours in the USA–Mira Costa College
Study Tours in the USA–Oxnard
Study Tours in the USA–Southern Nevada

Flying G Ranch, Tomahawk Ranch–Girl Scouts Mile Hi Council
Flying G Ranch, Tomahawk Ranch

Flying Moose Lodge

Forest Ridge School of the Sacred Heart
Forest Ridge Summer Program

Forrestel Farm Riding and Sports Camp

4 Star Summer Camps at the University of Virginia
4 Star Academics Junior Camp at the University of Virginia
4 Star Academics Scholars at the University of Virginia
4 Star Academics Senior Camp at the University of Virginia
4 Star College Prep Tennis at the University of Virginia
4 Star Golf Camp at the University of Virginia
4 Star Golf Plus All Sports Camp at the University of Virginia
4 Star Tennis Camp at the University of Virginia
4 Star Tennis Plus Camp at the University of Virginia
4 Star Tennis Plus Golf Camp at the University of Virginia

Four Winds, Inc.
Four Winds * Westward Ho

The Fowler Center
Camp Fowler
Mah Meh Weh

Freed-Hardeman University
Freed-Hardeman Horizons for Ages 12-18

French Woods Festival of the Performing Arts

Friendly House
Hidden Hollow Camp

Friends Camp

Friendship Ventures
Camp Friendship
Eden Wood Camp
Ventures Travel Service–Arizona
Ventures Travel Service–California
Ventures Travel Service–Florida
Ventures Travel Service–Iowa
Ventures Travel Service–Kentucky
Ventures Travel Service–Minnesota
Ventures Travel Service–Missouri
Ventures Travel Service–New York
Ventures Travel Service–North Dakota
Ventures Travel Service–Oregon
Ventures Travel Service–South Carolina
Ventures Travel Service–South Dakota
Ventures Travel Service–Tennessee
Ventures Travel Service–Texas
Ventures Travel Service–Washington
Ventures Travel Service–Wisconsin

Friends Music Institute, Inc.
Friends Music Camp

FUN-damental Basketball Camp, Inc.
FUN-damental Basketball Camp–Morrisville, New York
FUN-damental Basketball Camp–The Sports Mall

Furman University
Furman University Summer Scholars Program

Genesis at Brandeis University

GENEVA Camp & Retreat Center
Camp Geneva

Geneva Glen Camp, Inc.
Geneva Glen Camp

Georgetown Preparatory School
Georgetown Prep School Summer English Program

Georgetown University
Georgetown University College Prep Program
Georgetown University International Relations Program for High School Students
Georgetown University Summer College for High School Juniors

George Washington University
George Washington University Summer Scholars Pre-college Program

Geronimo Program
Geronimo Program

Gettysburg College
Academic Camps at Gettysburg College–Astronomy
Academic Camps at Gettysburg College–College Prep & Preview
Academic Camps at Gettysburg College–Community Service
Academic Camps at Gettysburg College–Foreign Language Study (Spanish)
Academic Camps at Gettysburg College–U.S. Civil War
Academic Camps at Gettysburg College–Writer's Workshops

GIC Arg–Cultural Exchange Group of Argentina
GIC Arg–Argentinian Cooking
GIC Arg–Soccer
GIC Arg–Spanish Language
GIC Arg–Tango

Girl Scouts–Audubon Council
Marydale Resident Camp

Girl Scouts–Great Rivers Council, Inc.
Camp Butterworth
Camp Stonybrook
Explorer Day Camp

Girl Scouts of Genesee Valley
Girl Scouts of Genesee Valley Day Camp
Girl Scouts of Genesee Valley Resident Camp

Girl Scouts of Kennebec Council
Camp Kirkwold
Camp Pondicherry
Camp Scelkit

Girl Scouts of Mid-Continent Council
Girl Scouts of Mid-Continent–Camp Oakledge
Girl Scouts of Mid-Continent–Camp Prairie Schooner
Girl Scouts of Mid-Continent–Juliette Low Camp
Girl Scouts of Mid-Continent–Winding River Camp and Ranch

Girl Scouts of Shagbark Council
Camp Cedar Point

Girl Scouts of the Fox River Area, Inc.
Camp Birch Trails

Girl Scouts of the Western Reserve, Inc.
Camp Ledgewood

Girl Scouts of Washington Rock Council
Camp Lou Henry Hoover

Girl Scouts of Western North Carolina Pisgah Council
Camp Pisgah

Girl Scouts Susitna Council
Camp Togowoods

GLOBAL WORKS
GLOBAL WORKS–Adventure Travel-Pacific Northwest-3 weeks
GLOBAL WORKS–Cultural Exchange-Fiji Islands-4 weeks
GLOBAL WORKS–Cultural Exchange-Ireland-4 weeks
GLOBAL WORKS–Cultural Exchange-New Zealand and Fiji Islands-4 weeks
GLOBAL WORKS–Language Exposure-Costa Rica-4 weeks
GLOBAL WORKS–Language Exposure-Ecuador and the Galapagos-4 weeks
GLOBAL WORKS–Language Exposure-Puerto Rico-3 weeks
GLOBAL WORKS–Language Exposure-Yucatan Peninsula, Mexico-4 weeks
GLOBAL WORKS–Language Immersion-Costa Rica-4 weeks
GLOBAL WORKS–Language Immersion-Ecuador and the Galapagos-4 weeks
GLOBAL WORKS–Language Immersion-France-4 weeks
GLOBAL WORKS–Language Immersion-Puerto Rico-4 weeks
GLOBAL WORKS–Language Immersion-Spain-4 weeks
GLOBAL WORKS–Language Immersion-Yucatan Peninsula, Mexico-4 weeks

GLS German Language School Berlin
GLS Bavarian Summer School
GLS Berlin Summer School
GLS Potsdam Summer School
GLS Sports and Language Camp Inzell
GLS Summer Camp Blossin
GLS Summer Camp Loewenstein
GLS Summer Camp Schmoeckwitz

Gold Arrow Camp

Golf Academy of Hilton Head Island
International Junior Golf Academy

Gordon Kent's New England Tennis Camp
Gordon Kent's New England Tennis Camp

The Governor's Program for Gifted Children
The Governor's Program for Gifted Children

The Gow School
The Gow School Summer Program

The Grand River Academy
The Grand River Summer Academy

Greater Burlington YMCA
YMCA Camp Abnaki
YMCA Camp Abnaki–Counselor-in-Training Program
YMCA Camp Abnaki–Family Camp
YMCA Camp Abnaki–Mini Camp
YMCA Camp Abnaki–Teen Adventure Trips

Greater Green Bay YMCA
YMCA Camp U-Nah-Li-Ya
YMCA Camp Wabansi

Greenbrier River Outdoor Adventures
Greenbrier River Outdoor Adventures, Adventure Camp
Greenbrier River Outdoor Adventures, Camp Snowshoe
Greenbrier River Outdoor Adventures, Rock and River
Greenbrier River Outdoor Adventures, Wilderness Explorer

Green River Preserve
Green River Preserve

Grinnell College
Grinnell Summer Institute

The Groundwater Foundation
Groundwater University

Guitar Workshop Plus
Guitar Workshop Plus–Bass, Drums, Keyboards

Hamilton Learning Centre
Hamilton Learning Centre Summer Fun in the Sun Camp
Hamilton Learning Centre Summer School

Harand Camp of the Theatre Arts

Hargrave Military Academy
Hargrave Summer Program

The Harker School
Harker Summer English Language Institute
The Harker Summer Institute
Harker Summer Programs

Harmon's Pine View Camp

Harvard University
Harvard University Summer School: Secondary School Program

Hawaii Extreme Adventure Scuba Camp
Hawaii Extreme Adventure Scuba Camp

Hawaii Preparatory Academy
Big Island Volleyball Elite Camp
Big Island Volleyball Player Camp
Hawaii Preparatory Academy Summer Session

Haycock Camping Ministries
Haycock Camping Ministries–Adventure Trails
Haycock Camping Ministries–Battalion Program
Haycock Camping Ministries–Stockade Program
Haycock Camping Ministries–Trailbuilders Program

Hidden Valley Camp
Hidden Valley Camp

Hidden Villa Trust
Hidden Villa Summer Camp

High Cascade Snowboard Camp
High Cascade Snowboard Camp
High Cascade Snowboard Camp Photography Workshop
Vans Skateboard Camp

Hillsdale College
Hillsdale College Summer Science Camps

Hillside School
Camp Hillside
Camp Hillside Soccer Program

The Hill Top Preparatory School
Hill Top Summer Programs

Historical Experiences
Fort Union Civil War Camp

Hobart and William Smith Colleges
Environmental Studies Summer Youth Institute

The Hockaday School
The Hockaday School Summer Session

Hockey Opportunity Camp

Holiday Trails, Inc.
Camp Holiday Trails

Hollins University
Hollinsummer

The Hollows Camp, Ltd.
The Hollows Camp
Summer Music at The Hollows

Horizon Adventures, Inc.
Horizon Adventures Inc.

Horizons for Youth, Inc.
Horizons for Youth

Houghton Academy
Houghton Academy Summer ESL

Howard Community College
Kids on Campus

Howling Wolf Adventures
Canadian Rockies Adventurer Camp
Canadian Rockies Outdoor Leader Camp

Humanities Spring in Assisi
Humanities Spring in Assisi
Humanities Spring on the Road

Humboldt State University
Sequoia Chamber Music Workshop

The Hun School of Princeton
Bridge to the Future
The Hun School of Princeton American Culture and Language Institute
The Hun School of Princeton Boys' Basketball Camp
The Hun School of Princeton Girls' Basketball Camp
The Hun School of Princeton–Summer Academic Session
The Hun School of Princeton Summer Day Camp
The Hun School of Princeton Summer Theatre Classics

Hurricane Island Outward Bound/Outward Bound, USA
Hurricane Island Outward Bound–Maine Coast and Western Maine Canoeing and Sailing
Hurricane Island Outward Bound–Maine Coast and Western Maine Sailing and Backpacking
Hurricane Island Outward Bound–Maine Coast and Western Maine Sea Kayaking and Backpacking
Hurricane Island Outward Bound–Maine Coast Sailing/Sailing and Rock Climbing
Hurricane Island Outward Bound–Maine Coast Schooner Sailing
Hurricane Island Outward Bound–Maine Coast Sea Kayaking
Hurricane Island Outward Bound–Maine Woods High School Summer Semester
Hurricane Island Outward Bound–Mid-Atlantic Canoeing, Backpacking, and Rock Climbing
Hurricane Island Outward Bound–North Woods Maine Allagash and Appalachian Trail Canoeing and Backpacking
Hurricane Island Outward Bound–North Woods Maine Canoeing and Backpacking
Hurricane Island Outward Bound–North Woods Maine Expedition Canoeing
Hurricane Island Outward Bound–Ocean Bound: Tall Ship Sailing and Sea Kayaking Semester
Hurricane Island Outward Bound–Western Maine and New Hampshire Canoeing and Backpacking
Hurricane Island Outward Bound–Western Maine Backpacking and Rock Climbing
Hurricane Island Outward Bound–Western Maine Woods Expedition Canoeing

Hyde School
Hyde School Summer Challenge Program–Bath, ME
Hyde School Summer Challenge Program–Woodstock, CT

iD Tech Camps
iD Tech Camps–Cal Lutheran University, Thousand Oaks, CA
iD Tech Camps–Carnegie Mellon University, Pittsburgh, PA
iD Tech Camps–Colorado College, Colorado Springs, CO
iD Tech Camps–Documentary Filmmaking and Cultural Immersion at the University of Cádiz, Spain
iD Tech Camps–Dominican University, San Rafael, CA
iD Tech Camps–Emerson College, Boston, MA
iD Tech Camps–Emory University, Atlanta, GA
iD Tech Camps–Georgetown University, Washington, DC
iD Tech Camps–Lake Forest College, Evanston, IL
iD Tech Camps–Merrimack College, North Andover, MA
iD Tech Camps–MIT, Cambridge, MA
iD Tech Camps–Northwestern University, Chicago, IL
iD Tech Camps–Pepperdine University, Malibu, CA
iD Tech Camps–Princeton University, Princeton, NJ
iD Tech Camps–Sacred Heart University, Fairfield, CT
iD Tech Camps–Santa Clara University, Santa Clara, CA
iD Tech Camps–Smith College, Northampton, MA
iD Tech Camps–Southern Methodist University, Dallas, TX
iD Tech Camps–Stanford University, Palo Alto, CA
iD Tech Camps–St. Mary's College, Moraga, CA
iD Tech Camps–UC Berkeley, Berkeley, CA
iD Tech Camps–UC Irvine, Irvine, CA
iD Tech Camps–UCLA, Westwood, CA
iD Tech Camps–UC San Diego, La Jolla, CA

iD Tech Camps–UC Santa Cruz, Santa Cruz, CA
iD Tech Camps–University of Denver, Denver, CO
iD Tech Camps–University of Miami, Coral Gables, FL
iD Tech Camps–University of Michigan, Ann Arbor, MI
iD Tech Camps–University of Minnesota, Minneapolis, MN
iD Tech Camps–University of North Carolina at Chapel Hill, Chapel Hill, NC
iD Tech Camps–University of Virginia, Charlottesville, VA
iD Tech Camps–University of Washington, Seattle, WA
iD Tech Camps–UT Austin, Austin, TX
iD Tech Camps–Vassar College, Poughkeepsie, NY
iD Tech Camps–Villanova University, Villanova, PA

Idyllwild Arts Foundation
Idyllwild Arts Summer Program–American Experience for International Students
Idyllwild Arts Summer Program–Children's Center
Idyllwild Arts Summer Program–Family Week
Idyllwild Arts Summer Program–Junior Artists' Center
Idyllwild Arts Summer Program–Youth Arts Center

Indiana University School of Music Office of Special Programs
Indiana University School of Music College Audition Preparation Workshop
Indiana University School of Music Piano Academy
Indiana University School of Music Recorder Academy
Indiana University School of Music String Academy

Indian Head Camp

Institut auf dem Rosenberg
Institut auf dem Rosenberg

Institute for Arts and Humanities Education
PixelNation

Institute for Mathematics & Computer Science (IMACS)
IMACS–Full Day Summer Camp–Connecticut
IMACS–Full Day Summer Camp–Florida
IMACS–Full Day Summer Camp–Missouri
IMACS–Full Day Summer Camp–North Carolina
IMACS–Full Day Summer Camp–Pennsylvania
IMACS–Full Day Summer Camp–South Carolina
IMACS–Individual Summer Programs–Connecticut
IMACS–Individual Summer Programs–Florida
IMACS–Individual Summer Programs–Missouri
IMACS–Individual Summer Programs–North Carolina
IMACS–Individual Summer Programs–Pennsylvania
IMACS–Individual Summer Programs–South Carolina

The Institute for Rehabilitation, Research, and Recreation, Inc.
Meadowood Springs Speech and Hearing Camp

Instituto de Idiomas Geos
Instituto de Idiomas Geos–Costa Rica
Instituto de Idiomas Geos–Granada, Spain
Instituto de Idiomas Geos–Marbella, Spain

Interamerican University Studies Institute
Artes en Mexico
Costa Rica ¡Pura Vida!

Interlochen Center for the Arts
Interlochen Arts Camp

Interlocken at Windsor Mountain
Windsor Mountain: Adventures in Filmmaking
Windsor Mountain: Alaska
Windsor Mountain: Bonjour Quebec
Windsor Mountain: California Community Service
Windsor Mountain: Coast of Australia
Windsor Mountain: Crossroads France
Windsor Mountain: Cuba Friendship Exchange
Windsor Mountain: Driftwood Stables Ranch Camp
Windsor Mountain: European Traveling Minstrels
Windsor Mountain: Experiential Summer School
Windsor Mountain: Family Camp
Windsor Mountain: Hawaii
Windsor Mountain: International Summer Camp
Windsor Mountain: Leaders in Action
Windsor Mountain: Mexico Community Service
Windsor Mountain: New England Adventure
Windsor Mountain: New England Traveling Minstrels
Windsor Mountain: Puerto Rico
Windsor Mountain: Random Acts of Kindness
Windsor Mountain: Voices of the Wind River, Wyoming

International Bicycle Fund
Bicycle Africa Tours
Ibike Cultural Tours–Ecuador
Ibike Cultural Tours–Guyana
Ibike Cultural Tours–Washington/British Columbia

International Cultural Adventures
The Nepal Cultural Immersion Experience
The Peru Cultural Immersion Experience
The Sikkim Cultural Immersion Experience

International Music Camp

International Riding Camp

International School of Beijing–Shunyi
ISB Chinese Language Camp

International Seminar Series
Service-Learning in Paris

International Summer Camp Montana, Switzerland
International Summer Camp Montana, Switzerland

Intern Exchange International, Ltd.
IEI–Digital Media Plus Programme
IEI–Fashion and Design Plus Programme
IEI–Fine Arts Plus Programme
IEI–Photography Plus Programme
IEI–Print and Broadcast Journalism
IEI Student Travel–Internship Program in London
IEI–Theatre Plus Programme

Irish American Cultural Institute
Irish Way

Iroquois Springs
Iroquois Springs

Ithaca College Division of Continuing Education and Summer Sessions
Ithaca College Summer College for High School Students: Session I
Ithaca College Summer College for High School Students: Session II
Ithaca College Summer College for High School Students: Minicourses
Ithaca College Summer Piano Institute

Jewish Community Center of Greater Buffalo
Camp Lakeland

Jewish Community Center of Greater Monmouth
Jewish Community Center Day Camp

Jewish Community Center of Houston
JCC Houston: Art Camp
JCC Houston: Camp Bami
JCC Houston: Camp Kaleidoscope
JCC Houston: Counselor-In-Training
JCC Houston: Gordon Campsite
JCC Houston: Gymnastics Camp

▶ Jewish Community Center of Houston

JCC Houston: Kindercamp
JCC Houston: Sports Camp
JCC Houston: Teen Trek
JCC Houston: Tennis Camp
JCC Houston: Theater Camp

Joel Ross Tennis & Sports Camp

Joe Machnik's No. 1 Camps

Joe Machnik's No. 1 Academy One and Premier Programs–Aston, Pennsylvania
Joe Machnik's No. 1 Academy One and Premier Programs–Brooklyn, Michigan
Joe Machnik's No. 1 Academy One and Premier Programs–Claremont, California
Joe Machnik's No. 1 Academy One and Premier Programs–Colorado Springs, Colorado
Joe Machnik's No. 1 Academy One and Premier Programs–Columbus, Ohio
Joe Machnik's No. 1 Academy One and Premier Programs–Dyke, Virginia
Joe Machnik's No. 1 Academy One and Premier Programs–Fort Worth, Texas
Joe Machnik's No. 1 Academy One and Premier Programs–Kenosha, Wisconsin
Joe Machnik's No. 1 Academy One and Premier Programs–Newtown, Pennsylvania
Joe Machnik's No. 1 Academy One and Premier Programs–Olympia, Washington
Joe Machnik's No. 1 Academy One and Premier Programs–Rohnert Park, California
Joe Machnik's No. 1 Academy One and Premier Programs–Rome, Georgia
Joe Machnik's No. 1 Academy One and Premier Programs–Vero Beach, Florida
Joe Machnik's No. 1 Academy One and Premier Programs–Windsor, Connecticut
Joe Machnik's No. 1 College Prep Academy–Colorado Springs, Colorado
Joe Machnik's No. 1 College Prep Academy–Fort Worth, Texas
Joe Machnik's No. 1 College Prep Academy–Kenosha, Wisconsin
Joe Machnik's No. 1 College Prep Academy–Newtown/Aston, Pennsylvania
Joe Machnik's No. 1 College Prep Academy–Windsor, Connecticut
Joe Machnik's No. 1 Mighty Mini, Goalkeeper and Striker Camp–Aston, Pennsylvania
Joe Machnik's No. 1 Mighty Mini, Goalkeeper and Striker Camp–Brooklyn, Michigan
Joe Machnik's No. 1 Mighty Mini, Goalkeeper and Striker Camp–Claremont, California
Joe Machnik's No. 1 Mighty Mini, Goalkeeper and Striker Camp–Colorado Springs, Colorado
Joe Machnik's No. 1 Mighty Mini, Goalkeeper and Striker Camp–Columbus, Ohio
Joe Machnik's No. 1 Mighty Mini, Goalkeeper and Striker Camp–Dyke, Virginia
Joe Machnik's No. 1 Mighty Mini, Goalkeeper and Striker Camp–Newtown, Pennsylvania
Joe Machnik's No. 1 Mighty Mini, Goalkeeper and Striker Camp–Olympia, Washington
Joe Machnik's No. 1 Mighty Mini, Goalkeeper and Striker Camp–Rohnert Park, California
Joe Machnik's No. 1 Mighty Mini, Goalkeeper and Striker Camp–Rome, Georgia
Joe Machnik's No. 1 Mighty Mini, Goalkeeper and Striker Camp–Vero Beach, Florida
Joe Machnik's No. 1 Mighty Mini, Goalkeeper and Striker Camp–Windsor, Connecticut
Joe Machnik's No. 1 Mighty Mini, Goalkeeper and Striker Camp–Fort Worth, Texas
Joe Machnik's No. 1 Mighty Mini, Goalkeeper and Striker Camp–Kenosha, Wisconsin

The John Cooper School

The John Cooper School Academic Camps
The John Cooper School Discovery Camps
The John Cooper School Recreational Activities and Sports

The Johns Hopkins University

Johns Hopkins University Zanvyl Krieger School of Arts and Sciences Summer Programs

Joy Outdoor Education Center

Camp Joy

Julian Krinsky Camps and Programs

Julian Krinsky Business School at Haverford College
Julian Krinsky Business School at Wharton (Leadership in the Business World)
Julian Krinsky California Teen Tours
Julian Krinsky/Canyon Ranch Young Adult Summer Program " for Smarter Minds and Bodies"
Julian Krinsky Creative and Performing Arts Camp at The Shipley School/Bryn Mawr
Julian Krinsky Exploring the Majors at the University of Pennsylvania
Julian Krinsky Golf Camp at Cabrini College
Julian Krinsky Golf Camp at Haverford College
Julian Krinsky Golf Tours
Julian Krinsky Junior Enrichment Camp at Cabrini College
Julian Krinsky Senior Enrichment Camp at Haverford College
Julian Krinsky Super Sports Camp at The Shipley School
Julian Krinsky Tennis Camp at Cabrini College
Julian Krinsky Tennis Camp at Haverford College
Julian Krinsky Yesh Shabbat California Teen Tour
Julian Krinsky Yesh Shabbat Summer Camp

Junior Statesmen Foundation

Junior Statesmen Summer School–Georgetown University
Junior Statesmen Summer School–Northwestern University
Junior Statesmen Summer School–Princeton University
Junior Statesmen Summer School–Stanford University
Junior Statesmen Summer School–Yale University
Junior Statesmen Symposium on California State Politics and Government
Junior Statesmen Symposium on Los Angeles Politics and Government
Junior Statesmen Symposium on New Jersey State Politics and Government
Junior Statesmen Symposium on Ohio State Politics and Government
Junior Statesmen Symposium on Texas Politics and Leadership
Junior Statesmen Symposium on Washington State Politics and Government

Kabbalah Children's Academy-Spirituality for Kids Academy

Miracle Makers Summer Camp

Kamp Kohut

Kamp Kohut

Kansas Cosmosphere and Space Center

Future Astronaut Training Program
Mars Academy

Kawkawa Camp and Retreat

Kawkawa Summer Camps

Keewaydin Camps Corporation

Keewaydin Canoe Camp

Keewaydin Foundation

Keewaydin Dunmore
Keewaydin Temagami
Songadeewin of Keewaydin

Kendall College

Kendall College Culinary Camp

Kent School

Kent School Summer Writers Camp

Kenyon College/The Kenyon Review

Kenyon Review Young Writers

Keystone Camp

Keystone Science School

Discovery Camp
Keystone Counselor Assistant Program
Keystone Science Adventures

Kickapoo Kamp

KidsMakeADifference.org

Alien Adventure Overnight Camp
California Cruzin' Overnight Camp
Camp Exploration Travel Day Camp
Hiker's Heaven Overnight Camp
Mountain Retreat Overnight Camp

Kildonan School

Dunnabeck at Kildonan

Killooleet

Kingsley Pines Camp

Kingsley Pines Camp

Kinhaven Music School
Kinhaven Music School

Kippewa for Girls

The Kiski School
Kiski Summer Camp–Junior Division-Boys Grades 5-8
Kiski Summer Camp–Senior Division-Boys Grades 9-12
Kiski Summer Camp–Senior Division-Girls Grades 9-12

Knowledge Exchange Institute
Knowledge Exchange Institute–African Safari Program
Knowledge Exchange Institute–Artist Abroad Program in Italy
Knowledge Exchange Institute–Discover Spain and Portugal Program
Knowledge Exchange Institute–European Capitals Program
Knowledge Exchange Institute–Research Abroad in Russia
Knowledge Exchange Institute–Spanish on the Road in Mexico Program

Kostopulos Dream Foundation
Camp Kostopulos

Kroka Expeditions of Vermont
Kroka Expeditions–Advanced Rock Climbing
Kroka Expeditions–Adventures for Small People
Kroka Expeditions–Cape Cod Triple Surfing Bonanza
Kroka Expeditions–Coastal Sea Kayaking
Kroka Expeditions–Coming of Age for Young Women
Kroka Expeditions–Expedition Pre-Columbus
Kroka Expeditions–Introduction to Adventure Day Camp
Kroka Expeditions–Introduction to Adventure Residential Camp
Kroka Expeditions–Introduction to Rock Climbing
Kroka Expeditions–Introduction to White Water
Kroka Expeditions–Paddlers Journey Up North
Kroka Expeditions–Rock 'n Road
Kroka Expeditions–Vermont Underground Trail
Kroka Expeditions–Wild Arts and Canoe Adventure
Kroka Expeditions–Wild World of White Water

Kutsher's Sports Academy

Lacunza–ih-San Sebastian
Lacunza Junior Summer Spanish Course

Lake Ann Baptist Camp

Lake of the Woods Camp for Girls and Greenwoods Camp for Boys
The Glen at Lake of the Woods
Greenwoods Camp for Boys
The Grove at Greenwoods
Lake of the Woods Camp for Girls

Lancaster Family YMCA
YMCA Camp Shand

Landmark School
Landmark School Summer Academic Program

Landmark Volunteers, Inc.
Landmark Volunteers: Arizona
Landmark Volunteers: California
Landmark Volunteers: Colorado
Landmark Volunteers: Connecticut
Landmark Volunteers: Idaho
Landmark Volunteers: Maine
Landmark Volunteers: Massachusetts
Landmark Volunteers: Michigan
Landmark Volunteers: Minnesota
Landmark Volunteers: Montana
Landmark Volunteers: New Hampshire
Landmark Volunteers: New Mexico
Landmark Volunteers: New York
Landmark Volunteers: North Carolina
Landmark Volunteers: Ohio
Landmark Volunteers: Rhode Island
Landmark Volunteers: Vermont
Landmark Volunteers: Virginia
Landmark Volunteers: Washington
Landmark Volunteers: Wyoming

Langskib Wilderness Programs
Excalibur
Langskib Wilderness Programs

Language Liaison
Global Teen–French Summer Camp in Monte Carlo
Global Teen–German in Bavaria
Global Teen–German Plus Web Design, Video/Theatre in Berlin
Global Teen–German Summer Camp in Potsdam
Global Teen–Italian and Soccer in Rome
Global Teen–Learn French in Biarritz
Global Teen–Learn French in Nice
Global Teen–Learn French in Paris
Global Teen–Learn German in Berlin, Ages 12-15 on Lake Schmockwitz
Global Teen–Learn German in Berlin-City Centre, Ages 16-19
Global Teen–Learn German in Vienna, Summer Camp-Ages 12-18
Global Teen–Learn German in Vienna, Young Adult Summer Camp, Ages 16-18
Global Teen–Learn Italian in Italy
Global Teen–Learn Spanish in Andalusia
Global Teen–Learn Spanish in Costa Rica
Global Teen–Learn Spanish in Marbella, Ages 6-14
Global Teen–Learn Spanish in Marbella-Young Adult
Global Teen–Learn Spanish in Mexico
Global Teen–Learn Spanish in Salamanca, Ages 11-18
Global Teen–Learn Spanish in Salamanca, Ages 13-16
Global Teen–Learn Spanish in Sevilla
Global Teen–Spanish in Ecuador
Global Teen–Spanish in Madrid, Ages 6-14
Global Teen–Spanish in Malaga-Young Adult, Ages 16-20
Global Teen–Spanish in Palma de Mallorca
Global Teen–Spanish Summer Camp in San Sebastian
Global Teen–Summer Camp in Barcelona
Global Teen–Summer Camp in Marbella, Ages 14-18
Global Teen–Summer Language Adventure in Montreal
Global Teen Summer Sports Camp in Berlin
Global Teen–Vejer Beach Spectacular in Spain
Global Teen–Young Adult Summer Camp in Madrid, Ages 14-18
Global Teen–Young Adult Summer Program in Malaga, Ages 16-20

Language Studies Abroad, Inc.
LSA Alicante, Spain
LSA Almuñecar, Spain
LSA Amboise, France
LSA Antibes, France
LSA Antigua, Guatemala
LSA Argelés-Gazost, France
LSA Ascoli, Italy
LSA Barcelona, Spain
LSA Berlin, Germany
LSA Biarritz, France
LSA Blossin, Germany
LSA Bordeaux, France
LSA Buenos Aires, Argentina
LSA Cannes, France
LSA Cologne, Germany
LSA Cordoba, Argentina
LSA Cuernavaca, Mexico
LSA Cuzco, Peru
LSA El Puerto de Santa Maria, Spain
LSA Ensenada, Mexico
LSA Flamingo Beach, Costa Rica
LSA Florence, Italy
LSA Granada, Spain
LSA Hamburg, Germany
LSA Holzkirchen, Germany
LSA Hyères, France
LSA Inzell, Germany
LSA Kanazawa, Japan
LSA La Rochelle, France
LSA Lausanne, Switzerland
LSA Lignano, Italy–Active Junior Italian Summer Program
LSA Lisbon, Portugal
LSA Livorno, Italy
LSA Loewenstein, Germany
LSA Madrid, Spain
LSA Màlaga, Spain
LSA Marbella, Spain
LSA Mérida, Mexico
LSA Milan, Italy
LSA Montreal, Canada–English/French
LSA Moscow, Russia
LSA Munich, Germany
LSA Nerja, Spain
LSA Nice, France
LSA Oaxaca, Mexico
LSA Orvieto, Italy
LSA Paris, France
LSA Playa Del Carmen, Mexico
LSA Potsdam, Germany
LSA Puebla, Mexico
LSA Puerto Vallarta, Mexico
LSA Quito, Ecuador
LSA Rimini, Italy
LSA Rome, Italy

▶ Language Studies Abroad, Inc.

LSA St. Petersburg, Russia
LSA Salamanca, Spain
LSA San José, Costa Rica
LSA San Sebastian, Spain
LSA Schmoeckwitz, Germany
LSA Sevilla, Spain
LSA Siena, Italy
LSA Stuttgart, Germany
LSA Sucre, Bolivia
LSA Taormina, Italy
LSA Tenerife, Spain
LSA Tours, France
LSA Treviso, Italy
LSA Valencia, Spain
LSA Vienna, Austria
LSA Viña del Mar, Chile

Learning Programs International

Learning Programs International–Argentina
Learning Programs International–Chile
Learning Programs International–Costa Rica
Learning Programs International–Mexico
Learning Programs International–Spain

Learning Theatre, Inc.

Encore! Ensemble Theatre Workshop

Lebanon Valley College

Daniel Fox Youth Scholars Institute
Lebanon Valley College Summer Music Camp

Les Elfes International Summer/Winter Camp

Les Elfes–International Summer/Winter Camp

Leysin American School in Switzerland

Summer in Switzerland

Lifeschool Wilderness Adventures and Learning Program

Lifeschool Wilderness Adventures–Summer Adventures

Lifeway Christian Resources

Camp Crestridge for Girls
Camp Ridgecrest for Boys

LIFEWORKS International

LIFEWORKS with the Australian Red Cross
LIFEWORKS with the British Virgin Islands Marine Parks and Conservation Department
LIFEWORKS with the DPF Foundation in Thailand
LIFEWORKS with the Galapagos Islands' National Parks

Ligonier Camp and Conference Center

Adventure Camps
Ligonier Camp
Next Level Camp

Linden Hill School

Linden Hill Summer Program

Lions Club Organization

Lions Camp Merrick Deaf/HOH/KODA Program
Lions Camp Merrick Diabetes Program

Litchfield Performing Arts

Greenhouse: Litchfield Jazz Festival Summer Dance Institute
Litchfield Jazz Festival Summer Music School Program

Little Keswick School

Little Keswick School Summer Session

Little Palm Family Theatre

Camp Little Palm for the Performing Arts

Lochearn Camp for Girls

Longacre Expeditions

Longacre Expeditions, Adventure 28
Longacre Expeditions, Alaska
Longacre Expeditions, Belize
Longacre Expeditions, Blue Ridge
Longacre Expeditions, British Columbia
Longacre Expeditions, British Isles
Longacre Expeditions, Downeast
Longacre Expeditions, Hawaii
Longacre Expeditions, Iceland
Longacre Expeditions, Laurel Highlands
Longacre Expeditions, Leadership Training
Longacre Expeditions, New England/Canada
Longacre Expeditions, Pacific Coast and Inlands
Longacre Expeditions, Peak to Peak
Longacre Expeditions, Photography
Longacre Expeditions, Surf Oregon
Longacre Expeditions, Virgin Islands
Longacre Expeditions, Volcanoes
Longacre Expeditions, Western Challenge
Longacre Expeditions, Whales
Longacre Expeditions, Wind and Waves

Longacre Farm

Longacre Leadership Program

The Loomis Chaffee School

The Loomis Chaffee Summer in France
The Loomis Chaffee Summer in Spain

Loras College

Loras All-Sports Camp

Louisiana College

Lady Wildcat Basketball Camp
Louisiana College Center for Academically Talented Students (CATS)
Louisiana College Summer Superior Program
Wildcat Basketball Camp

Lynn University

Kampus Kampers
Pine Tree Camps at Lynn University

Mad River Glen Cooperative

Mad River Glen Naturalist Adventure Camp

Maine College of Art

Maine College of Art Early College Program

Maine Golf and Tennis Academy

Maine Golf Academy–Family Camp
Maine Golf Academy–Junior Golf Camp
Maine Golf and Tennis Academy–Serve and Turf
Maine Tennis Academy–Junior Tennis Camp

Maine Teen Camp

Maine Teen Camp

Manchester, NH Lions and Boston, MA Kiwanis Clubs

Camp Allen

Maplebrook School

Maplebrook School's Summer Program

Marbridge Foundation, Inc.

Marbridge Summer Camp

Marine Military Academy

Marine Military Academy English as a Second Language (ESL)
Marine Military Academy Summer Military Training Camp

The Marvelwood School

Marvelwood Summer

Marywood University

Pathways at Marywood University

Massachusetts College of Art

Massachusetts College of Art/Creative Vacation
Massachusetts College of Art/Summer Studios

Massachusetts Institute of Technology

MIT MITE^{2}S (Minority Introduction to Engineering, Entrepreneurship and Science)

Massanutten Military Academy

Massanutten Military Academy Summer Cadet Program
Summer Leadership Education and Training

Maui Surfer Girls

Maui Surfer Girls
Maui Surfer Girls–Advanced Surf Camp on Kauai
Maui Surfer Girls–Mother/Daughter

The McCallie School

McCallie Sports Camp
McCallie Academic Camp
McCallie Lacrosse Camp

McGaw YMCA

Camp Echo

Medeba

Medeba Leader in Training Program
Medeba Summer Camp

Med-O-Lark Camp

Mercer County Community College
Camp College–Institute for Arts and Sciences

Mercersburg Academy Summer and Extended Programs
Mercersburg Academy Blue Storm Boys Basketball School
Mercersburg Academy Blue Storm Football Camp
Mercersburg Academy Junior Adventure Camp
Mercersburg Academy Summer Study in France
Mercersburg Academy Young Writer's Camp
Mercersburg Adventure Camp
Mercersburg All-American Wrestling Camp & Junior All-American Wrestling Camp
Mercersburg ESL Plus Program
Mercersburg Onstage! Young Actors Workshop
Mercersburg Academy Summer Study in Spain
Mercersburg Teen Adventure Camp
Mercersburg The World's A Stage Theatre Workshop

MexArt
MexArt: Art and Spanish
MexArt Dance: Dance and Spanish

Miami University
Miami University Junior Scholars Program
Miami University Summer Sports School

Michigan State University
Michigan State University High School Engineering Institute

Michigan Technological University
Michigan Technological University American Indian Workshop
Michigan Technological University Explorations in Engineering Workshop
Michigan Technological University Honors Orchestra Program
Michigan Technological University Summer Youth Program
Michigan Technological University Women in Engineering Workshop

Middlesex County College
Camp Middlesex

Millennium Entrepreneurs
Millennium Entrepreneurs Camp CEO
Millennium Entrepreneurs "Training Tomorrow's Business Leaders Today"

Millersville University of Pennsylvania
Millersville University of Pennsylvania–Summer Language Camps for High School Students

Milwaukee School of Engineering
Milwaukee School of Engineering (MSOE)–Discover the Possibilities
Milwaukee School of Engineering (MSOE)–Focus on Nursing
Milwaukee School of Engineering (MSOE)–Focus on the Possibilities

MIMC
MIMC–Intensive Music Camp
MIMC–Language Camp
MIMC–Music and Sports Camp

Mississippi University for Women
Mississippi Governor's School

Miss Porter's School
Miss Porter's School Athletic Experience
Miss Porter's School Summer Challenge
Miss Porter's School Arts Alive!
The Sarah Porter Leadership Institute

The Monarch School
The Monarch School Summer Camp
The Monarch School Summer Course

Montclair State University
Montclair State University Hi Jump Program
Montclair State University Summer Camp for Academically Gifted and Talented Youth

Monte Vista Christian School
Monte Vista ESL Intensive Language Institute

Montgomery Bell Academy
Montgomery Bell Academy–All-Sports Camps
Montgomery Bell Academy–LEAD Program
Montgomery Bell Academy–Specialty Sports Camps
Montgomery Bell Academy–Summer Cooking Camp
Montgomery Bell Academy–Summer Music Camp
Montgomery Bell Academy–Summer School
Montgomery Bell Academy–Summer Science Experience
Montgomery Bell Academy–Summer Theater Camp

Montgomery College Workforce Development & Continuing Education Youth Programs
Montgomery College WDCE–Aspiring Filmmakers
Montgomery College WDCE–Biotechnology and Diversity Camp
Montgomery College WDCE–Computer Programming Camp–Co-ed
Montgomery College WDCE–Computer Programming Camp for Middle School Girls
Montgomery College WDCE–Culinary Arts–Kids Cook
Montgomery College WDCE–Entrepreneurship Camp 2005
Montgomery College WDCE–FIT Summer Camp
Montgomery College WDCE–GURL Power
Montgomery College WDCE–Hands on Art
Montgomery College WDCE–Inventor's Workshop
Montgomery College WDCE–Joy of Art
Montgomery College WDCE–Language in Motion
Montgomery College WDCE–Leadership Skills Camp
Montgomery College WDCE–Mathematics Enrichment Program
Montgomery College WDCE–Science Adventures
Montgomery College WDCE–Summer Dinner Theatre
Montgomery College WDCE–Summer Science Camp for Girls
Montgomery College WDCE–Summer Student Writing Institute
Montgomery College WDCE–Summer Youth Programs
Montgomery College WDCE–Super Sleuths–Meet the Challenge
Montgomery College WDCE–Web Design Camp for Girls and Boys
Montgomery College WDCE–World Events 2005
Montgomery College WDCE–Young Scientist Academy

Montverde Academy
Montverde Academy Summer School

Morning Cheer, Inc.
Camp Sandy Cove
The Marsh
Summer Family Conference

The Morris Farm Trust
Summer Days at the Morris Farm

Mountain Adventure Guides
Mountain Adventure Guides: Summer Adventure Camp–Blue Ridge Expedition I
Mountain Adventure Guides: Summer Adventure Camp–Blue Ridge Expedition II
Mountain Adventure Guides: Summer Adventure Camp–Jr. Adventure Camp

Mountain Camp
Mountain Camp

Mountain Meadow Ranch
Mountain Meadow Ranch

Mountain Workshop
Mountain Workshop–Graduate Plus Awesome Adventures
Mountain Workshop–Awesome 5: North Woods of Maine
Mountain Workshop–Awesome 4: Pennsylvania
Mountain Workshop–Awesome 1: Adirondacks
Mountain Workshop–Awesome 6: Quebec
Mountain Workshop–Awesome 3: Maine Coast
Mountain Workshop–Awesome 2: Vermont
Mountain Workshop–Bike 1: Martha's Vineyard and Nantucket
Mountain Workshop–Bike Touring Days 1
Mountain Workshop–Bike 2

Mountain Workshop/Dirt Camp: Dirt Camp Junior Killington
Mountain Workshop/Dirt Camp–Mountain Bike Days 1
Mountain Workshop/Dirt Camp–Mountain Bike Days 3
Mountain Workshop/Dirt Camp–Mountain Bike Days 2
Mountain Workshop–Graduate Awesome Adventures
Mountain Workshop–Junior Awesome Adventures
Mountain Workshop–Leadership Through Adventure: Adirondacks
Mountain Workshop–Original Awesome Adventures
Mountain Workshop–Trailblazer Awesome Adventures

Mount Holyoke College

Mount Holyoke College SEARCH (Summer Explorations and Research Collaborations for High School Girls) Program
Mount Holyoke College SummerMath Program

The Museum of Flight

Aerospace Camp Experience

Musiker Tours

Discovery Works New England Community Service Experience
Musiker Tours: Action Europe
Musiker Tours: Action USA
Musiker Tours: Alaska Aloha
Musiker Tours: America Coast to Coast
Musiker Tours: Cali-Pacific Passport
Musiker Tours: ComboCamp America
Musiker Tours: Discover America
Musiker Tours: Eastcoaster
Musiker Tours: Westcoaster

Nantahala Outdoor Center

Nantahala Outdoor Center–Kids Adventure Sports Camp
Nantahala Outdoor Center–Kids Kayaking Courses

National Computer Camps

National Computer Camps at Fairfield University
National Computer Camps at La Roche College
National Computer Camps at Notre Dame College
National Computer Camps at Oglethorpe University
National Computer Camps at San Francisco State University

National Guitar Workshop

National Guitar Workshop–Austin, TX
National Guitar Workshop–Chicago, IL
National Guitar Workshop–Los Angeles, CA
National Guitar Workshop–Murfreesboro, TN
National Guitar Workshop–New Milford, CT
National Guitar Workshop–New Orleans, LA
National Guitar Workshop–San Francisco, CA
National Guitar Workshop–Seattle, WA
The National Music Workshop Day Jams–Alexandria, VA
The National Music Workshop Day Jams–Ann Arbor, MI
The National Music Workshop Day Jams–Baltimore, MD
The National Music Workshop Day Jams–Boston, MA
The National Music Workshop Day Jams–Chicago, IL
The National Music Workshop Day Jams–Long Island, NY
The National Music Workshop Day Jams–Los Angeles, CA
The National Music Workshop Day Jams–Manhattan, NY
The National Music Workshop Day Jams–Philadelphia, PA
The National Music Workshop Day Jams–Purchase, NY
The National Music Workshop Day Jams–Rockville, MD

National Student Leadership Conference

National Student Leadership Conference: Business and Commerce
National Student Leadership Conference: International Diplomacy
National Student Leadership Conference: Law and Advocacy–California
National Student Leadership Conference: Law and Advocacy–Washington, DC
National Student Leadership Conference: Mastering Leadership
National Student Leadership Conference: Medicine and Health Care

The Navigators

Eagle Lake Bike Camp
Eagle Lake Camp Crew Program
Eagle Lake Camp–East
Eagle Lake Camp Jaunts–Kenya Mission Adventure
Eagle Lake Camp Jaunts–Minnesota Boundary Waters
Eagle Lake Camp Jaunts–Norway Mission Adventure
Eagle Lake Horse Camp
Eagle Lake Resident Camp
Eagle Lake Wilderness Program

NAWA Academy

NAWA Academy–Girls on the Go
NAWA Academy–Great Challenge
NAWA Academy–Lassen Expedition
NAWA Academy–Trinity Challenge

NBC Camps

NBC Camps–Basketball–Adult & Child Hoops–Spokane, WA
NBC Camps–Basketball–Crowell's Intensity–Spokane, WA
NBC Camps–Basketball Individual Training–Alaska
NBC Camps–Basketball Individual Training (Boys)–Auburn, WA
NBC Camps–Basketball Individual Training–CA
NBC Camps–Basketball Individual Training (Girls)–Auburn, WA
NBC Camps–Basketball Individual Training–La Grande, OR
NBC Camps–Basketball Individual Training–Montana
NBC Camps–Basketball Individual Training–Newberg, OR
NBC Camps–Basketball Individual Training–Olds, AB Canada
NBC Camps–Basketball Individual Training–Spangle, WA
NBC Camps–Basketball Individual Training–Spokane, WA
NBC Camps–Basketball Individual Training–Three Hills, AB Canada
NBC Camps–Basketball Point Guard Play–Spangle, WA
NBC Camps–Basketball Post & Shooting–Spokane, WA
NBC Camps–Basketball Speed–Alaska
NBC Camps–Basketball Speed Explosion–California
NBC Camps–Basketball Speed Explosion–Spokane, WA
NBC Camps–Basketball–Team–Billings, MT
NBC Camps–Basketball–Team (Boys)–Alaska
NBC Camps–Basketball–Team (Girls)–Alaska
NBC Camps–Basketball–Team (Girls)–Spangle, WA
NBC Camps–Basketball–Team–La Grande, OR
NBC Camps–Soccer–Spangle, WA
NBC Camps–Soccer Speed Explosion–Spokane, WA
NBC Camps–Volleyball–Alaska
NBC Camps–Volleyball–California
NBC Camps–Volleyball–Oregon
NBC Camps–Volleyball Speed Explosion–California
NBC Camps–Volleyball Speed Explosion–Spokane, WA
NBC Camps–Basketball Individual Training–Isle of Man

Nelson/Feller Tennis Camp

Nelson/Feller Tennis Camp–Lakeland College
Nelson/Feller Tennis Camp–University of Wisconsin–Oshkosh

New Camps, Inc.

Camp Mishawaka for Boys
Camp Mishawaka for Girls

New England Vacation Tours Inc.

Teen Tour USA and Canada

The Newgrange School

Newgrange Summer Program
Newgrange Summer Tutoring Program

New Haven/León Sister City Project

Summer Delegation to León, Nicaragua

New Jersey YMHA–YWHA Camps

New Jersey YMHA–YWHA Camp Mountaintop
New Jersey YMHA–YWHA Camp Nah-jee-wah
New Jersey YMHA–YWHA Camp Nesher
New Jersey YMHA–YWHA Cedar Lake Camp
New Jersey YMHA–YWHA Round Lake Camp

New Jersey YMHA–YWHA Teen Camp

The Newman School
Newman School Summer Session

New Mexico Institute of Mining and Technology
New Mexico Tech Summer Mini-Course

New York Film Academy
The New York Film Academy, Disney-MGM Studios, FL
The New York Film Academy, Harvard University, Cambridge, MA
The New York Film Academy in Florence, Italy
The New York Film Academy in London
The New York Film Academy in Paris
The New York Film Academy, Princeton University, Princeton, NJ
The New York Film Academy, The Dalton School, New York, NY
The New York Film Academy, Universal Studios, Hollywood, Ca

New York Military Academy
New York Military Academy–JROTC Summer Program
Summer School at New York Military Academy

New York University
Tisch School of the Arts–International High School Program–Dublin
Tisch School of the Arts–International High School Program–Paris
Tisch School of the Arts–Summer High School Programs

Nicaragua/Costa Rica High School Summer Exchange
Spanish Through Leadership–Nicaragua
Spanish Through Leadership–Nicaragua/Costa Rica

92nd Street YM–YWHA
92nd Street Y Camps–Camp Bari Tov
92nd Street Y Camps–Camp Haverim
92nd Street Y Camps–Camp Kesher
92nd Street Y Camps–Camp Kesher Junior
92nd Street Y Camps–Camp K'Ton Ton
92nd Street Y Camps–Camp Tevah for Science and Nature
92nd Street Y Camps–Camp Tova
92nd Street Y Camps–Camp Yaffa for the Arts
92nd Street Y Camps–Camp Yomi
92nd Street Y Camps–Fantastic Gymnastics
92nd Street Y Camps–The TIYUL
92nd Street Y Camps–Trailblazers

North Carolina Outward Bound/Outward Bound, USA
North Carolina Outward Bound–Outer Banks
North Carolina Outward Bound–Southern Appalachian Mountains

North Carolina School of the Arts
North Carolina School of the Arts Summer Session

North Carolina State University
Young Investigators Program in Nuclear Science & Technology

North Country Camps
North Country Camps—Camp Lincoln for Boys
North Country Camps—Camp Whippoorwill for Girls

North Country School
Camp Treetops

Northern Sports and Recreation
Camp Brandon for Boys

Northfield Mount Hermon School
Northfield Mount Hermon Summer Session

Northwaters Wilderness Programs
Northern Lights
Northwaters Wilderness Programs

Northwestern University
Northwestern University's College Preparation Program
Northwestern University's National High School Institute

Northwestern University's Center for Talent Development
Center for Talent Development Summer Academic Program

The Northwest School
The Northwest School Summer Program

Northwest Youth Corps
Summer Conservation Corps
Teens-n-Trails
Youth Forest Camps

Norwich University
Future Leader Camp

Oak Creek Ranch School
Oak Creek Ranch Summer School

Oak Hill Academy
Oak Hill Academy Summer Program

Oak Ridge Military Academy
Oak Ridge Academic Summer Camp
Oak Ridge Summer Leadership Camp

Ocean Educations, Ltd.
Marine and Environmental Science Program

Offense-Defense Golf Camp, Massachusetts

Offense-Defense Tennis Camp

Ojai Valley School
Ojai Valley School Summer Programs

OMNI Camp
OMNI Camp

Onaway Camp Trust
Camp Onaway

Operafestival Roma, Inc.
Operafestival di Roma

Oregon Episcopal School
OES–Challenge Workshops
OES–Summer Adventure Camp
OES–Summer Discovery
OES–Summer Mini Camps
OES–Summer Wonder

Oregon Museum of Science and Industry
Cascade Science School
Hancock Field Station
Pacific Marine Science Camp
Redwood National Park Camps
Salmon Camp for Native Americans
Salmon Camp Research Team for Native Americans–Oregon
Salmon Camp Research Team for Native Americans–Redwoods
Salmon Camp Research Team for Native Americans–San Juan Island
San Juan Island Camps
Shizen Kyampu-Japanese Language Science Camp

Oregon State University
Adventures in Learning
Expeditions

Outpost Wilderness Adventure
Outpost Wilderness Adventure–Adventure Skills
Outpost Wilderness Adventure–Alpine Rock and Ice
Outpost Wilderness Adventure–Copper Canyon Project
Outpost Wilderness Adventure–Mountain Bike/Rock Camp
Outpost Wilderness Adventure–Wind River Expedition

Outreach Program Office at Auburn University
American Allstar Dance Camp
Architecture Summer Camp
Auburn University Design Workshop
Dance Magic
Half–Time USA
Josten Yearbook Summer Workshop
National Cheerleaders Association Cheerleader Camps
Universal Cheerleaders Association and Universal Dance Association Camps
World Affairs Youth Seminar

Outward Bound West/Outward Bound, USA

Outward Bound West–Backpacking and Whitewater Rafting, Oregon
Outward Bound West–Backpacking, Climbing, and Rafting–Boys
Outward Bound West–Backpacking, Climbing, and Rafting–Colorado
Outward Bound West–Cataract Canyon Rafting
Outward Bound West–Climbing and Backpacking–High Sierra, CA
Outward Bound West–Climbing, Backpacking, and Canoeing–North Cascades, WA
Outward Bound West–Colorado Rockies Lightweight Backpacking
Outward Bound West–Mountaineering and Rafting, Oregon
Outward Bound West–Mountaineering–Colorado
Outward Bound West–Mountaineering–North Cascades, WA
Outward Bound West–Mountaineering, Rafting, and Climbing-XT, Oregon
Outward Bound West–Sea Kayaking and Mountaineering–Alaska
Outward Bound West–Sea Kayaking, Backpacking, and Mountaineering–Washington
Outward Bound West–Service Course–North Cascades
Outward Bound West–Sierra Nevada Mountaineering
Outward Bound West–Southwest Mountaineering, Rafting, and Canyoneering
Outward Bound West–Southwest Mystery Expedition
Outward Bound West–Utah Summer Semester
Outward Bound West–Volcanoes Mountaineering–Oregon
Outward Bound West–Wyoming Rock Climbing

Overland Travel, Inc.

Overland: Acadia and Prince Edward Island Bicycle Touring and Sea-Kayaking
Overland: Adventure Camp for 5th and 6th Grade Boys
Overland: Adventure Camp for 5th and 6th Grade Girls
Overland: Alaskan Expedition Hiking, Sea-Kayaking, and Rafting
Overland: American Challenge Coast-to-Coast Bicycle Touring
Overland: American Community Service, Alaska
Overland: American Community Service, Hawaii
Overland: American Community Service, New England
Overland: American Community Service, Southwest
Overland: Appalachian Trail Challenge Hiking
Overland: Blue Ridge Explorer Hiking, Rafting and Kayaking
Overland: Cape Cod and the Islands Bicycle Touring
Overland: Colorado and Utah Mountain Biking and Rafting
Overland: Costa Rica Explorer Hiking, Rafting, and Sea-Kayaking
Overland: European Challenge Bicycle Touring from Paris to Rome
Overland: European Explorer Hiking, Rafting, and Sea Kayaking
Overland: Hawaii Explorer Hiking, Kayaking, Sailing and Snorkeling
Overland: Language Study Abroad in Costa Rica
Overland: Language Study Abroad in France
Overland: Language Study Abroad in Spain
Overland: New England Explorer Hiking, Mountain Biking, and Rafting
Overland: Pacific Coast Bicycle Touring and Rafting
Overland: Paris to the Sea Bicycle Touring
Overland: Rocky Mountain Explorer Hiking, Mountain Biking, and Rafting
Overland: Shasta & the Sierras Backpacking, Climbing and Rafting
Overland: Teton Challenge Hiking, Climbing and Kayaking
Overland: The Alpine Challenge Leadership Course Backpacking and Hiking
Overland: Vermont & Montreal Bicycle Touring
Overland: World Service, Costa Rica
Overland: Yellowstone Explorer Backpacking, Rock Climbing, and Rafting

Oxbridge Academic Programs

L' Académie de Paris
The Cambridge Prep Experience
The Cambridge Tradition
The Oxford Prep Experience
The Oxford Tradition

The Oxford Academy

The Oxford Academy Summer Program

Oxford Media School

Oxford Media School–Film
Oxford Media School–Film Master Class
Oxford Media School–Newsroom in Europe
Oxford Media School–Newsroom in Europe, Master Class

Oxford School

Oxford School Summer Camp

Oxford Tutorial College

Oxford Advanced Studies Program

Pacific Village Institute

China's Frontiers: Diverse Landscapes and Peoples
Tibetan Culture of Northern India

Padua Franciscan High School

Padua Franciscan High School Sports Camps
Padua Summer Experience

Pali Overnight Adventures

Acting Academy at Pali Overnight Adventures
Battlebot Mania at Pali Overnight Adventures
Culinary Institute at Pali Overnight Adventures
Film Institute at Pali Overnight Adventures
Gymnastics Academy at Pali Overnight Adventures
Hollywood Stunt Camp at Pali Overnight Adventures
Horseback Riding Academy at Pali Overnight Adventures
Leadership Training at Pali Overnight Adventures
Pali Overnight Adventures Camp
Rock Star Camp at Pali Overnight Adventures
Scuba Adventures at Pali Overnight Adventures
Secret Agent Camp at Pali Overnight Adventures
Skateboarding Academy at Pali Overnight Adventures
Watersports Extravaganza at Pali Overnight Adventures

Palm Beach Photographic Centre

Fotocamp

PANIM: The Institute for Jewish Leadership and Values

Summer JAM (Judaism, Activism, and Mitzvah Work)

Parsons School of Design

Parsons Pre-College Academy
Parsons Summer Intensive Studies–New York
Parsons Summer Intensive Studies–Paris

Passage: Project for International Education

Ladakh Summer Passage
Lower Mustang Summer Passage
Personal Passage
Tibetan Summer Passage

Paul Hogan Sports Camps

Paul Hogan's Shooter's Gold Basketball Camp–Alton
Paul Hogan's Shooter's Gold Basketball Camp–Gilford
Paul Hogan's Shooter's Gold Basketball Camp–Laconia
Paul Hogan's Shooter's Gold Basketball Camp–Lancaster
Paul Hogan's Shooter's Gold Basketball Camp–Littleton
Paul Hogan's Shooter's Gold Basketball Camp–Manchester
Paul Hogan's Shooter's Gold Basketball Camp–Meredith
Paul Hogan's Shooter's Gold Basketball Camp–Tilton
Paul Hogan's Shooter's Gold Basketball Camp–Woodsville
Paul Hogan's Specialty Basketball Camp

PAX Abroad

PAX Abroad–Brazil
PAX Abroad–Ecuador Rainforest Adventure
PAX Abroad–Ecuador–Spanish Language Immersion
PAX Abroad–Summer Spain
PAX Abroad to Australia

Peace Works International
Peace Works International–Costa Rica
Peace Works International–Peru
Peace Works International–Ecuador

The Peddie School
The Peddie School Summer Day School

The Pennsylvania State University at Erie, The Behrend College
College for Kids
Teen Challenge

The Pennsylvania State University–WISE
Women in Science & Engineering Camp

Pepperdine University
Pepperdine University Summer College for High School Students

Performance PLUS
Performance PLUS–Positive Learning Using the Stage+Studio+Screen

Perry-Mansfield Performing Arts School and Camp
Perry-Mansfield Performing Arts School and Camp

The Phelps School
The Phelps School Summer Program

Phillips Academy (Andover)
Phillips Academy Summer Session

Phillips Exeter Academy
Phillips Exeter Academy French Study Tour
Phillips Exeter Academy Summer School
Phillips Exeter Academy Taiwan and Beijing Summer Study Tour

Pine Island Camp
Pine Island Camp

Pine Manor College
Leadership Adventure in Boston
Summer Summit on Leadership

Pine Ridge School
Pine Ridge Summer Program

The Pingry School
Pingry Academic Camps
Pingry Day Camps
Pingry Lacrosse Camp–Martinsville Campus
Pingry Lacrosse Camp–Short Hills Campus
Pingry Soccer Camp
Pingry Softball Camp
Pingry Summer Enrichment Experience

Plato College
Plato College–English/French Intensive Courses

Point CounterPoint Chamber Music Camp

Point O' Pines Camp
Point O' Pines Camp for Girls

Portsmouth Abbey School
Portsmouth Abbey Summer School

The Potomac School
Potomac School Summer Programs

Poulter Colorado Camps
Poulter Colorado Camps
Poulter Colorado Camps: Adventures Planet Earth–Austria
Poulter Colorado Camps: Adventures Planet Earth–Costa Rica
Poulter Colorado Camps: Adventures Planet Earth–New Zealand
Poulter Colorado Camps: Adventures Planet Earth–Spain

Power Chord Academy
Power Chord Academy–Chicago
Power Chord Academy–Los Angeles
Power Chord Academy–New York City

Pratt Institute
Pratt Institute Summer Pre-College Program for High School Students

Presbyterian Clearwater Forest

Presbytery of Eastern Virginia
Camp Jordan for Children with Diabetes
Makemie Woods Summer Camp

Prescott College
Four Corners School of Outdoor Education: Southwest Ed-Venture

Princeton Ballet School
Princeton Ballet School's Ballet Plus Junior
Princeton Ballet School's Ballet Plus Senior
Princeton Ballet School's Summer Intensive

Prince William Sound Science Center
From the Forest to the Sea

Pripstein's Camp

Professional Sports Camps
Professional Sports Camps–Big League Baseball Camp
Professional Sports Camps–Hall of Fame Basketball Camp
Professional Sports Camps–Hall of Fame Soccer Camp

Programs Abroad Travel Alternatives
Programs Abroad Travel Alternatives–Canada
Programs Abroad Travel Alternatives–Costa Rica
Programs Abroad Travel Alternatives–Ecuador
Programs Abroad Travel Alternatives–France
Programs Abroad Travel Alternatives–Germany
Programs Abroad Travel Alternatives–Guatemala
Programs Abroad Travel Alternatives–Ireland
Programs Abroad Travel Alternatives–Italy
Programs Abroad Travel Alternatives–Mexico
Programs Abroad Travel Alternatives–Peru
Programs Abroad Travel Alternatives–Russia
Programs Abroad Travel Alternatives–Spain

ProShot Basketball Camp
ProShot Basketball Camp–Boys Camp
ProShot Basketball Camp–Girls Camp

Purcell Marian High School
Purcell Marian High School Cavalier Basketball Camp
Purcell Marian High School Summer School

Purchase College, State University of New York
Purchase Youth Theatre
Shakespeare at Purchase
Visual Arts Institute for High School Students
Young Actors and Playwrights Workshop
Young Artists at Purchase
Young Filmmakers at Purchase
Young Photographers

The Putney School
The Putney School Summer Arts Program
The Putney School Summer Program for International Education (ESL)
The Putney School Summer Writing Program

Putney Student Travel
Excel at Amherst College and Williams College
Excel at Madrid/Barcelona
Excel at Oxford/Tuscany
Excel at UC Santa Cruz
Excel Cuba
Putney Student Travel–Community Service–Alaska
Putney Student Travel–Community Service–Brazil
Putney Student Travel–Community Service–Costa Rica
Putney Student Travel–Community Service–Dominican Republic
Putney Student Travel–Community Service–Dominica, West Indies
Putney Student Travel–Community Service–Ecuador
Putney Student Travel–Community Service–Hawaii
Putney Student Travel–Community Service-India
Putney Student Travel–Community Service–Montana
Putney Student Travel–Community Service-Nicaragua
Putney Student Travel–Community Service–Nusa Penida and Bali
Putney Student Travel–Community Service–Tanzania
Putney Student Travel–Cultural Exploration–Australia, New Zealand, and Fiji
Putney Student Travel–Cultural Exploration-Creative Writing in Cuba

▶ Putney Student Travel

Putney Student Travel–Cultural Exploration–Eastern European Heritage
Putney Student Travel–Cultural Exploration–France, Holland, and England
Putney Student Travel–Cultural Exploration–Switzerland, Italy, France, and Holland
Putney Student Travel–Cultural Exploration–Thailand and Cambodia
Putney Student Travel–Cultural Exploration–Theatre in Britain
Putney Student Travel–Language Learning–Costa Rica
Putney Student Travel–Language Learning–France
Putney Student Travel–Language Learning–Spain

Quest Scholars Program
Quest Scholars Program at Stanford/QuestLeadership

Ramey Tennis and Equestrian Schools
Ramey Summer Riding Camps
Ramey Summer Tennis Camps

The Ranch–Lake Placid Academy
The Ranch–Lake Placid Academy
The Ranch–Lake Placid Teen Travel Camp
The Ranch–National Golf Camp–Lake Placid

Randolph-Macon Academy
Randolph-Macon Academy Summer Programs

Rassias Programs
Rassias Programs–Arles, France
Rassias Programs–Gijón, Spain
Rassias Programs–Pontevedra, Spain
Rassias Programs–Segovia, Spain
Rassias Programs–Tours, France

Rawhide Ranch
Rawhide Ranch

The Rectory School
Rectory School Summer Session

Red Bank Regional High School
Summer Academy for the Visual and Performing Arts

Red Pine Camp for Girls

Rein Teen Tours
Rein Teen Tours–American Adventure
Rein Teen Tours–California Caper
Rein Teen Tours–Crossroads
Rein Teen Tours–Eastern Adventure
Rein Teen Tours–Grand Adventure
Rein Teen Tours–Hawaiian/Alaskan Adventure
Rein Teen Tours–Western Adventure

Rhode Island School of Design
Rhode Island School of Design Pre-College Program

Rhodes College
Rhodes Summer Writing Institute

Rider University
Rider University Opportunity for Academically Gifted and Talented High School Students

Ridgewood YMCA
YMCA Camp Bernie

Ringling School of Art and Design
Ringling School of Art and Design Pre-College Perspective
Ringling School of Art and Design's Teen Studio

Riverside Military Academy
Riverside Military Academy High Adventure Camp
Riverside Military Academy Summer Opportunity and Academic Review
Riverside Military Academy Young Cadet Camp

River Way Ranch Camp

Road's End Farm
Road's End Farm Horsemanship Camp

Roaring Brook Camp for Boys

Rochester Institute of Technology
Graphic Media Experience

Rockbrook Camp

Rocky Mountain Bird Observatory
On the Wing

Rowe Camp and Conference Center, Inc.
Rowe Camp

Rowland Hall-St. Mark's School
SummerWorks

Rumsey Hall School
Rumsey Hall School Summer Session

Rust College
Rust College Study Abroad in Africa

Rustic Pathways
RUSTIC PATHWAYS–ACCELERATED SPANISH IMMERSION
RUSTIC PATHWAYS–ADVENTURE IN AMERICA'S SOUTHWEST
RUSTIC PATHWAYS–AWESOME AUSSIE EXPLORER
RUSTIC PATHWAYS–BIG FIJI EXPLORER
RUSTIC PATHWAYS–BUDDHIST LIFE & ANGKOR WAT
RUSTIC PATHWAYS–COSTA RICA ADVENTURER
RUSTIC PATHWAYS–COSTA RICA EXTREME
RUSTIC PATHWAYS–COSTA RICA NATURAL WONDERS
RUSTIC PATHWAYS–DIVER'S DREAM IN THE FIJI ISLANDS
RUSTIC PATHWAYS–ELEPHANTS & AMAZING THAILAND
RUSTIC PATHWAYS–EXTENDED COMMUNITY SERVICE IN THE FIJI ISLANDS
RUSTIC PATHWAYS–EXTREME PLANET
RUSTIC PATHWAYS–HAWAIIAN ISLANDS ADVENTURE
RUSTIC PATHWAYS–HIGH ADRENALINE AUSSIE
RUSTIC PATHWAYS–HIGHLANDS COMMUNITY SERVICE IN FIJI
RUSTIC PATHWAYS–INTRO TO COMMUNITY SERVICE IN FIJI
RUSTIC PATHWAYS–INTRO TO COMMUNITY SERVICE IN THAILAND
RUSTIC PATHWAYS–LEARN TO DIVE IN THE FIJI ISLANDS
RUSTIC PATHWAYS–OUTBACK 4-WHEEL DRIVE SAFARI
RUSTIC PATHWAYS–PHOTOGRAPHY & ADVENTURE IN THAILAND
RUSTIC PATHWAYS–RAMP UP YOUR SPANISH
RUSTIC PATHWAYS–RHYTHM IN THE RICEFIELDS
RUSTIC PATHWAYS–RICEFIELDS, MONKS & SMILING CHILDREN
RUSTIC PATHWAYS–SKI AND SNOWBOARD ADVENTURE IN NEW ZEALAND
RUSTIC PATHWAYS–SNAPSHOT OF FIJI
RUSTIC PATHWAYS–SPANISH LANGUAGE IMMERSION
RUSTIC PATHWAYS–SURF THE SUMMER–COSTA RICA
RUSTIC PATHWAYS–SURF THE SUMMER–THE FIJI ISLANDS
RUSTIC PATHWAYS–THE AMAZING THAILAND ADVENTURE
RUSTIC PATHWAYS–THE CANO NEGRO SERVICE PROJECT
RUSTIC PATHWAYS–THE SUNSHINE COAST & SYDNEY
RUSTIC PATHWAYS–THE THAI ELEPHANT CONSERVATION PROJECT
RUSTIC PATHWAYS–THE TURTLE CONSERVATION PROJECT
RUSTIC PATHWAYS–THE WONDERS & RICHES OF THAILAND
RUSTIC PATHWAYS–TOTALLY DOWNUNDER ADVENTURE
RUSTIC PATHWAYS–TROPICAL AUSSIE ADVENTURE
RUSTIC PATHWAYS–ULTIMATE AUSTRALIAN ADVENTURE
RUSTIC PATHWAYS–VOLCANOES AND RAINFORESTS

Rutgers Cooperative Extension System/Rutgers University
Lindley G. Cook 4-H Camp

Sagamore Institute of the Adirondacks
Grandparents' and Grandchildren's Camp

Sail Caribbean
Sail Caribbean–All Levels of Scuba Certification with Sailing
Sail Caribbean–British Virgin Islands
Sail Caribbean–Community Service
Sail Caribbean–Leeward Islands
Sail Caribbean–Marine Biology

St. Andrew's Episcopal School
St. Andrew's Summer Programs

St. George's School
St. George's Summer Session

St. Johns Country Day School
St. Johns Summer Camp

St. John's Northwestern Military Academy
Camp St. John's Northwestern
St. John's Northwestern Academic Camp
St. John's Northwestern ESL Camp

St. John's University
St. John's University Scholars Program

St. Louis County Promotional Bureau
St. Louis County 4-H Camp

St. Louis Jewish Community Center
Camp Sabra

St. Margaret's School
St. Margaret's School International Summer ESL Programme

St. Paul's Preparatory Academy
St. Paul's Preparatory Academy Summer Program

St. Stephen's Episcopal School
Arts on the Lake

Saint Thomas More School
Saint Thomas More School–Summer Academic Camp

Saint Vincent College
Saint Vincent College Challenge Program

Salisbury School
Salisbury Summer School of Reading and English

San Antonio Academy
Summer at the Academy

Sanborn Western Camps
Sanborn Western Camps: Big Spring Ranch for Boys
Sanborn Western Camps: High Trails Ranch for Girls

The San Francisco Shakespeare Festival
Bay Area Shakespeare Camp

Santa Catalina School
Santa Catalina School Summer Camp

Sargent Center Adventure Camp
Sargent Center Adventure Camp

Scandinavian Seminar
Environmental Studies and Solutions
Peace in the Modern World

The School for Field Studies
SFS: Community Wildlife Management
SFS: Conserving Coastal Diversity
SFS: Marine Parks Management Studies
SFS: Sustaining Tropical Ecosystems
SFS: Tropical Reforestation Studies

The School for Film and Television
"Summer in the City"

School of Engineering and Technology/Lake Superior State University
Robotics Camp
Women in Technology

Seacamp

SEACAMP San Diego
SEACAMP San Diego

Seattle Youth Symphony Orchestras
Marrowstone-in-the-City
Marrowstone Music Festival

SeaWorld Adventure Park
SeaWorld/Busch Gardens Tampa Bay Adventure Camp
SeaWorld Orlando Adventure Camp
SeaWorld San Antonio Adventure Camp
SeaWorld San Diego Adventure Camp

Seton Hill University
Science Quest

76ers Basketball Camp

Shaffer's High Sierra Camp, Inc.
Shaffer's High Sierra Camp

Shane (Trim-Down) Camp

Shattuck-St. Mary's School
Shattuck–St. Mary's Girls Elite Hockey Camp
Shattuck-St. Mary's Summer Discovery and English Language Institute
Shattuck-St. Mary's Boys Elite Hockey Camp

Shippensburg University of Pennsylvania
Shippensburg University Academic Camps–Acting & Theatre Arts
Shippensburg University Academic Camps–Government in Real Life
Shippensburg University Academic Camps–Science Academy for Girls
Shippensburg University Sports Camps–Baseball–Regular Camp
Shippensburg University Sports Camps–Baseball–Specialist Camp
Shippensburg University Sports Camps–Boys Basketball
Shippensburg University Sports Camps–Cross Country
Shippensburg University Sports Camps–Fast Pitch Softball
Shippensburg University Sports Camps–Father/Son Basketball Camp
Shippensburg University Sports Camps–Field Hockey
Shippensburg University Sports Camps–Football
Shippensburg University Sports Camps–Girls Basketball
Shippensburg University Sports Camps–Jumps
Shippensburg University Sports Camps–Soccer–Boys Camp
Shippensburg University Sports Camps–Soccer–Day Camp
Shippensburg University Sports Camps–Soccer–Girls Camp
Shippensburg University Sports Camps–Swimming
Shippensburg University Sports Camps–Tennis
Shippensburg University Sports Camps–Throws Camp
Shippensburg University Sports Camps–Track & Field
Shippensburg University Sports Camps–Volleyball–Girls Camp

Shodor Education Foundation, Inc.
Project SUCCEED

Sidwell Friends School
Sidwell Friends Basketball Camp
Sidwell Friends Bethesda Day Camp
Sidwell Friends Camp Corsica
Sidwell Friends DaVinci Days Art Studios, Young Artist Academy and Young Scientist Academy
Sidwell Friends Drama and Dance Workshops with BAPA
Sidwell Friends Explorer Day Camp, Explorer Voyagers and ExploreStar
Sidwell Friends Overnight Sea Kayaking Trip
Sidwell Friends Riverview Programs
Sidwell Friends Service Expedition to Hawaii
Sidwell Friends Soccer Program with American Soccer Academy
Sidwell Friends Summer Community Service Programs
Sidwell Friends Summer Program: Costa Rica
Sidwell Friends Summer Studies
Sidwell Friends Tennis Camp

Sidwell Friends Women's Leadership–St. Margaret's School

Signature Music Camp

Signature Music Teen Camp
Signature Music Youth Camp

SILC

International Summer Centre at Biarritz
International Summer Centre at Chatel
International Summer Centre at Paris-Brétigny

Simon's Rock College of Bard

Simon's Rock College of Bard Young Writers Workshop

SJ Ranch, Inc.

SJ Ranch Riding Camp

Skidmore College

Skidmore College–Acceleration Program in Art for High School Students
Skidmore College–Pre-College Program in the Liberal Arts for High School Students

Skylake Yosemite Camp

Skyland Camp for Girls

Smith College

Smith College Summer Science and Engineering Program

Snow Farm: The New England Craft Program

Snowy Owl Camp for Girls

Snowy Owl Camp for Girls

SoccerPlus Camps

SoccerPlus FieldPlayer Academy–Charleston, IL
SoccerPlus FieldPlayer Academy–Easthampton, MA
SoccerPlus FieldPlayer Academy–Hamilton, NY
SoccerPlus FieldPlayer Academy–Kent, CT
SoccerPlus FieldPlayer Academy–Pottstown, PA
SoccerPlus FieldPlayer Academy–Rome, GA
SoccerPlus FieldPlayer Academy–Slippery Rock, PA
SoccerPlus Goalkeeper School–Advanced National Training Center–Connecticut
SoccerPlus Goalkeeper School–Challenge Program–Brunswick, ME
SoccerPlus Goalkeeper School–Challenge Program–Charleston, IL
SoccerPlus Goalkeeper School–Challenge Program–Delaware, OH
SoccerPlus Goalkeeper School–Challenge Program–Fayetteville, NC
SoccerPlus Goalkeeper School–Challenge Program–Franklin, MA
SoccerPlus Goalkeeper School–Challenge Program–Hamilton, NY
SoccerPlus Goalkeeper School–Challenge Program–Kent, CT
SoccerPlus Goalkeeper School–Challenge Program–Pottstown, PA
SoccerPlus Goalkeeper School–Challenge Program–Rome, GA
SoccerPlus Goalkeeper School–Challenge Program–San Diego, CA
SoccerPlus Goalkeeper School–Challenge Program–Slippery Rock, PA
SoccerPlus Goalkeeper School–Challenge Program–Stockton, CA
SoccerPlus Goalkeeper School–Challenge Program–Suffield, CT
SoccerPlus Goalkeeper School–Challenge Program–Waco, TX
SoccerPlus Goalkeeper School–Competitive Program–Charleston, IL
SoccerPlus Goalkeeper School–Competitive Program–Easthampton, MA
SoccerPlus Goalkeeper School–Competitive Program–Hamilton, NY
SoccerPlus Goalkeeper School–Competitive Program–Kent, CT
SoccerPlus Goalkeeper School–Competitive Program–Pottstown, PA
SoccerPlus Goalkeeper School–Competitive Program–Rome, GA
SoccerPlus Goalkeeper School–Competitive Program–Slippery Rock, PA
SoccerPlus Goalkeeper School–Competitive Program–Suffield, CT
SoccerPlus Goalkeeper School–National Training Center–Brunswick, ME
SoccerPlus Goalkeeper School–National Training Center–Charleston, IL
SoccerPlus Goalkeeper School–National Training Center–Delaware, OH
SoccerPlus Goalkeeper School–National Training Center–Fayetteville, NC
SoccerPlus Goalkeeper School–National Training Center–Franklin, MA
SoccerPlus Goalkeeper School–National Training Center–Hamilton, NY
SoccerPlus Goalkeeper School–National Training Center–Kent, CT
SoccerPlus Goalkeeper School–National Training Center–Pottstown, PA
SoccerPlus Goalkeeper School–National Training Center–Rome, GA
SoccerPlus Goalkeeper School–National Training Center–San Diego, CA
SoccerPlus Goalkeeper School–National Training Center–Slippery Rock, PA
SoccerPlus Goalkeeper School–National Training Center–Stockton, CA
SoccerPlus Goalkeeper School–National Training Center–Waco, TX

Society for Christian Activities

Camp Good News for Young People and Teens

Sonatina Enterprises

Summer Sonatina International Piano Camp

South Carolina Governor's School for Science and Math

Summer Science Program at the South Carolina Governor's School for Science and Math

Southern Methodist University

Southern Methodist University–College Experience
Southern Methodist University TAG (Talented and Gifted)

Southern Oregon University Youth Programs

Academy

Southern Utah University

Camp Shakespeare

South Mountain YMCA

Camp Conrad Weiser

South Shore YMCA Camps

Camp Burgess
Camp Hayward
Great Escapes (Adventure Trips for Teens)–California Beach Escape
Great Escapes (Adventure Trips for Teens)–Canadian Adventure
Great Escapes (Adventure Trips for Teens)–Canadian Canoe and Kayak Adventure
Great Escapes (Adventure Trips for Teens)–Cape Cod Sail Adventure
Great Escapes (Adventure Trips for Teens)–Cape Cod Underwater Adventure
Great Escapes (Adventure Trips for Teens)–Cape Escapes
Great Escapes (Adventure Trips for Teens)–Colorado River and Canyons Adventure
Great Escapes (Adventure Trips for Teens)–Costa Rica Rainforest Adventure
Great Escapes (Adventure Trips for Teens)–Maine Waterways
Great Escapes (Adventure Trips for Teens)–Rock and Rapids
Great Escapes (Adventure Trips for Teens)–Rocky Mountain Horsepacking Adventure
Great Escapes (Adventure Trips for Teens)–Saddle and Sail
Great Escapes (Adventure Trips for Teens)–White Mountain Adventure
South Shore YMCA Specialty Camp

Southwestern Academy

Southwestern Academy International Summer Semester
Southwestern Adventures

Southwestern Safaris and Camps and Tours

High Sierra Wilderness Camps

Space Camp Turkey

Space Camp Turkey 6-Day International Program

Spoleto Study Abroad

Spoleto Study Abroad

Sports and Arts Center at Island Lake

Sports International, Inc.

Alex Brown and Dustin Lyman Football Camp/Sports International
Andy McCollum Football Camp
Antwaan Randle Football Camp/Sports International
Art Monk Football Camp/Sports International–Maryland
Art Monk Football Camp/Sports International–Virginia
Brad Hoover and Will Witherspoon Football Camp/Sports International
Damon Huard and Matt Light Football Camp/Sports International
Deuce McCallister Football Camp
Dhani Jones Football Camp/Sports International
James Thrash and Hollis Thomas Football Camp/Sports International
Jay Novacek Football Camp/Sports International
Joe Krivak Quarterback Camp, Maryland/Sports International
Joe Krivak Quarterback Camp, North Carolina/Sports International
Joe Krivak Quarterback Camp, Pennsylvania/Sports International
Joe Krivak Quarterback Camp, Rhode Island/Sports International
Keenan McCardell and Jimmy Smith Football Camp/Sports International
Keenan McCardell Football Camp
Tice Brothers Football Camp
William Henderson Football Camp/Sports International

Sprachkurse Ariana AG

Sprachkurse Ariana, Aldenham
Sprachkurse Ariana, Arosa
Sprachkurse Ariana, Lenk
Sprachkurse Ariana, Seefeld-Austria

Springfield College

Springfield College Allied Health Career Exploration Program
Springfield College Athletic Trainer Workshop
Springfield College Sports Management Career Exploration Program

Springfield Technical Community College

Springfield Technical Community College–College for Kids

Sprucelands Equestrian Center and Summer Camp

Sprucelands Camp

Stagedoor Manor Performing Arts Training Center/Theatre and Dance Camp

Stanford Debate Society

Stanford National Forensic Institute

Stanford Jazz Workshop

Stanford Jazz Workshop
Stanford Jazz Workshop: Jazz Camp
Stanford Jazz Workshop: Jazz Residency

Stanford University Summer Session

Stanford Discovery Institutes
Stanford University Summer College for High School Students

Stanstead College

Stanstead College–English as a Second Language
Stanstead College–French as a Second Language

Star Programs, Inc.

Star Ranch Summer Camp

Stevens Institute of Technology

ECOES: Exploring Career Options in Engineering and Science

Stevenson School

Stevenson School Summer Camp

Stoneleigh–Burnham School

Bonnie Castle Riding Camp
Stoneleigh–Burnham School: Camp $tart-Up
Stoneleigh–Burnham School: Science Camp for Middle School Girls
Stoneleigh–Burnham School Softball Camp
Stoneleigh–Burnham School Summer Dance Camp
Stoneleigh–Burnham School: Summer Debate and Public Speaking Camp

Stony Brook University, State University of New York

Stony Brook Summer Music Festival
Stony Brook University–Biotechnology Summer Camp
Stony Brook University–Environmental Education Summer Camp
Stony Brook University–Science Exploration Camp
Stony Book University–Summer Camp at Stony Brook
Stony Brook University Summer Sessions College Program

Streamside Foundation, Inc./BCM International

Camp Streamside
Streamside Camp and Conference Center
Streamside Family Camp
Streamside Pathfinder Adventure Camp

Student Conservation Association (SCA)

Student Conservation Association–Conservation Crew Program (Alabama)
Student Conservation Association–Conservation Crew Program (Alaska)
Student Conservation Association–Conservation Crew Program (Arizona)
Student Conservation Association–Conservation Crew Program (Arkansas)
Student Conservation Association–Conservation Crew Program (California)
Student Conservation Association–Conservation Crew Program (Colorado)
Student Conservation Association–Conservation Crew Program (Connecticut)
Student Conservation Association–Conservation Crew Program (Delaware)
Student Conservation Association–Conservation Crew Program (Florida)
Student Conservation Association–Conservation Crew Program (Georgia)
Student Conservation Association–Conservation Crew Program (Hawaii)
Student Conservation Association–Conservation Crew Program (Idaho)
Student Conservation Association–Conservation Crew Program (Illinois)
Student Conservation Association–Conservation Crew Program (Indiana)
Student Conservation Association–Conservation Crew Program (Iowa)
Student Conservation Association–Conservation Crew Program (Kansas)
Student Conservation Association–Conservation Crew Program (Kentucky)
Student Conservation Association–Conservation Crew Program (Louisiana)
Student Conservation Association–Conservation Crew Program (Maine)
Student Conservation Association–Conservation Crew Program (Maryland)
Student Conservation Association–Conservation Crew Program (Massachusetts)
Student Conservation Association–Conservation Crew Program (Michigan)
Student Conservation Association–Conservation Crew Program (Minnesota)
Student Conservation Association–Conservation Crew Program (Mississippi)
Student Conservation Association–Conservation Crew Program (Missouri)
Student Conservation Association–Conservation Crew Program (Montana)
Student Conservation Association–Conservation Crew Program (Nebraska)
Student Conservation Association–Conservation Crew Program (Nevada)
Student Conservation Association–Conservation Crew Program (New Hampshire)
Student Conservation Association–Conservation Crew Program (New Jersey)
Student Conservation Association–Conservation Crew Program (New Mexico)
Student Conservation Association–Conservation Crew Program (New York)
Student Conservation Association–Conservation Crew Program (North Carolina)
Student Conservation Association–Conservation Crew Program (North Dakota)
Student Conservation Association–Conservation Crew Program (Ohio)
Student Conservation Association–Conservation Crew Program (Oklahoma)
Student Conservation Association–Conservation Crew Program (Oregon)

▶ Student Conservation Association (SCA)

Student Conservation Association–Conservation Crew Program (Pennsylvania)
Student Conservation Association–Conservation Crew Program (Rhode Island)
Student Conservation Association–Conservation Crew Program (South Carolina)
Student Conservation Association–Conservation Crew Program (South Dakota)
Student Conservation Association–Conservation Crew Program (Tennessee)
Student Conservation Association–Conservation Crew Program (Texas)
Student Conservation Association–Conservation Crew Program (Utah)
Student Conservation Association–Conservation Crew Program (Vermont)
Student Conservation Association–Conservation Crew Program (Virginia)
Student Conservation Association–Conservation Crew Program (Washington)
Student Conservation Association–Conservation Crew Program (West Virginia)
Student Conservation Association–Conservation Crew Program (Wisconsin)
Student Conservation Association–Conservation Crew Program (Wyoming)
Student Conservation Association–Conservation Leadership Corps, Bay Area
Student Conservation Association–Conservation Leadership Corps–Northwest
Student Conservation Association–Conservation Leadership Corps–Washington, DC Metropolitan Area

Success Oriented Achievement Realized (SOAR)

Success Oriented Achievement Realized (SOAR)–North Carolina
Success Oriented Achievement Realized (SOAR)–Wyoming

Suffield Academy

The Summer Academy at Suffield

Summer Camp for the Young Actor, Inc.

Young Actors Camp

Summer Discovery

Summer Discovery at Australia
Summer Discovery at Cambridge
Summer Discovery at Georgetown
Summer Discovery at Michigan
Summer Discovery at UCLA
Summer Discovery at UC San Diego
Summer Discovery at UC Santa Barbara
Summer Discovery at Vermont

Summer Institute for the Gifted

The Summer Institute for the Gifted at Amherst College
The Summer Institute for the Gifted at Bryn Mawr College
The Summer Institute for the Gifted at Drew University
The Summer Institute for the Gifted at Fairfield University
The Summer Institute for the Gifted at Hofstra University
The Summer Institute for the Gifted at Moorestown Friends School
The Summer Institute for the Gifted at Oberlin College
The Summer Institute for the Gifted at Princeton University
The Summer Institute for the Gifted at Purchase College
The Summer Institute for the Gifted at UCLA
The Summer Institute for the Gifted at University of California, Berkeley
The Summer Institute for the Gifted at Vassar College

Summer Science Program, Inc.

The Summer Science Program–California Campus
The Summer Science Program–New Mexico Campus

Summer Study Programs

Summer Study at Penn State
Summer Study at The University of Colorado at Boulder
Summer Study in Paris at The American University of Paris

Summit Camp

Summit Camp
Summit Travel Program

SuperCamp

SuperCamp–Claremont Colleges
SuperCamp–Colorado College
SuperCamp–Dominican Republic
SuperCamp–Hampshire College
SuperCamp–Hong Kong
SuperCamp–Mexico
SuperCamp–Singapore
SuperCamp–Stanford University
SuperCamp–Switzerland
SuperCamp–Thailand
SuperCamp–University of Wisconsin at Parkside
SuperCamp–Wake Forest University

Surprise Lake Camp

Susquehanna University

Susquehanna University Advanced Writers Workshop for High School Students

Swift Nature Camp

Swift Nature Camp–Adventure Camp
Swift Nature Camp–Canadian Canoe Trip
Swift Nature Camp–Discovery Camp
Swift Nature Camp–Explorer Camp

Swiss Challenge

Swiss Challenge

Syracuse University

Syracuse University Summer College

Tabor Academy

Tabor Academy Summer Program

The Taft School

Taft Summer School
Taft Summer School Abroad–France
Taft Summer School Abroad–Spain

Talisman Summer Programs

Talisman–Academics
Talisman–INSIGHT
Talisman Mini-Camp
Talisman Open Boat Adventures (TOBA)
Talisman–SIGHT
Talisman Summer Camp
Talisman–Trek Hiking Program
Talisman–Tri-Adventures

Tampa Preparatory School

Tampa Prep–Academic Credit and Enrichment Courses
Tampa Prep–Boys Athletic Camps
Tampa Prep–Girls Athletic Camps
Tampa Prep–Terrapin Day Camp

Tanager Lodge

Tannen's Magic, Inc.

Tannen's Summer Magic Camp

TASC for Teens

TASC Canadian Wilderness Fishing Camps

TASIS The American School in England

TASIS Arts and Architecture in the South of France
TASIS England Summer Program
TASIS Spanish Summer Program

TASIS The American School in Switzerland

TASIS French Language Program in Château–d'Oex, Switzerland
TASIS Le Château des Enfants
TASIS Middle School Program
TASIS Summer Program for Languages, Arts, and Outdoor Pursuits
TASIS Tuscan Academy of Art and Culture

Teen Tours of America

Teen Tours of America–Alaskan Expedition
Teen Tours of America–Aloha Hawaii
Teen Tours of America–Golf Camp–Florida Swing
Teen Tours of America–New England Journey
Teen Tours of America–Western Adventure
Teen Tours of America–Western Sprint

TENNIS: EUROPE

TENNIS: EUROPE
TENNIS: EUROPE & MORE–North American Teams

Teton Valley Ranch Camp Education Foundation

Teton Valley Ranch Camp–Boys Camp
Teton Valley Ranch Camp–Girls Camp

Texas A&M University at Galveston

Sea Camp

Texas Tech University
Clark Scholars Program

Texas Woman's University
Access to Careers in the Sciences (ACES) Camps

Thomas More College of Liberal Arts
Collegiate Summer Program for High School Students

Thompson Island Outward Bound/Outward Bound, USA
Outward Bound–Connecting with Courage
Outward Bound–Environmental Expeditions
Outward Bound–Passages

Thunderbird Ranch

Towering Pines Camp
Towering Pines Camp
Woodland

Trail Blazers

Trailmark Outdoor Adventures
Trailmark Outdoor Adventures–Colorado–West Elks with Backpack
Trailmark Outdoor Adventures–Colorado–West Elks with Horseback
Trailmark Outdoor Adventures–New England–Acadia
Trailmark Outdoor Adventures–New England–Camden
Trailmark Outdoor Adventures–New England–Downeast
Trailmark Outdoor Adventures–New England–Jr. Acadia
Trailmark Outdoor Adventures–New England–Mahoosoc
Trailmark Outdoor Adventures–New England–Moose River
Trailmark Outdoor Adventures–New England–Mt. Desert
Trailmark Outdoor Adventures–New England–Rangeley Coed
Trailmark Outdoor Adventures–Northern Rockies–Tetons with Backpack
Trailmark Outdoor Adventures–Northern Rockies–Tetons with Horseback

Trailridge Mountain Camp, Inc.
Trailridge Mountain Camp

Traveling Players Ensemble, Inc.
Traveling Players Ensemble Camp

Tufts University
Tufts Summer Study
Tufts Summit

Tufts University School of Veterinary Medicine
Adventures in Veterinary Medicine

Tuskegee University College of Veterinary Medicine
Tuskegee University Vet Step I
Tuskegee University Vet Step II

Union for Reform Judaism
Crane Lake Camp

United Soccer Academy, Inc.
United Soccer Academy–Goal Keeping Training Camp, Connecticut
United Soccer Academy–Goal Keeping Training Camp, Delaware
United Soccer Academy–Goal Keeping Training Camp, Maryland
United Soccer Academy–Goal Keeping Training Camp, New Jersey
United Soccer Academy–Goal Keeping Training Camp, New York
United Soccer Academy–Goal Keeping Training Camp, Pennsylvania
United Soccer Academy–Junior Soccer Squirts, Connecticut
United Soccer Academy–Junior Soccer Squirts, Delaware
United Soccer Academy–Junior Soccer Squirts, Maryland
United Soccer Academy–Junior Soccer Squirts, New Jersey
United Soccer Academy–Junior Soccer Squirts, New York
United Soccer Academy–Junior Soccer Squirts, Pennsylvania
United Soccer Academy–Recreation Soccer Community Camp, Connecticut
United Soccer Academy–Recreation Soccer Community Camp, Delaware
United Soccer Academy–Recreation Soccer Community Camp, Maryland
United Soccer Academy–Recreation Soccer Community Camp, New Jersey
United Soccer Academy–Recreation Soccer Community Camp, New York
United Soccer Academy–Recreation Soccer Community Camp, Pennsylvania
United Soccer Academy–Regional Academy Camp, New Jersey
United Soccer Academy–Regional Academy Camp, New York
United Soccer Academy–Regional Academy Camp, Pennsylvania
United Soccer Academy–Senior Soccer Squirts, Connecticut
United Soccer Academy–Senior Soccer Squirts, Delaware
United Soccer Academy–Senior Soccer Squirts, Maryland
United Soccer Academy–Senior Soccer Squirts, New Jersey
United Soccer Academy–Senior Soccer Squirts, New York
United Soccer Academy–Senior Soccer Squirts, Pennsylvania
United Soccer Academy–Team Training Camp, Connecticut
United Soccer Academy–Team Training Camp, Delaware
United Soccer Academy–Team Training Camp, Maryland
United Soccer Academy–Team Training Camp, New Jersey
United Soccer Academy–Team Training Camp, New York
United Soccer Academy–Team Training Camp, Pennsylvania
United Soccer Academy–Travel Soccer Community Camp, Connecticut
United Soccer Academy–Travel Soccer Community Camp, Delaware
United Soccer Academy–Travel Soccer Community Camp, Maryland
United Soccer Academy–Travel Soccer Community Camp, New Jersey
United Soccer Academy–Travel Soccer Community Camp, New York
United Soccer Academy–Travel Soccer Community Camp, Pennsylvania

The University of Alabama
Alabama Museum of Natural History Summer Expedition

University of California, San Diego
UC San Diego Academic Connections

University of California, Santa Barbara Alumni Association
UCSB Alumni Association Santa Barbara Family Vacation Center

University of Chicago
University of Chicago–ChicaGO! The Traveling Academy
University of Chicago–Insight
University of Chicago–Research in the Biological Sciences
University of Chicago–Stones and Bones
University of Chicago–Summer Quarter for High School Students

University of Connecticut
University of Connecticut Mentor Connection

University of Connecticut American English Language Institute
UCAELI Summer Camp

University of Connecticut College of Continuing Studies–Community School of the Arts
University of Connecticut Community School of the Arts–Music Camps
University of Connecticut Community School of the Arts–World Arts Camps

University of Dayton
Women in Engineering Summer Camp

University of Delaware
University of Delaware Summer College

University of Evansville College of Engineering and Computer Science
OPTIONS for Young Women

The University of Iowa
Iowa Young Writers' Studio

University of Kansas
Bill Self Kansas Summer Basketball Camp
Jayhawk Debate Institute
Kansas Journalism Institute
KU Jazz Workshop
KU Marching Band Camps
University of Kansas–Boys Soccer Camp
University of Kansas–Duke University Talent Identification Program
University of Kansas–Girls Golf Camp
University of Kansas–Girls Soccer Camp
University of Kansas–Jayhawk Baseball Camps–Little League, Super Skills, and All-Star
University of Kansas–Jayhawk Boys and Girls Tennis Camp
University of Kansas–Jayhawk Golf Camp–Boys
University of Kansas–Jayhawk Swim Camp
University of Kansas–Jayhawk Track and Field/Cross Country Camps
University of Kansas–Jayhawk Volleyball Camp
University of Kansas–Midwestern Music Camp–Junior and Senior Divisions
University of Kansas–Natural History Museum Summer Workshops
University of Kansas–Project Discovery
University of Kansas–School of Pharmacy Summer Camp
University of Kansas–Sertoma-Schiefelbush Communication Camp
University of Kansas–Softball–Teen and Advanced Camps
University of Kansas–Sports Skills and Fitness Camp

University of Maryland, Office of Continuing and Extended Education
The Arts! at Maryland
University of Maryland Young Scholars Program

University of Miami
University of Miami Summer Scholar Programs

University of Oregon
Oregon Summer Music Camps

University of Pennsylvania
University of Pennsylvania–Penn Summer Art Studio
University of Pennsylvania–Penn Summer Science Academy
University of Pennsylvania–Precollege Program

University of Rhode Island
Alton Jones Day Camp
Alton Jones Earth Camp
Teen Expeditions

University of St. Andrews Summer Studies
University of St. Andrews Creative Writing Summer Program
University of St. Andrews Scottish Studies Summer Program

University of San Diego Sports Camps
University of San Diego Sports Camps–Baseball Camp
University of San Diego Sports Camps–Boys Basketball High School Team Camp
University of San Diego Sports Camps–Boys High School Basketball Camp
University of San Diego Sports Camps–Boys High School Elite Baseball Camp
University of San Diego Sports Camps–Boys High School Soccer Camp
University of San Diego Sports Camps–Boys Junior Basketball Camp
University of San Diego Sports Camps–Coed Junior Soccer Camp
University of San Diego Sports Camps–Coed Water Polo Camp
University of San Diego Sports Camps–Competitive Swim Camp
University of San Diego Sports Camps–Girls Basketball Fundamentals Camp
University of San Diego Sports Camps–Girls Basketball High School Elite Camp
University of San Diego Sports Camps–Girls Basketball High School Team Camp
University of San Diego Sports Camps–Girls Soccer Camp
University of San Diego Sports Camps–Girls Softball Advanced Camp
University of San Diego Sports Camps–Girls Softball Beginner/Intermediate Camp
University of San Diego Sports Camps–Girls Volleyball Camp
University of San Diego Sports Camps–Sherri Stephens High School Tennis Camp
University of San Diego Sports Camps–Sherri Stephens Junior Tennis Camp
University of San Diego Sports Camps–Sports–N–More All Sports Camp
University of San Diego Sports Camps–Sports–N–More Team Sports Camp
University of San Diego Sports Camps–Sports–N–More Wet & Wild Sports Camp

The University of Scranton
Arts Unite
High School Scholars (Summer Courses)
Time Travelers Program

University of South Carolina Continuing Education
Carolina Master Scholars Adventure Series

University of Southern California, School of Architecture
Exploration of Architecture

University of Southern California–Summer and Special Programs
Science Program for High School Girls
Science Program for Middle School Boys on Catalina
Science Program for Middle School Girls on Catalina
University of Southern California Summer Seminars

The University of Texas at Austin, School of Music
Longhorn Music Camp: All-State Choir Camp
Longhorn Music Camp: Harp Solo and Ensemble Camp
Longhorn Music Camp: High School Band Camp
Longhorn Music Camp: Middle School Band Camp
Longhorn Music Camp: Middle School String Orchestra Camp
Longhorn Music Camp: Piano Performance Workshop

The University of the Arts
Pre-College Summer Institute, The University of the Arts

University of Vermont, College of Engineering and Mathematics
University of Vermont Summer Institute for High School Students Discovering Engineering, Computers, and Mathematics

University of Wisconsin–Green Bay
University of Wisconsin–Green Bay Biz 4 Youth Camp
University of Wisconsin–Green Bay Computer Camp
University of Wisconsin–Green Bay Ecosystem Investigations
University of Wisconsin–Green Bay Space Trek Camp
University of Wisconsin–Green Bay Summer Art Studio
University of Wisconsin–Green Bay Summer Discovery
University of Wisconsin–Green Bay Summer Music Camps
University of Wisconsin–Green Bay Summer Spanish Immersion

University of Wisconsin–Madison
Summer Music Clinic

University of Wisconsin–Stevens Point
Point Arts Camp–Music

University of Wisconsin–Superior
University of Wisconsin–Superior Youthsummer 2005

The University School for the Gifted, Creative and Talented
The Festival of Creative Youth

Urban League of Springfield, Inc.
Camp Atwater–Boys Session
Camp Atwater–Girls Session

Usdan Center for the Creative and Performing Arts

Valley Forge Military Academy and College
Valley Forge Military Academy Extreme Tennis Camp
Valley Forge Military Academy Summer Band Camp
Valley Forge Military Academy Summer Camp for Boys
Valley Forge Military Academy Summer Coed Day Camp

Valley View Ranch Equestrian Camp
Valley View Ranch Equestrian Camp

Vanderbilt University
Preparatory Academics for Vanderbilt Engineers (PAVE)

Vassar College
Vassar College Coed Basketball Camp
Vassar College Coed Soccer Camp
Vassar College Coed Swim Camp
Vassar College Girl's Field Hockey Camp

Vermont Arts Institute at Lyndon Institute
Vermont Arts Animation Institute
Vermont Arts Dance Institute
Vermont Arts Filmmaking Institute
Vermont Arts Screenwriting Institute
Vermont Arts Theatre Camp Institute
Vermont Arts Theatre Institute
Vermont Arts Visual Arts Institute

Village Camps
Village Camps–Austria
Village Camps–England
Village Camps–France
Village Camps–Switzerland

Visions
Visions–Alaska
Visions–Australia
Visions–British Virgin Islands
Visions–Dominica
Visions–Dominican Republic
Visions–Ecuador
Visions–Guadeloupe
Visions–Montana
Visions–Peru
Visions–South Carolina
Visions–Trinidad

Vista Camps
Camp Rio Vista for Boys
Camp Sierra Vista for Girls

Volunteers for Peace International Work Camps
Volunteers for Peace International Work Camp–Armenia
Volunteers for Peace International Work Camp–Belarus
Volunteers for Peace International Work Camp–Belgium
Volunteers for Peace International Work Camp–Czech Republic
Volunteers for Peace International Work Camp–Estonia
Volunteers for Peace International Work Camp–France
Volunteers for Peace International Work Camp–Germany
Volunteers for Peace International Work Camp–Italy
Volunteers for Peace International Work Camp–Lithuania
Volunteers for Peace International Work Camp–Russia
Volunteers for Peace International Work Camp–Slovakia
Volunteers for Peace International Work Camp–Turkey

Voyageur Outward Bound/ Outward Bound, USA
Voyageur Outward Bound–Boundary Waters Wilderness Canoeing
Voyageur Outward Bound–Boundary Waters Wilderness Canoeing and Climbing XT
Voyageur Outward Bound–Greater Yellowstone Whitewater and Backpacking
Voyageur Outward Bound–Lake Superior Freshwater Kayaking
Voyageur Outward Bound–Lake Superior Freshwater Kayaking and Backpacking
Voyageur Outward Bound–Lewis and Clark Alpine Backpacking
Voyageur Outward Bound–Lewis and Clark Alpine Backpacking-Girls
Voyageur Outward Bound–Manitoba to Montana Summer Semester
Voyageur Outward Bound–Montana High Alpine Backpacking
Voyageur Outward Bound–Montana Rock Climbing XT
Voyageur Outward Bound–Northern Rockies Backpacking Family Adventure
Voyageur Outward Bound–Northwoods Wilderness Canoeing and Backpacking

Washington and Lee University
Washington and Lee University Summer Scholars

Washington International School
Washington International School Passport to Summer

Washington University in St. Louis
Washington University High School Summer Scholars Program

Washington University in St. Louis, School of Art
Washington University in St. Louis, School of Art–Portfolio Plus

Washington Workshops Foundation
The Congressional Seminar
Diplomacy and Global Affairs Seminar
Washington Internship Experience

Weather Research Center
WRC Weather Camp

Wediko Children's Services
Wediko Summer Program

Weissman Teen Tours
Weissman Teen Tours–"Aloha–Welcome to Hawaiian Paradise"
Weissman Teen Tours–European Experience
Weissman Teen Tours–U.S. and Western Canada, 4 Weeks
Weissman Teen Tours–U.S. and Western Canada, 6 Weeks

Wentworth Military Academy and Junior College
Wentworth Military Academy Pathfinder Adventure Camp
Wentworth Military Academy Summer School
Wentworth Military Academy Summer School–Camp LEAD

Wesleyan College
MidSummer Macon

Westcoast Connection
Westcoast Connection–American Voyageur
Westcoast Connection–Australian Outback Plus Hawaii
Westcoast Connection–Californian Extravaganza
Westcoast Connection–Community Connections Alaska
Westcoast Connection–Community Service
Westcoast Connection–Florida Swing Junior Touring Golf Camp
Westcoast Connection–Hawaiian Spirit
Westcoast Connection/On Tour– Australian Outback
Westcoast Connection Travel/On Tour–Northwestern Odyssey
Westcoast Connection Travel–Adventure California
Westcoast Connection Travel–California and the Canyons
Westcoast Connection Travel–Canadian Mountain Magic
Westcoast Connection Travel–Eastcoast Encounter
Westcoast Connection Travel–European Discovery
Westcoast Connection Travel–European Escape
Westcoast Connection Travel–Great West Challenge
Westcoast Connection Travel–Northwestern Odyssey

Westcoast Connection Travel/On Tour–Canadian Adventure
Westcoast Connection Travel/On Tour–European Experience
Westcoast Connection Travel–Quebec Adventure
Westcoast Connection Travel–Ski and Snowboard Sensation
Westcoast Connection Travel–Southwesterner
Westcoast Connection Travel–Western Canadian Adventure
Westcoast Connection–U.S. Explorer

Western Washington University
Adventures in Science and Arts
College Quest
Outdoor Adventure

Westminster Choir College of Rider University
Westminster Choir College Composition Week
Westminster Choir College High School Solo Pianist
Westminster Choir College High School Solo Vocal Artist: A Performance Workshop for Singers
Westminster Choir College Middle School Music Theater
Westminster Choir College Middle School Piano Camp
Westminster Choir College Middle School Vocal Camp
Westminster Choir College Music Theater Workshop
Westminster Choir College Organ Week
Westminster Choir College Piano Camp
Westminster Choir College Vocal Institute

Westminster Conservatory of Music
Westminster Conservatory of Music–Flute Camp
Westminster Conservatory of Music–Musical Jamboree
Westminster Conservatory of Music–Summer Ensemble
Westminster Conservatory of Music–Try It Out
Westminster Conservatory of Music–Youth Opera Workshop

Westminster Presbyterian Church of Grand Rapids, MI/Camp Henry Board of Directors
Camp Henry
Camp Henry Offsite: Teen Challenge

West River United Methodist Center

West Virginia Wesleyan College
Wesleyan Summer Gifted Program

The Whale Camp
The Whale Camp–Youth Programs

Where There Be Dragons
Where There Be Dragons: China
Where There Be Dragons: Guatemala
Where There Be Dragons: India Culture and Philosophy
Where There Be Dragons: India Zanskar Trek
Where There Be Dragons: Mexico
Where There Be Dragons: Mongolia
Where There Be Dragons: Peru
Where There Be Dragons: Silk Road
Where There Be Dragons: Thailand
Where There Be Dragons: Tibet
Where There Be Dragons: Vietnam

White Water Learning Center of Georgia
White Water Learning Center of Georgia Kids Kayaking Summer Day Camp

Whitman College
Whitman National Debate Institute

Wilderness Adventure at Eagle Landing

Wilderness Dance Camp, Inc.
Wilderness Dance Camp

Wilderness Education Institute
Organic Farm Camp
WEI Leadership Training
Wilderness Adventure
Wildlife Camp

Wilderness Experiences Unlimited, Inc.
Kayak Adventures Unlimited
Wilderness Experiences Unlimited–Explorers Camp
Wilderness Experiences Unlimited–Leaders In Training Camp
Wilderness Experiences Unlimited–Pathfinders Day Camp
Wilderness Experiences Unlimited–Trailblazers Camp
Wilderness Experiences Unlimited/Westfield Water Sports: Scuba Camp

Wilderness Ventures
Wilderness Ventures–Alaska Leadership
Wilderness Ventures–Alaska Service
Wilderness Ventures–Alaska Southcentral
Wilderness Ventures–Alaska Southeast
Wilderness Ventures–Australia
Wilderness Ventures–California
Wilderness Ventures–Cascade-Olympic
Wilderness Ventures–Colorado/Utah Mountain Bike
Wilderness Ventures–Costa Rica
Wilderness Ventures–Ecuador and Galapagos
Wilderness Ventures–European Alps
Wilderness Ventures–Grand Teton
Wilderness Ventures–Great Divide
Wilderness Ventures–Great Divide Bike
Wilderness Ventures–Hawaii
Wilderness Ventures–High Sierra
Wilderness Ventures–Jackson Hole
Wilderness Ventures–Northwest
Wilderness Ventures–Oregon
Wilderness Ventures–Pacific Coast Bike
Wilderness Ventures–Pacific Northwest
Wilderness Ventures–Puget Sound
Wilderness Ventures–Rocky Mountain
Wilderness Ventures–Spanish Pyrenees
Wilderness Ventures–Teton Adventure
Wilderness Ventures–Washington Alpine
Wilderness Ventures–Washington Mountaineering
Wilderness Ventures–Wyoming Mountaineering
Wilderness Ventures–Yellowstone Fly Fishing

Williwaw Adventures
Williwaw Adventures–Maine Mountains and Coast
Williwaw Adventures–Maine Wilderness
Williwaw Adventures–Pacific Northwest Expedition

Willow Hill Farm Camp

The Winchendon School
The Winchendon School Summer Session

Windridge Tennis Camps
Windridge Tennis Camp at Craftsbury Common
Windridge Tennis Camp at Teela-Wooket, Vermont

The Windsor School
JHS/HS Academic Summer School Program

Winona Camp for Boys

Wisconsin World Affairs Council, Inc.
World Affairs Seminar

Wohelo-Luther Gulick Camps

Wolfeboro: The Summer Boarding School

Woodberry Forest School
Woodberry Forest Basketball Camp
Woodberry Forest Golf Camp
Woodberry Forest Junior Adventure
Woodberry Forest Lacrosse Camp
Woodberry Forest Senior Adventure
Woodberry Forest Sports Camp
Woodberry Forest Summer School–England
Woodberry Forest Summer School–France
Woodberry Forest Summer School–Japan
Woodberry Forest Summer School–Scotland
Woodberry Forest Summer School–Spain

Woodward Camp, Inc.
Woodward Freestyle BMX Bicycle, Inline Skate, Skateboarding Camp
Woodward Gymnastics Camp

Worcester Polytechnic Institute
Frontiers Program
Gems: Girls in Engineering, Math and Science
Strive: Exploring Engineering, Math and Science

World Horizons International
World Horizons International–Costa Rica
World Horizons International–Dominica
World Horizons International–Fiji
World Horizons International–Iceland
World Horizons International–Kanab, Utah
World Horizons International–Mexico
World Horizons International–Oahu, Hawaii
World Horizons International–Puerto Rico

Wright State University Pre-College Programs
Wright State University Residential Camps and Institutes

Wyoming Seminary College Preparatory School
The Performing Arts Institute of Wyoming Seminary
Wyoming Seminary–Sem Summer 2005

Xi'an Jiao Tong University Campus/Xi'an Winning Training Center
China Summer Learning Adventures

YMCA Camp Fitch
YMCA Camp Fitch Summer Camp

YMCA Camping Services of Greater New York
Camp Greenkill–Conservation/Adventure
Camp Greenkill–Gymnastics
Camp Greenkill–Judo
Camp Greenkill–Volleyball
Camp McAlister
Camp Talcott

YMCA Camp Lincoln
YMCA Camp Lincoln–Junior CIT Program
YMCA Camp Lincoln–On the Road
YMCA Camp Lincoln–Outdoor Adventure Camp: Backpacking
YMCA Camp Lincoln–Outdoor Adventure Camp: Canadian Adventure
YMCA Camp Lincoln–Outdoor Adventure Camp: Everything Outdoors
YMCA Camp Lincoln–Outdoor Adventure Camp: Mountain Bike
YMCA Camp Lincoln–Outdoor Adventure Camp: River Runners
YMCA Camp Lincoln–Senior CIT Program
YMCA Camp Lincoln–Specialty Camps: Archaeology Camp
YMCA Camp Lincoln–Specialty Camps: Arts & Drama
YMCA Camp Lincoln–Specialty Camps: Horse Camp
YMCA Camp Lincoln–Specialty Camps: Sports Camp
YMCA Camp Lincoln–Traditional Day Camp
YMCA Camp Lincoln–Travel Camp

YMCA Camp Ockanickon, Inc.
YMCA Camp Matollionequay
YMCA Camp Ockanickon
YMCA Lake Stockwell

YMCA Camp Pendalouan
YMCA Camp Pendalouan–Bugs and Bunks
YMCA Camp Pendalouan–Counselor-in-Training
YMCA Camp Pendalouan–Resident Camp
YMCA Camp Pendalouan–Ropers and Wranglers Horse Camp
YMCA Camp Pendalouan–Teen Xtreme

YMCA Camp Seymour
YMCA Camp Seymour Summer Camp

YMCA Camp Surf
YMCA Camp Surf

YMCA Camp Widjiwagan
YMCA Camp Widjiwagan

YMCA of Central Stark County
YMCA Camp Tippecanoe–Adventure Camp
YMCA Camp Tippecanoe–Bike Camp
YMCA Camp Tippecanoe–Equine Camp
YMCA Camp Tippecanoe–Girl's & Guy's Corral
YMCA Camp Tippecanoe–Horse Pals
YMCA Camp Tippecanoe–Jr. Counselor
YMCA Camp Tippecanoe–Teen Camp

YMCA of Greater Bergen County
YMCA Camp Michikamau

YMCA of Greater Boston–Camping Services Branch
North Woods Camp for Boys
Pleasant Valley Camp for Girls
Ponkapoag Outdoor Center Day Camps
Sandy Island Camp for Families

YMCA of Greater High Point, North Carolina, Inc.
Camp Cheerio YMCA
Cheerio Adventures–Appalachian Adventure
Cheerio Adventures–Cave/Raft
Cheerio Adventures–5 Rivers in 5 Days
Cheerio Adventures–Mountains to the Sea
Cheerio Adventures–Ocean Odyssey
Cheerio Adventures–Rock Climb/Raft
Cheerio Adventures–Sampler
Cheerio Adventures–Seekers
Cheerio Adventures–Standard

YMCA of Greater Long Beach
YMCA Camp Oakes Rangers
YMCA Camp Oakes Teen Leadership

YMCA of Hamilton/Burlington
YMCA Wanakita Summer Family Camp
YMCA Wanakita Summer Resident and Day Camp

YMCA of Metropolitan Milwaukee
YMCA Camp Minikani

YMCA of Metropolitan Minneapolis
YMCA Camp Icaghowan
YMCA Camp Ihduhapi
YMCA Camp Warren for Boys
YMCA Camp Warren for Girls
YMCA Wilderness Camp Menogyn

YMCA of the Triangle
YMCA Camp Kanata

YM-YWHA of North Jersey
Camp Veritans

Yo! Basecamp Rock Climbing Camps
Yo! Basecamp Rock Climbing Camps

Yosemite Institute
Yosemite Backpacking Adventures

Young Judea
Israel Discovery

Young Musicians & Artists
Young Musicians & Artists

Youth for Understanding USA
Youth for Understanding USA–Argentina
Youth for Understanding USA–Australia
Youth for Understanding USA–Brazil
Youth for Understanding USA–Chile
Youth for Understanding USA–China
Youth for Understanding USA–Denmark
Youth for Understanding USA–Ecuador
Youth for Understanding USA–Estonia/Latvia-Baltic Summer
Youth for Understanding USA–France
Youth for Understanding USA–Germany
Youth for Understanding USA–Ghana
Youth for Understanding USA–Greece
Youth for Understanding USA–Hungary
Youth for Understanding USA–Ireland
Youth for Understanding USA–Italy
Youth for Understanding USA–Japan
Youth for Understanding USA–Kazakhstan
Youth for Understanding USA–Kenya
Youth for Understanding USA–Poland
Youth for Understanding USA–Russia
Youth for Understanding USA–South Africa
Youth for Understanding USA–South Korea
Youth for Understanding USA–Spain
Youth for Understanding USA–Sweden
Youth for Understanding USA–Thailand
Youth for Understanding USA–Uruguay
Youth for Understanding USA–Venezuela
Youth for Understanding USA–Vietnam

Youth Theatre of New Jersey's Teen Program in Residence at Columbia University, NYC
Summer Theatre Institute–2005

▶ Academic Programs

Academic Programs

AAVE–Costa Rica, Costa Rica
AAVE–Inmersión en España, Spain
AAVE–Vivons le Français, France
Abbey Road Overseas Programs–French Immersion and Homestay, France
Abbey Road Overseas Programs–French Study Abroad in Cannes, France
Abbey Road Overseas Programs–Italy Study Abroad: Language and Culture, Italy
Abbey Road Overseas Programs–Spanish Immersion and Homestay, Spain
Academic Camps at Gettysburg College–Astronomy, PA
Academic Camps at Gettysburg College–College Prep & Preview, PA
Academic Camps at Gettysburg College–Community Service, PA
Academic Camps at Gettysburg College–Foreign Language Study (Spanish), PA
Academic Camps at Gettysburg College–U.S. Civil War, PA
Academic Camps at Gettysburg College–Writer's Workshops, PA
Academic Study Associates–ASA at the University of California, Berkeley, CA
Academic Study Associates–ASA at the University of Massachusetts Amherst, MA
Academic Study Associates–Barcelona, Spain
Academic Study Associates–Florence, Italy
Academic Study Associates–Nice, France
Academic Study Associates–Pathways Program at Amherst College, MA
Academic Study Associates–Royan, France
Academic Study Associates–Spanish in España, Spain
L' Académie de Paris, France
Academy, OR
Academy by the Sea, CA
Acadia Institute of Oceanography, ME
Access to Careers in the Sciences (ACES) Camps, TX
A.C.E. Intercultural Institute, WA
ACTIONQUEST: Tropical Marine Biology Voyages, British Virgin Islands
Adventure Ireland–English Learning Option, Ireland
Adventures in Learning, OR
Adventures in Science and Arts, WA
Adventures in Veterinary Medicine, MA
Aerospace Camp Experience, WA
AFS-USA–Homestay–Argentina, Argentina
AFS-USA–Homestay–Chile, Chile
AFS-USA–Homestay–France, France
AFS-USA–Homestay Language Study–Canada, Canada
AFS-USA–Homestay Language Study–Latvia, Latvia
AFS-USA–Homestay–Paraguay, Paraguay
AFS-USA–Homestay–Thailand, Thailand
AFS-USA–Team Mission–China, China
Alabama Museum of Natural History Summer Expedition, AL
Alexander Muss High School in Israel, Israel
Alexander-Smith Academy Summer School, TX
Alfred University Summer Institute in Astronomy, NY
Alfred University Summer Institute in Entrepreneurial Leadership, NY
Alfred University Summer Institute in Writing, NY
All Arts and Sciences Camp–George Mason University, VA
All Arts and Sciences Camp–North Carolina State University, NC
All Arts and Sciences Camp–The College of William and Mary, VA
All Arts and Sciences Camp–The University of North Carolina at Greensboro, NC
All Arts and Sciences Camp–Virginia Tech, VA
American Association of Teachers of German, German Summer Study Program, Germany
American Collegiate Adventures–Italy, Italy
American Collegiate Adventures–Spain, Spain
American Collegiate Adventures–Wisconsin, WI
American Legal Experience by Education Unlimited–Berkeley, CA, CA
American Legal Experience by Education Unlimited–Stanford, CA, CA
American Youth Foundation Leadership Conference, MI
Appleby College Summer Academy, Canada
Arrowsmith Academy Arts and Academics, CA
Artes en Mexico, Mexico
Asheville School Summer Academic Adventures, NC
Audubon Vermont Youth Camp, VT
Austin Nature and Science Center, TX
Ball State University Summer Journalism Workshops, IN
Barat Foundation Summer Program in Provence and Paris, France
Bark Lake Leadership Through Recreation Camp, Canada
Barnard's Summer in New York City: A Pre-College Program, NY
Barnard's Summer in New York City: One-Week Mini-Course, NY
Barnard's Summer in New York City: Young Women's Leadership Institute, NY
Baylor University High School Summer Science Research Program, TX
Beekman School Summer Session, NY
Birmingham-Southern College Summer Scholar Program, AL
Bishop's College School Summer School, Canada
Blyth Education–Summer Study in Costa Rica, Costa Rica
Blyth Education–Summer Study in Cozumel, Mexico
Blyth Education–Summer Study in London and Oxford University, United Kingdom
Blyth Education–Summer Study in Paris and the South of France, France
Blyth Education–Summer Study in Rome and Siena, Italy
Blyth Education–Summer Study in the Amazon and the Galapagos Islands, Ecuador
Boston University High School Honors Program, MA
Boston University Institute for Television, Film, and Radio Production, MA
Boston University Promys Program, MA
Boston University Summer Challenge Program, MA
Bravo Spain–Barcelona, Spain
Brewster Academy Summer Session, NH
Bridge to the Future, NJ
Brighton College Admissions Prep at Tufts University, MA
Brighton College Admissions Prep at UCLA, CA
Brighton in Cannes, France
Brighton in Costa Rica, Costa Rica
Brighton in Paris, France
Brighton in Tuscany, Italy
BROADREACH Academic Treks–Language Exposure and Service Learning, Chile
BROADREACH Academic Treks–Marine Mammal Studies, Canada
BROADREACH Academic Treks–Marine Park Management
BROADREACH Academic Treks–Sea Turtle Studies, Costa Rica
BROADREACH Academic Treks–Spanish Immersion in Mexico, Mexico
BROADREACH Academic Treks–Spanish Language Immersion in Ecuador, Ecuador
BROADREACH Academic Treks–Wilderness Emergency Medicine, Belize
BROADREACH Honduras Eco-Adventure, Honduras
BROADREACH Marine Biology Accredited, Bahamas
Brown University Summer Programs–Pre-College Program, RI
Bryn Mawr College–Writing for College, PA
Buckswood: English Language (ESL) and Activities–Bradfield, England, United Kingdom
Buckswood: English Language (ESL) and Activities–Plumpton, England, United Kingdom
Buckswood: English Language (ESL) and Activities–West Virginia, WV
Bugs to Biospheres, CO
California Campus Tours, CA
California National Debate Institute, CA
Cal Poly State University Young Scholars Prepare for the PSAT & SAT I, CA
Cambridge College Programme, United Kingdom
The Cambridge Prep Experience, United Kingdom
The Cambridge Tradition, United Kingdom
Camden Military Academy Summer Session/Camp, SC
Camp Buckskin, MN
Camp College–Institute for Arts and Sciences, NJ
Camp Discovery–Madison, NJ
Camp Discovery–Teaneck, NJ
Camp Hillside, MA
Camp Kodiak, Canada
Camp Lee Mar, PA
Camp Middlesex, NJ
Camp Shakespeare, UT
Timber-lee Science Camp, WI
Camp Watonka, PA
Canadian College Italy/The Renaissance School Summer Academy, Italy
The Cardigan Mountain School Summer Session, NH
Career Explorations, NY
Carleton College Summer Writing Program, MN
Carnegie Mellon University Advanced Placement Early Admission, PA
Carolina Master Scholars Adventure Series, SC
Carson-Newman College–EXCEL Program, TN

▶ Academic Programs

Cybercamps–University of Michigan, MI
Cybercamps–University of Minnesota, MN
Cybercamps–University of Washington, WA
Cybercamps–University of Washington, Bothell, WA
Cybercamps–Washington University, MO
Daniel Fox Youth Scholars Institute, PA
Davidson College July Experience, NC
Deep River Science Academy–Deep River Campus, Canada
Deep River Science Academy–Whiteshell Campus, Canada
Delphi's Summer Session, OR
Denver Academy Summer Program, CO
Dickinson College Research and Writing Workshop, PA
Dickinson College Spanish Language and Cultural Immersion Program, Mexico
Dickinson College Young Writer's Workshop, PA
Dickinson Summer College Program, PA
DigiPen Institute of Technology Junior Game Developer Workshop, WA
DigiPen Institute of Technology Robotics Workshop, WA
DigiPen Institute of Technology 3D Computer Animation Workshop, WA
DigiPen Institute of Technology Video Game Programming Workshop, WA
Diplomacy and Global Affairs Seminar, DC
Discovery Camp, CO
Duke Action: Science Camp for Young Women, NC
Duke Creative Writers' Workshop, NC
Duke Young Writers Camp, NC
Dunnabeck at Kildonan, NY
Dwight-Englewood Summer Academic Session, NJ
Dwight-Englewood Weekly Enrichment, NJ
Eaglebrook Summer Semester, MA
Eagle Hill School Summer Session, MA
EARTHWATCH INSTITUTE–Medicinal Plants of Antiquity, Italy
East Coast College Tour by Education Unlimited
ECOES: Exploring Career Options in Engineering and Science, NJ
EF International Language School–Barcelona, Spain
EF International Language School–Malaga, Spain
EF International Language School–Munich, Germany
EF International Language School–Nice, France
EF International Language School–Paris, France
EF International Language School–Rome, Italy
EF International Language School–Quito, Ecuador
EF International Language School–St. Petersburg, Russian Federation
EF International Language School–Shanghai, China
EKOCAMP International, Canada
Elite Educational Institute Elementary Enrichment, CA
Elite Educational Institute Elementary Enrichment–Korea, Republic of Korea
Elite Educational Institute Junior High/PSAT Program, CA
Elite Educational Institute Junior High/PSAT Program–Korea, Republic of Korea
Elite Educational Institute SAT Bootcamp–Korea, Republic of Korea
Elite Educational Institute SAT I and II Preparation, CA
Elite Educational Institute SAT Preparation–Korea, Republic of Korea
Elite Educational Institute SAT Summer Bootcamp, CA
Emagination Computer Camps–Georgia, GA
Emagination Computer Camps–Illinois, IL
Emagination Computer Camps–Massachusetts, MA
Embry-Riddle Aeronautical University–Aerospace Summer Camp, FL
Embry-Riddle Aeronautical University–Aviation Career Exploration, FL
Embry-Riddle Aeronautical University–Flight Exploration, FL
Embry-Riddle Aeronautical University–Sun Flight, FL
Emerging Leaders 2005, SC
Enforex–General Spanish–Almuñecar, Spain
Enforex–General Spanish–Barcelona, Spain
Enforex–General Spanish–Granada, Spain
Enforex–General Spanish–Madrid, Spain
Enforex–General Spanish–Marbella, Spain
Enforex–General Spanish–Salamanca, Spain
Enforex–General Spanish–Valencia, Spain
Enforex Hispanic Culture: Civilization, History, Art, and Literature–Barcelona, Spain
Enforex Hispanic Culture: Civilization, History, Art, and Literature–Granada, Spain
Enforex Hispanic Culture: Civilization, History, Art, and Literature–Madrid, Spain
Enforex Homestay Program–Almuñecar, Spain
Enforex Homestay Program–Barcelona, Spain
Enforex Homestay Program–Granada, Spain
Enforex Homestay Program–Madrid, Spain
Enforex Homestay Program–Marbella, Spain
Enforex Homestay Program–Salamanca, Spain
Enforex Spanish and Golf, Spain
Enforex Spanish and Tennis, Spain
Enforex Study Tour Vacational Program–Madrid, Spain
Environmental Studies Summer Youth Institute, NY
Episcopal High School Academic Camp, FL
Excel at Amherst College and Williams College, MA
Excel at Madrid/Barcelona, Spain
Excel at Oxford/Tuscany
Excel at UC Santa Cruz, CA
Excel Cuba, Cuba
Expeditions, OR
The Experiment in International Living–France, Homestay, Language Training, and Cooking, France
The Experiment in International Living–Spain, Five-Week Language Training, Travel, and Homestay, Spain
The Experiment in International Living–Spain, Four-Week Language Study and Homestay, Spain
Exploration Intermediate Program at Wellesley College, MA
Exploration Junior Program at St. Mark's School, MA
Exploration of Architecture, CA
Exploration Senior Program at Yale University, CT
Explore-A-College, IN
Fairfax Collegiate School Summer Enrichment Program, VA
Fay Summer School, MA
The Fessenden School Summer ESL Program, MA
The Festival of Creative Youth, ME
Fir Acres Workshop in Writing and Thinking, OR
Fishburne Summer Session, VA
Flint Hill School–"Summer on the Hill"–Academics on the Hill–English and Math Review, VA
Flint Hill School–"Summer on the Hill"–Academics on the Hill–Geometry for Credit, VA
Flint Hill School–"Summer on the Hill"–Academics on the Hill–The Reading Clinic, VA
Flint Hill School–"Summer on the Hill"–Counselor-in-Training Day Camp, VA
Flint Hill School–"Summer on the Hill"–Enrichment on the Hill–Gee, Whiz!, VA
Flint Hill School–"Summer on the Hill"–Enrichment on the Hill–Junior Great Books, VA
Flint Hill School–"Summer on the Hill"–Enrichment on the Hill–Scientific Super Sleuths, VA
Flint Hill School–"Summer on the Hill"–Enrichment on the Hill–Spanish Immersion Camp, VA
Flint Hill School–"Summer on the Hill"–Enrichment on the Hill–Study Skills for 9th Graders, VA
Flint Hill School–"Summer on the Hill"–Trips from the Hill–Ecological Study of Coral Reefs, Bahamas, Bahamas
Florida Air Academy Summer Session, FL
4 Star Academics Junior Camp at the University of Virginia, VA
4 Star Academics Scholars at the University of Virginia, VA
4 Star Academics Senior Camp at the University of Virginia, VA
From the Forest to the Sea, AK
Frontiers Program, MA
Furman University Summer Scholars Program, SC
Future Astronaut Training Program, KS
Gems: Girls in Engineering, Math and Science, MA
Genesis at Brandeis University, MA
Georgetown Prep School Summer English Program, MD
Georgetown University College Prep Program, DC
Georgetown University International Relations Program for High School Students, DC
Georgetown University Summer College for High School Juniors, DC
George Washington University Summer Scholars Pre-college Program, DC
Geronimo Program
GIC Arg–Spanish Language, Argentina
GirlSummer at Emma Willard School, NY
Global Teen–French Summer Camp in Monte Carlo, Monaco
Global Teen–German in Bavaria, Germany

Global Teen–German Plus Web Design, Video/Theatre in Berlin, Germany
Global Teen–German Summer Camp in Potsdam, Germany
Global Teen–Italian and Soccer in Rome, Italy
Global Teen–Learn French in Biarritz, France
Global Teen–Learn French in Nice, France
Global Teen–Learn French in Paris, France
Global Teen–Learn German in Berlin, Ages 12-15 on Lake Schmockwitz, Germany
Global Teen–Learn German in Berlin-City Centre, Ages 16-19, Germany
Global Teen–Learn German in Vienna, Summer Camp-Ages 12-18, Austria
Global Teen–Learn German in Vienna, Young Adult Summer Camp, Ages 16-18, Austria
Global Teen–Learn Italian in Italy, Italy
Global Teen–Learn Spanish in Andalusia, Spain
Global Teen–Learn Spanish in Costa Rica, Costa Rica
Global Teen–Learn Spanish in Marbella, Ages 6-14, Spain
Global Teen–Learn Spanish in Marbella-Young Adult, Spain
Global Teen–Learn Spanish in Mexico, Mexico
Global Teen–Learn Spanish in Salamanca, Ages 11-18, Spain
Global Teen–Learn Spanish in Salamanca, Ages 13-16, Spain
Global Teen–Learn Spanish in Sevilla, Spain
Global Teen–Spanish in Ecuador, Ecuador
Global Teen–Spanish in Madrid, Ages 6-14, Spain
Global Teen–Spanish in Malaga-Young Adult, Ages 16-20, Spain
Global Teen–Spanish in Palma de Mallorca, Spain
Global Teen–Spanish Summer Camp in San Sebastian, Spain
Global Teen–Summer Camp in Barcelona, Spain
Global Teen–Summer Camp in Marbella, Ages 14-18, Spain
Global Teen–Summer Language Adventure in Montreal, Canada
Global Teen Summer Sports Camp in Berlin, Germany
Global Teen–Vejer Beach Spectacular in Spain, Spain
Global Teen–Young Adult Summer Camp in Madrid, Ages 14-18, Spain
Global Teen–Young Adult Summer Program in Malaga, Ages 16-20, Spain
GLS Bavarian Summer School, Germany
GLS Berlin Summer School, Germany
GLS Potsdam Summer School, Germany
GLS Sports and Language Camp Inzell, Germany
GLS Summer Camp Blossin, Germany
GLS Summer Camp Loewenstein, Germany
GLS Summer Camp Schmoeckwitz, Germany
The Governor's Program for Gifted Children, LA
The Gow School Summer Program, NY
The Grand River Summer Academy, OH
Graphic Media Experience, NY
Grinnell Summer Institute, IA
Groundwater University, NE
Guitar Workshop Plus–Bass, Drums, Keyboards, Canada
Hamilton Learning Centre Summer Fun in the Sun Camp, Canada
Hamilton Learning Centre Summer School, Canada
Hancock Field Station, OR
Hargrave Summer Program, VA
Harker Summer English Language Institute, CA
The Harker Summer Institute, CA
Harker Summer Programs, CA
Harvard University Summer School: Secondary School Program, MA
Hawaii Preparatory Academy Summer Session, HI
High School Scholars (Summer Courses), PA
Hillsdale College Summer Science Camps, MI
Hill Top Summer Programs, PA
The Hockaday School Summer Session, TX
Hollinsummer, VA
Houghton Academy Summer ESL, NY
Humanities Spring in Assisi, Italy
Humanities Spring on the Road, Italy
The Hun School of Princeton American Culture and Language Institute, NJ
The Hun School of Princeton–Summer Academic Session, NJ
Hyde School Summer Challenge Program–Bath, ME, ME
Hyde School Summer Challenge Program–Woodstock, CT, CT
Idaho Engineering Science Camp, ID
iD Tech Camps–Cal Lutheran University, Thousand Oaks, CA, CA
iD Tech Camps–Carnegie Mellon University, Pittsburgh, PA, PA
iD Tech Camps–Colorado College, Colorado Springs, CO, CO
iD Tech Camps–Documentary Filmmaking and Cultural Immersion at the University of Cádiz, Spain, Spain
iD Tech Camps–Dominican University, San Rafael, CA, CA
iD Tech Camps–Emerson College, Boston, MA, MA
iD Tech Camps–Emory University, Atlanta, GA, GA
iD Tech Camps–Georgetown University, Washington, DC, DC
iD Tech Camps–Lake Forest College, Evanston, IL, IL
iD Tech Camps–Merrimack College, North Andover, MA, MA
iD Tech Camps–MIT, Cambridge, MA, MA
iD Tech Camps–Northwestern University, Chicago, IL, IL
iD Tech Camps–Pepperdine University, Malibu, CA, CA
iD Tech Camps–Princeton University, Princeton, NJ, NJ
iD Tech Camps–Sacred Heart University, Fairfield, CT, CT
iD Tech Camps–Santa Clara University, Santa Clara, CA, CA
iD Tech Camps–Smith College, Northampton, MA, MA
iD Tech Camps–Southern Methodist University, Dallas, TX, TX
iD Tech Camps–Stanford University, Palo Alto, CA, CA
iD Tech Camps–St. Mary's College, Moraga, CA, CA
iD Tech Camps–UC Berkeley, Berkeley, CA, CA
iD Tech Camps–UC Irvine, Irvine, CA, CA
iD Tech Camps–UCLA, Westwood, CA, CA
iD Tech Camps–UC San Diego, La Jolla, CA, CA
iD Tech Camps–UC Santa Cruz, Santa Cruz, CA, CA
iD Tech Camps–University of Denver, Denver, CO, CO
iD Tech Camps–University of Miami, Coral Gables, FL, FL
iD Tech Camps–University of Michigan, Ann Arbor, MI, MI
iD Tech Camps–University of Minnesota, Minneapolis, MN, MN
iD Tech Camps–University of North Carolina at Chapel Hill, Chapel Hill, NC, NC
iD Tech Camps–University of Virginia, Charlottesville, VA, VA
iD Tech Camps–University of Washington, Seattle, WA, WA
iD Tech Camps–UT Austin, Austin, TX, TX
iD Tech Camps–Vassar College, Poughkeepsie, NY, NY
iD Tech Camps–Villanova University, Villanova, PA, PA
IEI–Print and Broadcast Journalism, United Kingdom
IEI Student Travel–Internship Program in London, United Kingdom
IMACS–Full Day Summer Camp–Connecticut, CT
IMACS–Full Day Summer Camp–Florida, FL
IMACS–Full Day Summer Camp–Missouri, MO
IMACS–Full Day Summer Camp–North Carolina, NC
IMACS–Full Day Summer Camp–Pennsylvania, PA
IMACS–Full Day Summer Camp–South Carolina, SC
IMACS–Individual Summer Programs–Connecticut, CT
IMACS–Individual Summer Programs–Florida, FL
IMACS–Individual Summer Programs–Missouri, MO
IMACS–Individual Summer Programs–North Carolina, NC
IMACS–Individual Summer Programs–Pennsylvania, PA
IMACS–Individual Summer Programs–South Carolina, SC
Institut auf dem Rosenberg, Switzerland
Instituto de Idiomas Geos–Costa Rica, Costa Rica
Instituto de Idiomas Geos–Granada, Spain, Spain
Instituto de Idiomas Geos–Marbella, Spain, Spain
International Junior Golf Academy, SC
Iowa Young Writers' Studio, IA
Irish Way, Ireland
ISB Chinese Language Camp, China
Ithaca College Summer College for High School Students: Session I, NY
Ithaca College Summer College for High School Students: Session II, NY
Ithaca College Summer College for High School Students: Minicourses, NY
Jayhawk Debate Institute, KS
JHS/HS Academic Summer School Program, NY
The John Cooper School Academic Camps, TX

▶ Academic Programs

Johns Hopkins University Zanvyl Krieger School of Arts and Sciences Summer Programs, MD
Julian Krinsky Business School at Haverford College, PA
Julian Krinsky Business School at Wharton (Leadership in the Business World), PA
Julian Krinsky Exploring the Majors at the University of Pennsylvania, PA
Julian Krinsky Junior Enrichment Camp at Cabrini College, PA
Julian Krinsky Senior Enrichment Camp at Haverford College, PA
Julian Krinsky Yesh Shabbat Summer Camp, PA
Junior Institute, WA
Junior Statesmen Summer School–Georgetown University, DC
Junior Statesmen Summer School–Northwestern University, IL
Junior Statesmen Summer School–Princeton University, NJ
Junior Statesmen Summer School–Stanford University, CA
Junior Statesmen Summer School–Yale University, CT
Junior Statesmen Symposium on California State Politics and Government, CA
Junior Statesmen Symposium on Los Angeles Politics and Government, CA
Junior Statesmen Symposium on New Jersey State Politics and Government, NJ
Junior Statesmen Symposium on Ohio State Politics and Government, OH
Junior Statesmen Symposium on Texas Politics and Leadership, TX
Junior Statesmen Symposium on Washington State Politics and Government, WA
Kansas Journalism Institute, KS
Kent School Summer Writers Camp, CT
Kenyon Review Young Writers, OH
Keystone Science Adventures, CO
Kids on Campus, MD
Kiski Summer Camp–Junior Division-Boys Grades 5-8, PA
Kiski Summer Camp–Senior Division-Boys Grades 9-12, PA
Kiski Summer Camp–Senior Division-Girls Grades 9-12, PA
Knowledge Exchange Institute–Artist Abroad Program in Italy, Italy
Knowledge Exchange Institute–Research Abroad in Russia, Russian Federation
Knowledge Exchange Institute–Spanish on the Road in Mexico Program, Mexico
Lacunza Junior Summer Spanish Course, Spain
Ladakh Summer Passage, India
Landmark School Summer Academic Program, MA
Lead 2005, SC
Learn English and Discover Canada, Canada
Learning Programs International–Argentina, Argentina
Learning Programs International–Chile, Chile
Learning Programs International–Costa Rica, Costa Rica
Learning Programs International–Mexico, Mexico
Learning Programs International–Spain, Spain
Les Elfes–International Summer/Winter Camp, Switzerland
Linden Hill Summer Program, MA
The Loomis Chaffee Summer in France, France
The Loomis Chaffee Summer in Spain, Spain
Louisiana College Center for Academically Talented Students (CATS), LA
Louisiana College Summer Superior Program, LA
Lower Mustang Summer Passage, Nepal
LSA Alicante, Spain, Spain
LSA Almuñecar, Spain, Spain
LSA Antibes, France, France
LSA Antigua, Guatemala, Guatemala
LSA Argelés-Gazost, France, France
LSA Ascoli, Italy, Italy
LSA Barcelona, Spain, Spain
LSA Berlin, Germany, Germany
LSA Biarritz, France, France
LSA Blossin, Germany, Germany
LSA Bordeaux, France, France
LSA Buenos Aires, Argentina, Argentina
LSA Cannes, France, France
LSA Cordoba, Argentina, Argentina
LSA Cuernavaca, Mexico, Mexico
LSA Cuzco, Peru, Peru
LSA El Puerto de Santa Maria, Spain, Spain
LSA Flamingo Beach, Costa Rica, Costa Rica
LSA Florence, Italy, Italy
LSA Granada, Spain, Spain
LSA Hamburg, Germany, Germany
LSA Holzkirchen, Germany, Germany
LSA Hyères, France, France
LSA Inzell, Germany, Germany
LSA Kanazawa, Japan, Japan
LSA Lausanne, Switzerland, Switzerland
LSA Lignano, Italy–Active Junior Italian Summer Program, Italy
LSA Lisbon, Portugal, Portugal
LSA Livorno, Italy, Italy
LSA Loewenstein, Germany, Germany
LSA Madrid, Spain, Spain
LSA Màlaga, Spain, Spain
LSA Marbella, Spain, Spain
LSA Mérida, Mexico, Mexico
LSA Milan, Italy, Italy
LSA Montreal, Canada–English/French, Canada
LSA Moscow, Russia, Russian Federation
LSA Munich, Germany, Germany
LSA Nerja, Spain, Spain
LSA Nice, France, France
LSA Oaxaca, Mexico, Mexico
LSA Orvieto, Italy, Italy
LSA Paris, France, France
LSA Playa Del Carmen, Mexico, Mexico
LSA Potsdam, Germany, Germany
LSA Puebla, Mexico, Mexico
LSA Puerto Vallarta, Mexico, Mexico
LSA Quito, Ecuador, Ecuador
LSA Rimini, Italy, Italy
LSA Rome, Italy, Italy
LSA St. Petersburg, Russia, Russian Federation
LSA Salamanca, Spain, Spain
LSA San José, Costa Rica, Costa Rica
LSA San Sebastian, Spain, Spain
LSA Schmoeckwitz, Germany, Germany
LSA Sevilla, Spain, Spain
LSA Siena, Italy, Italy
LSA Stuttgart, Germany, Germany
LSA Sucre, Bolivia, Bolivia
LSA Treviso, Italy, Italy
LSA Valencia, Spain, Spain
LSA Vienna, Austria, Austria
LSA Viña del Mar, Chile, Chile
Maine College of Art Early College Program, ME
Maplebrook School's Summer Program, NY
Marine and Environmental Science Program, Canada
Marine Military Academy English as a Second Language (ESL), TX
Mars Academy, KS
Marvelwood Summer, CT
Massanutten Military Academy Summer Cadet Program, VA
McCallie Academic Camp, TN
Mercersburg Academy Summer Study in France, France
Mercersburg Academy Young Writer's Camp, PA
Mercersburg ESL Plus Program, PA
Mercersburg Academy Summer Study in Spain, Spain
MexArt: Art and Spanish, Mexico
MexArt Dance: Dance and Spanish, Mexico
Miami University Junior Scholars Program, OH
Michigan State University High School Engineering Institute, MI
Michigan Technological University American Indian Workshop, MI
Michigan Technological University Explorations in Engineering Workshop, MI
Michigan Technological University Summer Youth Program, MI
Michigan Technological University Women in Engineering Workshop, MI
Millennium Entrepreneurs Camp CEO, CA
Millennium Entrepreneurs "Training Tomorrow's Business Leaders Today", CA
Millersville University of Pennsylvania–Summer Language Camps for High School Students, PA
Milwaukee School of Engineering (MSOE)–Discover the Possibilities, WI
Milwaukee School of Engineering (MSOE)–Focus on Nursing, WI
Milwaukee School of Engineering (MSOE)–Focus on the Possibilities, WI
MIMC–Intensive Music Camp, Canada
MIMC–Language Camp, Canada
Mississippi Governor's School, MS
Miss Porter's School Summer Challenge, CT
Miss Porter's School Arts Alive!, CT
MIT MITE^{2}S (Minority Introduction to Engineering, Entrepreneurship and Science), MA
The Monarch School Summer Course, TX
Montclair State University Hi Jump Program, NJ
Montclair State University Summer Camp for Academically Gifted and Talented Youth, NJ
Monte Vista ESL Intensive Language Institute, CA
Montgomery Bell Academy–LEAD Program, TN
Montgomery Bell Academy–Summer Cooking Camp, TN
Montgomery Bell Academy–Summer School, TN
Montgomery Bell Academy–Summer Science Experience, TN
Montgomery College WDCE–Biotechnology and Diversity Camp, MD

Academic Programs

St. Andrew's Summer Programs, MD
St. George's Summer Session, RI
St. John's Northwestern Academic Camp, WI
St. John's Northwestern ESL Camp, WI
St. John's University Scholars Program, NY
St. Margaret's School International Summer ESL Programme, Canada
St. Paul's Preparatory Academy Summer Program, AZ
Saint Thomas More School–Summer Academic Camp, CT
Saint Vincent College Challenge Program, PA
Salisbury Summer School of Reading and English, CT
The Sarah Porter Leadership Institute, CT
Science Program for High School Girls, CA
Science Program for Middle School Boys on Catalina, CA
Science Program for Middle School Girls on Catalina, CA
Science Quest, PA
Sciencescape, MO
Sea Camp, TX
Seacamp, FL
SEACAMP San Diego, CA
SeaWorld San Antonio Adventure Camp, TX
SeaWorld San Diego Adventure Camp, CA
Service-Learning in Paris, France
SFS: Community Wildlife Management, Kenya
SFS: Conserving Coastal Diversity, Mexico
SFS: Marine Parks Management Studies, Turks and Caicos Islands
SFS: Sustaining Tropical Ecosystems, Costa Rica
SFS: Tropical Reforestation Studies, Australia
Shattuck-St. Mary's Summer Discovery and English Language Institute, MN
Shippensburg University Academic Camps–Government in Real Life, PA
Shippensburg University Academic Camps–Science Academy for Girls, PA
Shizen Kyampu-Japanese Language Science Camp, OR
Sidwell Friends Explorer Day Camp, Explorer Voyagers and ExploreStar, DC
Sidwell Friends Riverview Programs, VA
Sidwell Friends Summer Program: Costa Rica, Costa Rica
Sidwell Friends Summer Studies, DC
Sidwell Friends Women's Leadership–St. Margaret's School, VA
Simon's Rock College of Bard Young Writers Workshop, MA
Skidmore College–Pre-College Program in the Liberal Arts for High School Students, NY
Smith College Summer Science and Engineering Program, MA
Southern Methodist University–College Experience, TX
Southern Methodist University TAG (Talented and Gifted), TX
Southwestern Academy International Summer Semester, CA
Southwestern Adventures, AZ
Space Camp Turkey 6-Day International Program, Turkey
Spanish Language and Flamenco Enforex–Granada, Spain
Spanish Language and Flamenco Enforex–Madrid, Spain
Spanish Language and Flamenco Enforex–Marbella, Spain
Spoleto Study Abroad, Italy
Sports and Arts Center at Island Lake, PA
Sprachkurse Ariana, Aldenham, United Kingdom
Sprachkurse Ariana, Arosa, Switzerland
Sprachkurse Ariana, Lenk, Switzerland
Sprachkurse Ariana, Seefeld-Austria, Austria
Springfield College Allied Health Career Exploration Program, MA
Springfield College Athletic Trainer Workshop, MA
Springfield College Sports Management Career Exploration Program, MA
Springfield Technical Community College–College for Kids, MA
Squirrel Hollow Learning Camp, GA
Stanford Discovery Institutes, CA
Stanford National Forensic Institute, CA
Stanford University Summer College for High School Students, CA
Stanstead College–English as a Second Language, Canada
Stanstead College–French as a Second Language, Canada
Star Ranch Summer Camp, TX
Stevenson School Summer Camp, CA
Stoneleigh–Burnham School: Camp $tart-Up, MA
Stoneleigh–Burnham School: Science Camp for Middle School Girls, MA
Stoneleigh–Burnham School: Summer Debate and Public Speaking Camp, MA
Stony Brook University–Biotechnology Summer Camp, NY
Stony Brook University–Environmental Education Summer Camp, NY
Stony Brook University–Science Exploration Camp, NY
Stony Book University–Summer Camp at Stony Brook, NY
Stony Brook University Summer Sessions College Program, NY
Strive: Exploring Engineering, Math and Science, MA
Study Tours and Hotel and Tourism Management in the USA–Southern Nevada College, NV
Study Tours and Leisure Sports in the USA–Citrus College, CA
Study Tours in the USA–Citrus, CA
Study Tours in the USA–Dean College, MA
Study Tours in the USA–Lock Haven, PA
Study Tours in the USA–Mira Costa College, CA
Study Tours in the USA–Oxnard, CA
Study Tours in the USA–Southern Nevada, NV
Study Tour Vacational Program Enforex–Barcelona, Spain
The Summer Academy at Suffield, CT
Summer Academy for the Visual and Performing Arts, NJ
Summer Academy of Mathematics and Sciences, PA
Summer at Altamont, AL
Summer Biotechnology Institute for High School and Middle School Teachers and Students, OH
Summer Discovery at Australia, Australia
Summer Discovery at Cambridge, United Kingdom
Summer Discovery at Georgetown, DC
Summer Discovery at Michigan, MI
Summer Discovery at UCLA, CA
Summer Discovery at UC San Diego, CA
Summer Discovery at UC Santa Barbara, CA
Summer Discovery at Vermont, VT
Summer Focus at Berkeley, CA
The Summer Institute for the Gifted at Amherst College, MA
The Summer Institute for the Gifted at Bryn Mawr College, PA
The Summer Institute for the Gifted at Drew University, NJ
The Summer Institute for the Gifted at Fairfield University, CT
The Summer Institute for the Gifted at Hofstra University, NY
The Summer Institute for the Gifted at Moorestown Friends School, NJ
The Summer Institute for the Gifted at Oberlin College, OH
The Summer Institute for the Gifted at Princeton University, NJ
The Summer Institute for the Gifted at Purchase College, NY
The Summer Institute for the Gifted at UCLA, CA
The Summer Institute for the Gifted at University of California, Berkeley, CA
The Summer Institute for the Gifted at Vassar College, NY
Summer in Switzerland, Switzerland
"Summer in the City", NY
Summer JAM (Judaism, Activism, and Mitzvah Work), DC
Summer Leadership Education and Training, VA
Summer Programs on the River; Skills Program, VA
Summer School at New York Military Academy, NY
Summer Science Program at the South Carolina Governor's School for Science and Math, SC
The Summer Science Program–California Campus, CA
The Summer Science Program–New Mexico Campus, NM
SummerSkills at Albany Academy for Girls, NY
Summer Study at Penn State, PA
Summer Study at The University of Colorado at Boulder, CO
Summer Study in Paris at The American University of Paris, France
Summer Vet, CO
SuperCamp–Claremont Colleges, CA
SuperCamp–Colorado College, CO
SuperCamp–Dominican Republic, Dominican Republic
SuperCamp–Hampshire College, MA
SuperCamp–Hong Kong, Hong Kong
SuperCamp–Mexico, Mexico
SuperCamp–Singapore, Singapore
SuperCamp–Stanford University, CA
SuperCamp–Switzerland, Switzerland
SuperCamp–Thailand, Thailand
SuperCamp–University of Wisconsin at Parkside, WI
SuperCamp–Wake Forest University, NC
Susquehanna University Advanced Writers Workshop for High School Students, PA
Syracuse University Summer College, NY
Tabor Academy Summer Program, MA
Taft Summer School, CT

Taft Summer School Abroad–France, France
Taft Summer School Abroad–Spain, Spain
Talisman–Academics, NC
Talisman Summer Camp, NC
Tampa Prep–Academic Credit and Enrichment Courses, FL
TASIS England Summer Program, United Kingdom
TASIS French Language Program in Château–d'Oex, Switzerland, Switzerland
TASIS Le Château des Enfants, Switzerland
TASIS Middle School Program, Switzerland
TASIS Spanish Summer Program, Spain
TASIS Summer Program for Languages, Arts, and Outdoor Pursuits, Switzerland
Teen Challenge, PA
Teen Tour USA and Canada
Tibetan Summer Passage
Time Travelers Program, PA
Tisch School of the Arts–International High School Program–Dublin, Ireland
Tisch School of the Arts–International High School Program–Paris, France
Tisch School of the Arts–Summer High School Programs, NY
Tufts Summer Study, MA
Tufts Summit, France
Tuskegee University Vet Step I, AL
Tuskegee University Vet Step II, AL
UCAELI Summer Camp, CT
UC San Diego Academic Connections, CA
University of Chicago–ChicaGO! The Traveling Academy, France
University of Chicago–Insight, IL
University of Chicago–Research in the Biological Sciences, IL
University of Chicago–Stones and Bones, WY
University of Chicago–Summer Quarter for High School Students, IL
University of Connecticut Mentor Connection, CT
University of Delaware Summer College, DE
University of Kansas–Duke University Talent Identification Program, KS
University of Kansas–Natural History Museum Summer Workshops, KS
University of Kansas–Project Discovery, KS
University of Kansas–School of Pharmacy Summer Camp, KS
University of Maryland Young Scholars Program, MD
University of Miami Summer Scholar Programs, FL
University of Pennsylvania–Penn Summer Science Academy, PA
University of Pennsylvania–Precollege Program, PA
University of St. Andrews Creative Writing Summer Program, United Kingdom
University of St. Andrews Scottish Studies Summer Program, United Kingdom
University of Southern California Summer Seminars, CA
University of Vermont Summer Institute for High School Students Discovering Engineering, Computers, and Mathematics, VT
University of Wisconsin–Green Bay Biz 4 Youth Camp, WI
University of Wisconsin–Green Bay Computer Camp, WI
University of Wisconsin–Green Bay Ecosystem Investigations, WI
University of Wisconsin–Green Bay Space Trek Camp, WI
University of Wisconsin–Green Bay Summer Discovery, WI
University of Wisconsin–Green Bay Summer Spanish Immersion, WI
University of Wisconsin–Superior Youthsummer 2005, WI
Village Camps–Austria, Austria
Village Camps–England, United Kingdom
Village Camps–Switzerland, Switzerland
Washington and Lee University Summer Scholars, VA
Washington International School Passport to Summer, DC
Washington Internship Experience, DC
Washington University High School Summer Scholars Program, MO
Wentworth Military Academy Summer School, MO
Wentworth Military Academy Summer School–Camp LEAD, MO
Wesleyan Summer Gifted Program, WV
The Whale Camp–Youth Programs, Canada
Where There Be Dragons: China, China
Where There Be Dragons: Guatemala, Guatemala
Where There Be Dragons: India Culture and Philosophy, India
Where There Be Dragons: India Zanskar Trek, India
Where There Be Dragons: Mexico, Mexico
Where There Be Dragons: Mongolia, Mongolia
Where There Be Dragons: Peru, Peru
Where There Be Dragons: Silk Road, China
Where There Be Dragons: Thailand, Thailand
Where There Be Dragons: Tibet, China
Where There Be Dragons: Vietnam, Vietnam
Whitman National Debate Institute, WA
The Winchendon School Summer Session, MA
Windsor Mountain: Crossroads France, France
Windsor Mountain: Experiential Summer School
Wolfeboro: The Summer Boarding School, NH
Women in Engineering Summer Camp, OH
Women in Science & Engineering Camp, PA
Women in Technology, MI
Woodberry Forest Junior Adventure, VA
Woodberry Forest Senior Adventure, VA
Woodberry Forest Summer School–England, United Kingdom
Woodberry Forest Summer School–France, France
Woodberry Forest Summer School–Japan, Japan
Woodberry Forest Summer School–Scotland, United Kingdom
Woodberry Forest Summer School–Spain, Spain
World Affairs Seminar, WI
World Affairs Youth Seminar, AL
WRC Weather Camp, TX
Wright State University Residential Camps and Institutes, OH
Wyoming Seminary–Sem Summer 2005, PA
YMCA Camp Fitch Summer Camp, PA
Young Investigators Program in Nuclear Science & Technology, NC
Youth for Understanding USA–Argentina, Argentina
Youth for Understanding USA–Australia, Australia
Youth for Understanding USA–Brazil, Brazil
Youth for Understanding USA–Chile, Chile
Youth for Understanding USA–China, China
Youth for Understanding USA–Denmark, Denmark
Youth for Understanding USA–Ecuador, Ecuador
Youth for Understanding USA–Estonia/Latvia-Baltic Summer
Youth for Understanding USA–France, France
Youth for Understanding USA–Germany, Germany
Youth for Understanding USA–Ghana, Ghana
Youth for Understanding USA–Greece, Greece
Youth for Understanding USA–Hungary, Hungary
Youth for Understanding USA–Ireland, Ireland
Youth for Understanding USA–Italy, Italy
Youth for Understanding USA–Japan, Japan
Youth for Understanding USA–Kazakhstan, Kazakhstan
Youth for Understanding USA–Poland, Poland
Youth for Understanding USA–Russia, Russian Federation
Youth for Understanding USA–South Africa, South Africa
Youth for Understanding USA–South Korea, Republic of Korea
Youth for Understanding USA–Spain, Spain
Youth for Understanding USA–Sweden, Sweden
Youth for Understanding USA–Thailand, Thailand
Youth for Understanding USA–Uruguay, Uruguay
Youth for Understanding USA–Venezuela, Venezuela
Youth for Understanding USA–Vietnam, Vietnam
Youth Program in Spain, Spain

Adventure Programs

AAVE–Africa
AAVE–Alaska, AK
AAVE–Alps Rider
AAVE–Australia, Australia
AAVE–Belize, Belize
AAVE–Bike France, France
AAVE–Bold Europe
AAVE–Bold West
AAVE–Boot/Saddle/Paddle
AAVE–Border Cross
AAVE–Costa Rica, Costa Rica
AAVE–Ecuador and Galapagos, Ecuador
AAVE–Hawaii, HI
AAVE–Inmersión en España, Spain
AAVE–Peru and Machu Picchu, Peru
AAVE–Rock & River
AAVE–Rocky Mountain Adventure, CO
AAVE–Thailand, Thailand
AAVE–Vietnam, Vietnam
AAVE–Vivons le Français, France
AAVE–Wild Isles
AAVE–X–Five
Abilene Christian University–Cross Training, NM
ACTIONQUEST: Advanced PADI Scuba Certification and Specialty Voyages, British Virgin Islands
ACTIONQUEST: Australian and Great Barrier Reef Adventures, Australia

Adventure Programs

ACTIONQUEST: British Virgin Islands–Sailing and Scuba Voyages, British Virgin Islands
ACTIONQUEST: British Virgin Islands-Sailing Voyages, British Virgin Islands
ACTIONQUEST: Galapagos Archipelago Expeditions, Ecuador
ACTIONQUEST: Junior Advanced Scuba with Marine Biology, British Virgin Islands
ACTIONQUEST: Leeward and French Caribbean Island Voyages
ACTIONQUEST: Mediterranean Sailing Voyage
ACTIONQUEST: Rescue Diving Voyages, British Virgin Islands
ACTIONQUEST: Tahiti and French Polynesian Island Voyages, French Polynesia
ACTIONQUEST: Tropical Marine Biology Voyages, British Virgin Islands
Adventure Ireland–English Learning Option, Ireland
Adventure Ireland–Surf Camp/Activity Camp, Ireland
Adventure Links
Adventure Links–Appalachian Odyssey
Adventure Links–North Carolina Expeditions, NC
Adventure Links–The Costa Rica Experience, Costa Rica
Adventure Links–Ultimate Adventure Camps, VA
!ADVENTURES–AFLOAT: Advanced Scuba Adventure Voyages–British Virgin Islands, British Virgin Islands
!ADVENTURES–AFLOAT: Advanced Scuba Adventure Voyages–Caribbean Islands
!ADVENTURES–AFLOAT: Scuba and Sailing Discovery Voyages–British Virgin Islands, British Virgin Islands
!ADVENTURES–AFLOAT: Scuba and Sailing Discovery Voyages–Caribbean Islands
Adventures Cross-Country, Alaska Adventure, AK
Adventures Cross-Country, Australia/Fiji Adventure
Adventures Cross-Country, Caribbean Adventure
Adventures Cross-Country, Colorado Adventure, CO
Adventures Cross-Country, Costa Rica Adventure, Costa Rica
Adventures Cross-Country, Extreme British Columbia Adventure, Canada
Adventures Cross-Country, Hawaii Adventure, HI
Adventures Cross-Country,Southern Europe Adventure
Adventures Cross-Country, Thailand Adventure, Thailand
Adventures Cross-Country, Western Adventure
Adventure Treks–Alaska Adventures, AK
Adventure Treks–California Challenge Adventures
Adventure Treks–California 19 Adventures, CA
Adventure Treks–Canadian Rockies Adventures, Canada
Adventure Treks–Montana Adventures, MT
Adventure Treks–Pacific Northwest Adventures, WA
Adventure Treks–PAC 16, OR
Adventure Treks–Summit Fever
Adventure Treks–Ultimate Northwest Adventures
AFS-USA–Homestay Plus–Brazil, Brazil
Alpengirl–Alaska, AK
Alpengirl–Hawaii, HI
Alpengirl–Montana, MT
Alpengirl–Montana Art
Alpengirl–Montana Fitness, MT
Alpengirl–Montana Horse, MT
Alpengirl–Scandinavia
Alpengirl–Washington, WA
Alpengirl–Washington Alpenguide Training, WA
Alpengirl–Washington Lil' Alpengirl, WA
Apogee Outdoor Adventures–Burlington to Boston
Apogee Outdoor Adventures–Coast to Quebec
Apogee Outdoor Adventures–New England Mountains and Coast
Apogee Outdoor Adventures–Montana Service Adventure, MT
Apogee Outdoor Adventures–Cape Cod and the Islands, MA
ATW: Action America West
ATW: Adventure Roads
ATW: American Horizons
ATW: California Sunset
ATW: Camp Inn 42
ATW: Discoverer
ATW: European Adventures
ATW: Fire and Ice
ATW: Mini Tours
ATW: Pacific Paradise
ATW: Skyblazer
ATW: Sunblazer
ATW: Wayfarer
Audubon Journeys, VT
Bark Lake Leadership Through Recreation Camp, Canada
Bicycle Africa Tours
BICYCLE TRAVEL ADVENTURES–Student Hosteling Program–Amsterdam to Paris
BICYCLE TRAVEL ADVENTURES–Student Hosteling Program–A Thousand Miles: Massachusetts to Nova Scotia
BICYCLE TRAVEL ADVENTURES–Student Hosteling Program–Canadian Rockies to California
BICYCLE TRAVEL ADVENTURES–Student Hosteling Program–Cape Cod, MA
BICYCLE TRAVEL ADVENTURES–Student Hosteling Program–Cross-Country America
BICYCLE TRAVEL ADVENTURES–Student Hosteling Program–France and Italy
BICYCLE TRAVEL ADVENTURES–Student Hosteling Program–Ireland and England
BICYCLE TRAVEL ADVENTURES–Student Hosteling Program–Maine Coast, ME
BICYCLE TRAVEL ADVENTURES–Student Hosteling Program–Maine-Nova Scotia Coast Loop
BICYCLE TRAVEL ADVENTURES–Student Hosteling Program–Niagara Falls to Montreal
BICYCLE TRAVEL ADVENTURES–Student Hosteling Program–Off-Road Vermont
BICYCLE TRAVEL ADVENTURES–Student Hosteling Program–Pacific Coast Adventure: Washington, Oregon, and California
BICYCLE TRAVEL ADVENTURES–Student Hosteling Program–Province du Québec, Canada
BICYCLE TRAVEL ADVENTURES–Student Hosteling Program–Province du Québec (short program), Canada
BICYCLE TRAVEL ADVENTURES–Student Hosteling Program–Spain and France
BICYCLE TRAVEL ADVENTURES–Student Hosteling Program–Vermont
BICYCLE TRAVEL ADVENTURES–Student Hosteling Program–Vermont to the Atlantic Ocean
Blue Ridge School–Adventure Camps, VA
Blue Ridge School–Rock Climbing Camp, VA
Blyth Education–Summer Study in the Amazon and the Galapagos Islands, Ecuador
BROADREACH Academic Treks–Marine Mammal Studies, Canada
BROADREACH Academic Treks–Marine Park Management
BROADREACH Academic Treks–Sea Turtle Studies, Costa Rica
BROADREACH Academic Treks–Spanish Immersion in Mexico, Mexico
BROADREACH Academic Treks–Spanish Language Immersion in Ecuador, Ecuador
BROADREACH Adventures Down Under, Australia
BROADREACH Adventures in Scuba and Sailing–Underwater Discoveries
BROADREACH Adventures in the Grenadines–Advanced Scuba, Saint Vincent and The Grenadines
BROADREACH Adventures in the Windward Islands–Advanced Scuba
BROADREACH Adventures Underwater–Advanced Scuba
BROADREACH Amazon and Galapagos Encounter, Ecuador
BROADREACH Arc of the Caribbean Sailing Adventure
BROADREACH Baja Extreme–Scuba Adventure, Mexico
BROADREACH Costa Rica Experience, Costa Rica
BROADREACH Fiji Solomon Quest
BROADREACH Honduras Eco-Adventure, Honduras
BROADREACH Red Sea Scuba Adventure, Egypt
California Campus Tours, CA
Camp Arowhon–Voyageur Canoe Trip Program, Canada
Camp Berachah Ministries–Leadership Expedition Camp, WA
Camp Chewonki Eco-Kayak Australia, Australia
Camp Chewonki for Girls, ME
Camp Chewonki Wilderness Expeditions, ME
Camp Chi Teenage Adventure Trips
Camp Echo, MI
Camp Henry Offsite: Teen Challenge, MI
Camp Tawonga–Call of the Wild, CA
Camp Tawonga–Magical Mystery Tour, CA
Camp Tawonga–Surf 'n Turf Quest, CA
Camp Tawonga–Teen Quest: Canada, Canada
Camp Tawonga–Teen Quest: High Sierra, CA
Camp Tawonga–Teen Quest: Northwest
Camp Tawonga–Teen Quest: Southwest
Camp Tawonga–Teen Quest: Yosemite, CA

Camp Tawonga–Teen Service Learning to Alaska, AK
Camp Winding Gap, NC
Canadian Rockies Adventurer Camp, Canada
Canadian Rockies Outdoor Leader Camp, Canada
Cheerio Adventures–Appalachian Adventure, VA
Cheerio Adventures–Cave/Raft, VA
Cheerio Adventures–5 Rivers in 5 Days
Cheerio Adventures–Mountains to the Sea, VA
Cheerio Adventures–Ocean Odyssey, VA
Cheerio Adventures–Rock Climb/Raft, VA
Cheerio Adventures–Sampler, VA
Cheerio Adventures–Seekers, VA
Cheerio Adventures–Standard, VA
Cheley Colorado Camps, CO
Costa Rica Rainforest Outward Bound School–Multi-Element, Costa Rica
Costa Rica Rainforest Outward Bound School–Summer Semester, Costa Rica
Costa Rica Rainforest Outward Bound School–Surf Adventure, Costa Rica
Costa Rica Rainforest Outward Bound School–Tri-Country/Tri-Mester
Cottonwood Gulch Mountain Desert Challenge, NM
Cottonwood Gulch Prairie Trek Expedition, NM
Cottonwood Gulch Turquoise Trail Expedition, NM
Cottonwood Gulch Wild Country Trek, NM
Darrow Wilderness Trips–Maine, ME
Darrow Wilderness Trips–Quebec: Mistassini, Canada
Darrow Wilderness Trips–St. Croix, ME
Darrow Wilderness Trips–Voyageurs, ME
Darrow Youth Backpacking, ME
Discovery Works New England Community Service Experience
Eagle Lake Camp–East, NC
Eagle Lake Wilderness Program, CO
EARTHWATCH INSTITUTE–Argentina's Pampas Carnivores, Argentina
EARTHWATCH INSTITUTE–Bahamian Reef Survey, Bahamas
EARTHWATCH INSTITUTE–Baltic Island Wetlands and Wildlife, Estonia
EARTHWATCH INSTITUTE–Butterflies of Vietnam, Vietnam
EARTHWATCH INSTITUTE–Cacti and Orchids of the Yucatan, Mexico
EARTHWATCH INSTITUTE–Canyonland Creek Ecology, UT
EARTHWATCH INSTITUTE–Caring for Chimpanzees, WA
EARTHWATCH INSTITUTE–Carnivores of Madagascar, Madagascar
EARTHWATCH INSTITUTE–Cheetah, Namibia
EARTHWATCH INSTITUTE–China's Ancestral Temples, China
EARTHWATCH INSTITUTE–Climate Change at Arctic's Edge, Canada
EARTHWATCH INSTITUTE–Coastal Ecology of the Bahamas, Bahamas
EARTHWATCH INSTITUTE–Community Health in Cameroon, Cameroon
EARTHWATCH INSTITUTE–Conservation Research Initiative–Restoring Wild Salmon, WA
EARTHWATCH INSTITUTE–Crocodiles of the Okavango, Botswana
EARTHWATCH INSTITUTE–Dolphins and Whales of Abaco Island, Bahamas
EARTHWATCH INSTITUTE–Dolphins of Brazil, Brazil
EARTHWATCH INSTITUTE–Early Man at Olduvai Gorge, United Republic of Tanzania
EARTHWATCH INSTITUTE–Early Man in Spain, Spain
EARTHWATCH INSTITUTE–Echidnas and Goannas of Kangaroo Island, Australia
EARTHWATCH INSTITUTE–Ecuador Forest Birds, Ecuador
EARTHWATCH INSTITUTE–England's Hidden Kingdom, United Kingdom
EARTHWATCH INSTITUTE–Europe–Africa Songbird Migrations–Hungary, Hungary
EARTHWATCH INSTITUTE–Europe–Africa Songbird Migrations–Italy, Italy
EARTHWATCH INSTITUTE–Frontier Fort in Virginia, VA
EARTHWATCH INSTITUTE–Icelandic and Alaskan Glaciers, Iceland
EARTHWATCH INSTITUTE–Inner Mongolia's Lost Water, China
EARTHWATCH INSTITUTE–Itjaritjari: the Outback's Mysterious Marsupial, Australia
EARTHWATCH INSTITUTE–Jackson Hole Bison Dig, WY
EARTHWATCH INSTITUTE–Kenya's Black Rhino, Kenya
EARTHWATCH INSTITUTE–Koala Ecology, Australia
EARTHWATCH INSTITUTE–Lakes of the Rift Valley, Kenya
EARTHWATCH INSTITUTE–Lions of Tsavo, Kenya
EARTHWATCH INSTITUTE–Mallorca's Copper Age, Spain
EARTHWATCH INSTITUTE–Mammoth Cave, KY
EARTHWATCH INSTITUTE–Mammoth Graveyard, SD
EARTHWATCH INSTITUTE–Moose and Wolves, MI
EARTHWATCH INSTITUTE–Mountain Waters of Bohemia, Czech Republic
EARTHWATCH INSTITUTE–New Zealand Dolphins, New Zealand
EARTHWATCH INSTITUTE–Orca, WA
EARTHWATCH INSTITUTE–Pine Marten of the Ancient Forest, Canada
EARTHWATCH INSTITUTE–Puerto Rico's Rainforest, Puerto Rico
EARTHWATCH INSTITUTE–Rare Plants of Kenya, Kenya
EARTHWATCH INSTITUTE–Rivers of the Peruvian Amazon, Peru
EARTHWATCH INSTITUTE–Roman Fort on the Danube, Romania
EARTHWATCH INSTITUTE–Roman Fort on Tyne, United Kingdom
EARTHWATCH INSTITUTE–Saving the Leatherback Turtle, U.S. Virgin Islands
EARTHWATCH INSTITUTE–Sea Turtles of Baja, Mexico
EARTHWATCH INSTITUTE–South African Penguins, South Africa
EARTHWATCH INSTITUTE–South African Wildlife, South Africa
EARTHWATCH INSTITUTE–Spanish Dolphins, Spain
EARTHWATCH INSTITUTE–Sri Lanka's Temple Monkeys, Sri Lanka
EARTHWATCH INSTITUTE–Wild Dolphin Societies, FL
EARTHWATCH INSTITUTE–Wildlife Conservation in West Africa, Ghana
Excalibur, Canada
The Experiment in International Living–Argentina Homestay, Community Service, and Outdoor Ecological Program, Argentina
The Experiment in International Living–Australia Homestay, Australia
The Experiment in International Living–Botswana Homestay, Botswana
The Experiment in International Living–Brazil–Ecological Preservation, Brazil
The Experiment in International Living–Chile North Homestay, Community Service, Chile
The Experiment in International Living–China North and East Homestay, China
The Experiment in International Living–China South and West Homestay, China
The Experiment in International Living–Costa Rica Homestay, Costa Rica
The Experiment in International Living–Ecuador Homestay, Ecuador
The Experiment in International Living–France, Biking and Homestay, France
The Experiment in International Living–France, Four-Week Homestay and Photography, France
The Experiment in International Living–France, Four-Week Homestay and Theatre, France
The Experiment in International Living–France, Four–Week Homestay and Travel through Alps, France
The Experiment in International Living–France, Three-Week Homestay and Travel–Borders, France
The Experiment in International Living–Germany, Four-Week Homestay, Travel, Community Service, Germany
The Experiment in International Living–Ireland/Northern Ireland Homestay and Peace Studies, Ireland
The Experiment in International Living–Morocco Four-Week Arts and Culture Program, Morocco
The Experiment in International Living–Navajo Nation, NM
The Experiment in International Living–Poland, Homestay, Community Service, and Travel, Poland
The Experiment in International Living–South Africa Homestay and Community Service, South Africa
The Experiment in International Living–Spain, Five-Week Homestay, Travel, Ecology, Spain
The Experiment in International Living–Spain, Four-Week Homestay and Trekking Program, Spain
The Experiment in International Living–Switzerland French Language Immersion, Homestay, and Alpine Adventure, Switzerland
The Experiment in International Living–Thailand Homestay, Thailand

▶ Adventure Programs

The Experiment in International Living–The United Kingdom Celtic Odyssey, United Kingdom
The Experiment in International Living–United Kingdom Filmmaking Program and Homestay, United Kingdom
ExploraMar: Marine Biology Sailing Expeditions–Sea of Cortez, Baja, Mexico
Flint Hill School–"Summer on the Hill"–Into the Woods Day Camp, VA
Flying Moose Lodge, ME
Four Corners School of Outdoor Education: Southwest Ed-Venture
French Immersion Kayak Expedition, Canada
Geronimo Program
GLOBAL WORKS–Adventure Travel-Pacific Northwest-3 weeks, WA
GLOBAL WORKS–Cultural Exchange-Fiji Islands-4 weeks, Fiji
GLOBAL WORKS–Cultural Exchange-Ireland-4 weeks, Ireland
GLOBAL WORKS–Cultural Exchange-New Zealand and Fiji Islands-4 weeks
GLOBAL WORKS–Language Exposure-Costa Rica-4 weeks, Costa Rica
GLOBAL WORKS–Language Exposure-Ecuador and the Galapagos-4 weeks, Ecuador
GLOBAL WORKS–Language Exposure-Puerto Rico-3 weeks, Puerto Rico
GLOBAL WORKS–Language Exposure-Yucatan Peninsula, Mexico-4 weeks, Mexico
GLOBAL WORKS–Language Immersion-Costa Rica-4 weeks, Costa Rica
GLOBAL WORKS–Language Immersion-Ecuador and the Galapagos-4 weeks, Ecuador
GLOBAL WORKS–Language Immersion-France-4 weeks, France
GLOBAL WORKS–Language Immersion-Puerto Rico-4 weeks, Puerto Rico
GLOBAL WORKS–Language Immersion-Spain-4 weeks, Spain
GLOBAL WORKS–Language Immersion-Yucatan Peninsula, Mexico-4 weeks, Mexico
Great Escapes (Adventure Trips for Teens)–Canadian Adventure
Great Escapes (Adventure Trips for Teens)–Canadian Canoe and Kayak Adventure, Canada
Great Escapes (Adventure Trips for Teens)–Cape Escapes, MA
Great Escapes (Adventure Trips for Teens)–Colorado River and Canyons Adventure
Great Escapes (Adventure Trips for Teens)–Costa Rica Rainforest Adventure, Costa Rica
Great Escapes (Adventure Trips for Teens)–Maine Waterways, ME
Great Escapes (Adventure Trips for Teens)–Rock and Rapids
Great Escapes (Adventure Trips for Teens)–Rocky Mountain Horsepacking Adventure, CO
Great Escapes (Adventure Trips for Teens)–Saddle and Sail
Great Escapes (Adventure Trips for Teens)–White Mountain Adventure, NH
Hante School, NC
Horseback Riding Academy at Pali Overnight Adventures, CA
Hulbert Voyageurs Youth Wilderness Trips
Hurricane Island Outward Bound–Maine Coast and Western Maine Canoeing and Sailing, ME
Hurricane Island Outward Bound–Maine Coast and Western Maine Sailing and Backpacking, ME
Hurricane Island Outward Bound–Maine Coast and Western Maine Sea Kayaking and Backpacking, ME
Hurricane Island Outward Bound–Maine Coast Sailing/Sailing and Rock Climbing, ME
Hurricane Island Outward Bound–Maine Coast Schooner Sailing, ME
Hurricane Island Outward Bound–Maine Coast Sea Kayaking, ME
Hurricane Island Outward Bound–Maine Woods High School Summer Semester, ME
Hurricane Island Outward Bound–Mid-Atlantic Canoeing, Backpacking, and Rock Climbing
Hurricane Island Outward Bound–North Woods Maine Allagash and Appalachian Trail Canoeing and Backpacking, ME
Hurricane Island Outward Bound–North Woods Maine Canoeing and Backpacking, ME
Hurricane Island Outward Bound–North Woods Maine Expedition Canoeing, ME
Hurricane Island Outward Bound–Ocean Bound: Tall Ship Sailing and Sea Kayaking Semester
Hurricane Island Outward Bound–Western Maine and New Hampshire Canoeing and Backpacking
Hurricane Island Outward Bound–Western Maine Backpacking and Rock Climbing, ME
Hurricane Island Outward Bound–Western Maine Woods Expedition Canoeing, ME
Ibike Cultural Tours–Ecuador, Ecuador
Ibike Cultural Tours–Washington/British Columbia
Instituto de Idiomas Geos–Costa Rica, Costa Rica
Irish Way, Ireland
Israel Discovery
Jumonville Adventure Camps, PA
Keewaydin Canoe Camp, Canada
Keewaydin Temagami, Canada
Keystone Science Adventures, CO
Knowledge Exchange Institute–African Safari Program, Kenya
Kroka Expeditions–Adventures for Small People, VT
Kroka Expeditions–Coastal Sea Kayaking, ME
Kroka Expeditions–Introduction to Adventure Residential Camp, VT
Kroka Expeditions–Introduction to White Water, VT
Kroka Expeditions–Paddlers Journey Up North
Kroka Expeditions–Rock 'n Road, VT
Kroka Expeditions–Wild World of White Water, VT
Ladakh Summer Passage, India
Langskib Wilderness Programs, Canada
Leadership Training at Pali Overnight Adventures, CA
Lifeschool Wilderness Adventures–Summer Adventures, CA
LIFEWORKS with the British Virgin Islands Marine Parks and Conservation Department, British Virgin Islands
LIFEWORKS with the DPF Foundation in Thailand, Thailand
LIFEWORKS with the Galapagos Islands' National Parks, Ecuador
Longacre Expeditions, Adventure 28
Longacre Expeditions, Alaska, AK
Longacre Expeditions, Belize, Belize
Longacre Expeditions, Blue Ridge, PA
Longacre Expeditions, British Columbia
Longacre Expeditions, British Isles, United Kingdom
Longacre Expeditions, Downeast, ME
Longacre Expeditions, Hawaii, HI
Longacre Expeditions, Iceland, Iceland
Longacre Expeditions, Laurel Highlands, PA
Longacre Expeditions, Leadership Training, CO
Longacre Expeditions, New England/Canada
Longacre Expeditions, Pacific Coast and Inlands
Longacre Expeditions, Peak to Peak, OR
Longacre Expeditions, Photography, ME
Longacre Expeditions, Surf Oregon, OR
Longacre Expeditions, Virgin Islands
Longacre Expeditions, Volcanoes
Longacre Expeditions, Western Challenge
Longacre Expeditions, Whales, ME
Longacre Expeditions, Wind and Waves, OR
Lower Mustang Summer Passage, Nepal
Luna Adventures with AAG SummerSkills
Maine Wilderness Adventure Trip, ME
Mountain Adventure Guides: Summer Adventure Camp–Blue Ridge Expedition I, NC
Mountain Adventure Guides: Summer Adventure Camp–Blue Ridge Expedition II, NC
Mountain Adventure Guides: Summer Adventure Camp–Jr. Adventure Camp, NC
Mountain Workshop–Graduate Plus Awesome Adventures, NY
Mountain Workshop–Awesome 5: North Woods of Maine, ME
Mountain Workshop–Awesome 4: Pennsylvania, PA
Mountain Workshop–Awesome 1: Adirondacks, NY
Mountain Workshop–Awesome 6: Quebec, Canada
Mountain Workshop–Awesome 3: Maine Coast, ME
Mountain Workshop–Awesome 2: Vermont, VT
Mountain Workshop–Bike 1: Martha's Vineyard and Nantucket, MA
Mountain Workshop–Bike 2, MA
Mountain Workshop–Leadership Through Adventure: Adirondacks, NY
Musiker Tours: Action Europe
Musiker Tours: Action USA
Musiker Tours: Alaska Aloha
Musiker Tours: America Coast to Coast
Musiker Tours: Cali-Pacific Passport
Musiker Tours: ComboCamp America
Musiker Tours: Discover America
Musiker Tours: Eastcoaster
Musiker Tours: Westcoaster
NAWA Academy–Girls on the Go, CA
NAWA Academy–Great Challenge, CA
NAWA Academy–Lassen Expedition, CA
NAWA Academy–Trinity Challenge, CA

The Nepal Cultural Immersion Experience, Nepal
North Carolina Outward Bound–Outer Banks, NC
North Carolina Outward Bound–Southern Appalachian Mountains, NC
Northern Lights, Canada
Northwaters Wilderness Programs, Canada
Oak Ridge Summer Leadership Camp, NC
ODYSSEY EXPEDITIONS: Tropical Marine Biology Voyages–British Virgin Islands, British Virgin Islands
ODYSSEY EXPEDITIONS: Tropical Marine Biology Voyages–Caribbean Islands
Outpost Wilderness Adventure–Adventure Skills, CO
Outpost Wilderness Adventure–Alpine Rock and Ice, CO
Outpost Wilderness Adventure–Copper Canyon Project, Mexico
Outpost Wilderness Adventure–Mountain Bike/Rock Camp, CO
Outpost Wilderness Adventure–Wind River Expedition, WY
Overland: Acadia and Prince Edward Island Bicycle Touring and Sea-Kayaking
Overland: Adventure Camp for 5th and 6th Grade Boys, MA
Overland: Adventure Camp for 5th and 6th Grade Girls, MA
Overland: Alaskan Expedition Hiking, Sea-Kayaking, and Rafting, AK
Overland: American Challenge Coast-to-Coast Bicycle Touring
Overland: Appalachian Trail Challenge Hiking
Overland: Blue Ridge Explorer Hiking, Rafting and Kayaking, NC
Overland: Cape Cod and the Islands Bicycle Touring, MA
Overland: Colorado and Utah Mountain Biking and Rafting
Overland: Costa Rica Explorer Hiking, Rafting, and Sea-Kayaking, Costa Rica
Overland: European Challenge Bicycle Touring from Paris to Rome
Overland: European Explorer Hiking, Rafting, and Sea Kayaking
Overland: Hawaii Explorer Hiking, Kayaking, Sailing and Snorkeling, HI
Overland: New England Explorer Hiking, Mountain Biking, and Rafting
Overland: Pacific Coast Bicycle Touring and Rafting
Overland: Paris to the Sea Bicycle Touring, France
Overland: Rocky Mountain Explorer Hiking, Mountain Biking, and Rafting
Overland: Shasta & the Sierras Backpacking, Climbing and Rafting
Overland: Teton Challenge Hiking, Climbing and Kayaking, WY
Overland: The Alpine Challenge Leadership Course Backpacking and Hiking
Overland: Vermont & Montreal Bicycle Touring
Overland: Yellowstone Explorer Backpacking, Rock Climbing, and Rafting
PAX Abroad–Ecuador Rainforest Adventure, Ecuador
Peace Works International–Costa Rica, Costa Rica
Peace Works International–Peru, Peru
Peace Works International–Ecuador, Ecuador
The Peru Cultural Immersion Experience, Peru
Poulter Colorado Camps: Adventures Planet Earth–Austria
Poulter Colorado Camps: Adventures Planet Earth–New Zealand, New Zealand
Poulter Colorado Camps: Adventures Planet Earth–Spain, Spain
Putney Student Travel–Cultural Exploration–Australia, New Zealand, and Fiji
Putney Student Travel–Cultural Exploration–France, Holland, and England
Putney Student Travel–Cultural Exploration–Switzerland, Italy, France, and Holland
Rein Teen Tours–American Adventure
Rein Teen Tours–California Caper
Rein Teen Tours–Crossroads
Rein Teen Tours–Eastern Adventure
Rein Teen Tours–Grand Adventure
Rein Teen Tours–Hawaiian/Alaskan Adventure
Rein Teen Tours–Western Adventure
Riverside Military Academy High Adventure Camp, GA
RUSTIC PATHWAYS–ADVENTURE IN AMERICA'S SOUTHWEST
RUSTIC PATHWAYS–AWESOME AUSSIE EXPLORER, Australia
RUSTIC PATHWAYS–BIG FIJI EXPLORER, Fiji
RUSTIC PATHWAYS–COSTA RICA ADVENTURER, Costa Rica
RUSTIC PATHWAYS–COSTA RICA EXTREME, Costa Rica
RUSTIC PATHWAYS–COSTA RICA NATURAL WONDERS, Costa Rica
RUSTIC PATHWAYS–DIVER'S DREAM IN THE FIJI ISLANDS, Fiji
RUSTIC PATHWAYS–ELEPHANTS & AMAZING THAILAND, Thailand
RUSTIC PATHWAYS–EXTREME PLANET
RUSTIC PATHWAYS–HAWAIIAN ISLANDS ADVENTURE, HI
RUSTIC PATHWAYS–HIGH ADRENALINE AUSSIE, Australia
RUSTIC PATHWAYS–LEARN TO DIVE IN THE FIJI ISLANDS, Fiji
RUSTIC PATHWAYS–OUTBACK 4-WHEEL DRIVE SAFARI, Australia
RUSTIC PATHWAYS–PHOTOGRAPHY & ADVENTURE IN THAILAND, Thailand
RUSTIC PATHWAYS–SKI AND SNOWBOARD ADVENTURE IN NEW ZEALAND, New Zealand
RUSTIC PATHWAYS–SNAPSHOT OF FIJI, Fiji
RUSTIC PATHWAYS–SURF THE SUMMER–COSTA RICA, Costa Rica
RUSTIC PATHWAYS–THE AMAZING THAILAND ADVENTURE, Thailand
RUSTIC PATHWAYS–THE SUNSHINE COAST & SYDNEY, Australia
RUSTIC PATHWAYS–THE WONDERS & RICHES OF THAILAND, Thailand
RUSTIC PATHWAYS–TOTALLY DOWNUNDER ADVENTURE, Australia
RUSTIC PATHWAYS–TROPICAL AUSSIE ADVENTURE, Australia
RUSTIC PATHWAYS–ULTIMATE AUSTRALIAN ADVENTURE, Australia
Sail Caribbean–All Levels of Scuba Certification with Sailing, British Virgin Islands
Sail Caribbean–British Virgin Islands, British Virgin Islands
Sail Caribbean–Community Service, British Virgin Islands
Sail Caribbean–Leeward Islands
Sail Caribbean–Marine Biology, British Virgin Islands
Sargent Center Adventure Camp, NH
Sea Kayak Expedition (English), Canada
SeaWorld/Busch Gardens Tampa Bay Adventure Camp, FL
Sidwell Friends Overnight Sea Kayaking Trip, MD
The Sikkim Cultural Immersion Experience, India
Skateboarding Academy at Pali Overnight Adventures, CA
Streamside Pathfinder Adventure Camp, PA
Success Oriented Achievement Realized (SOAR)–North Carolina, NC
Success Oriented Achievement Realized (SOAR)–Wyoming, WY
Talisman–Trek Hiking Program, NC
Teen Tours of America–Alaskan Expedition
Teen Tours of America–Aloha Hawaii
Teen Tours of America–New England Journey
Teen Tours of America–Western Adventure
Teen Tours of America–Western Sprint
Tibetan Summer Passage
Timber-lee Creation Camp, WI
Timber-lee Wilderness Trips, WI
Trailmark Outdoor Adventures–Colorado–West Elks with Backpack, CO
Trailmark Outdoor Adventures–Colorado–West Elks with Horseback, CO
Trailmark Outdoor Adventures–New England–Acadia
Trailmark Outdoor Adventures–New England–Camden
Trailmark Outdoor Adventures–New England–Downeast
Trailmark Outdoor Adventures–New England–Jr. Acadia
Trailmark Outdoor Adventures–New England–Mahoosoc
Trailmark Outdoor Adventures–New England–Moose River
Trailmark Outdoor Adventures–New England–Mt. Desert
Trailmark Outdoor Adventures–New England–Rangeley Coed
Trailmark Outdoor Adventures–Northern Rockies–Tetons with Backpack
Trailmark Outdoor Adventures–Northern Rockies–Tetons with Horseback
Trailridge Mountain Camp
Voyageur Outward Bound–Lake Superior Freshwater Kayaking and Backpacking
Wentworth Military Academy Pathfinder Adventure Camp, MO
Westcoast Connection–American Voyageur
Westcoast Connection–Australian Outback Plus Hawaii
Westcoast Connection–Californian Extravaganza
Westcoast Connection–Hawaiian Spirit
Westcoast Connection/On Tour– Australian Outback, Australia
Westcoast Connection Travel/On Tour–Northwestern Odyssey
Westcoast Connection Travel–Adventure California, CA

▶ Adventure Programs

Westcoast Connection Travel–California and the Canyons
Westcoast Connection Travel–Canadian Mountain Magic
Westcoast Connection Travel–Eastcoast Encounter
Westcoast Connection Travel–European Discovery
Westcoast Connection Travel–European Escape
Westcoast Connection Travel–Great West Challenge
Westcoast Connection Travel–Northwestern Odyssey
Westcoast Connection Travel/On Tour–Canadian Adventure
Westcoast Connection Travel/On Tour–European Experience
Westcoast Connection Travel–Quebec Adventure, Canada
Westcoast Connection Travel–Southwesterner
Westcoast Connection Travel–Western Canadian Adventure, Canada
Westcoast Connection–U.S. Explorer
The Whale Camp–Youth Programs, Canada
Where There Be Dragons: China, China
Where There Be Dragons: Guatemala, Guatemala
Where There Be Dragons: India Culture and Philosophy, India
Where There Be Dragons: India Zanskar Trek, India
Where There Be Dragons: Mexico, Mexico
Where There Be Dragons: Mongolia, Mongolia
Where There Be Dragons: Peru, Peru
Where There Be Dragons: Silk Road, China
Where There Be Dragons: Thailand, Thailand
Where There Be Dragons: Tibet, China
Wilderness Experiences Unlimited–Explorers Camp, MA
Wilderness Experiences Unlimited–Leaders In Training Camp, MA
Wilderness Experiences Unlimited–Trailblazers Camp, MA
Wilderness Ventures–Alaska Leadership, AK
Wilderness Ventures–Alaska Service, AK
Wilderness Ventures–Alaska Southcentral, AK
Wilderness Ventures–Alaska Southeast, AK
Wilderness Ventures–Australia, Australia
Wilderness Ventures–California, CA
Wilderness Ventures–Cascade-Olympic, WA
Wilderness Ventures–Colorado/Utah Mountain Bike
Wilderness Ventures–Costa Rica, Costa Rica
Wilderness Ventures–Ecuador and Galapagos, Ecuador
Wilderness Ventures–European Alps
Wilderness Ventures–Grand Teton, WY
Wilderness Ventures–Great Divide
Wilderness Ventures–Great Divide Bike
Wilderness Ventures–Hawaii, HI
Wilderness Ventures–High Sierra, CA
Wilderness Ventures–Jackson Hole, WY
Wilderness Ventures–Northwest
Wilderness Ventures–Oregon, OR
Wilderness Ventures–Pacific Coast Bike
Wilderness Ventures–Pacific Northwest
Wilderness Ventures–Puget Sound, WA
Wilderness Ventures–Rocky Mountain
Wilderness Ventures–Spanish Pyrenees, Spain
Wilderness Ventures–Teton Adventure, WY
Wilderness Ventures–Washington Alpine, WA
Wilderness Ventures–Washington Mountaineering, WA
Wilderness Ventures–Wyoming Mountaineering, WY
Wilderness Ventures–Yellowstone Fly Fishing
Windsor Mountain: Alaska, AK
Windsor Mountain: Bonjour Quebec, Canada
Windsor Mountain: California Community Service, CA
Windsor Mountain: Crossroads France, France
Windsor Mountain: Experiential Summer School
Windsor Mountain: Hawaii, HI
Windsor Mountain: New England Adventure
Windsor Mountain: Puerto Rico, Puerto Rico
YMCA Camp Abnaki–Teen Adventure Trips, VT
YMCA Camp Lincoln–On the Road, NH
YMCA Camp Lincoln–Outdoor Adventure Camp: Backpacking, NH
YMCA Camp Lincoln–Outdoor Adventure Camp: Canadian Adventure, Canada
YMCA Camp Lincoln–Outdoor Adventure Camp: Everything Outdoors, NH
YMCA Camp Lincoln–Outdoor Adventure Camp: Mountain Bike, NH
YMCA Camp Lincoln–Outdoor Adventure Camp: River Runners, NH
YMCA Camp Lincoln–Specialty Camps: Archaeology Camp, NH
YMCA Camp Lincoln–Travel Camp, NH
Yo! Basecamp Rock Climbing Camps, CA
Yosemite Backpacking Adventures, CA
Youth for Understanding USA–Australia, Australia
Youth for Understanding USA–Kenya, Kenya

Arts Programs

AAC–Aloha Adventure Photo Camp, HI
Abbey Road Overseas Programs–French Immersion and Homestay, France
Abbey Road Overseas Programs–French Study Abroad in Cannes, France
Abbey Road Overseas Programs–Italy Study Abroad: Language and Culture, Italy
Abbey Road Overseas Programs–Spanish Immersion and Homestay, Spain
L' Académie de Paris, France
Acteen August Academy, NY
Acteen July Academy, NY
Acteen June Academy, NY
Acteen Summer Saturday Academy, NY
Acting Academy at Pali Overnight Adventures, CA
The Actor's Workshop by Education Unlimited, CA
Adventures in Science and Arts, WA
AFS-USA–Homestay Plus–Hungary, Hungary
All Arts and Sciences Camp–George Mason University, VA
All Arts and Sciences Camp–North Carolina State University, NC
All Arts and Sciences Camp–The College of William and Mary, VA
All Arts and Sciences Camp–The University of North Carolina at Greensboro, NC
All Arts and Sciences Camp–Virginia Tech, VA
Alpengirl–Montana Art
American Academy of Dramatic Arts Summer Program at Hollywood, California, CA
American Academy of Dramatic Arts Summer Program at New York, NY
Appel Farm Summer Arts Camp, NJ
Architecture Summer Camp, AL
Arrowsmith Academy Arts and Academics, CA
Art Center College of Design Art Center for Kids, CA
Artes en Mexico, Mexico
The Art Institute of Boston Pre-College Program, MA
The Art Institute of Seattle–Studio 101, WA
The Arts! at Maryland, MD
Arts on the Lake, TX
Arts Unite, PA
Atelier des Arts, Switzerland
Atlanta College of Art–Pre-College Program, GA
Auburn University Design Workshop, AL
Barat Foundation Summer Program in Provence and Paris, France
Battlebot Mania at Pali Overnight Adventures, CA
Bay Area Shakespeare Camp, CA
Belvoir Terrace, MA
Berklee Business of Music Program, MA
Berklee College of Music Summer Performance Program, MA
Berklee in L.A. Summer Performance Program, CA
Berklee Music Production Workshop, MA
Berklee Summer Basslines Program, MA
Berklee Summer Brass Weekend, MA
Berklee Summer Guitar Sessions, MA
Berklee Summer Saxophone Weekend, MA
Berklee Summer Songwriting Workshop, MA
Berklee Summer String Fling, MA
Berklee World Percussion Festival, MA
Blue Lake Fine Arts Camp, MI
Blue Lake International Exchange Program
Boston University Institute for Television, Film, and Radio Production, MA
Boston University Summer Theatre Institute, MA
Boston University Tanglewood Institute, MA
Brant Lake Camp's Dance Centre, NY
Brevard Music Center, NC
Bristol Hills Music Camp, NY
Buck's Rock Performing and Creative Arts Camp, CT
Burklyn Ballet Edinburgh Connection
Burklyn Ballet Theatre, VT
Burklyn Ballet Theatre II, The Intermediate Program, VT
California College of the Arts Pre-College Program, CA
California State Summer School for the Arts/Inner Spark, CA
The Cambridge Prep Experience, United Kingdom
The Cambridge Tradition, United Kingdom
Camp Ballibay for the Fine and Performing Arts, PA
Camp College–Institute for Arts and Sciences, NJ
Camp Curtain Call, VA
Camp Encore-Coda for a Great Summer of Music, Sports, and Friends, ME
Camp Hawthorne Creative Arts Camp, ME
Camp Horizons Specialty Camp, VA
Camp Little Palm for the Performing Arts, FL
Camp Middlesex, NJ
Camp Rim Rock–Arts Camp, WV
Camp Shakespeare, UT
Camp Togowoods, AK
Career Explorations, NY

Arts Programs

Litchfield Jazz Festival Summer Music School Program, CT
Longhorn Music Camp: All-State Choir Camp, TX
Longhorn Music Camp: Harp Solo and Ensemble Camp, TX
Longhorn Music Camp: High School Band Camp, TX
Longhorn Music Camp: Middle School Band Camp, TX
Longhorn Music Camp: Middle School String Orchestra Camp, TX
Longhorn Music Camp: Piano Performance Workshop, TX
LSA Ascoli, Italy, Italy
LSA Loewenstein, Germany, Germany
LSA Rome, Italy, Italy
LSA Treviso, Italy, Italy
Maine College of Art Early College Program, ME
Marrowstone-in-the-City, WA
Marrowstone Music Festival, WA
Massachusetts College of Art/Creative Vacation, MA
Massachusetts College of Art/Summer Studios, MA
Med-O-Lark Camp, ME
Mercersburg Onstage! Young Actors Workshop, PA
Mercersburg The World's A Stage Theatre Workshop, PA
MexArt: Art and Spanish, Mexico
MexArt Dance: Dance and Spanish, Mexico
Michigan Technological University Honors Orchestra Program, MI
Michigan Technological University Summer Youth Program, MI
Midsummer in London, United Kingdom
MidSummer Macon, GA
MIMC–Intensive Music Camp, Canada
MIMC–Music and Sports Camp, Canada
Miss Porter's School Arts Alive!, CT
Montclair State University Summer Camp for Academically Gifted and Talented Youth, NJ
Montgomery Bell Academy–Summer Music Camp, TN
Montgomery Bell Academy–Summer Theater Camp, TN
Montgomery College WDCE–Aspiring Filmmakers, MD
Montgomery College WDCE–Culinary Arts–Kids Cook, MD
Montgomery College WDCE–GURL Power, MD
Montgomery College WDCE–Hands on Art, MD
Montgomery College WDCE–Inventor's Workshop, MD
Montgomery College WDCE–Joy of Art, MD
Montgomery College WDCE–Summer Dinner Theatre, MD
Montgomery College WDCE–Summer Student Writing Institute, MD
Montgomery College WDCE–Summer Youth Programs, MD
Montgomery College WDCE–Super Sleuths–Meet the Challenge, MD
Montgomery College WDCE–Web Design Camp for Girls and Boys, MD
Music and Dance Summer Workshops, MO
National Guitar Workshop–Austin, TX, TX
National Guitar Workshop–Chicago, IL, IL
National Guitar Workshop–Los Angeles, CA, CA
National Guitar Workshop–Murfreesboro, TN, TN
National Guitar Workshop–New Milford, CT, CT
National Guitar Workshop–New Orleans, LA, LA
National Guitar Workshop–San Francisco, CA, CA
National Guitar Workshop–Seattle, WA, WA
The National Music Workshop Day Jams–Alexandria, VA, VA
The National Music Workshop Day Jams–Ann Arbor, MI, MI
The National Music Workshop Day Jams–Baltimore, MD, MD
The National Music Workshop Day Jams–Boston, MA, MA
The National Music Workshop Day Jams–Chicago, IL, IL
The National Music Workshop Day Jams–Long Island, NY, NY
The National Music Workshop Day Jams–Los Angeles, CA, CA
The National Music Workshop Day Jams–Manhattan, NY, NY
The National Music Workshop Day Jams–Philadelphia, PA, PA
The National Music Workshop Day Jams–Purchase, NY, NY
The National Music Workshop Day Jams–Rockville, MD, MD
The New York Film Academy, Disney-MGM Studios, FL, FL
The New York Film Academy, Harvard University, Cambridge, MA, MA
The New York Film Academy in Florence, Italy, Italy
The New York Film Academy in London, United Kingdom
The New York Film Academy in Paris, France
The New York Film Academy, Princeton University, Princeton, NJ, NJ
The New York Film Academy, The Dalton School, New York, NY, NY
The New York Film Academy, Universal Studios, Hollywood, Ca, CA
92nd Street Y Camps–Camp Yaffa for the Arts, NY
North Carolina School of the Arts Summer Session, NC
Northwestern University's National High School Institute, IL
The Northwest School Summer Program, WA
Operafestival di Roma, Italy
Oregon Summer Music Camps, OR
Oxford Media School–Film, United Kingdom
Oxford Media School–Film Master Class, United Kingdom
Oxford Media School–Newsroom in Europe, United Kingdom
Oxford Media School–Newsroom in Europe, Master Class, United Kingdom
The Oxford Prep Experience, United Kingdom
The Oxford Tradition, United Kingdom
Parsons Pre-College Academy, NY
Parsons Summer Intensive Studies–New York, NY
Parsons Summer Intensive Studies–Paris, France
Performance PLUS–Positive Learning Using the Stage+Studio+Screen, NH
The Performing Arts Institute of Wyoming Seminary, PA
Perry-Mansfield Performing Arts School and Camp, CO
PixelNation, NJ
Point Arts Camp–Music, WI
Point CounterPoint Chamber Music Camp, VT
Power Chord Academy–Chicago, IL
Power Chord Academy–Los Angeles, CA
Power Chord Academy–New York City, NY
Pratt Institute Summer Pre-College Program for High School Students, NY
Pre-College Summer Institute, The University of the Arts, PA
Princeton Ballet School's Ballet Plus Junior, NJ
Princeton Ballet School's Ballet Plus Senior, NJ
Princeton Ballet School's Summer Intensive, NJ
Purchase Youth Theatre, NY
The Putney School Summer Arts Program, VT
The Putney School Summer Writing Program, VT
Putney Student Travel–Cultural Exploration-Creative Writing in Cuba, Cuba
Putney Student Travel–Cultural Exploration–Theatre in Britain, United Kingdom
Rhode Island School of Design Pre-College Program, RI
Ringling School of Art and Design Pre-College Perspective, FL
Ringling School of Art and Design's Teen Studio, FL
Rock Star Camp at Pali Overnight Adventures, CA
RUSTIC PATHWAYS–PHOTOGRAPHY & ADVENTURE IN THAILAND, Thailand
Santa Catalina School Summer Camp, CA
Saturday High at Art Center College of Design, CA
Sequoia Chamber Music Workshop, CA
Shakespeare at Purchase, NY
Shippensburg University Academic Camps–Acting & Theatre Arts, PA
Sidwell Friends DaVinci Days Art Studios, Young Artist Academy and Young Scientist Academy, DC
Sidwell Friends Drama and Dance Workshops with BAPA, DC
Signature Music Teen Camp, NY
Signature Music Youth Camp, NY
Simon's Rock College of Bard Young Writers Workshop, MA
Skidmore College–Acceleration Program in Art for High School Students, NY
Skidmore College–Pre-College Program in the Liberal Arts for High School Students, NY
Snow Farm: The New England Craft Program, MA
Spoleto Study Abroad, Italy
Sports and Arts Center at Island Lake, PA
Stagedoor Manor Performing Arts Training Center/Theatre and Dance Camp, NY
Stanford Discovery Institutes, CA
Stanford Jazz Workshop, CA
Stanford Jazz Workshop: Jazz Camp, CA
Stanford Jazz Workshop: Jazz Residency, CA
Stoneleigh–Burnham School Summer Dance Camp, MA
Stony Brook Summer Music Festival, NY
Study Tours and Cinema Program in the USA–Oxnard College, CA

Study Tours and Dance/Theater Camp in the USA–Dean College, MA
The Summer Academy at Suffield, CT
Summer Academy for the Visual and Performing Arts, NJ
Summer Dance '05, MA
Summer in Switzerland, Switzerland
"Summer in the City", NY
Summer Music at The Hollows, Canada
Summer Music Clinic, WI
Summer Sonatina International Piano Camp, VT
Summer Theatre Institute–2005, NY
Suzuki Family Camp, MI
Syracuse University Summer College, NY
Tannen's Summer Magic Camp, NY
TASIS Arts and Architecture in the South of France, France
TASIS Tuscan Academy of Art and Culture, Italy
Technology Encounters–Video Encounter/ Computer Encounter–California, CA
Technology Encounters–Video Encounter/ Computer Encounter–Colorado, CO
Technology Encounters–Video Encounter/ Computer Encounter–Florida, FL
Technology Encounters–Video Encounter/ Computer Encounter–New York, NY
Technology Encounters–Video Encounter/ Computer Encounter–Pennsylvania, PA
Timber-lee Drama Camp, WI
Tisch School of the Arts–International High School Program–Dublin, Ireland
Tisch School of the Arts–International High School Program–Paris, France
Tisch School of the Arts–Summer High School Programs, NY
Traveling Players Ensemble Camp, MD
University of Connecticut Community School of the Arts–Music Camps, CT
University of Connecticut Community School of the Arts–World Arts Camps, CT
University of Kansas–Midwestern Music Camp–Junior and Senior Divisions, KS
University of Pennsylvania–Penn Summer Art Studio, PA
University of Wisconsin–Green Bay Summer Art Studio, WI
University of Wisconsin–Green Bay Summer Music Camps, WI
Usdan Center for the Creative and Performing Arts, NY
Valley Forge Military Academy Summer Band Camp, PA
Vermont Arts Animation Institute, VT
Vermont Arts Dance Institute, VT
Vermont Arts Filmmaking Institute, VT
Vermont Arts Screenwriting Institute, VT
Vermont Arts Theatre Camp Institute, VT
Vermont Arts Theatre Institute, VT
Vermont Arts Visual Arts Institute, VT
Visual Arts Institute for High School Students, NY
Washington University in St. Louis, School of Art–Portfolio Plus, MO
Westminster Choir College Composition Week, NJ
Westminster Choir College High School Solo Pianist, NJ
Westminster Choir College High School Solo Vocal Artist: A Performance Workshop for Singers, NJ
Westminster Choir College Middle School Music Theater, NJ
Westminster Choir College Middle School Piano Camp, NJ
Westminster Choir College Middle School Vocal Camp, NJ
Westminster Choir College Music Theater Workshop, NJ
Westminster Choir College Organ Week, NJ
Westminster Choir College Piano Camp, NJ
Westminster Choir College Vocal Institute, NJ
Westminster Conservatory of Music–Flute Camp, NJ
Westminster Conservatory of Music–Musical Jamboree, NJ
Westminster Conservatory of Music–Summer Ensemble, NJ
Westminster Conservatory of Music–Try It Out, NJ
Westminster Conservatory of Music–Youth Opera Workshop, NJ
Wilderness Dance Camp, MN
Windsor Mountain: Adventures in Filmmaking, Saint Vincent and The Grenadines
Windsor Mountain: European Traveling Minstrels
Windsor Mountain: New England Traveling Minstrels
Wright State University Residential Camps and Institutes, OH
YMCA Camp Lincoln–Specialty Camps: Arts & Drama, NH
Young Actors and Playwrights Workshop, NY
Young Actors Camp, CA
Young Artists at Purchase, NY
Young Filmmakers at Purchase, NY
Young Musicians & Artists, OR
Young Photographers, NY

Bible Camps

Abilene Christian University–Cross Training, NM
Abilene Christian University–Kadesh Life Camp, TX
Abilene Christian University–Learning to Lead, TX
Abilene Christian University–MPulse, TX
Abiliene Christian University–KidQuest Day Camp, TX
Camp Berachah Ministries–Counselor-In-Training, WA
Camp Berachah Ministries–Day Camp, WA
Camp Berachah Ministries–Horse Day Camp, WA
Camp Berachah Ministries–Junior Camp, WA
Camp Berachah Ministries–Leadership Expedition Camp, WA
Camp Berachah Ministries–Legend Teen Camp, WA
Camp Berachah Ministries–Overnight Horse Camp, WA
Camp Berachah Ministries–Primary Camp, WA
Camp Berachah Ministries–Soccer Camp, WA
Camp Berachah Ministries–Teen Leadership, WA
Camp Berachah Ministries–Wrangler-In-Training, WA
Camp Echoing Hills, OH
Camp Ganadaoweh, Canada
Camp Geneva, MI
Camp Good News for Young People and Teens, MA
Camp Modin, ME
Camp Mt. Luther, PA
Camp Rockmont for Boys, NC
Camp Roger, MI
Camp Sandy Cove, WV
Camp Streamside, PA
Camps with Meaning–Advanced Horsemanship I & II, Canada
Camps with Meaning–Boys Camp, Canada
Camps with Meaning–Girls Camp, Canada
Camps with Meaning–Junior High/Junior Youth Camp, Canada
Camps with Meaning–PreJunior/Junior/ Intermediate Camp, Canada
Camps with Meaning–Youth Camp, Canada
Timber-lee Science Camp, WI
Catholic Youth Camp, MN
Christikon, MT
Eagle Lake Bike Camp, CO
Eagle Lake Camp Crew Program, CO
Eagle Lake Camp–East, NC
Eagle Lake Camp Jaunts–Kenya Mission Adventure, Kenya
Eagle Lake Camp Jaunts–Minnesota Boundary Waters, MN
Eagle Lake Camp Jaunts–Norway Mission Adventure, Norway
Eagle Lake Horse Camp, CO
Eagle Lake Resident Camp, CO
Eagle Lake Wilderness Program, CO
Freed-Hardeman Horizons for Ages 12-18, TN
Genesis at Brandeis University, MA
Haycock Camping Ministries–Adventure Trails, PA
Haycock Camping Ministries–Battalion Program, PA
Haycock Camping Ministries–Stockade Program, PA
Haycock Camping Ministries–Trailbuilders Program, PA
Israel Discovery
Jumonville Adventure Camps, PA
Jumonville Baseball/Softball Camp, PA
Jumonville Basketball Camp, PA
Jumonville Creative and Performing Arts Camps, PA
Jumonville Discovery Camp, PA
Jumonville Golf Camp, PA
Jumonville Sampler Camps, PA
Jumonville Soccer Camp, PA
Jumonville Spirit and Sport Spectacular–Soccer Camp, PA
Jumonville Spirit and Sport Spectacular–Swim Camp, PA
Jumonville Spirit and Sport Spectacular–Tennis Camp, PA
Jumonville Spirit and Sport Spectacular–Volleyball Camp, PA
Jumonville Sports Camp, PA
Jumonville Youth Mission Work Camp, PA
Kawkawa Summer Camps, Canada
KidzZone Summer Camp, GA
Lake Ann Baptist Camp, MI
Ligonier Camp, PA
Makemie Woods Summer Camp, VA
The Marsh, MD
Medeba Leader in Training Program, Canada
Medeba Summer Camp, Canada
Next Level Camp, PA
92nd Street Y Camps–The TIYUL
Presbyterian Clearwater Forest, MN

▶ Bible Camps

Shwayder Camp, CO
Star Ranch Summer Camp, TX
Streamside Camp and Conference Center, PA
Streamside Family Camp, PA
Streamside Pathfinder Adventure Camp, PA
Summer Family Conference, MD
Timber-lee Creation Camp, WI
Timber-lee Drama Camp, WI
Timber-lee Horsemanship Camps, WI
Timber-lee Wilderness Trips, WI
Timber-lee Youth Camp, WI

Community Service Programs

AAVE–Belize, Belize
AAVE–Border Cross
AAVE–Costa Rica, Costa Rica
Academic Camps at Gettysburg College–Community Service, PA
Adventure Links–The Costa Rica Experience, Costa Rica
AFS-USA–Community Service–Argentina, Argentina
AFS-USA–Community Service–Bolivia, Bolivia
AFS-USA–Community Service–Costa Rica, Costa Rica
AFS-USA–Community Service–Panama, Panama
AFS-USA–Community Service–Paraguay, Paraguay
AFS-USA–Community Service–Thailand, Thailand
AFS-USA–Community Service–United Kingdom, United Kingdom
AFS-USA–Team Mission–China, China
AFS-USA–Team Mission–Ghana, Ghana
AFS-USA–Team Mission–Russia, Russian Federation
American Youth Foundation Leadership Conference, MI
Apogee Outdoor Adventures–Burlington to Boston
Apogee Outdoor Adventures–Coast to Quebec
Apogee Outdoor Adventures–Montana Service Adventure, MT
Apogee Outdoor Adventures–Cape Cod and the Islands, MA
Barat Foundation Summer Program in Provence and Paris, France
Birmingham-Southern College Student Leaders in Service Program, AL
BROADREACH Academic Treks–Language Exposure and Service Learning, Chile
BROADREACH Academic Treks–Sea Turtle Studies, Costa Rica
BROADREACH Academic Treks–Spanish Language Immersion in Ecuador, Ecuador
BROADREACH Academic Treks–Wilderness Emergency Medicine, Belize
Camp Tawonga–Teen Service Learning to Alaska, AK
China's Frontiers: Diverse Landscapes and Peoples, China
Cottonwood Gulch Prairie Trek Expedition, NM
Cottonwood Gulch Turquoise Trail Expedition, NM
Cushing Academy Summer Session, MA
Deer Hill Expeditions, Arizona, AZ
Deer Hill Expeditions, Colorado, CO
Deer Hill Expeditions, Costa Rica, Costa Rica
Deer Hill Expeditions, New Mexico, NM
Deer Hill Expeditions, Utah, UT
Discovery Works New England Community Service Experience
Eagle Lake Camp Crew Program, CO
Eagle Lake Camp Jaunts–Kenya Mission Adventure, Kenya
Eagle Lake Camp Jaunts–Norway Mission Adventure, Norway
EARTHWATCH INSTITUTE–Health and Nutrition in Botswana, Botswana
EARTHWATCH INSTITUTE–Maternal and Child Healthcare in India, India
The Experiment in International Living–Argentina Homestay, Community Service, and Outdoor Ecological Program, Argentina
The Experiment in International Living–Belize Homestay, Belize
The Experiment in International Living–Botswana Homestay, Botswana
The Experiment in International Living–Brazil Homestay and Community Service, Brazil
The Experiment in International Living–Chile North Homestay, Community Service, Chile
The Experiment in International Living–Chile South Homestay, Chile
The Experiment in International Living–Costa Rica Homestay, Costa Rica
The Experiment in International Living–Germany, Four-Week Homestay, Travel, Community Service, Germany
The Experiment in International Living–Ghana Homestay, Ghana
The Experiment in International Living–Ireland/Northern Ireland Homestay and Peace Studies, Ireland
The Experiment in International Living–Mexico, Community Service, Travel, and Homestay, Mexico
The Experiment in International Living–Morocco Four-Week Arts and Culture Program, Morocco
The Experiment in International Living–Navajo Nation, NM
The Experiment in International Living–New Zealand Homestay, New Zealand
The Experiment in International Living–Poland, Homestay, Community Service, and Travel, Poland
The Experiment in International Living–South Africa Homestay and Community Service, South Africa
The Experiment in International Living–Thailand Homestay, Thailand
The Experiment in International Living–Turkey Homestay, Community Service, and Travel, Turkey
Farm and Wilderness Camps–Tamarack Farm, VT
Flint Hill School–"Summer on the Hill"–Enrichment on the Hill–Summer Service, VA
Four Corners School of Outdoor Education: Southwest Ed-Venture
Genesis at Brandeis University, MA
GLOBAL WORKS–Adventure Travel-Pacific Northwest-3 weeks, WA
GLOBAL WORKS–Cultural Exchange-Fiji Islands-4 weeks, Fiji
GLOBAL WORKS–Cultural Exchange-Ireland-4 weeks, Ireland
GLOBAL WORKS–Cultural Exchange-New Zealand and Fiji Islands-4 weeks
GLOBAL WORKS–Language Exposure-Costa Rica-4 weeks, Costa Rica
GLOBAL WORKS–Language Exposure-Ecuador and the Galapagos-4 weeks, Ecuador
GLOBAL WORKS–Language Exposure-Puerto Rico-3 weeks, Puerto Rico
GLOBAL WORKS–Language Exposure-Yucatan Peninsula, Mexico-4 weeks, Mexico
GLOBAL WORKS–Language Immersion-Costa Rica-4 weeks, Costa Rica
GLOBAL WORKS–Language Immersion-Ecuador and the Galapagos-4 weeks, Ecuador
GLOBAL WORKS–Language Immersion-France-4 weeks, France
GLOBAL WORKS–Language Immersion-Puerto Rico-4 weeks, Puerto Rico
GLOBAL WORKS–Language Immersion-Spain-4 weeks, Spain
GLOBAL WORKS–Language Immersion-Yucatan Peninsula, Mexico-4 weeks, Mexico
Greek Summer, Greece
Groundwater University, NE
Israel Discovery
Jumonville Youth Mission Work Camp, PA
Landmark Volunteers: Arizona, AZ
Landmark Volunteers: California, CA
Landmark Volunteers: Colorado, CO
Landmark Volunteers: Connecticut, CT
Landmark Volunteers: Idaho, ID
Landmark Volunteers: Maine, ME
Landmark Volunteers: Massachusetts, MA
Landmark Volunteers: Michigan, MI
Landmark Volunteers: Minnesota, MN
Landmark Volunteers: Montana, MT
Landmark Volunteers: New Hampshire, NH
Landmark Volunteers: New Mexico, NM
Landmark Volunteers: New York, NY
Landmark Volunteers: North Carolina, NC
Landmark Volunteers: Ohio, OH
Landmark Volunteers: Rhode Island, RI
Landmark Volunteers: Vermont, VT
Landmark Volunteers: Virginia, VA
Landmark Volunteers: Washington, WA
Landmark Volunteers: Wyoming, WY
Leadership Adventure in Boston, MA
LIFEWORKS with the Australian Red Cross, Australia
LIFEWORKS with the British Virgin Islands Marine Parks and Conservation Department, British Virgin Islands
LIFEWORKS with the DPF Foundation in Thailand, Thailand
LIFEWORKS with the Galapagos Islands' National Parks, Ecuador
Longacre Leadership Program, PA
Millennium Entrepreneurs Camp CEO, CA
Millennium Entrepreneurs "Training Tomorrow's Business Leaders Today", CA
The Nepal Cultural Immersion Experience, Nepal
New Jersey YMHA–YWHA Teen Camp, PA
New Strides Day Camp, Canada
92nd Street Y Camps–The TIYUL
Outpost Wilderness Adventure–Copper Canyon Project, Mexico
Overland: American Community Service, Alaska, AK

Overland: American Community Service, Hawaii, HI
Overland: American Community Service, New England
Overland: American Community Service, Southwest, NM
Overland: World Service, Costa Rica, Costa Rica
Peace Works International–Costa Rica, Costa Rica
Peace Works International–Peru, Peru
Peace Works International–Ecuador, Ecuador
The Peru Cultural Immersion Experience, Peru
Programs Abroad Travel Alternatives–Peru, Peru
Putney Student Travel–Community Service–Alaska, AK
Putney Student Travel–Community Service–Brazil, Brazil
Putney Student Travel–Community Service–Costa Rica, Costa Rica
Putney Student Travel–Community Service–Dominican Republic, Dominican Republic
Putney Student Travel–Community Service–Dominica, West Indies, Dominica
Putney Student Travel–Community Service–Ecuador, Ecuador
Putney Student Travel–Community Service–Hawaii, HI
Putney Student Travel–Community Service-India, India
Putney Student Travel–Community Service–Montana, MT
Putney Student Travel–Community Service-Nicaragua, Nicaragua
Putney Student Travel–Community Service–Nusa Penida and Bali, Indonesia
Putney Student Travel–Community Service–Tanzania, United Republic of Tanzania
Quest Scholars Program at Stanford/QuestLeadership, CA
RUSTIC PATHWAYS–BIG FIJI EXPLORER, Fiji
RUSTIC PATHWAYS–BUDDHIST LIFE & ANGKOR WAT
RUSTIC PATHWAYS–ELEPHANTS & AMAZING THAILAND, Thailand
RUSTIC PATHWAYS–EXTENDED COMMUNITY SERVICE IN THE FIJI ISLANDS, Fiji
RUSTIC PATHWAYS–EXTREME PLANET
RUSTIC PATHWAYS–HIGHLANDS COMMUNITY SERVICE IN FIJI, Fiji
RUSTIC PATHWAYS–INTRO TO COMMUNITY SERVICE IN FIJI, Fiji
RUSTIC PATHWAYS–INTRO TO COMMUNITY SERVICE IN THAILAND, Thailand
RUSTIC PATHWAYS–RHYTHM IN THE RICEFIELDS, Thailand
RUSTIC PATHWAYS–RICEFIELDS, MONKS & SMILING CHILDREN, Thailand
RUSTIC PATHWAYS–THE CANO NEGRO SERVICE PROJECT, Costa Rica
RUSTIC PATHWAYS–THE THAI ELEPHANT CONSERVATION PROJECT, Thailand
RUSTIC PATHWAYS–THE TURTLE CONSERVATION PROJECT, Costa Rica
RUSTIC PATHWAYS–VOLCANOES AND RAINFORESTS, Costa Rica
Sail Caribbean–Community Service, British Virgin Islands
Sail Caribbean–Marine Biology, British Virgin Islands
Service-Learning in Paris, France
SFS: Community Wildlife Management, Kenya
SFS: Conserving Coastal Diversity, Mexico
SFS: Marine Parks Management Studies, Turks and Caicos Islands
SFS: Sustaining Tropical Ecosystems, Costa Rica
Sidwell Friends Service Expedition to Hawaii, HI
Sidwell Friends Summer Community Service Programs, DC
Sidwell Friends Summer Program: Costa Rica, Costa Rica
The Sikkim Cultural Immersion Experience, India
Spanish Through Leadership–Nicaragua, Nicaragua
Spanish Through Leadership–Nicaragua/Costa Rica
Student Conservation Association–Conservation Crew Program (Alabama), AL
Student Conservation Association–Conservation Crew Program (Alaska), AK
Student Conservation Association–Conservation Crew Program (Arizona), AZ
Student Conservation Association–Conservation Crew Program (Arkansas), AR
Student Conservation Association–Conservation Crew Program (California), CA
Student Conservation Association–Conservation Crew Program (Colorado), CO
Student Conservation Association–Conservation Crew Program (Connecticut), CT
Student Conservation Association–Conservation Crew Program (Delaware), DE
Student Conservation Association–Conservation Crew Program (Florida), FL
Student Conservation Association–Conservation Crew Program (Georgia), GA
Student Conservation Association–Conservation Crew Program (Hawaii), HI
Student Conservation Association–Conservation Crew Program (Idaho), ID
Student Conservation Association–Conservation Crew Program (Illinois), IL
Student Conservation Association–Conservation Crew Program (Indiana), IN
Student Conservation Association–Conservation Crew Program (Iowa), IA
Student Conservation Association–Conservation Crew Program (Kansas), KS
Student Conservation Association–Conservation Crew Program (Kentucky), KY
Student Conservation Association–Conservation Crew Program (Louisiana), LA
Student Conservation Association–Conservation Crew Program (Maine), ME
Student Conservation Association–Conservation Crew Program (Maryland), MD
Student Conservation Association–Conservation Crew Program (Massachusetts), MA
Student Conservation Association–Conservation Crew Program (Michigan), MI
Student Conservation Association–Conservation Crew Program (Minnesota), MN
Student Conservation Association–Conservation Crew Program (Mississippi), MS
Student Conservation Association–Conservation Crew Program (Missouri), MO
Student Conservation Association–Conservation Crew Program (Montana), MT
Student Conservation Association–Conservation Crew Program (Nebraska), NE
Student Conservation Association–Conservation Crew Program (Nevada), NV
Student Conservation Association–Conservation Crew Program (New Hampshire), NH
Student Conservation Association–Conservation Crew Program (New Jersey), NJ
Student Conservation Association–Conservation Crew Program (New Mexico), NM
Student Conservation Association–Conservation Crew Program (New York), NY
Student Conservation Association–Conservation Crew Program (North Carolina), NC
Student Conservation Association–Conservation Crew Program (North Dakota), ND
Student Conservation Association–Conservation Crew Program (Ohio), OH
Student Conservation Association–Conservation Crew Program (Oklahoma), OK
Student Conservation Association–Conservation Crew Program (Oregon), OR
Student Conservation Association–Conservation Crew Program (Pennsylvania), PA
Student Conservation Association–Conservation Crew Program (Rhode Island), RI
Student Conservation Association–Conservation Crew Program (South Carolina), SC
Student Conservation Association–Conservation Crew Program (South Dakota), SD
Student Conservation Association–Conservation Crew Program (Tennessee), TN
Student Conservation Association–Conservation Crew Program (Texas), TX
Student Conservation Association–Conservation Crew Program (Utah), UT
Student Conservation Association–Conservation Crew Program (Vermont), VT
Student Conservation Association–Conservation Crew Program (Virginia), VA

▶ Community Service Programs

Student Conservation Association–Conservation Crew Program (Washington), WA
Student Conservation Association–Conservation Crew Program (West Virginia), WV
Student Conservation Association–Conservation Crew Program (Wisconsin), WI
Student Conservation Association–Conservation Crew Program (Wyoming), WY
Student Conservation Association–Conservation Leadership Corps, Bay Area, CA
Student Conservation Association–Conservation Leadership Corps–Northwest, WA
Student Conservation Association–Conservation Leadership Corps–Washington, DC Metropolitan Area, VA
Summer Delegation to León, Nicaragua, Nicaragua
Summer JAM (Judaism, Activism, and Mitzvah Work), DC
Summer Summit on Leadership, MA
Tibetan Culture of Northern India, India
Visions–Alaska, AK
Visions–Australia, Australia
Visions–British Virgin Islands, British Virgin Islands
Visions–Dominica, Dominica
Visions–Dominican Republic, Dominican Republic
Visions–Ecuador, Ecuador
Visions–Guadeloupe, Guadeloupe
Visions–Montana, MT
Visions–Peru, Peru
Visions–South Carolina, SC
Visions–Trinidad, Trinidad and Tobago
Volunteers for Peace International Work Camp–Armenia, Armenia
Volunteers for Peace International Work Camp–Belarus, Belarus
Volunteers for Peace International Work Camp–Belgium, Belgium
Volunteers for Peace International Work Camp–Czech Republic, Czech Republic
Volunteers for Peace International Work Camp–Estonia, Estonia
Volunteers for Peace International Work Camp–France, France
Volunteers for Peace International Work Camp–Germany, Germany
Volunteers for Peace International Work Camp–Italy, Italy
Volunteers for Peace International Work Camp–Lithuania, Lithuania
Volunteers for Peace International Work Camp–Russia, Russian Federation
Volunteers for Peace International Work Camp–Slovakia, Slovakia
Volunteers for Peace International Work Camp–Turkey, Turkey
WEI Leadership Training, CO
Westcoast Connection–Community Connections Alaska, AK
Westcoast Connection–Community Service, WA
Where There Be Dragons: Guatemala, Guatemala
Where There Be Dragons: India Culture and Philosophy, India
Where There Be Dragons: India Zanskar Trek, India
Where There Be Dragons: Mexico, Mexico
Where There Be Dragons: Mongolia, Mongolia
Where There Be Dragons: Peru, Peru
Where There Be Dragons: Thailand, Thailand
Where There Be Dragons: Tibet, China
Where There Be Dragons: Vietnam, Vietnam
Wilderness Ventures–Alaska Service, AK
Windsor Mountain: Alaska, AK
Windsor Mountain: California Community Service, CA
Windsor Mountain: Crossroads France, France
Windsor Mountain: Cuba Friendship Exchange, Cuba
Windsor Mountain: Hawaii, HI
Windsor Mountain: Leaders in Action, NH
Windsor Mountain: Mexico Community Service, Mexico
Windsor Mountain: Puerto Rico, Puerto Rico
Windsor Mountain: Random Acts of Kindness
Windsor Mountain: Voices of the Wind River, Wyoming, WY
World Horizons International–Costa Rica, Costa Rica
World Horizons International–Dominica, Dominica
World Horizons International–Fiji, Fiji
World Horizons International–Iceland, Iceland
World Horizons International–Kanab, Utah, UT
World Horizons International–Mexico, Mexico
World Horizons International–Oahu, Hawaii, HI
World Horizons International–Puerto Rico, Puerto Rico
Youth for Understanding USA–Ghana, Ghana
Youth for Understanding USA–Ireland, Ireland

Cultural Programs

AAC–Aloha Adventure Photo Camp, HI
AAC–Aloha Adventure Surf Camp, HI
AAVE–Africa
AAVE–Alps Rider
AAVE–Belize, Belize
AAVE–Bike France, France
AAVE–Bold Europe
AAVE–Costa Rica, Costa Rica
AAVE–Ecuador and Galapagos, Ecuador
AAVE–Inmersión en España, Spain
AAVE–Peru and Machu Picchu, Peru
AAVE–Thailand, Thailand
AAVE–Vietnam, Vietnam
AAVE–Vivons le Français, France
AAVE–Wild Isles
Abbey Road Overseas Programs–French Immersion and Homestay, France
Abbey Road Overseas Programs–French Study Abroad in Cannes, France
Abbey Road Overseas Programs–Italy Study Abroad: Language and Culture, Italy
Abbey Road Overseas Programs–Spanish Immersion and Homestay, Spain
A.C.E. Intercultural Institute, WA
ACTIONQUEST: Australian and Great Barrier Reef Adventures, Australia
ACTIONQUEST: Galapagos Archipelago Expeditions, Ecuador
ACTIONQUEST: Leeward and French Caribbean Island Voyages
ACTIONQUEST: Mediterranean Sailing Voyage
ACTIONQUEST: Tahiti and French Polynesian Island Voyages, French Polynesia
Adventure Ireland–English Learning Option, Ireland
Adventure Ireland–Irish Studies, Ireland
Adventure Ireland–Surf Camp/Activity Camp, Ireland
Adventure Links–The Costa Rica Experience, Costa Rica
AFS-USA–Community Service–Argentina, Argentina
AFS-USA–Community Service–Bolivia, Bolivia
AFS-USA–Community Service–Costa Rica, Costa Rica
AFS-USA–Community Service–Panama, Panama
AFS-USA–Community Service–Paraguay, Paraguay
AFS-USA–Community Service–Thailand, Thailand
AFS-USA–Community Service–United Kingdom, United Kingdom
AFS-USA–Homestay–Argentina, Argentina
AFS-USA–Homestay–Chile, Chile
AFS-USA–Homestay–Ecuador, Ecuador
AFS-USA–Homestay–Finland, Finland
AFS-USA–Homestay–France, France
AFS-USA–Homestay Language Study–Canada, Canada
AFS-USA–Homestay Language Study–Costa Rica, Costa Rica
AFS-USA–Homestay Language Study–Japan, Japan
AFS-USA–Homestay Language Study–Latvia, Latvia
AFS-USA–Homestay, Outdoor Adventure Amazon–Brazil, Brazil
AFS-USA–Homestay–Paraguay, Paraguay
AFS-USA–Homestay Plus–Australia, Australia
AFS-USA–Homestay Plus–Brazil, Brazil
AFS-USA–Homestay Plus–Costa Rica, Costa Rica
AFS-USA–Homestay Plus–Hungary, Hungary
AFS-USA–Homestay Plus–Italy, Italy
AFS-USA–Homestay Plus–Netherlands, Netherlands
AFS-USA–Homestay Plus–New Zealand, New Zealand
AFS-USA–Homestay–Spain, Spain
AFS-USA–Homestay–Thailand, Thailand
AFS-USA–Homestay–Turkey, Turkey
AFS-USA–Team Mission–China, China
AFS-USA–Team Mission–Ghana, Ghana
AFS-USA–Team Mission–Russia, Russian Federation
Alexander Muss High School in Israel, Israel
Alien Adventure Overnight Camp
Alpengirl–Scandinavia
American Association of Teachers of German, German Summer Study Program, Germany
American Collegiate Adventures–Spain, Spain
Artes en Mexico, Mexico
ATW: European Adventures
ATW: Mini Tours
Barat Foundation Summer Program in Provence and Paris, France
Bicycle Africa Tours
BICYCLE TRAVEL ADVENTURES–Student Hosteling Program–Amsterdam to Paris

BICYCLE TRAVEL ADVENTURES–Student Hosteling Program–France and Italy
BICYCLE TRAVEL ADVENTURES–Student Hosteling Program–Ireland and England
BICYCLE TRAVEL ADVENTURES–Student Hosteling Program–Province du Québec, Canada
BICYCLE TRAVEL ADVENTURES–Student Hosteling Program–Province du Québec (short program), Canada
BICYCLE TRAVEL ADVENTURES–Student Hosteling Program–Spain and France
Blue Lake International Exchange Program
Blyth Education–Summer Study in Costa Rica, Costa Rica
Blyth Education–Summer Study in London and Oxford University, United Kingdom
Blyth Education–Summer Study in Paris and the South of France, France
Blyth Education–Summer Study in Rome and Siena, Italy
Blyth Education–Summer Study in the Amazon and the Galapagos Islands, Ecuador
Bravo Spain–Barcelona, Spain
BROADREACH Academic Treks–Spanish Immersion in Mexico, Mexico
BROADREACH Academic Treks–Spanish Language Immersion in Ecuador, Ecuador
BROADREACH Academic Treks–Wilderness Emergency Medicine, Belize
BROADREACH Amazon and Galapagos Encounter, Ecuador
BROADREACH Arc of the Caribbean Sailing Adventure
BROADREACH Fiji Solomon Quest
BROADREACH Red Sea Scuba Adventure, Egypt
Buckswood: English Language (ESL) and Activities–Bradfield, England, United Kingdom
Buckswood: English Language (ESL) and Activities–Plumpton, England, United Kingdom
Buckswood: English Language (ESL) and Activities–West Virginia, WV
Cambridge College Programme, United Kingdom
Camp Chewonki Eco-Kayak Australia, Australia
Camp Tawonga–Teen Service Learning to Alaska, AK
Celtic Learning and Travel Services–Edinburgh and Dublin
Celtic Learning and Travel Services–London and Dublin
Celtic Learning and Travel Services–Summer in Ireland, Ireland
Center for Cultural Interchange–Argentina Independent Homestay, Argentina
Center for Cultural Interchange–Australia High School Abroad, Australia
Center for Cultural Interchange–Brazil High School Abroad, Brazil
Center for Cultural Interchange–Chile Independent Homestay, Chile
Center for Cultural Interchange–France High School Abroad, France
Center for Cultural Interchange–France Independent Homestay, France
Center for Cultural Interchange–France Language School, France
Center for Cultural Interchange–Germany High School Abroad, Germany
Center for Cultural Interchange–Germany Independent Homestay, Germany
Center for Cultural Interchange–Germany Language School, Germany
Center for Cultural Interchange–Ireland High School Abroad, Ireland
Center for Cultural Interchange–Ireland Independent Homestay Program, Ireland
Center for Cultural Interchange–Italy Language School, Italy
Center for Cultural Interchange–Japan High School Abroad, Japan
Center for Cultural Interchange–Mexico High School Abroad, Mexico
Center for Cultural Interchange–Mexico Language School, Mexico
Center for Cultural Interchange–Netherlands High School Abroad, Netherlands
Center for Cultural Interchange–South Africa High School Abroad, South Africa
Center for Cultural Interchange–Spain High School Abroad, Spain
Center for Cultural Interchange–Spain Independent Homestay, Spain
Center for Cultural Interchange–Spain Language School, Spain
Center for Cultural Interchange–Spain Sports and Language Camp, Spain
Center for Cultural Interchange–Switzerland Language Camp, Switzerland
Center for Cultural Interchange–United Kingdom Independent Homestay, United Kingdom
China's Frontiers: Diverse Landscapes and Peoples, China
China Summer Learning Adventures, China
Choate Rosemary Hall Summer in China, China
Choate Rosemary Hall Summer in Paris, France
Choate Rosemary Hall Summer in Spain, Spain
Columbia University Continuing Education–The Barcelona Experience, Spain
Concordia Language Villages–Chinese, MN
Concordia Language Villages–Danish, MN
Concordia Language Villages–English, MN
Concordia Language Villages–Finnish, MN
Concordia Language Villages–France, France
Concordia Language Villages–French–Bemidji, MN
Concordia Language Villages–French–Camp Holiday, MN
Concordia Language Villages–French–Fosston, MN
Concordia Language Villages–French–Savannah, GA, GA
Concordia Language Villages–French Voyageur, MN
Concordia Language Villages–German–Bemidji, MN
Concordia Language Villages–German–Camp Trowbridge, MN
Concordia Language Villages–Germany, Germany
Concordia Language Villages–Italian, MN
Concordia Language Villages–Japan, Japan
Concordia Language Villages–Japanese, MN
Concordia Language Villages–Korean, MN
Concordia Language Villages–Norwegian, MN
Concordia Language Villages–Russian, MN
Concordia Language Villages–Spain, Spain
Concordia Language Villages–Spanish–Bemidji, MN
Concordia Language Villages–Spanish–Maplelag, MN
Concordia Language Villages–Spanish–Wilder Forest, MN
Concordia Language Villages–Swedish, MN
Costa Rica ¡Pura Vida!, Costa Rica
Costa Rica Rainforest Outward Bound School–Multi-Element, Costa Rica
Costa Rica Rainforest Outward Bound School–Summer Semester, Costa Rica
Costa Rica Rainforest Outward Bound School–Surf Adventure, Costa Rica
Costa Rica Rainforest Outward Bound School–Tri-Country/Tri-Mester
Cottonwood Gulch Family Trek, NM
Cottonwood Gulch Mountain Desert Challenge, NM
Cottonwood Gulch Outfit Expedition, NM
Cottonwood Gulch Prairie Trek Expedition, NM
Cottonwood Gulch Turquoise Trail Expedition, NM
Crow Canyon Archaeological Center High School Excavation Program, CO
Crow Canyon Archaeological Center High School Field School, CO
Crow Canyon Archaeological Center Middle School Archaeology Program, CO
Cuernavaca Summer Program for Teens, Mexico
Deer Hill Expeditions, Arizona, AZ
Deer Hill Expeditions, Colorado, CO
Deer Hill Expeditions, Costa Rica, Costa Rica
Deer Hill Expeditions, New Mexico, NM
Deer Hill Expeditions, Utah, UT
Dickinson College Spanish Language and Cultural Immersion Program, Mexico
Eagle Lake Camp Jaunts–Kenya Mission Adventure, Kenya
EARTHWATCH INSTITUTE–Argentina's Pampas Carnivores, Argentina
EARTHWATCH INSTITUTE–Bahamian Reef Survey, Bahamas
EARTHWATCH INSTITUTE–Baltic Island Wetlands and Wildlife, Estonia
EARTHWATCH INSTITUTE–Butterflies of Vietnam, Vietnam
EARTHWATCH INSTITUTE–Cacti and Orchids of the Yucatan, Mexico
EARTHWATCH INSTITUTE–Canyonland Creek Ecology, UT
EARTHWATCH INSTITUTE–Carnivores of Madagascar, Madagascar
EARTHWATCH INSTITUTE–Cheetah, Namibia
EARTHWATCH INSTITUTE–China's Ancestral Temples, China
EARTHWATCH INSTITUTE–Climate Change at Arctic's Edge, Canada
EARTHWATCH INSTITUTE–Coastal Ecology of the Bahamas, Bahamas
EARTHWATCH INSTITUTE–Community Health in Cameroon, Cameroon
EARTHWATCH INSTITUTE–Conservation Research Initiative–Restoring Wild Salmon, WA
EARTHWATCH INSTITUTE–Conservation Research Initiative–Samburu: Communities and Water Resources, Kenya

▶ Cultural Programs

EARTHWATCH INSTITUTE–Conservation Research Initiative–Samburu: Communities and Wildlife Habitat, Kenya
EARTHWATCH INSTITUTE–Crocodiles of the Okavango, Botswana
EARTHWATCH INSTITUTE–Dolphins and Whales of Abaco Island, Bahamas
EARTHWATCH INSTITUTE–Dolphins of Brazil, Brazil
EARTHWATCH INSTITUTE–Early Man at Olduvai Gorge, United Republic of Tanzania
EARTHWATCH INSTITUTE–Early Man in Spain, Spain
EARTHWATCH INSTITUTE–Echidnas and Goannas of Kangaroo Island, Australia
EARTHWATCH INSTITUTE–Ecuador Forest Birds, Ecuador
EARTHWATCH INSTITUTE–England's Hidden Kingdom, United Kingdom
EARTHWATCH INSTITUTE–Europe–Africa Songbird Migrations–Hungary, Hungary
EARTHWATCH INSTITUTE–Europe–Africa Songbird Migrations–Italy, Italy
EARTHWATCH INSTITUTE–Frontier Fort in Virginia, VA
EARTHWATCH INSTITUTE–Guatemala's Ancient Maya, Guatemala
EARTHWATCH INSTITUTE–Hawksbill Turtles of Barbados, Barbados
EARTHWATCH INSTITUTE–Health and Nutrition in Botswana, Botswana
EARTHWATCH INSTITUTE–Hopi Ancestors, AZ
EARTHWATCH INSTITUTE–Icelandic and Alaskan Glaciers, Iceland
EARTHWATCH INSTITUTE–Inner Mongolia's Lost Water, China
EARTHWATCH INSTITUTE–Itjaritjari: the Outback's Mysterious Marsupial, Australia
EARTHWATCH INSTITUTE–Jackson Hole Bison Dig, WY
EARTHWATCH INSTITUTE–Kenya's Black Rhino, Kenya
EARTHWATCH INSTITUTE–Koala Ecology, Australia
EARTHWATCH INSTITUTE–Lakes of the Rift Valley, Kenya
EARTHWATCH INSTITUTE–Lions of Tsavo, Kenya
EARTHWATCH INSTITUTE–Mallorca's Copper Age, Spain
EARTHWATCH INSTITUTE–Mammoth Cave, KY
EARTHWATCH INSTITUTE–Mammoth Graveyard, SD
EARTHWATCH INSTITUTE–Manatees in Belize, Belize
EARTHWATCH INSTITUTE–Maternal and Child Healthcare in India, India
EARTHWATCH INSTITUTE–Mountain Waters of Bohemia, Czech Republic
EARTHWATCH INSTITUTE–New Zealand Dolphins, New Zealand
EARTHWATCH INSTITUTE–Pine Marten of the Ancient Forest, Canada
EARTHWATCH INSTITUTE–Prehistoric Pueblos of the American Southwest, NM
EARTHWATCH INSTITUTE–Rainforest Caterpillars–Costa Rica, Costa Rica
EARTHWATCH INSTITUTE–Rare Plants of Kenya, Kenya
EARTHWATCH INSTITUTE–Rivers of the Peruvian Amazon, Peru
EARTHWATCH INSTITUTE–Roman Fort on the Danube, Romania
EARTHWATCH INSTITUTE–Roman Fort on Tyne, United Kingdom
EARTHWATCH INSTITUTE–Saving the Leatherback Turtle, U.S. Virgin Islands
EARTHWATCH INSTITUTE–Sea Turtles of Baja, Mexico
EARTHWATCH INSTITUTE–Singing Russia, Russian Federation
EARTHWATCH INSTITUTE–South African Penguins, South Africa
EARTHWATCH INSTITUTE–South African Wildlife, South Africa
EARTHWATCH INSTITUTE–Spanish Dolphins, Spain
EARTHWATCH INSTITUTE–Sri Lanka's Temple Monkeys, Sri Lanka
EARTHWATCH INSTITUTE–Wildlife Conservation in West Africa, Ghana
EF International Language School–Barcelona, Spain
EF International Language School–Malaga, Spain
EF International Language School–Munich, Germany
EF International Language School–Nice, France
EF International Language School–Paris, France
EF International Language School–Rome, Italy
EF International Language School–Quito, Ecuador
EF International Language School–St. Petersburg, Russian Federation
EF International Language School–Shanghai, China
EKOCAMP International, Canada
Environmental Studies and Solutions, Norway
Excel at Madrid/Barcelona, Spain
Excel at Oxford/Tuscany
Excel Cuba, Cuba
The Experiment in International Living–Argentina Homestay, Community Service, and Outdoor Ecological Program, Argentina
The Experiment in International Living–Australia Homestay, Australia
The Experiment in International Living–Belize Homestay, Belize
The Experiment in International Living–Botswana Homestay, Botswana
The Experiment in International Living–Brazil–Ecological Preservation, Brazil
The Experiment in International Living–Brazil Homestay and Community Service, Brazil
The Experiment in International Living–Chile North Homestay, Community Service, Chile
The Experiment in International Living–Chile South Homestay, Chile
The Experiment in International Living–China North and East Homestay, China
The Experiment in International Living–China South and West Homestay, China
The Experiment in International Living–Costa Rica Homestay, Costa Rica
The Experiment in International Living–Ecuador Homestay, Ecuador
The Experiment in International Living–France, Biking and Homestay, France
The Experiment in International Living–France, Five-Week Art and Adventure in Provence, France
The Experiment in International Living–France, Four-Week Brittany Discovery, France
The Experiment in International Living–France, Four-Week Homestay and Photography, France
The Experiment in International Living–France, Four-Week Homestay and Theatre, France
The Experiment in International Living–France, Four-Week Homestay and Travel–Borders, France
The Experiment in International Living–France, Four–Week Homestay and Travel through Alps, France
The Experiment in International Living–France, Homestay, Language Training, and Cooking, France
The Experiment in International Living–France, Three-Week Camargue Homestay, France
The Experiment in International Living–France, Three-Week Homestay and Travel–Borders, France
The Experiment in International Living–Germany, Four-Week Homestay, Travel, Community Service, Germany
The Experiment in International Living–Ghana Homestay, Ghana
The Experiment in International Living–Ireland/Northern Ireland Homestay and Peace Studies, Ireland
The Experiment in International Living–Italy Homestay, Italy
The Experiment in International Living–Japan Homestay, Japan
The Experiment in International Living–Mexico, Community Service, Travel, and Homestay, Mexico
The Experiment in International Living–Mexico Homestay and Travel, Mexico
The Experiment in International Living–Morocco Four-Week Arts and Culture Program, Morocco
The Experiment in International Living–Navajo Nation, NM
The Experiment in International Living–New Zealand Homestay, New Zealand
The Experiment in International Living–Poland, Homestay, Community Service, and Travel, Poland
The Experiment in International Living–South Africa Homestay and Community Service, South Africa
The Experiment in International Living–Spain, Five-Week Homestay, Travel, Ecology, Spain
The Experiment in International Living–Spain, Five-Week Language Training, Travel, and Homestay, Spain
The Experiment in International Living–Spain, Four-Week Homestay and Trekking Program, Spain
The Experiment in International Living–Spain, Four-Week Language Study and Homestay, Spain

The Experiment in International Living–Spain–Spanish Culture and Folklore, Spain
The Experiment in International Living–Spain, Three-Week Homestay, Spain
The Experiment in International Living–Switzerland French Language Immersion, Homestay, and Alpine Adventure, Switzerland
The Experiment in International Living–Thailand Homestay, Thailand
The Experiment in International Living–The United Kingdom Celtic Odyssey, United Kingdom
The Experiment in International Living–Turkey Homestay, Community Service, and Travel, Turkey
The Experiment in International Living–United Kingdom Filmmaking Program and Homestay, United Kingdom
The Experiment in International Living–United Kingdom Theatre Program, United Kingdom
The Fessenden School Summer ESL Program, MA
Flint Hill School–"Summer on the Hill"–Enrichment on the Hill–Spanish Immersion Camp, VA
Four Corners School of Outdoor Education: Southwest Ed-Venture
Georgetown Prep School Summer English Program, MD
Global Teen–Vejer Beach Spectacular in Spain, Spain
GLOBAL WORKS–Cultural Exchange-Fiji Islands-4 weeks, Fiji
GLOBAL WORKS–Cultural Exchange-Ireland-4 weeks, Ireland
GLOBAL WORKS–Cultural Exchange-New Zealand and Fiji Islands-4 weeks
GLOBAL WORKS–Language Exposure-Costa Rica-4 weeks, Costa Rica
GLOBAL WORKS–Language Exposure-Ecuador and the Galapagos-4 weeks, Ecuador
GLOBAL WORKS–Language Exposure-Puerto Rico-3 weeks, Puerto Rico
GLOBAL WORKS–Language Exposure-Yucatan Peninsula, Mexico-4 weeks, Mexico
GLOBAL WORKS–Language Immersion-Costa Rica-4 weeks, Costa Rica
GLOBAL WORKS–Language Immersion-Ecuador and the Galapagos-4 weeks, Ecuador
GLOBAL WORKS–Language Immersion-France-4 weeks, France
GLOBAL WORKS–Language Immersion-Puerto Rico-4 weeks, Puerto Rico
GLOBAL WORKS–Language Immersion-Spain-4 weeks, Spain
GLOBAL WORKS–Language Immersion-Yucatan Peninsula, Mexico-4 weeks, Mexico
Greek Summer, Greece
Hante School, NC
Hidden Villa Summer Camp, CA
Houghton Academy Summer ESL, NY
Humanities Spring in Assisi, Italy
Humanities Spring on the Road, Italy
The Hun School of Princeton American Culture and Language Institute, NJ
Ibike Cultural Tours–Ecuador, Ecuador
Ibike Cultural Tours–Guyana, Guyana
Ibike Cultural Tours–Washington/British Columbia
iD Tech Camps–Documentary Filmmaking and Cultural Immersion at the University of Cádiz, Spain, Spain
Instituto de Idiomas Geos–Costa Rica, Costa Rica
Instituto de Idiomas Geos–Granada, Spain, Spain
Instituto de Idiomas Geos–Marbella, Spain, Spain
International Summer Camp Montana, Switzerland, Switzerland
International Summer Centre at Biarritz, France
International Summer Centre at Chatel, France
International Summer Centre at Paris-Brétigny, France
Irish Way, Ireland
ISB Chinese Language Camp, China
Israel Discovery
Julian Krinsky California Teen Tours, CA
Julian Krinsky Yesh Shabbat California Teen Tour, CA
Junior Institute, WA
Knowledge Exchange Institute–African Safari Program, Kenya
Knowledge Exchange Institute–Discover Spain and Portugal Program
Knowledge Exchange Institute–European Capitals Program
Knowledge Exchange Institute–Spanish on the Road in Mexico Program, Mexico
Lacunza Junior Summer Spanish Course, Spain
Ladakh Summer Passage, India
Learn English and Discover Canada, Canada
Learning Programs International–Argentina, Argentina
Learning Programs International–Chile, Chile
Learning Programs International–Costa Rica, Costa Rica
Learning Programs International–Mexico, Mexico
Learning Programs International–Spain, Spain
LIFEWORKS with the Australian Red Cross, Australia
LIFEWORKS with the British Virgin Islands Marine Parks and Conservation Department, British Virgin Islands
LIFEWORKS with the DPF Foundation in Thailand, Thailand
LIFEWORKS with the Galapagos Islands' National Parks, Ecuador
The Loomis Chaffee Summer in France, France
The Loomis Chaffee Summer in Spain, Spain
Lower Mustang Summer Passage, Nepal
LSA Alicante, Spain, Spain
LSA Almuñecar, Spain, Spain
LSA Amboise, France, France
LSA Antibes, France, France
LSA Antigua, Guatemala, Guatemala
LSA Argelés-Gazost, France, France
LSA Ascoli, Italy, Italy
LSA Barcelona, Spain, Spain
LSA Berlin, Germany, Germany
LSA Biarritz, France, France
LSA Blossin, Germany, Germany
LSA Bordeaux, France, France
LSA Buenos Aires, Argentina, Argentina
LSA Cannes, France, France
LSA Cologne, Germany, Germany
LSA Cordoba, Argentina, Argentina
LSA Cuernavaca, Mexico, Mexico
LSA Cuzco, Peru, Peru
LSA El Puerto de Santa Maria, Spain, Spain
LSA Ensenada, Mexico, Mexico
LSA Flamingo Beach, Costa Rica, Costa Rica
LSA Florence, Italy, Italy
LSA Granada, Spain, Spain
LSA Hamburg, Germany, Germany
LSA Holzkirchen, Germany, Germany
LSA Hyères, France, France
LSA Inzell, Germany, Germany
LSA Kanazawa, Japan, Japan
LSA La Rochelle, France, France
LSA Lausanne, Switzerland, Switzerland
LSA Lignano, Italy–Active Junior Italian Summer Program, Italy
LSA Lisbon, Portugal, Portugal
LSA Livorno, Italy, Italy
LSA Loewenstein, Germany, Germany
LSA Madrid, Spain, Spain
LSA Màlaga, Spain, Spain
LSA Marbella, Spain, Spain
LSA Mérida, Mexico, Mexico
LSA Milan, Italy, Italy
LSA Montreal, Canada–English/French, Canada
LSA Moscow, Russia, Russian Federation
LSA Munich, Germany, Germany
LSA Nerja, Spain, Spain
LSA Nice, France, France
LSA Oaxaca, Mexico, Mexico
LSA Orvieto, Italy, Italy
LSA Paris, France, France
LSA Playa Del Carmen, Mexico, Mexico
LSA Potsdam, Germany, Germany
LSA Puebla, Mexico, Mexico
LSA Puerto Vallarta, Mexico, Mexico
LSA Quito, Ecuador, Ecuador
LSA Rimini, Italy, Italy
LSA Rome, Italy, Italy
LSA St. Petersburg, Russia, Russian Federation
LSA Salamanca, Spain, Spain
LSA San José, Costa Rica, Costa Rica
LSA San Sebastian, Spain, Spain
LSA Schmoeckwitz, Germany, Germany
LSA Sevilla, Spain, Spain
LSA Siena, Italy, Italy
LSA Stuttgart, Germany, Germany
LSA Sucre, Bolivia, Bolivia
LSA Taormina, Italy, Italy
LSA Tenerife, Spain, Spain
LSA Tours, France, France
LSA Treviso, Italy, Italy
LSA Valencia, Spain, Spain
LSA Vienna, Austria, Austria
LSA Viña del Mar, Chile, Chile
Maui Surfer Girls, HI
MexArt: Art and Spanish, Mexico
MexArt Dance: Dance and Spanish, Mexico
Millersville University of Pennsylvania–Summer Language Camps for High School Students, PA
Mountain Workshop–Awesome 6: Quebec, Canada
Musiker Tours: Action Europe
The Nepal Cultural Immersion Experience, Nepal

▶ Cultural Programs

Outpost Wilderness Adventure–Copper Canyon Project, Mexico
Overland: Costa Rica Explorer Hiking, Rafting, and Sea-Kayaking, Costa Rica
Overland: European Challenge Bicycle Touring from Paris to Rome
Overland: Language Study Abroad in Costa Rica, Costa Rica
Overland: Language Study Abroad in France, France
Overland: Language Study Abroad in Spain, Spain
Overland: Paris to the Sea Bicycle Touring, France
Overland: The Alpine Challenge Leadership Course Backpacking and Hiking
Overland: Vermont & Montreal Bicycle Touring
Overland: World Service, Costa Rica, Costa Rica
Oxford Advanced Seminars Programme, United Kingdom
Oxford Advanced Studies Program, United Kingdom
Oxford School Summer Camp, CA
PAX Abroad–Ecuador Rainforest Adventure, Ecuador
PAX Abroad–Ecuador–Spanish Language Immersion, Ecuador
PAX Abroad–Summer Spain, Spain
PAX Abroad to Australia, Australia
Peace in the Modern World, Denmark
Peace Works International–Costa Rica, Costa Rica
Peace Works International–Peru, Peru
Peace Works International–Ecuador, Ecuador
Personal Passage, Nepal
The Peru Cultural Immersion Experience, Peru
Phillips Exeter Academy French Study Tour, France
Phillips Exeter Academy Taiwan and Beijing Summer Study Tour
Poulter Colorado Camps: Adventures Planet Earth–Austria
Poulter Colorado Camps: Adventures Planet Earth–Costa Rica, Costa Rica
Poulter Colorado Camps: Adventures Planet Earth–New Zealand, New Zealand
Poulter Colorado Camps: Adventures Planet Earth–Spain, Spain
Programs Abroad Travel Alternatives–Costa Rica, Costa Rica
Programs Abroad Travel Alternatives–Ecuador, Ecuador
Programs Abroad Travel Alternatives–France, France
Programs Abroad Travel Alternatives–Germany, Germany
Programs Abroad Travel Alternatives–Italy, Italy
Programs Abroad Travel Alternatives–Mexico, Mexico
Programs Abroad Travel Alternatives–Peru, Peru
Programs Abroad Travel Alternatives–Russia, Russian Federation
Programs Abroad Travel Alternatives–Spain, Spain
Putney Student Travel–Community Service–Brazil, Brazil
Putney Student Travel–Community Service–Costa Rica, Costa Rica
Putney Student Travel–Community Service–Dominican Republic, Dominican Republic
Putney Student Travel–Community Service–Dominica, West Indies, Dominica
Putney Student Travel–Community Service–Ecuador, Ecuador
Putney Student Travel–Community Service-India, India
Putney Student Travel–Community Service–Montana, MT
Putney Student Travel–Community Service–Tanzania, United Republic of Tanzania
Putney Student Travel–Cultural Exploration–Australia, New Zealand, and Fiji
Putney Student Travel–Cultural Exploration–Eastern European Heritage
Putney Student Travel–Cultural Exploration–France, Holland, and England
Putney Student Travel–Cultural Exploration–Switzerland, Italy, France, and Holland
Putney Student Travel–Cultural Exploration–Thailand and Cambodia
Putney Student Travel–Language Learning–Costa Rica, Costa Rica
Putney Student Travel–Language Learning–France, France
Putney Student Travel–Language Learning–Spain, Spain
Quest Scholars Program at Stanford/ QuestLeadership, CA
Rassias Programs–Arles, France, France
Rassias Programs–Gijón, Spain, Spain
Rassias Programs–Pontevedra, Spain, Spain
Rassias Programs–Segovia, Spain, Spain
Rassias Programs–Tours, France, France
RUSTIC PATHWAYS–ACCELERATED SPANISH IMMERSION, Costa Rica
RUSTIC PATHWAYS–ADVENTURE IN AMERICA'S SOUTHWEST
RUSTIC PATHWAYS–AWESOME AUSSIE EXPLORER, Australia
RUSTIC PATHWAYS–BIG FIJI EXPLORER, Fiji
RUSTIC PATHWAYS–BUDDHIST LIFE & ANGKOR WAT
RUSTIC PATHWAYS–COSTA RICA ADVENTURER, Costa Rica
RUSTIC PATHWAYS–COSTA RICA EXTREME, Costa Rica
RUSTIC PATHWAYS–DIVER'S DREAM IN THE FIJI ISLANDS, Fiji
RUSTIC PATHWAYS–ELEPHANTS & AMAZING THAILAND, Thailand
RUSTIC PATHWAYS–EXTENDED COMMUNITY SERVICE IN THE FIJI ISLANDS, Fiji
RUSTIC PATHWAYS–EXTREME PLANET
RUSTIC PATHWAYS–HAWAIIAN ISLANDS ADVENTURE, HI
RUSTIC PATHWAYS–HIGH ADRENALINE AUSSIE, Australia
RUSTIC PATHWAYS–HIGHLANDS COMMUNITY SERVICE IN FIJI, Fiji
RUSTIC PATHWAYS–INTRO TO COMMUNITY SERVICE IN FIJI, Fiji
RUSTIC PATHWAYS–INTRO TO COMMUNITY SERVICE IN THAILAND, Thailand
RUSTIC PATHWAYS–OUTBACK 4-WHEEL DRIVE SAFARI, Australia
RUSTIC PATHWAYS–PHOTOGRAPHY & ADVENTURE IN THAILAND, Thailand
RUSTIC PATHWAYS–RAMP UP YOUR SPANISH, Costa Rica
RUSTIC PATHWAYS–RHYTHM IN THE RICEFIELDS, Thailand
RUSTIC PATHWAYS–RICEFIELDS, MONKS & SMILING CHILDREN, Thailand
RUSTIC PATHWAYS–SNAPSHOT OF FIJI, Fiji
RUSTIC PATHWAYS–SPANISH LANGUAGE IMMERSION, Costa Rica
RUSTIC PATHWAYS–THE AMAZING THAILAND ADVENTURE, Thailand
RUSTIC PATHWAYS–THE CANO NEGRO SERVICE PROJECT, Costa Rica
RUSTIC PATHWAYS–THE SUNSHINE COAST & SYDNEY, Australia
RUSTIC PATHWAYS–THE THAI ELEPHANT CONSERVATION PROJECT, Thailand
RUSTIC PATHWAYS–THE WONDERS & RICHES OF THAILAND, Thailand
RUSTIC PATHWAYS–TOTALLY DOWNUNDER ADVENTURE, Australia
RUSTIC PATHWAYS–TROPICAL AUSSIE ADVENTURE, Australia
RUSTIC PATHWAYS–ULTIMATE AUSTRALIAN ADVENTURE, Australia
Sail Caribbean–Leeward Islands
Service-Learning in Paris, France
SFS: Tropical Reforestation Studies, Australia
Shizen Kyampu-Japanese Language Science Camp, OR
The Sikkim Cultural Immersion Experience, India
Space Camp Turkey 6-Day International Program, Turkey
Spanish Through Leadership–Nicaragua, Nicaragua
Spanish Through Leadership–Nicaragua/ Costa Rica
Spoleto Study Abroad, Italy
Summer Delegation to León, Nicaragua, Nicaragua
Summer in Switzerland, Switzerland
Summer Study in Paris at The American University of Paris, France
Summer Summit on Leadership, MA
TASIS Le Château des Enfants, Switzerland
TASIS Middle School Program, Switzerland
TASIS Spanish Summer Program, Spain
TASIS Summer Program for Languages, Arts, and Outdoor Pursuits, Switzerland
TASIS Tuscan Academy of Art and Culture, Italy
Teen Tour USA and Canada
TENNIS: EUROPE
Tibetan Culture of Northern India, India
Tibetan Summer Passage
Tisch School of the Arts–International High School Program–Dublin, Ireland
Tisch School of the Arts–International High School Program–Paris, France
Tufts Summit, France
UCAELI Summer Camp, CT
University of Chicago–ChicaGO! The Traveling Academy, France
University of St. Andrews Creative Writing Summer Program, United Kingdom
University of St. Andrews Scottish Studies Summer Program, United Kingdom
University of Wisconsin–Green Bay Summer Spanish Immersion, WI
Visions–Alaska, AK
Visions–Australia, Australia

Visions–British Virgin Islands, British Virgin Islands
Visions–Dominica, Dominica
Visions–Dominican Republic, Dominican Republic
Visions–Ecuador, Ecuador
Visions–Guadeloupe, Guadeloupe
Visions–Montana, MT
Visions–Peru, Peru
Visions–South Carolina, SC
Visions–Trinidad, Trinidad and Tobago
Weissman Teen Tours–"Aloha–Welcome to Hawaiian Paradise"
Weissman Teen Tours–European Experience
Weissman Teen Tours–U.S. and Western Canada, 4 Weeks
Westcoast Connection Travel–European Discovery
Westcoast Connection Travel–European Escape
Westcoast Connection Travel/On Tour–European Experience
Where There Be Dragons: China, China
Where There Be Dragons: Guatemala, Guatemala
Where There Be Dragons: India Culture and Philosophy, India
Where There Be Dragons: India Zanskar Trek, India
Where There Be Dragons: Mexico, Mexico
Where There Be Dragons: Mongolia, Mongolia
Where There Be Dragons: Peru, Peru
Where There Be Dragons: Silk Road, China
Where There Be Dragons: Thailand, Thailand
Where There Be Dragons: Tibet, China
Where There Be Dragons: Vietnam, Vietnam
Wilderness Ventures–Australia, Australia
Wilderness Ventures–Costa Rica, Costa Rica
Wilderness Ventures–Ecuador and Galapagos, Ecuador
Wilderness Ventures–European Alps
Wilderness Ventures–Spanish Pyrenees, Spain
Windsor Mountain: Adventures in Filmmaking, Saint Vincent and The Grenadines
Windsor Mountain: Alaska, AK
Windsor Mountain: Bonjour Quebec, Canada
Windsor Mountain: Coast of Australia, Australia
Windsor Mountain: Crossroads France, France
Windsor Mountain: Cuba Friendship Exchange, Cuba
Windsor Mountain: European Traveling Minstrels
Windsor Mountain: Mexico Community Service, Mexico
Windsor Mountain: Puerto Rico, Puerto Rico
Windsor Mountain: Random Acts of Kindness
Windsor Mountain: Voices of the Wind River, Wyoming, WY
World Affairs Seminar, WI
World Horizons International–Costa Rica, Costa Rica
World Horizons International–Dominica, Dominica
World Horizons International–Fiji, Fiji
World Horizons International–Iceland, Iceland
World Horizons International–Kanab, Utah, UT
World Horizons International–Mexico, Mexico
World Horizons International–Oahu, Hawaii, HI
World Horizons International–Puerto Rico, Puerto Rico
Youth for Understanding USA–Argentina, Argentina
Youth for Understanding USA–Australia, Australia
Youth for Understanding USA–Brazil, Brazil
Youth for Understanding USA–Chile, Chile
Youth for Understanding USA–China, China
Youth for Understanding USA–Denmark, Denmark
Youth for Understanding USA–Ecuador, Ecuador
Youth for Understanding USA–Estonia/Latvia-Baltic Summer
Youth for Understanding USA–France, France
Youth for Understanding USA–Germany, Germany
Youth for Understanding USA–Ghana, Ghana
Youth for Understanding USA–Greece, Greece
Youth for Understanding USA–Hungary, Hungary
Youth for Understanding USA–Ireland, Ireland
Youth for Understanding USA–Italy, Italy
Youth for Understanding USA–Japan, Japan
Youth for Understanding USA–Kazakhstan, Kazakhstan
Youth for Understanding USA–Kenya, Kenya
Youth for Understanding USA–Poland, Poland
Youth for Understanding USA–Russia, Russian Federation
Youth for Understanding USA–South Africa, South Africa
Youth for Understanding USA–South Korea, Republic of Korea
Youth for Understanding USA–Spain, Spain
Youth for Understanding USA–Sweden, Sweden
Youth for Understanding USA–Thailand, Thailand
Youth for Understanding USA–Uruguay, Uruguay
Youth for Understanding USA–Venezuela, Venezuela
Youth for Understanding USA–Vietnam, Vietnam
Youth Program in Spain, Spain

Family Programs

Alford Lake Family Camp, ME
Cal Poly State University Young Scholars–Find the College for You!, CA
Camp Lincoln for Boys/Camp Lake Hubert for Girls Family Camp, MN
Camp Lookout, MI
Camp Tawonga–Summertime Family Camp, CA
Cazadero Family Camp, CA
Cheley Colorado Camps, CO
Christikon, MT
Clara Barton Family Camp, MA
Cottonwood Gulch Family Trek, NM
Crossroads School–Aquatics, CA
Double "H" Hole in the Woods Ranch Summer Camp, NY
Embry-Riddle Aeronautical University–Generations, FL
Explore Nor'wester, WA
Four Corners School of Outdoor Education: Southwest Ed-Venture
Grandparents' and Grandchildren's Camp, NY
Idyllwild Arts Summer Program–Family Week, CA
Jumonville Creative and Performing Arts Camps, PA
Kawkawa Summer Camps, Canada
Maine Golf Academy–Family Camp, ME
Maui Surfer Girls–Mother/Daughter, HI
NBC Camps–Basketball–Adult & Child Hoops–Spokane, WA, WA
Parent/Youth Golf School, TX
Rainbow Club–Greenwich, Connecticut, CT
River Way Ranch Camp, CA
Sandy Island Camp for Families, NH
SeaWorld San Antonio Adventure Camp, TX
Shippensburg University Sports Camps–Father/Son Basketball Camp, PA
Streamside Family Camp, PA
Summer Family Conference, MD
UCSB Alumni Association Santa Barbara Family Vacation Center, CA
Windsor Mountain: Family Camp, NH
YMCA Camp Abnaki–Family Camp, VT
YMCA Wanakita Summer Family Camp, Canada

Outdoor Programs

AAC–Aloha Adventure Photo Camp, HI
AAVE–Africa
AAVE–Alaska, AK
AAVE–Alps Rider
AAVE–Australia, Australia
AAVE–Belize, Belize
AAVE–Bike France, France
AAVE–Bold Europe
AAVE–Bold West
AAVE–Boot/Saddle/Paddle
AAVE–Border Cross
AAVE–Costa Rica, Costa Rica
AAVE–Ecuador and Galapagos, Ecuador
AAVE–Hawaii, HI
AAVE–Inmersión en España, Spain
AAVE–Peru and Machu Picchu, Peru
AAVE–Rock & River
AAVE–Rocky Mountain Adventure, CO
AAVE–Thailand, Thailand
AAVE–Vietnam, Vietnam
AAVE–Vivons le Français, France
AAVE–Wild Isles
AAVE–X-Five
Abilene Christian University–Cross Training, NM
ACTIONQUEST: Advanced PADI Scuba Certification and Specialty Voyages, British Virgin Islands
ACTIONQUEST: Australian and Great Barrier Reef Adventures, Australia
ACTIONQUEST: British Virgin Islands–Sailing and Scuba Voyages, British Virgin Islands
ACTIONQUEST: British Virgin Islands-Sailing Voyages, British Virgin Islands
ACTIONQUEST: Galapagos Archipelago Expeditions, Ecuador
ACTIONQUEST: Junior Advanced Scuba with Marine Biology, British Virgin Islands
ACTIONQUEST: Leeward and French Caribbean Island Voyages
ACTIONQUEST: Mediterranean Sailing Voyage
ACTIONQUEST: Rescue Diving Voyages, British Virgin Islands

Outdoor Programs

ACTIONQUEST: Tahiti and French Polynesian Island Voyages, French Polynesia
ACTIONQUEST: Tropical Marine Biology Voyages, British Virgin Islands
Adirondack Alpine Adventures, NY
Adventure Camps, PA
Adventure Ireland–Surf Camp/Activity Camp, Ireland
Adventure Links
Adventure Links–Appalachian Odyssey
Adventure Links–Ultimate Adventure Camps, VA
!ADVENTURES–AFLOAT: Advanced Scuba Adventure Voyages–British Virgin Islands, British Virgin Islands
!ADVENTURES–AFLOAT: Advanced Scuba Adventure Voyages–Caribbean Islands
!ADVENTURES–AFLOAT: Scuba and Sailing Discovery Voyages–British Virgin Islands, British Virgin Islands
!ADVENTURES–AFLOAT: Scuba and Sailing Discovery Voyages–Caribbean Islands
Adventures Cross-Country, Alaska Adventure, AK
Adventures Cross-Country, Australia/Fiji Adventure
Adventures Cross-Country, Caribbean Adventure
Adventures Cross-Country, Colorado Adventure, CO
Adventures Cross-Country, Costa Rica Adventure, Costa Rica
Adventures Cross-Country, Extreme British Columbia Adventure, Canada
Adventures Cross-Country, Hawaii Adventure, HI
Adventures Cross-Country,Southern Europe Adventure
Adventures Cross-Country, Thailand Adventure, Thailand
Adventures Cross-Country, Western Adventure
Adventure Treks–Alaska Adventures, AK
Adventure Treks–California Challenge Adventures
Adventure Treks–California 19 Adventures, CA
Adventure Treks–Canadian Rockies Adventures, Canada
Adventure Treks–Montana Adventures, MT
Adventure Treks–Pacific Northwest Adventures, WA
Adventure Treks–PAC 16, OR
Adventure Treks–Summit Fever
Adventure Treks–Ultimate Northwest Adventures
AFS-USA–Homestay, Outdoor Adventure Amazon–Brazil, Brazil
AFS-USA–Homestay Plus–Australia, Australia
AFS-USA–Homestay Plus–Brazil, Brazil
AFS-USA–Homestay Plus–New Zealand, New Zealand
AFS-USA–Team Mission–Russia, Russian Federation
Alabama Museum of Natural History Summer Expedition, AL
Alien Adventure Overnight Camp
Alpengirl–Alaska, AK
Alpengirl–Hawaii, HI
Alpengirl–Montana, MT
Alpengirl–Montana Art
Alpengirl–Montana Fitness, MT
Alpengirl–Montana Horse, MT
Alpengirl–Washington, WA
Alpengirl–Washington Alpenguide Training, WA
Alpengirl–Washington Lil' Alpengirl, WA
Alton Jones Day Camp, RI
Alton Jones Earth Camp, RI
American Youth Foundation–Camp Merrowvista, NH
American Youth Foundation–Camp Miniwanca, MI
Anderson Camps' Colorado River Ranch for Boys/Hilltop Ranch for Girls, CO
Anderson Camps' Wilderness Pioneer Camp, CO
Apogee Outdoor Adventures–Burlington to Boston
Apogee Outdoor Adventures–Montana Service Adventure, MT
Appalachian Mountain Club–Teen Crews–Alpine Trail, Berkshires, MA
Appalachian Mountain Club–Teen Crews–Mount Greylock, MA
Appalachian Mountain Club–Teen Crews–Pinkham Notch, NH
Appalachian Mountain Club–Teen Crews–Spike, NH
Appalachian Mountain Club–Teen Crews–Two-week Teen Spike, NH
Appalachian Mountain Club–Teen Stewardship Training, NH
Appalachian Mountain Club–Trail Crew–Berkshires, MA
Appalachian Mountain Club–Trail Crew–Mount Everett/Alpine Trail, MA
Appalachian Mountain Club–Trail Crew–White Mountains, NH
Appalachian Mountain Club–Volunteer Trail Crew–Alpine/Mount Washington, NH
Appalachian Mountain Club–Volunteer Trail Crew–Crawford Notch, NH
Appalachian Mountain Club–Volunteer Trail Crew–Grafton Loop, ME
Appalachian Mountain Club–Volunteer Trail Crew–Hut Crew, NH
Appalachian Mountain Club–Volunteer Trail Crew–Mount Greylock, MA
Appalachian Mountain Club–Wild New Hampshire Trail Crew, NH
Appalachian Mountain Club–Women's Trail Crew, NH
Audubon Journeys, VT
Audubon Vermont Youth Camp, VT
Austin Nature and Science Center, TX
Bark Lake Leadership Through Recreation Camp, Canada
Barton Adventure Camp
Bicycle Africa Tours
BICYCLE TRAVEL ADVENTURES–Student Hosteling Program–Amsterdam to Paris
BICYCLE TRAVEL ADVENTURES–Student Hosteling Program–A Thousand Miles: Massachusetts to Nova Scotia
BICYCLE TRAVEL ADVENTURES–Student Hosteling Program–Canadian Rockies to California
BICYCLE TRAVEL ADVENTURES–Student Hosteling Program–Cape Cod, MA
BICYCLE TRAVEL ADVENTURES–Student Hosteling Program–Cross-Country America
BICYCLE TRAVEL ADVENTURES–Student Hosteling Program–France and Italy
BICYCLE TRAVEL ADVENTURES–Student Hosteling Program–Ireland and England
BICYCLE TRAVEL ADVENTURES–Student Hosteling Program–Maine Coast, ME
BICYCLE TRAVEL ADVENTURES–Student Hosteling Program–Maine-Nova Scotia Coast Loop
BICYCLE TRAVEL ADVENTURES–Student Hosteling Program–Niagara Falls to Montreal
BICYCLE TRAVEL ADVENTURES–Student Hosteling Program–Off-Road Vermont
BICYCLE TRAVEL ADVENTURES–Student Hosteling Program–Pacific Coast Adventure: Washington, Oregon, and California
BICYCLE TRAVEL ADVENTURES–Student Hosteling Program–Province du Québec, Canada
BICYCLE TRAVEL ADVENTURES–Student Hosteling Program–Province du Québec (short program), Canada
BICYCLE TRAVEL ADVENTURES–Student Hosteling Program–Spain and France
BICYCLE TRAVEL ADVENTURES–Student Hosteling Program–Vermont
BICYCLE TRAVEL ADVENTURES–Student Hosteling Program–Vermont to the Atlantic Ocean
Blue Ridge School–Adventure Camps, VA
Blue Ridge School–Rock Climbing Camp, VA
Brewster Academy Summer Session, NH
BROADREACH Academic Treks–Language Exposure and Service Learning, Chile
BROADREACH Academic Treks–Marine Mammal Studies, Canada
BROADREACH Academic Treks–Marine Park Management
BROADREACH Academic Treks–Sea Turtle Studies, Costa Rica
BROADREACH Academic Treks–Spanish Immersion in Mexico, Mexico
BROADREACH Academic Treks–Spanish Language Immersion in Ecuador, Ecuador
BROADREACH Academic Treks–Wilderness Emergency Medicine, Belize
BROADREACH Adventures Down Under, Australia
BROADREACH Adventures in Scuba and Sailing–Underwater Discoveries
BROADREACH Adventures in the Grenadines–Advanced Scuba, Saint Vincent and The Grenadines
BROADREACH Adventures in the Windward Islands–Advanced Scuba
BROADREACH Adventures Underwater–Advanced Scuba
BROADREACH Amazon and Galapagos Encounter, Ecuador
BROADREACH Arc of the Caribbean Sailing Adventure
BROADREACH Baja Extreme–Scuba Adventure, Mexico
BROADREACH Costa Rica Experience, Costa Rica
BROADREACH Fiji Solomon Quest
BROADREACH Honduras Eco-Adventure, Honduras
BROADREACH Marine Biology Accredited, Bahamas
BROADREACH Red Sea Scuba Adventure, Egypt

Burgundy Center for Wildlife Studies Summer Camp, WV
California Cruzin' Overnight Camp, CA
Camp AK-O-MAK, Canada
Camp Berachah Ministries–Leadership Expedition Camp, WA
Camp Burgess, MA
Camp Chewonki, ME
Camp Chewonki Adventure Camps, ME
Camp Chewonki for Girls, ME
Camp Chewonki Wilderness Expeditions, ME
Camp Chosatonga for Boys, NC
Camp Conrad Weiser, PA
Camp Craig Horse Residential Summer Camp, Canada
Camp Exploration Travel Day Camp, CA
Camp Fire Camp Wi-Ta-Wentin, LA
Camp Fowler, MI
Camp Ganadaoweh, Canada
Camp Glen Brook, NH
Camp Green Cove, NC
Camp Greenkill–Conservation/Adventure, NY
Camp Hawthorne, ME
Camp Hitaga, IA
Camp Hitaga–Stirrups and Saddles, IA
Camp Horizons Adventure, VA
Camp Horizons Explorer, VA
Camp Horizons Pathfinder, VA
Camp Horizons Specialty Camp, VA
Camp Kostopulos, UT
Camp La Jolla, CA
Camp Ledgewood, OH
Camp Maromac, Canada
Camp Mondamin, NC
Camp Mt. Luther, PA
Camp Mowglis, School of the Open, NH
Camp Niwana, TX
Camp Nominingue, Canada
Camp Northway, Canada
Camp Nor'wester, WA
Camp O-AT-KA, ME
Camp O'Bannon, OH
Camp Oweki Summer Day Camp, MI
Camp Pocono Ridge, PA
Camp Roger, MI
Camp Sandy Cove, WV
Camps with Meaning–Advanced Horsemanship I & II, Canada
Camps with Meaning–Boys Camp, Canada
Camps with Meaning–Girls Camp, Canada
Camps with Meaning–Junior High/Junior Youth Camp, Canada
Camps with Meaning–PreJunior/Junior/ Intermediate Camp, Canada
Camps with Meaning–Youth Camp, Canada
Camp Tawonga–Magical Mystery Tour, CA
Camp Tawonga–Summer Camp, CA
Timber-lee Science Camp, WI
Camp Togowoods, AK
Camp Treetops, NY
Camp Wendigo, Canada
Canadian Rockies Adventurer Camp, Canada
Canadian Rockies Outdoor Leader Camp, Canada
Cascade Science School, OR
Center for Cultural Interchange–Spain Sports and Language Camp, Spain
Center for Cultural Interchange–Switzerland Language Camp, Switzerland
Central Wisconsin Environmental Station–Natural Resources Careers Camp, WI
Central Wisconsin Environmental Station–Sunset Lake Adventures, WI
Cheley Colorado Camps, CO
Christikon, MT
College Settlement of Philadelphia, PA
Colvig Silver Camps, CO
Community Sailing of Colorado–Advanced Sailing, CO
Community Sailing of Colorado–Learn to Sail, CO
Community Sailing of Colorado–Sailboat Racing Camp, CO
Costa Rica ¡Pura Vida!, Costa Rica
Costa Rica Rainforest Outward Bound School–Multi-Element, Costa Rica
Costa Rica Rainforest Outward Bound School–Summer Semester, Costa Rica
Costa Rica Rainforest Outward Bound School–Surf Adventure, Costa Rica
Costa Rica Rainforest Outward Bound School–Tri-Country/Tri-Mester
Cottonwood Gulch Family Trek, NM
Cottonwood Gulch Mountain Desert Challenge, NM
Cottonwood Gulch Outfit Expedition, NM
Cottonwood Gulch Prairie Trek Expedition, NM
Cottonwood Gulch Turquoise Trail Expedition, NM
Cottonwood Gulch Wild Country Trek, NM
The Country School Farm, OH
Darlington School Summer Camps, GA
Deerfoot Lodge, NY
Deer Hill Expeditions, Arizona, AZ
Deer Hill Expeditions, Utah, UT
Discovery Camp, CO
Discovery Works New England Community Service Experience
Eagle Lake Bike Camp, CO
Eagle Lake Camp–East, NC
Eagle Lake Camp Jaunts–Minnesota Boundary Waters, MN
Eagle Lake Wilderness Program, CO
Eagle's Nest Camp, NC
EARTHWATCH INSTITUTE–Archaeology at West Point Foundry, NY
EARTHWATCH INSTITUTE–Argentina's Pampas Carnivores, Argentina
EARTHWATCH INSTITUTE–Bahamian Reef Survey, Bahamas
EARTHWATCH INSTITUTE–Baltic Island Wetlands and Wildlife, Estonia
EARTHWATCH INSTITUTE–Biodiversity of the Grenadines, Grenada
EARTHWATCH INSTITUTE–Bogs of Belarus, Belarus
EARTHWATCH INSTITUTE–Brazil's Marine Wildlife, Brazil
EARTHWATCH INSTITUTE–Butterflies and Orchids of Spain, Spain
EARTHWATCH INSTITUTE–Butterflies of Vietnam, Vietnam
EARTHWATCH INSTITUTE–Cacti and Orchids of the Yucatan, Mexico
EARTHWATCH INSTITUTE–Canyonland Creek Ecology, UT
EARTHWATCH INSTITUTE–Caring for Chimpanzees, WA
EARTHWATCH INSTITUTE–Carnivores of Madagascar, Madagascar
EARTHWATCH INSTITUTE–Cheetah, Namibia
EARTHWATCH INSTITUTE–Chilean Coastal Archaeology, Chile
EARTHWATCH INSTITUTE–China's Ancestral Temples, China
EARTHWATCH INSTITUTE–Climate Change at Arctic's Edge, Canada
EARTHWATCH INSTITUTE–Coastal Archaeology of Maine, ME
EARTHWATCH INSTITUTE–Coastal Ecology of the Bahamas, Bahamas
EARTHWATCH INSTITUTE–Community Health in Cameroon, Cameroon
EARTHWATCH INSTITUTE–Conservation Research Initiative–Climate Change in the Rainforest, Australia
EARTHWATCH INSTITUTE–Conservation Research Initiative–Conserving the Pantanal, Brazil
EARTHWATCH INSTITUTE–Conservation Research Initiative–Hawksbill Turtles of the Great Barrier Reef, Australia
EARTHWATCH INSTITUTE–Conservation Research Initiative–Mountain Meadows of the North Cascades, WA
EARTHWATCH INSTITUTE–Conservation Research Initiative–Queensland Tropical Fish Ecology, Australia
EARTHWATCH INSTITUTE–Conservation Research Initiative–Restoring Wild Salmon, WA
EARTHWATCH INSTITUTE–Conservation Research Initiative–Salmon Hotspots of the Skagit River, WA
EARTHWATCH INSTITUTE–Conservation Research Initiative–Salmon of the Pacific Northwest, WA
EARTHWATCH INSTITUTE–Conservation Research Initiative–Samburu: Communities and Water Resources, Kenya
EARTHWATCH INSTITUTE–Conservation Research Initiative–Samburu: Communities and Wildlife Habitat, Kenya
EARTHWATCH INSTITUTE–Conservation Research Initiative–Traditions of Cedar, Salmon, and Gold, WA
EARTHWATCH INSTITUTE–Coral Reefs of the Virgin Islands, U.S. Virgin Islands
EARTHWATCH INSTITUTE–Crocodiles of Cuba, Cuba
EARTHWATCH INSTITUTE–Crocodiles of the Okavango, Botswana
EARTHWATCH INSTITUTE–Desert Elephants of Namibia, Namibia
EARTHWATCH INSTITUTE–Dolphins and Whales of Abaco Island, Bahamas
EARTHWATCH INSTITUTE–Dolphins of Brazil, Brazil
EARTHWATCH INSTITUTE–Dolphins of Costa Rica, Costa Rica
EARTHWATCH INSTITUTE–Early Man at Olduvai Gorge, United Republic of Tanzania
EARTHWATCH INSTITUTE–Early Man in Spain, Spain
EARTHWATCH INSTITUTE–Echidnas and Goannas of Kangaroo Island, Australia
EARTHWATCH INSTITUTE–Ecuador Forest Birds, Ecuador
EARTHWATCH INSTITUTE–England's Hidden Kingdom, United Kingdom
EARTHWATCH INSTITUTE–Europe–Africa Songbird Migrations–Hungary, Hungary
EARTHWATCH INSTITUTE–Europe–Africa Songbird Migrations–Italy, Italy

▶ Outdoor Programs

EARTHWATCH INSTITUTE–Frontier Fort in Virginia, VA
EARTHWATCH INSTITUTE–Guatemala's Ancient Maya, Guatemala
EARTHWATCH INSTITUTE–Hawksbill Turtles of Barbados, Barbados
EARTHWATCH INSTITUTE–Hopi Ancestors, AZ
EARTHWATCH INSTITUTE–Icelandic and Alaskan Glaciers, Iceland
EARTHWATCH INSTITUTE–India's Sacred Groves, India
EARTHWATCH INSTITUTE–Inner Mongolia's Lost Water, China
EARTHWATCH INSTITUTE–Itjaritjari: the Outback's Mysterious Marsupial, Australia
EARTHWATCH INSTITUTE–Jackson Hole Bison Dig, WY
EARTHWATCH INSTITUTE–Jamaica's Coral Reefs, Jamaica
EARTHWATCH INSTITUTE–Kenya's Black Rhino, Kenya
EARTHWATCH INSTITUTE–Koala Ecology, Australia
EARTHWATCH INSTITUTE–Lakes of the Rift Valley, Kenya
EARTHWATCH INSTITUTE–Lions of Tsavo, Kenya
EARTHWATCH INSTITUTE–Maine's Island Ecology, ME
EARTHWATCH INSTITUTE–Malaysian Bat Conservation, Malaysia
EARTHWATCH INSTITUTE–Mallorca's Copper Age, Spain
EARTHWATCH INSTITUTE–Mammoth Cave, KY
EARTHWATCH INSTITUTE–Mammoth Graveyard, SD
EARTHWATCH INSTITUTE–Manatees in Belize, Belize
EARTHWATCH INSTITUTE–Mangroves of the Kenyan Coast, Kenya
EARTHWATCH INSTITUTE–Medicinal Plants of Vietnam, Vietnam
EARTHWATCH INSTITUTE–Meerkats of the Kalahari, South Africa
EARTHWATCH INSTITUTE–Mexican Mangroves and Wildlife, Mexico
EARTHWATCH INSTITUTE–Mexican Megafauna, Mexico
EARTHWATCH INSTITUTE–Mojave Desert Tortoises, CA
EARTHWATCH INSTITUTE–Mongolian Argali, Mongolia
EARTHWATCH INSTITUTE–Moose and Wolves, MI
EARTHWATCH INSTITUTE–Moundbuilders on the Mississippi, IL
EARTHWATCH INSTITUTE–Mountain Waters of Bohemia, Czech Republic
EARTHWATCH INSTITUTE–Namibian Black Rhinos, Namibia
EARTHWATCH INSTITUTE–Namibian Wildlife Survey, Namibia
EARTHWATCH INSTITUTE–New Zealand Dolphins, New Zealand
EARTHWATCH INSTITUTE–Orca, WA
EARTHWATCH INSTITUTE–Pine Marten of the Ancient Forest, Canada
EARTHWATCH INSTITUTE–Poland's Ancient Burials, Poland
EARTHWATCH INSTITUTE–Prehistoric Pueblos of the American Southwest, NM
EARTHWATCH INSTITUTE–Puerto Rico's Rainforest, Puerto Rico
EARTHWATCH INSTITUTE–Rainforest Caterpillars–Costa Rica, Costa Rica
EARTHWATCH INSTITUTE–Rare Plants of Kenya, Kenya
EARTHWATCH INSTITUTE–Restoring Costa Rica's Rainforest, Costa Rica
EARTHWATCH INSTITUTE–Restoring the Sagebrush Steppe, ID
EARTHWATCH INSTITUTE–Restoring Vietnam's Forests, Vietnam
EARTHWATCH INSTITUTE–Rivers of the Peruvian Amazon, Peru
EARTHWATCH INSTITUTE–Roman Fort on the Danube, Romania
EARTHWATCH INSTITUTE–Roman Fort on Tyne, United Kingdom
EARTHWATCH INSTITUTE–Saving the Leatherback Turtle, U.S. Virgin Islands
EARTHWATCH INSTITUTE–Sea Otters of Alaska, AK
EARTHWATCH INSTITUTE–Sea Turtles of Baja, Mexico
EARTHWATCH INSTITUTE–South African Penguins, South Africa
EARTHWATCH INSTITUTE–South African Wildlife, South Africa
EARTHWATCH INSTITUTE–Spanish Dolphins, Spain
EARTHWATCH INSTITUTE–Sri Lanka's Temple Monkeys, Sri Lanka
EARTHWATCH INSTITUTE–Triassic Park, Argentina
EARTHWATCH INSTITUTE–Trinidad's Leatherback Sea Turtles, Trinidad and Tobago
EARTHWATCH INSTITUTE–Wild Dolphin Societies, FL
EARTHWATCH INSTITUTE–Wildlife Conservation in West Africa, Ghana
EARTHWATCH INSTITUTE–Wildlife Trails of the American West, UT
EDUCO Summer Adventure Programs, CO
EKOCAMP International, Canada
Elk Creek Ranch and Trek Program, WY
Environmental Studies and Solutions, Norway
Environmental Studies Summer Youth Institute, NY
Excalibur, Canada
The Experiment in International Living–Argentina Homestay, Community Service, and Outdoor Ecological Program, Argentina
The Experiment in International Living–Australia Homestay, Australia
The Experiment in International Living–Belize Homestay, Belize
The Experiment in International Living–Botswana Homestay, Botswana
The Experiment in International Living–Brazil–Ecological Preservation, Brazil
The Experiment in International Living–Chile North Homestay, Community Service, Chile
The Experiment in International Living–Chile South Homestay, Chile
The Experiment in International Living–Costa Rica Homestay, Costa Rica
The Experiment in International Living–Ecuador Homestay, Ecuador
The Experiment in International Living–France, Biking and Homestay, France
The Experiment in International Living–France, Four-Week Homestay and Travel–Borders, France
The Experiment in International Living–France, Four–Week Homestay and Travel through Alps, France
The Experiment in International Living–Navajo Nation, NM
The Experiment in International Living–New Zealand Homestay, New Zealand
The Experiment in International Living–South Africa Homestay and Community Service, South Africa
The Experiment in International Living–Spain, Five-Week Homestay, Travel, Ecology, Spain
The Experiment in International Living–Spain, Four-Week Homestay and Trekking Program, Spain
The Experiment in International Living–Switzerland French Language Immersion, Homestay, and Alpine Adventure, Switzerland
The Experiment in International Living–Thailand Homestay, Thailand
ExploraMar: Marine Biology Sailing Expeditions–Sea of Cortez, Baja, Mexico
Farm and Wilderness Camps–Barn Day Camp, VT
Farm and Wilderness Camps–Flying Cloud, VT
Farm and Wilderness Camps–Indian Brook, VT
Farm and Wilderness Camps–Saltash Mountain, VT
Farm and Wilderness Camps–Tamarack Farm, VT
Farm and Wilderness Camps–Timberlake, VT
Fenn School Summer Day Camp, MA
The Fessenden School Summer ESL Program, MA
Flint Hill School–"Summer on the Hill"–A Biking Odyssey Day Camp, VA
Flint Hill School–"Summer on the Hill"–Boys Outdoor Adventures! Day Camp, VA
Flint Hill School–"Summer on the Hill"–Into the Woods Day Camp, VA
Flint Hill School–"Summer on the Hill"–Trips from the Hill–Ecological Study of Coral Reefs, Bahamas, Bahamas
Flint Hill School–"Summer on the Hill"–Trips from the Hill–Tanzania Safari, United Republic of Tanzania
Flying Moose Lodge, ME
Fort Union Civil War Camp, MN
Four Corners School of Outdoor Education: Southwest Ed-Venture
French Immersion Kayak Expedition, Canada
French Immersion Summer Camp, Canada
From the Forest to the Sea, AK
Future Leader Camp, VT
Geronimo Program
Girl Scouts of Mid-Continent–Camp Oakledge, MO
Great Escapes (Adventure Trips for Teens)–California Beach Escape, CA
Great Escapes (Adventure Trips for Teens)–Canadian Adventure
Great Escapes (Adventure Trips for Teens)–Canadian Canoe and Kayak Adventure, Canada
Great Escapes (Adventure Trips for Teens)–Cape Cod Sail Adventure, MA

Great Escapes (Adventure Trips for Teens)–Cape Cod Underwater Adventure, MA
Great Escapes (Adventure Trips for Teens)–Cape Escapes, MA
Great Escapes (Adventure Trips for Teens)–Colorado River and Canyons Adventure
Great Escapes (Adventure Trips for Teens)–Costa Rica Rainforest Adventure, Costa Rica
Great Escapes (Adventure Trips for Teens)–Maine Waterways, ME
Great Escapes (Adventure Trips for Teens)–Rock and Rapids
Great Escapes (Adventure Trips for Teens)–Rocky Mountain Horsepacking Adventure, CO
Great Escapes (Adventure Trips for Teens)–Saddle and Sail
Great Escapes (Adventure Trips for Teens)–White Mountain Adventure, NH
Greenbrier River Outdoor Adventures, Adventure Camp, WV
Greenbrier River Outdoor Adventures, Camp Snowshoe, WV
Greenbrier River Outdoor Adventures, Rock and River, WV
Greenbrier River Outdoor Adventures, Wilderness Explorer, WV
Green River Preserve, NC
Groundwater University, NE
Hancock Field Station, OR
Hante School, NC
Hargrave Summer Program, VA
Hawaii Extreme Adventure Scuba Camp, HI
Haycock Camping Ministries–Adventure Trails, PA
Haycock Camping Ministries–Battalion Program, PA
Haycock Camping Ministries–Stockade Program, PA
Haycock Camping Ministries–Trailbuilders Program, PA
Hidden Villa Summer Camp, CA
High Cascade Snowboard Camp Photography Workshop, OR
Hiker's Heaven Overnight Camp
Horizon Adventures Inc., CO
Hulbert Voyageurs Youth Wilderness Trips
Hyde School Summer Challenge Program Bath, ME, ME
Hyde School Summer Challenge Program–Woodstock, CT, CT
Ibike Cultural Tours–Ecuador, Ecuador
Ibike Cultural Tours–Guyana, Guyana
Ibike Cultural Tours–Washington/British Columbia
International Summer Camp Montana, Switzerland, Switzerland
Israel Discovery
JCC Houston: Gordon Campsite, TX
Julian Krinsky/Canyon Ranch Young Adult Summer Program " for Smarter Minds and Bodies", PA
Jumonville Adventure Camps, PA
Kayak Adventures Unlimited
Keewaydin Canoe Camp, Canada
Keewaydin Dunmore, VT
Keewaydin Temagami, Canada
Keystone Counselor Assistant Program, CO
Keystone Science Adventures, CO
Knowledge Exchange Institute–African Safari Program, Kenya
Kooch-I-Ching, MN
Kroka Expeditions–Advanced Rock Climbing
Kroka Expeditions–Adventures for Small People, VT
Kroka Expeditions–Cape Cod Triple Surfing Bonanza, MA
Kroka Expeditions–Coastal Sea Kayaking, ME
Kroka Expeditions–Coming of Age for Young Women, VT
Kroka Expeditions–Expedition Pre-Columbus, VT
Kroka Expeditions–Introduction to Adventure Day Camp, VT
Kroka Expeditions–Introduction to Adventure Residential Camp, VT
Kroka Expeditions–Introduction to Rock Climbing, VT
Kroka Expeditions–Introduction to White Water, VT
Kroka Expeditions–Paddlers Journey Up North
Kroka Expeditions–Rock 'n Road, VT
Kroka Expeditions–Vermont Underground Trail, VT
Kroka Expeditions–Wild Arts and Canoe Adventure, VT
Kroka Expeditions–Wild World of White Water, VT
Ladakh Summer Passage, India
Landmark Volunteers: Arizona, AZ
Landmark Volunteers: California, CA
Landmark Volunteers: Colorado, CO
Landmark Volunteers: Connecticut, CT
Landmark Volunteers: Idaho, ID
Landmark Volunteers: Maine, ME
Landmark Volunteers: Massachusetts, MA
Landmark Volunteers: Michigan, MI
Landmark Volunteers: Minnesota, MN
Landmark Volunteers: Montana, MT
Landmark Volunteers: New Hampshire, NH
Landmark Volunteers: New Mexico, NM
Landmark Volunteers: New York, NY
Landmark Volunteers: North Carolina, NC
Landmark Volunteers: Ohio, OH
Landmark Volunteers: Vermont, VT
Landmark Volunteers: Virginia, VA
Landmark Volunteers: Washington, WA
Landmark Volunteers: Wyoming, WY
Langskib Wilderness Programs, Canada
Leadership Adventure in Boston, MA
Learn English and Discover Canada, Canada
Les Elfes–International Summer/Winter Camp, Switzerland
Lifeschool Wilderness Adventures–Summer Adventures, CA
LIFEWORKS with the Australian Red Cross, Australia
LIFEWORKS with the British Virgin Islands Marine Parks and Conservation Department, British Virgin Islands
LIFEWORKS with the Galapagos Islands' National Parks, Ecuador
Ligonier Camp, PA
Longacre Expeditions, Adventure 28
Longacre Expeditions, Alaska, AK
Longacre Expeditions, Belize, Belize
Longacre Expeditions, Blue Ridge, PA
Longacre Expeditions, British Columbia
Longacre Expeditions, British Isles, United Kingdom
Longacre Expeditions, Downeast, ME
Longacre Expeditions, Hawaii, HI
Longacre Expeditions, Iceland, Iceland
Longacre Expeditions, Laurel Highlands, PA
Longacre Expeditions, Leadership Training, CO
Longacre Expeditions, New England/Canada
Longacre Expeditions, Pacific Coast and Inlands
Longacre Expeditions, Peak to Peak, OR
Longacre Expeditions, Photography, ME
Longacre Expeditions, Surf Oregon, OR
Longacre Expeditions, Virgin Islands
Longacre Expeditions, Volcanoes
Longacre Expeditions, Western Challenge
Longacre Expeditions, Whales, ME
Longacre Expeditions, Wind and Waves, OR
Longacre Leadership Program, PA
Lower Mustang Summer Passage, Nepal
LSA Argelés-Gazost, France, France
LSA Lignano, Italy–Active Junior Italian Summer Program, Italy
LSA Marbella, Spain, Spain
LSA Treviso, Italy, Italy
Luna Adventures with AAG SummerSkills
Mad River Glen Naturalist Adventure Camp, VT
Maine Conservation School Summer Camps, ME
Maine Wilderness Adventure Trip, ME
Marine and Environmental Science Program, Canada
Marine Military Academy Summer Military Training Camp, TX
Maritime Camp, NJ
The Marsh, MD
Maui Surfer Girls, HI
Medeba Leader in Training Program, Canada
Medeba Summer Camp, Canada
Mercersburg Academy Young Writer's Camp, PA
Michigan Technological University Summer Youth Program, MI
Mountain Meadow Ranch, CA
Mountain Retreat Overnight Camp, CA
Mountain Workshop–Graduate Plus Awesome Adventures, NY
Mountain Workshop–Awesome 5: North Woods of Maine, ME
Mountain Workshop–Awesome 4: Pennsylvania, PA
Mountain Workshop–Awesome 1: Adirondacks, NY
Mountain Workshop–Awesome 6: Quebec, Canada
Mountain Workshop–Awesome 3: Maine Coast, ME
Mountain Workshop–Awesome 2: Vermont, VT
Mountain Workshop–Bike 1: Martha's Vineyard and Nantucket, MA
Mountain Workshop–Bike Touring Days 1, CT
Mountain Workshop–Bike 2, MA
Mountain Workshop/Dirt Camp: Dirt Camp Junior Killington
Mountain Workshop/Dirt Camp–Mountain Bike Days 1, CT
Mountain Workshop/Dirt Camp–Mountain Bike Days 3, CT
Mountain Workshop/Dirt Camp–Mountain Bike Days 2, CT
Mountain Workshop–Graduate Awesome Adventures, CT
Mountain Workshop–Junior Awesome Adventures, CT
Mountain Workshop–Leadership Through Adventure: Adirondacks, NY

▶ Outdoor Programs

Mountain Workshop–Original Awesome Adventures, CT
Mountain Workshop–Trailblazer Awesome Adventures, CT
Musiker Tours: Action USA
Musiker Tours: America Coast to Coast
Musiker Tours: Cali-Pacific Passport
Musiker Tours: ComboCamp America
Musiker Tours: Discover America
Musiker Tours: Eastcoaster
Musiker Tours: Westcoaster
Nantahala Outdoor Center–Kids Adventure Sports Camp, NC
Nantahala Outdoor Center–Kids Kayaking Courses, NC
NAWA Academy–Girls on the Go, CA
NAWA Academy–Great Challenge, CA
NAWA Academy–Lassen Expedition, CA
NAWA Academy–Trinity Challenge, CA
New England Camping Adventures, ME
Next Level Camp, PA
92nd Street Y Camps–Camp Tevah for Science and Nature, NY
North Carolina Outward Bound–Outer Banks, NC
North Carolina Outward Bound–Southern Appalachian Mountains, NC
Northern Lights, Canada
Northwaters Wilderness Programs, Canada
North Woods Camp for Boys, NH
Oak Creek Ranch Summer School, AZ
Oak Ridge Summer Leadership Camp, NC
ODYSSEY EXPEDITIONS: Tropical Marine Biology Voyages–British Virgin Islands, British Virgin Islands
ODYSSEY EXPEDITIONS: Tropical Marine Biology Voyages–Caribbean Islands
OES–Summer Adventure Camp, OR
On the Wing, CO
Organic Farm Camp, CO
Outdoor Adventure, WA
Outpost Wilderness Adventure–Adventure Skills, CO
Outpost Wilderness Adventure–Alpine Rock and Ice, CO
Outpost Wilderness Adventure–Copper Canyon Project, Mexico
Outpost Wilderness Adventure–Mountain Bike/Rock Camp, CO
Outpost Wilderness Adventure–Wind River Expedition, WY
Outward Bound–Connecting with Courage, MA
Outward Bound–Environmental Expeditions, MA
Outward Bound–Passages, MA
Outward Bound West–Backpacking and Whitewater Rafting, Oregon, OR
Outward Bound West–Backpacking, Climbing, and Rafting–Boys, CO
Outward Bound West–Backpacking, Climbing, and Rafting–Colorado, CO
Outward Bound West–Cataract Canyon Rafting
Outward Bound West–Climbing and Backpacking–High Sierra, CA, CA
Outward Bound West–Climbing, Backpacking, and Canoeing–North Cascades, WA, WA
Outward Bound West–Colorado Rockies Lightweight Backpacking, CO
Outward Bound West–Mountaineering and Rafting, Oregon, OR
Outward Bound West–Mountaineering–Colorado, CO
Outward Bound West–Mountaineering–North Cascades, WA, WA
Outward Bound West–Mountaineering, Rafting, and Climbing-XT, Oregon, OR
Outward Bound West–Sea Kayaking and Mountaineering–Alaska, AK
Outward Bound West–Sea Kayaking, Backpacking, and Mountaineering–Washington, WA
Outward Bound West–Service Course–North Cascades, WA
Outward Bound West–Sierra Nevada Mountaineering, CA
Outward Bound West–Southwest Mountaineering, Rafting, and Canyoneering, UT
Outward Bound West–Southwest Mystery Expedition, UT
Outward Bound West–Utah Summer Semester, UT
Outward Bound West–Volcanoes Mountaineering–Oregon, OR
Outward Bound West–Wyoming Rock Climbing, WY
Overland: Acadia and Prince Edward Island Bicycle Touring and Sea-Kayaking
Overland: Adventure Camp for 5th and 6th Grade Boys, MA
Overland: Adventure Camp for 5th and 6th Grade Girls, MA
Overland: Alaskan Expedition Hiking, Sea-Kayaking, and Rafting, AK
Overland: American Challenge Coast-to-Coast Bicycle Touring
Overland: Appalachian Trail Challenge Hiking
Overland: Blue Ridge Explorer Hiking, Rafting and Kayaking, NC
Overland: Cape Cod and the Islands Bicycle Touring, MA
Overland: Colorado and Utah Mountain Biking and Rafting
Overland: Costa Rica Explorer Hiking, Rafting, and Sea-Kayaking, Costa Rica
Overland: European Challenge Bicycle Touring from Paris to Rome
Overland: European Explorer Hiking, Rafting, and Sea Kayaking
Overland: Hawaii Explorer Hiking, Kayaking, Sailing and Snorkeling, HI
Overland: New England Explorer Hiking, Mountain Biking, and Rafting
Overland: Pacific Coast Bicycle Touring and Rafting
Overland: Paris to the Sea Bicycle Touring, France
Overland: Rocky Mountain Explorer Hiking, Mountain Biking, and Rafting
Overland: Shasta & the Sierras Backpacking, Climbing and Rafting
Overland: Teton Challenge Hiking, Climbing and Kayaking, WY
Overland: The Alpine Challenge Leadership Course Backpacking and Hiking
Overland: Vermont & Montreal Bicycle Touring
Overland: Yellowstone Explorer Backpacking, Rock Climbing, and Rafting
Pacific Marine Science Camp, OR
PAX Abroad–Ecuador Rainforest Adventure, Ecuador
Pine Island Camp, ME
Ponkapoag Outdoor Center Day Camps, MA
Poulter Colorado Camps, CO
Poulter Colorado Camps: Adventures Planet Earth–Austria
Poulter Colorado Camps: Adventures Planet Earth–Costa Rica, Costa Rica
Poulter Colorado Camps: Adventures Planet Earth–New Zealand, New Zealand
Poulter Colorado Camps: Adventures Planet Earth–Spain, Spain
Presbyterian Clearwater Forest, MN
Program of Audubon Research for Teens (Take P.A.R.T.), VT
Putney Student Travel–Community Service–Alaska, AK
Putney Student Travel–Community Service–Montana, MT
The Ranch–Lake Placid Academy, NY
The Ranch–Lake Placid Teen Travel Camp
Rawhide Ranch, CA
Redwood National Park Camps, CA
Rein Teen Tours–American Adventure
Rein Teen Tours–California Caper
Rein Teen Tours–Crossroads
Rein Teen Tours–Eastern Adventure
Rein Teen Tours–Grand Adventure
Rein Teen Tours–Hawaiian/Alaskan Adventure
Rein Teen Tours–Western Adventure
Riverside Military Academy High Adventure Camp, GA
RUSTIC PATHWAYS–COSTA RICA NATURAL WONDERS, Costa Rica
RUSTIC PATHWAYS–DIVER'S DREAM IN THE FIJI ISLANDS, Fiji
RUSTIC PATHWAYS–LEARN TO DIVE IN THE FIJI ISLANDS, Fiji
RUSTIC PATHWAYS–THE TURTLE CONSERVATION PROJECT, Costa Rica
RUSTIC PATHWAYS–VOLCANOES AND RAINFORESTS, Costa Rica
Sail Caribbean–All Levels of Scuba Certification with Sailing, British Virgin Islands
Sail Caribbean–British Virgin Islands, British Virgin Islands
Sail Caribbean–Community Service, British Virgin Islands
Sail Caribbean–Leeward Islands
Sail Caribbean–Marine Biology, British Virgin Islands
Sailing Program at NE Camping Adventures, ME
Salmon Camp for Native Americans, OR
Salmon Camp Research Team for Native Americans–Oregon, OR
Salmon Camp Research Team for Native Americans–Redwoods, CA
Salmon Camp Research Team for Native Americans–San Juan Island, WA
Sanborn Western Camps: Big Spring Ranch for Boys, CO
Sanborn Western Camps: High Trails Ranch for Girls, CO
Sandy Island Camp for Families, NH
San Juan Island Camps, WA
Sargent Center Adventure Camp, NH
Scuba Adventures at Pali Overnight Adventures, CA
Sea Camp, TX
Seacamp, FL
SEACAMP San Diego, CA
Sea Kayak Expedition (English), Canada

▶ Outdoor Programs

Trailmark Outdoor Adventures–New England–Acadia
Trailmark Outdoor Adventures–New England–Camden
Trailmark Outdoor Adventures–New England–Downeast
Trailmark Outdoor Adventures–New England–Jr. Acadia
Trailmark Outdoor Adventures–New England–Mahoosoc
Trailmark Outdoor Adventures–New England–Moose River
Trailmark Outdoor Adventures–New England–Mt. Desert
Trailmark Outdoor Adventures–New England–Rangeley Coed
Trailmark Outdoor Adventures–Northern Rockies–Tetons with Backpack
Trailmark Outdoor Adventures–Northern Rockies–Tetons with Horseback
Traveling Players Ensemble Camp, MD
University of Chicago–Stones and Bones, WY
Valley Forge Military Academy Summer Camp for Boys, PA
Valley Forge Military Academy Summer Coed Day Camp, PA
Valley View Ranch Equestrian Camp, GA
Village Camps–France, France
Visions–Alaska, AK
Visions–Australia, Australia
Visions–British Virgin Islands, British Virgin Islands
Visions–Dominica, Dominica
Visions–Dominican Republic, Dominican Republic
Visions–Guadeloupe, Guadeloupe
Visions–Montana, MT
Visions–Peru, Peru
Visions–South Carolina, SC
Visions–Trinidad, Trinidad and Tobago
Voyageur Outward Bound–Boundary Waters Wilderness Canoeing, MN
Voyageur Outward Bound–Boundary Waters Wilderness Canoeing and Climbing XT, MN
Voyageur Outward Bound–Greater Yellowstone Whitewater and Backpacking, MT
Voyageur Outward Bound–Lake Superior Freshwater Kayaking, Canada
Voyageur Outward Bound–Lake Superior Freshwater Kayaking and Backpacking
Voyageur Outward Bound–Lewis and Clark Alpine Backpacking, MT
Voyageur Outward Bound–Lewis and Clark Alpine Backpacking-Girls, MT
Voyageur Outward Bound–Manitoba to Montana Summer Semester
Voyageur Outward Bound–Montana High Alpine Backpacking, MT
Voyageur Outward Bound–Montana Rock Climbing XT, MT
Voyageur Outward Bound–Northern Rockies Backpacking Family Adventure, MT
Voyageur Outward Bound–Northwoods Wilderness Canoeing and Backpacking, MN
WEI Leadership Training, CO
Weissman Teen Tours–"Aloha–Welcome to Hawaiian Paradise"
Weissman Teen Tours–European Experience
Weissman Teen Tours–U.S. and Western Canada, 4 Weeks
Weissman Teen Tours–U.S. and Western Canada, 6 Weeks
Westcoast Connection–American Voyageur
Westcoast Connection–Australian Outback Plus Hawaii
Westcoast Connection–Californian Extravaganza
Westcoast Connection/On Tour– Australian Outback, Australia
Westcoast Connection Travel/On Tour–Northwestern Odyssey
Westcoast Connection Travel–Adventure California, CA
Westcoast Connection Travel–California and the Canyons
Westcoast Connection Travel–Canadian Mountain Magic
Westcoast Connection Travel–Eastcoast Encounter
Westcoast Connection Travel–Great West Challenge
Westcoast Connection Travel–Northwestern Odyssey
Westcoast Connection Travel/On Tour–Canadian Adventure
Westcoast Connection Travel–Quebec Adventure, Canada
Westcoast Connection Travel–Southwesterner
Westcoast Connection Travel–Western Canadian Adventure, Canada
Westcoast Connection–U.S. Explorer
The Whale Camp–Youth Programs, Canada
Where There Be Dragons: China, China
Where There Be Dragons: Guatemala, Guatemala
Where There Be Dragons: India Culture and Philosophy, India
Where There Be Dragons: India Zanskar Trek, India
Where There Be Dragons: Mexico, Mexico
Where There Be Dragons: Mongolia, Mongolia
Where There Be Dragons: Peru, Peru
Where There Be Dragons: Silk Road, China
Where There Be Dragons: Thailand, Thailand
Where There Be Dragons: Tibet, China
Where There Be Dragons: Vietnam, Vietnam
White Water Learning Center of Georgia Kids Kayaking Summer Day Camp, GA
Wilderness Adventure, CO
Wilderness Adventure at Eagle Landing, VA
Wilderness Experiences Unlimited–Explorers Camp, MA
Wilderness Experiences Unlimited–Leaders In Training Camp, MA
Wilderness Experiences Unlimited–Pathfinders Day Camp, MA
Wilderness Experiences Unlimited–Trailblazers Camp, MA
Wilderness Experiences Unlimited/Westfield Water Sports: Scuba Camp, MA
Wilderness Ventures–Alaska Leadership, AK
Wilderness Ventures–Alaska Service, AK
Wilderness Ventures–Alaska Southcentral, AK
Wilderness Ventures–Alaska Southeast, AK
Wilderness Ventures–Australia, Australia
Wilderness Ventures–California, CA
Wilderness Ventures–Cascade-Olympic, WA
Wilderness Ventures–Colorado/Utah Mountain Bike
Wilderness Ventures–Costa Rica, Costa Rica
Wilderness Ventures–Ecuador and Galapagos, Ecuador
Wilderness Ventures–European Alps
Wilderness Ventures–Grand Teton, WY
Wilderness Ventures–Great Divide
Wilderness Ventures–Great Divide Bike
Wilderness Ventures–Hawaii, HI
Wilderness Ventures–High Sierra, CA
Wilderness Ventures–Jackson Hole, WY
Wilderness Ventures–Northwest
Wilderness Ventures–Oregon, OR
Wilderness Ventures–Pacific Coast Bike
Wilderness Ventures–Pacific Northwest
Wilderness Ventures–Puget Sound, WA
Wilderness Ventures–Rocky Mountain
Wilderness Ventures–Spanish Pyrenees, Spain
Wilderness Ventures–Teton Adventure, WY
Wilderness Ventures–Washington Alpine, WA
Wilderness Ventures–Washington Mountaineering, WA
Wilderness Ventures–Wyoming Mountaineering, WY
Wilderness Ventures–Yellowstone Fly Fishing
Wildlife Camp, CO
Williwaw Adventures–Maine Mountains and Coast, ME
Williwaw Adventures–Maine Wilderness
Williwaw Adventures–Pacific Northwest Expedition
Windsor Mountain: Alaska, AK
Windsor Mountain: Bonjour Quebec, Canada
Windsor Mountain: California Community Service, CA
Windsor Mountain: Coast of Australia, Australia
Windsor Mountain: Crossroads France, France
Windsor Mountain: Driftwood Stables Ranch Camp, NH
Windsor Mountain: Experiential Summer School
Windsor Mountain: Hawaii, HI
Windsor Mountain: New England Adventure
Windsor Mountain: Random Acts of Kindness
Windsor Mountain: Voices of the Wind River, Wyoming, WY
Wolfeboro: The Summer Boarding School, NH
World Horizons International–Iceland, Iceland
World Horizons International–Kanab, Utah, UT
World Horizons International–Mexico, Mexico
World Horizons International–Puerto Rico, Puerto Rico
YMCA Camp Abnaki, VT
YMCA Camp Abnaki–Counselor-in-Training Program, VT
YMCA Camp Abnaki–Teen Adventure Trips, VT
YMCA Camp Lincoln–Outdoor Adventure Camp: Backpacking, NH
YMCA Camp Lincoln–Outdoor Adventure Camp: Canadian Adventure, Canada
YMCA Camp Lincoln–Outdoor Adventure Camp: Everything Outdoors, NH
YMCA Camp Lincoln–Outdoor Adventure Camp: Mountain Bike, NH
YMCA Camp Lincoln–Outdoor Adventure Camp: River Runners, NH
YMCA Camp Lincoln–Specialty Camps: Horse Camp, NH
YMCA Camp Minikani, WI
YMCA Camp Oakes Rangers, CA
YMCA Camp Oakes Teen Leadership, CA
YMCA Camp Widjiwagan, MN
Yosemite Backpacking Adventures, CA
Youth Forest Camps, OR

Special Needs Programs

Ability First–Camp Joan Mier, CA
Ability First–Camp Paivika, CA
Barton Adventure Camp
Barton Day Camp–Long Island, NY
Barton Day Camp–New York, NY
Barton Day Camp–Worcester, MA
Camp Aldersgate–Kota Camp, AR
Camp Aldersgate–Med Camps, AR
Camp Aldersgate–Respite Care, AR
Camp Allen, NH
Camp Bon Coeur, LA
Camp Brandon for Boys, NH
Camp Buckskin, MN
Camp Courageous of Iowa, IA
Camp Echoing Hills, OH
Camp Fowler, MI
Camp Friendship, MN
Camp Heartland Summer Camp–California, CA
Camp Heartland Summer Camp–Minnesota, MN
Camp Holiday Trails, VA
Camp Jordan for Children with Diabetes, VA
Camp Kingsmont, MA
Camp Kodiak, Canada
Camp Kostopulos, UT
Camp La Jolla, CA
Camp Lee Mar, PA
Camp O'Bannon, OH
Camp Sky Ranch, Inc., NC
Camp Starfish, NH
Camp Superkids–Camp Crosley, IN
Camp Superkids–Happy Hollow Children's Camp, IN
Carroll Center for the Blind–Computing for College: Computer and Communication Skills, MA
Carroll Center for the Blind–Real World Work Experience, MA
Carroll Center for the Blind–Youth in Transition, MA
Clara Barton Camp, MA
Clara Barton Family Camp, MA
Double "H" Hole in the Woods Ranch Summer Camp, NY
Dunnabeck at Kildonan, NY
Eden Wood Camp, MN
Girl Scouts of Mid-Continent–Juliette Low Camp, MO
Hamilton Learning Centre Summer Fun in the Sun Camp, Canada
Hamilton Learning Centre Summer School, Canada
Jewish Community Center Day Camp, NJ
Jumonville Discovery Camp, PA
Landmark School Summer Academic Program, MA
Linden Hill Summer Program, MA
Lions Camp Merrick Deaf/HOH/KODA Program, MD
Lions Camp Merrick Diabetes Program, MD
Little Keswick School Summer Session, VA
Maplebrook School's Summer Program, NY
Marbridge Summer Camp, TX
Meadowood Springs Speech and Hearing Camp, OR
Missouri Children's Burn Camp, MO
The Monarch School Summer Camp, TX
The Monarch School Summer Course, TX
Newgrange Summer Program, NJ
Newgrange Summer Tutoring Program, NJ
New Jersey YMHA–YWHA Round Lake Camp, PA
New Strides Day Camp, Canada
92nd Street Y Camps–Camp Bari Tov, NY
92nd Street Y Camps–Camp Tova, NY
Pine Ridge Summer Program, VT
Rainbow Club–Greenwich, Connecticut, CT
Rocky Mountain Village, CO
Shane (Trim-Down) Camp, NY
South Shore YMCA Specialty Camp, MA
Squirrel Hollow Learning Camp, GA
Star Ranch Summer Camp, TX
Success Oriented Achievement Realized (SOAR)–North Carolina, NC
Success Oriented Achievement Realized (SOAR)–Wyoming, WY
Summit Camp, PA
Summit Travel Program
Talisman–Academics, NC
Talisman–INSIGHT, NC
Talisman Mini-Camp, NC
Talisman Open Boat Adventures (TOBA), NC
Talisman–SIGHT, NC
Talisman Summer Camp, NC
Talisman–Trek Hiking Program, NC
Talisman–Tri-Adventures, NC
University of Kansas–Sertoma-Schiefelbush Communication Camp, KS
Ventures Travel Service–Arizona, AZ
Ventures Travel Service–California, CA
Ventures Travel Service–Florida, FL
Ventures Travel Service–Iowa, IA
Ventures Travel Service–Kentucky, KY
Ventures Travel Service–Minnesota, MN
Ventures Travel Service–Missouri, MO
Ventures Travel Service–New York, NY
Ventures Travel Service–North Dakota, ND
Ventures Travel Service–Oregon, OR
Ventures Travel Service–South Carolina, SC
Ventures Travel Service–South Dakota, SD
Ventures Travel Service–Tennessee, TN
Ventures Travel Service–Texas, TX
Ventures Travel Service–Washington, WA
Ventures Travel Service–Wisconsin, WI
Wediko Summer Program, NH
YMCA Wanakita Summer Resident and Day Camp, Canada

Sports Camps

AAC–Aloha Adventure Surf Camp, HI
Alex Brown and Dustin Lyman Football Camp/Sports International, IL
American Allstar Dance Camp, AL
Andy McCollum Football Camp, IL
Antwaan Randle Football Camp/Sports International, PA
Art Monk Football Camp/Sports International–Maryland, MD
Art Monk Football Camp/Sports International–Virginia, VA
Big Island Volleyball Elite Camp, HI
Big Island Volleyball Player Camp, HI
Bill Self Kansas Summer Basketball Camp, KS
Black River Farm and Ranch, MI
Bonnie Castle Riding Camp, MA
Brad Hoover and Will Witherspoon Football Camp/Sports International, NC
Britannia Soccer Camp, CA
Cage Scope/High Potential "Blue-Chip" Basketball Camp, KY
Camp AK-O-MAK, Canada
Camp All-Star, ME
Camp Berachah Ministries–Soccer Camp, WA
Camp Carysbrook Equestrian, VA
Camp Greenkill–Gymnastics, NY
Camp Greenkill–Judo, NY
Camp Greenkill–Volleyball, NY
Camp Hillside Soccer Program, MA
Camp Lincoln Fishing Camp, MN
Camp Lincoln for Boys/Camp Lake Hubert for Girls Golf Camp, MN
Camp Lincoln for Boys/Camp Lake Hubert for Girls Tennis Camp, MN
Camp Olympia Junior Golf Academy, TX
Camp Pacific's Surf and Bodyboard Camp, CA
Camp Rim Rock–Horseback Riding Camp, WV
Camp Rim Rock–Tennis Camp, WV
Camp Skyline–Equestrian Program, AL
Carmel Valley Tennis Camp, CA
Cedar Lodge, MI
Center for Cultural Interchange–Spain Sports and Language Camp, Spain
Community Sailing of Colorado–Advanced Sailing, CO
Community Sailing of Colorado–Learn to Sail, CO
Community Sailing of Colorado–Sailboat Racing Camp, CO
Craftsbury Running Camps, VT
Craftsbury Sculling Camps, VT
Crossroads School–Aquatics, CA
Crossroads School– Basketball Camps, CA
Crossroads School–Soccer Camps, CA
Culver Summer Camps/Culver Specialty Camp–Equestrian Arts, IN
Culver Summer Camps/Culver Specialty Camp–Fencing, IN
Culver Summer Camps/Culver Specialty Camp–Golf, IN
Culver Summer Camps/Culver Specialty Camp–Ice Hockey, IN
Culver Summer Camps/Culver Specialty Camp–Sailing, IN
Culver Summer Camps/Culver Specialty Camp–Scuba, IN
Culver Summer Camps/Culver Specialty Camp–Soccer, IN
Culver Summer Camps/Culver Specialty Camp–Tennis, IN
Culver Summer Camps/Culver Specialty Camp–Water Ski, IN
Damon Huard and Matt Light Football Camp/Sports International, RI
Dance Magic, AL
Davidson Academy–Sports Camps, TN
Deuce McCallister Football Camp, LA
Dhani Jones Football Camp/Sports International, PA
Dwight-Englewood Summer Sports Clinics, NJ
Episcopal High School Sports Camp, FL
Falcon Horse Lover Camp, OH
Falcon Horse Lover Camp for Girls, OH
Flint Hill School–"Summer on the Hill"–Enrichment on the Hill–Summer Chess Camp, VA
Flint Hill School–"Summer on the Hill"–Sports on the Hill–Coed, VA
Flint Hill School–"Summer on the Hill"–Sports on the Hill for Boys, VA
Flint Hill School–"Summer on the Hill"–Sports on the Hill for Girls, VA
4 Star College Prep Tennis at the University of Virginia, VA

▶ Sports Camps

4 Star Golf Camp at the University of Virginia, VA
4 Star Golf Plus All Sports Camp at the University of Virginia, VA
4 Star Tennis Camp at the University of Virginia, VA
4 Star Tennis Plus Camp at the University of Virginia, VA
4 Star Tennis Plus Golf Camp at the University of Virginia, VA
FUN-damental Basketball Camp–Morrisville, New York, NY
FUN-damental Basketball Camp–The Sports Mall, FL
GIC Arg–Soccer, Argentina
Global Teen–Italian and Soccer in Rome, Italy
Global Teen Summer Sports Camp in Berlin, Germany
GLS Sports and Language Camp Inzell, Germany
Gordon Kent's New England Tennis Camp, NY
Gymnastics Academy at Pali Overnight Adventures, CA
Hargrave Summer Program, VA
High Cascade Snowboard Camp, OR
Hockey Opportunity Camp, Canada
The Hun School of Princeton Boys' Basketball Camp, NJ
The Hun School of Princeton Girls' Basketball Camp, NJ
International Junior Golf Academy, SC
International Riding Camp, NY
James Thrash and Hollis Thomas Football Camp/Sports International, PA
Jay Novacek Football Camp/Sports International, TX
JCC Houston: Gymnastics Camp, TX
JCC Houston: Sports Camp, TX
JCC Houston: Tennis Camp, TX
Joe Krivak Quarterback Camp, Maryland/ Sports International, MD
Joe Krivak Quarterback Camp, North Carolina/Sports International, NC
Joe Krivak Quarterback Camp, Pennsylvania/ Sports International, PA
Joe Krivak Quarterback Camp, Rhode Island/Sports International, RI
Joel Ross Tennis & Sports Camp, CT
Joe Machnik's No. 1 Academy One and Premier Programs–Aston, Pennsylvania, PA
Joe Machnik's No. 1 Academy One and Premier Programs–Brooklyn, Michigan, MI
Joe Machnik's No. 1 Academy One and Premier Programs–Claremont, California, CA
Joe Machnik's No. 1 Academy One and Premier Programs–Colorado Springs, Colorado, CO
Joe Machnik's No. 1 Academy One and Premier Programs–Columbus, Ohio, OH
Joe Machnik's No. 1 Academy One and Premier Programs–Dyke, Virginia, VA
Joe Machnik's No. 1 Academy One and Premier Programs–Fort Worth, Texas, TX
Joe Machnik's No. 1 Academy One and Premier Programs–Kenosha, Wisconsin, WI
Joe Machnik's No. 1 Academy One and Premier Programs–Newtown, Pennsylvania, PA
Joe Machnik's No. 1 Academy One and Premier Programs–Olympia, Washington, WA
Joe Machnik's No. 1 Academy One and Premier Programs–Rohnert Park, California, CA
Joe Machnik's No. 1 Academy One and Premier Programs–Rome, Georgia, GA
Joe Machnik's No. 1 Academy One and Premier Programs–Vero Beach, Florida, FL
Joe Machnik's No. 1 Academy One and Premier Programs–Windsor, Connecticut, CT
Joe Machnik's No. 1 College Prep Academy–Colorado Springs, Colorado, CO
Joe Machnik's No. 1 College Prep Academy–Fort Worth, Texas, TX
Joe Machnik's No. 1 College Prep Academy–Kenosha, Wisconsin, WI
Joe Machnik's No. 1 College Prep Academy–Newtown/Aston, Pennsylvania, PA
Joe Machnik's No. 1 College Prep Academy–Windsor, Connecticut, CT
Joe Machnik's No. 1 Mighty Mini, Goalkeeper and Striker Camp–Aston, Pennsylvania, PA
Joe Machnik's No. 1 Mighty Mini, Goalkeeper and Striker Camp–Brooklyn, Michigan, MI
Joe Machnik's No. 1 Mighty Mini, Goalkeeper and Striker Camp–Claremont, California, CA
Joe Machnik's No. 1 Mighty Mini, Goalkeeper and Striker Camp–Colorado Springs, Colorado, CO
Joe Machnik's No. 1 Mighty Mini, Goalkeeper and Striker Camp–Columbus, Ohio, OH
Joe Machnik's No. 1 Mighty Mini, Goalkeeper and Striker Camp–Dyke, Virginia, VA
Joe Machnik's No. 1 Mighty Mini, Goalkeeper and Striker Camp–Newtown, Pennsylvania, PA
Joe Machnik's No. 1 Mighty Mini, Goalkeeper and Striker Camp–Olympia, Washington, WA
Joe Machnik's No. 1 Mighty Mini, Goalkeeper and Striker Camp–Rohnert Park, California, CA
Joe Machnik's No. 1 Mighty Mini, Goalkeeper and Striker Camp–Rome, Georgia, GA
Joe Machnik's No. 1 Mighty Mini, Goalkeeper and Striker Camp–Vero Beach, Florida, FL
Joe Machnik's No. 1 Mighty Mini, Goalkeeper and Striker Camp–Windsor, Connecticut, CT
Joe Machnik's No. 1 Mighty Mini, Goalkeeper and Striker Camp–Fort Worth, Texas, TX
Joe Machnik's No. 1 Mighty Mini, Goalkeeper and Striker Camp–Kenosha, Wisconsin, WI
The John Cooper School Recreational Activities and Sports, TX
Julian Krinsky California Teen Tours, CA
Julian Krinsky/Canyon Ranch Young Adult Summer Program " for Smarter Minds and Bodies", PA
Julian Krinsky Golf Camp at Cabrini College, PA
Julian Krinsky Golf Camp at Haverford College, PA
Julian Krinsky Golf Tours
Julian Krinsky Super Sports Camp at The Shipley School, PA
Julian Krinsky Tennis Camp at Cabrini College, PA
Julian Krinsky Tennis Camp at Haverford College, PA
Julian Krinsky Yesh Shabbat Summer Camp, PA
Jumonville Baseball/Softball Camp, PA
Jumonville Basketball Camp, PA
Jumonville Golf Camp, PA
Jumonville Soccer Camp, PA
Jumonville Spirit and Sport Spectacular–Soccer Camp, PA
Jumonville Spirit and Sport Spectacular–Swim Camp, PA
Jumonville Spirit and Sport Spectacular–Tennis Camp, PA
Jumonville Spirit and Sport Spectacular–Volleyball Camp, PA
Jumonville Sports Camp, PA
Keenan McCardell and Jimmy Smith Football Camp/Sports International, FL
Keenan McCardell Football Camp, FL
Lady Wildcat Basketball Camp, LA
Lenny Armuth Soccer Academy, NJ
Loras All-Sports Camp, IA
Maine Golf Academy–Family Camp, ME
Maine Golf Academy–Junior Golf Camp, ME
Maine Golf and Tennis Academy–Serve and Turf, ME
Maine Tennis Academy–Junior Tennis Camp, ME
Maui Surfer Girls, HI
Maui Surfer Girls–Advanced Surf Camp on Kauai, HI
Maui Surfer Girls–Mother/Daughter, HI
McCallie Sports Camp, TN
McCallie Lacrosse Camp, TN
Mercersburg Academy Blue Storm Boys Basketball School, PA
Mercersburg Academy Blue Storm Football Camp, PA
Mercersburg All-American Wrestling Camp & Junior All-American Wrestling Camp, PA
Miami University Summer Sports School, OH
MIMC–Music and Sports Camp, Canada
Miss Porter's School Athletic Experience, CT
Montgomery Bell Academy–All-Sports Camps, TN
Montgomery Bell Academy–Specialty Sports Camps, TN
Montgomery College WDCE–FIT Summer Camp, MD
National Cheerleaders Association Cheerleader Camps, AL
NBC Camps–Basketball–Adult & Child Hoops–Spokane, WA, WA
NBC Camps–Basketball–Crowell's Intensity–Spokane, WA, WA
NBC Camps–Basketball Individual Training–Alaska, AK
NBC Camps–Basketball Individual Training (Boys)–Auburn, WA, WA
NBC Camps–Basketball Individual Training–CA, CA
NBC Camps–Basketball Individual Training (Girls)–Auburn, WA, WA
NBC Camps–Basketball Individual Training–La Grande, OR, OR
NBC Camps–Basketball Individual Training–Montana, MT
NBC Camps–Basketball Individual Training–Newberg, OR, OR

NBC Camps–Basketball Individual Training–Olds, AB Canada, Canada
NBC Camps–Basketball Individual Training–Spangle, WA, WA
NBC Camps–Basketball Individual Training–Spokane, WA, WA
NBC Camps–Basketball Individual Training–Three Hills, AB Canada, Canada
NBC Camps–Basketball Point Guard Play–Spangle, WA, WA
NBC Camps–Basketball Post & Shooting–Spokane, WA, WA
NBC Camps–Basketball Speed–Alaska, AK
NBC Camps–Basketball Speed Explosion–California, CA
NBC Camps–Basketball Speed Explosion–Spokane, WA, WA
NBC Camps–Basketball–Team–Billings, MT, MT
NBC Camps–Basketball–Team (Boys)–Alaska, AK
NBC Camps–Basketball–Team (Girls)–Alaska, AK
NBC Camps–Basketball–Team (Girls)–Spangle, WA, WA
NBC Camps–Basketball–Team–La Grande, OR, OR
NBC Camps–Soccer–Spangle, WA, WA
NBC Camps–Soccer Speed Explosion–Spokane, WA, WA
NBC Camps–Volleyball–Alaska, AK
NBC Camps–Volleyball–California, CA
NBC Camps–Volleyball–Oregon, OR
NBC Camps–Volleyball Speed Explosion–California, CA
NBC Camps–Volleyball Speed Explosion–Spokane, WA, WA
NBC Camps–Basketball Individual Training–Isle of Man, United Kingdom
Nelson/Feller Tennis Camp–Lakeland College, WI
Nelson/Feller Tennis Camp–University of Wisconsin–Oshkosh, WI
92nd Street Y Camps–Fantastic Gymnastics, NY
Offense-Defense Golf Camp, Massachusetts, MA
Offense-Defense Tennis Camp, MA
Padua Franciscan High School Sports Camps, OH
Parent/Youth Golf School, TX
Paul Hogan's Shooter's Gold Basketball Camp–Alton, NH
Paul Hogan's Shooter's Gold Basketball Camp–Gilford, NH
Paul Hogan's Shooter's Gold Basketball Camp–Laconia, NH
Paul Hogan's Shooter's Gold Basketball Camp–Lancaster, NH
Paul Hogan's Shooter's Gold Basketball Camp–Littleton, NH
Paul Hogan's Shooter's Gold Basketball Camp–Manchester, NH
Paul Hogan's Shooter's Gold Basketball Camp–Meredith, NH
Paul Hogan's Shooter's Gold Basketball Camp–Tilton, NH
Paul Hogan's Shooter's Gold Basketball Camp–Woodsville, NH
Paul Hogan's Specialty Basketball Camp, NH
PAX Abroad–Brazil, Brazil
Pingry Lacrosse Camp–Martinsville Campus, NJ
Pingry Lacrosse Camp–Short Hills Campus, NJ
Pingry Soccer Camp, NJ
Pingry Softball Camp, NJ
Professional Sports Camps–Big League Baseball Camp, NJ
Professional Sports Camps–Hall of Fame Basketball Camp, NJ
Professional Sports Camps–Hall of Fame Soccer Camp, NJ
ProShot Basketball Camp–Boys Camp, PA
ProShot Basketball Camp–Girls Camp, PA
Purcell Marian High School Cavalier Basketball Camp, OH
Ramey Summer Riding Camps, IN
Ramey Summer Tennis Camps, KY
The Ranch–National Golf Camp–Lake Placid, NY
RUSTIC PATHWAYS–SURF THE SUMMER–COSTA RICA, Costa Rica
RUSTIC PATHWAYS–SURF THE SUMMER–THE FIJI ISLANDS, Fiji
76ers Basketball Camp, PA
Shattuck–St. Mary's Girls Elite Hockey Camp, MN
Shattuck-St. Mary's Boys Elite Hockey Camp, MN
Shippensburg University Sports Camps–Baseball–Regular Camp, PA
Shippensburg University Sports Camps–Baseball–Specialist Camp, PA
Shippensburg University Sports Camps–Boys Basketball, PA
Shippensburg University Sports Camps–Cross Country, PA
Shippensburg University Sports Camps–Fast Pitch Softball, PA
Shippensburg University Sports Camps–Father/Son Basketball Camp, PA
Shippensburg University Sports Camps–Field Hockey, PA
Shippensburg University Sports Camps–Football, PA
Shippensburg University Sports Camps–Girls Basketball, PA
Shippensburg University Sports Camps–Jumps, PA
Shippensburg University Sports Camps–Soccer–Boys Camp, PA
Shippensburg University Sports Camps–Soccer–Day Camp, PA
Shippensburg University Sports Camps–Soccer–Girls Camp, PA
Shippensburg University Sports Camps–Swimming, PA
Shippensburg University Sports Camps–Tennis, PA
Shippensburg University Sports Camps–Throws Camp, PA
Shippensburg University Sports Camps–Track & Field, PA
Shippensburg University Sports Camps–Volleyball–Girls Camp, PA
Sidwell Friends Basketball Camp, DC
Sidwell Friends Soccer Program with American Soccer Academy, DC
Sidwell Friends Tennis Camp, DC
SJ Ranch Riding Camp, CT
SoccerPlus FieldPlayer Academy–Charleston, IL, IL
SoccerPlus FieldPlayer Academy–Easthampton, MA, MA
SoccerPlus FieldPlayer Academy–Hamilton, NY, NY
SoccerPlus FieldPlayer Academy–Kent, CT, CT
SoccerPlus FieldPlayer Academy–Pottstown, PA, PA
SoccerPlus FieldPlayer Academy–Rome, GA, GA
SoccerPlus FieldPlayer Academy–Slippery Rock, PA, PA
SoccerPlus Goalkeeper School–Advanced National Training Center–Connecticut, CT
SoccerPlus Goalkeeper School–Challenge Program–Brunswick, ME, ME
SoccerPlus Goalkeeper School–Challenge Program–Charleston, IL, IL
SoccerPlus Goalkeeper School–Challenge Program–Delaware, OH, OH
SoccerPlus Goalkeeper School–Challenge Program–Fayetteville, NC, NC
SoccerPlus Goalkeeper School–Challenge Program–Franklin, MA, MA
SoccerPlus Goalkeeper School–Challenge Program–Hamilton, NY, NY
SoccerPlus Goalkeeper School–Challenge Program–Kent, CT, CT
SoccerPlus Goalkeeper School–Challenge Program–Pottstown, PA, PA
SoccerPlus Goalkeeper School–Challenge Program–Rome, GA, GA
SoccerPlus Goalkeeper School–Challenge Program–San Diego, CA, CA
SoccerPlus Goalkeeper School–Challenge Program–Slippery Rock, PA, PA
SoccerPlus Goalkeeper School–Challenge Program–Stockton, CA, CA
SoccerPlus Goalkeeper School–Challenge Program–Suffield, CT, CT
SoccerPlus Goalkeeper School–Challenge Program–Waco, TX, TX
SoccerPlus Goalkeeper School–Competitive Program–Charleston, IL, IL
SoccerPlus Goalkeeper School–Competitive Program–Easthampton, MA, MA
SoccerPlus Goalkeeper School–Competitive Program–Hamilton, NY, NY
SoccerPlus Goalkeeper School–Competitive Program–Kent, CT, CT
SoccerPlus Goalkeeper School–Competitive Program–Pottstown, PA, PA
SoccerPlus Goalkeeper School–Competitive Program–Rome, GA, GA
SoccerPlus Goalkeeper School–Competitive Program–Slippery Rock, PA, PA
SoccerPlus Goalkeeper School–Competitive Program–Suffield, CT, CT
SoccerPlus Goalkeeper School–National Training Center–Brunswick, ME, ME
SoccerPlus Goalkeeper School–National Training Center–Charleston, IL, IL
SoccerPlus Goalkeeper School–National Training Center–Delaware, OH, OH
SoccerPlus Goalkeeper School–National Training Center–Fayetteville, NC, NC
SoccerPlus Goalkeeper School–National Training Center–Franklin, MA, MA
SoccerPlus Goalkeeper School–National Training Center–Hamilton, NY, NY
SoccerPlus Goalkeeper School–National Training Center–Kent, CT, CT
SoccerPlus Goalkeeper School–National Training Center–Pottstown, PA, PA

▶ Sports Camps

SoccerPlus Goalkeeper School–National Training Center–Rome, GA, GA
SoccerPlus Goalkeeper School–National Training Center–San Diego, CA, CA
SoccerPlus Goalkeeper School–National Training Center–Slippery Rock, PA, PA
SoccerPlus Goalkeeper School–National Training Center–Stockton, CA, CA
SoccerPlus Goalkeeper School–National Training Center–Waco, TX, TX
Sports and Arts Center at Island Lake, PA
Springfield College Athletic Trainer Workshop, MA
Sprucelands Camp, NY
Stoneleigh–Burnham School Softball Camp, MA
Study Tours and Leisure Sports in the USA–Citrus College, CA
Summer Programs on the River; Crew/Rowing Camp, VA
Summer Programs on the River; Sailing Camp, VA
Swiss Challenge, Switzerland
Tampa Prep–Boys Athletic Camps, FL
Tampa Prep–Girls Athletic Camps, FL
Teen Tours of America–Golf Camp–Florida Swing, FL
TENNIS: EUROPE
TENNIS: EUROPE & MORE–North American Teams
Tice Brothers Football Camp, MN
Timber-lee Horsemanship Camps, WI
United Soccer Academy–Goal Keeping Training Camp, Connecticut, CT
United Soccer Academy–Goal Keeping Training Camp, Delaware, DE
United Soccer Academy–Goal Keeping Training Camp, Maryland, MD
United Soccer Academy–Goal Keeping Training Camp, New Jersey, NJ
United Soccer Academy–Goal Keeping Training Camp, New York, NY
United Soccer Academy–Goal Keeping Training Camp, Pennsylvania, PA
United Soccer Academy–Junior Soccer Squirts, Connecticut, CT
United Soccer Academy–Junior Soccer Squirts, Delaware, DE
United Soccer Academy–Junior Soccer Squirts, Maryland, MD
United Soccer Academy–Junior Soccer Squirts, New Jersey, NJ
United Soccer Academy–Junior Soccer Squirts, New York, NY
United Soccer Academy–Junior Soccer Squirts, Pennsylvania, PA
United Soccer Academy–Recreation Soccer Community Camp, Connecticut, CT
United Soccer Academy–Recreation Soccer Community Camp, Delaware, DE
United Soccer Academy–Recreation Soccer Community Camp, Maryland, MD
United Soccer Academy–Recreation Soccer Community Camp, New Jersey, NJ
United Soccer Academy–Recreation Soccer Community Camp, New York, NY
United Soccer Academy–Recreation Soccer Community Camp, Pennsylvania, PA
United Soccer Academy–Regional Academy Camp, New Jersey, NJ
United Soccer Academy–Regional Academy Camp, New York, NY
United Soccer Academy–Regional Academy Camp, Pennsylvania, PA
United Soccer Academy–Senior Soccer Squirts, Connecticut, CT
United Soccer Academy–Senior Soccer Squirts, Delaware, DE
United Soccer Academy–Senior Soccer Squirts, Maryland, MD
United Soccer Academy–Senior Soccer Squirts, New Jersey, NJ
United Soccer Academy–Senior Soccer Squirts, New York, NY
United Soccer Academy–Senior Soccer Squirts, Pennsylvania, PA
United Soccer Academy–Team Training Camp, Connecticut, CT
United Soccer Academy–Team Training Camp, Delaware, DE
United Soccer Academy–Team Training Camp, Maryland, MD
United Soccer Academy–Team Training Camp, New Jersey, NJ
United Soccer Academy–Team Training Camp, New York, NY
United Soccer Academy–Team Training Camp, Pennsylvania, PA
United Soccer Academy–Travel Soccer Community Camp, Connecticut, CT
United Soccer Academy–Travel Soccer Community Camp, Delaware, DE
United Soccer Academy–Travel Soccer Community Camp, Maryland, MD
United Soccer Academy–Travel Soccer Community Camp, New Jersey, NJ
United Soccer Academy–Travel Soccer Community Camp, New York, NY
United Soccer Academy–Travel Soccer Community Camp, Pennsylvania, PA
Universal Cheerleaders Association and Universal Dance Association Camps, AL
University of Kansas–Boys Soccer Camp, KS
University of Kansas–Girls Golf Camp, KS
University of Kansas–Girls Soccer Camp, KS
University of Kansas–Jayhawk Baseball Camps–Little League, Super Skills, and All-Star, KS
University of Kansas–Jayhawk Boys and Girls Tennis Camp, KS
University of Kansas–Jayhawk Golf Camp–Boys, KS
University of Kansas–Jayhawk Swim Camp, KS
University of Kansas–Jayhawk Track and Field/Cross Country Camps, KS
University of Kansas–Jayhawk Volleyball Camp, KS
University of Kansas–Softball–Teen and Advanced Camps, KS
University of Kansas–Sports Skills and Fitness Camp, KS
University of San Diego Sports Camps–Baseball Camp, CA
University of San Diego Sports Camps–Boys Basketball High School Team Camp, CA
University of San Diego Sports Camps–Boys High School Basketball Camp, CA
University of San Diego Sports Camps–Boys High School Elite Baseball Camp, CA
University of San Diego Sports Camps–Boys High School Soccer Camp, CA
University of San Diego Sports Camps–Boys Junior Basketball Camp, CA
University of San Diego Sports Camps–Coed Junior Soccer Camp, CA
University of San Diego Sports Camps–Coed Water Polo Camp, CA
University of San Diego Sports Camps–Competitive Swim Camp, CA
University of San Diego Sports Camps–Girls Basketball Fundamentals Camp, CA
University of San Diego Sports Camps–Girls Basketball High School Elite Camp, CA
University of San Diego Sports Camps–Girls Basketball High School Team Camp, CA
University of San Diego Sports Camps–Girls Soccer Camp, CA
University of San Diego Sports Camps–Girls Softball Advanced Camp, CA
University of San Diego Sports Camps–Girls Softball Beginner/Intermediate Camp, CA
University of San Diego Sports Camps–Girls Volleyball Camp, CA
University of San Diego Sports Camps–Sherri Stephens High School Tennis Camp, CA
University of San Diego Sports Camps–Sherri Stephens Junior Tennis Camp, CA
University of San Diego Sports Camps–Sports–N–More All Sports Camp, CA
University of San Diego Sports Camps–Sports–N–More Team Sports Camp, CA
University of San Diego Sports Camps–Sports–N–More Wet & Wild Sports Camp, CA
Valley Forge Military Academy Extreme Tennis Camp, PA
Valley View Ranch Equestrian Camp, GA
Vans Skateboard Camp, OR
Vassar College Coed Basketball Camp, NY
Vassar College Coed Soccer Camp, NY
Vassar College Coed Swim Camp, NY
Vassar College Girl's Field Hockey Camp, NY
Watersports Extravaganza at Pali Overnight Adventures, CA
Westcoast Connection–Florida Swing Junior Touring Golf Camp, FL
Westcoast Connection Travel–Ski and Snowboard Sensation
Wildcat Basketball Camp, LA
William Henderson Football Camp/Sports International, WI
Willow Hill Farm Camp, NY
Windridge Tennis Camp at Craftsbury Common, VT
Windridge Tennis Camp at Teela-Wooket, Vermont, VT
Woodberry Forest Basketball Camp, VA
Woodberry Forest Golf Camp, VA
Woodberry Forest Lacrosse Camp, VA
Woodberry Forest Sports Camp, VA
Woodward Freestyle BMX Bicycle, Inline Skate, Skateboarding Camp, PA
Woodward Gymnastics Camp, PA
YMCA Camp Lincoln–Specialty Camps: Sports Camp, NH

Traditional Camps

A.C.E. Intercultural Institute, WA
Acting Academy at Pali Overnight Adventures, CA
Adirondack Camp, NY
Adventure Camps, PA
Agassiz Village, ME
Alford Lake Camp, ME
Alford Lake Family Camp, ME
Aloha Camp, VT

Alpine Camp for Boys, AL
American Youth Foundation–Camp Merrowvista, NH
American Youth Foundation–Camp Miniwanca, MI
Anderson Camps' Colorado River Ranch for Boys/Hilltop Ranch for Girls, CO
Appleby College Summer Camps, Canada
Applejack Teen Camp, NY
Bark Lake Leadership Through Recreation Camp, Canada
Bar 717 Ranch/Camp Trinity, CA
Barton Day Camp–Long Island, NY
Barton Day Camp–New York, NY
Barton Day Camp–Worcester, MA
Battlebot Mania at Pali Overnight Adventures, CA
Birch Trail Camp for Girls, WI
Blue Star Camps, NC
Boulder Ridge Day Camp, CT
Breezy Point Day Camp, PA
Brown Ledge Camp, VT
Buckswood: English Language (ESL) and Activities–Bradfield, England, United Kingdom
Buckswood: English Language (ESL) and Activities–Plumpton, England, United Kingdom
Buckswood: English Language (ESL) and Activities–West Virginia, WV
California Cruzin' Overnight Camp, CA
Camden Military Academy Summer Session/ Camp, SC
Camp Airy, MD
Camp AK-O-MAK, Canada
Camp Aloha Hive, VT
Camp Androscoggin, ME
Camp Arcadia, ME
Camp Arowhon–Boys and Girls Camp, Canada
Camp Atwater–Boys Session, MA
Camp Atwater–Girls Session, MA
Camp Avoda, MA
Camp Awosting, CT
Camp Barney Medintz, GA
Camp Berachah Ministries–Counselor-In-Training, WA
Camp Berachah Ministries–Day Camp, WA
Camp Berachah Ministries–Horse Day Camp, WA
Camp Berachah Ministries–Junior Camp, WA
Camp Berachah Ministries–Legend Teen Camp, WA
Camp Berachah Ministries–Overnight Horse Camp, WA
Camp Berachah Ministries–Primary Camp, WA
Camp Berachah Ministries–Teen Leadership, WA
Camp Berachah Ministries–Wrangler-In-Training, WA
Camp Betsey Cox, VT
Camp Billings, VT
Camp Birch Trails, WI
Camp Brandon for Boys, NH
Camp Brookwoods and Deer Run, NH
Camp Buckskin, MN
Camp Burgess, MA
Camp Butterworth, OH
Camp Canadensis, PA
Camp Canonicus, RI
Camp Carysbrook, VA
Camp Catherine Capers, VT
Camp Cayuga, PA
Camp Cedar Point, IL
Camp Chateaugay, NY
Camp Chatuga, SC
Camp Cheerio YMCA, NC
Camp Chen-A-Wanda, PA
Camp Chewonki, ME
Camp Chi, WI
Camp Chikopi for Boys, Canada
Camp Chinqueka, CT
Camp Chippewa for Boys, MN
Camp Chosatonga for Boys, NC
Camp Conrad Weiser, PA
Camp Courageous of Iowa, IA
Camp Craig Horse Residential Summer Camp, Canada
Camp Craig Sports and Recreation Summer Camp, Canada
Camp Crestridge for Girls, NC
Camp Curtain Call, VA
Camp Discovery–Madison, NJ
Camp Discovery–Teaneck, NJ
Camp Dudley, NY
Camp Echo, MI
Camp Echo in Coleman High Country, NY
Camp Exploration Travel Day Camp, CA
Camp Fire Camp Wi-Ta-Wentin, LA
Camp Fowler, MI
Camp Friendship, VA
Camp Ganadaoweh, Canada
Camp Geneva, MI
Camp Glen Arden for Girls, NC
Camp Glen Brook, NH
Camp Good News for Young People and Teens, MA
Camp Greenbrier for Boys, WV
Camp Green Cove, NC
Camp Greylock for Boys, MA
Camp Hawthorne, ME
Camp Hawthorne Creative Arts Camp, ME
Camp Hayward, MA
Camp Heartland Summer Camp–California, CA
Camp Heartland Summer Camp–Minnesota, MN
Camp Henry, MI
Camp Highlands for Boys, WI
Camp High Rocks, NC
Camp Hillside, MA
Camp Hilltop, NY
Camp Hitaga, IA
Camp Hitaga–Stirrups and Saddles, IA
Camp Horizons Discover, VA
Camp Horizons Explorer, VA
Camp Horizons Pathfinder, VA
Camp Horseshoe, WI
Camp Illahee for Girls, NC
Camp James Summer Day Camp, CA
Camp JCA Shalom, CA
Camp Jordan for Children with Diabetes, VA
Camp Joy, OH
Camp Kahdalea for Girls, NC
Camp Kawanhee for Boys, ME
Camp Kennybrook, NY
Camp Kingsmont, MA
Camp Kiniya, VT
Camp Kirkwold, ME
Camp Kodiak, Canada
Camp Kostopulos, UT
Camp La Junta, TX
Camp Lakeland, NY
Camp Lanakila, VT
Camp Laney for Boys, AL
Camp Laurel, ME
Camp Laurel South, ME
Camp Ledgewood, OH
Camp Lee Mar, PA
Camp Lincoln for Boys/Camp Lake Hubert for Girls, MN
Camp Lindenmere, PA
Camp Lohikan in the Pocono Mountains, PA
Camp Lookout, MI
Camp Louemma, NJ
Camp Lou Henry Hoover, NJ
Camp Louise, MD
Camp Maplehurst, MI
Camp Maromac, Canada
Camp Matoaka for Girls, ME
Camp McAlister, NY
Camp Menominee, WI
Camp Merrie-Woode, NC
Camp Mi-A-Kon-Da, Canada
Camp Micah, ME
Camp Middlesex, NJ
Camp Mishawaka for Boys, MN
Camp Mishawaka for Girls, MN
Camp Modin, ME
Camp Mondamin, NC
Camp Monroe, NY
Camp Mt. Luther, PA
Camp Mowglis, School of the Open, NH
Camp Nakanawa, TN
Camp Namanu, OR
Camp Nashoba North, ME
Camp Nawaka, MA
Camp Niwana, TX
Camp Nock-A-Mixon, PA
Camp Nominingue, Canada
Camp North Star for Boys, WI
Camp Northway, Canada
Camp Nor'wester, WA
Camp O-AT-KA, ME
Camp O'Bannon, OH
Camp Olympia, TX
Camp Onaway, NH
Camp Ouareau, Canada
Camp Oweki Summer Day Camp, MI
Camp Pacific's Recreational Camp, CA
Camp Pasquaney, NH
Camp Pinehurst, ME
Camp Pisgah, NC
Camp Pocono Ridge, PA
Camp Pok-O-MacCready, NY
Camp Ponacka, Canada
Camp Pondicherry, ME
Camp Quinebarge, NH
Camp Redwood, NY
Camp Regis, NY
Camp Ridgecrest for Boys, NC
Camp Rim Rock–General Camp, WV
Camp Rim Rock–Mini Camp, WV
Camp Rio Vista for Boys, TX
Camp Robin Hood for Boys and Girls, NH
Camp Rockmont for Boys, NC
Camp Runoia, ME
Camp Sabra, MO
Camp Saginaw, PA
Camp St. John's Northwestern, WI
Camp Sandy Cove, WV
Camp Sangamon for Boys, VT
Camp Scatico, NY
Camp Scelkit, ME
Camp Seagull for Girls, MI
Camp Shohola, PA
Camp Sierra Vista for Girls, TX
Camp Skylemar, ME

▶ Traditional Camps

Camp Skyline, AL
Camp Sky Ranch, Inc., NC
Camp Stanislaus, MS
Camp Starfish, NH
Camp Stonybrook, OH
Camp Streamside, PA
Camp Susquehannock for Boys, PA
Camp Susquehannock for Girls, PA
Camps with Meaning–Advanced Horsemanship I & II, Canada
Camps with Meaning–Boys Camp, Canada
Camps with Meaning–Girls Camp, Canada
Camps with Meaning–Junior High/Junior Youth Camp, Canada
Camps with Meaning–PreJunior/Junior/Intermediate Camp, Canada
Camps with Meaning–Youth Camp, Canada
Camp Talcott, NY
Camp Tall Timbers, WV
Camp Tapawingo, ME
Camp Tawonga–Summer Camp, CA
Camp Timanous, ME
Timber-lee Science Camp, WI
Camp Tioga, PA
Camp Togowoods, AK
Camp Tohkomeupog, NH
Camp Towanda, PA
Camp Treetops, NY
Campus Kids–CT, CT
Campus Kids–Minisink, NY
Campus Kids–NJ, NJ
Camp Veritans, NJ
Camp Wah-Nee, CT
Camp Walden, NY
Camp Walt Whitman, NH
Camp Watitoh, MA
Camp Watonka, PA
Camp Wawenock, ME
Camp Wayne for Boys, PA
Camp Wayne for Girls, PA
Camp Waziyatah, ME
Camp Wekeela for Boys and Girls, ME
Camp Westmont, PA
Camp Wicosuta, NH
Camp Wilvaken, Canada
Camp Winding Gap, NC
Camp Wing, MA
Camp Wingate Kirkland, MA
Camp Wing Day Camp, MA
Camp Winnebago, ME
Camp WinShape for Boys, GA
Camp WinShape for Girls, GA
Cape Cod Sea Camps–Monomoy/Wono, MA
The Cardigan Mountain School Summer Session, NH
Carmel Valley Tennis Camp, CA
Carousel Day School, NY
Castilleja Summer Day Camp, CA
Catalina Island Camps, CA
Catholic Youth Camp, MN
Cedar Lodge, MI
Center for Cultural Interchange–Switzerland Language Camp, Switzerland
Central Wisconsin Environmental Station–Sunset Lake Adventures, WI
Channel 3 Kids Camp, CT
Cheley Colorado Camps, CO
Cheshire Academy Summer Program, CT
Children's Creative and Performing Arts Academy Archaeology Adventure Camp, CA
Children's Creative and Performing Arts Academy Summer Elementary Program, CA
Children's Creative and Performing Arts Academy Summer Middle School Program, CA
Children's Creative and Performing Arts Academy Summer Programs for High School Students, CA
Chop Point Camp, ME
Christikon, MT
Circle Pines Center Summer Camp, MI
Clara Barton Camp, MA
Clara Barton Family Camp, MA
Clearwater Camp for Girls, WI
Cloverleaf Ranch Summer Camp, CA
Coleman Country Day Camp, NY
College for Kids, PA
College Settlement of Philadelphia, PA
Colorado Academy Summer Programs, CO
The Colorado Mountain Ranch, CO
Colvig Silver Camps, CO
The Community Center Going Places Camp, MD
Cragged Mountain Farm, NH
Crane Lake Camp, MA
Cross Keys, United Kingdom
Crystalaire Camp, MI
Cuernavaca Summer Program for Teens, Mexico
Culinary Institute at Pali Overnight Adventures, CA
Culver Summer Camps/Culver Specialty Camp– Aviation, IN
Culver Summer Camps/Culver Specialty Camp–Equestrian Arts, IN
Culver Summer Camps/Upper Camp–Boys, IN
Culver Summer Camps/Upper Camp–Girls, IN
Culver Summer Woodcraft Camp, IN
CYO Boys Camp, MI
CYO Girls Camp, MI
Darlington School Summer Camps, GA
Davidson Academy–Bear Country Day Camp, TN
Deerfoot Lodge, NY
Deerkill Day Camp, NY
Delphi's Summer Session, OR
Douglas Ranch Camps, CA
Dwight-Englewood Summer Adventures, NJ
Dwight-Englewood Weekly Enrichment, NJ
Eagle Lake Horse Camp, CO
Eagle Lake Resident Camp, CO
Eagle's Nest Camp, NC
Eden Wood Camp, MN
EKOCAMP International, Canada
Enforex Residential Youth Summer Camp–Madrid, Spain
Enforex Residential Youth Summer Camp–Marbella, Spain
Enforex Residential Youth Summer Camp–Salamanca, Spain
Explorer Day Camp, OH
Falcon Camp, OH
Falcon Young Adventure Camp, OH
Falling Creek Camp, NC
Farm and Wilderness Camps–Barn Day Camp, VT
Farm and Wilderness Camps–Indian Brook, VT
Farm and Wilderness Camps–Tamarack Farm, VT
Farm and Wilderness Camps–Timberlake, VT
Fay School Day Camp, MA
Fenn School Summer Day Camp, MA
Film Institute at Pali Overnight Adventures, CA
Fleur de Lis Camp, NH
Flint Hill School–"Summer on the Hill"–Counselor-in-Training Day Camp, VA
Flint Hill School–"Summer on the Hill"–Junior Day/Day Camps, VA
Flint Hill School–"Summer on the Hill"–Trips and Travel Day Camp, VA
Flying G Ranch, Tomahawk Ranch, CO
Flying Moose Lodge, ME
Forest Ridge Summer Program, WA
Forrestel Farm Riding and Sports Camp, NY
4 Star Academics Junior Camp at the University of Virginia, VA
4 Star Academics Senior Camp at the University of Virginia, VA
Four Winds * Westward Ho, WA
French Immersion Summer Camp, Canada
Friends Camp, ME
Geneva Glen Camp, CO
Girl Scouts of Genesee Valley Day Camp, NY
Girl Scouts of Genesee Valley Resident Camp, NY
Girl Scouts of Mid-Continent–Camp Prairie Schooner, MO
Girl Scouts of Mid-Continent–Winding River Camp and Ranch, MO
The Glen at Lake of the Woods, MI
Global Teen Summer Sports Camp in Berlin, Germany
GLS Summer Camp Blossin, Germany
GLS Summer Camp Loewenstein, Germany
GLS Summer Camp Schmoeckwitz, Germany
Gold Arrow Camp, CA
The Gow School Summer Program, NY
Grandparents' and Grandchildren's Camp, NY
Greenbrier River Outdoor Adventures, Adventure Camp, WV
Greenbrier River Outdoor Adventures, Camp Snowshoe, WV
Greenwoods Camp for Boys, MI
Griffith Park Boys Camp, CA
The Grove at Greenwoods, MI
Gymnastics Academy at Pali Overnight Adventures, CA
Hamilton Learning Centre Summer Fun in the Sun Camp, Canada
Harker Summer Programs, CA
Harmon's Pine View Camp, OH
Haycock Camping Ministries–Adventure Trails, PA
Haycock Camping Ministries–Battalion Program, PA
Haycock Camping Ministries–Stockade Program, PA
Haycock Camping Ministries–Trailbuilders Program, PA
Hidden Hollow Camp, OH
Hidden Villa Summer Camp, CA
Hill Top Summer Programs, PA
The Hockaday School Summer Session, TX
The Hollows Camp, Canada
Hollywood Stunt Camp at Pali Overnight Adventures, CA
Horizons for Youth, MA
Horseback Riding Academy at Pali Overnight Adventures, CA
The Hun School of Princeton Summer Day Camp, NJ
Indian Head Camp, PA

Instituto de Idiomas Geos–Granada, Spain, Spain
International Summer Centre at Biarritz, France
International Summer Centre at Chatel, France
International Summer Centre at Paris-Brétigny, France
Iroquois Springs, NY
JCC Houston: Camp Bami, TX
JCC Houston: Camp Kaleidoscope, TX
JCC Houston: Counselor-In-Training, TX
JCC Houston: Gordon Campsite, TX
JCC Houston: Kindercamp, TX
JCC Houston: Teen Trek, TX
Jewish Community Center Day Camp, NJ
The John Cooper School Discovery Camps, TX
Jumonville Sampler Camps, PA
Junior Institute, WA
Kamp Kohut, ME
Kampus Kampers, FL
Kawkawa Summer Camps, Canada
Keewaydin Dunmore, VT
Keystone Camp, NC
Kickapoo Kamp, TX
KidzZone Summer Camp, GA
Killooleet, VT
Kingsley Pines Camp, ME
Kippewa for Girls, ME
Kiski Summer Camp–Junior Division-Boys Grades 5-8, PA
Kiski Summer Camp–Senior Division-Boys Grades 9-12, PA
Kiski Summer Camp–Senior Division-Girls Grades 9-12, PA
Kooch-I-Ching, MN
Kutsher's Sports Academy, NY
Lake Ann Baptist Camp, MI
Lake of the Woods Camp for Girls, MI
Leadership Adventure in Boston, MA
Leadership Training at Pali Overnight Adventures, CA
Les Elfes–International Summer/Winter Camp, Switzerland
Ligonier Camp, PA
Linden Hill Summer Program, MA
Lindley G. Cook 4-H Camp, NJ
Lions Camp Merrick Deaf/HOH/KODA Program, MD
Lions Camp Merrick Diabetes Program, MD
Little Keswick School Summer Session, VA
Lochearn Camp for Girls, VT
Mah Meh Weh, MI
Maine Golf Academy–Junior Golf Camp, ME
Maine Golf and Tennis Academy–Serve and Turf, ME
Maine Teen Camp, ME
Maine Tennis Academy–Junior Tennis Camp, ME
The Marsh, MD
Marydale Resident Camp, LA
Medeba Leader in Training Program, Canada
Medeba Summer Camp, Canada
Med-O-Lark Camp, ME
Mercersburg Academy Junior Adventure Camp, PA
Mercersburg Adventure Camp, PA
Mercersburg Teen Adventure Camp, PA
Millennium Entrepreneurs Camp CEO, CA
Millennium Entrepreneurs "Training Tomorrow's Business Leaders Today", CA
Mini-Camp in the Pocono Mountains, PA
Mini Minors, United Kingdom
Miracle Makers Summer Camp, CA
Montgomery College WDCE–Computer Programming Camp–Co-ed, MD
Montgomery College WDCE–FIT Summer Camp, MD
Montgomery College WDCE–Summer Youth Programs, MD
Moose River Outpost, ME
Mountain Camp, CA
Mountain Meadow Ranch, CA
New Jersey YMHA–YWHA Camp Mountaintop, PA
New Jersey YMHA–YWHA Camp Nah-jee-wah, PA
New Jersey YMHA–YWHA Camp Nesher, PA
New Jersey YMHA–YWHA Cedar Lake Camp, PA
New Jersey YMHA–YWHA Teen Camp, PA
New Strides Day Camp, Canada
Next Level Camp, PA
92nd Street Y Camps–Camp Bari Tov, NY
92nd Street Y Camps–Camp Haverim, NY
92nd Street Y Camps–Camp Kesher, PA
92nd Street Y Camps–Camp Kesher Junior, PA
92nd Street Y Camps–Camp K'Ton Ton, NY
92nd Street Y Camps–Camp Tevah for Science and Nature, NY
92nd Street Y Camps–Camp Tova, NY
92nd Street Y Camps–Camp Yaffa for the Arts, NY
92nd Street Y Camps–Camp Yomi, NY
92nd Street Y Camps–Trailblazers, NY
North Country Camps—Camp Lincoln for Boys, NY
North Country Camps—Camp Whippoorwill for Girls, NY
North Woods Camp for Boys, NH
Oak Ridge Academic Summer Camp, NC
OES–Summer Discovery, OR
OES–Summer Mini Camps, OR
OES–Summer Wonder, OR
Ojai Valley School Summer Programs, CA
OMNI Camp, ME
OPTIONS for Young Women, IN
Outdoor Adventure, WA
Padua Summer Experience, OH
Pali Overnight Adventures Camp, CA
Pine Island Camp, ME
Pine Tree Camps at Lynn University, FL
Pingry Day Camps, NJ
Pleasant Valley Camp for Girls, NH
Point O' Pines Camp for Girls, NY
Ponkapoag Outdoor Center Day Camps, MA
Potomac School Summer Programs, VA
Poulter Colorado Camps, CO
Presbyterian Clearwater Forest, MN
Pripstein's Camp, Canada
The Ranch–Lake Placid Academy, NY
Rawhide Ranch, CA
Red Pine Camp for Girls, WI
Riverside Military Academy Young Cadet Camp, GA
River Way Ranch Camp, CA
Road's End Farm Horsemanship Camp, NH
Rockbrook Camp, NC
Rock Star Camp at Pali Overnight Adventures, CA
Rocky Mountain Village, CO
Rowe Camp, MA
Sailing Program at NE Camping Adventures, ME
St. Andrew's Summer Programs, MD
St. John's Northwestern Academic Camp, WI
St. John's Northwestern ESL Camp, WI
St. Johns Summer Camp, FL
Saint Thomas More School–Summer Academic Camp, CT
St. Louis County 4-H Camp, MN
Saint Vincent College Challenge Program, PA
Sanborn Western Camps: Big Spring Ranch for Boys, CO
Sanborn Western Camps: High Trails Ranch for Girls, CO
Sandy Island Camp for Families, NH
Santa Catalina School Summer Camp, CA
Scuba Adventures at Pali Overnight Adventures, CA
Secret Agent Camp at Pali Overnight Adventures, CA
Shaffer's High Sierra Camp, CA
Shwayder Camp, CO
Sidwell Friends Bethesda Day Camp, MD
Sidwell Friends Camp Corsica, MD
Sidwell Friends Explorer Day Camp, Explorer Voyagers and ExploreStar, DC
Sidwell Friends Riverview Programs, VA
SJ Ranch Riding Camp, CT
Skateboarding Academy at Pali Overnight Adventures, CA
Skylake Yosemite Camp, CA
Skyland Camp for Girls, NC
Snowy Owl Camp for Girls, ME
Songadeewin of Keewaydin, VT
South Shore YMCA Specialty Camp, MA
Southwestern Adventures, AZ
Springfield Technical Community College–College for Kids, MA
Sprucelands Camp, NY
Stevenson School Summer Camp, CA
Stony Book University–Summer Camp at Stony Brook, NY
Streamside Camp and Conference Center, PA
Streamside Family Camp, PA
Summer at Altamont, AL
Summer at the Academy, TX
Summer Horizons Day Camp, VT
Summer in Switzerland, Switzerland
Summer Music at The Hollows, Canada
SummerWorks, UT
Surprise Lake Camp, NY
Swift Nature Camp–Adventure Camp, WI
Swift Nature Camp–Discovery Camp, WI
Swift Nature Camp–Explorer Camp, WI
Tabor Academy Summer Program, MA
Talisman Summer Camp, NC
Tampa Prep–Terrapin Day Camp, FL
Tanager Lodge, NY
TASIS Le Château des Enfants, Switzerland
TASIS Middle School Program, Switzerland
Teton Valley Ranch Camp–Boys Camp, WY
Teton Valley Ranch Camp–Girls Camp, WY
Thunderbird Ranch, CA
Timber-lee Creation Camp, WI
Timber-lee Drama Camp, WI
Timber-lee Youth Camp, WI
Towering Pines Camp, WI
University of Kansas–Sertoma-Schiefelbush Communication Camp, KS
University of Wisconsin–Green Bay Summer Discovery, WI
University of Wisconsin–Superior Youthsummer 2005, WI
Valley Forge Military Academy Summer Band Camp, PA

▶ Traditional Camps

Valley Forge Military Academy Summer Camp for Boys, PA
Valley Forge Military Academy Summer Coed Day Camp, PA
Village Camps–Austria, Austria
Village Camps–England, United Kingdom
Village Camps–France, France
Village Camps–Switzerland, Switzerland
Washington International School Passport to Summer, DC
Watersports Extravaganza at Pali Overnight Adventures, CA
West River United Methodist Center, MD
Wilderness Experiences Unlimited–Pathfinders Day Camp, MA
Wildlife Camp, CO
Windsor Mountain: International Summer Camp, NH
Winona Camp for Boys, ME
Wohelo-Luther Gulick Camps, ME
Woodland, WI
XUK, United Kingdom
YMCA Camp Abnaki, VT
YMCA Camp Abnaki–Counselor-in-Training Program, VT
YMCA Camp Abnaki–Family Camp, VT
YMCA Camp Abnaki–Mini Camp, VT
YMCA Camp Bernie, NJ
YMCA Camp Fitch Summer Camp, PA
YMCA Camp Icaghowan, WI
YMCA Camp Ihduhapi, MN
YMCA Camp Kanata, NC
YMCA Camp Lincoln–Junior CIT Program, NH
YMCA Camp Lincoln–Senior CIT Program, NH
YMCA Camp Lincoln–Traditional Day Camp, NH
YMCA Camp Matollionequay, NJ
YMCA Camp Michikamau, NY
YMCA Camp Minikani, WI
YMCA Camp Oakes Rangers, CA
YMCA Camp Oakes Teen Leadership, CA
YMCA Camp Ockanickon, NJ
YMCA Camp Pendalouan–Bugs and Bunks, MI
YMCA Camp Pendalouan–Counselor-in-Training, MI
YMCA Camp Pendalouan–Resident Camp, MI
YMCA Camp Pendalouan–Ropers and Wranglers Horse Camp, MI
YMCA Camp Pendalouan–Teen Xtreme, MI
YMCA Camp Seymour Summer Camp, WA
YMCA Camp Shand, PA
YMCA Camp Surf, CA
YMCA Camp Tippecanoe–Adventure Camp, OH
YMCA Camp Tippecanoe–Bike Camp, OH
YMCA Camp Tippecanoe–Equine Camp, OH
YMCA Camp Tippecanoe–Girl's & Guy's Corral, OH
YMCA Camp Tippecanoe–Horse Pals, OH
YMCA Camp Tippecanoe–Jr. Counselor, OH
YMCA Camp Tippecanoe–Teen Camp, OH
YMCA Camp U-Nah-Li-Ya, WI
YMCA Camp Wabansi, WI
YMCA Camp Warren for Boys, MN
YMCA Camp Warren for Girls, MN
YMCA Lake Stockwell, NJ
YMCA Wanakita Summer Family Camp, Canada
YMCA Wanakita Summer Resident and Day Camp, Canada

Wilderness Programs

AAVE–Africa
AAVE–Alaska, AK
AAVE–Alps Rider
AAVE–Australia, Australia
AAVE–Belize, Belize
AAVE–Bold Europe
AAVE–Bold West
AAVE–Boot/Saddle/Paddle
AAVE–Border Cross
AAVE–Hawaii, HI
AAVE–Inmersión en España, Spain
AAVE–Peru and Machu Picchu, Peru
AAVE–Rock & River
AAVE–Rocky Mountain Adventure, CO
AAVE–Wild Isles
AAVE–X–Five
Adirondack Alpine Adventures, NY
Adventure Camps, PA
Adventure Links
Adventure Links–Appalachian Odyssey
Adventure Links–North Carolina Expeditions, NC
Adventure Links–The Costa Rica Experience, Costa Rica
Adventure Links–Ultimate Adventure Camps, VA
Adventures Cross-Country, Alaska Adventure, AK
Adventures Cross-Country, Australia/Fiji Adventure
Adventures Cross-Country, Colorado Adventure, CO
Adventures Cross-Country, Costa Rica Adventure, Costa Rica
Adventures Cross-Country, Extreme British Columbia Adventure, Canada
Adventures Cross-Country, Hawaii Adventure, HI
Adventures Cross-Country,Southern Europe Adventure
Adventures Cross-Country, Western Adventure
Adventure Treks–Alaska Adventures, AK
Adventure Treks–California Challenge Adventures
Adventure Treks–California 19 Adventures, CA
Adventure Treks–Canadian Rockies Adventures, Canada
Adventure Treks–Montana Adventures, MT
Adventure Treks–Pacific Northwest Adventures, WA
Adventure Treks–PAC 16, OR
Adventure Treks–Summit Fever
Adventure Treks–Ultimate Northwest Adventures
Alien Adventure Overnight Camp
Alpengirl–Alaska, AK
Alpengirl–Hawaii, HI
Alpengirl–Montana, MT
Alpengirl–Montana Art
Alpengirl–Montana Fitness, MT
Alpengirl–Montana Horse, MT
Alpengirl–Scandinavia
Alpengirl–Washington, WA
Alpengirl–Washington Alpenguide Training, WA
Alpengirl–Washington Lil' Alpengirl, WA
Anderson Camps' Wilderness Pioneer Camp, CO
Apogee Outdoor Adventures–Burlington to Boston
Apogee Outdoor Adventures–Coast to Quebec
Apogee Outdoor Adventures–New England Mountains and Coast
Appalachian Mountain Club–Teen Crews–Alpine Trail, Berkshires, MA
Appalachian Mountain Club–Teen Crews–Pinkham Notch, NH
Appalachian Mountain Club–Teen Crews–Spike, NH
Appalachian Mountain Club–Teen Crews–Two-week Teen Spike, NH
Appalachian Mountain Club–Teen Stewardship Training, NH
Appalachian Mountain Club–Trail Crew–Berkshires, MA
Appalachian Mountain Club–Trail Crew–Mount Everett/Alpine Trail, MA
Appalachian Mountain Club–Trail Crew–White Mountains, NH
Appalachian Mountain Club–Volunteer Trail Crew–Alpine/Mount Washington, NH
Appalachian Mountain Club–Volunteer Trail Crew–Crawford Notch, NH
Appalachian Mountain Club–Volunteer Trail Crew–Grafton Loop, ME
Appalachian Mountain Club–Volunteer Trail Crew–Hut Crew, NH
Appalachian Mountain Club–Wild New Hampshire Trail Crew, NH
Appalachian Mountain Club–Women's Trail Crew, NH
Audubon Journeys, VT
Barton Adventure Camp
Blue Ridge School–Adventure Camps, VA
Blue Ridge School–Rock Climbing Camp, VA
BROADREACH Adventures Down Under, Australia
BROADREACH Amazon and Galapagos Encounter, Ecuador
BROADREACH Costa Rica Experience, Costa Rica
BROADREACH Honduras Eco-Adventure, Honduras
Camp Chewonki Adventure Camps, ME
Camp Chewonki Eco-Kayak Australia, Australia
Camp Chewonki for Girls, ME
Camp Chewonki Wilderness Expeditions, ME
Camp Friendship Challenge Program
Camp Tawonga–Call of the Wild, CA
Camp Tawonga–Teen Quest: Canada, Canada
Camp Tawonga–Teen Quest: High Sierra, CA
Camp Tawonga–Teen Quest: Northwest
Camp Tawonga–Teen Quest: Southwest
Camp Tawonga–Teen Quest: Yosemite, CA
Camp Wendigo, Canada
Camp Winding Gap, NC
Canadian Rockies Adventurer Camp, Canada
Canadian Rockies Outdoor Leader Camp, Canada
Central Wisconsin Environmental Station–Natural Resources Careers Camp, WI
Central Wisconsin Environmental Station–Sunset Lake Adventures, WI
Cheerio Adventures–Appalachian Adventure, VA
Cheerio Adventures–Cave/Raft, VA
Cheerio Adventures–5 Rivers in 5 Days
Cheerio Adventures–Mountains to the Sea, VA
Cheerio Adventures–Ocean Odyssey, VA
Cheerio Adventures–Rock Climb/Raft, VA
Cheerio Adventures–Sampler, VA
Cheerio Adventures–Seekers, VA

Cheerio Adventures–Standard, VA
Cheley Colorado Camps, CO
Christikon, MT
Concordia Language Villages–French Voyageur, MN
Costa Rica Rainforest Outward Bound School–Multi-Element, Costa Rica
Costa Rica Rainforest Outward Bound School–Summer Semester, Costa Rica
Costa Rica Rainforest Outward Bound School–Surf Adventure, Costa Rica
Costa Rica Rainforest Outward Bound School–Tri-Country/Tri-Mester
Cottonwood Gulch Mountain Desert Challenge, NM
Cottonwood Gulch Prairie Trek Expedition, NM
Cottonwood Gulch Turquoise Trail Expedition, NM
Cottonwood Gulch Wild Country Trek, NM
Darrow Wilderness Trips–Kayak, ME
Darrow Wilderness Trips–Maine, ME
Darrow Wilderness Trips–Quebec: Mistassini, Canada
Darrow Wilderness Trips–St. Croix, ME
Darrow Wilderness Trips–Voyageurs, ME
Darrow Youth Backpacking, ME
Deer Hill Expeditions, Arizona, AZ
Deer Hill Expeditions, Colorado, CO
Deer Hill Expeditions, Costa Rica, Costa Rica
Deer Hill Expeditions, New Mexico, NM
Deer Hill Expeditions, Utah, UT
Eagle Lake Bike Camp, CO
Eagle Lake Camp–East, NC
Eagle Lake Camp Jaunts–Minnesota Boundary Waters, MN
Eagle Lake Wilderness Program, CO
EARTHWATCH INSTITUTE–Conservation Research Initiative–Mountain Meadows of the North Cascades, WA
EARTHWATCH INSTITUTE–Hawksbill Turtles of Barbados, Barbados
EARTHWATCH INSTITUTE–Malaysian Bat Conservation, Malaysia
EARTHWATCH INSTITUTE–Manatees in Belize, Belize
EARTHWATCH INSTITUTE–Moose and Wolves, MI
EARTHWATCH INSTITUTE–Puerto Rico's Rainforest, Puerto Rico
EARTHWATCH INSTITUTE–Rainforest Caterpillars–Costa Rica, Costa Rica
EARTHWATCH INSTITUTE–Rivers of the Peruvian Amazon, Peru
EARTHWATCH INSTITUTE–Sea Otters of Alaska, AK
EDUCO Summer Adventure Programs, CO
Elk Creek Ranch and Trek Program, WY
Excalibur, Canada
Farm and Wilderness Camps–Flying Cloud, VT
Farm and Wilderness Camps–Indian Brook, VT
Farm and Wilderness Camps–Saltash Mountain, VT
Farm and Wilderness Camps–Timberlake, VT
Flying Moose Lodge, ME
Four Corners School of Outdoor Education: Southwest Ed-Venture
French Immersion Kayak Expedition, Canada
From the Forest to the Sea, AK
Greenbrier River Outdoor Adventures, Adventure Camp, WV
Greenbrier River Outdoor Adventures, Rock and River, WV
Greenbrier River Outdoor Adventures, Wilderness Explorer, WV
Hante School, NC
High Sierra Wilderness Camps, CA
Hiker's Heaven Overnight Camp
Horizon Adventures Inc., CO
Hulbert Voyageurs Youth Wilderness Trips
Hurricane Island Outward Bound–Maine Coast and Western Maine Canoeing and Sailing, ME
Hurricane Island Outward Bound–Maine Coast and Western Maine Sailing and Backpacking, ME
Hurricane Island Outward Bound–Maine Coast and Western Maine Sea Kayaking and Backpacking, ME
Hurricane Island Outward Bound–Maine Coast Sailing/Sailing and Rock Climbing, ME
Hurricane Island Outward Bound–Maine Coast Schooner Sailing, ME
Hurricane Island Outward Bound–Maine Coast Sea Kayaking, ME
Hurricane Island Outward Bound–Maine Woods High School Summer Semester, ME
Hurricane Island Outward Bound–Mid-Atlantic Canoeing, Backpacking, and Rock Climbing
Hurricane Island Outward Bound–North Woods Maine Allagash and Appalachian Trail Canoeing and Backpacking, ME
Hurricane Island Outward Bound–North Woods Maine Canoeing and Backpacking, ME
Hurricane Island Outward Bound–North Woods Maine Expedition Canoeing, ME
Hurricane Island Outward Bound–Ocean Bound: Tall Ship Sailing and Sea Kayaking Semester
Hurricane Island Outward Bound–Western Maine and New Hampshire Canoeing and Backpacking
Hurricane Island Outward Bound–Western Maine Backpacking and Rock Climbing, ME
Hurricane Island Outward Bound–Western Maine Woods Expedition Canoeing, ME
Kayak Adventures Unlimited
Keewaydin Canoe Camp, Canada
Keewaydin Temagami, Canada
Kooch-I-Ching, MN
Kroka Expeditions–Advanced Rock Climbing
Kroka Expeditions–Cape Cod Triple Surfing Bonanza, MA
Kroka Expeditions–Coastal Sea Kayaking, ME
Kroka Expeditions–Coming of Age for Young Women, VT
Kroka Expeditions–Expedition Pre-Columbus, VT
Kroka Expeditions–Introduction to Adventure Residential Camp, VT
Kroka Expeditions–Introduction to Rock Climbing, VT
Kroka Expeditions–Introduction to White Water, VT
Kroka Expeditions–Paddlers Journey Up North
Kroka Expeditions–Rock 'n Road, VT
Kroka Expeditions–Vermont Underground Trail, VT
Kroka Expeditions–Wild Arts and Canoe Adventure, VT
Kroka Expeditions–Wild World of White Water, VT
Landmark Volunteers: California, CA
Landmark Volunteers: Colorado, CO
Landmark Volunteers: New York, NY
Landmark Volunteers: Washington, WA
Langskib Wilderness Programs, Canada
Lifeschool Wilderness Adventures–Summer Adventures, CA
Longacre Expeditions, Adventure 28
Longacre Expeditions, Alaska, AK
Longacre Expeditions, Belize, Belize
Longacre Expeditions, Blue Ridge, PA
Longacre Expeditions, British Columbia
Longacre Expeditions, Downeast, ME
Longacre Expeditions, Hawaii, HI
Longacre Expeditions, Iceland, Iceland
Longacre Expeditions, Laurel Highlands, PA
Longacre Expeditions, Leadership Training, CO
Longacre Expeditions, New England/Canada
Longacre Expeditions, Pacific Coast and Inlands
Longacre Expeditions, Peak to Peak, OR
Longacre Expeditions, Photography, ME
Longacre Expeditions, Surf Oregon, OR
Longacre Expeditions, Virgin Islands
Longacre Expeditions, Volcanoes
Longacre Expeditions, Western Challenge
Longacre Expeditions, Whales, ME
Longacre Expeditions, Wind and Waves, OR
Maine Conservation School Summer Camps, ME
Maine Wilderness Adventure Trip, ME
Mountain Adventure Guides: Summer Adventure Camp–Blue Ridge Expedition I, NC
Mountain Adventure Guides: Summer Adventure Camp–Blue Ridge Expedition II, NC
Mountain Adventure Guides: Summer Adventure Camp–Jr. Adventure Camp, NC
Mountain Workshop–Graduate Plus Awesome Adventures, NY
Mountain Workshop–Awesome 5: North Woods of Maine, ME
Mountain Workshop–Awesome 4: Pennsylvania, PA
Mountain Workshop–Awesome 1: Adirondacks, NY
Mountain Workshop–Awesome 6: Quebec, Canada
Mountain Workshop–Awesome 3: Maine Coast, ME
Mountain Workshop–Awesome 2: Vermont, VT
Mountain Workshop–Leadership Through Adventure: Adirondacks, NY
New England Camping Adventures, ME
North Carolina Outward Bound–Outer Banks, NC
North Carolina Outward Bound–Southern Appalachian Mountains, NC
Northern Lights, Canada
Northwaters Wilderness Programs, Canada
Outpost Wilderness Adventure–Adventure Skills, CO
Outpost Wilderness Adventure–Alpine Rock and Ice, CO
Outpost Wilderness Adventure–Copper Canyon Project, Mexico

▶ Wilderness Programs

Outpost Wilderness Adventure–Mountain Bike/Rock Camp, CO
Outpost Wilderness Adventure–Wind River Expedition, WY
Outward Bound–Connecting with Courage, MA
Outward Bound–Environmental Expeditions, MA
Outward Bound–Passages, MA
Outward Bound West–Backpacking and Whitewater Rafting, Oregon, OR
Outward Bound West–Backpacking, Climbing, and Rafting–Boys, CO
Outward Bound West–Backpacking, Climbing, and Rafting–Colorado, CO
Outward Bound West–Cataract Canyon Rafting
Outward Bound West–Climbing and Backpacking–High Sierra, CA, CA
Outward Bound West–Climbing, Backpacking, and Canoeing–North Cascades, WA, WA
Outward Bound West–Colorado Rockies Lightweight Backpacking, CO
Outward Bound West–Mountaineering and Rafting, Oregon, OR
Outward Bound West–Mountaineering–Colorado, CO
Outward Bound West–Mountaineering–North Cascades, WA, WA
Outward Bound West–Mountaineering, Rafting, and Climbing-XT, Oregon, OR
Outward Bound West–Sea Kayaking and Mountaineering–Alaska, AK
Outward Bound West–Sea Kayaking, Backpacking, and Mountaineering–Washington, WA
Outward Bound West–Service Course–North Cascades, WA
Outward Bound West–Sierra Nevada Mountaineering, CA
Outward Bound West–Southwest Mountaineering, Rafting, and Canyoneering, UT
Outward Bound West–Southwest Mystery Expedition, UT
Outward Bound West–Utah Summer Semester, UT
Outward Bound West–Volcanoes Mountaineering–Oregon, OR
Outward Bound West–Wyoming Rock Climbing, WY
Overland: Alaskan Expedition Hiking, Sea-Kayaking, and Rafting, AK
Overland: Appalachian Trail Challenge Hiking
Overland: Blue Ridge Explorer Hiking, Rafting and Kayaking, NC
Overland: Colorado and Utah Mountain Biking and Rafting
Overland: Costa Rica Explorer Hiking, Rafting, and Sea-Kayaking, Costa Rica
Overland: European Explorer Hiking, Rafting, and Sea Kayaking
Overland: Hawaii Explorer Hiking, Kayaking, Sailing and Snorkeling, HI
Overland: New England Explorer Hiking, Mountain Biking, and Rafting
Overland: Rocky Mountain Explorer Hiking, Mountain Biking, and Rafting
Overland: Shasta & the Sierras Backpacking, Climbing and Rafting
Overland: Teton Challenge Hiking, Climbing and Kayaking, WY
Overland: The Alpine Challenge Leadership Course Backpacking and Hiking
Overland: Yellowstone Explorer Backpacking, Rock Climbing, and Rafting
Poulter Colorado Camps, CO
Program of Audubon Research for Teens (Take P.A.R.T.), VT
Putney Student Travel–Community Service–Alaska, AK
Roaring Brook Camp for Boys, VT
Sea Kayak Expedition (English), Canada
Streamside Pathfinder Adventure Camp, PA
Student Conservation Association–Conservation Crew Program (Alabama), AL
Student Conservation Association–Conservation Crew Program (Alaska), AK
Student Conservation Association–Conservation Crew Program (Arizona), AZ
Student Conservation Association–Conservation Crew Program (Arkansas), AR
Student Conservation Association–Conservation Crew Program (California), CA
Student Conservation Association–Conservation Crew Program (Colorado), CO
Student Conservation Association–Conservation Crew Program (Connecticut), CT
Student Conservation Association–Conservation Crew Program (Delaware), DE
Student Conservation Association–Conservation Crew Program (Florida), FL
Student Conservation Association–Conservation Crew Program (Georgia), GA
Student Conservation Association–Conservation Crew Program (Hawaii), HI
Student Conservation Association–Conservation Crew Program (Idaho), ID
Student Conservation Association–Conservation Crew Program (Illinois), IL
Student Conservation Association–Conservation Crew Program (Indiana), IN
Student Conservation Association–Conservation Crew Program (Iowa), IA
Student Conservation Association–Conservation Crew Program (Kansas), KS
Student Conservation Association–Conservation Crew Program (Kentucky), KY
Student Conservation Association–Conservation Crew Program (Louisiana), LA
Student Conservation Association–Conservation Crew Program (Maine), ME
Student Conservation Association–Conservation Crew Program (Maryland), MD
Student Conservation Association–Conservation Crew Program (Massachusetts), MA
Student Conservation Association–Conservation Crew Program (Michigan), MI
Student Conservation Association–Conservation Crew Program (Minnesota), MN
Student Conservation Association–Conservation Crew Program (Mississippi), MS
Student Conservation Association–Conservation Crew Program (Missouri), MO
Student Conservation Association–Conservation Crew Program (Montana), MT
Student Conservation Association–Conservation Crew Program (Nebraska), NE
Student Conservation Association–Conservation Crew Program (Nevada), NV
Student Conservation Association–Conservation Crew Program (New Hampshire), NH
Student Conservation Association–Conservation Crew Program (New Jersey), NJ
Student Conservation Association–Conservation Crew Program (New Mexico), NM
Student Conservation Association–Conservation Crew Program (New York), NY
Student Conservation Association–Conservation Crew Program (North Carolina), NC
Student Conservation Association–Conservation Crew Program (North Dakota), ND
Student Conservation Association–Conservation Crew Program (Ohio), OH
Student Conservation Association–Conservation Crew Program (Oklahoma), OK
Student Conservation Association–Conservation Crew Program (Oregon), OR
Student Conservation Association–Conservation Crew Program (Pennsylvania), PA
Student Conservation Association–Conservation Crew Program (Rhode Island), RI
Student Conservation Association–Conservation Crew Program (South Carolina), SC
Student Conservation Association–Conservation Crew Program (South Dakota), SD
Student Conservation Association–Conservation Crew Program (Tennessee), TN
Student Conservation Association–Conservation Crew Program (Texas), TX
Student Conservation Association–Conservation Crew Program (Utah), UT
Student Conservation Association–Conservation Crew Program (Vermont), VT
Student Conservation Association–Conservation Crew Program (Virginia), VA
Student Conservation Association–Conservation Crew Program (Washington), WA
Student Conservation Association–Conservation Crew Program (West Virginia), WV
Student Conservation Association–Conservation Crew Program (Wisconsin), WI
Student Conservation Association–Conservation Crew Program (Wyoming), WY

Student Conservation Association–Conservation Leadership Corps, Bay Area, CA
Success Oriented Achievement Realized (SOAR)–North Carolina, NC
Success Oriented Achievement Realized (SOAR)–Wyoming, WY
Swift Nature Camp–Canadian Canoe Trip
Talisman Open Boat Adventures (TOBA), NC
Talisman–Trek Hiking Program, NC
Teen Expeditions, RI
Teton Valley Ranch Camp–Boys Camp, WY
Teton Valley Ranch Camp–Girls Camp, WY
Timber-lee Wilderness Trips, WI
Trail Blazers, NJ
Trailmark Outdoor Adventures–Colorado–West Elks with Backpack, CO
Trailmark Outdoor Adventures–Colorado–West Elks with Horseback, CO
Trailmark Outdoor Adventures–New England–Acadia
Trailmark Outdoor Adventures–New England–Camden
Trailmark Outdoor Adventures–New England–Downeast
Trailmark Outdoor Adventures–New England–Mahoosoc
Trailmark Outdoor Adventures–New England–Moose River
Trailmark Outdoor Adventures–New England–Mt. Desert
Trailmark Outdoor Adventures–New England–Rangeley Coed
Trailmark Outdoor Adventures–Northern Rockies–Tetons with Backpack
Trailmark Outdoor Adventures–Northern Rockies–Tetons with Horseback
Voyageur Outward Bound–Boundary Waters Wilderness Canoeing, MN
Voyageur Outward Bound–Boundary Waters Wilderness Canoeing and Climbing XT, MN
Voyageur Outward Bound–Greater Yellowstone Whitewater and Backpacking, MT
Voyageur Outward Bound–Lake Superior Freshwater Kayaking, Canada
Voyageur Outward Bound–Lake Superior Freshwater Kayaking and Backpacking
Voyageur Outward Bound–Lewis and Clark Alpine Backpacking, MT
Voyageur Outward Bound–Lewis and Clark Alpine Backpacking-Girls, MT
Voyageur Outward Bound–Manitoba to Montana Summer Semester
Voyageur Outward Bound–Montana High Alpine Backpacking, MT
Voyageur Outward Bound–Montana Rock Climbing XT, MT
Voyageur Outward Bound–Northern Rockies Backpacking Family Adventure, MT
Voyageur Outward Bound–Northwoods Wilderness Canoeing and Backpacking, MN
Where There Be Dragons: Guatemala, Guatemala
Where There Be Dragons: India Zanskar Trek, India
Where There Be Dragons: Mexico, Mexico
Where There Be Dragons: Mongolia, Mongolia
Where There Be Dragons: Peru, Peru
Where There Be Dragons: Tibet, China
Wilderness Adventure, CO
Wilderness Adventure at Eagle Landing, VA
Wilderness Experiences Unlimited–Explorers Camp, MA
Wilderness Experiences Unlimited–Leaders In Training Camp, MA
Wilderness Experiences Unlimited–Trailblazers Camp, MA
Wilderness Experiences Unlimited/Westfield Water Sports: Scuba Camp, MA
Wilderness Ventures–Alaska Leadership, AK
Wilderness Ventures–Alaska Service, AK
Wilderness Ventures–Alaska Southcentral, AK
Wilderness Ventures–Alaska Southeast, AK
Wilderness Ventures–Australia, Australia
Wilderness Ventures–California, CA
Wilderness Ventures–Cascade-Olympic, WA
Wilderness Ventures–Colorado/Utah Mountain Bike
Wilderness Ventures–Costa Rica, Costa Rica
Wilderness Ventures–Ecuador and Galapagos, Ecuador
Wilderness Ventures–European Alps
Wilderness Ventures–Grand Teton, WY
Wilderness Ventures–Great Divide
Wilderness Ventures–Great Divide Bike
Wilderness Ventures–Hawaii, HI
Wilderness Ventures–High Sierra, CA
Wilderness Ventures–Jackson Hole, WY
Wilderness Ventures–Northwest
Wilderness Ventures–Oregon, OR
Wilderness Ventures–Pacific Coast Bike
Wilderness Ventures–Pacific Northwest
Wilderness Ventures–Puget Sound, WA
Wilderness Ventures–Rocky Mountain
Wilderness Ventures–Spanish Pyrenees, Spain
Wilderness Ventures–Teton Adventure, WY
Wilderness Ventures–Washington Alpine, WA
Wilderness Ventures–Washington Mountaineering, WA
Wilderness Ventures–Wyoming Mountaineering, WY
Wilderness Ventures–Yellowstone Fly Fishing
Williwaw Adventures–Maine Mountains and Coast, ME
Williwaw Adventures–Maine Wilderness
Williwaw Adventures–Pacific Northwest Expedition
YMCA Camp Lincoln–Outdoor Adventure Camp: Backpacking, NH
YMCA Camp Lincoln–Outdoor Adventure Camp: Everything Outdoors, NH
YMCA Camp Lincoln–Outdoor Adventure Camp: Mountain Bike, NH
YMCA Camp Lincoln–Outdoor Adventure Camp: River Runners, NH
YMCA Camp Widjiwagan, MN
YMCA Wilderness Camp Menogyn, MN
Yo! Basecamp Rock Climbing Camps, CA
Yosemite Backpacking Adventures, CA

Alabama

ATW: Action America West
Overland: American Challenge Coast-to-Coast Bicycle Touring

Alaska

AAVE–Alaska
Adventure Treks–Alaska Adventures
Alpengirl–Alaska
ATW: Fire and Ice
Camp Tawonga–Teen Service Learning to Alaska
Longacre Expeditions, Alaska
Musiker Tours: Alaska Aloha
Outward Bound West–Sea Kayaking and Mountaineering–Alaska
Overland: Alaskan Expedition Hiking, Sea-Kayaking, and Rafting
Overland: American Community Service, Alaska
Rein Teen Tours–Hawaiian/Alaskan Adventure
Teen Tours of America–Alaskan Expedition
Visions–Alaska
Westcoast Connection–Community Connections Alaska
Wilderness Ventures–Alaska Leadership
Wilderness Ventures–Alaska Service
Wilderness Ventures–Alaska Southcentral
Wilderness Ventures–Alaska Southeast
Windsor Mountain: Alaska

Anguilla

Sail Caribbean–Leeward Islands

Antigua and Barbuda

ACTIONQUEST: Leeward and French Caribbean Island Voyages
BROADREACH Adventures in Scuba and Sailing–Underwater Discoveries
BROADREACH Adventures Underwater–Advanced Scuba
BROADREACH Arc of the Caribbean Sailing Adventure

Arizona

AAVE–Boot/Saddle/Paddle
Adventures Cross-Country, Western Adventure
Alien Adventure Overnight Camp
ATW: Action America West
ATW: American Horizons
ATW: California Sunset
ATW: Camp Inn 42
ATW: Discoverer
ATW: Pacific Paradise
ATW: Skyblazer
ATW: Sunblazer
ATW: Wayfarer
Camp Tawonga–Teen Quest: Southwest
Flint Hill School–"Summer on the Hill"–Enrichment on the Hill–Women Writers' Adventure
Four Corners School of Outdoor Education: Southwest Ed-Venture
Musiker Tours: Action USA
Musiker Tours: America Coast to Coast
Musiker Tours: ComboCamp America
Musiker Tours: Discover America
Musiker Tours: Westcoaster
Overland: American Challenge Coast-to-Coast Bicycle Touring
Rein Teen Tours–American Adventure
Rein Teen Tours–California Caper
Rein Teen Tours–Crossroads
Rein Teen Tours–Grand Adventure
Rein Teen Tours–Western Adventure
RUSTIC PATHWAYS–ADVENTURE IN AMERICA'S SOUTHWEST
Summit Travel Program
Teen Tours of America–Western Adventure
Teen Tours of America–Western Sprint
Ventures Travel Service–Arizona
Weissman Teen Tours–U.S. and Western Canada, 6 Weeks
Westcoast Connection–American Voyageur
Westcoast Connection–Californian Extravaganza
Westcoast Connection Travel–California and the Canyons
Westcoast Connection Travel–Southwesterner
Westcoast Connection–U.S. Explorer

Arkansas

Overland: American Challenge Coast-to-Coast Bicycle Touring

Australia

AAVE–Australia
ACTIONQUEST: Australian and Great Barrier Reef Adventures
Adventures Cross-Country, Australia/Fiji Adventure
BROADREACH Adventures Down Under
Camp Chewonki Eco-Kayak Australia
LIFEWORKS with the Australian Red Cross
PAX Abroad to Australia
Putney Student Travel–Cultural Exploration–Australia, New Zealand, and Fiji
RUSTIC PATHWAYS–AWESOME AUSSIE EXPLORER
RUSTIC PATHWAYS–EXTREME PLANET
RUSTIC PATHWAYS–HIGH ADRENALINE AUSSIE
RUSTIC PATHWAYS–OUTBACK 4-WHEEL DRIVE SAFARI
RUSTIC PATHWAYS–THE SUNSHINE COAST & SYDNEY
RUSTIC PATHWAYS–TOTALLY DOWNUNDER ADVENTURE
RUSTIC PATHWAYS–TROPICAL AUSSIE ADVENTURE
RUSTIC PATHWAYS–ULTIMATE AUSTRALIAN ADVENTURE
Visions–Australia
Westcoast Connection–Australian Outback Plus Hawaii
Westcoast Connection/On Tour– Australian Outback
Wilderness Ventures–Australia
Windsor Mountain: Coast of Australia
Youth for Understanding USA–Australia

Austria

Blue Lake International Exchange Program
Knowledge Exchange Institute–European Capitals Program
Poulter Colorado Camps: Adventures Planet Earth–Austria
TENNIS: EUROPE

Bahamas

Flint Hill School–"Summer on the Hill"–Trips from the Hill–Ecological Study of Coral Reefs, Bahamas
Geronimo Program

Belgium

ATW: European Adventures
BICYCLE TRAVEL ADVENTURES–Student Hosteling Program–Amsterdam to Paris
Blue Lake International Exchange Program
Knowledge Exchange Institute–European Capitals Program
Musiker Tours: Action Europe
Weissman Teen Tours–European Experience
Westcoast Connection Travel–European Discovery

Belize

AAVE–Belize
BROADREACH Academic Treks–Wilderness Emergency Medicine
Longacre Expeditions, Belize

Benin

Bicycle Africa Tours

Bermuda

Geronimo Program

Brazil

PAX Abroad–Brazil

British Virgin Islands

ACTIONQUEST: Advanced PADI Scuba Certification and Specialty Voyages
ACTIONQUEST: British Virgin Islands–Sailing and Scuba Voyages
ACTIONQUEST: British Virgin Islands-Sailing Voyages
ACTIONQUEST: Junior Advanced Scuba with Marine Biology
ACTIONQUEST: Leeward and French Caribbean Island Voyages
ACTIONQUEST: Rescue Diving Voyages
ACTIONQUEST: Tropical Marine Biology Voyages
Adventures Cross-Country, Caribbean Adventure
LIFEWORKS with the British Virgin Islands Marine Parks and Conservation Department
Longacre Expeditions, Virgin Islands
Sail Caribbean–All Levels of Scuba Certification with Sailing
Sail Caribbean–British Virgin Islands
Sail Caribbean–Community Service
Sail Caribbean–Marine Biology
Visions–British Virgin Islands

California

AAVE–Bold West
Adventures Cross-Country, Western Adventure
Adventure Treks–California Challenge Adventures
Adventure Treks–California 19 Adventures
Adventure Treks–Summit Fever
Alien Adventure Overnight Camp
ATW: Action America West
ATW: American Horizons

ATW: California Sunset
ATW: Camp Inn 42
ATW: Discoverer
ATW: Fire and Ice
ATW: Pacific Paradise
ATW: Skyblazer
ATW: Sunblazer
ATW: Wayfarer
BICYCLE TRAVEL ADVENTURES–Student Hosteling Program–Canadian Rockies to California
BICYCLE TRAVEL ADVENTURES–Student Hosteling Program–Pacific Coast Adventure: Washington, Oregon, and California
California Campus Tours
California Cruzin' Overnight Camp
Camp Tawonga–Call of the Wild
Camp Tawonga–Magical Mystery Tour
Camp Tawonga–Surf 'n Turf Quest
Camp Tawonga–Teen Quest: High Sierra
Camp Tawonga–Teen Quest: Northwest
Camp Tawonga–Teen Quest: Yosemite
ExploraMar: Marine Biology Sailing Expeditions–Sea of Cortez, Baja, Mexico
Great Escapes (Adventure Trips for Teens)–California Beach Escape
Hiker's Heaven Overnight Camp
Julian Krinsky California Teen Tours
Julian Krinsky Yesh Shabbat California Teen Tour
Lifeschool Wilderness Adventures–Summer Adventures
Musiker Tours: Action USA
Musiker Tours: Alaska Aloha
Musiker Tours: America Coast to Coast
Musiker Tours: Cali-Pacific Passport
Musiker Tours: ComboCamp America
Musiker Tours: Discover America
Musiker Tours: Westcoaster
Outward Bound West–Climbing and Backpacking–High Sierra, CA
Outward Bound West–Sierra Nevada Mountaineering
Overland: American Challenge Coast-to-Coast Bicycle Touring
Overland: Pacific Coast Bicycle Touring and Rafting
Overland: Shasta & the Sierras Backpacking, Climbing and Rafting
Rein Teen Tours–American Adventure
Rein Teen Tours–California Caper
Rein Teen Tours–Crossroads
Rein Teen Tours–Grand Adventure
Rein Teen Tours–Hawaiian/Alaskan Adventure
Rein Teen Tours–Western Adventure
Summer Conservation Corps
Summit Travel Program
Teen Tours of America–Alaskan Expedition
Teen Tours of America–Aloha Hawaii
Teen Tours of America–Western Adventure
TENNIS: EUROPE & MORE–North American Teams
Ventures Travel Service–California
Weissman Teen Tours–"Aloha–Welcome to Hawaiian Paradise"
Weissman Teen Tours–U.S. and Western Canada, 4 Weeks
Weissman Teen Tours–U.S. and Western Canada, 6 Weeks
Westcoast Connection–American Voyageur
Westcoast Connection–Californian Extravaganza
Westcoast Connection–Hawaiian Spirit
Westcoast Connection Travel–Adventure California
Westcoast Connection Travel–California and the Canyons
Westcoast Connection Travel–Great West Challenge
Westcoast Connection–U.S. Explorer
Wilderness Ventures–California
Wilderness Ventures–High Sierra
Wilderness Ventures–Pacific Coast Bike
Windsor Mountain: California Community Service
Yosemite Backpacking Adventures

Cambodia

RUSTIC PATHWAYS–BUDDHIST LIFE & ANGKOR WAT

Cameroon

Bicycle Africa Tours

Canada

AAVE–Border Cross
Adventure Treks–Canadian Rockies Adventures
Apogee Outdoor Adventures–Coast to Quebec
ATW: Adventure Roads
ATW: American Horizons
ATW: Camp Inn 42
ATW: Fire and Ice
ATW: Mini Tours
ATW: Pacific Paradise
ATW: Skyblazer
ATW: Wayfarer
BICYCLE TRAVEL ADVENTURES–Student Hosteling Program–A Thousand Miles: Massachusetts to Nova Scotia
BICYCLE TRAVEL ADVENTURES–Student Hosteling Program–Canadian Rockies to California
BICYCLE TRAVEL ADVENTURES–Student Hosteling Program–Maine-Nova Scotia Coast Loop
BICYCLE TRAVEL ADVENTURES–Student Hosteling Program–Niagara Falls to Montreal
BICYCLE TRAVEL ADVENTURES–Student Hosteling Program–Province du Québec
BICYCLE TRAVEL ADVENTURES–Student Hosteling Program–Province du Québec (short program)
BICYCLE TRAVEL ADVENTURES–Student Hosteling Program–Vermont to the Atlantic Ocean
BROADREACH Academic Treks–Marine Mammal Studies
Camp Chi Teenage Adventure Trips
Camp Tawonga–Teen Quest: Canada
Darrow Wilderness Trips–Quebec: Mistassini
French Immersion Kayak Expedition
Great Escapes (Adventure Trips for Teens)–Canadian Adventure
Great Escapes (Adventure Trips for Teens)–Canadian Canoe and Kayak Adventure
Hulbert Voyageurs Youth Wilderness Trips
Hurricane Island Outward Bound–Ocean Bound: Tall Ship Sailing and Sea Kayaking Semester
Ibike Cultural Tours–Washington/British Columbia
Longacre Expeditions, Adventure 28
Longacre Expeditions, British Columbia
Longacre Expeditions, New England/Canada
Longacre Expeditions, Pacific Coast and Inlands
Longacre Expeditions, Western Challenge
Mountain Workshop–Awesome 6: Quebec
Musiker Tours: Alaska Aloha
Musiker Tours: America Coast to Coast
Musiker Tours: Cali-Pacific Passport
Musiker Tours: ComboCamp America
Musiker Tours: Discover America
Musiker Tours: Eastcoaster
Overland: Acadia and Prince Edward Island Bicycle Touring and Sea-Kayaking
Overland: Vermont & Montreal Bicycle Touring
Programs Abroad Travel Alternatives–Canada
The Ranch–Lake Placid Teen Travel Camp
Rein Teen Tours–American Adventure
Rein Teen Tours–Crossroads
Rein Teen Tours–Eastern Adventure
Rein Teen Tours–Grand Adventure
Rein Teen Tours–Hawaiian/Alaskan Adventure
Sea Kayak Expedition (English)
Summit Travel Program
Swift Nature Camp–Canadian Canoe Trip
Teen Tours of America–Alaskan Expedition
Teen Tours of America–New England Journey
Teen Tours of America–Western Adventure
Teen Tours of America–Western Sprint
Teen Tour USA and Canada
TENNIS: EUROPE & MORE–North American Teams
Voyageur Outward Bound–Lake Superior Freshwater Kayaking
Voyageur Outward Bound–Lake Superior Freshwater Kayaking and Backpacking
Voyageur Outward Bound–Manitoba to Montana Summer Semester
Weissman Teen Tours–U.S. and Western Canada, 4 Weeks
Weissman Teen Tours–U.S. and Western Canada, 6 Weeks
Westcoast Connection–American Voyageur
Westcoast Connection Travel/On Tour–Northwestern Odyssey
Westcoast Connection Travel–Canadian Mountain Magic
Westcoast Connection Travel–Eastcoast Encounter
Westcoast Connection Travel–Great West Challenge
Westcoast Connection Travel–Northwestern Odyssey
Westcoast Connection Travel/On Tour–Canadian Adventure
Westcoast Connection Travel–Quebec Adventure
Westcoast Connection Travel–Ski and Snowboard Sensation
Westcoast Connection Travel–Western Canadian Adventure
Westcoast Connection–U.S. Explorer
Windsor Mountain: Bonjour Quebec
YMCA Camp Lincoln–Outdoor Adventure Camp: Canadian Adventure

Chile

BROADREACH Academic Treks–Language Exposure and Service Learning
Youth for Understanding USA–Chile

▶ China

China
EF International Language School–Shanghai
Phillips Exeter Academy Taiwan and Beijing Summer Study Tour
Tibetan Summer Passage
Where There Be Dragons: China
Where There Be Dragons: Silk Road
Where There Be Dragons: Tibet

Colorado
AAVE–Boot/Saddle/Paddle
AAVE–Rock & River
AAVE–Rocky Mountain Adventure
AAVE–X–Five
Adventures Cross-Country, Western Adventure
ATW: American Horizons
ATW: Discoverer
ATW: Skyblazer
ATW: Wayfarer
BICYCLE TRAVEL ADVENTURES–Student Hosteling Program–Cross-Country America
Flint Hill School–"Summer on the Hill"–Enrichment on the Hill–Women Writers' Adventure
Four Corners School of Outdoor Education: Southwest Ed-Venture
Great Escapes (Adventure Trips for Teens)–Colorado River and Canyons Adventure
Great Escapes (Adventure Trips for Teens)–Rocky Mountain Horsepacking Adventure
Longacre Expeditions, Leadership Training
Musiker Tours: Action USA
Musiker Tours: America Coast to Coast
Outpost Wilderness Adventure–Alpine Rock and Ice
Outward Bound West–Backpacking, Climbing, and Rafting–Boys
Outward Bound West–Backpacking, Climbing, and Rafting–Colorado
Outward Bound West–Cataract Canyon Rafting
Outward Bound West–Colorado Rockies Lightweight Backpacking
Outward Bound West–Mountaineering–Colorado
Overland: Colorado and Utah Mountain Biking and Rafting
Overland: Rocky Mountain Explorer Hiking, Mountain Biking, and Rafting
RUSTIC PATHWAYS–ADVENTURE IN AMERICA'S SOUTHWEST
Summit Travel Program
TENNIS: EUROPE & MORE–North American Teams
Trailmark Outdoor Adventures–Colorado–West Elks with Backpack
Trailmark Outdoor Adventures–Colorado–West Elks with Horseback
Weissman Teen Tours–U.S. and Western Canada, 4 Weeks
Weissman Teen Tours–U.S. and Western Canada, 6 Weeks
Westcoast Connection–Californian Extravaganza
Westcoast Connection Travel–Southwesterner
Wilderness Ventures–Colorado/Utah Mountain Bike

Connecticut
College Impressions
East Coast College Tour by Education Unlimited
Mountain Workshop/Dirt Camp: Dirt Camp Junior Killington
92nd Street Y Camps–The TIYUL
The Ranch–Lake Placid Teen Travel Camp
Teen Tours of America–New England Journey
Teen Tour USA and Canada

Costa Rica
AAVE–Costa Rica
Adventure Links–The Costa Rica Experience
BROADREACH Academic Treks–Sea Turtle Studies
BROADREACH Costa Rica Experience
Costa Rica ¡Pura Vida!
Costa Rica Rainforest Outward Bound School–Multi-Element
Costa Rica Rainforest Outward Bound School–Summer Semester
Costa Rica Rainforest Outward Bound School–Surf Adventure
Costa Rica Rainforest Outward Bound School–Tri-Country/Tri-Mester
GLOBAL WORKS–Language Exposure-Costa Rica-4 weeks
GLOBAL WORKS–Language Immersion-Costa Rica-4 weeks
Great Escapes (Adventure Trips for Teens)–Costa Rica Rainforest Adventure
Overland: Costa Rica Explorer Hiking, Rafting, and Sea-Kayaking
Peace Works International–Costa Rica
Poulter Colorado Camps: Adventures Planet Earth–Costa Rica
Programs Abroad Travel Alternatives–Costa Rica
RUSTIC PATHWAYS–COSTA RICA ADVENTURER
RUSTIC PATHWAYS–COSTA RICA EXTREME
RUSTIC PATHWAYS–COSTA RICA NATURAL WONDERS
RUSTIC PATHWAYS–EXTREME PLANET
Sidwell Friends Summer Program: Costa Rica
Spanish Through Leadership–Nicaragua/Costa Rica
Wilderness Ventures–Costa Rica

Cuba
Windsor Mountain: Cuba Friendship Exchange

Czech Republic
Knowledge Exchange Institute–European Capitals Program

Denmark
Blue Lake International Exchange Program
Peace in the Modern World
TENNIS: EUROPE

District Of Columbia
ATW: Adventure Roads
East Coast College Tour by Education Unlimited
Hurricane Island Outward Bound–Mid-Atlantic Canoeing, Backpacking, and Rock Climbing
Julian Krinsky Golf Tours
Musiker Tours: Eastcoaster
Teen Tour USA and Canada
Trailridge Mountain Camp
Westcoast Connection Travel–Eastcoast Encounter

Dominica
BROADREACH Arc of the Caribbean Sailing Adventure
Kayak Adventures Unlimited
Visions–Dominica

Dominican Republic
Visions–Dominican Republic

Ecuador
AAVE–Ecuador and Galapagos
ACTIONQUEST: Galapagos Archipelago Expeditions
BROADREACH Academic Treks–Spanish Language Immersion in Ecuador
BROADREACH Amazon and Galapagos Encounter
EF International Language Schools–Quito
GLOBAL WORKS–Language Exposure-Ecuador and the Galapagos-4 weeks
GLOBAL WORKS–Language Immersion-Ecuador and the Galapagos-4 weeks
Ibike Cultural Tours–Ecuador
LIFEWORKS with the Galapagos Islands' National Parks
PAX Abroad–Ecuador Rainforest Adventure
PAX Abroad–Ecuador–Spanish Language Immersion
Peace Works International–Ecuador
Programs Abroad Travel Alternatives–Ecuador
Visions–Ecuador
Wilderness Ventures–Ecuador and Galapagos

Egypt
BROADREACH Red Sea Scuba Adventure

Eritrea
Bicycle Africa Tours

Estonia
Youth for Understanding USA–Estonia/Latvia-Baltic Summer

Ethiopia
Bicycle Africa Tours

Fiji
Adventures Cross-Country, Australia/Fiji Adventure
BROADREACH Fiji Solomon Quest
GLOBAL WORKS–Cultural Exchange-Fiji Islands-4 weeks
GLOBAL WORKS–Cultural Exchange-New Zealand and Fiji Islands-4 weeks
Putney Student Travel–Cultural Exploration–Australia, New Zealand, and Fiji
RUSTIC PATHWAYS–BIG FIJI EXPLORER
RUSTIC PATHWAYS–EXTREME PLANET
RUSTIC PATHWAYS–HIGHLANDS COMMUNITY SERVICE IN FIJI
RUSTIC PATHWAYS–LEARN TO DIVE IN THE FIJI ISLANDS
RUSTIC PATHWAYS–SNAPSHOT OF FIJI

Florida
ATW: Adventure Roads
ATW: Mini Tours
Musiker Tours: Eastcoaster

Rein Teen Tours–Eastern Adventure
Teen Tours of America–Golf Camp–Florida Swing
Trailridge Mountain Camp
Ventures Travel Service–Florida
Westcoast Connection–Florida Swing Junior Touring Golf Camp
Westcoast Connection Travel–Eastcoast Encounter

France
AAVE–Alps Rider
AAVE–Bike France
AAVE–Bold Europe
AAVE–Vivons le Français
Abbey Road Overseas Programs–French Immersion and Homestay
Abbey Road Overseas Programs–French Study Abroad in Cannes
ACTIONQUEST: Mediterranean Sailing Voyage
Adventures Cross-Country,Southern Europe Adventure
ATW: European Adventures
Barat Foundation Summer Program in Provence and Paris
BICYCLE TRAVEL ADVENTURES–Student Hosteling Program–Amsterdam to Paris
BICYCLE TRAVEL ADVENTURES–Student Hosteling Program–France and Italy
BICYCLE TRAVEL ADVENTURES–Student Hosteling Program–Spain and France
Blue Lake International Exchange Program
Blyth Education–Summer Study in Paris and the South of France
Concordia Language Villages–France
EF International Language School–Nice
EF International Language School–Paris
Excel at Oxford/Tuscany
GLOBAL WORKS–Language Immersion-France-4 weeks
Knowledge Exchange Institute–European Capitals Program
Mercersburg Academy Summer Study in France
Musiker Tours: Action Europe
Overland: European Challenge Bicycle Touring from Paris to Rome
Overland: European Explorer Hiking, Rafting, and Sea Kayaking
Overland: Language Study Abroad in France
Overland: Paris to the Sea Bicycle Touring
Overland: The Alpine Challenge Leadership Course Backpacking and Hiking
Phillips Exeter Academy French Study Tour
Programs Abroad Travel Alternatives–France
Putney Student Travel–Cultural Exploration–France, Holland, and England
Putney Student Travel–Cultural Exploration–Switzerland, Italy, France, and Holland
Rassias Programs–Arles, France
Rassias Programs–Tours, France
Taft Summer School Abroad–France
TENNIS: EUROPE
University of Chicago–ChicaGO! The Traveling Academy
Weissman Teen Tours–European Experience
Westcoast Connection Travel–European Discovery
Westcoast Connection Travel–European Escape
Westcoast Connection Travel/On Tour–European Experience
Wilderness Ventures–European Alps
Windsor Mountain: Crossroads France
Windsor Mountain: European Traveling Minstrels

French Polynesia
ACTIONQUEST: Tahiti and French Polynesian Island Voyages

Gambia
Bicycle Africa Tours
Rust College Study Abroad in Africa

Georgia
ATW: Adventure Roads
Cheerio Adventures–5 Rivers in 5 Days
92nd Street Y Camps–The TIYUL
Overland: American Challenge Coast-to-Coast Bicycle Touring
Trailridge Mountain Camp

Germany
Blue Lake International Exchange Program
EF International Language School–Munich
Knowledge Exchange Institute–European Capitals Program
Poulter Colorado Camps: Adventures Planet Earth–Austria
Programs Abroad Travel Alternatives–Germany
TENNIS: EUROPE

Ghana
Bicycle Africa Tours
Rust College Study Abroad in Africa

Greece
Greek Summer
TENNIS: EUROPE

Grenada
!ADVENTURES–AFLOAT: Advanced Scuba Adventure Voyages–Caribbean Islands
!ADVENTURES–AFLOAT: Scuba and Sailing Discovery Voyages–Caribbean Islands
BROADREACH Adventures in the Windward Islands–Advanced Scuba
ODYSSEY EXPEDITIONS: Tropical Marine Biology Voyages–Caribbean Islands

Guadeloupe
ACTIONQUEST: Leeward and French Caribbean Island Voyages
BROADREACH Academic Treks–Marine Park Management
BROADREACH Adventures in Scuba and Sailing–Underwater Discoveries
BROADREACH Adventures Underwater–Advanced Scuba
BROADREACH Arc of the Caribbean Sailing Adventure
Visions–Guadeloupe

Guatemala
Programs Abroad Travel Alternatives–Guatemala
Where There Be Dragons: Guatemala

Guinea
Bicycle Africa Tours

Guyana
Ibike Cultural Tours–Guyana

Hawaii
AAVE–Hawaii
Alpengirl–Hawaii
ATW: Camp Inn 42
ATW: Fire and Ice
Longacre Expeditions, Hawaii
Musiker Tours: Alaska Aloha
Musiker Tours: ComboCamp America
Overland: American Community Service, Hawaii
Overland: Hawaii Explorer Hiking, Kayaking, Sailing and Snorkeling
Rein Teen Tours–Hawaiian/Alaskan Adventure
RUSTIC PATHWAYS–HAWAIIAN ISLANDS ADVENTURE
Sidwell Friends Service Expedition to Hawaii
Teen Tours of America–Aloha Hawaii
Weissman Teen Tours–"Aloha–Welcome to Hawaiian Paradise"
Westcoast Connection–Australian Outback Plus Hawaii
Westcoast Connection–Hawaiian Spirit
Wilderness Ventures–Hawaii
Windsor Mountain: Hawaii

Honduras
BROADREACH Honduras Eco-Adventure

Iceland
Longacre Expeditions, Iceland

Idaho
Alpengirl–Montana Art
BICYCLE TRAVEL ADVENTURES–Student Hosteling Program–Cross-Country America
Musiker Tours: Action USA
Musiker Tours: America Coast to Coast
Musiker Tours: ComboCamp America
Musiker Tours: Discover America
Overland: Yellowstone Explorer Backpacking, Rock Climbing, and Rafting
Summer Conservation Corps
TENNIS: EUROPE & MORE–North American Teams
Wilderness Ventures–Great Divide
Wilderness Ventures–Great Divide Bike
Wilderness Ventures–Rocky Mountain
Wilderness Ventures–Yellowstone Fly Fishing

Illinois
ATW: American Horizons
ATW: Wayfarer
BICYCLE TRAVEL ADVENTURES–Student Hosteling Program–Cross-Country America
Musiker Tours: America Coast to Coast
Rein Teen Tours–American Adventure
Rein Teen Tours–Crossroads
Westcoast Connection–U.S. Explorer

India
Ladakh Summer Passage
The Sikkim Cultural Immersion Experience
Tibetan Summer Passage
Where There Be Dragons: India Culture and Philosophy
Where There Be Dragons: India Zanskar Trek

Indiana
BICYCLE TRAVEL ADVENTURES–Student Hosteling Program–Cross-Country America

Iowa
Ventures Travel Service–Iowa

Ireland
AAVE–Wild Isles
BICYCLE TRAVEL ADVENTURES–Student Hosteling Program–Ireland and England
Celtic Learning and Travel Services–Edinburgh and Dublin
Celtic Learning and Travel Services–London and Dublin
Celtic Learning and Travel Services–Summer in Ireland
GLOBAL WORKS–Cultural Exchange-Ireland-4 weeks
Irish Way
Programs Abroad Travel Alternatives–Ireland

Israel
Alexander Muss High School in Israel
Israel Discovery

Italy
AAVE–Alps Rider
AAVE–Bold Europe
Abbey Road Overseas Programs–Italy Study Abroad: Language and Culture
ACTIONQUEST: Mediterranean Sailing Voyage
Adventures Cross-Country,Southern Europe Adventure
ATW: European Adventures
BICYCLE TRAVEL ADVENTURES–Student Hosteling Program–France and Italy
Blue Lake International Exchange Program
EF International Language School–Rome
Excel at Oxford/Tuscany
Humanities Spring in Assisi
Humanities Spring on the Road
Israel Discovery
Musiker Tours: Action Europe
Overland: European Challenge Bicycle Touring from Paris to Rome
Overland: The Alpine Challenge Leadership Course Backpacking and Hiking
Programs Abroad Travel Alternatives–Italy
Putney Student Travel–Cultural Exploration–Switzerland, Italy, France, and Holland
TENNIS: EUROPE
Weissman Teen Tours–European Experience
Westcoast Connection Travel–European Discovery
Westcoast Connection Travel–European Escape
Westcoast Connection Travel/On Tour–European Experience
Wilderness Ventures–European Alps
Windsor Mountain: European Traveling Minstrels

Kansas
BICYCLE TRAVEL ADVENTURES–Student Hosteling Program–Cross-Country America
Rein Teen Tours–American Adventure

Kentucky
BICYCLE TRAVEL ADVENTURES–Student Hosteling Program–Cross-Country America
Trailridge Mountain Camp
Ventures Travel Service–Kentucky

Kenya
Bicycle Africa Tours
Eagle Lake Camp Jaunts–Kenya Mission Adventure
Knowledge Exchange Institute–African Safari Program
Youth for Understanding USA–Kenya

Latvia
Youth for Understanding USA–Estonia/Latvia-Baltic Summer

Louisiana
ATW: Adventure Roads

Luxembourg
Knowledge Exchange Institute–European Capitals Program

Maine
Apogee Outdoor Adventures–Burlington to Boston
Apogee Outdoor Adventures–Coast to Quebec
Apogee Outdoor Adventures–New England Mountains and Coast
ATW: Mini Tours
Barton Adventure Camp
BICYCLE TRAVEL ADVENTURES–Student Hosteling Program–A Thousand Miles: Massachusetts to Nova Scotia
BICYCLE TRAVEL ADVENTURES–Student Hosteling Program–Maine Coast
BICYCLE TRAVEL ADVENTURES–Student Hosteling Program–Maine-Nova Scotia Coast Loop
BICYCLE TRAVEL ADVENTURES–Student Hosteling Program–Vermont to the Atlantic Ocean
Camp Friendship Challenge Program
College Impressions
Darrow Wilderness Trips–Maine
Darrow Wilderness Trips–St. Croix
Darrow Wilderness Trips–Voyageurs
Darrow Youth Backpacking
Discovery Works New England Community Service Experience
Geronimo Program
Great Escapes (Adventure Trips for Teens)–Maine Waterways
Hulbert Voyageurs Youth Wilderness Trips
Hurricane Island Outward Bound–Maine Coast and Western Maine Canoeing and Sailing
Hurricane Island Outward Bound–Maine Coast and Western Maine Sailing and Backpacking
Hurricane Island Outward Bound–Maine Coast and Western Maine Sea Kayaking and Backpacking
Hurricane Island Outward Bound–Maine Coast Sailing/Sailing and Rock Climbing
Hurricane Island Outward Bound–Maine Coast Schooner Sailing
Hurricane Island Outward Bound–Maine Coast Sea Kayaking
Hurricane Island Outward Bound–Maine Woods High School Summer Semester
Hurricane Island Outward Bound–North Woods Maine Allagash and Appalachian Trail Canoeing and Backpacking
Hurricane Island Outward Bound–North Woods Maine Canoeing and Backpacking
Hurricane Island Outward Bound–North Woods Maine Expedition Canoeing
Hurricane Island Outward Bound–Ocean Bound: Tall Ship Sailing and Sea Kayaking Semester
Hurricane Island Outward Bound–Western Maine and New Hampshire Canoeing and Backpacking
Hurricane Island Outward Bound–Western Maine Backpacking and Rock Climbing
Hurricane Island Outward Bound–Western Maine Woods Expedition Canoeing
Kroka Expeditions–Coastal Sea Kayaking
Kroka Expeditions–Paddlers Journey Up North
Longacre Expeditions, Adventure 28
Longacre Expeditions, Downeast
Longacre Expeditions, New England/Canada
Longacre Expeditions, Photography
Longacre Expeditions, Whales
Luna Adventures with AAG SummerSkills
Maine Wilderness Adventure Trip
Mountain Workshop–Awesome 5: North Woods of Maine
Mountain Workshop–Awesome 3: Maine Coast
New England Camping Adventures
92nd Street Y Camps–The TIYUL
Overland: Acadia and Prince Edward Island Bicycle Touring and Sea-Kayaking
Overland: New England Explorer Hiking, Mountain Biking, and Rafting
Rein Teen Tours–Eastern Adventure
Teen Tours of America–New England Journey
Teen Tour USA and Canada
Trailmark Outdoor Adventures–New England–Acadia
Trailmark Outdoor Adventures–New England–Camden
Trailmark Outdoor Adventures–New England–Downeast
Trailmark Outdoor Adventures–New England–Jr. Acadia
Trailmark Outdoor Adventures–New England–Mahoosoc
Trailmark Outdoor Adventures–New England–Moose River
Trailmark Outdoor Adventures–New England–Mt. Desert
Trailmark Outdoor Adventures–New England–Rangeley Coed
Westcoast Connection Travel–Eastcoast Encounter
Williwaw Adventures–Maine Mountains and Coast
Williwaw Adventures–Maine Wilderness
Windsor Mountain: Experiential Summer School
Windsor Mountain: New England Adventure
Windsor Mountain: New England Traveling Minstrels
Windsor Mountain: Random Acts of Kindness

Malawi
Bicycle Africa Tours

Mali
Bicycle Africa Tours

Martinique
BROADREACH Arc of the Caribbean Sailing Adventure

Maryland
ATW: Mini Tours
East Coast College Tour by Education Unlimited
Hurricane Island Outward Bound–Mid-Atlantic Canoeing, Backpacking, and Rock Climbing
Julian Krinsky Golf Tours
Teen Tour USA and Canada
Trailridge Mountain Camp

Massachusetts
Apogee Outdoor Adventures–Burlington to Boston
Apogee Outdoor Adventures–New England Mountains and Coast
Apogee Outdoor Adventures–Cape Cod and the Islands
ATW: Adventure Roads
ATW: Mini Tours
Barton Adventure Camp
BICYCLE TRAVEL ADVENTURES–Student Hosteling Program–A Thousand Miles: Massachusetts to Nova Scotia
BICYCLE TRAVEL ADVENTURES–Student Hosteling Program–Cape Cod
BICYCLE TRAVEL ADVENTURES–Student Hosteling Program–Cross-Country America
BICYCLE TRAVEL ADVENTURES–Student Hosteling Program–Maine-Nova Scotia Coast Loop
BICYCLE TRAVEL ADVENTURES–Student Hosteling Program–Niagara Falls to Montreal
BICYCLE TRAVEL ADVENTURES–Student Hosteling Program–Off-Road Vermont
BICYCLE TRAVEL ADVENTURES–Student Hosteling Program–Vermont
BICYCLE TRAVEL ADVENTURES–Student Hosteling Program–Vermont to the Atlantic Ocean
College Impressions
Discovery Works New England Community Service Experience
East Coast College Tour by Education Unlimited
Geronimo Program
Great Escapes (Adventure Trips for Teens)–Cape Cod Sail Adventure
Great Escapes (Adventure Trips for Teens)–Cape Cod Underwater Adventure
Great Escapes (Adventure Trips for Teens)–Cape Escapes
Great Escapes (Adventure Trips for Teens)–Rock and Rapids
Great Escapes (Adventure Trips for Teens)–Saddle and Sail
Hurricane Island Outward Bound–Ocean Bound: Tall Ship Sailing and Sea Kayaking Semester
Mountain Workshop–Bike 1: Martha's Vineyard and Nantucket
Mountain Workshop–Bike 2
Musiker Tours: Eastcoaster
92nd Street Y Camps–The TIYUL
Overland: American Community Service, New England
Overland: Appalachian Trail Challenge Hiking
Overland: Cape Cod and the Islands Bicycle Touring
Overland: New England Explorer Hiking, Mountain Biking, and Rafting
Overland: Vermont & Montreal Bicycle Touring
Rein Teen Tours–Eastern Adventure
Teen Tours of America–New England Journey
Teen Tour USA and Canada
Westcoast Connection Travel–Eastcoast Encounter
Wilderness Experiences Unlimited–Trailblazers Camp
Williwaw Adventures–Maine Wilderness
Windsor Mountain: New England Traveling Minstrels
Windsor Mountain: Random Acts of Kindness

Mexico
Artes en Mexico
BROADREACH Academic Treks–Spanish Immersion in Mexico
BROADREACH Baja Extreme–Scuba Adventure
Dickinson College Spanish Language and Cultural Immersion Program
ExploraMar: Marine Biology Sailing Expeditions–Sea of Cortez, Baja, Mexico
GLOBAL WORKS–Language Exposure-Yucatan Peninsula, Mexico-4 weeks
GLOBAL WORKS–Language Immersion-Yucatan Peninsula, Mexico-4 weeks
Knowledge Exchange Institute–Spanish on the Road in Mexico Program
Outpost Wilderness Adventure–Copper Canyon Project
Programs Abroad Travel Alternatives–Mexico
Weissman Teen Tours–"Aloha–Welcome to Hawaiian Paradise"
Weissman Teen Tours–U.S. and Western Canada, 4 Weeks
Weissman Teen Tours–U.S. and Western Canada, 6 Weeks
Where There Be Dragons: Mexico
Windsor Mountain: Mexico Community Service

Michigan
ATW: American Horizons
ATW: Wayfarer
Camp Henry Offsite: Teen Challenge
Musiker Tours: America Coast to Coast
Rein Teen Tours–American Adventure
Rein Teen Tours–Crossroads
Westcoast Connection–U.S. Explorer

Minnesota
ATW: American Horizons
ATW: Wayfarer
Camp Chi Teenage Adventure Trips
Eagle Lake Camp Jaunts–Minnesota Boundary Waters
Musiker Tours: America Coast to Coast
Rein Teen Tours–American Adventure
Rein Teen Tours–Crossroads
Swift Nature Camp–Canadian Canoe Trip
Ventures Travel Service–Minnesota
Voyageur Outward Bound–Boundary Waters Wilderness Canoeing and Climbing XT
Voyageur Outward Bound–Lake Superior Freshwater Kayaking and Backpacking
Voyageur Outward Bound–Northwoods Wilderness Canoeing and Backpacking
Westcoast Connection–U.S. Explorer
YMCA Wilderness Camp Menogyn

Mississippi
Overland: American Challenge Coast-to-Coast Bicycle Touring

Missouri
BICYCLE TRAVEL ADVENTURES–Student Hosteling Program–Cross-Country America
Rein Teen Tours–American Adventure
Ventures Travel Service–Missouri

Monaco
ACTIONQUEST: Mediterranean Sailing Voyage
Westcoast Connection Travel–European Discovery
Westcoast Connection Travel/On Tour–European Experience

Mongolia
Where There Be Dragons: Mongolia

Montana
Adventure Treks–Montana Adventures
Alpengirl–Montana
Alpengirl–Montana Art
Alpengirl–Montana Fitness
Alpengirl–Montana Horse
Apogee Outdoor Adventures–Montana Service Adventure
ATW: Camp Inn 42
ATW: Pacific Paradise
ATW: Skyblazer
BICYCLE TRAVEL ADVENTURES–Student Hosteling Program–Cross-Country America
Camp Chi Teenage Adventure Trips
Musiker Tours: Action USA
Musiker Tours: America Coast to Coast
Musiker Tours: ComboCamp America
Musiker Tours: Discover America
Overland: Yellowstone Explorer Backpacking, Rock Climbing, and Rafting
Rein Teen Tours–Grand Adventure
Teen Tours of America–Western Adventure
Visions–Montana
Voyageur Outward Bound–Greater Yellowstone Whitewater and Backpacking
Voyageur Outward Bound–Lewis and Clark Alpine Backpacking
Voyageur Outward Bound–Lewis and Clark Alpine Backpacking-Girls
Voyageur Outward Bound–Manitoba to Montana Summer Semester
Voyageur Outward Bound–Montana High Alpine Backpacking
Voyageur Outward Bound–Montana Rock Climbing XT
Voyageur Outward Bound–Northern Rockies Backpacking Family Adventure
Weissman Teen Tours–U.S. and Western Canada, 4 Weeks
Weissman Teen Tours–U.S. and Western Canada, 6 Weeks
Westcoast Connection–American Voyageur
Westcoast Connection Travel/On Tour–Northwestern Odyssey
Westcoast Connection Travel–Northwestern Odyssey
Wilderness Ventures–Great Divide
Wilderness Ventures–Great Divide Bike

▶ MONTANA

Wilderness Ventures–Rocky Mountain
Wilderness Ventures–Yellowstone Fly Fishing

Namibia

AAVE–Africa

Nepal

Lower Mustang Summer Passage
The Nepal Cultural Immersion Experience
Personal Passage
Tibetan Summer Passage

Netherlands

BICYCLE TRAVEL ADVENTURES–Student Hosteling Program–Amsterdam to Paris
Knowledge Exchange Institute–European Capitals Program
Musiker Tours: Action Europe
Putney Student Travel–Cultural Exploration–France, Holland, and England
Putney Student Travel–Cultural Exploration–Switzerland, Italy, France, and Holland
TENNIS: EUROPE
Weissman Teen Tours–European Experience
Westcoast Connection Travel–European Discovery

Netherlands Antilles

ACTIONQUEST: Leeward and French Caribbean Island Voyages
BROADREACH Academic Treks–Marine Park Management
BROADREACH Adventures in Scuba and Sailing–Underwater Discoveries
BROADREACH Adventures Underwater–Advanced Scuba
BROADREACH Arc of the Caribbean Sailing Adventure
Kayak Adventures Unlimited
Sail Caribbean–Leeward Islands

Nevada

AAVE–Bold West
Alien Adventure Overnight Camp
ATW: Action America West
ATW: American Horizons
ATW: California Sunset
ATW: Camp Inn 42
ATW: Discoverer
ATW: Pacific Paradise
ATW: Skyblazer
ATW: Sunblazer
ATW: Wayfarer
Camp Tawonga–Teen Quest: Southwest
Hiker's Heaven Overnight Camp
Musiker Tours: Action USA
Musiker Tours: America Coast to Coast
Musiker Tours: Cali-Pacific Passport
Musiker Tours: ComboCamp America
Musiker Tours: Discover America
Musiker Tours: Westcoaster
Rein Teen Tours–American Adventure
Rein Teen Tours–California Caper
Rein Teen Tours–Crossroads
Rein Teen Tours–Grand Adventure
Rein Teen Tours–Western Adventure
Teen Tours of America–Western Adventure
Teen Tours of America–Western Sprint
Weissman Teen Tours–U.S. and Western Canada, 6 Weeks
Westcoast Connection–American Voyageur
Westcoast Connection–Californian Extravaganza
Westcoast Connection Travel–California and the Canyons
Westcoast Connection Travel–Southwesterner
Westcoast Connection–U.S. Explorer

New Hampshire

Apogee Outdoor Adventures–Burlington to Boston
Apogee Outdoor Adventures–New England Mountains and Coast
ATW: Mini Tours
Barton Adventure Camp
BICYCLE TRAVEL ADVENTURES–Student Hosteling Program–A Thousand Miles: Massachusetts to Nova Scotia
BICYCLE TRAVEL ADVENTURES–Student Hosteling Program–Vermont
BICYCLE TRAVEL ADVENTURES–Student Hosteling Program–Vermont to the Atlantic Ocean
College Impressions
Discovery Works New England Community Service Experience
Great Escapes (Adventure Trips for Teens)–Canadian Adventure
Great Escapes (Adventure Trips for Teens)–White Mountain Adventure
Hulbert Voyageurs Youth Wilderness Trips
Hurricane Island Outward Bound–Western Maine and New Hampshire Canoeing and Backpacking
Kroka Expeditions–Advanced Rock Climbing
Musiker Tours: Eastcoaster
Overland: Appalachian Trail Challenge Hiking
Overland: New England Explorer Hiking, Mountain Biking, and Rafting
Rein Teen Tours–Eastern Adventure
Teen Tours of America–New England Journey
Teen Tour USA and Canada
Trailmark Outdoor Adventures–New England–Acadia
Trailmark Outdoor Adventures–New England–Camden
Trailmark Outdoor Adventures–New England–Downeast
Trailmark Outdoor Adventures–New England–Jr. Acadia
Trailmark Outdoor Adventures–New England–Mahoosoc
Trailmark Outdoor Adventures–New England–Moose River
Trailmark Outdoor Adventures–New England–Mt. Desert
Trailmark Outdoor Adventures–New England–Rangeley Coed
Westcoast Connection Travel–Eastcoast Encounter
Williwaw Adventures–Maine Wilderness
Windsor Mountain: Experiential Summer School
Windsor Mountain: New England Adventure
Windsor Mountain: New England Traveling Minstrels
Windsor Mountain: Random Acts of Kindness
YMCA Camp Lincoln–Outdoor Adventure Camp: Backpacking
YMCA Camp Lincoln–Outdoor Adventure Camp: Everything Outdoors
YMCA Camp Lincoln–Outdoor Adventure Camp: Mountain Bike
YMCA Camp Lincoln–Outdoor Adventure Camp: River Runners

New Jersey

BICYCLE TRAVEL ADVENTURES–Student Hosteling Program–Cross-Country America
College Impressions
Maritime Camp
Teen Tour USA and Canada

New Mexico

Alien Adventure Overnight Camp
Cottonwood Gulch Mountain Desert Challenge
Cottonwood Gulch Prairie Trek Expedition
Cottonwood Gulch Turquoise Trail Expedition
Cottonwood Gulch Wild Country Trek
Flint Hill School–"Summer on the Hill"–Enrichment on the Hill–Women Writers' Adventure
Four Corners School of Outdoor Education: Southwest Ed-Venture
Overland: American Challenge Coast-to-Coast Bicycle Touring
Overland: American Community Service, Southwest
RUSTIC PATHWAYS–ADVENTURE IN AMERICA'S SOUTHWEST

New York

ATW: American Horizons
ATW: Mini Tours
ATW: Wayfarer
Barton Adventure Camp
BICYCLE TRAVEL ADVENTURES–Student Hosteling Program–Niagara Falls to Montreal
BICYCLE TRAVEL ADVENTURES–Student Hosteling Program–Off-Road Vermont
College Impressions
East Coast College Tour by Education Unlimited
Great Escapes (Adventure Trips for Teens)–Saddle and Sail
Hulbert Voyageurs Youth Wilderness Trips
Kroka Expeditions–Advanced Rock Climbing
Mountain Workshop–Graduate Plus Awesome Adventures
Mountain Workshop–Awesome 1: Adirondacks
Mountain Workshop–Leadership Through Adventure: Adirondacks
Musiker Tours: America Coast to Coast
Musiker Tours: Eastcoaster
92nd Street Y Camps–The TIYUL
92nd Street Y Camps–Trailblazers
The Ranch–Lake Placid Teen Travel Camp
Rein Teen Tours–American Adventure
Rein Teen Tours–Crossroads
Rein Teen Tours–Eastern Adventure
Teen Tours of America–New England Journey
Teen Tour USA and Canada
Ventures Travel Service–New York
Westcoast Connection Travel–Eastcoast Encounter
Westcoast Connection–U.S. Explorer

New Zealand

GLOBAL WORKS–Cultural Exchange-New Zealand and Fiji Islands-4 weeks
Poulter Colorado Camps: Adventures Planet Earth–New Zealand
Putney Student Travel–Cultural Exploration–Australia, New Zealand, and Fiji

RUSTIC PATHWAYS–EXTREME PLANET
RUSTIC PATHWAYS–SKI AND SNOWBOARD ADVENTURE IN NEW ZEALAND

Nicaragua

Costa Rica Rainforest Outward Bound School–Tri-Country/Tri-Mester
Spanish Through Leadership–Nicaragua
Spanish Through Leadership–Nicaragua/Costa Rica
Summer Delegation to León, Nicaragua

North Carolina

Adventure Links
Adventure Links–North Carolina Expeditions
Camp Friendship Challenge Program
Cheerio Adventures–5 Rivers in 5 Days
Hante School
Mountain Adventure Guides: Summer Adventure Camp–Blue Ridge Expedition I
Mountain Adventure Guides: Summer Adventure Camp–Blue Ridge Expedition II
Mountain Adventure Guides: Summer Adventure Camp–Jr. Adventure Camp
North Carolina Outward Bound–Outer Banks
North Carolina Outward Bound–Southern Appalachian Mountains
Overland: Blue Ridge Explorer Hiking, Rafting and Kayaking
Trailridge Mountain Camp

North Dakota

Ventures Travel Service–North Dakota

Norway

Alpengirl–Scandinavia
Eagle Lake Camp Jaunts–Norway Mission Adventure
Environmental Studies and Solutions

Ohio

ATW: American Horizons
BICYCLE TRAVEL ADVENTURES–Student Hosteling Program–Cross-Country America
Rein Teen Tours–American Adventure
Rein Teen Tours–Crossroads

Oklahoma

Overland: American Challenge Coast-to-Coast Bicycle Touring

Oregon

Adventure Treks–California Challenge Adventures
Adventure Treks–PAC 16
Adventure Treks–Summit Fever
Adventure Treks–Ultimate Northwest Adventures
ATW: Skyblazer
BICYCLE TRAVEL ADVENTURES–Student Hosteling Program–Canadian Rockies to California
BICYCLE TRAVEL ADVENTURES–Student Hosteling Program–Pacific Coast Adventure: Washington, Oregon, and California
Camp Tawonga–Teen Quest: Northwest
Longacre Expeditions, Peak to Peak
Longacre Expeditions, Surf Oregon
Longacre Expeditions, Volcanoes
Longacre Expeditions, Western Challenge
Musiker Tours: Alaska Aloha
Outward Bound West–Backpacking and Whitewater Rafting, Oregon
Outward Bound West–Mountaineering and Rafting, Oregon
Outward Bound West–Mountaineering, Rafting, and Climbing-XT, Oregon
Overland: Pacific Coast Bicycle Touring and Rafting
Overland: Shasta & the Sierras Backpacking, Climbing and Rafting
Pacific Marine Science Camp
Rein Teen Tours–Hawaiian/Alaskan Adventure
Summer Conservation Corps
Teen Tours of America–Alaskan Expedition
Teen Tours of America–Aloha Hawaii
Ventures Travel Service–Oregon
Westcoast Connection–American Voyageur
Westcoast Connection–Hawaiian Spirit
Westcoast Connection Travel/On Tour–Northwestern Odyssey
Westcoast Connection Travel–Great West Challenge
Westcoast Connection Travel–Northwestern Odyssey
Westcoast Connection Travel–Ski and Snowboard Sensation
Wilderness Ventures–Great Divide
Wilderness Ventures–Northwest
Wilderness Ventures–Oregon
Wilderness Ventures–Pacific Coast Bike
Wilderness Ventures–Pacific Northwest
Williwaw Adventures–Pacific Northwest Expedition

Panama

Costa Rica Rainforest Outward Bound School–Tri-Country/Tri-Mester

Pennsylvania

Adventure Links
ATW: Adventure Roads
ATW: American Horizons
ATW: Mini Tours
BICYCLE TRAVEL ADVENTURES–Student Hosteling Program–Cross-Country America
College Impressions
East Coast College Tour by Education Unlimited
Great Escapes (Adventure Trips for Teens)–Rock and Rapids
Hurricane Island Outward Bound–Mid-Atlantic Canoeing, Backpacking, and Rock Climbing
Julian Krinsky Golf Tours
Longacre Expeditions, Blue Ridge
Longacre Expeditions, Laurel Highlands
Mountain Workshop–Awesome 4: Pennsylvania
Musiker Tours: Eastcoaster
Rein Teen Tours–American Adventure
Rein Teen Tours–Eastern Adventure
Teen Tour USA and Canada

Peru

AAVE–Peru and Machu Picchu
Peace Works International–Peru
The Peru Cultural Immersion Experience
Programs Abroad Travel Alternatives–Peru
Visions–Peru
Where There Be Dragons: Peru

Portugal

BICYCLE TRAVEL ADVENTURES–Student Hosteling Program–Spain and France
Knowledge Exchange Institute–Discover Spain and Portugal Program
TENNIS: EUROPE

Puerto Rico

GLOBAL WORKS–Language Exposure-Puerto Rico-3 weeks
GLOBAL WORKS–Language Immersion-Puerto Rico-4 weeks
Windsor Mountain: Puerto Rico

Rhode Island

College Impressions
Discovery Works New England Community Service Experience
East Coast College Tour by Education Unlimited
Geronimo Program

Russian Federation

EF International Language Schools–St. Petersburg
Programs Abroad Travel Alternatives–Russia

Saint Kitts and Nevis

ACTIONQUEST: Leeward and French Caribbean Island Voyages
BROADREACH Academic Treks–Marine Park Management
BROADREACH Adventures in Scuba and Sailing–Underwater Discoveries
BROADREACH Adventures Underwater–Advanced Scuba
BROADREACH Arc of the Caribbean Sailing Adventure
Sail Caribbean–Leeward Islands

Saint Lucia

!ADVENTURES–AFLOAT: Advanced Scuba Adventure Voyages–Caribbean Islands
!ADVENTURES–AFLOAT: Scuba and Sailing Discovery Voyages–Caribbean Islands
BROADREACH Adventures in the Windward Islands–Advanced Scuba
BROADREACH Arc of the Caribbean Sailing Adventure
ODYSSEY EXPEDITIONS: Tropical Marine Biology Voyages–Caribbean Islands

Saint Vincent and The Grenadines

!ADVENTURES–AFLOAT: Advanced Scuba Adventure Voyages–Caribbean Islands
!ADVENTURES–AFLOAT: Scuba and Sailing Discovery Voyages–Caribbean Islands
BROADREACH Adventures in the Grenadines–Advanced Scuba
BROADREACH Adventures in the Windward Islands–Advanced Scuba
BROADREACH Arc of the Caribbean Sailing Adventure
ODYSSEY EXPEDITIONS: Tropical Marine Biology Voyages–Caribbean Islands
Windsor Mountain: Adventures in Filmmaking

Senegal
Bicycle Africa Tours
Rust College Study Abroad in Africa

Solomon Islands
BROADREACH Fiji Solomon Quest

South Africa
AAVE–Africa
Bicycle Africa Tours

South Carolina
ATW: Adventure Roads
Cheerio Adventures–5 Rivers in 5 Days
Musiker Tours: Eastcoaster
Rein Teen Tours–Eastern Adventure
Trailridge Mountain Camp
Ventures Travel Service–South Carolina
Visions–South Carolina

South Dakota
ATW: American Horizons
ATW: Discoverer
ATW: Skyblazer
ATW: Wayfarer
Camp Chi Teenage Adventure Trips
Musiker Tours: America Coast to Coast
Rein Teen Tours–American Adventure
Rein Teen Tours–Crossroads
Rein Teen Tours–Grand Adventure
Rein Teen Tours–Western Adventure
Teen Tours of America–Western Adventure
Ventures Travel Service–South Dakota
Westcoast Connection–U.S. Explorer

Spain
AAVE–Bold Europe
AAVE–Inmersión en España
Abbey Road Overseas Programs–Spanish Immersion and Homestay
American Collegiate Adventures–Spain
BICYCLE TRAVEL ADVENTURES–Student Hosteling Program–Spain and France
Bravo Spain–Barcelona
Choate Rosemary Hall Summer in Spain
Concordia Language Villages–Spain
EF International Language School–Barcelona
EF International Language Schools–Malaga
GLOBAL WORKS–Language Immersion-Spain-4 weeks
iD Tech Camps–Documentary Filmmaking and Cultural Immersion at the University of Cádiz, Spain
Israel Discovery
Knowledge Exchange Institute–Discover Spain and Portugal Program
Mercersburg Academy Summer Study in Spain
Overland: European Explorer Hiking, Rafting, and Sea Kayaking
Overland: Language Study Abroad in Spain
PAX Abroad–Summer Spain
Poulter Colorado Camps: Adventures Planet Earth–Spain
Programs Abroad Travel Alternatives–Spain
Rassias Programs–Gijón, Spain
Rassias Programs–Pontevedra, Spain
Rassias Programs–Segovia, Spain
Taft Summer School Abroad–Spain
TENNIS: EUROPE
Wilderness Ventures–Spanish Pyrenees
Youth Program in Spain

Sweden
Alpengirl–Scandinavia
TENNIS: EUROPE

Switzerland
AAVE–Alps Rider
Adventures Cross-Country,Southern Europe Adventure
ATW: European Adventures
Knowledge Exchange Institute–European Capitals Program
Musiker Tours: Action Europe
Overland: European Challenge Bicycle Touring from Paris to Rome
Overland: European Explorer Hiking, Rafting, and Sea Kayaking
Overland: The Alpine Challenge Leadership Course Backpacking and Hiking
Putney Student Travel–Cultural Exploration–Switzerland, Italy, France, and Holland
Swiss Challenge
TENNIS: EUROPE
Weissman Teen Tours–European Experience
Westcoast Connection Travel–European Discovery
Westcoast Connection Travel–European Escape
Westcoast Connection Travel/On Tour–European Experience
Wilderness Ventures–European Alps

Taiwan
Phillips Exeter Academy Taiwan and Beijing Summer Study Tour

Tennessee
Cheerio Adventures–5 Rivers in 5 Days
Trailridge Mountain Camp
Ventures Travel Service–Tennessee

Texas
JCC Houston: Teen Trek
Ventures Travel Service–Texas

Thailand
AAVE–Thailand
LIFEWORKS with the DPF Foundation in Thailand
RUSTIC PATHWAYS–BUDDHIST LIFE & ANGKOR WAT
RUSTIC PATHWAYS–ELEPHANTS & AMAZING THAILAND
RUSTIC PATHWAYS–EXTREME PLANET
RUSTIC PATHWAYS–PHOTOGRAPHY & ADVENTURE IN THAILAND
RUSTIC PATHWAYS–THE AMAZING THAILAND ADVENTURE
RUSTIC PATHWAYS–THE WONDERS & RICHES OF THAILAND
Where There Be Dragons: Thailand

Togo
Bicycle Africa Tours

Trinidad and Tobago
BROADREACH Arc of the Caribbean Sailing Adventure
Visions–Trinidad

Tunisia
Bicycle Africa Tours

U.S. Virgin Islands
Adventures Cross-Country, Caribbean Adventure
Longacre Expeditions, Virgin Islands

Uganda
Bicycle Africa Tours

United Kingdom
AAVE–Wild Isles
ATW: European Adventures
BICYCLE TRAVEL ADVENTURES–Student Hosteling Program–Ireland and England
Burklyn Ballet Edinburgh Connection
Cambridge College Programme
Celtic Learning and Travel Services–Edinburgh and Dublin
Celtic Learning and Travel Services–London and Dublin
Excel at Oxford/Tuscany
Knowledge Exchange Institute–European Capitals Program
Longacre Expeditions, British Isles
Musiker Tours: Action Europe
Putney Student Travel–Cultural Exploration–France, Holland, and England
TENNIS: EUROPE
Weissman Teen Tours–European Experience
Westcoast Connection Travel–European Discovery
Westcoast Connection Travel/On Tour–European Experience

United Republic Of Tanzania
Bicycle Africa Tours
Flint Hill School–"Summer on the Hill"–Trips from the Hill–Tanzania Safari

Utah
AAVE–Bold West
AAVE–Boot/Saddle/Paddle
AAVE–Rock & River
AAVE–X–Five
ATW: Action America West
ATW: American Horizons
ATW: Camp Inn 42
ATW: Discoverer
ATW: Pacific Paradise
ATW: Skyblazer
ATW: Sunblazer
ATW: Wayfarer
Camp Tawonga–Teen Quest: Southwest
Flint Hill School–"Summer on the Hill"–Enrichment on the Hill–Women Writers' Adventure
Four Corners School of Outdoor Education: Southwest Ed-Venture
Great Escapes (Adventure Trips for Teens)–Colorado River and Canyons Adventure
Hiker's Heaven Overnight Camp
Musiker Tours: Action USA
Musiker Tours: America Coast to Coast
Musiker Tours: ComboCamp America
Musiker Tours: Discover America
Musiker Tours: Westcoaster
Outward Bound West–Cataract Canyon Rafting
Outward Bound West–Southwest Mountaineering, Rafting, and Canyoneering
Outward Bound West–Southwest Mystery Expedition

Outward Bound West–Utah Summer Semester
Overland: Colorado and Utah Mountain Biking and Rafting
Overland: Rocky Mountain Explorer Hiking, Mountain Biking, and Rafting
Rein Teen Tours–American Adventure
Rein Teen Tours–California Caper
Rein Teen Tours–Crossroads
Rein Teen Tours–Grand Adventure
Rein Teen Tours–Western Adventure
RUSTIC PATHWAYS–ADVENTURE IN AMERICA'S SOUTHWEST
Summit Travel Program
Teen Tours of America–Western Adventure
Teen Tours of America–Western Sprint
TENNIS: EUROPE & MORE–North American Teams
Trailmark Outdoor Adventures–Northern Rockies–Tetons with Backpack
Trailmark Outdoor Adventures–Northern Rockies–Tetons with Horseback
Weissman Teen Tours–U.S. and Western Canada, 4 Weeks
Weissman Teen Tours–U.S. and Western Canada, 6 Weeks
Westcoast Connection–American Voyageur
Westcoast Connection–Californian Extravaganza
Westcoast Connection Travel/On Tour–Northwestern Odyssey
Westcoast Connection Travel–California and the Canyons
Westcoast Connection Travel–Southwesterner
Westcoast Connection–U.S. Explorer
Wilderness Ventures–Colorado/Utah Mountain Bike

Vanuatu

BROADREACH Fiji Solomon Quest

Vermont

Apogee Outdoor Adventures–Burlington to Boston
BICYCLE TRAVEL ADVENTURES–Student Hosteling Program–A Thousand Miles: Massachusetts to Nova Scotia
BICYCLE TRAVEL ADVENTURES–Student Hosteling Program–Off-Road Vermont
BICYCLE TRAVEL ADVENTURES–Student Hosteling Program–Vermont
BICYCLE TRAVEL ADVENTURES–Student Hosteling Program–Vermont to the Atlantic Ocean
Burklyn Ballet Edinburgh Connection
College Impressions
Discovery Works New England Community Service Experience
Great Escapes (Adventure Trips for Teens)–Saddle and Sail
Hulbert Voyageurs Youth Wilderness Trips
Kroka Expeditions–Paddlers Journey Up North
Luna Adventures with AAG SummerSkills
Mountain Workshop–Awesome 2: Vermont
Mountain Workshop/Dirt Camp: Dirt Camp Junior Killington
Overland: American Community Service, New England
Overland: Appalachian Trail Challenge Hiking
Overland: New England Explorer Hiking, Mountain Biking, and Rafting
Overland: Vermont & Montreal Bicycle Touring
The Ranch–Lake Placid Teen Travel Camp
Teen Tours of America–New England Journey
Teen Tour USA and Canada
Windsor Mountain: Experiential Summer School
Windsor Mountain: New England Adventure
Windsor Mountain: New England Traveling Minstrels
Windsor Mountain: Random Acts of Kindness
YMCA Camp Abnaki–Teen Adventure Trips

Vietnam

AAVE–Vietnam
Where There Be Dragons: Vietnam

Virginia

Adventure Links
Adventure Links–Appalachian Odyssey
ATW: Adventure Roads
ATW: Mini Tours
Camp Friendship Challenge Program
Musiker Tours: Eastcoaster
Rein Teen Tours–Eastern Adventure
Teen Tour USA and Canada
Trailridge Mountain Camp
Westcoast Connection Travel–Eastcoast Encounter

Washington

AAVE–Border Cross
Adventure Treks–Pacific Northwest Adventures
Adventure Treks–Summit Fever
Adventure Treks–Ultimate Northwest Adventures
Alpengirl–Washington
Alpengirl–Washington Alpenguide Training
Alpengirl–Washington Lil' Alpengirl
ATW: Camp Inn 42
ATW: Fire and Ice
ATW: Pacific Paradise
ATW: Skyblazer
BICYCLE TRAVEL ADVENTURES–Student Hosteling Program–Canadian Rockies to California
BICYCLE TRAVEL ADVENTURES–Student Hosteling Program–Cross-Country America
BICYCLE TRAVEL ADVENTURES–Student Hosteling Program–Pacific Coast Adventure: Washington, Oregon, and California
Camp Chi Teenage Adventure Trips
GLOBAL WORKS–Adventure Travel-Pacific Northwest-3 weeks
Ibike Cultural Tours–Washington/British Columbia
Longacre Expeditions, British Columbia
Longacre Expeditions, Pacific Coast and Inlands
Longacre Expeditions, Volcanoes
Longacre Expeditions, Western Challenge
Musiker Tours: Alaska Aloha
Musiker Tours: Cali-Pacific Passport
Musiker Tours: ComboCamp America
Musiker Tours: Discover America
Outward Bound West–Climbing, Backpacking, and Canoeing–North Cascades, WA
Outward Bound West–Mountaineering–North Cascades, WA
Outward Bound West–Sea Kayaking, Backpacking, and Mountaineering–Washington
Outward Bound West–Service Course–North Cascades
Rein Teen Tours–Grand Adventure
Rein Teen Tours–Hawaiian/Alaskan Adventure
Summer Conservation Corps
Teen Tours of America–Alaskan Expedition
Teen Tours of America–Aloha Hawaii
Teen Tours of America–Western Adventure
TENNIS: EUROPE & MORE–North American Teams
Ventures Travel Service–Washington
Weissman Teen Tours–U.S. and Western Canada, 4 Weeks
Weissman Teen Tours–U.S. and Western Canada, 6 Weeks
Westcoast Connection–American Voyageur
Westcoast Connection–Community Service
Westcoast Connection–Hawaiian Spirit
Westcoast Connection Travel/On Tour–Northwestern Odyssey
Westcoast Connection Travel–Canadian Mountain Magic
Westcoast Connection Travel–Great West Challenge
Westcoast Connection Travel–Northwestern Odyssey
Westcoast Connection Travel/On Tour–Canadian Adventure
Westcoast Connection Travel–Ski and Snowboard Sensation
Wilderness Ventures–Cascade-Olympic
Wilderness Ventures–Northwest
Wilderness Ventures–Pacific Coast Bike
Wilderness Ventures–Pacific Northwest
Wilderness Ventures–Puget Sound
Wilderness Ventures–Washington Alpine
Wilderness Ventures–Washington Mountaineering
Williwaw Adventures–Pacific Northwest Expedition

West Virginia

Adventure Links
Adventure Links–Appalachian Odyssey
BICYCLE TRAVEL ADVENTURES–Student Hosteling Program–Cross-Country America
Camp Friendship Challenge Program
Great Escapes (Adventure Trips for Teens)–Rock and Rapids
92nd Street Y Camps–The TIYUL

Wisconsin

Camp Chi Teenage Adventure Trips
Musiker Tours: America Coast to Coast
Timber-lee Wilderness Trips
Ventures Travel Service–Wisconsin

Wyoming

Alpengirl–Montana Art
ATW: Action America West
ATW: American Horizons
ATW: Camp Inn 42
ATW: Discoverer
ATW: Pacific Paradise
ATW: Skyblazer
ATW: Wayfarer
BICYCLE TRAVEL ADVENTURES–Student Hosteling Program–Cross-Country America
Musiker Tours: Action USA

▶ Wyoming

Musiker Tours: America Coast to Coast
Musiker Tours: ComboCamp America
Musiker Tours: Discover America
Outpost Wilderness Adventure–Wind River Expedition
Outward Bound West–Wyoming Rock Climbing
Overland: Rocky Mountain Explorer Hiking, Mountain Biking, and Rafting
Overland: Teton Challenge Hiking, Climbing and Kayaking
Overland: Yellowstone Explorer Backpacking, Rock Climbing, and Rafting
Rein Teen Tours–American Adventure
Rein Teen Tours–Crossroads
Rein Teen Tours–Grand Adventure
Rein Teen Tours–Western Adventure
Summit Travel Program
Teen Tours of America–Western Adventure
TENNIS: EUROPE & MORE–North American Teams
Trailmark Outdoor Adventures–Northern Rockies–Tetons with Backpack
Trailmark Outdoor Adventures–Northern Rockies–Tetons with Horseback
University of Chicago–Stones and Bones
Weissman Teen Tours–U.S. and Western Canada, 4 Weeks
Weissman Teen Tours–U.S. and Western Canada, 6 Weeks
Westcoast Connection–American Voyageur
Westcoast Connection–Californian Extravaganza
Westcoast Connection Travel/On Tour–Northwestern Odyssey
Westcoast Connection Travel–Northwestern Odyssey
Westcoast Connection–U.S. Explorer
Wilderness Ventures–Grand Teton
Wilderness Ventures–Great Divide
Wilderness Ventures–Great Divide Bike
Wilderness Ventures–Jackson Hole
Wilderness Ventures–Rocky Mountain
Wilderness Ventures–Teton Adventure
Wilderness Ventures–Wyoming Mountaineering
Wilderness Ventures–Yellowstone Fly Fishing

Zimbabwe

Bicycle Africa Tours

AD/HD
Camp Buckskin, MN
Camp Courageous of Iowa, IA
Camp Kodiak, Canada
New Jersey YMHA–YWHA Round Lake Camp, PA
Oak Creek Ranch Summer School, AZ
St. Paul's Preparatory Academy Summer Program, AZ
Star Ranch Summer Camp, TX
Success Oriented Achievement Realized (SOAR)–North Carolina, NC
Success Oriented Achievement Realized (SOAR)–Wyoming, WY
Talisman–Academics, NC
Talisman Mini-Camp, NC
Talisman Open Boat Adventures (TOBA), NC
Talisman Summer Camp, NC
Talisman–Trek Hiking Program, NC
The Winchendon School Summer Session, MA

ADD
Camp Courageous of Iowa, IA
Camp Kodiak, Canada
Eagle Hill School Summer Session, MA
New Jersey YMHA–YWHA Round Lake Camp, PA
Oak Creek Ranch Summer School, AZ
St. Paul's Preparatory Academy Summer Program, AZ
Star Ranch Summer Camp, TX
Success Oriented Achievement Realized (SOAR)–North Carolina, NC
Success Oriented Achievement Realized (SOAR)–Wyoming, WY
Summit Camp, PA
Summit Travel Program
The Winchendon School Summer Session, MA

Arthritis
Camp Holiday Trails, VA

Aspergers Syndrome
Camp Buckskin, MN
Camp Lee Mar, PA
Summit Camp, PA
Summit Travel Program
Talisman–Academics, NC
Talisman–INSIGHT, NC
Talisman–SIGHT, NC

Asthma
Camp Aldersgate–Kota Camp, AR
Camp Aldersgate–Med Camps, AR
Camp Aldersgate–Respite Care, AR
Camp Holiday Trails, VA
Camp Namanu, OR
Camp Superkids–Camp Crosley, IN
Camp Superkids–Happy Hollow Children's Camp, IN
YMCA Camp Abnaki, VT

Autistic
Camp Courageous of Iowa, IA
Talisman–Academics, NC
Talisman–INSIGHT, NC
Talisman–SIGHT, NC

Brain Injured
Camp Courageous of Iowa, IA
Camp Fowler, MI

Burn Survivor
Missouri Children's Burn Camp, MO

Cancer
Camp Aldersgate–Kota Camp, AR
Camp Aldersgate–Med Camps, AR
Camp Aldersgate–Respite Care, AR
Camp Holiday Trails, VA
Double "H" Hole in the Woods Ranch Summer Camp, NY
YMCA Camp Oakes Rangers, CA

Cerebral Palsy
Camp Aldersgate–Kota Camp, AR
Camp Aldersgate–Med Camps, AR
Camp Aldersgate–Respite Care, AR

Cystic Fibrosis
Camp Holiday Trails, VA

Developmentally Challenged
Ability First–Camp Joan Mier, CA
Ability First–Camp Paivika, CA
Bark Lake Leadership Through Recreation Camp, Canada
Camp Aldersgate–Kota Camp, AR
Camp Aldersgate–Med Camps, AR
Camp Aldersgate–Respite Care, AR
Camp Allen, NH
Camp Barney Medintz, GA
Camp Berachah Ministries–Day Camp, WA
Camp Berachah Ministries–Horse Day Camp, WA
Camp Berachah Ministries–Junior Camp, WA
Camp Berachah Ministries–Leadership Expedition Camp, WA
Camp Berachah Ministries–Legend Teen Camp, WA
Camp Berachah Ministries–Overnight Horse Camp, WA
Camp Berachah Ministries–Primary Camp, WA
Camp Berachah Ministries–Soccer Camp, WA
Camp Berachah Ministries–Teen Leadership, WA
Camp Berachah Ministries–Wrangler-In-Training, WA
Camp Cedar Point, IL
Camp Courageous of Iowa, IA
Camp Echoing Hills, OH
Camp Fowler, MI
Camp Friendship, MN
Camp Joy, OH
Camp Kostopulos, UT
Camp Lee Mar, PA
Camp O'Bannon, OH
Camp Oweki Summer Day Camp, MI
Camp Sky Ranch, Inc., NC
Camp Starfish, NH
Camp Veritans, NJ
Christikon, MT
The Colorado Mountain Ranch, CO
Double "H" Hole in the Woods Ranch Summer Camp, NY
Eden Wood Camp, MN
Fotocamp, FL
French Immersion Kayak Expedition, Canada
Girl Scouts of Mid-Continent–Juliette Low Camp, MO
Horizons for Youth, MA
The Hun School of Princeton Summer Day Camp, NJ
ISB Chinese Language Camp, China
JCC Houston: Art Camp, TX
JCC Houston: Camp Bami, TX
JCC Houston: Camp Kaleidoscope, TX
Jewish Community Center Day Camp, NJ
Kamp Kohut, ME
Little Keswick School Summer Session, VA
Marbridge Summer Camp, TX
Meadowood Springs Speech and Hearing Camp, OR
Medeba Summer Camp, Canada
The Monarch School Summer Camp, TX
The Monarch School Summer Course, TX
New Jersey YMHA–YWHA Round Lake Camp, PA
New Strides Day Camp, Canada
92nd Street Y Camps–Camp Bari Tov, NY
Purcell Marian High School Summer School, OH
Rocky Mountain Village, CO
Star Ranch Summer Camp, TX
Ventures Travel Service–Arizona, AZ
Ventures Travel Service–California, CA
Ventures Travel Service–Florida, FL
Ventures Travel Service–Iowa, IA
Ventures Travel Service–Kentucky, KY
Ventures Travel Service–Minnesota, MN
Ventures Travel Service–Missouri, MO
Ventures Travel Service–New York, NY
Ventures Travel Service–North Dakota, ND
Ventures Travel Service–Oregon, OR
Ventures Travel Service–South Carolina, SC
Ventures Travel Service–South Dakota, SD
Ventures Travel Service–Tennessee, TN
Ventures Travel Service–Texas, TX
Ventures Travel Service–Washington, WA
Ventures Travel Service–Wisconsin, WI
Wediko Summer Program, NH
XUK, United Kingdom
YMCA Camp Oakes Rangers, CA
YMCA Camp Oakes Teen Leadership, CA
YMCA Wanakita Summer Family Camp, Canada
YMCA Wanakita Summer Resident and Day Camp, Canada

Diabetic
Barton Adventure Camp
Barton Day Camp–Long Island, NY
Barton Day Camp–New York, NY
Barton Day Camp–Worcester, MA
Camp Aldersgate–Kota Camp, AR
Camp Aldersgate–Med Camps, AR
Camp Aldersgate–Respite Care, AR
Camp Holiday Trails, VA
Camp Jordan for Children with Diabetes, VA
Clara Barton Camp, MA
Clara Barton Family Camp, MA
Lions Camp Merrick Diabetes Program, MD
Rainbow Club–Greenwich, Connecticut, CT

Emotionally Challenged
Ability First–Camp Joan Mier, CA
Ability First–Camp Paivika, CA
Bark Lake Leadership Through Recreation Camp, Canada
BICYCLE TRAVEL ADVENTURES–Student Hosteling Program–Amsterdam to Paris
BICYCLE TRAVEL ADVENTURES–Student Hosteling Program–A Thousand Miles: Massachusetts to Nova Scotia

▶ Emotionally Challenged

BICYCLE TRAVEL ADVENTURES–Student Hosteling Program–Canadian Rockies to California
BICYCLE TRAVEL ADVENTURES–Student Hosteling Program–Cape Cod, MA
BICYCLE TRAVEL ADVENTURES–Student Hosteling Program–Cross-Country America
BICYCLE TRAVEL ADVENTURES–Student Hosteling Program–France and Italy
BICYCLE TRAVEL ADVENTURES–Student Hosteling Program–Ireland and England
BICYCLE TRAVEL ADVENTURES–Student Hosteling Program–Maine Coast, ME
BICYCLE TRAVEL ADVENTURES–Student Hosteling Program–Maine-Nova Scotia Coast Loop
BICYCLE TRAVEL ADVENTURES–Student Hosteling Program–Niagara Falls to Montreal
BICYCLE TRAVEL ADVENTURES–Student Hosteling Program–Off-Road Vermont
BICYCLE TRAVEL ADVENTURES–Student Hosteling Program–Pacific Coast Adventure: Washington, Oregon, and California
BICYCLE TRAVEL ADVENTURES–Student Hosteling Program–Province du Québec, Canada
BICYCLE TRAVEL ADVENTURES–Student Hosteling Program–Province du Québec (short program), Canada
BICYCLE TRAVEL ADVENTURES–Student Hosteling Program–Spain and France
BICYCLE TRAVEL ADVENTURES–Student Hosteling Program–Vermont
BICYCLE TRAVEL ADVENTURES–Student Hosteling Program–Vermont to the Atlantic Ocean
Camp Echoing Hills, OH
Camp Fowler, MI
Camp Joy, OH
Camp Kostopulos, UT
Camp O'Bannon, OH
Camp Oweki Summer Day Camp, MI
Camp Starfish, NH
Camp Veritans, NJ
The Colorado Mountain Ranch, CO
Cornell University Summer College Programs for High School Students, NY
Crane Lake Camp, MA
Double "H" Hole in the Woods Ranch Summer Camp, NY
Horizons for Youth, MA
JCC Houston: Art Camp, TX
JCC Houston: Camp Bami, TX
JCC Houston: Camp Kaleidoscope, TX
Little Keswick School Summer Session, VA
New Jersey YMHA–YWHA Round Lake Camp, PA
New Strides Day Camp, Canada
92nd Street Y Camps–Camp Tova, NY
Star Ranch Summer Camp, TX
Summit Camp, PA
Summit Travel Program
Swift Nature Camp–Adventure Camp, WI
Swift Nature Camp–Discovery Camp, WI
Swift Nature Camp–Explorer Camp, WI
Talisman Open Boat Adventures (TOBA), NC
Talisman Summer Camp, NC
Talisman–Trek Hiking Program, NC
Wediko Summer Program, NH
XUK, United Kingdom
YMCA Camp Oakes Rangers, CA
YMCA Camp Oakes Teen Leadership, CA
YMCA Camp Tippecanoe–Adventure Camp, OH
YMCA Camp Tippecanoe–Bike Camp, OH
YMCA Camp Tippecanoe–Equine Camp, OH
YMCA Camp Tippecanoe–Girl's & Guy's Corral, OH
YMCA Camp Tippecanoe–Horse Pals, OH
YMCA Camp Tippecanoe–Jr. Counselor, OH
YMCA Camp Tippecanoe–Teen Camp, OH
YMCA Wanakita Summer Family Camp, Canada
YMCA Wanakita Summer Resident and Day Camp, Canada

Encopresis

Camp Brandon for Boys, NH

Enuresis

Camp Brandon for Boys, NH

Epileptic

Camp Aldersgate–Kota Camp, AR
Camp Aldersgate–Med Camps, AR
Camp Aldersgate–Respite Care, AR
Camp Holiday Trails, VA

Hearing Impaired

Ability First–Camp Joan Mier, CA
Ability First–Camp Paivika, CA
Adventures in Science and Arts, WA
Ball State University Summer Journalism Workshops, IN
Bark Lake Leadership Through Recreation Camp, Canada
Burklyn Ballet Edinburgh Connection
Burklyn Ballet Theatre, VT
Burklyn Ballet Theatre II, The Intermediate Program, VT
Camp Aldersgate–Kota Camp, AR
Camp Aldersgate–Med Camps, AR
Camp Aldersgate–Respite Care, AR
Camp Allen, NH
Camp Berachah Ministries–Day Camp, WA
Camp Berachah Ministries–Horse Day Camp, WA
Camp Berachah Ministries–Junior Camp, WA
Camp Berachah Ministries–Leadership Expedition Camp, WA
Camp Berachah Ministries–Legend Teen Camp, WA
Camp Berachah Ministries–Overnight Horse Camp, WA
Camp Berachah Ministries–Primary Camp, WA
Camp Berachah Ministries–Soccer Camp, WA
Camp Berachah Ministries–Teen Leadership, WA
Camp Berachah Ministries–Wrangler-In-Training, WA
Camp Courageous of Iowa, IA
Camp Echoing Hills, OH
Camp Fowler, MI
Camp Kostopulos, UT
Camp Sky Ranch, Inc., NC
Center for Talent Development Summer Academic Program, IL
College Quest, WA
The Colorado Mountain Ranch, CO
Community Sailing of Colorado–Advanced Sailing, CO
Community Sailing of Colorado–Learn to Sail, CO
Community Sailing of Colorado–Sailboat Racing Camp, CO
Cornell University Summer College Programs for High School Students, NY
Double "H" Hole in the Woods Ranch Summer Camp, NY
The Experiment in International Living–Australia Homestay, Australia
Exploration Intermediate Program at Wellesley College, MA
Exploration Junior Program at St. Mark's School, MA
Exploration Senior Program at Yale University, CT
Girl Scouts of Mid-Continent–Juliette Low Camp, MO
Harvard University Summer School: Secondary School Program, MA
JCC Houston: Art Camp, TX
JCC Houston: Camp Bami, TX
JCC Houston: Camp Kaleidoscope, TX
Johns Hopkins University Zanvyl Krieger School of Arts and Sciences Summer Programs, MD
Lions Camp Merrick Deaf/HOH/KODA Program, MD
Meadowood Springs Speech and Hearing Camp, OR
Mississippi Governor's School, MS
New Strides Day Camp, Canada
Outdoor Adventure, WA
Preparatory Academics for Vanderbilt Engineers (PAVE), TN
Project SUCCEED, NC
Rocky Mountain Village, CO
Stanford Discovery Institutes, CA
Stanford University Summer College for High School Students, CA
Star Ranch Summer Camp, TX
Summer Dance '05, MA
The Summer Institute for the Gifted at Amherst College, MA
The Summer Institute for the Gifted at Bryn Mawr College, PA
The Summer Institute for the Gifted at Drew University, NJ
The Summer Institute for the Gifted at Fairfield University, CT
The Summer Institute for the Gifted at Moorestown Friends School, NJ
The Summer Institute for the Gifted at UCLA, CA
University of Kansas–Sertoma-Schiefelbush Communication Camp, KS
University of Southern California Summer Seminars, CA
Volunteers for Peace International Work Camp–Armenia, Armenia
Volunteers for Peace International Work Camp–Belarus, Belarus
Volunteers for Peace International Work Camp–Belgium, Belgium
Volunteers for Peace International Work Camp–Czech Republic, Czech Republic
Volunteers for Peace International Work Camp–Estonia, Estonia
Volunteers for Peace International Work Camp–France, France
Volunteers for Peace International Work Camp–Germany, Germany

Volunteers for Peace International Work Camp–Italy, Italy
Volunteers for Peace International Work Camp–Lithuania, Lithuania
Volunteers for Peace International Work Camp–Russia, Russian Federation
Volunteers for Peace International Work Camp–Slovakia, Slovakia
Volunteers for Peace International Work Camp–Turkey, Turkey
West River United Methodist Center, MD
YMCA Camp Oakes Rangers, CA
YMCA Camp Oakes Teen Leadership, CA
YMCA Camp Tippecanoe–Adventure Camp, OH
YMCA Camp Tippecanoe–Bike Camp, OH
YMCA Camp Tippecanoe–Equine Camp, OH
YMCA Camp Tippecanoe–Girl's & Guy's Corral, OH
YMCA Camp Tippecanoe–Horse Pals, OH
YMCA Camp Tippecanoe–Jr. Counselor, OH
YMCA Camp Tippecanoe–Teen Camp, OH
YMCA Wanakita Summer Family Camp, Canada
YMCA Wanakita Summer Resident and Day Camp, Canada

Heart Defects

Camp Aldersgate–Med Camps, AR
Camp Bon Coeur, LA
Camp Holiday Trails, VA

Hemophilia

Camp Aldersgate–Med Camps, AR
Camp Holiday Trails, VA
Double "H" Hole in the Woods Ranch Summer Camp, NY

HIV/AIDS

Camp Fowler, MI
Camp Heartland Summer Camp–California, CA
Camp Heartland Summer Camp–Minnesota, MN
Camp Holiday Trails, VA
Double "H" Hole in the Woods Ranch Summer Camp, NY
YMCA Camp Matollionequay, NJ

Kidney Disorders

Camp Aldersgate–Kota Camp, AR
Camp Aldersgate–Med Camps, AR
Camp Aldersgate–Respite Care, AR
Camp Holiday Trails, VA

Learning Disabled

Ability First–Camp Joan Mier, CA
Ability First–Camp Paivika, CA
Bark Lake Leadership Through Recreation Camp, Canada
Barnard's Summer in New York City: A Pre-College Program, NY
Barnard's Summer in New York City: One-Week Mini-Course, NY
Barnard's Summer in New York City: Young Women's Leadership Institute, NY
Beekman School Summer Session, NY
BICYCLE TRAVEL ADVENTURES–Student Hosteling Program–Amsterdam to Paris
BICYCLE TRAVEL ADVENTURES–Student Hosteling Program–A Thousand Miles: Massachusetts to Nova Scotia
BICYCLE TRAVEL ADVENTURES–Student Hosteling Program–Canadian Rockies to California
BICYCLE TRAVEL ADVENTURES–Student Hosteling Program–Cape Cod, MA
BICYCLE TRAVEL ADVENTURES–Student Hosteling Program–Cross-Country America
BICYCLE TRAVEL ADVENTURES–Student Hosteling Program–France and Italy
BICYCLE TRAVEL ADVENTURES–Student Hosteling Program–Ireland and England
BICYCLE TRAVEL ADVENTURES–Student Hosteling Program–Maine Coast, ME
BICYCLE TRAVEL ADVENTURES–Student Hosteling Program–Maine-Nova Scotia Coast Loop
BICYCLE TRAVEL ADVENTURES–Student Hosteling Program–Niagara Falls to Montreal
BICYCLE TRAVEL ADVENTURES–Student Hosteling Program–Off-Road Vermont
BICYCLE TRAVEL ADVENTURES–Student Hosteling Program–Pacific Coast Adventure: Washington, Oregon, and California
BICYCLE TRAVEL ADVENTURES–Student Hosteling Program–Province du Québec, Canada
BICYCLE TRAVEL ADVENTURES–Student Hosteling Program–Province du Québec (short program), Canada
BICYCLE TRAVEL ADVENTURES–Student Hosteling Program–Spain and France
BICYCLE TRAVEL ADVENTURES–Student Hosteling Program–Vermont
BICYCLE TRAVEL ADVENTURES–Student Hosteling Program–Vermont to the Atlantic Ocean
Brewster Academy Summer Session, NH
Bridge to the Future, NJ
Camp Aldersgate–Kota Camp, AR
Camp Aldersgate–Med Camps, AR
Camp Aldersgate–Respite Care, AR
Camp Buckskin, MN
Camp Conrad Weiser, PA
Camp Courageous of Iowa, IA
Camp Echoing Hills, OH
Camp Fowler, MI
Camp Hillside, MA
Camp Kodiak, Canada
Camp Kostopulos, UT
Camp Lee Mar, PA
Camp O'Bannon, OH
Camp Oweki Summer Day Camp, MI
Camp Sky Ranch, Inc., NC
Camp Starfish, NH
Camp Veritans, NJ
The Cardigan Mountain School Summer Session, NH
Cheshire Academy Summer Program, CT
Coleman Country Day Camp, NY
The Colorado Mountain Ranch, CO
Cornell University Summer College Programs for High School Students, NY
Crane Lake Camp, MA
Cushing Academy Summer Session, MA
Daniel Fox Youth Scholars Institute, PA
Denver Academy Summer Program, CO
Double "H" Hole in the Woods Ranch Summer Camp, NY
Dunnabeck at Kildonan, NY
Eagle Hill School Summer Session, MA
Excel at Amherst College and Williams College, MA
Exploration Intermediate Program at Wellesley College, MA
Exploration Junior Program at St. Mark's School, MA
Exploration Senior Program at Yale University, CT
Fay Summer School, MA
Fotocamp, FL
French Woods Festival of the Performing Arts, NY
The Gow School Summer Program, NY
Hamilton Learning Centre Summer Fun in the Sun Camp, Canada
Hamilton Learning Centre Summer School, Canada
Harvard University Summer School: Secondary School Program, MA
High Sierra Wilderness Camps, CA
Hill Top Summer Programs, PA
Horizons for Youth, MA
The Hun School of Princeton Summer Day Camp, NJ
JCC Houston: Art Camp, TX
JCC Houston: Camp Bami, TX
JCC Houston: Camp Kaleidoscope, TX
Jewish Community Center Day Camp, NJ
Johns Hopkins University Zanvyl Krieger School of Arts and Sciences Summer Programs, MD
Kamp Kohut, ME
Kroka Expeditions–Cape Cod Triple Surfing Bonanza, MA
Kroka Expeditions–Coastal Sea Kayaking, ME
Kroka Expeditions–Coming of Age for Young Women, VT
Kroka Expeditions–Introduction to Adventure Day Camp, VT
Kroka Expeditions–Introduction to Adventure Residential Camp, VT
Kroka Expeditions–Introduction to White Water, VT
Kroka Expeditions–Paddlers Journey Up North
Kroka Expeditions–Rock 'n Road, VT
Kroka Expeditions–Wild World of White Water, VT
Landmark School Summer Academic Program, MA
Linden Hill Summer Program, MA
Little Keswick School Summer Session, VA
Loras All-Sports Camp, IA
Maplebrook School's Summer Program, NY
Meadowood Springs Speech and Hearing Camp, OR
Medeba Summer Camp, Canada
The Monarch School Summer Camp, TX
The Monarch School Summer Course, TX
NAWA Academy–Girls on the Go, CA
NAWA Academy–Great Challenge, CA
NAWA Academy–Lassen Expedition, CA
NAWA Academy–Trinity Challenge, CA
Newgrange Summer Program, NJ
New Jersey YMHA–YWHA Round Lake Camp, PA
New Strides Day Camp, Canada
92nd Street Y Camps–Camp Tova, NY
Oak Creek Ranch Summer School, AZ
The Oxford Academy Summer Program, CT
The Phelps School Summer Program, PA
Pine Ridge Summer Program, VT

▶ Learning Disabled

Purcell Marian High School Summer School, OH
Rectory School Summer Session, CT
Rocky Mountain Village, CO
Rumsey Hall School Summer Session, CT
Sailing Program at NE Camping Adventures, ME
Saint Thomas More School–Summer Academic Camp, CT
Salisbury Summer School of Reading and English, CT
Sprucelands Camp, NY
Squirrel Hollow Learning Camp, GA
Stanford Discovery Institutes, CA
Stanford University Summer College for High School Students, CA
Star Ranch Summer Camp, TX
Success Oriented Achievement Realized (SOAR)–North Carolina, NC
Success Oriented Achievement Realized (SOAR)–Wyoming, WY
The Summer Institute for the Gifted at Amherst College, MA
The Summer Institute for the Gifted at Bryn Mawr College, PA
The Summer Institute for the Gifted at Drew University, NJ
The Summer Institute for the Gifted at Fairfield University, CT
The Summer Institute for the Gifted at Moorestown Friends School, NJ
The Summer Institute for the Gifted at UCLA, CA
The Summer Institute for the Gifted at Vassar College, NY
Summit Camp, PA
Summit Travel Program
Swift Nature Camp–Adventure Camp, WI
Swift Nature Camp–Canadian Canoe Trip
Swift Nature Camp–Discovery Camp, WI
Swift Nature Camp–Explorer Camp, WI
Talisman–Academics, NC
Talisman Open Boat Adventures (TOBA), NC
Talisman Summer Camp, NC
Talisman–Trek Hiking Program, NC
Wediko Summer Program, NH
The Winchendon School Summer Session, MA
XUK, United Kingdom
YMCA Camp Oakes Rangers, CA
YMCA Camp Oakes Teen Leadership, CA
YMCA Camp Tippecanoe–Adventure Camp, OH
YMCA Camp Tippecanoe–Bike Camp, OH
YMCA Camp Tippecanoe–Equine Camp, OH
YMCA Camp Tippecanoe–Girl's & Guy's Corral, OH
YMCA Camp Tippecanoe–Horse Pals, OH
YMCA Camp Tippecanoe–Jr. Counselor, OH
YMCA Camp Tippecanoe–Teen Camp, OH
YMCA Wanakita Summer Family Camp, Canada
YMCA Wanakita Summer Resident and Day Camp, Canada

Mentally Challenged

Jumonville Discovery Camp, PA

Muscular Dystrophy

Camp Aldersgate–Kota Camp, AR
Camp Aldersgate–Med Camps, AR
Camp Aldersgate–Respite Care, AR

Neurofibromatosis

Camp Kostopulos, UT

Organ Transplant Recipient

Camp Holiday Trails, VA
Camp Kostopulos, UT

Phenylketonuria

South Shore YMCA Specialty Camp, MA

Physically Challenged

Ability First–Camp Joan Mier, CA
Ability First–Camp Paivika, CA
Adventures in Science and Arts, WA
Agassiz Village, ME
Architecture Summer Camp, AL
The Art Institute of Seattle–Studio 101, WA
Auburn University Design Workshop, AL
Ball State University Summer Journalism Workshops, IN
Bark Lake Leadership Through Recreation Camp, Canada
California College of the Arts Pre-College Program, CA
Camp Aldersgate–Kota Camp, AR
Camp Aldersgate–Med Camps, AR
Camp Aldersgate–Respite Care, AR
Camp Allen, NH
Camp Courageous of Iowa, IA
Camp Echoing Hills, OH
Camp Fowler, MI
Camp Friendship, MN
Camp Kostopulos, UT
Camp Oweki Summer Day Camp, MI
Camp Sky Ranch, Inc., NC
Center for Talent Development Summer Academic Program, IL
College Quest, WA
The Colorado Mountain Ranch, CO
Columbia University Summer Program for High School Students, NY
Cordova 4-H Bluegrass and Old Time Music and Dance Camp, AK
Cordova 4-H Hawaiian Camp, AK
Cornell University Summer College Programs for High School Students, NY
Cuernavaca Summer Program for Teens, Mexico
Daniel Fox Youth Scholars Institute, PA
Double "H" Hole in the Woods Ranch Summer Camp, NY
ECOES: Exploring Career Options in Engineering and Science, NJ
Eden Wood Camp, MN
Exploration Intermediate Program at Wellesley College, MA
Exploration Junior Program at St. Mark's School, MA
Exploration of Architecture, CA
Exploration Senior Program at Yale University, CT
Fotocamp, FL
Georgetown Prep School Summer English Program, MD
Girl Scouts of Mid-Continent–Juliette Low Camp, MO
Harvard University Summer School: Secondary School Program, MA
JCC Houston: Art Camp, TX
JCC Houston: Camp Bami, TX
JCC Houston: Camp Kaleidoscope, TX
Johns Hopkins University Zanvyl Krieger School of Arts and Sciences Summer Programs, MD
Kroka Expeditions–Cape Cod Triple Surfing Bonanza, MA
Kroka Expeditions–Coastal Sea Kayaking, ME
Kroka Expeditions–Coming of Age for Young Women, VT
Kroka Expeditions–Introduction to Adventure Day Camp, VT
Kroka Expeditions–Introduction to Adventure Residential Camp, VT
Kroka Expeditions–Introduction to White Water, VT
Kroka Expeditions–Paddlers Journey Up North
Kroka Expeditions–Rock 'n Road, VT
Kroka Expeditions–Wild World of White Water, VT
Longhorn Music Camp: All-State Choir Camp, TX
Longhorn Music Camp: Harp Solo and Ensemble Camp, TX
Longhorn Music Camp: High School Band Camp, TX
Longhorn Music Camp: Middle School Band Camp, TX
Longhorn Music Camp: Middle School String Orchestra Camp, TX
Longhorn Music Camp: Piano Performance Workshop, TX
LSA Almuñecar, Spain, Spain
Mississippi Governor's School, MS
New Strides Day Camp, Canada
92nd Street Y Camps–Camp Tova, NY
Preparatory Academics for Vanderbilt Engineers (PAVE), TN
Purcell Marian High School Summer School, OH
Rocky Mountain Village, CO
St. John's University Scholars Program, NY
Stanford Discovery Institutes, CA
Stanford University Summer College for High School Students, CA
The Summer Institute for the Gifted at Amherst College, MA
The Summer Institute for the Gifted at Bryn Mawr College, PA
The Summer Institute for the Gifted at Drew University, NJ
The Summer Institute for the Gifted at Fairfield University, CT
The Summer Institute for the Gifted at Moorestown Friends School, NJ
The Summer Institute for the Gifted at UCLA, CA
The Summer Institute for the Gifted at Vassar College, NY
University of Southern California Summer Seminars, CA
University of Vermont Summer Institute for High School Students Discovering Engineering, Computers, and Mathematics, VT
University of Wisconsin–Superior Youthsummer 2005, WI
Ventures Travel Service–Arizona, AZ
Ventures Travel Service–California, CA
Ventures Travel Service–Florida, FL
Ventures Travel Service–Iowa, IA
Ventures Travel Service–Kentucky, KY
Ventures Travel Service–Minnesota, MN
Ventures Travel Service–Missouri, MO

Ventures Travel Service–New York, NY
Ventures Travel Service–North Dakota, ND
Ventures Travel Service–Oregon, OR
Ventures Travel Service–South Carolina, SC
Ventures Travel Service–South Dakota, SD
Ventures Travel Service–Tennessee, TN
Ventures Travel Service–Texas, TX
Ventures Travel Service–Washington, WA
Ventures Travel Service–Wisconsin, WI
Volunteers for Peace International Work Camp–Armenia, Armenia
Volunteers for Peace International Work Camp–Belarus, Belarus
Volunteers for Peace International Work Camp–Belgium, Belgium
Volunteers for Peace International Work Camp–Czech Republic, Czech Republic
Volunteers for Peace International Work Camp–Estonia, Estonia
Volunteers for Peace International Work Camp–France, France
Volunteers for Peace International Work Camp–Germany, Germany
Volunteers for Peace International Work Camp–Italy, Italy
Volunteers for Peace International Work Camp–Lithuania, Lithuania
Volunteers for Peace International Work Camp–Russia, Russian Federation
Volunteers for Peace International Work Camp–Slovakia, Slovakia
Volunteers for Peace International Work Camp–Turkey, Turkey
World Affairs Seminar, WI
World Affairs Youth Seminar, AL
YMCA Camp Oakes Rangers, CA
YMCA Camp Oakes Teen Leadership, CA
YMCA Wanakita Summer Family Camp, Canada
YMCA Wanakita Summer Resident and Day Camp, Canada

Sickle Cell Anemia

Camp Holiday Trails, VA
Double "H" Hole in the Woods Ranch Summer Camp, NY

Speech Impaired

Flint Hill School–"Summer on the Hill"–Academics on the Hill–The Reading Clinic, VA
Meadowood Springs Speech and Hearing Camp, OR
University of Kansas–Sertoma-Schiefelbush Communication Camp, KS

Tourette's Syndrome

Summit Camp, PA

Visually Impaired

Ability First–Camp Joan Mier, CA
Ability First–Camp Paivika, CA
Ball State University Summer Journalism Workshops, IN
Bark Lake Leadership Through Recreation Camp, Canada
Camp Aldersgate–Kota Camp, AR
Camp Aldersgate–Med Camps, AR
Camp Aldersgate–Respite Care, AR
Camp Allen, NH
Camp Courageous of Iowa, IA
Camp Echoing Hills, OH
Camp Fowler, MI
Camp Kostopulos, UT
Camp Sky Ranch, Inc., NC
Carroll Center for the Blind–Computing for College: Computer and Communication Skills, MA
Carroll Center for the Blind–Real World Work Experience, MA
Carroll Center for the Blind–Youth in Transition, MA
Center for Talent Development Summer Academic Program, IL
College Quest, WA
The Colorado Mountain Ranch, CO
Cordova 4-H Bluegrass and Old Time Music and Dance Camp, AK
Cordova 4-H Hawaiian Camp, AK
Cornell University Summer College Programs for High School Students, NY
Crane Lake Camp, MA
Cuernavaca Summer Program for Teens, Mexico
Double "H" Hole in the Woods Ranch Summer Camp, NY
The Experiment in International Living–Australia Homestay, Australia
Exploration Intermediate Program at Wellesley College, MA
Exploration Junior Program at St. Mark's School, MA
Exploration Senior Program at Yale University, CT
Girl Scouts of Mid-Continent–Juliette Low Camp, MO
Harvard University Summer School: Secondary School Program, MA
JCC Houston: Camp Bami, TX
JCC Houston: Camp Kaleidoscope, TX
Johns Hopkins University Zanvyl Krieger School of Arts and Sciences Summer Programs, MD
Mississippi Governor's School, MS
New Strides Day Camp, Canada
Rocky Mountain Village, CO
Stanford Discovery Institutes, CA
Stanford University Summer College for High School Students, CA
The Summer Institute for the Gifted at Amherst College, MA
The Summer Institute for the Gifted at Bryn Mawr College, PA
The Summer Institute for the Gifted at Drew University, NJ
The Summer Institute for the Gifted at Fairfield University, CT
The Summer Institute for the Gifted at Moorestown Friends School, NJ
The Summer Institute for the Gifted at UCLA, CA
The Summer Institute for the Gifted at Vassar College, NY
University of Southern California Summer Seminars, CA
YMCA Camp Oakes Rangers, CA
YMCA Camp Oakes Teen Leadership, CA

Weight Reduction

Camp Kingsmont, MA
Camp La Jolla, CA
Shane (Trim-Down) Camp, NY

Youth at Risk

Camp Wing, MA
Horizons for Youth, MA
St. Paul's Preparatory Academy Summer Program, AZ

▶ American Baptist Churches in the USA

American Baptist Churches in the USA
Camp Canonicus, RI

Baptist
Carson-Newman College–EXCEL Program, TN
Hargrave Summer Program, VA
Lady Wildcat Basketball Camp, LA
Lake Ann Baptist Camp, MI
Louisiana College Center for Academically Talented Students (CATS), LA
Louisiana College Summer Superior Program, LA
Wildcat Basketball Camp, LA

Buddhist Faith
RUSTIC PATHWAYS–BUDDHIST LIFE & ANGKOR WAT

Christian
Alpine Camp for Boys, AL
Camp Berachah Ministries–Counselor-In-Training, WA
Camp Berachah Ministries–Day Camp, WA
Camp Berachah Ministries–Horse Day Camp, WA
Camp Berachah Ministries–Junior Camp, WA
Camp Berachah Ministries–Leadership Expedition Camp, WA
Camp Berachah Ministries–Legend Teen Camp, WA
Camp Berachah Ministries–Overnight Horse Camp, WA
Camp Berachah Ministries–Primary Camp, WA
Camp Berachah Ministries–Soccer Camp, WA
Camp Berachah Ministries–Teen Leadership, WA
Camp Berachah Ministries–Wrangler-In-Training, WA
Camp Brookwoods and Deer Run, NH
Camp Burgess, MA
Camp Cheerio YMCA, NC
Camp Crestridge for Girls, NC
Camp Dudley, NY
Camp Hayward, MA
Camp Olympia, TX
Camp Olympia Junior Golf Academy, TX
Camp Ridgecrest for Boys, NC
Camp Roger, MI
Camp Sandy Cove, WV
Camp Streamside, PA
Camp WinShape for Boys, GA
Camp WinShape for Girls, GA
Cheerio Adventures–Appalachian Adventure, VA
Cheerio Adventures–Cave/Raft, VA
Cheerio Adventures–5 Rivers in 5 Days
Cheerio Adventures–Mountains to the Sea, VA
Cheerio Adventures–Ocean Odyssey, VA
Cheerio Adventures–Sampler, VA
Cheerio Adventures–Seekers, VA
Cheerio Adventures–Standard, VA
Davidson Academy–Academy Arts, TN
Davidson Academy–Bear Country Day Camp, TN
Davidson Academy–Sports Camps, TN
Eagle Lake Bike Camp, CO
Eagle Lake Camp Crew Program, CO
Eagle Lake Camp–East, NC
Eagle Lake Camp Jaunts–Kenya Mission Adventure, Kenya
Eagle Lake Camp Jaunts–Minnesota Boundary Waters, MN
Eagle Lake Camp Jaunts–Norway Mission Adventure, Norway
Eagle Lake Horse Camp, CO
Eagle Lake Resident Camp, CO
Eagle Lake Wilderness Program, CO
Freed-Hardeman Horizons for Ages 12-18, TN
Great Escapes (Adventure Trips for Teens)–California Beach Escape, CA
Great Escapes (Adventure Trips for Teens)–Canadian Adventure
Great Escapes (Adventure Trips for Teens)–Canadian Canoe and Kayak Adventure, Canada
Great Escapes (Adventure Trips for Teens)–Cape Cod Sail Adventure, MA
Great Escapes (Adventure Trips for Teens)–Cape Cod Underwater Adventure, MA
Great Escapes (Adventure Trips for Teens)–Cape Escapes, MA
Great Escapes (Adventure Trips for Teens)–Colorado River and Canyons Adventure
Great Escapes (Adventure Trips for Teens)–Costa Rica Rainforest Adventure, Costa Rica
Great Escapes (Adventure Trips for Teens)–Maine Waterways, ME
Great Escapes (Adventure Trips for Teens)–Rock and Rapids
Great Escapes (Adventure Trips for Teens)–Rocky Mountain Horsepacking Adventure, CO
Great Escapes (Adventure Trips for Teens)–Saddle and Sail
Great Escapes (Adventure Trips for Teens)–White Mountain Adventure, NH
KidzZone Summer Camp, GA
The Marsh, MD
McCallie Sports Camp, TN
Medeba Leader in Training Program, Canada
Medeba Summer Camp, Canada
Monte Vista ESL Intensive Language Institute, CA
Moose River Outpost, ME
South Shore YMCA Specialty Camp, MA
Star Ranch Summer Camp, TX
Streamside Camp and Conference Center, PA
Streamside Family Camp, PA
Streamside Pathfinder Adventure Camp, PA
Summer Family Conference, MD
YMCA Camp Minikani, WI

The Christian and Missionary Alliance
Kawkawa Summer Camps, Canada

Christian Churches and Churches of Christ
Camp Illahee for Girls, NC

Christian Non-Denominational
Camp Echoing Hills, OH
Camp Merrie-Woode, NC
Camp Skyline, AL
Camp Skyline–Equestrian Program, AL
Haycock Camping Ministries–Adventure Trails, PA
Haycock Camping Ministries–Battalion Program, PA
Haycock Camping Ministries–Stockade Program, PA
Haycock Camping Ministries–Trailbuilders Program, PA

Church of Christ
Abilene Christian University–Cross Training, NM
Abilene Christian University–Kadesh Life Camp, TX
Abilene Christian University–Learning to Lead, TX
Abilene Christian University–MPulse, TX
Abiliene Christian University–KidQuest Day Camp, TX
Pepperdine University Summer College for High School Students, CA

Episcopal
Episcopal High School Academic Camp, FL
Episcopal High School Eagle Arts Camp, FL
Episcopal High School Sports Camp, FL
OES–Challenge Workshops, OR
OES–Summer Adventure Camp, OR
OES–Summer Discovery, OR
OES–Summer Mini Camps, OR
OES–Summer Wonder, OR
St. Paul's Preparatory Academy Summer Program, AZ
Summer Programs on the River; Crew/Rowing Camp, VA
Summer Programs on the River; Marine Science Camp, VA
Summer Programs on the River; Sailing Camp, VA
Summer Programs on the River; Skills Program, VA

Evangelical Free Church of America
Timber-lee Science Camp, WI
Timber-lee Creation Camp, WI
Timber-lee Drama Camp, WI
Timber-lee Horsemanship Camps, WI
Timber-lee Wilderness Trips, WI
Timber-lee Youth Camp, WI

Evangelical Lutheran Church in America
Christikon, MT

Friends United Meeting
Applejack Teen Camp, NY
Camp Regis, NY

Interdenominational
Camp Good News for Young People and Teens, MA
Camp Rockmont for Boys, NC
Deerfoot Lodge, NY

Jewish
Alexander Muss High School in Israel, Israel
Blue Star Camps, NC
Camp Airy, MD
Camp Avoda, MA
Camp Barney Medintz, GA
Camp Canadensis, PA
Camp Chi, WI
Camp Chi Teenage Adventure Trips
Camp JCA Shalom, CA

Camp Lakeland, NY
Camp Louemma, NJ
Camp Louise, MD
Camp Micah, ME
Camp Modin, ME
Camp Monroe, NY
Camp Sabra, MO
Camp Tawonga–Call of the Wild, CA
Camp Tawonga–Magical Mystery Tour, CA
Camp Tawonga–Summer Camp, CA
Camp Tawonga–Summertime Family Camp, CA
Camp Tawonga–Surf 'n Turf Quest, CA
Camp Tawonga–Teen Quest: Canada, Canada
Camp Tawonga–Teen Quest: High Sierra, CA
Camp Tawonga–Teen Quest: Northwest
Camp Tawonga–Teen Quest: Southwest
Camp Tawonga–Teen Quest: Yosemite, CA
Camp Tawonga–Teen Service Learning to Alaska, AK
Camp Towanda, PA
Camp Veritans, NJ
Camp Walden, NY
Crane Lake Camp, MA
Genesis at Brandeis University, MA
Israel Discovery
JCC Houston: Art Camp, TX
JCC Houston: Camp Bami, TX
JCC Houston: Camp Kaleidoscope, TX
JCC Houston: Counselor-In-Training, TX
JCC Houston: Gordon Campsite, TX
JCC Houston: Gymnastics Camp, TX
JCC Houston: Kindercamp, TX
JCC Houston: Sports Camp, TX
JCC Houston: Teen Trek, TX
JCC Houston: Tennis Camp, TX
JCC Houston: Theater Camp, TX
Jewish Community Center Day Camp, NJ
Julian Krinsky Yesh Shabbat California Teen Tour, CA
Julian Krinsky Yesh Shabbat Summer Camp, PA
Miracle Makers Summer Camp, CA
New Jersey YMHA–YWHA Camp Mountaintop, PA
New Jersey YMHA–YWHA Camp Nah-jee-wah, PA
New Jersey YMHA–YWHA Cedar Lake Camp, PA
New Jersey YMHA–YWHA Round Lake Camp, PA
New Jersey YMHA–YWHA Teen Camp, PA
92nd Street Y Camps–Camp Bari Tov, NY
92nd Street Y Camps–Camp Haverim, NY
92nd Street Y Camps–Camp Kesher, PA
92nd Street Y Camps–Camp Kesher Junior, PA
92nd Street Y Camps–Camp K'Ton Ton, NY
92nd Street Y Camps–Camp Tevah for Science and Nature, NY
92nd Street Y Camps–Camp Tova, NY
92nd Street Y Camps–Camp Yaffa for the Arts, NY
92nd Street Y Camps–Camp Yomi, NY
92nd Street Y Camps–Fantastic Gymnastics, NY
92nd Street Y Camps–The TIYUL
92nd Street Y Camps–Trailblazers, NY
Shwayder Camp, CO
Summer JAM (Judaism, Activism, and Mitzvah Work), DC
Surprise Lake Camp, NY

Jewish (Orthodox)

New Jersey YMHA–YWHA Camp Nesher, PA

Lutheran

Camp Mt. Luther, PA

Mennonite

Camps with Meaning–Advanced Horsemanship I & II, Canada
Camps with Meaning–Boys Camp, Canada
Camps with Meaning–Girls Camp, Canada
Camps with Meaning–Junior High/Junior Youth Camp, Canada
Camps with Meaning–PreJunior/Junior/Intermediate Camp, Canada
Camps with Meaning–Youth Camp, Canada

Nondenominational

Camp St. John's Northwestern, WI
St. John's Northwestern Academic Camp, WI
St. John's Northwestern ESL Camp, WI

Presbyterian

Adventure Camps, PA
Camp Henry, MI
Camp Henry Offsite: Teen Challenge, MI
Camp Jordan for Children with Diabetes, VA
Ligonier Camp, PA
Makemie Woods Summer Camp, VA
Next Level Camp, PA
Presbyterian Clearwater Forest, MN

Reformed Church in America

Camp Geneva, MI

Roman Catholic

Camp Stanislaus, MS
Catholic University Benjamin T. Rome School of Music, DC
Catholic University Capitol Classic Debate Institute, DC
Catholic University College Courses for High School Students, DC
Catholic University Communication and Media Studies Workshops, DC
Catholic University Experiences in Architecture, DC
Catholic University Eye on Engineering, DC
Catholic University of America–Capitol Mock Trial Institute, DC
Catholic University of America–the Capitol Hill Lincoln-Douglas Debate Group, DC
Catholic Youth Camp, MN
Collegiate Summer Program for High School Students, NH
CYO Boys Camp, MI
CYO Girls Camp, MI
Georgetown Prep School Summer English Program, MD
Loras All-Sports Camp, IA
Portsmouth Abbey Summer School, RI
Purcell Marian High School Cavalier Basketball Camp, OH
Purcell Marian High School Summer School, OH
Saint Thomas More School–Summer Academic Camp, CT
Santa Catalina School Summer Camp, CA
Science Quest, PA
University of San Diego Sports Camps–Baseball Camp, CA
University of San Diego Sports Camps–Boys Basketball High School Team Camp, CA
University of San Diego Sports Camps–Boys High School Basketball Camp, CA
University of San Diego Sports Camps–Boys High School Elite Baseball Camp, CA
University of San Diego Sports Camps–Boys High School Soccer Camp, CA
University of San Diego Sports Camps–Boys Junior Basketball Camp, CA
University of San Diego Sports Camps–Coed Junior Soccer Camp, CA
University of San Diego Sports Camps–Coed Water Polo Camp, CA
University of San Diego Sports Camps–Competitive Swim Camp, CA
University of San Diego Sports Camps–Girls Basketball Fundamentals Camp, CA
University of San Diego Sports Camps–Girls Basketball High School Elite Camp, CA
University of San Diego Sports Camps–Girls Basketball High School Team Camp, CA
University of San Diego Sports Camps–Girls Softball Advanced Camp, CA
University of San Diego Sports Camps–Girls Softball Beginner/Intermediate Camp, CA
University of San Diego Sports Camps–Girls Volleyball Camp, CA
University of San Diego Sports Camps–Sherri Stephens High School Tennis Camp, CA
University of San Diego Sports Camps–Sherri Stephens Junior Tennis Camp, CA
University of San Diego Sports Camps–Sports–N–More All Sports Camp, CA
University of San Diego Sports Camps–Sports–N–More Team Sports Camp, CA
University of San Diego Sports Camps–Sports–N–More Wet & Wild Sports Camp, CA

Society of Friends

Explore-A-College, IN
Farm and Wilderness Camps–Barn Day Camp, VT
Farm and Wilderness Camps–Flying Cloud, VT
Farm and Wilderness Camps–Indian Brook, VT
Farm and Wilderness Camps–Saltash Mountain, VT
Farm and Wilderness Camps–Tamarack Farm, VT
Farm and Wilderness Camps–Timberlake, VT
Friends Camp, ME
Friends Music Camp, OH
Sidwell Friends Basketball Camp, DC
Sidwell Friends Bethesda Day Camp, MD
Sidwell Friends Camp Corsica, MD
Sidwell Friends Explorer Day Camp, Explorer Voyagers and ExploreStar, DC
Sidwell Friends Overnight Sea Kayaking Trip, MD
Sidwell Friends Riverview Programs, VA
Sidwell Friends Service Expedition to Hawaii, HI
Sidwell Friends Summer Community Service Programs, DC
Sidwell Friends Summer Studies, DC
Sidwell Friends Tennis Camp, DC
Sidwell Friends Women's Leadership–St. Margaret's School, VA

Southern Baptist

Oak Hill Academy Summer Program, VA

Unitarian Universalist

Rowe Camp, MA

United Church of Canada

Camp Ganadaoweh, Canada

United Church of Christ

Massanutten Military Academy Summer Cadet Program, VA
Summer Leadership Education and Training, VA

United Methodist

Jumonville Adventure Camps, PA
Jumonville Baseball/Softball Camp, PA
Jumonville Basketball Camp, PA
Jumonville Creative and Performing Arts Camps, PA
Jumonville Discovery Camp, PA
Jumonville Golf Camp, PA
Jumonville Sampler Camps, PA
Jumonville Soccer Camp, PA
Jumonville Spirit and Sport Spectacular–Soccer Camp, PA
Jumonville Spirit and Sport Spectacular–Swim Camp, PA
Jumonville Spirit and Sport Spectacular–Tennis Camp, PA
Jumonville Spirit and Sport Spectacular–Volleyball Camp, PA
Jumonville Sports Camp, PA
Jumonville Youth Mission Work Camp, PA
The Performing Arts Institute of Wyoming Seminary, PA
Randolph-Macon Academy Summer Programs, VA
West River United Methodist Center, MD
Wyoming Seminary–Sem Summer 2005, PA

Wesleyan Church

Houghton Academy Summer ESL, NY